Ethnologue

Volume 1

Languages of the World

Fourteenth Edition · Barbara F. Grimes, Editor
Consulting Editor · Joseph E. Grimes

SIL International
Dallas, Texas

Library of Congress Catalog Number 73–646678

Printed in the United States of America

Maps by

Irene Tucker, Bernard Wafukho, Matt Benjamin
Global Mapping International

Graphic Artist

Francisco Afanador

Previous editions

First edition	1951
Second edition	1951
Third edition	1952
Fourth edition	1953
Fifth edition	1958
Sixth edition	1965
Seventh edition	1969
Eighth edition	1974
Ninth edition	1978
Tenth edition	1984
Eleventh edition	1988
Twelfth edition	1992
Thirteenth edition	1996
Fourteenth edition	2000

ISBN 1–55671–106–9 (Set)
ISBN 1–55671–103–4 (Volume 1)
ISBN 1–55671–104–2 (Volume 2)
ISBN 1–55671–105–0 (CD)

Additional copies of the *Ethnologue, Volumes I and II* may be obtained from

SIL International
International Academic Bookstore
7500 West Camp Wisdom Road
Dallas, Texas 75236-5699 USA

Voice	(972) 708–7404
Fax	(972) 708–7363
Internet	academic_books@sil.org
Web	http//www.sil.org

TABLE OF CONTENTS

TABLE OF REGIONAL MAPS

No political statement is intended by the placement of any international or language boundary lines on any maps.

INTRODUCTION

Language can be a key to meaningful communication among persons or groups, or it can be a barrier to communication. In these days of ethnic pride and growing appreciation of minority groups, educators, government officials, and missionaries are realizing more than ever the importance of the first languages or 'mother tongues' of the peoples of the world, the languages through which communication is most effective.

How many languages are spoken in the world today? No one really knows. What is a language? The term has been used in many different senses. Popular usage often reserves the term 'language' for the major, prestigious speech forms of the world, and uses 'dialect' for everything else. Some people use 'language' to refer to speech forms that share a certain percentage of similar vocabulary, and 'dialect' to refer to speech forms that share higher percentages. Or they may consider varieties to constitute the same language which have similar grammatical and phonological systems. Many people, including some linguists, use the terms 'language' and 'dialect' without always clarifying the sense in which they are being used.

To those of us who are interested in cross-cultural communication and developing usable literature for speakers of many languages, however, it seems clear that one of the main factors that must be considered in distinguishing 'language' from 'dialect' is how well two linguistically close speech communities understand each other. Marginal intelligibility between two language communities does not allow their speakers to engage in meaningful communication beyond bare essentials.

Also to be considered in deciding which languages to use for educational and literary purposes is how well the vernacular speakers understand their national language, trade language, or other second language, their ability to use different languages in different social domains, differing levels of bilingual proficiency across a language population, and whether or not they will accept educational materials and other literature in those languages or dialects.

Sociological criteria such as the speakers' views concerning the relationship between language and identity, and between language and political or geographic factors, are also important in choosing which form of speech to use for educational and literary purposes. The nature and goals of such projects influence decisions about language choice.

Linguists recognize that many of the world's languages may cease to be spoken in coming decades. Our 'nearly extinct' category is only the tip of the iceberg. How to identify the other endangered languages, however, is not necessarily clear. Factors such as small population size (J. Grimes 1995), bilingualism, urbanization, modernization, migration, industrialization, the function of each language within a society, and speaker attitudes have different impacts on different groups. Such factors interact within a society in dynamic ways which are not necessarily predictable. Once a scholarly consensus forms that can be applied worldwide, we may be able to report more on language endangerment. In the meantime, we report information about the above factors in brief form as it becomes available.

The *Ethnologue* tries to bring together the best information available on the languages of the world. Language entries represent separate languages or probable languages (highly divergent 'dialects') according to our best sources. Variants of the language that are not distinct enough to need separate literature are treated as dialects, and are listed under the language entry and not as separate entries, unless attitudes or other social factors are strong enough that they need to be treated as separate sociolinguistic entities. For many language entries, however, we lack information on dialect intelligibility, and so have followed our best sources as to what they consider to be a language or a dialect.

The net gain of languages listed since the last edition is the result of better information, based on field investigation and other research by many trained individuals. In many cases the new languages are not languages previously unknown to outsiders, but ones which had been thought to be dialects of another language, and are now known to be distinct enough to be considered separate languages.

For each language entry, its alternate names, number of speakers, location, dialects, linguistic affiliation, multilingualism of speakers, availability of the Bible, and other demographic and sociolinguistic information is given if known. The information is given in concise form rather than in detail because of limited space.

Alternate names. Many languages are known by more than one name. Speakers may have one name for themselves, while neighboring groups may use different names for them. A French-speaking person may spell the name differently than an English-speaking person. The name of an ethnic group may differ from the name of its language; in that case the language name is preferred as the main name in the *Ethnologue*. An ethnic group may be made up of several groups speaking several languages, or the mother tongue speakers of a single language may be members of several different ethnic groups.

An entire language may be known by the name of one of its dialects. Some names in use by others are offensive to the speakers; we have attempted to identify those by double quotation marks. Names used in publications are included even when they are not entirely accurate. Alternate names are given in parentheses after the main name, and are separated from each other by commas. The "Language

Name Index" section in volume 2 lists all 41,806 such names included in the *Ethnologue, Volume I,* so you can look up the name you know to find out what it is listed under.

Language identification code. Each language entry in the world is assigned a unique three-letter code, which is the same in all countries in which that language is spoken. The code helps to distinguish the language from other languages with the same or similar names and ensures that each language is counted only once in world or area statistics. When different names are preferred for the same language in different countries, the identification code shows that the language is the same. This code is given in square brackets following the alternate names.

Number of speakers. The first population figure given refers to the estimated number of mother tongue speakers in the country in focus, unless it is followed by the words "in all countries", which indicates that it is an estimated figure for the total number of mother tongue speakers of that language in all countries. The date and source of the population estimate are given in parentheses. Some totals given do not equal the sum of the populations given for that language in each country because of differences among sources and differences in dates when the estimates were made. We do not try to extrapolate population estimates by some formula, because populations do not all increase at the same rate in all language groups, and because some starting estimates themselves turn out later to have been incorrect.

It is often difficult to get an accurate figure for the speakers of a language. All figures are only estimates—even census figures. Some sources do not include all dialects in their figures. Some sources count members of ethnic groups, whose membership does not always agree on a one-to-one basis with speakers of languages. Some sources do not make clear whether they refer to the total number of speakers in all countries, or only to those in one of the countries. Some do not distinguish first language speakers from second language speakers. We try to give the number of first language speakers wherever possible.

In cases where only a few elderly speakers are still living, the language entry includes the words "nearly extinct". In other cases where the language is no longer spoken as mother tongue it has the word "extinct" appended. In the latter case, there may be members of the ethnic group still living, but they now speak a different language as mother tongue. Their former language may still be used for ritual or other cultural purposes, but only as a second language. Many languages have become extinct; we have attempted to include only those which have ceased to be spoken recently, are considered by linguists to have special linguistic significance in their family relationships, or which have had some Scripture published. Total language statistics for the world or major areas do not include extinct languages.

Location. For purposes of carrying out field projects it is practical to organize the data by continents and countries. However, many languages are spoken in more than one country, and so are listed under several countries. One of the countries is considered primary; usually the country of origin or country where most of the speakers are located. More information about a language is given in the primary country than in the others. The primary country for each language is mentioned toward the end of the entry as "See...", and is listed first in the *Ethnologue Language Name Index* under the main name. When known, the region within each country where the language is spoken is given.

Nonindigenous languages. All languages spoken in a country are not necessarily listed as separate entries in the *Ethnologue*, especially nonindigenous or immigrant languages which are still spoken in the country of origin and apparently have no significant dialect differences between the two locations. Known nonindigenous languages are listed in the introduction at the beginning of each country's listing, with population estimate if known. They are not included in the language statistics for that country. Information about nonindigenous languages is incomplete, and may be incorrect. Corrections are welcomed. Some languages listed in the country introductions may not be nonindigenous languages, but if the only unique thing known about a language in a given country is its presence, or its population; and it is listed with more information in another country, then it may also be listed only in the country introduction. This is especially true for the countries of the former USSR.

Summary chart. A summary chart of the number of languages in each major area of the world is given in an appendix. We distinguish five major regions: Africa, the Americas, Asia, Europe, and the Pacific.

In addition, a list of the known indigenous languages in each country is given in that country's heading. Greenberg's diversity index, the probability that any two people in the country picked at random will have different mother tongues, is also calculated for each country (Lieberson 1981). It ranges from near 1 for high diversity to zero for no diversity.

Changing world events. We have attempted to keep up with world events. Since the last edition, Aruba has been recognized as a separate nation, and Zaïre is now called the Democratic Republic of Congo (DRC). Since this edition went to press, East Timor has gained independence from Indonesia.

Dialects. Speech varieties which are functionally intelligible to each other's speakers because of linguistic similarity are considered dialects of one language and listed under that language, with alternate names of individual dialects in parentheses. Until we receive evidence to the contrary, we assume all dialects listed under a single language can use the same literature and educational materials.

Linguistic affiliation. All languages are slowly changing, and related varieties are diverging for the most part. Most languages are related to some other languages: to some more closely and to others more distantly. Linguists have used terms such as phylum, stock, family, branch, group, language, and dialect to refer to these relationships in increasing order of closeness.

The organization of linguistic relationships outlined in the Oxford University Press *International Encyclopedia of Linguistics*, 1992, William Bright, ed., is followed for most language families, because it is the most comprehensive and up-to-date guide available. For Austronesian languages, the *Comparative Austronesian Dictionary*, 1995, Darrell Tryon, ed., is followed. Some changes have been entered based on more recent comparative studies. In the *Ethnologue*, more inclusive group names are given first, followed by the names for less inclusive subgroups, separated by commas. The information about language family relationships is also given in outline form in *Ethnologue Volume 2: Maps and Indexes*, by Joseph E. Grimes and Barbara F. Grimes.

The traditional numbering system used to identify different subgroups of Bantu languages in Africa has been followed.

Bilingualism. If speakers can use a second language, different speakers usually have varying degrees of bilingual proficiency in it, ranging from being able to use only greetings or trade in it to complete freedom to express anything in it. Language groups are sometimes reported to be bilingual if a few of the speakers can use a second language to some degree, or if there are no monolinguals; whereas other sources would not classify groups as bilingual unless a large majority of their members could use the second language very well. Because second languages are usually learned later than first languages, bilingualism is usually not uniform across a community, as mentioned above. Leaders, the educated, men, traders, those who travel, those in population centers, and people in certain age groups may be more bilingual than others. Where we have the information, we describe these factors about bilingualism.

For some language groups, estimates of percentages of bilingual proficiency according to U.S. Foreign Service Institute levels are included (see the Second Language Proficiency Questionnaire in the appendices). In many areas of the world multilingualism is a factor.

Availability of the Bible. Information on published Scripture is given with the dates of the earliest and most recent published Bible, New Testament, or complete books (portions).

Ecological information. For some languages, information on the ecological and geological environment, altitude range, and subsistence type of the speakers is given. This is not a complete typology, but a rough guide to the physical setting and general economic adaptation of the society (see the Environmental Questionnaire in the appendices).

Linguistic typology. For some languages, a little information is given on constituent order (Subject, Object, Verb = SOV) and other features that have been helpful to linguists in understanding certain basic linguistic relationships (see the Language Typology Questionnaire in the appendices).

Grammars and dictionaries. There is some indication given of the existence of a grammar or a dictionary for individual languages, but the information is very incomplete at this time. More information is welcomed.

'Click' symbols. We have followed our sources in using certain symbols for 'click' sounds produced with ingressive mouth air, such as /, //, !,", [; used among Khoisan languages and a few others in southern Africa.

Blindness and Braille. There are reported to be from 23,000,000 to 40,000,000 or more blind people in the world. Information on the number of blind people in each country is given in the country heading. Information about the availability of Braille codes and Braille Scripture is given under specific languages. Readers are encouraged to submit additional information on the number of blind people in specific language groups, availability and standardization of Braille codes, and Scripture published or in progress. Please send information to the *Ethnologue* editor at the address below.

Deaf People and Deafness. There are millions of deaf and hearing impaired people in the world. Information on the number of deaf people in some countries, and an approximate count of the deaf institutions (schools, clubs, associations), is given in the country headings. The deaf sign languages listed are those used within deaf communities, rather than those which spell out the spoken languages used in those countries, like Signed English. The deaf sign languages we know of are listed under their respective countries and in the list of Languages of Special Interest in an appendix. Please send additional information on deafness and deaf sign languages to the *Ethnologue* editor.

Languages of Special Interest. Languages which are related by factors other than, or in addition to, linguistic or geographical similarities, and which are of special interest to investigators are listed in an appendix. These include Gypsy languages, Jewish languages, creole and pidgin languages, mixed languages, and deaf sign languages. The lists are probably not complete.

Second languages only. Languages which are used as special second languages with no mother tongue speakers, such as languages of initiation, languages of herb doctors, cants, jargons, and American Plains Indian Sign Language are listed in the body of the *Ethnologue* but not included among the world and major area statistical totals of living languages. This information is also incomplete.

Sources. The major sources of information for each country are given at the beginning of the country section. A fuller bibliography of sources used appears in an appendix. Sources not listed in the bibliography are from personal communication with scholars knowledgeable in the area.

Accuracy of individual language data. For some language entries, indication is given of types of investigation still needed, such as investigation of inherent intelligibility among related language varieties, degrees of bilingual proficiency and spread, or language attitudes. Each edition of the *Ethnologue* represents improvement in the information about many languages, as the result of the efforts of many people.

Accuracy code for country data. Also given with each country is an estimate of the overall accuracy of the data for that country. The rating does not reflect the accuracy of individual sources but rather the general presence or absence of information on intelligibility and other first-hand evaluation by linguists. The data accuracy estimate codes are as follows:

A1: Based on intelligibility testing
A2: Based on reliable field experience
B: Based on good published sources but with need for further investigation by linguists on the field for intelligibility, bilingualism, or speaker attitudes toward other languages
C: Needs extensive checking by linguists on the field and more research in published sources

Users. The information given here can be useful to linguists, translators, anthropologists, missionaries, bilingual educators, government officials, field administrators, potential field investigators, and interested lay people.

Corrections. The information is not complete or perfect; but if we waited until it were we would never publish. As far as we know, it is the most complete and accurate large scale collection of information of its kind available. This edition contains tens of thousands of changes from the previous one. A new edition is planned for publication approximately every four years. Readers are encouraged to submit corrections and additions (see questionnaires in the appendices) to:

Editor, *Ethnologue*
International Linguistics Center
7500 West Camp Wisdom Road
Dallas, Texas 75236, U.S.A.
or
info-sil@sil.org

Maps. Volume 2 contains language maps for many countries included in Volume 1. Continent maps and a world map are given to help orient the reader to the location of specific countries and continents. No political statement is intended by the placement of any boundary lines for any languages or countries on any map.

Ethnologue Language Name Index. Volume 2 also contains an index of language names, alternate language names, dialect names, and alternate dialect names used in the *Ethnologue*, Volume 1.

Ethnologue Language Family Index. Volume 2 also gives the *Ethnologue* information about language family relationships in outline form, showing the relationship of each language to other languages.

Computerized archive. The data given here are all taken from the Ethnologue Language Archive, a computerized data base on languages of the world. It was begun in 1971 by the Summer Institute of Linguistics, Inc., at the University of Oklahoma under a grant from the National Science Foundation, was continued at Cornell University, and is now operated by the SIL International. It is available on the World Wide Web at http://www.sil.org. The main input to the data base has been the research compiled by the *Ethnologue* editor. The fact that the entries are constructed by computer accounts for a certain redundancy or stiffness in the phrasing.

Acknowledgements. We mourn the passing of Richard S. Pittman, the founder and first Editor of the Ethnologue. He continued as a Consulting Editor until his death in 1998. His vision, scholarship, and encouragement guided the Ethnologue in its direction during its first forty-seven years.

The Consulting Editor, Joseph E. Grimes, has given valuable advice. Special thanks also goes to him for the mammoth amount of computer programming necessary for maintaining and updating the data base with new information and to Bonnie Brown and Judy Benjamin for preparing it for camera-ready printing. Laurie Nelson, Chuck Maggio, Larry Salge, and colleagues at the International Linguistics Center in Dallas helped guide the publication through the printing process. Irene Tucker, Bernard Wafukho, Matt Benjamin, and Global Mapping International, produced the maps with help from people in many countries. Many persons around the world have supplied information based on personal knowledge of, and research on, languages and dialects, both for this edition and previous ones. Many thanks to all of these people. Without their work, the *Ethnologue* would not be possible.

Languages of the World

LANGUAGES OF THE WORLD

EACH DOT REPRESENTS THE PRIMARY LOCATION
OF A LIVING LANGUAGE LISTED IN THE ETHNOLOGUE

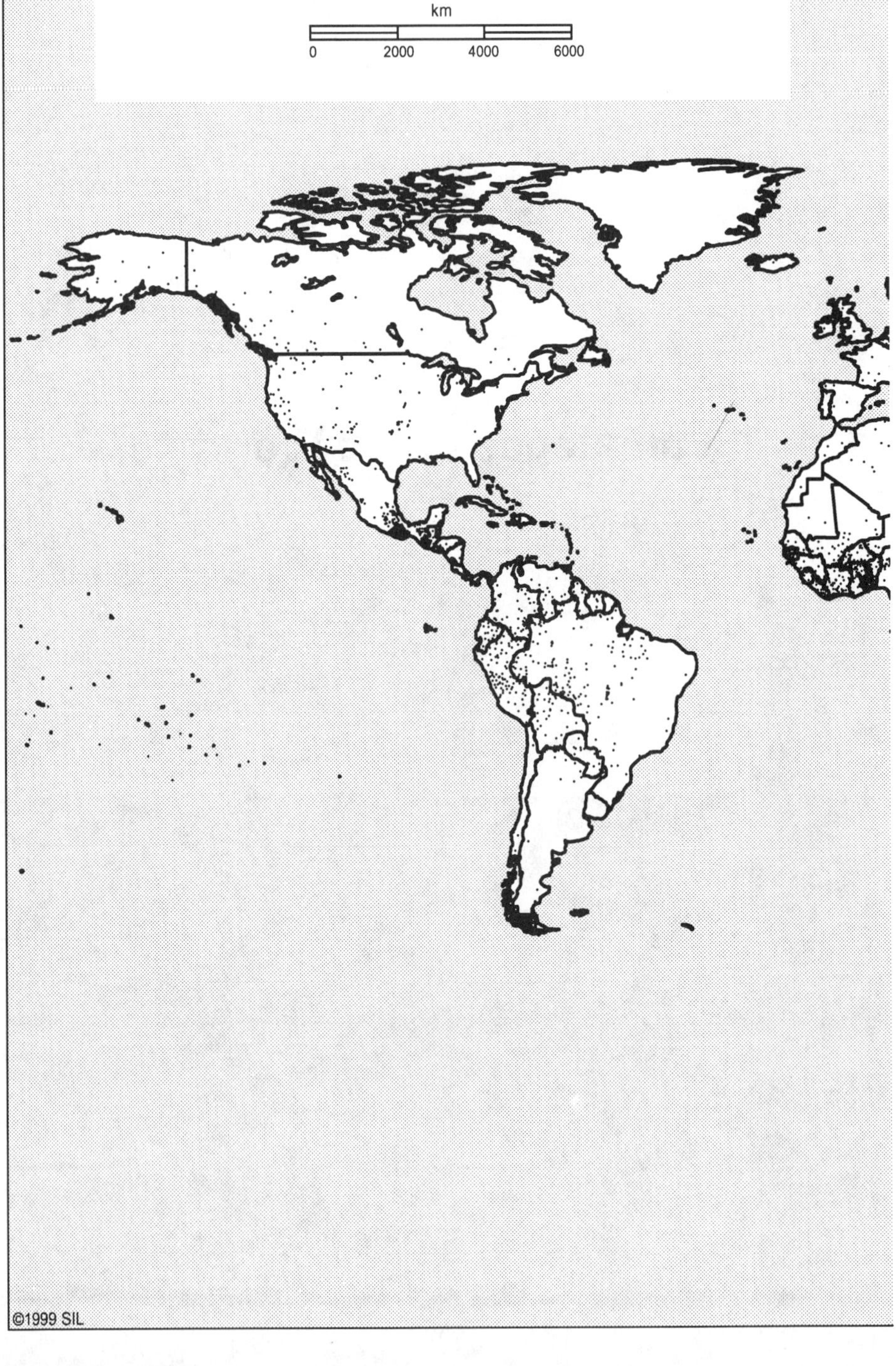

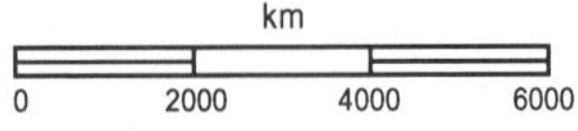

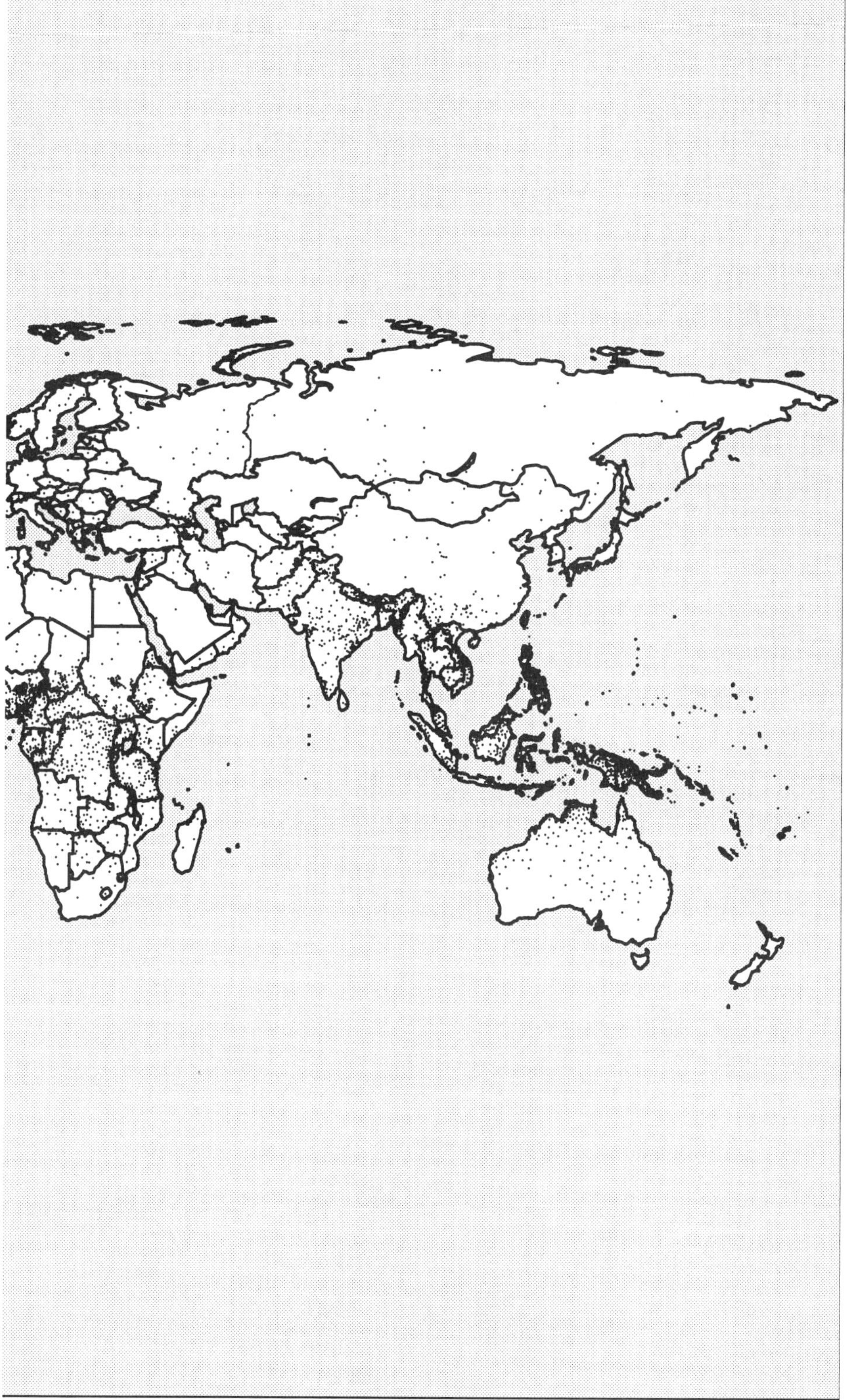

Africa

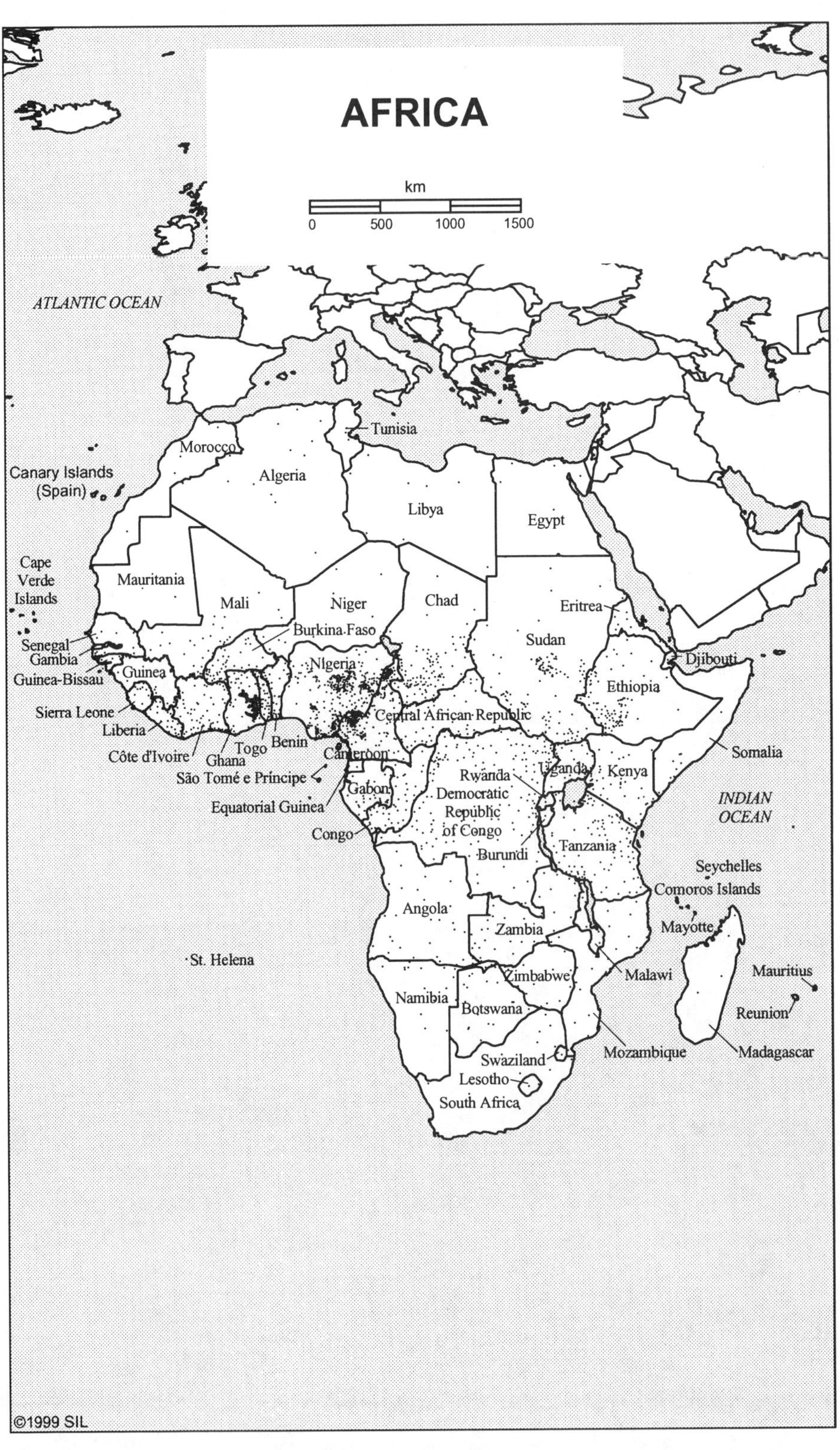
AFRICA
km
0
500
1000
1500
ATLANTIC OCEAN
Tunisia
Morocco
Canary Islands
(Spain)
Algeria
Libya
Egypt
Cape
Verde
Islands
Mauritania
Mali
Niger
Chad
Eritrea
Sudan
Burkina Faso
Senegal
Gambia
Guinea-Bissau
Guinea
Nigeria
Djibouti
Ethiopia
Sierra Leone
Liberia
Central African Republic
Côte d'Ivoire
Ghana
Togo
Benin
Cameroon
Somalia
São Tomé e Príncipe
Uganda
Kenya
Rwanda
Gabon
Democratic
Republic
of Congo
INDIAN
OCEAN
Equatorial Guinea
Congo
Burundi
Tanzania
Seychelles
Comoros Islands
Angola
Mayotte
Zambia
St. Helena
Malawi
Mauritius
Zimbabwe
Namibia
Botswana
Reunion
Mozambique
Madagascar
Swaziland
Lesotho
South Africa
©1999 SIL

ALGERIA

Democratic and Popular Republic of Algeria. al-Jumhuriya al-Jazãiriya ad-Dimuqratiya ash-Shabiya. National or official language: Standard Arabic. 30,081,000 (1998 UN). 14% speak Berber languages. Literacy rate 50% to 52%. Also includes Hassaniyya Arabic 150,000, Catalan-Valencian-Balear, Tadaksahak 1,800, Kidal Tamasheq. Information mainly from Y. Zavadovski, 1962; M. Bateson 1967; J. Applegate 1970; Ph. Marcais 1977; W. Fischer and O. Jastrow 1980; D. Cohen 1985. Sunni Muslim. Blind population 25,000. Deaf institutions: 3. Data accuracy estimate: B, C. The number of languages listed for Algeria is 18. Of those, all are living languages. Diversity index 0.31.

ALGERIAN SIGN LANGUAGE [ASP] Deaf sign language. It has influenced the deaf community in Oujda in northern Morocco.

ARABIC, ALGERIAN SAHARAN SPOKEN ***(SAHARAN ARABIC, TAMANRASSET ARABIC, TAMANGHASSET ARABIC)*** [AAO] 100,000 in Algeria (1996). Population total both countries 110,000. Moroccan border along the Atlas Mts., northeast to Medea (south of Algiers), southeast to the Righ Wadi, south to 28 degrees latitude, as far as Plateau du Tademait, including some in the town of Tamanrasset. Also spoken in Niger. Afro-Asiatic, Semitic, Central, South, Arabic. Structurally distinct from other Arabic.

ARABIC, ALGERIAN SPOKEN ***(ALGERIAN)*** [ARQ] 20,400,000 in Algeria (1996 Hunter), 83% of the population (1991). 2,000,000 outside of Algeria (1995 Hunter). Population total all countries 22,400,000. Also spoken in Belgium, France, Germany, Netherlands, St. Pierre and Miquelon. Afro-Asiatic, Semitic, Central, South, Arabic. Dialects: CONSTANTINE, ALGIERS, ORAN. Eastern Algerian and Tunisian dialects are close, and Western Algerian and Moroccan dialects are close, but speakers prefer their own varieties. The Ouled Nail of Biskra speak Arabic, but are ethnically separate. Sunni Muslim, Christian. Bible portions 1872-1964.

ARABIC, STANDARD [ABV] Middle East, North Africa. Afro-Asiatic, Semitic, Central, South, Arabic. Preserves the ancient grammar. Used for written materials, formal speeches. Not a mother tongue, but taught in schools. National language. Arabic script. Bible 1984-1991. See main entry under Saudi Arabia.

CHAOUIA ***(SHAWIYA, SHAWIA)*** [SHY] 1,400,000 (1993). South and southeast of Grand Kabylie in the Aurès Mts. Afro-Asiatic, Berber, Northern, Zenati, Shawiya. One of the major Berber languages. Muslim. Bible portions 1950.

CHENOUA [CHB] 15,000 to 75,000 (1996). Towns are Cherchell, Hamadia, Gouraya, Damous, Oued Damous, Larhat, Marceau, Sidi Amar, Nador, Tipaza, Sidi Mousa, Ain Tagourirt. Afro-Asiatic, Berber, Northern. 77% lexical similarity with Chaouia, 76% with Kabyle. Men and young people use Algerian Spoken Arabic as second language. Muslim.

FRENCH [FRN] 110,600 in Algeria (1993). Known more in the cities. Indo-European, Italic, Romance, Italo-Western, Western, Gallo-Iberian, Gallo-Romance, Gallo-Rhaetian, Oïl, French. 20% of the population can read and write French, and more can speak it. Bible 1530-1986. See main entry under France.

KABYLE [KYL] 2,537,000 or more in Algeria (1995), 8% of the population. Estimates by some sources are up to 6,000,000 in Algeria (1998). Population total all countries 3,074,000 or more. Grande Kabylie Mt. range, western Kabylia. Also spoken in Belgium, France. Afro-Asiatic, Berber, Northern, Kabyle. Dialects: GREATER KABYLE, LESSER KABYLE. French is often used by men in trade and correspondence. Arabic is also used as second language. Kabyle is used in the home and market. Speakers have pride in Kabyle and resistance to Arabic. The name 'Kabyle' is reported by some sources to derive from the Arabic word for 'tribesman', 'qabila'. Patrilineal and patrilocal. Roman script. Mountain slope. Peasant agriculturalists: olives, figs, pomegranates, peaches, apricots, pears, plums, vegetables. Muslim, secular, Christian. NT 1901-1995.

KORANDJE [KCY] Tabelbala oasis. They go to Libya from time to time to work. Nilo-Saharan, Songhai. The people are called 'Belbali'. Investigation needed: intelligibility with other Songhai languages.

TACHELHIT ***(TASHELHIT, TASHELHAIT, TASHELHAYT, TASOUSSIT, SHILHA, SOUTHERN SHILHA, TACHILHIT)*** [SHI] Southern Algeria near the Moroccan border around Tabelbala. Afro-Asiatic, Berber, Northern, Atlas. Dialect: SUSIUA (SUS, SOUSSE). Many men are bilingual in Arabic, but many women do not learn Arabic. One of the major Berber languages. Their name for their language is 'Tachelhit'. 'Shilha' is the Arabic name for Moroccan Berber varieties in general. Muslim. Bible portions 1906-1925. See main entry under Morocco.

TAGARGRENT ***(OUARGLA, OUARGLI, WARGLA)*** [OUA] 5,000 (1995). South of Constantine, near Mzab. Ouargla and Ngouça are the main centers. Afro-Asiatic, Berber, Northern, Zenati, Mzab-Wargla. Dialects: OUEDGHIR (WADI), TEMACIN, TARIYIT. Related to Tumzabt, Temacine Tamazight, and Taznatit.

Status as a language or dialect is not defined. Tariyit is a possible dialect spoken by the Haratine (former slaves of the Ouargli people. Healthy language and cultural attitudes. Dictionary. Muslim.

TAMAHAQ, TAHAGGART ***(TAMACHEK, TAMASHEKIN, TOMACHEK, TUAREG, TOUAREG, TOURAGE)*** [THV] 25,000 in Algeria, including 20,000 Hoggar, 5,000 Ghat (1987). Population total all countries 62,000. Hoggar dialect in south Hoggar (Ajjer) Mountain area around Tamanghasset and south into Niger. The Ghat dialect is in southeast Algeria around Ganet and west Libyan oases around Ghat. Also spoken in Libya, Niger. Afro-Asiatic, Berber, Tamasheq, Northern. Dialects: HOGGAR (AHAGGAREN, AJJER, TAHAGGART), GHAT (GANET, DJANET). 'Tuareg' are the people, 'Targi' is the singular, 'Tamahaq' is the language. Volcanic mountains. Inaden: blacksmiths, jewelry craftsmen. Muslim. Bible portions 1948-1965.

TAMAZIGHT, CENTRAL ATLAS ***(MIDDLE ATLAS BERBER, CENTRAL SHILHA)*** [TZM] Western Algeria mountain area of Atlas and adjacent valleys to Taza, in the vicinity of Rabat, south near the Moroccan border. Afro-Asiatic, Berber, Northern, Atlas. Dialect: SOUTH ORAN. One of the major Berber languages. 'Tamazight' is the name of the language, 'Berber' of the people. VSO. Muslim. Bible portions 1919-1981. See main entry under Morocco.

TARIFIT ***(TIRIFIE, RIFF, RIFI, RUAFA, FIFIA, RIF, NORTHERN SHILHA, SHILHA)*** [RIF] Along the coast, eastern Alteria to Arzeu. Afro-Asiatic, Berber, Northern, Zenati, Riff. Dialects: ARZEU, IGZENNAIAN, IZNACEN (BENI IZNASSEN). Muslim. Bible portions 1887-1890. See main entry under Morocco.

TAZNATIT [GRR] 40,000 (1995). Isolated, around Timimoun, near the Touat region and around 400 miles southwest of the Mzab. Afro-Asiatic, Berber, Northern, Zenati, Mzab-Wargla. Dialects: GOURARA (GURARA), TOUAT (TUAT, TUWAT). Related to Tumzabt, Tagargrent, and Temacine Tamazight. Low intelligibility with other Tamazight speech forms, including Tumzabt and Tagargrent. Vigorous use. Speakers call their language 'Taznatit'. Muslim.

TEMACINE TAMAZIGHT ***(TOUGOURT, TOUGGOURT, TUGURT)*** [TJO] 6,000 (1995). Vicinity of Temacine, Tamelhat, Ghomra, and Meggarin. Afro-Asiatic, Berber, Northern, Zenati, Mzab-Wargla. Related to Tumzabt, Tagargrent and Taznatit. Possibly a dialect of Tagargrent, but not likely. People may have shifted to Arabic. Muslim.

TIDIKELT TAMAZIGHT [TIA] 9,000 (1995). Tidikelt, in the vicinity of Salah, and Tit in southern Algeria. Afro-Asiatic, Berber, Northern, Zenati, Tidikelt. Dialects: TIDIKELT, TIT. People may have shifted to Arabic. Muslim.

TUMZABT ***(MZAB, MZABI, GHARDAIA)*** [MZB] 70,000 (1995). Mzab region, 330 miles south of Algiers. 7 oases; Ghardaia being the principal one. Afro-Asiatic, Berber, Northern, Zenati, Mzab-Wargla. Only minor dialect variations. Related to Tagargrent, Temacine Tamzight, and Taznatit. Some speakers are probably bilingual in Arabic, French, or Spanish. Women virtually monolingual in Tumzabt. Vigorous use. 'Tumzabt' is their name for their language. Strong cultural vitality. Tumzabt villages are interspersed among Arabic-speaking villages. Dictionary. Known as traders throughout Algeria. Muslim (Kharedjite).

ANGOLA

People's Republic of Angola. República Popular de Angola. National or official language: Portuguese. 12,092,000 (1998 UN). Literacy rate 30%. Information mainly from Redinha 1970; J. Bendor-Samuel 1989. Christian, traditional religion. Blind population 12,000. Data accuracy estimate: C. The number of languages listed for Angola is 42. Of those, 41 are living languages and 1 is extinct. Diversity index 0.76.

'AKHOE ***(AUKWE, AUEN, //AU//EN, //AU//EÌ, KAU-//-EN, KAUKAU, //K"AU-//EN, KOKO)*** [AKE] Khoisan, Southern Africa, Northern. Bible portions 1975-1980. See main entry under Namibia.

BOLO ***(LIBOLO, LUBOLO, HAKA)*** [BLV] Southeast of Luanda. Niger-Congo, Atlantic-Congo, Volta-Congo, Benue-Congo, Bantoid, Southern, Narrow Bantu, Central, H, Mbundu (H.20). Related to Loanda Mbundu, Nsongo, and Sama.

CHOKWE ***(CIOKWE, COKWE, SHIOKO, KIOKO, QUIOCO, DJOK, TSHOKWE, TSCHIOKLOE)*** [CJK] 455,800 in Angola (1991). Northeastern Lunda District, and some in eastern Bie, western Moxico, and central Cuando Cubango. Niger-Congo, Atlantic-Congo, Volta-Congo, Benue-Congo, Bantoid, Southern, Narrow Bantu, Central, K, Chokwe-Luchazi (K.20). Dialect: MINUNGO. Traditional religion, Christian. Bible 1970-1990. See main entry under DRC.

DIRIKU ***(MBOGEDO, SHIMBOGEDU, DIRIKO, GCIRIKU, RUGCIRIKU)*** [DIU] Southeastern border with Namibia, between Kwangali and Ndonga. Niger-Congo, Atlantic-Congo, Volta-Congo, Benue-Congo, Bantoid, Southern, Narrow Bantu, Central, K, Diriku (K.70). Close to Kwangali, but separate. NT 1988. See main entry under Namibia.

HOLU ***(KIHOLU, HOLO, KIHOLO)*** [HOL] Population total both countries 12,000 (1971 Welmers). Kwango River area. Also spoken in DRC. Niger-Congo, Atlantic-Congo, Volta-Congo, Benue-Congo, Bantoid, Southern, Narrow Bantu, Central, K, Holu (K.10). Dialect: YECI. Closely related to Samba. Different from Holoholo of DRC and Tanzania. Bible portions 1943-1956.

KONGO ***(KIKONGO, KIKOONGO, CONGO, CABINDA)*** [KON] 1,144,000 in Angola (1990), 13% of the population (1990 WA). Northwestern corner. Niger-Congo, Atlantic-Congo, Volta-Congo, Benue-Congo, Bantoid, Southern, Narrow Bantu, Central, H, Kongo (H.10). Dialects: SOUTH KONGO, SOUTH EAST KONGO, WEST KONGO (FIOTE, FIOTI), NDINGI, MBOKA, LAADI. Ndingi and Mboka may be separate languages. Investigation needed: intelligibility with Ndingi, Mboka, Vili. Christian, traditional religion. Bible 1905-1933. See main entry under DRC.

KONGO, SAN SALVADOR ***(KIKONGO, CONGO, KISIKONGO, KIKOONGO)*** [KWY] Northern Angola and DRC along the Congo River below Kinshasa. Niger-Congo, Atlantic-Congo, Volta-Congo, Benue-Congo, Bantoid, Southern, Narrow Bantu, Central, H, Kongo (H.10). Fioti and San Salvador are different enough to need separate literature. Bible 1916-1926. See main entry under DRC.

KUNG-EKOKA ***(EKOKO-!XÛ, !KUNG, !KU, !XU, !HU, QXÛ)*** [KNW] Primarily Namibia, Okavango and Ovamboland Territory. Khoisan, Southern Africa, Northern. Traditional religion, Christian. Bible portions 1980. See main entry under Namibia.

KWADI ***(CUEPE, CUANHOCA, CUROCA, KOROKA, BAKOROKA, MAKOROKO, MUCOROCA)*** [KWZ] Southwest corner, south of Moçamedes. Khoisan, Southern Africa, Central, Kwadi. Dialect: ZOROTUA (VASORONTU). J. C. Winter (1981) says it is extinct. There were 3 speakers in 1971 who used it regularly (E. O. J. Westphal). Extinct.

KWANGALI ***(SIKWANGALI, RUKWANGALI, KWANGARI, KWANGARE, CUANGAR)*** [KWN] South central. Niger-Congo, Atlantic-Congo, Volta-Congo, Benue-Congo, Bantoid, Southern, Narrow Bantu, Central, K, Kwangwa (K.40). Dialect: SAMBYU (SHISAMBYU, SAMBIU, SAMBIO). Traditional religion, Christian. Bible 1987. See main entry under Namibia.

KWANYAMA ***(OCHIKWANYAMA, KUANYAMA, KWANJAMA, KWANCAMA, CUANHAMA, OVAMBO, HUMBA)*** [KUY] 421,000 in Angola (1993 Johnstone). Population total both countries 421,000 or more. South central. Also spoken in Namibia. Niger-Congo, Atlantic-Congo, Volta-Congo, Benue-Congo, Bantoid, Southern, Narrow Bantu, Central, R, Ndonga (R.20). Bible 1974.

KXOE ***(XUN, HUKWE, !HUKWE, XUHWE, XU, ZAMA, VAZAMA, CAZAMA, "MBARAKWENGO", "MBARAKWENA", GLANDA-KHWE, BLACK BUSHMAN, WATER BUSHMEN, SCHEKERE)*** [XUU] 500 to 700 in Angola (1998 Brenzinger). Huthembo (Wuthembo), northeast of Likuwa, and Lukamba (Lukanga) west of Rivungu, southeast corner of Angola. Khoisan, Southern Africa, Central, Tshu-Khwe, Northwest. Dialect: BUMA-KXOE. Traditional religion, Christian. See main entry under Namibia.

LUCHAZI ***(CHILUCHAZI, LUJAZI, LUJASH, LUTSHASE, LUXAGE, LUCAZI, LUTCHAZ, PONDA)*** [LCH] 240,000 in Angola (1993 Johnstone). Population total both countries 294,400. Southeast, adjacent areas. Also spoken in Zambia. Niger-Congo, Atlantic-Congo, Volta-Congo, Benue-Congo, Bantoid, Southern, Narrow Bantu, Central, K, Chokwe-Luchazi (K.20). Christian, traditional religion. Bible 1963.

LUIMBI ***(CHILUIMBI, LUIMBE, LWIMBE, LWIMBI)*** [LUM] 20,000 (1972 Nida). Central, Cuanza River area. Niger-Congo, Atlantic-Congo, Volta-Congo, Benue-Congo, Bantoid, Southern, Narrow Bantu, Central, K, Chokwe-Luchazi (K.20). Related to Nkangala and Mbwela. Bible portions 1935.

LUNDA ***(CHILUNDA)*** [LVN] 90,000 in Angola (1993 Johnstone). Northeastern. Niger-Congo, Atlantic-Congo, Volta-Congo, Benue-Congo, Bantoid, Southern, Narrow Bantu, Central, K, Salampasu-Ndembo (K.30). Bible 1962. See main entry under Zambia.

LUVALE ***(LUENA, LWENA, CHILUVALE, LOVALE, LUBALE)*** [LUE] 155,000 in Angola (1993 Johnstone). Moxico, southeast provinces. Niger-Congo, Atlantic-Congo, Volta-Congo, Benue-Congo, Bantoid, Southern, Narrow Bantu, Central, K, Chokwe-Luchazi (K.20). Christian, traditional religion. Bible 1955-1961. See main entry under Zambia.

LUYANA ***(LUYI, LOUYI, LUI, ROUYI, LUANA, LUANO)*** [LAV] Southwestern, east of Moçamedes (Namibe). Niger-Congo, Atlantic-Congo, Volta-Congo, Benue-Congo, Bantoid, Southern, Narrow Bantu, Central, K, Kwangwa (K.40). Dialects: KWANDI, MBOWE (ESIMBOWE), MDUNDULU (NDUNDULU, IMILANGU), MISHULUNDU. A cluster of dialects. Mbowe may be a separate language. Imilangu may be a dialect of Simaa. See main entry under Zambia.

MALIGO [MWJ] Khoisan, Southern Africa, Northern.

MASHI ***(MASI)*** [MHO] Niger-Congo, Atlantic-Congo, Volta-Congo, Benue-Congo, Bantoid, Southern, Narrow Bantu, Central, K, Kwangwa (K.40). Dialects: NORTH KWANDU, SOUTH KWANDU, MASHI. Dialect cluster. Speakers are called 'a kwa Kwando', 'people of the Kwando River'. Nomadic. Different from Mashi (Shi) which is related to Havu of DRC. Traditional religion. See main entry under Zambia.

MBANGALA ***(CIMBANGALA, BANGALA)*** [MXG] North central, east of Luanda. Niger-Congo, Atlantic-Congo, Volta-Congo, Benue-Congo, Bantoid, Southern, Narrow Bantu, Central, H, Yaka (H.30). Dialects: MBANGALA, YONGO. Related to Yaka, Suku, Hungu, Sinji.

MBUKUSHU ***(MBUKUSHI, MAMBUKUSH, MAMPUKUSH, MBUKUHU, THIMBUKUSHU, GOVA, KUSO, CUSSO)*** [MHW] 4,000 in Angola (1997 Andersson and Janson). Southeastern corner, northern bank of the Okavango River. Niger-Congo, Atlantic-Congo, Volta-Congo, Benue-Congo, Bantoid, Southern, Narrow Bantu, Central, K, Kwangwa (K.40). Close to Kwangali, but a separate language. Traditional religion, Christian. NT 1986. See main entry under Namibia.

MBUNDA ***(CHIMBUNDA, MBUUNDA)*** [MCK] 100,000 in Angola (1993 Johnstone). Southeastern. Niger-Congo, Atlantic-Congo, Volta-Congo, Benue-Congo, Bantoid, Southern, Narrow Bantu, Central, K, Chokwe-Luchazi (K.20). Different from Mbunda (Gimbunda, Kimbunu, Mbunu) which is a dialect of Yans (Iyans) in DRC and Zambia and is in Tende-Yanzi group. Dictionary. NT 1983. See main entry under Zambia.

MBUNDU, LOANDA ***(LUANDA, LUNDA, LOANDE, KIMBUNDU, KIMBUNDO, NORTH MBUNDU, NBUNDU, N'BUNDO, DONGO, NDONGO, KINDONGO)*** [MLO] 3,000,000 (1999 WA) or 25% of the population (1990 WA), including 41,000 Ngola (1977 Voegelin and Voegelin). Northwest, Luanda Province. Niger-Congo, Atlantic-Congo, Volta-Congo, Benue-Congo, Bantoid, Southern, Narrow Bantu, Central, H, Mbundu (H.20). Dialects: NJINGA (GINGA, JINGA), MBAMBA (KIMBAMBA, BAMBEIRO), MBAKA (AMBAQUISTA), NGOLA. Related to Songo, Sama, Bolo. Other related languages, dialects, ethnic, or alternate names: Amboim (Mbuiyi), Kibala (Quibala), Lengue (Quilengue), Ngage, Dembo of Cacuta Caenda, Ngengu, Bondo, Quembo, Mussende, Makamba (Macamba). Mbamba may be a separate language. Bible 1980.

MBWELA ***(MBWERA, SHIMBWERA, MBUELA, AMBUELLA, AMBUELA)*** [MFU] 172,000 (1993 Johnstone). Central, east of Benguela. Niger-Congo, Atlantic-Congo, Volta-Congo, Benue-Congo, Bantoid, Southern, Narrow Bantu, Central, K, Chokwe-Luchazi (K.20). Traditional religion, Christian.

NDOMBE ***(DOMBE)*** [NDQ] South and southeast of Benguela. Niger-Congo, Atlantic-Congo, Volta-Congo, Benue-Congo, Bantoid, Southern, Narrow Bantu, Central, R, South Mbundu (R.10).

NDONGA ***(OSHINDONGA, OSIDONGA, AMBO, OCHINDONGA)*** [NDG] Southeast corner, Ovamboland. Niger-Congo, Atlantic-Congo, Volta-Congo, Benue-Congo, Bantoid, Southern, Narrow Bantu, Central, R, Ndonga (R.20). Ngandyera may be a separate language. Partially intelligible with Kwanyama. Highly acculturated. Literacy rate in second language: 75%. Christian, traditional religion. Bible 1954-1986. See main entry under Namibia.

NGANDYERA [NNE] Southeast corner. Niger-Congo, Atlantic-Congo, Volta-Congo, Benue-Congo, Bantoid, Southern, Narrow Bantu, Central, R, Ndonga (R.20). Related to Kwanyama, Ndonga, Kwambi.

NKANGALA ***(CANGALA, NGANGALA)*** [NKN] Central, southeast of Mbwela. Niger-Congo, Atlantic-Congo, Volta-Congo, Benue-Congo, Bantoid, Southern, Narrow Bantu, Central, K, Chokwe-Luchazi (K.20).

NKHUMBI ***(NKUMBI, KHUMBI, HUMBE, NGUMBI, OTJINGUMBI)*** [KHU] 150,000 (1996 UBS). Population total both countries 150,000 or more. Southwestern, between Zemba, Luyana, Umbundu, Nyemba, and Nyaneka. Also spoken in Namibia. Niger-Congo, Atlantic-Congo, Volta-Congo, Benue-Congo, Bantoid, Southern, Narrow Bantu, Central, R, South Mbundu (R.10). Bible portions 1985-1987.

NSONGO ***(SONGO, SUNGU)*** [NSX] 50,000 (1978 UBS). North central, Cuanza River area south of Malanje. Niger-Congo, Atlantic-Congo, Volta-Congo, Benue-Congo, Bantoid, Southern, Narrow Bantu, Central, H, Mbundu (H.20). Related to Loanda Mbundu, Sama, Bolo. Bible portions 1936-1978.

NYANEKA ***(LUNYANEKA, NHANEKA, NHANECA)*** [NYK] 300,000 (1996 UBS). Southwestern. Niger-Congo, Atlantic-Congo, Volta-Congo, Benue-Congo, Bantoid, Southern, Narrow Bantu, Central, R, South Mbundu (R.10). Dialects: HUMBE, MWILA (OLUMUILA, MUILA, HUILA).

NYEMBA ***(GANGUELA, GANGUELLA, NGANGELA, NHEMBA, GANGELA)*** [NBA] 172,000 in Angola (1993 Johnstone). Population total all countries 181,540 or more. South central, Cuchi River area, southeast. Also spoken in Namibia, Zambia. Niger-Congo, Atlantic-Congo, Volta-Congo, Benue-Congo, Bantoid, Southern, Narrow Bantu, Central, K, Chokwe-Luchazi (K.20). Bible portions 1955.

NYENGO ***(NHENGO)*** [NYE] 5,000 (1977 Voegelin and Voegelin). Southeast corner. Niger-Congo, Atlantic-Congo, Volta-Congo, Benue-Congo, Bantoid, Southern, Narrow Bantu, Central, K, Chokwe-Luchazi (K.20).

!OIUNG ***(!OIKUNG)*** [OUN] 1,000 to 5,000 (1977 Voegelin and Voegelin). Southern border with Namibia, surrounded by Luchazi. Khoisan, Southern Africa, Northern.

PORTUGUESE [POR] 57,600 in Angola (1993). Indo-European, Italic, Romance, Italo-Western, Western, Gallo-Iberian, Ibero-Romance, West Iberian, Portuguese-Galician. Official language. Bible 1751, in press (1993). See main entry under Portugal.

RUUND ***(URUUND, NORTHERN LUNDA, LUUNDA, CHILU WUNDA, MUATIAMVUA)*** [RND] Northeastern. Niger-Congo, Atlantic-Congo, Volta-Congo, Benue-Congo, Bantoid, Southern, Narrow Bantu, Central, K, Salampasu-Ndembo (K.30). NT 1933-1996. See main entry under DRC.

SAMA ***(KISSAMA, QUISSAMA)*** [SMD] 17,000 (1990 Atlas of the World's Languages). Coastal, south of Luanda. Niger-Congo, Atlantic-Congo, Volta-Congo, Benue-Congo, Bantoid, Southern, Narrow Bantu, Central, H, Mbundu (H.20). Related to Loanda Mbundu, Nsongo, Bolo.

UMBUNDU ***(UMBUNDO, M'BUNDO, QUIMBUNDO, OVIMBUNDU, SOUTH MBUNDU, NANO, MBALI, MBARI, MBUNDU BENGUELLA)*** [MNF] 4,000,000 (1995 WA) or 38% of the population (1990 WA). Population total both countries 4,003,000. West, Benguela District. Also spoken in Namibia. Niger-Congo, Atlantic-Congo, Volta-Congo, Benue-Congo, Bantoid, Southern, Narrow Bantu, Central, R, South Mbundu (R.10). Related to Nkhumbi, Ndombe, Nyaneka. 'Umbundu' is a better name than 'Mbundu Benguella'. Trade language. Dictionary. Grammar. Christian, traditional religion. Bible 1963.

YAKA ***(KIYAKA, IAKA, IYAKA, IACA)*** [YAF] 80,000 in Angola (1993 Johnstone). North central corner, east of the Kongo. Niger-Congo, Atlantic-Congo, Volta-Congo, Benue-Congo, Bantoid, Southern, Narrow Bantu, Central, H, Yaka (H.30). Dialects: YAKA, NGOONGO. Bible portions 1938-1957. See main entry under DRC.

YAUMA [YAX] Southeast, Kwando (Cuando) River area. Also spoken in Zambia. Unclassified. Bible portions 1978.

YOMBE ***(KIYOMBE, KIOMBI, IOMBE, BAYOMBE)*** [YOM] Cabinda. Niger-Congo, Atlantic-Congo, Volta-Congo, Benue-Congo, Bantoid, Southern, Narrow Bantu, Central, H, Kongo (H.10). Dialects: MBALA (MUMBALA), VUNGUNYA (KIVUNGUNYA, YOMBE CLASSIQUE). Distinct enough from Kongo-Fioti to need separate literature. Christian, traditional religion. See main entry under DRC.

ZEMBA ***(DHIMBA, DIMBA, OTJIDHIMBA, HIMBA, TJIMBA, SIMBA, CHIMBA, OLUTHIMBA)*** [DHM] 18,000 in Angola (1996 UBS). Population total both countries 30,000. Southwest corner. Also spoken in Namibia. Niger-Congo, Atlantic-Congo, Volta-Congo, Benue-Congo, Bantoid, Southern, Narrow Bantu, Central, R, Herero (R.30). Bible portions 1970-1984.

BENIN

Republic of Benin. République du Benin. Formerly Dahomey. National or official language: French. 5,781,000 (1998 UN). Literacy rate 28%. Also includes Kyenga 1,000, Mòoré, Ngangam. Information mainly from SIL 1972-1999; J. Bendor-Samuel 1989. Traditional religion, Christian, Muslim. Blind population 175. Deaf institutions: 1. Data accuracy estimate: A2, B. The number of languages listed for Benin is 51. Of those, all are living languages. Diversity index 0.90.

AGUNA ***(AWUNA, AGUNACO)*** [AUG] 3,470 (1992 census). Zou Province. Niger-Congo, Atlantic-Congo, Volta-Congo, Kwa, Left Bank, Gbe. Bilingualism in Fon-Gbe. Traditional religion.

AJA-GBE ***(AJA, ADJA, HWÈ)*** [AJG] 360,000 in Benin (1993 Johnstone). Population total both countries 474,800. Mono and Atlantique provinces. Also spoken in Togo. Niger-Congo, Atlantic-Congo, Volta-Congo, Kwa, Left Bank, Gbe, Aja. Dialects: DÒGBÓ-GBÈ, HWÈGBÈ. Bilingualism in Ewe, French. Literacy rate in first language: 1% to 5%. Traditional religion, Christian.

ANII ***(GISIDA, BASILA, BASSILA, BASECA, WINJI-WINJI, OUINJI-OUINJI)*** [BLO] 7,000 in Benin (1991). Population total both countries 11,100. Around Bassila, Atakora Province. Also spoken in Togo. Niger-Congo, Atlantic-Congo, Volta-Congo, Kwa, Nyo, Potou-Tano, Basila-Adele. Dialects: GIKOLODJYA, GILEMPLA, GISEDA. Closely related to Akpe of Togo. Bilingualism in French. Literacy rate in second language: 1%. Muslim.

ANUFO ***(CHOKOSI, CHAKOSI, CHOKOSSI, TCHOKOSSI)*** [CKO] 10,000 in Benin (1991). Atakora Province. Niger-Congo, Atlantic-Congo, Volta-Congo, Kwa, Nyo, Potou-Tano, Tano, Central, Bia, Northern. Bilingualism in French. Speakers' name for themselves is 'Anufo'. Literacy rate in first language: 1% to 5%. Traditional religion, Muslim. Bible portions 1993. See main entry under Ghana.

AYIZO-GBE ***(AYIZO, AYZO)*** [AYB] 227,000 (1993 Johnstone). Mono and Atlantique provinces. Niger-Congo, Atlantic-Congo, Volta-Congo, Kwa, Left Bank, Gbe, Aja. Dialect: KADAGBE (KADA-GBE). Toli-gbe may be inherently intelligible. Bilingualism in Ewe, Fon. Traditional religion.

BARIBA ***(BAATONU, BAATOMBU, BARUBA, BARGU, BURGU, BERBA, BARBA, BOGUNG, BARGAWA, BARGANCHI)*** [BBA] 460,000 in Benin (1995 R. Jones). Population total both countries 560,000 (1995 R. Jones SIM). Central, north, Borgou Province. Also spoken in Nigeria. Niger-Congo, Atlantic-Congo, Volta-Congo, North, Gur, Bariba. Bilingualism in French. The people's name for themselves is 'Baatonu', plural 'Baatombu', for the language 'Baatonum'. Distinct from Biali (Berba). Literacy rate in first language: 1% to 30%. Muslim, traditional religion, Christian. Bible, in press (1997).

BASA [BQA] 1,000 (1991 Vanderaa). Zou Province, three villages. Niger-Congo, Atlantic-Congo, Volta-Congo, Kwa, Nyo, Potou-Tano, Tano, Central, Akan. Related to Ashanti in Ghana. All people are trilingual in Cabe and Fon-gbe. Different from Bassa of Nigeria or Bassa of Liberia and Sierra Leone. Traditional religion.

BIALI ***(BIERI, BJERI, BJERB, BERBA)*** [BEH] 64,500 in Benin (1991). Population total both countries 66,000 (1991 L. Vanderaa). Atakora Province. Also spoken in Burkina Faso. Niger-Congo, Atlantic-Congo, Volta-Congo, North, Gur, Central, Northern, Oti-Volta, Eastern. Close to Nateni. Many monolinguals. Others use French as second language. The language is called 'Biali' or 'Bieri', the people 'Bialaba'. 'Berba' is the French name. Historical accounts claim they originated in the F'ada Ngourma area of Burkina Faso. Different from Bariba (Berba). Literacy rate in first language: Below 1%. Traditional religion, Christian.

BOKO ***(BOKONYA, BOKKO, BOO, BUSA-BOKO)*** [BQC] 70,000 in Benin (1995). Population total both countries 110,000 (1995 Ross Jones SIM). Borgu Province. Also spoken in Nigeria. Niger-Congo, Mande, Eastern, Eastern, Busa. Closely related languages: Busa-Bisã (Nigeria), Bokobaru (Nigeria), Shanga (Nigeria). Difficult intelligibility causes them to require separate literature. 90% lexical similarity between Busa-Bisã, Bokobaru, Shanga. Bilingual level estimates for French are 0 80%, 1 10%, 2 4%, 3 3%, 4 2%, 5 1%. Speakers use French (Benin), English (Nigeria), Hausa, Yoruba, Bariba, or Fulfulde as second language when speaking to people from those groups. Each of the related languages has strong ethnic pride. SOV; genitives before noun heads; articles, adjectives, numerals, relatives after noun heads; question word initial or final; 4 suffixes; word order distinguishes subject, object, indirect object; postpositions; person, number, aspect indicated in subject pronoun; tone indicates verb aspect; passives; CV, CCV; tonal. Literacy rate in second language: 6%. Savannah. Interfluvial. Peasant agriculturalists. Traditional religion, Muslim, Christian. Bible 1992.

BOULBA ***(BULBA, NOOTRE, NOTRE, BURUSA)*** [BLY] 800 (1991 SIL). Atakora Province, Tanguieta town. Niger-Congo, Atlantic-Congo, Volta-Congo, North, Gur, Central, Northern, Oti-Volta, Western, Nootre. Bilingualism in French. Traditional religion.

CABE ***(CAABE, EDE CABE)*** [CBJ] 80,000 (1991 L. Vanderaa). Borgou and Zou provinces. Niger-Congo, Atlantic-Congo, Volta-Congo, Benue-Congo, Defoid, Yoruboid, Edekiri. Bilingualism in Ewe, Fon, Yoruba. Literacy rate in first language: Below 1%. Traditional religion, Christian.

CENKA [CEN] Borgou Province, Kasa town only. Niger-Congo, Atlantic-Congo, Volta-Congo, Kwa, Unclassified. Bilingualism in Dendi, French. Speakers are shifting to Dendi. Investigation needed: bilingual proficiency in Dendi. Literacy rate in second language: Below 1%.

CI-GBE ***(CI)*** [CIB] Mono Province. Niger-Congo, Atlantic-Congo, Volta-Congo, Kwa, Left Bank, Gbe. Bilingualism in Ewe, Fon, French. Literacy rate in first language: Below 1%. Traditional religion.

DENDI ***(DANDAWA)*** [DEN] 30,000 in Benin (1995 R. Jones SIM). Population total both countries 31,000. Atakora and Borgou provinces, along the Niger River, from the Medru River to the Nigeria border, and down to Kandi. Many at Djogou. Also spoken in Nigeria. Nilo-Saharan, Songhai, Southern. Closely related language to Zarma and Songai, They form a dialect continuum. Bilingualism in French. Literacy rate in first language: 1% to 30%. Radio programs. Muslim, Christian. NT 1995.

DITAMMARI ***(DITAMARI, TAMARI, SOMBA)*** [TBZ] 120,000 (1991 UBS). From the Togo border toward Natitingou, Atakora Province. Niger-Congo, Atlantic-Congo, Volta-Congo, North, Gur, Central, Northern, Oti-Volta, Eastern. 65% intelligibility with Tamberma of Togo. 'Somba' is an ethnic name applied to several related dialect groups; mainly to the Ditammari. Bilingualism in Bariba, French. Literacy rate in first language: 1% to 5%. Muslim, traditional religion, Christian. NT 1989.

FON-GBE ***(FO, FON, FONNU, FOGBE, DAHOMEEN, DJEDJI)*** [FOA] 1,400,000 in Benin (1993 Johnstone). Population total both countries 1,436,000. South central, Weme, Atlantique, and Zou provinces. Also spoken in Togo. Niger-Congo, Atlantic-Congo, Volta-Congo, Kwa, Left Bank, Gbe, Fon. Dialects: FO, KOTAFOU. Bilingualism in Gun-Gbe, French. Language of wider communication. Literacy rate in first language: 1% to 30%. Traditional religion, Christian. NT 1993.

FOODO [FOD] 12,425 in Benin (1979). Population total both countries 13,425. Atakora Province, Semere town. Also spoken in Ghana. Niger-Congo, Atlantic-Congo, Volta-Congo, Kwa, Nyo, Potou-Tano, Tano, Guang, North Guang. Bilingualism in French, Hausa. Originally from Ghana; probably from the village of Salaga. Literacy rate in first language: 1% to 5%. Muslim.

FRENCH [FRN] 16,700 in Benin (1993 Johnstone). Indo-European, Italic, Romance, Italo-Western, Western, Gallo-Iberian, Gallo-Romance, Gallo-Rhaetian, Oïl, French. Official language. Bible 1530-1986. See main entry under France.

FULFULDE, BENIN-TOGO ***(PEULH, PEUL)*** [FUE] 280,000 in Benin (1993 Johnstone). Population total all countries 328,000 or more. Atakora and Borgou provinces, villages and encampments. Also spoken in Nigeria, Togo. Niger-Congo, Atlantic-Congo, Atlantic, Northern, Senegambian, Fula-Wolof, Fulani,

West Central. Dialect: FULBE-BORGU. Bilingualism in French. The Gando people speak Fulfulde, but are ethnically Boko and Baatonu (Bariba). Literacy rate in first language: 1%. Herdsmen, sell milk and cheese. Muslim, traditional religion, Christian.

GEN-GBE ***(GE, MINA-GEN, MINA, GUIN, GEGBE, POPO)*** [GEJ] 126,000 in Benin (1993 Johnstone). Mono and Atlantique provinces. Niger-Congo, Atlantic-Congo, Volta-Congo, Kwa, Left Bank, Gbe, Mina. Bilingualism in Ewe, Fon, French. The name of the people is 'Mina'. Trade language. Literacy rate in first language: 1% to 5%. Traditional religion, Christian. NT 1962. See main entry under Togo.

GOURMANCHÉMA ***(GOURMANTCHE, GURMA, GOULMANCEMA, GULIMANCEMA, MIGULIMANCEMA)*** [GUX] 50,000 in Benin (1993 Johnstone). Northern, Atakora and Borgou provinces. Niger-Congo, Atlantic-Congo, Volta-Congo, North, Gur, Central, Northern, Oti-Volta, Gurma. Bilingualism in Mòoré. Literacy rate in first language: 5% to 10%. Traditional religion, Christian. NT 1958-1990. See main entry under Burkina Faso.

GUN-GBE ***(ALADA, ALADA-GBE, GUN-ALADA, GUN, GOUN, EGUN, GU, GUGBE)*** [GUW] 320,000 in Benin (1993 Johnstone). Population total both countries 500,000 (1991 UBS). Southeast, Alada to Porto Novo, Weme Province. Also spoken in Nigeria. Niger-Congo, Atlantic-Congo, Volta-Congo, Kwa, Left Bank, Gbe, Aja. Bilingualism in Fon, Ewe, French. Literacy rate in first language: 1% to 5%. Traditional religion, Christian. Bible 1923-1972.

HAUSA [HUA] Atacora and Borgou provinces. Afro-Asiatic, Chadic, West, A, A.1. Trade language. Muslim, traditional religion, Christian. Bible 1932-1996. See main entry under Nigeria.

ICA ***(EDE ICA)*** [ICA] 39,000 in Benin (1991 L. Vanderaa). Population total both countries 39,000 or more. Zou Province. Also spoken in Togo. Niger-Congo, Atlantic-Congo, Volta-Congo, Benue-Congo, Defoid, Yoruboid, Edekiri. Literacy rate in first language: Below 1%. Traditional religion.

IDACA ***(IDAACA, EDE IDACA)*** [IDD] 30,000 (1991 L. Vanderaa). Zou Province. Niger-Congo, Atlantic-Congo, Volta-Congo, Benue-Congo, Defoid, Yoruboid, Edekiri. Bilingualism in Yoruba. Many loan words from Fon-gbe. Literacy rate in first language: Below 1%. Traditional religion.

IFÈ ***(BAATE, ANA, ANA-IFE, ANAGO, EDE IFE)*** [IFE] 80,000 in Benin (1990 SIL). Population total both countries 155,000. Zou Province. Also spoken in Togo. Niger-Congo, Atlantic-Congo, Volta-Congo, Benue-Congo, Defoid, Yoruboid, Edekiri. Bilingualism in Yoruba. Literacy rate in first language: Below 1%. Traditional religion. Bible portions 1995.

IJE ***(HOLI, EDE IJE)*** [IJJ] 20,000 (1991 L. Vanderaa). Zou Province. Niger-Congo, Atlantic-Congo, Volta-Congo, Benue-Congo, Defoid, Yoruboid, Edekiri. Bilingualism in Yoruba. Traditional religion.

KABIYÉ ***(KABRE, KABYE, KABURE, CABRAIS, CABRAI)*** [KBP] 30,000 in Benin (1991 Vanderaa). North, Atakora Province. Niger-Congo, Atlantic-Congo, Volta-Congo, North, Gur, Central, Southern, Grusi, Eastern. Traditional religion. NT 1996. See main entry under Togo.

KO-GBE ***(KO)*** [KQK] 20,000 (1991 L. Vanderaa). Mono Province. Niger-Congo, Atlantic-Congo, Volta-Congo, Kwa, Left Bank, Gbe. Bilingualism in Ewe, Fon, French. Traditional religion.

LAMA ***(LAMBA, LOSSO)*** [LAS] 60,000 in Benin (1993 Johnstone). Atakora Province. Niger-Congo, Atlantic-Congo, Volta-Congo, North, Gur, Central, Doghosie-Gurunsi, Grusi-Gouin, Grusi, Central, Southern, Grusi, Eastern. Dialects: KANTE, KADJALLA. Related to Tem and Kabre. Bilingualism in French, Kabiye. 'Lama' is their name for the people and language, 'Lamba' is the French name. 'Losso' refers to people on the Losso Plain and to Nawdm. Literacy rate in first language: 1% to 5%. Traditional religion. NT 1993. See main entry under Togo.

LUKPA ***(LOKPA, LOGBA, LEGBA, LUGBA, DOMPAGO)*** [DOP] 42,000 in Benin (1993 Johnstone). Population total both countries 125,000 (1992 UBS). West Djougou and border areas, Atakora Province. Primarily around Kémérida. Also spoken in Togo. Niger-Congo, Atlantic-Congo, Volta-Congo, North, Gur, Central, Southern, Grusi, Eastern. Different from Logba of Ghana. Literacy rate in first language: 5% to 30%. Traditional religion, Christian, Muslim. NT 1977.

MAXI-GBE ***(MAXI, MAHI)*** [MXL] 66,000 in Benin (1993 Johnstone). Population total both countries 91,000 (1993 Johnstone). Zou Province. Also spoken in Togo. Niger-Congo, Atlantic-Congo, Volta-Congo, Kwa, Left Bank, Gbe, Fon. Bilingualism in Ewe, Fon, French. Traditional religion.

MBELIME ***(MBILME, "NIENDI", "NIENDE")*** [MQL] 24,500 (1991 L. Vanderaa). Atakora Province. Niger-Congo, Atlantic-Congo, Volta-Congo, North, Gur, Central, Northern, Oti-Volta, Eastern. Related to Ditamari and Tamberma of Togo. Bilingualism in French. "Niende" is derogatory. Traditional religion.

MOKOLE ***(MOKOLLÉ, MOKWALE, MONKOLE, FÉRI)*** [MKL] 65,500 (1991 L. Vanderaa). Borgou Province, Kandi and villages to the north and east. Niger-Congo, Atlantic-Congo, Volta-Congo, Benue-Congo, Defoid, Yoruboid, Edekiri. Language related to Yoruba, but culture to Baatonu (Bariba), among whom they live. Bilingualism in French. Literacy rate in first language: Below 1%. Traditional religion, Muslim, a few Christian. NT 1994.

NAGO ***(NAGOTS, NAGOT, EDE NAGO)*** [NQG] 175,000 (1991 L. Vanderaa). Weme and Atakora provinces. Niger-Congo, Atlantic-Congo, Volta-Congo, Benue-Congo, Defoid, Yoruboid, Edekiri. Some speakers are bilingual in Yoruba. Muslim, Christian.

NATENI [NTM] 45,000 (1993 Johnstone). Atakora Province. The Natemba are in Toukountouna District, Tayaba in Tanguiéta District, Kuntemba in Kobly, Matiri, and Tanguiéta districts, Okoma in Tanguiéta and Kouandé districts. Tayakou is the center of traditional beliefs and practices. Niger-Congo, Atlantic-Congo, Volta-Congo, North, Gur, Central, Northern, Oti-Volta, Gurma. Dialects: NATENI (NATEMBA, NATIMBA), TAYARI (TAYABA), KUNTENI (KUNTEMBA), OKONI (OKOMA). Close to Bimoba. Dialect names in parentheses are for the speakers. Bilingualism in Bariba, French. Literacy rate in first language: 1% to 5%. Traditional religion, Christian.

PILA ***(PILAPILA, KPILAKPILA, YOM)*** [PIL] 70,000 (1993 Johnstone). Northwest, Djougou area, Atakora Province. Niger-Congo, Atlantic-Congo, Volta-Congo, North, Gur, Central, Northern, Oti-Volta, Yom-Nawdm. Close to Nawdm of Togo. 10% speak Dendi and 3% speak Dompago as second language. Ethnic groups: Temba (upland), Yoba (lowland). Literacy rate in first language: 2%. Traditional religion, Muslim, Christian. NT 1985.

SAXWE-GBE ***(SAXWE)*** [SXW] Mono Province. Niger-Congo, Atlantic-Congo, Volta-Congo, Kwa, Left Bank, Gbe. Bilingualism in Ewe, Fon, French. Traditional religion.

SETO-GBE ***(SETO)*** [STS] Ouéme (Weme) Province. Also spoken in Nigeria. Niger-Congo, Atlantic-Congo, Volta-Congo, Kwa, Left Bank, Gbe, Aja. Bilingualism in Ewe, French, Fon. Traditional religion.

SOLA ***(SORUBA, BIJOBE, BIYOBE, SOROUBA, SOLLA, UYOBE, MIYOBE, MEYOBE, KAYOBE, KUYOBE, SOLAMBA)*** [SOY] 7,000 in Benin (1991). Population total both countries 8,700 (1996 UBS). Atakora Province. Also spoken in Togo. Niger-Congo, Atlantic-Congo, Volta-Congo, North, Gur, Central, Northern, Oti-Volta, Gurma. Bilingualism in French, Bariba. Literacy rate in first language: Below 1%. Traditional religion, a few Christian.

TEM ***(KOTOKOLI, COTOCOLI, TIM, TIMU, TEMBE)*** [KDH] 43,000 in Benin (1993 Johnstone). Niger-Congo, Atlantic-Congo, Volta-Congo, North, Gur, Central, Southern, Grusi, Eastern. Bilingualism in French, Kabiye. Literacy rate in first language: 1% to 5%. Muslim. See main entry under Togo.

TOFIN-GBE ***(TOFIN)*** [TFI] 66,000 (1993 Johnstone). Weme and Atlantique provinces. Niger-Congo, Atlantic-Congo, Volta-Congo, Kwa, Left Bank, Gbe, Aja. Bilingualism in Ewe, Fon, French. Traditional religion, Christian.

TOLI-GBE ***(TOLI)*** [TLH] Weme and Atlantique provinces. Niger-Congo, Atlantic-Congo, Volta-Congo, Kwa, Left Bank, Gbe, Aja. A dialect or closely related language to Ayizo-gbe and Kadagbe. Bilingualism in Ewe, Fon, French. Traditional religion.

WAAMA ***(YOABU, YOABOU)*** [WWA] 40,000 (1989 SIL). Atakora Province, at least 20 villages. Niger-Congo, Atlantic-Congo, Volta-Congo, North, Gur, Central, Northern, Oti-Volta, Eastern. Dialects: WAAMA, TANGAMMA. Bilingualism in Bariba. Literacy rate in first language: 1% to 10%. NT 1994.

WACI-GBE ***(WATYU, WACI, OUATCHI)*** [WCI] 110,000 in Benin (1993 Johnstone). Mono Province. Niger-Congo, Atlantic-Congo, Volta-Congo, Kwa, Left Bank, Gbe. Bilingualism in Ewe, French, Fon. Investigation needed: intelligibility. Literacy rate in first language: Below 1%. Traditional religion. See main entry under Togo.

WEME-GBE ***(WEME)*** [WEM] 60,000 (1991 L. Vanderaa). Weme and Atlantique provinces. Niger-Congo, Atlantic-Congo, Volta-Congo, Kwa, Left Bank, Gbe, Aja. Bilingualism in Ewe, French, Fon. Traditional religion.

XWEDA-GBE ***(XWEDA)*** [XWD] 54,000 (1991 L. Vanderaa). Atlantique Province. Niger-Congo, Atlantic-Congo, Volta-Congo, Kwa, Left Bank, Gbe. Bilingualism in Ewe, French, Fon. Traditional religion.

XWELA-GBE ***(PHERA, XWELA)*** [XWE] Mono Province. Niger-Congo, Atlantic-Congo, Volta-Congo, Kwa, Left Bank, Gbe. Bilingualism in Ewe, French, Fon. Traditional religion.

XWLA-GBE ***(PHLA, XWLA)*** [XWL] 30,000 (1991 L. Vanderaa). Mono, Weme, and Atlantique provinces. Niger-Congo, Atlantic-Congo, Volta-Congo, Kwa, Left Bank, Gbe, Aja. Bilingualism in Ewe, French, Fon. Traditional religion.

YORUBA ***(YOOBA, YARIBA, EDE-YORUBA)*** [YOR] 465,000 in Benin (1993 Johnstone). Zou and Ouéme provinces. Niger-Congo, Atlantic-Congo, Volta-Congo, Benue-Congo, Defoid, Yoruboid, Edekiri. Dialect: EGBA. Bilingualism in French. Literacy rate in first language: 1% to 30%. Traditional religion, Christian, Muslim. Bible 1884-1966. See main entry under Nigeria.

ZARMA ***(DYERMA, DJERMA, ZERMA)*** [DJE] Borgou Province. Nilo-Saharan, Songhai, Southern. Bilingualism in French. Literacy rate in first language: 1% to 30%. Muslim. Bible 1990. See main entry under Niger.

BOTSWANA

Republic of Botswana. Formerly Bechuanaland. National or official languages: English, Tswana. 1,570,000 (1998 UN). 220,000 sq. miles. Capital: Gaborone. Literacy rate 68.9% over 15 years old in Tswana (1997 Central Statistics Office), 25% to 30% in English. Also includes Bemba 2,000, Hindi, Lozi 14,000, Nyanja, Shona, Northern Sotho 700, Southern Sotho, Urdu, Xhosa, Zulu, Chinese 1,000 (1999). Information mainly from J. Bendor-Samuel 1989; Andersson and Janson 1997; Sue Hasselbring LBT 1995-9. Christian, traditional religion, Muslim, Baha'i. Blind population 3,347 blind, 11,211 seeing impaired (1991 census). Deaf population 990 deaf, 6,477 hearing impaired (1991 census). Data accuracy estimate: B. The number of languages listed for Botswana is 26. Of those, all are living languages. Diversity index 0.44.

AFRIKAANS [AFK] 20,000 in Botswana (1995 LBT). Spoken as mother tongue mainly in commercial farms and Ghanzi village, Ghanzi District, in the southern half of Kgalagadi District, especially near the South Africa border, and in Takatokwane village, Kweneng District. Indo-European, Germanic, West, Low Saxon-Low Franconian, Low Franconian. Spoken as mother tongue by Afrikaners (Ghanzi District) and by people of mixed racial background (Kweneng and Kgalagadi districts). Literacy rate in first language: 100% in Ghanzi, 50% in Kweneng and Kgalagadi. Literacy rate in second language: 75% in Kweneng and Kgalagadi districts in Tswana, 50% in English; few in Ghanzi District in Tswana, most in English. Christian. Bible 1933-1983. See main entry under South Africa.

/ANDA ***(HANDÁ, //ANI, HANDÁDAM, HANDAKWE-DAM, HANDA-KHWE, TS'ÉXA, TS'EXA)*** [HNH] 1,000 (1997 Brenzinger). Northwest District, Khwai River, Mababe. Near the Kxoe. Khoisan, Southern Africa, Central, Tshu-Khwe, Northwest. Related to Kxoe. Literacy rate in second language: 15-29 years 70% Tswana, 50% English; 30-54 years 40% Tswana, 10% English. Traditional religion, Christian.

BIRWA [BRL] 10,000 (1993 Johnstone). Population total both countries 10,000 or more. Central District, Bobonong Subdistrict. East of Selebi-Phikwe in the villages: Bobonong, Kobojango, Semolale, Motalatau, and Mathathane. Also spoken in South Africa. Niger-Congo, Atlantic-Congo, Volta-Congo, Benue-Congo, Bantoid, Southern, Narrow Bantu, Central, S, Sotho-Tswana (S.30), Sotho. The population reported is for 'Shona' in Botswana.

DETI ***(DETI-KHWE, TETE, TETI, TLETLE)*** [DET] Central District, Boteti Subdistrict, in the villages along the Boteti River. Khoisan, Southern Africa, Central, Tshu-Khwe, Central. Dialects: K'ERE-KHWE, TSH'EREKHWE. Related to Shua. Reported to be endangered. The Deti are more acculturated to Tswana than the Shua and other Khoisan groups.

ENGLISH ***(SEKGOA)*** [ENG] Indo-European, Germanic, West, English. International trade, medium of western influences, language of instruction from fifth grade, written language, official purposes, as second language. Official language. Taught as a subject from the beginning of primary school as a required subject. Officially becomes the language of instruction in Standard 5. Standard 7 exams are written in English. Medium of instruction. Newspapers, magazines, radio programs, TV. Bible 1535-1989. See main entry under United Kingdom.

//GANA ***(G//ANA, G//ANA-KHWE, GXANA, GXANNA, DXANA, KANAKHOE)*** [GNK] 1,000 (1998 Hasselbring). Ghanzi District, New Xadi and Ghanzi villages, Ghanzi commercial farms, Central Kalahari Game Reserve. Central District, Boteti Subdistrict, cattleposts south and west of Rakops village. East of Naro, north of /Gwi. Khoisan, Southern Africa, Central, Tshu-Khwe, Northwest. Dialects: DOMKHOE, G//AAKHWE (G//AA), G//ANAKHWE (KANAKHOE), /KHESSÁKHOE. May be inherently intelligible with /Gwi. Investigation needed: intelligibility with /Gwi. Literacy rate in second language: 15-29 years 40% Tswana, 2% English; 30-54 years 2% Tswana, 0% English; 55+ years 0%. Hunter-gatherers, herders employed by cattleowners.

GANÁDI ***(GANÁDE)*** [GNE] Northeastern. Khoisan, Southern Africa, Central, Tshu-Khwe, North Central. Related to Shua.

/GWI ***(G//WIKHWE, G//WI, G/WI, GCWI, G!WIKWE, G/WIKHWE, DCUI)*** [GWJ] 800 (1998 Hasselbring). Kweneng District: Dutlwe, Serinane, Takotokwane, Kautwane, Khekhenye, Letihakeng, Morwamosu, and Tsetseng villages. Ghanzi District: New Xade, East Hanahai, and Kacgae villages. Khoisan, Southern Africa, Central, Tshu-Khwe, Southwest. Dialect: KHUTE. May be inherently intelligible with //Gana. Investigation needed: intelligibility with //Gana. Literacy rate in second language: 15-29 years 40% Tswana, 2% English; 30-54 years 2% Tswana, 0% English; 55+ years 0%. Hunter-gatherers.

HERERO ***(OTJIHERERO, OCHIHERERO)*** [HER] 31,000 in Botswana (1997 Andersson and Janson). Scattered among many ethnic groups, usually having their own areas within larger towns and villages: Northwest District (Maun, Gomare, Sehitwa, Makakung, Nokaneng, Shakawe, Nxaunxau, and western cattleposts), Central District (Mahalapye, Toromoja, Rakops, Mokoboxane, Letlhakane),

Ghanzi District (Charles Hill, Ghanzi, Makunda, Dryhoek, New Kanagas, Dekar), Kgalagadi District (Tsabong, Omaweneno, Werda), Kgatleng District (Morwa). Niger-Congo, Atlantic-Congo, Volta-Congo, Benue-Congo, Bantoid, Southern, Narrow Bantu, Central, R, Herero (R.30). All ages. Some older speakers are moving back to Namibia. Spoken by the Ovaherero and Ovambanderu peoples. Erroneously called 'Damara'. Most came to Botswana as refugees from Namibia in the early 1900s. Dictionary. Grammar. Literacy rate in first language: Nearly 60%. Literacy rate in second language: Nearly 60% in Tswana. Christian, traditional religion. Bible 1987. See main entry under Namibia.

HIETSHWARE ***(CHWARE, TSHWA, CUA, KUA, TYUA, TYHUA, SARWA, SESARWA, HAITSHUARI, HIOTSHUWAU, HIOCHUWAU, TSHUWAU, CHUWAU, GABAKE-NTSHORI, G//ABAKE, MASARWA, TATI, TATI BUSHMAN, KWE-ETSHORI KWEE, KWE, KWE-TSHORI)*** [HIE] 3,000 in Botswana (1976 P. Johnstone). Population total both countries 4,600. Central District, especially Mahalapye, Serowe subdistricts and Northeast District. Primarily on cattleposts and in 'settlements'. Also spoken in Zimbabwe. Khoisan, Southern Africa, Central, Tshu-Khwe, Northeast. Many children speak only Tswana, some only Hietshware, some both. Nomadic. Literacy rate in second language: 15-29 years 25% in Tswana, 20% in English; 30-54 years 2% in Tswana, 2% in English; 55+ years 0%. Herdsmen on cattleposts for owners; some gathering. Traditional religion, Christian.

ǂHUA ***(ǂHUA-OWANI, /HUA, /HÛ)*** [HUC] 1,000 to 1,500 (GR). Southern Kalahari Desert, Kweneng District. Sasi are in southwestern Mahalapye Subdistrict of the Central District. Khoisan, Southern Africa, Southern, Hua. Dialects: ǂHUA, SASI. Related to !Xóõ. Most over 50 years old. Reported to be diminishing in number.

JU/'HOAN ***(KUNG-TSUMKWE, XÛ, XUN, KUNG, !XO, JU'OASI, ZHU'OASI, DZU'OASI, TSUMKWE)*** [KTZ] 4,000 to 8,000 in Botswana (1995 LBT). Population total both countries 4,000 to 8,000 or more. Northwest District, on Namibia and Angola borders, north of ǂKx'au//'ein. Also spoken in Namibia. Khoisan, Southern Africa, Northern. Dialects: DZU'OASI (SSU GHASSI, ZHU'OASE), NOGAU (AGAU). May be intelligible with ǂKx'au//'ein. Speakers use the name 'Ju/'hoan' for themselves. Traditional religion, Christian. Bible portions 1974.

KALANGA ***(CHIKALANGA, KALAKA, SEKALAÑA, SEKALAKA)*** [KCK] 160,000 in Botswana (1993 P. Johnstone). Population total both countries 321,000. The entire Northeast District, and the eastern third of Central district. Also spoken in Zimbabwe. Niger-Congo, Atlantic-Congo, Volta-Congo, Benue-Congo, Bantoid, Southern, Narrow Bantu, Central, S, Shona (S.10). Dialects: NYAI, IKALANGA, TALAHUNDRA, LILIMA (HUMBE), PERI, NAJWA. Najwa speakers were Nambya speakers from Zimbabwe who moved to Botswana and settled along the Boteti River. Some Kalanga speakers also moved there. Najwa is now more similar to Kalanga than to Nambya. But the Najwa are borrowing many Tswana words. The Kalanga spoken in Boteti is more like Najwa than other Kalanga dialects. Bilingualism in Tswana. Resistance to pressures to adopt Tswana language and culture is led by men. Different from Kalanga (KiKalanga, Holoholo) of DRC. Dictionary. Grammar. Literacy rate in first language: 90%. Literacy rate in second language: 70% in Tswana, 85% in English. NT 1999.

KGALAGADI ***(KHALAGARI, KHALAKADI, KXHALAXADI, QHALAXARZI, SHEKGALAGADI)*** [XKV] 35,000 in Botswana (1995 LBT). Population total both countries 35,000 or more. South and central, along the South Africa border, northern half of Kgalagadi District, western half of Kweneng and western half of Southern districts. Ghanzi District: Ghanzi, Kanagas, Tsotsha, Kuke, Karakobis, Ncojane, Kule, Charles Hill, New Xade, Dekar, and Grootlaagte villages. Northwest District: Sehitwa and Maun. Also spoken in Namibia. Niger-Congo, Atlantic-Congo, Volta-Congo, Benue-Congo, Bantoid, Southern, Narrow Bantu, Central, S, Sotho-Tswana (S.30), Kgalagadi. Dialects: NGOLOGA, SHAGA, KGALAGADI, BOLAONGWE, PEDI, PHALENG. Ngologa is the largest dialect. It may be 2 separate languages. A separate language from Tswana. Bilingualism in Tswana, English, Afrikaans. Investigation needed: intelligibility with dialects. SVO; genitives, articles, adjectives, numerals, relatives after noun heads; question word final; word order distinguishes Subject, Object, Indirect Object; Verb Affixes mark person and number; passives formed by suffix *-w*; causatives formed by suffix *-is*; comparative locatives; CV; tonal. Literacy rate in second language: 15-29 85% Tswana, 55% English; 30-54 50% Tswana, 15% English; 55+ 20% Tswana, 2% English. Semi-arid desert. Plains. Sedentary pastoralists. Christian.

ǂKX'AU//'EIN ***(KUNG-GOBABIS, //AU//EI, //X'AU//'E, =KX'AU//'EI, AUEN, KAUKAU, KOKO)*** [AUE] 3,000 in Botswana (1999 Hasselbring). Ghanzi District: Grootelaagte, Kanagas, Ghanzi villages and on the commercial farms. Khoisan, Southern Africa, Northern. Dialect: NOGAU. Most bilinguals use Naro as second language; next most common is Tswana. The people call themselves and their language 'ǂkx'au//'ein'. Literacy rate in second language: 14-29 years 40% Tswana, 10% English; 30-54 years 2% Tswana, English 0%; 55+ years 0%. Traditional religion, Christian. Bible Y. See main entry under Namibia.

KXOE ***(KHOE, XUN, "WATER BUSHMEN", "MBARAKWENA")*** [XUU] 1,700 to 2,000 or more in Botswana (1998 Brenzinger). Northwest District: Gan, Cadikarauwe, Mohembo, Shakawe, Kaputura,

/Ao-Kyao, Sikondomboro, Ngarange, Sekanduko, Xongoa, Cauwe, Moxatce, Dungu, Seronga, Beyetca, Gudigoa, Sicokora, Geixa, /Qom-ca, Tobere, ǂUmbexa, Djaxo, Kangwara villages. Khoisan, Southern Africa, Central, Tshu-Khwe, Northwest. Dialect: BUGA-KXOE (BOGA, BUGA-KHWE, BUKAKHWE, "RIVER BUSHMAN", [[ANIKXOE, //ANI-KHOE, TANNEKWE, GANI-KHWE). Related to //Ani and /Anda. Investigation needed: intelligibility with related varieties. Literacy rate in second language: Buga: 15-29 years 70% Tswana, 50% English; 30-54 years 40% Tswana, 10% English. Hunter-gatherers, fishermen. Traditional religion, Christian. See main entry under Namibia.

MBUKUSHU ***(MBUKUSHI, MAMBUKUSH, MAMPUKUSH, MBUKUHU, THIMBUKUSHU, GOVA, KUSSO)*** [MHW] 12,000 in Botswana (1995 LBT). Northwest District, in all villages north of Gomare which are within 30 km. of the Okavango River. Niger-Congo, Atlantic-Congo, Volta-Congo, Benue-Congo, Bantoid, Southern, Narrow Bantu, Central, K, Kwangwa (K.40). Close to Kwangali, but a separate language. All ages. Vigorous use. Used as first language by a majority of families in the ethnic group. Dictionary. Grammar. Literacy rate in second language: 15-29 years 90% Tswana, 50% English; 30-54 3% in Tswana, 10% English; 55+ 0%. Traditional religion, Christian. NT 1986. See main entry under Namibia.

NAMA ***(NAMAN, NAMAKWA, NAMAQUA, DAMA, DAMARA, DAMAQUA, TAMA, TAMMA, TAMAKWA, BERDAMA, BERGDAMARA, KAKUYA BUSHMAN NASIE, ROOI NASIE, "HOTTENTOT", "KUPKAFFER", "KUPKAFERRN", KOEKHOEGOWAP)*** [NAQ] 200 to 1,000 in Botswana (1995 LBT). Kgalagadi District: Tsabong, Makopong, Omaweneno, Tshane villages. Ghanzi District: villages along the Ghanzi-Mamuno road. Khoisan, Southern Africa, Central, Nama. Dictionary. Grammar. SOV. Literacy rate in second language: 80% Tswana, 10% English. Bible 1966. See main entry under Namibia.

NARO ***(NHARO, NHARON, NHAURU, NHAURUN, //AIKWE, /AIKWE, //AI//EN, //AISAN, //AI//E)*** [NHR] 8,000 in Botswana (1996 Hasselbring). Population total both countries 12,000. Ghanzi District: Ghanzi, Bere, Dekar, East Hanahai, West Hanahai, Kuke, New Kanagas, Tshobokwane, Makunda, Grootelaagte, Karakobis, Kanagas, Charles Hill villages and on commercial farms. Also spoken in Namibia. Khoisan, Southern Africa, Central, Tshu-Khwe, Southwest. Dialects: /AMKWE, /ANEKWE, G!INKWE, !GINGKWE, G!OKWE, QABEKHOE (QABEKHO, !KABBAKWE), TS'AOKHOE (TSAUKWE, TSAOKHWE), TSEREKWE, TSOROKWE, N/HAI-NTSE'E (N//HAI, TS'AO). Trade language. Dictionary. Literacy rate in second language: 15-29 years 70% Tswana, 15% English; 30-54 years 10% Tswana 2% English; 55+ year 2% Tswana, 0% English. Savannah, scrub forest. Plains. Herdsmen on cattle ranches, nannies, cooks, laborers, gatherers. Traditional religion, Christian.

NDEBELE ***(TABELE, TEBELE, ISINDE'BELE, SINDEBELE, NORTHERN NDEBELE)*** [NDF] 10,000 (1998 S. Hasselbring). Northeast District, a few villages. Niger-Congo, Atlantic-Congo, Volta-Congo, Benue-Congo, Bantoid, Southern, Narrow Bantu, Central, S, Nguni (S.40). Close to Zulu. Different from Ndebele of Transvaal, South Africa, which is related to Northern Sotho. Dictionary. Bible 1978. See main entry under Zimbabwe.

SHUA ***(SHUA-KHWE, MASHUAKWE, TSHUMAKWE)*** [SHG] 19,000 in Botswana together with the Tshwa group (1995 LBT), including 100 Danisi (1977 Voegelin and Voegelin). Central District, Tutume Subdistrict: Nata, Gweta; Boteti Subdistrict: Motopi, Popipi, Mokoboxane, Mmatshumu, Letlhakane. Khoisan, Southern Africa, Central, Tshu-Khwe, North Central. Dialects: SHUA-KHWE (MASHUAKWE), N/OO-KHWE (N/OO, N//OOKHWE), /OREE-KHWE (/OREE, /KOREE-KHOE), //'AIYE (/AAYE), /XAISE (/HAISE, /TAISE, /HAIS, /AIS), TSHIDI-KHWE (TSH'ITI, TCAITI, SILI, SHETE TSERE), DANISI (DANISIS, DANISA, DEMISA, MADENASSE, MADENASSA, MADINNISANE), CARA. Bible portions 1978.

SUBIYA ***(ECHISUBIA, SUBIA, SUPIA, KWAHANE, KUAHANE, SESUBEA)*** [SBS] 12,000 in Botswana (1993 Johnstone). Northwest District, Chobe Subdistrict. Niger-Congo, Atlantic-Congo, Volta-Congo, Benue-Congo, Bantoid, Southern, Narrow Bantu, Central, K, Subia (L.50). 61% lexical similarity with Luyana, about 60% with Tonga. Their name for their language is 'Chikwahane'; 'Subiya' is the Tswana name. Grammar. Traditional religion, Christian. See main entry under Namibia.

TSWANA ***(CHUANA, COANA, CUANA, SETSWANA, SECHUANA, BEETJUANS)*** [TSW] 1,070,000 in Botswana (1993 Johnstone), 70% of the population. Population total all countries 4,000,000 (1999 WA). Spoken throughout the country as lingua franca, and as mother tongue primarily in the South-east and Kgatleng districts, the eastern half of Southern and Kweneng districts, in the Serowe-Palapye and Mahalapye subdistricts of Central District, and around Maun village in Northwest District. Also spoken in Namibia, South Africa, Zimbabwe. Niger-Congo, Atlantic-Congo, Volta-Congo, Benue-Congo, Bantoid, Southern, Narrow Bantu, Central, S, Sotho-Tswana (S.30), Tswana. Dialects: TLAHAPING (TLAPI), ROLONG, KWENA, KGATLA, NGWATU (NGWATO), TAWANA, LETE, NGWAKETSE, TLOKWA. Southern Sotho, Northern Sotho, and Tswana are largely inherently intelligible but have generally been considered separate languages. Standard Tswana uses Kgatla dialect. Used among the educated. Used more for spoken purposes than written. All ages. Vigorous use. 90% to 95% of children complete standard 7 in primary school. National language. Dictionary. Grammar. Literacy rate in first language: 80% to 90%. Officially used as language of instruction in grades 1-4 in all government primary schools. Often used for explanations through Standard 7 and first 2 years of secondary. Taught as a required subject in all secondary schools. Newspapers, magazines, radio programs, TV. Agriculturalists, pastoralists: cattle. Christian, traditional religion. Bible 1857-1993.

TSWAPONG ***(SETSWAPONG)*** [TWO] Several thousand (1997 Andersson and Janson). Central District, Mahalapye Subdistrict: all villages east of Mahalapye. Niger-Congo, Atlantic-Congo, Volta-Congo, Benue-Congo, Bantoid, Southern, Narrow Bantu, Central, S, Sotho-Tswana (S.30). Some similarities to Pedi (N. Sotho) and some to Tswana, but it is not clearly a dialect of either. Some intelligibility to speakers of a northern dialect of Tswana (Sengwato and Setawana), and to speakers of a northwestern dialect of Pedi (Hananwa and Setokwa). Some speakers of Birwa and Tswapong have said that their varieties are closer to one another than to Tswana or Pedi. Several groups: the Ramokgonami, Maifela, Chadibe, Sefbare, Tupsa.

!XÓÕ ***(NG/AMANI, TSASI)*** [NMN] 3,000 to 4,000 in Botswana (1995 LBT). Population total both countries 3,200 to 4,200 (1995). Southern Gantsi district, northern Kgalagadi District, western Southern and western Kweneng districts. Also spoken in Namibia. Khoisan, Southern Africa, Southern, Hua. Dialects: AUNI (/AUNI, /AUO), KAKIA (MASARWA), KI/HAZI, NG/U//EN (NU//EN, /U//EN, NG/U/EI, /NU//EN, //U//EN), NUSAN (NG/USAN, NU-SAN, NOOSAN), XATIA (KATIA, KATTEA, KHATIA, VAALPENS, /KUSI, /EIKUSI), !KWI. People older than 10 who have been to school or have lived with speakers of other languages use Tswana, Kgalagadi, Herero, Naro, or /Gwi as second languages for common topics. Nusan are in Botswana. Dictionary. SVO; prepositions; genitives, adjectives, numerals, relatives after noun heads; question word initial; 2 prefixes, 3 suffixes; word order distinguishes subjects, objects, indirect objects; verb affixes mark number, gender of Subject and Object, and is obligatory; passives; reduplication on periphrastics for causatives; periphrastic comparatives; CV, CVV, CVCV, CVN; tonal. Savannah. Plains. Sedentary hunter-gatherers. 1,100 meters. Nusan: traditional religion, Christian.

YEYI ***(SHIYEYI, YEEI, YEI, CIYEI, KOBA, KUBA)*** [YEY] 27,000 in Botswana (1997 Richard Cook LBT). Probably another 20,000 ethnic BaYeyi who do not speak Yeyi. Population total both countries 32,200. North West District, Maun, Shorobe up to Mababe, Sankoyo, Daunara, Nokaneng, Gumare, Sepopo, Ikoga, Shakawe, and Seronga. Central District, Letihakane, Xumu, Rakops, Motopi. Capitals for Wayei Maun and Gumare. Also spoken in Namibia. Niger-Congo, Atlantic-Congo, Volta-Congo, Benue-Congo, Bantoid, Southern, Narrow Bantu, Central, R, Yeye (R.40). Dialect: SHIRWANGA. Not closely related to other languages. 47% lexical similarity with Luyana, 30% with Herero. All speakers use Tswana as second language. 73% of respondents say they speak Tswana well. Young people who have attended secondary school also speak English. 12% of respondents say they speak only Yeyi to their children, 9% speak Yeyi and Tswana to their children. In some villages children speak Yeyi, including Seronga, Sepopa, Ikoga, Jau. In many villages only those over 40 and over 60 speak Yeyi. 43% of those who learned Yeyi from their parents say they speak Yeyi best, 57% say they speak Tswana best. Few speak Yeyi as second language. Dictionary. SVO; postpositions; articles, adjectives, numerals after noun heads; relatives before or after; question word initial; 4 prefixes, one suffix; word order distinguishes subjects, objects, indirect objects; noun affixes indicate case; verb affixes mark person, number, gender; CVC; nontonal. Literacy rate in second language: Age 15-29 95% Tswana, 68% English; age 30-54 33% Tswana, 20% English; age 55 and over 33% Tswana, 6% English. Motivation for literacy is high. Delta. Plains. Fishermen, hunters, peasant agriculturalists. 850 to 1,000 meters. Christian.

BRITISH INDIAN OCEAN TERRITORY

National or official language: English. 2,000 (1987). Chagos Archipelago including Diego Garcia. Also includes a few from the Philippines and Mauritius. The number of languages listed for British Indian Ocean Territory is 1. Diversity index 0.00.

ENGLISH [ENG] Indo-European, Germanic, West, English. The indigenous population no longer resides in the islands. Current residents include members of the USA military, a small detachment of British officials, and support staff, mainly of Mauritian and Philippine origin. Official language. Bible 1535-1989. See main entry under United Kingdom.

BURKINA FASO

Formerly Upper Volta. National or official languages: Mòoré, Fulfuldé, Jula, French. 11,305,000 (1998 UN). Literacy rate 19.2%: 29.5% males, 9.2% females (1998 UNESCO). Also includes Jowulu 1,000. Information mainly from J. Bendor-Samuel 1989; SIL 1973-1999. Muslim, Christian, traditional religion, other. Blind population 50,000. Data accuracy estimate: A2, B. The number of languages listed for Burkina Faso is 66. Of those, all are living languages. Diversity index 0.76.

BAMBARA ***(BAMANA, BAMANAKAN)*** [BRA] 300 in Burkina Faso (1991 L. Vanderaa CRC). Kénédougou Province, near N'Dorola. Niger-Congo, Mande, Western, Central-Southwestern, Central, Manding-Jogo, Manding-Vai, Manding-Mokole, Manding, Manding-East, Northeastern Manding, Bamana. Muslim. Bible 1961-1987. See main entry under Mali.

BIALI ***(BIERI, BJERI, BJERB, BERBA, BURBA)*** [BEH] 1,500 in Burkina Faso (1991). Tapoa and Gourma provinces, at the Benin border, south of Arli. Niger-Congo, Atlantic-Congo, Volta-Congo, North, Gur, Central, Northern, Oti-Volta, Eastern. 30% to 40% are monolingual. All ages. Different from Bariba (Berba). Literacy rate in second language: 9%. Traditional religion, Muslim, Christian. See main entry under Benin.

BIRIFOR, MALBA ***(BIRIFO, MALBA-BIRIFOR, NORTHERN BIRIFOR)*** [BFO] 108,000 in Burkina Faso (1993). Population total both countries 110,500. Southwestern Burkina Faso, Poni Province. Also spoken in Côte d'Ivoire. Niger-Congo, Atlantic-Congo, Volta-Congo, North, Gur, Central, Northern, Oti-Volta, Western, Northwest, Dagaari-Birifor, Birifor. Dialects: WILE, BIRIFOR. Bilingualism in Lobi, Mòoré, Jula, French. All ages. Dagaari, Wali, and Birifor of Ghana are separate languages. Many monolinguals. Traditional religion, Christian, Muslim. NT 1994.

BISSA ***(BISA)*** [BIB] 350,000 in Burkina Faso(1999 SIL), 5% of the population (1991 SIL). Does not include the Bissa southern Barka region. Population total all countries 535,000. South central, Boulgou and Zoundweogo provinces, in the cities of Garango, Zabré, Gomboussougou, Tenkodogo. Also spoken in Côte d'Ivoire, Ghana, Togo. Niger-Congo, Mande, Eastern, Eastern, Bissa. Dialects: BARKA, LEBIR, LERE. Related to Samo. Some people are bilingual in Mòoré, some in French. All ages. Not the same as Busa of Benin and Nigeria. The Mòoré name for the people is 'Boussanse'. Grammar. Muslim, traditional religion, Christian. Bible portions 1996.

BLÉ ***(DYALA, DYALANU, JALKUNA)*** [BXL] 500 speakers out of an ethnic group of 800 to 1,000 (1995 SIL). Village of Blédougou, west of Banfora, near the town of Sindou, Leraba Province. Niger-Congo, Mande, Western, Central-Southwestern, Central, Manding-Jogo, Jogo-Jeri, Jeri-Jalkuna. 19% lexical similarity with Jula, 17% with Bolon. The people say that everyone speaks Jula, all ages and sexes. Jula is used to people of other ethnic groups and for government administrative purposes. Blé is used in the homes and to other Blé. All ages. Tonal. Government literacy program in Jula. Savannah, scrub forest. Plains. Peasant agriculturalists. 300 to 400 meters. Muslim.

BOBO MADARÉ, NORTHERN ***(BOBO FING, BOBO FIGN, BOBO FI, BLACK BOBO, BOBO)*** [BBO] 35,000 speakers in Burkina Faso out of 47,000 to 57,000 in the ethnic group (1995 SIL). Population total both countries 50,000 to 55,000. Banwa Province. Tansilla is the center, with a radius of about 25 km. Also spoken in Mali. Niger-Congo, Mande, Western, Northwestern, Samogo, Soninke-Bobo, Bobo. Dialects: YABA, SANKUMA (SAROKAMA), JÈRÈ, TANKRI, KURE, KUKOMA. Northern Bobo Madaré has 20% to 30% intelligibility of Southern Bobo Madaré. All dialects of Northern understand Yaba, centered in Tansilla. Tankri is difficult for others to understand. Jula is also used by most men with good proficiency, and some women for common topics and trade. French is spoken by those who have been to school. Bobo Madaré is spoken at home and with other Bobo Madaré, Jula used for trade, government, and to other ethnic groups. Koma, a simplified form of Kukoma, has some negative attitudes held toward it. Bobo Fing call themselves 'Bobo' and their language 'Boboda'. The government calls them 'Bobo Madaré'. 'Bobo' is the general Bambara word for Bobo Madaré, Bwamu or Bomu. CV, CVC, CVV, CCV; tonal. Literacy rate in second language: 5% or less. Savannah, scrub forest. Plains. Peasant agriculturalists. 400 to 500 meters. Traditional religion, Muslim, Christian.

BOBO MADARÉ, SOUTHERN ***(BOBO FING, BOBO FI, BLACK BOBO, BOBO)*** [BWQ] 150,000 to 180,000 speakers out of 160,000 to 190,000 in the ethnic group, including 15,000 speakers of Zara (1999 SIL). Mainly Houet Province, from 20 km. west of Bobo Dioulasso to 40 km. east, north to Kouka region in Kossi Province. Niger-Congo, Mande, Western, Northwestern, Samogo, Soninke-Bobo, Bobo. Dialects: BENGE, SOGOKIRÉ, VORÉ, SYABÉRÉ (SYA), ZARA (BOBO DIOULA, BOBO JULA). Jula is also used by most men and some women, with varying proficiency. French is spoken by those who have been to school. All ages. Syabéré in Bobo Dioulasso region is the prestige dialect, and the one used for literature. They call themselves 'Bobo' and their language 'Boboda'. The government calls them 'Bobo Madaré'. 'Bobo' is the general Bambara word for Bobo Fing, Bwamu or Bomu. Tonal. Literacy rate in second language: 10% Jula. Savannah, scrub forest. Plains. Peasant agriculturalists. 200 to 500 meters. Traditional religion, Muslim, Christian. NT 1981.

BOLON *(BOKA, BO)* [BOF] 17,000 (1998 SIL). Kénédougou and Houet provinces, 12 villages around N'Dorola and Samorogouan. Niger-Congo, Mande, Western, Central-Southwestern, Central, Manding-Jogo, Manding-Vai, Manding-Mokole, Manding. Dialects: BLACK BOLON (NORTHERN BOLON), WHITE BOLON (SOUTHERN BOLON). White Bolon has higher inherent intelligibility with Jula (81%) than Black Bolon (52%). High bilingualism in Jula. All ages. Muslim, traditional religion.

BOMU *(BOOMU, BORE, WESTERN BOBO WULE, BOBO OULE)* [BMQ] 56,000 in Burkina Faso (1991). Kossi Province, Djibasso Subprefecture. Niger-Congo, Atlantic-Congo, Volta-Congo, North, Gur, Central, Northern, Bwamu. Bilingual level estimates for Jula are 0 0%, 1 58%, 2 20%, 3 20%, 4 2%, 5 0%. Men can speak Jula for common topics with outsiders, women for trading. All ages. Distinct language from Bwamu. The people are called 'Bonuu' (sg.) or 'Bwa' (pl.). Grammar. SOV; postpositions; genitives, relatives before noun heads; articles, adjectives, numerals after noun heads; word order distinguishes subjects, objects, indirect objects; V, CV, CVV; tonal. Literacy rate in first language: Adults over 30: 2%, young people: 20%. Literacy rate in second language: Young people 10% in Jula; 2% in French. Different orthography used in Mali. Savannah. Plains. Peasant agriculturalists. Burkina Faso: traditional religion, Christian. Bible, in press (1999). See main entry under Mali.

BWAMU *(EASTERN BOBO WULE, EASTERN BOBO OULE, RED BOBO, BWA, BWABA, BOUAMOU)* [BOX] 135,000 to 175,000 (1995 SIL). Kossi, Mouhoun, Houet, Bougouriba, and Sourou provinces. The boundary runs north-south through Solenzo and between Nouna and Djibasso. None in Mali. Niger-Congo, Atlantic-Congo, Volta-Congo, North, Gur, Central, Northern, Bwamu. Dialect: OUARKOYE. Bilingualism in Jula, French. 'Bwa' is their name for themselves ('Bwaba' is plural) in the Dedougou dialect. 'Bwamu' (Bouamou) is the language. 'Bobo' is the general Bambara name for Bwamu, Bomo, or Bobo Fing, but properly applies only to the Bobo Fing. Pwe is the name of a town, not a dialect (D. Shady CMA 1973). Literacy rate in second language: 2%. Traditional religion, Christian, Muslim. Bible portions 1957-1996.

BWAMU, CWI *(COO, CWI, TWI)* [BWY] 24,000 (1999 SIL). South of Boromo, border area between Bougouriba and Sissili provinces, area 10 km. north to south, and 40 km. east to west, from Founzan (Bougouriba Province) to Kabourou (Sissili Province). Niger-Congo, Atlantic-Congo, Volta-Congo, North, Gur, Central, Northern, Bwamu. Intelligibility within Cwi area is over 90%, 50% to 70% with Láá Láá Bwamu, 30% with Ouarkoye Bwamu, and 65% to 70% with Dakwi Bwamu. Some over 7 years old speak limited Jula (trade, common topics) or French as second language (greetings, weather). Cwi is used in the home and with other Twi speakers. All ages. Tonal. Literacy rate in second language: 3% Jula. Unable to use other Bwamu literature. Motivation for literacy is high. Savannah, scrub forest. Plains. Peasant agriculturalists. 250 meters. Traditional religion, Christian, Muslim.

BWAMU, LÁÁ LÁÁ *(KÀDENBÀ, YERE)* [BWJ] 50,000 to 60,000 (1985 census). Mouhoun and Houet provinces, in and around the villages of Bagassi, Pâ, and Boni. Niger-Congo, Atlantic-Congo, Volta-Congo, North, Gur, Central, Northern, Bwamu. Close to Ouarkoye dialect of Bwamu and Bwamu Twi. Speakers unable to use other Bwamu dialects for literature. Speakers over 7 years old can speak some Jula as second language for trade, government services, and common topics with people from other ethnic groups; and French for government services. Spoken by people in their homes and with other Bwaba. All ages. Grammar. Tonal. Literacy rate in first language: 1% to 2% are fluent readers of Ouarkoye Bwamu. Literacy rate in second language: 1% to 2% are fluent readers of French or Jula. Motivation for literacy is high. Scrub forest. Plains. Peasant agriculturalists. 250 meters. Traditional religion, Christian, Muslim. Bible portions 1977-1995.

CERMA *(GOUIN, GWE, GWEN, KIRMA)* [GOT] 61,400 in Burkina Faso (1991). Population total both countries 63,100. From just north of Ouangolodougou, Côte d'Ivoire, along the main road to Banfora, Comoé Province. Also spoken in Côte d'Ivoire. Niger-Congo, Atlantic-Congo, Volta-Congo, North, Gur, Central, Southern, Kirma-Tyurama. Dialects: BANFORA-SIENENA, NIANGOLOKO-DIARABAKOKO, SOUBAKANEDOUGOU, GOUINDOUGOUBA. The Gouindougouba dialect is spoken in 1 or 2 villages. Turka is the closest language, but not inherently intelligible. Most people use Jula as second language. Those who have been to school speak some French. All ages. The people are called 'Gouin' or 'Ciramba'. Investigation needed: intelligibility with Soubaka. Dictionary. SVO, postpositions, articles, numerals, relatives after noun heads; question word final, no more than one affix per word, word order distinguishes objects and indirect objects; verb changes with tense and aspect; causatives by sentence order; comparatives; CV, CVC, CVV, VV, V, tonal. Literacy rate in second language: 15% Jula or French. Government and SIL literacy program. Savannah. Plains. Peasant agriculturalists. Traditional religion, Muslim, Christian. Bible portions 1995.

DAGAARI DIOULA ***(DAGARI DYOULA, DAGAARI JULA, JARI, YARI, WALA)*** [DGD] 21,000 (1999 SIL). Population total both countries 21,000 or more. Diébougou, To, Boromo, Soukoulaye, Silly, Pa, Dano, Leo, Gao, Dissin, Wessa, Fara, French Hamele. Also spoken in Ghana. Niger-Congo, Atlantic-Congo, Volta-Congo, North, Gur, Central, Northern, Oti-Volta, Western, Northwest, Dagaari-Birifor, Dagaari. Not inherently intelligible with Dagaare, Jula, or Mòoré. 65% to 70% lexical similarity with Dagaare. West of the Mouhoun River some men have routine proficiency in Jula, but women have lower proficiency. In some western locations some people speak Mòoré as second language. Muslim.

DAGARA, NORTHERN ***(NORTHERN DAGAARE, DAGARI, DEGATI, DAGATI, DOGAARI, DAGAARI, DAGAARE)*** [DGI] 287,000 (1993 Johnstone). Southwest Burkina Faso, Poni, Bougouriba, Sissili, Mouhoun provinces. Niger-Congo, Atlantic-Congo, Volta-Congo, North, Gur, Central, Northern, Oti-Volta, Western, Northwest, Dagaari-Birifor, Dagaari. Dialects: LOBER (LOBR), WULE, NURA (LAWRA LOBI). Dagara and Birifor are partly intelligible. All ages. Dagara is more prominent politically and socially. The people are called 'Dagaaba'. Different from Southern Dagaare in Ghana. Dictionary. Grammar. Radio programs, TV. Traditional religion, Christian, Muslim.

DOGON ***(DOGOSO)*** [DOG] 138,000 in Burkina Faso (1995). Border area. Niger-Congo, Atlantic-Congo, Volta-Congo, Dogon. Not close to other languages. Several varieties are inherently unintelligible to each others' speakers, but are called 'dialects'. Different from Dogoso [DGS] and Dogosé [DOS]. All ages. Investigation needed: intelligibility with related varieties. Traditional religion, Muslim, Christian. NT 1957-1994. See main entry under Mali.

DOGOSÉ ***(DOROSIE, DORHOSYE, DOKHOSIÉ, DOGHOSIÉ, DOKHOBE, DOROBÉ, DOGHOSE, DORHOSSIÉ, DOROSSÉ)*** [DOS] 20,000 (1991 Ouattara). Villages of Ouo, Sidéradougou, Kouere, Koro, and Sirakoro, Comoé Province, Sidéradougou Subdistrict, southwest Burkina Faso. Niger-Congo, Atlantic-Congo, Volta-Congo, North, Gur, Central, Southern, Gan-Dogose. Dialects: KLAMAASISE, MESISE, LUTISE, GBEYÃSE, SUKURASE, GBOGOROSE,. Closely related to Lepatogoso. Different from Bambadion dialects Dogoso and Kheso. The regional dialects are inherently intelligible with each other. 82% lexical similarity with Khisa, 69% with Kpatogo, 68% with Kaanse, 15% with Dogoso, 14% with Khe. Bilingualism in Jula. All ages. Clans are Ouattara or Coulibaly. Muslim, traditional religion.

DOGOSO ***(DOROSSIÉ-FING, DORHOSIÉ-FINNG, BLACK DOGOSE, DORHOSIÉ-NOIRS, BAMBADION-DOGOSO, BAMBADION-DOKHOSIÉ)*** [DGS] 9,000 (1999 SIL). Population total both countries 9,000 or more. Villages are Dandougou, Torokoro, Sokoura, Bondokoro, Tolandougou, Sakédougou. Near the Dogo, Khi, and Khe. Also spoken in Côte d'Ivoire. Niger-Congo, Atlantic-Congo, Volta-Congo, North, Gur, Central, Southern, Dogoso-Khe. 56% lexical similarity with Khe, 15% with Dogosé, 16% with Khisa. Speakers are somewhat bilingual in Jula. All ages. Traditional religion.

DYAN ***(DIAN, DYA, DYANE, DYANU, DAN)*** [DYA] 14,100 (1991 Vanderaa). Bougouriba Province, Dolo, near Diébougou. Niger-Congo, Atlantic-Congo, Volta-Congo, North, Gur, Central, Southern, Dyan. Dialect: ZANGA. Zanga is a dialect or closely related language. Not close enough to Lobi to be intelligible, although they seem to adapt after awhile to Lobi. Distinct from Dan (Gio, Yacouba). Limited bilingualism in Jula. Traditional religion, Muslim.

DZÙÙNGOO ***(SAMOGHO, SAMOGO, SAMORO, KPANGO, EASTERN DUUN)*** [DNN] 13,400 (1998 Solomiac, Entz). Kénédougou Province, Samorogouan and Samogohiri departments, west of Bobo-Dioulasso near the town of Orodara; villages of Samogo-Iri, Saraba, Diomou, Gnalé, Sokouraba, Todié, and Samogogouan. Niger-Congo, Mande, Western, Northwestern, Samogo, Dzuun-Seeku, Dzuun. Dialects: KPANGO (SAMOROGOUAN), DZÙÙNGOO (SAMOGOHIRI). The two dialects are intelligible to each other's speakers. Bilingual level estimates for Jula are 0 0%, 1 10%, 2 10%, 3 30%, 4 40%, 5 10%. They speak Jula to outsiders. All men are fluent in Jula, all women are not. Some men also speak French. All ages. The speakers are unified, with pride in their language. 'Dzuun' is the name for the people, 'Dzùùngoo' for the language. 'Samogo' is the Jula name. SOV; postpositions; genitives before noun heads; articles, adjectives, numerals, relatives after noun heads; question word final; 2 suffixes; word order distinguishes subjects, objects, topic; causatives; comparatives; V, CV, CCV; tonal. Literacy rate in second language: 5% French. Scrub forest. Plains. Peasant agriculturalists. 500 meters. Muslim.

FRAFRA ***(GURENNE)*** [GUR] 25,100 in Burkina Faso (1991). Nahouri Province, subdistrict of Zecco and Ziou. Niger-Congo, Atlantic-Congo, Volta-Congo, North, Gur, Central, Northern, Oti-Volta, Western, Southeast. Dialects: GUDENI, NANKANI, BOONI, FRAFRA, NANKANA. All ages. Traditional religion, Christian, Muslim. NT 1986. See main entry under Ghana.

FRENCH [FRN] Indo-European, Italic, Romance, Italo-Western, Western, Gallo-Iberian, Gallo-Romance, Gallo-Rhaetian, Oïl, French. Official language. Bible 1530-1986. See main entry under France.

FULFULDE, NORTHEASTERN BURKINA FASO [FUH] 750,000 (1999 SILi. Northeastern Burkina Faso corner. Niger-Congo, Atlantic-Congo, Atlantic, Northern, Senegambian, Fula-Wolof, Fulani, West Central. Dialects: BARANI (BARAIN, BARANIIRE), GOURMANTCHE, BOGANDÉ, JELGOORE,

LIPTAAKOORE, BARKOUNDOUBA, SEEBA-YAGA (YAAGA) OUHIGUYUA, FADA NGURMA. Pastoralists: cattle. Muslim. See main entry under Niger.

GOURMANCHÉMA ***(GOURMA, GOURMANTCHE, GURMA, MIGULIMANCEMA, GOULMACEMA, GULMANCEMA, GULIMANCEMA)*** [GUX] 600,000 in Burkina Faso (1999 SIL). Population total all countries 800,000. Eastern Burkina Faso, Gourma, Tapoa, Gnagna, Komandjari, Yagha, and Kompienga provinces, just below the scrub land that blends into the Sahara. Also spoken in Benin, Niger, Togo. Niger-Congo, Atlantic-Congo, Volta-Congo, North, Gur, Central, Northern, Oti-Volta, Gurma. Dialects: NORTHERN GOURMANCHEMA, CENTRAL GOURMANCHEMA, SOUTHERN GOURMANCHEMA. Central and eastern dialects are inherently intelligible, northern only with difficulty. Bilingual level estimates for Mooré are 0 90%, 1 3%, 2 3%, 3 2%, 4 1%, 5 0%. Those who have been to school or live in town (about 10%) can use French for common topics. Some use Zarma or Fulfulde. All ages. Central is the prestige dialect, and used for writing. The people are called 'Bigulimanceba' or 'Gourma'. SVO; postpositions; genitives, articles before noun heads; numerals after; CV; 3 tones. Literacy rate in second language: 5% to 10%. Newspapers, radio programs, films. Savannah. Plains. Peasant agriculturalists: over 90% are able to meet all their food requirements. Traditional religion, Muslim, Christian. NT 1958-1990.

HAUSA ***(HAOUSSA)*** [HUA] 500 in Burkina Faso (1991 Vanderaa). Boulgou and Gourma provinces. Afro-Asiatic, Chadic, West, A, A.1. Muslim. Bible 1932-1996. See main entry under Nigeria.

JULA ***(DYULA, DYOULA, DIULA, DIOULA, DJULA)*** [DYU] 1,000,000 or more first language users in Burkina Faso, 3,000,000 to 4,000,000 second language users (1990 SIL). Population total all countries 2,520,000 first language speakers, 3,000,000 to 4,000,000 second language speakers (1990 SIL). Comoé, Kénédougou, Houet, and Leraba provinces. Also spoken in Côte d'Ivoire, Mali. Niger-Congo, Mande, Western, Central-Southwestern, Central, Manding-Jogo, Manding-Vai, Manding-Mokole, Manding, Manding-East, Northeastern Manding, Bamana. Jula is a trade language of western Burkina Faso and northern Côte d'Ivoire. It is a separate language from Bambara and Malinke, and ethnically distinct. All ages. Different than Jola (Diola) of Senegal. Trade language. Radio programs, films. Muslim. NT 1993-1997.

KAANSA ***(KAANSE, KÃASA, KAN, KAAN, GAN, GÃ, GANE)*** [GNA] 6,000 (1990 S. Showalter). Poni Province, Gaoua Subdistrict, Loropéni Department, bounded by Loropéni on the west, Derbi on the east, Djigoué on the south, and Yérifoula on the north. Obiré, ten km. northwest of Loropéni, is the cultural center and residence of the Kaan king. Niger-Congo, Atlantic-Congo, Volta-Congo, North, Gur, Central, Southern, Gan-Dogose. Dialect: KPATOGO (KPATOGOSO, GBADOGO, PADORO, PADOGHO, PADORHO, BODORO). 81% lexical similarity with Kpatogo, 71% with Khisa, 68% with Doghosié. Bilingual level estimates for Jula are 0 0%, 1 9%, 2 12%, 3 43%, 4 37%, 5 0%. All speakers can use Jula as second language, 30% to 50% can use Lobi, less than 20% French. All ages. The people are called 'Kamba' (pl.), 'Kaan' (sg.). Four clans: Farma, Suwa, Khama, Thaama. The Kpatogo separated politically and geographically from the Kambe. 5 primary schools in the area. Literacy rate in second language: 3%. Gallery forest. Interfluvial. Swidden or peasant agriculturalists. 150 to 400 meters. Traditional religion, Christian.

KALAMSÉ ***(KALEMSÉ, KALENGA, SÀMÒMÁ, SÀMÓ)*** [KNZ] 9,568 (1985 census). Population total both countries 11,000. Sourou Province, Tougan Subdistrict, 540 square km. bordering Mali. Also spoken in Mali. Niger-Congo, Atlantic-Congo, Volta-Congo, North, Gur, Central, Southern, Grusi, Northern. Dialects: KASOMA (EAST KALAMSÉ), LOGREMMA (LOGMA, WEST KALAMSÉ). All ages. Speakers call their language 'Samoma' and themselves 'Sàmó' (sg.) or 'Sàmóyá' (pl.). The administrative name is 'Kalemse' (pl.) or 'Kalenga' (sg.). Distinct from other languages called 'Samo'. Grammar. Traditional religion, Muslim, Christian.

KARABORO, EASTERN ***(KAR, KER, KLER)*** [KAR] 35,000 in Burkina Faso (1995 SIL). Population total both countries 40,000 to 41,000. East of the main Ferké to Bobo-Dioulosso road and Banfora, southern Burkina Faso. Comoé Province. Also spoken in Côte d'Ivoire. Niger-Congo, Atlantic-Congo, Volta-Congo, North, Gur, Senufo, Karaboro. Kar averages 70% comprehension by Tenyer and Syer speakers, but the reverse is 30%; probably some bilingualism involved. Some bilingualism in Jula. All ages. Dictionary. Grammar. Agriculturalists: maize, millet, peanuts. Traditional religion, Muslim, Christian. NT 1994.

KARABORO, WESTERN ***(SYER-TENYER)*** [KZA] 30,200 (1991 Vanderaa). West of the main Ferké to Bobo-Dioulosso road and Banfora, southern Burkina Faso. Niger-Congo, Atlantic-Congo, Volta-Congo, North, Gur, Senufo, Karaboro. Dialects: TENYER, SYER. Kar averages 70% comprehension by Tenyer and Syer speakers, but the reverse is 30%; probably some bilingualism involved. High bilingual proficiency in Jula. Muslim, traditional religion.

KASEM ***(KASSEM, KASIM, KASENA, KASSENA)*** [KAS] 120,000 in Burkina Faso (1998 SIL). Population total both countries 220,000. Nahouri Province, Po and Tiébélé towns. Also spoken in Ghana. Niger-Congo, Atlantic-Congo, Volta-Congo, North, Gur, Central, Southern, Grusi, Northern.

Dialects: EAST KASEM, WEST KASEM. West and East Kasem are inherently intelligible to each other's speakers. Closest to Nuni and Lyélé. Bilingual level estimates for Mòoré are 0 60%, 1 20%, 2 10%, 3 5%, 4 3%, 5 2%. French also used. All ages. The people are Kasena, the language is Kasem. East Kasem is more prestigious. Loan words from French and Mòoré in Burkina Faso, English, and Ashanti in Ghana. SVO; postpositions; genitives, articles, adjectives, numerals after noun heads; relatives after or without noun heads; no more than one affix per word; word order distinguishes subjects, objects, indirect objects, topic and comment; causatives; comparatives; CV, CVC, CVV; tonal. Literacy rate in first language: 15% Kasem. Literacy rate in second language: 15% French, 15% Mòoré. Orthography in Burkina Faso is from French, versus English for speakers in Ghana. Savannah, scrub forest. Plains. Peasant agriculturalists. 200 to 300 meters. Traditional religion, Christian, Muslim. NT 1988-1997.

KHE ***(KHESO, BAMBADION-KHESO)*** [KQG] 1,300 (1983 SIL). Population total both countries 1,300 or more. Near the Dogo, Khi, and Dogoso. Villages are Noumoukiedougou, Tiébata, Moromoro, Boli, Sessagbo, and Lobo. Also spoken in Côte d'Ivoire. Niger-Congo, Atlantic-Congo, Volta-Congo, North, Gur, Central, Southern, Dogoso-Khe. 56% lexical similarity to Dogoso (Bambadion-Dogoso), 14% with Dogosié, 13% with Khisa. Investigation needed: bilingual proficiency in Jula, attitudes toward Jula. Traditional religion.

KHISA ***(KOMONO, KHI, KHI KHIPA, KUMWENU)*** [KQM] 3,000 in Burkina Faso (1991 S. Showalter SIL). Comoé Province, around Mangodara Prefecture, in southwest Burkina Faso near the Côte d'Ivoire border. 25 villages. Niger-Congo, Atlantic-Congo, Volta-Congo, North, Gur, Central, Southern, Gan-Dogose. Speakers say they can understand Kaanse after a time. Also reported to be Senoufo. 82% lexical similarity with Doghosié, 72% with Kpatogo, 71% with Kaanse, 16% with Dogoso, 13% with Khe. Quite bilingual in Jula. The people in Dabokiri village have shifted to Jula. 'Komono' is the Jula name. Agriculturalists: millet, maize, yams. Muslim. See main entry under Côte d'Ivoire.

KOROMFÉ ***(KURUMFE, FULA, FULSE)*** [KFZ] 151,000 (1993 Johnstone). Population total both countries 151,000 or more. Yatenga Province, Titao Subdistrict, Soum and Oudalan provinces, Djibi-Aribinda Subdistrict. A few in Mali at Bandiagara and Yoro, several villages. The Koromba are east, the Fulse west. Also spoken in Mali. Niger-Congo, Atlantic-Congo, Volta-Congo, North, Gur, Central, Northern, Kurumfe. They use Mòoré or Fulfuldé as second language. Dictionary. Grammar. Savannah. Plains. Agriculturalists. Koromba: Muslim, Christian; Fulse: Muslim, Christian.

KUSAAL ***(KUSALE, KUSASI, KOUSSASSÉ)*** [KUS] 17,000 in Burkina Faso (1998 SIL). Nahouiri, Boulgou provinces, some villages south of Zabré, south central. Niger-Congo, Atlantic-Congo, Volta-Congo, North, Gur, Central, Northern, Oti-Volta, Western, Southeast, Kusaal. Dialect: TOENDE (WESTERN KUSAAL). Possible marginal intelligibility with Eastern (Angole) Kusaal. Many claim to be able to understand the related languages: Mòoré, Dagbani, Mampruli, Frafra (Gurenne). Kusaal is a member of the Mòoré-Dagbani cluster. All ages. Traditional religion, Muslim, Christian. NT 1976-1995. See main entry under Ghana.

LOBI ***(LOBIRI, MIWA)*** [LOB] 285,500 in Burkina Faso (1991 L. Vanderaa). Population total all countries 441,300. Poni Province, southwest border area around Gaoua. A few villages in northwest Ghana along the Volta River; known as Miwa. Also spoken in Côte d'Ivoire, Ghana. Niger-Congo, Atlantic-Congo, Volta-Congo, North, Gur, Lobi. Dialect: GONGON LOBI. Bilingualism in Jula, French. All ages. Traditional religion, Christian, Muslim. NT 1965-1985.

LYÉLÉ ***(LELE)*** [LEE] 225,000 (1993 Johnstone). Northern and central two-thirds of Sanguié Province: Réo, Kyon, Tenado, Dassa, Didyr, Godyr, and Kordie subdistricts, with principal center in Réo. Thousands of migrants in neighboring countries, especially Côte d'Ivoire. Niger-Congo, Atlantic-Congo, Volta-Congo, North, Gur, Central, Southern, Grusi, Northern. Dialects: SOUTHERN LYÉLÉ (REO), CENTRAL LYÉLÉ, NORTHERN LYÉLÉ, KANDÉRÉ. Most Central and Northern Lyélé speakers have nearly 100% comprehension of the Southern Lyélé, the one being developed. Kandéré speakers have 75% comprehension of Southern Lyélé. Southern Lyélé speakers understand all dialects except Kandéré well. Closely related to Nuni, but inherent intelligibility between them is low. A few speakers who have been in Jula-speaking areas can use Jula as second language. Under 20% have been to school, and they can use some French. Mòoré is used to some extent for trading and other contact with the Mossi, mainly by those living near the edges of the Lyélé region. About 50% of speakers are age 15 or under. The ethnic group is called 'Lyela' or 'Lela'. 'Gurunsi' is also used, but that applies more properly to the wider grouping. SVO; postpositions; genitives before noun heads; articles, adjectives, numerals, relatives after noun heads; question word initial; 1 prefix, 2 suffix; word order distinguishes subject and object; causatives; comparatives; CV, CVV; tonal. Literacy rate in first language: growing number in Lyélé. Literacy rate in second language: 18% mainly in French, some in Mòoré. Government coordinated literacy program, 110 classes (1998). Savannah. Plains. Peasant agriculturalists. 300 meters. Traditional religion over, Christian or less, Muslim or less, considerable syncretism. Bible portions 1968-1999.

MARKA ***(MARKA DAFING, MEKA)*** [MWR] 200,000 in Burkina Faso (1992 CMA). Population total both countries 225,000. Kossi and Mouhoun provinces, northwest, around Nouna, Dédougou. Also spoken in Mali. Niger-Congo, Mande, Western, Central-Southwestern, Central, Manding-Jogo, Manding-Vai, Manding-Mokole, Manding, Manding-East, Marka-Dafin. Dialects: SAFANÉ, NOUNA, GASSAN. Speakers of most dialects have more than 80% inherent intelligibility of the southeastern dialect around Safané, except for those in the northwestern dialect region, who have 70% intelligibility of it. The central dialect around Dembo village is also well understood. Reported to be close to Bambara or a variant of Jula. B. Coulibaly, a Bambara speaker and linguist, says it is harder for him to understand than the Jula on Radio Abidjan. Men who travel speak Jula to outsiders, but women and children do not speak Jula. Understanding of Jula ranged from 45% in a southeastern village to 85% in the northwest. All ages. 'Marka' is used for followers of the traditional religion, 'Dafing' for Muslim speakers. Different from the Marka dialect of Soninke. Grammar. SOV; postpositions; genitives, articles, adjectives, numerals, relatives after noun heads; question word final; word order distinguishes subject, object, indirect object; CV. Literacy rate in second language: 5% haltingly in French, some in Jula. Radio programs. Savannah. Plains. Peasant agriculturalists. Muslim, traditional religion, Christian. Bible portions.

MOBA ***(MOA, MOAB, MOARE, BEN)*** [MFQ] 1,800 in Burkina Faso (1991). Boulgou Province, Ouargaye Subdistrict. Niger-Congo, Atlantic-Congo, Volta-Congo, North, Gur, Central, Northern, Oti-Volta, Gurma, Moba. Related to Bimoba in Ghana, but not inherently intelligible. All ages. Bible portions 1941-1984. See main entry under Togo.

MÒORÉ ***(MOOSE, MORE, MOLE, MOSSI, MOSHI)*** [MHM] 5,000,000 in Burkina Faso, 53% of the population (1998), including 15,700 Yana (1991). Population total all countries 5,050,000 or more. Central Ouagadougou area and throughout the country. Also spoken in Benin, Côte d'Ivoire, Ghana, Mali, Togo. Niger-Congo, Atlantic-Congo, Volta-Congo, North, Gur, Central, Northern, Oti-Volta, Western, Northwest. Dialects: SAREMDÉ, TAOLENDÉ, YAADRÉ, OUAPADOUPOU, YAANDE, ZAORE (JOORE), YANA (YANGA, JAAN). Yana has over 90% intelligibility with Ouagadougou Mòoré, 75% to 80% with Joore. Joore with Ouagadougou varies from 88% in Tibga to 95% in Diabo. Some who have travelled outside the area speak Jula as second language. All ages. Dominant African language of Burkina Faso. 'Moose' is the name of the people (pl.) or 'Moaaga' (sg.); 'Mòoré' of the language. Other spellings reflect obsolete spellings or pronunciations of nonspeakers. Dictionary. Grammar. SOV; postpositions; genitives, articles, adjectives, numerals after noun heads; question word final; word order distinguishes subjects, objects; CV, CVC, CVV, CCV; tonal. More literacy materials needed. Radio programs. Savannah. Peasant agriculturalists. Traditional religion, Muslim, Christian. Bible 1983, in press (1998).

NATIORO ***(KOO'RA, NATYORO, NATJORO)*** [NTI] 2,400 (1991 Vanderaa). Léraba Province, Sindou Subdistrict, extreme west, almost due west of Banfora, around the town of Sindou; and in Dinaoro, Timba, and Kawara. The presence of Natioro in Mali or Côte d'Ivoire is unconfirmed. Niger-Congo, Atlantic-Congo, Volta-Congo, North, Gur, Wara-Natioro. Dialects: KAOUARA-TIMBA-SINDOU-KORONI, GINAOUROU. Similar to Wara but not inherently intelligible. They live mixed with the Jula, Sénufo, and blacksmiths, are intermarrying, and are quite bilingual in Jula. All ages. Muslim, traditional religion.

NUNI, NORTHERN ***(NOUNI, NUNUMA, NOUNOUMA, NUNA, NUNE, NIBULU, NURUMA)*** [NUV] 45,000 to 55,000, including 15,000 to 25,000 in Northwestern Nuni, 25,000 to 35,000 in Northeastern Nuni (1995 SIL). Sissili and Sanguié provinces, near Boromo. The dividing line between the dialects is the Mouhoun River. Niger-Congo, Atlantic-Congo, Volta-Congo, North, Gur, Central, Southern, Grusi, Northern. Dialect: NORTHWESTERN NUNI. NORTHEASTERN NUNI. Speakers of Northern Nuni cannot understand Southern Nuni. Closely related to Kasem and Lyélé. Jula is used by children and those older as a second language by Northwestern dialect speakers; Lyélé by Northeastern dialect speakers who trade at local markets; French by leaders and young people who have been to school. All ages. The people are called 'Nuna'. SVO; postpositions; genitives before noun heads; articles, adjectives, numerals, relatives after noun heads; question word initial; 1 prefix, 1 suffix; word order distinguishes subject and object; causatives; comparatives; CV, CVV, CVCV tonal. Literacy rate in first language: 1%. Literacy rate in second language: 5% in French. High motivation for literacy. Government coordinated literacy program in Sanguié and Sissili provinces. Savannah. Plains. Peasant agriculturalists. 250 meters. Traditional religion, Muslim, Christian.

NUNI, SOUTHERN ***(NOUNI, NUNUMA, NOUNOUMA, NUNA, NUNE, NIBULU, NURUMA)*** [NNW] 100,000 to 200,000 (1995 SIL). Sissili Province, around Léo, in eastern Mouhoun Province, southern Boulkiemdé and Sanguié provinces, western Nahouri and Kossi provinces. Over 100 villages. Niger-Congo, Atlantic-Congo, Volta-Congo, North, Gur, Central, Southern, Grusi, Northern. Dialects: MICARI,

BASINYARI (SUNDONI), YATINI, GORI, BWANA, SANKURA. Closely related to Kasena and Lyélé. Mòoré is sometimes used as a second language mainly by men; French by leaders and young people. All ages. The people are called 'Nuna'. SVO; postpositions; genitives before noun heads; articles, adjectives, numerals, relatives after noun heads; question word initial; 1 prefix, 1 suffix; word order distinguishes subject and object; causatives; comparatives; CV, CVV, CVCV tonal. Literacy rate in first language: 10%. Literacy rate in second language: 5% in French. Savannah. Plains. Peasant agriculturalists. 300 meters. Traditional religion, Muslim, Christian. NT, in press (1999).

PANA ***(SAMA)*** [PNQ] 5,000 in Burkina Faso (1998). Population total both countries 7,800. Sourou Province, Kassoum Subdistrict, around the town of Oué in the valley of the Sourou River where it enters from Mali, on the border due north of Dédougou. Also spoken in Mali. Niger-Congo, Atlantic-Congo, Volta-Congo, North, Gur, Central, Southern, Grusi, Northern. Dialects: PANA NORTH, PANA SOUTH. Bambara or Jula are used as second languages. Young people are free to use Jula and Marka-Dafin in the home. All ages. The people call themselves and their language 'Pana'. Muslim, traditional religion, Christian.

PWĨẼ ***(PUGULI, BUGULI, POUGOULI, PWIEN, PWẼ, PWA, PWO, BUGURI)*** [PUG] 13,000 to 15,000 (1998 SIL). Tuy, Ioba, and Bougouriba provinces. One area is between 10 and 50 km. north and west of Diébougou, the other is between 25 and 40 km. northeast of Dano. Other villages are scattered throughout the Dagaari territory. 450 sq. km. Niger-Congo, Atlantic-Congo, Volta-Congo, North, Gur, Central, Southern, Grusi, Western. Pwĩẽ is closely related to Winye and Sisala. The degree of bilingualism in Northern Dagaari (women more fluent, used in markets), Jula (men more fluent, used for trade, common topics), and French (those who have been to school) varies among villages and speakers. All ages. Vigorous. They are strongly attached to their language. 'Pwĩẽ' is their name for the language, 'Puguli' is used by outsiders, 'Phu' is their name for one person , 'Phuo' for the people. Tonal. Literacy rate in second language: 1% in French. Motivation for Pwĩẽ literacy is high. Scrub forest, savannah. Plains. Peasant agriculturalists. 250 meters. Traditional religion, Muslim, Christian.

SAMO, MATYA ***(TOUGAN, WEST CENTRAL GOE, SAN, SANE, NORTHWESTERN SAMO)*** [STJ] Population total both countries 105,000 in Tougan (1995 R. Jones SIM). Sourou Province, concentrations in Mouna and Solenzo areas, and Ouaga, Bobo, Dedougou, and Koudougou cities. Also spoken in Mali. Niger-Congo, Mande, Eastern, Eastern, Samo. Speakers of other dialects tend to use Jula with speakers from Tougan. Jula is used in some churches. Reciprocal bilingualism with Mòoré along the eastern border of the area. The Rimaïbé are Samo who were former Fula slaves, now speak Fulfulde as second language, and live in Kawara, Kassan, Zoumou, Teri, in the Tougan area. Other Rimaïbe in Biba and Sankoe in the Toma area no longer speak Fulfulde. Tougan is a large and politically important dialect. Motivation to read French is high. A literacy center near Tougan teaches Jula. Traditional religion, Christian.

SAMO, MAYA ***(SAN, SA, NORTHEASTERN SAMO)*** [SYM] 38,000 (1999). North central Burkina Faso, Sourou Province. Niger-Congo, Mande, Eastern, Eastern, Samo. Dialects: BOUNOU, KIEMBARA (NORTHEASTERN GOE), BANGASSOGO, GOMBORO. Intelligibility with Matya Samo varies between 28% and 50%, depending on the village and text tested; with Southern Samo it is less than 10%. Less than 10% are monolingual. In the east, young people learn Mòoré well and it is the trade language; in the west Jula is the more important trade language. French is used in elementary and secondary schools. Samo is used at home, with friends and relatives, and in the village. All ages. Vigorous. Literacy rate in first language: Below 2%. Literacy rate in second language: Below 20% French, below 10% Mòoré. Fairly successful literacy program in the early 1990s by RC no longer in progress. Savannah. Plains. Peasant agriculturalists. 200 to 400 meters. Muslim, traditional religion, Christian.

SAMO, SOUTHERN ***(SAN, SANE)*** [SBD] 85,000 (1998). Nayala Province, concentrations in Nouna and Solenzo areas, and Ouaga, Bobo, Dedougou, and Koudougou cities. Toma dialect is in Toma, Yaba, Gossina, Ye, Kougny, and Gassan departments. Niger-Congo, Mande, Eastern, Eastern, Samo. Dialect: TOMA (NYAANA, MAKAA). Some serious difficulty in intelligibility among Samo varieties. Northern Samo speakers have below 10% inherent intelligibility with Southern Samo. Toma speakers are more bilingual in French; the other Southern Samo speakers in Jula. Older men who have traveled a lot are bilingual in Jula; otherwise it is mainly youth who are bilingual in Jula. Jula is used in commerce, especially with non-Samo. Jula is used in some churches. Reciprocal bilingualism with Mòoré along the eastern border of the area. The Rimaïbé are Samo who were former Fula slaves, now speak Fulfulde as second language, and live in Kawara, Kassan, Zoumou, Teri, in the Tougan area. Other Rimaïbe in Biba and Sankoe in the Toma area no longer speak Fulfulde. All ages. Toma is the larger and more politically important dialect. Grammar. Literacy rate in second language: Higher among Toma. Motivation to read French and Toma Samo is high. A literacy center in Toma teaches Toma. Traditional religion, Muslim, Christian. NT 1995.

SEEKU ***(SAMBLA, SEMBLA, SOUTHERN SAMO, SAMOGHO)*** [SOS] 17,000 including 5,000 in the northern dialect, 4 villages, 12,000 in the southern, 7 villages. Houet Province, Bobo-Dioulasso Department, west of Bobo-Dioulasso, villages of Karankasso, Bouendé, Torosso, Banzo, Tiara, Bama. Niger-Congo, Mande, Western, Northwestern, Samogo, Dzuun-Seeku, Seeku. Dialects: NORTHERN SEEKU (TIMIKU), SOUTHERN SEEKU (GBENEKU). Dialects have good inherent intelligibility. Close to Dzùùngo. 3 minor dialects. Prost says lexical correspondence to Samogho Gouan and Samogho Ire is 50%. Bilingual proficiency in Jula is uneven across the population; higher in adults. French is used mainly by the young people. Seeku is used at home and with other Seemogo. All ages. 'Seeku' is their own name for the language, 'Seemogo' for the people. Mixed with Toussian speakers in the south and Bobo Dioula in the north. SOV; tonal. Literacy rate in second language: Below 5%. Motivation for literacy is high. Savannah. Plains. Peasant agriculturalists. 400 meters. Muslim, Christian.

SÉNOUFO, NANERIGÉ ***(NANDERGÉ, NANERGÉ, NANERGUÉ, NANDEREKE, NAANI)*** [SEN] 50,000 (1985 census). Northern 2/3 of Kénédougou Province, from Djigouéra and north. Niger-Congo, Atlantic-Congo, Volta-Congo, North, Gur, Senufo, Suppire-Mamara. Some intelligibility with Tagba. No significant dialects or subgroups. Most men speak Jula for trade and contact with non-Senoufo, though not all speak it in the home or village. Most women speak minimal Jula and seldom use it. French is spoken only by those who have been to school, but is not used in the home or village. All ages. 'Nanerige' is the name of the people. Investigation needed: intelligibility with Mali dialects. Literacy rate in second language: Some in Jula or French. Savannah. Plains. Peasant agriculturalists. Traditional religion, Muslim, Christian.

SÉNOUFO, SENARA ***(SÉNOUFO, NIANGOLO)*** [SEQ] 50,000 (1995 SIL). Southwest Burkina Faso, Leraba Province. Niger-Congo, Atlantic-Congo, Volta-Congo, North, Gur, Senufo, Senari. Intelligibility testing with Cebaara varies from 51% in Konadougou to 71% in Niankorodougou; with Pomoro of Mali varies from 42% in Konadougou to 74% in Niankorodougou. All ages. Traditional religion, Muslim.

SÉNOUFO, SÌCÌTÉ ***(SÌCÌTÉ, SÌPÌÌTÉ, SÌCÌRÉ, SUCITE, TAGBA)*** [SEP] 35,000 (1999 SIL). Population total all countries 35,000 or more. Kénédougou Province, Tagouara Plateau, Koloko and Ouelaní prefectures, west of Bobo-Dioulasso, to the Mali border. Also spoken in Côte d'Ivoire, Mali. Niger-Congo, Atlantic-Congo, Volta-Congo, North, Gur, Senufo, Suppire-Mamara. Difficult intelligibility with Nanerige. Bilingual level estimates for Jula are 0 5%, 1 13%, 2 55%, 3 12%, 4 9%, 5 6%. Most adults know enough Jula to meet routine social needs and discuss most common topics, but it is used only with strangers, as in the market. Those who have been to school use French only if a stranger does not know Jula. All ages. They call their language 'Sénoufo Sìcìté', themselves 'Sìcijuubíí' (pl.), or 'Sìcijuungé' (sg.), and their region 'Tagba'. 'Tagba' is used by outsiders for them. Little intermarriage with others in the southern area. SOV, postpositions, genitives before nouns, articles, adjectives, numerals after nouns, question word initial, 1 prefix, 2 suffixes, word order distinguishes subjects, objects, indirect objects; CV, CVV; 3 tones. Literacy rate in first language: A few. Literacy rate in second language: 20% Jula or French. Radio programs. Scrub forest, gallery forest. Plateau, interfluvial. Swidden agriculturalists. Traditional religion, Muslim, Christian. Bible portions 1995.

SIAMOU ***(SIÉMOU, SIEMU, SYÉMOU, SÉMU, SEME)*** [SIF] 20,000 in Burkina Faso (1999). Population total all countries 40,000 or more. Kénédougou Province, 80 km. west of Bobo-Dioulasso, centering in Orodara, plus several small villages: Tin, Diossogou, Diéri, Kotoudéni, Diéridéni, Didéri, Lidara, and Bandougou. Also spoken in Côte d'Ivoire, Mali. Niger-Congo, Atlantic-Congo, Volta-Congo, Kru, Seme. Dialect: BANDOUGOU. Minor dialect differences between villages and within Orodara. The Bandougou dialect is considered different, but intelligibility among dialects seems adequate. No closely related languages. Bilingual level estimates for Jula are 0 1%, 1 4%, 2 10%, 3 30%, 4 50%, 5 5%. A few also speak French as second language. Vigorous. They are reserved toward people who cannot speak Siamou. Previously classified as Mande. Their tradition says they came from the south. SOV; postpositions; genitives, articles, personal pronouns before noun heads; adjectives, numerals after noun heads; question word final for yes-no questions; content question words appear in normal position: e.g., S-O-adverbial-O of prep; word order distinguishes subjects and objects; CV, CVC, CCV; tonal. Literacy rate in second language: A few in Jula, some in French. Savannah, scrub forest. Plains, interfluvial. Swidden agriculturalists, peasant agriculturalists. Traditional religion, Muslim, Christian.

SININKERE ***(SILINKERE, SILANKE)*** [SKQ] 6,000 (1999 SIL). Sanmatenga Province, near Pensa. Niger-Congo, Mande, Western, Central-Southwestern, Central, Manding-Jogo, Manding-Vai, Manding-Mokole, Manding. Ability in Fulfulde is good community-wide. Some prefer to speak Fulfulde. A lot of intermarriage with the Fulfulde. Proficiency in Mòoré is less. Not everyone learns Mòoré well. All ages. Muslim.

SISSALA ***(SISAALI)*** [SLD] 13,000 (1991 SIL). Sissili Province, between Léo and Hamale. 30 villages. Niger-Congo, Atlantic-Congo, Volta-Congo, North, Gur, Central, Southern, Grusi, Western. All one dialect in Burkina Faso. A separate language from the Sisaala languages in Ghana, although closest to Busilli (Western Sisaala). All ages. Traditional religion, Muslim, Christian. NT 1999.

SONGHAY ***(SONGHAI, SONGAI, SONGAY, SONGOY, SONGOI, SONGHOY, SONRAI, SONRHAI, CENTRAL SONGAI)*** [HMB] 125,000 in Burkina Faso (1999). Séno Province around Dori. Nilo-Saharan, Songhai, Southern. Dialect: MARENSÉ. Closest to Humburi Senni Songhay or Zarma. All ages. Investigation needed: intelligibility. Marensé: Indigo dyeing. Muslim. See main entry under Mali.

TAMASHEQ, KIDAL ***(TIMBUKTU, TOMACHECK, TAMASHEKIN, TUAREG)*** [TAQ] 20,000 to 30,000 in Burkina Faso (1991 SIL). Oudalan Province. Afro-Asiatic, Berber, Tamasheq, Southern. Dialects: TIMBUKTU (TOMBOUCTOU, TANASLAMT), TADGHAQ (KIDAL). The two dialects may be separate languages. People are called 'Tuareg' ('Targi', singular), language 'Tamasheq'. Muslim. Bible portions 1953. See main entry under Mali.

TÉÉN ***(TÉNHÉ, TEGESIE, LORHON, LOGHON, LORON, NABE)*** [LOR] 2,000 in Burkina Faso (1999). Poni Province, Kampti Subdistrict, two pockets just west of Kampti. Niger-Congo, Atlantic-Congo, Volta-Congo, North, Gur, Teen. Closest to Loma, then Kulango, Nabanj, but a separate language. Bilingualism in Lobi, Jula, Loma, French. The people are called 'Ténsé' (sg.), 'Ténbo' (pl.). Savannah. Traditional religion, some Christian. See main entry under Côte d'Ivoire.

TIÉFO ***(TYEFO, TYEFORO, KIEFO)*** [TIQ] 1,000 speakers (1995 SIL), out of 12,000 to 15,000 in ethnic group (1995 SIL). Comoé Province, east of Toussiana, Dramandougou Tiéfo, one village. Other ethnic Tiéfo in about 20 villages, extending into Houet Province, speak Jula as mother tongue. Niger-Congo, Atlantic-Congo, Volta-Congo, North, Gur, Tiefo. Dialects: NOUMOUDARA-KOUMOUDARA, DRAMANDOUGOU-NYARAFO. They use Jula to those who do not speak Tiéfo. Tiéfo is used in the home and in every domain. All ages. Noumoudara-Koumoudara dialect is extinct. Five of nine respondents are not upset when Tiéfo young people use Jula in the home. They are endogamous within the village. Investigation needed: attitudes. Tonal. Literacy rate in second language: 1% in French. Nine of ten respondents state they would prefer to learn to read and write Tiéfo. Savannah, scrub forest. Plains. Peasant agriculturalists. 300 to 400 meters. Traditional religion.

TOUSSIAN, NORTHERN ***(TUSIA, TUSIAN)*** [TSP] 19,500 including 1,000 in Wenteene dialect, 18,500 in the other dialects (1995 SIL). Comoé Province, north, east, and south of Oradara. Niger-Congo, Atlantic-Congo, Volta-Congo, North, Gur, Tusia. Dialects: TER, TRU, KEBEENTON, WENTEENE. Dialects in the northern region are inherently intelligible to their speakers, but the speakers have 45% inherent intelligibility of Southern Toussian. Jula is used as second language with high competence among all subgroups to outsiders, for government, and for trade. French is used some for government contacts. Toussian is used in the home and ethnic group. All ages. SOV; postpositions; genitives, articles, adjectives, numerals, relatives after noun heads; word order distinguishes subjects, objects, indirect objects, passives; V, CV, CVC, CCV; tonal. Literacy rate in second language: 5% in French, 3% in Jula. Savannah. Plains. Peasant agriculturalists. 400 to 700 meters. Traditional religion, Muslim, Christian.

TOUSSIAN, SOUTHERN ***(WIN, TUSIA, TUSIAN)*** [WIB] 19,500 (1995 SIL). Population total both countries 19,500 or more. Comoé and Houet provinces, about half way between Banfora and Bobo-Dioulasso, around center of Toussiana. Also spoken in Côte d'Ivoire. Niger-Congo, Atlantic-Congo, Volta-Congo, North, Gur, Tusia. 40% inherent intelligibility of Northern Toussian. Nianha dialect is central. Each village has a separate dialect. The people are fairly fluent in Jula (all ages and sexes, adults more than young people, men more than women), and some in French (only those who have been to school, used for trade, and discussing weather). Toussian is used at home and with other Toussian. All ages. SOV; post-positions; genitives before noun heads; articles, adjectives, numerals, relatives after noun heads; word order distinguishes subjects, objects, indirect objects, passives; causatives; comparatives; V, CV, CVC, CCV; tonal. Literacy rate in second language: 5% in French, 3% in Jula. Savannah. Plains. Peasant agriculturalists. 400 to 500 meters. Traditional religion, Muslim, Christian.

TURKA ***(TOURKA, TURUKA, CURAMA, TYURAMA)*** [TUZ] 37,000 (1998 Suggett SIL). Population total both countries 37,000 or more. Comoé Province, north and west of Banfora. The principal villages are the dialects named. Also spoken in Côte d'Ivoire. Niger-Congo, Atlantic-Congo, Volta-Congo, North, Gur, Central, Southern, Kirma-Tyurama. Dialects: DOUNA, BEREGADOUGOU-TOUMOUSSENI. Cerma is the closest language, but it is not inherently intelligible with Turka. Bilingualism in Jula. All ages. Muslim, traditional religion, Christian.

VIEMO ***(VIGUÉ, VIGE, VIGYE)*** [VIG] 8,000 (1995 SIL). Houet Province, Karankasso Vigué Department, 40 km. southeast of Bobo Dioulasso. Niger-Congo, Atlantic-Congo, Volta-Congo, North, Gur, Viemo.

The second language of all is Jula, used for trade, most topics to outsiders. Few have learned French, or go very far in school. Viemo is used in the homes and for all village domains, with other Viemo. All ages. Vigorous. Tonal. Literacy rate in second language: 5% in Jula, 1% in French. Savannah, scrub forest. Plains. Peasant agriculturalists. 200 to 400 meters. Traditional religion, Muslim.

WARA ***(OUARA, OUALA, SAMOE)*** [WBF] 4,500 (1993 Johnstone). Comoé Province, west of Banfora, near the town of Sindou. The main village is Néguéni. Niger-Congo, Atlantic-Congo, Volta-Congo, North, Gur, Wara-Natioro. Dialects: NEGUENI-KLANI, OUATOUROU-NIASOGONI, SOULANI, FANIAGARA. Negueni has over 95% intelligibility with Niansogoni, but the reverse is below 80%. No intelligibility with Natioro. They speak Wara among themselves and Jula to outsiders. Everyone but the youngest children speaks Jula, but proficiency is limited. All ages. Pride in Wara. Traditional religion, Muslim, Christian.

WINYÉ ***(KÕ, KOLS, KOLSI)*** [KST] 20,000 (1999 SIL). Bali Province, Boromo Subdistrict, around Boromo, about half way between Bobo-Dioulosso and Ouagadougou on main route. 17 to 18 villages. Niger-Congo, Atlantic-Congo, Volta-Congo, North, Gur, Central, Southern, Grusi, Western. Close to Sisaala. Almost entirely monolingual. Traditional religion, Christian, Muslim.

ZARMA ***(DYERMA, DYARMA, DYABARMA, ZABARMA, ADZERMA, DJERMA, ZARBARMA)*** [DJE] 600 in Burkina Faso (1987 SIL). Nilo-Saharan, Songhai, Southern. Muslim. Bible 1990. See main entry under Niger.

BURUNDI

Republic of Burundi. Republika y'Uburundi. Formerly part of Ruanda-Urundi. National or official languages: Rundi, French. 6,457,000 (1998 UN). Literacy rate 14% to 30%. Also includes Rwanda. Information mainly from J. Bendor-Samuel 1989. Christian, traditional religion, Muslim. Blind population 11,000 (1982 WCE). Data accuracy estimate: B. The number of languages listed for Burundi is 3. Of those, all are living languages. Diversity index 0.00.

FRENCH [FRN] Indo-European, Italic, Romance, Italo-Western, Western, Gallo-Iberian, Gallo-Romance, Gallo-Rhaetian, Oïl, French. Official language. Bible 1530-1986. See main entry under France.

RUNDI ***(KIRUNDI, URUNDI)*** [RUD] 4,600,000 in Burundi (1986). Population total all countries 6,000,000 (1999 WA). Also spoken in Rwanda, Tanzania, Uganda. Niger-Congo, Atlantic-Congo, Volta-Congo, Benue-Congo, Bantoid, Southern, Narrow Bantu, Central, J, Rwanda-Rundi (J.60). Dialects of the Hutu and Tutsi are similar. Twa is more different but all are inherently intelligible, and also intelligible with Kinyarwanda (Rwanda). Some speakers use Swahili as a lingua franca. Hima is an ethnic group speaking Rundi or Rwanda. Ethnic groups: Hutu 80% to 85%, Tutsi 14% to 15%, Twa (Gesera, pygmy) 1% (30,000; 1972 Barrett). National language. Literacy rate in first language: 55%. Christian, traditional religion, Muslim; Twa: traditional religion, Christian. Bible 1967.

SWAHILI [SWA] Widely spoken in the capital. Spoken as first language in Buyenzi, Quartier asiatique, Muslim neighborhoods, and Congolese neighborhoods (probably Congo Swahili). Spoken by Muslims in other cities like Gitega. Niger-Congo, Atlantic-Congo, Volta-Congo, Benue-Congo, Bantoid, Southern, Narrow Bantu, Central, G, Swahili (G.40). Used in some churches (especially Congolese). Radio programs, TV. Muslim. Bible 1891-1996. See main entry under Tanzania.

CAMEROON

Republic of Cameroon. Formerly French Cameroun and British Cameroons. National or official languages: English, French. 14,305,000 (1998 UN). Literacy rate 63.4%, including 75% males, 52.1% females (1995 Encyclopedia Britannica). Also includes Efai, Herde. Information mainly from J. Bendor-Samuel 1989; R. Breton 1991; SIL 1973-1999. Christian, Muslim, traditional religion, Baha'i. Blind population 15,630 (1982 WCE). Data accuracy estimate: A2, B. The number of languages listed for Cameroon is 286. Of those, 279 are living languages, 3 are second languages without mother tongue speakers, and 4 are extinct. Diversity index 0.97.

ABO ***(BO, ABAW)*** [ABB] North of Douala and west of the Wouri River, and Dibombari, Moungo Division, Littoral Province. Niger-Congo, Atlantic-Congo, Volta-Congo, Benue-Congo, Bantoid, Southern, Narrow Bantu, Northwest, A, Basaa (A.40). Dialect: BANKON. Close to Barombi. Investigation needed: intelligibility with Barombi, bilingual proficiency.

AFADE ***(AFFADE, AFADEH, MANDAGE)*** [AAL] Centered around Afade in the southern part of Makari Subdivision, Logone-and-Chari Division, Far North Province. Afro-Asiatic, Chadic, Biu-Mandara, B, B.1, Kotoko Proper. It is unclear if the high comprehension of Mpade is because of dialect closeness or bilingualism. The name 'Mandage', etc., is applied to the northern Kotoko languages. Investigation needed: intelligibility with Mpade, bilingual proficiency in Mpade. Literacy rate in first language: Below 1%. Literacy rate in second language: 5% to 15%. See main entry under Nigeria.

AGHEM ***(WUM, YUM)*** [AGQ] 20,000 to 25,000 (1993 SIL). In and around Wum, Wum Central Subdivision, Menchum Division, North West Province. Niger-Congo, Atlantic-Congo, Volta-Congo, Benue-Congo, Bantoid, Southern, Wide Grassfields, Narrow Grassfields, Ring, West. May be intelligible with Isu or Weh. Regional differences in speech are minimal. English is used as second language. Some use Cameroon Pidgin. Speakers consider Weh and Isu to be separate languages. There appears to be multilingualism with Weh and Isu. Low comprehension of Kom and Essimbi. Aghem Cultural and Development Association interested in language development. Investigation needed: intelligibility with dialects. Literacy rate in first language: Below 1%. Literacy rate in second language: 15% to 25%. Traditional religion, Christian.

AKOOSE ***(BAKOSSI, BEKOOSE, AKOSI, KOOSE, KOSI, NKOSI, NKOOSI)*** [BSS] 70,000 (1998 R. Hedinger SIL). Bangem and Tombel subdivisions, Kupe-Muanenguba Division, South West Province, Manjo Subdivision, and Moungo Division, Littoral Province. Niger-Congo, Atlantic-Congo, Volta-Congo, Benue-Congo, Bantoid, Southern, Narrow Bantu, Northwest, A, Lundu-Balong (A.10), Ngoe. Dialects: NORTHERN BAKOSSI, WESTERN BAKOSSI, SOUTHERN BAKOSSI, MWAMBONG, NINONG, ELUNG (ELONG, ALONG, NLONG), MWAMENAM (MOUAMENAM). Dictionary. Literacy rate in first language: Below 1%. Literacy rate in second language: 25%. Bible portions 1998.

AKUM ***(ANYAR)*** [AKU] 600 (1986 R. Breton). Population total both countries 600 or more. Near the Nigerian border, Akum village, Furu-Awa Subdivision, Menchum Division, North West Province. 3 villages in Nigeria (Manga, Ekban, Konkom). Also spoken in Nigeria. Niger-Congo, Atlantic-Congo, Volta-Congo, Benue-Congo, Cross River, Unclassified. Not Bendi; may be Jukunoid. Bilingualism in Jukun is limited. Cameroons Pidgin is spoken in the area also. The people are called 'Anyar'. Mountain slope.

AMBELE [AEL] In about 10 villages in eastern Batibo Subdivision, Momo Division, North West Province. Niger-Congo, Atlantic-Congo, Volta-Congo, Benue-Congo, Bantoid, Southern, Wide Grassfields, Western Momo. May be related to Busamor Atong.

ARABIC, SHUWA ***(ARABE CHOA, SHUA ARABIC, CHOA, CHOWA, SHUA, CHADIAN SPOKEN ARABIC)*** [SHU] 63,600 in Cameroon (1982 SIL). Mayo-Sava, Diamere, Mayo-Danay and Logone and Chari Division, Far North Province. Mostly between Lake Chad and Kousseri, with some pockets of speakers south of Kousseri. Afro-Asiatic, Semitic, Central, South, Arabic. Trade language. Muslim. NT 1967-1991. See main entry under Chad.

ATONG [ATO] Extreme northwestern part of Batibo Subdivision, Momo Division, Northwest Province. Niger-Congo, Atlantic-Congo, Volta-Congo, Benue-Congo, Bantoid, Southern, Wide Grassfields, Western Momo. Related to Ambele and Busam.

AWING ***(AWI, BAMBULUWE)*** [AZO] Awing-Bambaluwe village, Mezam Division, North West Province. Niger-Congo, Atlantic-Congo, Volta-Congo, Benue-Congo, Bantoid, Southern, Wide Grassfields, Narrow Grassfields, Mbam-Nkam, Ngemba. Dialect: MBWE'WI. Also related to Bafut, Bambili, Kpati, Mendankwe, Ngemba, and Pinyin. 74% lexical similarity with Bamukumbit.

BABA ***(PAPIA, BAPA, BAPAKUM)*** [BBW] 12,750 (1982 SIL). East of Ndop on Ndop Plain, Mezam Division, North West Province. Niger-Congo, Atlantic-Congo, Volta-Congo, Benue-Congo, Bantoid, Southern, Wide Grassfields, Narrow Grassfields, Mbam-Nkam, Nun. Related to Mungaka. Speakers refer to their language as 'Papia'.

BABANKI ***(KIDZEM, KIDZOM, FINGE, KEJENG, KEDJOM)*** [BBK] Centered around village of Babanki, Tuba Subdivision, Mezam Division, North West Province. Niger-Congo, Atlantic-Congo, Volta-Congo, Benue-Congo, Bantoid, Southern, Wide Grassfields, Narrow Grassfields, Ring, Center. Babanki people refer to themselves as 'Kedjom Keku' (Big Babanki) and 'Kedjom ke Tinguh' (Babanki Tungo).

BAFANJI ***(BAFANYI, BAFANGI, CHUUFI)*** [BFJ] 8,500 (1982 SIL). South of Ndop on Ndop Plain, Ngo-Ketunjia Division, North West Province. Niger-Congo, Atlantic-Congo, Volta-Congo, Benue-Congo, Bantoid, Southern, Wide Grassfields, Narrow Grassfields, Mbam-Nkam, Nun. Closely related to Bamali, Bamenyam, and Bambalang. Speakers refer to their language as 'Chuufi'.

BAFAW-BALONG ***(NGOE)*** [BWT] 8,400 (1982 SIL). North of Kumba along Kumba-Mamfe Road, Meme Division, South West Province; and southeast of Ekondo-Titi, Meme Division, South West Province and Moungo Division, Littoral Province. Niger-Congo, Atlantic-Congo, Volta-Congo, Benue-Congo, Bantoid, Southern, Narrow Bantu, Northwest, A, Lundu-Balong (A.10), Ngoe. Dialects: BAFAW (BAFO, BAFOWU, AFO, NHO, LEFO'), BALONG (BALON, BALUNG, NLONG, VALONGI, BAYI, BAI). Some linguists consider this to be 2 languages. Fairly bilingual in Duala. Language community is heterogeneous.

BAFIA ***(RIKPA, LEFA', RIPEY, RIKPA', BEKPAK)*** [KSF] 60,000 (1991 UBS). Deuk and Bafia subdivisions, Mbam Division, Center Province. Niger-Congo, Atlantic-Congo, Volta-Congo, Benue-Congo, Bantoid, Southern, Narrow Bantu, Northwest, A, Bafia (A.50). Dialects: BALOM (FAK), KPA, BAPE. Speakers refer to their language as 'Rikpa' and to themselves as 'Bekpak'. NT 1996.

BAFUT ***(BUFE, FU, FUT, BEFE)*** [BFD] 50,000 (1987 Mfonyam). In Bafut, Tuba Subdivision, Mezam Division; and around the village of Beba, Wum Subdivision, Menchum Division, North West Province. Niger-Congo, Atlantic-Congo, Volta-Congo, Benue-Congo, Bantoid, Southern, Wide Grassfields, Narrow Grassfields, Mbam-Nkam, Ngemba. Dialects: BUFE (AFUGHE, BAFUT), BEBA' (MUBADJI, BATADJI, BABADJI, BEBADJI, BAZHI, BABA'ZHI, BIBA, SHISHONG, BOMBE). Literacy programs in about 10 schools and 30 churches. Traditional religion, Christian. NT, in press (1999).

BAKA ***(PYGMY-E, PYGMEE, BEBAYAKA, BEBAYAGA, BIBAYA, PYGMEES DE L'EST, BABINGA)*** [BKC] 25,000 in Cameroon (1980 Phillips). Population total both countries 28,200. Scattered in the southeast of East Province: Boumba and Ngoko, Kadey, and Upper Nyong divisions; Dja and Lobo Division, South Province. Also spoken in Gabon. Niger-Congo, Atlantic-Congo, Volta-Congo, North, Adamawa-Ubangi, Ubangi, Sere-Ngbaka-Mba, Ngbaka-Mba, Ngbaka, Western, Baka-Gundi. Bayanga of CAR may be a dialect. Nomadic but being encouraged by the government to settle along the roadways. Different from Baka of DRC and Sudan. Dictionary. Tropical forest.

BAKAKA ***(CENTRAL MBO)*** [BQZ] 30,000 (1998 R. Hedinger SIL). Nlonako, Manjo, western Loum and southern Nkongsamba subdivisions, Moungo Division, Littoral Province. Niger-Congo, Atlantic-Congo, Volta-Congo, Benue-Congo, Bantoid, Southern, Narrow Bantu, Northwest, A, Lundu-Balong (A.10), Ngoe. Dialects: BABONG (IHOBE MBOG, IHOBE MBOONG), BANEKA (MWANEKA), BAKAKA (EHOB MKAA, KAA, KAKA), MANEHAS (MWAHED, MWAHET, MVAE), BALONDO (EHOBE BELON), BAFUN (MBWASE NGHUY, MIAMILO, PENDIA). Related to Akoose, Bassossi, and Mbo. Dictionary. Literacy rate in first language: Below 1%. Literacy rate in second language: 25%.

BAKOKO ***(BASOO)*** [BKH] 50,000 (1982 SIL). Scattered communities in Littoral Province, south of Douala, Wouri Division; south of Dibombari, Moungo Division; around Nkondjok, Nkam Division; and southwest of Edea, Sanaga-Maritime Division; northwest area of Ocean Division, South Province. Niger-Congo, Atlantic-Congo, Volta-Congo, Benue-Congo, Bantoid, Southern, Narrow Bantu, Northwest, A, Basaa (A.40). Dialects: ADIE (ELOG MPOO, BASOO BA DIE, BASOO D'EDEA), BISOO (BASSO, BASOO BA LIKOL, ADIANGOK), MBANG (DIMBAMBANG), YABYANG (YABYANG-YAPEKE), YAKALAK (YAKALAG), YAPOMA, YASSUKU (YASOUKOU, YASUG, YASUKU).

BAKOLE ***(BAKOLLE, KOLE, BAMUSSO)*** [KME] 300 (1982 SIL). Around Bamusso, south of the Meme estuary, Ndian Division, South West Province. Niger-Congo, Atlantic-Congo, Volta-Congo, Benue-Congo, Bantoid, Southern, Narrow Bantu, Northwest, A, Duala (A.20). May be intelligible with or bilingual in Mokpwe.

BAKUNDU-BALUE ***(OROKO-EAST)*** [BDU] 65,000 (1982 SIL). West, north, and south of Kumba, South West Province: Kumba Subdivision, Meme Division; and eastern Ekondo-Titi Subdivision, Ndian Division. Niger-Congo, Atlantic-Congo, Volta-Congo, Benue-Congo, Bantoid, Southern, Narrow Bantu, Northwest, A, Lundu-Balong (A.10), Oroko. Dialects: BAKUNDU (KUNDU, LAKUNDU, BEKUNDE, BAWO, NKUNDU), BALUE (LOLUE, BARUE, BABUE, WESTERN KUNDU, LUE), MBONGE, EKOMBE (BEKOMBO, EKUMBE). The language community is heterogeneous. The most homogeneous of the subgroups listed are the Bakundu and Balue, for whom separate literature may be needed. It is reported that the Ekombe do not want to be classified with Bakundu. It may be two or three languages. Investigation needed: intelligibility with dialects. Traditional religion.

BALDAMU ***(MBAZLA)*** [BDN] Diamare Division, Far North Province. Afro-Asiatic, Chadic, Biu-Mandara, A, A.5.

BALO [BQO] Akwaya Subdivision. Niger-Congo, Atlantic-Congo, Volta-Congo, Benue-Congo, Bantoid, Southern, Tivoid. 60% lexical similarity with Osatu, 40% with Ipulo and Caka, 35% with Esimbi and Mesaka. Bilingualism in Pidgin. Literacy is in English, as it is with all languages in NW and SW provinces. Mountains. Traditional religion.

BALUNDU-BIMA ***(OROKO WEST)*** [NGO] 20,000 (1982 SIL). Central part of Ndian Division, southeast and northeast of Mundemba, South West Province. Niger-Congo, Atlantic-Congo, Volta-Congo, Benue-Congo, Bantoid, Southern, Narrow Bantu, Northwest, A, Lundu-Balong (A.10), Oroko. Dialects: BALUNDU (BARONDO, LONDO, LUNDU), BIMA, DOTANGA (BATANGA-BAKOKO, TANGA), NGOLO (NGORO). Batanga is distinct from Batanga (Banoho) of Bantu A.30, and the Batanga dialect of Caka; Bakoko is distinct from Bakoko of Bantu A.40. The language community is heterogeneous.

BAMALI ***(NGOOBECHOP)*** [BBQ] 5,300 (1982 SIL). South of Ndop, Ngo-Ketunjia Division, North West Province. Niger-Congo, Atlantic-Congo, Volta-Congo, Benue-Congo, Bantoid, Southern, Wide

Grassfields, Narrow Grassfields, Mbam-Nkam, Nun. Related to Bafanji, Bamenyam, Bambalang, Bangolan. Speakers refer to their language as 'Ngoobechop'.

BAMBALANG ***(BAMBOLANG, TSHIRAMBO, MBOYAKUM)*** [BMO] 14,500 (1982 SIL). Southeast of Ndop, Ngdo-Ketunjia Division, North West Province. Niger-Congo, Atlantic-Congo, Volta-Congo, Benue-Congo, Bantoid, Southern, Wide Grassfields, Narrow Grassfields, Mbam-Nkam, Nun. Related to Bafanji, Bamenyam, Bamun, Bamali, Bangolan. Speakers refer to their language as 'Mboyakum'.

BAMBILI ***(BAMBUI)*** [BAW] 10,000 or fewer (1984 ALCAM). Bambili and Bambui villages east of Bamenda, along Ring Road, Tuba Subdivision, Mezam Division, North West Province. Niger-Congo, Atlantic-Congo, Volta-Congo, Benue-Congo, Bantoid, Southern, Wide Grassfields, Narrow Grassfields, Mbam-Nkam, Ngemba. Dialects: BAMBILI (MBILI, MBELE, MBOGOE), BAMBUI (MBUI). Inherent intelligibility is low between them and Nkwen and Mendankwe. They associate more with Bafut than with Nkwen and Mendankwe. Grammar. Literacy rate in first language: Below 1%. Literacy rate in second language: 15% to 25%.

BAMENYAM ***(MAMENYAN, PAMENYAN, BAMENYAN, MENGAMBO)*** [BCE] 4,000 (1994 SIL). Around Bamenyam, northwestern Galim Subdivision, Bamboutos Division, West Province; and southeastern Mezam Division, West Province. Niger-Congo, Atlantic-Congo, Volta-Congo, Benue-Congo, Bantoid, Southern, Wide Grassfields, Narrow Grassfields, Mbam-Nkam, Nun. Bati may be a dialect of Bamenyam. Closely related to Bamali, Bafanji, Bambalang. Some bilingualism in French and Cameroons Pidgin. Stronger commercial links with Mbouda than with Ndop. Traditional religion, Christian.

BAMUKUMBIT ***(BAMUNKUM, BAMOUKOUMBIT, BAMENKOUMBIT, BAMENKOMBIT, MANGKONG)*** [BQT] 7,300 including 4,500 in the village (1987 census). Southwest of Ndop on Ndop Plain, Ngo-Ketunjia Division, Balikumbat Subdivision, North West Province, Bamukumbit village. Niger-Congo, Atlantic-Congo, Volta-Congo, Benue-Congo, Bantoid, Southern, Wide Grassfields, Narrow Grassfields, Mbam-Nkam, Ngemba. 74% lexical similarity with Awin. Adults can use Bafanji and Bamali. The few educated beyond primary level can use English as a second language. Cameroons Pidgin is generally spoken and understood. Traditional religion, Christian.

BAMUN ***(BAMOUN, BAMOUM, BAMUM, SHUMPAMEM)*** [BAX] 215,000 (1982 SIL). Most of Noun Division around Foumban, plus the extreme north of Mifi Division and the extreme southeast of Bamboutos Division, West Province. Niger-Congo, Atlantic-Congo, Volta-Congo, Benue-Congo, Bantoid, Southern, Wide Grassfields, Narrow Grassfields, Mbam-Nkam, Nun. Related to Bafanji, Bamali, Bambalang, Bangolan. Trade language. Has its own script, though not used for current orthography. Bible 1988.

BAMUNKA ***(NDOP-BAMUNKA, BAMUNKUN, NIEMENG, MBIKA, MUKA)*** [NDO] 15,200 (1982 SIL). Around village of Bamunka, Ndop Subdivision, Mezam Division, North West Province. Niger-Congo, Atlantic-Congo, Volta-Congo, Benue-Congo, Bantoid, Southern, Wide Grassfields, Narrow Grassfields, Ring, North. Speakers refer to the language as 'Niemeng'.

BANA ***(BAZA, KOMA, KA-BANA, PAROLE DES BANA, MIZERAN)*** [BCW] 13,000 including 8,000 Gamboura and 5,000 Guili (1987 SIL). On Nigerian border, north and northeast of Bourrah, Bourrah Subdivision, Mayo-Tsanaga Division, Far North Province. Afro-Asiatic, Chadic, Biu-Mandara, A, A.3. Dialects: GAMBOURA, GILI (GUILI). Closely related to Psikye and Hya in Cameroon and Kamwe in Nigeria.

BANGANDU ***(BAGANDO, BANGANDO, BANGANTU, SOUTHERN BANGANTU)*** [BGF] Population total both countries 2,700 (1977 Voegelin and Voegelin). Moloundou Subdivision, Boumba and Ngoko Division, East Province. Also spoken in Congo. Niger-Congo, Atlantic-Congo, Volta-Congo, North, Adamawa-Ubangi, Ubangi, Gbaya-Manza-Ngbaka, Southwest. May be related to Ngombe in CAR. Investigation needed: intelligibility with Southwest Gbaya, Ngombe [NMJ].

BANGOLAN [BGJ] 6,300 to 15,000 (1994 SIL). East of Ndop and south of Jakiri, Ngo-Ketunjia Division, North West Province. Niger-Congo, Atlantic-Congo, Volta-Congo, Benue-Congo, Bantoid, Southern, Wide Grassfields, Narrow Grassfields, Mbam-Nkam, Nun. The most distinct linguistically and culturally of the Ndop languages. Most closely related to Bambalang. Bilingualism in Cameroons Pidgin. Traditional religion, Muslim, Christian.

BAROMBI ***(LOMBI, LAMBI, ROMBI, RAMBI, LOMBE)*** [BBI] 1,300 (1982 SIL). South West Province, north of Mount Cameroon around Lake Barombi-Koto and west of Kumba around Lake Barombi-Mbo, Meme Division; and northeast of Ekondo-Titi, Ndian Division. Niger-Congo, Atlantic-Congo, Volta-Congo, Benue-Congo, Bantoid, Southern, Narrow Bantu, Northwest, A, Basaa (A.40). May be intelligible with Abo. Investigation needed: intelligibility with Abo.

BASAA ***(BASSA, BASA, BISAA, NORTHERN MBENE, MVELE, MBELE, MEE, TUPEN, BIKYEK, BICEK)*** [BAA] 230,000 (1982 SIL). Spread all over Nyong-and-Kelle Division, Center Province; and Nkam and Sanaga-Maritime divisions, Littoral Province. Niger-Congo, Atlantic-Congo, Volta-Congo,

Benue-Congo, Bantoid, Southern, Narrow Bantu, Northwest, A, Basaa (A.40). Dialects: BAKEM, BON, BIBENG, DIBOUM, LOG, MPO, MBANG, NDOKAMA, BASSO, NDOKBELE, NDOKPENDA, NYAMTAM. Dictionary. Literacy rate in first language: 5% to 10%. Literacy rate in second language: 25% to 50%. Bible 1969.

BASSOSSI ***(BASOSI, BASOSSI, SOSI, NSWASE, NSWOSE, NSOSE, SWOSE, ASOBSE, NGEN)*** [BSI] Central part of Nguti Subdivision, in Nguti town and east and south of it, Kupe-Muanenguba Division, South West Province. Niger-Congo, Atlantic-Congo, Volta-Congo, Benue-Congo, Bantoid, Southern, Narrow Bantu, Northwest, A, Lundu-Balong (A.10), Ngoe. Dialect: MIENGE (LOWER MBO). Related to Mbo.

BATA ***(GBWATA, BATTA, GWATE, DII)*** [BTA] 2,500 in Cameroon. Along the Nigerian border (30 km. northeast of Garoua), along the Benoue River, west of Garoua and along a small section of the Faro River, Benoue Division, North Province. Afro-Asiatic, Chadic, Biu-Mandara, A, A.8. Dialect: NDEEWE (BATA-NDEEWE). 'Demsa' may be an alternate name or dialect. Bacama dialect is only in Nigeria. See main entry under Nigeria.

BATANGA ***(BANOHO, BANO'O, NOHO, NOKU, BANOO)*** [BNM] 6,000 in Cameroon (1982 SIL). Ocean Division, South Province, scattered along the coast around Kribi. Niger-Congo, Atlantic-Congo, Volta-Congo, Benue-Congo, Bantoid, Southern, Narrow Bantu, Northwest, A, Bube-Benga (A.30). Dialects: BANO'O (BANOO, BANAKA, BANOKO), BAPUKU (PUKU, NAKA, BAPUU), BATANGA. Different from Batanga of South West Province (Balundu-Bima). Bible portions 1953. See main entry under Equatorial Guinea.

BATI ***(BATI BA NGONG, BATI DE BROUSSE)*** [BTC] 800 (1975 census). 4 villages in the Bati Canton, Ndom Subdivision, Sanaga-Maritime Division, Littoral Province. Niger-Congo, Atlantic-Congo, Volta-Congo, Benue-Congo, Bantoid, Southern, Mbam, West (A.40). Most older Bati adults have little problem understanding Basaa, because their schooling used to be in that, and Basaa is used in church. The younger Bati children cannot understand Basaa, because it is not inherently intelligible with Bati. Basaa is not interpreted into Bati in church. Children up to 14 years old are exposed to French for primary education. Markets are in Bakoko and Yambassa-speaking areas, so those languages are used. All ages. Investigation needed: bilingual proficiency in Basaa, French.

BEBE ***(YI BE WU)*** [BZV] West of Nkambe and north of Ring Road, west part of Ako Subdivision, Donga-Mangung Division, North West Province. Niger-Congo, Atlantic-Congo, Volta-Congo, Benue-Congo, Bantoid, Southern, Beboid, Eastern.

BEBELE ***(BAMVELE)*** [BEB] 24,000 (1971 Welmers). Minta Subdivision, Upper Sanaga, Center Province, and Diang Subdivision, Lom-and Djeram Division, East Province. Niger-Congo, Atlantic-Congo, Volta-Congo, Benue-Congo, Bantoid, Southern, Narrow Bantu, Northwest, A, Yaunde-Fang (A.70). Dialects: EKI, MANYOK. Related to Beti, Bulu, Eton, Ewondo, Fang, Mengisa. Bilingualism in Beti. Investigation needed: intelligibility with Bulu, Ewondo, bilingual proficiency in Beti.

BEBIL ***(BOBILIS, GBIGBIL)*** [BXP] 6,000 (1991 SIL). Around Belabo, Belabo Subdivision, Lom-and-Djerem Division, East Province. Niger-Congo, Atlantic-Congo, Volta-Congo, Benue-Congo, Bantoid, Southern, Narrow Bantu, Northwest, A, Yaunde-Fang (A.70). Different from Bebele, although related. Bilingualism in Beti, Bebele.

BEEZEN [BNZ] 400 (1986 R. Breton). Kpwep (Beezen) village, Furu-Awa Subdivision, Menchum Division, North West Province. Niger-Congo, Atlantic-Congo, Volta-Congo, Benue-Congo, Unclassified. May be Jukunoid. Bilingualism in Jukun is limited. Cameroon Pidgin is spoken in the area. Mountain slope.

BEFANG ***(MENCHUM, BIFANG, BEBA-BEFANG, BIBA-BIFANG)*** [BBY] Around Befang, straddling Mezam Division, Tuba Subdivision, and Menchum Division, Wum Subdivision, North West Province. Niger-Congo, Atlantic-Congo, Volta-Congo, Benue-Congo, Bantoid, Southern, Wide Grassfields, Menchum. Dialects: MODELE (BEEKURU, IKU, AKU, USHEIDA, MODELLE, MODELI, IDELE, AMBABIKO), USHAKU (MUKURU, MOKURU), BEFANG (GE, BEBA-BEFANG, BIFANG, ABEFANG), BANGUI (BANGWE, BANGWI), OBANG, OKOMANJANG (OKOROMANDJANG).

BEKWEL ***(BAKWELE, BAKWIL, BEKWIL, OKPELE)*** [BKW] Along the north side of the Ngoko River, at and near Moloundou, Boumba-and-Ngoko Division, East Province. Niger-Congo, Atlantic-Congo, Volta-Congo, Benue-Congo, Bantoid, Southern, Narrow Bantu, Northwest, A, Makaa-Njem (A.80). Dialect: ESEL (ESSEL). Closely related to Konabembe. 85% lexical similarity with Koozime. Bilingualism in Pongpong. Literacy rate in first language: Below 1%. Literacy rate in second language: 5% to 15%. Traditional religion, Christian. See main entry under Congo.

BETI [BTB] (2,000,000 including Fang, Ewondo, Bulu, Mengisa, etc.). Major part of Center and South Provinces; and in Lom-and-Djerem, and Upper Nyong divisions, East Province. Niger-Congo, Atlantic-Congo, Volta-Congo, Benue-Congo, Bantoid, Southern, Narrow Bantu, Northwest, A, Yaunde-Fang (A.70). Consists of a set of 'languages' (Bebele, Bebil, Bulu, Eton, Ewondo, Fang, Mengisa) which are partially intelligible but ethnically distinct. Different from Bette-Bende of Nigeria or the Bété languages of Côte d'Ivoire. Trade language. Bible 1970.

BIKYA ***(FURU)*** [BYB] 1 speaker, plus 3 others who have limited proficiency (1986 R. Breton). Furubana village, Furu-Awa Subdivision, Menchum Division, North West Province. Niger-Congo, Atlantic-Congo, Volta-Congo, Benue-Congo, Bantoid, Southern, Unclassified. May be Eastern Beboid. 24% lexical similarity with Nsaa and Noone (Beboid), 14% with Akum. Bilingualism in Jukun. The speaker is over 70 years old (1986 R. Breton). The people are now called 'Furu', and speak Jukun. They were formerly called 'Bikya'. Mountain slope. Nearly extinct.

BISHUO ***(BIYAM, FURU)*** [BWH] 1 speaker, plus 1 partial speaker (1986 R. Breton). Ntjieka, Furu-Turuwa, and Furu-Sambari villages, Furu-Awa Subdivision, Menchum Division, North West Province. Niger-Congo, Atlantic-Congo, Volta-Congo, Benue-Congo, Bantoid, Southern, Unclassified. May be Jukunoid. 16% to 17% lexical similarity with Nsaa and Noone, 11% with Bikya. Bilingualism in Jukun. The speaker is over 60 years old (1986 R. Breton). The people are called 'Furu' and now speak Jukun. They were formerly called 'Biyam'. Mountain slope. Nearly extinct.

BITARE ***(NJWANDE, YUKUTARE)*** [BRE] 3,700 in Cameroon (1982 SIL). Near Banyo, Mayo-Banyo Division, Adamawa Province. Niger-Congo, Atlantic-Congo, Volta-Congo, Benue-Congo, Bantoid, Southern, Tivoid. See main entry under Nigeria.

BOKYI ***(BOKI, BYOKI, NKI, OKII, UKI, NFUA, OSIKOM, OSUKAM, VAANEROKI)*** [BKY] 3,700 in Cameroon. Along Nigerian border northwest of Mamfe, Akwaya Subdivision, Manyu Division, South West Province. Niger-Congo, Atlantic-Congo, Volta-Congo, Benue-Congo, Cross River, Bendi. Dialects: BASUA, BOKI, IRUAN. Bible 1987. See main entry under Nigeria.

BOMWALI ***(BOMALI, BOUMOALI, BUMALI, LINO, "SANGASANGA")*** [BMW] 5,000 or fewer in Cameroon (1991 SIL). Malapa village, east of Moloundou. Niger-Congo, Atlantic-Congo, Volta-Congo, Benue-Congo, Bantoid, Southern, Narrow Bantu, Northwest, A, Makaa-Njem (A.80). A distinct language from Bekwel. See main entry under Congo.

BONKENG ***(BONGKEN, BONKENGE, BONKENG-PENDIA)*** [BVG] Moungo Division, Loun Subdivision, Littoral Province. Niger-Congo, Atlantic-Congo, Volta-Congo, Benue-Congo, Bantoid, Southern, Narrow Bantu, Northwest, A, Lundu-Balong (A.10). Literacy rate in first language: Below 1%. Literacy rate in second language: 15% to 25%.

BU [BOE] Villages of Bu, Za, and Ngwen, northeast of Wum, Wum Subdivision, Menchum Division, North West Province. Niger-Congo, Atlantic-Congo, Volta-Congo, Benue-Congo, Bantoid, Southern, Beboid, Western.

BUBIA ***(BOBE, BOBEA, WOVEA, BOTA, EWOTA)*** [BBX] 600 (1977 Voegelin and Voegelin). Limbe Subdivision, Fako Division, South West Province. Niger-Congo, Atlantic-Congo, Volta-Congo, Benue-Congo, Bantoid, Southern, Narrow Bantu, Northwest, A, Duala (A.20). Bilingualism in Duala. Investigation needed: bilingual proficiency in Duala.

BUDUMA ***(BOUDOUMA, YEDINA, YADENA, YEDIMA)*** [BDM] 200 in Cameroon. Islands of Lake Chad, Logone and Chari Division, Far North Province. Afro-Asiatic, Chadic, Biu-Mandara, B, B.1, Buduma. Muslim, traditional religion. See main entry under Chad.

BULU ***(BOULOU)*** [BUM] 174,000 (1982 SIL). Second language for as many as 800,000 (1991 UBS). Covers the entire Ntem and Dja-and-Lobo divisions, South Province; the south of Upper Sanaga Division; the north of Nyong-and-Mfoumou Division, Center Province; part of Upper Nyong Division, East Province. Niger-Congo, Atlantic-Congo, Volta-Congo, Benue-Congo, Bantoid, Southern, Narrow Bantu, Northwest, A, Yaunde-Fang (A.70). Dialects: YELINDA, YEMBANA, YENGONO, ZAMAN, BENE. Intelligible with Eton, Ewondo, and Fang as part of the Beti group. Formerly used for education, religion, and commerce, but now in decline. Different from Bulu (Sekiyani) of Gabon. Language of wider communication. Literacy rate in first language: 1% to 5%. Literacy rate in second language: 5% to 15%. Bible 1940.

BUM ***(BOM)*** [BMV] Northern part of Fundong Subdivision, mainly in the villages of Su-Bum and Laa-Bum, Menchum Division, North West Province. Niger-Congo, Atlantic-Congo, Volta-Congo, Benue-Congo, Bantoid, Southern, Wide Grassfields, Narrow Grassfields, Ring, Center.

BUNG [BQD] 3 (1995 Bruce Connell). Near the Kwanja language. Unclassified. It may have been a form of Kwanja. No one uses the language any longer. Nearly extinct.

BUSAM [BXS] In villages of Bifang, Ambambo, and Dinku, Batibo Subdivision, Momo Division, North West Province. Niger-Congo, Atlantic-Congo, Volta-Congo, Benue-Congo, Bantoid, Southern, Wide Grassfields, Western Momo. Related to Ambele and Atong.

BUSUU ***(AWA, FURU)*** [BJU] 8 (1986 R. Breton). Furu-Awa and Furu-Nangwa villages, Furu-Awa Subdivision, Menchum Division, North West Province. Niger-Congo, Atlantic-Congo, Volta-Congo, Benue-Congo, Bantoid, Unclassified. May be Jukunoid. 10% lexical similarity with Jukun languages, 7% to 8% with Beboid languages. Only used by older people for reunions. Children learn only Jukun. People are called 'Furu', and now speak Jukun. Formerly called 'Awa'. Mountain slope. Nearly extinct.

BUWAL ***(MA BUWAL, BUAL, GADALA)*** [BHS] 5,000 or fewer (1983 ALCAM). In and around Gadala, Mokolo Subdivision, Mayo-Tsanaga Division, Far North Province. Afro-Asiatic, Chadic, Biu-Mandara, A, A.7. May be intelligible with Gavar. Speakers closer to Mofu or Gavar regions claim to understand those languages. Fulfulde and French bilingualism is limited. Buwal is used in church. Investigation needed: intelligibility with Gavar.

BYEP ***(NORTH MAKAA, MEKA, MAKA, MAKYA, MEKYE, MEKAE, MEKAY, MEKEY, MOKA, MIKA)*** [MKK] 9,500 (1988 SIL). Essentially the whole northern part of Upper Nyong Division (Messamena, Abong-Mbang, Doume, Nguelemendouka subdivisions); eastern Diang Subdivision (west of Bertoua), Lom and Djerem Division, East Province. Niger-Congo, Atlantic-Congo, Volta-Congo, Benue-Congo, Bantoid, Southern, Narrow Bantu, Northwest, A, Makaa-Njem (A.80). Dialects: BYEP, BESEP (BESHA, BINDAFUM). Not intelligible with South Makaa. Related to South Makaa and Kol.

CAKA [CKX] 5,000 or fewer (1984 ALCAM). Asaka, Basaka, and Batanga villages, Akwaya Subdivision, Manyu Division, South West Province. Niger-Congo, Atlantic-Congo, Volta-Congo, Benue-Congo, Bantoid, Southern, Tivoid. Dialects: ASSAKA (ADZU BALAKA), BATANGA (ADZU BATANGA). 50% lexical similarity with Ipulo, 40% with Balo, Osatu, Icheve, and Otanga, 35% with Esimbi, 30% with Mesaka. Assaka and Batanga have 80% lexical similarity. Pidgin and English used as second languages. English is used for literacy. Some Ipulo use Caka as second language. Different from Batanga in the Bube-Benga group and the Batanga dialect of Balundu-Bima. Mountains. Traditional religion.

CUNG [CUG] Northeast of Wum, west of Nkambe, Menchum Division, North West Province. Niger-Congo, Atlantic-Congo, Volta-Congo, Benue-Congo, Bantoid, Unclassified. May be Eastern Beboid.

CUVOK ***(TCHOUVOK)*** [CUV] 5,000 or fewer (1983 ALCAM). In and around Tchouvok, Matakam South Canton, near Zamay, Mokolo Subdivision, Maya-Tsanaga Division, Far North Province. Afro-Asiatic, Chadic, Biu-Mandara, A, A.5. There is interpretation from Fulfulde into Cuvok in churches. Limited use of Fulfulde with outsiders and French by the few who have gone to school. Most do not know nearby languages well (Mefele, Mofu South, Mafa). Cuvok used in home, village, and market. Investigation needed: bilingual proficiency in Mofu.

DABA ***(DABBA)*** [DAB] 35,700 (1982 SIL). Population total both countries 36,700. Northwest of Guider in Mayo-Oulo and Guider subdivisions, Mayo-Louti Division, North Province; southwestern corner of Diamare Division (Ndoukoula region) and Mayo-Tsanaga Division (Hina and Bourrah subdivisions), Far North Province. Also spoken in Nigeria. Afro-Asiatic, Chadic, Biu-Mandara, A, A.7. Dialects: NIVE, POLOGOZOM, KOLA (DABA KOLA, KPALA), MUSGOI (MUSGOY, MAZAGWAY, DABA MOUSGOY). Literacy rate in first language: 5% to 10%. Literacy rate in second language: 5% to 15%. NT 1992.

DAMA [DMM] Small group in Rey-Bouba Subdivision, Benoue Division, North Province. Niger-Congo, Atlantic-Congo, Volta-Congo, North, Adamawa-Ubangi, Adamawa, Mbum-Day, Mbum, Northern, Dama-Galke. May be a dialect of Mono.

DEK [DEK] North Province. Niger-Congo, Atlantic-Congo, Volta-Congo, North, Adamawa-Ubangi, Adamawa, Mbum-Day, Mbum, Unclassified. It may be intelligible with Kari or Mbum. Investigation needed: intelligibility with Kari, Mbum.

DENYA ***(ANYANG, AGNANG, ANYAN, ANYAH, EYAN, TAKAMANDA, OBONYA, NYANG)*** [ANV] 11,200 (1982 SIL). Central and southern parts of Akwaya Subdivision and northern part of Mamfe Central Subdivision, Manyu Division, South West Province. Partially in Takamanda Forest Reserve. Niger-Congo, Atlantic-Congo, Volta-Congo, Benue-Congo, Bantoid, Southern, Mamfe. Dialects: BASHO, BITIEKU, TAKAMANDA, BAJWO. Dialect cluster. Kendem is linguistically between Denya and Kenyang. Around 70% to 80% lexical similarity between dialects. Speakers refer to their language as 'Denya'. Literacy rate in first language: Below 1%. Literacy rate in second language: 15% to 25%.

DII ***(DURU, DOUROU, DURRU, NYAG DII, YAG DII, ZAA)*** [DUR] 47,000 (1982 SIL). Tchollire Subdivision of Mayo-Rey Division, North Province; north and east of Ngaoundere, Ngaoundere Subdivision, Vina Division, Adamawa Province. Niger-Congo, Atlantic-Congo, Volta-Congo, North, Adamawa-Ubangi, Adamawa, Leko-Nimbari, Duru, Dii. Dialects: MAMBE', MAMNA'A, GOOM, BOOW, NGBANG, SAGZEE (SAADJE, SAAKYE), VAAZIN, HOME, NYOK. Goom is a related dialect or language. Speakers refer to themselves as 'Yag Dii'. Dictionary. Grammar. Literacy rate in first language: Below 1%. Literacy rate in second language: 5% to 15%. Traditional religion. Bible portions 1966.

DIMBONG ***(BUMBONG, KALONG, KAALONG, LAKAALONG, MBONG, LAMBONG, BAPE, PALONG)*** [DII] 140 (1992 SIL). Northwest of Bafia, Mbam Division, Center Province, 2 villages. Niger-Congo, Atlantic-Congo, Volta-Congo, Benue-Congo, Bantoid, Southern, Narrow Bantu,

Northwest, A, Bafia (A.50). Related to Bafia, Hijuk, and Tibea. Comprehension of Bafia is generally acquired at an early age. Comprehension of Yambeta is generalized.

DOYAYO ***(DOOHYAAYO, DOWAYAYO, DOYAAYO, DOYAU, DONYAYO, DONYANYO, DOAYO, DOOYAYO, DOOYAAYO, DOWAYO, DOOWAAYO, TUNGA, TUUNO, TUNGBO, NOMAI, "NAMSHI", "NAMCHI", "NAMCI")*** [DOW] 18,000 (1985 EELC). Northern Poli Subdivision and around Poli, Benoue Division, North Province. Niger-Congo, Atlantic-Congo, Volta-Congo, North, Adamawa-Ubangi, Adamawa, Leko-Nimbari, Duru, Voko-Dowayo, Vere-Dowayo, Dowayo. Dialects: MARKE, TEERE (POLI), SEWE. Perhaps 20% of the men are fairly bilingual in Bilkire Fulani for trading and everyday conversation. Perhaps 5% are bilingual in French. "Namshi" is a derogatory name sometimes used for them. People are called 'Doowaayo'. Literacy rate in first language: 1% to 5%. Literacy rate in second language: 5% to 15%. Traditional religion, Christian, Muslim. NT 1991.

DUALA ***(DOUALA, DIWALA, DWELA, DUALLA, DWALA)*** [DOU] 87,700 (1982 SIL). Towards Yabassi and along the Wouri River, Nkam Division; around Dibombari, Moungo Division; around Cameroon estuary, Wouri Division, Littoral Province; and both sides of the Mungo River, Fako Division, South West Province. Niger-Congo, Atlantic-Congo, Volta-Congo, Benue-Congo, Bantoid, Southern, Narrow Bantu, Northwest, A, Duala (A.20). Dialects: BODIMAN, MUNGO (MUNGU, MUUNGO), OLI (EWODI, OURI, ULI, WURI, WOURI, KOLI), PONGO. Related to Malimba. Trade language. Dictionary. Grammar. Literacy rate in first language: 1% to 5%. Literacy rate in second language: 25% to 50%. Coastal. Christian. Bible 1872-1970.

DUGWOR ***(DOUGOUR)*** [DME] West of Tchere Canton between Maroua and Meri, Meri Subdivision, Diamare Division, Far North Province. Afro-Asiatic, Chadic, Biu-Mandara, A, A.5. Dialect: MIKERE.

DULI ***(DUI)*** [DUZ] Near Pitoa, Benoue Division, North Province. Niger-Congo, Atlantic-Congo, Volta-Congo, North, Adamawa-Ubangi, Adamawa, Leko-Nimbari, Duru, Duli. Might have been the same as Gey, as reported by Barreteau, Breton, and Dieu 1984. Extinct.

DUUPA ***(NDUUPA, DOUPA, DUPA)*** [DAE] 5,000 (1991 UBS). East of Poli, Faro and Benoue divisions, North Province. Niger-Congo, Atlantic-Congo, Volta-Congo, North, Adamawa-Ubangi, Adamawa, Leko-Nimbari, Duru, Dii. Related to Pape. Literacy rate in second language: 5% to 15%. Traditional religion, Christian, Muslim. Bible portions 1982.

DZODINKA ***(ADERE, ADIRI, ARDERI, DZODZINKA)*** [ADD] 2,000 to 2,500 (1994 SIL). Population total both countries 2,000 to 2,500. Village of Adere, extreme northern part of Nwa Subdivision, Donga-Mantung Division, North West Province, 1 village. Also spoken in Nigeria. Niger-Congo, Atlantic-Congo, Volta-Congo, Benue-Congo, Bantoid, Southern, Wide Grassfields, Narrow Grassfields, Mbam-Nkam, Nkambe. Speakers consider themselves to be ethnically Mfumte. Different from Adele of Ghana and Togo. Bible portions 1923-1932.

EJAGHAM ***(EJAHAM, EKOI, ETUNG, EJWE, EDJAGAM, KEAKA, KWA, OBANG, EJAGAM)*** [ETU] 45,000 to 50,000 in Cameroon (1998 John Watters SIL). Whole of Eyumodjok Subdivision and southern part of Mamfe Subdivision west of Mamfe, Manyu Division, South West Province in Cameroon. Niger-Congo, Atlantic-Congo, Volta-Congo, Benue-Congo, Bantoid, Southern, Ekoid. Dialects: WESTERN EJAGHAM, EASTERN EJAGHAM, SOUTHERN EJAGHAM (EKIN, KWA, QUA, AQUA, ABAKPA). Western Ejagham includes Bendeghe Etung (Bindege, Dindiga, Mbuma), Northern Etung, Southern Etung, Ekwe, Akamkpa-Ejagham. Eastern Ejagham includes Keaka (Keaqa, Kejaka, Edjagam), Obang (Eeafeng). Literacy rate in first language: Below 1%. Literacy rate in second language: 15% to 25%. NT 1997. See main entry under Nigeria.

ELIP ***(BELIP, BELIBI, LIBIE)*** [EKM] 6,400 (1982 SIL). In Yambasa, southeast of Bokito towards the Mbam and Sanaga rivers, Elip canton, Mbam Division, Center Province. Niger-Congo, Atlantic-Congo, Volta-Congo, Benue-Congo, Bantoid, Southern, Mbam, Yambasa (A.60). It may be possible to standardize a written form with Mmala and Yangben, related languages. French is the language of instruction in primary and secondary education. Ewondo or Bulu are used in some churches, without interpretation. Speakers acquire understanding of Mmala and Yangben in early adulthood. Interpretation is made into Elip in RC church services. People do not think French will replace Elip.

EMAN ***(EMANE)*** [EMN] 800 (1990 SIL). Towns of Amayo, Amanavil, Akalabo, and Akalam Gomo in Akwaya Subdivision, Manyu Division, South West Province. No permanent settlements in Nigeria. Niger-Congo, Atlantic-Congo, Volta-Congo, Benue-Congo, Bantoid, Southern, Tivoid. Dialects: AMAYO, AMANAVIL (AMAN, AMANA, AMANI, ELAKA). 70% lexical similarity with Caka, 60% with Ipulo, 40% with Icheve and Otanga, 35% with Esimbi, 30% with Mesaka. Amayo and Amanavil have 80% lexical similarity. Speakers have high bilingualism in Ipulo. Pidgin is also used. Investigation needed: intelligibility with dialects, Emane, bilingual proficiency in Ipulo. Mountains. Traditional religion.

ENGLISH [ENG] Used mainly in South West and North West provinces. Indo-European, Germanic, West, English. Official language. Bible 1535-1989. See main entry under United Kingdom.

ESIMBI ***(ESSIMBI, ISIMBI, SIMPI, AGE, AAGE, BOGUE, MBURUGAM)*** [AGS] 20,000 (1982 SIL). Western part of Wum Subdivision, centered around Benakuma, Menchum Division, North West Province. Niger-Congo, Atlantic-Congo, Volta-Congo, Benue-Congo, Bantoid, Southern, Tivoid. 35% lexical similarity with Balo, Ipulo, and Icheve. Literacy rate in first language: Below 1%. Literacy rate in second language: 5% to 15%.

ETON [ETO] 52,000 (1982 SIL). Almost all of Lekie Division, Center Province. Niger-Congo, Atlantic-Congo, Volta-Congo, Benue-Congo, Bantoid, Southern, Narrow Bantu, Northwest, A, Yaunde-Fang (A.70). Dialects: ESSELE, MVOG-NAMVE, MVO-NANGKOK, BEYIDZOLO. Intelligible with Bulu, Ewondo, and Fang as part of the Beti language. Investigation needed: intelligibility with Ewondo.

EVANT ***(EVAND, AVAND, AVANDE, OVANDE, OVAND, OVANDO, BALEGETE, BELEGETE)*** [BZZ] 1,000 or fewer in Cameroon (1996 SIL). Atolo and Matene I villages, Akwaya Subdivision, Manyu Division, South West Province. Niger-Congo, Atlantic-Congo, Volta-Congo, Benue-Congo, Bantoid, Southern, Tivoid. 50% lexical similarity with Tiv, Icheve, and Otank. Bilingualism in Pidgin. Literacy is in English. Mountains. Traditional religion. See main entry under Nigeria.

EWONDO ***(EWUNDU, JAUNDE, YAOUNDE, YAUNDE)*** [EWO] 577,700 (1982 SIL). All except the eastern part of Mefou Division; the entire Mfoundi and Nyong-and-So divisions; the southern half of Nyong-and-Mfoumou Division, Center Province; the northern part of Ocean Division, South Province. Niger-Congo, Atlantic-Congo, Volta-Congo, Benue-Congo, Bantoid, Southern, Narrow Bantu, Northwest, A, Yaunde-Fang (A.70). Dialects: BADJIA (BAKJO), BAFEUK, BAMVELE (MVELE, YEZUM, YESOUM), BANE, BETI, FONG, MBIDA-BANI, MVETE, MVOG-NIENGUE, OMVANG, YABEKOLO (YEBEKOLO), YABEKA, YABEKANGA, ENOAH, EVOUZOK. It is intelligible with Bulu, Eton, and Fang as part of the Beti language. Trade language. Literacy rate in first language: 5% to 10%. Literacy rate in second language: 15% to 25%. NT 1959-1962.

FALI, NORTH [FLL] 16,000 (1982 SIL). Around Dourbeye and Mayo-Oulo, Mayo-Oulo Subdivision, Mayo-Louti Division, North Province. Niger-Congo, Atlantic-Congo, Volta-Congo, North, Adamawa-Ubangi, Adamawa, Fali. Dialects: DOURBEYE (FALI-DOURBEYE), BOSSOUM (FALI-BOSSOUM, BONUM), BVERI (FALI DU PESKE-BORI, PESKE, BORI). Speakers are rapidly shifting to Adamawa Fulfulde. Investigation needed: bilingual proficiency in Fulfulde. Muslim, traditional religion.

FALI, SOUTH [FAL] 20,000 (1982 SIL). Around Hossere Bapara, Tsolaram, Hossere Toro and Ndoudja; south of Dembo, Pitoa Subdivision northeast of Garoua, Benoue Division, North Province. Niger-Congo, Atlantic-Congo, Volta-Congo, North, Adamawa-Ubangi, Adamawa, Fali. Dialects: FALI-TINGUELIN (NDOUDJA, MANGO, RAM, TORO), KANGOU (KAANG, KANGU, FALI KANGOU), BELE (NGOUTCHOUMI, FALI-BELE, FALI DU BELE-FERE). Different from North Fali, or Fali (Bana) of Nigeria and Cameroon, which is Chadic; or Vin of Nigeria. Literacy rate in first language: 1% to 5%. Literacy rate in second language: 5% to 15%. NT 1975.

FANG ***(PAMUE, PAHOUIN)*** [FNG] 67,800 in Cameroon (1982 SIL). Half of Dja-and-Lobo Division (south of Djoum) and southeastern part of Ntem Division (south of Mvangan), as well as between Lolodorf and Kribi, Ocean Division, South Province. Niger-Congo, Atlantic-Congo, Volta-Congo, Benue-Congo, Bantoid, Southern, Narrow Bantu, Northwest, A, Yaunde-Fang (A.70). Dialects: FANG (OKAK), MVAE (MVAN, MVAY), NTOUMOU (NTUMU). Intelligible with Bulu and Ewondo as part of the Beti language group. Literacy rate in first language: 5% to 10%. Literacy rate in second language: 15% to 25%. Bible 1951. See main entry under Gabon.

FE'FE' ***(FE'EFE'E, FEEFEE, FEFE, FOTOUNI, BAFANG, BAMILEKE-FE'FE', NUFI)*** [FMP] 123,700 (1982 SIL). Upper Nkam Division (except for the vicinity of Kekem and a small section in the southeast corner), some in Mifi Division (Bangam), West Province. Niger-Congo, Atlantic-Congo, Volta-Congo, Benue-Congo, Bantoid, Southern, Wide Grassfields, Narrow Grassfields, Mbam-Nkam, Bamileke. Dialects: FA' (BAFANG), NKA' (BANKA), NEE (BANA), NJEE-POANTU (BANDJA-BABOUNTOU), NTII (FONDANTI), MKWET (FONDJOMEKWET), LA'FI (BALAFI), TUNGI' (FOTOUNI), NGAM (BANGAN), CA'. First 4 dialects listed belong to Central Fe'fe', next 5 belong to North Fe'fe'. Literacy rate in second language: 25% to 50%. Bible portions 1960.

FRENCH [FRN] Used mainly in the Littoral, West, Center, South, East, Adamawa, North, and Far North provinces. Indo-European, Italic, Romance, Italo-Western, Western, Gallo-Iberian, Gallo-Romance, Gallo-Rhaetian, Oïl, French. Official language. Bible 1530-1986. See main entry under France.

FULFULDE, ADAMAWA ***(ADAMAWA FULANI, PEUL, PEULH, FUL, FULA, FULBE, BOULBE, EASTERN FULANI, FULFULDE, FOULFOULDE, PULLO, GAPELTA, PELTA HAY, DOMONA, PLADINA, PALATA, PALDIDA, PALDENA, DZEMAY, ZEMAY, ZAAKOSA, PULE, TAAREYO, SANYO, BIIRA)*** [FUB] 668,700 in Cameroon, 7% of the population (1986). 5,000,000 in Cameroon including second language speakers (1987 UBS). Population total all countries 760,000 or more for Adamawa. Possibly 13,000,000 speakers of all Fulfulde. It is spread all over the Far North, North, and Adamawa provinces. Also spoken in Chad, Nigeria, Sudan. Niger-Congo, Atlantic-Congo, Atlantic, Northern, Senegambian, Fula-Wolof, Fulani, Eastern. Dialects: MAROUA, GAROUA, NGAONDÉRÉ, KAMBARIIRE, NOMADIC FULFULDE, BILKIRE FULANI (BILKIRI). There are some serious problems in intelligibility among Cameroon dialects, and elsewhere with Cameroon dialects. Bilkire is spoken by second language Fulfulde speakers. 'Fulfulde' is the language, 'Fulbe' the people. Adamawa is one of the major Fula geo-political states. Trade language. Dictionary. Grammar. SVO. Literacy rate in first language: 1% to 5%. Literacy rate in second language: 5% to 15%. Traditional religion, Muslim. Bible 1983.

FULFULDE, KANO-KATSINA-BORORRO ***(PEUL, FULBE)*** [FUV] Northern Cameroon. Niger-Congo, Atlantic-Congo, Atlantic, Northern, Senegambian, Fula-Wolof, Fulani, East Central. Dialects: KANO-KATSINA, BORORRO (BORORO, MBORORO, AKO, NOMADIC FULFULDE). Muslim. See main entry under Nigeria.

FUNGOM ***(NORTHERN FUNGOM, WE)*** [FUG] 1,000 (1994 SIL). In Fungom, northeast of Wum, Fungom Subdivision, Menchum Division, North West Province. Niger-Congo, Atlantic-Congo, Volta-Congo, Benue-Congo, Bantoid, Southern, Wide Grassfields, Narrow Grassfields, Ring, West. Apparently distinct from Oso (Southern Fungom). May be intelligible with Oso or a dialect of Mmen. Investigation needed: intelligibility with Mmen. Literacy rate in first language: Below 1%. Literacy rate in second language: 15% to 25%. Traditional religion, Christian.

GADUWA [GDW] Southwest corner of Mayo-Sava Division, Far North Province. Afro-Asiatic, Chadic, Biu-Mandara, A, A.5. A newly discovered language (1987).

GAVAR ***(GAWAR, GOUWAR, GAUAR, RTCHI, KORTCHI)*** [GOU] 5,000 (1992 SIL). Around Gawar, Mogode Canton, Mokolo Subdivision, Mayo-Tsanaga Division, Far North Province. One group of Gavar Hossere live among the Gavar-Fulfulde, and another in relative isolation in the mountains around Kortchi village. Afro-Asiatic, Chadic, Biu-Mandara, A, A.7. Gavar may be intelligible with Buwal, but speakers consider them to be different. The Gavar Hossere use Fulfulde in the market and for outside contacts. French is learned by the few who go to school. Comprehension of surrounding languages is limited (Mofu South, Mafa, Daba). The Gavar Hossere use their language in home and village. The Gavar Hossere speak Gavar; the Gavar Fulfulde speak Fulfulde. Investigation needed: intelligibility with Buwal. Literacy rate in first language: Below 1%. Literacy rate in second language: 5% to 15%. Traditional religion, a few Christian.

GBAYA, NORTHWEST ***(BAYA)*** [GYA] 65,000 to 80,000 or more in Cameroon (1980). Vast area spread out between Mayo-Rey Division (south of Touboro), North Province; Mbere Division (Meiganga Subdivision), Djerem Division (Ngaoundal and Tibati subdivisions), Faro and Deo Division (Tignere Subdivision), Adamawa Province; Lom and Djerem Division (Garoua Boulay, Betare-Oya, and Bertoua subdivisions), Kadey Division (Kette Subdivision), Boumba and Ngoko Division (Gari-Gombo Subdivision), East Province. Niger-Congo, Atlantic-Congo, Volta-Congo, North, Adamawa-Ubangi, Ubangi, Gbaya-Manza-Ngbaka, Northwest. Dialects: BANGINDA, MBAI, GAYMONA, LAI (LAY), LOMBU, MBERE, MOMBE, YAÁYUWEE (YAIWE, KALLA). Primer. Dictionary. Grammar. Literacy rate in first language: 1% to 5%. Literacy rate in second language: 5% to 15%. Bible, in press (1992). See main entry under CAR.

GBAYA, SOUTHWEST [MDO] 13,000 to 18,000 including 5,000 to 8,000 Dooka, 8,000 to 10,000 Mbodomo (1998 R. Hedinger). Yangamo-Garga-Sarali subdialect has the largest population. Ngoura District, Bétaré-Oya Subdivision, Lom and Djerem Division, East Province. Niger-Congo, Atlantic-Congo, Volta-Congo, North, Adamawa-Ubangi, Ubangi, Gbaya-Manza-Ngbaka, Southwest. Dialects: DOOKA, MBODOMO (GBAYA-MBODOMO, BODOMO). Mbodomo has subdialects Yangamo-Garga-Sarali, Petit-Belo-Doumba. They have high inherent intelligibility with each other. Minimal Fulfulde is used in the markets. Proficiency is greater where there are more Fulani people: Yangamo has a 30% Fulani population. French is used as second language by a relatively small population, mainly men who have been educated. Vigorous language use. Traditional religion, Christian. Bible portions 1980. See main entry under CAR.

GEMZEK ***(GEMJEK, GUEMSHEK)*** [GND] 8,000 to 10,000 (1992 SIL). Eastern edge of Mandara Mts., north of Meri, Tokombere Subdivision, Mayo-Sava Division, Far North Province, 16 villages. Afro-Asiatic, Chadic, Biu-Mandara, A, A.5. Slight dialect differences between villages. Related to Zulgwa. Fulfulde often used in church, but interpreted into Gemzek or Zulgwa. If Zulgwa is used in church, interpretation is not given into Gemzek. Speakers appear to be quite bilingual in Zulgwa. The Meri, Mbuko, Muyang, and Mada languages are in the surrounding area. Investigation needed: bilingual proficiency in Zulgwa. Literacy rate in first language: Below 1%. Literacy rate in second language: 5% to 15%.

GEY ***(GUEVE, GEWE)*** [GUV] Ethnic group has 1,900 (1982 SIL). East of Pitoa, Benoue Division, North Province. Niger-Congo, Atlantic-Congo, Volta-Congo, North, Adamawa-Ubangi, Adamawa, Gueve.

The people are ethnically still somewhat distinct, but the language is extinct. They now speak Fulfulde. Extinct.

GHOMÁLÁ' ***(BANJUN, BANDJOUN, BANJOUN-BAHAM, BALOUM, BATIE, BAMILEKE-BANDJOUN, MANDJU, MAHUM)*** [BBJ] 260,000 (1982 SIL). Most of Mifi Division (except the extreme south and pockets in the north and west), eastern part of Menoua Division, a pocket in southern Bamboutos Division, and Bamendjou Subdivision, Mifi Division, West Province. Niger-Congo, Atlantic-Congo, Volta-Congo, Benue-Congo, Bantoid, Southern, Wide Grassfields, Narrow Grassfields, Mbam-Nkam, Bamileke. Dialects: GHOMÁLÁ' CENTRAL (BANDJOUN, JO, WE, HOM, YOGAM, BAHAM), GHOMÁLÁ' NORTH (FUSAP, LANG), GHOMÁLÁ' SOUTH (TE, PA, DENGKWOP), NGEMBA (BAMENJOU, FU'DA, SA, MONJO, MEKA, MUGUM). Based on inherent intelligibility, Bameka, Bansoa, and Balessing are subdialects of South Ghomálá', North Ghomálá' has 2 subdialects, Central Ghomálá' 4, and Ngemba 5. Taught informally to adults since the early 1900s. Adopted by UNESCO in the 1960s and 1970s as one of 9 languages of wider communication for Cameroon, one of 2 in west Cameroon. Taught formally in 6 RC schools since 1995. Literacy rate in first language: 5% to 10%. Literacy rate in second language: 25% to 50%. Traditional religion, Christian. Bible portions 1964.

GIDAR ***(GUIDER, GUIDAR, GIDDER, KADA, BAYNAWA)*** [GID] 54,000 in Cameroon. Population total both countries 65,600 (1982 SIL). Guider and Figuil subdivisions, Mayo-Louti Division, North Province; a small section of Diamare Division, Far North Province. Also spoken in Chad. Afro-Asiatic, Chadic, Biu-Mandara, C. Dialect: LAM. Literacy rate in second language: 5% to 15%. NT 1986.

GIMME ***(KOMPARA, KOMPANA, KOMA KOMPANA, PANBE, GIMMA)*** [KMP] 3,000 (1982 SIL). West of Poli along the Nigerian border in the Alantika Mountains, on Saptou Plain, Faro Division, North Province. Niger-Congo, Atlantic-Congo, Volta-Congo, North, Adamawa-Ubangi, Adamawa, Leko-Nimbari, Duru, Voko-Dowayo, Vere-Dowayo, Vere-Gimme, Gimme. Fulfulde is used as second language. French proficiency is low. Church activities in Fulfulde. Distinct from Koma (Koma Ndera) and Gimnime (Komlama). Their name for the language is 'Gimma'.

GIMNIME ***(KADAM, KOMLAMA, GIMBE, KOMA KADAM, LAAME, YOTUBO)*** [KMB] 3,000 (1982 SIL). Northwest of Poli along Nigerian border, around Wangay in the Atlantika Mountains, Faro Division, North Province. Niger-Congo, Atlantic-Congo, Volta-Congo, North, Adamawa-Ubangi, Adamawa, Leko-Nimbari, Duru, Voko-Dowayo, Vere-Dowayo, Vere-Gimme, Gimme. Dialect: RITIME. Close to Gimme. Different from Koma (Koma Ndera) of Cameroon.

GIZIGA, NORTH ***(GUIZIGA, GISIGA, GISIKA, TCHERE, MI MARVA, GIZIGA DE MAROUA, DOGBA)*** [GIS] 20,000 (1982 SIL). North and west of Maroua, in Tchere and Mogazang massifs and neighboring Dogba plains, Meri Subdivision, Diamare Division, Far North Province. Afro-Asiatic, Chadic, Biu-Mandara, A, A.5. Traditional religion, Christian.

GIZIGA, SOUTH ***(GUIZIGA, GISIGA, GISIKA)*** [GIZ] 60,000 (1991 UBS). Southwest of Maroua, in Diamare plains, Diamare and Kaele divisions, Far North Province. Afro-Asiatic, Chadic, Biu-Mandara, A, A.5. Dialects: MUTURAMI (MUTURWA, MUTURUA, GIZIGA DE MOUTOUROUA, LOULOU), MI MIJIVIN (GIZIGA DE MIDJIVIN), RUM. Traditional religion, Christian. NT 1996.

GLAVDA ***(GELVAXDAXA, GALVAXDAXA, GUELEBDA, GALAVDA, VALE)*** [GLV] 2,800 in Cameroon (1982 SIL). Around the village of Gelvaxdaxa, south of Ashigashia, on the Nigerian Border, Koza Subdivision, Mayo-Tsanaga Division, Far North Province. Afro-Asiatic, Chadic, Biu-Mandara, A, A.4, Mandara Proper, Glavda. Wolff (1971) separates Glavda from Guduf and Gvoko. Closely related to Guduf. Different from Vale of Chad and CAR, which is Central Sudanic. Bible portions 1967. See main entry under Nigeria.

GUDE ***(GOUDE, MUBI, TCHADE, SHEDE, MAPODI, MUDAYE, MOCIGIN, MOTCHEKIN, CHEKE, TCHEKE)*** [GDE] 28,000 in Cameroon. North and northwest of Dourbeye, straddling the southern part of Bourrah Subdivision, Mayo-Tsanaga Division, Far North Province; and the extreme eastern part of Mayo-Oulo Subdivision, Mayo-Louti Division, North Province. Afro-Asiatic, Chadic, Biu-Mandara, A, A.8. Different dialects are spoken in Cameroon and Nigeria but they are inherently intelligible. Literacy rate in first language: 1% to 5%. Literacy rate in second language: 5% to 15%. Traditional religion. Bible portions 1974-1995. See main entry under Nigeria.

GUDUF ***(GUDUPE, AFKABIYE)*** [GDF] 2,500 in Cameroon (1982 SIL). On the Nigerian border, Cikide and Guduf, Mokolo Subdivision, Mayo-Tsanaga Division, Far North Province. Afro-Asiatic, Chadic, Biu-Mandara, A, A.4, Mandara Proper, Glavda. Dialects: CIKIDE (CHIKIDE), GUDUF, GAVA (YAGHWATADAXA, YAWOTATAXA). Wolff (1971) separates Guduf from Gvoko and Glavda. Closely related to Glavda. Hedi speakers have 35% intelligibility of Guduf. 56% lexical similarity with Hedi, 50% with Lamang and Mabas. Bible portions 1966. See main entry under Nigeria.

GVOKO ***(GEVOKO, GHBOKO, GAVOKO, KUVOKO, NGOSSI, NGOSHI, NGOSHE-NDHANG)*** [NGS] Ngoshi village (different from Nggoshe), north of Tourou, Mololo Subdivision, Mayo-Tsanaga

Division, Far North Province. Afro-Asiatic, Chadic, Biu-Mandara, A, A.4, Mandara Proper, Glavda. Wolff (1971) separates Gvoko from Guduf and Glavda. See main entry under Nigeria.

GYELE ***(GIELE, GIELI, GYELI, BAGYELE, BAGIELE, BAJELI, BAJELE, BOGYELI, BOGYEL, BONDJIEL, BAKO, BEKOE, BAKOLA, BAKUELE, LIKOYA, BABINGA)*** [GYI] Population total both countries 30 or more. In forests around Kribi and along the road from Kribi to Lolodorf, Kribi and Lolodorf subdivisions, Ocean Division, South Province. Also spoken in Equatorial Guinea. Niger-Congo, Atlantic-Congo, Volta-Congo, Benue-Congo, Bantoid, Southern, Narrow Bantu, Northwest, A, Makaa-Njem (A.80). Pygmies, dispersed in small groups in the forest. Forest. Bible portions 1969.

HAUSA ***(HAOUSSA, HAWSA)*** [HUA] 23,500 in Cameroon (1982 SIL). Scattered. Afro-Asiatic, Chadic, West, A, A.1. Dictionary. Grammar. Muslim. Bible 1932-1996. See main entry under Nigeria.

HDI ***(XEDI, HEDI, HIDE, TURU-HIDE, XADI)*** [TUR] 1,000 in Cameroon. Village of Tourou on Nigerian border northwest of Mokolo, Mokolo Subdivision, Mayo-Tsanaga Division, Far North Province. Afro-Asiatic, Chadic, Biu-Mandara, A, A.4, Lamang. Dialect: TUR (TURU, TOUROU, FTOUR). 51% intelligibility of Mabas, 48% of Lamang, 35% of Gvoko. 78% lexical similarity with Mabas, 64% with Lamang, 56% with Gvoko. Literacy rate in first language: Below 1%. Literacy rate in second language: 5% to 15%. See main entry under Nigeria.

HIJUK [HIJ] 400 (1992 SIL). Southwest of Bokito, Bokito Subdivision, Mbam Division, Center Province, part of 1 village. Niger-Congo, Atlantic-Congo, Volta-Congo, Benue-Congo, Bantoid, Southern, Narrow Bantu, Northwest, A, Bafia (A.50). ALCAM says it is lexically and morphologically related to the Bafia group (Bafia, Dimbong, and Tibea). It appears to have 45% lexical similarity with Bafia and 84% with Basaa. Speakers understand Yangben, spoken by part of the people in their village. Some understanding of Basaa and Yambasa. High degree of generalized bilingualism in French. Investigation needed: bilingual proficiency in Basaa, Yangben, French, Yambasa.

HYA ***(GHYE, ZA)*** [HYA] Only in Amsa on the Nigerian border, Mokolo Subdivision, Mayo-Tsanaga Division, Far North Province. Afro-Asiatic, Chadic, Biu-Mandara, A, A.3. Closely related to Kamwe of Nigeria and Psikye of Cameroon.

ICEVE-MACI ***(ICHEVE, BECHEVE, BECHERE, BACHEVE, OCHEBE, OCEBE, OCHEVE, UTSE, UTSER, UTSEU)*** [BEC] 7,000 in Cameroon (1990). Population total both countries 12,000. North and south of Akwaya, Manyu Division, South West Province. Also spoken in Nigeria. Niger-Congo, Atlantic-Congo, Volta-Congo, Benue-Congo, Bantoid, Southern, Tivoid. Dialects: ICHEVE (BACHEVE), OLITI (MACI, MATCHI, OLITI-AKWAYA, OLITHI, OLIT, KWAYA, AKWAYA MOTOM, MOTOMO, IHEKWOT). 80% lexical similarity, between Maci and Bacheve, 60% with Otanga, 50% with Evand and Tiv, 40% with Eman and Mesaka, 35% with Esimbi. Some use Evand, and older males can speak some Denya-Kenyang. Pidgin is also used. Literacy rate in first language: Below 1%. Literacy rate in second language: Below 5% English. Mountains. Traditional religion.

IPULO ***(ASSUMBO, ASUMBO, BADZUMBO)*** [ASS] 2,500 (1990 SIL). Southeast of Akwaya, Akwaya Subdivision, Manyu Division, South West Province. Niger-Congo, Atlantic-Congo, Volta-Congo, Benue-Congo, Bantoid, Southern, Tivoid. Dialects: OLULU, TINTA, ETONGO. Olulu and Tinta have 90% lexical similarity. 60% lexical similarity with Eman, 50% with Caka, 40% with Balo and Osatu, 35% with Esimbi. Some speakers are bilingual in Pidgin, Eman, or Caka. Communications are difficult in the area. Literacy rate in first language: Below 1%. Literacy rate in second language: Below 5%. Mountains. Agriculturalists. Traditional religion.

ISU [ISU] 10,400 (1994 SIL). Isu is the main town, Wum Central Subdivision, Menchum Division, North West Province. Reported to be spread over a wide area up to the Nigerian border. Niger-Congo, Atlantic-Congo, Volta-Congo, Benue-Congo, Bantoid, Southern, Wide Grassfields, Narrow Grassfields, Ring, West. Little dialect variation. Considered to be a distinct language from Aghem and Weh; some comprehension of those languages. Bilingualism in Pidgin, English. Isu is used in local churches and at home. Not the same as Isu (Subu, Bimbia) which is Narrow Bantu A.20. Investigation needed: intelligibility with Aghem, Weh. Traditional religion, Christian.

ISU ***(SU, ISUBU, ISUWU, SUBU, BIMBIA)*** [SZV] 800 (1982 SIL). Around Bimbia estuary east of Limbe and west of Douala, Tiko Subdivision, Fako Division, South West Province. Niger-Congo, Atlantic-Congo, Volta-Congo, Benue-Congo, Bantoid, Southern, Narrow Bantu, Northwest, A, Duala (A.20). Distinct from Isu which is Grassfields Bantu. Bible portions 1843-1852.

IYIVE ***(UIVE, YIIVE)*** [UIV] 1,000 or fewer and decreasing in Cameroon (1996 WT). Population total both countries 2,000 (1992 Crozier and Blench). Yive village, northeast of Akwaya on the Nigerian border, Manyu Division, South West Province. Also spoken in Nigeria. Niger-Congo, Atlantic-Congo, Volta-Congo, Benue-Congo, Bantoid, Southern, Tivoid. 75% lexical similarity with Tiv.

JIMI ***(DJIMI, JIMJIMEN, 'UM FALIN)*** [JIM] 3,500 (1982 SIL). On Nigerian border in and around Bourrha, Mayo-Tsanaga Division, Far North Province. Afro-Asiatic, Chadic, Biu-Mandara, A, A.8. Dialects: DJIMI, ZUMO (ZUMU, ZOMO, ZAME), JIMO, WADI (WA'I), MALABU. Different from Jimi of Nigeria in Bauchi State, which is West Chadic. Muslim, traditional religion.

JINA *(ZINA)* [JIA] Around Zina and east of Waza near the south of Logone-Birni Subdivision, Logone-and-Chari Division, Far North Province. Afro-Asiatic, Chadic, Biu-Mandara, B, B.1, Jina. Dialects: JINA (ZINE), SARASSARA, TCHIDE (SEDE), MUXULE (MUXULI, NGODENI), MAE. People in Zina say they understand Lagwan and Musgu better than Muxule. Muxule may be a separate language. Literacy rate in first language: Below 1%. Literacy rate in second language: Below 5%.

JUKUN TAKUM *(NJIKUM, JUKUN, DIYU)* [JBU] 1,700 in Cameroon (1986 R. Breton). Ntjieka, Furu-Turuwa, and Furu-Sambari villages, Furu-Awa Subdivision, Menchum Division, North West Province. Niger-Congo, Atlantic-Congo, Volta-Congo, Benue-Congo, Platoid, Benue, Jukunoid, Central, Kpan-Icen, Kpan. Dialects: TAKUM, DONGA (AKPANZHI). Trade language for 6,000 people in the area. The name 'Njikum' is preferred in Cameroon. People are called 'Jukun'. Trade language. Mountain slope. NT 1980. See main entry under Nigeria.

KAKO *(YAKA, KAKA, NKOXO, DIKAKA, MKAKO)* [KKJ] Population total all countries 70,500 (1982 SIL). Major part of Kadey Division (Batouri and Ndelele subdivisions), East Province. Also spoken in CAR, Congo. Niger-Congo, Atlantic-Congo, Volta-Congo, Benue-Congo, Bantoid, Southern, Narrow Bantu, Northwest, A, Kako (A.90). Dialects: MBONJOKU, BESEMBO, BERA, NGBAKO. Different from Kaka (Yamba) which is Grassfields Bantu. Dictionary. Literacy rate in first language: 1% to 5%. Literacy rate in second language: 15% to 25%. Bible portions 1990-1993.

KAMKAM *(BUNGNU, BUNU, BUNGUN, GBUNHU, KAKABA, MBONGNO)* [BGU] On the Mambila Plateau. Niger-Congo, Atlantic-Congo, Volta-Congo, Benue-Congo, Bantoid, Northern, Mambiloid, Mambila-Konja, Magu-Kamkam-Kila. Muslim (mainly), traditional religion. See main entry under Nigeria.

KANURI, CENTRAL *(YERWA KANURI, KOLE, KOLERE, SIRATA, "BARIBARI", "BERIBERI", KANOURI, KANOURY, BORNU, BORNOUANS, BORNOUAN)* [KPH] 56,500 in Cameroon (1982 SIL). Mainly north of Mora between Limani and Bounderi and in Kolofata Subdivision, Mayo-Sava Division; also in Diamare Division (Maroua and Bogo subdivisions); Kaele and Mayo-Danay divisions (as far as Mindif and Guirvidig), Far North Province. Nilo-Saharan, Saharan, Western, Kanuri. Dialects: MOVAR, DAGARA, KAGA (KAGAMA), SUGURTI, LARE, KWAYAM, NJESKO, KABARI (KUVURI), NGAZAR, GUVJA, MAO, TEMAGERI, FADAWA, MAIDUGURI. "Beriberi" is considered a derogatory name. Ajami script. Muslim. NT, in press (1997). See main entry under Nigeria.

KARANG *(KARENG, MBUM, MBUM-EAST, LAKA, LAKKA)* [KZR] 17,000 in Cameroon, including 7,000 in Sakpu (1991 SIL). Population total both countries 17,000 or more. In Padjama and from Tcholliere to Touboro, Mayo-Rey Division, North Province. Not in Nigeria. Also spoken in Chad. Niger-Congo, Atlantic-Congo, Volta-Congo, North, Adamawa-Ubangi, Adamawa, Mbum-Day, Mbum, Central, Karang. Dialects: SAKPU (PANDAMA, TU'BORO), KARANG, NGOMI, MBERE. Related to Sakpu and Pana. Different from Laka (Kabba Laka) of CAR and Chad, and from Laka of Nigeria. Investigation needed: intelligibility with Laka of Nigeria. Dictionary. Literacy rate in first language: 1% to 5%. Literacy rate in second language: 5% to 15%. Christian, traditional religion, Muslim.

KARE *(KARRÉ, KARI, KALI)* [KBN] Around Belel, Vina Division, Adamawa Province, and Mayo-Rey Division, North Province. Niger-Congo, Atlantic-Congo, Volta-Congo, North, Adamawa-Ubangi, Adamawa, Mbum-Day, Mbum, Central, Karang. Dialects: TALE, KARI. Intelligible with Mbum. Different from the Kari of DRC, which is Benue-Congo. Literacy rate in first language: 1% to 5%. Literacy rate in second language: 5% to 15%. NT 1947. See main entry under CAR.

KEMEZUNG *(DUMBO, DZUMBO, KUMAJU)* [DMO] Northwest of Nkambe, southwest corner of Ako Subdivision, Donga-Mantung Division, North West Province. Niger-Congo, Atlantic-Congo, Volta-Congo, Benue-Congo, Bantoid, Southern, Beboid, Eastern.

KENDEM *(BOKWA-KENDEM)* [KVM] 1,000 (1983 SIL). Villages of Kendem and Bokwa east of Mamfe, Mamfe Subdivision, Manyu Division, South West Province. Niger-Congo, Atlantic-Congo, Volta-Congo, Benue-Congo, Bantoid, Southern, Mamfe. A separate language, between Denya and Kenyang. Some people are bilingual in Kenyang and certain dialects of Denya. Investigation needed: bilingual proficiency in Kenyang, Denya.

KENSWEI NSEI *(BAMESSING, NDOP-BAMESSING, MELAMBA, NSEI, VETENG, VETWENG, CALEBASSES, BEFI, MESING, KENSENSE)* [NDB] 12,500 (1982 SIL). Centered around the village of Bamessing, west of Ndop on Ndop Plain, Ndop Subdivision, Mezam Division, North West Province. Niger-Congo, Atlantic-Congo, Volta-Congo, Benue-Congo, Bantoid, Southern, Wide Grassfields, Narrow Grassfields, Ring, North. Closely related languages: Vengo, Wushi, Bamunka. Speakers refer to the language as 'Nsei'.

KENYANG *(NYANG, BAYANGI, BANYANG, BANYANGI, BANJANGI, MANYANG)* [KEN] 65,000 (1992 SIL). Around and southwest of Mamfe, Mamfe Central Subdivision and Upper Banyang Subdivision, Manyu Division; and eastern corner of Nguti Subdivision, Meme Division, South West

Province. Niger-Congo, Atlantic-Congo, Volta-Congo, Benue-Congo, Bantoid, Southern, Mamfe. Dialects: UPPER KENYANG (HAUT-KENYANG), LOWER KENYANG (BAS-KENYANG), BAKONI (UPPER BALONG, NORTHERN BALONG, MANYEMEN, KICWE, KITWII, TWII, MANYEMAN). Upper Balong is distinct from Bafaw-Balong. Dictionary. Literacy rate in first language: Below 1%. Literacy rate in second language: 15% to 25%.

KERA [KER] 6,000 in Cameroon. Southeast of Doukoula, Mayo-Danay Division, Far North Province. Afro-Asiatic, Chadic, East, A, A.3. 42% lexical similarity with Kwang. SVO. Literacy rate in first language: 1% to 5%. Literacy rate in second language: 5% to 25%. Bible portions 1988-1995. See main entry under Chad.

KOL *(BIKELE-BIKENG, BIKELE-BIKAY, BEKOL)* [BIW] 12,000 (1988 SIL), including 1,000 in Bikeng. Vicinity of Messamena, Upper Nyong Division, East Province. Niger-Congo, Atlantic-Congo, Volta-Congo, Benue-Congo, Bantoid, Southern, Narrow Bantu, Northwest, A, Makaa-Njem (A.80). Dialects: BIKELE, BIKENG, KOL NORTH, KOL SOUTH. Bilingualism in Makaa, Koozime. Investigation needed: intelligibility, bilingual proficiency, attitudes toward Makaa, Koozime.

KOLBILA *(KOLBILARI, KOLBILLA, KOLENA, KOLBILI, ZOONO)* [KLC] 2,500 (1997 Lars Lode). North Province, Faro Division, Bantadje Canton, southeast of Poli, and some to the east on the main road between Ngaoundere and Garoua. Not in Nigeria. Niger-Congo, Atlantic-Congo, Volta-Congo, North, Adamawa-Ubangi, Adamawa, Leko-Nimbari, Leko. Related to Chamba Leko. Bilingualism in French. Mountain slope. Traditional religion, Christian, Muslim. Bible portions 1982-1985.

KOM *(NKOM, BIKOM, BAMEKON, ITANGIKOM, KONG)* [BKM] 127,000 (1982 SIL). Southern part of Fundong Subdivision, Menchum Division, North West Province. Niger-Congo, Atlantic-Congo, Volta-Congo, Benue-Congo, Bantoid, Southern, Wide Grassfields, Narrow Grassfields, Ring, Center. Dialect: MBIZENAKU (MBESA, ITANGIMBESA). Tonal. Literacy rate in first language: Below 1%. Literacy rate in second language: 15% to 25%. Bible portions 1998.

KOMA *(KUMA)* [KMY] 3,000 in Cameroon (1984 SIL). Northwest of Tchamba in Atlantika Mts. along Nigerian border, Faro Division, North Province. Niger-Congo, Atlantic-Congo, Volta-Congo, North, Adamawa-Ubangi, Adamawa, Leko-Nimbari, Duru, Voko-Dowayo, Vere-Dowayo, Vere-Gimme, Vere. Dialects: KOMA NDERA, KOMA DAMTI, LEELU, BANGRU, ZANU, LIU, YERU. Related to Vere (Kobo). Different from Gimme (Kompara), Gimnime (Komlama), Komo of Ethiopia and Central Koma of Sudan. See main entry under Nigeria.

KOONZIME *(NZIME, DJIMU, ZIMU, KOOZIME, KOOZHIME, KOONCIMO, DZIMOU)* [NJE] 45,000 in Cameroon (1987 SIL). Population total all countries 45,000 or more. Around Lomie (north and northwest, south and southeast in Ngoila Subdivision), Upper Nyong Division, East Province. Also spoken in Congo. Niger-Congo, Atlantic-Congo, Volta-Congo, Benue-Congo, Bantoid, Southern, Narrow Bantu, Northwest, A, Makaa-Njem (A.80). Dialects: NZIME (KOONZIME), BADWE'E (BADJOUE, BAJWE'E, KOOZIME), NJEME (NDJEME, NGYEME), NDJEM (NJEM, NDZEM, DJEM, DZEM, NYEM). Many Pygmies speak it as a second language. 'Koonzime' refers to the Nzime dialect, 'Koozime' to the Badwe'e dialect. Dictionary. Literacy rate in first language: 1% to 5%. Literacy rate in second language: 5% to 15%. NT 1998.

KOROP *(ODODOP, DUROP, DYUROP, ERORUP)* [KRP] Northwest of Mundemba, along Nigerian border, Ndian Division, South West Province. Niger-Congo, Atlantic-Congo, Volta-Congo, Benue-Congo, Cross River, Delta Cross, Upper Cross, Kiong-Korop. See main entry under Nigeria.

KOSKIN *(KOSHIN, KOSIN, KAW)* [KID] Villages of Koshin and Fang, Wum and Menchum subdivisions, North West Province. Niger-Congo, Atlantic-Congo, Volta-Congo, Benue-Congo, Bantoid, Southern, Beboid, Western.

KUO *(KO, KOH)* [KHO] Between Sorombeo and Chad border, and around Garoua, North Province. Niger-Congo, Atlantic-Congo, Volta-Congo, North, Adamawa-Ubangi, Adamawa, Mbum-Day, Mbum, Central, Koh. Closely related to Karang. Different from Kuo which is Grassfields Bantu. Second generation speakers and refugees only in Cameroon. Literacy rate in first language: 1% to 5%. Literacy rate in second language: 25% to 50%. Bible portions 1987-1993. See main entry under Chad.

KUTEP *(KUTEB, KUTEV, MBARIKE, ZUMPER, ATI, "JOMPRE")* [KUB] 1,400 in Cameroon (1986 R. Breton). Baji and Lubu villages near the Nigerian border, Furu-Awa Subdivision, Menchum Division, North West Province. Niger-Congo, Atlantic-Congo, Volta-Congo, Benue-Congo, Platoid, Benue, Jukunoid, Yukuben-Kuteb. Dialects: JENUWA, LISSAM, FIKYU, KUNABE, KENTIN. Fikyu has subdialects. High bilingualism in Jukun Takum. Pidgin is also spoken in the area. People are called 'Ati'. "Jompre" is an offensive name. Literacy rate in first language: 1% to 5%. Literacy rate in second language: 15% to 25%. Mountain slope. Christian, traditional religion. NT 1986. See main entry under Nigeria.

KWA' *(BAKWA, BAKOA, BAMILEKE-KWA)* [BKO] 1,000 (1998 estimate). Eastern Nkondjok Subdivision, Nkam Division, Littoral Province, and southwest corner of Nde Division, West Province.

Niger-Congo, Atlantic-Congo, Volta-Congo, Benue-Congo, Bantoid, Southern, Wide Grassfields, Narrow Grassfields, Mbam-Nkam, Bamileke. Dialects: KWA' (BEKWA', BAKOUA, BABWA, MIPA), MBYAM. 'Bamaha' may be an alternate name. Distinct from Kwa (Ba) of Nigeria in the Adamawa branch.

KWAJA [KDZ] Nkambe Subdivision, Donga-Mentung Division, North West Province. Niger-Congo, Atlantic-Congo, Volta-Congo, Benue-Congo, Bantoid, Southern, Wide Grassfields, Narrow Grass-fields, Mbam-Nkam, Nkambe. Possibly intelligible with or bilingual in other Mfumte languages. Bilingualism in French. Speakers consider themselves to be ethnically Mfumte. Investigation needed: intelligibility, bilingual proficiency.

KWAKUM ***(AKPWAKUM, ABAKOUM, PAKUM, KPAKUM, BAKUM, ABAKUM)*** [KWU] 3,700 (1982 SIL). Dimako and Doume subdivisions, Upper Nyong Division; north of Bertoua and in Belabo Subdivision, Lom-and-Djerem Division, East Province. Niger-Congo, Atlantic-Congo, Volta-Congo, Benue-Congo, Bantoid, Southern, Narrow Bantu, Northwest, A, Kako (A.90). Dialects: KWAKUM, BETEN (BETHEN, PETEM), TIL, BAKI (MBAKI).

KWANJA ***(KONJA, KONDJA)*** [KNP] 20,000 (1991 UBS). South of Mayo-Darle, between Banyo and Bankim in the northeastern Tikar Plain, Mayo-Banyo Division, Adamawa Province. Niger-Congo, Atlantic-Congo, Volta-Congo, Benue-Congo, Bantoid, Northern, Mambiloid, Mambila-Konja, Konja. Dialects: NYASUNDA, NYANDUNG, NYANJANG (NJANG, NJANGA). Speakers include a few old people who speak the Njanga dialect (1995 Bruce Connell). Literacy rate in first language: Below 1%. Literacy rate in second language: 5% to 15%.

LA'BI [LBI] Touboro Subdivision, Mayo-Rey Division, North Province. Niger-Congo, Atlantic-Congo, Volta-Congo, North, Adamawa-Ubangi, Adamawa, La'bi. The language of initiation rites practiced by the Gbaya, Mbum, and some Sara-Laka. Samarin says the vocabulary is borrowed from Sara languages. Second language only.

LAGWAN ***(KOTOKO-LOGONE, LOGONE, LAGWANE, LAGOUANE)*** [KOT] Population total all countries 38,500 (1982 SIL). All Kotoko languages: 167,471. North of Waza National Park in Logone-Birni Subdivision, from the bank of the Logone River across to the Nigerian border, Logone-and-Chari Division, Far North Province. There may be none in Nigeria. Also spoken in Chad, Nigeria. Afro-Asiatic, Chadic, Biu-Mandara, B, B.1, Kotoko Proper. Dialects: LOGONE-BIRNI, LOGONE-GANA (KOTOKO-GANA). Related to Afade, Mser, Malgbe, Maslam, and Mpade. Literacy rate in first language: Below 1%. Literacy rate in second language: Below 5%. Muslim.

LAIMBUE [LMX] 5,000 (1994 SIL). Several villages, Wum Central Subdivision, Menchum Division, North West Province, and Fundong Subdivision, Boyo Division, North West Province. Niger-Congo, Atlantic-Congo, Volta-Congo, Benue-Congo, Bantoid, Southern, Wide Grassfields, Narrow Grass-fields, Ring, West. Dialects: CHA', NYOS. Speakers in Wum Central Subdivision have some knowledge of Aghem. Investigation needed: intelligibility with other Laimbue villages, bilingual proficiency in Kom in Fundong Subdivision. Traditional religion, Christian.

LAMNSO' ***(NSO, NSO', NSAW, NSHO', LAMSO, LAMNSOK, BANSO, BANSO', BANSAW, PANSO)*** [NSO] 125,000 (1987 SIL). Population total both countries 125,000 or more. Northeast of Bamenda around Kumbo, eastern Kumbo and Jakiri subdivisions, Bui Division, North West Province. Also spoken in Nigeria. Niger-Congo, Atlantic-Congo, Volta-Congo, Benue-Congo, Bantoid, Southern, Wide Grassfields, Narrow Grassfields, Ring, East. Literacy rate in first language: 5% to 10%. Literacy rate in second language: 15% to 25%. NT 1990.

LETI [LEO] Along the bend of the Sanaga River, northern Sa'a Subdivision, Lekie Division, Center Province. Niger-Congo, Atlantic-Congo, Volta-Congo, Benue-Congo, Bantoid, Southern, Mbam, Sanaga (A.60). The Mangisa people are reported to speak two languages: Mengisa-Njowi, spoken daily, and Leti, a secret language of tradition (see Mengisa). Second language only.

LIMBUM ***(LIMBOM, NSUNGLI, NDZUNGLE, NDZUNGLI, NJUNGENE, NSUNGALI, NSUNGNI, LLIMBUMI, WIMBUM, BOJIIN)*** [LIM] 73,000 in Cameroon (1982 SIL). Population total both countries 73,000 or more. Entire Nkambe Subdivision around Nkambe and Ndu, Donga-Mantung Division, North West Province. Also spoken in Nigeria. Niger-Congo, Atlantic-Congo, Volta-Congo, Benue-Congo, Bantoid, Southern, Wide Grassfields, Narrow Grassfields, Mbam-Nkam, Nkambe. Dialects: WIYEH, TANG, WAT. Trade language. Grammar. Literacy rate in first language: 1% to 5%. Literacy rate in second language: 15% to 25%. Literacy classes in 6 villages (1995). Bible portions 1997.

LONGTO ***(VOKO, WOKO, BOKO, LONTO, LONGBO, LONGA, GOBEYO)*** [WOK] 2,400 (1982 SIL). Around Voko, southwest of Poli to Faro Reserve, Faro Division, North Province. Possibly in Nigeria. Niger-Congo, Atlantic-Congo, Volta-Congo, North, Adamawa-Ubangi, Adamawa, Leko-Nimbari, Duru, Voko-Dowayo, Voko. Muslim, Christian.

LUO [LUW] 1 (1995 Bruce Connell). A section of Atta. Unclassified. Nearly extinct.

MADA [MXU] 17,000 (1982 SIL). Mada massif at edge of Mandara Mts. and neighboring plain, Tokombere Subdivision, Mayo-Sava Division, Far North Province. Afro-Asiatic, Chadic, Biu-Mandara, A, A.5. Distinct from Mada of Nigeria, which is Benue-Congo. Bible portions 1989.

MAFA *("MATAKAM", MOFA, NATAKAN)* [MAF] 136,000 in Cameroon (1982 SIL). Population total both countries 138,000. From Mokolo north in Mayo-Tsanaga Division, Far North Province. Also spoken in Nigeria. Afro-Asiatic, Chadic, Biu-Mandara, A, A.5. Dialects: WEST MAFA, CENTRAL MAFA, EAST MAFA. Muktele may be a separate language. Subdialects of West Mafa: Magoumaz, Mavoumay; Central Mafa: Ouzal, Koza, Mokola, Mokolo, Ldamtsai; East Mafa: Soulede, Roua. The name "Matakam" has a derogatory connotation in Cameroon. Dictionary. Literacy rate in first language: Below 1%. Literacy rate in second language: 5% to 15%. Traditional religion, Christian. Bible 1978-1989.

MAJERA *(MIDAH, MIDA'A, DA'A)* [XMJ] 5,000 or fewer in Cameroon (1984 ALCAM). Population total both countries 5,000 or more. Around Majera in extreme southern Logone-Birni Subdivision, Logone-and-Chari Division, Far North Province. Also spoken in Chad. Afro-Asiatic, Chadic, Biu- Mandara, B, B.1, Jina. Dialects: MAJERA (MAZRA), KAJIRE-'DULO, HWALEM (HOLOM). Included in what the Mandage call 'Mida'a' and 'Da'a'. Investigation needed: bilingual proficiency in Lagwan, Musgu. Literacy rate in first language: Below 1%. Literacy rate in second language: Below 5%.

MAKAA *(MEKAA, SOUTH MAKAA, SOUTH MEKAA)* [MCP] 80,000 (1987 SIL). Essentially the whole northern part of Upper Nyong Division (Messamena, Abong-Mbang, Doume, Nguelemendouka subdivisions), East Province. Niger-Congo, Atlantic-Congo, Volta-Congo, Benue-Congo, Bantoid, Southern, Narrow Bantu, Northwest, A, Makaa-Njem (A.80). Dialects: BEBENT (BEBENDE, BIKEN, BEWIL, BEMINA), MBWAANZ, SEKUNDA. Related to Byep and Kol. Dictionary. Literacy rate in first language: Below 1%. Literacy rate in second language: 5% to 15%. Bible portions.

MALGBE *(MALGWE, GULFE, GULFEI, GOULFEI, SANBALBE, MALBE, NGWALKWE)* [MXF] Population total both countries 36,000 (1977 Bendor-Samuel). North of Kousseri in a town of Goulfey and Goulfey Subdivision, along the Chari River, Logone-and-Chari Division, Far North Province. Also spoken in Chad. Afro-Asiatic, Chadic, Biu-Mandara, B, B.1, Kotoko Proper. Dialects: MALGBE (GOULFEI), MARA, DRO, DOUGUIA. Related to Afade, Mser, Lagwan, Maslam, and Mpade. Literacy rate in first language: Below 1%. Literacy rate in second language: 5% to 15%.

MALIMBA *(MULIMBA, MUDIMA, LIMBA, LEMBA)* [MZD] 4,500 (1982 SIL). Small pocket north of Edea, and around the mouth of the Sanaga River, Sanaga-Maritime Division, Littoral Province. Niger-Congo, Atlantic-Congo, Volta-Congo, Benue-Congo, Bantoid, Southern, Narrow Bantu, Northwest, A, Duala (A.20). May be intelligible with Duala. Investigation needed: intelligibility, bilingual proficiency in Duala.

MAMBAI *(MANGBAI, MANGBEI, MANBAI, MAMBAY, MAMGBAY, MAMGBEI, MONGBAY)* [MCS] Population total both countries 2,500 (1982 SIL). Along Mayo-Kebi River near the Chad border in extreme northern Bibemi Subdivision, Benoue Division, North Province. Also spoken in Chad. Niger-Congo, Atlantic-Congo, Volta-Congo, North, Adamawa-Ubangi, Adamawa, Mbum-Day, Mbum, Northern, Tupuri-Mambai. Speakers are reported to be bilingual in Mundang. Investigation needed: bilingual proficiency in Mundang.

MAMBILA, CAMEROON *(MAMBILLA, MAMBERE, NOR, TORBI, LAGUBI, TAGBO, TONGBO, BANG, BLE, JULI, BEA)* [MYA] 30,000 (1993 UBS). On Nigerian border in northwestern Mayo-Banyo Division (Banyo and Bankim subdivisions), Adamawa Province. Niger-Congo, Atlantic-Congo, Volta-Congo, Benue-Congo, Bantoid, Northern, Mambiloid, Mambila-Konja, Mambila. Dialects: JU BA, SUNU TORBI (TORBI), JU NAARE (MAMBILA DE GEMBU). Closely related language: Mvanlip (Magu) in Nigeria. Close to Mambila of Nigeria, but different. Dialects form a chain; one end unintelligible to speakers of the other. At least four dialects in Cameroon. Dictionary. Literacy rate in first language: Below 1%. Literacy rate in second language: Below 5%. Traditional religion, Muslim. Bible portions 1992.

MANTA *(MENTA, AMASI, AMASSI, BANTAKPA, BANTA, ANTA)* [MYG] 13,600 (1982 SIL). Approximately 20 villages in a 40 km. stretch in Manyu Division northeast of Mamfe, from the border of Mom (Akwaya Subdivision) to Manta (Mamfe Subdivision), South West Province. Niger-Congo, Atlantic-Congo, Volta-Congo, Benue-Congo, Bantoid, Southern, Tivoid.

MASANA *(MASA, MASSA, WALIA, "BANANA")* [MCN] 103,000 in Cameroon (1982 SIL). Around Yagoua, southeastern Mayo-Danay Division, Far North Province. Afro-Asiatic, Chadic, Masa. Dialects: YAGWA (YAGOUA), DOMO, WALYA, BONGOR, WINA (VIRI), GIZAY (GUISSEY), BUDUGUM. All dialects understand Yagoua well. The first three dialects listed are West Masa, Wina and Gizay are Central Masa. Budugum has 97% lexical similarity to the closest other dialect. Literacy rate in first language: Below 1%. Literacy rate in second language: Below 5%. Traditional religion, Christian, Muslim. NT 1950-1955. See main entry under Chad.

MASLAM [MSV] 5,000 or fewer in Cameroon (1984 ALCAM). Population total both countries 5,000. In Maltam and Saho northwest of Kousseri, Makari Subdivision, Logone-and-Chari Division, Far North Province. Also spoken in Chad. Afro-Asiatic, Chadic, Biu-Mandara, B, B.1, Kotoko Proper. Dialects: MASLAM (MALTAM), SAO (SAHU). Related to Afade, Mser, Lagwan, Malgbe, and Mpade. Speakers may be able to use literature in one of those languages. Investigation needed: intelligibility with Afade, Mser, Lagwan, Malgbe, Mpade.

MATAL ***(MOUKTELE, MUKTILE, MUKTELE, BALDA)*** [MFH] 18,000 (1982 SIL). Eastern edge of Mandara Mountains, to the south, southwest of Mora, Mora Subdivision, Mayo-Sava Division, Far North Province. Afro-Asiatic, Chadic, Biu-Mandara, A, A.5. NT 1989.

MBE' ***(MBO, MBAW)*** [MTK] Canton of Mbo, Nwa Subdivision, Donga-Mantung Division, North West Province. Niger-Congo, Atlantic-Congo, Volta-Congo, Benue-Congo, Bantoid, Southern, Wide Grassfields, Narrow Grassfields, Mbam-Nkam, Nkambe. Bilingualism in Tikari. People are shifting to Tikari outside of the home. Distinct from Mbe of Nigeria, which is in the Ekoid group.

MBEDAM [XMD] Northeast of Hina, Mokolo Subdivision, Mayo-Tsanaga Division, Far North Province. Afro-Asiatic, Chadic, Biu-Mandara, A, A.7.

MBEMBE, TIGON ***(TIGUM, TIGON, TIGONG, TIGUN, TIKUN, AKONTO)*** [NZA] 36,000 in Cameroon (1982 SIL). Population total both countries 56,000. North of Nkambe, Ako Subdivision, Donga-Mantung Division, North West Province. Also spoken in Nigeria. Niger-Congo, Atlantic-Congo, Volta-Congo, Benue-Congo, Platoid, Benue, Jukunoid, Central, Jukun-Mbembe-Wurbo, Mbembe. Dialects: ASHUKU (KITSIPKI), NAMA (DAMA, NAMU), NZARE (NDZALE, NSARE, IZALE, IZARE, NJARI), KPORO, ENEEME. Entirely different from Mbembe of Nigeria which is in Cross River group. Literacy rate in first language: Below 1%. Literacy rate in second language: 15% to 25%. Traditional religion.

MBO ***(MBOO, SAMBO)*** [MBO] 45,000 (1995 Ewane). Mbo plain: Nkongsamba and Melong subdivisions, Moungo Division, Littoral Province; Santchou Subdivision, Menoua Division and Kekem Subdivision, Upper Nkam Division, West Province. Niger-Congo, Atlantic-Congo, Volta-Congo, Benue-Congo, Bantoid, Southern, Narrow Bantu, Northwest, A, Lundu-Balong (A.10), Ngoe. Dialects: MELONG (EHO MBO), BAREKO (EHOW MBA, MINAHE), KEKEM (NLEMBUU), SANTCHOU (NLA MBOO). Related to Akoose and Bassossi. Different from Mbo of DRC, which is Bantu D.30. Literacy rate in first language: Below 1%. Literacy rate in second language: 25%.

MBONGA ***(MBOA)*** [XMB] Near Betare-Oya, Lom-and-Djerem Division, East Province. Niger-Congo, Atlantic-Congo, Volta-Congo, Benue-Congo, Bantoid, Southern, Jarawan, Cameroon.

MBUKO ***(MBUKU, MBOKU, MBOKOU)*** [MQB] 6,700 (1982 SIL). Mbuko massif and neighboring Mayo-Raneo plain, Meri Subdivision east of Meri, Diamare Division, Far North Province. Afro-Asiatic, Chadic, Biu-Mandara, A, A.5. 'Mbuko' is the name speakers use. Literacy rate in first language: Below 1%. Literacy rate in second language: 5% to 15%.

MBULE ***(DUMBULE, MBOLA)*** [MLB] Mbola village in southern part of Bokito Subdivision, Mbam Division, Center Province. Niger-Congo, Atlantic-Congo, Volta-Congo, Benue-Congo, Bantoid, Southern, Mbam, Yambasa (A.60). Intelligibility with Yangben and Nu Baca is not fully determined. Related to Nu Baca, Elip, and Mmaala. Investigation needed: intelligibility with Yangben, Nu Baca.

MBUM ***(MBOUM, MBOUMTIBA, WUNA, BUNA)*** [MDD] 38,600 in Cameroon (1982 SIL). Population total both countries 51,000. West Mbum is spread out in isolated groups: south and southwest of Ngaoundere (Vina and Djerem divisions, Adamawa Province); around Ngaoundere to border of Faro Reserve in Faro Division, North Province. Gbete is in Belabo Subdivision, Lom-and-Djerem Division, East Province. Not in Chad. Also spoken in CAR. Niger-Congo, Atlantic-Congo, Volta-Congo, North, Adamawa-Ubangi, Adamawa, Mbum-Day, Mbum, Southern. Dialects: MBOUM (WEST MBUM, BUM), GBETE (KEPERE, KPERE, PERE, RIPERE, BYRRE, PONO, VANA). Speakers are rapidly becoming bilingual in Fulani. Primer. Dictionary. Grammar. Literacy rate in first language: 1% to 5%. Literacy rate in second language: 5% to 15%. Muslim, traditional religion. NT 1965.

MEDUMBA ***(BAGANGTE, BANGANGTE, BAMILEKE-MEDUMBA)*** [BYV] 210,000 (1991 UBS). Major part of Nde Division (Tonga Subdivision and Bangangte Subdivision east of Bangangte), West Province. Niger-Congo, Atlantic-Congo, Volta-Congo, Benue-Congo, Bantoid, Southern, Wide Grassfields, Narrow Grassfields, Mbam-Nkam, Bamileke. Dialect: BATONGTOU. Literacy rate in first language: Below 1%. Literacy rate in second language: 15% to 25%. Traditional religion, Christian. Bible 1992.

MEFELE ***(BULA, BULAHAI, BOULAHAY)*** [MFJ] 10,000 or more (1992 SIL). South and east of Mokolo, Mokolo Subdivision, Mayo-Tsanaga Division, Far North Province, 6 villages. Afro-Asiatic, Chadic, Biu-Mandara, A, A.5. Dialects: MEFELE, SERAK (SIRAK), MUHURA (MOUHOUR), SHUGULE (CHOUGOULE). Bilingualism in Fulfulde is increasing by those who travel, and in French by the few children in school. Bilingualism in Mafa appears to be increasing among the children, who learn it at school and market. Vigorous in family and village life. Investigation needed: bilingual proficiency in Mafa.

MELOKWO ***(MOLOKWO, MOLOKO, MOKYO, MOLKOA, MOLKWO, MOLKO)*** [MLW] 8,500 (1992 SIL). On Melokwo Mountain and in the plains around its base, Makalingay Canton, Tokombere Subdivision, Mayo-Sava Division, Far North Province. Afro-Asiatic, Chadic, Biu-Mandara, A, A.5. Only one dialect. Surrounded by 4 related languages (including Muyang, Giziga North, and the Mikiri dialect of Dugwor) plus one other. Little bilingualism except in outlying areas where there has been intermarriage with speakers of other languages. Fulfulde is used in the market, but interpretation is necessary when it is used in church. A few educated speakers can use French. Melokwo is used in all domains of daily living. Christian.

MENDANKWE ***(MANDANKWE)*** [MFD] 10,000 or more (1984 ALCAM). North and east of Bamenda, either side of Ring Road and in the mountainous circle of Menda Nkwe, Tuba Subdivision, Mezam Division, North West Province. Niger-Congo, Atlantic-Congo, Volta-Congo, Benue-Congo, Bantoid, Southern, Wide Grassfields, Narrow Grassfields, Mbam-Nkam, Ngemba. Dialects: NKWEN (BAFRENG), MENDANKWE (MUNDA, BAMENDA). Related to Ngemba, Bafut, Pinyin, Awing, and Bambili. Speakers may have functional intelligibility of the Mankon dialect of Ngemba. Literacy rate in first language: Below 1%. Literacy rate in second language: 15% to 25%.

MENGAKA ***(GHAP, BENZING, MEGAKA, BAMILEKE-MENGAKA)*** [XMG] 20,000 (1993 SIL). Bagam, Galim, and Bamendjing, Southern Galim Subdivision, Bamboutos Division, West Province. Niger-Congo, Atlantic-Congo, Volta-Congo, Benue-Congo, Bantoid, Southern, Wide Grassfields, Narrow Grassfields, Mbam-Nkam, Bamileke. Dialects: BAGAM, BAMENDJING (BAMENDJIN). 91% lexical similarity among villages, but speakers report no dialect differences. Some bilingualism in French among younger speakers and Bamun among older ones. They call themselves 'Eghap'. Outsiders call them 'Bagam'. Distinct from Mungaka (Bali) which is Mbam-Nkam, Nun. Investigation needed: bilingual proficiency in Bamun, French. Interest in language development for schools and individual literacy. Bagam script.

MENGISA ***(MANGISA, MENGISA-NJOWE)*** [MCT] 20,000 (1979 SIL). Along the bend of the Sanaga River between the river and Sa'a, Sa'a Subdivision, Lekie Division, Center Province. Niger-Congo, Atlantic-Congo, Volta-Congo, Benue-Congo, Bantoid, Southern, Narrow Bantu, Northwest, A, Yaunde-Fang (A.70). May be intelligible with Ewondo. The Mangisa people are reported to speak 2 languages: Mengisa Njowi, spoken daily and Leti, a secret language of tradition. Investigation needed: intelligibility with Ewondo.

MENKA [MEA] 12,500 (1982 SIL). West of Mbwengi, northwest of Batibo, Batibo Subdivision, Momo Division, North West Province. Niger-Congo, Atlantic-Congo, Volta-Congo, Benue-Congo, Bantoid, Southern, Wide Grassfields, Narrow Grassfields, Momo.

MEREY ***(MERI, MERE, MOFU DE MERI)*** [MEQ] 10,000 (1982 SIL). West of Meri on Meri Massif, Diamare Division, Far North Province. Afro-Asiatic, Chadic, Biu-Mandara, A, A.5. Dialect: DUGUR. Literacy rate in first language: Below 1%. Literacy rate in second language: 5% to 15%. Bible portions 1986.

MESAKA ***(UGARE, MESSAGA, MESSAGA-EKOL, MESSAKA, IYON, BANAGERE)*** [IYO] 14,000 (1982 SIL). On the Nigerian border northeast of Akwaya, Manyu Division, South West Province, in an isolated area. Niger-Congo, Atlantic-Congo, Volta-Congo, Benue-Congo, Bantoid, Southern, Tivoid. Dialect: BATOMO (BABASI). Batomo may be a separate language, or may be the same as Motomo (Oliti, Matchi), a dialect of Icheve. 70% lexical similarity with Tiv. Bilingualism in Tiv, Pidgin. 'Banagere' is the name used by the people for themselves, 'Ugare' for their language. 'Mesaka' is used by the government, 'Iyon' by the Tiv. Literacy rate in first language: Below 1%. Literacy rate in second language: 5% to 15%. Mountains. Traditional religion.

META' ***(MOGHAMO-MENEMO, MENEMO-MOGAMO, WIDIKUM-TADKON, CHUBO, BATIBO, METTA, BAMETA, MUTA, MITAA)*** [MGO] 87,000 (1982 SIL). Eastern and southeastern Mbengwi and eastern Batibo subdivisions, Momo Division; around villages of Bafuchu and Nja, Bamenda Subdivision, North West Province. Niger-Congo, Atlantic-Congo, Volta-Congo, Benue-Congo, Bantoid, Southern, Wide Grassfields, Narrow Grassfields, Momo. Dialects: MENEMO (METTA, META', UTA', BAMETA), MOGHAMO (MUYWI, IYIRIKUM, WIDEKUM, TIWIRKUM, BATIBO, BESI, KUGWE). Ngamambo is a separate language. Literacy rate in first language: Below 1%. Literacy rate in second language: 50% to 75%.

MFUMTE ***(NFUMTE)*** [NFU] 24,700 (1982 SIL). 14 villages, mostly in canton of Mfumte north of Nwa and east of Nkambe, Nwa Subdivision, Donga-Mantung Division, North West Province. Niger-Congo, Atlantic-Congo, Volta-Congo, Benue-Congo, Bantoid, Southern, Wide Grassfields, Narrow Grassfields, Mbam-Nkam, Nkambe. Dialects: LUS, KOM, MBALLA, BANG, KOFFA (KOFA), JUI, MBAT, MANANG, MBIBJI, MBAH. Literacy rate in first language: Below 1%. Literacy rate in second language: 5% to 15%. Christian, traditional religion.

MINA *(HINA, BESLERI)* [HNA] 8,000 to 10,000 (1992 SIL). South of Mokolo, Hina Subdivision, Mayo-Tsanaga Division, Far North Province, 20 villages. Afro-Asiatic, Chadic, Biu-Mandara, A, A.7. Dialects: BESLERI, JINGJING (DZUMDZUM), GAMDUGUN. Fulfulde is used at the market. French is learned in school, but few children attend school. Speakers are not generally bilingual in Daba. All ages. Vigorous in daily life. Muslim, traditional religion.

MISSONG *(MIJONG)* [MIJ] Centered around village of Missong, including villages of Munken, Aba, Mundabi, Mufu; Wum Subdivision, Menchum Division, North West Province. Niger-Congo, Atlantic-Congo, Volta-Congo, Benue-Congo, Bantoid, Southern, Beboid, Western. 'Dzaiven Boka' may be an alternate name.

MMAALA *(MMALA, BENYI)* [MMU] 5,300 (1982 SIL). In and south of Bokito, Mmala canton, Mbam Division, Center Province. Niger-Congo, Atlantic-Congo, Volta-Congo, Benue-Congo, Bantoid, Southern, Mbam, Yambasa (A.60). A standardized written form may be possible with Elip and Yangben, related languages. French is used for instruction in primary and secondary school. Ewondo or Bulu are used in other churches. Speakers acquire understanding of Elip and Yangben in early adulthood. Interpretation into Mmaala is made in RC church services. Speakers do not think French will replace Mmaala.

MMEN *(BAFMEN, BAFUMEN, BAFMENG, BAFOUMENG, MME)* [BFM] 63,500 (1998 Gabriel Ndong). Along the Fundong Road northwest of Fundong, Wum Subdivision, Menchum Division, North West Province. Niger-Congo, Atlantic-Congo, Volta-Congo, Benue-Congo, Bantoid, Southern, Wide Grassfields, Narrow Grassfields, Ring, Center. Possibly intelligible with other Center Ring languages. Investigation needed: intelligibility with Ring languages.

MOFU, NORTH *(MOFU-DOUVANGAR, DOUVANGAR, MOFU-NORD)* [MFK] 27,500 (1982 SIL). Massifs south of Meri, Diamare Division, Far North Province. Afro-Asiatic, Chadic, Biu-Mandara, A, A.5. Dialects: DOUROUN (MOFU DE DOUROUM, DURUM), WAZAN (WAZANG). Literacy rate in first language: Below 1%. Literacy rate in second language: 5% to 15%. NT 1975.

MOFU-GUDUR *(MOFOU, MOFOU DE GOUDOUR, MOFU-SUD, MOFU SOUTH)* [MIF] 60,000 (1998 K. Hollingsworth SIL). Massifs south of Tsanaga River to the Mayo-Louti, Mokolo Subdivision, Mayo-Tsanaga Division extending into Diamare Division, Far North Province. Afro-Asiatic, Chadic, Biu-Mandara, A, A.5. Dialects: MOKONG, GUDUR, ZIDIM, DIMEO, MASSAGAL (MASSAKAL), NJELENG. Dictionary. Literacy rate in first language: 1% to 5%. Literacy rate in second language: 5% to 15%. Bible portions 1985-1995.

MOKPWE *(BAKWERI, BEKWIRI, BAKPWE, BAKWEDI, BAKWELE, VAKWELI, KWEDI, KWELI, KWILI, KWIRI, MOKPE, VAMBENG, UJUWA)* [BRI] 32,200 (1982 SIL). A large part of the Fako Division (Muyuka, Tiko, Buea, and Limbe subdivisions), South West Province. Niger-Congo, Atlantic-Congo, Volta-Congo, Benue-Congo, Bantoid, Southern, Narrow Bantu, Northwest, A, Duala (A.20). Reported to include Wumboko. Literature may serve Wumboko, Bubia, and Isu. Widespread use of Pidgin and Duala. Literacy rate in first language: Below 1%. Literacy rate in second language: 15% to 25%.

MOM JANGO *(VERE, VERRE, WERE, KOBO)* [VER] 4,000 in Cameroon. North of Tchamba on Nigerian border, Beka Subdivision, Faro Division, North Province. Niger-Congo, Atlantic-Congo, Volta-Congo, North, Adamawa-Ubangi, Adamawa, Leko-Nimbari, Duru, Voko-Dowayo, Vere-Dowayo, Vere-Gimme, Vere. See main entry under Nigeria.

MONO *(MON-NON)* [MRU] 1,100 (1982 SIL). North of Rey-Bouba around Kongrong along the Mayo-Godi River, Mayo-Rey Division, North Province. Niger-Congo, Atlantic-Congo, Volta-Congo, North, Adamawa-Ubangi, Adamawa, Mbum-Day, Mbum, Northern, Dama-Galke. Related to Dama. Distinct from Mono in DRC in Banda group.

MPADE *(MAKARI, MAKARY, MENDAGE, MANDAGE, MANDAGUÉ)* [MPI] Population total all countries 12,000 (1992 SIL). Centered around Makari next to Lake Chad and Goulfey along the Chari River, Logone-and-Chari Division, Far North Province. Also spoken in Chad, Nigeria. Afro-Asiatic, Chadic, Biu-Mandara, B, B.1, Kotoko Proper. Dialects: SHOE (SHAWE, CHAOUE, SCHOE, MANI), MPADE (MAKARI), BODO, WOULKI, DIGAM. Shoe dialect is only in Cameroon. Close to Lagwan. Related to Afade, Mser, Malgbe, and Maslam. Literacy rate in first language: Below 1%. Literacy rate in second language: 5% to 15%.

MPIEMO *(MBIMU, MBIMOU, MPYEMO, MPO, BIMU)* [MCX] 5,000 in Cameroon (1991 SIL). Gari-Gombo Subdivision along the road from Gribi to Yokadouma, Boumba-and-Ngoko Division, East Province. Niger-Congo, Atlantic-Congo, Volta-Congo, Benue-Congo, Bantoid, Southern, Narrow Bantu, Northwest, A, Makaa-Njem (A.80). Dialects: JASUA (JASOA), BIDJUKI (BIDJOUKI). The Jasua dialect is spoken by most people and is well understood by others. The people are functionally monolingual. Used in church together with Pongpong. Literacy rate in first language: Below 1%. Literacy rate in second language: 5% to 15%. Traditional religion, Christian. See main entry under CAR.

MPONGMPONG ***(MPOMPO, BOMBO, MPOPO, MBOMBO, PONGPONG)*** [MGG] 45,000 (1991 SIL). Menzime and Bangantu are south of Batouri in Mbang Subdivision, Kadey Division, and the other dialects are south and west of Yokadouma, covering most of the Boumba-and-Ngoko Division, East Province. Niger-Congo, Atlantic-Congo, Volta-Congo, Benue-Congo, Bantoid, Southern, Narrow Bantu, Northwest, A, Makaa-Njem (A.80). Dialects: MBOBYENG (POBYENG), MENZIME (MEDZIME, MEZIME, MENDZIME), BAGETO (BAAGATO, BANGANTU, NORTHERN BANGANTU), KUNABEMBE (KONABEMBE, NKUMABEM, KUNABEEB, KONABEM), MPOMAM (BOMAN, MBOMAN). The people are functionally monolingual. Few understand Ewondo. Literacy rate in first language: Below 1%. Literacy rate in second language: 5% to 15%. Radio programs.

MSER ***(KOTOKO-KUSERI, KUSERI, KOUSERI, KOUSSERI, MANDAGE)*** [KQX] Population total both countries 2,100 (1982 SIL). Kousseri Subdivision, Logone-and-Chari Division, Far North Province. Also spoken in Chad. Afro-Asiatic, Chadic, Biu-Mandara, B, B.1, Kotoko Proper. Dialects: MSER (KOUSSERI), KALO (KALAKAFRA), GAWI, HOULOUF, KABE. Related to Afade, Lagwan, Malgbe, Maslam, and Mpade. Literacy rate in first language: Below 1%. Literacy rate in second language: 5% to 15%. Muslim.

MUMUYE ***(MOME, NAY KOPO)*** [MUL] Benoue Division, North Province. Uncertain if spoken in Cameroon. Niger-Congo, Atlantic-Congo, Volta-Congo, North, Adamawa-Ubangi, Adamawa, Leko-Nimbari, Mumuye-Yandang, Mumuye. Literacy rate in first language: Below 1%. Literacy rate in second language: 15% to 25%. Traditional religion, Muslim, Christian. NT 1995. See main entry under Nigeria.

MUNDANG ***(MOUNDANG, MOUNDAN, KAELE, NDA, MARHAY, MUSEMBAN)*** [MUA] 44,700 in Cameroon (1982 SIL). Near Chad border to north and west of Kaili, Kaili Subdivision, Kaili Division, Far North Province; south of Mayo-Kebi near Chad border, Benoue Division, North Province. The Torrock-Kaili subdialect of Zasing is spoken in Kaili and Torrock, Cameroon. Niger-Congo, Atlantic-Congo, Volta-Congo, North, Adamawa-Ubangi, Adamawa, Mbum-Day, Mbum, Northern, Tupuri-Mambai. Dialects: KIZIERE, IMBANA (BANA, MBANA, IMBARA), ZASING (YASSING, DJASING, YASING, JASING, ZAZING), GELAMA. Gelama may be a separate language. Investigation needed: intelligibility with Gelama. Literacy rate in first language: 1% to 5%. Literacy rate in second language: 5% to 15%. Traditional religion, Christian. Bible 1983. See main entry under Chad.

MUNDANI [MUN] 34,000 (1987 SIL). South of Batibo, Mamfe and northern Fontem subdivisions, Manyu Division, South West Province. Niger-Congo, Atlantic-Congo, Volta-Congo, Benue-Congo, Bantoid, Southern, Wide Grassfields, Narrow Grassfields, Momo. Dialects: BAMUMBO (BAMUMBU), BECHATI, BESALI, BANTI, FOLEPI, IGUAMBO (IGUMBO), BANGANG, NKO (NKONG). Dictionary. Literacy rate in first language: 5% to 10%. Literacy rate in second language: 25% to 50%. Mountain slope. Bible portions 1989-1990.

MUNGAKA ***(BALI, LI, NGAAKA, NGA'KA, MUNGA'KA)*** [MHK] 50,100 (1982 SIL). Bali Subdivision, Mezam Division, North West Province; southeastern Galim Subdivision, Bamboutos Division and northern Bafoussam Subdivision, Mifi Division, West Province. Niger-Congo, Atlantic-Congo, Volta-Congo, Benue-Congo, Bantoid, Southern, Wide Grassfields, Narrow Grassfields, Mbam-Nkam, Nun. Dialects: BALI NYONGA (BALI), TI (BATI), NDE (BANDENG). It may be a dialect of Bamenyam. Related to Baba. People are called 'Bali'. Different from three languages in DRC called 'Bali', Bali of Nigeria, or Bali which is a dialect of Chamba of Nigeria and Cameroon, although many of these people have Chamba ethnic origins. Literacy rate in first language: 1% to 5%. Literacy rate in second language: 25% to 50%. Traditional religion, Christian. Bible 1961.

MUNGONG ***(MUNGOM)*** [XMN] Northeast of Wum, west of Nkambe, Menchum Division, North West Province. Niger-Congo, Atlantic-Congo, Volta-Congo, Benue-Congo, Bantoid, Southern, Unclassified. May be Eastern Beboid.

MUSEY ***(MUSIINA, MUSAYA, MUSOI, MOUSSEI, MUSEI, MUSSOI, MOUSSEY, MUSSOY, MOSI, BANANNA, BANANNA HO, HO, MUSEYNA)*** [MSE] 20,000 in Cameroon. East of Guere on Chad border, Mayo-Danay Division, Far North Province. Afro-Asiatic, Chadic, Masa. Dialect: PE. Pe dialect is in Cameroon. Literacy rate in first language: Below 1%. Literacy rate in second language: 5% to 15%. Traditional religion. NT 1996. See main entry under Chad.

MUSGU ***(MOUSGOU, MOUSGOUN, MUSGUM, MOUSGOUM, MUSUK, MUZUK, MUNJUK, MULWI)*** [MUG] 61,500 in Cameroon (1982 SIL). Population total both countries 85,908. Entire Maga Subdivision, Mayo-Danay Division, Far North Province. Also spoken in Chad. Afro-Asiatic, Chadic, Biu-Mandara, B, B.2. Dialects: MPUS (PUS, POUSS, MOUSGOUM DE POUSS), BEEGE (JAFGA), VULUM (VLUM, MULWI), NGILEMONG, LUGGOY, MANILING (MANI-ILING), MUZUK (MOUSGOUM DE GUIRVIDIG). Vulum dialect is mainly in Chad. They call themselves 'Mulwi'. Literacy rate in first language: 1% to 5%. Literacy rate in second language: 5% to 15%. Traditional religion, Muslim. NT 1964.

MUYANG ***(MYAU, MYENGE, MUYENGE, MOUYENGE, MOUYENGUE)*** [MUY] 15,000 (1982 SIL). Muyang, Mougouba, Gouadagouada, and Palbarar massifs, northeast of Tokombere, Mayo-Sava Division, Far North Province. Afro-Asiatic, Chadic, Biu-Mandara, A, A.5.

NAGUMI ***(BAMA, MBAMA)*** [NGV] Formerly spoken in Garoua Subdivision between Benoue and Faro rivers and Poli Mts., Benoue Division, North Province. Niger-Congo, Atlantic-Congo, Volta-Congo, Benue-Congo, Bantoid, Southern, Jarawan, Cameroon. Voegelin and Voegelin (1977.55) say this was the same as Ngong. Extinct.

NAKI ***(MEKAF, MUNKAF, NKAP, BUNAKI)*** [MFF] 3,000 including 300 in Nse chiefdom (1986 R. Breton). Bukpang II and Lebo villages, Nse chiefdom, Furu-Awa Subdivision, Menchum Division, North West Province. Niger-Congo, Atlantic-Congo, Volta-Congo, Benue-Congo, Bantoid, Southern, Beboid, Western. In Nse chiefdom they speak Nsaa and are called 'Bunsaa'. Limited bilingualism in Nse and Lebo, although Jukun is the trade language. In Bukpang II few speak Jukun. Pidgin is used in the area. The people are called 'Bunaki'.

NCANE ***(NCHANTI, NTSHANTI, CANE)*** [NCR] In and south of Misaje village, western Nkambe Subdivision, Donga-Mantung Division, North West Province. Niger-Congo, Atlantic-Congo, Volta-Congo, Benue-Congo, Bantoid, Southern, Beboid, Eastern.

NDAI ***(GALKE, PORMI)*** [GKE] Only a few speakers left. Tchollire, Mayo-Rey Division, North Province. Niger-Congo, Atlantic-Congo, Volta-Congo, North, Adamawa-Ubangi, Adamawa, Mbum-Day, Mbum, Northern, Dama-Galke. Nearly extinct.

NDAKTUP [NCP] Northeast of Nkambe, Donga-Mantung Division, North West Province. Niger-Congo, Atlantic-Congo, Volta-Congo, Benue-Congo, Bantoid, Southern, Wide Grassfields, Narrow Grassfields, Mbam-Nkam, Nkambe. Dialects: NCHA, BITUI (BITWI). Possibly intelligible with or bilingual in other Mfumte languages. Speakers consider themselves to be ethnically Mfumte. Investigation needed: intelligibility, bilingual proficiency.

NDA'NDA' ***(BAMILEKE-NDA'NDA')*** [NNZ] 10,000 or more (1984 ALCAM). Straddling Upper Nkam (east of Bana), Nde (north and west of Bangante), and Mifi (south of Bangou) divisions, West Province. Niger-Congo, Atlantic-Congo, Volta-Congo, Benue-Congo, Bantoid, Southern, Wide Grassfields, Narrow Grassfields, Mbam-Nkam, Bamileke. Dialects: UNDIMEHA (EAST NDA'NDA'), UNGAMEHA (WEST NDA'NDA'-SOUTH NDA'NDA'). Batoufam is a subdialect of East Nda'nda'. Bilingualism in French. Literacy rate in first language: Below 1%. Literacy rate in second language: 15% to 25%.

NDEMLI ***(NDEMBA, BANDEM, BAYONG)*** [NML] Between Yabassi, Yingui, and Nkondjok, Nkam Division, Littoral Province. Niger-Congo, Atlantic-Congo, Volta-Congo, Benue-Congo, Bantoid, Southern, Ndemli. Related to Tikar and Bandobo. May be the same as Bandobo.

NDOOLA ***(NDORO, NJOYAME, NUNDORO)*** [NDR] 1,300 in Cameroon. Dodeo village near the Nigerian border, on the upper Mayo-Deo River, southern Mayo-Baleo Subdivision, Faro-and-Deo Division, Adamawa Province; and north of Nkambe, Donga-Mantung Division, North West Province. Niger-Congo, Atlantic-Congo, Volta-Congo, Benue-Congo, Bantoid, Northern, Mambiloid, Ndoro. See main entry under Nigeria.

NGAMAMBO ***(MBU, MUNGYEN, BAFUCHU, BANJA, NGA, NGEMBO)*** [NBV] Eastern and south-eastern Mbengwi and eastern Batibo subdivisions, Momo Division; around villages of Bafuchu and Nja, Bamenda Subdivision, North West Province. Niger-Congo, Atlantic-Congo, Volta-Congo, Benue-Congo, Bantoid, Southern, Wide Grassfields, Narrow Grassfields, Momo. A separate language from Meta'. Literacy rate in first language: Below 1%. Literacy rate in second language: 50% to 75%.

NGAMBAY ***(SARA, SARA NGAMBAI, GAMBA, GAMBAYE, GAMB-LAI, NGAMBAI, GAMBAI)*** [SBA] Near the Chad border east of Tchollire, Rey-Bouba Subdivision, Mayo-Rey Division, along the route to Garoua, in Garoua, Benoue Division, North Province. Primarily in Chad, some in Nigeria. Nilo-Saharan, Central Sudanic, West, Bongo-Bagirmi, Sara-Bagirmi, Sara, Sara Proper. Literacy rate in first language: Below 1%. Literacy rate in second language: 5% to 15%. Bible 1993. See main entry under Chad.

NGEMBA ***(MEGIMBA, MOGIMBA, NGOMBA, NGUEMBA)*** [NGE] 70,000 (1982 SIL). Tuba and western Bamenda subdivisions, Mezam Division, North West Province. Niger-Congo, Atlantic-Congo, Volta-Congo, Benue-Congo, Bantoid, Southern, Wide Grassfields, Narrow Grassfields, Mbam-Nkam, Ngemba. Dialects: BAGANGU (AKUM), NJONG (BANJONG), MBUTU (BAMBUTU, ALAMATU, MBOTU), SONGWA (NSONGWA, BANGWA, NGWA), MANKON (BIDA), MOMBU, SHOMBA (BAMECHOM, ALMATSON), MANGKUNGE (NGEMBA, BANDENG, BANDE, BANDE', NKUNE, MUKOHN), MBREREWI (MUNDUM 1, BAMUNDUM 1), ANYANG (MUNDUM 2, BAMUNDUM 2), ALATENING (ALATINING). Related to Bafut, Mandankwe, Pinyin, Awing. Distinct from Ngyemboon (Nguemba). Bilingualism in Cameroon Pidgin. Investigation needed: bilingual proficiency in Pidgin, intelligibility with Mundum, Mbrerewi, Anyang.

NGIE ***(NGI, ANGIE, BANINGE, BAMINGE, MINGI, UGIE, UNGIE)*** [NGJ] 31,000 (1982 SIL). Western Mbengwi Subdivision around Andek, Momo Division, North West Province. Niger-Congo, Atlantic-Congo, Volta-Congo, Benue-Congo, Bantoid, Southern, Wide Grassfields, Narrow Grassfields, Momo. Literacy rate in first language: Below 1%. Literacy rate in second language: 15% to 25%.

NGIEMBOON ***(NGUEMBA, NGYEMBOON, BAMILEKE-NGYEMBOON)*** [NNH] 100,000 (1987 SIL). Batcham Subdivision and in Balatchi in western Mbouda Subdivision, Bamboutos Division; north of Penka-Michel, Menoua Division, West Province. Niger-Congo, Atlantic-Congo, Volta-Congo, Benue-Congo, Bantoid, Southern, Wide Grassfields, Narrow Grassfields, Mbam-Nkam, Bamileke. Dialects: BATCHAM, BALATCHI, BAMOUNGONG. Distinct from Ngemba. Literacy rate in first language: Below 1%. Literacy rate in second language: 25% to 50%. Bible portions 1984.

NGISHE ***(OSHIE)*** [NSH] 5,000 (1984 ALCAM). Eastern Njikwa Subdivision, Momo Division, North West Province. Niger-Congo, Atlantic-Congo, Volta-Congo, Benue-Congo, Bantoid, Southern, Wide Grassfields, Narrow Grassfields, Momo. Dialects: MISE, OSHIE. Literacy rate in first language: Below 1%. Literacy rate in second language: 15% to 25%.

NGOMBA ***(NDAA, NDA'A, BAMILEKE-NGOMBA)*** [NNO] 63,000 (1999 SIL). Southeast of Mbouda, southern Mbouda Subdivision, Bamboutos Division, West Province. 5 villages; each a separate dialect. Niger-Congo, Atlantic-Congo, Volta-Congo, Benue-Congo, Bantoid, Southern, Wide Grassfields, Narrow Grassfields, Mbam-Nkam, Bamileke. Dialects: BAMENDJINDA, BAMENKUMBO, BAMESSO, BABETE (BAMETE), BAMENDJO. Dialect speakers appear to understand each other well. Bamendjinda, Bamesso, and Bamenkumbo are the most similar. Second languages are French and Pidgin. Church languages are Ngomba, French, Ngyembong, Medumba, or Bafunda. Ngomba is used by all in the 5 towns in all domains. Interest expressed in language development. 'Nda'a' is their name for themselves. Bafounda is a separate town and language (see Ghomala), but ethnically Nda'a. Different from Ngumba in the Maka-Njem group. Literacy rate in first language: Below 1%. Literacy rate in second language: 15% to 25%.

NGOMBALE ***(BAMILEKE-NGOMBALE)*** [NLA] 45,000 (1993 SIL). Northwest of Mbouda, northern Mbouda Subdivision, Bamboutos Division, West Province. Niger-Congo, Atlantic-Congo, Volta-Congo, Benue-Congo, Bantoid, Southern, Wide Grassfields, Narrow Grassfields, Mbam-Nkam, Bamileke. Dialects: BABADJOU (BASSO, NCHOBELA), BAMESSINGUE (BASSING). Many adults are reported to be bilingual in Ngomba and Ngyemboon, and young people in French. Pidgin is also used. Ngombale is used in all domains, including church. Interest expressed in language development. Literacy rate in first language: Below 1%. Literacy rate in second language: 15% to 25%. Traders. Traditional religion, Christian.

NGONG ***(GONG, PUURI)*** [NNX] 2 (1983 Atlas Linguistique du Cameroun). Ngong village, south of Garoua on road to Ngaoundere, Benoue Division, North Province. Niger-Congo, Atlantic-Congo, Volta-Congo, Benue-Congo, Bantoid, Southern, Jarawan, Cameroon. Voegelin and Voegelin (1977:55) say this is the same as Nagumi. Nearly extinct.

NGUMBA [NMG] Population total both countries 17,500 (1982 SIL). In forests around Kribi and along the road from Kribi to Lolodorf, Kribi and Lolodorf subdivisions, Ocean Division, South Province. Also spoken in Equatorial Guinea. Niger-Congo, Atlantic-Congo, Volta-Congo, Benue-Congo, Bantoid, Southern, Narrow Bantu, Northwest, A, Makaa-Njem (A.80). Dialects: KWASIO (KWASSIO, BISIO), MVUMBO (NGUMBA, NGOUMBA, MGOUMBA, MEKUK), MABI (MABEA). Distinct from Ngomba, which is in West Province. Literacy rate in first language: 1% to 5%. Literacy rate in second language: 5% to 15%. Christian, traditional religion. Bible portions 1957.

NGWE ***(NWE, FONTEM, FOTO, FONGONDENG, FOMOPEA, BAMILEKE-NGWE)*** [NWE] 50,000 (1992 SIL). Most of Fontem Subdivision, Manyu Division, South West Province. Niger-Congo, Atlantic-Congo, Volta-Congo, Benue-Congo, Bantoid, Southern, Wide Grassfields, Narrow Grassfields, Mbam-Nkam, Bamileke. Part of a language continuum which includes Yemba and Ngyemboon.

NGWO ***(NGWAW)*** [NGN] 31,000 together with Ngishe (1982 SIL). Njikwa Subdivision, Momo Division, North West Province. Niger-Congo, Atlantic-Congo, Volta-Congo, Benue-Congo, Bantoid, Southern, Wide Grassfields, Narrow Grassfields, Momo. Dialects: NGWO (NGUNI, NGWAW, MIGUHNI, NGUNU), KONDA, BASA (BASSA), IKWERI (EKPERI), BANYA, BAKO, OKOROBI, ZANG. Literacy rate in first language: Below 1%. Literacy rate in second language: 15% to 25%.

NIMBARI ***(NYAMNYAM, NIAMNIAM, BARI, NIMBARI-KEBI, NYAM-NYAM DU MAYO-KEBI)*** [NMR] Near Pitoa, Benoue and Mayo-Louti divisions, North Province. None in Chad or Nigeria. Niger-Congo, Atlantic-Congo, Volta-Congo, North, Adamawa-Ubangi, Adamawa, Leko-Nimbari, Nimbari. Different from Suga (Nyamnyam).

NJEN ***(NYEN)*** [MEN] Southeast of Batibo, Momo Division, North West Province. Niger-Congo, Atlantic-Congo, Volta-Congo, Benue-Congo, Bantoid, Southern, Wide Grassfields, Narrow Grassfields, Momo. Investigation needed: intelligibility, bilingual proficiency in Mundani, Meta'.

NKONGHO ***(KINKWA, LEKONGO, UPPER MBO)*** [NKC] Nguti Subdivision, Kupe-Muanenguba Division, South West Province. Niger-Congo, Atlantic-Congo, Volta-Congo, Benue-Congo, Bantoid, Southern, Narrow Bantu, Northwest, A, Lundu-Balong (A.10). Literacy rate in first language: Below 1%. Literacy rate in second language: 15% to 25%.

NOMAANDE ***(NOOMAANTE, NUMAND, LEMANDE, MANDI, MANDE, PIMENC)*** [LEM] 6,000 (1982 SIL). Southwest of Bafia, western and northern Bokito Subdivision, Mbam Division, Center Province. Niger-Congo, Atlantic-Congo, Volta-Congo, Benue-Congo, Bantoid, Southern, Mbam, West (A.40). Literacy rate in first language: Below 1%. Literacy rate in second language: 25% to 50%. Bible portions 1994-1998.

NOONE ***(NONI, NOORI)*** [NHU] 35,000 (1991 D. Lux SIL). Northwestern Kumbo Subdivision, Bui Division, North West Province. Niger-Congo, Atlantic-Congo, Volta-Congo, Benue-Congo, Bantoid, Southern, Beboid, Eastern. Dictionary. Literacy rate in first language: Below 1%. Literacy rate in second language: 25% to 50%.

NSARI ***(AKWETO, PESAA, SALI)*** [ASJ] On both sides of Ring Road between Misaje and Nkambe, western part of Nkambe Subdivision, Donga-Mantung Division, North West Province. Niger-Congo, Atlantic-Congo, Volta-Congo, Benue-Congo, Bantoid, Southern, Beboid, Eastern. May be intelligible with or bilingual in other Eastern Beboid languages. Investigation needed: intelligibility, bilingual proficiency.

NUBACA ***(BANGO, BONGO, BACA, NU BACA)*** [BAF] 800 (1994 SIL). 4 quarters, village of Bongo, south of Yangben, Yangben Canton, Bokito Subdivision, Mbam Division, Center Province. Niger-Congo, Atlantic-Congo, Volta-Congo, Benue-Congo, Bantoid, Southern, Mbam, Yambasa (A.60). No significant dialect differences. Not intelligible with other Yambassa language varieties. Related to Elip, Dumbule, and Mmaala. Ewondo is understood by most of the older generation. Basaa is mainly only used by the older generation, not young people. French is learned and spoken from early childhood in school, and in nearly every aspect of daily life, including the family, although interpretation into Nubaca is made in church. Investigation needed: bilingual proficiency in French.

NUGUNU ***(GUNU, GOUNOU, NU GUNU, YAMBASSA, YAMBASA, OMBESSA, BEKE, BEHIE)*** [YAS] 35,000 (1987 SIL). In and around Ombessa to southwest in Ombessa and Bokito subdivisions, Mbam Division, Center Province. Niger-Congo, Atlantic-Congo, Volta-Congo, Benue-Congo, Bantoid, Southern, Mbam, Yambasa (A.60). Dialects: NORTHERN GUNU, SOUTHERN GUNU. Literacy rate in first language: Below 1%. Literacy rate in second language: 50% to 75%.

NYONG ***(DAGANYONGA, DAGANONGA, NYONGNEPA, MUMBAKE, MUBAKO, NDAGAM, SAMBA BALI)*** [MUO] 17,000 in Cameroon (1987 census). Population total both countries 17,000 or more. Near the Ndop Plain in Balikuumbat, Baligansin, and Baligashu villages in Ngo-Ketunjia Division, Baligham in Mezam Division. Also spoken in Nigeria. Niger-Congo, Atlantic-Congo, Volta-Congo, North, Adamawa-Ubangi, Adamawa, Leko-Nimbari, Leko. They consider themselves to be the same ethnically as speakers of Samba Leko, but there is significant difficulty in inherent intelligibility. Speakers use Cameroons Pidgin (generally spoken and understood) or Standard English (by those educated beyond primary level) as second languages. The people are called 'Chamba', 'Samba', 'Chamba-Bali', or 'Samba-Bali'. Traditional religion, Christian (small).

NZAKAMBAY ***(NZAKMBAY, MBAY, NZAK MBAI, NZAK MBAY)*** [NZY] 10,000 to 15,000 (1998 SIL). Around Touboro, Touboro Subdivision, Mayo-Rey Division, North Province. Niger-Congo, Atlantic-Congo, Volta-Congo, North, Adamawa-Ubangi, Adamawa, Mbum-Day, Mbum, Central. Dialect: GONGE (NGONGE). Literacy rate in first language: Below 1%. Literacy rate in second language: 15% to 25%. NT 1968-1994. See main entry under Chad.

NZANYI ***(NJANYI, NZANGI, ZANI, ZANY, NJENY, JENG, NJEGN, NJENG, NJAI, NJEI, MZANGYIM, KOBOCHI, KOBOTSHI)*** [NJA] 9,000 in Cameroon. West of Dourbeye near Nigerian border in Doumo region, Mayo-Oulo Subdivision, Mayo-Louti Division, North Province. Afro-Asiatic, Chadic, Biu-Mandara, A, A.8. Dialect: HOLMA. Muslim, traditional religion. See main entry under Nigeria.

OBLO [OBL] Near Tchollire, Mayo-Rey Division, North Province. Niger-Congo, Atlantic-Congo, Volta-Congo, North, Adamawa-Ubangi, Adamawa, Unclassified.

OKU ***(KUO, EBKUO, EKPWO, BVUKOO, UKU, UKFWO)*** [OKU] 40,000 (1991 L. Davis SIL). Around Mt. Oku and Lake Oku, western Jakiri Subdivision, Bui Division, North West Province. Niger-Congo, Atlantic-Congo, Volta-Congo, Benue-Congo, Bantoid, Southern, Wide Grassfields, Narrow Grassfields, Ring, Center. Distinct from Kuo which is Adamawa. Literacy rate in first language: Below 1%. Literacy rate in second language: 5% to 15%.

OSATU ***(OSSATU, IHATUM)*** [OST] Southeast of Asumbo, Akwaya Subdivision, Manyu Division, South West Province. Niger-Congo, Atlantic-Congo, Volta-Congo, Benue-Congo, Bantoid, Southern, Tivoid. 60% lexical similarity with Balo, 40% with Ipulo and Caka, 35% with Mesaka and Esimbi. Bilingualism in Pidgin. Literacy is in English. Mountains. Traditional religion.

OSO ***(SOUTHERN FUNGOM, OSSO, NDUM)*** [OSO] 31,000 (1982 SIL). East of Wum, North West Province, spoken at Esu. Niger-Congo, Atlantic-Congo, Volta-Congo, Benue-Congo, Bantoid, Southern, Wide Grassfields, Narrow Grassfields, Ring, West. Distinctiveness from Fungom and Bum is not clear. Investigation needed: intelligibility.

PAM [PMN] Near Tchollire, Mayo-Rey Division, North Province. Niger-Congo, Atlantic-Congo, Volta-Congo, North, Adamawa-Ubangi, Adamawa, Mbum-Day, Mbum, Unclassified.

PANA ***(PANI)*** [PNZ] Touboro Subdivision, Mayo-Rey Division, North Province. Some are in urban areas. Niger-Congo, Atlantic-Congo, Volta-Congo, North, Adamawa-Ubangi, Adamawa, Mbum-Day, Mbum, Central, Karang. Dialect: MAN. Man may be a separate language. Investigation needed: intelligibility with Man. Literacy rate in first language: Below 1%. Literacy rate in second language: 5% to 15%. Bible portions 1953. See main entry under CAR.

PAPE ***(PANON, PA'NON, DUGUN, PANI)*** [NDU] 7,000 (1997 Lars Lode). Southeast of Poli, Poli Subdivision, Faro Division, North Province. Niger-Congo, Atlantic-Congo, Volta-Congo, North, Adamawa-Ubangi, Adamawa, Leko-Nimbari, Duru, Dii. Dialects: SAAN, NAAN. Close to Duupa and Saa. 80% lexical similarity with Dii. They refer to themselves as 'Dugun'. EELC primer.

PARKWA ***(PODOKO, PADUKO, PODOKWO, PODOGO, PADOGO, PADOKWA, PAWDAWKWA, PAREKWA, GWADI PAREKWA, KUDALA)*** [PBI] 30,000 (1993 SIL). West and southwest of Mora, Mora Subdivision, Mayo-Sava Division, Far North Province. Afro-Asiatic, Chadic, Biu-Mandara, A, A.4, Mandara Proper, Podoko. Dictionary. Literacy rate in first language: 1% to 5%. Literacy rate in second language: 5% to 15%. Traditional religion. NT 1992.

PEERE ***(PERE, PEER, KUTIN, KOUTIN, KOUTINE, KUTINE, KUTINN, KOTOPO, KOTOFO, KOTPOJO, POTOPO, POTOPORE, PATAPORI)*** [KUT] 15,000 in Cameroon (1993). Population total both countries 20,000. Northwestern Tignere Subdivision between Tignere and Nigerian border, Faro and Deo Division; northeast of Banyo, Mayo-Banyo Division, Adamawa Province. Also spoken in Nigeria. Niger-Congo, Atlantic-Congo, Volta-Congo, North, Adamawa-Ubangi, Adamawa, Leko-Nimbari, Duru, Voko-Dowayo, Kutin. Dialects: PEER MUURE, ZONGBI (DJONBI), DAN MUURE (POTOPO, KOTOPO, KPOTOPO, KOTOFO). Primer. 'Peer' is the name the people use for themselves. Dictionary. Grammar. Traditional religion. NT 1985.

PELASLA ***(MASLAVA, VAME)*** [MLR] 8,500 (1992 SIL). Southern Mora massif south of Mora, Mora and Tokombere subdivisions, Mayo-Sava Division, Far North Province. Afro-Asiatic, Chadic, Biu-Mandara, A, A.5. Dialects: MAYO-PLATA (PELASLA, PLASLA, PLATLA, PLATA, GWENDELE, DAMLALE), MBEREM (MBREME, MASLAVA), DEMWA (DMWA, DOUME), HURZA (HURZO, OURZA, OURZO, OUZZA), NDREME. The 5 dialects are inherently intelligible to each other's speakers. Mayo-Plata is closer to Wuzlam than the other dialects are to Wuzlam. Few know Fulfulde except a few in the Hurza area. Wandala is also used. 'Pelasla' is their own name. Ethnic groups are Pelasla, Mbreme, Ndereme, Afem, Dumwa, Hurzo.

PEVÉ ***(KA'DO, LAMÉ)*** [LME] 3,000 to 5,000 in Cameroon (1982 SIL). Northeast of Tchollire around Bouba-Ndjida Park, Mayo-Rey Division, North Province. Afro-Asiatic, Chadic, Masa. Primer. Different from Lame of Nigeria. NT 1986. See main entry under Chad.

PIDGIN, CAMEROON ***(WES COS, CAMEROON CREOLE ENGLISH)*** [WES] (2,000,000 mainly second language users; 1989 UBS). Primarily in South West and North West provinces, and widespread elsewhere. Creole, English based, Atlantic, Krio. Similar to Krio of Sierra Leone and Pidgin English of various West African countries; probably an offshoot of 19th century Krio. Also similar to Sranan (Ian Hancock). There are dialect variations. A growing number of first language speakers. Used by the police, prisons, urban school children at play since 1884. Now the most widespread lingua franca in Cameroon, used by about half the population (Todd and Hancock 1986). Trade language. Literacy rate in first language: Below 1%. Literacy rate in second language: Below 5%. Bible portions 1966.

PINYIN [PNY] 16,000 (1982 SIL). Southwest of Bamenda, southwestern Bamenda Subdivision, Mezam Division, North West Province. Niger-Congo, Atlantic-Congo, Volta-Congo, Benue-Congo, Bantoid, Southern, Wide Grassfields, Narrow Grassfields, Mbam-Nkam, Ngemba. Dialect: PINYIN (BAPINYI, PELIMPO). May be inherently intelligible with the Mankon dialect of Ngemba. Related to Awing, Ngemba, Bafut, and Mendankwe. Investigation needed: intelligibility with Mankon. Literacy rate in first language: Below 1%. Literacy rate in second language: 15% to 25%.

POL ***(PORI, POMO, PUL, CONGO POL)*** [PMM] East of Doume, Dimako Subdivision, Upper Nyong Division; east of Belabo, Belabo Subdivision, Lom and Djerem Division, East Province. Not in CAR. Niger-Congo, Atlantic-Congo, Volta-Congo, Benue-Congo, Bantoid, Southern, Narrow Bantu, Northwest, A, Kako (A.90). Dialects: AZOM (PORI ASOM, ASOM), BOBILI, DONDI, MAMBAYA, PORI KINDA (KINDA). Literacy rate in first language: Below 1%. Literacy rate in second language: 5% to 15%. See main entry under Congo.

PSIKYE ***(KAPSIKI, KAMSIKI, PTSAKE)*** [KVJ] 40,500 (1982 SIL). Population total both countries 52,500. Southwestern part of Mokolo Subdivision, Mayo-Tsanaga Division, Far North Province. Some in Nigeria. Also spoken in Nigeria. Afro-Asiatic, Chadic, Biu-Mandara, A, A.3. Dialects: PSIKYE (KAPSIKI, KAMU), ZLENGE, WULA (OULA, ULA-XANGKU). Closely related to Hya and Kamwe of Nigeria. Literacy rate in first language: Below 1%. Literacy rate in second language: 5% to 15%. Traditional religion. NT 1988.

SAA ***(SARI, SAAPA, YINGA)*** [SZR] 3,500 (1982 SIL). In the middle of a massif with difficult access, southeast of Poli, Yinga Canton, Faro Division, North Province. Niger-Congo, Atlantic-Congo, Volta-Congo, North, Adamawa-Ubangi, Adamawa, Leko-Nimbari, Duru, Dii. Related to Pape.

SAMBA LEKO ***(CHAMBA LEEKO, SAMBA)*** [NDI] Population total both countries 50,000 (1971 Welmers). West of Poli and south of Beka Subdivision along the Nigerian border, approximately between Chamba and the Mayo-Louti River, Faro Division, North Province. Also spoken in Nigeria. Niger-Congo, Atlantic-Congo, Volta-Congo, North, Adamawa-Ubangi, Adamawa, Leko-Nimbari, Leko. Dialects: SAMBA LEKO (NDII, LEKON, LEGO, LEKO, LAEKO, SUNTAI), DEENU (KOOLA), BANGLA, SAMBA DE WANGAI, SAMPARA. Closely related to Kolbila. Different from Samba Daka.

SHARWA ***(TCHEVI, SHERWIN)*** [SWQ] Southern Bourrah Subdivision, Mayo-Tsanaga Division, Far North Province; a few in Mayo-Louti Division, North Province. Afro-Asiatic, Chadic, Biu-Mandara, A, A.8. Different from Sarua (Sarwa) of Chad.

SO ***(SSO, SHWO, FO)*** [SOX] 9,000 (1992 D. Bradley SIL). Melan and Emvane cantons, Akonolinga Subdivision, Nyong-and-Mfoumou Division, Center Province; a few in Upper Nyong Division, East Province. Niger-Congo, Atlantic-Congo, Volta-Congo, Benue-Congo, Bantoid, Southern, Narrow Bantu, Northwest, A, Makaa-Njem (A.80). Dialects: MELAN SO, EMVANE SO. The two dialects have vocabulary and pronunciation differences, but no reported problem with intelligibility between them. Melan So has been influenced by Beti (Ewondo and Bulu). Beti is also used in home and village. Children are increasingly learning Beti and French. Beti is used in church and the marketplace. There is a lot of intermarriage with the Beti. French is used in schools and government offices. So is used in the home and village. Different from So (Heso) of DRC. Investigation needed: bilingual proficiency in Beti.

SUGA ***(NIZAA, SSUGA, GALIM, "NYAMNYAM", "NJEMNJEM", "JEMJEM")*** [SGI] 10,000 (1985 EELC). Around Galim southwest of Tignhre, Faro-and-Deo Division; and around Sambolabbo, northern Banyo Subdivision, Mayo-Banyo Division, Adamawa Province. Niger-Congo, Atlantic-Congo, Volta-Congo, Benue-Congo, Bantoid, Northern, Mambiloid, Suga-Vute, Suga. Different from Nimbari (Nyamnyam) of Cameroon. 'Sewe' may be an alternate name. 'Baghap' is their name for themselves; 'Nizaa' for their language. Dictionary. Grammar. Literacy rate in second language: A few adults in Fulfulde, Arabic script. Few can read Roman script. Agriculturalists. Muslim, traditional religion, Christian.

TIBEA ***(NGAYABA, NYABEA, MINJANTI, ZANGNTE, DJANTI, NJANTI)*** [NGY] 1,400 (1992 SIL). Northeast of Bafia in extreme northern Ngoro Subdivision, Mbam Division, Center Province, 3 villages. Niger-Congo, Atlantic-Congo, Volta-Congo, Benue-Congo, Bantoid, Southern, Narrow Bantu, Northwest, A, Bafia (A.50). Speakers not bilingual in nearby languages. Younger people learning French.

TIKAR ***(TIKAR-EAST, TIKARI, TIKALI, NDOB, TINGKALA, NDOME)*** [TIK] 25,000 (1989 SIL). Scattered over a wide area northwest of Yoko and northeast of Foumban, Center Province (Ngambe-Tikar Subdivision, Mbam Division), Adamawa Province (Bankim Subdivision, Mayo-Banyo Division), West Province (Magba Subdivision, Noun Division). Niger-Congo, Atlantic-Congo, Volta-Congo, Benue-Congo, Bantoid, Southern, Tikar. Dialects: TWUMWU (TUMU, TIKAR DE BANKIM), TIGE (TIKAR DE NGAMBE), NDITAM, KONG, MANKIM, GAMBAI, BANDOBO. Bandobo is a dialect or closely related language. The Bankim call their dialect 'Twumwu', the Ngambe call theirs 'Tige'. Literacy rate in first language: 1% to 5%. Literacy rate in second language: 25% to 50%. NT 1989.

TIV [TIV] A few in Cameroon. Only in the village of Njobo (Njawbaw) northeast of Akwaya on the Nigerian border, Manyu Division, South West Province. Niger-Congo, Atlantic-Congo, Volta-Congo, Benue-Congo, Bantoid, Southern, Tivoid. Literacy rate in first language: 1% to 5%. Literacy rate in second language: 15% to 25%. Christian, traditional religion. Bible 1964. See main entry under Nigeria.

TO [TOZ] Touboro Subdivision, Mayo-Rey Division, North Province. Also spoken in CAR. Niger-Congo, Atlantic-Congo, Volta-Congo, North, Adamawa-Ubangi, Adamawa, Mbum-Day, Mbum, Unclassified. An ancient secret male initiation language of the Gbaya. Second language only.

TSUVAN ***(TERKI, TELEKI, TCHEDE)*** [TSH] Northeast of Dourbeye in the village of Teleki, southeastern Bourrah Subdivision, Mayo-Tsanaga Division, Far North Province; some in Mayo-Louti Division, North Province. Afro-Asiatic, Chadic, Biu-Mandara, A, A.8.

TUKI ***(SANAGA, BETSINGA, BETZINGA, BACENGA, BATCHENGA, OKI, BAKI, KI, OSA NANGA)*** [BAG] 26,000 (1982 SIL). Along the Sanaga River north of Saa, and north of the Sanaga River between Ombessa and Ntui, Mbam Division, Center Province. Niger-Congo, Atlantic-Congo, Volta-Congo, Benue-Congo, Bantoid, Southern, Mbam, Sanaga (A.60). Dialects: KOMBE (TUKOMBE, WAKOMBE, BAKOMBE), TOCENGA (TIKI, BACENGA), TSINGA (CHINGA, TUTSINGO, BATSINGO), BUNDUM, TONJO (BUNJU, BOUDJOU), NGORO (TU NGORO, UKI, AKI), MBERE (TUMBELE, MBELE, BAMBELE, MVELE, BAMVELE). Literacy rate in first language: Below 1%. Literacy rate in second language: 5% to 15%.

TUNEN ***(BANEN, BANEND, PENIN, PENYIN, NENNI NYO'O)*** [BAZ] 35,300 (1982 SIL). Ndikinimeki and Makenene subdivisions, Mbam Division, Center Province; south to the eastern part of Yingui Subdivision, Nkam Division, Littoral Province. Niger-Congo, Atlantic-Congo, Volta-Congo, Benue-Congo, Bantoid, Southern, Mbam, West (A.60). Dialects: ELING (ALINGA, TULING), ITUNDU, LOGANANGA, NDOGBANG, NDOKBIAKAT, NDOKTUNA, NI NYO'O (NYO'ON, NYOKON, FUNG), MESE (PANINGESEN, NINGUESSEN, SESE). May be in Bantu A.60. Distinct from Pinyin in the Ngemba group. Dictionary. Grammar. Literacy rate in first language: Below 1%. Literacy rate in second language: 5% to 15%. Mountain slope. Traditional religion, Christian.

TUOTOMB ***(PONEK, BONEK)*** [TTF] 1,000 or fewer (1984 ALCAM). Village of Bonek near Ndikinemeki, Bafia Subdivision, Mbam Division, Center Province. Many live in urban areas. Niger-Congo, Atlantic-Congo, Volta-Congo, Benue-Congo, Bantoid, Southern, Mbam, West (A.40). Speakers are bilingual in Tunen, and some in Yambeta or Cameroon Pidgin.

TUPURI ***(TOUPOURI, TUBURI, TOUBOURI, NDORE, NDOORE, WINA, TONGOYNA, HONYA, DEMA, MATA)*** [TUI] 125,000 in Cameroon. Population total both countries 216,000. Southeastern Moulvouday plain east of Kaele, Kaele Division; Kar-Hay Subdivision, Mayo-Danay Division, Far North Province. Also spoken in Chad. Niger-Congo, Atlantic-Congo, Volta-Congo, North, Adamawa-Ubangi, Adamawa, Mbum-Day, Mbum, Northern, Tupuri-Mambai. Literacy rate in first language: Below 1%. Literacy rate in second language: 5% to 15%. Traditional religion, Christian. NT 1988.

TWENDI [TWN] 1,000 or fewer (1991 SIL). 35 or fewer in the villages of Sanga and Chamba on the Nyamboya to Somie road, and some in other villages. Sanga village, north of Bankim, Mayo-Banyo Division, Adamawa Province. Niger-Congo, Atlantic-Congo, Volta-Congo, Benue-Congo, Bantoid, Northern, Mambiloid, Mambila-Konja, Konja. Bilingualism in Kwanja. The language appears to be diminishing in use.

USAGHADE ***(USAKADE, USAKEDET, ISANGELE)*** [USK] 10,000 in Cameroon (1990 Bruce Connell). Population total both countries 10,000 or more. Mainly in Cameroon, Isangele Subdivision. Also spoken in Nigeria. Niger-Congo, Atlantic-Congo, Volta-Congo, Benue-Congo, Cross River, Delta Cross, Lower Cross, Obolo, Usaghade. A separate language from Efik (B. Connell 1998, Crozier and Blench 1992).

VEMGO-MABAS [VEM] 5,000 or fewer in Cameroon (1984 ALCAM). Village of Mabas on Nigerian border northwest of Mokolo, Mayo-Tsanaga Division, Far North Province. Afro-Asiatic, Chadic, Biu-Mandara, A, A.4, Lamang. Dialects: VEMGO, MABAS. 56% intelligibility of Lamang, 36% of Xedi. Possibly intelligible with Mafa. 78% lexical similarity with Xedi, 64% with Lamang, 50% with Gevoko. Speakers may be bilingual in Mafa or Lamang. Some people speak Xedi. Different from Maba of Chad. 'Maya' may be an alternate name. Investigation needed: intelligibility with Mafa, bilingual proficiency in Mafa, Lamang. See main entry under Nigeria.

VENGO ***(BABUNGO, VENGOO, VENGI, PENGO, NGO, NGUU, NGWA, NGE)*** [BAV] 13,500 (1982 SIL). North of Ndop on the Ndop Plain, Mezam Division, North West Province. Niger-Congo, Atlantic-Congo, Volta-Congo, Benue-Congo, Bantoid, Southern, Wide Grassfields, Narrow Grassfields, Ring, North. Closely related languages: Wushi, Kenswei-Nsei, Bamunka. Their name for themselves is 'Vengoo'. Dictionary. Grammar. Literacy rate in first language: Below 1%. Literacy rate in second language: 25% to 50%. NT 1993.

VUTE ***(VOUTE, WOUTE, BABOUTE, BUTE, PUTE, WUTE, BAMBOUTE, FOUTE, BOUTE, VOUTERE, BUBURE, LUVURE, BULE, NBULE, 'ABOTEE, 'ABWETEE)*** [VUT] 20,000 in Cameroon (1997 Lars Lode) including 300 in Banyo (1995 Bruce Connell). Population total both countries 21,000. North-eastern Mbam Division and near Nanga-Eboko and Mbandjok, Upper Sanaga Division, Center Province; Mayo-Banyo and Djerem divisions (near Tibati and Banyo), Adamawa Province; some in western Lom and Djerem Division, East Province. Also spoken in Nigeria. Niger-Congo, Atlantic-Congo, Volta-Congo, Benue-Congo, Bantoid, Northern, Mambiloid, Suga-Vute, Vute. Dialects: BUTE BAMNYO (VUTE DE BANYO), VUTE MBANJO (VUTE DE MBANDJOK), NUDOO (VUTE DE YANGBA), NUJUM (VUTE DE LINTE), NDUVUM (VUTE DE TIBATI), NUGANE (VUTE DE DOUME), KUMBERE (VUTE DE SANGBE), NGORO (VUTE DE NGORRO). Banyo Vute is still used daily, but seems heavily influenced by Fulfulde. Literacy rate in first language: Below 1%. Literacy rate in second language: 15% to 25%. Traditional religion, Christian. Bible portions 1988.

WANDALA ***(MANDARA, NDARA, MANDARA MONTAGNARD)*** [MFI] 23,500 in Cameroon (1982 SIL). Population total both countries 42,800. In a belt starting east of Mora, around it to the north in a semicircle, and northwest to the Nigerian border, Mayo-Sava Division, Far North Province. Also spoken in Nigeria. Afro-Asiatic, Chadic, Biu-Mandara, A, A.4, Mandara Proper, Mandara. Dialects: KAMBURWAMA, MASFEIMA, JAMPALAM, ZIOGBA, MAZAGWA, GWANJE, WANDALA (MANDARA), MURA (KIRDI-MORA, MORA BROUSSE, MORA MASSIF, DUWE), GAMARGU (GAMERGOU, GAMERGU, MALGO, MALGWA). A dialect cluster. Trade language. Literacy rate in first language: 1% to 5%. Literacy rate in second language: 5% to 15%. Muslim. NT 1988.

WAWA [WWW] 3,000 (1991 SIL). West of Banyo, Bankim Subdivision, Mayo-Banyo Division, Adamawa Province, 13 villages. There may be some in Nigeria. Niger-Congo, Atlantic-Congo, Volta-Congo, Benue-Congo, Bantoid, Northern, Mambiloid, Suga-Vute, Vute. Dialect: GANDUA. Bilingualism in Fulfulde. Investigation needed: bilingual proficiency in Fulfulde. Literacy rate in first language: Below 1%. Literacy rate in second language: Below 5%.

WEH [WEH] 6,900 (1994 SIL). Village of Weh, Wum Central Subdivision, Menchum Division, North West Province. Niger-Congo, Atlantic-Congo, Volta-Congo, Benue-Congo, Bantoid, Southern, Wide Grassfields, Narrow Grassfields, Ring, West. Little dialect variation. Closely related to Aghem, but considered to be a separate language. Some speakers use Cameroon Pidgin as second language; some multilingualism with Isu. Weh is used to some extent in church services. Investigation needed: intelligibility with Aghem, bilingual proficiency in Isu. Traditional religion, Christian.

WUMBOKO ***(BAMBOKO, BOMBOKO, BAMBUKU, BUMBOKO, WOMBOKO, MBOKO)*** [BQM] 2,500 (1977 Voegelin and Voegelin). Buea Subdivision, Fako Division, and Kumba Subdivision, Meme Division, South West Province. Niger-Congo, Atlantic-Congo, Volta-Congo, Benue-Congo, Bantoid, Southern, Narrow Bantu, Northwest, A, Duala (A.20). Probably intelligible with Mokpwe, but different enough from Duala to possibly need separate literature. Investigation needed: intelligibility with Mokpwe.

WUSHI ***(BABESSI, VESI, PESII, SII)*** [BSE] 12,350 (1982 SIL). East of Ndop, Ndop Subdivision, Mezam Division, North West Province. Niger-Congo, Atlantic-Congo, Volta-Congo, Benue-Congo, Bantoid, Southern, Wide Grassfields, Narrow Grassfields, Ring, North. Closely related to Vengo, Kenswei-Nsei, and Bamunka. 'Wushi' is their name for themselves.

WUZLAM ***(ULDEME, OULDEME, UZAM, UDLAM, UZLAM, MIZLIME)*** [UDL] 10,500 (1982 SIL). Wuzlam Massif south of Mora, Tokombere Subdivision, Mayo-Sava Division, Far North Province. Afro-Asiatic, Chadic, Biu-Mandara, A, A.5. 'Wuzlam' is the speakers' own name.

YAMBA ***("KAKA", MBEM, MBUBEM, KAKAYAMBA, BEBAROE, BOENGA KO MUZOK, SWE'NGA)*** [YAM] 30,000 to 40,000 in Cameroon (1993 SIL). Population total both countries 30,000 to 40,000 or more. Central Nwa Subdivision, Donga-Mantung Division, North West Province. Seasonal immigrants in Nigeria, Mambila Plateau. Also spoken in Nigeria. Niger-Congo, Atlantic-Congo, Volta-Congo, Benue-Congo, Bantoid, Southern, Wide Grassfields, Narrow Grassfields, Mbam-Nkam, Nkambe. Dialects: NTEM, MFE, NKOT, NTONG, KWAK. Literacy rate in first language: 1% to 5%. Literacy rate in second language: 15% to 25%. NT 1992.

YAMBETA ***(YAMBETTA, NJAMBETA)*** [YAT] 3,700 (1982 SIL). Bafia Subdivision northwest of Bafia, Mbam Division, Center Province. Niger-Congo, Atlantic-Congo, Volta-Congo, Benue-Congo, Bantoid, Southern, Mbam, West (A.40). Dialects: NEDEK, NIGII (NIGI, BEGI-NIBUM, KIBUM). Related to Bati, Dumbule, Elip, Leti, Mmaala, Nubaca, Nugunu, Tuki, and Yangben. Literacy rate in first language: Below 1%. Literacy rate in second language: 15% to 25%.

YANGBEN [YAV] 2,300 (1994 SIL), 14,000 together with Elip and Mmaala (1994 SIL). Yangben Canton south of Bokito, Bokito Subdivision, Mbam Division, Center Province. Niger-Congo, Atlantic-Congo, Volta-Congo, Benue-Congo, Bantoid, Southern, Mbam, Yambasa (A.60). A standardized written form may be possible with Mmaala and Elip, related languages. French is used in primary and secondary education. Ewondo or Bulu are used in other than RC churches. Speakers acquire understanding of Mmaala and Elip in early adulthood. Interpretation is made into Yangben in RC church services. Speakers do not think French will replace Yangben.

YASA ***(YASSA, LYAASA, MAASA, BONGWE)*** [YKO] Population total all countries 1,500 (1982 SIL). On the coast near Equatorial Guinea, Campo Subdivision, Ocean Division, South Province. Also spoken in Equatorial Guinea, Gabon. Niger-Congo, Atlantic-Congo, Volta-Congo, Benue-Congo, Bantoid, Southern, Narrow Bantu, Northwest, A, Bube-Benga (A.30), Yasa. Grammar.

YEMBA ***(TCHANG, DSCHANG, BAFOU, ATSANG-BANGWA, BANGWA, BAMILEKE-YEMBA)*** [BAN] 300,000 or more. Major part of Menoua Division, centered around Dschang, West Province. Niger-Congo, Atlantic-Congo, Volta-Congo, Benue-Congo, Bantoid, Southern, Wide Grassfields, Narrow Grassfields, Mbam-Nkam, Bamileke. Dialects: YEMBA, FOREKE DSCHANG (DSCHANG,

TCHANG). Part of a language continuum which includes Ngwe and Ngyemboon. Literacy rate in first language: Below 1%. Literacy rate in second language: 15% to 25%.

YENI [YEI] Not far north of Mayo Darle village in Nyalang area. Unclassified. Apparently all that remains of the language is a song, known by speakers of Sandani (Kwanja). Extinct.

YUKUBEN ***(NYIKUBEN, NYIKOBE, AYIKIBEN, BORITSU, BALAABE, BALAABEN, GOHUM, UUHUM, UUHUM-GIGI)*** [YBL] 950 in Cameroon (1986 R. Breton). Near Nigerian border, west of Furu-Awa, Menchum Division, North West Province. Niger-Congo, Atlantic-Congo, Volta-Congo, Benue-Congo, Platoid, Benue, Jukunoid, Yukuben-Kuteb. High bilingualism in Jukun Takum. Pidgin is also spoken in the area. Speakers in Cameroon want to have their language written and form a language committee. The name 'Uuhum Gigi' is preferred in Cameroon. The people are called 'Yukuben'. Mountain slope. See main entry under Nigeria.

ZIZILIVAKAN ***(ZIZILIVEKEN, ZILIVA, ÀMZÍRÍV, FALI OF JILBU)*** [ZIZ] A few hundred in Cameroon (1992 Crozier and Blench). Near Nigerian border, Bourrah Subdivision, Mayo-Tsanaga Division, Far North Province. Also spoken in Nigeria. Afro-Asiatic, Chadic, Biu-Mandara, A, A.8. People are called 'Fali of Jilbu'.

ZULGWA ***(ZULGO, ZOULGO, ZELGWA, MINEO, MINEW)*** [ZUL] 18,000 (1982 SIL). Eastern edge of Mandara Mts. northwest of Meri, Mayo-Sava Division, (Tokombere Subdivision) and Mayo-Tsanaga Division (Mokolo Subdivision), Far North Province. Afro-Asiatic, Chadic, Biu-Mandara, A, A.5. Dialects: ZELGWA, MINEW (ZULGWA, ZULGO, MUKUNO, MINEWE, MINEO). Literacy rate in first language: 1% to 5%. Literacy rate in second language: 5% to 15%. Agriculturalists: millet. NT 1988.

ZUMAYA [ZUY] Only a few speakers left (1987 SIL). Ouro-Lamorde, Maroua Subdivision, Diamare Division, Far North Province. Afro-Asiatic, Chadic, Masa. Nearly extinct.

CANARY ISLANDS

1,170,224 (1978 Hammond World Atlas). An autonomous region of Spain. See Spain.

CAPE VERDE ISLANDS

Republic of Cape Verde. República de Cabo Verde. National or official languages: Portuguese, Kabuverdianu. 408,000 (1998 UN). Literacy rate 37% to 70%. Information mainly from J. Holm 1989; S. and T. Graham 1998. Christian, secular. Data accuracy estimate: B. The number of languages listed for Cape Verde Islands is 2. Of those, both are living languages. Diversity index 0.00.

KABUVERDIANU ***(CABOVERDIANO)*** [KEA] 393,943 including 255,101 in Sotavento or 65% of the speakers, 138,842 in Barlavento or 35% of the speakers (SIL Steve and Trina Graham 1999). Population total all countries 934,000. Sotavento dialect is on Santiago, Maio, Fogo, and Brava islands; Barlavento dialect is on Santo Antão, São Vicente, São Nicolau, Sal, and Boa Vista islands. Also spoken in France, Germany, Italy, Luxembourg, Netherlands, Portugal, Senegal, Spain, USA. Creole, Portuguese based. Dialects: SOTAVENTO, BARLAVENTO. 59% lexical similarity with the Gulf of Guinea creoles. 29% are comfortable in Portuguese, 36% uncomfortable, 34% block up. Since independence in 1975, the domains of spoken Portuguese have receded in favor of Creole. Portuguese used primarily on TV and radio, in Congress, classrooms, churches, and with foreigners. Portuguese is the primary language of instruction in 12 grades. Used in most domains, and some in Congress, classrooms, churches. There is a creole continuum and some decreolization. National language. Dictionary. Grammar. Literacy rate in second language: 29% Portuguese. Radio programs. Christian. Bible portions 1936.

PORTUGUESE [POR] Indo-European, Italic, Romance, Italo-Western, Western, Gallo-Iberian, Ibero-Romance, West Iberian, Portuguese-Galician. Official language. Bible 1751, in press (1993). See main entry under Portugal.

CENTRAL AFRICAN REPUBLIC

République Centrafricaine, RCA, CAR. Formerly Central African Empire. National or official languages: Sango, French. 3,485,000 (1998 UN). 500,000 to 600,000 did not indicate their mother tongue in the 1988 census. Literacy rate 27%. Also includes Shuwa Arabic 63,000, Bangi, Bomitaba 224, Gbaya, Hausa 20,000, Lingala 9,100, Mbandja 1,400, Ngbaka 3,000, Northern Ngbandi 294, Ngundi, Sere 28. Information mainly from Atlas Linguistique de l'Afrique Central 1984; Moñino 1988; J. Bendor-Samuel 1989; SIL 1972-1999. Christian, traditional religion, Muslim. Blind population 27,000 (1982 WCE). Data accuracy estimate: B. The number of languages listed for Central African Republic is 69. Of those, 68 are living languages and 1 is a second language without mother tongue speakers. Diversity index 0.96.

ALI [AIY] 35,000 (1996). Boali, Bimbo, Boda, and Yaloke subprefectures. Niger-Congo, Atlantic-Congo, Volta-Congo, North, Adamawa-Ubangi, Ubangi, Gbaya-Manza-Ngbaka, East. Bilingualism in Sango. Many children learn Sango as their first language.

BANDA, MID-SOUTHERN ***(BANDA CENTRAL SUD)*** [BJO] 100,000 in CAR (1996). Population total all countries 102,000 or more. Alindao, Mobaye, Mingala, Kembe, Kouango subprefectures. Also spoken in DRC, Sudan. Niger-Congo, Atlantic-Congo, Volta-Congo, North, Adamawa-Ubangi, Ubangi, Banda, Central, Central Core, Mid-Southern. Dialects: BONGO, DUKPU, YAKPA (YACOUA, YAKPWA, YAKWA, BAYAKA), WASA (OUASSA). Speakers use Sango as second language in CAR, Lingala in DRC. Investigation needed: intelligibility with Banda-Bambari, Mono.

BANDA, SOUTH CENTRAL [LNL] 150,000 in CAR including 55,000 Langba, 95,000 Ngbugu (1996). Population total both countries 153,000. Sibut, Mobaye, Alindao, Kembe, Mingala subprefectures. Also spoken in DRC. Niger-Congo, Atlantic-Congo, Volta-Congo, North, Adamawa-Ubangi, Ubangi, Banda, South Central. Dialects: LANGBA (LAGBA), NGBUGU (NGBOUGOU). May be intelligible with Langbashe. Investigation needed: intelligibility with Langbashe.

BANDA, TOGBO-VARA [TOR] 12,000 in CAR (1996). Bria (Togbo) and Bambari (Vara) subprefectures. Niger-Congo, Atlantic-Congo, Volta-Congo, North, Adamawa-Ubangi, Ubangi, Banda, Central, Central Core, Togbo-Vara. Dialects: TOGBO (TOHGBOH, TAGBO, TAGBWALI), VARA (VORA, VERA). Bilingualism in Sango. Different from Tagbu (Tagbo, Tagba) of DRC in Sere group. They view themselves as very different from Mono. Investigation needed: intelligibility with Banda-Bambari. See main entry under DRC.

BANDA, WEST CENTRAL [BBP] 4,500 in CAR including 1,000 Wojo, mainly Dakpa (1996). Population total both countries 7,500 or more. Bambari, Bakala (Dakpa), Grimari (Gbi, Wojo), Kaga Bandoro (Wojo), Bamingui (Gbaga-Nord) subprefectures. Also spoken in Sudan. Niger-Congo, Atlantic-Congo, Volta-Congo, North, Adamawa-Ubangi, Ubangi, Banda, West Central. Dialects: DAKPA, GBAGA-NORD (GBAGA 2), GBI, VITA, WOJO (HODJO). Bilingualism in Sango. Investigation needed: intelligibility with Mbanza, Langbashe.

BANDA-BAMBARI ***(BANDA OF BAMBARI)*** [LIY] 183,000 including 4,000 Gbende, 2,000 Joto, mainly Linda (1996). Bambari, Ippy, Grimari, Bakala, Alindao subprefectures. Niger-Congo, Atlantic-Congo, Volta-Congo, North, Adamawa-Ubangi, Ubangi, Banda, Central, Central Core, Banda-Bambari. Dialects: LINDA, JOTO (JETO), NDOKPA, NGAPO (NGAPU), GBENDE. Bilingualism in Sango.

BANDA-BANDA [BPD] 102,000 in CAR (1996). Population total both countries 102,000 or more. Bria (Bereya), Yalinga (Vidiri), Bakouma, Sibut (Ka, Gbaga-South), Dekoa, Damara, Grimari (Mbi), Bossangoa (Gbambiya), Bozoum, Bocarangoa, Paoua (Hai) subprefectures. Also spoken in Sudan. Niger-Congo, Atlantic-Congo, Volta-Congo, North, Adamawa-Ubangi, Ubangi, Banda, Central, Central Core, Banda-Banda. Dialects: BANDA-BANDA, BEREYA (BRIA, BANDA OF BRIA, BANDA DE BRIA), BURU, GBAGA-SOUTH (GBAGA 1), GBAMBIYA, HAI, KA, MBI (MBIYI), NDI (NDRI), NGALABO, NGOLA, VIDIRI (MVEDERE, VODERE, VIDRI, VADARA). May be intelligible with Banda-Bambari. Bilingualism in Sango. Investigation needed: intelligibility with Banda-Bambari.

BANDA-MBRÈS ***(BANDA OF MBRÈS, BANDA-MBRE)*** [BQK] 42,500 in CAR (1996). Population total both countries 42,500 or more. Mbrès Subprefecture (Mbre, Moruba), Kaga Bandoro, Bouca (Buka), Bakala (Sabanga, Moruba). Also spoken in Sudan. Niger-Congo, Atlantic-Congo, Volta-Congo, North, Adamawa-Ubangi, Ubangi, Banda, Central, Central Core, Banda-Mbres. Dialects: BUKA (BOUKA), MBRE (MBERE, MBELE), MORUBA (MOROUBA, MARABA), SABANGA (SANGBANGA), WADA (OUADDA). Investigation needed: intelligibility with Banda-Bambari.

BANDA-NDÉLÉ ***(BANDA OF NDÉLÉ, NYELE)*** [BFL] 35,500 (1996). Population total both countries 35,500 or more. Ndili, Bamingui, Ouadda, Kaga Bandoro subprefectures. Also spoken in Sudan. Niger-Congo, Atlantic-Congo, Volta-Congo, North, Adamawa-Ubangi, Ubangi, Banda, Central, Central Core, Banda-Ndele. Dialects: BANDA-NDÉLÉ, JUNGURU (DJINGBURU, NGURU), TANGBAGO (TAMBOLO, TAMBAGGO, TOMBAGGO, TANGAGO), NGAO (NGAU, BANDANGAO), NGBALA. Bilingualism in Sango.

BANDA-YANGERE ***(YANGERE, YANGUERE)*** [YAJ] 26,500 (1996). Nola, Bambio, Berberati, and Carnot subprefectures. Niger-Congo, Atlantic-Congo, Volta-Congo, North, Adamawa-Ubangi, Ubangi, Banda, Central, Western. Bilingualism in Sango. Investigation needed: intelligibility with Banda-Bambari.

BIRRI ***(BIRI, VIRI, BVIRI)*** [BVQ] 200 (1996) out of 5,000 in the ethnic group. Extinct in Sudan (1993). Scattered throughout southwestern corner of CAR, and formerly in Deim Zubeir, Bahr el Ghazal Province, Sudan. Nilo-Saharan, Central Sudanic, West, Bongo-Bagirmi, Sara-Bagirmi. Dialects: MBOTO, MUNGA. Only one dialect spoken in CAR. The people are bilingual in Zande. They may be assimilated by the larger Zande people through marriage. Different from Viri, Biri, Bviri [BVI].

BODO [BOY] 15 (1996). Haut-Mbomou Prefecture, eastern tip of CAR. Scattered throughout CAR—not more than 3 speakers in the same village. None in the original area or Sudan. Niger-Congo, Atlantic-Congo, Volta-Congo, Benue-Congo, Bantoid, Southern, Narrow Bantu, Central, D, Bira-Huku (D.30). Nearly extinct.

BOFI ***(BOFFI)*** [BFF] 23,500 (1996). Boda and Bimbo subprefectures. Niger-Congo, Atlantic-Congo, Volta-Congo, North, Adamawa-Ubangi, Ubangi, Gbaya-Manza-Ngbaka, East. Speakers are fairly bilingual in Sango. Those in Bimbo Subprefecture are reported to be mostly pygmies.

BOKOTO ***(BOKODO, BOGOTO, BOGODO, BOKPOTO)*** [BDT] 130,000 (1996). Baoro, Carnot, Boda subprefectures. Niger-Congo, Atlantic-Congo, Volta-Congo, North, Adamawa-Ubangi, Ubangi, Gbaya-Manza-Ngbaka, Central. Dialects: GBAYA OF BODA (GBAYA DE BODA), BOKPAN, BOKOTO. May be intelligible with Northwest Gbaya. Use Sango as lingua franca. Investigation needed: intelligibility with Northwest Gbaya.

BURAKA ***(BOURAKA, BORAKA, BOLAKA)*** [BKG] 2,500 in CAR (1996). Population total both countries 2,500 or more. Mobaye Subprefecture, along the Ubangi River. Also spoken in DRC. Niger-Congo, Atlantic-Congo, Volta-Congo, North, Adamawa-Ubangi, Ubangi, Sere-Ngbaka-Mba, Ngbaka-Mba, Ngbaka, Western, Gbanzili. May not be inherently intelligible with Gbanziri.

DAGBA [DGK] 40,000 in CAR (1996). Population total both countries 40,000 or more. Batangafo, Kabo, and Bossangoa subprefectures. Also spoken in Chad. Nilo-Saharan, Central Sudanic, West, Bongo-Bagirmi, Sara-Bagirmi, Sara, Sara Proper. May be intelligible with Kaba. Investigation needed: intelligibility with Kaba.

DENDI [DEQ] 10,000 (1996). Ouango Subprefecture. Niger-Congo, Atlantic-Congo, Volta-Congo, North, Adamawa-Ubangi, Ubangi, Ngbandi. High intelligibility with Yakoma. Ngbandi and Mbangi may be inherently intelligible with Dendi. High bilingualism in Sango. Different from Dendi in Benin, Nigeria, and Niger. Investigation needed: intelligibility with Ngbandi, Mbangi, Yakoma, bilingual proficiency in Sango.

FRENCH [FRN] 9,000 in CAR (1996). Scattered. Indo-European, Italic, Romance, Italo-Western, Western, Gallo-Iberian, Gallo-Romance, Gallo-Rhaetian, Oïl, French. Official language. Bible 1530-1986. See main entry under France.

FULFULDE, BAGIRMI ***(BAGHIRMI PEUL, BAGIRMI FULA)*** [FUI] 156,000 in CAR (1996). Scattered. Niger-Congo, Atlantic-Congo, Atlantic, Northern, Senegambian, Fula-Wolof, Fulani, Eastern. May be close to Bororo Fulfulde; reported to be a nomadic group of Mbororo. Bilingualism in Sango. Spoken by people of Wodaabe lineage who are also in northern Niger and northern Cameroon. Nomadic. Different from the Bagirmi language of Chad, which is Nilo-Saharan. Investigation needed: intelligibility with Bororro. See main entry under Chad.

FURU ***(BAGERO, BAGIRO, BAGUERO, BAGUIRO)*** [FUU] 4,000 in CAR (1996). Mobaye Subprefecture, 11 villages. Nilo-Saharan, Central Sudanic, West, Bongo-Bagirmi, Kara. Bilingualism in Sango, Mono. See main entry under DRC.

GANZI [GNZ] 1,400 (1996). Scattered throughout CAR. Niger-Congo, Atlantic-Congo, Volta-Congo, North, Adamawa-Ubangi, Ubangi, Sere-Ngbaka-Mba, Ngbaka-Mba, Ngbaka, Western, Baka-Gundi. Dialects: GANZI, YAKA. May be intelligible with Baka. Pygmies.

GBANU ***(GBANOU, BANU)*** [GBV] 95,000 (1996). Carnot and Bossembélé subprefectures, north of Bogangolo. Niger-Congo, Atlantic-Congo, Volta-Congo, North, Adamawa-Ubangi, Ubangi, Gbaya-Manza-Ngbaka, Central. Dialects: GBANU, GBAGIRI (GBAGILI, BAGILI, BAGUILI), BUDIGRI (BIDIKILI). Have relatively high bilingualism in Sango. Investigation needed: bilingual proficiency in Sango. Bible portions 1932-1939.

GBANZIRI ***(GBANZILI, BANZIRI, GBANDERE)*** [GBG] 14,500 in CAR (1996). Population total both countries 17,500. Kouango Subprefecture, along the Ubangi River. Also spoken in DRC. Niger-Congo, Atlantic-Congo, Volta-Congo, North, Adamawa-Ubangi, Ubangi, Sere-Ngbaka-Mba, Ngbaka-Mba, Ngbaka, Western, Gbanzili. Bilingualism in Sango. Investigation needed: intelligibility with Bulaka.

GBAYA, NORTHWEST ***(GBAYA NORD-OUEST, GBAYA)*** [GYA] 200,000 in CAR (1996). Population total all countries 267,000 to 282,000 or more. Bouar, Baboua, Bocaranga, Paoua subprefectures. Also spoken in Cameroon, Congo, Nigeria. Niger-Congo, Atlantic-Congo, Volta-Congo, North, Adamawa-Ubangi, Ubangi, Gbaya-Manza-Ngbaka, Northwest. Dialects: GBAYA KARA (GBAYA DE BOUAR, BOAR), BODOE, LAI (LAY), YAÁYUWEE (YAIWE, KALLA). They use Sango as lingua franca. Primer. Dictionary. Grammar. Christian, traditional religion, Muslim. Bible 1994.

GBAYA, SOUTHWEST ***(GBAYA SUD-OUEST)*** [MDO] 164,000 in CAR (1996). Population total all countries 177,000. Berberati, Carnot, Gamboula, Nola subprefectures. Also spoken in Cameroon, Congo. Niger-Congo, Atlantic-Congo, Volta-Congo, North, Adamawa-Ubangi, Ubangi, Gbaya-Manza-Ngbaka, Southwest. Dialects: BIYANDA (BIANDA), BULI (BOLI), MBONDOMO (MBODOMO), BOKARE (BOKARI), MBOUNDJA (MBUNZA), BOSOKO (BOSSOUKA, MBUSUKU), TOONGO,

YANGELE, MBAKOLO (YASUA), BUDAMONO, MBOMBELENG. Use Sango as lingua franca. Bible portions 1980.

GBAYA-BOSSANGOA ***(GBAYA OF BOSSANGOA, GBAYA DE BOSANGOA, GBEA, GBEYA, GBAYA OF BORRO, GBAYA-BORRO)*** [GBP] 176,000 (1996). Bossangoa, Batangafo (Gbabana) subprefectures. Niger-Congo, Atlantic-Congo, Volta-Congo, North, Adamawa-Ubangi, Ubangi, Gbaya-Manza-Ngbaka, Central. Dialects: GBABANA, BOSSANGOA. May be inherently intelligible with Gbaya-Bosoum or Suma. Speakers use Sango as lingua franca, but women have low proficiency outside towns. Investigation needed: intelligibility with Gbaya-Bozoum, Suma. Bible portions 1934-1952.

GBAYA-BOZOUM ***(GBAYA DE BOZOUM, BOZOM)*** [GBQ] 32,500 (1996). Bozoum Subprefecture. Niger-Congo, Atlantic-Congo, Volta-Congo, North, Adamawa-Ubangi, Ubangi, Gbaya-Manza-Ngbaka, Central. Dialects: DIABE, BOYALI, BOZOM. May be inherently intelligible with Gbaya- Bossangoa. Use Sango as lingua franca. Investigation needed: intelligibility with Gbaya of Bossangoa.

GBAYI ***(KPASIYA)*** [GYG] 5,000 (1996). Northern Mingala Prefecture. Niger-Congo, Atlantic-Congo, Volta-Congo, North, Adamawa-Ubangi, Ubangi, Ngbandi. Related to Ngbandi. Ethnically Kpatili, but not intelligible with Kpatili. Investigation needed: intelligibility with Ngbandi.

GEME ***(JEME, NGBA GEME, GUEME)*** [GEQ] 550 (1996). Ndélé Subprefecture, 2 villages north of Ndélé. Niger-Congo, Atlantic-Congo, Volta-Congo, North, Adamawa-Ubangi, Ubangi, Zande, Zande-Nzakara. Dialects: GEME TULU, GEME KULAGBOLU. Bilingualism in Sango. Investigation needed: intelligibility with Zande.

GUBU ***(GOBU, NGOBO, NGOBU, GABOU, GABU)*** [GOX] Few in CAR. Niger-Congo, Atlantic-Congo, Volta-Congo, North, Adamawa-Ubangi, Ubangi, Banda, Central, Central Core, Mid-Southern. Closest to Togbo and Mono. Bilingualism in Sango. Investigation needed: intelligibility with Togbo, bilingual proficiency in Mono. See main entry under DRC.

GULA ***(KARA OF SUDAN, KARA DE SOUDAN, KARA, TAR GULA, GULA DU MAMOUN, GOULA, YAMEGI)*** [KCM] 13,000 in CAR (1996). Population total both countries 13,000 to 15,000. Birao Subprefecture, near Sudan border at Kafia Kingi. Also spoken in Sudan. Nilo-Saharan, Central Sudanic, West, Bongo-Bagirmi, Kara. Dialects: MOLO, MELE, MOT-MAR (MOTO-MARA), SAR (SARA), MERE, ZURA (KOTO). Different from Kara of CAR, Kare of Chad, or Gula of Chad. Muslim.

GUNDI ***(NGUNDI, NGONDI)*** [GDI] 9,000 (1988 census). Nola Subprefecture, south and east of Nola. The Sangha River is the border to the Yaka region. Niger-Congo, Atlantic-Congo, Volta-Congo, North, Adamawa-Ubangi, Ubangi, Sere-Ngbaka-Mba, Ngbaka-Mba, Ngbaka, Western, Baka-Gundi. May be intelligible with Baka. Bayanga may be a subgroup of Gundi or Baka. Most Pygmies have not been contacted by census takers. Different from Ngundi of Congo, and CAR, which is Bantu. Pygmies. Investigation needed: intelligibility with Baka.

KABA ***(KABBA, SARA KABA, SARA)*** [KSP] 72,000 in CAR (1996). Population total both countries 84,000. Paoua and Marounda subprefectures. Also spoken in Chad. Nilo-Saharan, Central Sudanic, West, Bongo-Bagirmi, Sara-Bagirmi, Sara, Sara Proper. Different from Kaba Deme, Kaba Na, Kulfa (Kaba So), Sara Kaba, Laka (Kabba Laka), or Kaba of Ethiopia, a dialect of Bench. Investigation needed: intelligibility with Dagba.

KAKO ***(KAKA, YAKA, NKOXO)*** [KKJ] 10,400 in CAR (1996). Gambula town at the Cameroon border near Berberati, west CAR. Niger-Congo, Atlantic-Congo, Volta-Congo, Benue-Congo, Bantoid, Southern, Narrow Bantu, Northwest, A, Kako (A.90). See main entry under Cameroon.

KARA ***(FER, DAM FER, FERTIT)*** [KAH] 4,800 (1996). Birao Subprefecture. Unclassified. Different from Gula (Kara of Sudan). Muslim.

KARE ***(KARRÉ, KARI, KALI)*** [KBN] 93,000 in CAR, including 57,500 Kare, 35,500 Tale (1996). Population total both countries 93,000 or more. Boxoum and Bocaranga subprefectures. Also spoken in Cameroon. Niger-Congo, Atlantic-Congo, Volta-Congo, North, Adamawa-Ubangi, Adamawa, Mbum-Day, Mbum, Central, Karang. Dialects: TALE (TALI), KARI. Intelligible with Mbum. Different from the Kari of DRC, which is Benue-Congo. NT 1947.

KPAGUA ***(KPAGWA)*** [KUW] 3,000 to 4,000 (1996). Not in DRC. Niger-Congo, Atlantic-Congo, Volta-Congo, North, Adamawa-Ubangi, Ubangi, Banda, Central, Central Core, Mid-Southern. Closest to Ngundu. Investigation needed: intelligibility with Ngundu.

KPATILI ***(KPATIRI, KPATERE, NGINDERE)*** [KYM] 4,500 (1996). Southern Mingala Prefecture. Niger-Congo, Atlantic-Congo, Volta-Congo, North, Adamawa-Ubangi, Ubangi, Zande, Zande-Nzakara. Related to Nzakara. Not intelligible with Gbayi, who are ethnically Kpatili.

LAKA ***(KABBA LAKA)*** [LAM] 2,050 in CAR (1996). Bocaranga Subprefecture, 9 villages at the Chad border. Nilo-Saharan, Central Sudanic, West, Bongo-Bagirmi, Sara-Bagirmi, Sara, Sara Proper. Some consider it to be a dialect of Ngambai. Different from Laka of Nigeria, which is Adamawa-Ubangi, and from Kaba of CAR and Chad. NT 1960. See main entry under Chad.

LANGBASHE ***(LANGBASHI, LANGBASE, LANGBASI, LANGWASI, LANGBWASSE)*** [LNA] 40,000 in CAR (1996). Population total both countries 43,000. Kouango Subprefecture. Also spoken in DRC.

Niger-Congo, Atlantic-Congo, Volta-Congo, North, Adamawa-Ubangi, Ubangi, Banda, South Central. May be intelligible with South Central Banda. Investigation needed: intelligibility with Ngbugu, Langba.

LUTOS ***(RUTO)*** [NDY] 17,000 in CAR (1996). Population total both countries 19,000. Ndélé, Kaga Andoro, and Kabo subprefectures. Also spoken in Chad. Nilo-Saharan, Central Sudanic, West, Bongo- Bagirmi, Sara-Bagirmi, Sara, Vale. Dialects: NDUKA (NDOUKA, NDOUKWA), LUTOS (RUTO, ROUTO, RITO, LUTO, LOUTO), WADA (WAD), NDUGA (NGOUGUA), KONGA.

MANZA ***(MANDJA, MANJA)*** [MZV] 220,000 (1996). Bouca, Kaga Bandoro, Mbrès, Dekoa, Sibut, Grimari subprefectures. Possibly in Chad or DRC. Niger-Congo, Atlantic-Congo, Volta-Congo, North, Adamawa-Ubangi, Ubangi, Gbaya-Manza-Ngbaka, East. Close to Ngbaka-Minangende of DRC. Speakers use Sango as lingua franca. Christian, traditional religion, Muslim.

MBANGI ***(MBANGUI)*** [MGN] 2,750 (1996). Bangassou, Ouango, and Alindao subprefectures. Niger-Congo, Atlantic-Congo, Volta-Congo, North, Adamawa-Ubangi, Ubangi, Ngbandi. High intelligibility with Yakoma. May be intelligible with Ngbandi or Dendi. Reported to be highly bilingual in Sango. Investigation needed: intelligibility with Ngbandi, Dendi, Yakoma, bilingual proficiency in Sango.

MBATI ***(SONGO, LISONGO, ISONGO, ISSONGO, LISSONGO)*** [MDN] 60,000 (1996). Mbaiki Subprefecture. Niger-Congo, Atlantic-Congo, Volta-Congo, Benue-Congo, Bantoid, Southern, Narrow Bantu, Northwest, C, Ngundi (C.20). Dialects: BOLEMBA, MBATI OF MBAÏKI, BWAKA, BONZIO. Speakers have high bilingual proficiency in Sango.

MBAY ***(MBAI)*** [MYB] 8,300 in CAR (1996). Markounda and Batangafo subprefectures. Nilo-Saharan, Central Sudanic, West, Bongo-Bagirmi, Sara-Bagirmi, Sara, Sara Proper. Different from Mbai, a dialect of Nandi of Kenya. Literacy rate in second language: Fair. Bible 1980. See main entry under Chad.

MBUM ***(MBOUM)*** [MDD] 12,500 in CAR (1996). Bocaranga Subprefectue, along the Cameroon border. Not in Chad. Niger-Congo, Atlantic-Congo, Volta-Congo, North, Adamawa-Ubangi, Adamawa, Mbum-Day, Mbum, Southern. Primer. Dictionary. Grammar. NT 1965. See main entry under Cameroon.

MONZOMBO ***(MONJOMBO, MONDJEMBO, MONZUMBO)*** [MOJ] 1,600 in CAR (1996). Mongoumba Subprefecture. Niger-Congo, Atlantic-Congo, Volta-Congo, North, Adamawa-Ubangi, Ubangi, Sere-Ngbaka-Mba, Ngbaka-Mba, Ngbaka, Western, Monzombo. See main entry under Congo.

MPIEMO ***(MPO, MBIMU, BIMU, MBIMOU, MPYEMO, MBYEMO)*** [MCX] 24,000 in CAR (1996). Population total both countries 29,000. Nola Subprefecture. Also spoken in Cameroon. Niger-Congo, Atlantic-Congo, Volta-Congo, Benue-Congo, Bantoid, Southern, Narrow Bantu, Northwest, A, Makaa-Njem (A.80). Dialects: JASOA (JASUA), BIDJUKI (BIDJOUKI), MPYEMO. Speakers have low bilingual proficiency in Sango. Traditional religion, Christian, Muslim.

NGAM ***(NGAMA)*** [NMC] 17,700 in CAR (1996). Kabo Subprefecture. Nilo-Saharan, Central Sudanic, West, Bongo-Bagirmi, Sara-Bagirmi, Sara, Sara Proper. Different from Ndam of Chad. See main entry under Chad.

NGANDO ***(DINGANDO, BODZANGA, BANGANDOU, BAGANDOU, NGANDO-KOTA)*** [NGD] 5,000 or fewer (1996). Mbaïki Subprefecture. Niger-Congo, Atlantic-Congo, Volta-Congo, Benue-Congo, Bantoid, Southern, Narrow Bantu, Northwest, C, Ngando (C.10). Dialects: DIKUTA, DIKOTA (KOTA). Close to Yaka. Kota may be a separate language. Not related to Ngando of DRC or Bangandu of Congo and Cameroon. Investigation needed: intelligibility with Mbati.

NGBAKA MA'BO ***(NGBAKA LIMBA, MBAKA, MBACCA, BWAKA, BOUAKA, NBWAKA, GBAKA, MA'BO)*** [NBM] 88,000 in CAR (1996). Population total all countries 150,000 (1972 Nida). Mbaiki, Bimbo, and Mongoumba subprefectures. Also spoken in Congo, DRC. Niger-Congo, Atlantic-Congo, Volta-Congo, North, Adamawa-Ubangi, Ubangi, Sere-Ngbaka-Mba, Ngbaka-Mba, Ngbaka, Western, Bwaka. Close to Gilima. Speakers in CAR have high bilingual proficiency in Sango. Investigation needed: intelligibility, bilingual proficiency in Gilima. Bible portions 1936-1937.

NGBAKA MANZA [NGG] 29,000 (1996). Damara, Bogangolo, and Boali subprefectures. Niger-Congo, Atlantic-Congo, Volta-Congo, North, Adamawa-Ubangi, Ubangi, Gbaya-Manza-Ngbaka, East. May be intelligible with Manza. Speakers use Sango as lingua franca. Investigation needed: intelligibility with Manza.

NGOMBE ***(NGOMBE-KAKA, BAGANDO-NGOMBE, BANGANDO-NGOMBE)*** [NMJ] 1,450 (1996). Mambere Kadeï Prefecture. Niger-Congo, Atlantic-Congo, Volta-Congo, North, Adamawa-Ubangi, Ubangi, Sere-Ngbaka-Mba, Ngbaka-Mba, Ngbaka, Western, Baka-Gundi. May be intelligible with Southwest Gbaya. The younger generation in CAR seems to not be using or controlling Ngombe. Different from Ngombe in DRC. May not be Baka-Gundi group but Gbaya group. Investigation needed: intelligibility with Baka, Southwest Gbaya.

NZAKARA ***(ANSAKARA, N'SAKARA, SAKARA, ZAKARA)*** [NZK] 50,000 in CAR (1996). Population total both countries 50,000 or more. Bangassou, Bakouma, and Gambo subprefectures. Also spoken in DRC. Niger-Congo, Atlantic-Congo, Volta-Congo, North, Adamawa-Ubangi, Ubangi, Zande, Zande-Nzakara.

PANA ***(PANI)*** [PNZ] 82,000 in CAR including 63,000 Pana, 10,000 Pondo, 9,000 Gonge (1996). Population total all countries 83,000. Bocaranga Subprefecture. Also spoken in Cameroon, Chad, Nigeria. Niger-Congo, Atlantic-Congo, Volta-Congo, North, Adamawa-Ubangi, Adamawa, Mbum-Day, Mbum, Central, Karang. Dialects: PANA, PONDO, GONGE. Investigation needed: intelligibility with Kare, Mbum. Traditional religion, Christian. Bible portions 1953.

PANDE ***(IPANDE)*** [BKJ] 9,700 (1996). Nola and Berberati subprefectures. Niger-Congo, Atlantic-Congo, Volta-Congo, Benue-Congo, Bantoid, Southern, Narrow Bantu, Northwest, C, Ngundi (C.20). Dialects: PANDE (NDJELI, NJELI, LINYELI, LINZELI, NGILI), BOGONGO (BUGONGO, BUKONGO). Bilingualism in Sango.

RUNGA ***(ROUNGA, RUNGA DE NDELE, AYKI, AYKINDANG)*** [ROU] 21,500 in CAR (1996). Bamingui-Bangoran Prefecture, capital city of Bangui. Nilo-Saharan, Maban, Mabang, Runga-Kibet. Bilingualism in Shua Arabic. Several villages of ethnic Runga near Ndélé speak Arabic as mother tongue: 3,280 (1988 census). Agriculturalists: sorghum; hunter-gatherers; fishermen; traders. Traditional religion, Muslim. See main entry under Chad.

SANGO ***(SANGHO)*** [SAJ] 350,000 mother tongue speakers in CAR, including 24,573 Sango Riverain (1988 census). Population total all countries 400,000 or more. Including second language speakers: 5,000,000 (1997 UBS). Scattered. Not in Cameroon. Also spoken in Chad, Congo, DRC. Creole, Ngbandi based. 51% lexical similarity with French, 49% from African languages. However, the African-based words are used more frequently. Spoken and written for informal use, used for instruction in community schools, in public schools when students do not understand French, church and mission publications. More men than women speak it as second language. A rapidly spreading creole derived from Ngbandi. National language. SVO. Radio programs, TV. Bible 1966.

SANGO, RIVERAIN [SNJ] 34,500 (1996). Mobaye Subprefecture, along the Ubangi River. Creole, Ngbandi based. High intelligibility with Sango. Investigation needed: intelligibility with Sango.

SARA DUNJO ***(KABA DUNJO, SARA DINJO)*** [KOJ] 4,000 (1996). Ndélé Subprefecture, close to the Chadian border. 9 villages. Nilo-Saharan, Central Sudanic, West, Bongo-Bagirmi, Sara-Bagirmi, Sara, Sara Proper, Sara Kaba. May be the same as Kaba Na [KWV] of Chad. May be intelligible with Sara. Investigation needed: intelligibility with Sara.

SARA KABA ***(TA SARA)*** [SBZ] 13,600 (1996). Ndélé and Birao subprefectures. Nilo-Saharan, Central Sudanic, West, Bongo-Bagirmi, Sara-Bagirmi, Sara, Sara Proper, Sara Kaba. May be intelligible with Sara Dunjo [KOJ] of CAR or Kaba Na [KWV] of Chad. Investigation needed: intelligibility with Sara Dunjo.

SUMA ***(SOUMA)*** [SQM] 50,000 (1996). Bossangoa, Markounda, and Paoua subprefectures. Niger-Congo, Atlantic-Congo, Volta-Congo, North, Adamawa-Ubangi, Ubangi, Gbaya-Manza-Ngbaka. May be intelligible with Gbaya-Bossangoa. Investigation needed: intelligibility with Gbaya-Bossangoa.

TO [TOZ] Niger-Congo, Atlantic-Congo, Volta-Congo, North, Adamawa-Ubangi, Adamawa, Mbum-Day, Mbum, Unclassified. Ancient secret male initiation language of the Gbaya practiced in Cameroon and CAR. Second language only. See main entry under Cameroon.

UKHWEJO ***(BENKONJO)*** [UKH] 1,000 to 2,000 (1996 K. Beavon SIL). Sangha Province, south of Nola. Ukhwejo dialect at Ngulo; Bikaka at Nalimo, Salo, Bayanga, and Gbaso; Piiga at Koola, Ambasila; Kamsili at Bomanzoku, Linjombo. 7 villages on both sides of the Sanga River. Niger-Congo, Atlantic-Congo, Volta-Congo, Benue-Congo, Bantoid, Southern, Narrow Bantu, Northwest, A, Makaa-Njem (A.80). Dialects: UKHWEJO, BIKAKA, PIIGA, KAMSILI (NGAMSILE). Close to Koozime, Mpiemo, Bomwali, and Makaa. Investigation needed: intelligibility with Bomwali.

VALE [VAE] 5,400 Vale (1996), few Tana (1996). Batangafo, Kabo, and Kaga Bandoro subprefectures. Not in Chad. Nilo-Saharan, Central Sudanic, West, Bongo-Bagirmi, Sara-Bagirmi, Sara, Vale. Dialects: VALE, TANA (TANE, TELE). Related to Lutos. Not intelligible with Sara or Ngambai. High bilingualism in Sango. Investigation needed: intelligibility with Lutos, bilingual proficiency in Sango.

YAKA ***(AKA, NYOYAKA, BEKÁ, PYGMÉE DE MONGOUMBA, PYGMÉE DE LA LOBAYE, PYGMÉES DE LA SANGHAS, "BABINGA", "BAMBENGA")*** [AXK] 15,000 in CAR (1996). Population total both countries 30,000 (1985 Bahuchet). Nola, Bambio, Mbaïki, Mongoumba subprefectures, all along the Congo border in the forest. The Sangha River is the border with the Baka region. Also spoken in Congo. Niger-Congo, Atlantic-Congo, Volta-Congo, Benue-Congo, Bantoid, Southern, Narrow Bantu, Northwest, C, Ngando (C.10). Dialects: BEKA (GBAYAKA, BAYAKA, MOYAKA), NZARI. "Babinga" is derogatory. The people are 'Bayaka' or 'Biaka'. Different from Baka, which is Ubangi. Pygmies. Forest. Hunter-gatherers. Traditional religion.

YAKOMA [YKY] 100,000 in CAR (1996). Population total both countries 110,000. Kembi and Ouango subprefectures. Mainly along the Ubangi River, and in administrative centers throughout CAR. Also spoken in DRC. Niger-Congo, Atlantic-Congo, Volta-Congo, North, Adamawa-Ubangi, Ubangi, Ngbandi. High intelligibility with Ngbandi and Sango. Bilingualism in Sango. Investigation needed: intelligibility with Ngbandi, Sango.

YULU ***(YOULOU)*** [YUL] 4,000 in CAR (1996). Population total all countries 7,000 or more. Ouadda-Djaléi and Ouadda subprefectures. Yulu are in CAR and Sudan; Binga are in Sudan and DRC. Also spoken in DRC, Sudan. Nilo-Saharan, Central Sudanic, West, Bongo-Bagirmi, Kara. Dialects: BINGA, YULU. Aja is not a dialect of Yulu, but of Kresh (R. Brown SIL). Many are bilingual in Kresh or Arabic in Sudan.

ZANDE ***(AZANDE, ZANDI, PAZANDE, SANDE, BADJANDE)*** [ZAN] 62,000 in CAR (1996). Rafaï, Zémio, and Obo subprefectures. Niger-Congo, Atlantic-Congo, Volta-Congo, North, Adamawa-Ubangi, Ubangi, Zande, Zande-Nzakara. Bilingualism in Sango. Traditional religion, Christian. Bible 1978. See main entry under DRC.

CHAD

Republic of Chad. République du Tchad. National or official languages: Standard Arabic, French. 7,270,000 (1998 UN). Literacy rate 11%. Also includes Hausa 100,000. Information mainly from P. Boyeldieu 1977, 1985; J. P. Caprile 1977; D. Barreteau 1978; H. Jungraithmayr 1981; P. Doornbos and M. L. Bender 1983; J. Bendor-Samuel 1989; SIL 1971-1999. Muslim, Christian, traditional religion. Blind population 110,000 to 175,000. Data accuracy estimate: B. The number of languages listed for Chad is 134. Of those, 132 are living languages and 2 are extinct. Diversity index 0.95.

AMDANG ***(MIMI, MIMA, MUTUTU, BILTINE, ANDANG, ANDANGTI)*** [AMJ] 15,000 (1956 Tucker and Bryan). East. Biltine Prefecture, Biltine Subprefecture, Southeast of Biltine. Nilo-Saharan, Fur. Thoroughly Arabicized. Often confused with other languages called 'Mimi' (M. L. Bender). Called 'Mima' by the Arabs and 'Mututu' by the Maba. They call themselves 'Andang'. Muslim.

ARABIC, BABALIA CREOLE ***(BABALIA, BUBALIA, BABALIYA)*** [BBZ] 3,937 (1993 census). West. Chari Baguirmi Prefecture, N'Djamena Subprefecture. North of Djermaya and between Karal and Tourba. Possibly also in the Bokoro Subprefecture around Ngoura. 23 villages. Creole, Arabic based. A creole developed from Chadian Arabic (90% of the vocabulary) and Berakou (10%; Decobert). The original language of the ethnic group was Berakou. Babalia shares structural similarities with Juba Arabic. There is a post-creole continuum from Chadian Arabic to the Bagirmian basilect. The ethnic group is called 'Babalia'. Muslim.

ARABIC, CHADIAN SPOKEN ***(ARABE CHOA, SHUWA ARABIC, SHUA ARABIC, SHUA, CHOWA, CHAD ARABIC, CHADIAN ARABIC, SUWA, L'ARABE DU TCHAD)*** [SHU] 754,590 speakers in Chad, 12% of the population (1993 census). Probably spoken by half the population including second language speakers (1977 J. Bendor-Samuel). Population total all countries 986,200. Salamat, Ouaddai, Biltine, center of the Batha region and to the west, much of Chari-Baguirmi. Beginning to be more widely used in the Mayo-Kebbi, in the north of the Tandjilé and in the Guéra. Also spoken in Cameroon, CAR, Niger, Nigeria. Afro-Asiatic, Semitic, Central, South, Arabic. Dialects: BATHA (BILTINE), CHARI-BAGUIRMI (SALAMAT). A pidginized variety of this, commonly called 'Bongor Arabic', is spoken as a second language by many people in the Mayo-Kebbi and other parts of south Chad. No diglossia with Modern Standard Arabic. 'Shuwa Arabic' is the name used in various other countries for the variety near Lake Chad. Language of wider communication, trade language. Dictionary. Grammar. Muslim. NT 1967-1991.

ARABIC, STANDARD [ABV] Middle East, North Africa. Afro-Asiatic, Semitic, Central, South, Arabic. Official language. Bible 1984-1991. See main entry under Saudi Arabia.

ASSANGORI ***(SUNGOR, SOUNGOR, ASSOUNGOR, AZANGURI, ASONG, ASUNGORE, BOGNAK-ASUNGORUNG, MADUNGORE, SHAALE)*** [SUN] 23,479 in Chad (1993 census). Population total both countries 38,500. East, Ouaddaï Prefecture, Adré Subprefecture, northwest of Adré and of the Masalit. Also spoken in Sudan. Nilo-Saharan, Eastern Sudanic, Western, Tama, Tama-Sungor. Dialects: SUNGOR, WALAD DULLA, GIRGA. 90% lexical similarity with Tama. The majority use Chadian Arabic as second language, although at a low proficiency level. Investigation needed: intelligibility with Tama. Muslim.

BAGIRMI ***(BAGUIRMI, BAGHIRMI, BAGUIRME, TAR BARMA, BARMA, MBARMA, TAR BAGRIMMA, BAGRIMMA, LIS, LISI)*** [BMI] 44,761 in Chad (1993 census). Population total both countries 44,761 or more. West. Chari Baguirmi Prefecture. Two groups: Massénya Subprefecture around Massénya; Bousso Subprefecture around Bousso. The Gol are at Massénya, the Kibar east of Massénya, the Bangri west of Massénya and along the Chari River between Guélendeng and N'Djaména, and the Dam along the Chari River from Bousso to Gezlendeng. Also spoken in Nigeria. Nilo-Saharan, Central Sudanic, West, Bongo-Bagirmi, Sara-Bagirmi, Bagirmi. Dialects: GOL, KIBAR, BANGRI, DAM. Many dialects. The majority use Arabic as second language. It was the language of the ancient Bagirmi kingdom. It is widely spoken as a second language. Trade language. Grammar. Muslim.

BAREIN ***(BARAÏN, GUILIA, JALKIA)*** [BVA] 4,100 (1993 SIL and census). South central. North Guera Prefecture, Melfi Subprefecture, west (Jalkia), south, southwest (Komi), and east (Sakaya) of Melfi. Afro-Asiatic, Chadic, East, B, B.3. Dialects: JALKIA, GUILIA, SAKAYA (DAGNE, JELKIN), KOMI. 92% lexical similarity between Jalkia and Guilia, 70% between Sakaya and both Jalkia and Guilia. Bilingualism in Chadian Arabic. Muslim.

BEDJOND ***(MBAY BEDIONDO, MBAY BEJONDO, BEDIONDO MBAI, BÉDJONDE, BEDJONDO, BEDIONDO, NANGNDA)*** [MAP] 36,000 (1969 Caprile and Fedry). Southwest, Moyen-Cahri Prefecture, Koumra and Moïssala subprefectures, centered around Bediondo. West of the Day. Nilo-Saharan, Central Sudanic, West, Bongo-Bagirmi, Sara-Bagirmi, Sara, Sara Proper. Dialects: BEDJOND, BÉBOTE, YOM. A distinct language from Sar or Ngambai.

BERAKOU ***(BABALIA, BUBALIA)*** [BXV] 2 speakers (1995 Djarangar). West. Chari Baguirmi Prefecture. 3 groups: N'Djamena Subprefecture, north of Djermaya and between Karal and Tourba; Bokoro Subprefecture, around Ngoura. 23 villages. Nilo-Saharan, Central Sudanic, West, Bongo-Bagirmi, Sara-Bagirmi, Bagirmi. Dialects: BOLO DJARMA, MONDOGOSSOU, MANAWADJI, YIRYO. Bilingualism in Chadian Arabic, Babalia Arabic. Speakers in their 60s (1995). During the last century the Babalia have been shifting to Chadian Arabic or Kotoko languages. The people are called 'Babalia', the language 'Berakou'. Muslim. Nearly extinct.

BERNDE ***(MOROM, TAR MURBA)*** [BDO] 2,000 (1999 J. Roberts SIL). Central, Guéra Prefecture, Bitkine Subprefecture, west of the village of Bolong to the border of Chari Baguirmi Prefecture. Nilo-Saharan, Central Sudanic, West, Bongo-Bagirmi, Sara-Bagirmi, Bagirmi. Dialects: MOROM, MORBO, BAYO, BOLONG (TAR BOLONGO). 59% lexical similarity with Bagirmi, 52% with Kenga, 51% with Jaya, 47% with Naba. Bolong may be a separate language.

BESME ***(HUNER, HOUNAR, 'UNAR, BESEME, BESEMME, BODOR)*** [BES] 1,228 (1993 census). Southwest, Tandjilé Prefecture, Kélo and Laï subprefectures, in Besmé, Bodor, and 3 other villages along the Logone River northwest of Laï. Niger-Congo, Atlantic-Congo, Volta-Congo, North, Adamawa-Ubangi, Adamawa, Mbum-Day, Kim. 51% lexical similarity with Kim. Some bilingualism in Nancere and Chadian Arabic, but not universal nor at a high level. Christian, traditional religion (a few).

BIDEYAT ***(BAELE, ANNA, AWE, TERAWIA, BERIA, BERI)*** [BIH] 3,000 (1982). North. B.E.T. Prefecture, Ennedi Subprefecture, east of Fada. The Sahara is on three sides. Nilo-Saharan, Saharan, Eastern. Probably not a dialect of Zaghawa, although sometimes considered to be one. Bilingualism in Chadian Arabic. Also known as 'Beria' together with Zaghawa. Mountains. Animal husbandry; gatherers; agricultural; traders: livestock, hides and skins, butter, salt. 600 meters. Muslim.

BIDIYO ***(BIDYO, BIDIO, 'BIDIO, 'BIDIYO, BIDIYO-WAANA, BIDIYA)*** [BID] 14,000 (1981 Jungraithmayr). South central, north Guéra Prefecture, Mongo Subprefecture, south of Mongo and west of Abou Telfane. Afro-Asiatic, Chadic, East, B, B.1, 1. Dialects: GARAWGINO, JEKKINO, BIGAWGUNO, NALGUNO, 'OBOYGUNO. The first 2 dialects listed are eastern, the others western. The majority use Chadian Arabic as second language. Dictionary. Grammar. Muslim.

BIRGIT ***(BERGIT, BIRGID, BERGUID)*** [BTF] 3,600 (1952). Southeast, Salamat Prefecture, Abou Déïa and Am Timan subprefectures, and Ouaddaï Prefecture, Am Dam Subprefecture. South of the Mubi, centered in Abgué. Afro-Asiatic, Chadic, East, B, B.1, 2. Dialects: ABGUE, EASTERN BIRGIT, DUGURI, AGRAB. All sources since Greenberg list it as a separate language from other Dangla languages. Different from Birked (Birgit) of Sudan, a Nilo-Saharan language.

BOLGO [BVO] 1,800 (1993 SIL and census). South central, Guéra Prefecture, Melfi Subprefecture, east of the Barain, southeast of Melfi. Niger-Congo, Atlantic-Congo, Volta-Congo, North, Adamawa-Ubangi, Adamawa, Mbum-Day, Bua. Dialects: BOLGO DUGAG (SMALL BOLGO), BOLGO KUBAR (BIG BOLGO). 68% lexical similarity between the two 'dialects' and between Bolgo Dugag and a form of Koke spoken in Daguéla. Most use Chadian Arabic as second language. Vigorous. Investigation needed: intelligibility with dialects. Traditional religion, Muslim.

BON GULA ***(TAATAAL, POUN, BON, BUN, GULA GUERA, BON GOULA)*** [GLC] 1,200 or more (1997 SIL). Southeast, Guéra Prefecture, Melfi Subprefecture. North of Lake Iro, northeast of Zan. Bon and Ibir villages. Niger-Congo, Atlantic-Congo, Volta-Congo, North, Adamawa-Ubangi, Adamawa, Mbum-Day, Bua. 46% lexical similarity with Zan Gula. The majority use Chadian Arabic as second language. Vigorous. Bon Gula and Zan Gula are referred to together as 'Gula Guera'. Traditional religion, Muslim.

BOOR ***(BWARA, DAMRAW)*** [BVF] 100 or fewer (1999 J. Roberts SIL). South, Chari-Baguirmi Prefecture, Bousso Subprefecture, and Moyen-Chari Prefecture, Sarh Rural Subprefecture, in and around Dumraw (Bwara) village on the north bank of the Chari River, just east of Miltu. Afro-Asiatic, Chadic, East, A, A.1, 2. Some have classified it as a dialect of Miltu. 36% lexical similarity with Miltu (closest). There may be a high degree of bilingualism in Bagirmi.

BUA ***(BOA, BOUA, BWA, 'BA)*** [BUB] 7,708 (1993 census). South. Moyen-Chari Prefecture, Sarh Subprefecture, around and to the northeast of Korbol; Guéra Prefecture, Melfi Subprefecture. Niger-Congo, Atlantic-Congo, Volta-Congo, North, Adamawa-Ubangi, Adamawa, Mbum-Day, Bua. A separate language from Niellim, Fania, Tounia, and Day. 'Mana' or 'Kobe' may be an alternate name or dialect. Bilingualism in Arabic is limited. Different from Bua (Bwa) of DRC, which is Benue-Congo. Traditional religion, Muslim.

BUDUMA ***(BOUDOUMA, YIDENA, YEDIMA, YEDINA, YIDANA)*** [BDM] 51,600 in Chad (1993 SIL and census). Population total all countries 58,800. West, Lac Prefecture, Bol Subprefecture, islands and northern shore of Lake Chad. No longer in Niger. Also spoken in Cameroon, Nigeria. Afro-Asiatic, Chadic, Biu-Mandara, B, B.1, Buduma. Dialects: SOUTHERN BUDUMA, NORTHERN BUDUMA. 90% inherent intelligiblity between the dialects. 2/3 have good to excellent oral proficiency in Kanembu as second language, about 50% in Kanuri. Some can use Arabic. Used in the home and traditional livelihoods. Vigorous. Investigation needed: intelligibility with Kuri. Grammar. Literacy rate in first language: Below 1%. Literacy rate in second language: Below 5%. Fishermen, agriculturalists. Muslim, traditional religion.

BUSO ***(BUSSO, DAM DE BOUSSO, BOUSSO)*** [BSO] 40 to 50 (1971 Welmers). West, Chari-Baguirmi Prefecture, Bousso Subprefecture, in Maffaling and Bousso. Afro-Asiatic, Chadic, East, A, A.1. Boyeldieu says it is not in the Bua group, but Chadic. Nearly extinct.

CHADIAN SIGN LANGUAGE [CDS] 390 or more users out of a large deaf population (1989 Mokommbay Yonadjiel KATA). Schools and an association for the deaf in N'Djamena, Sarh, and Moundou. Deaf sign language. Influences from American Sign Language. Some signs are traditional. Teachers were trained in Nigeria. Muslim, Christian.

DAGBA [DGK] Nilo-Saharan, Central Sudanic, West, Bongo-Bagirmi, Sara-Bagirmi, Sara, Sara Proper. May be intelligible with Kaba. Investigation needed: intelligibility with Kaba. See main entry under CAR.

DAJU, DAR DAJU ***(DADJO, DADJU, DAJOU, DAJU, DAJO, DAJU MONGO, DAJU OUM HADJER, SAARONGE)*** [DJC] 23,100 (1993 SIL and census). Central, Guera Prefecture, Mongo Subprefecture, around Mongo and Eref. Nilo-Saharan, Eastern Sudanic, Western, Daju, Western Daju. Not inherently intelligible with Dar Sila Daju. 64% lexical similarity with Dar Sila Daju. The majority use Chadian Arabic as second language. They call themselves 'Saaronge'. Muslim.

DAJU, DAR SILA ***(SILA, SULA, DAJU, DADJO, DAJOU, BOKORUGE, BOKORIKE)*** [DAU] Population total both countries 33,000 (1971 Welmers). Eastern, Ouaddaï Prefecture, Goz-Beïda Subprefecture, around Goz-Beïda and east to the Sudan border. Also spoken in Sudan. Nilo-Saharan, Eastern Sudanic, Western, Daju, Western Daju. Not inherently intelligible with Dar Daju Daju. 64% lexical similarity with Dar Daju Daju. The majority use Chadian Arabic as second language. They call themselves 'Bokoruge'. Muslim.

DANGALÉAT ***(DANGLA, DANAL, DANGAL)*** [DAA] 45,000 including 30,000 in Dangaléat Canton (1999 L. Burke SIL). Central, Guera Prefecture, Mongo and Bitkine subprefectures, west of Mongo. The western dialect is around Korbo; central dialect around Barlo, Koubo Adougoul; eastern dialect around Korlongo. Afro-Asiatic, Chadic, East, B, B.1, 1. Dialects: WEST DANGALÉAT (KORBO, KARBO), CENTRAL DANGALÉAT, EAST DANGALÉAT. Intelligibility between speakers of the eastern and western dialects is low, but both understand the central dialect well. The majority use Arabic as second language. Dictionary. Grammar. Literacy rate in first language: 1% to 5%. Literacy rate in second language: Below 5%. Traditional religion (Margai), some Muslim, some Christian.

DAY ***(DAI)*** [DAI] 49,916 (1993 census). Southwest, Moyen-Chari Prefecture, Sarh and Moïssala subprefectures, southwest of Sarh. Niger-Congo, Atlantic-Congo, Volta-Congo, North, Adamawa-Ubangi, Adamawa, Mbum-Day, Day. Dialects: BOUNA, BANGOUL, NGALO, TAKAWA-BÉNGORO. The dialects are inherently intelligible to each others' speakers. Dictionary. Grammar. NT 1989.

DAZAGA ***(DAZA, DASA, DAZZA)*** [DAK] 282,281 in Chad (1993 census). Population total both countries 312,300. North, Kanem and B.E.T. prefectures, Borkou and Ennedi subprefectures, north of Lake Chad and in the area of Largeau. Also spoken in Niger. Nilo-Saharan, Saharan, Western, Tebu. The majority use Arabic as second language. 'Daza' is the name for the people, 'Dazaga' for the language. Different from Daza in Nigeria, which is Chadic. Muslim.

DISA [DIV] South, Moyen-Chari Prefecture, Kyabé Subprefecture, northwest of Lake Iro. Nilo-Saharan, Central Sudanic, West, Bongo-Bagirmi, Sara-Bagirmi, Bagirmi. Little is known about it. It is probably similar or related to Gula (Sara Gula, GLU) of Chad. Probably fewer than 5,000 speakers. Investigation needed: intelligibility.

FANIA ***(FAGNIA, FANYA, FANYAN, FANA, FANIAN, MANA, KOBE)*** [FAN] 1,100 or more (1997 SIL). Southeast, Guéra Prefecture, Melfi Subprefecture, west of Lake Iro, and north of Sarh, around Mouraye, Sengué, Malakonjo, Rim, Sisi, Karo villages. Niger-Congo, Atlantic-Congo, Volta-Congo, North, Adamawa-Ubangi, Adamawa, Mbum-Day, Bua. Dialects: NORTHERN FANIA, SOUTHERN

FANIA. A separate language from Bua. 79% lexical similarity between dialects. Most use Chadian Arabic as second language. Vigorous. Traditional religion, Muslim.

FONGORO ***(GELE, KOLE)*** [FGR] 1,000 or fewer (1983 Doornbos and Bender). East, Ouaddai Prefecture, Goz Beida Subprefecture, Canton Fongoro, along the Sudan border in the Dar Fongoro region south of Mongororo and the Sinyar, in a rather inaccessible area. Nilo-Saharan, Central Sudanic, West, Bongo-Bagirmi, Sara-Bagirmi. The people have shifted to Fur linguistically and culturally. There may be a few elderly speakers left and some living in isolated places. Apparently extinct in Sudan. The tse-tse fly is a problem in the area. Mountains. Hunter-gatherers: honey, hides and skins; fishermen: dried fish.

FRENCH [FRN] 3,000 in Chad (1993). Indo-European, Italic, Romance, Italo-Western, Western, Gallo-Iberian, Gallo-Romance, Gallo-Rhaetian, Oïl, French. Official language. Bible 1530-1986. See main entry under France.

FULFULDE, ADAMAWA ***(ADAMAWA FULANI, PEUL, PEULH, PULLO, PULE, FUL, FULA FULBE, BOULBE, EASTERN FULANI, FOULFOULDE, NAGAPELTA, PELTA HAY, DOMONA, PLADINA, PALATA, PALDIDA, PALDENA, DZEMAY, ZEMAY, TAAREYO, ZAAKOSA, BIIRA, SANYO)*** [FUB] 128,000 in Chad, with Kano-Katsina-Bororro Fulfulde; 152,146 all Fulfulde varieties in Chad (1993 census). Southwest, Mayo-Kebbi Prefecture, around Léré. Niger-Congo, Atlantic-Congo, Atlantic, Northern, Senegambian, Fula-Wolof, Fulani, Eastern. Dialects: MAROUA, GAROUA, NGAOUNDÉRÉ, KAMBARIIRE, NOMADIC FULFULDE, BILKIRE FULANI (BILKIRI). Fulfulde is the language, Fulbe the people. Dictionary. Grammar. Traditional religion, Muslim. Bible 1983. See main entry under Cameroon.

FULFULDE, BAGIRMI ***(BAGHIRMI PEUL, BAGIRMI FULA)*** [FUI] 24,000 in Chad. Population total both countries 180,000. West, Chari-Baguirmi Prefecture, Massénya and Bokoro subprefectures, between Bokoro and Massénya. Also spoken in CAR. Niger-Congo, Atlantic-Congo, Atlantic, Northern, Senegambian, Fula-Wolof, Fulani, Eastern. May be close to Bororo Fulfulde; reported to be a nomadic group of Mbororo. Spoken by people of Wodaabe lineage who are also in northern Niger, northern Cameroon, CAR. Nomadic. Different from the Bagirmi language of Chad, which is Nilo-Saharan. Trade language.

FULFULDE, KANO-KATSINA-BORORRO ***(FULBE, PEUL)*** [FUV] Mayo-Kebbi Prefecture, in the area of Pala and Léré; Chari-Baguirmi Prefecture, between Massakory and Massénya, and Lac Prefecture, north of Lake Chad near Rig-Rig. Nomadic Bororro travel along the banks of the Chari River and elsewhere. Niger-Congo, Atlantic-Congo, Atlantic, Northern, Senegambian, Fula-Wolof, Fulani, East Central. Dialects: KANO-KATSINA, BORORRO (BORORO, MBORORO, AKO, NOMADIC FULFULDE). Muslim. See main entry under Nigeria.

FUR ***(FOR, FOUR, KONJARA, KONDJARA)*** [FUR] 1,800 in Chad. Nilo-Saharan, Fur. Several small groups. Grammar. Muslim. See main entry under Sudan.

GABRI ***(GABERI, GABERE, NGABRE, SOUTHERN GABRI)*** [GAB] 25,000 to 30,000 (1999). South-west, Tandjilé Prefecture, Laï Subprefecture, northwest of Laï around Dormo and Darbé villages. Afro-Asiatic, Chadic, East, A, A.2, 2. Dialects: DARBÉ, DORMON. Dormo and Chiri are Gabri villages, erroneously listed as languages in some sources. Traditional religion, Christian.

GADANG [GDK] 2,500 (1997 SIL). Southwest, Chari-Baguirmi Prefecture, Bousso Subprefecture, southeast of Bousso, along the N'Djaména-Sarh road, between Mogo and Mbarlé, Somrai region. Afro-Asiatic, Chadic, East, A, A.1, 2. Related to Sarwa and Miltu. Bilingualism in Bagirmi.

GIDAR ***(GUIDAR, GIDDER, KADA, "BAYNAWA")*** [GID] 11,687 in Chad (1993 census). Southwest, Mayo-Kebbi Prefecture, Léré Subprefecture, northwest of Léré in Chad to Guider in Cameroon, at least 25 villages. Afro-Asiatic, Chadic, Biu-Mandara, C. NT 1986. See main entry under Cameroon.

GOR ***(BODO)*** [GQR] 75,000 (1999 J. Roberts SIL). Logone Oriental Prefecture, Doba Subprefecture, centered around Bodo. Nilo-Saharan, Central Sudanic, West, Bongo-Bagirmi, Sara-Bagirmi, Sara, Sara Proper. Dialects: BODO, YAMOD. Close to Bedjond and Gor, with high inherent intelligibility. There is a Gor Language Committee. The speakers have a clear understanding of their identity as separate from Mango and Bedjond. Primer, literacy classes. Christian, traditional religion.

GOUNDO [GOY] 30 (1998). Tanjilé Prefecture, Laï and Kélo subprefectures, Goundo-Bengli, Goundo-Nangom, and Goundo-Yila villages. Niger-Congo, Atlantic-Congo, Volta-Congo, North, Adamawa-Ubangi, Adamawa, Mbum-Day, Kim. Lexical similarity with Besmé 60%, Kim 51%. Bilingualism in Kabalay, Nancere. Over 40 years old. Younger people have shifted to Kabalay and Nancere. Nearly extinct.

GULA ***(SARA GOULA, SARA GULA, GOULA)*** [GLU] Moyen-Chari Prefecture, Kyabé Subprefecture, northwest of Lake Iro. Nilo-Saharan, Central Sudanic, West, Bongo-Bagirmi, Sara-Bagirmi, Bagirmi. Probably related to Disa. Different from Gula Iro of Chad which is Adamawa and from Gula [KCM] of CAR and Sudan. May be smaller than 10,000 speakers.

GULA IRO ***(GOULA IRO, GOULA D'IRO, KULAAL)*** [GLJ] 3,500 (1991 SIL), including 2,000 Pongaal, 725 Tiaala, 200(?) Tiitaal, 350 Patool, 165 Korintal. Southeast, Moyen-Chari and Salamat prefectures, Kyabe and Am Timan subprefectures. Around Lake Iro, in and around Boum Kabir, northeast of Sarh. Pongaal dialect is in Boum Kabir, Boum Saher, Madjok, Teonen, and Karou; Tiaala in Masidjanga (Cheroba), Bouni, and Kore; Patool in Badi and Foundouk; Korintal in Cheou (Tieou); Tiitaal in western Salamat Prefecture. Niger-Congo, Atlantic-Congo, Volta-Congo, North, Adamawa-Ubangi, Adamawa, Mbum-Day, Bua. Dialects: PONGAAL (PONAAL), TIAALA, TIITAAL, PATOOL, KORINTAL. Not intelligible with Bon Gula or Zan Gula. Bilingualism in Arabic is limited, and there is almost none in Sara. 'Kulaal' is their name for themselves. Different from Gula of Chad and Sudan which is Nilo-Saharan, and from Gula of CAR. Traditional religion, Christian.

GULAY ***(GOULAI, GOULEI, GULEI, GULAI, GOULAYE)*** [GVL] 163,271 (1993 census), including 23,500 Pen in 26 villages (1995 Djarangar). Southwest, Moyen-Chari (6 cantons), Logone Oriental (1 canton) and Tandjilé (1 canton) prefectures, between Koumra, Laï, and Doba. Nilo-Saharan, Central Sudanic, West, Bongo-Bagirmi, Sara-Bagirmi, Sara, Sara Proper. Dialects: GULAY, PEN (PENI). Sar is the lingua franca. The Pen do not like to be called 'Gulay'. Bible portions 1956.

HERDÉ ***(KA'DO HERDÉ, HE'DÉ, "KADO", ZIME)*** [HED] 40,000 in Chad (1999 SIL). Population total both countries 40,000 or more. Southwest, Mayo-Kebbi Prefecture, Pala and Léré subprefectures. Around Pala and Lamé. Near the Pevé, west of the Ngueté. Also spoken in Cameroon. Afro-Asiatic, Chadic, Masa. Linguistic and sociolinguistic differences make separate literature from Pevé and Ngueté necessary. NT 1980.

HORO ***(HOR)*** [HOR] Béhor north of Sarh on the Chari River. Nilo-Saharan, Central Sudanic, West, Bongo-Bagirmi, Sara-Bagirmi, Sara, Sara Proper. Extinct. They now speak the Kle dialect of Ngam. Extinct.

JAYA [JYY] 2,200 (1993 census). Central, Guéra Prefecture, Bitkine Subprefecture, 50 km. north-northwest of Bitkine. Nilo-Saharan, Central Sudanic, West, Bongo-Bagirmi, Sara-Bagirmi, Bagirmi. Not inherently intelligible with Kenga. 44% lexical similarity with Naba.

JONKOR BOURMATAGUIL ***(DJONGOR BOURMATAGUIL, DOUGNE, KARAKIR)*** [JEU] 1,500 (1993 SIL). Reduced numerically in the last 25 years. Salamat Prefecture, Abou Deïa Subprefecture, west of Abou Deïa. Originally centered in Bourmataguil village, now centered in Ader-Ader. Afro-Asiatic, Chadic, East, B, B.1, 1. Dialects: DOUGNE, MUSUNYE. Relationship with other Dangla languages needs investigation, especially Toram and Mogum. A large number of the ethnic group have given up the traditional language for Chadian Arabic, but in two villages the children still learn Jonkor Bourmataguil. 'Karakir' means 'cave-dwellers' in Arabic. The name 'Jegu' has been applied to this language, but Jegu is a dialect of Mogum. Investigation needed: intelligibility with Toram, Mogum.

KABA ***(KABBA, KABA DE PAOUA, KABA DE BAIBOKOUM, WESTERN KABA)*** [KSP] 11,000 (1971 Welmers). Southwest, Logone Oriental Prefecture, Goré Subprefecture, around Goré and to the southeast. Nilo-Saharan, Central Sudanic, West, Bongo-Bagirmi, Sara-Bagirmi, Sara, Sara Proper. Different from Kaba Deme, Kaba Na, Kaba So (Kulfa), or Kabba Laka (Laka). Investigation needed: bilingual proficiency in Ngambai. See main entry under CAR.

KABA DEME ***(KABA DEMI, KABA 'DEM, TÀ SÀRA)*** [KWG] 40,000 (1993 UBS). Southeast, Moyen-Chari Prefecture, Sarh and Kyabé subprefectures, between Sarh and Kyabé. Along the Chari River, Bobé, Hélibongo, Banda, Moussafoyo, Kemata villages. Nilo-Saharan, Central Sudanic, West, Bongo-Bagirmi, Sara-Bagirmi, Sara, Sara Proper, Sara Kaba. Dialects: SIIME, MARA, KURUWER. Different from Kaba, Kaba So (Kulfa), Kaba Na, or Kabba Laka (Laka). Fishermen.

KABA NA ***(KABA NAR, KABA NAA, NA, DANA, SARA KABA)*** [KWV] 35,000 (1993 UBS) including 5,564 in Bale village, 4,937 in Koskabo, 4,548 in Kyabé. Southeast, Moyen-Chari Prefecture, Kyabé Subprefecture, centered in Kyabé. Nilo-Saharan, Central Sudanic, West, Bongo-Bagirmi, Sara-Bagirmi, Sara, Sara Proper, Sara Kaba. Dialects: DUNJE (DENDJE, DINDJE, DINJE, DENJE, DOUNJE), NA, BANGA (MBANGA), TIE (TIYE). Dunje may be the same as Kaba Dunjo [KOJ] of CAR. Kaba Na may be the same as Sara Kaba [SBZ] of CAR. Not the same as Kaba, Kaba Deme, Kaba So (Kulfa), or Kabba Laka (Laka). NT 1988.

KABALAI ***(KABA-LAI, KABALAY, KABALAYE, KEB-KAYE, GABLAI, LAY, LAI)*** [KVF] 17,885 (1993 census). Southwest Chad, Tandjile Prefecture, Lai Subprefecture; Lai and to the south on the eastern bank of the Logone River. Not in CAR. Afro-Asiatic, Chadic, East, A, A.2, 2. May be intelligible with Nancere. Erroneously called 'Sara' or 'Kaba of Lai'.

KAJAKSE ***(KADJAKSE, KAJESKE, KUJARKE, MINI, KAWA TADIMINI)*** [CKQ] 10,000 (1983 Bender). East, Ouaddaï Prefecture, Am Dam Subprefecture. South and southeast of Am Dam. Some refugees in Sudan near the border. Afro-Asiatic, Chadic, East, B, B.1, 2. Partially intelligible with Mesmedje and Mubi. Hills. Hunter-gatherers; little livestock; traders: hides.

KANEMBU ***(KANAMBU, KANEMBOU)*** [KBL] 389,028 (1993 census), including 168,441 in Lac Prefecture, 68,032 in Chari-Baguirmi Prefecture. Northwest, Kanem, Lac, prefectures, and Chari-Baguirmi Prefecture, Massakory Subprefecture, northeast of Lake Chad. Nilo-Saharan, Saharan, Western, Kanuri. Dialects: KARKAWU, MANDO, NGURI. There is a gradual differentiation between dialects of Kanembu and Kanuri. The majority use Arabic as second language. Ethnic groups: Badé (Badde 2,646), Baribu, Chiroa, Diabu, Galabu, Kadjidi (5,638), Kankena, Kanku, Kenguina (1,944), Koubri (Koubouri 2,817), Maguirmi (1,825), Nguiguim (7,233). Investigation needed: intelligibility with east and west varieties. Muslim, traditional religion.

KANURI, CENTRAL ***(YERWA KANURI, KANOURY, KANOURI, BORNU, BORNOUANS, BORNOUAN, AGA, KOLE, KOLERE, SIRATA, "BARIBARI", "BERIBERI")*** [KPH] 93,638 in Chad including 34,549 in Chari-Baguirmi and 23,287 in N'Djaména (1993 census). Communities of speakers in Chari-Baguirmi, Batha, Guéra, and Mayo-Kebbi prefectures. Nilo-Saharan, Saharan, Western, Kanuri. Dialects: DAGARA, KAGA (KAGAMA), SUGURTI, LARE, KWAYAM, NJESKO, KABARI (KUVURI), NGAZAR, GUVJA, MAO, TEMAGERI, FADAWA. "Beriberi" is considered a derogatory name. Ajami script. Muslim. NT, in press (1997). See main entry under Nigeria.

KARANG ***(LAKA, LAKKA, KARENG, EASTERN MBUM, LAKKA MBUM, MBUM BAKAL, NZ#AK KÀRÁNG)*** [KZR] 1,000 in Chad (1995 SIL). Southwest, Logone Oriental Prefecture, Baibokoum Subprefecture, northwest of Baïbokoum along the Cameroon border: Loumbogo, Lawtiko I, Lawtiko II, Sarkaluki villages, and possibly another, as well as two Sakpu villages. Niger-Congo, Atlantic-Congo, Volta-Congo, North, Adamawa-Ubangi, Adamawa, Mbum-Day, Mbum, Central, Karang. Dialects: KARANG, SAKPU, NGOMI, MBERE. Closely related to Nzakambay and Kuo. Different from Laka (Kabba Laka) of CAR and Chad, and from Laka of Nigeria. Traditional religion. See main entry under Cameroon.

KARANGA ***(KURUNGA)*** [KTH] 10,000 including 4,696 Karanga and 1,419 Bakha (1999 J. Roberts SIL). East, Ouaddaï Prefecture, Abéché and Am Dam subprefectures. Around Am Dam and between Am Dam and Abéché, south of the Maba. The Bakha are southwest of Am Dam, and the Karanga and the Koniéré are northeast of Am Dam. The Kashmere are south of Abéché and north of the Karanga. Nilo-Saharan, Maban. Dialects: KARANGA (KURUNGA), KASHMERE (KACHMERE), BAKHA (BAXA, BAKHAT, FAALA, FALA), KONIÉRÉ (KONYARE, KOGNERE, MOOYO, MOYO). 73% lexical similarity with Maba, 94% between Karanga and Kashmere dialects. The four dialects are distinct ethnic groups. Muslim.

KENDEJE ***(YAALI)*** [KLF] 1,000 to 2,000 (1995 SIL). East, Ouaddaï Prefecture, rural Abéché and Adré subprefectures, north and west of Hadjer Hadid. Nilo-Saharan, Maban, Mabang. Dialects: YAALI, FARANGA. 89% lexical similarity between the dialects with little contact between them. Reported high bilingualism in Maba and Masalit. Investigation needed: bilingual proficiency, attitudes. Muslim.

KENGA ***(KENGE, CENGE)*** [KYQ] 40,000 (1997 Testardi SIL). Central, Guera Prefecture, Bitkine Subprefecture, around Bitkine, 52 villages, including Bolongo, Bokiyo. Nilo-Saharan, Central Sudanic, West, Bongo-Bagirmi, Sara-Bagirmi, Bagirmi. Dialects: CENGE (TAR CENGE), BANAMA (TAR BANAMA), BIDJIR, BANALA (TAR BANALA). Related to Naba and Jaya, but not inherently intelligible. 62% lexical similarity with Jaya. The majority of men use Chadian Arabic as second language for trade. Speakers have a positive attitude toward Kenga and Kenga literacy. Grammar. SVO. Literacy rate in first language: 1% to 5%. Literacy rate in second language: Men: 15% or below in French, 1% in Arabic; women: below 1%. Muslim, Christian, traditional religion.

KERA [KER] 44,523 in Chad (1993 census). Population total both countries 51,000. Southwest, Mayo-Kebbi Prefecture, Fianga Subprefecture, south of Fianga, near Lake Tikem. Also spoken in Cameroon. Afro-Asiatic, Chadic, East, A, A.3. 42% lexical similarity with Kwang. It has been confused with neighboring Tupuri in some publications. Literacy rate in first language: 1% to 5%. Literacy rate in second language: Below 5%. Bible portions 1988-1991.

KIBET ***(KIBEIT, KIBEET, KABEN, KABENTANG)*** [KIE] 18,500 (1983 Bender) to 22,000 (1977 Voegelin and Voegelin). East, Salamat Prefecture, Am Timan Subprefecture, and Ouaddaï Prefecture, Goz Beïda Subprefecture. Northeast of Am Timan and southwest of Goz Beïda. Nilo-Saharan, Maban, Mabang, Runga-Kibet. Dialects: DAGEL (DAGGAL), MURRU (MURO, MOURRO), KIBET. Closely related to Runga. The dialects listed, including Murru, may be separate languages. Not a Tama variety, as reported in some sources. The majority are bilingual in Arabic. The area is flooded for 6 months each year. The tse-tse fly is a problem. Investigation needed: intelligibility with dialects. Agriculturalists: sorghum, peanuts; animal husbandry; fishermen; hunter-gatherers. Muslim.

KIM [KIA] 15,354 (1993 census). Southwest, Mayo-Kebbi Prefecture, Bongor Subprefecture, Logone River area, southeast of Bangor. Niger-Congo, Atlantic-Congo, Volta-Congo, North, Adamawa-Ubangi, Adamawa, Mbum-Day, Kim. Dialects: GARAP (ÉRÉ), GEREP (DJOUMAN, JUMAM), KOLOP (KILOP, KOLOBO), KOSOP (KWASAP, KIM). Dialects listed may be closely related languages. Formerly classified as Chadic. Incorrectly called 'Masa'. Investigation needed: intelligibility with dialects. NT 1955.

KIMRÉ ***(GABRI-KIMRÉ)*** [KQP] 15,000 (1990 census), including 700 Tchere-Aïba. Southwest Chad, Tandjilé Prefecture, Kélo Subprefecture, east of Laï, including Tchere-Aïba village. Afro-Asiatic, Chadic, East, A, A.2, 1. Dialects: KIMRUWA (KIM-RUWA, KIMRÉ), BURUWA (BORDO), TCHIRE (TCHERE-AÏBA). Popularly called 'Gabri', but it is not intelligible with Gabri. The 'Kimre' name is also used for Tobanga and Southern Gabri.

KOKE ***(KHOKE)*** [KOU] 600 (1993 SIL and census). Southeast, Guéra Prefecture, Melfi Subprefecture, southeast of Melfi; around Daguéla, Sengué, and Djourab villages. Niger-Congo, Atlantic-Congo, Volta-Congo, North, Adamawa-Ubangi, Adamawa, Mbum-Day, Bua. 60% lexical similarity with Bolgo Dugag. The majority may be bilingual in Chadian Arabic or Fania. Investigation needed: intelligibility, bilingual proficiency.

KUJARGE [VKJ] 1,000 (1983 Bender). Dar Fongoro, 7 villages near Jebel Mirra, and scattered among the Fur and Sinyar in Sudanese villages along the lower Wadis Salih and Azum rivers. The Daju Galfigé are to the west, Sinyar to the north, Fur-Dalinga, Fongoro, Formono, and Runga to the east and south. Unclassified. Fur is used as second language and some use Daju. A few groups. Hunter-gatherers: honey; little agriculture or animal husbandry.

KULFA ***(KULFE, KURMI, KURUMI, "KABA SO")*** [KXJ] Southeast, Moyen Chari Prefecture, Kyabé Subprefecture, southwest of Lake Iro. Centered in Alako, Male, and Moufa. Nilo-Saharan, Central Sudanic, West, Bongo-Bagirmi, Sara-Bagirmi, Sara, Sara Proper, Sara Kaba. Dialects: KURMI, SO (SUKA, SOUKA, SOKO). 80% lexical similarity with Kaba Na. Not the same as Kaba, Kaba Deme, Kaba Na, or Laka (Kabba Laka). The name "Kaba So" is considered to be derogatory by the speakers. Investigation needed: intelligibility with Kaba group, bilingual proficiency in Shuwa Arabic, Sara.

KUO ***(KO, KOH)*** [KHO] Population total both countries 15,000 (1995 SIL). Southwest, Logone Oriental Prefecture, Baibokoum Subprefecture, near Baibokoum, Pao and Bouroum cantons. The villages are on the north-south road from Pao to Laramanay, on the road northwest from Pao, and on the road northwest from Laramanay to Bouroum. Also spoken in Cameroon. Niger-Congo, Atlantic-Congo, Volta-Congo, North, Adamawa-Ubangi, Adamawa, Mbum-Day, Mbum, Central, Koh. Closely related to Karang and Nzakambay. Literacy rate in first language: 1% to 5%. Literacy rate in second language: Below 5%. Bible portions 1987.

KWANG ***(KUANG, KOUANG, KWONG)*** [KVI] 16,805 (1993 census), including 10,000 or more Kwang, 2,000 Mobou, 250 Aloa. Southwest Chad, Tandjilé Prefecture, Laï Subprefecture. North of Laï, east of Bongor, southwest of Bousso. The Mobou are in Mobou, south of Bousso. The Aloa are in Mogo. Afro-Asiatic, Chadic, East, A, A.3. Dialects: KWANG, MOBOU (MOBU), NGAM (GAM, MODGEL), TCHAGIN (TCHAKIN), ALOA, KAWALKÉ, GAYA, MINDÉRA. The dialects listed are inherently intelligible to each other's speakers. Includes Midigil village, sometimes erroneously listed as a language named 'Modgel' (Medegel) in some sources. 42% lexical similarity with Kera. The Aloa are Muslim and fully bilingual in Baguirmi. The Ngam use Sara as second language. Ngam is different from Ngam of Chad and CAR in the Sara group of Nilo-Saharan. Traditional religion, Christian, Muslim.

LAAL ***(GORI)*** [GDM] 300 to 500 (1977 Boyeldieu). Damtar village had its own dialect, called 'Laabe' with 3 speakers left in 1977. Southwest, Moyen-Chari Prefecture, Sarh Subprefecture, between Korbol and Dik. Centered in Gori, villages of Gori, Damtar, and Mailao near Kouno, northwest of Sarh. Unclassified. Dialects: LAAL, LAABE. Some lexical relationship to the Bua group, but Boyeldieu says it should not be classified with Bua. Probably Adamawa, some sources say Chadic. Further study needed.

LAGWAN ***(KOTOKO-LOGONE, LOGONE, LAGWANE, LAGOUANE)*** [KOT] West, Chari-Baguirmi Prefecture, N'Djaména Subprefecture, south of N'Djaména along the Logone River, in the vicinity of Logone-Gana. Afro-Asiatic, Chadic, Biu-Mandara, B, B.1, Kotoko Proper. Dialects: LOGONE-BIRNI, LOGONE-GANA (KOTOKO-GANA). A member of the Kotoko ethnic and linguistic group: Afade, Mser, Malgbe, Maslam, Mpade, and Jilbe (in Nigeria). Grammar. Muslim. See main entry under Cameroon.

LAKA ***(KABBA LAKA)*** [LAM] 55,143 in 310 villages in Chad (1991 census). Population total both countries 57,200. Southwest, Logone Oriental Prefecture, Baïbokoum and Goré subprefectures. Mang is in Ngadjibian Canton, north of Bessao, and in parts of the Békan and Timbéri cantons, Goré Subprefecture. Bémour is in Bessao and Pandzangué cantons south of Moundou. Maïngao is along the Ngamadja-Dodang II axis, and along the Bessao-Oudoumian axis. Goula is in Andoum Canton, and in the area around Pan in Pandzangué Canton. Paï is at Oudoumian. Also spoken in CAR. Nilo-Saharan, Central Sudanic, West, Bongo-Bagirmi, Sara-Bagirmi, Sara, Sara Proper. Dialects: MANG, BÉMOUR, MAÏNGAO, GOULA, PAÏ. Some consider it to be a dialect of Ngambai. Different from Laka of Nigeria, which is Adamawa-Ubangi, and from Kaba of CAR and Chad. NT 1960.

LELE [LLN] 26,000 (1991 UBS). Southwest Chad, Tandjilé Prefecture, Kélo Subprefecture, south of Kélo. Afro-Asiatic, Chadic, East, A, A.2, 1. Different from Lele of DRC and Lele (Kasena) of Ghana and Burkina Faso. NT 1991.

LUTOS [NDY] 1,978 in Chad (1993 census). Southwest, Moyen-Chari Prefecture, Maro Subprefecture, south of the Ngam. Nilo-Saharan, Central Sudanic, West, Bongo-Bagirmi, Sara-Bagirmi, Sara, Vale. Dialect: RUTO (ROUTO, RITO, LOUTO, LUTO). Only Lutos dialect is in Chad; Ruto and Nduka dialects are in CAR. Not intelligible with Sar or Ngambai. See main entry under CAR.

MABA ***(MABANG, MABANGI, MABAN, MABAA, MABAK, BURA MABANG, BORA MABANG, KANA MABANG, OUADDAO, OUADDAIEN, WADDAYEN, WADAI, WADAIKNS, BOURGU, BORGU, BORGOTKE)*** [MDE] 250,000 (1999 J. Roberts SIL). East, Ouaddaï Prefecture, Abéché and Am Dam subprefectures, and Biltine Prefecture, Biltine Subprefecture; almost all of Abéché Subprefecture and the area around Biltine. Over 200 villages, many with over 500 inhabitants. Nilo-Saharan, Maban, Mabang, Maba. Dialects: BAKHA, ABKAR, KAJANGA (KAJANGAN), KELINGAN, MALANGA, MANDABA (MA NDABA), MANDALA (MA DALA), NYABADAN, KODOO, OULED DJEMMA, KUJINGA, DONDONGO. 73% lexical similarity with Karanga and Kachmere, 63% with Marfa. Ethnic groups: Kondongo, Kujinga, Uled Djemma (Aulad Djema, Awlad Djema), Kabga, Ganyanga. Trade language. Mountains. Agriculturalists. Muslim.

MAJERA ***(MAZERA, MIDAH, MIDA'A, DA'A)*** [XMJ] (5,000 or fewer in Cameroon; 1984 ALCAM). West, Mayo-Kebbi Prefecture, Bongor Subprefecture, north of Gelengdeng, Dogwea village. Afro-Asiatic, Chadic, Biu-Mandara, B, B.1, Jina. Dialects: MAJERA (MAZRA), KAJIRE-'DULO, HWALEM (HOLOM). Included in what the Mandage call 'Mida'a' and 'Da'a'. Investigation needed: bilingual proficiency in Lagwan, Musgu. See main entry under Cameroon.

MALGBE ***(GULFEI, GOULFEI, GOULFEY, MALBE, MALGWE, NGWALKWE, MANDAGE, SANBALBE, KOTOKO-GULFEI)*** [MXF] West, Chari-Baguirmi Prefecture, N'Djamena Subprefecture, north of N'Djamena along the Chari River. Douguia, Malalie, and Oulio (Walia) villages, and others. Afro-Asiatic, Chadic, Biu-Mandara, B, B.1, Kotoko Proper. Dialects: GOULFEY, WALIA, MARA, DOUGUIA. Related to other Kotoko ethnic and linguistic groups: Afade, Lagwan, Maslam, Mpade, Mser, and Jilbe (of Nigeria). It appears to be a distinct language. 'Mandage' is a name applied to the northern Kotoko languages. See main entry under Cameroon.

MAMBAI ***(MANGBAI, MANGBEI, MANBAI, MAMBAY, MAMGBAY, MAMGBEI, MONGBAY, MANGBAÏ DE BIPARÉ, MOMBOI)*** [MCS] 2,067 in Chad (1993 census). Southwest, Mayo-Kebbi Prefecture, Lere Subprefecture, Cameroon border west of Lere. Niger-Congo, Atlantic-Congo, Volta-Congo, North, Adamawa-Ubangi, Adamawa, Mbum-Day, Mbum, Northern, Tupuri-Mambai. Speakers are reported to understand Mundang. Investigation needed: intelligibility. See main entry under Cameroon.

MANGO ***(MONGO, MBAY DOBA, DOBA)*** [MGE] 50,000 (1981 Bernard Lanne). Logone Oriental Prefecture, Doba Subprefecture, centered around Bodo. Nilo-Saharan, Central Sudanic, West, Bongo-Bagirmi, Sara-Bagirmi, Sara, Sara Proper. Close to Bedjond and Gor, with high inherent intelligibility. There is a Mango Language Committee. The speakers have a clear understanding of their identity as separate from Gor and Bedjond. Primer, literacy classes. Christian, traditional religion. Bible portions 1968.

MARARIT ***(MARARET, MERARIT, ABIYI, ABIRI, EBIRI)*** [MGB] 42,388 including 15,376 Mararit, 27,012 Abou Charib (1993 census). East, Biltine Prefecture, Am Zoer Subprefecture (Abou Charib), and Ouaddaï Prefecture, Adré Subprefecture, Mabrone Canton (Mararit). Nilo-Saharan, Eastern Sudanic, Western, Tama, Mararit. Dialects: MARARIT, ABOU CHARIB (ABU SHARIB, ABU SHARIN). Limited intelligibility between Abou Charib and Mararit. Very difficult intelligibility with Tama. Not intelligible with Sungor. 62% lexical similarity with Tama, 75% between Abou Charib and Mararit. The majority use Chadian Arabic as second language. The Abou Charib live north of the Mararit, and trace their ancestry to them. Investigation needed: intelligibility with Abou Charib. Mountains. Agriculturalists; pastoralists: cattle, camels. Muslim.

MARBA ***('AZUMEINA, AZUMEINA, MARABA, KOLONG, KULUNG)*** [MPG] 124,357 (1993 census). Southwest, Tandjilé Prefecture, Kélo Subprefecture, north of Kélo. Afro-Asiatic, Chadic, Masa. 'Kulung' is a place in the Marba-speaking area, not a dialect or language. Different from Marfa (Marba) of Chad, which is Maban. Bible, in press (1997).

MARFA ***(MARBA)*** [MVU] 5,000 to 10,000 (1999 J. Roberts). East, Ouaddaï Prefecture, Abéché Subprefecture, south of Abéché. Nilo-Saharan, Maban, Mabang, Maba. Not a dialect of Masalit, as some have implied. 63% lexical similarity with Maba, 69% with Karanga, 45% with Masalit. Chadian Arabic is used as second language, and the majority use Maba. Different from Marba which is Chadic.

MASALIT ***(MASSALIT, MASSOLIT, KAANA MASALA, MASARA, MASALE)*** [MSA] 50,847 in Chad (1993 census). East, Ouaddaï Prefecture, Adré Subprefecture, around Adré. Northern Masalit is north and east of Geneina in Sudan, Western Masalit in Ouaddaï, Southern Masalit in Sudan.

Nilo-Saharan, Maban, Mabang, Masalit. Dialects: NORTHERN MASALIT, WESTERN MASALIT, SOUTHERN MASALIT. 36% lexical similarity with Karanga, 42% with Maba, 45% with Marfa. The majority use Chadian Arabic as second language. Literacy rate in first language: Below 1%. Literacy rate in second language: Below 5%. Muslim. See main entry under Sudan.

MASANA ***(MASA, MASSA, "BANANA")*** [MCN] 109,093 in Chad (1993 census). Population total both countries 212,000. Southwest, Mayo-Kebbi Prefecture, Bongo Subprefecture, along the Logone River, Bongor region. Also spoken in Cameroon. Afro-Asiatic, Chadic, Masa. Dialects: YAGWA (YAGOUA), BONGOR, WINA (VIRI), WALIA (WALYA), DOMO, GIZAY (GUISSEY, GISEY), BUGUDUM (BUDUGUM), GUMAY (GOUMAYE), HAM. All dialects understand Yagoua well, although Gizay and Yagoua have 80% intelligibility. "Banana" has been used perjoratively by some neighboring groups. Dictionary. Traditional religion, Christian, Muslim. NT 1950-1955.

MASLAM ***(MANDAGE, MENDAGE, MANDAGUÉ, MALTAM, KOTOKO-MALTAM)*** [MSV] Possibly only a few hundred in Chad (1995). West, Chari-Baguirmi Prefecture, N'Djamena Subprefecture. North of N'Djamena, along the Chari River. Maltam is in Miskini and Blabli villages, Sao in Farcha-Milezi and Ngara-Mandju (or 'Gourmadjo') villages. Afro-Asiatic, Chadic, Biu-Mandara, B, B.1, Kotoko Proper. Dialects: MASLAM (MALTAM), SAO (SAHU). In the Kotoko ethnic and linguistic group. Closest to Afade. 'Mandage', etc., is applied to the northern Kotoko languages. Investigation needed: intelligibility with related languages. See main entry under Cameroon.

MASMAJE ***(MASMADJE, MESMEDJE)*** [MES] 25,727 (1993 census). Central, Batha Prefecture, Oum Hadjer Subprefecture, southwest of Oum Hadjer, north of the Mubi. Afro-Asiatic, Chadic, East, B, B.1, 2. Arabicized and Islamicized.

MASSALAT [MDG] 10 speakers or fewer (1991 R. Blench), out of an ethnic group of 29,836 (1993 census). East Batha Prefecture, Oum Hadjer Subprefecture, and Ouaddaï Prefecture, Am Dam Subprefecture. Nilo-Saharan, Maban, Mabang, Masalit. Nearly all now speak Chadian Arabic. The Massalat originally separated from the Masalit along the Sudan border and moved west. Muslim. Nearly extinct.

MAWA ***(MAHWA, MAHOUA)*** [MCW] 3,000 to 5,000 (1997 SIL). Central, north Guéra Prefecture, Bitkine Subprefecture, about 30 km. south of Bitkine, centered around the village of Mahoua. Southeast of the Mukulu. Afro-Asiatic, Chadic, East, B, B.1, 1. 'Gurara' and 'Roffono' ('Reupan') are villages, whose speech is hardly different from that of Mahoua. 48% lexical similarity with Ubi. The majority use Shuwa Arabic as second language, some use Kenga.

MBARA ***(MASSA DE GUELENGDENG, GUELENGDENG, G'KELENDENG, G'KELENDEG)*** [MPK] 1,000 or fewer (1980 Tourneux). East, Chari-Baguirmi Prefecture, Massénya Subprefecture, and Mayo-Kebbi Prefecture, Bongor Subprefecture, along the Chari River, around Guélengdeng. Afro-Asiatic, Chadic, Biu-Mandara, B, B.2.

MBAY ***(MBAI, MBAYE, SARA MBAI, MOISSALA MBAI, MBAY MOISSALA)*** [MYB] Population total all countries 100,000 (1981 UBS). Southwest, Moyen-Chari Prefecture, Moïssala Subprefecture. Around Moïssala. The traditional area is on the border of Chad and CAR. Also spoken in CAR, Nigeria. Nilo-Saharan, Central Sudanic, West, Bongo-Bagirmi, Sara-Bagirmi, Sara, Sara Proper. Dialects: BÉDJOU, KAN (MBAY-KAN), NGOKA (MBANG), BÉDÉGUÉ, MOUGO, BBATE. Dictionary. Traditional religion, Christian, Muslim. Bible 1980.

MESME ***(ZIME, DJIME, DJIWE)*** [ZIM] 20,120 (1993 census). Southwest, Tandjilé Prefecture, Kélo Subprefecture, south and west of Kélo, between Kélo and Pala. Afro-Asiatic, Chadic, Masa. Dialects: BERO, ZAMRE. Mesmé is a separate but related language to Pévé, Nguеté, and Herdé. They call themselves 'Zime', but that name is commonly used by outsiders to refer to all languages and dialects of this group. The name 'Mesmé' is used by outsiders to distinguish this group from the other groups they call 'Zime'. NT 1995.

MIGAAMA ***(MIGAMA, JONGOR, DJONKOR, DIONKOR, DYONGOR, DJONKOR ABOU TELFANE)*** [MMY] 23,000 (1991 census). Central, Guera Prefecture, Mongo Subprefecture, east of Mongo, centered in Baro, around Abu Telfan. Migaama dialect is in Baro, Doga in Fityari, Gamiya in Game and Julkulkili, and Dambiya in Mala. Afro-Asiatic, Chadic, East, B, B.1, 1. Dialects: MIGAAMA, DOGA, GAMIYA, DAMBIYA (NDAMBIYA). Dialect cluster. The majority use Chadian Arabic as second language, although at a low proficiency level. Muslim. Bible portions.

MILTU ***(MILTOU)*** [MLJ] 272 (1993 census). Southwest, Chari-Baguirmi Prefecture, Bousso Subprefecture, around the town of Miltou. Afro-Asiatic, Chadic, East, A, A.1, 2. 27% lexical similarity with Sarua, Somrai, Gadang, and Ndam; 36% with Boor. Speakers are shifting to Bagirmi in all domains.

MIMI ***(MIME)*** [MIV] 5,000 speakers (1983) out of an ethnic group of 39,945 (1993 census). Eastern, north of Biltine, near Jebels Batran and Agán, and scattered through Ouaddaï. Possibly in Sudan, in Dar Fur. Nilo-Saharan, Fur. May be the same as Amdang. This Mimi is different from the Mimi of Gaudefroy-Demombynes and the Mimi of Nachtigal (hitherto unidentified), which may be Maban

(Doornbos and Bender 1983). Most people are bilingual in Chadian Arabic. Investigation needed: intelligibility with Amdang. Mountains, plains. Pastoralists; agriculturalists. Muslim.

MIRE [MVH] 1,400 (1990 census). Southwest, Tandjile Prefecture, Lai Subprefecture, between the Ndam and the Kimré language areas. Afro-Asiatic, Chadic, East, A, A.1, 1. 65% lexical similarity with Ndam, 32% with Kimré. Most use Kimré or Ndam as second language. Traditional religion, Christian.

MOGUM *(MOGOUM)* [MOU] 7,000 (1997 SIL). South central Chad, north Guera Prefecture, Bitkine, Melfi, and Mongo subprefectures, south of the Bidiyo. Afro-Asiatic, Chadic, East, B, B.1, 1. Dialects: JEGU, KOFFA (KOFA), MOGUM DÉLE, MOGUM DIGUIMI, MOGUM URMI. Dialect cluster. Dialects listed are inherently intelligible with each other. Mogum Diguimi may not be a separate dialect. Above 96% lexical similarity among dialects.

MONOGOY [MCU] Southwest, Tandjilé Prefecture, Kélo Subprefecture, northwest of Kélo. Afro-Asiatic, Chadic, Masa. Investigation needed: intelligibility with Marba.

MPADE *(MAKARI, MENDAGE, MANDAGE, MANDAGUE, KOTOKO-MAKARI)* [MPI] West, Chari-Baguirmi Prefecture, N'Djaména Subprefecture, south of Lake Chad, in and around Mani on the Logone River, north of N'Djaména. Afro-Asiatic, Chadic, Biu-Mandara, B, B.1, Kotoko Proper. Dialects: MAKARI, SHOE (SHAWE, CHAOUE, MANI), BODO, WOULKI, DIGAM. In the Kotoko ethnic and linguistic group. 'Mandage', etc., is applied to the northern Kotoko languages (Afade, Malgbe, Maslam, Mpade, Mser). See main entry under Cameroon.

MSER *(KOTOKO-KUSERI, KUSERI, KOUSSERI, KLESEM, MANDAGE, MANDAGUE, MENDAGE)* [KQX] West, Chari-Baguirmi Prefecture, N'Djaména Subprefecture, Cameroon border near N'Djaména. Afro-Asiatic, Chadic, Biu-Mandara, B, B.1, Kotoko Proper. Dialects: MSER (KOUSSERI, MSIR), KALO (KALAKAFRA), GAWI, HOULOUF, KABE. The majority are bilingual in Chadian Arabic. Kanuri is also used. The people of Klesem village no longer speak Mser. The term 'Mandage', etc. is applied to all the northern Kotoko languages (Afade, Malgbe, Maslam, Mpade, Mser). Muslim. See main entry under Cameroon.

MUBI *(MOUBI, MONJUL)* [MUB] 35,277 (1993 census). Central, Guéra Prefecture, Mangalmé Subprefecture, east of Mongo, centered in and around Mangalmé. 135 villages. There may be some in Sudan. Afro-Asiatic, Chadic, East, B, B.1, 2. Dialects: MUBI, MINJILE. The majority use Arabic as second language. Different from Mubi (Gude) of Cameroon and Nigeria. Investigation needed: intelligibility. Muslim.

MUKULU *(MOKULU, MOKOULOU, DJONKOR GUERA, DYONGOR GUERA, DIONGOR GUERA, JONKOR-GERA, MOKILKO)* [MOZ] 12,000 (1990 SIL). Central, Guéra Prefecture, Bitkine Subprefecture, at the foot of the Guéra Massif: Moukoulou, Séguine, Doli, Morgué, Djarkatché (Mezimi), and Gougué villages. Afro-Asiatic, Chadic, East, B, B.2. Dialects: MOKILKO, SEGINKI, DOLIKI, MORIKO, MEZIMKO, GUGIKO. Dialects are inherently intelligible with each other. Bilingualism in Arabic is limited. Literacy rate in first language: Below 1%. Literacy rate in second language: Below 5%. Traditional religion, some Christian, Muslim.

MUNDANG *(MOUNDAN, MOUNDANG, KAELE, NDA)* [MUA] 160,880 in Chad (1993 census). Population total both countries 205,000. Southwest, Mayo-Kebbi Prefecture, Léré, Pala, and Fianga subprefectures, centered around Léré. The Kieziere subdialect is on the border with Pévé. The Torrock-Kaélé subdialect is in Torrock and in Kaélé Cameroon. Also spoken in Cameroon. Niger-Congo, Atlantic-Congo, Volta-Congo, North, Adamawa-Ubangi, Adamawa, Mbum-Day, Mbum, Northern, Tupuri-Mambai. Dialects: KABI, ZASING (YASING). A subdialect of Kabi is Kiziere, of Zasing is Torrock-Kaélé. Bible 1983.

MUSEY *(MOUSSEI, MUSEI, MUSSOI, MOUSSEY, MUSSOY, MOSI, BANANNA, BANANNA HO HO, MUSEYNA)* [MSE] 175,640 in Chad (1993 census). Population total both countries 195,640. Southwest, Mayo-Kebbi Prefecture, Fianga and Gounou Gaya subprefectures, and Tandjilé Prefecture, Kélo Subprefecture, southeast of Fianga. Gounou Gaya is the commercial and administrative center. Also spoken in Cameroon. Afro-Asiatic, Chadic, Masa. Dialects: BONGOR-JODO-TAGAL-BEREM-GUNU, PE-HOLOM-GAMÉ, JARAW-DOMO, LEW. Some intelligibility with Masa. Marba (Azumeina) is closest linguistically. The Lew dialect is closest to Marba. All dialects are intelligible with each other. Dialect names are village names. The Pe dialect is in Cameroon. Bilingual level estimates for French are 0 0%, 1 20%, 2 30%, 3 30%, 4 19%, 5 1%. Kera and other nearby groups are bilingual in Musey. Traditional religion. NT 1995.

MUSGU *(MOUSGOU, MUSGUM, MOUSGOUM, MUSUK, MOUSGOUN, MUNJUK, MOULOUI, MULWI)* [MUG] 24,408 (1993 census). West Chad, Mayo-Kebbi Prefecture, Bongor Subprefecture, and Chari-Baguirmi Prefecture, N'Djaména Subprefecture. Between the Chari and Logone rivers, west of Guélengdeng. Afro-Asiatic, Chadic, Biu-Mandara, B, B.2. Dialects: MPUS (PUS, POUSS, MOUSGOUM DE POUSS, MUSGUM-POUSS), BEEGE (JAFGA), VULUM (VLUM, MULWI-MOGROUM), MUZUK (MOUSGOUM DE GUIRVIDIG, MOUSGOUM DE GUIRVIDIK, GUIRVIDIG).

The Vulum dialect is mainly in Chad. Their name for themselves is 'Mulwi'. Distinct from the Muskum language in Mouskoun village. NT 1964. See main entry under Cameroon.

MUSKUM ***(MUZGUM)*** [MJE] West, Mayo-Kebbi Prefecture, Bongor Subprefecture. Along the Logone River, west of Guélengdeng, village of Muskum (Mouskoun), 10 km. north of Katoa. Afro-Asiatic, Chadic, Biu-Mandara, B, B.2. 40% lexical similarity with Musgu. There was 1 speaker in 1976. Because of intermarriage, speakers eventually shifted to the Vulum dialect of Musgu. Extinct.

NABA [MNE] 232,448 including 136,629 Bilala, 76,660 Kuka, and 19,159 Medogo (1993 census). Central, Batha Prefecture, Ati and Oum subprefectures, and Chari-Baguirmi Prefecture, Bokoro Subprefecture. The Bilala are around Lake Fitri and toward the east to Ati. The Kuka are between Moïto and Bokoro in Bokoro Subprefecture, and between Ati and Oum Hadjer. The Medogo are southwest of Ati. Nilo-Saharan, Central Sudanic, West, Bongo-Bagirmi, Sara-Bagirmi, Bagirmi. Dialects: BILALA (BOULALA, BULALA, MAGE, MA), KUKA (KOUKA, LISI), MEDOGO (MODOGO, MUD). Related but not inherently intelligible with Berakou or Kenga. Lexical similarity between Bilala, Kuka, and Medogo is 99%. Some use Chadian Arabic as second language. One part of the Kuka ethnic group, who live near Oum Hadjer, have shifted from the Naba language to Chadian Arabic. Bilala, Kuka, and Medogo are 3 ethnic groups who share a common culture and speak essentially the same language, called 'Naba' by all 3 groups. Muslim.

NANCERE ***(NANJERI, NANCHERE, NANTCERE, NANGJERE, NANGCERE)*** [NNC] 71,609 (1993 census). Southwest, Tandjilé Prefecture, Béré and Kélo subprefectures. Afro-Asiatic, Chadic, East, A, A.2, 1. Traditional religion, Christian. Bible 1986.

NDAM ***(DAM, NDAMM)*** [NDM] 6,500 (1990 census). Southwest, Tandjilé Prefecture, Laï Subprefecture, northeast of Laï, and southeast of Bousso. Afro-Asiatic, Chadic, East, A, A.1, 1. Dialects: NDAM-NDAM (SOUTHERN NDAM), NDAM DIK (NORTHERN NDAM). Distinct from Dam of Bousso. Traditional religion (primarily), Muslim, Christian.

NGAM ***(NGAMA, SARNGAM, NGAHM)*** [NMC] 43,743 (1993 census). Population total both countries 61,400. Southwestern Chad, Moyen-Chari Prefecture, Maro and Dembo subprefectures, centered in Maro. Ngam Tel is in Maro Canton and Moussafoyo. Ngam Tira is at Maro, Moyo, and Danamadji. Kon Ngam is in Djéké Canton. Kle is at Nara in Djéké Canton. Ngam Gir Bor is in Kabo in CAR. Also spoken in CAR. Nilo-Saharan, Central Sudanic, West, Bongo-Bagirmi, Sara-Bagirmi, Sara, Sara Proper. Dialects: NGAM TEL, NGAM TIRA, KON NGAM, KLE, NGAM GIR BOR. Sara Madjingay is the lingua franca. The Horo (Hor) are reported to have lost their language, and now speak the Kle dialect of Ngam. They consecrate the traditional chiefs of the Ngam.

NGAMBAY ***(SARA, SARA NGAMBAI, GAMBA, GAMBAYE, GAMBLAI, NGAMBAI)*** [SBA] 750,000 in Chad (1999 SIL). Population total all countries 750,000 or more. Southwest, all of Logone Occidental Prefecture; also Logone Oriental Prefecture, Bébedjia and Goré subprefectures, and Mayo-Kebbi Prefecture, Pala Subprefecture. Centered in and around Moundou. Also spoken in Cameroon, Nigeria. Nilo-Saharan, Central Sudanic, West, Bongo-Bagirmi, Sara-Bagirmi, Sara, Sara Proper. Dialects: LARA, BENOYE, MURUM (MOUROUM), KERE, BEMAR (DABA DE GORÉ). The dialects are reported to be completely intelligible with each other. The Laka language is considered by some to be a dialect of Ngambay. Largest language of the Sara-Bagirmi group. Trade language. Traditional religion, Christian, Muslim. Bible 1993.

NGETE ***(NGUETÉ, NGUETTÉ, NGE'DÉ, KA'DO NGUETÉ, ZIME)*** [NNN] 10,000 (1991 UBS). Southwest, Mayo-Kebbi Prefecture, Pala Subprefecture, east of Pala around Ngeté village; near the Pévé, east of the Herdé. Afro-Asiatic, Chadic, Masa. Linguistic and sociolinguistic differences with Pévé and Herdé make separate literature necessary. Also close to Marba. The term 'Zime' is used by outsiders to refer to this and related languages: Herdé, Pévé, Mesmé.

NIELLIM ***(MJILLEM, NYILEM, NIELIM, LUA)*** [NIE] 5,157 (1993 census), including 1,000 in the city of Sarh, and 400 in Niou dialect. Southwest, Moyen-Chari Prefecture, Sarh Subprefecture, around Niellim town, on the southwest bank of the Chari River. Niou dialect is in Niou on the northeast bank. Niger-Congo, Atlantic-Congo, Volta-Congo, North, Adamawa-Ubangi, Adamawa, Mbum-Day, Bua. Dialects: NIELLIM, TCHINI (CUNI, CINI), NIOU. Tchini dialect is extinct. The government calls them 'Niellim'. Their own name is 'Lua'. Traditional religion.

NOY ***(LOO)*** [NOY] 36 (1993 census). South, Moyen-Chari Prefecture, Sarh and Koumra subprefectures, in the area between Sarh, Djoli, Bédaya, Koumra, and Koumogo villages. Niger-Congo, Atlantic-Congo, Volta-Congo, North, Adamawa-Ubangi, Adamawa, Mbum-Day, Bua. Boyd (1989) indicates speakers are shifting to Sar. Nearly extinct.

NZAKAMBAY ***(NZAKMBAY, NZAK MBAI, NZAKA MBAY, MBUM, MBOUM, NJAKAMBAI, MBUM NZAKAMBAY)*** [NZY] 15,000 to 20,000 (1999 SIL). Population total both countries 25,000 to 35,000. Southwest, Logone Oriental Prefecture, Baïbokoum Subprefecture, Cameroon border, near Baïbokoum. Zoli is in the Monts de Lam area. Also spoken in Cameroon. Niger-Congo, Atlantic-Congo, Volta-Congo, North, Adamawa-Ubangi, Adamawa, Mbum-Day, Mbum, Central, Karang. Dialects: NZAKAMBAY,

ZOLI. Closely related to Karang and Kuo. Different from Mbai, which is Nilo-Saharan, and from Mbum of Cameroon. Traditional religion. NT 1968-1994.

PANA ***(PANI)*** [PNZ] 1,000 or fewer (1999 SIL). The Pana dialect is in Makele village, and the Gonge dialect in Giriwon and Diahoke villages. Niger-Congo, Atlantic-Congo, Volta-Congo, North, Adamawa-Ubangi, Adamawa, Mbum-Day, Mbum, Central, Karang. Dialects: PANA, GONGE. Investigation needed: intelligibility with Man. Bible portions 1953. See main entry under CAR.

PÉVÉ ***(KA'DO PEVÉ, LAMÉ, "KADO", ZIME)*** [LME] 30,000 in Chad (1999 SIL). Population total both countries 33,000 to 35,000. Southwest near the Cameroon border, Mayo-Kebbi Prefecture, Pala and Léré subprefectures. Lamé is the largest village, home of the Chef de Canton, and administrative center. Also spoken in Cameroon. Afro-Asiatic, Chadic, Masa. Dialects: LAMÉ, DOE (DOUÉ), DARI. Related to Herdé and Nguetè, but phonology and grammar differences and ethnic attitudes make separate literature necessary. Different from Lame of Nigeria. 'Zime' is used by outsiders to refer to Herdé, Ngeté, Pévé, and Mesmé. NT 1986.

RUNGA ***(ROUNGA, ROUNGO, AIKI, AYKI, AYKINDANG)*** [ROU] 21,479 in Chad (1993 census). Population total both countries 43,000. Southeast, Salamat Prefecture, Haraze-Mangueigne Subprefecture, and Ouaddaï Prefecture, Goz-Beïda Subprefecture, along the border of CAR. Also spoken in CAR. Nilo-Saharan, Maban, Mabang, Runga-Kibet. The majority of the men use Arabic as second language. The area is flooded for 6 months each year. The tse-tse fly is a problem. Investigation needed: intelligibility with Runga, Aiki. Agriculturalists: sorghum; hunter-gatherers; fishermen. Traditional religion, Muslim.

SABA ***(JELKUNG)*** [SAA] 1,000 to 1,200 (1997 SIL). South central, Guéra Prefecture, Melfi Subprefecture, northeast of Melfi. Afro-Asiatic, Chadic, East, B, B.3. Chadian Arabic is the second language of speakers, but with low proficiency. Arid. Plains. Agriculturalists: millet. Muslim, traditional religion.

SANGO ***(SANGHO)*** [SAJ] Southern Chad. Creole, Ngbandi based. A trade language derived from Ngbandi, with decreasing usage in Chad. Probably no mother tongue speakers in Chad. Trade language. Bible 1966. See main entry under CAR.

SAR ***(SARA, SARA MADJINGAY)*** [MWM] 183,471 (1993 census) including 74,670 Madjingay (1964), 16,260 No (1964), 32,000 Nar (1977). Southwest, Moyen-Chari prefecture, Sarh, Koumra, and Moïssala subprefectures, in and around Sarh, Koumra, Balimba, Bessada, Bédaya, Djoli, Matékaga, and Koumogo cantons. Nilo-Saharan, Central Sudanic, West, Bongo-Bagirmi, Sara-Bagirmi, Sara, Sara Proper. Dialects: MAJINGAI (MAJINNGAY, MADJINGAYE, MADJINGAY, MADJA NGAI), NAR, NO. The principal language of Sarh. Trade language. Dictionary. Traditional religion, Christian, Muslim. NT 1972-1986.

SARUA ***(SARWA, SAROUA)*** [SWY] 2,000 or more (1997 SIL). Southwest, Chari-Baguirmi Prefecture, Bousso Subprefecture, between Bousso and Miltou, along the Chari River. Afro-Asiatic, Chadic, East, A, A.1, 2. 42% lexical similarity with Gadang, 27% with Miltu. The majority use Bagirmi as second language. Different from Sharwa in Cameroon. Traditional religion, Christian.

SINYAR ***(SINYA, SHEMYA, SHAMYA, SYMIARTA, SHAMYAN, ZIMIRRA, TAAR SHAMYAN)*** [SYS] East, Ouaddaï Prefecture, Goz-Beïda Subprefecture, north of Mongororo, near the confluence of the Kaja, Azum, and Salih rivers. Nilo-Saharan, Central Sudanic, West, Bongo-Bagirmi, Sinyar. People are generally trilingual in Sinyar, Fur, and Chadian Arabic. Many speak Daju or Masalit. The language is not dying out. They are culturally Fur. Little education. It is geographically cut off from languages of the Bongo-Bagirmi group. Agriculturalists: grain; little livestock. Muslim. See main entry under Sudan.

SOKORO [SOK] 5,000 (1994 SIL). Central, Guéra Prefecture, Melfi Subprefecture, north and northwest of Melfi, from Gogmi to Badanga. Afro-Asiatic, Chadic, East, B, B.3. Dialects: SOKORO, BEDANGA. Closely related languages: Saba, Barein. 55% lexical similarity with Tamki. Most men speak Chadian Arabic as second language. A group called the 'Tunjur of Melfi' in the area around Djebren may have spoken a now extinct dialect of Sokoro, and are reported to mainly speak Arabic now. Muslim.

SOMRAI ***(SOUNRAI, SOMREI, SOMRE, SOUMRAY, SOUMRAI, SUMRAI, SIBINE, SHIBNE)*** [SOR] 7,414 (1993 census). Southwest, Tandjilé Prefecture, Laï Subprefecture, northeast of Laï, centered at Domogou. Afro-Asiatic, Chadic, East, A, A.1, 1. Not intelligible with any other language. 47% lexical similarity with Ndam, 39% with Sarua, 35% with Gadang, 33% with Tumak, 28% with Miltu. Speakers are not bilingual. They call themselves 'Shibne' or 'Sibine'. Traditional religion, Christian, Muslim.

SURBAKHAL ***(SOURBAKHAL)*** [SBJ] 5,000 to 7,000 (1993 SIL). East, Ouaddaï Prefecture, Adré Subprefecture, between Hadjer Hadid and Alacha. Nilo-Saharan, Maban, Mabang, Masalit. 74% lexical similarity with Masalit. The majority use Maba or Masalit as second language. Investigation needed: bilingual proficiency. Muslim.

TAMA ***(TAMONGOBO, TAMOK, TAMOT)*** [TMA] 62,931 (1993 census). Eastern, Biltine Prefecture, Guéréda Subprefecture, around Guéréda. and Gimr dialect is east of the Tama. Jabaal dialect is west of Jabal Muun in Sudan, centered in Sali'a. Nilo-Saharan, Eastern Sudanic, Western, Tama, Tama-Sungor. Dialects: TAMA, GIMR (ORRA, QIMR, HAURA), JABAAL (MILEERE, MISSIRII, MIISIIRII, MILRI), ERENGA. 90% to 95% lexical similarity with Assangori. The majority use Chadian Arabic as second language, although at a low proficiency level. Some also use Masalit. The Gimr now speak Chadian Arabic as mother tongue. Investigation needed: intelligibility with Assangori. Muslim.

TAMKI ***(TEMKI)*** [TAX] 500 (1999 J. Roberts SIL). Central, Guéra Prefecture, Melfi Subprefecture, about 60 km. northeast of Melfi, Tamki village. Afro-Asiatic, Chadic, East, B, B.3. Not inherently intelligible with Sokoro. Lexical similarity 62% with Saba, 55% with Sokoro, 32% with Mawa. Most speak Chadian Arabic, Kenga, or Saba as second languages. Speakers are positive toward Tamki. They consider themselves to be ethnically Sokoro, but their attitudes are not more positive toward Sokoro than toward other neighboring languages. Traditional religion.

TEDAGA ***(TEDA, TODA, TODAGA, TODGA, TUDA, TUDAGA, TUBU, TEBU, TEBOU, TIBBU, TOUBOU)*** [TUQ] 28,501 in Chad (1993 census). Population total all countries 40,500. Far northern desert, B.E.T. Prefecture, primarily in the Tibesti Subprefecture around Bardai. Also spoken in Libya, Niger, Nigeria. Nilo-Saharan, Saharan, Western, Tebu. 67% lexical similarity with Daza. The majority use Dazaga as a second language, although at a low proficiency level. Some bilingualism in Chadian Arabic. 'Teda' is the name for the people, 'Tedaga' for the language. Many separate groups. Semi-nomadic. Investigation needed: intelligibility with Aza. Well diggers; pastoralists: camels; warriors (Tubu). Muslim.

TOBANGA ***(GABRI-NORTH, GABRI-NORD, NORTHERN GABRI, GABRI)*** [TNG] 30,000 (1999 SIL). Southwest,Tandjilé Prefecture, Laï Subprefecture, around Deressia. Afro-Asiatic, Chadic, East, A, A.2, 2. Dialects: TOBANGA (DERESSIA), MOONDE. A separate language from Gabri (Southern Gabri). Traditional religion, Christian. NT 1978.

TORAM ***(TOROM, TORUM)*** [TRJ] 4,000 (1971 Fedry). Central, Salamat Prefecture, Abou Deïa Subprefecture, southeast of Abou Deïa, south of the Birgit, in and west of Ter. Afro-Asiatic, Chadic, East, B, B.1, 2. A separate language from other Dangla languages. Speakers seem to be shifting to Chadian Arabic. Investigation needed: bilingual proficiency. Muslim.

TUMAK ***(TOUMAK, TUMMOK, TUMAC, DIJE, SARA TOUMAK, TUMAG)*** [TMC] 25,249 (1993 census). Southwest, Moyen-Chari Prefecture, Koumra Subprefecture, around Goundil; southwest of Niellim. Afro-Asiatic, Chadic, East, A, A.1, 1. Dialects: TUMAK, MOTUN (MAWER, MODEN, MODIN, MOD, MOT, MOTIN). 71% lexical similarity between Motun and Tumak. Most Motun speak Sara as second language, but with low proficiency. Erroneously called 'Sara Toumak'. Investigation needed: attitudes toward Motun. Dictionary. NT 1988.

TUNIA ***(TOUNIA, TUNYA, TUN)*** [TUG] 2,255 (1993 census). South, Moyen-Chari Prefecture, Sarh Subprefecture, in Sarh and about three small villages north of Sarh. Niger-Congo, Atlantic-Congo, Volta-Congo, North, Adamawa-Ubangi, Adamawa, Mbum-Day, Bua. Dialects: TUNYA, PERIM. Not intelligible with other Bua languages. 25% are bilingual in Niellim, others in Sara (the majority, but with low proficiency), Chadian Arabic, or French. Perim dialect is extinct. Traditional religion, Christian.

TUPURI ***(TUBURI, TOUBOURI, TOUPOURI, NDORE)*** [TUI] 90,785 in Chad (1993 census). Southwest, Mayo-Kebbi Prefecture, Fianga Subprefecture, around Fianga. Niger-Congo, Atlantic-Congo, Volta-Congo, North, Adamawa-Ubangi, Adamawa, Mbum-Day, Mbum, Northern, Tupuri-Mambai. Dialects: BANG-LING, BANG-WERE, FAALE-PIYEW, PODOKGE, BANG-GO, KAELE, MATA. The first 4 dialects listed are spoken in Chad. Dictionary. NT 1988. See main entry under Cameroon.

UBI ***(OUBI)*** [UBI] 1,100 (1995 SIL). Central, Guéra Prefecture, Mongo Subprefecture, southwest of Tounkoul, around Oubi village. Afro-Asiatic, Chadic, East, B, B.1, 1. 48% lexical similarity with Mawa (closest).

ZAGHAWA ***(SOGHAUA, ZEGGAOUA, ZAGAOUA, ZORHAUA, ZAGAWA, ZEGHAWA, BERRI, BERI-AA, BERIA, BERI, MERIDA, KEBADI, KUYUK, ZAUGE)*** [ZAG] 77,834 in Chad including the Bideyat (1993 census). East, Biltine Prefecture, Iriba Subprefecture, and B.E.T. Prefecture, Ennedi Subprefecture. Nilo-Saharan, Saharan, Eastern. Dialects: TUER-GALA, KOBE-KAPKA, DIRONG-GURUF. The dialects may be spoken on different hills. Bideyat may not be a dialect. The majority use Arabic as second language. Bideyat and Zaghawa are sometimes called 'Beria' (Beri). Muslim. See main entry under Sudan.

ZAN GULA ***(GULA GUERA, GOULA, MORIIL)*** [ZNA] 4,000 (1997 SIL). Southeast, Guéra Prefecture, Melfi Subprefecture, north of Lake Iro, around and to the northwest of Zan. Niger-Congo, Atlantic-Congo, Volta-Congo, North, Adamawa-Ubangi, Adamawa, Mbum-Day, Bua. Dialects: ZAN, CHINGUIL. 46% lexical similarity with Bon Gula. The majority use Chadian Arabic as second language. Together with Bon Gula called 'Gula Guera'. The Gula Iro call the two groups 'Moriil'. Traditional religion, Muslim.

COMOROS ISLANDS

Federal Islamic Republic of the Comoros. Jumhuriyat al-Qumural-Itthadiyah Al-Islamiyah, Comores. National or official language: French. 658,000 (1998 UN). Islands of Grande Comore, Mohéli, and Anjouan. Literacy rate 15% to 46%. Also includes Reunion Creole French 500, Arabic 500. Information mainly from M. Chamanga and N. Guernie 1966-1967; H. and M. Ottenheimer 1976; H. Chagnoux and A. Naribou 1980. Muslim, Christian. Data accuracy estimate: A2. The number of languages listed for Comoros Islands is 5. Of those, all are living languages. Diversity index 0.01.

ARABIC, STANDARD [ABV] Middle east, north Africa, other Muslim countries. Afro-Asiatic, Semitic, Central, South, Arabic. Not a mother tongue. National language. Bible 1984-1991. See main entry under Saudi Arabia.

COMORIAN *(COMORES SWAHILI, KOMORO, COMORO)* [SWB] 493,220 in Comoros Islands together with Shingazidja Comorian (1993 Johnstone). Population total all countries 628,000. Anjouan Island. Also spoken in Madagascar, Mayotte, Réunion. Niger-Congo, Atlantic-Congo, Volta-Congo, Benue-Congo, Bantoid, Southern, Narrow Bantu, Central, G, Swahili (G.40). Dialects: SHINDZWANI (ANJOUAN, SHINDZUANI), SHIMAORE (MAYOTTE). Bilingualism in Swahili, French, Arabic. Literacy rate in second language: 25%. Vanilla, perfume production. Muslim, Christian. NT 1995.

COMORIAN, SHINGAZIDJA [SWS] Shingazidja is on Grande Comore Island (Ngazidja), Shimwali on Mohéli (Mwali). Niger-Congo, Atlantic-Congo, Volta-Congo, Benue-Congo, Bantoid, Southern, Narrow Bantu, Central, G, Swahili (G.40). Dialects: SHIMWALI (MOHÉLI), SHINGAZIDJA (GRANDE COMORE). Nationalism affects language attitudes. Muslim. Bible portions 1976.

FRENCH [FRN] 1,700 in Comoros Islands (1993). Indo-European, Italic, Romance, Italo-Western, Western, Gallo-Iberian, Gallo-Romance, Gallo-Rhaetian, Oïl, French. Language of all formal education except Koranic. Official language. Bible 1530-1986. See main entry under France.

MALAGASY [MEX] 700 in Comoros Islands (1993 Johnstone). Austronesian, Malayo-Polynesian, Western Malayo-Polynesian, Borneo, Barito, East, Malagasy. Most are bilingual in Comorian. It is spoken by a substantial number of residents of Madagascar origin. Traditional religion, Christian, Muslim. Bible 1835-1938. See main entry under Madagascar.

CONGO

People's Republic of the Congo. République Populaire du Congo. Formerly Congo Brazzaville. National or official languages: Lingala, Munukutuba, French. 2,785,000 (1998 UN). Literacy rate 63% to 80% (1996). Also includes Southwest Gbaya, Greek 400, Hausa 4,000, Portuguese 600, Sango 54,000. Information mainly from A. Jacquot 1971; J. Bendor-Samuel 1989; SIL 1982-1998. Christian, traditional religion, Muslim. Blind population 4,000 (1982 WCE). Data accuracy estimate: A2, B. The number of languages listed for Congo is 61. Of those, all are living languages. Diversity index 0.61.

AKWA [AKW] Cuvette Region, Makoua District. Niger-Congo, Atlantic-Congo, Volta-Congo, Benue-Congo, Bantoid, Southern, Narrow Bantu, Northwest, C, Mbosi (C.30).

BABOLE *(SOUTHERN BOMITABA)* [BVX] 4,000 (1989 SIL). Southern half of the Epena District, north-eastern Congo. Niger-Congo, Atlantic-Congo, Volta-Congo, Benue-Congo, Bantoid, Southern, Narrow Bantu, Northwest, C, Ngundi (C.20). Dialects: NORTHERN BABOLE (DZEKE), CENTRAL BABOLE (KINAMI), SOUTHERN BABOLE (BOUANILA). Traditional religion, Christian.

BANGANDU *(BAGANDO, BANGANDO)* [BGF] Niger-Congo, Atlantic-Congo, Volta-Congo, North, Adamawa-Ubangi, Ubangi, Gbaya-Manza-Ngbaka, Southwest. Dialects: BAAGATO, NORTH BANGATO. Investigation needed: intelligibility with Southwest Gbaya. See main entry under Cameroon.

BANGI *(BUBANGI, LOBOBANGI, REBU, DZAMBA, BUNGI, BOBANGI)* [BNI] On Congo river, Cuvette Region, Mossaka District. Niger-Congo, Atlantic-Congo, Volta-Congo, Benue-Congo, Bantoid, Southern, Narrow Bantu, Northwest, C, Bangi-Ntomba (C.40). NT 1909-1922, out of print. See main entry under DRC.

BEEMBE *(KIBEEMBE, BEMBE)* [BEJ] Bouenza Region, east of Madingou. Niger-Congo, Atlantic-Congo, Volta-Congo, Benue-Congo, Bantoid, Southern, Narrow Bantu, Central, H, Kongo (H.10). Dialect: KEENGE (KIKEENGE). Dialect cluster. Differemt from Bembe of DRC.

BEKWEL *(BAKWELE, BAKWIL, BEKWIL)* [BKW] Population total all countries 8,000 to 16,000 (1990 CMA). Sangha Region, parallel to the border with Cameroon, from close to the Gabon border almost to Ouesso. Also spoken in Cameroon, Gabon. Niger-Congo, Atlantic-Congo,

Volta-Congo, Benue-Congo, Bantoid, Southern, Narrow Bantu, Northwest, A, Makaa-Njem (A.80). Different from Baakpe (Bakwiri) of Cameroon. Traditional religion, Christian.

BOMITABA ***(MBOMITABA, MBOMOTABA, BAMITABA)*** [ZMX] 7,000 in Congo (1989 SIL). Population total both countries 7,224. Likouala Region, Epena District, along Likouala-aux-Herbes River. Also spoken in CAR. Niger-Congo, Atlantic-Congo, Volta-Congo, Benue-Congo, Bantoid, Southern, Narrow Bantu, Northwest, C, Ngundi (C.20). Dialects: NORTHERN BOMITABA (MATOKI), CENTRAL BOMITABA (EPENA). Related to Bongili. Traditional religion, Christian.

BOMWALI ***(BOMALI, BOUMOALI, BUMALI, LINO, SANGASANGA)*** [BMW] Population total both countries 5,000 or fewer. Sangha Region, around Ouesso. Also spoken in Cameroon. Niger-Congo, Atlantic-Congo, Volta-Congo, Benue-Congo, Bantoid, Southern, Narrow Bantu, Northwest, A, Makaa-Njem (A.80).

BONGILI ***(BONGIRI, BUNGILI, BUNGIRI)*** [BUI] 4,000. Sangha Region, on and near Sangha River, southeast of Ouesso, as far as Pikounda area, and southwest of Ouesso, Liouesso area. Niger-Congo, Atlantic-Congo, Volta-Congo, Benue-Congo, Bantoid, Southern, Narrow Bantu, Northwest, C, Ngundi (C.20). Different from Bukongo of CAR. NT 1947.

BONJO [BOK] Likouala Region, on and near Oubangui, Motaba, and Ibenga rivers, Dongou and Impfondo districts. Niger-Congo, Atlantic-Congo, Volta-Congo, North, Adamawa-Ubangi, Ubangi, Gbaya-Manza-Ngbaka, East.

BWISI ***(IBWISI, MBWISI)*** [BWZ] Niari Region, Kibangou District, Banda area, on Gabon border. Also spoken in Gabon. Niger-Congo, Atlantic-Congo, Volta-Congo, Benue-Congo, Bantoid, Southern, Narrow Bantu, Northwest, B, Sira (B.40). Different from Talinga-Bwisi of DRC and Uganda.

DOONDO ***(KIDOONDO, DONDO)*** [DOD] Bouenza Region; Nkayi, Madingou, Mfouati, and Boko-Songho districts. Niger-Congo, Atlantic-Congo, Volta-Congo, Benue-Congo, Bantoid, Southern, Narrow Bantu, Central, H, Kongo (H.10). Dialect: KAAMBA (KIKAAMBA). Dialect cluster.

FANG ***(PAMUE, PAHOUIN)*** [FNG] A few in Congo. Small area in extreme northwest. Niger-Congo, Atlantic-Congo, Volta-Congo, Benue-Congo, Bantoid, Southern, Narrow Bantu, Northwest, A, Yaunde-Fang (A.70). Dialects: MAKE, NTUM, OGOWE. Close to Bulu. Bible 1951. See main entry under Gabon.

FRENCH [FRN] 28,000 in Congo (1993). Indo-European, Italic, Romance, Italo-Western, Western, Gallo-Iberian, Gallo-Romance, Gallo-Rhaetian, Oïl, French. Sole language of formal education. Official language. Bible 1530-1986. See main entry under France.

GBAYA, NORTHWEST ***(BAYA)*** [GYA] 2,000 in Congo (1993 Johnstone). Sangha Region, a few scattered areas on Cameroon border. Niger-Congo, Atlantic-Congo, Volta-Congo, North, Adamawa-Ubangi, Ubangi, Gbaya, Gbaya. Bible 1994. See main entry under CAR.

KAKO ***(KAKA, YAKA, NKOXO)*** [KKJ] Scattered areas in extreme north of Likouala Region, on Ibenga and Motaba rivers. Niger-Congo, Atlantic-Congo, Volta-Congo, Benue-Congo, Bantoid, Southern, Narrow Bantu, Northwest, A, Kako (A.90). See main entry under Cameroon.

KÉLÉ ***(AKELE, DIKELE, WESTERN KELE)*** [KEB] Niger-Congo, Atlantic-Congo, Volta-Congo, Benue-Congo, Bantoid, Southern, Narrow Bantu, Northwest, B, Kele (B.20). Bible portions 1855-1879. See main entry under Gabon.

KONGO ***(KIKONGO, CONGO, KIKOONGO)*** [KON] Pool Region, west and northwest of Brazzaville. Niger-Congo, Atlantic-Congo, Volta-Congo, Benue-Congo, Bantoid, Southern, Narrow Bantu, Central, H, Kongo (H.10). Dialects: LAADI (LARI), SUUNDI (CISUUNDI), GHAANGALA (KIGHAANGALA, HANGALA). Other languages of the Kongo group are sometimes regarded as dialects of Kongo (see separate entries for Beembe, Doondo, Kunyi, Vili, Monokutuba, and Kituba). Christian, Muslim. Bible 1905-1933. See main entry under DRC.

KOONZIME ***(NZIME, DJIMU, ZIMU, KONZIME, KOOZIME)*** [NJE] Sangha Region, Souanke District, along Cameroon Border. Niger-Congo, Atlantic-Congo, Volta-Congo, Benue-Congo, Bantoid, Southern, Narrow Bantu, Northwest, A, Makaa-Njem (A.80). Dialects: NZIME, BADJOUE, NDJEM (NJEM), NJEME. NT 1998. See main entry under Cameroon.

KOTA ***(IKOTA, IKUTA)*** [KOQ] Cuvette Region, west of Mbomo; Sangha Region, Liouesso area. Primarily in Gabon. Niger-Congo, Atlantic-Congo, Volta-Congo, Benue-Congo, Bantoid, Southern, Narrow Bantu, Northwest, B, Kele (B.20). Bible portions 1938-1948. See main entry under Gabon.

KOYO [KOH] Cuvette Region, Owando District, around Owando. Niger-Congo, Atlantic-Congo, Volta-Congo, Benue-Congo, Bantoid, Southern, Narrow Bantu, Northwest, C, Mbosi (C.30). SVO.

KUNYI ***(KIKUNYI, KUGNI)*** [KNF] 52,000 (1984 census). Bouenza and Niari regions, south and southeast from Makabana to the DRC border. Niger-Congo, Atlantic-Congo, Volta-Congo, Benue-Congo, Bantoid, Southern, Narrow Bantu, Central, H, Kongo (H.10). Dialects: SUUNDI (KISUUNDI), NYAANGA (KINYAANGA). A dialect cluster.

LIKUBA ***(KUBA)*** [KXX] Cuvette Region, on the Congo River, just above the mouth of the Sangha River. Niger-Congo, Atlantic-Congo, Volta-Congo, Benue-Congo, Bantoid, Southern, Narrow Bantu, Northwest, C, Mbosi (C.30).

LIKWALA ***(LIKOUALA, KWALA)*** [KWC] 28,000 (1984 census). Cuvette Region, on lower reaches of the Likouala-Mossaka, Sangha, and Likouala-aux-Herbes rivers. Niger-Congo, Atlantic-Congo, Volta-Congo, Benue-Congo, Bantoid, Southern, Narrow Bantu, Northwest, C, Mbosi (C.30).

LINGALA ***(NGALA)*** [LIN] 300,000 in Congo (1993 SIL). Center and north. Niger-Congo, Atlantic-Congo, Volta-Congo, Benue-Congo, Bantoid, Southern, Narrow Bantu, Northwest, C, Bangi-Ntomba (C.40), Lusengo. National language. Literacy rate in first language: 10% to 30%. Literacy rate in second language: 25% to 75%. Bible 1970. See main entry under DRC.

LOBALA [LOQ] (40,000 in DRC; 1986 SIL). Niger-Congo, Atlantic-Congo, Volta-Congo, Benue-Congo, Bantoid, Southern, Narrow Bantu, Northwest, C, Bangi-Ntomba (C.40). See main entry under DRC.

LUMBU ***(ILUMBU)*** [LUP] Niari Region, Kibangou District, between Kibangou and Gabon border. Primarily in Gabon. Niger-Congo, Atlantic-Congo, Volta-Congo, Benue-Congo, Bantoid, Southern, Narrow Bantu, Northwest, B, Sira (B.40). Bible portions 1933-1966. See main entry under Gabon.

MANGALA ***(NGALA)*** [MGH] Likouala Region, on the west bank of the Oubangui River, upstream from the confluence with the Congo River. Niger-Congo, Atlantic-Congo, Volta-Congo, Benue-Congo, Bantoid, Southern, Narrow Bantu, Northwest, C, Bangi-Ntomba (C.40), Lusengo. Investigation needed: intelligibility with Lingala, Bangala, Lusengo.

MBAMA ***(LEMBAAMBA, MBAMBA, MBAAMA, OBAMBA)*** [MBM] Lekoumou Region, Bambama District. Niger-Congo, Atlantic-Congo, Volta-Congo, Benue-Congo, Bantoid, Southern, Narrow Bantu, Northwest, B, Mbere (B.60). 81% lexical similarity with Teghe, 77% with Mbere, 66% with Tsaayi. See main entry under Gabon.

MBANDJA ***(MBANZA, MBANJA)*** [ZMZ] A few in Congo. Extreme north of Likouala Region, close to Oubangui River. Niger-Congo, Atlantic-Congo, Volta-Congo, North, Adamawa-Ubangi, Ubangi, Banda, Southern. NT 1998. See main entry under DRC.

MBANGWE ***(MBAHOUIN, M'BAHOUIN)*** [ZMN] Population total both countries 2,000 to 7,000 (1990 CMA). Lekoumou Region, small groups in Bambama District. Also spoken in Gabon. Niger-Congo, Atlantic-Congo, Volta-Congo, Benue-Congo, Bantoid, Southern, Narrow Bantu, Northwest, B, Kele (B.20).

MBERE ***(MBÉDÉ, MBÉTÉ, LIMBEDE)*** [MDT] Population total both countries 45,000 to 60,000 (1990 CMA). Cuvette Region, Kelle and northern Ewo districts. Also spoken in Gabon. Niger-Congo, Atlantic-Congo, Volta-Congo, Benue-Congo, Bantoid, Southern, Narrow Bantu, Northwest, B, Mbere (B.60). Dialect: NGWII. 77% lexical similarity with Mbamba, 76% with Ngungwel, 74% with Teghe, 70% with Tsaayi. The people are called 'Ambede'. Different from Mbre (Mbere) in CAR. Traditional religion, Christian.

MBOKO ***(MBOXO, MBUKU)*** [MDU] Cuvette Region, western part of Makoua District. Niger-Congo, Atlantic-Congo, Volta-Congo, Benue-Congo, Bantoid, Southern, Narrow Bantu, Northwest, C, Mbosi (C.30). Dialect: NGARE. A dialect cluster.

MBOSI ***(MBOSHI, MBOCHI, MBOSHE, EMBOSI)*** [MDW] 70,000 to 100,000 (1998). Cuvette Region, Owando and Mossaka districts, but not as far north as Owando. Plateaux Region, Abala District. Niger-Congo, Atlantic-Congo, Volta-Congo, Benue-Congo, Bantoid, Southern, Narrow Bantu, Northwest, C, Mbosi (C.30).

MOI ***(LEMOI)*** [MOW] West bank of Oubangui River, at mouth of Alima River, south of Mossaka. Niger-Congo, Atlantic-Congo, Volta-Congo, Benue-Congo, Bantoid, Southern, Narrow Bantu, Northwest, C, Bangi-Ntomba (C.40).

MONZOMBO ***(MONJOMBO, MONDJEMBO, MONZUMBO)*** [MOJ] 6,000 in Congo (1993 Johnstone). Population total all countries 13,000. Extreme northeast, on Oubangui River. Also spoken in CAR, DRC. Niger-Congo, Atlantic-Congo, Volta-Congo, North, Adamawa-Ubangi, Ubangi, Sere-Ngbaka-Mba, Ngbaka-Mba, Ngbaka, Western, Monzombo.

MUNUKUTUBA [MKW] 1,156,800 or 60% of the population (1987 SIL). Mainly along roads and railroads westwards from Brazzaville and northwards to Mayoko. Creole, Kongo based. Close to Kituba of DRC. The main language of the south. National language. Literacy rate in first language: 5% to 10%. Literacy rate in second language: 15% to 25%. Bible portions 1989.

NCHINCHEGE [NCQ] Plateaux Region, Lekana District, between the Leketi River and the Gabon border. Possibly also in Gabon. Niger-Congo, Atlantic-Congo, Volta-Congo, Benue-Congo, Bantoid, Southern, Narrow Bantu, Northwest, B, Teke (B.70).

NDASA ***(ANDASA)*** [NDA] Population total both countries 5,000 (1990 CMA). Lekoumou Region, west of Zanaga. Also spoken in Gabon. Niger-Congo, Atlantic-Congo, Volta-Congo, Benue-Congo, Bantoid, Southern, Narrow Bantu, Northwest, B, Kele (B.20).

NDUMU ***(LENDUMU, MINDUUMO, MINDUMBU, ONDOUMBO)*** [NMD] Lekoumou Region, Bambama District. Niger-Congo, Atlantic-Congo, Volta-Congo, Benue-Congo, Bantoid, Southern, Narrow Bantu, Northwest, B, Mbere (B.60). Dialects: EPIGI, KANANDJOHO, KUYA, NYANI. See main entry under Gabon.

NGBAKA [NGA] 2,000 to 3,000 in Congo (1987 SIL). Likouala Region, small group on west bank of Oubangui River, midway between Impfondo and confluence with the Congo River. Niger-Congo, Atlantic-Congo, Volta-Congo, North, Adamawa-Ubangi, Ubangi, Gbaya-Manza-Ngbaka, East. Related to Gbaya of CAR and Cameroon. Different from Ngbaka Ma'bo. Bible 1995. See main entry under DRC.

NGBAKA MA'BO ***(NGBAKA LIMBA, MBAKA, MBACCA, BWAKA, BOUAKA, NBWAKA, GBALA, MA'BO)*** [NBM] Niger-Congo, Atlantic-Congo, Volta-Congo, North, Adamawa-Ubangi, Ubangi, Sere-Ngbaka-Mba, Ngbaka-Mba, Ngbaka, Western, Bwaka. Close to Gilima. Bilingualism in Lingala. Investigation needed: intelligibility with Gilima. Bible portions 1936-1937. See main entry under CAR.

NGOM ***(UNGOM, ANGOM, BANGOM, BANGOMO, ONGOM)*** [NRA] Population total both countries 11,000 (1977 Voegelin and Voegelin). Cuvette Region, northwest of Mbomo. Also spoken in Gabon. Niger-Congo, Atlantic-Congo, Volta-Congo, Benue-Congo, Bantoid, Southern, Narrow Bantu, Northwest, B, Kele (B.20). Bible portions 1910.

NGUNDI ***(INGUNDI, NGONDI)*** [NDN] Sangha Region, east of Ouesso. Also spoken in CAR. Niger-Congo, Atlantic-Congo, Volta-Congo, Benue-Congo, Bantoid, Southern, Narrow Bantu, Northwest, C, Ngundi (C.20). Different from Gundi of CAR, which is Adamawa-Ubangi.

NGUNGWONI ***(NGU NGWONI)*** [NGF] Southwest corner of Plateaux Region, southwest of Djambala. Niger-Congo, Atlantic-Congo, Volta-Congo, Benue-Congo, Bantoid, Southern, Narrow Bantu, Northwest, B, Teke (B.70).

NJEBI ***(NZEBI, INJEBI, NDJABI, NJEVI, BINZABI, NJABI, YINZEBI, YINJEBI)*** [NZB] Niari Province, Mayoko District. Niger-Congo, Atlantic-Congo, Volta-Congo, Benue-Congo, Bantoid, Southern, Narrow Bantu, Northwest, B, Njebi (B.50). NT 1968-1979. See main entry under Gabon.

POL ***(POMO, PORI, PUL, CONGO POL)*** [PMM] Population total both countries 27,000 (1982 SIL). Sangha Region, north of Ouesso, on borders with Cameroon and CAR. Not in CAR. Also spoken in Cameroon. Niger-Congo, Atlantic-Congo, Volta-Congo, Benue-Congo, Bantoid, Southern, Narrow Bantu, Northwest, A, Kako (A.90).

PUNU ***(IPUNU, YIPUNU, PUNO, POUNO, IPOUNOU)*** [PUU] Total of all Sira-Punu languages in Congo 80,000 or 4% of the population (1993 Johnstone). Niger-Congo, Atlantic-Congo, Volta-Congo, Benue-Congo, Bantoid, Southern, Narrow Bantu, Northwest, B, Sira (B.40). NT 1977. See main entry under Gabon.

TEKE, CENTRAL ***(KITEKE)*** [TEC] 35,000 or more in Congo (1984). 490,000 all Teke languages in Congo (1993 Johnstone). Population total both countries 35,000 or more (1988 SIL). Tyoo in Pool Region, Ngabe District. Boo and Njyunjyu in Plateaux Region, Djambala District; Njyunjyu around Djambala, Boo eastwards to Congo River. Also spoken in DRC. Niger-Congo, Atlantic-Congo, Volta-Congo, Benue-Congo, Bantoid, Southern, Narrow Bantu, Northwest, B, Teke (B.70). Dialects: TYOO (ITYOO, TEO, TIO, TIOO, TYO), BOO (BOÕ, EBOO, EBOOM, BAMBOMA), NJYUNJYU (NJIUNJIU). The Aboo speak the dialect of the ancient Teke kings. Boõ has 63% lexical similarity with Yaa, 69% with Laali, 75% with Tsaayi, 85% with Tyee (West Teke), 86% with Kukua (South Teke), 89% with Ngungwel (Northeastern Teke), 79% with Tege (Northern Teke). Speakers of Eboo called 'Aboo'.

TEKE, EASTERN ***(KITEKE, IBALI)*** [TEK] On Congo River, Pool region, close to Brazzaville. Niger-Congo, Atlantic-Congo, Volta-Congo, Benue-Congo, Bantoid, Southern, Narrow Bantu, Northwest, B, Teke (B.70). Bible portions 1889-1905. See main entry under DRC.

TEKE, NORTHEASTERN ***(NGUNGWEL, NGUNGULU, NGANGOULOU)*** [NGZ] 45,000 (1988 SIL). Plateaux Province, Gamboma District. Niger-Congo, Atlantic-Congo, Volta-Congo, Benue-Congo, Bantoid, Southern, Narrow Bantu, Northwest, B, Teke (B.70). Dialect: MPU (MPUMPUM). 89% lexical similarity with Boo, 81% with Kukua, 77% with Teghe, 76% with Tsaayi and Mbere, 75% with Tyee, 68% with Laali, 61% with Yaa. The speakers would not accept Eboo (Central Teke) or Kikukua (Southern Teke) literature. They consider themselves a distinct people from other Teke groups. The people are called 'Angungwel'.

TEKE, NORTHERN ***(TEGHE, ITEGHE, TEGE)*** [TEG] 30,000 in Congo (1987 SIL), including 9,000 Nzkini, 15,000 Teghe. Population total both countries 40,000 to 50,000. Cuvette Region, Ewo and Okoyo districts. Some in Plateaux Region, Abala District, west of Mpama River. Also spoken in Gabon. Niger-Congo, Atlantic-Congo, Volta-Congo, Benue-Congo, Bantoid, Southern, Narrow Bantu, Northwest, B, Teke (B.70). Dialects: KATEGHE (NZIKINI), KETEGHE. 81% lexical similarity with Mbamba, 79% with Kukua, 77% with Ngungwel, 76% with Boo, 75% with Tyee, 74% with Mbere, 73% with Laali and Tsaayi, 67% with Teghe.

TEKE, SOUTH CENTRAL ***(KITEKE)*** [IFM] 5,000 or more (1988 SIL). Pool Region. Fuumu is immediately north of Brazzaville; Wuumu extends north and northwest to the Lefini River. Niger-Congo, Atlantic-Congo, Volta-Congo, Benue-Congo, Bantoid, Southern, Narrow Bantu, Northwest, B, Teke (B.70). Dialects: FUUMU (IFUUMU, MFUMU), WUUMU (IWUUMU, WUMBU).

TEKE, SOUTHERN ***(KUKWA, KUKUYA, KIKUWA, CHIKUYA, KOUKOUYA)*** [KKW] 21,800 (1984). Plateaux Province, Lekana District, east of Leketi River. Niger-Congo, Atlantic-Congo, Volta-Congo, Benue-Congo, Bantoid, Southern, Narrow Bantu, Northwest, B, Teke (B.70). 86% lexical similarity with Boo, 85% with Tyee, 81% with Ngungwel, 80% with Tsaayi, 79% with Teghe, 75% with Laali, 70% with Yaa. They would not accept Ngungwel (Northeastern Teke) literature. Strong ethnic pride.

TEKE, WESTERN ***(WEST TEKE)*** [TEZ] 60,000 or more in Congo including 10,000 Yaka (1988). Population total both countries 92,000. Lekoumou Region, in arc to west, south and east of Mbama, east and northeast from Mossendjo. Also spoken in Gabon. Niger-Congo, Atlantic-Congo, Volta-Congo, Benue-Congo, Bantoid, Southern, Narrow Bantu, Northwest, B, Teke (B.70). Dialects: TSAAYI (GETSAAYI, TSAYA, TSAYE, TSAYI), LAALI (ILAALI), YAA (IYAA, IYAKA, YAKA), TYEE (ETYEE). Yaa has 91% lexical similarity with Laali, 74% with Tsaayi, 69% with Tyee; Laali has 81% with Tsaayi, 78% with Tyee; Tsaayi has 76% with Tyee, 80% with Kukua; Tyee has 85% with Kukua and Boo. Bible portions 1933.

TSAANGI ***(ITSANGI, TCENGUI, TCHANGUI, ICAANGI)*** [TSA] Niari Region, north and northwest of Mossendjo. Niger-Congo, Atlantic-Congo, Volta-Congo, Benue-Congo, Bantoid, Southern, Narrow Bantu, Northwest, B, Njebi (B.50). See main entry under Gabon.

VILI ***(TSIVILI, CIVILI, FIOTE, FIOT)*** [VIF] Population total both countries 5,000 to 6,000 (1990 CMA). Kouilou Province, along the coast between the Angola and Gabon borders. Yoombe Island. Also spoken in Gabon. Niger-Congo, Atlantic-Congo, Volta-Congo, Benue-Congo, Bantoid, Southern, Narrow Bantu, Central, H, Kongo (H.10). Dialect: YOOMBE (YOMBE, CIYOOMBE). A dialect cluster. The people are called 'Bavili'. Coastal.

WUMBVU ***(WUMVU)*** [WUM] Population total both countries 4,000 to 24,000 (1990 CMA). Also spoken in Gabon. Niger-Congo, Atlantic-Congo, Volta-Congo, Benue-Congo, Bantoid, Southern, Narrow Bantu, Northwest, B, Kele (B.20).

YAKA ***(AKA, BABINGA, BINGA, BEKA, MÒÁKA)*** [AXK] 15,000 in Congo (1986 Cavalli-Storza). Northeast corner. Niger-Congo, Atlantic-Congo, Volta-Congo, Benue-Congo, Bantoid, Southern, Narrow Bantu, Northwest, C, Ngando (C.10). Dialects: BASESE (EASTERN AKA), BAMBENZELE (WESTERN AKA). Mraka is singular, Beka plural. Different from the Baka language of Cameroon and Gabon, which is Ubangi. There may be more than one pygmy language in Congo. Nomadic. Pygmies. Forest. Hunter-gatherers. Traditional religion. See main entry under CAR.

YOMBE ***(KIYOMBE, KIOMBI, BAYOMBE)*** [YOM] Niger-Congo, Atlantic-Congo, Volta-Congo, Benue-Congo, Bantoid, Southern, Narrow Bantu, Central, H, Kongo (H.10). Dialects: MBALA (MUMBALA), VUNGUNYA (KIVUNGUNYA, YOMBE CLASSIQUE). Distinct enough from Kongo-Fioti to need separate literature. Christian, traditional religion. See main entry under DRC.

CÔTE D'IVOIRE

Ivory Coast. République de la Côte d'Ivoire. National or official language: French. 14,292,000 (1998 UN). Literacy rate 42.4% to 45%. Also includes Malba Birifor, Bissa 63,000, Dogoso, Maasina Fulfulde 1,200, Glaro-Twabo, Eastern Karaboro 5,000, Khe, Mòoré, Nafaanra, Sìcìté Sénoufo, Siamou, Southern Toussian, Turka, Vietnamese, people from Burkina Faso 1,600,000, from Mali 754,000, from Guinea 238,000, from Liberia 200,000 or more, others 345,000 (1993). Information mainly from M. Delafosse 1904; J. Bendor-Samuel 1989; SIL 1973-1999. Muslim, traditional religion, Christian. Blind population 50,000 (1982 WCE). Deaf institutions: 1. Data accuracy estimate: A2. The number of languages listed for Côte d'Ivoire is 78. Of those, 77 are living languages and 1 is extinct. Diversity index 0.91.

ABÉ ***(ABBÉ, ABBEY, ABI)*** [ABA] 170,000 (1995 SIL), including perhaps 10,000 to 20,000 in Abidjan (1991 S. Beasley SIL). Southern Department, Subprefecture of Agboville (except Krobou Canton) and Abbe Canton of Tiassale Subprefecture. 70 villages. Niger-Congo, Atlantic-Congo, Volta-Congo, Kwa, Nyo, Agneby. Dialects: TIOFFO, MORIE, ABBEY-VE, KOS. SVO, postpositions, tonal. Literacy rate in first language: 5% to 10%. Literacy rate in second language: 50% to 75%. Tropical forest. Coastal plains. Agriculturalists: manioc, yams, plantains, tomatoes, hot peppers; cash crops: cocoa, coffee; palm oil; some professionals. Sea level to 100 feet. Christian, traditional religion, Muslim, Other. Bible portions 1967-1980.

ABIDJI ***(ABIJI)*** [ABI] 50,500 (1993 SIL). Department of Abidjan, Subprefecture of Sikensi (12 villages) and a few villages in Subprefecture of Dabou. Niger-Congo, Atlantic-Congo, Volta-Congo, Kwa, Nyo, Agneby. Dialects: ENYEMBE, OGBRU. Bilingualism in French, Jula, Baoule, Adioukrou. Tonal, nasalization on syllable. Literacy rate in first language: 1% to 5%. Literacy rate in second language: 25% to 50%. Christian, other. Bible portions 1978-1988.

ABRON ***(BRONG, BRON, DOMA)*** [ABR] 131,700 in Côte d'Ivoire (1993 SIL). Eastern Department, subprefectures of Tanda and Bondoukou. Niger-Congo, Atlantic-Congo, Volta-Congo, Kwa, Nyo,

Potou-Tano, Tano, Central, Akan. Some are bilingual in Kulango or Jula. Most have good comprehension of Asante Twi in Ghana. Called 'Abron' in Côte d'Ivoire and 'Brong' in Ghana. Christian, Muslim, traditional religion, other. See main entry under Ghana.

ABURE *(ABOURÉ, ABULE, AKAPLASS, ABONWA)* [ABU] 55,120 (1993 SIL). Southern Department, Subprefecture of Bonoua, some in Subprefecture of Grand Bassam, many in Abidjan. Niger-Congo, Atlantic-Congo, Volta-Congo, Kwa, Nyo, Potou-Tano, Tano, Western. Closest to Anyin. Also close to Baule and Nzema. Many speakers are bilingual in Anyin. Ethnic subgroups: Eyive (majority), Ehie, Ossouon. Literacy rate in first language: 5% to 10%. Literacy rate in second language: 25% to 50%. Christian, traditional religion, Muslim, other.

ADIOUKROU *(ADYUKRU, ADJUKRU, ADYOUKROU, AJUKRU)* [ADJ] 100,000 or more (1999 SIL). Southern Department, Subprefecture of Dabou, in 49 villages. Niger-Congo, Atlantic-Congo, Volta-Congo, Kwa, Nyo, Agneby. Literacy rate in first language: 30% to 60%. Literacy rate in second language: 25% to 50%. Christian, Muslim, other. NT 1998.

AIZI, APROUMU *(AHIZI, APRWE, APROU, OPROU, APROUMU)* [AHP] 6,500 (1999 SIL). Southern Department, on both banks of the Ebrié Lagoon in Jacqueville Subprefecture (villages of Attoutou A-new quarter, Attoutou B, Tefredji, Koko, Bapo-Allaba B, Taboth) and in the village of Allaba in Dabou Subprefecture. Niger-Congo, Atlantic-Congo, Volta-Congo, Kru, Aizi. Those born before independence are more likely to know Adioukrou than younger Aizi. Young people learn French in school. Their name for the Aizi people: 'Aproin'. They call Lélémrin (Tiagbamrin) 'Chicalé', and Mobumrin 'Amaboué'. 'Akabu', 'Opro', 'Saptomrin', and 'Tchavamrin' are names used in different Mobu and Lélé villages to refer to Apro. The Adioukrou say 'Ed-eyng' and Alladian 'Ezibo" to refer to all the Aizi groups. Literacy rate in second language: 25% to 50%. Fishermen, fish merchants. Christian, Muslim, other.

AIZI, MOBUMRIN *(AHIZI)* [AHM] 2,000 (1999 SIL). Southern Department, Jacqueville Subprefecture, 2 villages (Abraco and Abraniamiambo) on the north bank of the Ebrié Lagoon. Niger-Congo, Atlantic-Congo, Volta-Congo, Kru, Aizi. Those born before independence are more likely to know Adioukru than younger Aizi. Young people learn French in school. Speakers are 'Mouin'. Their name for the Aizi people: 'Frukpu'. The Adioukrou say 'Ed-eyng' and the Alladian 'Ezibo' to refer to all the Aizi groups. Literacy rate in second language: 25% to 50%. Fish merchants. Christian, Muslim, other.

AIZI, TIAGBAMRIN *(AHIZI, TIAGBA, LÉLÉMRIN)* [AHI] 9,000 (1999 SIL). Southern Department, Jacqueville Subprefecture, both banks of the Ebrié Lagoon, in the villages of Tiagba, Nigui-Assoko, Nigui-Saff, Tiémié, and Attoutou B, old quarter. Niger-Congo, Atlantic-Congo, Volta-Congo, Kru, Aizi. Not intelligible with Mobumrin Aizi, even though both are Kru languages. Those born before independence are more likely to know Adioukru than younger speakers. Young people learn French in school. Their name for the Aizi people is 'Prokpo' ('Krokpo' in Tiagba town). 'Tiagbamrin' means 'language of Tiagba'. People in other villages say they speak 'Lélémrin'. The Adioukrou say 'Ed-eyng' and the Alladian 'Ezibo' to refer to all the Aizi groups. Literacy rate in second language: 25% to 50%. Fishermen, fish merchants. Christian, Muslim, other.

ALLADIAN *(ALLADYAN, ALLAGIA, ALLAGIAN)* [ALD] 23,000 (1993 SIL). Southern Department, along the plain between the coast and the Ebrie Lagoon in 21 villages in the Subprefecture of Jacqueville. Niger-Congo, Atlantic-Congo, Volta-Congo, Kwa, Nyo, Avikam-Alladian. Literacy rate in second language: 25% to 50%. Christian, Muslim, traditional religion, other. Bible portions 1937-1968.

ANYIN *(ANYI, AGNI)* [ANY] 610,000 in Côte d'Ivoire (1993 SIL), 10,000 to 100,000 second language users in Côte d'Ivoire. Population total both countries 810,000. Southern Region, Abidjan and Aboisso departments; East-Central Region, Abengourou and Agnibilekrou departments; North-East Region, Bondoukou and Tanda departments; North-Central Region, M'bahiakro Department; and Central Region, Bongouanou and Daoukro departments. Between Kulango and Abron to the north; Nzema, Abure, and the Lagoon languages to the south; Baulé to the west; Twi in Ghana to the east. Also spoken in Ghana. Niger-Congo, Atlantic-Congo, Volta-Congo, Kwa, Nyo, Potou-Tano, Tano, Central, Bia, Northern. Dialects: SANVI, INDENIE, BINI, BONA, MORONOU, DJUABLIN, ANO, ABE, BARABO, ALANGUA. Closest to Baoulé. Also close to Nzema. Bilingualism in French, Jula, Twi. Literacy rate in first language: 1% to 5%. Literacy rate in second language: 25% to 50%. Radio programs. Christian, traditional religion, Muslim, other. NT 1997.

ANYIN, MOROFO *(MOROFO)* [MTB] Southern, Eastern, and Central departments, Moronou. Niger-Congo, Atlantic-Congo, Volta-Congo, Kwa, Nyo, Potou-Tano, Tano, Central, Bia, Northern. 'Morofue' refers to a Morofo speaker.

ATTIÉ *(ATIE, AKYE, AKIE, ATCHE, ATSHE)* [ATI] 381,000 (1993 SIL). 34,000 live in Abidjan. Abidjan Department, subprefectures of Anyama, and Alepe; and Adzope Department, subprefectures of Adzope, Affery, Agou, Akoupe, Yakasse-Attobrou. Niger-Congo, Atlantic-Congo, Volta-Congo, Kwa, Nyo, Attie. Dialects: NAINDIN, KETIN, BODIN. The Bodin dialect is the most prestigious and numerous. Bilingualism in French, Jula, Anyin, Ebrie, Abbey, Baoule. Literacy rate in first language: 1% to 5%. Literacy rate in second language: 50% to 75%. Radio programs. Christian, traditional religion, other. NT 1995.

AVIKAM ***(AVEKOM, BRIGNAN, BRINYA, GBANDA, KWAKWA, LAHU)*** [AVI] 21,000 (1993 SIL). Southern Department, along the coastal plain of Grand Lahou, Avikam Canton. Niger-Congo, Atlantic-Congo, Volta-Congo, Kwa, Nyo, Avikam-Alladian. Literacy rate in second language: 25% to 50%. Christian, traditional religion, Muslim, other. Bible portions 1957.

BAKWÉ [BAK] 10,300 (1993 SIL). Southern and West Central departments, prefectures of Sassandra, Soubre, San Pedro. Niger-Congo, Atlantic-Congo, Volta-Congo, Kru, Eastern, Bakwe. Dialects: DEFA, DEPLE, DAFA, NIGAGBA, NYINAGBI. Closest to Godié. Literacy rate in first language: Below 1%. Literacy rate in second language: 5% to 15%. Christian, traditional religion, Muslim, other.

BAMBARA ***(BAMANA, BAMANAKAN)*** [BRA] 5,500 in Côte d'Ivoire (1993 SIL). Niger-Congo, Mande, Western, Central-Southwestern, Central, Manding-Jogo, Manding-Vai, Manding-Mokole, Manding, Manding-East, Northeastern Manding, Bamana. Trade language. Traders. Muslim, Christian, traditional religion, other. Bible 1961-1987. See main entry under Mali.

BAOULÉ ***(BAULE, BAWULE)*** [BCI] 2,130,000 (1993 SIL). Central Department, widespread throughout southern Côte d'Ivoire. Niger-Congo, Atlantic-Congo, Volta-Congo, Kwa, Nyo, Potou-Tano, Tano, Central, Bia, Northern. Closely related to Anyin. Many sub-groups, but all claim to understand the standard variety. Largest ethnic group in Côte d'Ivoire. Literacy rate in first language: 10% to 30%. Literacy rate in second language: 25% to 50%. Radio programs. Traditional religion, Christian, Muslim, other. Bible 1998.

BENG ***(NGAIN, NGAN, NGUIN, NGIN, NGEN, GAN, BEN)*** [NHB] 17,000 (1993 SIL). Central Department. 20 villages in the northeast corner of M'bahiakro Subprefecture, and 2 villages in Prikro Subprefecture. Niger-Congo, Mande, Eastern, Southeastern, Nwa-Ben, Ben-Gban. Somewhat bilingual in Baoulé, Jula, or French. Literacy rate in first language: Below 1%. Literacy rate in second language: Below 5%. Traditional religion, Muslim, Christian.

BÉTÉ, DALOA ***(DALOUA BÉTÉ, NORTHERN BÉTÉ)*** [BEV] 130,000 (1993 SIL). All Bété varieties: 532,000 (1995). West Central Department, Daloa Subprefecture. Niger-Congo, Atlantic-Congo, Volta-Congo, Kru, Eastern, Bete, Western. Literacy rate in first language: 1% to 5%. Literacy rate in second language: 25% to 50%. Christian, traditional religion, Christian, Muslim, other. NT 1996.

BÉTÉ, GAGNOA ***(GAGNOUA-BÉTÉ, SHYEN, EASTERN BÉTÉ)*** [BTG] 150,000 (1989 SIL). Gagnoa Subprefecture. Niger-Congo, Atlantic-Congo, Volta-Congo, Kru, Eastern, Bete, Eastern. Dialects: NEKEDI, ZADIE, NIABRE, KPAKOLO, ZEBIE, GUEBIE, GBADI (GBADIE, BADIE). Literacy rate in first language: Below 1%. Literacy rate in second language: 25% to 50%. Christian, traditional religion, Muslim, other.

BÉTE, GUIBEROUA ***(CENTRAL BÉTÉ, WESTERN BÉTÉ)*** [BET] 130,000 (1993 SIL). All Biti: 532,000 (1993 SIL). West Central Department, Daloua, Issia, Guiberoua, Soubre, Buyo, Gregbeu, and Ouaragahio subprefectures. Niger-Congo, Atlantic-Congo, Volta-Congo, Kru, Eastern, Bete, Western. Dialects: SOUBRÉ, GUIBEROUA. Closest to Godie. There are 18 dialects. Different from Bete of Nigeria and Cameroon. Literacy rate in first language: Below 1%. Literacy rate in second language: 15% to 25%. Christian, traditional religion, Muslim, other. NT 1982.

BETI ***(EOTILE)*** [EOT] 3,181 (1988 census). Southern Department, villages of Vitre I and Vitre II, Subprefecture of Grand Bassam. Niger-Congo, Atlantic-Congo, Volta-Congo, Kwa, Nyo, Potou-Tano, Tano, Western. Bilingualism in Anyi, Nzema, Abure, Ebrie, Mbato, Attie. Only a few old men remember a few words from the 'pure' Beti dialect. The last speaker of the 'pure' form of Beti died about 1993. Present speakers use a variety that is heavily influenced by surrounding languages. Investigation needed: bilingual proficiency in Anyin, Nzema. Christian, traditional religion, other.

BIRIFOR, SOUTHERN ***(BIRIFO)*** [BIV] 4,308 in Côte d'Ivoire (1993 SIL). Northeast corner. Niger-Congo, Atlantic-Congo, Volta-Congo, North, Gur, Central, Northern, Oti-Volta, Western, Northwest, Dagaari-Birifor, Birifor. A separate language from Wali, Dagaari, and Malba-Birifor of Burkina Faso, and not inherently intelligible with them. Traditional religion, Christian, Muslim, other. Bible portions 1993. See main entry under Ghana.

CERMA ***(GOUIN, GUIN, GWE, GWEN, KIRMA)*** [GOT] 1,700 in Côte d'Ivoire (1991). Five villages around Ouangolodougo, north of Ferkessedougou. Niger-Congo, Atlantic-Congo, Volta-Congo, North, Gur, Central, Southern, Kirma-Tyurama. Traditional religion. Bible portions 1995. See main entry under Burkina Faso.

DAHO-DOO [DAS] 4,000 (1996 SIL). Western Department, just north of Tai, and south of the Guéré. Niger-Congo, Atlantic-Congo, Volta-Congo, Kru, Western, Wee, Guere-Krahn. Preliminary intelligibility testing indicates Doo could understand Wobe of Kouibli well, and Daho could understand Guéré of Guiglo well. The closest lexical similarity they have to any Guéré variety is 80%, and the lowest is 30%. Lexical similarity between Daho and Doo is 92%. The Daho and Doo consider themselves to be Guéré.

DAN ***(YACOUBA, YAKUBA, DA, GIO, GIO-DAN)*** [DAF] 800,000 in Cote d'Ivoire (1993 M. Bolli SIL) including 400,000 in Eastern Dan, 400,000 in western Dan. Population total all countries 1,020,000 to 1,220,000. Prefectures of Man (except Kouibly and Facoubly), Danané, Biankouma (except Toura), plus 19 villages in the Prefecture of Touba. Also spoken in Guinea, Liberia. Niger-Congo, Mande, Eastern, Southeastern, Guro-Tura, Tura-Dan-Mano, Tura-Dan. Dialects: GWEETAAWU (EASTERN DAN), BLOWO (WESTERN DAN). At least 20 subdialects. Bilingualism in Jula, French. Called 'Gio' in Liberia. Literacy rate in first language: 1% or more. Literacy rate in second language: 25% to 50%. Agriculturalists: rice, manioc, coffee, cocoa. Traditional religion, Christian, Muslim, other. NT 1981-1993.

DEG ***(DEGHA, ACULO, JANELA, MO, BURO, MMFO)*** [MZW] 1,100 in Côte d'Ivoire (1991). Niger-Congo, Atlantic-Congo, Volta-Congo, North, Gur, Central, Southern, Grusi, Western. NT 1990. See main entry under Ghana.

DIDA, LAKOTA ***(DIEKO, GABO, SATRO, GUÉBIE, BRABORI, ZIKI)*** [DIC] 93,800 (1993 SIL). All Dida: 195,400 (1993 SIL). Region around the town of Lakota. Niger-Congo, Atlantic-Congo, Volta-Congo, Kru, Eastern, Dida. Dialect: VATA. A separate language from Yocoboué Dida. Literacy rate in first language: Below 1%. Literacy rate in second language: 25% to 50%. Traditional religion.

DIDA, YOCOBOUÉ [GUD] 101,600 (1993 SIL), including 7,100 Guitry, 94,500 Divo. Southern Department, Guitry Subprefecture, area around town of Guitry. Niger-Congo, Atlantic-Congo, Volta-Congo, Kru, Eastern, Dida. Dialects: LOZOUA (GUITRY, YOCOBOUE, YOKOUBOUÉ, GAKPA, GOUDOU, KAGOUÉ), DIVO. Lakota Dida is marginally intelligible with Yocoboué. Bilingualism in French. Guitry is prestigious. More survey is needed in Dida area. Literacy rate in first language: 1% to 5%. Literacy rate in second language: 25% to 50%. Radio programs, TV. Christian, Muslim, traditional religion, other. Bible portions 1930-1972.

EBRIÉ ***(TYAMA, KYAMA, TSAMA, CAMA, CAMAN, TCHAMAN)*** [EBR] 75,859 (1988 census). Abidjan Department, urban Abidjan, the Subprefecture of Dabou, and the Subprefecture of Bingerville. 57 villages, including 27 in Abidjan. Niger-Congo, Atlantic-Congo, Volta-Congo, Kwa, Nyo, Potou-Tano, Potou. Low lexical similarity and structurally different from surrounding languages. People are more bilingual in French than other groups because of their proximity to the capital. Literacy rate in second language: 50% to 75%. Radio programs. Christian, other. NT 1998.

EGA ***(DIÉS, EGWA)*** [DIE] 291 to 3,000. Southern Department, Diés Canton, Borondoukou village near Gly. Niger-Congo, Atlantic-Congo, Volta-Congo, Kwa, Nyo, Potou-Tano, Ega. The ethnic group is growing, but they are shifting to the Dida language because of intermarriage and other influences. Traditional religion, Christian, Muslim, other.

ESUMA ***(ESSOUMA)*** [ESM] Ethnic population of 164 (1988 census). Southern Department, Essouma Canton of Adiake Subprefecture. Two villages of Assinie and Mafia. Niger-Congo, Atlantic-Congo, Volta-Congo, Kwa, Nyo, Unclassified. Became extinct about 200 years ago. The ethnic group now speaks Anyin and Nzema (J. Burmeister SIL 1982). Christian, Muslim, other. Extinct.

FRENCH [FRN] 17,470 in Côte d'Ivoire (1988 census). Indo-European, Italic, Romance, Italo-Western, Western, Gallo-Iberian, Gallo-Romance, Gallo-Rhaetian, Oïl, French. Official language. Grammar. Bible 1530-1986. See main entry under France.

GAGU ***(GAGOU, GBAN)*** [GGU] 36,595 (1993). West Central Department, Oume Subprefecture. Niger-Congo, Mande, Eastern, Southeastern, Nwa-Ben, Ben-Gban. Dialects: BOKWA, N'DA, BOKABO, TUKA. N'da dialect is central. Bilingualism in French, Bété, Gouro, Dida, Jula. Christian, traditional religion, Muslim, other. NT, in press (1999).

GLIO-OUBI ***(OUBI, UBI, GLIO)*** [OUB] 2,500 in Côte d'Ivoire (1991). Western Department. Tai Canton, Tai Subprefecture. 6 towns on each side of the border. Niger-Congo, Atlantic-Congo, Volta-Congo, Kru, Western, Grebo, Glio-Oubi. Closest lexical similarity is 75% with Twabo of Liberia (see Glaro-Twabo). High bilingualism with several surrounding languages in Côte d'Ivoire. They are called 'Glio' in Liberia. Traditional religion. See main entry under Liberia.

GODIÉ ***(GODYE)*** [GOD] 26,448 (1993 SIL). Southern Department, Sassandra and Fresco subprefectures. Koyo dialect is in Kotrohou Canton. Niger-Congo, Atlantic-Congo, Volta-Congo, Kru, Eastern, Bete, Western. Dialects: TIGLU, GLIBE, KAGBO, DAGLI, NUGBO, DLOGO, JLUKO, NYAGO, KOYO. The Koyo dialect may be closer to Dida than to Godié. Kagbo is the most widely understood dialect. Radio programs, TV. Christian, traditional religion, Muslim, other. Bible portions 1977.

GREBO, SOUTHERN [GRJ] Niger-Congo, Atlantic-Congo, Volta-Congo, Kru, Western, Grebo, Liberian. Dialect: SEASIDE GREBO. Mainly refugees in Côte d'Ivoire. Traditional religion. See main entry under Liberia.

GURO ***(GOURO, KWENI, LO, KWÉNDRÉ)*** [GOA] 332,100 (1993 SIL). West Central and Central departments, subprefectures of Zuénoula, Vavoua, Gouitafla, Bouafle, Sinfra, Oumé. Niger-Congo, Mande, Eastern, Southeastern, Guro-Tura, Guro-Yaoure. Literacy rate in second language: 25%. Radio programs. Muslim, Christian, other. Bible 1979.

JULA ***(DYULA, DYOULA, DIULA, DIOULA, DJULA)*** [DYU] 179,100 first language speakers in Côte d'Ivoire (1991). Northern Region, Ferkessédougou Department, Kong Subprefecture, and major cities throughout Côte d'Ivoire. Niger-Congo, Mande, Western, Central-Southwestern, Central, Manding-Jogo, Manding-Vai, Manding-Mokole, Manding, Manding-East, Northeastern Manding, Bamana. Dialects: KONG JULA, TAGBOUSSIKAN, DIOULA VÉHICULAIRE (TRADE JULA). Many varieties formerly thought to be dialects have been found to be closer to Mahou or other Jula language entries. Designated by the government as one of five languages to be developed for literature. Trade language. Dictionary. Grammar. Literacy rate in first language: Below 1%. Literacy rate in second language: 15% to 25%. Muslim. NT 1993. See main entry under Burkina Faso.

JULA, KORO [KFO] 40,000 (1999 SIL). Mankono Department, Tiéningboué Subprefecture. Niger-Congo, Mande, Western, Central-Southwestern, Central, Manding-Jogo, Manding-Vai, Manding-Mokole, Manding, Manding-East, Southeastern Manding, Maninka-Mori. They appear to have good understanding of Koyaga Jula. They have their own ethnic identity, although they live near the Koyaga Jula. Investigation needed: attitudes toward Koyaga Jula. Muslim.

JULA, KOYAGA ***(KOYAGA, KOYAKA, KOYARA, KOYAA, KOYA, KOYAGAKAN)*** [KGA] 60,000 (1999 SIL). Mankono Department, western four subprefectures. Niger-Congo, Mande, Western, Central-Southwestern, Central, Manding-Jogo, Manding-Vai, Manding-Mokole, Manding, Manding-East, Southeastern Manding, Maninka-Mori. Dialects: KOYAGA, SIAKA, SAGAKA, NIGBI. They appear to have good understanding of Koro Jula. They have their own ethnic identity, although they live near the Koro Jula. Investigation needed: attitudes toward Koro Jula. Muslim, Christian, traditional religion, other.

JULA, ODIENNÉ ***(ODIENNEKAKAN, MALINKÉ)*** [JOD] 120,000 including 15,000 Wasulu (1999 SIL). Northwest Region, Odienné Department. Niger-Congo, Mande, Western, Central-Southwestern, Central, Manding-Jogo, Manding-Vai, Manding-Mokole, Manding, Manding-East, Southeastern Manding, Maninka-Mori. Dialects: ODIENNEKA, SIENKOKA, NAFANA, BODOUGOUKA, TOUDOUGOUKA, VANDOUGOUKA, WASULU (WASSULUNKA, WASSOULOUNKA, WASSULUNKE, FOREST MANINKA). Some of the dialects listed may be separate languages. Forest Maninka may be Folongakan, a dialect of Odienné Jula. Barala may be a dialect of Odienné Jula. Wasulu are ethnic Fulani who have adopted a Manding language. In Côte d'Ivoire this may be Kankan Maninka, Odienné Jula, or separate from both. Muslim.

JULA, WORODOUGOU ***(WORODOUGOU, OUORODOUGOU, WORODUGU, WORODOUGOUKAKAN, BAKOKAN)*** [JUD] 80,000 (1999 SIL). Northwest Region, Séguéla Department. Niger-Congo, Mande, Western, Central-Southwestern, Central, Manding-Jogo, Manding-Vai, Manding-Mokole, Manding, Manding-East, Southeastern Manding, Maninka-Mori. Dialects: WORODOUGOUKA, KARANJAN, KANIKA. Karanja may be a separate language. Called 'Bakokan' by people in Mankono Department. Muslim.

KHISA ***(KOMONO, KHI KHIPA, KUMWENU)*** [KQM] 5,000 in Côte d'Ivoire (1991 L. Vanderaa CRC). Population total both countries 8,000. Also spoken in Burkina Faso. Niger-Congo, Atlantic-Congo, Volta-Congo, North, Gur, Central, Southern, Gan-Dogose. Muslim.

KODIA ***(KWADIA, KWADYA)*** [KWP] 837 (1993 SIL). South central. Niger-Congo, Atlantic-Congo, Volta-Congo, Kru, Eastern, Kwadia. Literacy rate in first language: Below 1%. Literacy rate in second language: 15% to 25%. Déima (African syncretism), Christian, traditional religion, Muslim.

KOUYA ***(KOWYA, SOKYA, KUYA)*** [KYF] 10,117 (1993 SIL). West Central Department, Kouya Canton of Vavoua Subprefecture, 12 villages. Niger-Congo, Atlantic-Congo, Volta-Congo, Kru, Eastern, Bete, Eastern. Closest to Gbadi Bété and Dida. 50% of speakers are somewhat bilingual in Guro. Literacy rate in first language: Below 1%. Literacy rate in second language: 15% to 25%. Tropical forest, savannah. Subsistence agriculturalists. Traditional religion, Christian, Muslim, other. Bible portions 1992.

KRAHN, WESTERN ***(KRAHN, NORTHERN KRAHN)*** [KRW] 12,200 in Côte d'Ivoire (1993 SIL). Western Côte d'Ivoire, around Toulépleu. Niger-Congo, Atlantic-Congo, Volta-Congo, Kru, Western, Wee, Guere-Krahn. Dialects: PEWA (PEEWA), BIAI. Dialects in Liberia are Gbo, Gbaeson, Plo, Biai, and Gbobo. There are influences from local French, but in Liberia from Liberian English. Literacy rate in first language: Below 1%. Literacy rate in second language: 25% to 50%. There are orthographic differences from Liberia. Traditional religion, Christian, Muslim. NT 1992-1995. See main entry under Liberia.

KROBU ***(KROBOU)*** [KXB] 9,920 (1993 SIL). Southern Department, Subprefecture of Agboville. Four villages. Niger-Congo, Atlantic-Congo, Volta-Congo, Kwa, Nyo, Potou-Tano, Tano, Krobu. Bilingualism in Baule, Abe. Investigation needed: bilingual proficiency. Christian, Muslim, traditional religion, other.

KRUMEN, PLAPO ***(PLAPO)*** [KTJ] Southwest corner of Côte d'Ivoire, between Bapo and Honpo dialects of Tepo Krumen. Niger-Congo, Atlantic-Congo, Volta-Congo, Kru, Western, Grebo, Ivoirian. Coastal. NT, in press (1999).

KRUMEN, PYE ***(KROUMEN, SOUTHEASTERN KRUMEN, NORTHEASTERN KRUMEN)*** [PYE] 20,000 (1993 SIL). All Krumen: 48,300 (1993 SIL). Southwestern Côte d'Ivoire between San Pedro and Tai, subprefectures of Tai, Bereby, and part of San Pedro. Niger-Congo, Atlantic-Congo, Volta-Congo, Kru, Western, Grebo, Ivorian. Dialects: TREPO, WLUWE-HAWLO (HAOULO), GBOWE-HRAN, WLEPO, DUGBO, YREWE (GIRIWE), YAPO, PIE (PYE, PIE-PLI-MAHON-KUSE-GBLAPO-HENEKWE). Literacy rate in first language: Below 1%. Literacy rate in second language: 25% to 50%. Christian, traditional religion, Muslim, other.

KRUMEN, TEPO ***(SOUTHERN KRUMEN, SOUTHWESTERN KROUMEN, KRUMEN, KROUMEN, KRU)*** [TED] 28,300 (1993 SIL). All Krumen: 48,300 (1993 SIL). Population total both countries 28,300 or more. Southwest corner of Côte d'Ivoire, subprefectures of Tabou and Grabo. Glawlo dialect is in Liberia. Also spoken in Liberia. Niger-Congo, Atlantic-Congo, Volta-Congo, Kru, Western, Grebo, Ivorian. Dialects: TEPO, BAPO, WLOPO (ROPO), DAPO, HONPO, YREPO (KAPO), GLAWLO. Bilingualism in French, Jula. Grammar. Literacy rate in first language: 1% to 5%. Literacy rate in second language: 25% to 50%. Christian, traditional religion, Muslim, other. NT 1995.

KULANGO, BONDOUKOU [KZC] 77,000 in Côte d'Ivoire (1993 SIL). Population total both countries 87,000. Eastern Department, Subprefecture of Bondoukou. Also spoken in Ghana. Niger-Congo, Atlantic-Congo, Volta-Congo, North, Gur, Kulango. Literacy rate in first language: Below 1%. Literacy rate in second language: 15% to 25%. Roman. Muslim, Christian, traditional religion, other. NT 1975.

KULANGO, BOUNA ***(KOULANGO, KULANGE, NKURAENG, NKURANGE)*** [NKU] 142,000 in Côte d'Ivoire (1993). Population total both countries 157,500. Eastern Department, Subprefecture of Nassian. Also spoken in Ghana. Niger-Congo, Atlantic-Congo, Volta-Congo, North, Gur, Kulango. Dialect: NABANJ. Speakers of the Bouna dialect understand Bondoukou, but the reverse is not true. Literacy rate in first language: Below 1%. Literacy rate in second language: 15% to 25%. Traditional religion, Christian, Muslim.

LIGBI ***(LIGWI, NIGBI, NIGWI, TUBA, BANDA, JOGO)*** [LIG] 4,000 in Côte d'Ivoire (1991 L. Vanderaa CRC). Eastern Department, one large village called Bineto, one community at Bouna, the town of Slil near Boundoukou, some at Ourodougou on the edge of Malinke territory. Niger-Congo, Mande, Western, Central-Southwestern, Central, Manding-Jogo, Jogo-Jeri, Jogo. In other countries, blacksmiths speaking Manding languages are also called 'Noumou', but in Côte d'Ivoire and Ghana, the Noumou speak Ligbi. 'Numu' (Noumou, Numun) is the name of a caste of blacksmiths; not a separate language. 'Banda' is the name for the people, which is also the name for speakers of the Nafaanra language. Literacy rate in first language: Below 1%. Literacy rate in second language: 15% to 25%. Traditional religion, Muslim. See main entry under Ghana.

LOBI ***(LOBIRI, MIWA)*** [LOB] 155,800 in Côte d'Ivoire (1993 SIL). Eastern Department, northern strip. Niger-Congo, Atlantic-Congo, Volta-Congo, North, Gur, Lobi. Moru may be a dialect. Literacy rate in first language: Below 1%. Literacy rate in second language: 5% to 15%. Traditional religion, Christian, Muslim, other. NT 1965-1985. See main entry under Burkina Faso.

LOMA ***(LOMAKKA, LOMASSE, LOMAPO, MALINKE)*** [LOI] Near Tèèn and Kulango areas. Niger-Congo, Atlantic-Congo, Volta-Congo, North, Gur, Teen. Closely related to Tèèn and Kulango, but not inherently intelligible. Closer to Kulango than Tèèn is to Kulango. Bilingualism in Tèèn. The people are called 'Lomapo'. Different from Loma of Liberia. Investigation needed: bilingual proficiency in Tèèn.

MAHOU ***(MAOU, MAU, MAHU, MAUKA, MAUKE)*** [MXX] 169,100 (1993 SIL). Northwest Region, Touba Department. Niger-Congo, Mande, Western, Central-Southwestern, Central, Manding-Jogo, Manding-Vai, Manding-Mokole, Manding, Manding-East, Southeastern Manding, Maninka-Mori. Dialects: MAHOUKA, KOROKA, TENENGA, FINANGA, BARALAKA (BARALA). Speakers of some listed dialects may not be able to use Mahou literature. Barala may be a dialect of Odienné Jula. Literacy rate in first language: Below 1%. Literacy rate in second language: 5% to 15%. Muslim, traditional religion, other.

MANINKA, FOREST [MYQ] 15,000. Northwest Region, Odienné Department, near Mali and Guinea borders. Niger-Congo, Mande, Western, Central-Southwestern, Central, Manding-Jogo, Manding-Vai, Manding-Mokole, Manding, Manding-East, Southeastern Manding, Maninka-Mori. Dialect: WASULU (WASSULUNKA, WASSOULOUNKA, WASSULUNKE). This may be the same language as Kankan Maninka, Odienné Jula, or different from both. Ethnic Fulani who now speak a Manding language. Investigation needed: intelligibility. Muslim.

MBATO ***(GWA, M'BATO, MGBATO, POTU, N-BATTO)*** [GWA] 25,000 (1993 SIL). Southern Department, Subprefecture of Petit Alépé. Niger-Congo, Atlantic-Congo, Volta-Congo, Kwa, Nyo, Potou-Tano, Potou. Related to Ebrii. Some bilingualism with Attié or Anyin. Literacy rate in first language: Below 1%. Literacy rate in second language: 25% to 50%. Christian, traditional religion, Muslim, other.

MORU [MXZ] 10,000 (1971 Welmers). Niger-Congo, Atlantic-Congo, Volta-Congo, North, Gur, Unclassified. Perhaps related to Lobi. Different from Moru of Sudan. Unconfirmed.

MWAN ***(MUAN, MONA, MOUAN, MUANA, MWA)*** [MOA] 17,000 (1993 SIL). Kongasso Subprefecture and the southern part of Mankono Subprefecture. Niger-Congo, Mande, Eastern, Southeastern, Nwa-Ben, Wan-Mwan. Bilingualism in Jula, Guro. Literacy rate in first language: Below 1%. Literacy rate in second language: 15% to 25%. Traditional religion, Muslim, Christian, other. Bible portions 1982-1995.

NEYO ***(GWIBWEN, TOWI)*** [NEY] 9,200 (1993 SIL). Southern Department, Sassandra Subprefecture, Neyo, and Kébé cantons, from Niégba in the west to Dagbégo in the east and Niabayo in the north. Niger-Congo, Atlantic-Congo, Volta-Congo, Kru, Eastern, Dida. Closest to Kagbo dialect of Godié, but they consider themselves to be a separate ethnic group. May be closer to Dida than to Bété. 'Neyo' is their name for themselves. Literacy rate in first language: Below 1%. Literacy rate in second language: 25% to 50%. Christian, traditional religion, Muslim, other.

NYABWA ***(NYABOA, NIABOUA, NYABWA-NYÉDÉBWA)*** [NIA] 42,700 including 32,500 Nyabwa, 7,700 Nyedebwa, 2,500 Kouzié (1993 SIL). West Central Department, northwest corner, subprefectures of Vavoua (Nyedebwa), Issia, Buyo, Zoukougbeu (Nyabwa), Daloua. Niger-Congo, Atlantic-Congo, Volta-Congo, Kru, Western, Wee, Nyabwa. Dialects: NYABWA, NYEDEBWA (NIÉDÉBOUA). 90% lexical similarity between Nyabwa and Nyedebwa. 74% to 80% between them and Guéré and Wobe dialects. Bilingualism in French, Dioula, Guéré, Wobe, Biti. They do not want to be called 'Bété'. Kouzii is an ethnic subgroup of Nyabwa, not a dialect. Literacy rate in first language: 5% to 10%. Literacy rate in second language: 15% to 25%. Christian, traditional religion, Muslim, other. NT 1991.

NZEMA ***(NZIMA, APPOLO)*** [NZE] 66,700 in Côte d'Ivoire (1993 SIL). Aboisso Department, Tiapoum Subprefecture, southeastern coast. Many in Abidjan. Niger-Congo, Atlantic-Congo, Volta-Congo, Kwa, Nyo, Potou-Tano, Tano, Central, Bia, Southern. Literacy rate in first language: 1% to 5%. Literacy rate in second language: 25% to 50%. Christian, traditional religion, Muslim, other. Bible 1999. See main entry under Ghana.

SENOUFO, CEBAARA ***(SENADI, SENARI, SYENERE, TIEBAARA, TYEBALA)*** [SEF] 862,000 (1993 SIL). Northern, around Korhogo. Niger-Congo, Atlantic-Congo, Volta-Congo, North, Gur, Senufo, Senari. Dialects: KAFIRE, KASARA, KUFURU, TAGBARI (MBENGUI-NIELLÉ), PATARA, POGARA, TYEBARA, TAGARA, TENERE, TAKPASYEERI (MESSENI), SOUTHWEST SENARI, KANDERE (TENGRELA), PAPARA, FODARA, KULERE, NAFARA. Korhogo dialect is central. The Kulele speak the Kulere dialect scattered throughout the Senoufo area. Bilingualism in Jula. The Tyelibele (Tyeliri) are leather workers scattered throughout the Senoufo area, speaking the various Senoufo languages where they live as mother tongue. Literacy rate in first language: 1% to 5%. Literacy rate in second language: 5% to 15%. Tyeliri: leather workers, Kulere: wood carvers. Traditional religion, Muslim, Christian. NT 1982-1995.

SENOUFO, DJIMINI ***(DYIMINI, DJIMINI, JINMINI)*** [DYI] 95,500 (1993 SIL). Dabakala Department, northwest corner. Niger-Congo, Atlantic-Congo, Volta-Congo, North, Gur, Senufo, Tagwana-Djimini. Dialects: DIAMALA (DJAMALA, DYAMALA), DJAFOLO, DOFANA, FOOLO, SINGALA. Singala is the prestige dialect of Dabakala. 76% to 81% lexical similarity with Tagwana. Bilingualism in Djoula. Literacy rate in first language: Below 1%. Literacy rate in second language: 5% to 15%. Muslim, Christian, traditional religion, other. NT 1993.

SENOUFO, NYARAFOLO ***(NYARAFOLO-NIAFOLO)*** [SEV] 42,000 (1995 SIL). Northeast around Ferkessédougou. Niger-Congo, Atlantic-Congo, Volta-Congo, North, Gur, Senufo, Senari. Literacy rate in first language: Below 1%. Literacy rate in second language: 5% to 15%. Traditional religion, Muslim.

SENOUFO, PALAKA ***(PALARA, PALAKA, KPALAGHA, PALLAKHA, PILARA)*** [PLR] 8,000 (1995 SIL). Central Department, area around Sikolo, north of Djimini. Niger-Congo, Atlantic-Congo, Volta-Congo, North, Gur, Senufo, Kpalaga. 65% to 70% lexical similarity with other Senufo languages and dialects. Literacy rate in first language: Below 1%. Literacy rate in second language: 5% to 15%. Traditional religion, Muslim.

SENOUFO, SHEMPIRE ***(SYEMPIRE, SHENPIRE)*** [SEB] 100,000 (1996). North of Tingréla. Niger-Congo, Atlantic-Congo, Volta-Congo, North, Gur, Senufo, Suppire-Mamara. 3 or 4 dialects. Relationship to Supyire Senoufo in Mali is undetermined. Literacy rate in first language: 0%. Literacy rate in second language: Below 5%.

SENOUFO, TAGWANA ***(TAGBANA, TAGWANA, TAGOUNA)*** [TGW] 138,100 (1993 SIL). Central Department, north central area, west of Djimini. Niger-Congo, Atlantic-Congo, Volta-Congo, North, Gur, Senufo, Tagwana-Djimini. Dialects: GBO (ZORO), TAFIRE, NIEDIEKAHA, NIANGBO, NIAKARAMADOUGOU, FONDEBOUGOU, DJIDANAN, FOURGOULA, KATIARA, KATIOLA. 76% to 81% lexical similarity with Djimini dialects. Literacy rate in first language: Below 1%. Literacy rate in second language: 15% to 25%. Christian, Muslim, traditional religion, other. NT 1987.

SONINKE ***(MARKA, SARAKOLE, SARAWULE, TOUBAKAI, WAKORE, GADYAGA, SERAHULI, ASWANIK, SILABE)*** [SNN] 100,000 in Côte d'Ivoire (1991 L. Vanderaa CRC). Niger-Congo, Mande, Western, Northwestern, Samogo, Soninke-Bobo, Soninke-Boso, Soninke. Dialect: AZER (ADJER, ASER). Muslim. See main entry under Mali.

TÈÈN ***(TÉNHÉ, TEGESIE, LORHON, LORON, LOGHON, NABE)*** [LOR] 6,100 in Côte d'Ivoire (1991). Population total both countries 7,300. Bouna Department, mainly Téhini Subprefecture. Also spoken in Burkina Faso. Niger-Congo, Atlantic-Congo, Volta-Congo, North, Gur, Teen. Different from Kulango. Closest to Loma, Kulango, and Nabanj. Bilingualism in Lobi, Jula, Loma, French. The name of the people is 'Ténbó' (pl.), 'Ténsé' (sg.); the language 'Tèèn'. Literacy rate in first language: Below 1%. Literacy rate in second language: Below 5%. Savannah. Traditional religion, some Christian. Bible portions 1985-1995.

TOURA ***(TURA, WEEN)*** [NEB] 38,500 (1993 SIL). Department of Biankouma, eastern part, mountainous region east of the main road from Man to Touba, north of the main road from Man to Seguela, a little north of the Bafing River, otherwise the Bafing and Sassandra rivers from the northern and eastern borders. Niger-Congo, Mande, Eastern, Southeastern, Guro-Tura, Tura-Dan-Mano, Tura-Dan. Dialects: NAÒ, BOO, YILIGELE, GWÉÒ, WÁÁDÚ. Probably closest to Dan. Also close to Gouro, Gban, Mano (in Liberia). Bilingualism in Dan, Wobe, Jula, French. Literacy rate in first language: Below 1%. Literacy rate in second language: 5% to 15%. Traditional religion. NT 1986.

WAN ***(NWA)*** [WAN] 22,000 (1993 UBS). Subprefectures of Kounahiri and the western part of Beoumi. Niger-Congo, Mande, Eastern, Southeastern, Nwa-Ben, Wan-Mwan. Dialects: MIAMU, KEMU. Bilingualism in French, Jula, Muan. Traditional religion, Christian, Muslim, other.

WANÉ ***(NGWANÉ, HWANE)*** [HWA] 2,100 (1993 SIL). Southwestern coast. Niger-Congo, Atlantic-Congo, Volta-Congo, Kru, Eastern, Bakwe. Some young people understand Bakwe, and they seem to understand French. They do not like to be identified as Bakwe, and are vocal about their identity as separate. They intermarry frequently with the Bakwe. Literacy rate in first language: Below 1%. Literacy rate in second language: 15% to 25%. Traditional religion, Christian, Muslim, other.

WÈ NORTHERN ***(WOBÉ, OUOBE, WÈÈ)*** [WOB] 156,300 (1993 SIL). About 25% live outside the main territory. Western Department, subprefectures of Kouibly, Bangolo, and Fakobly. Niger-Congo, Atlantic-Congo, Volta-Congo, Kru, Western, Wee, Wobe. Dialects: TAO, PÉOMÉ, SÉMIEN (GBÉAN). Kouibly dialect is intelligible for about half of the Wè Southern speakers. Wè Northern dialects have 90% to 94% lexical similarity with each other. Kouibly dialect (Tao and Gbean) has 84% to 89% lexical similarity with Wè Southern dialects. Bilingualism in French. Grammar. Literacy rate in first language: 1% to 5%. Literacy rate in second language: 15% to 25%. Christian, traditional religion, Muslim, other. NT 1984.

WÈ SOUTHERN ***(GUÉRÉ, CENTRAL GUÉRÉ, GERE, WÈÈ)*** [GXX] 292,500 (1999 SIL), including 20,000 Niao (1995 SIL). Western Department, subprefectures of Guiglo, Duékoué, Bangolo, Tai. Niger-Congo, Atlantic-Congo, Volta-Congo, Kru, Western, Wee, Guere-Krahn. Dialects: ZIBIAO, ZAGNE, ZAGNA, BEU (ZARABAON), ZAA (ZAHA), NEAO (NIABO, NEABO), GBOO (GBOBO), FLEO, NYEO. Most bilingual comprehension in French and Jula is limited to greetings and trade. 'Wèè' is their name for people and language. Literacy rate in first language: Below 1%. Literacy rate in second language: 25% to 40%. Radio programs, TV. Christian, traditional religion, Muslim, other. NT 1982.

WÈ WESTERN ***(GUÉRÉ, GERE, WÈÈ)*** [WEC] 25,188 (1998 SIL), including 20,000 Kaoro (1995 SIL). Western Department, Subprefecture of Toulépleu. Niger-Congo, Atlantic-Congo, Volta-Congo, Kru, Western, Wee, Guere-Krahn. Dialects: NIDROU (NIDRU), KAORO (KAAWLU, KAOWLU). Most bilingual comprehension in French and Jula is limited to greetings and trade. 'Wèè' is their name for people and language. Literacy rate in first language: Below 1%. Literacy rate in second language: 15% to 25%. Christian, traditional religion. NT 1991.

YAOURÉ ***(YAURE, YOHOWRÉ, YOURÉ)*** [YRE] 24,600 (1991 L. Vanderaa CRC) including about 13,000 in villages, 7,000 in cities (1982 SIL). Bouaflé Department, Yaoure Canton of Bouafli Subprefecture, bounded on the south by Red Bandama, the east by White Bandama, the north by Lake Kossou, the west by Bouaflé. Niger-Congo, Mande, Eastern, Southeastern, Guro-Tura, Guro-Yaoure. Dialects: KLAN, YAAN, TAAN, YOO, BHOO. Closest to Guro. Bilingualism in Gouro, Baoule, Jula. Literacy rate in first language: 1% to 5%. Literacy rate in second language: 25% to 50%. Traditional religion. NT, in press (1999).

DEMOCRATIC REPUBLIC OF CONGO

Democratic Republic of the Congo, DRC. Formerly Belgian Congo, Congo-Leopoldville, Congo-Kinshasa, Republic of Zaïre. National or official languages: Kongo, Lingala, Luba-Kasai, Congo Swahili, French. 49,139,000 (1998 UN). Literacy rate 55% to 61%. Also includes Fanagolo, Greek, people from India. Information mainly from Y. Bastin 1978; K. S. Olson 1996; John Bendor-Samuel 1989; SIL 1977-1999. Christian, traditional religion, Muslim. Blind population 73,000 (1982 WCE). Deaf institutions: 12 (CMD). Data accuracy estimate: B. The number of languages listed for Democratic Republic of Congo is 219. Of those, 218 are living languages and 1 is extinct. Diversity index 0.92.

ALUR *(LUR, ALORO, ALUA, ALULU, LURI, DHO ALUR, JO ALUR)* [ALZ] 500,000 in DRC (1991 UBS). Population total both countries 920,000. Orientale Province: Mahagi Territory and northwest to Djalasiga area. Also spoken in Uganda. Nilo-Saharan, Eastern Sudanic, Nilotic, Western, Luo, Southern, Luo-Acholi, Alur-Acholi, Alur. Investigation needed: intelligibility. Christian in DRC. Bible 1936-1955.

AMBA *(KWAMBA, KUAMBA, RWAMBA, HAMBO, RUWENZORI KIBIRA, HUMU, KIHUMU)* [RWM] 4,500 in DRC (1991 SIL). Nord-Kivu Province, Uganda border area south of Lake Albert, northern foot-hills of Ruwenzori. Niger-Congo, Atlantic-Congo, Volta-Congo, Benue-Congo, Bantoid, Southern, Narrow Bantu, Central, D, Bira-Huku (D.30). Dialects: KIGUMU (KUAMBA, HAMBA, LUBULEBULE), KIHYANZI, KUSUWA. 70% lexical similarity to Bera, 57% to 59% with Bila, Kaiku, Komo, and Bhele, 25% with Nandi. 34% with Talinga-Bwisi may indicate convergence. Many are bilingual in Talinga-Bwisi. See main entry under Uganda.

ASOA *(ASUA, ASUATI, ASUAE, AKA)* [ASV] Orientale Province, Rungu Territory, Ituri Forest, among Mangbetu groups Maele, Meje, Aberu, and Popoi. Nilo-Saharan, Central Sudanic, East, Mangbetu. Not inherently intelligible to Mangbetu-Meje speakers. Some Asoa learn Mangbetu-Meje. Mangbetu men sometimes take Asoa wives, but Mangbetu women do not ordinarily marry Asoa men. A pygmy group. 'Aka' may be derogatory. Hunter-gatherers.

AUSHI *(AVAUSHI, VOUAOUSI, USHI, USI, UZHILI)* [AUH] Haut Katanga Province to the east of Lumbumbashi. Niger-Congo, Atlantic-Congo, Volta-Congo, Benue-Congo, Bantoid, Southern, Narrow Bantu, Central, M, Bemba (M.40). Language of wider communication. SVO. See main entry under Zambia.

AVOKAYA *(ABUKEIA, AVUKAYA)* [AVU] 25,000 in DRC, including 2,000 Ojila, 10,000 Northern Ogambi (1989 SIL). Population total both countries 40,000. Orientale Province, Faradje Territory, close to Sudan border. Also spoken in Sudan. Nilo-Saharan, Central Sudanic, East, Moru-Madi, Central. Dialects: OJILA, AJIGU (AJUGU), NORTHERN OGAMBI, AVOKAYA PUR. Avokaya Pur near Faradje is closer to Logo than to the Ojila dialect of Sudan. Bible portions 1986.

BABANGO *(MOBANGO)* [BBM] Orientale Province, Basoko Territory. Niger-Congo, Atlantic-Congo, Volta-Congo, Benue-Congo, Bantoid, Southern, Narrow Bantu, Northwest, C, Bangi-Ntomba (C.40), Lusengo. Closely related to Budza which is immediately down river; possibly a dialect. Investigation needed: intelligibility with Budza.

BAKA *(TARA BAAKA)* [BDH] 1,300 in DRC (1993 UBS). Orientale Province, between Garamba National Park and Sudan border. A few among the Logo. Nilo-Saharan, Central Sudanic, West, Bongo-Bagirmi, Bongo-Baka, Baka. Different from Baka of Cameroon. Refugees in DRC. Bible portions 1990-1993. See main entry under Sudan.

BALI *(KIBALI, KIBAALI, BAALI, KIBALA, LIBAALI, DHIBALI)* [BCP] 42,000 (1987 UBS) to 50,000 (1988 Huddleston PBT). Orientale Province, Tshopo District, Bafwasende Territory, between the Tshopo River to the south and the Ituri River to the north, and on the north bank of the Ituri River. Niger-Congo, Atlantic-Congo, Volta-Congo, Benue-Congo, Bantoid, Southern, Narrow Bantu, Central, D, Lega-Kalanga (D.20). Dialects: BEMILI, BAKUNDUMU, BAFWANDAKA, BEKENI. Dialects are inherently intelligible with each other; Bemili is central linguistically and geographically. 52% lexical similarity with Lika, 40% to 45% with Bwa and Pagibete; 46% with Komo, 40% Bhele, Bila, and Bera; 30% with Budu and Ndaka, 25% with Lega languages and Lingala. Bilingual level estimates for Lingala are 0 10%, 1 15%, 2 30%, 3 30%, 4 10%, 5 5%. 5% to 10% monolingual. Congo Swahili is spoken by (1) all leaders, nearly all young people and men (speak well in certain domains), (2) most women and older men (less fluent), (3) many older women and young children (limited everyday fluency). Lingala is used mainly by those who travel or have been in military service. French is spoken by those with secondary school education, less than 5%. 'Kibali' is the official name. 'Dhibali' is their own name. Speakers are called 'Babali'. SVO, prepositions, genitives before nouns; articles, adjectives, numerals, relatives after nouns; question word sentence final; 1-3 prefixes; 1-5 suffixes; word order distinguishes role; affixes mark person, number of subject and object in one noun group; active, passive, reflexive; 2 causatives; aspect; comparatives; 3 tones; stress; 9 vowels. Literacy rate in first language: 1% to 2%. Literacy rate in second language: 30% to 40% in Congo Swahili. Tropical forest. Riverine. Swidden agriculturalists. 500 meters.

BALOI ***(LOI, BOLOI, BAATO BALOI, REBU)*** [BIZ] Equateur Province, south, west, and east of Bomongo. Niger-Congo, Atlantic-Congo, Volta-Congo, Benue-Congo, Bantoid, Southern, Narrow Bantu, Northwest, C, Bangi-Ntomba (C.40), Ngiri. Dialects: LOI, DZAMBA (JAMBA), MAKUTU, MAMPOKO. Dialects or closely related languages: Balobo (Likila), Ndobo.

BAMWE [BMG] 20,000 (1983 census). Equateur Province, Sud Ubangi, Kungu Territory, in Mwanda Collectivité, upper reaches of Ngiri River between the villages of Limpoko and Sombe, including villages of Moniongo, Libobi, Likata, Mondongo, Lifunga, Bomole, Lokutu, Botunia; 10 villages. Niger-Congo, Atlantic-Congo, Volta-Congo, Benue-Congo, Bantoid, Southern, Narrow Bantu, Northwest, C, Bangi-Ntomba (C.40). All village dialects are highly intelligible to each other. Dzando and Ndolo are the most closely related languages. Nearly everyone speaks Lingala except oldest women. Many other women speak only market Lingala. Literacy rate in second language: 30% to 50% in Lingala. Riverine.

BANDA, MID-SOUTHERN [BJO] 2,000 in DRC (1986 SIL). Equateur Province, Bosobolo Territory in a few villages north of Dubulu, and Mobaye Territory. Niger-Congo, Atlantic-Congo, Volta-Congo, North, Adamawa-Ubangi, Ubangi, Banda, Central, Central Core, Mid-Southern. Dialect: YAKPA (YACOUA, YAKPWA, YAKWA, BAYAKA). Closest to Gubu, but speakers have better relations with Mbanza speakers. Many villages in DRC where Yakpa was formerly spoken now speak Mono or Mbanza. All speakers are bilingual in Mono, Mbanza, or Lingala. Investigation needed: intelligibility with Gubu, bilingual proficiency in Mono, Mbanza, Lingala. See main entry under CAR.

BANDA, SOUTH CENTRAL [LNL] 3,000 in DRC. Equateur Province. Niger-Congo, Atlantic-Congo, Volta-Congo, North, Adamawa-Ubangi, Ubangi, Banda, South Central. Dialect: NGBUGU (NGUBU, NGBOUGOU). Closest to Langbashe. Some men are fluent in Lingala and Sango. Some use Mono, but they may not accept Mono literature. Investigation needed: intelligibility with Langbashe, bilingual proficiency in Mono. Literacy rate in second language: Low. Fishermen. See main entry under CAR.

BANDA, TOGBO-VARA [TOR] 12,000 in DRC (1984 census). Population total all countries 24,000 or more. Equateur Province, Nord Ubangi, Bosobolo Territory mainly, around towns of Badja and Baya, between villages of Vongba II and Bandema, on the road as far as Gwara II, and scattered villages in the area. Also spoken in CAR, Sudan. Niger-Congo, Atlantic-Congo, Volta-Congo, North, Adamawa-Ubangi, Ubangi, Banda, Central, Central Core, Togbo-Vara. Dialect: TOGBO (TOHGBOH, TAGBO). High bilingualism in Mono, but they view themselves as very different from Mono. Many men, especially younger ones, speak Lingala and Sango. Different from Tagbu of DRC in Sere group. Investigation needed: intelligibility with Vara. Literacy rate in second language: Low in Lingala and not increasing.

BANGALA ***(NGALA)*** [BXG] Used by 3,500,000 as second language (1991 UBS). Orientale Province. Niger-Congo, Atlantic-Congo, Volta-Congo, Benue-Congo, Bantoid, Southern, Narrow Bantu, Northwest, C, Bangi-Ntomba (C.40), Lusengo. Related to Lusengo and Lingala. There is a trend toward becoming more like Lingala. Trade language. Bible 1953-1995.

BANGBA ***(ABANGBA)*** [BBE] 11,000 (1993 SIL). Orientale Province, Kopa Collectivité of the Niangara Territory, and the area around Tora in the Watsa Territory. Niger-Congo, Atlantic-Congo, Volta-Congo, North, Adamawa-Ubangi, Ubangi, Sere-Ngbaka-Mba, Ngbaka-Mba, Ngbaka, Eastern, Mayogo-Bangba. Dialects: KOPA, TORA. Dialects have 90% lexical similarity. Approximately 70% lexical similarity with Mayogo, 72% with Mündü.

BANGI ***(BOBANGI, BUBANGI, LOBOBANGI, REBU, DZAMBA)*** [BNI] Population total all countries 70,000 (1990 UBS). Equateur Province, east of Congo River from Bolobo to Mbandaka. Also spoken in CAR, Congo. Niger-Congo, Atlantic-Congo, Volta-Congo, Benue-Congo, Bantoid, Southern, Narrow Bantu, Northwest, C, Bangi-Ntomba (C.40). NT 1909-1922, out of print.

BANGUBANGU ***(KIBANGUBANGU, BANGOBANGO, KIBANGOBANGO)*** [BNX] 171,000 including 85,000 Bangubangu, 30,000 Mikebwe, 20,000 Kasenga, 32,000 Nonda, 4,000 Hombo (1995 SIL). Maniema Province, Kasongo District, Kabambare Territory. Niger-Congo, Atlantic-Congo, Volta-Congo, Benue-Congo, Bantoid, Southern, Narrow Bantu, Central, L, Songye (L.20). Dialects: BANGUBANGU, MIKEBWE, KASENGA, NONDA, HOMBO. Dialects listed are probably separate languages. Dialect or closely related language: KiSanzi. Most closely related to Hemba (67% lexical similarity), and Songe (58%). Bangubangu has 81% lexical similarity with Mikebwe, 80% with Kasenga, 80% with Nonda, 71% with Hombo. Investigation needed: intelligibility with dialects. Muslim, Christian, traditional religion.

BARAMBU ***(BARAMBO, AMIANGBA, AMIANGBWA, BALAMBU, ABARAMBO, DUGA)*** [BRM] 25,570 (1990 census). A few hundred living among the Bangba (1996). Orientale Province, Poko Territory, between the Bomokandi and Uélé rivers. Niger-Congo, Atlantic-Congo, Volta-Congo, North,

Adamawa-Ubangi, Ubangi, Zande, Barambo-Pambia. Unconfirmed reports of a 'Pamiaangba' dialect near Dungu in Niangara Territory. Extinct linguistically in Sudan in 1975.

BEEKE ***(BEKE, IBEEKE)*** [BKF] 1,000 or fewer (1994 SIL). Orientale Province, Ituri District, Mambasa Territory, one village in each of the Bandaka and Bombo collectivités. Niger-Congo, Atlantic-Congo, Volta-Congo, Benue-Congo, Bantoid, Southern, Narrow Bantu, Central, D, Lega-Kalanga (D.20). 65% lexical similarity with Bali, 46% with Lika and Bila, 40% with Bera, 38% with Ndaka. Nearly all are bilingual in Ndaka. They are losing their language. Probably ethnic Bali who moved away from Bali territory, first to 2 villages south of the Ituri River, and in the 1960s to Ndaka and Mbo territory along the main road from Mambasa to Kisangani. Investigation needed: bilingual proficiency in Ndaka.

BEMBA ***(ICHIBEMBA, WEMBA, CHIWEMBA)*** [BEM] 120,000 in Shila (1972 Barrett). Near southeastern border of Katanga Province. Possibly in Zimbabwe. Niger-Congo, Atlantic-Congo, Volta-Congo, Benue-Congo, Bantoid, Southern, Narrow Bantu, Central, M, Bemba (M.40). Dialects: LEMBUE, LOMOTUA (LOMOTWA), NGOMA, NWESI, SHILA. Language of wider communication. Shila: traditional religion, Christian. Bible 1956-1983. See main entry under Zambia.

BEMBA ***(KINYABEMBA)*** [BMY] Southern Kivu Province. Niger-Congo, Atlantic-Congo, Volta-Congo, Benue-Congo, Bantoid, Southern, Narrow Bantu, Unclassified. Distinct from Bemba (IchiBemba) in southeastern Shaba Region, Zambia, and Tanzania; or Bembe (IBembe) in Kivu Province, Fizi Territory.

BEMBE ***(IBEMBE, BEEMBE, EBEMBE)*** [BMB] 252,000 in DRC (1991 UBS). Population total both countries 252,000 or more. Sud-Kivu Province, Fizi Territory, west of Lake Tanganyika. Also spoken in Tanzania. Niger-Congo, Atlantic-Congo, Volta-Congo, Benue-Congo, Bantoid, Southern, Narrow Bantu, Central, D, Bembe (D.50). 76% to 84% lexical similarity with Lega-Mwenga dialects, 68% with Buyu, about 60% with Lega-Shabunda, 55% with Zimba, 50% with Enya, 45% with Nyanga, 40% with Tembo, 30% with Lengola. Bryan classifies it with the Lega group. Different from Beembe (Bembe) of Congo-Brazzaville. Traditional religion, Christian, Muslim. Bible 1991.

BENDI ***(MABENDI, MABENI)*** [BCT] 32,000 (1991 SIL). Orientale Province, Djugu Territory, midway between Bunia and Djalasiga. Nilo-Saharan, Central Sudanic, East, Lendu. Also reported to be Mangbutu-Efe. Different from Ngiti (Bindi) or Bendi which is a dialect of Banda. Investigation needed: intelligibility.

BERA ***(KIBIRA, PLAINS BIRA)*** [BRF] 120,000 (1992 SIL). Orientale Province, Ituri District, Irumu Territory. Niger-Congo, Atlantic-Congo, Volta-Congo, Benue-Congo, Bantoid, Southern, Narrow Bantu, Central, D, Bira-Huku (D.30). One dialect, but some variation around Solenyama. 70% lexical similarity with Amba, 56% to 59% with Bila, Kaiku, Bhele, and Komo; about 47% with Bwa, Lika, and Bali, 22% with Nyali and Budu. Older people do not understand Congo Swahili, but others do. Investigation needed: bilingual proficiency in Congo Swahili. Bible portions 1930.

BHELE ***(EBHELE, KIPERE, IPERE, PERE, PERI, PIRI, PILI, BILI, KIPILI)*** [PER] 15,000 (1989 estimate). Nord-Kivu Province, Lubero Territory, west of Butembo. Southern Bhele is in Munjoa. Niger-Congo, Atlantic-Congo, Volta-Congo, Benue-Congo, Bantoid, Southern, Narrow Bantu, Central, D, Bira-Huku (D.30). Dialect: BUGOMBE (EBUGOMBE). About 80% lexical similarity with Kaiku and Komo, 70% with Bila, less than 60% with Bera and Amba, about 40% with Bali and Lika. Swahili is their main second language, then KiNandi. Different from Peri, which is a dialect of ChiKalanga of Zimbabwe. Names of ethnic groups: Babeka, Baleje, Batike, Babhogombe (Bapakombe, Bugombe, Ebugombe), Babhaidhomba, Babhogala (Bapokara). Bible portions 1939-1986.

BILA ***(KIBILA, FOREST BIRA, EBILA, WESTERN BILA)*** [BIP] 40,000 (1993 SIL). Orientale Province, Ituri District, Irumu Territory. Niger-Congo, Atlantic-Congo, Volta-Congo, Benue-Congo, Bantoid, Southern, Narrow Bantu, Central, D, Bira-Huku (D.30). Dialects: BOMBI-NGBANJA, NYAKU. 94% lexical similarity between dialects. Closely related to other 'Bira' languages: 80% lexical similarity with Kaiku, 72% with Bhele, 70% with Komo, nearly 60% with Bera and Amba, 46% with Beeke, about 45% with Bwa, 40% with Lika and Bali, 26% with Mbo, 22% with Budu and Ndaka. About 25% of men, 10% to 15% of women have routine proficiency in Congo Swahili, older people have none. Investigation needed: intelligibility with Kaiku. Traditional religion, Christian, Muslim.

BINJI ***(BINDJI)*** [BIN] 64,000 (1971 Welmers). Kasaï Occidental Province, Kazumba Territory. Niger-Congo, Atlantic-Congo, Volta-Congo, Benue-Congo, Bantoid, Southern, Narrow Bantu, Central, L, Songye (L.20). NT 1962.

BOGURU ***(KOGURU, KOGORO, BUGURU)*** [BQU] 494 in DRC (1997). Orientale Province, west of Garamba National Park, Dungu. Niger-Congo, Atlantic-Congo, Volta-Congo, Benue-Congo, Bantoid, Southern, Narrow Bantu, Central, D, Bira-Huku (D.30). Dialects: BOGURU, BUKUR (BUKUM, BUKURU), KOGURU. Speakers in DRC are Sudan refugees. See main entry under Sudan.

BOKO *(IBOKO)* [BKP] Equateur Province, on Congo River, upstream from Mbandaka. Niger-Congo, Atlantic-Congo, Volta-Congo, Benue-Congo, Bantoid, Southern, Narrow Bantu, Northwest, C, Bangi-Ntomba (C.40). Different from Boko (Woko) of Cameroon, and Boko (Busa) of Benin and Nigeria.

BOLIA *(BULIA, BOKOKI)* [BLI] 45,000 (1977 Voegelin and Voegelin). Bandundu Province, north of Lake Mai-Ndombe. Niger-Congo, Atlantic-Congo, Volta-Congo, Benue-Congo, Bantoid, Southern, Narrow Bantu, Northwest, C, Bangi-Ntomba (C.40). Closely related to, or possibly a dialect of Ntomba. Investigation needed: intelligibility with Ntomba. Bible portions 1936.

BOLOKI *(BALOKI, BULUKI, BOLEKI, RIVER RUKI)* [BKT] Equateur Province, both sides of the Congo River, upstream from Mbandaka. Niger-Congo, Atlantic-Congo, Volta-Congo, Benue-Congo, Bantoid, Southern, Narrow Bantu, Northwest, C, Bangi-Ntomba (C.40), Lusengo. Bilingualism in Lingala. The language is being replaced by Lingala. Investigation needed: intelligibility with Lingala. Bible portions 1895-1904.

BOLONDO [BZM] 3,000 (1983 census). Equateur Province, Sud Ubangi, Budjala Territory on the Saw River south of Budjala, around the village of Bamba. Niger-Congo, Atlantic-Congo, Volta-Congo, Benue-Congo, Bantoid, Southern, Narrow Bantu, Northwest, C, Bangi-Ntomba (C.40). Most closely related to Motembo. Lingala is used widely in the main market towns among 'Water People', but hardly at all in the other villages, where comprehension is fair. Many villagers also speak Ngbandi. Riverine.

BOMA *(BUMA, KIBOMA, BOMA KASAI)* [BOH] 8,000 (1971 Welmers). Bandundu Province. Niger-Congo, Atlantic-Congo, Volta-Congo, Benue-Congo, Bantoid, Southern, Narrow Bantu, Northwest, B, Yanzi (B.80).

BOMASSA *(BOMASA, BAMASSA)* [BME] Niger-Congo, Atlantic-Congo, Volta-Congo, North, Adamawa-Ubangi, Ubangi, Sere-Ngbaka-Mba, Ngbaka-Mba, Ngbaka, Western, Baka-Gundi. Reported to be a pygmy group.

BOMBOLI *(BOMBONGO)* [BML] 2,500 (1986 SIL). Equateur Province, Sud Ubangi, Kungu Territory, Dongo Collectivité, north of Bomongo on one of the canals flowing into the Ngiri River, between the villages of Bokondo and Bodjinga. Niger-Congo, Atlantic-Congo, Volta-Congo, Benue-Congo, Bantoid, Southern, Narrow Bantu, Northwest, C, Bangi-Ntomba (C.40). Closest to Bozaba and Lobala. 3 dialects. Use of Lobala is receptive only. They use Lingala as second language. They consider themselves ethnically distinct from the Lobala. They may accept Lobala literature. Investigation needed: intelligibility, attitudes toward Lobala. Riverine.

BOMBOMA *(BOBA)* [BWS] 23,000 (1983 census) including 1,279 in Lingonda (1983 census). Equateur Province, Sud Ubangi, Kungu Territory, Bomboma Collectivité on the southern Roa Dongo between the villages of Bomboma and Bokonzi, and including the villages of Lingonda, Ebuku, Makengo, Ndzubele, Motuba: 7 villages. Niger-Congo, Atlantic-Congo, Volta-Congo, Benue-Congo, Bantoid, Southern, Narrow Bantu, Northwest, C, Bangi-Ntomba (C.40). Dialects: LIKAW, LINGONDA, EBUKU, BOKONZI. The Likaw in Budjala Territory, southwest of Budjala, are reported to be ethnically one with Bomboma and to have good intercomprehension. Ebuku and Lingonda have 93% lexical similarity with Bomboma. Lingala is widely spoken by nearly everyone. Riverine (Lingonda).

BORNA *(EBORNA)* [BXX] Niger-Congo, Atlantic-Congo, Volta-Congo, Benue-Congo, Bantoid, Southern, Unclassified. May not exist (J. Ellington UBS 1982) or may be same as Boma.

BOZABA *(BUZABA, BUDZABA)* [BZO] 5,500 (1983 census). Equateur Province, Sud Ubangi, Kungu Territory, Mwanda Collectivité, on the islands and canals northwest of the confluence of the Ngiri and Mwanda rivers. Niger-Congo, Atlantic-Congo, Volta-Congo, Benue-Congo, Bantoid, Southern, Narrow Bantu, Northwest, C, Bangi-Ntomba (C.40). Most closely related to Bomboli, then Bomboma and Lobala. Bilingual in Lingala but largely only for market use. Riverine.

BUDU *(EBUDU, KIBUDU, BODO)* [BUU] 180,000 or more (1991 SIL). Orientale Province, Wamba Territory, 8 collectivités. Niger-Congo, Atlantic-Congo, Volta-Congo, Benue-Congo, Bantoid, Southern, Narrow Bantu, Central, D, Bira-Huku (D.30). Dialects: INETA (TIMONIKO), WADIMBISA (ISOMBI), MAKODA, WEST BAFWANGADA (BAFANIO), EAST BAFWANGADA, BAFWAKOYI, MALAMBA, MAHAA. The first four dialects listed are on the Ibambi side of the Nepoko River; the last four on the Wamba side. The Ibambi group and the Wamba group consider themselves to be one people and language. 92% lexical similarity within dialects, 85% lexical similarity with Ndaka; 78% with Mbo, 74% with Nyali and Vanuma, about 30% with Bali, Lika, and Komo, 20% to 25% with Bhele, Kaiku, Bila, and Bera, about 14% with Swahili. They are in both Swahili and Bangala-speaking areas; mainly Swahili. People are fairly bilingual. Traditional religion, Christian.

BUDZA *(EBUJA, BUJA, BUDJA, MBUDJA, EMBUDJA, LIMBUDZA)* [BJA] 226,000 (1985 census). Equateur Province, Mongala, Bumba and parts of Bongandanga territories. Niger-Congo, Atlantic-Congo, Volta-Congo, Benue-Congo, Bantoid, Southern, Narrow Bantu, Northwest, C, Bangi-Ntomba (C.40), Lusengo. Dialects: MBILA, MONZAMBOLI, BOSAMBI, YALIAMBI. Dialect or closely related language: Babango. 89% lexical similarity with Babango, 59% with Ngombe, 48% with Lingala, 35% to 40% with Pagibete and Bwa. Lingala is the lingua franca, spoken by all ages and sexes. Some young people only speak Lingala. Literacy rate in second language: High in Lingala.

BURAKA ***(BOURAKA, BORAKA)*** [BKG] Equateur Province, scattered groups along the Ubangi River, north and northeast of Bosobolo. Niger-Congo, Atlantic-Congo, Volta-Congo, North, Adamawa-Ubangi, Ubangi, Sere-Ngbaka-Mba, Ngbaka-Mba, Ngbaka, Western, Gbanzili. See main entry under CAR.

BUSHOONG ***(BUSHONG, BUSOONG, BUSHONGO, SHONGO, MBALE, BAMONGO, MONGO, KUBA, GANGA)*** [BUF] 50,000 to 100,000 (1977 W. Washburn PR). Kasaï Occidental Province, Mweka and northern Ilebo territories. Niger-Congo, Atlantic-Congo, Volta-Congo, Benue-Congo, Bantoid, Southern, Narrow Bantu, Northwest, C, Bushong (C.90). Dialects: DJEMBE, NGENDE, NGOMBE (NGOMBIA), NGONGO, PIANGA (PANGA, TSOBWA, SHOBWA, SHOBA). Traditional religion, Christian. Bible 1927.

BUYA ***(IBUYA)*** [BYY] Niger-Congo, Atlantic-Congo, Volta-Congo, Benue-Congo, Bantoid, Southern, Unclassified.

BUYU ***(BUYI, KIBUYU, BUJWE)*** [BYI] On Lake Tanganyika, on the border between Sud-Kivu and Katanga provinces. Niger-Congo, Atlantic-Congo, Volta-Congo, Benue-Congo, Bantoid, Southern, Narrow Bantu, Central, D, Bembe (D.50). 68% lexical similarity with Bembe, about 60% with Lega-Mwenga, 55% with Lega-Shabunda, 50% with Zimba and Enya, 40% with Bangubangu.

BWA ***(BOA, BUA, BOUA, LIBUA, LIBWALI, LIBENGE, KIBUA, KIBWA)*** [BWW] 200,000 (1994 SIL). Orientale Province, Buta, Bambesa, Banalia, Aketi, and Bondo territories. Buta is considered the center. Most people in Buta and Bambesa territories speak similar dialects. Kiba is in Banalia Territory, Benge and Bati in Aketi and Bondo territories. Niger-Congo, Atlantic-Congo, Volta-Congo, Benue-Congo, Bantoid, Southern, Narrow Bantu, Northwest, C, Ngombe (C.50). Dialects: LEBOALE, YEWU, KIBA, BENGE, BATI (BAATI). The first 3 dialects listed have 90% lexical similarity to Benge and Bati, 80% to 85% with Pagibete, 60% to 80% with Kango, 60% to 65% with Ngelima, 55% to 60% with Lika, 48% with Komo, 43% with Bali, 37% with Ngombe, 35% with Budza, 30% with Lingala. Clan names: Bangingita, Bagunzulu, Bokipa. Different from Bua of Chad. The Ngombe group is sometimes called Bantu C.40. Investigation needed: intelligibility with dialects. Some noun classes have suffixes in addition to the usual prefixes. Bible portions 1938.

BWELA ***(BUELA, LINGI)*** [BWL] Niger-Congo, Atlantic-Congo, Volta-Congo, Benue-Congo, Bantoid, Southern, Narrow Bantu, Northwest, C, Ngombe (C.50).

BWILE [BWC] Haut Katanga Province, north of Aushi in Pweto area at the north end of Lake Mweru. Niger-Congo, Atlantic-Congo, Volta-Congo, Benue-Congo, Bantoid, Southern, Narrow Bantu, Central, L, Bwile (L.10). Not closely related to other languages. See main entry under Zambia.

CHOKWE ***(COKWE, CIOKWE, TSHOKWE, TSCHIOKWE, SHIOKO, DJOK, IMO)*** [CJK] 504,000 in DRC (1990 UBS). Population total all countries 1,009,600. Close to Angola border in southeastern Bandundu, Kasaï Occidental, and Katanga provinces. Also spoken in Angola, Namibia, Zambia. Niger-Congo, Atlantic-Congo, Volta-Congo, Benue-Congo, Bantoid, Southern, Narrow Bantu, Central, K, Chokwe-Luchazi (K.20). Bible 1970-1990.

DENGESE ***(NDENGESE, ILEO)*** [DEZ] 4,000 (1977 Voegelin and Voegelin). Kasaï Occidental Province, Dekese Territory. Niger-Congo, Atlantic-Congo, Volta-Congo, Benue-Congo, Bantoid, Southern, Narrow Bantu, Northwest, C, Bushong (C.90).

DING ***(DI, DIN, DZING)*** [DIZ] Bandundu Province, Idofa Territory, on the Kasaï River. Niger-Congo, Atlantic-Congo, Volta-Congo, Benue-Congo, Bantoid, Southern, Narrow Bantu, Northwest, B, Yanzi (B.80). Close to, but separate from Yans.

DONGO ***(DONGA)*** [DOO] 5,000 (1971 Welmers). Orientale Province, east of Watsa. Niger-Congo, Atlantic-Congo, Volta-Congo, North, Adamawa-Ubangi, Ubangi, Sere-Ngbaka-Mba, Ngbaka-Mba, Mba. Different from Dongo which is a dialect of Kresh of Sudan, Dong (Donga) of Nigeria which is in the Chamba group of Adamawa, and Ndo which is Nilo-Saharan.

DZANDO [DZN] 6,000 (1983 census). Equateur Province, Sud Ubangi, Kungu Territory, Mwanda Collectivité, between the Ngiri and Mwanda rivers in the swamp lands in the villages of Lokay, Molunga, Maboko, and Moliba. Niger-Congo, Atlantic-Congo, Volta-Congo, Benue-Congo, Bantoid, Southern, Narrow Bantu, Northwest, C, Bangi-Ntomba (C.40). Dialects: LOKAY, MOLUNGA, MABOKO, MOLIBA. Comprehension of Lifunga dialect of Bamwe is very high. 86% lexical similarity with Lifunga dialect of Bamwe. Nearly everyone speaks Lingala except the oldest women. Other women speak only market Lingala. Riverine.

EFE [EFE] 20,000 (1991 SIL). Orientale Province, Mambasa, Watsa, Irumu, and Djugu territories. Nilo-Saharan, Central Sudanic, East, Mangbutu-Efe. Related to Lese. A separate language from Mamvu. They live among the BaLese, and trade with them. A pygmy group. Forest, savannah. Hunter-gatherers: honey, meat. Traditional religion.

ENYA ***(TSHEENYA, ENA, GENYA)*** [GEY] 7,000 (1977 J. Carrington BAP). On Lualaba River from Kisangani upriver to Kongolo, Orientale Province, Ubundu Territory. Niger-Congo, Atlantic-Congo, Volta-Congo, Benue-Congo, Bantoid, Southern, Narrow Bantu, Central, D, Enya (D.10). 67% lexical similarity with Mituku, 54% with Lega-Shabunda, about 50% with Lega-Mwenga, Bembe, Buyu, and Zimba, 47% with Nyanga, 40% with Lengola, 30% with Komo and Lingala. Fishermen.

FOMA ***(LIFOMA, FUMA)*** [FOM] Orientale Province, on the north side of the Congo River upstream from Basoko. Niger-Congo, Atlantic-Congo, Volta-Congo, Benue-Congo, Bantoid, Southern, Narrow Bantu, Northwest, C, Kele (C.60). Also called 'Pseudo-Bambole'.

FRENCH [FRN] Indo-European, Italic, Romance, Italo-Western, Western, Gallo-Iberian, Gallo-Romance, Gallo-Rhaetian, Oïl, French. Official language. Bible 1530-1986. See main entry under France.

FULIIRU ***(FULIRU, KIFULIRU, FULERO, KIFULERO)*** [FLR] 300,000 (1999 SIL). Sud-Kivu Province, Uvira Territory, north and northwest of Uvira. Niger-Congo, Atlantic-Congo, Volta-Congo, Benue-Congo, Bantoid, Southern, Narrow Bantu, Central, J, Shi-Havu (J.50). 70% lexical similarity with Mashi, 90% with KiNyindu and Joba (KiVira). Bilingualism in Swahili. NT 1998.

FURU ***(BAGERO, BAGIRO, BAGUERO, BAGUIRO)*** [FUU] 12,000 in DRC (1984 census). Population total both countries 16,000. Equateur Province, Nord Ubangi, east of Bosobolo in Bosobolo and Mobaye territories. Also spoken in CAR. Nilo-Saharan, Central Sudanic, West, Bongo-Bagirmi, Kara. Most are bilingual in Lingala, Sango, Mono, or Gbanziri. Lingala comprehension is limited.

GBANZIRI ***(GBANZILI, BANZIRI, GBANDERE)*** [GBG] 3,000 in DRC (1986 SIL). Equateur Province, Nord Ubangi, Bosobolo Territory, a few villages along Ubangi River. Niger-Congo, Atlantic-Congo, Volta-Congo, North, Adamawa-Ubangi, Ubangi, Sere-Ngbaka-Mba, Ngbaka-Mba, Ngbaka, Western, Gbanzili. Bilingualism in Lingala, Mono. See main entry under CAR.

GBATI-RI ***(GBOTE)*** [GTI] Orientale Province, between Isiro and Watsa, north of Mungbere. Niger-Congo, Atlantic-Congo, Volta-Congo, Benue-Congo, Bantoid, Southern, Narrow Bantu, Central, J, Konzo (J.40). Part of a cluster with Nyanga-li and Mayeka.

GILIMA [GIX] 12,000 (1984 census). Equateur Province, Sud Ubangi, in the north of the Libenge Territory in 3 groups: Bogon in the north, Mbanza-Balakpa in the southeast, and Bandi in the southwest. It may also be in CAR. Niger-Congo, Atlantic-Congo, Volta-Congo, North, Adamawa-Ubangi, Ubangi, Sere-Ngbaka-Mba, Ngbaka-Mba, Ngbaka, Western, Bwaka. Closely related to Ngbaka Ma'bo. Very low bilingualism in Lingala. Gilima has recently taken over from Mbanza, Ngbaka, and Ma'bo in the Libenge Zone north of Zongo. Older people speak Mbanza or Ngbaka. Literacy rate in second language: Low.

GOBU ***(GUBU, NGOBO, NGOBU, GABOU, GABU)*** [GOX] 12,000 in DRC (1984 census). Population total both countries 12,000 or more. Equateur Province, Nord Ubangi, Bosobolo Territory, in two areas, north of Bili between Duguru and Borunu on the Sidi road, and in a wide area around Pandu between the villages of Denbili and Bele II. Also spoken in CAR. Niger-Congo, Atlantic-Congo, Volta-Congo, North, Adamawa-Ubangi, Ubangi, Banda, Central, Central Core, Mid-Southern. Closest to Togbo and Mono. High bilingualism in Mono. Most younger men are bilingual in Lingala or Sango. Ethnic attitudes may hinder use of Mono literature. Investigation needed: intelligibility with Togbo, bilingual proficiency in Mono. Literacy rate in second language: Low in Lingala.

HAMBA [HBA] Kasaï Oriental Province, Lodja Territory. Niger-Congo, Atlantic-Congo, Volta-Congo, Benue-Congo, Bantoid, Southern, Narrow Bantu, Central, D, Lega-Kalanga (D.20). Different from Hamba which is a dialect of EkiHaya of Tanzania and Uganda.

HAVU ***(KIHAVU, HAAVU)*** [HAV] Sud-Kivu Province, Kalehe Territory. Niger-Congo, Atlantic-Congo, Volta-Congo, Benue-Congo, Bantoid, Southern, Narrow Bantu, Central, J, Shi-Havu (J.50). Shi has about 70% lexical similarity with Havu. Havu learn Shi, but not vice versa.

HEMA ***(HEMA-SUD, SOUTHERN HEMA, CONGO NYORO, NYORO, RUNYORO)*** [NIX] Population total all countries 160,000 (1996 SIL). Orientale Province, Ituri District, Irumu Territory, around Geti. Also spoken in Rwanda, Uganda. Niger-Congo, Atlantic-Congo, Volta-Congo, Benue-Congo, Bantoid, Southern, Narrow Bantu, Central, J, Nyoro-Ganda (J.10). Dialect: TORO (ORUTORO, TOORO). Toro dialect in DRC is quite different from Nyoro of Uganda. Hema-Sud is different from Hema-Nord (see Lendu). Toro has 78% lexical similarity with Nyoro. Entirely different from Hima in the Haya-Jita subgroup, or the Hima dialect of Nyankore in Uganda.

HEMBA ***(KIHEMBA, EMBA, KIEMBA, LUBA-HEMBA, EASTERN LUBA)*** [HEM] 85,000 (1976). Katanga Province, eastern Kongolo Territory. Niger-Congo, Atlantic-Congo, Volta-Congo, Benue-Congo, Bantoid, Southern, Narrow Bantu, Central, L, Luba (L.30). 67% lexical similarity with Bangubangu, 64% with Songe, higher than 67% with Mikebwe and Hombo.

HOLOHOLO ***(KIHOLOHOLO, HOROHORO, GUHA, KALANGA, KIKALANGA)*** [HOO] Katanga Province, area northwest of Kalemie. Niger-Congo, Atlantic-Congo, Volta-Congo, Benue-Congo, Bantoid, Southern, Narrow Bantu, Central, D, Lega-Kalanga (D.20). KiKaranga may be separate. Different from Holu (Kiholo, Holo). Bible portions 1948. See main entry under Tanzania.

HOLU ***(KIHOLU, HOLO, KIHOLO)*** [HOL] Extreme southwest corner of Bandundu Province. Niger-Congo, Atlantic-Congo, Volta-Congo, Benue-Congo, Bantoid, Southern, Narrow Bantu, Central, K, Holu (K.10). Closely related to Samba. Different from Holoholo. Yeci is a related dialect or language. Bible portions 1943-1956. See main entry under Angola.

HUNDE ***(KIHUNDE, KOBI, RUKOBI)*** [HKE] 200,000 (1980 UBS). Nord-Kivu Province, Masisi and Rutshuru territories. Apparently none in Uganda. Niger-Congo, Atlantic-Congo, Volta-Congo, Benue-Congo, Bantoid, Southern, Narrow Bantu, Central, J, Shi-Havu (J.50). 75% lexical similarity with Tembo, 65% with Nandi, 57% with Nyanga and Shi, about 50% with Lega-Shabunda. Traditional religion, Christian. NT 1987.

HUNGANA ***(HUNGANNA, HUANA, KIHUNGANA, HUNGAAN)*** [HUM] Small. Bandundu Province, Bulungu Territory. Niger-Congo, Atlantic-Congo, Volta-Congo, Benue-Congo, Bantoid, Southern, Narrow Bantu, Central, H, Hungana (H.40). SVO. Bible portions 1920-1935.

JOBA ***(KIJOBA, VIRA, KIVIRA)*** [JOB] 10,000 (1989 SIL). Sud-Kivu Province, Uvira Territory, north and northwest of Uvira. Niger-Congo, Atlantic-Congo, Volta-Congo, Benue-Congo, Bantoid, Southern, Narrow Bantu, Central, J, Shi-Havu (J.50). May be the same as Zyoba of Tanzania and DRC. Speakers are highly bilingual in Fuliiru. Investigation needed: bilingual proficiency in Fuliiru.

KABWARI [KCW] Sud-Kivu or Katanga provinces. Niger-Congo, Atlantic-Congo, Volta-Congo, Benue-Congo, Bantoid, Southern, Narrow Bantu, Central, J, Shi-Havu (J.50).

KAIKU ***(IKAIKU, KAIKO)*** [KKQ] Orientale Province, Ituri District, Mambasa Territory, Babombi Collectivité. Niger-Congo, Atlantic-Congo, Volta-Congo, Benue-Congo, Bantoid, Southern, Narrow Bantu, Central, D, Bira-Huku (D.30). Closest to Bila and Bhele. About 80% lexical similarity with Bhele and Bila, 70% with Komo, 56% with Bera, 20% to 25% with Mbo, Ndaka, and Budu. The people are considered to be Bila.

KAKWA ***(BARI KAKWA)*** [KEO] 20,000 in DRC. Orientale Province, Aru Territory, north of Aru, and Faradje Territory. Nilo-Saharan, Eastern Sudanic, Nilotic, Eastern, Bari. Christian in DRC. Bible 1983. See main entry under Uganda.

KALIKO ***(KELIKO, KALIKO-MA'DI, MA'DI, MADITI)*** [KBO] 7,500 in DRC (1989 SIL). Orientale Province, northern Aru Territory, along the Sudan border. Nilo-Saharan, Central Sudanic, East, Moru-Madi, Central. Dialects: DIDI, DOGO. The two dialects in DRC are inherently intelligible. Dogo dialect is more like Sudanese Kaliko. See main entry under Sudan.

KANGO ***(DIKANGO, KANGO PIGMY)*** [KBI] Orientale Province, Tshopo District, Bafwasende Territory, among the Bali. Niger-Congo, Atlantic-Congo, Volta-Congo, Benue-Congo, Bantoid, Southern, Narrow Bantu, Central, D, Lega-Kalanga (D.20). 78% lexical similarity with Komo, 72% with Bila, 60% with Bali, 50% with Lika. Bilingualism in Bali. Evidently a combination of Komo and Bali, with some borrowings from the Bila-based Mbuti pygmy language. Pygmies, different from riverine Kango [KTY] to the north, who are fishermen. Investigation needed: bilingual proficiency in Bali. Tropical forest. Hunter-gatherers. Traditional religion.

KANGO ***(LIKANGO)*** [KTY] Orientale Province, Bas-Uélé District, along the banks of the Uélé River and its tributaries. Niger-Congo, Atlantic-Congo, Volta-Congo, Benue-Congo, Bantoid, Southern, Narrow Bantu, Northwest, C, Ngombe (C.50). Dialects: BOMOKANDI, UÉLÉ. One dialect has 70% to 75% lexical similarity with Pagibete, 66% with Ngelima, 75% to 80% with Bwa, 60% with Lika. Bomokandi has 60% to 65% with Bwa and Pagibete, 68% with Lika, 58% with Ngelima. Both dialects have 50% with Bali and Komo. Said to be a pidginized language. It may be a cover term for a variety of dialects spoken by fishermen, called 'Bakango'. Different from Dikango, a pygmy language spoken among the Bali. The Ngombe group is sometimes called Bantu C.40 rather than C.50.

KANGO ***(DIKANGO, KANGO PYGMY, LIKANGO, KIKANGO, "KIBATCHUA", "DIBATCHUA")*** [KZY] 2,000 (1998 T. Harvey) to 5,000 (1998 J. Farmer). Orientale Province, Tshopo District, Bafwasende Territory, among the Bali, primarily in the Bakundumu and Bemili collectivités. The smaller dialect has 7 villages just to the south of where the Nepoki River meets the Ituri to become the Aruwimi River. Niger-Congo, Atlantic-Congo, Volta-Congo, Benue-Congo, Bantoid, Southern, Narrow Bantu, Central, D, Bira-Huku (D.30). 2 dialects, inherently intelligible with each other. Related to Bali and Komo. They speak Bali as second language. Lingala is preferred by those whose permanent villages are to the north, and Congo Swahili by those whose permanent villages are to the south. No monolinguals. The people call themselves 'Bakango', and their language 'Dikango'. Different from the riverine Kango to the north, who are fishermen. Those who attend school have completed Standard 1 or 2. 5 vowels. Literacy rate in second language: 1%. Riverine. 500 meters. Traditional religion, Christian.

KANU ***(LIKANU, KAANU, KANO)*** [KHX] 3,500 (1971 Welmers). Nord-Kivu Province, Walikale Territory, Kabunga area. Niger-Congo, Atlantic-Congo, Volta-Congo, Benue-Congo, Bantoid, Southern, Narrow Bantu, Central, D, Lega-Kalanga (D.20). Probably a dialect of Lega-Shabunda.

KANYOK ***(KANYOKA, KANIOKA)*** [KNY] 200,000 (1991 UBS). Kasaï Oriental Province, Mwene-Ditu Territory, between the Bushimaie and Luembe rivers. Niger-Congo, Atlantic-Congo, Volta-Congo, Benue-Congo, Bantoid, Southern, Narrow Bantu, Central, L, Luba (L.30). NT, in press (1997).

KAONDE ***(CHIKAONDE, KAWONDE, CHIKAHONDE)*** [KQN] 36,000 in DRC (1995 estimate). Katanga Province, eastern part of Kolwezi Territory. Niger-Congo, Atlantic-Congo, Volta-Congo, Benue-Congo, Bantoid, Southern, Narrow Bantu, Central, L, Kaonde (L.40). Bible 1975. See main entry under Zambia.

KARI ***(KARE, LI-KARI-LI)*** [KBJ] 1,000. Scattered groups in northwestern Orientale Province, north of Uele River. Only scattered speakers in CAR (1996). Niger-Congo, Atlantic-Congo, Volta-Congo, Benue-Congo, Bantoid, Southern, Narrow Bantu, Central, D, Bira-Huku (D.30).

KELA ***(OKELA, IKELA, LEMBA)*** [KEL] 180,000 (1972 Barrett). Kasaï Oriental Province, Lomela Territory. Niger-Congo, Atlantic-Congo, Volta-Congo, Benue-Congo, Bantoid, Southern, Narrow Bantu, Northwest, C, Tetela (C.80). Traditional religion, Christian. Bible portions 1940.

KELE ***(LOKELE, EKELE, KILI, LIKELO, YAKUSU)*** [KHY] 160,000 (1980 UBS) including 7,000 Yalikoka (1977 Voegelin and Voegelin). Orientale Province, Isangi Territory, on Lomami and Congo rivers. Niger-Congo, Atlantic-Congo, Volta-Congo, Benue-Congo, Bantoid, Southern, Narrow Bantu, Northwest, C, Kele (C.60). Distinct from Kele (Dikele) of Gabon. Ethnic groups: Lileko, Mbooso, Yalikoka, Yaokandja, Yawemba. Trade language. Christian, traditional religion. NT 1918-1958.

KETE ***(LUKETE, KIKETE)*** [KCV] Kasaï Occidental Provice, northeast of Mweka. Niger-Congo, Atlantic-Congo, Volta-Congo, Benue-Congo, Bantoid, Southern, Narrow Bantu, Central, L, Songye (L.20).

KITUBA ***(KIKONGO-KUTUBA, KIKONGO SIMPLIFIÉ, KIKONGO YA LETA, KILETA, KIKONGO COMMERCIAL, KIBULAMATADI)*** [KTU] 4,200,000 (1990 UBS), 5,000,000 including second language users (1989 Mufwene). Orientale and southern Bandundu provinces. Creole, Kongo based. Dialects: IKELEVE, WESTERN KITUBA, EASTERN KITUBA. A creole based on the KiKongo dialect spoken in Manianga area (Bas-Congo), but unintelligible to speakers of it or other Kikongo dialects. Influenced by Lingala, French, restructured Swahili, Portuguese, and other local dialects. Munukutuba of Congo is closely related. Means of communication among various language groups. Bible 1990.

KOMO ***(KIKOMO, KIKUMU, KIKUUMU, KIKUMO, KUUMU, KUMU, KUMO)*** [KMW] 400,000 (1998 SIL). Maniema Province, and into Orientale and Nord-Kivu provinces, as far as Walikale, Opienge, and Punia. Lubutu is the center. Niger-Congo, Atlantic-Congo, Volta-Congo, Benue-Congo, Bantoid, Southern, Narrow Bantu, Central, D, Bira-Huku (D.30). No dialects, but speech varieties have the following differences: up to 10% lexical differences, whether or not the shape of the alienable possessive markers is used. Lubutu differed the most from other dialects in lexicon. 80% lexical similarity with Bhele, 70% with Bila, 58% with Bera, 48% with Bwa, 46% with Bali, Lika, and Pagibete, about 30% with Lingala, Lega-Shabunda, and Budu. Bilingual level estimates for Congo Swahili are 0 %, 1 %, 2 5%, 3 10%, 4 60%, 5 15%. Many Komo are fairly fluent in Congo Swahili. Those around Kisangani are more likely to know Lingala than Congo Swahili (more than 10% of the men). All ages except in population centers where the first language is Congo Swahili, and then it is 7 and older for boys. Used by Lengola speakers as their second language. SVO; prepositions; noun head followed by genitive and relative clause; question word initial; 7 prefixes; 4 suffixes; word order distinjguishes subject, object, indirect object; human-animate-inanimate contrast in plural and adjective agreement (no Bantu concord); verb affixes obligatorily mark person and number of subject and object; some ergativity in gerund phrase; middle, stative, unaccusative marked by suffix; causatives marked by suffix; comparisons; CV, V, Nasal CV, CV Nasal, Nasal; tonal. Literacy rate in first language: 1%. Literacy rate in second language: 50% older men (born before 1970), 30% younger men, less than 10% women. Poetry. Tropical forest. Interfluvial, mountain valley. Swidden agriculturalists. 450 to 600 meters. Christian, traditional religion, Muslim, other. Bible portions 1991.

KONGO ***(KIKONGO, CONGO)*** [KON] 1,000,000 in DRC (1986 UBS). Population total all countries 3,217,000 (1991 UBS). Bas-Congo Province. Cataract dialect in Bas-Congo Province and around Mbanza Manteke, Fioti north of Boma and scattered communities along the Congo River from Brazzaville to its mouth. Also spoken in Angola, Congo. Niger-Congo, Atlantic-Congo, Volta-Congo, Benue-Congo, Bantoid, Southern, Narrow Bantu, Central, H, Kongo (H.10). Dialects: SOUTH CONGO, CENTRAL KONGO, WEST KONGO (FIOTE, FIOTI), BWENDE (BUENDE), LAADI, EAST KONGO, SOUTHEAST KONGO, NZAMBA (DZAMBA). Fioti and San Salvador are distinct enough to need separate literature. Fioti is also spoken by the Buende and Vili peoples. National language. SVO (for Dzamba). Christian. Bible 1905-1933.

KONGO, SAN SALVADOR ***(KIKONGO, CONGO, KISIKONGO, KIKOONGO)*** [KWY] Population total both countries 1,500,000 (1989 UBS). Along the Congo River below Kinshasa in DRC and northern Angola. Also spoken in Angola. Niger-Congo, Atlantic-Congo, Volta-Congo, Benue-Congo, Bantoid, Southern, Narrow Bantu, Central, H, Kongo (H.10). Bible 1916-1926.

KPALA ***(KWALA, KPWAALA, GBAKPWA)*** [KPL] 3,000 (1986 SIL). Equateur Province, small groups in Libenge and Bosobolo territories. Niger-Congo, Atlantic-Congo, Volta-Congo, North, Adamawa-Ubangi, Ubangi, Sere-Ngbaka-Mba, Ngbaka-Mba, Ngbaka, Western, Monzombo. Closely related to Monzombo. Bilingualism in Lingala. Active language use. Different from Kpala which is a dialect of Kresh of Sudan.

KUSU ***(KIKUSU, KUTSU, LOKUTSU, KONGOLA, FULUKA)*** [KSV] 26,000 (1971 Welmers). Southwestern corner of Maniema Province, Kibombo Territory. Niger-Congo, Atlantic-Congo, Volta-Congo, Benue-Congo, Bantoid, Southern, Narrow Bantu, Northwest, C, Tetela (C.80).

KWAMI ***(KIKWAMI, KIKWAME, KWAME)*** [KTF] Small. Maniema and Nord-Kivu provinces, between Kasese and Walikale. Niger-Congo, Atlantic-Congo, Volta-Congo, Benue-Congo, Bantoid, Southern, Narrow Bantu, Central, D, Lega-Kalanga (D.20). 70% lexical similarity with Nyanga, 68% with Lega-Shabunda, 66% with Kanu and Enya, 61% with Mituku, 57% with Zimba, 55% with Bembe, 52% with Lega-Mwenga, 49% with Hunde and Shi, 48% with Buyu, 47% with Tembo, 46% with Nande, 41% with Lengola, 34% with Komo. More influence from Lega than from Komo.

KWESE ***(PINDI, KIKWESE, UKWESE)*** [KWS] 60,000. Eastern Bandundu Province, west of Kikwit. Niger-Congo, Atlantic-Congo, Volta-Congo, Benue-Congo, Bantoid, Southern, Narrow Bantu, Central, K, Holu (K.10). Bible portions 1929.

LALA-BISA [LEB] Extreme southeast corner of Katanga Province. Niger-Congo, Atlantic-Congo, Volta-Congo, Benue-Congo, Bantoid, Southern, Narrow Bantu, Central, M, Bisa-Lamba (M.50), Bisa. Dialects: AMBO (BAMBO, KAMBONSENGA), LUANO, SWAKA, WULIMA, LALA (ICHILALA), BISA (ICHIBISA, WIZA). NT 1947-1977. See main entry under Zambia.

LALIA [LAL] 55,000 or more (1993 estimate). Southeast corner of Equateur Province, Ikela Territory, collectivités of Tumbenga, Lokina, Lofume, Tshwapa, and Loile. Yalosaka is the center. Niger-Congo, Atlantic-Congo, Volta-Congo, Benue-Congo, Bantoid, Southern, Narrow Bantu, Northwest, C, Mongo (C.70). Mongo and Lingala are used in church. Young people continue to use Lalia. Distinct from Mongo.

LAMBA ***(ICHILAMBA, CHILAMBA)*** [LAB] Southeast corner of Katanga Province. Niger-Congo, Atlantic-Congo, Volta-Congo, Benue-Congo, Bantoid, Southern, Narrow Bantu, Central, M, Bisa-Lamba (M.50), Lamba. Bible 1959. See main entry under Zambia.

LANGBASHE ***(LANGBASHI, LANGBASE, LANGBASI, LANGWASI, LANGBWASSE)*** [LNA] 3,000 in DRC (1984 census). Equateur Province, Nord Ubangi, Bosobolo Territory, along the Ubangi River, villages of Sidi, Bada, Zimango, Banga, Boduna, and a few other villages elsewhere in the territory. Niger-Congo, Atlantic-Congo, Volta-Congo, North, Adamawa-Ubangi, Ubangi, Banda, South Central. Investigation needed: intelligibility with Ngbugu, Langba, South Central Banda. See main entry under CAR.

LEGA-MWENGA ***(SHILE, KILEGA, REGA, KIREGA, LEKA-SHILE, LEKA-SILE, ISHILE, ILEKA ISHILE)*** [LGM] 35,000 to 40,000 or more (1994 ACM). Sud-Kivu Province, Mwenga Territory. Niger-Congo, Atlantic-Congo, Volta-Congo, Benue-Congo, Bantoid, Southern, Narrow Bantu, Central, D, Lega-Kalanga (D.20). Dialects: IYOKO, IBANDA, ISOPO, LUSENGE, BILEMBO-MANGO, MIZULO. There are about 20 dialects. Speakers say Lega-Shabunda and Bembe are difficult to understand. 96% to 88% lexical similarity among dialects, 84% to 76% with Bembe, 81% to 67% with Lega-Shabunda, about 60% with Buyu, 50% with Zimba, Enya, and Mituku, 45% with Nyanga. Congo Swahili is the language of instruction in school.

LEGA-SHABUNDA ***(KILEGA, REGA, KIREGA, ILEKA-IGONZABALE, LEKA-IGONZABALE, IGONZABALE)*** [LEA] 400,000 (1982 UBS). Sud-Kivu and Maniema provinces, Shabunda, and Pangi territories. The first 5 dialects are in Shabunda Territory, Kinyamunsange is in Pangi Territory. Niger-Congo, Atlantic-Congo, Volta-Congo, Benue-Congo, Bantoid, Southern, Narrow Bantu, Central, D, Lega-Kalanga (D.20). Dialects: KIGALA, KIGYOMA, LILIGA, KISEDE, KINYABANGA, KINYAMUNSANGE (PANGI). Kanu is probably a dialect with 92% similarity. 67% to 81% lexical similarity with Lega-Mwenga, about 65% with Kwami, 60% with Bembe, 55% with Budu, Mituku and Enya, 50% with Zimba, Nyanga, and Hunde, 45% with Nandi, 30% with Komo. Traditional religion, Christian. NT 1957.

LELE ***(USILELE, BASHILELE)*** [LEL] 26,000 (1971 Welmers). Western edge of Kasaï Occidental Province, Ilebo and Tshikapa territories, and extreme east of Bandundu Province, Idiofa and Gungu territories. Niger-Congo, Atlantic-Congo, Volta-Congo, Benue-Congo, Bantoid, Southern, Narrow Bantu, Northwest, C, Bushong (C.90). Intelligible with Wongo. Different from Lele of CAR and Chad.

LENDU ***(BBADHA, BBALEDHA, KILENDU, BALETHA, BATHA, BALENDRU, BALE, HEMA-NORD, KIHEMA-NORD)*** [LED] 750,000 in DRC (1996 C. Kutsch Lojenga SIL). Population total both countries 760,000. Orientale Province, Ituri District, Djugu Territory, west and northwest of Lake Albert. Also spoken in Uganda. Nilo-Saharan, Central Sudanic, East, Lendu. Dialects: DJADHA, TADHA, PIDHA, DDRALO, NJAWLO, GEGERE. Tadha is the standard dialect. Djadha is the largest dialect and the one used for literature. Gegere is spoken by the ethnic Hema. Bilingualism in Swahili. Spoken as mother tongue by people from 4 ethnic backgrounds: Lendu, Hema-North, Alur, and Okebu. Investigation needed: intelligibility with Tadha with other dialects. Christian. NT 1936-1989.

LENGOLA ***(KILENGOLA, LENGORA)*** [LEJ] 100,000 or fewer (1998). Orientale Province, Ubundu Territory, Maniema Province, Lubutu and Punia territories, both sides of the Lualaba River, but more on the west side within a triangle between Opienge, Lowa, and a point called 'Km 100' on the Kisangani-Lubutu road. Niger-Congo, Atlantic-Congo, Volta-Congo, Benue-Congo, Bantoid, Southern, Narrow Bantu, Central, D, Enya (D.10). There are reported to be 2 dialects which differ in pronunciation. About 40% lexical similarity with Enya and Mituku, 35% to 40% with Budu and Komo, 30% to 35% with Lega-Shabunda, Lega-Mwenga, and Zimba, 25% to 30% with Bembe, Buyu, and Bali. Some Congo Swahili or Komo is used as second language. Riverine. Agriculturalists, fishermen, hunters. Christian, Muslim.

LESE ***(LESA, LESSE, LISSI, WALISI, WALESE, BALESE, MBUTI)*** [LES] 50,000 (1991 SIL). Orientale Province, Watsa, Djugu, Irumu, and Mambasa territories. Nilo-Saharan, Central Sudanic, East, Mangbutu-Efe. Dialects: LESE KARO, ARUMBI (UPSTREAM LESE), NDESE (LESE DESE), VUKUTU (VONKUTU, OBI), FARE. Closely related to Mamvu, Bendi, Mangbutu, and Efe. Congo Swahili (Kingwana) and Bangala are the lingua francas, but their use is somewhat limited, especially among the women. Agriculturalists. Traditional religion, Christian.

LIBINZA ***(LIBINJA)*** [LIZ] 10,000 (1986 SIL). Equateur Province, Sud Ubangi and Equateur districts, in Kungu and northern Bomongo districts, on the Ngiri and Mwanda rivers, from the villages of Monia and Boniange southwards, on islands as far as Bomongo. Niger-Congo, Atlantic-Congo, Volta-Congo, Benue-Congo, Bantoid, Southern, Narrow Bantu, Northwest, C, Bangi-Ntomba (C.40), Ngiri. Dialects: MONIA, BONIANGE, KUTU. There are other dialects besides those listed. Dialects or closely related languages: Balobo (Likila), Ndobo. Different from the Libinja dialect of Ngombe.

LIGENZA ***(GENDJA, DIGENJA, GENDZA-BALI)*** [LGZ] 43,000 (1986 SIL). Equateur Province, Bumba Territory, 3 or 4 small areas. Niger-Congo, Atlantic-Congo, Volta-Congo, Benue-Congo, Bantoid, Southern, Narrow Bantu, Northwest, C, Ngombe (C.50). Dialects: BOKOY, ELOWA, BENZA, BOLUPI. High bilingualism in Lingala for all speakers. Literacy rate in second language: High in Lingala.

LIKA ***(KILIKA, TORIKO, KPONGO, MABITI)*** [LIK] 60,000 including 57,000 in Wamba District, 3,000 in Rungu District (1989 SIL). Orientale Province, Upper-Uele District, Wamba Territory, Balika-Toriko Collectivité. Some in Rungu Territory, Mongomasi Collectivité. Niger-Congo, Atlantic-Congo, Volta-Congo, Benue-Congo, Bantoid, Southern, Narrow Bantu, Central, D, Lega-Kalanga (D.20). Dialects: LIKÓ (IKÓ), LILIKÓ, LILIKÁ (LIKÁ). 65% to 70% lexical similarity with Bomokandi Kango, 55% to 60% with Pagibete, Bwa,and Uélé Kango, 52% with Bali, 51% with Ngelima, 46% with Komo, about 40% with Bhele, Bila, and Bera, 30% with Budu, 25% with Lega languages and Lingala. Swahili is used as second language in southern Wamba Zone, Bangala in Rungu Zone, some Meje, and Budu is also used. Ethnic groups: Mabiti and Maliko. 2 secondary schools, 15 primary schools, but Lika is not used in the schools. Forest. Agriculturalists: coffee, manioc, peanuts, bananas, palm oil, rice, papaya, pineapple, sugar cane, sweet potatoes, yams, eggplant; chickens; fishermen. Christian, Muslim.

LIKILA ***(BANGELA, BALOBO)*** [LIE] Equateur Province, around Makanza town on the northern bank of the Congo River. Niger-Congo, Atlantic-Congo, Volta-Congo, Benue-Congo, Bantoid, Southern, Narrow Bantu, Northwest, C, Bangi-Ntomba (C.40), Ngiri. Dialect or closely related language to Libinza or Baloi.

LINGALA ***(NGALA)*** [LIN] Second language speakers together with Bangala: 7,000,000 (1999 WA). Population total all countries 309,100 or more. Widely used in Bandundu, Equateur, and Orientale provinces, except the southeast of Orientale. Also spoken in CAR, Congo. Niger-Congo, Atlantic-Congo, Volta-Congo, Benue-Congo, Bantoid, Southern, Narrow Bantu, Northwest, C, Bangi-Ntomba (C.40), Lusengo. Close to Lusengo and Bangala. 33% lexical similarity with Bobangi. Degree of effective understanding and use varies with location, age, rural versus urban and commercial centers, ethnically mixed areas, formal education. Variation in communities. National language. Dictionary. SVO. Bible 1970.

LOBALA [LOQ] 40,000 in DRC (1983 census). Population total both countries 40,000 or more. Equateur Province, Sud Ubangi and Equateur districts, Kungu and Bomongo territories, on the road northeast of Dongo as far as the village of Mokusi, and on the road south from Dongo following the Ubangi River, and forest south and west of this road. Also spoken in Congo. Niger-Congo, Atlantic-Congo, Volta-Congo, Benue-Congo, Bantoid, Southern, Narrow Bantu, Northwest, C, Bangi-Ntomba (C.40). Dialects: POKO, SOUTH LOBALA, TANDA, LIKOKA. Closest to Bomboma and Libinza in DRC. 65% lexical similarity with Lingala. Bilingualism in Lingala.

LOGO ***(LOGOTI)*** [LOG] 210,000 (1989 SIL) including 100,000 Ogambi. Orientale Province, Faradje Territory and Watsa town. Nilo-Saharan, Central Sudanic, East, Moru-Madi, Central. Dialects:

OGAMBI (OGAMARU, NORTHERN LOGO), DOKA, LOLYA, OBILEBHA (OBELEBHA, OBILEBA), BHAGIRA (BAGELA), BARI (BARI-LOGO, BARITI). A dialect cluster, with Lolya as central. Closely related to Avokaya and Omi. Avokaya in DRC spoken in the northern Ogambi Area, may be closer to Logo than to Avokaya in Sudan. Christian, traditional religion. Bible portions 1924-1927.

LOMBI ***(LUMBI, ROMBI, RUMLI, ODYALOMBITO)*** [LMI] 12,000 (1993 SIL). Orientale Province, Tshopo District, Bafwasende Territory, Barumi and Bekeni collectivités. Opienge, Banguruye, and Bangolu are centers. Nilo-Saharan, Central Sudanic, East, Mangbetu. Closely related to Mangbetu, but not as close as Mangbetu dialects are to each other. Different than the Lombi dialect of Basa in Cameroon.

LOMBO ***(OLOMBO, ULUMBU, TURUMBU)*** [LOO] 10,000 (1971 Welmers). Orientale Province, both sides of Congo River in Isangi area. Niger-Congo, Atlantic-Congo, Volta-Congo, Benue-Congo, Bantoid, Southern, Narrow Bantu, Northwest, C, Kele (C.60). Reported to readily understand Kele. Investigation needed: intelligibility, bilingual proficiency.

LONZO [LNZ] Small. Bandundu Province, Kenge Territory. Niger-Congo, Atlantic-Congo, Volta-Congo, Benue-Congo, Bantoid, Southern, Narrow Bantu, Central, H, Yaka (H.30).

LUBA-KASAI ***(LUBA-LULUA, TSHILUBA, WESTERN LUBA, LUVA)*** [LUB] 6,300,000 (1991 UBS). Used throughout Kasaï Occidental and Kasaï Oriental provinces. Niger-Congo, Atlantic-Congo, Volta-Congo, Benue-Congo, Bantoid, Southern, Narrow Bantu, Central, L, Luba (L.30). Significant dialect differences between East Kasai Region (Baluba people) and West Kasai Region (Bena Lulua people). Hemba is a closely related language. National language. Literacy rate in second language: Over 60% among Christians. Christian; over 1/3. Bible 1927-1996.

LUBA-KATANGA ***(LUBA-SHABA, KILUBA)*** [LUH] 1,505,000 (1991 UBS). Katanga Province, Haut-Lomami District. Niger-Congo, Atlantic-Congo, Volta-Congo, Benue-Congo, Bantoid, Southern, Narrow Bantu, Central, L, Luba (L.30). Bible 1951.

LUGBARA ***(HIGH LUGBARA)*** [LUG] 288,000 in DRC (1993 Johnstone). Orientale Province, Aru Territory, 6 collectivités. Nilo-Saharan, Central Sudanic, East, Moru-Madi, Central. Dialects: ZAKI, ABEDJU-AZAKI, LU, ALURU, NIO, OTSHO. Aluru is reported to be influenced by Ndo; Nio and Otsho are similar to Uganda Lugbara. Christian in DRC. Bible 1966. See main entry under Uganda.

LUNA ***(INKONGO, KUBA, NORTHERN LUBA)*** [LUJ] 50,000. Kasaï Oriental Province, Lusambo Territory. Niger-Congo, Atlantic-Congo, Volta-Congo, Benue-Congo, Bantoid, Southern, Narrow Bantu, Central, L, Songye (L.20). Bible 1927-1932, out of print.

LUNDA ***(CHILUNDA)*** [LVN] Southern and southwestern Katanga Province, Lualaba District; extreme south of Bandundu Province, Kahemba Territory. Niger-Congo, Atlantic-Congo, Volta-Congo, Benue-Congo, Bantoid, Southern, Narrow Bantu, Central, K, Salampasu-Ndembo (K.30). Dialects: LUNDA NDEMBU, LUNDA KALUNDA, LUNDA KAMBOVE. Ruund is a closely related language. Bible 1962. See main entry under Zambia.

LUSENGO ***(LOSENGO)*** [LUS] Primarily on the Congo River in Equateur Province, Mankanza, Lisala, and Bumba territories. Niger-Congo, Atlantic-Congo, Volta-Congo, Benue-Congo, Bantoid, Southern, Narrow Bantu, Northwest, C, Bangi-Ntomba (C.40), Lusengo. Dialects: KANGANA, ILIKU (ELEKO, LEKO, ELEKU, LOLEKO, LEKU), LIMPESA, LIPOTO (UPOTO, KELE, INGUNDJI), BUMWANGI, BUSU DJANGA, EMPESA POKO, ESUMBU, KUNDA, KUMBA, LUSENGO POTO, MONGALA POTO, NGUNDI, MONGO. Bible portions 1898-1920.

LWALU [LWA] 21,000 (1971 Welmers). Kasaï Occidental Province, Luiza Territory. Niger-Congo, Atlantic-Congo, Volta-Congo, Benue-Congo, Bantoid, Southern, Narrow Bantu, Central, L, Luba (L.30).

MA ***(AMADI, MADI, MADYO)*** [MSJ] 4,700 (1977 Voegelin and Voegelin). Orientale Province, north of Niangara, close to Kapili River. Niger-Congo, Atlantic-Congo, Volta-Congo, North, Adamawa-Ubangi, Ubangi, Sere-Ngbaka-Mba, Ngbaka-Mba, Mba. Closest to Dongo.

MABAALE ***(LOMABAALE, MABALE, MBALI)*** [MMZ] Equateur Province, Ngiri River area. Niger-Congo, Atlantic-Congo, Volta-Congo, Benue-Congo, Bantoid, Southern, Narrow Bantu, Northwest, C, Bangi-Ntomba (C.40). Dialects: BEMBE, LIPANJA, BANZA, MBINGA, LOBO (BALOBO).

MAMVU ***(TENGO)*** [MDI] 60,000 (1991 SIL). Orientale Province, west and southwest of Watsa in Watsa Territory. Possibly some in Uganda. Nilo-Saharan, Central Sudanic, East, Mangbutu-Efe. Dialects: AMENGI, MAMVU (MOMVU, MOMFU). They call their language 'Tengo'. A separate language from Efe. Bible portions 1931.

MANGBETU ***(NEMANGBETU, MANGBETTU, MAMBETTO, AMANGBETU, KINGBETU)*** [MDJ] 620,000. Population total both countries 650,000 (1985 UBS). Orientale Province, Rungu, Niangara, Poko, Watsa, Wamba and northeast corner of Banalia territories. The Popoi group is in Banalia Territory, and the Aberu group is in Wamba Territory. None in Uganda. Also spoken in Uganda. Nilo-Saharan, Central Sudanic, East, Mangbetu. Dialects: MEJE (MEDJE), MANGBETU, MAKERE, MALELE, POPOI. The Medje dialect is reported to have the most speakers, and is the most widely understood. Lombi and Asua are related separate languages. Perhaps 50% know Bangala, another 10% know a limited amount. Popoi and Aberu are in Swahili-speaking areas. Names of ethnic groups: Mangbetu, Mabisanga (clan name), Medje, Makere, Aberu, Popoi, Malele. Investigation needed: intelligibility.

MANGBUTU ***(MOMBUTTU, WAMBUTU, MANGU-NGUTU)*** [MDK] 15,000 including 1,200 Andinai (1991 SIL). Orientale Province, south of the Kibali River and east of the Moto River in Watsa Territory. Nilo-Saharan, Central Sudanic, East, Mangbutu-Efe. Dialects: ANDINAI, MAKUTANA, ANGWE (ANDALI). The Andinai are separated from the other Mangbutu by the Lese. The Andali are a clan speaking the Angwe dialect. Savannah. Christian.

MAYEKA [MYC] Vicinity of Congo, CAR, DRC borders. Not in CAR. Niger-Congo, Atlantic-Congo, Volta-Congo, Benue-Congo, Bantoid, Southern, Narrow Bantu, Central, J, Konzo (J.40). Part of the same dialect cluster as Nyanga-li, Gbati-ri.

MAYOGO ***(MAIGO, MAIKO, MAYKO, KIYOGO, MAJUGU, MAYUGO)*** [MDM] 100,000 (1991 McCord SIL). Orientale Province, Isiro area. Most are in the Rungu and Wamba territories. Niger-Congo, Atlantic-Congo, Volta-Congo, North, Adamawa-Ubangi, Ubangi, Sere-Ngbaka-Mba, Ngbaka-Mba, Ngbaka, Eastern, Mayogo-Bangba. Dialects: MADIMADOKO, MADIPIA (MABOZO, MAGBAI, MABODESE, MADJEDJE). Between 70% to 75% lexical similarity with Bangba, 62% with Mündü. Bangala is the main lingua franca, then Lingala. Bangba used by the older generation. Increasingly the young are using Lingala. Speakers use Mayogo when in the village or city. Ethnic groups: Bakango, Dai (Day, Angai), Maambi, Mangbele. Christian, traditional religion.

MBA ***(KIMANGA, MANGA, KIMBANGA)*** [MFC] 14,000 to 20,000 (1977 UFM). Orientale Province, Banalia Territory, Banjwade area. Niger-Congo, Atlantic-Congo, Volta-Congo, North, Adamawa-Ubangi, Ubangi, Sere-Ngbaka-Mba, Ngbaka-Mba, Mba. Bilingualism in Congo Swahili. Vigorous. Children have difficulty with Congo Swahili. Perhaps 45% of children are in school. SVO, SOV.

MBALA ***(GIMBALA, RUMBALA)*** [MDP] 200,000 (1972 Nida). Bandundu Province, Bagata and Bulungu territories, between Kwango and Kwilu rivers. Niger-Congo, Atlantic-Congo, Volta-Congo, Benue-Congo, Bantoid, Southern, Narrow Bantu, Central, K, Mbala (K.60). Speakers are fairly bilingual in Kituba. Bible portions 1931-1968.

MBANDJA ***(MBANZA, MBANJA, MBANDZA)*** [ZMZ] Population total all countries 200,000 (1982 M. Hill). Equateur Province, various areas in Sud Ubangi, Nord Ubangi, and western Mongala districts, to west, southwest, and east of the Ngbaka language. Also spoken in CAR, Congo. Niger-Congo, Atlantic-Congo, Volta-Congo, North, Adamawa-Ubangi, Ubangi, Banda, Southern. Dialects: KALA, GBADO. Lingala is the lingua franca; in some areas up to 60% speak it and 40% understand it in varying degrees. NT 1998.

MBESA ***(MOMBESA, MOBESA)*** [ZMS] Orientale Province, northern Yahuma Territory, south of Congo River. Niger-Congo, Atlantic-Congo, Volta-Congo, Benue-Congo, Bantoid, Southern, Narrow Bantu, Northwest, C, Kele (C.60).

MBO ***(KIMBO, IMBO)*** [ZMW] 11,000 (1994 SIL). Orientale Province, Ituri District, Mambasa Territory, Bombo Collectivité. Niger-Congo, Atlantic-Congo, Volta-Congo, Benue-Congo, Bantoid, Southern, Narrow Bantu, Central, D, Bira-Huku (D.30). Speakers Ndaka, Budu, Vanuma, Nyali, and Mbo agree that their languages are closer to each other than to other border Bantu languages. One dialect. 87% lexical similarity with Ndaka, 78% with Budu, 77% with Vanuma, 76% with Nyali, 30% with Komo, 25% with Bhele, Kaiku, Bila, Bera. Different from Mbo of Cameroon, which is Bantu A.10. Investigation needed: intelligibility with Ndaka. Traditional religion, Muslim.

MBOLE ***(LOMBOLE)*** [MDQ] 100,000 (1971 Welmers). Orientale Province, southwest of Kisangani. Niger-Congo, Atlantic-Congo, Volta-Congo, Benue-Congo, Bantoid, Southern, Narrow Bantu, Central, D, Enya (D.10). Dialects: KEEMBO, NKIMBE (NKEMBE), YANGONDA, YAISU, INJA, BOTUNGA, YAAMBA, YAIKOLE. Closely related to Mituku. Apparently different from the Mbole dialect of Ombo.

MFINU ***(EMFINU, FUNIKA, MFUNUNGA)*** [ZMF] Bandundu Province. Niger-Congo, Atlantic-Congo, Volta-Congo, Benue-Congo, Bantoid, Southern, Narrow Bantu, Northwest, B, Yanzi (B.80). Dialects: NTSIAM, NTSWAR.

MITUKU ***(KINYA-MITUKU, METOKO)*** [ZMQ] Orientale Province, Ubundu Territory, west of Lualaba River. Niger-Congo, Atlantic-Congo, Volta-Congo, Benue-Congo, Bantoid, Southern, Narrow Bantu, Central, D, Enya (D.10). Closely related to Mbole. 67% lexical similarity with Enya, about 55% with Lega-Shabunda, 50% with Nyanga, Lega-Mwenga, Bembe, Buyu, and Zimba, about 40% with Lengola.

MOINGI [MWZ] Orientale Province, Yahuma Territory, south of Congo River, opposite the town of Basoko. Niger-Congo, Atlantic-Congo, Volta-Congo, Benue-Congo, Bantoid, Southern, Unclassified.

MONGO-NKUNDU ***(MONGO, LOMONGO)*** [MOM] 400,000 or more (1995 estimate). 4,800,000 (1993 Johnstone) or 17% of the population (1978 WA) all Mongo languages in DRC. Southern half of Equateur Province and northeastern part of Bandundu Province. Niger-Congo, Atlantic-Congo, Volta-Congo,

Benue-Congo, Bantoid, Southern, Narrow Bantu, Northwest, C, Mongo (C.70). Dialects: MPAMA, WANGATA, PANGA (IPANGA, TITU, BULI, SOUTH NKUNDO), BUKALA (KALA), YALIMA (YAJIMA), KUTU (BAKUTU), EKONDA MONGO (LOMONGO), LONGO (BOLONGO), NKUNDO (NKUNDU, LONKUNDU, LONKUNDO, LOLO), NTOMBA-INONGO, NTOMBA-BIKORO, KONDA (EKONDA, LOKONDA, LOKWALA), LONGOMBE. Cluster of dialects or languages: Lalia, Mongo-Nkundu, Ngando, Ombo. The Longombe dialect is spoken along the road between Boende and Wema, is closest to the Bakutu dialect, and is distinct from the Lingombe language. Ntomba-Inongo, Ntomba-Bikoro, and Konda may be separate languages. Konda is in Equateur Province, Equateur District, Mai-Ndombe District, Kiri Territory. In Mbandaka, speakers called their dialect 'Lonkundo'. Lingala is increasing in use. Bible 1930.

MONO ***(AMONO)*** [MNH] 65,000 (1984 census). Equateur Province, Nord Ubangi, Bosobolo Territory and some in Libenge Territory. Bili is the center. Niger-Congo, Atlantic-Congo, Volta-Congo, North, Adamawa-Ubangi, Ubangi, Banda, Central, Central Core, Mid-Southern. Dialects: BILI, BUBANDA, GALABA, KAGA, MPAKA. Closest linguistically to Togbo and Gobu, but quite different ethnically from Togbo. Lingala is widely understood by men and most young people, but poorly understood by women. Sango is understood by many. Literacy rate in second language: Low in Lingala, women less than 10%.

MONZOMBO ***(MONJOMBO, MONO-JEMBO, MONZUMBO)*** [MOJ] 5,000 in DRC (1986 SIL). Equateur Province, on east bank of Ubangi River south of Libenge. Niger-Congo, Atlantic-Congo, Volta-Congo, North, Adamawa-Ubangi, Ubangi, Sere-Ngbaka-Mba, Ngbaka-Mba, Ngbaka, Western, Monzombo. Bilingualism in Lingala. Fishermen. See main entry under Congo.

MPUONO [ZMP] 165,000 (1972 Nida). Bandundu Province, Idiofa Territory. Niger-Congo, Atlantic-Congo, Volta-Congo, Benue-Congo, Bantoid, Southern, Narrow Bantu, Northwest, B, Yanzi (B.80). Dialects: MPUONO, MPUUN (MBUUN, KIMBUUN, MBUNDA, GIMBUNDA). Closely related to Yans. Different from Mbunda of DRC and Angola in Chokwe-Luchazi group. Bible portions 1935-1951.

MÜNDÜ ***(MUNDO, MOUNTOU, MONDO)*** [MUH] 2,800 in DRC. Orientale Province, north and northeast of Faradje. Niger-Congo, Atlantic-Congo, Volta-Congo, North, Adamawa-Ubangi, Ubangi, Sere-Ngbaka-Mba, Ngbaka-Mba, Ngbaka, Eastern, Mundu. Closest to Mayogo and Bangba. Bangala is the lingua franca, but people have difficulty understanding it. Bible portions 1984-1995. See main entry under Sudan.

MVUBA ***(MBUBA, BAMBUBA, BAMVUBA, MVUBA-A, OBIYE)*** [MXH] Population total both countries 5,000 (1981 Hurlburt). Nord-Kivu Province, Beni Territory, around Oicha. Also spoken in Uganda. Nilo-Saharan, Central Sudanic, East, Mangbutu-Efe. Closely related to Lese.

NANDI ***(KINANDI, KINANDE, NANDE, NORTHERN NANDE, NDANDE, ORUNDANDE)*** [NNB] 903,000 (1991 UBS). Nord-Kivu Province, mainly in Beni and Lubero territories. Niger-Congo, Atlantic-Congo, Volta-Congo, Benue-Congo, Bantoid, Southern, Narrow Bantu, Central, J, Konzo (J.40). Dialects: NANDI, KUMBULE (EKIKUMBULE), MATE (EKIMATE), TANGI (EKITANGI), SANZA (EKISANZA), SHU (EKISHU), EKISONGOORA (SONGOLA, NYANGALA), SWAGA (EKISWAGA, EKIKIRA), YIRA (EKIYIRA). Over 75% lexical similarity with Konjo, about 65% with Hunde, 55% with Tembo and Shi, 45% with Nyoro, Nyanga, and Lega-Shabunda, 40% with Talinga-Bwisi, 30% with Bhele, 25% with Amba. Different from Nandi dialect of Kalenjin of Kenya. Christian. Bible 1980-1996.

NDAKA ***(NDAAKA, INDAAKA)*** [NDK] 25,000 (1994 SIL). Orientale Province, Ituri District, Mambasa Territory, Bandaka Collectivité, along the road between Bunia and NiaNia. Roads also go to Kisangani and Isiro. Niger-Congo, Atlantic-Congo, Volta-Congo, Benue-Congo, Bantoid, Southern, Narrow Bantu, Central, D, Bira-Huku (D.30). Only one dialect. Speakers of Mbo, Budu, Vanuma, Nyali, and Ndaka agree that their languages are closer to each other than to other border Bantu languages. 87% lexical similarity with Mbo, 85% with Budu, 76% with Vanuma, 73% with Nyali, 30% with Komo, 22% with Bhele, Kaiku, Bila, and Bera. Literacy rate in second language: 25% to 40%. Traditional religion.

NDO ***(KE'BU, OKE'BU, KEBUTU, NDU)*** [NDP] 100,000. Population total both countries 300,000 (1991 UBS). Orientale Province, Mahagi and Aru territories, south of the Lowa River, west and northwest of Djalasiga, a pocket of Okebu on the border with Uganda. Also spoken in Uganda. Nilo-Saharan, Central Sudanic, East, Mangbutu-Efe. Dialects: AVARI (AVARE, AVERE, AVIRITU), OKE'BU, MEMBI (MEMBITU, MEEMBI, MOMBI, NDO). Bilingualism in Bangala, Swahili. Vigorous. In some areas Bangala is the lingua franca, in others Swahili. Blacksmiths. Christian in DRC. NT, in press (1994).

NDOBO ***(NDOOBO)*** [NDW] Equateur Province, between Bomongo and the Congo River. Niger-Congo, Atlantic-Congo, Volta-Congo, Benue-Congo, Bantoid, Southern, Narrow Bantu, Northwest, C, Bangi-Ntomba (C.40), Ngiri. It may be a dialect of Baloi or Libinza.

NDOLO ***(NDOOLO, MOSANGE, TANDO)*** [NDL] 8,000 (1983 census). Equateur Province, Sud Ubangi, Budjala Territory, Ndolo-Liboko Collectivité, on the Moeko River, south of Budjala between Ndama and Bokala villages, and in Tando and Lisombo villages. Niger-Congo, Atlantic-Congo, Volta-Congo,

Benue-Congo, Bantoid, Southern, Narrow Bantu, Northwest, C, Bangi-Ntomba (C.40), Lusengo. Bilingualism in Lingala. Might not accept Bamwe literature. Investigation needed: attitudes. Riverine.

NDUNGA ***(MONDUNGA, MONDUGU, BONDONGA, MODUNGA)*** [NDT] 2,500 (1977 Voegelin and Voegelin). Equateur Province, 8 villages in Lisala Territory. Niger-Congo, Atlantic-Congo, Volta-Congo, North, Adamawa-Ubangi, Ubangi, Sere-Ngbaka-Mba, Ngbaka-Mba, Mba. Close to Mba (Kimanga).

NGANDO ***(NGANDU, LONGANDU)*** [NXD] 220,000 or more (1995 estimate). Equateur Province, Maringa River area, north of Ikela. Niger-Congo, Atlantic-Congo, Volta-Congo, Benue-Congo, Bantoid, Southern, Narrow Bantu, Northwest, C, Mongo (C.70). Related to Lalia. Not related to Ngando of CAR. NT 1941.

NGBAKA ***(NGBAKA MINANGENDE, NGBAKA GBAYA)*** [NGA] 1,000,000 in DRC (1999). Population total all countries 1,005,000 or more. Equateur Province, Gemena Territory and surrounding area, 850 villages. Also spoken in CAR, Congo. Niger-Congo, Atlantic-Congo, Volta-Congo, North, Adamawa-Ubangi, Ubangi, Gbaya-Manza-Ngbaka, East. Dialect differences are minor. Many do not speak Lingala. All ages. Vigorous. Ngbaka is a different language from Gbaya or Ngbaka Ma'bo. Bible 1995.

NGBAKA MA'BO ***(NGBAKA LIMBA, MBAKA, MBACCA, BWAKA, BOUAKA, NBWAKA, GBAKA, GWAKA, MBWAKA, MA'BO)*** [NBM] 11,000 in DRC (1984 census). Equateur Province, Libenge District, and Zongo Territory, on the road north and south of Zongo, and in a belt just north of Libenge. Niger-Congo, Atlantic-Congo, Volta-Congo, North, Adamawa-Ubangi, Ubangi, Sere-Ngbaka-Mba, Ngbaka-Mba, Ngbaka, Western, Bwaka. Close to Gilima. Most people are bilingual in Lingala. Investigation needed: intelligibility with or bilingual proficiency in Gilima. Bible portions 1936-1937. See main entry under CAR.

NGBANDI, NORTHERN ***(NGWANDI, MONGWANDI, BAZA)*** [NGB] 105,000 (1989). Population total both countries 105,000 or more. Equateur Province, Mobaye and Yakoma territories, extending into Orientale Province, Bondo Territory. Also spoken in CAR. Niger-Congo, Atlantic-Congo, Volta-Congo, North, Adamawa-Ubangi, Ubangi, Ngbandi. 2 dialects, about equal in size. Sango is derived from Ngbandi. Speakers are fairly bilingual in Lingala. Vigorous. Ethnic groups: Abasango, Bwato, Mbaati, Nzomboy (Monjomboli). NT 1988.

NGBANDI, SOUTHERN ***(MONGBANDI, MBATI, NGBANDI-SUD, NGBANDI-NGIRI, NGWANDI, MONGWANDI)*** [NBW] 105,000. Equateur Province, Businga, Budjala, Kungu, and Libenge territories. Niger-Congo, Atlantic-Congo, Volta-Congo, North, Adamawa-Ubangi, Ubangi, Ngbandi. Different enough from Northern Ngbandi that separate literature is needed. Bible portions 1984.

NGBEE ***(LINGBEE, LINGBE, MANGBELE, MAJUU)*** [NBL] Orientale Province, scattered in Rungu, Niangara, Wamba, and Watsa territories. Niger-Congo, Atlantic-Congo, Volta-Congo, Benue-Congo, Bantoid, Southern, Narrow Bantu, Central, D, Bira-Huku (D.30). The people have adopted the language of the people they live among. Some speak Mangbetu and some Mayogo. The language shift is apparent from the fact that although there is no Mangbele dialect of either language, they both list a Mangbele people among the speakers of their languages. Extinct.

NGBINDA ***(BUNGBINDA, BANGBINDA)*** [NBD] Few speakers. Niger-Congo, Atlantic-Congo, Volta-Congo, Benue-Congo, Bantoid, Southern, Narrow Bantu, Central, D, Bira-Huku (D.30). Became extinct linguistically in Sudan by 1975.

NGBUNDU [NUU] 16,000 (1984 census). Equateur Province, Sud Ubangi, Libenge Territory. Northern group is north of Libenge from the Boyabo crossroads east to Budu and north to Oro. Southern group is south of Libenge, mixed with Mbanza and other language groups. Not in CAR. Niger-Congo, Atlantic-Congo, Volta-Congo, North, Adamawa-Ubangi, Ubangi, Banda, Southwestern. Bilingual in Lingala. Use of Mono, Mbanza, or Ngbaka is receptive only. Investigation needed: bilingual proficiency in Lingala.

NGELIMA ***(BANGELIMA, BANGALEMA, ANGBA, LEANGBA)*** [AGH] Orientale Province, Banalia and Basoko territories. Niger-Congo, Atlantic-Congo, Volta-Congo, Benue-Congo, Bantoid, Southern, Narrow Bantu, Northwest, C, Ngombe (C.50). Dialects: BEO, BURU (BORO, LEBORO), TUNGU, HANGA. May be more than one language. Closely related to Bwa. The Ngombe group is sometimes called Bantu C.40. 60% to 65% lexical similarity to Bwa, Kango, and Pagibete, about 50% with Lika and Komo, 40% with Ngombe, Benza, and Budza. Investigation needed: intelligibility with dialects.

NGIRI ***(NGUILI, NGWILI, LOI-NGIRI)*** [NGR] 6,000 (1977 SIL). Equateur Province, southern part of Bomongo Territory, between Ubangi River and Congo River. Niger-Congo, Atlantic-Congo, Volta-Congo, Benue-Congo, Bantoid, Southern, Narrow Bantu, Northwest, C, Bangi-Ntomba (C.40), Ngiri. Dialects: NUNU, MANGANJI, NGIRI. Dialect or closely related language: Balobo (Likila). Traditional religion, Christian.

NGITI ***(KINGITI, NGETI, KINGETI, NDRUNA, DRUNA, BINDI, LENDU-SUD)*** [NIY] 100,000 (1991 SIL). Orientale Province, Irumu Territory, south of Bunia. Nilo-Saharan, Central Sudanic, East, Lendu. 'Ndruna' is the name speakers use for their language. Different from Bendi.

NGOMBE ***(LINGOMBE)*** [NGC] 150,000 (1971 Welmers). Equateur Province, extensive area along both sides of Congo River, primarily in Mongala District and in adjacent parts of Southern Ubangi and Equateur districts. Binja is in Orientale Province, Aketi Territory. Niger-Congo, Atlantic-Congo, Volta-Congo, Benue-Congo, Bantoid, Southern, Narrow Bantu, Northwest, C, Ngombe (C.50). Dialects: BINJA (BINZA, LIBINDJA, LIBINJA), WIINDZA-BAALI, DOKO. Dialects or closely related languages: Bwela (Lingi), Doko, Libale. 78% lexical similarity between standard Ngombe and Binja, 59% with Ngombe, about 40% with Lingala, Pagibete, and Ngelima, 37% with Bwa. Different from Ngombe in CAR. NT 1915-1956.

NGONGO [NOQ] Bandundu Province. Niger-Congo, Atlantic-Congo, Volta-Congo, Benue-Congo, Bantoid, Southern, Narrow Bantu, Central, H, Yaka (H.30). Speakers are quite bilingual in Kituba.

NGUL ***(NGOLI, INGUL, NGULI, NGULU)*** [NLO] Western Bandundu Province along the Kasaï River north of Idiofa. Niger-Congo, Atlantic-Congo, Volta-Congo, Benue-Congo, Bantoid, Southern, Narrow Bantu, Northwest, B, Mbere (B.60).

NGUNDU [NUE] Niger-Congo, Atlantic-Congo, Volta-Congo, North, Adamawa-Ubangi, Ubangi, Banda, Central, Central Core, Mid-Southern. Closest to Kpagua. Investigation needed: intelligibility with Kpagua.

NKUTU ***(NKUCHU, NKUTSHU, BANKUTU)*** [NKW] 40,000 (1972 Nida). Maniema Province, Kibombo Territory. Niger-Congo, Atlantic-Congo, Volta-Congo, Benue-Congo, Bantoid, Southern, Narrow Bantu, Northwest, C, Tetela (C.80). Dialects: ELEMBE, HAMBA, LOKALO (KALO), KONGOLA-MENO, NGONGO, SAKA (LOSAKA). Descendants of the ancient Mongo empire. Traditional religion. Bible portions 1937-1940.

NTOMBA ***(LONTOMBA, NTUMBA, LUNTUMBA, NTOMBA-BOLIA)*** [NTO] 100,000 (1980 UBS). Bandundu Province, northeast of Lake Tumba. Niger-Congo, Atlantic-Congo, Volta-Congo, Benue-Congo, Bantoid, Southern, Narrow Bantu, Northwest, C, Bangi-Ntomba (C.40). Dialects: IMONA, MPONGO, NKOLE, NTOMBA, SAKANYI, SOKO, SAW. Dialects or closely related languages: Saw, Bolia (Bokoki). Bible portions 1916-1947.

NYALI ***(LINYALI, NYARI, HUKU, NYALI-KILO, NORTH NYALI)*** [NLJ] 43,000 (1993 SIL). Orientale Province, Ituri District, Djugu Territory, Kilo Collectivité. Niger-Congo, Atlantic-Congo, Volta-Congo, Benue-Congo, Bantoid, Southern, Narrow Bantu, Central, D, Bira-Huku (D.30). Only one dialect, since 'Nyali-South' is actually Vanuma. Speakers of Vanuma, Mbo, Ndaka, Budu, and Nyali agree with Bryan that their languages are closer to each other than to other border Bantu languages. 85% lexical similarity with Vanuma, 76% with Mbo, 73% with Ndaka and Budu. A local language committee has been promoting Nyali since 1982, in order to preserve their language. The name 'Huku' is reported to be a Hema term used for anyone who is not a Hema.

NYANGA ***(KINYANGA, INYANGA)*** [NYA] 150,000 (1994 census). Nord-Kivu Province, Walikale Territory, Wanyanga Collectivité. Niger-Congo, Atlantic-Congo, Volta-Congo, Benue-Congo, Bantoid, Southern, Narrow Bantu, Central, D, Nyanga (D.40). Dialects: INYANGA, IFUNA, IKUMBURE, ITIRI. The dialects do not differ much. Itiri appears to be the most divergent. The dialect around Bana-Bangi is reported to be the best understood. 70% lexical similarity with Kwami, 57% with Hunde, 54% with Kanu, about 50% with Lega-Shabunda and Tembo, 45% with Nandi, Lega-Mwenga, and Bembe, 42% with Shi, 40% with Buyu and Zimba, 30% with Komo. Many speakers are bilingual in Congo Swahili. Different from Nyanga-li. Literacy rate in second language: 20% to 30%. Agriculturalists: rice, beans, greens, manioc, tomato, onion, banana, avocado, papaya, pineapple, mango. Traditional religion, Christian, Muslim.

NYANGA-LI ***(LINYANGA-LE)*** [NYC] Orientale Province, Watsa Territory, southwest of Watsa. Niger-Congo, Atlantic-Congo, Volta-Congo, Benue-Congo, Bantoid, Southern, Narrow Bantu, Central, J, Konzo (J.40). Part of the same dialect cluster as Gbati-ri, Mayeka. Different from Nyanga.

NYINDU [NYG] Sud-Kivu Province, west of Lake Kivu. Niger-Congo, Atlantic-Congo, Volta-Congo, Benue-Congo, Bantoid, Southern, Narrow Bantu, Central, J, Shi-Havu (J.50). Many Nyindu speakers consider themselves to be Lega-Mwenda, but Lega and Shi speakers consider them to be Shi. Their speech is reported to be a mixture of Lega-Mwenga and Shi.

NZAKARA ***(N'SAKARA, SAKARA, ZAKARA, ANSAKARA)*** [NZK] Orientale Province, northwestern part of Bondo Territory, on the border with CAR. Niger-Congo, Atlantic-Congo, Volta-Congo, North, Adamawa-Ubangi, Ubangi, Zande, Zande-Nzakara. See main entry under CAR.

OMBO ***(LOOMBO, HOMBO, SONGOLA)*** [OML] Maniema Province, northwest of Kindu. Niger-Congo, Atlantic-Congo, Volta-Congo, Benue-Congo, Bantoid, Southern, Narrow Bantu, Northwest, C, Mongo (C.70). Dialect: MBULI (MBOLE). Jongo and Langa may be dialects. Mbole is apparently distinct from Mbole in the Enya group.

OMI ***(KALIKO-OMI)*** [OMI] 39,500 (1989 SIL). Orientale Province, Aru Territory, between the Nzoro and Lowa rivers along the Aru to Aba road. Nilo-Saharan, Central Sudanic, East, Moru-Madi, Central.

Closely related to Kaliko, but not close enough to Kaliko or Ma'di to use literature in those languages. Previously considered to be a Kaliko dialect. An important language.

PAGIBETE ***(APAKABETI, APAKIBETI, APAGIBETE, APAGIBETI, PAGABETE)*** [PAG] 25,000 (1985 SIL), including about 6,000 Momveda, 4,500 Mongbapele. Equateur Province, Businga, Yakoma, and Bumba territories. Mongbapele is along the road south of Businga. Momveda is in the area around Ngakpo on the north side of the Dua River, across from Gumba, and in Butu, Yakoma Territory. Ndundusana is to the south of Butu and at Ndundu-Sana in the northern Bumba Territory. Niger-Congo, Atlantic-Congo, Volta-Congo, Benue-Congo, Bantoid, Southern, Narrow Bantu, Northwest, C, Ngombe (C.50). Dialects: MOMVEDA, MONGBAPELE, NDUNDUSANA (GEZON, EGEZON, EGEZO, EGEJO). Momveda and Mongbapele are similar, and have 90% lexical similarity with Ndundusana. Momveda and Mongbapele have 80% lexical similarity with Bwa, Ndundusana has 85%. Dialects have 60% to 75% with Kango, 60% to 65% with Ngelima, 55% to 60% with Lika, 46% with Komo, 40% to 45% with Bali, 35% to 40% with Ngombe and Budza, 30% with Lingala. Most are partially bilingual in Lingala, some in Ngbandi. Vigorous.

PAMBIA ***(APAMBIA)*** [PAM] 21,000 (1982 SIL). Northern Orientale Province. Niger-Congo, Atlantic-Congo, Volta-Congo, North, Adamawa-Ubangi, Ubangi, Zande, Barambo-Pambia. None in Sudan or CAR.

PELENDE [PPP] Bandundu Province, Kenge Territory. Niger-Congo, Atlantic-Congo, Volta-Congo, Benue-Congo, Bantoid, Southern, Narrow Bantu, Central, H, Yaka (H.30). Similar to Lonzo, Ngongo.

PHENDE ***(KIPENDE, GIPHENDE, PENDE, GIPENDE, PINDI, PINJI)*** [PEM] 420,000 (1991 UBS). Bandundu Province, Idiofa and Gungu territories, south of the Kasaï River. Niger-Congo, Atlantic-Congo, Volta-Congo, Benue-Congo, Bantoid, Southern, Narrow Bantu, Central, K, Holu (K.10). Kituba is the lingua franca. Traditional religion. Bible, in press (1997).

POKE ***(TOPOKE, TOFOKE, TOVOKE, PUKI)*** [POF] 46,000 (1971 Welmers). Orientale Province, Isangi Territory, south of Congo River downstream from Kisangani. Niger-Congo, Atlantic-Congo, Volta-Congo, Benue-Congo, Bantoid, Southern, Narrow Bantu, Northwest, C, Kele (C.60). Dialects: BALUOMBILA, LIKOLO, LIUTWA, LOMBOOKI. May be able to use Lokele literature. Also called 'Pseudo-Lokele'. Christian, traditional religion. Bible portions 1923.

RUUND ***(URUUND, NORTHERN LUNDA, LUUNDA, CHILUWUNDA, MUATIAMVUA, LUWUNDA, LUNDA-KAMBORO, LUNDA KAMBOVE)*** [RND] Population total both countries 238,000 (1991 UBS). Katanga Province, Lualaba District. Also spoken in Angola. Niger-Congo, Atlantic-Congo, Volta-Congo, Benue-Congo, Bantoid, Southern, Narrow Bantu, Central, K, Salampasu-Ndembo (K.30). NT 1933-1996.

RWANDA ***(KINYARWANDA, RUANDA)*** [RUA] 250,000 possibly in DRC (UBS). Nord-Kivu Province, Rwanda border area between Lakes Edward and Kivu and extending westward. Niger-Congo, Atlantic-Congo, Volta-Congo, Benue-Congo, Bantoid, Southern, Narrow Bantu, Central, J, Rwanda-Rundi (J.60). Dialects: BWISHA (KINYABWISHA), MULENGE (KINYAMULENGE), TWA. Dialects in DRC may need separate literature. Twa: traditional religion, Christian. Bible 1954-1993. See main entry under Rwanda.

SAKATA ***(KISAKATA, SAKA, LESA, ODUAL)*** [SAT] 75,000 (1982 UBS). Bandundu Province, Kutu, Mushie and Inongo territories, Lukenie River and Semendua area. Niger-Congo, Atlantic-Congo, Volta-Congo, Benue-Congo, Bantoid, Southern, Narrow Bantu, Northwest, C, Bangi-Ntomba (C.40). Dialects: SAKATA, DJIA (KIDJIA, DIA, DJA), BAI (KIBAI). A cluster of dialects. Descendants of the ancient Mongo empire. Lingala is the lingua franca. All ages. Bible portions 1932-1951.

SALAMPASU ***(CHISALAMPASU)*** [SLX] 60,000 (1977 Voegelin and Voegelin). Southeastern part of Kasaï Occidental Province, east of Luiza. Niger-Congo, Atlantic-Congo, Volta-Congo, Benue-Congo, Bantoid, Southern, Narrow Bantu, Central, K, Salampasu-Ndembo (K.30). Dialect: LUNTU. Bible portions 1938.

SAMBA ***(TSAMBA, USAMBA, TSAAM, SHANKADI)*** [SMX] Bandundu Province, northern part of Kasongo-Lunda Territory. Niger-Congo, Atlantic-Congo, Volta-Congo, Benue-Congo, Bantoid, Southern, Narrow Bantu, Central, K, Holu (K.10). Closely related to Holu.

SANGA ***(KISANGA, SOUTHERN LUBA, LUBA-SANGA, LUBA-GARENGANZE)*** [SNG] 431,000 (1991 UBS). Katanga Province, north of Likasi, widely dispersed in Lubudi, Mitwaba, and Pweto territories. Niger-Congo, Atlantic-Congo, Volta-Congo, Benue-Congo, Bantoid, Southern, Narrow Bantu, Central, L, Luba (L.30). Bible 1928-1994.

SANGO ***(SANGHO)*** [SAJ] Only a few in DRC. Extreme northern border of Equateur Province (Oubangui River). Creole, Ngbandi based. A rapidly spreading language derived from Ngbandi with loans from Bantu languages and French. Trade language. Bible 1966. See main entry under CAR.

SEBA ***(SEWA, SHISHI, KUNDA)*** [KDG] Katanga Province, Kasenga Territory. Niger-Congo, Atlantic-Congo, Volta-Congo, Benue-Congo, Bantoid, Southern, Narrow Bantu, Central, M, Bisa-Lamba (M.50), Bisa. Distinct from Kunda dialect of Lusengo, the Kunda of Zimbabwe and Mozambique in the Senga-Sena group, the Kunda dialect of Nyanja, and the Konda dialect or language in Mongo group.

SENGELE ***(KESENGELE, SENGERE)*** [SZG] Bandundu Province, west of Lake Mai-Ndombe. Niger-Congo, Atlantic-Congo, Volta-Congo, Benue-Congo, Bantoid, Southern, Narrow Bantu, Northwest, C, Bangi-Ntomba (C.40). Bible portions 1915-1917.

SERE ***(SHERE, SHERI, CHERE, SERRE, SHAIRE, SIRI, SILI, BASIRI, BASILI)*** [SWF] 2,500 in DRC. Population total both countries 2,525. Groups live among the Zande in Orientale Province, northeast of Ango. No speakers in Sudan. Also spoken in CAR. Niger-Congo, Atlantic-Congo, Volta-Congo, North, Adamawa-Ubangi, Ubangi, Sere-Ngbaka-Mba, Sere, Sere-Bviri, Ndogo-Sere. Closest to Ndogo and Tagbu. Slight dialect differences in DRC and CAR.

SHI ***(MASHI)*** [SHR] 654,000 (1991 UBS). Sud-Kivu Province, north, west, and south of Bukavu. Niger-Congo, Atlantic-Congo, Volta-Congo, Benue-Congo, Bantoid, Southern, Narrow Bantu, Central, J, Shi-Havu (J.50). Dialects: LINDJA, HWINDJA (LWINDJA), ZIBA, LONGE-LONGE. About 70% lexical similarity to Havu and Tembo, 57% with Hunde, 55% with Nandi, 44% with Lega-Shabunda, 42% with Nyanga. Different from Mashi of Zambia. Bible, in press (1997).

SO ***(HESO, ESO, SOKO, SOA)*** [SOC] 6,000 (1971 Welmers). Orientale Province, north of Basoko. Niger-Congo, Atlantic-Congo, Volta-Congo, Benue-Congo, Bantoid, Southern, Narrow Bantu, Northwest, C, Kele (C.60). Distinct from So of Cameroon. Turumba and Gesogo may be names for So. NT 1920, out of print.

SONDE ***(KISONDE, SOONDE, KISOONDE)*** [SHC] Southeastern Bandundu Province, Feshi Territory. Niger-Congo, Atlantic-Congo, Volta-Congo, Benue-Congo, Bantoid, Southern, Narrow Bantu, Central, H, Yaka (H.30). 'Kilua' may be a name of the language.

SONGA ***(KISONGA)*** [SGO] Southern Kivu Province. Niger-Congo, Atlantic-Congo, Volta-Congo, Benue-Congo, Bantoid, Southern, Narrow Bantu, Unclassified.

SONGE ***(SONGYE, KISONGYE, LUSONGE, KALEBWE, NORTHEAST LUBA, YEMBE, KISONGE, LUBA-SONGI, KISONGI)*** [SOP] 1,000,000 (1991 WA) including 150,000 in Western Kalebwe (1982 UBS). Kasaï Oriental Province, between Sankuru and Lualaba rivers, mainly in Kabinda Zone and eastward into Kongolo and Kabolo territories of Katanga Province. Niger-Congo, Atlantic-Congo, Volta-Congo, Benue-Congo, Bantoid, Southern, Narrow Bantu, Central, L, Songye (L.20). Dialects: WESTERN KALEBWE (ESAMBI KIPYA, SONGE), EASTERN KALEBWE (KILOMBENO KIBYA, IKALEBWE), MBAGANI. Dialect or closely related language: Mbagani. Ethnic subgroups are Bena Tshofwe, Bekalebwe, Beneki, Belande. Investigation needed: intelligibility with Mbagani. NT 1952-1978.

SONGO ***(KISONGO, ITSONG)*** [SOO] Bandundu Province, Bulungu Territory. Possibly also in Angola. Niger-Congo, Atlantic-Congo, Volta-Congo, Benue-Congo, Bantoid, Southern, Narrow Bantu, Central, Unclassified. Possibly same as Nsongo (Songo) of Angola.

SONGOMENO [SOE] 50,000 (1972 Barrett). Kasaï Occidental Province, Dekese Territory. Niger-Congo, Atlantic-Congo, Volta-Congo, Benue-Congo, Bantoid, Southern, Narrow Bantu, Northwest, C, Bushong (C.90). Traditional religion, Christian.

SONGOORA ***(SONGOLA, KESONGOLA, BINJA)*** [SOD] 1,300 (1971 Welmers). Maniema Province, Punia, Kindu, and Shabunda territories. Gengele is in Kindu Territory. Niger-Congo, Atlantic-Congo, Volta-Congo, Benue-Congo, Bantoid, Southern, Narrow Bantu, Central, D, Lega-Kalanga (D.20). Dialects: GENGELE (KEGENGELE), NORTH BINJA, SOUTH BINJA. North and South Binja may be separate languages. Gengele is reported to be a creole based on Lega-Shabunda, Kusu, and other languages (Mwangati W. B. 1991). Apparently different from the Songoora (Edi Songoora) dialect of Nandi.

SUKU ***(KISUKU)*** [SUB] 50,000 (1980 UBS). Southern Bandundu Province, west of Feshi, in areas of Moanza and Mwela. Niger-Congo, Atlantic-Congo, Volta-Congo, Benue-Congo, Bantoid, Southern, Narrow Bantu, Central, H, Yaka (H.30). One report says that it is not in the Yaka (H.30) subgroup, but in the Kongo subgroup (H.10). Another says it is in Holu (K.10). Kituba is the lingua franca but its use seems limited. Vigorous. Bible portions 1973.

SWAHILI, CONGO ***(ZAÏRE SWAHILI)*** [SWC] There may be a few mother tongue speakers in cities. Second language for 9,100,000 (1991 UBS). Throughout the Katanga, Nord-Kivu, Sud-Kivu, and Maniema provinces and the southeastern part of the Orientale Province. There are other varieties of Swahili in East Africa. Niger-Congo, Atlantic-Congo, Volta-Congo, Benue-Congo, Bantoid, Southern, Narrow Bantu, Central, G, Swahili (G.40). Dialects: ITURI KINGWANA, LUALABA KINGWANA, KATANGA SWAHILI, KIVU SWAHILI. Kingwana is a pidgin Swahili which functions sociolinguistically as a dialect. There are several regional dialects, with that of eastern Kivu being closest to Swahili of Kenya and Tanzania. About 30% lexical similarity to Lingala and to the Lega group, 15% to 20% with Bira-Huku group, Bali, and Lika. National language. Bible 1960-1997.

TAABWA ***(RUNGU, ICHITAABWA, TABWA)*** [TAP] 250,000 in DRC (1972 Barrett). Population total both countries 250,000 or more. Katanga Province, on Lake Tanganyika, south of Moba. Also spoken in Zambia. Niger-Congo, Atlantic-Congo, Volta-Congo, Benue-Congo, Bantoid, Southern, Narrow Bantu, Central, M, Bemba (M.40). Dialect: SHILA. Traditional religion, Christian, Muslim.

TAGBU ***(TAGBO, TAGBA)*** [TBM] Widely scattered. None in Sudan or CAR. Niger-Congo, Atlantic-Congo, Volta-Congo, North, Adamawa-Ubangi, Ubangi, Sere-Ngbaka-Mba, Sere, Sere-Bviri, Ndogo-Sere. Closest to Sere and Ndogo. Different from Togbo (Tagbo) of DRC in Banda group.

TALINGA-BWISI ***(KITALINGA, LUBWISI, OLUBWISI, BWISSI, MAWISSI, LUBWISSI)*** [TLJ] 20,000 to 30,000 in DRC (1993 WHM). Nord-Kivu Province, Beni Territory, Butalinga County, within the boundaries of the Virunga National Park, up to the Uganda border. Niger-Congo, Atlantic-Congo, Volta-Congo, Benue-Congo, Bantoid, Southern, Narrow Bantu, Central, J, Haya-Jita (J.20). Approximately 40% lexical similarity with Nandi. Congo Swahili is the lingua franca in the area. Different from Bwisi of Congo-Brazzaville and Gabon. The name 'Talinga' is used in DRC and 'Bwisi' in Uganda. See main entry under Uganda.

TEKE, CENTRAL ***(KITEKE)*** [TEC] Bandundu Province, Mushie Territory. Niger-Congo, Atlantic-Congo, Volta-Congo, Benue-Congo, Bantoid, Southern, Narrow Bantu, Northwest, B, Teke (B.70). Dialects: KWE, NJINJU (NJYUNJYU, NDZIKOU, NDZINDZIJU, NZIKU, NZINZIHU), WUO, BOMA (BOO, EBOO, EBOOM, BOMA MBALI, BAMBOMA). See main entry under Congo.

TEKE, EASTERN ***(KITEKE, IBALI)*** [TEK] Population total both countries 71,000. Kwamouth, Masia, Kinshasa, near Banbana on road to Kenga. Upstream from Kinshasa to Kwa (Kasaï) River and inland to Fatunda area. Also spoken in Congo. Niger-Congo, Atlantic-Congo, Volta-Congo, Benue-Congo, Bantoid, Southern, Narrow Bantu, Northwest, B, Teke (B.70). Dialects: MOSIENO, NGEE (ESINGEE), BALI (AMBALI, TEO, TIO, TYO). Lingala or Kituba are trade languages. Fairly bilingual. Literacy rate in second language: 65% to 85%. Bible portions 1889-1905.

TEMBO ***(KITEMBO, CHITEMBO, NYABUNGU)*** [TBT] 150,000 (1994 SIL). Sud-Kivu and Nord-Kivu provinces, almost all in Kalehe Territory. Niger-Congo, Atlantic-Congo, Volta-Congo, Benue-Congo, Bantoid, Southern, Narrow Bantu, Central, J, Shi-Havu (J.50). Dialects: TEMBO (KITEMBO), RHINYIHINYI. No major dialect differences. Related to Havu, Hunde, Shi, and Fuliiru. 75% lexical similarity with Hunde, about 70% with Shi, 55% with Nande, 50% with Nyanga, 45% with Lega Shabunda. Different from LiTembo in the Ngombe group, Tembo (Tambo) in the Nyika-Safwa group, and Tembo in the Yaka group. Bible portions 1977.

TEMBO ***(MOTEMBO, LITEMBO)*** [TMV] 5,000 (1986 SIL). Equateur Province, Sud Ubangi and Equateur districts, Budjala and Bomongo districts, villages or Libanza, Bokele, and Bosanga on the Banga-Melo River, at 1 or 2 villages on the Mongala River southwest of Akula, and Sumba Island. Niger-Congo, Atlantic-Congo, Volta-Congo, Benue-Congo, Bantoid, Southern, Narrow Bantu, Northwest, C, Ngombe (C.50). There may be wide dialect variations. Bilingualism in Lingala. Riverine.

TETELA ***(OTETELA, SUNGU)*** [TEL] 750,000 (1991 UBS). Northern Kasaï Oriental Province. Niger-Congo, Atlantic-Congo, Volta-Congo, Benue-Congo, Bantoid, Southern, Narrow Bantu, Northwest, C, Tetela (C.80). Christian, traditional religion, Muslim. Bible 1966.

TIENE ***(KITIENE, KITIINI, TENDE)*** [TII] 24,500 or more (1977 SIL). Bandundu Province, Bolobo area on Congo River and inland savannah and forest. Niger-Congo, Atlantic-Congo, Volta-Congo, Benue-Congo, Bantoid, Southern, Narrow Bantu, Northwest, B, Yanzi (B.80). Lingala is the lingua franca, but its use is limited.

VANUMA ***(BVANUMA, LIVANUMA, BAMBUTUKU)*** [VAU] 6,700 (1993 SIL). Orientale Province, Ituri District, Irumu Territory, Tchabi Collectivité. Niger-Congo, Atlantic-Congo, Volta-Congo, Benue-Congo, Bantoid, Southern, Narrow Bantu, Central, D, Bira-Huku (D.30). 85% lexical similarity with Nyali, about 75% with Budu, Ndaka, and Mbo, 76% about 20% with Bila. Investigation needed: bilingual proficiency. Literacy rate in second language: 30%.

WONGO ***(GONGO, NDJEMBE, TUKKONGO, TUKONGO, BAKONG)*** [WON] 2,000 to 8,000 (1971 Welmers). Kasaï Occidental Province, Ilebo and Tshikapa territories. Bandundu Province, Guagu and Idiofa territories, in area of Lubue River. Niger-Congo, Atlantic-Congo, Volta-Congo, Benue-Congo, Bantoid, Southern, Narrow Bantu, Northwest, C, Bushong (C.90). Intelligible with Lele. Bible portions 1938-1940.

YAKA ***(KIYAKA, IAKA, IYAKA)*** [YAF] Population total both countries 150,000 to 200,000 (1977 SIL). Bandundu Province, Popokabaka and Kasongo Lunda territories. Also spoken in Angola. Niger-Congo, Atlantic-Congo, Volta-Congo, Benue-Congo, Bantoid, Southern, Narrow Bantu, Central, H, Yaka (H.30). Dialect: NGOONGO. Kituba is the lingua franca. Bible portions 1938-1957.

YAKOMA [YKY] 10,000. Niger-Congo, Atlantic-Congo, Volta-Congo, North, Adamawa-Ubangi, Ubangi, Ngbandi. Partly intelligible with Ngbandi. See main entry under CAR.

YAMONGERI ***(YAMONGIRI)*** [YMG] Equateur Province, south of the Congo River. Niger-Congo, Atlantic-Congo, Volta-Congo, Benue-Congo, Bantoid, Southern, Narrow Bantu, Northwest, C, Bangi-Ntomba (C.40). Dialect or closely related language to Buja.

YANGO ***(GBENDERE)*** [YNG] 3,000 (1986 SIL). Equateur Province, Kungu and Libenge districts, around Esobe River and in village of Gbendere. Niger-Congo, Atlantic-Congo, Volta-Congo, North, Adamawa-Ubangi, Ubangi, Sere-Ngbaka-Mba, Ngbaka-Mba, Ngbaka, Western, Monzombo. Closely related to Monzombo. It may be the same as Bayanga. Lingala is widely spoken; also Ngbandi and Mbanza.

YANSI ***(YANZI, EYANZI, KIYANZI, EYANSI)*** [YNS] 100,000 or more (1997 Salikoko Mufwene). Bandundu Province, Bulungu Territory, Loange River area. Niger-Congo, Atlantic-Congo, Volta-Congo, Benue-Congo, Bantoid, Southern, Narrow Bantu, Northwest, B, Yanzi (B.80). Dialect: YEEI (YEY). Related to Ding, Mbuun. 75% of the speakers are fairly bilingual in Kituba.

YELA ***(BOYELA, KUTU)*** [YEL] 33,000 (1977 Voegelin and Voegelin). Equateur Province, mainly in Bokungu Territory. Niger-Congo, Atlantic-Congo, Volta-Congo, Benue-Congo, Bantoid, Southern, Narrow Bantu, Northwest, C, Tetela (C.80).

YOMBE ***(KIYOMBE, KIOMBI, BAYOMBE)*** [YOM] Western Bas-Congo Province, Mayombe Forest. Also spoken in Angola, Congo. Niger-Congo, Atlantic-Congo, Volta-Congo, Benue-Congo, Bantoid, Southern, Narrow Bantu, Central, H, Kongo (H.10). Dialects: MBALA (MUMBALA), VUNGUNYA (KIVUNGUNYA, YOMBE CLASSIQUE). Distinct enough from Kongo-Fioti to need separate literature. Forest. Christian, traditional religion.

YULU ***(YOULOU)*** [YUL] Binga are in DRC and Sudan; Yulu are in Sudan and CAR. Nilo-Saharan, Central Sudanic, West, Bongo-Bagirmi, Kara. Dialects: BINGA, YULU. Aja is not a dialect of Yulu, but of Kresh (R. Brown SIL). Many in Sudan are bilingual in Kresh or Arabic. See main entry under CAR.

ZANDE ***(PAZANDE, ZANDI, AZANDE, SANDE, ASANDE, BADJANDE, BAZENDA)*** [ZAN] 730,000 in DRC. Population total all countries 1,142,000. Far north of Orientale Province, Bas-Uele District. Also spoken in CAR, Sudan. Niger-Congo, Atlantic-Congo, Volta-Congo, North, Adamawa-Ubangi, Ubangi, Zande, Zande-Nzakara. SVO, VSO. Traditional religion, Christian. Bible 1978.

ZIMBA [ZMB] 120,000 (1994 census). Maniema Province, Kasongo Territory, Mulu and Maringa collectivités. Niger-Congo, Atlantic-Congo, Volta-Congo, Benue-Congo, Bantoid, Southern, Narrow Bantu, Central, D, Lega-Kalanga (D.20). Dialects: BINJA (SOE, SOLE), SEMULU (SEMOLO, NYEMBOMBO, KISEMBOMBO), SEMALINGA, KWANGE, MAMBA (KYENYEMAMBA). Kwange and Mamba may be separate languages. About 55% lexical similarity with Bembe, 50% with Lega-Mwenga, Lega-Shabunda, Buyu, Mituku, Enya, 40% with Nyanga, 34% with Bangubangu, 32% with Komo. Many are bilingual in Congo Swahili. The majority speak Binja dialect. Semulu is spoken in the northeast, Semalinga in the west. Agriculturalists: rice, beans, greens, tomato, onion, cabbage, peanuts, papaya, pineapple, mango. Christian, Muslim, Kimbanguist, traditional religion.

ZYOBA ***(ZOBA)*** [ZYO] Niger-Congo, Atlantic-Congo, Volta-Congo, Benue-Congo, Bantoid, Southern, Narrow Bantu, Central, D, Lega-Kalanga (D.20). Dialects: VIRA, MASANZE. May be the same as Joba. See main entry under Tanzania.

DJIBOUTI

Republic of Djibouti. Jumhouriyya Djibouti. Formerly part of Somaliland and French Territory of the Afars and the Issas. National or official language: French. 623,000 (1998 UN). Literacy rate 20% to 34% (1996). Also includes Greek 1,600. Sunni Muslim, Christian. Data accuracy estimate: B. The number of languages listed for Djibouti is 4. Of those, all are living languages. Diversity index 0.58.

AFAR ***(AFARAF, "DANAKIL")*** [AFR] 300,000 in Djibouti (1996), 55.23% of the population (1996). May also be in Somalia. Afro-Asiatic, Cushitic, East, Saho-Afar. Saho is a distinct language. The people are called "Danakil" by others, but this is considered offensive. Nomadic. Literacy rate in second language: Largely none. Radio programs. Desert. Mountains. Pastoralists. Muslim. NT 1994. See main entry under Ethiopia.

ARABIC, TA'IZZI-ADENI ***(DJIBOUTI ARABIC)*** [ACQ] 52,000 in Djibouti, 11% of the population (1995). Afro-Asiatic, Semitic, Central, South, Arabic. Muslim. See main entry under Yemen.

FRENCH [FRN] 15,440 in Djibouti, 2.84% of the population (1988). Indo-European, Italic, Romance, Italo-Western, Western, Gallo-Iberian, Gallo-Romance, Gallo-Rhaetian, Oïl, French. Official language. Bible 1530-1986. See main entry under France.

SOMALI [SOM] 181,420 in Djibouti, 33.4% of the population (1996). Afro-Asiatic, Cushitic, East, Somali. Various dialects. Nomadic. 3 clans: Issa, Gadaboursi, Issaq. Radio programs. Pastoralists. Muslim. Bible 1979. See main entry under Somalia.

EGYPT

National or official language: Standard Arabic. 65,978,000 (1998 UN). Literacy rate 55% (1993 govt. figure). Also includes Adyghe, Tosk Albanian, Amharic, Moroccan Spoken Arabic, South Levantine Spoken Arabic 50,000, Sudanese Spoken Arabic 1,000,000, Armenian 100,000, Bedawi 77,000, Italian, West-Central Oromo. Information mainly from Applegate 1970; J Milton Cowan 1973. Muslim, Christian, secular. Blind population 1,000,000. Deaf institutions: 4. Data accuracy estimate: B. The number of languages listed for Egypt is 11. Of those, 10 are living languages and 1 is extinct. Diversity index 0.46.

ARABIC, EASTERN EGYPTIAN BEDAWI SPOKEN ***(BEDAWI, LEVANTINE BEDAWI ARABIC)*** [AVL] 780,000 in Egypt (1996). Population total all countries 1,610,000. Bedouin regions in Sinai and along parts of the Red Sea coast, most of the way to the southern border, along the whole east bank until it reaches the Bedawi language. Also spoken in Israel, Jordan, Palestinian West Bank and Gaza, Syria. Afro-Asiatic, Semitic, Central, South, Arabic. Dialects: NORTHEAST EGYPTIAN BEDAWI ARABIC, SOUTH LEVANTINE BEDAWI ARABIC, NORTH LEVANTINE BEDAWI ARABIC. Similar to some Hijazi dialects in northwestern Saudi Arabia. Sunni Muslim.

ARABIC, EGYPTIAN SPOKEN ***(LOWER EGYPT ARABIC, NORMAL EGYPTIAN ARABIC)*** [ARZ] 44,406,000 in Egypt (1998). Population total all countries 46,306,000. Also spoken in Iraq, Israel, Jordan, Kuwait, Libya, Saudi Arabia, UAE, Yemen. Afro-Asiatic, Semitic, Central, South, Arabic. Dialects: NORTH DELTA ARABIC, SOUTH CENTRAL DELTA ARABIC, CAIRENE ARABIC. The media have established a normal Egyptian Spoken Arabic based on Cairo speech. Cairene is the most widely understood dialect used for nonprint media, both in Egypt and throughout the sedentary Arab world. It is an amalgam of Delta Arabic and Middle Egypt Arabic, with borrowings from literary Arabic. Bilingualism in French, English. Used for political speeches. National language. Radio programs, TV. Muslim. NT 1932, out of print.

ARABIC, SA<IDI SPOKEN ***(SA<IDI UPPER EGYPT ARABIC)*** [AEC] 18,900,000 (1996). Southern Egypt from the edge of Cairo to the Sudan border. The Middle Egypt dialect is in Bani Sweef, Fayyuum, and Gizeh. Upper Egypt dialect is from Asyuut to Edfu and south. Some might be in Libya or the Gulf. Afro-Asiatic, Semitic, Central, South, Arabic. Dialects: MIDDLE EGYPT ARABIC, UPPER EGYPT ARABIC. Speakers of Cairene do not understand Sa<idi, but speakers of Sa<idi understand Cairene, and some use it as second language. Speakers prefer Cairene over Sudanese. Similar to Sudanese Arabic, especially in the south, but heavily influenced by Cairene Arabic.

ARABIC, STANDARD [ABV] Middle East, North Africa. Afro-Asiatic, Semitic, Central, South, Arabic. Preserves ancient grammar. Used for nearly all written materials and formal speeches. Not a mother tongue, but taught in schools. National language. Bible 1984-1991. See main entry under Saudi Arabia.

ARABIC, WESTERN EGYPTIAN BEDAWI SPOKEN ***(BEDAWI, LIBYAN SPOKEN ARABIC, SULAIMITIAN ARABIC, MAGHREBI ARABIC)*** [AYL] 300,000 in Egypt (1996). Bedouin regions from the edge of Alexandria west to the Libyan border. Some in western oases. Afro-Asiatic, Semitic, Central, South, Arabic. Dialects: WESTERN EGYPTIAN BEDAWI ARABIC, TRIPOLITANIAN ARABIC, SOUTHERN LIBYAN ARABIC, EASTERN LIBYAN ARABIC. Sunni Muslim. See main entry under Libya.

COPTIC ***(NEO-EGYPTIAN)*** [COP] Afro-Asiatic, Egyptian. Dialects: BOHAIRIC, SAHIDIC. Liturgical language of the Coptic Church, Bohairic dialect. No first language speakers; it probably became extinct in the 16th century. Estimated 6,500,000 Coptic Christians worldwide. Extinct. NT 1716-1924.

DOMARI [RMT] Muslim Gypsies in Egypt: 1,080,000, or 2% of the population, including 864,000 Helebi, 216,000 Ghagar (1993 Johnstone). The Ghagar live mainly in Dakahlia Governorate, north of Cairo. Indo-European, Indo-Iranian, Indo-Aryan, Central zone, Dom. Dialects: NAWAR (GHAGAR), HELEBI. Reports that many now speak Arabic. Muslim. See main entry under Iran.

GREEK [GRK] 60,000 in Egypt (1977 Voegelin and Voegelin). Alexandria. Indo-European, Greek, Attic. Bible 1840-1994. See main entry under Greece.

KENUZI-DONGOLA ***(DONGOLA-KENUZ, NILE NUBIAN, DONGOLAWI, METOKI)*** [KNC] 100,000 in Egypt in the ethnic group. There may be fewer speakers (1996). 40% in the Upper Nile valley, mainly at Kom Ombo, the rest in various cities. Nilo-Saharan, Eastern Sudanic, Eastern, Nubian, Central, Dongolawi. Dialects: DONGOLA, KENUZ (KENUZI, KUNUZI, KENZI). Not intelligible with Nobiin. 67% lexical similarity with Nobiin. The ethnic group is larger in Egypt than Sudan, but many are now monolingual in Egyptian or Saidi Arabic. The shift to Arabic is expected to continue in the cities. The language is the central feature of Nubian identity. Over 70% of the men can read Arabic script. Many can read Roman script. Muslim. Bible portions 1912. See main entry under Sudan.

NOBIIN ***(FIADIDJA-MAHAS, MAHAS-FIADIDJA, FADICCA, FADICHA, FEDIJA, FADIJA, FIADIDJA, FIYADIKKYA, FEDICCA, NILE NUBIAN, MAHAS, SUKOT)*** [FIA] 200,000 in Egypt

(1996). 40% in the Upper Nile Valley, mainly near Kom Ombo; the rest in various cities. Nilo-Saharan, Eastern Sudanic, Eastern, Nubian, Northern. Not intelligible with Kenuzi-Dongola. 67% lexical similarity with Kenuzi-Dongola. The ethnic group is larger in Egypt than Sudan, but most are now monolingual in Egyptian or Saidi Arabic. The shift to Arabic is expected to continue in the cities. The language is the center of Nubian identity. Spoken by the Fedicca in Egypt and the Mahas in Sudan. 70% of the men can read Arabic script. Many can read Roman script. Muslim. Bible portions 1860-1899. See main entry under Sudan.

SIWI ***(SIWA, SIOUA, OASIS BERBER, ZENATI)*** [SIZ] 5,000 (1995). Northwestern desert, Siwa Oasis, several isolated villages in the western oasis. Afro-Asiatic, Berber, Eastern, Siwa. Not closely related to other Berber languages. Bilingualism in Arabic. Muslim.

EQUATORIAL GUINEA

Republic of Equatorial Guinea. República de Guinea Ecuatorial. Formerly Spanish Guinea. National or official language: Spanish. 431,000 (1998 UN). Literacy rate 55% to 72%. Also includes people from Nigeria, Europe, India. Information mainly from A. Jacquot 1978; J. Holm 1989; J. Bendor-Samuel 1989; A. Iyanga Pendi 1991; SIL 1987-1999. Christian, traditional religion, secular. Blind population 800 (1982 WCE). Data accuracy estimate: C. The number of languages listed for Equatorial Guinea is 13. Of those, all are living languages. Diversity index 0.36.

BATANGA ***(BANOHO, BANO'O, NOHO, NOHU, NOKU, BANOO)*** [BNM] 6,600 Puku in Equatorial Guinea (1993 Johnstone). Population total both countries 12,600. Also spoken in Cameroon. Niger-Congo, Atlantic-Congo, Volta-Congo, Benue-Congo, Bantoid, Southern, Narrow Bantu, Northwest, A, Bube-Benga (A.30). Dialect: BAPUKU (PUKU, NAKA, BAPUU). The Puku are one of the Ndowe coastal peoples. Different from Batanga of South West Province in Cameroon (Balundu-Bima), and the Batanga dialect of Caka. Tropical forest. Coastal. Fishermen. 0 to 50 meters. Bible portions 1953.

BENGA [BEN] 3,000 in Equatorial Guinea, including 400 on Corisco Island (1995). Population total both countries 3,000 or more. Rio Muni. Corisco Island. 80% have moved to Libreville, Gabon to Bata in EG. Also spoken in Gabon. Niger-Congo, Atlantic-Congo, Volta-Congo, Benue-Congo, Bantoid, Southern, Narrow Bantu, Northwest, A, Bube-Benga (A.30). Related to Batanga. One of the Ndowe 'coastal' peoples. Tropical forest. Coastal and volcanic island. Fishermen, coconut palms. 1 to 30 meters. Christian. Bible 1898.

BUBE ***(BOOMBE, BOBE, BUBI, EDIYA, ADIJA, ADEEYAH, BOOBE, FERNANDIAN)*** [BVB] 40,000 or more (1995 UBS). Fernando Po, Biombo Island. Niger-Congo, Atlantic-Congo, Volta-Congo, Benue-Congo, Bantoid, Southern, Narrow Bantu, Northwest, A, Bube-Benga (A.30). Dialects: NORTH BOBE, SOUTHWEST BOBE, SOUTHEAST BOBE. Tropical forest. Volcanic island. Swidden agriculturalists, fishermen. 0 to 1500 meters. Bible portions 1849.

FA D'AMBU ***(ANNOBONÉS, ANNOBONESE, ANNOBONENSE)*** [FAB] 2,500 (1999 SIL). Population total both countries 2,500 or more. Annobón Island, isolated from the mainland by 360 km. of ocean (2,000), and in a community from Annobón living in Malabo on Bioko Island (500), a few on continental Equatorial Guinea. Also spoken in Spain. Creole, Portuguese based. Different from Fernando Po Krio and Crioulo of Guinea-Bissau and Kabuverdianu. Little variation between Annobonese in Annobón and Malabo. 62.5% lexical similarity with São Tomense. About 10% of the lexicon comes from Spanish. Many on Bioko learn Spanish, but less so on Annobón. Women on Annobón seem uncomfortable in Spanish. Spanish is used in government and education. Many on Bioko learn the local trade language, Fernando Po Creole English. Non-creolized Portuguese used as liturgical language by local Catholics. Used in the home and with other Annobonese, all contexts except government and education. Vigorous use in Annobón and Malabo. Language closely related to cultural identity and solidarity. The Portuguese took slaves from São Tomé and Angola to establish a population on Annobón. It was later traded to Spain. Also influenced by the Creole English of Bioko. They are famed swimmers, fishermen, and whalers. Possible vowel length, vowel harmony, tone sandhi. Tropical forest. Volcanic island. Fishermen, agricultural laborers, coconut palms, whalers. 0 to 500 meters. Christian.

FANG ***(PAMUE, PAHOUN)*** [FNG] 350,000 or more in Equatorial Guinea, 75% of the population (1995). Interior. Niger-Congo, Atlantic-Congo, Volta-Congo, Benue-Congo, Bantoid, Southern, Narrow Bantu, Northwest, A, Yaunde-Fang (A.70). Dialects: MAKE, NTUM (NTUMU). Ethnic groups are Okak, Ntumu. They are known as 'warriors of the jungle'. Their knowledge of jungle plants, animals, survival is legendary. Tropical forest. Interfluvial. Sedentary hunter-gatherers. 0 to 700 meters. Christian, traditional religion. Bible 1951. See main entry under Gabon.

FERNANDO PO CREOLE ENGLISH ***(PIDGINGLIS, FERNANDINO, FERNANDO PO KRIO, CRIOLLO)*** [FPE] 5,000 mother tongue speakers (1998 S. Smith SIL), 1.25% of the population, plus 70,000 or

17.5% who speak it as trade language. North central Bioko Island (Fernando Po), 6 communities in or near Malabo: Musola, Las Palmas, Sampaca, Basupu, Fiston, Balveri de Cristo Rey. Creole, English based, Atlantic, Krio. Pidginglis may be a separate language from Krio. About 1,000 are monolingual. Language of instruction in school is Spanish. English and some Bubi are also used. Speakers came from Sierra Leone in 1827. Investigation needed: intelligibility with Krio, attitudes. Trade language. Literacy rate in second language: 75% in Spanish, none in Krio. Tropical forest. Volcanic island. Agriculturalists. 0 to 1,000 feet. Christian.

GYELE ***(GIELE, GIELI, GYELI, BAGYELE, BAGIELE, BAJELI, BAJELE, BOGYELI, BOGYEL, BONDJIEL, BAKO, BEKOE, BAKOLA, BAKUELE, LIKOYA, BABINGA)*** [GYI] 29 in Equatorial Guinea (1998 govt.). Near the coast, northwest corner of Equatorial Guinea. Niger-Congo, Atlantic-Congo, Volta-Congo, Benue-Congo, Bantoid, Southern, Narrow Bantu, Northwest, A, Makaa-Njem (A.80). Pygmies, dispersed in small groups in the forest. Forest. Bible portions 1969. See main entry under Cameroon.

MOLENGUE ***(MOLENDJI, BALENGUE)*** [BXC] Southern, just inland from coast, about 4/9 of the way up, between the southern tip of the country and the Rio Benito. Unclassified. One of 3 groups known as 'semi-playeros', who function well on the coast and in the jungle. Tropical forest. Coastal, riverine. Swidden agriculturalists. 0 to 100 meters.

NGUMBA ***(MVUMBO, NGOUMBA, MGOUMBA, MABI, MABEA, BUJEBA)*** [NMG] 8,900 in Equatorial Guinea (1993 Johnstone), or 2% of the population. Rio Muni). Niger-Congo, Atlantic-Congo, Volta-Congo, Benue-Congo, Bantoid, Southern, Narrow Bantu, Northwest, A, Makaa-Njem (A.80). Dialect: KWASIO (BISIO, BISSIO, BISIWO). One of 3 groups known as 'semi-playeros', because they function well on the coast and in the jungle. Tropical forest. Coastal, riverine. Swidden agriculturalists. 0 to 100 meters. Bible portions 1957. See main entry under Cameroon.

NGUMBI ***(COMBE, KOMBE)*** [NUI] 4,000 (1995). Rio Muni coast, including Ecuco village. Niger-Congo, Atlantic-Congo, Volta-Congo, Benue-Congo, Bantoid, Southern, Narrow Bantu, Northwest, A, Bube-Benga (A.30), Yasa. Dialects: ASONGA, BOMUDI, MOGANDA. In Yasa (Bongwe) cluster. May be a dialect of Yasa. One of the Ndowe coastal peoples. Tropical forest. Coastal. Fishermen, swidden agriculturalists. 0 to 50 meters. Christian. NT 1940.

SEKI ***(SEKYANI, SEKIANI, SEKIYANI, SEKIANA, SHEKIYANA, SHEKE, SEKE, BESEKI, BULU)*** [SYI] 11,000 in Equatorial Guinea (1993 Johnstone). Population total both countries 12,000 to 15,000. Coastal. Also spoken in Gabon. Niger-Congo, Atlantic-Congo, Volta-Congo, Benue-Congo, Bantoid, Southern, Narrow Bantu, Northwest, B, Kele (B.20). Different from Bulu of Cameroon. One of 3 groups known as 'semi-playeros' because they function well on the coast and in the jungle. Tropical forest. Coastal, riverine. Swidden agriculturalists. 0 to 100 meters.

SPANISH [SPN] 11,500 in Equatorial Guinea (1993 Johnstone). Mainly on Biombo Island. Indo-European, Italic, Romance, Italo-Western, Western, Gallo-Iberian, Ibero-Romance, West Iberian, Castilian. Official language. Bible 1553-1979. See main entry under Spain.

YASA ***(YASSA, LYASSA, MAASA, BONGWE)*** [YKO] Rio Muni. Yasa dialect is in Cameroon and 1 village (Rio Ntem) in EG, The other dialects are in EG. Niger-Congo, Atlantic-Congo, Volta-Congo, Benue-Congo, Bantoid, Southern, Narrow Bantu, Northwest, A, Bube-Benga (A.30), Yasa. Dialects: IYASA, BWEKO, VENDO, BODELE, MARRY, ONE, ASONGA, BOMUI, MOGANA, MOOMA, MAPANGA. A cluster of dialects. One of the Ndowe coastal peoples. Grammar. Tropical forest. Coastal. Fishermen. 1 to 50 meters. See main entry under Cameroon.

ERITREA

National or official language: English. 3,577,000 (1998 UN). Capital: Asmara. Independence from Ethiopia 1993. Literacy rate 37%. Also includes Western Agaw, Hadrami Spoken Arabic 100,000, Sudanese Spoken Arabic 100,000, Taizzi-Adeni Spoken Arabic 18,000, Hausa, Central Kanuri. Data accuracy estimate: B. The number of languages listed for Eritrea is 13. Of those, 12 are living languages and 1 is extinct. Diversity index 0.69.

AFAR ***(AFARAF, "DANAKIL", "DENKEL")*** [AFR] 300,000 in Eritrea (1993 Johnstone). Southern Eritrea. May also be in Somalia. Afro-Asiatic, Cushitic, East, Saho-Afar. Dialects: CENTRAL AFAR, NORTHERN AFAR, AUSSA, BA'ADU. Saho is related but distinct. Bilingualism in Arabic. The people are called "Danakil" by others, but that is considered to be offensive by the Afar. Nomadic. People have suffered from recent famines. SOV. Literacy rate in second language: 8%. Muslim, Christian. NT 1994. See main entry under Ethiopia.

ARABIC, HIJAZI SPOKEN ***(HIJAZI)*** [ACW] Red Sea coast. Afro-Asiatic, Semitic, Central, South, Arabic. Rashaydah nomadic camel-herders migrated from Arabia to the Red Sea hills of Sudan and Eritrea in the middle of the 19th century. See main entry under Saudi Arabia.

ARABIC, STANDARD [ABV] Middle East, North Africa. Afro-Asiatic, Semitic, Central, South, Arabic. Used in some schools. Official language. Newspapers, radio programs. Bible 1984-1991. See main entry under Saudi Arabia.

BEDAWI ***(BEDÀWIE, BEJA, BEDAWIYE, BEDAWYE, BEDAUYE, BEDWI, BEDYA, BEDJA, LOBAT)*** [BEI] 120,000 in Eritrea (1993 Johnstone), including 20,000 Hadendoa (1970 Bendor). Afro-Asiatic, Cushitic, North. Dialects: HADAREB (HADAAREB), BISHARIN (BISARIN, BISARIAB), HADENDOA (HADENDOWA), BENI-AMIR, ABABDA, AMARA. The Beja people call their language 'Bedàwie'. SOV, postpositions, causatives, reciprocals, reflexives, subject suffixes distinguish person, number, gender. Muslim. See main entry under Sudan.

BILEN ***(BOGO, BOGOS, BILAYN, BILIN, BALEN, BELENI, BELEN, BILEIN, BILENO, NORTH AGAW)*** [BYN] 70,000 (1995). Central Eritrea, in and around the town of Keren. Afro-Asiatic, Cushitic, Central, Northern. 60% of the Christians are partly bilingual in Tigrinya, 70% of the Muslims appear to be bilingual in Tigré. The younger generation mixes their speech with Arabic. Some are bilingual in Nara or Kunama. SOV. Muslim, Christian. Bible portions 1882-1984.

ENGLISH [ENG] Indo-European, Germanic, West, English. Language of higher education and many technical fields. National language. Bible 1535-1989. See main entry under United Kingdom.

GEEZ ***(ANCIENT ETHIOPIC, ETHIOPIC, GE'EZ, GIIZ)*** [GEE] Afro-Asiatic, Semitic, South, Ethiopian, North. Liturgical language. Not otherwise used. VSO. Christian. Extinct. Bible 1918. See main entry under Ethiopia.

ITALIAN [ITN] Indo-European, Italic, Romance, Italo-Western, Italo-Dalmatian. Spoken as a second language. A few monolinguals. Bible 1471-1985. See main entry under Italy.

KUNAMA ***(BAZA, BAAZA, BAZEN, BAAZEN, BAAZAYN, BADEN, BAADEN, BADA, BAADA, CUNAMA, DIILA)*** [KUM] 140,000 in Eritrea (1993 Johnstone), including 1,000 in Ilit, 600 in Odasa. Population total both countries 142,000. Western Eritrea, on the Gash and Setit rivers, Sudan border and into Tigray Province. Barka is south of Barentu; Marda is north, northeast and east of Barentu and in Barentu; Aimara is west of Barentu; Laki-Tukura is south of Aimara, west of Barka; Tika is south of Laki-Tukura, west of Barka. None in Sudan. Also spoken in Ethiopia. Nilo-Saharan, Kunama. Dialects: BARKA (BERKA), MARDA, AIMARA (AAIMASA, AYMASA, ODASA), TIKA (TIIKA, LAKATAKURA-TIKA), ILIT (ILIIT, IILIIT, IILIT), BITAMA (BITAAMA), SOKODASA (SOGODAS, SOGADAS), TAKAZZE-SETIIT (SETIIT, SETIT), TIGRAY. Bitama and Ilit are nearly unintelligible to speakers of other Kunama. Barka is the largest dialect and intelligible to speakers of all others. Laka-Takura and Tika have been influenced by Arab culture and by the Beni-Amer. Investigation needed: intelligibility with Bitama, Ilit. SOV, postpositions, case suffixes. Literacy rate in second language: Low. Mountains, savannah, thorn trees. Agriculturalists: sorghum, millet, sesame; animal husbandry: cattle, sheep, goats, donkeys, chickens. Traditional religion, Muslim (Ilit, Bitama). NT 1927.

NARA ***(NERA, "BAREA", "BARYA", "BARIA", HIGIR, KOYTA, MOGAREB, SANTORA)*** [NRB] 63,000 (1993 Johnstone). In and north of Barentu, western Eritrea, adjoining Kunama territory which is to the south. Nilo-Saharan, Eastern Sudanic, Eastern, Nara. Considerable dialect variation within the four main tribal sections: Higir, Mogareb, Koyta, Santora. Little intelligibility with Kunama. They use Tigré for intercommunication, or Arabic. The Koyta use Kunama. "Barya" is a derogatory name. SOV, case suffixes, passive verbs, reciprocal verbs. Muslim, traditional religion.

SAHO ***(SAO, SHAHO, SHOHO, SHIHO)*** [SSY] 144,000 in Eritrea (1993 Johnstone). Population total both countries 166,750. Southern Eritrea. Also spoken in Ethiopia. Afro-Asiatic, Cushitic, East, Saho-Afar. Very close to Afar. The Irob dialect is only in Ethiopia. Ethnic group names are Asa'orta, Hadu (Hazu), Miniferi. Nomadic. They do not accept outsiders. They have suffered from recent famines. Dictionary. SOV. Literacy rate in first language: Below 1%. Literacy rate in second language: Below 5%. Muslim, Christian.

TIGRÉ ***(KHASA, XASA)*** [TIE] 800,000 in Eritrea (1997 census). Population total both countries 800,000 or more. Also spoken in Sudan. Afro-Asiatic, Semitic, South, Ethiopian, North. Dialect: MANSA' (MENSA). Used as second language by the Tukrir. Spoken by some Beni-Amer called 'Lobot'. Other ethnic groups are Ad Aha, Geden Sikta, Iddifer, Teroa Beit Mushe. Believed by some to be the direct linguistic descendant of Ge'ez. Incorrectly called 'Ge'ez'. People have suffered from recent famines. SOV. Muslim. Bible 1988.

TIGRIGNA ***(TIGRINYA, TIGRAY)*** [TGN] 1,900,000 in Eritrea (1993 Johnstone). South and central Eritrea. Afro-Asiatic, Semitic, South, Ethiopian, North. People have suffered from recent famines. Official language. Literacy rate in first language: 1% to 10%. Literacy rate in second language: 5% to 25%. Ethiopic script. Christian, Muslim. Bible 1956. See main entry under Ethiopia.

ETHIOPIA

Republic of Ethiopia. Federal Democratic Republic of Ethiopia. Ye Etiyop'iya Hizbawi Dimokrasiyawi Ripublik. National or official languages: Amharic, Tigrigna, English. 59,882,000 (1998 Central Statistical Authority [CSA]). Literacy rate 23.4% (1998 CSA). Also includes Sudanese Spoken Arabic, Kunama 1,883. Information mainly from M. L. Bender 1971, 1975, 1976, 1983, 1989; Ralph Siebert 1998-1999. Christian (including Orthodox), Muslim, traditional religion, other (1998 CSA). Blind population 117,739 totally blind, 201,455 partially blind (1998 census). Deaf population 131,359 hearing problems, 58,415 hearing and speaking problems (1998 census). Deaf institutions: 7. Data accuracy estimate: A2, B. The number of languages listed for Ethiopia is 86. Of those, 82 are living languages and 4 are extinct. Diversity index 0.84.

AARI ***(ARI, ARA, ARO, AARAI, "SHANKILLA", "SHANKILLINYA", "SHANKILLIGNA")*** [AIZ] 158,857 mother tongue speakers, 13,319 second language users, 155,002 in the ethnic group, 129,350 monolinguals (1998 census). North central Omo region, southern tip of Ethiopian plateau, near the Hamer-Banna. Afro-Asiatic, Omotic, South. Dialects: GOZZA, BAKO (BACO), BIYO (BIO), GALILA, LAYDO, SEYKI, SHANGAMA, SIDO, WUBAHAMER (UBAMER), ZEDDO. Galila is a significantly divergent dialect. Some bilingualism in Amharic and Gofa (Wolaytta). 95% speak Aari in the home and market. "Shankilla" is a derogatory name. Patrilineal. SOV. Literacy rate in first language: Below 1%. Literacy rate in second language: 8.3%. Plateau. Agriculturalists, traders, cottage industries. Traditional religion; Christian. NT (no date given).

AFAR ***(AFARAF, "DANAKIL", "DENKEL", <AFAR AF, ADAL)*** [AFR] 979,367 mother tongue speakers, 22,848 second language users, 979,367 in the ethnic group, 905,872 monolinguals in Ethiopia (1998 census). Population total all countries 1,579,000. Eastern lowlands, Afar Region. May also be in Somalia. Also spoken in Djibouti, Eritrea. Afro-Asiatic, Cushitic, East, Saho-Afar. Dialects: NORTHERN AFAR, CENTRAL AFAR, AUSSA, BAADU (BA<ADU). Saho is related but distinct. Bilingualism in Arabic. The people are called "Danakil" in Arabic and by others, but that is considered to be offensive by the Afar; called 'Adal' in Amharic. Nomadic. People have suffered from recent famines. Dictionary. Grammar. SOV. Literacy rate in first language: Below 1%. Literacy rate in second language: 3%. Desert. Coastal. Muslim, Christian. NT 1994.

AGAW, WESTERN [QIM] 1,650 mother tongue speakers, 3,181 second language users, out of 172,327 in the ethnic group, 170,747 ethnic Western Agaw are monolingual in Amharic in Ethiopia (1998 census). Population total both countries 1,650 or more. Northwest Amhara Region, north of Lake Tana. Communities of Qwara or Kayla are near Addis Ababa and in Eritrea. None in Sudan. Also spoken in Eritrea. Afro-Asiatic, Cushitic, Central, Western. Dialects: QIMANT (KEMANT, KIMANT, KEMANAT, KAMANT, CHEMANT, QEMANT), DEMBIYA (DEMBYA, DAMBYA), HWARASA (QWARA, QWARINA, "KARA"), KAYLA, SEMYEN, ACHPAR, KWOLASA (KWOLACHA). A separate language from Awngi, Bilen, and Xamtanga. It is reported that all Qimant are bilingual in Amharic. Ge'ez is used as liturgical language, but many use a few Hebrew words in prayer. Qwara is extinct. Kayla or Qwara people are called 'Falashi', the so-called 'Black Jews'. No evidence of a distinct Jewish language. The remaining 'Falasha' went to Israel in 1999. 'Kara' is an incorrect spelling. SOV. Literacy rate in second language: 14.7%. Christian (Qimant), Jewish (Kayla). Bible portions 1885.

ALABA ***(ALLAABA, HALABA)*** [ALB] 126,257 mother tongue speakers, 25,271 second language users, 125,900 in the ethnic group, 95,388 monolinguals (1998 census). Rift Valley southwest of Lake Shala. Separated by a river from the Kambatta. Afro-Asiatic, Cushitic, East, Highland. 81% lexical similarity with Kambaata, 64% with Sidamo, 56% with Libido, 54% with Hadiyya. There is interest in using Alaba for primary education. SOV. Literacy rate in first language: Below 1%. Literacy rate in second language: 8.6%. Muslim, Christian.

AMHARIC ***(ABYSSINIAN, ETHIOPIAN, AMARINYA, AMARIGNA)*** [AMH] 17,372,913 mother tongue speakers, 5,104,150 second language users, 16,007,933 in the ethnic group, 14,743,556 monolinguals in Ethiopia, (1998 census). Population total all countries 17,413,000 or more. 21,000,000 including second language users (1999 WA). North central Ethiopia, Amhara Region, and in Addis Ababa. Also spoken in Egypt, Israel, Sweden. Afro-Asiatic, Semitic, South, Ethiopian, South, Transversal, Amharic-Argobba. Bilingualism in English, Arabic, Oromo, Tigrinya. Used in government, public media, national business, education to seventh grade in many areas, wide variety of literature (fiction, poetry, plays, magazines). People have suffered from recent famines. National language. Dictionary. Grammar. SOV, prepositions, postpositions, genitives, articles, and relatives precede noun heads, question word initial, case affixes, verb suffixes show person, number, gender of subject and (optionally) object, passives including deponents, causatives, CV, CVC, V, CVCC. Literacy rate in first language: 28.1%. Literacy rate in second language: 28.1%. Radio programs, TV. Christian, Jewish. Bible 1840-1988.

ANFILLO ***(SOUTHERN MAO)*** [MYO] 500 speakers out of an ethnic group of 1,000 (1990 SIL). Anfillo Forest, west of Dembi Dolo. Afro-Asiatic, Omotic, North, Gonga-Gimojan, Gonga, Central. 53% lexical similarity with Shakacho. Members of the ethnic group mainly speak Western Oromo. All speakers are older. SOV. Literacy rate in second language: 5%.

ANUAK ***(ANYWAK, ANYUAK, ANYWA, YAMBO, JAMBO, YEMBO, BAR, BURJIN, MIROY, MOOJANGA, NURO)*** [ANU] 45,646 mother tongue speakers, 2,114 second language users, 45,665 in the ethnic group, 34,311 monolinguals in Ethiopia (1998 census). Gambela Region in the southwest. Along the Baro, Alworo, and Gilo rivers and on the right bank of the Akobo River. Gambela town is the main center. Nilo-Saharan, Eastern Sudanic, Nilotic, Western, Luo, Northern, Anuak. Dialects: ADOYO, CORO, LUL, OPËNO. Four main dialect areas, but only slight differences. Closer to Acholi and Luo of Uganda than to Shilluk. SVO, prepositions, tonal. Literacy rate in second language: 36.9%. Agriculturalists: maize, sorghum; animal husbandry; fishermen; hunters. Traditional religion. NT 1962-1965. See main entry under Sudan.

ARBORE ***(ARBORA, ERBORE, IRBORE)*** [ARV] 4,441 mother tongue speakers, 3,108 second language users, 6,559 in the ethnic group, 3,907 monolinguals (1998 census). Extreme southwest, Omo Region, near Lake Stefanie. Afro-Asiatic, Cushitic, East, Western Omo-Tana. Komso is the lingua franca. SOV. Literacy rate in second language: 13.9%.

ARGOBBA [AGJ] 10,860 mother tongue speakers, 3,236 second language speakers, 62,831 in the ethnic group. 44,737 monolinguals, including 47,285 in Amharic, 3,771 in Oromo, 541 in Tigrigna (1999 census). Fragmented areas along the Rift Valley in settlements like Yimlawo, Gusa, Shonke, Berket, Keramba, Mellajillo, Metehara, Shewa Robit and surrounding rural villages. Afro-Asiatic, Semitic, South, Ethiopian, South, Transversal, Amharic-Argobba. Dialects: ANKOBER, SHONKE. It is reported that the "purest" Argobba is spoken in Shonke and T'olaha. 75% to 85% lexical similarity to Amharic. Bilingualism in Amharic, Oromo. The ethnic group near Ankober mainly speaks Amharic; the group near Harar mainly speaks Oromo. The ethnic group is working to foster ethnic recognition. Investigation needed: bilingual proficiency in Amharic (Ankober). Literacy rate in second language: 16.4%. Traders, agriculturalists. Muslim.

AWNGI ***(AWIYA, AWI, AGAW, AGAU, AGEW, AGOW, AWAWAR, DAMOT, KWOLLANYOCH)*** [AWN] 356,980 mother tongue speakers, 64,425 second language speakers, 397,491 in the ethnic group, 279,326 monolinguals (1998 census). Amhara Region. Widely scattered parts of Agew Midir and Metekel, southwest of Lake Tana. Afro-Asiatic, Cushitic, Central, Southern. A separate language. 80% to 90% of speakers use Amharic as second language. SOV. Agriculturalists.

BAISO ***(BAYSO, ALKALI)*** [BSW] 1,010 (1995 SIL) out of a larger ethnic group. Alge village near Merab Abaya, half way between Soddo and Arba Minch (390); Gidicho Island, Baiso and Shigima villages (200); and Welege (420) Island on Lake Abaya, and the western shore of the lake. Afro-Asiatic, Cushitic, East, Western Omo-Tana. Older people speak Oromo as second language, younger people have better proficiency in Wolaytta. Speakers use Baiso in most domains. Most children learn Bayso. The people have resisted extinction for at least 1,000 years (Brenzinger, Heine, and Sommer 1991). They are positive toward the idea of Baiso literature. Investigation needed: bilingual proficiency in Oromo, Wolaytta. SOV. Fishermen, agriculturalists, weavers, hippo hunters.

BAMBASSI ***(BAMBESHI, SIGGOYO, AMAM, FADIRO, NORTHERN MAO, DIDESSA)*** [MYF] 5,000 (1982 SIL). Beni Shangul Region, in and around Bambesi. Afro-Asiatic, Omotic, North, Mao, East. Dialects: KERE, BAMBASSI. 31% lexical similarity with other Omotic languages, 17% with Hozo-Sezo (Bender 1983). Limited bilingualism in Oromo, Arabic, and almost none in Amharic. Attitudes toward Oromo vary. SOV. Literacy rate in second language: 5,3%. Muslim.

BASKETTO ***(BASKETO, BASKATTA, MESKETO)*** [BST] 57,805 mother tongue speakers, 8,961 second language speakers, 51,097 in the ethnic group, 42,726 monolinguals (1998 census). North Omo Region, on a plateau west of Bulki. Afro-Asiatic, Omotic, North, Gonga-Gimojan, Gimojan, Ometo-Gimira, Ometo, West. Not adequately intelligible with Wolaytta. 61% lexical similarity with Oyda. The average Basketo is monolingual and could not understand anything important in any language except Basketo. Limited bilingualism in Wolaytta. SOV. Literacy rate in first language: Below 1%. Literacy rate in second language: 10.2%. Plateau. Christian.

BENCH ***(GIMIRA, GHIMARRA, GIMARRA, DIZU)*** [BCQ] 173,586 mother tongue speakers, 22,640 second language speakers, 173,123 in the ethnic group, 149,293 monolinguals including 10,002 She, 1,070 Mer (1998 census). Kafa Region, in and around Mizan Teferi and Shewa Bench towns. Afro-Asiatic, Omotic, North, Gonga-Gimojan, Gimojan, Ometo-Gimira, Gimira. Dialects: BENCH (BENCHO, BENESHO), MER (MIERU), SHE (SCE, KABA). Bilingualism in Amharic. SOV, 5 level tones, 1 glide. Literacy rate in first language: Below 1%. Literacy rate in second language: 12.0%

Amharic. Forest, savannah. Agriculturalists: wheat, barley, maize, sorgum. 1,700 to 2,000 meters. Traditional religion, Christian. NT 1990.

BERTA ***(BENI SHANGUL, BERTHA, BARTA, BURTA, WETAWIT, JEBELAWI)*** [WTI] 124,799 mother tongue speakers including 8,715 Fadashi; 16,533 second language speakers including 795 of Fadashi; 125,853 in the ethnic group including 7,323 Fadashi in Ethiopia; 99,689 monolinguals including 4,146 Fadashi (1998 census). Population total both countries 147,000. Beni Shangul Region, the corner formed by the Blue Nile River and Sudan border north of Asosa, and Dalati, a village east of the Dabus River. Also spoken in Sudan. Nilo-Saharan, Berta. Dialects: SHURU, BAKE, UNDU, MAYU, FADASHI, DABUSO, GOBATO. Fadashi may be a separate language. "Beni Shangul" is the Arabic name, and is reported to be derogatory. Investigation needed: intelligibility with Fadashi. SVO, case suffixes, passive, causative, tonal, prepositions. Literacy rate in second language: Berta: 9.7%, Gobato: 55.4%. Agriculturalists. Muslim.

BIRALE ***('ONGOTA, BIRELLE, IFA'ONGOTA, "SHANQILLA")*** [BXE] 20 speakers out of an ethnic group of 70 (1990 SIL). One village on the west bank of the Weyt'o River, southeast Omo Region. Afro-Asiatic, Unclassified. Members of the ethnic group who do not speak Birale conduct their affairs in Tsamai. All speakers are old. Not supportive to language maintenance. SOV; postpositions; genitives follow noun heads; suffixes indicate noun case; verb affixes mark subject person, number, and gender; passive; causative. Agriculturalists, hunters. Nearly extinct.

BORO ***(BWORO, SHINASHA, SCINACIA)*** [BWO] 19,878 mother tongue speakers including 144 Gamila; 2,276 second language speakers including 45 Gamila; 32,894 in the ethnic group including 186 Gamila; 18,567 monolinguals including 77 Gamila (1998 census). Southwest Amhara Region, near the Blue Nile River. Afro-Asiatic, Omotic, North, Gonga-Gimojan, Gonga, North. Dialects: AMURU, WAMBERA, GAMILA, GUBA. Related to Kafa. Scattered dialect groups. 46% lexical similarity with Shakako. Bilingualism in Amharic, Oromo. Investigation needed: bilingual proficiency in Amharic, Oromo. SOV. Literacy rate in second language: 25.1%.

BURJI ***(BAMBALA, BEMBALA, DAASHI)*** [BJI] 35,731 mother tongue speakers, 3,045 second language speakers, 46,565 in the ethnic group, 29,259 monolinguals in Ethiopia (1998 census). Population total both countries 42,730. South of Lake Ciamo. Also spoken in Kenya. Afro-Asiatic, Cushitic, East, Highland. 41% lexical similarity with Sidamo (closest). Many speakers in Ethiopia are older. Dictionary. SOV, passives, middle voice, causatives, subject suffixes distinguish person, number, gender. Literacy rate in first language: Below 1%. Literacy rate in second language: 29.1%. Christian, Muslim. NT 1993.

BUSSA ***(DOBASE, D'OOPACE, D'OPAASUNTE, LOHU, MASHILE, MASHELLE, MASHOLLE, MOSIYE, MUSIYE, GOBEZE, GOWASE, GORAZE, ORASE)*** [DOX] 6,624 mother tongue speakers, 920 second language speakers, 9,207 in the ethnic group, 4,955 monolinguals (1998 census). Omo Region, west of Lake Chamo. Afro-Asiatic, Cushitic, East, Dullay. There is a dialect chain with Komso-Dirasha-Dobase. 78% lexical similarity with Gawwada, 51% with Komso, 86% with Gollango, 80% with Harso, 61% with Tsamai. Bilingualism reinforces intelligibility of Komso and Dirasha. SOV. Literacy rate in second language: 13.8%. Deciduous forest. Mountain slope. Peasant agriculturalists.

CHARA ***(CIARA)*** [CRA] 6,932 mother tongue speakers, 668 second language speakers, 6,984 in the ethnic group, 5,556 monolinguals (1998 census). Central Kafa Region, just north of the Omo River. Afro-Asiatic, Omotic, North, Gonga-Gimojan, Gimojan, Ometo-Gimira, Chara. 54% lexical similarity with Wolaytta, which can be understood after some months. Some are bilingual in Wolaytta to the east or Kafa to the west. They use Chara in village and family life. SOV, noun case suffixes, postpositions. Literacy rate in second language: 0.8%. Agriculturalists: small grain. Traditional religion.

DAASANACH ***(DASENECH, DAASANECH, DATHANAIK, DATHANAIC, DATHANIK, GHELEBA, GELEBA, GELEB, GELEBINYA, GALLAB, GALUBA, GELAB, GELUBBA, DAMA, MARILLE, MERILE, MERILLE, MORILLE, RESHIAT, RUSSIA, "SHANGILLA")*** [DSH] 32,064 mother tongue speakers, 231 second language speakers, 32,099 in the ethnic group, 31,368 monolinguals in Ethiopia (1998 census). Population total both countries 34,560. Lower Omo River, along Lake Turkana, extending into Kenya. Also spoken in Kenya. Afro-Asiatic, Cushitic, East, Western Omo-Tana. An ethnic group name is 'Reshiat' (Russia). SOV. Literacy rate in second language: 1.7%. Semi-arid, desert. Plains. Pastoralists, agriculturalists: sorghum. Traditional religion, Christian. Bible portions 1997.

DIME ***(DIMA)*** [DIM] 6,501 mother tongue speakers, 529 second language speakers, 6,197 in the ethnic group, 4,785 monolinguals (1998 census). Kafa Region, north of the Omo River, just before it turns south. Afro-Asiatic, Omotic, South. 47% lexical similarity with Banna. Not bilingual in neighboring languages, except possibly Aari. Population has diminished because of disease and war. SOV. Literacy rate in first language: Below 1%. Literacy rate in second language: Below 9.9%.

DIRASHA ***(DHIRASHA, DIRAASHA, DIRAYTA, GARDULLA, GHIDOLE, GIDOLE)*** [GDL] 50,328 mother tongue speakers, 1,974 second language speakers, 54,354 in the ethnic group, 41,685 monolinguals (1998 census). Omo Region, in the hills west of Lake Chamo, around Gidole town. Afro-Asiatic, Cushitic, East, Konso-Gidole. Part of a dialect chain with Komso and Bussa. 55% lexical similarity with Komso. Many are bilingual in Oromo or Komso. SOV, verb suffix morphology shows causative, reflexive, subject person, number, gender.

DIZI ***(MAJI, DIZI-MAJI, SIZI, TWOYU)*** [MDX] 21,075 mother tongue speakers, 2,054 second language speakers, 21,894 in the ethnic group, 17,583 monolinguals (1998 census). Kafa Region, near Maji town. Afro-Asiatic, Omotic, North, Dizoid. Related to Sheko, Nayi. SOV, tonal. Literacy rate in first language: Below 1%. Literacy rate in second language: 16.8%. Traditional religion, Christian.

DORZE [DOZ] 20,782 mother tongue speakers, 3,597 second language speakers, 28,990 in the ethnic group, 9,905 monolinguals (1998 census). Mostly in North Omo Region in and around Chencha, but a significant community is in Addis Ababa. Afro-Asiatic, Omotic, North, Gonga-Gimojan, Gimojan, Ometo-Gimira, Ometo, Central. 82% to 87% lexical similarity with Gamo, 77% to 81% with Gofa, 80% with Wolaytta, 73% to 75% with Kullo, 54% with Koorete, 48% with Male. Investigation needed: intelligibility. SOV. Literacy rate in second language: 56.8%. Weavers.

ENGLISH [ENG] 1,986 mother tongue speakers, 169,726 second language users (1998 census). Indo-European, Germanic, West, English. Language of higher education, many technical fields, and international communication. Official language. Bible 1535-1989. See main entry under United Kingdom.

ETHIOPIAN SIGN LANGUAGE [ETH] Deaf sign language. There are several sign languages used in different schools for the deaf. Little research. Used since 1971. There have been elementary schools for deaf children since 1956. There is a manual alphabet for spelling.

GAFAT [GFT] South Blue Nile area. Afro-Asiatic, Semitic, South, Ethiopian, South, Outer, n-Group. No longer spoken. The people now speak Amharic. Extinct. Bible portions 1945.

GAMO-GOFA-DAWRO [GMO] 1,236,637 mother tongue speakers including 690,069 Gamo, 313,228 Dawro, 233,340 Gofa; 77,883 second language users including 24,438 Gamo, 19,996 Dawro, 33,449 Gofa; 1,292,860 in the ethnic group including 719,847 Gamo, 331,483 Dawro, 241,530 Gofa; 1,046,084 monolinguals including 597,130 Gamo, 259,633 Dawro, 189,321 Gofa (1998 census). Omo Region, in and around Arba Minch, and in the mountains west to Lake Abaya. Dache is a place name, not a language. Afro-Asiatic, Omotic, North, Gonga-Gimojan, Gimojan, Ometo-Gimira, Ometo, Central. Dialects: GAMO (GEMU), GOFA (GOFFA), DAWRO (DAURO, KULLO, CULLO, OMETAY). Subdialects of Dawro are Konta (Conta) and Kucha (Kusha, Koysha). Gamo has 79% to 91% lexical similarity with Gofa, 79% to 89% with Wolaytta, 82% to 87% with Dorze, 73% to 80% with Dawro, 49% with Koorete, 44% with Male. Dawro has 76% with Gofa, 80% with Wolaytta, 73% to 75% with Dorze, 48% with Koorete, 43% with Male. The government is developing joint educational materials for these 3 groups. SOV; tonal; derived nouns formed by suffixation of verbs; passives; case suffixes; postpositions. Literacy rate in first language: Below 1%. Literacy rate in second language: Gamo: 18.2%, Gofa: 18.5%, Dawro: 23.8%.

GANZA ***(GANZO, KOMA)*** [GZA] Western Oromo, near the Blue Nile. Afro-Asiatic, Omotic, North, Mao, West. Related to Hozo-Sezo, but a separate language (Ruhlen 1987.322). 14% lexical similarity with Omotic languages; 6% with Mao. Oromo-Wellega is the lingua franca of the area, but possibly not for Ganza. Different from Gumuz. SOV. Nearly extinct.

GAWWADA ***(GAUWADA, GAWATA, KAWWAD'A, KAWWADA)*** [GWD] 32,698 mother tongue speakers, 1,367 second language speakers, 33,971 in the ethnic group, 27,477 monolinguals (1998 census). Omo Region, west of Lake Chamo. Afro-Asiatic, Cushitic, East, Dullay. Dialects: DIHINA (TIHINA, TIHINTE), GERGERE (K'ARK'ARTE), GOBEZE, GOLLANGO (KOLLANKO), GOROSE (GORROSE, KORROSE), HARSO (WORASE). Gawwada has 78% lexical similarity with Bussa, 73% with Tsamai, 77% with Harso, 92% with Gollango, 41% with Komso. Harso has 80% with Dobase, 56% with Tsamai. Amharic and Oromo are used as second language. Leaders use Komso. Investigation needed: intelligibility with Harso. SOV. Literacy rate in first language: Below 1%. Literacy rate in second language: 22.3%. Deciduous forest. Mountain slope. Peasant agriculturalists.

GEDEO ***(GEDDEO, DERESA, DERASA, DARASA, DERASANYA, DARASSA)*** [DRS] 637,082 mother tongue speakers, 47,950 second language speakers, 639,905 in the ethnic group, 438,958 monolinguals (1998 census). Central highland area, southwest of Dilla and east of Lake Abaya. Afro-Asiatic, Cushitic, East, Highland. 60% lexical similarity with Sidamo (closest), 57% with Alaba, 54% with Kambaata, 51% with Hadiyya. SOV, causative, middle, passive verbs. Literacy rate in first language: Below 1%. Literacy rate in second language: 5.2%. Traditional religion, Christian, Muslim. NT 1986.

GEEZ ***(ANCIENT ETHIOPIC, ETHIOPIC, GE'EZ, GIIZ)*** [GEE] Also spoken in Eritrea. Afro-Asiatic, Semitic, South, Ethiopian, North. Liturgical language. Not otherwise used. VSO. Christian. Extinct. Bible 1918.

GUMUZ ***(GUMIS, GOMBO, "SHANKILLINYA", "SHANQILLA", MENDEYA, DEBATSA, DEBUGA, DEHENDA, BEGA, "SHANKILLIGNA")*** [GUK] 120,424 mother tongue speakers, 4,379 second language speakers, 121,487 in the ethnic group, 88,192 monolinguals in Ethiopia (1998 census). Population total both countries 160,400. Near Metemma on Sudan border south through Gondar and Gojjam, across Blue Nile in Wellaga into Didessa Valley to Leqemt-Gimbi Road, and villages southwest of Addis Ababa, around Welqite (possibly 1,000). Also spoken in Sudan. Nilo-Saharan, Komuz, Gumuz. Dialects: DAKUNZA (DUKUNA, DUGUNZA, DUKUNZA, DUGUNZ, GUNZA, GANZA, DEGOJA), SAI, SESE (SAYSAY), DISOHA (DESUA). There are noticeable dialect differences but all are inherently intelligible. Limited Oromo comprehension. "Shankillinya" is a derogatory name. There are connections between villages for intermarriage and trade. SVO, 3 tones, verb affixes show person, number of subject, first plural inclusive and exclusive. Literacy rate in first language: Below 1%. Literacy rate in second language: 6.2%. Traditional religion, Muslim, Christian.

GURAGE, EAST [GRE] 827,764 mother tongue speakers, 89,042 second language speakers, 900,348 in the ethnic group (1998 census). About 150 kms. south of Addis Ababa. Afro-Asiatic, Semitic, South, Ethiopian, South, Transversal, Harari-East Gurage. Dialects: ENNEQOR (INNEQOR), SILTI (SELTI), ULBARAG (URBAREG), WOLANE (WALANE). Not intelligible with West or North Gurage. 40% or less intelligible with Chaha (Central West Gurage). Zay or Mesmes may be dialects. Investigation needed: intelligibility with Zay, Mesmes. Dictionary. SOV; prepositions and postpositions; genitives, adjectives, numerals, relatives before noun heads, articles after; passives; causatives; CV, CVC; nontonal. Literacy rate in first language: Below 1%. Literacy rate in second language: 16.6%. Bible portions 1981.

GURAGE, SODDO ***(KISTANE, SODDO, NORTH GURAGE)*** [GRU] 254,682 mother tongue speakers, 60,538 second language speakers, 363,867 in the ethnic group (1998 census). 4,000 Gogot. Gurage, Kambaata, Hadiyya Region, just southwest of Addis Ababa. Afro-Asiatic, Semitic, South, Ethiopian, South, Outer, n-Group. Dialects: SODDO (AYMALLAL, AYMELLEL, KESTANE, KISTANE), GOGOT (GOGGOT, DOBI, DOBBI). Not intelligible with East Gurage or West Gurage. Soddo and Gogot may not be inherently intelligible. People along the roads have contact with Amharic; some men are partially bilingual. People in the interior are not very bilingual (B. Denboba 1989). Investigation needed: intelligibility with Gogot. SOV. Literacy rate in second language: 21.5%. Christian.

GURAGE, WEST ***(CENTRAL WEST GURAGE, GURAGIE, GOURAGHIE, GURAGUE)*** [GUY] 798,202 mother tongue speakers, 58,694 second language speakers, 1,022,089 in the ethnic group (1998 census). All Gurage languages including Soddo: 1,881,574 mother tongue speakers, 208,358 second language speakers, 2,290,274 in the ethnic group, 1,248,415 monolinguals (1998 census). West Gurage Region. Afro-Asiatic, Semitic, South, Ethiopian, South, Outer, tt-Group. Dialects: CHAHA (CHEHA), INOR (ENNEMOR), EZHA (EZA, IZHA), GUMER (GWEMARRA), GURA, ENEGEGNY, MASQAN (MESQAN, MESKAN), MUHER. R. Hetzron divides Western Gurage as follows: (a) Masqan, (b) 3-tense Gurage, (i) Central Western (Ezha, Chaha, Gumer, Gura), (ii) Peripheral Western (Gyeto, Inor (Ennemor), Engegeny, Ener). Not intelligible with East Gurage or Soddo. SOV. Literacy rate in first language: Below 1%. Literacy rate in second language: 25.3%. NT 1983.

HADIYYA ***(ADIYA, ADIYE, HADIYA, HADYA, ADEA, HADIA)*** [HDY] 923,958 mother tongue speakers, 150,889 second language speakers, 927,933 in the ethnic group, 595,107 monolinguals (1998 census). Gurage, Kambaata, Hadiyya Region, between the Omo and Billate rivers, in and around Hosaina town. Afro-Asiatic, Cushitic, East, Highland. Dialects: LEEMO, SORO. 82% lexical similarity with Libido, 56% with Kambaata, 54% with Alaba, 53% with Sidamo. Bilingualism in Amharic. SOV, passive, reflexive, causative, middle verbs. Literacy rate in first language: Below 1%. Literacy rate in second language: 34.4%. Christian, Muslim. NT 1992.

HAMER-BANNA ***(HAMAR-KOKE, HAMMERCOCHE, AMARCOCCHE, COCCHE, BESHADA, HAMER, HAMMER, HAMAR, AMER, AMAR, AMMAR, BANNA, BANA, KARA KERRE)*** [AMF] 42,838 mother tongue speakers, 7,120 second language speakers, 42,466 in the ethnic group, 38,354 monolinguals (1998 census). South Omo Region, near the Omo River, and north of Lake Turkana, in the southwest corner, near the Kenya, Uganda, Sudan borders. Afro-Asiatic, Omotic, South. Hamer and Banna are separate ethnic groups who speak virtually the same language. SOV. Literacy rate in first language: Below 1%. Literacy rate in second language: 1.4%. Pastoralists. Traditional religion, Christian.

HARARI ***(HARARRI, ADARE, ADERE, ADERINYA, ADARINNYA, GEY SINAN)*** [HAR] 21,283 mother tongue speakers, 7,766 second language speakers, 21,757 in the ethnic group, 2,351 monolinguals (1998 census). Today 20,000 in Addis Ababa, outside Harar city (Hetzron 1997:486). Homeland Eastern, traditionally within the walled city of Harar. Large communities in Addis Ababa, Nazareth and Dire Dawa. Afro-Asiatic, Semitic, South, Ethiopian, South, Transversal, Harari-East Gurage.

The language has prestige. Dictionary. SOV. Literacy rate in first language: Below 1%. Literacy rate in second language: 81.3%. Muslim.

HOZO ***(BEGI-MAO)*** [HOZ] 3,000 (1995 SIL). Western Oromo Region, Begi area, 50 or more villages. Afro-Asiatic, Omotic, North, Mao, West. Related to Bambassi, but a separate language (Bender 1975). Western Oromo is the lingua franca of the area, but there are some negative attitudes toward it. Bilingual proficiency in Amharic and Arabic is low. Literacy rate in second language: 5.1%.

KACHAMA-GANJULE ***(GATS'AME, GET'EME)*** [KCX] 4,072 mother tongue speakers including 2,682 Kachama,1,390 Ganjule; 419 second language speakers including 223 Kachama, 196 Ganjule; 3,886 in the ethnic group including 2,740 Kachama, 1,146 Ganjule; 1,002 monolinguals including 816 Kachama, 186 Ganjule (1998 census). Kachama is on Gidicho Island in Lake Abaya. Ganjule originally on a small island in Lake Chamo. Ganjule have recently relocated to Shela-Mela on the west shore of Lake Chamo. Afro-Asiatic, Omotic, North, Gonga-Gimojan, Gimojan, Ometo-Gimira, Ometo, East. Dialects: GANJULE (GANJAWLE), GANTA, KACHAMA. 46% lexical similarity with Wolaytta. Some people are bilingual in Wolaytta. SOV. Literacy rate in second language: Kachama: 35.2%.

KACIPO-BALESI [KOE] 2,000 to 3,000 in Ethiopia (1982 SIL). Southern Ethiopia-Sudan border, Boma Plateau in Sudan (Kacipo). Nilo-Saharan, Eastern Sudanic, Eastern, Surmic, South, Southwest, Kacipo-Balesi. Dialects: BALESI (BAALE, BALE), ZILMAMU (SILMAMO, ZELMAMU, ZULMAMU, TSILMANO), KACIPO (KACHEPO, SURI, WESTERN SURI). Pronoun differences between Balesi and Zilmamu. 40% to 54% lexical similarity with Murle, 35% with Mursi. Some use Surma as second language. VSO. Literacy rate in first language: Below 1%. Literacy rate in second language: Below 0.6%. See main entry under Sudan.

KAFICHO ***(KAFA, KEFA, KEFFA, KAFFA, CAFFINO, MANJO)*** [KBR] 569,626 mother tongue speakers, 46,720 second language speakers, 599,188 in the ethnic group, 445,018 monolinguals (1998 census). Kafa Region, in and around the town of Bonga. There may be some in Sudan. Afro-Asiatic, Omotic, North, Gonga-Gimojan, Gonga, South. Dialects: KAFA, BOSHA (GARO). Related to Shakacho. Bosha may be a separate language. Manjo is an argot based on Kafa (Bender 1983). SOV. Literacy rate in second language: 22.2%. Agriculturalists. Traditional religion, Christian, Muslim. Bible portions 1934-1986.

KAMBAATA ***(KAMBATTA, KAMBATA, KEMBATA, KEMATA, KAMBARA, DONGA)*** [KTB] 606,241 mother tongue speakers including 487,655 Kambaata, 82,803 Timbaro, 35,783 Qebena; 83,750 second language speakers including 68,607 Kambaata, 10,715 Timbaro. 4,428 Qebena; 621,407 in the ethnic group including 499,825 Kambaata, 86,510 Timbaro, 35,072 Qebena; 345,797 monolinguals including 278,567 Kambaata, 51,541 Timbaro, 15,689 Qebena (1998 census). Southwest Gurage, Kambaata, Hadiyya Region. Durame is the main town. Afro-Asiatic, Cushitic, East, Highland. Dialects: TAMBARO, TIMBARO (TIMBARA, TIMBAARO), QEBENA (QABENA, KEBENA, K'ABENA). Qebena may be a separate language. 95% lexical similarity with Timbaro dialect, 81% with Allaaba, 62% with Sidamo, 57% with Libido, 56% with Hadiyya. Investigation needed: intelligibility with Qebena. SOV, passive, middle, causative verbs, subject suffixes distinguish person, number, gender. Literacy rate in first language: Below 1%. Literacy rate in second language: 43.7%. Christian, some Muslim. NT 1992.

KARO ***(KERRE, CHERRE, KERE)*** [KXH] 200 (1998 M. Yigezu). South Omo Region, upstream from the Daasanech, riverside settlements near the Hamer-Banna. Afro-Asiatic, Omotic, South. Dialect or closely related language to Hamer-Banna. 81% lexical similarity with Hamer-Banna. Many use Nyangatom as second language. Different from Kara of Sudan which is Central Sudanic. They have a service relationship with the Banna. Investigation needed: intelligibility with Hamer-Banna, bilingual proficiency in Nyangatom. SOV. Literacy rate in second language: 1.5%. Agriculturalists.

KOMO ***(MADIIN, KOMA, SOUTH KOMA, CENTRAL KOMA)*** [KOM] 1,500 in Ethiopia (1975 Bender). South and west of Kwama. Nilo-Saharan, Komuz, Koman. Dialects: KOMA OF BEGI, KOMA OF DAGA. 52% lexical similarity with Uduk (Twampa). Different from Koma of Cameroon. Literacy rate in second language: 12.8%. See main entry under Sudan.

KOMSO ***(KONSO, CONSO, GATO, AF-KARETI, KARATE, KARETI)*** [KXC] 149,508 mother tongue speakers, 5,658 second language speakers, 153,419 in the ethnic group, 138,696 monolinguals (1998 census). South of Lake Ciamo in the bend of the Sagan River. A few migrants in Kenya. Afro-Asiatic, Cushitic, East, Konso-Gidole. 51% lexical similarity with Bussa, 41% with Gawwada, 31% with Tsamai. SOV. Literacy rate in first language: Below 1%. Literacy rate in second language: 7.2%. Deciduous forest. Mountain slope. Peasant agriculturalists. Traditional religion. Bible portions 1996.

KOORETE ***(AMARRO, AMAARRO, BADITTU, NUNA, KOYRA)*** [KQY] 103,879 mother tongue speakers, 2,371 second language speakers, 107,595 in the ethnic group, 84,388 monolinguals (1998 census). About 60 Harro families in Harro village on Gidicho (Gidicció) Island. In the Amaro mountains east of Lake Abaya, Sidama Region. Afro-Asiatic, Omotic, North, Gonga-Gimojan, Gimojan, Ometo-Gimira, Ometo, East. 54% lexical similarity with Dorze, 53% with Wolaytta, 52% with Gofa, 49% with Gamo, 48% with Kullo, 45% with Male. 'Koorete' is their name for themselves. 'Amaro' is the name of the mountain area where they live. SOV. Literacy rate in first language: Below 1%. Literacy rate in second language: 24.1%.

KUNFAL ***(KUNFEL, KUMFEL)*** [XUF] East of Lake Tana. Afro-Asiatic, Cushitic, Central, Southern. Related to Awngi. The people are fairly bilingual in Amharic. Investigation needed: bilingual proficiency in Amharic. SOV.

KWAMA ***(TAKWAMA, GWAMA, GOMA, GOGWAMA, KOMA OF ASOSA, NORTH KOMA, NOKANOKA, AFAN MAO, AMAM, T'WA KWAMA)*** [KMQ] 15,000 (1982 SIL). Along Sudan border in southern Beni Shangul Region, from south of Asosa to Gidami, and in Gambela and Bonga. 19 villages, including one (Yabus) in Sudan. Nilo-Saharan, Komuz, Koman. Oromo is their second language. Arabic has some influence, and speakers have low to moderate proficiency in it. Amharic has little influence. Kwama is the dominant language. Children learn Kwama first. Literacy rate in second language: 68.4%. Muslim.

KWEGU ***(KOEGU, KWEGI, BACHA, MENJA)*** [YID] 103 mother tongue speakers, 51 second language speakers, 173 in the ethnic group, 73 monolinguals (1998 census). Kuchur village on the western bank of the Omo River in southwestern Ethiopia. Nilo-Saharan, Eastern Sudanic, Eastern, Surmic, South, Southeast, Kwegu. Dialects: YIDINICH (YIDINIT, YIDI), MUGUJI. The dialects listed may not be inherently intelligible with Kwegu; it may be a name for several hunter groups. 36% lexical similarity with Mursi. The Kwegu use the Bodi dialect of Me'en or Mursi as second language, depending on the area. Diminishing among adults. They are under the Bodi and Mursi, and looked down on by them. Mursi and Bodi men may marry Kwegu women. Investigation needed: intelligibility with Yidinich, Muguji. SVO, postpositions. Hunter-gatherers: hippopotamus, wild fruit, honey; flood and rain cultivation: maize, durra.

LIBIDO ***(MARAQO, MARAKO)*** [LIQ] 36,612 mother tongue speakers, 9,208 second language speakers, 38,096 in the ethnic group, 14,623 monolinguals (1998 census). Hadiyya, Kambaata, Gurage Region, northeast of Hosaina. Afro-Asiatic, Cushitic, East, Highland. Syntactic, morphological, and lexical differences from Hadiyya. 82% lexical similarity with Hadiyya, 57% with Kambaata, 56% with Allaaba, 53% with Sidamo. SOV, passive, reflexive, causative, middle voice verbs. Literacy rate in first language: Below 1%. Literacy rate in second language: 15.7%. Muslim.

MAJANG ***(MESENGO, MASONGO, MASANGO, MAJANJIRO, TAMA, OJANJUR, AJO, ATO MAJANG, ATO MAJANGER-ONK)*** [MPE] 15,341 mother tongue speakers, 438 second language speakers, 15,341 in the ethnic group, 10,752 monolinguals (1998 census). Southwest. Mainly within a long, narrow belt between Bure (east of Gambela) and Guraferda to the south. Covers part of Gambela, Oromo, and Kafa administrative regions. They have been scattered, but are now settling in villages. Nilo-Saharan, Eastern Sudanic, Eastern, Surmic, North, Majang. Minor dialect variation. The people are called 'Majang' or 'Majangir'. VSO; postpositions; genitives, articles, adjectives, numerals, relatives after noun heads; question words final; suffixes indicate case; verb affixes mark person, number, subject, object; passives, causative prefix; reciprocal verb forms; many syllable patterns; tonal. Literacy rate in first language: Below 1%. Literacy rate in second language: 21.1%. Rain forest. Mountains. Swidden agriculturalists, beekeepers, hunters. Traditional religion, Christian.

MALE [MDY] 53,779 mother tongue speakers, 6,730 second language speakers, 46,458 in the ethnic group, 40,660 monolinguals (1998 census). Omo Region, southeast of Jinka. Afro-Asiatic, Omotic, North, Gonga-Gimojan, Gimojan, Ometo-Gimira, Ometo. 48% lexical similarity with Dorze, 46% with Gofa, 45% with Koorete, 44% with Gamo, 43% with Wolaytta and Kullo. Male is spoken in the home. Different from Malo (see Zayse). SOV. Literacy rate in second language: 4.5%. Interest in Male literature.

ME'EN ***(MEKAN, MIE'EN, MIEKEN, MEQAN, MEN)*** [MYM] 56,585 mother tongue speakers including 4,570 Bodi; 6,300 second language speakers including 342 Bodi; 57,501 in the ethnic group including 4,686 Bodi; 51,446 monolinguals including 4,553 Bodi (1998 census). Central Kafa region, the Tishena in and around Bachuma, the Bodi in lowlands to the south, near the Omo River. Not in Sudan. Nilo-Saharan, Eastern Sudanic, Eastern, Surmic, South, Southeast, Pastoral, Me'en. Dialects: BODI (PODI), TISHENA (TESHINA, TESHENNA). Tishena is inherently intelligible with Bodi. Closely related to Mursi. 65% lexical similarity with Surma, 30% with Murle. Geographical names: Bachuma, Bachuman, Golda, Goldea, Goldiya, Guldiya. SVO; postpositions; genitives, adjective, articles, and relatives follow noun heads; question word final; prefixes and suffixes; verbs inflected; tonal. Literacy rate in first language: Below 1%. Literacy rate in second language: 3.3%. The number of literates is increasing. Highland (Me'en), Lowland (Bodi). Tishena, Me'en: agriculturalists, Bodi (nomadic): pastoralists: cattle. Traditional religion, Christian.

MELO ***(MALO)*** [MFX] 20,151 mother tongue speakers, 4,657 second language users, 20,189 in the ethnic group, 13,264 monolinguals (1998 census). North Omo Region, in and around Malo-Koza, northeast of the Basketo. Afro-Asiatic, Omotic, North, Gonga-Gimojan, Gimojan, Ometo-Gimira, Ometo, Central. Related to Gamo-Gofa-Dawro, but may not be inherently intelligible. The Language Academy said it should be considered a separate speech variety. 70% lexical similarity with the majority of Ometo language varieties. Literacy rate in second language: 9.5%.

MESMES [MYS] Gurage, Hadiyya, Kambatta Region. Afro-Asiatic, Semitic, South, Ethiopian, South, Outer, tt-Group. Related to West Gurage. Investigation needed: intelligibility with West Gurage. SOV.

MURLE ***(MURELE, MERULE, MOURLE, MURULE, BEIR, AJIBBA)*** [MUR] 200 in Ethiopia (1975 Tournay). South of the Akobo River. Olam is in southwest Ethiopia and on the Sudan border. It is between Murle and Majang culturally and linguistically (Bender 1983). Nilo-Saharan, Eastern Sudanic, Eastern, Surmic, South, Southwest, Didinga-Murle, Murle. Dialect: OLAM (NGALAM, BANGALAM). Related to Didinga. Subgroups: Lotilla, Boma, Olam (Ngalam). Maacir may be a dialect or ethnic group. They speak Nyangatom as second language. There is a lot of intermarriage with the Nyangatom. VSO, postpositions; genitives and relatives follow heads, suffixes indicate case, question words final, verbal affixes (prefixes and suffixes) distinguish subject person and number. Pastoralists, agriculturalists. Traditional religion. NT 1996. See main entry under Sudan.

MURSI ***(MURZI, MURZU, MERDU, MERITU, DAMA)*** [MUZ] 3,278 mother tongue speakers, 34 second language users, 3,258 in the ethnic group, 3,155 monolinguals (1998 census). Central Omo Region, lowlands southwest of Jinka. Nilo-Saharan, Eastern Sudanic, Eastern, Surmic, South, Southeast, Pastoral, Suri. Closely related to Suri of Sudan. SVO, postpositions, tonal, case suffixes, verb affixes show subject person and number, question words final. Literacy rate in first language: Below 1%. Literacy rate in second language: 1.2%. Pastoralists. Traditional religion.

NAYI ***(NA'O, NAO)*** [NOZ] 3,656 mother tongue speakers, 1,876 second language users, 4,005 in the ethnic group, 1,137 monolinguals (1998 census). Decha Awraja, Kafa Region, and scattered in other parts of Kafa. The nearest town is Bonga. A few in Dulkuma village of the Shoa Bench Wereda, and Aybera, Kosa, and Jomdos villages of Sheko Wereda. Afro-Asiatic, Omotic, North, Dizoid. Related to Dizi, Sheko. 58% lexical similarity with Dizi. Kaficho is the trade language. Spoken by adults. Young people speak only Kaficho. Investigation needed: bilingual proficiency in Kaficho. SOV. Literacy rate in second language: 6.5%. Agriculturalists.

NUER ***(NAATH)*** [NUS] 64,907 mother tongue speakers, 1,122 second language speakers, 64,534 in the ethnic group, 61,640 monolinguals in Ethiopia (1998 census). Along the Baro River, in Gambela Region. Nilo-Saharan, Eastern Sudanic, Nilotic, Western, Dinka-Nuer, Nuer. Dialect: EASTERN NUER (JI, KANY, JIKANY, DOOR, ABIGAR). Bilingualism in Arabic. 'Naath' is their name for themselves. Severe disruption in residence patterns caused by fighting in Ethiopia and Sudan. Many are refugees or homeless (1991). Literacy rate in second language: 7.9%. Traditional religion. NT 1968. See main entry under Sudan.

NYANGATOM ***(INYANGATOM, DONYIRO, DONGIRO, IDONGIRO)*** [NNJ] 14,177 mother tongue speakers, 123 second language speakers, 14,201 in the ethnic group, 13,797 monolinguals (1998 census). Extreme southwest corner of Ethiopia, Omo Region. Two settlement centers: Omo River and Kibish River. Transhumance into the region of Moru Angipi in Sudan. Nilo-Saharan, Eastern Sudanic, Nilotic, Eastern, Lotuxo-Teso, Teso-Turkana, Turkana. Inherently intelligible with Toposa and Turkana. Ethnic identity attitudes are strong. Mutual nonagression pact with the Toposa. Occasionally hostile with the Turkana and Sudan Jiye. Semi-nomadic. Investigation needed: intelligibility, attitudes. VSO; highly inflectional; grammatical tone (tense, case); vowel harmony; voiceless vowels. Literacy rate in second language: 1.9%. Pastoralists: cattle herders; subsistence agriculturalists: sorghum, beans. Traditional religion.

OPUUO ***(OPO-SHITA, OPO, OPUO, CITA, CIITA, SHITA, SHIITA, ANSITA, KINA, KWINA, "LANGA")*** [LGN] 301 mother tongue speakers, 72 second language speakers, 307 in the ethnic group, 235 monolinguals (1998 census). Population total both countries 301 or more. 5 villages along the Sudan border north of the Anuak and Nuer. Also spoken in Sudan. Nilo-Saharan, Komuz, Koman. 24% lexical similarity with Koma. West-Central Oromo is the lingua franca of the area. "Langa" is a derogatory name used by the Anuak for them. Literacy rate in second language: 35.9%.

OROMO, BORANA-ARSI-GUJI ***(AFAN OROMO, SOUTHERN OROMO, "GALLA", "GALLINYA", "GALLIGNA")*** [GAX] 3,634,000 mother tongue speakers in Ethiopia. Population total all countries 3,786,000. South Oromo Region. Also spoken in Kenya, Somalia. Afro-Asiatic, Cushitic, East, Oromo. Dialects: BORANA (BORAN, BORENA), ARSI (ARUSSI, ARUSI), GUJI (GUJJI, JEMJEM), KEREYU, SALALE (SELALE), GABRA (GABBRA, GEBRA). Harar is closely related, but distinct enough to need separate literature. Called 'Borana' in Kenya. The name "Galla" is derogatory. SOV. Literacy rate in first language: Below 1%. Literacy rate in second language: 16%. Muslim, traditional religion. Bible 1995.

OROMO, EASTERN ***("QOTU" OROMO, HARAR, HARER, "QOTTU", "QUOTTU", "QWOTTU", "KWOTTU", ITTU)*** [HAE] 4,526,000 (1998 census). Eastern and western Hararghe zone in northern Bale zone. Afro-Asiatic, Cushitic, East, Oromo. Closely related to Borana Oromo, but divergent. Bilingualism in Amharic. SOV. Literacy rate in second language: 15%. Muslim.

OROMO, WEST-CENTRAL ***(GALLA, OROMOO)*** [GAZ] 8,920,000 (1998 census). Population total both countries 8,920,000 or more. Oromo Region, West and Central Ethiopia, and along the Rift Valley escarpment east of Dessie and Woldiya. Also spoken in Egypt. Afro-Asiatic, Cushitic, East, Oromo. Dialects: WESTERN OROMO, CENTRAL OROMO. Subdialects are Mecha (Maccha, Wellaga, Wallaga, Wollega), Raya, Wello (Wollo), Tulema (Tulama, Shoa, Shewa). Trade language. Dictionary. Grammar. SOV. Literacy rate in first language: 1% to 5%. Literacy rate in second language: 22.4%. Newspapers, radio programs, TV. Traditional religion, Christian, Muslim. Bible 1899-1998.

OYDA [OYD] 16,597 mother tongue speakers, 4,040 second language speakers, 14,075 in the ethnic group, 6,244 monolinguals (1998 census). Northwest Omo Region, southwest of Sawla. Afro-Asiatic, Omotic, North, Gonga-Gimojan, Gimojan, Ometo-Gimira, Ometo, Central. 69% lexical similarity with Wolaytta, 61% with Basketto. Some people are reported to be bilingual in Wolaytta. Investigation needed: bilingual proficiency in Wolaytta. SOV. Literacy rate in second language: 18.7%.

RER BARE ***(REREBERE, ADONA)*** [RER] Wabi Shebelle River around Gode, eastern Ogaden, near Somali border, and along the Ganale and Dawa rivers. Unclassified. Bilingualism in Somali. They speak Somali. It is uncertain if they spoke a different language earlier. They are called 'Rer Bare' in Somali, which means 'tribe Bare'. Extinct.

SAHO ***(SAO, SHAHO, SHOHO, SHIHO)*** [SSY] 22,759 first language speakers in Ethiopia, 3,378 second language speakers (1998 census). Tigray. Afro-Asiatic, Cushitic, East, Saho-Afar. Dialect: IROB. Very close to Afar. The Irob dialect is only in Tigray. They do not accept outsiders. Ethnic group names are Asa'orta, Hadu (Hazu), Miniferi. They have suffered from recent famines. The Irob are not nomadic. SOV. Literacy rate in second language: High. Irob: Christian. See main entry under Eritrea.

SEZE ***(SEZO)*** [SZE] 3,000 (1995 SIL). Western Oromo Region, near Begi, north of the Hozo. Afro-Asiatic, Omotic, North, Mao, West. Related to Bambassi, but a separate language (Bender 1975). Oromo-Wellega is the lingua franca of the area, but there are some negative attitudes toward it. Bilingual proficiency in Amharic and Arabic is low. Literacy rate in second language: 5%.

SHABO ***(SHAKO, "MEKEYER", "MIKEYIR", "MIKAIR")*** [SBF] 400 to 1,000 (1986) out of a larger ethnic population. Kafa Region, between Godere and Mashi, among the Majang and Shakacho. Nilo-Saharan, Unclassified. A distinct language, apparently a hybrid. Distinct from Sheko. 30% lexical similarity with Majang, 12% with other West Cushitic (Omotic) languages. They are bilingual in Majang or Shakacho. Shabo used in most domains. About half the children learn Shabo. They do not like the name "Mekeyer" used by outsiders. They live in family units, not villages. Investigation needed: bilingual proficiency in Majang, Mocha. SOV, postpositions, gender in all 3 persons. Hunter-gatherers, beekeepers. Traditional religion, Christian.

SHAKACHO ***(MOC'HA, MOCHA, SHEKKA)*** [MOY] 54,894 mother tongue speakers, 3,476 second language speakers, 53,897 in the ethnic group, 36,449 monolinguals (1998 census). North Kafa Region, in and around Maasha. Afro-Asiatic, Omotic, North, Gonga-Gimojan, Gonga, South. Closely related to Kaficho. 'Shakacho' is their self name. SOV, tonal. Literacy rate in first language: Below 1%. Literacy rate in second language: 38.9%. Traditional religion, Christian.

SHEKO ***(SHEKKO, SHEKKA, TSCHAKO, SHAKO, SHAK)*** [SHE] 23,785 mother tongue speakers, 4,920 second language speakers, 23,785 in the ethnic group, 13,611 monolinguals (1998 census). Kafa Region, Shako District. Gaizek'a is a monolingual community. Bajek'a, Selale, and Shimi are multilingual. Afro-Asiatic, Omotic, North, Dizoid. Dialects: DORSHA, BULLA (DAAN, DAN, DAANYIR). Some bilingualism in Amharic and Gimira. Sheko is the primary language of the home, religion, and public use. SOV; postpositions, genitives, articles, adjectives, numerals, relatives after noun heads; question word initial; 1 prefix, 5 suffixes; word order distinguishes subjects, objects, indirect objects; affixes indicate case of noun phrases; verb affixes mark person, number, gender of subject; passives, causatives, comparatives; CV, CVC, CVV, CV:C, CVCC; 3 tones. Literacy rate in first language: Below 1%. Literacy rate in second language: 16.3%. Agriculturalists. Traditional religion, Christian.

SIDAMO ***(SIDÁMO 'AFÓ, SIDAMINYA)*** [SID] 1,876,329 mother tongue speakers, 101,340 second language speakers, 1,842,314 in the ethnic group, 1,632,902 monolinguals (1998 census). South central Ethiopia, northeast of Lake Abaya and southeast of Lake Awasa (Sidamo Awraja). Awasa is the capital of the Sidama Region. Afro-Asiatic, Cushitic, East, Highland. 64% lexical similarity with Allaaba, 62% with Kambaata, 53% with Hadiyya. Dictionary. Grammar. SOV. Literacy rate in first language: 1% to 5%. Literacy rate in second language: 20.3%. NT 1990.

SOMALI ***(STANDARD SOMALI, COMMON SOMALI)*** [SOM] 3,187,053 mother tongue speakers, 95,572 second language speakers, 3,160,540 in the ethnic group, 2,878,371 monolinguals in Ethiopia (1998 census). Southeast Ethiopia, Somali Region. Afro-Asiatic, Cushitic, East, Somali. 10% use Amharic or Arabic as second language. Daarood, Ogaadeen, Dir, Gadabuursi, Hawiye, and Isxaaq are major clan families in Ethiopia. SOV. Literacy rate in second language: 7.3%. Agriculturalists. Muslim, Christian. Bible 1979. See main entry under Somalia.

SURI ***(SURMA, SHURI, CHURI, DHURI, SHURO, EASTERN SURI)*** [SUQ] 19,622 mother tongue speakers, 212 second language speakers, 19,632 in the ethnic group, 19,269 monolinguals in Ethiopia (1998 census). Population total both countries 20,600. Southwestern Kafa Region toward the Sudan border. Some are west of Mizan Teferi. Also spoken in Sudan. Nilo-Saharan, Eastern Sudanic, Eastern, Surmic, South, Southeast, Pastoral, Suri. Dialects: TIRMA (TIRIMA, TEREMA, TERNA, DIRMA, CIRMA, TIRMAGA, TIRMAGI, TID), CHAI (CAI, CACI). Related to Mursi; 81% lexical similarity. Names of ethnic groups: Dama, Dhuak. Dictionary. SVO. Literacy rate in first language: Below 1%. Literacy rate in second language: 0.6%. Savannah, scrub forest. Mountain valley. Transhumant pastoralists, swidden agriculturalists. 800 to 1,800 meters. Traditional religion.

TIGRIGNA ***(TIGRINYA, TIGRAY)*** [TGN] 3,224,875 mother tongue speakers, 146,933 second language speakers, 3,284,568 in the ethnic group, 2,819,755 monolinguals in Ethiopia (1998 census). Population total all countries 5,135,000. Tigray province. Also spoken in Eritrea, Israel. Afro-Asiatic, Semitic, South, Ethiopian, North. Speakers are called 'Tigrai'. National language. Grammar. Literacy rate in first language: 1% to 10%. Ethiopic script. Christian. Bible 1956.

TSAMAI ***(TS'AMAY, S'AMAI, TAMAHA, TSAMAKO, TSAMAKKO, BAGO S'AAMAKK-ULO, KUILE, KULE, CULE)*** [TSB] 8,621 mother tongue speakers, 1,200 second language speakers, 9,702 in the ethnic group, 5.298 monolinguals (1998 census). Omo Region, lowlands west of Lake Chamo. Afro-Asiatic, Cushitic, East, Dullay. The Tsamai say Gawwada is difficult to understand. Possibly related to Birale. The most aberrant Dullay variety. 56% to 73% lexical similarity with Gawwada dialects, 61% with Bussa, 31% with Komso. They use Komso for trade. SOV. Literacy rate in first language: Below 1%. Literacy rate in second language: 2.8%. Deciduous forest. Mountain slope. Peasant agriculturalists.

UDUK ***(TWAMPA, KWANIM PA, BURUN, KEBEIRKA, OTHAN, KORARA, KUMUS)*** [UDU] Population total both countries 20,000 (1995 W. James). Large refugee camp at Bonga, near Gambela town, Gambela Region. Some still in Sudan (1995). Also spoken in Sudan. Nilo-Saharan, Komuz, Koman. Most have come from Sudan. SVO. Traditional religion, Christian. NT 1963.

WEYTO ***(WAYTO, WEYT'O)*** [WOY] Ethnic population: 1,631: 1,519 (93%) speak Amharic as mother tongue, others speak other mother tongues. 1,532 speak no other language. Lake Tana region. Unclassified. The former language was possibly Eastern Sudanic or an Awngi variety (Bender 1983), or Cushitic (Bender, Bowen, Cooper and Ferguson 1976:14). The people now speak Amharic. Literacy rate in second language: 16.2%. Hunters: hippopotamus. Extinct.

WOLAYTTA ***(WELLAMO, WELAMO, WOLLAMO, WALLAMO, WALAMO, UALAMO, UOLLAMO, WOLAITTA, WOLAITA, WOLAYTA, WOLATAITA, BORODDA, UBA, OMETO)*** [WBC] 1,231,673 mother tongue speakers, 89,801 second language speakers, 1,269,216 in the ethnic group, 999,694 monolinguals (1998 census). Wolaytta Region, Lake Abaya area. Afro-Asiatic, Omotic, North, Gonga-Gimojan, Gimojan, Ometo-Gimira, Ometo, Central. Dialect: ZALA. Dorze, Melo, Oyda may be dialects of Wolaytta or of Gamo-Gofa-Dawro. 79% to 93% lexical similarity with Gamo, 84% with Gofa, 80% with Kullo and Dorze, 48% with Koorete, 43% with Male. Geographic names: Balta, Borodda, Ganta, Otschollo, Uba. SOV. Literacy rate in first language: 1% to 5%. Literacy rate in second language: 29.6%. Traditional religion, Christian. NT 1981.

XAMTANGA ***(KHAMTANGA, SIMT'ANGA, AGAWINYA, XAMTA, XAMIR)*** [XAN] 143,369 mother tongue speakers, 11,026 second language speakers, 158,231 in the ethnic group, 93,889 monolinguals (1998 census). North Amhara Region, Avergele District and Lasta and Waag zones, 100 kms. north of Weldiya. Afro-Asiatic, Cushitic, Central, Eastern. Inherent intelligibility is inadequate with Qemant. About 45% lexical similarity with Qemant. The monolinguals are older people or women. Others are bilingual in Amharic. A few Xamir do not speak Xamtanga, but most do, and have a strong desire to have literature. There is an association of Xamtanga speakers in Weldiya. Surrounded by Amharic and Tigrigna speakers. A different language from Awngi, also sometimes called 'Agaw'. The people are called 'Xamir'. Area badly disrupted by war. SOV. Literacy rate in second language: 6.5%. Agriculturalists: wheat, sorghum. 2,000 to 3,000 meters. Christian.

YEMSA ***(YEM, YEMMA, "JANJERO", "JANJERINYA", "JANJOR", "YANGARO", "ZINJERO")*** [JNJ] 81,613 mother tongue speakers, 4,356 second language speakers, 165,184 in the ethnic group, 114,701 monolinguals (1998 census). Oromo Region, recognized as separate district, northeast of Jimma, southwestern Ethiopia, Fofa, and mixed with the Oromo in their villages; Sokoru, Saja, Deedoo, Sak'a, Jimma. Afro-Asiatic, Omotic, North, Gonga-Gimojan, Gimojan, Janjero. Dialects:

FUGA OF JIMMA, TOBA. Fuga of Jimma may be a separate language. 24% lexical similarity with Mocha. Young people are bilingual in Amharic, older people in Oromo. The primary language of the ethnic group. Some negative attitudes toward Oromo. Speakers want literature in their language. 'Yemma' is the name for the ethnic group, 'Yemsa' for the language. "Janjero" is derogatory. SOV, tonal. Literacy rate in second language: 24.2%. Traditional religion, Christian.

ZAY ***(ZWAY, LAK'I, LAQI, GELILLA)*** [ZWA] 4,880 (1994 SIL). Shores of Lake Zway and eastern islands in Lake Zway. Afro-Asiatic, Semitic, South, Ethiopian, South, Transversal, Harari-East Gurage. No dialect variations. 61% lexical similarity with Harari, 70% with East Gurage (M. L. Bender 1971). Bilingualism in Oromo, Amharic. 'Zway' refers to the lake and town, 'Zay' to the people and language. 'Lak'i' ('Laqi') is the Oromo name for the people. Investigation needed: bilingual proficiency in Amharic. Agriculturalists, fishermen.

ZAYSE-ZERGULLA ***(ZAYSSE)*** [ZAY] 17,797 mother tongue speakers including 10,172 Zayse, 7,625 Zergulla; 2,815 second language speakers including 1,017 Zayse, 1,798 Zergulla; 11,232 in the ethnic group including 10,842 Zayse, 390 Zergulla; 7,530 monolinguals including 7,371 Zayse, 159 Zergulla (1998 census). Omo Region, west of Lake Chamo. Afro-Asiatic, Omotic, North, Gonga-Gimojan, Gimojan, Ometo-Gimira, Ometo, East. Dialects: ZERGULLA (ZERGULLINYA), ZAYSE. Close to the Gidicho dialect of Koorete. Vigorous. Approximately 7,000 ethnic Gamo speak Zergulla as mother tongue, which is reflected in the figures above. The culture is vigorous. SOV. Literacy rate in second language: 32.5%.

GABON

Gabonese Republic. République Gabonaise. National or official language: French. 1,167,000 (1998 UN). Literacy rate 70% to 77%. Also includes people from Lebanon 1,000, from Cameroon, Equatorial Guinea, and West Africa 12% of the population. Information mainly from A. Jacquot 1978; J. Bendor-Samuel 1989. Christian, traditional religion, Muslim. Blind population 1,300 (1982 WCE). Data accuracy estimate: A2, B. The number of languages listed for Gabon is 41. Of those, all are living languages. Diversity index 0.53.

BAKA ***(BABINGA)*** [BKC] 3,200 in Gabon (1990 CMA). Cameroon border area. Niger-Congo, Atlantic-Congo, Volta-Congo, North, Adamawa-Ubangi, Ubangi, Sere-Ngbaka-Mba, Ngbaka-Mba, Ngbaka, Western, Baka-Gundi. 'Babinga' is used for the Baka, Aka, and Gieli; separate Pygmy languages; it means 'Pygmy'. The name 'Aka' may not be used in Gabon. Dispersed in small groups. Nomadic. Tropical forest. Hunter-gatherers, fishermen. Traditional religion. See main entry under Cameroon.

BARAMA ***(GIBARAMA, GHIBARAMA, BAVARAMA, YIBARAMBU)*** [BBG] 6,000 (1990 CMA). Ogooue Maritime Province, east of Omboue. Nyanga Province, west of Moabi. Niger-Congo, Atlantic-Congo, Volta-Congo, Benue-Congo, Bantoid, Southern, Narrow Bantu, Northwest, B, Sira (B.40). The people are called 'Yibarambu'. Traditional religion.

BEKWEL ***(BEKWIL, BEKWIE, BAKWELE, BAKWIL)*** [BKW] Extreme northeast corner, Ogooue Ivindo Province, northeast of Mekambo. Niger-Congo, Atlantic-Congo, Volta-Congo, Benue-Congo, Bantoid, Southern, Narrow Bantu, Northwest, A, Makaa-Njem (A.80). Different from Bakwiri (Mokpwe) of Cameroon. Forest. Traditional religion, Christian. See main entry under Congo.

BENGA [BEN] North of Libreville. Niger-Congo, Atlantic-Congo, Volta-Congo, Benue-Congo, Bantoid, Southern, Narrow Bantu, Northwest, A, Bube-Benga (A.30). Bible 1898. See main entry under Equatorial Guinea.

BUBI ***(BHUBHI, IBUBI, IBHUBHI, POVE, EVIIA)*** [BUW] 5,000 (1990 CMA). Ogooue-Lolo Province, west of Koulamoutou, between M'Bigou and N'djoli. Niger-Congo, Atlantic-Congo, Volta-Congo, Benue-Congo, Bantoid, Southern, Narrow Bantu, Northwest, B, Tsogo (B.30). Speakers are reported to understand Getsogo. They are called 'Bapove'. Distinct from the Bubi dialect of Kele, and from Bube of Equatorial Guinea. Traditional religion.

BWISI ***(IBWISI, MBWISI)*** [BWZ] Far south, Nyanga Province, Ndende area on the border with Congo. Niger-Congo, Atlantic-Congo, Volta-Congo, Benue-Congo, Bantoid, Southern, Narrow Bantu, Northwest, B, Sira (B.40). Different from Talinga-Bwisi of DRC and Uganda. See main entry under Congo.

DUMA ***(LIDUMA, ADUMA, DOUMA, ADOUMA, BADOUMA)*** [DMA] 7,000 to 10,000 (1990 CMA). Upper Ogooue Province, Franceville area near Lastourville. Niger-Congo, Atlantic-Congo, Volta-Congo, Benue-Congo, Bantoid, Southern, Narrow Bantu, Northwest, B, Njebi (B.50). They can understand Njebi.

FANG ***(PAMUE, PAHOUIN)*** [FNG] 427,000 in Gabon (1993 Johnstone), 29% of population (1982 Barrett). Population total all countries 858,000. Northwest, Estuary and Woleu-Ntem Provinces. Also spoken in Cameroon, Congo, Equatorial Guinea, São Tomé e Príncipe. Niger-Congo, Atlantic-Congo,

Volta-Congo, Benue-Congo, Bantoid, Southern, Narrow Bantu, Northwest, A, Yaunde-Fang (A.70). Dialects: MAKE, NTUM, OGOWE. Close to Bulu. Bible 1951.

FRENCH [FRN] 37,500 in Gabon (1993 Johnstone). Indo-European, Italic, Romance, Italo-Western, Western, Gallo-Iberian, Gallo-Romance, Gallo-Rhaetian, Oïl, French. The only language of formal education. Official language. Bible 1530-1986. See main entry under France.

KANDE ***(KANDA, OKANDE)*** [KBS] 1,000 or fewer (1990 CMA). Ogooue-Ivindo Province, west of Booue. Niger-Congo, Atlantic-Congo, Volta-Congo, Benue-Congo, Bantoid, Southern, Narrow Bantu, Northwest, B, Tsogo (B.30). The people are called 'Okande'. Traditional religion.

KANINGI ***(LEKANINGI, BAKANIKE)*** [KZO] 6,000 (1990 CMA). Upper Ogooue Province, south of Franceville. Niger-Congo, Atlantic-Congo, Volta-Congo, Benue-Congo, Bantoid, Southern, Narrow Bantu, Northwest, B, Mbere (B.60). Traditional religion.

KILI ***(AKELE, DIKELE, WESTERN KELE)*** [KEB] 4,000 in Bubi (j1977 Voegelin and Voegelin). Population total both countries 15,000 to 24,000 (1990 CMA). Scattered groups in or near Middle Ogooue Province, around Mimongo. Also spoken in Congo. Niger-Congo, Atlantic-Congo, Volta-Congo, Benue-Congo, Bantoid, Southern, Narrow Bantu, Northwest, B, Kele (B.20). Dialects: BUBI, WESTERN KELE. Closely related to Ngom. Also related to Kota, Mahongwe, Mbangwe, Ndasa, Sake, Seki, Sighu, Wumbvu. Not the same as Lokele of DRC. They interact with the Tsogo and the Sangu around Mimongo. Traditional religion. Bible portions 1855-1879.

KOTA ***(IKOTA, IKUTA, KOTU)*** [KOQ] Population total both countries 28,000 to 60,000 (1990 CMA). A large area in Ogooue-Iwindo Province. Also spoken in Congo. Niger-Congo, Atlantic-Congo, Volta-Congo, Benue-Congo, Bantoid, Southern, Narrow Bantu, Northwest, B, Kele (B.20). Many dialects. Traditional religion. Bible portions 1938-1948.

LUMBU ***(ILUMBU, BALOUMBOU)*** [LUP] Population total both countries 12,000 to 20,000 (1990). Nyanga Province, between the Nyanga and Bangua rivers, on the southwest coast and the Congo border. Also spoken in Congo. Niger-Congo, Atlantic-Congo, Volta-Congo, Benue-Congo, Bantoid, Southern, Narrow Bantu, Northwest, B, Sira (B.40). Some intermarriage with Vili women. Coastal. Fishermen, hunters. Traditional religion. Bible portions 1933-1966.

MAHONGWE [MHB] Northeast corner, Mekambo area. Niger-Congo, Atlantic-Congo, Volta-Congo, Benue-Congo, Bantoid, Southern, Narrow Bantu, Northwest, B, Kele (B.20).

MBAMA ***(LEMBAAMBA, GIMBAAMA, BAMBAAMA, MBAMBA, MBAAMA, OBAMBA, BAKOTA)*** [MBM] Population total both countries 10,000 to 12,000 (1990 CMA). Upper Ogooue Province, south of Okondja. Also spoken in Congo. Niger-Congo, Atlantic-Congo, Volta-Congo, Benue-Congo, Bantoid, Southern, Narrow Bantu, Northwest, B, Mbere (B.60). Intermarriage with the Sake. Traditional religion.

MBANGWE ***(MBAHOUIN, M'BAHOUIN)*** [ZMN] Upper Ogooue Province, south and west of Franceville. Niger-Congo, Atlantic-Congo, Volta-Congo, Benue-Congo, Bantoid, Southern, Narrow Bantu, Northwest, B, Kele (B.20). Traditional religion. See main entry under Congo.

MBERE ***(MBÉDÉ, LIMBEDE, MBÉTÉ, AMBEDE)*** [MDT] All Mbere languages in Gabon: 110,000 (1993 Johnstone) or 15% of the population (1982 Barrett). Upper Ogooue Province, Okondja area. Niger-Congo, Atlantic-Congo, Volta-Congo, Benue-Congo, Bantoid, Southern, Narrow Bantu, Northwest, B, Mbere (B.60). Dialect: NGWII. Related to Kaningi, Mbama, Ndumu, Yangho. The people are called 'Ambede'. Different from Mbre (Mbere) in CAR. Traditional religion. See main entry under Congo.

MYENE ***(OMYENE, PANGWE)*** [MYE] 35,000 to 69,000 or 5% of the population (1993), including 1,000 to 2,000 Dyumba, 1,000 to 5,000 Enenga, 2,000 to 11,000 Galwa, 1,000 to 4,000 Mpongwe, 10,000 Orungu, 20,000 Nkomi. Mainly in Ogooue-Maritime and Middle Ogooue provinces, from Lambarene area to coast. Mpongwe dialect is spoken on both sides of the Gabon Estuary, south of Libreville, Port Gentil area. Ajumba is north of Lambarene, Enenga northeast of Lambarene, Galwa in the Lambarene area and westward, Nkomi is on the coast, southeast of Port Gentil. Niger-Congo, Atlantic-Congo, Volta-Congo, Benue-Congo, Bantoid, Southern, Narrow Bantu, Northwest, B, Myene (B.10). Dialects: AJUMBA (DYUMBA, ADYUMBA, ADJUMBA), ENENGA, GALWA (GALOA, GALUA, GALLOA, OMYENE), MPONGWE (MPUNGWE, NPONGWE, PONGOUÉ, MPONGOUÉ, NPONGUÉ), NKOMI (N'KOMI), ORUNGU (RONGO, RUNGU). A dialect cluster. Reported to have been partly submerged by the Fang. Nkomi: fishermen, work in oil fields. Bible 1927.

NDASA ***(ANDASA, NDASH, NDASSA)*** [NDA] Upper Ogooue Province, south of Franceville. Niger-Congo, Atlantic-Congo, Volta-Congo, Benue-Congo, Bantoid, Southern, Narrow Bantu, Northwest, B, Kele (B.20). The people are called 'Bandasa'. Traditional religion. See main entry under Congo.

NDUMU ***(MINDUUMO, MINDOUMOU, LENDUMU, NDUMBU, NDUUMO, NDUMBO, ONDOUMBO, ONDUMBO, MINDUMBU, DOUMBOU, DUMBU, BANDOUMOU)*** [NMD] Population total both countries 4,000 to 7,000 (1990). Upper Ogooue Province, from Lastoursville to the north of Franceville. Also spoken in Congo. Niger-Congo, Atlantic-Congo, Volta-Congo, Benue-Congo, Bantoid, Southern,

Narrow Bantu, Northwest, B, Mbere (B.60). Dialects: EPIGI, KANANDJOHO, KUYA, NYANI. The people are called 'Bandoumu'. Riverine. Traditional religion.

NGOM ***(UNGOM, ANGOM, BANGOM, BANGOMO, ONGOM, NGOMO)*** [NRA] Extreme northeast, around Mekambo, and in Ogooue-Lolo Province, Koulamoutou area. Niger-Congo, Atlantic-Congo, Volta-Congo, Benue-Congo, Bantoid, Southern, Narrow Bantu, Northwest, B, Kele (B.20). Closely related to Kele. Bible portions 1910. See main entry under Congo.

NJEBI ***(NZEBI, INJEBI, YINZEBI, YINJEBI, NJABI, BANDZABI, NDJABI, NDJEVI)*** [NZB] Population total both countries 40,000 to 150,000 (1990 CMA). Ogooue-Lolo and Ngounie provinces, west of Franceville and extending to Lebamba area. Also spoken in Congo. Niger-Congo, Atlantic-Congo, Volta-Congo, Benue-Congo, Bantoid, Southern, Narrow Bantu, Northwest, B, Njebi (B.50). NT 1968-1979.

PINJI ***(GAPINJI, APINJI, APINDJI, APINDJE)*** [PIC] 5,000 (1990 CMA). Ngounie Province, east of Mouila, between Eleke and Fougamou. Niger-Congo, Atlantic-Congo, Volta-Congo, Benue-Congo, Bantoid, Southern, Narrow Bantu, Northwest, B, Tsogo (B.30). Bilingualism in Getsogo. Different from Pende of DRC. Investigation needed: intelligibility, bilingual proficiency in Tsogo. Forest. Traditional religion.

PUNU ***(IPUNU, YIPUNU, POUNO, PUNO, YIPOUNOU)*** [PUU] 10% of the population (1976 WA). 111,150 or 19% of the population, all Sira-Punu languages in Gabon (1982 Barrett). Population total both countries 50,000 (1991 UBS). Nyanga and Ngounie provinces, Tchibanga and Ndende areas. Also spoken in Congo. Niger-Congo, Atlantic-Congo, Volta-Congo, Benue-Congo, Bantoid, Southern, Narrow Bantu, Northwest, B, Sira (B.40). NT 1977.

SAKE ***(ASAKE, SHAKE)*** [SAG] Central, Ogooue-Iwindo Province, Booue area. Niger-Congo, Atlantic-Congo, Volta-Congo, Benue-Congo, Bantoid, Southern, Narrow Bantu, Northwest, B, Kele (B.20).

SANGU ***(ISANGU, YISANGU, CHANGO, SHANGO, YISANGOU)*** [SNQ] 10,000 to 30,000 (1990 CMA). Ngounie Province, Mimongo and Iboundji area. Niger-Congo, Atlantic-Congo, Volta-Congo, Benue-Congo, Bantoid, Southern, Narrow Bantu, Northwest, B, Sira (B.40). The people are called 'Masangu' or 'Massangou'. Not related to Sangu of Tanzania or Sango of CAR, Chad, and DRC. Traditional religion. Bible portions 1943-1959.

SEKI ***(SEKYANI, SEKIANI, SEKIYANI, SEKIANA, SHEKIYANA, SHEKE, SEKE, SESEKI)*** [SYI] 1,000 to 4,000 in Gabon (1990 CMA). Northwest coast around Cocobeach. Niger-Congo, Atlantic-Congo, Volta-Congo, Benue-Congo, Bantoid, Southern, Narrow Bantu, Northwest, B, Kele (B.20). Different from Bulu of Cameroon. See main entry under Equatorial Guinea.

SIGHU ***(LESIGHU, MISSISSIOU)*** [SXE] 1,000 (1990 CMA). Ogooue-Lolo Province, Koulamoutou-Lastourville area. Niger-Congo, Atlantic-Congo, Volta-Congo, Benue-Congo, Bantoid, Southern, Narrow Bantu, Northwest, B, Kele (B.20).

SIMBA ***(NSINDAK)*** [SBW] 3,000 (1990 CMA). Ogooue-Lolo Province, between Sindare and Mimongo. Niger-Congo, Atlantic-Congo, Volta-Congo, Benue-Congo, Bantoid, Southern, Narrow Bantu, Northwest, B, Tsogo (B.30). Traditional religion.

SIRA ***(GISIRA, ESHIRA, ISIRA, ICHIRA, ISHIRA, YICHIRA, SHIRA, SHIRE)*** [SWJ] 17,000 to 50,000 (1990 CMA). 250,000 in all Sira languages in Gabon (1993 Johnstone). Ngounie Province, west of Mouila, southwest of Fougamou and Mandji. Niger-Congo, Atlantic-Congo, Volta-Congo, Benue-Congo, Bantoid, Southern, Narrow Bantu, Northwest, B, Sira (B.40). They are reported to understand and to be able to use Punu quite well. The people are called 'Eshira'. Grammar. Traditional religion. Bible portions 1954.

TEKE, NORTHERN ***(TEGHE, KATEGE, ITEGHE, TEGE, TEKE, KETEGO)*** [TEG] 10,000 to 20,000 in Gabon (1990 CMA). Upper Ogooue Province, east of Franceville. Niger-Congo, Atlantic-Congo, Volta-Congo, Benue-Congo, Bantoid, Southern, Narrow Bantu, Northwest, B, Teke (B.70). Dialects: NJININGI (KANJININGI, NDJININI, NJIKINI, NZIKINI, DJIKINI), TEGEKALI (KATEGE, TEGE, TÉGUÉ). Traditional religion, Christian. See main entry under Congo.

TEKE, WESTERN ***(WEST TEKE, SOUTHWEST TEKE)*** [TEZ] 32,000 in Gabon (1990 CMA). Upper Ogooue Province, south of Franceville. Niger-Congo, Atlantic-Congo, Volta-Congo, Benue-Congo, Bantoid, Southern, Narrow Bantu, Northwest, B, Teke (B.70). Dialects: TSAAYI (TSAYI, NTSAAYI, TSAYE, GETSAAYI), YAKA (IYAKA, IYAA, YAA). Bible portions 1933. See main entry under Congo.

TSAANGI ***(ITSAANGI, TSANGI, ITSANGI, ICAANGUI, TCENGUI, TCHANGUI, BATSANGUI)*** [TSA] Population total both countries 10,000 (1971 Welmers). Upper Ogooue Province, west and southwest of Franceville. Also spoken in Congo. Niger-Congo, Atlantic-Congo, Volta-Congo, Benue-Congo, Bantoid, Southern, Narrow Bantu, Northwest, B, Njebi (B.50). The people are called 'Batsangui'. Traditional religion.

TSOGO ***(GETSOGO, GHETSOGO, MITSOGO)*** [TSV] 12,000 (1982 UBS) to 31,000 (1990 CMA). Ngounie Province, north and east of Mouila. Niger-Congo, Atlantic-Congo, Volta-Congo, Benue-

Congo, Bantoid, Southern, Narrow Bantu, Northwest, B, Tsogo (B.30). The people are called 'MiTsogo'. Grammar. NT 1983.

VILI ***(TSIVILI, CIVILI, FIOTE, FIOT)*** [VIF] Extreme south, on the coast near Mayumba. Niger-Congo, Atlantic-Congo, Volta-Congo, Benue-Congo, Bantoid, Southern, Narrow Bantu, Central, H, Kongo (H.10). Dialect: YOOMBE (CIYOOMBE). A dialect cluster. The people are called 'Bavili'. Some people are literate in Ipunu or Lumbu. Traditional religion, Christian. See main entry under Congo.

VUMBU ***(YIVOUMBOU)*** [VUM] Yetsou area, west of Mouila. Niger-Congo, Atlantic-Congo, Volta-Congo, Benue-Congo, Bantoid, Southern, Narrow Bantu, Northwest, B, Sira (B.40). Related to Yipunu. Distinct from Wumbvu in the Kele subgroup (B.20).

WANDJI ***(BAWANDJI)*** [WDD] 6,000 to 14,000 (1990 CMA). Ogooue-Lolo and Haut Ogooue. Niger-Congo, Atlantic-Congo, Volta-Congo, Benue-Congo, Bantoid, Southern, Narrow Bantu, Northwest, B, Njebi (B.50). May be a dialect of Njebi. Reported that speakers can understand Njebi. The people are called 'Bawandji'. Traditional religion.

WUMBVU ***(WUMVU)*** [WUM] Ngounie Province, east of Lebamba. Niger-Congo, Atlantic-Congo, Volta-Congo, Benue-Congo, Bantoid, Southern, Narrow Bantu, Northwest, B, Kele (B.20). Traditional religion. See main entry under Congo.

YANGHO ***(YONGHO, MIYANGHO, BAYONGHO)*** [YNH] 5,000 (1990 CMA). Haut Ogooue around Mamidi and Bakoumba. Niger-Congo, Atlantic-Congo, Volta-Congo, Benue-Congo, Bantoid, Southern, Narrow Bantu, Northwest, B, Mbere (B.60). Traditional religion.

YASA ***(YASSA, LYASSA, MAASA, BONGWE)*** [YKO] Niger-Congo, Atlantic-Congo, Volta-Congo, Benue-Congo, Bantoid, Southern, Narrow Bantu, Northwest, A, Bube-Benga (A.30), Yasa. Dialects: IYASA, BWEKO, VENDO, BODELE, MARRY, ONE, ASONGA, BOMUI, MOGANA, MOOMA, MAPANGA. A cluster of dialects. Some or all speakers are reported to be pygmies. Grammar. See main entry under Cameroon.

GAMBIA

The Gambia. Republic of The Gambia. National or official language: English. 1,229,000 (1998 UN). Literacy rate 35%. Also includes Bainouk-Gunyaamolo, Balanta-Kentohe, Bambara 5,100, Bayot, Upper Guinea Crioulo, Fuuta Jalon, Jola-Kasa, Karon 1,200, Krio 8,000, Mankanya 1,200, Mansoanka, Wolof, Xasonga. Information mainly from J. Bendor-Samuel 1989; Central Statistics Department, Banjul 1996. Muslim, traditional religion, Christian. Blind population 2,700 (1982 WCE). Data accuracy estimate: B. The number of languages listed for Gambia is 10. Of those, all are living languages. Diversity index 0.73.

ENGLISH [ENG] Indo-European, Germanic, West, English. Official language. Bible 1535-1989. See main entry under United Kingdom.

JOLA-FOGNY ***(DIOLA-FOGNY, YOLA, JOLA)*** [DYO] 53,000 in Gambia (1998 SIL). Southwestern districts. Niger-Congo, Atlantic-Congo, Atlantic, Northern, Bak, Jola, Jola Proper, Jola Central, Jola-Fogny. Fogny is the largest and most widely understood Jola variety. Muslim, traditional religion, Christian. See main entry under Senegal.

KALANKE [CKN] Niger-Congo, Mande, Western, Central-Southwestern, Central, Manding-Jogo, Manding-Vai, Manding-Mokole, Manding. 79% lexical similarity with Mandinka. Muslim.

MANDINKA ***(MANDINQUE, MANDINGO, MANDING, MANDÉ, SOCÉ)*** [MNK] 402,500 in Gambia (1998). Most of the western half of Gambia. Niger-Congo, Mande, Western, Central-Southwestern, Central, Manding-Jogo, Manding-Vai, Manding-Mokole, Manding, Manding-West. Significantly different from Maninka of Guinea and Malinke of Senegal (Church). Some related varieties may be distinct languages. 79% lexical similarity with Kalanke, 75% with Jahanka, 70% with Xasonga, 59% with Malinke, 53% with Mori, 48% with Bambara. The main language of middle Gambia. Literacy rate in second language: About 50% in Mandinka in Arabic script. Muslim. NT 1989. See main entry under Senegal.

MANDJAK ***(MANDJAQUE, MANJACA, MANJACO, MANJIAK, MANJACU, MANJACK, MANDYAK, NDYAK, KANYOP)*** [MFV] 17,100 in Gambia (1998). Western, south of the Gambia River. Niger-Congo, Atlantic-Congo, Atlantic, Northern, Bak, Manjaku-Papel. Dialects: BOK (BABOK), SARAR, TEIXEIRA PINTO, TSAAMO, LIKES-UTSIA (BARAA, KALKUS), CUR (CHURO), LUND, YU (PECIXE). Some dialects listed may be separate languages. Closely related to Mankanya and Papel. Investigation needed: intelligibility. Traditional religion, Christian. Bible portions 1968. See main entry under Guinea-Bissau.

MANINKA, WESTERN ***(NORTHWESTERN MANINKA, MALINKE, MALINKA)*** [MLQ] Eastern Gambia. Niger-Congo, Mande, Western, Central-Southwestern, Central, Manding-Jogo, Manding-Vai, Manding-Mokole, Manding, Manding-West. Dialect: JAHANKA. Jahanka in Gambia may be a dialect of Western

Maninka, or a separate language. 75% lexical similarity with Mandinka. Muslim. See main entry under Mali.

PULAAR ***(FULFULDE-PULAAR, PULAAR FULFULDE, PEUL, PEULH, FULBE JEERI, FULANI)*** [FUC] 233,300 in Gambia (1998). Niger-Congo, Atlantic-Congo, Atlantic, Northern, Senegambian, Fula-Wolof, Fulani, Western. Dialects: FULACUNDA (FULAKUNDA, FULKUNDA), TOUCOULEUR (TUKOLOR, TUKULOR, HALPULAAR, HAALPULAAR). Bilingualism in Mandinka. Fulbe Jeeri, Toucouleur, and Fulacunda are ethnic groups that speaks Pulaar. An official literacy committee is concerned with Pulaar. Muslim, Christian. NT 1997. See main entry under Senegal.

SERER-SINE ***(SERER, SERRER, SEEREER, SERER-SIN, SINE-SALOUM)*** [SES] 25,200 in Gambia (1998). Northwestern Gambia. Niger-Congo, Atlantic-Congo, Atlantic, Northern, Senegambian, Serer. Dialects: SEGUM, FADYUT-PALMERIN, SINE, DYEGUEME (GYEGEM). Traditional religion, Muslim, Christian. NT 1987. See main entry under Senegal.

SONINKE ***(MARKA, MARAKA, SARAHOLE, SARAWULE, SARAHULI, SILABE, TOUBAKAI, WAKORE, GADYAGA, ASWANIK)*** [SNN] 58,800 in Gambia (1998). Southeastern corner. Niger-Congo, Mande, Western, Northwestern, Samogo, Soninke-Bobo, Soninke-Boso, Soninke. Dialect: AZER (ADJER, ASER). Muslim, Christian. See main entry under Mali.

WOLOF, GAMBIAN [WOF] 146,650 (1998). Western Division, south bank of the Gambia River and central. Wolof on the north bank speak Wolof of Senegal. Niger-Congo, Atlantic-Congo, Atlantic, Northern, Senegambian, Fula-Wolof, Wolof. Wolof of Senegal not intelligible with that of Gambia. Tropical forest. Riverine. Fishermen, peasant agriculturalists. 46 meters. Muslim. Bible portions 1882-1967.

GHANA

Republic of Ghana. Formerly Gold Coast and British Togoland. National or official languages: Ga, English. Official recognition to be taught at the School of Ghanaian Languages at Ajumako, are on TV, radio, and taught in schools: Asante Twi, Akuapim Twi, Fante, Ewe, Nzema, Dagbani, Dagaari, Kasem. For the government's nonformal education efforts and radio: Frafra, Buli, Kusaal, Sisaala, Gonja. 19,162,000 (1998 UN). Literacy rate 36% (1992 UNESCO). Also includes Dagaari Dioula, Foodo 1,000, Klao, Lobi, Mòoré. Information mainly from E. Hall 1983; J. Bendor-Samuel 1989; GILLBT 1970-99. Christian, traditional religion, Muslim. Blind population 60,418. Deaf institutions: 20. Data accuracy estimate: A2. The number of languages listed for Ghana is 79. Of those, all are living languages. Diversity index 0.79.

ABRON ***(BRONG, BRON, DOMA)*** [ABR] 606,600 in Ghana (1991 L. Vanderaa CRC). Population total both countries 738,300. Southwestern Ghana, northwest of Asante Twi. Also spoken in Côte d'Ivoire. Niger-Congo, Atlantic-Congo, Volta-Congo, Kwa, Nyo, Potou-Tano, Tano, Central, Akan. Investigation needed: intelligibility, bilingual proficiency in Asante Twi. Literacy rate in first language: Below 1%. Literacy rate in second language: 25% to 50%. Largely Muslim.

ADAMOROBE SIGN LANGUAGE [ADS] 300 deaf in the village, 3,000 including hearing people (1998 GILLBT). Adamorobe, a village in the Eastern Region. The district capital is Aburi. Deaf sign language. All ages, evenly distributed. 15% deafness in the population; one of the highest percentages in the world, caused by genetic recessive autosome. The village has been settled for 200 years. It is an indigenous deaf sign language, also used by many hearing people. Most users have no contact with Ghanaian Sign Language. They are considered to be full citizens. Agriculturalists, firewood traders.

ADANGBE ***(DANGBE, ADANTONWI, AGOTIME, ADAN)*** [ADQ] Border area with Togo directly east of Ho. Agotime are mainly in Ghana. Volta region. Ghana towns are Kpoeta and Apegame, and others. Also spoken in Togo. Niger-Congo, Atlantic-Congo, Volta-Congo, Kwa, Left Bank, Kposo-Ahlo-Bowili. Close to Igo. Different from Adangme. The Adan and Agotime are separate ethnic groups who speak Adangbe.

ADELE ***(GIDIRE, BIDIRE)*** [ADE] 9,000 in Ghana (1995). East central border with Togo. Upper Adele is in Togo, Lower Adele in Ghana. Niger-Congo, Atlantic-Congo, Volta-Congo, Kwa, Nyo, Potou-Tano, Basila-Adele. Dialects: UPPER ADELE, LOWER ADELE. 85% to 90% inherent intelligibility between dialects, minor differences in tone and lexicon. Bilingualism in Twi. Speakers' name for their language is 'Gidire', for themselves, 'Bidire'. 'Adele' is the name used by others. Different from Adere of Cameroon. Grammar. Literacy rate in first language: Below 1%. Literacy rate in second language: 5% to 15%. Forest, savannah. River valley. Subsistence agriculturalists: crop diversity. Traditional religion, Christian. NT 1996. See main entry under Togo.

AHANTA [AHA] 100,000 (1993 SIL). Southwest coast. Niger-Congo, Atlantic-Congo, Volta-Congo, Kwa, Nyo, Potou-Tano, Tano, Central, Bia, Southern. Partial bilingualism in Fante and Nzema. Strong language community. Ahanta not used in schools or churches. Literacy rate in first language:

Below 1%. Literacy rate in second language: 5% to 15%. Radio programs. Agriculturalists. Traditional religion, Christian.

AKAN [TWS] 7,000,000 (1995 WA), 44% of the population (1990 WA). 1,170,000 Asante Twi, 4,300,000 Fante, 230,000 Akuapem Twi (1993 UBS). The Asante are south central, Ashanti Province. The Akuapem are southeast, in areas north of Accra. The Fante are south central, between Winneba, Takoradi, and Obuasi. Niger-Congo, Atlantic-Congo, Volta-Congo, Kwa, Nyo, Potou-Tano, Tano, Central, Akan. Dialects: FANTE (FANTI, MFANTSE), AKUAPEM (AKWAPEM TWI, TWI, AKUAPIM, AKWAPI), ASANTE (ASHANTE TWI, TWI, ASANTI, ACHANTI), AGONA, DANKYIRA, ASEN, AKYEM BOSOME, KWAWU, AHAFO. Dialects are largely inherently intelligible. The speech of the Asante and Akuapem is called 'Twi'. Dictionary. Grammar. SVO. Literacy rate in first language: 30% to 60%. Literacy rate in second language: 5% to 10%. Roman. Bible 1871-1964.

AKPOSO ***(KPOSO, IKPOSO, AKPOSSO)*** [KPO] 5,400 in Ghana (1991). Southern. Niger-Congo, Atlantic-Congo, Volta-Congo, Kwa, Left Bank, Kposo-Ahlo-Bowili. Dialects: AMOU OBLOU, IKPONU, IWI (UWI), LITIME (BADOU), LOGBO, UMA. Somewhat bilingual in Ewe. Speakers have a keen interest in their language. Literacy rate in first language: Below 1%. Literacy rate in second language: 5% to 15%. Community sponsored vernacular literacy materials are available. Traditional religion. See main entry under Togo.

ANIMERE ***(ANYIMERE, KUNDA)*** [ANF] 2,000 (1988 GILLBT). East central, Kecheibi and Kunda villages, remote location. None in Togo. Niger-Congo, Atlantic-Congo, Volta-Congo, Kwa, Left Bank, Kebu-Animere. Intelligibility with related varieties is not known. Twi may be the second language. Literacy rate in second language: 5% to 15%. Traditional religion.

ANUFO ***(CHOKOSI, CHAKOSI, KYOKOSI, TCHOKOSSI, TIOKOSSI)*** [CKO] 53,000 in Ghana (1995). Population total all countries 105,000 (1991 L. Vanderaa CRC). Northeast around Wawjayga. Also spoken in Benin, Togo. Niger-Congo, Atlantic-Congo, Volta-Congo, Kwa, Nyo, Potou-Tano, Tano, Central, Bia, Northern. Large migration across the border. 'Anufo' is the name the people use for themselves; 'Chokosi' is used by others. Dictionary. Grammar. Literacy rate in first language: Below 1%. Literacy rate in second language: Below 5%. Traditional religion, Muslim, Christian. Bible portions 1993.

ANYIN ***(ANYI, AGNI)*** [ANY] 200,000 in Ghana (1995 SIL). Between Abron to the north, Nzema to the south, Côte d'Ivoire to the west, Twi to the east. The Aowin dialect is in Ghana. Niger-Congo, Atlantic-Congo, Volta-Congo, Kwa, Nyo, Potou-Tano, Tano, Central, Bia, Northern. Dialect: AOWIN (BRISSA, BROSA). Closely related to Sehwi. Bilingualism in Twi. Literacy rate in second language: Below 5%. Possible orthography adaptation is needed for materials from Côte d'Ivoire for Aowin. Traditional religion. NT 1997. See main entry under Côte d'Ivoire.

AVATIME ***(AFATIME, SIDEME, SIA)*** [AVA] 11,600 (1991 L. Vanderaa CRC). Southeast, center at Amedzofe (Amajofe). Niger-Congo, Atlantic-Congo, Volta-Congo, Kwa, Left Bank, Avatime-Nyangbo. Closely related languages or dialects: Nyangbo, Tafi. Diminishing contact with Éwé. Understood somewhat as a second language by speakers of nearby languages. Grammar. Literacy rate in first language: Below 1%. Literacy rate in second language: 5% to 15%. Traditional religion.

AWUTU [AFU] 100,000 (1988 GILLBT). Coast, west of Accra. Niger-Congo, Atlantic-Congo, Volta-Congo, Kwa, Nyo, Potou-Tano, Tano, Guang, South Guang. Dialects: AWUTU, EFUTU, SENYA. Bilingualism in Fante. A high proportion of the people have school education. Literacy rate in first language: Below 1%. Literacy rate in second language: 5% to 15%. Christian, Muslim, traditional religion, secular.

BIMOBA ***(MOAR, MOOR)*** [BIM] 73,700 (1991 L. Vanderaa CRC). Northeast, Gambaga District, south of Kusaasi, north of Konkomba. Niger-Congo, Atlantic-Congo, Volta-Congo, North, Gur, Central, Northern, Oti-Volta, Gurma, Moba. Related to Moba of Togo, but not inherently intelligible with it. Grammar. Literacy rate in first language: 10% to 30%. Literacy rate in second language: 15% to 25%. Traditional religion, Muslim, Christian. NT 1986.

BIRIFOR, SOUTHERN ***(BIRIFO, GHANA BIRIFOR)*** [BIV] 100,000 in Ghana (1995 SIL). Population total both countries 104,000. Northwest corner. Also spoken in Côte d'Ivoire. Niger-Congo, Atlantic-Congo, Volta-Congo, North, Gur, Central, Northern, Oti-Volta, Western, Northwest, Dagaari-Birifor, Birifor. A separate language from Wali, Dagaari, and Malba-Birifor of Burkina Faso, and not inherently intelligible with them. Dictionary. Grammar. Literacy rate in first language: 1%. Literacy rate in second language: 5% or more. Traditional religion. Bible portions 1993.

BISSA ***(BISA)*** [BIB] 119,100 in Ghana (1991 Vanderaa). Northeast. Niger-Congo, Mande, Eastern, Eastern, Bissa. Dialects: LEBIR (WESTERN BISA), BARAKA (EASTERN BISA). It may include more than one distinct language. Related to Samo. Some bilingualism in Mòoré. Not the same as Busa of Benin and Nigeria. The name of the people is 'Busansi'. Dictionary. Grammar. Literacy rate in second language: 7%. Traditional religion, Muslim, Christian. Bible portions 1996. See main entry under Burkina Faso.

BULI ***(BUILSA, BULISA, KANJAGA, GURESHA)*** [BWU] 131,000 (1998 GILLBT). Sandema District. None in Burkina Faso. Niger-Congo, Atlantic-Congo, Volta-Congo, North, Gur, Central, Northern, Oti-Volta, Buli-Koma. Konni is the closest language. 77% lexical similarity with Mampruli. Bilingualism in Neighboring languages. The people call themselves 'Bulisa' or 'Builsa', and their language 'Buli'. 'Kanjaga' and 'Guresha' are names given by others. Dictionary. Grammar. Literacy rate in first language: Around 10%. Literacy rate in second language: 5% to 15%. Traditional religion, Christian, Muslim. NT 1995.

CHAKALI [CLI] 5,000 (1995 GILLBT). East of Wa. Ducie is largest village. Niger-Congo, Atlantic-Congo, Volta-Congo, North, Gur, Central, Southern, Grusi, Western. Lexical similarity is 62% with Tampulma, 68% with Vagla. People are reported to be bilingual in Wali. Chakali is used in the home. In Tuasa only older people. The Chakali seem to accept the Wali language, but do not approve of it being used in their homes. Muslim, traditional religion, Christian.

CHALA ***(TSHALA, CALA)*** [CHA] 2,000 (1988 GILLBT). Villages of Nkwanta, Odomi, Agoin the Volta Region. Jadigbe village near Seipe, south of Ekumdipe in the Northern Region is 35% Chala. None in Togo. Niger-Congo, Atlantic-Congo, Volta-Congo, North, Gur, Central, Southern, Grusi, Eastern. Some are bilingual in Gikyode; proficiency is higher than in Twi. Twi is spoken to outsiders. Different from Chala (Ron) of Nigeria. They are under the Gikyode paramount chief. Investigation needed: bilingual proficiency in Gichode, Twi. Traditional religion.

CHEREPON ***(OKERE, KYEREPONG, CHIRIPONG, CHIRIPON)*** [CPN] 66,000 (1998 GILLBT). A pocket between the Ga and Twi areas, north of Larteh. Niger-Congo, Atlantic-Congo, Volta-Congo, Kwa, Nyo, Potou-Tano, Tano, Guang, South Guang. Speakers are reported to use Twi (Akan) as second language. Investigation needed: intelligibility with dialects, bilingual proficiency in Twi. Literacy rate in first language: 1% to 5%. Literacy rate in second language: 5% to 15%. Traditional religion.

CHUMBURUNG ***(NCHUMBURUNG, NCHIMBURU, NCHUMMURU, KYONGBORONG)*** [NCU] 40,000 (1992 GILLBT), including 2,000 Yeji. A triangular area with Volta Lake on the south, Daka River on the northwest, Yeji south of the lake. Niger-Congo, Atlantic-Congo, Volta-Congo, Kwa, Nyo, Potou-Tano, Tano, Guang, North Guang. Dialects: NORTHERN CHUMBURUNG (BANDA), SOUTHERN CHUMBURUNG (LONTO, GURUBI, CHINDERI, BEJAMSE, BORAE), YEJI (YEDJI). Reported to be intelligible with Krache. 77% lexical similarity with Yeji, 79% with Kplang, 78% with Krache, 69% with Dwang, 67% with Nawuri and Gichode, 60% with Gonja. Most people speak Twi as second language. 'Chumburung' is the language, 'Nchumburung' the people. Dictionary. Grammar. Literacy rate in first language: Below 1%. Literacy rate in second language: Below 5%. Traditional religion, Christian, Muslim. NT 1988, out of print.

DAGAARE, SOUTHERN ***(SOUTHERN DAGARI, DAGARI, DAGARA, DEGATI, DAGATI, DOGAARI, DAGAARE)*** [DGA] 700,000 to 1,200,000 (1998). 1,000,000 to 1,500,000 including Northern Dagara in Burkina Faso (1998 A. B. Bodomo). Northwest corner of Ghana, western part of Upper West Region. Niger-Congo, Atlantic-Congo, Volta-Congo, North, Gur, Central, Northern, Oti-Volta, Western, Northwest, Dagaari-Birifor, Dagaari. Dagaare and Birifor are partially intelligible. It is distinct from Northern Dagara in Burkina Faso. All ages. The people are called 'Dagaaba'. Dagaare is more prominent politically and socially than Birifor. Dictionary. Grammar. Literacy rate in first language: 5% to 10%. Literacy rate in second language: 5% to 15%. Traditional religion, Christian, Muslim. Bible portions 1970.

DAGBANI ***(DAGBANE, DAGOMBA, DAGBAMBA)*** [DAG] 540,000 in Ghana (1995 SIL). Population total both countries 540,000 or more. Northeast around Tamale and as far as Yendi. Also spoken in Togo. Niger-Congo, Atlantic-Congo, Volta-Congo, North, Gur, Central, Northern, Oti-Volta, Western, Southeast. Dialect: NANUNI (NANUMBA). 95% lexical similarity with Mampruli, 90% with Talni, 89% with Kusaal. The people are called 'Dagbamba' or 'Dagomba', the language 'Dagbanli' ('Dagbani' by outsiders). Dictionary. Grammar. SVO. Literacy rate in first language: 3%. Literacy rate in second language: 2%. Agriculturalists. Muslim, traditional religion, Christian. NT 1974, in press (1995).

DANGME ***(ADANGME)*** [DGM] 825,900 in Ghana (1991 L. Vanderaa CRC). Population total both countries 825,900 or more. Southeast, coast east of Accra and inland. Also spoken in Togo. Niger-Congo, Atlantic-Congo, Volta-Congo, Kwa, Nyo, Ga-Dangme. Dialects: ADA, NINGO, OSU, SHAI, GBUGBLA, KROBO. Literacy rate in first language: 30% to 60%. Literacy rate in second language: 75% to 100%. Traditional religion. Bible In press (1997).

DEG ***(DEGHA, MO, MMFO, ACULO, JANELA, BURU)*** [MZW] 20,000 in Ghana (1993 UBS). Population total both countries 21,000. West central, west of Volta Lake. Also spoken in Côte d'Ivoire. Niger-Congo, Atlantic-Congo, Volta-Congo, North, Gur, Central, Southern, Grusi, Western. Dialects: LONGORO, MANGUM, BOE. 78% lexical similarity with Vagla. Twi (Akan) is widely spoken as second language. English is also used. 'Deg' is their name for themselves; 'Mo' is used by outsiders. Literacy rate in first language: 5% to 10%. Literacy rate in second language: 5% to 15%. Traditional religion, Christian. NT 1990.

DELO ***(NTRUBO, NTRIBU, NTRIBOU)*** [NTR] 6,000 in Ghana (1998 GILLBT). Population total both countries 11,400. East central border with Togo. The paramount chief is at Brewaniase, 20 miles south of Nkwanta. Also spoken in Togo. Niger-Congo, Atlantic-Congo, Volta-Congo, North, Gur, Central, Southern, Grusi, Eastern. It has been reclassified from Kwa to Gur family. Bilingualism in Twi, English. 'Delo' is the language name; 'Ntrubo' the people. Literacy rate in first language: Below 1%. Literacy rate in second language: 5% to 15%. Traditional religion, Christian. Bible portions.

DOMPO ***(DUMPO, NDMPO)*** [DOY] 60 to 70 speakers, 10 households (1999 Roger Blench). Brong-Ahafo Region, a quarter of Banda called Dompofie. Niger-Congo, Atlantic-Congo, Volta-Congo, Kwa, Nyo, Potou-Tano, Tano, Guang, North Guang. Bilingualism in Nafaanra. 'Dompo' is the name of people and language.

DWANG ***(DWAN, NCHUMUNU)*** [NNU] 10,000 (1988 GILLBT). South of Volta Lake and the Chumburung, east of Atebubu. Niger-Congo, Atlantic-Congo, Volta-Congo, Kwa, Nyo, Potou-Tano, Tano, Guang, North Guang. Dialects: KWAME-DANSO, BASSA, EWOASE. A dialect continuum. Closest to Kplang. 75% comprehension of Chumburung. Krache is understood well because of contact. Most people are bilingual in Twi (Akan). The people were historically known as 'Bassa'.

ENGLISH [ENG] Second language speakers: 1,000,000 (1977 Voegelin and Voegelin). Indo-European, Germanic, West, English. Official language. Bible 1535-1989. See main entry under United Kingdom.

ÉWÉ ***(EIBE, EBWE, EVE, EFE, EUE, VHE, GBE, KREPI, KREPE, POPO)*** [EWE] 1,615,700 in Ghana (1991), 13% of the population (1990 WA). Population total both countries 2,477,600 (1991 L. Vanderaa CRC). Including second language users: 3,000,000 (1999 WA). Southeast corner. Also spoken in Togo. Niger-Congo, Atlantic-Congo, Volta-Congo, Kwa, Left Bank, Gbe. Dialects: ANGLO, AWUNA, HUDU, KOTAFOA. Language of wider communication. Grammar. Literacy rate in first language: 30% to 60%. Literacy rate in second language: 75% to 100%. Roman. Christian, traditional religion. Bible 1913-1931.

FRAFRA ***(FAREFARE, GURENNE, GURUNE, NANKANI)*** [GUR] 526,300 in Ghana (1991 L. Vanderaa CRC) including 400,000 in the Upper East Region, perhaps 100,000 in various towns and cities in other regions (1988 SIL). Population total both countries 551,400 (1991 L. Vanderaa CRC). Northeast Ghana, Upper East Region around Bolgatanga, Frafra District, and as far west as Navrongo. Also spoken in Burkina Faso. Niger-Congo, Atlantic-Congo, Volta-Congo, North, Gur, Central, Northern, Oti-Volta, Western, Northwest. Dialects: GUDENI (GUDENNE, GURENNE, GURUNE), NANKANI (NAANI, NANKANSE), BOONI, TALNI (TALENSI, TALENE), NABT (NABIT, NABDE, NABTE, NABDAM, NABDUG, NABRUG, NABNAM, NAMNAM). The dialects are named after towns or localities. They consider Dagaare in particular to be a sister language. 5 major dialects and many minor ones, all able to use the published materials. They call themselves their clan or dialect name, and their language 'Farefare'. Speakers of Talni are called 'Talensi'. Dictionary. Grammar. Literacy rate in first language: 1% to 5%. Literacy rate in second language: 5% to 15%. Roman. Taught at the University of Ghana. Radio programs, videos. Traditional religion, Christian, Muslim. NT 1986.

FULFULDE, MAASINA ***(PEUL, FULBE, MAACINA)*** [FUL] 7,300 in Ghana (1991). Northern, in small groups. Niger-Congo, Atlantic-Congo, Atlantic, Northern, Senegambian, Fula-Wolof, Fulani, West Central. Bilingualism in Hausa. Nomadic. They are considered to be foreigners by Ghanaians. Pastoralists. Muslim. Bible portions 1934. See main entry under Mali.

GA ***(AMINA, GAIN, ACCRA, ACRA)*** [GAC] 300,000 in Ghana (1993 UMS). Population total both countries 300,000 or more. Southeast, coast around Accra. Also spoken in Togo. Niger-Congo, Atlantic-Congo, Volta-Congo, Kwa, Nyo, Ga-Dangme. Ga is the major language of Accra, the capital. Literacy rate in first language: 30% to 60%. Literacy rate in second language: 75% to 100%. Traditional religion. Bible 1866, in press (1997).

GHANAIAN SIGN LANGUAGE [GSE] Deaf sign language. Related to American and Nigerian sign languages. Brought in 1957 by missionary Andrew Foster. Differs from American Sign Language in lexicon. There are new and local signs, and some modified from ASL. 9 deaf schools. Other deaf people use home signs. Elementary schools for deaf children since 1957. Sign language interpreters are required for deaf people in court. Little research. Some sign language classes for hearing people. There is a manual alphabet for signing. Investigation needed: intelligibility with American Sign Language, Nigerian Sign Language.

GIKYODE [ACD] 8,000 speakers (1998 SIL). East central, on the border with Togo. Remote. 9 villages. Niger-Congo, Atlantic-Congo, Volta-Congo, Kwa, Nyo, Potou-Tano, Tano, Guang, North Guang. Closest to Anyanga of Togo; 75% lexical similarity. Twi (Akan) is used for trade. The name of the people is 'Akyode' (Achode), the language is 'Gikyode' (correct spelling), 'Gichode' is the correct

English pronunciation. Literacy rate in first language: 1% to 2% first language literates, 5% second language literates. Literacy rate in second language: 5% to 20%. Forest, savannah. Foothills, mountain slope. Subsistence agriculturalists: cassava, yam. Traditional religion, Christian. Bible portions 1986-1988.

GONJA ***(NGBANYITO)*** [DUM] 250,000 (1995 SIL). In the southern part of the Northern Region, west central Ghana, around the upper branches of the Volta Lake, and from the Black Volta River to the area on both sides of the White Volta. Niger-Congo, Atlantic-Congo, Volta-Congo, Kwa, Nyo, Potou-Tano, Tano, Guang, North Guang. Dialects: GONJA, CHORUBA (CHOROBA). It is not intelligible with Chumburung. Dictionary. Grammar. Literacy rate in first language: 1% to 5%. Literacy rate in second language: Below 5%. Traditional religion, Muslim, Christian. NT 1984.

GUA ***(ANUM-BOSO, GWA)*** [GWX] 36,500 (1998 GILLBT). A pocket in Éwé area. Niger-Congo, Atlantic-Congo, Volta-Congo, Kwa, Nyo, Potou-Tano, Tano, Guang, South Guang. Dialects: ANU (ANUM), BOSO. Speakers of all dialects use Twi (Akan) as second language. Grammar. Literacy rate in first language: 1% to 5%. Literacy rate in second language: 5% to 15%. Traditional religion.

HANGA ***(ANGA)*** [HAG] 5,000 including 3,000 in the traditional area, 2,000 elsewhere (1992 GILLBT). North central, southeast of the Mole Game Reserve, Damongo District. The biggest village is Murugu. Niger-Congo, Atlantic-Congo, Volta-Congo, North, Gur, Central, Northern, Oti-Volta, Western, Southeast. Dialects: NORTHERN HANGA, SOUTHERN HANGA. Kamara is a separate language. Subdialects of Southern Hanga are Langantere, Murugu, Damongo; subdialects of Northern Hanga are Yazori and Bowena. 84% lexical similarity with Dagaare and Frafra. Bilingualism in Gonja. Politically a subgroup of the Gonja. Literacy rate in first language: 10% to 30%. Literacy rate in second language: 5% to 15%. Savannah. Agriculturalists: maize, sorghum, millet, yams, cassava. NT 1983.

HAUSA [HUA] Afro-Asiatic, Chadic, West, A, A.1. Trade language. Muslim. Bible 1932-1996. See main entry under Nigeria.

JWIRA-PEPESA ***(PEPESA-JWIRA)*** [JWI] 14,500 (1995 SIL). Southwest corner. The Jwira live north of Axim from Bamiankaw to Humjibere along the Ankobra River (18 villages). The Pepesa live on Wasa land between Agona Junction and Tarkwa. Dompim is the main town. A mountain range separates the two groups. Niger-Congo, Atlantic-Congo, Volta-Congo, Kwa, Nyo, Potou-Tano, Tano, Central, Bia, Southern. Dialects: JWIRA, PEPESA. 60% intelligibility of Nzema. In the north, some Jwira speak Wasa; in the south some speak Nzema. The Pepesa use Wasa as second language. Literacy rate in second language: 50% to 75%. Traditional religion, Christian.

KABIYÉ ***(KABIRE, CABRAI, KABURE, KABYE, CABRAIS)*** [KBP] North. Niger-Congo, Atlantic-Congo, Volta-Congo, North, Gur, Central, Southern, Grusi, Eastern. Traditional religion. NT 1996. See main entry under Togo.

KAMARA [JMR] 1,000 in Ghana (1997 G. Hunt SIL). Larabanga village, about 10 miles along the road west of Damongo, in the middle of the Northern Region, on the edge of the Hanga area. Safaliba sources report another small village about 15 to 20 miles south of Bole. Some ethnic Kamara in Mandari speak Safaliba, not Kamara. J. Becuwe reports a population of 3,000 in Bouna, Côte d'Ivoire (1981). Niger-Congo, Atlantic-Congo, Volta-Congo, North, Gur, Central, Northern, Oti-Volta, Western, Southeast. Significantly different from Hanga, and distinct culturally. Closer to Dagbani than to Hanga (G. Hunt 1997). The Kamara in Larabanga speak Kamara. Those in Mandari are bilingual or speak only Safaliba. It is not known if those in Côte d'Ivoire speak Kamara. Investigation needed: intelligibility, bilingual proficiency. Muslim.

KANTOSI ***(KANTONSI, YARE, YARSI)*** [XKT] 2,000 possibly in Ghana, including 250 to 350 in Sandema District, probably about 250 in Kpaliwongo (1998 P. Schaefer SIL). North central Ghana, Sandema District, among the Bulsa (Buli language). Other settlements near Wa, in Navrongo, Bolgatonga, Nalerigu, and Kpaliwogo. They say Kpaliwongo, a village southeast of Funsi (Upper West Region) is their place of origin. After being destroyed during the days of slave-raiding, it was rebuilt and Kantosis have moved back. They may also be in Burkina Faso. Niger-Congo, Atlantic-Congo, Volta-Congo, North, Gur, Central, Northern, Oti-Volta, Western, Southeast. Closer to Kamara, Frafra, Dagbani. Those in Sandema use Buli as second language. Endangered because people in some of the settlements now speak the language of those they have settled among: those in Funsi now speak Pasaale, those near Wa now speak Wali. One source says they are from Niger or Mali. Kantosi is referred to as 'Yare' or 'Yarsi' by the Bulsa from 'Yadasi' (pl.), 'Yadakala' (sg.), which means 'Muslim'. A school in Wa uses Kantosi. Muslim.

KASEM ***(KASENA, KASSENA, KASSENE)*** [KAS] 100,000 in Ghana (1995 SIL). North central (Navrongo District). Niger-Congo, Atlantic-Congo, Volta-Congo, North, Gur, Central, Southern, Grusi, Northern. Dialects: NUNUMA, LELA, KASEM, FERE. The people are Kasena, the language Kasem. Grammar. Literacy rate in first language: 1% to 5%. Literacy rate in second language: 15% to 25%. Traditional religion, Christian, secular, Muslim. NT 1988-1997. See main entry under Burkina Faso.

KONKOMBA ***(LIKPAKPALN, KPANKPAM, KOM KOMBA)*** [KOS] 400,000 in Ghana (1995 SIL). Population total both countries 450,000. Northeast border area around Guerin, Yendi District. Many groups are scattered throughout north central Ghana. Also spoken in Togo. Niger-Congo, Atlantic-Congo, Volta-Congo, North, Gur, Central, Northern, Oti-Volta, Gurma. Dialects: LICHABOOL-NALONG, LIMONKPEL, LINAFIEL, LIKOONLI, LIGBELN. Bilingualism in Twi, Bassari, Hausa, English. 'Likpakpaln' is the self name for the language, 'Bikpakpaln' for the people. Patrilineal, patrilocal. Dictionary. Literacy rate in first language: 1% to 10%. Literacy rate in second language: 5% to 15%. Agriculturalists: yams. Traditional religion, Muslim, Christian. Bible 1998.

KONNI ***(KONI, KOMA, KOMUNG)*** [KMA] 2,500 (1995 SIL). Remote and isolated. Southeast of the Sisaala and west of the Mamprusi. No roads. 5 villages; Yikpabongo is the main one, Nangurima is another. Niger-Congo, Atlantic-Congo, Volta-Congo, North, Gur, Central, Northern, Oti-Volta, Buli-Koma. It has some linguistic features common to Mampruli, Hanga, and Buli. 60% lexical similarity with Buli. They also speak several nearby languages including Mampruli and Sisaala. Politically under the Mampruli chief. The people are called 'Koma', the language 'Komung' or 'Konni'. A high percentage of blindness from onchocerciasis. Literacy rate in first language: 0%. Literacy rate in second language: 0%. Agriculturalists: yams, cassava, millet, guinea corn, maize, peanuts. Traditional religion, Christian, Muslim.

KPLANG ***(PRANG)*** [PRA] 7,700 (1991 L. Vanderaa CRC). South of Volta Lake, south of Yeji (Chumburung). Niger-Congo, Atlantic-Congo, Volta-Congo, Kwa, Nyo, Potou-Tano, Tano, Guang, North Guang. 73% intelligibility of Chumburung. 96% comprehension of Yeji (Chumburung dialect) because of proximity. 92% lexical similarity with Yeji Chumburung, 79% with Chumburung. Most people are bilingual in Twi (Akan). Traditional religion.

KRACHE ***(KRACHI, KRAKYE, KAAKYI)*** [KYE] 60,000 (1988 GILLBT). Central, near Nchimburu, area of Kete Krachi. Niger-Congo, Atlantic-Congo, Volta-Congo, Kwa, Nyo, Potou-Tano, Tano, Guang, North Guang. A portion of the population is bilingual in Twi (Akan). High level of school attendance. Community sponsored literacy materials available. Traditional religion.

KULANGO, BONDOUKOU ***(NKURAENG, NKURANGE, KOULANGO, KULANGE, KOLANGO, BONDUKU KULANGO)*** [KZC] 10,000 in Ghana (1991). West central, west of Wenchi. Niger-Congo, Atlantic-Congo, Volta-Congo, North, Gur, Kulango. Traditional religion. NT 1975. See main entry under Côte d'Ivoire.

KULANGO, BOUNA ***(NKURAENG, BUNA KULANGO, BOUNA KOULANGO)*** [NKU] 15,500 in Ghana (1991). West central border area. Niger-Congo, Atlantic-Congo, Volta-Congo, North, Gur, Kulango. Dialects: SEKWA, NABANJ. Mainly traditional religion. See main entry under Côte d'Ivoire.

KUSAAL ***(KUSALE, KUSASI)*** [KUS] 500,000 in Ghana including 417,000 Angole (1995 SIL), 83,000 Toende (1995 SIL). Population total both countries 517,000. Northeast corner, Bawku District. Also spoken in Burkina Faso. Niger-Congo, Atlantic-Congo, Volta-Congo, North, Gur, Central, Northern, Oti-Volta, Western, Southeast, Kusaal. Dialects: ANGOLE (EASTERN KUSAAL), TOENDE (WESTERN KUSAAL). Further investigation of Toende in Burkina Faso is needed, including inherent intelligibility and language attitudes. Bilingualism in Hausa. 'Kusasi' are the people, 'Kusaal' is the language. Dictionary. Grammar. Literacy rate in first language: 1% to 5%. Literacy rate in second language: 15% to 25%. Roman. Traditional religion, Muslim, Christian. NT 1976-1995.

LAMA ***(LAMBA, LOSSO)*** [LAS] Several hundred or perhaps thousands in Ghana (1996). About 100 km. south of Bassar, over to Yendi, an even as far as Tamale. Niger-Congo, Atlantic-Congo, Volta-Congo, North, Gur, Central, Southern, Grusi, Eastern. May be called Kabiye or Losso in Ghana. NT 1993. See main entry under Togo.

LARTEH ***(LATE, LETE, GUA)*** [LAR] 44,000 (1998 GILLBT). A pocket in the Ga and Twi areas, south of Cherepon. Niger-Congo, Atlantic-Congo, Volta-Congo, Kwa, Nyo, Potou-Tano, Tano, Guang, South Guang. Speakers are reported to use Twi (Akan) as second language. Investigation needed: intelligibility with dialects, bilingual proficiency in Twi. Literacy rate in first language: 1% to 5%. Literacy rate in second language: 5% to 15%. Traditional religion.

LELEMI ***(LEFANA, LAFANA, BUEM)*** [LEF] 38,500 (1998 SIL). Southeast, town of Jasikan. Niger-Congo, Atlantic-Congo, Volta-Congo, Kwa, Nyo, Potou-Tano, Lelemi, Lelemi-Akpafu. Some bilingualism in Twi (Akan). The people are called 'Buem', the language 'Lelemi'. Grammar. SVO. Literacy rate in first language: Below 1%. Literacy rate in second language: 5% to 15%. Christian, traditional religion. NT 1995.

LIGBI ***(LIGWI, NIGBI, NIGWI, TUBA, BANDA, DZOWO, NAMASA, TSIE, WEILA, WIILA, WEELA)*** [LIG] 10,000 in Ghana (1988 GILLBT). Population total both countries 14,000. Numasa, northwest Brong-Ahafo, East of Sampa and northwest of Wenchi. Also spoken in Côte d'Ivoire. Niger-Congo, Mande, Western, Central-Southwestern, Central, Manding-Jogo, Jogo-Jeri, Jogo. Dialects: BUNGASE, GYOGO, HWELA (WEILA, WIILA, WEELA, VWELA), DWERA (MANJI-KASA), ATUMFUOR (ATUMFUOR-KASA), NTOLEH. Bilingualism in Twi Asante. Blacksmiths in other countries speaking Manding languages are also called 'Noumou', but in Ghana and Côte d'Ivoire the Noumou speak Ligbi. 'Banda' is the name of the people, which also refers to speakers of the Nafaanra language. 'Numu' is a caste of blacksmiths who speak the same dialect as others. Grammar. Muslim, traditional religion.

LOGBA [LGQ] 5,000 (1988 SIL). Southeast. Niger-Congo, Atlantic-Congo, Volta-Congo, Kwa, Nyo, Potou-Tano, Logba. A population sample averaged 87% comprehension of Éwé mixed discourse types. Different from Dompago (Logba) of Benin and Togo.

MAMPRULI ***(MAMPRULE, MANPELLE, NGMAMPERLI)*** [MAW] 226,800 Mamprusi (1991 L. Vanderaa CRC). Population total both countries 226,800 or more. East and west of Gambaga, northeast Northern Region. Also spoken in Togo. Niger-Congo, Atlantic-Congo, Volta-Congo, North, Gur, Central, Northern, Oti-Volta, Western, Southeast. Dialects: EASTERN MAMPRULI, WESTERN MAMPRULI. 50% intelligibility with Dagbani. 95% lexical similarity with Dagbani, 90% with Frafra. Bilingualism in Frafra, Bimoba, Bissa. The people are called 'Mamprusi'. Dictionary. Literacy rate in first language: Below 1%. Literacy rate in second language: 5% to 15%. Traditional religion, Muslim. Bible portions 1943-1998.

NAFAANRA ***(NAFANA, NAFAARA, PANTERA-FANTERA, BANDA, DZAMA, GAMBO)*** [NFR] 45,000 (1992 GILLBT). Population total both countries 45,000 or more. Western border, east of Bondoukou in Côte d'Ivoire. Also spoken in Côte d'Ivoire. Niger-Congo, Atlantic-Congo, Volta-Congo, North, Gur, Senufo, Nafaanra. Dialects: PANTERA, FANTERA. Bilingual level estimates for Twi (Akan) are 0 15%, 1 15%, 2 50%, 3 20%, 4 0%, 5 0%. 'Banda', 'Banafo', or 'Nafana' are names for the people. Different from Nafara Senoufo of Côte d'Ivoire. Grammar. SOV; postpositions; genitives before noun heads; articles, adjectives, numerals, relatives after noun heads; question word initial; word order distinguishes subject, object, indirect object; ergativity; causatives; comparatives; CV, CVV; tonal. Literacy rate in first language: 1% to 5%. Literacy rate in second language: 15% to 25%. Savannah, tropical forest. Plains, low rocky mountains. Intensive agriculturalists: tobacco, yams, cotton, peanuts. Cattle guarded by Fulani. 200 to 300 meters. Traditional religion, Muslim, Christian. NT 1984.

NAWDM ***(NAUDM, NAWDAM, NAOUDEM)*** [NMZ] In Accra, Ho, Kpandu, and Volta Region. Niger-Congo, Atlantic-Congo, Volta-Congo, North, Gur, Central, Northern, Oti-Volta, Yom-Nawdm. Bible portions 1992. See main entry under Togo.

NAWURI [NAW] 14,000 (1998 GILLBT). East central, mostly on the western bank of the Oti River branch of Lake Volta. Niger-Congo, Atlantic-Congo, Volta-Congo, Kwa, Nyo, Potou-Tano, Tano, Guang, North Guang. Closest inherent intelligibility with Gikyode. Not intelligible with Chumburung. Highest lexical similarity with the Buipe dialect of Gonja (72%). Grammar. SVO; postpositions; genitives before noun heads; articles, adjectives, numerals, relatives after noun heads; question word initial; word order distinguishes subjects, objects, indirect objects, given and new information, topic and comment; subject pronouns are clitics, objects (postverbal) can be treated as independent words; subject and object pronouns indicate person and number; limited noun class agreement of head nouns with modifiers; verb agreement with prefix concord marker which is usually a copy of the head noun (agreement both within noun phrase and subject-verb), but less extensive than in many Bantu languages; semi-productive causative suffix on verbs; comparison typically indicated by a serial verb or serial clause construction; CV, CVC, limited V(C); tonal. Literacy rate in first language: Below 1%. Literacy rate in second language: 5% to 15%. Traditional religion, Christian. Bible portions 1999.

NCHUMBULU [NLU] 1,300 (1991 L. Vanderaa CRC). Three villages west of Volta Lake near Kplang. Niger-Congo, Atlantic-Congo, Volta-Congo, Kwa, Nyo, Potou-Tano, Tano, Guang, North Guang. May use Chumburung or Dwan literature. Bilingualism in Twi. Investigation needed: intelligibility with Chumburung, Dwan.

NKONYA [NKO] 20,000 (1988 GILLBT). Southeast Ghana, northwest of the Éwé. Some among the Gua. Niger-Congo, Atlantic-Congo, Volta-Congo, Kwa, Nyo, Potou-Tano, Tano, Guang, North Guang. Bilingualism in Éwé, Twi. Literacy rate in first language: Below 1%. Literacy rate in second language: 5% to 15%. Traditional religion. Bible portions.

NTCHAM ***(TOBOTE, NCHAM, BASSAR, BASSARI, BASARI, BASAR, BASARE)*** [BUD] 47,700 in Ghana (1998 P. Schaefer SIL). Niger-Congo, Atlantic-Congo, Volta-Congo, North, Gur, Central, Northern, Oti-Volta, Gurma, Ntcham. Dialect: BITAAPUL. Grammar. Literacy rate in first language: Below 1%. Literacy rate in second language: 15% to 25%. Traditional religion. NT 1986-1990. See main entry under Togo.

NYANGBO ***(TUTRUGBU)*** [NYB] 3,900 (1991 L. Vanderaa CRC). Southeast. Niger-Congo, Atlantic-Congo, Volta-Congo, Kwa, Left Bank, Avatime-Nyangbo. People who have had no contact with Tafi had 67% intelligibility of it on tests; people 30 to 50 years old had near perfect comprehension. There are reported to be only phonological differences. A population sample averaged 72% comprehension of Éwé mixed discourse types. Investigation needed: intelligibility with Tafi. Traditional religion.

NZEMA ***(NZIMA, APPOLO)*** [NZE] 285,800 in Ghana (1991 L. Vanderaa CRC). Population total both countries 352,500. Southwest corner and into Côte d'Ivoire. Also spoken in Côte d'Ivoire. Niger-Congo, Atlantic-Congo, Volta-Congo, Kwa, Nyo, Potou-Tano, Tano, Central, Bia, Southern. Bilingualism in Fante. Literacy rate in first language: 1% to 5%. Literacy rate in second language: 50% to 75%. Traditional religion. Bible 1999.

SAFALIBA ***(SAFALI, SAFALABA, SAFALBA)*** [SAF] 3,200 (1998 P. Schaefer SIL). Immediately west and south of Bole, western Northern Region. Villages of Mandari, Tanyire, Manfuli, and Gbenfu, and settlements in the nearby towns of Bote, Sawla, Kalba. Speakers also reported in Vonkoro and Bouna, Côte d'Ivoire. Niger-Congo, Atlantic-Congo, Volta-Congo, North, Gur, Central, Northern, Oti-Volta, Western, Northwest. 79% lexical similarity with Dagaari. Bilingualism in Gonja. Literacy rate in first language: Below 1%. Literacy rate in second language: 8% English, Gonja. Savannah. Plains, some hills. Subsistence agriculturalists: yam, maize. Traditional religion, Muslim, Christian.

SEHWI ***(SEFWI, ASAHYUE)*** [SFW] 200,000 (1995 SIL). Southwest. Niger-Congo, Atlantic-Congo, Volta-Congo, Kwa, Nyo, Potou-Tano, Tano, Central, Bia, Northern. Closely related to Anyin of Côte d'Ivoire. Bilingualism in Twi. Traditional religion, Christian. Bible portions 1998.

SEKPELE ***(LIKPE, MU)*** [LIP] 15,000 (1991 L. Vanderaa CRC). Southeast, north of Hohoe. Niger-Congo, Atlantic-Congo, Volta-Congo, Kwa, Nyo, Potou-Tano, Lelemi, Likpe-Santrokofi. Dialects: SEKWA, SEKPELE. A population sample averaged 75% comprehension of Éwé mixed discourse types. Twi is also used. Literacy rate in first language: Below 1%. Literacy rate in second language: 5% to 15%. Community sponsored vernacular literacy materials are available. Traditional religion.

SELE ***(SANTROKOFI, SENTROKOFI, BALE)*** [SNW] 6,000 (1988 GILLBT). Southeast, villages of Benua, Bume, Gbodome. Niger-Congo, Atlantic-Congo, Volta-Congo, Kwa, Nyo, Potou-Tano, Lelemi, Likpe-Santrokofi. Diminishing contact with Éwé. The language is called 'Sele'; the people 'Bale'. Outsiders call them 'Santrokofi'. Literacy rate in first language: Below 1%. Literacy rate in second language: 5% to 15%. Community sponsored vernacular literacy materials are available. Traditional religion, Christian.

SISAALA, PASAALE ***(PASAALE, FUNSILE, SOUTHERN SISAALA)*** [SIG] 26,000 to 30,000 (1996 SIL). Upper West Region, 80 km. south of Tumu, 105 km. east of Wa, about 18 villages. Niger-Congo, Atlantic-Congo, Volta-Congo, North, Gur, Central, Southern, Grusi, Western. Dialects: GILBAGALA, PASAALI. Gilbagala is closer to Pasaale than to Tumulung Sisaala. The dialect in Funsi Kundogo is predominant among the Pasaale villages. There are 4 dialects. Bilingualism in Wali, Sisaala, Hausa, English. Grammar. SVO; prepositions; articles, adjectives, numerals after noun heads; question word initial; word order distinguishes object; ergativity; CV, CVC, CVV; tonal. Literacy rate in first language: 1% to 2%. Literacy rate in second language: 5% to 15%. About 50% of children begin school; 10% to 20% complete Junior Secondary School. Savannah. Plains. Subsistence agriculturalists: guinea corn. Traditional religion, Muslim, Christian. Bible portions 1994-1996.

SISAALA, TUMULUNG ***(SISAI, ISSALA, HISSALA, SISALA TUMU, ISAALUNG)*** [SIL] 121,200 (1991 L. Vanderaa CRC). North central, Tumu District. Niger-Congo, Atlantic-Congo, Volta-Congo, North, Gur, Central, Southern, Grusi, Western. Dialects: ISALA, GIL BAGALE (GALEBAGLA), NSIHAA, POTULE. Bilingualism in Twi, Hausa. Dictionary. Literacy rate in first language: 1% to 5%. Literacy rate in second language: 5% to 15%. Traditional religion, Muslim, Christian. NT 1984.

SISAALA, WESTERN ***(BUSILLU SISALA, SISAI, ISSALA, HISSALA)*** [SSL] 20,000 (1988 GILLBT). North central, Lambusie and surrounding towns. Niger-Congo, Atlantic-Congo, Volta-Congo, North, Gur, Central, Southern, Grusi, Western. Close to Sissala of Burkina Faso, but distinct. Investigation needed: intelligibility with Tumulung Sisaala, Burkina Faso Sisaala. Traditional religion, Muslim.

SIWU ***(AKPAFU-LOLOBI, LOLOBI-AKPAFU, SIWUSI)*** [AKP] 16,100 (1991 L. Vanderaa CRC). Southeast, north of Hohoé. Niger-Congo, Atlantic-Congo, Volta-Congo, Kwa, Nyo, Potou-Tano, Lelemi, Lelemi-Akpafu. Dialects: AKPAFU, LOLOBI. Lolobi and Akpafu are inherently intelligible, but have been politically separate since the 1800s. A population sample averaged 66% comprehension of Éwé mixed discourse types. 'Lolobi' and 'Akpafu' are names for town and people. Their own name for their language is 'Siwu'. Literacy rate in second language: 25% to 50%. Community sponsored vernacular literacy materials are available. Traditional religion, Christian.

TAFI ***(TEGBO)*** [TCD] 2,900 (1991 L. Vanderaa CRC). East central, near the Togo border. None in Togo. Niger-Congo, Atlantic-Congo, Volta-Congo, Kwa, Left Bank, Avatime-Nyangbo. Bilingualism in Éwé. A population sample averaged 73% comprehension of Éwé mixed discourse types. 83% understand Nyangbo narrative well. Muslim, traditional religion.

TAMPULMA ***(TAMPRUSI, TAMPOLE, TAMPOLEM, TAMPOLENSE, TAMPLIMA, TAMPELE)*** [TAM] 40,000 (1993 GILLBT). North central, south of Sisala, Damongo District, 25 villages. Niger-Congo, Atlantic-Congo, Volta-Congo, North, Gur, Central, Southern, Grusi, Western. Two inherently intelligible dialects. 62% lexical similarity with Chakali. 'Tamprusi' is the name of the people,

'Tampulma' of the language. Literacy rate in first language: 1% to 5%. Literacy rate in second language: 15% to 25%. Roman. Agriculturalists: guinea corn, millet, yams; fishermen. Christian, traditional religion. Bible, in press (1998).

TEM ***(KOTOKOLI, COTOCOLI, TIM, TIMU, TEMBA)*** [KDH] 53,000 in Ghana. Most in Accra. Niger-Congo, Atlantic-Congo, Volta-Congo, North, Gur, Central, Southern, Grusi, Eastern. Muslim. See main entry under Togo.

TUWILI ***(BOWIRI, BOWILI, LIWULI, SIWURI, BAWULI)*** [BOV] 10,000 (1988 GILLBT). Volta Region, from Volta Lake eastward to Amanfro on the Hohoe-Jasikan road. Not found in Togo. Niger-Congo, Atlantic-Congo, Volta-Congo, Kwa, Left Bank, Kposo-Ahlo-Bowili. Diminishing contact with Éwé. Literacy rate in second language: 25% to 50%. Traditional religion.

VAGLA ***(VAGALA, SITI, SITIGO, KIRA, KONOSAROLA, PAXALA)*** [VAG] 10,000 (1992 GILLBT). West central near Sawla, Northern Province, Damongo District. Niger-Congo, Atlantic-Congo, Volta-Congo, North, Gur, Central, Southern, Grusi, Western. Dialects: BOLE, BUGE. 68% lexical similarity with Chakali. 75% use Waali as second language. Dictionary. Literacy rate in first language: 1% to 5%. Literacy rate in second language: 15% to 25%. Roman. Traditional religion, Muslim. NT 1977.

WALI ***(WAALI, WALA, ALA, OUALA)*** [WLX] 99,100 (1991 L. Vanderaa CRC). Northwest corner. Niger-Congo, Atlantic-Congo, Volta-Congo, North, Gur, Central, Northern, Oti-Volta, Western, Northwest. Dialects: FUFULA, YERI WAALI, CHERII, 'BULENGEE, 'DOLIMI. Separate language from Birifor and Dagaari. The Chakali are reported to be bilingual in Wali. The ' before dialect names indicates a change in vowel quality. Literacy rate in first language: Below 1%. Literacy rate in second language: 15% to 25%. Traditional religion, Muslim, Christian. NT 1984.

WASA ***(WASAW, WASSA)*** [WSS] 175,000 (1991 L. Vanderaa CRC). Southwestern. Niger-Congo, Atlantic-Congo, Volta-Congo, Kwa, Nyo, Potou-Tano, Tano, Central, Akan. Dialects: AMENFI, FIANSE. Some intelligibility with Abron. Twi (Akan) is used as second language. Low Asante and Fante comprehension in rural areas. Investigation needed: intelligibility with Abron. Literacy rate in first language: Below 1%. Literacy rate in second language: 5% to 15%. Traditional religion.

GUINEA

Republic of Guinea. République de Guinée. National or official languages: Fuuta Jalon, French. 7,337,000 (1998 UN). Literacy rate 28% to 35%. Also includes Bambara, Bandi 50,000, Krio, Loko 4,000, Soninke, Wolof, people from Lebanon and Europe. Information mainly from J. Bendor-Samuel 1989. Muslim, traditional religion, Christian. Blind population 45,000 (1982 WCE). Deaf institutions: 3. Data accuracy estimate: B, C. The number of languages listed for Guinea is 35. Of those, 33 are living languages and 2 are extinct. Diversity index 0.75.

BADJARA ***(BADARA, BADIAN, BADYARANKE, PAJADE, PAJADINKA, GOLA, BIGOLA)*** [PBP] 6,300 in Guinea (1998 NTM). Population total all countries 11,550. Koundara region. Also spoken in Guinea-Bissau, Senegal. Niger-Congo, Atlantic-Congo, Atlantic, Northern, Eastern Senegal-Guinea, Tenda. Biafada is the closest language, with 52% lexical similarity. They maintain cultural autonomy. Beekeepers, agriculturalists, cotton cloth weavers. Muslim.

BAGA BINARI ***(BARKA, BINARI, KALUM, MBORIN)*** [BCG] Coast east of the Nunez River in Boké region. Niger-Congo, Atlantic-Congo, Atlantic, Southern, Mel, Temne, Baga. Close to Landoma and Temne. Bilingualism in Susu. Muslim, traditional religion.

BAGA KALOUM [BQF] Niger-Congo, Atlantic-Congo, Atlantic, Southern, Mel, Temne, Baga. The people now speak Susu. Muslim, traditional religion. Extinct.

BAGA KOGA ***(BARKA, KOGA, KOBA)*** [BGO] Coast between the Pongo and Konkouré rivers, extending to the Île de Kito. Niger-Congo, Atlantic-Congo, Atlantic, Southern, Mel, Temne, Baga. Close to Landoma and Temne. Bilingualism in Susu. Muslim, traditional religion. Nearly extinct.

BAGA MANDURI ***(BARKA, MANDARI, MADURI, MANDURI)*** [BMD] Islands in Nunez River delta, around Dobale, Kanfarande Subprefecture. Niger-Congo, Atlantic-Congo, Atlantic, Southern, Mel, Temne, Baga. Close to Landoma and Temne. Bilingualism in Susu. Investigation needed: intelligibility with Baga, bilingual proficiency in Susu. Muslim, traditional religion.

BAGA MBOTENI [BGM] Niger-Congo, Atlantic-Congo, Atlantic, Northern, Mbulungish-Nalu. Related to Nalu and Mbulungish. Bilingualism in Susu. Investigation needed: intelligibility with Nalu, Mbulungish, bilingual proficiency in Susu. Muslim, traditional religion. Nearly extinct.

BAGA SITEMU ***(BARKA, SITEMUÚ, TCHITEM, STEM BAGA, RIO PONGO BAGA)*** [BSP] 32,100 all Baga languages. Southern bank of the Nunez River in the Boké and Boffa regions. Baga Marara is spoken on Marara islands south of the Rio Pongo Inlet. Niger-Congo, Atlantic-Congo, Atlantic, Southern, Mel, Temne, Baga. Dialect: MARARA. Close to Landoma and Temne. Bilingualism in Susu. Investigation needed: intelligibility with Baga Marara. Muslim, traditional religion.

BAGA SOBANÉ ***(BARKA, SOBANÉ, BAGA KAKISSA)*** [BSV] Between the Kapatchez and Pongo rivers. Niger-Congo, Atlantic-Congo, Atlantic, Southern, Mel, Temne, Baga. Was close to Landoma and Temne. Susu is the language used now. Muslim, traditional religion. Extinct.

BASARI ***(BASSARI, ONIAN, AYAN, BIYAN, WO, TENDA BASARI)*** [BSC] 8,600 in Guinea (1991 Vanderaa). Niger-Congo, Atlantic-Congo, Atlantic, Northern, Eastern Senegal-Guinea, Tenda. Matrilineal. Traditional religion. NT 1988. See main entry under Senegal.

DAN ***(YACOUBA, YAKUBA, GIO, GYO, GIO-DAN, DA)*** [DAF] 70,600 in Guinea (1991 Vanderaa). Niger-Congo, Mande, Eastern, Southeastern, Guro-Tura, Tura-Dan-Mano, Tura-Dan. Traditional religion, Christian. NT 1981-1993. See main entry under Côte d'Ivoire.

FRENCH [FRN] Indo-European, Italic, Romance, Italo-Western, Western, Gallo-Iberian, Gallo-Romance, Gallo-Rhaetian, Oïl, French. Official language. Bible 1530-1986. See main entry under France.

FULFULDE, PULAAR ***(PULAAR, PEUL, PEULH, HAALPULAAR)*** [FUC] 24,000 in Guinea (1991). One community near Dinguiray (Pulaar), and a few communities in the north near Sareboido. Niger-Congo, Atlantic-Congo, Atlantic, Northern, Senegambian, Fula-Wolof, Fulani, Western. Dialects: TOUCOULEUR (TUKULOR, TUKOLOR, PULAAR), FULACUNDA (FULAKUNDA, FULKUNDA, FULA PRETO). Guinea has an extensive literature in Pulaar. All of the primary and some secondary schools are taught in Pulaar. Many Arabic loans. The official orthography is different from that used elsewhere. Muslim. NT 1997. See main entry under Senegal.

FUUTA JALON ***(FUTA JALLON, FOUTA DYALON, FULBE, FULLO FUUTA, FUTA FULA, FOULA FOUTA, FULFULDE JALON, JALON, PULAR, PULAAR)*** [FUF] 2,550,000 in Guinea (1991 Vanderaa), 40% of the population (1986). Population total all countries 2,900,000. Northwest, Fouta Djallon area. Also spoken in Gambia, Guinea-Bissau, Mali, Senegal, Sierra Leone. Niger-Congo, Atlantic-Congo, Atlantic, Northern, Senegambian, Fula-Wolof, Fulani, West Central. Dialects: KEBU FULA, FULA PETA. Many monolinguals. Maninka and Susu used as second language by others. Guinea has had an extensive literature in Pular, but little still exists. Used in schools. Fuuta Jalon in Guinea is a major Fula geo-political state. Heavy borrowing from Arabic. National language. Muslim, Christian. Bible portions 1929-1975.

GUINEAN SIGN LANGUAGE [GUS] Conakry. Deaf sign language. Used in the deaf school in Conakry. Appears to be heavily influenced by, or based on, ASL, with some influence from French Sign Language. Investigation needed: intelligibility with American Sign Language.

JAHANKA ***(JAHANQUE, JAHONQUE, DIAKKANKE, DIAKHANKE, DYAKANKE)*** [JAD] 12,600 in Guinea (1991). Population total both countries 12,600 or more. Around Touba and Toubadinque near Gaoua, border area of Mali and Guinea. Also spoken in Mali. Niger-Congo, Mande, Western, Central-Southwestern, Central, Manding-Jogo, Manding-Vai, Manding-Mokole, Manding. Jahanka in Gambia may be the same as this, or a dialect of Western Maninka. Jahanka in Senegal and Guinea-Bissau is a dialect of Western Maninka. 75% lexical similarity with Mandinka. They are reported to have come from Mali in the 18th century. They trace their origins to Soninke, but now speak a separate language. Arabic script. Merchants of Gao rice; Muslim scholars. Muslim.

KISSI, NORTHERN ***(GIZI, KISI, KISSIEN, KISIE)*** [KQS] 286,500 in Guinea (1991 Vanderaa). Population total both countries 326,500. South central, Kissidougou region. Also spoken in Sierra Leone. Niger-Congo, Atlantic-Congo, Atlantic, Southern, Mel, Bullom-Kissi, Kissi. Dialects: LIARO, KAMA, TENG, TUNG. Closely related to Sherbro. Southern Kissi of Liberia and Sierra Leone is different. Many loan words from Malinke. Literacy rate in second language: 10% in French. Traditional religion, Muslim, Christian. NT 1966-1986.

KPELLE, GUINEA ***(KPELE, GUERZE, GERZE, GERSE, GBESE, PESSA, PESSY, KPWESSI, AKPESE, KPELESE, KPELESETINA, KPESE, KPERESE, NORTHERN KPELE)*** [GKP] 308,000 (1991 Vanderaa). Southeast at Liberia border. Niger-Congo, Mande, Western, Central-Southwestern, Southwestern, Kpelle. Dialect: KONO. Different enough from Kpelle of Liberia to need separate materials. 'Guerzé' is the French name. The Kono dialect of Kpelle in Guinea is different from the Kono language of Sierra Leone. The government recently changed the orthography. Traditional religion, Christian, Muslim. Bible portions 1945-1969.

KURANKO ***(KORANKO)*** [KHA] 55,200 in Guinea (1991). Between Faranah and Kissidougou. Niger-Congo, Mande, Western, Central-Southwestern, Central, Manding-Jogo, Manding-Vai, Manding-Mokole, Mokole. Dialects: SENGBE, NEYA, DIANG. Sengbe dialect is used for literature. All dialects are inherently intelligible with each other. Ethnically separate from Maninka. Mountain slope. Traditional religion, Muslim. NT 1972. See main entry under Sierra Leone.

LANDOMA ***(LANDOUMAN, LANDUMA, TYAPI, TYOPI, TIAPI, COCOLI)*** [LAO] 14,400 (1991 Vanderaa). Between the upper Rio Nunez and the upper Rio Pongas. Not in Guinea-Bissau. Niger-Congo, Atlantic-Congo, Atlantic, Southern, Mel, Temne, Baga. Dialect: TIAPI (TAPESSI). Close to Baga and Temne. Traditional religion, Muslim.

LELE [LLC] 23,000, including 12,000 in Kissidougou Prefecture and 11,000 in Guekedou (1998 Brad Willets PBT). Kissidougou vicinity, with Mato River on the west. Main centers are Yombiro, Tangalto, and Kassadou, west and southwest of Kissidou. Not in Sierra Leone. Niger-Congo, Mande, Western, Central-Southwestern, Central, Manding-Jogo, Manding-Vai, Manding-Mokole, Mokole. Dialects: YOMBIRO LELE (NORTH LELE), TANGALTO LELE (EAST LELE), KASSADOU LELE (SOUTH LELE), KOUNTE LELE (CENTRAL LELE). Kassadou people cannot understand Tangalto dialect. 55% lexical similarity with Maninka and Mixifore, 73% with Kuranko of Sierra Leone. They seem to have a strong ethnic conscience. Muslim.

LIMBA, EAST ***(YIMBA, YUMBA)*** [LMA] 4,000 in Guinea (1993 Johnstone), including 2,000 speakers of the Ke subdialect of Northern Limba (1991 J. Kaiser LBT). Population total both countries 4,000 or more. Also spoken in Sierra Leone. Niger-Congo, Atlantic-Congo, Atlantic, Southern, Limba. Dialect: NORTHERN LIMBA (WARAWARA, KE-WOYA-YAKA). Quite different from West-Central Limba of Sierra Leone. Traditional religion, Muslim.

MANINKA, KANKAN ***(MANINKA, MANDE, SOUTHERN MANINKA)*** [MNI] 1,890,000 in Guinea, 25% of the population (1986), including 73,500 Wasulu. Population total all countries 2,255,000. Central, Kankan Region, all over upper Guinea, and the forest region near Liberia. Also spoken in Liberia, Sierra Leone. Niger-Congo, Mande, Western, Central-Southwestern, Central, Manding-Jogo, Manding-Vai, Manding-Mokole, Manding, Manding-East, Southeastern Manding. Dialects: BÖ, AMANA (KOUROUSA), KOULOUNKALAN, MANINKA-MORI (MORI), WASULU (WASSULU, WASSULUNKA, WASSULUNKE). Maninka of Liberia is the same as Maninka of Guinea (southern Maninka), Bambara of Mali and parts of Senegal is not vastly different. Southeastern Maninka of Côte d'Ivoire is close to Bambara; Western Maninka of south central and southeast Senegal is considerably different. Wasulu is a dialect of Kankan Maninka in Guinea, but of Bambara in Mali. Kankan variety has 92% lexical similarity with Wasulu, 79% with Sankaran, 72% with Konyanka. Investigation needed: intelligibility with Mori. Dictionary. Nko script is popular, created in 1948 by Sulemana Kante, with about 50 publications, and schools teaching it. Only uses Nko script. Muslim. NT 1932-1966.

MANINKA, KONYANKA ***(KONYA, KONYAKAKAN)*** [MKU] 128,400 (1986). Beyla region. Niger-Congo, Mande, Western, Central-Southwestern, Central, Manding-Jogo, Manding-Vai, Manding-Mokole, Manding, Manding-East, Southeastern Manding. 72% lexical similarity with Kankan. Muslim.

MANINKA, SANKARAN ***(FARANAH, SANKARKAN)*** [MSC] Niger-Congo, Mande, Western, Central-Southwestern, Central, Manding-Jogo, Manding-Vai, Manding-Mokole, Manding, Manding-East, Southeastern Manding. 79% lexical similarity with Kankan. Muslim.

MANINKA, WESTERN ***(NORTHWESTERN MANINKA, MALINKE, MALINKA)*** [MLQ] Niger-Congo, Mande, Western, Central-Southwestern, Central, Manding-Jogo, Manding-Vai, Manding-Mokole, Manding, Manding-West. 59% lexical similarity with Mandinka of Gambia and Senegal. Muslim, traditional religion. See main entry under Mali.

MANO ***(MAA, MAH, MAWE)*** [MEV] 71,022 in Guinea (1997 Moise Mamy). East of Kpelle in Nzérékore Prefecture (40,536), Lola Prefecture (16,486), Yomou Prefecture (14,000). Niger-Congo, Mande, Eastern, Southeastern, Southern, Kweni-Tura, Tura-Dan-Mano, Mano. Traditional religion. NT 1978. See main entry under Liberia.

MANYA ***(MANYA KAN, MANDINGO, MANIYA)*** [MZJ] 25,000 in Guinea (1997 PBT). Macenta Prefecture. Niger-Congo, Mande, Western, Central-Southwestern, Central, Manding-Jogo, Manding- Vai, Manding-Mokole, Manding, Manding-East, Southeastern Manding. Related to Maninka, but distinct. 70% lexical similarity with Konyanka, 66% with Kankan Maninka. Speakers do not consider themselves to be Maninka. Muslim, Christian. See main entry under Liberia.

MBULUNGISH ***(BAGA FORÉ, BAGA MONSON, MONSHON, MONCHON, BULUNITS, LONGICH, BLACK BAGA)*** [MBV] 5,000 (1998 Brad Willetts 1998). 22 villages. Niger-Congo, Atlantic-Congo, Atlantic, Northern, Mbulungish-Nalu. Related to Nalu and Baga Mboteni. Children were reported to be speaking the language actively in 1995-1996. Investigation needed: intelligibility with Nalu, bilingual proficiency in Susu. Muslim, traditional religion.

MIXIFORE ***(MOGOFIN, MIKIFORE)*** [MFG] 3,600 (1991). Central. Niger-Congo, Mande, Western, Central-Southwestern, Central, Manding-Jogo, Manding-Vai, Manding-Mokole, Mokole. It seems to be close to the Vai-Kono-Kuranko subgroup (Valentin Vydrine). 51% lexical similarity with Maninka of Kankan, 55% with Lele, 54% to 58% with varieties of Kuranko. 'Mixifore' means 'black person' in Susu. 'Mogofin' means the same thing, and is their name for themselves. Muslim.

NALU ***(NALOU)*** [NAJ] 13,000 in Guinea (1993 Johnstone). Population total both countries 20,250. Near Boke. Also spoken in Guinea-Bissau. Niger-Congo, Atlantic-Congo, Atlantic, Northern, Mbulungish-Nalu. Related to Mbulungish and Baga Mboteni. Muslim, traditional religion.

PAPEL ***(PEPEL, PAPEI, MOIUM, OIUM)*** [PBO] 2,400 in Guinea (1991 Vanderaa). Bissao Island. Niger-Congo, Atlantic-Congo, Atlantic, Northern, Bak, Manjaku-Papel. Closely related to Mankanya and Mandyak. 3 dialects. Traditional religion. NT 1996. See main entry under Guinea-Bissau.

SUSU ***(SOSO, SUSOO, SOUSSOU, SOSE)*** [SUD] 800,000 in Guinea (1993 Johnstone), 10% of the population (1986). Population total all countries 923,500. Western Guinea, and mainly in the southwest. Also spoken in Guinea-Bissau, Sierra Leone. Niger-Congo, Mande, Western, Central-Southwestern, Central, Susu-Yalunka. A separate language from Yalunka. Krio is used as second language. People have limited bilingualism in French in Guinea. Many people write Susu in both Roman and Arabic scripts. Muslim, traditional religion, Christian. NT 1884-1988.

TOMA ***(TOA, TOALE, TOALI, TOOMA)*** [TOD] 143,800 (1991 Vanderaa). Southern, between Macenta and Kissidougou. Niger-Congo, Mande, Western, Central-Southwestern, Southwestern, Mende -Loma, Loma. Distinct enough from Loma of Liberia to need separate literature. Traditional religion, Muslim, Christian. NT 1981.

WAMEI ***(KONYAGI, CONIAGUI, COGNIAGUI, KONIAGI, CONHAGUE, TENDA, DUKA)*** [COU] 4,000 in Guinea (1996). Koundara region and around Youkounkoun, extending to the Senegal border. Niger-Congo, Atlantic-Congo, Atlantic, Northern, Eastern Senegal-Guinea, Tenda. 'Wamei' is their own name. Nomadic. Over 3,000 migrate from Guinea to Senegal annually. Many stay longer. Traditional religion, Christian, Muslim (less than). See main entry under Senegal.

YALUNKA ***(DJALLONKE, DYALONKE, DIALONKE, JALONKE, YALUNKE)*** [YAL] 81,000 in Guinea (1997 Pruett). Population total all countries 129,000. West of Faranah, villages around the edge of the Futa Jalon, and Koubia, northeast Guinea near the Sierra Leone border. Also spoken in Mali, Senegal, Sierra Leone. Niger-Congo, Mande, Western, Central-Southwestern, Central, Susu-Yalunka. Dialects: SULIMA, FIRIA. Close to Susu, but only marginally intelligible. Muslim. NT 1976.

GUINEA-BISSAU

Republic of Guinea-Bissau. República da Guiné-Bissau. Formerly Portuguese Guinea. National or official language: Portuguese. 1,161,000 (1998 UN). Literacy rate 6%. Also includes Fuuta Jalon, Western Maninka, Susu 3,450, Wolof, people from Cape Verde, Guinea, Europe. Information mainly from J. Bendor-Samuel 1989; J. Holm 1989. Traditional religion, Muslim, Christian. Blind population 5,000 (1982 WCE). Data accuracy estimate: B. The number of languages listed for Guinea-Bissau is 20. Of those, all are living languages. Diversity index 0.85.

BADJARA ***(BADYARA, BADIAN, BADYARANKE, PAJADE, PAJADINCA, PAJADINKA, GOLA, BIGOLA)*** [PBP] 3,750 in Guinea-Bissau (1998). Northeast corner. Niger-Congo, Atlantic-Congo, Atlantic, Northern, Eastern Senegal-Guinea, Tenda. Biafada is the closest language, with 52% lexical similarity. The speakers may be bilingual in Mandinka. Investigation needed: intelligibility. Muslim. See main entry under Guinea.

BAINOUK-GUNYUÑO ***(BANYUM, BANYUN, BAGNOUN, BANHUM, BAINUK, BANYUK, BANYUNG, ELOMAY, ELUNAY)*** [BAB] 7,260 (1998). South of the Casamance River. Niger-Congo, Atlantic-Congo, Atlantic, Northern, Eastern Senegal-Guinea, Banyun. A distinct language from Bainouk-Gunyamoolo of Senegal and Gambia. Related to Kobiana and Kasanga of Senegal and Guinea-Bissau. More closely related to the Tenda languages of eastern Senegal than to Diola and Balanta. Investigation needed: intelligibility. Muslim, traditional religion.

BALANTA-KENTOHE ***(BALANTA, BALANT, BALANTE, BALANDA, BALLANTE, BELANTE, BULANDA, BRASSA, ALANTE, FRASE)*** [BLE] 326,700 in Guinea-Bissau (1998). Population total both countries 326,700 or more. North central and central coast. Also spoken in Gambia. Niger-Congo, Atlantic-Congo, Atlantic, Northern, Bak, Balant-Ganja. Dialects: FORA, KANTOHE (KENTOHE, QUEUTHOE), NAGA, MANE. Naga, Mane, and Kantohe may be separate languages. A separate language from Balanta-Ganja in Senegal. Not intelligible with Mansoanka. Investigation needed: intelligibility with Naga, Mane. Traditional religion, Christian, Muslim. NT 1998.

BASARI ***(ONIAN, AYAN, BIYAN, WO, BASSARI)*** [BSC] 450 in Guinea-Bissau (1998). Northeastern. Niger-Congo, Atlantic-Congo, Atlantic, Northern, Eastern Senegal-Guinea, Tenda. Traditional religion, Christian. NT 1988. See main entry under Senegal.

BAYOT ***(BAYOTE, BAIOT, BAYOTTE)*** [BDA] 1,800 in Guinea-Bissau (1998). Northwestern, along the border with Senegal. Niger-Congo, Atlantic-Congo, Atlantic, Northern, Bak, Jola, Bayot. 15% lexical similarity with other Jola varieties. Traditional religion. See main entry under Senegal.

BIAFADA ***(BEAFADA, BIAFAR, BIDYOLA, BEDFOLA, DFOLA, FADA)*** [BIF] 36,800 (1998). Central south, north of the Nalu. Niger-Congo, Atlantic-Congo, Atlantic, Northern, Eastern Senegal-Guinea, Tenda. 52% lexical similarity with Badjara. Muslim.

BIDYOGO ***(BIJAGO, BIJOGO, BIJOUGOT, BUDJAGO, BUGAGO, BIJUGA)*** [BJG] 24,500 (1998). Roxa and Bijago islands. Niger-Congo, Atlantic-Congo, Atlantic, Bijago. Dialects: ORANGO, ANHAQUI. Some intelligibility problems are reported between dialects. Investigation needed: intelligibility with dialects. Little literacy work has been done. Traditional religion, Christian. NT 1975.

CRIOULO, UPPER GUINEA ***(PORTUGUESE CREOLE, KRIULO)*** [POV] 159,000 first language speakers in Guinea-Bissau (1996) and 600,000 second language users (Chataigner ms.) Population total all countries 361,500 or more. Also Bijagos Islands. Also spoken in Gambia, Senegal, USA. Creole, Portuguese based. Dialects: BISSAU-BOLAMA CREOLE, BAFATÁ CREOLE, CACHEU-ZIGUINCHOR CREOLE. The Senegal dialect is a little different, but they are intelligible to each other's speakers. Portuguese not well known. The lingua franca in much of Guinea-Bissau, more in the west than in the east. Trade language. Grammar. Bible, in press (1997).

EJAMAT ***(EDIAMAT, FULUP, FELOUP, FELUP, FELUPE, FLOUP, FLUP)*** [EJA] 19,550 in Guinea-Bissau (1998). Population total both countries 21,350. Northwest corner, San Domingo District. Also spoken in Senegal. Niger-Congo, Atlantic-Congo, Atlantic, Northern, Bak, Jola, Jola Proper, Jola Central, Her-Ejamat. Investigation needed: intelligibility with Kerak, bilingual proficiency in Bayot. Muslim, traditional religion.

KASANGA ***(CASSANGA, KASSANGA, I-HADJA, HAAL)*** [CCJ] 600 (1998). A remnant is living near Felupe, northwest, in a sparsely populated border area. None in Senegal. Niger-Congo, Atlantic-Congo, Atlantic, Northern, Eastern Senegal-Guinea, Nun. Close to Banyun. Traditional religion.

KOBIANA ***(COBIANA, UBOI, BUY)*** [KCJ] 600 (1998). Population total both countries 600 or more. Near Banyun. Also spoken in Senegal. Niger-Congo, Atlantic-Congo, Atlantic, Northern, Eastern Senegal-Guinea, Nun. Closely related to Bainouk and Kasanga. Speakers are bilingual in Mandyak, but not vice versa. Traditional religion.

MANDINKA ***(MANDINGA, MANDINGUE, MANDINGO, MANDINQUE, MANDING)*** [MNK] 137,000 in Guinea-Bissau (1998). North central, central, and northeastern. Niger-Congo, Mande, Western, Central-Southwestern, Central, Manding-Jogo, Manding-Vai, Manding-Mokole, Manding, Manding-West. Significantly different from Maninka of Guinea and Malinke of Senegal (Church). Some varieties thought to be dialects may be separate languages. 79% lexical similarity with Kalanke, 75% with Jahanka, 70% with Kassonke, 59% with Malinke, 53% with Mori, 48% with Bambara. An important language. Muslim. NT 1989. See main entry under Senegal.

MANDJAK ***(MANDJAQUE, MANJACA, MANJACO, MANJIAK, MANDYAK, MANJAKU, MANJACK, NDYAK, MENDYAKO, KANYOP)*** [MFV] 151,250 in Guinea-Bissau (1998). Half speak the central dialect, 25% speak dialects which are inherently intelligible with that. Population total all countries 253,350. West and northwest of Bissau. Also spoken in France, Gambia, Senegal. Niger-Congo, Atlantic-Congo, Atlantic, Northern, Bak, Manjaku-Papel. Dialects: BOK (BABOK, SARAR, TEIXEIRA PINTO, TSAAM), LIKES-UTSIA (BARAA, KALKUS), CUR (CHURO), LUND, YU (PECIXE, SIIS, PULHILH). Some dialects listed may be separate languages. Closely related to Mankanya and Papel. Important politically. Thousands have emigrated to France. Investigation needed: intelligibility. Nominal prefixes, 2 plural forms; complex auxiliary verbs and aspect particles; verb suffixes; relative clauses functioning as adjectives, with nominal markers at beginning and end; pitch distinction on verbal and nominal forms; emphatic markers. Traditional religion, Christian, Muslim. Bible portions 1968.

MANKANYA ***(MANKANHA, MANCANHA, MANCAGNE, MANCANG, BOLA)*** [MAN] 36,300 in Guinea-Bissau (1998). Population total all countries 61,000. Northwest of Bissau. Also spoken in Gambia, Senegal. Niger-Congo, Atlantic-Congo, Atlantic, Northern, Bak, Manjaku-Papel. Dialects: BURAMA (BULAMA, BURAM, BRAME), SHADAL (SADAR). Speakers are fairly well educated. Traditional religion.

MANSOANKA ***(MANSOANCA, MASWANKA, SUA, KUNANT, KUNANTE)*** [MSW] 12,700 in Guinea-Bissau (1998). Population total both countries 12,700 or more. North central. Also spoken in Gambia. Niger-Congo, Atlantic-Congo, Atlantic, Southern, Sua. Not inherently intelligible with Balanta or Mandinka, although called 'Mandinkanized Balanta'. Investigation needed: intelligibility. Muslim.

NALU ***(NALOU)*** [NAJ] 7,250 in Guinea-Bissau (1998). Southwest near the coast. Niger-Congo, Atlantic-Congo, Atlantic, Northern, Mbulungish-Nalu. Many are bilingual in Susu. Intermarriage in the border area with another group. Reported to be closed to outsiders. Muslim, traditional religion. See main entry under Guinea.

PAPEL ***(PEPEL, PAPEI, MOIUM, OIUM)*** [PBO] 111,550 in Guinea-Bissau (1998). Population total both countries 114,000. Bissau Island. Also spoken in Guinea. Niger-Congo, Atlantic-Congo, Atlantic, Northern, Bak, Manjaku-Papel. Closely related to Mankanya and Mandyak. 3 dialects. Traditional religion, Christian. NT 1996.

PORTUGUESE [POR] Indo-European, Italic, Romance, Italo-Western, Western, Gallo-Iberian, Ibero-Romance, West Iberian, Portuguese-Galician. Official language. Bible 1751, in press (1993). See main entry under Portugal.

PULAAR ***(FULFULDE-PULAAR, PULAAR FULFULDE, PEUL, PEULH)*** [FUC] 217,800 in Guinea-Bissau (1998). North central and northeastern Guinea-Bissau. Niger-Congo, Atlantic-Congo, Atlantic, Northern, Senegambian, Fula-Wolof, Fulani, Western. Dialect: FULACUNDA (FULAKUNDA, FULKUNDA, FULA PRETO, FULA FORRO). There are five Fulfulde varieties in Guinea-Bissau. Fula Forro are 'free' Fulas; Fulacunda are 'slave' Fulas. Muslim. NT 1997. See main entry under Senegal.

SONINKE ***(SARAKOLE, MARKA)*** [SNN] 5,750 in Guinea-Bissau (1998). Niger-Congo, Mande, Western, Northwestern, Samogo, Soninke-Bobo, Soninke-Boso, Soninke. Dialect: AZER (ADJER, ASER, AJER, MASIIN, TAGHDANSH). They live among the Fula and Mandinka and speak those languages as second languages. Ethnic groups: Aser, Aswanik, Gadyaga, Marka, Markanka, Nono, Saracole, Serahuli, Sarawule, Tonbakai, Wakove. Muslim. See main entry under Mali.

KENYA

Republic of Kenya. Jamhuriya Kenya. National or official languages: Swahili, English. 29,008,000 (1998 UN). Literacy rate 45% (1987 official government figure). Also includes Hadrami Spoken Arabic 10,000, Taizzi-Adeni Spoken Arabic 10,000, Hindi, 1,892 from Pakistan (1989 census). Information mainly from W. Whiteley 1969, 1974; Heine and Möhlig 1980; J. Bendor-Samuel 1989; BTL 1983-1999. Christian, traditional religion, Muslim, Baha'i. Blind population 70,000. Deaf institutions: 25. Data accuracy estimate: A1, A2. The number of languages listed for Kenya is 61. Of those, all are living languages. Diversity index 0.90.

ARABIC, OMANI SPOKEN [ACX] 15,000 in Kenya (1995). Up and down the coast. Afro-Asiatic, Semitic, Central, South, Arabic. Swahili is the mother tongue of most or all. It is reported that they came to Kenya as early as 900 A.D., originally from Yemen and Oman. SVO. Literacy is in Arabic. Muslim. See main entry under Oman.

BONI ***(AWEERA, AWEER, WAATA, WATA, SANYE, WASANYE, WABONI, BON, OGODA, WATA-BALA)*** [BOB] 3,500 in Kenya (1994). Population total both countries 5,000 (1980). In forest hinterland behind Lamu, Lamu and Tana River districts, Coast Province; Garissa District, North-Eastern Province. At least 11 villages. Also spoken in Somalia. Afro-Asiatic, Cushitic, East, Rendille-Boni. Close to Garre of Somalia. Many are monolingual. Some are bilingual in Somali, Orma, or Swahili. Different from Sanye (Waat) of the Oromo Group or Dahalo (Sanye) of Southern Cushitic. Vernacular literature is desired. They are being settled in scattered villages and encouraged to switch to farming. Literacy rate in first language: 10% to 30%. Literacy rate in second language: 50% to 75%. Forest. Hunter-gatherers, limited agriculturalists: maize, beans. Traditional religion, Muslim.

BORANA ***(BORAN, BOORAN, BORAAN, SOUTHERN OROMO, OROMO, "GALLA")*** [GAX] 152,000 in Kenya (1994 I. Larsen BTL), including 96,000 Borana (1994), 43,000 Gabra (1994), 13,000 Sakuye (1994). Marsabit and Isiolo Districts, Eastern Province. Afro-Asiatic, Cushitic, East, Oromo. Dialects: BORAN, GABRA (GABBRA, GEBRA), SAKUYE (SAGUYE). Gabra and Sakuye may have significant dialect and language attitude differences from Borana. Also spoken by the younger Burji population around Marsabit and Moyale. The name 'Borana' is used almost exclusively in Kenya, but 'Oromo' is used in Ethiopia. Semi-nomadic. Investigation needed: intelligibility, attitudes toward Gabra, Sakuye. Desert. Pastoralists: camel, cattle. Boran: Muslim, Christian; Gabra: mainly traditional religion, Christian, some Muslim; Sakuye: Muslim, Christian. Bible 1995. See main entry under Ethiopia.

BUKUSU ***(LUBUKUSU)*** [BUL] 565,000 (1987 BTL), including 47,000 Tachon (1980 Heine and Möhlig). Western Province, Bungoma District, Mt. Elgon. Niger-Congo, Atlantic-Congo, Volta-Congo, Benue-Congo, Bantoid, Southern, Narrow Bantu, Central, J, Masaba-Luyia (J.30), Luyia. Dialects: BUKUSU, TACHONI (TACHON), KABRAS. Literacy rate in first language: 1% to 5%. Literacy rate in second language: 25% to 50%. Mountain slope. Christian. NT 1993.

BURJI ***(BAMBALA)*** [BJI] 7,000 in Kenya (1994 I. Larsen BTL). Mainly around Marsabit township, Moyale. Afro-Asiatic, Cushitic, East, Highland. Kenyan resident Burji below 40 years are apparently functionally bilingual in Boran. Above 20 years. Below 20 people do not speak Burji. Ethiopia is considered the traditional home territory, but some migration occurs between the two countries. Brought from Ethiopia in the 1930s to build roads from Moyale to other north Kenya towns. Literacy rate in first language: Below 1%. Literacy rate in second language: 15% to 25%. Mountain slope. Businessmen, agriculturalists. Christian, traditional religion. NT, in press (1995). See main entry under Ethiopia.

CHONYI ***(CHICHONYI)*** [COH] 121,000 (1994 I. Larsen BTL). Kilifi District, Coast Province. Niger-Congo, Atlantic-Congo, Volta-Congo, Benue-Congo, Bantoid, Southern, Narrow Bantu, Central, E, Nyika (E.40), Mijikenda. Chonyi speakers may understand Giryama. Investigation needed: intelligibility with Giryama. Christian, Muslim.

CHUKA ***(SUKA, CHUKU)*** [CUH] 70,000 (1980 SIL). Southern Meru District, Eastern Province. Niger-Congo, Atlantic-Congo, Volta-Congo, Benue-Congo, Bantoid, Southern, Narrow Bantu, Central, E, Kikuyu-Kamba (E.20), Meru. Comprehension of northern Meru dialects is borderline. Close to Tharaka. 73% lexical similarity with Embu, 70% with Gikuyu, 67% with Meru, 63% with Kamba. Speakers in different regions are bilingual in Meru, Gikuyu, Kamba, or Swahili. Christian.

CUTCHI-SWAHILI ***(ASIAN SWAHILI)*** [CCL] Also spoken in Tanzania. Creole, Swahili based. May be adequately intelligible to speakers of standard Swahili. Cutchi-Swahili and Asian Swahili may not be the same. Bilingualism in English. Asian Swahili is used by other Asians in communicating with non-English speaking Africans and other Asians who share no other common language. The first language of some Gujarati Muslims who have come from Zanzibar. It has regular but distinct phonology, lexical, and grammatical differences from Swahili, described by Whitely (1974.73-79). Literacy rate in first language: Below 1%. Literacy rate in second language: 15% to 25%. Ismaili and Ithnasheri Muslim.

DAASANACH ***(GELEB, DAMA, MARILLE, RESHIAT, "SHANGILLA", DAASANECH, DASENECH, DATHANAIK, GELEBA, GHELEBA)*** [DSH] 2,500 in Kenya (1980 SIL). Northeastern shore of Lake Turkana, around Illeret, Marsabit District, Eastern Province. Afro-Asiatic, Cushitic, East, Western Omo-Tana. "Shangilla" is a derogatory name. 8 ethnic groups: Inkabelo (7,000), Inkoria (2,000), Naritch (Naarich 1,800), Elele (1,500), Randal (1,000), Oro (800), Koro (500), Riele (400). SOV. Literacy rate in first language: Below 1%. Literacy rate in second language: Below 5%. Semi-arid desert. Plains. Pastoralists: cattle; agriculturalists: millet, tobacco; fishermen. Traditional religion, Christian. Bible portions 1997. See main entry under Ethiopia.

DAHALO ***(SANYE, GUO GARIMANI)*** [DAL] 3,000 possibly (1987 SIL). Near the mouth of the Tana River, Lamu and Tana River districts, Coast Province. Afro-Asiatic, Cushitic, South. The language has clicks, although unrelated to Khoisan languages. Highly assimilated and bilingual in Swahili. Different from Sanye (Waata). The name "Dahalo" is derogatory. Traditional religion.

DIGO ***(KIDIGO, CHIDIGO)*** [DIG] 217,000 in Kenya (1994 I. Larsen BTL), .8% of the population. Population total both countries 305,000. Kwale District, Coast Province, south of Mombasa. Also spoken in Tanzania. Niger-Congo, Atlantic-Congo, Volta-Congo, Benue-Congo, Bantoid, Southern, Narrow Bantu, Central, E, Nyika (E.40), Mijikenda. Partially intelligible with Giryama but the most remote from Giryama of the Mijikenda Subgroup. 74% lexical similarity with Duruma, 72% with Chonyi and Swahili, 71% with Swahili dialects Mrima and Mvita, 67% with Amu, 62% with Bajun, 58% with Lower Pokomo. Bilingualism in Swahili. Vigorous. A fair degree of Swahili influence. Literacy rate in first language: Below 1%. Literacy rate in second language: 45% in Swahili. Coastal. Agriculturalists, fishermen, traders, industry workers. Muslim, traditional religion, Christian. Bible portions 1982-1997.

DURUMA [DUG] 247,000 (1994 I. Larsen SIL). West Kwale District, Coast Province, south of Mombasa to the Tanzanian border. Niger-Congo, Atlantic-Congo, Volta-Congo, Benue-Congo, Bantoid, Southern, Narrow Bantu, Central, E, Nyika (E.40), Mijikenda. Of the nine Mijikenda dialects, Duruma is the second most remote from Giryama linguistically. 74% lexical similarity with Digo, 66% with Swahili. Comprehension of Swahili and Digo is low. Vigorous. Language attitudes toward Giryama indicate the need for separate Duruma literature. Literacy rate in first language: Below 1%. Literacy rate in second language: 13%. Traditional religion, Christian, Muslim. NT, in press (1999).

EL MOLO ***(ELMOLO, FURA-PAWA, LDES, DEHES, "NDOROBO")*** [ELO] 8 speakers out of 4,000 in the ethnic group (1994 I. Larsen BTL). Southeastern shore of Lake Turkana, Elmolo Bay, Marsabit District, Eastern Province. Afro-Asiatic, Cushitic, East, Western Omo-Tana. The original language is close to Daasanech. Most of the ethnic group now speak Samburu. They are affiliated with the Samburu. All over 50 years old (1994). Semi-arid desert. Plains, lake shore. Fishermen. Traditional religion, Christian. Nearly extinct.

EMBU ***(KIEMBU)*** [EBU] 429,000 (1994 I. Larsen BTL) including 150,000 in Embu, 61,725 in Mbeere (1980 Heine and Möhlig), 1.2% of the population. Embu District, Eastern Province. Niger-Congo, Atlantic-Congo, Volta-Congo, Benue-Congo, Bantoid, Southern, Narrow Bantu, Central, E, Kikuyu-Kamba (E.20). Dialects: MBEERE (MBERE, KIMBEERE), EMBU. Mbeere is reported to have adequate intelligibility of Embu. The population estimate may include Chuka and Mwimbi-Muthambi. 85% lexical similarity with Mbeere, 73% with Gikuyu and Chuka, 66% with Kamba, 63% to 65% with Meru. There is bilingualism in Gikuyu because of previous teaching in the schools, but it is limited in rural areas. Up to 70% have limited bilingualism in Swahili. Comprehension of Meru is limited. 'Embo' is an incorrect spelling. Literacy rate in first language: Below 1%. Literacy rate in second language: 25% to 50%. There are government literacy materials in Embu. Embu: Christian, traditional religion; Mbeere: traditional religion, Christian.

ENDO ***(ENDO-MARAKWET, MARAKUET, MARKWETA)*** [ENB] 80,000 (1997 SIL). Rift Valley Province, Elgeyo Marakwet District. Nilo-Saharan, Eastern Sudanic, Nilotic, Southern, Kalenjin, Nandi-Markweta,

Markweta. Dialects: ENDO, SAMBIRIR. Low intelligibility with major Kalenjin dialects and Talai. Marakwet is a cover term for Endo-Sambirir and Talai. Literacy rate in first language: Below 1%. Literacy rate in second language: 5% to 15%. Orthography problems. Pastoralists: cattle, goats, sheep; hunters; agriculturalists. Traditional religion, Christian. 18 churches. Bible portions 1998.

ENGLISH [ENG] Mainly second language speakers. Indo-European, Germanic, West, English. Official language. Bible 1535-1989. See main entry under United Kingdom.

GARREH-AJURAN [GGH] 128,000 including 96,000 Garreh, 32,000 Ajuran (1994 I. Larsen BTL). Mandera and Wajir districts, North-Eastern Province. Afro-Asiatic, Cushitic, East, Oromo. Dialects: GARREH (GURREH, GARRE, GARI), AJURAN (AJUURAAN, UJUURAAN). Part of a dialect cluster. 85% lexical similarity with Boran on a short word list. The Ajuran in Kenya speak Somali as second language. Swahili is also used, and some can also speak the Garre of Somalia, which their ancestors spoke. In Somalia (not Kenya) the Ajuran ethnic group speak a variety of Common Somali as mother tongue, and the Garre ethnic group apparently speak a language related to Somali. Semi-nomadic. Investigation needed: intelligibility with Ajuran. Literacy rate in second language: 2%. Pastoralists. Muslim, Christian.

GIKUYU ***(KIKUYU, GEKOYO, GIGIKUYU)*** [KIU] 5,347,000 (1994 I. Larsen BTL) or 19.8% of the population (1987). West central Kenya, in Kiambu, Murang'a, Nyeri, and Kirinyaga districts, Central Province. Niger-Congo, Atlantic-Congo, Volta-Congo, Benue-Congo, Bantoid, Southern, Narrow Bantu, Central, E, Kikuyu-Kamba (E.20). Dialects: SOUTHERN GIKUYU (KIAMBU, SOUTHERN MURANG'A), NDIA (SOUTHERN kIRINYAGA), GICHUGU (NORTHERN kIRINYAGA), MATHIRA (KARATINA), NORTHERN GIKUYU (NORTHERN MURANG'A, NYERI). 73% lexical similarity with Embu, 70% with Chuka, 67% with Kamba, 63% with Meru. Bilingualism in Swahili, English. The first consonant of the name 'Gikuyu' or 'Gekoyo' is a voiced velar fricative; the vowels are mid. Grammar. Literacy rate in first language: 30% to 60%. Literacy rate in second language: 75% to 100%. 95% of the children are in school. Mountain slope, hills, plains. Agriculturalists: sorghum, millet, beans, sweet potatoes, maize, potatoes, cassava, bananas, sugar cane, yams, fruit, tobacco, coffee, castor oil, tea, pyrethium, peas; animal husbandry: goats, sheep, cattle. Christian, traditional religion. Bible 1951-1965.

GIRYAMA ***(GIRIAMA, AGIRYAMA, KIGIRIAMA, NIKA, NYIKA, KINYIKA)*** [NYF] 623,000 (1994 I. Larsen BTL), including 496,000 Giryama, 17,000 Kauma, 19,000 Jibana, 13,000 Kambe, 72,000 Rabai, 6,000 Ribe. 2.3% of the population. North of Mombasa, Kilifi and Kwale districts, Coast Province. Niger-Congo, Atlantic-Congo, Volta-Congo, Benue-Congo, Bantoid, Southern, Narrow Bantu, Central, E, Nyika (E.40), Mijikenda. Dialects: KAUMA, RIBE (RIHE), JIBANA (DZIHANA), KAMBE, GIRYAMA, CHWAKA, RABAI. Digo and Duruma are the most distinct from Giryama. Dialect speakers may understand Chonyi. 72% lexical similarity with Digo, 63% with Mrima, 62% with Mvita, 61% with Amu, 59% with Lower Pokomo and Bajun. Most speak Swahili fairly well. Many school children are learning English. Different from Nyiha (Nyika) of Tanzania and Zambia. Strong traditional social system. Nine ethnic groups, all called 'Mijikenda'. Literacy rate in first language: Below 1%. Literacy rate in second language: 15% to 25%. Coastal. Subsistence agriculturalists, cash crops. Traditional religion, Christian, Muslim. Bible 1901.

GUJARATI [GJR] 50,000 in Kenya (1995 SIL). Mainly in Nairobi. Indo-European, Indo-Iranian, Indo-Aryan, Central zone, Gujarati. Most have lived in Kenya for several generations. Hindu, Jain, Muslim. Bible 1823-1998. See main entry under India.

GUSII ***(KISII, KOSOVA, GUZII, EKEGUSII)*** [GUZ] 1,582,000 (1994 I. Larsen BTL), 6.3% of the population. 2,000,000 probably including second language users (1999 WA). Southwestern, south of Kavirondo Gulf, Kisii District, Nyanza Province. Niger-Congo, Atlantic-Congo, Volta-Congo, Benue-Congo, Bantoid, Southern, Narrow Bantu, Central, E, Kuria (E.10). Different from Kisi of Tanzania. Literacy rate in first language: Below 1%. Literacy rate in second language: 15% to 25%. Christian, traditional religion. Bible 1988.

IDAKHO-ISUKHA-TIRIKI [IDA] 306,000 (1987 BTL), including Idakho 65,000, Isukha 90,000, Tiriki 100,000 (1980 Heine and Möhlig). Kakamega District, Western Province. Niger-Congo, Atlantic -Congo, Volta-Congo, Benue-Congo, Bantoid, Southern, Narrow Bantu, Central, J, Masaba-Luyia (J.30), Luyia. Dialects: IDAKHO (IDAXO, ITAKHO, KAKAMEGA, KAKUMEGA), ISUKHA (ISUXA, LWISUKHA), TIRIKI. Speakers have high comprehension of Logooli, but there is resistance to each other's pronunciation. 70% lexical similarity with Logooli, 52% with Masaba (Uganda) and Saamia. Literacy rate in first language: Below 1%. Literacy rate in second language: 15% to 25%. Christian.

KACHCHI ***(CUTCHI, KACCHI, KATCHI, CUTCH)*** [KFR] 10,000 in Kenya (1995 SIL). Nairobi, Mombasa, and main trade routes. Indo-European, Indo-Iranian, Indo-Aryan, Northwestern zone, Sindhi. Bilingualism in Gujarati, English, Swahili. A community language and spoken in the home. Not used in schools. Masons, merchants (70% of Kenyan Asians). Swami Narayan Hindu, Memon and Shi'a Ismaili Muslim, Christian. Bible portions 1834. See main entry under India.

KALENJIN [KLN] 2,458,123 (1989 census), including 471,459 Kipsigis, 261,969 Nandi, 110,908 Keiyo, 130,249 Tugen (1980 Heine and Möhlig). Mainly Nandi, Kericho, and Uasin Gishu districts, Rift Valley Province. Nilo-Saharan, Eastern Sudanic, Nilotic, Southern, Kalenjin, Nandi-Markweta, Nandi. Dialects: NANDI (NAANDI, CEMUAL), TERIK (NYANG'ORI), KIPSIGIS (KIPSIIKIS, KIPSIKIS, KIPSIKIIS), KEIYO (KEYO, ELGEYO), SOUTH TUGEN (TUKEN), CHERANGANY. 60% lexical similarity with Omotik, 50% with Datooga. VSO. Literacy rate in first language: Below 1%. Literacy rate in second language: 15% to 25%. Orthography problems. Agriculturalists: millet, maize, potatoes, beans, pumpkins, tobacco, bananas, tea, sweet potatoes, sugar cane, peas, fruit, coffee, pyrethrum; animal husbandry: cattle, goats, sheep, fowl. Keiyo: Christian, traditional religion; Kipsigis: Christian, traditional religion; Nandi: Christian, traditional religion. Bible 1939-1969.

KAMBA ***(KIKAMBA, KEKAMBA)*** [KIK] 2,448,302 (1989 census) or 11.2% of the population (1987). 3,000,000 including second language users (1999 WA). South central, Machakos and Kitui Districts, Eastern Province. Some in Kwale District, Coast Province. Niger-Congo, Atlantic-Congo, Volta-Congo, Benue-Congo, Bantoid, Southern, Narrow Bantu, Central, E, Kikuyu-Kamba (E.20). Dialects: MASAKU, SOUTH KITUI, NORTH KITUI, MUMONI. 67% lexical similarity with Gikuyu, 66% with Embu, 63% with Chuka, 57% to 59% with Meru. Literacy rate in first language: Below 1%. Literacy rate in second language: 25% to 50%. Mountain slope. Agriculturalists: sorghum, millet, maize, beans, peas, sweet potatoes, yams, cassava, sugar cane, bananas, tobacco; animal husbandry: cattle, sheep, goats; traders; woodcarvers. 1,500 to 5,000 feet. Christian, traditional religion, Muslim. Bible 1956.

KENYAN SIGN LANGUAGE [XKI] Students in primary schools in 1990: 2,600. There are around 200,000 deaf people in Kenya. It is not known how many know KSL. 32 primary schools for the deaf in Hola, Kapsabet, Karatina, Karen, Kerugoya, Kilifi, Kisumu, Kitui, Kwale, Meru, Mombasa, Mumias, Murang'a, Nairobi, Nakuru, North Kinangop, Ruiru, Sakwa. Schools under the Kenya Institute of Education (KIE) use a Kenyan version of (American) Exact Signed English, including one at Machakos. KSL is used at Nyangoma School at Bondo, a primary and boys' technical school (Sakwa), and in one girl's school. A school in Mombasa uses British Sign Language. Some Belgian brothers use Belgian Sign language in a school near Oyugis. 4 churches in Nairobi: 2 use KIE Signed English, 1 a mixture of that and KSL, the other uses a mixture of Korean, American, and Kenyan Sign Languages. Deaf sign language. Mainly unrelated to other sign languages. It has become standardized with slight variations since 1961, when elementary schools for deaf children were begun. The deaf from Kisumu (western Kenya) to the deaf in Mombasa (eastern Kenya) can understand each other completely even with some dialect differences. The deaf in Uganda and Tanzania do not really understand KSL, though they have much in common. Used in court cases involving deaf people. The Kenya National Association of the Deaf, which has 12 branches. The government is using KIE Signed English. The University of Nairobi backs KSL. Little research. Communication with those who do not know KSL is superficial only. KSL fits Kenyan culture and ties students back to their families and friends who know it. There is a manual alphabet for spelling. Dictionary.

KONKANI, GOANESE ***(GOMATAKI, GOAN, GOANESE)*** [GOM] 3,900 in Kenya or 9% to 10% of Asians (1987). Nairobi. Indo-European, Indo-Iranian, Indo-Aryan, Southern zone, Unclassified. Bilingualism in English. A community and home language. Used by many Asians whose ancestors came from Goa or north India. Not used in schools. NT 1818-1976. See main entry under India.

KURIA ***(KIKURIA, IGIKURIA, EKIGURIA, KURYA, TENDE)*** [KUJ] 135,000 in Kenya (1994 I. Larsen BTL), .6% of population. The first four dialects listed are in Kenya, Kuria District, Nyanza Province. The last three dialects are in Tanzania. Niger-Congo, Atlantic-Congo, Volta-Congo, Benue-Congo, Bantoid, Southern, Narrow Bantu, Central, E, Kuria (E.10). Dialects: NYABASI, BUGUMBE, BUKIRA, BWIREGE, KIROBA, SIMBITI, SWETA. The Kenya dialects are very closely related. 'Koria' is not a good spelling. Christian, traditional religion. NT 1996. See main entry under Tanzania.

LOGOOLI ***(RAGOLI, ULURAGOOLI, LLUGULE, LUGOOLI, MARAGOOLI, LURAGOLI, LLOGOLE, MARAGOLI)*** [RAG] 197,000 (1987 BTL). Kakamega District, Western Province. Niger-Congo, Atlantic-Congo, Volta-Congo, Benue-Congo, Bantoid, Southern, Narrow Bantu, Central, J, Masaba-Luyia (J.30), Luyia. 70% to 80% lexical similarity with Idakho-Isukha-Tiriki. The people are called 'Avalogoli'. 'Mulogoli' is a person from Maragoli. Literacy rate in first language: 10% to 30%. Literacy rate in second language: 50% to 75%. Bible 1951.

LUO ***(DHOLUO, NILOTIC KAVIRONDO, KAVIRONDO LUO)*** [LUO] 3,185,000 in Kenya (1994 I. Larsen BTL) or 13.8% of the population (1987). Population total both countries 3,408,000. Nyanza Province. Also spoken in Tanzania. Nilo-Saharan, Eastern Sudanic, Nilotic, Western, Luo, Southern, Luo-Acholi, Luo. Different from Lwo of Uganda or Lwo (Luo, Jur Lwo) of Sudan. Literacy rate in first language: 10% to 30%. Literacy rate in second language: 50% to 75%. Fishermen. Christian, traditional religion, Muslim. Bible 1953-1977.

LUYIA ***(LULUYIA, LUHYA)*** [LUY] 3,418,083 (1989 census), or 13.1% of the population, including 135,000 Wanga, 65,000 Marama, 45,000 Tsotso 60,000 Kisa, 105,000 Kabras, 35,000 East Nyala, 50,000 Saamia, 35,000 West Nyala, 60,000 Khayo, 60,000 Marachi (1980 SIL). Population total both countries 3,643,461. Lake Victoria area, Western Province. Saamia and Songa dialects are in Uganda. Also spoken in Uganda. Niger-Congo, Atlantic-Congo, Volta-Congo, Benue-Congo, Bantoid, Southern, Narrow Bantu, Central, J, Masaba-Luyia (J.30), Luyia. Dialects: KISA (SHISA, LUSHISA), MARAMA, WANGA (HANGA, LUHANGA, OLUHANGA, KAWANGA, OLUWANGA), TSOTSO, SAAMIA (SAMIA, OLUSAMIA, LUSAMIA, LUSAAMIA, SAMYA), WEST NYALA (NYALA-B), KHAYO, SONGA, MARACHI. Saamia has 88% lexical similarity with Wanga, 62% with Masaba, 52% with Isuxa, 51% with Gwere. The people are called 'Abaluyia', singular 'Muluyia'. Literacy rate in first language: 10% to 30%. Literacy rate in second language: 25% to 75%. Christian, traditional religion, Muslim. Bible 1975.

MAASAI ***(MASAI)*** [MET] 453,000 in Kenya (1994 I. Larsen BTL), 1.5% of the population. Population total both countries 883,000. Kajiado and Narok districts, Rift Valley Province. Also spoken in Tanzania. Nilo-Saharan, Eastern Sudanic, Nilotic, Eastern, Lotuxo-Teso, Lotuxo-Maa, Ongamo-Maa. Dialects: KAPUTIEI, KEEKONYOKIE, MATAPO, LAITOKITOK, ILOODOKILANI, DAMAT, PURKO, LOITAI, SIRIA, MOITANIK (WUASINKISHU), KORE, ARUSA (ARUSHA), BARAGUYU, KISONKO. Purko is the largest dialect in Kenya and centrally located. The last three dialects listed are in Tanzania. Kwavi may be a dialect. Purko has 91% to 96% lexical similarity with other Kenya dialects, 82% with Baraguyu, 86% with Arusha in Tanzania, 77% to 89% with Samburu, 82% to 89% with Chamus, 60% with Ngasa (Ongamo). The Kore now speak Somali as first language. Semi-nomadic. VSO. Literacy rate in first language: Below 1%. Literacy rate in second language: 18%. Pastoralists: cattle, goats; agriculturalists. Traditional religion, Christian. Bible 1991.

MALAKOTE ***(ILWANA)*** [MLK] 8,000 (1994 I. Larsen BTL). Tana River north of Pokomo, between Bura and Garissa, Tana River District, Coast Province. Niger-Congo, Atlantic-Congo, Volta-Congo, Benue-Congo, Bantoid, Southern, Narrow Bantu, Central, E, Nyika (E.40), Malakote. Not intelligible with Upper Pokomo or Lower Pokomo. 57% lexical similarity with Lower Pokomo; 55% with Upper Pokomo. Cushitic influence. Literacy rate in first language: Below 1%. Literacy rate in second language: Below 5%. Agriculturalists, fishermen. Muslim.

MERU ***(KIMERU)*** [MER] 1,305,000 (1994 I. Larsen BTL), or 5.6% of the population including 540,000 Meru, 26,400 Igoji (1980 Berne and Mölig). Meru District, Eastern Province, northeast of Mt. Kenya. Niger-Congo, Atlantic-Congo, Volta-Congo, Benue-Congo, Bantoid, Southern, Narrow Bantu, Central, E, Kikuyu-Kamba (E.20), Meru. Dialects: MERU, IGEMBE, TIGANIA, IMENTI, MIUTINI, IGOJI. 85% lexical similarity between Imenti and Tigania. 67% similarity with Chuka, 63% with Embu and Gikuyu, 57% with Kamba. 'Mero' is not a correct spelling. Different from Meru (Rwo) of Tanzania. Literacy rate in first language: 5% to 10%. Literacy rate in second language: 25% to 50%. Traditional religion, Christian, Muslim. Bible 1964.

MWIMBI-MUTHAMBI [MWS] 70,000 (1980 SIL). Central Meru District, Eastern Province. Niger-Congo, Atlantic-Congo, Volta-Congo, Benue-Congo, Bantoid, Southern, Narrow Bantu, Central, E, Kikuyu-Kamba (E.20), Meru. Dialects: MWIMBI (KIMWIMBI), MUTHAMBI. People may be able to use Meru literature. Investigation needed: intelligibility, bilingual proficiency, attitudes toward Meru. Christian.

NUBI ***(KI-NUBI, KINUBI)*** [KCN] 10,000 in Kenya, including 3,000 to 6,000 in Kibera. Kibera, outside Nairobi. Creole, Arabic based. Formerly a soldier language, which split off from Sudanese Pidgin Arabic about 1900. There are conflicting reports of intelligibility with Sudanese Creole Arabic. 90% of the lexicon comes from Arabic. Speakers use Swahili for out-group communication and Nubi for in-group communication, with a stable bilingualism. 30% can also use English. Non-Nubi wives of Nubi men are expected to learn Nubi. Investigation needed: intelligibility with Sudanese Creole Arabic. Grammar. Literacy rate in first language: Below 1%. Literacy rate in second language: Below 5%. Muslim. See main entry under Uganda.

NYALA, EAST [NLE] 35,000 (1980 SIL). Lake Victoria area, Western Province. Niger-Congo, Atlantic-Congo, Volta-Congo, Benue-Congo, Bantoid, Southern, Narrow Bantu, Central, J, Masaba-Luyia (J.30), Luyia.

NYORE ***(OLUNYORE, LUNYORE, NYOLE, NYOOLE, LUNYOLE, OLUNYOLE)*** [NYD] 120,000 (1980 Heine and Möhlig). Above Kavirondo Gulf, Kakamega District, Western Province. Niger-Congo, Atlantic-Congo, Volta-Congo, Benue-Congo, Bantoid, Southern, Narrow Bantu, Central, J, Masaba-Luyia (J.30), Luyia. 61% lexical similarity with Nyole of Uganda. SVO. Christian. Bible, in press (1998).

OKIEK ***(AKIEK, "NDOROBO")*** [OKI] A few speakers out of an ethnic group of 20,000 in Kenya (1980 Heine and Möhlig). On East Mau Escarpment, Nakuru District, Rift Valley Province. Possibly in Tanzania. Nilo-Saharan, Eastern Sudanic, Nilotic, Southern, Kalenjin, Okiek. Dialects: SUIEI, SOGOO. People may be bilingual Nandi. Most or all "Ndorobo" are highly bilingual in an adopted language. "The language is remembered by a few old men married to Kikuyu women and living in Kikuyu communities" (Dimmendaal 1989). Some "Ndorobo" languages are nearly extinct. The Akiek in northern Tanzania now speak Maasai. The Akiek of Kinare in Kenya now speak Kikuyu. Those in Tanzania and Kenya are not in contact with each other. "Ndorobo" is a derogatory cover term for several small hunter or forest groups, not linguistically related (El Molo, Yaaku, Okiek, Omotik). Forest, mountain slope. Hunter-gatherers (formerly), beekeepers. Some Christian.

OMOTIK ***(LAAMOOT, "NDOROBO")*** [OMT] 50 or fewer (1980). 24,363 "Dorobo" (1989 census). Around Lolgorien, Lemek, and Entasekera, Narok District, Rift Valley Province. Nilo-Saharan, Eastern Sudanic, Nilotic, Southern, Tatoga. Dialect: SUIEI. 60% lexical similarity with Kalenjin, 50% with Datooga. The majority of ethnic group now speak Maasai. Most or all Ndorobo language speakers are highly bilingual in an adopted language. All over 40 years old (1980). "Ndorobo" is a derogatory cover term for several small hunter or forest groups, not linguistically related (El Molo, Yaaku, Okiek, Omotik). Some are nearly extinct. Investigation needed: bilingual proficiency in Kipsigis, Nandi. Traditional religion.

ORMA ***(UARDAI, WADAI, WARDAY, WARDEI)*** [ORC] 55,000 (1994 I. Larsen BTL), including 5,000 Munyo. Garissa and Tana River districts, Northeastern and Coast provinces. The Oromo spoken in the Lower Jubba Region of Somalia may actually be Orma. The Orma controlled that area until the mid or late 19th century. They move from the lower Tana River inland toward Kitui District during rainy season. Afro-Asiatic, Cushitic, East, Oromo. Dialects: MUNYO (KOROKORO, MUNYO YAYA), WAATA (SANYE), ORMA. A distinct language from Boran. Munyoyaya is an ethnic group speaking a dialect of Orma. Savannah, semi-arid. Orma: pastoralists: cattle, sheep, goats; Munyo: agriculturalists, fishermen. Muslim.

PANJABI, EASTERN ***(PUNJABI, GURMUKHI, GURUMUKHI)*** [PNJ] 10,000 in Kenya (1995 SIL). Nairobi. Indo-European, Indo-Iranian, Indo-Aryan, Central zone, Panjabi. Dialect: PANJABI PROPER. Most came to Kenya with the building of the railroad at the turn of the 20th century. Sikh, Hindu, Muslim. Bible 1959-1984. See main entry under India.

POKOMO, LOWER ***(KIPOKOMO, PFOKOMO, MALACHINI)*** [POJ] 29,000 (1994 I. Larsen BTL). Lower Tana River, Tana River District, Coast Province. Niger-Congo, Atlantic-Congo, Volta-Congo, Benue-Congo, Bantoid, Southern, Narrow Bantu, Central, E, Nyika (E.40), Pokomo. Dialects: MWINA, BUU I, BUU II, BUU III, KULESA, NGATANA, DZUNZA, KALINDI. 76% lexical similarity with Upper Pokomo, 63% with Mvita, 61% with Amu, 60% with Mrima, 59% with Giryama, 58% with Digo, 57% with Bajun. 75% of the speakers have some degree of bilingual proficiency in Swahili. Literacy rate in first language: Below 1%. Literacy rate in second language: 25% to 50%. Agriculturalists, fishermen. Traditional religion, Christian. NT 1902, out of print.

POKOMO, UPPER [PKB] 34,000 (1994 I. Larsen BTL), including 5,000 Malalulu, 6,000 Zubaki, 2,100 Ndura, 2,600 Kinakomba, 1,500 Gwano, 6,150 Ndera. Upper Tana River, Tana River District, Coast Province. Niger-Congo, Atlantic-Congo, Volta-Congo, Benue-Congo, Bantoid, Southern, Narrow Bantu, Central, E, Nyika (E.40), Pokomo. Dialects: MALALULU, ZUBAKI, NDURA, KINAKOMBA, GWANO, NDERA. Investigation needed: intelligibility with Lower Pokomo. Literacy rate in first language: Below 1%. Literacy rate in second language: 15% to 25%. Flood plain. Agriculturalists, fishermen. Mainly Muslim.

PÖKOOT ***(PÖKOT, SUK, PAKOT)*** [PKO] 264,000 in Kenya (1994 I. Larsen BTL). Population total both countries 264,000 or more. Baringo and West Pokot districts, Rift Valley Province. Also spoken in Uganda. Nilo-Saharan, Eastern Sudanic, Nilotic, Southern, Kalenjin, Pokot. Dialects: EAST POKOT, WEST POKOT. Semi-nomadic. Literacy rate in first language: Below 1%. Literacy rate in second language: 15% to 25%. Mountain slope, plains. Half pastoralists: cattle, sheep, goats; half agriculturalists. Traditional religion, Christian. NT 1967, in press (1996).

RENDILLE ***(RENDILE, RANDILE)*** [REL] 32,000 (1994 I. Larsen BTL). Marsabit District, between Lake Turkana and Marsabit Mt., Eastern Province. Afro-Asiatic, Cushitic, East, Rendille-Boni. Nomadic. The Ariaal Rendille people live in interdependent relationship with the Samburu and speak Samburu. SOV. Literacy rate in first language: Below 1%. Literacy rate in second language: 5% to 15%. Semi-arid desert. Pastoralists: camels, sheep, goats, cattle. Traditional religion, Muslim, Christian. Bible portions 1993.

SABAOT ***(MT. ELGON MAASAI)*** [SPY] 143,000 (1994 I. Larsen BTL). Mt. Elgon District, Western Province. Also Trans-Nzoia District in Rift Valley Province. Nilo-Saharan, Eastern Sudanic, Nilotic, Southern, Kalenjin, Elgon. Dialects: BONG'OMEEK (BONG'OM, PONG'OM), KOONY (KONY), BOOK (BOK, POK). Related to Sebei of Uganda. Bung'omek is being absorbed by Bukusu. Literacy rate in first language: Below 1%. Literacy rate in second language: 15% to 25%. Pastoralists: cattle; agriculturalists. Christian, traditional religion. NT 1998.

SAGALLA ***(KISAGALA, KISAGALLA, SAGALA, TERI, SAGHALA)*** [TGA] 10,000 (1980 Heine and Möhlig). Taita Hills, slopes of Sagala Hill, Taita District, Coast Province. Niger-Congo, Atlantic-Congo,

Volta-Congo, Benue-Congo, Bantoid, Southern, Narrow Bantu, Central, E, Nyika (E.40), Taita. Dialects: DAMBI, MUGANGE, TERI, KISHAMBA, GIMBA, KASIGAU. 62% lexical similarity with Taita. Distinct from Sagala of Tanzania. Literacy rate in first language: Below 1%. Literacy rate in second language: 15% to 25%. Traditional religion, Christian, Muslim. NT 1994.

SAMBURU ***(SAMBUR, SAMPUR, BURKENEJI, LOKOP, E LOKOP, NKUTUK)*** [SAQ] 147,000 (1994 I. Larsen BTL) including 128,000 Samburu, 19,000 Chamus. Samburu District, and south and east shores of Lake Baringo, Baringo District, Rift Valley Province (Chamus). Nilo-Saharan, Eastern Sudanic, Nilotic, Eastern, Lotuxo-Teso, Lotuxo-Maa, Ongamo-Maa. Dialect: CHAMUS (ILCAMUS, NJEMPS). 94% to 88% lexical similarity with Chamus, 89% to 77% with Maasai, 59% with Ngasa (Ongamo). Chamus has 82% with Maasai. The El Molo mainly speak Samburu now, a slightly different dialect. Nomadic. Literacy rate in first language: Below 1%. Literacy rate in second language: Samburu: 15% to 25%, Chamus: 41%. Pastoralists: cattle, goats, sheep. Samburu: traditional religion, Christian; Chamus: traditional religion, Christian.

SANYE ***(SANYA, WASANYE, ARIANGULU, LANGULO, WAATA, WAAT)*** [SSN] 5,000 (1980 SIL). Lower parts of Tana River, Lamu District, Coast Province. Afro-Asiatic, Cushitic, East, Oromo. They have maintained their language in spite of change in economy and pressure from other languages. Distinct language from Dahalo (Sanye) or Boni. Literacy rate in first language: Below 1%. Literacy rate in second language: 15% to 25%. Forest dwellers. Formerly hunter-gatherers, now agriculturalists. Largely Muslim, some Christian.

SOMALI ***(STANDARD SOMALI)*** [SOM] 312,339 in Kenya (1989 census), including 45,098 Somali, 27,244 Hawiyah, 100,400 Degodia,139,597 Ogaden (1989 census). Northeastern Province around Wajir. Afro-Asiatic, Cushitic, East, Somali. Dialects: DEGODIA, OGADEN. Dialect differences cut across clan differences. Daarood, Dir, Hawiye, Ogaadeen are clan families in Kenya. The people are nomadic. Investigation needed: intelligibility with dialects. Literacy rate in first language: Below 1%. Literacy rate in second language: Somali: 15% to 25%, Ogaadeen: 1%. Pastoralists: camel, sheep, goats. Muslim. Bible 1979. See main entry under Somalia.

SUBA [SUH] 129,000 in Kenya (1994 I. Larsen BTL), including 37,000 Mfangano, 32,000 Gwasi, 22,000 Kaksingri, 15,000 Muhuru, 10,000 Suna, 8,000 Wiregi, 5,000 Ungoe (1997). Population total both countries 159,000. Eastern shores of Lake Victoria, and Mfangano and Rusinga Islands. Also spoken in Tanzania. Niger-Congo, Atlantic-Congo, Volta-Congo, Benue-Congo, Bantoid, Southern, Narrow Bantu, Central, E, Kuria (E.10). Dialects: MFANGANO, GWASI, KAKSINGRI, MUHURU, SUNA, WIREGI, UNGOE. The majority use Luo as second language. Vigorous use of Suba in Kaksingiri and Mfangano Island. Literacy rate in first language: Below 1%. Literacy rate in second language: 25% to 50%. Bible portions 1993-1999.

SWAHILI ***(KISWAHELI, SUAHILI, KISUAHILI, ARAB-SWAHILI)*** [SWA] 131,000 in Kenya, including 66,000 Bajuni (1994 I. Larsen BTL), 6,000 Siyu, 3,000 Pate, 15,000 Amu, 25,000 to 30,000 Mvita, 13,900 Shirazi (1989 census), 2,000 Vumba (1980 Heine and Möhlig). Coast Province. Niger-Congo, Atlantic-Congo, Volta-Congo, Benue-Congo, Bantoid, Southern, Narrow Bantu, Central, G, Swahili (G.40). Dialects: AMU, MVITA (KIMVITA, MOMBASA), BAJUNI (BAJUN, T'IK'UU, TIKULU, TUKULU, GUNYA, MBALAZI, CHIMBALAZI), PATE, PEMBA (PHEMBA, HADIMU, TAMBATU), MRIMA, FUNDI, SIU (SIYU), SHAMBA (KISHAMBA), MATONDONI. The dialects listed are in Kenya. Bajuni is the most divergent. Bajuni and Pemba may be separate languages. Bajun has 85% lexical similarity with Amu, 78% with Mvita, 72% with Mrima; Mvita has 86% with Amu, 79% with Mrima; Mrima has 79% with Amu. Classical and modern literature. In the Mombasa area they call themselves 'Arab' or 'Shirazi', in Lamu area they call themselves 'Bajun'. Investigation needed: intelligibility with Bajun, Pemba. National language. Literacy rate in second language: 51%. Swahili is compulsory in primary education. Coastal, mountain valley. Traders, small businessmen; Bajun: fishermen, agriculturalists. Muslim. Bible 1891-1996. See main entry under Tanzania.

TAITA ***(DABIDA, DAVIDA, KIDABIDA, TEITA, KITAITA, DAWIDA)*** [DAV] 203,389 (1989 census). Taita hills, Taita District, Coast Province. Niger-Congo, Atlantic-Congo, Volta-Congo, Benue-Congo, Bantoid, Southern, Narrow Bantu, Central, E, Nyika (E.40), Taita. Dialects: MBOLOLO, WERUGHA, MBALE, CHAWIA, BURA, MWANDA. 62% lexical similarity with Sagalla, 46% with Gweno, 41% to 44% with Chagga. Speakers are highly bilingual in Swahili. Literacy rate in first language: 1% to 5%. Literacy rate in second language: 25% to 50%. Christian, traditional religion, Muslim. Bible, in press (1997).

TALAI ***(MARAKWET)*** [TLE] 25,000 to 30,000 (1987 estimate). Rift Valley Province. Nilo-Saharan, Eastern Sudanic, Nilotic, Southern, Kalenjin, Nandi-Markweta, Markweta. Low intelligibility with basic Kalenjin dialects and Endo. 'Marakwet' is a cover term for Talai and Endo. Literacy rate in first language: Below 1%. Literacy rate in second language: 15% to 25%. Traditional religion, Christian.

TAVETA ***(KITAVETA, KITUBETA, TUBETA)*** [TVS] 14,358 in Kenya (1989 census). Population total both countries 14,358 or more. Around Taveta in adjacent areas of Kenya and Tanzania. Taita

District, Coast Province. Also spoken in Tanzania. Niger-Congo, Atlantic-Congo, Volta-Congo, Benue-Congo, Bantoid, Southern, Narrow Bantu, Central, G, Shambala (G.20). Those younger than 30 years old in Kenya are highly bilingual in Swahili. Literacy rate in first language: 1% to 5%. Literacy rate in second language: 25% to 50%. Christian or more. NT 1906, out of print.

TESO ***(ATESO)*** [TEO] 217,000 in Kenya (1993 Johnstone). Busia District, Western Province. Nilo-Saharan, Eastern Sudanic, Nilotic, Eastern, Lotuxo-Teso, Teso-Turkana, Teso. Christian, traditional religion. Bible 1961. See main entry under Uganda.

THARAKA ***(KITHARAKA, SARAKA, SHAROKA)*** [THA] 112,000 (1994 I. Larsen BTL). Eastern Meru District, Embu District, and some in Kitui District, Eastern Province. Niger-Congo, Atlantic-Congo, Volta-Congo, Benue-Congo, Bantoid, Southern, Narrow Bantu, Central, E, Kikuyu-Kamba (E.20), Meru. Dialects: GATUE (NORTH THARAKA), THAGICHU (KITUI), NTUGI (CENTRAL THARAKA), THARAKA (SOUTH THARAKA). Thagichu dialect has extensive Kamba borrowings. Gatue dialect is influential. Difficult intelligibility with northern Meru dialects. Some Meru words have offensive meanings in Tharaka. Close to Chuka. English is used in schools and offices; Swahili in churches, schools, jobs, and sometimes in the home. Gikuyu and Meru also used. Older people's dialect is more prestigious because of lack of borrowings, but few people use it. Literacy rate in first language: Below 1%. Literacy rate in second language: 30% Swahili or English. Agriculturalists: millet, sorghum. Traditional religion, Christian. Bible portions 1934-1996.

TUGEN, NORTH ***(NORTH TUKEN, TUKEN)*** [TUY] 144,000 (1987 BTL). West central, west of the Kalenjin. Nilo-Saharan, Eastern Sudanic, Nilotic, Southern, Kalenjin, Nandi-Markweta, Nandi. People may not be able to use Kalenjin literature. Investigation needed: intelligibility, bilingual proficiency, attitudes toward Kalenjin. Traditional religion, Christian.

TURKANA ***(BUME, BUMA, TURKWANA)*** [TUV] 340,000 (1994 I. Larsen BTL). Turkana, Samburu, Trans-Nzoia, Laikipia, Isiolo districts, Rift Valley Province, west and south of Lake Turkana, and Turkwel and Kerio rivers. Nilo-Saharan, Eastern Sudanic, Nilotic, Eastern, Lotuxo-Teso, Teso-Turkana, Turkana. Dialects: NORTHERN TURKANA, SOUTHERN TURKANA. Inherently intelligible with Toposa, but hostile toward the speakers. Also partially intelligible with Karamojong, Jie, and Nyangatom, but all five are ethnically distinct. There are a few phonological, lexical, and discourse marker differences between them. Northern Turkana and Eastern Toposa are closer; Southern Turkana and Western Toposa are farther apart linguistically. The four varieties form a continuum divided in the middle by the Kenya-Sudan border. 85% lexical similarity with Karamojong, 76% with Teso. Most people are monolingual. Only a few adults have mastered upcountry Swahili as lingua franca. More are learning Swahili because of a new road. A few can speak Pokot or Daasenech. Vigorous. Hostile toward the Karamojong and Pokot; friendly with Jie. A few Somali and Gikuyu have shops in the area. VSO; highly inflectional; grammatical tone; vowel harmony; voiceless vowels. Literacy rate in first language: 5% to 10%. Literacy rate in second language: 25% to 50%. Semi-arid desert. Plains. Pastoralists (semi-nomadic): cattle, sheep, goats, camels, donkeys; fishermen. 1,200 to 6,000 feet. Traditional religion, Christian. Bible, in press (1998).

YAAKU ***(MUKOGODO, MOGOGODO, MUKOQUODO, SIEGU, YAAKUA, "NDOROBO")*** [MUU] 50 speakers out of 250 ethnic group (1983). Laikipia District, Mukogodo Division, Mukogodo Forest west of Doldol, foothills north of Mt. Kenya. Afro-Asiatic, Cushitic, East, Yaaku. Yaaku may be Konsoid, Dullay rather than Oromo. Most or all "Ndorobo" groups are highly bilingual in an adopted language. Yaaku not used in many domains. All over 40 years old (1983). Negative attitude toward Yaaku. "Ndorobo" is a derogatory cover term for several small hunter or forest groups, which are not linguistically related (El Molo, Yaaku, Okiek, Omotik). Forest. Hunter-gatherers, pastoralists. Christian. Nearly extinct.

LESOTHO

Kingdom of Lesotho. Formerly Basutoland. National or official languages: South Sotho, English. 2,062,000 (1998 UN). Literacy rate 59% to 74%. Also includes Afrikaans, Xhosa 18,000, Zulu 248,000, people from France, India, Pakistan. Information mainly from J. Bendor-Samuel 1989. Christian, traditional religion, Baha'i. Blind population 3,000 (1982 WCE). Deaf institutions: 1. Data accuracy estimate: B. The number of languages listed for Lesotho is 2. Of those, both are living languages. Diversity index 0.26.

ENGLISH [ENG] Indo-European, Germanic, West, English. Official language. Bible 1535-1989. See main entry under United Kingdom.

SOTHO, SOUTHERN ***(SUTO, SUTHU, SOUTO, SESOTHO, SISUTHO)*** [SSO] 1,493,000 in Lesotho (1993 Johnstone), 85% of the population. Population total all countries 4,197,000. Also spoken in Botswana, South Africa. Niger-Congo, Atlantic-Congo, Volta-Congo, Benue-Congo, Bantoid, Southern, Narrow

Bantu, Central, S, Sotho-Tswana (S.30), Sotho, Southern. National language. Christian, traditional religion. Bible 1878-1989.

LIBERIA

Republic of Liberia. National or official language: English. 2,666,000 (1998 UN). Literacy rate 25% (1989 WA). Also includes Kankan Maninka 33,800, people from Lebanon, elsewhere in West Africa. Information mainly from J. Bendor-Samuel 1989; TILL 1973-1998. Traditional religion, Muslim, Christian. Blind population 15,000 (1982 WCE). Deaf institutions: 1. Data accuracy estimate: A1, A2. The number of languages listed for Liberia is 29. Of those, all are living languages. Diversity index 0.91.

BANDI ***(BANDE, GBANDI, GBANDE, GBUNDE)*** [GBA] 70,800 in Liberia (1991 L. Vanderaa CRC). 50,000 have fled to Guinea (1993 Johnstone). Population total both countries 121,000. Lofa County, northwest Liberia. Also spoken in Guinea. Niger-Congo, Mande, Western, Central-Southwestern, Southwestern, Mende-Loma, Mende-Bandi, Bandi. Dialects: TAHAMBA, WAWANA, WULUKOHA, HASALA, LUKASA, HEMBEH. Tahamba dialect used for literature. 96% lexical similarity among the 6 dialects; 83% with the closest Mende dialect. Erroneously but often called 'Gbandi' or 'Gbande'. Grammar. Traditional religion, Muslim, Christian. Bible portions 1954-1995.

BASSA [BAS] 347,600 in Liberia (1991 L. Vanderaa). Population total both countries 353,000. Grand Bassa, Rivercess, and Montserrado counties, central Liberia. Gbii overlaps into Nimba County. Also spoken in Sierra Leone. Niger-Congo, Atlantic-Congo, Volta-Congo, Kru, Western, Bassa. Dialects: GBOR, GBA SOR, MABAHN, HWEN GBA KON, CENTRAL BASSA, RIVERCESS BASSA. Bilingualism in Liberian English. Different from Bassa of Nigeria or Bassa (Basaa) of Cameroon. SVO. Indigenous Vah script, developed around 1900 by Dr. Lewis, alphabetical, with tone marked, is still used by older men. Tropical forest. Hills, marshes. Agriculturalists: upland rice. Christian, traditional religion. NT 1970.

DAN ***(YACOUBA, YAKUBA, GIO, GYO, DA, GIO-DAN)*** [DAF] 150,800 to 200,000 in Liberia (1993 M. Bolli SIL). Nimba County, north central Liberia. Niger-Congo, Mande, Eastern, Southeastern, Guro-Tura, Tura-Dan-Mano, Tura-Dan. Dialects: UPPER GIO, LOWER GIO, RIVER CESS GIO. Speakers in Garplay understood Côte d'Ivoire Yacouba dialect tapes as follows: Danane, Koulinle, Kale: very well; Blosse: quite well; Bloundo: reasonably well; dialects east of Blouno: considerable difficulty (M. Bolli SIL 1971). Traditional religion. NT 1981-1993. See main entry under Côte d'Ivoire.

DEWOIN ***(DE, DEY, DEI, DEWOI)*** [DEE] 8,100 (1991 L. Vanderaa CRC). Montserrado County near the coast and Monrovia, primarily between the Lofa and St. Paul rivers. Niger-Congo, Atlantic-Congo, Volta-Congo, Kru, Western, Bassa. No significant dialect differences. 72% lexical similarity with Bassa. Many speak English. Many loans from other languages. Investigation needed: bilingual proficiency in Gola, Vai. Literacy rate in second language: 5%. Muslim, traditional religion, Christian.

ENGLISH [ENG] 69,000 or 2.5% of the population are Americo-Liberian (1993). Indo-European, Germanic, West, English. Dialect: LIBERIAN STANDARD ENGLISH. Official language. Bible 1535-1989. See main entry under United Kingdom.

GBII ***(GBI-DOWLU, GBEE)*** [GGB] 5,600 (1991 L. Vanderaa CRC). Nimba County, central Liberia, west of Cestos River. Niger-Congo, Atlantic-Congo, Volta-Congo, Kru, Western, Bassa. Dialects: KPLOR, DORBOR. 78% lexical similarity with Bassa. Many understand Bassa, but the reverse is not true. Many understand English. Liberian English is also used. Traditional religion.

GLARO-TWABO [GLR] Population total both countries 3,900 (1991). Grand Gedeh County, northeastern Liberia. Refugees in Côte d'Ivoire. Also spoken in Côte d'Ivoire. Niger-Congo, Atlantic-Congo, Volta-Congo, Kru, Western, Wee, Guere-Krahn. Dialects: GLARO, TWABO. Minimal intelligibility between Twabo and some Eastern Krahn dialects, but not between Glaro and Eastern Krahn. Glaro and Twabo have 87% lexical similarity. 82% lexical similarity with some Eastern Krahn dialects. Tropical forest. Traditional religion.

GLIO-OUBI ***(GLIO, OUBI, UBI)*** [OUB] 3,500 in Liberia (1991). Population total both countries 6,000. Northeast. Six towns on each side of the border. Also spoken in Côte d'Ivoire. Niger-Congo, Atlantic-Congo, Volta-Congo, Kru, Western, Grebo, Glio-Oubi. Closest lexical similarity is 75% with Twabo of Liberia and 73% with Trepo of Côte d'Ivoire. Called 'Glio' in Liberia and 'Oubi' in Côte d'Ivoire. Traditional religion.

GOLA [GOL] 99,300 in Liberia (1991 L. Vanderaa CRC). Population total both countries 107,300. Western Liberia, between the Mano and St. Paul rivers. Also spoken in Sierra Leone. Niger-Congo, Atlantic-Congo, Atlantic, Southern, Mel, Gola. Dialects: DENG (TODII), KONGBA, SENJE. Different from Gola of Nigeria or Gola (Badyara) of Guinea and Guinea-Bissau. SVO, tonal, CV. Mainly Muslim, Christian, traditional religion. Bible portions.

GREBO, BARCLAYVILLE ***(WEDEBO GREBO)*** [GRY] 23,700 (1991 L. Vanderaa CRC). 223,000 all Grebo languages in Liberia (1993 Johnstone). Grand Gedeh County. Southeast coast and inland, between Klao and Jabo Grebo. Niger-Congo, Atlantic-Congo, Volta-Congo, Kru, Western, Grebo, Liberian. Dialects: WEDEBO, KPLEBO. A dialect cluster. Dialects are quite distinct. Many phonological differences with Jabo, which would make literacy difficult if they were combined. They identify with Klao, but understand Grebo better. There are strong ethnocentric attitudes between subgroups. Traditional religion.

GREBO, CENTRAL [GRV] Eastern border, including Barrobo. Niger-Congo, Atlantic-Congo, Volta- Congo, Kru, Western, Grebo, Liberian. Dialects: GLOBO, NYENEBO, DOROBO, BOROBO, TREMBO. Distinct from Gboloo. Dialects may be quite distinct. Traditional religion.

GREBO, GBOLOO ***(GBOLOO, GBLOU GREBO)*** [GEC] 56,300 (1991 L. Vanderaa CRC). Eastern Province, Maryland County, eastern border, north of Jabo Grebo. Niger-Congo, Atlantic-Congo, Volta-Congo, Kru, Western, Grebo, Liberian. Dialects: GEDEROBO, NYANOUN, TUOBO, BIABO, DEDIEBO. Tropical forest. Traditional religion.

GREBO, NORTHERN [GRB] 84,500 (1999 LBT). Southeast, Grand Gedeh, Maryland, and Kru Coast counties near the Côte d'Ivoire border, south of Krahn, north of Klao, west of Glaro. Niger-Congo, Atlantic-Congo, Volta-Congo, Kru, Western, Grebo, Liberian. Dialects: CHEDEPO, E JE (EH JE), PALIPO, GBEPO (GBEAPO), JEDEPO, TIENPO, KLEPO, FOPO-BUA, NORTHEASTERN GREBO. Dialect cluster. Dialects are quite distinct. Subdialects of Northeastern dialect are Nitiabo, Sabo, Tuobo, Ketiepo, Webo. Ethnocentric attitudes are strong between different subgroups. Traditional religion. NT 1989.

GREBO, SOUTHERN [GRJ] 28,700 or more (1999 LBT). Population total both countries 28,700 or more. Eastern Province, Grand Gedeh and Maryland counties, southeastern coast and inland. Also spoken in Côte d'Ivoire. Niger-Congo, Atlantic-Congo, Volta-Congo, Kru, Western, Grebo, Liberian. Dialects: GLEBO (SEASIDE GREBO), JABO, NYABO, WRELPO. A dialect cluster. Dialects are quite distinct. Ethnocentric attitudes are strong between subgroups. Traditional religion.

KISI, SOUTHERN ***(KISSI, GIZI, GISI, KISSIEN)*** [KSS] 115,000 in Liberia (1995). Population total both countries 200,000. Lofa County, extreme northwest corner of Liberia. Also spoken in Sierra Leone. Niger-Congo, Atlantic-Congo, Atlantic, Southern, Mel, Bullom-Kissi, Kissi. Dialects: LUANGKORI, TENGIA, WARN. Different from Northern Kissi of Guinea. Literacy rate in second language: 20%. Traditional religion, Christian, Muslim. NT 1991.

KLAO ***(KRU, KROO, KLAOH, KLAU)*** [KLU] 184,000 in Liberia (1991 L. Vanderaa CRC). Population total all countries 192,000. Coastal and inland, Eastern Province. Also spoken in Ghana, Nigeria, Sierra Leone, USA. Niger-Congo, Atlantic-Congo, Volta-Congo, Kru, Western, Klao. Dialects: WESTERN KLAOH, WEST CENTRAL KLAOH, CENTRAL KLAOH, EASTERN KLAOH. SVO main clause; SOV embedded clause. Traditional religion. NT 1999.

KPELLE, LIBERIA ***(KPELE, GBESE, PESSA, PESSY, KPWESSI)*** [KPE] 487,400 (1991 L. Vanderaa CRC). Central. Niger-Congo, Mande, Western, Central-Southwestern, Southwestern, Kpelle. Dialect differences are slight. Different enough from Kpelle of Guinea to need separate literature. Largest group in Liberia. Traditional religion, Christian. NT 1967.

KRAHN, EASTERN [KQO] 47,000 (1991 L. Vanderaa CRC), including 20,000 Tchien (1992 UBS). Northeast near Côte d'Ivoire border. Niger-Congo, Atlantic-Congo, Volta-Congo, Kru, Western, Wee, Konobo. Dialects: GORBO, KANNEH, KONOBO, TCHIEN (CHIEHN). Minimal intelligibility between some dialects and Twabo. Gorbo and Kanneh have 93% lexical similarity with each other and 87% with Konobo. Traditional religion, Christian, Muslim. NT, in press (1996).

KRAHN, WESTERN ***(KRAHN, NORTHERN KRAHN)*** [KRW] 47,800 in Liberia (1991). Population total both countries 60,000. Near the border of Côte d'Ivoire, Grand Gedeh County. Also spoken in Côte d'Ivoire. Niger-Congo, Atlantic-Congo, Volta-Congo, Kru, Western, Wee, Guere-Krahn. Dialects: GBO, GBAESON (GBAISON, GBARZON), PLO, BIAI, GBARBO, GBORBO (GBOBO), KPEAPLY. Dialects in Côte d'Ivoire are Pewa, Biai. They have French influences. Dialects in Côte d'Ivoire have orthography differences from Liberia. Traditional religion, Christian, Muslim. NT 1992-1995.

KRUMEN, TEPO ***(SOUTHERN KRUMEN, KRUMEN, KROUMEN, KRU)*** [TED] Glawlo dialect is in southeastern Liberia. Other dialects are in southwestern Côte d'Ivoire. Niger-Congo, Atlantic-Congo, Volta-Congo, Kru, Western, Grebo, Ivorian. Dialects: TEPO, BAPO, PLAPO, WLOPO (ROPO), DAPO, HONPO, YREPO (KAPO), GLAWLO. Traditional religion. NT 1995. See main entry under Côte d'Ivoire.

KUWAA ***(KWAA, KOWAAO, BELLEH, BELLE)*** [BLH] 12,800 (1991 L. Vanderaa CRC). Lofa County, south of Bandi and Loma, north of Kpelle. Niger-Congo, Atlantic-Congo, Volta-Congo, Kru, Kuwaa. Only minor pronunciation differences exist between the two Kuwaa clans; Lubaisu and Gbade. Many of the Kuwaa also speak the nearby languages Bandi, Loma, and Kpelle. Literacy rate in second language: 5%. Traditional religion, Christian, Muslim. NT 1989.

LIBERIAN ENGLISH ***(LIBERIAN PIDGIN ENGLISH)*** [LIR] (1,500,000 second language users; 1984 census). Pidgin, English based, Atlantic. Dialect: KRU PIDGIN ENGLISH. Regional dialects. Used as a second language for communication between different language groups. As different from Standard English as is Sierra Leone Krio. Repidginized from American Black English of the 1800s (J. Holm). Trade language. Radio programs.

LOMA ***(LOOMA, LOGHOMA, LORMA, "BUZI", "BUSY", "BOUZE")*** [LOM] 141,800 (1991 L. Vanderaa CRC). Northwest Liberia Loffa County, border area. Niger-Congo, Mande, Western, Central-Southwestern, Southwestern, Mende-Loma, Loma. Dialects: GIZIMA, WUBOMEI, ZIEMA, BUNDE, BULUYIEMA. Distinct enough from Toma of Guinea to need separate literature. "Buzi" is an offensive name. Different from Loma of Côte d'Ivoire. Literature and literacy program in progress. Traditional religion, Christian. NT 1971.

MANO ***(MAA, MAH, MAWE)*** [MEV] 185,000 in Liberia (1995). Population total both countries 256,022. Nimba County, north central Liberia. Also spoken in Guinea. Niger-Congo, Mande, Eastern, Southeastern, Guro-Tura, Tura-Dan-Mano, Mano. Traditional religion, Christian. NT 1978.

MANYA ***(MANYA KAN, MANDINGO)*** [MZJ] 45,400 (1991 L. Vanderaa CRC). Population total both countries 70,400. Also spoken in Guinea. Niger-Congo, Mande, Western, Central-Southwestern, Central, Manding-Jogo, Manding-Vai, Manding-Mokole, Manding, Manding-East, Southeastern Manding. An indigenous Liberian language related to Maninka, but distinct. Muslim, Christian.

MENDE ***(BOUMPE, HULO, KOSSA, KOSSO)*** [MFY] 19,700 in Liberia (1991 L. Vanderaa CRC). Niger-Congo, Mande, Western, Central-Southwestern, Southwestern, Mende-Loma, Mende-Bandi, Mende-Loko. Muslim. Bible 1959. See main entry under Sierra Leone.

SAPO ***(SOUTHERN KRAHN, SARPO)*** [KRN] 31,600 (1991 L. Vanderaa CRC). Eastern, Sinoe County, and Grand-Gedeh County (Putu). Adjacent to Eastern Krahn, Tchien dialect. Niger-Congo, Atlantic-Congo, Volta-Congo, Kru, Western, Wee, Guere-Krahn. Dialects: NOMOPO (NIMPO), WAYA (WEDJAH), JUARZON, SINKON (SENKON), PUTU, KABADE (KARBARDAE). All Guéré and Sapo dialects are related by 84% to 97% lexical similarity, including some Guéré dialects in Côte d'Ivoire. Traditional religion, Christian. Bible portions 1956.

TAJUASOHN ***(TAJUOSOHN, TAJUOSO, TAJUASON)*** [KRU] 9,600 (1991 L. Vanderaa CRC). Sino County, north of Greenville. Niger-Congo, Atlantic-Congo, Volta-Congo, Kru, Western, Klao. Five clans speaking inherently intelligible dialects. Many can understand Klao, but the reverse is not true. Traditional religion.

VAI ***(VEI, VY, GALLINAS, GALLINES)*** [VAI] 89,500 in Liberia (1991). Population total both countries 105,000 (1991 L. Vanderaa CRC). Western. Also spoken in Sierra Leone. Niger-Congo, Mande, Western, Central-Southwestern, Central, Manding-Jogo, Manding-Vai, Vai-Kono. Not intelligible with Kono. 20% use English, 10% Mende, 5% Gola as second language. Grammar. SOV. Literacy rate in second language: 10%. Indigenous script; a syllabary invented by Duala Bukare in the 1820s or 1830s. Muslim, traditional religion, Christian. Bible portions 1995.

LIBYA

Socialist People's Libyan Arab Jamahiriya. al-Jamahiriyah al-Arabiya al-Libya al-Shabiya al-Ishtirakiya. National or official language: Standard Arabic. 5,339,000 (1998 UN). 500,000 resident foreign workers (1986 USA Today). Literacy rate 22% to 60%. Also includes Egyptian Spoken Arabic 1,000,000, Western Cham, Italian, Tedaga 2,000, Zaghawa 7,000, Many laborers from Sudan, North Africa, Chad, Korea, Pakistan, Bangladesh, Europe. Information mainly from J. Applegate 1970; D. Cohen 1985. Sunni Muslim, Christian, Buddhist. Deaf institutions: 2. Data accuracy estimate: B, C. The number of languages listed for Libya is 9. Of those, all are living languages. Diversity index 0.35.

ARABIC, LIBYAN SPOKEN ***(LIBYAN VERNACULAR ARABIC, SULAIMITIAN ARABIC)*** [AYL] 4,200,000 (1995), 96% of population (1991). Population total all countries 4,505,000. Especially in the northern half of Libya. Also spoken in Egypt, Niger. Afro-Asiatic, Semitic, Central, South, Arabic. Dialects: TRIPOLITANIAN ARABIC, SOUTHERN LIBYAN ARABIC, EASTERN LIBYAN ARABIC, NORTHEAST EGYPTIAN BEDAWI ARABIC. Similar to the bedouin Arabic of southern Tunisia. French is used as second language. 20% use Italian. Literacy rate in second language: 50%. Agriculturalists: wheat, barley, olives, citrus, dates, livestock. Sunni Muslim.

ARABIC, STANDARD [ABV] Afro-Asiatic, Semitic, Central, South, Arabic. Preserves ancient grammar. Used for nearly all written materials, formal speeches. Not a mother tongue, but taught in schools. National language. Bible 1984-1991. See main entry under Saudi Arabia.

AWJILAH ***(AUJILA, AUGILA, AOUDJILA)*** [AUJ] 2,000 (1993). Cyrenaica, eastern Libya. Afro-Asiatic, Berber, Eastern, Awjila-Sokna. Most men are bilingual in Libyan Spoken Arabic. Women are monolingual. The language may be extinct. They cultivate small gardens using subsoil water from 6 to 12 meters below the surface. Sunni Muslim.

DOMARI [RMT] Indo-European, Indo-Iranian, Indo-Aryan, Central zone, Dom. Dialect: HELEBI. Muslim. See main entry under Iran.

GHADAMÈS [GHA] 2,000 in Libya. Population total both countries 4,000. Ghadamès, a small oasis near the Algeria-Tunisia border. Also spoken in Tunisia. Afro-Asiatic, Berber, Northern, Zenati, East. Dialects: AYT WAZITEN, ELT ULID. Muslim.

LIBYAN SIGN LANGUAGE [LBS] Deaf sign language.

NAFUSI ***(DJERBI, NEFUSI, JABAL NAFUSI, JEBEL NEFUSI, JBEL NAFUSI)*** [JBN] 141,000 in Libya (1998). Population total both countries 167,000. Tripolitania, western Libya, isolated area around the towns of Nalut and Yafran, Jabal Nafusah region, coastal area around Zuara, west of Tripoli. Also spoken in Tunisia. Afro-Asiatic, Berber, Northern, Zenati, East. Dialects: ZUARA (ZOUARA, ZUWARAH, ZWARA, ZURAA), TAMEZRET (DUWINNA), JERBI (JERBA). Zuara dialect well known in Jebel Nafusa area and in Jerba Tunisia. Some visit Zuara, but not vice versa. Dialect of Matmata and Tatawine area less well understood by speakers in Jerba or Zuara. Speakers in Zuara and Jebel areas understand Jerba stories well. Pre-school children are monolingual in Nafusi. In Nafusi villages they speak Nafusi among themselves. In towns they speak it among friends and families, most exclusively at home. All ages. They are not ashamed of Nafusi. Most live apart from Arabized inhabitants of the region. They built dams and terraces for cultivation. Semi-arid. Ibadite Muslim.

SAWKNAH ***(SOKNA)*** [SWN] Tripolitania. Afro-Asiatic, Berber, Eastern, Awjila-Sokna. The language may be extinct. Muslim.

TAMAHAQ, TAHAGGART ***(TAMASHEKIN, TOURAGE, TOMACHEK, TAMACHEK, TUAREG, TOUREG)*** [THV] 17,000 in Libya (1993 Johnstone). The Hoggar dialect is in the south Hoggar (Ajjer) Mountain area around Tamanrasset and south into Niger. The Ghat dialect is in southeast Algeria around Ganet and west Libyan oases around Ghat. Afro-Asiatic, Berber, Tamasheq, Northern. Dialects: HOGGAR (AHAGGAREN, AJJER, TAHAGGART), GHAT (GANET, DJANET). 'Tuareg' are the people ('Targi' is the singular); 'Tamahaq' is the language. Volcanic mountains. Inadan: blacksmiths, jewelry craftsmen. Muslim. Bible portions 1948-1965. See main entry under Algeria.

MADAGASCAR

Democratic Republic of Madagascar. Repoblika Demokratika Malagasy. National or official languages: Malagasy, French. 15,057,000 (1998 UN). Literacy rate 46%. Also includes Makhuwa, Morisyen 4,000, Reunion Creole French 40,000, Arabic 20,000, Chinese 16,000. Information mainly from P. Verin, Kottak, and Gorlin 1969; A. Ramer 1995. Traditional religion, Christian, Muslim. Blind population 40,000 (1982 WCE). Deaf institutions: 2. Data accuracy estimate: B. The number of languages listed for Madagascar is 7. Of those, all are living languages. Diversity index 0.50.

BUSHI ***(SHIBUSHI, KIBUSHI, KIBUKI, SHIBUSHI SHIMAWORE, SAKALAVA, ANTALAOTRA)*** [BUC] 767,000 in Madagascar (1995). Population total both countries 806,200. Also spoken in Mayotte. Austronesian, Malayo-Polynesian, Western Malayo-Polynesian, Borneo, Barito, East, Malagasy. VOS.

COMORIAN ***(COMORES SWAHILI, KOMORO, COMORO)*** [SWB] 25,000 in Madagascar (1993 Johnstone). Niger-Congo, Atlantic-Congo, Volta-Congo, Benue-Congo, Bantoid, Southern, Narrow Bantu, Central, G, Swahili (G.40). Dialects: SHINZWANI (ANJOUAN), SHIMAORE (MAYOTTE). All dialects sufficiently distinct from mainland Swahili to warrant separate translation. Vanilla, perfume production. Muslim. NT 1995. See main entry under Comoros Islands.

FRENCH [FRN] 18,000 in Madagascar (1993 Johnstone). Indo-European, Italic, Romance, Italo-Western, Western, Gallo-Iberian, Gallo-Romance, Gallo-Rhaetian, Oïl, French. Official language. Bible 1530-1986. See main entry under France.

MALAGASY ***(MALGACHE, STANDARD MALAGASY)*** [MEX] 9,390,000 in Madagascar, including 3,200,000 Merina, 1,800,000 Betsimisaraka, 1,400,000 Betsileo, 635,000 Antandroy, 473,000 Tanala, 422,000 Antaimoro (1993 Johnstone). Population total all countries 9,398,700. The central part of the Island. Also spoken in Comoros Islands, Réunion. Austronesian, Malayo-Polynesian, Western Malayo-Polynesian, Borneo, Barito, East, Malagasy. Dialects: MERINA, TAISAKA (ANTAISAKA, TESAKA), TANOSY (ANTANOSY), TAIMANAMBONDRO (ANTAIMANAMBONDRO), SAHAFATRA, TAIFASY (TEFASY, ANTAIFASY), TAMBAHOAKA (ANTAMBAHOAKA), ZAFISORO, BETSIMISARAKA, SIHANAKA, BEZANOZANO (ANTAIVA, ANTANKA, TANKAY), TANALA (ANTANALA, MENABE-IKONGO), BARA, BETSILEO, VEZO, MAHAFALY, TAÑALAÑA, ANTANDROY 1 (TANDROY), ANTANDROY 2, TANKARANA, TAIMORO (ANTAIMORO, TEMORO). The closest language outside of Madagascar is Ma'anyan in south Borneo (Kalimantan, Indonesia). Loans from Bantu languages, Swahili, Arabic, English, French. National language. Dictionary. Grammar. VOS. The Merina dialect was the first to be written in Latin characters and it has become the literary dialect. Subsistence agriculturalists: coffee, cloves, vanilla, rice; perfume. Traditional religion, Christian, Muslim. Bible 1835-1938.

MALAGASY, ANTANKARANA ***(ANTANKARANA)*** [XMV] 88,000 or .637% of the population (1996). Northern tip, Antananarivo. Austronesian, Malayo-Polynesian, Western Malayo-Polynesian, Borneo, Barito, East, Malagasy. 71% lexical similarity with Merina. VOS. Subsistence agriculturalists.

MALAGASY, SOUTHERN [XMU] 2,606,000 or 18.802% of the population (1996). Southern tip. Austronesian, Malayo-Polynesian, Western Malayo-Polynesian, Borneo, Barito, East, Malagasy. 61% lexical similarity with Merina. VOS. Subsistence agriculturalists.

MALAGASY, TSIMEHETY ***(TSIMIHETY, TSIMIHETRY)*** [XMW] 1,016,000 or 7.33% of the population (1996). North central. Austronesian, Malayo-Polynesian, Western Malayo-Polynesian, Borneo, Barito, East, Malagasy. 68% lexical similarity with Merina. VOS. Subsistence agriculturalists. Bible portions 1924.

MALAWI

Republic of Malawi. Formerly Nyasaland. National or official languages: Nyanja (Chewa), Tumbuka, English. 10,346,000 (1998 UN). Literacy rate 25% to 41%. Also includes Bemba, Bengali, Fipa, Greek 2,000, Gujarati 5,000, Portuguese 9,000, Shona, Urdu. Information mainly from R. B. Boeder; Patai 1972; J. Bendor-Samuel 1989. Christian, Muslim, traditional religion. Blind population 18,000 (1982 WCE). Data accuracy estimate: A2, B. The number of languages listed for Malawi is 15. Of those, all are living languages. Diversity index 0.70.

AFRIKAANS [AFK] Indo-European, Germanic, West, Low Saxon-Low Franconian, Low Franconian. Spoken by people of Dutch descent from South Africa. Bible 1933-1983. See main entry under South Africa.

ENGLISH [ENG] 16,000 in Malawi (1993). Indo-European, Germanic, West, English. Official language. Bible 1535-1989. See main entry under United Kingdom.

KACHCHI ***(KATCHI, KACCHI, KACHI, CUCHI, CUTCH)*** [KFR] Indo-European, Indo-Iranian, Indo-Aryan, Northwestern zone, Sindhi. Spoken by the majority of Asians in Malawi. They have been here for many generations. Muslim. Bible portions 1834. See main entry under India.

KOKOLA ***(KOKHOLA)*** [KZN] 74,466 (1966 census). Population total both countries 75,000 or more. Southeastern border, south of Mlanje and Cholo, north of Chiromo. Also spoken in Mozambique. Niger-Congo, Atlantic-Congo, Volta-Congo, Benue-Congo, Bantoid, Southern, Narrow Bantu, Central, P, Makua (P.30). One source says they are a subgroup of Lolo, which is a subgroup of Lomwe. Most speakers use Chewa (Nyanja) as second language. Investigation needed: intelligibility with Lomwe.

LAMBYA ***(ICHILAMBYA, LAMBIA, LAMBWA, RAMBIA)*** [LAI] 41,000 in Malawi (1993 Johnstone). Northwestern tip, bordering Tanzania and Zambia. Niger-Congo, Atlantic-Congo, Volta-Congo, Benue-Congo, Bantoid, Southern, Narrow Bantu, Central, N, Tumbuka (N.20). Sukwa (1,000 to 3,000 in 1992) in the Sukwa Hills, northern Malawi, came from Tanzania, and may be intelligible with Lambya. See main entry under Tanzania.

LOMWE ***(NGULU, INGULU, NGURU, MIHAVANE, MIHAVANI, MIHAWANI, WESTERN MAKUA, ILOMWE, LOMUE, CHILOWE, LOLO)*** [NGL] 1,550,000 in Malawi (1993 Johnstone). Southeastern, south of Lake Kilwa, south of the Yao, northeast of the Sena. Niger-Congo, Atlantic-Congo, Volta-Congo, Benue-Congo, Bantoid, Southern, Narrow Bantu, Central, P, Makua (P.30). Bilingualism in Nyanja (Chewa). Different from Ngulu (Kingulu) of Tanzania. Traditional religion. NT 1930-1983. See main entry under Mozambique.

MPOTO ***(CHIMPOTO, KINYASA, NYASA)*** [MPA] 40,000 in Malawi (1993 Johnstone). Niger-Congo, Atlantic-Congo, Volta-Congo, Benue-Congo, Bantoid, Southern, Narrow Bantu, Central, N, Manda (N.10). Both Mpoto and Manda of Tanzania have alternate names of 'Nyasa'. May not be in Malawi, or may be an alternate name for another language. Investigation needed: intelligibility with Manda. Christian. Bible portions 1913-1924. See main entry under Tanzania.

NGONI ***(CHINGONI, KINGONI, ANGONI, KISUTU, SUTU)*** [NGU] Small remote pockets. Niger-Congo, Atlantic-Congo, Volta-Congo, Benue-Congo, Bantoid, Southern, Narrow Bantu, Central, N, Manda (N.10). Distinct from 'Ngoni', an alternate name for Zulu, the Ngoni dialect of Nsenga, the Ngoni dialect of Nyanja, or the Ngoni dialect of Tumbuka. Low lexical similarity percentage with Zulu. Most Ngoni people in Malawi speak Chewa or Tumbuka. Speakers formerly spoke Zulu. Muslim. Bible portions 1891-1898. See main entry under Tanzania.

NYAKYUSA-NGONDE ***(KINYAKYUSA, IKINYIKYUSA, NYEKYOSA, NGONDE, IKINGONDE, KONDE, NKONDE, NKHONDE, MOMBE, SOCHILE, SOKILE, KUKWE, NYAKUSA)*** [NYY] 300,000 Ngonde in Malawi (1993 Johnstone). Northern tip, south of the Lambya, west of Lake Malawi. Niger-Congo,

Atlantic-Congo, Volta-Congo, Benue-Congo, Bantoid, Southern, Narrow Bantu, Central, M, Nyakyusa (M.30). Dialects: NYAKYUSA, NKONDE. Bible 1993. See main entry under Tanzania.

NYANJA ***(CHINYANJA, CHEWA)*** [NYJ] 3,958,000 in Malawi (1993 Johnstone). Population total all countries 5,622,000 (1998). Including second language speakers: 6,000,000 (1999 WA). West central and southwestern. Also spoken in Botswana, Mozambique, Tanzania, Zambia, Zimbabwe. Niger-Congo, Atlantic-Congo, Volta-Congo, Benue-Congo, Bantoid, Southern, Narrow Bantu, Central, N, Nyanja (N.30). Dialects: CHEWA (CHICHEWA, CHEVA, SHEVA), NGONI, MANGANJA (WAGANGA, CIMANGANJA), NYASA, PETA (CIPETA, MARAVI, MARAVE, MALAWI). Most Ngoni in Malawi speak Chewa or Tumbuka. National language. Dictionary. Grammar. SVO. Traditional religion, Christian. Bible 1905, in press (1997).

SENA, MALAWI ***(CISENA, CHISENA)*** [SWK] 255,000 (1993 Johnstone). Southern tip bordering Mozambique. Niger-Congo, Atlantic-Congo, Volta-Congo, Benue-Congo, Bantoid, Southern, Narrow Bantu, Central, N, Senga-Sena (N.40), Sena. Different enough from Sena in Mozambique to require separate literature. Dialect or closely related language: ChiKunda.

TONGA ***(CHITONGA, SISKA, SISYA, WESTERN NYASA, KITONGA)*** [TOG] 220,000 (1993 Johnstone). North of Bandawe, west shore of Lake Malawi, Northern Province. Niger-Congo, Atlantic-Congo, Volta-Congo, Benue-Congo, Bantoid, Southern, Narrow Bantu, Central, N, Manda (N.10). Different from Chitonga of Zimbabwe and Zambia and GiTonga of Mozambique. Bible 1987.

TUMBUKA ***(TUMBOKA, CHITUMBUKA, TAMBOKA, TAMBUKA, TIMBUKA, TOMBUCAS)*** [TUW] 662,000 in Malawi (1993 Johnstone). Population total all countries 2,000,000 (1999 WA). Northern Province, west shore of Lake Malawi, south of the Ngonde, north of the Tonga and Ngoni. Also spoken in Tanzania, Zambia. Niger-Congo, Atlantic-Congo, Volta-Congo, Benue-Congo, Bantoid, Southern, Narrow Bantu, Central, N, Tumbuka (N.20). Dialects: CHITUMBUKA, CHIKAMANGA (KAMANGA, HENGA), NENYA, POKA (CHIPOKA, PHOKA), YOMBE, SENGA, NTHALI, FUNGWE, WENYA, HEWE (HEWA). Most Ngoni in Malawi speak Tumbuka or Chewa. Kandawire and Fulirwa are clans, not dialects. National language. Christian, some traditional religion. Bible 1957-1980.

YAO ***(CHIYAO, ACHAWA, ADSAWA, ADSOA, AJAWA, AYAWA, AYO, AYAO, DJAO, HAIAO, HIAO, HYAO, JAO, VEIAO, WAJAO)*** [YAO] 1,003,000 in Malawi (1993 Johnstone). Population total all countries 1,597,000. Around the southeastern tip of Lake Malawi, bordering Mozambique. Also possibly in Zimbabwe. Also spoken in Mozambique, Tanzania, Zambia. Niger-Congo, Atlantic-Congo, Volta-Congo, Benue-Congo, Bantoid, Southern, Narrow Bantu, Central, P, Yao (P.20). Dialect: MANGOCHE. Literacy rate in first language: 5%. Literacy rate in second language: 60% Chewa, 30% Arabic. Yao in Tanzania use a different orthography than Malawi. Muslim, Christian, traditional religion. Bible 1920.

ZULU ***(NGONI, KINGONI, ISIZULU, ZUNDA)*** [ZUU] 37,480 in Malawi (1966 census). Niger-Congo, Atlantic-Congo, Volta-Congo, Benue-Congo, Bantoid, Southern, Narrow Bantu, Central, S, Nguni (S.40). Ngoni is a dialect of Zulu or Swazi spoken in Malawi. 'Ngoni' also used as an alternate name for Chichewa and possibly for Matengo. Bible 1883-1959. See main entry under South Africa.

MALI

Republic of Mali. République du Mali. Formerly French Sudan. National or official languages: Bamanankan, Bomu, Bozo, Dogoso, Fulfulde, Hasanya, Mamara, Maninkakan, Songhay, Soninke, Syenara, Tamasheq, Xaasongaxanno, French. 10,694,000 (1998 UN). Literacy rate Men 26.64%, women 11.35% (1987). Also includes North Levantine Spoken Arabic, Koromfe, Matya Samo, Siamou 20,000, Wolof. Information mainly from G. Manessy 1961, 1975, 1981; J. Capron 1973; R. Nicolai 1979, 1981, 1983; J. Bendor-Samuel 1989. Muslim, traditional religion, Christian. Blind population 110,000 (1982 WCE). Data accuracy estimate: A2, B. The number of languages listed for Mali is 40. Of those, all are living languages. Diversity index 0.86.

ARABIC, HASANYA ***(MAURE, MAURI, MOOR, SURAKA, SURAXXÉ, HASSANIYYA, HASSANI)*** [MEY] 106,100 in Mali (1991). Nioro and Nara. Afro-Asiatic, Semitic, Central, South, Arabic. 5,000 ethnic Fulani refugees from Mauritania are reported to be Hassaniyya speakers. Speakers are called 'Maures' ('Moors'). The 'Nemadi' are an ethnic group that speaks Hasanya, and do not have their own language. National language. Radio programs. Muslim. See main entry under Mauritania.

BAMAKO SIGN LANGUAGE [BOG] Bamako school for deaf children, separated into 3 grade classes. It is not known if it is widely used elsewhere or not. Deaf sign language. Not related to other sign languages. They have some knowledge of French, and possibly Bambara. 6 to 50 years old. Some hearing people use it to communicate with deaf people. Another community of deaf people in Bamako use a West African variety of American Sign Language. Dictionary.

BAMANANKAN ***(BAMBARA, BAMANAKAN)*** [BRA] 2,700,000 in Mali (1995), including 75,000 Gan (1991 Vanderaa), 41,200 Wasulu (1991 Vanderaa). Population total all countries 2,777,400 or more. Also spoken in Burkina Faso, Côte d'Ivoire, Gambia, Guinea, Mauritania, Senegal. Niger-Congo, Mande, Western, Central-Southwestern, Central, Manding-Jogo, Manding-Vai, Manding-Mokole, Manding, Manding-East, Northeastern Manding, Bamana. Dialects: STANDARD BAMBARA, SOMONO, SEGOU, SAN, BELEDUGU, GANADUGU, WASULU (WASUU, WASSULUNKA, WASSULUNKE), SIKASSO. There are many local dialects. The main division is Standard Bambara, influenced heavily by Maninka, and rural dialects. Bamanankan dialects are spoken in varying degrees by 80% of the population. Wasulu is a dialect of Bamanankan in Mali, but of Western Maninka in Guinea. Used for adult education. Wasulu are former Fulbe. National language. Dictionary. Grammar. Radio programs. Muslim, traditional religion, Christian. Bible 1961-1987.

BANKAGOMA ***(BANKA)*** [BXW] 5,085 (1995 SIL). North of Sikasso in Danderesso Administrative District, towns of Nougoussouala (Nonko), Fourouma, Mamarasso (Mora), Famsara, and Zantiguila. Niger-Congo, Mande, Western, Northwestern, Samogo, Dzuun-Seeku, Banka. Bilingualism in Bambara. Spoken by children and adults as first language. Bankagoma is no longer spoken in Bambadougou (Faijanta), Nyaradougou (Jaata), Samogossoni, and possibly other towns, where the people now speak Bambara.

BOBO MADARÉ, NORTHERN ***(BOBO FING, BOBO FIGN, BOBO FI, BOBO, BLACK BOBO, FINNG, BOBO DA)*** [BBO] 15,000 to 20,000 in Mali (1995 SIL). An approximate rectangle in Mali around Bura and Mafune. Niger-Congo, Mande, Western, Northwestern, Samogo, Soninke-Bobo, Bobo. Dialects: BENGE, SOGOKIRI, SYA (SIA), VORE. Different from other Mande languages, particularly in the plural system. Separate literature may be needed for the Mali dialect. Some linguists treat Bobo as a separate major branch of Mande. Sya is the prestige dialect, and used for literature. Bilingualism in Jula, French. The term 'Bobo' has been carelessly applied to the Bwa people or their languages Bwamu and Boomu. The Bambara names 'Black Bobo' (Bobo Fing) and 'Red Bobo' (Bobo Oule for Bwamu and Bomu) only add confusion. Grammar. Traditional religion, Muslim. See main entry under Burkina Faso.

BOMU ***(BOOMU, BORE, WESTERN BOBO OULE, WESTERN RED BOBO, WESTERN BWAMU, BOBO WULE)*** [BMQ] 102,000 in Mali (1976 census). Population total both countries 158,000. A triangle between San and Sofara on the Bani River in Mali, and Soumbara, west of Nouna, in Burkina Faso. The Mao subdialect is separate from the others and straddles the Mali-Burkina Faso border about 40 kms. east-west by 20 kms. north-south, and is on the main San to the Bobo-Dioulasso road. Also spoken in Burkina Faso. Niger-Congo, Atlantic-Congo, Volta-Congo, North, Gur, Central, Northern, Bwamu. Dialects: DWEMU, DAHANMU. Dwemu subdialects are Terekongo (Terekoungo), Wahu (between Téné and the Bani River), Togo. Dahanmu subdialects are Koniko, Mandiakuy, Bomborokuy, Mao (Mahou). 'Bomu' is the official spelling. The people call themselves 'Bo' (sg.), 'Bwa' (pl.), and their language 'Bomu' or 'Boré'. The so-called 'Bobo Gbe (White Bobo, Kyan, Tian, Tyan)' were a mistakenly identified group of Bwa. Investigation needed: intelligibility with Mao dialect. National language. Traditional religion. Bible, in press (1999).

BOZO, HAINYAXO ***(HAINYAXO, HANYAXO, XANYAXO, XAN, HAIN, KELENGA, KÉLINGA, KÉLLINGUA, BOSO)*** [BZX] (117,696 all mother tongue Boso speakers; 1987 census). From Miérou (near Ke-Maacina) to Tamani on the Niger River. They can be found working the major rivers in much of West Africa. Niger-Congo, Mande, Western, Northwestern, Samogo, Soninke-Bobo, Soninke-Boso, Boso, Eastern. 48% lexical similarity with Tieyaxo Boso (closest). Bilingualism in Bambara. All Bozo speakers 6 years and older (1987). They call themselves 'Hain' (Xan; sg.) and their language 'Hainyaxo'. They accept the Bambara term 'Boso' to refer to all ethnic Boso. National language. Fishermen. Muslim.

BOZO, SOROGAMA ***(SOROGAMA, COROGAMA, SORKO, SARKANCI, SARKAWA, JENAMA, NONONKE, BOSO)*** [BZE] 100,000 (1991 Vanderaa). Population total both countries 100,000 or more. Administrative circles of Djenné and Mopti. Between the Bani and Niger rivers (Pondori dialects), between the Diaka and Niger rivers (Kotya dialect), along the Niger River from Mopti to Lake Débo (Kouakourou and Débo dialects). Some in Côte d'Ivoire around the Ayamé, Kosson, and Ayamé dams. Also spoken in Nigeria. Niger-Congo, Mande, Western, Northwestern, Samogo, Soninke-Bobo, Soninke-Boso, Boso, Sorogama. Dialects: NORTHERN PONDORI (JANAMA), SOUTHERN PONDORI (JANAMA), KOTYA (KOTYAXO), NORTHERN KORONDOUGOU, SOUTHERN KORONDOUGOU, DÉBO. 53% lexical similarity with Tieyaxo Boso (closest). Speakers of the northern dialects are somewhat bilingual in Songai and Fulfulde; of the southern dialects in Bambara. Some ethnic Marka and Somono live among them and speak Sorogama as mother tongue. They call themselves 'Sorogo' (sg.), 'Sorogoye' (pl.), and their language 'Sorogama'. They accept the Bambara term 'Boso' to refer to the entire ethnic group. National language. Fishermen (traditionally), sedentary agriculturalists. Muslim.

BOZO, TIÈMA CIÈWÈ ***(TIÈMA CIÈWÈ, TIÉ, BOSO)*** [BOO] 2,500 including 831 in Enguem, 1,315 in Aouré (1991). Administrative circle of Youwarou, Arrondissement Guidio Saré; Enghem (Enguem), Aouré (Aoré), and Kamago Sébi villages, where the Niger River leaves Lake Debo. Niger-Congo, Mande, Western, Northwestern, Samogo, Soninke-Bobo, Soninke-Boso, Boso, Eastern. 60% lexical similarity with Tieyaxo Boso. Bilingualism in Fulfulde, Songai. They call themselves 'Tié' (sg.) and their language 'Tièma Cèwè'. The Bambara term 'Boso' is accepted to refer to the entire ethnic group. Investigation needed: bilingual proficiency in Fulfulde, Songai. National language. Fishermen. Muslim.

BOZO, TIÉYAXO ***(TIEYAXO, TIGEMAXO, TIEMAXO, TYEYAXO, TIÉYAKHO, TIGUÉMAKHO, TIE, TÉGUÉ, BOSO)*** [BOZ] (117,696 all mother tongue Boso speakers; 1987 census). From Koa to Miérou on the Niger River, and Diafarabié to Sendédaga on the Diaka River (a tributary). They work the major rivers in much of West Africa. Niger-Congo, Mande, Western, Northwestern, Samogo, Soninke-Bobo, Soninke-Boso, Boso, Eastern. 53% lexical similarity with Sorogama Boso (closest), 30% with Soninke. Some of the people are bilingual in Bambara or Fulfulde, depending on the region. 6 years and older (1987). Some ethnic Marka and Somono live among them and speak Tiéyaxo as their mother tongue. They call themselves 'Tié' (sg.), 'Tieye' (pl.), and their language 'Tiéyaxo'. The term 'Boso' (Bambara term meaning 'house of bamboo') is accepted to refer to their ethnic group. National language. Swamp. Fishermen. Muslim.

DOGON ***(DOGOSO)*** [DOG] 462,000 in Mali (1995). Population total both countries 600,000 (1995 V. Plungian). Around Bandiagara, southern edge of the Sahara. Also spoken in Burkina Faso. Niger-Congo, Atlantic-Congo, Volta-Congo, Dogon. Dialects: TOROSO, TOMBO (TOMMO-SO), JAMSAI, BANKASA. Not close to other languages. More than 15 'dialects', most inherently unintelligible to each others' speakers, especially Jamsai and Bankasa. Different from Dogoso [DGS] and Dogosé [DOS] in Burkina Faso. Cliff dwellers. Investigation needed: intelligibility with Dogon varieties. National language. Radio programs. Agriculturalists. Traditional religion, Muslim, Christian. NT 1957-1994.

DUUNGOMA ***(SAMOGHO, SAMOGO, SAMORO, DU, MALI DUUN, DUUNGO, WESTERN DUUN)*** [DUX] 70,000 (1991 Vanderaa). 3rd Region (Sikasso), Circles of Kadiolo and Sikasso. The Mali dialect has over 40,000, with Kai the largest town. Niger-Congo, Mande, Western, Northwestern, Samogo, Dzuun-Seeku, Dzuun. Nearly everyone can speak Bambara. Students also speak French. 'Samogho' is the ethnic name used in Bambara, and is a cover term to include Duungoma, Bankagoma, and Jowulu speakers. Muslim, traditional religion.

FRENCH [FRN] 9,000 in Mali (1993 Johnstone). Indo-European, Italic, Romance, Italo-Western, Western, Gallo-Iberian, Gallo-Romance, Gallo-Rhaetian, Oïl, French. Official language for instruction in schools. Official language. Bible 1530-1986. See main entry under France.

FULFULDE, MAASINA ***(PEUL, MACINA)*** [FUL] 911,200 in Mali (1991). Population total all countries 919,700. Central Mali. The western dialect is spoken around Segou and Macina. The eastern dialect is spoken from north of Mopti to Timbuctou. Also spoken in Côte d'Ivoire, Ghana. Niger-Congo, Atlantic-Congo, Atlantic, Northern, Senegambian, Fula-Wolof, Fulani, West Central. Dialects: WESTERN MACINA, EASTERN MACINA. There are some dialect differences, but popular opinion is that all dialects in Mali are inherently intelligible. Substantial Bambara influence. There is skewing between the ethnic and linguistic relationships. Bilingualism in Bambara. Maasina in Mali is a major Fula geo-political state. The people are called 'Fulbe' in English, the language 'Peul' or 'Toucouleur' in French, 'Fulani' in English. National language. Dictionary. Grammar. Pastoralists. Muslim, Christian. Bible portions 1934.

FUUTA JALON ***(FUTA JALLON, FOUTA DYALON, FULFULDE JALON, FULLO FUUTA, FUTA FULA, FOULA FOUTA)*** [FUF] 50,000 in Mali (1991). Western Mali from Guinea up to about Keniéba, especially in the administrative arrondissements of Faléa and Faraba. Niger-Congo, Atlantic-Congo, Atlantic, Northern, Senegambian, Fula-Wolof, Fulani, West Central. Mali variety is completely intelligible with variety in Guinea. Muslim. Bible portions 1929-1975. See main entry under Guinea.

JAHANKA ***(JAHANQUE, JAHONQUE, DIAKKANKE, DIAKHANKE, DYAKANKE)*** [JAD] Kotema and Niebore villages, near the Guinea border. Possibly more villages farther east. Niger-Congo, Mande, Western, Central-Southwestern, Central, Manding-Jogo, Manding-Vai, Manding-Mokole, Manding. Jahanka in Gambia may be the same as this, or a dialect of Western Maninka. Jahanka in Senegal and Guinea-Bissau is a dialect of Western Maninka. 75% lexical similarity with Mandinka. They are reported to have originated in Mali. They trace their origins to Soninke, but now speak a separate language. Arabic script. Muslim. See main entry under Guinea.

JALUNGA ***(YALUNKA, DJALLONKE, DYALONKE, DIALONKE, JALONKE, YALUNKE)*** [YAL] 10,000 in Mali (1991). Extreme southwest corner along the Guinea border, Faleya region, to where the Baafing River comes to the Mali-Guinea border. Niger-Congo, Mande, Western, Central-Southwestern, Central,

Susu-Yalunka. Close to Susu, but only marginally intelligible. Muslim. NT 1976. See main entry under Guinea.

JOWULU ***(JO, SAMOGHO)*** [JOW] 9,100 (1991). Population total both countries 9,100 or more. 3rd Region, Circle of Kadiolo, Arrondissement of Loulouni. Also spoken in Burkina Faso. Niger-Congo, Mande, Western, Northwestern, Samogo, Dzuun-Seeku, Dzuun. Not closely related to Duungo. The men speak Bambara fairly well. The few who have been to school speak and read French. The name of the language is 'Jowulu', of the people 'Jotoni'. 'Samogho' is a cover term including the Duungo, Samo, Jowulu languages and possibly others. Traditional religion.

JULA ***(DYOULA, DIULA, DIOULA, DJULA, DYULA)*** [DYU] 50,000 in Mali (1991). Niger-Congo, Mande, Western, Central-Southwestern, Central, Manding-Jogo, Manding-Vai, Manding-Mokole, Manding, Manding-East, Northeastern Manding, Bamana. Dialects: MALINKE, KONG JULA. Trade language. Muslim. NT 1994. See main entry under Burkina Faso.

KAGORO ***(KAKOLO)*** [XKG] 15,000 speakers (1998 Valentin Vydrine) out of an ethnic group of 21,500 (1991 Vanderaa). Kaarta-Bine and Gumbu regions, about 70 ethnic Kagoro villages (Vydrine 1998). Niger-Congo, Mande, Western, Central-Southwestern, Central, Manding-Jogo, Manding-Vai, Manding-Mokole, Manding, Manding-West. Close to Khasonke. Bamanankan speakers have poor understanding of Kagoro. 86% lexical similarity with Kita Maninka. Most can use Bamanankan, Soninke, or Hasanya as second language (1998 Vydrine). Being replaced by Bambara. Kagoro now spoken only in a few corners of Kaarta. Some lexical influence from Soninke. Recent heavy Bambara influence. Investigation needed: intelligibility. Muslim (most), traditional religion.

MANINKAKAN, KITA ***(MALINKE, KITA MANINKA)*** [MWK] 200,000 (1998). Kita area. Niger-Congo, Mande, Western, Central-Southwestern, Central, Manding-Jogo, Manding-Vai, Manding-Mokole, Manding, Manding-West. Kita speakers have 64% intelligibility of Bambara. Investigation needed: intelligibility, attitudes toward Kangaba area, Kankan Maninkakan, Bamanankan. Grammar. Muslim.

MANINKAKAN, WESTERN ***(NORTHWESTERN MANINKA, MALINKE, MALINKA)*** [MLQ] 626,800 in Mali (1993 Johnstone), including 50,000 Fulanke (1991 Vanderaa). Population total all countries 967,000 or more. Borders of Mali and Guinea. Also spoken in Gambia, Guinea, Guinea-Bissau, Senegal. Niger-Congo, Mande, Western, Central-Southwestern, Central, Manding-Jogo, Manding-Vai, Manding-Mokole, Manding, Manding-West. Dialects: FULANKE, KENIEBA MANINKA, NYOXOLONKAN. 59% lexical similarity with Mandinka of Gambia and Senegal. The Fulanke live in the Kita area and have a Fulbe background. Investigation needed: intelligibility with dialects, attitudes. National language. Grammar. Muslim, traditional religion, Christian.

MARKA ***(MARKA-DAFIN, DAFING, MEKA)*** [MWR] 25,000 in Mali (1991). Around the villages of Koula, Diarani, Yelené, Kuna; Dialassagou, Ouenkoro, Bai. Niger-Congo, Mande, Western, Central-Southwestern, Central, Manding-Jogo, Manding-Vai, Manding-Mokole, Manding, Manding-East, Marka-Dafin. Most Pana people also speak Marka-Dafin very well. 'Marka' is used for followers of the traditional religion, 'Dafing' for Muslim speakers. Different from the Marka name for Soninke, and the Marka-Jalan who speak the San dialect of Bamanankan. Grammar. SOV; postpositions; genitives, articles, adjectives, numerals, relatives after noun heads; question word final; word order distinguishes subject, object, indirect object; CV. Traditional religion, Muslim, Christian. Bible portions. See main entry under Burkina Faso.

MÒORÉ ***(MORE, MOLE, MOSSI, MOSHI)*** [MHM] 17,000 in Mali (1980). Some villages in the Dogon area near the Burkina Faso border, and elsewhere. Niger-Congo, Atlantic-Congo, Volta-Congo, North, Gur, Central, Northern, Oti-Volta, Western, Northwest. Speakers came into Mali from Burkina Faso during the colonial period. Traditional religion, Muslim. Bible 1983, in press (1998). See main entry under Burkina Faso.

PANA ***(SAMA)*** [PNQ] 2,800 in Mali (1982 SIL). South of Bandiagara, straddling the Mali-Burkina Faso border east of the Sourou River, due north of Kassoum in Burkina Faso. Niger-Congo, Atlantic-Congo, Volta-Congo, North, Gur, Central, Southern, Grusi, Northern. Dialects: PANA NORTH, PANA SOUTH. They are reported to be bilingual in Jula. Speakers are favorable toward using Marka-Dafin, Jula, or Bamanankan. The people call themselves and their language 'Pana'. See main entry under Burkina Faso.

PULAAR ***(PULAAR FULFULDE, PEUL, PEUHL)*** [FUC] 175,000 in Mali, including 40,000 Fulbe Jeeri (1995). Settled primarily around Bandiagara and Ségou. Niger-Congo, Atlantic-Congo, Atlantic, Northern, Senegambian, Fula-Wolof, Fulani, Western. Dialect: TOUCOULEUR (TUKOLOR, TUKULOR, PULAAR, HALPULAAR, HAALPULAAR, FULBE JEERI). Related to Maasina Fulfulde but distinct. Fulbe Jeeri is an ethnic group which speaks this language as mother tongue. Muslim. NT 1997. See main entry under Senegal.

SÀMÒMÁ ***(KALAMSÉ, KALEMSÉ, KALENGA, SÀMÓ)*** [KNZ] Lògrèmmá dialect spoken in at least six villages in Mali: Dian, Sougou, Zon, Ponghon, Gako, Soyma. Niger-Congo, Atlantic-Congo, Volta- Congo, North, Gur, Central, Southern, Grusi, Northern. Dialect: LOGREMMA (LOGMA, WEST KALAMSÉ).

Several Mali villages have given up Sàmòmá in favor of Dogon. Speakers call their language 'Sàmòmá' and themselves 'Sàmó' (sg.) or 'Sàmóyá' (pl.). Different from other languages called 'Samo'. Traditional religion, Muslim, Christian. See main entry under Burkina Faso.

SENOUFO, MAMARA ***(MINIYANKA, MINYA, MIANKA, MINIANKA, MAMARA, TUPIIRE)*** [MYK] 500,000 to 900,000 (1999 SIL). Niger-Congo, Atlantic-Congo, Volta-Congo, North, Gur, Senufo, Suppire-Mamara. Dialects: SÕGHOO, BÀJII, NAFÃÃ, MÌJUU, KLE NOEHMÕ, NEJUU, KOLOO, KUJAA, SUÕÕ. Close to Supyire Senoufo, but intercomprehension is difficult. Bilingualism in Bambara. Their name for themselves is 'Bamana', but this is different from the Bambara dialect called 'Bamana'. National language. Grammar. Traditional religion, Muslim, Christian. Bible portions 1967-1975.

SÉNOUFO, SÌCÌTÉ ***(SÌCÌTÉ, SÌPÌÌTÉ, SÌCÌRÉ, SUCITE, TAGBA)*** [SEP] Villages of Bakoronidougou, Gouaniéresso Finkolo-Zanso, and Missidougou, east of Sikasso near the Burkina Faso border. Niger-Congo, Atlantic-Congo, Volta-Congo, North, Gur, Senufo, Suppire-Mamara. Difficult intelligibility with Nanerige. They call their language 'Sénoufo Sìcìté', themselves 'Sìcijuubíí' (pl.), or 'Sìcijuungé' (sg.), and their region 'Tagba'. 'Tagba' is used by outsiders for them. Little intermarriage with others in the southern area. Scrub forest, gallery forest. Plateau, interfluvial. Swidden agriculturalists. Traditional religion, Muslim. Bible portions 1995. See main entry under Burkina Faso.

SENOUFO, SUPYIRE ***(SUPYIRE, SUP'IDE, SUPPIRE)*** [SPP] 364,000 (1991). At Sikasso. Niger-Congo, Atlantic-Congo, Volta-Congo, North, Gur, Senufo, Suppire-Mamara. Traditional religion, Muslim. Bible portions 1979-1998.

SENOUFO, SYENARA ***(SYENARA, SHENARA, SENARE,SENARI)*** [SHZ] 136,500 (1991 Vanderaa). South of the Duun language area. Niger-Congo, Atlantic-Congo, Volta-Congo, North, Gur, Senufo, Senari. Investigation needed: intelligibility with Senoufo. Traditional religion, Muslim.

SONGHAY, HUMBURI SENNI ***(SONGHAI, SONGAI, SONGAY, SONGOI, SONGOY, SONGHOY, SONRAI, SONRHAI, CENTRAL SONGAI, HOMBORI SONGHAY)*** [HMB] 15,000 in Mali (1999 J. Heath). Population total both countries 140,000. Hombori area, halfway between Gao and Mopti. Also spoken in Burkina Faso. Nilo-Saharan, Songhai, Southern. Closely related languages: Koyraboro Senni Songhay, Koyra Senni Songhay, Zarma, Dendi. Another separate Songhay variety is in Kikara (=Kiira) village near Douentza (J. Heath). Investigation needed: intelligibility, attitudes. Dictionary. Grammar. SOV, tonal. Muslim, traditional religion.

SONGHAY, KOYRA CHIINI ***(SONGHAI, SONGAI, SONGAY, SONGOI, SONGOY, SONGHOY, SONRAI, SONRHAI, WEST SONGHOY, TIMBUKTU SONGHOY)*** [KHQ] 200,000 (1999 Dan Stauffer). On the Niger River from Djenné to just east of Timbuktu. Nilo-Saharan, Songhai, Southern. Dialects: KOYRA CHIINI, DJENNÉ CHIINI. The main dialect division is between Timbuktu and the upriver towns from Diré to Niafunké. A very distinct dialect is in Djenné city. Closely related languages: Koyraboro Senni Songhay, Humburi Senni Songhay, Zarma, Dendi. Kaado (Zarma dialect) is SOV, West Songhay SVO; Kaado has 3 tones, West Songhay no tones. 77% lexical similarity between Gao and Timbuktu dialects, 50% lexical similarity with Tadaksahak. In Timbuktu they are mainly monolingual, some French, Tamashek, Arabic; In Djenné most are bilingual or multilingual in French, Bambara, or other languages. All ages. Timbuktu has more prestige than other West Songhoy dialects. Dictionary. Grammar. Djenné Chiini phonology, lexicon, basic inflection almost identical to Koyra Chiini, but syntax (especially relativization and focalization) very different; Djenné has 7 vowels to 5 for Koyra Chinni (J. Heath). Muslim, traditional religion. NT 1936.

SONGHAY, KOYRABORO SENNI ***(SONGHAI, SONGAY, SONGAI, SONGOI, SONGOY, SONGHOY, SONRAI, SONRHAI, KOROBORO SENNI SONGHAY, SONGAY SENNI, EAST SONGHAY, GAO SONGHAY, KOYRA SENNI SONGHAY)*** [SON] 400,000 (1999 Dan Stauffer). Southeast, on the Niger River from Gourma Rharous, just east of Timbuktu, through Bourem, Gao, and Ansongo on to the Mali-Niger border. Borders Kaado (Zarma) in Niger, but boundary zone not well studied. Nilo-Saharan, Songhai, Southern. Intelligibility is good with all dialects on the Niger River. Fulan Kirya variety has more limited intelligibility because of heavy lexical borrowing from Fulfulde and Humburi Senni Songay. Closely related languages: Koyra Chiini Songhay, Humburi Senni Songhay, Zarma, Dendi. 77% lexical similarity between Gao and Timbuktu varieties, 50% lexical similarity with Tadaksahak. Many are monolingual. Some know Bambara, French, or Tamasheq, but there is no extensive bilingualism (J. Heath 1999). All ages. Gao variety is dominant in all respects. Trade language. Dictionary. Grammar. SOV, nontonal. Gao Songai is being actively promoted by the government through adult literacy classes and as the language of instruction at primary level in some experimental schools throughout the Songhay area. Some French literacy. Language of instruction at primary level in some experimental schools. Muslim, traditional religion.

SONINKE ***(MARKA, MARAKA, SARAKOLE, SARAKULE, SARAWULE, SERAHULI, SILABE, TOUBAKAI, WAKORE, GADYAGA, ASWANIK, DIAWARA)*** [SNN] 700,000 in Mali (1991), including 125,000 Diawara (1991 Vanderaa), 374,042 mother tongue Marka speakers (1987 census).

Population total all countries 1,067,000. Nioro, Nara, Banamba, Yélémané, Kayes are principal towns in Mali. Also possibly Niger. Also spoken in Côte d'Ivoire, Gambia, Guinea, Guinea-Bissau, Mauritania, Senegal. Niger-Congo, Mande, Western, Northwestern, Samogo, Soninke-Bobo, Soninke-Boso, Soninke. Dialects: AZER (ADJER, ASER), KINBAKKA, XENQENNA. Bilingualism in Bambara, Fula. 6 years and older (1987). The Diawara (125,000 in 1993; Johnstone) live among the Soninke and speak Sarakole, but consider themselves to be separate from the Soninke. Their own name for the language is 'Soninkanxaane'. The 'Marka' name used for Soninke is different from the Marka language [MWR]. Radio programs, TV. Muslim.

TADAKSAHAK ***(DAUSAHAQ, DAOUSSAK, DAOUSSAHAQ, DAWSAHAQ, DAOSAHAQ)*** [DSQ] 30,000 to 40,000 in Mali (1995). Population total both countries 32,000 to 42,000. 7th region, about 300 km. east-west by 200 km. north-south with Ménaka as geographic center. They travel into Niger and Algeria. Also spoken in Algeria. Nilo-Saharan, Songhai, Northern. 50% lexical similarity with Gao Songai and 51% with Timbuktu Songai. Lexical similarity is higher with Tamasheq in the domain of breeding and animal husbandry. People are reported to be bilingual in Tamasheq, although women and children in isolated encampments understand very little. All ages. Vigorous. They call themselves 'Idaksahak' (pl.), and their language 'Tadaksahak'. The culture is shared with Tamasheq. SVO, stress system. Traditionally nomadic herdsmen for the Iwellemmeden Tuareg nobility.

TAMAJAQ ***(TAMAJEQ, TAMASHEQ, TOMACHECK, TAMASHEKIN, "TUAREG", "TOURAGE", TAHOUA, TAJAG)*** [TTQ] 190,000 in Mali (1991). East Mali, Menaka and Gao regions. Afro-Asiatic, Berber, Tamasheq, Southern. Dialects: TAWALLAMMET TAN DANNAG (IOULLEMMEDEN), TAWALLAMMAT TAN ATARAM. The people call themselves 'Kal Tamajaq'. Muslim. Bible portions 1979-1985. See main entry under Niger.

TAMASHEQ ***(KIDAL TAMASHEQ, TOMACHECK, TAMASHEKIN, "TUAREG", TIMBUKTU, KIDAL)*** [TAQ] 250,000 or more in Mali (1991). Population total all countries 270,000 or more. Central, Timbuktu area, and northeast Mali. Also spoken in Algeria, Burkina Faso. Afro-Asiatic, Berber, Tamasheq, Southern. Dialects: TIMBUKTU (TOMBOUCTOU, TANASLAMT), TADHAQ (KIDAL). It may be two separate languages. The people are called 'Kel Tamasheq', the language 'Tamasheq'. The Bellah were formerly under the Tuareg economically. Investigation needed: intelligibility with dialects. The government is actively promoting the language through adult literacy classes. Language of instruction at primary level in some experimental schools. Pastoralists: cattle, goats, camels, donkeys. Muslim. Bible portions 1953-1998.

XAASONGAXANGO ***(XASONGA, KASSONKE, KHASSONKA, KHASSONKÉ, KHASONKE, KASONKE, KASSON, KASSO, XAASONGA, XASONKE)*** [KAO] 120,000 in Mali (1991). Population total all countries 127,300. Principal towns are Bafoulabé, Kayes. Also spoken in Gambia, Senegal. Niger-Congo, Mande, Western, Central-Southwestern, Central, Manding-Jogo, Manding-Vai, Manding-Mokole, Manding, Manding-West. Highly intelligible with Western Maninka and a bit less with Bambara, but for sociolinguistic reasons they are not considered dialects. 70% lexical similarity with Mandinka of Gambia and Senegal. Most Xasonga and Bambara manage to understand each other. The people call themselves 'Xasongo' or 'Xasonga' (sg.), 'Xasongolu' (pl.), and their language 'Xasongaxango' (velar nasal between the n and the final o). The French spelling is Khassonké. Grammar. Muslim, traditional religion. Bible portions 1997.

ZARMACI ***(ZARMA, DYERMA, DYARMA, DYABARMA, ADZERMA, DJERMA, ZABARMA, ZARBARMA)*** [DJE] Tabankort and Akabar villages south of Menaka at Niger border. Nilo-Saharan, Songhai, Southern. Dictionary. Muslim, traditional religion. Bible 1990. See main entry under Niger.

MAURITANIA

Islamic Republic of Mauritania. République Islamique de Mauritanie. National or official language: Arabic. 2,529,000 (1998 UN). There are many tribes, castes, or clans of whom little is known. Literacy rate 17% to 28%. Also includes Bambara, French, Korean 60,000, Tamasheq. Information mainly from A. Gerteiny 1967; Applegate 1970. Muslim. Data accuracy estimate: B, C. The number of languages listed for Mauritania is 6. Of those, all are living languages. Diversity index 0.19.

HASSANIYYA ***(KLEM EL BITHAN, HASANYA, HASSANI, HASSANIYA)*** [MEY] 2,200,000 in Mauritania, 66% of the population (1998). 3% per year growth. Population total all countries 2,511,000. Throughout the country. Also spoken in Algeria, Mali, Morocco, Niger, Senegal. Afro-Asiatic, Semitic, Central, South, Arabic. Not intelligible with other Arabic varieties. Speakers are called 'Maures' ('Moors'). White Maure are called 'Bithan', which may also be used for the Maure in general. Black Maure are called 'Haratine'. The 'Nemadi' are an ethnic group that speak Hassaniyya, and do not have their own language. Pastoralists, traders. Muslim.

IMERAGUEN ***(IMRAGUEN)*** [IME] 120 (1967 Gerteiny). Near Nouakchott, the region stretching from Cape Timiris to Nouadhibou. Unclassified. The language is reported to be a variety of Hassaniyya structured on an Azer (Soninke) base. Vassals to important Hassan tribes, especially the Oulad Bou Sba. Reported to be remnants of the Bafours. They use nets for fishing. Coastal. Fishermen.

PULAAR ***(PEUL)*** [FUC] 150,000 in Mauritania. Niger-Congo, Atlantic-Congo, Atlantic, Northern, Senegambian, Fula-Wolof, Fulani, Western. Dialect: TOUCOULEUR (TUKULOR, PULAAR, HAALPULAAR). Fuuta Tooro (Fouta Toro) was a major Toucouleur geo-political state, which has its seat in northern Senegal and is also in Mauritania. Muslim. NT 1997. See main entry under Senegal.

SONINKE ***(MARKA, SARAKOLE, SARAWULE, TOUBAKAI, WAKORE, GADYAGA, SERAHULI, ASWANIK, SILABE)*** [SNN] 30,000 in Mauritania. Chamama region. Niger-Congo, Mande, Western, Northwestern, Samogo, Soninke-Bobo, Soninke-Boso, Soninke. Dialect: AZER (ADJER, ASER). Muslim. See main entry under Mali.

WOLOF ***(OUOLOF, YALLOF, WALAF, VOLOF)*** [WOL] 10,000 in Mauritania (1993 Johnstone). Niger-Congo, Atlantic-Congo, Atlantic, Northern, Senegambian, Fula-Wolof, Wolof. Dialects: BAOL, CAYOR, DYOLOF (DJOLOF, JOLOF), LEBOU, NDYANGER. Different from Wolof of Gambia. Language of wider communication. Muslim. NT 1988. See main entry under Senegal.

ZENAGA [ZEN] 200 to 300 (1998). Between Mederdra and the Atlantic coast, southern Mauritania. Afro-Asiatic, Berber, Zenaga. The language is related to other Berber languages in basic structure though specific features are quite different. Bilingualism in Hassaniyya. It is reported that adult speakers are not teaching it to their children. People are bedouins, reported to travel mainly in caravans. Racially they are both white and black; the latter are descendants of slaves captured centuries ago. Pastoralists. Muslim.

MAURITIUS

National or official language: English. 1,141,111 (1998 UN). Ethnically 685,170 or 69% of the population from India. Includes Rodrigues; 4 islands. Literacy rate 90% to 94%. Also includes Hakka Chinese 35,000, Mandarin Chinese, Yue Chinese, Gujarati, Marathi, Eastern Panjabi, Telugu. Information mainly from P. Baker 1972; P. Baker and R. Ramnak 1985; R. Barz and J. Siegel 1988; T. Eriksen 1990. Hindu, Christian, Muslim, secular. Blind population 250. Deaf institutions: 2. Data accuracy estimate: B. The number of languages listed for Mauritius is 6. Of those, all are living languages. Diversity index 0.60.

BHOJPURI [BHJ] 330,000 in Mauritius (1993 Johnstone). Urban and rural areas. Indo-European, Indo-Iranian, Indo-Aryan, Central zone, Western Hindi, Hindustani. Dialects: MAURITIAN BHOJPURI, BOJPURY. Often used in government and politics. Although often called 'Hindi', the language is Bhojpuri. Hindu. Bible portions 1911-1982. See main entry under India.

ENGLISH [ENG] 3,000 in Mauritius (1993 Johnstone). Indo-European, Germanic, West, English. Used in secondary school, courts, for road signs. Not widely known. Official language. Bible 1535-1989. See main entry under United Kingdom.

FRENCH [FRN] 37,000. Indo-European, Italic, Romance, Italo-Western, Western, Gallo-Iberian, Gallo-Romance, Gallo-Rhaetian, Oïl, French. Used in stores. Widely used by young people as second language. The elderly tend to use creole. Newspapers, radio programs, TV. Bible 1530-1986. See main entry under France.

MORISYEN ***(MAURITIUS CREOLE FRENCH, KREOLE, KREOL, MAURITIAN, MAURYSEN)*** [MFE] 600,000 first language speakers in Mauritius (1989). Population total both countries 604,000. Also spoken in Madagascar. Creole, French based. Dialect: RODRIGUES CREOLE. Closer to French creoles of the Caribbean than to Reunion Creole (Philip Baker). Nearly identical to Rodrigues. Bilingualism in French. The mother tongue of virtually the entire population (D. Bickerton). Lower prestige than French or English. Trade language. Dictionary. Grammar. Bible portions 1885-1900.

TAMIL [TCV] 22,000 in Mauritius (1993 Johnstone). Dravidian, Southern, Tamil-Kannada, Tamil-Kodagu, Tamil-Malayalam, Tamil. Often used in government and politics. Hindu. Bible 1727-1995. See main entry under India.

URDU [URD] 64,000 in Mauritius (1993 Johnstone). Indo-European, Indo-Iranian, Indo-Aryan, Central zone, Western Hindi, Hindustani. Often used in government and politics. Muslim. Bible 1843-1998. See main entry under Pakistan.

MAYOTTE

National or official language: French. 98,000 (1995). A French department. Literacy rate 32% to 58.4%. Muslim, Christian. Data accuracy estimate: B. The number of languages listed for Mayotte is 4. Of those, all are living languages. Diversity index 0.46.

BUSHI ***(SHIBUSHI, KIBUSHI, KIBUKI, SHIBUSHI SHIMAWORE, SAKALAVA, ANTALAOTRA)*** [BUC] 39,200 in Mayotte (1995), 40% of the population (1980). Austronesian, Malayo-Polynesian, Western Malayo-Polynesian, Borneo, Barito, East, Malagasy. Kibushi is the Malagasy variety spoken in Mayotte. There are 2 to 4 subdialects. VOS. See main entry under Madagascar.

COMORIAN ***(COMORES SWAHILI, KOMORO, COMORO)*** [SWB] 92,806 in Mayotte (1993 Johnstone). Niger-Congo, Atlantic-Congo, Volta-Congo, Benue-Congo, Bantoid, Southern, Narrow Bantu, Central, G, Swahili (G.40). Dialects: SHINZWANI (ANJOUAN), SHIMAWORE (SHIMAORE, SHIMAORI, MAYOTTE). Vanilla, perfume production. Muslim. NT 1995. See main entry under Comoros Islands.

FRENCH [FRN] 2,450 in Mayotte (1993 Johnstone). Indo-European, Italic, Romance, Italo-Western, Western, Gallo-Iberian, Gallo-Romance, Gallo-Rhaetian, Oïl, French. Official language. Bible 1530-1986. See main entry under France.

SWAHILI [SWA] 2,744 in Mayotte (1993 Johnstone). Niger-Congo, Atlantic-Congo, Volta-Congo, Benue-Congo, Bantoid, Southern, Narrow Bantu, Central, G, Swahili (G.40). Muslim. Bible 1891-1996. See main entry under Tanzania.

MOROCCO

Kingdom of Morocco. al-Mamlaka al-Maghrebia. National or official language: Standard Arabic. 27,377,000 (1998 UN). Literacy rate 30% to 50%. Also includes French 80,000. Information mainly from C. Coon 1931; Y. Zavadovskii 1962; D. Cohen 1963, 1985; J. Applegate 1970; J. Chetrit 1985. Sunni Muslim. Blind population 35,000 (1982 WCE). Deaf institutions: 1. Data accuracy estimate: B, C. The number of languages listed for Morocco is 11. Of those, 9 are living languages and 2 are extinct. Diversity index 0.47.

ARABIC, HASSANIYYA ***(SAHRAWI, MAURE, MAURI, MOOR, SULAKA, HASANYA, HASSANI)*** [MEY] 40,000 in Morocco (1995). Southern Morocco, from Laayoune on down. Afro-Asiatic, Semitic, Central, South, Arabic. Not intelligible with other Arabic varieties. See main entry under Mauritania.

ARABIC, JUDEO-MOROCCAN [AJU] 4,000 to 6,000 speakers in Morocco, including 90% in Casablanca (1997 World Jewish Congress). Casablanca. Afro-Asiatic, Semitic, Central, South, Arabic. Many dialects. May be inherently intelligible with Moroccan Arabic. Has medium inherent intelligibility with Tunisian Judeo-Arabic, some with Libyan Judeo-Arabic, but none with Iraqi Judeo-Arabic. Many of the elderly speak Spanish or French as mother tongue. Some bilingualism in Spanish, French, and Hebrew. Most in Morocco are elderly. The younger generation uses French as mother tongue. Their Arabic is closer to Moroccan Arabic than to Moroccan Judeo-Arabic. A large number of borrowings from Spanish, Ladino, and French. In Casablanca, the Jewish community is well educated and well off. Several Jewish schools taught almost exclusively in Hebrew. Jewish. See main entry under Israel.

ARABIC, MOROCCAN SPOKEN ***(MAGHREBI ARABIC, MAGHRIBI COLLOQUIAL ARABIC)*** [ARY] 18,800,000 in Morocco (1995), 65% of the population (1991). Perhaps another 20% speak it as second language. Population total all countries 19,542,000. Northern Morocco and southern Morocco south of the Atlas Mts., and including the port cities of the Sahara. Also spoken in Belgium, Egypt, France, Germany, Gibraltar, Netherlands, United Kingdom. Afro-Asiatic, Semitic, Central, South, Arabic. Dialects: RABAT-CASABLANCA ARABIC, FEZ. MEKNES, TANGIER ARABIC, OUJDA, JEBLI (JEBELIA, JBALA), SOUTHERN MOROCCO ARABIC, MARRAKECH ARABIC. Speakers prefer their own variety to Algerian Arabic, Tunisian Arabic, and Libyan Arabic. Speakers across North Africa call their spoken Arabic varieties 'darija' or 'darijah', so it is not specific for this variety. Sunni Muslim. NT 1932.

ARABIC, STANDARD [ABV] Afro-Asiatic, Semitic, Central, South, Arabic. Used for education, official purposes, communication among Arabic speaking countries. National language. Newspapers. Bible 1984-1991. See main entry under Saudi Arabia.

GHOMARA [GHO] North and west of Tamazight, a small region near Chechaouen, western Rif mountains, Oued Laou Valley. Afro-Asiatic, Berber, Northern, Zenati, Ghomara. Coon says Ghomara is intelligible with Tarifit. The ethnic group now speaks only Moroccan Spoken Arabic. Muslim. Extinct.

MOROCCAN SIGN LANGUAGE [XMS] Used in Tetouan and other cities. Deaf sign language. Algerian Sign Language has influenced the strong deaf community of 60 to 70 men in the city of Oujda in the north. Less than 50% lexical similarity with American Sign Language. Most deaf people cannot read or write or understand Arabic. Many deaf women do not leave their homes, or do not sign in the streets, so it is difficult to determine numbers. Association Nanane, a school in the north, had about 30 students, ages 4-21. MSL used in 3 programs for the deaf. Communities in Rabat, Tangier, and Casa Blanca do not use MSL. Used by USA Peace Corps. Developed from local signs and introduced signs. Dictionary.

SENHAJA DE SRAIR ***(SANHAJA OF SRAIR)*** [SJS] Northern, west of Tarifit. Afro-Asiatic, Berber, Northern, Zenati, Riff. Coon (1939) says it was a separate language from Tarifit. The ethnic group now speaks only Moroccan Spoken Arabic. Muslim. Extinct.

SPANISH [SPN] 20,000 in Morocco (1993 Johnstone). Melilla and scattered across the north coast. Indo-European, Italic, Romance, Italo-Western, Western, Gallo-Iberian, Ibero-Romance, West Iberian, Castilian. Bible 1553-1979. See main entry under Spain.

TACHELHIT ***(TASHILHEET, TACHILHIT, TASHELHIT, TASOUSSIT, SHILHA, SUSIUA, SOUTHERN SHILHA)*** [SHI] 3,000,000 in Morocco (1998). Population total all countries 3,500,000. Southwestern Morocco, from coast south to Ifni and north to near Agadir, northeast to outskirts of Marrakech, and east to Draa, including the valley of the Sous, and south near the border. Also spoken in Algeria, France. Afro-Asiatic, Berber, Northern, Atlas. Many men are bilingual in Arabic. Many women do not learn Arabic. 'Tachelhit' is their name for their language. 'Shilha' is the Arabic name for Moroccan Berber language varieties in general. Soussi are known as shop owners throughout Morocco. Muslim. Bible portions 1906-1925.

TAMAZIGHT, CENTRAL ATLAS ***(CENTRAL SHILHA, MIDDLE ATLAS BERBER, SHILHA)*** [TZM] 3,000,000 in Morocco (1998). Population total all countries 3,500,000. Middle Atlas, High Atlas, eastern High Atlas Mountains. 1,200,000 in rural areas between Taza, Khemisset, Azilal, Errachidia; 100,000 outside the language area. Also spoken in Algeria, France. Afro-Asiatic, Berber, Northern, Atlas. Dialects: CENTRAL ATLAS, SOUTH ORAN. 40% monolingual. Others use Arabic as second language. 65% live in rural areas, 10% live outside the traditional area. VSO (for Berber). Literacy rate in second language: Men 25%, women 5%. Bible portions 1919-1981.

TARIFIT ***(RIFI, RIFIA, NORTHERN SHILHA, SHILHA)*** [RIF] 1,500,000 in Morocco (1991). Population total all countries 2,000,000 (1991). Northern Morocco. The dialects listed are near Al Hoceima. Also spoken in Algeria, France, Netherlands. Afro-Asiatic, Berber, Northern, Zenati, Riff. Dialects: URRIGHEL, BENI IZNASSEN. The chief differences among dialects are phonological. There may be other dialects. Coon (1939) said Senhaja de Srair is a separate language. 'Rifia' is the Arabic name for their language, 'Rifi' (sg.) or 'Ruafa' (pl.) are names for the people, 'Rif' or 'Riff' geographical names. Muslim. Bible portions 1887-1890.

MOZAMBIQUE

Republic of Mozambique. República de Moçambique. National or official language: Portuguese. 18,880,000 (1998 UN). Literacy rate 20%. Also includes Chinese 7,000 or fewer, people from India 15,000. Information mainly from J. Rennie 1973; R. B. Boeder n.d.; P. Afido et al. 1989. Traditional religion, Christian, Muslim, secular. Blind population 28,000 (1982 WCE). Data accuracy estimate: B. The number of languages listed for Mozambique is 39. Of those, all are living languages. Diversity index 0.92.

BARWE ***(BALKE, CIBALKE)*** [BWG] 15,000 (1999). Tete Province. Niger-Congo, Atlantic-Congo, Volta-Congo, Benue-Congo, Bantoid, Southern, Narrow Bantu, Central, N, Senga-Sena (N.40), Sena. Between Nyungwe and Sena. Probably has good understanding of Nyungwe. Investigation needed: intelligibility with Nyungwe, Sena.

CHOPI ***(SHICHOPI, COPI, CICOPI, SHICOPI, TSCHOPI, TXOPI, TXITXOPI)*** [CCE] 760,000 (1993 Johnstone). Southern coast, north of Limpopo River. Center is Quissico, southern part of Zavala District, approximately 100 km. coastal strip between Inharrime and Chidunguela. Niger-Congo, Atlantic-Congo, Volta-Congo, Benue-Congo, Bantoid, Southern, Narrow Bantu, Central, S, Chopi (S.60). Dialects: COPI, NDONGE, LENGUE (LENGE, KILENGE), TONGA, LAMBWE, KHAMBANI. Many dialects, all inherently intelligible with each other. 44% lexical similarity with GiTonga. About half of the speakers understand Tswa. Distinct from Chopi (Dhopaluo), a dialect of Acholi of Uganda. Dictionary. Grammar. Literacy rate in second language: About 10%. Bible portions 1910-1986.

CHUWABO ***(CHWABO, CUWABO, CUABO, CHUABO, CHUAMBO, CHWAMPO, CUAMBO, CHICHWABO, CICUABO, TXUWABO, ECHUWABO, ECHUABO, LOLO)*** [CHW] 664,279 (1980 census). Central coast between Quelimane and the Mlanje Mts. Niger-Congo, Atlantic-Congo, Volta-Congo, Benue-Congo, Bantoid, Southern, Narrow Bantu, Central, P, Makua (P.30). Dialects: CENTRAL CHUWABO, ECKARUMGU, NYARINGA, MAINDO. Chuwabo of Makusi District and Marrare have 78% lexical similarity with each other (closest). Investigation needed: intelligibility with Makusi Dist Chuwabo, Marrare Chuwabo. Grammar. Traditional religion, Christian, Muslim. NT 1978.

GITONGA ***(TONGA, INHAMBANE, SHENGWE, BITONGA, TONGA-INHAMBANE)*** [TOH] 223,971 (1980 census). South, Inhambane area up to Morrumbane. Niger-Congo, Atlantic-Congo, Volta-Congo, Benue-Congo, Bantoid, Southern, Narrow Bantu, Central, S, Chopi (S.60). Dialects: GITONGA GY KHOGANI,

NYAMBE (CINYAMBE), SEWI (GISEWI). 44% lexical similarity with Chopi. Different from ChiTonga of Malawi, ChiTonga of Zambia and Zimbabwe, or Tonga dialect of Ndau. NT 1890-1996.

KOKOLA [KZN] Western Zambezia Province. Niger-Congo, Atlantic-Congo, Volta-Congo, Benue-Congo, Bantoid, Southern, Narrow Bantu, Central, P, Makua (P.30). May be intelligible with Lomwe. One source says they are a subgroup of Lolo, which is a subgroup of Lomwe, Close to Marendje and Takwane. Investigation needed: intelligibility with Lomwe. See main entry under Malawi.

KOTI *(COTI, EKOTI, AKOTI, ANGOCHE, ANGOXE)* [EKO] 41,287 (1980 census). Nampula Province, Angoche District, coastal around Angoche Island and other islands of the Archipelago from Moma to Angoche. Also a community in Nampula City. Niger-Congo, Atlantic-Congo, Volta-Congo, Benue-Congo, Bantoid, Southern, Narrow Bantu, Central, P, Makua (P.30). Probably a separate language within the Makua group. Close to Maka and Makhuwa. Those above 15 can use Makhuwa or Maka (trading, contacts with neighbors), Portuguese (school, church, government), but little Swahili or Arabic. Koti used in home, market, and trading. All ages. Lexicon heavily influenced by Swahili. Grammar. Literacy rate in second language: 20% Portuguese. Muslim, Christian.

KUNDA *(CHIKUNDA, CIKUNDA, CHICUNDA)* [KDN] 3,258 in Mozambique (1980 census). Around confluence of the Luangwe and Zambezi rivers. Niger-Congo, Atlantic-Congo, Volta-Congo, Benue-Congo, Bantoid, Southern, Narrow Bantu, Central, N, Senga-Sena (N.40), Sena. Closer to Nyungwe than to Sena. Different from Kunda which is a dialect of Nyanja, and apparently different from Kunda of DCR. Traditional religion, Christian. Bible portions 1988. See main entry under Zimbabwe.

LOLO [LLB] Western Zambezia Province. Niger-Congo, Atlantic-Congo, Volta-Congo, Benue-Congo, Bantoid, Southern, Narrow Bantu, Central, P, Makua (P.30). May be a dialect of Lomwe or Makhuwa.

LOMWE *(NGULU, INGULU, NGURU, MIHAVANE, MIHAVANI, MIHAWANI, WESTERN MAKUA, LOMUE, ILOMWE, ELOMWE, ALOMWE, WALOMWE, CHILOWE, CILOWE, ACILOWE)* [NGL] 1,300,000 in Mozambique (1991). Population total both countries 2,850,000. Northeast and central, most of Zambezia Province, southern Nampula Province. The prestige center is Alto Molocue, Zambezia. Also spoken in Malawi. Niger-Congo, Atlantic-Congo, Volta-Congo, Benue-Congo, Bantoid, Southern, Narrow Bantu, Central, P, Makua (P.30). Closest to Makhuwa, Chwabo. Different from Ngulu (Kingulu) of Tanzania. Traditional religion, Christian, Muslim. NT 1930-1983.

MAKHUWA *(CENTRAL MAKHUWA, MAKHUWA-MAKHUWANA, MACUA, EMAKUA, MAKUA, MAKOANE, MAQUOUA, MAKHUWWA OF NAMPULA)* [VMW] 2,500,000 (1996). Population total both countries 2,500,000 or more. Nampula, south of Meeto area. Also spoken in Madagascar. Niger-Congo, Atlantic-Congo, Volta-Congo, Benue-Congo, Bantoid, Southern, Narrow Bantu, Central, P, Makua (P.30). Dialects: MAKHUWANA (MAKUANA, EMAKHUWANA), NAHARRA (MACA, MAKA, EMAKA, ENAHARRA, MAHARRA, NAHARA, NORTH MACA), EMPAMELA (NAMPAMELA), ENLAI (MULAI). Traditional religion, Muslim Christian. Bible 1982.

MAKHUWA-MARREVONE *(MACA, MAKA, COASTAL MAKHUWA, SOUTH MACA, EMAKA, MAREVONE, MARREVONE)* [XMC] 300,000 to 400,000 (1989). Coast of central Delgado Province from Moma to Angoche. Niger-Congo, Atlantic-Congo, Volta-Congo, Benue-Congo, Bantoid, Southern, Narrow Bantu, Central, P, Makua (P.30). Dialects: MAKHUWANA (EMAKHUWANA), NAHARRA (ENAHARRA), ENLAI, NAMPAMELA (EMPAMELA). Probably a separate language within the Makua group. Appears to be significantly different from Makhuwa. Muslim.

MAKHUWA-MEETTO *(MEETTO, KIMAKUA, MAKUA, MACUA)* [MAK] 800,000 in Mozambique (1997). Population total both countries 1,160,000. North central, Cabo Delgado. Also spoken in Tanzania. Niger-Congo, Atlantic-Congo, Volta-Congo, Benue-Congo, Bantoid, Southern, Narrow Bantu, Central, P, Makua (P.30). Dialects: MEETTO (METO, METTO, EMETO, IMEETTO, MEDO), SAAKA (ESAAKA, SAKA), SAANGA (ISAANGA, ISHANGA, SANGA). Imeetto has 81% to 88% lexical similarity with Esaaka, 78% to 82% with Enahara, 78% to 80% with Makhuwana, 66% to 68% with Lomwe. Dictionary. Grammar. Traditional religion, Muslim, Christian. Bible portions 1927.

MAKHUWA-SHIRIMA *(WEST MAKUA, XIRIMA, ESHIRIMA, CHIRIMA, SHIRIMA, MAKHUWA-NIASSA, MAKHUWA-XIRIMA)* [VMK] 500,000 (1996). Center may be Maúa, south of the Lugenda River in Niassa Province. Niger-Congo, Atlantic-Congo, Volta-Congo, Benue-Congo, Bantoid, Southern, Narrow Bantu, Central, P, Makua (P.30). Probably not intelligible with the Metto, Makhuwa, or Lomwe.

MAKONDE *(CHIMAKONDE, CHINIMAKONDE, CIMAKONDE, KONDE, MAKONDA, MACONDE, SHIMAKONDE, MATAMBWE)* [KDE] 360,000 in Mozambique (1993 Johnstone) including 12,000 Ndonde (1980). Northeast Mozambique. Maviha is in Mueda, Mozambique. Niger-Congo, Atlantic-Congo, Volta-Congo, Benue-Congo, Bantoid, Southern, Narrow Bantu, Central, P, Yao (P.20). Dialects: VADONDE (DONDE, NDONDE), VAMWALU (MWALU), VAMWAMBE (MWAMBE), VAMAKONDE (MAKONDE), MAVIHA (CHIMAVIHA, KIMAWIHA, MAVIA, MABIHA, MAWIA). Speakers are reserved toward outsiders. Grammar. Woodcarvers, agriculturalists. Muslim, traditional religion, Christian. See main entry under Tanzania.

MAKWE ***(KIMAKWE, PALMA, MACUE)*** [YMK] 20,000 to 22,000 in Mozambique (1997). Population total both countries 28,000 to 32,000. Cabo Delgado Province, on the coast from the Tanzania border south to Quionga, Palma, until just south of Olumbe; and in the interior along the Rovuma River until Pundanhar. Also spoken in Tanzania. Niger-Congo, Atlantic-Congo, Volta-Congo, Benue-Congo, Bantoid, Southern, Narrow Bantu, Central, G, Swahili (G.40). Dialects: COASTAL MAKWE (PALMA), INTERIOR MAKWE. Not inherently intelligible with Swahili. 60% lexical similarity with Swahili, 57% with Mwani, 48% with Yao. All men appear to speak Swahili, not all women understand it well. Most Palma men can speak Mwani. Most Rovuma people can speak Makonde. Those who have been to school can read Portuguese or Swahili. Investigation needed: bilingual proficiency in Swahili, Mwani, Makonde. Literacy rate in second language: 20%. Motivation for literacy is high. Muslim.

MANYAWA [MNY] 150,000 (1999). Western Zambezia Province, including Lugela District. Niger-Congo, Atlantic-Congo, Volta-Congo, Benue-Congo, Bantoid, Southern, Narrow Bantu, Central, P, Makua (P.30). Their proficiency in Lomwe is limited. In Lugela District, 85% of the people are monolingual.

MANYIKA ***(CHIMANYIKA, MANIKA)*** [MXC] 100,000 to 200,000 in Mozambique (1998). 759,923 Shona in Mozambique (1980 census) probably included Manyika, Ndau, Tewe, Tawala. Northern half of Manica Province, north of Ndau, west of Tewe. Niger-Congo, Atlantic-Congo, Volta-Congo, Benue-Congo, Bantoid, Southern, Narrow Bantu, Central, S, Shona (S.10). Dialects: BOCHA (BOKA), BUNJI, BVUMBA, DOMBA, GUTA, HERE, HUNGWE, JINDWI, KAROMBE, NYAMUKA, NYATWE, UNYAMA. Manyika has 74% to 81% lexical similarity with Ndau. Traditional religion, Christian, Muslim. NT 1908. See main entry under Zimbabwe.

MARENJE ***(EMARENDJE, MARENDJE)*** [VMR] 402,861 (1980 census). Western Zambezia. Niger-Congo, Atlantic-Congo, Volta-Congo, Benue-Congo, Bantoid, Southern, Narrow Bantu, Central, P, Makua (P.30). Related to Takwane and Kokola. Probably has good inherent intelligibility with Takwane.

MOZAMBICAN SIGN LANGUAGE [MZY] In at least the 3 largest cities: Maputo, Beira, and Nampula. Deaf sign language. Some dialectal variation. Standardization efforts are in progress (1999). Not related to or based on Portuguese nor Portuguese Sign Language. Being taught and developed.

MWANI ***(KIMWANI, MWANE, MUANE, QUIMUANE, IBO)*** [WMW] 100,000 (1990 S. J. Floor), and 20,000 second language users. Cabo Delgado Province, on the coast north of Pemba from Arimba to Palma, including Ibo and Mocimboa da Praia, and the offshore Querimba Archipelago. Niger-Congo, Atlantic-Congo, Volta-Congo, Benue-Congo, Bantoid, Southern, Narrow Bantu, Central, G, Swahili (G.40). Dialects: WIBO (KIWIBO), KISANGA (KIKISANGA, QUISSANGA), NKOJO (KINKOJO), NSIMBWA (KINSIMBWA). Not intelligible with Swahili. Kiwibo is the prestige dialect. Kinsimbwa, the northernmost Mocimboa da Praia dialect is inherently intelligible with others, even though it is the most different. 60% lexical similarity with Swahili; 48% with Yao. 30% to 40% of the people use Portuguese as second language, 30% Swahili (mainly in the north), 30% to 40% Makhuwa. Men are more bilingual than women. Traders and schoolchildren can use Portuguese. Portuguese is used for school, government, and trading. Swahili is used for trading in the north. People use KiMwani in the home, for social purposes, religion, and trading. People are called 'Namwaní' or 'Mwaní' by Portuguese speakers. Dictionary. Literacy rate in second language: 30% to 40% Arabic script, 30% to 40% in Portuguese. Traders. Muslim.

NATHEMBO ***(SAKAJI, ESAKAJI, SANKAJI, SANAGAGE, SANGAJI, THEITHEI)*** [NTE] 18,000 (1993 Johnstone). Southeastern Nampula Province, just north of Angohe, on the Sangange Peninsula, at Zubairi, Charamatane, Amisse, Mutembua, Namaeca, Namaponda, up to Mogincual and Khibulani. Niger-Congo, Atlantic-Congo, Volta-Congo, Benue-Congo, Bantoid, Southern, Narrow Bantu, Central, P, Makua (P.30). Similar to Makhuwa and Swahili, but Prata says it is distinct. 'Nathembo' is the language name. 'Sakaji' is a place name. Coastal.

NDAU ***(CHINDAU, NJAO, NDZAWU, SOUTHEAST SHONA, SOFALA)*** [NDC] 500,000 in Mozambique (1999). South central region, south of Beira in Sofala and Manica Province. Niger-Congo, Atlantic-Congo, Volta-Congo, Benue-Congo, Bantoid, Southern, Narrow Bantu, Central, S, Shona (S.10). Dialects: NDAU (CINDAU), SHANGA (CIMASHANGA, MASHANGA, CHICHANGA, CHIXANGA, XANGA, CHANGA, SENJI, CHISENJI), DANDA (CIDANDA, NDANDA, CINDANDA, VADANDA, WATANDE), DONDO (CIDONDO, WADONDO, CHIBABAVA), GOVA (CIGOVA). Closer to Manyika, and much more divergent from Union Shona. Danda and Ndanda may be the same. Danda and Dondo dialects have 92% lexical similarity; 85% between Dondo and Shanga; 74% to 81% Ndau dialects with Manyika. Other geographical or ethnic names: Dzika, Hijo, Buzi (Buji), Tomboji, Mukwilo. Traditional religion, Christian. Bible 1957. See main entry under Zimbabwe.

NDONDE ***(KIMAWANDA, MAWANDA, NDOMDE)*** [NDS] From the Tanzania border through Mueda, down to Macomia. Niger-Congo, Atlantic-Congo, Volta-Congo, Benue-Congo, Bantoid, Southern,

Narrow Bantu, Central, P, Yao (P.20). Related to Yao. Reported to be very bilingual in Makhuwa-Metto. See main entry under Tanzania.

NGONI ***(CHINGONI, KINGONI, ANGONI, KISUTU, SUTU)*** [NGU] 35,000 in Mozambique (1989). Central Cabo Delgado Province, around Macuaida in Niassa Province, in northeast Tete Province. Niger-Congo, Atlantic-Congo, Volta-Congo, Benue-Congo, Bantoid, Southern, Narrow Bantu, Central, N, Manda (N.10). Distinct from 'Ngoni', an alternate name for Zulu, the Ngoni dialect of Nsenga, the Ngoni dialect of Nyanja, or the Ngoni dialect of Tumbuka. Low lexical similarity percentage with Zulu. Speakers formerly spoke Zulu. Muslim. Bible portions 1891-1898. See main entry under Tanzania.

NSENGA ***(CHINSENGA, SENGA)*** [NSE] 141,000 in Mozambique (1993 Johnstone). Niger-Congo, Atlantic-Congo, Volta-Congo, Benue-Congo, Bantoid, Southern, Narrow Bantu, Central, N, Sena-Senga (N.40), Senga. Dialect: PIMBI. Different from Senga dialect of Tumbuka of Zambia, Malawi, and Tanzania. Traditional religion, Christian. NT 1923. See main entry under Zambia.

NYANJA ***(CHINYANJA)*** [NYJ] 423,000 in Mozambique (1993 Johnstone). Niassa, Zambezia and Tete provinces. CiChewa is in Macanga district, Tete; CiNgoni is in Sanga and Lago in Niassa, Angonia in Tete; CiNsenga is in Zumbo in Tete; CiNyanja is along Lake Niassa in Niassa and Tete. Niger-Congo, Atlantic-Congo, Volta-Congo, Benue-Congo, Bantoid, Southern, Narrow Bantu, Central, N, Nyanja (N.30). Dialects: CHEWA (CEWA, CHICHEWA, CICEWA), NGONI (CINGONI), NSENGA (CINSENGA), NYANJA (CINYANJA). Eastern dialect in Mozambique. Dictionary. Grammar. SVO. Traditional religion, Christian. Bible 1905, in press (1997). See main entry under Malawi.

NYUNGWE ***(CHINYUNGWI, CINYUNGWE, NYONGWE, TETA, TETE, YUNGWE, PHIMBI, PIMBI)*** [NYU] 262,455 (1980 census). Central, banks of Zambezi River above the Sena. Niger-Congo, Atlantic-Congo, Volta-Congo, Benue-Congo, Bantoid, Southern, Narrow Bantu, Central, N, Senga-Sena (N.40), Sena. Closely related to Sena. Dictionary. Grammar. Bible portions 1897.

PORTUGUESE [POR] 30,000 or more in Mozambique (1998 SIL), 27% speak it as second language (1980 census). Indo-European, Italic, Romance, Italo-Western, Western, Gallo-Iberian, Ibero-Romance, West Iberian, Portuguese-Galician. Official language. Bible 1751, in press (1993). See main entry under Portugal.

RONGA ***(SHIRONGA, XIRONGA, GIRONGA)*** [RON] 423,797 in Mozambique (1980 census). Population total both countries 500,000 (1991 UBS). South of Maputo Province, coastal areas. Also spoken in South Africa. Niger-Congo, Atlantic-Congo, Volta-Congo, Benue-Congo, Bantoid, Southern, Narrow Bantu, Central, S, Tswa-Ronga (S.50). Dialects: KONDE, PUTRU, KALANGA. Partially intelligible with ShiTsonga and ShiTswa. Grammar. Bible 1923.

SENA ***(CISENA, CHISENA)*** [SEH] 1,086,040 (1980 census). 86,000 Podzo in Mozambique (1993 Johnstone). Northwest, Sofala, Tete, and Zambezia provinces, lower Zambezi River region. Sena Central is in Tete and northern Sofala. Niger-Congo, Atlantic-Congo, Volta-Congo, Benue-Congo, Bantoid, Southern, Narrow Bantu, Central, N, Senga-Sena (N.40), Sena. Dialects: SENA CENTRAL, SENA-CARE (CARE, SARE, NORTH SENA), SENA BANGWE (BANGWE, SOUTH SENA), RUE (CHIRUE), GOMBE, SANGWE, PODZO (CHIPODZO, CIPODZO, PUTHSU, SHIPUTHSU), GORONGOSA. Different literature needed for Malawi. Close to Nyungwe, Nyanja, and Kunda. Podzo and Sena-Sare have 92% lexical similarity. People have limited bilingual comprehension of Ndau in Beira region. Ndau is the church language in Beira; Shona and Nyanja are used in Tâte. They use Ndau to Ndau speakers, Portuguese to other non-Sena. Sena Central is the prestige dialect. Dictionary. Grammar. Traditional religion, Christian, Muslim. NT 1983.

SWAHILI [SWA] Northern. Niger-Congo, Atlantic-Congo, Volta-Congo, Benue-Congo, Bantoid, Southern, Narrow Bantu, Central, G, Swahili (G.40). Second language speakers in Mozambique. Bible 1891-1996. See main entry under Tanzania.

SWATI ***(SWAZI, SISWAZI, SISWATI, TEKELA, TEKEZA)*** [SWZ] 731 in Mozambique (1980 census). Niger-Congo, Atlantic-Congo, Volta-Congo, Benue-Congo, Bantoid, Southern, Narrow Bantu, Central, S, Nguni (S.40). Bible 1996. See main entry under Swaziland.

TAKWANE ***(THAKWANI)*** [TKE] Western Zambezia Province. Niger-Congo, Atlantic-Congo, Volta-Congo, Benue-Congo, Bantoid, Southern, Narrow Bantu, Central, P, Makua (P.30). Related to Marenje and Kokola.

TAWARA ***(TAWALA)*** [TWL] 50,000 (1997). Far western Mozambique, just north of Zimbabwe. Niger-Congo, Atlantic-Congo, Volta-Congo, Benue-Congo, Bantoid, Southern, Narrow Bantu, Central, S, Shona (S.10). The northernmost variety related to Korekore. It appears to have been influenced by Nyungwe.

TEWE ***(CIUTE, CHIUTE, TEVE, VATEVE, WATEVE)*** [TWX] 250,000 (1998). Manyika Province, east of Manyika language. Not in Zimbabwe. Niger-Congo, Atlantic-Congo, Volta-Congo, Benue-Congo, Bantoid, Southern, Narrow Bantu, Central, S, Shona (S.10). Considered by many to be a Manyika dialect, but appears to be a separate, closely related language.

TSHWA *(SHITSHWA, KITSHWA, SHEETSHWA, XITSHWA)* [TSC] 695,212 in Mozambique (1980 census). Population total all countries 700,000. Southern region, most of Inhambane Province. Also spoken in South Africa, Zimbabwe. Niger-Congo, Atlantic-Congo, Volta-Congo, Benue-Congo, Bantoid, Southern, Narrow Bantu, Central, S, Tswa-Ronga (S.50). Dialects: HLENGWE (LENGWE, SHILENGWE, LHENGWE, MAKWAKWE-KHAMBANA, KHAMBANA-MAKWAKWE, KHAMBANI), TSHWA (DZIBI-DZONGA, DZONGA-DZIBI, DZIVI, XIDZIVI), MANDLA, NDXHONGE, NHAYI. Partially intelligible with Ronga and Tsonga. Dictionary. Grammar. Bible 1910-1955.

TSONGA *(SHITSONGA, XITSONGA, THONGA, TONGA, GWAMBA)* [TSO] 1,500,000 in Mozambique (1989 UBS). South of Maputo, most of Maputo and Gaza provinces. Niger-Congo, Atlantic-Congo, Volta-Congo, Benue-Congo, Bantoid, Southern, Narrow Bantu, Central, S, Tswa-Ronga (S.50). Dialects: BILA (VILA), CHANGANA (XICHANGANA, CHANGA, SHANGAAN, HLANGANU, HANGANU, LANGANU, SHILANGANU, SHANGANA), JONGA (DJONGA, DZONGA), NGWALUNGU (SHINGWALUNGU). 'Tsonga' is used to describe XiChangana, XiTswa, and XiRonga, although it is often used interchangeably with Changana, the most prestigious of the three. All are recognized as languages, although they are inherently intelligible. Dictionary. Grammar. Christian, traditional religion, Muslim. Bible 1907-1989. See main entry under South Africa.

YAO *(CHIYAO, CIYAO, ACHAWA, ADSAWA, ADSOA, AJAWA, AYAWA, AYO, DJAO, HAIAO, HIAO, HYAO, JAO, VEIAO, WAJAO)* [YAO] 194,107 in Mozambique (1980 census). North central, area south of Lake Nyasa. Also possibly Zimbabwe. Niger-Congo, Atlantic-Congo, Volta-Congo, Benue-Congo, Bantoid, Southern, Narrow Bantu, Central, P, Yao (P.20). Dialects: MAKALE (CIMAKALE), MASSANINGA (CIMASSANINGA). Dictionary. Grammar. Yao in Tanzania use different orthography than Malawi. Muslim, Christian, traditional religion. Bible 1920. See main entry under Malawi.

ZULU *(ISIZULU, ZUNDA)* [ZUU] 1,798 in Mozambique (1980 census). Niger-Congo, Atlantic-Congo, Volta-Congo, Benue-Congo, Bantoid, Southern, Narrow Bantu, Central, S, Nguni (S.40). Bible 1883-1959. See main entry under South Africa.

NAMIBIA

Republic of Namibia. Formerly South West Africa. National or official language: English. 1,660,000 (1998 UN). Literacy rate 16% (1989 WA). Also includes Chokwe 5,580, Fanagolo, Standard German 12,827, Kgalagadi, Luyana, Nkhumbi, Nyemba 9,540, Portuguese, Umbundu 2,880. Information mainly from G. Stanley 1968; M. Brenzinger 1997; W. Haacke and E. Elderkin 1997; T. Güldemann 1998; J. Maho 1998. Christian, traditional religion, secular. Blind population 1,400 (1982 WCE). Data accuracy estimate: B, C. The number of languages listed for Namibia is 29. Of those, all are living languages. Diversity index 0.84.

AFRIKAANS [AFK] 133,324 in Namibia (1991 census). Used by 25% of the population in Windhoek in their homes (1995 census). Not known in the north, in the Owambo tribes, and the Kavango and Caprivi regions. Indo-European, Germanic, West, Low Saxon-Low Franconian, Low Franconian. It formerly had official status. Bible 1933-1983. See main entry under South Africa.

'AKHOE *(//AUKWE, AUEN, //AU//EN, //AU//EI, /AU-//EN, //KAU-//-EN, KAUKAU, //K"AU-//EN, KOKØ/ //AU-KWE, /AUKWE)* [AKE] Population total both countries 5,000 (1985 UBS). Ovamboland Territory, north, Ekoka. Also spoken in Angola. Khoisan, Southern Africa, Northern. Probably the same as Ekoka Kung and maybe Vasekela. Bible portions 1975-1980.

DIRIKU *(DIRIKO, GCIRIKU, RUGCIRIKU, MBOGEDO, MBOGEDU, SHIMBOGEDU)* [DIU] 29,400 (1982 Prinloo et al.) Population total both countries 29,400 or more. Okavango. Also spoken in Angola. Niger-Congo, Atlantic-Congo, Volta-Congo, Benue-Congo, Bantoid, Southern, Narrow Bantu, Central, K, Diriku (K.70). May be close to Sambya and Kwangali. Used in schools, administration, broadcasting. National language. Dictionary. Radio programs. NT 1988.

ENGLISH [ENG] 10,941 in Namibia (1991 census). Indo-European, Germanic, West, English. Not understood or spoken by everyone. Official language. Bible 1535-1989. See main entry under United Kingdom.

FWE [FWE] 7,400 (1998). About 1/3 of the population of East Caprivi speak it. Western East Caprivi. Niger-Congo, Atlantic-Congo, Volta-Congo, Benue-Congo, Bantoid, Southern, Narrow Bantu, Central, K, Subia (K.50). Close to Subiya. Not the same as the We dialect of Tonga [TOI].

HAI//OM *("SAN", "SAAN")* [HGM] 16,000 or fewer (1995 A. Miller-Ockhuizen). Population total both countries 16,000 or fewer. Mangetti Dune, Omataku, Grootfontein, Baghani, Tsintsabis. 'Maroelaboom' is the area of Namibia next to the Agricultural gate entering the former Bushmanland. Some moved to Kimberley, South Africa. Possibly in Angola, where they are reported to have come from. Also spoken in South Africa. Khoisan, Southern Africa, Central, Hain//um. Dialects: KEDI (KEDDE, KEDDI), CHWAGGA, HAIN//UM (HEI//OM, HEIKOM, HEIKUM, HEIKOM BUSHMAN). Somewhat intelligible with Kung-Tsumkwe (Ju/'hoan), but a different language. Also reported to speak a language or dialect similar to Nama and Damara. They speak Afrikaans, English, Damara, or Kwangali as second languages. Afrikaans is more widely known than English, but English is now learned in school instead of Afrikaans. Used for inter-language contact. Many men speak Afrikaans well. Many who live near the Damara or Kwangali speak those languages well or at least understand them. The language is used by all members of the ethnic group. "San" is a derogatory Nama name for all bushmen. Literacy rate in second language: Low in Afrikaans. Hunter-gatherers. Traditional religion, Christian.

HERERO ***(OTJIHERERO, OCHIHERERO)*** [HER] 113,000 in Namibia (1991 census). Population total both countries 144,000. Damaraland and northwest Ovamboland territory, Kaokoveld. Also spoken in Botswana. Niger-Congo, Atlantic-Congo, Volta-Congo, Benue-Congo, Bantoid, Southern, Narrow Bantu, Central, R, Herero (R.30). Dialect: MBANDIERU. Erroneously called 'Damara'. The people are 'Ovaherero'. National language. Dictionary. Grammar. Traditional religion, Christian. Bible 1987.

JU/'HOAN ***(KUNG-TSUMKWE, X[, XUN, KUNG, !XO, JU/'HOAN, JU'OASI, ZHU'OASI, DZU'OASI, TSHUMKWE)*** [KTZ] (25,000 to 30,000 together with the Vasekela, the !Xung, and the ǂKx'au//ein; 1998 J. F. Maho p.113). Northeast. Khoisan, Southern Africa, Northern. Dialects: DZU'OASI (SSU GHASSI, ZHU'OASE), NOGAU (AGAU). Speakers use the name 'Ju/'hoan' for themselves. Dictionary. Grammar. Nyaenyae Development Trust is teaching reading in Namibia. Traditional religion, Christian. Bible portions 1974. See main entry under Botswana.

KUNG-EKOKA ***(EKOKA-!XÛ, KUNG, !KUNG, !KU, !XU, !HU, QXÜ, !XUN, !KHUNG)*** [KNW] Population total both countries 5,000 (1985 UBS). Okavango and Ovamboland Territory. Also spoken in Angola. Khoisan, Southern Africa, Northern. Probably the same as Akhoe and maybe Vasekela. Traditional religion, Christian. Bible portions 1980.

KWAMBI [KWM] 30,000 (1972 Nida). Ovamboland north. Possibly also in Angola. Niger-Congo, Atlantic-Congo, Volta-Congo, Benue-Congo, Bantoid, Southern, Narrow Bantu, Central, R, Ndonga (R.20). NT 1951.

KWANGALI ***(SIKWANGALI, RUKWANGALI, KWANGARI, KWANGARE)*** [KWN] Population total both countries 79,000 including 2,000 Sambyu (1991 in J. F. Maho 1998). Okavango. Also spoken in Angola. Niger-Congo, Atlantic-Congo, Volta-Congo, Benue-Congo, Bantoid, Southern, Narrow Bantu, Central, K, Kwangwa (K.40). Dialect: SAMBYU (SHISAMBYU, SAMBIU, SAMBIO). Sambyu may be intelligible with Diriku. Recognized for education, administration, and broadcasting. National language. Dictionary. Grammar. Bible 1987.

KWANYAMA ***(OCHIKWANYAMA, KUANYAMA, OVAMBO, HUMBA, KWANJAMA, KWANCAMA, OTJIWAMBO, OWAMBO)*** [KUY] (713,919 in Namibia together with Ndonga and Kwambi; 1991 census). Northern Okavangoland. Niger-Congo, Atlantic-Congo, Volta-Congo, Benue-Congo, Bantoid, Southern, Narrow Bantu, Central, R, Ndonga (R.20). Intelligible with Ndonga and Kwambi. Called 'Otjiwambo' and 'Owambo' together with Ndonga. National language. Literacy rate in second language: 50%. Bible 1974. See main entry under Angola.

ǂKX'AU//'EIN ***(KUNG-GOBABIS, //AU//EI, //X'AU//'E, =KX'AU//'EI, AUEN, KAUKAU, KOKO)*** [AUE] Population total both countries 5,000 (1993 UBS). Ovamboland Territory, Ekoka. Also spoken in Botswana. Khoisan, Southern Africa, Northern. Dialect: NOGAU. The people call themselves and their language 'ǂkx'au//'ein'. Traditional religion, Christian. Bible (no date given).

KXOE ***(KXOEDAM, KHOE, XUN, "WATER BUSHMEN", "MBARAKWENA", "BARAKWENA", "BARAKWENGO")*** [XUU] 4,000 in the Caprivi Strip, including 3,600 in West Caprivi, and 400 in East Caprivi. Population total all countries 8,000 or more. West Caprivi in Namibia is recognized as the 'core land' of the Kxoe people by the Kxoe and the Namibian government. They also live in East Caprivi. Also spoken in Angola, Botswana, South Africa, Zambia. Khoisan, Southern Africa, Central, Tshu-Khwe, Northwest. Dialects: [[XO-KXOE, [[XOM-KXOE, BUMA-KXOE, BUGA-KXOE. Minor dialect differences within Kxoe. Many young people in West Caprivi claim not to understand Mbukushu at all. English, Afrikaans, and Kxoe used for oral teaching in schools, textbooks are in English. Vigorous. Kxoe speakers want Kxoe teachers and learning materials used in schools. Many non-Kxoe learn Kxoe for interaction with Kxoe. Dictionary. Grammar. Hunter-gatherers; fishermen: they still get 25% to 50% of their food this way; agriculturalists.

LOZI ***(SILOZI, ROZI, TOZVI, ROTSE, RUTSE, KOLOLO)*** [LOZ] 25,200 in Namibia (1982 Prinsloo et al.) East Caprivi Strip. Niger-Congo, Atlantic-Congo, Volta-Congo, Benue-Congo, Bantoid, Southern, Narrow Bantu, Central, S, Sotho-Tswana (S.30). Used in education, administration, radio broadcasting. Spoken as lingua franca by all East Caprivians. National language. Dictionary. Grammar. Radio programs. Bible 1951-1987. See main entry under Zambia.

MASHI ***(MASI)*** [MHO] A few in Namibia. East Caprivi. Niger-Congo, Atlantic-Congo, Volta-Congo, Benue-Congo, Bantoid, Southern, Narrow Bantu, Central, K, Kwangwa (K.40). Dialects: NORTH KWANDU, SOUTH KWANDU, MASHI. Dialect cluster. Nomadic. Different from Mashi (Shi) which is related to Havu of DRC. Traditional religion. See main entry under Zambia.

MBALANHU ***(MBALANTU, MBAANHU, MBALUNTU)*** [LNB] Northern. Niger-Congo, Atlantic-Congo, Volta-Congo, Benue-Congo, Bantoid, Southern, Narrow Bantu, Central, R, Ndonga (R.20).

MBUKUSHU ***(MBUKUSHI, MAMBUKUSH, MAMPUKUSH, MBUKUHU, THIMBUKUSHU, GOVA, KUSSO)*** [MHW] 20,000 in Namibia (1997 Andersson and Janson). Population total all countries 35,000 to 40,000 (1997). Northwest Ovambo and northeast Okavango area, Andara. Also spoken in Angola, Botswana, Zambia. Niger-Congo, Atlantic-Congo, Volta-Congo, Benue-Congo, Bantoid, Southern, Narrow Bantu, Central, K, Kwangwa (K.40). Close to Kwangali, but separate. National language. Traditional religion, Christian. NT 1986.

NAMA ***(NAMAN, NAMAKWA, NAMAQUA, MAQUA, TAMA, TAMMA, TAMAKWA, BERDAMA, BERGDAMARA, KAKUYA BUSHMAN NASIE, ROOI NASIE, "HOTTENTOT", "KLIPKAFFER", "KLIPKAFFERN", "KHOEKHOEGOWAP", "KHOEKHOEGOWAB")*** [NAQ] 176,201 in Namibia (1992 Barnard), including 70,000 Nama, 105,000 Damara (1998 J. F. Maho). Population total all countries 233,000. South central to the Orange River, Great Namaland. Also spoken in Botswana, South Africa. Khoisan, Southern Africa, Central, Nama. Dialects: DAMARA, SESFONTEIN DAMARA, NAMIDAMA, CENTRAL DAMARA, NAMA. Sesfontein Damara is reported to be unintelligible to speakers of other dialects. Offered as a school subject. Can be studied up to doctoral level at U. of Namibia. Also used in administration and radio broadcasting. National language. Dictionary. Grammar. SOV. Radio programs. Pastoralist. Bible 1966.

NAMIBIAN SIGN LANGUAGE [NBS] Deaf sign language. Dictionary.

NARO ***(NHARO)*** [NHR] 4,000 in Namibia (1998 Maho). Eastern Namibia. Khoisan, Southern Africa, Central, Tshu-Khwe, Southwest. Dictionary. Grammar. Agriculturalists. See main entry under Botswana.

NDONGA ***(OCHINDONGA, OSHINDONGA, OSINDONGA, OTJIWAMBO, OWAMBO, AMBO)*** [NDG] (713,919 in Namibia together with Kwanyama and Kwambi; 1991 census). Population total both countries 240,000 (1987 UBS). Ovamboland. Also spoken in Angola. Niger-Congo, Atlantic-Congo, Volta-Congo, Benue-Congo, Bantoid, Southern, Narrow Bantu, Central, R, Ndonga (R.20). Dialects: NGANDYERA, EUNDA KOLONKADHI, KWALUDHI. Ngandyera may be a separate language. Partially intelligible with Kwanyama. Called 'Otjiwambo' and 'Owambo' together with the Kwanyama and Kwambi. Highly acculturated. National language. Dictionary. Grammar. Literacy rate in second language: 75%. Christian, traditional religion. Bible 1954-1986.

SUBIYA ***(ECHISUBIA, SUBIA, SUPIA, CHIKWAHANE, CHIKUAHANE, CIIKUHANE, MBALANGWE)*** [SBS] 24,500 in Namibia (1991). 37.1% of population in East Caprivi (1982 Prinloo et al.) Population total all countries 42,000. East Caprivi. Also spoken in Botswana, Zambia. Niger-Congo, Atlantic-Congo, Volta-Congo, Benue-Congo, Bantoid, Southern, Narrow Bantu, Central, K, Subia (K.50). Their name for their language is 'Chikwahane'. 'Subiya' is the Tswana name. Tonga is a separate language. 'Mbalangwe' is applied to Subiya speakers living in the Mafwe area (Anton Bredell, J. F. Maho 1998:51). Grammar. Traditional religion, Christian.

TOTELA ***(ECHITOTELA)*** [TTL] East Caprivi. Niger-Congo, Atlantic-Congo, Volta-Congo, Benue-Congo, Bantoid, Southern, Narrow Bantu, Central, K, Subia (K.50). Apparently no linguistic descriptions have been written. See main entry under Zambia.

TSWANA [TSW] 6,050 in Namibia (1991 census). East central Namibia and Eastern Caprivi. Niger-Congo, Atlantic-Congo, Volta-Congo, Benue-Congo, Bantoid, Southern, Narrow Bantu, Central, S, Sotho-Tswana (S.30), Tswana. Dialects: TLHARO, TLHAPING, TAWANA. Education, administration, radio broadcasting. National language. Radio programs. Pastoral: cattle, agriculturalists. Bible 1857-1993. See main entry under Botswana.

VASEKELA BUSHMAN ***(!'O-!KHUNG)*** [VAJ] Western Caprivi area. Khoisan, Southern Africa, Northern. May be the same as 'Akhoe or Kung-Ekoka. Large numbers migrated to Namibia and South Africa because of the war in Angola.

!XÓÕ [NMN] 200 in Namibia (1985 Traill). Along the east central Botswana border in the vicinity of Aranos and Leonardville. Khoisan, Southern Africa, Southern, Hua. Dialects: AUNI (/AUNI, /AUO), KAKIA (MASARWA), KI/HAZI, NG/U/EN (NU//EN, /U//EN, NG/U/EI, /NU//EN, //U//EN), NUSAN (NG/USAN, NU-SAN, NOOSAN), XATIA (KATIA, KHATIA, KATTEA, VAALPENS, /KUSI, /EIKUSI), !KWI. The N/gamani, /Nu//en, /'Auni, and Ki/hazi are extinct. Grammar. See main entry under Botswana.

YEYI ***(SHIYEYI, YEI, YEEI, CIYEI, KOBA, KUBA)*** [YEY] 5,200 in Namibia (1998 Maho). East Caprivi strip. Niger-Congo, Atlantic-Congo, Volta-Congo, Benue-Congo, Bantoid, Southern, Narrow Bantu, Central, R, Yeye (R.40). Dialect: SHIRWANGA. Second languages are Subiya, Mbukushu, Mashi, Lozi. They speak many languages of the Caprivi with those speakers. Speakers are from 2 years to over 65 years old. Literacy rate in second language: 45% in Lozi. Christian. See main entry under Botswana.

ZEMBA ***(DHIMBA, OTJIDHIMBA, HIMBA, SIMBA, OLUTHIMBA, LUZIMBA)*** [DHM] 12,000 in Namibia (1996 UBS). Kunene Region, northwest Namibia, especially around Etoto and Ruacana, near the Herero. Niger-Congo, Atlantic-Congo, Volta-Congo, Benue-Congo, Bantoid, Southern, Narrow Bantu,

Central, R, Herero (R.30). Himba may be a different language. Speakers are called 'Luzimba', 'Ovazemba', or 'Ovazimba'. Bible portions 1970-1984. See main entry under Angola.

NIGER

Republic of Niger. République du Niger. National or official languages: Official: French; National: Arabic, Fulfulde, Gourmanchéma, Hausa, Kanuri, Tamajaq, Tubu, Zarma. 10,078,000 (1998 UN). Literacy rate 17%. Information mainly from J. Lukas 1937; J. Applegate 1970; D. Sapir 1971; R. Nicolai 1979, 1981, 1983; J. Bendor-Samuel 1989; K. Isaac 1998. Muslim, traditional religion, Christian. Blind population 30,000 (1998). Deaf population 20,000 (1998). Data accuracy estimate: A2, B. The number of languages listed for Niger is 20. Of those, all are living languages. Diversity index 0.64.

ARABIC, ALGERIAN SAHARAN SPOKEN [AAO] 10,000 in Niger (1998). Around Agadez and northwest Niger. Afro-Asiatic, Semitic, Central, South, Arabic. Bilingualism in Tamajaq. Originally from Algeria. Muslim. See main entry under Algeria.

ARABIC, HASSANIYYA *(MAURE, MAURI, MOOR, SULAKA, HASANYA, HASSANI)* [MEY] 10,000 in Niger (1998). Afro-Asiatic, Semitic, Central, South, Arabic. Muslim. See main entry under Mauritania.

ARABIC, LIBYAN SPOKEN *(LIBYAN VERNACULAR ARABIC, SULAIMITIAN ARABIC)* [AYL] 5,000 in Niger (1998). Eastern Niger north of N'guigmi near Ngourti. Afro-Asiatic, Semitic, Central, South, Arabic. Similar to the bedouin Arabic of southern Tunisia. Investigation needed: intelligibility. Muslim. See main entry under Libya.

ARABIC, SHUWA *(ARABE CHOA, SHUWA ARABIC, SHUA, CHADIC ARABIC)* [SHU] 5,000 in Niger (1998). Eastern Niger. Afro-Asiatic, Semitic, Central, South, Arabic. Muslim. NT 1967-1991. See main entry under Chad.

DAZAGA *(DASA, DAZZA, DAZA, TUBU, TEBU, TIBBU, TOUBOU)* [DAK] 30,000 in Niger (1998 SIL). Eastern Niger in the south near the Chad border. Nilo-Saharan, Saharan, Western, Tebu. Dialects: DAZAGA, AZZAGA (AZZA, AZA). Closely related to Tedaga. Azzaga, the speech of the Azza, a caste division, is different from Dazaga. Its relation to Dazaga and to the speech of the Azza among the Teda is not known. Low bilingualism in Arabic. The government plans to develop Dazaga for formal and informal education. 'Daza' is the name for the people, 'Dazaga' for the language. In Niger the outsider term 'Tubu' groups Dazaga and Tedaga. Different from Daza in Nigeria, which is Chadic. National language. Muslim. See main entry under Chad.

FRENCH [FRN] 6,000 in Niger (1993 Johnstone). Indo-European, Italic, Romance, Italo-Western, Western, Gallo-Iberian, Gallo-Romance, Gallo-Rhaetian, Oïl, French. Official language. Bible 1530-1986. See main entry under France.

FULFULDE, CENTRAL-EASTERN NIGER *(PEUL, PEULH, FULANI, FULA, FULBE)* [FUQ] 450,000 (1998). Central and eastern Niger, from around Dogondoutchi on eastward to the Chad border. Niger-Congo, Atlantic-Congo, Atlantic, Northern, Senegambian, Fula-Wolof, Fulani, East Central. Dialect: WODAABE. Woodabe culture is distinct from other Fulfulde varieties. Many use Hausa as second language. The Fulbe (15,000,000) from Senegal to Sudan consider themselves to be one ethnic group and to speak one language, while acknowledging differences in speech. The people are 'Pullo' (sg.) or 'Fulbe' (pl.), the language 'Fulfulde'. The English name is 'Fulani' and the French 'Peul'. Many loan words from Hausa. Investigation needed: attitudes. National language. SVO; prepositions and postpositions; genitives, articles, adjectives, numerals, relatives after noun heads; question word final; 1 prefix, 9 suffixes; word order distinguishes subjects, objects, indirect objects, given and new information, topic and comment; verb affixes mark number, subject (obligatory); class marking with participle obligatory; middle and passive voice; causatives; CV, CVC, CVV, CVVC; nontonal. Radio programs, TV. Muslim, traditional religion.

FULFULDE, WESTERN NIGER *(PEUL, PEULH, FULANI, FULA, FULBE)* [FUH] 400,000 in Niger (1998). Population total both countries 1,150,000. Western Niger, from Burkina Faso border east to around Dogondoutchi. Also spoken in Burkina Faso. Niger-Congo, Atlantic-Congo, Atlantic, Northern, Senegambian, Fula-Wolof, Fulani, East Central. Dialects: DALLOL, BITINKOORE. Many use Zarma as second language. The Fulbe from Senegal to Sudan consider themselves to be one ethnic group and to speak one language, while acknowledging differences in speech. The Fulbe call their language 'Fulfulde' and the people 'Fulbe' (pl.), 'Pullo' (sg.). National language. SVO; prepositions and postpositions; genitives, articles, adjectives, numerals, relatives after noun heads; question word final; 1 prefix, 9 suffixes; word order distinguishes subjects, objects, indirect objects, given and new information, topic and comment; verb affixes mark number, subject (obligatory); class marking with participle obligatory; middle and passive voice; causatives; CV, CVC, CVV, CVVC; nontonal. Radio programs, TV. Muslim.

GOURMANCHÉMA ***(GOURMA, GURMA, GOURMANTCHE, GOULIMANCEMA)*** [GUX] 30,000 in Niger (1998). Southwest, near Burkina Faso border. Niger-Congo, Atlantic-Congo, Volta-Congo, North, Gur, Central, Northern, Oti-Volta, Gurma. National language. Radio programs, TV. Traditional religion, Muslim, Christian. NT 1958-1990. See main entry under Burkina Faso.

HAUSA ***(HAUSSA, HAOUSSA, HAUSAWA)*** [HUA] 5,000,000 first language speakers in Niger (1998). Mother tongue speakers in central Niger along the Nigeria border. Spoken in cities throughout Niger. Afro-Asiatic, Chadic, West, A, A.1. Dialects: DAWRA, KATSINA, DAMAGARAM, GOBIRAWA, ADERAWA, AREWA, KURFEY, GAYA. Spoken by 55% of the population as mother tongue, by 25% as second language. The main trade language of Niger. National language. Dictionary. Radio programs, TV. Muslim. Bible 1932-1996. See main entry under Nigeria.

KANURI, CENTRAL ***(YERWA KANURI, KANOURY, KANOURI, BORNU, BORNOUANS, KOLE, SIRATA, "BERIBERI")*** [KPH] 80,000 in Niger (1998). Eastern Niger along the Nigeria border, also at Bilma and Fachi oases in northeastern Niger. Nilo-Saharan, Saharan, Western, Kanuri. Dialects: MOVAR (MOBER, MOBBER, MAVAR), BILMA, FACHI. Yerwa in Nigeria is the central dialect. Part of a dialect chain that includes other Kanuri dialects and Kanembu in Chad. "Beriberi" is considered a derogatory name. Dictionary. Grammar. Ajami script used. Muslim. NT, in press (1997). See main entry under Nigeria.

KANURI, MANGA ***(MANGA, KANOURI, KANOURY)*** [KBY] 280,000 in Niger (1998). Population total both countries 480,000. Eastern Niger along the Nigeria border. Also spoken in Nigeria. Nilo-Saharan, Saharan, Western, Kanuri. Dialects: MANGA, DAGARA. Part of a dialect chain that includes other Kanuri varieties and Kanembu in Chad. National language. Literacy rate in second language: 30% possibly. 4 experimental schools. Radio programs, TV. Muslim. Bible portions.

KANURI, TUMARI ***(KANEMBU, KANAMBU)*** [KRT] 40,000 (1998). Tumari in N'guigmi and the other dialects in neighboring villages. Nilo-Saharan, Saharan, Western, Kanuri. Dialects: TUMARI, SUGURTI (SUWURTI), KUBARI. Not the same as Kanembu in Chad, although referred to as 'Kanembu' in Niger. There is a gradual differentiation between Kanembu in Chad and Kanuri dialects. About half the population use Hausa as second language. A few use Dazaga. 50% reported themselves to be monolingual. Muslim, traditional religion.

TAGDAL ***(TIHISHIT)*** [TDA] 25,000 (1998 SIL). Central Niger, Tahoua to Agadez. Nilo-Saharan, Songhai, Northern. Dialects: TABAROG, TAGDAL. Closely related to Tasawaq and Tadaksahak (Algeria, Mali). Bilingualism in Tamajaq. Shares features of Songai and Tamajaq. Ethnic group names are Iberogan (speak Tabarog) and Igdalen (speak Tagdal). Muslim.

TAMAHAQ, TAHAGGART ***(TAMASHEQ, TAMACHEK, TAMASHEKIN, TOMACHEK, TUAREG, TOUAREG, TOURAGE)*** [THV] 20,000 (1998). The Hoggar dialect is in the south Hoggar (Ajjer) Mountain area around Tamanrasset and south into Niger. The Ghat dialect is in southeast Algeria around Ganet and west Libyan oases around Ghat. Afro-Asiatic, Berber, Tamasheq, Northern. Dialects: HOGGAR (AHAGGAREN, AJJER, TAHAGGART), GHAT (GANET, DJANET). 'Tamahaq' is the speakers' name for their language. 'Tuareg' is an Arabic name for the people. Nomadic. Traditional script called 'Shifinagh'. Volcanic mountains. Nomadic. Inadan caste: blacksmiths, jewelry craftsmen. Muslim. Bible portions 1948-1965. See main entry under Algeria.

TAMAJAQ, TAWALLAMMAT ***(TAMASHEQ, TAMACHEK, TOMACHECK, TAMASHEKIN, TUAREG, TOUAREG, TOURAGE, AMAZIGH, TAHOUA, TEWELLEMET, TAHOUA TAMAJEQ)*** [TTQ] 450,000 in Niger (1998). Population total all countries 640,000. The eastern dialect is in central Niger, around Tahoua from Ingal to the Mali border. The western dialect is in western Niger, north and northwest of Niamey and in eastern Mali, Menaka region. Also spoken in Mali, Nigeria. Afro-Asiatic, Berber, Tamasheq, Southern. Dialects: TAWALLAMMAT TAN DANNAG (IOULLEMMEDEN), TAWALLAMMAT TAN ATARAM. 'Tuareg' is an Arabic name for the people. They call their language 'Tamajaq' and themselves 'Kel Tamajaq'. Nomadic. National language. Traditional script called 'Shifinagh'. Radio programs. Pastoralists, agriculturalists. Muslim. Bible portions 1979-1985.

TAMAJEQ, TAYART ***(TAMACHEK, TOMACHECK, AMAZIGH, TUAREG, TOUAREG)*** [THZ] 250,000 (1998). Central, Agadez area. Afro-Asiatic, Berber, Tamasheq, Southern. Dialects: AIR (AGADEZ, TAYART, TAYERT, TAMESTAYERT), TANASSFARWAT (TAMAGARAST). The speakers' name for their language is 'Tamajeq'. Nomadic. Traditional script called 'Shifinagh'. Radio programs. Muslim. NT 1990.

TASAWAQ ***(INGELSHI)*** [TWQ] 8,000 (1998 SIL). Central Niger, Ingal and Teguidda-n-Tessoumt, near Agadez. Nilo-Saharan, Songhai, Northern. Closely related to Tagdal and Tadaksahak (Algeria, Mali). Bilingualism in Hausa. Shares features of Songai and Tamajaq. The people call themselves 'Ingalkoyyu', 'The lords of Ingal'. Muslim.

TEDAGA ***(TEDA, TUBU, TEBU, TIBBU, TOUBOU)*** [TUQ] 10,000 in Niger (1998 SIL). Seguedine, Bilma, Termit-Kaoboul. Nilo-Saharan, Saharan, Central. Closely related to Dazaga. Azzaga, the speech of the Azza, a caste division, is different from Tedaga, but its relation to Tedaga and to the speech of the Azza among the Daza is not known. Speakers are bilingual in Dazaga. The majority are bilingual in Arabic. 'Teda' is the name for the people, 'Tedaga' for the language. In Niger the outsider term 'Tubu' groups Dazaga and Tedaga. Semi-nomadic. Well diggers, pastoralists: camels. Muslim. See main entry under Chad.

ZARMA ***(DYERMA, DYARMA, DYABARMA, ADZERMA, DJERMA, ZABARMA, ZARBARMA, ZARMACI)*** [DJE] 2,100,000 in Niger (1998). Population total all countries 2,151,000. Southwestern Niger. Also spoken in Benin, Burkina Faso, Mali, Nigeria. Nilo-Saharan, Songhai, Southern. Dialect: KAADO. In Niger, dialects from Dendi and Songai blend into Zarma. Intelligibility is high, although they use ethnic names 'Dendi' or 'Songai' for themselves. Speakers cannot understand Gao Songai in Mali. Ethnic groups include Kurtey (32,000), Wogo (28,000), Songai (400,000), Dendi (40,000). National language. Dictionary. Radio programs, TV. Muslim, traditional religion, some Christian. Bible 1990.

NIGERIA

Federal Republic of Nigeria. National or official languages: Edo, Efik, Adamawa Fulfulde, Hausa, Idoma, Igbo, Yerwa Kanuri, Yoruba, English. 106,409,000 (1998 UN). Literacy rate 42% to 51%. Also includes Bagirmi, Klao, Mbay, Mpade, Ngambay, Pana, people from Lebanon, Europe. Information mainly from K. Hansford, J. Bendor-Samuel, and R. Stanford 1976; J. Bendor-Samuel 1989; D. Crozier and R. Blench 1992; R. Blench 1998-1999; B. Connell 1998-1999; U. Siebert 1998-1999. Christian, Muslim, traditional religion. Blind population 800,000 (1982 WCE). Deaf institutions: 22. Data accuracy estimate: A2, B. The number of languages listed for Nigeria is 515. Of those, 505 are living languages, 2 are second languages without mother tongue speakers, and 8 are extinct. Diversity index 0.88.

ABANYOM ***(ABANYUM, BEFUN, BOFON, MBOFON)*** [ABM] 12,500 (1986). Cross River State, Ikom LGA, Abangkang the main village. Niger-Congo, Atlantic-Congo, Volta-Congo, Benue-Congo, Bantoid, Southern, Ekoid.

ABON ***(ABONG, ABÕ, BA'BAN)*** [ABO] 1,000 (1973 SIL). Taraba State, Sardauna LGA, Abong town, east of Baissa. Niger-Congo, Atlantic-Congo, Volta-Congo, Benue-Congo, Bantoid, Southern, Tivoid. Investigation needed: bilingual proficiency in Hausa, attitudes.

ABUA ***(ABUAN)*** [ABN] 25,000 (1989 Faraclas). Rivers State, Degema and Ahoada LGAs. Niger-Congo, Atlantic-Congo, Volta-Congo, Benue-Congo, Cross River, Delta Cross, Central Delta, Abua-Odual. Dialects: CENTRAL ABUAN, EMUGHAN, OTABHA (OTAPHA), OKPEDEN. The central dialect is understood by all others. Odual is the most closely related language. About 70% lexical similarity with Odual. Dictionary. NT 1978.

ACIPA, EASTERN ***(ACIPANCI, ACHIPA, SAGAMUK)*** [AWA] 5,000 (1993). Niger State, Kontagora LGA; Kaduna State, Birnin Gwari LGA. Towns include Randeggi and Bobi. Niger-Congo, Atlantic-Congo, Volta-Congo, Benue-Congo, Kainji, Western, Kamuku. Dialect: BOROMA (TABOROMA). 83% lexical similarity between Randeggi and Bobi; 52% with Shama, 47% to 50% with Kamuku, 42% to 44% with Hungworo, 15% to 20% with Western Acipa. The influence of the Hausa language is slight. The people are called 'Acipawa'. Traditional religion.

ACIPA, WESTERN ***(ACIPANCI, ACHIPA, SAGAMUK)*** [AWC] 20,000 (1995 CAPRO). Niger State, Kontagora LGA; Kebbi State, Sakaba LGA. Towns include Kumbashi, Kakihum, and Karisen. Niger-Congo, Atlantic-Congo, Volta-Congo, Benue-Congo, Kainji, Western, Kamuku. Dialect: CEP (TOCHIPO, TACEP, WESTERN ACIPANCI). Morphological evidence suggests its affiliation with the Kamuku language cluster. 89% to 95% lexical similarity among the dialects; 15% to 20% with Eastern Acipa, 18% with Hungworo, 16% to 17% with Shama, 15% to 17% with Kamuku. The influence of the Hausa language is slight. The people are called 'Acipawa'. Traditional religion.

ADUGE [ADU] 1,904 (1992 Crozier and Blench). Anambra State, Oyi LGA. Niger-Congo, Atlantic-Congo, Volta-Congo, Benue-Congo, Edoid, Northwestern. Investigation needed: bilingual proficiency in Igbo, attitudes. Grammar.

AFADE ***(AFFADE, AFADEH, AFADA, KOTOKO, MOGARI)*** [AAL] 25,000 in Nigeria (1998 R. M. Blench). Population total both countries 25,000 or more. Borno State, Ngala LGA, 12 rather dense villages. Also spoken in Cameroon. Afro-Asiatic, Chadic, Biu-Mandara, B, B.1, Kotoko Proper. All Kotoko-language speakers in Nigeria may speak Afade. Investigation needed: bilingual proficiency in Hausa, attitudes.

AGATU ***(NORTH IDOMA, OCHEKWU)*** [AGC] 70,000 (1987 UBS). Benue State, Otuko Divison, districts of Agatu, Ochekwu, and Adoka; Nasarawa State, Awe and Nasarawa LGAs. Niger-Congo, Atlantic-Congo, Volta-Congo, Benue-Congo, Idomoid, Akweya, Etulo-Idoma, Idoma. In Idoma dialect cluster. NT 1984.

AGOI ***(WAGOI, RO BAMBAMI, WA BAMBANI, IBAMI)*** [IBM] 12,000 (1989 Faraclas). Cross River State, Obubra LGA, Agoi-Ekpo, Ekom-Agoi, Agoi-Ibami, and Itu-Agoi towns. Niger-Congo, Atlantic-Congo,

Volta-Congo, Benue-Congo, Cross River, Delta Cross, Upper Cross, Agoi-Doko-Iyoniyong. Dialect: IKO.

AGWAGWUNE ***("AKUNAKUNA", AGWAGUNA, GWUNE, AKURAKURA, OKURIKAN)*** [YAY] 20,000 (1973 SIL). Cross River State, Akamkpa LGA. Niger-Congo, Atlantic-Congo, Volta-Congo, Benue- Congo, Cross River, Delta Cross, Upper Cross, Central, North-South, Ubaghara-Kohumono, Kohumono. Dialects: ABAYONGO (BAYONO, BAYINO), ABINI (OBINI, ABIRI), ADIM (ODIM, DIM), ORUM, EREI (ENNA, EZEI), AGWAGWUNE, ETONO (ETUNO). A dialect cluster. Bible portions 1894.

ÀHÀN ***(AHAAN)*** [AHN] A few hundred (1998 Blench). Ondo State, Ekiti LGA, Ajowa, Igashi, and Omou towns. Niger-Congo, Atlantic-Congo, Volta-Congo, Benue-Congo, Defoid, Ayere-Ahan.

AJAWA ***(AJA, AJANCI)*** [AJW] Bauchi State. Afro-Asiatic, Chadic, West, B, B.2. Related to Miya. Became extinct between 1920 and 1940. The people now speak Hausa. Extinct.

AKE ***(AIKE, AKYE)*** [AIK] 2,000 (1999 R. Blench). Nasarawa State, Lafia LGA, 3 villages. Niger-Congo, Atlantic-Congo, Volta-Congo, Benue-Congo, Platoid, Plateau, Western, Southwestern, B. The closest language is Eggon. Bilingualism in Hausa. There is concern in the largest village that people are losing their language to Hausa.

AKPA ***(AKWEYA)*** [AKF] 5,500 (1952 Robert G. Armstrong). Benue State, Otukpo LGA. Niger-Congo, Atlantic-Congo, Volta-Congo, Benue-Congo, Idomoid, Yatye-Akpa. Dialect cluster. 84% lexical similarity with Ekpari.

AKPES ***(IBARAM-EFIFA)*** [IBE] 10,000 or more (1992 Crozier and Blench). Ondo State, Akoko North LGA. Niger-Congo, Atlantic-Congo, Volta-Congo, Benue-Congo, Akpes. Dialects: AKUNNU (AKPES), ASE, DAJA, EFIFA, ESUKU (ECHUKU), GEDEGEDE, IKOROM, IBARAM, IYANI. A dialect cluster. Yoruba is the lingua franca. Investigation needed: bilingual proficiency in Yoruba, attitudes.

AKUM ***(ANYAR)*** [AKU] Taraba State, near the Cameroon border, 3 villages in Nigeria (Manga, Ekban, Konkom). Niger-Congo, Atlantic-Congo, Volta-Congo, Benue-Congo, Cross River, Unclassified. Not Bendi; may be Jukunoid. Bilingualism in Jukun is limited. Cameroons Pidgin is spoken in the area also. The people are called 'Anyar'. Mountain slope. See main entry under Cameroon.

ALAGO ***(ARAGU, ARAGO, ARGO, IDOMA NOKWU)*** [ALA] 35,000 (1973 SIL). Nasarawa State, Awe and Lafia LGAs. Niger-Congo, Atlantic-Congo, Volta-Congo, Benue-Congo, Idomoid, Akweya, Etulo-Idoma, Idoma. Dialects: DOMA, AGWATASHI, KEANA, ASSAIKIO. Bilingualism in Hausa. Literacy rate in second language: 5%. Traditional religion, Muslim, Christian. Bible portions 1929.

ALEGE ***(ALEGI, UGE, UGBE)*** [ALF] 1,200 (1973 SIL). Cross River State, Obudu LGA. Niger-Congo, Atlantic-Congo, Volta-Congo, Benue-Congo, Cross River, Bendi. Related to Gayi (Bisu of Obanliku cluster) of Nigeria and Cameroon.

AMBO [AMB] 1,000 or fewer. Taraba State, Sardauna LGA, 1 village east of Baissa. Niger-Congo, Atlantic-Congo, Volta-Congo, Benue-Congo, Bantoid, Southern, Tivoid.

AMO ***(AMON, AMONG, TIMAP, BA)*** [AMO] 3,550 (1950). Plateau State, Bassa LGA; Kaduna State, Saminaka LGA. Niger-Congo, Atlantic-Congo, Volta-Congo, Benue-Congo, Kainji, Eastern, Amo. Not close to other languages. 'Timap' is the language, 'Kumap' a speaker, 'Amap' the people. Investigation needed: bilingual proficiency in Hausa, attitudes. Grammar.

ANAANG ***(ANANG, ANNANG)*** [ANW] 1,000,000 (1990). Akwa Ibom State, Ikot Ekpene, Essien Udim, Abak, Ukanafun, and Oruk-Anam LGAs. Niger-Congo, Atlantic-Congo, Volta-Congo, Benue-Congo, Cross River, Delta Cross, Lower Cross, Obolo, Efik. Dialects: IKOT EKPENE, ABAK, UKANAFUN. Referred to locally as 'Ekpene', 'Abak', and 'Ukanafun'. Used as a medium of instruction in the schools. TV.

ÁNCÁ ***(BUNTA)*** [ACB] Taraba State, Sardauna LGA, Antere, Nca village. Niger-Congo, Atlantic-Congo, Volta-Congo, Benue-Congo, Bantoid, Unclassified. May be the same as Manta.

ARABIC, SHUWA ***(ARABE CHOA, SHUWA, SHUA ARABIC, CHADIAN ARABIC)*** [SHU] 100,000 in Nigeria (1973 SIL). Borno State, Dikwa, Konduga, Ngala, and Bama LGAs, and ranging widely across Borno and Yobe states on transhumance. Afro-Asiatic, Semitic, Central, South, Arabic. No diglossia with Modern Standard Arabic. The term 'Shua' is considered perjorative by some people. Trade language. Muslim. NT 1967-1991. See main entry under Chad.

ARIGIDI ***(NORTH AKOKO)*** [AKK] 48,000 or more, including 45,000 Igasi, 3,000 Uro (1986 in Crozier and Blench 1992). Ondo State, Akoko North LGA; Kogi State, Kogi LGA. Niger-Congo, Atlantic-Congo, Volta-Congo, Benue-Congo, Defoid, Akokoid. Dialects: OYIN, URO, ARIGIDÍ, ERÚSÚ (ERUSHU), OJO, UDO (IDO, ÒWÒN ÙDÒ, OKE-AGBE), AFA (AFFA, ÒWÒN ÀFÁ, OKE-AGBE), ÒGE (ÒWÒN ÒGÈ), AJE, ESE (ÒWÒN ÈSÉ), IGASI (ÌGÀSHÍ, ÒWÒN ÌGÁSÍ). A dialect cluster.

ARUM-TESU ***(ARUM-CESU, ARUM-CHESSU, ALUMU)*** [AAB] 4,000 to 5,000 (1999 Blench). Nasarawa State, Akwanga LGA, near Wamba. Arum is 7 villages and Tesu is 1. Niger-Congo, Atlantic-Congo, Volta-Congo, Benue-Congo, Platoid, Unclassified. Dialects: ARUM, TESU. Related to Toro. The two dialects are reported to have only intonation differences. Language spoken fluently by young people. Investigation needed: bilingual proficiency in Hausa, attitudes.

ASHE *(KORON ACHE, ACHE, ALA, KORON ALA, KORO MAKAMA)* [AHS] (35,000 including Begbere-Ejar; 1972 Barrett). Kaduna State, Kachia LGA. Niger-Congo, Atlantic-Congo, Volta-Congo, Benue-Congo, Platoid, Plateau, Western, Northwestern, Koro. Related to Begbere-Ejar.

ASU *(ABEWA, EBE)* [AUM] 5,000 or fewer (1998 R. Blench). Niger State, Mariga LGA, several villages south of Kontagora. Niger-Congo, Atlantic-Congo, Volta-Congo, Benue-Congo, Nupoid, Nupe-Gbagyi, Nupe. Bilingualism in Nupe. Vigorous. Vocabulary has been heavily influenced by Nupe in recent years (Blench 1991). Investigation needed: bilingual proficiency in Nupe, attitudes.

ATEN *(GANAWURI, ETIEN, JAL, TEN, NITEN)* [GAN] 40,000 (1988 Kjenstad). Plateau State, Barakin Ladi LGA; Kaduna State, Jema'a LGA. Niger-Congo, Atlantic-Congo, Volta-Congo, Benue-Congo, Platoid, Plateau, Central, North-Central. The language is 'Ten', a speaker 'Aten', the people 'Niten'. Bible portions 1940.

ATSAM *(CAWAI, CAWE, CAWI, CHAWAI, CHAWE, CHAWI)* [CCH] 30,000 (1972 Barrett). Kaduna State, Kachia LGA. Niger-Congo, Atlantic-Congo, Volta-Congo, Benue-Congo, Kainji, Eastern, Piti-Atsam. Closest to Piti. Investigation needed: intelligibility with Hausa, attitudes. Traditional religion. Bible portions 1923-1932.

AUYOKAWA *(AUYAKAWA, AWIAKA)* [AUO] Jigawa State, Keffin Hausa and Auyo LGAs. Afro-Asiatic, Chadic, West, B, B.1. Extinct.

AWAK *(AWOK, YEBU)* [AWO] 6,000 (1995 CAPRO). Gombe State, Kaltungo LGA. Niger-Congo, Atlantic-Congo, Volta-Congo, North, Adamawa-Ubangi, Adamawa, Waja-Jen, Waja, Awak. Investigation needed: bilingual proficiency in Hausa, attitudes. Agriculturalists: millet, maize, peanuts, Guinea corn. Christian, traditional religion.

AYERE [AYE] 3,000 or more (Blench 1992:18). Kwara State, Oyi LGA, Kabba district. Niger-Congo, Atlantic-Congo, Volta-Congo, Benue-Congo, Defoid, Ayere-Ahan.

AYU *(AYA)* [AYU] 4,000 (1976 SIL). Kaduna State, Jema'a LGA. Niger-Congo, Atlantic-Congo, Volta-Congo, Benue-Congo, Platoid, Plateau, Ayu. Investigation needed: bilingual proficiency in Hausa, attitudes.

BAAN *(BAAN-OGOI, GOI, OGOI)* [BVJ] 5,000 or fewer (1990). Rivers State, Gokana, Tai, and Eleme LGAs, Ban-Ogoi plus villages. Niger-Congo, Atlantic-Congo, Volta-Congo, Benue-Congo, Cross River, Delta Cross, Ogoni, West. Dialects: KA-BAN, KESARI.

BAANGI *(CIBAANGI)* [BQX] 15,000 estimate (1996). Northern Niger State. Niger-Congo, Atlantic-Congo, Volta-Congo, Benue-Congo, Kainji, Western, Kambari.

BACAMA *(BACHAMA, BASHAMMA, ABACAMA, BESEMA, BWAREBA, GBOARE)* [BAM] 150,000 (1992 CAPRO). Adamawa State, Numan and Guyuk LGAs, Kaduna State, northeast of Kaduna town. Afro-Asiatic, Chadic, Biu-Mandara, A, A.8. Dialects: MULYEN (MULWYIN, MWULYIN), OPALO, WA-DUKU. In Bata dialect cluster. Bacama fishermen migrate long distances down the Benue with camps as far as the confluence. Trade language. Grammar. Agriculturalists, fishermen. Bible portions 1915.

BADA *(BADAWA, BADANCHI, BAT, MBADA, MBAT, MBADAWA, KANNA, JAR, JARAWAN KOGI, GARAKA, RIVER JARAWA, PLAINS JARAWA)* [BAU] 10,000 (SIL). Plateau State, Kanam LGA; Bauchi State, Tafawa Balewa LGA. Niger-Congo, Atlantic-Congo, Volta-Congo, Benue-Congo, Bantoid, Southern, Jarawan, Nigerian. Dialect: GAR. A member of the Jarawa dialect cluster. Traditional religion, Christian, Muslim.

BADE *(BEDDE, BEDE, GIDGID)* [BDE] 250,000 (1993). Yobe State, Bade LGA; Jigawa State, Hadejia LGA. Afro-Asiatic, Chadic, West, B, B.1, Bade Proper. Dialects: GASHUA BADE (MAZGARWA), SOUTHERN BADE (BADE-KADO), WESTERN BADE (MAGWARAM. MAAGWARAM), SHIRAWA. Closely related to Duwai and Ngizim, but separate languages. Fair degree of bilingualism in Hausa, Kanuri, or Fulani. Large ethnic population, but finding competent speakers of Bade is becoming difficult because of a shift to Hausa. Shirawa dialect is extinct. Muslim, traditional religion, Christian.

BAKPINKA *(BEGBUNGBA, UWET, IYONGIYONG, IYONIYONG)* [BBS] Cross River State, Akamkpa LGA. Niger-Congo, Atlantic-Congo, Volta-Congo, Benue-Congo, Cross River, Delta Cross, Upper Cross, Agoi-Doko-Iyoniyong. Reported to be dying out.

BALI *(BIBAALI, MAYA, ABAALI, IBAALI)* [BCN] 2,000 (1991 Blench). Adamawa State, Numan LGA, at Bali, 30 km. from Numan on the road to Jalingo. Niger-Congo, Atlantic-Congo, Volta-Congo, North, Adamawa-Ubangi, Adamawa, Leko-Nimbari, Mumuye-Yandang, Yandang. Closely related to Kpasam. They speak Hausa as second language, and some Bacama or Fulfulde. 'Maya' or 'Abaali' is their name for the language, 'Ibaali' for the people. Investigation needed: bilingual proficiency in Hausa, attitudes. Agriculturalists: Guinea corn, peanuts, rice. Christian, traditional religion, Muslim.

BANGWINJI *(BANGUNJI, BANGJINGE)* [BSJ] 6,000 or fewer (1992 Crozier and Blench). Bauchi State, Balanga, Billiri, and Kaltungo LGAs. Niger-Congo, Atlantic-Congo, Volta-Congo, North, Adamawa-Ubangi, Adamawa, Waja-Jen, Waja, Tula. Dialects: KAALO, NAABAN. Noun class system is closer to Waja and Tula. Investigation needed: bilingual proficiency in Hausa, attitudes. Agriculturalists: Guinea corn, beans, millet, beniseed, cotton, peanuts. Traditional religion.

BARIBA ***(BAATONUN, BATONNUM, BATONU, BAATONUN-KWARA, BARGU, BURGU, BORGU, BORGAWA, BERBA, BARBA, BOGUNG, ZANA)*** [BBA] 100,000 in Nigeria (1995 R. Jones SIM). Kwara State, Borgu LGA; Niger State. Niger-Congo, Atlantic-Congo, Volta-Congo, North, Gur, Bariba. Investigation needed: bilingual proficiency in Boko. Traditional religion, Muslim, Christian. Bible, in press (1997). See main entry under Benin.

BARIKANCHI [BXO] Pidgin, Hausa based. Used in military barracks. Second language only.

BASA ***(BASA-BENUE, RUBASA, RUBASSA, "BASSA-KWOMU", "BASSA-KOMO", ABATSA, ABACHA)*** [BZW] 100,000 (1973 SIL). Kogi State, Bassa and Ankpa LGAs; Plateau State, Nasarawa LGA; Federal Capital Territory, Yaba and Kwali LGAs; Benue State, Makurdi LGA. Niger-Congo, Atlantic-Congo, Volta-Congo, Benue-Congo, Kainji, Western, Basa. North-south dialect division along the Benue River. Bilingualism in Hausa. Speakers do not like the name "Bassa-Kwomu" or "Basa-Komo". Literacy rate in second language: 5%. Traditional religion, Christian, Muslim. NT 1972, out of print.

BASA-GUMNA ***(BASA-KADUNA, BASSA-KADUNA, GWADARA BASA, BASA KUTA)*** [BSL] Niger State, Chanchaga LGA; Plateau State, Nasarawa LGA. Niger-Congo, Atlantic-Congo, Volta-Congo, Benue-Congo, Kainji, Western, Basa. No fluent speakers left in 1987. The ethnic group speaks Hausa. Extinct.

BASA-GURMANA ***(KOROMBA)*** [BUJ] 2,000 or more (Blench 1987). Niger State, border of Rafi and Chanchaga LGAs, Kafin Gurmana. Niger-Congo, Atlantic-Congo, Volta-Congo, Benue-Congo, Kainji, Western, Basa.

BASSA-KONTAGORA [BSR] 10 speakers (1987). Niger State, Mariga LGA, northeast of Kontagora. Niger-Congo, Atlantic-Congo, Volta-Congo, Benue-Congo, Kainji, Western, Basa. Nearly extinct.

BATA ***(GBWATA, BATTA, DEMSA BATA, GBOATI, GBWATE, BETE, BIRSA, DUNU)*** [BTA] 150,000 in Nigeria (1992). Population total both countries 152,500. Adamawa State, Numan, Song, Fufore, and Mubi LGAs. Also spoken in Cameroon. Afro-Asiatic, Chadic, Biu-Mandara, A, A.8. Dialects: ZUMU (ZOMO, JIMO), WADI (WA'I), MALABU, KOBOTACHI, RIBAW, DEMSA, GAROUA, JIRAI. Closely related languages: Bacama, Gude, Nzanyi, Vin, Ziziliveken. They have joined with the Bacama in the Bwatiye Association. Agriculturalists, fishermen, animal husbandry: pigs, goats. Traditional religion, Muslim, Christian.

BATU [BTU] 25,000. Taraba State, Sardauna LGA, several villages east of Baissa, below the Mambila escarpment. Niger-Congo, Atlantic-Congo, Volta-Congo, Benue-Congo, Bantoid, Southern, Tivoid. Dialects: AMANDA-AFI, ANGWE, KAMINO. A language cluster.

BAUCHI ***(BAUCI, BAUSHI, KUSHI)*** [BSF] 20,000 or fewer (1988 Blench). Niger State, Rafi and Shiroro LGAs. Niger-Congo, Atlantic-Congo, Volta-Congo, Benue-Congo, Kainji, Western, Baushi-Gurmana. Dialects: WAYAM-RUBU, MADAKA (ADEKA), SUPANA.

BEELE ***(BELE, ÀBÉÉLÉ, BELLAWA)*** [BXQ] 120 (1922 Temple). Bauchi State, near the Bole, a few villages. Afro-Asiatic, Chadic, West, A, A.2, Bole, Bole Proper. A separate language from Bole. Investigation needed: bilingual proficiency in Hausa, attitudes. Muslim.

BEGBERE-EJAR ***(KORO AGWE, AGERE, KORO MAKAMA, KORO MYAMYA, MIAMIA, MIAMIYA)*** [BQV] 35,000 including Ashe (1972 Barrett). Kaduna State, Kachia LGA, Plateau State, Keffi LGA. Niger-Congo, Atlantic-Congo, Volta-Congo, Benue-Congo, Platoid, Plateau, Western, Northwestern, Koro. Dialects: KORON PANDA, KORON ACHE, EJAR. The alternate names listed refer to the people. 'Koro' is used as a cover term for several groups. Investigation needed: intelligibility with Ejar. Traditional religion, Muslim, Christian.

BEKWARRA ***(EBEKWARA, BEKWORRA, YAKORO)*** [BKV] 100,000 (1989 SIL). Cross River State, Ogoja LGA. Niger-Congo, Atlantic-Congo, Volta-Congo, Benue-Congo, Cross River, Bendi. Grammar. Radio programs, TV. NT 1983.

BENA ***(EBINA, BINNA, GBINNA, EBUNA, BUNA, YONGOR, YUNGUR, YANGERU, PURRA, "LALA")*** [YUN] 95,000 (1992). Adamawa State, Guyuk, Gombi, and Song LGAs, new settlements along the road from Song to Yola. Niger-Congo, Atlantic-Congo, Volta-Congo, North, Adamawa-Ubangi, Adamawa, Waja-Jen, Yungur, Yungur-Roba. Bilingualism in Fulfulde, Kanakuru, Hausa. The name "Lala" is offensive. 'Purra' is a cover term for the northern clans. 17 clans. Traditional religion, Christian, Muslim.

BEROM ***(BIROM, BERUM, GBANG, KIBO, KIBBO, KIBBUN, KIBYEN, "SHOSHO", ABORO, BORO-ABORO, AFANGO, CHENBEROM, CEN BEROM)*** [BOM] 300,000 (1993 SIL). Plateau State, Berakin Ladi and Jos LGAs; Kaduna State, Jema'a LGA; Bauchi State. Niger-Congo, Atlantic-Congo, Volta-Congo, Benue-Congo, Platoid, Plateau, Southern. Dialects: GYELL-KURU-VWANG (NGELL-KURU-VWANG), FAN-FORON-HEIKPANG, BACHIT-GASHISH, DU-ROPP-RIM, HOSS. The language is Cen Berom, a speaker Worom, the people Berom. "Shosho" is an offensive name. Grammar. Literacy rate in first language: 10% to 30%. Literacy rate in second language: 25% to 50%. NT 1984.

BETE [BYF] Few speakers out of 3,000 population (1992). Taraba State, Takum LGA, Bete town, at the foot of Bete mountain. Unclassified. Reported to have been close to Lufu and Bibi. The language is dying out. The people now speak Jukun. 6 subgroups: Aphan (Afan), Ruke, Osu, Agu, Botsu, Humiyan. Formerly had land disputes with the Tiv. Christian, traditional religion. Nearly extinct.

BETE-BENDI ***(BETTE-BENDI, DAMA)*** [BTT] 36,800 (1963). Cross River State, Obudu LGA. Niger-Congo, Atlantic-Congo, Volta-Congo, Benue-Congo, Cross River, Bendi. Dialects: BETE (BETTE, MBETE), BENDI. Not the same as Bete of Nigeria in Gongola State, Bete of Cameroon, or Bété of Côte d'Ivoire. NT 1982.

BILE ***(BILLE, BILLANCHI, KUNBILLE, BILI)*** [BIL] 30,000 (1992). East of Numan, along Benue River, Adamawa State, Numan LGAs, southwest of Numan. Niger-Congo, Atlantic-Congo, Volta-Congo, Benue-Congo, Bantoid, Southern, Jarawan, Nigerian. Related to Mbula-Bwazza. Bilingualism in Hausa, Fulfulde. Investigation needed: bilingual proficiency in Hausa, attitudes. Traditional religion, Christian, Muslim.

BINA ***(BOGANA, BINAWA)*** [BYJ] 2,000 (1973 SIL). Kaduna State, Saminaka LGA. Niger-Congo, Atlantic-Congo, Volta-Congo, Benue-Congo, Kainji, Eastern, Northern Jos, Kauru. Investigation needed: bilingual proficiency in Hausa, attitudes.

BISENI ***(BUSENI, AMEGI, NORTHEAST CENTRAL IJO)*** [IJE] 4,800 (1977 Voegelin and Voegelin). Biyelsa State, Yenagoa LGA. Niger-Congo, Atlantic-Congo, Ijoid, Ijo, Central, Oruma-Northeast Central, Northeast Central. Not intelligible with other languages in the Ijo language cluster.

BITARE ***(NJWANDE, YUKUTARE)*** [BRE] 46,300 in Nigeria. Population total both countries 50,000 (1971 Welmers). Taraba State, Sardauna LGA, near Baissa. Also spoken in Cameroon. Niger-Congo, Atlantic-Congo, Volta-Congo, Benue-Congo, Bantoid, Southern, Tivoid. Closely related to Abong.

BO-RUKUL ***(MABO-BARKUL, MABO-BARUKUL, "KALERI")*** [MAE] 1,000 to 2,000, including 1,000 in each dialect (1998 Daniel Nettle). Plateau State, Bokkos LGA, Barkul, Mabo, Richa, Horom, Mwa villages. Niger-Congo, Atlantic-Congo, Volta-Congo, Benue-Congo, Platoid, Plateau, Southeastern. Dialects: BO, RUKUL. A language cluster. They speak Hausa and Kulere outside the village. Hausa is the lingua franca. English is restricted to young people, especially men, used in education and government. They speak Bo and Rukul within the village. Vigorous. *ma-* (sg.) and *ba-* (pl.) are prefixes referring to speakers. Culturally they are considered to be Kulere, but the language is different. "Kaleri" is a derogatory name. Investigation needed: bilingual proficiency in Hausa, attitudes. Literacy rate in second language: 50% of young people read Hausa haltingly. Christian (most).

BOGA ***(BOKA)*** [BOD] Adamawa State, Gombi LGA. Afro-Asiatic, Chadic, Biu-Mandara, A, A.1, Eastern. Investigation needed: intelligibility with Ga'anda.

BOGHOM ***(BOGGHOM, BOHOM, BUROM, BURUM, BURRUM, BURMA, BORROM, BOGHOROM, BOKIYIM)*** [BUX] 50,000 (1973 SIL). Plateau State, Kanam, Wase, and Shendam LGAs. Afro-Asiatic, Chadic, West, B, B.3, Boghom. Related to Mangas. Bible portions 1955.

BOKO ***(BOKKO, BOKONYA, BOO)*** [BQC] 40,000 in Nigeria (1995 R. Jones). Niger State, Borgu LGA; Kebbi State, Bagudo LGA, from Senji in the north to Kenugbe and Kaoje, 150 km. to the south and Demmo, 50 km. to the east, 35 villages. Niger-Congo, Mande, Eastern, Eastern, Busa. Other Busa languages in Nigeria require separate literature: Bokobaru, Busa-Bisa, Shanga, Tyenga. 86% lexical similarity with Bokobaru, 85% with Busa, 52% with Kyenga, 51% with Bissa in Burkina Faso. Bilingualism in Bariba, Hausa, English. Pride in their language. They call their language 'Boo'; the Hausa call all Busa languages 'Busanchi' and the people 'Busawa'. Dictionary. Grammar. Adult literacy program. Muslim, traditional religion, Christian. Bible 1992. See main entry under Benin.

BOKOBARU ***(BUSA-BOKOBARU, ZONGBEN, ZÕGB□)*** [BUS] 30,000 (1997 Ross Jones SIM), including 6,000 in Kaiama, 24,000 in other villages. Kwara State, primarily Kaiama LGA, some in Baruten LGA. 35 villages. Niger-Congo, Mande, Eastern, Eastern, Busa. Dialects: KAIAMA, VILLAGE BOKOBARU. Speakers of Kaiama and dialect in other villages have good inherent intelligibility of each other's dialects. The Bokobaru variety is distinct enough to require separate literature from Boko of Benin. The Busa variety of Nigeria may also require separate literature. 86% lexical similarity with Boko, 91% with Busa, 53% with Kyenga, 50% with Bissa of Burkina Faso and Ghana. Bilingual level estimates for English are 0 80%, 1 10%, 2 4%, 3 3%, 4 2%, 5 1%. Some speakers use Hausa, Yoruba, English, Bariba, Fulfulde as second languages to speakers from those groups. Some use Hausa or English among themselves. Kaiama has more prestige and is used for literature. Speakers have pride in Bokobaru. The people are Bussawa. They call their language 'Bussagwe'. The Hausa call their language 'Busanchi'. Dictionary. Grammar. SOV; genitives before noun heads; articles, adjective, numerals, relatives after noun heads; question word initial or final; 4 suffixes; word order distinguishes subject, object, indirect object; postpositions; person, number, aspect included in subject pronouns; tone changes some verb aspect; passives; CV, CVV, CCV; tonal. Literacy rate in second language: 10%. High motivation for literacy. Adult literacy program. Savannah. Interfluvial. Peasant agriculturalists. Muslim, traditional religion, Christian. Bible portions 1972-1998.

BOKYI ***(BOKI, NKI, OKII, UKI, NFUA, OSIKOM, OSUKAM, VAANEROKI)*** [BKY] 140,000 in Nigeria (1989 SIL). Population total both countries 144,000. Cross River State, Ikom, Obudu, and Ogoja LGAs. Also spoken in Cameroon. Niger-Congo, Atlantic-Congo, Volta-Congo, Benue-Congo, Cross River, Bendi. Dialects: BASUA (BASHUA), IRRUAN (ERWAN, EERWEE), BOJE (BOJIE), KWAKWAGOM, NSADOP, OSOKOM, WULA (BASWO, OKUNDI, KECWAN), OKU, BOORIM, OYOKOM, ABO (ABU), EASTERN BOKYI (EAST BOKI). Important district language. Ethnic groups: Ndir, Ukwese, Utang, Yon. Bible 1987.

BOLE ***(BOLANCHI, AMPIKA, BORPIKA, BOLEWA, BOLAWA)*** [BOL] 100,000 (1990). Bauchi State, Dukku, Alkaleri, and Darazo LGAs; Gombe State, Dukku LGA; Yobe State, Fika LGA; Plateau State, Wase LGA. Afro-Asiatic, Chadic, West, A, A.2, Bole, Bole Proper. Dialects: BARA, FIKA (FIKANKAYEN, ANPIKA). Speakers are called 'Bolewa' or 'Bolawa'. Bele is a separate language. The Ngara (2,000 in 1993) claim to be part of Bole, but the Bolewa disagree. Investigation needed: bilingual proficiency in Hausa, attitudes. Grammar. Muslim.

BOZO, SOROGAMA ***(SOROGAMA, COROGAMA, SORKO, SARKANCI, SARKAWA, JENAMA, NONONKE, "BOSO")*** [BZE] Niger, Kwara, and Kebbi states, Lake Kainji. Niger-Congo, Mande, Western, Northwestern, Samogo, Soninke-Bobo, Soninke-Boso, Boso, Sorogama. Bilingualism in Hausa. Those in Nigeria mainly speak Hausa as mother tongue. In Nigeria, 'Sorko' is preferred. Fishermen. Muslim. See main entry under Mali.

BU ***(JIDA-ABU, JIDDA-ABU, JIDA, IBUT, NAKARE)*** [JID] 6,000 including 4,000 Bu and 2,000 Ninkada (1999 R. Blench). Nasarawa State, Akwanga LGA, 4 villages. Niger-Congo, Atlantic-Congo, Volta-Congo, Benue-Congo, Platoid, Plateau, Western, Southwestern, A. Dialects: BU (ABU), NINKADA (JIDA). The 2 dialects are ethnically and geographically distinct, but linguistically similar. Closely related to Ninzam. Investigation needed: bilingual proficiency in Hausa, attitudes.

BUDUMA ***(BOUDOUMA, YEDINA, YEDIMA, YIDANA)*** [BDM] 3,000 in Nigeria. Borno State, on islands in Lake Chad. Afro-Asiatic, Chadic, Biu-Mandara, B, B.1, Buduma. Dialects: BUDUMA, KURI (KOURI, KAKAA). Semi-nomadic. Grammar. Pastoralists, fishermen. Muslim, traditional religion. See main entry under Chad.

BUKWEN [BUZ] Taraba State, near Takum, 1 village. Niger-Congo, Atlantic-Congo, Volta-Congo, Benue-Congo, Bantoid, Southern, Beboid.

BUMAJI [BYP] Cross River State, Obudu LGA, Bumaji town. Niger-Congo, Atlantic-Congo, Volta-Congo, Benue-Congo, Cross River, Bendi.

BURA-PABIR ***(BURA, BURRA, BOURRAH, PABIR, BABIR, BABUR, BARBURR, MYA BURA, KWOJEFFA, HUVE, HUVIYA)*** [BUR] 250,000 (1987 UBS), including 200,000 Pabir (1993). 32,000 in Adamawa State (1992). Borno State, Biu and Askira-Uba LGAs; Adamawa State, Gombi LGA. Afro-Asiatic, Chadic, Biu-Mandara, A, A.2, 1. Dialects: PELA (BURA PELA, HILL BURA), HYIL HAWUL (BURA HYILHAWUL, PLAIN BURA). Kofa may be a related language. Ngohi is a small subgroup. Dictionary. Grammar. Literacy rate in second language: 3%. Agriculturalists, weavers, hunters, fishermen, wood carvers. Traditional religion, Muslim, Christian. NT 1937-1987.

BURAK ***(BUURAK)*** [BYS] 4,000 (1992 Crozier and Blench). Bauchi State, Billiri and Kaltungo LGAs, Burak town. Niger-Congo, Atlantic-Congo, Volta-Congo, North, Adamawa-Ubangi, Adamawa, Waja-Jen, Jen. Investigation needed: bilingual proficiency in Hausa, attitudes. Mountain slope. Traditional religion, Christian.

BURE ***(BUBURE)*** [BVH] Bauchi State, Darazo LGA, one village southeast of Darazo town. Afro-Asiatic, Chadic, West, A, A.2, Bole. Investigation needed: bilingual proficiency in Hausa, attitudes.

BURU [BQW] Taraba State, Sardauna LGA, east of Baissa, a village near Batu. Niger-Congo, Atlantic-Congo, Volta-Congo, Benue-Congo, Bantoid, Unclassified.

BUSA ***(BISÃ, BISAYÃ, BUSA-BISÃ, BUSANO, BUSSANCHI)*** [BQP] 20,000 first language speakers, 20,000 second language users (1998 Ross Jones SIM). Niger State, Borgu LGA, Kebbi State, Bagudo LGA, 35 villages. Niger-Congo, Mande, Eastern, Eastern, Busa. Dialects: NEW BUSA, WAWA, ILLO. The two dialects are inherently intelligible to each other's speakers. Busa has more prestige, but Wawa viewed as purer, and used for literature. New Busa has Hausa influenced phonology. Illo Busa has Boko influence. Other Busa languages (Boko, Bokobaru) require separate literature. 91% lexical similarity with Bokobaru, 85% with Boko, 54% with Kyenga, 50% with Bissa in Burkina Faso. Bilingual level estimates for Hausa are 0 30%, 1 40%, 2 13%, 3 10%, 4 5%, 5 2%. Speakers use Hausa and Kambari as second languages when speaking to non-Busa people, and Hausa in public places. Hausa is used in school. English also used. Pride in language and history. Speakers call themselves 'Bisã'. Different from Bissa of Burkina Faso and Ghana. Dictionary. Grammar. SOV; postpositions; genitives before noun heads; articles, adjectives, numerals, relatives after noun heads; question word initial or final; 4 suffixes; word order distinguishes subject, object, direct object; person, number, aspect included in subject pronouns; tone indicates some verb aspect; passive; CV, CVV, CCV; 3 level tones, grammatical tone affects NPs, verbs, and pronouns. Literacy rate in second language: 5%. Busa and Hausa adult literacy programs. Busa literature is available. Savannah. Riverine. Peasant agriculturalists. Muslim, Christian. Bible portions 1993-1998.

CAKFEM-MUSHERE ***(CHAKFEM, CHOKFEM)*** [CKY] 5,000 (1990 SIL). Plateau State, Mangu LGA. Afro-Asiatic, Chadic, West, A, A.3, Angas Proper, 1. Dialects: KADIM-KABAN, JAJURA.

CARA ***(CHARA, FACHARA, NFACHARA, FAKARA, PAKARA, TERA, TERIYA, TERRI, TARIYA)*** [CFD] 3,000 or fewer (1999 R. Blench). Plateau State, Bassa LGA, Teriya village. Niger-Congo, Atlantic-Congo, Volta-Congo, Benue-Congo, Platoid, Plateau, Central, North-Central. They tend to know Hausa, and some younger people also speak English. They generally do not speak the languages of their neighbors. The older people think that younger people are shifting to Hausa. Complex morphology. Investigation needed: bilingual proficiency in Hausa, attitudes.

CENTÚÚM ***(CEN TUUM)*** [CET] Small (1992 Crozier and Blench). Bauchi State, Balanga LGA, Cham town, among the Dijim. Unclassified. Older people. The Dijim call the people 'Jalabe' or 'Jaabe'. Nearly extinct.

CHE ***(RUKUBA, KUCHE, BACHE, INCHAZI, SALE)*** [RUK] 50,000 (1973 SIL). Plateau State, Bassa LGA. Niger-Congo, Atlantic-Congo, Volta-Congo, Benue-Congo, Platoid, Plateau, Western, Southwestern, A. The language is 'Kuche', a speaker 'Ache', the people 'Bache'. Bible portions 1924-1931.

CIBAK ***(CHIBUK, CHIBOK, CHIBBAK, CHIBBUK, KYIBAKU, KIBBAKU, KIKUK)*** [CKL] 100,000 (1993 CAPRO). Borno State, Damboa LGA. Afro-Asiatic, Chadic, Biu-Mandara, A, A.2, 1. Investigation needed: intelligibility with Hausa, attitudes.

CINDA-REGI-TIYAL ***(KAMUKU)*** [KAU] 30,000 or more (1995 S. and S. Dettweiler). Niger State, Chanchaga, Rafi, and Mariga LGAs; Kaduna State, Birnin Gwari LGA. Niger-Congo, Atlantic-Congo, Volta-Congo, Benue-Congo, Kainji, Western, Kamuku. Dialects: CINDA (UCINDA, JINDA, MAJINDA, TEGINA, MAKANGARA), REGI, TIYAL (TIYAR, KUKI). Most speakers say they can easily understand the other dialects. 90% to 95% lexical similarity among the three dialects. Bilingualism in Hausa. Clans are Uregi, Urogo, Tiyar (Kuki), Ucinda (Jinda), and Ushana. Laka, or Kamuku Laka, are Hausa-speaking ethnic Kamuku. Literacy rate in second language: 10%. Traditional religion, Muslim, Christian.

CINENI [CIE] 3,000 or more (1998). Borno State, Gwoza LGA, Cineni village. Afro-Asiatic, Chadic, Biu-Mandara, A, A.4, Mandara Proper, Glavda. Closely related to Guduf, but it appears to be a separate language.

CISHINGINI ***(ASHAGANNA, ASHINGINI, ASCHINGINI, CHISINGINI, "MAUNCHI", "MAWANCHI", KAMBARI, KAMBERRI, KAMBERCHI, YAURI, AGWARA KAMBARI)*** [ASG] 80,000 (1996). Niger State, Borgu and Agwara LGAs, just west of the Niger River and north of the Kainji game park; and Kebbi State, east of the Niger River from the Yelwa area south to Ngaski and Nasko. Niger-Congo, Atlantic-Congo, Volta-Congo, Benue-Congo, Kainji, Western, Kambari. Dialect: ROFIA. Close to Tsishingini and Tsikimba, but a separate language. Speakers can use Hausa, and some can use English or other Kambari languages. Speakers are called 'Ashingini'. Traditional religion, Christian, Muslim. Bible portions 1994.

CIWOGAI ***(TSAGU, SAGO)*** [TGD] 2,000 (1995 CAPRO). Bauchi State, Ganjuwa LGA, Tsagu village and farms in the vicinity. Near the Diri. Afro-Asiatic, Chadic, West, B, B.2. Related to Diri, but a separate language. Investigation needed: bilingual proficiency in Hausa, attitudes. Traditional religion.

C'LELA ***(LELA, LALAWA, C'LELA, KOLELA, CALA-CALA, CHILELA, CHILALA, DAKARKARI, DAKAKARI, DAKKARKARI)*** [DRI] 90,000 or more (1993 Dettweiler SIL). Eastern Kebbi State, Zuru, Sakaba, and Donko-Wasagu LGAs; Niger State, Rijau LGA; and migrants farther south. Niger-Congo, Atlantic-Congo, Volta-Congo, Benue-Congo, Kainji, Western, Duka. Dialects: LILA (ZURU, SENCHI, SOUTHERN LELA), DABAI (CENTRAL LELA), RIBAH, ADOMA (AROMA, ROMA-NA, ROMA, YELMO, NORTHERN LELA). Lexical similarity among dialects at Rade, Ribah, Dabai, and Senchi were between 93% and 98%. 55% lexical similarity with Duka, 54% with the Fakai cluster, 47% with Gwamhi-Wuri, 20% with Acipa. Bilingualism in Hausa. 'Dakarkari' is the Hausa name for the people. 'Lela' is their own name for people and language. Orthography needs revision. Radio programs. Savannah. Stony hills, plains. Agriculturalists: guinea corn, millet, maize, acha, peanuts, beans, sugar cane, cotton; brewing alcohol, blacksmiths, mat makers, smelting, potters. 800 to 1600 feet. Traditional religion, Muslim, Christian. Bible portions 1931.

COMO KARIM ***(CHOMO, SHOMONG, SHOMOH, NUADHU, SHOMO KARIM, KIRIM, KIYU, KINZIMBA, ASOM)*** [CFG] Taraba State, Jalingo, Karim Lamido LGAs, near Lau. Niger-Congo, Atlantic-Congo, Volta-Congo, Benue-Congo, Platoid, Benue, Jukunoid, Central, Jukun-Mbembe-Wurbo, Wurbo. Called

'Bakula' together with Shoo-Minda-Nyem, Jiru, and Jessi. Hunters, fishermen. Traditional religion, Muslim, Christian.

CORI ***(CHORI)*** [CRY] Kaduna State, Jema'a LGA, one village and associated hamlets. Niger-Congo, Atlantic-Congo, Volta-Congo, Benue-Congo, Platoid, Plateau, Western, Northwestern, Jaba.

DABA ***(DABBA)*** [DAB] 1,000 or fewer (1992 Crozier and Blench). Adamawa State, Mubi LGA, between Mubi and Bahuli, 1 village. Afro-Asiatic, Chadic, Biu-Mandara, A, A.7. NT 1992. See main entry under Cameroon.

DADIYA ***(DADIA, DAADIYA, LOODIYA)*** [DBD] 30,000 (1998). Bauchi State, Balanga LGA; Taraba State, Karim Lamido LGA; Adamawa State, Numan LGA, between Dadiya and Bambam. Niger-Congo, Atlantic-Congo, Volta-Congo, North, Adamawa-Ubangi, Adamawa, Waja-Jen, Waja, Dadiya. Dialects: TUNGA (BOLERI), LOOFIYO, KOOKWILA, LOOFAA. The dialect names are also names of settlements. Investigation needed: bilingual proficiency in Hausa, attitudes. Mountains, plains. Agriculturalists: grain, peanuts, beans, rice, cotton. Traditional religion.

DASS ***(BARAWA)*** [DOT] 8,830 including 1,130 Lukshi, 4,700 Durr-Baraza, 700 Wandi and Zumbul, 2,300 Dot (1971 census). Bauchi State, Akleri, Toro, and Dass LGAs; Plateau State, Shendam LGA. Afro-Asiatic, Chadic, West, B, B.3. Dialects: LUKSHI (DEKSHI), DURR-BARAZA (BANDAS), ZUMBUL (BOODLA), WANDI (WANGDAY), DOT (DWAT, ZODI, DOTT). A dialect cluster. Investigation needed: bilingual proficiency in Hausa, attitudes.

DAZA ***(DAZAWA)*** [DZD] Bauchi State, Darazo LGA, a few villages. Afro-Asiatic, Chadic, West, A. Different from Dazaga in Chad and Niger, which is Saharan. Investigation needed: bilingual proficiency in Hausa, attitudes.

DEFAKA ***(AFAKANI)*** [AFN] 1,000 or fewer (1992 Crozier and Blench). Rivers State, Bonny LGA, in the Niger Delta, town of Nkoro. Niger-Congo, Atlantic-Congo, Ijoid, Defaka. Related to, but a separate language from the Ijo group. Investigation needed: bilingual proficiency.

DEGEMA [DEG] 10,000 (SIL). Rivers State, Degema LGA, Usokun-Degema (Usokun) and Degema Town (Atala) communities. Niger-Congo, Atlantic-Congo, Volta-Congo, Benue-Congo, Edoid, Delta. Dialects: ATALA, USOKUN (KALA DEGEMA). There is no standard variety of Degema. 'Degema' refers to the people, the area, and the language. The Obonoma (Ekomburu) in Akuku-Toru LGA shifted from Degema to Kalabari in the past.

DENDI ***(DANDAWA)*** [DEN] 839 in Nigeria (1925 Meek). Kebbi State, Argungu and Bagudo LGAs, on upper Niger River. Nilo-Saharan, Songhai, Southern. A closely related language to Zarma and Songai. They form a dialect continuum. Dictionary. Grammar. NT 1995. See main entry under Benin.

DENO ***(DENAWA, DENWA, BE)*** [DBB] 6,000 (1995 CAPRO). Bauchi State, Darazo LGA, 45 km. northeast of Bauchi town. Afro-Asiatic, Chadic, West, A, A.2, Bole, Bole Proper. The language is rapidly being replaced by Hausa and Fulfulde. Investigation needed: bilingual proficiency in Hausa, attitudes. Agriculturalists: guinea corn, maize, millet, cassava, beans, rice. Traditional religion, Muslim.

DERA ***(KANAKURU)*** [KNA] 20,000 (1973 SIL). Gongola State, Guyuk LGA; Borno State, Biu LGA. Afro-Asiatic, Chadic, West, A, A.2, Tangale, Dera. Dialects: SHANI, SHELLEN, GASI. Some speakers use Hausa, Bura, Lala, Fulfulde, Longuda, or English as second language. Investigation needed: bilingual proficiency in Hausa, attitudes. Grammar. Many are educated. Most villages have primary schools. Agriculturalists: guinea corn, peanuts, cotton; hunters, fishermen. Traditional religion, Muslim, Christian. Bible portions 1937.

DGHWEDE ***(HUDE, JOHODE, TRAUDE, DEHOXDE, TGHUADE, TOGHWEDE, WA'A, AZAGHVANA, ZAGHVANA)*** [DGH] 30,000 (1980 UBS). Borno State, Gwoza LGA. Afro-Asiatic, Chadic, Biu-Mandara, A, A.4, Mandara Proper, Glavda. NT 1980.

DIBO ***(SHITAKO, ZITAKO, ZHITAKO. GANAGANA, GANAGAWA)*** [DIO] 100,000 or fewer (1992 Crozier and Blench). Niger State, Lapai LGA; Federal Capital Territory; Plateau State, Nasarawa LGA. Niger-Congo, Atlantic-Congo, Volta-Congo, Benue-Congo, Nupoid, Nupe-Gbagyi. An unknown number living among the Gbari no longer speak their own language (Blench 1990). 'Ganagana' and 'Ganagawa' are names for the people. Investigation needed: bilingual proficiency in Hausa, attitudes. Muslim, traditional religion, Christian few.

DIJIM-BWILIM [CFA] 25,000 (1998). Bauchi State, Balanga LGA; Gongola State, Numan LGA. Niger-Congo, Atlantic-Congo, Volta-Congo, North, Adamawa-Ubangi, Adamawa, Waja-Jen, Waja, Cham-Mona. Dialects: DIJIM (CHAM, CAM), BWILIM (MWANO, MWONA, MWOMO, MONA, MWANA, FITILAI). Related to Lotsu-Piri. Investigation needed: bilingual proficiency in Hausa, attitudes. Traditional religion, Christian.

DIRI ***(DIRYA, DIRIYA, DIRYAWA)*** [DWA] 3,750 (1971). Bauchi State, Ningi and Darazo LGAs. Afro-Asiatic, Chadic, West, B, B.2. A separate language from Tsagu. Investigation needed: bilingual proficiency in Hausa, attitudes.

DIRIM ***(DIRIN, DIRRIM, DAKA, DAKKA)*** [DIR] 9,000 (1992). Taraba State, Bali LGA. Niger-Congo, Atlantic-Congo, Volta-Congo, Benue-Congo, Bantoid, Northern, Dakoid. Closely related to Samba Daka—may be a dialect. Many blind people, caused by filaria. Traditional religion, Muslim, Christian.

DOKA [DBI] Kaduna State, Kachia LGA, 1 village. Niger-Congo, Atlantic-Congo, Volta-Congo, Benue-Congo, Platoid, Plateau, Northern. Distinct from Duka. Investigation needed: bilingual proficiency in Hausa, attitudes.

DOKO-UYANGA ***(UYANGA, DOSANGA, BASANGA, IKO)*** [UYA] A few. Cross River State, Akamkpa LGA, several towns. Niger-Congo, Atlantic-Congo, Volta-Congo, Benue-Congo, Cross River, Delta Cross, Upper Cross, Agoi-Doko-Iyoniyong.

DONG ***(DONGA)*** [DOH] 5,000 or fewer (Blench 1998). Taraba State, Zing LGA; Adamawa State, Mayo Belwa LGA. Niger-Congo, Atlantic-Congo, Volta-Congo, Benue-Congo, Bantoid, Northern, Dakoid. Distinct from Dongo (Donga) of DRC, which is in the Amadi group of Ubangi (Adamawa-Ubangi). Investigation needed: bilingual proficiency in Hausa, attitudes.

DUGURI ***(DUGURAWA, DUGARWA, DUGURANCHI, DUKURI)*** [DBM] 20,000 (1995 CAPRO). Bauchi State, Alkaleri and Tafawa Balewa LGAs; Plateau State, Kanam LGA. Niger-Congo, Atlantic-Congo, Volta-Congo, Benue-Congo, Bantoid, Southern, Jarawan, Nigerian. Dialects: GAR DUGURI, BADARA DUGURI, NORTHEAST DUGURI, SOUTHWEST DUGURI. A member of the Jarawa dialect cluster. 21 elementary schools, a senior and a junior secondary school. Literacy rate in second language: 20%. Agriculturalists: guinea corn, peanuts, millet, beans, rice; animal husbandry. Traditional religion, Muslim, Christian.

DUGUZA ***(DUGUSA)*** [DZA] 2,000 (1973 SIL). Bauchi State, Toro LGA; Plateau State, Jos South LGA. Niger-Congo, Atlantic-Congo, Volta-Congo, Benue-Congo, Kainji, Eastern, Northern Jos, Jera. Investigation needed: bilingual proficiency in Hausa, attitudes.

DUHWA ***(KARFA, KERIFA, NZUHWI)*** [KBZ] 800 (1973 SIL). Nasarawa State, Akwanga LGA, Kerifa village. Afro-Asiatic, Chadic, West, A, A.4, Ron Proper. 'Duhwa' is their own name. Investigation needed: bilingual proficiency in Hausa, attitudes.

DULBU [DBO] 100 (1993). Bauchi State, Bauchi LGA, Dulbu village southeast of Bauchi town. Niger-Congo, Atlantic-Congo, Volta-Congo, Benue-Congo, Bantoid, Southern, Jarawan, Nigerian. Investigation needed: bilingual proficiency in Hausa, attitudes.

DUNGU ***(DUNGI, DINGI, DWINGI, DUNJAWA)*** [DBV] 310 (1949). Kaduna State, Saminaka LGA, Dungi town. Niger-Congo, Atlantic-Congo, Volta-Congo, Benue-Congo, Kainji, Eastern, Northern Jos, Kauru. Investigation needed: bilingual proficiency in Hausa, attitudes.

DUWAI ***(EVJI, EASTERN BADE)*** [DBP] Yobe State, Bade LGA; Kano State, Hadejia LGA. Afro-Asiatic, Chadic, West, B, B.1, Duwai. In Bade language cluster. Investigation needed: intelligibility with Bade, bilingual proficiency in Hausa, attitudes.

DZA ***(JANJO, JENJO, JEN)*** [JEN] 6,100 (1952). Taraba State, Karim Lamido LGA, and Adamawa State, Numan LGA, Jen town, east of Karim-Lamido town, south of Bambuka town, by the Benue River bank. Niger-Congo, Atlantic-Congo, Volta-Congo, North, Adamawa-Ubangi, Adamawa, Waja-Jen, Jen. Dialects: KAIGAMA, LAREDO (ARDIDO), JAULE (JOOLE). Agriculturalists, hunters. Traditional religion, Christian, Muslim.

DZODINKA ***(ADERE, ADIRI)*** [ADD] Taraba State, Sardauna LGA, 1 village on the Cameroon border. Niger-Congo, Atlantic-Congo, Volta-Congo, Benue-Congo, Bantoid, Southern, Wide Grassfields, Narrow Grassfields, Mbam-Nkam, Nkambe. Different from Adele of Ghana and Togo. Bible portions 1923-1932. See main entry under Cameroon.

EBIRA ***(IGBIRRA, IGBARRA, IBARA, KOTOKORI, KATAWA, KWOTTO, IGBIRA, EGBIRA, EGBURA)*** [IGB] 1,000,000 (1989 J. Adive). Kwara State, Okene, Okehi, and Kogi LGAs; Nasarawa State, Nasarawa LGA; Edo State, Akoko-Edo LGA. Niger-Congo, Atlantic-Congo, Volta-Congo, Benue-Congo, Nupoid, Ebira-Gade. Dialects: OKENE (HIMA, IHIMA), IGARA (ETUNO), KOTO (IGU, EGU, IKA, BIRA, BIRI, PANDA). A dialect cluster. Grammar. Literacy rate in first language: 5% to 10%. Literacy rate in second language: 25%. Ebira is used in schools. Agriculturalists. Muslim, traditional religion, Christian. NT 1981.

EBUGHU ***(ORON)*** [EBG] 5,000 or more (1988). Akwa Ibom State, Mbo and Oron LGAs. Niger-Congo, Atlantic-Congo, Volta-Congo, Benue-Congo, Cross River, Delta Cross, Lower Cross, Obolo, Ebughu. Listed separately in Crozier and Blench 1992.

EDO ***(BINI, BENIN, ADDO, OVIEDO, OVIOBA)*** [EDO] 1,000,000 (1987 UBS). Bendel State, Ovia, Oredo, and Orhionmwon LGAs. Niger-Congo, Atlantic-Congo, Volta-Congo, Benue-Congo, Edoid, North-Central, Edo-Esan-Ora. Used in adult education, history text. National language. Dictionary. Roman. Radio programs, TV. Bible 1996.

EFAI ***(EFFIAT)*** [EFA] 5,000 or more (1988). Population total both countries 5,000 or more. Akwa Ibom State, Mbo LGA. Also spoken in Cameroon. Niger-Congo, Atlantic-Congo, Volta-Congo, Benue-Congo, Cross

River, Delta Cross, Lower Cross, Obolo, Efai. Listed separately in Crozier and Blench 1992. Investigation needed: intelligibility with Efik, attitudes.

EFIK ***(CALABAR)*** [EFK] 400,000 first language speakers (1998), 2,400,000 including second language users (1998). Cross River State, Calabar Municipality, Odukpani and Akamkpa LGAs. Niger-Congo, Atlantic-Congo, Volta-Congo, Benue-Congo, Cross River, Delta Cross, Lower Cross, Obolo, Efik. The major dialect and language of the Ibibio-Efik group. Used in adult education, university courses. Decreasing in use as a second language. National language. Dictionary. Grammar. SVO. Roman. Radio programs, TV. Bible 1868-1995.

EFUTOP ***(OFUTOP, AGBARAGBA)*** [OFU] 10,000 (1973 SIL). Cross River State, Ikom LGA. Niger-Congo, Atlantic-Congo, Volta-Congo, Benue-Congo, Bantoid, Southern, Ekoid. Investigation needed: intelligibility with Ekajuk, attitudes.

EGGON ***(EGON, MO EGON, MADA EGGON, HILL MADA, MADA DUTSE)*** [EGO] 140,368 (1990). Nasarawa State, Nasarawa Eggon, Akwanga, Lafia, Awe, and Obi LGAs. Niger-Congo, Atlantic-Congo, Volta-Congo, Benue-Congo, Platoid, Plateau, Western, Southwestern, B. 25 dialects are locally recognized, but their status is unclear. Bilingualism in Hausa. Dictionary. Traditional religion, Christian, Muslim. NT 1974.

EHUEUN ***(EKPIMI, EKPENMEN, EPIMI)*** [EHU] 5,766 (1963). Ondo State, Akoko South LGA. Niger-Congo, Atlantic-Congo, Volta-Congo, Benue-Congo, Edoid, Northwestern, Osse. Related to Ukue. Investigation needed: intelligibility with Ukue, attitudes.

EJAGHAM ***(EKOI)*** [ETU] 60,000 to 70,000 in Nigeria (1998 John Watters SIL). Population total both countries 105,000 to 120,000. Cross River State, Akampka, Idom, Odukpani, Calabar LGAs. Also spoken in Cameroon. Niger-Congo, Atlantic-Congo, Volta-Congo, Benue-Congo, Bantoid, Southern, Ekoid. Dialects: SOUTHERN EJAGHAM (EKIN, QUA, KWA, AQUA, ABAKPA), WESTERN EJAGHAM, EASTERN EJAGHAM. Western Ejagham includes Bendeghe Etung (Bindege, Dindiga, Mbuma), Northern Etung, Southern Etung, Ekwe, Akamkpa-Ejagham. Eastern Ejagham includes Keaka (Keaqa, Kejaka, Edjagam), Obang (Eeafeng). Grammar. Radio programs, TV. NT 1997.

EKAJUK ***(AKAJO, AKAJUK)*** [EKA] 30,000 (1986 Asinya). Cross River State, Ogoja LGA, Bansara, Nwang, Ntara 1, 2, and 3, and Ebanibim towns. Niger-Congo, Atlantic-Congo, Volta-Congo, Benue-Congo, Bantoid, Southern, Ekoid. NT 1971.

EKI [EKI] 5,000 or more (1988, in Crozier and Blench 1992:36). Cross River State, northeast of Efik, south of Idere. Niger-Congo, Atlantic-Congo, Volta-Congo, Benue-Congo, Cross River, Delta Cross, Lower Cross, Obolo. Listed separately in Crozier and Blench 1992. Probably Central Lower Cross, related to Anaang. Close to Idere (B. Connell 1998). Investigation needed: intelligibility with Efik, Anaang, Idere, attitudes.

EKIT ***(EKET)*** [EKE] 200,000 (1989). Akwa Ibom State, Uquo Ibeno and Eket LGAs. Niger-Congo, Atlantic-Congo, Volta-Congo, Benue-Congo, Cross River, Delta Cross, Lower Cross, Obolo, Ekit. Listed separately in Crozier and Blench 1992. Some dialect variation. Investigation needed: intelligibility with Efik, attitudes.

EKPEYE ***(EKPABYA, EKKPAHIA, EKPAFFIA)*** [EKP] 30,000 (1973 SIL). Rivers State, Ahoada LGA; Bayelsa State, Yenagoa LGA. Niger-Congo, Atlantic-Congo, Volta-Congo, Benue-Congo, Igboid, Ekpeye. Dialects: AKO, UPATA, UBYE, IGBUDUYA. Related to Igbo but not inherently intelligible with it. Investigation needed: bilingual proficiency in Igbo, attitudes. Grammar.

ELEME [ELM] 58,000 (1990 UBS). Rivers State, Otelga LGA. Niger-Congo, Atlantic-Congo, Volta-Congo, Benue-Congo, Cross River, Delta Cross, Ogoni, West. Bible portions 1988.

ELOYI ***(AFO, AFU, AHO, AFAO, EPE, KEFFI)*** [AFO] 25,000 (SIL). Plateau State, Awe and Nasarawa LGAs; Benue State, Otukpo LGA. Niger-Congo, Atlantic-Congo, Volta-Congo, Benue-Congo, Idomoid, Akweya, Eloyi. Dialects: MBECI, MBAMU. Bilingualism in Hausa. Literacy rate in second language: 5% Hausa. Traditional religion, Muslim Christian.

EMAI-IULEHA-ORA ***(KUNIBUM, IVBIOSAKON)*** [EMA] 100,000 (1987 Schaefer). Edo State, Owan LGA. Niger-Congo, Atlantic-Congo, Volta-Congo, Benue-Congo, Edoid, North-Central, Edo-Esan-Ora. Dialects: IVHIMION, EMAI, IULEHA, ORA. Dialect cluster. Dictionary. Ora is used in initial primary education. Traditional religion. Bible portions 1908-1910.

ENGENNI ***(NGENE, EGENE)*** [ENN] 20,000 (1980 UBS). Rivers State, Ahoada LGA; Bayelsa State, Yenagoa LGA. Niger-Congo, Atlantic-Congo, Volta-Congo, Benue-Congo, Edoid, Delta. Dialects: EDIRO, INEDUA, OGUA. Grammar. NT 1977.

ENGLISH [ENG] Second language speakers: 1,000,000 (1977 Voegelin and Voegelin). Indo-European, Germanic, West, English. Used in government, education. Official language. Bible 1535-1989. See main entry under United Kingdom.

ENWAN ***(ORON)*** [ENW] 15,000 (1998 B. Connell). Akwa Ibom State, Mbo LGA. Niger-Congo, Atlantic-Congo, Volta-Congo, Benue-Congo, Cross River, Delta Cross, Lower Cross, Obolo, Enwang-Uda. Listed separately in Crozier and Blench 1992. Incorrectly referred to as 'Oron'.

EPIE ***(EPIE-ATISSA)*** [EPI] 12,000 (1973 SIL). Rivers State, Yenagoa LGA. Niger-Congo, Atlantic-Congo, Volta-Congo, Benue-Congo, Edoid, Delta. Dialect: ATISA (ATISSA). Most speakers are bilingual in Ijo. Investigation needed: bilingual proficiency in Ijo, attitudes.

ERUWA ***(EROHWA, ERAKWA, AROKWA)*** [ERH] Delta State, Isoko LGA. Niger-Congo, Atlantic-Congo, Volta-Congo, Benue-Congo, Edoid, Southwestern. Related to Urhobo. Not intelligible with any Isoko dialect. Most speakers are bilingual in Central Isoko, which is replacing Eruwa. Investigation needed: bilingual proficiency in Central Isoko, attitudes.

ESAN ***(ISHAN, ISA, ESA, ANWAIN)*** [ISH] 200,000 (1973 SIL) including 7,000 Ekpon in 7 villages (1998). Edo State, Agbazko, Okpebho, Owan, and Etsako LGAs. Niger-Congo, Atlantic-Congo, Volta-Congo, Benue-Congo, Edoid, North-Central, Edo-Esan-Ora. Dialects: EKPON, IGUEBEN. Many dialects, apparently inherently intelligible. 90% speak or understand Nigerian Pidgin English. English and possibly Ika are also used as second languages. A regionally important language. Used in initial primary education. Radio programs, TV. Tropical forest. Plains. Peasant agriculturalists: yams, bananas, oranges, plantains, cassava; hunters. Christian, traditional religion, Muslim. Bible portions 1974.

ETEBI [ETB] 15,000 (1989). Akwa Ibom State, Uquo Ibeno LGA. Niger-Congo, Atlantic-Congo, Volta-Congo, Benue-Congo, Cross River, Delta Cross, Lower Cross, Obolo, Ekit. Listed separately in Crozier and Blench 1992. 'Oron' and 'Ekit' are incorrect names.

ETKYWAN ***(ICEN, ICHEN, ITCHEN, ETEKWE, KYATO, KYANTON, KENTU, NYIDU)*** [ICH] 40,000 to 50,000 (1992). Taraba State, Takum, Sardauna, Bali, and part of Wukari LGAs. Niger-Congo, Atlantic-Congo, Volta-Congo, Benue-Congo, Platoid, Benue, Jukunoid, Central, Kpan-Icen. Some speak Hausa as second language. Christian, traditional religion, Muslim.

ETULO ***(ETURO, UTUR, TURUMAWA)*** [UTR] 10,000 (1988 Shain). Benue State, Gboko LGA; Taraba State, Wukari LGA. Niger-Congo, Atlantic-Congo, Volta-Congo, Benue-Congo, Idomoid, Akweya, Etulo-Idoma, Etulo. Traditional religion, Christian (small).

EVANT ***(EVAND, AVAND, AVANDE, OVAND, OVANDE, OVANDO, BALEGETE, BELEGETE)*** [BZZ] 10,000 or fewer in Nigeria (1996 R. Hedinger). Population total both countries 11,000 or fewer. Cross River State, Obudu LGA. Also spoken in Cameroon. Niger-Congo, Atlantic-Congo, Volta-Congo, Benue-Congo, Bantoid, Southern, Tivoid. 50% lexical similarity with Icheve, Tiv, and Otanga. Mountain slope. Traditional religion.

FALI ***(FALI OF MUBI, FALI OF MUCHELLA, VIMTIM, YIMTIM)*** [FLI] 20,000 or more (1990 in Crozier and Blench 1992:39), including 5,000 or fewer in Vin (1995 SIL). Adamawa State, Mubi and Michjika LGAs, 4 principal villages. Afro-Asiatic, Chadic, Biu-Mandara, A, A.8. Dialects: VIN (UROOVIN, UVIN, VIMTIM), HULI (BAHULI, URAHULI), MADZARIN (URA MADZARIN, MUCHELLA), BWEEN (URAMBWEEN, BAGIRA). Dialects are named after villages. Bilingualism in Fulfulde, Hausa. Investigation needed: bilingual proficiency in Hausa, Fulfulde, attitudes. Little formal education. Hills, plains. Africulturalists: guinea corn, maize, peanuts, bambara nuts, tiger nuts, rice; animal husbandry: cows, sheep, goats, chickens. Traditional religion.

FALI OF BAISSA [FAH] Some speakers left (1992 Crozier and Blench). Southern Taraba State, Falinga Plateau region. Niger-Congo, Atlantic-Congo, Volta-Congo, Benue-Congo, Unclassified. Nearly extinct.

FAM [FAM] 1,000 or fewer (1984). Taraba State, Bali LGA, 17 km. east of Kungana. Niger-Congo, Atlantic-Congo, Volta-Congo, Benue-Congo, Bantoid, Northern, Fam. Not closely related to other languages.

FIRAN ***(FARAN, FORON, YES FIRAN, KWAKWI)*** [FIR] 1,500 or fewer (1991 C. Regnier). Plateau State, Barkin Ladi LGA, Kwakwi Station south of Jos. Niger-Congo, Atlantic-Congo, Volta-Congo, Benue-Congo, Platoid, Plateau, Central, South-Central. A separate, but related language to Izere. Investigation needed: intelligibility with Izere, bilingual proficiency in Hausa, attitudes.

FULFULDE, ADAMAWA ***(EASTERN FULFULDE, FULATANCHI, FULANI, FULA, FILLANCI)*** [FUB] All Fulfulde in Nigeria: 7,611,000 or 8.6% of the population (1991 SIL). East central Nigeria, Taraba and Adamawa States, center in Yola. Niger-Congo, Atlantic-Congo, Atlantic, Northern, Senegambian, Fula-Wolof, Fulani, Eastern. The language is 'Fulatanchi', 'Fillanci', or 'Fula'; a speaker is 'Pullo'; the people are 'Fulbe' or 'Fulani'. National language. Grammar. Muslim, traditional religion. Bible 1983. See main entry under Cameroon.

FULFULDE, BENIN-TOGO [FUE] South and west of the Niger River, from the corner where Nigeria, Niger, and Benin meet, down to about 50 km. south of where a big tributary joins the Niger River from the east, and following the Niger River south to the delta. The southern boundary is a rough east-west line from a point below the intersection of the rivers to about 75 km. south of the angle in the Benin-Nigeria border, where the border bends from almost straight north-south to about 30 km. nearly due east. Niger-Congo, Atlantic-Congo, Atlantic, Northern, Senegambian, Fula-Wolof, Fulani, West Central. See main entry under Benin.

FULFULDE, NIGERIAN ***(KANO-KATSINA-BORORRO FULFULDE)*** [FUV] 7,611,000 all Fulfulde in Nigeria (1991 SIL), including 340,000 in Sokoto. Population total all countries 7,611,000 or more.

Kano-Katsina dialect is spoken in the area of Kano, Katsina, Zaria, Jos Plateau and southeast to Bauchi; Gombe is the center. The Bororro dialect is in Bornu State; Maiduguri is the center. Sokoto is in Sokoto State. Also spoken in Cameroon, Chad. Niger-Congo, Atlantic-Congo, Atlantic, Northern, Senegambian, Fula-Wolof, Fulani, East Central. Dialects: KANO-KATSINA, BORORRO (BORORO, MBORORO, AKO, NOMADIC FULFULDE), SOKOTO. Sokoto is a major Fulbe geo-political unit. Muslim.

FUM [FUM] Taraba State, Sardauna LGA, Antere, on the Cameroon border. Niger-Congo, Atlantic-Congo, Volta-Congo, Benue-Congo, Bantoid, Southern, Wide Grassfields, Narrow Grassfields. May be the same as Mfumte in Cameroon.

FUNGWA *(TUFUNGWA, AFUNGWA, URA, ULA)* [ULA] 1,000 (1992 Blench). Niger State, Rafi LGA. Niger-Congo, Atlantic-Congo, Volta-Congo, Benue-Congo, Kainji, Western, Kamuku. Investigation needed: bilingual proficiency, attitudes.

FYAM *(FYEM, PYEM, PAIEM, GYEM, FEM, PEM)* [PYM] 12,000 (1998 Daniel Nettle). Plateau State, Jos, Barkin Ladi, and Mangu LGAs. Niger-Congo, Atlantic-Congo, Volta-Congo, Benue-Congo, Platoid, Plateau, Southeastern. Closest to Horom. Chadic influence. Hausa is used generally, English in education and government. English is restricted to young people, especially men. Fyam is used at home and in the village in some cases. In some villages, young people use Fyam only in special contexts. Shift to Hausa in progress. Grammar. 50% of the young read haltingly in Hausa. Radio programs. Muslim, Christian.

FYER *(FIER)* [FIE] 20,000 to 30,000 (1999 R. Blench). Plateau State, Mangu LGA, Fyer District. Afro-Asiatic, Chadic, West, A, A.4, Fyer. Language maintenance is good. Investigation needed: bilingual proficiency in Hausa, attitudes. Grammar.

GAA *(TIBA)* [TTB] 10,000 or fewer (1997 Boyd). Adamawa State, Ganye LGA; Tiba Plateau, between Garba Sbege and Jada, north of the Shebshi Mountains. Niger-Congo, Atlantic-Congo, Volta-Congo, Benue-Congo, Bantoid, Northern, Dakoid.

GA'ANDA *(GA'ANDU, GANDA, MOKAR, MAKWAR)* [GAA] 43,000 (1992). Adamawa State, Gombi LGA. Some also in Song, Guyuk, and Mubi LGAs, and Borno State, Biu LGA. Afro-Asiatic, Chadic, Biu-Mandara, A, A.1, Eastern. Dialects: GA'ANDA, GABIN. Bilingualism in Hausa, Fulfulde. 14 villages have primary schools, and Ga'anda has a secondary school. Speakers are becoming more interested in education. Investigation needed: intelligibility with Boga. Grammar. Traditional religion, Christian, Muslim.

GADE *(GEDE)* [GED] 60,000 (1977 Sterk). Federal Capital Territory and Nasarawa State, Nasarawa LGA. Niger-Congo, Atlantic-Congo, Volta-Congo, Benue-Congo, Nupoid, Ebira-Gade. Considered to be conservative by neighbors. Important district language. Dictionary. Grammar. Traditional religion, Muslim.

GALAMBU *(GALAMBI, GALAMBE, GALEMBI)* [GLO] 20,000 (1993). Bauchi State, Bauchi LGA. Afro-Asiatic, Chadic, West, A, A.2, Bole, Bole Proper. Most do not speak Galambu. Investigation needed: bilingual proficiency in Hausa, attitudes. Agriculturalists: guinea corn, maize, beans. Muslim.

GAMO-NINGI [BTE] Ethnic group of 15,000 (1992 Crozier and Blench). Bauchi State, Ningi LGA. Niger-Congo, Atlantic-Congo, Volta-Congo, Benue-Congo, Kainji, Eastern, Northern Jos, Jera. Dialects: GAMO (BUTA, MBUTA, MBOTU, BA-BUCHE, BA-MBUTU), NINGI. Formerly a dialect cluster. The people now speak Hausa. Muslim, traditional religion. Extinct.

GBAGYI *(IBAGYI, GBAGYE, GWARI, EAST GWARI, GWARI MATAI)* [GBR] 700,000 (1991 SIL). Niger State, Rafi, Chanchaga, Shiroro, Suleija LGAs; Kaduna State, Kachia LGA; Nasarawa State, Keffi, Nasarawa LGAs; Federal Capital Territory. Niger-Congo, Atlantic-Congo, Volta-Congo, Benue-Congo, Nupoid, Nupe-Gbagyi, Gbagyi-Gbari. Dialects: TAWARI, KUTA, DIKO, KARU, KADUNA, LOUOME, VWEZHI, NGENGE (GENGE, GYANGE, GYENGYEN). Agriculturalists, pastoralists. Traditional religion, Christian, Muslim. NT 1956, in press (1995).

GBAGYI NKWA [GBW] 50,000 or more (1992 Crozier and Blench). Niger State, Rafi LGA. Niger-Congo, Atlantic-Congo, Volta-Congo, Benue-Congo, Nupoid, Nupe-Gbagyi, Gbagyi-Gbari. Listed separately by Crozier and Blench 1992. Investigation needed: bilingual proficiency in Hausa, attitudes.

GBARI *(GBARI YAMMA, GWARI YAMMA, WEST GWARI, NKWA)* [GBY] 300,000 (1991 SIL). From Zungeru in Niger State to the Kaduna River in the north, southeast through Minna and Paiko to a little past Kwali in the Federal Capital Territory. Niger State, Chanchaga, Suleija, Agaie, and Lapai LGAs; Nasarawa State, Nasarawa LGA. Niger-Congo, Atlantic-Congo, Volta-Congo, Benue-Congo, Nupoid, Nupe-Gbagyi, Gbagyi-Gbari. Dialects: KWALI, IZEM, GAYEGI, PAIKO, BOTAI, JEZHU, KONG, KWANGE (KANGYE, AGBAWI, WAKE, WI), WAHE. Dialects share 89% to 98% lexical similarity; 66% to 78% with Gbagyi dialects. Speakers do not want to be considered Gbagyi. Dictionary. Grammar. Literacy rate in first language: Below 1%. Literacy rate in second language: 5% to 15%. Mountains. Agriculturalists. Traditional religion, some Muslim. Bible portions 1925-1926.

GBAYA, NORTHWEST ***(BAYA)*** [GYA] Very few in Nigeria. Taraba State, Bali LGA. Niger-Congo, Atlantic-Congo, Volta-Congo, North, Adamawa-Ubangi, Ubangi, Gbaya, Gbaya. Dialect: GBEYA (GBEA). Bible 1994. See main entry under CAR.

GBIRI-NIRAGU ***(GURE-KAHUGU)*** [GRH] 5,000 (1952 Westermann and Bryan). Kaduna State, Saminaka LGA. Niger-Congo, Atlantic-Congo, Volta-Congo, Benue-Congo, Kainji, Eastern, Northern Jos, Kauru. Dialects: GBIRI (IGBIRI, AGARI, AGBIRI, GURA, GURE), NIRAGU (KAHUGU, KAPUGU, KAFUGU, KAGU, ANIRAGO). Investigation needed: bilingual proficiency in Hausa, attitudes.

GEJI ***(GEZAWA, GEJAWA, KAYAURI)*** [GEZ] 6,000 (1995 CAPRO). Bauchi State, Toro LGA. Afro-Asiatic, Chadic, West, B, B.3, Zaar Proper. Dialects: BOLU (MAGANG, PELU), GEJI (GYAAZI, GEZAWA, GAEJAWA), ZARANDA (BUU). Geji dialect cluster, in Barawa language cluster. Investigation needed: bilingual proficiency in Hausa, attitudes. Agriculturalists: Guinea corn, maize, millet, rice, peanuts, cassava. Traditional religion.

GENGLE ***(WEGELE, MOMU, YAGELE)*** [GEG] Adamawa State, Mayo Belwa and Fufore LGAs. Niger-Congo, Atlantic-Congo, Volta-Congo, North, Adamawa-Ubangi, Adamawa, Leko-Nimbari, Mumuye-Yandang, Mumuye. Bilingualism in Hausa. Not the same as Gongla. Investigation needed: bilingual proficiency in Hausa, attitudes. Traditional religion, Christian, Muslim.

GERA ***(GERAWA)*** [GEW] 200,000 (1995 CAPRO). Bauchi State, Bauchi and Ganjuwa LGAs, Bauchi town. Afro-Asiatic, Chadic, West, A, A.2, Bole, Bole Proper. Many Gera villages no longer speak the language. Investigation needed: bilingual proficiency in Hausa, attitudes. Traditional religion, Muslim.

GERUMA ***(GEREMA, GERMA)*** [GEA] 4,700 (1971). Bauchi State, Toro, Ganjuwa, Bauchi, and Southern Ningi LGAs. Afro-Asiatic, Chadic, West, A, A.2, Bole, Bole Proper. Dialects: SUM, DUURUM. Gamsawa (Gamshi) mentioned by Temple 1922 could be another dialect. Geruma is rapidly being replaced by Hausa. Investigation needed: bilingual proficiency in Hausa, attitudes. Agriculturalists: Guinea corn, millet, maize, peanuts, beans, rice. Muslim, traditional religion.

GHOTUO ***(OTWA, OTUO)*** [AAA] 9,000 (1952). Edo State, Owan and Akoko-Edo LGAs. Niger-Congo, Atlantic-Congo, Volta-Congo, Benue-Congo, Edoid, North-Central, Ghotuo-Uneme-Yekhee.

GIBANAWA ***(GEMBANAWA, GIMBANAWA, JEGA)*** [GIB] Sokoto State, Jega LGA, near the Dukawa. Pidgin, Hausa based. Hausa-speaking Fulani. The largest group in Jega LGA. They use Gibanawa as a contact language. Second language only.

GIIWO ***(BU GIIWO, KIRFI, KIRIFI, KIRIFAWA)*** [KKS] 14,000 (1998 SIL). Bauchi State, Alkaleri, Bauchi, and Darazo LGAs. Afro-Asiatic, Chadic, West, A, A.2, Bole, Bole Proper. Bilingualism in Hausa. Investigation needed: bilingual proficiency in Hausa, attitudes. Agriculturalists: Guinea corn, beans, peanuts, maize. Muslim.

GLAVDA ***(GALAVDA, GELEBDA, GLANDA, GUELEBDA, GALVAXDAXA)*** [GLV] 20,000 in Nigeria (1963). Population total both countries 22,800. Borno State, Gwoza LGA, mainly in Nggoshe village (different from Ngoshi), and in Agapalawa, Amuda, Vale, Ashigashiya, Kerawa, Pelekwa villages. Also spoken in Cameroon. Afro-Asiatic, Chadic, Biu-Mandara, A, A.4, Mandara Proper, Glavda. Dialects: BOKWA, NGOSHIE (NGWESHE), GLAVDA. Closely related to Guduf. Dictionary. Literacy rate in second language: 5%. Traditional religion, Christian, Muslim. Bible portions 1967.

GOEMAI ***(ANKWAI, ANKWEI, ANKWE, KEMAI)*** [ANK] 200,000 or more (1995). Plateau State, Shendam; Nasarawa State, Lafia and Awe LGAs. Afro-Asiatic, Chadic, West, A, A.3, Angas Proper, 2. Hausa is used as lingua franca. Dictionary. Grammar. Radio programs. Traditional religion, Muslim.

GOKANA [GKN] 100,000 (1989). Rivers State, Gokana, Tai, and Eleme LGAs. Niger-Congo, Atlantic-Congo, Volta-Congo, Benue-Congo, Cross River, Delta Cross, Ogoni, East. NT 1996.

GUDE ***(GOUDE, CHEKE, TCHADE, SHEDE, MAPODI, MAPUDA, MUDAYE, MOCIGIN, MOTCHEKIN)*** [GDE] 68,000 in Nigeria (1987). Population total both countries 96,000. Adamawa State, Mubi LGA; Borno State, Askira-Uba LGA. Also spoken in Cameroon. Afro-Asiatic, Chadic, Biu-Mandara, A, A.8. Different dialects are spoken in Cameroon and Nigeria but they are inherently intelligible. Bilingualism in Hausa, Nzanyi, Fulfulde, English. Grammar. Literacy program in progress. Muslim, traditional religion, Christian. Bible portions 1974-1995.

GUDU ***(GUDO, GUTU)*** [GDU] 5,000 (1993). Adamawa State, Song LGA. Afro-Asiatic, Chadic, Biu-Mandara, A, A.8. Dialect: KUMBI. Formerly the culture and religion were similar to the Ngwaba. Investigation needed: bilingual proficiency in Hausa, attitudes. Muslim.

GUDUF-GAVA ***(GUDUPE, AFKABIYE)*** [GDF] 20,000 in Nigeria (1963). Population total both countries 22,500. Borno State, Gwoza LGA, mainly in Gava, Cikide, and Guduf. Also spoken in Cameroon. Afro-Asiatic, Chadic, Biu-Mandara, A, A.4, Mandara Proper, Glavda. Dialects: CIKIDE (CHIKIDE), GUDUF, GAVA (YAGHWATADAXA, YAWOTATAXA). Closely related to Glavda. Hedi speakers have 35% intelligibility of Guduf. Wolff (1971) separates Guduf from Gvoko and Glavda. 56% lexical similarity with Hedi, 50% with Lamang and Mabas. Investigation needed: intelligibility with Cineni, attitudes. Mountain slope. Bible portions 1966.

GUN-GBE ***(GŨGBE, GUN-ALADA)*** [GUW] 180,000 to 300,000 in Nigeria. Lagos State, Badagry LGA. Niger-Congo, Atlantic-Congo, Volta-Congo, Kwa, Left Bank, Gbe, Aja. Dialects: ALADA (ALADA-GBE), ASENTO, GBEKON, GUN (Gũ, EGUN, GOUN), PHELA, SAVI, WEME. Bible 1923-1972. See main entry under Benin.

GUPA-ABAWA [GPA] 15,000 or more including 10,000 or more Gupa, 5,000 Abawa (1989). Niger State, Lapai LGA, around Gupa and Edzu villages. Niger-Congo, Atlantic-Congo, Volta-Congo, Benue-Congo, Nupoid, Nupe-Gbagyi, Nupe. Dialects: GUPA, ABAWA. Closely related to Nupe. Listed separately by Crozier and Blench 1992. Investigation needed: intelligibility with Nupe.

GURMANA [GRC] 3,000 (1989). Niger State, Shiroro LGA, Gurmana town and nearby hamlets. Niger-Congo, Atlantic-Congo, Volta-Congo, Benue-Congo, Kainji, Western, Baushi-Gurmana.

GURUNTUM-MBAARU ***(GURUNTUM, GURDUNG)*** [GRD] 15,000 (1993). Bauchi State, Bauchi and Alkaleri LGAs. Afro-Asiatic, Chadic, West, B, B.3, Guruntum. Dialects: DOOKA, GAR, GAYAR, KARAKARA, KUUKU, MBAARU. Investigation needed: bilingual proficiency in Hausa, attitudes. Agriculturalists: beans, maize, millet. Muslim.

GVOKO ***(GEVOKO, GHBOKO, GAVOKO, KUVOKO, NGOSSI, NGOSHI, NGOSHE-NDHANG, NGWESHE-NDAGHAN, NGOSHE SAMA, NGGWESHE)*** [NGS] 20,000 or more in Nigeria (1990). Population total both countries 20,000 or more. Borno State, Gwoza LGA; Adamawa State, Michika LGA. Also spoken in Cameroon. Afro-Asiatic, Chadic, Biu-Mandara, A, A.4, Mandara Proper, Glavda. A separate but related language to Glavda and Guduf.

GWA [GWB] 1,000 or fewer (1971). Bauchi State, Toro LGA. Niger-Congo, Atlantic-Congo, Volta-Congo, Benue-Congo, Bantoid, Southern, Jarawan, Nigerian. Related to Lame. Bilingualism in Hausa. Investigation needed: intelligibility with Lame, bilingual proficiency, attitudes.

GWAMHI-WURI ***(LYASE, LYASE-NE)*** [BGA] 8,000 (1973 SIL). Kebbi State, Wasugu LGA, Danko-Maga area, and Niger State, Magama LGA, Dusai and Kwimu. The Gwamfawa are around Danko and the Wurawa around Maga. Migrants are in Niger State. Niger-Congo, Atlantic-Congo, Volta-Congo, Benue-Congo, Kainji, Western, Duka. Dialects: GWAMHI (GWAMFANCI, GWAMFI GWAMFAWA, ABAANGI, BANGA, BANGANCI, BANGAWA), WURI (WURANCI, WURAWA). The two dialects have slight lexical and tonal differences. 57% lexical similarity with Puku-Geeri-Keri-Wipsi, 47% with Duka, 43% with Lela. Bilingualism in Lela, Hausa. Many Gwamfawa are assimilating to Lela culture and language, while the Wurawa are assimilating to Hausa. 'Bangawa' is the Hausa name for the people, 'Banganci' for the language; 'Lyase' means 'mother tongue'.

GWANDARA ***(KWANDARA)*** [GWN] 30,000 (1973 SIL). Niger State, Suleija LGA; Federal Capital Territory; Kaduna State, Kachia LGA; Nasarawa State, Keffi, Lafia, Nasarawa, and Akwanga LGAs. Afro-Asiatic, Chadic, West, A, A.1. Dialects: GWANDARA KARASHI, GWANDARA KORO, GWANDARA SOUTHERN (KYAN KYAR), GWANDARA EASTERN (TONI), GWANDARA GITATA, NIMBIA. Bilingualism in Hausa. Dictionary. Traditional religion, Muslim.

GYEM ***(GYEMAWA, GEMA, GEMAWA, GYAM)*** [GYE] 1,000 (1995 CAPRO). Bauchi State, Toro LGA. Niger-Congo, Atlantic-Congo, Volta-Congo, Benue-Congo, Kainji, Eastern, Northern Jos, Jera. Bilingualism in Hausa. Different from Fyam (Gyem). Investigation needed: bilingual proficiency in Hausa, attitudes. Agriculturalists. Traditional religion.

HAM ***(HYAMHUM, JABA, JABBA, JEBA)*** [JAB] 100,000 (1994 UBS). Kaduna State, Kachia and Jema'a LGAs; Nasarawa State, Keffi LGA. Niger-Congo, Atlantic-Congo, Volta-Congo, Benue-Congo, Platoid, Plateau, Western, Northwestern, Jaba. A dialect cluster. Traditional religion. Bible portions 1921-1923.

HASHA ***(YASHI)*** [YBJ] 3,000 (1999 Blench). Nasarawa State, Akwanga LGA, 3 villages: Hashasu, Kusu, and Bwora. Niger-Congo, Atlantic-Congo, Volta-Congo, Benue-Congo, Platoid, Plateau, Western, Southwestern, B. Hasha spoken by young people. Hausa widely known. English spoken by some secondary school students. Investigation needed: bilingual proficiency in Hausa.

HAUSA ***(HAUSAWA, HAOUSSA, ABAKWARIGA, MGBAKPA, HABE, KADO)*** [HUA] 18,525,000 in Nigeria (1991 SIL). Population total all countries 24,200,000 first language speakers, 39,000,000 including second language speakers (1999 WA). Spoken as a first language in large areas of Sokoto, Kaduna, Katsina, Kano, Bauchi, Jigawa, Zamfara, Kebbi, and Gombe states. Spoken as a second language in the northern half of Nigeria. Also spoken in Benin, Burkina Faso, Cameroon, CAR, Chad, Congo, Eritrea, Germany, Ghana, Niger, Sudan, Togo. Afro-Asiatic, Chadic, West, A, A.1. Dialects: KANO, KATAGUM, HADEJIYA, SOKOTO, GOBIRAWA, ADARAWA, KEBBAWA, ZAMFARAWA, KATSINA, AREWA. Barikanchi is a Hausa pidgin used in military barracks. There is a pidgin or market Hausa. Subdialects of Eastern Hausa: Kano, Katagum, Hadejiya; of Western Hausa: Sokoto, Katsina, Gobirawa, Adarawa, Kebbawa, Zamfarawa; of North Hausa: Arewa, Arawa. Abakwariga is a subgroup. Official regional language in the north. Official language. Dictionary. Grammar. SVO.

Roman and Ajami scripts used. Radio programs. Muslim, traditional religion (Maguzawa), Christian. Bible 1932-1996.

HAUSA SIGN LANGUAGE [HSL] Deaf sign language.

HOLMA ***(DA HOLMACI, BALI HOLMA)*** [HOD] 4 (1987 Blench in 1992 Crozier and Blench). Adamawa State, north of Sorau on the Cameroon border. Afro-Asiatic, Chadic, Biu-Mandara, A, A.8. Related to Nzanyi. Being replaced by Fulfulde (Blench). Nearly extinct.

HOROM ***("KALERI")*** [HOE] 1,500 or fewer (1998 Blench). Plateau State, Bokkos LGA. Niger-Congo, Atlantic-Congo, Volta-Congo, Benue-Congo, Platoid, Plateau, Southeastern. Horom is the name of a village in the Kulere-speaking area, therefore they have been erroneously referred to as "Kaleri", which is a derogatory name. Investigation needed: bilingual proficiency in Hausa, attitudes.

HUBA ***(KILBA, CHOBBA)*** [KIR] 175,000 (1992). Adamawa State, Hong, Maiha, Gombi, and Mubi LGAs. Afro-Asiatic, Chadic, Biu-Mandara, A, A.2, 2. Dialect: LUWA. Bilingualism in Hausa, Fulfulde. Nearly all villages have primary schools; some have secondary schools. Literacy program in progress. Mountain slope. Agriculturalists; animal husbandry: cattle; weavers, cloth dyers. Bible portions 1976.

HUN-SAARE ***(DUKA, DUKAWA, DUKWA, DUKANCI, DUKANCHI)*** [DUD] 73,000 including 10,000 outside the traditional area (1985 Patience Ahmed). Kebbi State, Wasagu and Yauri LGAs; Niger State, Rijau LGA, and migrants farther south. Dialect centers are Rijau-Senjir, Dukku-Iri, Zente-Dogo, and Darengi. Niger-Congo, Atlantic-Congo, Volta-Congo, Benue-Congo, Kainji, Western, Duka. Dialects: EASTERN DUKA (HUN, ET-HUN, HUNE), WESTERN DUKA (ES-SAARE). 85% lexical similarity between Rijau and Dukku dialects; 63% Duka with Puku-Geeri-Keri-Wipsi, 50% with Lela, 47% with Gwamhi-Wuri. Dukawa from the west refer to the speech of the east as 'Es-Saare', just as they refer to their own. Literacy rate in first language: Below 1%. Literacy rate in second language: 2%. Savannah. Plains, hills. Peasant agriculturalists, hunters. 200 to 500 meters. Traditional religion, Muslim, Christian. Bible portions 1974-1979.

HUNGWORO ***(NGWOI, NKWOI, NGWE, INGWO, INGWE, UNGWE)*** [NAT] 1,000 (1949; 1956 H. D. Gunn). Niger State, Rafi LGA, around Kagara and Maikujeri towns. Niger-Congo, Atlantic-Congo, Volta-Congo, Benue-Congo, Kainji, Western, Kamuku. 50% to 52% lexical similarity with Kamuku dialects. Investigation needed: bilingual proficiency in Hausa, attitudes.

HWANA ***(HWONA, HONA, TUFTERA, FITERYA)*** [HWO] 32,000 (1992). Adamawa State, Gombi LGA, and some in Song and Hong LGAs. Afro-Asiatic, Chadic, Biu-Mandara, A, A.1, Eastern. Bilingualism in Fulfulde, Hausa, Kilba, Gaanda. 'Tuftera' is their name for their language, 'Fiterya' for themselves. Four divisions: Hwana Guyaku, Hwana Tawa, Ngithambara, and Hwana Barni. Agriculturalists, animal husbandry: cattle, goats; hunters. Traditional religion, Christian, Muslim.

IBANI ***(BONNY, UBANI)*** [IBY] 60,000 (1989 UBS). Rivers State, Bonny and Degema LGAs. Niger-Congo, Atlantic-Congo, Ijoid, Ijo, Eastern, Northeastern, Ibani-Okrika-Kalabari. A member of Koin cluster within the Ijo cluster. Bible portions 1892-1986.

IBIBIO [IBB] 1,500,000 to 2,000,000 (1998 B. Connell). Akwa Ibom State, Itu, Uyo, Etinan, Ikot Abasi, Ikono, Ekpe-Atai, Uruan, Onna, Nsit-Ubium, and Mkpat Enin LGAs. Niger-Congo, Atlantic-Congo, Volta-Congo, Benue-Congo, Cross River, Delta Cross, Lower Cross, Obolo, Efik. Dialects: ENYONG, CENTRAL IBIBIO, ITAK, NSIT. Several dialects. Efik is decreasing in use as literary language. Ibibio is the main trade language of Akwa Ibom State. Used in university courses. Trade language. Dictionary. Grammar. SVO. Roman. Radio programs, TV. Christian.

IBILO [IBO] Edo State. Niger-Congo, Atlantic-Congo, Volta-Congo, Benue-Congo, Edoid, North-Central, Edo-Esan-Ora.

IBINO ***(IBENO, IBUNO)*** [IBN] 10,000 (1989 Faraclas). Akwa Ibom State, Uquo-Ibeno LGA. Niger-Congo, Atlantic-Congo, Volta-Congo, Benue-Congo, Cross River, Delta Cross, Lower Cross, Obolo, Ibino. Listed separately in Crozier and Blench 1992.

IBUORO [IBR] 5,000 or more (1988). Akwa Ibom State, Itu and Ikono LGAs. Niger-Congo, Atlantic-Congo, Volta-Congo, Benue-Congo, Cross River, Delta Cross, Lower Cross, Obolo, Ibuoro. Listed separately in Crozier and Blench 1992.

ICEVE-MACI ***(ICHEVE, OCHEBE, OCHEVE, OCEVE, UTSE, UTSER, UTSEU)*** [BEC] 5,000 in Nigeria (1990). Cross River State, Obudu LGA. Niger-Congo, Atlantic-Congo, Volta-Congo, Benue-Congo, Bantoid, Southern, Tivoid. Dialects: MACI (MATCHI, OLITI, OLITHI, OLIT, KWAYA, OLITI-AKWAYA, MOTOM, MOTOMO), BACHEVE (BECHEVE, BECHERE, BEHEVE, BACEVE). Maci and Bacheve have 80% lexical similarity. See main entry under Cameroon.

IDERE [IDE] 5,000 or more (1988). Akwa Ibom State, Itu LGA. Niger-Congo, Atlantic-Congo, Volta-Congo, Benue-Congo, Cross River, Delta Cross, Lower Cross, Obolo. Listed separately in Crozier and Blench 1992. Probably Central Lower Cross, related to Anaang. Close to Eki (B. Connell 1998).

IDOMA [IDO] 600,000 (1991 UBS). Benue State, Otukpo and Okpokwu LGAs. Niger-Congo, Atlantic-Congo, Volta-Congo, Benue-Congo, Idomoid, Akweya, Etulo-Idoma, Idoma. Dialects:

IDOMA CENTRAL (OTURKPO, AKPOTO), IDOMA WEST, IDOMA SOUTH (IGUMALE, IGWAALE, IJIGBAM), OKPOGU. Dialect cluster. Used in adult education. National language. Grammar. Used in primary education. Radio programs, TV. Agriculturalists: yam, Guinea corn, cassava, maize, beniseed, rice, millet; hunters, fishermen. Bible, in press (1997).

IDON ***(IDONG)*** [IDC] Small. Kaduna State, Kachia LGA. Niger-Congo, Atlantic-Congo, Volta-Congo, Benue-Congo, Platoid, Plateau, Northern.

IDUN ***(LUNGU, UNGU, ADONG)*** [LDB] 10,000 (1972 Barrett). Kaduna State, Jema'a LGA. Niger-Congo, Atlantic-Congo, Volta-Congo, Benue-Congo, Platoid, Plateau, Western, Northwestern, Koro. Different from Idon. Traditional religion.

IGALA ***(IGARA)*** [IGL] 800,000 (1989 UBS). Kogi State, Ankpa, Idah, Dekina, and Bassa LGAs; Edo State, Oshimili LGA; Anambra State, Anambra LGA. Niger-Congo, Atlantic-Congo, Volta-Congo, Benue-Congo, Defoid, Yoruboid, Igala. Dialects: EBU, IDAH, ANKPA, OGUGU, IBAJI, IFE, ANYUGBA. They are able to converse in most common topics in Idoma and Agatu. Agatu, Idoma, and Bassa people use Igala for attending Ika Bible School. Used in initial primary education. Traditional religion, Christian, Muslim. Bible 1968.

IGBO ***(IBO)*** [IGR] 18,000,000 or 16.6% of the population (1999 WA). Abia State, Anambra State, Aguata, Anambra, Awka, Idemili, Ihiala, Njikoka, Nnewi, and Onitsha LGAs; Enugu State, Awgu, Enugu, Ezeagu, Igo-Etiti, Igbo-Eze, Isi-Uzo, Nkanu, Nsukka, Udi, and Uzo-Uwani LGAs; Imo State; Rivers State, Ikwerre, Bonny, and Ahoada LGAs; Delta State, Oshimili, Anoicha, and Ndokwa LGAs; Akwa Ibom State, Ika LGA. Niger-Congo, Atlantic-Congo, Volta-Congo, Benue-Congo, Igboid, Igbo. Dialects: OWERRI (ISUAMA), ONITSHA, UMUAHIA (OHUHU), ORLU, NGWA, AFIKPO, NSA, OGUTA, ANIOCHA, ECHE, EGBEMA, OKA (AWKA), BONNY-OPOBO, MBAISE, NSUKA, OHUHU, UNWANA. 30 dialects vary in inherent intelligibility. A standard literary form is developing from the dialect of Owerri and Umuahia. The main trade language of Anambra and Imo States. Used for government notices. Official language. Dictionary. Grammar. Roman. Radio programs, TV. Christian, traditional religion. Bible 1906-1988.

IGEDE ***(IGEDDE, EGEDE)*** [IGE] 250,000 (1991 UBS). Benue State, Oju, Otukpo, and Okpokwu LGAs; Cross River State, Ogoja LGA. Niger-Congo, Atlantic-Congo, Volta-Congo, Benue-Congo, Idomoid, Akweya, Etulo-Idoma, Idoma. Dialects: ITO, OJU (CENTRAL IGEDE), WORKU, GABU. Grammar. NT 1981.

IGUTA ***(NARAGUTA, ANAGUTA)*** [NAR] 6,123 (1990). Plateau State, Bassa LGA. Niger-Congo, Atlantic-Congo, Volta-Congo, Benue-Congo, Kainji, Eastern, Northern Jos, Jera. 'Iguta' is the language, 'Unaguta' a speaker, 'Anaguta' or 'Naragutawa' the people. Investigation needed: bilingual proficiency in Hausa, attitudes.

IJO, SOUTHEAST ***(IJAW, BRASS IJO)*** [IJO] 71,500 (1977 Voegelin and Voegelin) including 66,600 Nembe, 4,900 Akassa. Bayelsa State, Brass LGA. Niger-Congo, Atlantic-Congo, Ijoid, Ijo, Eastern, Southeastern. Dialects: NEMBE (NIMBE), AKASSA (AHASA). A separate language within the Ijo cluster. Dictionary. Literacy rate in second language: 60%. Christian, traditional religion. Bible 1956.

IKA [IKK] Akwa Ibom State, Ika LGA; Edo State, Orhionwon LGAs. Niger-Congo, Atlantic-Congo, Volta-Congo, Benue-Congo, Igboid, Igbo. A separate language in the Igbo language cluster. The dialect around Agbor, the administrative and commercial center, appears to be developing into a standard form. Further east and south from there, the varieties become more similar to Igbo (Report of the Committee on Languages of Midwestern State: 12). Investigation needed: intelligibility with Igbo, bilingual proficiency, attitudes. Grammar.

IKO [IKI] 5,000 or more (1988). Akwa Ibom State, Ikot Abasi LGA, 3 villages. Niger-Congo, Atlantic-Congo, Volta-Congo, Benue-Congo, Cross River, Delta Cross, Lower Cross, Obolo, Iko. Culturally they consider themselves Obolo, but they cannot use Obolo literature. The language is closer to other Lower Cross languages than to Obolo. Listed separately by Crozier and Blench 1992.

IKPESHI ***(IKPESHE, EKPESHE)*** [IKP] 1,826 (1957 Bradbury). Bendel State, Etsako LGA. Niger-Congo, Atlantic-Congo, Volta-Congo, Benue-Congo, Edoid, North-Central, Ghotuo-Uneme-Yekhee.

IKU-GORA-ANKWA ***(IKU)*** [IKV] Kaduna State, Kachia LGA. Niger-Congo, Atlantic-Congo, Volta-Congo, Benue-Congo, Platoid, Plateau, Northern.

IKULU ***(IKOLU, ANKULU)*** [IKU] 50,000 (1998). Kaduna State, Kachia LGA. Niger-Congo, Atlantic-Congo, Volta-Congo, Benue-Congo, Platoid, Plateau, Northern. Investigation needed: bilingual proficiency in Hausa, attitudes.

IKWERE ***(IKWERRE, IKWERRI)*** [IKW] 200,000 probably (1973 SIL). Rivers State, Ikwerre, Port Harcourt, and Obio-Akpor LGAs. The Odegnu are in 5 villages. Niger-Congo, Atlantic-Congo, Volta-Congo, Benue-Congo, Igboid, Igbo. Dialects: APANI, AKPO-MGBU-TOLU, OGBAKIRI, EMOWHUA, NDELE, ELELE, OMERELU, EGBEDNA, ALUU, IGWURUTA, IBAA, ISIOKPO, OMAGWNA, UBIMA, IPO, OMUDIOGA, OBIO, RUMUJI. A separate language in the Igbo language cluster. An important language. Clan name: Odegnu. Considerable local interest in language and literacy.

ILUE ***(IDUA)*** [ILE] 5,000 or less (1988). Akwa Ibom State, Oron LGA. Niger-Congo, Atlantic-Congo, Volta-Congo, Benue-Congo, Cross River, Delta Cross, Lower Cross, Obolo, Ilue. Listed separately in Crozier and Blench 1992. Generally not used by younger people. Diminishing in size.

IRIGWE ***(IREGWE, AREGWE, RIGWE, NNERIGWE, KWOLL, KWAL, MIANGO, NYANGO, IDAFAN, KWAN, NKARIGWE)*** [IRI] 40,000 (1985 UBS). Plateau State, Bassa and Barakin Ladi LGAs; Kaduna State, Saminaka LGA. Niger-Congo, Atlantic-Congo, Volta-Congo, Benue-Congo, Platoid, Plateau, Central, South-Central. The language is 'Nkarigwe' or 'Rigwe', the people are 'Nnerigwe' or 'Miyango'. Bible portions 1923-1935.

ISEKIRI ***(ITSEKIRI, ISHEKIRI, SHEKIRI, JEKRI, CHEKIRI, IWERE, IRHOBO, WARRI, ISELEMA-OTU, SELEMO)*** [ITS] 510,000 (1991 UBS). Delta State, Warri, Bomadi, and Ethiope LGAs. Niger-Congo, Atlantic-Congo, Volta-Congo, Benue-Congo, Defoid, Yoruboid, Edekiri. Closely related to Yoruba. Grammar. Used in initial primary education. NT 1985.

ISOKO ***("IGABO", "SOBO", "BIOTU")*** [ISO] 321,000 (1993 Johnstone). Delta State, Isoko and Ndokwa LGAs. Niger-Congo, Atlantic-Congo, Volta-Congo, Benue-Congo, Edoid, Southwestern. Dialects: OZORO, OFAGBE, EMEDE, OWE (OWHE), ELU, AVIARA, IYEDE, IMIV, ENHWE, UME, IWIRE (IGBIDE), OLOMORO, IYEDE-AMI, UNOGBOKO, ITEBIEGE, UTI, IYOWO, IBIEDE, OYEDE, UZERE, IRRI (IRI) OLE (OLEH). A regionally important language. "Sobo" and "Igabo" are offensive names. "Biotu" not recommended. Official orthography. Used in initial primary education. Bible 1977.

ITO [ITW] 5,000 or more (1988). Akwa Ibom State, Akamkpa LGA. Niger-Congo, Atlantic-Congo, Volta-Congo, Benue-Congo, Cross River, Delta Cross, Lower Cross, Obolo, Ibuoro. Listed separately in Crozier and Blench 1992.

ITU MBON UZO ***(ITU MBON USO, ITU MBUZO)*** [ITM] 5,000 or more (1988). Akwa Ibom State, Ikono and Itu LGAs. Niger-Congo, Atlantic-Congo, Volta-Congo, Benue-Congo, Cross River, Delta Cross, Lower Cross, Obolo, Ibuoro. Listed separately in Crozier and Blench 1992.

IVBIE NORTH-OKPELA-ARHE [ATG] 20,000 possibly (1973 SIL). Edo State, Etsako and Akoko-Edo LGAs. Niger-Congo, Atlantic-Congo, Volta-Congo, Benue-Congo, Edoid, North-Central, Ghotuo-Uneme-Yekhee. Dialects: IVBIE NORTH (IBIE NORTH), OKPELA (OKPELLA, UKPELLA, UPELLA), ARHE (ATTE, ATE). Dialect cluster.

IYAYU ***(IDOANI)*** [IYA] 9,979 (1963). Ondo State, one-quarter of Idoani town. Niger-Congo, Atlantic-Congo, Volta-Congo, Benue-Congo, Edoid, Northwestern, Osse. Listed separately from Uhami in Crozier and Blench 1992. The people are sometimes called 'Idoani'.

IYIVE ***(UIVE, YIIVE, NDIR, ASUMBO)*** [UIV] 1,000 in Nigeria (1992 Crozier and Blench). Benue State, Kwande LGA, near Turan. Niger-Congo, Atlantic-Congo, Volta-Congo, Benue-Congo, Bantoid, Southern, Tivoid. 75% lexical similarity with Tiv. The people's name for themselves is 'Ndir'. Investigation needed: bilingual proficiency in Tiv, attitudes. See main entry under Cameroon.

IZERE ***(IZAREK, FIZERE, FEZERE, FESEREK, AFIZAREK, AFIZARE, AFUSARE, JARI, JARAWA, JARAWAN DUTSE, HILL JARAWA, JOS-ZARAZON)*** [FIZ] 50,000 (1993 SIL). Southern dialects: Plateau State, Birikin Ladi LGA; Northern dialects: Plateau State, Jos LGA; Bauchi State, Toro LGA; and Kaduna State, Jema'a LGA. Niger-Congo, Atlantic-Congo, Volta-Congo, Benue-Congo, Platoid, Plateau, Central, South-Central. Dialects: NORTHWEST IZERE, NORTHEAST IZERE, SOUTH IZERE, GANANG-FAISHANG. The Fobor dialect is prestigious. Northwest Izere subdialects: Fobor (Fobur) and Shere; Northeast Izere: Fedare (Zandi, Zendi), Jarawan Kogi (Maigemu), and Fursom (Fursum); South Izere: Forom (Ichen); Ganang and Faishang. Firan is a separate language. The language is called 'Izarek', 'Izere', or 'Izer'; a speaker 'Bajari', the people 'Jarawa', 'Afizarek', 'Afizere', 'Afudelek', 'Fizere', 'Feserek', 'Fezere', 'Hill Jarawa', 'Jarawan Dutse'. 'Jos-Zarazon' is the name of indigenous speakers in Jos. Literacy rate in first language: Below 1%. Literacy rate in second language: 25% to 50%. Radio programs. Bible portions 1940.

IZI-EZAA-IKWO-MGBO [IZI] 593,000 (1973 SIL) including 200,000 Izi, 180,000 Ezaa, 150,000 Ikwo, 63,000 Mgbo. Ebonyi State, Abakaliki, Ezza, Ohaozara, and Ishielu LGAs; Benue State, Okpokwu LGA. Niger-Congo, Atlantic-Congo, Volta-Congo, Benue-Congo, Igboid, Igbo. Dialects: IZI (IZZI), EZAA (EZA), IKWO, MGBO (NGBO). Dialect cluster within the Igbo language cluster. Grammar. NT 1980.

IZON ***(IZO, UZO, IJO, IJAW, CENTRAL-WESTERN IJO)*** [IJC] 1,000,000 (1989 Williamson) including 100,000 Kolokuma (1991 UBS). 1,770,000 all Ijo languages, 2% of the population (1991 SIL). Bayelsa State, Yenagoa and Sagbama LGAs; Delta State, Burutu, Warri, and Ughelli LGAs; Ondo State, Ilaje Ese-Odo LGAs; Ekiti State, Ikole LGA. Niger-Congo, Atlantic-Congo, Ijoid, Ijo, Central, Central Western. Dialects: IDUWINI, OGULAGHA, OPOROZA (GBARANMATU), AROGBO, EGBEMA, OLODIAMA EAST, OLODIAMA WEST, FURUPAGHA, KABO (PATANI), KUMBO, TARAKIRI EAST, TARAKIRI WEST, MEIN (NORTHWEST IZON), TUOMO, OPEREMOR, SEIMBRI, OGBOIN, OIAKIRI, OPOROMA, APOI, GBANRAIN, KOLUKUMA (KOLOKUMA, NORTH IZON), BUMO (SOUTH CENTRAL IZON), EKPETIAMA, IKIBIRI, BOMA, OGBE IJO. The Ijo (Ijaw) group is made up of seven separate languages.

Izon has about 30 inherently intelligible dialects. The Kolokuma dialect is used in adult and primary education. Dictionary. Grammar. Radio programs, TV. Bible portions 1912-1924.

IZORA ***(CHOKOBO, COKOBO, CIKOBU, CHIKOBO, COKOBANCI, AZORA)*** [CBO] 4,000 to 5,000 (1998 CAPRO). Plateau State, Bassa LGA. Niger-Congo, Atlantic-Congo, Volta-Congo, Benue-Congo, Kainji, Eastern, Northern Jos, Jera. The language is 'Izora' or 'Cokobanci'; a speaker is 'Bacokobi'; the speakers are 'Cokobawa' or 'Ndazora'. Investigation needed: bilingual proficiency in Hausa, attitudes.

JANJI ***(ANAFEJANZI, JENJI, TIJANJI, AJANJI)*** [JNI] 360 (1950). Plateau State, Bassa LGA. Niger-Congo, Atlantic-Congo, Volta-Congo, Benue-Congo, Kainji, Eastern, Northern Jos, Jera. 'Tijanji' is the language, 'Ujanji' a speaker, 'Ajanji' the people. Investigation needed: bilingual proficiency in Hausa, attitudes.

JARA ***(JERA)*** [JAF] 4,000 (1973). Borno State, Biu and Kwaya-Kusar LGAs; Gombei State, Akko and Yamaltu-Deba LGAs. Afro-Asiatic, Chadic, Biu-Mandara, A, A.1, Western. Jara is being replaced by Fulfulde and Hausa. Different from Jera, which is Benue-Congo. Investigation needed: bilingual proficiency in Hausa, Fulfulde, attitudes.

JARAWA ***(JARANCHI, JAR, JARA, JARAWAN KOGI)*** [JAR] 150,000 (1978 MARC), including 20,000 Bankal, 19,000 Gingwak. Bauchi, Adamawa, and Plateau States. Niger-Congo, Atlantic-Congo, Volta-Congo, Benue-Congo, Bantoid, Southern, Jarawan, Nigerian. Dialects: BANKAL (BANKALA, BARANCI, ZHAR), LIGRI, KANAM, BOBAR, GINGWAK (GWAK, JARAWAN BUNUNU, JARACIN KASA). Dialect cluster. Most men speak Hausa but most women understand little Hausa. Investigation needed: bilingual proficiency in Hausa, attitudes. Agriculturalists: Guinea corn, maize, millet. Traditional religion, Muslim, Christian. Bible portions 1940.

JERE ***(JEERE, JERA)*** [JER] 64,850 (1998 CAPRO) including 15,000 Buji (1998), 15,000 Gusu (1998), 30,000 Jere (1998), 4,000 Ribina (1996 CAPRO), 850 Gurrum (1936). Plateau State, Bassa LGA; Bauchi State, Toro LGA; Kaduna State, Saminaka LGA. Niger-Congo, Atlantic-Congo, Volta-Congo, Benue-Congo, Kainji, Eastern, Northern Jos, Jera. Dialects: BUJI (EBOZE, ANABEZE), GUSU (GUSAWA, GUSSUM, GESAWA, GUZAWA, ISANGA, ASANGA, ANIBAU, ANOSANGOBARI), JERE (JERIYAWA, EZELLE, AZELLE, JENGRE), RIBINA (REBINA, BUNU, IBUNU, NARABUNU, ANORUBUNA, GURRUM, ANEGOROM). A dialect cluster. For Ezelle dialect, a speaker is 'Ozelle' or 'Bajere'; the speakers are 'Azelle' or 'Jarawa'. For Eboze dialect, a speaker is 'Unabeze', speakers are 'Anabeze'. Different from Jara, which is Chadic. Investigation needed: bilingual proficiency in Hausa, attitudes. Agriculturalists: Guinea corn, maize, potatoes, cocoyam, tomatoes. Traditional religion, Christian.

JIBU ***(JIBAWA, JIBANCI)*** [JIB] 30,000 (1997 SIL). Taraba State, Gashaka and Bali LGA. Niger-Congo, Atlantic-Congo, Volta-Congo, Benue-Congo, Platoid, Benue, Jukunoid, Central, Jukun-Mbembe-Wurbo, Jukun. Dialects: GAYAM, GARBABI, GALAMJINA. Some living near the main roads also speak Fulfulde and Hausa. Literacy rate in first language: 1% to 3%. Literacy rate in second language: 5% to 7%. Few have finished secondary school. Mountain slope, plains. Agriculturalists. Traditional religion, Christian, Muslim. NT 1996.

JILBE ***(ZOULBOU)*** [JIE] 100 (H. Tourneux). Borno State, Jilbe town, on the border of Cameroon across from the town of Dabanga. 1 village only. Afro-Asiatic, Chadic, Biu-Mandara, B, B.1. Speakers of Kotoko languages in Cameroon and Chad consistently report low intelligibility with Jilbe. Not the same as Zizilivakan. Muslim.

JIMI ***(BI-GIMU)*** [JMI] 1,000 (1995 CAPRO). Bauchi State, Ganjuwa LGA, Jimi village. Afro-Asiatic, Chadic, West, B, B.3, Eastern. Dialect: ZUMO. Only elders. Different from Jimi in Cameroon in the Biu-Mandara group. Investigation needed: bilingual proficiency in Hausa, attitudes. Muslim.

JIRU ***(WIYAP, KIR, ATAK, ZHIRU)*** [JRR] Taraba State, Karim Lamido LGA. Niger-Congo, Atlantic-Congo, Volta-Congo, Benue-Congo, Platoid, Benue, Jukunoid, Central, Jukun-Mbembe-Wurbo, Wurbo. Traditional religion, Muslim, Christian.

JJU ***(KAJE, KAJJI, KACHE)*** [KAJ] 300,000 (1988 C. McKinney SIL). Kaduna State, Kachia and Jema'a LGAs. Niger-Congo, Atlantic-Congo, Volta-Congo, Benue-Congo, Platoid, Plateau, Central, South-Central. Literacy rate in first language: 10% to 30%. Literacy rate in second language: 50% to 75%. Literacy program in progress. Official orthography. NT 1982.

JORTO [JRT] 4,876 (1934 Ames). Plateau State, Shendam LGA, at Dokan Kasuwa. Afro-Asiatic, Chadic, West, A, A.3, Angas Proper, 1. Investigation needed: bilingual proficiency in Hausa, attitudes.

JU [JUU] 900 (1993). Bauchi State, Bauchi LGA, Ju village. Afro-Asiatic, Chadic, West, B, B.3, Guruntum. Investigation needed: bilingual proficiency in Hausa, attitudes. Agriculturalists: sweet potato, millet, maize; animal husbandry; hunters. Traditional religion, Christian.

JUKUN TAKUM ***(DIYI, NJIKUM, JUKUN)*** [JBU] Second language speakers in Nigeria: 40,000 (1979 UBS). No first language speakers in Nigeria. Population total both countries 1,700. Taraba State, Takum, Sardauna, and Bali LGAs. Also spoken in Cameroon. Niger-Congo, Atlantic-Congo, Volta-Congo,

Benue-Congo, Platoid, Benue, Jukunoid, Central, Jukun-Mbembe-Wurbo, Jukun. Dialects: TAKUM, DONGA (AKPANZHI). The name 'Njikum' is preferred in Cameroon. Formerly founders of the Kwararafa Kingdom, which existed from the 16th to the 19th centuries. Trade language. Dictionary. Grammar. Literacy program in progress. Christian, traditional religion, Muslim. NT 1980.

KAAN ***(LIBO, LIBBO, KAN)*** [LDL] 10,000 (1992). Adamawa State, Shellen, Song, and Numan LGAs. Niger-Congo, Atlantic-Congo, Volta-Congo, North, Adamawa-Ubangi, Adamawa, Waja-Jen, Yungur, Libo. Most adults speak Hausa, Fulfulde, Mbula-Bwaza, Tambo, or Kanakuru as second language. Investigation needed: bilingual proficiency in Hausa, Fulfulde, attitudes. No primary schools in the area. Many desire education. Agriculturalists. Traditional religion, Christian, Muslim.

KADARA ***(ADARA)*** [KAD] 40,000 (1972 Barrett). Kaduna State, Kachia LGA; Niger State, Chanchaga LGA. Niger-Congo, Atlantic-Congo, Volta-Congo, Benue-Congo, Platoid, Plateau, Northern. Dialects: KAJURU (AJURE), MINNA, KACHIA, IRI. Literacy rate in second language: 20%. Traditional religion, Christian, Muslim.

KAG-FER-JIIR-KOOR-ROR-US-ZUKSUN ***(FAKANCI, FAKKANCI, PUKU-GEERI-KERI-WIPSI)*** [GEL] 36,000 or more (1992 SIL). Kebbi State, Zuru LGA, Fakai District, with migrants farther south. Kur is also in Kebbi State, Sakaba LGA. Niger-Congo, Atlantic-Congo, Volta-Congo, Benue-Congo, Kainji, Western, Duka. Dialects: KAG (PUKU, FAKANCHI, ET-KAG), JIIR (GELANCHI, ET-JIIR), KUR (KERE, KAR, KERI-NI, KELLI-NI, KELANCHI, KELINCI), ZUKSUN (ZUSSUN, WIPSI-NI, ET-ZUKSUN), ROR (ET-MAROR, TUDANCHI, FAKANCHI, ER-GWAR), FER (FERE. ET-FER, WIPSI-NI, KUKUM), US (ET-US), KOOR (KULU). Kag, Ker, Jiir, and Fer speakers have 79% to 92% inherent intelligibility of Ror. Ror and Kag are the largest dialects, Koor and Us the smallest. 81% to 97% lexical similarity among dialects, 63% with Duka, 50% with Lela, 57% with Gwamhi-Wuri. Hausa bilingual proficiency differs regionally. Speakers are interested in literature in their language. Traditional religion, Muslim, Christian.

KAGOMA ***(GWONG, GYONG, KWONG, AGOMA)*** [KDM] 6,250 (1934, 1956 H. D. Gunn). Kaduna State, Jema'a LGA. Niger-Congo, Atlantic-Congo, Volta-Congo, Benue-Congo, Platoid, Plateau, Western, Northwestern, Jaba. Investigation needed: bilingual proficiency in Hausa, attitudes. Grammar.

KAIVI ***(KAIBI)*** [KCE] 650 (1949). Kaduna State, Saminaka LGA. Niger-Congo, Atlantic-Congo, Volta-Congo, Benue-Congo, Kainji, Eastern, Northern Jos, Kauru. Investigation needed: bilingual proficiency in Hausa, attitudes.

KAKANDA ***(AKANDA, HYABE, ADYAKTYE)*** [KKA] 20,000 (1989 Blench). Niger State, Agaie and Lapai LGAs; Kwara State, Kogi LGA, and communities along the Niger River centered on Budã. Niger-Congo, Atlantic-Congo, Volta-Congo, Benue-Congo, Nupoid, Nupe-Gbagyi, Nupe. Dialects: BUDON KAKANDA, GBANMI-SOKUN KAKANDA.

KAKIHUM [KXE] 15,000 estimate (1996). Northern Niger State. Niger-Congo, Atlantic-Congo, Volta-Congo, Benue-Congo, Kainji, Western, Kambari.

KALABARI [IJN] 257,764 (1989 Jenewari). Rivers State, Degema, Bonny, Asari Toru LGAs. Niger-Congo, Atlantic-Congo, Ijoid, Ijo, Eastern, Northeastern, Ibani-Okrika-Kalabari. A dialect cluster within the Ijo language cluster. Okrika and Ibani are closely related. Grammar. NT, in press (1996).

KAM ***(YIMWOM, NYIWOM, NYINGWOM)*** [KDX] 5,000 (1993). Taraba State, Bali LGA, 18 villages between Mayo Kam and Garba Chede. Niger-Congo, Atlantic-Congo, Volta-Congo, North, Adamawa-Ubangi, Adamawa, Kam. Bilingualism in Hausa, Fulfulde. Investigation needed: bilingual proficiency in Hausa, attitudes. Traditional religion, Christian, Muslim.

KAMANTAN ***(KAMANTON, ANGAN)*** [KCI] 10,000 (1972 Barrett). Kaduna State, Kachia LGA. Niger-Congo, Atlantic-Congo, Volta-Congo, Benue-Congo, Platoid, Plateau, Western, Northwestern, Jaba. Investigation needed: bilingual proficiency in Hausa, attitudes. Traditional religion.

KAMI [KMI] 5,000 or more (1992 Crozier and Blench). Niger State, Lapai LGA, Ebo town and 11 villages. Niger-Congo, Atlantic-Congo, Volta-Congo, Benue-Congo, Nupoid, Nupe-Gbagyi, Nupe. Investigation needed: intelligibility with Nupe, attitudes.

KAMO ***(KAMU, NUBAMA, NYIMA, MA)*** [KCQ] 20,000 (1995 CAPRO). Gombe State, Billiri, Kaltungo and Akko LGAs. Niger-Congo, Atlantic-Congo, Volta-Congo, North, Adamawa-Ubangi, Adamawa, Waja-Jen, Waja, Awak. Typologically closer to Awak (no singular/plural noun suffixes). 5 primary schools, 1 junior secondary school. Investigation needed: bilingual proficiency in Hausa, attitudes. Agriculturalists: Guinea corn, rice, millet, peanuts. Traditional religion, Christian.

KAMWE ***(HIGI, HIJI, HIGGI, VACAMWE)*** [HIG] 300,000 (1992). Adamawa State, Michika LGA, in the Mandara Mts. Afro-Asiatic, Chadic, Biu-Mandara, A, A.3. Dialects: NKAFA, DAKWA (BAZZA), SINA, WULA, FUTU, TILI PTE, FALI OF KIRIYA, FALI OF MIJILU. Closely related to Psikye and Hya of Cameroon. Primary schools. People in lowland towns have more education. Mountain slope. Agriculturalists: Guinea corn, peanuts, beans, sweet potato, millet; animal husbandry; hunters. Traditional religion, Christian, Muslim. NT 1975.

KANINGDON-NINDEM [KDP] 2,291 or more (1934). Kaduna State, Jema'a LGA. Niger-Congo, Atlantic-Congo, Volta-Congo, Benue-Congo, Platoid, Plateau, Western, Southwestern, A. Dialects: KANINGDOM (KANINKON, KANINGKWOM, KANINGKON), NINDEM (INIDEM, NIDEM). Dialect cluster. Investigation needed: bilingual proficiency in Hausa, attitudes.

KANUFI *(KARSHI)* [KNI] Kaduna State, Jema'a LGA. Niger-Congo, Atlantic-Congo, Volta-Congo, Benue-Congo, Platoid, Plateau, Western, Southwestern, A. Investigation needed: bilingual proficiency in Hausa, attitudes.

KANURI, CENTRAL *(YERWA KANURI, KANOURI, BERIBERI, BORNU, KANOURY)* [KPH] 3,000,000 or more in Nigeria (1985 Gunnemark and Kenrick). Population total all countries 3,500,000 (1987 UBS). All Kanuri in all countries including second language speakers: 4,000,000 (1999 WA). Borno State, Kukawa, Kaga, Konduga, Maiduguri, Monguno, Ngala, Bama, Gwoza LGAs; Yobe State, Nguru, Geidam, Damaturu, Fika, Fune, and Gujba LGAs; Jigawa State, Hadejia LGA. Also spoken in Cameroon, Chad, Eritrea, Niger, Sudan. Nilo-Saharan, Saharan, Western, Kanuri. Dialects: KAGA (KAGAMA), LARE (LERE), KWAYAM, NJESKO, KABARI (KUVURI), NGAZAR, GUVJA, MAO, TEMAGERI, FADAWA. Lukas says Kwayam is not understood by other Kanuri. All can understand the Maiduguri dialect. Closest to Manga Kanuri and Kanembu. Used in adult education. The people of Ngala no longer speak a Kotoko language. National language. Dictionary. Grammar. SOV. Ajami script. Radio programs, TV. Muslim. NT, in press (1997).

KANURI, MANGA *(MANGA, KANOURI, KANOURY)* [KBY] 200,000 in Nigeria (1993). Mainly Yobe State, some in Jigawa and Bauchi states. Nilo-Saharan, Saharan, Western, Kanuri. Dialects: DAGARA, MANGA. Trade language. Muslim. Bible portions. See main entry under Niger.

KAPYA [KLO] Taraba State, Takum LGA, at Kapya. Niger-Congo, Atlantic-Congo, Volta-Congo, Benue-Congo, Platoid, Benue, Jukunoid, Yukuben-Kuteb. Close to Kutep, but listed separately in Crozier and Blench. Investigation needed: intelligibility with Kutep.

KAREKARE *(KARAIKARAI, KARAI KARAI, KEREKERE, KERRIKERRI)* [KAI] 150,000 to 200,000 (1993 CAPRO). Bauchi State, Gamawa and Misau LGAs; Yobe State, Fika and Nangere LGAs. Afro-Asiatic, Chadic, West, A, A.2, Bole, Karekare. Dialects: JALALAM (WEST KAREKARE), BIRKAI, KWARTA MATACI. Investigation needed: bilingual proficiency in Hausa, attitudes. Grammar. Muslim, traditional religion, Christian.

KARIYA *(KARIYU, KAUYAWA, LIPKAWA, VINAHE, WIHE)* [KIL] 2,000 (1995 CAPRO). Bauchi State, Ganjuwa LGA, Kariya village near Miya town. Afro-Asiatic, Chadic, West, B, B.2. Investigation needed: bilingual proficiency in Hausa, attitudes. Agriculturalists: maize, Guinea corn, peanuts, millet. Muslim, traditional religion.

KHANA *(KANA, OGONI)* [KEH] 200,000 (1989). Rivers State, Khana, Gokana, and Iyigbo LGAs. Niger-Congo, Atlantic-Congo, Volta-Congo, Benue-Congo, Cross River, Delta Cross, Ogoni, East. Dialects: TAI, YEGHE, NORKHANA, KEN-KHANA, BOÚE. Closely related to Gokana, Eleme. Important district language. Bible 1968.

KHOLOK *(KODE, KOODE, KWOODE, PIA, PITIKO, WIDALA, WURKUM)* [KTC] 2,500 (1977 Voegelin and Voegelin). Taraba State, Karim Lamido LGA, near Didango. Afro-Asiatic, Chadic, West, A, A.2, Bole, Bole Proper. Investigation needed: bilingual proficiency in Hausa, attitudes.

KINUKU *(KINUKA, KINUGU)* [KKD] 500 (1973 SIL). Kaduna State, Saminaka LGA. Niger-Congo, Atlantic-Congo, Volta-Congo, Benue-Congo, Kainji, Eastern, Northern Jos, Kauru. Investigation needed: bilingual proficiency in Hausa, attitudes.

KIONG *(AKAYON, AKOIYANG, OKONYONG, OKOYONG, IYONIYONG)* [KKM] Cross River State, Odukpani and Akampka LGAs. Niger-Congo, Atlantic-Congo, Volta-Congo, Benue-Congo, Cross River, Delta Cross, Upper Cross, Kiong-Korop. Bilingualism in Efik. Spoken only by elderly people; the younger generation speaks Efik. For several generations before now the people were bilingual in Kiong and Efik. Nearly extinct.

KIR-BALAR *(KIR, KIRR)* [KKR] 3,050 (1993). Bauchi State, Bauchi LGA, Kir Bengbet and Kir Bajang'le villages. Afro-Asiatic, Chadic, West, B, B.3, Boghom. Dialects: KIR, BALAR (LARBAWA). Investigation needed: intelligibility with Boghom, bilingual proficiency in Hausa, attitudes. Muslim.

KIRIKE *(OKRIKA)* [OKR] 248,000 (1995 UBS). Rivers State, Okrika, Opobo-Nkoro, Bonny, and Degema LGAs. Niger-Congo, Atlantic-Congo, Ijoid, Ijo, Eastern, Northeastern, Ibani-Okrika-Kalabari. NT, in press (1997).

KOENOEM *(KANAM)* [KCS] 3,000 (1973 SIL). Plateau State, Shendam LGA. Afro-Asiatic, Chadic, West, A, A.3, Angas Proper, 2. Investigation needed: bilingual proficiency in Hausa, attitudes.

KOFA *(KOTA)* [KSO] Adamawa State, Song LGA, north of Betul road. Afro-Asiatic, Chadic, Biu-Mandara, A, A.2, 1. Reported to be a separate language from Bura-Pabir. Investigation needed: intelligibility with Bura.

KOFYAR [KWL] 72,946 (1963 census). Plateau State, Qua'an Pan and Mangu LGAs; Nasarawa State, Lafia LGA. Afro-Asiatic, Chadic, West, A, A.3, Angas Proper, 1. Dialects: KOFYAR (KWONG),

KWAGALLAK (KWA'ALANG, KWALLA), DIMMUK (DIMUK, DOEMAK), MIRRIAM (MERNYANG), BWOL (BWAL, MBOL), GWORAM (GIVEROM, GORAM), JIPAL (JEPEL, JEPAL, JIBYAL). Dialect cluster. Traditional religion.

KOHUMONO ***(BAHUMONO, OHUMONO, EDIBA, HUMONO, EKUMURU)*** [BCS] 30,000 (1989). Cross River State, Obubra LGA. Niger-Congo, Atlantic-Congo, Volta-Congo, Benue-Congo, Cross River, Delta Cross, Upper Cross, Central, North-South, Ubaghara-Kohumono, Kohumono.

KOMA ***(KUMA)*** [KMY] 32,000 in Nigeria (1989). Population total both countries 35,000. Adamawa State, Ganye and Fufore LGAs, Koma Vomni, Alantika Mountains. Also spoken in Cameroon. Niger-Congo, Atlantic-Congo, Volta-Congo, North, Adamawa-Ubangi, Adamawa, Leko-Nimbari, Duru, Voko-Dowayo, Vere-Dowayo, Vere-Gimme, Vere. Dialects: GOMME (DAMTI, KOMA KAMPANA, PANBE), GOMNOME (MBEYA, GIMBE, KOMA KADAM, LAAME, YOUTUBO), NDERA (VOMNI, DOOME, DOOBE). A language cluster. 3 subdialects: Koma Vomni, Koma Beiya, and Koma Damti. Ndera and Gomnome speakers barely understand each other, but both understand Gomme. Some speakers understand Hausa, especially those on the plains, but the majority speak only Koma. 'Koma' is a Fulfulde cover term for the languages listed. Different from Koma of Ethiopia and Sudan. 7 primary schools. Literacy rate in second language: Low. Mountain slope, plains. Traditional religion, Christian, Muslim.

KONA ***(JUKUN KONA, JIBI, JIBA)*** [JUO] 2,000 (1977 Voegelin and Voegelin). Taraba State, Wukari and Karim Lamido LGAs; Plateau State, Langtang and Wase LGAs; Bauchi State, Alkaleri and Akko LGAs; villages north and west of Kalingo. Niger-Congo, Atlantic-Congo, Volta-Congo, Benue-Congo, Platoid, Benue, Jukunoid, Central, Jukun-Mbembe-Wurbo, Kororofa. In Kororofa language cluster. Traditional religion. Bible portions 1927-1950.

KONO ***(KONU, KWONO)*** [KLK] 1,550 (1949). Kaduna State, Saminaka LGA, Kona village. Niger-Congo, Atlantic-Congo, Volta-Congo, Benue-Congo, Kainji, Eastern, Northern Jos, Kauru.

KORO IJA ***(KORO AFIKI)*** [VKI] Federal Capital Territory, south of Abuja, north of the Minna Suleja road. Niger-Congo, Atlantic-Congo, Volta-Congo, Benue-Congo, Unclassified. Listed separately in Crozier and Blench 1992. Different from Koro Zuba, Koro of Lafia, Begbere-Ejar, or Tanjijili. 'Koro' is used as a cover term for several languages.

KORO ZUBA [VKZ] Federal Capital Territory, near Zuba, north of the Minna Suleja road. Niger-Congo, Atlantic-Congo, Volta-Congo, Benue-Congo, Unclassified. Listed separately in Crozier and Blench 1992. Different from Koro Ija, Koro of Lafia, Begbere-Ejar, or Tanjijili. 'Koro' is used as a cover term for several languages.

KOROP ***(ODODOP, DUROP, KUROP)*** [KRP] Population total both countries 12,500 (1982 SIL). Cross River State, Odukpani and Akampka LGAs. Also spoken in Cameroon. Niger-Congo, Atlantic-Congo, Volta-Congo, Benue-Congo, Cross River, Delta Cross, Upper Cross, Kiong-Korop. Speakers in Nigeria are reported to mostly be bilingual in Efik. Investigation needed: bilingual proficiency in Efik.

KPAN ***(YORDA, IBUKWO, KPWATE, HWAYE, HWASO, NYATSO, KPANTEN, IKPAN, ABAKAN, NYONYO)*** [KPK] Taraba State, Wukari, Takum, and Sardauna LGAs, Kato Bagha, Wukari, Suntai, Gayan, Gindin Dutse, Likam. Niger-Congo, Atlantic-Congo, Volta-Congo, Benue-Congo, Platoid, Benue, Jukunoid, Central, Kpan-Icen. Dialects: BISSAULA, KUMBO (KPANZON), TAKUM, DONGA (AKPANZHI), APA, KENTE (KENTU, KYENTU, ETKYE), EREGBA. Related to Icen. Bissaula is extinct. Investigation needed: intelligibility with Icen, attitudes.

KPASAM ***(PASSAM, KPASHAM, NYISAM, 'BALO)*** [PBN] 15,000 (1992). Adamawa State, Numan LGA, Kpasham town, on the Numan-Jalingo road. Niger-Congo, Atlantic-Congo, Volta-Congo, North, Adamawa-Ubangi, Adamawa, Leko-Nimbari, Mumuye-Yandang, Yandang. Bilingualism in Hausa, Fulfulde, Bacama. There are primary schools in the villages, and speakers want to send their children to school. One junior secondary school. Investigation needed: bilingual proficiency in Hausa, attitudes. Agriculturalists. Christian, traditional religion, Muslim.

KPATI [KOC] Taraba State, Wukari, Takum LGAs. Niger-Congo, Atlantic-Congo, Volta-Congo, Benue-Congo, Bantoid, Southern, Wide Grassfields, Narrow Grassfields, Mbam-Nkam, Ngemba. Extinct.

KUBI ***(KUBA, KUBAWA)*** [KOF] Ethnic group has 1,500 (1995 CAPRO). Bauchi State, Gunjawa LGA, Kubi town. Afro-Asiatic, Chadic, West, A, A.2, Bole, Bole Proper. They now speak Hausa. Muslim. Extinct.

KUDU-CAMO ***(KUDA-CHAMO, KUDAWA)*** [KOV] 2,000 to 4,000 (1977 Voegelin and Voegelin). Bauchi State, Ningi LGA. Niger-Congo, Atlantic-Congo, Volta-Congo, Benue-Congo, Kainji, Eastern, Northern Jos, Jera. Dialects: KUDU (KUDA), CAMO (CHAMO). Related to Butu-Ningi. A dialect cluster. The language is reported to be dying out. Investigation needed: bilingual proficiency in Hausa, attitudes.

KUGAMA ***(KUGAMMA, WEGAM, YAMALE, YAMALO)*** [KOW] 5,000 or more (1995). Adamawa State, Fufore LGA. Niger-Congo, Atlantic-Congo, Volta-Congo, North, Adamawa-Ubangi, Adamawa, Leko-Nimbari, Mumuye-Yandang, Yandang. Bilingualism in Hausa, Gengle, Yandang, Kumba, Kona, Poli. Investigation needed: intelligibility with Yendang, attitudes. Traditional religion, Christian, Muslim.

KUGBO [KES] 2,000 (1973 SIL). Rivers State, Brass LGA. Niger-Congo, Atlantic-Congo, Volta-Congo, Benue-Congo, Cross River, Delta Cross, Central Delta, Kugbo.

KUKELE ***(UKELE, BAKELE)*** [KEZ] 95,000 (1989). Cross River State, Ogoja LGA; Ebonyi State, Abakaliki LGA; Benue State, Okpokwu and Oju LGAs. Niger-Congo, Atlantic-Congo, Volta-Congo, Benue-Congo, Cross River, Delta Cross, Upper Cross, Central, North-South, Koring-Kukele, Kukele. Dialects: MTEZI, UGBALA, ITEEJI. Four dialects in the north, three in the south, besides those named. Literacy program in progress. NT 1979.

KULERE ***(TOF, KOROM BOYE, AKANDI, AKANDE, KANDE)*** [KUL] 15,570 (1990). Plateau State, Bokkos LGA. Afro-Asiatic, Chadic, West, A, A.4, Ron Proper. Dialects: TOF, RICHA, KAMWAI-MARHAI. Different from Kulere of Côte d'Ivoire, a trade dialect of Senoufo. Investigation needed: bilingual proficiency in Hausa, attitudes. Grammar.

KULUNG ***(BAMBUR, KULUNO, BAKULUNG, BAKULU, BAKULI, KULU, KUKULUNG, WO, WURKUM)*** [BBU] 15,000 (1973 SIL). Taraba State, Karim Lamido LGA, at Balasa, Bambur, and Kirim; Wukari LGA at Gada Mayo. Niger-Congo, Atlantic-Congo, Volta-Congo, Benue-Congo, Bantoid, Southern, Jarawan, Nigerian. 4 clans: Bambur, Balassa, Banyam, Bamingun. Different from Kulung of Chad which is Chadic. Similar in culture to Piya, Kodei, Kwanchi, Pelang, and Pero. Agriculturalists. Traditional religion, Christian, Muslim. Bible portions 1950.

KUMBA ***(SATE, YOFO, ISARO)*** [KSM] Adamawa State, Mayo Belwa and Fufore LGAs. Niger-Congo, Atlantic-Congo, Volta-Congo, North, Adamawa-Ubangi, Adamawa, Leko-Nimbari, Mumuye-Yandang, Mumuye. Bilingualism in Fulfulde, Hausa. Investigation needed: bilingual proficiency in Hausa, Fulfulde, attitudes. No schools. Agriculturalists, animal husbandry: cows. Traditional religion, Christian, Muslim.

KUPA [KUG] 20,000 or fewer (1998 Blench). Kwara State, Kogi LGA, around Abugi. 52 villages. Niger-Congo, Atlantic-Congo, Volta-Congo, Benue-Congo, Nupoid, Nupe-Gbagyi, Nupe. Investigation needed: intelligibility with Nupe, attitudes.

KURAMA ***(TIKURAMI, AKURUMI, BAGWAMA, AKURMI, AZUMU, BUKURUMI)*** [KRH] 11,300 (1949). Kaduna State, Saminaka and Ikara LGAs; Kano State, Tudun Waya LGA. Niger-Congo, Atlantic-Congo, Volta-Congo, Benue-Congo, Kainji, Eastern, Northern Jos, Kauru. 'Tukurami' is the language, 'Bukurumi' a speaker, 'Akurumi' the people. Investigation needed: bilingual proficiency in Hausa, attitudes.

KUSHI ***(CHONG'E, KUSHE, GOJI)*** [KUH] 11,000 (1995 CAPRO). Bauchi State, Billiri, and Kaltungo LGAs, Kushi village. Afro-Asiatic, Chadic, West, A, A.2, Tangale, Tangale Proper. Investigation needed: attitudes toward Hausa. Agriculturalists: guinea corn, maize, beans, peanuts, cotton, rice.

KUTEP ***(KUTEB, KUTEV, MBARIKE, ZUMPER, "JOMPRE", ATI)*** [KUB] 30,000 to 50,000 in Nigeria (1992). Population total both countries 31,000 to 51,000. Taraba State, Takum LGA. Also spoken in Cameroon. Niger-Congo, Atlantic-Congo, Volta-Congo, Benue-Congo, Platoid, Benue, Jukunoid, Yukuben-Kuteb. Dialects: JENUWA, LISSAM, FIKYU, KUNABE, KENTIN. Fikyu has subdialects. Bilingualism in Hausa, Jukun. "Jompre" is an offensive name. Grammar. Literacy program in progress. Christian, traditional religion. NT 1986-1995.

KUTTO ***(KUPTO, KÚTTÒ)*** [KPA] 3,000 or fewer (1995). Bauchi State, Bajoga LGA; Borno State, Gujba LGA, 2 villages. Afro-Asiatic, Chadic, West, A, A.2, Tangale, Tangale Proper. Investigation needed: bilingual proficiency in Hausa, attitudes.

KUTURMI ***(ADA)*** [KHJ] 2,950 (1949). Kaduna State, Kachia LGA. Niger-Congo, Atlantic-Congo, Volta-Congo, Benue-Congo, Platoid, Plateau, Northern. Investigation needed: bilingual proficiency in Hausa, attitudes.

KWA ***(KWAH, BAA)*** [KWB] 7,000 (1992). Adamawa State, Numan LGA, Gyakan and Kwa towns, near Munga. Niger-Congo, Atlantic-Congo, Volta-Congo, North, Adamawa-Ubangi, Adamawa, Kwa. Dialects: GYAKAN, KWA. Bilingualism in Bacama. Different from Kwa' of Cameroon in the Bamileke group. Tradesmen. Traditional religion, Christian.

KWAAMI ***(KWAMI, KWAM, KWAMANCHI, KWOM, KOMAWA)*** [KSQ] 10,000 (1990). Bauchi State, Gombe LGA. Afro-Asiatic, Chadic, West, A, A.2, Tangale, Tangale Proper. Investigation needed: bilingual proficiency in Hausa, attitudes. Grammar.

KWAK ***(BÙKWÁK)*** [KWQ] Taraba State, Sardauna LGA, Antere. Niger-Congo, Atlantic-Congo, Volta-Congo, Benue-Congo, Bantoid, Unclassified. May be the same as Yamba.

KYAK ***(BAMBUKA, NYAKYAK)*** [BKA] 5,000 or fewer (1995 Adelberger). Taraba State, Karim Lamido LGA. Niger-Congo, Atlantic-Congo, Volta-Congo, North, Adamawa-Ubangi, Adamawa, Waja-Jen, Jen. Agriculturalists. Traditional religion, Christian.

KYENGA ***(TYANGA, TIENGA, TYENGA, KENGA)*** [TYE] 4,000 in Nigeria (1995 Ross Jones SIM). Population total both countries 5,000. Kebbi State, Geshuru, Kaele, Saufu, and Tuni villages, all west of Illo, and in the Boko villages of Maze, Samia, Baikinrua, and Pisa. Also spoken in Benin. Niger-Congo, Mande, Eastern, Eastern, Busa. Kyenga and Shanga have 70% lexical similarity with each other, 38% to 40% with the Busa group. Those who do speak Kyenga are bilingual in Hausa. It is reported that nearly all Kyenga do not speak their language any longer but Hausa or Dendi. Investigation needed: intelligibility with Shanga, bilingual proficiency in Hausa, Dendi. Traditional religion, Muslim.

LABIR ***(JAKU, JAKUN, JAKANCI)*** [JKU] Bauchi State, Bauchi and Alkaleri LGAs. Niger-Congo, Atlantic-Congo, Volta-Congo, Benue-Congo, Bantoid, Southern, Jarawan, Nigerian. Investigation needed: bilingual proficiency in Hausa, attitudes. Agriculturalists. Muslim, some Christians.

LAGWAN ***(KOTOKO-LOGONE, LOGONE, LAGWANE, LAGOUANE)*** [KOT] 25,000 in Nigeria (1993). Borno State, Dikwa and Ngala LGAs. May not be in Nigeria. Afro-Asiatic, Chadic, Biu-Mandara, B, B.1, Kotoko Proper. Dialects: LOGONE-BIRNI, LOGONE-GANA (KOTOKO-GANA). Related to Afade, Mser, Malgbe, Maslam, and Mpade. Grammar. Muslim. See main entry under Cameroon.

LAKA ***(LAKKA, LAU, LAO HABE, GODOGODO)*** [LAK] 5,000 or more (1995). Taraba State, Karim Lamido LGA; Adamawa State, Yola LGA. Niger-Congo, Atlantic-Congo, Volta-Congo, North, Adamawa-Ubangi, Adamawa, Mbum-Day, Mbum, Unclassified. Related to Karang. Different than Laka (Kabba Laka) of CAR and Chad, or from Karang (Laka) of Cameroon and Chad. Muslim, Christian.

LALA-ROBA ***(GWORAM)*** [LLA] 46,000 (1993). Adamawa State, Gombi LGA, and Borno State. Niger-Congo, Atlantic-Congo, Volta-Congo, North, Adamawa-Ubangi, Adamawa, Waja-Jen, Yungur, Yungur-Roba. Dialects: LALA (LALLA), ROBA (ROBBA), EBODE. Bilingualism in Fulfulde, Gaanda, Hausa. Hunters (January to April); agriculturalists (May to December): peanuts, Guinea corn, bambara nuts, tiger nuts; animal husbandry: goats, chickens, sheep, dogs. Traditional religion, Christian.

LAMANG ***(LAAMANG, GBUHWE, WAHA)*** [HIA] 40,000 (1993). Borno State, Gwoza LGA; Adamawa State, Michika LGA. Afro-Asiatic, Chadic, Biu-Mandara, A, A.4, Lamang. Dialects: NORTH LAAMANG, CENTRAL LAAMANG, SOUTH LAAMANG. Speakers have 37% intelligibility of Mabas, 31% of Hedi. Subdialects of North Lamang: Zaladeva (Alataghwa), Dzuba, Leghva (Luhuva), Gwoza-Wakane; of Central Lamang: Hedkala (Hidkala, Xidkala, Hitkala, Hitkalanchi), Waga (Waha, Woga, Wagga), Dlige; of South Lamang: Ghudavan. 64% lexical similarity with Hedi and Mabas, 50% with Gevoko. Grammar. Literacy rate in first language: Below 1%. Literacy rate in second language: 25% to 50%. Bible portions 1992.

LAME [BMA] 10,000 (1995 CAPRO). Bauchi State, Toro LGA, Lame District. Niger-Congo, Atlantic-Congo, Volta-Congo, Benue-Congo, Bantoid, Southern, Jarawan, Nigerian. Dialects: RUHU (RUFU, RUFAWA), MBARU (BAMBARO, BOMBARO, BOMBERAWA, BUNBERAWA, BAMBARA, BAMBURO), GURA (TUGURA, AGARI, AGBIRI). Dialect cluster. There were reported to be no speakers of Ruhu left in 1987 (Blench). Different from Peve (Lame) of Cameroon and Chad. Investigation needed: bilingual proficiency in Hausa, attitudes.

LAMJA-DENGSA-TOLA [LDH] Adamawa State, Mayo Belwa LGA, around Ganglamja (Lamja Mt.), near the road between Mayo Belwa and Tola. 13 villages of Lamja and Dengsa. The central town of the Lamja is Ganglamja. The Dengsa live south of the Lamja. Niger-Congo, Atlantic-Congo, Volta-Congo, Benue-Congo, Bantoid, Northern, Dakoid. Dialects: LAMJA, DENGSA, TOLA. A dialect cluster. The three dialects are inherently intelligible to each others' speakers. They may not be sufficiently distinct from Samba Daka to be a separate language. 8 primary schools. Investigation needed: intelligibility with Samba Daka. Literacy rate in second language: Low. Agriculturalists: Guinea corn, peanuts, maize, rice, cassava; hunters (dry season). Muslim, traditional religion, Christian.

LAMNSO' ***(NSHO', LAMSO, LAMNSOK, BANSO, BANSO', BANSAW, PANSO, NSO, NSO', NSAW)*** [NSO] Taraba State, Sardauna LGA, in settlements sometimes mixed with speakers of other languages. Niger-Congo, Atlantic-Congo, Volta-Congo, Benue-Congo, Bantoid, Southern, Wide Grassfields, Narrow Grassfields, Ring, East. Bilingualism in Fulfulde. Agriculturalists. Traditional religion, Christian. NT 1990. See main entry under Cameroon.

LARU ***(LARAWA, LARANCHI, LARO)*** [LAN] 5,000 (1995 Ross Jones SIM). Niger State, Borgu LGA, on the banks of the Niger River, Karabonde, Monnai, Leshigbe, Luma, Sansanni, Shagunu villages. Niger-Congo, Atlantic-Congo, Volta-Congo, Benue-Congo, Kainji, Western, Kainji Lake. They are reported to be assimilating to Bisã language and culture. Investigation needed: bilingual proficiency in Bisa, attitudes. Muslim.

LEELAU ***(LELAU, LELO, MUNGA LELAU, MUNGA)*** [LDK] 5,000 or fewer (1995 Adelberger). Taraba State, Karim Lamido LGA, between Bambuka and Karim-Lamido town, near Lake Mungah. Niger-Congo, Atlantic-Congo, Volta-Congo, North, Adamawa-Ubangi, Adamawa, Waja-Jen, Jen. In the Munga dialect cluster. In the Bikwin ethnic cluster. Clan names: Tanyam, Munzigah, Brem, Gopi. Agriculturalists, animal husbandry, fishermen. Traditional religion, Christian.

LEGBO ***(AGBO, GBO, IGBO, IMABAN, ITIGIDI)*** [AGB] 60,000 (1989). Cross River State, Obubra LGA; Ebonyi State, Afikpo LGA. Niger-Congo, Atlantic-Congo, Volta-Congo, Benue-Congo, Cross River, Delta Cross, Upper Cross, Central, East-West, Mbembe-Legbo, Legbo.

LEMORO ***(LIMORO, LIMORRO, EMORO, ANEMORO, ANOWURU)*** [LDJ] 10,000 (1998 CAPRO). Plateau State, Bassa LGA; Bauchi State, Toro LGA. Niger-Congo, Atlantic-Congo, Volta-Congo, Benue-Congo, Kainji, Eastern, Northern Jos, Jera. The language is 'Emoro', a speaker is 'Limoro', the speakers are 'Anemoro'. Investigation needed: bilingual proficiency in Hausa, attitudes. Traditional religion, Christian, few Muslims.

LENYIMA ***(ANYIMA, INYIMA)*** [LDG] Cross River State, Obubra LGA. Niger-Congo, Atlantic-Congo, Volta-Congo, Benue-Congo, Cross River, Delta Cross, Upper Cross, Central, East-West, Mbembe-Legbo, Legbo. The people are 'Anyima', the language 'Lenyima'.

LERE [GNH] Bauchi State, Toro LGA. Niger-Congo, Atlantic-Congo, Volta-Congo, Benue-Congo, Kainji, Eastern, Northern Jos, Jera. Dialects: SI (RISHUWA, KAURU, KUZAMANI), GANA, TAKAYA (TAURA). Language cluster. There may be few speakers left. Nearly extinct.

LEYIGHA ***(ASIGA, ASSIGA, AYIGHA, AYIGA, YIGHA)*** [AYI] 10,000 (1989). Cross River State, Obubra LGA. Niger-Congo, Atlantic-Congo, Volta-Congo, Benue-Congo, Cross River, Delta Cross, Upper Cross, Central, East-West, Mbembe-Legbo, Legbo. The people are called 'Ayigha', the language 'Leyigha'.

LIJILI ***(LIGILI, MIJILI, MIGILI, MEGILI, KORO LAFIA, KORO OF LAFIA)*** [MGI] 50,000 (1985 UBS). Nasarawa State, Awe and Lafia LGAs. Niger-Congo, Atlantic-Congo, Volta-Congo, Benue-Congo, Platoid, Plateau, Southern. 'Ligili' or 'Lijili' is the name of the language; 'Migili' of the people. Grammar. NT 1986.

LIMBUM ***(WIMBUM, KAMBU)*** [LIM] A few in Nigeria (1992 Crozier and Blench). Taraba State, Sardauna LGA, Mambila uplands. Niger-Congo, Atlantic-Congo, Volta-Congo, Benue-Congo, Bantoid, Southern, Wide Grassfields, Narrow Grassfields, Mbam-Nkam, Nkambe. See main entry under Cameroon.

LOKAA ***(YAKURR, YAKÖ, LOKO, LOKE, LUKO)*** [YAZ] 120,000 (1989). Cross River State, Obubra LGA. Niger-Congo, Atlantic-Congo, Volta-Congo, Benue-Congo, Cross River, Delta Cross, Upper Cross, Central, East-West, Loko. Dialects: UGEP, NKPAM. Grammar. Agriculturalists: yams. Bible portions 1967-1984.

LONGUDA ***(NUNGUDA, NUNGURABA, NUNGURA, LANGUDA, LONGURA)*** [LNU] 32,000 (1973 SIL). Adamawa State, Guyuk LGA; Bauchi State, Balanga LGA. Niger-Congo, Atlantic-Congo, Volta-Congo, North, Adamawa-Ubangi, Adamawa, Waja-Jen, Longuda. Dialects: NYA CERIYA (BANJIRAM, CIRIMBA), NYA GWANDA (NYUWAR, GWANDABA), NYA GUYUWA (GUYUK, PLAIN, TURUBA), NYA DELE (JESSU), NYA TARIYA (TARABA). Bilingualism in Hausa, Fulfulde, Kanakuru, Waja, English. Literacy rate in second language: 20% Hausa. Traditional religion, Christian. NT 1978.

LOO ***(LO, LOH, SHUNHU, SHUNGO)*** [LDO] 8,000 (1992 Crozier and Blench). Gombe State, Kaltungo LGA; Taraba State, Karim Lamido LGA, northeast of Karim Lamido town, off the Bambuka to Karim-Lamido road. Niger-Congo, Atlantic-Congo, Volta-Congo, North, Adamawa-Ubangi, Adamawa, Waja-Jen, Jen. Clan names: Fore (Kyilayo), Bene, Tamu, Bana, Talau, Tadam, Wawa. Agriculturalists, animal husbandry, fishermen. Traditional religion, Christian.

LOPA ***(LOPAWA, LUPA, KIRIKJIR, DJIRI)*** [LOP] 5,000 (1996 Blench). Niger State, Borgu LGA, Amboshidi and Tungan Bori, islands in the Niger River; Kebbi State, Yauri LGA. Niger-Congo, Atlantic-Congo, Volta-Congo, Benue-Congo, Kainji, Western, Kainji Lake. Those in Borgu LGA are reported to be assimilating to Bisã language and culture.

LUBILA ***(LUBILO, KABILA, KABIRE, OJOR, OFOR)*** [KCC] Cross River State, Akamkpa LGA, at Ojo Nkomba and Ojo Akangba. Niger-Congo, Atlantic-Congo, Volta-Congo, Benue-Congo, Cross River, Delta Cross, Upper Cross, Central, East-West, Loko.

LUFU [LDQ] Ethnic group: 2,000 to 3,000 (1992). Taraba State, Takum LGA, Lufu and Lufu Jauro. Unclassified. One report says the language is mostly spoken by elders (1992). The people now speak Jukun. Culture and religion similar to the Jukun Kapya. Language reported to have been close to Bete and Bibi. Former speakers at Arufu near Wukari have lost the language. Christian, traditional religion. Nearly extinct.

LURI [LDD] 30 (1973 SIL). Bauchi State, Bauchi LGA, Kayarda and Luri villages. Afro-Asiatic, Chadic, West. Investigation needed: bilingual proficiency in Hausa. Muslim.

MAAKA ***(MAHA, MAKA, MAGA, MAGHA)*** [MEW] 10,000 (1993). Borno State, Gujba LGA, Bara town and associated hamlets. Afro-Asiatic, Chadic, West, A, A.2, Bole, Bole Proper. Investigation needed: bilingual proficiency in Hausa, attitudes. Muslim, traditional religion.

MADA ***(MADDA, YIDDA)*** [MDA] 100,000 (1993 SIL). Nasarawa State, Akwanga LGA; Kaduna State, Jema'a LGA. Niger-Congo, Atlantic-Congo, Volta-Congo, Benue-Congo, Platoid, Plateau, Western, Southwestern, A. Different from Mada of Cameroon. Literacy rate in first language: Below 1%.

Literacy rate in second language: 25% to 50%. Traditional religion, Christian, Muslim. NT, in press (1999).

MAFA *("MATAKAM", NATAKAN, BULAHAI, BULA)* [MAF] 2,000 in Nigeria (1963). Borno State, Gwoza LGA. Afro-Asiatic, Chadic, Biu-Mandara, A, A.5. Dialect: MAFA. "Matakam" is disliked. Dictionary. Bible 1978-1989. See main entry under Cameroon.

MÁGHDÌ *(TALA, WIDALA)* [GMD] 2,000 or fewer (1992). Taraba State, Karim Lamido LGA, a section of the Widala. Niger-Congo, Atlantic-Congo, Volta-Congo, North, Adamawa-Ubangi, Adamawa, Waja-Jen, Jen. 'Widala' applies to the people. Kholok is also called 'Widala'.

MAK *(PANYAM, PANYA, LEEMAK, LEMAK, ZO)* [PBL] Taraba State, Karim Lamido LGA, northeast of Karim Lamido town, off the Banbuka to Karim-Lamido road. Niger-Congo, Atlantic-Congo, Volta-Congo, North, Adamawa-Ubangi, Adamawa, Waja-Jen, Jen. Dialects: PANYA, ZO. In the Bikwin ethnic cluster. Clan names: Guma, Zidah, Togon, Mungok, Tawok, Tagwam. Traditional religion, Christian.

MALA *(RUMAYA, RUMAIYA, AMALA, TUMALA)* [RUY] 1,800 (1948). Kaduna State, Saminaka LGA. Niger-Congo, Atlantic-Congo, Volta-Congo, Benue-Congo, Kainji, Eastern, Northern Jos, Kauru. Investigation needed: bilingual proficiency in Hausa, attitudes.

MAMA *(KANTANA, KWARRA)* [MMA] 20,000 (1973 SIL). Nasarawa State, Akwanga LGA. Niger-Congo, Atlantic-Congo, Volta-Congo, Benue-Congo, Bantoid, Southern, Jarawan, Nigerian.

MAMBILA, NIGERIA *(MAMBILLA, MABILA, MAMBERE, NOR, NOR TAGBO, LAGUBI, TONGBO, BANG)* [MZK] 99,000 (1993). Taraba State, Sardauna LGA, Mambila Plateau. Niger-Congo, Atlantic-Congo, Volta-Congo, Benue-Congo, Bantoid, Northern, Mambiloid, Mambila-Konja, Mambila. Dialect: BARUP. Nearly every village has a separate dialect, forming a chain. Dialect centers are Bang, Dorofi, Gembu, Hainari, Kabri, Mayo Ndaga, Mbamnga, 'tamien, Tepo, Warwar. Close to Mambila of Cameroon, but distinct. Bilingualism in Fulfulde, English. Traditional religion, Christian, Muslim. NT 1977.

MANGAS [MAH] 100 or fewer (1995 CAPRO). Bauchi State, Bauchi LGA. Mangas town. Afro-Asiatic, Chadic, West, B, B.3, Boghom. Bilingualism in Hausa. Investigation needed: bilingual proficiency in Hausa, attitudes. Muslim, traditional religion, Christian.

MARGHI CENTRAL *(MARGHI, MARGI)* [MAR] 135,000 in Marghi Central, Marghi South, and Putai languages (1999). Borno State, Askira-Uba and Damboa LGAs; Adamawa State, Mubi and Michika LGAs. Afro-Asiatic, Chadic, Biu-Mandara, A, A.2, 2. Dialects: LASSA (BABAL), GULAK (DZERNGU), MADUBE (GWARA), MULGWE (MALGWA), WURGA. Marghi South, Marghi Central, and Putai form a language cluster. Grammar. SVO. NT 1987.

MARGHI SOUTH [MFM] Borno State, Askira-Uba LGA; Adamawa State, Mubi and Michika LGAs. Afro-Asiatic, Chadic, Biu-Mandara, A, A.2, 2. Dialects: WAMDIU, HILDI. Marghi South, Marghi Central, and Putai form a language cluster. Hoffman (1963) relates Marghi South to Huba rather than to Margi. Investigation needed: intelligibility with Marghi Central, bilingual proficiency in Hausa, attitudes.

MASHI [JMS] Taraba State, near Takum. Niger-Congo, Atlantic-Congo, Volta-Congo, Benue-Congo, Bantoid, Southern, Beboid.

MAWA [WMA] Ethnic population is small (1982 Shimizu). Bauchi State, Toro LGA, possibly Mara village. Unclassified. Apparently different from the Mawa language of Chad, which is Chadic. Extinct.

MBE *(WESTERN MBUBE, KETUEN)* [MFO] 14,300 (1973 SIL). Cross River State, Ogoja LGA. Niger-Congo, Atlantic-Congo, Volta-Congo, Benue-Congo, Bantoid, Southern, Mbe. Dialects: IDUM, IKUMTALE, ODAJE. Distinct from Mbe' of Cameroon, a Grassfields language. Bible portions 1992.

MBEMBE, CROSS RIVER *(OKAM, ODERIGA, WAKANDE, IFUNUBWA, EKOKOMA, OFUNOBWAM)* [MFN] 100,000 (1982 UBS). Cross River State, Obubra and Ikom LGAs; Anambra State, Abakaliki LGA. Niger-Congo, Atlantic-Congo, Volta-Congo, Benue-Congo, Cross River, Delta Cross, Upper Cross, Central, East-West, Mbembe-Legbo, Mbembe. Dialects: OKOM (EGHOM, OHANA-ONYEN), APIAPUM, ADUN, OSOPONG (OSOPHONG, EZOPONG), OFOMBONGA (EWUMBONGA), OFONOKPAN, EKAMA (EKAMU), OFERIKPE. Different than Tigon Mbembe. Grammar. NT 1985.

MBEMBE, TIGON *(AKONTO, AKWANTO, TIGON, TIGONG, TIGIM, TUKUN, NOALE)* [NZA] 20,000 in Nigeria (1987). Taraba State, Sardauna LGA, Kurmi district. Niger-Congo, Atlantic-Congo, Volta-Congo, Benue-Congo, Platoid, Benue, Jukunoid, Central, Jukun-Mbembe-Wurbo, Mbembe. Dialects: ASHUKU (KITSIPKI), NAMA (DAMA, NAMU, NZARE, KPORO, ENEEME). A dialect cluster. Bilingualism in Hausa. Entirely different from Mbembe of Nigeria in the Cross River group. Every village has a primary school. Forest. Hills. Agriculturalists: palm nuts, palm oil. Traditional religion, Christian. See main entry under Cameroon.

MBOI *(MBOIRE, MBOYI, GENA)* [MOI] 19,000 (1992). Adamawa State, Song, Fufore, and Gombi LGAs. Niger-Congo, Atlantic-Congo, Volta-Congo, North, Adamawa-Ubangi, Adamawa, Waja-Jen, Yungur, Mboi. Dialects: BANGA, MBOI, HANDA. Dialect cluster. Bilingualism in Hausa, Fulfulde, Bwatiye, Yungur, Gudu, Gaanda. Investigation needed: bilingual proficiency in Hausa, attitudes.

Primary schools are in all the major villages. They desire education. Traditional religion, Christian, Muslim.

MBONGNO ***(BUNGNU, BUNU, BUNGUN, GBUNHU, KAKABA, KAMKAM)*** [BGU] Population total both countries 1,300 (1982 SIL). Taraba State, Sardauna LGA, Kamkam town. Also spoken in Cameroon. Niger-Congo, Atlantic-Congo, Volta-Congo, Benue-Congo, Bantoid, Northern, Mambiloid, Mambila-Konja, Magu-Kamkam-Kila. Several minor dialects. Bilingualism in Fulfulde, Hausa, Mambila. Investigation needed: bilingual proficiency in Mambila. Agriculturalists. Muslim (mainly), traditional religion.

MBULA-BWAZZA [MBU] 35,000 to 40,000, including 10,000 Bwazza, 20,000 Tambo, 5,000 to 10,000 Mbula (1993). Adamawa State, Numan, Guyuk, Song, Demsa LGAs. Niger-Congo, Atlantic-Congo, Volta-Congo, Benue-Congo, Bantoid, Southern, Jarawan, Nigerian. Dialects: BWAZZA (BWAZA, BWA'ZA, BARE, BERE, TAMBO), MBULA. Many also speak Kanakuru, Longuda, Bacama, or Bata. In some areas they live with the Libo and also speak Libo. Some older ones also speak Hausa or Fulfulde. Some speak English. Primary schools in the major villages, and a few secondary schools. Agriculturalists: maize, millet, Guinea corn, peanuts, cassava, sweet potatoes, cocoyam, bananas, sugar cane; fishermen; animal husbandry: horses, goats, sheep, pigs. Traditional religion, Christian.

MBURKU ***(BARKE, BARKO, BURKANAWA, MBURKANCI, LIPKAWA, WUDUFU, KARIYA WUUFU)*** [BBT] 4,000 (1977 Skinner). Bauchi State, Darazo LGA. Afro-Asiatic, Chadic, West, B, B.2. Speakers are known as 'Lipkawa' or 'Burkunawa'. Investigation needed: bilingual proficiency in Hausa, attitudes.

MINGANG DOSO ***(MUNGA DOSO, NGWAI MUNGÀN, DOSO)*** [MKO] 3,000 or fewer (1995 SIL). Taraba State, Karim Lamido LGA, 15 km. east of Karim Lamido town. 1 village and associated hamlets. Niger-Congo, Atlantic-Congo, Volta-Congo, North, Adamawa-Ubangi, Adamawa, Waja-Jen, Jen. Investigation needed: bilingual proficiency in Hausa, attitudes. Traditional religion.

MINI [MGJ] Rivers State, Brass LGA, 3 villages. Niger-Congo, Atlantic-Congo, Volta-Congo, Benue-Congo, Cross River, Delta Cross, Central Delta, Kugbo.

MISHIP ***(CHIP, CIP, SHIP)*** [CHP] 6,000 (1976 SIL). Plateau State, Pankshin, Mangu, Shendam LGAs. Afro-Asiatic, Chadic, West, A, A.3, Angas Proper, 1. Dialect: DOKA. Investigation needed: bilingual proficiency in Hausa, attitudes.

MIYA ***(MIYAWA, MUYA)*** [MKF] 30,000 (1995 CAPRO). Bauchi State, Ganjuwa LGA, Miya town. Afro-Asiatic, Chadic, West, B, B.2. Dialects: GALA, FAISHANG, FURSUM, DEMSHIN, FEDERE. Bilingualism in Hausa. Investigation needed: intelligibility with Gala with Warji, bilingual proficiency in Hausa, attitudes. Grammar. Agriculturalists: Guinea corn, maize, rice, millet, peanuts. Traditional religion, Muslim, Christian.

MOM JANGO ***(VERE, VERRE, WERE, KOBO)*** [VER] 84,000 in Nigeria. Population total both countries 88,000 (1992). Adamawa State, Yola and Fufore LGAs, Verre hills. Also spoken in Cameroon. Niger-Congo, Atlantic-Congo, Volta-Congo, North, Adamawa-Ubangi, Adamawa, Leko-Nimbari, Duru, Voko-Dowayo, Vere-Dowayo, Vere-Gimme, Vere. Dialects: MOM JANGO, MOMI (ZIRI). Mom Jango and Momi are probably separate languages. 90% use Fulfulde as second language. Investigation needed: intelligibility with Momi. Traditional religion, Christian, Muslim.

MONTOL ***(MONTAL, BALTAP, TEEL)*** [MTL] 21,858 (1990). Plateau State, Shendam LGA. Afro-Asiatic, Chadic, West, A, A.3, Angas Proper, 2. Dialects: MONTOL, BALTAP-LALIN. Related to Tal. Investigation needed: bilingual proficiency in Hausa, attitudes.

MOO ***(GWOMU, GWOMO, GWOM, GOMU, NGWAA MÓÒ, YÁÁ MÒÒ)*** [GWG] 5,000 (1998). Taraba State, Karim Lamido LGA, northeast of Karim Lamido town, off the Bambuka to Karim-Lamido road, close to Gomu Mountain. Niger-Congo, Atlantic-Congo, Volta-Congo, North, Adamawa-Ubangi, Adamawa, Waja-Jen, Jen. In the Bikwin ethnic cluster. Investigation needed: intelligibility with Jen. Agriculturalists, animal husbandry, fishermen. Traditional religion, Christian.

MUMUYE ***(YORO)*** [MUL] 400,000 in Nigeria (1993 SIL). Population total both countries 400,000 or more. Taraba State, Jalingo, Zing, Karim Lamido, Yorro, Bali LGAs; Adamawa State, Ganye, Fufore, Yola, Numan, and Mayo Belwa LGAs. Also spoken in Cameroon. Niger-Congo, Atlantic-Congo, Volta-Congo, North, Adamawa-Ubangi, Adamawa, Leko-Nimbari, Mumuye-Yandang, Mumuye. Dialects: ZINNA, DONG, YORO, LANKAVIRI, GOLA (BAJAMA), GONGLA, KASAA, SAAWA, JALINGO, NYAAJA, JENG, GNOORE, YAA, SAGBEE, SHAARI, KUGONG, MANG, KWAJI, MEEKA, YAKOKO. Lankaviri dialect is sufficiently different from Zing to need separate literature. Grammar. Literacy rate in first language: Below 1%. Literacy rate in second language: 25% to 50%. Agriculturalists. Traditional religion, Muslim, Christian. NT 1995.

MUNDAT [MMF] 1,000 (1998 Uwe Seibert SIL). Plateau State, Bokkos LGA, Mundat village near Sha. Afro-Asiatic, Chadic, West, A, A.4, Ron Proper. Closely related to Sha and Karfa. Investigation needed: bilingual proficiency in Hausa, attitudes.

MVANIP ***(MVANÖP, MVANON, MVANLIP, MVANO, MAGU)*** [MCJ] 100 (1999 Connell and Blench). Taraba State, Sardauna LGA, 1/4 of Zongo Ajiya and related hamlets in the northwest of the Mambila Plateau. Niger-Congo, Atlantic-Congo, Volta-Congo, Benue-Congo, Bantoid, Northern, Mambiloid, Mambila-Konja, Magu-Kamkam-Kila. Bilingualism in Vehicular Fulfulde. All ages. Vigorous.

MWAGHAVUL ***(SURA)*** [SUR] 295,000 (1993 SIL). Plateau State, Barakin-Ladi and Mangu LGAs. Afro-Asiatic, Chadic, West, A, A.3, Angas Proper, 1. Dialects: MUPUN (MAPAN, MAPUN), PANYAM. Several smaller language groups nearby use Mwaghavul as second language. Trade language. Dictionary. Grammar. Literacy rate in first language: 10% to 30%. Literacy rate in second language: 50% to 75%. NT 1991-1995.

NANDU-TARI ***(TARI)*** [NAA] 4,000 (1973 SIL). Kaduna State, Jema'a LGA. Niger-Congo, Atlantic-Congo, Volta-Congo, Benue-Congo, Platoid, Plateau, Central, West-Central. Investigation needed: bilingual proficiency in Hausa, attitudes.

NDE-GBITE ***(BITI, BÖTÖ)*** [NED] Taraba State, Sardauna LGA, Antere. Niger-Congo, Atlantic-Congo, Volta-Congo, Benue-Congo, Bantoid, Southern, Wide Grassfields, Narrow Grassfields, Unclassified.

NDE-NSELE-NTA [NDD] 19,500 (1987), including 12,000 Nde, 3,000 Nsele, 4,500 Nsa. Cross River State, Ikom LGA. Niger-Congo, Atlantic-Congo, Volta-Congo, Benue-Congo, Bantoid, Southern, Ekoid. Dialects: NDE (EKAMTULUFU, MBENKPE, UDOM, MBOFON, BEFON), NSELE, NTA (ATAM, AFUNATAM).

NDOE [NBB] 3,000 (1953). Cross River State, Ikom LGA. Niger-Congo, Atlantic-Congo, Volta-Congo, Benue-Congo, Bantoid, Southern, Ekoid. Dialects: EKPARABONG (AKPARABONG), BALEP (ANEP, ANYEP).

NDOOLA ***(NDORO, NUNDORO, NJOYAME, NDOLA)*** [NDR] 48,700 in Nigeria. Population total both countries 50,000 (1992). Taraba State, Bali, Gashaka, Sardauna LGAs. Also spoken in Cameroon. Niger-Congo, Atlantic-Congo, Volta-Congo, Benue-Congo, Bantoid, Northern, Mambiloid, Ndoro. Bilingualism in Fulfulde, Hausa. Investigation needed: bilingual proficiency in Hausa, attitudes. Traditional religion, Christian, Muslim.

NDUNDA [NUH] 300 to 400 (1999 Blench and Connell). Taraba State, Sardauna LGA, near Mvanip, 5 km. from Yerimaru, past Kakara on the tea estate road, northwest of Gembu. Niger-Congo, Atlantic-Congo, Volta-Congo, Benue-Congo, Bantoid, Northern, Mambiloid, Mambila-Konja, Magu-Kamkam-Kila. A separate language from Mvanip. All ages.

NGAMO ***(NGAMAWA, GAMO, GAMAWA)*** [NBH] 60,000 (1993). Yobe State, Fika LGA; Gambe State, Nafada-Bajoga LGA. Afro-Asiatic, Chadic, West, A, A.2, Bole, Bole Proper. Traditional religion, Muslim, Christian.

NGAS ***(ANGAS, KERANG, KARANG)*** [ANC] 400,000 (1998 SIL). Plateau State, Pankshin, Kanam, and Langtang LGAs. Afro-Asiatic, Chadic, West, A, A.3, Angas Proper, 1. Dialects: HILL ANGAS, PLAIN ANGAS. The people are called 'Kerang' or 'Karang'. Speakers prefer 'Ngas' as language name. Dictionary. Grammar. NT 1979.

NGGWAHYI ***(NGWAXI, NGWOHI)*** [NGX] 2,000 or fewer (1995). Borno State, Askira-Uba LGA. Afro-Asiatic, Chadic, Biu-Mandara, A, A.2.

NGIZIM ***(NGIZMAWA, NGEZZIM)*** [NGI] 80,000 (1993). Yobe State, Damaturu LGA. Afro-Asiatic, Chadic, West, B, B.1, Bade Proper. Dictionary. Grammar. Muslim, traditional religion, Christian.

NGWABA ***(GOMBI, GOBA)*** [NGW] 10,000 (1993 CAPRO). Adamawa State, Gombi LGA at Fachi and Guduniya, and Hong LGA. Afro-Asiatic, Chadic, Biu-Mandara, A, A.8. Bilingualism in Fulfulde, Hausa, Gudu, Nzanyi. Investigation needed: intelligibility with Nzanyi, attitudes. Agriculturalists, hunters, butchers. Traditional religion, Christian, Muslim.

NIGERIAN SIGN LANGUAGE [NSI] Deaf sign language. Influences from American and Ghanaian sign languages. Originated in 1960.

NINGYE [NNS] 3,000 to 4,000 (1999 Blench). Kaduna State, Jema'a LGA, Ningeshen Kurmi village and 3 small settlements: Akwankwan, Kobin, and Ningeshen Dutse. Niger-Congo, Atlantic-Congo, Volta-Congo, Benue-Congo, Platoid, Plateau, Western, Southwestern, A. Numana and Gwantu are the main second languages. Hausa widely known. Some young people also speak English. Language is spoken fluently by young people and others.

NINZAM ***(NINZO, NUNZO, GBHU D AMAR RANDFA, AMAR TITA, ANCHA, INCHA, KWASU, AKIZA, SAMBE, FADAN WATE, HATE)*** [NIN] 35,000 (1973 SIL). Kaduna State, Jema'a LGA; Nasarawa State, Akwanga LGA. Niger-Congo, Atlantic-Congo, Volta-Congo, Benue-Congo, Platoid, Plateau, Western, Southwestern, A. Speakers have a considerable degree of bilingualism in Hausa. Grammar.

NJEREP ***(NJERUP)*** [NJR] 2 (1987 Blench and Williamson). Southeast, near the Mambila. Not used in Cameroon any longer. Niger-Congo, Atlantic-Congo, Volta-Congo, Benue-Congo, Bantoid, Northern, Mambiloid, Mambila-Konja, Njerup. Nearly extinct.

NKARI [NKZ] 5,000 (1998 B. Connell). Akwa Ibom State, Ikono LGA. Niger-Congo, Atlantic-Congo, Volta-Congo, Benue-Congo, Cross River, Delta Cross, Lower Cross, Obolo, Ibuoro. Formerly thought to be a dialect of Ibibio. Ibibio is the main trade language of Akwa Ibom State.

NKEM-NKUM [ISI] 34,500 (1987 Asinya), including 18,000 Nkem, 16,500 Nkum. Cross River State, Ogoja LGA. Niger-Congo, Atlantic-Congo, Volta-Congo, Benue-Congo, Bantoid, Southern, Ekoid. Dialects: NKEM (NKIM, OGOJA, ISHIBORI, ISIBIRI, OGBOJA), NKUM. Dialect cluster.

NKOROO ***(NKORO)*** [NKX] 4,550 (1989 UBS). Rivers State, Bonny LGA. Niger-Congo, Atlantic-Congo, Ijoid, Ijo, Eastern, Northeastern, Nkoroo. A separate language within the Ijo cluster. Investigation needed: bilingual proficiency.

NKUKOLI ***(LOKOLI, LOKUKOLI, NKOKOLLE, EKURI)*** [NBO] 1,000 (1973 SIL). Cross River State, at the juncture of Ikom, Obubra and Akamkpa LGAs, Iko Ekperem Development Area. Niger-Congo, Atlantic-Congo, Volta-Congo, Benue-Congo, Cross River, Delta Cross, Upper Cross, Central, East-West, Loko.

NKWAK [NKQ] Kaduna State, Birnin Gwari LGA, further location data imprecise. Niger-Congo, Atlantic-Congo, Volta-Congo, Benue-Congo, Platoid, Unclassified. All the alternate names listed except 'Tanjijili' are names of the people. Listed separately in Crozier and Blench 1992. Investigation needed: bilingual proficiency in Hausa, attitudes.

NNAM ***(NDEM)*** [NBP] 3,000 (1987 Asinya). Cross River State, Ikom and Ogoja LGAs. Niger-Congo, Atlantic-Congo, Volta-Congo, Benue-Congo, Bantoid, Southern, Ekoid.

NSHI [NSC] Taraba State, Sardauna LGA, Antere, Nkiri. Niger-Congo, Atlantic-Congo, Volta-Congo, Benue-Congo, Bantoid, Unclassified. May be the same as Wushi.

NUMANA-NUNKU-GWANTU-NUMBU ***(SANGA)*** [NBR] 15,000 (SIL). Kaduna State, Jema'a LGA; Plateau State, Akwanga LGA. Niger-Congo, Atlantic-Congo, Volta-Congo, Benue-Congo, Platoid, Plateau, Western, Southwestern, A. Dialects: NUNKU, NUMANA (NIMANA), GWANTU (GWANTO), NUMBU. Dialect cluster. Different from Sanga in Bauchi State. Investigation needed: bilingual proficiency in Hausa, attitudes.

NUNGU ***(RINDRE, RENDRE, RINDIRI, LINDIRI)*** [RIN] 50,000 (1999). Plateau State, Akwanga LGA. Niger-Congo, Atlantic-Congo, Volta-Congo, Benue-Congo, Platoid, Plateau, Western, Southwestern, B. Dialects: RINDRE, GUDI. Investigation needed: bilingual proficiency in Hausa, attitudes.

NUPE-NUPE-TAKO ***(NUPE, NUFAWA, NUPECI, NUPENCHI, NUPECIDJI, NUPENCIZI)*** [NUP] 800,000 (1990). Niger State, Mariga, Gbako, Agaie, and Lapai LGAs; Kwara State, Edu LGA; KoGi State, KogiLGA; Federal Capital Territory. Niger-Congo, Atlantic-Congo, Volta-Congo, Benue-Congo, Nupoid, Nupe-Gbagyi, Nupe. Dialects: NUPE CENTRAL (NIFE, ANUPE, NUPECIZI, NUPENCIZI, AMPEYI, ANUPECWAYI, ANUPERI, TAPA, TAPPAH, TAKPA), NUPE TAKO (BASSA NGE). Nupe Central has become the literary norm. A regionally important language. Investigation needed: intelligibility with dialects. Trade language. Dictionary. Grammar. Literacy rate in second language: 60%. Fishermen. Muslim, traditional religion, Christian. Bible 1953-1989.

NYAM ***(NYAMBOLO)*** [NMI] Taraba State, Karim Lamido LGA, at Andami village. 1 village. Afro-Asiatic, Chadic, West, A, A.2, Bole, Bole Proper.

NYONG ***(MUMBAKE, MUBAKO, NYONGNEPA, NYOKING, DAGANYONGA, TETEKA, CHUKKOL, YAPELI, PETI)*** [MUO] Adamawa State, Mayo Belwa LGA, 6 villages. Niger-Congo, Atlantic-Congo, Volta-Congo, North, Adamawa-Ubangi, Adamawa, Leko-Nimbari, Leko. Bilingualism in Hausa, Fulfulde, Samba, Yendang, Kumba, Mumuye. Growing interest in education. Agriculturalists, traders, hunters. Traditional religion, Christian, Muslim. See main entry under Cameroon.

NZANYI ***(NJANYI, NZANGI, NJAI, NJENY, ZANI, ZANY, JENG, JENGE, NJEI, NJEING, KOBOTSHI)*** [NJA] 77,000 in Nigeria (1993). Population total both countries 86,000. Adamawa State, Maiha LGA. Also spoken in Cameroon. Afro-Asiatic, Chadic, Biu-Mandara, A, A.8. Dialects: PAKA, ROGEDE, NGGWOLI, HOODE, MAIHA, MAGARA, DEDE, MUTIDI, LOVI. Schools in nearly every village, but enrollment is usually low. Agriculturalists. Muslim, traditional religion, Christian.

OBANLIKU ***(ABANLIKU)*** [BZY] 65,000 (1989 Faraclas). Cross River State, Obudu LGA. Niger-Congo, Atlantic-Congo, Volta-Congo, Benue-Congo, Cross River, Bendi. Dialects: BEBI, BUSI, BASANG, BISU (GAYI), BISHIRI. Dialect cluster. Related to Alege.

OBOLO ***(ANDONI, ANDONE, ANDONNI)*** [ANN] 100,000 (1990 Uche E. Aaron). Rivers State, Bonny LGA; Akwa Ibom State, Ikot Abasi LGA, islands off southern coast. Bounded on the east and north-east by the Ibibio, on the northwest by the Ogoni, on the west by the Kalabari, on the south by the Atlantic Ocean. Niger-Congo, Atlantic-Congo, Volta-Congo, Benue-Congo, Cross River, Delta Cross, Lower Cross, Obolo. Dialects: NGO, ATABA, UNYEADA, OKOROETE, IBOT OBOLO. Ngo is the prestige dialect. Ibibio and Ibo are the trade languages. English is learned in school. In the east there is a movement toward establishing a stronger Obolo ethnic identity and getting rid of borrowed words from Ibibio. 'Obolo' is their own name, 'Andoni' is the government's name. Grammar. Literacy rate in first language: 5% to 10%. Literacy rate in second language: 25% to 50%. There are church adult literacy classes all over the area. Taught in primary schools. Taught in junior secondary schools. Magazines. Riverine. Fishermen, agriculturalists. NT 1991.

OBULOM ***(ABULOMA)*** [OBU] Rivers State, Okrika LGA, Abuloma town. Niger-Congo, Atlantic-Congo, Volta-Congo, Benue-Congo, Cross River, Delta Cross, Central Delta, Kugbo.

ODUAL ***(SAKA)*** [ODU] 18,000 (1989). Rivers State, Ahoada LGA. Niger-Congo, Atlantic-Congo, Volta-Congo, Benue-Congo, Cross River, Delta Cross, Central Delta, Abua-Odual. Dialects: ARUGHAUNYA, ADIBOM. Most closely related to Abua; about 70% lexical similarity. NT 1981.

ODUT [ODA] 700 (1940, 1950 Forde and Jones). Cross River State, Odukpani LGA. Niger-Congo, Atlantic-Congo, Volta-Congo, Benue-Congo, Cross River, Delta Cross, Upper Cross, Kiong-Korop. It may be extinct.

OGBAH ***(OGBA)*** [OGC] 170,000 (1993 A. Ahiamadu). Rivers State, Ogbah-Egbema-Ndoni LGA, northern Niger Delta. Niger-Congo, Atlantic-Congo, Volta-Congo, Benue-Congo, Igboid, Igbo. Dialects: EGNIH, IGBURU-USOMINI. A separate language in the Igbo language cluster. The dialects have 81% to 94% lexical similarity with each other. Ogbah has 45% lexical similarity with Ndoni, 41% with Egbema, 32% with Ikwere, 23% with Ekpeye. Bilingualism in Igbo, Nigerian Pidgin, English. About 64 primary schools, 8 post-primary schools, technical college in the area. Literacy rate in first language: Low. Swamps, waterways. Agriculturalists, fishermen, traders. Christian, traditional religion. Bible portions 1999.

OGBIA ***(OGBINYA)*** [OGB] 200,000 (1989). Bayelsa State, Brass LGA. Niger-Congo, Atlantic-Congo, Volta-Congo, Benue-Congo, Cross River, Delta Cross, Central Delta, Kugbo. Dialects: KOLO, OLOIBIRI, ANYAMA. Dialect cluster but all inherently intelligible. English making little impact.

OGBOGOLO ***(OBOGOLO)*** [OGG] 10,000 or fewer (1995). Rivers State, Ahoada LGA, 1 town. Niger-Congo, Atlantic-Congo, Volta-Congo, Benue-Congo, Cross River, Delta Cross, Central Delta, Kugbo.

OGBRONUAGUM ***(BUKUMA)*** [OGU] Rivers State, Degema LGA, Bukuma village near Buguma. Niger-Congo, Atlantic-Congo, Volta-Congo, Benue-Congo, Cross River, Delta Cross, Central Delta, Kugbo.

OKO-ENI-OSAYEN ***(OKO, OGORI-MAGONGO)*** [OKS] 10,000 including 4,000 in Ogori, 3,000 in Magongo, 3,000 in Eni (1989 Williamson). Kogi State, Okene LGA, Ogori and Magongo towns, ten miles south southwest of Okene. Niger-Congo, Atlantic-Congo, Volta-Congo, Benue-Congo, Oko. Dialects: OKO (OGORI, UKU), OSAYEN (MAGONGO, OSANYIN), ENI. A dialect cluster. It seems to be equally distantly related to Yoruba, Ebira, Edo, Igbo, and Idoma.

OKOBO [OKB] 50,000 (1991 Connell). Akwa Ibom State, Okobo LGA. Niger-Congo, Atlantic-Congo, Volta-Congo, Benue-Congo, Cross River, Delta Cross, Lower Cross, Obolo, Okobo. Possibly two dialects.

OKODIA ***(OKORDIA)*** [OKD] 3,600 (1977 Voegelin and Voegelin). Bayelsa State, Yenagoa LGA. Niger-Congo, Atlantic-Congo, Ijoid, Ijo, Central, Oruma-Northeast Central, Northeast Central. Not intelligible with Biseni or other Ijo languages. Investigation needed: bilingual proficiency.

OKPAMHERI ***(OPAMERI)*** [OPA] 30,000 (1973 SIL). Edo State, Akoko-Edo LGA. Niger-Congo, Atlantic-Congo, Volta-Congo, Benue-Congo, Edoid, Northwestern, Southern. Dialects: OKULOSHO (OKUROSHO), WESTERN OKPAMHERI, EMHALHE (EMARLE, SOMORIKA, SEMOLIKA). Subdialects of Okulosho: Ojirami (Eekunu), Dagbala (Dangbala), Oja (Oza), Makeke (Uuma), Oma. Subdialects of Western Okpamheri: Ekpe, Bekuma, Lankpese (Lampese, Lankpeshi), Ibillo (Ibilo), Imoga (Imorga, Uma), Eko (Ekon, Ekor), Ikaran-Oke (Ikeram-Oke), Ebunn-Oke, Ikaran-Ele (Ikeran-Ile, Ebunn-Ugbo, Ikpesa, Igbo-Ola-Sale (Ugboshi-Sale), Aiyegunle (Oshi), Igbo-Ola-Oke (Ugboshi-Oke), Onumo (Onumu), Ogugu, Ogbe-Sale, Ogbe-Oke. Investigation needed: intelligibility with Emhalhe. Traditional religion, Christian.

OKPE [OKE] 8,722 (1957 Bradbury). Edo State, Okpe LGA. Niger-Congo, Atlantic-Congo, Volta-Congo, Benue-Congo, Edoid, Southwestern. Distinct from Okpe-Idesa-Oloma-Akuku, which is Northwestern Edoid.

OKPE-IDESA-AKUKU [OKP] Edo State, Akoko-Edo LGA. Niger-Congo, Atlantic-Congo, Volta-Congo, Benue-Congo, Edoid, Northwestern, Southern. Dialects: OKPE, IDESA, AKUKU. Related to Oloma. Different from Okpe which is Southwestern Edoid. Investigation needed: intelligibility with Oloma.

OLOMA [OLM] Edo State, Akoko-Edo LGA. Niger-Congo, Atlantic-Congo, Volta-Congo, Benue-Congo, Edoid, Northwestern, Southern. Related to Okpe-Idesa-Akuku.

OLULUMO-IKOM ***(LULUMO)*** [IKO] 30,000 (1989 Faraclas), including 5,000 Olulumo, 25,000 Ikom. Cross River State, Ikom LGA. May also be in Cameroon. Niger-Congo, Atlantic-Congo, Volta-Congo, Benue-Congo, Cross River, Delta Cross, Upper Cross, Central, East-West, Ikom. Dialects: OKUNI, OLULUMO, IKOM.

ORING ***(ORRI, ORRIN, ORRINGORRIN, KORING)*** [ORI] 75,000 (1989), including 12,300 Ufia, 3,000 Effium, 6,350 Okpoto (1955 R. G. Armstrong). Benue State, Okpokwu LGA; Ebonyi State, Ishielu LGA. Niger-Congo, Atlantic-Congo, Volta-Congo, Benue-Congo, Cross River, Delta Cross, Upper

Cross, Central, North-South, Koring-Kukele, Koring. Dialects: OKPOTO, UFIA (UTONKON), UFIOM (EFFIUM).

ORO ***(ORON)*** [ORX] 75,000 (1989). Akwa-Ibom State, Oron LGA. Niger-Congo, Atlantic-Congo, Volta-Congo, Benue-Congo, Cross River, Delta Cross, Lower Cross, Obolo, Oro. Some dialect variation. Grammar.

ORUMA [ORR] 5,000 or fewer (1995). Bayelsa State, Brass LGA, 1 town. Niger-Congo, Atlantic-Congo, Ijoid, Ijo, Central, Oruma-Northeast Central, Oruma. A separate language within the Ijo cluster. Investigation needed: bilingual proficiency.

OSOSO [OSS] 6,532 (1957 Bradbury). Edo State, Akoko-Edo LGA. Niger-Congo, Atlantic-Congo, Volta-Congo, Benue-Congo, Edoid, North-Central, Ghotuo-Uneme-Yekhee.

OTANK ***(OTANGA, UTANGA, UTANGE, OTANG, UTANK)*** [UTA] 3,000 (1973 SIL). Cross River State, Obudu LGA; Benue State, Kwande LGA. Niger-Congo, Atlantic-Congo, Volta-Congo, Benue-Congo, Bantoid, Southern, Tivoid. 70% lexical similarity with Tiv, 60% with Icheve, 50% with Evand, 40% with Mesaka and Eman. Mountains. Traditional religion.

PA'A ***(AFAWA, AFANCI, PALA, PA'AWA, FA'AWA, FONI, AFA, FUCAKA)*** [AFA] 8,000 (1995 CAPRO). Bauchi State, Ningi and Bauchi LGAs. Afro-Asiatic, Chadic, West, B, B.2. Bilingualism in Hausa. Speakers are shifting to Hausa. Investigation needed: bilingual proficiency in Hausa, attitudes. Grammar. Literacy rate in second language: 1%. Agriculturalists: Guinea corn, millet, maize, peanuts, beans; fishermen. Traditional religion, Muslim, Christian.

PAI ***(DALONG)*** [PAI] 2,000 to 3,000 (1996 Blench). Plateau State, Pankshin LGA, 17 km. south of the main road from Jos-Amper, turning a few kms. before Amper. 7 villages. Niger-Congo, Atlantic-Congo, Volta-Congo, Benue-Congo, Platoid, Benue, Tarokoid. All children apparently fluent. Language use vigorous.

PANGSENG [PAN] Taraba State, Karim Lamido LGA. Niger-Congo, Atlantic-Congo, Volta-Congo, North, Adamawa-Ubangi, Adamawa, Leko-Nimbari, Mumuye-Yandang, Mumuye. Dialects: PANGSENG, KOMO, JEGA. Investigation needed: intelligibility with Mumuye.

PEERE ***(PERE, PEER, PARE, POTOPO, POTOPORE, PATAPORI, KUTIN, KOUTIN, KUTINE, KUTINN, KOTOPO, KOTOFO, KOTPOJO)*** [KUT] 5,000 in Nigeria (1993). Adamawa State, Ganye LGA. Niger-Congo, Atlantic-Congo, Volta-Congo, North, Adamawa-Ubangi, Adamawa, Leko-Nimbari, Duru, Voko-Dowayo, Kutin. Bilingualism in Fulfulde. It is reported that all Peere speakers have moved to Cameroon since Gashaka-Gumti National Park was created. Dictionary. Hunters. Muslim, traditional religion, Christian. NT 1986. See main entry under Cameroon.

PERO ***(PIPERO, FILIYA)*** [PIP] 25,000 (1995 CAPRO). Bauchi State, Kaltungo LGA, Gwandum, Gundalf, Kushi, Yapito, Burak and Bangunji. Afro-Asiatic, Chadic, West, A, A.2, Tangale, Tangale Proper. They use Hausa as lingua franca. Investigation needed: bilingual proficiency in Hausa, attitudes. Dictionary. Grammar. Agriculturalists: Guinea corn, peanuts, beniseed, millet, maize, cotton, beans, fruit. Christian. Bible portions 1936-1938.

PIDGIN, NIGERIAN ***(NIGERIAN CREOLE ENGLISH, NIGERIAN PIDGIN ENGLISH)*** [PCM] Southern states and in Sabon Garis of the northern states, coastal and urban areas. Creole, English based, Atlantic, Krio. Dialects: LAGOS PIDGIN, DELTA PIDGIN, CROSS RIVER PIDGIN, BENIN PIDGIN. No unified standard. The dialects listed may be very different from each other. Partially intelligible with Krio of Sierra Leone and Cameroon Pidgin. Used in novels, plays, advertising. Increasing in importance and use. It is a creole with native speakers, as well as used as a pidgin between Africans and Europeans, and Africans from different languages. Trade language. Grammar. No unified orthography. Poetry, radio programs, TV. Bible portions 1957.

PITI ***(PITTI, ABISI, BISI)*** [PCN] 1,600 (1950). Kaduna State, Saminaka LGA. Niger-Congo, Atlantic-Congo, Volta-Congo, Benue-Congo, Kainji, Eastern, Piti-Atsam. Dialect: RIBAN (RIBAM). Investigation needed: bilingual proficiency, attitudes.

PIYA-KWONCI ***(PIYA, PIA, PITIKO, WURKUM, AMBANDI)*** [PIY] 5,000 or more (1992). Taraba State, Karim Lamido LGA; and some in Bauchi State. 21 villages or more. Afro-Asiatic, Chadic, West, A, A.2, Tangale, Tangale Proper. Dialects: PIYA, KWONCI. Speakers use Hausa, Kulung, Pelang, Tangale or some English as second language. Similar in culture to the Kulung, Kodei, Kwanchi, Pelang, and Pero. 'Ambandi' is their name for themselves. Investigation needed: bilingual proficiency in Hausa, attitudes. Agriculturalists. Christian, Muslim. Bible portions 1950.

POLCI ***(PALCI, PALCHI, POLCHI)*** [POL] 22,000 (1995 CAPRO) including 2,000 Zul (1995), 4,000 Buli (1993), 400 Langas (1993), 15,000 Polci, 250 Baram (1993), 800 Dir (1993). Bauchi State, Dass, Toro, and Bauchi LGAs. Afro-Asiatic, Chadic, West, B, B.3, Zaar Proper. Dialects: ZUL (MBARMI, BARMA), BARAM (MBARAM, BARANG), DIR (DIIR, DRA, BARAM DUTSE), BULI, LANGAS (NYAMZAX, LUNDUR), POLCI (POSA, POLSHI, PALCI). Polci dialect cluster in Barawa language cluster. Investigation needed: bilingual proficiency in Hausa, attitudes. Grammar. Agriculturalists: Guinea corn, peanuts, acha, maize; animal husbandry: fowl, goats; hunters.

PONGU ***(PONGO, PANGU, ARRINGEU, TARYA)*** [PON] 20,000 or more speakers (1988 Roger Blench). Niger State, Rafi LGA, Gumna and Tegina districts, widespread small villages between Kusheriki in the north, Zungeru in the south, and along the new road to the southwest, with center in Sabon Gari Pangu. Bordered by the Kamuku, Ngwoi, Ura, Basa-Kaduna, Baushi, Basa-Gurmana, Gurmana, and Gbari. Small numbers are in Kaduna, Minna, Kontagora, and Bida towns. Niger-Congo, Atlantic-Congo, Volta-Congo, Benue-Congo, Kainji, Western, Kamuku. Dialects: AKWA, ASEBI, AWEGE, AZHIGA, CAGERE, CAMAJERE, CANSU, CAUNDU, UBWEBWE. Dialect variation is slight, with 94% to 99% similarity. Hausa is used as second language with outsiders. English is used in education and for national government purposes. Pongu always used to other Pongu. Also used in church when only Pongu are present. They call their language 'Tarya', themselves 'Arya'. Sister exchange pattern in marriage. Some children and adults are literate in Hausa or English. Savannah. Peasant agriculturalists. 200 to 500 meters. Muslim, traditional religion (Mai-Giro), Christian.

PSIKYE ***(KAPSIKI, KAMSIKI, PTSAKE)*** [KVJ] 12,000 in Nigeria (1992). Adamawa State, north and east of Michika, south of Madagali, in the Mandara Mts. Afro-Asiatic, Chadic, Biu-Mandara, A, A.3. Dialects: PSIKYE (KAPSIKI, KAMU), ZLENGE, WULA (OULA, ULA-XANGKU, LYING). The Wula dialect is in Nigeria. Closely related to Hya and Kamwe of Nigeria. Literacy rate in second language: Low. Mountain slope. Agriculturalists: Guinea corn, peanuts, rice, beans; animal husbandry. Traditional religion, Christian, Muslim. NT 1988. See main entry under Cameroon.

PUTAI ***(MARGHI WEST)*** [MFL] Few speakers. Borno State, Damboa LGA. Afro-Asiatic, Chadic, Biu-Mandara, A, A.2, 1. Bilingualism in Kanuri. The language is dying out in favor of Kanuri, but the ethnic population is large. Nearly extinct.

PUTUKWAM ***(UTUGWANG, MBE AFAL, MBUBE EASTERN)*** [AFE] 12,000 (1973 SIL), including 3,500 Afrike (1953). Cross River State, Obudu and Ogoja LGAs. Niger-Congo, Atlantic- Congo, Volta-Congo, Benue-Congo, Cross River, Bendi. Dialects: UTUGWANG (OTUKWANG), OKOROGUNG, OKOROTUNG, AFRIKE (AFERIKE), OBE (MBE EAST), OBOSO. Member of the Obe cluster. Speakers are reported to understand Bekwarra well. Investigation needed: bilingual proficiency in Bekwarra. Traditional religion, Christian.

PYAPUN [PCW] 4,635 (1934 Ames). Plateau State, Shendam LGA. Afro-Asiatic, Chadic, West, A, A.3, Angas Proper, 2. Related to Tal and Montol. Investigation needed: bilingual proficiency in Hausa, attitudes.

RANG [RAX] Taraba State, Zing LGA. Niger-Congo, Atlantic-Congo, Volta-Congo, North, Adamawa-Ubangi, Adamawa, Leko-Nimbari, Mumuye-Yandang, Mumuye. Close to Mumuye.

RESHE ***(TSURESHE, TSUREJA, BARESHE, GUNGA, GUNGAWA, GUNGANCHI, YAURAWA)*** [RES] 44,000 (1993 SIL). Kebbi State, Yauri LGA; Niger State, Borgu LGA; southern Kebbi State, western Niger State, banks of the Niger River, north of Busa. Niger-Congo, Atlantic-Congo, Volta-Congo, Benue-Congo, Kainji, Western, Reshe. Blench says it is the most divergent of the Western Kainji languages. 43% lexical similarity with Lopa, 33% with Laru, 20% with Duka, 11% with Kamabari (Salka). There is a strong association between wrestling, the traditional religion, and ethnic identity. The people are BaReshe, the language Reshe or TsuReshe. Ethnic subgroups: Gungawa, Yaurawa (Yauri). Investigation needed: intelligibility with Laru, Lopa, attitudes. Agriculturalists: Guinea corn, beans, rice, onions; fishermen; canoe makers; mat makers. 180 to 300 meters. Muslim, traditional religion, Christian less than. Bible portions 1970.

ROGO ***(UROGO, BUROGO, UCANJA KAMUKU)*** [ROD] POPULATION? Niger State, Rafi and Mariga LGAs, around Ucanja town, 30 km. northwest of Kagara; Kaduna State, Birnin Gwari LGA. Niger-Congo, Atlantic-Congo, Volta-Congo, Benue-Congo, Kainji, Western, Kamuku.

RON ***("CHALLA", "CHALA")*** [CLA] 115,000 (1995) including 20,000 Shagawu. Plateau State, Bokkos, Barakin-Ladi and Mangu LGAs. Afro-Asiatic, Chadic, West, A, A.4, Ron Proper. Dialects: BOKKOS (ALIS I RUN), DAFFO-BUTURA (LIS MA RUN), MONGUNA (SHAGAWU, SHAGAU, NAFUNFIA, MALENI). Grammar. Radio programs.

RUMA ***(RURUMA, RURAMA, TURAMA, BAGWAMA)*** [RUZ] 2,200 (1948). Kaduna State, Saminaka LGA. Niger-Congo, Atlantic-Congo, Volta-Congo, Benue-Congo, Kainji, Eastern, Northern Jos, Kauru.

SAMBA DAKA ***(CHAMBA DAKA, TSAMBA, TCHAMBA, SAMA, SAMBA, JAMA, DAKA, DAKKA, DEKKA, NAKANYARE, DENG, TIKK)*** [CCG] 60,000 (1973 SIL). 500,000 all Samba varieties (1993). Taraba State, Gashaka, Jalingo, Bali, Zing LGAs, and Adamawa State, Ganye and Mayo Belwa LGAs. Niger-Congo, Atlantic-Congo, Volta-Congo, Benue-Congo, Bantoid, Northern, Dakoid. Dialects: SAMBA DAKA, SAMBA JANGANI, SAMBA NNAKENYARE, SAMBA OF MAPEO, TARAM, DIRIM. A dialect cluster. Together with Lamja-Dengsa-Tola it may form a dialect cluster or language cluster. Close to Dirim. Bilingualism in Fulfulde, Hausa. Different from Samba Leko or Chamba (Akaselem) of Togo. Literacy rate in second language: 3%. Traditional religion, Muslim, Christian. Bible portions 1933.

SAMBA LEKO ***(CHAMBA LEKO, SAMBA LEEKO, SAMBA, NDI, LEKON, LEGO, LEKO, SUNTAI)*** [NDI] Adamawa State, Ganye, Fufore, Wukari, and Takum LGAs. Niger-Congo, Atlantic-Congo, Volta-Congo, North, Adamawa-Ubangi, Adamawa, Leko-Nimbari, Leko. Those in Donga now speak Jukun. Traditional religion, Christian, Muslim. See main entry under Cameroon.

SANGA ***(ISANGA, ASANGA)*** [SGA] 15,000 to 20,000 (1995 CAPRO), including 1,600 Bujiyel (1995 CAPRO). Bauchi State, Toro LGA. Niger-Congo, Atlantic-Congo, Volta-Congo, Benue-Congo, Kainji, Eastern, Northern Jos, Jera. Dialect: BUJIYEL. The language is 'Isanga', a speaker 'Osanga', the speakers 'Asanga'. Distinct from Numana-Nunku-Gwantu (Sanga) of Kaduna and Plateau states. Traditional religion, Christian.

SASARU-ENWAN-IGWE [SSC] 3,775 (1952). Edu State, Akoko-Edo LGA. Niger-Congo, Atlantic-Congo, Volta-Congo, Benue-Congo, Edoid, North-Central, Ghotuo-Uneme-Yekhee. Dialects: SASARU, ENWAN, IGWE.

SAYA ***(SAYAWA, SEYA, SEYAWA, SAYANCI, SEIYARA, SAYARA)*** [SAY] 50,000 (1973 SIL), including 7,000 Sigdi (1995 CAPRO). Bauchi State, Tafawa Balewa LGA. Afro-Asiatic, Chadic, West, B, B.3, Zaar Proper. Dialects: SIGIDI (SUGUDI, SIGDI, SEGIDDI), ZAAR (VIKZAR, VIGZAR, KAL, GAMBAR LEERE, LUSA). Saya dialect cluster in Barawa language cluster. Mountain slope. Agriculturalists: Guinea corn, peanuts, sweet potato, acha, rice, yams, cocoyam, maize, cotton, onions, tomato, pepper; weavers; basket makers; gourd carvers; sculptors; leatherwork; hunters. Traditional religion, Christian.

SETO-GBE [STS] Lagos State, Badagry LGA. Niger-Congo, Atlantic-Congo, Volta-Congo, Kwa, Left Bank, Gbe, Aja. See main entry under Benin.

SHA [SCW] 3,000 (1998 Seibert SIL). Plateau State, Bokkos LGA, Sha district. Afro-Asiatic, Chadic, West, A, A.4, Ron Proper. Investigation needed: bilingual proficiency in Hausa, attitudes. Grammar.

SHALL-ZWALL [SHA] Bauchi State, Dass LGA. Niger-Congo, Atlantic-Congo, Volta-Congo, Benue-Congo, Platoid, Plateau, Western, Southwestern, A. Dialects: SHALL (SHAL), ZWALL. Dialect cluster. Investigation needed: bilingual proficiency in Hausa, attitudes.

SHAMA-SAMBUGA ***(TUSHAMA, BUSHAMA)*** [SQA] 5,000 or fewer (1995 S. and S. Dettweiler). Niger State, Rafi and Mariga LGAs; Kaduna State, Birnin Gwari LGA. Niger-Congo, Atlantic-Congo, Volta-Congo, Benue-Congo, Kainji, Western, Kamuku. Dialects: SHAMA, SAMBUGA. 64% to 66% lexical similarity with the three Kamuku dialects, 69% with Hungworo, 52% with Eastern Acipa, 16% to 17% with Western Acipa. Bilingualism in Hausa. Investigation needed: bilingual proficiency in Hausa, attitudes.

SHAMANG ***(SAMBAN, SAMANG)*** [SGN] Kaduna State, Kachia and Jema'a LGAs. Niger-Congo, Atlantic-Congo, Volta-Congo, Benue-Congo, Platoid, Plateau, Western, Northwestern, Jaba. Related to Ham. Investigation needed: bilingual proficiency in Hausa, attitudes.

SHANGA ***(SHANGAWA, SHONGA, SHONGAWA)*** [SHO] 5,000 to 10,000 (1995 Ross Jones SIM). Kebbi State between Kaoje and Yauri, on both sides of the Niger River, but especially on the north bank; Gante, Lafugu, Zaria, Besse, Shanga, Dugu Raha, Dugu Tsofo, Bakin Turu villages. Niger-Congo, Mande, Eastern, Eastern, Busa. Not inherently intelligible with the Busa group. Tyenga and Shanga have 70% lexical similarity, 38% to 40% lexical similarity with the Busa group. It is reported that most Shanga do not speak Shanga any longer but Hausa, and those who do speak Shanga are bilingual in Hausa, some in Dendi. Investigation needed: intelligibility with Tyenga, bilingual proficiency in Hausa, Dendi. Traditional religion, Muslim.

SHAU ***(SHO, LÌSHÁÙ)*** [SQH] Bauchi State, Toro LGA, Shau an Mana villages. Niger-Congo, Atlantic-Congo, Volta-Congo, Benue-Congo, Kainji, Eastern, Northern Jos, Jera. Nearly extinct.

SHENI ***(SHANI, SHAINI)*** [SCV] 200 (1925). Kaduna State, Saminaka LGA. Niger-Congo, Atlantic-Congo, Volta-Congo, Benue-Congo, Kainji, Eastern, Northern Jos, Jera. Nearly extinct.

SHIKI ***(GUBI, GUBA, GUBAWA, MASHIKI)*** [GUA] Bauchi State, Bauchi LGA. Gubi and Guru towns north of Bauchi town. Niger-Congo, Atlantic-Congo, Volta-Congo, Benue-Congo, Bantoid, Southern, Jarawan, Nigerian. Dialects: GUBI, GURU. Bilingualism in Gera, Hausa. Reported to be spoken only by elders (CAPRO 1995:153). Literacy rate in second language: 30% or less. Agriculturalists: Guinea corn, peanuts, rice, maize, yams; animal husbandry: cattle, sheep. Muslim.

SHOO-MINDA-NYE [BCV] 10,000 (1973 SIL). Taraba State, Karim Lamido LGA, villages on the banks of the Benue River. Niger-Congo, Atlantic-Congo, Volta-Congo, Benue-Congo, Platoid, Benue, Jukunoid, Central, Jukun-Mbembe-Wurbo, Unclassified. Dialects: SHOO (BANDA, BANDAWA), MINDA (JINLERI), NYE (KUNINI). Some bilingualism in Fulfulde, Hausa, and Jenjo. All 3 dialects are of equal status. Called 'Bakula' together with Como Karim, Munga, Jiru, and Jessi. Ethnic groups: Banda, Kunini, Lau Habe. Fishermen. Christian, traditional religion, Muslim.

SHUWA-ZAMANI ***(KUZAMANI, RISHUWA, KAURU)*** [KSA] 1,000 (1973 SIL). Bauchi State, Toro LGA. Niger-Congo, Atlantic-Congo, Volta-Congo, Benue-Congo, Kainji, Eastern, Northern Jos, Kauru.

SIRI ***(SIRAWA)*** [SIR] Bauchi State, Ningi LGA. Afro-Asiatic, Chadic, West, B, B.2. Reported to be spoken by only a few elders. Agriculturalists: Guinea corn, millet, maize, orchards. Muslim, Christian.

SOMYEWE ***(KILA)*** [KGT] 100 speakers or fewer (1992 Crozier and Blench). Taraba State, Sardauna LGA, Kila Yang, Njike, Kuma, Jabu, Kikau, and Mayo Daga towns. Apparently extinct in Cameroon. Niger-Congo, Atlantic-Congo, Volta-Congo, Benue-Congo, Bantoid, Northern, Mambiloid, Mambila-Konja, Magu-Kamkam-Kila. They live among the Mambila. Blacksmiths. Muslim.

SUKUR ***(SUGUR, ADIKIMMU SUKUR, GEMASAKUN, SAKUL)*** [SUK] 14,779 (1992). Northern tip of Adamawa State, Michika LGA, Mandara Mts. Perhaps in Cameroon. Afro-Asiatic, Chadic, Biu-Mandara, A, A.6. Speakers use Fulfulde, Hausa, Wula (Psikyye), Kamwe, or some English as second languages. Hausa used in most churches. Investigation needed: intelligibility with Hausa, attitudes. Mountain slope. Agriculturalists, animal husbandry. Traditional religion, Christian, Muslim.

SURUBU ***(SRUBU, FITI, SKRUBU, ZURUBU)*** [SDE] 1,950 (1948). Kaduna State, Saminaka LGA. Niger-Congo, Atlantic-Congo, Volta-Congo, Benue-Congo, Kainji, Eastern, Northern Jos, Kauru.

TAL ***(AMTUL, KWABZAK)*** [TAL] 10,000 (1973 SIL). Plateau State, Pankshin LGA. Afro-Asiatic, Chadic, West, A, A.3, Angas Proper, 2. Related to Montol, Goemai, Pyapun, Koenoem. Investigation needed: bilingual proficiency in Hausa, attitudes.

TALA [TAK] 1,000 (1993). Bauchi State, Bauchi LGA, Kuka and Talan Kasa villages. Afro-Asiatic, Chadic, West, B, B.3, Guruntum. Investigation needed: intelligibility with Guruntum, bilingual proficiency in Hausa, attitudes. Agriculturalists: Guinea corn, maize; animal husbandry: livestock. Traditional religion, Christian over.

TAMAJAQ, TAWALLAMMAT ***(TAMASHEQ, TOMACHECK, TAHOUA TAMAJEQ, TUAREG, BUZU, AZBINAWA)*** [TTQ] Few in Nigeria. Afro-Asiatic, Berber, Tamasheq, Southern. Dialect: IOULLEMMEDEN. It may be the eastern rather than the western dialect in Nigeria. Only seasonal migrants and laborers. No resident villages. Muslim. Bible portions 1979-1985. See main entry under Niger.

TAMBAS ***(TAMBES, TEMBIS)*** [TDK] 8,000 (1999 Blench). Plateau State, Pankshin LGA. Afro-Asiatic, Chadic, West, A, A.4, Fyer. Investigation needed: intelligibility with Fyer, bilingual proficiency in Hausa.

TANGALE ***(TANGLE)*** [TAN] 130,000 (1995 CAPRO). Gombe State, Billiri, Kaltungo, Akko, and Balanga LGAs. Afro-Asiatic, Chadic, West, A, A.2, Tangale, Tangale Proper. Dialects: KALTUNGO, BILIRI, SHONGOM, TURE. Dictionary. Agriculturalists: Guinea corn, peanuts, maize, beans, millet, cotton, rice; small businesses. Christian, traditional religion. NT 1932-1963.

TANJIJILI ***(JIJILI, UJIJILI, KORO FUNTU OF KAFIN KORO, KORO FUNTU OF MINNA, KORO OF SHAKOYI)*** [UJI] 7,000 to 8,000 (1999 R. Blench). Niger State, Chanchaga and Suleija LGAs, on the road from Minna to Abuja at Kafin Koro, aout 10 villages. Niger-Congo, Atlantic-Congo, Volta-Congo, Benue-Congo, Platoid, Plateau, Southern. All the alternate names listed except 'Tanjijili' are names of the people.

TAPSHIN ***(TAPSHINAWA, SURU, MYET, NSUR, DISHILI)*** [TDL] 5,000 or fewer (1998 Blench). Bauchi State, Tafawa Balewa LGA; Plateau State, Pankshin LGA. Niger-Congo, Atlantic-Congo, Volta-Congo, Benue-Congo, Platoid, Benue, Tarokoid. Bilingualism in Angas. Investigation needed: bilingual proficiency in Angas, attitudes. Traditional religion.

TAROK ***(YERGAM, YERGUM, APPA)*** [YER] 300,000 (1998 Blench). Plateau State, Kanam, Wase, and Langtang LGAs; Gongola State, Wukari LGA. Niger-Congo, Atlantic-Congo, Volta-Congo, Benue-Congo, Platoid, Benue, Tarokoid. Dialects: IZINI (HILL TAROK), ITAROK (PLAIN TAROK), SELYER, ITAROK OGA ASA, IGYANG. Dictionary. Literacy rate in first language: 5% to 10%. Literacy rate in second language: 50% to 75%. Literacy program in progress. NT 1988.

TEDAGA [TUQ] 2,000 or fewer in Nigeria (1990 Blench). Borno State, northeastern LGAs, a few villages. Nilo-Saharan, Saharan, Central. Dialects: KECHERDA, AZA, TEDA, TUBU (TEBU, TEBOU, TIBBU, TOUBOU). Kecherda dialect is in Nigeria. 'Teda' is the name for the people, 'Tedaga' for the language. Muslim. See main entry under Chad.

TEME ***(TEMA)*** [TDO] 4,000 or fewer (1995). Adamawa State, Mayo Belwa LGA, along the banks of the Mayo Belwa River. Niger-Congo, Atlantic-Congo, Volta-Congo, North, Adamawa-Ubangi, Adamawa, Leko-Nimbari, Mumuye-Yandang, Mumuye. Speakers use Hausa or Fulfulde as second language. Some can speak Sate (Kumba), Yendang, or Gengle. Investigation needed: bilingual proficiency in Hausa, attitudes. Literacy rate in second language: Low. Agriculturalists. Traditional religion, Muslim.

TERA [TER] 50,000 (1970 P. Newman). Bauchi State, Yamaltu-Deba LGA; Borno State, Kwayakusar LGA. Afro-Asiatic, Chadic, Biu-Mandara, A, A.1, Western. Dialects: NYIMATLI (NYEMATHI, YAMALTU, NIMALTO, NYIMATALI), PIDLIMDI (HINA, HINNA, GHUNA, GHENA), BURA KOKURA. Dialect cluster. Bilingualism in Hausa. Investigation needed: bilingual proficiency in Hausa, attitudes. Grammar. Agriculturalists: Guinea corn, millet, maize, rice, wheat, orchards; fishermen; weavers. Bible portions 1930.

TESHENAWA [TWC] Jigawa State, Keffin Hausa LGA, Teshena town. Afro-Asiatic, Chadic, West, B, B.1, Bade Proper. Extinct.

THA ***(JOOLE MANGA, KAPAWA)*** [THY] 1,000 or fewer (1998 Kleinewillinghöfer). Taraba State, near Lau. Niger-Congo, Atlantic-Congo, Volta-Congo, North, Adamawa-Ubangi, Adamawa, Waja-Jen, Jen.

TITA ***(HOAI PETEL)*** [TDQ] Taraba State, Jalingo LGA, at Hoai Petel. Niger-Congo, Atlantic-Congo, Volta-Congo, Benue-Congo, Platoid, Benue, Jukunoid, Central, Jukun-Mbembe-Wurbo, Wurbo.

TIV ***("MUNSHI")*** [TIV] 2,212,000 in Nigeria (1991 UBS), 2.5% of the population (1991 SIL). Population total both countries 2,212,000 or more. Benue State, Makurdi, Gwer, Gboko Kwande, Vandeikya, and Katsina Ala LGAs; Plateau State, Lafia LGA; Taraba State, Bali, Takum, and Wukari LGAs. A few in Cameroon. Also spoken in Cameroon. Niger-Congo, Atlantic-Congo, Volta-Congo, Benue-Congo, Bantoid, Southern, Tivoid. Regionally important language. "Munshi" is a perjorative name. Dictionary. Grammar. Used in initial primary education. Christian, traditional religion. Bible 1964.

TORO ***(TURKWAM)*** [TDV] 3,000 to 4,000 (1996 Blench). Nasarawa State, Akwanga LGA, northeast of Wamba, Turkwam village. Niger-Congo, Atlantic-Congo, Volta-Congo, Benue-Congo, Platoid, Plateau. Language maintenance good. They identify culturally with the Kantana.

TSIKIMBA ***(AGAUSHI, AUNA, KIMBA, AKIMBA, KAMBARI, KAMBERRI, KAMBERCHI)*** [KDL] 50,000 (1996). Niger State, Magama and Mariga LGAs, Auna and Wara areas, just west of Kainji Lake on the Niger River. Niger-Congo, Atlantic-Congo, Volta-Congo, Benue-Congo, Kainji, Western, Kambari. Dialects: AGAUNSHE, ASHEN. Part of the Kambari cluster. Closest to Tsishingini and Cishingini, but a separate language. Bilingualism in Hausa, some English, other Kambari languages. All ages. Speakers are called 'Akimba'. Literacy rate in second language: 20% Hausa. Muslim, traditional religion, Christian.

TSISHINGINI ***(KAMBARI, KAMBERRI, KAMBERCHI, SALKA, ASHINGINI)*** [KAM] 80,000 (1996 SIL). Niger State, Magama and Mariga LGAs, Salka area. Niger-Congo, Atlantic-Congo, Volta-Congo, Benue-Congo, Kainji, Western, Kambari. Dialect: IBETO. Speakers have little or no intelligibility with Cishingini and Tsikimba. Bilingualism in Hausa, some English, other Kambari languages. All ages. An important language in the Kambari language cluster, including Cishingini and Tsikimba. Speakers are called 'Ashingini'. Area opened by large dam. Primarily rural. Grammar. Literacy rate in first language: Below 1%. Literacy rate in second language: 15% to 20% Hausa. Christian, Muslim, traditional religion. Bible portions 1933.

TSO ***(LOTSU-PIRI, CIBBO, TSÓBÓ, CUYI TSÓ, PIRE, PIRI, KITTA)*** [LDP] 16,000 (1992 CAPRO). Adamawa State, Numan LGA; Bauchi State, Kaltungo LGA. Niger-Congo, Atlantic-Congo, Volta-Congo, North, Adamawa-Ubangi, Adamawa, Waja-Jen, Waja, Cham-Mona. Dialects: BERBOU, GUSUBOU, SWABOU. Investigation needed: bilingual proficiency in Hausa, attitudes.

TSUVADI ***(AVADI, ABADI, EVADI, KAMBERI, IBETO)*** [TVD] 150,000 (1998). Niger State, Bangi, Kontagora, and Rijau LGAs. Niger-Congo, Atlantic-Congo, Volta-Congo, Benue-Congo, Kainji, Western, Kambari. The people are called 'Avadi'. Literacy rate in second language: 2%. New orthography has been developed. Bible portions 1997.

TULA ***(KOTULE, KUTULE)*** [TUL] 30,000 (1998 Kleinewillinghöfer). Gombe State, Kaltungo LGA, 30 km. east of Billiri. Niger-Congo, Atlantic-Congo, Volta-Congo, North, Adamawa-Ubangi, Adamawa, Waja-Jen, Waja, Tula. Dialects: KUTULE, BAULE, YILI. Several primary and secondary schools. Grammar. Agriculturalists: Guinea corn, maize, peanuts, millet, beans, fruits. Bible portions 1929.

TUMI ***(TUTUMI, KITIMI)*** [KKU] 635 (1949). Kaduna State, Saminaka LGA. Niger-Congo, Atlantic-Congo, Volta-Congo, Benue-Congo, Kainji, Eastern, Northern Jos, Kauru.

TYAP ***(KATAB, KATAF)*** [KCG] 130,000 (1993 SIL). Kaduna State, Kachia, Saminaka, and Jema'a LGAs. Niger-Congo, Atlantic-Congo, Volta-Congo, Benue-Congo, Platoid, Plateau, Central, South-Central. Dialects: KAFANCHAN (FANTUAN, KPASHAN), KACHICHERE (ATICHERAK, DARORO), KATAB (ATYAP, TYAP), KAGORO (AGWOLOK, AGOLOK, AGWOT, AGURO), ATAKAT (ATAKAR, ATTAKA, ATTAKAR, TAKAT), SHOLIO (ASHOLIO, ASOLIO, OSHOLIO, AHOLIO, MARWA, MORWA, MOROA, MARUWA, MAROA). An important district language. Literacy rate in first language: Below 1%. Literacy rate in second language: 25% to 50%. Bible portions 1940.

UBAGHARA [BYC] 30,000 (1985 UBS), including 24,000 Biakpan (1991 UBS). Cross River State, Akampka LGA. Niger-Congo, Atlantic-Congo, Volta-Congo, Benue-Congo, Cross River, Delta Cross, Upper Cross, Central, North-South, Ubaghara-Kohumono, Ubaghara. Dialects: BIAKPAN, IKUN, ETONO, UGBEM, UTUMA (UTAMA, UTAMU). Dialect cluster. Bible portions 1984.

UBANG [UBA] Cross River State, Obudu LGA. Niger-Congo, Atlantic-Congo, Volta-Congo, Benue-Congo, Cross River, Bendi.

UDA [UDA] 10,000 or more (1988). Akwa Ibom State, Mbo LGA. Niger-Congo, Atlantic-Congo, Volta-Congo, Benue-Congo, Cross River, Delta Cross, Lower Cross, Obolo, Enwang-Uda. Listed separately in Crozier and Blench 1992.

UHAMI ***(ISHUA)*** [UHA] 5,498 (1963). Ondo State, Akoko South and Owo LGAs. Niger-Congo, Atlantic-Congo, Volta-Congo, Benue-Congo, Edoid, Northwestern, Osse. Listed separately from Iyayu by Crozier and Blench 1992.

UKAAN ***(IKAN, ANYARAN, AUGA, KAKUMO)*** [KCF] 18,000 (1973 SIL). Ondo State, Akoko North LGA, towns of Kakumo-Akoko, Auga, Ishe; Edo State, Akoko Edo LGA, town of Anyaran, Kakumo-Aworo. Niger-Congo, Atlantic-Congo, Volta-Congo, Benue-Congo, Ukaan. Dialects: ISHE, KAKUMO, AUGA. Yoruba is lingua franca. Investigation needed: bilingual proficiency in Yoruba, attitudes.

UKPE-BAYOBIRI [UKP] 12,000 (1973 SIL). Cross River State, Obudu and Ikom LGAs. Niger-Congo, Atlantic-Congo, Volta-Congo, Benue-Congo, Cross River, Bendi. Dialects: UKPE, BAYOBIRI. Dialect cluster.

UKPET-EHOM ***(AKPET-EHOM)*** [AKD] Cross River State, Akamkpa LGA. Niger-Congo, Atlantic-Congo, Volta-Congo, Benue-Congo, Cross River, Delta Cross, Upper Cross, Akpet. Dialects: UKPET (AKPET), EHOM (UBETENG, EBETENG). A dialect cluster.

UKUE ***(UKPE, EKPENMI, EKPENMEN, EPINMI)*** [UKU] 5,702 (1963). Ondo State, Akoko South LGA. Niger-Congo, Atlantic-Congo, Volta-Congo, Benue-Congo, Edoid, Northwestern, Osse. Related to Ehuen.

UKWA [UKQ] Cross River State, Akampka LGA. Niger-Congo, Atlantic-Congo, Volta-Congo, Benue-Congo, Cross River, Delta Cross, Lower Cross, Obolo, Efik. Listed separately in Crozier and Blench 1992.

UKWUANI-ABOH-NDONI [UKW] 150,000 (1973 SIL). Delta State, Ndokwa LGA; Rivers State, Ahoada LGA. Niger-Congo, Atlantic-Congo, Volta-Congo, Benue-Congo, Igboid, Igbo. Dialects: UKWUANI (UKWANI, UKWALI, KWALE), ABOH (EBOH), NDONI. A dialect cluster within the Igbo language cluster. Investigation needed: bilingual proficiency in Igbo, attitudes. Grammar.

ULUKWUMI [ULB] 10,000 or fewer (1992 Crozier and Blench). Delta State, Aniocha and Oshimili LGAs. Niger-Congo, Atlantic-Congo, Volta-Congo, Benue-Congo, Defoid, Yoruboid, Edekiri.

UMON ***(AMON)*** [UMM] 20,000 or fewer (1995). Cross River State, Akampka LGA, 25 villages. Niger-Congo, Atlantic-Congo, Volta-Congo, Benue-Congo, Cross River, Delta Cross, Upper Cross, Central, North-South, Ubaghara-Kohumono, Kohumono. Bible portions 1895.

UNEME ***(ULEME, ILEME, INEME)*** [UNE] 6,000 (1952). Edo State, Etsako, Agbazko, and Akoko-Edo LGAs. Niger-Congo, Atlantic-Congo, Volta-Congo, Benue-Congo, Edoid, North-Central, Ghotuo-Uneme-Yekhee.

URHOBO ***(BIOTU, "SOBO")*** [URH] 546,000 (1993 Johnstone). Delta State, Ethiope and Ughelli LGAs. Niger-Congo, Atlantic-Congo, Volta-Congo, Benue-Congo, Edoid, Southwestern. Dialect: AGBARHO. Formerly called "Sobo", which is offensive. Used in initial primary education. Bible 1977.

USAGHADE ***(USAKADE, USAKEDET, ISANGELE)*** [USK] Cross River State, Odukpani LGA, half of a village. In and around Calabar. Niger-Congo, Atlantic-Congo, Volta-Congo, Benue-Congo, Cross River, Delta Cross, Lower Cross, Obolo, Usaghade. Listed separately in Crozier and Blench 1992. See main entry under Cameroon.

UVBIE ***("EVHRO", UVHRIA, UVWIE, EVRIE, EFFURUN)*** [EVH] 6,000 (1952). Delta State, Ethiope LGA. Niger-Congo, Atlantic-Congo, Volta-Congo, Benue-Congo, Edoid, Southwestern. Related to Urhobo. The name "Evhro" is offensive. Investigation needed: intelligibility with Urhobo, attitudes.

UZEKWE ***(EZEKWE)*** [EZE] 5,000 (1973 SIL). Cross River State, Ogoja LGA. Niger-Congo, Atlantic-Congo, Volta-Congo, Benue-Congo, Cross River, Delta Cross, Upper Cross, Central, North-South, Koring-Kukele, Kukele.

VAGHAT-YA-BIJIM-LEGERI ***(KWANKA)*** [BIJ] 223,859 (1990). Plateau State, Mangu and Pankshin LGAs; Bauchi State, Tafawa Balewa LGA. Niger-Congo, Atlantic-Congo, Volta-Congo, Benue-Congo, Platoid, Plateau, Western, Southwestern, A. Dialects: VAGHAT (TIVAGHAT, KADUN, KWANKA), YA (TIYA, BOI), BIJIM, LEGERI. Dialect cluster. Investigation needed: bilingual proficiency in Hausa, attitudes. Traditional religion, Christian.

VEMGO-MABAS [VEM] 10,000 in Nigeria (1993). Population total both countries 15,000 or fewer. Adamawa State, Michika LGA, Madagali district. Also spoken in Cameroon. Afro-Asiatic, Chadic, Biu-Mandara, A, A.4, Lamang. Dialects: VEMGO, MABAS, VISIK (VIZIK). 56% intelligibility of Lamang, 36% intelligibility of Hedi. 78% lexical similarity with Hedi, 64% with Lamang, 50% with Gevoko. Speakers use Fulfulde, Mafa, or Wula (Psikye) as second language. Some speak Hedi. 'Maya' may be an alternate name. Different from Maba of Chad. Investigation needed: bilingual proficiency in Mafa, Hedi, Fulfulde, attitudes. Pastoralists, agriculturalists. Traditional religion, Christian.

VITI ***(VÖTÖ)*** [VIT] Taraba State, Sardauna LGA, Antere. Niger-Congo, Atlantic-Congo, Volta-Congo, Benue-Congo, Bantoid, Southern, Wide Grassfields, Narrow Grassfields, Unclassified.

VONO ***(KIBALLO, KIWOLLO)*** [KCH] 500 (1973 SIL). Kaduna State, Saminaka LGA. Niger-Congo, Atlantic-Congo, Volta-Congo, Benue-Congo, Kainji, Eastern, Northern Jos, Kauru. Investigation needed: bilingual proficiency in Hausa, attitudes.

VORO ***(EBINA, EBUNA, BUNA, BENA, WORO, YUNGUR)*** [VOR] Adamawa State, Guyuk and Song LGAs, south of the Dumne road, Waltande and associated hamlets. Niger-Congo, Atlantic-Congo, Volta-Congo, North, Adamawa-Ubangi, Adamawa, Waja-Jen, Yungur, Yungur-Roba.

VUTE ***(MBUTE, MBUTERE, BUTE, WUTE, FUTE, BUTI, BABUTE, MFUTI, WETERE, VUTERE)*** [VUT] 1,000 or fewer in Nigeria (1973 SIL). Taraba State, Sardauna LGA, Northeast Mambila Plateau. Niger-Congo, Atlantic-Congo, Volta-Congo, Benue-Congo, Bantoid, Northern, Mambiloid, Suga-Vute, Vute. Bible portions 1988. See main entry under Cameroon.

WAJA ***(WIYAA, WUYA, NYAN WIYAU)*** [WJA] 60,000 (1989 Kleinewillinghöfer). Gombe State, Balanga, Akko, Yamaltu Deba LGAs; Adamawa State, northern Michika LGA; Borno State, Gwoza LGA; Taraba State, Bali LGA. Niger-Congo, Atlantic-Congo, Volta-Congo, North, Adamawa-Ubangi, Adamawa, Waja-Jen, Waja, Tula. Dialects: DERUWO (WAJAN DUTSE), WAJA (WAJAN KASA). Only small dialect differences. Bilingualism in Fulfulde. Grammar. Agriculturalists: wheat, Guinea corn, maize, rice; hunters; animal husbandry: cattle, goats, sheep. Traditional religion, Christian, Muslim. Bible portions 1926-1935.

WAKA [WAV] 5,000 or more (1992). Taraba State, Karim Lamido LGA. Niger-Congo, Atlantic-Congo, Volta-Congo, North, Adamawa-Ubangi, Adamawa, Leko-Nimbari, Mumuye-Yandang, Mumuye.

WANDALA ***(MANDARA, NDARA)*** [MFI] 20,000 in Nigeria (1993), including 10,000 Gamargu, 9,300 Kirawa. Borno State, Damboa, Bama, Gwoza, and Konduga LGAs. Afro-Asiatic, Chadic, Biu-Mandara, A, A.4, Mandara Proper, Mandara. Dialects: KAMBURWAMA, MASFEIMA, JAMPALAM, ZIOGBA, MAZAGWA, GWANJE, GAMARGU (GAMERGU, MALGO, MALGWA), KIRAWA. Dialect cluster. Grammar. Muslim, traditional religion. NT 1988. See main entry under Cameroon.

WANNU ***(ABINSI, JUKUN ABINSI, RIVER JUKUN)*** [JUB] A few thousand (1998 Storch). Gongola State, Makurdi Division, Iharev District at Abinsi. Niger-Congo, Atlantic-Congo, Volta-Congo, Benue-Congo, Platoid, Benue, Jukunoid, Central, Jukun-Mbembe-Wurbo, Kororofa. In Kororofa language cluster. Investigation needed: bilingual proficiency in Hausa, attitudes. Traditional religion.

WAPAN ***(JUKUN WUKARI, WUKARI, WAKARI, WAPÃ, JUKUN WAPAN, JUKU, JUKUM, JUKON, JUKU JUNKUN, JINKUM)*** [JUK] 100,000 (1994 UBS). Taraba State, Wukari LGA; Plateau State, Shendam and Langtang LGAs; Nasarawa State, Lafia and Awe LGAs. Niger-Congo, Atlantic-Congo, Volta-Congo, Benue-Congo, Platoid, Benue, Jukunoid, Central, Jukun-Mbembe-Wurbo, Kororofa. Dialect: WUKAN. In the Kororofa language cluster. Traditional religion. NT 1994.

WARJI ***(WARJA, WARJAWA, SAR, SARAWA)*** [WJI] 65,000 to 70,000 (1995 CAPRO). Bauchi State, Ningi LGA; Jigawa State, Birnin Kudu LGA. Afro-Asiatic, Chadic, West, B, B.2. Gala may be a dialect. Speakers are shifting to Hausa. Investigation needed: bilingual proficiency in Hausa, attitudes. Literacy rate in second language: 10%. Agriculturalists: Guinea corn, maize, peanuts, beans, rice, millet, wheat, onions, pepper, tomato. Traditional religion, Muslim, Christian.

WASE ***(JUKUN WASE)*** [JUW] 1,000 to 2,000 (1998 Storch). Plateau State, Shendam, Wase, and Langtang LGAs. Niger-Congo, Atlantic-Congo, Volta-Congo, Benue-Congo, Platoid, Benue, Jukunoid, Central, Jukun-Mbembe-Wurbo, Jukun. In Jukun language cluster. Investigation needed: bilingual proficiency in Hausa, attitudes. Traditional religion.

WOM ***(PERE, PEREMA, PEREBA)*** [WOM] 5,000 (1992 Crozier and Blench). Adamawa State, Fufore LGA. Niger-Congo, Atlantic-Congo, Volta-Congo, North, Adamawa-Ubangi, Adamawa, Leko-Nimbari, Leko. Closely related to Samba Leko. It is reported that they intermarry with Mom Jango speakers. 'Wom' is a town name. Investigation needed: intelligibility with Samba Leko, attitudes. Traditional religion, Christian, Muslim.

XEDI ***(HDI, HEDI, HIDE, TURU-HIDE, TUR, TURU, TOUROU, FTOUR)*** [TUR] 9,000 in Nigeria (1992 CAPRO). Population total both countries 10,000. Borno State, Gwoza LGA; Adamawa State, Michika LGA; along the Cameroon border, across from Tourou; part of one village. Also spoken in Cameroon. Afro-Asiatic, Chadic, Biu-Mandara, A, A.4, Lamang. In Nigeria the name 'Xedi' is preferred, in Cameroon 'Hdi'. Little education. 1 primary school. Mountain slope. Agriculturalists: Guinea corn, beans, millet. Traditional religion, Christian, Muslim.

YACE ***(YACHE, YATYE, IYACE, EKPARI)*** [EKR] 10,000 (1982 UBS). Cross River State, Ogoja LGA. Niger-Congo, Atlantic-Congo, Volta-Congo, Benue-Congo, Idomoid, Yatye-Akpa. Dialects: ALIFOKPA, IJIEGU. 84% lexical similarity with Akpa. Bible portions 1980.

YALA ***(IYALA)*** [YBA] 50,000 (1973 SIL). Cross River State, Ogoja, Obubra, and Ikom LGAs. Niger-Congo, Atlantic-Congo, Volta-Congo, Benue-Congo, Idomoid, Akweya, Etulo-Idoma, Idoma. Dialects: NKUM (YALA IKOM), NKUM AKPAMBE (YALA OBUBRA), YALA OGOJA. Grammar. NT 1979.

YAMBA ***(MBEM, "KAKA")*** [YAM] A few in Nigeria (1990 Blench). Taraba State, Sardauna and Gashaka LGAs, Antere and other border villages. Niger-Congo, Atlantic-Congo, Volta-Congo, Benue-Congo, Bantoid, Southern, Wide Grassfields, Narrow Grassfields, Mbam-Nkam, Nkambe. NT 1992. See main entry under Cameroon.

YANGKAM ***(YANKAM, BASHARAWA, BASHIRI, BASHAR)*** [BSX] 100 (1996 Blench). Plateau State, Kanam, Langtang, and Wase LGAs, west of Bashar, 25 km. north of Jarme on the Amper-Bashar road. 4 villages: Tukur, Bayar, Pyaksam, and Kiram; and 2 elderly men in Yuli, 15 km. northwest of Bashar. Niger-Congo, Atlantic-Congo, Volta-Congo, Benue-Congo, Platoid, Benue, Tarokoid. Closely related to Pe. Bilingualism in Hausa. All over 50 years old (1996). Most have shifted to Hausa, while still retaining their Bashar identity. Heavily influenced by 19th century slave raids. Muslim.

YEKHEE ***(ETSAKO, ETSAKOR, AFENMAI, IYEKHEE, "KUKURUKU")*** [ETS] 274,000 (1995 UBS). Edo State, Etsako, Agbako, and Okpebho LGAs. Niger-Congo, Atlantic-Congo, Volta-Congo, Benue-Congo, Edoid, North-Central, Ghotuo-Uneme-Yekhee. Dialects: AUCHI, UZAIRUE, SOUTH IBIE (SOUTH IVBIE), UWEPA-UWANO (WEPPA WANO), AVIANWU (FUGAR), AVIELE, IVHIADAOBI, EKPERI. Not all speakers of the language recognize 'Yekhee' as the name of the language; some prefer 'Etsako'. However, 'Etsako' is not the only language listed as being spoken in Etsako LGA. The name "Kukuruku" is derogatory. NT, in press (1997).

YENDANG ***(YENDAM, YANDANG, NYANDANG, YUNDUM)*** [YEN] 62,640 (1987). Adamawa State, Mayo Belwa and Numan LGAs; Taraba State, Yoro, Jalingo, Zing, and Karim Lamido LGAs. Niger-Congo, Atlantic-Congo, Volta-Congo, North, Adamawa-Ubangi, Adamawa, Leko-Nimbari, Mumuye-Yandang, Yandang. Dialects: KUSEKI, YOFO, POLI (AKULE, YAKULE), YOTI. Bilingualism in Hausa, Fulfulde, Mumuye, English. Investigation needed: bilingual proficiency in Hausa, attitudes. Agriculturalists, animal husbandry.

YESKWA ***(YASGUA)*** [YES] 13,000 (1973 SIL). Kaduna State, Jema'a LGA; Nasarawa State, Keffi LGA. Niger-Congo, Atlantic-Congo, Volta-Congo, Benue-Congo, Platoid, Plateau, Western, Northwestern, Koro.

YIWOM ***(GERKA, GERKAWA, GERKANCHI, GURKA)*** [GEK] 8,000 (1973 SIL). Plateau State, Shendam and Langtang South LGAs. Afro-Asiatic, Chadic, West, A, A.3, Yiwom. Investigation needed: bilingual proficiency in Hausa, attitudes. Radio programs.

YORUBA ***(YOOBA, YARIBA)*** [YOR] 18,850,000 in Nigeria (1993 Johnstone). Population total all countries 20,000,000 (1991 UBS). Including second language speakers: 22,000,000 (1999 WA). Most of Oyo, Ogun, Ondo Osun, Kwara, and Lagos states; and western LGAs of Kogi State. Also spoken in Benin, Togo, United Kingdom, USA. Niger-Congo, Atlantic-Congo, Volta-Congo, Benue-Congo, Defoid, Yoruboid, Edekiri. Dialects: OYO, IJESHA, ILA, IJEBU, ONDO, WO, OWE, JUMU, IWORRO, IGBONNA, YAGBA, GBEDDE, EGBA, AKONO, AWORO, BUNU (BINI), EKITI, ILAJE, IKALE, AWORI. Official language. Grammar. SVO. Literacy rate in second language: 35%. Roman. Newspapers, radio programs, TV. Christian, Muslim, traditional religion. Bible 1884-1966.

YUKUBEN ***(NYIKUBEN, NYIKOBE, AYIKIBEN, BORITSU, BALAABE, BALAABEN, OOHUM, UUHUM, UUHUM-GIGI, UHUMKHEGI)*** [YBL] 15,000 in Nigeria (1992). Population total both countries 16,000. Taraba State, Takum LGA, between the Katsina Ala and Gamana rivers. About 20 villages in Nigeria. Also spoken in Cameroon. Niger-Congo, Atlantic-Congo, Volta-Congo, Benue-Congo, Platoid, Benue, Jukunoid, Yukuben-Kuteb. Speakers use Jukun, Kuteb (in areas close to Kuteb), or Hausa as second languages. Many women, especially in the mountains, do not understand Hausa. Trade language. Traditional religion, Christian.

ZANGWAL ***(ZWANGAL, TWAR)*** [ZAH] 100 (1993). Bauchi State, Bauchi LGA. Afro-Asiatic, Chadic, West, B, B.3, Guruntum. Investigation needed: bilingual proficiency in Hausa, attitudes. Agriculturalists: millet, peanuts, Guinea corn. Muslim.

ZARI ***(ZARIWA)*** [ZAZ] 21,000 or more including 20,000 Zakshi (1995 CAPRO), 1,000 Boto (1950). Bauchi State, Toro, Dass, and Tafawa Balewa LGAs, and Plateau State. Afro-Asiatic, Chadic, West, B, B.3, Zaar Proper. Dialects: ZAKSHI (ZAKSA), BOTO (BOOT, BIBOT), ZARI (KOPTI, KWAPM). In the Zari dialect cluster in the Barawa language cluster. Investigation needed: bilingual proficiency in Hausa, attitudes. Traditional religion, Muslim, Christian.

ZARMA ***(DYERMA, DYARMA, DYABARMA, ZABARMA, ADZERMA, DJERMA, ZARBARMA, ZERMA)*** [DJE] 50,000 in Nigeria (1973 SIL). Kebbi State, Argungu, Birnin Kebbi, and Bunza LGAs; Niger State. Nilo-Saharan, Songhai, Southern. Muslim. Bible 1990. See main entry under Niger.

ZEEM [ZUA] Bauchi State, Toro LGA. Afro-Asiatic, Chadic, West, B, B.3, Zaar Proper. Dialects: ZEEM (TULAI), DANSHE (CHAARI), LUSHI (LUKSHI, DOKSHI). The Zeem dialect cluster in the Barawa language cluster. Investigation needed: bilingual proficiency in Hausa, attitudes.

ZHIRE ***(KENYI)*** [ZHI] Kaduna State, Kachia and Jema'a LGAs. Niger-Congo, Atlantic-Congo, Volta-Congo, Benue-Congo, Platoid, Plateau, Western, Northwestern, Jaba. Related to Ham. Investigation needed: bilingual proficiency in Hausa, attitudes.

ZIRIYA ***(JIRIYA)*** [ZIR] Bauchi State, Toro LGA, Kere and Ziriya. Niger-Congo, Atlantic-Congo, Volta-Congo, Benue-Congo, Kainji, Eastern, Northern Jos, Jera. Nearly extinct.

ZIZILIVAKAN ***(ZIZILIVEKEN, ZILIVA, ÀMZÍRÍV, FALI OF JILBU)*** [ZIZ] Adamawa State, Mubi LGA, Jilbu town, near Cameroon border. Afro-Asiatic, Chadic, Biu-Mandara, A, A.8. People are called 'Fali of Jilbu'. Muslim. See main entry under Cameroon.

ZUMBUN ***(JIMBIN, JIMBINAWA)*** [JMB] 2,000 (1995 CAPRO). Bauchi State, Darazo LGA, Jimbim settlement. Afro-Asiatic, Chadic, West, B, B.2. Investigation needed: bilingual proficiency in Hausa, attitudes. Traditional religion.

REUNION

French Department of Réunion. National or official language: French. 682,000 (1998 UN). Literacy rate 61.2% (1975 WA). Also includes Comorian 17,000, Gujarati, Malagasy 8,000, Chinese 21,000. Information mainly from J. Holm 1989. Christian, Muslim. Data accuracy estimate: B. The number of languages listed for Reunion is 3. Of those, all are living languages. Diversity index 0.09.

FRENCH [FRN] 2,400 in Réunion (1993 Johnstone). Including second language speakers: 160,500 in Réunion, 30% of the population (1986). Indo-European, Italic, Romance, Italo-Western, Western, Gallo-Iberian, Gallo-Romance, Gallo-Rhaetian, Oïl, French. Official language. Bible 1530-1986. See main entry under France.

RÉUNION CREOLE FRENCH [RCF] 554,500 in Réunion (1987 estimate), or 91% of the population (1982 Barrett). Population total all countries 595,000. Also spoken in Comoros Islands, Madagascar. Creole, French based. Two dialects: urban and popular; the former is closer to French, the latter more similar to Bantu and West African languages. Education is in French. 25% of the speakers are white, poor, living in the mountainous interior, and speak archaic highland varieties. 25% are Indian, live in the coastal lowlands, and speak the basilect or deep creole. 45% are African and mixed, live in the coastal lowlands, and speak the basilect. The creole is gaining status on Réunion. Dictionary. Sugar, perfume production.

TAMIL [TCV] Possibly including second language speakers: 120,000 in Réunion (1991 Froise). Dravidian, Southern, Tamil-Kannada, Tamil-Kodagu, Tamil-Malayalam, Tamil. 90% describe themselves as of Indian origin. Hindu. Bible 1727-1995. See main entry under India.

RWANDA

Republic of Rwanda. Republika y'u Rwanda. Formerly part of Ruanda-Urundi. National or official languages: Rwanda, English, French. 6,604,000 (1998 UN). Literacy rate 50%. Also includes Hema, Rundi, Swahili. Information mainly from J. Bendor-Samuel 1989. Christian, Muslim, traditional religion. Blind population 12,000 (1982 WCE). Data accuracy estimate: B. The number of languages listed for Rwanda is 3. Of those, all are living languages. Diversity index 0.00.

ENGLISH [ENG] Mainly second language speakers. Indo-European, Germanic, West, English. There may be more users of English than of French. Official language. Bible 1535-1989. See main entry under United Kingdom.

FRENCH [FRN] Indo-European, Italic, Romance, Italo-Western, Western, Gallo-Iberian, Gallo-Romance, Gallo-Rhaetian, Oïl, French. Official language. Bible 1530-1986. See main entry under France.

RWANDA ***(RUANDA, KINYARWANDA, IKINYARWANDA, ORUNYARWANDA, URUNYARUANDA)*** [RUA] 6,491,700 in Rwanda, 98.3% (1998). Population total all countries 7,362,800. Also spoken in Burundi, DRC, Tanzania, Uganda. Niger-Congo, Atlantic-Congo, Volta-Congo, Benue-Congo, Bantoid, Southern, Narrow Bantu, Central, J, Rwanda-Rundi (J.60). Dialects: IGIKIGA (KIGA, TSHIGA), BUFUMBWA, HUTU (LERA, ULULERA, HERA, NDARA, SHOBYO, TSHOGO, NDOGO), RUTWA (TWA). Intelligible with Rundi. Hima is an ethnic group speaking Rwanda or Rundi, not a language. Ethnic groups: Hutu 89%, Tutsi 10%, Twa (pygmies, 30,000; 1972 Barrett) 1%. Possibly 75% of the BaTwa killed in the 1994 war. National language. SVO. Christian, traditional religion, Muslim; Twa: traditional religion, Christian. Bible 1954-1993.

SÃO TOMÉ E PRÍNCIPE

Democratic Republic of São Tomé and Príncipe. República Democrática de São Tomé e Príncipe. National or official languages: Portuguese, Sãotomense, Principense. 141,000 (1998 UN). Literacy rate 50% to 74%. Also includes Fang 12,000, people from Angola, Cape Verde, Mozambique. Information mainly from J. Holm 1989; P. Maurer 1995; G. Lorenzino 1999; S. and T. Graham 1998. Christian. Data accuracy estimate: B. The number of languages listed for São Tomé e Príncipe is 4. Of those, all are living languages. Diversity index 0.37.

ANGOLAR ***(NGOLA)*** [AOA] 5,000 (1998 S. and T. Graham). Angolar is spoken on the southern tip of São Tomé Island. Most are around the town of São João dos Angolares, and some in the southern region of Caué. Creole, Portuguese based. The substratum was largely Kwa and Western Bantu languages; quite distinct from the creoles of Guinea-Bissau, Senegal, Gambia, and Cape Verde. The 33% of the Angolar lexicon not shared with São Tomense is largely of Bantu origin, apparently KiMbundu of Angola, with some from Kongo, Bini, and Ndingi. Angolar shares 70% lexical similarity with São Tomense, 67% with Principense, 53% with Annobonese. Some Angolares speak São Tomense also, and are tending to be absorbed into the Forros. Many speak Portuguese, but many are not comfortable in speaking it. Home and community social life. The Angolares are a distinct ethnolinguistic group from the Forros ('freedmen'). Grammar. Tonal. Literacy rate in second language: 50% Portuguese. Christian.

PORTUGUESE [POR] 2,580 in São Tomé (1993). Indo-European, Italic, Romance, Italo-Western, Western, Gallo-Iberian, Ibero-Romance, West Iberian, Portuguese-Galician. Used by many people as their primary language until their late 20s, when they become more active in São Tomense society, and relearn São Tomense, the language of social networks above age 30. Used as a second language by some people. Official language. Bible 1751, in press (1993). See main entry under Portugal.

PRINCIPENSE ***(LUN'GWIYE, "MONCÓ")*** [PRE] Few speakers out of 1,558 Principenses on Príncipe (1999 S. Graham). On Príncipe Island. Creole, Portuguese based. The substratum was largely Kwa and Western Bantu languages; quite distinct from the creoles of Guinea-Bissau, Senegal, Gambia, and Cape Verde. Principense shares 77% lexical similarity with São Tomense, 67% with Angolar, 62% with Annobonese. Most speak Portuguese, and some learn Sãotomense. Speakers are elderly. National language. Nearly extinct.

SÃOTOMENSE ***(SÃO TOMENSE)*** [CRI] 69,899 (1999 S. Graham). São Tomense is spoken on São Tomé Island, all but the southern tip. Creole, Portuguese based. The substratum was largely Kwa and Western Bantu languages; quite distinct from the creoles of Guinea-Bissau, Senegal, Gambia, and Cape Verde. Sãotomense shares 77% lexical similarity with Principense, and 62% with Fa D'Ambu (Annobonese), 70% with Angolar. Most speak Portuguese. Some elderly women may not understand Portuguese adequately. The language of social identity in most São Tomé social networks for age 30 and above. The Angolares are a distinct ethnolinguistic group from the Forros ('freedmen'), Sãotomense speakers also on São Tomé Island. Most Angolares speak Sãotomense also, and are tending to be absorbed into the Forros. National language. Literacy rate in second language: 50% Portuguese.

SENEGAL

Republic of Senegal. République du Sénégal. National or official languages: National: Jola-Fogny, Malinke, Mandinka, Pulaar, Serer-Sine, Soninke, Wolof; Official: French. 9,003,000 (1998 UN). Literacy rate 21.7% (1988 census), 28.6% men, 15.6% women. Also includes Bambara 66,500, Hassaniyya 5,000, Kabuverdianu 25,000, Krio, Vietnamese. Information mainly from D. Sapir 1971; Atlas National du Senegal 1977; J. Lopis 1980; A. Barry 1987; J. Bendor-Samuel 1989; G. Williams 1993; B. Hopkins 1995. Muslim, traditional religion, Christian. Blind population 22,000 (1982 WCE). Deaf institutions: 6. Data accuracy estimate: A2, B. The number of languages listed for Senegal is 36. Of those, all are living languages. Diversity index 0.77.

BADJARA ***(BADYARA, BADIAN, BADJARANKE, PAJADE, PAJADINCA, PAJADINKA, GOLA, BIGOLA)*** [PBP] 1,500 in Senegal (1998). South central, one village that is all Bajara. Niger-Congo, Atlantic-Congo, Atlantic, Northern, Eastern Senegal-Guinea, Tenda. Biafada is the closest language, with 52% lexical similarity. The speakers may use Mandinka as second language. Muslim. See main entry under Guinea.

BAINOUK-GUNYAAMOLO ***(BANYUM, BANYUN, BAGNOUN, BANHUM, BAINUK, BANYUK, BANYUNG, ELOMAY, ELUNAY, ÑUÑ)*** [BCZ] 5,000 in Senegal (1998). North of the Casamance River in the triangle formed by the towns of Bignona, Tobor, and Niamone, north of Ziguinchor, across the Casamance River. Also spoken in Gambia. Niger-Congo, Atlantic-Congo, Atlantic, Northern, Eastern Senegal-Guinea, Banyun. Dialects: GUJAAXET, GUNYAMOOLO. Two dialects are intelligible to each other's speakers: the one around Niamone (Gunyaamolo) and the other around Tobor. Closely related to Kobiana and Kasanga of Guinea-Bissau. More closely related to the Tenda languages of eastern Senegal than to the neighboring Diola and Balanta. Gunyuño in Guinea-Bissau is distinct. Literacy rate in first language: Below 1%. Muslim, traditional religion, Christian.

BAINOUK-SAMIK [BCB] 1,500 (1998). Mainly in Samik and surrounding villages, on the south side of the Casamance River, about 20 km. east of Ziguinchor; also in some scattered villages north and east of Samik. Niger-Congo, Atlantic-Congo, Atlantic, Northern, Eastern Senegal-Guinea, Banyun. A different language from Gunyaamolo-Bainouk in Senegal and Gambia, and Bainouk-Gunyuño in Guinea-Bissau.

BALANTA-GANJA ***(FJAA, BALANT, BALANTE, BALANDA, BALLANTE, BELANTE, BULANDA, BRASSA, ALANTE, FRAASE)*** [BJT] 94,500 (1998). Southwest corner of Senegal, south of the Casamance River, between Goudomp and Tanaff, and south from there. Niger-Congo, Atlantic-Congo, Atlantic, Northern, Bak, Balant-Ganja. Dialects: FGANJA (GANJA), FJAALIB (BLIP). A separate language from Balanta-Kentohe in Guinea-Bissau. Speakers are fairly bilingual in Mandinka. Investigation needed: intelligibility with Naga, Mane. Literacy rate in first language: Below 1%. Traditional religion, Christian.

BANDIAL ***(BANJAAL)*** [BQJ] 9,000 (1998 B. Hopkins). Villages of Affiniam, Badiate-Grand, Bandial, Brin, Enampor, Essil, Etama, Kamobeul, and Seleky. The area is bounded by the Casamance River on the north, the Komobeul Bôlon on the west, the Ziguinchor-Oussouye road on the south, and the Brin-Nyassia road on the east. The only village north of the Casamance River is Affiniam. Niger-Congo, Atlantic-Congo, Atlantic, Northern, Bak, Jola, Jola Proper, Jola Central, Gusilay. Dialects: AFFINIAM, ELUN (HULON, KULUUNAAY). More intelligible with Bandial than with Gusilay. Affiniam has 74% lexical similarity with Bandial and 66% with Gusilaay. Bilingualism in Jola Fogny, Jola Kasa, Mandinka, Pulaar, Wolof. Literacy rate in first language: Below 1%.

BASARI ***(BASSARI, TENDA BASARI, BIYAN, ONIAN, AYAN, WO)*** [BSC] 7,850 in Senegal (1998). Population total all countries 16,900. Southeastern, Upper Casamance, around Edun, border areas, Kedougou, Tambacounda. Also spoken in Guinea, Guinea-Bissau. Niger-Congo, Atlantic-Congo, Atlantic, Northern, Eastern Senegal-Guinea, Tenda. Closely related language: Budik. 'Tenda' is used as a cover term for Basari, Badjara, Konyagi, Budik. High mortality rate. Women intermarry with men from Fulbe and other groups; children become part of the other group. Trading is carried on with the Fulbe. Literacy rate in first language: Below 1%. Traditionally hunter-gatherers; now agriculturalists: millet, peanuts, fonyo, beans; in cities: bamboo fence makers, domestic help. Traditional religion, Christian. NT 1988.

BAYOT ***(BAIOTE, BAIOT, BAYOTTE)*** [BDA] 13,000 in Senegal (1999). Population total all countries 14,800. A cluster of villages about 12 km. southwest of Ziguinchor, grouped around the village of Nyassia. Also spoken in Gambia, Guinea-Bissau. Niger-Congo, Atlantic-Congo, Atlantic, Northern, Bak, Jola, Bayot. Dialect: ESSIN. 15% to 18% lexical similarity with other Jola varieties (closest). Essin and Bayot form a cluster that needs further investigation. Speakers use Jola-Kasa as second language, some Wolof, and perhaps Mankanya or Mandjak. Investigation needed: intelligibility with Essin. Literacy rate in first language: Below 1%. Traditional religion, Christian.

BUDIK ***(BEDIK, TANDANKE, TENDANKE, TENDA, BANDE, BASARI DU BANDEMBA)*** [TNR] 3,000 (1998 NTM). Southeastern. Niger-Congo, Atlantic-Congo, Atlantic, Northern, Eastern Senegal-Guinea, Tenda. Close to Basari. Reported to be a creole with elements from Basari, Peul, and other languages. Dictionary. Literacy rate in first language: Below 1%. Traditional religion, Christian. Bible portions 1997.

CRIOULO, UPPER GUINEA ***(PORTUGUESE CREOLE, KRIULO)*** [POV] 46,500 in Senegal (1998). Ziguinchor, Bignona, and Kolda. It overlaps from Guinea-Bissau and the Bijagos Islands. Creole, Portuguese based. Dialect: CACHEU-ZIGUINCHOR CREOLE. The Senegal dialect is a little different than Guinea-Bissau, with some Pidgin French vocabulary. Intelligible with Guinea-Bissau Creole. Literacy rate in first language: Below 1%. Christian. Bible, in press (1997). See main entry under Guinea-Bissau.

EJAMAT ***(EDIAMAT, FULUP, FELOUP, FELUP, FELUPE, FLOUP, FLUP)*** [EJA] 1,800 in Senegal (1998 B. Hopkins SIL). Extreme southern Senegal, a handful of villages 5 to 7 km. due south of Oussouye, including Kahem, Efok, Youtou. Niger-Congo, Atlantic-Congo, Atlantic, Northern, Bak, Jola, Jola Proper, Jola Central, Her-Ejamat. A distinct language from other Jola varieties. 63% lexical similarity between Her-Ejamat and Jola-Fogny or Jola-Kasa; 50% with Gusilay or Elun. They may use Jola-Kasa and Wolof as second languages. Investigation needed: bilingual proficiency. Literacy rate in first language: Below 1%. See main entry under Guinea-Bissau.

FRENCH [FRN] Indo-European, Italic, Romance, Italo-Western, Western, Gallo-Iberian, Gallo-Romance, Gallo-Rhaetian, Oïl, French. Official language. Bible 1530-1986. See main entry under France.

FUUTA JALON ***(FUTA JALLON, FOUTA DYALON, FULLO FUUTA, FUTA FULA)*** [FUF] 121,000 in Senegal (1998). Niger-Congo, Atlantic-Congo, Atlantic, Northern, Senegambian, Fula-Wolof, Fulani, West Central. Looked upon as outsiders in Senegal. Large numbers from Guinea have settled or work seasonally in Casamance, eastern Senegal, and Dakar. Grammar. Literacy rate in first language: Below 1%. Muslim. Bible portions 1929-1975. See main entry under Guinea.

GUSILAY ***(KUSIILAAY, GUSILAAY, GUSIILAY, KUSILAY)*** [GSL] 12,400 (1998). Village of Tionk Essil, between Tendouck and Mlomp-North. Niger-Congo, Atlantic-Congo, Atlantic, Northern, Bak, Jola, Jola Proper, Jola Central, Gusilay. Bilingualism in Jola-Fogny, Wolof, Mandinka, Pulaar. Investigation needed: intelligibility with dialects. Literacy rate in first language: Below 1%.

JALUNGA ***(YALUNKA, YALUNKE, JALONKÉ, DYALONKE, DJALLONKE, DIALONKÉ)*** [YAL] 10,000 in Senegal (1998 S. Hejnar NTM). Southeastern, intersection of Mali, Guinea, and Senegal borders. Niger-Congo, Mande, Western, Central-Southwestern, Central, Susu-Yalunka. Close to Susu, but only marginally intelligible. Called 'Yalunka' in other countries. Muslim. NT 1976. See main entry under Guinea.

JOLA-FOGNY ***(DIOLA-FOGNY, DYOLA, JÓOLA, JOLA, YOLA)*** [DYO] 260,000 in Senegal including 186,000 Fogny, 74,000 Buluf (1998 B. Hopkins SIL). Population total both countries 313,000 (1998). Area surrounding the city of Bignona, bounded on the south by the Casamance River, on the north by a strip just north of the Senegal-Gambia border, on the west by the Diouloulou Marigot tributary, and on the east by the Soungrougrou River. Also in an area 15 to 20 km. east and southeast of Ziguinchor, the regional capital. Also spoken in Gambia. Niger-Congo, Atlantic-Congo, Atlantic, Northern, Bak, Jola, Jola Proper, Jola Central, Jola-Fogny. Dialects: BULUF, FOGNY, KOMBO, KALOUNAYE, NARANG. Gusilaay, Kwatay, Karon, Mlomp, Kerak, Ejamat, and Bayot are more distantly related languages, but they are close geographically. Jola-Fogny is the largest Jola variety and the most widely understood. 68% lexical similarity with Jola-Kasa. Recognized by the government as one of six national languages. Buluf seems to have many lexical items different from Fogny, but Buluf speakers are willing to learn to read Fogny. A different language from Jula (Dioula, Dyoula, Dyula) of Mali, Burkina Faso, and Côte d'Ivoire, which is Mande. National language. Dictionary. Grammar. Literacy rate in first language: Below 1%. Intensive agriculturalists: wet rice, millet, peanuts. Traditional religion, Muslim, Christian.

JOLA-KASA ***(DIOLA-KASA, CASA, JÓOLA-KASA)*** [CSK] 36,300 (1998). Villages around the city of Oussouye and north to the Casamance River, bounded by the Kamobeul Bôlon tributary on the east and the Kachiouane Bôlon on the west. It also includes the villages of Hitou and Niamoun north of the Casamance River. Also spoken in Gambia. Niger-Congo, Atlantic-Congo, Atlantic, Northern, Bak, Jola, Jola Proper, Jola Central, Jola-Kasa. Dialects: AYUN, ESULALU (ESUULAALUR, OUSSOUYE, MLOMP SOUTH), FLUVIAL, HULUF, SELEK, BLISS (NIOMOUN). Closely related to, but a distinct language from Jola-Fogny. Grammar. Literacy rate in first language: Below 1% to 5%. Bible portions 1961-1995.

KARON [KRX] 8,060 (1998). Population total both countries 9,300. Southwest Senegal along the coast, south of Diouloulou and surrounding the town of Kafountine. Bounded on the west by the Atlantic Ocean, on the south by the Kalisseye Inlet, on the east by the Diouloulou Marigot Estuary, and on the north by the Senegal-Gambia border. Also spoken in Gambia. Niger-Congo, Atlantic-Congo, Atlantic, Northern, Bak, Jola, Jola Proper, Karon-Mlomp. 42% lexical similarity between Karon-Mlomp and the closest Jola language. Bilingualism in Jola-Fogny, Wolof. Literacy rate in first language: Below 1%.

KERAK ***(HER, KEERAK, KEERAKU)*** [HHR] 10,600 (1998). Kabrousse village, extreme southwestern corner of Senegal just before crossing into Guinea-Bissau, and possibly other nearby villages in both countries. Niger-Congo, Atlantic-Congo, Atlantic, Northern, Bak, Jola, Jola Proper, Jola Central, Her-Ejamat. A distinct language from other Jola varieties. 63% lexical similarity between Her-Ejamat and closest Jola language. Speakers may use French and Wolof as second languages. Literacy rate in first language: Below 1%.

KOBIANA ***(COBIANA, UBOI, BUY)*** [KCJ] Niger-Congo, Atlantic-Congo, Atlantic, Northern, Eastern Senegal-Guinea, Nun. Closely related to Bainouk and Kasanga. Speakers are bilingual in Mandyak, but not vice versa. Traditional religion. See main entry under Guinea-Bissau.

KUWAATAAY ***(KWATAY)*** [CWT] 5,000 (1998). In Diembering, Bouyouye, Nyikine, Boukot-Diola, and some other villages along the coast just south of the mouth of the Casamance River, and Dakar. Niger-Congo, Atlantic-Congo, Atlantic, Northern, Bak, Jola, Jola Proper, Kwatay. A distinct language from other Jola varieties. 40% lexical similarity with closest Jola language. Most speakers can speak or understand Jola-Kasa, Jola-Fogny, and some Wolof. Dictionary. Grammar. Literacy rate in first language: Below 1%. NT, in press (1999).

LEHAR ***(LALA)*** [CAE] 10,000 (1999). North of Thies in west central Senegal, around the towns of Panbal, Mbaraglov, Dougnan. Niger-Congo, Atlantic-Congo, Atlantic, Northern, Cangin. 52% intelligibility of Non. 84% lexical similarity with Non, 74% with Safen, 68% with Ndut and Palor, 22% with Serer-Sine. Bilingual level estimates for Wolof are 0 %, 1 5%, 2 15%, 3 60%, 4 15%, 5 5%. Some speakers are also bilingual in Non, Ndut, or French. Their name for themselves is 'Lala'. SVO, nontonal. Literacy rate in first language: Below 1%. Savannah. Plains. Peasant agriculturalists: peanuts, manioc, tomatoes. Muslim, traditional religion, Christian.

MALINKE ***(MANINKA-WESTERN, WESTERN MANINKA, MANINGA, MALINKA)*** [MLQ] 340,000 in Senegal (1998). Eastern Senegal. Niger-Congo, Mande, Western, Central-Southwestern, Central, Manding-Jogo, Manding-Vai, Manding-Mokole, Manding, Manding-West. Dialect: JAHANKA (JAHANQUE, JAHONQUE, DIAKKANKE, DIAKHANKE, KYAKANKE). The Jahanka are reported to have come from Mali in the 18th century. They trace their origins to Soninke, but now speak a dialect of Malinke in Senegal (Western Maninka). Vocabulary and grammar differences with Mandinka. 59% lexical similarity with Mandinka. Recognized by the government as one of six national languages. National language. Literacy rate in first language: Below 1%. Arabic script used by Jahanka. Muslim, traditional religion. Bible portions 1997. See main entry under Mali.

MANDINKA ***(MANDING, MANDINGO, MANDINGUE, MANDINQUE, MANDE, SOCÉ)*** [MNK] 539,000 in Senegal (1998). Population total all countries 1,178,500. Southeastern and south central. Also spoken in Gambia, Guinea-Bissau. Niger-Congo, Mande, Western, Central-Southwestern, Central, Manding-Jogo, Manding-Vai, Manding-Mokole, Manding, Manding-West. Mandinka and Malinke are separate languages. 65% to 75% lexical similarity with Malinke. National language. Literacy rate in first language: Below 1%. Muslim. NT 1989.

MANDJAK ***(MANDJAQUE, MANJACA, MANJACO, MANJAK, MANJAKU, MANJACK, MANDYAK, MAJAK, NDJAK, KANYOP)*** [MFV] 85,000 in Senegal (1998). Southwest Senegal. Niger-Congo, Atlantic-Congo, Atlantic, Northern, Bak, Manjaku-Papel. Dialects: BOK (KABOK, SARA, TEIXEIRA PINTO, TSAAM), LIKES-UTSIA (BARAA, KALKUS), CUR (CHURO), LUND, YU (PECIXE). Some dialects listed may be separate languages. Closely related to Mankanya and Papel. Investigation needed: intelligibility with Senegal, Guinea-Bissau. Literacy rate in first language: Below 1%. Traditional religion, Christian. Bible portions 1968. See main entry under Guinea-Bissau.

MANKANYA ***(MANCAGNE, MANCANG, MANCANHA, MANKANHA, BOLA)*** [MAN] 23,500 in Senegal (1998). Scattered. Niger-Congo, Atlantic-Congo, Atlantic, Northern, Bak, Manjaku-Papel. Dialects: BURAMA (BULAMA, BURAM, BRAME), SHADAL (SADAR). Related to Mandjak. Extensive bilingualism in Mandjak. Speakers have a language association (PKUMEL), are developing an orthography and standardizing their language. Grammar. Literacy rate in first language: Below 1%. Traditional religion, Christian. See main entry under Guinea-Bissau.

MLOMP ***(MLOMP NORTH, GULOMPAAY)*** [QML] 4,350 (1998 B. Hopkins SIL). Mainly in Mlomp village north of the Casamance River, 25 km. due east of Bignona, on the road between Tendouck and Tiobon, Bignona Department, several surrounding villages, and scattered around the country. Niger-Congo, Atlantic-Congo, Atlantic, Northern, Bak, Jola, Jola Proper, Karon-Mlomp. 64% lexical similarity with Karon (closest), 42% between Karon-Mlomp and the closest other Jola language. Many speak and understand Jola-Fogny as second language, some know Wolof, and a few may know Mandinka or Pulaar. Investigation needed: intelligibility, bilingual proficiency. Literacy rate in first language: Below 1%.

NDUT ***(NDOUTE)*** [NDV] 25,350 (1998). West central, northwest of Thiès. Niger-Congo, Atlantic-Congo, Atlantic, Northern, Cangin. 32% intelligibility of Palor. 84% lexical similarity with Palor, 68% with Safen, Non, and Lehar, 22% with Serer-Sine. Bilingual level estimates for Wolof are 0 <1%, 1 5%, 2 15%, 3 60%, 4 15%, 5 5%. Some speakers are also bilingual in Lehar, Safen, or French. 'Ndut' is their name for themselves. SVO, nontonal. Literacy rate in first language: Below 1%. Savannah. Plains. Peasant agriculturalists: peanuts, manioc, tomatoes, corn. Muslim, Christian, traditional religion.

NOON ***(NONE, NON, SERER-NOON)*** [SNF] 26,500 (1998). Surrounding Thiès and in Thiès. Padee is in Fandene, Cangin in Thiès, Saawii north of Thiès. Niger-Congo, Atlantic-Congo, Atlantic, Northern, Cangin. Dialects: PADEE, CANGIN, SAAWII. Noon is very different from Serer-Sine. 68% intelligibility of Lehar. 84% lexical similarity with Lehar, 74% with Safen, 68% with Ndut and Palor, 22% with Serer-Sine. Bilingual level estimates for Wolof are 0 <1%, 1 5%, 2 15%, 3 60%, 4 15%, 5 5%. They use Wolof to communicate with Lehar speakers, and others. Some are also bilingual in French. 'Noon' is their name for themselves. 'Dyoba' is an alternate name for a family name, not for Noon. 'Serer-Noon' is only used to distinguish them from other languages in a context of the larger cultural group of Serer languages. SVO, nontonal. Literacy rate in first language: Below 1%. Savannah. Plains. Peasant agriculturalists. Christian, Muslim.

PALOR ***(FALOR, SILI, SILI-SILI, WARO)*** [FAP] 8,600 (1998). West central, west southwest of Thiès. Niger-Congo, Atlantic-Congo, Atlantic, Northern, Cangin. 55% intelligibility of Ndut, 27% of Safen. 84% lexical similarity with Ndut, 74% with Safen, 68% with Non and Lehar, 22% with Serer-Sine. Bilingual level estimates for Wolof are 0 <1%, 1 5%, 2 15%, 3 60%, 4 15%, 5 5%. Some are also bilingual in Safen and French. Palor is used in the home. 'Waro' is their name for themselves. There are no schools in the area. SVO, nontonal. Literacy rate in first language: Below 1%. Savannah. Plains. Peasant agriculturalists: peanuts, manioc, mangos, tomatoes. Muslim, traditional religion.

PULAAR ***(PULAAR FULFULDE, PEUL, PEULH)*** [FUC] 2,121,140 in Senegal (1998). Population total all countries 2,921,300. Fulbe Jeeri and Toucouleur are primarily in the Senegal River Valley and Mauritania. Fulacunda is in the Upper Casamance region, from 40 miles west of Kolda to the headwaters of the Gambia River in the east, from the southern border of Senegal in the south to the Gambian border in the north. Also spoken in Gambia, Guinea, Guinea-Bissau, Mali, Mauritania. Niger-Congo, Atlantic-Congo, Atlantic, Northern, Senegambian, Fula-Wolof, Fulani, Western.

Dialects: TOUCOULEUR (TUKOLOR, TUKULOR, TOKILOR, PULAAR, HAALPULAAR, FULBE JEERI), FULACUNDA (FULAKUNDA, FULKUNDA). Fulbe Jeeri and Toucouleur (Haalpulaar'en) are separate ethnic groups speaking this form of Pulaar. Jeeri is a geographical region in which a large number of diverse lineages still follow a semi-nomadic life. There are 3 families subdivided into at least 20 lineages, each of which has some dialect differences; all are inherently intelligible. Bunndu is a Fula geo-political state composed of a mix of Toucouleur and Fulbe Jeeri. Fuuta Tooro (Fouta Toro) was a major Toucouleur geo-political state, which has its seat in northern Senegal, and is also in Mauritania. Fulacunda is an ethnic group speaking a closely related dialect of Pulaar. Their region is called Fuladu in the Upper Casamance area of Senegal. National language. Grammar. Literacy rate in first language: 10% to 30%. Literacy rate in second language: 15% to 25%. Desert. Fulbe Jeeri: semi-nomadic pastoralists. Muslim. NT 1997.

SAAFI-SAAFI ***(SERER-SAFEN, SERERE-SAFEN, SAFI, SAAFI, SAFI-SAFI, SAFEN)*** [SAV] 104,000 (1998). Southwest of and near Thiès, and to the ocean. Niger-Congo, Atlantic-Congo, Atlantic, Northern, Cangin. 74% lexical similarity with Noon, Lehar, and Palor; 68% with Ndut; 22% with Serer-Sine. Bilingual level estimates for Wolof are 0 <1%, 1 5%, 2 15%, 3 60%, 4 15%, 5 5%. Some speakers are also bilingual in Ndut or French. 'Safen' is their name for the people, 'Saafi-Saafi' for the language. Trade language. SVO, nontonal. Literacy rate in first language: Below 1%. Savannah. Plains. Peasant agriculturalists: peanuts, manioc, beans, tomatoes. Muslim, traditional religion, Christian.

SERER-SINE ***(SÉRÈRE-SINE, SERER, SERRER, SEREER, SEEREER, SERER-SIN, SINE-SALOUM, SEEX, SINE-SINE)*** [SES] 1,026,000 in Senegal (1998). Population total both countries 1,051,200. West central Senegal and the Sine and Saloum River valleys. Also spoken in Gambia. Niger-Congo, Atlantic-Congo, Atlantic, Northern, Senegambian, Serer. Dialects: SEGUM, FADYUT-PALMERIN, SINE, DYEGUEME (GYEGEM), NIOMINKA. Niominka and Serer-Sine are inherently intelligible to each other's speakers. 'Sereer' is their name for themselves. National language. Literacy rate in first language: Below 1%. Traditional religion, Muslim, Christian. NT 1987.

SONINKE ***(MARKA, MARAKA, SARAHOLE, SARAWULE, SERAHULI, SILABE, TOUBAKAI, WALPRE)*** [SNN] 172,500 in Senegal (1998). Principally north and south of Bakel along the Senegal River. Bakel, Ouaoundé, Moudéri, and Yaféra are the principal towns. Niger-Congo, Mande, Western, Northwestern, Samogo, Soninke-Bobo, Soninke-Boso, Soninke. Dialects: AZER (ADJER, ASER), GADYAGA. Dialects in Mali, Senegal, Mauritania, and possibly Gambia are close enough to use the same literature. National language. Dictionary. Grammar. Literacy rate in first language: Below 1%. Radio programs. Muslim. See main entry under Mali.

WAMEI ***(KONYAGI, CONIAGUI, CONHAGUE, KONIAGUI)*** [COU] 14,850 in Senegal (1998). Population total both countries 18,850. Southeast. Migration from Guinea no longer taking place. Also spoken in Guinea. Niger-Congo, Atlantic-Congo, Atlantic, Northern, Eastern Senegal-Guinea, Tenda. 'Wamei' is their own name for their language. Literacy rate in first language: Below 1%. Traditional religion, Christian.

WOLOF ***(OUOLOF, YALLOF, WALAF, VOLOF, WARO-WARO)*** [WOL] 3,170,200 in Senegal (1998). Population total all countries 3,215,000 or more first language speakers (1998); 7,000,000 including second language speakers (1999 WA). Western and central, left bank of Senegal River to Cape Vert. May also be in Mali. Also spoken in France, Gambia, Guinea, Guinea-Bissau, Mali, Mauritania. Niger-Congo, Atlantic-Congo, Atlantic, Northern, Senegambian, Fula-Wolof, Wolof. Dialects: BAOL, CAYOR, DYOLOF (DJOLOF, JOLOF), LEBOU (LEBU), JANDER. Different from Wolof of Gambia. Bilingualism in French, Arabic. The main African language of Senegal. Predominantly urban. 'Wolof' is their name for themselves. National language. Dictionary. Grammar. Literacy rate in first language: 10%. Literacy rate in second language: 30%. Radio programs. Muslim. NT 1988.

XASONGA ***(KASSONKE, KHASONKE, KASONKE, KASSON, KASSO, XAASONGA, XASONKE, XAASONGAXANGO)*** [KAO] 7,260 in Senegal (1998). Niger-Congo, Mande, Western, Central-Southwestern, Central, Manding-Jogo, Manding-Vai, Manding-Mokole, Manding, Manding- West. 90% inherent intelligibility with Malinke of eastern Senegal. 70% lexical similarity with Mandinka of Gambia and Senegal. Literacy rate in first language: Below 1%. Muslim. Bible portions 1997. See main entry under Mali.

SEYCHELLES

Republic of Seychelles. National or official languages: English, French. 76,000 (1998 UN). Includes Aldabra, Farquhar, Des Roches; 92 islands. Literacy rate 62% to 80%. Information mainly from J. Holm 1989; D. Bickerton 1988. Christian, secular, Hindu, Muslim, Baha'i. Blind population 150 (1982 WCE).

Data accuracy estimate: A2. The number of languages listed for Seychelles is 3. Of those, all are living languages. Diversity index 0.07.

ENGLISH [ENG] 1,601 in Seychelles (1971 census). Indo-European, Germanic, West, English. Principal language of the schools. Official language. Bible 1382-1989. See main entry under United Kingdom.

FRENCH [FRN] 977 in Seychelles (1971 census). Indo-European, Italic, Romance, Italo-Western, Western, Gallo-Iberian, Gallo-Romance, Gallo-Rhaetian, Oïl, French. Spoken by the French settler families, 'grands blancs'. Official language. Bible 1530-1986. See main entry under France.

SESELWA CREOLE FRENCH *(SEYCHELLOIS CREOLE, SEYCHELLES CREOLE FRENCH, KREOL, CREOLE)* [CRS] 69,000 (1995), 95.7% of the population (1982 Barrett). Creole, French based. Seychelles dialect is reported to be the same as Chagos. Structural differences with Mauritius are relatively minor. Not adequately intelligible with Reunion Creole. It is heard everywhere on the streets, in the shops and homes. The native language of virtually all its citizens (D. Bickerton 1988). It is gaining rapidly in status. Dictionary. Grammar. The first 4 years of education are in Seselwa. Used for some subjects for 5 more years. Radio programs. Fishermen. Christian. NT, in press (1998).

SIERRA LEONE

Republic of Sierra Leone. National or official language: English. 4,568,000 (1998 UN). Literacy rate 15%. Also includes Greek 700, people from Lebanon, India, Pakistan, Liberia. Information mainly from D. Dalby 1962; TISSL 1995. Muslim, traditional religion, Christian. Blind population 28,000 (1982 WCE). Deaf institutions: 5. Data accuracy estimate: A2. The number of languages listed for Sierra Leone is 23. Of those, all are living languages. Diversity index 0.82.

BASSA [BAS] 5,000 in Sierra Leone (1991 D. Slager UBS). Freetown. Niger-Congo, Atlantic-Congo, Volta-Congo, Kru, Western, Bassa. Traditional religion. NT 1970. See main entry under Liberia.

BOM *(BOME, BUM, BOMO)* [BMF] 250 speakers out of an ethnic group of 5,000 (1991 D. Slager UBS). Along the Bome River. Niger-Congo, Atlantic-Congo, Atlantic, Southern, Mel, Bullom-Kissi, Bullom, Northern. Bilingualism in Mende. They are being absorbed into the Mende group. Traditional religion.

BULLOM SO *(NORTHERN BULLOM, BOLOM, BULEM, BULLUN, BULLIN, MMANI, MANDINGI)* [BUY] Few speakers out of 6,800 in the ethnic group (1988 L. Vanderaa). Along the coast from the Guinea border to the Sierra Leone River. Niger-Congo, Atlantic-Congo, Atlantic, Southern, Mel, Bullom- Kissi, Bullom, Northern. Dialects: MMANI, KAFU. Bom is closely related. Little intelligibility with Sherbro, none with Krim. Bom has 66% to 69% lexical similarity with Sherbro dialects, 34% with Krim. The people are intermarried with the Temne and the Susu. Traditional religion. Nearly extinct. Bible portions 1816.

ENGLISH [ENG] Indo-European, Germanic, West, English. Used in administration, law, education, commerce. Official language. Bible 1535-1989. See main entry under United Kingdom.

FUUTA JALON *(FUTA JALLON, FOUTA DYALON, FULBE, PULAR, FULLO FUUTA, FUTA FULA)* [FUF] 178,400 in Sierra Leone (1991). Throughout the country but especially in the north. Niger-Congo, Atlantic-Congo, Atlantic, Northern, Senegambian, Fula-Wolof, Fulani, West Central. Dialects: KRIO FULA, KEBU FULA. Recent immigrants from Guinea speak the original Futa Jalon or the Kebu dialect (Dalby 1962). It is intelligible with Fula Peta of Guinea and with dialects of Guinea, Guinea-Bissau, and Senegal. A slightly modified form of Futa Jalon is known as Krio Fula with many loans from Sierra Leone languages. People live in settled and migrant communities. Muslim. Bible portions 1929-1975. See main entry under Guinea.

GOLA *(GULA)* [GOL] 8,000 in Sierra Leone, or 0.2% of the population (1989 TISLL). Along the border and a few miles into Sierra Leone. Niger-Congo, Atlantic-Congo, Atlantic, Southern, Mel, Gola. Dialects: DE (DENG), MANAGOBLA (GOBLA), KONGBAA, KPO, SENJE (SENE), TEE (TEGE), TOLDIL (TOODII). Most Gola in Sierra Leone have become Mende speakers. Different from Gola of Nigeria (dialect of Mumuye) or Gola (Badyara) of Guinea-Bissau and Guinea. Muslim, Christian. Bible portions. See main entry under Liberia.

KISI, SOUTHERN *(KISI, GISSI, KISSIEN)* [KSS] 85,000 in Sierra Leone (1995). Niger-Congo, Atlantic-Congo, Atlantic, Southern, Mel, Bullom-Kissi, Kissi. Different from Northern Kissi. Literacy rate in second language: 3%. Traditional religion, Muslim, Christian. NT 1991. See main entry under Liberia.

KISSI, NORTHERN *(GIZI, KISI, KISSIEN, KISIE)* [KQS] 40,000 in Sierra Leone (1991 LBT). Niger-Congo, Atlantic-Congo, Atlantic, Southern, Mel, Bullom-Kissi, Kissi. Dialects: LIARO, KAMA, TENG, TUNG. Closely related to Sherbro. Southern Kissi is different. Bilingualism in Krio, Mende. Traditional religion. NT 1966-1986. See main entry under Guinea.

KLAO ***(KRU, KROO, KLAOH, KLAU)*** [KLU] 8,000 in Sierra Leone, or 0.2% of the population (1989 TISLL). Freetown. Originally from Liberia. Niger-Congo, Atlantic-Congo, Volta-Congo, Kru, Western, Klao. Traditional religion. NT, in press (1996). See main entry under Liberia.

KONO ***(KONNOH)*** [KNO] 190,000 first language speakers, or 4.8% of the population (1989 TISLL), 25,000 second language speakers (1981 Cranmer UBS). Northeast. Niger-Congo, Mande, Western, Central-Southwestern, Central, Manding-Jogo, Manding-Vai, Vai-Kono. Dialects: NORTHERN KONO (SANDO), CENTRAL KONO (FIAMA, GBANE, GBANE KANDO, GBENSE, GORAMA KONO, KAMARA, LEI, MAFINDO, NIMI KORO, NIMI YAMA, PENGUIA, SOA, TANKORO, TOLI). Not intelligible with Vai. The dialects have minor differences, and can use the same literature. Different from the Kono dialect of Kpelle in Guinea. Hills. Agriculturalists: rice, greens, cassava, yams, coffee, cacao; diamond miners. Traditional religion, Muslim, Christian. Bible portions 1919-1993.

KRIM ***(KIM, KITTIM, KIRIM, KIMI)*** [KRM] 500 speakers or fewer out of an ethnic group of 10,000 (1990 CRC). On the coast between Sherbro and Vai, along the Krim River. Niger-Congo, Atlantic-Congo, Atlantic, Southern, Mel, Bullom-Kissi, Bullom, Southern. 44% to 45% lexical similarity with Sherbo, 34% with Northern Bullom. The people are bilingual in Sherbro, and being absorbed into the Mende group. There are 7 or 8 towns where children and others speak Krim. Traditional religion, Muslim.

KRIO ***(CREOLE, PATOIS)*** [KRI] 472,600 in Sierra Leone (1993), or 10% of the population are first language speakers (1987 Frederick Jones). Possibly 4,000,000 or 95% of the remainder are second language users (1987 F. Jones). Population total all countries 478,000 or more. Communities in Freetown, on the Peninsula, on the Banana Islands, York Island, in Bonthe, by de-tribalized Sierra Leoneans and as the lingua franca throughout the country. Also spoken in Gambia, Guinea, Senegal. Creole, English based, Atlantic, Krio. Dialect: AKU. Krio and Jamaican Creole, and Krio and Sea Islands Creole may have some interintelligibility. Domains of use include education, urban and town living, everyday life. Dominant language of the younger generation. Vigorous. Spoken more in provincial towns than in villages, and for inter-ethnic communication. Possibly half the speakers use Krio in their workplace. It is the formal language for those who do not speak English. Second language users prefer their indigenous languages for informal situations. Mother tongue Krio speakers are mainly descendents of repatriated slaves from Jamaica. There is linguistic influence from Yoruba (I. Hancock 1987). Language of wider communication. Literacy rate in second language: Fewer than 15% in English. Taught as an elective from primary to college level. Traditional religion, Christian. NT 1986-1992.

KURANKO ***(KORANKO)*** [KHA] 250,000 in Sierra Leone (1995), 3.7% of the population (1991 J. Kaiser TISLL). Population total both countries 305,000. Northern Province around Kabala. Also spoken in Guinea. Niger-Congo, Mande, Western, Central-Southwestern, Central, Manding-Jogo, Manding-Vai, Manding-Mokole, Mokole. Dialects: BARRAWA, NIENI, MANKALIYA, SAMBAYA, NEY, SENGBE, MONGO. The dialect near the Guinea border is more similar to Maninka, so some have called Kuranko a dialect of Maninka. Farther south, the dialects are more different from Maninka. Literacy rate in second language: 5%. Traditional religion, Muslim, Christian. NT 1972.

LIMBA, EAST ***(YIMBA, YUMBA)*** [LMA] North central. Niger-Congo, Atlantic-Congo, Atlantic, Southern, Limba. Dialects: NORTHERN LIMBA (WARAWARA, KE-WOYA-YAKA), SOUTHERN LIMBA (BIRIWA-SAROKO-KALANTUBA-SUNKO). Traditional religion, Muslim. See main entry under Guinea.

LIMBA, WEST-CENTRAL ***(YIMBA, YUMBA)*** [LIA] 335,000 in Sierra Leone including East Limba, or 8.4% of the population (1989 J. Kaiser TISLL). North central area north of Makeni. Niger-Congo, Atlantic-Congo, Atlantic, Southern, Limba. Dialects: WESTERN LIMBA (TONKO, SELA), CENTRAL (TAMISO, GBONGOGBO). It is quite different from East Limba of Sierra Leone and Guinea. Traditional religion, Muslim, Christian. NT 1966-1983.

LOKO ***(LANDOGO)*** [LOK] 115,000 in Sierra Leone, or 3% of the population (1989 J. Kaiser TISLL) 4,000 in Guinea (1993 Johnstone). Population total both countries 119,000. Two separate areas; parts of the Koya, Ribbi, and Bumpe chiefdoms; Sanda Loko chiefdom. Also spoken in Guinea. Niger-Congo, Mande, Western, Central-Southwestern, Southwestern, Mende-Loma, Mende-Bandi, Mende-Loko. Dialects: MAGBIAMBO, GBENDEMBU, NGOAHU, NAGBANMBA, SANDA, LAIA, LIBISEGAHUN, KOYA, RIBBI, BUYA. Closely related to Mende. Traditional religion, Muslim, Christian. NT 1983.

MANINKA, KANKAN ***(MANDINGO, MADINGO, MANDE, MANINKA-MORI, SOUTHERN MANINKA)*** [MNI] 90,000 in Sierra Leone, or 2.3% of the population (1989 J. Kaiser TISLL). Kabala area and small groups throughout the country. Niger-Congo, Mande, Western, Central-Southwestern, Central, Manding-Jogo, Manding-Vai, Manding-Mokole, Manding, Manding-East, Southeastern Manding. Trade language. Traders. Muslim. NT 1932-1966. See main entry under Guinea.

MENDE ***(BOUMPE, HULO, KOSSA, KOSSO)*** [MFY] 1,460,000 in Sierra Leone (1987 UBS), 30.9% of the population (1989 TISLL). Population total both countries 1,480,000. South central. Expanding along the coast and to the south and east. Also spoken in Liberia. Niger-Congo, Mande, Western,

Central-Southwestern, Southwestern, Mende-Loma, Mende-Bandi, Mende-Loko. Dialects: KPA, KO, WAANJAMA, SEWAWA. Bandi, mainly in Liberia, is considered to be a separate language. Dialects have 92% to 98% lexical similarity with each other. There are a number of monolinguals. Others use Krio as second language. Trade language. Dictionary. Grammar. An indigenous script called Kikakui still in use. Taught as an elective from primary to college levels. Traditional religion, Muslim, Christian. Bible 1959.

SHERBRO ***(SOUTHERN BULLOM, SHIBA, AMAMPA, MAMPA, MAMPWA)*** [BUN] 135,000 or 3.4% of the population (1989 J. Kaiser TISLL). Southern Province adjoining the Western Area; York District on western peninsula, Ribbi Shenge, Dima, Sicie, Timdel, Benducha, Nongoba. Niger-Congo, Atlantic-Congo, Atlantic, Southern, Mel, Bullom-Kissi, Bullom, Southern. Dialects: SHENGE SHERBRO, SITIA SHERBRO, NDEMA SHERBRO, PENINSULA SHERBRO. Not intelligible with Krim or Bullom So. 83% to 89% lexical similarity among dialects; 66% to 69% with Bullom So, 44% to 45% with Krim. Shenge is the prestige dialect. Traditional religion, Muslim, Christian.

SUSU ***(SUSOO, SOUSSOU, SOSO, SOSE)*** [SUD] 120,000 in Sierra Leone, or 3.1% of the population (1989 J. Kaiser TISLL). Northern Province, interspersed throughout western sections. Niger-Congo, Mande, Western, Central-Southwestern, Central, Susu-Yalunka. A separate language from Yalunka. People have limited bilingualism in Krio or English in Sierra Leone. Muslim. NT 1884-1988. See main entry under Guinea.

THEMNE ***(TEMNE, TIMNE, TIMENE, TIMMANNEE, TEMEN)*** [TEJ] 1,200,000 first language speakers, or 29.8% of the population (1989 J. Kaiser TISLL). 240,000 second language users (1981 D. Cranmer). Northern Province, west of Sewa River to Little Scarcie. Niger-Congo, Atlantic-Congo, Atlantic, Southern, Mel, Temne, Temne-Banta. Dialects: BANTA, KONIKE, YONI, BOMBALI, WESTERN TEMNE (PIL), SANDA, RIBIA, KHOLIFA, KOYA, MASINGBI, MALAL. The people claim to understand all dialects. Lexical similarity between Masingbi and Malal is 74%; between Konike and western varieties 70%. 25% use Krio, 5% use English as second language. A number of monolinguals. Used as a second language in parts of neighboring tribes. The primary language of central Sierra Leone. Trade language. Literacy rate in second language: 6%. Taught as an elective from primary to college level. Agriculturalists: rice. Traditional religion, Muslim, Christian. NT 1868-1955.

VAI ***(VEI, VY, GALLINAS, GALLINES)*** [VAI] 15,500 in Sierra Leone (1991), or 0.3% of the population (1989 J. Kaiser TISLL). Niger-Congo, Mande, Western, Central-Southwestern, Central, Manding-Jogo, Manding-Vai, Vai-Kono. Not intelligible with Kono. Bilingualism in Mende. Most are Mende speakers in Sierra Leone. SOV. Indigenous script. Muslim. See main entry under Liberia.

YALUNKA ***(YALUNKE, DJALLONKE, KJALONKE, DIALONKE, JALONKE)*** [YAL] 28,000 in Sierra Leone, or 0.7% of the population (1989 J. Kaiser TISLL). Northern Province, Balaki Subprefecture around Yifin, Falaba area; Balaki, Kunsi, Bouria, Solia, Foulaya, Jouloubaya villages. Niger-Congo, Mande, Western, Central-Southwestern, Central, Susu-Yalunka. Dialects: MUSAIA, FIRIA, SULIMA. Close to Susu, but only marginally intelligible. Most people are monolingual. Dialects have 83% to 92% lexical similarity. Bilingualism in Maninka, Krio. They want literature in Yalunka. Literacy rate in second language: 2%. Muslim, traditional religion, Christian. NT 1976. See main entry under Guinea.

SOMALIA

Somali Democratic Republic, Jamhuriyadda Dimugradiga Somaliya. Formerly British and Italian Somaliland. National or official languages: Somali, Standard Arabic, English. 9,237,000 (1998 UN). Most of the Arabic and all of the people from India and Italy have left. Literacy rate 24% to 40% (1977 C. M. Brann). Information mainly from B. W. Andrzejewski 1975, 1978; D. Biber 1984; M. Lamberti 1986; A. O. Mansur 1986; K. Menkhaus 1989. Muslim. Blind population 10,000 (1982 WCE). Data accuracy estimate: B. The number of languages listed for Somalia is 13. Of those, all are living languages. Diversity index 0.20.

ARABIC, STANDARD [ABV] Afro-Asiatic, Semitic, Central, South, Arabic. Most Somalis have very limited or no ability in Arabic. Not used as a medium of communication by the government. National language. Bible 1984-1991. See main entry under Saudi Arabia.

BONI [BOB] Few if any, in Somalia (1991). Afro-Asiatic, Cushitic, East, Rendille-Boni. Reported to be linguistically close to Garre of Somalia, but not close in culture or appearance. Hunters. Muslim. See main entry under Kenya.

BOON ***(AF-BOON)*** [BNL] Jilib District, Middle Jubba Region, scattered in the bush and live in settlements of 2 or 3 houses with their closest relatives. Afro-Asiatic, Cushitic, East. There are similarities to Somali. All speakers over 60 years old (1986 M. Lamberti). In recent decades they have shifted to the Maay dialect of Jilib. Not the same as Boni. 'Boon' means low caste, including

Yibir, Midgaan (Midgo, language Af-Midgood), Madiban, Tumal, Yahar, Yihir, and other clans. Hunter-gatherers, leather workers. Nearly extinct.

DABARRE ***(AF-DABARRE)*** [DBR] 20,000 to 50,000 (1992). Spoken by the Dabarre clan around Dhiinsoor District, May Region, and the Iroole Clan in nearby Baraawe District, Lower Shabeelle Region, and in Qansax Dheere. Afro-Asiatic, Cushitic, East, Somali. Dialects: DABARRE, IROOLE (AF-IROOLE). A very distinctive language in the Digil clan family. Muslim.

ENGLISH [ENG] Indo-European, Germanic, West, English. Used more in the north. Official language. Bible 1535-1989. See main entry under United Kingdom.

GARRE ***(AF-GARRE)*** [GEX] 50,000 or more (1992). Possibly several hundred thousand in the ethnic group. Dominate areas of southern Somalia, especially in the Wanle Weyn-Buur Hakaba area; Baydhaba, Dhiinsoor, Buurhakaba, and Qoryooley districts; Middle and Lower Shabeelle and Bay regions. Afro-Asiatic, Cushitic, East, Somali. Reported to be linguistically close to Boni. Part of the Hawiye clan family. They consider themselves to be one people with the Garreh in Kenya, although they now speak different languages. Some ethnic Garre in Somalia speak Maay as mother tongue. Muslim.

JIIDDU ***(JIDDU, AF-JIIDDU)*** [JII] 20,000 to 60,000 (1992). Lower Shabeelle Bay and Middle Jubba regions, Qoryooley, Dhiinsoor, Jilib, and Buurhakaba districts. Afro-Asiatic, Cushitic, East, Somali. A distinct language from Somali and Tunni, usually grouped under the Digil dialects or languages. Different sentence structure and phonology from Somali. Closer to Somali than to Baiso. Some similarities to Konsoid languages, and to Gedeo, Alaba, Hadiyya, and Kambaata. Spoken by the Jiiddu clan. Ethnic Jiiddu in Bale Province, Ethiopia speak Oromo as mother tongue. Muslim.

MAAY ***(AF-MAAY TIRI, AF-MAAY, AF-MAY, AF-MAYMAY, RAHANWEEN, RAHANWEYN)*** [QMA] 500,000 to 1,000,000 (1992). 700,000 to 1,500,000 including the Digil dialects or languages. Southern Somalia, Gedo Region, Middle and Lower Shabeelle, Middle and Lower Jubba, Baay, and Bakool regions. Afro-Asiatic, Cushitic, East, Somali. Dialect: AF-HELLEDI. It may be more than one language; the dialects form a continuum. Standard Somali is difficult or unintelligible to Maay speakers, except for those who have learned it through mass communications, urbanization, and internal movement. Different sentence structure and phonology from Somali. The Rahanwiin (Rahanweyn) clan confederacy speak various Maay dialects or languages. Af-Helledi is a Maay secret language used by hunters. Used by the Tunni, Jiiddu, Garre, and Dabarre as second language. They tend to not travel much. Muslim.

MUSHUNGULU ***(KIMUSHUNGULU, MUSHUNGULI)*** [XMA] 20,000 to 50,000 (1992). Southern Somalia, Jamaame District of Lower Jubba Region, centered in Jamaame District, and some in urban areas in nearby Kismaayo and in Muqdisho. Niger-Congo, Atlantic-Congo, Volta-Congo, Benue-Congo, Bantoid, Southern, Narrow Bantu, Central, G, Zigula-Zaramo (G.30). May be the same as, or intelligible with, Zigula or Shambaa. They do not mingle with other peoples of Somalia, so the women do not learn Somali. The men learn Maay or Somali as second language. Descended from fugitive slaves who escaped from their Somali masters in the Middle Shabeelle region around 1840. In northeast Tanzania, they were called 'WaZegua' (see Zigula). Investigation needed: intelligibility with Zigula, Shambaa. Agriculturalists. Muslim, traditional religion.

OROMO, BORANA-ARSI-GUJI ***(SOUTHERN OROMO)*** [GAX] Gedo Region. Afro-Asiatic, Cushitic, East, Oromo. Dialect: BORANA (BOORAN, BORAN). The Oromo variety in Gedo is probably Borana; that in the Lower Jubba Region is probably Orma. Muslim. Bible 1995. See main entry under Ethiopia.

SOMALI ***(AF-SOOMAALI, AF-MAXAAD TIRI, COMMON SOMALI, STANDARD SOMALI)*** [SOM] 5,400,000 to 6,700,000 in Somalia (1991). Population total all countries 9,472,000 to 10,770,000. Throughout the country. Also spoken in Djibouti, Ethiopia, Finland, Italy, Kenya, Oman, Saudi Arabia, Sweden, UAE, United Kingdom, Yemen. Afro-Asiatic, Cushitic, East, Somali. Dialects: NORTHERN SOMALI, BENAADIR, AF-ASHRAAF (ASHRAAF). Northern Somali is the basis for Standard Somali. It is readily intelligible to speakers of Benaadir Somali, but difficult or unintelligible to Maay and Digil speakers, except for those who have learned it through mass communications, urbanization, and internal movement. The Rahanwiin (Rahanweyn) are a large clan confederacy in southern Somalia, speaking various Maay dialects or languages (Central Somali). The Digil are a clan confederacy speaking Central Somali varieties. Daarood is a large clan family in northeast Somalia and the Ogaadeen region of Ethiopia, extreme southern Somalia and northeast Kenya which speaks several different dialects. Dir is a clan family with various clans in Djibouti, Ethiopia, throughout Somalia and northeast Kenya. The Gadabuursi are a section of the Dir living in northwest Somalia and adjoining parts of Djibouti and Ethiopia, and speaking Northern Common Somali. The Isxaaq are a major clan grouping in northeast Somalia, some in Djibouti and Ethiopia, speaking Northern Common Somali. The Hawiye are a major clan family living in central southern Somalia, parts of Ethiopia, and extreme northeast Kenya. Hawiye northern clans (Habar Gidir) speak a dialect of Common Somali similar to the adjacent Daarood clans, while Hawiye southern clans (especially Abgaal and Gaaljaal) speak the

Benaadir dialect of Common Somali. Ogaadeen is the largest clan within the Daarood clan family, living in eastern Ethiopia, extreme southern Somalia and northeast Kenya, speaking various forms of Northern Common Somali. 'Sab' is an ambiguous term used by some scholars to refer to various lower caste clans. 'Medibaan' is a low caste clan within the Hawiye. 'Benaadir' as an ethnic group refers to the residents of the coastal cities. Those in Merka and Muqdisho speak Af-Ashraaf, a distinct variety which may have limited inherent intelligibility to speakers of Standard Somali. Most of these fled to Kenya during the recent fighting. Bilingualism in Arabic, Italian. The language of most of the people of the country. Investigation needed: intelligibility with Af-Ashraaf. National language. Dictionary. Grammar. Literacy rate in second language: 25% in cities, 10% rural. The government adopted the Roman script in 1972. The Osmania script no longer used. Standard Somali used. Pastoralists; agriculturalists: sugar, bananas, sorghum, corn, gum, incense; miners: iron, tin, gypsum, bauxite, uranium. Muslim, Christian. Bible 1979.

SWAHILI [SWA] 40,000 Baraawe in Somalia (1992). The Mwini live in Baraawe (Brava), Lower Shabeelle, and were scattered in cities and towns of southern Somalia. Most have fled to Kenya because of the civil war. The Bajun live in Kismaayo District and the neighboring coast. Niger-Congo, Atlantic-Congo, Volta-Congo, Benue-Congo, Bantoid, Southern, Narrow Bantu, Central, G, Swahili (G.40). Dialects: MWINI (MWIINI, CHIMWIINI, AF-CHIMWIINI, BARWAANI, BRAVANESE), BAJUNI (KIBAJUNI, BAJUN, AF-BAJUUN, MBALAZI, CHIMBALAZI). Reported to have come centuries ago from Zanzibar. Mwini: artisans (leather goods); Bajun: fishermen. Bible 1891-1996. See main entry under Tanzania.

TUNNI ***(AF-TUNNI)*** [TQQ] 20,000 to 60,000 (1992). Lower Shabeelle and Middle Jubba regions, Dhiinsoor, Baraawe, and Jilib districts. Afro-Asiatic, Cushitic, East, Somali. A distinct language from Somali or Jiiddu, usually grouped under the Digil dialects or languages. Different sentence structure and phonology from Somali. Maay language influences. Nomadic. Pastoralists: cattle, sheep, goats. Muslim.

SOUTH AFRICA

Republic of South Africa. Republiek van Suid-Afrika. National or official languages: Afrikaans, Ndebele, Northern Sotho, Southern Sotho, Swati, Tsonga, Tswana, Venda, Xhosa, Zulu, English. 39,357,000 (1998 UN), including 24,100,000 Africans (73.8%), 5,000,000 Whites (14.8%), 2,800,000 'Coloreds' (8.7%), 890,292 Asians (2.7%) (1987 USA Today). 11 official languages. Literacy rate 50% Africans, 62% 'Coloureds', 69% Asians, 99% Whites (1990 WA). Also includes Angloromani, Hakka Chinese 5,000, Yue Chinese 15,000, Standard German 45,000, Greek 70,000, Gujarati, Haiom, Portuguese 617,000, Tamil 250,000, Eastern Yiddish, Workers from nearby countries 2,700,000. Information mainly from F. Anderson 1987; J. Holm 1989; L-G Andersson and T. Janson 1997; M. Brenzinger 1997. Christian, traditional religion, secular, Hindu, Muslim. Blind population 62,000 (1982 WCE). Deaf population 12,100 (1986 Gallaudet University). Deaf institutions: 43. Data accuracy estimate: B. The number of languages listed for South Africa is 31. Of those, 25 are living languages, 3 are second languages without mother tongue speakers, and 3 are extinct. Diversity index 0.87.

AFRIKAANS [AFK] 6,200,000 in South Africa (1991 Christos van Rensburg), of whom 1,000,000 are native bilinguals with English (1989 J. Holm), 15.1% of the population (1995 The Economist). 4,000,000 in South Africa use it as a second or third language (1989 J. Holm). Population total all countries 6,381,000. Including second language users: 10,000,000 (1999 WA). Pretoria and Bloemfontein are principal centers of population. Cape Malays live mainly in Capetown, with some in Johannesburg, Pretoria, Durban, and Port Elizabeth. Also spoken in Australia, Botswana, Canada, Lesotho, Malawi, Namibia, New Zealand, Zambia, Zimbabwe. Indo-European, Germanic, West, Low Saxon-Low Franconian, Low Franconian. Dialects: CAPE AFRIKAANS (WEST CAPE AFRIKAANS), ORANGE RIVER AFRIKAANS, EAST CAPE AFRIKAANS. A variant of the Dutch spoken by the 17th century colonists, with some lexical and syntactic borrowings from Malay, Bantu languages, Khoisan languages, Portuguese, and other European languages. Their ancestors were brought from Java 300 years ago. 150,000 Cape Malays speak Afrikaans; some also speak English. National language. Cape Malays: builders, carpenters. Cape Malay: Muslim, Christian. Bible 1933-1983.

BIRWA [BRL] (10,000 in Botswana; 1993). Niger-Congo, Atlantic-Congo, Volta-Congo, Benue-Congo, Bantoid, Southern, Narrow Bantu, Central, S, Shona (S.10). See main entry under Botswana.

CAMTHO ***(ISICAMTHO, ISCAMTHO)*** [CMT] Soweto, Johannesburg, urban settings. Mixed Language, Zulu-Bantu. A development in the 1980s from the original Tsotsitaal, and sometimes called 'Tsotsitaal'. Also described as a basically Zulu or Sotho language with heavy code-switching and a lot of English and Afrikaans content morphemes. Mainly used by young people. Second language only.

ENGLISH [ENG] 3,500,000 in South Africa (1991 Christos van Rensburg), 9.1% of the population (1995 The Economist). Indo-European, Germanic, West, English. The main means of communication in urban areas. Many second generation people from India, Portugal, Germany, and Greece speak English as first language. Official language. Bible 1382-1989. See main entry under United Kingdom.

FANAGOLO ***("FANAKALO", "FANEKOLO", "KITCHEN KAFFIR", "MINE KAFFIR", PIKI, ISIPIKI, "ISIKULA", LOLOLO, ISILOLOLO, PIDGIN BANTU, BASIC ZULU, SILUNGUBOI)*** [FAO] Several hundred thousand speakers (1975 Reinecke). Also spoken in DRC, Namibia, Zambia, Zimbabwe. Pidgin, Zulu based. The dialect in Zambia is called 'Cikabanga', that in Zimbabwe is called 'Chilapalapa'. About 70% of the vocabulary comes from Zulu, 24% from English, 6% from Afrikaans. Used widely in towns and gold, diamond, coal, and copper mining areas. Originated in the 19th century. "Fanagolo" and most or all other names are pejorative. Trade language. Dictionary. Second language only.

GAIL [GIC] Used by an estimated 20,000 as second or third language. Mainly in Johannesburg, Pretoria, Cape Town, Durban, Bloemfontein, and Port Elizabeth. Unclassified. In Johannesburg it is more English based, in Pretoria more Afrikaans based. Reported to be related to Polari in the United Kingdom. The first language of users is English or Afrikaans. An in-group language among some people. Second language only.

HINDI [HND] 890,292 including all Indian languages (1986 USA Today). 2,000,000 speakers of Western Hindi languages in all Africa (1977 Voegelin and Voegelin). Mainly in Natal. Indo-European, Indo-Iranian, Indo-Aryan, Central zone, Western Hindi, Hindustani. Has features of Bhojpuri in South Africa. Hindu. Bible 1818-1987. See main entry under India.

KORANA ***(KORANNA, !ORA, !KORA, KORAQUA, GORACHOUQUA)*** [KQZ] 50 (1977 Voegelin and Voegelin), out of an ethnic group of 10,000 (1972 Barrett). Western. Possibly also Botswana. Khoisan, Southern Africa, Central, Nama. Slowly dying out. May be extinct. Nomads. Christian, traditional religion. Bible 1933.

KXOE ***(KHOE, XUN, WATER BUSHMEN, MBARAKWENA, MBARAKWENGO)*** [XUU] 1,600 (1998 Brenzinger). Smithsdrift. Khoisan, Southern Africa, Central, Tshu-Khwe, Northwest. Dialect: //ANI. Kxoedam is the language used. Refugees from Caprivi since 1991 living in tents. See main entry under Namibia.

NAMA ***(NAMAN, NAMAKWA, NAMAQUA, DAMA, DAMARA, DAMAQUA, TAMA, TAMMA, TAMAKWA, KHOEKHOE, BERDAMA, BERGDAMARA, KHOI, "HOTTENTOT", ROOI NASIE, KAKUYA BUSHMAN NASIE, "KLIPKAFFER", "KLIPKAFFERN")*** [NAQ] 56,000 in South Africa (1989 UBS). Khoisan, Southern Africa, Central, Nama. Dialect: GIMSBOK NAMA. Language of secondary education. SOV. Radio programs. Bible 1966. See main entry under Namibia.

NDEBELE ***(NREBELE, NDZUNDZA, TRANSVAAL NDEBELE, SOUTHERN NDEBELE)*** [NEL] 588,000 (1995), 1.5% of the population (1995 The Economist). Transvaal, south and central. Niger-Congo, Atlantic-Congo, Volta-Congo, Benue-Congo, Bantoid, Southern, Narrow Bantu, Central, S, Sotho-Tswana (S.30), Sotho, Northern. Sometimes called a dialect of Northern Sotho. Different from Ndebele of Zimbabwe. National language. Grammar. NT 1986.

N/U ***(=KHOMANI, NG'UKI,)*** [NGH] 20 mother tongue speakers out of 500 in the ethnic group (1998 Nigel Crawhall, South African San Institute). 3 in Swartkop, a township outside Upington, 1 in Sesbrugge outside Upington, 1 in Keimoes, 3 in Rosedale township in Upington, 1 in Raaswater outside Upington (!Kabee), 1 in Rietfontein (/'Auni), 1 partial speaker in Welkom (village in Kalahari, not Free State). Possibly 5 in Botswana. All varieties were spoken in the southern Kalahari before the speakers were displaced in the 1930s, whereupon most moved to urban townships. Khoisan, Southern Africa, Southern, !Kwi. Dialects: N/U, !KABEE, /'AUNI, //KXAU, //NG!KE (NG//-/E, //NG, /ING/KE). Closely related to /Xam. Speakers use Afrikaans and Nama (Khoekhoegowab) fluently. N/u is used with other N/u speakers, Nama with Nama friends and children, Afrikaans with adults and outsiders, sometimes with children, and for church. 60 to 96. Speakers are very upset that N/u is dying out. Younger people have a strong loyalty to Nama, not shared by N/u speakers. '=Khomani' is the name for the ethnic group. 'Ng'uki' is an incorrect name. Literacy is in Afrikaans. Nearly extinct.

OORLAMS [OOR] Creole, Afrikaans based. There are mother tongue speakers. It also includes some Bantu words. There are a large number of small colonies of Africans.

RONGA ***(SHIRONGA)*** [RON] Niger-Congo, Atlantic-Congo, Volta-Congo, Benue-Congo, Bantoid, Southern, Narrow Bantu, Central, S, Tswa-Ronga (S.50). Dialect: KONDE. Partially intelligible with ShiTsonga and ShiTswa. Bible 1923. See main entry under Mozambique.

SEROA [KQU] Also was in Lesotho. Khoisan, Southern Africa, Southern, !Kwi. Dialects: !GÃ!NGE (!GÃ!NE), //KU//E. Had three dialects. Extinct.

SOTHO, NORTHERN ***(PEDI, SEPEDI, TRANSVAAL SOTHO)*** [SRT] 3,840,000 in South Africa (1995 The Economist). Population total both countries 3,851,000. Transvaal, south and central. Also spoken in Botswana. Niger-Congo, Atlantic-Congo, Volta-Congo, Benue-Congo, Bantoid, Southern, Narrow Bantu, Central, S, Sotho-Tswana (S.30), Sotho, Northern. Dialects: MASEMOLA (MASEMULA, TAU), KGAGA (KXAXA, KHAGA), KONI (KONE), TSWENE (TSWENI), GANANWA (XANANWA, HANANWA), PULANA, PHALABORWA (PHALABURWA, THEPHALABORWA), KHUTSWE (KHUTSWI, KUTSWE),

LOBEDU (LUBEDU, LOVEDU, KHELOBEDU), TLOKWA (TLOKOA, TOKWA, DOGWA), PAI, DZWABO (THABINE-ROKA-NARENG), KOPA, MATLALA-MOLETSHI. Dialects Pai, Kutswe, and Pulana are more divergent and sometimes called 'Eastern Sotho'. National language. Newspapers, radio programs. Bible 1904-1951.

SOTHO, SOUTHERN ***(SUTO, SUTHU, SESOTHO, SOUTO, SISUTHO)*** [SSO] 2,704,000 in South Africa (1995), 6.9% of the population (1995 The Economist). Niger-Congo, Atlantic-Congo, Volta-Congo, Benue-Congo, Bantoid, Southern, Narrow Bantu, Central, S, Sotho-Tswana (S.30), Sotho, Southern. Dialects: TAUNG, PHUTHI. Sotho, Pedi, and Tswana are largely inherently intelligible but have generally been considered separate languages. National language. Literacy rate in second language: Fair. Language of secondary education. Newspapers, radio programs. Bible 1878-1989. See main entry under Lesotho.

SOUTH AFRICAN SIGN LANGUAGE [SFS] (12,100 deaf persons including 6,000 Black, 2,000 English white, 2,000 Afrikaans white, 1,200 Coloured, 900 Indian; 1986 Gallaudet Univ.). Deaf sign language. The North British sign system was used for the deaf in white English speaking families. In 1881 a school for Afrikaans speaking families was begun using British Sign Language. Several dialects are used unofficially in different schools. There are 9 sign language systems, 60% related to British or Australian sign languages, few to American Sign Language. Sign language is understood to some degree by most deaf people. Some interpreters are provided in courts. The first deaf school was established about 1846. Now there are 29 schools for 4,000 children. There is a Signed Afrikaans.

SWAHILI ***(KISWAHELI, SUAHILI, KISUAHILI, ARAB-SWAHILI)*** [SWA] 1,000 in South Africa (1987 Schreck and Barrett). Chatsworth, an urban area close to Durban on the Natal coast. Niger-Congo, Atlantic-Congo, Volta-Congo, Benue-Congo, Bantoid, Southern, Narrow Bantu, Central, G, Swahili (G.40). Zanzibaris brought from Zanzibar and northern Mozambique from 1873 to 1878. Coastal. Market gardeners. Muslim. Bible 1891-1996. See main entry under Tanzania.

SWATI ***(SWAZI, SISWAZI, SISWATI, TEKELA, TEKEZA)*** [SWZ] 1,019,000 in South Africa (1995), 2.6% of the population (1995 The Economist). Niger-Congo, Atlantic-Congo, Volta-Congo, Benue-Congo, Bantoid, Southern, Narrow Bantu, Central, S, Nguni (S.40). Dialects: BACA, HLUBI, PHUTHI. National language. Radio programs. Bible 1996. See main entry under Swaziland.

TSHWA ***(SHITSHWA, KITSHWA, XITSHWA, SHEETSHWA)*** [TSC] Niger-Congo, Atlantic-Congo, Volta-Congo, Benue-Congo, Bantoid, Southern, Narrow Bantu, Central, S, Tswa-Ronga (S.50). Dialects: HLENGWE (MAKAWE-KHAMBANA), TSHWA (DZIBI-DZONGA). Partially intelligible with Ronga and Tsonga. Bible 1910-1955. See main entry under Mozambique.

TSONGA ***(SHITSONGA, THONGA, TONGA, SHANGANA, SHANGAAN)*** [TSO] 1,646,000 in South Africa (1995), 4.2% of the population (1995 The Economist). Population total all countries 3,165,000. Transvaal. Also spoken in Mozambique, Swaziland, Zimbabwe. Niger-Congo, Atlantic-Congo, Volta-Congo, Benue-Congo, Bantoid, Southern, Narrow Bantu, Central, S, Tswa-Ronga (S.50). Dialects: LULEKE (XILULEKE), GWAMBA (GWAPA), CHANGANA, HLAVE, KANDE, N'WALUNGU (SHINGWALUNGU), XONGA, JONGA (DZONGA), NKUMA, SONGA, NHLANGANU (SHIHLANGANU). Partially intelligible with Ronga and Tswa. National language. A language of secondary education. Newspapers, radio programs. Christian, traditional religion. Bible 1907-1989.

TSOTSITAAL ***(FLY TAAL, FLAAI TAAL)*** [FLY] It had tens of thousands of primary users; hundreds of thousands of second language users (1984 Gilbert and Makhudu). In African townships around Johannesburg, Pretoria, Bloemfontein and other cities. Creole, Afrikaans based. Not intelligible to Afrikaans speakers. Uses many Afrikaans, English, and Bantu words, and others of unknown origin. Originated in the gold mines in Transvaal from 1886. Creolized by 1930. Used until the 1970s or 1980s. 'Tsotsitaal' means 'speech of young gang member, criminal, or thug'. Nearly extinct.

TSWANA ***(TSIWAHA, BEETJUANS, CHUANA, COANA, CUANA, SECHUANA)*** [TSW] 2,822,000 in South Africa (1995), 7.2% of the population (1995 The Economist). Niger-Congo, Atlantic-Congo, Volta-Congo, Benue-Congo, Bantoid, Southern, Narrow Bantu, Central, S, Sotho-Tswana (S.30), Tswana. Dialects: TAWANA, HURUTSHE, NGWAKETSE, THLARO, KWENA, NGWATO, TLOKWA, MELETE, KGATLA, THLAPING (TLAPI), ROLONG. Close to Southern and Northern Sotho. National language. Newspapers, radio programs. Bible 1857-1993. See main entry under Botswana.

URDU [URD] 170,000 South Asian Muslims in South Africa (1987). Along the Natal coast and urban areas around Durban, Transvaal surrounding Johannesburg, and scattered smaller towns. Indo-European, Indo-Iranian, Indo-Aryan, Central zone, Western Hindi, Hindustani. Most speak English. Merchants, traders, industrial, professional (medicine, computers), clerical workers, craftsmen. Muslim. Bible 1843-1998. See main entry under Pakistan.

VENDA ***(CHIVENDA)*** [VEN] 666,000 in South Africa (1995), 1.7% of the population (1995 The Economist). Population total both countries 750,000. Transvaal, north. Also spoken in Zimbabwe. Niger-Congo, Atlantic-Congo, Volta-Congo, Benue-Congo, Bantoid, Southern, Narrow Bantu, Central, S, Venda (S.20). Dialects: PHANI, TAVHA-TSINDI. The Lembaa are a Venda-speaking Jewish people claiming Falasha descent. National language. Literacy rate in second language: Fairly low. Traditional religion, Christian, Jewish (Lembaa). Bible 1936, in press (1997).

/XAM ***(/KHAM-KA-!K'E, /KAMKA!E, /XAM-KA-!K'E)*** [XAM] Khoisan, Southern Africa, Southern, !Kwi. Extinct.

//XEGWI ***(//XEGWE, //XEKWI, BATWA, BUSH-C, ABATHWA, BOROA, TLOUE, TLOUTLE, KLOUKLE, LXLOUKXLE, AMANKGQWIGQWI, NKQESHE, AMABUSMANA, GI/KXIGWI, KI//KXIGWI)*** [XEG] Near the Swaziland border. Khoisan, Southern Africa, Southern, !Kwi. Extinct.

XHOSA ***(ISIXHOSA, XOSA, KOOSA, "KAFFER", "KAFFIR", "CAFFRE", "CAFRE", "CAUZUH")*** [XOS] 6,858,000 in South Africa (1995), 17.5% of the population (1995 The Economist). Population total all countries 6,876,000. Southwest Cape Province and Transkei. Also spoken in Botswana, Lesotho. Niger-Congo, Atlantic-Congo, Volta-Congo, Benue-Congo, Bantoid, Southern, Narrow Bantu, Central, S, Nguni (S.40). Dialects: GEALEKA, NDLAMBE, GAIKA (NCQIKA), THEMBU, BOMVANA, MPONDOMSE (MPONDOMISI), MPONDO, XESIBE. 15% of the vocabulary is estimated to be of Khoekhoe (Khoisan) origin. Many understand Zulu, Swati, Southern Sotho. "Cauzuh" is an obsolete name. Somewhat acculturated. National language. Clicks. Literacy rate in second language: Fair rate. Newspapers, radio programs. Bible 1859, in press (1997).

XIRI ***(GRIKWA, GRIQUA, XRIKWA, XIRIKWA, GRY, CAPE HOTTENTOT)*** [XII] Khoisan, Southern Africa, Central, Nama. May be extinct. Nearly extinct.

ZULU ***(ISIZULU, ZUNDA)*** [ZUU] 8,778,000 in South Africa (1995), 22.4% of the population (1995 The Economist). Population total all countries 9,142,000. Zululand and northern Natal. Also spoken in Botswana, Lesotho, Malawi, Mozambique, Swaziland. Niger-Congo, Atlantic-Congo, Volta-Congo, Benue-Congo, Bantoid, Southern, Narrow Bantu, Central, S, Nguni (S.40). Dialects: LALA, QWABE. Close to Swazi and Xhosa. National language. Dictionary. Grammar. Literacy rate in second language: 70%. Newspapers, radio programs. Christian, traditional religion. Bible 1883-1959.

ST. HELENA

National or official language: English. 6,000 (1998 UN), including 5,400 St. Helena (1985 WA), 262 Tristen de Cunha (1983 WA), 1,500 Ascension (1985 WA). British dependencies. Data accuracy estimate: A2. The number of languages listed for St. Helena is 1. Diversity index 0.00.

ENGLISH [ENG] Indo-European, Germanic, West, English. National language. Bible 1535-1989. See main entry under United Kingdom.

SUDAN

Republic of the Sudan. Jamhuryat as-Sudan. National or official language: Standard Arabic. 28,292,000 (1998 UN). Literacy rate 20% to 27%. Information mainly from M. L. Bender 1976, 1983, 1989; T. Schadeberg 1981; P. Doornbos and M. L. Bender 1983; R. Stevenson 1984; J. Bendor-Samuel 1989. Sunni Muslim, traditional religion, Christian, secular. Blind population 110,000 (1982 WCE). Deaf institutions: 1. Data accuracy estimate: A2, B. The number of languages listed for Sudan is 142. Of those, 134 are living languages and 8 are extinct. Diversity index 0.56.

ACHERON ***(GARME)*** [ACZ] Northern Sudan, Kordofan Province, southern Nuba Hills. Niger-Congo, Kordofanian, Kordofanian Proper, Talodi, Talodi Proper, Tocho. Dialects: EASTERN ACHERON, WESTERN ACHERON. Not a dialect of Moro.

ACHOLI ***(ACOLI, ATSCHOLI, SHULI, GANG, LWO, AKOLI, ACOOLI, LOG ACOLI, DOK ACOLI)*** [ACO] 27,000 in Sudan (1978 SIL). Southern Sudan, Opari District, Acholi Hills. Nilo-Saharan, Eastern Sudanic, Nilotic, Western, Luo, Southern, Luo-Acholi, Alur-Acholi, Lango-Acholi. Bible 1986. See main entry under Uganda.

AFITTI ***(DITTI, UNIETTI, AFFITTI, DINIK)*** [AFT] 4,512 (1984 R. C. Stevenson). Northern Sudan, Nuba Hills, eastern Jebel ed Dair. Main center is Sidra. Nilo-Saharan, Eastern Sudanic, Western, Nyimang. Not inherently intelligible with Nyimang. 59% lexical similarity with Nyimang. Investigation needed: bilingual proficiency. Muslim.

AJA ***(AJJA, ADJA)*** [AJA] 200 (1993 R. Brown SIL). Southern Sudan, Western Bahr el Ghazal Province. Along the Sudan border, near the Shinko and Sapo rivers. Nilo-Saharan, Central Sudanic, West, Kresh. They consider themselves to be a Kresh tribe, but their language is not intelligible to the Kresh. Santandrea reports it to be half-way between Banda and Kresh; nearer to Banda in vocabulary and Kresh in structure. Speakers are mostly bilingual in Kresh. Investigation needed: bilingual proficiency in Gbaya (Kresh). Wooded savannah. Rolling plains with granite domes. Swidden agriculturalists.

AKA ***(SILLOK, JEBELS SILLOK, JEBEL SILAK, FA-C-AKA)*** [SOH] A few hundred (1989 Bender). Northern Sudan, Sillok (Silak) Hills, west of the main Berta-speaking people. Nilo-Saharan, Eastern Sudanic, Eastern, Eastern Jebel, Aka-Kelo-Molo. Bilingualism in Arabic, Berta. Heavily Arabicized and influenced by Berta. A remnant group (1983 Bender). They call themselves 'Fa-c-aka', 'people of Aka'.

AMA ***(NYIMANG, INYIMANG, NYIMA, NYIMAN)*** [NYI] 70,000 (1982 SIL). Northern Sudan, Kordofan Province, northwest of Dilling on range of hills of which Jebel Nyimang is a part, and on the Mandal range. Nilo-Saharan, Eastern Sudanic, Western, Nyimang. 59% lexical similarity with Afitti. Education is in Arabic. Muslim, Christian. Bible portions 1950.

ANUAK ***(ANYWAK, ANYWA, YAMBO, JAMBO, NURO, ANYUAK, DHO ANYWAA)*** [ANU] 52,000 in Sudan (1991 UBS). Population total both countries 98,000. Upper Nile Province, Pibor and Lower Akobo Rivers. From Akobo Post to latitude 6.45N. Also spoken in Ethiopia. Nilo-Saharan, Eastern Sudanic, Nilotic, Western, Luo, Northern, Anuak. Riverine. Traditional religion, Christian, Muslim. NT 1962-1965.

ARABIC, STANDARD [ABV] Middle East, North Africa. Afro-Asiatic, Semitic, Central, South, Arabic. Preserves ancient grammar. Not intelligible with Sudanese Spoken Arabic or Sudanese Creole Arabic. Used for nearly all written materials and formal speeches. Not a mother tongue, but taught in schools. Very little known and even less used in the south. Serious educational and sociolinguistic problems in the north also. National language. Bible 1984-1991. See main entry under Saudi Arabia.

ARABIC, SUDANESE CREOLE ***(JUBA ARABIC, SOUTHERN SUDAN ARABIC, PIDGIN ARABIC)*** [PGA] 20,000 first language and 44,000 second language speakers in Juba alone (1987 estimate). Southern Sudan, in the towns and many villages all over Equatoria Region, and up into Bahr al Ghazal and Upper Nile regions. Refugees have gone to other countries. Creole, Arabic based. Difficult intelligibility with Nubi, Sudanese Arabic, or Modern Standard Arabic. Also used as the major language of communication among speakers of different languages in Equatoria, south of Wau and Malakal. Used in many church services as first or second language in Juba and a few other towns. Many school teachers use it at least part of the time. Most people in towns speak at least two languages, and it is common for them to speak Creole Arabic, English, and 1, 2, or 3 vernaculars. Creole Arabic is gaining at the expense of English and the vernaculars, although most people keep their vernaculars as first, or at least second language. Trade language. SVO, tonal. Muslim, Christian. Bible portions 1983-1985.

ARABIC, SUDANESE SPOKEN ***(KHARTOUM ARABIC)*** [APD] 15,000,000 or more in Sudan, 51% of population (1991). Population total all countries 16,000,000 to 19,000,000. Northern Sudan primarily. Also spoken in Egypt, Eritrea, Ethiopia, Saudi Arabia. Afro-Asiatic, Semitic, Central, South, Arabic. Dialects: KHARTOUM, WESTERN SUDANESE, NORTH KORDOFAN ARABIC, JA'ALI, SHUKRI. Western Sudan Spoken Arabic, Juba Arabic, and Khartoum Arabic have little compatibility (Alan S. Kaye 1988). Trade language. Muslim, some Christian. NT 1978.

AVOKAYA ***(ABUKEIA, AVUKAYA)*** [AVU] 15,000 in Sudan (1982 SIL), including 2,800 Ajigu and 12,000 Ojila. Southern Sudan, Western Equatoria Province. The Ajiga dialect is north of Yei and south of Maridi, the Ojila dialect is mainly between the Naam (Era) and Olo rivers and farther east. Nilo-Saharan, Central Sudanic, East, Moru-Madi, Central. Dialects: OJILA (ODZILA, ODZILIWA), AJIGU (ADJIGA, OJIGA, AGAMORU). Closely related to Logo. There is intermarriage and bilingualism with the Baka and Mundu, especially near Maridi. Some speakers are bilingual in Zande. Bible portions 1986-1990. See main entry under DRC.

BAI ***(BARI)*** [BDJ] 2,500 (1971 Welmers). Southern Sudan, Western District, on Wau-Deim Zubeir road, west of Sere. A few north of Tembura. 2 villages. Niger-Congo, Atlantic-Congo, Volta-Congo, North, Adamawa-Ubangi, Ubangi, Sere-Ngbaka-Mba, Sere, Sere-Bviri, Bai-Viri. Speakers are reported to be bilingual in Ndogo.

BAKA ***(TARA BAAKA)*** [BDH] 25,000 in Sudan (1993 UBS). Population total both countries 26,300. Southern Sudan, Western Equatoria Province, south and west of Maridi, northwest of Yei. Also spoken in DRC. Nilo-Saharan, Central Sudanic, West, Bongo-Bagirmi, Bongo-Baka, Baka. Sudanese Creole Arabic is the main second language. Zande is taught in school and used in EP church. Some speakers intermarry with the Avokaya and Mundu, and are bilingual in those languages. Moru also used. Different from, and unrelated to, Baka of Cameroon. Literacy rate in first language: Below 1%. Literacy rate in second language: 5% to 25%. Christian, traditional religion, Muslim. Bible portions 1990-1993.

BANDA, MID-SOUTHERN [BJO] Southern Sudan, town of Sopo, near CAR border, and refugees in Khartoum. Niger-Congo, Atlantic-Congo, Volta-Congo, North, Adamawa-Ubangi, Ubangi, Banda, Central, Central Core, Mid-Southern. Dialects: DUKPU, WASA. See main entry under CAR.

BANDA, TOGBO-VARA [TOR] Southern Sudan. Niger-Congo, Atlantic-Congo, Volta-Congo, North, Adamawa-Ubangi, Ubangi, Banda, Central, Central Core, Togbo-Vara. Dialect: TOGBO (TOHGBOH, TAGBO). Not intelligible with other Banda languages or dialects in Sudan. They view themselves as very different from Mono. Different from Tagbu (Tagbo, Tagba) of DRC in Sere group. See main entry under DRC.

BANDA, WEST CENTRAL ***(GOLO)*** [BBP] 3,000 in Sudan (1982 SIL). Between Wau and Mboro. Niger-Congo, Atlantic-Congo, Volta-Congo, North, Adamawa-Ubangi, Ubangi, Banda, West Central. Speakers are reported to be bilingual in Ndogo in Sudan. Investigation needed: bilingual proficiency in Ndogo. See main entry under CAR.

BANDA-BANDA [BPD] Southern Sudan, town of Sopo near CAR border. Refugees in Khartoum. Niger-Congo, Atlantic-Congo, Volta-Congo, North, Adamawa-Ubangi, Ubangi, Banda, Central, Central Core, Banda-Banda. Dialects: GOVORO (GOVHOROH), VIDIRI (MVEDERE, VODERE, VIDRI, VADARA), WUNDU. See main entry under CAR.

BANDA-MBRÈS ***(BANDA OF MBRÉS, BANDA-MBRE)*** [BQK] Southern Sudan, town of Sopo, near the CAR border, and refugees in Khartoum. Niger-Congo, Atlantic-Congo, Volta-Congo, North, Adamawa-Ubangi, Ubangi, Banda, Central, Central Core, Banda-Mbres. Dialects: BUKA (BOUKA), MBRE (MBERE, MBELE), MORUBA (MOROUBA, MARABA), SABANGA (SANGBANGA), WADA (OUADDA). Investigation needed: intelligibility with Banda-Bambari. See main entry under CAR.

BANDA-NDÉLÉ ***(BANDA OF NDÉLÉ, NYELE)*** [BFL] Southern Sudan, town of Sopo near the CAR border, and refugees in Khartoum. Niger-Congo, Atlantic-Congo, Volta-Congo, North, Adamawa-Ubangi, Ubangi, Banda, Central, Central Core, Banda-Ndele. Dialects: JUNGURU (DJINGBURU, NGURU), TANGBAGO (TAMBOLO, TAMBAGGO, TOMBAGGO, TANGAGO), BANDA-KPAYA. Muslim, Christian, traditional religion. See main entry under CAR.

BARI ***(BERI)*** [BFA] 226,000 in Sudan (1978 SIL), including 26,400 in Kuku, 18,000 in Nyangbara, 3,400 in Nyepu, 25,000 in Pojulu. Population total both countries 286,000 or more. Southern Sudan, both banks of the Nile, south of Terakeka on the west bank, south of Mongalla on the east bank, as far as the Kajo Kaji Escarpment, from 5.30N on left bank, 5.15N on right bank to just south of latitude 4.15N. Also spoken in Uganda. Nilo-Saharan, Eastern Sudanic, Nilotic, Eastern, Bari. Dialects: KUKU, NYANGBARA (NYANGWARA, NYAMBARA), NYEPU (NYEFU, NYEPO, NYPHO, NGYEPU), PÖJULU (PAJULU, FADJULU, FAJELU, MADI), LIGO (LIGGO). 86% lexical similarity with Ngyepu, 85% with Pöjulu, 81% with Kuku, 80% with Nyanggwara, 71% with Mondari, 73% with Kakwa. Ethnic groups: Dupi (serfs), Kulu'ba, Liggi, Lui (free men), Tomonok (fishing, smithing). The Marshia (Marsanit) are professional smiths within the Bari group, who live in and around Rimo (Remo), and keep to themselves. Ethnic Bari in DRC now speak a dialect of Logo, and not Bari. Bushy, savannah, swamps, forests. Plains, shallow ravines, mountains. Blacksmiths: iron ore; pastoralists: cattle, goats, sheep; agriculturalists: millet, eleusine, simsim, peanuts, cassava, sweet potatoes. 1,700 to 3,000 feet. Traditional religion. Bible 1979.

BAYGO ***(BAIGO, BEGO, BEKO, BEIGO, BEYGO)*** [BYG] Ethnic group 850 (1978 GR). Northern Sudan, Southern Dar Fur, in the hills east of Kube (Kubbi). Jebel Beygo. Nilo-Saharan, Eastern Sudanic, Western, Daju, Western Daju. Was close to Daju of Dar Fur. They did not use the name 'Daju'. Muslim. Extinct.

BEDAWI ***(BEJA, BEDAWIYE, BEDAUYE, TO-BEDAWIE, BEDJA)*** [BEI] 951,000 in Sudan (1982 SIL) including 30,000 Hadendoa, 15,000 Bisharin (1992). Population total all countries 1,148,000. Northeastern Sudan along the Red Sea coast. Also spoken in Egypt, Eritrea. Afro-Asiatic, Cushitic, North. Dialects: HADENDOA (HADENDOWA, HADENDIWA), HADAREB (HADAAREB), BISHARIN (BISARIAB), BENI-AMIR. Little vocabulary in common with other Cushitic languages, but a great deal of the verbal morphology is similar. Bilingualism in Arabic, Tigre. 'Bedàwie' is their name for their language. Halenga and Arteiga are ethnic groups. Investigation needed: intelligibility with dialects. Dictionary. Grammar. Desert, coastal. Pastoralists. Sunni Muslim.

BELANDA BOR ***(DE BOR)*** [BXB] 8,000 (1983 SIL). Southern Sudan, on the main road south of Wau. Nilo-Saharan, Eastern Sudanic, Nilotic, Western, Luo, Northern, Bor. Most people are bilingual in Belanda Viri. There is much intermarriage between the two groups. Traditional religion, Christian, Muslim.

BELANDA VIRI ***(VIRI, BVIRI, BIRI, GUMBA, GAMBA, MBEGUMBA, MVEGUMBA, BELANDA)*** [BVI] 16,000 (1971 Welmers). Southern Sudan, scattered, around Raffili, on the Wau road, on the Kuru River, 40 miles from Deim Zubeir, around Tembura among the Zande, on the Iba River near Yambio. Niger-Congo, Atlantic-Congo, Volta-Congo, North, Adamawa-Ubangi, Ubangi, Sere-Ngbaka-Mba, Sere, Sere-Bviri, Bai-Viri. Some bilingualism in Belanda Bor. They call themselves 'Viri'.

BELI ***(BEHLI, BEILI, JUR BELI, 'BELI)*** [BLM] 6,600 including 5,000 Beli, 1,600 Sopi (1982 SIL). Southern Sudan. One group is southwest of Rumbek, at Wulu, westward along the road to Bahr Gel and south toward the southern border of Lakes Province. In some areas they are heavily intermingled with Dinka. Another group lives east of Mvolo and has no links with the first group. They are centered around Bahri Girinti (Lake Nyiropo) just west of Yei River. Nilo-Saharan, Central Sudanic, West, Bongo-Bagirmi, Bongo-Baka, Morokodo-Beli. Dialects: WULU, BAHRI GIRINTI,

SOPI (SUPI). 46% lexical similarity with Jur Modo, 45% with Bongo, 41% with Mo'da and Morokodo, 39% with Baka. Using Jur Modo literacy materials (1998). Christian, traditional religion.

BERTA ***(BARTA, BURTA, "BENI SHANGUL", WETAWIT)*** [WTI] 22,000. Northern Sudan. Nilo-Saharan, Berta. Dialects: SHURU, BAKE, UNDU, MAYU, FADASHI. Probably two or more languages. Fadashi may be separate. "Beni Shangul" is the Arabic name, and is reported to be derogatory. Investigation needed: intelligibility with Fadashi. Agriculturalists. Traditional religion, Muslim. See main entry under Ethiopia.

BERTI [BYT] Northern Sudan. Tagabo Hills, Dar Fur, and in Kordofan. Nilo-Saharan, Saharan, Eastern. Muslim. Extinct.

BIRKED ***(BIRGUID, BIRGID, BIRKIT, BIRQED, MURGI, KAJJARA)*** [BRK] Northern Sudan, north Dar Fur, north and east of Daju and Baygo, east of Jebel Marra between Jebel Harayt and the Rizaykat (Arab) country. Also north of Nyala. A few in north Kordofan south of El Obeid. Nilo-Saharan, Eastern Sudanic, Eastern, Nubian, Central, Birked. 60% lexical similarity with Kadaru; 51% with Meidob (closest). Muslim. Extinct.

BOGURU ***(KOGURU, KOGORO, BUGURU)*** [BQU] Population total both countries 494 and more (1997). Mariko, Baambu, Ibba, Bagasu. Also spoken in DRC. Niger-Congo, Atlantic-Congo, Volta-Congo, Benue-Congo, Bantoid, Southern, Narrow Bantu, Central, D, Bira-Huku (D.30). Dialects: BOGURU, BUKUR (BUKUM, BUKURU). Speakers in exile in DRC are organized and wanting help with language revival.

BONGO ***(BUNGU, DOR)*** [BOT] 5,000 to 10,000 (1987 SIL). A large sparsely populated area reaching from Tonj and Wau on the north, the Beli on the east, the Zande on the south, and the Bor on the west. Nilo-Saharan, Central Sudanic, West, Bongo-Bagirmi, Bongo-Baka, Bongo. Dialects: BUSERE BONGO, TONJ BONGO, BUNGO. Slight dialect differences between those on the River Busere, who have had Zande influence, and those around Tonj. Bungo dialect has minor differences. Close to the Jur Beli cluster. Bilingualism in Jur Beli is low. Generally, adults understand Zande, and adult males understand Dinka Rek. Younger people do not understand Zande or Dinka because education is mostly in Arabic with some English. Many students drop out of school because they cannot understand the language being used. Different from Bongo which is a dialect or closely related language to Banda of CAR and DRC. SVO. Hunters. Traditional religion, Muslim, Christian.

BURUN ***(BARUN, LANGE, CAI, BORUN)*** [BDI] 18,000 (1977 Voegelin and Voegelin). Northern Sudan, Blue Nile Province. Nilo-Saharan, Eastern Sudanic, Nilotic, Western, Luo, Northern, Maban-Burun, Burun. Dialects: RAGREIG, ABULDUGU (BOGON, MUGO-MBORKOINA), MAIAK, MUFWA (MOPO), MUGHAJA (MUGAJA, MUMUGHADJA). Some southern dialects are intelligible with Mabaan.

DAGIK ***(MASAKIN, MASAKIN DAGIG, DAGIG, REIKHA, DENGEBU)*** [DEC] (38,000 with Ngile; 1982 SIL). Northern Sudan, Kordofan Province, Nuba Mts., on some outlying hills in Mesakin Hills, Reika village. Niger-Congo, Kordofanian, Kordofanian Proper, Talodi, Talodi Proper, Ngile-Dengebu. 80% lexical similarity with Ngile (closest).

DAIR ***(DAIER, THAMINYI)*** [DRB] 1,000 (1978 GR). Northern Sudan, west and south parts of Jebel Dair, Kordofan. Nilo-Saharan, Eastern Sudanic, Eastern, Nubian, Central, Hill, Unclassified. SOV.

DAJU, DAR FUR ***(NYALA-LAGOWA, FININGA, DAGU, DAJU FERNE, BEKE)*** [DAJ] 70,000 to 90,000 all Daju in Dar Fur (1983 Bender). Northern Sudan, Dar Fur Province, in the Daju Hills 25 miles northeast of Nyala. Also in Geneina District in Dar Masalit. The West Kordofan dialect is in the Daju Hills near Lagowa, with main settlements at Dar el Kabira, Nyukri, and Tamanyik and other hills. Nilo-Saharan, Eastern Sudanic, Western, Daju, Western Daju. Dialects: NYALA, LAGOWA. 83% lexical similarity between Nyala and Lagowa, 74% with Sila, 62% with Shatt, 56% with Logorik. Muslim.

DAJU, DAR SILA ***(SILA, SULA, MONGO-SILA, BOKOR, BOKORUGE, BOKORIKE)*** [DAU] Northern Sudan. Nearly all those Daju of Dar Sila who are in Sudan have migrated into Dar Fur and settled there in recent times. Nilo-Saharan, Eastern Sudanic, Western, Daju, Western Daju. Dialects: MONGO, SILA. 74% lexical similarity with Daju of Dar Fur (Nyala and Lagowa), 60% with Shatt, 57% with Logorik. Little education. Traditional religion, some Muslim. See main entry under Chad.

DIDINGA ***('DI'DINGA, XAROXA, TOI, LANGO)*** [DID] 58,000 (1978 SIL). Southern Sudan, Didinga Hills and north of Nagishot. Nilo-Saharan, Eastern Sudanic, Eastern, Surmic, South, Southwest, Didinga-Murle, Didinga-Longarim. Ethnic groups: Chukudum, Lowudo. Slight differences in speech between Chukudum and Lowudo, apparently mainly phonetic. 83% lexical similarity with Longarim, 71% with Murle. Different from Lango which is related to Lotuko. Traditional religion. Bible portions 1994.

DILLING ***(DELEN, WARKI, WARKIMBE)*** [DIL] 5,295 (1984 R. C. Stevenson). Northern Sudan, Southern Kordofan, town of Dilling and surrounding hills, including Kudr. Nilo-Saharan, Eastern Sudanic, Eastern, Nubian, Central, Hill, Unclassified. Dialects: DILLING, DEBRI. 94% lexical similarity with Debri, 93% with Kadaru. SOV.

DINKA, NORTHEASTERN ***(PADANG, WHITE NILE DINKA)*** [DIP] 320,000 (1986 UBS) including 7,200 Abialang, 9,000 Dongjol, 2,500 Luac, 16,000 Ngok-Sobat, 20,000 Jok, 13,500 Ageer, 2,000 Rut, 400 Thoi. Southern Sudan, northeast of the Sudd, along both sides of the White Nile, and along the Sobat River. Nilo-Saharan, Eastern Sudanic, Nilotic, Western, Dinka-Nuer, Dinka. Dialects: ABILIANG (DINKA IBRAHIM, AKOON, BAWOM, BOWOM), DONGJOL, LUAC (LUAIC), NGOK-SOBAT (NGORK, JOK), AGEER (AGER, AGEIR, ABUYA, BEER, NIEL, NYEL, PALOC, PALOIC), RUT, THOI. 92% lexical similarity with Northwestern Dinka, 88% with Southwestern Dinka, 88% with Southeastern Dinka, 86% with South Central Dinka. Bilingualism in Sudanese Arabic. 'Jaang' is a cover term for all Dinka languages. Traditional religion, Christian, Muslim. NT 1952.

DINKA, NORTHWESTERN [DIW] 80,000 Ruweng (1986). Southern Sudan, north of the Bahr el Ghazal River, and southern Kordofan around Abyei. Nilo-Saharan, Eastern Sudanic, Nilotic, Western, Dinka-Nuer, Dinka. Dialects: ALOR, NGOK-KORDOFAN, PAN ARU, RUWENG. A separate language from other Dinka (J. Duerksen SIL). 88% lexical similarity with Southwestern Dinka and Southeastern Dinka, 84% with South Central Dinka.

DINKA, SOUTH CENTRAL ***(AGAR, CENTRAL DINKA)*** [DIB] 250,000 including 2,000 Aker, 2,000 Thany, 22,000 Ciec, 25,000 Gok (Tucker and Bryan). Total Dinka 2,000,000 or more. Southern Sudan, west of the Nile, south of the Sudd. Aker is southeast of the Agar; Aliap is south of the Bor in a few fishing villages mainly on the east bank of the Nile. Ciec is in Lakes District on the west bank of the Nile. Gok is between the Agar and the Rek in Jur River and Lakes districts. Nilo-Saharan, Eastern Sudanic, Nilotic, Western, Dinka-Nuer, Dinka. Dialects: ALIAP (ALIAB, THANY, AKER), CIEC (CIEM, CIC, CHIECH, KWAC, AJAK, ADOR), GOK (GAUK, COK), AGAR. Gok is also influenced by Southwestern Dinka and has a number of Arabic loans. Agar is becoming accepted as the educational standard for South Central Dinka. 90% with Southeastern Dinka. Bilingualism in Sudanese Arabic. Pastoralists, agriculturalists: grain, corn, peanuts, beans. Traditional religion, Christian, Muslim. Bible portions 1866-1916.

DINKA, SOUTHEASTERN ***(BOR, EASTERN DINKA)*** [DIN] 250,000 including 21,000 Atoc, 9,000 Ghol, 4,000 Nyarueng, 35,000 Twi, 21,000 Bor Gok (Tucker and Bryan). 500,000 including South Central (Agar) and Southeastern (Bor) (1982 UBS). Southern Sudan, east of the Nile, around Bor and northwards. Nilo-Saharan, Eastern Sudanic, Nilotic, Western, Dinka-Nuer, Dinka. Dialects: BOR (BOR GOK), ATHOC (ATHOIC, ATOC, BORATHOI, BOR ATHOIC), GHOL, NYARWENG (NYARUENG, NARREWENG), TUIC (TWI). Sudanese Arabic is the second language. Speakers of some dialects also speak Nuer Gewaar and Nuer Lou. Traditional religion, Christian, Muslim. NT 1940.

DINKA, SOUTHWESTERN ***(REK, WESTERN DINKA)*** [DIK] 450,000 (1982 UBS) including 55,000 Abiem, 15,000 Luac, 40,000 Malual, 17,000 Paliet, 35,000 Palioupiny, 50,000 Tuic. Southern Sudan, north and northwest of Wau. Nilo-Saharan, Eastern Sudanic, Nilotic, Western, Dinka-Nuer, Dinka. Dialects: REK (RAIK), ABIEM (AJONG DIT, AJONG THI, AKANY KOK, AKERN JOK, APUOTH, APWOTH, ANEI), AGUOK (AGWOK), APUK, AWAN, LAU, LUAC, MALUAL (MALWAL, ATOKTOU, DULIIT, KOROK, MAKEM, PETH), PALIET (BALIET, AJAK, BUONCWAI, BON SHWAI, BWONCWAI, KONGDER, KONDAIR, THANY BUR, TAINBOUR), PALIOUPINY (PALIOPING, AKJUET, AKWANG, AYAT, CIMEL, GOMJUER), TUIC (TWIC, TWICH, TWIJ, ADHIANG, AMIOL, NYANG, THON). Luac dialect is different from Luac dialect in Northeastern Dinka. 89% lexical similarity with South Central Dinka, 90% with Southeastern Dinka. Bilingualism in Sudanese Arabic. Pastoralists: cattle. Traditional religion, Christian, Muslim.

DONGOTONO [DDD] Southern Sudan, eastern Equatoria Province, Dongotono Hills southeast of Torit. Nilo-Saharan, Eastern Sudanic, Nilotic, Eastern, Lotuxo-Teso, Lotuxo-Maa, Lotuxo. 60% lexical similarity with Otuho.

EL HUGEIRAT [ELH] 1,000 (1978 GR). Northern Sudan, West Kordofan on El Hugeirat Hills. Nilo-Saharan, Eastern Sudanic, Eastern, Nubian, Central, Hill, Unclassified. SOV.

FEROGE ***(FERROGE, FEROGHE, KALIGI, KALIKI, KALIGE, KALIKE)*** [FER] 8,000 (1982 SIL). Southern Sudan, Western Bahr el Ghazal at Khor Shamam, 8 miles northeast of Raga. Niger-Congo, Atlantic-Congo, Volta-Congo, North, Adamawa-Ubangi, Ubangi, Sere-Ngbaka-Mba, Sere, Feroge-Mangaya. Indri, Mangaya, and Togoyo are closely related languages. Many are bilingual in Sudanese Arabic. Their own name is 'Kaligi'. 'Feroge' is the Arabic name for the people. Muslim.

FULFULDE, ADAMAWA ***(FELLATA)*** [FUB] 90,000 in Sudan (1982 SIL). Northern Sudan, Blue Nile and Kordofan regions. Niger-Congo, Atlantic-Congo, Atlantic, Northern, Senegambian, Fula-Wolof, Fulani, Eastern. Dialect: GOMBE. Many speak Sudanese Arabic; some also speak Hausa and Songai as second languages. Mahdist group is bilingual in Fulfulde and Sudanese Spoken Arabic. Few monolinguals; most are children. Previous migrations from Sokoto, Nigeria; Maasina, Mali; Liptaako and Jelgooji, Burkina Faso; Adamawa and Gombe, Nigeria; and the Wodaabe lineage have settled in Sudan. Some also from Cameroon. Predominant Fulfulde in Sudan is Adamawa.

Influenced by Arabic. Muwalid group is monolingual in Sudanese Spoken Arabic. Muslim. Bible 1983. See main entry under Cameroon.

FUR ***(FOR, FORA, FORDUNGA, FURAWI, FURAKANG, FORTA, FOROK, KONJARA, KUNGARA, YERGE, ONAGE, KORRA, KADIRGI, KURKA, DALA, LALI)*** [FUR] 500,000 in Sudan (1983 Bender). Population total both countries 502,000. Northern Sudan, Dar Fur. Also spoken in Chad. Nilo-Saharan, Fur. Largely uniform with some dialect differences. Those in urban situations are shifting to Arabic. SOV. Mountains, foothills, lowland. Agriculturalists: millet, sorghum, peanuts, vegetables, spices, fruit; cattle. Muslim.

GAAM ***(INGASSANA, INGESSANA, TABI, METABI, MUNTABI, MAMEDJA, MAMIDZA, KAMANIDI)*** [TBI] 40,000 to 80,000 (1997 M. L. Bender). Northern Sudan. The main center is in and around Jebel Tabi, on Tabi Massif and outlying hills. A small community in Khartoum. Not in Ethiopia. Nilo-Saharan, Eastern Sudanic, Eastern, Eastern Jebel, Gaam. Ethnic groups: Agadi, Bagis, Beek, Bulmut, Kilgu, Kukuli, Mugum, Sidak. Traditional religion, Christian.

GBAYA ***(KRESH, KREISH, KREICH, KREDJ, KPARLA, KPALA, KPARA)*** [KRS] 16,000 (1987 SIL). About 4,000 others speak Gbaya as second language. Population total both countries 16,000 or more. Southern Sudan, Western Bahr el Ghazal Province. At Kuru, Deim Zubeir, Raga, Angbanga, Kata, Menangba, Boro, Kafia Kingi. The Dongo are reported by Fr. Santandrea to be in Hobbinya District of Southern Dar Fur Province. Also communities in Wau and Khartoum. Largest numbers in Raga and Boro. A few refugees have settled in CAR and elsewhere. Also spoken in CAR. Nilo-Saharan, Central Sudanic, West, Kresh. Dialects: NAKA (KRESH-BORO), GBAYA-NDOGO (KRESH-NDOGO), GBAYA-NGBONGBO (KRESH-HOFRA), GBAYA-GBOKO, ORLO (WORO), GBAYA-DARA, DONGO. 8 tribes and dialects. Gbaya-Ndogo is prestigious and understood by all. Naka is largest and also well understood. Men and those who have been to school speak Sudanese Arabic as second language for most common topics. They do not accept Standard Arabic, except for a few who have been to school. 'Gbaya' is speakers' own name. Different from the Gbaya languages in the Niger-Congo family. SVO, prepositions, genitives and articles after noun heads, adjectives before, numerals usually before, relatives after, CV, V, CCV (CVC rare), 5 tones. Wooded savannah. Rolling plains with granite domes. Swidden agriculturalists; craftsmen in towns. 400 meters (Wau), 600 meters (Raga), 700 meters (Boro). Muslim, Christian.

GHULFAN ***(GULFAN, WUNCI, WUNCIMBE)*** [GHL] 16,000 (1984 R. C. Stevenson). Northern Sudan, Kordofan, in two hill ranges 25 to 30 miles south of Dilling: Ghulfan Kurgul and Ghulfan Morung. Nilo-Saharan, Eastern Sudanic, Eastern, Nubian, Central, Hill, Kadaru-Ghulfan. SOV.

GULA ***(KARA, KARA OF SUDAN, YAMEGI)*** [KCM] 200 to 2,000 in Sudan (1987 SIL). Southern Sudan at Kafia Kingi in extreme western Bahr el Ghazal Province and at Kata. Nilo-Saharan, Central Sudanic, West, Bongo-Bagirmi, Kara. Dialects: GULA (GOULA), NGURU (BUBU, KOYO). Many in Sudan are reported to be bilingual in Kresh or Arabic. Different from Kara of CAR, Kare of Chad, or Gula of Chad. See main entry under CAR.

GULE ***(ANEJ, HAMEJ, FECAKOMODIYO)*** [GLE] Northern Sudan, Jebel Gule, San and Roro hills north of the Gaam, west of Er Roseires. Nilo-Saharan, Komuz, Koman. The people now speak Arabic. The name 'Funj' is a cover term used by all the peoples of the southern Blue Nile area, and some Arabs from that area to identify their languages to outsiders. It also refers to the empire of the Funj that existed 500 years ago in that area. Muslim, traditional religion. Extinct.

GUMUZ ***(MENDEYA, DEBATSA, DEGUBA, DEHENDA, GUMIS, GOMBO, SHANKILLINYA, SHANQILLA)*** [GUK] 40,000 in Sudan. Northern Sudan, around Famaka, Roseires from Ethiopia border possibly as far as Fazoglo. Nilo-Saharan, Komuz, Gumuz. Dialects: DISOHA (DESUA), DAKUNZA (DEGOJA, DUKUNZA, GUNZA, GANZA, DUKUNA, DUGUNZA), SAI, SESE (SAYSAY), DEKOKA, DEWIYA, KUKWAYA, GOMBO, JEMHWA, MODEA. Dialects are inherently intelligible. See main entry under Ethiopia.

HAUSA [HUA] 418,000 in Sudan (1993 Johnstone). Northern Sudan. Afro-Asiatic, Chadic, West, A, A.1. In Sudan many speakers are probably ethnic Fulani who no longer speak Fulfulde. Trade language. Muslim. Bible 1932-1996. See main entry under Nigeria.

HEIBAN ***(EBANG, ABUL)*** [HEB] 4,412 (1984). Northern Sudan, around Heiban, Abul (Obul) and nearby hills. In Heiban town on the Abri-Talodi road. Niger-Congo, Kordofanian, Kordofanian Proper, Heiban, West-Central, Central, Ebang-Logol, Ebang-Laru. 90% lexical similarity with Laro (closest). NT 1966.

HOMA [HOM] Southern Sudan, around towns of Mopoi and Tambura. Niger-Congo, Atlantic-Congo, Volta-Congo, Benue-Congo, Bantoid, Southern, Narrow Bantu, Central, D, Bira-Huku (D.30). Extinct linguistically in 1975. Extinct.

INDRI ***(YANDERIKA, YANDIRIKA)*** [IDR] 700. Southern Sudan, southwest, in a small area around Raga. Niger-Congo, Atlantic-Congo, Volta-Congo, North, Adamawa-Ubangi, Ubangi, Sere-Ngbaka-Mba, Sere, Indri-Togoyo. Closest to Feroge. Speakers are reported to be bilingual in Arabic or Feroge.

JUMJUM ***(BERIN, OLGA, WADEGA)*** [JUM] 25,000 to 50,000 (1987 SIL). Northern Upper Nile Province, along Khor Jumjum on Jebels Tunga, Terta, and Wadega. Nilo-Saharan, Eastern Sudanic, Nilotic, Western, Luo, Northern, Maban-Burun, Maban.

JUR MODO [BEX] 15,400 (1982 SIL). Southern Sudan, vicinity of Mvolo and on the Naam (Olo) River. Nilo-Saharan, Central Sudanic, West, Bongo-Bagirmi, Bongo-Baka, Morokodo-Beli. Dialects: LORI, MODO (JUR MODO, MODO LALI), WIRA, WETU. The Wetu dialect is not extinct. NT 1998.

KACIPO-BALESI [KOE] 5,000 in Sudan (1983 SIL). Population total both countries 7,000 to 8,000. Southern Sudan, on the Boma Plateau among the Murle, near the Ethiopian border. Also spoken in Ethiopia. Nilo-Saharan, Eastern Sudanic, Eastern, Surmic, South, Southwest, Kacipo-Balesi. Dialects: KICHEPO, SURI, WESTERN SURI. Related to Murle and Didinga. Almost completely monolingual. They have little contact with the outside world. They call themselves 'Kacipo'. Traditional religion.

KADARU ***(KADARO, KADERO, KADERU, KODORO, KODHIN, KODHINNIAI)*** [KDU] 7,000 including Western Kadaru (1978 GR). Northern Sudan, Kordofan Province, Nuba mountains, north and east part of the Kadaru Hills between Dilling and Delami. Nilo-Saharan, Eastern Sudanic, Eastern, Nubian, Central, Hill, Kadaru-Ghulfan. Dialect: WESTERN KADARU. 93% lexical similarity with Dilling; 92% to 87% with Debri; 60% with Birked. SOV.

KAKWA ***(BARI KAKWA, KAKUA, KWAKWAK, KAKWAK)*** [KEO] 40,000 in Sudan (1978 SIL). Southern Sudan, Yei District, extending into DRC in the west at Aba and in the south around Mahagi. Nilo-Saharan, Eastern Sudanic, Nilotic, Eastern, Bari. The DRC and Sudan dialects differ only slightly. Some treat Kakwa as a dialect of Bari, but they are separate (SIL 1978). Agriculturalists: maize, eleusine, peanuts, simsim, sweet potatoes, cassava, honey; pastoralists: goats, few sheep, cattle. Traditional religion. Bible 1983. See main entry under Uganda.

KANGA ***(KUFO, KUFA)*** [KCP] 8,000 (1989). Northern Sudan, Miri Hills, west and southwest of Kadugli. Niger-Congo, Kordofanian, Kadugli, Central. Dialects: ABU SINUN, CHIRORO-KURSI, KUFA-LIMA. 85% lexical similarity with Tumma (closest).

KANURI, CENTRAL ***(YERWA KANURI, KANOURI, BORNU, BORNOUANS, KANOURY, KOLE, SIRATA, "BERIBERI")*** [KPH] 195,000 in Sudan (1993 Johnstone). Northern. Nilo-Saharan, Saharan, Western, Kanuri. Dialects: DAGARA, KAGA (KAGAMA), SUGURTI, LARE, KWAYAM, NJESKO, KABARI (KUVURI), NGAZAR, GUVJA, MAO, TEMAGERI, FADAWA, MAIDUGURI. "Beriberi" is considered a derogatory name. Ajami script used. Muslim. NT, in press (1997). See main entry under Nigeria.

KARKO ***(GARKO, KITHONIRISHE)*** [KKO] 12,986 (1984 R. C. Stevenson). Northern Sudan, Kordofan, in Karko Hills 20 miles west of Dilling, including Dulman. May also be spoken on Abu Jinik to the west (1,000) and El Tabaq southwest of Katla (800). Nilo-Saharan, Eastern Sudanic, Eastern, Nubian, Central, Hill, Unclassified. SOV.

KATCHA-KADUGLI-MIRI [KAT] 74,935 including 48,864 Kadugli and Katcha, 26,071 Miri (1984 R. C. Stevenson). Northern Sudan, Kordofan Province, in the southern hills of the Nuba Hills area. Katcha is in villages a short distance south of Kadugli and southeast of the Miri Hills. Kadugli is also in villages surrounding Kadugli. Miri is in Miri villages south of Kadugli. Niger-Congo, Kordofanian, Kadugli, Central. Dialects: KATCHA (TOLUBI, DHOLUBI, TUNA, KACA), KADUGLI (DAKALLA, TALLA, DHALLA, TOMA MA DALLA, KUDUGLI, MORTA), MIRI, DAMBA. R. C. Stevenson treats them as dialects of one language. Ruhlen (1987) and Schadeberg (1989) treat them as separate. 85% lexical similarity between Katcha, Kadugli, and Miri. Some Daju live among the Kadugli. Orthography in use developed by Stevenson in Katcha.

KATLA ***(AKALAK, KALAK)*** [KCR] 14,208 (1984 R. C. Stevenson). Northern Sudan, Nuba Hills, Katla Hills 35 miles southwest of Dilling. Niger-Congo, Kordofanian, Kordofanian Proper, Katla. Dialects: BOMBORI, KATEIK, KIDDU, KIRKPONG, KAROKA, KOLDRONG, JULUD (GULUD). Tima is a related, but separate language. The dialects listed are place names where variations are spoken.

KEIGA ***(YEGA, KEIGA-TIMERO, KEIGA-AL-KHEIL, DEMIK, AIGANG)*** [KEC] 6,072 (1984 R. C. Stevenson) out of a larger ethnic population. Northern Sudan, Nuba Hills area, Jebel Demik, north of Miri. Niger-Congo, Kordofanian, Kadugli, Western. Dialects: DEMIK (ROFIK), KEIGA (AIGANG). 60% lexical similarity with closest Kadugli languages. Keiga used in most domains. About half the children learn the language.

KELIKO ***(KALIKO)*** [KBO] 10,000 in Sudan (1998 SIL). Population total all countries 22,500. Southern Sudan, southern part of Yei District. Also spoken in DRC, Uganda. Nilo-Saharan, Central Sudanic, East, Moru-Madi, Central. Dialects: EASTERN KALIKO, WESTERN KALIKO. The two dialects in Sudan are inherently intelligible to each other's speakers. The name 'Keliko' is preferred in Sudan, 'Kaliko' in the other countries. Traditional religion, Christian.

KELO ***(TORNASI, KELO-BENI SHEKO, NDU-FAA-KEELO)*** [TSN] Northern Sudan, Tornasi Hills; Jebels Tornasi (Keeli village) and Beni Sheko. West of Berta speaking people. Nilo-Saharan,

Eastern Sudanic, Eastern, Eastern Jebel, Aka-Kelo-Molo. Dialects: BENI SHEKO, KELO. M. L. Bender reports that they are not extinct (1997). Muslim.

KENUZI-DONGOLA ***(DONGOLA-KENUZ, NILE NUBIAN, DONGOLAWI)*** [KNC] 180,000 in Sudan (1996). Population total both countries 280,000. Northern Sudan, mainly at Dongola and surrounding regions, Northern Province. Also spoken in Egypt. Nilo-Saharan, Eastern Sudanic, Eastern, Nubian, Central, Dongolawi. Dialects: DONGOLA, KENUZI (KENUZ, KUNUZI). Not intelligible with Mahas-Fiadidja. 67% lexical similarity with Nobiin. 56% with Debri. Bible portions 1912.

KO ***(KAU, FUNGOR, FUNGUR)*** [FUJ] 2,683 (1984 R. C. Stevenson). Northern Sudan, on small isolated hills in the extreme eastern part of the Nuba hills, between Talodi and the White Nile. Niger-Congo, Kordofanian, Kordofanian Proper, Heiban, Eastern. Dialects: KAU (KO), NYARO. Nyaro and Kau may be the same dialect. 67% lexical similarity with Warnang (closest). Traditional religion.

KOALIB ***(KAWALIB, KOWALIB, NGIRERE, NIRERE, RERE, LGALIGE, ABRI)*** [KIB] 44,258 (1984 R. C. Stevenson). Northern Sudan, southern Kordofan Province, Nuba Mountains, around Delami, including Umm Berumbita and Turum (Nguqwurang), south and southwest of Abri around Koalib range (Ngunduna), at and around Nyukwur, also at Umm Heitan and Hadra (Nginyukwur), in villages scattered over the plain around Abri (Ngirere). Niger-Congo, Kordofanian, Kordofanian Proper, Heiban, West-Central, Central, Rere. Dialects: NGUQWURANG, NGUNDUNA, NGINYUKWUR, NGIRERE, NGEMERE. 75% lexical similarity with closest Heiban languages. Traditional religion, Muslim, Christian. NT 1967-1994.

KOMO ***(KOMA OF DAGA, COMO, CENTRAL KOMA, GOKWOM, HAYAHAYA, MADIIN)*** [KOM] 10,000 in Sudan (1979 James). Population total both countries 11,500. Northern Sudan, around Ahmar, Tombak, and Yabus rivers, in southern Funj region of Blue Nile Province. Also spoken in Ethiopia. Nilo-Saharan, Komuz, Koman. Dialects: BEILLA, CHALI. Those listed as dialects may be separate languages. 52% lexical similarity with Uduk. Different from Koma of Cameroon. Dictionary.

KRONGO ***(KORONGO, KURUNGU, KADUMODI, TABANYA, DIMODONGO)*** [KGO] 21,688 (1984 R. C. Stevenson). Northern Sudan, Krongo Hills, south of Masakin range and west of Talodi, Kordofan Province. Niger-Congo, Kordofanian, Kadugli, Eastern. Dialect: FAMA-TEIS-KUA. 85% lexical similarity with Tumtum. 'Nuba' is a goegraphical term which is applied ethnically to the 40 or more people groups, including Krongo, living in the Nuba Hills. 'Nubian' is basically an ethnic term referring to the groups who live along the Nile from around Dongola north into Egypt (speaking the 'Nile Nubian' languages, Nobiin and Kenuzi-Dongola). 'Nubian' is also used linguistically for the group of languages related to the Nile Nubian ones, some of which (the Hill Nubian languages) are spoken in the Nuba Hills. Traditional religion, Muslim, Christian. NT 1963.

LAFOFA ***(KIDIE, TEGEM)*** [LAF] 5,140 (1984 R. C. Stevenson). Northern Sudan, Nuba Hills, central Eliri range and on two hills to the south and east. Niger-Congo, Kordofanian, Kordofanian Proper, Talodi, Tegem. Dialects: JEBEL EL AMIRA (EL AMIRA), JEBEL TEKEIM (JEBEL, TEKEIM, TEGEM), LAFOFA. 25% lexical similarity with closest languages.

LANGO ***(LANGGO)*** [LNO] 20,000 possibly (1987 SIL). Southern Sudan, eastern Equatoria Province, Torit District. Nilo-Saharan, Eastern Sudanic, Nilotic, Eastern, Lotuxo-Teso, Lotuxo-Maa, Lotuxo. A separate language from Otuho. The people are bilingual in Otuho. Different language from Lango of Uganda, or Lango, an alternate name for Didinga of Sudan. Pastoralists: cattle; agriculturalists: millet, beans, sweet potatoes, tobacco, bananas. Traditional religion.

LARO ***(LARU, AALEIRA, YILLARO, NGWULLARO)*** [LRO] 40,000 (1998 local estimate). Northern Sudan, Nuba Hills on the hills of Laro (Alleira) and a few small hills nearby. Niger-Congo, Kordofanian, Kordofanian Proper, Heiban, West-Central, Central, Ebang-Logol, Ebang-Laru. Dialects: TUNDULI, LARO. 90% lexical similarity with Heiban (closest). Christian, Muslim, traditional religion.

LOGOL ***(LUKHA)*** [LOF] 2,600 (1956 Tucker and Bryan). Northern Sudan, on small isolated hills in the extreme eastern part of the Nuba Hills, between Talodi and the White Nile. Niger-Congo, Kordofanian, Kordofanian Proper, Heiban, West-Central, Central, Ebang-Logol, Logol. 85% lexical similarity with Otoro (closest). Traditional religion.

LOGORIK ***(LIGURI)*** [LIU] 2,000 (1971 Welmers). Northern Sudan, central Nuba Mts., Jebel Liguri and other hills northeast of Kadugli. Nilo-Saharan, Eastern Sudanic, Western, Daju, Eastern Daju. Dialects: SABURI, TALLAU (TALAU, TALO), LIGURI. 64% lexical similarity with Shatt, 56% with Daju of Dar Fur (Nyala and Lagowa), 57% with Sila. Christian, Muslim, traditional religion.

LOKOYA ***(LOKOIYA, LOKOJA, LOQUIA, LOWOI, OWOI, LOIRYA, OIRYA, ELLYRIA, OXORIOK, KOYO)*** [LKY] 12,392 (1952). Southern Sudan, eastern Equatoria, Torit District. Nilo-Saharan, Eastern Sudanic, Nilotic, Eastern, Lotuxo-Teso, Lotuxo-Maa, Lotuxo. 64% lexical similarity with Otuho, 57% with Lopit, 56% with Dongotono. Speakers are reported to be bilingual in Otuho. Ethnic groups: Irya and Owe. Investigation needed: bilingual proficiency in Otuho. Animal husbandry: sheep, goats, cattle, fowl; agriculturalists: millet, simsim, beans, tobacco. Traditional religion.

LONGARIM ***(NARIM, LARIM, LARIMINIT, BOYA)*** [LOH] 3,623 (1983 K. Fukui survey). Southern Sudan, western Boya Hills, around Mt. Kosodek and Mt. Lobuli. Nilo-Saharan, Eastern Sudanic, Eastern, Surmic, South, Southwest, Didinga-Murle, Didinga-Longarim. 74% lexical similarity with Murle, 83% with Didinga. 'Narim' is their name for themselves.

LOPPIT ***(LOPIT, LOPID, LOFIT, LAFITE, LAFIT, LAFIIT)*** [LPX] 50,000 (1995 Scott Randal). Southern Sudan, eastern Equatoria Province, Lopit Hills, northeast of Torit. Nilo-Saharan, Eastern Sudanic, Nilotic, Eastern, Lotuxo-Teso, Lotuxo-Maa, Lotuxo. 63% lexical similarity with Otuho. Blacksmiths, swidden agriculturalists, cattle raisers.

LULUBO ***(LULUBA, OLUBOGO, OLUBOTI, OLU'BO, ONDOE, LOLUBO)*** [LUL] 15,000 (1985 SIL). Southern Sudan, eastern Equatoria Province, about 30 miles east of the Nile River. Nilo-Saharan, Central Sudanic, East, Moru-Madi, Southern. Many are bilingual in Bari. There is strong interest in using Lulubo for education. Pastoralists; traders. Traditional religion.

LUMUN ***(LOMON, KUKU-LUMUN)*** [LMD] Northern Sudan, Talodi, Moro Hills. Niger-Congo, Kordofanian, Kordofanian Proper, Talodi, Talodi Proper, Tocho. 70% lexical similarity with closest Talodi languages.

LUWO ***(LWO, JUR LUO, JUR LWO, JO LWO, DHE LWO, DHE LUWO, GIUR)*** [LWO] 80,000 (1983 census). Southern Sudan, north of Wau toward Aweil, southeast of Wau as far as Tonj. Nilo-Saharan, Eastern Sudanic, Nilotic, Western, Luo, Northern, Jur. Different from Lwo of Uganda, or Luo of Kenya and Tanzania, but related. Bible portions 1954-1995.

MABAAN ***(MAABAN, MEBAN, SOUTHERN BURUN, GURA, TUNGAN, BARGA, TONKO, ULU)*** [MFZ] 25,000 to 50,000 (1987 SIL). On the border of Blue Nile and Upper Nile provinces, between Yabus and Tombak rivers in the north and Khor Daga in the south. Not in Ethiopia. Nilo-Saharan, Eastern Sudanic, Nilotic, Western, Luo, Northern, Maban-Burun, Maban. Partially intelligible with some southern dialects of Burun. Traditional religion, Christian. NT 1988.

MA'DI ***(MA'ADI, MA'DITI, MA'DI)*** [MHI] 18,000 in Sudan (1982 SIL). Southern Sudan, Equatoria Province, Madi Subdistrict, Opari District, West Nile District. Nilo-Saharan, Central Sudanic, East, Moru-Madi, Southern. Dialects: PANDIKERI, LOKAI, 'BURULO. NT 1977. See main entry under Uganda.

MANDARI ***(MONDARI, MUNDARI, SHIR, CHIR, KIR)*** [MQU] 35,812 (1952). Southern Sudan, near Bari; 1 division around Tali, the other on both sides of the Nile between Tombe and Mongalla. Nilo-Saharan, Eastern Sudanic, Nilotic, Eastern, Bari. A different language and culture from Bari. 75% lexical similarity with Nyanggwara, 71% with Bari and Ngyepu, 70% with Pöjulu, 66% with Kuku, 61% with Kakwa. Nomadic. Ethnic groups: Mondari Boronga, Sere, Böri. Arid, acacia and scrub forest. Plain. Pastoralists: cattle, goats; agriculturalists: peanuts, beans, millet, simsim, maize, sugar cane, cassava, tobacco, Indian hemp, honey; gatherers: wild vegetables; fishermen; hunters. Traditional religion.

MANGAYAT ***(MANGAYA, MONGAIYAT, BUG)*** [MYJ] 400 (1987 SIL). Southern Sudan, in Western Bahr el Ghazal, some in Raga, most in Mangayat, 18 miles southeast of Raga. Niger-Congo, Atlantic-Congo, Volta-Congo, North, Adamawa-Ubangi, Ubangi, Sere-Ngbaka-Mba, Sere, Feroge-Mangaya. Many are bilingual in Kresh or Arabic. They call themselves 'Bug'.

MASALIT ***(MASSALIT, KAANA MASALA, JWISINCE)*** [MSA] 145,000 in Sudan. Population total both countries 250,000 (1983 Doornbos and Bender). Northern Sudan, Dar Fur Province, Dar Masalit and Nyala District, scattered colonies in Dar Fongoro and to the south and east, and Gedaref region; Geneina, Mistere, and Habila Kajangise. Also spoken in Chad. Nilo-Saharan, Maban, Mabang, Masalit. Dialect: SURBAKHAL. The dialect in Dar Masalit in Dar Fur differs from that spoken in Nyala District. The majority use Arabic as second language; however, people in the central area and women know only limited Arabic. Muslim.

MIDOB ***(MEIDOB, MIDOBI, TIDDA, TID, TID-N-AAL)*** [MEI] 50,000 (1993 R. Werner). Northern Sudan, Dar Fur Province, Jebel Midob, and settled communities in Omdurman and Gezira Aba. The center is Malha. Nilo-Saharan, Eastern Sudanic, Eastern, Nubian, Western. Dialects: SHELKOTA (SHALKOTA), KAAGEDDI, URRTI (UURTI). The dialects are inherently intelligible. 51% lexical similarity with Birgid (closest). Pastoralists. Muslim.

MITTU [MWU] Southern Sudan. Nilo-Saharan, Central Sudanic, West, Bongo-Bagirmi, Bongo-Baka, Morokodo-Beli. Extinct.

MO'DA ***(GBERI, GWERI, GBARA, MUDA)*** [GBN] 600 (1977 Voegelin and Voegelin). Southern Sudan, northwest of Mvolo on both sides of the border of Lakes and Western Equatoria provinces. Nilo-Saharan, Central Sudanic, West, Bongo-Bagirmi, Bongo-Baka, Morokodo-Beli, Morokodo-Mo'da. 64% lexical similarity with Morokodo, 58% with Jur Modo, 41% with Beli, 49% with Bongo, 38% with Baka. Investigation needed: intelligibility with Jur Modo.

MOLO ***(MALKAN, TURA-KA-MOLO)*** [ZMO] 100 (1988 M. L. Bender). At Jebel Malkan, near the Berta language, south of the Blue Nile, near the Ethiopian border. Nilo-Saharan, Eastern Sudanic, Eastern,

Eastern Jebel, Aka-Kelo-Molo. Reported to be bilingual in Arabic and Berta. They call themselves 'Tura-Ka-Molo', meaning 'speech of Molo'. Muslim.

MORO ***(DHIMORONG)*** [MOR] 30,000 (1982 SIL) including 4,100 Abu Leila and Lebu, 460 Umm Dore, 9,000 Umm Gabralla (1977 Voegelin and Voegelin). Northern Sudan, eastern Nuba Mountains, Kordofan Province. Niger-Congo, Kordofanian, Kordofanian Proper, Heiban, West-Central, Western. Dialects: UMM DOREIN (LOGORBAN), UMM GABRALLA (TOBERELDA), NDERRE, LAIYEN, NUBWA, ULBA, WERRIA. 75% lexical similarity with Tira (closest). NT 1965-1994.

MOROKODO ***(MA'DI)*** [MGC] 3,400 or more, including 280 Biti (1977 Voegelin and Voegelin). Southern Sudan, in the area between Amadi and Maridi. Nilo-Saharan, Central Sudanic, West, Bongo-Bagirmi, Bongo-Baka, Morokodo-Beli, Morokodo-Mo'da. Dialects: BITI, MA'DU, MOROKODO. A dialect cluster. 63% lexical similarity with Jur Modo, 41% with Beli, 45% with Bongo, 43% with Baka. Many use Moru as second language. Ma'du may be extinct (1984).

MORU ***(KALA MORU)*** [MGD] 70,000 (1982 SIL), including 1,200 Agi, 2,500 Andri, 5,000 Kadiro, 9,000 Miza, 400 Wa'di. Southern Sudan, Mundri District, Equatoria Province. Nilo-Saharan, Central Sudanic, East, Moru-Madi, Northern. Dialects: AGI, ANDRI, 'BALI'BA, KADIRO, LAKAMA'DI, MIZA, MORUWA'DI. Andri and 'Bali'ba dialects are similar, Kadiro and Lakama'di are nearly identical. SVO, SOV. Literacy rate in second language: 85%. Orthography problems. Bible, in press (1998).

MÜNDÜ ***(MUNDO, MOUNTOU, MONDU, MONDO)*** [MUH] 23,000 in Sudan. Population total both countries 25,800. Southern Sudan, western Equatoria Province northwest of Yei and in Moru District south of Maridi. Also spoken in DRC. Niger-Congo, Atlantic-Congo, Volta-Congo, North, Adamawa-Ubangi, Ubangi, Sere-Ngbaka-Mba, Ngbaka-Mba, Ngbaka, Eastern, Mundu. Dialect: SHATT. Closest to Mayogo and Bangba of DRC. There is intermarriage with the Avokaya and Baka, and bilingualism in those languages. Some bilingualism also in Bangala and Arabic. Literacy rate in first language: 10% to 15%. Literacy rate in second language: 25% to 50%. Bible portions 1984-1995. NT nearly complete (2000).

MURLE ***(MURELEI, MERULE, MOURLE, MURULE, BEIR, AJIBBA, AGIBA, ADKIBBA)*** [MUR] 60,000 in Sudan (1982 SIL). Population total both countries 60,200. Southern Sudan, Upper Nile Province, Pibor District, south of the Akobo River, Boma Plateau, and to east and north. Also spoken in Ethiopia. Nilo-Saharan, Eastern Sudanic, Eastern, Surmic, South, Southwest, Didinga-Murle, Murle. 74% lexical similarity with Longarim, 71% with Didinga. Ethnic groups: Lotilla, Boma, Olam (Ngalan). Dictionary. Grammar. Flood plains, savannah. Semi-nomadic pastoralists. Traditional religion, Christian. NT 1996.

NDING ***(ELIRI)*** [ELI] 3,513 (1984 Stevenson). Northern Sudan, southern Eliri range. Niger-Congo, Kordofanian, Kordofanian Proper, Talodi, Talodi Proper, Nding. 70% lexical similarity with closest Talodi languages.

NDOGO [NDZ] 20,000 (1993). Southern Sudan, Western District along Wau-Deim Zubeir Road between Mboro and Kpango rivers. A few are north of Tembura among the Zande. Not in CAR. Niger-Congo, Atlantic-Congo, Volta-Congo, North, Adamawa-Ubangi, Ubangi, Sere-Ngbaka-Mba, Sere, Sere-Bviri, Ndogo-Sere. Spoken as a second language by the Golo and Gbaya at Deim Zubeir. Gbaya-Ndogo is a different language. Bible portions 1985-1990.

NGILE ***(MASAKIN, MESAKIN, DALOKA, TALOKA, DARRA)*** [MAS] 38,000 including Dagik (1982 SIL). Northern Sudan, Kordofan Province, Nuba Mountains, in Mesakin Hills on some outlying hills. Niger-Congo, Kordofanian, Kordofanian Proper, Talodi, Talodi Proper, Ngile-Dengebu. Dialects: AHEIMA (EL AKHEIMAR), DALOKA (TALOKA), MASAKIN GUSAR (MESAKIN QUSAR, MASAKIN BURAM), MASAKIN TUWAL (TIWAL, TOWAL).

NJALGULGULE ***(NYOLGE, NYOOLNE, NGULGULE, BEGI, BEGE, BEKO, NJANGULGULE)*** [NJL] 900 (1977 Voegelin and Voegelin). Southern Sudan, on the Sopo River just above the Sopo-Boro confluence, and west of the Dinka. 1 village. Nilo-Saharan, Eastern Sudanic, Western, Daju, Western Daju. Bilingualism in Arabic. Muslim.

NOBIIN ***(MAHAS-FIADIDJA, MAHAS-FIYADIKKYA, FIADIDJA-MAHAS)*** [FIA] 295,000 in Sudan (1996). Population total both countries 545,000. Northern Sudan, between Dongola and the Egyptian border, Wadi Halfa, Khashim el Ghirba. Also spoken in Egypt. Nilo-Saharan, Eastern Sudanic, Eastern, Nubian, Northern. Dialects: MAHAS (MAHASI, MAHASS), FIYADIKKA (FEDICCA, FADICHA, FADICCA, FADIJA, FIADIDJA). Not intelligible with Kenuzi-Dongola. 67% lexical similarity with Kenuzi-Dongola. Spoken by the Mahas in Sudan and the Fedicca in Egypt. Called 'Fiadidja-Mahas' in Egypt. Muslim. Bible portions 1860-1899.

NUER ***(NAATH, NAADH)*** [NUS] 740,000 in Sudan (1982 SIL), including 2,935 Western Jikany, 12,500 Lou, 1,100 Nyuong, 2,500 Thiang, 5,900 Bul, 2,400 Jagai, 6,700 Laak, 4,900 Leik, 1,600 Door, 17,600 Eastern Jikany (1977 Voegelin and Voegelin). Population total both countries 805,000. Southern Sudan, east Upper Nile Province, in the region of Nasir on the upper Sobat River, in and around a triangle formed between Bahr el Zeraf and Bahr el Jebel, and extending up the Sobat River across the Ethiopian border.

Also spoken in Ethiopia. Nilo-Saharan, Eastern Sudanic, Nilotic, Western, Dinka-Nuer, Nuer. Dialects: DOR (DOOR), EASTERN JIKANY (JIKAIN, JEKAING), ABIGAR, WESTERN JIKANY, CIEN, THOGNAATH (THOK NATH), LOU (LAU), NYUONG, THIANG (BUL, GAWAAR, JAGAI, LAAK, LEIK). Dialects correspond mainly to geographic divisions. Bilingualism in Arabic. They call themselves 'Naath'. Severe disruption in residence patterns caused by fighting in Sudan and Ethiopia. Many are refugees or homeless (1991). Plains. Pastoralists: cattle; fishermen. Traditional religion, Christian. Bible, in press (1998).

NYAMUSA-MOLO [NYO] 1,200 Nyamusa (1977 Voegelin and Voegelin). Southern Sudan, western Equatoria Province, southeast of Beli, northeast of Morokodo. Nilo-Saharan, Central Sudanic, West, Bongo-Bagirmi, Bongo-Baka, Morokodo-Beli, Morokodo-Mo'da. Dialects: NYAMUSA, MOLO. 84% lexical similarity between Nyamusa and Molo, 70% to 75% with Jur Modo dialect cluster. Investigation needed: intelligibility with Jur Modo.

OPUUO *(OPO-SHITA, OPO, OPUO, LANGA, SHITA, SHITTA, CITA, CIITA, ANSITA, KINA, KWINA)* [LGN] Northern Sudan. Nilo-Saharan, Komuz, Koman. 24% lexical similarity with Koma. See main entry under Ethiopia.

OTORO *(UTORO, DHITORO, LITORO, KAWAMA, KAWARMA)* [OTR] 13,000 (1989). Northern Sudan, Kordofan Province, Nuba Mountains region, Otoro Hills south of Heiban and west of the Heiban-Talodi road. Niger-Congo, Kordofanian, Kordofanian Proper, Heiban, West-Central, Central, Ebang-Logol, Utoro. Dialects: DIJAMA, DUGWUJUR, DOKWARA, DOROMBE, DOGORINDI, DAGARRO, DUGURILA. All Otoro dialects are inherently intelligible. NT 1966.

OTUHO *(LOTUKO, LOTUHO, LOTUXO, LOTUKA, LATTUKA, LATUKO, LATUKA, LATOOKA, OTUXO, OLOTORIT)* [LOT] 135,000 including Dongotono (1998), 2,500 Koriot, 1,000 Lomya (1977 Voegelin and Voegelin). Southern Sudan, Torit District, eastern Equatoria Province, east and southeast of the Luluba and the Lokoya. Nilo-Saharan, Eastern Sudanic, Nilotic, Eastern, Lotuxo-Teso, Lotuxo-Maa, Lotuxo. Dialects: KORIOK, LOGIRI (LOGIR), LOMYA (LOMIA), LORWAMA, LOWUDO (LOUDO, LAUDA), LOGOTOK. 64% lexical similarity with Lokoya, 63% with Lopit, 60% with Dongotono. Literacy rate in second language: 10%. Agriculturalists: millet, eleusine, maize, simsim, peanuts, sweet potatoes, tobacco; pastoralists: cattle, sheep; hunters; fishermen. Traditional religion, Christian, Muslim. NT 1969.

PÄRI *(LOKORO)* [LKR] 28,000 (1987 SIL). Southern Sudan, Upper Nile Province. Nilo-Saharan, Eastern Sudanic, Nilotic, Western, Luo, Northern, Unclassified.

REEL *(ATUOT, ATWOT, THOK CIENG REEL)* [ATU] 50,000 (1998 Atuot community). Bordering Ciec Dinka in the north near Panekar, Agar Dinka on the west near Lake Nyibor, Jur Modo on the south, and Ador Dinka in the east near Yirol. Nilo-Saharan, Eastern Sudanic, Nilotic, Western, Dinka-Nuer, Nuer. No dialect differences. 77% lexical similarity with Nuer, 49% with Dinka. The Apak are fully bilingual in the Ciec dialect of South Central Dinka. The other subtribes are less bilingual. The Kuek and Rorkec have many monolinguals and are regarded as having the purest form of the language. They live among the Dinka, 100 km. from the Nuer, but have common grazing grounds with the Nuer. They are culturally Dinka. Subtribes: Apak, Luac, Jilek, Rorkec, Akot, Kuek. 'Atuot' is the Dinka name for them. The Apak call themselves 'Atuot'. Pastoralists.

SHATT *(CANING)* [SHJ] 15,000 (1984 R. C. Stevenson). Northern Sudan, Shatt Hills southwest of Kadugli (Shatt Daman, Shatt Safia, Shatt Tebeldia) and parts of Abu Hashim and Abu Sinam. Nilo-Saharan, Eastern Sudanic, Western, Daju, Eastern Daju. 64% lexical similarity with Liguri, 62% with Daju of Dar Fur (Nyala and Lagowa), 60% with Sila. 'Caning' is their own name for themselves. 'Shatt' is applied by Arabic speakers to inhabitants of the Kordofan Hills. It means 'dispersed', 'scattered', and is applied to various groups. Distinct from Shatt (Thuri) in the Lwo group, or the Shatt dialect of Mundu. SVO.

SHILLUK *(COLO, DHOCOLO, CHULLA, SHULLA)* [SHK] 175,000 (1982 SIL). Southern Sudan, Upper Nile Province, between Nile and Kordofan Province boundary, from Latitude 11 in the north to about 80 miles west of Tonga; also on the east bank of the Nile around the junction of the Nile and Sobat rivers, and for about 20 miles up the Sobat River. Nilo-Saharan, Eastern Sudanic, Nilotic, Western, Luo, Northern, Shilluk. 60% lexical similarity with Anuak, Pari, Luwo. Grammar. Literacy rate in second language: 20%. Roman. Traditional religion, Christian. NT 1977.

SHWAI *(SHIRUMBA, SHUWAY, LUDUMOR, CWAYA)* [SHW] 3,500 (1989). Northern Sudan, Kordofan Province, Nuba Mountains, in villages in the Shwai Hills, northwest of Otoro near Heiban-Kadugli road. Niger-Congo, Kordofanian, Kordofanian Proper, Heiban, West-Central, Shirumba. Dialects: SHABUN, CERUMBA (SHIRUMBA), NDANO. They call themselves 'Cwaya'.

SINYAR *(SINYA, SHEMYA)* [SYS] Population total both countries 5,000 to 10,000 (1983 Bender). The main center is at Foro Boranga. Also spoken in Chad. Nilo-Saharan, Central Sudanic, West, Bongo-Bagirmi, Sinyar. They are geographically cut off from speakers of other Bongo-Bagirmi languages. Muslim.

SUNGOR ***(SOUNGOR, ASSAGORI, AZANGORI, ASONGORI, ASUNGORE, ERENGA, MADUNGORE, SHAALE)*** [SUN] 15,000 in Sudan. Northern Sudan, Dar Fur, Melmele in Dar Masalit. Bounded on the west by the Tama, south by the Masalit, east by Arabic-speaking nomadic groups, north by the Gimr and Jebel Mun. Nilo-Saharan, Eastern Sudanic, Western, Tama, Tama-Sungor. Dialects: GIRGA, WALAD DULLA, ERENGA. Girga and Walad Dulla are ethnic groups which may or may not speak different dialects. Culturally Maba. Agriculturalists; cattle. Muslim. See main entry under Chad.

SURI ***(SURMA)*** [SUQ] 1,000 Tirma in Sudan (1983 SIL). Southern Sudan, Boma Plateau near the Ethiopian border. Nilo-Saharan, Eastern Sudanic, Eastern, Surmic, South, Southeast, Pastoral, Suri. Dialects: TIRMA (TIRIMA, TEREMA, TERNA, DIRMA, CIRMA, TIRMAGA, TIRMAGI, TID), CHAI (CACI, CAI). Closely related to Mursi of Ethiopia. See main entry under Ethiopia.

TAGOI ***(TAGOY)*** [TAG] 13,000 (1982 SIL) including 2,000 Tagoi, 552 Moreb, 1,100 Tumale (1977 Voegelin and Voegelin). Northern Sudan, Kordofan Province, Nuba Mountains, at Moreb, Tagoi, Turjok, Tumale Hill, possibly Tuling village. Tukum and Turum are places where Tagoi dialects are spoken (1956 Tucker and Bryan). Niger-Congo, Kordofanian, Kordofanian Proper, Rashad. Dialects: MOREB, TUMALE, TAGOI.

TALODI ***(GAJOMANG, AJOMANG, JOMANG)*** [TLO] 1,500 (1989). Northern Sudan, Nuba Hills, in Talodi town and hill, including the villages of Tasomi and Tata. Niger-Congo, Kordofanian, Kordofanian Proper, Talodi, Talodi Proper, Jomang. The dialects are nearly identical. 70% lexical similarity with closest Talodi languages.

TEGALI ***(TAGALE, TEGELE, TOGOLE, TEKELE)*** [RAS] 35,738 (1984 R. C. Stevenson). Northern Sudan, Kordofan Province, Nuba Mountains, Tegali Range, Rashad hills and town of Rashad. Niger-Congo, Kordofanian, Kordofanian Proper, Rashad. Dialects: RASHAD (KOM, NGAKOM, KOME), TEGALI. Tegali and Rashad are nearly identical. SOV. Muslim.

TEMEIN ***(TEMAINIAN, RONE, RONGE)*** [TEQ] 10,000 (1984 R. C. Stevenson). Northern Sudan, Nuba Hills in the Temein hills southwest of Dilling, between Jebels Ghulfan Morung and Julud (Gulud). Nilo-Saharan, Eastern Sudanic, Western, Temein. 67% lexical similarity with Tese.

TENNET ***(TENET)*** [TEX] 4,000 (1994 SIL). Southern Sudan, Equatoria Province, Lopit Hills, northeast of Torit, 5 villages. Nilo-Saharan, Eastern Sudanic, Eastern, Surmic, South, Southwest, Didinga-Murle, Tennet. Some intelligibility with Murle, Longarim, and Didinga (in descending order). Most Tennet are fluent in Loppit, from which they borrow most of their songs. Many over 20 years old know Toposa, which is used for ox names and a few songs. Many can also understand some Otuho, which is closely related to Loppit. Those with schooling know a little Arabic. All ages. A strong sense of Tenet ethnic identity. They have a number of Loppit loan words. Grammar. VSO; genitives, adjectives, numerals, relatives after noun heads; question word final; 4 suffixes; word order distinguishes given and new information; noun affixes indicate case; verb affixes mark person, number; agreement obligatory; passives; antipassives; causatives; comparatives; (C)(G)V(:)(C) or (C)V(G)(C); tonal. Literacy rate in first language: 1%. Literacy rate in second language: 1% Arabic. Motivation for literacy is high. Savannah, surrounding plain, tropical forest on the hill. Mountain slope. Swidden agriculturalists; cattle raisers; Blacksmiths. 600 to 1,200 meters. Traditional religion, Christian. Bible portions 1994-1996.

TESE ***(TEIS-UMM-DANAB, KEIGA JIRRU, KEIGA GIRRU)*** [KEG] 1,400 (1971 Welmers). Northern Sudan, Nuba Hills, Keiga Jirru west of Debri, and in 6 villages, northeast of Kadugli. Nilo-Saharan, Eastern Sudanic, Western, Temein. 67% lexical similarity with Temein.

THURI ***(DHE THURI, JO THURI, WADA THURI, SHATT)*** [THU] 6,600 (1956 Tucker and Bryan). Southern Sudan between Wau and Aweil, between Jur and Lol rivers, on Raga-Nyamlell road, and on Wau-Deim Zubeir road. Nilo-Saharan, Eastern Sudanic, Nilotic, Western, Luo, Northern, Thuri. Dialects: BODHO (DHE BOODHO, DEMBO, DEMEN, DOMBO), COLO (DHE COLO, JUR SHOL, JO COLO), MANANGEER (JUR MANANGEER). It is reported that all Thuri groups speak Dinka and Luwo. Different from Shatt in the Daju group. Investigation needed: bilingual proficiency in Dinka, Luwo.

TIGRÉ ***(KHASA, XASA)*** [TIE] Northern Sudan. Afro-Asiatic, Semitic, South, Ethiopian, North. Dialect: MANSA' (MENSA). Believed by some to be a direct linguistic descendant of Ge'ez. Muslim. Bible 1988. See main entry under Eritrea.

TIMA ***(LOMORIK, LOMURIKI, TAMANIK, YIBWA)*** [TMS] 1,100 ? (1956). Northern Sudan, Nuba Hills in villages on and near Jebel Tima, 10 miles southwest of Katla, West Kordofan District. Niger-Congo, Kordofanian, Kordofanian Proper, Katla.

TINGAL ***(KAJAKJA, KAJAJA)*** [TIG] 8,000 (1982 SIL). Northern Sudan, Tegali Hills. Niger-Congo, Kordofanian, Kordofanian Proper, Rashad.

TIRA ***(TIRO, THIRO, LITHIRO)*** [TIR] 40,000 (1982 SIL). Northern Sudan, Nuba Hills in villages extending from near Otoro to the neighborhood of Talodi. Niger-Congo, Kordofanian, Kordofanian Proper, Heiban, West-Central, Western. Dialects: KINDERMA (KANDERMA), TIRA EL AKHDAR (TIRA

DAGIG), TIRA LUMUM (LUMAN), TIRA MANDI. There are slight variations among the dialects. 75% lexical similarity with Moro (closest). Traditional religion, Christian.

TOCHO ***(TOICHO, TACHO)*** [TAZ] 3,800 (1977 Voegelin and Voegelin). Northern Sudan, Talodi, Moro Hills. Niger-Congo, Kordofanian, Kordofanian Proper, Talodi, Talodi Proper, Tocho. 70% lexical similarity with closest Talodi languages.

TOGOYO ***(TOGOY)*** [TGY] Southern Sudan, west, in a small area around Raga. Niger-Congo, Atlantic-Congo, Volta-Congo, North, Adamawa-Ubangi, Ubangi, Sere-Ngbaka-Mba, Sere, Indri-Togoyo. Extinct.

TOPOSA ***(TAPOSA, TOPOTHA, AKARA, KARE, KUMI)*** [TOQ] 100,000 (1984 M. Schroeder). Southern Sudan, along both sides of Singaita and Lokalyen rivers. The southern boundary is 4.30' N, northern 5 N, western 33.22' E, eastern 34 E. Ritual center at Loyooro River. They migrate as far as Moruangipi (34.30 E, 5.10 N), and occasionally farther east into the disputed Ilemi Triangle at the Ethiopian border for seasonal grazing. They have no permanent settlements there. The Jiye live at 5.20 N 33.45 E. Nilo-Saharan, Eastern Sudanic, Nilotic, Eastern, Lotuxo-Teso, Teso-Turkana, Turkana. Dialects: EASTERN TOPOSA, WESTERN TOPOSA, JIYE. Eastern Toposa and Jiye are linguistically closer to Turkana; Western Toposa to Karamajong. Inherently intelligible with Nyangatom, Karamojong, and Turkana, but each has strong ethnic attitudes. Separate literature is needed also because of loans from different second languages, and different discourse structures. Limited intelligibility with Teso. Most are monolingual. A small number speak Southern Sudanese Arabic for trading. The Toposa are peaceful with the Karamojong, have a mutual nonagression pact with the Nyangatom, are intermittenly hostile to the Jiye of Sudan, permanently hostile to the Turkana, and to the Murle-Didinga group (Murle, Didinga, Boya-Longarim). Semi-nomadic. Dictionary. Grammar. VSA (morphologically ergative); highly inflectional; grammatical tone (tense, case); vowel harmony; voiceless vowels; questions: yes and no sentence final, content questions sentence initial and final. Cattle breeding, limited agriculture. Traditional religion, Christian.

TORONA [TQR] Northern Sudan, Talodi, Moro Hills. Niger-Congo, Kordofanian, Kordofanian Proper, Talodi, Talodi Proper, Tocho. The ethnic group now speaks Tira. Extinct.

TULISHI ***(TULESH, THULISHI, KUNTULISHI)*** [TEY] 8,628 (1977 Voegelin and Voegelin), including 3,000 Kamdang, 2,500 Tulishi. Northern Sudan, hills south of the Nuba Hills on Jebel Tulishi south of Katla, on Jebel Kamdang north of Lagowa, south of Tulishi. Niger-Congo, Kordofanian, Kadugli, Central. Dialects: TULISHI, KAMDANG (KAMDA), DAR EL KABIRA (TURUJ, TRUJ, LOGOKE, MINJIMMINA). Dar el Kabira and Kamdang dialects are similar.

TUMMA ***(SANGALI)*** [TBQ] 6,500 (1956 census). Northern Sudan, hills south of Nuba Hills between the Katla range and Miri. Niger-Congo, Kordofanian, Kadugli, Central. Dialects: BELANYA, KRONGO ABDALLAH, TUMMA. 85% lexical similarity with Kanga (closest).

TUMTUM [TBR] 7,300 including 6,000 in Karondi, 1,300 in Tumtum. Northern Sudan, Upper Nile Province; Kurondi south of Eliri, Talassa in the northern part of Eliri. Niger-Congo, Kordofanian, Kadugli, Eastern. Dialects: KARONDI (KURONDI, KORINDI), TALASSA (TALASA), TUMTUM. 85% lexical similarity with Krongo (closest).

UDUK ***(TWAMPA, KWANIM PA, BURUN, KEBEIRKA, OTHAN, KORARA, KUMUS)*** [UDU] Northern Sudan, Upper Nile Province from Belila in the north, southwards along Blue Nile Province boundary to Yabus River. Most now in a refugee camp in Ethiopia. Nilo-Saharan, Komuz, Koman. SVO. Christian, traditional religion. NT 1963. See main entry under Ethiopia.

WALI ***(WALARI, WALARISHE)*** [WLL] 487 (1977 Voegelin and Voegelin). Northern Sudan, in the Wali Hills, south of Karko Hills. Nilo-Saharan, Eastern Sudanic, Eastern, Nubian, Central, Hill, Unclassified. SOV.

WARNANG ***(WERNI)*** [WRN] 1,100 (1956 census). Northern Sudan, on small isolated hills in the extreme eastern part of the Nuba Hills between Talodi and the White Nile. Niger-Congo, Kordofanian, Kordofanian Proper, Heiban, Eastern. 67% lexical similarity with Ko (closest). Traditional religion.

YULU ***(YOULOU)*** [YUL] 3,000 in Sudan, including 2,000 Yulu and 1,000 Binga (1987 SIL). Southern Sudan. The Yulu are at Khor Buga, 2 miles west of Raga in Western Bahr el Ghazal Province, and in Habbaniya District of Dar Fur. The Binga are at Menangba, west of Raga and in DRC. Nilo-Saharan, Central Sudanic, West, Bongo-Bagirmi, Kara. Dialects: BINGA, YULU. Aja is not a dialect of Yulu, but of Kresh (R. Brown SIL). Many people are reported to be bilingual in Kresh or Arabic. See main entry under CAR.

ZAGHAWA ***(SOGHAUA, ZEGGAOUA, ZAGAOUA, ZORHAUA, ZAGAWA, ZEGHAWA, ZAUGE, BERRI, BERI, BERI-AA, MERIDA, KEBADI, KUYUK)*** [ZAG] 102,000 in Sudan (1982 SIL). Population total all countries 186,800. Northern Sudan, northwest Dar Fur (northern Magdumate and Dar Kabja), and scattered farther south. Also in Kordofan. Surrounded on three sides by the Sahara. Also spoken in Chad, Libya. Nilo-Saharan, Saharan, Eastern. Ethnic subgroups are Kobe, Dor, Anka, with slight dialect differences. Semi-nomadic. Groups in Sudan are Arabic speaking. Better educated than other groups. Mountains. Animal husbandry; gatherers; agriculturalists; traders: livestock, hides and skins, butter, salt. 600 meters. Muslim, traditional religion.

ZANDE ***(SOGHAUA, ZEGGAOUA, ZAGAOUA, ZORHAUA, ZAGAWA, ZEGHAWA, ZAUGE, BERRI, BERI, BERI-AA, MERIDA, KEBADI, KUYUKI)*** [ZAN] 350,000 in Sudan (1982 SIL). Southern Sudan, DRC primarily, and CAR in an elongated semicircle with Uele River as its base. Some projections south. Niger-Congo, Atlantic-Congo, Volta-Congo, North, Adamawa-Ubangi, Ubangi, Zande, Zande-Nzakara. Dialects: DIO, MAKARAKA (ODIO). The speech of the Zande in Sudan is fairly uniform except for the Mbomu, Sueh-Meridi, Bile, Bandiya, Bamboy, Bomokandi, Anunga. Agriculturalists. Traditional religion, Christian. Bible 1978. See main entry under DRC.

SWAZILAND

Kingdom of Swaziland. National or official languages: Swati, English. 952,000 (1998 UN). Literacy rate 65% to 67%. Information mainly from J. Bendor-Samuel 1989. Christian, traditional religion. Blind population 1,000 (1982 WCE). Deaf institutions: 1. Data accuracy estimate: B. The number of languages listed for Swaziland is 4. Of those, all are living languages. Diversity index 0.23.

ENGLISH [ENG] Indo-European, Germanic, West, English. Taught in all government and private schools. National language. Bible 1535-1989. See main entry under United Kingdom.

SWATI ***(SWAZI, ISISWAZI, SISWATI, TEKELA, TEKEZA)*** [SWZ] 650,000 in Swaziland (1993 Johnstone), or 90% of the population. Population total all countries 1,670,000. Also spoken in Mozambique, South Africa. Niger-Congo, Atlantic-Congo, Volta-Congo, Benue-Congo, Bantoid, Southern, Narrow Bantu, Central, S, Nguni (S.40). Dialects: BACA, HLUBI, PHUTHI. The people are highly educated. National language. Literacy rate in first language: High. Taught in all national schools. Christian, traditional religion. Bible 1996.

TSONGA ***(SHITSONGA, XITSONGA, CHANGANA, XICHANGANA)*** [TSO] 19,000 in Swaziland (1993 Johnstone). Niger-Congo, Atlantic-Congo, Volta-Congo, Benue-Congo, Bantoid, Southern, Narrow Bantu, Central, S, Tswa-Ronga, (S.50). Bible 1907, in press (1989). See main entry under South Africa.

ZULU ***(ISIZULU, ZUNDA)*** [ZUU] 76,000 in Swaziland, 2.3% of the population (1993 Johnstone). Niger-Congo, Atlantic-Congo, Volta-Congo, Benue-Congo, Bantoid, Southern, Narrow Bantu, Central, S, Nguni (S.40). Close to Swati and Xhosa. Bible 1883-1959. See main entry under South Africa.

TANZANIA

United Republic of Tanzania. Jamhuri ya Mwungano wa Tanzania. Formerly German East Africa, Tanganyika. National or official language: Swahili. 32,102,000 (1998 UN). Some population figures updated from 1957 census. Literacy rate 80% to 85%. Also includes Konkani, Panjabi, Urdu, Chinese, people from Europe 70,000, Rwanda 25,000, Mozambique. Information mainly from F. Huntingford 1953; B. Taylor 1962; R. Willis 1966; W. Whiteley 1969; E. Polomé and C. Hill 1980; F. Rottland 1981; D. Nurse 1982; G. Dimmendaal 1989. Christian, Muslim, traditional religion. Blind population 40,000 (1982 WCE). Deaf institutions: 7. Data accuracy estimate: A2, B. The number of languages listed for Tanzania is 137. Of those, 135 are living languages and 2 are extinct. Diversity index 0.95.

AASÁX ***(ASAX, ASÁ, ASAK)*** [AAS] Northern Tanzania near the Maasai. Afro-Asiatic, Cushitic, South. Became linguistically extinct in 1976. They were dependent on the Maasai and became absorbed into it and nearby Bantu groups. Hunter-gatherers. Extinct.

ARABIC, OMANI SPOKEN [ACX] 195,000 in Tanzania (1993 Johnstone). Afro-Asiatic, Semitic, Central, South, Arabic. Second and third generation in Tanzania, originally from Yemen and Oman. Some or all may speak Swahili as first language. Investigation needed: intelligibility. SVO. Literacy is in Arabic. Muslim. See main entry under Oman.

ARABIC, STANDARD [ABV] Middle East, north Africa. Afro-Asiatic, Semitic, Central, South, Arabic. Bible 1984-1991. See main entry under Saudi Arabia.

ARAMANIK ***(LARAMANIK, "NDOROBO", "DOROBO")*** [AAM] Nilo-Saharan, Eastern Sudanic, Nilotic, Southern, Kalenjin, Nandi-Markweta, Nandi. Speakers have limited comprehension of other languages. Kisankasa, Mediak, and Mosiro are also called "Ndorobo".

ASU ***(CHIASU, CHASU, ATHU, CASU, PARE)*** [ASA] 400,000 (1993 Johnstone). Northeastern, Kilimanjaro Region, Pare Mountains, Mwanga and Same districts. Niger-Congo, Atlantic-Congo, Volta-Congo, Benue-Congo, Bantoid, Southern, Narrow Bantu, Central, G, Shambala (G.20). Welmers says Asu is the same as Pare. Related to Taveta. 5% monolingual, 63% bilingual in Swahili,

32% trilingual in Swahili and English. Asu used in home and worship. 'Wapare' is an ethnic group name. Literacy rate in second language: 80%. Mountain slope. Christian, Muslim. NT 1922-1967.

BEMBA ***(CHIBEMBA, ICHIBEMBA, WEMBA, CHIWEMBA)*** [BEM] 28,600 in Tanzania (1987). Niger-Congo, Atlantic-Congo, Volta-Congo, Benue-Congo, Bantoid, Southern, Narrow Bantu, Central, M, Bemba (M.40). Traditional religion, Christian. Bible 1956-1983. See main entry under Zambia.

BEMBE ***(IBEMBE, BEEMBE, EBEMBE)*** [BMB] Lake Tanganyika coast, fishing villages from the Burundi border south to the southern border of the Kigoma region. Niger-Congo, Atlantic-Congo, Volta-Congo, Benue-Congo, Bantoid, Southern, Narrow Bantu, Central, D, Bembe (D.50). Church services in Swahili. Some are Tanzanian citizens, others are recent immigrants and citizens of DRC. Different from Beembe (Bembe) of Congo. Fishermen. Traditional religion, Christian. Bible 1991. See main entry under DRC.

BENA ***(EKIBENA)*** [BEZ] 568,000 (1993 Johnstone). Southwest central. Niger-Congo, Atlantic-Congo, Volta-Congo, Benue-Congo, Bantoid, Southern, Narrow Bantu, Central, G, Bena-Kinga (G.60). 71% lexical similarity with Pangwa, 65% with Hehe, 55% with Sangu, 53% with Kinga, 51% with Wanji, 47% with Kisi. NT 1914-1920.

BENDE [BDP] 20,000 (1987). Southwest and west of Konongo. Niger-Congo, Atlantic-Congo, Volta-Congo, Benue-Congo, Bantoid, Southern, Narrow Bantu, Central, F, Tongwe (F.10). Reported to be bilingual in Swahili. Investigation needed: bilingual proficiency in Swahili.

BONDEI ***(KIBONDEI, BONDE)*** [BOU] 80,000 (1987). Usambara Mountains, northeastern, inland from Tanga. Niger-Congo, Atlantic-Congo, Volta-Congo, Benue-Congo, Bantoid, Southern, Narrow Bantu, Central, G, Shambala (G.20). It has been influenced linguistically by Doe and Kwere, and it has influenced them. 75% lexical similarity with Shambala and Zigula, 73% with Ngulu. Some bilingualism in Swahili. Muslim, Christian. Bible portions 1887-1895.

BUNGU ***(WUNGU)*** [WUN] 36,000 (1987). Chunya District of Mbeya Region. Niger-Congo, Atlantic-Congo, Volta-Congo, Benue-Congo, Bantoid, Southern, Narrow Bantu, Central, F, Sukuma-Nyamwezi (F.20). Closely related to Kimbu and Sumbwa. Many people have below routine ability in Swahili. Investigation needed: intelligibility with Kimbu, Sumbwa, bilingual proficiency in Swahili. Semi-arid. Plateau. Traditional religion, Christian.

BURUNGE ***(BULUNGE, MBULUGWE)*** [BDS] 31,000 (1987). Central Province, Kondoa District, southeast of the Rangi, Goima, Chambalo, and Mirambu villages. Afro-Asiatic, Cushitic, South. Closely related to Wasi, Gorowa, Iraqw. They also speak Swahili and Rangi as second languages. SOV; prepositions; genitives, articles, adjectives, numerals, relatives after noun heads; 5 suffixes; word order distinguishes subjects, objects, indirect objects, given and new information (SOV already introduced object, SVO newly introduced object), topic and comment; preverbal clitics indicate case of noun phrase; verbal suffixes mark person, number, gender of subject; preverbal clitics mark person of subject; preverbal clitics mark person, number, and gender of nonsubject noun phrase; this agreement is obligatory; mediopassive is marked by verbal derivational suffix; subject indefinite is marked by preverbal clitic; causatives; CV, CVV, CVC (restriction on second C)CV; tonal. Arid, deciduous bush. 4,000 feet. Traditional religion, Muslim, Christian.

CHAGGA ***(KICHAGA, CHAGA, DSCHAGGA, KISHAKA, DJAGA)*** [KAF] 400,000 (1995). Northeastern slopes of Mt. Kilimanjaro, Mt. Meru, and Moshi area. Niger-Congo, Atlantic-Congo, Volta-Congo, Benue-Congo, Bantoid, Southern, Narrow Bantu, Central, E, Chaga (E.30). Dialects: KIHAI (MERU), KIBOMBO, SHIRA, MKUU, KENI, KIBOSHO, KILEMA, MAMBA, MASHATI, URU, SIHA. A dialect continuum from Siha to Usseri. Speakers say most of the Vunjo (central) dialects are intelligible with the Kibosho and Machame dialects of Hai (west). Hai and Rombo (east) are not inherently intelligible with each other (Polomé 1980). 54% to 56% lexical similarity with Gweno, 41% to 44% with Taita. Value placed on children learning Chagga (Whiteley). SVO. Roman script. NT 1964.

CUTCHI-SWAHILI ***(ASIAN SWAHILI)*** [CCL] Dar es Salaam, Dodoma, Mwanza, Arusha. Creole, Swahili based. May be adequately intelligible to speakers of standard Swahili. Cutchi-Swahili and Asian Swahili may not be identical. Bilingualism in English. The first language of some Gujarati Muslims who have come from Zanzibar. Asian Swahili is used by other Asians in communicating with non-English speaking Africans and other Asians who share no common language. It has a regular but distinct phonology and lexical and grammatical differences, described by Whitely (1974.73-79). Cutchi-Swahili and Asian Swahili may not be identical. Ismaili and Ithnasheri Muslim. See main entry under Kenya.

DATOOGA ***(DATOGA, DATOG, TATOGA, TATOG, TATURU, "MANGATI")*** [TCC] 150,000 to 200,000 (1993 SIL), including 28,000 Taturu (1987), 76,000 Barabaig (1987), a few thousand Gisamjanga (1982 F. Rottland), 370 Tsimajeega (1967 census), 740 Rootigaanga (1967 census), 4,099 Bianjiida (1948 census). Singida and Mbulu regions. The Barabaig are mainly in the northern volcanic highlands near Mt. Hanang. Nilo-Saharan, Eastern Sudanic, Nilotic, Southern, Tatoga. Dialects: BAJUTA, GISAMJANGA (KISAMAJENG, GISAMJANG), BARABAYIIGA (BARABAIG, BARABAIK, BARBAIG), TSIMAJEEGA

(ISIMIJEEGA), ROOTIGAANGA (ROTIGENGA), BURAADIIGA (BURADIGA), BIANJIIDA (UTATU). Sabaot is probably the closest language linguistically. Barabaik and Kisamajeng are very close and are completely inherently intelligible. There are several other dialects or ethnic groups: Darorajega, Gidang'odiga, Bisiyeda, Daragwajega, Salawajega, Ghumbiega, Mangatiga. 50% lexical similarity with Kalenjin and Omotik of Kenya. Bilingual level estimates for Swahili are 0 90%, 1 6%, 2 2%, 3 1%, 4 1%, 5 0%. Those who have been to school may speak Swahili at FSI level 2 or 3. A few use Iraqw, Iramba, or Nyaturu as second language for commerce. 'Mangati' or 'Ole-Mangati' is the Maasai name meaning 'enemies'. 'Taturu' is the Sukuma name. There is intermarriage with the Iraqw. VSO; prepositions; genitives, articles, adjectives, numerals after noun heads; question word final; 4 prefixes, 5 suffixes on verb; case marked by tone; verb affixes mark person, number; (C)(C)V(:), VC; tonal. Literacy rate in second language: 1%. Datoga orthography is different from Swahili. Savannah. Plains, mountain slope. Pastoralists: cattle, goats, sheep, donkeys; agriculturalists: maize, beans, millet; hunters. 3,800 to 6,000 feet. Traditional religion, Christian.

DHAISO ***(KIDHAISO, DAISO, DAISU, KISEGUJU)*** [DHS] 5,000 or fewer (1999). Bwiti and Magati villages at the base of the eastern Usambara Mts. on the northern side, Muheza District, Tanga region. Niger-Congo, Atlantic-Congo, Volta-Congo, Benue-Congo, Bantoid, Southern, Narrow Bantu, Central, E, Kikuyu-Kamba (E.20). Related to Kamba of Kenya. 32% lexical similarity with Digo. Self reported proficiency in Swahili is high. 47% of adults claimed Swahili as mother tongue on a questionnaire. Most older children and nearly all adults are able to speak Dhaiso, but they report speaking Swahili at least as often as Dhaiso, even at home. Most primary-school age children do not speak Dhaiso. Not being transmitted by adults to children. Muslim.

DIGO ***(KIDIGO, CHIDIGO)*** [DIG] 88,000 in Tanzania (1987). Northeastern coast area around Tanga. Niger-Congo, Atlantic-Congo, Volta-Congo, Benue-Congo, Bantoid, Southern, Narrow Bantu, Central, E, Nyika (E.40), Mijikenda. Muslim. Bible portions 1982-1997. See main entry under Kenya.

DOE ***(DOHE)*** [DOE] 24,000 (1987). North coast, north of the Kwere, south of the Nghwele. Niger-Congo, Atlantic-Congo, Volta-Congo, Benue-Congo, Bantoid, Southern, Narrow Bantu, Central, G, Zigula-Zaramo (G.30). Doe has influenced Zigula and Bondei linguistically, and it has been influenced by them. 74% lexical similarity with Kwere, 64% with Kami, 61% with Kutu and Zalamo, 70% with Zigula, 54% with Ruguru. Reported to be bilingual in Swahili. Investigation needed: bilingual proficiency in Swahili.

ENGLISH [ENG] Second language speakers in Tanzania: 1,500,000 (1977 Voegelin and Voegelin). Indo-European, Germanic, West, English. Used by some Asian residents as mother tongue. Taught in secondary school and university. Bible 1535-1989. See main entry under United Kingdom.

FIPA ***(ICHIFIPA, CIFIPA, FIBA)*** [FIP] 200,000 (1992 UBS). Population total both countries 200,000 or more. West central near southern Lake Tanganyika. Also spoken in Malawi. Niger-Congo, Atlantic-Congo, Volta-Congo, Benue-Congo, Bantoid, Southern, Narrow Bantu, Central, F, Tongwe (F.10). Dialects: KANDASI, SIWA, KWAFI, YANTILI (PEMBA), KWA, CILE. Bilingualism in Swahili. Savannah, scrub. Plateau, hills, coast, valleys. Agriculturalists: millet, maize, lima beans, sweet potatoes, cassava, peanuts, spinach, cucurbits, tomatoes, onions, potatoes, chiles, sorghum, bananas, papayas, oranges, limes, mangos, tobacco, coconuts, wheat, coffee; animal husbandry: cattle, sheep, goats, fowl, pidgeons; fishermen. 2,530 to 7,000 feet. Traditional religion. NT 1988.

GANDA ***(LUGANDA)*** [LAP] 9,459 in Tanzania (1957 census). Niger-Congo, Atlantic-Congo, Volta-Congo, Benue-Congo, Bantoid, Southern, Narrow Bantu, Central, J, Nyoro-Ganda (J.10). SVO. Bible 1896-1968. See main entry under Uganda.

GOGO ***(CHIGOGO)*** [GOG] 1,300,000 (1992 UBS). Southwest of Dodoma, east of Kimbu, Rift Valley. Niger-Congo, Atlantic-Congo, Volta-Congo, Benue-Congo, Bantoid, Southern, Narrow Bantu, Central, G, Gogo (G.10). 50% lexical similarity with Hehe and Sangu, 48% with Kimbu, 45% with Nilamba. Gogo is used in meetings by Anglicans. Semi-nomadic. Dry valley. Agriculturalists. Traditional religion, Christian, Muslim. Bible 1962.

GOROWA ***(GOROA, GORWAA, FIOME)*** [GOW] 30,000 (1987) to 50,000 (1999 R. Kiessling). Mbulu and Kondoa districts, Central Province, Arusha region around Mt. Ufiome, near Babati; Galapo, Gidas, Riroda, and Bereku villages. Afro-Asiatic, Cushitic, South. Closely related to Burunge, Wasi, and Iraqw. May be a dialect of Iraqw. They speak Iraqw and Swahili as second languages. Investigation needed: intelligibility with Iraqw. Forests. Hills. 4,500 feet. Christian, traditional religion.

GUJARATI [GJR] 250,000 in Tanzania from India, predominantly Gujarati (1993 Johnstone). Small communities. Indo-European, Indo-Iranian, Indo-Aryan, Central zone, Gujarati. Vigorous. They have their own religious institutions and evening schools. Bible 1823-1998. See main entry under India.

GWENO ***(KIGWENO)*** [GWE] Around Mt. Kilimanjaro. Niger-Congo, Atlantic-Congo, Volta-Congo, Benue-Congo, Bantoid, Southern, Narrow Bantu, Central, E, Chaga (E.30). 54% to 56% lexical similarity with Chagga dialects (closest), 46% with Taita.

HA ***(GIHA, KIHA, IKIHA)*** [HAQ] 800,000 (1993 Johnstone). Northwestern, Kigoma Province. Niger-Congo, Atlantic-Congo, Volta-Congo, Benue-Congo, Bantoid, Southern, Narrow Bantu, Central, J, Rwanda-Rundi (J.60). Dialects in border area near Burundi are reported to be intelligible with Rundi (Polomé 1980). 78% lexical similarity with Rundi, 77% with Hangaza and Shubi, 72% with Rwanda. Speakers upcountry do not know Swahili. Speakers upcountry are traditionally oriented. Traditional religion, Muslim, Christian. Bible portions 1960-1962.

HADZA ***(HATSA, HADZAPI, HADZABI, KINDIGA, "TINDIGA", WAKINDIGA, KANGEJU)*** [HTS] 200 (1987). Some distance northwest of the Sandawe, southeast of Lake Victoria, Singida, Arusha, and Shinyanga regions, near Lake Eyasi. Khoisan, Hatsa. Bali may be a dialect. Nomadic. Pressures from outside are resulting in less land, food, and more disease. Swamps, wilderness. Hunter-gatherers. Traditional religion, Christian.

HANGAZA ***(KIHANGAZA)*** [HAN] 150,000 (1987). Northwestern, southwest of Bukoba. Niger-Congo, Atlantic-Congo, Volta-Congo, Benue-Congo, Bantoid, Southern, Narrow Bantu, Central, J, Rwanda-Rundi (J.60). 85% lexical similarity with Shubi, 83% with Rundi, 77% with Ha, 72% with Rwand. Speakers have strong ethnic pride. Bible portions 1938.

HAYA ***(EKIHAYA, RUHAYA, ZIBA)*** [HAY] 1,200,000 (1991 UBS). Northwestern, west of Lake Victoria, Bukoba District of West Lake Province. Niger-Congo, Atlantic-Congo, Volta-Congo, Benue-Congo, Bantoid, Southern, Narrow Bantu, Central, J, Haya-Jita (J.20). Dialects: BUMBIRA, EDANGABO, HAMBA, HANGIRO, MWANI, NYAKISISA, EKIZIBA, YOZA. Agriculturalists: plantain, coffee, beans, maize; miners: tin, wolfram; animal husbandry: cattle, goats. Christian, traditional religion, Muslim. Bible, in press (1998).

HEHE ***(KIHEHE)*** [HEH] 750,000 (1994 UBS)). Southeast central, north of Pogolo. Niger-Congo, Atlantic-Congo, Volta-Congo, Benue-Congo, Bantoid, Southern, Narrow Bantu, Central, G, Bena-Kinga (G.60). 65% lexical similarity with Bena (closest), 59% with Pangwa, 56% with Sangu, 50% with Kinga, 48% with Wanji.

HOLOHOLO ***(HOROHORO, KALANGA, KIKALANGA)*** [HOO] Population total both countries 12,500 (1987). East central shore of Lake Tanganyika. Also spoken in DRC. Niger-Congo, Atlantic-Congo, Volta-Congo, Benue-Congo, Bantoid, Southern, Narrow Bantu, Central, D, Lega-Kalanga (D.20). KiKaranga may be separate. Different from Kiholo of DRC and Angola. Bible portions 1948.

IKIZU [IKZ] 28,000 (1987). East of Zanaki and Kerebe. Niger-Congo, Atlantic-Congo, Volta-Congo, Benue-Congo, Bantoid, Southern, Narrow Bantu, Central, E, Kuria (E.10). Limited bilingualism in Swahili.

IKOMA ***(NATA, IKINATA)*** [NTK] 15,000 (1987). East of Ikizu, Zanaki, and Kerebe. Niger-Congo, Atlantic-Congo, Volta-Congo, Benue-Congo, Bantoid, Southern, Narrow Bantu, Central, E, Kuria (E.10). Dialect: ISSENYI (ISENYI, IKISENYI). 81% lexical similarity with Zanaki, 73% with Ngurimi, 68% with Kuria, 44% with Gusii. Limited bilingualism in Swahili.

IRAQW ***(MBULU, MBULUNGE, EROKH, IRAKU)*** [IRK] 365,000 (1993 Johnstone). Mbulu District, highlands southwest of Arusha in north. Afro-Asiatic, Cushitic, South. Dialect: ASA. Asa may be a separate language. Investigation needed: intelligibility with Asa. Agriculturalists: maize, beans, red and white sorghum, sweet potatoes, millet; animal husbandry: cattle sheep. 6,000 feet. Traditional religion, Christian, Muslim. NT 1977.

ISANZU [ISN] 32,400 (1987). Iramba District of Singida Region. Niger-Congo, Atlantic-Congo, Volta-Congo, Benue-Congo, Bantoid, Southern, Narrow Bantu, Central, Unclassified. Investigation needed: intelligibility with Nyaturu, Nilamba, bilingual proficiency in Swahili. Christian, traditional religion, Muslim.

JIJI [JIJ] 12,000 (1987). In Kigoma, Ujiji. Niger-Congo, Atlantic-Congo, Volta-Congo, Benue-Congo, Bantoid, Southern, Narrow Bantu, Central, Unclassified. May be Ha in the Ujiji area, not a separate language. Limited bilingualism in Swahili. Investigation needed: intelligibility with Ha. Muslim.

JITA ***(ECHIJITA, ECIJITA)*** [JIT] 217,000 (1987). Southeastern shore of Lake Victoria, between the Zanaki and Kerebe. Niger-Congo, Atlantic-Congo, Volta-Congo, Benue-Congo, Bantoid, Southern, Narrow Bantu, Central, J, Haya-Jita (J.20). 83% lexical similarity with Kwaya, 81% with Kara, 62% with Kerewe. NT 1943-1960.

KABWA [CWA] North central. Niger-Congo, Atlantic-Congo, Volta-Congo, Benue-Congo, Bantoid, Southern, Narrow Bantu, Central, E, Kuria (E.10). Close to Kiroba (Kuria), but separate.

KACHCHI ***(CUTCHI, KACCHI, KACHI, KATCHI)*** [KFR] Cities. Indo-European, Indo-Iranian, Indo-Aryan, Northwestern zone, Sindhi. Speakers use Kachchi 52% of the time, Gujarati 14%, English 26%. Hindu, Muslim. Bible portions 1834. See main entry under India.

KAGULU ***(CHIKAGULU, KAGURU, NORTHERN SAGARA, KININGO, WETUMBA, SOLWA, MANGAHERI)*** [KKI] 217,000 (1987). East central, east of Dodoma. Niger-Congo, Atlantic-Congo, Volta-Congo, Benue-Congo, Bantoid, Southern, Narrow Bantu, Central, G, Gogo (G.10). Dialect: MEGI. 63% lexical similarity with Sagala, 56% with Gogo. Speakers are reported to be bilingual in Swahili. Investigation needed: bilingual proficiency in Swahili. Savannah, scrub, deciduous forest.

Lowland, plateau, rolling hills, mountain slope. Agriculturalists: maize, beans, peanuts, banana, cassava, mango, papaya, limes, cotton, sugarcane, potatoes, plantains, tobacco, coffee, citrus, pumpkins, castor, sunflowers; animal husbandry: chickens, ducks, sheep, goats, cattle. 2,000 to 7,000 feet. Christian, traditional religion, Muslim. Bible portions 1885-1894.

KAHE [HKA] 2,700 (1987). Northeastern slopes of Mt. Kilimanjaro. Niger-Congo, Atlantic-Congo, Volta-Congo, Benue-Congo, Bantoid, Southern, Narrow Bantu, Central, E, Chaga (E.30). Investigation needed: intelligibility with Chagga. SVO.

KAMI *(KIKAMI)* [KCU] 10,000 to 20,000 (1998 PBT). About 30 km. north and northeast of Morogoro, on and south of the main road to Dar es Salaam, and on for about 20 km. The farthest village is about 60 km. south of this road. Niger-Congo, Atlantic-Congo, Volta-Congo, Benue-Congo, Bantoid, Southern, Narrow Bantu, Central, G, Zigula-Zaramo (G.30). 69% lexical similarity with Kutu and Kwere, 65% with Zalamo, 64% with Doe, 54% with Ruguru. Muslim.

KARA *(REGI)* [REG] 86,000 (1987). Southeastern shore of Lake Victoria, between the Zanaki and Kerebe, on the Ukerewe, and islands. A few in Mwanza. Niger-Congo, Atlantic-Congo, Volta-Congo, Benue-Congo, Bantoid, Southern, Narrow Bantu, Central, J, Haya-Jita (J.20). 81% lexical similarity with Jita, 80% with Kwaya. Younger speakers are bilingual in Swahili, but those over 35 are not; the majority do not know Swahili. Vigorous. 'Regi' is a tribal name. They do not travel much. Fishermen.

KEREBE *(EKIKEREBE, KEREWE)* [KED] 100,000 (1987). Northwestern Ukerewe Island, southern Lake Victoria, Kibara. North of Sukuma, across Speke Gulf. Niger-Congo, Atlantic-Congo, Volta-Congo, Benue-Congo, Bantoid, Southern, Narrow Bantu, Central, J, Haya-Jita (J.20). 76% lexical similarity with Zinza, 75% with Haya, 69% with Nyambo, 68% with Nyankole, 63% with Chiga and Toro, 62% with Nyoro. NT 1936-1946.

KIMBU *(KIKIMBU, IKIBUNGU, YANZI)* [KIV] 78,000 (1987). Southwest and west of the Konongo, south and southeast of the Nyamwezi; Chunya District, southern Highlands Province, Manyoni District, Central Province; 23% in traditional area. Niger-Congo, Atlantic-Congo, Volta-Congo, Benue-Congo, Bantoid, Southern, Narrow Bantu, Central, F, Sukuma-Nyamwezi (F.20). 61% lexical similarity with Nilamba, 57% with Sukuma, 53% with Nyaturu, 48% with Sumbwa, 47% with Langi. Limited bilingualism in Swahili. Moravians use Nyamwezi in church, a related but separate language; RC use Swahili. Semi-nomadic. Forest. Hunter-gatherers, beekeepers, agriculturalists: sorghum, millet, maize, rice, sweet potatoes, cassava, peanuts, beans, chick peas, gourds, sunflowers. Traditional religion, Christian, Muslim.

KINGA *(KIKINGA, EKIKINGA)* [KIX] 65,000 (1987). Livingston Mountains, northeastern shore of Lake Malawi. Niger-Congo, Atlantic-Congo, Volta-Congo, Benue-Congo, Bantoid, Southern, Narrow Bantu, Central, G, Bena-Kinga (G.60). NT 1961.

KISANKASA *("NDOROBO", "DOROBO")* [KQH] 4,670 (1987). Nilo-Saharan, Eastern Sudanic, Nilotic, Southern, Kalenjin, Nandi-Markweta, Nandi. A distinct language from others called "Dorobo": Aramanik, Mediak, Mosiro. Speakers have limited comprehension of other languages.

KISI [KIZ] 13,000 (1987). Southwest, north shore of Lake Malawi. Niger-Congo, Atlantic-Congo, Volta-Congo, Benue-Congo, Bantoid, Southern, Narrow Bantu, Central, G, Bena-Kinga (G.60). Different from Kisii (Gusii) of Kenya. May be the same as Kichi.

KONONGO [KCZ] 51,000 (1987). South of the Nyamwezi, across the Ugalla River, in the northwest corner of Mpanda District, Western Province; 25% live in the tribal area. Niger-Congo, Atlantic-Congo, Volta-Congo, Benue-Congo, Bantoid, Southern, Narrow Bantu, Central, F, Sukuma-Nyamwezi (F.20). Agriculturalists: sorghum, millet, maize, rice, sweet potatoes, cassava, peanuts, beans, chick peas, gourds, sunflowers.

KURIA *(IKIKURIA, IGIKURIA, TENDE, KURYA, KURYE)* [KUJ] 213,000 in Tanzania (1987). Population total both countries 348,000. North central near the Kenya border, east of Lake Victoria. Also spoken in Kenya. Niger-Congo, Atlantic-Congo, Volta-Congo, Benue-Congo, Bantoid, Southern, Narrow Bantu, Central, E, Kuria (E.10). Dialects: KIROBA, SIMBITI, SWETA. The dialects listed are in Tanzania; four others are in Kenya. Kiroba and Simbiti may be distinct languages. Koria is not a good spelling. Investigation needed: intelligibility with Kiroba, Simbiti. NT, in press (1997).

KUTU *(KIKUTU, KHUTU, ZIRAHA, QWADZA, NG'OMVIA)* [KDC] 45,000 (1987). South Morogodo and southeast Kilosa districts, Eastern Region. Niger-Congo, Atlantic-Congo, Volta-Congo, Benue-Congo, Bantoid, Southern, Narrow Bantu, Central, G, Zigula-Zaramo (G.30). 69% lexical similarity with Kami, 68% with Zalamo, 64% with Kwere, 61% with Doe. They are reported to be bilingual in Swahili. Matrilineal. Investigation needed: bilingual proficiency in Swahili. Low plains. Agriculturalists: tobacco, cotton, kapok, sorghum, maize; animal husbandry: sheep, goats, poultry; hunters; fishermen. Less than 500 feet.

KWADZA *(QWADZA)* [WKA] Mbulu District. Afro-Asiatic, Cushitic, South. Related to Iraqw, but a separate language. C. Ehret was reported to be working with the last speaker (M. L. Bender 1976:280). Confirmed by R. Kiessling (1999). Extinct.

KWAVI ***(PARAKUYO)*** [CKG] 7,378 (1957 census). Unclassified. Limited understanding of other languages. Not a Bantu language.

KWAYA [KYA] 102,000 (1987). Southeastern shore of Lake Victoria, between the Zanaki and Kerebe. Niger-Congo, Atlantic-Congo, Volta-Congo, Benue-Congo, Bantoid, Southern, Narrow Bantu, Central, J, Haya-Jita (J.20). Dialect: RURI. 83% lexical similarity with Jita, 80% with Kara. Investigation needed: intelligibility with Jita, Kara.

KWERE ***(KAKWERE, KWELE, NG'WERE)*** [CWE] 98,000 (1987). Western Bagamoyo District, northwest Kisarawe District, eastern Morogoro District, Eastern Region. Many live among the Zalamo and Ruguru. Niger-Congo, Atlantic-Congo, Volta-Congo, Benue-Congo, Bantoid, Southern, Narrow Bantu, Central, G, Zigula-Zaramo (G.30). 74% lexical similarity with Doe, 69% with Kami, 64% with Kutu, 61% with Zalamo, 62% with Zigula, 54% with Ruguru. Kwere has influenced Zigula linguistically, and has been influenced by Zigula and Bondei. Matrilineal. Rolling open bush, coastal. Agriculturalists: dry rice, maize, sorghum, peas, sesame, cotton, coconuts, fruit; fishermen; animal husbandry: small livestock; wood carvers. Traditional religion, Muslim, Christian.

LAMBYA ***(ICHILAMBYA, LAMBIA, LAMBWA, RAMBIA, IRAMBA)*** [LAI] 40,000 in Tanzania (1987). Population total both countries 81,000. Southwest border with Malawi, south of Nyiha. Also spoken in Malawi. Niger-Congo, Atlantic-Congo, Volta-Congo, Benue-Congo, Bantoid, Southern, Narrow Bantu, Central, N, Tumbuka (N.20).

LUO ***(DHOLUO, KAVIRONDO)*** [LUO] 223,000 in Tanzania (1993 Johnstone). North central near Kenya border, east of Lake Victoria. Nilo-Saharan, Eastern Sudanic, Nilotic, Western, Luo, Southern, Luo-Acholi, Luo. Different from Lwo (Lango) of Uganda or Lwo (Luo, Jur Luwo) of Sudan. Bible 1953-1977. See main entry under Kenya.

MAASAI ***(MASAI, MAA, LUMBWA)*** [MET] 430,000 in Tanzania (1993) including 170,000 Arusa, 30,000 Baraguyu (1987). North central, on Kenya border, east of Serengeti National Park. The Baraguyu are spread from the Indian Ocean nearly to Malawi. Nilo-Saharan, Eastern Sudanic, Nilotic, Eastern, Lotuxo-Teso, Lotuxo-Maa, Ongamo-Maa. Dialects: ENGUTUK-ELOIKOB, ARUSHA (IL-ARUSHA, L-ARUSHA), BARAGUYU, KISONKO. Arusha is distinct from the Bantu Chagga-related variety. One source reports that Arusha who are pastoralists dress like the Maasai and speak a Maasai-related variety, whereas those who are agriculturalists intermarry with the Chagga. Other sources say the Arusha originally spoke a Bantu language. The last 3 dialects listed are in Tanzania, and have 82% to 86% lexical similarity with Kenya dialects. Bilingualism in Swahili. The Baraguyu speak Maasai, but they consider themselves to be a separate ethnic group from the Maasai. Nomadic. Patrilineal. Some men marry women from other language groups. Pastoralists: cattle, sheep, goats; agriculturalists (Baraguyu, Il-Arusha, Il-Lumpua (Lumbwa), Il-Oikop, Wakuavi). Traditional religion, Christian; Arusha: traditional religion, Christian. Bible 1991. See main entry under Kenya.

MACHAMBE ***(MACHAME, KIMASHAMI)*** [JMC] 300,000 (1992 UBS). Chagga area. Niger-Congo, Atlantic-Congo, Volta-Congo, Benue-Congo, Bantoid, Southern, Narrow Bantu, Central, E, Chaga (E.30). A separate language from Chagga, Mochi, Rombo, and Vunjo. NT, in press (1997).

MACHINGA [MVW] 36,000 (1987). Along the coast, above the 10th parallel south, close to the Mwera and the Ngindo. Niger-Congo, Atlantic-Congo, Volta-Congo, Benue-Congo, Bantoid, Southern, Narrow Bantu, Central, P, Yao (P.20). Investigation needed: intelligibility with Mwera.

MAKHUWA-MEETTO ***(MAKUA, MAKHUA, IMAKUA, MAKOA, MATO, MAQUOUA, KIMAKUA, MAKUWA)*** [MAK] 360,000 in Tanzania (1993). Extreme southern Tanzania. Niger-Congo, Atlantic-Congo, Volta-Congo, Benue-Congo, Bantoid, Southern, Narrow Bantu, Central, P, Makua (P.30). Dialect: MEDO (METO, EMETO). See main entry under Mozambique.

MAKONDE ***(CHIMAKONDE, CHINIMAKONDE, KONDE, MATAMBWE)*** [KDE] 900,000 in Tanzania (1993 Johnstone). Population total both countries 1,260,000. Extreme southern section of Tanzania. Also spoken in Mozambique. Niger-Congo, Atlantic-Congo, Volta-Congo, Benue-Congo, Bantoid, Southern, Narrow Bantu, Central, P, Yao (P.20). Dialect: MAVIHA. Between Yao and Swahili. Muslim, Christian, traditional religion. Bible portions.

MAKWE ***(KIMAKWE, PALMA)*** [YMK] 8,000 to 10,000 in Tanzania (1997 SIL). Southeast Tanzania. Niger-Congo, Atlantic-Congo, Volta-Congo, Benue-Congo, Bantoid, Southern, Narrow Bantu, Central, G, Swahili (G.40). Not inherently intelligible with Swahili. 60% lexical similarity with Swahili, 57% with Mwani, 48% with Yao. All speak Swahili. Investigation needed: bilingual proficiency in Swahili. Motivation for literacy is high. Muslim. See main entry under Mozambique.

MALILA ***(MALILIA, ISHIMALILIA)*** [MGQ] 52,000 (1987). Southwest near Malawi, south of Safwa, north of Lambya. Niger-Congo, Atlantic-Congo, Volta-Congo, Benue-Congo, Bantoid, Southern, Narrow Bantu, Central, M, Nyika-Safwa (M.20). Reported to be bilingual in Swahili. Investigation needed: bilingual proficiency in Swahili.

MAMBWE-LUNGU [MGR] 97,000 in Tanzania, including 63,000 Mambwe and 34,000 Rungu (1987). Mambwe is southwest of Lake Rukwa; Lungu is on the southeast shore. Some in Bemba region.

Lungu covers 6,393 square miles. Niger-Congo, Atlantic-Congo, Volta-Congo, Benue-Congo, Bantoid, Southern, Narrow Bantu, Central, F, Tongwe (F.10). Dialects: MAMBWE (ICHIMAMBWE), RUNGU (LUNGU, CILUNGU). Forest, savannah. Agriculturalists: millet, sorghum, maize, peanuts, beans; animal husbandry: cattle, sheep, goats, fowl; fishermen. Traditional religion. NT 1901-1991. See main entry under Zambia.

MANDA ***(KIMANDA, KINYASA, NYASA)*** [MGS] 18,000 (1987). Northeast shore of Lake Malawi, western Ruvuma Province. Niger-Congo, Atlantic-Congo, Volta-Congo, Benue-Congo, Bantoid, Southern, Narrow Bantu, Central, N, Manda (N.10). NT 1937.

MATENGO ***(CHIMATENGO, KIMATENGO)*** [MGV] 150,000 (1987). Southwest just northeast of Nyasa. Also possibly in Malawi. Niger-Congo, Atlantic-Congo, Volta-Congo, Benue-Congo, Bantoid, Southern, Narrow Bantu, Central, N, Manda (N.10). Speakers have little comprehension of other languages.

MATUMBI ***(KIMATUMBI)*** [MGW] 72,000 (1978 MARC). On the banks of the Ruvuma, next to the Makonde and Makhuwa (Polomé and Hill 1980). Niger-Congo, Atlantic-Congo, Volta-Congo, Benue-Congo, Bantoid, Southern, Narrow Bantu, Central, P, Matumbi (P.10). Dialect: KUCHI. Speakers have little comprehension of Swahili or other languages. Muslim, traditional religion, Christian.

MBUGU ***(MA'A, MBOUGOU, VAMA'A, WA MAATHI, KIBWYO)*** [MHD] 32,000 (1987). Eastern Province in Usambara. Mixed Language, Pare-Cushitic. People call themselves 'Va-Ma'a'. A hybrid language; Bantu inflectional (prefix and concord) system with Cushitic vocabulary. Derivational morphemes are Bantu and Cushitic (or non-Bantu). The Bantu influence is from Pare (Shambaa).

MBUGWE [MGZ] 24,000 (1999). Babati District, Arusha Region. Niger-Congo, Atlantic-Congo, Volta-Congo, Benue-Congo, Bantoid, Southern, Narrow Bantu, Central, F, Nyilamba-Langi (F.30). 52% lexical similarity with Rangi. All ages. Investigation needed: bilingual proficiency in Rangi.

MBUNGA [MGY] 29,000 (1987). South central, southeast of the Hehe, north of the Pogolo. Niger-Congo, Atlantic-Congo, Volta-Congo, Benue-Congo, Bantoid, Southern, Narrow Bantu, Central, P, Matumbi (P.10). 69% lexical similarity with Ndamba, 57% with Pogolu. There may be two varieties called 'Mbunga', one Bantu P.10, and one Bantu G.50.

MEDIAK ***(NDOROBO, DOROBO)*** [MWX] Nilo-Saharan, Eastern Sudanic, Nilotic, Southern, Kalenjin, Nandi-Markweta, Nandi. A distinct language from others called 'Dorobo': Aramanik, Kisankasa, Mosiro. Limited comprehension of other languages.

MOCHI ***(MOSHI, KIMOSHI, MOSI)*** [OLD] 240,000 (1972 Bendor-Samuel). Northeast corner, Chaga area. Niger-Congo, Atlantic-Congo, Volta-Congo, Benue-Congo, Bantoid, Southern, Narrow Bantu, Central, E, Chaga (E.30). NT 1939.

MOSIRO ***(NDOROBO, DOROBO)*** [MWY] Nilo-Saharan, Eastern Sudanic, Nilotic, Southern, Kalenjin, Nandi-Markweta, Nandi. A distinct language from others called 'Dorobo': Aramanik, Mediak, Kisankasa. Speakers have limited comprehension of other languages.

MPOTO ***(CHIMPOTO, KINYASA, NYASA)*** [MPA] Population total both countries 80,000 (1977 Voegelin and Voegelin). Southwestern, along northeast shore of Lake Malawi, western Ruvuma Province. Also spoken in Malawi. Niger-Congo, Atlantic-Congo, Volta-Congo, Benue-Congo, Bantoid, Southern, Narrow Bantu, Central, N, Manda (N.10). Both Mpoto and Manda have alternate names of 'Kinyasa'. Bible portions 1913-1924.

MWANGA ***(CHINAMWANGA, NYAMWANGA, NAMWANGA, KINAMWANGA)*** [MWN] 87,000 in Tanzania (1987). Southwest of Lake Rukwa. Saisi Valley in the northwest to forested plateau in the southeast. Niger-Congo, Atlantic-Congo, Volta-Congo, Benue-Congo, Bantoid, Southern, Narrow Bantu, Central, M, Nyika-Safwa (M.20). Dialect: TAMBO. Agriculturalists: millet, peanuts, beans, maize; animal husbandry: cattle, sheep, goats, fowl, pidgeons. Traditional religion. Bible 1982. See main entry under Zambia.

MWERA ***(CHIMWERA, CIMWERA, MWELA)*** [MWE] 400,000 (1993 Johnstone). Southeast, north of Makonde. Niger-Congo, Atlantic-Congo, Volta-Congo, Benue-Congo, Bantoid, Southern, Narrow Bantu, Central, P, Yao (P.20). Muslim.

NDALI [NDH] 150,000 (1987). South border with Malawi, between Lambya and Nyakyusa. Niger-Congo, Atlantic-Congo, Volta-Congo, Benue-Congo, Bantoid, Southern, Narrow Bantu, Central, M, Nyika-Safwa (M.20). Different from Ndali which is a dialect of Zanaki.

NDAMBA [NDJ] 55,000 (1987). South central, northeast of Bena, southeast of Hehe, west of Pogolo, southwest of Mbunga. Niger-Congo, Atlantic-Congo, Volta-Congo, Benue-Congo, Bantoid, Southern, Narrow Bantu, Central, G, Pogoro (G.50). 69% lexical similarity with Mbunga, 56% with Pogolo. Reported to be bilingual in Swahili. Investigation needed: bilingual proficiency in Swahili.

NDENDEULE ***(NDENDEULI)*** [DNE] 79,000 (1987). Inland, east of the main Ngoni territory south of the 10th parallel. Niger-Congo, Atlantic-Congo, Volta-Congo, Benue-Congo, Bantoid, Southern, Unclassified. Speakers have little understanding of other languages.

NDENGEREKO ***(KINGENGEREKO, NDENGELEKO)*** [NDE] 110,000 (1987). Central coast, south of the Zalamo, north of the Rufiji. Niger-Congo, Atlantic-Congo, Volta-Congo, Benue-Congo, Bantoid, Southern, Narrow Bantu, Central, P, Matumbi (P.10). Limited bilingualism in Swahili.

NDONDE ***(KIMAWANDA, MAWANDA, NDOMDE)*** [NDS] 33,000 (1987). Population total both countries 33,000 or more. From the Tanzania border through Mueda in Mozambique, down to Macomia. Also spoken in Mozambique. Niger-Congo, Atlantic-Congo, Volta-Congo, Benue-Congo, Bantoid, Southern, Narrow Bantu, Central, P, Yao (P.20). Reported to be very bilingual in Makhuwa-Metto.

NGASA ***(SHAKA, ONGAMO)*** [NSG] 200 to 300 speakers out of an ethnic group of 2,500 (1983). Eastern slopes of Mt. Kilimanjaro. Nilo-Saharan, Eastern Sudanic, Nilotic, Eastern, Lotuxo-Teso, Lotuxo-Maa, Ongamo-Maa. 60% lexical similarity with Maasai, 59% with Samburu, 58% with Chamus. Bilingualism in Chaga. Only elderly speakers left. The young people speak Chaga. It began to diminish in the 1950s.

NGHWELE ***(KINGHWELE, NGWELE)*** [NHE] Coast north of the Doe, east and south of the Zigula. Niger-Congo, Atlantic-Congo, Volta-Congo, Benue-Congo, Bantoid, Southern, Narrow Bantu, Central, G, Zigula-Zaramo (G.30).

NGINDO ***(KINGINDO, NJINDO)*** [NNQ] 220,000 (1987). East central, south of the Rufiji, west of the Mwera. Niger-Congo, Atlantic-Congo, Volta-Congo, Benue-Congo, Bantoid, Southern, Narrow Bantu, Central, P, Matumbi (P.10). Reported to be bilingual in Swahili. Investigation needed: bilingual proficiency in Swahili.

NGONI ***(CHINGONI, KINGONI, ANGONI, KISUTU, SUTU)*** [NGU] 170,000 in Tanzania (1987). Population total all countries 205,000. South central, Ruvuma Province, south of Songea. Also spoken in Malawi, Mozambique. Niger-Congo, Atlantic-Congo, Volta-Congo, Benue-Congo, Bantoid, Southern, Narrow Bantu, Central, N, Manda (N.10). Different from 'Ngoni', an alternate name for Zulu, Ngoni dialect of Nsenga, Ngoni dialect of Nyanja, Ngoni dialect of Tumbuka. The people formerly spoke Zulu. Bible portions 1891-1898.

NGULU ***(KINGULU, NGURU, NGUU, WAYOMBA, GEJA)*** [NGP] 132,000 (1987). Northwest Morogodo District, Eastern Region, western Handeni District, Northern Region, northeast Kilosa District, Eastern Region, Mpwapwa District, Central Region, Ngulu Mts. Niger-Congo, Atlantic-Congo, Volta-Congo, Benue-Congo, Bantoid, Southern, Narrow Bantu, Central, G, Zigula-Zaramo (G.30). 83% lexical similarity with Zigula, 73% with Bondei, 68% with Shambala. Somewhat bilingual in Swahili. Different from Ngulu of Mozambique and Malawi. Matrilineal. Mountain slope, foothills, plains. Traders; agriculturalists: maize, millet, sorghum, beans, peas, bananas, sugarcane, cassava, castor, peanuts, sweet potatoes, pumpkins, fruit, mountain rice, tobacco, cotton, coffee; animal husbandry: poultry, sheep, goats, cattle. 1,000 feet and higher. Traditional religion.

NGURIMI ***(IKINGURIMI, NGOREME, NGRUIMI, NGURUIMI, DENGURUME)*** [NGQ] 32,000 (1987). North central border with Kenya, between the Maasai and the Kuria. Niger-Congo, Atlantic-Congo, Volta-Congo, Benue-Congo, Bantoid, Southern, Narrow Bantu, Central, E, Kuria (E.10). Limited comprehension of other languages. 84% lexical similarity with Kuria, 80% with Zanaki, 73% with Ikoma, 49% with Gusii.

NILAMBA ***(NYILAMBA, IKINILAMBA, IRAMBA, NILYAMBA, IKINIRAMBA, ILAMBA, NIRAMBA, KINIRAMBA)*** [NIM] 440,000 including 50,000 Iambi (1987). Northwest of Singida, north of the Nyaturu. Niger-Congo, Atlantic-Congo, Volta-Congo, Benue-Congo, Bantoid, Southern, Narrow Bantu, Central, F, Nyilamba-Langi (F.30). Dialect: IAMBI. 56% lexical similarity with Nyamwezi, 55% with Sukuma, 45% with Sumbwa. NT 1967.

NYAKYUSA-NGONDE ***(IKINYAKYUSA, MOMBE, NGONDE, IKINGONDE, KONDE, NKONDE, NYAKUSA, NYIKYUSA, SOCHILE, SOKILE, SOKILI, KUKWE, NYEKYOSA)*** [NYY] 750,000 Nyakyusa in Tanzania (1992 UBS). Population total both countries 1,050,000. North end, Lake Malawi. Also spoken in Malawi. Niger-Congo, Atlantic-Congo, Volta-Congo, Benue-Congo, Bantoid, Southern, Narrow Bantu, Central, M, Nyakyusa (M.30). Dialects: NYAKYUSA, KUKWE, MWAMBA (LUNGULU), NGONDE, SELYA (SALYA, SERIA). Traditional religion, Christian, Muslim. Bible 1993-1996.

NYAMBO ***(EKINYAMBO, KARAGWE, RUKARAGWE, URURAGWE, RAGWE, RUNYAMBO, KINYAMBO)*** [NYM] 7,000 (1987). Northwest corner, Uganda border, west of Lake Victoria, Karagwe District. Niger-Congo, Atlantic-Congo, Volta-Congo, Benue-Congo, Bantoid, Southern, Narrow Bantu, Central, J, Haya-Jita (J.20). Dialect: YAKAHANGA. 84% lexical similarity with Haya, 81% with Zinza, 75% with Kerewe, 78% with Nyankole, 72% with Chiga, 69% with Kerewe, 68% with Toro, 67% with Nyoro. People may be bilingual in Haya.

NYAMWEZI ***(KINYAMWEZI, KINYAMWESI, NYAMWESI, NAMWEZI)*** [NYZ] 926,000 (1993 Johnstone) or 4.2% of population (1971 Whiteley). 73% are in the traditional area. Northwest central, between Lake Victoria and Lake Rukwa. Niger-Congo, Atlantic-Congo, Volta-Congo, Benue-Congo, Bantoid, Southern, Narrow Bantu, Central, F, Sukuma-Nyamwezi (F.20). Dialects: NYANYEMBE, TAKAMA (GARAGANZA), MWERI (SUMBWA, KONONGO, KIYA). 84% lexical similarity with Sukuma, 61%

with Sumbwa, 56% with Nilamba. Agriculturalists: sorghum, millet, maize, rice, sweet potatoes, cassava, peanuts, beans, check peas, gourds, sunflowers. Traditional religion, Muslim, Christian. NT 1909-1951.

NYANJA ***(CINYANJA, CHEWA)*** [NYJ] A few in Tanzania. Niger-Congo, Atlantic-Congo, Volta-Congo, Benue-Congo, Bantoid, Southern, Narrow Bantu, Central, N, Nyanja (N.30). Dialects: CHICHEWA (CHEWA, CEWA), PETA (CIPETA, CHIPETA, MALAWI, MARAVI, MARAVE), CHINGONI (NGONI), MANGANJA (WAGANGA), NYASA, CHIKUNDA. Kuulwe (3,000 or fewer; Willis 1966:65-66) may be the same as Peta. Investigation needed: intelligibility with Kuulwe Peta. Bible 1905, in press (1997). See main entry under Malawi.

NYATURU ***(TURU, KINYATURU, RIMI, LIMI, KIRIMI, REMI, KIREMI, KEREMI, WANYATURU, WALIMI)*** [RIM] 556,000 (1993 Johnstone). North central, south of Singida, west of the Wembere River. Niger-Congo, Atlantic-Congo, Volta-Congo, Benue-Congo, Bantoid, Southern, Narrow Bantu, Central, F, Nyilamba-Langi (F.30). Dialects: GIRWANA (RIMI), CHAHI, GINYAMUNYINGANYI. 63% lexical similarity with Nilamba, 59% with Sukuma, 58% with Nyamwezi, 53% with Kimbu, 49% with Nyaturu, 44% with Sumbwa. Government name is 'Kinyaturu'. Traditional religion, Christian, Muslim. Bible portions 1956-1964.

NYIHA ***(ISHINYIHA, SHINYIHA, NYIKA, NYIXA)*** [NIH] 306,000 in Tanzania (1987). Population total both countries 626,000. South and west of Lake Rukwa. Also spoken in Zambia. Niger-Congo, Atlantic-Congo, Volta-Congo, Benue-Congo, Bantoid, Southern, Narrow Bantu, Central, M, Nyika-Safwa (M.20). Close to Lambya. Different from Nyika (Giryama) of Kenya. Traditionally weavers, iron workers, hunters; swidden agriculturalists: millet; animal husbandry: cattle, goats, fowl. NT 1913-1966.

PANGWA ***(EKIPANGWA)*** [PBR] 177,000 (1987). Northeast shore of Lake Malawi. Niger-Congo, Atlantic-Congo, Volta-Congo, Benue-Congo, Bantoid, Southern, Narrow Bantu, Central, G, Bena-Kinga (G.60). 71% lexical similarity with Bena, 62% with Kisi, 61% with Kinga, 59% with Hehe, 58% with Sangu, 55% with Wanji. Somewhat bilingual in Swahili.

PIMBWE ***(ICHIPIMBWE, CIPIMBWE)*** [PIW] 29,000 (1987). Rift Valley to the northwest of Lake Rukwa. Niger-Congo, Atlantic-Congo, Volta-Congo, Benue-Congo, Bantoid, Southern, Narrow Bantu, Central, F, Tongwe (F.10). A separate language. Somewhat bilingual in Swahili. Agriculturalists: millet, maize, sorghum, cassava, beans, peanuts; animal husbandry: goats, fowl. Traditional religion.

POGOLO ***(CHIPOGOLO, POGORO, POGORA, CHIPOGORO, POGOLU)*** [POY] 185,000 (1987). South central, south of the Mbunga, east of the Ndamba. Niger-Congo, Atlantic-Congo, Volta-Congo, Benue-Congo, Bantoid, Southern, Narrow Bantu, Central, G, Pogoro (G.50). 57% lexical similarity with Mbunga, 56% with Ndamba.

RANGI ***(KILANGI, IRANGI, LANGI)*** [LAG] 310,000 (1993 Johnstone), including some ethnic Burunge and Wasi (in Kolo and Mnenya) who are Rangi mother tongue speakers. West of the Maasai, northeast of the Sandawe. One community in Dodoma, and others in Mwanza and Dar es Salaam. Niger-Congo, Atlantic-Congo, Volta-Congo, Benue-Congo, Bantoid, Southern, Narrow Bantu, Central, F, Nyilamba-Langi (F.30). Close to Mbugwe. Limited comprehension of any other language. 74% lexical similarity with Mbugwe, 49% with Nyaturu and Sukuma, 48% with Nyamwezi, 47% with Kimbu and Nilamba, 40% with Sumbwa. Influenced by Cushitic languages. Speakers call their language 'Langi'; the Swahili pronunciation is 'Rangi'. Agriculturalists. Muslim, Christian.

ROMBO ***(USSERI)*** [ROF] Chaga area, eastern area. Niger-Congo, Atlantic-Congo, Volta-Congo, Benue-Congo, Bantoid, Southern, Narrow Bantu, Central, E, Chaga (E.30). Not intelligible with Hai, a western Chagga dialect (Potomé 1980).

RUFIJI ***(RUIHI, KIRUIHI, FIJI)*** [RUI] 200,000 (1987). Central coast, south of the Ndengereko, north of the Matumbi. Niger-Congo, Atlantic-Congo, Volta-Congo, Benue-Congo, Bantoid, Southern, Narrow Bantu, Central, P, Matumbi (P.10). Muslim.

RUGURU ***(LUGURU, LUGULU, IKIRUGURU, GURU)*** [RUF] 520,000 (1993 Johnstone). Morogodo, Bagamoyo, and Kilosa districts, Eastern Region, Luguru Mts., and Dar-es-Salaam. Niger-Congo, Atlantic-Congo, Volta-Congo, Benue-Congo, Bantoid, Southern, Narrow Bantu, Central, G, Zigula-Zaramo (G.30). People have little understanding of other languages. 54% lexical similarity with Kami, Kutu, Doe, Kwere (closest). Matrilineal. Rolling coastal plains, rough hills, mountain slope. Agriculturalists: hill rice, maize, sorghum, beans, peas, cassava, bananas, sweet potatoes, vegetables, coffee, fruit; animal husbandry: sheep, goats, chickens; fishermen, some wage earners. 1,000 to 3,000 feet. Traditional religion.

RUNDI [RUD] 150,000 refugees in Tanzania (1993 Johnstone). Burundi border, north of the Shubi. Niger-Congo, Atlantic-Congo, Volta-Congo, Benue-Congo, Bantoid, Southern, Narrow Bantu, Central, J, Rwanda-Rundi (J.60). Bible 1967. See main entry under Burundi.

RUNGI ***(IRUNGI)*** [RUR] 166,000 (1987). Southeast shore of Lake Tanganyika. Niger-Congo, Atlantic-Congo, Volta-Congo, Benue-Congo, Bantoid, Southern, Narrow Bantu, Central, Unclassified.

RUNGWA ***(ICHIRUNGWA, RUNGA, LUNGWA)*** [RNW] 18,000 (1987). South of the Konongo. Niger-Congo, Atlantic-Congo, Volta-Congo, Benue-Congo, Bantoid, Southern, Narrow Bantu, Central, F, Tongwe (F.10). People are somewhat bilingual in Swahili. Agriculturalists: millet, maize, cassava, simsim, peanuts; animal husbandry: goats, sheep, fowl. Traditional religion.

RWA ***(RWO, KIRWO, MERU)*** [RWK] 90,000 (1987). Northeastern border. Niger-Congo, Atlantic-Congo, Volta-Congo, Benue-Congo, Bantoid, Southern, Narrow Bantu, Central, E, Chaga (E.30). Distinct from Meru of Kenya. NT 1964.

RWANDA ***(RUNYARWANDA, RUANA)*** [RUA] 88,000 in Tanzania (1987). Northwest, bordering Rwanda. Niger-Congo, Atlantic-Congo, Volta-Congo, Benue-Congo, Bantoid, Southern, Narrow Bantu, Central, J, Rwanda-Rundi (J.60). Bible 1954-1993. See main entry under Rwanda.

SAFWA ***(ISHISAFWA, CISAFWA)*** [SBK] 158,000 (1987). Mbeya and Poroto mountain ranges in the Mbeya, Chunya, and Mbozi districts of Mbeya Region. Niger-Congo, Atlantic-Congo, Volta-Congo, Benue-Congo, Bantoid, Southern, Narrow Bantu, Central, M, Nyika-Safwa (M.20). Dialects: GURUKA, MBWILA, POROTO, SONGWE. A Swahili sentence repetition test was given to a stratified random population sample in 3 rural villages. 82% tested below routine proficiency. Grammar. Traditional religion, Christian.

SAGALA ***(KISAGALA, SOUTHERN KISAGALA, KISAGARA, SAGARA)*** [SBM] 79,000 (1987). South Kilosa District, Eastern Region, southwest Mpwapwa District, Central Region, northeast Iringa District, southern Highlands Region, north Ulanga District, Southern Region. Niger-Congo, Atlantic-Congo, Volta-Congo, Benue-Congo, Bantoid, Southern, Narrow Bantu, Central, G, Zigula-Zaramo (G.30). Dialects: ITUMBA, KONDOA (SOLWE), KWENY, NKWIFIYA (KWIFA, KWIVA). 63% lexical similarity with Kagulu, 60% with Gogo. Somewhat bilingual in Swahili. Different from KiSagala which is in Taita group of Kenya. Matrilineal. Mountain slope. Traditional religion, Muslim, Christian.

SANDAWE ***(SANDAUI, SANDAWI, SANDWE)*** [SBR] 70,000 (1987). Between the Bubu and Mponde rivers, Kondoa District. Khoisan, Sandawe. Monogamists. They have intermarried with the Gogo, Turu, and Maasai. People have limited understanding of other languages. SOV. Hunter-gatherers, fishermen, agriculturalists, pastoralists: cattle. Traditional religion, Christian, Muslim.

SANGU ***(SANGO, ESHISANGO, RORI)*** [SBP] 75,000 (1987). Southwestern, southeast of the Kimbu, north of the Safwa. Niger-Congo, Atlantic-Congo, Volta-Congo, Benue-Congo, Bantoid, Southern, Narrow Bantu, Central, G, Bena-Kinga (G.60). Somewhat bilingual in Swahili. Different from Sango of DRC, CAR, and Chad, or from Sanga of DRC, or from Sangu of Gabon.

SEGEJU ***(KISEGEJU, SAGEJU, SENGEJU)*** [SEG] 7,000 or fewer speakers out of an ethnic group of 15,000 (1999). Narrow strip of the northeast coast between Tanga and the Kenya border, Muheza District, Tanga region. Niger-Congo, Atlantic-Congo, Volta-Congo, Benue-Congo, Bantoid, Southern, Narrow Bantu, Central, E, Nyika (E.40), Mijikenda. Closely related to Digo. Self reported proficiency in Swahili is high. Many ethnic Segeju speak Swahili or Digo as mother tongue. Investigation needed: intelligibility with Digo, bilingual proficiency in Swahili. Muslim.

SHAMBALA ***(KISHAMBALA, KISHAMBAA, KISAMBAA, SAMBAA, SHAMBAA, SAMBALA, SAMBARA, SCHAMBALA)*** [KSB] 550,000 (1993 Johnstone). Northeastern, Usambara Mountains, Tanga Province. Niger-Congo, Atlantic-Congo, Volta-Congo, Benue-Congo, Bantoid, Southern, Narrow Bantu, Central, G, Shambala (G.20). 75% lexical similarity with Bondei, 68% with Ngulu and Zigula. Muslim, Christian, traditional religion. NT 1908.

SHUBI ***(SUBI, URUSHUBI, SINJA)*** [SUJ] 153,000 (1987). Northwest of Sumbwa, near Lake Victoria. Niger-Congo, Atlantic-Congo, Volta-Congo, Benue-Congo, Bantoid, Southern, Narrow Bantu, Central, J, Rwanda-Rundi (J.60). 85% lexical similarity with Hangaza, 77% with Rundi and Ha, 71% with Rwanda, 49% with Sumbwa. Traditional religion.

SIZAKI ***(SHASHI, SASI)*** [SZK] 82,000 (1987). Near Zanaki, northeast of Kerebe, near the southeast shore of Lake Victoria. Niger-Congo, Atlantic-Congo, Volta-Congo, Benue-Congo, Bantoid, Southern, Narrow Bantu, Central, E, Kuria (E.10). An important dialect or language related to Zanaki. Bilingualism in Swahili.

SUBA [SUH] 30,000 in Tanzania (1987). North central, south of Luo. Niger-Congo, Atlantic-Congo, Volta-Congo, Benue-Congo, Bantoid, Southern, Narrow Bantu, Central, E, Kuria (E.10). Speakers are somewhat bilingual in Swahili. Suba is a major part of the Kuria subgroup. Bible portions 1993. See main entry under Kenya.

SUKUMA ***(KISUKUMA)*** [SUA] 5,000,000 (1993 Johnstone) or 12.6% of population (1971 Whiteley). Northwest, between Lake Victoria and Lake Rukwa, Shinyanga to Serengeti Plain (Kiya); also Mwanza (Gwe). A small percentage in cities; 88% in the traditional area. Niger-Congo, Atlantic-Congo, Volta-Congo, Benue-Congo, Bantoid, Southern, Narrow Bantu, Central, F, Sukuma-Nyamwezi (F.20). Dialects: KIYA, GWE (KIGWE). Dialects contiguous with Nyamwezi are intelligible with it. 84% lexical similarity with Nyamwezi, 59% with Sumbwa and Nyaturu, 57% with Kimbu, 55% with Nilamba, 49% with Langi. Bilingualism in Swahili. A few young people in cities do not speak

Sukuma. In the country the young people borrow more Swahili in their Sukuma. Pastoralists: cattle; agriculturalists: sorghum, millet, maize, rice, sweet potatoes, cassava, peanuts, beans, chick peas, gourds, sunflowers, cotton, tobacco; fishermen. Traditional religion, Christian, Muslim. Bible 1960.

SUMBWA ***(KISUMBWA)*** [SUW] 191,000 (1987). Bukombe District of Shinyanga Region. Niger-Congo, Atlantic-Congo, Volta-Congo, Benue-Congo, Bantoid, Southern, Narrow Bantu, Central, F, Sukuma-Nyamwezi (F.20). 61% lexical similarity with Nyamwezi, 59% with Sukuma, 45% with Nilamba. Many speakers have below routine ability in Swahili. Investigation needed: bilingual proficiency in Swahili. Agriculturalists: sorghum, millet, maize, rice, sweet potatoes, cassava, peanuts, beans, chick peas, gourds, sunflowers, bananas. Christian, traditional religion, Muslim.

SWAHILI ***(KISWAHILI, KISUAHELI)*** [SWA] 313,200 monolinguals or 1.8%, 93.4% bilinguals in Tanzania (1982 Polomé). Population total all countries 5,000,000 first language speakers (1989 Holm); 30,000,000 second language users (1989 Holm). Zanzibar, coastal areas. Also spoken in Burundi, Kenya, Mayotte, Mozambique, Oman, Rwanda, Somalia, South Africa, Uganda, UAE, USA. Niger-Congo, Atlantic-Congo, Volta-Congo, Benue-Congo, Bantoid, Southern, Narrow Bantu, Central, G, Swahili (G.40). Dialects: MRIMA, UNGUJA (KIUNGUJA, ZANZIBAR), PEMBA, MGAO. Rural people are second language users; they use the local language for most activities, but Swahili with outsiders. National language. Dictionary. SVO. Used through secondary education and in some university courses. Muslim. Bible 1891-1996.

TANZANIAN SIGN LANGUAGE [TZA] Deaf sign language. Deaf people go to different schools, each using a different sign language. There have been elementary schools for deaf children since 1963. There is a committee on national sign language. Little research.

TAVETA ***(KITUBETA, TUBETA, KITAVETA)*** [TVS] Northeastern, around Taveta in adjacent areas of Tanzania and Kenya. Niger-Congo, Atlantic-Congo, Volta-Congo, Benue-Congo, Bantoid, Southern, Narrow Bantu, Central, G, Shambala (G.20). Highly bilingual in Swahili in Kenya; bilingualism is limited in Tanzania. NT 1906, out of print. See main entry under Kenya.

TEMI ***(SONJO, SONYO, WASONJO, WATEMI)*** [SOZ] 20,000 (1995 SIL). North central near the Kenya border, Maasai area, 2 to 4 hours by car from the Wasso-Loliondo area, on unimproved roads. 7 villages: Sale, Mdito, Samunge, Digodigo, Kisangiro, Mugholo, Oldonyo Sambu (Kura). Niger-Congo, Atlantic-Congo, Volta-Congo, Benue-Congo, Bantoid, Southern, Narrow Bantu, Central, E, Kuria (E.10). The language is reported to show some similarities to Sukuma. Reported to be bilingual in Swahili. The name 'Wasonjo' is a misnomer, referring to beans of the Batemi plant. They call their language 'KiTemi', and themselves the 'Batemi'. Traditional religion, Christian.

TONGWE ***(KITONGWE)*** [TNY] 22,000 (1987). East shore of Lake Tanganyika, south of the Vinza and Kogoma town, sharing some villages with the WaBembe. Niger-Congo, Atlantic-Congo, Volta-Congo, Benue-Congo, Bantoid, Southern, Narrow Bantu, Central, F, Tongwe (F.10). Somewhat bilingual in Swahili. Traditional religion, Muslim.

TUMBUKA ***(TUMBOKA, CHITUMBUKA, TAMBOKA, TAMBUKA, TIMBUKA, TOMBUCAS)*** [TUW] 1,000,000 in Tanzania. Niger-Congo, Atlantic-Congo, Volta-Congo, Benue-Congo, Bantoid, Southern, Narrow Bantu, Central, N, Tumbuka (N.20). Dialects: CHITUMBUKA, CHIKAMANGA (HENGA), CHIPOKA, YOMBE, SENGA, FUNGWE, WENYA, HEWE (HEWA), NENYA, NTHALI. The Senga dialect is distinct from Nsenga (Senga) of Zambia and Zimbabwe. Kandawire and Fulirwa are clans, not dialects. Bible 1957-1980. See main entry under Malawi.

VIDUNDA ***(CHIVIDUNDA, KIVIDUNDA, NDUNDA)*** [VID] 32,000 (1987). East central, east of the Hehe, west of the Kutu. Niger-Congo, Atlantic-Congo, Volta-Congo, Benue-Congo, Bantoid, Southern, Narrow Bantu, Central, G, Zigula-Zaramo (G.30). People are somewhat bilingual in Swahili. Matrilineal. Valleys, foothills, mountain slope. Animal husbandry: goats, sheep, fowl, few cattle; hunters; fishermen; agriculturalists: dry rice, maize, millet, beans, bananas, peas sugarcane, cassava, sweet potatoes, pumpkins, tobacco, cotton, vegetables, fruit. 1,000 to 6,000 feet. Traditional religion, Muslim, Christian.

VINZA [VIN] 10,000 (1987). West of the Nyamwezi, north of the Tongwe. Niger-Congo, Atlantic-Congo, Volta-Congo, Benue-Congo, Bantoid, Southern, Narrow Bantu, Central, J, Rwanda-Rundi (J.60). Somewhat bilingual in Swahili.

VUNJO ***(KIVUNJO, WUNJO, KIWUNJO, MARANGU)*** [VUN] 300,000 (1992 UBS). Chagga area, central variety. Niger-Congo, Atlantic-Congo, Volta-Congo, Benue-Congo, Bantoid, Southern, Narrow Bantu, Central, E, Chaga (E.30). Separate from Chagga, Machambe, Rombo, Mochi, but related. NT, in press (1998).

WANDA ***(ICHIWANDA, WANDIA)*** [WBH] 24,000 (1987). Mbozi District, Mbeya Region; Sumbawanga District, Rukwa Region. Niger-Congo, Atlantic-Congo, Volta-Congo, Benue-Congo, Bantoid, Southern, Narrow Bantu, Central, M, Nyika-Safwa (M.20). 68% lexical similarity with Mwanga. A significant percentage of speakers appear to have less than routine proficiency in Swahili. Investigation needed: bilingual proficiency in Swahili, intelligibility with Mwanga. Agriculturalists: millet, sorghum, simsim, peanuts, maize. Christian, traditional religion.

WANJI ***(KIVWANJI)*** [WBI] 60,000 (1987). South, west of the Bena, south of the Sangu, north of the Kinga. Niger-Congo, Atlantic-Congo, Volta-Congo, Benue-Congo, Bantoid, Southern, Narrow Bantu, Central, G, Bena-Kinga (G.60). Bible portions 1979-1985.

WARE [WRE] Niger-Congo, Atlantic-Congo, Volta-Congo, Benue-Congo, Bantoid, Southern, Narrow Bantu, Central, E, Kuria (E.10).

WASI ***(ALAGWASE, ALAGWA, ALAWA, CHASI, UWASSI, ASI)*** [WBJ] 10,000 (1989 Martin Mous). Kondoa District, Central Province, in the Rangi chiefdom, Kolo, Ee-Dinu, and Tlawi villages. Afro-Asiatic, Cushitic, South. Related to Iraqw, but not inherently intelligible. Also close to Burunge and Gorowa. Nearly all are bilingual in Rangi for trade and some in Swahili for administration. Children tend to speak Rangi among themselves. All members of the ethnic group have a fairly good command of the language. Their name for themselves is 'Alagwa'. Muslim.

YAO ***(CHIYAO, ACHAWA, ADSAWA, AJAWA, AYAWA, AYO, DJAO, HAJAO, HIAO, HYAO, JAO, VEIAO, WAJAO)*** [YAO] 400,000 in Tanzania (1993 Johnstone). South central, east of Lake Malawi, Mozambique border area. Also possibly in Zimbabwe. Niger-Congo, Atlantic-Congo, Volta-Congo, Benue-Congo, Bantoid, Southern, Narrow Bantu, Central, P, Yao (P.20). Yao in Tanzania use a Swahili based orthography different from Malawi and Mozambique. Muslim, Christian, traditional religion. Bible 1920. See main entry under Malawi.

ZALAMO ***(ZARAMO, KIZARAMO, DZALAMO, ZARAMU, SARAMO, MYAGATWA)*** [ZAJ] A few speakers (1991 Brenzinger, Heine, and Sommer). Ethnic group had 173,518 (1959 Bryan). East central coast, Kisarawe District, between Bagamoyo and Dar es Salaam. Niger-Congo, Atlantic-Congo, Volta-Congo, Benue-Congo, Bantoid, Southern, Narrow Bantu, Central, G, Zigula-Zaramo (G.30). 68% lexical similarity with Kutu, 65% with Kami, 61% with Kwere and Doe. Bilingualism in Swahili. All are elderly. Matrilineal. Forest, scrub. Coastal plain, low hills. Agriculturalists: rice, millet, sorghum, maize, cassava, peas, beans, yams, fruit, peanuts, cashews, sesame seed, tobacco, cotton, coconuts; animal husbandry: goats, sheep, fowl; fishermen. 500 to 3,000 feet. Muslim, traditional religion, Christian. NT 1975.

ZANAKI ***(IKIZANAKI)*** [ZAK] 62,000 (1987). Slightly inland, southeast shore, Lake Victoria above Speke Gulf. Niger-Congo, Atlantic-Congo, Volta-Congo, Benue-Congo, Bantoid, Southern, Narrow Bantu, Central, E, Kuria (E.10). Dialects: NDALI, SIORA, GIRANGO. 81% lexical similarity with Ikoma, 80% with Ngurimi, 78% with Kuria, 50% with Gusii. Limited bilingualism in Swahili and some other languages. Bible portions 1948.

ZIGULA ***(ZIGUA, ZIGWA, KIZIGULA, ZEGUHA, ZIGOUA, ZEGURA, SEGUHA, WAZEGUA, WAYOMBO)*** [ZIW] 355,000 (1993 Johnstone). Northeastern, Maasai Steppe, Tanga and Coast Provinces. Niger-Congo, Atlantic-Congo, Volta-Congo, Benue-Congo, Bantoid, Southern, Narrow Bantu, Central, G, Zigula-Zaramo (G.30). 83% lexical similarity with Ngulu, 75% with Bondei, 68% with Shambala, 70% with Doe, 62% with Kwere. The people are somewhat bilingual in a non-standard, 'street' Swahili. It has been influenced linguistically by Doe and Kwere, and has influenced them. May be the same as Mushungulu in Somalia. Coastal plain, rolling hills. Agriculturalists: sorghum, maize, beans, yams, manioc, pumpkins, cucumbers, sesame, peanuts, tobacco, hemp, castor, coconuts; animal husbandry: cattle, goats, sheep, donkeys, fowl; hunters; fishermen; wage laborers; traders. 500 to 1,000 feet. Muslim, Christian. Bible portions 1906.

ZINZA ***(ECHIJINJA, ECHIDZINDZA, ECIZINZA, DZINDA, JINJA, ZINJA)*** [JIN] 138,000 (1987). Southwest shore of Lake Victoria and neighboring islands. Niger-Congo, Atlantic-Congo, Volta-Congo, Benue-Congo, Bantoid, Southern, Narrow Bantu, Central, J, Haya-Jita (J.20). 81% lexical similarity with Nyambo and Nyankole, 78% with Haya, 76% with Kerewe, 75% with Chiga, 67% with Nyoro and Toro. Limited bilingualism in Swahili. Agriculturalists: millet, beans, plantains; fishermen; animal husbandry: cattle, sheep, goats. Traditional religion, Christian, Muslim. Bible portions 1930-1958.

ZYOBA ***(ZOBA)*** [ZYO] Most in Tanzania, near Lake Tanganyika. Also spoken in DRC. Niger-Congo, Atlantic-Congo, Volta-Congo, Benue-Congo, Bantoid, Southern, Narrow Bantu, Central, D, Lega-Kalanga (D.20). Dialects: VIRA, MASANZE.

TOGO

Republic of Togo. République Togolaise. National or official languages: Éwé, Kabiye, French. 4,397,000 (1998 UN). Literacy rate 39% all, 40% males. Also includes Dagbani, Ica, Mampruli, Yoruba, people from Lebanon 3,500. Information mainly from B. Heine 1968; J. Stewart 1971; G. Manessy 1975, 1981; J. Bendor-Samuel 1989. Traditional religion, Christian, Muslim. Blind population 12,052 (1981 census). Deaf institutions: 1. Data accuracy estimate: A2, B. The number of languages listed for Togo is 42. Of those, all are living languages. Diversity index 0.89.

ADANGBE ***(DANGBE, ADANTONWI, AGOTIME, ADAN)*** [ADQ] Border area with Togo directly east of Ho. Agotime are mainly in Ghana. Volta region. Ghana towns are Kpoeta and Apegame, and others. Niger-Congo, Atlantic-Congo, Volta-Congo, Kwa, Left Bank, Kposo-Ahlo-Bowili. Close to Igo. Different from Adangme. The Adan and Agotime are separate ethnic groups who speak Adangbe. See main entry under Ghana.

ADELE ***(BIDIRE, BEDERE, GIDIRE, GADRE)*** [ADE] 12,000 in Togo (1995 SIL). Population total both countries 21,000 (1995 SIL). West central. There is difficult access to the area. The main centers are Koué Mpotì, Yégué. Upper Adele is in Togo, Lower Adele in Ghana. Also spoken in Ghana. Niger-Congo, Atlantic-Congo, Volta-Congo, Kwa, Nyo, Potou-Tano, Basila-Adele. Dialects: UPPER ADELE, LOWER ADELE. Ghana and Togo dialects are different. Ethnic group: Lolo. Different from Adere of Cameroon. Literacy rate in first language: Below 1%. Traditional religion, Christian. NT 1996.

AJA-GBE ***(AJA, ADJA)*** [AJG] 114,800 in Togo (1991 Vanderaa CRC). Southeast Togo, north of Tabligbo. The main centers are Tado, Tohoun, Asrama, Togo-Benin border. Niger-Congo, Atlantic-Congo, Volta-Congo, Kwa, Left Bank, Gbe, Aja. Dialects: TÀGÓBÉ, HWÈGBÈ (HWE, EHOUÉ, HWEDA). Three dialects: Tàgóbé is only in Togo, Dògóbè is in Benin, Hwègbè is in both countries. Bilingualism in Éwé, French. Their ancestral place of origin is Tado. Literacy rate in first language: 1% to 5%. Traditional religion. See main entry under Benin.

AKASELEM ***(TCHAMBA, AKASELE, KASELE, KAMBA, CHAMBA, CEMBA)*** [AKS] 34,300 (1991 L. Vanderaa CRC). Tchamba is the main center. Central, near Kotokoli. Niger-Congo, Atlantic-Congo, Volta-Congo, North, Gur, Central, Northern, Oti-Volta, Gurma, Ntcham. The men are more bilingual in Tem than the women. Some also use French. Ethnic identity is strong. People desire the language to be written. Literacy rate in first language: Below 1%. Muslim, syncretism.

AKEBOU ***(AKEBU, KEBU, KABU, KEGBERIKE, EKBEBE)*** [KEU] 40,700 (1991 L. Vanderaa CRC). South, Canton Akebou of Préfecture de Wawa and into Ghana. Main centers Kougnohou, Veh-Nkougna, Kamina. Niger-Congo, Atlantic-Congo, Volta-Congo, Kwa, Left Bank, Kebu-Animere. Somewhat bilingual in Éwé. Some also know French. Speakers have a keen interest in their language. Investigation needed: bilingual proficiency. Literacy rate in first language: Below 1%. Traditional religion, Christian.

AKPOSO ***(KPOSO, IKPOSO, AKPOSSO)*** [KPO] 94,900 in Togo (1991). Population total both countries 100,300 (1991 L. Vanderaa CRC). West of Atakpamé in southern Togo. The main centers are Amlamé, Amou-Oblo, Atakpami. Also spoken in Ghana. Niger-Congo, Atlantic-Congo, Volta-Congo, Kwa, Left Bank, Kposo-Ahlo-Bowili. Dialects: AMOU OBLOU, IKPONU, IWI (UWI), LITIME (BADOU), LOGBO, UMA. Two dialects. Somewhat bilingual in Éwé or French. Speakers have a keen interest in their language. Literacy rate in first language: 1% to 5%. Traditional religion, Christian.

ANII ***(AKPE, GISIDA, BASILA, BASSILA, BASECA, WINJI-WINJI, OUNJI-OUNJI)*** [BLO] 4,100 in Togo (1991 Vanderaa CRC). Around Bassila. Niger-Congo, Atlantic-Congo, Volta-Congo, Kwa, Nyo, Potou-Tano, Basila-Adele. Dialects: GIKOLODJYA, GILEMPLA, GISEDA, GISÈME, ANANJUBI (ANANDJOOBI). Closely related to Akpe. Muslim. See main entry under Benin.

ANUFO ***(CHOKOSI, CHAKOSI, TCHOKOSSI, TIOKOSSI, CHOKOSSI)*** [CKO] 41,800 in Togo (1991 Vanderaa). Northwest around Mango (Nzara). Niger-Congo, Atlantic-Congo, Volta-Congo, Kwa, Nyo, Potou-Tano, Tano, Central, Bia, Northern. Bilingualism in Hausa, French. About 18,000 Ngangam speak it as a second language. 'Tchokossi' is the official name in Togo. 'Anufo' is their name for their language and people. Trade language. Literacy rate in first language: 1% to 5%. Some can read some French or Arabic. Motivation for literacy is high. Radio programs. Traditional religion, Muslim, Christian. Bible portions 1993. See main entry under Ghana.

ANYANGA ***(AGNAGAN)*** [AYG] 7,200 (1991 L. Vanderaa CRC). Central, west and south of Blitta. Niger-Congo, Atlantic-Congo, Volta-Congo, Kwa, Nyo, Potou-Tano, Tano, Guang, North Guang. 75% lexical similarity with Gichode. Somewhat bilingual in Éwé. Investigation needed: intelligibility, bilingual proficiency. Literacy rate in first language: Below 1%. Traditional religion.

BAGO ***(KOUSSOUNTOU)*** [BQG] 6,100 (1991 L. Vanderaa CRC). The main centers are Bagou, Koussountou. Niger-Congo, Atlantic-Congo, Volta-Congo, North, Gur, Central, Southern, Grusi, Eastern. Bilingualism in French. Literacy rate in first language: Below 1%. Muslim, some traditional religion.

BISSA ***(BISA)*** [BIB] 3,000 in Togo (1991 SIL). Border with Burkina Faso. Niger-Congo, Mande, Eastern, Eastern, Bissa. There are no dialect differences in Togo. Many speak Mòoré with Mossi who do not speak Bissa; on common topics. They also use French. Speakers are called 'Busansi'. Literacy rate in first language: Below 1%. Traditional religion. Bible portions 1996. See main entry under Burkina Faso.

DANGME ***(ADANGME)*** [DGM] Niger-Congo, Atlantic-Congo, Volta-Congo, Kwa, Nyo, Ga-Dangme. Dialects: ADA, NINGO, OSU, SHAI, GBUGBLA, KROBO. Traditional religion. Bible, in press (1997). See main entry under Ghana.

DELO ***(NTRUBO, NTRIBU, NTRIBOU)*** [NTR] 5,400 in Togo (1998). West central border with Ghana. Niger-Congo, Atlantic-Congo, Volta-Congo, North, Gur, Central, Southern, Grusi, Eastern. Bilingualism in French. Literacy rate in first language: Below 1%. Traditional religion. See main entry under Ghana.

ÉWÉ ***(EIBE, EHWE, EVE, VHE, KREPE, KREPI, POPO)*** [EWE] 861,900 in Togo (1991 Vanderaa CRC), 20% of the population. South of Atakpamé, coastal areas. Main centers in Kpalimé, Notsé, Tsévié. Closely related languages or dialects in Benin. Niger-Congo, Atlantic-Congo, Volta-Congo, Kwa, Left Bank, Gbe. Dialects: ANGLO, AWUNA, HUDU, KOTAFON. Bilingualism in French. Predominant language in southern Togo. National language. Literacy rate in first language: 10% to 60%. Christian, traditional religion. Bible 1913-1931. See main entry under Ghana.

FON-GBE ***(FO, FON, FONNU, FOGBE, DAHOMEEN, DJEDJI)*** [FOA] 35,500 in Togo (1991). They are widely scattered and form small minorities in most southern districts. Niger-Congo, Atlantic-Congo, Volta-Congo, Kwa, Left Bank, Gbe, Fon. Bilingualism in Éwé, French. Literacy rate in first language: 5% to 60%. Traditional religion, Christian. NT 1993. See main entry under Benin.

FRENCH [FRN] 3,000 in Togo (1993). Indo-European, Italic, Romance, Italo-Western, Western, Gallo-Iberian, Gallo-Romance, Gallo-Rhaetian, Oïl, French. Official language. Bible 1530-1986. See main entry under France.

FRENCH SIGN LANGUAGE ***(LANGUE DES SIGNES FRANÇAISE, LSF)*** [FSL] Deaf sign language. Taught in 1 school for the deaf in Togo. See main entry under France.

FULFULDE, BENIN-TOGO ***(PEULH, PEUL)*** [FUE] 48,200 in Togo (1993 Johnstone). North. Niger-Congo, Atlantic-Congo, Atlantic, Northern, Senegambian, Fula-Wolof, Fulani, West Central. Dialect: ATAKORA FULFULDE. Muslim. See main entry under Benin.

GA ***(AMINA, GAIN, ACCRA, ACRA)*** [GAC] Zio, Yoto, and Amou prefectures. Niger-Congo, Atlantic-Congo, Volta-Congo, Kwa, Nyo, Ga-Dangme. Bilingualism in French. Literacy rate in first language: Below 1%. Bible 1866, in press (1997). See main entry under Ghana.

GEN-GBE ***(GE, MINA-GEN, MINA, POPO, GUIN, GEBE)*** [GEJ] 200,900 in Togo (1991). Population total both countries 327,000. Southeast. Also spoken in Benin. Niger-Congo, Atlantic-Congo, Volta-Congo, Kwa, Left Bank, Gbe, Mina. Bilingualism in Éwé. The people are called 'Mina' by neighboring groups. Trade language. Literacy rate in first language: 1% to 5%. NT 1962.

GOURMANCHÉMA ***(GOURMANTCHE, GOURMA, GURMA, MIGULIMANCEMA, GULIMANCEMA)*** [GUX] 120,500 in Togo (1991 Vanderaa). Northern, main centers in Bidjanga, Dapaon, Korbongou. Niger-Congo, Atlantic-Congo, Volta-Congo, North, Gur, Central, Northern, Oti-Volta, Gurma. Numerous dialects, mainly east of Dapaong. Literacy rate in first language: 1% to 30%. Traditional religion. NT 1958-1990. See main entry under Burkina Faso.

HAUSA ***(HAUSSA, HAOUSSA)*** [HUA] 9,600 in Togo (1991 L. Vanderaa CRC). Afro-Asiatic, Chadic, West, A, A.1. Bilingualism in French. Widely spoken in Togo as second language. Trade language. Literacy rate in first language: 1% to 30%. Muslim. Bible 1932-1996. See main entry under Nigeria.

HWLA [HWL] 31,719 (1983 Togo Linguistic Atlas). Unknown region. Unclassified. Bilingualism in Éwé, French. May be the same as Hwe in Togo or Xwla-Gbe in Benin. Literacy rate in first language: Below 1%. Traditional religion.

IFÈ ***(ANA-IFÉ, ANA, BAATE)*** [IFE] 74,000 in Togo (1991 L. Vanderaa CRC). Southeast central, Ogou Province. The main centers are Atakpamé, Kamina, and Dadja. Also in the town of Ese-Ana in southern Togo. Niger-Congo, Atlantic-Congo, Volta-Congo, Benue-Congo, Defoid, Yoruboid, Edekiri. Dialects: TSCHETTI, DJAMA, DADJA. Some bilingualism in Éwé in the south and Yoruba in the north. Some also know French. 'Ana' is the government name. Literacy rate in first language: 1% to 5%. Literacy rate in second language: 15%. Traditional religion, Christian, Muslim. Bible portions 1995. See main entry under Benin.

IGO ***(AHLON, ACHLO, ANLO, AGO, AHLÕ, AHONLAN, AHLON-BOGO)*** [AHL] 6,300 (1991 L. Vanderaa CRC). South, border between Ghana and Togo around Dénou, Sassanou, Canton Bogo-Ahlon of Préfecture de Kloto. Niger-Congo, Atlantic-Congo, Volta-Congo, Kwa, Left Bank, Kposo-Ahlo-Bowili. Anlo may be a separate language. Speakers use French, and may use Éwé as second language. 'Ahlon' is the official name. They call themselves 'Igo'. Literacy rate in first language: 1% to 5%. Traditional religion.

KABIYÉ ***(KABRE, CABRAI, KABURE, KABYE, CABRAIS)*** [KBP] 700,000 in Togo (1998 SIL), 14% of population (1976 WA). Population total all countries 730,000 (1998). Kara region. Main centers in prefectures of Kozah and Binah. Many have settled in prefectures of Sotouboua, Kloto, Ogou, and Haho. Also spoken in Benin, Ghana. Niger-Congo, Atlantic-Congo, Volta-Congo, North, Gur, Central, Southern, Grusi, Eastern. Dialect: LAMA. Bilingualism in French. Second largest group in Togo. The Lama dialect is different from the Lama (Lamba) language of Togo. National language. Literacy rate in first language: 1% to 30%. Traditional religion, Christian, Muslim. NT 1996.

KAMBOLÉ ***(SOUTHWEST EDE)*** [XKB] 20,000 (1991 SIL). East central in the town of Kambolé and a few surrounding villages. Niger-Congo, Atlantic-Congo, Volta-Congo, Benue-Congo, Defoid, Yoruboid,

Edekiri. Closely related to Ifè. Bilingualism in French, Yoruba. Investigation needed: intelligibility with Ifè. Literacy rate in first language: Below 1%. Mainly Muslim, some Christian.

KONKOMBA [KOS] 50,100 in Togo (1991 L. Vanderaa CRC). Central. Main centers in Guérin-Kouka, Nawaré, Kidjaloum. Niger-Congo, Atlantic-Congo, Volta-Congo, North, Gur, Central, Northern, Oti-Volta, Gurma. Bilingualism in French, Yoruba. Literacy rate in first language: 1% to 5%. Traditional religion. Bible 1998. See main entry under Ghana.

KPESSI ***(KPESI, KPÉTSI)*** [KEF] 3,100 (1991 L. Vanderaa CRC). South. Main centers around Kpétsi, Langanbou. Niger-Congo, Atlantic-Congo, Volta-Congo, Kwa, Left Bank, Gbe. Bilingualism in French. Investigation needed: intelligibility with Éwé. Literacy rate in first language: Below 1%. Traditional religion.

LAMA ***(LAMBA, LOSSO)*** [LAS] 117,400 in Togo (1991 Vanderaa). Population total all countries 177,400 or more. Region of Kande, Lama. Also spoken in Benin, Ghana. Niger-Congo, Atlantic-Congo, Volta-Congo, North, Gur, Central, Southern, Grusi, Eastern. Dialects: KANTE, KADJALLA, DEFALE. It is related to Tem and Kabiyé. Leon and Yaka, and 2 to 4 other villages south of Kande, between Lama and Kabiyé, and west of Niamtougou (Nawdm) may need separate literature. Bilingualism in French, Kabiyé. 'Lama' is their name for the language and people. 'Lamba' is the French name. 'Losso' refers to people on the Losso Plain, including the Nawdeba (Nawdm). Investigation needed: intelligibility with Leon-Yaka villages. Literacy rate in first language: 1% to 5%. Literacy rate in second language: 20%. Roman. Traditional religion, Muslim, Christian. NT 1993.

LUKPA ***(LOKPA, LOGBA, LEGBA, LUGBA, DOMPAGO)*** [DOP] Niger-Congo, Atlantic-Congo, Volta-Congo, North, Gur, Central, Southern, Grusi, Eastern. Bilingualism in French. Different from Logba of Ghana. Literacy rate in first language: 1% to 5%. Traditional religion, Christian, Muslim. NT 1977. See main entry under Benin.

MAXI-GBE ***(MAHI)*** [MXL] 25,300 in Togo (1991). Niger-Congo, Atlantic-Congo, Volta-Congo, Kwa, Left Bank, Gbe, Fon. Bilingualism in Éwé, French. 'Mahi' is the name of the people. Similar to Fon-gbe of Benin and Togo. Literacy rate in first language: Below 1%. Traditional religion. See main entry under Benin.

MOBA ***(MOAB, MOARE, MOA, BEN)*** [MFQ] 189,400 in Togo (1991). Population total both countries 191,200 (1991 L. Vanderaa CRC). Northwest. The main centers are Dapaong and Bombouaka. Also spoken in Burkina Faso. Niger-Congo, Atlantic-Congo, Volta-Congo, North, Gur, Central, Northern, Oti-Volta, Gurma, Moba. Dialect: NATCHABA. Related to Bimoba in Ghana, but with only limited intelligibility. Diverse dialect situation, varying almost from family to family. Possible dialect continuum. Women almost exclusively monolingual. Men and women with more education can speak limited French. French is used to talk to those from another language group, or for a few, when discussing abstract concepts. Highly educated Moba use Moba among themselves. Literacy rate in first language: 1% to 30%. More interest in learning to read French than Moba. Traditional religion, Christian. Bible portions 1941-1984.

MÒORÉ ***(MOOSE, MOSSI, MORE, MOLE, MOSHI)*** [MHM] 19,700 in Togo (1991), including 7,155 in Moore, 7,908 in Yanga dialect (1981 census). Several villages in northwestern corner of Togo bordering Burkina Faso, Senkanssé, Timbou, Tabi. Niger-Congo, Atlantic-Congo, Volta-Congo, North, Gur, Central, Northern, Oti-Volta, Western, Northwest. Dialect: YANGA (YANA, YAN, YAM, YAAN, JAAN, TIMBOU). Yanga dialect is in Togo, completely intelligible with Central Moore. Many monolinguals. Some use French as second language. Literacy rate in second language: Many in the younger generation can read French. Bible 1983, in press (1998). See main entry under Burkina Faso.

NAWDM ***(NAUDM, NAWDAM, NAOUDEM, LOSSO, LOSU)*** [NMZ] 145,600 in Togo (1991 L. Vanderaa CRC). Population total both countries 145,600 or more. Around Niamtougou, Préfecture of Doufelgou. Many have settled in the préfectures of Sotouboua, Ogou, and Haho. There is an important minority in Lomé. Also spoken in Ghana. Niger-Congo, Atlantic-Congo, Volta-Congo, North, Gur, Central, Northern, Oti-Volta, Yom-Nawdm. Linguistically close to Yom. Bilingualism in French. 'Losso' is the name they use for themselves when talking to outsiders. Literacy rate in first language: Below 1%. Traditional religion, Christian. Bible portions 1992.

NGANGAM ***(DYE, GANGAM, GANGUM, NGANGAN, NBANGAM, MIGANGAM, MIJIEM)*** [GNG] 33,500 in Togo (1991 L. Vanderaa CRC). Population total both countries 33,500 or more. Northern Togo around Gando-Namoni, Mogou, Koumongou, and Kountouri. Also spoken in Benin. Niger-Congo, Atlantic-Congo, Volta-Congo, North, Gur, Central, Northern, Oti-Volta, Gurma. Dialects: MOTIEM (MOGOU), KOUMONGOU. Closely related to Konkomba, Ntcham, Moba, and Gurma, but they are not inherently intelligible. The dialect around Gando is the largest. Subdialects of Motiem are Mituom (Tiemanga) and Tontondi. Subdialects near the Benin border are Midokm and Mifelm. Two subdialects have low intelligibility with each other. Some people speak Anufo well enough to discuss abstract concepts. A small percentage of speakers, mainly men, have been educated in French.

'Migangam' is the correct language name, with 'Ngangam' as another pronunciation. There are Anufo villages in the area, and tensions between the two groups exist. Gando is considered to be the center of economic and religious life. Due to expansion of a game reserve, they have lost large tracts of land, and some have moved to other areas. In 1991 some of this land was given back to the Gangam people. Literacy rate in first language: Below 1%. Traditional religion.

NTCHAM ***(BASSAR, BASARE, BASSARI, BASARI, BASAR, NCHAM, NATCHAMBA, TOBOTE)*** [BUD] 100,000 in Togo (1993 SIL). Population total both countries 150,000. West central, Bassar, Kabou, Kalanga, and adjacent areas. Also spoken in Ghana. Niger-Congo, Atlantic-Congo, Volta-Congo, North, Gur, Central, Northern, Oti-Volta, Gurma, Ntcham. Dialects: NCANM, NTAAPUM, CEEMBA, LINANGMANLI. Dialects listed are in Togo. Bilingualism in French, Konkomba. Literacy rate in first language: 1% to 5%. Traditional religion, Christian, Muslim. NT 1986-1990.

SOLA ***(SORUBA, SOROUBA, BIJOBE, BIYOBE, UYOBE, MIYOBE, KYOBE, KUYOBE, SOLAMBA, SOLLA)*** [SOY] 1,700 in Togo (1991). Northeast of Kpagouda in Togo, bordering Benin. Main centers in Kouyoria, Sola. There are isolated groups in Kounacire (Massédéna) and Sola (Koutougou). Niger-Congo, Atlantic-Congo, Volta-Congo, North, Gur, Central, Northern, Oti-Volta, Gurma. A single dialect situation. Moba has 27% lexical similarity, Tamberma 25%, Ngangam 47%. Most people speak Kabiyé with the ability to discuss common topics. Some speakers in isolated groups can speak Lama as well as Sola. Some also speak French. 'Sola' is the official name, 'Bijobe' the ethnic name, 'Solla' the popular name. Literacy rate in first language: Below 1%. See main entry under Benin.

TAMBERMA ***(TAMARI, SOMA, SOME, "SOMBA")*** [SOF] 19,800 (1991 L. Vanderaa CRC). East of Kanté. The main centers are Nadoba, Wantema, Warengo, Koutougou. Niger-Congo, Atlantic-Congo, Volta-Congo, North, Gur, Central, Northern, Oti-Volta, Eastern. Dialect: NIENDE. 65% intelligibility with Ditammari of Benin. A little bilingualism in French. "Somba" is a derogatory name. 'Tamberma', 'Bataba', 'Batammaraba' are names for the people. Literacy rate in first language: Below 1%. Literacy rate in second language: none. Traditional religion, Muslim.

TEM ***(KOTOKOLI, COTOCOLI, TIM, TIMU, TEMBA)*** [KDH] 204,100 in Togo (1991). Population total all countries 300,000 (1987 SIL). Most are around Bafilo and Sokode. The main centers are in Tchaoudjo, Nyala, Sotouboua. Also spoken in Benin, Ghana. Niger-Congo, Atlantic-Congo, Volta-Congo, North, Gur, Central, Southern, Grusi, Eastern. Bilingualism in French, Kabiyé. Literacy rate in first language: 1% to 5%. Muslim, traditional religion, Christian.

WACI-GBE ***(WATYI, WACI, WACHI, OUATCHI)*** [WCI] 365,500 in Togo (1991). Population total both countries 475,000. The main centers are in Vogan, Tabligbo, Attitigon. Also spoken in Benin. Niger-Congo, Atlantic-Congo, Volta-Congo, Kwa, Left Bank, Gbe. Bilingualism in Éwé, French. Investigation needed: intelligibility with Iwi (Akposo), Éwé. Literacy rate in first language: Below 1%. Traditional religion, Christian.

WUDU [WUD] The main centers are Gbékon and Glitho. Niger-Congo, Atlantic-Congo, Volta-Congo, Kwa, Left Bank, Gbe. Bilingualism in Éwé, French. Investigation needed: intelligibility with Éwé. Traditional religion.

TUNISIA

Republic of Tunisia. alJumhuriyah at-Tunisiyah. National or official language: Standard Arabic. 9,335,000 (1998 UN). Literacy rate 42% to 62%. Also includes Ghadames, Greek, Italian, Maltese. Information mainly from J. Applegate 1970; D. Cohen 1985; J. Holm 1989. Muslim. Blind population 18,000. Deaf institutions: 1. Data accuracy estimate: B. The number of languages listed for Tunisia is 8. Of those, 6 are living languages and 2 are extinct. Diversity index 0.01.

ARABIC, JUDEO-TUNISIAN [AJT] 500 in Tunisia (1994 H. Mutzafi). Afro-Asiatic, Semitic, Central, South, Arabic. Dialects: FES, TUNIS. Medium intelligibility with Judeo-Moroccan Arabic and Judeo-Tripolitanian Arabic, but none with Judeo-Iraqi Arabic. A lexicon of 5,000 words in 1950 had 79% words of Arabic origin, 15% Romance loanwords, 4.4% Hebrew loanwords, 1.6% others (D. Cohen 1985.254). Most of the Jews in Tunisia now speak French. Formerly written in Hebrew script. Jewish. Bible portions 1897-1937. See main entry under Israel.

ARABIC, STANDARD [ABV] Afro-Asiatic, Semitic, Central, South, Arabic. Preserves ancient grammar. Used for written materials and formal speeches. Not a mother tongue, but taught in schools. National language. Bible 1984-1991. See main entry under Saudi Arabia.

ARABIC, TUNISIAN SPOKEN ***(TUNISIAN)*** [AEB] 9,000,000 in Tunisia (1995), 98% of the population (1986). Population total all countries 9,308,000. Also spoken in Belgium, France, Germany, Netherlands. Afro-Asiatic, Semitic, Central, South, Arabic. Dialects: NORTHERN TUNISIAN ARABIC, CENTRAL WESTERN TUNISIAN ARABIC, SOUTHERN TUNISIAN, SAHIL TUNISIAN.

Close to Eastern Algerian Arabic, but speakers prefer Tunisian. The Tunis dialect is used in media and in language textbooks for foreigners. Southern dialects are structurally similar to dialects in Libya. Muslim. Bible portions 1903-1928.

DJERBI ***(NAFUSI, JABAL NAFUSI)*** [JBN] 26,000 in Tunisia (1998). Southeastern Tunisia on Mediterranean islands (Jerba), isolated villages south of Jerba, southern Tunisia, and Pacha, old Medina, and Bab Souika streets in Tunis (Tamezret), Tamezret village near Zeraoua and Taoujjout, south of Gabès (Tamezret). Afro-Asiatic, Berber, Northern, Zenati, East. Dialects: TAMEZRET (DUWINNA), JERBA (DJERBA, GUELILI). Spoken only in the home. Many people from Chenini sell newspapers in Tunis. Muslim. See main entry under Libya.

FRENCH [FRN] 11,000 in Tunisia (1993). Indo-European, Italic, Romance, Italo-Western, Western, Gallo-Iberian, Gallo-Romance, Gallo-Rhaetian, Oïl, French. Bible 1530-1986. See main entry under France.

LINGUA FRANCA ***(PETIT MAURESQUE, FERENGHI, SABIR, 'AJNABI, ALJAMIA)*** [PML] Tunisia; Dodecanese Islands west bank, Greece; Cyprus; other major Mediterranean ports. Pidgin, Romance-based. Lexicon from Italian and Provençal. An earlier version may have been a pidginized Latin. On the Barbary Coast of North Africa in 1578, its lexicon came from Spanish and Portuguese. In Algeria in the 1830s, it drew increasingly from French, and later became the nonstandard French of that area. It may also have influenced other pidgins. There is a report of a present-day variety on the Aegean Islands, used as a pidgin in the southeastern Mediterranean region, to have mainly Arabic syntax, and vocabulary which is 65% to 70% Italian, 10% Spanish, and other Catalan, French, Ladino, and Turkish words. Documented in Djerba, Tunisia in 1353. Dictionary. Coastal. Craftsmen, urban workers. Sea level. Christian, Sunni Muslim. Extinct.

SENED [SDS] Sened and Tmagourt villages, northwest of Gabès. Southern Tunisia. Afro-Asiatic, Berber, Northern, Zenati, East. Dialects: TMAGOURT (TMAGURT), SENED. Only a few elderly people still remember a few words. Muslim. Extinct.

TUNISIAN SIGN LANGUAGE [TSE] Deaf sign language. Used in a school for the deaf. Used by USA Peace Corps. There are loans from French Sign Language and Italian Sign Language, but it is distinct.

UGANDA

Republic of Uganda. National or official language: English. 20,554,000 (1998 UN), including 16,072,548 of Ugandan citizenship (1993 SIL). Literacy rate 52% to 57%. Also includes Hema, Kaliko 5,000, Lendu 8,600, Mvuba, people from DRC, Rwanda, Kenya, Sudan. Information mainly from C. Stigand 1925; E. Ramponi 1937; J. Middleton 1955, 1960, 1965; A. Southall 1956; B. Taylor 1962; P. Ladefoged, R. Glick, C. Criper 1972; C. Turnbull 1972; R. Vossen 1981, 1983; M. L. Bender 1989; G. Dimmendaal 1989. Christian, traditional religion, Muslim, Baha'i. Blind population 175,000. Deaf institutions: 4. Data accuracy estimate: A2, B. The number of languages listed for Uganda is 45. Of those, 43 are living languages and 2 are extinct. Diversity index 0.93.

ACHOLI ***(ACOLI, ATSCHOLI, SHULI, GANG, LWO, LWOO, AKOLI, ACOOLI, LOG ACOLI, DOK ACOLI)*** [ACO] 746,796 in Uganda, including 12,089 speakers of Chopi (1991 census), 4.4% of the population (1972 Ladefoged et al.). Population total both countries 773,800. North central Acholi District. Also spoken in Sudan. Nilo-Saharan, Eastern Sudanic, Nilotic, Western, Luo, Southern, Luo-Acholi, Alur-Acholi, Lango-Acholi. Dialects: LABWOR, NYAKWAI, DHOPALUO (CHOPI, CHOPE). Ruhlen (1987) classifies Labwor as a separate language. Literacy campaign. Christian, traditional religion. Bible 1986.

ADHOLA ***(DHOPADHOLA, JOPADHOLA, LUDAMA)*** [ADH] 247,577 (1986). Eastern, Mbale District. Not in Kenya. Nilo-Saharan, Eastern Sudanic, Nilotic, Western, Luo, Southern, Adhola. The most distinct of the Western Nilotic languages in Uganda. The people are called 'Jopadhola' or 'Budama'. Literacy campaign. Newspapers, radio programs. Bible portions 1977-1979.

ALUR ***(LUR, LURI, ALORO, ALUA, ALULU, DHO ALUR, JO ALUR)*** [ALZ] 420,000 in Uganda (1993 Johnstone), 1.9% of the population. North of Lake Albert. Nilo-Saharan, Eastern Sudanic, Nilotic, Western, Luo, Southern, Luo-Acholi, Alur-Acholi, Alur. Dialects: JOKOT, JONAM, MAMBISA, WANYORO. The Jonam dialect has 96% lexical similarity with Ngora. Literacy campaign. Newspapers, radio programs. Christian in Uganda. Bible 1936-1955. See main entry under DRC.

AMBA ***(KWAMBA, KUAMBA, KU-AMBA, RWAMBA, LWAMBA, HAMBA, LUBULEBULE, RUWENZORI KIBIRA, HUMU, KIHUMU)*** [RWM] 16,000 in Uganda out of an ethnic group of 62,926 (1991 census), .5% of the population (1972 Ladefoged et al.) Population total both countries 20,500. DRC border south of Lake Albert, Ruwenzori Mts., Bundibugyo District. Also spoken in DRC. Niger-Congo, Atlantic-Congo, Volta-Congo, Benue-Congo, Bantoid, Southern, Narrow Bantu, Central, D, Bira-Huku (D.30). Dialects: KYANZI (KIHYANZI), SUWA (KUSUWA). Closely related to

Bera, Bila, Komo, and Bhele. They use LuBwisi as a second language. Proficiency in Runyoro-Rutooro, used in churches, is limited. Their name for themselves is 'Kwamba'. Called 'KiHumu' in DRC. The people are called 'BaAmba'. Literacy campaign. Savannah, forest. Agriculturalists: plantains, millet, maize, sweet potatoes, peanuts, rice, coffee, cotton, cassava; animal husbandry: goats, sheep. 2,400 to 3,400 feet. Traditional religion, Christian.

ARINGA ***(LOW LUGBARA)*** [LUC] 588,830 (1991 census). Northwest corner, north of Lake Albert, Aringa county, north of Lugbara, west of Ma'di. Not in Sudan. Nilo-Saharan, Central Sudanic, East, Moru-Madi, Central. The speakers of Lugbara and Ma'di both consider Aringa to be a separate but related language.

BARI ***(BERI)*** [BFA] 60,000 in Uganda. Northwest corner. Nilo-Saharan, Eastern Sudanic, Nilotic, Eastern, Bari. Dialects: KUKU, NYEPU (NGYEPU, NYEFU, NYEPO, NYPHO), PÖJULU (PAJULU, FADJULU, FAJULU, FAJELU), NYANGBARA (NYANGWARA, NYAMBARA), MONDARI (MANDARI, MUNDARI). Kakwa is a separate language. Trade language. Bible 1979. See main entry under Sudan.

CHIGA ***(OLUCHIGA, ORUKIGA, CIGA, KIGA, RUKIGA)*** [CHG] 1,391,442 (1991 census), 7.1% of the population. Extreme southwest, Ankole District, Western Province. Niger-Congo, Atlantic-Congo, Volta-Congo, Benue-Congo, Bantoid, Southern, Narrow Bantu, Central, J, Nyoro-Ganda (J.10). 72% intelligible with Nyankore. 84% to 94% lexical similarity with Nyankore, 77% with Nyoro, 75% with Zinza, 72% with Nyambo, 70% with Haya, 68% with Tooro, 63% with Kerewe. Hills, mountain lakes, swamps. Agriculturalists: millet, sorghum, sweet potatoes, beans, peas, maize, wheat, peanuts, sunflower seeds, potatoes, cassava, vegetables, plantains, tobacco, flax, coffee, peas; animal husbandry: cattle. 4,000 to 6,000 feet and above. Christian (most), traditional religion.

ENGLISH [ENG] Second language speakers: 1,000,000 (1977 Voegelin and Voegelin). Indo-European, Germanic, West, English. Used in primary schools, law courts. Official language. Newspapers, radio programs. Bible 1535-1989. See main entry under United Kingdom.

GANDA ***(LUGANDA)*** [LAP] 3,015,980 in Uganda (1991 census), a little more than 16% of the population (1972 Ladefoged et al.). Population total both countries 3,025,000. Including second language users: 4,000,000 (1999 WA). Southeast, from the northwest shore of Lake Victoria to Lake Kyoga and the Tanzania border; primarily Buganda Province. Also spoken in Tanzania. Niger-Congo, Atlantic-Congo, Volta-Congo, Benue-Congo, Bantoid, Southern, Narrow Bantu, Central, J, Nyoro-Ganda (J.10). Dialects: KOOKI (OLUKOOKI), SESE (OLUSESE), LUVUMA, LUDIOPA. Luvuma, Ludiope may be dialects. 71% to 86% lexical similarity with Soga, 68% with Gwere. The most widely spoken second language in Uganda next to English. Used in primary schools. The people are called 'Baganda'. Investigation needed: intelligibility with Luvuma, Ludiope. Language of wider communication. Dictionary. SVO. Newspapers, radio programs. Plateau, hills, swamps, valleys. Agriculturalists: bananas, tobacco, beans, millet, maize, sweet potatoes, peanuts, cassava, cotton; animal husbandry: cattle, goats, chicken; hunters. 4,000 feet. Bible 1896-1968.

GUJARATI [GJR] 147,000 or 1% of the population (1986). Indo-European, Indo-Iranian, Indo-Aryan, Central zone, Gujarati. The people migrated to Uganda during the early part of the 20th century. Newspapers. Hindu. Bible 1823-1998. See main entry under India.

GUNGU ***(RUGUNGU, LUGUNGU)*** [RUB] 25,000 (1991 census). Hoima and Masindi districts, primarily along the northeast shore of Lake Albert in the Rift Valley. Also in the hills above the valley. Niger-Congo, Atlantic-Congo, Volta-Congo, Benue-Congo, Bantoid, Southern, Narrow Bantu, Central, J, Nyoro-Ganda (J.10). 58% or lower inherent intelligibility of Nyoro-Tooro. Tooro is the closest language. 65% lexical similarity with Tooro. Speakers are not bilingual in Nyoro. Vigorous use. Lugungu Language Committee. The ethnic group is called 'BaGungu'. SVO; prepositions, genitives, adjectives, relatives after noun heads; question word initial; word order distinguishes subject and object; subject agreement obligatory, object agreement optional; verb suffixes mark passive and causative; V, CV, CVV, (C)C(C)V where first C is a nasal and last C a semivowel; tonal. Radio programs. Savannah, tropical forest. Shore, hills. Fishermen, peasant agriculturalists. Bible portions 1998.

GWERE ***(LUGWERE, OLUGWERE)*** [GWR] 275,608 (1991 census), 1.7% of population (1972 Ladefoged et al.). Pallisa District, dominating 2 of the district's 4 counties. Niger-Congo, Atlantic-Congo, Volta-Congo, Benue-Congo, Bantoid, Southern, Narrow Bantu, Central, J, Nyoro-Ganda (J.10). Closest to Lusiki in vocabulary. 68% lexical similarity with Ganda, 64% with Soga. LuGanda is used in church. Gwere used in the home, village, and market. Vigorous use. Medium of instruction in the first 2 years of primary school. Newspapers, radio programs.

HINDI [HND] 147,000 1% of the population (1986). Indo-European, Indo-Iranian, Indo-Aryan, Central zone, Western Hindi, Hindustani. The people migrated to Uganda in the early 20th century. Radio programs. Hindu. Bible 1818-1987. See main entry under India.

IK ***(ICIETOT, TEUSO, TEUTH, NGULAK)*** [IKX] 2,000 (1972 C. Turnbull). Northeast part of Karamoja. Nilo-Saharan, Eastern Sudanic, Kuliak, Ik. It is very different from other Eastern Sudanic languages.

Speakers are reported to use Karamojong as second language. They call their language 'Icietot'. Mountain slope. Hunters, some cultivation. Traditional religion.

KAKWA ***(BARI KAKWA, KAKUA, KWAKWAK)*** [KEO] 86,472 in Uganda (1991 census), .6% of population (1972 Ladefoged et al.) Population total all countries 146,500. Northwest corner, West Nile District. Also spoken in DRC, Sudan. Nilo-Saharan, Eastern Sudanic, Nilotic, Eastern, Bari. Dialects of Sudan, DRC, and Uganda differ little (Nida). Very different from other Eastern Nilotic languages of Uganda. 74% lexical similarity with Pöjulu, 73% with Bari, 72% with Ngyepu and Kuku, 68% with Nyanggwara, 61% with Mondari. Literacy campaign. Radio programs. 15,000 Christians in Uganda. Bible 1983.

KARAMOJONG ***(KARIMOJONG, KARIMONJONG)*** [KDJ] 370,000 (1994 UBS) or 2% of the population (1972 Ladefoged et al.), including 50,000 Jie (1986 MARC). East and northeast, Karamojo District around Moroto. Nilo-Saharan, Eastern Sudanic, Nilotic, Eastern, Lotuxo-Teso, Teso-Turkana, Turkana. Dialects: KARAMOJONG, JIE (JIYE), DODOS (DODOTH). The dialects have 83% to 95% lexical similarity. 85% lexical similarity with Turkana, 75% with Teso. People are friendly with the Toposa; hostile to the Turkana. Several subdivisions represent more than one ethnic group. Semi-nomadic. Dictionary. VSO; highly inflectional; grammatical tone; vowel harmony; voiceless vowels. Radio programs. Pastoralists: cattle, sheep, goats, donkeys; limited agriculture: sorghum. Traditional religion, Christian; Jie: traditional religion. NT 1974, in press (1997).

KENYI ***(LUKENYI)*** [LKE] 390,115. Between Lake Victoria and Lake Kyoga, Busoga Province. Niger-Congo, Atlantic-Congo, Volta-Congo, Benue-Congo, Bantoid, Southern, Narrow Bantu, Central, J, Nyoro-Ganda (J.10). Welmers lists Olusoga and Lukenyi separately. 81% lexical similarity with Soga, 71% to 86% with Ganda, 64% with Gwere, 58% with Saamia. Politically distinct from Ganda. The people are called 'BaKenyi'. They say they are a displaced people of Ganda origin. Investigation needed: intelligibility with Soga, Ganda. Low flat hills, swamps, valleys. Agriculturalists: bananas, beans, millet, coffee, cotton.

KONJO ***(RUKONJO, OLUKONJO, KONZO, OLUKONZO, LHUKONZO)*** [KOO] 361,709 (1992 census), 1.7% of the population (1972 Ladefoged et al.). Southwest, Ruwenzori Mountains. Niger-Congo, Atlantic-Congo, Volta-Congo, Benue-Congo, Bantoid, Southern, Narrow Bantu, Central, J, Konzo (J.40). Dialects: SANZA (EKISANZA), RUKONJO. Many dialects. 77% lexical similarity with Nandi. Radio programs. Mountain slope, rolling hills, plains. Agriculturalists: yams, beans, sweet potatoes, peanuts, soy beans, potatoes, rice, wheat, cassava, coffee, bananas, cotton; animal husbandry: goats, sheep, fowl. Up to 7,500 feet. Traditional religion (most), Christian. Bible portions 1914.

KUMAM ***(KUMAN, IKOKOLEMU, KUMUM, IKUMAMA, AKUM, AKOKOLEMU)*** [KDI] 112,629 (1991 census), 1% of the population (1972 Ladefoged et al.). South of Lake Kwania, western Teso District. Nilo-Saharan, Eastern Sudanic, Nilotic, Western, Luo, Southern, Kuman. 82% lexical similarity with Dhopaluo, 81% with Lango, 77% with Acholi. Ladefoged and Bender classify Kumam as Southern Luo; some linguists classify it in the Dinka group. Kumam oral tradition gives a Teso descent. Literacy campaign. Radio programs.

KUPSABINY ***(SEBEI, SAPEI)*** [KPZ] 120,000 (1994 UBS), .6% of the population (1972 Ladefoged). Eastern border area slightly north of Mbale, Sebei Province. Nilo-Saharan, Eastern Sudanic, Nilotic, Southern, Kalenjin, Elgon. Dialects: SABINY (SAPINY, KUPSABINY, KUPSAPINY), MBAI, SOR. People called 'Sebei', language 'Kupsabiny'. Literacy campaigns. Radio programs. NT 1996.

LANGO ***(LWO, LWOO, LEB-LANO, LANGI)*** [LAJ] 977,680 (1991 census), 5.6% of population (1972 Ladefoged et al.). Central, north of Lake Kyoga, Lango Province. Nilo-Saharan, Eastern Sudanic, Nilotic, Western, Luo, Southern, Luo-Acholi, Alur-Acholi, Lango-Acholi. Distinct from Acholi (Lwo), Lango of Sudan (related to Lotuko), or Lango (Didinga) of Sudan. Literacy campaign. Roman script. Newspapers, radio programs. Bible 1979.

LUGBARA ***(HIGH LUGBARA)*** [LUG] 200,000 in Uganda, including 140,000 in Arua, 60,000 in Maracha and Terego (1983 SIL). Population total both countries 488,000. Northwest, west Nile district. Also spoken in DRC. Nilo-Saharan, Central Sudanic, East, Moru-Madi, Central. Dialects: ARUA (STANDARD LUGBARA), MARACHA, TEREGO (OMUGO). Literacy campaign. Used in primary schools. Newspapers, radio programs. Few trees. Plateau, low ridges. Agriculturalists: eleusine, sorghum, simsim, peas, beans, peanuts, pumpkins, sugar cane, bananas, maize, cassava, tobacco; animal husbandry: cattle, goats, sheep, fowl. 4000 to 5000 feet. Traditional religion, Christian, Muslim, Baha'i. Bible 1966.

LUYIA ***(LULUYIA, LUHYA)*** [LUY] 225,378 in Uganda (1991 census), including 10,000 Songa, 40,074 of Lugwe. Lake Victoria area near Kenya border. Niger-Congo, Atlantic-Congo, Volta-Congo, Benue-Congo, Bantoid, Southern, Narrow Bantu, Central, J, Masaba-Luyia (J.30), Luyia. Dialects: SAAMIA, SONGA, LUGWE. Saamia has 88% lexical similarity with Wanga, 80% with Nyore, 62% with Masaba, 59% to 61% with Ganda, 52% with Isuxa, 51% with Gwere. Dialects in Uganda have

92% lexical similarity. Ganda is used in church. The people are called 'Abaluyia', singular 'Muluyia'. Christian, traditional religion. Bible 1975. See main entry under Kenya.

MA'DI ***(MA'ADI, MA'DITI, MA'DI)*** [MHI] 130,558 in Uganda (1991 census). Population total both countries 150,000. Northwestern Sudan border area near Nimule, West Nile District, Madi Province, Madi Subdistrict, and Madi County. Moyo is in the west, Adjumani in the east. Also spoken in Sudan. Nilo-Saharan, Central Sudanic, East, Moru-Madi, Southern. Dialects: MOYO, ADJUMANI (OYUWI). Literacy campaign. Newspapers, radio programs. NT 1977.

MA'DI, SOUTHERN ***(SOUTHERN MA'DI)*** [QMD] 48,000 (1983 SIL). Okollo County, on the west bank of the Nile River. Okollo town is the administrative center. Nilo-Saharan, Central Sudanic, East, Moru-Madi, Southern. Dialects: OKOLLO, OGOKO, RIGBO. Closer to Lugbara than to Madi (Moyo), which they do not understand. Ogoko and Rigbo are closer to Lugbara than Okollo is; intelligibility testing needed. Okollo dialect is considered more 'pure' than the others. Investigation needed: intelligibility with Lugbara.

MANGBETU [MDJ] 30,700 in Uganda including 17,500 Makere, 13,200 Meje. Northwest, DRC border north of Lake Albert. Nilo-Saharan, Central Sudanic, East, Mangbetu. Dialects: MAKERE (AMAKERE, NAMAKERE, NAMAKERETI), MEJE (MEDJE, MEDYE, MEGYE, EMEEJE, NEMEEJE, NAMEJETI). Only Makere and Meje dialects are in Uganda. See main entry under DRC.

MASABA ***(LUMASABA, MASAABA, GISU, LUGISU)*** [MYX] 751,253 (1991 census). Eastern, south of the Kupsabiny, Bugisu Province. Niger-Congo, Atlantic-Congo, Volta-Congo, Benue-Congo, Bantoid, Southern, Narrow Bantu, Central, J, Masaba-Luyia (J.30). Dialects: ULUBUKUSU, ULUBUYA, ULUDADIRI, LUGISU (GISHU), ULUKISU, SYAN. Syan is a related dialect or language. 62% lexical similarity with Saamia, 52% with Isuxa, 50% with Ragooli. Investigation needed: intelligibility with dialects. Literacy campaign. Radio programs. NT 1977-1992.

NDO ***(KEBU, OKE'BU, NDU)*** [NDP] 200,000 in Uganda (1994 UBS). Northwestern. Mahigi is the center. Nilo-Saharan, Central Sudanic, East, Mangbutu-Efe. Dialects: AVARI (AVIRITU, AVERE), OKE'BU (NDO OKE'BU, KEBUTU, KEBU), MEMBI. Blacksmiths. NT 1994. See main entry under DRC.

NUBI ***(KINUBI, KI-NUBI)*** [KCN] 14,739 in Uganda (1991 census). Population total both countries 25,000. Bombo, 30 miles north of Kampala, Arua, and elsewhere in Uganda. Also spoken in Kenya. Creole, Arabic based. Descendants of Emin Pasha's troops. Formerly a soldier language, which split off from Sudanese Pidgin Arabic about 1900. There are conflicting reports of intelligibility with Sudanese Creole Arabic. 90% of the lexicon is from Arabic. Traders. Muslim.

NYANG'I ***(NUANGEYA, NYUANGIA, NYANGIYA, NYANGIA, NGANGEA, GYANGIYA, NYANGEYA, NGIANGEYA, NIPORI, NIPOREN, POREN, NGAPORE, UPALE)*** [NYP] Eastern Uganda. Nilo-Saharan, Eastern Sudanic, Kuliak, Ngangea-So. A separate language from Ik. People now speak Dodos (Karamojong). Hunters, some cultivation. Traditional religion. Extinct.

NYANKORE ***(NKOLE, NYANKOLE, RUNYANKOLE, ULUNYANKOLE, ULUNYANKORE)*** [NYN] 1,643,193 including 141,668 Hororo, 1,643,193 Hima (1991 census) or 8.1% of the population. Western Province, Ankole District, east of Lake Edward. Niger-Congo, Atlantic-Congo, Volta-Congo, Benue-Congo, Bantoid, Southern, Narrow Bantu, Central, J, Nyoro-Ganda (J.10). Dialects: HORORO, ORUTAGWENDA, HIMA. Hima may be a separate language. Nyankole, Nyoro, and their dialects are considered by some to be one language (78% to 96% lexical similarity). 84% to 94% lexical similarity with Chiga, 75% to 86% with Tooro (Nyoro), 81% with Zinza, 78% with Nyambo, 74% with Haya, 68% with Kerewe. The standardization of the western languages (Nyankore-Chiga and Nyoro-Tooro) is called 'RuNyakitara', and is taught at the University. Ethnic groups: BaHima, BaIru. Investigation needed: intelligibility with Hima. Used in primary schools. Newspapers, radio programs. Savannah, acacia scrub, tropical forest, papyrus. Plains, hills, plateau, swamps, crater lakes. Agriculturalists: millet, sweet potatoes, plantains beans, peanuts, cassava, coffee, maize, sorghum; animal husbandry: goats, sheep, cattle; fishermen. 3,000 to 4,000 feet. Christian (most), Traditional religion, Muslim. Bible 1964-1989.

NYOLE ***(NYULE, NYULI, LUNYOLE)*** [NUJ] 228,918 (1991 census) or 1.4% of population (1972 Ladefoged et al.). Southeast Uganda in Tororo District. Niger-Congo, Atlantic-Congo, Volta-Congo, Benue-Congo, Bantoid, Southern, Narrow Bantu, Central, J, Masaba-Luyia (J.30). Dialects: MENYA (LUMENYA), HADYO (LUHADYO), SABI (LUSABI), WESA (LUWESA). 70% to 80% lexical similarity with LuSaamia, 82% with the Lugwe dialect of Saamia (closest), 67% with Ganda, 61% with Nyore of Kenya. Speakers have limited bilingualism in Ganda, which is used in church. Vigorous, widely used. There is a Lunyole Language Association. Dictionary. SVO. Radio programs. Tropical forest. Plains. Peasant agriculturalists.

NYORO ***(RUNYORO)*** [NYR] 495,443 (1991 census), 6.2% of the population. South and southeast of Lake Albert, Bunyoro and Toro provinces. Niger-Congo, Atlantic-Congo, Volta-Congo, Benue-Congo, Bantoid, Southern, Narrow Bantu, Central, J, Nyoro-Ganda (J.10). Dialects: RUTAGWENDA, ORUNYORO (NYORO). 73% inherent intelligibility with Gungu. Hema-Sud (Nyoro-Toro) In DRC is quite different. 78% to 93% lexical similarity with Toro, 77% with Nyankole and Ciga, 67% with Nyambo and Zinza, 66% with Haya, 62% with Kerewe. Literacy campaign. Roman script. Newspapers, radio programs. Savannah. Swamps, coastal, plateau, mountain slope. Animal husbandry: cattle; fishermen; agriculturalists: millet, sorghum, plantains, sweet potatoes, beans, pumpkins, cow peas, cassava, peanuts, cotton, tobacco; hunters. Christian, traditional religion, Muslim. Bible 1912.

PÖKOOT ***(POKOT, PAKOT, SUK)*** [PKO] East central, near Kupsabiny. Nilo-Saharan, Eastern Sudanic, Nilotic, Southern, Kalenjin, Pokot. Semi-nomadic. Traditional religion, Christian. NT 1967-1987. See main entry under Kenya.

RULI ***(RURULI, LUDUULI)*** [RUC] 68,010 (1991 census). East of Nyoro. Niger-Congo, Atlantic-Congo, Volta-Congo, Benue-Congo, Bantoid, Southern, Narrow Bantu, Central, J, Nyoro-Ganda (J.10). Dialects: EASTERN RULI, WESTERN RULI. Nakasongola (east) is influenced by Ganda, and in Kuyanoongo (west) by Nyoro. Eastern and Western Ruli have 79% lexical similarity. 71% lexical similarity with Nyoro (closest), 70% Eastern Ruli and Ganda. Ruli used the most in home and village. Investigation needed: intelligibility with dialects.

RUNDI [RUD] 100,903 in Uganda (1991 census), 2% of the population (1972 Ladefoged et al.). Most in Buganda. Niger-Congo, Atlantic-Congo, Volta-Congo, Benue-Congo, Bantoid, Southern, Narrow Bantu, Central, J, Rwanda-Rundi (J.60). Bible 1967. See main entry under Burundi.

RWANDA ***(RUNYARWANDA, RUANDA)*** [RUA] 532,692 in Uganda, including 203,030 speakers of Rufumbira, 329,662 Rwanda, 1,394 Twa (1991 census), 5.9% of the population (1972 Ladefoged et al.). Southwestern border with Rwanda. The largest group in Kisoro District. Niger-Congo, Atlantic-Congo, Volta-Congo, Benue-Congo, Bantoid, Southern, Narrow Bantu, Central, J, Rwanda-Rundi (J.60). Dialects: RUFUMBIRA, TWA. Rufumbira may be distinct and need separate literature. Widely spoken. Investigation needed: intelligibility with Rufumbira. Literacy campaign. Radio programs. Bible 1954-1993. See main entry under Rwanda.

SINGA ***(LUSINGA)*** [SGM] Rusinga Island. Niger-Congo, Atlantic-Congo, Volta-Congo, Benue-Congo, Bantoid, Southern, Narrow Bantu, Central, J, Nyoro-Ganda (J.10). Extinct.

SOGA ***(LUSOGA, OLUSOGA)*** [SOG] 1,370,845 (1991 census), 8% of the population. Between Lake Victoria and Lake Kyoga, Busoga Province. LuTenga is around Jjinja, LuLamogi farther north. Niger-Congo, Atlantic-Congo, Volta-Congo, Benue-Congo, Bantoid, Southern, Narrow Bantu, Central, J, Nyoro-Ganda (J.10). Dialects: TENGA (LUTENGA), LAMOGI (LULAMOGI), GABULA (LUGABULA). Welmers lists Soga and Kenyi separately. 81% lexical similarity with Kenyi, 71% to 86% with Ganda, 64% with Gwere, 58% with Saamia. Tenga has 82% with Ganda. Lamogi dialect has 79% to 82% lexical similarity with Tenga, 89% with Siki, 88% with Soga, 82% with Gwere. Politically distinct from Ganda. Investigation needed: intelligibility with Ganda, Kenyi, Lamogi. Literacy campaign. Radio programs. Low flat hills, swamps, valleys. Agriculturalists: bananas, beans, millet, coffee, cotton. Bible portions 1896-1899.

SOO ***(SO, TEPETH, TEPES)*** [TEU] 5,000 (1972 Ladefoged et al.). Karamoja District of eastern Uganda on Mt. Moroto on Kenya border. Nilo-Saharan, Eastern Sudanic, Kuliak, Ngangea-So. Bilingualism in Karamojong. In some areas used mainly by those over 40 years old. Younger people speak Karamojong as primary language. Dictionary.

SWAHILI ***(KISWAHILI, KISUAHELI)*** [SWA] Niger-Congo, Atlantic-Congo, Volta-Congo, Benue-Congo, Bantoid, Southern, Narrow Bantu, Central, G, Swahili (G.40). Dialect: SHAMBA (KISHAMBA). The government plans to make this a mandatory subject in schools. Used by the security forces and in some regions. Muslim. Bible 1891-1996. See main entry under Tanzania.

TALINGA-BWISI ***(KITALINGA, LUBWISI, OLUBWISI, BWISSI, MAWISSI, LUBWISSI)*** [TLJ] 53,467 in Uganda (1991 census). Population total both countries 75,000 to 85,000. DRC border, Bundibugyo District, southwest of Fort Portal, between Albert and Edward lakes, immediately next to the DRC border, near Kilembe. Also spoken in DRC. Niger-Congo, Atlantic-Congo, Volta-Congo, Benue-Congo, Bantoid, Southern, Narrow Bantu, Central, J, Haya-Jita (J.20). 68% inherent intelligibility of Tooro. Closest to Tooro (73% lexical similarity) and Nyoro (72%). Speakers use Tooro as second language. The BaTooro used to rule over the BaBwisi, but Tooro use seems to be decreasing. English is used by men and boys who have been to higher levels of school. LuBwisi is used in the home, in some churches, primary school, and market if both speakers are BaBwisi. RuTooro is used in some churches. English is used by men and boys who have been to higher levels of school. Called 'Bwisi' in Uganda, 'Talinga' in DRC. Different from Bwisi of Congo and Gabon. SVO; CV, V; tonal. Speakers desire written materials. Radio programs. Tropical forest. Mountain slope. Peasant agriculturalists. Christian, Muslim.

TESO ***(ATESO, IKUMAMA, BAKEDI, BAKIDI, ETOSSIO, ELGUMI, WAMIA)*** [TEO] 999,537 in Uganda (1991 census), 8.3% of the population (1972 Ladefoged et al.) Population total both countries 1,217,000. Sorot and Kumi region, southeast, Teso Province. Lokathan live around Madial at the north end of the Nangeya Mts. Also spoken in Kenya. Nilo-Saharan, Eastern Sudanic, Nilotic,

Eastern, Lotuxo-Teso, Teso-Turkana, Teso. Dialects: LOKATHAN (BIRI, KETEBO), OROM (ROM). Limited intelligibility with other varieties in the Teso-Turkana group. The dialect in Ngoro is considered standard. 76% lexical similarity with Turkana, 75% with Karamojong. The people are 'Iteso', the language 'Ateso'. VSO; highly inflectional; grammatical tone; vowel harmony. Literacy campaign. Used in primary schools. Newspapers, radio programs. Pastoralists; agriculturalists. Christian; traditional religion. Bible 1961.

TOORO ***(RUTOORO, ORUTORO, RUTORO, TORO)*** [TTJ] 488,024 (1991 census). South and southeast of Lake Albert, Toro province. Niger-Congo, Atlantic-Congo, Volta-Congo, Benue-Congo, Bantoid, Southern, Narrow Bantu, Central, J, Nyoro-Ganda (J.10). Dialect: TUKU. Hema-Sud (Nyoro-Toro) in DRC is quite different. 78% to 93% lexical similarity with Nyoro. Savannah. Swamps, coastal, plateau, mountain slope. Animal husbandry: cattle; fishermen; agriculturalists: millet, sorghum, plantains, sweet potatoes, beans, pumpkins, cow peas, cassava, peanuts, cotton, tobacco; hunters. Christian, traditional religion, Muslim.

UGANDAN SIGN LANGUAGE ***(USL)*** [UGN] All over Uganda, but mainly in the towns. Deaf sign language. Influences from Kenyan Sign Language and ASL. Knowledge of English is not widespread or deep. There have been elementary schools for deaf children since 1962. Several sign languages became one in 1988. The schools allow sign language in the classroom since 1988. The sign language used in the classroom and that used by adults outside is the same. Some sign language interpreters are provided for deaf people in court. There are a few sign language classes for hearing people. It was recognized as a minority language in 1995. Interpretation provided in parliament from a deaf member. Promotion by the Uganda National Association of the Deaf. USL's prestige is growing. There is a manual alphabet for spelling. Dictionary.

ZAMBIA

Republic of Zambia. Formerly Northern Rhodesia and Mozambique. National or official language: English. 8,781,000 (1998 UN). Literacy rate 25% to 76%. Also includes Hindi, Nyemba, Urdu, people from Europe 30,000, Asia 8,000, Angola, and Mozambique. Information mainly from S. Ohannessian and M. Kashoki 1978; A. Vitale 1980; J. Holm 1989; M. Brenzinger 1997. Christian, traditional religion. Blind population 38,000 (1982 WCE). Deaf institutions: 5. Data accuracy estimate: A2, B. The number of languages listed for Zambia is 43. Of those, 41 are living languages and 2 are second languages without mother tongue speakers. Diversity index 0.90.

AFRIKAANS [AFK] Indo-European, Germanic, West, Low Saxon-Low Franconian, Low Franconian. Language of wider communication. Bible 1933-1983. See main entry under South Africa.

AUSHI ***(AVAUSHI, VOUAOUSI, USHI, USI, UZHIL)*** [AUH] 90,204 in Zambia (1969 census). Population total both countries 90,204 or more. Northern, Luapula Province. Also spoken in DRC. Niger-Congo, Atlantic-Congo, Volta-Congo, Benue-Congo, Bantoid, Southern, Narrow Bantu, Central, M, Bemba (M.40). Language of wider communication. SVO.

BEMBA ***(CHIBEMBA, ICHIBEMBA, WEMBA, CHIWEMBA)*** [BEM] 2,000,000 in Zambia (1993 Johnstone), 25% of the population, including 741,114 Bemba, 32,022 Luunda, 5,190 Shila, 26,429 Tabwa, 16,833 Cishinga, 28,172 Kabende, 6,706 Mukulu, 42,298 Ng'umbo, 14,040 Twa-Unga (1969 census). Population total all countries 2,150,000 or more. Northern, Copperbelt and Luapula provinces. Possibly in Zimbabwe. Also spoken in Botswana, DRC, Malawi, Tanzania. Niger-Congo, Atlantic-Congo, Volta-Congo, Benue-Congo, Bantoid, Southern, Narrow Bantu, Central, M, Bemba (M.40). Dialects: LEMBUE, LOMOTUA (LOMOTWA), NGOMA, NWESI, TOWN BEMBA, LUUNDA (LUAPULA), CHISHINGA, KABENDE, MUKULU, NG'UMBO, TWA OF BANGWEULU, UNGA. Town Bemba has a Bemba base with heavy codeswitching with English and neighboring Bantu languages. Town Bemba is a widely used lingua franca in urban, not rural areas, and it has higher social status than other languages except English. Bemba is recognized for educational and administrative purposes. Language of wider communication. Dictionary. SVO. Newspapers, radio programs. Traditional religion, Christian. Bible 1956-1983.

BWILE [BWC] 12,362 in Zambia (1969 census). Population total both countries 12,362 or more. Also spoken in DRC. Niger-Congo, Atlantic-Congo, Volta-Congo, Benue-Congo, Bantoid, Southern, Narrow Bantu, Central, L, Bwile (L.10). Not closely related to other languages.

CHOKWE ***(CIOKWE, COKWE, SHIOKO, TSHOKWE, TSCHIOKWE, DJOK)*** [CJK] 44,200 in Zambia, .65% of the population (1986). Northwestern Province, east of the Mbunda. Niger-Congo, Atlantic-Congo, Volta-Congo, Benue-Congo, Bantoid, Southern, Narrow Bantu, Central, K, Chokwe-Luchazi (K.20). Dialect: MINUNGO. Bible 1970-1990. See main entry under DRC.

ENGLISH [ENG] 41,434 in Zambia (1969 census). Indo-European, Germanic, West, English. Spoken as mother tongue by Europeans mainly. A small minority of Zambian Africans speak it as a mother tongue. Used as a second language. The only language of Parliament. Official language. Bible 1535-1989. See main entry under United Kingdom.

FANAGOLO ***("FANAKALO", "FANEKOLO", PIKI, ISIPIKI, LOLOLO, ISILOLOLO, PIDGIN BANTU, BASIC ZULU, "KITCHEN KAFFIR", "MINE KAFFIR", "ISIKULA")*** [FAO] Several hundred speakers (1975 Reinecke). Towns and mining areas. Pidgin, Zulu based. Dialect: CIKABANGA. Influenced by Bemba in Zambia. Rejected by most Africans because it was imported from Zimbabwe and South Africa by Europeans who did not want Africans to learn English (Adler 1977). Trade language. Second language only. See main entry under South Africa.

GUJARATI [GJR] 12,000 in Zambia (1985 IEM). Indo-European, Indo-Iranian, Indo-Aryan, Central zone, Gujarati. Hindu. Bible 1823-1998. See main entry under India.

ILA ***(CHIILA, SHUKULUMBWE, SUKULUMBWE)*** [ILB] 61,200 or .9% of the population (1986). Central and Southern provinces, west of the Sala. With Tonga it predominates in the south. West bend of Kafue River. Niger-Congo, Atlantic-Congo, Volta-Congo, Benue-Congo, Bantoid, Southern, Narrow Bantu, Central, M, Lenje-Tonga (M.60), Tonga. Dialects: LUNDWE, LUMBU, ILA. Dictionary. Grammar. NT 1915-1945.

KAONDE ***(CHIKAONDE, CHIKAHONDE, KAWONDE, LUBA KAONDE)*** [KQN] 240,000 in Zambia (1993 Johnstone), 2.9% of the population (1986). Population total both countries 276,000. Northwest of Mumbwe, Northwestern and Central provinces. Also spoken in DRC. Niger-Congo, Atlantic-Congo, Volta-Congo, Benue-Congo, Bantoid, Southern, Narrow Bantu, Central, L, Kaonde (L.40). Not closely related to other languages. Literacy campaigns, agricultural extension services. Officially taught in primary schools. Newspapers, radio programs. Bible 1975.

KUNDA ***(CHIKUNDA)*** [KDN] Southeastern Central Province. Niger-Congo, Atlantic-Congo, Volta-Congo, Benue-Congo, Bantoid, Southern, Narrow Bantu, Central, N, Sena-Senga (N.40), Sena. Distinct from the Kunda dialect of Nyanja or Kunda of DRC. See main entry under Zimbabwe.

KXOE ***(XUN, HUKWE, !HUKWE, XUHWE, XU, ZAMA, VAZAMA, CAZAMA, MBARA KWENGO, MBARAKWENA, GLANDA-KHWE, BLACK BUSHMAN, WATER BUSHMEN, SCHEKERE)*** [XUU] 100 (1998 Brenzinger). Western Zambia, east of the Zambesi River near Luzu village, 6 villages. East of Luzu in Sakulinda village; and 250 km. to the northwest, in remote areas of southeastern Senaga District, and the 3 settlements Kashesha ki liwanika, Namafumbwana, and Sanze. Khoisan, Southern Africa, Central, Tshu-Khwe, Northwest. Dialect: [[XO-KXOE. Few speak Lozi, the lingua franca of the area. Many in Zambia have given up Kxoe to speak the language of their partners and parents. See main entry under Namibia.

LALA-BISA ***(BIZA-LALA)*** [LEB] 439,000 in Zambia (1993 Johnstone), 5.2% of the population (1986), including Lala 200,000 (1991 UBS). Population total both countries 439,000 or more. Eastern, along Luangwa River (Bisa), and southwest (Lala), Northern, Central, and Eastern provinces. Also spoken in DRC. Niger-Congo, Atlantic-Congo, Volta-Congo, Benue-Congo, Bantoid, Southern, Narrow Bantu, Central, M, Bisa-Lamba (M.50), Bisa. Dialects: AMBO, LUANO, SWAKA, BISA (ICHIBISA, BIISA, WISA, WIZA), LALA (ICHILALA). NT 1947-1977.

LAMBA ***(ICHILAMBA, CHILAMBA)*** [LAB] 211,000 in Zambia (1993 Johnstone), 2.5% of the population (1986), including 89,969 Lamba, 11,782 Lima (1969 census). Population total both countries 211,000 or more. Copperbelt, Central, and southeastern Northwestern provinces. Also spoken in DRC. Niger-Congo, Atlantic-Congo, Volta-Congo, Benue-Congo, Bantoid, Southern, Narrow Bantu, Central, M, Bisa-Lamba (M.50), Lamba. Dialects: LAMBA, LIMA. Different from Ilamba of Tanzania. Dictionary. Bible 1959.

LENJE ***(CHILENJE, LENJI, LENGI, MUKUNI, CHINAMUKUNI, CIINA)*** [LEH] 169,000 2% of the population (1993 Johnstone). Lukanga Swamp area, Central Province. Niger-Congo, Atlantic-Congo, Volta-Congo, Benue-Congo, Bantoid, Southern, Narrow Bantu, Central, M, Lenje-Tonga (M.60), Lenje. Dialects: TWA (LUKANGA), LENJE. Bible portions 1927-1994.

LOZI ***(SILOZI, ROZI, TOZVI, ROTSE, RUTSE, KOLOLO)*** [LOZ] 473,000 in Zambia (1993 Johnstone), 5.6% of the population (1986). Population total all countries 557,000. Barotseland, Western Province and Southern Province near Livingstone. Also spoken in Botswana, Namibia, Zimbabwe. Niger-Congo, Atlantic-Congo, Volta-Congo, Benue-Congo, Bantoid, Southern, Narrow Bantu, Central, S, Sotho-Tswana (S.30). Recognized for educational and administrative purposes. Newspapers, radio programs. Bible 1951-1987.

LUCHAZI ***(CHILUCHAZI, LUCAZI, CUJAZI, LUJASI, LUJASH, LUTSHASE, LUXAGE, PONDA)*** [LCH] 54,400 in Zambia, .8% of the population (1986). West central Northwestern Province. Niger-Congo, Atlantic-Congo, Volta-Congo, Benue-Congo, Bantoid, Southern, Narrow Bantu, Central, K, Chokwe-Luchazi (K.20). Bible 1963. See main entry under Angola.

LUNDA ***(CHILUNDA)*** [LVN] 220,000 in Zambia (1993 Johnstone), 2.6% of the population (1986). Population total all countries 310,000 or more. Northwestern Province, Copperbelt. Also spoken in Angola, DRC. Niger-Congo, Atlantic-Congo, Volta-Congo, Benue-Congo, Bantoid, Southern, Narrow Bantu, Central, K,

Salampasu-Ndembo (K.30). Dialects: KOSA (KOOSA), NDEMBU, HUMBU, KAWIKU. Distinct from Luunda, a dialect of Bemba. Literacy campaigns, agricultural extension services. Officially taught in primary schools. Newspapers, radio programs. Bible 1962.

LUVALE ***(LUENA, LWENA, CHILUVALE, LOVALE, LUBALE)*** [LUE] 203,000 in Zambia (1993 Johnstone), 2.4% of the population (1986). Population total both countries 358,000. Northwestern and Western Provinces. Also spoken in Angola. Niger-Congo, Atlantic-Congo, Volta-Congo, Benue-Congo, Bantoid, Southern, Narrow Bantu, Central, K, Chokwe-Luchazi (K.20). Recognized for educational and administrative purposes. A dominant regional language. Language of wider communication. Newspapers, radio programs. Traditional religion, Christian. Bible 1955-1961.

LUYANA ***(ESILUYANA, LOUYI, LUI, LUYI, ROUYI)*** [LAV] 74,800 in Zambia (1986), 1.1% of the population, including 12,114 Kwandi, 29,333 Kwanga, 2,692 Mbowe (1969 census). Population total all countries 100,000. Eastern Lozi-Luyana area, Western Province. Also spoken in Angola, Namibia. Niger-Congo, Atlantic-Congo, Volta-Congo, Benue-Congo, Bantoid, Southern, Narrow Bantu, Central, K, Kwangwa (K.40). Dialects: KWANDI, KWANGA, MBOWE (ESIMBOWE), MBUMI. Mbowe may be a separate language. Dictionary.

MAMBWE-LUNGU [MGR] 262,800 in Zambia (1993 Johnstone), 3.1% of the population (1986). Population total both countries 359,000. Northeastern Northern Province south of Lake Tanganyika. Also spoken in Tanzania. Niger-Congo, Atlantic-Congo, Volta-Congo, Benue-Congo, Bantoid, Southern, Narrow Bantu, Central, F, Tongwe (F.10). Dialects: MAMBWE (ICHIMAMBWE, KIMAMBWE), RUNGU (LUNGU, ICHIRUNGU, ADONG). There are minor dialect differences between Mambwe and Lungu. NT 1901-1991.

MASHI ***(MASI)*** [MHO] 20,795 in Zambia (1969 census). Population total all countries 50,000 or more (1996 A. M. Machipisa). Southwestern Western Province. Also spoken in Angola, Namibia. Niger-Congo, Atlantic-Congo, Volta-Congo, Benue-Congo, Bantoid, Southern, Narrow Bantu, Central, K, Kwangwa (K.40). Dialects: NORTH KWANDU, SOUTH KWANDU, MASHI. Dialect cluster. Nomadic. Different from Mashi (Shi) which is related to Havu of DRC. Traditional religion.

MBOWE ***(ESIMBOWE)*** [MXO] 2,692 (1969 census). North central Western Province. Niger-Congo, Atlantic-Congo, Volta-Congo, Benue-Congo, Bantoid, Southern, Narrow Bantu, Central, K, Kwangwa (K.40).

MBUKUSHU ***(MBUKUSHI, MAMBUKUSH, MAMPUKUSH, MBUKUHU, THIMUKUSHU, GOVA, KUSSO)*** [MHW] A small number. Southwestern corner of Western Province, along the Kwando River. Niger-Congo, Atlantic-Congo, Volta-Congo, Benue-Congo, Bantoid, Southern, Narrow Bantu, Central, K, Kwangwa (K.40). Close to Kwangali and Mashi, but a separate language. Schools, administration, radio broadcasting. National language. Dictionary. Grammar. Radio programs. Traditional religion, Christian. NT 1986. See main entry under Namibia.

MBUNDA ***(CHIMBUNDA, MBUUNDA, GIMBUNDA, KIMBUNDA)*** [MCK] 126,000 in Zambia (1993 Johnstone), 1.5% of the population (1986). Population total both countries 226,000. Northern Barotseland, western Northwestern Province. Also spoken in Angola. Niger-Congo, Atlantic-Congo, Volta-Congo, Benue-Congo, Bantoid, Southern, Narrow Bantu, Central, K, Chokwe-Luchazi (K.20). Different from Mbunda (Mbuun, Mbunu) which is a dialect of Mpuono in DRC in the Yanzi group. NT 1983.

MWANGA ***(ICHINAMWANGA, NYAMWANGA, NAMWANGA, INAMWANGA)*** [MWN] 169,000 in Zambia (1993 Johnstone), 2% of the population, including 14,698 Iwa and 7,171 Tambo (1969 census). Population total both countries 256,000. Eastern Northern Province to Lake Rukwa. Also spoken in Tanzania. Niger-Congo, Atlantic-Congo, Volta-Congo, Benue-Congo, Bantoid, Southern, Narrow Bantu, Central, M, Nyika-Safwa (M.20). Dialects: IWA, TAMBO (TEMBO). Dialects listed are inherently intelligible. Bible 1982.

NKOYA ***(SHINKOYA)*** [NKA] 70,000 (1995 UBS). Mankoya area, Western and Southern provinces. Niger-Congo, Atlantic-Congo, Volta-Congo, Benue-Congo, Bantoid, Southern, Narrow Bantu, Central, L, Nkoya (L.50). Dialects: NKOYA, MBOWELA (MBWELA, MBWERA, SHIMBWERA), LUSHANGI, SHASHA, LUKOLWE, MASHASHA. Dialects listed are all inherently intelligible. NT 1936-1991.

NSENGA ***(CHINSENGA, SENGA)*** [NSE] 427,000 in Zambia (1993 Johnstone). Population total all countries 584,000. Petauke District, Eastern and Central provinces. Also spoken in Mozambique, Zimbabwe. Niger-Congo, Atlantic-Congo, Volta-Congo, Benue-Congo, Bantoid, Southern, Narrow Bantu, Central, N, Senga-Sena (N.40), Senga. Dialects: NSENGA, NGONI (MPEZENI). Distinct from Senga dialect of Tumbuka of Zambia, Malawi, and Tanzania. Christian, traditional religion. NT 1923.

NYANJA ***(CHINYANJA)*** [NYJ] 989,000 in Zambia (1993 Johnstone), 11.7% of the population (1986), including 196,640 Chewa, 256,588 Ngoni, 8,032 ChiKunda (1969 census). Eastern and Central provinces. Niger-Congo, Atlantic-Congo, Volta-Congo, Benue-Congo, Bantoid, Southern, Narrow Bantu, Central, N, Nyanja (N.30). Dialects: CHICHEWA (CHEWA, CEWA), PETA (CIPETA, CHIPETA,

MALAWI, MARAVI, MARAVE), CHINGONI (NGONI), MANGANJA (WAGANGA), NYASA, CHIKUNDA. Western dialect in Zambia. Chewa, Ngoni, and Kunda are completely intelligible with each other's speakers. It is recognized for educational and administrative purposes. The Kunda dialect is distinct from Kunda of Mozambique in the Senga-Sena group. Official language. Newspapers, radio programs. Bible 1905, in press (1997). See main entry under Malawi.

NYIHA ***(ISHINYIHA, NYIKA, NYIXA)*** [NIH] 320,000 in Zambia (1993 Johnstone). Northeastern Northern Province near the Malawi border, Isoka and Chama districts. Niger-Congo, Atlantic-Congo, Volta-Congo, Benue-Congo, Bantoid, Southern, Narrow Bantu, Central, M, Nyika-Safwa (M.20). Dialect: WANDYA. May constitute one language with Ichilambya of Tanzania and Malawi. Different from Nyika (Nika, Giryama) of Kenya. NT 1913-1966. See main entry under Tanzania.

SALA [SHQ] 20,400 or .3% of the population (1986). South central Central Province. Niger-Congo, Atlantic-Congo, Volta-Congo, Benue-Congo, Bantoid, Southern, Narrow Bantu, Central, M, Lenje-Tonga (M.60), Tonga. Reported to be intelligible with Tonga and possibly Ila.

SETTLA ***(KISETTLA, KISETLA)*** [STA] May also be in Kenya. Pidgin, Swahili based. A 'despised' pidgin (M. Adler 1977.50). Limited vocabulary and grammar. Second language only.

SHONA ***(CHISHONA)*** [SHD] 15,000 Goba in Zambia, and several thousand Shona in Mumbwe (1969). Mumbwa, Central Province. Goba dialect is near the Zimbabwe border. Niger-Congo, Atlantic-Congo, Volta-Congo, Benue-Congo, Bantoid, Southern, Narrow Bantu, Central, S, Shona (S.10). Dialect: KOREKORE (KORIKORI, MAKOREKORE, WAKORIKORI, NORTHERN SHONA, GOBA, GOVA, GOWA). Korekore is the main dialect in Zambia, with subdialect Goba. Bible 1949-1980. See main entry under Zimbabwe.

SIMAA [SIE] 74,800 or 1.1% of the population (1986), including 8,000 in Makoma (1977 Voegelin and Voegelin). Western Lozi-Luyana area, Western Province. Niger-Congo, Atlantic-Congo, Volta-Congo, Benue-Congo, Bantoid, Southern, Narrow Bantu, Central, K, Kwangwa (K.40). Dialects: SIMAA, MULONGA, IMILANGU, MWENYI, NYENGO, MAKOMA, LIYUWA. Imigangu may be a dialect of Luyana.

SOLI ***(CHISOLI)*** [SBY] 54,400 or .8% of the population (1986). Central Province, east of Lusaka. Niger-Congo, Atlantic-Congo, Volta-Congo, Benue-Congo, Bantoid, Southern, Narrow Bantu, Central, M, Lenje-Tonga (M.60), Tonga. A more distinct language or dialect of the Tonga group. Bible portions.

SUBIYA ***(SUBIA, SUPIA, ECHISUBIA, CHIKWAHANE, CHIKUAHANE)*** [SBS] 5,485 (1969 census). Southeastern corner of Western Province. Niger-Congo, Atlantic-Congo, Volta-Congo, Benue-Congo, Bantoid, Southern, Narrow Bantu, Central, K, Subia (K.50). Traditional religion, Christian. See main entry under Namibia.

TAABWA ***(RUNGU, ICHITAABWA, TABWA)*** [TAP] Northwestern Northern Province. Niger-Congo, Atlantic-Congo, Volta-Congo, Benue-Congo, Bantoid, Southern, Narrow Bantu, Central, M, Bemba (M.40). Dialect: SHILA. See main entry under DRC.

TONGA ***(CHITONGA, ZAMBEZI, PLATEAU TONGA)*** [TOI] 990,000 in Zambia (1993 Johnstone), 11.7% of the population (1986). Includes 427,031 Tonga, 11,994 Toka, 7,874 Leya. Population total both countries 1,105,000 or more. With Ila it predominates in the south, Southern and Western provinces. Also spoken in Zimbabwe. Niger-Congo, Atlantic-Congo, Volta-Congo, Benue-Congo, Bantoid, Southern, Narrow Bantu, Central, M, Lenje-Tonga (M.60), Tonga. Dialects: CHITONGA, LEYA, TOKA (SOUTHERN TONGA), WE (VALLEY TONGA), SHANJO (SANJO), TWA OF KAFWE, MALA. Recognized for educational and administrative purposes. Different from ChiTonga of Malawi, GiTonga of Mozambique, or Tsonga (Tonga) of Mozambique. Newspapers, radio programs. Bible 1963, in press (1997).

TOTELA ***(ECHITOTELA)*** [TTL] 14,000 in Zambia (1971 Welmers). Population total both countries 14,000 or more. Southeastern Western Province, north of Subia. Also spoken in Namibia. Niger-Congo, Atlantic-Congo, Volta-Congo, Benue-Congo, Bantoid, Southern, Narrow Bantu, Central, K, Subia (K.50).

TUMBUKA ***(TUMBOKA, CHITUMBUKA, TEW, TAMBUKA, TIMBUKA, TOMBUCAS)*** [TUW] 406,000 in Zambia (1993 Johnstone), 4.8% of the population (1986) including 33,666 Senga, 1,720 Yombe. Northeastern Eastern Province. Niger-Congo, Atlantic-Congo, Volta-Congo, Benue-Congo, Bantoid, Southern, Narrow Bantu, Central, N, Tumbuka (N.20). Dialects: CHITUMBUKA, CHIKAMANGA (KAMANGA, HENGA), KANDAWIRE, CHIPOKA, YOMBE, SENGA, FUNGWE, WENYA, NENYA, NGONI (MAGODI), FILILWA (FILIRWA), HEWE (HEWA), NTHALI. Senga dialect is distinct from Nsenga of Petauke District. Bible 1957-1980. See main entry under Malawi.

YAO ***(CHIYAO, CIYAO, ACHAWA, ADSAWA, ADSOA, AJAWA, AYAWA, CHICHAWA, AYO, DJAO, HAIAO, HIAO, HYAO, JAO, VEIAO, WAJAO)*** [YAO] An estimated 200 families or more in the 1970s (Dr. Felix Banda). Eastern Province, Chipata District, Kapata Township, and Katete District. Niger-Congo, Atlantic-Congo, Volta-Congo, Benue-Congo, Bantoid, Southern, Narrow Bantu, Central, P, Yao (P.20). Dialects: MAKALE (CIMAKALE), MASSANINGA (CIMASSANINGA). Bilingualism in

Nyanja/Chewa. Dictionary. Grammar. Workers for Asian merchants. Muslim. Bible 1920. See main entry under Malawi.

YAUMA [YAX] Southwest corner, Kwando River area. Unclassified. Bible portions 1978. See main entry under Angola.

ZAMBIAN SIGN LANGUAGE [ZSL] Deaf sign language.

ZIMBABWE

Republic of Zimbabwe. Formerly Rhodesia and Southern Rhodesia. National or official language: English. 11,377,000 (1998 UN). Literacy rate 49% to 76%. Also includes Afrikaans, Gujarati 19,000, people from Europe 90,000, possibly Bemba. Information mainly from J. Bendor-Samuel 1989. Christian, traditional religion, secular, Muslim. Blind population 15,000 (1982 WCE). Deaf institutions: 6. Data accuracy estimate: A2, B. The number of languages listed for Zimbabwe is 20. Of those, 19 are living languages and 1 is a second language without mother tongue speakers. Diversity index 0.56.

DOMBE [DOV] Hwange District, around Lukosi. Niger-Congo, Atlantic-Congo, Volta-Congo, Benue-Congo, Bantoid, Southern, Narrow Bantu, Central, M, Lenja-Tonga (M.60), Tonga. Related to Tonga [TOI], with Nambya influences. Speakers of Nambya appear to understand it, and vice versa. Investigation needed: intelligibility with Tonga.

ENGLISH [ENG] 375,490 in Zimbabwe (1969 census). Indo-European, Germanic, West, English. Spoken by most Europeans and an increasing number of Africans. Used in all or most education. Official language. Newspapers. Bible 1535-1989. See main entry under United Kingdom.

FANAGOLO *("FANAKALO", "FANEKOLO", PIKI, ISIPIKI, LOLOLO, ISILOLOLO, PIDGIN BANTU, "KITCHEN KAFFIR", "MINE KAFFIR", "ISIKULA")* [FAO] Several hundred thousand speakers (1975 Reinecke). Pidgin, Zulu based. Dialect: CHILAPALAPA. About 70% of the vocabulary comes from Zulu, 24% from English, 6% from Afrikaans. Influenced by Shona in Zimbabwe. Used widely in towns and mining areas. Trade language. Second language only. See main entry under South Africa.

HIETSHWARE *(HIECHWARE, CHWARE, SARWA, SESARWA, TSHUWAU, HAITSHUWAU)* [HIE] 1,600 in Zimbabwe (1972 Barrett). Khoisan, Southern Africa, Central, Tshu-Khwe, Northeast. Nomadic. Traditional religion, Christian. See main entry under Botswana.

KALANGA *(CHIKALANGA, KANANA, SEKALAÑA, KALANA, WESTERN SHONA, BAKAA, MAKALAKA, WAKALANGA)* [KCK] 161,000 in Zimbabwe (1993 P. Johnstone). Southwest of Bulawayo and along the Botswana border. Niger-Congo, Atlantic-Congo, Volta-Congo, Benue-Congo, Bantoid, Southern, Narrow Bantu, Central, S, Shona (S.10). Dialects: LILIMA (HUMBE, LIMIMA), NYAI (ABANYAI, BANYAI, WANYAI), PERI, TALAHUNDRA. Bilingualism in Ndebele. Rapidly being absorbed by Ndebele, though most rural members speak Kalanga. In the fall of 1985 the government introduced Kalanga primers into schools in the Kalanga area. Grammar. NT 1999. See main entry under Botswana.

KUNDA *(CHIKUNDA, CIKUNDA)* [KDN] 29,000 in Zimbabwe (1993 Johnstone). Population total all countries 100,000 (1971 Welmers). Along the Mwazam'tanda River. Also spoken in Mozambique, Zambia. Niger-Congo, Atlantic-Congo, Volta-Congo, Benue-Congo, Bantoid, Southern, Narrow Bantu, Central, N, Senga-Sena (N.40), Sena. Different from Kunda which is a dialect of Nyanja. Bible portions 1988.

LOZI *(SILOZI, ROZI, ROTVI, TOZVI, ROTSE, RUTSE, KOLOLO)* [LOZ] 70,000 in Zimbabwe (1982). Niger-Congo, Atlantic-Congo, Volta-Congo, Benue-Congo, Bantoid, Southern, Narrow Bantu, Central, S, Sotho-Tswana (S.30). Bible 1951-1987. See main entry under Zambia.

MANYIKA *(CHIMANYIKA, MANIKA, BAMANYEKA, WAMANYIKA, WANYIKA)* [MXC] 348,350 in Zimbabwe (1969 census). Population total both countries 450,000 or more. Manicaland Province and adjacent areas, northeast of Umtali. Also spoken in Mozambique. Niger-Congo, Atlantic-Congo, Volta-Congo, Benue-Congo, Bantoid, Southern, Narrow Bantu, Central, S, Shona (S.10). Dialects: BOCHA (BOKA), BUNJI, BVUMBA, DOMBA, GUTA, HERE, HUNGWE, JINDWI, KAROMBE, NYAMUKA, NYATWE, UNYAMA. A little more divergent from Shona than Karanga, Zezuru, and Korekore. At least partially intelligible with Shona. NT 1908.

NAMBYA *(CHINAMBYA, NANZVA, NAMBZYA)* [NMQ] 64,000 (1993 P. Johnstone). Primarily Hwange District of Matabeleland North, with some speakers having migrated south and west into Lupane and Binga districts. Some in Bulawayo. Niger-Congo, Atlantic-Congo, Volta-Congo, Benue-Congo, Bantoid, Southern, Narrow Bantu, Central, S, Shona (S.10). Slight pronunciation difference in Jambezi area: [Cwi] versus [Cu]. Closest to Kalanga, but unintelligible to each other's speakers without several weeks of living together. Ndebele is taught in school. Educated young people speak it with varying fluency. Older, uneducated people rarely speak or understand it. Both young and old mostly speak and understand Dombe. Those who have had contact with Tonga are also comfortable in it. Intermarriage with Tonga is common. Few first language speakers of Shona in Hwange District, it is dominant in print and electronic media, and similar to Nambya, so most Nambya understand it. Nyanja is commonly spoken and understood. Educated people have varying degrees of English ability, but few would choose to use English outside of school or work. Since Nambya is rarely written and not taught in school, educated young people will often choose Ndebele as their mode of communication, unless speaking to other Nambya. 'Nanzva' is the Ndebele name for Nambya. 'BaNyai' is a name for the people. Ndebele and English. RC church in Hwange carrying on literacy work. Christian. NT 1993.

NDAU ***(CHINDAU, NDZAWU, NJAO, SOUTHEAST SHONA, SOFALA)*** [NDC] 391,000 in Zimbabwe (1991). Population total both countries 891,000. South of Umtali, Melsetter, and adjacent areas. Also spoken in Mozambique. Niger-Congo, Atlantic-Congo, Volta-Congo, Benue-Congo, Bantoid, Southern, Narrow Bantu, Central, S, Shona (S.10). Dialects: CHANGA (CHICHANGA, CHIXANGA, SHANGA), GARWE, TONGA (ABATONGA, ATONGA, BATOKA, BATONGA, WATONGA). Close to Manyika, and much more divergent from Union Shona. In the fall of 1985 the government introduced Ndau primers into schools in the Ndau area. Traditional religion, Christian. Bible 1957.

NDEBELE ***(TABELE, TEBELE, ISINDE'BELE, SINDEBELE, NORTHERN NDEBELE)*** [NDF] 1,485,000 (1993 Johnstone). Population total both countries 1,502,000. Matabeleland, around Bulawayo. Also spoken in Botswana. Niger-Congo, Atlantic-Congo, Volta-Congo, Benue-Congo, Bantoid, Southern, Narrow Bantu, Central, S, Nguni (S.40). Close to Zulu. One of the main languages of Zimbabwe. Different from Ndebele of Transvaal, South Africa, which is related to Northern Sotho. Dictionary. Literacy rate in second language: 55%. Bible 1978.

NSENGA ***(CHINSENGA, SENGA)*** [NSE] 16,100 in Zimbabwe (1969 census). Niger-Congo, Atlantic-Congo, Volta-Congo, Benue-Congo, Bantoid, Southern, Narrow Bantu, Central, N, Senga-Sena (N.40), Senga. Different from Senga dialect of Tumbuka of Zambia, Malawi, and Tanzania. NT 1923. See main entry under Zambia.

NYANJA ***(CHINYANJA)*** [NYJ] 251,800 in Zimbabwe (1969 census). Niger-Congo, Atlantic-Congo, Volta-Congo, Benue-Congo, Bantoid, Southern, Narrow Bantu, Central, N, Nyanja (N.30). Bible 1905, in press (1997). See main entry under Malawi.

SHONA ***("SWINA", CHISHONA)*** [SHD] 6,225,000 in Zimbabwe (1989) including 2,250,000 Karanga (1993 Johnstone), 300,000 Korekore (1993 Johnstone), 1,800,000 Zezuru (1993 Johnstone), 1,262,870 Shona. Population total all countries 7,000,000 (1990 UBS). Mashonaland, central, and dispersed over many areas of the country. Also spoken in Botswana, Malawi, Zambia. Niger-Congo, Atlantic-Congo, Volta-Congo, Benue-Congo, Bantoid, Southern, Narrow Bantu, Central, S, Shona (S.10). Dialects: KARANGA (CHIKARANGA), ZEZURU (CHIZEZURU, BAZEZURU, BAZUZURA, MAZIZURU, VAZEZURU, WAZEZURU), KOREKORE (NORTHERN SHONA, GOBA, GOVA). Subdialects: Karanga: Duma, Jena, Mhari (Mari), Ngova, Nyubi, Govera; Korekore: Budya, Gova, Tande, Tavara, Nyongwe, Pfunde, Shan Gwe; Zezuru: Shawasha, Gova, Mbire, Tsunga, Kachikwakwa, Harava, Nohwe, Njanja, Nobvu, Kwazwimba (Zimba); Shona: Toko, Hwesa. Rozvi (Rozwi, Ruzwi, Chirozwi) speak Karanga dialect and do not have their own language. Ndau and Manyika are partially intelligible with Shona. Shona is the dominant African language of Zimbabwe and is understood by a considerable number. It is primarily a written language apparently based chiefly on Karanga and Zezuru with lexical items also from Manyika and Korekore. "Swina" is a derogatory name. Dictionary. Grammar. SVO. Roman. Used in primary education, mother tongue authored literature. Bible 1949-1980.

TONGA ***(CHITONGA, ZAMBEZI)*** [TOI] 112,000 in Zimbabwe (1993 Johnstone). Niger-Congo, Atlantic-Congo, Volta-Congo, Benue-Congo, Bantoid, Southern, Narrow Bantu, Central, M, Lenje-Tonga (M.60), Tonga. Dialects: CHITONGA, LEYA, TOKA, WE. Dialects or closely related languages: Lundwe, Mala. Different from ChiTonga of Malawi or Tonga of Mozambique. Bible 1963, in press (1997). See main entry under Zambia.

TSHWA ***(SHITSHWA, KITSHWA, XITSHWA, SHEETSHWA)*** [TSC] South. Niger-Congo, Atlantic-Congo, Volta-Congo, Benue-Congo, Bantoid, Southern, Narrow Bantu, Central, S, Tswa-Ronga (S.50). Dialects: HLENGWE (MAKAKWE-KHAMBANA), TSHWA (DZIBI-DZONGA). It is partially intelligible with Ronga and Tsonga. Bible 1910-1955. See main entry under Mozambique.

TSONGA ***(SHITSONGA, XITSONGA, THONGA, TONGA, GWAMBA)*** [TSO] Southeastern near Mozambique border. Niger-Congo, Atlantic-Congo, Volta-Congo, Benue-Congo, Bantoid, Southern, Narrow Bantu, Central, S, Tswa-Ronga (S.50). Dialects: BILA (VILA), CHANGANA (CHANGA, XICHANGANA, SHANGAAN, HLANGANU, HANGANU, LANGANU, SHILANGANU, SHANGANA), JONGA (DJONGA, DZONGA), NGWALUNGU (SHINGWALUNGU). 'Tsonga' is used to describe XiChangana, XiTswa, and XiRonga, although it is often used interchangeably with Changana, the most prestigious of the three. All are recognized as languages, although they are inherently intelligible. Dictionary. Grammar. Bible 1907-1989. See main entry under South Africa.

TSWANA ***(CHUANA, SECHUANA, COANA, CUANA, TSHWANA, BEETJUANS, CHWANA)*** [TSW] 29,350 in Zimbabwe (1969 census). Niger-Congo, Atlantic-Congo, Volta-Congo, Benue-Congo, Bantoid, Southern, Narrow Bantu, Central, S, Sotho-Tswana (S.30), Tswana. Dialects: NGWATU (MANGWATO), TLHAPING. Spoken by the Bakaka. Bible 1857-1993. See main entry under Botswana.

VENDA ***(CHIVENDA, CEVENDA, TSHIVENDA)*** [VEN] 84,000 in Zimbabwe (1989). South-southeast along South Africa border. Niger-Congo, Atlantic-Congo, Volta-Congo, Benue-Congo, Bantoid, Southern, Narrow Bantu, Central, S, Venda (S.20). Dialects: PHANI, TAVHATSINDI. Traditional religion, Christian. Bible 1936, in press (1997). See main entry under South Africa.

ZIMBABWE SIGN LANGUAGE ***(ZIMSIGN)*** [ZIB] Deaf sign language. Dialects: ZIMBABWE SCHOOL SIGN, MASVINGO SCHOOL SIGN, ZIMBABWE COMMUNITY SIGN. The sign language used in Masvingo is different from that used in other schools. The sign language used in schools and that used by adults outside is different. It is not clear if they are inherently intelligible to each other. There is some desire for standardization among educators. There are rumors of relationships to sign languages from Germany, Ireland, Australia, England, South Africa. Deaf people go to different schools, each using a different sign language. There have been elementary schools for deaf children since the 1940s. The Ministry of Education has pushed to open more spaces for deaf students in special classes in local schools. There is little research on the sign language. The deaf community is quite strong in terms of individual identity. They live their lives around deaf social networks and activities. There is a manual alphabet used for spelling English, possibly related to that in South Africa. Literacy in English is better among some deaf people than others, but generally limited. It is quite limited in Shona, mainly known by those from Masvingo. TV.

The Americas

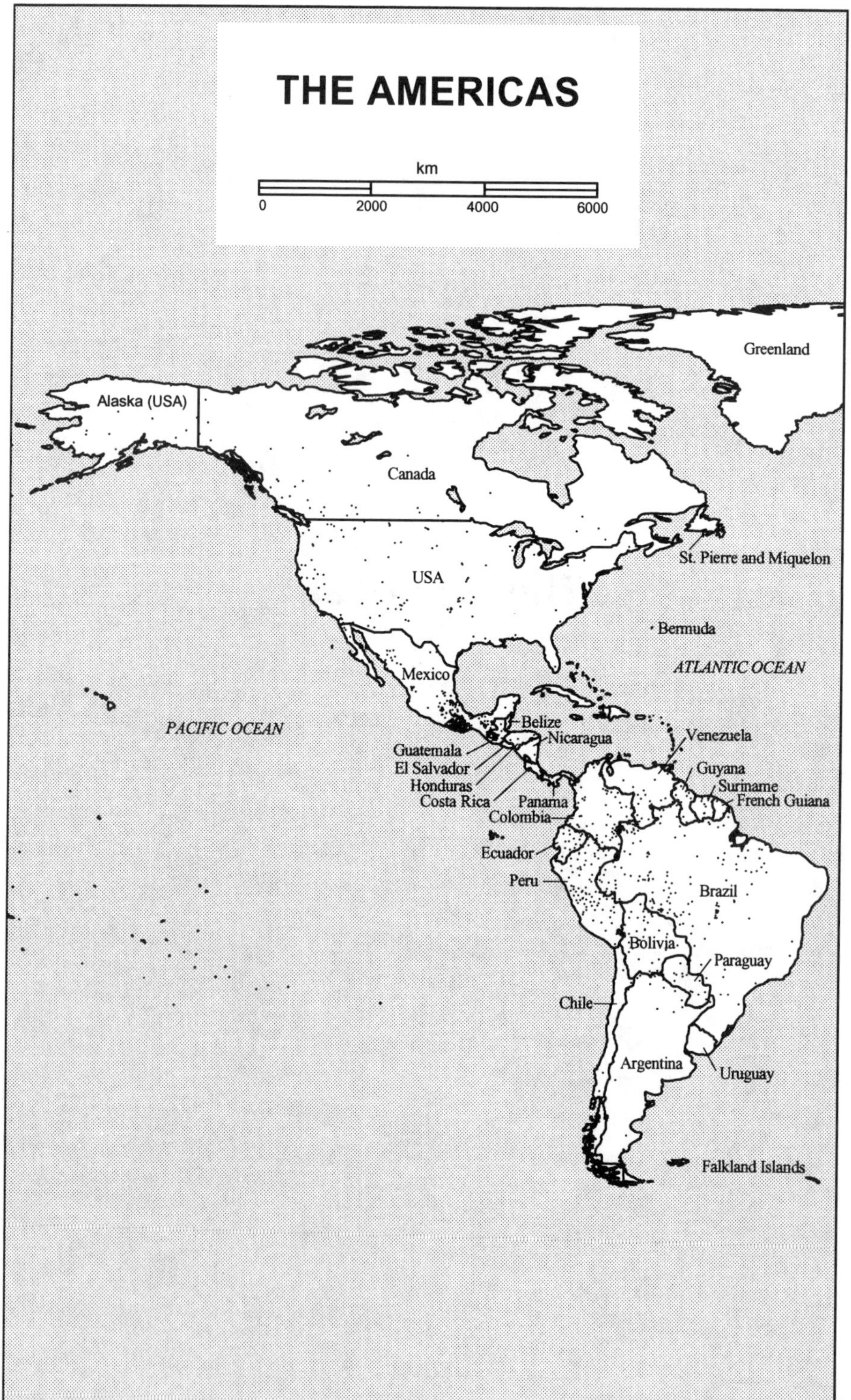

THE AMERICAS

km
0 2000 4000 6000

Greenland
Alaska (USA)
Canada
St. Pierre and Miquelon
USA
Bermuda
ATLANTIC OCEAN
Mexico
PACIFIC OCEAN
Belize
Nicaragua
Guatemala
El Salvador
Honduras
Costa Rica
Panama
Venezuela
Guyana
Suriname
French Guiana
Colombia
Ecuador
Peru
Brazil
Bolivia
Paraguay
Chile
Argentina
Uruguay
Falkland Islands

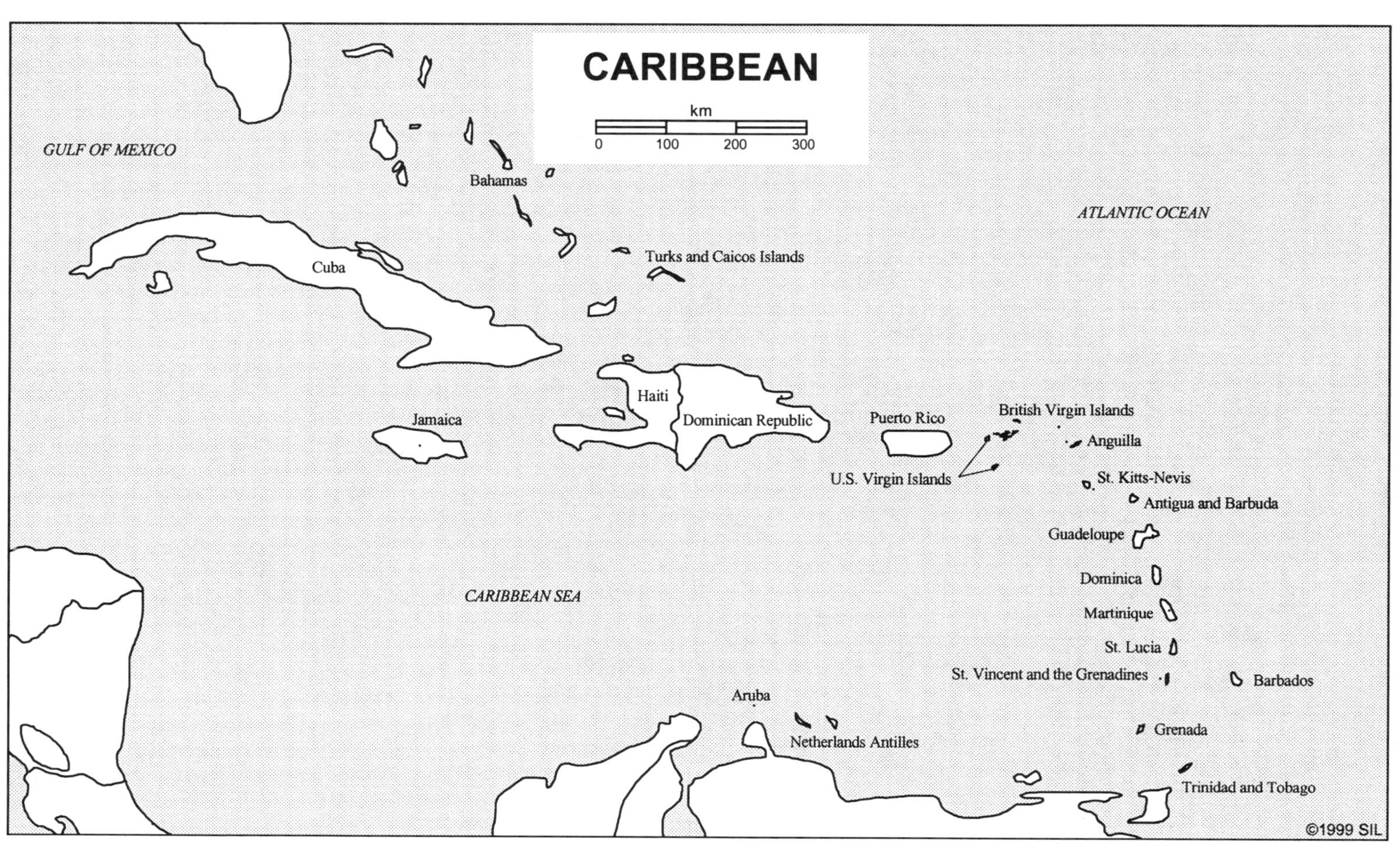
CARIBBEAN
km
0
100
200
300
GULF OF MEXICO
Bahamas
Cuba
Turks and Caicos Islands
ATLANTIC OCEAN
Haiti
Dominican Republic
Jamaica
Puerto Rico
British Virgin Islands
Anguilla
U.S. Virgin Islands
St. Kitts-Nevis
Antigua and Barbuda
Guadeloupe
Dominica
Martinique
St. Lucia
St. Vincent and the Grenadines
Barbados
CARIBBEAN SEA
Aruba
Netherlands Antilles
Grenada
Trinidad and Tobago
©1999 SIL

ANGUILLA

National or official language: English. 8,000 (1998 UN). Self governing part of British West Indies. Literacy rate 82% to 95%. Information mainly from J. Holm 1989; SIL 1977-99. Christian. Data accuracy estimate: A2. The number of languages listed for Anguilla is 2. Of those, both are living languages. Diversity index 0.00.

ENGLISH [ENG] Indo-European, Germanic, West, English. National language. Bible 1535-1989. See main entry under United Kingdom.

LEEWARD CARIBBEAN CREOLE ENGLISH [AIG] 7,000 in Anguilla (1998). Creole, English based, Atlantic, Eastern, Southern. Dialect: ANGUILLAN CREOLE ENGLISH. Reported to be close to the creoles of Antigua, St. Kitts, Nevis, Montserrat, and Barbuda (Holm 1989:450-1). Slightly intelligible with Jamaican and perhaps Bahamas creoles. Agriculturalists, fishermen. Christian. See main entry under Antigua and Barbuda.

ANTIGUA AND BARBUDA

National or official language: English. 67,000 (1998 UN), including 64,000 on Antigua, 1,200 on Barbuda (1997 govt. figures). Self governing part of British West Indies. Literacy rate 90%. Also includes North Levantine Spoken Arabic, Portuguese, people from India and Pakistan. Christian, traditional religion. Deaf institutions: 1. Data accuracy estimate: A2. The number of languages listed for Antigua and Barbuda is 2. Of those, both are living languages. Diversity index 0.00.

ENGLISH [ENG] Indo-European, Germanic, West, English. National language. Bible 1535-1989. See main entry under United Kingdom.

LEEWARD CARIBBEAN CREOLE ENGLISH [AIG] 65,100, including 64,000 in Antigua, 1,100 in Barbuda (1990). Population total all countries 120,370. Antigua and Barbuda. Also spoken in Anguilla, Dominica, Montserrat, St. Kitts-Nevis, United Kingdom. Creole, English based, Atlantic, Eastern, Southern. Dialects: ANTIGUAN CREOLE ENGLISH, BARBUDA CREOLE ENGLISH. Closest to Barbuda, St. Kitts, Montserrat, Nevis. Most villagers deny the existence of a creole, although they speak it. There is a creole continuum with Standard English. Agriculturalists: sugarcane.

ARGENTINA

Argentine Republic, República Argentina. National or official language: Spanish. 36,123,000 (1998 UN), including 100,000 to 150,000 American Indians (1997). Literacy rate 92% to 95%. Also includes North Levantine Spoken Arabic 1,000,000, South Levantine Spoken Arabic, Catalan-Valencian-Balear, Standard German 400,000, Paraguayan Guarani 200,000, Italian 1,500,000, Japanese 32,000, Lithuanian, Plautdietsch 140, Vlax Romani, Slovenian 10,000, Turoyo, Ukrainian, Welsh 25,000, Eastern Yiddish. Information mainly from A. Acebes 1966; A. Tovar 1961, 1966; SIL 1969-96; A. Buckwalter MEN 1981-83; Nick Drayson ANG 1982-84. Christian, Jewish, secular. Blind population 14,300 (1982 WCE) or 30,000 (1979 estimate). Deaf population 2,056,145. Deaf institutions: 17. Data accuracy estimate: B. The number of languages listed for Argentina is 26. Of those, 25 are living languages and 1 is extinct. Diversity index 0.21.

ARGENTINE SIGN LANGUAGE [AED] Deaf sign language. Deaf people go to different schools, each using a different sign language outside class. Sign language is not allowed in the classroom. Volunteer sign language interpreters are used at some important public events. There are sign language stories and drama on film. There is a committee for a national sign language, and organizations for sign language teachers and interpreters. Deaf schools were begun in 1885. Some research on the language. There is a manual alphabet for Spanish spelling. TV, videos.

AYMARA, CENTRAL [AYM] Aymaran. Quite a few have come from Bolivia looking for work. Sugar mill workers. Bible 1987-1993. See main entry under Bolivia.

CHANÉ [CAJ] Salta. Arawakan, Unclassified. Some have equated this name with 'Guana' (Kaskiha) of Paraguay of Mascoian affiliation, or Terena of Brazil of Arawakan affiliation, but they are distinct. The language has not been spoken for 300 years. Descendents are called 'Izoceño' and now speak a variety of Chiriguano (Eastern Bolivian Guaraní). Extinct.

CHIRIPÁ ***(TSIRIPÁ, TXIRIPÁ, NHANDEVA, ÑANDEVA, APYTARE)*** [NHD] Tupi, Tupi-Guarani, Guarani (I). Dialect: APAPOCUVA. Called 'Chiripá' in Paraguay, 'Nhandeva' in Brazil. 'Ñandeva' is used in the Paraguayan Chaco for the Tapiete. Bible portions 1991. See main entry under Paraguay.

CHOROTE, IYOJWA'JA ***(CHOROTI, YOFUAHA, EKLENJUY)*** [CRT] 800 all in Argentina (1982 Drayson ANG). Northeast Salta Province. Mataco-Guaicuru, Mataco. A distinct language from Iyo'wujwa Chorote (Drayson). Called 'Chorote' in Argentina, 'Choroti' in Paraguay, 'Eklenjuy' by the Chulupi. River dwellers. Traditional religion. NT 1997.

CHOROTE, IYO'WUJWA ***(CHOROTI, MANJUY, MANJUI)*** [CRQ] 1,500 in Argentina. Perhaps 50% monolinguals. Population total all countries 2,000. In Argentina they are mixed with the Iyojwa'ja Chorote. No more than a couple of families in Bolivia. Also spoken in Bolivia, Paraguay. Mataco-Guaicuru, Mataco. In Argentina all children have primary education in Spanish. Traditional religion. Bible portions 1992.

CHULUPÍ ***(CHURUPI, ASHLUSHLAY, CHULUPIE, CHULUPE, NIVAKLÉ, NIVACLÉ)*** [CAG] 200 in Argentina. Salta, northeast. Mataco-Guaicuru, Mataco. Dialects: FOREST CHULUPI, RIVER CHULUPI. Dialects are inherently intelligible. Traditional religion. Bible 1994. See main entry under Paraguay.

GUARANÍ, ARGENTINE, WESTERN ***(EASTERN BOLIVIAN GUARANÍ, "CHAWUNCU", "CHIRIGUANO")*** [GUI] 15,000 in Argentina. Jujuy, Salta. Tupi, Tupi-Guarani, Guarani (I). Dialects: CHANÉ, IZOCEÑO (IZOCENYO, ISOCENIO). Izoceño is a group that speaks a variety of this language. Chané is a group that formerly spoke an Arawakan language, but now speak a variety of Western Argentine Guaraní. 'Guarayo' is used in Argentina as a collective name; distinct from Guarayo of Bolivia. "Chawuncu", "Chabanco", "Chaguanco", "Chiriguano" are derogatory. Traditional religion. NT 1974. See main entry under Bolivia.

GUARANÍ, MBYÁ ***(MBUA, EASTERN ARGENTINA GUARANI, MBYÁ)*** [GUN] Northeast. Tupi, Tupi-Guarani, Guarani (I). Traditional religion. NT 1987. See main entry under Paraguay.

KAIWÁ ***(CAINGUA, CAIWÁ, KAYOVA)*** [KGK] 512 in Argentina. Northeast. Tupi, Tupi-Guarani, Guarani (I). 70% lexical similarity with Pai Tavytera of Paraguay. NT 1986. See main entry under Brazil.

MAPUDUNGUN ***(ARAUCANO, MAPUTONGO, MAPUCHE, MAPUDUNGU)*** [ARU] 40,000 or more in Argentina (1975 Golbert). Provinces of Neuquen, Rio Negro, Chubut, Buenos Aires, La Pampa. Araucanian. Dialect: PEHUENCHE. One or more dialects. Recent migration from Chile. NT 1997. See main entry under Chile.

MOCOVÍ ***(MOCOBÍ, MBOCOBÍ)*** [MOC] 3,000 to 4,000 (1981 Buckwalter). South Chaco, northeast Santa Fe. Mataco-Guaicuru, Guaicuruan. Traditional religion. NT 1988.

ONA ***(AONA, SELKNAM, SHELKNAM)*** [ONA] 1 to 3 speakers in Tierra del Fuego (1991 Adelaar). Patagonia, Tierra del Fuego. Also formerly in Chile. Chon. Bilingualism in Spanish. Steppe in the north, forest in the south. Island. Hunter-gatherers. Up to 800 meters. Nearly extinct.

PILAGÁ ***(PILACA)*** [PLG] 2,000 (1991 UBS). Along the valleys of the Bermejo and Pilcomayo rivers in central and western Formosa Province, Chaco and Salta Province. Mataco-Guaicuru, Guaicuruan. Dialects: TOBA-PILAGÁ (SOMBRERO NEGRO), CHACO PILAGÁ. Intelligibility between the dialects needs investigation. Traditional religion. NT 1993.

PUELCHE ***(GENNAKEN, PAMPA, NORTHERN TEHUELCHE)*** [PUE] 5 or 6 speakers. Extinct in Chile. Pampas. Language Isolate. Distinct from Pehuenche dialect of Mapudungun. Nearly extinct.

QUECHUA, NORTHWEST JUJUY ***(COLLA)*** [QUO] 5,000 possibly (1990 SIL). Northwest Jujuy Province, near the Bolivian border. Quechuan, Quechua II, C. Different from Santiago del Estero (R. Nardi). Probably intelligible with South Bolivian Quechua. Apparent high bilingualism in Spanish. Migratory. Investigation needed: intelligibility with South Bolivian Quechua, bilingual proficiency. SOV. Traditional religion.

QUECHUA, SOUTH BOLIVIAN ***(CENTRAL BOLIVIAN QUECHUA)*** [QUH] 850,000 in Argentina, including about 200,000 temporary laborers, about 100,000 looking for work, 500,000 living in Buenos Aires (1971 F. Hicks). Possibly 70,000 in Salta Province. Buenos Aires, some working on docks. Some in Salta Province. Quechuan, Quechua II, C. Bible 1986-1993. See main entry under Bolivia.

QUICHUA, SANTIAGO DEL ESTERO ***(SANTIAGUEÑO QUICHUA)*** [QUS] 60,000 (L. Stark). Santiago del Estero Province, north central Argentina, Departments of Figueroa, Moreno, Robles, Sarmiento, Brigadier J. F. Ibarra, San Martín, Silipica, Loreto, Atamisqui, Avellaneda, Salavina, Quebrachos, Mitre, Aguirre. Some in southeast Salta Province. Quechuan, Quechua II, C. Different from Bolivian (81% lexical similarity) or other Quechua (P. Landerman SIL 1968). Young men are becoming somewhat bilingual in Spanish because of serving in the armed forces; rural men are bilingual in Spanish; children are in Spanish language schools. Increased use by media, musical groups. There is a Chair of Quichua in the National University. Investigation needed: bilingual proficiency in Spanish. Dictionary. There is a decree authorizing promotion and teaching in schools. Radio programs. Agriculturalists, migrations to sugar cane harvest, cotton harvesters, carbon making industry.

SPANISH [SPN] 33,000,000 in Argentina (1995 estimate). Indo-European, Italic, Romance, Italo-Western, Western, Gallo-Iberian, Ibero-Romance, West Iberian, Castilian. National language. Bible 1553-1979. See main entry under Spain.

TAPIETÉ *(GUARAYO, GUASURANGUE, TIRUMBAE, YANAIGUA, ÑANAGUA)* [TAI] 100 in Argentina. Northeast, Tartagal, 1 village. Tupi, Tupi-Guarani, Guarani (I). See main entry under Paraguay.

TEHUELCHE *(AONIKEN, GUNUA-KENA, GUNUNA-KENA, INAQUEN)* [TEH] 30 (1983 Casamiquela, in Clairis). Patagonia. Chon. The people have come from Chile. Nearly extinct.

TOBA *(CHACO SUR, QOM, TOBA QOM)* [TOB] 15,000 to 20,000 in Argentina. Population total all countries 15,500 to 20,500. Eastern Formosa Province and Chaco Province. Also spoken in Bolivia, Paraguay. Mataco-Guaicuru, Guaicuruan. Dialects: SOUTHEAST TOBA, NORTHERN TOBA. Different from Toba of Paraguay (Toba-Maskoy) or Toba-Pilagá of Argentina. Traditional religion, Christian. NT 1980.

VILELA [VIL] Five families. Resistencia, east central Chaco province near Paraguay border. Lule-Vilela. Bilingualism in Toba. Any remaining Vilela are apparently being absorbed by the Toba or losing their Indian identity in the barrios of towns and cities (1981 Buckwalter). Nearly extinct.

WICHÍ LHAMTÉS GÜISNAY *("MATACO" GÜISNAY, GÜISNAY, "MATACO" PILCOMAYO, "MATACO")* [MZH] 15,000 (1999). Northern, Pilcomayo River area. Mataco-Guaicuru, Mataco. "Mataco" is derogatory. The self name of the people is 'Wichí'; the language 'Wichí Lhamtés'. Traditional religion.

WICHÍ LHAMTÉS NOCTEN *("MATACO" NOCTEN, NOCTEN, NOCTENES, OKTENAI)* [MTP] 100 in Argentina. Northern border down to Tartagal. Mataco-Guaicuru, Mataco. Traditional religion. See main entry under Bolivia.

WICHÍ LHAMTÉS VEJOZ *("MATACO" VEJOZ, VEJOS)* [MAD] Population total both countries 25,000 (1991 UBS). Northern area: Chaco, Formosa, Salta, Jujuy. Generally west of Toba, along upper Bermejo River Valley and Pilcomayo River. Also spoken in Bolivia. Mataco-Guaicuru, Mataco. Dialect: BERMEJO VEJOZ. Not intelligible with other Chaco languages. Bilingual level estimates for Spanish are 0 0%, 1 80%, 2-3 19%, 4-5 1%. Language family also called 'Mataco-Mataguayo'. Traditional religion. NT 1962-1993.

ARUBA

Aruba. National or official language: Dutch. 94,000 (1998 UN). Government has been autonomous since 1986 from Netherlands Antilles. By agreement of all parties, it remains part of the Kingdom of the Netherlands. Also includes Spanish, Sranan. Christian, Hindu, Muslim, Confucian, Jewish. The number of languages listed for Aruba is 3. Of those, all are living languages. Diversity index 0.00.

DUTCH [DUT] Indo-European, Germanic, West, Low Saxon-Low Franconian, Low Franconian. It is decreasing in importance. Official language. Bible 1522-1988. See main entry under Netherlands.

ENGLISH [ENG] Indo-European, Germanic, West, English. Dialect: ARUBA ENGLISH. The third most important language. Bible 1382-1989. See main entry under United Kingdom.

PAPIAMENTU *(PAPIAMENTO, PAPIAM, CURAÇOLEÑO, CURASSESE, PAPIAMENTOE)* [PAE] 70,000 in Aruba (1999 estimate). Creole, Iberian based. Three main dialects. The language is becoming more like Spanish, which is prestigious. Using both Papiamentu and Dutch is not considered an indication of lack of education. However, inability to use Dutch hinders social and political mobility, and leads to discontent. Bible 1997. See main entry under Netherlands Antilles.

BAHAMAS

The Commonwealth of the Bahamas. National or official language: English. 296,000 (1998 UN). 30 inhabited islands. Literacy rate 95% (1990). Also includes Greek 800, Haitian Creole French. Christian, secular, traditional religion. Deaf population 16,451. Deaf institutions: 2. Data accuracy estimate: A2. The number of languages listed for Bahamas is 3. Of those, 2 are living languages and 1 is extinct. Diversity index 0.01.

BAHAMAS CREOLE ENGLISH *(BAHAMIAN CREOLE ENGLISH, BAHAMIAN DIALECT)* [BAH] 225,000, or 86.5% of population (1987). Population total both countries 225,000 or more. Also spoken in USA. Creole, English based, Atlantic, Eastern, Northern. Intelligible with Sea Islands Creole good. Very close to Sea Islands Creole and Afro-Seminole of USA (Ian Hancock). The major differences with Sea Islands are in phonology, a few words, regional expressions, and a few grammatical differences (verbal markers). There is a spectrum of varieties from Standard USA English usage to the creole (Todd and Hancock 1986). Dictionary. Another orthography may be needed, since there were negative responses to the Sea Islands orthography presently in use. Christian.

ENGLISH [ENG] Indo-European, Germanic, West, English. National language. Bible 1535-1989. See main entry under United Kingdom.

TAINO [TNQ] Members of the ethnic group are also now in the USA, in Florida and New Jersey, in Puerto Rico, Santo Domingo, and Cuba. Arawakan, Maipuran, Northern Maipuran, Caribbean. They are bilingual in Spanish or English. The ethnic group now speak Spanish, or a Spanish-Taino mixed language, not understood by Spanish speakers. They estimate their present language to be 55% Taino and 45% Spanish. Extinct.

BARBADOS

National or official language: English. 268,000 (1998 UN). Literacy rate 98% to 99%. Christian, secular. Deaf institutions: 2. Data accuracy estimate: A2. The number of languages listed for Barbados is 2. Of those, both are living languages. Diversity index 0.09.

BAJAN ***(BARBADIAN CREOLE ENGLISH)*** [BJS] 259,000 (1995 estimate). Creole, English based, Atlantic, Eastern, Southern. There is a basilectal variety spoken in a fishing village (Roy 1986). The speech of the poor and less educated is similar to the mesolect in nearby countries. Increasingly influenced by USA rather than United Kingdom English (Todd and Hancock 1986). Fewer than 20 lexical items are traceable to African origin (Niles 1980:148). Shares lexical features with Caribbean creoles. Christian.

ENGLISH [ENG] 13,000 (1995). Indo-European, Germanic, West, English. National language. Bible 1535-1989. See main entry under United Kingdom.

BELIZE

National or official language: English. 230,000 (1998 UN). American Indians 11% (1991 census). Formerly British Honduras. Literacy rate 70%. Average years of schooling 7.53. Also includes North Levantine Spoken Arabic 187, Hindi 8,455, Caribbean Hindustani, Japanese, Korean, Chinese, Japanese, Korean. Information mainly from SIL 1973-99. Christian, traditional religion, Baha'i, Hindu, Muslim, other. Blind population 728 registered. Deaf population 12,671. Deaf institutions: 1. Data accuracy estimate: A1, A2. The number of languages listed for Belize is 8. Of those, all are living languages. Diversity index 0.70.

ENGLISH [ENG] Second language speakers: 55,998 in Belize (1991 census). Indo-European, Germanic, West, English. Used in education, government, and business. National language. Bible 1535-1989. See main entry under United Kingdom.

GARÍFUNA ***(CARIBE, CENTRAL AMERICAN CARIB, BLACK CARIB)*** [CAB] 12,274 in Belize (1991 census). Another estimate is 20,460 (1989). Stann Creek and Toledo along the coast. Arawakan, Maipuran, Northern Maipuran, Caribbean. Bilingualism in Creole. Dictionary. English-oriented orthography used in Belize, Spanish-oriented in Guatemala. NT 1983-1994. See main entry under Honduras.

KEKCHÍ ***(KETCHÍ, QUECCHÍ, CACCHÉ)*** [KEK] 9,000 in Belize (1995 SIL). Southern Belize. Mayan, Quichean-Mamean, Greater Quichean, Kekchi. Slightly different dialect from Guatemala, but comprehension of speakers is adequate. Bible 1990. See main entry under Guatemala.

MAYA, YUCATÁN ***(YUCATECO)*** [YUA] 5,000 in the ethnic group in Belize (1991). San Antonio and Succoths in Cayo District. It may still be spoken in the Orange Walk and Corozal districts near the Mexico border. Mayan, Yucatecan, Yucatec-Lacandon. Bilingualism in Spanish. Speakers in Belize are all older than 40. People in Succoths village say the older people speak Maya. They are concerned about language loss and are trying to start classes for the youth. Bible 1992. See main entry under Mexico.

MOPÁN MAYA ***(MAYA MOPÁN, MOPANE)*** [MOP] 7,000 to 7,750 in Belize. Population total both countries 9,600 to 10,350. Toledo, Stann Creek, and Cayo districts. Also spoken in Guatemala. Mayan, Yucatecan, Mopan-Itza. NT 1979.

NORTHERN CENTRAL AMERICA CREOLE ENGLISH [BZI] 55,051 first language speakers in Belize (1991 census). 158,000 including second language speakers (1990 estimate). Population total all countries 137,000 or more. Most live in Belize City, but nearly everyone else in Belize is either a first or second language speaker of Creole. Many of the rural villages are Creole-speaking. Creole people tend to live along the coast or other waterways. It is the lingua franca in much of the country. Also spoken in Colombia, Nicaragua, USA. Creole, English based, Atlantic, Western. Dialect: BELIZE CREOLE

ENGLISH (KRIOL, CREOLA). Reported to be very close to Miskito coast, Rama Cay, and Islander (San Andrés) creoles, Jamaican creole is different in grammar. Historically an extension of Miskito Coast Creole. Dahufra was a creole used in the 16th to 18th centuries. Spoken by creoles and people of East Indian descent, used everywhere in most areas of life. Used in advertisements. People have a positive attitude toward Creole. There is popular support for development. Dictionary. Jamaican creole is different in orthography. Newspapers, radio programs, TV. Timber, agriculturalists, fishermen, industrial workers, construction industry, business, commerce, government, teachers.

PLAUTDIETSCH ***(GERMAN, MENNONITE GERMAN)*** [GRN] 5,763 in Belize (1991 census), 4% of the population (1989 J. Holm). 110,735 or more in Latin America are fairly monolingual. Indo-European, Germanic, West, Low Saxon-Low Franconian, Low Saxon. 15% speak German, many speak English, and some speak Creole or Spanish as second language. Christian. NT 1987. See main entry under Canada.

SPANISH ***(ESPAÑOL, CASTELLANO)*** [SPN] 80,477 in Belize (1991 census). Northern and western districts, and scattered throughout the country. Indo-European, Italic, Romance, Italo-Western, Western, Gallo-Iberian, Ibero-Romance, West Iberian, Castilian. Radio programs, TV. Bible 1553-1979. See main entry under Spain.

BERMUDA

National or official language: English. 64,000 (1998 UN). 66% of African descent. British dependency. Literacy rate 97% to 99%. Christian. Data accuracy estimate: A2. The number of languages listed for Bermuda is 1. Diversity index 0.00.

ENGLISH [ENG] 58,800 in Bermuda (1989 estimate). Indo-European, Germanic, West, English. Dialect: BERMUDAN ENGLISH. Colloquial English may not be a creole but a regional variety of uncreolized English. National language. Bible 1535-1989. See main entry under United Kingdom.

BOLIVIA

Republic of Bolivia, República de Bolivia. National or official language: Spanish. 7,957,000 (1998 UN). Literacy rate 63% to 81%. Also includes Corsican 60,000, Standard German 160,000, Wichi Lhamtes Vejoz. Information mainly from SIL 1956-99. Christian, Baha'i, traditional religion, secular. Blind population 1,070. Deaf population 46,800. Deaf institutions: 9 or more. Data accuracy estimate: A2. The number of languages listed for Bolivia is 44. Of those, 37 are living languages, 1 is a second language without mother tongue speakers, and 6 are extinct. Diversity index 0.68.

ARAONA ***(CAVINA)*** [ARO] 87 (1994 H. Petersen NTM). Northwest, headwaters of Manupari River. Tacanan, Araona-Tacana, Araona. Knowledge of Spanish is increasing. All ages. Vigorous. Araona and Cavina are names of two moieties of the group. Dictionary. SOV. Bible portions 1974-1981.

AYMARA, CENTRAL [AYM] 1,785,000 in Bolivia (1987), 23.7% of the population. Population total all countries 2,200,000. Whole Altiplano west of eastern Andes. Some migration to the yungas and the lowlands. Also spoken in Argentina, Chile, Peru. Aymaran. Dictionary. Grammar. Churches are active in literacy. Openings in government schools for the use of Aymara literature. Radio programs. Traditional religion, Christian. Bible 1987-1993.

AYOREO ***(AYORÉ, MOROTOCO, MORO, PYETA, YOVAI)*** [AYO] 1,000 to 1,500 in Bolivia. Southeastern region. Zamucoan. Dialect: TSIRICUA. Called 'Morotoco' in Paraguay and Ayoreo in Bolivia. NT 1982. See main entry under Paraguay.

BAURE [BRG] Few speakers. More than 300 in the ethnic group. Beni Department, northwest of Magdalena. Arawakan, Maipuran, Southern Maipuran, Bolivia-Parana. Bilingualism in Spanish. Children and most adults were not using Baure 20 years ago. Nearly extinct. Bible portions 1960-1966.

BOLIVIAN SIGN LANGUAGE [BVL] 350 to 400 users (1988 E. Powlison). Cochabamba, La Paz, Riberalta, Santa Cruz. Deaf sign language. Based on American Sign Language with necessary changes for Spanish spelling. Some groups in La Paz and Santa Cruz use the same signs with some dialect signs from their own areas. Originated by missionaries. Other deaf schools use only the oralist approach. Investigation needed: intelligibility with American Sign Language.

CALLAWALLA ***(CALLAHUAYA)*** [CAW] 10 or 20 (1995 estimate SIL). Highlands and high valleys, eastern Andes north of La Paz, Charazani area north of Lake Titicaca. Unclassified. Their language seems to have Quechua affixes and syntactic patterns, but distinctive roots from a dialect of the extinct Puquina language (Girault 1990). Bilingualism in North Bolivia Quechua, Aymara, Spanish. Women and children do not speak Callawalla, but speak Spanish, North Bolivia Quechua, or

Aymara. Spoken only by the men. A special language used by the herb doctors of the Inca emperors; they continue as herb doctors. Second language only.

CANICHANA ***(KANICHANA)*** [CAZ] There may be 500 in the ethnic group (1991 Adelaar). Lowlands. Unclassified. Said to be of the Tucanoan family. Extinct.

CAVINEÑA [CAV] 2,000 (1995 MES). Northern Bolivia, southeast of Riberalta, along the Beni River, east of the Beni, and 500 in the Pando on the west side of the Beni. Tacanan, Araona-Tacana, Cavinena-Tacana, Cavinena. Bilingual level estimates for Spanish are 0 40%, 1 25%, 2 15%, 3 10%, 4 5%, 5 5%. Becoming increasingly bilingual in Spanish. 500 children in school (1995). High school in Galilea has 135 students and 15 teachers. Dictionary. SOV. Rubber and castaña nut gatherers, agriculturalists. NT 1985.

CAYUBABA ***(CAYUWABA, CAYUVAVA)*** [CAT] There may be 900 in the ethnic group (1991 W. H. Adelaar). Beni Department, west of Mamore River, north of Santa Ana. Language Isolate. Ruhlen and others classify it as Equatorial. Bilingualism in Spanish. The ethnic group speaks Spanish. Extinct.

CHÁCOBO [CAO] 520 (1994 MES). Northwest Beni, south of Riberalta. Panoan, Southern. Spanish bilingual schools have about 180 students, 4 teachers, 5 grades. 3 of the teachers are Chácobo. 50% are monolingual. NT 1979.

CHIPAYA [CAP] 2,000 (1995 R. Olson SIL). Department of Oruro, Province of Atahuallpa. Uru-Chipaya. May be Arawakan or distantly related to Mayan. Previously bilingualism was mainly in Aymara, now in Spanish. 400 children in school. 5% are monolingual. Now have a complete high school. SOV. Plains. Agriculturalists: grain; animal husbandry: sheep, llamas. 12,000 feet. Christian, traditional religion (8 to 10 families). NT 1978.

CHIQUITANO ***(CHIQUITO, TARAPECOSI)*** [CAX] 20,000 (1981 SIL) to 42,000 (1991 Adelaar). Eastern region east of Santa Cruz. Macro-Ge, Chiquito. Dialects: CONCEPCIÓN, SAN IGNACIO DE VELAZCO, SAN JAVIER (JAVIERANO, XAVIERANO), SANTIAGO, SAN MIGUEL. VO. Sedentary agriculturalists. Traditional religion, Christian. NT 1980.

CHOROTE, IYO'WUJWA ***(CHOROTI, MANJUY, MANJUI)*** [CRQ] No more than a couple of families in Bolivia (1982). Southeast, Tarija Department. Mataco-Guaicuru, Mataco. Estimated 80% monolingual. Bible portions 1992. See main entry under Argentina.

ESE EJJA ***(ESE EJA, ESE EXA, TIATINAGUA, "CHAMA", HUARAYO)*** [ESE] 600 to 650 in Bolivia (1976 SIL). Population total both countries 850 to 1,050. Northwestern region, and into the foothills on the Beni and Madre de Dios rivers in Bolivia, Tambopata and Heath rivers around Puerto Maldonado in Peru. Also spoken in Peru. Tacanan, Tiatinagua. Each clan has slight dialect differences; all seem inherently intelligible. Appears the most different from other Tacanan languages. Bilingual level estimates for Spanish are 0 40%, 1 20%, 2 30%, 3 10%, 4 0%, 5 0%. The name "Chama" is objectionable. Dictionary. SOV. NT 1984.

GUARANÍ, BOLIVIAN, EASTERN ***("CHIRIGUANO")*** [GUI] 15,000 in Bolivia. Population total all countries 32,000. South central Parapeti River area, Tarija. Also spoken in Argentina, Paraguay. Tupi, Tupi-Guarani, Guarani (I). Dialect: IZOCEÑO (IZOCENIO). Called 'Guarayo' in Paraguay and 'Guaraní Occidental', "Chiriguano", or "Chawuncu" in Argentina. "Chawuncu" and "Chiriguano" are derogatory names. Grammar. Radio programs. Tropical forest. Interfluvial. Swidden agriculturalists. Traditional religion, Christian. NT 1974.

GUARANÍ, BOLIVIAN, WESTERN ***(SIMBA, SIMBA GUARANÍ)*** [GNW] 5,000 or more (1995 R. Olson SIL). Chuquisaca Department, south to Pilcomayo River, east to Cuevo, north to Monte Agudo. Tupi, Tupi-Guarani, Guarani (I). Traditional religion, Christian. NT 1984.

GUARAYU ***("GUARAYO")*** [GYR] 7,000 to 8,000 (1995 R. Olson SIL). Northeastern Guarayos River area. Tupi, Tupi-Guarani, Guarayu-Siriono-Jora (II). Different from Guarayo of Paraguay (which is the same as Chiriguano) or Huarayo (Ese Ejja) of Peru and Bolivia. The name "Guarayo", used for several groups, means 'savage'. 950 children in school in Urubicha. 31 of 34 teachers are Guarayu (1995). SOV. Tropical forest. Traditional religion, Christian. NT 1985.

IGNACIANO ***(MOXO, MOXOS, MOJOS)*** [IGN] 4,000 (1982 SIL). South central Beni. Arawakan, Maipuran, Southern Maipuran, Bolivia-Parana. Bilingual level estimates for Spanish are 0 25%, 1 20%, 2 44%, 3 19%, 4 2%, 5 0%. Dictionary. Tropical forest, savannah. NT 1980.

ITENE ***(ITENEO, ITENEZ, MORE)*** [ITE] (100 in ethnic group in 1959). North central Beni Department at junction of Mamoré and Itenez rivers. Chapacura-Wanham, Guapore. Dialect: ITOREAUHIP. Children were not speaking Itene and only some of the older people were actively using it 30 years ago. They speak Spanish. Related languages: Chapacura, Quitemoca, Cujuna, Cumana, Mataua, Uanham, Urunumacan; probably all extinct. Extinct.

ITONAMA ***(MACHOTO, SARAMO)*** [ITO] (110 in ethnic group in 1969). Beni Department and Itonamas River. Language Isolate. Bilingualism in Spanish. Only a few speakers 25 years ago. Ruhlen classifies it as Paezan. Dictionary. Nearly extinct. Bible portions 1967.

JORÁ ***(HORA)*** [JOR] Tupi, Tupi-Guarani, Guarayu-Siriono-Jora (II). Has become extinct since 1963. Adelaar reports 5 to 10 speakers (1991). Extinct.

LECO [LEC] Some speakers out of possibly 200 in the ethnic group (1996 W. Adelaar). East of Lake Titicaca, some in Apolo area, scattered families. Unclassified. Reported to be Quechuan. Preserve some folklore, dances, and music. Reported to be recently extinct linguistically. Nearly extinct.

MOVIMA [MZP] Few speakers, probably 1,000 in ethnic group (1976 SIL). Central Beni Department, in and around Santa Ana on the Yacuma River. Unclassified. Bilingualism in Spanish. A few older people along the rivers may speak Movima. Reported to be Tucanoan. Dictionary. Nearly extinct. Bible portions 1967.

PACAHUARA ***(PACAWARA)*** [PCP] Individuals in one family (1986 SIL). Northwest Beni. Panoan, Southern. All are integrated into the Chácobo. Tropical forest. Rubber gatherers. Nearly extinct.

PAUSERNA ***(PAU CERNE, GUARAYU-TA, PAUSERNA-GUARASUGWÉ)*** [PSM] 25 to 30 (1991 Adelaar). Southeast Beni on Guapore River. Tupi, Tupi-Guarani, Pauserna. Elderly speakers. Nearly extinct.

PLAUTDIETSCH ***(GERMAN, MENNONITE GERMAN)*** [GRN] 28,567 in Bolivia (1996 editor, Menno-Bote). Indo-European, Germanic, West, Low Saxon-Low Franconian, Low Saxon. 6% speak Spanish or Standard German as second language. Christian. NT 1987. See main entry under Canada.

QUECHUA, NORTH BOLIVIAN ***(NORTH LA PAZ QUECHUA)*** [QUL] 116,483 in Bolivia, including 18,452 monolinguals, 65,649 bilinguals in Spanish, 32,382 trilinguals in Aymara and Spanish (1978 census). Population total both countries 116,500 or more. Apolo region, La Paz Department. Also spoken in Peru. Quechuan, Quechua II, C. Dialects: APOLO, CHARAZANI, CHUMA. SOV. Radio programs. NT 1985.

QUECHUA, SOUTH BOLIVIAN ***(CENTRAL BOLIVIAN QUECHUA, QUECHUA BOLIVIANO)*** [QUH] 2,782,500 in Bolivia, 37.1% of the population (1987). Population total both countries 3,632,500. Highland regions and lowland except around Apolo. Also spoken in Argentina. Quechuan, Quechua II, C. Dialects: SUCRE, COCHABAMBA, ORURO, POTOSÍ, CHUQUISACA. May be intelligible with Chilean Quechua, and Northwest Jujuy Quechua in Argentina. Dictionary. SOV. Traditional religion, Christian. Bible 1986-1993.

REYESANO ***(SAN BORJANO)*** [REY] There are perhaps 1,000 members of the ethnic group. Beni Department, west central around San Borja, near Reyes. Tacanan, Araona-Tacana, Cavinena-Tacana, Tacana Proper. There were a few speakers in 1961, including some children. Nearly extinct.

SARAVECA [SAR] Eastern jungle. Arawakan, Maipuran, Central Maipuran. Extinct.

SHINABO [SHN] Panoan, Southern. Existence improbable; contact has been attempted several times. Thought to have possibly been a Chácobo group. Extinct.

SIRIONÓ [SRQ] 500. Eastern Beni and northwestern Santa Cruz Departments. Tupi, Tupi-Guarani, Guarayu-Siriono-Jora (II). 5% to 10% are monolingual, others use Spanish as second language. Dictionary. NT 1977.

SPANISH [SPN] 3,483,700 in Bolivia (1995 estimate). Indo-European, Italic, Romance, Italo-Western, Western, Gallo-Iberian, Ibero-Romance, West Iberian, Castilian. National language. Bible 1553-1979. See main entry under Spain.

TACANA [TNA] 3,500. Beni and Madre de Dios rivers, jungle, some in foothills. Tacanan, Araona-Tacana, Cavinena-Tacana, Tacana Proper. Bilingualism in Spanish. Dictionary. Grammar. NT 1981.

TAPIETÉ ***(GUASURANGO, TIRUMBAE, YANAIGUA, ÑANAGUA)*** [TAI] 40 in Bolivia (1981 J. Alvarsson SFM). Southeast, towns of Samayhuate and Cutaiqui. Tupi, Tupi-Guarani, Guarani (I). Same as Guasurango in Paraguay. See main entry under Paraguay.

TOBA ***(QOM)*** [TOB] 100 possibly in Bolivia. Mataco-Guaicuru, Guaicuruan. Different from Toba-Pilagá of Argentina or Toba of Paraguay (Toba-Maskoy). NT 1980. See main entry under Argentina.

TOROMONO ***(TOROMONA)*** [TNO] Northwest, close to the Araona. Tacanan, Araona-Tacana, Cavinena-Tacana, Tacana Proper. They have not been located. May not still exist.

TRINITARIO ***(MOXOS, MOJOS)*** [TRN] 5,000. South central Beni. Arawakan, Maipuran, Southern Maipuran, Bolivia-Parana. Dialects: LORETO (LORETANO), JAVIERANO. NT 1979.

TSIMANÉ ***(CHIMANÉ, MOSETÉN)*** [CAS] 5,500 including 500 speakers of Mosetén. Southwestern Beni Department and along Maniqui River, and towns of San Miguel de Huachi and Santa Ana de Alto Beni. Mosetenan. Adelaar (1991) considers Mosetén and Tsimané to be 2 separate languages. Fishermen; swidden agriculturalists: bananas, manioc; hunters. Bible portions 1963-1986.

URU ***(MORATO, MURATU)*** [URE] In 1965 there were 5 to 10 (1998 R. Olson SIL). Department of Oruro, Province of Atahuallpa, near Lake Titicaca, near where the Desaguadero River comes out of Titicaca, near Iruitu. Uru-Chipaya. Bilingualism in Spanish, Aymara. A few older people 20 years ago. The others were assimilated to Spanish or Central Aymara. Those at the south end of Lake Poopo spoke only Aymara and Spanish 15 years ago. May be extinct. Nearly extinct.

WICHÍ LHAMTÉS NOCTEN ***("MATACO" NOCTEN, OKTENAI, NOCTEN, NOCTENES, BOLIVIAN "MATACO")*** [MTP] 1,427 in Bolivia (1978 SFM). Population total both countries 1,530 or more. North central Tarija Department, southwest of Pilcomayo River, Cordillera de Pirapo. Also spoken in Argentina. Mataco-Guaicuru, Mataco.

YAMINAHUA ***(YAMINAWA, JAMINAWA, YAMANAWA)*** [YAA] 150 in Bolivia (1976 SIL). Northwest corner Pando Department. Panoan, South-Central, Yaminahua-Sharanahua. Same dialect or close to that of Peru and Brazil. They came from Brazil. Bible portions 1987. See main entry under Peru.

YUQUI [YUQ] 155 (1996 NTM). Foothills north of Cochabamba, one location on the Chimoré River. Tupi, Unclassified. Nomadic. Bible portions.

YURACARE ***(YURA)*** [YUE] 500 to 2,500 speakers (1991 Adelaar) including 3,000 in the ethnic group (1996 NTM). Beni and Cochabamba departments, scattered primarily along the Chapare River. Language Isolate. Dialects: MANSINYO, SOLOTO. Bible portions 1956-1965.

BRAZIL

Federative Republic of Brazil. República Federativa do Brasil. National or official language: Portuguese. 165,851,000 (1998 UN), including 311,656 American Indians (1995 govt. figure). 155,000 speakers of American Indian languages (Rodrigues 1985). There are reports of up to 34 groups without peaceful contact. Literacy rate 76% (1989 WA). Also includes Assyrian Neo-Aramaic, Catalan-Valencian-Balear, Irish Gaelic, Standard German 1,500,000, Italian 500,000, Japanese 380,000, Korean 37,000, Latvian, Lithuanian, Vlax Romani, Turoyo, Ukrainian. Information mainly from D. Ribeiro 1957; A. Rodrigues 1958; J. Hopper 1967; A. Jensen 1985; D. Derbyshire and G. Pullum 1986; SIL 1957-1999. Christian, traditional religion, secular. Blind population 124,805. Deaf population 9,624,345. Deaf institutions: 60. Data accuracy estimate: A2, B. The number of languages listed for Brazil is 234. Of those, 192 are living languages and 42 are extinct. Diversity index 0.03.

ACROÁ ***(COROÁ)*** [ACS] Bahia area. Macro-Ge, Ge-Kaingang, Ge, Central. Extinct.

AGAVOTAGUERRA ***(AGAVOTOKUENG, AGAVOTOQUENG)*** [AVO] 100 (1986 SIL). Mato Grosso, Xingú Park, between the Curisevo and Culuene rivers, near the Kuikúro. Unclassified. May be Arawakan, related to Waurá and Yawalapiti.

AKAWAIO ***(ACEWAIO, AKAWAI, ACAHUAYO, INGARIKÓ)*** [ARB] 500 in Brazil. Roraima and Rio Branco. Carib, Northern, East-West Guiana, Macushi-Kapon, Kapon. Close to Macushi and Arecuna. Not intelligible with Macushi. Limited bilingualism. Bible portions 1873. See main entry under Guyana.

AMAHUACA ***(AMAWÁKA, AMAWACA, AMENGUACA, SAYACU)*** [AMC] 220 in Brazil (1995). Amazonas. Panoan, South-Central, Amahuaca. Dialects: INUVAKEN, VIWIVAKEU. Investigation needed: intelligibility, bilingual proficiency in Portuguese. Bible portions 1963-1997. See main entry under Peru.

AMANAYÉ ***(AMANAJÉ, MANAZE, AMANAGE, MANAXO, MANAJO, MANAZO, AMANYÉ)*** [AMA] 66 or fewer (1995 SIL). Pará. Tupi, Tupi-Guarani, Oyampi (VIII). Bilingualism in Portuguese. Integrated culturally and linguistically to Portuguese.

AMAPÁ CREOLE ***(LANC-PATÚA)*** [AMD] 25,000 (1995 SIL). Throughout State of Amapá, concentrated around the capital, Macapá. Creole, French based. Has English and French influences. Some Indian groups in Amapá speak other creoles, like the Karipuna.

AMIKOANA [AKN] A few. Northern Amapá. Unclassified.

AMONDAWA ***(AMUNDAWA, AMUNDAVA)*** [ADW] 50 (1994 SIL). Rondônia. Tupi, Tupi-Guarani, Kawahib (VI). Similar to Tenharim.

ANAMBÉ [AAN] 7 active speakers (1991 SIL) out of an ethnic group of 77 (1993 SIL). Pará. Tupi, Tupi-Guarani, Oyampi (VIII). Close to Asuriní. Some monolinguals. Most are bilingual in, and switching to, Portuguese. Some Brazilians who have intermarried with Anambé have learned Anambé. Nearly extinct.

APALAÍ ***(APARAI, APALAY)*** [APA] 450 (1993 SIL). Pará, mainly on the Paru Leste River with fringe groups on the Jari and Citare rivers. 20 villages. Carib, Northern, East-West Guiana, Wayana-Trio. 75% bilingual in Wayana, 25% monolingual. Dictionary. Grammar. OVS, SOV. Literacy rate in first language: 10% to 30%. Literacy rate in second language: 37%. NT 1986.

APIACÁ ***(APIAKE, APIAKÁ)*** [API] 40 to 70 (1998 SIL). Northern Mato Grosso, upper Rio Tapajos, near confluence of São Manoel. Tupi, Tupi-Guarani, Kawahib (VI). Bilingualism in Portuguese. Assimilated into Brazilian culture. Voegelin and Voegelin (1977) treat Carib Apiacá as distinct.

APINAYÉ ***(APINAJÉ, APINAGÉ)*** [APN] 800 (1994 SIL). Tocantins, near Tocantinópolis, 6 villages. Macro-Ge, Ge-Kaingang, Ge, Northwest, Apinaye. People are somewhat bilingual. Grammar. SOV. Literacy rate in first language: 5% to 10%. Literacy rate in second language: 15% to 25%. Between tropical forest and savannah. Hunter-gatherers, agriculturalists: manioc, sweet potatoes, gourds, cotton. Bible portions 1967-1989.

APURINÃ ***(IPURINÃN, KANGITE, POPENGARE)*** [APU] 2,000 (1994 SIL). Amazonas, Acre; scattered over a thousand miles of the Purus River from Rio Branco to Manaus. Arawakan, Maipuran, Southern Maipuran, Purus. OSV. Traditional religion, Christian. Bible portions 1993.

ARAPASO ***(ARAPAÇO, ARASPASO, KONEÁ)*** [ARJ] 268 (1992 ALEM). São Gabriel, Iauarete, Amazonas. Tucanoan, Eastern Tucanoan, Northern. Reported to be a dialect of Tucano. Bilingualism in Tucano. May only speak Tucano. Investigation needed: intelligibility, bilingual proficiency in Tucano.

ARÁRA, ACRE [AXA] 130 to 200 (1998 SIL). Acre, municipality of Cruziero do Sul, on Rio Humaitá off the Juará River. Panoan, Unclassified. May be a dialect of Panoan Katukina, or the same as Sharanahua in Peru.

ARÁRA, MATO GROSSO ***(ARARA DO BEIRADÃO, ARARA DO RIO BRANCO)*** [AXG] Ethnic group has 100 (1998). Mato Grosso. Unclassified. Members of the ethnic group speak only Portuguese. Extinct.

ARÁRA, PARÁ ***(AJUJURE)*** [AAP] 110 (1994 SIL). Pará in 2 villages. Carib, Northern, Northern Brazil. The closest extant languages are Txikão and Bakairí. A few can speak a little Portuguese. There are uncontacted groups. Hunter-gatherers, fishermen.

ARÁRA, RONDÔNIA ***(ARÁRA DO JIPARANÁ)*** [ARR] 92 (1986 SIL). Rondônia, Acre. Tupi, Ramarama. A separate language. Bilingualism is limited.

ARAWETÉ [AWT] 184 (1994 ALEM). Amazonas, at least one sizeable village, near Xingú River, near Altamira. Tupi, Tupi-Guarani, Kayabi-Arawete (V). Close to Asuriní, Parakanã, and Tapirapé. Nearly all speakers are monolingual (1986).

ARIKAPÚ ***(MAXUBÍ, ARICAPÚ)*** [ARK] 6 (1998 SIL). Rondônia, headwaters of the Rio Branco, tributary of the right bank of the Guaporé. Macro-Ge, Yabuti. Similar to Jabuti. Bilingualism in Portuguese. Integrated into Brazilian culture and language. Nearly extinct.

ARUA ***(ARAWÁ)*** [ARA] Arauan. Became extinct in 1877. Known from an 1869 word list. Different from Tupi Aruá and Ge Arua. Extinct.

ARUÁ [ARX] 12 (1990 YWAM). Rio Branco post, Rondônia. Tupi, Monde. Dialect: ARUÁSHI (ARUACHI). A few still remember the language. Most speak Portuguese. Said to be many in Mato Grosso. Voegelin and Voegelin treat as distinct from Arawak Arua (Aruan, Araua) and Ge Arua. Nearly extinct.

ARUMA ***(WAPITXÁNA, WAPISIANA, VAPIDIANA)*** [WAP] 1,500 in Brazil including 64 Mawayana (1986 SIL). Roraima. The Mawayana live with the Waiwai. Arawakan, Maipuran, Northern Maipuran, Wapishanan. Dialects: ATORADA (ATOR'TI, DAURI, ATORAI), AMARIBA, MAPIDIAN (MAOPITYAN, MAIOPITIAN, MAWAYANA, MAHUAYANA), TARUMA. People are somewhat bilingual. Taruma is nearly extinct. Amariba may be extinct. The dialect Atorada (Atorai) is not the same as the separate language Atroai (Atruahí). Bible portions 1975-1994. See main entry under Guyana.

ARUTANI ***(AUAQUÉ, AUAKE, AWAKE, AOAQUI, OEWAKU, URUAK, URUTANI)*** [ATX] 17 in Brazil (1986 SIL). Population total both countries 22. Roraima. Also spoken in Venezuela. Arutani-Sape. The remaining speakers are bilingual in Ninam. Most are intermarried with the Ninam, some with the Pemon (Arecuna) and a few with the Sapi and do not speak Arutani fluently. Nearly extinct.

ASHÉNINCA UCAYALI-YURUA ***(KAMPA, CAMPA)*** [CPB] 212 to 235 in Brazil (1983 SIL). Acre. Arawakan, Maipuran, Southern Maipuran, Campa. Intermittent contact in Brazil. See main entry under Peru.

ASURINÍ ***(ASSURINÍ, ASSURINÍ DO TOCANTINS, AKWAYA)*** [ASU] 191 (1995 AMTB). Trocará on the Tocantins River, Pará. Tupi, Tupi-Guarani, Tenetehara (IV). Closely related to Parakanã. Similar to Suruí do Pará. Bilingualism in Portuguese. Different from Asuriní do Xingú. Dictionary. Grammar. OVS. Literacy rate in first language: Below 1%. Literacy rate in second language: Below 5%. Agriculturalists: manioc, fishermen. Bible portions 1973.

ASURINÍ, XINGÚ ***(AWATÉ)*** [ASN] 63 (1994 ALEM). At least one sizeable village, on Rio Piçava off Xingú River near Altamira, Pará. Tupi, Tupi-Guarani, Kayabi-Arawete (V). A separate language, different from Asuriní of the Tocantins (Akwaya), and Arawete. Bilingualism is limited.

ATRUAHÍ ***(ATROAÍ, ATROARÍ, ATROWARI, ATROAHY, KI'NYA)*** [ATR] 350 (1995 SIL). On the Alalau and Camanau rivers on the border between the state of Amazonas and the territory of Roraima, and on the Jatapu and Jauaperi rivers. 24 villages. Carib, Northern, East-West Guiana, Waimiri. Dialects: ATRUAHI, WAIMIRÍ (UAIMIRÍ, WAHMIRÍ), JAWAPERI (YAUAPERI). Dialects or related languages: Sapara, Pauxiana. Piriutite and Tiquiriá. Contacted by Waiwai people in 1968. Traditional religion.

AVÁ-CANOEIRO ***(CANOEIROS, CANOE, CANOA, AVÁ, ABÁ, AWANA)*** [AVV] 56 (1995 SIL). Goiás, Island of Bananal, and the upper Tocantins River valley. Tupi, Tupi-Guarani, Tenetehara (IV). Monolingual. FUNAI contacted another group of 15 in 1983 close to the Tocantins River. Semi-nomadic. Traditional religion.

AWETÍ ***(AWETÖ, AUETO, AUITI, ARAUITE, ARAUINE)*** [AWE] 36 (1986 SIL). Xingú Park, Mato Grosso, Rio Culiseu. Tupi, Aweti. May be bilingual in Kamayurá. Tropical forest. Fishermen, hunter-gatherers, swidden agriculturalists: manioc, maize.

BAKAIRÍ ***(BACAIRÍ, KURÂ)*** [BKQ] 570 (1994 SIL). Mato Grosso in 9 or 10 villages. Carib, Southern, Xingu Basin. Speakers are somewhat bilingual in Portuguese. Grammar. SOV, OVS. Literacy rate in first language: Below 1%. Literacy rate in second language: 15% to 25%. Bible portions 1969-1976.

BANAWÁ ***(KITIYA, BANAVÁ, BANAUÁ, JAFÍ)*** [BNH] 70 (1994 SIL). Amazonas, upriver quite a distance from the Jamamadí. Half live on the Banawá River, others on small creeks and in scattered locations; 1 village and 2 extended family settlements. Arauan. Not as close to Jamamadí linguistically as previously thought. Some bilingualism in Jamamadí, and a little in Portuguese. They prefer their own language. They call themselves 'Kitiya'. Literacy rate in first language: Below 1%. Literacy rate in second language: Below 5%. Tropical forest.

BANIWA ***(BANIUA DO IÇANA, MANIBA, BANIVA, BANIBA, ISSANA, DAKENEI)*** [BAI] 5,460 in Brazil, including 4,057 Baniwa, 1,000 Hohodené, 403 Seuci (1983 SIL). Population total both countries 5,900 or more. Middle Içana River, Amazonas. They go to Colombia or Venezuela mainly to work or trade. Also spoken in Venezuela. Arawakan, Maipuran, Northern Maipuran, Inland. Dialects: HOHODENÉ (HOHODENA, KADAUPURITANA), SIUSY-TAPUYA (SEUCI, SIUCI, SIUSI). Related to Karutana and Kuripaco. Several groups on the middle Içana and Ayarí rivers who speak Baniwa: Hohodené, Kadaupuritana, Sucuriyu-Tapuya, Siusy-Tapuya, Irá-Tapuya, Kawá-Tapuya, Waliperedakenai (Ribeiro 1967). 'Kohoroxitari' may be another name for Baniwa. NT 1965-1985.

BORA ***(BORO)*** [BOA] Amazonas near the Solimões, between the Tefé and Caiçara rivers, and along the Brazilian part of the Rio Iça. Witotoan, Boran. Dialect: MIRANHA (MIRAÑA, MIRÃNIA). Miraña has 94% intelligibility with Bora. 457 Miran in Brazil (1986 SIL) no longer speak the language. SOV. Riverine. NT 1982. See main entry under Peru.

BORÔRO ***(BOE)*** [BOR] 850 (1994 SIL). Central Mato Grosso, 8 villages. Macro-Ge, Bororo, Bororo Proper. SOV. Literacy rate in first language: 10% to 30%. Literacy rate in second language: 15% to 25%. NT 1993.

BRAZILIAN SIGN LANGUAGE ***(LSB, SÃO PAULO SIGN LANGUAGE)*** [BZS] São Paulo, Rio de Janeiro, Minas Gerais, Santa Catarina, and elsewhere. Deaf sign language. The dialects appear to be inherently intelligible, although northern dialects above the Amazon are probably more different. Some relationship to North American and European sign languages. The fingerspelling used for proper names is similar to a European system. The first deaf school was begun in 1857 in Rio de Janeiro, then one in Porto Alegre. The deaf in São Paulo generally receive an oralist education. TV.

CAFUNDO CREOLE [CCD] 40 (1978 M. Gnerre, U. Estadual de Campinas). Cafundo, 150 miles from São Paulo. Creole, Portuguese based. Bilingualism in Portuguese. Bantu lexicon in Portuguese morphological and syntactic framework. The people are all fluent in Portuguese. The creole is considered a secret language. A similar creole has been recently discovered in Minas Gerais.

CALÓ ***(CALO, GITANO, IBERIAN ROMANI)*** [RMR] 10,000 in Latin America. Indo-European, Italic, Romance, Italo-Western, Western, Gallo-Iberian, Ibero-Romance, West Iberian, Castilian. Dialect: BRAZILIAN CALÃO. Very different from other Romani. A cryptolectal variety of Portuguese. Bilingualism in Portuguese. Christian. Bible portions 1837-1872. See main entry under Spain.

CANELA ***(KANELA)*** [RAM] 1,420 (1995 SIL), including 950 Ramkokamekra, 470 Apanjekra (1995 SIL). Maranhão, southeastern Pará. Macro-Ge, Ge-Kaingang, Ge, Northwest, Timbira. Dialects: APANJEKRA (APANHECRA, APANIEKRA), RAMKOKAMEKRA. Grammar. SOV. Hunters, agriculturalists: maize, yams. Traditional religion. NT 1990.

CARAPANA ***(CARAPANÃ, KARAPANÃ, MEXTÃ)*** [CBC] 50 in Brazil (1986 SIL). São Gabriel and Pari-Cachoeira, Amazonas. Tucanoan, Eastern Tucanoan, Central, Tatuyo. NT 1992. See main entry under Colombia.

CARIB ***(CARIBE, CARIÑA, KALIHNA, KALINYA, GALIBÍ, MARAWORNO, MARWORNO)*** [CRB] 100 or more in Brazil (1995 SIL). State of Amapá. Carib, Northern, Galibi. Dialect: TYREWUJU (EASTERN CARIB). Called 'Galibi' in Brazil. Portuguese-Carib creole people (Galibí do Uaça) also speak Crioulo (French Creole). Bible portions 1994. See main entry under Venezuela.

CARÚTANA ***(KARUTANA, ARARA DO AMAZONAS)*** [CRU] 250 (1977 Voegelin and Voegelin). Northwest Amazonas, near Curripaco. Arawakan, Maipuran, Northern Maipuran, Inland. Dialects: ADARU, ARARA, DZAUI (DZAWI), JAUARETE (YAWARETE TAPUYA), JURUPARI (YURUPARI TAPUYA), MAPACHE, UADZOLI (WADZOLI), URUBU. Close to Curripaco and Baniwa. Arara may be distinct. Investigation needed: intelligibility with Curripaco, Arara.

CASHINAHUA ***(CASHINAHUÁ, KAXINAWÁ, KAXINAUÁ, KAXYNAWA, CAXINAWÁ)*** [CBS] 775 in Brazil (1986 SIL). Acre. Panoan, Southeastern. Minor changes from Peruvian dialect. Somewhat bilingual. NT 1983. See main entry under Peru.

CHIRIPÁ ***(NHANDEVA, ÑANDEVA, TSIRIPÁ, TXIRIPÁ, APYTARE, GUARANÍ)*** [NHD] 4,900 in Brazil (1995 AMTB). Mato Grosso do Sul State, Paraná, Santa Catarina, Rio Grande do Sul, São Paulo. Tupi, Tupi-Guarani, Guarani (I). Dialect: APAPOCUVA. In Brazil it has been influenced by Paraguayan Guaraní, Mbyá, and Kaiwá. Most speakers are from the Apapocuva group, which has been described by ethnographers. Called 'Chiripá' in Paraguay, 'Nhandeva' in Brazil. The name 'Ñandeva' is used in the Paraguayan Chaco for Tapiete, a different but related language. In Brazil, speakers are over 40. In Brazil, the group is shifting to Portuguese. Bible portions 1991. See main entry under Paraguay.

CINTA LARGA [CIN] 1,000 (1995 SIL). Western Mato Grosso. Tupi, Monde. Some are still uncontacted. Rodrigues lists Zoró, Cinta Larga, and Gavião as separate languages (1986).

COCAMA-COCAMILLA ***(COCAMA, KOKAMA)*** [COD] Ethnic group: 176 in Brazil (1995 SIL). Amazonas. Tupi, Tupi-Guarani, Tupi (III). Dialects: COCAMA, COCAMILLA (KOKAMILLA, PAMBADEQUE), XIBITAONA. They speak only Portuguese in Brazil. SVO. Bible portions 1961-1967. See main entry under Peru.

CUBEO ***(CUVEO, CUBEU, KOBEUA, KOBEWA, KUBWA, KOBÉWA, HEHENAWA, PAMIWA)*** [CUB] 150 in Brazil (1986 SIL). Northwest Amazonas. Tucanoan, Central Tucanoan. NT 1970-1989. See main entry under Colombia.

CULINA ***(KULÍNA, KULYNA, CORINA, MADIJA, MADIHÁ)*** [CUL] 865 in Brazil (1995 SIL). Population total both countries 1,300. Amazonas, Acre. Also spoken in Peru. Arauan. Minor changes from Peruvian dialect. The Arawan languages may not be Arawakan. Bible portions 1965-1985.

CURRIPACO ***(CURIPACO, KURIPAKO, KORIPAKO, KORISPASO)*** [KPC] 810 in Brazil (1995 AMTB). Northwest Amazonas. Arawakan, Maipuran, Northern Maipuran, Inland. Dialects: KORRIPAKO (KARUPAKA), UNHUN (CADAUAPURITANA, ENHEN). Close to Baniwa and Carutana. NT 1959. See main entry under Colombia.

DENÍ ***(DANI)*** [DAN] 600 (1986 SIL). Amazonas. Arauan. Dialect: INAUINI. Sometimes called 'Jamamadí', but that is a separate language. Dictionary.

DESANO ***(DESÂNA, DESSANO, WINA, UINA, WIRÃ, BOLEKA, OREGU, KUSIBI)*** [DES] 960 in Brazil (1995 SIL), 800 in Colombia (1982 SIL). Population total both countries 1,760. Northwestern Amazonas. Also spoken in Colombia. Tucanoan, Eastern Tucanoan, Central, Desano. Desano in Brazil generally speak Tucano instead of Desano. NT 1984.

FULNIÔ ***(FURNIÔ, FORNIÓ, CARNIJÓ, IATÊ, YATÊ)*** [FUN] 2,788 (1995 SIL). Pernambuco. Macro-Ge, Fulnio. Bilingualism in Portuguese. Fulniô language is mainly used in 3-month annual religious retreat. Subsistence agriculturalists: beans, cotton.

GAVIÃO DO JIPARANÁ ***(GAVIÃO DO RONDÔNIA, DIGUT)*** [GVO] 472 including 220 Gavião (1986 SIL) and 252 Zoró (1995 AMTB). Rondônia (Gavião). Tupi, Monde. Dialects: GAVIÃO, ZORÓ (PANGINEY, CABEÇA SECA). Partially intelligible with Suruí. Rodrigues lists Zoró and Cinta Larga as separate languages from Gavião (1986). Different from Gavião of Pará, which is Je. Bible portions 1988.

GAVIÃO, PARÁ ***(PARAKATÊJÊ, PUKOBJÊ)*** [GAY] 180 in the main village and others scattered (1995 SIL). State of Pará, in a new village called 'Kaikoturé', near Marabá. Some live scattered in or near their original locations in Maranhão and Pará. Macro-Ge, Ge-Kaingang, Ge, Northwest, Timbira. Related to Krikati-Timbira, Canela, and Krahô. Increasing use of regional Portuguese as second language. Schools are in Portuguese. They prefer their language. They call themselves 'Parakatêjê Indian Community'. 'Gavião', meaning 'hawk', is used by outsiders. Not to be confused with the Gavião of Rondônia.

GUAJÁ ***(AWA GUAJÁ, AYAYA, WAZAIZARA, GUAXARE)*** [GUJ] 370 (1995 AMTB). Maranhão, babassu palm area near Gurupi and Upper Pindare rivers, some in Serra Canastra, Tocantins, and Guamá post in Pará. At least 6 isolated groups. Tupi, Tupi-Guarani, Oyampi (VIII). Related to Guajajara, but a separate language. Limited bilingualism. Hunter-gatherers.

GUAJAJÁRA ***(GUAZAZARA, TENETEHAR, TENETEHÁRA)*** [GUB] 10,000 (1986 C. Harrison SIL). Maranhão, 81 villages. Tupi, Tupi-Guarani, Tenetehara (IV). Dialects: PINDARE, ZUTIUA, MEARIM, TEMBE OF GURUPI. Three main dialects. Somewhat bilingual in Portuguese. Grammar. Literacy rate in first language: 30%. Literacy rate in second language: 30%. NT 1985.

GUANA ***(KINIKINAO, CHUALA, CHANA, EAST PARANÁ, KINIHINAO, EQUINAO)*** [QKS] Mato Grosso do Sul, near the Terêna. Arawakan, Maipuran, Southern Maipuran, Bolivia-Parana. Related to Ter^ena, Iranche. Extinct.

GUANANO ***(WANÂNA, WANANO, UANANA, ANANA, KÓTEDIA, KÓTIRYA)*** [GVC] 550 in Brazil (1995 AMTB). Population total both countries 1,000. Northwest Amazonas. Also spoken in Colombia. Tucanoan, Eastern Tucanoan, Northern. Close to Piratapuyo, but ethnically distinct. NT 1982.

GUARANÍ, MBYÁ ***(MBYÁ, MBUA, MBIÁ, BUGRE)*** [GUN] 5,000 or more in Brazil (1995 SIL). Southwestern Paraná, southeastern São Paulo, Santa Catarina, Rio Grande do Sul, Espíritu Santo, Minas Gerais. 35 villages in 7 states. Tupi, Tupi-Guarani, Guarani (I). Dialects: TAMBÉOPÉ, BATICOLA. 75% lexical similarity with Paraguayan Guaraní. Bilingual level estimates for Portuguese are Female: 0 30%, 1 50%, 2 18%, 3 2%, 4 0%, 5 0%; Male: 0 2%, 1 22%, 2 50%, 3 20%, 4 4%, 5 2%; Total: 0 16%, 1 36%, 2 34%, 3 11%, 4 2%, 5 1%. SVO. Literacy rate in first language: 10% to 30%. Literacy rate in second language: 15% to 25%. NT 1987. See main entry under Paraguay.

GUAREQUENA ***(UREQUEMA, WAREKÉNA, WEREKENA, UEREQUEMA, WERIKENA, AREQUENA)*** [GAE] 338 in Brazil (1983 NTM). Amazonas, Rio Chié (Xié) and Içana near Venezuelan border. Arawakan, Maipuran, Northern Maipuran, Inland. Many speak Nhengatu in Brazil. Those in centers are more bilingual. Spoken in remote areas. Most use Guarequena by preference. See main entry under Venezuela.

GUATÓ [GTA] 40 scattered speakers out of 382 in the ethnic group (1993 SIL). Mato Grosso do Sul and Bolivian border, banks of the Paraguai and going up the São Lourenço rivers. Macro-Ge, Guato.

HALÓ TÉ SÚ [HLO] 38 to 52 (1987 SIL). Mato Grosso. Nambiquaran. Speakers are bilingual in Southern Nambikuara. Recently contacted. Investigation needed: bilingual proficiency, intelligibility with Nambiquara.

HIMARIMÃ [HIR] Small. Amazonas, near the Jamamadi and Jarawara. Unclassified.

HIXKARYÁNA ***(HIXKARIANA, HISHKARYANA, PARUKOTO-CHARUMA, PARUCUTU, CHAWIYANA, KUMIYANA, SOKAKA, WABUI, FARUARU, SHEREWYANA, XEREWYANA, XEREU, HICH-KARYANA)*** [HIX] 550 (1994 SIL), including 89 Xereuyana (1986 SIL). Amazonas, upper Nhamunda River to Mapuera and Jatapú rivers. Carib, Southern, Southern Guiana. Close to Waiwai. No dialectal variation. The Sherewyana speak the same language but some live with the Waiwai. Bilingual level estimates for Portuguese are 0 85%, 1 10%, 2 5%, 3 0%, 4 0%, 5 0%. Grammar. OVS. Literacy rate in first language: 30% to 60%. Literacy rate in second language: 25% to 50%. NT 1976.

HUPDË ***("HUPDÁ MAKÚ", "JUPDÁ MACÚ", "MAKÚ-HUPDÁ", "MACÚ DE TUCANO", UBDÉ)*** [JUP] 1,208 in Brazil (1995 SIL). Population total both countries 1,350. Rio Auari, northwestern Amazonas. Also spoken in Colombia. Maku. Dialects: HUPDË, TUHUP, NËHUP. Ruhlen and others classify it as Puinave, Macro-Tucanoan. Intelligibility among Yahup, Tuhup, and Nëhup needs investigation. Possibly 50% are bilingual in Tucano or some other Tucanoan language. They are subservient to the Tucano and other Tucanoan Indians. The name "Macu" is offensive. Some are nomadic between Brazil and Colombia. Tropical forest.

IAPAMA [IAP] Border region of Pará and Amapá. Unclassified. Existence uncertain.

IPEKA-TAPUIA ***(PATO-TAPUYA, PATO TAPUIA, CUMATA, IPECA, PACU, PAKU-TAPUYA, PAYULIENE, PAYUALIENE, PALIOARIENE)*** [PAJ] 135 (1976 RC). Içana, Amazonas. Arawakan, Maipuran, Northern Maipuran, Inland. Dialect: WALIPERI (VELIPERI). Voegelin and Voegelin (1997) treat it as a dialect of Siuci (see Baniwa). They may all speak Tucano.

IRÁNTXE ***(IRANXE, IRANCHE, MÜNKÜ)*** [IRA] 191 (1995 AMTB). Mato Grosso, headwaters of the Rio Cravari, tributary of the Rio Sangue, which is a tributary of the Rio Juruena. Arawakan, Maipuran, Southern Maipuran, Unclassified. Dialects: MÜNKÜ (MYNKY, MENKU, KENKÜ, MYY), IRÁNTXE. Most are bilingual in Portuguese. 'Münkü' is a self designation.

ITOGAPÚK ***(ITOGAPUC, NTOGAPIG, NTOGAPID, RAMARAMA, ITANGA)*** [ITG] 95 (1986 SIL). Mato Grosso. Tupi, Ramarama.

JABUTÍ ***(YABUTÍ)*** [JBT] 5 (1990 YWAM). Rio Branco Post, Rondônia. Macro-Ge, Yabuti. Nearly extinct.

JAMAMADÍ ***(YAMAMADÍ, KANAMANTI, CANAMANTI)*** [JAA] 195 (1994 SIL) including 12 Mamoria. Amazonas, scattered over 200,000 square miles. Arauan. Dialects: BOM FUTURO, JURUA, PAUINI, MAMORIA (MAMORI), CUCHUDUA (MAIMA), TUKURINA. Other groups are called 'Jamamadí' which are closer to Culina or Dení. Tukurina may be a separate language. Dialects or related languages: Araua, Pama, Sewacu, Sipo, Yuberi. People want a school. OSV. Literacy rate in first language: 60% to 100%. Literacy rate in second language: 75% to 100%. Christian, traditional religion. Bible portions 1991.

JARUÁRA ***(JARAWARA)*** [JAP] 150 (1993 SIL). Amazonas, near the Jamamadí, 7 villages. Arauan. Formerly considered a dialect of Jamamadí. OSV. Literacy rate in first language: 5% to 10%. Literacy rate in second language: 5% to 15%.

JÚMA ***(YUMÁ, KATAUIXI, ARARA, KAGWAHIVA, KAGWAHIBM, KAGWAHIV, KAWAHIP, KAVAHIVA, KAWAIB, KAGWAHIPH)*** [JUA] 4 (1998). There were 300 in 1940. Amazonas, Rio Açuã, tributary of the Mucuim. Tupi, Tupi-Guarani, Kawahib (VI). Call themselves 'Kagwahiva'. SVO. Tropical forest. Nearly extinct.

JURÚNA ***(YURÚNA, IURUNA, JARUNA)*** [JUR] 181 (1998 SIL). Xingú Park, northern Mato Grosso, near mouth of the Maritsauá-Mitau River, 2 villages. Tupi, Yuruna. A separate language. Bilingualism is limited. Agriculturalists: manioc; fishermen.

KABIXÍ ***(CABICHÍ, CABISHI)*** [KBD] 100 (1986 SIL). Slopes of Planalto dos Parecís, right bank of upper Guaporé, near Vila Bela, Mato Grosso. Chapacura-Wanham, Guapore. Related to Cujuna, Cumana, Mataua, Wanham, Urunumacan. Both people and language may be extinct. The name is also used for Parecís or Nambikuara.

KADIWÉU ***(MBAYA-GUAIKURU, CADUVÉO, EDIU-ADIG)*** [KBC] 1,200 (1995 SIL) to 1,800 (1995 Filomena Sandalo). Mato Grosso do Sul, around Serra da Bodoquena. 3 villages. Mataco-Guaicuru, Guaicuruan. 'Payagua' may be a term for 'enemy' applied to this group. SVO. Literacy rate in first language: 1% to 5%. Literacy rate in second language: 25% to 50%. NT, in press (1999).

KAIMBÉ [QKQ] (1,100 to 1,400 in ethnic group; 1986 SIL). Bahía. Unclassified. Ethnic group now speaks Portuguese. Extinct.

KAINGÁNG ***(COROADO, COROADOS, CAINGANG, BUGRE)*** [KGP] 18,000 (1989 U. Wiesemann SIL). São Paulo, Paraná, Santa Catarina, Rio Grande do Sul; 21 locations. Central Kaingang is in São Paulo and Santa Catarina. Macro-Ge, Ge-Kaingang, Kaingang, Northern. Dialects: PARANÁ KAINGANG, CENTRAL KAINGANG, SOUTHWEST KAINGANG, SOUTHEAST KAINGANG. 4 dialects. Somewhat bilingual in Portuguese. The name 'Bugre' is also used for Xokleng and Mbyá Guaraní. Dictionary. SOV. NT 1977.

KAINGÁNG, SÃO PAULO [ZKS] 80 (1989 U. Wiesemann SIL). São Paulo. Macro-Ge, Ge-Kaingang, Kaingang, Northern. Different enough from Kaingáng to need adapted literature. Most speakers use Portuguese as second language. Grammar.

KAIWÁ ***(CAIWA, CAINGUA, CAYUA, CAIUA, KAYOVA, KAIOVA)*** [KGK] 15,000 in Brazil (1994 SIL). Population total both countries 15,500 or more. Mato Grosso do Sul. Also spoken in Argentina. Tupi, Tupi-Guarani, Guarani (I). Dialects: TEÜI, TEMBEKUÁ, KAIWÁ. Somewhat intelligible with Paraguayan Guaraní. 70% lexical similarity with Pai Tavytera of Paraguay. Literacy rate in first language: 5% to 10%. Literacy rate in second language: 15% to 25%. NT 1986.

KAMÃ ***(KAMÃ MAKÚ, DÂW)*** [KWA] 83 (1994 ALEM). Amazonas, across the river from São Gabriel de Cochoeira, a county seat just below the confluence of the Vaupés and Negro rivers. Maku. They call themselves 'Dâw'.

KAMAKAN ***(EZESHIO)*** [VKM] Bahia area. Macro-Ge, Kamakan. Extinct.

KAMAYURÁ ***(KAMAIURÁ, CAMAIURA, KAMAYIRÁ)*** [KAY] 279 (1995 AMTB). Xingú Park, Mato Grosso. Tupi, Tupi-Guarani, Kamayura (VII). A separate language. Limited bilingualism. Hunters, fishermen, agriculturalists.

KAMBA ***(CAMBA)*** [QKZ] (2,000 in ethnic group; 1986 SIL). Mato Grosso do Sul, near Corumbá. Unclassified. May have been Tupí. Ethnic group came from Bolivia, and now speak Spanish. Extinct.

KAMBIWÁ [QKH] (1,108 in ethnic group; 1995 SIL). Pernambuco. Unclassified. Ethnic group now speaks Portuguese. Extinct.

KANAMARÍ ***(KANAMARÉ, CANAMARÍ)*** [KNM] 647 (1995 SIL). Amazonas, upper regions of Jurua, Jutai, Itaquai rivers. Katukinan. Dialect: TSHOM-DJAPA (TXUNHUÃ-DJAPÁ, TXUNHUÃ DYAPÁ).

KANOÉ ***(CANOÉ, GUARATÉGAYA, GUARATEGAJA, KOARATIRA, GUARATIRA, AMNIAPÉ, MEQUENS)*** [KXO] Ethnic group: 30 (1995 SIL). Rondônia, scattered locations. Tupi, Tupari. They speak only Portuguese. Distinct from Ava (Canoeiros). Extinct.

KAPINAWÁ [QKP] (354 in ethnic group; 1995 AMTB). Pernambuco. Unclassified. Ethnic group now speaks Portuguese. Extinct.

KARAHAWYANA [XKH] 40 (1995 SIL). Amazonas, near the Waiwai. Unclassified. Probably Cariban. Today some live with the Waiwai and some near the Hixkaryana, and speak those languages. Nearly extinct.

KARAJÁ ***(XAMBIOÁ, CHAMBOA, YNÃ)*** [KPJ] 1,700 (1995 SIL), including 383 Javaé (1986 SIL). Goiás, Pará, Mato Grosso, Araguaia River, Bananal Island, and Tocantins. Macro-Ge, Karaja. Dialect: JAVAÉ (JAVAHE). Men and women speak different dialects. Grammar. Literacy rate in second language: 70%. Agriculturalists, hunters. NT 1983.

KARIPÚNA ***(KARIPÚNA DO UAÇÁ, KARIPÚNA DO AMAPÁ)*** [KGM] Territory of Amapá, on French Guiana border. Unclassified. It has been suggested, but not demonstrated, that this was a Tupi-Guarani language. The descendants now speak Karipúna Creole French. Extinct.

KARIPUNÁ ***(KARIPUNÁ DO GUAPORÉ, CARIPUNA, JAU-NAVO, JUANAUO, KARIPUNÁ DE RONDÔNIA)*** [KUQ] 12 or more (1995 SIL). Rondônia, sides of Jaru, Jamery, Urupa, Cabecciras, Candeias rivers. Panoan, Southern. Dialects: JACARIA, PAMA (PAMANA). They may be bilingual in Tenharim. There may be more in the jungle. Investigation needed: bilingual proficiency in Tenharim.

KARIPÚNA CREOLE FRENCH ***(CRIOULO)*** [KMV] 672 (1995 SIL). Amapá, on French Guiana border. Creole, French based. There are conflicting reports about how different it is from French Guianese. It is different from Haitian Creole. Limited bilingualism. Speakers formerly spoke Karipúna, an unclassified language, possibly formerly from Marajó Island at the mouth of the Amazon.

Investigation needed: intelligibility with French Guianese, Amapa Creole. Grammar. SVO. Tropical forest. Islands, swamp. Fishermen, swidden agriculturalists: manioc. Traditional religion, Christian.

KARIRI-XOCÓ ***(KARIRÍ, KARIRI XUCÓ, KIPEÁ, XOKÓ-KARIRÍ, XUKURU KARIRI, XUKURÚ, XOCÓ, XOKÓ)*** [KZW] (1,062 in ethnic group; 1995 SIL). Alagoas. Unclassified. Dialects: KIPEÁ (QUIPEA), KAMURÚ (CAMURU), DZUBUKUÁ (DZUBUCUA), SABUJÁ (PEDRA BRANCA). Other dialects or languages are even less well attested. Classified as Equatorial (Greenberg 1959), Macro-Carib (Swadesh 1959), Macro-Ge (Rodrigues 1975), Isolate (Rivet and Loukotka 1952, Larsen 1984). The ethnic group is monolingual in Portuguese. Catechism (Mamiani 1698). Grammar. Extinct.

KARITIÂNA ***(CARITIANA)*** [KTN] 150 (1995 SIL). Rondônia. Tupi, Arikem. Dictionary. Grammar. SVO. Bible portions 1981.

KATAWIXI ***(CATAWIXI, CATAUIXI, CATAWISHI, CATAUICHI)*** [QKI] 10 (1986 SIL). Amazonas. Katukinan. Nearly extinct.

KATUKÍNA ***(KATUKINA DO JUTAÍ, PIDÁ-DJAPÁ, CATUQUINA)*** [KAV] 1 speaker (1976 SIL). 253 in the ethnic group (1986 SIL). Acre. Katukinan. Dialect: CUTIADAPA (KUTIA-DYAPA). Different from Panoan Katukina in Amazonas and Acre. Nearly extinct.

KATUKÍNA, PANOAN ***(CATUQUINA, WANINNAWA, KAMANAWA, KAMANNAUA, KATUKINA DO JURUÁ)*** [KNT] 196 (1995 AMTB). Amazonas, Acre. Panoan, Southeastern. Dialects: ARARA-SHAWANAWA (SHAWANAWA-ARARA), ARARAPINA, ARARAWA, SANAINAWA (SANINAWACANA). Possibly intelligible with Marubo. Different from other Katukína (Katukinan Family) in Acre.

KAXARARÍ ***(KAXARIRI)*** [KTX] 220 (1995 AMTB). Alto Rio Marmelo, tributary of Rio Abuna, Acre, Rondônia, Amazonas. Panoan, Eastern. Limited bilingualism. Different from Arawakan Casharari (Cacharari; Voegelin and Voegelin 1977.215).

KAXUIÂNA ***(KASHUYANA, KASHUJANA, KACHUANA, WARIKYANA, WARIKIANA, KAXÚYANA)*** [KBB] 434 including 300 Warikyana, 134 Kaxuiâna (1986 SIL). Imabu River near perimetral norte, on Trombetes River near junction with Mapuwera, northwestern Para. A few are living with the Hixkaryána; most with the Trió. Carib, Southern, Southern Guiana. Dialect: PAWIYANA (PAWIXI). There is a fair amount of bilingualism between some speakers of Trio and Kaxuiâna.

KAYABÍ ***(KAJABÍ, CAIABI, PARUA, MAQUIRI)*** [KYZ] 800 (1994 SIL). Northern Mato Grosso, Xingú Park, and southern Para; Teles Pires River and Tatui, many villages. Tupi, Tupi-Guarani, Kayabi-Arawete (V). Grammar. OSV. Literacy rate in first language: 1% to 5%. Literacy rate in second language: Below 5%. Bible portions 1986.

KAYAPÓ ***(KOKRAIMORO)*** [TXU] 4,000 (1994 SIL) including 469 Xikrin (1986 SIL). Xingú Park, Mato Grosso, southern Pará. 9 villages. Macro-Ge, Ge-Kaingang, Ge, Northwest, Kayapo. Dialects: XIKRIN (XUKRU, DIORE), KARARAÓ, KAYAPÓ-kRADAÚ. Those listed as dialects are only slightly different. Village names sometimes listed as dialects are: Txukuhamai (Txucarramãe), Gorotire, Kube-Kran-Kenh (Cabeca Pelada), Menkragnotire (Mentuktire, Kuben-Kragnotire, Gente Preta, Kubenkrangnoti, Kubenkrankegn, Menkrangnoti), Pacajá. Grammar. SOV. Literacy rate in first language: 5% to 10%. Literacy rate in second language: 5% to 15%. NT 1996.

KIRIRÍ-XOKÓ ***(XUKURÚ, SHOCU, SHOCO, KIRIRÍ)*** [XOO] (1,800 in the ethnic group; 1995 SIL). Pernambuco, Serra de Urubá (Arobá) near the city of Cimbres, Bahia. Unclassified. The people are monolingual in Portuguese. Apparently distinct from Karirí-Xocó. Extinct.

KOHOROXITARI [KOB] 622 (1976 RC). Amazonas, Prelazia Rio Negro. Unclassified. Possibly Tucanoan. May be the same as Baniwa.

KORUBO ***(CACETEIROS)*** [QKF] 500 (1995 AMTB). Amazonas. Unclassified. Possibly Panoan. May be the same as Marubo, or related to Yanomami.

KRAHÔ ***(CRAÔ, KRAÔ)*** [XRA] 1,200 (1988 SIL). Maranhão, southeastern Pará, Tocantins, 5 villages. Macro-Ge, Ge-Kaingang, Ge, Northwest, Timbira. Different from Canela, but may be able to use literature adapted from Canela. Limited bilingualism. The Krahô do not accept the name 'Canela'. SOV.

KREEN-AKARORE ***(KREN AKARORE, PANARÁ)*** [KRE] 122 (1995 AMTB). Xingú Park, northern Mato Grosso. Macro-Ge, Ge-Kaingang, Ge, Northwest, Kreen-Akarore. Not a dialect of Kayapó; possibly closer to Canela. Bilingualism is limited. Agriculturalists, hunter-gatherers.

KRENAK [KQQ] 80 approximately. At least 20 families in southern São Paulo (1989 U. Wiessemann SIL). Left margin of Doce River, on reservations in east São Paulo, Mato Grosso, Paraná. Macro-Ge, Botocudo. Bilingualism in Portuguese.

KREYE ***(KREM-YE, CRENGE, CRANGE, CREYE, CRENYE, TAZE, TAGE)*** [XRE] 30 or fewer (1995 SIL). Maranhão and Pará. Macro-Ge, Ge-Kaingang, Ge, Northwest, Timbira. Nearly extinct.

KRIKATI-TIMBIRA [XRI] 420 (1995 AMTB). Maranhão, southeastern Pará, Tocantins. The Timbira are in Governador Village, Municipality of Amarante. Macro-Ge, Ge-Kaingang, Ge, Northwest, Timbira. Dialects: KRINKATI (KARAKATI), TIMBIRA. The Krikati and Timbira are separate ethnic groups speaking related dialects. Limited bilingualism. SOV.

KUIKÚRO-KALAPÁLO ***(KUIKURU, GUICURÚ, KURKURO, CUICUTL, KALAPALO, APALAKIRI, APALAQUIRI)*** [KUI] 526 including 277 Kuikúro and 249 Kalapálo (1995 AMTB). Xingú Park, Mato Grosso. Carib, Southern, Xingu Basin. The Kuikúru and the Kalapálo speak the same language, but are separate ethnically. Limited bilingualism. Fishermen, hunters, swidden agriculturalists: manioc, maize.

KURUÁYA ***(XIPAIA, CARAVARE, CURUAIA)*** [KYR] 52 to 147 (1998). Pará. Tupi, Munduruku. The people use Portuguese almost exclusively now (1995).

MACHINERE ***(MANCHINERE, MANCHINERI, MANITENERÍ, MANITENÉRE, MAXINÉRI)*** [MPD] 400 (1995 AMTB). Acre. Arawakan, Maipuran, Southern Maipuran, Purus. Distinct enough from Yine (Piro) in Peru to need separate literature. Manitenére may be different from Machinere. Bible portions 1960.

MACUNA ***(MAKUNA, BUHAGANA, BAIGANA, WUHÁNA, JEPA-MATSI, YEPÁ-MAHSÁ, YEHPÁ MAJSÁ, YEPÁ MAXSÃ, YEBAMASÃ, PANEROA)*** [MYY] 100 in Brazil (1973 RC). Rio Chié, Amazonas. Tucanoan, Eastern Tucanoan, Central, Southern. NT 1989. See main entry under Colombia.

MACUSHI ***(MAKUXI, MACUSI, MAKUSHI, TEWEYA, TEUEIA)*** [MBC] 3,800 in Brazil. Contingo, Quino, Pium, and Mau rivers, northeast Roraima and Rio Branco. Carib, Northern, East-West Guiana, Macushi-Kapon, Macushi. Not intelligible with Arecuna or Patamona. Bilingualism increasing in Portuguese. OVS. NT 1981. See main entry under Guyana.

MAKURÁP ***(MAKURÁPI, MACURAP, MACURAPI, MASSAKA, KURATEG, SAKIRAP)*** [MAG] 114 (1995 AMTB). Pororoca Post, Rondônia, and scattered locations. Tupi, Tupari. Bilingualism in Portuguese. Children speak Portuguese as first language. Young adults speak Portuguese as second language. Intermarriage on same post with speakers of other languages. They call themselves 'Kurateg'.

MANDAHUACA ***(MANDAUACA, MANDAWÁKA, IHINI, MALDAVACA)*** [MHT] 3 in Brazil (1993 ALEM). Amazonas, upper Cauaboris, tributary of the Rio Negro, Colombian border. Arawakan, Maipuran, Northern Maipuran, Inland. Related to Adzaneni, Yabaana, Masaca. The name 'Baré' is also used as a cover term for separate languages: Baré, Mandahuaca, Guarekena, Baniwa, Piapoko. See main entry under Venezuela.

MAQUIRITARI ***(MAYONGONG, MAQUIRITARE, MAQUIRITAI, MAKIRITARE, PAWANA, SOTO)*** [MCH] 270 in Brazil (1986 SIL). Roraima. Carib, Southern, Southern Guiana. Dialects: CUNUANA, DE'CUANA (WAINUNGOMO), IHURUANA, MAITSI, MAYONGONG (YE'CUANA, YEKUANA). NT 1970. See main entry under Venezuela.

MARITSAUÁ ***(MANITSAWÁ, MANTIZULA, MARITSAUA)*** [MSP] Manitsaua-Missu, a tributary of the Upper Xingú, Xingú Park, Mato Grosso. Tupi, Yuruna. Dialect: ARUPAI (URUPAYA). Extinct.

MARÚBO ***(MARUBA, MAROVA, KANIUÁ)*** [MZR] 594 (1995 SIL). Amazonas, along the headwaters of the tributaries of the Curuçá, Ipixuna, and Javarí, near the Peru border. Panoan, North-Central. Speakers say they cannot understand Matsés (Mayoruna). Possibly intelligible with Panoan Katukína. Korubo may be the same.

MATIPUHY ***(MATIPU, MARIAPE-NAHUQUA)*** [MZO] 40 (1995 AMTB). Xingú Park, Mato Grosso. Carib, Southern, Xingu Basin. Dialects: MATIPUHY, NAHUKUÁ (NAKUKWA, NAFUKWÁ, NAHUQUA). Ruhlen says Kalapalo is a dialect of Nahukua. May also be intelligible with Kuikúro. Investigation needed: intelligibility with Kuikúro-Kalapálo. Fishermen, hunters, swidden agriculturalists: manioc, maize.

MATÍS [MPQ] 120 (1995 SIL). Amazonas, Javari Valley, Municipality of Atalaia do Norte, on the border with Peru. Panoan, Northern. Seems to be different from Matsés, although similar.

MATSÉS ***(MATSE, MAYORUNA)*** [MCF] 483 in Brazil (1995 SIL). Amazonas. Panoan, Northern. Different from Mayo, Marubo, or Maya. Matís seems to be different. NT 1993. See main entry under Peru.

MAXAKALÍ ***(CAPOSHO, CUMANASHO, MACUNI, MONAXO, MONOCHO)*** [MBL] 728 (1994 SIL). Minas Gerais, 100 miles inland from coast, 14 villages. Macro-Ge, Maxakali. The population is largely young. SOV. Literacy rate in first language: 37%. Literacy rate in second language: 37%. NT 1981.

MEHINÁKU ***(MEHINACO, MAHINAKU, MINACO)*** [MMH] 121 (1995 AMTB). Xingú Park, Mato Grosso. Arawakan, Maipuran, Central Maipuran. Somewhat intelligible with Waura, but probably needs adapted literature. Bilingualism is limited. Fishermen, hunters, swidden agriculturalists: manioc, maize.

MEKEM ***(MEQUEM, MEQUEN, MUKI)*** [XME] 50 (1995 AMTB). Rondônia. Tupi, Monde. May be the same as Kanoé (Mequens).

MIARRÃ [XMI] Xingú Park, Mato Grosso. Unclassified.

MIRITI ***(MIRITI-TAPUIA, MIRITI TAPUYO, NEENOÁ)*** [MMV] Ethnic group: 55 (1995 AMTB). Pari-Cachoeira, Taracua, Amazonas. Tucanoan, Miriti. All speak Tucano. 'Tapuya' comes from the Tupí word for 'enemy'. Extinct.

MONDÉ ***(SANAMAIKÁ, SANAMAYKÃ, SANAMAICA, SALAMÃI, SALAMAIKÃ)*** [MND] 30 (1995 AMTB). Apidia River, tributary of Igarape Tanaru, Rondônia. Tupi, Monde. May be Huarí, not Tupí. Related to Arua, Digüt. May be extinct. Nearly extinct.

MOREREBI [XMO] Amazonas, Rio Preto and Marmelos. Tupi, Tupi-Guarani, Kawahib (VI). May be a Tenharim dialect. A family group that has not lived with the Tenharim for many years, and does not want contact with outside culture. Existence not able to be confirmed in 1993.

MUNDURUKÚ ***(MUNDURUCU, WEIDYENYE, PAIQUIZE, PARI, CARAS-PRETAS)*** [MYU] 2,000 or more (1995 SIL). Pará, Amazonas. 22 villages. Tupi, Munduruku. Grammar. OV. Tropical forest, savannah. NT 1980.

MÚRA-PIRAHÃ ***(PIRAHÃ)*** [MYP] 150 (1986 SIL) out of an ethnic group of 1,500 (1995 SIL). The Pirahã are small, the Múra larger. Amazonas, along the Maici and Autaces rivers. Mura. Probably related to Matanawi, which is extinct. The Múra are mostly integrated into Portuguese. The Pirahã are quite monolingual. Semi nomadic. Grammar. SOV. Tropical forest. Riverine. Hunter-gatherers. 40 to 120 feet. Bible portions 1987.

NADËB ***(NADEB MACU, MAKÚ NADËB, MAKUNADÖBÖ, NADÖBÖ, ANODÖUB, KABORI, KABARI, XIRIWAI, XURIWAI)*** [MBJ] 300 (1986 SIL). Amazonas, three locations on the Uneiuxi River, a tributary of the Negro River, on the Japura and Negro rivers, and in other scattered places. Maku. Ruhlen and others classify it as Puinave in Macro-Tucanoan. The people are semi-nomadic. OSV. Hunter-gatherers.

NAMBIKUÁRA, NORTHERN ***(MAMAINDÉ)*** [MBG] 126 (1995 SIL). Mato Grosso (Mamaindé), Rondônia (Latundê). Nambiquaran. Dialects: MAMAINDÉ, NEGAROTE, TAWANXTE, TAXMAINITE, TAXWENSITE, YALAPMUNXTE (LACONDE, LATUNDÊ). The Latundê live with the Tubarão. Tropical forest. Rubber gatherers. Bible portions 1979-1980.

NAMBIKUÁRA, SOUTHERN ***(NAMBIQUARA, NAMBIKWARA)*** [NAB] 900 (1988 SIL), including 150 Galera (1983 SIL). Northwestern Mato Grosso, scattered along the Porto Velho-Cuiabá highway for about 300 km. 10 villages. Nambiquaran. Dialects: MANDUKA, KHITHAULHU, SERRA AZUL, HAHAINTESU, WASUSU, ALATESU, WAIKISU, GALERA. The Manduca are semi-integrated. The Nambikuára were reduced from 10,000 in the 1940s by measles. Manairisu is a subgroup. Grammar. SOV, tonal. Literacy rate in first language: 5% to 10%. Literacy rate in second language: 5% to 15%. Traditional religion, Christian. NT 1992.

NHENGATU ***(YERAL, GERAL, LÍNGUA GERAL, NYENGATÚ, NHEENGATU, NYENGATO, ÑEEGATÚ, WAENGATU, COASTAL TUPIAN, MODERN TUPÍ)*** [YRL] 3,000 in Brazil (1998). Population total all countries 8,000. Lower Vaupés, Içana, and Negro River areas, Amazonas. Also spoken in Colombia, Venezuela. Tupi, Tupi-Guarani, Tupi (III). All use Tucano as second language. Based on Tupinambá. Trade language. NT 1973.

NINAM ***(YANAM, XIRIANÁ, SHIRIANA CASAPARE, KASRAPAI, JAWAPERI, CRICHANA, JAWARI)*** [SHB] 466 (1976 UFM), 236 in southern dialect, 230 in northern. Population total both countries 566. Mucajai, upper Uraricáa, and Paragua rivers, Roraima. Also spoken in Venezuela. Yanomam. Dialects: SOUTHERN NINAM (MUKAJAI), NORTHERN NINAM (URARICAA-PARAGUA). Generally monolingual; a few children are beginning to learn Portuguese. All ages. Distinct from the Arawakan Xiriâna. Bible portions 1970.

NUKUINI ***(NUQUINI)*** [NUC] Acre, northwestern, from the upper Mõa to the Rio Sungarú in Juruá. Panoan, South-Central, Unclassified. Dialect: CUYANAWA. They have used mainly Portuguese for 3 generations. Some older people remember a little of the language. Extinct.

OMAGUA ***(CANGA-PEBA, AGUA, JANBEBA, COMPEVA, OMAGUA-YETE, ARIANA, PARIANA, ANAPIA, MACANIPA, YHUATA, UMAUA, CAMBEBA, CAMPEBA, CAMBELA)*** [OMG] There may be none left in Brazil (1995). Amazonas. Tupi, Tupi-Guarani, Tupi (III). Dialects: AIZUARE (AISSUARI), CURACIRARI (CURAZICARI), CURUCICURI (CURUZICARI), PAGUANA (PAGUARA). Closest to Cocama. Nearly extinct. See main entry under Peru.

OPAYÉ ***(OPAIÉ-SHAVANTE, OFAIÉ-XAVANTE, OFAYÉ)*** [OPY] Ethnic group: 37 (1995 AMTB). Mato Grosso do Sul, along the Verde, Vacaris, and Ivinhema rivers, and area of Brazilândia. Macro-Ge, Opaye. Laborers. Extinct.

ORO WIN [ORW] 5 speakers (1996 D. Everett SIL) out of 55 in the ethnic group (1998). Headwaters of the Pacaas-Novos River, a tributary of the Mamoré River, along the Brazil-Bolivia border. Chapacura-Wanham, Madeira. Related to Tora, Itene (More), and Wari (Pakaasnovos), but not inherently intelligible with them. Bilingualism in Wari. All speakers over 40 years old (1986 D. Everett SIL). VOS. Nearly extinct.

OTI ***(CHAVANTE, EUCHAVANTE)*** [OTI] São Paulo. Macro-Ge, Oti. Extinct.

OTUKE ***(OTUQUE, OTUQUI, LOUXIRU)*** [OTU] Mato Grosso lowlands into eastern Bolivia. Macro-Ge, Bororo, Otuke. Related dialects or languages: Covareca, Curuminaca, Coraveca (Curave), Curucaneca, Tapii; all are extinct. Extinct.

PAKAÁSNOVOS ***(JARU, UOMO, PAKAANOVAS, PACAAS-NOVOS, PAKAANOVA, PACAHANOVO, ORO WARI, WARI)*** [PAV] 1,833 (1994 D. Everett SIL). Rondônia, 7 villages. Chapacura-Wanham, Madeira. Bible portions 1975-1984.

PALIKÚR ***(PALIKOUR, PALICUR, PALIJUR)*** [PAL] 800 in Brazil. Population total both countries 1,400. Northern coastal tip along rivers, Amapá. Also spoken in French Guiana. Arawakan, Maipuran, Eastern Maipuran. Somewhat bilingual. Grammar. Literacy rate in second language: 25%. Riverine, island. Hunters, agriculturalists. NT 1982.

PANKARARÉ ***(PANKARÉ)*** [PAX] Ethnic group: 1,200 (1995 AMTB). Bahía. Unclassified. Monolingual in Portuguese. Extinct.

PANKARARÚ ***(PANKARARÁ, PANKARÚ, PANCARU, PANCARÉ, PANKARAVU, PANKARORU)*** [PAZ] Ethnic group: 3,676 (1995 AMTB). Pernambuco, Alagoas. Language Isolate. Possibly related to Kirirí. Highly acculturated. Monolingual in Portuguese. Extinct.

PAPAVÔ [PPV] Acre, Taramacá River. Unclassified. A separate language. Limited bilingualism. Existence unconfirmed.

PARAKANÃ ***(PARAKANÂN, PAROCANA)*** [PAK] 451 (1995 AMTB). Pará, Xingú Park, lower Xingú River. Tupi, Tupi-Guarani, Tenetehara (IV).

PARANAWÁT ***(PARANAUAT, PAWATÉ, MAJUBIM)*** [PAF] (50 to 100 in ethnic group; 1986 SIL). Rondônia, tributaries of the Jiparaná (Machado) River and Sono River. Tupi, Tupi-Guarani, Kawahib (VI). Extinct.

PARECÍS ***(PARESSÍ, PARESÍ, HALITI)*** [PAB] 1,200 (1994 SIL). Mato Grosso, 6,000 square kms. 15 to 20 villages. Arawakan, Maipuran, Central Maipuran. Somewhat bilingual. There are public schools in 7 villages. Dictionary. Grammar. SOV, OVS. Plateau. 650 meters. NT 1995.

PATAXÓ-HÃHAÃI ***(PATAXI, PATASHÓ, PATOXÓ, PATAXÓ-HÃHÃHÃE)*** [PTH] (2,950 in ethnic group; 1995 AMTB). Minas Gerais, Bahía, Pôsto Paraguassu in the municipality of Itabuna. Unclassified. The people are monolingual in Portuguese. Extinct.

PAUMARÍ ***(PURUPURÚ)*** [PAD] 700 or more (1994 SIL). Amazonas. 3 villages. Arauan. Dialects: PAUMARM (PAMMARI), KURUKURU (CURUCURU), UAIAI. Three inherently intelligible dialects. Speakers are fairly bilingual. Half the speakers are under 12 years of age (1984 SIL). Grammar. Literacy rate in first language: 10% to 30%. Literacy rate in second language: 15% to 25%. NT 1995.

PEMON ***(PEMONG, INGARIKÓ, INGARICÓ)*** [AOC] 679 in Brazil, including 220 Taulipang, 459 Ingariko. Rio Branco, near Guyana border, Roraima. Carib, Northern, East-West Guiana, Macushi-Kapon, Kapon. Dialects: TAULIPANG (TAUREPAN), CAMARACOTA (IPURICOTO), ARECUNA (ARICUNA, AREKUNA, JARICUNA). OVS. Bible portions 1990. See main entry under Venezuela.

PIRATAPUYO ***(WAIKINO, PIRA-TAPUYA, UAIKENA, UAICANA, WAIKHARA, WAINA, UAIANA, UAINANA)*** [PIR] 618 in Brazil (1986 SIL). Population total both countries 1,070. Amazonas. Also spoken in Colombia. Tucanoan, Eastern Tucanoan, Northern. Close to Guanano linguistically, ethnically distinct, but the two groups do not intermarry. Bilingualism in Tucano. NT 1991.

PLAUTDIETSCH ***(LOW GERMAN, MENNONITE GERMAN)*** [GRN] 5,955 in Brazil (1985 SIL). 110,735 or more in Latin America are fairly monolingual. Indo-European, Germanic, West, Low Saxon-Low Franconian, Low Saxon. Bilingualism in Portuguese, Standard German. Christian. NT 1987. See main entry under Canada.

POKANGÁ ***(PAKANG, POKANGÁ-TAPUYA, BARÁ, BARASANO, BARA SONA)*** [POK] 100 (1983 SIL). Upper Tiquie, tributary of Vaupés, Amazonas. Tucanoan, Eastern Tucanoan, Central, Bara. It may be the same as Barasana or Waimaha (Northern Barasano, Bará).

PORTUGUESE [POR] 158,000,000 in Brazil (1997 UBS). Throughout the country. Indo-European, Italic, Romance, Italo-Western, Western, Gallo-Romance, Ibero-Romance, West Iberian, Portuguese-Galician. National language. Literacy rate in first language: 71%. Christian, spiritism. Bible 1751-1996. See main entry under Portugal.

POTIGUÁRA ***(PITONARA)*** [POG] Ethnic group: 6,120 (1995 AMTB). Paraíba, Pôsto Nísia Brasileira on the Baía da Traição, in the municipality of Mamanguape. Tupi, Tupi-Guarani, Tupi (III). People speak only Portuguese and are culturally assimilated. Extinct.

POTURU ***(ZO'É, TUPÍ OF CUMINAPANEMA, POTURUJARA, BURÉ)*** [PTO] 136 (1995 SIL). State of Pará, Municipality of Obidos, on the Cuminapanema River. Tupi, Tupi-Guarani, Oyampi (VIII). Similar to Wayampi.

POYANÁWA ***(POIANÁUA, PUINAHUA)*** [PYN] 310 (1995 AMTB). Acre, upper Rio Môa, tributary of the Jumá. Panoan, South-Central, Yaminahua-Sharanahua. Pacified in 1913.

PURI ***(COROADO)*** [PRR] Espíritu Santo, Minas Gerais, and adjacent areas. Macro-Ge, Puri. Extinct.

PURUBORÁ ***(PURUBA, AURÃ, PUMBORA, PUROBORÁ, BURUBORA, KUYUBI, CUJUBI, MIGUELENO, MIGUELENHO)*** [PUR] 50 (1986 SIL). Rondônia, headwaters of the Rio São Miguel, tributary of the right bank of the Guaporé. Tupi, Purubora.

RIKBAKTSA ***(ARIPAKTSA, ERIKBATSA, ERIKPATSA, CANOEIRO)*** [ART] 800 or more (1994 SIL). Mato Grosso, confluence of Sangue and Juruena rivers, Japuira on the east bank of the Juruena between the Arinos and Sangue rivers, and Posto Escondido on the west bank of the Juruena 700 kms. north. 9 villages and 14 settlements. Macro-Ge, Rikbaktsa. Distinct from Avá-Canoeiro and Kanoé. SOV. Literacy rate in first language: 5% to 10%. Literacy rate in second language: 15% to 25%. Tropical forest. Bible portions 1977-1993.

SABANÊS ***(SABONES, SABANÊ)*** [SAE] 60 (1995 AMTB). Mato Grosso. Nambiquaran. Bilingualism in Portuguese, Northern Nambikuára. Integrated into Brazilian culture. Men are trilingual, understanding Portuguese and Northern Nambikuára.

SAKIRABIÁ ***(SAKIRIABAR, SAKIRABIAK, SAKIRAP)*** [SKF] 51 (1995 SIL). Rondônia, Municipality of Cerejeira and Colorado do Oeste, on the Mequens River. Unclassified.

SALUMÁ [SLJ] Northwest Pará, on the upper Anamu, source of the Trombetas, along the Suriname border. Carib, Northern, East-West Guiana, Waiwai, Sikiana. Different from Salumã in Mato Grosso.

SALUMÃ ***(ENAWENÉ-NAWÉ, ENEUENE-MARE)*** [UNK] 165 (1995 AMTB). Mato Grosso within northeast Nambiquara reserve. Arawakan, Maipuran, Central Maipuran. Related to Parecís. Another village of 30 to 50 people of totally different design is near this. Distinct from Carib Salumá in Pará.

SANUMÁ ***(TSANUMA, SANEMA, GUAIKA, SAMATARI, SAMATALI, XAMATARI)*** [SAM] 462 in Brazil (1976 UFM). Population total both countries 1,500 to 4,500. Auaris River, Roraima. Also spoken in Venezuela. Yanomam. Dialects: CAURA, ERVATO-VENTUARI, AUARIS. Dialects are closely related. In some areas up to 25% of the speakers are bilingual in Maquiritare.

SARARÉ ***(KABIXI, KAVIXI)*** [SRR] 150 (1983 SIL). Mato Grosso, Juina River. Nambiquaran. Bilingualism in Southern Nambikuára. Distinct from Kabixi which is Chapacuran.

SATERÉ-MAWÉ ***(MAUE, MABUE, MARAGUA, SATARÉ, ANDIRA, ARAPIUM)*** [MAV] 9,000 (1994 SIL). Pará, Andirá and other rivers. May also be in Amazonas. More than 14 villages. Tupi, Mawe-Satere. People are somewhat bilingual in Portuguese. Grammar. Literacy rate in first language: 12%. Literacy rate in second language: Below 5%. NT 1986.

SHARANAHUA [MCD] 350 in Brazil. Marináwa in Acre, along the upper Envira, tributary of the Tarauacá. Panoan, South-Central, Yaminahua-Sharanahua. Dialects: MARINAHUA (MARINÁWA), CHANDINAHUA. Bilingualism in Portuguese. The Marináwa are integrated into Brazilian society. There may be no speakers left. NT 1996. See main entry under Peru.

SIKIANA ***(SIKIÂNA, SHIKIANA, CHIQUIANA, CHIKENA, CHIQUENA, XIKUJANA, XIKIYANA)*** [SIK] 33 in Brazil (1986 SIL). Population total both countries 33 or more. Northwest Pará, between the Rio Cafuini and the headwaters of the Turuna and Itapi, near the Suriname border. Also spoken in Venezuela. Carib, Northern, East-West Guiana, Waiwai, Sikiana. Close to Salumá.

SIRIANO ***(SIRIANA, SIRIANE, SURYANA, SURIANÁ, SURIRÁ, SARIRÁ)*** [SRI] 10 in Brazil (1995 AMTB). São Gabriel, Amazonas. Tucanoan, Eastern Tucanoan, Central, Desano. Second languages are Tucano and Nhengatu, but they are ethnically distinct. NT 1998. See main entry under Colombia.

SURUAHÁ ***(SURUWAHÁ, ZURUAHÁ, MNDIOS DO COXODOÁ)*** [SWX] 130 (1995 AMTB). Amazonas. Arauan. First contact with the outside was 1980. Word minimality, word binarity, foot minimality. Tropical forest. Hunter-gatherers. Traditional religion.

SURUÍ ***(SURUÍ DO JIPARANÁ, SURUÍ DE RONDÔNIA, PAITER)*** [SRU] 800 (1994 SIL). A series of villages and scattered locations along the Rondônia-Mato Grosso border. 10 villages. Tupi, Monde. Related to Cinta Larga and Gavião do Jiparaná. SOV. Literacy rate in first language: 10% to 30%. Literacy rate in second language: 15% to 25%. Agriculturalists: coffee. Bible portions 1991.

SURUÍ DO PARÁ ***(AKEWERE, AKEWARA, "MUDJETÍRE", "MUDJETÍRE-SURUÍ", SURUÍ)*** [MDZ] 140 (1995 A. Graham SIL). Pará, 110 km. from Maraba, in municipio of São João Araguaia. Tupi, Tupi-Guarani, Tenetehara (IV). Probably fairly close linguistic relationship to Asuriní and Parakanã. Different from Suruí do Jiparaná. The name "Mudjetire" is offensive to the people. Literacy rate in first language: Below 1%. Literacy rate in second language: Below 5%.

SUYÁ [SUY] 196 including 31 Tapayuna (1995 AMTB). Xingu Park, Mato Grosso, headwaters of Rio Culuene. Macro-Ge, Ge-Kaingang, Ge, Northwest, Suya. Dialect: BEIÇO DE PAU (TAPAYÚNA). A separate language. Bilingualism is limited. Agriculturalists: manioc, maize; hunters, fishermen.

TAPEBA ***(TABEBA)*** [TBB] Ethnic group: 984 (1995 AMTB). Ceará. Unclassified. Monolingual in Portuguese. Extinct.

TAPIRAPÉ [TAF] 208 (1986 SIL). Mouth of the Tapirapé and Araguaia rivers, northeastern Mato Grosso. Tupi, Tupi-Guarani, Tenetehara (IV). Agriculturalists: manioc, maize, beans, pumpkins, peanuts, cotton; hunters, fishermen.

TARIANO ***(TARÎNA, TALIÁSERI)*** [TAE] 100 (1996 A. Aikhenvald) speakers out of an ethnic group of 1,500 in Brazil (1985 Rodrigues). Population total both countries 100 or more. Middle Vaupés River, Santa Rosa (Juquira), Iauarete, Periquitos, and Ji-Ponta, Amazonas. Also spoken in Colombia. Arawakan, Maipuran, Northern Maipuran, Inland. All are elderly in Brazil. No one has been located who speaks Tariano in Colombia, but the tribal identity is still maintained. The first language is Tucano or Nhengatu. Nearly extinct.

TEMBÉ [TEM] 100 speakers out of 853 ethnic Tembé (1995 SIL). Maranhão, Gurupi River and Guama. None in Guama speak Tembé, only Portuguese. In Gurupi about 100 of 170 speak Tembé. Tupi, Tupi-Guarani, Tenetehara (IV). The speech of most or all groups of this name is intelligible with Guajajara. Well integrated.

TENHARIM ***(TENHAREM, TENHARIN)*** [PAH] 345 including 13 Diahói (1994 SIL). Amazonas. The Diahói are on the Rio Marmelos, Karipuna on Jaci Paraná River Post in Rondônia, Morerebi on Rio Preto and Marmelos. 2 villages. Tupi, Tupi-Guarani, Kawahib (VI). Dialects: PARINTINTÍN, KAGWAHIV (KAWAIB), KARIPUNA JACI PARANÁ, MIALÁT, DIAHÓI (JAHUI, GIAHOI). Boca Negra is a related ethnic group. Tenharim and Kagwahiv are nearly identical. Eru-eu-wau-wau (Uru-eu-wau-wau) and Morerebi may be dialects. The Tenharim consider the Diahói to be relatives; slight dialect difference. The Morerebi are a family group who have not lived with the Tenharim for many years, and do not want contact with outside culture. The Kayabí, Parintintín, Tenharim, Júma, Karipuna, and Diahói all call themselves 'Kagwahiva' (Kagwahibm, Kagwahiv, Kawahip, Kavahiva, Kawaib, Kagwahiph). Speakers are fairly bilingual. Grammar. SVO. Literacy rate in first language: 10% to 30%. Literacy rate in second language: 15% to 25%. Fishermen, gatherers, agriculturalists. NT 1996.

TERÊNA ***(TERENO, ETELENA)*** [TEA] 15,000 (1991 SIL). Mato Grosso do Sul, in 20 villages and 2 cities. Arawakan, Maipuran, Southern Maipuran, Bolivia-Parana. Many speak limited Portuguese. Dictionary. Grammar. VOS. Literacy rate in first language: 20%. Literacy rate in second language: 80%. NT 1994.

TICUNA ***(TIKUNA, TUKUNA, MAGÜTA)*** [TCA] 12,000 in Brazil. West Amazonas. Language Isolate. NT 1986. See main entry under Peru.

TINGUI-BOTO ***(TINGUI, CARAPATÓ, KARAPATÓ)*** [TGV] (800 in ethnic group; 1986 SIL). Alagoas. Unclassified. People are monolingual in Portuguese. Extinct.

TORÁ ***(TORAZ)*** [TRZ] 40 out of an ethnic group of 120 (1990 YWAM). Amazonas, on the lower Rio Marmelos, tributary of the Rio Madeira. Chapacura-Wanham, Madeira. Nearly extinct.

TREMEMBÉ [TME] Ceará. Unclassified. Bilingualism in Portuguese. Probably linguistically and culturally integrated. There may be no speakers left (1995). Nearly extinct.

TRIÓ ***(TIRIÓ, TIRIYÓ)*** [TRI] 329 in Brazil (1995 AMTB). Pará, Rio Mapari. Carib, Northern, East-West Guiana, Wayana-Trio. Dialect: PIANOCOTÓ. Pianokotó is probably extinct; no reports since 1957. NT 1979. See main entry under Suriname.

TRUKÁ [TKA] Ethnic group 909 (1995 AMTB). Pernambuco, Bahía. Unclassified. People are monolingual in Portuguese. Extinct.

TRUMAÍ [TPY] 78 (1995 AMTB). Xingú Park, source of Xingú River, villages along banks, Mato Grosso. Language Isolate. Ruhlen and others classify it as Equatorial. They are intermarrying with speakers of other languages. They trade extensively with other groups. Agriculturalists: manioc, peppers, beans.

TUBARÃO ***(AIKANÃ, WARI, UARI, CORUMBIARA, KOLUMBIARA)*** [TBA] 90 (1986 SIL). Rondônia, west of Vilhena, near the Cuiabá-Porto Velho highway. Arawakan, Maipuran, Northern Maipuran, Unclassified. Dialect: MASAKÁ (MASSACA). Ione Vasconcelos of UNB is studying them.

TUCANO ***(TUKÁNA, TAKUNA, DAXSEA)*** [TUO] 2,631 in Brazil (1986 SIL). Population total both countries 5,000. Amazonas. Also spoken in Colombia. Tucanoan, Eastern Tucanoan, Northern. Dialects: YOHORAA (CURAUA), WASONA (UASONA). Used as a second language by many neighboring groups. Trade language. NT 1988.

TUKUMANFÉD [TKF] Rondônia, mouth of the Cacoal tributary of the Jiparaná. Tupi, Tupi-Guarani, Kawahib (VI). Extinct.

TUPARÍ [TUP] 56 or more (1986 SIL). Pororoca Post, Rondônia. Tupi, Tupari. There are reported to be others upstream on the Rio Branco. Tropical forest. Nearly extinct.

TUPINAMBÁ ***(OLD TUPÍ)*** [TPN] Tupi, Tupi-Guarani, Tupi (III). Modern descendent is Nhengatu. Extinct.

TUPINIKIN ***(TUPINAKI, TUPINIKIM)*** [TPK] Ethnic group: 820 (1995 AMTB). Espirito Santo, Bahia. Tupi, Tupi-Guarani, Tupi (III). People are monolingual in Portuguese. Extinct.

TURIWÁRA ***(TURIUARA)*** [TWT] Ethnic group: possibly 30 (1995 SIL). Pará, live with the Tembé. Tupi, Tupi-Guarani, Tenetehara (IV). Extinct.

TUXÁ ***(TUSHA, TODELA)*** [TUD] Ethnic group: 900 (1995 AMTB). Bahía, Pernambuco. Language Isolate. Ruhlen and others classify it as Equatorial. People are monolingual in Portuguese. Extinct.

TUXINÁWA ***(TUCHINAUA)*** [TUX] Acre. Panoan, South-Central, Yaminahua-Sharanahua. Extinct.

TUYUCA ***(TUYUKA, TUIUCA, DOCHKAFUARA, DOKA-POARA, DOXKÁ-POÁRÁ)*** [TUE] 465 in Brazil (1995 AMTB). Amazonas. Tucanoan, Eastern Tucanoan, Central, Bara. Dialect: TSOLA. Bilingualism in Tucano, Waimaha. Bible portions 1991-1994. See main entry under Colombia.

TXIKÃO ***(TXIKÂN, CHICAO, TUNULI, TONORE)*** [TXI] 146 (1995 AMTB). Xingú Park, Mato Grosso. Carib, Northern, Northern Brazil. A separate language, similar to Arara of Pará. Bilingualism is limited. Agriculturalists: maize, manioc, cotton, urucu, gourds; hunter-gatherers, fishermen.

UAMUÉ ***(ATICUM, ATIKUM, HUAMUÊ)*** [UAM] Ethnic group: 3,900 (1995 AMTB). Pernambuco, vicinity of Floresta. Unclassified. Ethnic group now speaks only Portuguese. Extinct.

UMOTÍNA ***(UMUTINA, BARBADOS)*** [UMO] In the ethnic group: 160 (1993). Mato Grosso, along the Paraguay River. Macro-Ge, Bororo, Bororo Proper. Bilingualism in Portuguese. The last speaker died in 1988. The people now speak Portuguese. Extinct.

URU-EU-UAU-UAU ***(URUEWAWAU, ERU-EU-WAU-WAU)*** [URZ] 100 (1995 AMTB). Rondônia. Tupi, Tupi-Guarani, Kawahib (VI).

URU-PA-IN [URP] 200 (1995 SIL). Rondônia, Municipality of Ariquemes. Unclassified. No permanent contact.

URUBÚ-KAAPOR [URB] 500 (1988 SIL). Maranhão, 8 to 10 villages scattered over 2,800 sq. mi. Tupi, Tupi-Guarani, Oyampi (VIII). Dictionary. Grammar. SOV, OSV. Literacy rate in first language: 6%. Literacy rate in second language: 6%. NT 1986.

URUBÚ-KAAPOR SIGN LANGUAGE ***(URUBÚ SIGN LANGUAGE)*** [UKS] 7 first language users, 500 second language users (1986 J. Kakumasu). Maranhão. Deaf sign language. The deaf are monolingual in sign language. About one out of every 75 persons is deaf. Urubu hearing children grow up knowing both the verbal and the sign systems. OSV.

WAIMAHA ***(WAIMAJA, NORTHERN BARASANO, "BARÁ")*** [BAO] 100 in Brazil (1998). Prelazia Rio Negro, Amazonas. Tucanoan, Eastern Tucanoan, Central, Bara. Bible portions 1975-1994. See main entry under Colombia.

WAIWAI ***(UAIUAI, UAIEUE, OUAYEONE)*** [WAW] 571 in Brazil (1995 AMTB). Population total both countries 770. Amazonas, Pará, Roraima. Also spoken in Guyana. Carib, Northern, East-West Guiana, Waiwai. Dialect: KATAWIAN (KATWENA, KATAWINA, CATAWIAN, CATAUIAN, PARUCUTU, PARUKUTU, KATUENA, CACHUENA). Dialect or related language: Salumá. Voegelin and Voegelin (1977) treat Katawian as a separate language. Hunters, fishermen. NT 1984.

WAKONÁ [WAF] Ethnic group: 500 to 1,000 (1995 SIL). Alagoas. Unclassified. They may not live together as a group. Extinct.

WASU ***(WAÇU)*** [WSU] Ethnic group: 1,024 (1995 AMTB). Alagoas. Unclassified. People are monolingual in Portuguese. Extinct.

WAURÁ ***(UAURA, AURA)*** [WAU] 240 (1994 SIL). Xingú Park, Mato Grosso. Arawakan, Maipuran, Central Maipuran. Partially intelligible with Mehinacu. Literacy rate in first language: 1% to 5%. Literacy rate in second language: 5% to 15%.

WAYAMPI, AMAPARI ***("OIAMPIPUCU", "OYAMPIPUKU")*** [OYM] 350 (1993 C Jensen SIL). Along tributaries of the upper Amapari River, west central Amapá. 8 villages. Tupi, Tupi-Guarani, Oyampi (VIII). Inherently intelligible with Oiapoque Wayampi. Bilingual level estimates for Portuguese are 0 63%, 1 21%, 2 13%, 3 2.5%, 4 .5%, 5 0%. Language attitudes indicate the need for separate literature from Oiapoque Wayampi. Dictionary. Grammar. Literacy rate in first language: 10% to 30%. Literacy rate in second language: Below 5%.

WAYAMPI, OIAPOQUE ***(OIAMPÍ, OYAMPÍ, WAYÃPI, WAYAPÍ, OYANPÍK, OYAPÍ, WAIAMPI)*** [OYA] 10 in Brazil (1986 A. Jensen SIL). Northern Pará. Tupi, Tupi-Guarani, Oyampi (VIII). Inherently intelligible with Amapari Wayampi. Not intelligible with Emerillon. Bilingualism in Portuguese. Language attitudes indicate need for separate literature from Amapari Wayampi. SOV. See main entry under French Guiana.

WAYANA ***(OAYANA, OYANA, OIANA, UAIANA, WAYÂNA, UPURUI, ALUKUYANA)*** [WAY] 150 in Brazil. Amapá, among the Apalaí. Carib, Northern, East-West Guiana, Wayana-Trio. Dialects: RUCUYEN (ROUCOUYENNE), URUCUIANA (URUCENA). Partially intelligible with Apalaí. NT 1979. See main entry under Suriname.

WAYORÓ ***(WAYURÚ, AYURÚ, AJURÚ, UAIORA, WAJARU)*** [WYR] 40 possibly (1986 SIL). Pororoca Post, Rondônia, Guapore River. Tupi, Tupari.

WIRAFÉD ***(WIROFÉD, UIRAFED)*** [WIR] Rondônia, on the Riosinho and Muquí tributaries of the Jiparaná. Tupi, Tupi-Guarani, Kawahib (VI). Permanent contact reported in late 1950s. Extinct.

XAKRIABÁ ***(CHAKRIABA, SHACRIABA, CHIKRIABA)*** [XKR] Ethnic group: 4,643 (1995 AMTB). Minas Gerais. Macro-Ge, Ge-Kaingang, Ge, Central, Acua. People are monolingual in Portuguese. Extinct.

XAVÁNTE ***(AKUÊN, AKWEN, A'WE, CHAVANTE, SHAVANTE, CRISCA, PUSCITI, TAPACUA)*** [XAV] 8,000 (1994 SIL). Mato Grosso, 60 villages. Macro-Ge, Ge-Kaingang, Ge, Central, Acua. Dictionary. Grammar. OSV. Literacy rate in first language: 10% to 30%. Literacy rate in second language: 25% to 50% (most men, few women). Hunter-gatherers. Bible portions 1970-1993.

XERÉNTE ***(SHERENTÉ)*** [XER] 1,200 (1993 SIL). Tocantins, between the Rio do Sono and Rio Tocantins. Macro-Ge, Ge-Kaingang, Ge, Central, Acua. People are somewhat bilingual in Portuguese. Bible portions 1970-1990.

XETÁ ***(ARÉ, SETA, SHETA, CHETA)*** [XET] 3 speakers (1990 R. Dooley) out of an ethnic population of 100 to 250 (1986 SIL). Paraná, among the Kaingang. Tupi, Tupi-Guarani, Guarani (I). Nearly extinct.

XIPINÁWA ***(SHIPINAHUA)*** [XIP] Southern Amazonas and Acre. Panoan, South-Central, Yaminahua-Sharanahua. Both people and language are thought to be extinct.

XIRIÂNA [XIR] Tributaries of Demeni and Rio Negro, Amazonas, near Venezuela border. Arawakan, Unclassified. Distinct from the Yanomam language, Ninam (Xirianá).

XOKLENG ***(AWEIKOMA, BUGRE, BOTOCUDOS)*** [XOK] 250 speakers (1975) out of ethnic group of 634 (1986 SIL). Santa Catarina, along tributary of the Itajaí River. Macro-Ge, Ge-Kaingang, Kaingang, Northern. A separate language. People are fairly bilingual in Portuguese. The name 'Bugre' is also used for Kaingang and Brazilian Guaraní. The name 'Kaingang' is sometimes used for Xokleng. SOV.

YABAÂNA ***(JABAANA, YABARANA)*** [YBN] (90 in ethnic group; 1986 SIL). Amazonas, headwaters of the Marauia and Cauaboris, tributaries of the left bank of Rio Negro. Arawakan, Maipuran, Northern Maipuran, Unclassified. Distinct from Yabarana of Venezuela. People are monolingual in Portuguese. Extinct.

YAMINAHUA ***(YAMINÁWA, JAMINAWÁ, YAMANAWA)*** [YAA] 357 in Brazil (1986 SIL). Acre. Panoan, South-Central, Yaminahua-Sharanahua. Same dialect as Bolivia, and the same as, or close to, that of Peru. Bible portions 1987. See main entry under Peru.

YANOMÁMI ***(WAICÁ, WAIKÁ, YANOAM, YANOMAM, YANOMAMÉ, SURARA, XURIMA, PARAHURI)*** [WCA] 9,000 (1994 SIL). Waicá post, Uraricuera River, Roraima, Toototobi post, Amazonas, Catrimani River, Roraima. Yanomam. Dialects: YANAMAM (PATIMITHERI, WAIKA), YANOMAM (NAOMAM, GUADEMA, WADEMA, WAREMA), YANOMAY (TOOTOTOBI), NANOMAM (KARIME), JAUARI (JOARI, YOARI, AICA). Distinct from but related to Yanomamö of Brazil and Venezuela. Monolingual. Semi-nomadic. SOV.

YANOMAMÖ ***(GUAICA, GUAHARIBO, YANOMA, YANOMAMI, SHAMATRI, SHAATHARI)*** [GUU] 1,500 to 2,000 in Brazil. Amazonas, upper tributaries of Rio Negro. Yanomam. Dialects: EASTERN YANOMAMI (PARIMA), WESTERN YANOMAMI (PADAMO-ORINOCO). Related to, but distinct from Yanomami of Brazil. Monolingual. NT 1984. See main entry under Venezuela.

YARUMÁ ***(JARUMÁ, WAIKU)*** [YRM] Mato Grosso, Xingú Park. Carib, Southern, Xingu Basin. May be extinct.

YAWALAPITÍ ***(JAULAPITI, YAULAPITI)*** [YAW] 140 (1995 AMTB). Xingú Park, Mato Grosso. Arawakan, Maipuran, Central Maipuran. Related to but not intelligible with Waurá and Mehinaku. Many understand another language of the Xingú because they have lived in other villages. Fishermen, hunter-gatherers, swidden agriculturalists: manioc, maize.

YAWANAWA ***(IAUANAUÁ, JAWANAUA, YAHUANAHUA)*** [YWN] 310 (1994 SIL). Acre. 1 village of 100 people, with the remainder living along a river. Panoan, South-Central, Yaminahua-Sharanahua. Portuguese is used only with outsiders. Vigorous. Bible portions.

YUHUP ***(MAKÚ-YAHUP, YËHUP, YAHUP, YAHUP MAKÚ, "MAKU")*** [YAB] 360 in Brazil (1995 AMTB). Population total both countries 600. Amazonas, on a tributary of the Vaupés River. Also spoken in Colombia. Maku. Limited intelligibility with Hupdë. Ruhlen and other classify it as related to Puinave. South of the Hupdë. The name "Maku" is offensive. OSV.

YURUTI ***(JURUTI, JURUTI-TAPUIA, LURUTY-TAPUYA, JURITI, YURITI, YURITI-TAPUIA)*** [YUI] 50 in Brazil (1991 SIL). Iauarete, Amazonas. Tucanoan, Eastern Tucanoan, Central, Bara. Bible portions 1985. See main entry under Colombia.

BRITISH VIRGIN ISLANDS

National or official language: English. 20,000 (1998 UN). 60 islands, 15 are inhabited. Main islands: Tortola, Virgin Gorda, Anegada, Jost Van Dyke. Literacy rate 98%. Christian. Data accuracy estimate: B. The number of languages listed for British Virgin Islands is 2. Of those, both are living languages. Diversity index 0.24.

ENGLISH [ENG] 2,000 (1998). Indo-European, Germanic, West, English. National language. Bible 1535-1989. See main entry under United Kingdom.

VIRGIN ISLANDS CREOLE ENGLISH [VIB] 12,000 in British Virgin Islands (1987). Creole, English based, Atlantic, Eastern, Southern. Coexists with English in a fairly stable diglossic relationship (Holm 1989:455). See main entry under U.S. Virgin Islands.

CANADA

National or official languages: English, French. 30,563,040 (1998 UN). Indian (800,000) and Eskimo (32,000) ethnic total (1993): 146,285 mother tongue speakers (1981 census). 4,120,770 non-English or French mother tongue, or 15.3% (1991 census). Literacy rate 96% to 99%. Also includes Afrikaans 2,353, Tosk Albanian 29, Judeo-Moroccan Arabic, Najdi Spoken Arabic 28,550, Armenian 2,265, Assyrian Neo-Aramaic 5,000, Belarusan 2,280, Bulgarian 1,630, Chaldean Neo-Aramaic, Yue Chinese 250,000, Corsican, Czech 27,780, Danish 27,395, Dutch 159,000, Estonian 14,520, Western Farsi 15,000, Finnish 36,725, Western Frisian, Irish Gaelic, Scots Gaelic 5,000, Standard German 470,505, Greek 104,455, Haitian Creole French 12,317, Hebrew, Hungarian 86,835, Icelandic, Italian 514,410, Iu Mien 100, Japanese 43,000, Kashubian, Korean 73,000, Lao, Latvian 15,000, Lithuanian, Macedonian 3,995, Maltese, Bokmaal Norwegian 27,405, Nung, Eastern Panjabi 214,530, Western Panjabi, Plains Indian Sign Language, Polish 222,355, Pontic, Portuguese 222,870, Vlax Romani, Romanian 11,300, Russian 31,745, Serbo-Croatian 93,860, Sinhala 3,004, Slovak 17,370, Slovenian 6,415, Southwestern Caribbean Creole English, Spanish 228,580, Swedish 21,650, Tagalog 158,210, Turkish 8,863, Turoyo, Ukrainian 174,830, Vietnamese 60,000, Welsh 3,160, Eastern Yiddish 49,890, Arabic 166,150 (1998), Chinese 736,015 (1998), from India and Pakistan 280,000, speakers of many European languages. Information mainly from W. Chafe 1962, 1965; SIL 1951-1999. Christian, secular, Muslim, Jewish. Blind population 27,184. Deaf population 1,704,551. Deaf institutions: many. Data accuracy estimate: A1, A2. The number of languages listed for Canada is 90. Of those, 85 are living languages and 5 are extinct. Diversity index 0.55.

ABNAKI, WESTERN ***(ABENAKI, ABENAQUI, ST. FRANCIS)*** [ABE] 20 speakers (1991 M. Krauss) out of 1,800 ethnic population including Eastern Abnaki in USA (1982 SIL). Quebec on St. Lawrence River between Montreal and Quebec City. Algic, Algonquian, Eastern. Bilingualism in French. All elderly. Dictionary. Grammar. Nearly extinct. Bible portions 1844.

ALGONQUIN ***(ALGONKIN)*** [ALG] 2,275 mother tongue speakers (1998 Statistics Canada) out of 5,000 population (1987 SIL). Southwestern Quebec, northwest of Ottawa and in adjacent areas of Ontario (Golden Lake and Maniwaki). Algic, Algonquian, Central, Ojibwa. Several dialects. In the east Algonquin is the principal means of communication, and spoken by the majority of all ages. In the west most adults speak Algonquin, young adults may prefer the national language, and children prefer the national language, although some may speak Algonquin. Literacy rate in first language: 30% to 60%. Literacy rate in second language: 75% to 100%. NT 1998.

AMERICAN SIGN LANGUAGE ***(ASL, AMESLAN)*** [ASE] English-speaking areas of Canada. Deaf sign language. Dialect differences with USA ASL, and regional differences in Canada from east to west. Structurally and grammatically distinct from Quebec Sign Language (LSQ). Has grammatical characteristics independent of English. A few adults know both ASL and LSQ. Most signers from eastern Canada use ASL with some British Sign Language vocabulary, a remnant from Maritime Sign Language, which came from British Sign Language. Sign language interpreters are required for deaf people in court. Used for deaf college students, important public functions, job training, social service programs, sign language instruction for parents of deaf children, classes for hearing people, organization for sign language teachers, committee on national sign language. Manual alphabet. Dictionary. TV, videos. Bible portions 1982-1987. See main entry under USA.

ASSINIBOINE ***(ASSINIBOIN)*** [ASB] Population total both countries 150 to 200 fluent speakers, out of 3,500 population (1986 SIL). West central and southeastern Saskatchewan (Mosquito-Grizzly Bear's Head) and southern Saskatchewan (part of Carry-the-Kettle and Whitebear). Also spoken in USA. Siouan, Siouan Proper, Central, Mississippi Valley, Dakota. Very close to the Assiniboine of Montana. 94% lexical similarity with Dakota of Manitoba, 90% with Dakota of North Dakota, 89% with Lakota and Stoney. English is spoken extensively. Over 40 years old, most over 60.

ATIKAMEKW ***(TÊTE DE BOULE, ATTIMEWK, ATTIKAMEK, ATIHKAMEKW, ATIKAMEK)*** [TET] 3,995 mother tongue speakers (1998 Statistics Canada). Three isolated communities on reservations of Manuane, Obedjiwan, Weymontachie, between La Tuque, Quebec, and Senneterre, Quebec, 200 to 400 km. north of Montreal in south central Quebec, along the upper reaches of the St. Maurice River. Algic, Algonquian, Central, Cree-Montagnais-Naskapi. Very different from Montagnais and Naskapi in the nearby area. Language complex or dialect continuum within Cree-Montagnais-Naskapi. Non-palatalized r-dialect. Bilingualism in French. Vigorous. Three subgroups: Manawan, Wemotaci, Opitciwan. Literacy rate in first language: 10% to 30%. Literacy rate in second language: 50% to 75%. Roman orthography, based on French. Hunters, trappers. Bible portions 1980-1983.

BABINE ***(BABINE CARRIER, NORTHERN CARRIER)*** [BCR] 1,600 speakers out of 2,200 population (1982 SIL). Areas of Burns Lake, Babine Lake, Moricetown, Takla Lake area, west central British

Columbia. Na-Dene, Nuclear Na-Dene, Athapaskan-Eyak, Athapaskan, Canadian, Carrier-Chilcotin, Babine-Carrier. Babine is still the principal means of communication among middle-aged adults and older. Children and young adults may speak Babine but prefer English. Literacy rate in first language: 1% to 5%. Literacy rate in second language: 50% to 75%. Bible portions 1978.

BEAVER [BEA] 300 speakers (1991 M. Dale Kinkade) out of 600 population (1987 SIL). Prophet River area of north eastern British Columbia and northwestern Alberta, Chateh (Assumption) on the Hay River, and Prophet River south of Fort Nelson. Na-Dene, Nuclear Na-Dene, Athapaskan-Eyak, Athapaskan, Canadian, Beaver-Sekani. The remaining speakers are reported to be highly bilingual in English. Literacy rate in first language: 5% to 15%. Literacy rate in second language: 25% to 50%. Bible portions 1886-1989.

BELLA COOLA *(NUXALK)* [BEL] 200 or fewer speakers out of 700 population (1991 M. D. Kinkade). Inlet on the central British Columbia coast. Salishan, Bella Coola. Bilingualism in English. There is a language course in Bella Coola (1991). Dictionary. Grammar.

BEOTHUK *(BEOTHUC, BETHUCK, BETHUK, NEWFOUNDLAND, RED INDIANS)* [BUE] Newfoundland. Unclassified. The theory that it was an Algonquian language is not accepted by all Algonquianists. Became extinct in 1829. Extinct.

BLACKFOOT *(PIKANII, BLACKFEET)* [BLC] 4,745 mother tongue speakers in Canada (1998 Statistics Canada) out of 15,000 population including USA (1977 SIL). Population total both countries 5,800. Blackfoot, Piegan, and Blood Reserves in southern Alberta. Also spoken in USA. Algic, Algonquian, Plains. Dialects: PIEGAN, BLOOD. In some places Blackfoot is the principal language for older adults. Children and young adults tend to prefer English. Dictionary. Grammar. Bible portions 1890-1980.

CARRIER *(CENTRAL CARRIER)* [CAR] 1,500 speakers out of 2,100 population (1987 SIL). Both Carrier languages have 2,190 mother tongue speakers (1998 Statistics Canada). All Athapaskan language family mother tongue speakers in Canada 20,090 (1998 Statistics Canada). Central British Columbia, Stuart and Fraser Lake area. Na-Dene, Nuclear Na-Dene, Athapaskan-Eyak, Athapaskan, Canadian, Carrier-Chilcotin, Babine-Carrier. Bilingualism in English. Mainly adults. In some communities vigorous among adults. Most children and young adults prefer English. Dictionary. Grammar. Literacy rate in first language: 5% to 10%. Literacy rate in second language: 50% to 75%. Bilingual literacy materials used in schools. NT 1995.

CARRIER, SOUTHERN [CAF] 500 (1987 SIL). Central British Columbia, west of Quesnel and south of Cheslatta Lake, towards the Fraser and its tributaries, and Anahim Lake-Ulkatcho. Na-Dene, Nuclear Na-Dene, Athapaskan-Eyak, Athapaskan, Canadian, Carrier-Chilcotin, Babine-Carrier. Can use literature adapted from Central Carrier. 90% lexical similarity with Central Carrier. Limited bilingualism. Vigorous. Literacy rate in first language: Below 1%. Literacy rate in second language: 50% to 75%. Bible portions 1997.

CAYUGA [CAY] 360 speakers in Canada. Population total both countries 370. Six Nations, Ontario. Also spoken in USA. Iroquoian, Northern Iroquoian, Five Nations, Seneca-Onondaga, Seneca-Cayuga. English is the first or second language for the ethnic group. In Ontario most speakers are middle-aged or older.

CHILCOTIN *(TZILKOTIN)* [CHI] 705 mother tongue speakers (1998 Statistics Canada) out of 1,800 population (1982 SIL). West of Williams Lake, south central British Columbia. Na-Dene, Nuclear Na-Dene, Athapaskan-Eyak, Athapaskan, Canadian, Carrier-Chilcotin, Chilcotin. Vigorous among adults. Many children prefer English. SOV. Literacy rate in first language: Below 1%. Literacy rate in second language: 25% to 50%. Bible portions 1993.

CHINOOK WAWA *(CHINOOK JARGON, CHINOOK PIDGIN)* [CRW] Population total both countries 100 speakers, all over 50 years old (1962 Chafe). British Columbia. Also spoken in USA. Pidgin, Amerindian. Bilingualism in English. Formerly used along the Pacific coast from Oregon to Alaska, between Indian and white, and between speakers of different languages. All speakers are now probably scattered. Nearly extinct. Bible portions 1912.

CHIPEWYAN *(DENE)* [CPW] 4,000 speakers out of 6,000 population (1995 M. Krauss). Northern Alberta, Saskatchewan, Manitoba, southeastern Northwest Territories (Snowdrift and Fort Resolution). Communities of Fort Smith, Fort Chipewyan, Buffalo Narrows, Brochet, and Reindeer Lake are some of the communities. Na-Dene, Nuclear Na-Dene, Athapaskan-Eyak, Athapaskan, Canadian, Hare-Chipewyan, Chipewyan. Dialect: YELLOWKNIFE. Speakers include children in some places (1995). Dictionary. Grammar. Literacy rate in first language: 1% to 5%. Literacy rate in second language: 25% to 50%. NT 1881.

COMOX *(COMOX-SLIAMMON)* [COO] 400 speakers or fewer, including 1 speaker of Island Comox, fewer than 400 of Sliammon (1991 M. Dale Kinkade), out of a population of 850 (1983). British Columbia, Vancouver Island and the coast north of Powell River. Salishan, Central Salish, Northern. Dialects: ISLAND COMOX, SLIAMMON. Speakers all speak the Sliammon (mainland) dialect. No speakers of Island Comox left. Some members of the ethnic group speak English as mother tongue. Speakers primarily middle-aged and older. Grammar.

CREE, MOOSE ***(YORK CREE, WEST SHORE CREE, WEST MAIN CREE)*** [CRM] 4,500 speakers out of 5,000 population (1982 SIL). All Cree mother tongue speakers in Canada 87,555 (1998 Statistics Canada). Southern tip of James Bay, Moosonee, Ontario. This community and surrounding area (Moose Factory, Ontario). Has speakers of both Moose Cree and Swampy Cree in it. Algic, Algonquian, Central, Cree-Montagnais-Naskapi. Language complex or dialect continuum within Cree-Montagnais-Naskapi. Nonpalatalized l-dialect. Bilingualism in English. Vigorous. Grammar. Literacy rate in first language: 5% to 10%. Literacy rate in second language: 75% to 100%. Cree syllabary, eastern finals. NT 1876.

CREE, NORTHERN EAST ***(COASTAL EAST CREE, EAST COASTAL CREE, EAST CREE)*** [CRL] 5,308 speakers (1997 Quebec Ministere de la Sante et des Services Sociaux). West central Quebec, east coast of lower Hudson Bay and James Bay, communities of Whapmagoostui, Chisasibi, Wemindji, and most people in Eastmain. Algic, Algonquian, Central, Cree-Montagnais-Naskapi. Language complex or dialect continuum within Cree-Montagnais-Naskapi. Sometimes classified as Montagnais. Palatalized y-dialect. Bilingualism in English. Vigorous. Dictionary. Literacy rate in first language: 5% to 10%. Literacy rate in second language: 50% to 75%. Cree syllabary, eastern finals. Bible portions 1921.

CREE, PLAINS ***(WESTERN CREE)*** [CRP] 34,000 or more in Canada. Population total both countries 35,000 or more speakers out of 53,000 or more population (1982 SIL). North central Manitoba westward across Saskatchewan and central Alberta to the foot of the Rocky Mountains. Also spoken in USA. Algic, Algonquian, Central, Cree-Montagnais-Naskapi. Dialects: PLAINS CREE, WESTERN YORK CREE. Language complex or dialect continuum within Cree-Montagnais-Naskapi. Non-palatalized y-dialect. Bilingualism in English. All ages. Vigorous. Grammar. Literacy rate in first language: 1% to 5%. Literacy rate in second language: 75% to 100%. Cree syllabary, western finals. Bible 1861-1908.

CREE, SOUTHERN EAST ***(INLAND EAST CREE, EAST INLAND CREE, EAST CREE)*** [CRE] 7,306 speakers (1997 Quebec Ministere de la Sante et des Services Sociaux). Quebec, southeastward from James Bay, inland to the height of land (watershed) east of Lake Mistissini. Coastal communities of Waskaganish, some speakers in Eastmain, Inland, in Mistissini, Waswanipi, Nemaska, and Ouje-Bougoumo. Algic, Algonquian, Central, Cree-Montagnais-Naskapi. Language complex or dialect continuum within Cree-Montagnais-Naskapi. Sometimes classified as Montagnais. Palatalized y-dialect. Bilingualism in English. Vigorous. Dictionary. Literacy rate in second language: 75% to 100%. Cree syllabary, eastern finals. Language of instruction in over half the communities, taught as a subject in others. NT, in press (1999).

CREE, SWAMPY ***(YORK CREE, WEST SHORE CREE, WEST MAIN CREE)*** [CSW] 4,500 speakers out of 5,000 population (1982 SIL). All Cree mother tongue speakers in Canada 60,000 (1991 M. Dale Kinkade). Ontario, along the coast of Hudson Bay and northern west coast of James Bay, and inland. Algic, Algonquian, Central, Cree-Montagnais-Naskapi. Dialects: EASTERN SWAMPY CREE, WESTERN SWAMPY CREE. Language complex or dialect continuum within Cree-Montagnais-Naskapi. Nonpalatalized n-dialect. Bilingualism in English. Vigorous. Dictionary. Grammar. Literacy rate in first language: 5% to 10%. Literacy rate in second language: 75% to 100%. Cree syllabary, western finals. NT 1976.

CREE, WOODS [CWD] Far north Manitoba and Saskatchewan, almost to the border with Northwest Territories. Only in Canada. Algic, Algonquian, Central, Cree-Montagnais-Naskapi. Language complex or dialect continuum within Cree-Montagnais-Naskapi. Nonpalatalized th-dialect. Bilingualism in English. All ages. Vigorous. Literacy rate in first language: 1% to 5%. Literacy rate in second language: 75% to 100%. Cree syllabary, western finals.

DAKOTA ***(SIOUX)*** [DHG] 5,000 in Canada (1991 M. Dale Kinkade). Southern Manitoba and Saskatchewan, Oak River and Oak Lake, Long Plain west of Winnipeg, Standing Buffalo, Birdtail, Stony Wahpeton, and Moose Woods. May be at Wood Mountain. Siouan, Siouan Proper, Central, Mississippi Valley, Dakota. Dialects: DAKOTA (SANTEE), NAKOTA (YANKTON). 83% to 86% lexical similarity with Stoney, 89% to 94% with Assiniboine, 90% to 95% among dialects. All ages in some communities. Vigorous in some communities. In some communities children and young adults may not speak Dakota or may prefer English. Literacy rate in first language: Below 1%. Literacy rate in second language: 50% to 75%. Bible 1879. See main entry under USA.

DOGRIB [DGB] 2,085 mother tongue speakers (1998 Statistics Canada) out of 2,965 population (1994 J. Feenstra SIL). Between Great Slave Lake and Great Bear Lake, Northwest Territories, 5 communities (Rae, Detah, Rae Lakes, Lac la Martre, Snare Lake) and a subdivision of Yellowknife. Rae is the center. Na-Dene, Nuclear Na-Dene, Athapaskan-Eyak, Athapaskan, Canadian, Hare-Chipewyan, Hare-Slavey. Dialect: DETAH-NDILO. The Detah-Ndilo dialect developed from intermarriage between the Yellowknife subdivision of the Chipewyan and the Dogrib. 84% lexical similarity with Southern Slavey, 82% with Northern Slavey. 16% speak a little English; 37% speak both Dogrib and English, but speak Dogrib better; 14% speak both languages equally; 9% speak both, but speak English better; 7% speak English and a little Dogrib; 3% are monolingual in English (children), 12% are monolingual in Dogrib. All ages. Monolinguals include children and the elderly. Adults prefer to use Dogrib in most contexts. One Dogrib band has frequent contact and close relationships with the Bear Lake (North Slavey) people of Fort Franklin. Relations with the Inuit and the Chipewyan have traditionally been strained. Dictionary. Grammar. SOV. Literacy rate in first language: 1% to 5%. Literacy rate in second language: 25% to 50%. There is bilingual education. Canadian shield, rocks, lakes. Hunters, trappers. 300 feet.

ENGLISH [ENG] 17,100,000 mother tongue speakers in Canada, or 60% of the population (1998 Statistics Canada). 820,000 mother tongue speakers in Quebec (1995 Statistics Canada); plus another 1,500,000 in Quebec whose first or second language is English (1995 Statistics Canada). Indo-European, Germanic, West, English. Dialect: NEWFOUNDLAND ENGLISH. National language. Bible 1382-1989. See main entry under United Kingdom.

FRENCH *(FRANÇAIS)* [FRN] 6,700,000 mother tongue speakers in Canada, or less than 24% (1998 Statistics Canada). Mother tongue of over 80% of Quebec's population (1997 DiverCite Langues). 300,000 speak Acadien, 500,000 speak Franco-Ontariens. Québécois is in Québéc, Franco-Ontariens in Ontario, Acadian is in Caraquet, Shippagan, the east coast of New Brunswick, pockets in Nova Scotia and Prince Edward Island. Some Québécois speakers in Manitoba. Indo-European, Italic, Romance, Italo-Western, Western, Gallo-Iberian, Gallo-Romance, Gallo-Rhaetian, Oïl, French. Dialects: QUÉBÉICOIS, FRANCO-ONTARIEN, ACADIAN (ACADIEN). Difficult intelligibility between speakers of Québécois and Acadian for speakers not fluent in Standard French. National language. Bible 1530-1986. See main entry under France.

GERMAN, HUTTERITE *(TYROLESE, TIROLEAN, HUTTERIAN GERMAN)* [GEH] 15,000 in western Canada, including 7,000 in Alberta (1981 P. Fast SIL). Population total both countries 30,000 (1982 V. Peters). Other estimates up to 100,000. 76 colonies in Alberta, 12 or 13 in Saskatchewan, 27 in Manitoba, some in British Columbia, 30 in USA, with about 100 people in each, an estimated 300 colonies around the world. Also spoken in USA. Indo-European, Germanic, West, High German, German, Upper German, Bavarian-Austrian. About 70% intelligible to a speaker of Pennsylvania German; about 50% to a speaker of Plautdietsch and Standard German. Although it is called 'Tirolean', it is not a Tirolean dialect. In addition to attendance at public schools, children attend supplemental private schools with instruction in religion and Standard German. Some reports say adults are usually equally fluent in English and Standard German, others that most understand English better and have limited understanding in Standard German. They all use Standard German in church for written sermons and for Scriptures. All ages in the home. Strict communal living. Communal groups in New York, Connecticut, Pennsylvania, and Japan have affiliated recently with the Hutterians, but are not ethnically Hutterian (Victor Peters 1982). Intensive agriculturalists. Christian.

GERMAN, PENNSYLVANIA *(PENNSYLVANISCH, PENNSYLVANIA DUTCH)* [PDC] 15,000 in Canada (1995). Kitchener-Waterloo area, Ontario. Indo-European, Germanic, West, High German, German, Middle German, West Middle German. Dialects: AMISH PENNSYLVANIA GERMAN, NON-AMISH PENNSYLVANIA GERMAN (PENNSYLVANISCH DEITSCH). Christian. NT 1994. See main entry under USA.

GITXSAN *(GITKSAN, GITYSKYAN, GIKLSAN)* [GIT] 400 including 220 in the west, 180 in the east (1999 Jay Powell). Gitxsan on middle Skeena River in west central British Columbia. Penutian, Tsimshian. Dialects: GITXSAN (EASTERN GITXSAN), GITSKEN (WESTERN GITSKEN). High degree of inherent intelligibility between Nisga'a and Gitxsan. About 1,500 speak Nisga'a as second or third language. Speakers consider Nisga'a and Gitxsan to be politically distinct. Dictionary. VSO; prepositions; genitives after noun heads; articles, adjectives, numerals before noun heads; relatives without noun heads; question word initial in sentence; 3 or 4 prefixes, 1 inflectional suffix; word order distinguishes subjects, objects, indirect objects, given and new information, topic and comment; verb affixes mark person and number of subject and object unless obscured by phonological rule; pronominal system is fully ergative; morphological passives, but not by construction; direct causatives indicated by suffixes, indirect (jussive) by prefix; CVC; nontonal. Pine and cedar forest with some deciduous trees. Riverine. Fishermen, hunter-gatherers. 0 to 300 meters. Christian. Bible portions 1906.

GWICH'IN *(KUTCHIN, LOUCHEUX)* [KUC] 430 mother tongue speakers (1998 Statistics Canada) including 300 in Northwest Territories out of 1,500 population, and 100 in Yukon out of 400 population (1995 M. Krauss). Population total both countries 700. Between Old Crow, Yukon, and the lower Mackenzie River, Northwest Territories. Also spoken in USA. Na-Dene, Nuclear Na-Dene, Athapaskan-Eyak, Athapaskan, Canadian, Han-Kutchin. Dialects: FORT YUKON GWICH'IN, ARCTIC VILLAGE GWICH'IN, WESTERN

CANADA GWICH'IN (TAKUDH, TUKUDH, LOUCHEUX), ARCTIC RED RIVER. Most adults speak the language. In a few communities use of the language is vigorous by all ages. Elsewhere younger ones may speak the language, but tend to prefer English. Vigorous in a few communities. Dictionary. Grammar. Literacy rate in first language: 1% to 5%. Literacy rate in second language: 50% to 75%. Bible 1898.

HAIDA, NORTHERN ***(MASSET)*** [HAI] 30 mother tongue speakers out of 1,100 population in Canada (1995 M. Krauss). Population total both countries 45. Queen Charlotte Islands and southern half of Prince of Wales Island, British Columbia. Also spoken in USA. Na-Dene, Haida. Borderline inherent intelligibility with Southern Haida. Bilingualism in English. Speakers are 60 or 70 or older. There are language courses in Haida (1991). Dictionary. Grammar. Nearly extinct. Bible portions 1891-1899.

HAIDA, SOUTHERN ***(SKIDEGATE)*** [HAX] 10 fluent speakers out of 500 population (1995 M. Krauss). Queen Charlotte Islands, Skidegate. Na-Dene, Haida. Borderline intelligibility with Northern Haida. Nearly extinct.

HAISLA [HAS] 25 fluent speakers, fewer than 200 speakers (1991 M. Dale Kinkade), out of 1,000 population (1977 SIL). Inlet on central British Columbia coast. Wakashan, Northern. Dialect: KITIMAT (KITAMAT). Related to Heiltsuk and Kwakiutl. Bilingualism in English. Most or all speakers are middle-aged or older. Dictionary.

HALKOMELEM [HUR] 500 speakers out of 6,700 population (1977 SIL). Southwestern British Columbia. Salishan, Central Salish, Halkomelem. Dialects: CHILIWACK, COWICHAN, MUSQUEAM, NANAIMO. Bilingualism in English. Speakers are middle-aged or older. Language courses in Halkomelem (1991). Dictionary. Grammar.

HAN ***(HAN-KUTCHIN, MOOSEHIDE, DAWSON)*** [HAA] Yukon River area in Alaska-Canada border, Dawson. Na-Dene, Nuclear Na-Dene, Athapaskan-Eyak, Athapaskan, Canadian, Han-Kutchin. Bilingualism in English. All are elderly (1995). Nearly extinct. See main entry under USA.

HEILTSUK [HEI] 300 speakers (1991 M. Dale Kinkade) out of 1,200 population (1977 SIL). Central British Columbia coast including Ooweekeeno on Rivers Inlet. Wakashan, Northern. Dialects: BELLA BELLA (NORTHERN HEILTSUK), OOWEEKEENO (SOUTHERN HEILTSUK). Related to Haisla and Kwakiutl. Bilingualism in English. Most or all speakers are middle-aged or older. Dictionary.

INUKTITUT, EASTERN CANADIAN ***(EASTERN CANADIAN "ESKIMO", EASTERN ARCTIC "ESKIMO", INUIT)*** [ESB] 14,000 speakers out of 17,500 population (1991 L. Kaplan). West of Hudson Bay and east through Baffin Island, Quebec, and Labrador. Eskimo-Aleut, Eskimo, Inuit. Dialects: BAFFINLAND "ESKIMO", LABRADOR "ESKIMO", QUEBEC "ESKIMO". In Labrador the youngest speakers average over 20 years old, except for possibly a few children at Nain. Vigorous except in Labrador, where less than half are speakers. In Northern Quebec and the Northwest Territories to the Central Arctic, it is spoken by over 90% of the population. Inuit is the name of the people, Inuktitut of the language. Literacy rate in first language: 10% to 30%. Literacy rate in second language: 75% to 100%. Bible 1826-1871.

INUKTITUT, WESTERN CANADIAN [ESC] 4,000 speakers out of a population of 7,500 (1981). All Eskimo mother tongue speakers in Canada 18,840 (1981 census). Central Canadian Arctic, and west to the Mackenzie Delta and coastal area, including Tuktoyaktuk on the Arctic coast north of Inuvik (but not Inuvik and Aklavik, and coastal area. Eskimo-Aleut, Eskimo, Inuit. Dialects: COPPER INUKTITUT (COPPER ESKIMO, COPPER INUIT), CARIBOU ESKIMO (KEEWATIN), NETSILIK, SIGLIT. Caribou dialect may need separate literature. In Commer and farther west, parent and grandparent generations speak the language (M. Krauss 1995). Vigorous in Caribou and Netsilik. Literacy rate in first language: 25% to 50%. Literacy rate in second language: 50% to 75%. NT 1983.

INUPIATUN, NORTH ALASKAN ***(NORTH ALASKAN INUPIAT, INUPIAT, INUPIAQ, "ESKIMO")*** [ESI] Mackenzie delta region including Aklavik and Inuvik, into Alaska, USA. Eskimo-Aleut, Eskimo, Inuit. Dialects: WEST ARCTIC INUPIATUN (MACKENZIE INUPIATUN, MACKENZIE DELTA INUPIATUN), NORTH SLOPE INUPIATUN. Bilingualism in English. Most speakers are over 30. Younger speakers often prefer English. Literacy rate in first language: Below 1%. Literacy rate in second language: 50% to 75%. NT 1968. See main entry under USA.

KASKA ***(CASKA, EASTERN NAHANE, NAHANE, NAHANI)*** [KKZ] 400 speakers (1995 M. Krauss) out of 900 population (1995). Southeastern Yukon Territory and northern British Columbia border area, Watson Lake and Lower Post. Na-Dene, Nuclear Na-Dene, Athapaskan-Eyak, Athapaskan, Tahltan-Kaska. Closely related to Tahltan. Bilingualism in English. Speakers are nearly middle aged, except at Ross River, where there may be younger speakers.

KUTENAI ***(KTUNAXA, KOOTENAI, KOOTENAY)*** [KUN] 120 mother tongue speakers in Canada (1998 Statistics Canada). Population total both countries 222. Southeastern British Columbia. Also spoken in USA. Language Isolate. Bilingualism in English. All speakers are middle-aged or elderly. Columbia Lake Reserve EKCC is offering Kutenai as a second language course (1991). Dictionary. Grammar.

KWAKIUTL ***(KWAGIUTL, KWAK'WALA)*** [KWK] 250 or fewer good speakers in Canada (1991 M. Dale Kinkade) out of 3,300 population (1977 SIL). Population total both countries 295 or fewer. Northern Vancouver Island and adjacent mainland, British Columbia. Also spoken in USA. Wakashan, Northern. Related to Haisla and Heiltsuk. Bilingualism in English. Most or all speakers are middle-aged or older. Dictionary. Grammar. Bible portions 1882-1900.

LAKOTA ***(LAKHOTA, TETON)*** [LKT] Wood Mountain. Those at Wood Mountain may be Dakota. Siouan, Siouan Proper, Central, Mississippi Valley, Dakota. See main entry under USA.

LAURENTIAN ***(ST. LAWRENCE IROQUOIAN)*** [LRE] Along the St. Lawrence River. Iroquoian, Northern Iroquoian. A group of languages, at least one with no modern descendents. Encountered by Jacques Cartier in 1534 and 1535. Extinct.

LILLOOET ***(ST'AT'IMCETS)*** [LIL] 300 to 400 speakers (1990 M. D. Kinkade) out of a population of 2,800 (1977 SIL). In area of Lillooet and middle Fraser rivers, southern British Columbia. Salishan, Interior Salish, Northern. Extensive bilingualism in English. Most speakers are middle aged or older. Language courses in Lillooet (1991). Dictionary. Grammar.

MALECITE-PASSAMAQUODDY [MAC] 655 mother tongue speakers of Malecite in Canada (1998 Statistics Canada). Population total both countries 1,500 speakers out of 3,000 to 4,000 ethnic population (1998 SIL). New Brunswick, villages along the Saint John River. Malecite mainly in Canada, Passamaquoddy in Maine, USA. Also spoken in USA. Algic, Algonquian, Eastern. Dialects: MALECITE (MALISEET), PASSAMAQUODDY. English is preferred by most younger ones. Most speakers are older, but in some communities younger ones may speak it. Interest in the language is increasing in some places. Dictionary. Grammar. Bible portions 1870.

MARITIME SIGN LANGUAGE ***(NOVA SCOTIAN SIGN LANGUAGE)*** [NSR] Nova Scotia, New Brunswick, and Prince Edward Island. Deaf sign language. Now remembered only by older deaf people. Based on British Sign Language. Distinct from American and Quebec sign languages. Nearly extinct.

MICHIF ***(FRENCH CREE, METIS)*** [CRG] Scattered locations in Canada. Mixed Language, French-Cree. Closest to Plains Cree. Several varieties. Bilingualism in English. Most or all speakers are middle-aged or older. Grammar. Formerly buffalo hunters. See main entry under USA.

MICMAC ***(MI'GMAW, MIIGMAO, MI'KMAW, RESTIGOUCHE)*** [MIC] 7,310 mother tongue speakers (1998 Statistics Canada) out of 14,200 population in Canada (1998 SIL). In Canada, 1,500 are in mainland Nova Scotia, 4,000 on Cape Breton Island, Nova Scotia, 800 on Prince Edward Island and Lennox Island, 4,550 on the east coast of New Brunswick, 3,150 on the Gaspe Peninsula, Quebec, 200 in Newfoundland. Population total both countries 8,500. Central and northern Nova Scotia. The mainland has 6 major villages: Afton, Picto, Truro, Shubanakati, Bear River, and Yarmouth, and some small communities; Cape Breton Island of Nova Scotia with 5 major villages: Memberto, Eskasoni, Chapel Island, Wakmatkug, and Waikoqomaq; and one small village: Prince Edward Island; the east coast of New Brunswick: Fort Folly, Big Cove, Indian Island, Burnt Church, Eel Ground, Red Bank, Pabino Falls, and Eel River Bar; and eastern Gaspe Peninsula, Quebec, with 3 villages: Gespe'q, Gesgapeqiaq, and Listuguj; and Newfoundland with 1 major village: Conn River. Also spoken in USA. Algic, Algonquian, Eastern. Dialects: NORTHERN MICMAC, SOUTHERN MICMAC. Speakers of Mi'gmaw (Restigouche) Quebec dialect have difficulty understanding other dialects. Bilingualism in English. Most adults speak Micmac. Many adults below 35 do not speak it. Younger ones may prefer English. Most children learn English first, but there is an effort in many communities to teach children Micmac. In some communities usage is more vigorous. Dictionary. Grammar. Literacy rate in first language: 1% to 5%. Literacy rate in second language: 50% to 75%. 3 major writing systems used in teaching and writing. NT 1874, in press (1999).

MOHAWK [MOH] 350 mother tongue speakers in Canada (1998 Statistics Canada) out of 30,000 population including USA (1999 SIL). Population total both countries 2,000 to 4,000. Southwestern Quebec, southern Ontario. Also spoken in USA. Iroquoian, Northern Iroquoian, Five Nations, Mohawk-Oneida. Bilingualism in English. Most speakers are middle-aged or over. In some areas younger ones may speak the language. Dictionary. Grammar. Literacy rate in second language: 75% to 100%. Bible portions 1787-1991.

MONTAGNAIS ***(INNU AIMUN, INNU)*** [MOE] 8,483 speakers (1987 Quebec Ministere de la Sante el des Services Sociaux), 5,866 in Western Montagnais, and 2,617 in Eastern Montagnais. 10,000 ethnic population (1996 D. Myers SIL). 9,070 mother tongue speakers of Montagnais and Naskapi (1998 Statistics Canada). 11 communities in Quebec and Labrador, from Lake St. John eastward along the Saquenay Valley to the north shore of the St. Lawrence River and Gulf of St. Lawrence eastward to St. Augustin, northward to the height of land at Schefferville and inland Labrador (Goose Bay, Lake Melville). Western Montagnais is in 4 communities: Mashteueiash (near Roberval, Quebec), Betsiamites, Uashat or Maliotenam (near Sept-Iles, Quebec), and Matimekush (near Schefferville, Quebec). The others speak Eastern Montagnais: Natashquan, Mingan, La Romaine,

Pakuashipi (St. Augustine, Quebec, sometimes called Pakuashipu), and Sheshatshit (North-West River, Labrador). Algic, Algonquian, Central, Cree-Montagnais-Naskapi. Dialects: WESTERN MONTAGNAIS, EASTERN MONTAGNAIS. There are 2 or possibly 3 dialects based on the shifting of Proto-Algonuian /l/ (Southern Montagnais) to /n/ (Eastern Montagnais). Language complex or dialect continuum within Cree-Montagnais-Naskapi. Mashteuiatsh nearly all French-speaking. Speakers are fluent in Quebec English (Sheshatshiu) or French (other communities). All ages. Women of all ages and men over 55 are mainly not fluent in national languages: 3,000 people. Vigorous in all but 2 communities. Rapid shift occurring in communities close to national language cities. Strong use in lower north shore communities and Schefferville. The language is also called 'Innu' in northeast Quebec and Labrador. Culture was and is for the most part based on designated family hunting grounds visited seasonally. Hunting exploited a large variety of animals and fish, including extensive salt-water fishing. Dictionary. Grammar. Literacy rate in first language: 5%. Literacy rate in second language: 50% to 75% in French or English. Standardized Roman orthography, based on French. Montagnais has been used as language of instruction in Betsiamites in recent past, and is taught as a subject in other classess. Taught as second language in 2 communities. Traditionally hunters, trappers, fishermen. NT 1990.

MUNSEE ***(DELAWARE, ONTARIO DELAWARE)*** [UMU] 7 or 8 speakers out of 400 population (1991 M. Dale Kinkade). Southern Ontario, Moraviantown Reserve. Algic, Algonquian, Eastern. Close to Unami in USA, but a separate language. Bilingualism in English. Only elderly speakers left. Dictionary. Grammar. Nearly extinct. Bible portions 1818-1821.

NASKAPI ***(INNU AIMUUN)*** [NSK] 1,177 including 677 Western Naskapi, 500 Eastern Naskapi (1996 Ministere de la Sante el des Services Sociaux). 9,070 mother tongue speakers of Naskapi and Montagnais (1998 Statistics Canada). 2 communities in Quebec and Labrador. Those in Kawawachikamach are about 10 km. northeast of Schefferville in northeastern Quebec at the height of land. The Mushuau Innu presently live at Utshimassits (Davis Inlet), Labrador, an island on the Labrador Coast, but are planning (1998) to construct and relocate nearby on the mainland. Algic, Algonquian, Central, Cree-Montagnais-Naskapi. Dialects: WESTERN NASKAPI, EASTERN NASKAPI (INNU). Language complex or dialect continuum within Cree-Montagnais-Naskapi. Closely related to Montagnais, but distinct. Palatalized y- (Western Naskapi) or n- (Eastern Naskapi). Bilingualism in English. Vigorous in both dialects. Slow shift occurring. Naskapi culture was nomadic and completely dependent on the migratory habits of the caribou. Many still use caribou in important ways. Dictionary. Grammar. Literacy rate in first language: 1% to 5%. Literacy rate in second language: 50% to 75%. Western Naskapi: modified Cree syllabary, Eastern Naskapi: Roman orthography based on French. Western Naskapi as language of instruction in school at Kawawachikamach, elsewhere as a subject in school. Subsistence hunting in the bush in watersheds north from Schefferville and west from Davis Inlet.

NISGA'A ***(NASS, NISKA, NISHKA, NISK'A, NISHGA)*** [NCG] 1,500 to 2,000 speakers of Nisga'a (1998 Wilp Wilxo'oskwhl Nisga'a, School District #92 Nisga'a, and Nisga'a Tribal Council Ayuukhl Nisga'a, and Deanna Nyce) out of 5,400 ethnic population (1997 M. Krauss). Lower Nass River Valley, villages of Aiyansh (Ay'ans), Canyon City (Gitwinksihlkw), Greenville (Laxtalts'ap or Gitxat'in), Kincolith (Gingolx), British Columbia. Penutian, Tsimshian. Variation within Nass not great enough to be considered dialects. High degree of inherent intelligibility between Nisga'a and Gitxsan. Some older Nisga'a speak Tsimshian as second language; English mostly used. Fluent: 22 to 95. Children learn Nisga'a in School District #92. Many young adults prefer English. Some children speak the language but most prefer English. About 1,500 speak Nisga'a as second or third language. Speakers consider Nisga'a and Gitxsan to be ethnically distinct. Schools try to teach oral and written Nisga'a. Dictionary. Grammar. VSO; prepositions; genitives after noun heads; articles, adjectives, numerals before noun heads; relatives without noun heads; question word initial in sentence; 3 or 4 prefixes, 1 inflectional suffix; word order distinguishes subjects, objects, indirect objects, given and new information, topic and comment; verb affixes mark person and number of subject and object unless obscured by phonological rule; pronominal system is fully ergative; morphological passives, but not by construction; direct causatives indicated by suffixes, indirect (jussive) by prefix; CVC; nontonal. Pine and cedar forest with some deciduous trees. Riverine. Fishermen, hunter-gatherers. 0 to 300 meters. Christian. Bible portions 1906.

NOOTKA ***(NUTKA, NUUCHAHNULTH)*** [NOO] 590 mother tongue speakers (1998 Statistics Canada), out of 3,500 population (1977 SIL). Nitinat has about 30 speakers (1991 M. Dale Kinkade). South-western British Columbia, Nitinat along Pacific side of Vancouver Island and on Nitinat Lake. Wakashan, Southern. Dialects: NITINAT (NITINAHT), NOOTKA. Bilingualism in English. Most or all speakers are middle-aged or older. People are called 'West Coast People'. Dictionary. Grammar.

OJIBWA, CENTRAL ***(CENTRAL OJIBWE, OJIBWAY, OJIBWE)*** [OJC] Central Ontario from Lake Nipigon in the west to Lake Nipissing in the east. Algic, Algonquian, Central, Ojibwa. An area of transitional dialects (see Lisa Valentine, 1995, Making it their own: Severn Ojibwe communicative practices, Univ. of Toronto Press, p.22).

OJIBWA, EASTERN ***(OJIBWE, OJIBWAY)*** [OJG] Southern Ontario, north of Lake Ontario and east of Georgian Bay. East of a north-south line through the base of the Bruce Peninsula (Rhodes 1976:131). Algic, Algonquian, Central, Ojibwa. Probably all speakers are bilingual in English, some in other Ojibwa varieties. Dying out in many areas. Concerted effort via language teaching in public schools and other efforts to reverse the decline. Dictionary. Grammar.

OJIBWA, NORTHWESTERN ***(NORTHERN OJIBWA, OJIBWAY, OJIBWE)*** [OJB] Southern northwest Ontario into Manitoba. Algic, Algonquian, Central, Ojibwa. Dialects: BERENS RIVER OJIBWA (SAULTEAUX), LAC SEUL OJIBWA, ALBANY RIVER OJIBWA, LAKE OF THE WOODS OJIBWA, RAINY RIVER OJIBWA. Vigorous use. Concerted effort via language teaching in public schools and other efforts to reverse decline in use. Grammar. Literacy rate in first language: 50% to 75%. NT 1988.

OJIBWA, SEVERN ***(NORTHERN OJIBWA, OJIBWAY, OJIBWE, OJICREE, CREE)*** [OJS] 8,000 or fewer out of 8,000 or fewer population, possibly including some Northwestern Ojibwa (1999 SIL). Northern northwest Ontario into Manitoba. Algic, Algonquian, Central, Ojibwa. Dialects: WINISK RIVER OJIBWA, SEVERN RIVER OJIBWA. 50 and older. Vigorous use. Concerted effort via language teaching in public schools and other efforts to reverse decline in use. Grammar. Literacy rate in first language: 50% to 75%. Bible portions 1974-1986.

OJIBWA, WESTERN ***(SAULTEAUX, PLAINS OJIBWAY, OJIBWAY, OJIBWE)*** [OJI] 35,000. Westward from Lake Winnipeg into Saskatchewan with outlying groups as far west as British Colombia. Algic, Algonquian, Central, Ojibwa. All ages in most areas. Vigorous in most areas. In some areas young people and children may prefer English. Literacy rate in first language: 30% to 60%. Some primers by the Federation for Saskatchewan Indian Nations.

OKANAGAN ***(OKANAGAN-COLVILLE, OKANAGON, OKANOGAN)*** [OKA] 500 total speakers out of 3,000 population including USA (1977 SIL). Population total both countries 612 speakers out of 3,000 population (1977 SIL). Another source says 10,000 in the ethnic group (1996 Peter Stark). Colville has fewer than 200 (1999 R. McDonald). South central British Columbia. Also spoken in USA. Salishan, Interior Salish, Southern. Dialects: SOUTHERN OKANOGAN, SANPOIL. Bilingualism in English. Most speakers are middle-aged or older. Language courses in Okanagan (1991). Dictionary. Grammar.

ONEIDA [ONE] 200 speakers in Canada (1991 H. Dale Kincade). Population total both countries 250. Southern Ontario. Also spoken in USA. Iroquoian, Northern Iroquoian, Five Nations, Mohawk-Oneida. Bilingualism in English. In Canada most or all speakers are middle-aged or older. Grammar. Bible portions 1880-1942.

ONONDAGA ***(ONANDAGA)*** [ONO] 50 to 100 speakers in Canada (1991 H. Dale Kinkade). Population total both countries 65 to 115 speakers out of 1,500 population (1977 SIL). Southern Ontario. Also spoken in USA. Iroquoian, Northern Iroquoian, Five Nations, Seneca-Onondaga, Onondaga. Bilingualism in English. Most or all speakers are middle-aged or older. Grammar.

OTTAWA ***(ODAWA, OJIBWE, OJIBWAY)*** [OTW] Including Ottawa, Eastern and Central Ojibwa and USA: 8,000 speakers. All Ojibwa mother tongue speakers in Canada: 25,885 (1998 Statistics Canada). Including Ottawa and all Ojibwa in Canada: 30,000 (1999 C. Fiero SIL). Total of 35,000 speakers out of an ethnic population of 60,000 in all Ojibwa, Chippewa, and Ottawa in Canada and USA (1999 C. Fiero). Islands in, and areas surrounding, Lake Huron, from the region of Manitoulin Island to southern Ontario north of Lake Erie. West of a north south line through the base of Bruce Peninsula (Rhodes 1976:131). Also spoken in USA. Algic, Algonquian, Central, Ojibwa. Probably all speakers are bilingual in English, some in other Ojibwa varieties. Most adults and some younger ones in a large population on Manitoulin Island. Vigorous on Manitoulin Island. Dying out in many areas. Concerted effort via language teaching in public schools and other efforts to reverse the decline. Called Eastern Ojibwa in Bloomfield's grammar. In southern Ontario also called Chippewa. Dictionary. Grammar. Bible portions 1841-1844.

PENTLATCH ***(PUNTLATCH)*** [PTW] No speakers out of population of 40 (1977 SIL). South Vancouver Island, British Columbia. Salishan, Central Salish, Northern. Extinct since about 1940. Extinct.

PLAUTDIETSCH ***(LOW GERMAN, MENNONITE GERMAN, MENNONITEN PLATT)*** [GRN] 80,000 or more first language speakers and 20,000 second language speakers in Canada (1978 Kloss and McConnell). Total German mother tongue speakers in Canada including standard German, 561,000 (J. A. Hawkins in B. Comrie 1986). Population total all countries 400,000, of whom 150,000 use it habitually. 110,735 or more in Latin America are fairly monolingual. Southern Canada; Ontario, Saskatchewan, Manitoba, Alberta, British Columbia. Also spoken in Argentina, Belize, Bolivia, Brazil, Costa Rica, Germany, Kazakhstan, Mexico, Paraguay, Russia (Asia), Uruguay, USA. Indo-European, Germanic, West, Low Saxon-Low Franconian, Low Saxon. Not intelligible with many other Low German languages, Standard German, Pennsylvania German or Hutterite German.

110,735 or more speakers in Latin America are mainly monolingual in Plautdietsch. 50% of speakers in Canada speak Standard German and 95% speak English as second language. Literacy rate in second language: 95%. Christian. NT 1987.

POTAWATOMI ***(POTTAWOTTOMI)*** [POT] Southern Ontario. Algic, Algonquian, Central. Bilingualism in English. Most or all speakers are middle-aged or older. Bible portions 1844. See main entry under USA.

QUEBEC SIGN LANGUAGE ***(LANGUE SIGNE QUEBECARS, LANGUE DES SIGNES QUÉBÉCOISE, LSQ)*** [FCS] Québéc, except northern Québéc, Ottawa, Northern Ontario, Bathurst New Brunswick, and a few in Vancouver and Edmonton. Deaf sign language. Related to French Sign Language (LSF). In northern Québéc, deaf people use ASL, with English the second language. Some use Signed French. Segregated deaf education by sex resulted in some lexical differences between the sexes; female use more influenced by ASL and LSQ; male by Signed French and LSQ. It is rare for a deaf child to learn both LSQ and ASL. A few adults have a working knowledge of both.

SALISH, STRAITS ***(STRAITS)*** [STR] Population total both countries 30 speakers or fewer (1990 M. D. Kinkade) out of a population of 3,000 (1977 SIL). Southeastern tip of Vancouver Island, British Columbia. Also spoken in USA. Salishan, Central Salish, Straits. Dialects: SAANICH, LUMMI, SAMISH, SOOKE, SONGISH. Most speakers are of the Saanich dialect. Bilingualism in English. Most are middle aged or older. The last three dialects listed are linguistically extinct. Dictionary. Grammar.

SARSI ***(SARCEE)*** [SRS] 50 speakers or fewer (1991 M. Dale Kinkade), out of 600 population (1977 SIL). Alberta, near Calgary. Na-Dene, Nuclear Na-Dene, Athapaskan-Eyak, Athapaskan, Canadian, Sarcee. Bilingualism in English. All speakers are middle-aged or older. Grammar.

SECHELT [SEC] 40 or fewer speakers (1990 M. D. Kinkade) out of a population of 550 (1977 SIL). British Columbia coast north of Vancouver. Salishan, Central Salish, Northern. Bilingualism in English. All speakers are middle-aged or older. Dictionary. Grammar. Nearly extinct.

SEKANI [SEK] 100 to 500 speakers (1991 M. Dale Kinkade) out of 600 population (1982 SIL). McLeod Lake and Ware (Finlay River), north central British Columbia. Na-Dene, Nuclear Na-Dene, Athapaskan-Eyak, Athapaskan, Canadian, Beaver-Sekani. The majority are bilingual in English. Most speakers are middle-aged or older. Bible portions 1969.

SENECA [SEE] 25 in Canada (1991 M. Dale Kinkade). Six Nations Reserve, Ontario. Iroquoian, Northern Iroquoian, Five Nations, Seneca-Onondaga, Seneca-Cayuga. Bilingualism in English. Most or all speakers are middle-aged or older. Dictionary. Grammar. Bible portions 1829-1874. See main entry under USA.

SHUSWAP ***(SECWEPEMC)*** [SHS] 745 mother tongue speakers (1998 Statistics Canada) out of 6,500 population (1990 M. D. Kinkade). British Columbia, south central. Salishan, Interior Salish, Northern. Dialects: EASTERN SHUSWAP, WESTERN SHUSWAP. Bilingualism in English. Most speakers are middle-aged or older. Language courses in Shuswap (1991). Dictionary. Grammar.

SLAVEY, NORTH ***(SLAVI, DENÉ, MACKENZIAN, "SLAVE")*** [SCS] 290 mother tongue speakers (1998 Statistics Canada) out of 1,600 population (1995 M. Krauss). Mackenzie District, along the middle Mackenzie River from Fort Norman north, around Great Bear Lake, Northwest Territories, and in the Mackenzie Mts. Na-Dene, Nuclear Na-Dene, Athapaskan-Eyak, Athapaskan, Canadian, Hare-Chipewyan, Hare-Slavey. Dialects: HARE, BEARLAKE, MOUNTAIN. A separate language from South Slavey. All ages in some communities. 4 or 5 communities have vigorous language use. Dictionary.

SLAVEY, SOUTH ***(SLAVI, "SLAVE", DENÉ, MACKENZIAN)*** [SLA] 2,620 mother tongue speakers (1998 Statistics Canada) out of 3,600 population (1995 M. Krauss). Great Slave Lake, upper Mackenzie River and drainage in Mackenzie District, northeast Alberta, northwest British Columbia. Na-Dene, Nuclear Na-Dene, Athapaskan-Eyak, Athapaskan, Canadian, Hare-Chipewyan, Hare-Slavey. North and South Slavey are separate languages. Adults still use South Slavey in smaller, isolated communities, but there is serious attrition among children and young people. Dictionary. Grammar. Literacy rate in first language: Below 1%. Literacy rate in second language: 25% to 50%. NT 1891, out of print.

SQUAMISH [SQU] 20 or fewer speakers (1990 M. D. Kinkade) out of a population of 2,300. Southwestern British Columbia, north of Vancouver. Salishan, Central Salish, Squamish. Bilingualism in English. All speakers are middle-aged or older. Dictionary. Grammar. VSO. Nearly extinct.

STONEY ***(STONY, NAKODA)*** [STO] 1,000 to 1,500 speakers out of 3,200 population (1987 SIL). Southern Alberta, west and northwest of Calgary, and central Alberta, west of Edmonton. Southern Stoney occupy 3 reserves represented on the Stoney Tribal Council at Morley, Alberta: Eden Valley, west of Longview, Alberta, the southernmost reserve and principally Bearspaw Band members (about 400 speakers); Morley, west of Calgary, the main administrative center of Stoney Country, with about 2,700 people of all three southern bands; the Bearspaw, Chiniki, and Wesley Bands; and the Big Horn Reserve west of Rocky Mountain House, the most northerly of the 3, with about 100 people, mostly Wesley Band. The other dialect is spoken at Paul and Alexis Bands. Siouan, Siouan Proper, Central, Mississippi Valley, Dakota. Dialects: SOUTHERN STONEY, NORTHERN STONY. Dialects nearly 100% intelligible with each other. 89% lexical similarity with Assiniboine, 86% with Dakota of Manitoba, 85% with Dakota of North Dakota, 83% with Lakota. Many children prefer English. Vigorous use. Literacy rate in first language: Below 1%. Literacy rate in second language: 75% to 100%. They want provincially published school curriculum about their language, culture, and history. Bible portions 1970.

TAGISH [TGX] 2 speakers out of a possible population of 400 (1995 M. Krauss). Southern Yukon, west or west-northwest of the Tlingit, with some at Carcross. Na-Dene, Nuclear Na-Dene, Athapaskan-Eyak, Athapaskan, Tahltan-Kaska. Speakers are also fluent in Tlingit and speak English as second language. All are elderly. Tagish label was also applied to inland Tlingit. Nearly extinct.

TAHLTAN [TAH] 40 speakers (1991 M. Dale Kinkade), out of 750 population (1977 SIL). Telegraph Creek, northwest British Columbia. Na-Dene, Nuclear Na-Dene, Athapaskan-Eyak, Athapaskan, Tahltan-Kaska. Closely related to Kaska. Bilingualism in English. Only elderly speakers left (1991). Tahltan is seldom used. Nearly extinct.

TANANA, UPPER *(NABESNA)* [TAU] 10 speakers out of 40 population (1995 M. Krauss). Southwestern Yukon Territory, Beaver Creek. Na-Dene, Nuclear Na-Dene, Athapaskan-Eyak, Athapaskan, Tanana-Upper Kuskokwim, Tanana. Speakers are bilingual in English. Bible portions 1970-1982. See main entry under USA.

THOMPSON *(NTLAKAPMUK, NKLAPMX)* [THP] 595 mother tongue speakers (1998 Statistics Canada) out of a population of 3,000 (1977 SIL). British Columbia, south central. Fraser River north of Yale, and the lower Thompson River and tributaries. Salishan, Interior Salish, Northern. Bilingualism in English. Most speakers are middle-aged or older. Language courses in Thompson (1991). Dictionary. Grammar.

TLINGIT *(THLINGET, TLINKIT)* [TLI] 145 mother tongue speakers in Canada (1998 Statistics Canada) out of 1,000 population in Canada (1995 M. Krauss). Northwestern British Columbia and southern Yukon, communities of Carcross and Teslin. Na-Dene, Nuclear Na-Dene, Tlingit. English is the first or second language of the ethnic group. Speakers are generally 55 or older, but many in the 40 to 55 range understand a certain amount of Tlingit. Dictionary. Grammar. In Teslin. Bible portions 1969. See main entry under USA.

TSETSAUT [TXC] Portland Canal area, borderline to southwest Alaska and British Columbia. Na-Dene, Nuclear Na-Dene, Athapaskan-Eyak, Athapaskan. Became extinct about 1930. Extinct.

TSIMSHIAN *(TSIMPSHEAN, ZIMSHIAN, CHIMMEZYAN)* [TSI] 432 speakers out of 3,200 ethnic population in Canada, including 2 or 3 Southern Tsimshian, 430 Coast Tsimshian (1995 M. Krauss). Population total both countries 500. Northern coast of British Columbia. Southern Tsimshian is at the southern end on the coast at Klemtu. Also spoken in USA. Penutian, Tsimshian. Dialects: SOUTHERN TSIMSHIAN (SGUXS, OLD KLEMTU), COAST TSIMSHIAN (SM'ALGYAX). Bilingualism in English. Speakers are middle-aged or older. Southern Tsimshian is very divergent. Dictionary. Grammar. Bible portions 1885-1898.

TUSCARORA [TUS] 7 or 8 speakers in Canada (1991 M. Dale Kinkade). Population total both countries 17. Six Nations Reserve, Ontario. Also spoken in USA. Iroquoian, Northern Iroquoian, Tuscarora-Nottoway. Bilingualism in English. Only elderly speakers left. Dictionary. Grammar. Nearly extinct.

TUTCHONE, NORTHERN *(SELKIRK)* [TUT] 200 speakers out of 1,000 population (1995 M. Krauss). Central Yukon, Mayo-Stewart, Selkirk-Pelly, Carmacks, and White River areas. Na-Dene, Nuclear Na-Dene, Athapaskan-Eyak, Athapaskan, Tutchone. Dialect: MASSET. Bilingualism in English. Youngest speakers are 30 to 40.

TUTCHONE, SOUTHERN [TCE] 200 speakers out of 1,400 population (1995 M. Krauss). Southwestern Yukon Territory, Whitehorse, Aishihik-Champagne-Klukwan, and Kluane-Burwash areas. Na-Dene, Nuclear Na-Dene, Athapaskan-Eyak, Athapaskan, Tutchone. Dialect: SKIDEGATE. Bilingualism in English. The youngest fluent speakers are 40 or 50.

WYANDOT *(WENDAT)* [WYA] Near Quebec City, Wendake Reserve. Iroquoian, Northern Iroquoian, Huron. Wyandot became extinct after 1961, Huron in the mid-19th century or 1912. Dictionary. Extinct. See main entry under USA.

CAYMAN ISLANDS

National or official language: English. 36,000 (1998 UN). Literacy rate over age 15: 97.5%. Also includes Haitian Creole French, Spanish 2,212. Christian. Deaf institutions: 1. Data accuracy estimate: B. The number of languages listed for Cayman Islands is 2. Of those, both are living languages. Diversity index 0.58.

CAYMAN ISLANDS ENGLISH [CYE] 10,770 (1995). Indo-European, Germanic, West, English. The colloquial English seems to have borrowed creole features similar to Jamaica and Central America without having undergone creolization (John Holm 1989:479-80). Structurally similar to a creole language. May be close to Northern Central America Creole English. Agriculturalists: cotton.

ENGLISH [ENG] 9,200 (1993). Indo-European, Germanic, West, English. National language. Bible 1535-1989. See main entry under United Kingdom.

CHILE

Republic of Chile, República de Chile. National or official language: Spanish. 14,824,000 (1998 UN). Literacy rate 92% to 95%. Also includes Catalan-Valencian-Balear, Standard German 35,000, Vlax Romani. Information mainly from A. Tovar 1961, 1966; Grete Mostny 1965; S. Wurm and S. Hattori 1981; N. Besnier OIEL 1992; SIL 1969-99. Christian, secular, traditional religion. Blind population 100,000. Deaf population 845,849. Deaf institutions: 7. Data accuracy estimate: A2, B. The number of languages listed for Chile is 11. Of those, 9 are living languages and 2 are extinct. Diversity index 0.06.

AYMARA, CENTRAL [AYM] 899 (1994 Hans Gundermann K.) speakers in Chile out of 20,000 population (1983 SIL). Mountains of extreme north, first region (Tarapacá); Arica, Parinacota, Iquique. Aymaran. Chilean Aymara is very close to La Paz, Bolivia dialect. Bilingualism in Spanish. Bible 1987-1993. See main entry under Bolivia.

CHILEAN SIGN LANGUAGE [CSG] Deaf sign language.

HUILLICHE ***(VELICHE, HUILICHE)*** [HUH] Several thousand speakers (1982 SIL R. Croese). South of the Mapuche, Tenth Region, from Valdivia to Chiloé. Araucanian. Dialect: TSESUNGÚN. Related to Mapudungun, but barely intelligible with it. Most of the ethnic group speaks Spanish as first language. Used mainly among friends and for ceremonial purposes. Mountain valleys.

KAKAUHUA ***(KAUKAUE, CACAHUE)*** [KBF] Alacalufan. Extinct.

KUNZA ***(LIKANANTAÍ, LIPE, ULIPE, ATACAMEÑO)*** [KUZ] A few speakers were located in 1949 and since by anthropologists. Peine, Socaire (Salar de Atacama), and Caspana. Unclassified. Greenberg places it in Macro-Chibchan. Group now speaks Spanish. Dictionary. Extinct.

MAPUDUNGUN ***(MAPUDUNGU, "ARAUCANO", MAPUCHE)*** [ARU] 400,000 in Chile, 200,000 of whom are active users of the language (1982 R. Croese SIL). Population total both countries 440,000. Between the Itata and Tolten rivers. Also spoken in Argentina. Araucanian. Dialects: MOLUCHE (NGOLUCHE, MANZANERO), PICUNCHE, PEHUENCHE. Easy intelligibility among all dialects. Pehuenche and Moluche are very close. Bilingual level estimates for Spanish are 0 0%, 1 8%, 2 50%, 3 30%, 4 10%, 5 2%. Partly bilingual in Spanish. The language is called 'Mapudungun'; the people 'Mapuche'. SVO. Literacy rate in first language: Below 1%. Literacy rate in second language: 21%. 85,000 are reported to be literate in Spanish. Deciduous forest, rolling farm land. Mountain slope, coastal, plains, riverine. Peasant agriculturalists. 0 to 2,000 meters. Traditional religion, Christian. NT 1997.

QAWASQAR ***(KAWESKAR, KAWESQAR, ALACALUFE, ALACALUF, HALAKWULUP)*** [ALC] 20 including 10 in Puerto Edin (1996 Oscar Aguilera). Channel region, western Patagonia, Isle of Wellington off south Chilean coast, 49 degrees south with center in Puerto Edin. Speakers of the extinct Aksanás dialect also lived in Puerto Edén. Alacalufan. Dialect: AKSANÁS (AKSANA). Reports are that speakers are not bilingual in Spanish (Christos Clairis, M. Ruhlen 1987, personal communication). They are 20% monolingual in Qawasqar (O. Aguilera 1996, personal communication. The youngest speakers are from 3 to 20 years old (1996). Speakers have positive language attitudes. J. Suarez says Aksanás vocabulary differences might be explained by word taboo. Dictionary. Grammar. Fishermen.

QUECHUA, CHILEAN [QUE] Northern second region. Quechuan, Quechua II, C. May be intelligible with, or the same as, Bolivian Quechua or Northwest Jujuy Quechua of Argentina. There may be no Quechua speakers in Chile.

RAPA NUI ***(EASTER ISLAND, PASCUENSE)*** [PBA] 2,400 to 2,500 including 2,200 on Easter Island; 200 to 300 on Chile mainland, Tahiti, and USA (1982 R. Weber SIL). Population total all countries 2,400 to 2,500. Easter Island, 3,800 km. from Chile, 4,000 km. from Tahiti. Also spoken in French Polynesia, USA. Austronesian, Malayo-Polynesian, Central-Eastern, Eastern Malayo-Polynesian, Oceanic, Central-Eastern Oceanic, Remote Oceanic, Central Pacific, East Fijian-Polynesian, Polynesian, Nuclear, East, Rapanui. 64% lexical similarity with Hawaiian, Mangareva, Rarotonga; 63% with Marquesas; 62% with Tahitian, Paumotu. Bilingualism in Spanish. Difficult cultivation. Grammar. VSO. Literacy rate in first language: Below 1%. Literacy rate in second language: 25% to 50%. Tropical. Volcanic island. Fishermen, craftsmen.

SPANISH ***(ESPAÑOL, CASTELLANO)*** [SPN] 13,800,000 in Chile, including 25% Spanish, 66% mestizo (1995). Indo-European, Italic, Romance, Italo-Western, Western, Gallo-Iberian, Ibero-Romance, West Iberian, Castilian. National language. Bible 1553-1979. See main entry under Spain.

YÁMANA ***(YAGHAN, YAGÁN, TEQUENICA, HÁUSI KÚTA)*** [YAG] 3 women speakers (Anne Chapmen), who are married to Spanish men and raised their children as Spanish speakers (1990 A. Salas and A. Valencia). Patagonia, Isla Navarino, Puerto Williams, Ukika hamlet. Extinct in Argentina. Language Isolate. Tovar (1961) says it was closest to Qawasqar, and had some relationship to Ona. Earlier there were up to five dialects. Bilingualism in Spanish. Speakers from 56 to 70 years old (1990). One report says that there are still speakers near the Beagle Canal Naval Base in Chile. Their name for their language is 'Háusi Kúta'. Dictionary. Nearly extinct. Bible portions 1881-1886.

COLOMBIA

Republic of Colombia, República de Colombia. National or official language: Spanish. 40,803,000 (1998 UN). 500,000 speakers of American Indian languages (Centro Colombiano de Estudios de Lenguas Aborigenes 1997). Literacy rate 70% to 80%. Also includes Catalan-Valencian-Balear, Yagua, Yuhup. Information mainly from S. H. Levinsohn 1976 a,b,c; SIL 1964-99. Christian, secular, traditional religion. Blind population 30,000 (1982 WCE). Deaf population 300,000 to 2,157,094 in Colombia (1998), 50,000 in Bogotá, half school-aged (1992). Deaf institutions: 8. Data accuracy estimate: A1, A2. The number of languages listed for Colombia is 98. Of those, 78 are living languages and 20 are extinct. Diversity index 0.03.

ACHAGUA ***(AJAGUA, XAGUA)*** [ACA] 400 (1994 SIL). Rio Meta near Puerto Gaitan. Not in Venezuela. Arawakan, Maipuran, Northern Maipuran, Inland. Close to Piapoco. Speakers are trilingual in Achuagua, Spanish, and Piapoco. They speak Achagua in the home. Fair degree of acculturation. Literacy rate in first language: 1% to 5%. Literacy rate in second language: 5% to 25%.

ANDAQUI ***(ANDAKI)*** [ANA] Southern highlands. Barbacoan, Andaqui. Not the same as Andoque, which is in Amazonas. Extinct.

ANDOQUE ***(ANDOKE)*** [ANO] 518 to 600 speakers in Colombia, all of whom are reported to understand it, but few speak it (1998 Arango and Sánchez). Extinct in Peru (1992 SIL). There were 10,000 in 1908 (Landaburu 1979). Aduche River (tributary of Caqueta) 15 km. down river from Araracuara, Amazonas. Language Isolate. Mason (1950:246 with disclaimer), Tax (1960:433), and Kaufman (1990:43 tentatively) say this is Witotoan. Tovar (1961:150), Witte (1981:1), and Aschmann (1993:2) say it is an isolate. 80% speak fair Spanish, 10% are monolingual. People are somewhat acculturated. Tropical forest. Rubber gatherers.

ANSERMA ***(ANSERNA)*** [ANS] Choco. Related to Cauca, Arma (both extinct), and Caramanta. Extinct.

ARMA [AOH] Choco. People spoke either Cenu or Cauca (both extinct). Extinct.

AWA-CUAIQUER ***(COAIQUER, QUAIQUER, KWAIKER, AWA, AWA PIT, CUAIQUER)*** [KWI] 20,000 in Colombia (1986 SIL). Population total both countries 21,000. Pacific slopes of the Andes, Nariño, from Ecuador border north, near Barbacoas. Also spoken in Ecuador. Barbacoan, Pasto. Bilingual level estimates for Spanish are 0 55%, 1 30%, 2 10%, 3 5%, 4 0%, 5 0%. It is mainly women and children that are monolingual. Grammar. SOV. Literacy rate in first language: Below 1%. Literacy rate in second language: Below 5%. Tropical forest. Mountain slope. Swidden agriculturalists. 200 to 300 meters. Bible portions 1979-1982.

BARASANA ***(SOUTHERN BARASANO, PANEROA, EDURIA, EDULIA)*** [BSN] 350 (1990 SIL). Pira-Paraná River and tributaries, southern Vaupés region. Jepa Matsi in Brazil may be the same as this. Tucanoan, Eastern Tucanoan, Central, Southern. Dialects: TAIWANO (TAIBANO, TAIWAENO), JANERA, COMEMATSA. 5 dialects. Taiwano is treated culturally as a separate language. Dictionary. Grammar. OVS. Literacy rate in first language: 1% to 5%. Literacy rate in second language: 5% to 15%. Tropical forest. Interfluvial. Swidden agriculturalists. 200 meters. Bible portions 1973.

BARBACOAS [BPB] Near the coastal town of Barbacoas, Nariño. Barbacoan, Pasto. Extinct.

BORA ***(BORO)*** [BOA] 500 in Colombia, including 100 or more Miraña and 400 other Bora. Bora are in Providencia on the Igaraparana (tributary of the Putumayo). Miraña are on the lower Caquetá River, near the mouth of the Cabinari River, Amazonas. Witotoan, Boran. Dialects: MIRAÑA (MIRANHA), BORA. Miraña has 94% intelligibility with Bora. The Miraña want a school. SOV. Riverine. NT 1982. See main entry under Peru.

CABIYARÍ ***(CABIUARÍ, CAUYARÍ, KAUYARÍ, CUYARE, KAWILLARY)*** [CBB] 50 (1976 Bourgue). Cananarí River (tributary of the Apaporis and Vaupés). Arawakan, Maipuran, Northern Maipuran, Inland. They continue to speak their language. High degree of intermarriage with Barasana. Nearly extinct.

CACUA ***(MACU DE CUBEO, MACU DE GUANANO, MACU DE DESANO, BÁDA, KÁKWA)*** [CBV] 150 (1982 SIL). Wacará, 30 kms. east of Mitú, Lower Vaupés region. Maku. Dialects: VAUPÉS CACUA, MACÚ-PARANÁ CACUA. Related to Jupda and Nukak. Some bilingualism in Cubeo, Desano, and Guanano, but none in Spanish. Many are monolingual, especially children. Vigorous. SOV, OSV. Literacy rate in first language: 10%. Literacy rate in second language: Below 5% in Spanish. Tropical forest. Interfluvial. Hunter-gatherers (nomadic), swidden agriculturalists. 200 meters. Bible portions 1975.

CAGUA [CBH] Unclassified. Extinct.

CAMSÁ ***(KAMSA, COCHE, SIBUNDOY, KAMEMTXA, KAMSE, CAMËNTSËÁ)*** [KBH] 4,022 (1998 Arango and Sánchez). Sibundoy Valley, Putumayo region. Language Isolate. Ruhlen and others classify it as Equatorial. Literacy rate in first language: 40%. Literacy rate in second language: 85%. Mountain slope. NT 1990.

CARABAYO ***("AMAZONAS MACUSA")*** [CBY] 150 estimate. Amazonas Department, half way between the San Bernardo and Pure rivers. 3 long houses, at least. Unclassified. The name "Macusa" or "Macú" means 'savage', and is arbitrarily applied to uncontacted groups.

CARAPANA ***(MOCHDA, MOXDOA, KARAPANÁ, KARAPANO, CARAPANA-TAPUYA, MEXTÃ)*** [CBC] 600 in Colombia (1990 SIL). Population total both countries 650. Caño Tí (tributary of the middle Vaupés River) and upper Papurí and Pirá-Paraná rivers, Vaupés region. Also spoken in Brazil. Tucanoan, Eastern Tucanoan, Central, Tatuyo. Due to intermarriage with neighboring groups, almost all Tatuyo and Waimajã Indians speak Carapana as well as their mother tongue. Grammar. Literacy rate in first language: 50%. Literacy rate in second language: 50%. Tropical forest. Riverine, interfluvial. Swidden agriculturalists. NT 1992.

CARIJONA ***(KARIJONA, CARIHONA, OMAGUA, UMAWA, HIANACOTO-UMAUA)*** [CBD] 140 (1993 SIL). Upper Vaupés, Yarí, and lower Caquetá rivers, 1 hour by motorized canoe; 2-3 hours by canoe south of Miraflores, around Puerto Nare. Carib, Southern, Southeastern Colombia. M. Durbin says there are possibly two separate languages, Hianacoto-Umaua and Carijona. The two groups have not had contact for many years. Some bilingualism in Spanish. Intermarrying with other tribes. All worked for one rubber hunter. Reported to have come from the Yarí Indian area originally. Male descent groups, exogamous. Investigation needed: intelligibility, bilingual proficiency. OVS. Interest in literacy. Hunters, fishermen, agriculturalists: manioc. Rubber hunters in the past.

CHIBCHA ***(MUISCA, MOSCA)*** [CBF] Almost one million before extinction in the 18th century. Central highlands. Chibchan, Chibchan Proper. The Chibcha people are still located near the towns of Tocancipa, Cota, Gachancipa and Tenjo. No speakers are left. SOV. Extinct.

CHIMILA ***(CACA WERANOS, SAN JORGE, SHIMIZYA)*** [CBG] 2,000 (1993 census). Lowlands south and west of Fundación, and scattered in the central part of Magdalena Department. Chibchan, Unclassified. Limited Spanish is used as second language. Vigorous. Its classification as Aruak is questionable. There are two major separated groups. Literacy rate in first language: 1% to 2%. Literacy rate in second language: 5%. Work for local settlers.

CHIPIAJES [CBE] Unclassified. A Sáliba last name. Many Guahibo have that last name. Extinct.

COCAMA-COCAMILLA ***(COCAMA, KOKAMA)*** [COD] Ethnic group: 20 in Colombia. Lower Putumayo. Tupi, Tupi-Guarani, Tupi (III). Bilingualism in Spanish. Bible portions 1961-1967. See main entry under Peru.

COFÁN ***(KOFAN, KOFANE, A'I)*** [CON] 520 in Colombia. Colombia-Ecuador border area. Chibchan, Cofan. Dialects: AGUARICO, SANTA ROSA. Chibchan with Western Tucanoan features (Ferndon, Borman), Barbacoan (J. A. Mason), or Jivaroan (Ruhlen 1987). Fairly monolingual. Traditional religion, Christian. NT 1980-1991. See main entry under Ecuador.

COGUI ***(KOGUI, COGHUI, KOGI, KAGABA, KAGGABA)*** [KOG] 4,000 to 6,000 (1996 SIL). Northern, eastern, and western slopes of Sierra Nevada de Santa Marta. Chibchan, Aruak. Bilingual level estimates for Spanish are 0 92%, 1 7%, 2 1%, 3 0%, 4 0%, 5 0%. Malayo also used. SOV. Literacy rate in first language: Below 1%. Literacy rate in second language: Below 5%. Tropical forest. Mountain slope. Swidden agriculturalists. 750 to 1750 meters. Bible portions.

COLOMBIAN SIGN LANGUAGE [CSN] (50,000 deaf in Bogotá in 1992). Deaf sign language. Some signs are similar to those in sign languages of El Salvador, Spain, and the USA. Half of school age. There are at least 4 deaf schools (begun in 1924); 2 in Bogotá and 2 in Medellín, and 3 other deaf institutions. Some schools use sign language in the classroom. Interpreters are provided at important public events, and for college students. Many sign language classes for hearing people. There is a committee on the national sign language, and an organization for sign language teachers. Little research. It is not clear how many deaf persons know a sign language. Begun in 1929. There is a manual alphabet for spelling. Dictionary. Grammar. TV.

COXIMA ***(KOXIMA)*** [KOX] Unclassified. Extinct.

COYAIMA [COY] Tolima region. Carib, Northern, Coastal. Ruhlen says it was a Yukpa variety. The tribe still exists as an entity, but has not spoken the language for several generations. Spanish is now spoken. Extinct.

CUBEO ***(CUVEO, KOBEUA, KUBWA, KOBEWA, PAMIWA, HEHENAWA)*** [CUB] 6,000 in Colombia (1994 SIL). Population total both countries 6,150. Vaupés, Cuduyari, Querarí rivers and tributaries, Vaupés region. Also spoken in Brazil. Tucanoan, Central Tucanoan. 10%, women and children, cannot speak Spanish. About 5% of the population are 7 years old or younger. Trade language. SOV. Literacy rate in first language: 35%. Literacy rate in second language: 60%. Tropical forest. Riverine. Swidden agriculturalists. 200 to 500 meters. NT 1970-1989.

CUIBA ***(CUIVA, CUIBA-WÁMONAE)*** [CUI] 2,000 in Colombia (1979 SIL). Population total both countries 2,650. Meta Casanare and Capanapara rivers and tributaries. Also spoken in Venezuela. Guahiban. Dialects: CHIRICOA, MASIWARE (MASIGUARE), CHIRIPO (WUPIWI, SIRIPU), YARAHUURAXI-CAPANAPARA, MAYAYERO, MOCHUELO-CASANARE-CUIBA, TAMPIWI (MARIPOSAS), AMARUWA (AMORUA). 8 dialects; 2 in Venezuela, 7 in Colombia. 50% in Colombia are monolingual. Semi-nomadic bands. Grammar. Literacy rate in first language: 45%. Literacy rate in second language: 45%. Savannah. Hunter-gatherers, swidden agriculturalists. NT 1988.

CUMERAL [CUM] Arawakan, Unclassified. Extinct.

CURRIPACO ***(CURIPACO, KURIPACO, KURRIPACO, KORIPAKO)*** [KPC] 2,000 to 2,500 in Colombia. Population total all countries 3,000 to 3,500. Guainia, Isana, and Inirida rivers. Also spoken in Brazil, Venezuela. Arawakan, Maipuran, Northern Maipuran, Inland. Close to Baniwa and Carutana. NT 1959.

DESANO ***(DESÁNA, DESSANA, WINA, BOLEKA, OREGU, KUSIBI)*** [DES] 800 in Colombia (1995 SIL). Papurí and Abiyu rivers (tributary of the Vaupés), Pacá River (tributary of the Papurí), and Macú Parana River (tributary of the Papurí), plus other tributaries of the Papurí. Tucanoan, Eastern Tucanoan, Central, Desano. All speak at least one other Tucanoan language. Spanish is also used. Desano in Brazil generally speak Tucano instead of Desano. Literacy rate in first language: 30%. Literacy rate in second language: 25% to 35%. NT 1984. See main entry under Brazil.

EMBERÁ, NORTHERN ***(EMPERÃ, EBERÃ BED'EA, EPERÃ PEDEA, ATRATO, DARIÉN, DARIENA, PANAMA EMBERA, EBERÃ, CHOLO)*** [EMP] 13,000 to 15,000 in Colombia (1988 Aguirre and Pardo-Rojas). Atrato River basin in Chocó Department, Pacific coastal rivers from Cabo Corrientes (5'30"N), to Antioquia (Rio Verde) Department. Choco, Embera, Northern. Related languages in order of closeness: Emberá-Catío, Emberá-Baudó, Emberá-Tadó, Epena Saija, Embera-Chamí, and Wounmeu. Panama and Colombia dialects are inherently intelligible. Northern Embera of the Upper Baudó area and downriver Embera-Baudó are inherently intelligible. 'Embena' (Embera, Epena), meaning 'people' is used by all Choco peoples except Waunana to refer to themselves. Dictionary. Grammar. Traditional religion, Christian. NT 1993. See main entry under Panama.

EMBERÁ-BAUDÓ ***(BAUDÓ, CATRÚ)*** [BDC] 5,000 (1995 SIL). Baudó River basin and Pacific (north) coastal rivers between Cabo Corrientes and the south of the San Juan River, near Northern Emberá. Choco, Embera, Southern. Somewhat intelligible with Northern Embera and other southern Embera languages. Investigation needed: intelligibility.

EMBERÁ-CATÍO ***(CATIO, KATIO, EMBENA, EYABIDA)*** [CTO] 15,000 to 20,000 in Colombia (1992 SIL). Population total both countries 15,000 to 20,000. Upper Sinu, San Jorge, San Pedro, Murri Rivers. Also spoken in Panama. Choco, Embera, Northern. 90% to 95% are monolingual, a few use Spanish as second language. The term 'Catio' is sometimes used for other Choco groups. Literacy rate in first language: Below 1%. Literacy rate in second language: 5% to 15%. Bible portions 1975-1987.

EMBERÁ-CHAMÍ ***(CHAMI)*** [CMI] 11,000 (1995 SIL). Departments of Risaralda, Caldas, Antioquía, Valle, including the Municipio of Caramanta. Choco, Embera, Southern. Fairly monolingual. Literacy rate in first language: Below 1%. Literacy rate in second language: 5% to 15%. Mountain slopes. Bible portions 1989.

EMBERÁ-SAIJA ***(SAIJA, EPENÁ SAIJA, EPEA PEDÉE, SOUTHERN EMBERA, SOUTHERN EMPERA, CHOLO)*** [SJA] 3,500 (1992 SIL). Population total both countries 3,500 or more. Southern Pacific coast, Caucá, Nariño, Chocó departments. Also spoken in Panama. Choco, Embera, Southern. Dialect: BASURUDO. Bilingual level estimates for Spanish are 0 0%, 1 20%, 2 30%, 3 50%, 4 0%, 5 0%. Saija is used in the home. Vernacular language and culture strong. Investigation needed: intelligibility with Basurudó. Grammar. SOV. Literacy rate in first language: 1% to 5%. Literacy rate in second language: 25% to 50%. Tropical forest. Coastal, riverine. Fishermen, agriculturalists. 0 to 70 meters. Bible portions 1991.

EMBERÁ-TADÓ *(EMBENÁ TADÓ)* [TDC] 1,000 possibly (1991 SIL). Upper San Juan River Region, Andes, Risaralda region, near the Chamí. Choco, Embera, Southern. Secluded. Literacy rate in first language: Below 1%. Literacy rate in second language: Below 5%.

GUAHIBO *(GUAJIBO, GOAHIBO, GUAIGUA, GUAYBA, WAHIBO, GOAHIVA, "SICUANI")* [GUH] 15,000 in Colombia. Population total both countries 20,000. Casanare, eastern Meta, Vichada, Guaviare, Guainia states, plains regions. Also spoken in Venezuela. Guahiban. Dialects: GUAHIBO (SIKUANI), AMORUA (RIO TOMO GUAHIBO), TIGRERO. The Guahiban languages may not be within Arawakan. The Guahibo range from good bilinguals to about 40% completely monolingual. Rio Tomo Guahibo are nomadic. The name "Sicuani" is derogatory, and is disliked by most Guahibo. Dictionary. Grammar. SOV, SVO. Literacy rate in first language: 45%. Literacy rate in second language: 45%. Available in most areas. Available for some. Newspapers. Savannah, gallery forest. Plains, riverine, interfluvial. Swidden agriculturalists, fishermen, hunters-gatherers, limited animal husbandry. 200 meters. Traditional religion, Christian, secular. NT 1982.

GUAMBIANO *(GUAMBIA, MOGUEX)* [GUM] 9,000 (1977 SIL). Central Andes Range near Popayán, Caucá. Barbacoan, Coconucan. Bilingualism in Spanish. Grammar. Literacy rate in first language: 10% to 20%. Literacy rate in second language: 50% to 75%. Agriculturalists. NT, in press (2000).

GUANANO *(WANANA, UANANO, KOTIRIA, ANANA, KÓTEDIA)* [GVC] 450 in Colombia (1983 SIL). Lower Vaupés River region. Tucanoan, Eastern Tucanoan, Northern. Close to Piratapuyo linguistically, but the two groups do not intermarry. SOV. Literacy rate in first language: 5% to 10%. Literacy rate in second language: 25% to 50%. Tropical forest. Riverine. Fishermen, swidden agriculturalists. NT 1982. See main entry under Brazil.

GUAYABERO *(JIW, CUNIMÍA, MÍTUS, MÍTIA)* [GUO] 1,200 (1991 Adelaar). Upper Guaviaré River, Metá and Guaviaré states. Guahiban. Bilingual level estimates for Spanish are 0 33%, 1 50%, 2 15%, 3 2%, 4 0%, 5 0%. Young children and older women are monolingual in Guayabero. Others know varying degrees of Spanish. SOV. Literacy rate in first language: Few. Literacy rate in second language: 15% to 20%. Available in most villages. Savannah, tropical forest. Riverine. Hunter-gatherers, swidden agriculturalists. Traditional religion. Bible portions 1961-1995.

HUITOTO, MɨNɨCA *(MɨNɨCA, MENECA, MINICA)* [HTO] 1,700 in Colombia (1995 SIL). Population total both countries 1,700 or more. Upper Igara-Parana. Caquetá River at Isla de los Monos, Caguan River near Sanvicente del Caguan. Also spoken in Peru. Witotoan, Witoto, Witoto Proper, Minica-Murui. Dictionary. Grammar. Literacy rate in first language: 75%. Literacy rate in second language: 85%. NT 1985.

HUITOTO, MURUI *(BUE, WITOTO)* [HUU] 1,900 in Colombia (1995 SIL), 1,000 in Peru (1982 SIL). Caraparana, Putumayo, and Leticia rivers. None left in Brazil. Witotoan, Witoto, Witoto Proper, Minica-Murui. NT 1978. See main entry under Peru.

HUPDË *(UBDÉ, "HUPDÁ MAKÚ", "JUPDÁ MACÚ", "MACÚ DE TUCANO", "MAKÚ-HUPDÁ")* [JUP] 150 in Colombia (1991 SIL). Papurí and Tiquié river systems. Maku. A related but separate language from Yahup. Tuhup and Nehup may be related dialects, and may be extinct. Possibly half the speakers use Tucano or another Tucano language as second language. Subservient to the Tucano and other Tucanoan Indians. The name "Macu" is offensive. Some are nomadic between Colombia and Brazil. Investigation needed: intelligibility with Nehup, Yuhup, Tuhup. Tropical forest. See main entry under Brazil.

ICA *(ARUACO, ARHUACO, BINTUK, BÍNTUKUA, BINTUCUA, IJCA, IJKA, IKA, IKE)* [ARH] 14,301 (1998 Arango and Sánchez). Southern slopes of Sierra Nevada de Santa Marta. Chibchan, Aruak. 90% are monolingual. A few use Spanish as second language. The people use the name 'Ica'. Strong traditional culture. Grammar. SOV. Literacy rate in first language: 1% to 5%. Literacy rate in second language: 15% to 25%.

INGA *(HIGHLAND INGA)* [INB] 10,000 (1995 SIL). Population total both countries 14,000. Sibundoy Valley, in and around Santiago, San Andrés, and Colón; Aponte, Department of Nariño. 1,000 in Bogotá, small numbers in regional capitals. None in Ecuador. Also spoken in Venezuela. Quechuan, Quechua II, B. Dialects: SANTIAGO INGA, SAN ANDRÉS INGA, APONTE INGA. Partially intelligible with Imbabura Quichua of Ecuador. Aponte Inga may need separate literature. Bilingual level estimates for Spanish are 0 0%, 1 10%, 2 10%, 3 20%, 4 40%, 5 20%. Dictionary. Grammar. SOV. Literacy rate in first language: 10% to 60%. Literacy rate in second language: 25% to 50%. Deciduous forest. Mountain mesa. Intensive agriculturalists, craftsmen. 2,100 to 2,500 meters. NT 1996.

INGA, JUNGLE *(LOWLAND INGA, MOCOA, INGANO)* [INJ] 5,000 to 8,000 (1987 SIL). Upper Caquetá and Putumayo rivers. Quechuan, Quechua II, B. Dialects: YUNGUILLO-CONDAGUA, GUAYUYACO. Closest to Highland Inga. Distinct from Napo Quechua. Bilingualism in Spanish. SOV. Literacy rate in first language: 10% to 30%. Literacy rate in second language: 25% to 50%. Tropical forest. Rolling hills, close to major rivers. Intensive agriculturalists. 200 to 1,000 meters.

KOREGUAJE ***(COREGUAJE, CORREGUAJE, KO'REUAJU, CAQUETÁ, CHAOCHA PAI)*** [COE] 2,000 (1995 SIL). Orteguaza and Caquetá rivers and tributaries, Caquetá region. Tucanoan, Western Tucanoan, Northern, Coreguaje. 90% use Spanish as second language. The Tama ethnic group now speak Koreguaje. 'Caquetá' is the name of the river, not of the people. Literacy rate in first language: 10% to 30%. Literacy rate in second language: 25% to 40%. Agriculturalists. NT 1991.

KUNA, BORDER ***(COLOMBIA CUNA, CAIMAN NUEVO, CUNA, PAYA-PUCURO)*** [KUA] 600 to 800 in Colombia (1991 SIL). Population total both countries 1,300 to 1,500. North coastal region near the Panama isthmus. Also spoken in Panama. Chibchan, Kuna. NT 1993.

MACAGUAJE [MCL] Lower Putumayo, tributaries of Caquetá River. Tucanoan, Western Tucanoan, Northern, Siona-Secoya. Bilingualism in Siona, Coreguaje. Siona and Coreguaje are the languages used. A few still maintain tribal identity. Extinct.

MACAGUÁN ***(MACAGUANE, AGUALINDA GUAHIBO, HITNÜ)*** [MBN] 130 or more (1981 SIL). Arauca, Agualinda, and San José de Lipa between the Lipa, Ele, and Cuiloto rivers and Caño Colorado, and other scattered locations. Guahiban. Unintelligible to speakers of other Guahibo varieties. Most are monolingual. Vigorous. Small groups. Semi-nomadic. Dictionary. Grammar. Hunter-gatherers.

MACUNA ***(MAKUNA, BUHAGANA, ROEA, EMOA, IDE, YEBA, SUROA, TABOTIRO JEJEA, UMUA, WUHÁNA, PANEROA, JEPA-MATSI, YEPÁ-MAHSÁ)*** [MYY] 450 in Colombia (1991 SIL). Population total both countries 550. Lower Pira-Parana, Vaupés region; Apaporis tributaries and Miriti-Parana. Also spoken in Brazil. Tucanoan, Eastern Tucanoan, Central, Southern. Dictionary. OVS. Literacy rate in first language: 5% to 10%. Literacy rate in second language: 15% to 25%. Tropical forest. Interfluvial. Swidden agriculturalists. NT 1989.

MALAYO ***(MAROCASERO, MARACASERO, SANJA, SANKA, SANCÁ, AROSARIO, ARSARIO, GUAMAKA, GUAMACA, WIWA)*** [MBP] 3,225 (1993 Organización Gonawindu Tayrona). Southern and eastern slopes of Sierra Nevada de Santa Marta. Chibchan, Aruak. Literacy rate in first language: Below 1%. Literacy rate in second language: Below 5%.

MOTILÓN ***(BARI, MOTILONE)*** [MOT] Population total both countries 1,500 to 2,000. Oro River and Catatumbo River region. Also spoken in Venezuela. Chibchan, Motilon. Bible portions.

MUINANE ***(MUINANA, MUINANI, MUENAME)*** [BMR] 150 in Colombia (1982 SIL). Upper Cahuinarí, (tributary Caquetá) Amazonas. Witotoan, Boran. All are bilingual in Bora or Huitotoan languages. Not to be confused with Muinane Huitoto. Literacy rate in first language: 1% to 5%. Literacy rate in second language: Below 5%. NT 1981.

NATAGAIMAS [NTS] Tolima region. Unclassified. The group still exists as a tribal entity, but the language has not been spoken for several generations. Spanish is used. Extinct.

NHENGATU ***(YERAL, GERAL, NHEENGATU, NYENGATO, WAENGATU, MODERN TUPI)*** [YRL] 3,000 in Colombia. Vaupés. Tupi, Tupi-Guarani, Tupi (III). NT 1973. See main entry under Brazil.

NORTHERN CENTRAL AMERICA CREOLE ENGLISH [BZI] 12,000 to 18,000 (1981 SIL) out of total San Andrés population of 30,000 (1989 J. Holm). San Andrés and Providencia Islands. Creole, English based, Atlantic, Western. Dialect: ISLANDER CREOLE ENGLISH (SAN ANDRÉS CREOLE, BENDE). There is reported to be a 'deep Creole'. Very close to Belize Creole English. Standard English is used among the most highly educated. Probably the first language of the majority of the Islanders. Creole is considered appropriate for oral purposes only in popular thinking. Literacy rate in second language: 90% Spanish, 80% English. Providencia: mountains, San Andrés: plains. See main entry under Belize.

NUKAK MAKÚ ***(MACZSA, GUAVIARE)*** [MBR] 300 possibly. Jungle region between Guaviare and Inirida rivers, up to Maparipan. Near Charco Caimán. Maku. Evasive hunters.

OCAINA ***(OKAINA)*** [OCA] (3 or 4 families in Colombia; 1982 SIL). Upper Igara-Paraná and tributaries, Amazonas region. Witotoan, Witoto, Ocaina. Dialects: DUKAIYA, IBO'TSA. Bilingualism in Murui Huitoto, Bora, Spanish. Bible portions 1964-1971. See main entry under Peru.

OMEJES [OME] Arawakan, Unclassified. Extinct.

PÁEZ ***(NASA YUWE)*** [PBB] 118,845 in the ethnic group (1998 Arango). Central Andes Range near Popayán, Cauca. Paezan. Dialects: PITAYO, PANIQUITA (PANIKITA). Bilingual level estimates for Spanish are 0 50%, 1 25%, 2 13%, 3 10%, 4 2%, 5 0%. Spanish is the predominant language of instruction in schools. It is reported that not all members of the ethnic group speak Páez (1999). Dictionary. Grammar. SOV. Literacy rate in first language: 10% to 30%. Literacy rate in second language: 25% to 50%. Scrub forest. Mountain mesa and slope. Peasant agriculturalists. 2,500 to 3,000 meters. NT 1980.

PALENQUERO ***(PALENQUE, LENGUA)*** [PLN] The ethnic group is 2,500 (1989 J. Holm). Village of San Basilio de Palenque southeast of Cartagena, and 2 neighborhoods in Barranquilla. Creole, Spanish based. Entirely unintelligible to Spanish speakers. Linguistic influences from Kongo in Democratic Republic of Congo (I. Hancock 1987). Most members of the ethnic group speak Spanish as mother tongue, but some old people have limited proficiency in Spanish. 10% of those under 25 speak it (1998 Armin Schwegler). Most speakers are older. Everyone values Palenquero. People are culturally distinct from nearby Spanish speakers. Investigation needed: bilingual proficiency in Spanish, attitudes toward Spanish. Grammar.

PIAPOCO [PIO] 3,000 in Colombia. Population total both countries 3,100. Tributaries and lower Vichada River region, and Meta and Guaviare rivers. Also spoken in Venezuela. Arawakan, Maipuran, Northern Maipuran, Inland. Bilingual level estimates for Spanish are 0 60%, 1 20%, 2 10%, 3 10%, 4 0%, 5 0%. Dictionary. SVO. Literacy rate in first language: 30% to 40%. Literacy rate in second language: 20% to 40%. Savannah. Plains. Hunter-gatherers, swidden agriculturalists. 800 to 1,000 feet. NT 1966-1987.

PIAROA *(KUAKUA, GUAGUA, QUAQUA)* [PID] 80 in Colombia (1991 Adelaar). Near the Sáliba. Salivan. Dialects: MACO (MAKO, ITOTO), PIAROA. Maco is reported to be a separate language, with speakers of each bilingual in the other. 'Ature' (Adole) may be an alternate name. Investigation needed: intelligibility with Maco. NT 1986. See main entry under Venezuela.

PIJAO *(PIAJAO)* [PIJ] Tolima region. Unclassified. M. Durbin said there is not enough data to classify it linguistically. They still exist as a tribal entity, but there have been no speakers since the 1950s. Spanish is used. Extinct.

PIRATAPUYO *(WAIKINO, URUBU-TAPUYA, UAIKENA)* [PIR] 450 in Colombia. Papurí River and lower Vaupés, Amazonas. Most near RC mission at Teresita. Others in small groups. Tucanoan, Eastern Tucanoan, Northern. 75% intelligibility with Guanano (N. Waltz). 99% lexical similarity with Guanano (N. Waltz). All are bilingual in at least one other Tucanoan language, especially Desano or Tucano. Spanish also used. Distinct ethnically from the Guanano, but the exogamy system does not permit the two groups to intermarry. Literacy rate in first language: 5% to 10%. Literacy rate in second language: 40% to 60%. NT 1991. See main entry under Brazil.

PLAYERO *(RIO ARAUCA GUAHIBO)* [GOB] 150 to 160 (1983 SIL). Arauca River, Venezuela border, Arauca Division, on the banks of the Arauca River from Gaviotas Island to Arauca. Guahiban. Low intelligibility with other Guahibo. Somewhat acculturated and bilingual in Spanish for trading purposes. Many have fields in Venezuela. Interested in literacy.

PONARES [POD] Arawakan, Unclassified. A Sáliba last name. Might have been a Piapoco or Achagua subgroup. Extinct.

PROVIDENCIA SIGN LANGUAGE [PRO] Known by most people on the Island including 19 born deaf out of 2,500 to 3,000 population (1986 W. Washabaugh). Providencia Island off the coast of Nicaragua. Deaf sign language. They have not been exposed to other sign languages. East differs from west with some variation between villages. The high deaf population is probably caused by in-breeding. The deaf are fairly well integrated into daily activities. The system is about 100 years old. They are illiterate and untutored, do not use finger spelling.

PUINAVE *(PUINABE)* [PUI] 2,000 in Colombia (1977 NTM). Population total both countries 2,240. Inírida River and tributaries, Territory of Guainia. Also spoken in Venezuela. Language Isolate. Ruhlen and others classify it as related to Macú. Plains. NT 1964.

QUICHUA, LOWLAND, NAPO *(LOWLAND NAPO QUECHUA)* [QLN] Undetermined number in Colombia. Putumayo River. Quechuan, Quechua II, B. Bible portions 1972-1987. See main entry under Ecuador.

ROMANI, VLAX [RMY] 39,000 Gypsies in Colombia (1993 Johnstone); Several hundred thousand in Latin America (1984 Ian Hancock). Indo-European, Indo-Iranian, Indo-Aryan, Central zone, Romani, Vlax. Christian. NT 1984-1986. See main entry under Romania.

RUNA [RUN] Choco. Extinct.

SÁLIBA *(SÁLIVA)* [SLC] 2,000 in Colombia (1982 T. Benaissa SIL). Population total both countries 2,250. Meta and Casanare rivers. Also spoken in Venezuela. Salivan. Bilingualism in Spanish. Those 50 and older use Sáliba as mother tongue. Younger members use Spanish. SOV. Literacy rate in first language: 1% to 5%. Literacy rate in second language: 15% to 25%. Tropical forest. Plains, interfluvial. Swidden agriculturalists. lower than 200 meters.

SIONA *(SIONI, PIOJE, PIOCHE-SIONI)* [SIN] 300 total including Ecuador (1982 SIL). Population total both countries 300 or more (1982 SIL). Live on both sides of the Putumayo River. Also spoken in Ecuador. Tucanoan, Western Tucanoan, Northern, Siona-Secoya. Bilingual level estimates for Spanish are 0 0%, 1 5%, 2 20%, 3 60%, 4 10%, 5 5%. Those in Ecuador consider themselves Colombians. Distinct from Secoya (Siona-Secoya). SOV. Literacy rate in first language: 5% to 10%. Literacy rate in second language: 15% to 25%. Tropical forest. Interfluvial. Swidden agriculturalists. 320 meters. NT 1982.

SIRIANO [SRI] 250 to 300 in Colombia (1992 SIL). Population total both countries 260 to 310. Paca and Vina Rivers, Vaupés region. Also spoken in Brazil. Tucanoan, Eastern Tucanoan, Central, Desano. Different from Desano. All speak at least one other Tucanoan language. Spanish is also used. Ethnic differences are important because of the system of exogamy, and persons are identified by first language of father. SOV. Literacy rate in first language: 5% to 30%. Literacy rate in second language:

15% to 25%. Tropical forest. Riverine. Swidden agriculturalists. 100 to 200 meters. Traditional religion, Christian. NT 1998.

SPANISH [SPN] 34,000,000 in Colombia (1995 estimate). Indo-European, Italic, Romance, Italo-Western, Western, Gallo-Iberian, Ibero-Romance, West Iberian, Castilian. National language. Bible 1553-1979. See main entry under Spain.

TAMA [TEN] Vicente, Orteguaza River, Caquetá region. Tucanoan, Western Tucanoan, Northern, Tama. Ruhlen says it is a Koreguaje dialect. Those living on the Orteguaza River have completely integrated with the Coreguaje. Possibly no one speaks Tama now. Extinct.

TANIMUCA-RETUARÃ ***(RETUAMA, RETUARÃ, LETUAMA, LETUHAMA, UFAINA, UAIRÃ)*** [TNC] 300 (1976 SIL), including 180 Tanimuca. Guacayá, Oiyaka rivers (tributaries of the Mirití-Parana), Mirití-Parana, Apaporis, and Popeyaka rivers near the mouth of the Pira River below Popeyaca, Amazonas region. Tucanoan, Western Tucanoan, Tanimuca. Dialects: TANIMUCA, RETUARÃ. The Tanimuca and Retuarã are two ethnic groups living close together who speak the same language. Possibly Eastern Tucanoan. Quite a few from the Apaporis and Popeyaka understand Macuna; those in other areas are often fluent in Yucuna. The Retuarã are more monolingual than the Tanimuca. All work for one rubber hunter. Grammar. Literacy rate in first language: 1% to 5%. Literacy rate in second language: Below 5%. Tropical forest. Swidden agriculturalists. Bible portions.

TARIANO ***(TARIÁNA)*** [TAE] Members of the ethnic group in Colombia: 332 (1998 Arango and Sánchez). Lower Papurí, Vaupés region. Arawakan, Maipuran, Northern Maipuran, Inland. No one has been located who speaks Tariano in Colombia, but the tribal identity is still maintained. All speak Tuca. Nearly extinct. See main entry under Brazil.

TATUYO ***(PAMOA, OA, TATUTAPUYO, JUNA)*** [TAV] 350 (1983 SIL). Pira-Paraná headwaters and Upper Papurí, Vaupés region. Tucanoan, Eastern Tucanoan, Central, Tatuyo. All speak at least one other Tucanoan language. The majority marry Carapana, Northern Barasano, or Barasana women. Literacy rate in first language: 1% to 5%. Literacy rate in second language: Below 5%. Tropical forest. Interfluvial. Swidden agriculturalists. 235 to 245 meters. NT 1987.

TICUNA ***(TIKUNA, TUKÚNA, TUCUNA)*** [TCA] 4,000 in Colombia. Amazon River. Language Isolate. NT 1986. See main entry under Peru.

TOMEDES ***(TAMUDES)*** [TOE] Arawakan, Unclassified. Extinct.

TOTORO [TTK] Only a few speakers in the mid 1970s. 17 km. west of Silvia, Cauca, in town of Totoro. Barbacoan, Coconucan. Extinct.

TUCANO ***(DAXSEA, DACHSEA, DASEA, BETOYA, BETAYA, TUKANA)*** [TUO] 2,000 in Colombia. Upper Papurí River and tributaries. Tucanoan, Eastern Tucanoan, Northern. 6 regional dialects. All speak at least one other Tucanoan language or Spanish as second language. Tucano is the second language of many neighboring groups, especially south and east of Mitú. Trade language. Grammar. SOV. Literacy rate in first language: 30% to 40%. Literacy rate in second language: 30% to 40%. Tropical forest. Riverine, hills. Swidden agriculturalists. 200 to 250 meters. NT 1988. See main entry under Brazil.

TUNEBO, ANGOSTURAS [TND] Very small. Chibchan, Chibchan Proper, Tunebo. 71% intelligibility between Eastern and Angosturas Tunebo. Somewhat bilingual. Nearly extinct.

TUNEBO, BARRO NEGRO ***(EASTERN TUNEBO)*** [TBN] 300 or more (1981 SIL). Isolated, on the edge of the eastern plains in the Andes foothills above Paz de Ariporo, in Barro Negro, San Lope (Casanare), and Tabías (Casanare), south of Tame Arauca. Chibchan, Chibchan Proper, Tunebo. 62% intelligibility with Cobarma Tunebo. Partly bilingual, somewhat acculturated. Tunebo is used exclusively in the home. Swidden agriculturalists: maize; hunter-gatherers, fishermen. 4,000 to 5,000 feet.

TUNEBO, CENTRAL ***(COBARÍA TUNEBO)*** [TUF] 1,500 in Colombia (1982 SIL). Population total both countries 1,500 or more. North slopes of Sierra Nevada de Cocuy, Boyaca and Arauca regions; Satocá, Calafita, Tegría (Boyaca), Cobaría (Boyacá). Also spoken in Venezuela. Chibchan, Chibchan Proper, Tunebo. Bilingual level estimates for Spanish are 0 65%, 1 20%, 2 10%, 3 4%, 4 .5%, 5 .5%. They have a taboo on the use of paper. Dictionary. SOV. Literacy rate in first language: 1% to 5%. Literacy rate in second language: 5% to 25%. Tropical forest. Mountain slope. Swidden agriculturalists. 500 to 1,500 meters. NT 1987.

TUNEBO, WESTERN ***(AGUAS BLANCAS)*** [TNB] 700 (1998). Santander del Sur. Chibchan, Chibchan Proper, Tunebo. The most divergent of the Tunebo languages. Limited bilingualism. Swidden agriculturalists: maize; hunter-gatherers, fishermen. Bible portions.

TUYUCA ***(DOCHKAFUARA, TEJUCA, TUYUKA)*** [TUE] 350 in Colombia (1995 SIL). Population total both countries 815. Inambu, Tiquie, and Papurí rivers. Also spoken in Brazil. Tucanoan, Eastern Tucanoan, Central, Bara. All speak at least one other Tucanoan language. Second language is Tucano or Waimaha. Spanish used in schools in the area. Dictionary. Grammar. Literacy rate in first language: 10%. Literacy rate in second language: 60%. Bible portions 1991-1994.

WAIMAHA ***(WAIMAJA, "BARÁ", NORTHERN BARASANO, BARASANO)*** [BAO] 600 in Colombia (1995 SIL). Population total both countries 700. Tributaries of mid and upper Pira-Paraná, upper Papurí and Tiquié, southeastern Vaupés region. Also spoken in Brazil. Tucanoan, Eastern Tucanoan, Central, Bara. 40% to 50% speak Spanish as second language. All speak 2 to 4 of these: Tucano, Tatuyo, Tuyuca, Taiwano, Barasana, Yuruti, Macuna, Carapana. The name "Bará" has derogatory connotations to some speakers. SOV. Literacy rate in first language: 25%. Literacy rate in second language: 25% to 40%. Tropical forest. Riverine, interfluvial. Swidden agriculturalists. Bible portions 1975-1994.

WAYUU ***(GUAJIRO, GOAJIRO, GUAJIRA)*** [GUC] 135,000 in Colombia (1995 SIL). Population total both countries 305,000. Guajira Peninsula on the Caribbean coast. Also spoken in Venezuela. Arawakan, Maipuran, Northern Maipuran, Caribbean. VSO. Literacy rate in first language: Below 1%. Literacy rate in second language: 5% to 15%. Desert. Coastal. Sedentary pastoralists. Sea level. Bible portions 1944-1989.

WOUN MEU ***(WAUN MEO, WAUMEO)*** [NOA] 3,000 possibly in Colombia. San Juan River basin. Choco. The people's name for themselves is 'Wounaan', and for their language 'Woun Meo'. NT 1988. See main entry under Panama.

YAHUNA ***(YAÚNA, YAYUNA)*** [YNU] Fewer than 23 in ethnic group, fewer than 20 on Umana River, 3 on Apaporis River (1988). Umuqa River, a tributary of the Piraparana River. Tucanoan, Eastern Tucanoan, Unclassified. Dialects: OPAINA, DATUANA. All now speak Macuna. Extinct.

YARÍ [YRI] Yarí River, Caquetá region, above El Capitán waterfalls near the Yarí River. About 50 years ago 140 of them migrated to the Apaporis River, and settled on the upper Vaupés River near Puerto Nare. Unclassified. Possibly a dialect of Carijona (Carib), a Western Tucanoan language, or Huitoto. They were given the name 'Yarí' by outsiders because of their location on the Yarí River. Investigation needed: intelligibility.

YUCUNA ***(MATAPI, YUKUNA)*** [YCN] 800 to 1,000 (1992 SIL). Miriti-Parana (tributary Caquetá), Amazonas region. Arawakan, Maipuran, Northern Maipuran, Inland. Bilingualism in Spanish. SVO. Literacy rate in first language: 5% to 10%. Literacy rate in second language: 15% to 25%. Tropical forest. Riverine. Swidden agriculturalists. 300 meters. NT 1982.

YUKPA ***(YUKO, YUPA, YUCPA, NORTHERN MOTILÓN, CARIB MOTILÓN)*** [YUP] 2,500 in Colombia (1976 SIL). Population total both countries 3,000. Serranía de Perijá, Cesar Department, Municipio of Augustín Codazzi and neighboring municipios north and south, Colombia-Venezuela border. Río Cascará dialect is in the Municipio of Agustín Codassi along the Casacará River and the Caño Iroka. Caqo Padilla-La Laguna is small and farther north. Río Maracas is to the south in the Municipio of Becerril. Also spoken in Venezuela. Carib, Northern, Coastal. Dialects: RÍO CASACARÁ (IROKA), RÍO MARACAS, CAÑO PADILLA-LA LAGUNA, COYAIMA. At least five extant dialects including two in Venezuela. Ruhlen says Coyaima was a dialect. Río Cascará and Río Maracas dialects are probably the largest ones, and different enough to probably be separate languages. Venezuela dialects seem more similar to Río Maracas. Relations between speakers of different dialects have sometimes been hostile in the past. Presently they have little contact with each other. Unrelated to Chibchan Motilón (Bari). Low lexical similarity with Japreira of Venezuela (Luis Oquendo (U. of Zulia-Venezuela). Men can use Spanish for buying and selling only. Vigorous.

YURUTI ***(JURUTI, YURUTI-TAPUYA, LURUTY-TAPUYA, YURITI, JURITI, JURITI-TAPUIA, WAYHARA, PATSOKA)*** [YUI] 200 to 250 in Colombia (1991 R. Kinch SIL). Population total both countries 250 or more. Upper Pacá River (tributary of Papurí) and Caño Yi River, Vaupés. Also spoken in Brazil. Tucanoan, Eastern Tucanoan, Central, Bara. Yuriti and Juriti are incorrect spellings. Literacy rate in first language: Below 1%. Literacy rate in second language: 15% to 25%. Tropical forest. Agriculturalists: manioc; fishermen, hunter-gatherers. 900 feet. Bible portions 1985.

COSTA RICA

Republic of Costa Rica, República de Costa Rica. National or official language: Spanish. 3,841,000 (1998 UN). Literacy rate 93% (1989 WA). Also includes Basque, Ngäbere 5,000. Information mainly from SIL 1967-98. Christian. Blind population 2,500. Deaf population 202,625. Deaf institutions: 9. Data accuracy estimate: A1, A2. The number of languages listed for Costa Rica is 11. Of those, 10 are living languages and 1 is extinct. Diversity index 0.04.

BORUCA ***(BORUNCA, BURUNCA, BRUNCA, BRUNKA)*** [BRN] 5 women (1986 SIL) out of an ethnic group of 1,000 (1991). Southern coast between Playa Bonita and Golfito. Chibchan, Talamanca. Nearly all speak only Spanish. SOV. Agriculturalists: maize, beans, vegetables; hunter-gatherers. Nearly extinct.

BRIBRI ***(TALAMANCA)*** [BZD] 6,000 speakers (1995 UBS). Southern, along Lari, Telire, and Uren rivers, Canton of Talamanca, Limón Province; Canton of Buenos Aires, Puntarenas Province. Chibchan, Talamanca. Dialects: SALITRE-CABAGRA, AMUBRE-KATSI, COROMA. Closest to, but unintelligible to speakers of Cabécar, Guatuso, and Teribe. At least 3 major dialects which are inherently intelligible to each others' speakers. Bilingualism in Spanish. Speak Bribri in the home. All ages. SOV. Literacy rate in first language: 2% to 3%. Literacy rate in second language: 50% read halting Spanish. Bible portions 1905-1994.

CABÉCAR ***(CHIRRIPÓ)*** [CJP] 3,000 (1986 UBS). Turrialba region. Chibchan, Talamanca. Dialects: CHIRRIPÓ, TELIRE, ESTRELLA, UJARRÁS. Bilingual level estimates for Spanish are 0 80%, 1-5 20%. 80% monolingual. Identified historically with the Huetares. Dictionary. Grammar. SOV. NT 1993.

CHINESE, YUE ***(YUE, YUEH, CANTONESE)*** [YUH] 4,500 including Mandarin and Hakka speakers (1981 MARC). Limón, Guanacaste, Puntarenas, San José. Sino-Tibetan, Chinese. Bible 1894-1981. See main entry under China.

CHOROTEGA ***(CHOLUTECA, MANGUE, DIRIA, OROTINA)*** [CJR] Some from the ethnic group live near Tuturrialba, but do not maintain the language. A few elderly people may remember a few words. They were originally from the Guanacaste region near the Nicaraguan border. Some are also in El Salvador and Honduras. Oto-Manguean, Chiapanec-Mangue. Dialects: CHOROTEGA, DIRIA, NAGRANDAN, NICOYA, ORISI, OROTINYA (OROTINA). Reported to have been quite similar to Chiapaneco of Mexico. Extinct.

COSTA RICAN SIGN LANGUAGE [CSR] Deaf sign language. May be related to Providencia Sign Language. Reported to have about 60% lexical similarity with ASL.

MALÉKU JAÍKA ***(GUATUSO)*** [GUT] 365 (1985 SIL). Northern. Chibchan, Rama. Bilingual level estimates for Spanish are 0 0%, 1 0%, 2 4%, 3 58%, 4 37%, 5 1%. Agriculturalists: tubers, bananas, white cacao; hunters.

PLAUTDIETSCH ***(LOW GERMAN, MENNONITE GERMAN)*** [GRN] 100 in Costa Rica (1974 Minnich). Sarapiqui area. Indo-European, Germanic, West, Low Saxon-Low Franconian, Low Saxon. Bilingualism in Spanish. People speak Plautdietsch in the home. Church services are in Spanish. Christian. NT 1987. See main entry under Canada.

SOUTHWESTERN CARIBBEAN CREOLE ENGLISH [JAM] 55,100 in Costa Rica, 2% of the population (1986). East of San José, principally along the railroad between Siquirres and Limón, and south of Limón along the road. Creole, English based, Atlantic, Western. Dialect: LIMÓN CREOLE ENGLISH (LIMONESE CREOLE, MEKITELYU). Jamaican migrants settled in Limón about the middle of the 19th Century, as they also did in Panama, so those varieties are close. Some say they do not understand Islander Creole of San Andrés. Comprehension of Standard English is somewhat limited. All ages. Vigorous among themselves. Creole is not considered proper for literary purposes. They consider Jamaican Creole to be more 'broken' than their own. See main entry under Jamaica.

SPANISH ***(ESPAÑOL, CASTELLANO)*** [SPN] 3,300,000 in Costa Rica (1995 estimate). Indo-European, Italic, Romance, Italo-Western, Western, Gallo-Iberian, Ibero-Romance, West Iberian, Castilian. National language. Bible 1553-1979. See main entry under Spain.

TERIBE ***(TERRABA)*** [TFR] 5 in Costa Rica out of an ethnic group of 35 to 300 (1991 SIL), 1,500 in Panama (1991 SIL). Southeastern, north coast. Chibchan, Talamanca. Terraba in Costa Rica who know only a little Teribe want to relearn the language and culture (1991). Bible portions 1979-1984. See main entry under Panama.

CUBA

Republic of Cuba, República de Cuba. National or official language: Spanish. 11,116,000 (1998 UN). Literacy rate 94% (1991 National Geographic). Also includes Catalan-Valencian-Balear, Corsican. Secular 57, Christian, traditional religion. Deaf population 670,810. Deaf institutions: 4. Data accuracy estimate: A2. The number of languages listed for Cuba is 2. Of those, 1 is a living language and 1 is a second language without mother tongue speakers. Diversity index 0.00.

LUCUMI [LUQ] Niger-Congo, Atlantic-Congo, Volta-Congo, Benue-Congo, Defoid, Yoruboid, Edekiri. A secret language used for ritual by the Santeria religion. The people are sometimes called 'Yoruba'. Santeria. Second language only.

SPANISH [SPN] 10,000,000 in Cuba (1995 estimate). Indo-European, Italic, Romance, Italo-Western, Western, Gallo-Iberian, Ibero-Romance, West Iberian, Castilian. National language. Bible 1553-1979. See main entry under Spain.

DOMINICA

Commonwealth of Dominica. National or official language: English. 71,000 (1998 UN). Self governing part of British West Indies. Literacy rate 80% to 94%. Christian. Deaf population 5,335. Data accuracy estimate: A1. The number of languages listed for Dominica is 4. Of those, 3 are living languages and 1 is extinct. Diversity index 0.00.

CARIB, ISLAND [CAI] Formerly also in Lesser Antilles, excluding Trinidad. Also spoken in St. Vincent and the Grenadines. Arawakan, Maipuran, Northern Maipuran, Caribbean. Was not intelligible with Black Carib (D. Taylor 1959). Vincentian on St. Vincent may have been closer to Black Carib than to Island Carib. Became extinct in Dominica about 1920. Used a special language of Cariban origin to address men (Berend Hoff). Extinct.

ENGLISH [ENG] Indo-European, Germanic, West, English. Dialect: DOMINICAN ENGLISH. National language. Bible 1535-1989. See main entry under United Kingdom.

LEEWARD CARIBBEAN CREOLE ENGLISH [AIG] Kokoy dialect is in 2 villages: Marigot and Wesley in northeast Dominica. Creole, English based, Atlantic, Eastern, Southern. Dialect: KOKOY. Grammar closest to basilectal Antiguan or Jamaican (Pauline Christie 1998). People use it with Jamaicans and some other Caribbean people, but not with non-Caribbean people. See main entry under Antigua and Barbuda.

LESSER ANTILLEAN CREOLE FRENCH [DOM] 42,600 in Dominica (1998), 60% of the population (M. Parkvall). Creole, French based. Dialect: DOMINICA CREOLE FRENCH (PATWA, PATOIS, KWÈYÒL). The dialect of Dominica is virtually the same as St. Lucia. Most people are bilingual in English or English dominant, especially younger people. Standard French understood by no more than 10% of the population (M. Adler 1977). Loan words from Island Carib and Arawak. Dictionary. Christian. NT 1999. See main entry under St. Lucia.

DOMINICAN REPUBLIC

República Dominicana. National or official language: Spanish. 8,232,000 (1998 UN). Literacy rate 68% to 94%. Also includes North Levantine Spoken Arabic 3,000, Catalan-Valencian-Balear, Japanese 1,500, Southwestern Caribbean Creole English 22,000, Chinese 25,000. Christian, traditional religion, secular. Blind population 5,000. Deaf population 474,490. Deaf institutions: 3. Data accuracy estimate: B. The number of languages listed for Dominican Republic is 4. Of those, all are living languages. Diversity index 0.05.

DOMINICAN SIGN LANGUAGE [DOQ] Deaf sign language. Reported to have 85% to 90% lexical similarity with ASL, and to use most of the features of ASL, such as absent referent and reduplication. Many are not fluent or use home sign.

HAITIAN CREOLE FRENCH [HAT] 159,000 or 2% of the population in Dominican Republic (1987). Creole, French based. Bible 1985. See main entry under Haiti.

SAMANÁ ENGLISH [SAX] 8,000 (1989 J. Holm). Samaná Peninsula, northeastern Dominican Republic. Creole, English based, Atlantic, Unclassified. Spanish is used as second language. Some use Haitian Creole. A community of descendants of ex-USA slaves settled in 1824. It is reported that there was a settlement of African slaves here in the early 1500s. It may not be a creole, but a regional variety of uncreolized English. There are features of creolization and archaic Black English.

SPANISH [SPN] 6,886,000 in Dominican Republic (1995 estimate), 87% of the population. Indo-European, Italic, Romance, Italo-Western, Western, Gallo-Romance, Ibero-Romance, West Iberian, Castilian. National language. Bible 1553-1979. See main entry under Spain.

ECUADOR

Republic of Ecuador, República del Ecuador. National or official language: Spanish. 12,175,000 (1998 UN). 2,300,000 speakers of American Indian languages (Adelaar 1991). Literacy rate 70% to 90%. Also includes English 65,000, Standard German 32,000, Bokmaal Norwegian 11,000, Arabic 1,800, Chinese 7,000. Information mainly from SIL 1955-99. Christian, secular, traditional religion. Blind population 10,000 (1982 WCE). Deaf population 64,692 to 150,000 or more (1986 Gallaudet University). Deaf institutions: 3. Data accuracy estimate: A1, A2. The number of languages listed for Ecuador is 23. Of those, 22 are living languages and 1 is extinct. Diversity index 0.26.

ACHUAR-SHIWIAR ***(ACHUAR, ACHUAL, ACHUARA, ACHUALE, JIVARO, MAINA)*** [ACU] 2,000 in 7 villages in Ecuador. Pastaza and Bobonaza river areas. Jivaroan. Bilingual level estimates for Shuar are 0 60%, 1 20%, 2 10%, 3 7%, 4 3%, 5 0%. Many people in the Ecuador group seem to be fairly bilingual in Shuar, but their comprehension is limited. SOV. Tropical forest. Interfluvial. Swidden agriculturalists, hunters-gatherers, fishermen. 150 to 500 meters. Traditional religion. NT 1981. See main entry under Peru.

AWA-CUAIQUER ***(AWA, CUAIQUER)*** [KWI] 1,000 in Ecuador (1991 Adelaar). Extreme north, on the western slopes of the Andes, Colombia-Ecuador border, Carchi Province. Barbacoan, Pasto. More distantly related to Chachi and Colorado. Speakers call themselves 'Awa' in Ecuador. Bible portions 1979-1982. See main entry under Colombia.

CHACHI ***(CAYAPA, CHA' PALAACHI)*** [CBI] 5,000 (1987 N. Wiebe SIL). North coastal jungle, Esmeraldas Province, Cayapas River and its tributaries (Onzole, Canandé, Sucio, Cojimíes, and others). Barbacoan, Cayapa-Colorado. Bilingual level estimates for Spanish are 0 6%, 1 25.5%, 2 26.5%, 3 34.5%, 4 6%, 5 1.5%. Women, older people, and those living in the isolated headwaters of the river are less bilingual in Spanish. The name of the people is 'Chachilla'. Dictionary. SOV. Tropical forest. Coastal, riverine. Swidden agriculturalists: plantain; fishermen: shrimp, fish; hunters. 10 to 400 meters. Traditional religion, Christian. Bible portions 1964-1980. NT nearly ready for press (2000).

COFÁN ***(KOFÁN, A'I, KOFANE)*** [CON] 780 in Ecuador. Population total both countries 1,300. Both sides of the Colombia and Ecuador border, Napo Province near Santa Rosa de Sucumbios, and Aguarico River. Also spoken in Colombia. Chibchan, Cofan. Chibchan with Western Tucanoan features (Ferndon, Borman), Barbacoan (J. A. Mason), or Jivaroan (Ruhlen 1987). Bilingual level estimates for Spanish are 0 1%, 1 33%, 2 28%, 3 25%, 4 12%, 5 1%. SOV. Radio programs. Tropical forest. Riverine. Swidden agriculturalists. 200 to 1,000 meters. Traditional religion, Christian. NT 1980-1991.

COLORADO ***(TSACHILA)*** [COF] 2,100 (1999 SIL). Northwestern jungle west of Quito, around Santo Domingo de los Colorados. Barbacoan, Cayapa-Colorado. Dictionary. SOV. Tropical forest. Interfluvial. Peasant agriculturalists. 550 to 600 meters. Traditional religion, Christian. NT 1980-1990.

ECUADORIAN SIGN LANGUAGE [ECS] (188,000 deaf persons, 2% of the population; 1986 Gallaudet Univ.). Deaf sign language. Slight regional variants in sign languages. Some influences from USA Peace Corps, others from people educated in Spain or Argentina. Some deaf schools use total communication; speaking and signing.

MEDIA LENGUA [MUE] 1,000 first and second language speakers (1999 Peter Bakker). A few villages. Mixed Language, Spanish-Quechua. Has a Quechua grammatical system and a Spanish vocabulary.

QUICHUA, HIGHLAND, CALDERÓN ***(CALDERÓN QUICHUA, PICHINCHA QUICHUA, CAYAMBE QUICHUA)*** [QUD] 25,000 to 30,000 (1987 SIL). Calderón and Cayambe areas of Pichincha Province around Quito. Quechuan, Quechua II, B. Distinct from Chimborazo, Imbabura, and Tungurahua lexically. Spoken in the home. All ages. A strong Quichua-speaking area. All Quichua are called 'Quechua' in most other countries. SOV.

QUICHUA, HIGHLAND, CAÑAR [QQC] 100,000 (1991 UBS). Southern highlands, Cañar Province. Quechuan, Quechua II, B. Lexical differences and a strong sense of linguistic and cultural identity make separate literature necessary. Strong use of Quichua, especially away from the road. They consider Chimborazo to be a separate language. SOV. Traditional religion, Christian. NT, in press (1997).

QUICHUA, HIGHLAND, CHIMBORAZO [QUG] 1,000,000 (1990 UBS). 4,320,000 all Quichua in Ecuador, or 41.3% of the population (1987). Central highlands, Chimborazo and Bolivar provinces. Dialects of Cotopaxi (large) and the rest of Tungurahua (large towns around Ambato not called Salasaca). Quechuan, Quechua II, B. High percentage of monolinguals. SOV. Traditional religion, Christian. Bible 1989.

QUICHUA, HIGHLAND, IMBABURA ***(OTAVALO QUICHUA)*** [QHO] 300,000 (1977 SIL). Northern highlands, Imbabura Province. Quechuan, Quechua II, B. Many monolinguals; especially women. Children speak Quichua as first language. All ages. Vigorous. SOV. Traditional religion, Christian. Bible 1994.

QUICHUA, HIGHLAND, LOJA ***(SARAGURO QUICHUA, LOJA QUICHUA)*** [QQU] 10,000 to 25,000 (1976 SIL). Northern area of Loja Province in southern highlands. Quechuan, Quechua II, B. Lexically more distinct from Chimborazo and Imbabura. They claim little comprehension of Chimborazo. Lexical differences and a strong sense of linguistic and cultural identity make separate literature necessary. SOV. Traditional religion, Christian.

QUICHUA, HIGHLAND, TUNGURAHUA ***(SALASACA QUICHUA, TUNGURAHUA QUICHUA)*** [QQS] 7,000 to 10,000 (1977 SIL). South and east of Ambato in Tungurahua Province. At least 15 towns in the Salasaca area, not counting other varieties of Quichua. Quechuan, Quechua II, B. Lexically distinct from Chimborazo, Imbabura, and Calderón. SOV. Traditional religion, Christian.

QUICHUA, LOWLAND, NAPO ***(INGANO, LOWLAND NAPO QUICHUA, NAPO QUICHUA)*** [QLN] 5,000 in Ecuador. Population total all countries 11,000 to 15,000. Eastern jungle along the Napo, Aguarico, and Putomayo rivers. Also spoken in Colombia, Peru. Quechuan, Quechua II, B. Dialect: SANTA ROSA QUECHUA. Bilingual level estimates for Spanish are 0 15%, 1 21%, 2 50%, 3 10%, 4 3%, 5 1%. 'Ingano' is a name for all lowland Quichua. SOV. Radio programs. Tropical forest. Riverine. Swidden agriculturalists. 280 meters. Traditional religion, Christian. Bible portions 1972-1987.

QUICHUA, LOWLAND, TENA ***(YUMBO)*** [QUW] 5,000 (1976 SIL). Eastern jungle, Tena, Arajuno, Shandia area. Quechuan, Quechua II, B. SOV. Tropical forest. Interfluvial. Swidden agriculturalists. 600 meters. Traditional religion, Christian. NT 1972.

QUICHUA, PASTAZA, NORTHERN ***(BOBONAZA QUICHUA, NORTHERN PASTAZA QUICHUA, PASTAZA QUICHUA, ALAMA, CANELOS QUICHUA, SARAYACU QUICHUA)*** [QLB] 4,000 in Ecuador. Population total both countries 6,000. Eastern jungle along Bobonaza and Conambo rivers, Pastaza Province. Tigre Quechua is in Peru. Also spoken in Peru. Quechuan, Quechua II, B. Dialect: TIGRE QUECHUA. Distinct from Southern Pastaza Quechua of Peru. SOV. Tropical forest. Riverine. Swidden agriculturalists. 300 to 600 meters. Traditional religion, Christian. NT 1992.

SECOYA [SEY] 290 in Ecuador (170 Secoya Angotero, 120 Ecuadorian Siona). Population total both countries 435. Northeastern jungle Aguarico, Cuyabeno, and Eno rivers, near Colombian border. Also spoken in Peru. Tucanoan, Western Tucanoan, Northern, Siona-Secoya. Dialects: ECUADORIAN SIONA, ANGOTERO. Identical to Secoya in Peru. Ecuadorian Siona is distinct from Siona of Colombia. Bilingual level estimates for Spanish are 0 55%, 1 23%, 2 15%, 3 36%, 4 1%, 5 0%. Once used as a wider contact language by the Spanish colonial administration. SOV. Tropical forest. Riverine. Swidden agriculturalists. 300 to 350 meters. Traditional religion, Christian. NT 1990.

SHUAR ***(JIVARO, XIVARO, JIBARO, CHIWARO, SHUARA)*** [JIV] 30,000 to 32,000 (1981 SIL). Southeastern jungle, Morona-Santiago Province. Jivaroan. Bilingual level estimates for Spanish are 0 14%, 1 30%, 2 25%, 3 20%, 4 10%, 5 1%. Different from Achuar Jivaro of Peru. The people prefer to be called 'Shuar'. SOV. Tropical forest. Mountain slope, plains, interfluvial. Swidden, peasant agriculturalists. 500 to 1,000 meters. Traditional religion, Christian. NT 1976-1983.

SIONA [SIN] Putumayo River. Tucanoan, Western Tucanoan, Northern, Siona-Secoya. Distinct from Secoya (Siona-Secoya). SOV. Tropical forest. Riverine. Swidden agriculturalists. 300 to 350 meters. NT 1982. See main entry under Colombia.

SPANISH [SPN] 9,500,000 in Ecuador (1995 estimate). Indo-European, Italic, Romance, Italo-Western, Western, Gallo-Iberian, Ibero-Romance, West Iberian, Castilian. National language. Christian. Bible 1553-1979. See main entry under Spain.

TETETE [TEB] Near the Colombian border, eastern jungle in Cofán area. Tucanoan, Western Tucanoan, Northern, Tetete. Closely related to Secoya but intelligible only with difficulty. Recently extinct. Extinct.

WAORANI ***("AUCA", HUAORANI, WAODANI, HUAO, SABELA, AUISHIRI)*** [AUC] 800 (1993 SIL). Eastern jungle between the Napo and Curaray rivers. Unclassified. Bilingual level estimates for Quichua, Spanish are 0 94%, 1 5%, 2 1%, 3 0%, 4 0%, 5 0%. "Auca" means 'savage' in Quichua. SOV. Tropical forest. Riverine. Swidden agriculturalists. 300 to 400 meters. Traditional religion, Christian. NT 1992.

ZÁPARO ***(ZÁPARA, KAYAPWE)*** [ZRO] 5 or 6 (1996 SIL). Extinct in Peru. Pastaza Province, Peru border, between the Curaray and Bobonaza rivers. Zaparoan. Bilingualism in Quichua. A large ethnic group, which is integrated with the Quichua. Quichua is used exclusively in the home. Distinct from Andoa (Shimagae) of Peru. SOV. Tropical forest. Riverine. Swidden agriculturalists. 300 to 400 meters. Nearly extinct.

EL SALVADOR

Republic of El Salvador, República de El Salvador. National or official language: Spanish. 6,032,000 (1998 UN). Literacy rate 55% to 63%. Also includes Central Pokomam, Turkish 500, Chinese 1,300. Christian, secular. Blind population 8,000. Deaf population 150,000 to 348,804 (1998). Deaf institutions: 4. Data accuracy estimate: A1, A2. The number of languages listed for El Salvador is 6. Of those, 5 are living languages and 1 is extinct. Diversity index 0.00.

CACAOPERA [CCR] Department of Morazán. Misumalpan. Closely related to Matagalpa. In 1974 several elderly men could remember a few words and fixed phrases, but none had been native speakers. Extinct.

KEKCHÍ ***(QUECCHÍ, CACCHÉ)*** [KEK] 12,286 in El Salvador. Mayan, Quichean-Mamean, Greater Quichean, Kekchi. SVO. Bible 1990. See main entry under Guatemala.

LENCA [LEN] (36,858 in ethnic group in El Salvador, 1987; or .6% of the population; 1982 Barrett). Town of Chilango. Unclassified. A different dialect of Lenca is in Honduras. Some classify this as Macro-Chibchan. Bilingualism in Spanish. Nearly extinct. See main entry under Honduras.

PIPIL ***(NAHUAT, NAWAT)*** [PPL] 20 speakers approximately, all older people, out of 196,576 in ethnic group (1987). Population total both countries 20 or more. Municipio of Dolores, Ocotepeque Department, near the El Salvador border. A few ethnic Pipil in Honduras. Also spoken in Honduras. Uto-Aztecan, Southern Uto-Aztecan, Aztecan, General Aztec, Pipil. Perhaps intelligible with Isthmus Nahuatl of Mexico (Otto Schumann 1969). High level of bilingualism in Spanish. Speakers are all older (1987). Investigation needed: intelligibility with Isthmus Nahuatl of Mexico. Has been taught in some schools for several years (D. Stewart 1994). Nearly extinct.

SALVADORAN SIGN LANGUAGE ***(EL SALVADORAN SIGN LANGUAGE)*** [ESN] Deaf sign language. Different from French or Spanish sign languages.

SPANISH ***(ESPAÑOL, CASTELLANO)*** [SPN] 5,900,000 in El Salvador (1995), or 92.3% of the population (1982 Barrett). Indo-European, Italic, Romance, Italo-Western, Western, Gallo-Iberian, Ibero-Romance, West Iberian, Castilian. National language. Bible 1553-1979. See main entry under Spain.

FALKLAND ISLANDS

Islas Malvinas. National or official language: English. 2,000 (1998 UN). A British dependency. About 200 islands. Christian, secular, other. Data accuracy estimate: A2. The number of languages listed for Falkland Islands is 1. Diversity index 0.00.

ENGLISH [ENG] 1,991 in Falkland Islands (1993 Johnstone). Indo-European, Germanic, West, English. National language. Bible 1535-1989. See main entry under United Kingdom.

FRENCH GUIANA

National or official language: French. 167,000 (1998 UN). Literacy rate 78% to 82%. Also includes North Levantine Spoken Arabic 800, Aukan 6,000, Haitian Creole French, Hmong Njua 2,000, Saramaccan 3,000. Information mainly from A. Butt 1966; SIL 1965-99. Christian, secular, traditional religion, Chinese traditional religion, Muslim, Baha'i. Data accuracy estimate: B. The number of languages listed for French Guiana is 10. Of those, all are living languages. Diversity index 0.47.

ARAWAK ***(LOKONO)*** [ARW] 150 to 200 in French Guiana. Coastal areas. Arawakan, Maipuran, Northern Maipuran, Caribbean. Reported to be used only by the elderly. Investigation needed: bilingual proficiency in French Guiana. Bible portions 1850-1978. See main entry under Suriname.

CARIB ***(CARIBE, CARIÑA, KALIHNA, KALINYA, GALIBI)*** [CRB] 1,200 in French Guiana. Coastal areas. Carib, Northern, Galibi. Dialect: TYREWUJU (EASTERN CARIB). Bible portions 1994. See main entry under Venezuela.

CHINESE, HAKKA [HAK] 5,000 in French Guiana. Sino-Tibetan, Chinese. Bilingual. They have preserved their language. Bible 1916. See main entry under China.

EMERILLON ***(EMERILON, MEREO, MEREYO, EMEREÑON, TECO)*** [EME] 200 (1987 Cheryl Jensen). Southern border area. None in Brazil. Tupi, Tupi-Guarani, Oyampi (VIII). Probably not intelligible with Wayampí. Heavy borrowing from Wayana.

FRENCH [FRN] Indo-European, Italic, Romance, Italo-Western, Western, Gallo-Iberian, Gallo-Romance, Gallo-Rhaetian, Oïl, French. National language. Bible 1530-1986. See main entry under France.

FRENCH GUIANESE CREOLE FRENCH ***(GUYANAIS, GUYANE, GUYANE CREOLE, PATOIS, PATWA)*** [FRE] 50,000 (1977 SIL). Creole, French based. Intelligibility of St. Lucia Creole is 78%, of Karipuna Creole of Brazil 77%. Most speakers are bilingual in French to some degree. Over one-third of the population in the capital speaks Creole as mother tongue. It is the most important rural language. Educated people can all speak it, but try to avoid it. Low status. Not taught in schools. A counter-movement is beginning. Some decreolization is taking place. Trade language. Dictionary. Grammar.

JAVANESE, CARIBBEAN [JVN] Coastal area. Austronesian, Malayo-Polynesian, Western Malayo-Polynesian, Sundic, Javanese. Most are bilingual. They have preserved their language. Muslim. NT 1999. See main entry under Suriname.

PALIKÚR ***(PALIKOUR, PALICUR)*** [PAL] 600 in French Guiana. Eastern border area. Arawakan, Maipuran, Eastern Maipuran. NT 1982. See main entry under Brazil.

WAYAMPI, OIAPOQUE ***(OIAMPÍ, OYAPÍ, OYAMPÍ, WAYÃPI, WAYAPI, WAJAPI, OIUMPIAN)*** [OYA] 400 in French Guiana (1987 C. Jensen SIL), including 120 Camopí and Masikilí on the middle Oyapock River, and 180 in 3 villages on upper Oyapock around Trois-Sauts (1980 Françoise

Grenand). Population total both countries 410. Southern border area. Also spoken in Brazil. Tupi, Tupi-Guarani, Oyampi (VIII). Monolinguals include children under 6, more than half the women, most men over 45, and all of those recently from Brazil. Everyone on the middle Oyapock and a few on the upper Oyapock can understand Emerillon, but no one will speak it. 7 people on upper Oyapock and 8 on middle Oyapock speak French well. Half can partially understand French Guianese Creole; 30 speak it well around Camopí. A few speak Portuguese passably. 20 on the upper Oyapock River speak imperfect Wayana. 2 schools since 1956 and 1971. Grammar.

WAYANA *(OAYANA, GUAYANA, UAIANA, ALUKUYANA, UPURUI)* [WAY] 200 in French Guiana. Southwestern border area. Carib, Northern, East-West Guiana, Wayana-Trio. NT 1979. See main entry under Suriname.

GREENLAND

Kalaallit Nunaat. National or official languages: Greenlandic Inuktitut, Danish. 56,000 (1998 UN). Affiliated with Denmark; home rule since 1979. Literacy rate 93%. Christian. Data accuracy estimate: A2. The number of languages listed for Greenland is 2. Of those, both are living languages. Diversity index 0.27.

DANISH [DNS] 7,830 in Greenland, 14.5% of the population (1986). Indo-European, Germanic, North, East Scandinavian, Danish-Swedish, Danish-Bokmal, Danish. National language. Bible 1550, in press (1993). See main entry under Denmark.

INUKTITUT, GREENLANDIC *(GREENLANDIC ESKIMO, GREENLANDIC, KALAALLISUT)* [ESG] 40,000 in Greenland (1990 L. D. Kaplan), including 3,000 East Greenlandic, 44,000 West Greenlandic, 800 North Greenlandic. Population total both countries 47,000. Greenland. About 80 communities of populations over 10. Also spoken in Denmark. Eskimo-Aleut, Eskimo, Inuit. Dialects: WEST GREENLANDIC, EAST GREENLANDIC, POLAR ESKIMO (NORTH GREENLANDIC, THULE ESKIMO). Dialects border on being different languages (M. Krauss 1995). Bilingualism in Danish. Vigorous in Greenland. National language. West Greenlandic and Danish used in schools. Fishermen, fur export. Bible 1900.

GRENADA

National or official language: English. 93,000 (1998 UN). Grenada, Carriacou, and Petit Martinique Islands. Literacy rate 95% (1991 WA). Also includes East Indian 3,300 (1993). Deaf population 5,699. Deaf institutions: 1. Data accuracy estimate: B. The number of languages listed for Grenada is 3. Of those, all are living languages. Diversity index 0.00.

ENGLISH [ENG] Indo-European, Germanic, West, English. Dialect: GRENADIAN ENGLISH. Post-creole English with French Creole influences (M. Alleyne). National language. Bible 1535-1989. See main entry under United Kingdom.

LESSER ANTILLEAN CREOLE FRENCH [DOM] Carriacou Island. On northern Grenada island it is in scattered pockets, mainly in rural areas. Creole, French based. Dialect: GRENADA CREOLE FRENCH (PATWA, PATOIS). Mainly older people on Grenada Island. The same as, or similar to, that spoken in St. Lucia (M. Alleyne). NT 1999. See main entry under St. Lucia.

WINDWARD CARIBBEAN CREOLE ENGLISH [SVG] 113,000 (Holm 1989:458). Creole, English based, Atlantic, Eastern, Southern. Dialect: GRENADA CREOLE ENGLISH (CARRIACOU CREOLE ENGLISH). Closest to St. Vincent and the Grenadines, and Tobago. M. Alleyne says it is a post-creole English with French creole influence, no longer a creole. R. Kephart says Carriacou is a creole English. J. Holm says the creole predominates in Grenada (1989:458). Grammar. See main entry under St. Vincent and the Grenadines.

GUADELOUPE

National or official language: French. 443,000 (1998 UN). A French department in the Leeward Islands. Two large islands: Basse Terre, Grande Terre; also Marie Galante, the Saintes group, Desirade, St. Barthélemy, most of St. Martin. Literacy rate 89% to 90%. Christian, secular. Data accuracy estimate: A1. The number of languages listed for Guadeloupe is 3. Of those, all are living languages. Diversity index 0.00.

FRENCH [FRN] Indo-European, Italic, Romance, Italo-Western, Western, Gallo-Iberian, Gallo-Romance, Gallo-Rhaetian, Oïl, French. There is a variety on the northwest end of St. Barthélemy, west of but not including Gustavia, similar to Cajun French of the USA, which may or may not be a French dialect (Julianne Maher 1997). National language. Bible 1530-1986. See main entry under France.

LESSER ANTILLEAN CREOLE FRENCH [DOM] 335,000 in Guadeloupe (1975). Guadeloupe, eastern St. Barthélemy, northern St. Martin, Marie Galante islands. Creole, French based. Dialects: GUADELOUPE CREOLE FRENCH (PATWA, PATOIS, KREYOL), ST. MARTIN CREOLE FRENCH, MARIE GALANTE CREOLE FRENCH, ST. BARTH CREOLE FRENCH. Very close to Martinique Creole. St. Barth Creole is distinct in grammatical, phonological, and lexical features, and may not be a dialect (J. Maher 1989). Investigation needed: intelligibility with St. Barth Creole, St. Martin Creole, Marie Galante Creole. Dictionary. Grammar. NT 1999. See main entry under St. Lucia.

VIRGIN ISLANDS CREOLE ENGLISH [VIB] St. Barthélemy Island. Creole, English based, Atlantic, Eastern, Southern. Dialect: ST. BARTH CREOLE ENGLISH. See main entry under U.S. Virgin Islands.

GUATEMALA

Republic of Guatemala, República de Guatemala. National or official language: Spanish. 10,801,000 (1998 UN). Indian 55%, Mestizo 44% (1990 WA). Literacy rate 48% to 55%; Indian 0-25%, Mestizo 75-85%. Information mainly from M. K. Mayers 1965a, b; SIL 1952-1999. Christian, secular. Blind population 6,000 (1982 WCE). Deaf population 100,000 to 650,014 (1998). Deaf institutions: 5. Data accuracy estimate: A1, A2. The number of languages listed for Guatemala is 56. Of those, 54 are living languages and 2 are extinct. Diversity index 0.60.

ACHÍ, CUBULCO [ACC] 45,000 to 50,000 (1999 Gary Desterke FREF). Central area west of Rabinal, Baja Verapaz Department. Mayan, Quichean-Mamean, Greater Quichean, Quichean, Quiche-Achi. All ages. Dictionary. Grammar. SVO. Literacy rate in first language: 1% to 5%. Literacy rate in second language: 11%. NT 1984.

ACHÍ, RABINAL *(RABINAL QUICHÉ)* [ACR] 37,300 (1990 SIL). Central Rabinal area, Baja Verapaz Department. Mayan, Quichean-Mamean, Greater Quichean, Quichean, Quiche-Achi. Closest linguistically to Cubulco Achí. Possibly 20% of speakers can discuss more than common topics in Spanish. All ages. Dictionary. SVO. Literacy rate in first language: 15% to 20%. Literacy rate in second language: 25% to 40%. Bible portions 1966-1993.

AGUACATECO *(AGUACATEC)* [AGU] 18,000 (1998 SIL). Western Huehuetenango Department. Mayan, Quichean-Mamean, Greater Mamean, Ixilan. All ages. Dictionary. Grammar. VSO. Literacy rate in first language: 10%. Literacy rate in second language: 29%. NT 1971-1993.

AMERICAN SIGN LANGUAGE *(ASL, AMESLAN)* [ASE] Deaf sign language. There may be other sign languages besides ASL. Dictionary. Videos. Bible portions 1982-1987. See main entry under USA.

CAKCHIQUEL, CENTRAL *(KAQCHIQUEL)* [CAK] 132,200 (1990 SIL). Southern Guatemala, Chimaltenango Department. Mayan, Quichean-Mamean, Greater Quichean, Quichean, Cakchiquel. All ages. Dictionary. Grammar. SVO. Literacy rate in first language: 5% to 10%. Literacy rate in second language: 25% to 39%. NT 1931-1980.

CAKCHIQUEL, EASTERN [CKE] 100,000 (1998 SIL). Northwest of and near Guatemala City, San Juan Sacatepequez. Mayan, Quichean-Mamean, Greater Quichean, Quichean, Cakchiquel. All ages. SVO. Literacy rate in first language: 3%. Literacy rate in second language: 45%. NT 1986.

CAKCHIQUEL, NORTHERN [CKC] 16,000 (1982 SIL). Central highlands, San Martín Jilotepeque. Mayan, Quichean-Mamean, Greater Quichean, Quichean, Cakchiquel. Bilingualism in Spanish. 45 and older. SVO. Literacy rate in first language: Below 1%. Literacy rate in second language: 10%. Bible portions 1982-1991.

CAKCHIQUEL, SANTA MARÍA DE JESÚS [CKI] 15,000 (1998 SIL). Southeast of Antigua. Mayan, Quichean-Mamean, Greater Quichean, Quichean, Cakchiquel. Literacy rate in first language: Below 1%. Literacy rate in second language: 54%.

CAKCHIQUEL, SANTO DOMINGO XENACOJ *(SANTO DOMINGO XENACOJ, XENACOJ)* [CKJ] 5,200 (1991 SIL). West of Guatemala City on the Pan American highway. Mayan, Quichean-Mamean, Greater Quichean, Quichean, Cakchiquel. All ages. SVO. Literacy rate in first language: 2%. Literacy rate in second language: 50%. Bible portions 1982-1998.

CAKCHIQUEL, SOUTH CENTRAL [CKD] 43,000 (1998 SIL). Pan American highway west of Guatemala City. Mayan, Quichean-Mamean, Greater Quichean, Quichean, Cakchiquel. All ages. SVO. Literacy rate in first language: 1% to 5%. Literacy rate in second language: 25% to 63%. Bible portions 1982-1997.

CAKCHIQUEL, SOUTHERN [CKF] 43,000 (1993 SIL). Area south of Antigua. Mayan, Quichean-Mamean, Greater Quichean, Quichean, Cakchiquel. Some shift to Spanish. 30 and older. SVO. Literacy rate in first language: 3% to 65%. Literacy rate in second language: 73%. NT 1993.

CAKCHIQUEL, SOUTHWESTERN, ACATENANGO [CKK] Few speakers (1997 SIL). Municipio of Acatenango, town of Acatenango. Mayan, Quichean-Mamean, Greater Quichean, Quichean,

Cakchiquel. People understand Cakchiquel, but seem to mainly speak Spanish. Literacy rate in second language: 38%. Agriculturalists: maize, beans, squash, coffee.

CAKCHIQUEL, SOUTHWESTERN, YEPOCAPA [CBM] 8,000 speakers out of 15,000 in the ethnic group (1991 SIL). Municipio of Yepocapa. Mayan, Quichean-Mamean, Greater Quichean, Quichean, Cakchiquel. 40 and older. SVO. Literacy rate in first language: 1% to 5%. Literacy rate in second language: 25%. NT 1990.

CAKCHIQUEL, WESTERN [CKW] 77,000 (1998 SIL). Northern and eastern shores of Lake Atitlán, Departamento de Sololá. Mayan, Quichean-Mamean, Greater Quichean, Quichean, Cakchiquel. 25 and older. Dictionary. Grammar. SVO. Literacy rate in first language: 1% to 5%. Literacy rate in second language: 25% to 43%. Swidden agriculturalists: maize, beans, squash. NT 1996.

CAKCHIQUEL-QUICHE MIXED LANGUAGE ***(CAUQUE MIXED LANGUAGE)*** [CKZ] 2,000 (1998 SIL). Santiago, Sacatepaquez, Santa María Cauque aldea. Mixed Language, Cakchiquel-Quiche. Speakers came from the Quiché area in the colonial period. Older speakers show a base of Quiché. Speakers are fully bilingual in South Central Cakchiquel and becoming bilingual in Spanish. 30 and above. The language is changing to become more like South Central Cakchiquel.

CHICOMUCELTEC ***(CAKCHIQUEL MAM)*** [COB] Ethnic group: 100 in Guatemala (1982 GR). Mayan, Huastecan. Bilingualism in Spanish. Reported to be extinct in current Mayanist literature. Extinct. See main entry under Mexico.

CHORTÍ [CAA] 31,500 (1990 SIL). Population total both countries 31,500 or more. Eastern border with Honduras, and into Honduras. Also spoken in Honduras. Mayan, Cholan-Tzeltalan, Cholan, Chorti. All ages. 'Chorté' is not correct. Not the same as the extinct language called 'Choltí' formerly spoken in the Quirigua and Isabal area. Dictionary. Grammar. VOS. Literacy rate in first language: 15%. Literacy rate in second language: 30%. NT 1997.

CHUJ, SAN MATEO IXTATÁN ***(CHUH, CHUJE, CHUHE)*** [CNM] 22,130 in Guatemala (1991 SIL). Population total both countries 31,630. Western Huehuetenango Department. Also spoken in Mexico. Mayan, Kanjobalan-Chujean, Chujean. VOS. Literacy rate in first language: 20% to 40%. Literacy rate in second language: 25%. NT 1970-1994.

CHUJ, SAN SEBASTIÁN COATÁN [CAC] 19,458 (1991 SIL). Central western Coatán River area, western Huehuetenango Department. Mayan, Kanjobalan-Chujean, Chujean. VSO. Literacy rate in first language: 30% to 60%. Literacy rate in second language: 25%. NT 1969.

GARÍFUNA ***(BLACK CARIB, CARIBE, CENTRAL AMERICAN CARIB)*** [CAB] 16,700 in Guatemala. Two villages on the northeast coast: Livingston and Puerto Barrios. Arawakan, Maipuran, Northern Maipuran, Caribbean. Related to Island Carib with Spanish, English, and French borrowings. Ancestors brought from St. Vincent Island in 1796-1797. VSO. Literacy rate in first language: 1% to 5%. Literacy rate in second language: 15% to 20%. NT 1983-1994. See main entry under Honduras.

GUATEMALAN SIGN LANGUAGE [GSM] Deaf sign language.

ITZÁ ***(PETÉN ITZÁ MAYA, YUCATEC MAYA, ICAICHE MAYA, MAYA)*** [ITZ] 12 speakers (1986 SIL). North central, north of Lake Petén Itzá in San José Petén, 15 minutes by auto from Flores. The language is extinct in Belize. Mayan, Yucatecan, Mopan-Itza. All are elderly (1986). The language is nearly extinct in Guatemala, but the ethnic group retains the Indian culture. The ethnic group in Belize speaks Spanish. Nearly extinct.

IXIL, CHAJUL [IXJ] 18,000 (1998 SIL). Quiché Department. Mayan, Quichean-Mamean, Greater Mamean, Ixilan. Dialect: ILOM. All ages. Dictionary. Grammar. VSO. Literacy rate in first language: 10% to 30%. Literacy rate in second language: 16%. Bible portions 1981-1984.

IXIL, NEBAJ [IXI] 35,000 (1991 SIL). Nebaj area, Quiché Department. Mayan, Quichean-Mamean, Greater Mamean, Ixilan. All ages. Dictionary. Grammar. VSO. Literacy rate in first language: 10%. Literacy rate in second language: 7%. Bible portions 1960-1997.

IXIL, SAN JUAN COTZAL [IXL] 16,000 (1998 SIL). Quiché Department. Mayan, Quichean-Mamean, Greater Mamean, Ixilan. 70% to 75% intelligibility among the three Ixil languages. Little bilingualism in Spanish. All ages. VOS. Literacy rate in first language: 10% to 30%. Literacy rate in second language: 15% to 25%. Bible portions 1978-1993.

JACALTECO, EASTERN [JAC] 11,000 (1998 SIL). Huehuetenango Department near México border, Concepción Huista area. Mayan, Kanjobalan-Chujean, Kanjobalan, Kanjobal-Jacaltec. Allo ages. Dictionary. VSO. Literacy rate in first language: 5% to 10%. Literacy rate in second language: 15% to 28%. NT 1997.

JACALTECO, WESTERN [JAI] 77,700 in Guatemala (1998). Population total both countries 88,000. Huehuetenango Department, around Jacaltenango. Also spoken in Mexico. Mayan, Kanjobalan-Chujean, Kanjobalan, Kanjobal-Jacaltec. Eastern and Western Jacalteco understand each other's spoken languages, but not written text. VSO. Literacy rate in first language: 5% to 10%. Literacy rate in second language: 52%. NT 1979.

KANJOBAL, EASTERN ***(SANTA EULALIA KANJOBAL, KANHOBAL, CONOB)*** [KJB] 77,700 in Guatemala (1998). Population total both countries 88,200. Huehuetenango Department, Santa Eulalia. Also spoken in USA. Mayan, Kanjobalan-Chujean, Kanjobalan, Kanjobal-Jacaltec. VSO. Literacy rate in first language: 5% to 10%. Literacy rate in second language: 26%. Bible 1981-1989.

KANJOBAL, WESTERN ***(ACATECO, ACATEC, SAN MIGUEL ACATÁN KANJOBAL, CONOB)*** [KNJ] 48,500 in Guatemala (1998). Population total all countries 58,600. San Miguel Acatán. Also spoken in Mexico, USA. Mayan, Kanjobalan-Chujean, Kanjobalan, Kanjobal-Jacaltec. All ages. VOS. Literacy rate in first language: 5% to 10%. Literacy rate in second language: 20%. NT 1981.

KEKCHÍ ***(QUECCHÍ, CACCHÉ)*** [KEK] 400,000 in Guatemala (1998 SIL). Population total all countries 421,300. Northern Alta Verapaz, southern Petén departments in Guatemala. Also spoken in Belize, El Salvador. Mayan, Quichean-Mamean, Greater Quichean, Kekchi. Only slight dialect differences. Prestige dialect is Cobán, Alta Verapaz. All ages. Dictionary. Grammar. SVO. Literacy rate in first language: 10% to 30%. Literacy rate in second language: 22%. Traditional religion, Christian. Bible 1988.

MAM, CENTRAL ***(COMITANCILLO MAM, WESTERN MAM, MAM OCCIDENTAL, MAM MARQUENSE, SAN MARCOS COMITANCILLAS MAM)*** [MVC] 100,000 (1992 Wes Collins SIL). San Marcos Department (10 towns). The towns of San Miguel Ixtahuacán (18,000) and Concepción Tutapa (30,000) could be considered dialects of Northern Mam. Mayan, Quichean-Mamean, Greater Mamean, Mamean. 77% lexical similarity between Tajumulco and Comitancillo. All ages. Dictionary. Grammar. Literacy rate in first language: 1% to 5%. Literacy rate in second language: 25% to 32% Spanish. NT 1998.

MAM, NORTHERN ***(HUEHUETENANGO MAM)*** [MAM] 180,000 to 200,000 in Guatemala (1998 SIL). Population total both countries 180,000 to 200,000. Western Huehuetenango Department (San Sebastián and other towns) and San Marcos Department; 17 towns. Also spoken in Mexico. Mayan, Quichean-Mamean, Greater Mamean, Mamean. VSO. Literacy rate in first language: 1% to 5%. Literacy rate in second language: 21%. Bible 1993.

MAM, SOUTHERN ***(SAN JUAN OSTUNCALCO MAM, OSTUNCALCO MAM, QUETZALTENANGO MAM, MAM QUETZALTECO)*** [MMS] 125,000 (1991 SIL). Quetzaltenango Department (9 towns), Retalhuleu Department (1 town); Western Ostuncalco area (San Juan Ostuncalco, San Martín Sacatepéquez, and other towns). Mayan, Quichean-Mamean, Greater Mamean, Mamean. Dialect: SAN MARTÍN SACATEPÉQUEZ MAM (SAN MARTÍN CHILE VERDE MAM). VSO. Literacy rate in first language: 1% to 5%. Literacy rate in second language: 37%. NT 1939-1980.

MAM, TAJUMULCO [MPF] 35,000 (1992 W. Collins SIL). San Marcos Department, Tajumulco and Ixchiguán towns. Mayan, Quichean-Mamean, Greater Mamean, Mamean. Investigation of acceptability of literature in other Mam varieties in progress. 77% lexical similarity with Comitancillo. Ethnic pride is strong. Literacy rate in first language: Below 1%. Literacy rate in second language: 5% to 15%.

MAM, TODOS SANTOS CUCHUMATÁN [MVJ] 50,000 in Guatemala (1998 SIL). Population total both countries 60,000. Huehuetenango Department, town of Todos Santos Cuchumatán. Also spoken in Mexico. Mayan, Quichean-Mamean, Greater Mamean, Mamean. VSO. Literacy rate in first language: Below 1%. Literacy rate in second language: 15% to 21%. NT 1997.

MOPÁN MAYA ***(MAYA MOPÁN, MOPANE)*** [MOP] 2,600 in Guatemala (1990 SIL). Petén Department. Mayan, Yucatecan, Mopan-Itza. VOS. Literacy rate in first language: Below 1%. Literacy rate in second language: 5% to 15%. NT 1979. See main entry under Belize.

POKOMAM, CENTRAL ***(CENTRAL POCOMAM, POCOMÁN)*** [POC] 8,600 (1990 SIL). Population total both countries 8,600 or more. 9 kms. northwest of Guatemala City, Chinautla. Also spoken in El Salvador. Mayan, Quichean-Mamean, Greater Quichean, Pocom. Speakers are becoming more bilingual in Spanish. SVO. Literacy rate in first language: Below 1%. Literacy rate in second language: 25% to 32%. Bible portions 1981-1982.

POKOMAM, EASTERN ***(POCOMAM ORIENTAL)*** [POA] 12,500 (1990 SIL). Eastern Guatemala, Jalapa Department, San Luis Jilotepeque. Mayan, Quichean-Mamean, Greater Quichean, Pocom. Possibly 50% intelligibility with Central Pocomam. Bilingualism in Spanish. SVO. Literacy rate in first language: Below 1%. Literacy rate in second language: 27%. Bible portions 1966-1982.

POKOMAM, SOUTHERN ***(PALÍN POCOMAM)*** [POU] 27,912 (1991 SIL). 20 kms. south of Guatemala City. Mayan, Quichean-Mamean, Greater Quichean, Pocom. Bilingualism in Spanish. Literacy rate in first language: Below 1%. Literacy rate in second language: 25% to 30%.

POKOMCHÍ, EASTERN ***(TACTIC POKOMCHÍ, POCOMCHÍ, POCONCHÍ, POKONCHÍ)*** [POH] 35,000 to 45,000 (1998 SIL). Atla Verapaz Department. Mayan, Quichean-Mamean, Greater Quichean, Pocom. Bilingualism in Spanish. K'ekchi also used. Literacy rate in first language: Below 1%. Literacy rate in second language: 21%. NT 1983.

POKOMCHÍ, WESTERN ***(WESTERN POCOMCHÍ, POCOMCHÍ)*** [POB] 50,000 (1998 SIL). Around San Cristobal. Mayan, Quichean-Mamean, Greater Quichean, Pocom. Dialect: SANTA CRUZ VERAPAZ POKOMCHÍ. All ages. Dictionary. Grammar. SVO. Literacy rate in first language: 5% to

10%. Literacy rate in second language: 35%. Swidden agriculturalists: maize, black beans, bananas; rope makers. Bible portions 1957-1979.

QUICHÉ, CENTRAL [QUC] 216,910 (1990 SIL). Central highlands. Mayan, Quichean-Mamean, Greater Quichean, Quichean, Quiche-Achi. Dictionary. Grammar. SVO. Literacy rate in first language: Below 1%. Literacy rate in second language: 25% to 35%. Roman. Radio programs, videos. Bible 1995.

QUICHÉ, CUNÉN ***(NORTHERN QUICHÉ, CHUIL QUICHÉ, CUNENTECO QUICHÉ)*** [CUN] 6,500 (1992 census). Quiché Department. Mayan, Quichean-Mamean, Greater Quichean, Quichean, Quiche-Achi. Literacy rate in second language: 24%. Swidden agriculturalists: maize, beans, squash.

QUICHÉ, EASTERN, CHICHICASTENANGO ***(EAST CENTRAL QUICHÉ)*** [QUU] 100,000 (1991 SIL). Includes Chichicastenango and Chiché. Mayan, Quichean-Mamean, Greater Quichean, Quichean, Quiche-Achi. All ages. Dictionary. Literacy rate in first language: 5% to 10%. Literacy rate in second language: 15% to 25%.

QUICHÉ, JOYABAJ [QUJ] 54,298 (1991 SIL). Quiché Department. Mayan, Quichean-Mamean, Greater Quichean, Quichean, Quiche-Achi. SVO. Literacy rate in first language: Below 1%. Literacy rate in second language: 12%. NT 1984.

QUICHÉ, SAN ANDRÉS ***(SAN ANDRÉS SAJCABAJÁ QUICHÉ)*** [QIE] 19,728 (1991 SIL). Quiché Department. Mayan, Quichean-Mamean, Greater Quichean, Quichean, Quiche-Achi. All ages. Grammar. Literacy rate in first language: 5%. Literacy rate in second language: 10% to 15%. Swidden agriculturalists: maize, beans, squash. Bible portions 1997.

QUICHÉ, WEST CENTRAL ***(SOUTHWESTERN QUICHÉ, CANTEL QUICHÉ)*** [QUT] 250,000 (1994 SIL). Southwest of Lake Atitlán, Quezaltenango, and Totonicapan departments. Mayan, Quichean-Mamean, Greater Quichean, Quichean, Quiche-Achi. Dialects: COASTAL QUICHÉ, WESTERN QUICHÉ. All ages. Dictionary. Grammar. SVO. Literacy rate in first language: 5% to 10%. Literacy rate in second language: 25% to 55%. NT 1997.

SACAPULTECO ***(SACAPULAS QUICHÉ)*** [QUV] 36,823 (1991 SIL). Quiché Department, and some speakers in Guatemala City. Mayan, Quichean-Mamean, Greater Quichean, Sacapulteco. Bilingualism in Spanish. Literacy rate in first language: Below 1%. Literacy rate in second language: 16%. Bible portions 1980.

SIPACAPENSE ***(SIPACAPEÑO, SIPACAPA QUICHÉ)*** [QUM] 6,000 (1991 SIL). San Marcos Department. Mayan, Quichean-Mamean, Greater Quichean, Sipacapeno. All ages. Dictionary. Grammar. Literacy rate in first language: 1%. Literacy rate in second language: Possibly 20% in Spanish. Traditional religion, Christian. Bible portions 1992-1998.

SPANISH ***(ESPAÑOL, CASTELLANO)*** [SPN] 4,673,000 in Guatemala (1995 estimate). Indo-European, Italic, Romance, Italo-Western, Western, Gallo-Iberian, Ibero-Romance, West Iberian, Castilian. National language. Bible 1553-1979. See main entry under Spain.

TACANECO ***(TACANÁ MAM, WESTERN MAM, TILÓ, MAMÉ)*** [MTZ] 20,000 in Guatemala (1991 SIL). Population total both countries 21,200. Western San Marcos Department; rural areas west of the town of Tacaná, western Guatemala border, and in Sibinal and Tectitán. Also spoken in Mexico. Mayan, Quichean-Mamean, Greater Mamean, Mamean. The most distinctive of all the Mam varieties. All speakers are highly bilingual in Spanish. Very few speakers under 25 years old. VSO. Literacy rate in second language: 25%. Mountain slope. Agriculturalists: maize, beans, potatoes, cabbage, wheat. 8000 feet.

TECTITECO ***(TECO, TECTITÁN MAM)*** [TTC] 1,200 in Guatemala (1998 SIL). Population total both countries 2,200 or more. Area of Tectitán, western Guatemala border. Also spoken in Mexico. Mayan, Quichean-Mamean, Greater Mamean, Mamean. All ages. Some parents tend to discourage younger children from Tectiteco usage. Dictionary. Grammar. VSO. Literacy rate in first language: 10% to 20%. Literacy rate in second language: 15% to 20%.

TZUTUJIL, EASTERN ***(TZUTUJIL ORIENTAL, SANTIAGO ATITLÁN TZUTUJIL, TZUTUHIL)*** [TZJ] 50,000 (1998 SIL). Southern shore of Lake Atitlán. Mayan, Quichean-Mamean, Greater Quichean, Quichean, Tzutujil. All ages. Grammar. Literacy rate in first language: 10%. Literacy rate in second language: 25%. Agriculturalists. NT 1992.

TZUTUJIL, WESTERN [TZT] 33,800 (1990 SIL). Southern Sololá area, southwestern shore of Lake Atitlán. Mayan, Quichean-Mamean, Greater Quichean, Quichean, Tzutujil. All ages. Grammar. SVO. Literacy rate in first language: 3% to 4%. Literacy rate in second language: 50%. Agriculturalists. NT 1981-1989.

USPANTECO [USP] 3,000 (1998 SIL). Quiché Department. Mayan, Quichean-Mamean, Greater Quichean, Uspantec. All ages. Grammar. SVO. Literacy rate in first language: Below 1%. Literacy rate in second language: 16%. Bible portions 1978-1993.

XINCA ***(SZINCA)*** [XIN] Southeastern. Unclassified. Language may be related to Lenca. All members of the ethnic group now speak Spanish. Extinct.

GUYANA

Co-operative Republic of Guyana. Formerly British Guiana. National or official language: English. 850,000 (1998 UN). 43,000 Amerindians (1990 Janette Forte). Literacy rate 91%. Also includes Lesser Antillean Creole French 250, Portuguese, Urdu, Chinese 1,500. Information mainly from J. Forte 1990; SIL 1965-99. Christian, Hindu, Muslim, traditional religion, secular. Blind population 1,300 (1982 WCE). Deaf population 44,199. Deaf institutions: 6. Data accuracy estimate: A2, B. The number of languages listed for Guyana is 14. Of those, 13 are living languages and 1 is extinct. Diversity index 0.07.

AKAWAIO ***(ACEWAIO, AKAWAI, ACAHUAYO, KAPON)*** [ARB] 3,800 in Guyana, 9% of the Amerindians (1990 J. Forte). Population total all countries 4,300 or more. West central, north of Patamona. Also spoken in Brazil, Venezuela. Carib, Northern, East-West Guiana, Macushi-Kapon, Kapon. Important differences in vocabulary from Patamona. Language attitudes indicate separate literature is needed. They and the Patamona call themselves 'Kapon'. Tropical forest. Upland. Hunter-gatherers, fishermen. Traditional religion. Bible portions 1873.

ARAWAK ***(AROWAK, LOKONO)*** [ARW] 1,500 speakers (1984) out of 15,000 in the ethnic group in Guyana (1990 J. Forte). West coast and northeast along the Corantyne River. Arawakan, Maipuran, Northern Maipuran, Caribbean. Others in the ethnic group are bilingual. Reported to be used only primarily by the elderly in Guyana and Suriname. The ethnic group in Guyana represents 33% of the Amerindians. Bible portions 1850-1978. See main entry under Suriname.

ARUMA ***(WAPITXANA, WAPISIANA, VAPIDIANA, WAPIXANA)*** [WAP] 6,000 in Guyana (1990 J. Forte), 14% of the Amerindians (1990 J. Forte). Population total both countries 7,500. Southwest Guyana, south of the Kanuku Mts., northwest of the Waiwai; a few villages. Also spoken in Brazil. Arawakan, Maipuran, Northern Maipuran, Wapishanan. Dialects: ATORADA (ATOR'TI, DAURI, ATORAI), MAPIDIAN (MAOPITYAN, MAWAYANA), AMARIBA. English is taught in school. 40 Mapidian are intermarried with Waiwai speakers and speak fluent Waiwai. Amariba may be extinct, Taruma is nearly extinct. Savannah. Swidden agriculturalists: cassava. Traditional religion, Christian. Bible portions 1975-1994.

BERBICE CREOLE DUTCH [BRC] 4 or 5 speakers (1993 S. Kouwenberg), 15 with limited competence (1989 J. Holm). Berbice River area. Creole, Dutch based. Speakers claim it is not inherently intelligible with Skepi or Rupununi. About 1/3 of the basic lexicon and, most of the productive morphology is from Eastern Ijo in Nigeria; most of the rest of the lexicon is from Dutch, 10% loans from Arawak and Guyanese Creole English. Speakers are bilingual in Guyanese, which has influenced Berbice considerably. Grammar. SVO. Nearly extinct.

CARIB ***(CARIBE, CARIÑA, KALIHNA, KALINYA, GALIBI)*** [CRB] 475 or more in Guyana (1991) out of 2,700 in the ethnic group (1990 J. Forte). West coast and northwest. Carib, Northern, Galibi. Dialect: MURATO (MYRATO, WESTERN CARIB). The ethnic group in Guyana represents 6% of the Amerindians. Bible portions 1994. See main entry under Venezuela.

ENGLISH [ENG] Indo-European, Germanic, West, English. Dialect: GUYANESE ENGLISH. Spoken as first language by some Blacks and some Hindustanis. National language. Bible 1535-1989. See main entry under United Kingdom.

GUYANESE CREOLE ENGLISH ***(CREOLESE, GUYANESE CREOLE)*** [GYN] 650,000 possibly (250,000 Blacks and 400,000 Hindustanis). Population total all countries 700,000. Georgetown, coast, and Rupununi River area. There may be some in French Guiana. Also spoken in Suriname, USA. Creole, English based, Atlantic, Eastern, Southern. Dialects: AFRO-GUYANESE CREOLE, RUPUNUNI, INDO-GUYANESE CREOLE. It may be intelligible with other English based creoles of the Caribbean. Closest to creoles of Windward and Leeward Islands and Tobago. Rupununi may be a separate language. Speakers of Rupununi, Berbice Creole Dutch, and Skepi Creole Dutch claim they are not inherently intelligible with each other. It will remain the home language and be used alongside Standard English (M. Adler 1977). There is a creole continuum with Standard English. The first or second language of most people, but it has no official status. Grammar.

HINDUSTANI, CARIBBEAN ***(AILI GAILI)*** [HNS] Ethnic group: 538,500 Hindustanis in Guyana. Indo-European, Indo-Iranian, Indo-Aryan, Eastern zone, Bihari. Closer to Bhojpuri than to Hindi. Similar dialect to Suriname and Trinidad-Tobago. Those closer to Georgetown use a more standard English than Guyanese. A few are learning Hindi for religious purposes. Only a few older people of Guyanese origin in Guyana speak Caribbean Hindustani. Many Hindustanis in Guyana speak Guyanese as first language. Coastal. Agriculturalists. Hindu. NT 1997. See main entry under Suriname.

MACUSHI ***(MAKUSHI, MAKUXI, MACUSI, MACUSSI, TEWEYA, TEUEIA)*** [MBC] 7,000 in Guyana, 16% of the Amerindians (1990 J. Forte). Population total all countries 11,400 to 13,000. Southwestern border area, Rupununi north savannahs. Spread out in small settlements up to the foothills of the Pakaraima Mts. Also spoken in Brazil, Venezuela. Carib, Northern, East-West Guiana, Macushi-Kapon, Macushi. Close to, but not intelligible with, Patamona. The second language is English in Guyana, Portuguese in Brazil, Spanish in Venezuela. OVS. NT 1981.

PATAMONA ***(INGARIKO, EREMAGOK, KAPON)*** [PBC] 4,700 10% of the Amerindians (1990 J. Forte). West central, about 13 villages. Carib, Northern, East-West Guiana, Macushi-Kapon, Kapon. Close to Macushi but not inherently intelligible. Marginally intelligible with Arecuna. Closest to Akawaio, but vocabulary differences and language attitudes make separate literature necessary. The Akawaio are less acculturated than Patamona. 'Ingariko' is the Macushi term for 'bush people'. People in the village of Paramakatoi are literate in English and Patamona. Some in other villages are literate in English. NT 1974.

PEMON ***(PEMONG)*** [AOC] 475 Arekuna in Guyana, 1% of the Amerindians (1990 J. Forte). Paruima Settlement. Carib, Northern, East-West Guiana, Macushi-Kapon, Kapon. Dialects: CAMARACOTO, TAUREPAN (TAULIPANG), ARECUNA (ARICUNA, AREKUNA, JARICUNA). Marginally intelligible with Patamona and Akawaio. Camaracoto may be distinct. OVS. Bible portions 1990. See main entry under Venezuela.

SKEPI CREOLE DUTCH [SKW] Essequibo region. Creole, Dutch based. Dialect: ESSEQUIBO. Speakers said it was not inherently intelligible with Berbice or Rupununi. 52% lexical similarity with Berbice. Became extinct by 1998. Extinct.

WAIWAI ***(UAIUAI, UAIEUE, OUAYEONE, PARUKOTA)*** [WAW] 200 in Guyana (1990 J. Forte). Southwest Guyana, headwaters of the Essequibo River. Carib, Northern, East-West Guiana, Waiwai. Dialect: KATAWIAN (KATWENA, KATAWINA). Tropical forest. NT 1984. See main entry under Brazil.

WARAO ***(WARAU, WARRAU, GUARAO, GUARAUNO)*** [WBA] A few speakers in Guyana out of 4,700 in the ethnic group (1990 J. Forte). Northwestern, at Oreala, Guyana near coast, mixed with Arawak and Carib speakers. Language Isolate. Bilingualism in Guyanese. In Guyana only the older people speak the language. NT 1974. See main entry under Venezuela.

HAITI

Republic of Haiti, République d'Haiti. National or official languages: Haitian Creole French, French. 7,952,000 (1998 UN). Literacy rate 23% to 33%. Traditional religion, Christian, secular. Blind population 60,000. Deaf population 93,549. Deaf institutions: 4. Data accuracy estimate: A2. The number of languages listed for Haiti is 3. Of those, 2 are living languages and 1 is a second language without mother tongue speakers. Diversity index 0.00.

FRENCH [FRN] Second language speakers in Haiti: 400,000. Indo-European, Italic, Romance, Italo-Western, Western, Gallo-Iberian, Gallo-Romance, Gallo-Rhaetian, Oïl, French. National language. Bible 1530-1986. See main entry under France.

HAITIAN CREOLE FRENCH [HAT] 7,410,000 in Haiti (1998). Population total all countries 7,800,000. Throughout the country. Also spoken in Bahamas, Canada, Cayman Islands, Dominican Republic, French Guiana, Puerto Rico, USA. Creole, French based. Dialects: FABLAS, PLATEAU HAITIAN CREOLE. Linguistic influences from Wolof (Benjamin 1956), Fon, and Ewe (C. Lefebvre) of West Africa. Bilingualism in French. Mother tongue of the entire population; the only language of 95% of the population (Nida 1972). Strong, with strong basilect. In 1961 it was granted legal and educational status in Haiti. A growing literature, including poetry. Lower social status than Standard French. National language. Dictionary. Grammar. SVO; prepositions; articles after noun heads. Faublas-Pressoir orthography is standard since 1979. Newspapers, radio programs, TV. Bible 1985.

HAITIAN VODOUN CULTURE LANGUAGE ***(LANGAY, LANGAJ)*** [HVC] Unclassified. Used for religion, song, dance. It uses some Haitian creole words, and others which may have African or American Indian influence. Second language only.

HONDURAS

Republic of Honduras, República de Honduras. National or official language: Spanish. 6,147,000 (1998 UN). Literacy rate 56% to 60%. Also includes Armenian 900, Yue Chinese 1,000, Turkish 900, Arabic 42,000, Chinese 2,000. Information mainly from D. Oltrogge 1977; L. Campbell and D. Oltrogge 1980. Christian. Blind population 1,000 (1982 WCE). Deaf population 322,248. Deaf institutions: 2. Data accuracy estimate: A1, A2. The number of languages listed for Honduras is 11. Of those, all are living languages. Diversity index 0.05.

BAY ISLANDS CREOLE ENGLISH [BYH] 13,000 first language speakers, including 10,000 on the Bay Islands, and 3,000 on the north coast (1998 estimate). Bay Islands (Guanaja, Roatán, Utila), north coast including La Ceiba and Puerto Cortes, and some in the Mosquitia. Creole, English based, Atlantic, Western. Dialect: CALABASH BIGHT. Ross Graham says creole influence is wider than has been reported and still needs to be addressed (1996). They understand at least some of San Andrés Creole (Colombia). They may not understand Limón Creole (Costa Rica), and they say Jamaican is different. A 'stronger dialect' in Calabash Bight needs investigation. The variety on the north coast is reported to be a creole. Investigation needed: intelligibility with Calabash Bight, North Coast, San Andres, Limón, Belize.

CHORTÍ [CAA] 10 speakers out of 4,200 in the ethnic group (1997 R. Reeck). Cofan Department, along the Guatemala border. Mayan, Cholan-Tzeltalan, Cholan, Chorti. NT 1996. See main entry under Guatemala.

ENGLISH [ENG] 9,000 first language speakers in Honduras. Indo-European, Germanic, West, English. Bible 1535-1989. See main entry under United Kingdom.

GARÍFUNA ***(CARIBE, CENTRAL AMERICAN CARIB, BLACK CARIB)*** [CAB] 98,000 in Honduras (1993 Ramon D. Rivas). Population total all countries 190,000 possibly (1997 SIL). Mainly of the north coast between Masca, Cortes department and Plaplaya, Gracias a Dios Department. 40 towns in Honduras, at least 54 in Central America. Also spoken in Belize, Guatemala, Nicaragua, USA. Arawakan, Maipuran, Northern Maipuran, Caribbean. Dictionary. Literacy rate in first language: 1% to 5%. Literacy rate in second language: 5% to 15%. Coastal. Christian, traditional religion. NT 1983-1994.

LENCA [LEN] Only a few speakers out of 100,000 or more ethnic population (1993 Ramon D. Rivas). La Paz, Intibucá, Lempira, Comayagua, Santa Bárbara, Valle and Francisco Morozan departments. Also spoken in El Salvador. Unclassified. Some consider it to be Macro-Chibchan. The dialect in El Salvador is different from Honduras. Bilingualism in Spanish. Nearly extinct.

MÍSKITO ***(MÍSQUITO, MARQUITO, MÍSKITU, MOSQUITO)*** [MIQ] 29,000 in Honduras (1993 Ramon D. Rivas). Gracias a Dios Department. Misumalpan. Trade language. Literacy rate in first language: 1% to 10%. Literacy rate in second language: 5% to 25%. Bible 1999. See main entry under Nicaragua.

PECH ***(PAYA, SECO)*** [PAY] 994 speakers out of 2,586 in the ethnic group (1993 Ramon D. Rivas). North central coast, Municipio Dulce Nombre de Culmí, Olancho Department,Santa María del Carbón. Speakers also in Las Marias, Gracias a Dios, Silin, Colon. Chibchan, Paya. Bilingualism in Spanish. The youngest speakers are 40 years old, but most are over 60. More active in using Pech in Agua Amarilla and La Laguna in El Carbón, and less in using Spanish. There is a lot of interest in the community in preserving the Pech language, and some work is being done to preserve it. Investigation needed: bilingual proficiency in Spanish. SOV.

PIPIL ***(NAHUAT)*** [PPL] No speakers in Honduras. Municipio of Dolores, Ocotepeque Department, near El Salvador border. Uto-Aztecan, Southern Uto-Aztecan, Aztecan, General Aztec, Pipil. The language is called 'Nahuat', the people 'Pipil'. Nearly extinct. See main entry under El Salvador.

SPANISH ***(ESPAÑOL, CASTELLANO)*** [SPN] 5,600,000 in Honduras (1996). Indo-European, Italic, Romance, Italo-Western, Western, Gallo-Iberian, Ibero-Romance, West Iberian, Castilian. National language. Bible 1553-1979. See main entry under Spain.

SUMO TAWAHKA ***(SUMO, SUMU, SOUMO, SUMOO)*** [SUM] 700 in Honduras (1997 SIL). 800 to 1,000 in the ethnic group (1993 Ramon D. Rivas. Banks of the Patuca River, Gracias a Dios and parts of Olanco departments. Misumalpan. Dialects: TAWAHKA, ULWA. Same language as in Nicaragua, but different dialect. Honduran Tawahka is reported to be closer to Nicaraguan Panamahka than to Nicaraguan Tawahka. Bilingualism in Mískito. The name 'Sumo' is not used by speakers. Investigation needed: intelligibility with Nicaraguan Tawahka. SOV. Literacy rate in first language: 10% to 30%. Literacy rate in second language: 25% to 50%. NT, in press (1999). See main entry under Nicaragua.

TOL ***(TOLPAN, JICAQUE, XICAQUE)*** [JIC] 350 speakers (1997) out of an ethnic group of 593 (1990 Educación Comunitaria para la Salud-Honduras). Also 19,000 ethnic Tolpan in the Department of Yoro, including some speakers. Montaña de la Flor, northern Francisco Morazán Department, north central Honduras. Language Isolate. No distinct dialects. It may be distantly related to Subtiaba of Nicaragua (extinct linguistically), Tlapaneco of Mexico, or the Hokan languages. Varying degrees of bilingualism in Spanish; adult male leaders are more fluent, women and children are more limited. Ethnic Tolpan who do not speak Tol speak Spanish. All ages. SOV. Literacy rate in first language: 5% to 10%. Literacy rate in second language: 5% to 15%. Christian, traditional religion. NT 1993.

JAMAICA

National or official language: English. 2,538,000 (1998 UN). Literacy rate 82% to 89%. Also includes North Levantine Spoken Arabic 2,000, Portuguese 5,000, Spanish 8,000, Chinese 31,000. Christian, traditional religion, secular. Deaf population 154,909. Deaf institutions: 26. Data accuracy estimate: B. The number of languages listed for Jamaica is 3. Of those, all are living languages. Diversity index 0.01.

ENGLISH [ENG] Indo-European, Germanic, West, English. National language. Bible 1535-1989. See main entry under United Kingdom.

JAMAICAN COUNTRY SIGN LANGUAGE ***(COUNTRY SIGN)*** [JCS] Deaf sign language. There is no standardized sign language, but 'Country Sign' differs from region to region. Signed English is used in at least one deaf school, but students do not understand many of the function words. It is used for all communication needs outside the classroom. Many deaf children do not attend school.

SOUTHWESTERN CARIBBEAN CREOLE ENGLISH [JAM] 2,544,000 in Jamaica (1995 estimate). Population total all countries 2,699,000 or more. Also spoken in Canada, Costa Rica, Dominican Republic, Panama, United Kingdom, USA. Creole, English based, Atlantic, Western. Dialect: JAMAICAN CREOLE ENGLISH (PATWA, PATOIS, BONGO TALK, QUASHIE TALK). The extreme varieties and Standard English are inherently unintelligible to each other's speakers (Voegelin and Voegelin, LePage, Adler). It may be partly intelligible to speakers of Cameroons Pidgin and Krio of Sierra Leone, spoken by descendants of Jamaicans repatriated between 1787 and 1860. Inherently intelligible to speakers of creoles in Panama and Costa Rica. Reported to be very close to Creole of Belize, close to Grenada, St. Vincent, different from Tobago, very different from Guyana, Barbados, Leeward and Windward Islands. 25% lexical similarity with Guyanese, 13% with Belizean, 9% with Trinidadian, 8% with Barbadian, 5% with Nicaraguan. Most speakers have some competence in Standard English. Education is in Standard English. Extreme vitality. Creole is the dominant language and gaining in prestige. Continuum of speech from the distinct creole to provincial Standard English of town dwellers. Most speakers believe that they speak Standard English. Linguistic influences from Akan in Ghana and Bantu (I. Hancock 1988). Dictionary. Grammar. Literacy rate in second language: High in English.

MARTINIQUE

National or official language: French. 389,000 (1998 UN). A French department in the Windward Islands. Literacy rate 89% to 93%. Also includes Vietnamese 330, Arabic 500, Chinese 500. Christian, secular. Data accuracy estimate: A1. The number of languages listed for Martinique is 2. Of those, both are living languages. Diversity index 0.00.

FRENCH [FRN] Indo-European, Italic, Romance, Italo-Western, Western, Gallo-Iberian, Gallo-Romance, Gallo-Rhaetian, Oïl, French. National language. Bible 1530-1986. See main entry under France.

LESSER ANTILLEAN CREOLE FRENCH [DOM] 325,000 in Martinique (1975). Creole, French based. Dialect: MARTINIQUE CREOLE FRENCH (PATWA, PATOIS). Dialect of Guadeloupe is close to Martinique. Comprehension of St. Lucia Creole is 89%. NT 1999. See main entry under St. Lucia.

MEXICO

Estados Unidos Mexicanos. National or official language: Spanish. 95,831,000 (1998 UN). 8% of the population speak American Indian languages. Literacy rate 87% to 88%. Also includes Basque, Catalan-Valencian-Balear, English 350,000, Japanese 35,000, O'odham, Vlax Romani 5,000, Arabic 400,000, Chinese 31,000. Information mainly from S. Gudschinsky 1953, 1959; R. Longacre 1957; A. Wares 1965; D. Bartholomew 1965; C. Rensch 1966, 1968; C. H. Bradley 1968; P. Kirk 1970; E. Casad 1974; W. R. Miller 1975; S. Egland, D. Bartholomew, and S. Ramos 1983; SIL 1951-1999. Christian, secular. Blind population 200,000. Deaf population 1,300,000 to 5,590,207 (1998). Deaf institutions: 30. Data accuracy estimate: A1, A2. The number of languages listed for Mexico is 295. Of those, 288 are living languages and 7 are extinct. Diversity index 0.13.

AFRO-SEMINOLE CREOLE ***(AFRO-SEMINOLE, AFRO-SEMINOL CRIOLLO)*** [AFS] Several hundred (1990). Nacimiento de los Negros, Coahuila, México. Creole, English based, Atlantic, Eastern, Northern. Dialect: MEXICO AFRO-SEMINOLE. Separated from coastal Sea Islands Creole between 1690 and 1760. "The variety in Mexico has not been described" (J. Holm 1989:496). Similar to Bahamas Creole. 90% lexical similarity with Sea Islands Creole. Bilingualism in Spanish. Only spoken by older people in Nacimiento. See main entry under USA.

AMUZGO, GUERRERO [AMU] 23,000 including 10,000 monolinguals (1990 census). Southeastern Guerrero, Xochistlahuaca municipio, Zacoalpan, Cochoapa, Huehuetonoc, Tlacoachistlahuaca, Guadalupe Victoria, Cozoyoapan. Oto-Manguean, Amuzgoan. 67% intelligibility of San Pedro Amuzgos Amuzgo. Bilingual level estimates for Spanish are 0 50%, 1 37%, 2 10%, 3 2.5%, 4 .5%, 5 0%. VSO, tonal, short word, affixes, clitics. Literacy rate in first language: 10% adults, 15% children. Literacy rate in second language: 30% adults, 40% children. Subtropical deciduous. Mountain slope. Peasant agriculturalists. 400 to 1,600 meters. NT 1973, in press (1999).

AMUZGO, IPALAPA ***(SANTA MARÍA IPALAPA AMUZGO)*** [AZM] 1,200 including 60 monolinguals (1990 census). May be up to 2,000 speakers, including more than 60 monolinguals (1992 C. Stewart SIL). Oaxaca, Putla district, about 8 to 10 miles northeast of San Pedro Amuzgos; five locations around Santa María Ipalapa. Just off the highway from Tlaxiaco to the coast. Oto-Manguean, Amuzgoan. Not intelligible with other Amuzgo. Some bilingualism in Spanish. All ages. Primary and secondary education available. Tonal. Savannah, scrub or gallery forest. Mountain slope, inland coastal. Swidden agriculturalists: maize, beans, squash, chile peppers, tomatoes. 2,000 feet.

AMUZGO, SAN PEDRO AMUZGOS ***(AMUZGO, OAXACA, AMUZGO DE SAN PEDRO AMUZGOS)*** [AZG] 4,000 including monolinguals (1990 census). Southwestern Oaxaca, Putla district, San Pedro Amuzgos. One town with outlying settlements. Oto-Manguean, Amuzgoan. 76% intelligibility of Amuzgo of Guerrero. Bilingual level estimates for Spanish are 0 50%, 1 35%, 2 15%, 3 0%, 4 0%, 5 0%. Dictionary. Grammar. VSO, tonal, affixes. Gallery forest. Mountain slope. Peasant agriculturalists. 350 to 500 meters. NT 1992.

CHATINO, NOPALA [CYA] 11,000 including 2,300 monolinguals (1990 census). Southeastern Oaxaca, Juquila district, Santos Reyes Nopala, Santa María Texmaxcaltepec, San María Magdalena Tiltepec, Teotepec, Cerro el Aire, Santiago Cuixtla, Atotonilco, San Gabriel Mixtepec. Oto-Manguean, Zapotecan, Chatino. 59% intelligibility of Panixtlahuaca, 73% of Yaitepec, 13% of Tataltepec. Bilingualism in Spanish. VSO, tonal, short words, affixes, clitics. Tropical forest. Coastal, mountain slope. Peasant agriculturalists, craftsmen. 480 to 1,600 meters.

CHATINO, SIERRA OCCIDENTAL ***(CHATINO DE LA ZONA ALTA OCCIDENTAL, WESTERN HIGHLAND CHATINO)*** [CTP] 10,000 (1999 L. Pride SIL) including 900 monolinguals in Yaitepec (1990 census). Southeastern Oaxaca, Juquila district, towns of Panixtlahuaca, San Juan Quiahije, and Yaitepec; villages of Ixtapan, Tepenixtelahuaca, Ixpantepec, and Amialtepec, plus various rancherías. Oto-Manguean, Zapotecan, Chatino. Dialects: PANIXTLAHUACA CHATINO, SAN JUAN QUIAHIJE CHATINO, YAITEPEC CHATINO. 71% intelligibility of Yaitepec, 66% of Nopala, 46% of Zacatepec, 32% of Tataltepec. Yaitepec has 80% intelligibility of Nopala, 78% of Panixtlahuaca, 20% of Tataltepec. Bilingual level estimates for Spanish are 0 60%, 1 30%, 2 9.95%, 3 .05%, 4 0%, 5 0%. Yaitepec is one of the most monolingual Chatino towns. The economic situation varies from poor in Ixtapan to some wealthy families in Panixtlahuaca and San Juan Quiahije. VSO, tonal, short words, affixes, clitics. Tropical, pine forest. Mountain slope. Swidden agriculturalists, coffee culture, timber, cattle. 650 to 2,335 meters. NT 1992.

CHATINO, SIERRA ORIENTAL ***(EASTERN HIGHLAND CHATINO, LACHAO-YOLOTEPEC CHATINO)*** [CLY] 2,000 (1993 SIL). Southeastern Oaxaca, villages of Lachao Pueblo Nuevo and Santa María Yolotepec. Oto-Manguean, Zapotecan, Chatino. One dialect. Uses lengthened word forms similar to Zenzontepec Chatino. Similar to Zacatepec, but geographically and socioeconomically separated. 87% intelligibility of Yaitepec, 83% of Nopala, 77% of Panixtlahuaca, 21% of Tataltepec. 30% to 40% of the speakers have limited to routine ability in Spanish. VSO, tonal, long words, affixes, clitics. Mountains, coastal range. Subsistence agriculturalists: coffee; timber. 6,000 to 8,000 feet.

CHATINO, TATALTEPEC ***(LOWLAND CHATINO)*** [CTA] 4,000 including 470 monolinguals (1990 census). Southeastern Oaxaca, Juquila district, extreme west lowland Chatino area, in the towns of Tataltepec de Valdez and San Pedro Tututepec, and a few speakers in nearby Spanish population centers. Oto-Manguean, Zapotecan, Chatino. 38% intelligibility of Yaitepec, 35% of Panixtlahuaca, 33% of Nopala, 27% of Zacatepec. Bilingual level estimates for Spanish are 0 1%, 1 9%, 2 70%, 3 20%, 4 5%, 5 0%. Dictionary. Grammar. VSO, tonal, long words, affixes, clitics. Scrub forest, tropical forest. Coastal, foothills. Swidden agriculturalists. 300 to 500 meters. NT 1981.

CHATINO, ZACATEPEC ***(SAN MARCOS ZACATEPEC CHATINO)*** [CTZ] 1,000 (1990 census). Southeastern Oaxaca, village of San Marcos Zacatepec and Juquila. Oto-Manguean, Zapotecan, Chatino. 66% intelligibility of Nopala, 61% of Panixtlahuaca, 57% of Yaitepec, 6% of Tataltepec. Lengthened word forms are like Zenzontepec Chatino. Similar to Lachao-Yolotepec Chatino in some respects, but geographically and socioeconomically separated. Spoken in Zacatepec. Virtually extinct in Juquila with 2 elderly men speakers. Tropical forest. Mountain slope. Agriculturalists: maize, coffee, palm nuts, fruit. 500 to 600 meters.

CHATINO, ZENZONTEPEC ***(NORTHERN CHATINO)*** [CZE] 8,000 including 2,000 monolinguals (1990 census). Southeastern Oaxaca, Juquila district, various sectors in the municipios of Santa Cruz

Zenzontepec and San Jacinto Tlacotepec, and parts of the former municipio of Santa María Tlapanalquiahuitl. It does not include the adjacent Zapoteco areas of Texmelucan or Zaniza. Oto-Manguean, Zapotecan, Chatino. Some dialect differences in Santa María Tlapanalquiahuitl area. One of the most isolated and conservative groups in Oaxaca. Bilingual level estimates for Spanish are 0 50%, 1 20%, 2 20%, 3 10%, 4 0%, 5 0%. Economically marginal. SVO, tonal, long words, affixes. Scrub forest. Mountain slope, inland. Swidden agriculturalists. 1,000 to 1,500 meters.

CHIAPANECO [CIP] 150 including 17 speakers out of 32 ethnic population in Chiapas (1990 census). State of Chiapas, El Bosque (2), Las Margaritas (2), Ocosingo (4), Palenque (2), Sabanilla (7). Oto-Manguean, Chiapanec-Mangue. Reported to be quite similar to Chorotega of Costa Rica and El Salvador. Nearly extinct.

CHICHIMECA-JONAZ ***(CHICHIMECO, CHICHIMECA, MECO, JONAZ)*** [PEI] 200 speakers (1993 K. Olson Instituto Betania). State of Guanajuato, San Luís de la Paz, Jonáz village. Oto-Manguean, Otopamean, Chichimec. Bilingualism in Spanish.

CHICOMUCELTEC ***(CAC'CHIQUEL MAM, CAKCHIQUEL MAM, CHICOMULCELTECO)*** [COB] Ethnic group: 1,500 in Mexico; 100 in Guatemala (1982 GR). Chiapas, towns of Mazapa de Madero, Amatenango, and Chicomuselo. Also spoken in Guatemala. Mayan, Huastecan. Reported to be extinct in recent Mayanist literature, but the 1990 Mexico census lists 275 speakers. Extinct.

CHINANTECO, CHILTEPEC [CSA] 1,000 or fewer (1994), including some possible monolinguals. They live in villages with speakers of other Chinanteco varieties, so it is difficult to know how many there are. 4,000 in Chiltepec municipio with 250 monolinguals (1990 census). Oaxaca, San José Chiltepec. Oto-Manguean, Chinantecan. 76% intelligibility of Tlacoatzintepec (closest), 20% of Usila and Ojitlán, 13% of Valle Nacional. Speakers use Spanish as second language, but outlying towns are not as bilingual as the center. Riverine. below 3,000 feet.

CHINANTECO, COMALTEPEC [CCO] 2,000 including 145 monolinguals (1990 census). North Oaxaca, Santiago Comaltepec, Soledad Tectitlán, La Esperanza, San Martín Soyolapan, Vista Hermosa (Quiotepec), San Pedro Yolox, Rosario Temextitlán, Maninaltepec. Oto-Manguean, Chinantecan. 69% intelligibility of Quiotepec (closest), 7% of Tepetotutla. Bilingual level estimates for Spanish are 0 5%, 1 15%, 2 30%, 3 30%, 4 19%, 5 1%. VSO, tonal, short words, affixes. Literacy rate in first language: 1%. Literacy rate in second language: 75%. Pine forest. Mountain slope. Swidden agriculturalists. 1,300 to 1,500 meters. Bible portions 1976-1990.

CHINANTECO, LALANA [CNL] 10,500 including 2,500 monolinguals (1998). Oaxaca-Veracruz border, 25 towns. Oto-Manguean, Chinantecan. 87% intelligibility of Tepinapa (closest, but lower in outlying areas), 43% of Ozumacín, 24% of Lealao. Bilingual level estimates for Spanish are 0 50%, 1 29%, 2 10%, 3 10%, 4 1%, 5 0%. VOS, tonal, short words, affixes, clitics. Tropical. Mountain slope, inter-fluvial. Peasant agriculturalists. 100 to 2,000 meters. NT 1974-1994.

CHINANTECO, LEALAO ***(SAN JUAN LEALAO CHINANTECO)*** [CLE] 2,000 including monolinguals (1990 census). North Oaxaca, San Juan Lealao, Latani, and Tres Ríos. Oto-Manguean, Chinantecan. Considered the most divergent of the Chinantec languages. Bilingual level estimates for Spanish are 0 5%, 1 45%, 2 50%, 3 0%, 4 0%, 5 0%. There is also some bilingualism in Zapoteco. Dictionary. VOS, tonal, short words, affixes. Tropical. Mountain slope. Swidden agriculturalists. 50 to 500 meters. NT 1980.

CHINANTECO, OJITLÁN [CHJ] 22,000 including 2,800 monolinguals (1990 census). Northern Oaxaca, San Lucas Ojitlán, including 4 towns and 15 rancherías, and Veracruz, Hidalgotitlán and Minatitlán municipios. Most speakers have been relocated because a dam flooded their land in 1991. Oto-Manguean, Chinantecan. 49% intelligibility of Sochiapan (closest), 43% of Usila, 39% of Palantla, 31% of Chiltepec. NT 1968, out of print.

CHINANTECO, OZUMACÍN [CHZ] 3,500 (1998 SIL) including 260 monolinguals (1990 census). North Oaxaca, 3 towns: San Pedro Ozumacín, Auyotzintepec, Santiago Progreso. Oto-Manguean, Chinantecan. Dialect: AYOTZINTEPEC. 63% intelligibility of Palantla (closest), 22% of Lalana and Valle Nacional. Literacy rate in first language: Below 1%. Literacy rate in second language: 50% to 75%. Forests. Mountain slope. Agriculturalists: maize, pigs, poultry. Bible portions 1990-1995.

CHINANTECO, PALANTLA [CPA] 12,000 including 1,500 monolinguals (1990 census). Oaxaca, San Juan Palantla plus 13 towns. Oto-Manguean, Chinantecan. 78% intelligibility of Tepetotutla (closest), 72% of Valle Nacional, 69% of Usila, 54% of Ozumacín. Bilingual level estimates for Spanish are 0 10%, 1 25%, 2 35%, 3 25%, 4 5%, 5 0%. Dictionary. VSO, tonal, short words. Literacy rate in first language: Below 1%. Literacy rate in second language: 50%. Tropical. Mountain slope. Swidden agriculturalists. 50 to 500 meters. NT 1973.

CHINANTECO, QUIOTEPEC ***(HIGHLAND CHINANTECO)*** [CHQ] 8,000 including 1,750 monolinguals (1998). Oaxaca, Ixtlán District: San Juan Quiotepec, Reforma, Maninaltepec, San Pedro Yolox, Rosario Temextitlán; Oaxaca, Etla District: San Juan Bautista Atatlah. Oto-Manguean, Chinantecan. Dialect: YOLOX CHINANTECO. 87% intelligibility of Comaltepec (closest, lower in outlying areas),

7% of Tepetotutla. The highland Chinanteco languages share a complexity of vowel length and tone extensions that Tepetotutla and Palantla do not have. Bilingual level estimates for Spanish are 0 35%, 1 20%, 2 15%, 3 15%, 4 10%, 5 5%. VSO, tonal, short words, affixes. Deciduous forest, pine forest. Mountain slope. Peasant agriculturalists. 1,000 to 2,400 meters. NT 1983.

CHINANTECO, SOCHIAPAN [CSO] 3,700 including 725 monolinguals (1990 census). North Oaxaca, Cuic: San Pedro Sochiapan, Retumbadeo, San Juan Zautla, Santiago Quetzalapa, San Juan Zapotitlán. Oto-Manguean, Chinantecan. 66% intelligibility of Tlacoatzintepec (closest), 56% of Chiltepec, 45% of Usila, 11% of Tepetotutla. Bilingual level estimates for Spanish are 0 15%, 1 15%, 2 30%, 3 30%, 4 9%, 5 1%. VSO, tonal, short words, affixes, clitics. Tropical forest. Mountain slope. Swidden agriculturalists. 800 to 2,000 meters. NT 1986.

CHINANTECO, TEPETOTUTLA [CNT] 2,000 (1990 census). North Oaxaca, Santa Cruz Tepetotutla, San Antonio del Barrio, San Pedro Tlatepusco, Santo Tomás Texas, Vega del Sol, El Naranjal. Oto-Manguean, Chinantecan. 60% intelligibility of Quiotepec, 59% of Palantla, 48% of Yolox. Grammar. VSO, tonal, short words, affixes, clitics. Tropical forest, mountain slope. Agriculturalists: coffee. 4,000 feet. NT 1994.

CHINANTECO, TEPINAPA [CTE] 8,000 including 2,500 monolinguals (1990 census). Oaxaca, Choapan District, Santiago Jocotepec Municipio: San Pedro Tepinapa; San Juan Petlapa Municipio: Santa María Lovani, San Juan Toavela, and Santa Isabel Cajonos. Very remote area. Oto-Manguean, Chinantecan. 79% intelligibility of Comaltepec, 87% to 68% of Lalana, 24% of Lealao, 23% of Ozumacín. Limited bilingualism in Spanish. Most children are monolingual when they start school. Vigorous. Most villages have less than 6 grades of primary school. Mountain slope. Agriculturalists: maize, coffee, ixtle. 1,000 to 3,000 feet.

CHINANTECO, TLACOATZINTEPEC [CTL] 2,000 including 550 monolinguals (1990 census). Oaxaca, San Juan Bautista Tlacoatzintepec, San Pedro Alianza, Santiago Quetzalapa, San Juan Zapotitlán. Oto-Manguean, Chinantecan. 85% intelligibility of Chiltepec (closest, lower in outlying areas), 84% of Usila, 74% of Sochiapan, 15% of Tepetotutla. Bilingual level estimates for Spanish are 0 50%, 1 40%, 2 9%, 3 1%, 4 0%, 5 0%. VSO, tonal, short words, affixes, clitics. Tropical forest. Mountain slope. Swidden agriculturalists. 3,200 feet.

CHINANTECO, USILA [CUS] 9,000 including 2,200 monolinguals (1990 census). Oaxaca, San Felipe Usila plus 12 towns, and 1 in Veracruz (Pueblo Doce). Oto-Manguean, Chinantecan. 48% intelligibility of Tlacoatzintepec (closest), 33% of Palantla, 32% of Sochiapan, 31% of Ojitlán. Bilingual level estimates for Spanish are 0 50%, 1 30%, 2 10%, 3 7%, 4 2%, 5 1%. VSO, tonal, short words, affixes, clitics. Literacy rate in first language: 1%. Literacy rate in second language: 20%. Tropical. Riverine. Swidden, peasant agriculturalists. 100 to 400 meters. NT 1983.

CHINANTECO, VALLE NACIONAL [CHV] 1,000 to 2,000 (1990 census). North Oaxaca, San Juan Bautista Valle Nacional and mainly in San Mateo Yetla. Oto-Manguean, Chinantecan. 71% intelligibility of Chiltepec (closest), 70% of Palantla, 53% of Ozumacín, 40% of Tepetotutla. Bilingualism in Spanish. Investigation needed: bilingual proficiency in Spanish.

CHOCHOTECO *(CHOCHO)* [COZ] 770 (1998). Oaxaca, Nochixtlán district, Santa María Nativitas (428 out of 764 population), San Juan Bautista Coixtlahuaca (272 out of 3,111 population), San Martín Toxpalán (207 out of 2,462 population), San Miguel Tulancingo (72 out of 553 population). Oto-Manguean, Popolocan, Chocho-Popolocan, Chocho. Bilingualism in Spanish. "Chocho" speakers were also reported in the 1990 census in Puebla and other parts of Mexico, apparently referring to Popoloca speakers. Investigation needed: bilingual proficiency in Spanish.

CH'OL, TILA [CTI] 35,000 to 40,000 (1990 census) including 10,000 monolinguals (1998). Chiapas, Tila, Vicente Guerrero, Chvioalito, Limar. Mayan, Cholan-Tzeltalan, Cholan, Chol-Chontal. 86% intelligibility of Sabanilla, 82% of Tumbalá. Dictionary. Grammar. NT 1976.

CH'OL, TUMBALÁ [CTU] 90,000 including 30,000 monolinguals and 10,000 in Sabanilla (1992). North central Chiapas, Tumbalá, Sabanilla, Misijá, Limar, Chivalita, Vicente Guerrero. Mayan, Cholan-Tzeltalan, Cholan, Chol-Chontal. Bilingual level estimates for Spanish are 0 50%, 1 25%, 2 20%, 3 4.7%, 4 .2%, 5 .1%. Dictionary. Grammar. SVO, VOS, nontonal, long words, affixes, clitics. Tropical, deciduous forest. Mountain slope, interfluvial. Peasant agriculturalists. 100 to 1,600 meters. Christian, traditional religion. Bible 1977-1992.

CHONTAL DE OAXACA, COSTA *(LOWLAND OAXACA CHONTAL, HUAMELULA CHONTAL, COASTAL CHONTAL OF OAXACA, HUAMELULTECO)* [CLO] 950 (1990 census). No monolinguals. Southern Oaxaca, Tehuantepec district, San Pedro Huamelula and Santiago Astata. Hokan, Tequistlatecan. Bilingual level estimates for Rural Spanish are 0 0%, 1 0%, 2 0%, 3 40%, 4 30%, 5 30%. VSO, nontonal, medium long words, affixes, clitics. Scrub forest. Coastal. Swidden agriculturalists. 300 meters. Bible portions 1955.

CHONTAL DE OAXACA, SIERRA *(HIGHLAND OAXACA CHONTAL, MOUNTAIN TEQUISTLATECO, TEQUISTLATEC)* [CHD] 3,600 (1990 census). Southernmost part of Oaxaca, west of the Isthmus of

Tehuantepec, San José Chiltepec, San Lucas Ixcatepec, plus 15 towns. Hokan, Tequistlatecan. Bilingual level estimates for Spanish are 0 1%, 1 2%, 2 70%, 3 22%, 4 5%, 5 0%. 'Tequistlateco' has been used in publications, but the true Tequistlateco was spoken in the town of Tequisistlán, and is now extinct. VS, SV, or VO, nontonal, medium long words, affixes. Literacy rate in first language: 60% to 100%. Literacy rate in second language: 75% to 100%. Tropical, deciduous forest, pine forest. Mountain slope. Swidden agriculturalists. 1,500 to 2,300 meters. NT 1991.

CHONTAL, TABASCO ***(YOCOT'AN)*** [CHF] 55,000 (1995 census). North central and southern Tabasco, 21 towns. Mayan, Cholan-Tzeltalan, Cholan, Chol-Chontal. Dialects: TAMULTÉ DE LAS SÁBANAS CHONTAL, BUENA VISTA CHONTAL, MIRAMAR CHONTAL. Speakers of all dialects understand San Carlos Macuspana 80% to 94%. Dictionary. NT 1977.

CHUJ, SAN MATEO IXTATÁN ***(CHAPAI)*** [CNM] 9,500 in Mexico including 8,000 refugees (1991 Schumann). Municipio of Trinitaria, Chiapas; villages of Tziscau and Cuauhtémoc. Mayan, Kanjobalan-Chujean, Chujean. The Mexican group is reported to be bilingual in Spanish. NT 1970. See main entry under Guatemala.

COCHIMÍ ***(COCHIMTEE, COCHETIMI, COCHIMA, CADEGOMO, CADEGOMEÑO, DIDIU, LAIMON, LAYMONEM, LAYMON-COCHIMI, SAN JAVIER, SAN XAVIER, SAN JOAQUÍN, SAN FRANCESCO SAVERIO MISSION, SAN FRANCISCO XAVIER DE VIGGÉ-BIAUNDO MISSION)*** [COJ] Baja California Norte, north of Loreto to the northern part of the peninsula. Hokan, Esselen-Yuman, Yuman, Cochimi. Troike (1970) regards it as two distinct languages. Kumiai (Tipai) in La Huerta now call themselves 'Cochimí'. Old Cochimí is extinct (Mixco 1978). Extinct.

COCOPA ***(COCOPÁ, COCOPAH, CUCUPÁ, CUCAPÁ, KWIKAPÁ, KIKIMÁ)*** [COC] 200 in Mexico (1998 Peter Larson). Population total both countries 520. Baja California, El Mayor, San Poza de Aroizú (to the south of Río San Luis Colorado). Also spoken in USA. Hokan, Esselen-Yuman, Yuman, Delta-Californian. Hunter-gatherers, agriculturalists: maize. Bible portions 1972.

CORA [COR] 8,000 (1993 SIL). Population total both countries 8,000 or more. North central Nayarit. Also spoken in USA. Uto-Aztecan, Southern Uto-Aztecan, Sonoran, Corachol. Dialects: JESÚS MARÍA CORA (EL NAYAR), LA MESA DEL NAYAR CORA (MESA DEL NAYAR), SAN FRANCISCO CORA, PRESIDIO DE LOS REYES CORA. Santa Teresa Cora is distinct enough to need separate literature. Bilingual level estimates for Spanish are 0 5%, 1 10%, 2 25%, 3 35%, 4 15%, 5 10%. VSO, VOS, tonal, short nouns, long verbs, affixes, clitics. Scrub forest, tropical forest, pine forest. Mountain mesa, mountain slope. Swidden agriculturalists: maize, beans, squash. 100 to 2,300 meters. NT, in press (1999).

CORA, SANTA TERESA [COK] 7,000 (1993 SIL). North central Nayarit, Santa Teresa, Dolores, San Blasito. Uto-Aztecan, Southern Uto-Aztecan, Sonoran, Corachol. Dialects: SANTA TERESA CORA, DOLORES CORA, SAN BLASITO CORA, SAN JUAN CORAPAN CORA, ROSARITO CORA. Difficult intelligibility with other Cora varieties.

CUICATECO, TEPEUXILA [CUX] 8,500 including 850 monolinguals (1990 census). Northwestern Oaxaca, 16 towns. Oto-Manguean, Mixtecan, Mixtec-Cuicatec, Cuicatec. Dialect: SANTA MARÍA PÁPALO. 88% intelligibility of Teutila. Bilingual level estimates for Spanish are 0 .01%, 1 .10%, 2 9%, 3 9%, 4 80%, 5 0%. VSO, tonal, short words, affixes, clitics. Pine forest. Mountain slope. Swidden agriculturalists. 2,000 to 2,500 meters. NT 1974.

CUICATECO, TEUTILA [CUT] 10,000 including 260 monolinguals (1990 census). Teutila, Oaxaca, 8 towns. Oto-Manguean, Mixtecan, Mixtec-Cuicatec, Cuicatec. 79% intelligibility of Tepeuxila. Bilingual level estimates for Spanish are 0 3%, 1 22%, 2 5%, 3 10%, 4 50%, 5 10%. Tonal, VSO, short words, affixes. Pine forest. Mountain slope. Peasant agriculturalists. 1,700 to 2,300 meters. NT 1972.

HUARIJÍO ***(GUARIJÍO, WARIHÍO, VARIHÍO)*** [VAR] 5,000 (1994 SIL). Nearly all are monolingual. Western Sierra Madre Mts., west central Chihuahua, from Río Chinipas on the east to the Sonora border, to the headwaters of the Río Mayo in Sonora, more than 17 villages. Uto-Aztecan, Southern Uto-Aztecan, Sonoran, Tarahumaran, Guarijio. Dialects: HIGHLAND HUARIJÍO, LOWLAND HUARIJÍO. Intelligibility with Tarahumara is less than 50%. Possible dialect or separate language: Maculai. Bilingual level estimates for Spanish are 0 50%, 1 20%, 2 19%, 3 10%, 4 <1%, 5 0%. OVS, nontonal, long words, affixes, clitics. Literacy rate in first language: Below 1%. Literacy rate in second language: 5% adults. Scrub forest. Riverine. Swidden agriculturalists. 300 to 800 meters. Bible portions 1995.

HUASTECO, SAN FRANCISCO CHONTLA ***(SOUTHEASTERN HUASTECO, SAN FRANCISCO CHONTLA HUASTEC)*** [HAU] Northern Veracruz, directly east of Huasteco Veracruz, including Cerro Azul on the southeastern edge, Tepetzintla on the southern edge, Tantima on the northern edge, Santa María Ixcatepec on the western edge, San Francisco Chontla, Tancoco, Amatlán Tuxpan, Galeana y Zaragoza Vieja, Tamiahua. Mayan, Huastecan. Inadequate intelligibility of other Veracruz Huasteco. Bilingualism in Spanish. Eastern Huasteca Náhuatl also used. Scrub forest. Mountain slope. Peasant agriculturalists. 500 to 700 meters.

HUASTECO, SAN LUÍS POTOSÍ ***(POTOSINO HUASTEC)*** [HVA] 70,000 (1990 census). San Luís Potosí, 12 villages. Mayan, Huastecan. Intelligibility tests indicate one Huasteco language, but sociological factors require literature in the Veracruz variety. Bilingual level estimates for Spanish are 0 25%, 1 40%, 2 15%, 3 10%, 4 6%, 5 4%. SVO, nontonal, short words, affixes. Newspapers. Semi-tropical. Coastal, mountain slope. Peasant agriculturalists. 93 meters. NT 1971.

HUASTECO, TANTOYUCA ***(TANTOYUCA HUASTEC)*** [HUS] 50,000 (1990 census). Northern Veracruz, 60 villages. Mayan, Huastecan. 84% intelligibility of San Luís Potosí Huasteco. Bilingual level estimates for Spanish are 0 5%, 1 15%, 2 30%, 3 25%, 4 0%, 5 0%. Eastern Huasteca Náhuatl also used. SVO, nontonal, short words, affixes, clitics. Literacy rate in first language: Below 1%. Literacy rate in second language: 52%. Scrub forest. Mountain slope. Peasant agriculturalists. 500 to 700 meters. Bible portions 1994.

HUAVE, SAN DIONISIO DEL MAR [HVE] 3,000 to 5,000 speakers (1993 G. Stairs SIL). Southeastern coast, Oaxaca, Juchitán Distrct, San Dionisio del Mar. Huavean. 98% intelligibility of Santa María del Mar Huave, 88% of San Mateo del Mar Huave. Bilingualism in Spanish. Investigation needed: bilingual proficiency. Nontonal. Desert. Coastal. Fishermen. 0 to 60 meters.

HUAVE, SAN FRANCISCO DEL MAR [HUE] 900 speakers out of an ethnic population of 3,900 (1990 census). Southeastern coast, Oaxaca, Juchitán District, San Francisco del Mar, old town and new town. Huavean. 38% intelligibility of San Mateo del Mar Huave. The most divergent variety of Huave. Only fishermen were tested, and they are familiar with the other varieties. Younger speakers use Spanish as second language. 2,000 to 3,000 in the new San Francisco town have shifted from Huave to Spanish. 30% to 40% monolingual in the old village. Nontonal. Desert. Coastal. Fishermen. 0 to 60 meters.

HUAVE, SAN MATEO DEL MAR [HUV] 12,000 including 1,800 monolinguals (1990 census). Southeastern coast, Oaxaca, San Mateo del Mar. Huavean. Only very limited intelligibility of other Huave varieties; 88% of San Dionicio del Mar. Bilingual level estimates for Spanish are 0 0.5%, 1 14.5%, 2 40%, 3 35%, 4 10%, 5 0%. Their legend says they came from Central America. SVO, nontonal, short words, affixes. Literacy rate in first language: 60%. Literacy rate in second language: 40%. Desert. Coastal. Fishermen, agriculturalists. Sea level. NT 1972-1996.

HUAVE, SANTA MARÍA DEL MAR [HVV] 500 speakers in 100 families (1993 G. Stairs SIL). Southeastern coast, Oaxaca, Santa María del Mar. Huavean. Very limited intelligibility of other Huave, although closest to San Dionisio. Bilingualism in Spanish. Children learn Spanish first, but learn Huave by adulthood, because adults speak Huave. Investigation needed: bilingual proficiency in Spanish. Nontonal. Desert. Coastal. Fishermen. 0 to 60 meters.

HUICHOL [HCH] 20,000 (1990 census). Northeastern Nayarit and northwestern Jalisco. The main centers are Guadalupe Ocotán, Nay., San Andrés Cohamiata, Jal., San Sebastián, Jal., Santa Catarina, Jal., Tuxpan de Bolaños, Jal. Uto-Aztecan, Southern Uto-Aztecan, Sonoran, Corachol. Dialects: SAN ANDRÉS COHAMIATA (WESTERN HUICHOL), SAN SEBASTIÁN-SANTA CATARINA (EASTERN HUICHOL), COYULTITA. All dialects are easily inherently intelligible. 58% cognate with Cora, closest (Wick Miller 1984). Bilingual level estimates for Spanish are 0 10%, 1 50%, 2 30%, 3 9%, 4 1%, 5 0%. All ages. Vigorous. Few schools, clinics. Dictionary. Grammar. SOV, tonal, long words, affixes, clitics. Literacy rate in first language: 5% to 10%. Literacy rate in second language: 5% to 15%. Roman. Scrub forest. Mountain slope. Swidden agriculturalists: maize, beans, squash, vegetables; animal husbandry: chickens, pigs, donkeys, horses, cattle. 500 to 2,500 meters. Traditional religion, Christian. NT 1967.

IXCATECO [IXC] 119 speakers (1983 Jorge Suárez). Santa María Ixcatlán, Oaxaca is the original town, surrounded by Mixteco speakers. Oto-Manguean, Popolocan, Ixcatecan. Primer, description of phonology, tone. Dictionary.

JACALTECO, WESTERN [JAI] 10,300 in Mexico including 1,300 long-term residents (1990 census) and 10,000 refugees (1991 Schumann). Concepción Saravia near the municipio of Comalapa de la Frontera, and Amatenango de la Frontera, Chiapas. Mayan, Kanjobalan-Chujean, Kanjobalan, Kanjobal-Jacaltec. Mexican group is bilingual in Spanish. NT 1979. See main entry under Guatemala.

KANJOBAL, WESTERN ***(ACATECO, ACATEC, SAN MIGUEL ACATÁN KANJOBAL, CONOB)*** [KNJ] 100 Acatec and 10,000 refugees in Mexico (1991 Schumann). Trinitaria, Comalapa, and Mazapa de Madero, Chiapas, and Quintana Roo. Mayan, Kanjobalan-Chujean, Kanjobalan, Kanjobal-Jacaltec. VSO. NT 1981. See main entry under Guatemala.

KIKAPÚ ***(KICKAPOO, KICAPUS, KIKAPAUX, KICAPOUX, KIKABEEUX, QUICAPAUSE)*** [KIC] 300 in Mexico (1992 SIL). Coahuila: Nacimiento de Kikapú, 25 miles northeast of Muzquiz. Algic, Algonquian, Central. Vigorous in Mexico. Most speakers spend part of the year in the USA working. Literacy rate in first language: 5%. Literacy rate in second language: 1% Spanish, 45% English. See main entry under USA.

KILIWA ***(KILIWI, QUILIGUA)*** [KLB] 24 to 32 (1994 Stoltzfus SIL), 6 to 8 households (1994 SIL). Arroyo León (4 or 5 houses), Agua Escondida (1 house), La Parra (1 or 2 houses) southeast of Ensenada, Baja California Norte. South of the Paipai, Tipai, and Cocopa. Hokan, Esselen-Yuman, Yuman, Kiliwa. Linguistically distinct from Paipai, Tipai, and Cocopa (A. Wares). A Kiliwa population sample understood Paipai at 87%, but a Paipai sample understood no Kiliwa. Nearly extinct.

KUMIÁI ***(DIEGUEÑO, TIPÁI, TIPAI', TIPÉI, COCHIMÍ, CUCHIMÍ, KAMIA, KAMIAI, QUEMAYÁ, COMEYA, KUMEYAAI, KAMIYAI, KAMIYAHI, KI-MIAI, KUMIA, KUMEYAAY, CAMPO,KO'AL, KU'AHL, KW'AAL)*** [DIH] 220 in Mexico (1991 Garza and Lastra). Population total both countries 320. Baja California, Rancho Nejí, in the mountains southeast of Tecate, 60 kms. east of Ensenada, in La Huerta de los Indios, San Antonio Nécua, San José de la Zorra, Cañon de los Encinos, and Ja'áa. Also spoken in USA. Hokan, Esselen-Yuman, Yuman, Delta-Californian. It is not clear how the above names group into different dialects. Speakers in Neji call themselves 'Kumiai', in La Huerta call themselves 'Cochimí'. Bilingualism in Spanish. Different from the extinct language called 'Cochimí'. Grammar.

LACANDÓN [LAC] 700 to 800 (1997 P. Baer SIL), including 69 at Lake Metzaboc, Chiapas. There were 178 in 1942, all monolingual. Southeastern Chiapas, Najá, Lacanjá San Quintín, Metzaboc, Betel. Mayan, Yucatecan, Yucatec-Lacandon. Dialects: LACANJÁ, NAJÁ. Bilingual level estimates for Tzeltal are 0 49%, 1 20%, 2 20%, 3 10%, 4 1%, 5 0%. Chol, Spanish also used. Dictionary. SVO, nontonal, short words, affixes, clitics. Tropical forest. Interfluvial. Swidden agriculturalists. 500 to 1,200 meters. NT 1978.

MAM, NORTHERN [MAM] 1,000 or more in Mexico. Total Mam in Mexico: 28,000 (1980 census). Chiapas, outside of Pacayal near La Mesilla border, and in Ojo de Agua near Guadalupe. Mayan, Quichean-Mamean, Greater Mamean, Mamean. These are two colonies of Northern Mam Indians from Guatemala. Most are native of either Cuilco or San Ildefonso Ixtahuacan. Bible 1993. See main entry under Guatemala.

MAM, TODOS SANTOS CUCHUMATÁN [MVJ] 10,000 in Mexico (1991 SIL). Cacahuatán and Tapachula, Chiapas. Mayan, Quichean-Mamean, Greater Mamean, Mamean. NT 1997. See main entry under Guatemala.

MATLATZINCA, ATZINGO ***(OCUILTECO, OCUILTEC, ATZINTECO, TLAHURA, TLAHUICA)*** [OCU] 50 to 100 fluent speakers (1993 SIL), 642 in the ethnic group, no monolinguals (1990 census). State of México, Ocuilan municipio, San Juan Atzingo, Santa Lucía del Progreso. Oto-Manguean, Otopamean, Matlatzincan. Closely related to Matlatzinca of Francisco de los Ranchos, but not inherently intelligible. Bilingualism in Spanish. Mountain slope. Nearly extinct.

MATLATZINCA, SAN FRANCISCO DE LOS RANCHOS ***(MATLATZINCA)*** [MAT] State of México, 1 village: San Francisco de los Ranchos. Oto-Manguean, Otopamean, Matlatzincan. Bilingualism in Spanish. Those 30 and over still use the language; those under 30 use Spanish as first language. About half the people are working in Mexico City or elsewhere most of the time. Nearly extinct.

MAYA, CHAN SANTA CRUZ [YUS] 40,000 (1990 census). East central Quintana Roo. Mayan, Yucatecan, Yucatec-Lacandon. Speakers are bilingual in Maya of Yucatán, but not in Spanish.

MAYA, YUCATÁN ***(PENINSULAR MAYA)*** [YUA] 700,000 in Mexico (1990 census). Population total both countries 700,000 or more (1990). Campeche, Quintana Roo, Yucatán. Also spoken in Belize. Mayan, Yucatecan, Yucatec-Lacandon. SVO. Bible 1992.

MAYO [MAY] 40,000 (1990 census). Southern Sonora around Navojoa along the coast (Huatabampo), and a few in northern Sinaloa (Los Mochis, Guasave, San José Ríos, north of Guamuchil). Uto-Aztecan, Southern Uto-Aztecan, Sonoran, Cahita. 90% intelligibility with Yaqui. Bilingual level estimates for Spanish are 0 2%, 1 10%, 2 40%, 3 35%, 4 8%, 5 5%. Speakers prefer Mayo. Dictionary. Nontonal, SOV, medium word length, clitics, and affixes. Literacy rate in first language: 1%. Literacy rate in second language: 10%. Desert, gallery forest. Coastal plains. Peasant agriculturalists, pastoralists, fishermen. 0 to 100 meters. Traditional religion, Christian. Bible portions 1962-1998.

MAZAHUA CENTRAL [MAZ] 350,000 (1993 SIL). Western and northwestern State of México and some in D. F. Oto-Manguean, Otopamean, Otomian, Mazahua. Dialects: ATLACOMULCO-TEMASCALCINGO, SANTA MARÍA CITENDEJÉ-BANOS, SAN MIGUEL TENOXTITLÁN. The Atlacomulco-Temascalcingo dialect uses different kinship terms, has phonological differences, grammatical variation among towns, and may need further adaptation of literature. 85% to 100% intelligibility among dialects. Bilingual level estimates for Spanish are 0 7%, 1 40%, 2 37%, 3 12%, 4 3%, 5 1%. VSO, (usually VS or VO), tonal, short words, affixes, clitics. Literacy rate in first language: Below 1%. Literacy rate in second language: 35%. Savannah, gallery forest, deciduous forest, pine forest. Mountain mesa and slope, riverine. Pastoralists, peasant agriculturalists. 1,500 to 2,750 meters. Traditional religion, Christian. NT 1970.

MAZAHUA, MICHOACÁN [QMN] 15,000 to 20,000 (1993 SIL). Eastern Michoacán. Oto-Manguean, Otopamean, Otomian, Mazahua. Bilingualism in Spanish. VSO, (usually VS or VO), tonal, short words, affixes, clitics. Savannah, gallery forest, deciduous forest, pine forest. Mountain mesa and slope, riverine. Pastoralists, peasant agriculturalists. 1,500 to 2,750 meters. Traditional religion, Christian. Bible portions 1987.

MAZATECO, AYAUTLA [VMY] 3,500 speakers including 2,800 monolinguals, others somewhat bilingual (1994 SIL). Oaxaca, southeastern Teotitlán District, San Bartolomé Ayautla. Oto-Manguean, Popolocan, Mazatecan. 80% intelligibility of Huautla, 79% of San Miguel Hualtepec, 40% of Soyaltepec, 37% of Jalapa, 24% of Ixcatlán. All. All ages. A prestige variety. Children play in the language. There is a secondary school. People are interested in literature. There is a bilingual school. Agriculturalists: maize, beans, chile, coffee, vanilla. 2,000 feet.

MAZATECO, CHIQUIHUITLÁN ***(SAN JUAN CHIQUIHUITLÁN MAZATECO)*** [MAQ] 2,500 including 340 monolinguals (1990 census). Oaxaca. Oto-Manguean, Popolocan, Mazatecan. 47% intelligibility of Huautla (closest), 37% of Ayautla, 29% of Soyaltepec, 20% of Ixcatlán. Bilingual level estimates for Spanish are 0 3%, 1 3%, 2 23.5%, 3 60%, 4 10%, 5 .5%. Dictionary. Grammar. VSO, (with fronting of S or O for focus), tonal, clitics, affixes. Tropical forest. Mountain slope. Swidden, peasant agriculturalists. 1,300 meters. NT 1991.

MAZATECO, HUAUTLA ***(MAZATECO, HUAUTLA DE JIMENEZ MAZATECO, HIGHLAND MAZATECO)*** [MAU] 72,000 including 27,000 (37.5%) monolinguals (1990 census). Northern Oaxaca, Huautla and vicinity. Oto-Manguean, Popolocan, Mazatecan. Dialects: SAN MATEO, SAN MIGUEL. 90% intelligibility of San Jerónimo (closest, lower in outlying areas), 60% of Mazatlán, 35% of Jalapa. 94% lexical similarity with San Miguel, 93% with San Mateo, 80% with Soyaltepec, 78% with San Pedro Ixcatlán, 74% with Jalapa de Díaz. They use a whistle speech, which distinguishes tones of the spoken language, described by G. Cowan (1948, 1952). Dictionary. Tonal, short words. NT 1961.

MAZATECO, IXCATLÁN ***(SAN PEDRO IXCATLÁN MAZATECO)*** [MAO] 11,000 including 3,150 monolinguals (1990 census). Oaxaca, towns of Chichicazapa, Nuevo Ixcatlán, San Pedro Ixcatlán. Oto-Manguean, Popolocan, Mazatecan. 76% intelligibility of Huautla (closest), 78% lexical similarity; 86% lexical similarity with San Mateo Eloxochitlán, 85% with San Miguel Hualtepec and Soyaltepec, 82% with Jalapa de Díaz. Most speakers use Spanish as second language.

MAZATECO, JALAPA DE DÍAZ ***(SAN FELIPE JALAPA DE DÍAZ MAZATECO, LOWLAND MAZATECO)*** [MAJ] 15,500 including 4,600 monolinguals (1990 census). Northern Oaxaca and Veracruz, 13 towns. Oto-Manguean, Popolocan, Mazatecan. 73% intelligibility with Huautla (closest), 62% with Ixcatlán, 51% with Soyaltepec, 46% with San Jerónimo, 35% with Mazatlán. 82% lexical similarity with Ixcatlán, San Mateo Eloxochitlán, and San Miguel Hualtepec; 80% with Soyaltepec, 74% with Huautla. Bilingual level estimates for Spanish are 0 75%, 1-5 25%. VSO, tonal, short words, affixes, clitics. Literacy rate in first language: Below 1%. Literacy rate in second language: 5%. Tropical. Coastal, slope. Swidden, peasant. 150 meters. NT, in press (1998).

MAZATECO, MAZATLÁN ***(MAZATLÁN VILLA DE FLORES MAZATECO)*** [VMZ] 13,000 including 2,200 monolinguals (1990 census). Oaxaca, southern Teotitlán District, Mazatlán Villa de Flores, plus 32 towns and villages, and others in D.F. Oto-Manguean, Popolocan, Mazatecan. Dialects: LOMA GRANDE, ZOYALTITLA. 80% intelligibility of San Jerónimo, 78% of Huautla, 16% of Jalapa de Díaz, 8% of Chiquihuitlán. A significant number of monolinguals are 5 to 9 years old. Over half the children do not know Spanish when entering school. Every village has a primary school, and some have secondary schools. Agriculturalists: maize, coffee, mango, zapote, banana. 4,000 feet.

MAZATECO, SAN JERÓNIMO TECÓATL ***(SAN JERÓNIMO MAZATECO, NORTHERN HIGHLAND MAZATECO)*** [MAA] 34,000 including 8,000 in Puebla (1990 census). Oaxaca, San Jerónimo Tecóatl, San Lucas Zoquiapan, Santa Cruz Acatepec, San Antonio Eloxochitlán, San Pedro Ocopetatillo, San Lorenzo, Santa Ana municipios, and a few in Puebla. 12 towns. Oto-Manguean, Popolocan, Mazatecan. Dialects: SAN JERÓNIMO TECÓATL MAZATECO, SAN ANTONIO ELOXOCHITLÁN MAZATECO, SAN LUCAS ZOQUIAPAN MAZATECO, SANTA CRUZ OCOPETATILLO MAZATECO, SAN LORENZO CUANECUILTITLA MAZATECO, SANTA ANA ATEIXTLAHUACA MAZATECO, SAN FRANCISCO HUEHUETLÁN MAZATECO. 76% intelligibility of Huautla (closest), 26% of Jalapa. Bilingual level estimates for Spanish are 0 30%, 1 30%, 2 25%, 3 5%, 4 5%, 5 5%. VSO, tonal, nouns up to 2 syllables, verbs long, affixes, clitics. Mixed forest. Mountain slope. Peasant agriculturalists. 1,700 to 2,700 meters. Bible portions 1995-1999.

MAZATECO, SOYALTEPEC ***(SAN MIGUEL SOYALTEPEC MAZATEC, TEMASCAL MAZATEC, NUEVO SOYALTEPEC MAZATEC)*** [VMP] 23,000 speakers in the Municipio, including 6,000 monolinguals (1990 census). However, the original Soyaltepec variety may only be 900 speakers, most of whom are monolingual. Oaxaca, northwestern Tuxtepec District, part of Soyaltepec Municipio, towns of Santa María Jacatepec and San Miguel Soyaltepec, Soyaltepec Island. Oto-Manguean, Popolocan, Mazatecan. 5% intelligibility of Chiquihuitlán. A separate language from other Mazateco. Bilingualism in Spanish. Description of phonology, tone, primers. A dam built in 1954, so this Municipio includes many speakers of other Mazateco varieties. Soyaltepec Island has the least mixture of dialects. A bilingual primary school and a secondary school on the Island. Agriculturalists: maize, beans, bananas, squash; fishermen; embroidery. less than 1000 feet.

MEXICAN SIGN LANGUAGE ***(EL LENGUAJE MEXICANO DE LAS MANOS, EL LENGUAJE MANUAL DE MÉXICO, LA LENGUA MANUAL MEXICANA, EL LENGUAJE DE SEÑAS MEXICANAS)*** [MFS] 87,000 to 100,000 mainly monolingual users (1986 T. C. Smith-Stark), out of 1,300,000 deaf persons in Mexico (1986 Gallaudet University). Used throughout Mexico, except in some American Indian areas (see Yucatec Maya Sign Language): Mexico D.F. Guadalajara, Monterrey, Hermosillo, Morelia, Veracruz, Oaxaca, San Luis Potosí, Querétaro, Puebla, Cuernavaca, Torreón, Saltillo, Toluca. Deaf sign language. Influence from French Sign Language. Users of ASL have 14% intelligibility of MSL. Preliminary investigation indicates lexical similarities from 85% to 100% among regional dialects; nearly all above 90% (A. Bickford SIL 1989). Most deaf schools use the oralist method, but some use signs. At least 3 deaf churches in Mexico City, 3 in Guadalajara. 19 schools for the deaf in Saltillo, Torreón, Guadalajara (3), Mexico City (6), Morelia, Cuernavaca, Monterrey, Ciudad Obregón, Hermosillo, Villahermosa, Matamoros, Veracruz; athletic clubs, craft schools, rehabilitation institutions. It does not follow Spanish grammar. The deaf are called 'sordos, sordomudos, los silentes'. Dictionary.

MIXE, COATLÁN ***(SOUTHEASTERN MIXE)*** [MCO] 5,000 (1993 SIL). Speakers of all Mixe languages: 90,000 (1993 SIL). East central Oaxaca, including Coatlán, Camotlán, San José, Santa Isabel, Ixcuintepec. Mixe-Zoque, Mixe, Eastern Mixe. Dialects: COATLÁN MIXE, CAMOTLÁN MIXE. Bilingual level estimates for Spanish are 0 10%, 1 50%, 2 25%, 3 10%, 4 5%, 5 0%. Dictionary. Nontonal, long words, affixes, clitics. Videos. Tropical forest, deciduous forest, pine forest. Mountain slope. Swidden agriculturalists. 500 to 2,500 meters. NT 1976.

MIXE, ISTMO ***(ISTHMUS MIXE, EASTERN MIXE, GUICHICOVI MIXE)*** [MIR] 20,000 (1990 SIL). Northeastern Oaxaca, throughout the Municipio of San Juan Guichicovi, near the border of Veracruz, on the Isthmus of Tehuantepec, 3 towns. Mixe-Zoque, Mixe, Eastern Mixe. SOV, nontonal, long words, affixes, clitics, prepositions, genitives and demonstratives before noun heads, relative clauses after head, question words initial. Literacy rate in first language: 10%. Literacy rate in second language: 30%. Traditional religion, Christian. NT 1988.

MIXE, JUQUILA ***(SOUTH CENTRAL MIXE)*** [MXQ] 15,000 (1993 SIL). East central Oaxaca, including the municipios of Juquila, Quetzaltepec, Ocotepec, and 1 or 2 other towns. Mixe-Zoque, Mixe, Eastern Mixe. Dialects: JUQUILA MIXE, OCOTEPEC MIXE. NT 1980.

MIXE, MAZATLÁN ***(EAST CENTRAL MIXE, TUTLA MIXE)*** [MZL] 15,000 to 20,000 (1993 SIL). Eastern Oaxaca, including 7 towns. Mixe-Zoque, Mixe, Eastern Mixe.

MIXE, QUETZALTEPEC ***(CENTRAL MIXE)*** [MVE] 20,500 (1990 census). Northeastern Oaxaca, several towns in the northeastern part of the Mixe District, including those listed as dialects. Mixe-Zoque, Mixe, Eastern Mixe. Dialects: QUETZALTEPEC MIXE, PUXMETECÁN MIXE, SAN JUAN COTZOCÓN MIXE, OLOTEPEC MIXE, MIXIXTLÁN MIXE, TAMAZULAPAM MIXE, ZACATEPEC MIXE, ATITLÁN MIXE. Puxmetecán, Mixistlán and Tamazulapan may not be dialects of this. Tropical forest. Mountain foothills. Swidden agriculturalists, some cash crops. Bible portions 1994.

MIXE, TLAHUITOLTEPEC ***(WEST CENTRAL MIXE)*** [MXP] 5,000 (1991 SIL). Northeastern Oaxaca. Some have moved into central Oaxaca, in the area of Albarradas Zapoteco, 3 towns. Mixe-Zoque, Mixe, Western Mixe. Bilingual level estimates for Spanish are 0 10%, 1 50%, 2 30%, 3 9%, 4 1%, 5 0%. SOV, VOS, nontonal, long words, affixes. Pine forest. Mountain slope. Swidden agriculturalists. 1,845 to 3,380 meters. NT 1988.

MIXE, TOTONTEPEC ***(NORTHWESTERN MIXE)*** [MTO] 5,200 speakers including 870 monolinguals (1990 census). Northeastern Oaxaca, 10 towns. Mixe-Zoque, Mixe, Western Mixe. The most distinct of the Mixe varieties. 89% intelligibility of Acatepec, 79% of Alotepec, 72% of Tlahuitoltepec, 70% of Mixistlán. Bilingual level estimates for Spanish are 0 15%, 1 15%, 2 20%, 3 25%, 4 20%, 5 5%. Dictionary. SOV, nontonal, long words, affixes, clitics. Literacy rate in first language: Below 1%. Literacy rate in second language: 50%. Forest. Mountain slope. Peasant agriculturalists. 1,200 to 2,300 meters. NT 1989.

MIXTECO, ALACATLATZALA ***(HIGHLAND GUERRERO MIXTECO, ALACATLATZALA MIXTEC)*** [MIM] 18,000 to 20,000 including 6,000 to 7,000 monolinguals (1990 census). Over 300,000 speakers in all Mixtecan languages (1995). Eastern Guerrero, towns of Alacatlatzala, Ocuapa, Potoichan. There are tiny communities in Acapulco, Guerrero; Cuautla, Morelos; and Culiacán, Sinaloa. Oto-Manguean, Mixtecan, Mixtec-Cuicatec, Mixtec. Dialects: POTOICHAN, PLAN DE GUADALUPE. 65% to 85% intelligibility with Metlatonoc. Some had 70% intelligibility of Silacayoapan. Bilingual level estimates for Spanish are 0 60%, 1 20%, 2 19%, 3 1%, 4 0%, 5 0%. They switch to Spanish when trying to communicate with people from Silacayoapan. About 20% (nearly all men) speak some Spanish for trade, travel, or work outside the area. Less than 5% are bilingual in Tlapaneco or Náhuatl resulting from intermarriage. Mixteco is the language of choice in nearly all domains; at home, in local shops, among officials in the town hall for business, for teaching in the classroom even though materials are in Spanish. High appreciation for Mixteco among speakers. Investigation needed: intelligibility with Coicoyán (San Martín Peras). Dictionary. VSO, tonal, short words, clitics. Literacy rate in first language: 5%. Literacy rate in second language: 30%. Desire for literacy in either language is somewhat limited. Some adaptation of materials for Potoichan may be needed. Scrub and pine forest. Mountain slope. Peasant agriculturalists. 1,076 to 2,153 meters. Bible portions 1990-1998.

MIXTECO, ALCOZAUCA ***(ALOCOCAUCA MIXTEC)*** [QMX] 10,000 speakers, including 4,000 monolinguals (1994 SIL) in 14 villages. Eastern Guerrero, near Metlatonoc. Oto-Manguean, Mixtecan, Mixtec-Cuicatec, Mixtec. Dialects: XOCHAPA MIXTECO, PETLACALANCINGO MIXTECO. 92% intelligibility of Metlatonoc. Metlatonoc has 70% intelligibility of Xochapa. A separate language from Metlatonoc. Mountain slope. Bible portions 1997.

MIXTECO, AMOLTEPEC ***(WESTERN SOLA DE VEGA MIXTEC, AMOLTEPEC MIXTEC)*** [MBZ] 5,000 (1992 SIL) including 1,200 monolinguals (1990 census). Oaxaca, western edge of Sola de Vega District, Santiago Amoltepec Municipio, and settlements (Las Cuevas, La Mesilla, El Armadillo, El Mamey, El Zapote, Colonia de Jesús, Barranca Oscura). Oto-Manguean, Mixtecan, Mixtec-Cuicatec, Cuicatec. 63% intelligibility of Northeastern Jamiltepec, 52% of Western Jamiltepec, 46% of Yosondúa, 42% of Nuyoo, 32% of Zacatepec, 25% of San Juan Colorado, 20% of Jamiltepec, 15% of Chayuco. Speakers in Amoltepec center are bilingual in Spanish, but those in the outlying rancherías are quite monolingual. Schools through 6th grade. Many men work outside the area. 4,600 feet.

MIXTECO, APASCO Y APOALA ***(NORTHERN NOCHIXTLÁN MIXTECO, SANTIAGO APOALA MIXTECO, CHOCHO MIXTECO, APOALA MIXTEC, APASCO MIXTEC)*** [MIP] 7,866 speakers, including 6,728 monolinguals (1990 census). Oaxaca, 40 km. north northwest of Nochixtlán. Includes towns of Santa Catarina Ocotlán, San Miguel Chicagua, San Miguel Chicahuastepec, Jocotepec, Santa María Apasco, San Miguel Huautla, Nduayaco, and 2 others. Oto-Manguean, Mixtecan, Mixtec-Cuicatec, Mixtec. 26% intelligibility with Southern Puebla Mixteco (closest). Good attitudes toward the language; desire for literature. Bible portions 1966.

MIXTECO, ATATLÁHUCA ***(SAN ESTEBAN ATATLÁHUCA MIXTECO, SOUTH CENTRAL TLAXIACO MIXTECO, ATATLÁHUCA MIXTEC)*** [MIB] 8,300 including 435 monolinguals (1995 census). West central Oaxaca, towns of San Esteban Atatláhuca, Santa Lucía Monteverde, and Santa Catarina Yosonotú. Oto-Manguean, Mixtecan, Mixtec-Cuicatec, Mixtec. 68% intelligibility of Yosondúa. San Agustín Tlacotepec may need separate literature (69% intelligibility of San Esteban; closest). Santa Lucía Monteverde Mixteco may also need separate literature. Bilingual level estimates for Spanish are 0 50%, 1 30%, 2 15%, 3 5%, 4 0%, 5 0%. Investigation needed: intelligibility with San Augustín Tlacotepec. VSO, tonal, short words, clitics. Pine forest. Mountain slope. Peasant agriculturalists. 3,000 meters. NT 1973.

MIXTECO, AYUTLA ***(COASTAL GUERRERO MIXTECO, AYUTLA MIXTEC)*** [MIY] 8,500 including 3,000 monolinguals (1990 census). Guerrero, Ayutla. Oto-Manguean, Mixtecan, Mixtec-Cuicatec, Mixtec. Literacy rate in first language: Below 1%. Literacy rate in second language: 75% to 100%. Coastal. Bible portions 1970-1972.

MIXTECO, CACALOXTEPEC ***(HUAJUAPAN MIXTECO, CACALOXTEPEC MIXTEC)*** [MIU] 848 speakers including 100 monolinguals (1990 census). 1,254 in the ethnic group. Oaxaca, town of Santiago Cacaloxtepec. Oto-Manguean, Mixtecan, Mixtec-Cuicatec, Mixtec. 59% intelligibility with Silacayoapan (closest). Bilingualism in Spanish. Most monolinguals are over 50.

MIXTECO, CHAYUCO ***(CHAYUCU MIXTECO, EASTERN JAMILTEPEC-CHAYUCO MIXTECO)*** [MIH] 30,000 (1977 SIL). Southwest Oaxaca. Oto-Manguean, Mixtecan, Mixtec-Cuicatec, Mixtec. 69% intelligibility with Western Jamiltepec. NT 1979.

MIXTECO, CHAZUMBA ***(CHAZUMBA MIXTEC, NORTHERN OAXACA MIXTECO)*** [QMB] 2,477 speakers including 32 monolinguals (1995 census). Oaxaca, close to the Puebla border, with a few in Puebla. Near Southern Puebla Mixteco. The largest group speaking Mixteco is in Santiago Chazumba. Some other villages with speakers are San Pedro y San Pablo Tequixtepec (in Oaxaca), Zapotitlán, Petlalcingo, and Totoltepec de Guerrero (in Puebla). Oto-Manguean, Mixtecan, Mixtec-Cuicatec, Mixtec. A distinct language. 65% inherent intelligibility of Xayacatlán, 53% of Cacaloxtepec, 24% of Chigmecatitlán, 19% of Cuyamecalco (Coatzospan). 75% of the speakers are over 50 years old. 75% of the speakers are scattered over a large area, with most villages having fewer than 15% of the population able to speak Mixteco. A large percentage of the populations of each village no longer speak Mixteco, but speak Spanish. Investigation needed: bilingual proficiency in Spanish.

MIXTECO, CHIGMACATITLÁN ***(SANTA MARÍA CHIGMECATITLÁN MIXTECO, CENTRAL PUEBLA MIXTECO, CHIGMACATITLÁN MIXTEC)*** [MII] 1,600 (1990 census). Puebla, straight south of Puebla city, about half way to Oaxaca border. Includes Santa Catarina Tlaltemplan. Oto-Manguean, Mixtecan, Mixtec-Cuicatec, Mixtec. 23% intelligibility with Chazumba (Southern Puebla; closest). An 'island' of

Mixteco surrounded by Popoloca and Náhuatl. Low intelligibility with all Mixteco; very different. A lot of bilingualism in Spanish. 217 speakers over 50 years old, 273 monolinguals (1990). 4,000 to 5,000 feet.

MIXTECO, COATZOSPAN ***(TEOTITLÁN MIXTECO, SAN JUAN COATZOSPAN MIXTECO, COATZOSPAN MIXTEC)*** [MIZ] 5,000 speakers, including 500 monolinguals (1994 SIL). Oaxaca. Oto-Manguean, Mixtecan, Mixtec-Cuicatec, Mixtec. 25% intelligibility with Chazumba. Cuyamecalco is close, but inherent intelligibility is inadequate. Bilingual level estimates for Spanish are Women: 0 90%, 1 5%, 2 2%, 3 1%, 4 1%, 5 1%; Men: 0 10%, 1 61%, 2 25%, 3 2%, 4 1%, 5 1%. Mazateco also used. Dictionary. VSO, tonal, short words, affixes, clitics. Literacy rate in first language: 5%. Literacy rate in second language: 60%. Scrub forest. Mountain slope. Pastoralists, swidden, peasant agriculturalists. 1,000 to 2,000 meters. Bible portions 1971-1978.

MIXTECO, CUYAMECALCO ***(CUYAMECALCO MIXTEC, CUICATLÁN MIXTEC)*** [QMZ] 2,600 speakers, including 143 monolinguals, 660 speakers in San Miguel, including 72 monolinguals (1994 SIL). Oaxaca, Cuyamecalco, San Miguel Santa Flor. Oto-Manguean, Mixtecan, Mixtec-Cuicatec, Mixtec. San Juan Coatzospan is close, but inherent intelligibility is inadequate. Bilingualism in Spanish. 17 monolinguals are between 5 and 14 years old (1994). Scrub forest. Mountain slope. Pastoralists, swidden, peasant agriculturalists. 1,000 to 2,000 meters.

MIXTECO, DIUXI-TILANTONGO ***(CENTRAL NOCHISTLÁN MIXTECO, DIUXI MIXTEC)*** [MIS] 8,500 including 300 monolinguals (1990 census). Oaxaca, 20 towns and villages in the Diuxi and Tilantongo area, Oaxaca City, Puebla City, Mexico City. Oto-Manguean, Mixtecan, Mixtec-Cuicatec, Mixtec. 37% intelligibility with Peñoles (Eastern); closer to Nuxaá. Bilingual level estimates for Spanish are 0 <20%, 1 <30%, 2 <20%, 3 <30%, 4 <3%, 5 <1%. VSO, tonal, short words, affixes, clitics, stems are CVCV or CVV. Savannah, scrub forest. Mountain mesa, slope. Peasant agriculturalists. 2,000 to 3,200 meters. NT, in press (1999).

MIXTECO, HUITEPEC ***(ZAACHILA MIXTECO, HUITEPEC MIXTEC, SAN ANTONIO HUITEPEC MIXTECO)*** [MXS] 4,000 including over 200 monolinguals, and 2,000 in the town of Huitepec (1990 census). Oaxaca, 60 km. west of Zaachila, 25 km. southwest of Peñoles, Huitepec Municipio, towns of San Antonio Huitepec, San Francisco Yucucundo, and San Francisco Infiernillo. Oto-Manguean, Mixtecan, Mixtec-Cuicatec, Mixtec. 77% intelligibility of Estetla (Eastern), 75% of Chalcatongo, 52% of Peñoles, 20% of Yosondúa, 8% of Tilantongo. Spoken in most homes in Huitepec town; more so in rural areas. Secondary school. Pine forest. Mountain slope. 7,000 to 8,000 feet.

MIXTECO, ITUNDUJIA ***(SANTA CRUZ ITUNDUJIA MIXTECO, ITUNDUJIA MIXTEC, EASTERN PUTLA MIXTECO)*** [MCE] 1,082 speakers including 33 monolinguals (1990 census). Oaxaca, Putla District, 10 km. southwest of Yosondua, 40 km. southeast of Putla. Most in Morelos and Guerrero villages. Oto-Manguean, Mixtecan, Mixtec-Cuicatec, Mixtec. 60% intelligibility of Yosondua, 59% of Chalcatongo, 25% of San Martín Peras, 15% of Amoltepec, 12% of Zacatepec, 10% of San Esteban Atatlahuca, Nuyoo, 0% of Ixtayutla. Bilingualism in Spanish. Nearly all of the monolinguals and over half of the speakers are over 50 years old.

MIXTECO, IXTAYUTLA ***(SANTIAGO IXTAYUTLA MIXTEC, IXTAYUTLA MIXTEC, NORTHEASTERN JAMILTEPEC MIXTECO)*** [VMJ] 5,500 speakers, including 2,800 monolinguals or more (1990 census). Oaxaca, Jamiltepec District, Santiago Ixtayutla and about 15 settlements (Nuyuku, Xiniyuva, La Humedad, Pueblo Viejo, Musko, Yukuyaa, Llano Verde, Yomuche, Carasul, Frutillo). Oto-Manguean, Mixtecan, Mixtec-Cuicatec, Cuicatec. 79% intelligibility of Amoltepec, 59% of Chayuco, 49% of Jamiltepec, 40% of San Juan Colorado, 30% of Zacatepec. School through 6th grade in Ixtayutla. Some settlements have schools. Subsistence agriculturalists: bananas, beans, maize; sell rope and goats. 1,800 feet. Christian, traditional religion.

MIXTECO, JAMILTEPEC ***(EASTERN JAMILTEPEC-SAN CRISTOBAL MIXTECO)*** [MXT] 10,000 (1983 SIL). Southwest Oaxaca. Oto-Manguean, Mixtecan, Mixtec-Cuicatec, Mixtec. Intelligibility and sociolinguistic attitudes make separate literature from Chayucu advisable. Bilingual level estimates for Spanish are 0 25%, 1 50%, 2 20%, 3 3%, 4 2%, 5 0%. VSO, tonal, short words, affixes, clitics. Semi-tropical. Mountain slope. Peasant agriculturalists. 750 to 1,000 feet. NT 1983.

MIXTECO, JUXTLAHUACA ***(JUXTLAHUACA MIXTEC, CENTRAL JUXTLAHUACA MIXTECO)*** [VMC] 16,000 speakers, including 5,500 monolinguals (1990 census). Oaxaca, central Santiago Juxtlahuaca, towns of San Sebastian Tecomaxtlahuaca, San Miguel Tlacotepec, Santos Reyes Tepejillo, Santa María Tindú, and Santa María Yucunicoco. Probably a few thousand in San Quintín Valley, Baja California. Oto-Manguean, Mixtecan, Mixtec-Cuicatec, Cuicatec. 84% intelligibility of Silacayoapan, 80% of Yucucani and San Miguel Peras, 63% of Santa Cruz Mixtepec, 48% of Coicoyán, 37% of Tezoatlán, 18% of Zacatepec, 10% of Ñumí. Secondary school. Many work in Culiacán or the USA. Little tillable land. Desert. Mountain slope. 4,000 to 6,000 feet.

MIXTECO, JUXTLAHUACA OESTE ***(WESTERN JUXTLAHUACA MIXTECO, COICOYÁN MIXTEC)*** [JMX] 25,000 including 7,000 in San Martín Peras, 2,000 in Santa Cruz Yucucani, 2,000 in San José Yoxocaño (1992 SIL). 7,000 monolinguals (1990 census). Oaxaca-Guerrero border due west of

Juxtlahuaca. In Oaxaca: San Martín Peras is at 17" 21' N Lat, 98" 14' W Long. Other municipios: Río Frijol, Santa Cruz Yucucani, San José Yoxocaño (all towns in these municipios). In Guerrero: Malvabisco, Rancho Limón, Río Aguacate, Boca de Mamey. Oto-Manguean, Mixtecan, Mixtec-Cuicatec, Mixtec. Dialects: SAN MARTÍN PERAS, COICOYÁN, SAN JUAN PIÑAS. 82% intelligibility of Metlatonoc, 80% of Silacayoapan, 65% of Juxtlahuaca, 19% of Cuatzoquitengo, 16% of Zacatepec. Very little comprehension or use of Spanish. There is a primary school in San Martín. Many work in Culiacán during the cold months. Pine forest. Mountain slope. Agriculturalists. 6,500 feet. Traditional religion, Christian.

MIXTECO, MAGDALENA PEÑASCO [QMP] 4,200 speakers, including over 1,050 monolinguals (1990 census). Oaxaca, Tlaxiaco District, municipios of Santa María Magdalena Peñasco, San Cristobal Amoltepec, and San Agustín Tlacotepec. Also includes the town of San Mateo Peñasco. Oto-Manguean, Mixtecan, Mixtec-Cuicatec, Mixtec. Dialects: SAN AGUSTÍN TLACOTEPEC, SAN CRISTÓBAL AMOLTEPEC MIXTECO, SAN MATEO PEÑASCO MIXTECO, SANTO DOMINGO HEUNDÍO MIXTECO, SAN MIGUEL ACHIUTLA MIXTECO. Speakers have 89% intelligibility of San Cristóbal Amoltepec, 76% of Tijaltepec and Sinicahua, 73% of San Miguel el Grande, 72% of Tlacotepec, 68% of Ocotepec, 64% of Nduaxico, 58% of Yucuañe. A distinct language, different from Santiago Amoltepec Mixteco. There is pride in the language and culture. Secondary school. Investigation needed: intelligibility with San Cristóbal Amoltepec, San Agustín Tlacotepec. Bilingual primary school. Agriculturalists: maize; weavers: tenates, hats. 6,600 feet.

MIXTECO, METLATONOC *(SAN RAFAEL MIXTECO)* [MXV] 42,000 to 44,000 including 14,000 to 15,000 monolinguals (1995 census). Eastern Guerrero, Metlatonoc, San Rafael, and towns further south. Oto-Manguean, Mixtecan, Mixtec-Cuicatec, Mixtec. 90% or higher intelligibility among nearby towns, but only 50% with most in the Alacatlatzala area. Xochapa Mixteco is a separate language. Investigation needed to determine if Chilistlahuaca and Ojo de Pescado are different. Mountain slope. Bible portions 1959-1998.

MIXTECO, MITLATONGO *(MITLATONGO MIXTEC)* [VMM] 1,800 speakers (1994 SIL). Oaxaca, Nochixtlán, Santiago Mitlatongo, Santa Cruz Mitlatongo. Oto-Manguean, Mixtecan, Mixtec-Cuicatec, Cuicatec. 70% intelligibility of Yutanduchi, 56% of Peñoles, 54% of San Juan Tamazola, 43% of Teita, 10% of Nuxaa, 8% of Diuxi. Children are learning Spanish, but it is limited. All children and adults speak Mixteco. Secondary school. Some men work outside, and a few in the USA. Mountain slope. Agriculturalists: maize, beans, anona (chirimoya, ice cream fruit), lima beans, dates. 7,000 feet.

MIXTECO, MIXTEPEC *(EASTERN JUXTLAHUACA MIXTECO, SAN JUAN MIXTEPEC MIXTECO, MIXTEPEC MIXTEC)* [MIX] 12,000 including 2,600 monolinguals (1990 census). Population total both countries 12,000 or more. Oaxaca, San Juan Mixtepec, and probably a few thousand in the San Quintín Valley of Baja California. Also spoken in USA. Oto-Manguean, Mixtecan, Mixtec-Cuicatec, Mixtec. Distinct from other Mixteco. Limited bilingualism in Spanish. Bible portions 1974.

MIXTECO, NOCHIXTLÁN SURESTE *(SOUTHEASTERN NOCHIXTLÁN MIXTEC, SANTO DOMINGO NUXAÁ MIXTECO, NUXAÁ MIXTECO)* [MXY] 7,000 including 4,075 monolinguals (1990 census). Oaxaca, Nochixtlán District, 30 km. along highway 190, starting 20 km. southeast of Nochixtlán, four turn-offs from highway 190. Well graded gravel road. Main towns are Santo Domingo Nuxaá, San Andrés Nuxiño, Santa Inez Zarogoza. Also Ojo de Agua Nuxaá, El Oro, La Herradura, La Unión Zaragoza, Reforma, La Paz, and other hamlets. Oto-Manguean, Mixtecan, Mixtec-Cuicatec, Mixtec. 60% to 70% intelligibility with Peñoles Mixteco. Speakers understand little of San Miguel Piedras or San Pedro Tidaá Mixteco. They speak the language in the home. Spanish is preferred in Santa Inez Zaragoza; elsewhere Mixteco is preferred. Dictionary. VSO, tonal. Literacy rate in first language: 5% to 10%. Literacy rate in second language: 75% to 100%. Pine forest in highest areas, mixed deciduous forest, scrub in lower areas. Mountain slope. Peasant agriculturalists. 1,800 to 2,500 meters.

MIXTECO, OAXACA NOROESTE *(NORTHWEST OAXACA MIXTEC)* [MXA] 2,500 including 2,195 monolinguals (1990 census). Northwest Oaxaca, towns of Santos Reyes Yucuná, Guadalupe Portezuelo, and San Simón Zahuatlán. Oto-Manguean, Mixtecan, Mixtec-Cuicatec, Mixtec. Bilingual level estimates for Spanish are 0 20%, 1 35%, 2 40%, 3 0%, 4 0%, 5 0%. Tonal, SVO, short words, clitics. Sparse to barren scrub or deciduous forest. Mountain slope. Peasant agriculturalists. 1,500 to 1,800 meters.

MIXTECO, OCOTEPEC *(SANTO TOMÁS OCOTEPEC MIXTECO, OCOTEPEC MIXTEC)* [MIE] 5,000 to 8,000 (1982 SIL). West central Oaxaca. Oto-Manguean, Mixtecan, Mixtec-Cuicatec, Mixtec. Dialect: SANTA CATARINA YOSONOTU. 80% intelligibility with Ñumí (Northwestern Tlaxiaco). Bilingual level estimates for Spanish are 0 40%, 1 30%, 2 25%, 3 5%, 4 0%, 5 0%. Investigation needed: intelligibility with dialect. VSO, tonal, short words, clitics. Pine forest. Mountain slope. Peasant agriculturalists. 2,500 meters. NT 1977.

MIXTECO, PEÑOLES *(EASTERN MIXTECO)* [MIL] 12,000 to 14,000 (1998 J. and M. Daly), including 2,000 monolinguals (1990 census). West central Oaxaca. Santa María Peñoles municipio, Monteflor,

San Mateo Tepantepec, Estetla and Cholula agencias; Santiago Tlazoyaltepec municipio; and Huazolotipac agencia in Huitepec municipio, Zaachila District, and San Mateo Sindihui town. Oto-Manguean, Mixtecan, Mixtec-Cuicatec, Mixtec. Dialects: SANTA MARÍA PEÑOLES (PEÑOLES), SANTIAGO TLAZOYALTEPEC (TLAZOYALTEPEC), SAN MATEO TEPANTEPEC (TEPANTEPEC). 14% intelligibility with Chalcatongo. Nuxaa has 30% intelligibility with Peñoles. Bilingual level estimates for Spanish are 0 25%, 1 20%, 2 30%, 3 20%, 4 4%, 5 1%. VSO, tonal, short words, clitics. Literacy rate in first language: 5%. Literacy rate in second language: 40%. Deciduous, pine forest. Mountain slope. Peasant agriculturalists, sedentary pastoralists. 1,500 to 2,600 meters. NT 1979.

MIXTECO, PINOTEPA NACIONAL ***(WESTERN JAMILTEPEC MIXTECO, COASTAL MIXTECO, LOWLAND JICALTEPEC MIXTECO)*** [MIO] 20,000 including 2,200 monolinguals (1990 census). Oaxaca, around Jamiltepec. Oto-Manguean, Mixtecan, Mixtec-Cuicatec, Mixtec. Investigation needed to determine how different Huazolititlán and Don Luís Pinotepa are. Bilingual level estimates for Spanish are 0 23%, 1 24%, 2 22%, 3 13%, 4 10%, 5 8%. VSO, tonal, short words, affixes, clitics. Scrub forest. Coastal plains. Swidden agriculturalists. 300 to 500 meters. NT 1980.

MIXTECO, PUEBLA SUR ***(SOUTHERN PUEBLA MIXTEC, ACATLÁN MIXTECO)*** [MIT] 1,330 speakers including 386 monolinguals (1990 census). Oaxaca, southwestern Puebla, town of Zapotitlán Palmas. Oto-Manguean, Mixtecan, Mixtec-Cuicatec, Mixtec. 53% intelligibility with Cacaloxtepec (Huajuapan; closest). Bilingual level estimates for Spanish are 0 0%, 1 5%, 2 20%, 3 60%, 4 10%, 5 5%. Most children under 16 have limited or no ability in Mixteco and are monolingual in Spanish. VSO, tonal, short words, clitics. Mountain slope. Sedentary pastoralists, peasant agriculturalists. 1,800 to 2,000 meters. NT 1978.

MIXTECO, SAN JUAN COLORADO [MJC] 13,500 including 3,100 monolinguals (1990 census). Oaxaca. Oto-Manguean, Mixtecan, Mixtec-Cuicatec, Mixtec. Bilingual level estimates for Spanish are 0 60%, 1 35%, 2 5%, 3 0%, 4 0%, 5 0%. VSO, tonal, short words, clitics, affixes. Semi-tropical. Mountain slope. Peasant agriculturalists. 500 to 700 feet. NT 1994.

MIXTECO, SAN JUAN TEITA ***(SAN JUAN TEITA MIXTEC, TEITA MIXTECO)*** [QMC] 550 (1994 SIL). Oaxaca, Tlaxiaco District, 30 km. southeast of Tlaxiaco, towns of San Juan Teita, San Agustín Tlacotepec. Oto-Manguean, Mixtecan, Mixtec-Cuicatec, Mixtec. May be closest to Diuxi Mixteco, but not close enough to any other Mixteco for adequate comprehension. All ages and sexes speak some Spanish; some women have only basic knowledge, and some young people and men are very fluent. In San Agustín Tlacotepec all but older people prefer and speak Spanish. All ages. Nearly everyone prefers Mixteco for family and informal usage. Literacy rate in second language: Possibly 40% in Spanish. Tropical forest, scrub forest desert. Mountain valley. Peasant agriculturalists, palm and cactus fiber gathering. 1,500 to 2,500 meters.

MIXTECO, SAN MIGUEL EL GRANDE [MIG] 14,453 including 10,000 in other dialects, 4,453 in Chalcatongo, 800 monolinguals in other dialects, 226 in Chalcatongo (1990 census). West central Oaxaca. Oto-Manguean, Mixtecan, Mixtec-Cuicatec, Mixtec. Dialects: SAN PEDRO MOLINOS, SAN MATEO PEÑASCO, SANTA MARÍA YOSOYÚA, SANTA CATARINA TICUÁ, SAN MIGUEL CHALCATONGO. 86% intelligibility with Yosondua (closest). Investigation needed: intelligibility with dialects. VSO, tonal, short words, clitics. Pine forest. Mountain slope. Peasant agriculturalists. 1,846 to 3,077 meters. NT 1951, out of print.

MIXTECO, SAN MIGUEL PIEDRAS [QMG] 448 speakers out of a population of 1,123 (1990 census). Oaxaca, Nochixtlán District, Yutanduchi de Guerrero. Oto-Manguean, Mixtecan, Mixtec-Cuicatec, Mixtec. 49% intelligibility of Estetla (Eastern), 29% of Soyaltepec, Yosondúa, 18% of Peñoles, 15% of Chalcatongo, 13% of Tilantongo, 11% of Chicahua. Bilingualism in Spanish. A few speakers are in the lower age categories, but most are over 50 years old.

MIXTECO, SANTA MARÍA ZACATEPEC ***(ZACATEPEC MIXTEC, SANTA MARÍA ZACATEPEC MIXTEC, SOUTHERN PUTLA MIXTECO, "TACUATE")*** [MZA] 6,000 including 3,000 in Zacatepec and 3,000 in surrounding rancherías and villages (1992 E. Farris SIL). Oaxaca, 45 km. south of Putla, on paved road from Tlaxiaco to Pinotepa Nacional. Towns of Tapanco, Nejapa, Atotonilco. Oto-Manguean, Mixtecan, Mixtec-Cuicatec, Mixtec. 64% intelligibility with Ixtayutla (closest) 63% with Jicaltepec (Western Jamiltepec Mixteco), 40% to 50% with Metlatonoc, 25% to 30% with Yoloxochitl. Called "Tacuates" by people in the area including Indians, which can be offensive depending on context and other signals. Literacy rate in first language: 1%. Literacy rate in second language: 30%. 4,000 feet. Bible portions 1995.

MIXTECO, SILACAYOAPAN [MKS] 15,000 to 17,000 including 1,500 monolinguals (1990 census). Oaxaca, including towns of Santo Domingo Tonala (5,704 in 1990 census) and San Jorge Nuchita (3,052), and Tijuana. Oto-Manguean, Mixtecan, Mixtec-Cuicatec, Mixtec. Dialect: SAN SIMÓN ZAHUATLÁN. 70% intelligibility with Metlatonoc, 68% with Santa María Peras. Cuatzoquitengo may need separate literature; testing incomplete; also Guadalupe Portezuelo (65% intelligibility with Silacayoapan). Bilingual level estimates for Spanish are 0 20%, 1 40%, 2 28%, 3 10%, 4 2%, 5 0%.

Grammar. VSO, tonal, short words, affixes, clitics. Desert, scrub forest. Mountain mesa. Swidden, peasant agriculturalists. 2,100 to 3,000 meters. NT 1999.

MIXTECO, SINDIHUI [QMH] 138 speakers (1990 census). West central Oaxaca. Oto-Manguean, Mixtecan, Mixtec-Cuicatec, Mixtec. Distinct from Yutanduchi. All over 50 years old (1990). Nearly extinct.

MIXTECO, SINICAHUA *(SINICAHUA MIXTEC, SAN ANTONIO SINICAHUA MIXTECO)* [QMI] 1,300 speakers, including 400 monolinguals or more (1990 census). Oaxaca, Tlaxiaco District, San Antonio Sinicahua, Siniyucu, and settlements of Sinicahua Municipio. Oto-Manguean, Mixtecan, Mixtec-Cuicatec, Mixtec. Speakers have 75% intelligibility of Yosoyúa, 73% of Ocotepec, 72% of San Miguel el Grande, and 51% of Nduaxico (Northern Tlaxiaco Mixteco). A distinct language. Speakers have extremely limited ability in Spanish. Primary and secondary schools. Agriculturalists: maize, wheat, peas. 8,600 feet.

MIXTECO, SOYALTEPEC *(SAN BARTOLO SOYALTEPEC MIXTECO, SOYALTEPEC MIXTEC)* [VMQ] 322 speakers out of 926 population (1990 census). Oaxaca, Teposcolula District, village of San Bartolo Soyaltepec and Guadalupe Gabilera. Oto-Manguean, Mixtecan, Mixtec-Cuicatec, Mixtec. 28% intelligibility of Tilantongo, 25% of Ñumi, 23% of Apoala. Bilingualism in Spanish. All ages in some places. Children are learning Mixteco in Guadalupe. Investigation needed: bilingual proficiency.

MIXTECO, TACAHUA *(TACAHUA MIXTEC, SANTA CRUZ TACAHUA MIXTECO)* [QMT] 585 speakers, including 78 monolinguals (1990 census). Oaxaca, Tlaxiaco District, east of Yosondúa, southeast of San Miguel el Grande. Oto-Manguean, Mixtecan, Mixtec-Cuicatec, Mixtec. 70% of the monolinguals are over 50 years old, none under 35.

MIXTECO, TAMAZOLA *(SAN JUAN TAMAZOLA MIXTEC, TAMAZOLA MIXTECO)* [VMX] 2,500 (1990 census). Oaxaca, Nochixtlán, San Juan Tamazola. Oto-Manguean, Mixtecan, Mixtec-Cuicatec, Mixtec. Bilingualism in Spanish.

MIXTECO, TEZOATLÁN *(TEZOATLÁN DE SEGURA Y LUNA MIXTECO)* [MXB] 6,200 including 850 monolinguals (1990 census). Oaxaca, Tezoatlán area, southwest of Huajuapan, about 40 to 50 km. off the highway by gravel road; 25 miles south of Cacaloxtepec; towns of Yucuquimi de Ocampo, San Andrés Yutatío, Yucuñuti de Benito Juárez, San Juan Diquiyú, San Marcos de Garzón, San Martín del Río, Santa Catarina Yotandu, San Isidro de Zaragoza, San Valentín. Oto-Manguean, Mixtecan, Mixtec-Cuicatec, Mixtec. Dialects: TEZOATLÁN, YUCU ÑUTI. 70% to 80% intelligibility with Silacayoapan and Atenango. Some are bilingual in Spanish. All ages. Speakers have pride in the language. Swidden agriculturalists: maize; basket weavers. Bible portions 1992.

MIXTECO, TIDAÁ *(TIDAÁ MIXTEC, NORTH CENTRAL NOCHIXTLÁN MIXTECO)* [MTX] 550 speakers out of a population of about 900 (1990 census). Oaxaca. Oto-Manguean, Mixtecan, Mixtec-Cuicatec, Mixtec. 60% intelligibility with Peñoles (Eastern); closest. Nuxaa is close. Bilingualism in Spanish. 2 monolinguals are over 50. Most speakers are over 40. 13% of children 5 to 15 years old are speakers (1990). Other children are not learning Mixteco. Investigation needed: bilingual proficiency in Spanish.

MIXTECO, TIJALTEPEC *(TIJALTEPEC MIXTEC, SAN PABLO TIJALTEPEC MIXTECO)* [QMJ] 3,300 to 3,500 speakers, including 800 to 900 monolinguals or more (1990 census). Oaxaca, southeastern Tlaxiaco District, towns of San Pablo Tijaltepec, Santa María Yosoyúa, and all their communities. Oto-Manguean, Mixtecan, Mixtec-Cuicatec, Mixtec. Speakers have 89% intelligibility of San Miguel el Grande and Yosoyúa, 82% of San Mateo Peñasco, 81% of Sinicahua and 66% of Teita. A distinct language. Primary schools, 1 secondary school. Some work outside in Veracruz or the USA. Investigation needed: intelligibility with San Felipe Tindaco, Sta. Catarina Yujía, Sta. María Yosoyúa. Agriculturalists: maize, wheat, beans, chilacayote squash. 7,500 feet.

MIXTECO, TLAXIACO NORTE *(NORTHERN TLAXIACO MIXTEC, SAN JUAN ÑUMÍ MIXTECO, ÑUMÍ MIXTECO)* [MOS] 14,000 (1990 census). Oaxaca, Tlaxiaco District, San Juan Ñumí and Santiago Nundichi municipios; Teposcolula District, San Antonino Monte Verde and San Sebastián Nicananduta municipios. Oto-Manguean, Mixtecan, Mixtec-Cuicatec, Mixtec. Dialects: MONTE VERDE MIXTECO, YOSOÑAMA. Literacy rate in first language: 20%. Literacy rate in second language: 40%. Bible portions 1995.

MIXTECO, TLAXIACO SUROESTE *(SOUTHWESTERN TLAXIACO MIXTEC, SANTIAGO NUYOO MIXTECO, NUYOO MIXTECO, SOUTHEASTERN OCOTEPEC MIXTECO)* [MEH] 6,000 including 1,000 monolinguals (1990 census). Oaxaca. Oto-Manguean, Mixtecan, Mixtec-Cuicatec, Mixtec. Dialects: NUYOO, YUCUHITI. 54% intelligibility with Atatláhuca (closest). Literacy rate in first language: 5%. Literacy rate in second language: 60%. Bible portions 1999.

MIXTECO, TUTUTEPEC *(SAN PEDRO TUTUTEPEC MIXTECO, TUTUTEPEC MIXTEC)* [MTU] 817 speakers out of 30,046 in the ethnic group (1990 census). Oaxaca, 10 km. north of coastal highway, on dirt road that turns off pavement 40 km. southeast of Jamiltepec. Includes San Pedro Tututepec, Santa María Acatepec, Santa Cruz Tututepec, other towns and villages. Oto-Manguean, Mixtecan, Mixtec-Cuicatec, Mixtec. Dialect: SANTA MARÍA ACATEPEC. 61% intelligibility with Ixtayutla (closest), 50% with Pinotepa. Bilingualism in Spanish. There are children and 2 monolingual speakers. Most speakers are over 50 years old (1990). Most vigorous in Acatepec, but young people not using Mixteco. 2,000 feet or less.

MIXTECO, YOLOXOCHITL ***(YOLOXOCHITL MIXTEC)*** [QMY] 2,540 speakers (1994 SIL). Southeastern Guerrero, San Luís Acatlán Municipio, just south of Tlapaneco, and about half way between Metlatonoc and Ayutla Mixteco; town of Yoloxochitl and possibly a few speakers in Cuanacastitlán. Oto-Manguean, Mixtecan, Mixtec-Cuicatec, Mixtec. Metlatonoc has 35% intelligibility of Yoloxochitl, and Ayutla has 30% intelligibility of it. There is a bilingual primary school with Spanish. Mixteco used for everything except speaking to outsiders. Coastal. Agriculturalists: maize, beans, tropical fruits, jamaica; embroidery. 1,600 feet.

MIXTECO, YOSONDÚA ***(SANTIAGO YOSONDÚA MIXTECO, YOSONDÚA MIXTEC, SOUTHERN TLAXIACO MIXTECO)*** [MPM] 5,000 including 240 monolinguals (1990 census). Oaxaca. Oto-Manguean, Mixtecan, Mixtec-Cuicatec, Mixtec. 70% intelligibility with San Miguel el Grande and Chalcatongo (closest). San Mateo Sindihui has 19% intelligibility with Yosondúa. Bilingual level estimates for Spanish are 0 15%, 1 20%, 2 35%, 3 20%, 4 5%, 5 5%. Investigation needed: intelligibility with San Mateo Sindihui. Gallery, pine forest. Mountain mesa, slope. Peasant agriculturalists. NT 1988.

MIXTECO, YUCUAÑE ***(SAN BARTOMOMÉ YUCUAÑE MIXTECO, YUCUAÑE MIXTEC)*** [MVG] 515 including 88 monolinguals (1990 census). Oaxaca, northeastern Tlaxiaco District, 30 km. southeast of Tlaxiaco, town of San Bartolomé Yucuañe. Many work in D.F. and USA. Oto-Manguean, Mixtecan, Mixtec-Cuicatec, Mixtec. May be closest to Diuxi Mixteco, but not close enough to any other Mixteco for adequate comprehension. Speakers have 87% intelligibility of San Cristobal Amoltepec, 86% of Yosoyúa, 85% of Magdalena Peñasco, 64% of Teita, 60% of Nduaxico (Northern Tlaxiaco Mixteco), 56% of Tlacotepec. 2 dialects in different halves of San Agustín Tlacotepec. All ages and sexes speak some Spanish; some women have only basic knowledge, and some young people and men are very fluent. In San Agustín Tlacotepec all but older people prefer and speak Spanish. All ages. Nearly everyone prefers Mixteco for family and informal usage. Primary and secondary schools. Literacy rate in second language: Possibly 40% in Spanish. Tropical forest, scrub forest desert. Mountain valley. Peasant agriculturalists: maize; palm and cactus fiber gathering. 6,000 feet.

MIXTECO, YUTANDUCHI ***(SOUTHERN NOCHIXTLÁN MIXTEC, YUTANDUCHI MIXTEC)*** [MAB] 1,800 including 38 monolinguals (1990 census). Oaxaca, Nochixtlán District, Yutanduchi de Guerrero. Oto-Manguean, Mixtecan, Mixtec-Cuicatec, Mixtec. 49% intelligibility of Estetla (Eastern), 48% of San Juan Tamazola, 20% of Yosondúa and Soyaltepec, 36% to 18% of Peñoles, 15% of Chalcatongo, 13% of Tilantongo. Bilingualism in Spanish. Primary and secondary school. Mountain slope. Agriculturalists; export palm leaf; make rope and woven mats. 5,000 feet.

MOCHO ***(MOTOZINTLECO)*** [MHC] 168 speakers, no monolinguals (1990 census). Chiapas, on border of Guatemala and Mexico (area of Tuzantán and Motozintla). Mayan, Kanjobalan-Chujean, Kanjobalan, Mocho. Dialects: MOTOZINTLECO, TUZANTECO. Not intelligible with Mam dialects (Paul Townsend SIL 1973). Tuzanteco and Mocho are two distinct dialects of the same language (Terrence Kaufman 1967). Bilingualism in Spanish. Only a few speakers still use the language in the home.

NÁHUATL CENTRAL ***(CENTRAL AZTEC, TLAXCALA-PUEBLA NÁHUATL)*** [NHN] 40,000 speakers with 1,000 monolinguals (1990 census). Ethnic population 63,000 in 1986. Speakers of all Náhuatl varieties: 1,376,898 (1980 census). States of Tlaxcala and Puebla. Uto-Aztecan, Southern Uto-Aztecan, Aztecan, General Aztec, Aztec. The most monolingual location is northeast of Puebla City about 15 km. Spanish is used by a few. There are some monolingual children.

NÁHUATL, CLASSICAL ***(CLASSICAL AZTEC)*** [NCI] Central México, Tenochtitlán, Aztec Empire. Uto-Aztecan, Southern Uto-Aztecan, Aztecan, General Aztec, Aztec. Extinct. NT 1833.

NÁHUATL, COATEPEC ***(COATEPEC AZTEC)*** [NAZ] 1,400 speakers including 15 monolinguals (1990 census). State of Mexico, Coatepec Costales, Tlacultlapa, Texcalco, Tonalapa, Maxela, Machito de las Flores, Chilacachapa, Miacacsingo, Los Sabinos, and Acapetlahuaya, all west of Iguala, Guerrero. The language has strongest usage in Coatepec Costales and Chilacachapa. Uto-Aztecan, Southern Uto-Aztecan, Aztecan, General Aztec, Aztec. 54% intelligibility of Santa Catarina (Morelos), 48% of Atliaca (Guerrero), 35% of Copalillo Guerrero, 28% of Zongolica (Orizaba). Bilingualism in Spanish. It is reported that only those over 40 speak the language. 11 monolinguals are over 50 (1990 census). Investigation needed: bilingual proficiency.

NÁHUATL, DURANGO ***(MEXICANERO, DURANGO AZTEC)*** [NLN] 1,000 (1990 census). Southern Durango, San Pedro de la Jicoras and San Juan de Buenaventura. One day trail from nearest air strip or highway. Uto-Aztecan, Southern Uto-Aztecan, Aztecan, General Aztec, Aztec. 76% intelligibility with Michoacán Náhuatl (closest). Moderate bilingualism in Spanish. All ages. Vigorous. 'Mexicanero' is the local name.

NÁHUATL, GUERRERO ***(GUERRERO AZTEC)*** [NAH] 150,000 to 200,000 (1998 SIL). Balsas River, Guerrero. Uto-Aztecan, Southern Uto-Aztecan, Aztecan, General Aztec, Aztec. Bilingual level estimates for Spanish are 0 5%, 1 20%, 2 40%, 3 20%, 4 10%, 5 5%. SVO, nontonal, long words, affixes, clitics. Desert. Mountain mesa. Peasant agriculturalists. 600 to 2,200 meters. Traditional religion, Christian. NT 1987.

NÁHUATL, HUASTECA, ESTE ***(EASTERN HUASTECA AZTEC, HIDALGO NÁHUATL, HUASTECA NÁHUATL)*** [NAI] 410,000 (1991 SIL). Huautla, Hidalgo is the center; also in Puebla and Veracruz. 1,500 villages. Uto-Aztecan, Southern Uto-Aztecan, Aztecan, General Aztec, Aztec. 85% intelligibility between Eastern and Western Huasteca Náhuatl. Survey of other dialects needed. Southeastern Huasteca Náhuatl may need separate materials. Bilingual level estimates for Spanish are 0 50%, 1 10%, 2 10%, 3 10%, 4 19%, 5 1%. Nontonal, SVO, long words, affixes. Radio programs. Scrub forest. Mountain mesa. Swidden agriculturalists. 0 to 2,000 meters. NT 1984.

NÁHUATL, HUASTECO OESTE ***(WESTERN HUASTECA AZTEC, TAMAZUNCHALE NÁHUATL, HUASTECA NÁHUATL)*** [NHW] 400,000 (1991 SIL). Tamazunchale, San Luis Potosí is the center; also in Hidalgo. 1,500 villages. Uto-Aztecan, Southern Uto-Aztecan, Aztecan, General Aztec, Aztec. Dialects: CENTRAL HUASTECA NÁHUATL, WESTERN HUASTECA NÁHUATL. 85% intelligibility between Eastern and Western Huasteco Náhuatl. Separate literature may be needed for 100,000 speakers of a Central dialect. Bilingual level estimates for Spanish are 0 50%, 1 10%, 2 10%, 3 10%, 4 19%, 5 1%. Investigation needed: intelligibility with Central Huasteca. Nontonal, SVO, long words, affixes. Radio programs. Scrub forest. Mountain mesa. Swidden agriculturalists. 0 to 2,000 meters. NT 1986.

NÁHUATL, HUAXCALECA ***(HUAXCALECA AZTEC, CHICHIQUILA NÁHUATL)*** [NHQ] 7,000 speakers, including 55 monolinguals (1990 census). 800 speakers are over 50. 2% under 20 speak Náhuatl. 40 of the monolinguals are over 50. The population in about 12 municipios no longer speak Náhuatl. Puebla, towns of Chichiquila and Chilchotla. Uto-Aztecan, Southern Uto-Aztecan, Aztecan, General Aztec, Aztec. 87% intelligibility of Sierra de Puebla Náhuatl, 85% on Orizaba Náhuatl.

NÁHUATL, ISTMO-COSOLEACAQUE ***(ISTHMUS NÁHUATL, COSOLEACAQUE AZTEC)*** [NHK] 5,144 speakers, including 12 monolinguals (1990 census). Veracruz, Cosoleacaque, Oteapan, Jáltipan de Morelos, Hidalgotitlán, Soconusco. Uto-Aztecan, Southern Uto-Aztecan, Aztecan, General Aztec, Aztec. 84% intelligibility of Pajapan, 83% of Mecayapan, 46% on Xoteapan. Bilingualism in Spanish. Most of the monolinguals are over 50 years old. Investigation needed: bilingual proficiency.

NÁHUATL, ISTMO-MECAYAPAN ***(ISTHMUS NAHUAT, ISTHMUS AZTEC, MECAYAPAN NAHUAT)*** [NAU] 20,000 (1994 SIL). Southern Veracruz, Mecayapan Municipio, Mecayapan and Tatahuicapan towns. Uto-Aztecan, Southern Uto-Aztecan, Aztecan, General Aztec, Aztec. It may be intelligible with Pipil of Honduras and El Salvador. Dictionary. Grammar. Bible portions 1952.

NÁHUATL, ISTMO-PAJAPAN ***(ISTHMUS NÁHUAT, PAJAPAN NÁHUAT)*** [NHP] 7,000 speakers, including 500 monolinguals (1990 census). Veracruz, Pajapan, San Juan Volador, Santanón, Sayultepec, Jicacal. Uto-Aztecan, Southern Uto-Aztecan, Aztecan, General Aztec, Aztec. 83% intelligibility of Mecayapan (Isthmus Náhuatl), 94% of Oteapan (Cosoleacaque). Bible portions 1990.

NÁHUATL, IXHUATLANCILLO [NHX] 4,000 speakers, including 600 monolinguals or more (1990 census). Veracruz, Ixhuatlancillo Municipio, town of Ixhuatlancillo, just 15 minutes north of Orizaba city. Uto-Aztecan, Southern Uto-Aztecan, Aztecan, General Aztec, Aztec. 67% intelligibility of Chilac (Southeastern Puebla), 60% of Zautla, 50% of Canoa and Teopoxco, 48% of Orizaba, low intelligibility of other Náhuatl. All ages. 50% of children are totally monolingual upon entering school. 60% to 70% of each age group is monolingual. There are primary schools and 1 secondary. Animal husbandry: cattle; agriculturalists: sugarcane; merchants. 4,500 feet.

NÁHUATL, MICHOACÁN ***(MICHOACÁN NAHUAL, MICHOACÁN AZTEC)*** [NCL] 3,000 (1990 census). Michoacán near the coast around Pómaro. Uto-Aztecan, Southern Uto-Aztecan, Aztecan, General Aztec, Aztec. Bilingual level estimates for Spanish are 0 0%, 1 0%, 2 0%, 3 45%, 4 50%, 5 5%. SVO, VSO, long words, affixes. Literacy rate in first language: 5% to 10% (mainly children). Literacy rate in second language: 35%. Scrub forest. Mountain slope. Sedentary pastoralists, swidden agriculturalists. 200 meters. NT 1998.

NÁHUATL, MORELOS [NHM] 15,000 speakers, including possibly 200 to 500 monolinguals (1990 census). Morelos, towns of Cuentepec, Santa Catarina Tepoztlán, Tetela del Volcán, Hueyapan, Temixco, Xocotitlán, Tepetlapa, Puente de Ixtla. Uto-Aztecan, Southern Uto-Aztecan, Aztecan, General Aztec, Aztec. 72% inherent intelligibility of Cuaohueyalta (Northern Puebla), 69% of Atliaca (Guerrero), 54% of Macuilocatl (Western Huasteca), 40% of Yahualica (Eastern Huasteca), 36% of Pómaro (Michoacán), 34% of Tetelcingo, 27% of Chilac (Southeast Puebla), 19% of Tatóscac (Highland Puebla), 0% on Mecayapan (Isthmus). Dialects in Canoa, Tlaxcala, and northern Puebla need to be compared with this. Bilingual level estimates for Spanish are 0 0%, 1 5%, 2 10%, 3 45%, 4 30%, 5 10%. Only a few children do not speak Náhuatl. Cuentepec has the most vigorous language use. There is a secondary school. Nontonal, SVO, long words, affixes. There is a bilingual primary school. Deciduous forest. Mountain mesa. Peasant agriculturalists. 4,000 feet or higher.

NÁHUATL, OAXACA NORTE ***(NORTHERN OAXACA NÁHUATL)*** [NHY] 9,000 including 1,400 monolinguals (1990 census). Northwestern Oaxaca, near Southeast Puebla Náhuatl, towns of Santa María Teopoxco, San Antonio Nanahuatipan, San Gabriel Casa Blanca, Teotitlán del Camino, San Martín Toxpalan, Ignacio Zaragosa, Apixtepec, El Manzano de Mazatlán, Cosolapa, Tesonapa (one of the last 2 towns is in Veracruz). In Puebla: Coxcatlán. Uto-Aztecan, Southern Uto-Aztecan, Aztecan, General Aztec, Aztec. 80% intelligibility of Orizaba Náhuatl, 76% of Southeast Puebla and Canoa, 75% of North Puebla, 48% of Tatóscac.

NÁHUATL, OMETEPEC ***(OMETEPEC AZTEC)*** [NHT] 433 (1990 census), 12 towns. Southern Guerrero, Arcelia, Acatepec, Quetzalapa de Azoyú, Rancho de Cuananchinicha, and El Carmen; and some in Oaxaca, Juxtlahuaca District, Cruz Alta and San Vicente Piñas towns; and Putla District, Concepción Guerrero town. Uto-Aztecan, Southern Uto-Aztecan, Aztecan, General Aztec, Aztec. Intelligibility testing in Quetzalapa yielded 77% on Santa Catarina, México (near Texcoco) and 70% on Atliaca, Guerrero. May be 3 languages. Bilingualism in Spanish. Investigation needed: intelligibility with dialects, bilingual proficiency.

NÁHUATL, ORIZABA ***(ORIZABA AZTEC, NÁHUATL DE LA SIERRA DE ZONGOLICA)*** [NLV] 120,000 (1991 SIL). Veracruz, Orizaba area. Uto-Aztecan, Southern Uto-Aztecan, Aztecan, General Aztec, Aztec. 79% intelligibility with closest Náhuatl (Morelos). Bible portions 1995.

NÁHUATL, PUEBLA CENTRAL ***(CENTRAL PUEBLA AZTEC, SOUTHWESTERN PUEBLA NÁHUATL)*** [NCX] 16,000 speakers, including 1,430 monolinguals, 800 in Teopantlán, 600 in Huatlatlauca (1998 SIL). South of Puebla City (97" 08' 56 W Long, 17" 10' 27 N Lat), Teopantlán, Tepatlaxco de Hidalgo, Tochimilco, Atoyatempan, Huatlathauca, Huehuetlán (near Molcaxac). Uto-Aztecan, Southern Uto-Aztecan, Aztecan, General Aztec, Aztec. 87% intelligibility of Zongolica, Ver.; 82% of Chilac, Pue. and Tlaxpanaloya, Pue.; 69% of Zautla, Pue.; 68% of Canoa, Pue.; 60% of Teopoxco, Oax. Bilingualism in Spanish. 70% to 80% of children entering school in some towns do not speak Spanish. In other towns the younger generation are not learning Náhuatl. There are schools in most towns. Agriculturalists, mat makers, laborers to other areas. 5,000 feet or more.

NÁHUATL, PUEBLA NORTE ***(NORTH PUEBLA AZTEC)*** [NCJ] 60,000 (1990 census). Naupan, northern Puebla. Uto-Aztecan, Southern Uto-Aztecan, Aztecan, General Aztec, Aztec. Bilingual level estimates for Spanish are 0 20%, 1 30%, 2 30%, 3 15%, 4 5%, 5 0%. SVO, nontonal, long words, affixes, clitics. Pine forest. Mountain slope. Swidden, peasant agriculturalists. 2,000 meters. NT 1979.

NÁHUATL, PUEBLA SURESTE ***(SOUTHEASTERN PUEBLA NÁHUATL, TEHUACÁN NÁHUATL)*** [NHS] 130,000 (1991 SIL). Southeast Puebla, Tehuacán region, Chilac and San Sebastián Zinacatepec area. Uto-Aztecan, Southern Uto-Aztecan, Aztecan, General Aztec, Aztec. Approximately 60% intelligibility with Morelos Náhuatl. Bilingual level estimates for Spanish are 0 30%, 1 20%, 2 20%, 3 20%, 4 10%, 5 10%. Nontonal, long words, affixes. Desert. Mountain slope, plains. Peasant, intensive agriculturalists with irrigation. Bible portions 1992-1995.

NÁHUATL, PUEBLA, SIERRA ***(SIERRA DE PUEBLA NÁHUAT, HIGHLAND PUEBLA NÁHUAT, SIERRA AZTEC, ZACAPOAXTLA NÁHUAT, ZACAPOAXTLA MEJICANO)*** [AZZ] 125,000 (1983). Northeast Puebla. Uto-Aztecan, Southern Uto-Aztecan, Aztecan, General Aztec, Aztec. Bilingual level estimates for Spanish, Totonaca are 0 20%, 1 30%, 2 30%, 3 10%, 4 5%, 5 5%. VSO, nontonal, long words, affixes. Tropical forest. Mountain slope. Pastoralists, peasant agriculturalists. 1,000 to 1,500 meters. NT 1979.

NÁHUATL, SANTA MARÍA LA ALTA ***(SANTA MARÍA NÁHUATL)*** [NHZ] 2,000 to 3,000 speakers, including at least 9 monolinguals (1992 SIL). Puebla, Santa María la Alta, Atenayuca. A pocket northwest of Tehuacán, off the Puebla-Tehuacán highway. Uto-Aztecan, Southern Uto-Aztecan, Aztecan, General Aztec, Aztec. 60% intelligibility of Pómaro (Michoacán), 53% of Huatlatlauca, Puebla; 50% of Zautla (Highland Puebla), Chilac (Southeastern Puebla); 40% of Zongolica (Orizaba); 33% of Mecayapan, Veracruz (Isthmus); 30% of Canoa, Puebla. Reported to be bilingual in Spanish. Investigation needed: bilingual proficiency in Spanish.

NÁHUATL, TABASCO ***(TABASCO AZTEC)*** [NHC] State of Tabasco, towns of Cupilco and Tecominoacan. Uto-Aztecan, Southern Uto-Aztecan, Aztecan, General Aztec, Aztec. Recently extinct. Extinct.

NÁHUATL, TEMASCALTEPEC ***(TEMASCALTEPEC AZTEC, ALMOMOLOYA NÁHUATL)*** [NHV] 311 speakers in 4 communities (1990 census). There may be fewer actual speakers. State of México, towns of San Mateo Almomoloa, Santa Ana, La Comunidad, and Potrero de San José, southwest of Toluca. Uto-Aztecan, Southern Uto-Aztecan, Aztecan, General Aztec, Aztec. 53% intelligibility of Coatepec, Guerrero; 45% of Pómaro, Michoacán; 40% of Santa Catarina, Morelos; 10% of Tlaxpanaloya, Puebla. Reported to be bilingual in Spanish. Investigation needed: bilingual proficiency.

NÁHUATL, TENANGO ***(SAN MIGUEL TENANGO NÁHUATL, TENANGO AZTEC)*** [NHI] 1,500 to 2,000 (1999 SIL). North of Puebla City, just south of Zacatlán, Puebla, 8 km. on a road which branches to the east. 6 towns: San Miguel Tenango, Yehuala, Cuacuila, Tetelatzingo, Zonotla, Zoquitla. Uto-Aztecan, Southern Uto-Aztecan, Aztecan, General Aztec, Aztec. Close to Southeastern Puebla Náhuatl, but mother tongue speakers of both discovered many differences over a 2-day period. About 50% to 60% intelligibility with Sierra Náhuatl and Northern Puebla Náhuatl, about 80% to 90% with Southeastern Puebla Náhuatl. Most speakers can apparently speak some Spanish, but are more comfortable in Náhuatl. Children play in Náhuatl. Positive attitudes toward Náhuatl. Agriculturalists: corn, peas, chilicayotes. 2,000 meters. Christian.

NÁHUATL, TETELCINGO ***(TETELCINGO AZTEC)*** [NHG] 3,500 (1990 census). State of Morelos, town of Tetelcingo. Uto-Aztecan, Southern Uto-Aztecan, Aztecan, General Aztec, Aztec. Distinct from Morelos Náhuatl. Bilingual level estimates for Spanish are 0 1%, 1 5%, 2 30%, 3 24%, 4 30%, 5 10%. Grammar. SVO, VSO, VOS (order of frequency), nontonal, long words, affixes, clitics. Savannah. Mountain slope, plains. Agriculture. 1,500 to 1,800 meters. NT 1980.

NÁHUATL, TLALITZLIPA [NHJ] 108 speakers (1990 census). Near Zacatlán, Puebla, 1 village. Uto-Aztecan, Southern Uto-Aztecan, Aztecan, General Aztec, Aztec. 77% inherent intelligibility of Tlaxpanaloya (North Puebla), 58% of Macuilocatl (Western Huasteco Náhuatl), 41% of Tatóscac (Highland Puebla). Nearly extinct.

NÁHUATL, TLAMACAZAPA [NUZ] 1,548, including 12 monolinguals (1990 census). Tlamacazapa, 1 hour from Taxco on a good road. Uto-Aztecan, Southern Uto-Aztecan, Aztecan, General Aztec, Aztec. Different from Morelos Náhuatl and Guerrero Náhuatl. 79% inherent intelligibility of Guerrero. Some young children are speakers.

ÓPATA [OPT] 15 speakers: 11 in Distrito Federal, 4 in State of México (1993 Instituto Nacional Indigenista). Sonora: Nacori, Bacahora, Suaqui, Sahuaripa, Arivechi, Onavas, Tecoripa is the traditional area. Uto-Aztecan, Southern Uto-Aztecan, Sonoran, Cahita. The last speakers had been reported to have died about 1930. Nearly extinct.

OTOMÍ, ESTADO DE MÉXICO ***(HÑATHO, STATE OF MEXICO OTOMÍ)*** [OTS] 10,000 including 400 monolinguals (1990 census). State of México. Oto-Manguean, Otopamean, Otomian, Otomi. Dialect: SAN FELIPE SANTIAGO OTOMÍ. 73% intelligibility with Mezquital Otomí (closest), lower in outlying areas. Bilingual level estimates for Spanish are Women: 0 0%, 1 20%, 2 40%, 3 40%, 4 0%, 5 0%; Men: 0 0%, 1 20%, 2 30%, 3 50%, 4 0%, 5 0%. VOS, tonal, short words, affixes, clitics. Savannah. Mountain mesa. Peasant agriculturalists: maize. 2,500 to 2,600 meters. Traditional religion, Christian. NT 1975.

OTOMÍ, IXTENCO ***(SOUTHEASTERN OTOMÍ)*** [OTA] 736 speakers including 4 monolinguals out of a population of 5,356 (1990 census). Tlaxcala, San Juan Bautista Ixtenco. Oto-Manguean, Otopamean, Otomian, Otomi. 41% intelligibility of State of Mexico Otomí (closest), 23% of Mezquital, and Eastern Otomí, 22% of Tenango Otomí. Bilingualism in Spanish. Speakers are over 50 years old.

OTOMÍ, MEZQUITAL ***(HÑÄHÑU, OTOMÍ DEL VALLE DE MEZQUITAL)*** [OTE] 100,000 (1990 census), including 100 in North Carolina, USA. Population total both countries 100,000 or more. Mezquital Valley, Hidalgo. Some in Florida, USA. Also spoken in USA. Oto-Manguean, Otopamean, Otomian, Otomi. Dictionary. Grammar. Desert, semi-arid. Plains, mountains. Pastoralists: sheep, goats; swidden agriculturalists: maize. 5,000 feet. Traditional religion, Christian. NT 1970.

OTOMÍ, NORTHWESTERN ***(HÑÄHÑO, QUERÉTARO OTOMÍ, WESTERN OTOMÍ, QUERÉTARO-MÉXICO OTOMÍ)*** [OTQ] 33,000 (1990 census). Querétaro, Guanajuato, Hidalgo, State of México, Amealco Municipio: towns of San Ildefonso, Santiago Mexquititlán; Acambay Municipio; Tolimán Municipio. Oto-Manguean, Otopamean, Otomian, Otomi. 78% intelligibility with Mezquital (closest), lower in outlying areas. Semi-arid, savannah. Mountain mesa. Pastoralists: sheep, goats, cattle; agriculturalists: maize. 7,000 feet. Traditional religion, Christian. Bible portions 1998.

OTOMÍ, SIERRA ORIENTAL ***(EASTERN OTOMÍ, SIERRA OTOMÍ, YUHU, HUEHUETLA OTOMÍ, OTOMÍ DEL ORIENTE)*** [OTM] 20,000 including 4,700 monolinguals (1990 census). Vicinity of Huehuetla and San Bartolo, Hidalgo; Tlachichilco and Ixhuatlán, Veracruz. Oto-Manguean, Otopamean, Otomian, Otomi. 81% intelligibility with Tenango (closest), 50% with Mezquital. Bilingual level estimates for Spanish are 0 16%, 1 59%, 2 20%, 3 3%, 4 1%, 5 1%. Dictionary. VOS, tonal, short words, affixes, clitics. Literacy rate in first language: 1%. Literacy rate in second language: 40%. Semi-tropical. Mountain slope. Peasant agriculturalists. 555 to 770 meters. NT 1974.

OTOMÍ, TEMOAYA [OTT] 37,000 (1990 census). State of México Temoyaya Municipio and 16 barrios, including San Pedro Arriba, San Pedro Abajo, Enthavi, Solalpan, and Jiquipilco el Viejo. Oto-Manguean, Otopamean, Otomian, Otomi. Bilingual level estimates for Spanish are Women: 0 0%, 1 0%, 2 20%, 3 40%, 4 30%, 5 10%; Men: 0 0%, 1 0%, 2 5%, 3 15%, 4 40%, 5 40%. 10% of the 850 monolinguals are under 10 years old (1990 census). It is mainly those over 40 years old who have difficulty with Spanish (1999). VOS, tonal, short words, affixes, clitics. Deciduous forest. Mountain slope. Peasant agriculturalists, laborers in city (men). 2,700 to 2,850 meters. Christian.

OTOMÍ, TENANGO [OTN] 10,000 (1990 census). San Nicolás, Hidalgo, and Puebla. Oto-Manguean, Otopamean, Otomian, Otomi. 53% intelligibility with Eastern Otomí (closest). NT 1975.

OTOMÍ, TEXCATEPEC *(NORTHEASTERN OTOMÍ)* [OTX] 12,000 including 3,000 monolinguals (1990 census). Northwestern Veracruz, Texcatepec Municipio: Texcatepec, Ayotuxtla, Zontecomatlán Municipio: Hueytepec, Amajac, Tzicatlán. Oto-Manguean, Otopamean, Otomian, Otomi. 70% to 79% intelligibility of Eastern Otomí, 57% of Ixmiquilpan, 44% of Tolimán, 40% of San Felipe, 20% of Ixtenco. Limited bilingualism in Spanish. Pastoralists: sheep. 6,000 feet. Christian, traditional religion.

OTOMÍ, TILAPA [OTL] 400 speakers (1990 census). Santiago Tilapa town between Mexico, D. F. and Toluca, State of Mexico. Oto-Manguean, Otopamean, Otomian, Otomi. Bilingualism in Spanish. Speakers mainly over 50 years old (1990). Linguistic island. Nearly extinct.

PAIPAI *(AKWA'ALA)* [PPI] 300 (1990 census). Santa Catarina (about 300 people), and some near Valle de la Trinidad in Los Pocitos, Estado Valle de la Trinidad (1 or 2 houses), and Rancho Aguascalientes or La Palmita (2 to 3 families), Ensenada, Baja California Norte, south of the Diegueño. Hokan, Esselen-Yuman, Yuman, Pai. A Kiliwa speaker sample understood Paipai at 87%, but Paipai speakers understood no Kiliwa. Only a few speakers use Paipai in the home. Mountain slope.

PAME CENTRAL *(CENTRAL PAME, SANTA MARÍA ACAPULCO PAME, CHICHIMECA-PAME CENTRAL)* [PBS] 4,350 (1990 census). San Luis Potosí, Santa María Acapulco. Oto-Manguean, Otopamean, Pamean. Bilingual level estimates for Spanish are 0 10%, 1 70%, 2 15%, 3 5%, 4 .1%, 5 0%. SVO, pitch-accent, short words, affixes. Desert, forest. Mountain slope, deep valleys, limestone. Pastoralists, peasant agriculturalists. 600 to 1,200 meters. Bible portions 1953-1998.

PAME NORTE [PMQ] 1,000 to 10,000 (1993). San Luis Potosí, north of Río Verde to the border with Tamaulipas. Includes Alaquines, Morales, Pasito de San Francisco, Las Crucitas, La Palma, Santa Catarina, Tamasopo, Rayón, Cuesta Blanca. Most speakers are in a natural corredor from the base of the Sierra del Mezquital along La Cañada River. Oto-Manguean, Otopamean, Pamean. 10% to 15% intelligibility of Santa María Acapulco; 87% intelligibility of Alaquines by La Palma speakers. Limited bilingualism in Spanish. 2 to 6 years of primary school in the 2 towns. Semi-arid. Agriculturalists: banana. 2,600 feet.

PAME SUR [PMZ] Jiliapan. Oto-Manguean, Otopamean, Pamean. Extinct.

PIMA BAJO, CHIHUAHUA *(LOWER PIMAN)* [PMB] 1,000 or more (1989 D. Saxton). Chihuahua-Sonoran border area, around Yepachic, scattered. Uto-Aztecan, Southern Uto-Aztecan, Sonoran, Tepiman. Not intelligible with Pima Bajo of Sonora. Limited bilingualism in Spanish. Agriculturalists: maize.

PIMA BAJO, SONORA *(NEBOME, MOUNTAIN PIMA, LOWER PIMAN)* [PIA] 1,000 or more (1989 D. Saxton SIL). Central Sonora-Chihuahua border, scattered. Uto-Aztecan, Southern Uto-Aztecan, Sonoran, Tepiman. Sonora Pima Bajo and Pima of the USA are close. Sonora and Chihuahua Pima Bajo are not inherently intelligible. 85% lexical similarity with Pima (O'odham) of USA and Northern Tepehuán. Somewhat bilingual in Spanish. Agriculturalists: maize, lumber mill workers. Bible portions 1994.

PLAUTDIETSCH *(LOW GERMAN, MENNONITE GERMAN)* [GRN] 40,000 in México (1996). Chihuahua (Cuauhtemoc, Virginias, Buenos Aires, Capulín), Durango (Nuevo Ideal, Canatlán), Campeche (Chávez, Progreso, Yalnon), Zacatecas (La Honda, La Batea). Indo-European, Germanic, West, Low Saxon-Low Franconian, Low Saxon. Not intelligible with other Low Saxon languages or Standard German. 22% speak Standard German, 5% speak English, 30% speak Spanish, 5% speak Russian as second language. Literacy rate in second language: 60%. Intensive agriculturalists, cheese production. Christian. NT 1987. See main entry under Canada.

POPOLOCA, COYOTEPEC [PBF] 500 speakers out of a town of about 7,000 (1990 census). State of Puebla, west of Tehuacán city, east of Ahuatempan, towns of Coyotepec and San Mateo (2 miles from Coyotepec). Oto-Manguean, Popolocan, Chocho-Popolocan, Popolocan. Dialects: SAN VICENTE COYOTEPEC POPOLOCA, SAN MATEO ZOYAMAZALCO POPOLOCA. 41% intelligibility of Otlaltepec, 23% of Atzingo, 15% of Tlacoyalco Northern Popoloca. San Mateo may be intelligible with Coyotepec, San Felipe, or may be a separate language. Bilingualism in Spanish. Fluent speakers are fewer than 500. Investigation needed: intelligibility with San Mateo, bilingual proficiency in Spanish.

POPOLOCA, MEZONTLA *(LOS REYES METZONTLA POPOLOCA, SOUTHERN POPOLOCA)* [PBE] 2,000 (1993 SIL). There may be fewer fluent speakers. State of Puebla, 1 town. Oto-Manguean, Popolocan, Chocho-Popolocan, Popolocan. 52% intelligibility with Atzingo Popoloca, 35% on Tlacoyalco (Northern Popoloca), 11% on Otlaltepec. Investigation needed: bilingual proficiency in Spanish. Grammar.

POPOLOCA, SAN FELIPE OTLALTEPEC *(OTLALTEPEC POPOLOCA, WESTERN POPOLOCA, POPOLOCA PONIENTE)* [POW] 6,000 (1993 SIL). State of Puebla, 3 towns: San Felipe Otlaltepec

(5,000), Santa María Nativitas (500), Huejonapan (500). Oto-Manguean, Popolocan, Chocho-Popolocan, Popolocan. Bilingualism in Spanish. SVO, nontonal, long words, affixes. Literacy rate in first language: 1% to 5%. Literacy rate in second language: 25% to 50%. Desert, deciduous forest. Mountain slope. Swidden agriculturalists. 2,000 meters. Bible portions 1955-1980.

POPOLOCA, SAN JUAN ATZINGO ***(ATZINGO POPOLOCA, EASTERN POPOLOCA, SOUTHERN POPOLOCA)*** [POE] 5,000 (1991 SIL). San Juan Atzingo, Puebla: 1 town. Oto-Manguean, Popolocan, Chocho-Popolocan, Popolocan. 76% intelligibility of Metzontla Popoloca (closest), 26% of San Felipe Popoloca. Bilingual level estimates for Spanish are 0 50%, 1 50%, 2 0%, 3 0%, 4 0%, 5 0%. Most men speak elementary Spanish as second language. Many women who cannot speak Spanish speak Náhuatl for trading in San Gabriel Chilac. Onyx and sugar cane workers have team leaders who speak Spanish for them. Dictionary. VSO, tonal, short words, affixes, clitics. Literacy rate in first language: 20%. Literacy rate in second language: 30%. Desert. Mountain slope. Sedentary pastoralists: goats; onyx miners; potters. 1,538 meters. NT 1982.

POPOLOCA, SAN LUÍS TEMALACAYUCA ***(TEMALACAYUCA POPOLOCA)*** [PPS] 4,729 (1999 SIL M. Kalstrom and J. Austin). San Luís Temalacayuca, Puebla. Oto-Manguean, Popolocan, Chocho-Popolocan, Popolocan. San Luís has 84% intelligibility of San Marcos, 22% of Atzingo, 8% of Otlaltepec. All children know a little Spanish when they enter school. Most people speak limited Spanish. All children speak Popoloca. Vigorous. Popoloca is the language of adults. Used in stores. Kindergarten, primary, and secondary schools. About 25% of the men work part of the year in the D. F. or USA. Desert, plains. Mountain mesa. Peasant agriculturalists. 6,000 feet.

POPOLOCA, SAN MARCOS TLALCOYALCO ***(NORTHERN POPOLOCA, TLALCOYALCO POPOLOCA)*** [PLS] 5,000 (1993 SIL). San Marcos Tlacoyalco, Puebla. Oto-Manguean, Popolocan, Chocho-Popolocan, Popolocan. San Luis has 90% intelligibility of San Marcos. Bilingual level estimates for Spanish are 0 5%, 1 30%, 2 60%, 3 5%, 4 0%, 5 0%. VSO, tonal, long words, affixes, clitics. Desert, plains. Mountain mesa. Peasant agriculturalists. 7,000 feet. NT 1983.

POPOLOCA, SANTA INÉS AHUATEMPAN ***(AHUATEMPAN POPOLOCA)*** [PCA] 7,500 including 6,000 in Ahuatempan (town of 10,000 to 15,000), 1,500 in Almolonga (1993 SIL). State of Puebla, west of Coyotepec and Tehuacán city, 2 towns. Oto-Manguean, Popolocan, Chocho-Popolocan, Popolocan. Dialects: AHUATEMPAN POPOLOCA, TODOS SANTOS ALMOLONGA POPOLOCA. 75% intelligibility of San Felipe Popoloca (closest). Bilingualism in Spanish. Some children do not speak Popoloca. Literacy rate in first language: Below 1%. Literacy rate in second language: 55%. Agriculturalists: maize, black beans, avocados, oranges, lemons, papaya. Traditional religion, Christian. Bible portions 1994.

POPOLUCA, OLUTA [PLO] 102 speakers out of a population of 10,000 (1990 census). Southeastern Veracruz, Oluta, inland, west of Texistepec. Mixe-Zoque, Mixe, Veracruz Mixe. Bilingualism in Spanish. Nearly all are over 50 years old. Dictionary.

POPOLUCA, SAYULA [POS] 4,000 including 14 monolinguals (1990 census). Sayula, Veracruz. Mixe-Zoque, Mixe, Veracruz Mixe. Bilingual level estimates for Spanish are 0 5%, 1 10%, 2 10%, 3 15%, 4 55%, 5 5%. Dictionary. SOV, VOS, nontonal, long words, affixes, clitics. Tropical. Coastal. Peasant agriculturalists. 10 to 600 meters. NT 1969.

POPOLUCA, SIERRA ***(HIGHLAND POPOLUCA)*** [POI] 30,000 (1991 SIL). Soteapan, Veracruz. Mixe-Zoque, Zoque, Veracruz Zoque. Closer to Zoque than to Mixe. Bilingual level estimates for Spanish are 0 5%, 1 45%, 2 20%, 3 20%, 4 10%, 5 10%. Náhuatl also used. VOS, nontonal, short words, affixes. Tropical, pine forest. Mountain slope, coastal. Swidden agriculturalists. 10 to 600 meters. NT 1977-1996.

POPOLUCA, TEXISTEPEC [POQ] 427 speakers out of a population of 15,779 (1990 census). Southeastern Veracruz, Texistepec, east of Oluta. Mixe-Zoque, Zoque, Veracruz Zoque. Bilingualism in Spanish. Speakers over 50 years old. Nearly extinct.

PURÉPECHA ***(TARASCO, TARASCAN, PHORHÉPECHA, PORHÉ)*** [TSZ] 120,000 (1990 census). Michoacán. Tarascan. Several varieties do not have functional intelligibility with each other. Dictionary. Grammar. NT 1969.

PURÉPECHA, SIERRA OCCIDENTAL ***(WESTERN HIGHLAND PURÉPECHA, TARASCO, TARASCAN)*** [PUA] Michoacán, western mountains, Zamora on the northern edge, Los Reyes de Salgado on the southwestern corner, Paracho on the eastern edge, including Pamatácuaro. Tarascan. All Purépecha varieties do not have functional intelligibility with some other Purépecha: the western mountain variety has 60% intelligibility with Pátzcuaro.

SERI [SEI] 700 (1992 M. Moser SIL). The population was 215 in 1951. Sonora coast, 2 villages. Hokan, Salinan-Seri. Bilingual level estimates for Spanish are 0 6%, 1 70%, 2 10%, 3 10%, 4 3%, 5 1%. Dictionary. SOV, nontonal, long words, affixes, clitics. Desert. Coastal. Fishermen; hunter-gatherers (traditionally); craftsmen: ironwood carvings, basketry, necklaces. 0 meters. NT 1982.

SPANISH ***(ESPAÑOL, CASTELLANO)*** [SPN] 86,211,000 first language speakers in Mexico (1995), 88% of the population. Indo-European, Italic, Romance, Italo-Western, Western, Gallo-Iberian, Ibero-Romance, West Iberian, Castilian. National language. Bible 1553-1979. See main entry under Spain.

TACANECO ***(TACANA MAM, MAMÉ)*** [MTZ] 1,200 in Mexico (1990 census). Buenos Aires, hills above Motozintla, and Mazapa, eastern Chiapas. Mayan, Quichean-Mamean, Greater Mamean, Mamean. Speakers are highly bilingual in Spanish in Mexico. All over 20 years old. Widespread seasonal migration to the Pacific coast for labor. See main entry under Guatemala.

TARAHUMARA BAJA ***(WESTERN TARAHUMARA, RALÁMULI DE LA TARAHUMARA BAJA, ROCOROIBO TARAHUMARA)*** [TAC] 15,000 (1990 census). Chihuahua. Uto-Aztecan, Southern Uto-Aztecan, Sonoran, Tarahumaran, Tarahumara. Bilingual level estimates for Spanish are 0 5%, 1 15%, 2 30%, 3 30%, 4 15%, 5 5%. Nontonal, SOV, long words, affixes. Pine forest. Mountain slope. Semi-nomadic pastoralists, swidden or peasant agriculturalists. 600 to 3,000 meters. Bible portions 1975-1985.

TARAHUMARA CENTRAL ***(CENTRAL TARAHUMARASAMACHIQUE TARAHUMARA)*** [TAR] 50,000 (1993 SIL). Southwestern Chihuahua. Uto-Aztecan, Southern Uto-Aztecan, Sonoran, Tarahumaran, Tarahumara. Literacy rate in first language: 1%. Literacy rate in second language: 20%. NT 1972.

TARAHUMARA NORTE ***(NORTHERN TARAHUMARA, ARISEACHI TARAHUMARA)*** [THH] 300 or fewer speakers out of a population of 1,500 (1993 SIL). Chihuahua, towns of Santa Rosa Ariseachi, Agua Caliente Ariseachi, Bilaguchi, Tomochi, La Nopalera. Uto-Aztecan, Southern Uto-Aztecan, Sonoran, Tarahumaran, Tarahumara. 45% intelligibility of Central Tarahumara, 25% of Tarahumara Baja. Bilingualism in Spanish. Speakers are all over 40 years old and few use it daily. May be extinct. Mountain slope. Agriculturalists: maize, beans, squash, potatoes; pastoralists: goats, sheep, cattle; hunters.

TARAHUMARA SURESTE ***(SOUTHEASTERN TARAHUMARA)*** [TCU] Chinatú, Chihuahua. Uto-Aztecan, Southern Uto-Aztecan, Sonoran, Tarahumaran, Tarahumara. Dialect: CHINATÚ TARAHUMARA.

TARAHUMARA SUROESTE ***(SOUTHWESTERN TARAHUMARA)*** [TWR] 100 or fewer (1983 D. Burgess). Chihuahua, town of Tubare. Uto-Aztecan, Southern Uto-Aztecan, Sonoran, Tarahumaran, Tarahumara. Bilingualism in Tarahumara, Spanish. May be the original town of the extinct Tubar language. Nontonal. Scrub forest. Mountain slope (canyon). Hunter-gatherers, agriculturalists. 1,200 to 5,000 feet.

TECTITECO ***(TECO, TECTITÁN MAM)*** [TTC] 1,000 or more in Mexico. Amatenango de la Frontera and Mazapa de Madero, Chiapas. Mayan, Quichean-Mamean, Greater Mamean, Mamean. Closely related to Mam. The Mexican group is highly bilingual in Spanish, but not the Guatemalan group. See main entry under Guatemala.

TEPECANO [TEP] Northwestern Jalisco near Bolaños. Uto-Aztecan, Southern Uto-Aztecan, Sonoran, Tepiman, Southern Tepehuan. No speakers found on SIL survey, 1972. Extinct.

TEPEHUA, HUEHUETLA ***(HIDALGO TEPEHUA)*** [TEE] 3,000 (1982 SIL). Northeastern Hidalgo, Huehuetla, and half the town of Mecapalapa in Puebla. Totonacan, Tepehua. 70% intelligibility with Pisa Flores (closest). Bilingual level estimates for Spanish are 0 10%, 1 37%, 2 25%, 3 10%, 4 10%, 5 8%. They use a whistle speech (G. Cowan 1952, 1972), which distinguishes consonants and vowels of the spoken language. SVO, nontonal, long words, affixes. Tropical. Mountain slope. Swidden, peasant agriculturalists. 300 meters. NT 1976.

TEPEHUA, PISA FLORES [TPP] 4,000 (1990 census). Veracruz, towns of Pisa Flores, Ixhuatlán de Madero, and one other town. Not in Puebla. Totonacan, Tepehua. 59% intelligibility with Huehuetla (closest), 40% or less with Tlachichilco. Limited bilingualism in Spanish. Bible portions 1998.

TEPEHUA, TLACHICHILCO [TPT] 3,000 (1990 SIL). Tlachichilco, Veracruz. Totonacan, Tepehua. 37% intelligibility with Pisa Flores (closest). Bilingual level estimates for Spanish are 0 5%, 1 20%, 2 50%, 3 20%, 4 4%, 5 1%. Otomí, Náhuatl also used. SVO, nontonal, long words, affixes, clitics. Literacy rate in first language: 2%. Literacy rate in second language: 10%. Tropical. Mountain slope. Swidden, peasant agriculturalists. 500 to 900 meters. Bible portions 1985-1999.

TEPEHUÁN NORTE ***(NORTHERN TEPEHUÁN)*** [NTP] 8,000 (1990 census). Southern Chihuahua, Baborigame area. Uto-Aztecan, Southern Uto-Aztecan, Sonoran, Tepiman. Related to Pima Bajo, O'odham, Southern Tepehuán. Bilingual level estimates for Spanish are 0 15%, 1 15%, 2 20%, 3 35%, 4 10%, 5 5%. Tarahumara also used. VSO, tonal, long words, affixes, clitics. Literacy rate in first language: 25%. Literacy rate in second language: 35%. Tropical, deciduous, pine forest. Mountain mesa, slope, canyons. Pastoralists. 700 to 4,000 meters. NT 1982.

TEPEHUÁN SURESTE ***(SOUTHEASTERN TEPEHUÁN)*** [STP] 8,000 to 9,000 (1990 census). Southeastern Durango. Uto-Aztecan, Southern Uto-Aztecan, Sonoran, Tepiman, Southern Tepehuan. 78% intelligibility with Southwestern Tepehuán. Bilingual level estimates for Spanish are 0 50%, 1 30%, 2 15%, 3 4%, 4 1%, 5 0%. VSO, VOS, nontonal, long words, affixes, clitics. Literacy rate in first language: 10%. Literacy rate in second language: 25%. Deciduous, pine forest. Mountain slope. Pastoralists, peasant agriculturalists. 1,500 to 3,000 meters. Christian, traditional religion. Bible portions 1991.

TEPEHUÁN SUROESTE ***(SOUTHWESTERN TEPEHUÁN)*** [TLA] 6,000 to 8,000 (1990 census). Southwestern Durango. Uto-Aztecan, Southern Uto-Aztecan, Sonoran, Tepiman, Southern Tepehuan. 55% intelligibility with Southeastern Tepehuán. Limited bilingualism in Spanish. Swidden agriculturalists: maize, beans, squash; pastoralists. Traditional religion.

TLAPANECO, ACATEPEC ***(WESTERN TLAPANEC, ME'PHAA)*** [TPX] 33,000 including over 10,000 monolinguals (1994 SIL). Acatepec, Guerrero, Zapotitlán Tablas Municipio: Huitzapula, Ayotoxtla, Excalerilla, Huiztlatzala; Acatepec Municipio: Acatepec, Apetzuca, Tenamazapa, Barranca Pobre, Mezcalapa, Metlapilapa, Tres Cruces, El Salto, Zochitepec, Caxitepec; Platanillo municipio: Nanzintla, Teocuitlapa. Subtiaba-Tlapanec. Dialects: ACATEPEC, ZAPOTITLÁN TABLAS, PLATANILLO. 83% intelligibility of Malinaltepec, 79% of Tlacoapa. Many bilingual school teachers from Malinaltepec. Primary schools in most villages, secondary schools in major centers. Investigation needed: intelligibility with dialects. Mountain slope. Swidden agriculturalists. 5,000 to 6,000 feet.

TLAPANECO, AZOYÚ [TPC] 682 speakers. 17,000 in the Municipio including Spanish-speaking mestizos (1990 census). No monolinguals. However, there are reports of 1,000 to 10,000 speakers. East and a little south of Chilpancingo, Guerrero, Azoyú, Maxnadi, Toxnene, Zapotitlán del Puente, San Isidro del Puente, El Carrizo. Subtiaba-Tlapanec. 50% intelligible with Malinaltepec. Reported to be bilingual in Spanish. Investigation needed: intelligibility with other Tlapaneco, bilingual proficiency.

TLAPANECO, MALINALTEPEC ***(MEPHÁA, EASTERN TLAPANECO, MALINALTEPEC TLAPANEC)*** [TLL] 33,000 speakers, including 6,000 monolinguals (1994 M. Weathers SIL). East and a little south of Chilpancingo, Guerrero. Subtiaba-Tlapanec. Dialects: TLACOAPA, MALINALTEPEC (HUIZAPULA), ZILACAYOTITLÁN. Tlacoapa Tlapaneco speakers can understand Malinaltepec, but the reverse is not true. Linguistically closest to Subtiaba of Nicaragua (extinct). It may be distantly related to Tol of Honduras. Investigation needed: intelligibility with dialects. Grammar. NT 1975.

TOJOLABAL ***(CHAÑABAL, COMITECO)*** [TOJ] 36,000 including 7,700 monolinguals (1990 census). Chiapas, Margaritas and Altamirano. Mayan, Kanjobalan-Chujean, Chujean. NT 1972-1994.

TOTONACA, COYUTLA [TOC] 30,000 to 40,000 (1982 SIL). Speakers of all Totonac languages: 196,003 (1980 census). Puebla, foot of the mountains north of the 'Sierra Totonaca' and the Olintla River. Totonacan, Totonac. Linguistically closest to Highland Totonaca with many similarities to Papantla. NT 1987.

TOTONACA, FILOMENO MATA-COAHUITLÁN ***(SANTO DOMINGO TOTONACA)*** [TLP] 10,000 to 12,000 (1982 SIL). Veracruz, highlands, in the middle of the main highlands dialect. Totonacan, Totonac. 93% intelligibility with Nonacatlán. Linguistically between Highland and Northern Totonaca. Speakers are bilingual in Coyutla Totonaca.

TOTONACA, OZUMATLÁN [TQT] 4,000 (1990 census) or fewer speakers (1999). Puebla, Ozumatlán, Tepetzintla, Tlapehuala, San Agustín. Totonacan, Totonac. 79% intelligibility of Highland Totonaca, 75% of Northern Totonaca, 67% of Zihuateutla, Puebla, 43% of Papantla. Speakers are not bilingual in Spanish. Agriculturalists: maize, squash, chicken, pigs. 5,000 feet.

TOTONACA, PAPANTLA ***(LOWLAND TOTONACA)*** [TOP] 80,000 (1982 SIL). Veracruz. Totonacan, Totonac. 40% intelligibility with Highland Totonaca (closest). Bilingual level estimates for Spanish are 0 5%, 1 10%, 2 50%, 3 15%, 4 10%, 5 10%. Dictionary. VSO, nontonal, long words, affixes, clitics. Savannah, tropical. Mountain slope, coastal, interfluvial. Peasant agriculturalists. 0 to 300 meters. Traditional religion, Christian. NT 1979.

TOTONACA, PATLA-CHICONTLA ***(PATLA-CHICONTLA TOTONAC)*** [TOT] 6,000 (1990 census). Northeastern Puebla, Patla, Chicontla, Tecpatlán, and 2 other villages. Totonacan, Totonac. It is difficult for speakers to read Northern Totonaca materials. Literacy rate in first language: 5%. Literacy rate in second language: 30%. NT, in press (1999).

TOTONACA, SIERRA ***(HIGHLAND TOTONACA)*** [TOS] 120,000 (1982 SIL). Zacatlán, Puebla area and Veracruz. Totonacan, Totonac. Bilingual level estimates for Spanish are 0 10%, 1 50%, 2 24%, 3 10%, 4 5%, 5 1%. Náhuatl also used. Dictionary. VSO, nontonal, long words, affixes, clitics. Tropical. Mountain slope, interfluvial. Peasant agriculturalists. 300 to 2,500 meters. NT 1959, in press (1999).

TOTONACA, XICOTEPEC DE JUÁREZ ***(NORTHERN TOTONACA, VILLA JUÁREZ TOTONACA)*** [TOO] 10,000 or more (1982 SIL). Northeastern Puebla, Xicotepec de Juárez, and Veracruz; 30 towns. Totonacan, Totonac. Dialect: ZIHUATEUTLA TOTONACA. 87% intelligibility with Ozumatlán (closest). Bilingual level estimates for Spanish are 0 3%, 1 7%, 2 35%, 3 40%, 4 10%, 5 5%. SVO, nontonal, long words, affixes, clitics. Literacy rate in first language: 20%. Literacy rate in second language: 60%. Tropical. Mountain slope. Peasant agriculturalists: coffee. 215 to 1,230 meters. NT 1978.

TOTONACA, YECUATLA [TLC] 500 (1994 SIL). Near southern coast, Veracruz, towns of Yecuatla (293 speakers out of 11,541 population) and Misantla (126 speakers out of 50,000 population). Totonacan, Totonac. Bilingualism in Spanish. Speakers are all over 50 years old.

TRIQUE, CHICAHUAXTLA ***(SAN ANDRÉS CHICAHUAXTLA TRIQUE, TRIQUI)*** [TRS] 6,000 (1982). Tlaxiaco area, Oaxaca. Oto-Manguean, Mixtecan, Trique. Dialect: LAGUNA. 74% intelligibility with Copala. 100% lexical similarity with Laguna, 87% with Itunyoso, 78% with Sabana. Bilingual level estimates for Spanish are 0 15%, 1 40%, 2 20%, 3 14%, 4 10%, 5 1%. Dictionary. Grammar. VSO, tonal, short words, affixes, clitics. Scrub forest. Mountain slope. Peasant agriculturalists. 1,200 to 2,500 meters. NT 1968.

TRIQUE, COPALA ***(SAN JUAN COPALA TRIQUE, TRIQUI)*** [TRC] 15,000 (1990 census). Oaxaca, San Juan Copala, and probably a few thousand in San Quintín Valley, Baja California. Oto-Manguean, Mixtecan, Trique. 56% intelligibility with Chicahuaxtla. Bilingual level estimates for Spanish are 0 40%, 1 30%, 2 15%, 3 10%, 4 5%, 5 0%. VSO, tonal, short words, affixes, clitics. Literacy rate in first language: 1%. Literacy rate in second language: 20%. Pine forest. Mountain slope. Swidden agriculturalists. 1,000 to 2,200 meters. NT 1988.

TRIQUE, SAN MARTÍN ITUNYOSO ***(SAN MARTÍN ITUNYOSO TRIQUI, TRIQUI)*** [TRQ] 2,000 (1983). Oaxaca. Oto-Manguean, Mixtecan, Trique. 87% lexical similarity with Laguna, Chicahuaxtla; 84% with Sabana, San Miguel. Bilingual level estimates for Spanish are 0 50%, 1 40%, 2 4%, 3 3%, 4 2%, 5 1%. Tonal, VSO, short words, affixes. Scrub forest. Mountain slope. Sedentary pastoralists, peasant agriculturalists. NT 1996.

TUBAR ***(TUBARE)*** [TBU] There may have been as many as 100 in 1970. Chihuahua, where the Río San Ignacio (Verde) and Río Urique meet in the southwest near the Sinaloa and Sonora borders. Uto-Aztecan, Southern Uto-Aztecan, Sonoran, Tubar. Extinct.

TZELTAL, BACHAJÓN ***(LOWLAND TZELTAL)*** [TZB] 100,000 (1993 SIL). Speakers of all Tzeltal varieties: 215,145 (1980 census). East central Chiapas. Mayan, Cholan-Tzeltalan, Tzeltalan. Dialect: AMATENANGO DEL VALLE. Dictionary. NT 1964.

TZELTAL, OXCHUC ***(HIGHLAND TZELTAL, TENEJAPA, CHANAL, CANCUC, TENANGO)*** [TZH] 200,000 (1993 SIL). East central Chiapas, Oxchuc area. Mayan, Cholan-Tzeltalan, Tzeltalan. VOS. Bible 1993.

TZOTZIL, CHAMULA ***(CHAMULA)*** [TZC] 130,000 (1990 census). Speakers of all Tzotzil languages: 265,000 (1990 census). West central Chiapas, San Juan Chamula, Huitiupan, Simojovel, San Juan del Bosque, San Cristóbal Las Casas, Bochil, Pueblo Nuevo Solistahuacan, Ocozocoautla, Ixtapa (Nibak), Jitotol, Teopisca, Amatan, Ishuatan. Mayan, Cholan-Tzeltalan, Tzeltalan. NT 1979-1988.

TZOTZIL, CH'ENALHÓ ***(CHENALÓ)*** [TZE] 35,000 (1990 census). Chenalhó region, Chiapas. Mayan, Cholan-Tzeltalan, Tzeltalan. Dialects: SAN PEDRO CHENALHÓ, SAN PABLO CHALCHIHUITAN, SANTA CATARINA PANTELHO, SAN MIGUEL MITONTIC. Partially intelligible with San Andrés Larrainzar Chamula. Bilingual level estimates for Spanish are 0 95%, 1 1%, 2 1%, 3 2%, 4 .5%, 5 0%. Nontonal, SVO or VOS, short and long words, affixes. Scrub forest. Mountain slope. Swidden agriculturalists. Bible, in press (1998).

TZOTZIL, HUIXTÁN ***(HUIXTECO)*** [TZU] 20,000 (1990 census). Huixtán region, Chiapas. Mayan, Cholan-Tzeltalan, Tzeltalan. Dialects: HUIXTÁN, ANGEL ALBINO CORZO, LA CONCORDIA, VILLA CORZO. Bilingual level estimates for Spanish are 0 98%, 1 .5%, 2 .5%, 3 .5%, 4 .3%, 5 .2%. SVO, VOS, nontonal, short words, affixes. Pine forest. Mountain slope. Sedentary pastoralists, swidden agriculturalists. 2,185 meters. NT 1975-1995.

TZOTZIL, SAN ANDRÉS LARRAINZAR ***(SAN ANDRÉS TZOTZIL)*** [TZS] 50,000 (1990 census). West central Chiapas. Mayan, Cholan-Tzeltalan, Tzeltalan. Dictionary. Pine forest. Mountain slope, plains. Swidden agriculturalists. 1,500 to 3,000 meters. NT 1983.

TZOTZIL, VENUSTIANO CARRANZA ***(SAN BARTOLOMÉ VENUSTIANO CARRANZA TZOTZIL)*** [TZO] 4,226 speakers including 58 monolinguals (1990 census). 60,000 in the ethnic group. Central Chiapas, Venustiano Carranza Municipio, towns of Venustiano Carranza, El Puerto, and El Paraiso de Grijalva. Mayan, Cholan-Tzeltalan, Tzeltalan. 66% intelligibility of Chenalhó Tzotzil, 65% of Zinacantán, 57% of Chamula, 56% of Huixtán. Spanish proficiency is limited. Primary schools and a secondary school. Agriculturalists: maize, beans; fishermen. 1,500 feet.

TZOTZIL, ZINACANTÁN ***(ZINACANTECO TZOTZIL)*** [TZZ] 25,000 (1990 census). West central Chiapas. Mayan, Cholan-Tzeltalan, Tzeltalan. Bilingual level estimates for Spanish are 0 94%, 1 3%, 2 2%, 3 1%, 4 0%, 5 0%. SVO or VOS, short and long words, affixes, nontonal. Scrub forest. Mountain slope. Pastoralists, swidden agriculturalists. NT 1987.

YAQUI [YAQ] 16,000 in Mexico (1993 SIL). Population total both countries 16,400. Sonora. Also spoken in USA. Uto-Aztecan, Southern Uto-Aztecan, Sonoran, Cahita. Partially intelligible with Mayo. Bilingual level estimates for Spanish are 0 0%, 1 0%, 2 1%, 3 55%, 4 35%, 5 4%. English also used. Grammar. SOV, tonal, long words, affixes, clitics. Literacy rate in first language: 1%. Literacy rate in second language: 5% to 10%. Desert, gallery forest. Coastal, riverine. Pastoralists, hunters, fishermen, agriculture. 0 to 100 meters. NT 1977.

YUCATEC MAYA SIGN LANGUAGE ***(NOHYA SIGN LANGUAGE)*** [MSD] 17 deaf people out of a village of 500 in the primary location (1999 H. Smith). All use sign (1989 Sacks), including hearing people in the village. Concentrated population in south central Yucatán and in smaller groups in the same region, and a sizeable concentration in northern Quintana Roo (1999 H. Smith). Chican, formerly called 'Nohya', Yucatán. An isolated village plus other villages (at least 2 in Oxkutzcab, 4 in Xyatil, 1 in Carillo Puerto) throughout a wide portion of the lowland Mayan region. Kinil is also mentioned (1997 H. Smith). Deaf sign language. Dialects of Yucatán and Quintana Roo probably differ, but users have no contact with each other. There is a report of a person in Guatemala who uses related signs. Not intelligible with Mexican Sign Language used elsewhere in Mexico, or other sign languages. 100% monolingual. 3 years old to 70 years old (1999 H. Smith). 13 adults and 3 children under 5 (1997 H. Smith), plus all hearing people (1989 Sacks). 400 to 500 who use it as a second or third language (1999 H. Smith). Congenital deafness. It is of some antiquity. Investigation needed: intelligibility with dialects. Literacy rate in second language: 0%. Lowland.

ZAPOTECO, ALBARRADAS ***(ALBARRADAS ZAPOTEC)*** [ZAS] 5,500 including 1,500 to 2,000 in Santo Domingo (1993 SIL). All Zapotec languages: 422,937 (1980 census). Central Oaxaca, Santa María Albarradas, Santo Domingo Albarradas, San Miguel Albarradas. Oto-Manguean, Zapotecan, Zapotec. 39% intelligibility with Mitla (closest). Santa Catarina Albarradas may need separate literature. Bilingual level estimates for Spanish are 0 3%, 1 17%, 2 40%, 3 30%, 4 9%, 5 1%. Speakers switch to Spanish for communication with Mitla Zapoteco speakers. Spanish is generally used between them and the Mixe in mixed marriages. Since 1979 speakers in Santo Domingo have shown increasing preference for Zapoteco, but in Santa María it is reported to be diminishing in use. Some immigrant Mixe have learned the local Zapoteco, but few Xapoteco have learned Mixe. Tonal, VSO, varying word length, clitics and affixes. Literacy rate in first language: 1%. Literacy rate in second language: 80%. Gallery forest. Mountain slope. Swidden agriculturalists. 4,000 to 6,000 feet.

ZAPOTECO, ALOÁPAM ***(ALOÁPAM ZAPOTEC)*** [ZAQ] Northern Oaxaca, San Miguel Aloápam, San Isidro Aloápam. Oto-Manguean, Zapotecan, Zapotec. Different from Teococuilco Zapoteco. People are not bilingual in Spanish. VSO, tonal, affixes, clitics. Pine forest. Sedentary pastoralists, peasant agriculturalists. Bible portions 1996.

ZAPOTECO, AMATLÁN ***(NORTHEASTERN MIAHUATLÁN, SAN FRANCISCO LOGUECHE ZAPOTECO, SAN CRISTÓBAL AMATLÁN ZAPOTECO, AMATLÁN ZAPOTEC)*** [ZPO] 5,000 to 6,000 (1993 SIL). Southern Oaxaca, east of Miahuatlán, 3 towns. Oto-Manguean, Zapotecan, Zapotec. Closest to Loxicha. Bilingual level estimates for Spanish are 0 60%, 1 20%, 2 15%, 3 4%, 4 1%, 5 0%. VSO, tonal, short words. Literacy rate in first language: 5%. Literacy rate in second language: 35%. Gallery forest. Mountain slope. Sedentary pastoralists, peasant agriculturalists. 1,690 meters. Bible portions 1992-1995.

ZAPOTECO, ASUNCIÓN MIXTEPEC ***(NORTH CENTRAL ZIMATLÁN ZAPOTECO, ASUNCIÓN MIXTEPEC ZAPOTEC)*** [ZOO] 100 or fewer speakers out of a population of 2,476 (1990 census). Southwest of Oaxaca City in central Oaxaca, Asunción Mixtepec and another town. Oto-Manguean, Zapotecan, Zapotec. 22% intelligibility of Ayoquesco (closest), and 3% of San Pedro el Alto. Bilingualism in Spanish. Nearly extinct.

ZAPOTECO, AYOQUESCO ***(WESTERN EJUTLA ZAPOTECO, SANTA MARÍA AYOQUESCO ZAPOTEC)*** [ZAF] 876 speakers, including 9 monolinguals (1990 census). Oaxaca, Santa María Ayoquesco, Santa Cruz Nexila, San Andrés Zabache, and San Martín Lachila. Oto-Manguean, Zapotecan, Zapotec. Closest to Western Ocotlán Zapoteco (23% intelligibility). Bilingualism in Spanish. All ages in Santa Cruz Nexila. Most vigorous in Nexila where 52% of the population speak Zapoteco. They have pride in their language.

ZAPOTECO, CAJONOS ***(SAN PEDRO CAJONOS ZAPOTECO, SOUTHERN VILLA ALTA ZAPOTECO, CAJONOS ZAPOTEC)*** [ZAD] 5,000 (1993 SIL). Population total both countries 5,000 or more. Northern Oaxaca, towns of San Pedro Cajonos, San Francisco Cajonos, San Mateo Cajonos, San Miguel Cajonos, San Pablo Yaganiza, Xagacía. Also spoken in USA. Oto-Manguean, Zapotecan, Zapotec. Dialects: CAJONOS ZAPOTECO, YAGANIZA-XAGACÍA ZAPOTECO. Yaganiza and Xagacía are similar. Major differences between those two towns and the other four towns; adaptation of literature will probably be needed. 73% intelligibility of San Pedro Cajonos with Zoogocho (closest other Zapoteco). Bilingual level estimates for Spanish are 0 10%, 1 20%, 2 15%, 3 25%, 4 10%, 5 10%. Many nearly monolingual speakers in Yaganiza. VSO, tonal, long words, affixes, clitics. The school is bilingual. Deciduous, pine forests. Mountain slope. Agriculturalists, craftsmen, merchants. 1,800 meters. Bible portions 1982.

ZAPOTECO, CHICHICAPAN ***(SAN BALTAZAR CHICHICAPAN ZAPOTEC, EASTERN OCOTLÁN ZAPOTECO)*** [ZPV] 4,000 (1993 SIL). Central Oaxaca. Oto-Manguean, Zapotecan, Zapotec. 59%

intelligibility with Western Ocotlán (closest). Bilingual level estimates for Spanish are 0 30%, 1 5%, 2 60%, 3 4%, 4 1%, 5 0%. Monolinguals are mainly women and older people. VSO, tonal, short words, affixes, clitics. Literacy rate in first language: Below 5%. Literacy rate in second language: 30% to 50%. Desert, scrub, gallery forest. Mountain slope. Peasant agriculturalists, sedentary pastoralists. 1,666 to 3,030 meters. NT 1990.

ZAPOTECO, CHOAPAN ***(CHOAPAN ZAPOTEC, CHOÁPAM ZAPOTECO)*** [ZPC] 24,000 (1991 SIL). North central Oaxaca and Veracruz, including Comaltepec. Oto-Manguean, Zapotecan, Zapotec. 60% intelligibility with Zoogocho (closest). Bilingual level estimates for Spanish are 0 10%, 1 25%, 2 30%, 3 20%, 4 12%, 5 3%. Dictionary. VSO, tonal, short words, affixes, clitics. Tropical. Mountain slope. Swidden agriculturalists. 840 meters. NT 1986.

ZAPOTECO, COATECAS ALTAS ***(SAN JUAN COATECAS ALTAS ZAPOTEC)*** [ZAP] 5,000 (1993 SIL) including 100 monolinguals (1990 census). Ejutla, Oaxaca. Oto-Manguean, Zapotecan, Zapotec. Closest to San Gregorio Ozolotepec (83% intelligibility) and Miahuatlán (Cuitla). Literacy rate in first language: Below 1%. Literacy rate in second language: 20% to 30%.

ZAPOTECO, COATLÁN ***(WESTERN MIAHUATLÁN ZAPOTECO, SANTA MARÍA COATLÁN ZAPOTECO, COATLÁN ZAPOTEC, SAN MIGUEL ZAPOTECO)*** [ZPS] 500 or fewer (1992 SIL). Southern Oaxaca near Chatino region, about 7 towns, but mainly in Santo Domingo Coatlán. Oto-Manguean, Zapotecan, Zapotec. 54% intelligibility of Loxicha (closest), 51% of San Gregorio Ozolotepec, 44% of Cuixtla, 29% of Logueche, 16% of San Juan Mixtepec, 1% of Santa Catalina Quierí. Speakers are reported to be bilingual in Spanish.

ZAPOTECO, EL ALTO ***(SOUTH CENTRAL ZIMATLÁN ZAPOTECO, SAN PEDRO EL ALTO ZAPOTECO, EL ALTO ZAPOTEC)*** [ZPP] 900 speakers, including 29 monolinguals (1990 census). Western Oaxaca, San Pedro el Alto, San Antonino el Alto, San Andrés el Alto. Oto-Manguean, Zapotecan, Zapotec. 20% intelligibility with Totomachapan (closest). Bilingualism in Spanish.

ZAPOTECO, ELOTEPEC ***(SAN JUAN ELOTEPEC ZAPOTEC, PAPABUCO)*** [ZTE] 200 speakers (1990 census). Western Oaxaca, west of Zimatlán, 1 village. Oto-Manguean, Zapotecan, Zapotec. 68% intelligibility of Santa María Zaniza (closest), 10% of Texmelucan. Bilingualism in Spanish. All are 50 years old and older (1990). Mountain slope. Nearly extinct.

ZAPOTECO, GUEVEA DE HUMBOLDT ***(NORTHERN ISTHMUS ZAPOTECO, GUEVEA DE HUMBOLDT ZAPOTEC)*** [ZPG] 7,000 (1977 SIL). Eastern Oaxaca. Oto-Manguean, Zapotecan, Zapotec. 49% intelligibility with Lachiguiri (Northwestern Tehuantepec; closest). VSO, tonal, short words, clitics, affixes. Literacy rate in first language: 2%. Literacy rate in second language: 20% to 30%. 1,760 to 2,500 feet. Bible portions 1982.

ZAPOTECO, GÜILÁ ***(SAN PABLO GÜILÁ ZAPOTEC)*** [ZTU] 9,500 (1990 census), including 2,300 monolinguals. San Pablo Güilá and San Dionisio Ocotepec municipios, Oaxaca. Oto-Manguean, Zapotecan, Zapotec. San Dionisio has 80% inherent intelligibility of Mitla. Güilá has 83% inherent intelligibility of Guelavía, 80% of Chichicapan, 69% of Tilquiapan, 41% of Mitla, 35% of Ocotlán, 5% of Santa María Albarradas.

ZAPOTECO, ISTMO ***(ZAPOTECO, ÍSTMO)*** [ZAI] 85,000 (1990 census). Tehuantepec and Juchitán, Oaxaca. Oto-Manguean, Zapotecan, Zapotec. 18% intelligibility of Santa María Petapa (closest). Bilingual level estimates for Spanish are 0 10%, 1 45%, 2 25%, 3 10%, 4 10%, 5 10%. Dictionary. Grammar. VSO, tonal, short words, affixes, clitics. Coastal. Fishermen, peasant agriculturalists, merchants. 0 meters. NT 1972.

ZAPOTECO, IXTLÁN SURESTE ***(SOUTHEASTERN IXTLÁN ZAPOTEC, YAVESÍA ZAPOTECO, LATUVI ZAPOTECO)*** [ZPD] 6,000 (1992 SIL). Northern Oaxaca, Santa María Yavesía (center), Carrizal, Latuvi, Benito Juárez, Ixtlán de Juárez, Santa Catarina Lachatao, Llano Grande, La Trinidad, Nevería, San Miguel Amatlán, Capulalpan de Morelos, Santiago Xiacui, Natividad, Guelatao de Juárez. Oto-Manguean, Zapotecan, Zapotec. 63% intelligibility of Atepec (Sierra de Juárez), 43% of Teococuilco. Bilingualism in Spanish.

ZAPOTECO, JUÁREZ, SIERRA ***(ATEPEC ZAPOTECO, IXTLÁN ZAPOTECO)*** [ZAA] 4,000 including 150 monolinguals (1990 census). Northern Oaxaca. Oto-Manguean, Zapotecan, Zapotec. Bilingual level estimates for Spanish are 0 25%, 1 25%, 2 25%, 3 18%, 4 5%, 5 1%. Dictionary. VSO, tonal, long words, affixes, clitics. Scrub, pine forests. Mountain slope. Sedentary pastoralists, swidden, peasant agriculturalists. 1,540 to 2,770 meters. NT 1970.

ZAPOTECO, LACHIGUIRI ***(NORTHWESTERN TEHUANTEPEC ZAPOTECO, SANTIAGO LACHIGUIRI ZAPOTECO, LACHIGUIRI ZAPOTEC)*** [ZPA] 5,000 (1977 SIL). Oaxaca, north of Isthmus, 15 km. southwest of Guevea de Humboldt. Includes towns in neighboring municipios, such as Santa María Totolapilla, Jalapa, and Magdalena. Oto-Manguean, Zapotecan, Zapotec. 62% intelligibility in Lachixila (Northeastern Yautepec) and Juchitán (Isthmus; closest). Although speakers are fairly bilingual in Spanish, there is a strong preference for Zapoteco. Mountains. 3,000 to 4,000 feet.

ZAPOTECO, LACHIRIOAG ***(LACHIRUAJ ZAPOTECO, SAN CRISTÓBAL LACHIRUAJ ZAPOTECO)*** [ZTC] 2,000 speakers (1999 SIL). Oaxaca, San Cristóbal Lachiruáj. Oto-Manguean, Zapotecan, Zapotec. Closest to Villa Alta Zapoteco and Yalalag Zapoteco, but different. Different from Yatee. Limited bilingualism in Spanish.

ZAPOTECO, LOXICHA ***(WESTERN POCHUTLA ZAPOTECO, LOXICHA ZAPOTEC)*** [ZTP] 50,000 (1990 census). Oaxaca, 120 km. south of Oaxaca city, west of highway 175, half way between Miahuatlán and Pochutla. Includes Candelaria Loxicha, Buena Vista, and San Bartolomé Loxicha. Oto-Manguean, Zapotecan, Zapotec. Dialects: SAN AGUSTÍN LOXICHA ZAPOTECO, CANDELARIA LOXICHA ZAPOTECO. Distinct from San Baltázar Loxicha and Santa Catarina Loxicha. People in town centers are fairly bilingual in Spanish. In many towns perhaps 70% of the men and 90% of the women are monolingual. Bible portions.

ZAPOTECO, MAZALTEPEC ***(SANTO TOMÁS MAZALTEPEC ZAPOTECO, ETLA ZAPOTECO, MAZALTEPEC ZAPOTEC)*** [ZPY] 2,200 including 24 monolinguals (1990 census). Western Oaxaca Valley, Etla District, 20 km. northwest of Oaxaca city; Santo Tomás Mazaltepec, San Pedro y San Pablo Etla, and a few in San Andrés Zautla. Oto-Manguean, Zapotecan, Zapotec. 10% intelligibility of Guelavía, none of other Zapoteco varieties. Speakers are somewhat bilingual in Spanish. Several bilingual school teachers. Zapoteco is used in the home. 25% of children do not speak Spanish when entering school. Vigorous. People have strong pride in the language. Kindergarten and primary school. Agriculturalists; adobe brick makers. 5,600 feet.

ZAPOTECO, MIAHUATLÁN CENTRAL ***(CENTRAL MIAHUATLÁN ZAPOTEC)*** [ZAM] 80,000 (1982 SIL). South central Oaxaca, Cuixtla. Oto-Manguean, Zapotecan, Zapotec. Bilingual level estimates for Spanish are 0 10%, 1 5%, 2 30%, 3 4%, 4 1%, 5 50%. Dictionary. SVO, tonal, short words, affixes, clitics. Desert, scrub forest. Mountain slope. Swidden, peasant agriculturalists. 1,800 meters. NT 1971.

ZAPOTECO, MITLA ***(EAST CENTRAL TLACOLULA ZAPOTECO, EAST VALLEY ZAPOTECO)*** [ZAW] 19,500 (1983 SIL), including 4,500 in Matatlán (1983 SIL). Mitla Valley, Oaxaca. Oto-Manguean, Zapotecan, Zapotec. Dialect: SANTIAGO MATATLÁN ZAPOTEC (MATATLÁN ZAPOTEC). 75% intelligibility with Guelavía (closest). Bilingual level estimates for Spanish are 0 5%, 1 30%, 2 30%, 3 15%, 4 15%, 5 5%. Dictionary. SVO or VSO, short and long words, clitics and affixes, tonal. Literacy rate in first language: 15%. Literacy rate in second language: 80% to 90%. Desert, gallery, scrub, deciduous, and pine forests. Mountain slope, plains. Pastoralists, peasant agriculturalists, craftsmen, merchants. 1,500 meters. NT 1981.

ZAPOTECO, MIXTEPEC ***(EASTERN MIAHUATLÁN ZAPOTECO, SAN JUAN MIXTEPEC ZAPOTECO, MIXTEPEC ZAPOTEC)*** [ZPM] 7,000 (1991 SIL). Southern Oaxaca. Oto-Manguean, Zapotecan, Zapotec. 80% intelligibility with Santiago Lapaguía (closest). A separate language from San Agustín Mixtepec Zapoteco. Bilingual level estimates for Spanish are 0 40%, 1 15%, 2 30%, 3 15%, 4 0%, 5 0%. VSO, tonal, short words, clitics. Pine forest. Mountain slope. Pastoralists, peasant agriculturalists, merchants. NT 1998.

ZAPOTECO, OCOTLÁN OESTE ***(WESTERN OCOTLÁN ZAPOTEC, OCOTLÁN ZAPOTEC, CENTRAL OCOTLÁN ZAPOTECO)*** [ZAC] 15,000 (1993 SIL). Ocotlán, central Oaxaca, around Santiago Apóstol. Oto-Manguean, Zapotecan, Zapotec. 67% intelligibility with Tilquiapan (closest). Bilingual level estimates for Spanish are 0 10%, 1 30%, 2 40%, 3 10%, 4 6%, 5 4%. VSO, tonal, short words, affixes. Literacy rate in first language: Below 1%. Literacy rate in second language: 50%. Deciduous forest. Plains. Peasant agriculturalists, merchants. 1,385 meters. NT 1983.

ZAPOTECO, OZOLOTEPEC [ZAO] 6,500 (1990 census); including the town of San Marcial (1,400 in 1973). Oaxaca, southeastern Miahuatlán, east side of highway 175, about half way between Miahuatlán and coast. The majority of towns with 'Ozolotepec' in the name are included. Oto-Manguean, Zapotecan, Zapotec. Dialects: SAN MARCIAL OZOLOTEPEC ZAPOTECO, SAN GREGORIO OZOLOTEPEC ZAPOTECO. 87% intelligibility with Cuixtla (Central Miahuatlán), 84% with Candelaria Loxicha (Northeastern Pochutla). Cuixtla literature not acceptable here. People in the towns of San Marcial, San Gregorio, San Esteban, and Santo Domingo are monolingual. 6,000 feet.

ZAPOTECO, PETAPA ***(SANTA MARÍA PETAPA ZAPOTECO, PETAPA ZAPOTEC)*** [ZPE] 8,000 speakers, including 220 monolinguals (1990 census). Oaxaca, north of the Isthmus, Juchitán District, Santa María Petapa and Santo Domingo Petapa. Oto-Manguean, Zapotecan, Zapotec. 55% intelligibility of Guevea (closest), 34% of Lachiguiri. Bilingualism in Spanish.

ZAPOTECO, QUIAVICUZAS ***(QUIAVICUZAS ZAPOTEC, SAN JUAN LACHIXILA ZAPOTECO, NORTHEASTERN YAUTEPEC ZAPOTECO)*** [ZPJ] 4,000 (1990 census). Oaxaca, northeast corner of Yautepec District, 45 km. northeast of Pan American highway, 75 km. east of Mitla. San Carlos Yautepec Municipio: Santiago Quiavicuzas; Nejapa de Madero Municipio: San Juan Lachixila, Corral de Piedra, Carrizal; Guevea de Humboldt Municipio: Guadalupe Guevea. Oto-Manguean, Zapotecan,

Zapotec. 59% intelligibility of Lachiguiri (Northwestern Tehuantepec; closest). Bilingualism in Spanish. 40 of the 180 monolinguals are between ages 5 to 9. Primary schools. Agriculturalists. 3,500 to 5,000 feet.

ZAPOTECO, QUIOQUITANI Y QUIERÍ [ZTQ] 4,000 (1991 SIL). Yautepec, Oaxaca, Quioquitani and Quierí municipios, and including Leapi. Oto-Manguean, Zapotecan, Zapotec. Dialects: QUIOQUITANI ZAPOTEC (SANTA CATARINA QUIOQUITANI ZAPOTECO), QUIERÍ ZAPOTEC (SANTA CATARINA QUIERI ZAPOTECO). Closest to Eastern Miahuatlán. Bible portions 1990-1995.

ZAPOTECO, RINCÓN ***(RINCÓN ZAPOTEC, YAGALLO ZAPOTECO, NORTHERN VILLA ALTA ZAPOTECO)*** [ZAR] 23,000 to 27,000 (1990 census). Northern Oaxaca. Oto-Manguean, Zapotecan, Zapotec. 64% intelligibility with Choapan (closest). Temaxcalapan may not be part of this language. Bilingual level estimates for Spanish are 0 50%, 1 35%, 2 10%, 3 3%, 4 2%, 5 0%. Investigation needed: intelligibility with Temaxcalapan. VOS, short words, affixes, clitics. Deciduous forest. Mountain slope. Peasant agriculturalists. 400 to 1,000 meters. NT 1971.

ZAPOTECO, RINCÓN SUR ***(RINCÓN-SUR ZAPOTEC)*** [ZSR] 12,000 (1990 census). Oaxaca. Oto-Manguean, Zapotecan, Zapotec. NT 1992.

ZAPOTECO, SAN AGUSTÍN MIXTEPEC [ZTM] 59 speakers (1994 SIL). Oaxaca, Miahuatlán, town of San Agustín Mixtepec. Oto-Manguean, Zapotecan, Zapotec. A separate language from San Juan Mixtepec Zapoteco [ZPM]. Nearly extinct.

ZAPOTECO, SAN BALTÁZAR LOXICHA ***(NORTHWESTERN POCHUTLA ZAPOTECO, SAN BALTÁZAR LOXICHA ZAPOTEC, LOXICHA ZAPOTECO)*** [ZPX] 1,500 including 19 monolinguals (1990 census). Oaxaca, 115 km. south of Oaxaca city. San Baltázar Loxicha and Santa Catarina Loxicha. Oto-Manguean, Zapotecan, Zapotec. 71% intelligibility with Santa María Coatlán (closest), 63% with Cuixtla (Central Miahuatlán), 46.5% with San Vicente Coatlán. Bilingualism in Spanish. Pre-coastal mountains. 4,000 feet.

ZAPOTECO, SAN JUAN GUELAVÍA ***(WESTERN TLACOLULA ZAPOTECO, GUELAVÍA ZAPOTEC)*** [ZAB] 28,000 (1990 census). Population total both countries 28,500. Central Oaxaca. Also spoken in USA. Oto-Manguean, Zapotecan, Zapotec. Dialects: JALIEZA ZAPOTECO, TEOTITLÁN DEL VALLE ZAPOTECO, SAN MARTÍN TILCAJETE ZAPOTECO. 20% intelligibility with Zegache (closest). Jalieza has 99% intelligibility of Guelavía. Teotitlán del Valle has 100% intelligibility of Guelavía, but Guelavía only 59% of Teotitlán del Valle. Bilingual level estimates for Spanish are 0 40%, 1 10%, 2 10%, 3 20%, 4 10%, 5 10%. Investigation needed: intelligibility with Teotitlán del Valle. Dictionary. VSO, tonal, affixes, clitics. Literacy rate in second language: 10%. Desert, scrub forest. Mountain valley. Peasant agriculturalists. 1,650 meters. NT 1995.

ZAPOTECO, SAN PEDRO QUIATONI ***(SAN PEDRO QUIATONI ZAPOTEC, QUIATONI ZAPOTECO, EASTERN TLACOLULA ZAPOTECO)*** [ZPF] 12,000 to 15,000 (1993 SIL). Central Oaxaca, San Pedro Quiatoni, Salinas, Unión Juárez, and nearby settlements. Oto-Manguean, Zapotecan, Zapotec. 76% intelligibility with Mitla; closest. Literacy rate in first language: 1%. Literacy rate in second language: 75%. Traditional religion.

ZAPOTECO, SAN VICENTE COATLÁN ***(SOUTHERN EJUTLA ZAPOTECO, SAN VICENTE COATLÁN ZAPOTEC, COATLÁN ZAPOTECO)*** [ZPT] 2,430 (1990 census). Oaxaca, Ejutla District, 90 km. south of Oaxaca city. San Vicente Coatlán, a municipio town. Oto-Manguean, Zapotecan, Zapotec. 75% intelligibility of San Baltázar Loxicha (closest, Northwestern Pochutla), 45% of Santa María Coatlán. 166 of the 584 monolinguals are 5 to 9 years old (1990). Vigorous. Primary school. Agriculturalists; mezcal makers.

ZAPOTECO, SANTA CATARINA ALBARRADAS [ZTN] 1,000 or fewer (1990 census). Oaxaca, Santa Catarina Albarradas. Oto-Manguean, Zapotecan, Zapotec. 80% intelligibility of Santo Domingo Albarradas; Santo Domingo 52% of Santa Catarina. Differences in phonology and grammar between them. About half the population can understand San Pedro Cajonos Zapoteco reasonably well because of trading with them.

ZAPOTECO, SANTA INÉS YATZECHI ***(SANTA INÉS ZEGACHE ZAPOTECO, SANTA INÉS YATZECHI ZAPOTEC, YATZECHI ZAPOTECO, ZEGACHE ZAPOTEC0, SOUTHEASTERN ZIMATLÁN ZAPOTECO)*** [ZPN] 2,235 speakers (1990 census). Central Oaxaca, Zimatlán District, 40 km. south of Oaxaca city, west of Ocotlán de Morelos. Oto-Manguean, Zapotecan, Zapotec. Dialect: ZAACHILA. 75% intelligibility with San Antonino Ocotlán (closest). Zaachila may need some separate literature. San Miguel Tilquiapan may be a dialect. 176 monolinguals. Zapoteco is apparently no longer spoken in Santa Ana Zegache, and going out of use in Zaachila. Vigorous use among children in Santa Inés, some of whom are monolinguals (1990). Bible portions 1989-1991.

ZAPOTECO, SANTA MARÍA QUIEGOLANI ***(SANTA MARÍA QUIEGOLANI ZAPOTEC, QUIEGOLANI ZAPOTEC, WESTERN YAUTEPEC ZAPOTECO)*** [ZPI] 3,000 (1990 census). Central Oaxaca. Oto-Manguean, Zapotecan, Zapotec. 60% intelligibility with San Juan Mixtepec (closest). Traditional religion, Christian.

ZAPOTECO, SANTIAGO LAPAGUÍA [ZTL] 4,200 (1983 SIL). Oaxaca, southeastern Miahuatlán, including four towns: Lapaguía (700, monolingual), San Felipe Lachillo (500, settled from Lapaguía), La Merced del Potrero (2,500, bilingual), San Juan Guivini (500, monolingual). Oto-Manguean, Zapotecan, Zapotec. 80% intelligibility with San Juan Mixtepec Zapoteco. Speakers are not very bilingual in Spanish.

ZAPOTECO, SANTIAGO XANICA ***(XANICA ZAPOTEC)*** [ZPR] 2,500 (1990 census). Oaxaca, southeastern Miahuatlán, including four towns: Santiago Xanica, Santa María Coixtepec, San Andrés Lovene, San Antonio Ozolotepec. Oto-Manguean, Zapotecan, Zapotec. 72% intelligibility with San Gregorio Ozolotepec, 70% with Cuixtla (Central Miahuatlán). Bilingualism in Spanish. Agriculturalists: coffee. 3,000 to 4,000 feet.

ZAPOTECO, SOLA DE VEGA ESTE ***(EASTERN SOLA DE VEGA ZAPOTEC, LACHIXÍO ZAPOTECO)*** [ZPL] 6,500 (1990 census). Western Oaxaca, eastern Sola de Vega, towns of Santa Marma Lachixío, San Vicente Lachixío. Oto-Manguean, Zapotecan, Zapotec. Southwestern Zimatlán dialect speakers need separate literature. 73% intelligibility with San Pedro el Alto. Bilingual level estimates for Spanish are 0 <60%, 1 <30%, 2 <15%, 3 <8%, 4 <5%, 5 0%. Dictionary. VSO, tonal, short words, affixes, clitics. Literacy rate in first language: 5%. Literacy rate in second language: 60%. Pine forest. Mountain slope. Peasant agriculturalists. 1,846 to 2,460 meters. Bible portions 1984-1989.

ZAPOTECO, TABAA ***(CENTRAL VILLA ALTA ZAPOTECO, TABAA ZAPOTECO, TABÁ ZAPOTEC)*** [ZAT] 2,000 (1992 SIL). Oaxaca. Oto-Manguean, Zapotecan, Zapotec. Bilingual level estimates for Spanish are 0 50%, 1 30%, 2 13%, 3 5%, 4 2%, 5 0%. VSO, tonal, long words, affixes, clitics. Scrub, pine forest. Mountain slope. Sedentary pastoralists, swidden, peasant agriculturalists. 300 to 800 meters. NT 1981.

ZAPOTECO, TEJALAPAN ***(SAN FELIPE TEJALAPAN ZAPOTEC, TEJALAPAN ZAPOTEC, TEJALÁPAM ZAPOTECO, SAN FELIPE ZAPOTECO)*** [ZTT] 124 (1990 census). The town has 4,656 people. Oaxaca, Etla District, town of San Felipe Tejalapan. Oto-Manguean, Zapotecan, Zapotec. A separate language from Santo Tomás Mazaltepec Zapoteco. Bilingualism in Spanish. 92 speakers are over 50 years old, including the 2 monolinguals. They came from Ixtepeji area 300 years ago. Nearly extinct.

ZAPOTECO, TEXMELUCAN ***(CENTRAL SOLA DE VEGA ZAPOTECO, SAN LORENZO TEXMELUCAN ZAPOTECO, PAPABUCO, TEXMELUCAN ZAPOTEC)*** [ZPZ] 4,100 (1992 SIL). Western Oaxaca. Oto-Manguean, Zapotecan, Zapotec. Closest to Western Sola de Vega (Zaniza). Bilingual level estimates for Spanish are 0 70%, 1 20%, 2 8%, 3 2%, 4 0%, 5 0%. Zaniza and Elotepec Zapoteco are also called 'Papabuco'. VSO, tonal, short words, affixes, clitics. Pine, tropical forest. Mountain slope. Swidden, peasant agriculturalists. 1,365 to 1,846 meters. NT 1989.

ZAPOTECO, TILQUIAPAN ***(TILQUIAPAN ZAPOTEC, SAN MIGUEL TILQUIAPAN ZAPOTECO)*** [ZTS] 2,700 speakers including 900 monolinguals (1990 census). Central Oaxaca, Ocotlán, San Miguel Tilquiapan town. Oto-Manguean, Zapotecan, Zapotec. 87% intelligibility of Yatzechi, 65% of Chichicapan, 59% of Ocotlán, 45% of Guelavía. Bilingualism in Spanish. Sociolinguistic differences with nearest Zapoteco. Primary school with bilingual teachers. Semi-arid, rocky. Agriculturalists. 5,000 feet.

ZAPOTECO, TLACOLULITA ***(SOUTHEASTERN YAUTEPEC ZAPOTECO, ASUNCIÓN TLACOLULITA ZAPOTECO, TLACOLULITA ZAPOTEC)*** [ZPK] 135 speakers out of a population of 904 (1990 census). Eastern Oaxaca, Asunción Tlacolulita and San Juan Alotepec. Oto-Manguean, Zapotecan, Zapotec. 15% intelligibility with Lachixila (closest), 10% on Mitla and Guelavía, 0% on Lachiguiri, Juchitán, Guevea de Humboldt, Petapa, San Juan Mixtepec, and Quiegolani. Bilingualism in Spanish. 111 speakers are 50 years old or older (1990). Nearly extinct.

ZAPOTECO, TOTOMACHAPAN ***(WESTERN ZIMATLÁN ZAPOTECO, SAN PEDRO TOTOMACHAPAN ZAPOTECO, TOTOMACHAPAN ZAPOTEC)*** [ZPH] 259 speakers out of a population of 1,009 (1990 census). Western Oaxaca, 2 towns. Oto-Manguean, Zapotecan, Zapotec. No intelligibility with other Zapoteco. Bilingualism in Spanish. Most speakers are over 50 years old (1990). Nearly extinct.

ZAPOTECO, XADANI ***(XADANI ZAPOTEC, SANTA MARÍA XADANI ZAPOTECO, EASTERN POCHUTLA ZAPOTECO)*** [ZAX] 338 speakers (1990 census). Oaxaca, Pochutla District, San Miguel del Puerto Municipio, Santa María Xadani, 16 towns or villages. Oto-Manguean, Zapotecan, Zapotec. Bilingualism in Spanish. 122 speakers over 50 years old, 90 between 35 and 50, 1 monolingual (1990). Coastal.

ZAPOTECO, XANAGUÍA ***(XANAGUÍA ZAPOTEC, SANTA CATARINA XANAGUÍA ZAPOTECO)*** [ZTG] 2,500 (1990 census). Oaxaca, southeastern Miahuatlán, including three towns: Santa Catarina Xanaguía, San Francisco Ozolotepec, and San José Ozolotepec. Oto-Manguean, Zapotecan, Zapotec. 6th grade education in Spanish available in Xanaguía. Most children finish third or fourth grade. Those finishing 6th grade, the highest available locally, still have limited Spanish proficiency. Zapoteco is used by all in the home. All ages. They have pride in their language. Many women over 40 and some men have no education. VSO. Literacy rate in first language: 1%. Literacy rate in second language: 10%. Swidden agriculturalists. Mountains. 6,000 feet. Bible portions 1996.

ZAPOTECO, YALÁLAG [ZPU] 5,000 (1990 census). 2,000 are in Yalálag, others are in D. F, Oaxaca City, Veracruz. Also in Los Angeles, California, USA. Population total both countries 5,000 or more. Oaxaca. Also spoken in USA. Oto-Manguean, Zapotecan, Zapotec. Bilingual level estimates for Spanish are 0 10%, 1 10%, 2 30%, 3 30%, 4 10%, 5 10%. VSO, tonal, short words, affixes, clitics. Literacy rate in first language: 1%. Literacy rate in second language: 60%. Pine, scrub forests. Mountain slope. Peasant agriculturalists, craftsmen. 1,400 meters. Bible portions 1988-1999.

ZAPOTECO, YARENI *(WESTERN IXTLÁN ZAPOTECO, TEOCOCUILCO DE MARCOS PÉREZ ZAPOTECO, SANTA ANA YARENI, ETLA ZAPOTEC)* [ZAE] 6,000 (1982 SIL). Northern Oaxaca. Oto-Manguean, Zapotecan, Zapotec. 80% intelligibility with Sierra de Juárez Zapoteco (closest). Bilingual level estimates for Spanish are 0 20%, 1 40%, 2 25%, 3 10%, 4 5%, 5 0%. VSO, tonal, affixes, clitics. Literacy rate in first language: Below 1%. Literacy rate in second language: 60% to 75%. Pine forest. Sedentary pastoralists, peasant agriculturalists. 1,900 to 2,300 meters. Bible portions 1966-1990.

ZAPOTECO, YATEE *(YATEE ZAPOTEC)* [ZTY] 3,000 (1999 SIL). Oaxaca, San Francisco Yatee, 4 towns. Oto-Manguean, Zapotecan, Zapotec. Closest to Villa Alta Zapoteco and Yalalag Zapoteco, but distinct. Different from Lachiruaj. Limited bilingualism in Spanish. Bible portions 1999.

ZAPOTECO, YATZACHI *(YATZACHI ZAPOTEC, VILLA ALTA ZAPOTECO)* [ZAV] 2,500 (1990 census). Population total both countries 2,500 or more. Villages of Yatzachi el Bajo, Yatzachi el Alto, Xoochixtepec, Yohueche, Zoochina, Zoochila, Yalina, north central Oaxaca; and Los Angeles, California, USA. Also spoken in USA. Oto-Manguean, Zapotecan, Zapotec. 90% intelligibility with Zoogocho on narrative, 85% with Cajonos (Southern Villa Alta) and Yalálag, and somewhat intelligible with Solaga and Tabaa. Bilingual level estimates for Spanish are 0 10%, 1 10%, 2 40%, 3 20%, 4 14%, 5 1%. Dictionary. Grammar. VSO, tonal, long words, affixes, clitics. Literacy rate in first language: 30%. Literacy rate in second language: 60%. Scrub forest. Mountain slope. Peasant agriculturalists in Oaxaca, wage laborers outside. 615 to 1,690 meters. NT 1971.

ZAPOTECO, YAUTEPEC *(SAN BARTOLO YAUTEPEC ZAPOTECO, NORTHWESTERN YAUTEPEC ZAPOTECO, YAUTEPEC ZAPOTEC)* [ZPB] 314 speakers (1990 census). Eastern Oaxaca, San Bartolo Yautepec. Oto-Manguean, Zapotecan, Zapotec. 10% intelligibility with Tlacolulita (closest), no intelligibility of other Zapoteco. Bilingualism in Spanish. 126 speakers between 35 and 50 years old, 138 over 50, 4 monolinguals over 50 (1990).

ZAPOTECO, ZAACHILA *(SAN RAYMUNDO JALPAN ZAPOTEC)* [ZTX] 550 speakers out of a population of over 10,000 (1990 census). Oaxaca, 15 km. south of the city of Oaxaca, past Xoxo, town of Zaachila (416 speakers out of 10,601 population) and San Raymundo Jalpan (116 speakers out of 1,270 population). A few in San Bartolo Coyotepec, San Pablo Cuatro Venados, and Santa María Coyotepec. Oto-Manguean, Zapotecan, Zapotec. 85% intelligibility of Zegeche, 75% of Tilquiapan, 72% of Guelavía, 10% of Ocotlán. Bilingualism in Spanish. Only those over 50 years of age understand but do not normally speak it, but this includes 3 women monolinguals (1990). No children speak it.

ZAPOTECO, ZANIZA *(ZANIZA ZAPOTEC, SANTA MARÍA ZANIZA ZAPOTECO, WESTERN SOLA DE VEGA ZAPOTECO, PAPABUCO)* [ZPW] 770 speakers including 4 monolinguals (1990 census). Western Oaxaca, Santa María Zaniza, Santiago Textitlán, Santiago Xochiltepec, El Frijol, Buenavista. Oto-Manguean, Zapotecan, Zapotec. 10% intelligibility with Texmelucan (closest). Bilingualism in Spanish. 35% of speakers are under 40. Texmelucan is also called 'Papabuco'.

ZAPOTECO, ZOOGOCHO *(SAN BARTOLOMÉ ZOOGOCHO ZAPOTECO, ZOOGOCHO ZAPOTEC)* [ZPQ] 1,000 in Mexico (1991 SIL). Population total both countries 1,400. Zoogocho, Yalina, Tabehua, and Oaxaca City, Oaxaca, and Mexico City. Also spoken in USA. Oto-Manguean, Zapotecan, Zapotec. Dialects: ZOOGOCHO, YALINA, TABEHUA. 57% intelligibility with Comaltepec (Choapan; closest). Zoogocho is the market town, so most Yatzachi people go there weekly, but Zoogocho people do not understand Yatzachi as well (80%). Bilingual level estimates for Spanish are 0 10%, 1 10%, 2 45%, 3 20%, 4 14%, 5 1%. The local economy is supported to a large extent by those working outside the area. Dictionary. VSO, tonal, long words, affixes, clitics. Literacy rate in first language: 30%. Literacy rate in second language: 60%. Scrub forest. Mountain slope. Peasant agriculturalists in Zoogocho, wage laborers outside. 900 to 1,800 meters. NT 1988.

ZOQUE, CHIMALAPA [ZOH] 4,500 including 15 monolinguals (1990 census). Oaxaca, Santa María Chimalapa and San Miguel Chimalapa. Mixe-Zoque, Zoque, Oaxaca Zoque. Bilingualism in Spanish. Bible portions.

ZOQUE, COPAINALÁ [ZOC] 10,000 (1990 census). Copainalá, Chiapas. Mixe-Zoque, Zoque, Chiapas Zoque. Dialects: OCOTEPEC, OSTUACÁN. 83% intelligibility with Francisco León (closest). Bilingual level estimates for Spanish are 0 0%, 1 5%, 2 5%, 3 30%, 4 50%, 5 10%. Dictionary. Grammar. VSO, nontonal, long words, affixes, clitics. Tropical. Mountain slope, riverine. Agriculturalists. 215 to 1,845 meters. NT 1967.

ZOQUE, FRANCISCO LEÓN ***(SANTA MAGDALENA ZOQUE)*** [ZOS] 20,000 (1990 census). Mezcalapa, Chiapas. Mixe-Zoque, Zoque, Chiapas Zoque. Dialects: CHAPULTENANGO, SAN PEDRO YASPAC. Close to Copainalá. Bilingual level estimates for Spanish are 0 40%, 1 35%, 2 10%, 3 10%, 4 3%, 5 2%. The eruption of El Chicón volcano in 1982 has necessitated relocation; the original town of Francisco León is buried. Dictionary. Nontonal, long words, affixes. Tropical. Mountain slope. Peasant agriculturalists. 200 to 800 meters. NT 1978.

ZOQUE, RAYÓN [ZOR] 2,000 to 2,300 speakers including about 20 monolinguals in a population of 10,400 (1990 census). Northwest Chiapas, Rayón and Tapilula. Mixe-Zoque, Zoque, Chiapas Zoque. Distinct from other Zoque. Bilingual level estimates for Spanish are 0 25%, 1 25%, 2 50%, 3 0%, 4 0%, 5 0%. Dictionary. Nontonal, VOS, short and long words, clitic and affixes. Scrub forest. Mountain mesa. Swidden or peasant agriculturalists. 1,337 meters.

ZOQUE, TABASCO ***(AYAPANEC)*** [ZOQ] 40 speakers (1971 García de León) out of 367 in the ethnic group (1960 census). Municipio of Jalapa de Méndez, Ayapa, Tabasco. Mixe-Zoque, Zoque, Veracruz Zoque. Bilingualism in Spanish. Nearly extinct.

MONTSERRAT

National or official language: English. 11,000 (1998 UN). Literacy rate 97%. Also includes Arabic 500, Chinese 500. Christian. Data accuracy estimate: B. The number of languages listed for Montserrat is 2. Of those, both are living languages. Diversity index 0.00.

ENGLISH [ENG] Indo-European, Germanic, West, English. National language. Bible 1535-1989. See main entry under United Kingdom.

LEEWARD CARIBBEAN CREOLE ENGLISH [AIG] 10,000. Creole, English based, Atlantic, Eastern, Southern. Dialect: MONTSERRAT CREOLE ENGLISH. Montserrat variety is closest to St. Kitts, Nevis, Antigua (Ian Hancock). Montserrat has a creole continuum with Standard English. Agriculturalists: cotton. See main entry under Antigua and Barbuda.

NETHERLANDS ANTILLES

National or official language: Dutch. 213,000 (1998 UN), including St. Eustatius 1,000, Saba 1,000, St. Maarten 10,000 (1995). Leeward islands: Curaçao, Bonaire; Windward islands: St. Maarten, Saba, St. Eustatius. Self-governing part of the Netherlands. By agreement of all parties, it remains in the Kingdom of the Netherlands (1996). Literacy rate 95%. Also includes Spanish, Sranan, Arabic, Chinese. Christian, secular. Blind population 500 (1982 WCE). Deaf institutions: 3. Data accuracy estimate: A2. The number of languages listed for Netherlands Antilles is 4. Of those, all are living languages. Diversity index 0.12.

DUTCH [DUT] Indo-European, Germanic, West, Low Saxon-Low Franconian, Low Franconian. It is decreasing in importance. Official language. Bible 1522-1988. See main entry under Netherlands.

ENGLISH [ENG] Dutch Virgin Islands. Indo-European, Germanic, West, English. Post-creole English is the dialect used (Alleyne). The third most important language in Netherlands Antilles. Bible 1382-1989. See main entry under United Kingdom.

PAPIAMENTU ***(PAPIAMENTO, PAPIAM, PAPIAMENTOE, PAPIAMEN, CURAÇOLEÑO, CURASSESE)*** [PAE] 179,000 in Netherlands Antilles (1998), 84% of the population (1995). Population total all countries 329,000. Curaçao, St. Maartens, Bonaire islands off Venezuela coast and islands off Nicaragua. Also spoken in Aruba, Netherlands, Puerto Rico, U.S. Virgin Islands. Creole, Iberian based. The language is becoming more like Spanish, which is prestigious. They use Dutch at school and with tourists, Spanish with Spanish-speaking persons, English with tourists. All domains. All ages. About 20,000 speak it as second language. Using both Papiamentu and Dutch is not considered an indication of lack of education. However, inability to use Dutch hinders social and political mobility, and leads to discontent. Dictionary. Grammar. Taught in first 2 years of primary school. Newspapers. Christian. Bible 1997.

VIRGIN ISLANDS CREOLE ENGLISH [VIB] 12,700 including 10,000 on St. Maarten, 1,100 on Saba, 1,600 on St. Eustatius. Southern St. Maarten, Saba, St. Eustatius. Creole, English based, Atlantic, Eastern, Southern. Dialect: ST. MAARTEN CREOLE ENGLISH. See main entry under U.S. Virgin Islands.

NICARAGUA

Republic of Nicaragua, República de Nicaragua. National or official language: Spanish. 4,807,000 (1998 UN). Literacy rate 66% to 74%. Also includes Arabic 400, Chinese 7,000. Christian, secular. Blind population 1,800 (1982 WCE). Deaf population 248,401. Data accuracy estimate: A1, A2. The number of languages listed for Nicaragua is 10. Of those, 7 are living languages and 3 are extinct. Diversity index 0.08.

GARÍFUNA ***(CARIBE, BLACK CARIB, CENTRAL AMERICAN CARIB)*** [CAB] 1,500 in Nicaragua (1982 Meso-America). Arawakan, Maipuran, Northern Maipuran, Caribbean. NT 1983-1994. See main entry under Honduras.

MATAGALPA ***(PANTASMAS)*** [MTN] No speakers out of an ethnic group of 18,000 to 20,000 (1981 MARC). The ethnic group is in the Central highlands, Matagalpa and Jinotega departments, and in Honduras, El Paraíso Department. Misumalpan. They now speak Spanish. Sedentary subsistence agriculturalists. Extinct.

MÍSKITO ***(MÍSQUITO, MÍSKITU, MOSQUITO, MARQUITO)*** [MIQ] 154,400 in Nicaragua (1993 census). Population total both countries 183,400. From Pearl Lagoon to Black River, coast and lowlands. Zalaya Department, North Atlantic Autonomous Region (RAAN) with a concentration in the city of Puerto Cabeza, and towns and villages of Prinzapolka, Tronquera, San Carlos (Río Coco), Waspam, Leimus, Bocana de Paiwas, Karawala, Sangnilaya, Wasla, Sisin, Rosita, Bonanza, Siuna, Bihmuna, and all along the Río Coco area. Also in South Atlantic Autonomous Region (RAAS). Also spoken in Honduras. Misumalpan. Dialects: HONDURAN MÍSKITO (MAM), TAWIRA (TAUIRA), BAYMUNA (BAYMUNANA, BALDAM), WANKI (WANGKI), CABO (KABO). All dialects are intelligible with each other. The language is closest to Sumo. Bilingual level estimates for Spanish are 0 0%, 1 2%, 2 3%, 3 15%, 4 70%, 5 10%. Secondary school children are taught in Spanish, Some English is known. All Mískito understand the language. Widespread use among older people. Many Hispanic people have learned Mískito. Educational materials are in Wangki, spoken around Puerto Cabeza. The other dialects are in settlements southwest of there. Trade language. SOV; articles, relatives after noun heads; word order distinguishes subject, object; verb affixes mark person, number; ergative; passive; CVC; nontonal. Literacy rate in first language: 52% to 58%. Widespread use in primary schools. Semi-tropical to tropical. Coastal. Agriculturalists, fishermen, government and education workers. Just above sea level. Christian. Bible 1999.

MONIMBO [MOL] No speakers out of an ethnic group of 10,000 (1981 MARC). Unclassified. Have retained few traits of their pre-conquest American Indian culture. Extinct.

NICARAGUAN SIGN LANGUAGE ***(IDIOMA DE SENAS DE NICARAGUA)*** [NCS] 3,000 deaf users plus other hearing people (1997 Asociacion Nacional de Sordos de Nicaragua). Managua and throughout the nation. Deaf sign language. Unrelated to El Salvadoran, Costa Rican, or other sign languages. Users know little Spanish. Officially used in school since 1992, and used outside the classroom. Dictionary.

NORTHERN CENTRAL AMERICA CREOLE ENGLISH [BZI] 30,000 or more (1986 Carrier Pidgin), 23.5% of the coastal population (1989 J. Holm). Includes 625 speakers of Rama Cay Creole (1989 Holm). Bluefields region including Rama Cay Island. Creole, English based, Atlantic, Western. Dialects: MÍSKITO COAST CREOLE ENGLISH (BLUEFIELDS CREOLE ENGLISH), RAMA CAY CREOLE ENGLISH. Bilingualism in English, Spanish. The first language of the Creole people and most Carib; the second language of most Miskito and some Spanish speakers. Speakers consider English to be their standard language, but identify with the creole. See main entry under Belize.

RAMA [RMA] 24 speakers out of 649 population (1989 Holm). Rama Cay, 30-mile radius. Chibchan, Rama. Most people now speak Rama Cay Creole. Nearly extinct.

SPANISH ***(ESPAÑOL, CASTELLANO)*** [SPN] 4,347,000 in Nicaragua (1995 estimate). Indo-European, Italic, Romance, Italo-Western, Western, Gallo-Iberian, Ibero-Romance, West Iberian, Castilian. National language. Bible 1553-1979. See main entry under Spain.

SUBTIABA [SUT] No speakers out of an ethnic group of 5,000 (1981 MARC). Plains of León, Pacific slope. Subtiaba-Tlapanec. Have retained few traits of their pre-conquest culture. Extinct.

SUMO TAWAHKA ***(SUMU, SOUMO, SUMOO, WOOLWA, SUMO, ULWA)*** [SUM] 6,700 in Nicaragua (1982 Mesoamerica). Population total both countries 7,400. Huaspuc (Waspuk) River and tributaries. Also spoken in Honduras. Misumalpan. Dialects: PANAMAHKA, TWAHKA, NICARAGUAN TAWAHKA, HONDURAN TAWAHKA (SOUTHERN SUMO). The same language as Honduras, but a different dialect. The first three dialects listed group together into Northern Sumo. SOV. Hunter-gatherers, fishermen, swidden agriculturalists: manioc. NT, in press (1999).

PANAMA

Republic of Panama, República de Panamá. National or official language: Spanish. 2,767,000 (1998 UN). Literacy rate 87% to 88%. Also includes Hebrew, Japanese 1,200, Korean, Eastern Yiddish, Arabic 15,000. Information mainly from P. Cohen 1976; SIL 1970-1998. Christian, Jewish, Muslim, traditional religion, Baha'i. Blind population 2,000 (1982 WCE). Deaf population 159,456. Data accuracy estimate: A1, A2. The number of languages listed for Panama is 14. Of those, all are living languages. Diversity index 0.23.

BUGLERE ***(BOKOTA, BOGOTA, BOFOTA, BOBOTA, BOCOTA, BUKUETA, NORTENYO, MURIRE, VERAGUAS SABANERO)*** [SAB] 2,500 (1986 SIL). Mountains of western Panama. Chibchan, Guaymi. Dialects: SABANERO, BOKOTÁ. Speakers of Sabanero are few and integrated among the Guaymí. NT 1988.

CHINESE, HAKKA [HAK] 6,000 speakers in Panama out of an ethnic group of 30,000 to 60,000 including Cantonese (1981 MARC). Panama City, Colón, larger towns of interior. Sino-Tibetan, Chinese. Bilingualism in Spanish. Merchants. Bible 1916. See main entry under China.

CHINESE, YUE ***(YUE, YUEH, CANTONESE)*** [YUH] Panama City, Colón, larger towns of interior. Sino-Tibetan, Chinese. Bilingualism in Spanish. Merchants. Bible 1894-1981. See main entry under China.

EMBERÁ, NORTHERN ***(EMPERA, EBERA BEDEA, ATRATO, DARIEN, DARIENA, PANAMA EMBERA, CHOLO, EERÃ)*** [EMP] 7,000 to 8,000 in Panama. Population total both countries 20,000 to 23,000. Southeastern Panama, Darién area, lowland jungle. Also spoken in Colombia. Choco, Embera, Northern. Bilingual level estimates for Spanish are 0 40%, 1 32%, 2 25%, 3 2.5%, 4 .5%, 5 0%. Dictionary. Grammar. SOV. Tropical forest. Interfluvial. Swidden agriculturalists. 100 to 400 meters. Traditional religion, Christian. NT 1993.

EMBERÁ-CATÍO ***(CATÍO, KATIO, EMBENA, EPERA)*** [CTO] 40 in Panama (1982 SIL). Choco, Embera, Northern. Bible portions 1975-1987. See main entry under Colombia.

EMBERÁ-SAIJA ***(SAIJA, EPENA SAIJA, EPEA PEDÉE, SOUTHERN EMBERA, SOUTHERN EMPERA, CHOLO)*** [SJA] Southern Pacific coast, Caucá, Nariño, Chocó departments. Choco, Embera, Southern. Dialect: BASURUDO. Bilingual level estimates for Spanish are 0 0%, 1 20%, 2 30%, 3 50%, 4 0%, 5 0%. Grammar. SOV. Tropical forest. Coastal, riverine. Fishermen, agriculturalists. 0 to 70 meters. Bible portions 1991. See main entry under Colombia.

KUNA, BORDER ***(PAYA-PUCURO KUNA, KUNA DE LA FRONTERA, COLUMBIA CUNA, CAIMAN NUEVO, LONG HAIR CUNA, CUNA)*** [KUA] 700 in Panama (1991 SIL). Southeastern Panama, villages of Paya and Pucuro. Chibchan, Kuna. Classification of Kuna is uncertain; it may be an isolate with certain Chibchan features. Bilingual level estimates for Spanish are 0 20%, 1 70%, 2 7%, 3 3%, 4 0%, 5 0%. SOV. Tropical forest. Riverine. Swidden agriculturalists. 300 to 400 feet. NT 1993. See main entry under Colombia.

KUNA, SAN BLAS ***(SAN BLAS CUNA)*** [CUK] 50,000 to 70,000 (1995 SIL), including about 10,000 in Panama City, Colón, and on banana plantations (1991 SIL). San Blas Islands and on the mainland. Chibchan, Kuna. Dialects: CHUANA, CUEVA, BAYANO (ALTO BAYANO, MAJE). Bilingual level estimates for Spanish are 0 60%, 1 20%, 2 12%, 3 2%, 4 3%, 5 3%. English also used. SOV. Tropical forest. Island, riverine. Swidden agriculturalists, fishermen. 0 to 200 feet. Christian. NT 1970-1995.

NGÄBERE ***(VALIENTE, CHIRIQUI, NGOBERE, NGÄBERE, GUAYMÍ)*** [GYM] 128,000 in Panama (1990 census). Population total both countries 133,000 or more. Northeastern Chiriqui, Bocas del Toro, western Veraguas (western provinces). Also spoken in Costa Rica. Chibchan, Guaymi. Dialects: VALIENTE, EASTERN GUAYMÍ (TOLÉ, CHIRIQUÍ). Bilingual level estimates for Spanish are 0 30%, 1 40%, 2 15%, 3 10%, 4 4.5%, 5 .5%. English creole also used. 'Ngäbere' is name preferred by speakers for language, 'Ngäbe' for themselves. SOV. Tropical forest. Slope, coastal. Swidden agriculturalists, hunters, fishermen. 100 to 6,000 feet. NT 1977.

SAN MIGUEL CREOLE FRENCH [SME] 3 or more speakers (1999 SIL). Creole, French based. Ancestors came from St. Lucia in mid-19th century as laborers. The Creole had Spanish influences. Nearly extinct.

SOUTHWESTERN CARIBBEAN CREOLE ENGLISH [JAM] 100,000 to 299,600 in Panama, 14% of the population (1986). Bocas del Toro, Colón, and Rio Abajo in Panama City. Creole, English based, Atlantic, Western. Dialect: PANAMANIAN CREOLE ENGLISH (PANAMA ENGLISH CREOLE, GUARI-GUARI). Ancestors came from Barbados and Jamaica in mid-19th century to work in fruit plantations, and later to build the railway and canal. Influences from both eastern and western Caribbean creole English. Formerly education was in English, but is now in Spanish. See main entry under Jamaica.

SPANISH ***(ESPAÑOL, CASTELLANO)*** [SPN] 2,100,000 in Panama (1995 estimate). Enclaves of speakers. Indo-European, Italic, Romance, Italo-Western, Western, Gallo-Iberian, Ibero-Romance, West Iberian, Castilian. National language. Bible 1553-1979. See main entry under Spain.

TERIBE ***(TERRABA, TIRIBI, TIRRIBI, NORTENYO, QUEQUEXQUE, NASO)*** [TFR] 3,000 in Panama (1996 SIL). Population total both countries 3,000 to 3,400. Northwestern area, Changuinola, Teribe River. Also spoken in Costa Rica. Chibchan, Talamanca. Bilingualism in Spanish. 'Naso' is the name preferred by speakers. OVS. Tropical forest. Interfluvial. Swidden agriculturalists. 200 feet. Bible portions 1979-1984.

WOUN MEU ***(WAUN MEO, WAUNANA, WAUMEO, WOUNMEU, WOUNAAN, NOANAMA, NOENAMA, NONAMA, CHOCAMA, CHANCO)*** [NOA] 3,000 in Panama. Population total both countries 6,000. Southeastern Panama, lowlands. Also spoken in Colombia. Choco. Bilingual level estimates for Spanish are 0 10%, 1 50%, 2 25%, 3 13.5%, 4 1.0%, 5 0.5%. The people call themselves 'Wounaan', and their language 'Woun Meo'. SOV. Tropical forest. Riverine. Swidden agriculturalists. 50 feet. NT 1988.

PARAGUAY

Republic of Paraguay, República del Paraguay. National or official languages: Paraguayan Guaraní, Spanish. 5,222,000 (1998 UN). 50,000 speakers of American Indian languages not counting Paraguayan Guaraní (Adelaar 1991). Literacy rate 81% to 90%. Also includes Greek 1,800, Italian 26,000, Japanese 12,000, Korean 6,000, Portuguese 636,000, Ukrainian 26,000, Chinese 7,500. Information mainly from SIL 1969-1999. Christian, secular, traditional religion. Blind population 4,000 (1982 WCE). Deaf population 316,214. Deaf institutions: 3. Data accuracy estimate: B. The number of languages listed for Paraguay is 22. Of those, 20 are living languages, 1 is a second language without mother tongue speakers, and 1 is extinct. Diversity index 0.33.

ACHÉ ***("GUAIAQUI", "GUAYAKÍ", "GUOYAGUI", GUAYAKI-ACHE, AXE, ACHE)*** [GUQ] 900 (1995). Eastern, Alto Paraná, Caaguazú, Chopa Pou, Cerro Moroti, and Puerto Barra reservations, and Tupa Renda. Tupi, Tupi-Guarani, Guarani (I). Reported to be four dialects, one of which is nearly extinct. Speakers are becoming bilingual in Paraguayan Guaraní. Scattered and nomadic. The name "Guayakí" is derogatory. Dictionary. Hunter-gatherers. Bible portions 1978.

AYOREO ***(MOROTOCO, MORO, AYORÉ, PYETA YOVAI)*** [AYO] 3,000 in Paraguay (1991). Population total both countries 4,000 to 4,500. Chaco and northern Alto Paraguay departments. Also spoken in Bolivia. Zamucoan. Dialect: TSIRACUA. Partially nomadic. NT 1982.

CHAMACOCO ***(ISHIRO, JEYWO)*** [CEG] 1,800 (1991 Ulrich SIL). Northeastern Chaco, eastern Alto Paraguay Department, Puerto Bahia Negra, Puerto Diana, Puerto Esperanza (On+ch+tah), Dos Estrellas, Potrerito, Fuerte Olimpo, along the Paraguay River. There may be some in Brazil. Zamucoan. Dialects: CHAMACOCO BRAVO (TOMARAHO, TOMARAXA), EBITOSO (ISHIRO). Bilingual proficiency in Spanish and Guaraní is limited. All ages. Vigorous. Traditionally hunter-gatherers. Presently agriculturalists; animal husbandry: sheep, goats, pigs, cows, horses, poultry; ranch hands; day laborers; maids; basketry; wood carvers; selling alligator skins. Bible portions 1992-1995.

CHIRIPÁ ***(TSIRIPÁ, TXIRIPÁ, AVA, AVA GUARANÍ, APYTARE, NHANDEVA, ÑANDEVA)*** [NHD] 7,000 in Paraguay (1991). Population total all countries 11,900 or more. Eastern Paraguay. Also spoken in Argentina, Brazil. Tupi, Tupi-Guarani, Guarani (I). Dialect: APAPOCUVA. Close to Paraguayan Guaraní, but a separate language. Many are assimilating to Guaraní. Most speakers are of the Apapocuva group, which has been described by ethnographers. Fewer Spanish loan words than Guaraní. Called 'Chiripá' in Paraguay, 'Nhandeva' in Brazil. 'Ñandeva' is used in the Chaco in Paraguay to refer to Tapiete, a different but related language. Bible portions 1991.

CHOROTE, IYO'WUJWA ***(MANJUY, MANJUI, CHOROTI)*** [CRQ] 500 in Paraguay (1991 SIL). Pilcomayo, Boquerón, Chaco. Mataco-Guaicuru, Mataco. Almost 100% are monolingual in Paraguay. Only leaders can speak some Guaraní or Spanish. All ages. Vigorous. Bible portions 1992. See main entry under Argentina.

CHULUPÍ ***(CHURUPI, CHULUPIE, CHULUPE, NIVACLÉ, ASHLUSHLAY, AXLUSLAY)*** [CAG] 18,000 in Paraguay (1991 SIL), 200 in Argentina. Population total both countries 18,200. Chaco, Presidente Hayes Department, Boquerón. Also spoken in Argentina. Mataco-Guaicuru, Mataco. Dialects are inherently intelligible with each other. Mataguayo languages in Paraguay are less similar than Mascoi languages in Paraguay (Fasold 1984). The home language is Chulupí. Vigorous by all Chulupí. Bilingual education in Chulupí. Radio programs. Bible 1995.

EMOK ***(TOBA-EMOK, TOBA, PARAGUAYAN TOBA)*** [EMO] (630 in ethnic group; 1981 census). Near Asunción. Eastern Chaco. Mascoian. They speak Toba mainly, but the women speak Lengua in the home. Agriculturalists, fishermen, hunters. Extinct.

GERMAN, STANDARD [GER] 166,000 in Paraguay including 19,000 who are also mother tongue speakers of Plautdietsch. Indo-European, Germanic, West, High German, German, Middle German, East Middle German. Bible 1466-1982. See main entry under Germany.

GUANA ***(KASKIHÁ, CASHQUIHA)*** [GVA] 500 to 600 (1991 SIL). Boquerón, Salado River, south of Chamacoco, north of Sanapaná, Loma Plata. Mascoian. Dialects: LAYANA (NIGUECACTEMIGI), ECHOALDI (ECHONOANA, CHARARANA). Closely related to Sanapaná. Increasing use of Paraguayan Guaraní as second language. A separate Guana (Kinikinao) is in Mato Grosso, Brazil, related to Chané of Argentina and Terena of Brazil (Arawakan; Voegelin and Voegelin 1977:284, 216; Ruhlen 1987:374, 375; Branislava Susnik). Unconfirmed reports of some Guana in Bolivia. Many live in large villages divided into two sections based on kinship; others live in scattered groups. Some intermarriage with other language groups. Investigation needed: intelligibility with Sanapana, bilingual proficiency in Paraguayan Guaraní. Agriculturalists: maize; hunters, fishermen.

GUARANÍ, BOLIVIAN, EASTERN ***(GUASURANGO, GUARAYO, EASTERN BOLIVIAN GUARANÍ, "CHAWUNCU", "CHIRIGUANO")*** [GUI] 2,000 in Paraguay. Chaco. Tupi, Tupi-Guarani, Guarani (I). Called 'Guasurango', 'Guarayo' or "Chiriguano" in Paraguay. Different from Guarayo of Bolivia or Huarayo (Ese Ejja) of Peru and Bolivia. "Chawuncu" and "Chiriguano" are derogatory names. NT 1974. See main entry under Bolivia.

GUARANÍ, MBYÁ ***(MBYÁ, MBUA)*** [GUN] 7,000 in Paraguay (1995 SIL). Population total all countries 12,000 or more. Also spoken in Argentina, Brazil. Tupi, Tupi-Guarani, Guarani (I). 75% lexical similarity with Paraguayan Guaraní. Some Chiripá may live among them. They use a special vocabulary, *ayvu porã*, for ritual purposes. Traditionally hunter-gatherers. NT 1987.

GUARANÍ, PARAGUAYAN ***(AVAÑE'E)*** [GUG] 4,648,000 in Paraguay (1995), 95% of the population. Population total both countries 5,000,000 (1999 WA). Also spoken in Argentina. Tupi, Tupi-Guarani, Guarani (I). Dialect: JOPARÁ (YOPARÁ). One speaker of Chiripá indicated it was bilingualism rather than linguistic closeness that made Paraguayan Guaraní intelligible to him. Jopará is the colloquial form mixed with Spanish loanwords, used by 90% of the population in and around Asunción. 80% lexical similarity with Chiriguano and 75% lexical similarity with Mbyá. 52% of rural Paraguayans are monolingual in Guaraní. Used some in education. National language. SVO. Bible 1997.

LENGUA ***(ENXET)*** [LEG] 10,000 (1991). Chaco, Presidente Hayes Department, Boquerón. Mascoian. Dialects: NORTHERN LENGUA (EENTHLIT, VOWAK, LENGUA NORTE), SOUTHERN LENGUA (LENGUA SUR). Differences between the two dialects are reported to be mainly phonological and orthographic. Southern Lengua are semi-nomadic. Southern Lengua women are less bilingual in Paraguayan Guaraní. Different orthography between Southern and Northern Lengua. Southern: agriculturalists; pastoralists: cattle, sheep, horses; hunter-gatherers, fishermen. Bible 1995.

MACA ***(TOWOLHI, MAKA, MAK'Á, ENIMACA, ENIMAGA)*** [MCA] 1,000 (1991 SIL). Southwestern, Presidente Hayes Department, Colonia Juan Belaieff Island in Paraguay River west of Asunción. Many were taken to Asunción. Mataco-Guaicuru, Mataco. Men are more proficient in Spanish than women. Vigorous by all Maca. Alternate names may be 'Nynaka', 'Toothle'. Artifact craftsmen, hunters, agriculturalists. Christian, traditional religion. Bible portions 1985.

MASKOY PIDGIN [MHH] Puerto Victoria. Pidgin, Mascoian based. Bilingualism in Paraguayan Guaraní. A mixed language formerly used in a tannin factory with Lengua, Sanapana, Angaite, Guana, and Toba-Maskoy influences. Speakers are reported to have returned to former areas and languages, or to Guaraní-speaking rural areas. Different from Toba-Maskoy. Second language only.

PAI TAVYTERA ***(PAI, TAVYTERA, AVA)*** [PTA] 10,000 to 12,000 (1991 SIL). Eastern, Colonia Juan Carlos. Tupi, Tupi-Guarani, Guarani (I). 70% lexical similarity with Kaiwá of Brazil.

PLAUTDIETSCH ***(LOW GERMAN)*** [GRN] 38,000 first language speakers in Paraguay, including 19,000 who speak Plautdietsch and Standard German both as mother tongue. Chaco and eastern Paraguay; towns of Filadelfia, Menno Colony, Loma Plata, Neuland. Indo-European, Germanic, West, Low Saxon-Low Franconian, Low Saxon. Bilingualism in Spanish, German. Agriculturalists: dairy, grain, cotton, peanuts. Christian. NT 1987. See main entry under Canada.

SANAPANÁ ***(QUIATIVIS, QUILYACMOC, LANAPSUA, SAAPA, SANAM)*** [SAP] 6,900 including 2,900 Sanapana and 4,000 Angaite (1991 SIL). Chaco. Sanapana are north of Angaite and Lengua; Boquerón, Presidente Hayes Department, Galbán River. Large concentrations at Salazar Ranch, La Patria, and Esperanza. Angaite are in the southeast Chaco, Presidente Hayes Department, Boquerón, San Carlos. Mascoian. Dialects: SANAPANA, ANGAITE (ANGATE, ENLIT, COVAVITIS, COVAHLOC). 85% lexical similarity with Northern Lengua. Very limited understanding of Lengua and Paraguayan Guaraní. Some older people are monolingual. Many young people speak only Guaraní, but understand Angaite. All ages. Some of the older people are monolingual. Vigorous. Children do not go to school. An alternate name may be 'Kasnatan'. Agriculturalists, plantation laborers, tannin factor workers, cattle hands. Bible portions 1994-1995.

SPANISH [SPN] 110,000 in Paraguay (1979 estimate). Mainly Asunción, urban areas. Indo-European, Italic, Romance, Italo-Western, Western, Gallo-Iberian, Ibero-Romance, West Iberian, Castilian. Used in education and government. National language. Bible 1553-1979. See main entry under Spain.

TAPIETÉ ***(GUASURANGO, GUASURANGUE, TIRUMBAE, YANAIGUA, ÑANAGUA)*** [TAI] 1,800 in Paraguay (1991 SIL). Population total all countries 2,000. Chaco, northwestern border area, Laguna Negra reservation. Also spoken in Argentina, Bolivia. Tupi, Tupi-Guarani, Guarani (I). Linguistically between Chiriguano and Paraguayan Guaraní. Reported to be bilingual in Paraguayan Guaraní. Some are bilingual in Spanish. Speakers have reservations about use of their language except within their culture. Investigation needed: bilingual proficiency in Paraguayan Guaraní.

TOBA ***(TOBA-QOM, QOM)*** [TOB] 700 in Paraguay (1991 SIL). 60 km. northwest of Asunción, Franciscan mission. Mataco-Guaicuru, Guaicuruan. Different from Toba-Maskoy and Toba-Pilagá. NT 1980. See main entry under Argentina.

TOBA-MASKOY ***(TOBA OF PARAGUAY, QUILYILHRAYROM, CABANATIT, MACHICUI, ENENLHIT)*** [TMF] 2,500 (1991 SIL). Reserve of 30,000 hectares near Puerto Victoria and Puerto Guaraní, eastern Chaco. Mascoian. Men 40 years and older speak Paraguayan Guaraní, others use it as second language, and it is used as the church language. They are reported to speak a 'poor' variety of Paraguayan Guaraní. Young people speak Toba-Maskoy and learn some Spanish in school. Different from Toba Qom, Toba-Pilagá of Argentina, Maskoy of Paraguay, or Maskoy Pidgin.

PERU

Republic of Peru, República del Perú. National or official languages: Spanish, Cuzco Quechua. 24,797,000 (1998 UN). Literacy rate 67% to 79%. Also includes Japanese 109,000, North Bolivian Quechua, Chinese 100,000. Information mainly from E. Loos 1973; M. R. Wise 1983; D. Payne 1988, 1991; SIL 1951-1999. Christian, traditional religion, secular. Blind population 30,000. Deaf population 1,433,960. Deaf institutions: 73 or more. Data accuracy estimate: A1, A2. The number of languages listed for Peru is 106. Of those, 92 are living languages and 14 are extinct. Diversity index 0.35.

ABISHIRA ***(ABIQUIRA, AUISHIRI, AGOUISIRI, AVIRXIRI, ABIGIRA, IXIGNOR, VACACOCHA, TEQURACA)*** [ASH] In 1925 there were 55 to 75 speakers. Puerto Elvira on Lake Vacacocha on the Napo River. Unclassified. Distinct from Aushiri (M. R. Wise SIL 1987). Extinct.

ACHUAR-SHIWIAR ***(ACHUAR, ACHUAL, ACHUARA, ACHUALE, JIVARO, MAINA)*** [ACU] 3,000 to 3,500 in Peru. Population total both countries 5,000 to 5,500. Morona, Macusari, Tigre, Huasaga, and Corrientes rivers. Also spoken in Ecuador. Jivaroan. Different from Shuar (Jivaro) of Ecuador. Bilingual level estimates for Spanish are 0 90%, 1 6%, 2 3%, 3 1%, 4 0%, 5 0%. Dictionary. Grammar. SOV. Literacy rate in first language: 10% to 30%. Literacy rate in second language: 1%. NT 1981-1994.

AGUANO ***(UGUANO, AGUANU, AWANO, SANTA CRUCINO)*** [AGA] In 1959 there were 40 families in Santa Cruz de Huallaga who did not use Aguano but were members of the ethnic group. Lower Huallaga and upper Samiria rivers, the right bank tributary of the Marañon River. Unclassified. Ruhlen says this is the same as Chamicuro (1987, personal communication). Chamicuro speakers say they were not the same, but the Aguano spoke Quechua (M. R. Wise SIL 1987, personal communication). Extinct.

AGUARUNA ***(AGUAJUN, AHUAJUN)*** [AGR] 35,000 to 39,000 (1998 SIL). Western upper Marañon River area, Potro, Mayo and Cahuapanas rivers. Jivaroan. Bilingual level estimates for Spanish are 0 35%, 1 20%, 2 20%, 3 15%, 4 9.9%, 5 .1%. Dictionary. Grammar. SOV. Literacy rate in first language: 60% to 100%. Literacy rate in second language: 50% to 75%. Tropical forest. Mountain slope. Swidden agriculturalists: manioc, bananas, peanuts, wild potatoes; hunter-gatherers. 200 to 1,000 meters. NT 1973.

AJYÍNINKA APURUCAYALI ***(ASHÉNINCA APURUCAYALI, APURUCAYALI CAMPA, AJYÉNINKA, CAMPA)*** [CPC] 5,000 (1995 SIL). Apurucayali tributary of the Pachitea River. Arawakan, Maipuran, Southern Maipuran, Campa. Not intelligible with other Campa languages. "Campa" is a derogatory name. VSO.

AMAHUACA ***(AMAWAKA, AMAGUACO, AMEUHAQUE, IPITINERI, SAYACO)*** [AMC] 300 in Peru (1998 SIL). Population total both countries 520. Sepahua, Curiuja, Upper Ucayali, Inuya, Mapuya, and Purus rivers. Also spoken in Brazil. Panoan, South-Central, Amahuaca. Closest to Cashinahua. 10% can speak Spanish fairly well. Some speak only Spanish. Most speak some Spanish. Children not learning Amahuaca (1999). The group is disintegrating and losing its tribal identity. Dictionary. Grammar. SOV. Literacy rate in first language: 1% to 5%. Literacy rate in second language: 5% to 15%. Hunters, fishermen, agriculturalists. Bible portions 1963-1997.

AMARAKAERI ***(AMARAKAIRE, AMARACAIRE, "MASHCO")*** [AMR] 500 (1987 SIL). Madre de Dios and Colorado rivers. Harakmbet. Dialect: KISAMBAERI. The Harakmbet languages are probably not within Arawakan. Bilingual level estimates for Spanish are 0 20%, 1 30%, 2 40%, 3 5%, 4 5%, 5 0%. "Mashco" is a derogatory term. Ethnic subgroups: Kochimberi, Küpondirideri, Wíntaperi, Wakitaneri, Kareneri. Dictionary. SOV. Literacy rate in first language: Below 1%. Literacy rate in second language: 5% to 15%. Gold panners. NT 1986.

ANDOA ***(SHIMIGAE, SEMIGAE, GAE, GAYE)*** [ANB] Pastaza River. None in Ecuador. Zaparoan. Some use Spanish as second language. The ethnic group speaks Pastaza Quechua. Integrated with the Quechua. A distinct language from Záparo (Kayapwe) of Ecuador, which is now extinct in Peru. Extinct.

ARABELA ***(CHIRIPUNO, CHIRIPUNU)*** [ARL] 100 speakers out of 400 ethnic population (1998 SIL). Arabela River, tributary of Napo. Zaparoan. Bilingual level estimates are Quechua: 0 0%, 1 0%, 2 20%, 3 60%, 4 20%, 5 0%; Spanish: 0 0%, 1 20%, 2 40%, 3 30%, 4 10%, 5 0%. SOV. Literacy rate in first language: 10% to 30%. Literacy rate in second language: 50% to 75%. Tropical forest. NT 1986.

ASHÁNINCA ***("CAMPA")*** [CNI] 25,000 (1998 SIL). Total Campa languages: 50,000 to 60,000. Apurimac, Ene, Perene, Tambo rivers and tributaries. Arawakan, Maipuran, Southern Maipuran, Campa. Closely related to other Campa and Machiguenga. "Campa" is a derogatory name. Dictionary. VSO. Literacy rate in first language: 10% to 30%. Literacy rate in second language: 15% to 25%. Swidden agriculturalists: manioc, hunter-gatherers. NT 1972.

ASHÉNINCA PAJONAL ***(ATSIRI, PAJONAL, CAMPA)*** [CJO] 16,000 (1998 SIL). Central Gran Pajonal area and western headwaters of the Ucayali River. Arawakan, Maipuran, Southern Maipuran, Campa. Bilingual level estimates for Spanish are 0 79%, 1 15%, 2 5%, 3 .5%, 4 .5%, 5 0%. "Campa" is a derogatory name. VSO. Literacy rate in first language: Below 1%. Literacy rate in second language: Below 5%. Bible portions 1976-1986.

ASHÉNINCA PERENÉ ***(PERENÉ, CAMPA)*** [CPP] 9,000 (1995 SIL). Perené tributary of the Pachitea River. Arawakan, Maipuran, Southern Maipuran, Campa. Not intelligible with other Campa languages. "Campa" is a derogatory name. VSO.

ASHÉNINCA PICHIS ***(PICHIS, ASHÉNINCA)*** [CPU] 3,000 to 5,000 (1986 SIL). Pichis and Sheshea tributaries of the Pachitea River. Arawakan, Maipuran, Southern Maipuran, Campa. Not intelligible with other Campa languages. Bilingual level estimates for Spanish are 0 40%, 1 25%, 2 20%, 3 10%, 4 3%, 5 2%. "Campa" is a derogatory name. Dictionary. Grammar. VSO. Literacy rate in first language: 10% to 30%. Literacy rate in second language: 15% to 25%. NT 1996.

ASHÉNINCA UCAYALI-YURÚA [CPB] 7,000 in Peru (1995 SIL). Population total both countries 7,235. Tributaries of the Ucayali River. Also spoken in Brazil. Arawakan, Maipuran, Southern Maipuran, Campa. Not intelligible with other Campa varieties. "Campa" is a derogatory name. VSO.

ATSAHUACA ***(YAMIACA)*** [ATC] In 1904 there were 20 speakers. Carama River, tributary of Tambopata, and Chaspa River, tributary of Inambari. Panoan, North-Central. Extinct.

AUSHIRI ***(AUXIRA)*** [AUS] Tributaries of the right bank of the Napo River, Escuelacocha. Zaparoan. Similar to Arabela. Distinct from Abishira (M. R. Wise SIL 1987). Extinct.

AYMARA, CENTRAL [AYM] 350,320 Aymara in Peru (1987 Cerrón-Palomino). Lake Titicaca area, Puno. Aymaran. Lupaca is the main literary dialect. Bible 1987-1993. See main entry under Bolivia.

AYMARA, SOUTHERN [AYC] From Lake Titicaca toward ocean. Aymaran. Some important verb forms and vocabulary differences from Central Aymara. Dialect intelligibility needs investigation in Tacna and Moquegua (P. Landerman 1984). Limited bilingualism. Investigation needed: intelligibility.

BORA [BOA] 2,000 to 2,500 in Peru (1998 SIL). Population total all countries 2,500 to 3,000. Northeast Yaguasyacu, Putumayo, Ampiyacu River area, five villages in Peru. Also spoken in Brazil, Colombia. Witotoan, Boran. Dialect: MIRAÑA. A distinct language from Bora Muinane but related. 94% intelligibility with Miraña. Dictionary. Grammar. SOV. Literacy rate in first language: 10% to 30%. Literacy rate in second language: 25% to 50%. NT 1982.

CAHUARANO [CAH] 5 (1976 SIL). Nanay River. Zaparoan. Bilingualism in Spanish. Speakers are middle-aged or older. It may be extinct. Nearly extinct.

CANDOSHI-SHAPRA ***(KANDOSHI, CANDOSHI, CANDOXI, MURATO)*** [CBU] 3,000 (1981 SIL). Morona, Pastaza, Huitoyacu and Chapuli rivers. Unclassified. Dialects: CHAPARA (SHAPRA), KANDOASHI. May be distantly related to Arawakan; probably not Jivaroan. Bilingual level estimates for Spanish are 0 88.5%, 1 10%, 2 1%, 3 .5%, 4 0%, 5 0%. Strong preference for Candoshi. Dictionary. SOV. Literacy rate in first language: 10% to 30%. Literacy rate in second language: 15% to 25%. NT 1979-1993.

CAPANAHUA ***(KAPANAWA)*** [KAQ] 350 to 400 (1998 SIL). Tapiche-Buncuya rivers area. Panoan, North-Central. Dialect: PAHENBAQUEBO. Closest language is Shipibo. Bilingual level estimates for Spanish are 0 0%, 1 0%, 2 15%, 3 50%, 4 30%, 5 5%. Use of Spanish to a Capanahua by a

Capanahua can be interpreted as rejecting the other as an outsider. SOV. Literacy rate in first language: Below 1%. Literacy rate in second language: 5% to 15%. NT 1978.

CAQUINTE ***(CAQUINTE CAMPA, POYENISATI, "CACHOMASHIRI")*** [COT] 200 to 300 (1998 SIL). Poyeni, Mayapo, and Picha rivers. Arawakan, Maipuran, Southern Maipuran, Campa. Closest to Asháninca Campa. Bilingual level estimates for Machiguenga are 0 85%, 1 5%, 2 8%, 3 2%, 4 0%, 5 0%. Almost none can converse at all in Spanish. Some use Asháninca as second language. The Caquinte do not like to be called 'Campa'. "Cachomashiri" is a derogatory name. Grammar. VSO. Literacy rate in first language: 30% to 60%. Literacy rate in second language: Below 5%. Bible portions 1984-1991.

CASHIBO-CACATAIBO ***(CAXIBO, CACIBO, CACHIBO, CAHIVO, MANAGUA, HAGUETI)*** [CBR] 1,500 to 2,000 (1998 SIL). Aguaytía and San Alejandro rivers. Panoan, Western. Dialects: CACATAIBO, CASHIBO. Bilingual level estimates for Spanish are 0 34%, 1 24%, 2 22%, 3 12%, 4 6%, 5 2%. Dictionary. SOV. Literacy rate in first language: 5% to 10%. Literacy rate in second language: 15% to 25%. NT 1978.

CASHINAHUA ***(KAXINAWÁ, KAXYNAWA, CAXINAWA, CAXINAWÁ)*** [CBS] 850 to 1,200 in Peru. Population total both countries 1,600 to 2,000. Curanja and Purus rivers. Also spoken in Brazil. Panoan, Southeastern. Dialect: SHEMINAHUA. It may be closest to Sharanahua. Dictionary. SOV. Literacy rate in first language: 5% to 10%. Literacy rate in second language: 5% to 15%. Tropical forest. NT 1980.

CHAMICURO ***(CHAMICURA, CHAMICOLO)*** [CCC] 5 speakers (1987) out of ethnic population of 100 to 150 (1976 SIL). Pampa Hermosa on a tributary of Huallaga. Arawakan, Maipuran, Western Maipuran. Bilingualism in Spanish. Ruhlen says Aguano is the same as this (1987, personal communication). Chamicuro speakers say it was different (SIL 1987). Dictionary. Nearly extinct.

CHAYAHUITA ***(CHAYAWITA, CHAWI, TSHAAHUI, CHAYHUITA, CHAYABITA, SHAYABIT, BALSAPUERTINO, PARANAPURA, CAHUAPA)*** [CBT] 10,000 to 12,000 (1998 SIL). Paranapura, Cahuapanas, Sillay and Shanusi rivers. Cahuapanan. Dialects: CHAYAHUITA, CAHUAPANA. Very slight intelligibility with Jebero. Bilingual level estimates for Spanish are 0 60%, 1 20%, 2 10%, 3 6%, 4 3%, 5 1%. Dictionary. SOV. Literacy rate in first language: 1% to 5%. Literacy rate in second language: 5% to 15%. NT 1978.

CHOLON ***(TINGANESES, SEEPTSA)*** [CHT] 1 or 2 speakers left (1986). Valley of the Huallaga River from Tingo María to Valle. Unclassified. Ruhlen says it is Andean. Many speak Quechua. Nearly extinct.

COCAMA-COCAMILLA ***(COCAMA, KOKAMA, UCAYALI, XIBITAOAN, HUALLAGA, PAMPADEQUE, PANDEQUEBO)*** [COD] Only older speakers left out of 15,000 to 18,000 in ethnic group in Peru (1981 SIL). Population total all countries 200 or more. Northeastern lower Ucayali, lower Marañon and Huallaga rivers area. Also spoken in Brazil, Colombia. Tupi, Tupi-Guarani, Tupi (III). Dialects: COCAMILLA, COCAMA. Closest to Omagua. Bilingual level estimates for Spanish are 0 0%, 1 0%, 2 2%, 3 28%, 4 60%, 5 10%. Only older speakers left (1981). Grammar. SOV. Bible portions 1961-1967.

CULINA ***(KULINA, KULINO, KULYNA, KURINA, KOLLINA, MADIJA, MADIHÁ)*** [CUL] 500 or fewer in Peru (1998 SIL). Southeast, near Brazilian border, upper Purus and Santa Rosa rivers. Arauan. The Arawan languages probably are not Arawakan. Bilingual level estimates for Spanish are 0 78%, 1 10%, 2 5%, 3 5%, 4 1.5%, 5 .5%. SOV. Literacy rate in first language: 1% to 5%. Literacy rate in second language: 5% to 15%. Bible portions 1965-1985. See main entry under Brazil.

ESE EJJA ***(ESE EXA, ESE EJA, ESE'EJJA, TIATINAGUA, TAMBOPATA-GUARAYO, HUARAYO, "CHAMA")*** [ESE] 250 to 400 in Peru (1977 Catholic University, Lima). Tambopata and Heath rivers around Maldonado. Tacanan, Tiatinagua. The Tambopata dialect in Peru is somewhat different. Almost all in Peru are bilingual in Spanish. "Chama" is a derogatory name. SOV. NT 1984. See main entry under Bolivia.

HIBITO ***(JIBITO, CHIBITO, ZIBITO, IBITO, XIBITA)*** [HIB] In 1851 there were 500. Bobonaje River, tributary of Jelache, tributary of Huayabamba, coming into Huallaga on the left side. Unclassified. Extinct.

HUACHIPAERI ***(HUACHIPAIRE, WACIPAIRE, "MASHCO")*** [HUG] 130 to 215 including about 12 Sapiteri, 10 Toyeri, 20 Arasairi, 50 Manuquiari, 36 to 50 Pukirieri (Puncuri) (1981 SIL). Upper Madre de Dios and Keros rivers. Harakmbet. Dialects: HUACHIPAIRE, SAPITERI, TOYERI (TOYOERI, TUYUNERI), ARASAIRI. Closely related to Amarakaeri but they probably cannot use the same literature. The Sapiteri are integrating with the Amarakaeri. Toyeri is similar to Sapiteri. Some Kisambaeri (Amarakaeri dialect) have integrated with the Toyeri and others with the Sapiteri. Manuquiari may be a subgroup of Toyeri or Huachipaeri. Pukirieri may be a subgroup of Toyeri or Arasairi. Arasairi is distinct from Amarakaeri or Huachipaeri; similar to Sapiteri. Speakers are somewhat bilingual in Spanish. "Mashco" is a derogatory name. SOV.

HUAMBISA ***(HUAMBIZA, WAMBISA)*** [HUB] 6,000 to 10,000 (1991 SIL). Morona and Santiago rivers. Jivaroan. Bilingual level estimates for Spanish are 0 20%, 1 25%, 2 25%, 3 20%, 4 9%, 5 1%.

Dictionary. SOV. Literacy rate in first language: 10% to 30%. Literacy rate in second language: 25% to 50%. Tropical forest. Hunter-gatherers. NT 1975-1997.

HUITOTO, MɨNIɨCA ***(MINICA HUITOTO)*** [HTO] 5 in Peru, 1,700 in Colombia (1995 SIL). Witotoan, Witoto, Witoto Proper, Minica-Murui. Dictionary. NT 1985. See main entry under Colombia.

HUITOTO, MURUI ***(BUE, WITOTO)*** [HUU] 1,000 in Peru (1995 SIL), 1,900 in Colombia (1995 SIL). Population total both countries 2,900. Ampiyacu, Putumayo, and Napo rivers. None left in Brazil. Also spoken in Colombia. Witotoan, Witoto, Witoto Proper, Minica-Murui. Bilingual level estimates for Spanish are 0 1%, 1 9%, 2 45%, 3 35%, 4 9%, 5 1%. 90% of those under 50 are fairly bilingual in Spanish. Huitoto has more prestige in Colombia than in Peru. Dictionary. Grammar. SOV. Literacy rate in first language: Below 1%. Literacy rate in second language: 15% to 25%. 95% of those under 40 are literate. NT 1978.

HUITOTO, NɨPODE ***(NIPODE WITOTO, MUINANE HUITOTO)*** [HUX] 100 possibly (1991 SIL). Witotoan, Witoto, Witoto Proper, Nipode. Bilingualism in Minica Huitoto, Murui Huitoto. Dictionary. Grammar. Bible portions 1961.

IÑAPARI ***(INAMARI)*** [INA] 4 speakers (1999 S. Parker SIL). Piedras River, at the mouth of Sabaluyo, near Puerto Maldonado. Extinct in Bolivia. Arawakan, Maipuran, Southern Maipuran, Purus. All are reported to be bilingual in Spanish. Dictionary. Nearly extinct.

IQUITO ***(IQUITA, IKITO, AMACACORE, HAMACORE, QUITURRAN, PUCA-UMA)*** [IQU] 150. Northern Nanay River area. Zaparoan. Widespread use of Spanish. Bible portions 1963.

ISCONAHUA ***(ISCOBAQUEBU)*** [ISC] 28 to 50 (1976 SIL). Callaria River. Panoan, North-Central. Most closely related to Shipibo. They live close to the Shipibo and are bilingual in Shipibo. Nearly extinct.

JAQARU ***(HAQEARU, HAQARU, HAQ'ARU, ARU)*** [JQR] 2,000 (1987 J. L. Rivarola). Lima Department, Yauyos Province, Tupe village (Jaqaru) and Cachuy village (Cauqui). Aymaran. Dialect: CAUQUI (KAWKI, CACHUY). Jaqaru has 73% lexical similarity with Aymara; Kawki 79% with Aymara. Most or all use Spanish as second language. There may still be a few monolinguals, all women. Cauqui dialect is nearly extinct. Investigation needed: intelligibility, bilingual proficiency.

JEBERO ***(XEBERO, CHEBERO, XIHUILA)*** [JEB] 2,300 to 3,000 (1976 SIL). District of Jeberos. Cahuapanan. Widespread use of Spanish. Bible portions 1959.

MACHIGUENGA ***(MATSIGANGA, MATSIGENKA, MAÑARIES)*** [MCB] 6,000 to 8,000 (1981 SIL). Urubamba, Camisea, Picha, Manu, Timpia, Tigompinia, Kompiroshiato, and Mishagua rivers. Arawakan, Maipuran, Southern Maipuran, Campa. Closest to Nomatsiguenga. There are minor dialects. Bilingual level estimates for Spanish are 0 60%, 1 25%, 2 8.3%, 3 4.6%, 4 1.6%, 5 .5%. Dictionary. VSO. Literacy rate in first language: 30% to 60%. Literacy rate in second language: 25% to 50%. NT 1976-1997.

MASHCO PIRO ***(CUJARENO, CUJAREÑO, "MASHCO")*** [CUJ] 20 to 100 speakers (1976 SIL). Manu Park, Dept. of Madre de Dios. Cujar, Purus, Tahuamanu, Mishagua, and Piedras rivers. Extinct in Bolivia. Arawakan, Maipuran, Southern Maipuran, Purus. About 60% inherent intelligibility with Piro. "Mashco" is a derogatory name. All are completely monolingual. Highly nomadic.

MATSÉS ***(MAYORUNA, MAXURUNA, MAJURUNA, MAYIRUNA, MAXIRONA, MAGIRONA, MAYUZUNA)*** [MCF] 1,500 in Peru (1998). Population total both countries 2,000. Yaquerana. Also spoken in Brazil. Panoan, Northern. Different from Mayo, or Maya and Marubo of Brazil. Bilingual level estimates for Spanish are 0 97%, 1 3%, 2 0%, 3 0%, 4 0%, 5 0%. Grammar. SOV. Literacy rate in first language: 1% to 5%. Literacy rate in second language: 5% to 15%. NT 1993.

MUNICHE ***(OTANAVE, OTANABE, MUNICHINO, MUNICHI)*** [MYR] 3 (1988 SIL). Town of Muniches on the Paranapura River. Unclassified. Bilingualism in Spanish. Dictionary. Grammar. Nearly extinct.

NANTI ***(COGAPACORI)*** [COX] 300 to 1,000 (1997 D. Payne SIL). 100 to 300 are still uncontacted (1998). Near the Machiguenga. Arawakan, Maipuran, Southern Maipuran, Campa. Close to Machiguenga. Need literature adapted from Machiguenga. They have remained separate from the Machiguenga.

NOCAMAN ***(NOCOMAN)*** [NOM] In 1925 there were 3 speakers. Headwaters of the Inuya River, Amueya River, Tamaya River. Panoan, Western. May have been a dialect of Cashibo. Extinct.

NOMATSIGUENGA ***(NOMATSIGUENGA CAMPA, ATIRI)*** [NOT] 4,500 (1998 SIL). South central Junín region. Arawakan, Maipuran, Southern Maipuran, Campa. Closely related to other Campa and Machiguenga. Bilingual level estimates are Spanish: 0 5%, 1 15%, 2 30%, 3 25%, 4 20%, 5 5%; Asháninca Campa: 0 5%, 1 10%, 2 15%, 3 20%, 4 25%, 5 25%. Dictionary. VSO. Literacy rate in first language: 10% to 30%. Literacy rate in second language: 25% to 50%. NT 1980.

OCAINA ***(OKAINA)*** [OCA] 150 to 250 in Peru (1982 SIL), 3 or 4 families in Colombia (1976 SIL). Population total both countries 165 to 265. Yaguasyacu, Ampuyacu, and Putumayo rivers, northeastern Peru. Also spoken in Colombia. Witotoan, Witoto, Ocaina. Dialects: DUKAIYA, IBO'TSA. Bilingualism in Bora, Murui Huitoto, Spanish. Dictionary. Bible portions 1964-1971.

OMAGUA ***(OMAGUA-YETE, ARIANA, PARIANA, ANAPIA, MACANIPA, KAMBEBA, YHUATA, UMAUA, CAMBEBA, CAMPEBA, CAMBELA, CANGA-PEBA, AGUA)*** [OMG] 10 to 100 in Peru (1976 SIL). Population total both countries 10 to 100. Omaguas near Iquitos. There may be none left in Brazil (1995). Also spoken in Brazil. Tupi, Tupi-Guarani, Tupi (III). Closest to Cocama. In Peru all are bilingual in Spanish or Cocama. Nearly extinct.

OMURANO ***(HUMURANA, ROAMAINA, NUMURANA, UMURANO, MAYNA)*** [OMU] Zaparoan. Became extinct by 1958. Extinct.

OREJÓN ***(COTO, KOTO, PAYAGUA, MAI JA, OREGON, ORECHON, TUTAPI)*** [ORE] 190 to 300 (1976 SIL). Yanayacu, Sucusari, Algodon, and Putumayo rivers. Tucanoan, Western Tucanoan, Southern. Dialect: NEBAJI. Bilingualism in Spanish. Dictionary. Bible portions 1967-1976.

PANOBO ***(MANOA, PANO, PANA, PELADO, WARIAPANO, HUARIAPANO)*** [PNO] The last speaker died in March 1991; 100 to 200 in 1925. Along the Ucayali River and mixed with the Shetebo. There are some reports of others. Panoan, Unclassified. Data obtained January 1991. Not a Shipibo-Conibo dialect. Extinct.

PERUVIAN SIGN LANGUAGE [PRL] Deaf sign language. There are over 70 deaf schools, but the oralist method is used by most in the classroom. The majority of students use sign language outside the classroom. The sign language used in the schools is different from what adults use outside. There is a manual alphabet for spelling. Investigation needed: intelligibility. Dictionary. TV.

PISABO ***(PISAGUA, PISAHUA)*** [PIG] Between the Tapíche and Blanco rivers. Panoan, Northern. Investigation needed: intelligibility with Matses, other Panoan languages.

PUQUINA [PUQ] South shore of Lake Titicaca, town of Puquina. Unclassified. Extinct for at least 200 years. Proposals for its classification are inconclusive. Extinct.

QUECHUA, ANCASH, CHIQUIAN [QEC] 25,000 (1993 SIL). Southeast Ancash Department, Bolognesi Province, Chiquian District. Quechuan, Quechua I. Possibly intelligible with Cajatambo Quechua. 95% cognate with Ocros, 94% with La Unión and Cajatambo. Rural areas are predominately monolingual. Investigation needed: intelligibility. SOV. Literacy rate in first language: Below 1%. Literacy rate in second language: 5% to 15%.

QUECHUA, ANCASH, CONCHUCOS, NORTHERN ***(CONCHUCOS QUECHUA, NORTHERN CONCHUCOS QUECHUA)*** [QED] 200,000 or fewer, including 65,000 monolinguals (1994 census). East Ancash Department, Pomabamba to San Luis, and Huacrachuco in northwest Huánuco Department. May include a small part of the northern Marañon area. Quechuan, Quechua I. Related to South Conchucos, Huamalíes, Sihuas. Rural areas are predominantly monolingual. SOV. Literacy rate in first language: Below 1%. Literacy rate in second language: 15% to 25%. Bible portions 1990-1995.

QUECHUA, ANCASH, CONCHUCOS, SOUTHERN ***(CONCHUCOS QUECHUA, SOUTHERN CONCHUCOS QUECHUA)*** [QEH] 250,000 or fewer, including 80,000 monolinguals (1994 census). East Ancash Department, Chavín to San Luis to Llamellín in East Ancash Department, and Huacaybamba, Huacrachuco, San Buenaventura, and Pinra in northwest Huánuco Department. Includes much of southern Marañon. Quechuan, Quechua I. Related to North Conchucos, Huamalíes, Huaylas. Rural areas are predominantly monolingual. SOV. Literacy rate in first language: Below 1%. Literacy rate in second language: 15% to 25%. Bible portions 1992-1995.

QUECHUA, ANCASH, CORONGO [QEE] 8,500 (1998N SIL). Northern Ancash Department, Sihuas and Corongo areas. Quechuan, Quechua I. Most closely related to Huaylas and Sihuas Quechua. Limited bilingualism in Spanish. SOV. Literacy rate in first language: Below 1%. Literacy rate in second language: 5% to 15%.

QUECHUA, ANCASH, HUAYLAS [QAN] 300,000 to 350,000 (1998 SIL). Central Ancash Department, provinces of Huaraz, Carhuaz, Caraz; in the Callejón de Huaylas. Quechuan, Quechua I. Dialects: HUARAZ, YUNGAY, HUAILAS (HUAYLAS). Parker says it is not intelligible with Cuzco, Ayacucho, Southern Junín (Huanca), Cajamarca, Amazonas (Chachapoyas), or San Martín Quechua. Rural areas are predominantly monolingual. Speakers use Spanish to communicate with Quechua speakers from Huánuco and Tarma because of differences in speech. Dictionary. Grammar. SOV. Literacy rate in first language: Below 1%. Literacy rate in second language: 25% to 50%. NT 1993.

QUECHUA, ANCASH, SIHUAS [QES] 10,000 (1991 SIL). Ancash Department. Quechuan, Quechua I. Investigation needed: intelligibility. Literacy rate in first language: Below 1%. Literacy rate in second language: 5% to 15%.

QUECHUA, APURIMAC [QEA] Ayamaraes, Chuquibambilla, and Anda provinces. Quechuan, Quechua II, C. Different from Cuzco Quechua and Ayacucho Quechua. Investigation needed: intelligibility, bilingual proficiency. Bible portions 1974.

QUECHUA, AREQUIPA-LA UNION ***(AREQUIPA QUECHUA, COTAHUASI QUECHUA)*** [QAR] 18,000 (1998 SIL. Arequipa Department, La Unión Province, Cotahuasi District. Quechuan, Quechua II, C. Dialects: COTAHUASI, NORTHERN AREQUIPA, HIGHLAND AREQUIPA, ANTABAMBA (APURIMAC). Closer linguistically to Cuzco than to Ayacucho. Many monolinguals. Dictionary. SOV. Literacy rate in first language: Below 1%. Literacy rate in second language: Below 5%. Bible portions 1993.

QUECHUA, AYACUCHO ***(CHANKA)*** [QUY] 1,000,000 (1976 Soto Ruiz). Southwestern Ayacucho region. Quechuan, Quechua II, C. Dialects: ANDAHUAYLAS, HUANCAVELICA. 96% lexical similarity with Surcubamba, Puquio, and Cuzco. Bilingual level estimates for Spanish are 0 31%, 1 20%, 2 20%, 3 20%, 4 8%, 5 1%. Dictionary. Grammar. SOV. Literacy rate in first language: 5% to 10%. Literacy rate in second language: 25% to 50%. Bible 1987.

QUECHUA, CAJAMARCA [QNT] 35,000 (1981 D. Coombs SIL). Cajamarca, Chetilla, and Los Baños districts. Quechuan, Quechua II, A. Dialect differences are minor. 94% lexical similarity with Lambayeque (closest), 92% with Pacaraos, Tarma. Bilingual level estimates are Standard Spanish: 0 30%, 1 10%, 2 15%, 3 25%, 4 15%, 5 5%; Peasant Spanish: 0 15%, 1 20%, 2 10%, 3 15%, 4 30%, 5 10%. Strong Quechua use in Chetilla and Porcón. Dictionary. Grammar. SOV. Literacy rate in first language: 1% to 5%. Literacy rate in second language: 15% to 25%. Bible portions 1985-1993.

QUECHUA, CHACHAPOYAS ***(AMAZONAS)*** [QUK] 3,000 to 5,000 (1976 SIL). Chachapoyas and Luya provinces, Amazonas Department. Quechuan, Quechua II, B. Dialects: LAMUD (WEST CHACHAPOYAS), GRENADA-MENDOZA (EAST CHACHAPOYAS), LA JALCA (SOUTH CHACHAPOYAS). Closest to San Martín. Some are still monolingual but are becoming bilingual in Spanish. All ages in Conila. SOV. Literacy rate in first language: Below 1%. Literacy rate in second language: 15% to 25%.

QUECHUA, CLASSICAL [QCL] Central Peru. Quechuan, Quechua II, C. Extinct. Bible portions 1880.

QUECHUA, CUZCO ***(CUSCO QUECHUA)*** [QUZ] 1,500,000 (1989 UBS). Central Cuzco, Arequipa regions. Quechuan, Quechua II, C. Dialect: CAYLLOMA QUECHUA. Some dialect differences, but not as distinct as elsewhere. Substantial phonological and morphological differences with Ayacucho Quechua. National language. Dictionary. Grammar. SOV. Literacy rate in first language: 1% to 5%. Literacy rate in second language: 25% to 50%. Bible 1988.

QUECHUA, HUÁNUCO, HUALLAGA [QUB] 40,000 (1993 SIL). Northeast Huánuco Department, including the city of Huánuco. Quechuan, Quechua I. 66% monolingual. Dictionary. Grammar. SOV. Literacy rate in first language: Below 1%. Literacy rate in second language: 15% to 25%. Radio programs. Bible portions 1917-1995.

QUECHUA, HUÁNUCO, HUAMALÍES-NORTHERN DOS DE MAYO [QEJ] 60,000 to 80,000 (1998 SIL). North central Huanuco Department. Quechuan, Quechua I. Dialects: MONZÓN, HUAMALÍES, NORTHERN DOS DE MAYO. 96% lexical similarity with La Unión and Panao Quechua. Dictionary. SOV. Literacy rate in first language: Below 1%. Literacy rate in second language: Below 5%. Bible portions 1986-1992.

QUECHUA, HUÁNUCO, PANAO ***(PACHITEA QUECHUA)*** [QEM] 17,540 including 10,000 monolinguals (1972 census). East central Huánuco Department. Quechuan, Quechua I. 98% lexical similarity with La Unión, 96% with Cajatambo Quechua. Dictionary. SOV. Literacy rate in first language: Below 1%. Literacy rate in second language: 15% to 25%. Bible portions 1994-1995.

QUECHUA, LAMBAYEQUE ***(FERREÑAFE)*** [QUF] 20,000 (1998 SIL). Lambayeque region, Inkawasi, Kañaris, and Miracosta districts, and the communities of Penachí and Santa Lucía, and in adjacent areas of other departments (Cajamarca, Piura). Quechuan, Quechua II, A. Dialects: INCAHUASI, CAÑARIS. 94% lexical similarity with Cajamarca Quechua. Dictionary. Grammar. SOV. Literacy rate in first language: Below 1%. Literacy rate in second language: Below 5%. Bible portions 1992.

QUECHUA, MARGOS-YAROWILCA-LAURICOCHA [QEI] 120,000 (1998 SIL); 15,000 monolinguals (1972 census). Southwest and south central Huánuco Department, Districts of La Unión, Ripan, Huallanca, Sillapata, Yanas, Obas, Chuquis, Chupan, Cahuac, Chavinillo, Chacabamba, Jacas Chico, Rondos, San Francisco, Jivia, Banos, Queropalca. Quechuan, Quechua I. Literature can be adapted from Huamalies. 98% lexical similarity with Panao, 96% with Corongo (Ancash), Sihuas, Monzón, Tarma, Ulcumayo Quechua. Dictionary. SOV. Literacy rate in first language: Below 1%. Literacy rate in second language: Below 5%. Bible portions 1987-1991.

QUECHUA, NORTH JUNÍN ***(TARMA-JUNÍN QUECHUA, JUNÍN QUECHUA)*** [QJU] 60,000 (1998) including 7,000 monolinguals (1972 census). Northern Junín Department, districts of Junín, Carhuamayo, Ondores, San Pedro de Cajas, southeast of Pasco. Quechuan, Quechua I. There are two dialects in Tarma Province which differ from the town of Junin. 97% lexical similarity with Cajatambo, 96% with La Unión Quechua. Bilingual level estimates for Spanish are 0 30%, 1 20%, 2 10%, 3 10%, 4 25%, 5 5%. Dictionary. Grammar. SOV. Literacy rate in first language: Below 1%. Literacy rate in second language: Below 5%. Mountain slope. Pastoralists, peasant agriculturalists. NT 1997.

QUECHUA, NORTH LIMA, CAJATAMBO [QNL] 16,525 (1974 SIL). Northeast Lima Department, especially rural Oyon, Pachangara, Andajes, Maráy, Copa, Huanacapón, Jucul, Cajatambo; Pacaraos in east central Lima Department. Quechuan, Quechua I. Literature probably needs to be adapted from Ancash. Cajatambo has 97% lexical similarity with Andajes, 96% with La Unión and Panao, 95% with Monzón, 94% with Chiquián. Pacaraos has 94% lexical similarity with Huarí, Cajatambo, Tarma, Carás Quechua. 7,650 in areas where it is used by all ages, 6,550 in others used by those 10 years or older, 250 in Pacaraos mainly 40 years or older (1974). Investigation needed: intelligibility, bilingual proficiency. SOV. Literacy rate in first language: Below 1%. Literacy rate in second language: 5% to 15%.

QUECHUA, PACAROAS [QCP] 250 (1974 SIL) speakers (1984 P. Adelaar). East central Lima Department, Pacaroas village. Quechuan, Quechua II, A. Divergent lexically, morphologically, and phonologically from other Quechua. By its archaic features it occupies an important position relative to the reconstruction of Proto-Quechua. 94% lexical similarity with Huarí, Cajatambo, Tarma, and Carás Quechua. All are elderly. SOV. Nearly extinct.

QUECHUA, PASCO, SANTA ANA DE TUSI [QEF] 10,000 (1993 SIL). Pasco Department, west of Huariaca. Quechuan, Quechua I. Probably a dialect of Ambo Quechua (San Rafael-Huariaca Quechua). Investigation needed: intelligibility with Ambo Quechua. SOV.

QUECHUA, PASCO-YANAHUANCA *(DANIEL CARRION)* [QUR] 20,500 (1972 census). Pasco Department, sparsely populated high country and more densely populated valleys, districts of Yanahuanca, Villcabamba, Tapoc, Chacayan, Paucar, San Pedro de Pillao, Goyllarisquizqa. Quechuan, Quechua I. Closely related to Junín Quechua. Many dialects intersect here. Literature in two or three dialects will need adaptation with Tusi and Huariaca. SOV. Literacy rate in first language: Below 1%. Literacy rate in second language: Below 5%.

QUECHUA, PASTAZA, SOUTHERN *(INGA)* [QUP] 1,000 to 2,000 (1998 SIL). Northern jungle, Anatico Lake, Pastaza and Huasaga rivers, and along the Urituyacu. Quechuan, Quechua II, B. Bilingual level estimates for Spanish are 0 60%, 1 20%, 2 10%, 3 10%, 4 0%, 5 0%. Distinct from Northern Pastaza Quechua of Peru and Ecuador. Dictionary. SOV. Literacy rate in first language: Below 1%. Literacy rate in second language: 5% to 15%. Tropical forest. NT 1997.

QUECHUA, PUNO [QEP] Puno Department and adjacent areas. Quechuan, Quechua II, C. Differs from Cuzco Quechua in its borrowing of lexicon and morphology from Aymara. Investigation needed: intelligibility. Literacy rate in first language: Below 1%. Literacy rate in second language: 25% to 50%.

QUECHUA, SAN MARTÍN *(UCAYALI, LAMISTA, LAMISTO, LAMA, LAMANO, MOTILÓN)* [QSA] 40,000 to 45,000 (1998 SIL). San Martín, Sisa, Lamas and other districts, and along parts of the Ucayali River. Quechuan, Quechua II, B. Several minor dialects. Bilingual level estimates for Spanish are 0 10%, 1 10%, 2 39%, 3 40%, 4 1%, 5 0%. Dictionary. Grammar. SOV. Literacy rate in first language: 1% to 5%. Literacy rate in second language: 50% to 75%. Mountain valleys. Agriculturalists. NT 1992.

QUECHUA, SAN RAFAEL-HUARIACA *(AMBO-PASCO QUECHUA)* [QEG] 90,000 (1998 SIL). Ambo, southern Huánuco, western Cerro de Pasco departments; districts of San Rafael, Mosca, Ambo, Huánuco, Pallanchacra, Huariaca, Yarusyacan, Ticlacayan, Yanacancha. Quechuan, Quechua I. Santa Ana de Tusi Quechua may be a dialect. 35% monolingual in southern Huanuco. Dictionary. SOV. Literacy rate in first language: Below 1%. Literacy rate in second language: 25% to 50%. Bible portions 1993.

QUECHUA, WANCA, HUAYLLA *(SOUTHERN HUANCAYO QUECHUA, HUANCA HUAYLLA QUECHUA)* [QHU] 300,000 (1998 SIL). Southern Junín Department, Huancayo and Concepción provinces. Quechuan, Quechua I. Dialects: WAYCHA (HUAYCHA, CENTRAL HUANCAYO), EAST WAYLLA, WEST WAYLLA. Waycha dialect is nearly extinct in Concepción. Dictionary. SOV. Literacy rate in first language: Below 1%. Literacy rate in second language: Below 5%. Radio programs. Bible portions 1991-1992.

QUECHUA, WANCA, JAUJA *(SHAUSHA WANKA QUECHUA, HUANCA JAUJA QUECHUA)* [QHJ] 14,549 to 31,501 (1962 census). Central Junín Department, Jauja Province. Quechuan, Quechua I. Considerable phonological differences with Tarma. Bilingualism in Spanish. Grammar. SOV.

QUECHUA, YAUYOS [QUX] 18,950 (1974 SIL). Lima Department, Yauyos Province. Quechuan, Quechua II, A. Dialects: SAN PEDRO DE HUACARPANA, APURÍ, MADEAN-VIÑAC (MADEÁN), AZÁNGARO-HUANGÁSCAR-CHOCOS (HUANGÁSCAR), CACRA-HONGOS, TANA-LINCHA (LINCHA), TOMÁS-ALIS (ALIS), HUANCAYA-VITIS, LARAOS. Speakers include 3,800 in areas where it is used by all ages, and 9,200 in others where it is used by teenage and older (1974). There are monolinguals in the Chincha area. Not a single language, but a cover term for a highly differentiated linguistic area with many one-village varieties, which will probably need separate materials. Investigation needed: intelligibility with dialects. SOV. Literacy rate in first language: Below 1%. Literacy rate in second language: Below 5%.

QUICHUA, LOWLAND, NAPO *(SANTA ROSA QUECHUA, SANTARROSINO, QUIXO, KICHO, QUIJO, NAPO, YUMBO, LOWLAND NAPO QUECHUA)* [QLN] 6,000 to 10,000 in Peru. Napo River region. Also communities on the Putumayo. Some were moved to Madre de Dios. Quechuan, Quechua II, B. SOV. Tropical forest. Bible portions 1972-1987. See main entry under Ecuador.

QUICHUA, PASTAZA, NORTHERN ***(TIGRE QUECHUA, ALAMA, BOBONAZA)*** [QLB] 2,000 in Peru. Alamos, Tigre River. Quechuan, Quechua II, B. Distinct from Southern Pastaza Quechua. Tropical forest. NT 1992. See main entry under Ecuador.

REMO ***(RHENO)*** [REM] Between the Tapiche and Calleria rivers. If they exist they are in Brazil at the headwaters of the Moa River; but there is no evidence of their existence in Brazil. Panoan, North-Central. Extinct.

RESÍGARO ***(RESÍGERO)*** [RGR] 14 (1976 SIL). Northeastern Peru, Loreto Department, in Bora and Ocaina villages. Arawakan, Maipuran, Northern Maipuran, Inland. Bilingualism in Ocaina, Bora, Murui Huitoto, Spanish. Dictionary. Nearly extinct.

SECOYA ***(ANGOTERO, ENCABELLAO)*** [SEY] 144 in Peru. Northern Peru, Boca de Angusilla and Santa Marta, a small river off the Napo River near the Ecuador border. Tucanoan, Western Tucanoan, Northern, Siona-Secoya. Dialects: ANGOTERO, PIOJÉ. NT 1990. See main entry under Ecuador.

SENSI ***(SENTI, TENTI, MANANAHUA)*** [SNI] In 1925 there were 100. Right bank of the Ucayali River. Panoan, North-Central. Subgroups: Ynubu (Inubu), Runubu, Casca. Extinct.

SHARANAHUA [MCD] 500 to 600 in Peru (1998 SIL). Population total both countries 850 to 950. Upper Purus River area. Also spoken in Brazil. Panoan, South-Central, Yaminahua-Sharanahua. Dialects: MARINAHUA (MARINAWA), CHANDINAHUA. Bilingual level estimates for Spanish are 0 7%, 1 67%, 2 25%, 3 1%, 4 0%, 5 0%. SOV. Literacy rate in first language: 10% to 30%. Literacy rate in second language: Below 5%. NT 1996.

SHIPIBO-CONIBO [SHP] 30,000 (1998 SIL). Northeastern middle Ucayali River area. Panoan, North-Central. Dialects: SHIPIBO, CONIBO (CONIBA), PISQUIBO, SHETEBO (SETEBO, SETIBO, XITIBO, MANOITA). Bilingual level estimates for Spanish are 0 10%, 1 20%, 2 23%, 3 30%, 4 15%, 5 2%. Dictionary. Grammar. Literacy rate in first language: 1% to 5%. Literacy rate in second language: 15% to 25%. NT 1983.

SPANISH ***(ESPAÑOL, CASTELLANO)*** [SPN] 20,000,000 in Peru (1995 estimate). Indo-European, Italic, Romance, Italo-Western, Western, Gallo-Iberian, Ibero-Romance, West Iberian, Castilian. National language. Bible 1553-1979. See main entry under Spain.

SPANISH, LORETO-UCAYALI ***(JUNGLE SPANISH)*** [SPQ] Loreto and Ucayali River areas. Indo-European, Italic, Romance, Italo-Western, Western, Gallo-Iberian, Ibero-Romance, West Iberian, Castilian. Some other speakers have limited understanding of colloquial standard Spanish. There are monolingual speakers.

TAUSHIRO ***(PINCHI, PINCHE)*** [TRR] 7 (1998 SIL). Off the Tigre River, Aucayacu River, tributary of the Ahuaruna River. Unclassified. Possibly Zaparoan. Ruhlen says it is related to Candoshi. Speakers are somewhat bilingual in Spanish or Bobonaza-Tigre Quechua. VSO. Nearly extinct.

TICUNA ***(TIKUNA, TUKUNA)*** [TCA] 8,000 in Peru (1998 SIL). Population total all countries 24,000. Northeastern Amazon River region, from Chimbote in Peru to San Antonio do Iça in Brazil. Also spoken in Brazil, Colombia. Language Isolate. SVO. Literacy rate in first language: 30% to 60%. Literacy rate in second language: 25% to 50%. Christian, traditional religion. NT 1986.

URARINA ***(SHIMACU, SIMACU, ITUCALI)*** [URA] 2,000 to 3,000 (1998 SIL). Urarinas District, Pucayacu, Chambira, and Urituyacu rivers. Unclassified. There are several dialects with minor differences, inherently intelligible. Ruhlen and others classify it as Andean. Bilingual level estimates for Spanish are 0 60%, 1 20%, 2 10%, 3 7%, 4 3%, 5 0%. Women are monolingual. Men range from monolingual to fairly bilingual in Spanish-the majority are able to handle commercial matters. OVS. Literacy rate in first language: Below 1%. Literacy rate in second language: Below 5%. Bible portions 1973-1990.

YAGUA ***(YAHUA, LLAGUA, YAVA, YEGUA)*** [YAD] 5,000 to 6,000 in Peru (1998 SIL). Population total both countries 5,000 to 6,000 or more. Northeastern Amazon River region, from Iquitos to the Brazil border. Some occasionally go into Brazil. Also spoken in Colombia. Peba-Yaguan. Two dialects. Bilingual level estimates for Spanish are 0 54%, 1 20%, 2 15%, 3 10%, 4 .95%, 5 .05%. Dictionary. VSO. Literacy rate in first language: Below 1%. Literacy rate in second language: 25% to 50%. NT 1994.

YAMEO [YME] In 1925 there were 50. Marañon and Amazon rivers from the mouth of the Tigre to the Nanay River. Peba-Yaguan. Extinct.

YAMINAHUA ***(YAMINAWA, JAMINAWÁ, YUMINAHUA, YAMANAWA)*** [YAA] 1,200 to 1,450 in Peru, including 850 to 1,050 Yaminahua (1998 SIL), 200 to 300 Mastanahua (1981 SIL), 150 Chitonahua (1997 SIL). Population total all countries 1,700 to 1,900. Huacapishtea and Mapuya. Chitonahua at the headwaters of the Embira River. Also spoken in Bolivia, Brazil. Panoan, South-Central, Yaminahua-Sharanahua. Dialects: YAMINAHUA, MASTANAHUA, CHITONAHUA (MORUNAHUA, MORONAHUA, FOREDAFA, HORUDAHUA, HORUNAHUA). Closest to Sharanahua. Bilingual level estimates for Spanish are 0 50%, 1 15%, 2 25%, 3 8%, 4 2%, 5 0%. Subgroups: Masronahua

(Masrodawa), Nishinahua (Nishidawa), Chitonahua (Chitodawa), Shaonahua (Shaodawa). Grammar. SOV. Literacy rate in first language: Below 1%. Literacy rate in second language: Below 5%. Bible portions 1987-1992.

YANESHA' ***(AMUESHA, AMUESE, AMUEIXA, AMOISHE, AMAGUES, AMAGE, OMAGE, AMAJO, LORENZO, AMUETAMO, AMAJE, YANESHA')*** [AME] 9,000 to 10,000 (1998 SIL). Central and eastern Pasco region and Junín, western jungle, headwaters of the Pachitea and Perene rivers. Arawakan, Maipuran, Western Maipuran. Bilingual level estimates for Spanish are 0 5%, 1 15%, 2 40%, 3 20%, 4 10%, 5 10%. The people prefer to be called 'Yanesha'. Dictionary. Grammar. VSO. Literacy rate in first language: 10% to 30%. Literacy rate in second language: 15% to 25%. NT 1978.

YINE ***(PIRO, PIRRO, PIRA, SIMIRINCHE, SIMIRANCH, CONTAQUIRO, YINE)*** [PIB] 1,500 to 2,000 (1991 SIL). East central Urubamba River area. Arawakan, Maipuran, Southern Maipuran, Purus. Machinére in Brazil is different enough to need separate literature. Dictionary. SOV. Literacy rate in first language: 30% to 60%. Literacy rate in second language: 50% to 75%. NT 1960.

YORA ***(YURA, MANU PARK PANOAN, PARQUENAHUA, NAHUA)*** [MTS] 350 to 400 (1998 SIL). Manu Park, Panagua River. Some are outside of the Park on the Mishagua River. Panoan, South-Central, Yora. Close to Yaminahua and Sharanahua. Literacy rate in first language: Below 1%. Literacy rate in second language: Below 5%.

PUERTO RICO

National or official languages: Spanish, English. 3,810,000 (1998 UN). Self governing part of USA. Literacy rate 89% to 90%. Also includes North Levantine Spoken Arabic, South Levantine Spoken Arabic, Corsican, French 2,624, Standard German 1,453, Haitian Creole French 438, Italian 1,556, Ladino, Papiamentu 200, Eastern Yiddish, Chinese 2,000. Christian, secular, Jewish, Muslim, Hindu, Buddhist, Baha'i. Deaf population 8,000 to 40,000 (1986 Gallaudet University). Deaf institutions: 5. Data accuracy estimate: A2. The number of languages listed for Puerto Rico is 3. Of those, all are living languages. Diversity index 0.05.

ENGLISH [ENG] 82,000 mother tongue speakers (1995), 376,371 second language users (1970 census). Indo-European, Germanic, West, English. National language. Bible 1535-1989. See main entry under United Kingdom.

PUERTO RICAN SIGN LANGUAGE ***(PRSL)*** [PSL] (8,000 to 40,000 deaf persons; 1986 Gallaudet Univ.). Deaf sign language. Related to American Sign Language but distinct. 4 varieties are used: Signed Spanish as a pidgin with hearing Spanish speakers, Signed English as a pidgin with deaf educated in USA and with hearing English speakers, American Sign Language with those who know only that, and PRSL. Some know only PRSL. Signs were introduced in 1907 by nuns. Some home signs are also used.

SPANISH [SPN] 3,437,120 speakers in Puerto Rico, 90% of the population (1996). Indo-European, Italic, Romance, Italo-Western, Western, Gallo-Iberian, Ibero-Romance, West Iberian, Castilian. Some dialects are considered to be archaic. National language. Bible 1553-1979. See main entry under Spain.

ST. KITTS-NEVIS

Federation of St. Kitts and Nevis. National or official language: English. 39,000 (1998 UN). Gained independence in 1983. Literacy rate 88% to 90%. Christian. Deaf institutions: 1. Data accuracy estimate: B. The number of languages listed for St. Kitts-Nevis is 2. Of those, both are living languages. Diversity index 0.00.

ENGLISH [ENG] Indo-European, Germanic, West, English. National language. Bible 1535-1989. See main entry under United Kingdom.

LEEWARD CARIBBEAN CREOLE ENGLISH [AIG] 39,000 in St. Kitts. St. Kitts. Creole, English based, Atlantic, Eastern, Southern. Dialect: ST. KITTS CREOLE ENGLISH (KITTITIAN CREOLE ENGLISH). Closest to Montserrat, Antigua, Barbuda. There is a creole continuum with Standard English. Investigation needed: intelligibility with St. Kitts and Nevis. Agriculturalists: sugarcane. See main entry under Antigua and Barbuda.

ST. LUCIA

National or official language: English. 150,000 (1998 UN). Independent member of the British Commonwealth. 238 sq. miles. Literacy rate 54%. Information mainly from L. Carrington 1984;

H. Simmons-McDonald 1994. Christian, traditional religion. Blind population 2,276 (1991 census). Deaf population 800 to 8,791. Deaf institutions: 1. Data accuracy estimate: A1. The number of languages listed for St. Lucia is 2. Of those, both are living languages. Diversity index 0.00.

ENGLISH [ENG] Indo-European, Germanic, West, English. Dialect: ST. LUCIAN ENGLISH. There is an emerging English vernacular on St. Lucia, in a certain rural area. It is significantly restructured, heavily French creole-influenced, English lexicon (Paul Garrett 1998). National language. Bible 1535-1989. See main entry under United Kingdom.

LESSER ANTILLEAN CREOLE FRENCH [DOM] 123,000 in St. Lucia (1995), 75% of the population (1997 M. Parkvall). Population total all countries 985,450. Also spoken in Dominica, France, Grenada, Guadeloupe, Guyana, Martinique, Trinidad and Tobago. Creole, French based. Dialect: ST. LUCIA CREOLE FRENCH (PATWA, PATOIS, KWÉYÒL). Guadeloupe dialect is similar to Haiti, close to Martinique; St. Lucia is close to Dominica (97% to 99% intelligibility). Goodman (1964) says all French creoles of the Caribbean are somewhat inherently intelligible to each other's speakers. Other sources also include those of the Indian Ocean and probably Southeast Asia and Oceania (Voegelin and Voegelin 1977). Standard French is understood by no more than 10% of the population in St. Lucia. Standard French is used in some church services. English is also used. Politicians give speeches in Creole. In the islands under French influence nearly all the population speaks creole as mother tongue, although there is a local variety of Standard French. In those under English influence, the creole has less standing, and its speakers are normally illiterate in the creole. Dictionary. Grammar. Literacy rate in second language: 36%. Has an orthography. Newspapers, radio programs. Christian. NT 1999.

ST. PIERRE AND MIQUELON

National or official language: French. 7,000 (1998 UN). French Department; islands off the southwest coast of Newfoundland, Canada. Also includes Algerian Spoken Arabic. Christian, other. Data accuracy estimate: A2. The number of languages listed for St. Pierre and Miquelon is 2. Of those, both are living languages. Diversity index 0.07.

ENGLISH [ENG] 188 in St. Pierre and Miquelon (1967 census). Indo-European, Germanic, West, English. Bible 1535-1989. See main entry under United Kingdom.

FRENCH [FRN] 5,114 out of 5,235 population in St. Pierre and Miquelon (1967 census). Indo-European, Italic, Romance, Italo-Western, Western, Gallo-Iberian, Gallo-Romance, Gallo-Rhaetian, Oïl, French. National language. Bible 1530-1986. See main entry under France.

ST. VINCENT AND THE GRENADINES

National or official language: English. 112,000 (1998 UN). Self governing part of British West Indies. Literacy rate 85%. Also includes Portuguese. Christian, traditional religion, Baha'i. Data accuracy estimate: B. The number of languages listed for St. Vincent and the Grenadines is 3. Of those, 2 are living languages and 1 is extinct. Diversity index 0.00.

CARIB, ISLAND [CAI] Formerly also in Dominica. Arawakan, Maipuran, Northern Maipuran, Caribbean. Dialect: VINCENTIAN. Not inherently intelligible with Garífuna in more than a limited way (D. Taylor IJAL 1959:67). Became extinct in Dominica and St. Vincent about 1920. Extinct. See main entry under Dominica.

ENGLISH [ENG] Indo-European, Germanic, West, English. National language. Bible 1535-1989. See main entry under United Kingdom.

WINDWARD CARIBBEAN CREOLE ENGLISH [SVG] 138,000 (1989 J. Holm). Population total both countries 251,000. Also spoken in Grenada. Creole, English based, Atlantic, Eastern, Southern. Dialect: VINCENTIAN CREOLE ENGLISH. Closest to Grenada, Tobago. Slightly intelligible with Jamaican and perhaps Bahamas creoles. May have some French influence, although the former French creole used here is virtually gone. J. Holm says it is the only folk language (1989:457).

SURINAME

Republic of Suriname. National or official language: Dutch. 414,000 (1998 UN). Literacy rate 65% to 95%. Also includes North Levantine Spoken Arabic, English, Korean, Portuguese. Information mainly from SIL 1964-1999. Christian, Hindu, Muslim, traditional religion, secular, Baha'i. Blind population 1,300 (1982 WCE). Deaf population 25,646. Deaf institutions: 1. Data accuracy estimate: A2. The number of languages listed for Suriname is 16. Of those, 15 are living languages and 1 is a second language without mother tongue speakers. Diversity index 0.79.

AKURIO ***(AKOERIO, AKURI, AKURIJO, AKURIYO, AKULIYO, WAMA, WAYARICURI, OYARICOULET, TRIOMETESEM, TRIOMETESEN)*** [AKO] 44 or 45 (1998 Eithne B. Carlin). Southeast jungle. Carib, Northern, East-West Guiana, Wama. Related to, but not inherently intelligible with, Trió. Dialects or related languages: Urukuyana, Kumayena. All but one group is living with the Trió and bilingual in Trió. Children speak Trió. The Trió respect the Akurio for their knowledge of the forest, but look down on them and their language. Contacted in 1969. Nearly extinct.

ARAWAK ***(LOKONO, AROWAK)*** [ARW] 700 speakers out of 2,051 in the ethnic group in Suriname (1980 census). Population total all countries 2,400. Scattered locations across the north of Suriname. Also spoken in French Guiana, Guyana, Venezuela. Arawakan, Maipuran, Northern Maipuran, Caribbean. Reported to be used only by the elderly in Suriname and Guyana. The young people use Sranan. Investigation needed: bilingual proficiency in Arawak (French Guiana, Venezuela). Dictionary. Grammar. Literacy rate in first language: Below 1%. Literacy rate in second language: 25% to 50%. Bible portions 1850-1978.

AUKAN ***(NDYUKA, NDJUKÁ, NJUKÁ, "DJUKA", "DJOEKA", AUKAANS, OKANISI)*** [DJK] 15,542 in Suriname, including 14,353 Aukan, 33 Aluku, 1,156 Paramaccan (1980 census). Population total both countries 21,500 or more. Eastern along the Marowijne and Tapanahony rivers, northeastern along the Cottica River. Aluku are along the French Guiana border and in French Guiana. Paramaccan are in northeast Suriname. Also spoken in French Guiana. Creole, English based, Atlantic, Suriname, Ndyuka. Dialects: AUKAN, ALUKU (ALOEKOE, BONI), PARAMACCAN. Kwinti is further removed from Aukan than are Aluku and Paramaccan. The society was formed by escaped slaves. Subsistence and economy is Amerindian, social culture and religion are West African. Aluku has more French influence than Paramaccan does. Any spelling of Ndyuka without the initial nasal is considered derogatory. 'Aukan' is English, 'Aukaans' is Dutch. Dictionary. Grammar. Tonal. Literacy rate in first language: Below 1%. Literacy rate in second language: 15% to 25%. Traditional religion, Christian. NT 1999.

CARIB ***(CARIBE, CARIÑA, KALIHNA, KALINYA, KALI'NA, GALIBÍ, MARAWORNO)*** [CRB] 2,390 in Suriname villages (1980 census). Various locations along the north coast. The eastern dialect in Suriname is primarily in the Albina area and in French Guiana, Brazil, and Venezuela; the western dialect is in the central and western areas of Suriname and in Guyana. Carib, Northern, Galibi. Dialects: MURATO (MYRATO, WESTERN CARIB), TYREWUJU (EASTERN CARIB). Speakers of the central dialect are reported to be bilingual and switching to Sranan. They also speak Dutch as second language. All ages in some areas. The eastern dialect is the prestige dialect in Suriname. Their own name for the language is 'Kari'na auran', 'Kari'na' for the people. The name in Dutch is 'Kara'ibs', in French 'Galibi', in Spanish 'Caribe', in English 'Carib'. Dictionary. Grammar. Literacy rate in first language: Below 1%. Literacy rate in second language: 25% to 50%. Bible portions 1992-1996. See main entry under Venezuela.

CHINESE, HAKKA [HAK] 6,000 in Suriname out of an ethnic group of 12,000 Chinese, including Yue. Sino-Tibetan, Chinese. Bible 1916. See main entry under China.

DUTCH [DUT] 200,000 mother tongue speakers in Suriname (1997 Christa DeKleine), many of whom are native bilingual speakers with Sranan or Sarnami Hindustani. Indo-European, Germanic, West, Low Saxon-Low Franconian, Low Franconian. National language. Bible 1522-1992. See main entry under Netherlands.

GUYANESE CREOLE ENGLISH ***(CREOLESE, GUYANESE CREOLE)*** [GYN] 50,000 in Suriname (1986 SIL). May be some in French Guiana. Creole, English based, Atlantic, Eastern, Southern. Literacy rate in second language: 25% to 50%. See main entry under Guyana.

HINDUSTANI, CARIBBEAN [HNS] 150,000 in Suriname, about 38% of population (1986). Population total all countries 165,600 or more. Coastal region. No speakers in French Guiana. Also spoken in Belize, Guyana, Netherlands, Trinidad and Tobago. Indo-European, Indo-Iranian, Indo-Aryan, Eastern zone, Bihari. Dialects: TRINIDAD BHOJPURI, SARNAMI HINDUSTANI (SARNAMI HINDI, AILI GAILI). There are monolingual speakers. Others use Sranan or Dutch as second language. Based on Bhojpuri, with influences from Awadhi. It has loans from Sranan, Dutch, and English. Literacy rate in first language: Below 1%. Literacy rate in second language: 50% to 75%. Hindu, Muslim. NT 1997.

JAVANESE, CARIBBEAN ***(SURINAME JAVANESE)*** [JVN] 60,000 in Suriname, about 15% of population (1986). Population total both countries 60,000 or more. Coastal area. Also spoken in French Guiana. Austronesian, Malayo-Polynesian, Western Malayo-Polynesian, Sundic, Javanese. Significantly different from the Javanese of Indonesia. Descended from plantation workers brought from Java between 1890-1939. Dictionary. Literacy rate in first language: Below 1%. Literacy rate in second language: 50% to 75%. Muslim, traditional religion. NT 1999.

KWINTI [KWW] 133 living in villages in Suriname (1980 census). North central, along the Coppename River, upstream from Carib villages in Kaimanstan and Witagron. Creole, English based, Atlantic, Suriname, Ndyuka. Further removed from Ndyuka than Aluku and Paramaccan. Probably needs literature adapted from Ndyuka. Traditional religion.

NDYUKA-TRIO PIDGIN [NJT] Southern Suriname, upper Tapanahonij River. Pidgin. Formerly used until the 1960s by the Ndyuka and Trió and Wayana peoples for trading. Increasing travel by the Indians to the coast at that time cut back on that trade, and also gave some of them opportunity to use Sranan in contact with the Ndyuka. Many Ndyuka men in their 30s or older now do not know it. Scarcely used at all now. Trade language. Second language only.

SARAMACCAN [SRM] 23,000 in Suriname including 1,000 Matawari (1995 N. Glock SIL). Population total both countries 26,000. Central, along Saramacca and upper Suriname rivers. Refugees are in Paramaribo. Also spoken in French Guiana. English-based creole. Dialect: MATAWARI (MATAWAI, MATUARI, MATOEWARI). Portuguese influenced. Also linguistic influences from KiKongo (Hancock 1988). 20% or more of the lexicon has an African component. A Bush Negro ethnic group with background similar to the Ndyuka. Dictionary. Grammar. Tonal, one tone per vowel. Literacy rate in first language: Below 1%. Literacy rate in second language: 15% to 25%. Traditional religion. NT 1991-1999.

SRANAN ***(SRANAN TONGO, TAKI-TAKI, SURINAAMS, SURINAMESE, SURINAME CREOLE ENGLISH)*** [SRN] 120,000 or more first language speakers in Suriname or 30% of the population (1993 SIL), 400,000 including second language speakers (1993). Population total all countries 120,000 or more. Mainly in Paramaribo and along the coast. Also spoken in Aruba, Netherlands, Netherlands Antilles. Creole, English based, Atlantic, Suriname. Similar to Ndyuka, but there are cultural differences. Also has many similarities to Krio of Sierra Leone. Bilingualism in Dutch. Some literature. The lingua franca of 80% of the population of the country, including the Hindustanis, Javanese, Chinese, American Indians, and Bush Negroes. Language of wider communication. Literacy rate in first language: 10%. Literacy rate in second language: 50% to 75%. Christian, traditional religion. Bible 1997.

TRIÓ ***(TIRIÓ)*** [TRI] 822 in Suriname villages (1980 census). Population total both countries 1,150. South central, villages of Tepoe and Alalapadu. Also spoken in Brazil. Carib, Northern, East-West Guiana, Wayana-Trio. All domains: home, school, playground, church, administration. Speakers have an attitude of pride toward Trió, but do not consider it to be appropriate for a subject or instruction in school. The purer Trió is considered to be spoken by the older men and storytellers, and not by most of the younger men, those who have lived in town, or children of mixed marriages (E. B. Carlin 1998). Literacy rate in first language: 10% to 30%. Literacy rate in second language: 25% to 50%. NT 1979.

WARAO ***(WARRAU, GUARAO, GUARAUNO)*** [WBA] A very small number of individuals in Suriname. Near Guyana border. Language Isolate. Bilingualism in Guyanese. All speakers in Suriname are elderly. NT 1974. See main entry under Venezuela.

WAYANA ***(OAYANA, WAJANA, UAIANA, OYANA, OIANA, ALUKUYANA, UPURUI, ROUCOUYENNE)*** [WAY] 397 in Suriname villages (1980 census). Population total all countries 750. Villages in southeastern Suriname. Also spoken in Brazil, French Guiana. Carib, Northern, East-West Guiana, Wayana-Trio. Literacy rate in first language: 10% to 30%. Literacy rate in second language: 25% to 50%. NT 1979.

TRINIDAD AND TOBAGO

Republic of Trinidad and Tobago. National or official language: English. 1,283,000 (1998 UN); Afro-Trinidadian 40%, East Indian 41%, mixed 14%, white 1%, Chinese 1%, other 1%. Literacy rate All 97%: male 98%, female 96%. Also includes North Levantine Spoken Arabic 2,600, Chinese 6,500. Information mainly from S. R. Sperl 1980; I. Hancock 1985; P. Mohan and P. Zador 1986; L. Winer 1993. Christian, Hindu, Muslim, Baha'i, other or unknown. Deaf institutions: 2. Data accuracy estimate: B. The number of languages listed for Trinidad and Tobago is 6. Of those, all are living languages. Diversity index 0.47.

ENGLISH [ENG] Indo-European, Germanic, West, English. National language. Bible 1535-1989. See main entry under United Kingdom.

HINDUSTANI, CARIBBEAN ***(TRINIDAD BHOJPURI)*** [HNS] 15,633 in Trinidad and Tobago, or 3% of the East Indians, who are 41% of the population (1996). Indo-European, Indo-Iranian, Indo-Aryan, Eastern zone, Bihari. Related to Bhojpuri. Bilingualism in English. 90% of the Hindustanis are reported to speak English as mother tongue. Literacy rate in second language: 70%. Hindu, Muslim, Christian. NT 1997. See main entry under Suriname.

LESSER ANTILLEAN CREOLE FRENCH [DOM] Trinidad, villages of the Northern Range, fishing communities in the islands and coastal settlements along the peninsula to the west of the capital especially (I. Hancock ms.). Creole, French based. Dialect: TRINIDADIAN CREOLE FRENCH (PATOIS,

TRINIDADIEN). Speakers have contact with French creoles from St. Lucia and elsewhere, which contributes to language maintenance. M. Alleyne and J. Holm say it is close to Lesser Antillean Creole French. Not intelligible with Standard French. In settlements around Dragon Mouths children under ten speak the language; elsewhere speakers are middle-aged and older (I. Hancock 1984). Fishermen. NT 1999. See main entry under St. Lucia.

SPANISH [SPN] Fishing villages and communities of the southern peninsula. Indo-European, Italic, Romance, Italo-Western, Western, Gallo-Iberian, Ibero-Romance, West Iberian, Castilian. Users seem to be second language users only. Frequent contact with Venezuelan fishing communities that lie nine miles off the coast of Trinidad. Bible 1553-1979. See main entry under Spain.

TOBAGONIAN CREOLE ENGLISH *(TOBAGONIAN DIALECT)* [TGH] 36,000 (1990 estimate). Not known if population is of speakers or the ethnic group. Tobago. Creole, English based, Atlantic, Eastern, Southern. Closest to Grenada, St. Vincent. Slightly intelligible with Jamaican and perhaps Bahamas creoles. Investigation needed: intelligibility with regional dialects, bilingual proficiency in English. Dictionary. Plains, hills, low mountains.

TRINIDADIAN CREOLE ENGLISH [TRF] Trinidad. Creole, English based, Atlantic, Eastern, Southern. Investigation needed: intelligibility with regional varieties, bilingual proficiency in English. Dictionary. Grammar. Plains, hills, low mountains.

TURKS AND CAICOS ISLANDS

National or official language: English. 16,000 (1998 UN). Literacy rate over age 15 86.7% (1985). Christian. Data accuracy estimate: B. The number of languages listed for Turks and Caicos Islands is 2. Of those, both are living languages. Diversity index 0.00.

ENGLISH [ENG] Indo-European, Germanic, West, English. National language. Bible 1535-1989. See main entry under United Kingdom.

TURKS AND CAICOS CREOLE ENGLISH [TCH] 10,730 (1995). Creole, English based, Atlantic, Eastern. This variety has not been studied, but it may be related to Bahamas creole (Holm 1989:489). Agriculturalists: cotton.

U.S. VIRGIN ISLANDS

National or official language: English. 94,000 (1998 UN). U.S. Territory. 50 small islands plus St. John, St. Croix, St. Thomas. Literacy rate 90% to 95%. Also includes Papiamentu 200, Spanish 4,444. Christian, secular. Deaf institutions: 2. Data accuracy estimate: B. The number of languages listed for U.S. Virgin Islands is 3. Of those, 2 are living languages and 1 is extinct. Diversity index 0.34.

DUTCH CREOLE *(NEGERHOLLANDS)* [DCR] Formerly in Leeward Islands, U.S. Virgin Islands, St. Thomas, St. John, Puerto Rico. Creole, Dutch based. The last speaker died recently. There may be some remaining second language speakers. Extinct. NT 1781-1833.

ENGLISH [ENG] 8,414 mother tongue speakers in U.S. Virgin Islands (1970 census). Indo-European, Germanic, West, English. National language. Bible 1535-1989. See main entry under United Kingdom.

VIRGIN ISLANDS CREOLE ENGLISH [VIB] 52,250 (1980 WA). Population total all countries 64,250. Also spoken in British Virgin Islands, Guadeloupe, Netherlands Antilles. Creole, English based, Atlantic, Eastern, Southern. Dialect: CRUZAN. St. Croix, St. Eustatius, St. John, and Saba are closest. Slightly intelligible with Jamaican and perhaps Bahamas Creole. Alleyne says it is post-creole English. Dictionary.

URUGUAY

Republic of Uruguay, República Oriental del Uruguay. National or official language: Spanish. 3,289,000 (1998 UN). Literacy rate 95% to 96%. Also includes Catalan-Valencian-Balear, Corsican, Standard German 28,000, Italian 79,000, Lithuanian, Plautdietsch 1,200, Portuguese 28,000, Russian 14,000, Eastern Yiddish. Christian, secular, Jewish. Deaf institutions: 4. Data accuracy estimate: A2. The number of languages listed for Uruguay is 2. Of those, both are living languages. Diversity index 0.09.

SPANISH [SPN] 3,000,000 in Uruguay (1995 estimate). Indo-European, Italic, Romance, Italo-Western, Western, Gallo-Iberian, Ibero-Romance, West Iberian, Castilian. National language. Bible 1553-1979. See main entry under Spain.

URUGUAYAN SIGN LANGUAGE [UGY] Deaf sign language. The sign language has been used since 1910. Used in schools. Sign language interpreters are required in court. Instruction for parents of deaf children. A committee on national sign language, and an organization for sign language teachers. There is a manual alphabet for spelling. Dictionary. TV, videos.

USA

United States of America. National or official languages: English (in Hawaii), Hawaiian (in Hawaii), Spanish (in New Mexico). 274,000,000 (1999 census), 1,900,000 American Indians, Eskimos, and Aleut, not all speaking indigenous languages (1990 census). Literacy rate 95% to 99%. Also includes Abaza 15, Adyghe 3,000, Gheg Albanian 17,382, Tosk Albanian, Judeo-Tunisian Arabic, Najdi Spoken Arabic 193,520, Armenian 1,100,000, Assyrian Neo-Aramaic 80,000, South Azerbaijani, Bahamas Creole English, Bahnar, Basque 8,108, Belarusan 10,000, Bengali, Brao 90, Breton 32,722, Western Bru, Bukharic, Bulgarian, Burmese 1,581, Catalan-Valencian-Balear 40,000, Cebuano, Chaldean Neo-Aramaic 80,000, Eastern Cham 10, Western Cham 3,000, Hakka Chinese, Mandarin Chinese, Min Nan Chinese, Yue Chinese, Chru 1, Cora, Corsican, Crimean Turkish, Upper Guinea Crioulo 156,000, Czech 1,452,812, Danish 194,000, Dutch 412,637, Estonian 20,507, Western Farsi 900,000, Finnish 214,168, French 1,100,000, Eastern Frisian, Western Frisian, Irish Gaelic, Scots Gaelic, Garifuna 50,000, Georgian 757, Standard German 6,093,054, Greek 458,699, Gujarati, Guyanese Creole English, Haitian Creole French 200,000, Hebrew, Hiligaynon, Hindi 26,253, Fijian Hindustani, Hmong Daw 70,000, Hmong Njua 100,000, Hulaula, Hungarian 447,497, Icelandic 9,768, Ilocano, Indonesian, Italian 906,000, Iu Mien 24,000, Japanese 804,000, Jarai, Kabardian 2,000, Kabuverdianu 400,000, Kalmyk-Oirat, Eastern Kanjobal, Western Kanjobal, Karachay-Balkar, Central Khmer 50,000, Khmu, Khuen, Klao, Koho, Korean 1,800,000, Kurdi, Kurmanji, Kwakiutl 45, Ladin, Ladino, Lahu Shi 2,000, Lamet 24, Lao 171,577, Latvian 50,000, Laven, Laz 1, Lithuanian, Lombard, Luri, Luxembourgeois 20,618, Mal, Malay 6,253, Ambonese Malay 20, Maltese, Mixtepec Mixteco, Eastern Mnong, Nhang 5, Northern Central America Creole English 40,000, Bokmaal Norwegian 612,862, Nung, Mezquital Otomí, Eastern Panjabi 100,000, Western Panjabi, Parsi 75,000, Phu Thai, Piemontese, Pingelapese 500, Polish 2,437,938, Pontic, Portuguese 365,000, Rade, Rapa Nui, Balkan Romani, Carpathian Romani 18,000, Vlax Romani 650,000, Romanian 56,590, Samoan 120,000, Senaya 400, Serbo-Croatian 249,257, Shelta 50,000, Sherpa 500, Sindhi, Slovak 510,366, Slovenian 82,321, Southwestern Caribbean Creole English, Swahili 3,991, Swedish 626,102, Tagalog 377,000, Tai Daeng, Tai Dam 3,000, Upper Taoih, Tatar 7,000, Tay, Thai 14,416, Tibetan 3,000, Tokelauan, Tondano 20, Tongan 3,000, Traveller Scottish, Turkish 24,123, Turkmen, Turoyo 5,000, Ukrainian 249,351, Uyghur, Northern Uzbek, Vietnamese 859,000, Yevanic 15, Eastern Yiddish 1,250,000, Yoruba, Cajonos Zapoteco, San Juan Guelavía Zapoteco 500, Yalalag Zapoteco, Yatzachi Zapoteco, Zoogocho Zapoteco 400, Arabic 3,000,000, Chinese 1,645,000, from the Philippines 1,405,000, South Asians 634,000, speakers of other African, Asian, European, Latin American, and Pacific languages. Approximately 1,000,000 Gypsies use a variety of Romani as first or second language (1980 census). Information mainly from W. Chafe 1962, 1965; M. Mithun and L. Campbell 1979; C. A. Callaghan 1998; M-L Tarpent and D. Kendall 1998; SIL 1951-1999. Christian, secular, Jewish, Muslim. Blind population 500,000. Deaf population nearly 2,000,000 (1988). Deaf institutions: many. Data accuracy estimate: A1, A2. The number of languages listed for USA is 231. Of those, 176 are living languages, 3 are second languages without mother tongue speakers, and 52 are extinct. Diversity index 0.35.

ABNAKI, EASTERN [AAQ] 1. Near Bangor, Maine, 1 village (Penobscot). Algic, Algonquian, Eastern. Dialect: PENOBSCOT. Bilingualism in English. Elderly. Nearly extinct.

ACHUMAWI *(ACHOMAWI, PITT RIVER)* [ACH] 10 speakers out of 800 in the ethnic group (1982 SIL), The 1990 census reports 81 speakers. Northeastern California. Hokan, Northern, Karok-Shasta, Shasta-Palaihninan, Palaihninan. Originally there were nine dialects. All are elderly. Nearly extinct.

AFRO-SEMINOLE CREOLE *(AFRO-SEMINOLE, SEMINOLE, BLACK SEMINOLE)* [AFS] Bracketville, Texas and El Nacimiento, Coahuila, Mexico. Creole, English based, Atlantic, Eastern, Northern. Dialects: TEXAS, MEXICO. Separated from coastal Sea Islands Creole between 1690 and 1760. Similar to Sea Islands Creole of USA and Bahamas Creole. 90% lexical similarity with Sea Islands Creole. Speakers use English or Spanish as second language. No speakers left in Oklahoma. "Probably absorbed by Bahamian on Andros Island, and by Spanish in Cuba."

AHTENA *(ATNA, AHTNA, COPPER RIVER, MEDNOVSKIY)* [AHT] 80 speakers out of 500 population (1995 M. Krauss). Copper River above the Eyak River at its mouth, and upper Susitna and Nenana drainages. 8 communities. Na-Dene, Nuclear Na-Dene, Athapaskan-Eyak, Athapaskan, Tanaina-Ahtna. Bilingualism in English. Speakers are in their 50s or 60s and older. There is a growing interest in the language among the population. Dictionary. Nearly extinct.

ALABAMA ***(ALIBAMU)*** [AKZ] 256 speakers (1990 census), out of an ethnic group of 500 to 600 (1990 Heather Hardy). Alabama-Coushatta Reservation near Livingston in southeastern Texas. No speakers left in Oklahoma. Muskogean, Eastern. Less than 50% cognate with Koasati. Bilingualism in English.

ALEUT [ALW] 300 speakers in USA out of 2,000 in the ethnic group (1995 M. Krauss). Population total both countries 305. Western Aleut on Atka Island (Aleutian Chain) and Commander Islands (Russia); Eastern Aleut on eastern Aleutian Islands, Pribilofs, and Alaskan Peninsula. Also spoken in Russia (Asia). Eskimo-Aleut, Aleut. Dialects: WESTERN ALEUT (ATKAN, ATKA, ATTUAN, UNANGANY, UNANGAN), EASTERN ALEUT (UNALASKAN, PRIBILOF ALEUT). All but 4 speakers can speak English well. Many school texts have been produced. Copper Island Aleut is a mixed Aleut-Russian language, or pidgin, spoken on Mednyj Island. Dictionary. Grammar. Finite verb morphology, kinship terms, acculturational words and some adverbs come from Russian; nonfinite verb morphology, and most of the lexicon and structure come from Aleut. Bible portions 1840-1903.

ALSEA ***(ALSÉYA)*** [AES] There were fewer than 10 in 1930 (1977 Voegelin and Voegelin). Oregon, on Alsea River and Bay. Penutian, Oregon Penutian, Coast Oregon, Yakonan. Dialect: YAQUINA (YAKWINA, YAKON, YAKONA). Extinct.

AMERAX [AEX] Unclassified. Spoken by Neo-Muslims in prisons. Reported to not have mother tongue speakers. It may have Arabic influences (J. M. Cowan 1990). Muslim. Second language only.

AMERICAN SIGN LANGUAGE ***(ASL, AMESLAN, THE LANGUAGE OF THE DEAF)*** [ASE] 100,000 to 500,000 primary users (1986 Gallaudet U.) out of nearly 2,000,000 profoundly deaf persons in USA (1988), 0.8% of the USA population. 15,000,000 hard of hearing persons in the USA (1989 Sacks). Population total all countries 100,000 to 500,000. Also used in varying degrees in Canada, Philippines, Ghana, Nigeria, Chad, Burkina Faso, Gabon, Democratic Republic of Congo, Central African Republic, Côte d'Ivoire, Mauritania, Kenya, Madagascar, Benin, Togo, Zimbabwe, Singapore, China (Hong Kong). Also spoken in Canada, Guatemala. Deaf sign language. Dialects: BLACK AMERICAN SIGN LANGUAGE, TACTILE SIGN LANGUAGE. Black American Sign Language developed in segregated schools in the south. It contains much sign vocabulary not in ASL and some different grammatical structure. Tactile Sign Language is used by over 900 persons in Louisiana who know ASL, but have lost their sight from a generic cause: Usher's Syndrome. They communicate by touch on each other's wrists. Some have migrated to Seattle. Some have learned Braille. ASL has 43% lexical similarity with French Sign Language in an 872-word list. Sign language interpreters provided in court, for college students, at important public events, in job training, at social services programs, in mental health service programs, some instruction for parents of deaf children, many sign language classes for hearing people. There is an organization for sign language teachers. Many hearing people are learning ASL as second language. Reported to be the third largest language in the USA (1993 Honolulu Advertiser). Used since 1817. ASL is different from 'English on the Hands' (Signed English, Siglish). There are several systems of manually coded English, including different ones in different countries. Also several systems called Pidgin Signed English. Pidgin Signed English is taught in schools in the USA rather than ASL. Investigation needed: intelligibility with Black American Sign Language. Dictionary. SOV; prepositions, genitives, articles, adjectives, numerals, relatives before noun heads; question word initial. The average deaf person graduates from high school with 3rd or 4th grade reading level in English. TV, videos. Bible portions 1982-1996.

ANGLOROMANI ***(ENGLISH ROMANI, ROMANI ENGLISH, ROMANICHAL, ROMANIS)*** [RME] 100,000 or fewer in North America. Indo-European, Germanic, West, English. A variety of English with heavy Romani lexical borrowing. See main entry under United Kingdom.

APACHE, JICARILLA [APJ] 812 speakers (1990 census), out of 2,000 population (1977 SIL). Northern New Mexico, area of Dulce. Na-Dene, Nuclear Na-Dene, Athapaskan-Eyak, Athapaskan, Apachean, Navajo-Apache, Eastern Apache. Many young adults may prefer English. Children tend to prefer English. Parents and the elderly speak the language (1998). Most adults speak the language. Some children may speak the language, many can understand it.

APACHE, KIOWA [APK] 18 speakers (1990 census), out of 1,000 population (1977 SIL). Western Oklahoma, Caddo County. Na-Dene, Nuclear Na-Dene, Athapaskan-Eyak, Athapaskan, Apachean, Kiowa Apache. Bilingualism in English. Nearly extinct.

APACHE, LIPAN [APL] 2 or 3 speakers (1981 R. W. Young) out of 100 ethnic population (1977 SIL). New Mexico, Mescalero Reservation. Na-Dene, Nuclear Na-Dene, Athapaskan-Eyak, Athapaskan, Apachean, Navajo-Apache, Eastern Apache. Bilingualism in English. All speakers were elderly in 1981. May be extinct. Nearly extinct.

APACHE, MESCALERO-CHIRICAHUA [APM] 1,800 speakers out of 2,000 population (1977 SIL), including 279 Chiricahua speakers (1990 census). Mescalero Reservation, New Mexico. A small number of Chiricahua at Ft. Sill, Oklahoma. Na-Dene, Nuclear Na-Dene, Athapaskan-Eyak, Athapaskan,

Apachean, Navajo-Apache, Eastern Apache. Dialects: CHIRICAHUA, MESCALERO. In Oklahoma most or all speakers are middle-aged or older. Vigorous in New Mexico. Dictionary.

APACHE, WESTERN ***(COYOTERO)*** [APW] 12,693 speakers (1990 census), including 303 San Carlos. East central Arizona, several reservations. Na-Dene, Nuclear Na-Dene, Athapaskan-Eyak, Athapaskan, Apachean, Navajo-Apache, Western Apache-Navajo. Dialects: WHITE MOUNTAIN, SAN CARLOS, CIBECUE, TONTO. Children being raised speaking the language (1998). Vigorous. Dictionary. NT 1966.

ARAPAHO ***(ARRAPAHOE)*** [ARP] 1,038 speakers (1990 census), out of 5,000 population (1977 SIL). Wind River Reservation, Wyoming, and associated with the Cheyenne in western Oklahoma. Algic, Algonquian, Plains, Arapaho. Bilingualism in English. Most or all speakers are middle-aged or older. Bible portions 1903.

ARIKARA ***(ARIKARI, ARIKARIS, ARIKAREE, REE, RIS)*** [ARI] 90 speakers (1990 census), out of 1,000 population (1977 SIL). Fort Berthold Reservation, North Dakota. Caddoan, Northern, Pawnee-Kitsai, Pawnee. Not inherently intelligible with Pawnee. Bilingualism in English. Most or all speakers are middle-aged or older. Arikara instructional material has been published for use in a language teaching program. Reported to be one of the groups Lewis and Clark met in 1804 in North Dakota. There had been 30,000 reduced to 6,000 because of smallpox. Dictionary. Grammar.

ASSINIBOINE ***(ASSINIBOIN, HOHE)*** [ASB] Fort Belknap and Fort Peck Reservations, Montana. Siouan, Siouan Proper, Mississippi Valley, Dakota. Very close to the Assiniboine of Saskatchewan. Closely related to Stoney. English is spoken extensively. All speakers are over 40 years old, most over 60 (1986). See main entry under Canada.

ATAKAPA [ALE] No speakers left out of a few individuals in the ethnic group (1977 SIL). Southwestern Louisiana and southeastern Texas. Gulf. Dictionary. Grammar. Extinct.

ATSUGEWI [ATW] 4 speakers (1962 Chafe), out of an ethnic group of 200 (1977 SIL). Northeastern California. Hokan, Northern, Karok-Shasta, Shasta-Palaihninan, Palaihninan. All over 50 years old (1962). There may be no speakers left (1982). Nearly extinct.

BARBAREÑO [BOI] Southern California, near Santa Barbara. Chumash. Was not intelligible with other Chumash varieties. Extinct.

BILOXI [BLL] Lower Mississippi Valley. Siouan, Siouan Proper, Southeastern, Biloxi-Ofo. Extinct.

BLACKFOOT ***(PIKANII, BLACKFEET)*** [BLC] 1,062 speakers in USA including 4 monolinguals (1990 census). Blackfeet Reservation, Montana. Algic, Algonquian, Plains. Dialects: PIEGAN, BLOOD. Bilingualism in English. In USA most or all speakers are middle-aged or older. In Missoula, Montana, summer language classes are offered in Blackfoot. Bible portions 1890-1980. See main entry under Canada.

CADDO ***(KADO, CADDOE, KADOHADACHO)*** [CAD] 141 speakers, including 6 monolinguals (1990 census), out of 1,800 population (1977 SIL). Western Oklahoma, Caddo County. Formerly in northeastern Texas, extending into southwestern Arkansas. Caddoan, Southern. Related to Pawnee, Wichita, and two extinct languages: Kitsai and Adai. Bilingualism in English. Most or all speakers are middle-aged or older. The tribes are Cahinnio, Hasinai, Kadohadacho, Nanatsoho, Upper Nasoni, Upper Natchitoches, Upper Yatasi.

CAHUILLA [CHL] 35 speakers (1990 census), out of 800 ethnic population (1977 SIL). Southern California, San Gorgonio Pass and Mohave Desert areas. Uto-Aztecan, Northern Uto-Aztecan, Takic, Cupan, Cahuilla-Cupeno. Bilingualism in English. All speakers are middle-aged or older. Nearly extinct.

CATAWBA [CHC] The last fluent speaker died in 1996, out of ethnic population of 500 (1977 SIL). Near Rock Hill, northern South Carolina. Siouan, Catawba. There were several dialects. Related to Woccon. Bilingualism in English. Nearly extinct.

CAYUGA [CAY] 10 speakers in USA (1991 M. Dale Kinkade). Cattaraugus Reservation, western New York, and formerly in northeastern Oklahoma. Iroquoian, Northern Iroquoian, Five Nations, Seneca-Onondaga, Seneca-Cayuga. Bilingualism in English. In the USA, only a few elderly speakers are left. See main entry under Canada.

CHEHALIS, LOWER [CEA] 5 or fewer speakers (1990 M. D. Kinkade). Southwestern coast of Washington. Salishan, Tsamosan, Inland. All speakers are elderly. Nearly extinct.

CHEHALIS, UPPER ***(CHEHALIS, KWAIAILK)*** [CJH] 2 or fewer speakers (1990 M. D. Kinkade and 1990 census) out of a population of 200 (1977 SIL). Washington, south of Puget Sound. Salishan, Tsamosan, Inland. A separate language from Lower Chehalis. Not to be confused with Halkomelem on the Chehalis River in British Columbia. Bilingualism in English. Dictionary. Nearly extinct.

CHEROKEE ***(TSALAGI, TSLAGI)*** [CER] 11,905 to 22,500 speakers, including 14,000 speakers out of 70,000 population on Oklahoma rolls (1986 Durbin Feeling, Cherokee Nation, OK), 8,500 in North Carolina. 11,905 speakers including 130 monolinguals, 308,132 ethnic Cherokee (1990 USA Census). Eastern and northeastern Oklahoma and Cherokee Reservation, Great Smokey Mts., western North Carolina. Iroquoian, Southern Iroquoian. Dialects: ELATI (LOWER CHEROKEE, EASTERN CHEROKEE),

KITUHWA (MIDDLE CHEROKEE), OTALI (UPPER CHEROKEE, WESTERN CHEROKEE, OVERHILL CHEROKEE), OVERHILL-MIDDLE CHEROKEE. In Oklahoma children are being raised speaking the language (1998). Vigorous in some Oklahoma communities. Elsewhere some younger ones prefer English. The Elati dialect is extinct. Dictionary. Grammar. Literacy rate in first language: 15% to 20% can read it, 5% can write it (1986 Cherokee Heritage Center). Sequoyah syllabary. Now being taught in schools, churches, and other classes (1986 Cherokee Advocate). Christian, traditional religion. NT 1850-1951.

CHETCO [CHE] 5 speakers or fewer (1962 Chafe) out of possible 100 population (1977 SIL). Southern coast, Oregon. Na-Dene, Nuclear Na-Dene, Athapaskan-Eyak, Athapaskan, Pacific Coast, Oregon, Tolowa-Galice. Bilingualism in English. Nearly extinct.

CHEYENNE [CHY] 1,721 speakers (1990 census), out of 5,000 population (1987 SIL). Northern Cheyenne Reservation, southeastern Montana; associated with Arapaho in western Oklahoma. Algic, Algonquian, Plains. In Montana most adults (parents and the elderly, 1998) speak the language but many younger ones prefer English. In Oklahoma most speakers are middle-aged or older. Northern Cheyenne in Montana have a summer camp for children, where 5 fluent speakers teach the language (1998). Literacy rate in first language: 1% to 5%. Literacy rate in second language: 50% to 100%. NT 1934.

CHICKASAW [CIC] 1,000 or fewer speakers (1987 Munro and Willmond) out of an ethnic group of 35,000 to 37,000 (1999 Chickasaw nation). Principally in south central Oklahoma, from Byng or Happyland (near Ada) in the north, and from Davis or Ardmore in the west to Fillmore and Wapanucka in the east. Some in Los Angeles, California. Muskogean, Western. Recent reports indicate that Choctaw speakers find Chickasaw to be unintelligible. Most speakers over 40 years old (1987 Munro and Willmond). Dictionary.

CHIMARIKO [CID] Northwest California. Hokan, Northern. Extinct.

CHINOOK ***(LOWER CHINOOK)*** [CHH] 12 speakers of Kiksht dialect (1996), out of a possible population of 300 (1977 SIL). Lower Columbia River, Oregon and Washington. Penutian, Chinookan. Dialects: KLATSOP (TLATSOP), CLACKAMA, KIKSHT. SVO, VSO. Nearly extinct.

CHINOOK WAWA ***(CHINOOK JARGON, CHINOOK PIDGIN, TSINUK WAWA)*** [CRW] 17 speakers in USA (1990 census). Formerly used along the Pacific coast from Oregon to Alaska. All speakers are probably now scattered. Pidgin, Amerindian. Consists mainly of words from Chinook, with a large admixture of words from Nootka, Canadian French, and English. Bilingualism in English. Formerly used widely during the 19th century between Indian and white, and between speakers of different languages. Trade language. Nearly extinct. Bible portions 1912. See main entry under Canada.

CHIPPEWA ***(SOUTHWESTERN OJIBWA, OJIBWE, OJIBWAY)*** [CIW] Ethnic Chippewa in USA: 103,826 (1990 Census Bureau). Upper Michigan westward to North Dakota, and unconfirmed groups in Montana. Algic, Algonquian, Central, Ojibwa. Dialects: UPPER MICHIAN-WISCONSIN CHIPPEWA, CENTRAL MINNESOTA CHIPPEWA, RED LAKE CHIPPEWA, MINNESOTA BORDER CHIPPEWA. Turtle Mountain in North Dakota shares features with Central Minnesota. Red Lake includes Northwest Angle on shore of Lake of the Woods. Nett Lake on the Minnesota border is closely related to Lac la Croix (Rainy River Ojibwa of Northwestern Ojibwa) in Ontario. Most or all speakers are middle-aged or older. Concerted effort via language teaching in public schools and other efforts to reverse decline. Dictionary. Grammar. NT 1833-1854, out of print.

CHITIMACHA [CHM] No speakers out of 300 population (1977 SIL). Southern Louisiana. Gulf. Extinct.

CHOCTAW [CCT] 17,890 speakers including 11,140 in Oklahoma (1998), 6,750 fluent speakers in Mississippi (1997). Ethnic group: 120,400 including 111,400 in Oklahoma (1998 Choctaw Language Department, Choctaw Nation of Oklahoma), 9,000 in Mississippi (1997 Mississippi Band of Choctaw Indians). Principally in southeastern Oklahoma (McCurtain County) and east central Mississippi. Some in Louisiana and Tennessee. Muskogean, Western. Recent reports indicate that Choctaw speakers find Chickasaw to be unintelligible. 24 years old and older in Oklahoma. Children are being raised speaking Choctaw in Mississippi. Vigorous in Mississippi, but some children prefer English. The Houma are 12,000 racially mixed descendents of a Choctaw subgroup in southern Louisiana who speak a dialect of Cajun French, and no longer speak Choctaw. More Choctaw are registering with the BIA now than previously (R. S. Williams). Literacy rate in first language: 5% to 10%. Literacy rate in second language: 75% to 100%. NT 1848.

CHUMASH [CHS] No speakers out of a possible 100 population (1977 SIL). Southern California coast near Santa Barbara. Chumash. Extinct since 1965. Inherently unintelligible Chumash varieties formerly spoken included Obispeño, Ineseño, Purisimeño, Barbareño, Ventureño, and Cruzeño (Island Chumash, Isleño), named after the missions to which they were brought. Marianne Mithun says it is not Hokan. Extinct.

CLALLAM ***(KLALLAM, S'KLALLAM, NA'KLALLAM)*** [CLM] 5 speakers (1990 census). Washington, northeastern Olympic Peninsula. Salishan, Central Salish, Straits. All speakers are elderly. Nearly extinct.

COCOPA ***(KIKIMA, CUCAPÁ, COCOPAH, KWIKAPA, DELTA RIVER YUMAN)*** [COC] 321 speakers including 6 monolinguals in the USA (1990 census). Lower Colorado River south of Yuma, Arizona. The majority live in Baja California, Mexico. Hokan, Esselen-Yuman, Yuman, Delta-Californian. Vigorous in the USA. Bible portions 1972. See main entry under Mexico.

COEUR D'ALENE [CRD] 5 or fewer speakers (1999 R. McDonald), out of a population of 800 (1977 SIL). Northern Idaho, Coeur d'Alene Reservation. Salishan, Interior Salish, Southern. They have language lessons in the school curriculum for children, and classes for adults. Nearly extinct.

COLUMBIA-WENATCHI ***(WENATCHI-COLUMBIA)*** [COL] 75 or fewer speakers (1990 M. D. Kinkade) out of a possible population of 500 (1977 SIL). 39 Columbia speakers (1990 census). North central Washington, Colville Reservation. Salishan, Interior Salish, Southern. Dialects: COLUMBIA (SINKIUSE, COLUMBIAN), WENATCHI (WENATCHEE, ENTIAT, CHELAN). Bilingualism in English. All speakers are middle-aged or older.

COMANCHE [COM] 854 speakers including 7 monolinguals (1990 census), out of 6,000 population (1977 SIL). Western Oklahoma. Uto-Aztecan, Northern Uto-Aztecan, Numic, Central. Closely related to Shoshoni, Panamint. Bilingualism in English. Most or all speakers are elderly (1998). Dictionary. Grammar. Bible portions 1958.

COOS ***(HANIS)*** [COS] 1 or 2 speakers (1962 Chafe) out of a possible 250 population (1977 SIL). Southern Oregon coast. Penutian, Oregon Penutian, Coast Oregon, Coosan. Bilingualism in English. All over 50 years old (1962). Possibly extinct. Nearly extinct.

COQUILLE ***(UPPER COQUILLE, MISHIKHWUTMETUNEE)*** [COQ] Probably no speakers left (1977 SIL). Southwestern Oregon, formerly on upper Coquille River. Na-Dene, Nuclear Na-Dene, Athapaskan-Eyak, Athapaskan, Pacific Coast, Oregon, Tolowa-Galice. Extinct.

COSTANOAN, NORTHERN ***(OHLONE)*** [CST] North central California from the head of the San Pablo Bay branch of San Francisco Bay to Southern Costanoan. Penutian, Yok-Utian, Utian, Costanoan. Dialects: EAST BAY, SAN FRANCISCO, SANTA CLARA, SANTA CRUZ, SOLEDAD. Became extinct in the 1950s. Subdialects of East Bay were Huchiun (Juichun), Niles (Chocheño), San José, San Lorenzo. Soledad may be transitional between Northern and Southern Costanoan. The name 'Costanoan' is reported to be insulting to the people. Coast and coastal valleys. Extinct.

COSTANOAN, SOUTHERN ***(OHLONE)*** [CSS] North central California from Northern Costanoan down to 30 miles south of Salinas. Penutian, Yok-Utian, Utian, Costanoan. Dialects: MONTEREY, MUTSUN (SAN JUAN BAUTISTA), RUMSEN (RUNSIEN, SAN CARLOS, CARMEL). Became extinct in the 1950s. The name 'Costanoan' is reported to be disliked by the people. Coast and coastal valleys. Extinct.

COWLITZ ***(LOWER COWLITZ)*** [COW] Possibly 2 speakers remaining from a population of about 200 (1990 M. D. Kinkade). Southwestern Washington. Salishan, Tsamosan, Inland. All speakers are elderly. Nearly extinct.

CREE, PLAINS ***(WESTERN CREE)*** [CRP] 1,070 speakers (1990 census). North central Montana. Algic, Algonquian, Central, Cree-Montagnais-Naskapi. Language complex or dialect continuum within Cree-Montagnais-Naskapi. Nonpalatalized y-dialect. Bilingualism in English. Most or all speakers in the USA are middle-aged or older. Grammar. Literacy rate in first language: 1% to 10%. Literacy rate in second language: 50% to 75%. Cree syllabary. Bible 1861-1908. See main entry under Canada.

CROW ***(APSAALOOKE)*** [CRO] 4,280 speakers (1990 census), out of a population of 9,840 enrolled in the Crow tribe (1999 BIA). Includes 8 to 20 monolinguals (1999). Southern Montana. Siouan, Siouan Proper, Missouri Valley. Close to Hidatsa. Bilingualism in English. Spoken by parents and the elderly (1998). Although almost all high school students and younger children can speak Crow, about 80% prefer to use English (1998). 77% of Crow people over 66 years old speak the language; 13% of preschoolers do. Language use is mainly vigorous. Literacy rate in first language: 1% to 5%. Literacy rate in second language: 75% to 100%. Bible portions 1980-1998.

CRUZEÑO ***(ISLAND CHUMASH, ISLEÑO)*** [CRZ] Southern California, near Santa Barbara. Chumash. Was not intelligible with other Chumash varieties. Had multiple dialects. Extinct.

CUPEÑO [CUP] 9 speakers (1990 census) out of a total population of 150 (1962 Chafe). Southern California, near the Pala Reservation, north of Valley Center. Uto-Aztecan, Northern Uto-Aztecan, Takic, Cupan, Cahuilla-Cupeno. Bilingualism in English. All over 50 years old (1962). Nearly extinct.

DAKOTA ***(SIOUX)*** [DHG] 15,355 speakers in USA including 31 monolinguals (1990 census). Population total both countries 20,355. Northern Nebraska, southern Minnesota, North and South Dakota, northeastern Montana. Also spoken in Canada. Siouan, Siouan Proper, Central, Mississippi Valley, Dakota. Dialects: DAKOTA (DAKHOTA, SANTEE, SANTEE-SISSETON), NAKOTA (NAKODA,

YANKTON, YANKTON-YANKTONAIS). Some children are being raised speaking the language in the northern Plains (1998). Many younger ones prefer English or do not speak the language. Bible 1879.

DEGEXIT'AN ***("INGALIK", "INGALIT", DEG XINAG, DEG XIT'AN)*** [ING] 40 or fewer speakers out of 250 to 300 population (1997 M. Krauss). Alaska, Shageluk, Anvik, and Athapaskans at Holy Cross, below Grayling on the Yukon River. Na-Dene, Nuclear Na-Dene, Athapaskan-Eyak, Athapaskan, Ingalik-Koyukon, Ingalik. Bilingualism in English. Speakers are in their 50s or older. The names "Ingalik" and "Ingalit" formerly applied to this language are unacceptable to its speakers.

DELAWARE, PIDGIN [DEP] Middle Atlantic region. Pidgin, Amerindian. Widely used in the 17th century between Algonquians and Europeans as a second language. Extinct.

ENGLISH [ENG] 210,000,000 first language speakers in USA (1984 estimate). 8,400,000 USA residents with no one 14 years old or older who speaks fluent English; 38% or 7,700,000 households headed by immigrants. Indo-European, Germanic, West, English. Dialect: BLACK ENGLISH. There are many regional dialects. Official language. Bible 1382-1989. See main entry under United Kingdom.

ESSELEN [ESQ] Central California coast near Carmel. Hokan, Esselen-Yuman, Esselen. Extinct.

EYAK [EYA] 1 speaker (1996 N. Barnes) out of 50 population (1995 M. Krauss). Mouth of the Copper River, Alaska. Last speaker lives in Anchorage. Na-Dene, Nuclear Na-Dene, Athapaskan-Eyak, Eyak. Bilingualism in English. The speaker is older (1996). Nearly extinct.

FRENCH, CAJUN ***(FRANÇAIS ACADIEN, ACADIAN, CAJUN, CAJAN, CADIEN)*** [FRC] 1,000,000 (M. Harris in B. Comrie 1988:212). Southern Louisiana west of the Mississippi as far north as Avoyelles, Evangeline, Allen, and Calcasieu parishes. Indo-European, Italic, Romance, Italo-Western, Western, Gallo-Iberian, Gallo-Romance, Gallo-Rhaetian, Oïl, French. Dialects: MARSH FRENCH, PRAIRIE FRENCH, BIG WOODS FRENCH. Ancestors came from French Canada in the 18th century. It is reported that Cajun speakers can partially understand Standard French, but Cajun is difficult for some Standard French speakers. Different from the variety of 'Broken French' used by 8,000 African Americans, or the 'Napoleanic Era French' (located around Houma and north of Theriot on Hwy. 315, speaking an archaic French and English). Many are reported to have limited proficiency in English. Some use Cajun English. Most under 50 speak English as first language, Cajun as second. There are children actively speaking Cajun to friends and family. Textbooks on Cajun, translations of some classics. Dictionary. Grammar. Literacy rate in second language: 60% English, 0% French. Radio programs. Swamps. Fishermen, fur trappers. Christian.

GALICE [GCE] Southwestern Oregon. Na-Dene, Nuclear Na-Dene, Athapaskan-Eyak, Athapaskan, Pacific Coast, Oregon, Tolowa-Galice. Extinct.

GERMAN, HUTTERITE ***(TYROLESE, TIROLEAN, HUTTERIAN GERMAN)*** [GEH] 5,000 in USA (1981 P. Fast SIL). 30 colonies in USA (South and North Dakota, Montana, 4 colonies in Washington State, a few in Minnesota); 115 or 116 in Canada, with about 100 people in each. Indo-European, Germanic, West, High German, German, Upper German, Bavarian-Austrian. Called 'Tirolean', but not a Tirolean dialect. Speakers use Standard German in church and for Scriptures. They are partly bilingual in English and Standard German. Have their own schools. Strict communal living. Communal groups in New York, Connecticut, Pennsylvania, and Japan have affiliated recently with Hutterians but are not ethnically Hutterian. Intensive agriculturalists. Christian. See main entry under Canada.

GERMAN, PENNSYLVANIA ***(PENNSYLVANISH, PENNSYLVANIA DUTCH)*** [PDC] 85,000 in USA, including 70,000 Old Order Amish, 15,000 Old Order Mennonites, fewer Pennsylvanisch (Lutheran). Population total both countries 100,000 out of an ethnic population of 200,000 (1978 Kloss and McConnell). Pennsylvania, Ohio, Indiana, Iowa, Kansas, Oklahoma, Virginia, West Virginia, and Florida. Also spoken in Canada. Indo-European, Germanic, West, High German, German, Middle German, West Middle German. Dialects: AMISH PENNSYLVANIA GERMAN (PLAIN PENNSYLVANIA GERMAN), NON-AMISH PENNSYLVANIA GERMAN (PENSYLVANISCH DEITSCH, NON-PLAIN PENNSYLVANIA GERMAN). Blending of several German dialects, primarily Rhenish Palatinate (Pfalzer) German, with syntactic elements of High German and English. Mostly incomprehensible now to a person from the Palatinate (H. Kloss 1978). Non-plain community: youngest fluent speakers 40 to 50 years old (M. Louden 1987). Plain community not shifting to English, but has stable bilingualism (M. Louden 1987). Separate orthographies for Pennsylvania and Ohio dialects. Christian. NT 1994.

GROS VENTRE ***(GROS VENTRES, ATSINA, WHITE CLAY PEOPLE, AHAHNELIN, AHE, FALL INDIANS, A' ANANIN)*** [ATS] 10 or fewer speakers out of 1,200 population (1977 SIL). The 1990 census reports 111 speakers. Fort Belknap Reservation, Milk River, north central Montana. Algic, Algonquian, Plains, Arapaho. Bilingualism in English. Nearly extinct.

GWICH'IN ***(KUTCHIN)*** [KUC] 300 speakers out of 1,100 population (1995 M. Krauss). Northeastern Alaska on Yukon River and tributaries. 6 villages. Na-Dene, Nuclear Na-Dene, Athapaskan-Eyak, Athapaskan, Canadian, Han-Kutchin. Dialects: FORT YUKON GWICH'IN, ARCTIC VILLAGE GWICH'IN, WESTERN

CANADA GWICH'IN (TAKUDH, TUKUDH, LOUCHEUX), ARCTIC RED RIVER. Many young people prefer English. Many children only speak English. Generally most adults speak the language (parents and the elderly, 1998), but many children do not speak Gwich'in. Vigorous in isolated communities. Literacy rate in first language: 1% to 5%. Literacy rate in second language: 75% to 100%. Bible 1898. See main entry under Canada.

HAIDA, NORTHERN ***(MASSET)*** [HAI] 15 fluent speakers out of 600 population in USA (1995 M. Krauss). Southern tip of Alaska panhandle, Hydaburg, Kasaan, Craig, and Ketchikan. Na-Dene, Haida. There is borderline intelligibility with Southern Haida. Bilingualism in English. Speakers are 60 or 70 or older. There is interest in reviving the language. Nearly extinct. Bible portions 1891-1899. See main entry under Canada.

HAN ***(HAN-KUTCHIN, MOOSEHIDE, DAWSON)*** [HAA] 7 or 8 speakers in Alaska (1995 M. Krauss) out of a total population of 300 (1995). Population total both countries 7 or 8. Yukon River in area of Alaska-Canada border, Eagle, Alaska. Also spoken in Canada. Na-Dene, Nuclear Na-Dene, Athapaskan-Eyak, Athapaskan, Canadian, Han-Kutchin. Bilingualism in English. Youngest speaker in Alaska below 60 years old (1997). There is a Han textbook with tapes for teaching the language. Grammar. Being taught in bush schools as an elective to native and non-native children. Nearly extinct.

HAVASUPAI-WALAPAI-YAVAPAI ***(UPPER COLORADO RIVER YUMAN, UPLAND YUMAN)*** [YUF] 1,007 speakers, including 404 Havasupai speakers (including 4 monolinguals), 440 Walapai speakers, 163 Yavapai speakers (1990 census), out of 1,500 population (1977 SIL). Central and northwestern Arizona. The Walapai are on top of the south rim of the Grand Canyon, the Havasupai at the bottom. Hokan, Esselen-Yuman, Yuman, Upland Yuman. Dialects: WALAPAI (HUALPAI), HAVASUPAI, YAVAPAI. 78% to 98% intelligibility among the dialects. 91% to 95% lexical similarity among the dialects. All ages: Havasupai. Most or all Yavapai speakers are middle-aged or older. Many younger Walapai prefer English and some do not speak Walapai. Children being raised speaking Havasupai and Walapai (1998). Vigorous: Havasupai. Literacy rate in first language: 1% to 5%. Literacy rate in second language: 75% to 100%. Bible portions 1980.

HAWAI'I CREOLE ENGLISH ***(PIDGIN, HAWAI'I PIDGIN, HCE)*** [HAW] 600,000 speakers or more, half of the state population (1986 M. Forman), including 100,000 to 200,000 who have limited control of Standard English and near Standard English (1986 M. Forman). Another 100,000 speakers on the USA mainland. There are many second language users. The population of Hawaii is 1,185,497 (1999 census). All the Hawaiian Islands, USA mainland (especially the west coast, Las Vegas, and Orlando). Creole, English based, Pacific. The basilect (heavy creole) is barely intelligible with Standard English (H. McKaughan and M. Forman 1982). Bilingualism in English, Hawaiian, Hakka, Cantonese, Japanese, Korean, Tagalog, Ilocano, Cebuano, Hiligaynon, Portuguese, Spanish, Samoan. 50% of children in Hawaii do not speak English as mother tongue when entering school. Most of these speak HCE as mother tongue. Used in courts by officers, jurors, plaintiffs, defendants, witnesses. Creative writing in it in some schools. A growing body of serious literature. Used in schools for many explanations, because many students do not control Standard English. There are some communication problems at university level. All ages. Vigorous use by 100,000 to 200,000. The native speech of a large number of those born or brought up in Hawaii, regardless of racial origin. There is a continuum of speech from the distinct creole to Standard English of Hawaii. Different speakers control different spans along the continuum; there are those whose only form of verbal communication is the creole. It is accepted by many as an important part of the local culture, a distinctive local language, but looked down on by others. Some official acknowledgement of it in print and public discussion. Grammar. Literacy rate in first language: 66% to 75%. Literacy rate in second language: 66% to 75%. Roman. Radio programs, TV. Tropical forest. Volcanic islands, coral reefs, coastal, mountain slope. Fishermen, agriculturalists, animal husbandry, white and blue collar workers, tourism, military. Sea level to 4,000 feet. Christian, Hawaiian traditional religion, Buddhist. Bible portions 1997.

HAWAI'I PIDGIN SIGN LANGUAGE ***(PIDGIN SIGN LANGUAGE)*** [HPS] A few users out of about 6,000 profoundly deaf people in Hawaii (1987 Honolulu Star-Bulletin), 72,000 deaf or hard of hearing people in Hawaii (1998 Honolulu Advertiser). Hawaiian Islands. Deaf sign language. Bilingualism in American Sign Language. Mainly 70 to 90 years old (1993). 9,600 deaf people in Hawaii now use American Sign Language with a few local signs for place names and cultural items (1998 Honolulu Advertiser). Nearly extinct.

HAWAIIAN ***('OLELO HAWAI'I, 'OLELO HAWAI'I MAKUAHINE)*** [HWI] 1,000 mother tongue speakers, 500 with Ni'ihau Island connections, another 500 in their 70s or 80s (1995 Laina Wong Univ. of Hawaii). 8,000 can speak and understand it (1993 Keith Haugen). 237,128 ethnic Hawaiians in Hawaii (1996 Hawaii State Dept. of Health), 18.8% of the population (1990 Hawaii State Dept. of Health), and 99,269 ethnic Hawaiians on the USA mainland (1990 census), including 24,245 in

California. In 1900 there were 37,000 mother tongue speakers (1995 Honolulu Advertiser). Ethnic Hawaiians include 8,244 pure Hawaiian, 72,809 between 50% and 99% Hawaiian, 127,523 less than 50% Hawaiian in Hawaii (1984 Office of Hawaiian Affairs). In 1778 there were believed to have been more than 500,000 pure Hawaiians (1995 Wayne Harada). Hawaiian Islands, mainly Ni'ihau Island and the Big Island of Hawai'i, some on all the other islands. Austronesian, Malayo-Polynesian, Central-Eastern, Eastern Malayo-Polynesian, Oceanic, Central-Eastern Oceanic, Remote Oceanic, Central Pacific, East Fijian-Polynesian, Polynesian, Nuclear, East, Central, Marquesic. 79% lexical similarity with Rarotongan, 77% with Tuamotuan, 76% with Tahitian (Elbert), 71% with Maori (Schütz), 70% with Marquesan, 64% with Rapa Nui. Speakers use Hawaii Creole English (Pidgin) or English as second language. 500 mother tongue speakers in their 70s or 80s (1995). People 2 years old and older are learning it as second language: 1,000 ages 0-15. 350 ages 15-25 (1997 Rosemary Henze). Official language. Dictionary. Grammar. VSO. Roman. Punana Leo private schools offer Hawaiian immersion programs (as a second language) for about 800 2-year-old ethnic Hawaiians into high school. The University of Hawaii offers a BA in the Hawaiian language. Christian, traditional religion. Bible 1838.

HIDATSA ***(MINITARI, HIRACA, HINATSA)*** [HID] 100 fluent speakers, 25-50 semi-fluent speakers, out of 1,200 population (1986 SIL). The 1990 census reports 451 speakers including 6 monolinguals. Fort Berthold Reservation, North Dakota. Siouan, Siouan Proper, Missouri Valley. Close to Crow. Bilingualism in English. Most speakers are elderly (1998). Bible portions.

HOCÁK ***(WINNEBAGO, HOCAK WAZIJACI, HOCANK, HOCHANK, HOCHUNK)*** [WIN] 250 speakers (1995 V. Zeps), out of 6,000 population (1995). 822 enrolled Hocák in Nebraska, with 535 speakers (1968 USA BIA). Scattered locations in central Wisconsin and Winnebago Reservation in eastern Nebraska. Siouan, Siouan Proper, Central, Mississippi Valley, Winnebago. Dialects: WISCONSIN, NEBRASKA. In 1968 10% were extremely limited in their use of English. Now reported to be bilingual in English. In Wisconsin most adults speak the language. In Nebraska most are elderly (1998). The name is written with a hook under the 'a' of 'Hocák', representing a nasalized vowel. The official name for the people is Hocák Nation. 'Winnebago' is the Algonguin name. There is a Language Program which plans a full-immersion Hocák school system, grades pre-school through community college. Bible portions 1907.

HOLIKACHUK [HOI] 12 speakers out of 200 population (1995 M. Krauss). Village of Grayling on lower Yukon River, Alaska. Na-Dene, Nuclear Na-Dene, Athapaskan-Eyak, Athapaskan, Ingalik-Koyukon, Koyukon-Holikachuk. Bilingualism in English. All speakers are probably over 60. Nearly extinct.

HOPI [HOP] 5,264 speakers who speak Hopi at home (1990 census), out of a 6,500 population (1977 SIL). Several villages in northeast Arizona, with small numbers in Utah and New Mexico. Uto-Aztecan, Northern Uto-Aztecan, Hopi. All ages, including 40 monolinguals (1990). 5,264 were over 5 years old, 989 of those were 5 to 17 years old, 3,390 were 18 to 54, 388 were 55 to 64, 578 were 65 and older (1990). Children being raised speaking the language (1998). Language use is vigorous except for some younger ones who prefer English. Dictionary. NT 1972.

HUPA ***(HOOPA)*** [HUP] 8 fluent speakers (1998 James Brook N.Y. Times, April 9, p. A1, A20), out of 2,000 population (1998 J. Brook). Hoopa Valley Reservation, northwestern California. Na-Dene, Nuclear Na-Dene, Athapaskan-Eyak, Athapaskan, Pacific Coast, California, Hupa. Bilingualism in English. Only elderly speakers left. Language revitalization effort is in progress. Dictionary. Nearly extinct.

INESEÑO [INE] Southern California, near Santa Barbara. Chumash. Was not intelligible with other Chumash varieties. Extinct.

INUPIATUN, NORTH ALASKAN ***(NORTH ALASKAN INUPIAT, INUPIAT, "ESKIMO")*** [ESI] Population total both countries 3,500 speakers out of an ethnic population of 8,000 (1990 L. D. Kaplan). Norton Sound and Point Hope, Alaska into Canada. Also spoken in Canada. Eskimo-Aleut, Eskimo, Inuit. Dialects: NORTH SLOPE INUPIATUN (POINT BARROW INUPIATUN), WEST ARCTIC INUPIATUN, POINT HOPE INUPIATUN, ANAKTUVIK PASS INUPIATUN. Most speakers are over 30. Younger speakers often prefer English. Dictionary. Grammar. NT 1968.

INUPIATUN, NORTHWEST ALASKA ***(NORTHWEST ALASKA INUPIAT, INUPIATUN, "ESKIMO")*** [ESK] 4,000 speakers out of 8,000 population (1978 SIL). Alaska, Kobuk River, Noatak River, Seward Peninsula, and Bering Strait. Eskimo-Aleut, Eskimo, Inuit. Dialects: NORTHERN MALIMIUT INUPIATUN, SOUTHERN MALIMIUT INUPIATUN, KOBUK RIVER INUPIATUN, COASTAL INUPIATUN, KOTZEBUE SOUND INUPIATUN, SEWARD PENINSULA INUPIATUN, KING ISLAND INUPIATUN (BERING STRAIT INUPIATUN). Most speakers of Seward Peninsula are over 40 (1990). Literacy rate in first language: 1% to 5%. NT 1997.

IOWA-OTO [IOW] Ethnic population of 2,400, including 1,000 Iowa, 1,400 Oto (1986 SIL). Last fluent speakers of Iowa and Oto died the end of 1996. There are others who have some degree of knowledge of the language (1997 Jimm G. GoodTracks). North central Oklahoma and Iowa Reservation, northeast

Kansas. Siouan, Siouan Proper, Central, Mississippi Valley, Chiwere. Dialects: IOWA (BAXOJE, IOWAY), OTO (JIWERE, OTOE, JIWELE, CHIWERE), NIUTAJI (NYUT'CHI, MISSOURI, MISSOURIA). Bilingualism in English. Iowa and Oto are effectively a single language, with some family variations cross-cutting the tribal affiliations. Speakers believe certain minor differences of pronunciation and vocabulary reflect original tribal dialect distinctions (J. E. Koontz 1996). Missouri dialect has been extinct for many years. Extinct.

JEMEZ ***(TOWA)*** [TOW] 1,301 speakers (1990 census), out of 1,488 population (1980 census). North central New Mexico. Kiowa Tanoan, Kiowa-Towa, Towa. 6 monolinguals (1990). 95% of the population under 18 years old were speakers (1980). Vigorous. Literacy rate in first language: Below 1%. Literacy rate in second language: 50% to 75%. Traditional religion, Christian.

KALAPUYA ***(SANTIAM, LUKAMIUTE, WAPATU)*** [KAL] 1 or 2 speakers (1962 Chafe). Northwest Oregon. Penutian, Oregon Penutian, Kalapuyan. Bilingualism in English. All over 50 years old (1962). Nearly extinct.

KALISPEL-PEND D'OREILLE ***(KALISPEL-"FLATHEAD", "FLATHEAD"-KALISPEL, SALISH)*** [FLA] 200 first language speakers, 6,800 ethnic population (1997). Kalispel Reservation, northeast Washington, Flathead Reservation, northwest Montana. Salishan, Interior Salish, Southern. Dialects: PEND D'OREILLE, KALISPEL. Bilingualism in English. Most or all mother tongue speakers are middle-aged or older. Spokane is a coordinate language variety. Nearly extinct.

KANSA ***(KAW, KONZE, KANZE)*** [KAA] 19 speakers (1990 census), out of 250 population (1986 SIL). Oklahoma, north central. Siouan, Siouan Proper, Central, Mississippi Valley, Dhegiha. Closely related to Omaha, Osage, Ponca, and Quapaw. Bilingualism in English. Nearly extinct.

KARKIN [KRB] North Central California. Penutian, Yok-Utian, Utian, Costanoan. Became extinct in the 1950's. Extinct.

KAROK ***(KARUK)*** [KYH] 126 speakers (1990 census), out of 3,781 population (1982 SIL). Northwestern California, along the banks of the Klamath River. Hokan, Northern, Karok-Shasta. No significant dialect differences. Bilingualism in English. Most or all speakers are middle-aged or over.

KASHAYA ***(SOUTHWESTERN POMO)*** [KJU] 50 (1977 Voegelin and Voegelin). 100 or fewer speakers, all Pomo varieties (1977 SIL). Hokan, Northern, Pomo, Russian River and Eastern, Russian River, Southern. Bilingualism in English. A separate language from other Pomo varieties. Nearly extinct.

KATO ***(CAHTO, BATEM-DA-KAI-EE, KAI PO-MO, TLOKEANG)*** [KTW] 10 speakers or fewer (1962 Chafe) out of 92 population (1982 SIL). Laytonville Reservation, northwestern California. Na-Dene, Nuclear Na-Dene, Athapaskan-Eyak, Athapaskan, Pacific Coast, California, Mattole-Wailaki. Bilingualism in English. All over 50 years old (1962). Nearly extinct.

KAWAIISU [KAW] 10 or fewer speakers (1962 Chafe) out of 150 population (1977 SIL). California, south, Tehachapi-Mojave area of the Mojave Desert. Uto-Aztecan, Northern Uto-Aztecan, Numic, Southern. Bilingualism in English. All over 50 years old (1962). Nearly extinct.

KERES, EASTERN ***(EASTERN KERES PUEBLO)*** [KEE] 4,580 speakers out of 5,701 population (80%), 463 Zia speakers out of 602 population, 229 Santa Ana speakers out of 374 population, 1,560 San Felipe speakers out of 1,789 population, 1,888 Santo Domingo speakers out of 2,140 population, 384 Cochiti speakers out of 796 population. North central New Mexico. Keres. Dialects: ZIA, SANTA ANA, SAN FELIPE, SANTO DOMINGO, COCHITI. Bilingualism in English. Language use is vigorous in some pueblos; in others some younger people prefer English. Literacy rate in first language: Below 1%. Literacy rate in second language: 75% to 100%. Bible portions 1933-1936.

KERES, WESTERN ***(WESTERN KERES PUEBLO)*** [KJQ] 3,391 speakers out of 5,880 population (57.7%) including 1,695 Laguna speakers out of 3,526 population, 1,696 Acoma out of 2,354 (1980 census). New Mexico, north central. Keres. Dialect: ACOMA (LAGUNA). In Acoma most adults speak the language but some younger people prefer English and many children do not speak the language. In Laguna most or all speakers are middle-aged or over. Percentage under 18 years old who are speakers: 47.7%, including Laguna 32.3%, Acoma 67.9%; above 18: 75.1%. Literacy rate in first language: Below 1%. Literacy rate in second language: 50% to 75%. Bible portions 1966-1997.

KICKAPOO ***(KIKAPOO, KIKAPU)*** [KIC] 539 speakers in the USA, including 6 monolinguals (1990 census). Population total both countries 850. Northeastern Kansas: Horton; central Oklahoma: McCloud, Jones; Texas: Nuevo Nacimiento. 6 hours by automobile between Kansas and Oklahoma locations, 10 hours to Texas, 3 hours to Mexico location. Also spoken in Mexico. Algic, Algonquian, Central. Possibly intelligible with Sac and Fox (Mesquakie). In Oklahoma some younger people prefer English, and in Kansas most or all speakers are middle-aged or over. Dictionary.

KIOWA [KIO] 1,092 speakers (1990 census), out of 6,000 population (1977 SIL). Oklahoma, west central. Kiowa Tanoan, Kiowa-Towa, Kiowa. Bilingualism in English. Most speakers are middle-aged or older. Dictionary.

KITSAI ***(KICHAI)*** [KII] No speakers out of 350 population (1977 SIL). West central Oklahoma among the Caddo, Caddo County. Caddoan, Northern, Pawnee-Kitsai, Kitsai. Closer to Pawnee than to Wichita. Extinct.

KLAMATH-MODOC [KLA] 1 speaker of Klamath (1998 N.Y. Times, April 9, p. A20) out of 2,000 population (1977 SIL). Oregon, south central, around and to the east and north of Klamath and Agency lakes; Modoc directly to the south. Penutian, Plateau Penutian, Klamath-Modoc. Closest to Molala and Sahaptian. Bilingualism in English. Elderly. Dictionary. Grammar. Nearly extinct.

KOASATI ***(COUSHATTA)*** [CKU] 600 speakers (1996 Geoff Kimball), including 100 in Texas and 500 speakers out of 600 in the ethnic group in Louisiana. Koasati reservation near Elton, Louisiana, and Alabama-Koasati reservation near Livingston, Texas. Others elsewhere; 1 family in Oregon. The language is no longer used in Oklahoma. Muskogean, Eastern. The grammars of Koasati and Alabama are significantly different. Less than 50% cognate with Alabama. 30 people have limited English proficiency (1992 D. Rising SIL). Others are quite bilingual in English. A few are more bilingual in Cajun French than in English. In Louisiana the people use Koasati in the home and for church services. More vigorous in Louisiana than Texas. Dictionary. Christian.

KOYUKON ***(TEN'A)*** [KOY] 300 speakers out of 2,300 population (1995 M. Krauss). Alaska, Koyukuk and middle Yukon rivers. Na-Dene, Nuclear Na-Dene, Athapaskan-Eyak, Athapaskan, Ingalik-Koyukon, Koyukon-Holikachuk. Bilingualism in English. Speakers are 35, 40, 60, or older. Dictionary. Nearly extinct. Bible portions 1974-1980.

KUMIÁI ***(DIEGUEÑO, CAMPO, KAMIA)*** [DIH] 97 speakers in USA (1990 census). Southern California east of San Diego, including some in Imperial Valley. Hokan, Esselen-Yuman, Yuman, Delta-Californian. Speakers in California are very bilingual in English. Spanish is the second language in Mexico. See main entry under Mexico.

KUSKOKWIM, UPPER ***(MCGRATH INGALIK, KOLCHAN)*** [KUU] 40 speakers out of 160 population (1995 M. Krauss). 3 households (1997). Nikolai, Telida, McGrath, Upper Kuskokwim River, central Alaska. Na-Dene, Nuclear Na-Dene, Athapaskan-Eyak, Athapaskan, Tanana-Upper Kuskokwim, Upper Kuskokwim. Bilingualism in English. Youngest speakers, average age 30. At one time the people were regarded as part of the Ingalik tribe.

KUTENAI ***(KTUNAXA, KOOTENAI)*** [KUN] 102 speakers in USA (1990 census). Northern Idaho, Flathead Reservation, Montana. Language Isolate. Bilingualism in English. All speakers are elderly. Columbia Lake Reserve in Canada is offering a Kutenai as a second language course (1991). See main entry under Canada.

LAKOTA ***(LAKHOTA, TETON)*** [LKT] 6,000 speakers out of 20,000 population (1987 SIL). 103,255 ethnic Sioux in USA (1990 Census Bureau). Population total both countries 6,000 or more. Northern Nebraska, southern Minnesota, North and South Dakota, northeastern Montana. Also spoken in Canada. Siouan, Siouan Proper, Central, Mississippi Valley, Dakota. Children are being raised speaking the language in the northern Plains (1998). Vigorous in some Lakota communities. Grammar.

LOUISIANA CREOLE FRENCH [LOU] 60,000 to 80,000 (1985 Neumann) out of an ethnic group of 1,500,000 (1977 M. Adler). Predominantly in St. Martin parish (St. Martinville, Breaux Bridge, Cecilia), New Roads and Edgard, Louisiana, parts of east Texas, small community in Sacramento, California. Creole, French based. Different from Standard French, the Cajun French also spoken in Louisiana, Haitian Creole French, and others of the Caribbean. Reports indicate that monolingual speakers may not be able to understand those other creoles. "Over 2/3 of the original slaves came from Senegambia, hardly any slaves arrived during the second decade of exploitation, and within just over two decades, 2/3 of the population was native-born. No slaves (and few if any of the slaveowners) appear to have come from the French Antilles...What we now need is a careful comparison between Louisiana Creole and other French Caribbean creoles, detailing the similarities and differences" (D. Bickerton, Carrier Pidgin 1995 23(2):2). People are reported to have a high degree of bilingualism in English. 4.6% in the older group are monolingual in Creole. Some in the younger group are monolingual in English. Those over 60 prefer Creole, and those under 30 prefer English. Investigation needed: intelligibility with French Caribbean Creoles, bilingual proficiency in English. Dictionary. Grammar.

LUISEÑO [LUI] 43 speakers (1990 census), out of 1,500 population (1977 SIL). Southern California. Uto-Aztecan, Northern Uto-Aztecan, Takic, Cupan, Luiseno. Dialects: JUANEÑO (AJACHEMA, AJACHEMEM, AGACHEMEM, ACGACHEMEM), LUISEÑO. Bilingualism in English. Most or all speakers are middle-aged or older. Grammar.

LUMBEE ***(CROATAN)*** [LUA] No speakers out of 30,000 population (1977 SIL). Southern North Carolina and into South Carolina and Maryland. Algic, Algonquian, Unclassified. Racially mixed descendents of a Pamlico group. Still a distinct ethnic group. Extinct.

LUSHOOTSEED [LUT] 60 speakers or fewer (1990 M. D. Kinkade) about evenly divided between the northern and southern dialects, from a population of 2,000. Washington, Puget Sound area. Salishan, Central Salish, Twana. Dialects: NORTHERN LUSHOOTSEED (NORTHERN PUGET SOUND SALISH), SOUTHERN LUSHOOTSEED (SOUTHERN PUGET SOUND SALISH). Northern Lushootseed includes subdialects Skagit, Snohomish, and Swinomish; southern Lushootseed includes Duwamish, Nisqually, Puyallup, and Suquamish. There are numerous programs starting up around Puget Sound teaching Lushootseed, in which children, parents, and elders are taking part. It is also being introduced as a language available at local colleges. Nearly extinct.

MAIDU, NORTHEAST ***(MOUNTAIN MAIDU)*** [NMU] 10 or fewer (1962 H. Landar in Sebeok 1977). 100 or more in the ethnic group (1990). California, northern Sierras, Plumas and Lassen counties. Penutian, Maiduan. A separate language from other Maidu varieties. Bilingualism in English. Only elderly speakers left. Nearly extinct.

MAIDU, NORTHWEST ***(HOLÓLUPAI, MAIDUAN, MEIDOO, MICHOPDO, NÁKUM, SECUMNE, SEKUMNE, TSAMAK, YUBA, KONKOW, KONKAU, CONCOW, "DIGGER")*** [MAI] 10 to 100 (1962 H. Landar in Sebeok 1977). Possibly 20 speakers of all Maidu varieties out of 200 population (1977 SIL). Lower foothills of the Sierras, central California. The ethnic group is scattered. Penutian, Maiduan. Bilingualism in English. Only elderly speakers are left. A separate language from other Maidu varieties. Alternate names listed apply to all Maidu except the last four. Dictionary. Nearly extinct.

MAIDU, VALLEY [VMV] California, between Sacramento and the Sierra foothills. Penutian, Maiduan. A separate language from other Maidu varieties. Dictionary. Extinct.

MAKAH ***(KWE-NEE-CHEE-AHT, KWEEDISHCHAAHT)*** [MYH] 10 to 30 speakers (1997), and others who use it as second language, out of 900 population on the reservation, and others not on the reservation (1995 Davissons). Northern tip of Olympic Peninsula, opposite Vancouver Island, Washington. Wakashan, Southern. Bilingualism in English. Most or all speakers are elderly (1998). There is a Makah Cultural Center. Grammar. Makah is taught bilingually in preschool on the reservation and is ongoing throughout grade school, although not heavily encouraged.

MALECITE-PASSAMAQUODDY [MAC] 887 speakers in USA (1990 census). Maine, New Brunswick border area. Malecite mainly in Canada, Passamaquoddy mainly in Maine. Algic, Algonquian, Eastern. Dialects: MALECITE (MALISEET), PASSAMAQUODDY. Bilingualism in English. Most speakers of Passamaquoddy are elderly (1998) with younger speakers in a few areas. English is preferred by most younger ones. Bible portions 1870. See main entry under Canada.

MANDAN [MHQ] 6 fluent speakers (1992 M. Krauss) out of 400 population (1986 SIL). Fort Berthold Reservation, North Dakota. Siouan, Siouan Proper, Central, Mandan. Bilingualism in English. All fluent speakers are elderly (1992), 2 semi-fluent over 60 (1986). Grammar. Nearly extinct.

MARICOPA ***(COCOMARICOPA)*** [MRC] 181 speakers (1990 census), out of 400 population (1977 SIL). Associated with the Pima on the Gila River and Salt River reservations near Phoenix, Arizona. Hokan, Esselen-Yuman, Yuman, River Yuman. 85% lexical similarity with Mohave, 58% with Havasupai, 57% with Walapai and Yavapai. Most or all speakers are middle-aged or older.

MARTHA'S VINEYARD SIGN LANGUAGE [MRE] Martha's Vineyard, Massachusetts. Deaf sign language. The early sign language was based on a regional one in Weald, England, where the deaf persons' ancestors had lived. French Sign Language was introduced to Martha's Vineyard in 1817. MVSL was later combined with American Sign Language, but never became identical to ASL. From 1692 to 1910 nearly all hearers on Martha's Vineyard were bilingual in English and sign language. The first deaf person arrived in 1692. From 1692 to 1950 there was a high rate of hereditary deafness. In the 19th century, 1/5700 of Americans were deaf, 1/155 in Martha's Vineyard, 1/25 in one town, 1/4 in one neighborhood. Extinct.

MATTOLE [MVB] Northern California. Na-Dene, Nuclear Na-Dene, Athapaskan-Eyak, Athapaskan, Pacific Coast, California, Mattole-Wailaki. Extinct.

MENOMINI ***(MENOMINEE)*** [MEZ] 39 first language speakers, 26 second language speakers, 15 others ages 30 to 50, who have learned Menominee in order to teach it, and 50 ages 20 and above who have learned it to understand it (1997 Menominee Historic Preservation Office), out of 3,500 population (1977 SIL). Northeastern Wisconsin, on what was formerly the Menomini Reservation. Algic, Algonquian, Central. Bilingualism in English. Only elderly first language speakers are left. Grammar. Nearly extinct.

MESQUAKIE ***(SAC AND FOX, SAUK-FOX)*** [SAC] 800 speakers out of 2,500 population (1977 SIL). 673 Fox speakers, including 2 monolinguals (1990 census). Mesquakie at Tama, Iowa; Sac and Fox at Sac and Fox Reservation on eastern Kansas-Nebraska border and central Oklahoma. Algic, Algonquian, Central. Dialects: FOX, SAC, MESQUAKIE. Kansas and Oklahoma groups are closely related to Kikapoo of Oklahoma and Mexico. Bilingualism in English. In Iowa it is spoken by parents and the elderly (1998). Outside Iowa most or all speakers are middle-aged or older. Vigorous in Iowa.

Literacy rate in first language: Below 1%. Literacy rate in second language: 75% to 100%. Bible portions 1986-1996.

MIAMI ***(MIAMI-ILLINOIS, MIAMI-MYAAMIA)*** [MIA] No speakers (1996), out of 2,000 ethnic population (1977 SIL). Miami in north central Indiana, Miami and Peoria in northeast Oklahoma. Algic, Algonquian, Central. Dialects: MIAMI, PEORIA. There are some who know a few words and phrases. A revitalization program is in progress. Extinct.

MICHIF ***(FRENCH CREE, MITCHIF)*** [CRG] 390 speakers in USA (1990 census). Population total both countries 390 or more. Turtle Mountain Reservation, North Dakota. Also spoken in Canada. Mixed Language, French-Cree. Closest to Plains Cree. Bilingualism in English. Most or all speakers are middle-aged or older. Dictionary.

MICMAC ***(MI'GMAW, MIIGMAO, MI'KMAW, RESTIGOUCHE)*** [MIC] 1,200 in the USA, including 200 in Maine, and 1,000 largely in Boston. Northern Maine near Fort Fairfield, Boston, Massachusetts, and small scattered places elsewhere in the USA. Algic, Algonquian, Eastern. Literacy rate in first language: 1% to 5%. Literacy rate in second language: 50% to 75%. NT 1874, in press (1999). See main entry under Canada.

MIKASUKI ***(HITCHITI, MIKASUKI SEMINOLE, MICCOSUKEE)*** [MIK] 496 speakers including 33 monolinguals (1990 census), out of 1,200 population (1977 SIL). Southern Florida. Muskogean, Eastern. Dialects: HITCHITI, MIKASUKI. Not intelligible with Creek, Alabama, or Koasati. There are monolinguals only among elderly women. Others use English as second language. Language use is vigorous except at Hollywood, where most younger ones do not speak Mikasuki. Bible portions 1980-1985.

MIWOK, BAY ***(SACLAN, SAKLAN)*** [MKQ] Northern California, San Francisco Bay. Penutian, Yok-Utian, Utian, Miwokan, Eastern. Extinct.

MIWOK, CENTRAL SIERRA [CSM] 5 or fewer (1962 H. Landar in Sebeok 1977). The 1990 census reports 105 speakers of 'Sierra Miwok'. California, upper valleys of the Stanislause and Tuolumne. Penutian, Yok-Utian, Utian, Miwokan, Eastern, Sierra. Bilingualism in English. A separate language from other Miwok varieties. Nearly extinct.

MIWOK, COAST [CSI] 1 (1962 H. Landar in Sebeok 1977). California, coast from San Francisco Bay to Bodega Bay. Penutian, Yok-Utian, Utian, Miwokan, Western. Dialects: BODEGA, HUIMEN, MARIN MIWOK. Bilingualism in English. A separate language from other Miwok varieties. Bodega and Marin Miwok were possibly separate languages. Nearly extinct.

MIWOK, LAKE [LMW] 8 (1965 H. Landar in Sebeok 1977). California, Clear Lake basin. Penutian, Yok-Utian, Utian, Miwokan, Western. Bilingualism in English. A separate language from other Miwok varieties. Nearly extinct.

MIWOK, NORTHERN SIERRA [NSQ] 10 or fewer. California, upper valleys of Mokelumne and Calaveras rivers. Penutian, Yok-Utian, Utian, Miwokan, Eastern, Sierra. Bilingualism in English. A separate language from other Miwok varieties. Nearly extinct.

MIWOK, PLAINS ***(VALLEY MIWOK)*** [PMW] 1 (1962 H. Landar in Sebeok 1977). California, deltas of the San Joaquin and Cosumnes rivers. Penutian, Yok-Utian, Utian, Miwokan, Eastern. Bilingualism in English. A separate language from other Miwok varieties. Nearly extinct.

MIWOK, SOUTHERN SIERRA ***(MEEWOC, MEWOC, ME-WUK, MIWOC, MIWOKAN, MOKÉLUMNE, MOQUELUMNAN, SAN RAPHAEL, TALATUI, TALUTUI, YOSEMITE)*** [SKD] 10 or fewer. California, along headwaters of the Merced and Chowchilla rivers and on Mariposa Creek. Penutian, Yok-Utian, Utian, Miwokan, Eastern, Sierra. Bilingualism in English. A separate language from other Miwok varieties. Alternate names listed refer to all Miwok except last three. Nearly extinct.

MOBILIAN ***(MOBILIAN JARGON)*** [MOD] No fluent speakers left. Lower Mississippi River valley area, south central USA. Pidgin, Amerindian. Muskogean based pidgin, formerly used as lingua franca. Loan words from Spanish, English, French, Creek, Alabama-Koasati, Choctaw, Chickasaw. Became extinct about 100 years ago. OSV. Extinct.

MOHAVE ***(MOJAVE)*** [MOV] 234 speakers (1990 census), out of 1,500 population (1977 SIL). Fort Mohave and Colorado River reservations, on the California-Arizona border. Hokan, Esselen-Yuman, Yuman, River Yuman. 85% lexical similarity with Maricopa, 63% with Walapai and Havasupai, 62% with Yavapai. Most adults speak the language but many younger ones do not.

MOHAWK ***(KANIEN'KEHAKA)*** [MOH] 1,667 speakers in the USA (1990 census) out of 30,000 in the ethnic group in both countries (1999 SIL). St. Regis Reservation, northern New York. Iroquoian, Northern Iroquoian, Five Nations, Mohawk-Oneida. Bilingualism in English. Most speakers are middle-aged or older. In some areas the younger ones may speak the language. Bible portions 1787-1991. See main entry under Canada.

MOHEGAN-MONTAUK-NARRAGANSETT [MOF] No speakers out of 1,400 population (1977 SIL). Connecticut, Rhode Island, Long Island, New York, Wisconsin. Algic, Algonquian, Eastern. Dialects:

PEQUOT-MOHEGAN, NARRANGANSETT, MONTAUK (SHINNECOCK-POOSEPATUCK), STOCKBRIDGE. Extinct.

MOLALE ***(MOLELE, MOLALA, MOLALLA)*** [MBE] Washington and Oregon in the valley of the Deschutes River, later west into the Molala and Santiam River valleys, and to the headwaters of the Umpqua and Rogue rivers. Penutian, Unclassified. Not close to Cayuse as formerly thought. Extinct.

MONO [MON] 20 speakers possibly, out of 200 population (1977 SIL). East central California. Uto-Aztecan, Northern Uto-Aztecan, Numic, Western. Related to Northern Paiute. Bilingualism in English. Only a few elderly speakers left. Nearly extinct.

MUSKOGEE ***(CREEK)*** [CRK] 6,213 speakers including 43 monolinguals (1990 census), out of 20,000 population (1977 SIL). Creek and Seminole of east central Oklahoma, Creek of southern Alabama, Seminole of Brighton Reservation, Florida. Muskogean, Eastern. Dialects: CREEK, SEMINOLE. Closely related to Mikasuki in Florida. The dialects are not very different. Most adults speak the language. Many younger ones may prefer English and some may not speak the language. NT 1886-1891, out of print.

NANTICOKE [NNT] No speakers out of 400 population (1977 SIL). Southern Delaware. Algic, Algonquian, Eastern. Extinct.

NATCHEZ [NCZ] No speakers left. Oklahoma. Gulf. There are some individuals of Natchez descent among the Creek and Cherokee in Oklahoma. Extinct.

NAVAJO ***(DINÉ, NAVAHO)*** [NAV] 148,530 speakers including 7,616 monolinguals (1990 census) out of 219,198 ethnic Navaho (1990 USA Census Bureau). Northeastern Arizona, northwestern New Mexico, southeastern Utah, and a few in Colorado. Na-Dene, Nuclear Na-Dene, Athapaskan-Eyak, Athapaskan, Apachean, Navajo-Apache, Western Apache-Navajo. Vigorous. But mother tongue speakers among first graders are 30% versus 90% in 1968 (1998 N.Y. Times, April 9, p. A20). The people prefer the name 'Dine'. Bible 1985.

NEZ PERCE [NEZ] 697 speakers (1990 census), out of 1,500 population (1977 SIL). The 1990 census also reports 878 Sahaptian speakers. Northern Idaho. Penutian, Plateau Penutian, Sahaptin. Bilingualism in English. Most speakers are elderly (1998). Conversational Nez Perce taught in Nespelem, Washington. Dictionary. Bible portions 1845-1876.

NISENAN ***(SOUTHERN MAIDU, NEESHENAM, NISHINAM, PUJUNI, WAPUMNI)*** [NSZ] 12 (1962 H. Landar in Sebeok 1977). Central California, scattered, foothills of the Sierras. Penutian, Maiduan. Bilingualism in English. Only elderly speakers are left. A separate language from other Maidu varieties. Nearly extinct.

NOOKSACK ***(NOOTSACK)*** [NOK] The ethnic group numbers about 350 (1977 SIL). Northwest corner of Washington. Salishan, Central Salish, Nooksack. Bilingualism in English. Extinct since about 1988. There are 2 or 3 elderly people who each know less than 30 or 40 words (1998). Extinct.

OBISPEÑO [OBI] Northernmost Chumash language, California, near Santa Barbara. Chumash. Not inherently intelligible with other Chumash varieties. Extinct.

OFO [OFO] Lower Mississippi Valley. Siouan, Siouan Proper, Southeastern, Biloxi-Ofo. Extinct.

OKANAGAN ***(OKANAGAN-COLVILLE, OKANAGON, OKANOGAN)*** [OKA] 112 speakers in USA (1990 census). Colville Reservation, Washington. Salishan, Interior Salish, Southern. Dialects: SOUTHERN OKANOGAN, SANPOIL, COLVILLE, LAKE. Bilingualism in English. Most speakers are middle-aged or older. Dictionary. Grammar. See main entry under Canada.

OMAHA-PONCA ***(MAHAIRI, PONKA, UMANHAN, PPANKKA)*** [OMA] 85 fluent speakers including 60 speakers of Omaha (1993 V. Zeps), out of 3,000 population (1993 C. Rudin), and 25 fluent speakers over 60 and a few semi-fluent speakers of Ponca out of 2,000 population (1986 SIL). Omaha Reservation, eastern Nebraska (Omaha), and north central Oklahoma (Ponca). Siouan, Siouan Proper, Central, Mississippi Valley, Dhegiha. Dialects: OMAHA, PONCA. Ponca and Omaha are completely inherently intelligible to each other's speakers, Closely related to Osage, Quapaw, and Kansa. In 1985 only a few older women seemed less than fully fluent in at least the regional English. Omaha is used formally for prayers, especially at funerals, for songs, powwow announcements, but usually translated into English for nonspeakers present. Most adults speak the language. Many young adults may prefer English. Children tend to prefer English, but many can understand Omaha and some may speak it. Christian, Native American Church, Mormon, Baha'i.

ONEIDA [ONE] 50 speakers in USA (1991 M. Dale Kincade). The 1990 census reports 6 monolinguals in the USA. Central New York, eastern Wisconsin. Iroquoian, Northern Iroquoian, Five Nations, Mohawk-Oneida. Bilingualism in English. Only a few elderly speakers remain in New York. Bible portions 1880-1942. See main entry under Canada.

ONONDAGA ***(ONANDAGA)*** [ONO] 15 speakers in USA (1993 V. Zeps), out of 1,000 population in USA (1993). Central New York south of Syracuse. Iroquoian, Northern Iroquoian, Five Nations, Seneca-Onondaga, Onondaga. Bilingualism in English. Most or all speakers are middle-aged or older. See main entry under Canada.

O'ODHAM ***(PAPAGO-PIMA, O'ODHAM, O'OTHHAM, NEVOME, NEBOME, UPPER PIMAN)*** [PAP] 11,819 speakers including 181 monolinguals (1990 census), out of 20,000 population (1977 SIL). Population total both countries 11,819 or more. South central Arizona. 60 villages on 7 reservations. Also spoken in Mexico. Uto-Aztecan, Southern Uto-Aztecan, Sonoran, Tepiman. Dialects: TOHONO O'ODAM ("PAPAGO"), AKIMEL O'ODHAM (PIMA). In the north and east some younger ones do not speak it or they prefer English. Most speakers are older than 25. Language use is vigorous in the west and south. Different from Pima Bajo of Mexico. Grammar. From elementary school on, schools on the Tohono O'Odham Nation teach the language. NT 1975.

OSAGE ***(WAZHAZHE)*** [OSA] 5 fluent speakers (1991 M. Krauss), and a few semi-fluent speakers, out of 2,500 population (1986 SIL). North central Oklahoma. Siouan, Siouan Proper, Central, Mississippi Valley, Dhegiha. Closely related to Omaha, Ponca, Quapaw, and Kansa. Bilingualism in English. Fluent speakers are elderly (1991). Nearly extinct. Bible portions.

OTTAWA ***(ODAWA, CHIPPEWA, EASTERN OJIBWA, OJIBWE)*** [OTW] 5,395 including 330 Ottawa, 5,065 Ojibwa in USA (1990 census), 10 monolinguals. 20,000 total ethnic Ojibwa (Ottawa and Chippewa) in USA (1991 M. Dale Kincade). Lower Michigan and upper Michigan near Sault Ste. Marie. Algic, Algonquian, Central, Ojibwa. Probably all speakers are bilingual in English, some in other Ojibwa varieties. Ottawa is dying out in many areas. Concerted effort via language teaching in public schools and other efforts to reverse the decline. Dictionary. Grammar. Bible portions 1841-1844. See main entry under Canada.

PAIUTE, NORTHERN ***(PAVIOTSO)*** [PAO] 1,631 speakers out of 6,000 population (1999 SIL). Northern Nevada and adjacent areas of Oregon, California, and Idaho. Spoken on about twenty reservations spread out over 1,000 miles. Uto-Aztecan, Northern Uto-Aztecan, Numic, Western. Dialects: BANNOCK, NORTH NORTHERN PAIUTE (MCDERMITT), SOUTH NORTHERN PAIUTE (YERINGTON- SCHURZ). Related to Mono. Almost every reservation has its own dialect. All dialects are inherently intelligible. Yerington-Schurz (one of the southern ones) is the dialect of cultural innovation. Most adults speak the language but some younger ones do not. Vigorous in McDermitt. NT 1985.

PANAMINT ***(PANAMINT SHOSHONE, TÜMPISA SHOSHONI, KOSO, COSO, KOSO SHOSHONE)*** [PAR] 20 speakers out of 100 population (1998 John E. McLaughlin). The Panamint are in south-eastern California, in and around southern Owens Valley around Owens Lake Coso Range, south-west of Darwin, and Little Lake area, southern Eureka Valley, southwest of Lida in Nevada, Saline Valley and eastern slopes of Inyo Mts., Argus Range south of Darwin, northern Panamint Valley and Panamint Mts. north and central Death Valley, Grapevine Mts. and Funeral Range on California-Nevada border, west and southwest of Beatty, Nevada, Amargosa Desert, and area around Beatty. Uto-Aztecan, Northern Uto-Aztecan, Numic, Central. Closely related to Shoshoni and Comanche. Not inherently intelligible with them. English is used in nearly all situations. Over 50 years old. Only used among oldest speakers to each other. They lament the loss of Panamint by younger people, and total use of English. Younger speakers attempting to revive interest in Panamint among the younger generations, but with little success. Grammar. Literacy rate in second language: 90%. Nearly extinct.

PAWNEE [PAW] 4 speakers (1996), out of 2,000 ethnic population (1977 SIL). North central Oklahoma. Caddoan, Northern, Pawnee-Kitsai, Pawnee. Dialects: SOUTH BAND, SKIRI (SKIDI). Closely related to Arikara, but not inherently intelligible with it. Kitsai is between Pawnee and Wichita, but closer to Pawnee. Bilingualism in English. All speakers are elderly. Nearly extinct.

PIRO ***(TOMPIRO)*** [PIE] Socorro, left bank of Rio Grande, USA, and Senecu, right bank, Mexico. Kiowa Tanoan, Tewa-Tiwa, Tiwa. Extinct.

PLAINS INDIAN SIGN LANGUAGE ***(PLAINS SIGH LANGUAGE)*** [PSD] Great Plains of the USA and Canada. Also spoken in Canada. Sign language. Some variation by ethnic group and region. Formerly used between nations in hunting, trade, by deaf people, and at every level of social interaction, and with non-Indians. Today used within nations in storytelling, rituals, legends, prayers, and by deaf people. Arose when horses were introduced from the south by the Spanish and guns from the east by the French. Second language only.

PLAUTDIETSCH ***(LOW GERMAN, MENNONITE GERMAN)*** [GRN] 10,000 in USA (1978 Kloss and McConnell). Hillsboro, Kansas; Reedley, California; and Corn, Oklahoma. Indo-European, Germanic, West, Low Saxon-Low Franconian, Low Saxon. Not inherently intelligible with Pennsylvania German, Hutterite German, many other Low German languages or Standard German. 5% speak Standard German, 98% speak English as second language. Literacy rate in second language: 95%. Christian. NT 1987. See main entry under Canada.

POMO, CENTRAL ***(BALLO-KAI-POMO, CABANAPO, HABENAPO, H'HANA, KÁBINAPEK, KHABENAPO, KHANA, KULANAPAN, KULANAPO, VENAAMBAKAIA, VENAMBAKAIIA, YOKAIA)*** [POO] 40 or fewer (1962 H. Landar in Sebeok 1977). 165 speakers (1990 census) out of 1,000 all ethnic Pomo (1977 SIL). Clear Lake area, northern California. Hokan, Northern, Pomo,

Russian River and Eastern, Russian River, Southern. Dialects: POINT ARENA, HOPLAND, UKIAH. Bilingualism in English. A separate language from other Pomo varieties. Nearly extinct.

POMO, EASTERN ***(CLEAR LAKE POMO)*** [PEB] California, Clear Lake area. Hokan, Northern, Pomo, Russian River and Eastern, Eastern. A separate language from other Pomo varieties. Extinct.

POMO, NORTHEASTERN ***(SALT POMO)*** [PEF] 1 (1962 H. Landar in Sebeok 1977). California, Coast Range Valley of Story Creek; a tributary of the Sacramento River. Hokan, Northern, Pomo, Russian River and Eastern, Russian River, Northeastern. Bilingualism in English. A separate language from other Pomo varieties. Nearly extinct.

POMO, NORTHERN [PEJ] California, Sherwood Valley area. Hokan, Northern, Pomo, Russian River and Eastern, Russian River, Northern. Dialects: GUIDIVILLE, SHERWOOD VALLEY. Bilingualism in English. Became extinct in 1994 (M. Krauss). A separate language from other Pomo varieties. Extinct.

POMO, SOUTHEASTERN ***(LOWER LAKE POMO)*** [PEO] 10 or fewer (1962 H. Landar in Sebeok 1977). California, eastern shores of Clear Lake. Hokan, Northern, Pomo, Southeastern. Bilingualism in English. A separate language from other Pomo varieties. Nearly extinct.

POMO, SOUTHERN ***(GALLINOMÉRO)*** [PEQ] 40 or fewer (1962 H. Landar in Sebeok 1977). California. Hokan, Northern, Pomo, Russian River and Eastern, Russian River, Southern. Bilingualism in English. A separate language from other Pomo varieties. Nearly extinct.

POTAWATOMI ***(POTTAWOTOMI)*** [POT] Population total both countries 50 (1995 Potawatomi Language Institute). Southwestern and northern Michigan, northern Wisconsin and northeastern Kansas. Also spoken in Canada. Algic, Algonquian, Central. Bilingualism in English. Most or all speakers are middle-aged or older. 85% have varying degrees of language retention. Grammar. Bible portions 1844.

POWHATAN ***(VIRGINIA ALGONKIAN)*** [PIM] No speakers out of 3,000 population (1977 SIL). Scattered in eastern Virginia, and Powhatan Renape Nation, Rankokus Indian Reservation, Rancocas, New Jersey. Algic, Algonquian, Eastern. Extinct.

PURISIMEÑO [PUY] Southern California, near Santa Barbara. Chumash. Was not intelligible with other Chumash varieties. Extinct.

QUAPAW ***(ARKANSAS, ALKANSEA, CAPA, OGAXPA)*** [QUA] 34 speakers (1990 census) out of 2,000 population (1986 SIL). Northeastern corner of Oklahoma. Siouan, Siouan Proper, Central, Mississippi Valley, Dhegiha. Closely related to Kansa, Omaha, Osage, and Ponca, all called 'Dhegiha'. Bilingualism in English. Nearly extinct.

QUECHAN ***(KECHAN, YUMA, QUECL)*** [YUM] 343 speakers (1990 census), out of 1,500 population (1977 SIL). Fort Yuma Reservation, southeastern corner of California. Hokan, Esselen-Yuman, Yuman, River Yuman. Closely related to Maricopa and Mohave. Bilingualism in English. Most speakers are elderly (1998).

QUILEUTE [QUI] 10 speakers possibly out of 300 population (1977 SIL). Pacific side of Olympic Peninsula in Washington. Chimakuan. Dialects: QUILEUTE, HOH. Bilingualism in English. Nearly extinct.

QUINAULT [QUN] 6 or fewer speakers (1990) out of a population of 1,500 (1977 SIL). Pacific side of the Olympic Peninsula in Washington. Salishan, Tsamosan, Maritime. Dialect: LOWER CHEHALIS. Bilingualism in English). Nearly extinct.

RUSSIAN ***(RUSSKI)*** [RUS] 334,615 in USA (1970 census). Indo-European, Slavic, East. The Doukhobors and Molokans are conservative religious groups who speak Standard Russian. Other Russian speakers in the USA have long-standing residence; still others have come more recently. Bible 1680-1993. See main entry under Russia.

SALINAN [SAL] California, central coast. Hokan, Salinan-Seri. Formerly there were two dialects. Extinct.

SALISH, SOUTHERN PUGET SOUND [SLH] 107 speakers including 5 monolinguals (1990 census), out of 2,000 population (1977 SIL). Southern end of Puget Sound, Washington. Salishan, Central Salish, Twana. Dialects: DUWAMISH, MUCKLESHOOT, NISQUALLY, PUYALLUP, SNOQUALMIE, SUQUH. Bilingualism in English. Only elderly speakers left. Nearly extinct.

SALISH, STRAITS ***(STRAITS)*** [STR] Southeastern Vancouver Island, British Columbia and adjoining portions of Washington, including the islands in between. Salishan, Central Salish, Straits. Dialects: SAANICH, LUMMI, SAMISH, SOOKE, SONGISH. Bilingualism in English. All speakers are middle-aged or over. The Samish, Sooke, and Songish dialects are linguistically extinct. Conversational Salish is taught in Nespelem, Washington, but it is not known which Salish. See main entry under Canada.

SEA ISLAND CREOLE ENGLISH ***(GULLAH, GEECHEE)*** [GUL] 125,000 speakers (1977 I. Hancock), including 7,000 to 10,000 monolinguals, and 10,000 in New York City (1989 J. Holm). Coastal region from Jacksonville, North Carolina to Jacksonville, Florida, and especially on the Sea Islands off the Georgia coast. Small clusters in New York City and Detroit. Creole, English based, Atlantic, Eastern,

Northern. Dialects: NORTHEAST FLORIDA COAST, GEORGIA, SOUTH CAROLINA. Intelligibility with other English based creoles is undetermined. Very close to Bahamas Creole and Afro-Seminole. 90% lexical similarity with Afro-Seminole. In limited contact with English, and barely understandable with Standard English. Government bilingual education program begun. Vigorous. Linguistic influences from Fula, Mende, upper Guinea coast, Gambia River area (I. Hancock 1987). Scholars have been predicting its demise for 100 years (W. Stewart). Investigation needed: intelligibility with Bahamas Creole, Afro-Seminole. Dictionary. Literacy rate in first language: 1% to 5%. Literacy rate in second language: 75% to 100%. Swamps, coastal plains. Agriculturalists: rice, cotton. Bible portions 1994.

SENECA [SEE] 200 speakers including Canada, out of 8,000 population (1977 SIL). Population total both countries 200 or more. Tonawanda, Cattaraugus, and Allegheny Reservations in western New York, and mixed with Cayuga in northeastern Oklahoma. Also spoken in Canada. Iroquoian, Northern Iroquoian, Five Nations, Seneca-Onondaga, Seneca-Cayuga. Bilingualism in English. Most speakers are elderly in New York (1998). Bible portions 1829-1874.

SERRANO [SER] 1 speaker (1994 C. J. Coker). Southern California, San Bernardino and San Gorgonio Pass area. Uto-Aztecan, Northern Uto-Aztecan, Takic, Serrano-Gabrielino. Bilingualism in English. The speaker is elderly (1994). Nearly extinct.

SHASTA ***(SASTEAN, SHASTAN)*** [SHT] 12 speakers (1990 census). Northern California. Hokan, Northern, Karok-Shasta, Shasta-Palaihninan, Shastan. Formerly there were four dialects. Bilingualism in English. All over 50 years old (1962 Chafe). Nearly extinct.

SHAWNEE [SJW] 234 speakers (1990 census), out of 2,000 population (1977 SIL). Central and northeastern Oklahoma. Algic, Algonquian, Central. Bilingualism in English. Most or all speakers are middle-aged or older. Dictionary. Bible portions 1842-1929.

SHOSHONI ***(SHOSHONE)*** [SHH] 2,284 speakers (1990 census), out of 7,000 population (1977 SIL). Wind River Shoshoni is the largest contingent of speakers (Jon Dayley). The Western Shoshoni are in central to northeastern Nevada, and Fort Hall Reservation in Idaho, Northern Shoshoni in Wyoming, Goshute in western Utah. Uto-Aztecan, Northern Uto-Aztecan, Numic, Central. Dialects: GOSIUTE (GOSHUTE), WESTERN SHOSHONI, NORTHERN SHOSHONI. Wind River Shoshoni is a subdialect of Northern Shoshoni, spoken at Wind River Reservation. Closely related to Comanche and Panamint, which are not inherently intelligible with Shoshoni. Bilingualism in English. In some locations only the older ones speak the language. Vigorous in some locations. Bible portions 1986.

SIUSLAW [SIS] Southern Oregon coast. Penutian, Oregon Penutian, Coast Oregon, Siuslawan. "There have been no speakers of Siuslaw for many years" (M. Dale Kinkade 1998). Extinct.

SKAGIT ***(SWINOMISH)*** [SKA] 100 speakers out of 350 population (1977 SIL). East side of Puget Sound, Washington. Salishan, Central Salish, Twana. Bilingualism in English. Most or all speakers are middle-aged or older.

SNOHOMISH [SNO] 10 or fewer speakers (1998 J. Brooke, New York Times 4/9/98), out of 800 population (1977 SIL). Tulalip Reservation, northwestern Washington. Salishan, Central Salish, Twana. Bilingualism in English. Only elderly speakers are left. Nearly extinct.

SPANISH ***(ESPAÑOL, CASTELLANO)*** [SPN] 22,400,000 in USA, 8.9% of the population (1990 census). San Antonio, Texas to Los Angeles; Miami, Florida area; New York City, Illinois, Denver, other areas. Indo-European, Italic, Romance, Italo-Western, Western, Gallo-Iberian, Ibero-Romance, West Iberian, Castilian. Population has increased 61% or more since 1970. Official language. Bible 1553-1979. See main entry under Spain.

SPOKANE ***(SPOKAN)*** [SPO] 50 or fewer speakers (1990) out of a population of 1,000 (1977 SIL). Northeastern Washington. Salishan, Interior Salish, Southern. Closely related to Kalispel-Pend d'Oreille. Bilingualism in English. Most speakers are middle-aged or older. They have developed a program to teach vocabulary to seventh-graders. They teach by songs and place names, and plan to teach prayers and hymns. Dictionary.

SUSQUEHANNOCK ***(SUSQUEHANNA, CONESTOGA, ANDASTE, MINQUA)*** [SQN] Along the Susquehanna River. Iroquoian. Became extinct about 1763. Extinct.

TAKELMA ***(TAKILMA, LOWLAND TAKELMA)*** [TKM] Middle course of the Rogue River, Oregon. Penutian, Oregon Penutian, Takelma. May be in a Takelma-Kalapuyan subgroup, but not conclusive yet. Extinct.

TANACROSS [TCB] 65 speakers out of 220 ethnic population (1995 M. Krauss). Central Alaska, near the Upper Tanana. Na-Dene, Nuclear Na-Dene, Athapaskan-Eyak, Athapaskan, Tanana-Upper Kuskokwim, Tanana. Bilingualism in English. Youngest speakers in their 30s. Recognized as a distinct language in the 1970s.

TANAINA ***(DENA'INA, KINAYSKIY)*** [TFN] 75 or fewer speakers, out of 900 population (1997 M. Krauss). Around Cook Inlet and adjacent area of southern Alaska. Na-Dene, Nuclear Na-Dene, Athapaskan-Eyak, Athapaskan, Tanaina-Ahtna. Dialects: KENAI PENINSULA, UPPER INLET,

COASTAL-INLAND, STONEY RIVER. Bilingualism in English. Youngest speakers in their 20s at Lime Village, but elsewhere in their 50s and older. Kenai dialect is nearly extinct. Nearly extinct.

TANANA, LOWER ***(TANANA)*** [TAA] 30 speakers out of 380 population (1995 M. Krauss). Tanana River below Fairbanks, Nenana and Minto, central Alaska. Na-Dene, Nuclear Na-Dene, Athapaskan-Eyak, Athapaskan, Tanana-Upper Kuskokwim, Tanana. Dialects: CHENA, SALCHA-GOODPASTER. Bilingualism in English. All speakers are near 60 or older. Chena River dialect became extinct in 1976 and Salcha-Goodpaster Rivers in 1993.

TANANA, UPPER ***(NABESNA)*** [TAU] 105 speakers (1995 M. Krauss), out of 300 population in Alaska (1995). Population total both countries 115. Area of upper Tanana River, east central Alaska. Also spoken in Canada. Na-Dene, Nuclear Na-Dene, Athapaskan-Eyak, Athapaskan, Tanana-Upper Kuskokwim, Tanana. Bilingualism in English. Youngest speakers are in their 20s at Tetlin, older elsewhere. Bible portions 1970-1982.

TENINO ***(WARM SPRINGS)*** [WAR] 200 speakers out of 1,000 population (1977 SIL). Warm Springs Reservation, Oregon. Penutian, Plateau Penutian, Sahaptin. Bilingualism in English. Most or all speakers are middle-aged or older.

TEWA [TEW] 1,298 speakers out of 2,383 population, 54.5% (1980 census). 50 Nambe speakers out of 175 population, 25 Pojoaque out of 37, 349 San Ildefonso out of 478, 495 San Juan out of 1,146, 207 Santa Clara out of 318, 172 Tesuque out of 229 (1980 census). 18 monolinguals (1990 census). North of Santa Fe, New Mexico and at Hano on the Hopi Reservation, Arizona. Kiowa Tanoan, Tewa-Tiwa, Tewa. Dialects: HANO, SAN JUAN, NAMBE, POJOAQUE, SANTA CLARA, SAN ILDEFONSO, TESUQUE. 49.8% of the population below 18 years are speakers, 70% above 18 (1980 census). Most adults speak the language. Many younger ones prefer English and some do not speak the language. Dictionary. Bible portions 1969-1984.

TILLAMOOK [TIL] Northwestern Oregon. Salishan, Tillamook. Bilingualism in English. The last speaker died in 1970. Extinct.

TIWA, NORTHERN [TAO] 927 speakers out of 1,166 population, 79.5% (1980 census). 803 Taos speakers out of 1,042 population, 101 Picuris speakers (1990 census) out of 124 population (1980 census), 67.3% of the Taos under 18 are speakers, 92.9% over 18 are speakers (1980 census). North central New Mexico. Kiowa Tanoan, Tewa-Tiwa, Tiwa. Dialects: TAOS, PICURIS. At Picuris speakers tend to be older. Vigorous at Taos. Literacy rate in first language: 1% to 5%. Literacy rate in second language: 50% to 75%. Bible portions 1976-1992.

TIWA, SOUTHERN [TIX] 1,631 speakers out of 2,469 population, 70.1% (1980 census). 1,588 Isleta speakers out of 2,249 population (1980 census), 43 Sandia speakers (1990 census) out of 220 population, 65.6% under 18 are speakers, 67% of Isleta, 46.7% of Sandia (1980 census). New Mexico, pueblos of Isleta and Sandia, north and south of Albuquerque. Kiowa Tanoan, Tewa-Tiwa, Tiwa. Dialects: SANDIA, ISLETA (ISLETA PUEBLO). Bilingualism in English. At Sandia most or all speakers are middle-aged or older. Vigorous at Isleta among adults. Many children prefer English. Bible portions 1981-1987.

TLINGIT ***(THLINGET, TLINKIT)*** [TLI] 700 speakers out of 10,000 population in USA (1995 M. Krauss). Population total both countries 775. Southeastern Alaska from Yakutat south to the Canadian border at Portland Canal, and inland through British Columbia into south central Yukon Territory between Tagish and Kaska northward. Also spoken in Canada. Na-Dene, Nuclear Na-Dene, Tlingit. Bilingualism in English. Youngest speakers are 60 to 65 and older, except in Angoon, Alaska, where they are nearly 50. There is growing interest in the language among the population. SOV. Coastal. Fishermen, lumbermen. Bible portions 1969.

TOLOWA ***(SMITH RIVER)*** [TOL] 5 speakers or fewer (1977 SIL). Southwestern Oregon. Na-Dene, Nuclear Na-Dene, Athapaskan-Eyak, Athapaskan, Pacific Coast, Oregon, Tolowa-Galice. Only a few elderly speakers are left. Chasta Costa was a separate tribe in Oregon; now extinct. Nearly extinct.

TONKAWA [TON] No fluent speakers left out of a population of 90 (1977 SIL). North central Oklahoma. Coahuiltecan. The ethnic group speak English as mother tongue. Extinct.

TSIMSHIAN ***(SM'ALGYAX, TSIMSHEAN, ZIMSHIAN, CHIMMEZYAN, COAST TSIMSHIAN)*** [TSI] 70 out of 1,300 ethnic population in USA (1995 M. Krauss). Tip of Alaska panhandle, (New) Metlakatla on Annette Island, some in Ketchikan. Penutian, Tsimshian. Bilingualism in English. Speakers are 60, 70, or older. Bible portions 1885-1898. See main entry under Canada.

TÜBATULABAL [TUB] 6 speakers or fewer out of an ethnic population of 50 (1972 SIL). South central California. Uto-Aztecan, Northern Uto-Aztecan, Tubatulabal. All over 50 years old (1972). May be extinct (1987). Nearly extinct.

TUNICA [TUK] No speakers left out of a population of 150 (1977 SIL). Central Louisiana. Gulf. Extinct.

TUSCARORA ***(SKAROHREH)*** [TUS] 10 or fewer speakers in USA (1998 James Brooke New York Times 4/9/98) out of 1,000 population including Canada (1977 SIL). Tuscarora Reservation near Niagara Falls, New York, eastern North Carolina. Iroquoian, Northern Iroquoian, Tuscarora- Nottoway.

Bilingualism in English. Only elderly speakers left. Children are being taught the Tuscarora language in eastern North Carolina. Dictionary. Nearly extinct. See main entry under Canada.

TUTELO ***(SAPONI)*** [TTA] Lower Mississippi Valley. Siouan, Siouan Proper, Southeastern, Tutelo. Saponi was either the same or very similar to Tutelo. Extinct.

TUTUTNI [TUU] 10 speakers or fewer (1962 Chafe). Southwestern Oregon. Na-Dene, Nuclear Na-Dene, Athapaskan-Eyak, Athapaskan, Pacific Coast, Oregon, Tolowa-Galice. All over 50 years old (1962). Nearly extinct.

TWANA ***(SKOKOMISH)*** [TWA] (350 in the ethnic population; 1977 SIL). East of Puget Sound, Washington. Salishan, Central Salish, Twana. Dialects: SKOKOMISH, QUILCENE. Bilingualism in English. Extinct since 1980. Extinct.

UMATILLA ***(COLUMBIA RIVER SAHAPTIN)*** [UMA] 50 possible speakers out of 120 population (1977 SIL). Umatilla Reservation, Oregon. Penutian, Plateau Penutian, Sahaptin. Bilingualism in English. Most or all speakers are middle-aged or older.

UNAMI ***(DELAWARE, LENNI-LENAPE, LENAPE, TLA WILANO)*** [DEL] 5 or fewer speakers (1996 John O'Meara) out of 2,000 population (1990, in OIEL 1992). Northeastern and west central Oklahoma, northern New Jersey and lower Delaware Valley. Algic, Algonquian, Eastern. Related to Munsee in Ontario. Bilingualism in English. Only elderly speakers are left. Nearly extinct.

UTE-SOUTHERN PAIUTE [UTE] 1,984 speakers including 20 monolinguals (1990 census), out of 5,000 population (1977 SIL), including 3 Chemehuevi (1990 census). Ute in southwestern Colorado and southeastern and northeastern Utah; Southern Paiute in southwestern Utah, northern Arizona, and southern Nevada; Chemehuevi on lower Colorado River, California. Uto-Aztecan, Northern Uto-Aztecan, Numic, Southern. Dialects: SOUTHERN PAIUTE, UTE, CHEMEHUEVI. Most adults speak the language but most younger ones do not. Literacy rate in first language: Below 1%. Literacy rate in second language: 75% to 100%.

VENTUREÑO [VEO] Southern California, near Santa Barbara. Chumash. Was not intelligible with other Chumash varieties. Had multiple dialects. Extinct.

WAILAKI [WLK] Round Valley Reservation, northern California. Na-Dene, Nuclear Na-Dene, Athapaskan-Eyak, Athapaskan, Pacific Coast, California, Mattole-Wailaki. Extinct.

WALLA WALLA ***(NORTHEAST SAHAPTIN)*** [WAA] 100 speakers out of 700 population (1977 SIL). Umatilla Reservation, Oregon. Penutian, Plateau Penutian, Sahaptin. Bilingualism in English. Most or all speakers are middle-aged or older.

WAMPANOAG ***(MASSACHUSETT, MASSACHUSETTS, NATICK)*** [WAM] Ethnic group: 1,200 (1977 SIL). Southeastern Massachusetts. Algic, Algonquian, Eastern. Bilingualism in English. Dictionary. Extinct. Bible 1663-1685.

WAPPO [WAO] 1 speaker (1977 Voegelin and Voegelin) out of a possible population of 50 (1977 SIL). California, north of the San Francisco Bay area. Yuki. Bilingualism in English. Nearly extinct.

WASCO-WISHRAM ***(UPPER CHINOOK)*** [WAC] 69 speakers including 7 monolinguals (1990 census), out of a possible population of 750 (1977 SIL). North central Oregon, south central Washington. Penutian, Chinookan. Bilingualism in English. Nearly extinct.

WASHO ***(WASHOE)*** [WAS] 10 or fewer speakers (1998 J. Brooke, New York Times 4/9/98), out of 1,000 population (1977 SIL). California-Nevada border southeast of Lake Tahoe. Hokan, Washo. Bilingualism in English. All speakers are elderly. Nearly extinct.

WICHITA [WIC] 10 or fewer speakers (1998 James Brook, New York Times 4/9/98), out of 750 population (1977 SIL). West central Oklahoma. Caddoan, Northern, Wichita. Dialects: WACO, TAWAKONI. Close to Kitsai and Pawnee. Bilingualism in English. All speakers are elderly. Nearly extinct.

WINTU ***(WINTUN)*** [WIT] 10 speakers (1990 census), out of 1,000 possible population (1982 SIL). California, Clear Lake and Colusa area and northward. Penutian, California Penutian, Wintuan. Dialects: WINTU, PATWIN, NOMLAKI. Bilingualism in English. Nearly extinct.

WIYOT [WIY] No speakers left out of a population of 120 (1977 SIL). Northwestern California. Algic, Wiyot. Last speaker died in 1962 (K. V. Teeter 1975). Dictionary. Grammar. Extinct.

WYANDOT ***(WENDAT, WYENDAT, WYANDOTTE)*** [WYA] Northeastern Oklahoma and Canada. Also spoken in Canada. Iroquoian, Northern Iroquoian, Huron. Dialects: HURON, WYANDOT. No mother tongue fluent speakers. Wyandot was spoken until quite recently near Sandwich, Ontario, and Wyandotte, Oklahoma. There were 2 elderly speakers in 1961. Huron was last spoken at Lorette, near Quebec City, in the mid-19th century, or 1912. Dictionary. The language is being taught to children in school (1999). Extinct.

YAKIMA [YAK] 3,000 speakers out of 8,000 population (1977 SIL). Yakima Valley, south central Washington. Penutian, Plateau Penutian, Sahaptin. Dialects: YAKIMA, KLIKITAT. Bilingualism in English. Most speakers are elderly (1998). Together with Cowlitz and Klikitat, sometimes called 'Northwest Sahaptin'.

YANA [YNN] Upper Sacramento Valley, California. Hokan, Northern, Yana. An extinct group of varieties, including Yahi. Extinct.

YAQUI [YAQ] 406 in USA including 2 monolinguals (1990 census). Tucson and Phoenix, Arizona area. Uto-Aztecan, Southern Uto-Aztecan, Sonoran, Cahita. Partially intelligible with Mayo. Bilingualism in English, Spanish. NT 1977. See main entry under Mexico.

YINGLISH *(AMERIDISH)* [YIB] Also spoken in United Kingdom. Indo-European, Germanic, West, English. Bilingualism in English. Professor Joshua A. Fishman says, "'Yinglish' is a variety of English influenced by Yiddish (lexically, particularly, but also grammatically and phonetically). Any good English dictionary will now include 50-100 or more 'borrowings from Yiddish' (=Yinglish)....These forms are now used not only by Jews but by others, inversely proportionally to their distance from NYC. In the case of non-Jews the original Yiddish meaning may no longer be known and a related metaphoric or contextual meaning is intended...Since the variety is only used...by speakers who can always speak 'proper English'. Yinglish is never a mother tongue acquired by the usual process of intergenerational transmission. French, Spanish, and Russian counterparts (also a Hebrew counterpart) also exist, but are more restricted in nature, both in size as well as in availability to non-Jews." Jewish. Second language only.

YOKUTS [YOK] 78 speakers of Northern Foothill Yokuts (1990 census), out of a possible total Yokuts population of 500 (1977 SIL). California, San Joaquin River and the slopes of the Sierra Nevada, San Joaquin Valley. Penutian, Yok-Utian, Yokuts. Dialects: NORTHERN FOOTHILL YOKUTS, SOUTHERN FOOTHILL YOKUTS, VALLEY YOKUTS. Many subdialects. Bilingualism in English. Southern Foothill and Valley Yokuts are extinct. Nearly extinct.

YUCHI *(UCHEAN)* [YUC] 12 to 19 fluent speakers (1997), out of 1,500 population (1977 SIL). Among Creek people in east central Oklahoma. Language Isolate. Bilingualism in English. All speakers are middle-aged or older. Dictionary. Nearly extinct.

YUKI [YUK] 6 speakers (1990 census). Round Valley Reservation, northern California. Yuki. Bilingualism in English. All over 50 years old (1962 Chafe). The speakers in 1962 were not fluent in the language. Probably extinct (1977 SIL). Nearly extinct.

YUPIK, CENTRAL *(CENTRAL ALASKAN YUPIK, WEST ALASKA "ESKIMO")* [ESU] 10,000 speakers out of 21,000 population (1995 M. Krauss). Nunivak Island, Alaska coast from Bristol Bay to Unalakleet on Norton Sound and inland along Nushagak, Kuskokwim, and Yukon rivers. Eskimo-Aleut, Eskimo, Yupik, Alaskan. Dialect: KUSKOKWIM "ESKIMO" (BETHEL YUPIK). There are 3 dialects, which are quite different. People are quite bilingual. All ages along the central coast and up the Kuskokwim River. In Bristol Bay, Yukon Delta, City of Bethel, and on Nunivak Island, the average age of youngest speakers is from 20 to 40. Investigation needed: intelligibility with dialects. Grammar. NT 1956.

YUPIK, CENTRAL SIBERIAN *(ST. LAWRENCE ISLAND "ESKIMO")* [ESS] 808 speakers (1990 census), out of 1,000 population in Alaska. Population total both countries 1,100. St. Lawrence Island, Alaska. Also spoken in Russia (Asia). Eskimo-Aleut, Eskimo, Yupik, Siberian. Dialect: CHAPLINO. In Alaska children are being raised speaking the language (1998). In Siberia only older people speak the language. Vigorous in Alaska. Children beginning to show signs of preferring English. Dictionary. Grammar. Literacy rate in first language: 1% to 10%. Literacy rate in second language: 40% to 50%. Bible portions 1974-1998.

YUPIK, PACIFIC GULF *(ALUTIIQ, SUGPIAK "ESKIMO", SUGPIAQ "ESKIMO", CHUGACH "ESKIMO", KONIAG-CHUGACH, SUK, SUGCESTUN, ALEUT, PACIFIC YUPIK, SOUTH ALASKA "ESKIMO")* [EMS] 400 speakers out of 3,000 population (1995 M. Krauss). Alaska Peninsula, Kodiak Island (Koniag dialect), Alaskan coast from Cook Inlet to Prince William Sound (Chugach dialect). 20 villages. Eskimo-Aleut, Eskimo, Yupik, Alaskan. Dialects: CHUGACH, KONIAG. Bilingualism in English. Most speakers are middle-aged or older. The youngest are in the late twenties at the tip of the Kenai Peninsula and the fifties or sixties on Kodiak Island. They call themselves 'Aleut'. Dictionary. Grammar. Bible portions 1848.

YUROK [YUR] 10 or fewer speakers out of a possible 3,000 to 4,500 population (1982 SIL). Northwestern California. Algic, Yurok. Bilingualism in English. Few if any full bloods younger than 20 years old. Nearly extinct.

ZUNI *(ZUÑI)* [ZUN] 6,413 speakers (1980 census). New Mexico, south of Gallup. Language Isolate. Includes 31 monolinguals (1980). Speakers were 85.5% of the population below 18 years of age, 6.2% above 18 (1980). Children are being raised speaking the language (1998). Vigorous. Literacy rate in first language: Below 1%. Literacy rate in second language: 75% to 100%. Bible portions 1941-1970.

VENEZUELA

República Bolivariana de Venezuela, Bolivarian Republic of Venezuela. National or official language: Spanish. 23,242,000 (1998 UN). 145,230 American Indians (Mosonyi 1987). Literacy rate 88% (1991 WA). Also includes Catalan-Valencian-Balear, Corsican, English 20,000, Inga 4,000, Latvian, Arabic 110,000, Chinese 400,000. Information mainly from M. Durbin and H. Seijas 1973; E. Migliazza 1977. Christian, secular. Deaf population 1,246,674. Deaf institutions: 3. Data accuracy estimate: B. The number of languages listed for Venezuela is 42. Of those, 40 are living languages and 2 are extinct. Diversity index 0.02.

AKAWAIO ***(ACEWAIO, AKAWAI, ACAWAYO, ACAHUAYO, WAICÁ)*** [ARB] A few in Venezuela. Bolivar State. Carib, Northern, East-West Guiana, Macushi-Kapon, Kapon. Close to Macushi but not inherently intelligible. Marginally intelligible with Arecuna. Limited bilingualism. Ethnic pride. The Akawaio and Patamona call themselves 'Kapon'. Bible portions 1873. See main entry under Guyana.

ARAWAK ***(AROWAK, LOKONO)*** [ARW] A few in Venezuela. Coastal area near Guyana, Delta Amacuro. Arawakan, Maipuran, Northern Maipuran, Caribbean. Investigation needed: bilingual proficiency. Bible portions 1850-1978. See main entry under Suriname.

ARUTANI ***(AUAQUÉ, AUAKE, AWAKÉ, URUAK, URUTANI, AOAQUI, OEWAKU)*** [ATX] 5 speakers out of a population of up to 30 in Venezuela (1977 Migliazza). Below the Sape of the Karum River area, Bolivar State, headwaters of the Paraqua and Uraricáa rivers. Arutani-Sape. The remaining speakers are bilingual in Ninam. Most are intermarried with the Ninam, some with the Pemon (Arecuna), a few with the Sape, and they do not speak Arutani fluently. Nearly extinct. See main entry under Brazil.

BANIVA ***(AVANI, AYANE, ABANE)*** [BVV] Colombian border area. Arawakan, Maipuran, Northern Maipuran, Inland. Dialects: BANIVA, QUIRRUBA. Distinct from Baniwa in Rio Negro region. Extinct.

BANIWA ***(BANIUA DO IÇANA, MANIBA, BANIVA, BANIBA)*** [BAI] 407 in Venezuela (1975 Gaceta Indigenista). Amazonas, between the Curipaco and the Guarequena, along the Colombian border. Arawakan, Maipuran, Northern Maipuran, Inland. Related to Carutana and Curripaco. NT 1965-1985. See main entry under Brazil.

BARÉ ***(BARAWANA, BARAUNA, BARAUANA, IHINI, ARIHINI, MALDAVACA, CUNIPUSANA, YAVITA, MITUA)*** [BAE] A few speakers in Venezuela, perhaps 238 in the ethnic group (1975 Gaceta Indigenista). Colombian border in extreme southwest, Amazonas, along the upper Rio Negro from Brazil-Venezuela border to the Casiquiare Canal, Maroa. Arawakan, Maipuran, Northern Maipuran, Inland. Bilingualism in Spanish, Nhengatu. All are elderly (1975). The name 'Baré' is also used as a cover term for separate languages: Baré, Mandahuaca, Guarekena, Baniwa, Piapoko. Nearly extinct.

CARIB ***(CARIBE, CARIÑA, KALIHNA, KALINYA, GALIBI)*** [CRB] 4,000 to 5,000 in Venezuela (1978 J. C. Mosonyi). Population total all countries 10,000 (1991). Monagas and Anzoategui states, northeast near Orinoco River mouth, plus a few communities in Bolivar State, just south of Orinoco. Also spoken in Brazil, French Guiana, Guyana, Suriname. Carib, Northern, Galibi. Dialects: TABAJARI, CHAYMA (CHAIMA, SAYMA, WARAPICHE, GUAGA-TAGARE). The Chayma people are probably bilingual or monolingual in Spanish. The very old and very young are monolingual. Quite well integrated into Venezuelan culture, though they do speak their own language among themselves. Bible portions 1994.

CUIBA ***(CUIVA)*** [CUI] 650 in Venezuela (1995 SIL). Apure Division. Guahiban. Dialects: CHIRICOA, AMARUWA (AMORUA), MASIGUARE, SIRIPU, YARAHUURAXI-CAPANAPARA, MELLA, PTAMO, SICUANE (SICUARI). Semi-nomadic bands. Nearly all are monolingual. Literacy rate in second language: 1%. Hunter-gatherers. NT 1988. See main entry under Colombia.

CURRIPACO ***(CURIPACO, KURIPAKO, KURRIPAKO)*** [KPC] 210 in Venezuela (1970 census). Amazonas. Arawakan, Maipuran, Northern Maipuran, Inland. An alternate name may be 'Yaverete-Tapuya'. NT 1959. See main entry under Colombia.

GERMAN, COLONIA TOVAR ***(ALEMÁN COLONEIRO)*** [GCT] Indo-European, Germanic, West, High German, German, Upper German, Alemannic. Developed from the Alemannisch (Oberdeutsch) of 1843 under the influence of many other dialects of south Germany, Austria, and Switzerland. Not intelligible with Standard German. Bilingualism in Spanish. Investigation needed: bilingual proficiency in Spanish. Newspapers.

GUAHIBO ***(GUAJIBO, WAHIBO)*** [GUH] 5,000 in Venezuela. Orinoco River from Caicaro de Orinoco on the upper Orinoco, Amazonas and Apure states. Guahiban. The Guahiban languages may or may not be within Arawakan. Plains. NT 1982. See main entry under Colombia.

GUAREQUENA ***(GUAREKENA, AREQUENA, UREQUEMA, UEREQUEMA, WAREKENA)*** [GAE] 367 in Venezuela. Population total both countries 705. Village of Guzmán Blanco, half an hour below Maroa. San Miguel River, Amazonas. Also possibly in Colombia. Also spoken in Brazil. Arawakan, Maipuran, Northern Maipuran, Inland. Bilingualism in Spanish. Only older people speak the language in Venezuela.

JAPRERÍA ***(YAPRERÍA)*** [JRU] 80 (1975 Gaceta Indigenista). Northern region of Sierra de Perija, Zulia State. Carib, Northern, Coastal. Not inherently intelligible with other Carib languages of the area (M. Durbin). Low lexical similarity with Yukpa (Luis Oquendo: U. of Zulia).

MACUSHI ***(MAKUXI, MAKUSHI, TEWEYA)*** [MBC] 600 in Venezuela. Eastern border area. Carib, Northern, East-West Guiana, Macushi-Kapon, Macushi. Close to, but not intelligible with Patamona (Ingariko). Some from Guyana in Bolivar State speak English as second language. NT 1981. See main entry under Guyana.

MANDAHUACA ***(MANDAUACA, MANDAWAKA, IHINI, ARIHINI, MALDAVACA, CUNIPUSANA, YAVITA, MITUA)*** [MHT] 3,000 in Venezuela (1975 Gaceta Indigenista). Population total both countries 3,000 or more. Colombian border in extreme southwest, Amazonas, east of the Baré on the Baria River and Casiquiare Canal. Also spoken in Brazil. Arawakan, Maipuran, Northern Maipuran, Inland. Related to Adzaneni, Yabaana, Masaca. The name 'Baré' is also used as a cover term for separate languages: Baré, Mandahuaca, Guarekena, Baniwa, Piapoko.

MAPOYO ***(MAPAYO, MAPOYE, MOPOI, NEPOYE, WANAI)*** [MCG] 2 speakers out of 120 population (1977 Migliazza). Suapure River, 100 kms. north of La Urbana, Amazonas. Carib, Northern, Western Guiana. Nearly extinct.

MAQUIRITARI ***(MAIONGONG, MAQUIRITARE, YEKUANA, DE'CUANA, YE'CUANA, MAQUIRITAI, SOTO, CUNUANA, PAWANA)*** [MCH] 4,970 in Venezuela (1975 Gaceta Indigenista). Population total both countries 5,240. Bolivar State and Amazonas, near the Brazilian border on the mid-Paragua, Caura, Erebato, upper Ventuari, upper Auaris, Matacuni, Cuntinano, Padamo, and Cunucunuma rivers. Also spoken in Brazil. Carib, Southern, Southern Guiana. Literacy rate in second language: 15%. NT 1970.

MOTILÓN ***(MOTILONE, BARÍ)*** [MOT] 850 in Venezuela (1980 Seely). Venezuelan and Colombian border, Zulia State. Chibchan, Motilon. M. Durbin questions its classification as Chibchan; Voegelin and Voegelin classify it as Arawakan. Unrelated to Carib Motilón (Yukpa). Tropical forest. Bible portions. See main entry under Colombia.

MUTÚS ***(LOCO, MUTÚ)*** [MUF] 200 or more (1977 Merrill Seely). Town of Mutús, a little above Pueblo Llano, Barinas State. Unclassified. Possibly a remnant of Cuica or Timote-a dialect of Timote was Mukutu. All speak their language and Spanish, but comprehension of abstract concepts through Spanish is inadequate. Civilized, prosperous farmers. Synchretistic religion.

NHENGATU ***(YERAL, GERAL, WAENGATU, MODERN TUPI)*** [YRL] 2,000 in Venezuela (1987 Mosonyi). Tupi, Tupi-Guarani, Tupi (III). Trade language. NT 1973. See main entry under Brazil.

NINAM ***(YANAM, XIRIANA)*** [SHB] 100 in Venezuela. Karun and Paragua rivers, Bolivar State. Yanomam. Dialects: NORTHERN NINAM, SOUTHERN NINAM. In Venezuela all speakers are bilingual in Spanish or Arecuna or both. Bible portions 1970. See main entry under Brazil.

PANARE ***(PANARI, ABIRA, EYE)*** [PBH] 1,200 in 20 or more villages. 150 mile perimeter south of Caicaro de Orinoco basin of the Cuchivero River; Bolivar State. Two groups: jungle and highland. Carib, Northern, Western Guiana. Communal life. Nearly all are monolingual. Grammar. SVO, OVS. Tropical forest, mountain slope. Bible portions 1984.

PARAUJANO ***(PARAHUJANO)*** [PBG] 20 or fewer speakers out of 4,306 population (1975 Gaceta Indigenista). Lake Maracaibo, near Guajiro, Zulia State. Arawakan, Maipuran, Northern Maipuran, Caribbean. Dialects: ALILE, TOA. All are bilingual. Most speakers are women. Nearly extinct.

PEMON ***(PEMONG)*** [AOC] 4,850 Pemon in Venezuela. Population total all countries 6,004. Bolivar State, Gran Sabana and adjacent areas. Also spoken in Brazil, Guyana. Carib, Northern, East-West Guiana, Macushi-Kapon, Kapon. Dialects: CAMARACOTO, TAUREPAN (TAULIPANG), ARECUNA (ARICUNA, AREKUNA, JARICUNA, PEMON, DAIGOK, POTSAWUGOK, PISHAUCO, PURUCOTO, KAMARAGAKOK). Marginally intelligible with Akawaio and Patamona. Camaracoto may be distinct. The large majority are monolingual. OVS. Bible portions 1990.

PIAPOCO ***(DZAZE)*** [PIO] 99 in Venezuela (1975 Gaceta Indigenista). Area of San Fernando de Atapapo, Amazonas along the Orinoco. Arawakan, Maipuran, Northern Maipuran, Inland. NT 1966-1987. See main entry under Colombia.

PIAROA ***(KUAKUA, GUAGUA, QUAQUA)*** [PID] 12,000 including 130 Maco (1987 UBS). Population total both countries 12,000 or more. South bank of the Orinoco River, inland from the Paguasa River to Manipiari, Amazonas. Large area. Also spoken in Colombia. Salivan. Dialects: MACO (MAKO, ITOTO), PIAROA. Possibly 50% of the men are bilingual in Maquiritare, Yabarana, or Spanish. 'Ature' (Adole) may be an alternate name. NT 1986.

PUINAVE ***(PUINARE)*** [PUI] 240 in Venezuela (1975 Gaceta Indigenista). Amazonas. Language Isolate. Ruhlen and others classify it as related to Macú. NT 1964. See main entry under Colombia.

SÁLIBA ***(SÁLIVA)*** [SLC] 250 in Venezuela (1991 Adelaar). Cedoño Department. Salivan. Very acculturated in Venezuela. See main entry under Colombia.

SANUMÁ ***(TSANUMA, SANEMA, GUAIKA, SAMATARI, SAMATALI, XAMATARI, CHIRICHANO)*** [SAM] 1,000 to 4,000 in Venezuela (1976 UFM). Caura and Ervato-Ventuari rivers. Yanomam. Three dialects. Nearly all are monolingual. See main entry under Brazil.

SAPÉ ***(KARIANA, KALIÁNA, CALIANA, CHIRICHANO)*** [SPC] 5 speakers out of a population of fewer than 25 (1977 Migliazza). 3 small settlements on Paragua and Karuna rivers. Arutani-Sape. Some lexical correspondences with Guinau (Arawak) and Warao (Chibchan) Greenberg classified it provisionally as Macro-Tucanoan. Most have intermarried with Arecuna (Pemon) and a few with Arutani and Ninam. There are conflicting reports on the number of speakers and degree of bilingualism. Nearly extinct. Bible portions.

SIKIANA ***(SIKIÁNA, SHIKIANA, CHIQUIANA, CHIKENA, CHIQUENA)*** [SIK] Carib, Northern, East-West Guiana, Waiwai, Sikiana. Possibly extinct in Venezuela. See main entry under Brazil.

SPANISH [SPN] 21,480,000 in Venezuela (1995 estimate). Indo-European, Italic, Romance, Italo-Western, Western, Gallo-Iberian, Ibero-Romance, West Iberian, Castilian. National language. Bible 1553-1979. See main entry under Spain.

TUNEBO, CENTRAL [TUF] A few speakers in Venezuela discovered by Roberto Lizarralde a few years ago. Apure State. Chibchan, Chibchan Proper, Tunebo. NT 1987. See main entry under Colombia.

VENEZUELAN SIGN LANGUAGE [VSL] Deaf sign language. The sign language used in the classroom is different from the one used by adults outside. There is a national bilingual education program for Venezuelan Sign Language and Spanish. There have been schools for the deaf since 1937, and they use sign language. Deaf people can attend college with a sign language interpreter. There is a manual alphabet for spelling. Dictionary. Grammar.

WARAO ***(GUARAUNO, GUARAO, WARRAU)*** [WBA] 18,000 in Venezuela (1993 UBS). Population total all countries 18,000 or more. On the delta of the Orinoco River, Delta Amacuro, Sucre, Monagas. Also spoken in Guyana, Suriname. Language Isolate. All ages. NT 1974.

WAYUU ***(GUAJIRO, GUAJIRA, GOAJIRO)*** [GUC] 170,000 in Venezuela (1995 SIL). Zulia State, western, Guajira Peninsula. Arawakan, Maipuran, Northern Maipuran, Caribbean. Bible portions 1944-1989. See main entry under Colombia.

YABARANA ***(YAUARANA)*** [YAR] 20 pure Yabarana and 34 mixed with Piaroa and Macú (1977 Migliazza). 64 (1975 Gaceta Indigenista). North central, Nueva Esparta, area of the Manapiare River basin above the village of San Juan de Manapiare. Amazonas. Carib, Northern, Western Guiana. Dialects: CURASICANA, WOKIARE (UAIQUIARE, GUAYQUERI). Distinct from Yabaana of Brazil. Nearly extinct.

YANOMAMÖ ***(YANOMAME, YANOMAMI, GUAICA, GUAHARIBO, GUAJARIBO)*** [GUU] 12,000 to 14,000 in Venezuela (1991 AP). Population total both countries 13,500 to 16,000. Orinoco-Mavaca area. The Eastern dialect is in the Parima Mountains, east of Batau River, Western dialect in Padamo River basin; Ocamo, Manaviche, and upper Orinoco rivers; and south of the Orinoco River up to headwaters of Marania and Cauaburi rivers, and a number of large villages in the Siapa River area in southern Venezuela. Also spoken in Brazil. Yanomam. Dialects: EASTERN YANOMAMI (PARIMA), WESTERN YANOMAMI (PADAMO-ORINOCO), COBARI (KOBALI, COBARIWA). Different from, but related to Yanomami (Waika) of Brazil. The Cobari dialect is easily intelligible with the others. Tropical forest. Hunters, agriculturalists: bananas, tubers, tobacco. NT 1984.

YARURO ***(LLARURO, YARURU, PUMÉ, YUAPÍN)*** [YAE] 2,000 to 3,000. Orinoco, Sinaruco, Meta, and Apure rivers, Amazonas and Apure states. Unclassified. Their name for themselves and the local name is 'Pumé'. Classified as Jivaroan and Macro-Chibchan. Plains.

YAVITERO ***(PARAENE)*** [YVT] Arawakan, Maipuran, Northern Maipuran, Inland. The last known speaker died in 1984. Extinct.

YUKPA ***(YUKO, YUCPA, YUPA, NORTHERN MOTILÓN)*** [YUP] 500. Areas adjacent to Colombia border, Zulia State. Carib, Northern, Coastal. Dialects: YRAPA, RÍO NEGRO. Low lexical similarity with Japreira (Luis Oquendo). Possible alternate name: 'Manso'. See main entry under Colombia.

YUWANA ***(YOANA, YUANA, WARUWARU, CHICANO, CHIKANO, JOTI, HOTI)*** [YAU] 300 (1970 census, Chicano). Central Venezuela. A northern group is in Bolivar Division on the Kaima River, a tributary of the Cuchivero River; an isolated southern group is in Amazonas on the Iguana, a tributary of the Asita River, and on the Parucito, a tributary of the Manapiare River. Unclassified. There are linguistic similarities to Yanomam and Piaroa (Salivan). The southern group is monolingual; the northern group is partially bilingual in Panare.

Asia

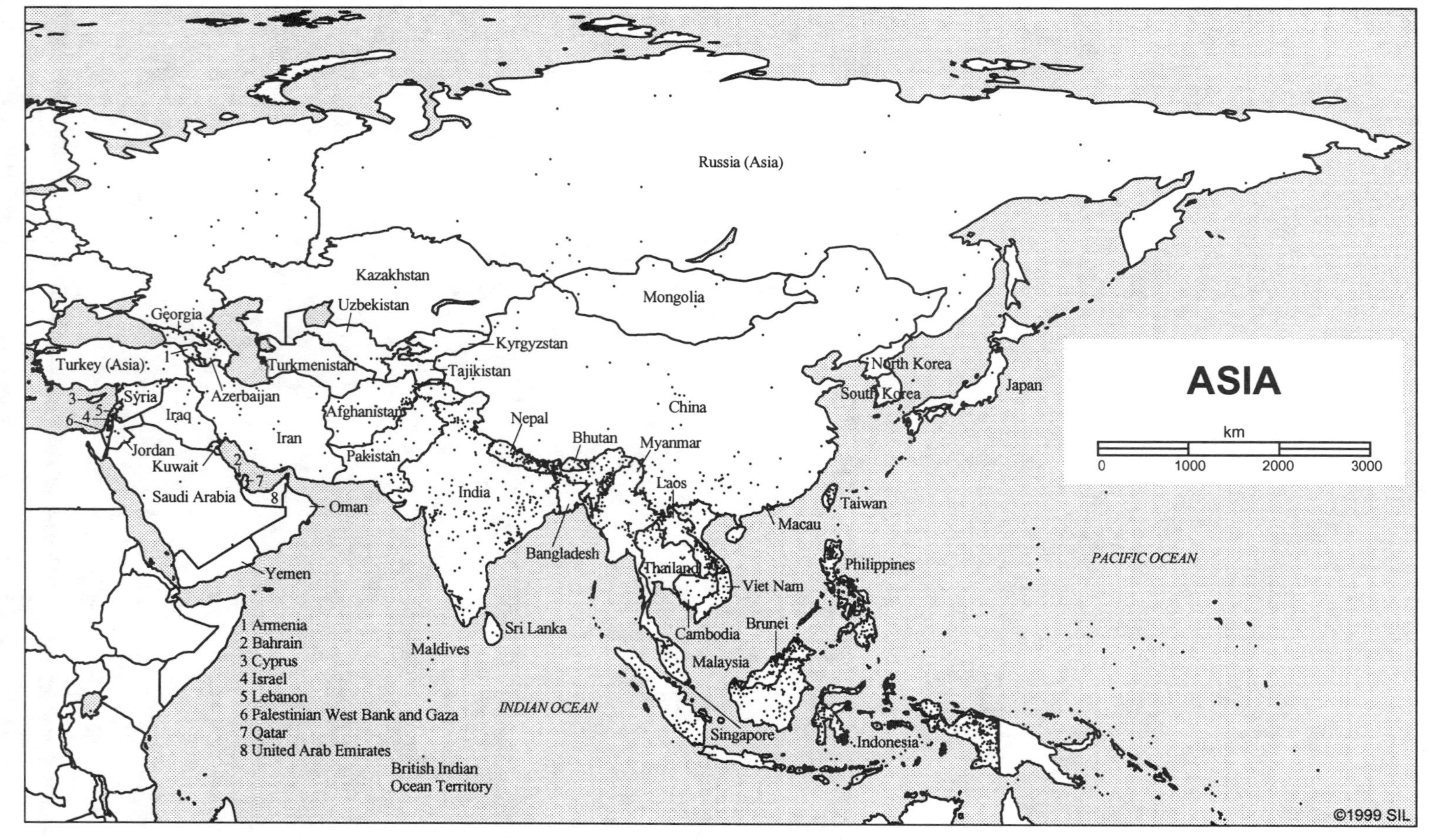
ASIA
km
0
1000
2000
3000
Russia (Asia)
Kazakhstan
Mongolia
Georgia
Uzbekistan
Kyrgyzstan
Turkey (Asia)
Turkmenistan
Tajikistan
North Korea
South Korea
Japan
Syria
Azerbaijan
Iraq
Afghanistan
China
Nepal
Iran
Bhutan
Myanmar
Jordan
Kuwait
Pakistan
Laos
Saudi Arabia
India
Oman
Taiwan
Macau
Bangladesh
PACIFIC OCEAN
Philippines
Thailand
Yemen
Viet Nam
Sri Lanka
Cambodia
Brunei
Maldives
Malaysia
INDIAN OCEAN
Singapore
Indonesia
British Indian
Ocean Territory
1 Armenia
2 Bahrain
3 Cyprus
4 Israel
5 Lebanon
6 Palestinian West Bank and Gaza
7 Qatar
8 United Arab Emirates
1
2
3
4
5
6
7
8
©1999 SIL

AFGHANISTAN

Republic of Afghanistan. De Afghanistan Jamhuriat. National or official languages: Eastern Farsi, Southern Pashto. 21,354,000 (1998 UN), including an estimated 2,500,000 nomads. Literacy rate 31.5% 15 years and older: male 47.2%, female 15%. Also includes Western Panjabi 35,000, Parsi-Dari 350,000, Tatar 350, Urdu. Information mainly from G. Buddress 1960; A. Farhadi 1967; A. Grjunberg 1968, 1971; T. Sebeok 1970; R. Strand 1973; G. Morgenstierne 1974; L. Dupree 1980; J. R. Payne 1987. Sunni Muslim, Shi'a Muslim, Hindu. Blind population 200,000 (1982 WCE). Data accuracy estimate: C. The number of languages listed for Afghanistan is 45. Of those, all are living languages. Diversity index 0.70.

AIMAQ ***(BARBARI, BERBERI, CHAHAR-AIMAQ, CHAR AIMAQ)*** [AIQ] 480,000 in Afghanistan (1993) including 1,000 Jamshidi (1978 MARC). Population total all countries 800,000 (1980 Dupree). West of the Hazara, central northwest Afghanistan, eastern Iran, and Tajikistan (Jamshidi and Khazara). Also spoken in Iran, Tajikistan. Indo-European, Indo-Iranian, Iranian, Western, Southwestern, Persian. Dialects: TAIMURI (TEIMURI, TIMURI, TAIMOURI), TAIMANI, ZOHRI (ZURI), JAMSHIDI (JAMSHEDI, DJAMCHIDI, YEMCHIDI, DZHEMSHID), FIROZKOHI, MALIKI, MIZMAST, CHINGHIZI, ZAINAL. Dialect names listed are as much or more ethnic names. Dari Persian dialects with some Turkic and Mongolian elements, possibly quite distinct. 'Barbari' and 'Berberi' are also applied to Hazara people in and around Mashad, Iran. Investigation needed: intelligibility with related varieties. Literacy rate in second language: 5% to 15%. Agriculturalists, pastoralists. Hanafi Sunni Muslim.

ARABIC, TAJIKI SPOKEN [ABH] 5,000 in Afghanistan (1967 Farhadi). Spoken in a few villages west of Daulatabad (Khushalabad), near Balkh (Yakhdan), Aq Chah (Sultan Aregh), Shibarghan (Hassanabad), and south of Talukan in Takhar Province; 4 northern provinces. Some in Uzbekistan. Afro-Asiatic, Semitic, Central, South, Arabic. Dialect: BALKH ARABIC. Speakers are reported to be bilingual in Tajiki. Reported to be declining in number. Persianized Arabic. Muslim. See main entry under Tajikistan.

ASHKUN ***(ASHKUND, ASHKUNI, WAMAYI, WAMAIS)*** [ASK] 7,000 195,000 in all Nuristani groups (1993). Pech Valley around Wama, northwest of Asadabad in Kunar Province. Indo-European, Indo-Iranian, Indo-Aryan, Nuristani. Dialects: ASHURUVERI (KOLATA, TITIN BAJAYGUL), GRAMSUKRAVIRI, SURUVIRI (WAMAI). Not written. Literacy rate in second language: 5% to 15%. Muslim.

AZERBAIJANI, SOUTH ***(AZERI)*** [AZB] Afshari dialect spoken in small groups north of Kabul, Chandaul quarter of Kabul city, also some in Herat city. Altaic, Turkic, Southern, Azerbaijani. Dialect: AFSHARI (AFSHAR, AFSAR). Significant differences from North Azerbaijani in the former USSR. Part of the Qizilbash merchant group speak the Afshari dialect, which is strongly influenced by Persian. Part of the Qizilbash speak Dari. All are bilingual in Persian or Pashto. Those under 35 do not know any Azerbaijani. Most do not know the Cyrillic script. Muslim. See main entry under Iran.

BALOCHI, WESTERN ***(BALUCHI, BALUCI, BALOCI)*** [BGN] 200,000 in Afghanistan (1979 estimate). Along Helmand River and Zaranj area, in the southwest desert region. Indo-European, Indo-Iranian, Iranian, Western, Northwestern, Balochi. Dialect: RAKHSHANI (RAXSHANI). Largely nomadic. Literacy rate in first language: 5% to 10%. Literacy rate in second language: 15% to 25%. Arabic script. Newspapers. Sunni Muslim. Bible portions 1984. See main entry under Pakistan.

BRAHUI ***(BRAHUIKI, BIRAHUI, KUR GALLI)*** [BRH] 200,000 in Afghanistan (1980 Dupree). Among the Baluchi in the south, from Shorawak to Chakhansoor. Dravidian, Northern. Literacy rate in first language: Below 1%. Literacy rate in second language: 15% to 25%. Pastoralists. Muslim. Bible portions 1905-1978. See main entry under Pakistan.

DARWAZI [DRW] 10,000 (1983). Town of Darwaz on the Amu Darya River, in the northernmost tip of Afghanistan. May also be in Tajikistan. Indo-European, Indo-Iranian, Iranian, Western, Southwestern, Persian. May be called Badakhshani. Literacy rate in first language: Below 1%. Literacy rate in second language: 15% to 25%. Muslim.

DOMARI [RMT] Indo-European, Indo-Iranian, Indo-Aryan, Central zone, Dom. Dialect: CHURI-WALI. Literacy rate in first language: Below 1%. Literacy rate in second language: Below 5%. Muslim. See main entry under Iran.

FARSI, EASTERN ***(PERSIAN, DARI, PARSI)*** [PRS] 5,600,000 25% to 50% of population (1996). Population total both countries 7,000,000. Various Dari dialects in Khorasan Province (Iran), and provinces of Herat, Hazarajat, Balkh, Ghor, Ghazni, Budaksham, Panjsher, and Galcha-Pamir Mountains and Kabul regions. Also spoken in Pakistan. Indo-European, Indo-Iranian, Iranian, Western, Southwestern, Persian. Dialects: DARI (AFGHAN FARSI, HERATI, TAJIKI, KABOLI, KABULI, KHORASANI), PARSIWAN. Radio Afghanistan broadcasts are promoting a standardized pronunciation of the literary language which is based on the old dictional tradition of the country, with its archaic phonetic characteristics. Formal style is closer to Tehrani Persian (Farsi); informal style in some parts of Afghanistan is closer to Tajiki of Tajikistan. Phonological and lexical differences between Iran and Afghanistan cause little difficulty in comprehension. Most Afghan dialects are closer to literary Persian than Iranian dialects are to literary Persian. Zargari (Morghuli) is a secret language used among goldsmiths and perhaps others, based on a dialect of Persian. See also Balkan Romani in Iran. National language. Arabic script. Taught in schools. Radio programs. Sunni and Shi'a Muslim. 70 Jews (1980) speak the same dialect as Muslims. NT 1982-1985.

GAWAR-BATI ***(GOWARI, NARSATI, NARISATI, ARANDUI, SATRE)*** [GWT] 8,000 in Afghanistan. Population total both countries 9,500 (1992). 8 or 9 villages in the Kunar Valley. Also spoken in Pakistan. Indo-European, Indo-Iranian, Indo-Aryan, Northwestern zone, Dardic, Kunar. 47% lexical similarity with Shumashti. Related to Grangali, Zemiaki, and Nangalami. Some bilingualism in Pashto. Literacy rate in first language: Below 1%. Literacy rate in second language: 5% to 15%. Mountain valleys. Sunni Muslim.

GRANGALI ***(GELANGALI, JUMIAKI)*** [NLI] 5,000 (1994). Grangali and Zemiaki in 2 small valleys on the south side of the Pech River at Kandai. Nangalami was in Ningalam village where the Waigal River meets the Pech River, but there may be no speakers left. Indo-European, Indo-Iranian, Indo-Aryan, Northwestern zone, Dardic, Kunar. Dialects: NANGALAMI (NINGALAMI), GRANGALI, ZEMIAKI (ZAMYAKI). Zemiaki may be related to Waigali. Nangalami had 63% lexical similarity with Shumashti, 42% with Gawar-Bati. Literacy rate in first language: Below 1%. Literacy rate in second language: 5% to 15%. Mountain valleys. Muslim.

GUJARI ***(GUJURI RAJASTHANI, GOJRI, GOJARI)*** [GJU] 2,000 or fewer in Afghanistan (1994). Nomads travelling in the summer in the valleys of eastern Afghanistan. Indo-European, Indo-Iranian, Indo-Aryan, Central zone, Rajasthani, Unclassified. Literacy rate in first language: Below 1%. Literacy rate in second language: Below 5%. Pastoralists. Muslim. See main entry under India.

HAZARAGI ***(AZARGI, HAZARA, HEZAREH)*** [HAZ] 1,403,000 in Afghanistan (1989), 9% of the population (1989). Population total all countries 1,756,000 to 6,000,000. Central Afghanistan mountains between Kabul and Herat (Hazarajat), in Kabul, in area between Maimana and Sari-Pul, in settlements in north Afghanistan and from immediately south of the IKoh i Baba mountain Range almost all the way to Mazar e Sharif, and in the area of Qunduz, in Baluchistan and near Quetta in Pakistan. Some have moved to northern Iran. Many are refugees. Also spoken in Iran, Pakistan, Tajikistan. Indo-European, Indo-Iranian, Iranian, Western, Southwestern, Persian. They speak a variety related to Dari; possibly distinct. Ethnic group names are (Central) Dai Kundi, Dai Zangi, Behsud, Yekaulang, (Southern) Polada, Urusgani, Jaguri, Ghazni Hazaras, Dai Miradad. Literacy rate in first language: Below 1%. Literacy rate in second language: Possibly 10% to 20%. In Hazarajat: agriculturalists, semi-sedentary pastoralists; in cities like Kabul and Mazar e Sharif: laborers, traders, shopkeepers, tradesmen, transportation workers. Muslim.

JAKATI ***(JATI, JATU, JAT, JATAKI, KAYANI, MUSALI)*** [JAT] 1,000 in Afghanistan (1967). Kabul (25 families); Jalalabad (50 families); Charikar (15 families). Indo-European, Indo-Iranian, Indo-Aryan, Northwestern zone, Lahnda. Related to Western Panjabi. Spoken by the Jats ('Gypsies' of Afghanistan). Different from Jadgali of Pakistan. Nomadic. Ironsmiths, fortune tellers. Muslim. See main entry under Ukraine.

KAMVIRI ***(KAMDESHI, LAMERTIVIRI, SHEKHANI, KAMIK)*** [QMV] 4,000 in Afghanistan (1973 R. Strand). Population total both countries 6,000. Lower Bashgal Valley, mainly around Kamdesh and Kishtoz villages. Also spoken in Pakistan. Indo-European, Indo-Iranian, Indo-Aryan, Nuristani. Dialects: KAMVIRI, SHEKHANI. Shekhani in Pakistan may be a separate language. Related to Kati. Bilingualism in Pashto. Literacy rate in first language: Below 1%. Literacy rate in second language: 15% to 25%. Mountain valleys.

KARAKALPAK ***(QARAQULPAQS)*** [KAC] 2,000 in Afghanistan. North of Jalalabad, also some south of Mazar-i Sharif. Altaic, Turkic, Western, Aralo-Caspian. Dialects: NORTHEAST KARAKALPAK, SOUTHWEST KARAKALPAK. Bilingualism in Eastern Farsi. There may be none now in Afghanistan; the reference to them is from many years ago. They may now speak closely related Uzbek, or have been absorbed into Farsi or Pashto. Literacy rate in first language: Below 1%. Literacy rate in second language: 5% to 15%. Muslim. Bible portions 1996. See main entry under Uzbekistan.

KATI ***(BASHGALI, KATIVIRI, NURISTANI)*** [BSH] 15,000 in Afghanistan (1994). Population total both countries 20,000. Western Kativiri is in Ramgal, Kulam, Ktivi, or Kantiwo, and Paruk or Papruk valleys. Mumviri is in Mangul, Sasku, Gabalgrom villages in the Bashgal Valley. Eastern Kativiri is in the upper Bashgal Valley. Also spoken in Pakistan. Indo-European, Indo-Iranian, Indo-Aryan, Nuristani. Dialects: EASTERN KATIVIRI (SHEKHANI), WESTERN KATIVIRI, MUMVIRI. Bilingual level estimates for Pashto are Western Kati Men: 0 50%, 1 <5%, 2 <5%, 3 <40%, 4 0%, 5 0%; Western Kati Women: 0-1 100%, 2-5 0%. Eastern Farsi also used. Shekhani is different from the Kamviri which is also called 'Shekhani' in Pakistan. Men take turns 20 days, taking goats to high summer pastures. CVC, CCVC, CV. Literacy rate in first language: Below 1%. Literacy rate in second language: 15% to 25%. Radio programs. Savannah, scrub forest. Mountain valley. Pastoralists: goats. 8,000 to 14,000 feet. Muslim.

KAZAKH ***(KAZAKHI, QAZAQI, QAZAQ)*** [KAZ] 2,000 in Afghanistan. Northern Afghanistan, especially Chahar Dara District west of Kunduz, and around Khanabad and Andkhoi. 500 in Herat city. Altaic, Turkic, Western, Aralo-Caspian. Dialects: NORTHEASTERN KAZAKH, SOUTHERN KAZAKH, WESTERN KAZAKH. Literacy rate in first language: Below 1%. Muslim. NT 1820-1910, out of print. See main entry under Kazakhstan.

KIRGHIZ ***(KIRGHIZI, KIRGIZ)*** [KDO] 500 in Afghanistan (445 in the Great Pamir, plus a few in Badakhshan). Great Pamir Valley east of 73E, in the very northeast. It is spoken by a few Kirghiz who wander across the Chinese and Kyrgyzstan frontiers. All from the Little Pamir went to Pakistan and then Turkey in 1982. Altaic, Turkic, Western, Aralo-Caspian. Literacy rate in first language: Below 1%. Afghan Kirghiz do not read Cyrillic. Sunni Muslim. NT 1991. See main entry under Kyrgyzstan.

MALAKHEL [MLD] 2,000 (1983). Southwest of Kabul in Logar, north of Baraki. Unclassified. May be the same as Ormuru. Literacy rate in first language: Below 1%. Literacy rate in second language: 5% to 15%. Muslim.

MOGHOLI ***(MOGHOL, MOGUL, MOGOL, MONGUL)*** [MLG] 200 or fewer speakers out of an ethnic group of a few thousand. Two villages near Herat: Kundur and Karez-i-Mulla. Altaic, Mongolian, Western. Dialects: KUNDUR, KAREZ-I-MULLA. Unintelligible to remaining body of Mongol speakers; linguistically relatively well explored. In the two villages Farsi is the common language, and is rapidly replacing Mogholi. Moghol people in northern Afghanistan now speak Pashto. Apparently only elderly speakers. Sunni Muslim. Nearly extinct.

MUNJI ***(MUNJANI, MUNJHAN, MUNJIWAR)*** [MNJ] 2,000 to 2,500 (1992). Northeastern Afghanistan in the Munjan and Mamalgha Valleys. Indo-European, Indo-Iranian, Iranian, Eastern, Southeastern, Pamir. Dialects: NORTHERN MUNJI, CENTRAL MUNJI, SOUTHERN MUNJI, MAMALGHA MUNJI. 68% lexical similarity among 'dialects', 56% to 80% with Yidgha in Pakistan. Bilingualism in Eastern Farsi. Little contact with Yidgha. Literacy rate in first language: Below 1%. Literacy rate in second language: 15% to 25%. Muslim.

ORMURI ***(BARGISTA, BARAKS, ORMUI)*** [ORU] 50 speakers out of 2,000 to 5,000 ethnic group members in Afghanistan. Spoken by a few families in Baraki-Barak in Logar. Indo-European, Indo-Iranian, Iranian, Western, Northwestern, Ormuri-Parachi. Dialects: KANIGURAMI, LOGAR. Literacy rate in first language: Below 1%. Literacy rate in second language: 5% to 15%. Muslim. See main entry under Pakistan.

PAHLAVANI [PHV] Spoken in village Haji Hamza Khan of Karim Kushta in Chakhansoor Province. Indo-European, Indo-Iranian, Iranian, Western, Southwestern, Persian. Similar to Dari Persian but still distinct. Literacy rate in first language: Below 1%. Muslim.

PARACHI [PRC] 500 to 600 speakers out of 5,000 to 6,000 members of the ethnic group. Villages in Nijrau and Tagau (600 families), Pachaghan, Shutul (400 families), Ghujulan (100 families), Hindu Kush Valley near Kabul. Indo-European, Indo-Iranian, Iranian, Western, Northwestern, Ormuri-Parachi. Dialects: SHUTUL, GHUJULAN, NIJRAU. Close affinity to Ormuri. Dialect diversity seems to be slight. Literacy rate in first language: Below 1%. Literacy rate in second language: 5% to 15%. Muslim.

PARYA ***(AFGHANA-YI NASFURUSH, AFGHANA-YI SIYARUI, LAGHMANI)*** [PAQ] Indo-European, Indo-Iranian, Indo-Aryan, Central zone, Unclassified. It may be related to Panjabi, or the Laghman dialect of Southeast Pashayi of Afghanistan. Bilingualism in Tajiki. Parya remains the exclusive language within the home. Literacy rate in first language: Below 1%. Literacy rate in second language: 5% to 15%. See main entry under Tajikistan.

PASHAYI, NORTHEAST [AEE] Side valleys between the Kunar and Pech rivers, in Kunar Province, west of Asadabad. Indo-European, Indo-Iranian, Indo-Aryan, Northwestern zone, Dardic, Kunar, Pashayi. Dialects: ARET, CHALAS (CHILAS), KANDAK, KURANGAL, KURDAR. Unintelligible to other Pashayi language speakers. The villages of Kandak, Shemul, Aret, Shumasht, and Kordar belong to the Chugani people; Chalas and Kurangal are separate. Literacy rate in first language: Below 1%. Literacy rate in second language: 5% to 15%. Muslim.

PASHAYI, NORTHWEST [GLH] From Gulbahar across Kapisa and Laghman provinces to Nuristan on the Alingar River, especially the Alisheng Valley and valleys north of Sarobi. Indo-European, Indo-Iranian, Indo-Aryan, Northwestern zone, Dardic, Kunar, Pashayi. Dialects: GULBAHAR, KOHNADEH, LAUROWAN, SANJAN, SHUTUL, BOLAGHAIN, PACHAGAN, ALASAI, SHAMAKOT, UZBIN, PANDAU, NAJIL, PARAZHGHAN, PASHAGAR, WADAU, NANGARACH. Unintelligible to other Pashayi language speakers. Literacy rate in first language: Below 1%. Literacy rate in second language: 5% to 15%. Muslim.

PASHAYI, SOUTHEAST ***(PASHAI)*** [DRA] Upper and Lower Darrai Nur Valley, Damench, Shale (Shari). North of Shewa in Nangarhar Province, and adjacent regions of the Alingar Valley in southern Laghman Province. Indo-European, Indo-Iranian, Indo-Aryan, Northwestern zone, Dardic, Kunar,

Pashayi. Dialects: DARRAI NUR, WEGAL, LAGHMAN, ALINGAR, KUNAR. Unintelligible to other Pashayi language speakers. In the upper Darrai Nur there are ten villages (including Bamba Kot, Lamatek, and Sutan) which form a single people group with their own dialect. Residents of the lower Darrai Nur (Nur River) are separate and perhaps not ethnically an organized people. Literacy rate in first language: Below 1%. Literacy rate in second language: 5% to 15%. Muslim.

PASHAYI, SOUTHWEST [PSH] 108,000 or .6% of the population (1982), including all Pashayi languages or dialects. Tagau (Tagab) Valley, north of Sarobi, northeast of Kabul. Indo-European, Indo-Iranian, Indo-Aryan, Northwestern zone, Dardic, Kunar, Pashayi. Dialects: TAGAU, ISHPI, ISKEN. Not intelligible with other Pashayi languages. All Pashayi peoples have rich folklore and songs preserved by oral tradition. Literacy rate in first language: Below 1%. Literacy rate in second language: 5% to 15%. Muslim.

PASHTO, NORTHERN ***(PAKTU, PAKHTU, PAKHTOO, AFGHAN)*** [PBU] Central Ghilzai area. Indo-European, Indo-Iranian, Iranian, Eastern, Southeastern, Pashto. Dialects: NORTHWESTERN PAKHTO, GHILZAI, DURANI. Bilingualism in Farsi. Since the early 1930s the Afghan government has been exerting considerable effort to standardize and publicize the language. One of the two official languages taught in schools. The Ghilzai speakers are nomadic and 24% of the national population. The Durani, 16%, live in permanent settlements. The people are called 'Pakhtoon' in the north, 'Pashtoon' in the south. Pashto clans are: Mohmandi, Ghilzai, Durani, Yusufzai, Afridi, Kandahari (Qandahari), Waziri, Chinwari (Shinwari), Mangal, Wenetsi. National language. Literacy rate in first language: 5% to 10%(?). Literacy rate in second language: 15% to 25%. Radio programs. Mainly Hanafi Sunni Muslim. Bible 1895. See main entry under Pakistan.

PASHTO, SOUTHERN [PBT] 8,000,000 all Pashto in Afghanistan (1989), 35% to 50% of the population (1996). Population total all countries 9,204,000 or more. All Pashto in all countries: 19,000,000 (1999 WA). Kandahar area. Also spoken in Iran, Pakistan, Tajikistan, UAE, United Kingdom. Indo-European, Indo-Iranian, Iranian, Eastern, Southeastern, Pashto. Dialects: SOUTHWESTERN PASHTO, KANDAHAR PASHTO, QANDAHAR PASHTO. There is generally an 80% lexical similarity between the northern and southern varieties of Pashto. Grammar. Perso-Arabic script used. Muslim.

PRASUNI ***(PRASUN, VERUNI, PARUN, WASI-VERI, VERON, VEROU)*** [PRN] 2,000. Prasun (Parun) Valley on the upper reaches of Pech River in Nuristan; villages of Shupu (Ishtivi, Shtevgrom), Sech, Ucu, Ushut, Zumu. Indo-European, Indo-Iranian, Indo-Aryan, Nuristani. Dialects: UPPER WASI-WERI, CENTRAL PRASUN, LOWER PRASUN (USHUT). Very closely related to Bashgali but more archaic. The most aberrant of the Nuristani languages. Literacy rate in first language: Below 1%. Literacy rate in second language: 5% to 15%. Muslim.

SANGLECHI-ISHKASHIMI [SGL] 2,000 in Afghanistan. Sanglech Valley, Ishkashim area. Ishkashimi spoken in 17 villages; Sanglechi in 2. Indo-European, Indo-Iranian, Iranian, Eastern, Southeastern, Pamir. Dialects: ZEBAK (ZEBAKI), SANGLECHI, ISHKASHIMI (ISHKASHMI, ISHKASHIM, ESHKASHIMI). Bilingualism in Persian. Spoken mainly in villages; formerly used more widely. Literacy rate in first language: Below 1%. Literacy rate in second language: 15% to 25%. Muslim. See main entry under Tajikistan.

SAVI ***(SAWI, SAUJI, SAU)*** [SDG] 3,000 (1983) or several thousand (1992). Population total both countries 3,000 or more. Sau village on the Kunar River. Some might still live in refugee camps in Pakistan. Probably most have returned to their home area now. Also spoken in Pakistan. Indo-European, Indo-Iranian, Indo-Aryan, Northwestern zone, Dardic, Shina. 56% to 58% lexical similarity with Phalura. Bilingualism in Pashto. Literacy rate in first language: Below 1%. Literacy rate in second language: 5% to 15%. Muslim.

SHUGHNI [SGH] 20,000 in Afghanistan (1994 GMI). Both sides of Afghan-Tajikistan border, some 30 miles north of Ishkashim, Pamir Mts. Indo-European, Indo-Iranian, Iranian, Eastern, Southeastern, Pamir, Shugni-Yazgulami. Dialects: ROSHANI (RUSHANI, RUSHAN, OROSHANI), SHUGHNI (SHUGNI, SHIGHNI, SHUGHNANI, SHUGAN, KHUGNI, KUSHANI, SAIGHANI, GHORANI), BARTANGI (BARTANG), OROSHOR (OROSHORI). Dialects listed may be separate languages. Grammar. Literacy rate in first language: Below 1%. Literacy rate in second language: 5% to 15%. Pastoralists. Muslim. See main entry under Tajikistan.

SHUMASHTI ***(SHUMASHT)*** [SMS] 1,000 (1994). Chitral frontier, 60 miles up the Kunar River from Gawar-Bati, on the west side, Darrai Mazar Valley. Shumast village has two languages; this Dardic Kunar language, and a Northeast Pashayi dialect. Indo-European, Indo-Iranian, Indo-Aryan, Northwestern zone, Dardic, Kunar. 63% lexical similarity with Nangalami (Grangali), 47% with Gawar-Bati. Heavily influenced by Pashayi. Literacy rate in first language: Below 1%. Literacy rate in second language: 5% to 15%. Muslim.

TANGSHEWI ***(TANGSHURI)*** [TNF] 10,000 (1994). East of Darwazi on the Amu Darya, far northeast of Badakhshan. May also be in Turkmenistan. Indo-European, Indo-Iranian, Iranian, Unclassified. May be Eastern Iranian. Probably closely related to Darwazi. May be called 'Tajiki'. Literacy rate in first language: Below 1%. Literacy rate in second language: 5% to 15%. Muslim.

TIRAHI [TRA] A few speakers out of possibly 5,000 members in the ethnic group. Southeast of Jalalabad, and west of the Khyber Pass; village of Nangarhar. Not in Pakistan. Indo-European, Indo-Iranian, Indo-Aryan, Northwestern zone, Dardic, Kohistani. Most closely related to Kohistani languages of Pakistan. All are elderly. Muslim. Nearly extinct.

TREGAMI ***(TRIGAMI)*** [TRM] 1,000 (1994). Nuristan, villages of Katar and Gambir. Indo-European, Indo-Iranian, Indo-Aryan, Nuristani. 76% to 80% lexical similarity with Waigali. Literacy rate in first language: Below 1%. Literacy rate in second language: 5% to 15%. Muslim.

TURKMEN ***(TURKOMAN, TRUKMEN, TURKMAN)*** [TCK] 500,000 in Afghanistan (1995). Along the border of Turkmenistan, especially the border regions of Fariab and Badghis provinces. Some in Andkhoi town and Herat city. Altaic, Turkic, Southern, Turkmenian. Dialects: SALOR, TEKE (TEKKE, CHAGATAI, JAGATAI), ERSARI, SARIQ, YOMUT. Sharp dialect differences. Probably mainly Ersari dialect in Afghanistan. Bilingualism in Pashtu. Refugee group in Kabul. People called 'Turkomen' in Syria are Azerbaijani speakers. Literacy rate in second language: 15% to 25%. Arabic script. Some better educated persons can read Cyrillic. Newspapers. Nomadic, cultivators, pastoralists, Persian lamb export, Persian rugs. Hanafi Sunni Muslim, occult. Bible portions 1880-1982. See main entry under Turkmenistan.

UYGHUR ***(UIGHUR, UYGHURI, WIGHOR, UIGHOR, UIGUIR)*** [UIG] 3,000 in Afghanistan. Spoken in a few villages in Badakshan and Abi-i-Barik. Also possibly in Iran and Taiwan. Altaic, Turkic, Eastern. Dialects: KASHGAR-YARKAND (YARKANDI), TARANCHI. Literacy rate in first language: Below 1%. Literacy rate in second language: 5% to 15%. Sunni Muslim. Bible 1950. See main entry under China.

UZBEK, SOUTHERN ***(UZBEKI, USBEKI, UZBAK)*** [UZS] 1,403,000 or 9% of population in Afghanistan (1991 WA). Population total all countries 1,455,000 or more. Many places in north Afghanistan, especially Fariab Province. Maimana town is largely Uzbek. Also possibly in Germany. Also spoken in Pakistan, Turkey (Asia). Altaic, Turkic, Eastern. Limited understanding of Northern Uzbek. Differences in grammar and loan words from Western Farsi. City dwellers are bilingual in Dari; village dwellers have limited ability in Dari. 20% use Dari as second language. Pashto is also used. The only literature is 2 journals, circulation 400. Literacy rate in first language: 10% to 30%(?). Literacy rate in second language: 15% to 25% in Dari. Arabic script, orthography not yet standardized. Mainly settled agriculturalists, some nomads, some craftsmen in gold, jewels, pottery, leather. Hanafi Sunni Muslim.

WAIGALI ***(WAIGELI, WAIGALA, ZHONJIGALI, SUKI, WAI-ALA, WAI, KALASHA-ALA)*** [WBK] 8,000 to 10,000 (1974 Jones). Southeast Nuristan, north of Pech in central Kunar Province. Varjan is in north Waigal Valley, villages of Waigal, Zonchigal, Jamach, Ameshdesh, and eastward in the Veligal Valley and villages there. Chima-Nishey is in villages in the lower valley. Indo-European, Indo-Iranian, Indo-Aryan, Nuristani. Dialects: VARJAN, CHIMA-NISHEY. 76% to 80% lexical similarity with Tregami. Literacy rate in first language: Below 1%. Literacy rate in second language: 15% to 25%. Muslim.

WAKHI ***(WAKHANI, WAKHIGI, VAKHAN, KHIK, GUHJALI)*** [WBL] 7,000 in Afghanistan (1979 estimate). East of Ishkashim, Pamir Mts., in 64 villages on the left bank of the Panj River in the Wakhan Corridor, as far as Sarhad village (about 73E). Center is Khandud. Most have scattered as refugees in Afghanistan or Pakistan. Indo-European, Indo-Iranian, Iranian, Eastern, Southeastern, Pamir. People are called 'Guhjali'. There may be none in Afghanistan now. Literacy rate in first language: Below 1%. Muslim. See main entry under Pakistan.

WARDUJI [WRD] 5,000 (1994). Werdoge River area west of Ishkashim, northeast Afghanistan. Unclassified. Probably a Persian dialect. May be Pamir. Literacy rate in first language: Below 1%. Literacy rate in second language: 5% to 15%. Muslim.

WOTAPURI-KATARQALAI [WSV] 2,000 (1994). South of Waigali area in Nuristan in the towns of Wotapuri and Katarqalai. Indo-European, Indo-Iranian, Indo-Aryan, Northwestern zone, Dardic, Kohistani. Literacy rate in first language: Below 1%. Literacy rate in second language: 15% to 25%. Muslim.

ARMENIA

National or official language: Armenian. 3,536,000 (1998 UN). Formerly part of USSR. Capital: Erevan. 11,306 square miles. Literacy rate 99%. Also includes Georgian 1,314, Greek 4,700, Karachay-Balkar 983, Russian 70,000, Ukrainian 8,000. Data accuracy estimate: B. The number of languages listed for Armenia is 6. Of those, all are living languages. Diversity index 0.16.

ARMENIAN ***(HAIEREN, SOMKHURI, ENA, ERMENICE, ERMENI DILI, ARMJANSKI YAZYK)*** [ARM] 3,197,000 in Armenia (1993 Johnstone). 91% of the ethnic group in the former USSR spoke it as mother tongue (1979 census). Population total all countries 6,000,000 (1999 WA). Throughout the country. Also spoken in 29 other countries including Azerbaijan, Bulgaria, Canada, Cyprus, Egypt, Estonia, France, Georgia, Greece, Honduras, Hungary, India, Iran, Iraq, Israel, Jordan, Kazakhstan, Kyrgyzstan, Lebanon. Indo-European, Armenian. Dialects: EASTERN ARMENIAN, EREVAN (ERIWAN), TBILISI (TIFLIS), KARABAGH, SHAMAKHI (SCHAMACHI), ASTRAKHAN (ASTRACHAN), DZHULFA (DSCHUGHA, DSCHULFA), AGULIS, KHVOY-SALMST (CHOI-SALMST), URMIA-MARAGHEH (URMIA-MARAGHA), ARTVIN (ARTWIN), KARIN (ERZURUM, ERZERUM), MUS (MUSCH), VAN (WAN), TIGRANAKERT (DIYARBAKIR, DIARBEKIR), KHARBERD (CHARBERD, ERZINCAN, ERZENKA), SHABIN-KARAHISSAR (SCHABIN-KARAHISSAR), TRABZON (TRAPEZUNT), HAMSHEN (HAMSCHEN), MALATYA (MALATIA), KILIKIEN, SYRIA (SYRIEN), ARABKIR, AKN, SEBASTE, EWDOKIA (TOKAT), SMYRNA (IZMIR), NORTH KOMEDIA, CONSTANTINOPLE (KONSTANTINOPEL, ISTANBUL), RODOSTO, CRIMEA (KRIM), ASHKHARIK. All dialects in all countries usually reported to be inherently intelligible. Russian (about 30% of Armenians in Armenia). Eastern Armenian (Ashkharik) spoken in Armenia, Turkey, Iran. National language. SVO. Unique alphabet. National Armenian Christian Church. Bible 1883-1994.

ARMENIAN SIGN LANGUAGE [AEN] Deaf sign language.

ASSYRIAN NEO-ARAMAIC ***(AISORSKI)*** [AII] 3,000 speakers in Armenia (1999) out of a reported population of 15,000. Erevan and scattered throughout Transcaucasia. Afro-Asiatic, Semitic, Central, Aramaic, Eastern, Central, Northeastern. Close linguistically to other Northeastern Aramaic varieties. Most speakers in Armenia elderly now. Many speakers use Russian as primary language. 'Aisor' is the Russian name for the people. The Assyrian and Chaldean separated denominationally during the 16th century. Syriac script is used. Christian (Nestorian). Bible 1852-1911. See main entry under Iraq.

AZERBAIJANI, NORTH ***(AZERI TURK, TURKLER, AZERBAYDZHANI)*** [AZE] 161,000 in Armenia (1993 Johnstone). In southern Dagestan, along the Caspian coast and beyond the Caucasian Mts. Altaic, Turkic, Southern, Azerbaijani. Dialects: KUBA, DERBENT, BAKU, SEMAKHA, SALIANY, LENKORAN, KAZAKH, AIRYM, BORCALA, TEREKEME, KYZYLBASH, NUKHA, ZAKATALY (MUGALY), KUTKASEN, EREVAN, NAKHICHEVAN, ORDUBAD, KIROVABAD, SUSA (KARABAKH), KARAPAPAK. Significant differences from South Azerbaijani in phonology, lexicon, morphology, and syntax. Used in schools, publications. Literacy rate in second language: High. Cyrillic script used in Azerbaijan. Radio programs. Shi'a Muslim. Bible 1891. See main entry under Azerbaijan.

KURMANJI ***(NORTHERN KURDISH, KERMANJI, KIRMANJI)*** [KUR] 58,000 in Armenia, including Yezid (1993 Johnstone), 84% speak it as mother tongue (1979). Indo-European, Indo-Iranian, Iranian, Western, Northwestern, Kurdish. Kurmanji is northern, Kurdi is southern. They are distinct languages. Kurmanji schools, texts. Language of wider communication. Cyrillic script. Newspapers, radio programs. Sunni Muslim, Shi'a Muslim, Christian. NT 1872. See main entry under Turkey.

LOMAVREN ***(ARMENIAN BOSHA, ARMENIAN BOSA, BOSHA, BOSA)*** [RMI] Armenia, southern Caucasus. Also spoken in Azerbaijan, Russia (Asia), Syria. Indo-European, Armenian. Gramatically restructured to be like Armenian with phonology and lexicon also influenced by Armenian. Investigation needed: intelligibility with Armenian.

AZERBAIJAN

National or official language: North Azerbaijani. 7,669,000 (1998 UN). Formerly part of USSR. Capital: Baku. 33,400 square miles. Literacy rate 98%. Also includes Aghul 32, Assyrian Neo-Aramaic 1,231, South Azerbaijani, Belarusan 4,782, Dargwa 863, Erzya 1,150, Western Farsi, Georgian 13,595, Karachay-Balkar 184, Lak 1,205, Lishan Didan 100, Lomavren, Osetin 2,315, Polish 1,264, Pontic, Romanian 1,397, Russian 475,000, Rutul 111, Tabassaran 279, Tatar 31,787, Turkish 18,000, Ukrainian 32,000. Information mainly from T. Sebeok 1963; A. Grjunberg 1963; Q. Voroshil 1972; A. Kibrik 1991. Muslim, Jewish. Data accuracy estimate: B. The number of languages listed for Azerbaijan is 14. Of those, all are living languages. Diversity index 0.37.

ARMENIAN ***(HAIEREN, SOMKHURI, ERMENICE, ARMJANSKI)*** [ARM] Nagorno-Karabakh region. Indo-European, Armenian. Dialect: WESTERN ARMENIAN. Christian, Monophysite. Bible 1853-1978. See main entry under Armenia.

AVAR ***(AVARO, DAGESTANI)*** [AVR] 44,000 in Azerbaijan (1989 census). Northwest, Zaqatala and Balakan regions. North Caucasian, Northeast, Avaro-Andi-Dido, Avar. Dialect: ZAQATALA (ZAKATALY, CHAR). Sunni Muslim. Bible portions 1979-1996. See main entry under Russia.

AZERBAIJANI, NORTH ***(AZERBAIJAN, AZERI TURK, AZERBAYDZHANI)*** [AZE] 6,069,453 in Azerbaijan. In the republics of the former USSR, 98% of the ethnic group speak Azerbaijani as mother tongue, 4,000,000 are monolingual (1989 census). Population total all countries 7,059,000. Including second language speakers: 15,000,000 (1999 WA). Azerbaijan, and southern Dagestan, along the Caspian coast in the southern Caucasian Mts. Also spoken in Armenia, Estonia, Georgia,

Kazakhstan, Kyrgyzstan, Russia (Asia), Turkmenistan, Uzbekistan. Altaic, Turkic, Southern, Azerbaijani. Dialects: QUBA, DERBEND, BAKU, SHAMAKHI, SALYAN, LENKARAN, QAZAKH, AIRYM, BORCALA, TEREKEME, QYZYLBASH, NUKHA, ZAQATALA (MUGALY), QABALA, YEREVAN, NAKHCHIVAN, ORDUBAD, GANJA, SHUSHA (KARABAKH), KARAPAPAK. Dialect differences are slight. The Qazakh dialect is not related to the Kazakh language. Significant differences from South Azerbaijani in phonology, lexicon, morphology, syntax, and loan words. Used in publications. Everyone is familiar with the standardized written and spoken forms. Taught as a second language in Russian language schools. They feel that North and South Azerbaijani are spoken by one people, one ethnic group, but recognize that there are differences in both the spoken and written forms. Each has problems accepting the written form of the other. National language. Dictionary. Grammar. Literacy rate in second language: High. Roman script official. Cyrillic script is widely used in Azerbaijan. Used in schools. Radio programs, TV. Shi'a Muslim, Sunni Muslim (Akiner). Bible 1891.

BUDUKH ***(BUDUX, BUDUG, BUKUKHI, BUDUGI)*** [BDK] 2,000 (1977 Voegelin and Voegelin). Quba region. North Caucasian, Northeast, Lezgian. Dialects: BUDUKH, YERGYUCH. Azerbaijani is used as the literary language. Used in everyday family communication. Traditional territory and way of life. Not a written language. Sunni Muslim.

JUDEO-TAT ***(JUDEO-TATIC, JEWISH TAT, BIK, DZHUHURIC, JUWRI, JUHURI)*** [TAT] 24,000 in Azerbaijan (1989 census). Northeast, especially Quba region, Baku, and Derbent (Russia). None in Iran. Indo-European, Indo-Iranian, Iranian, Western, Southwestern, Tat. Tats holding to the Gregorian (Armenian) church used to live in Madrasa village until the late 1980s, and spoke a variety of Tat similar to Judeo-Tat. They may have gone to Armenia or Russia. Jewish. Bible portions 1980. See main entry under Israel.

KHALAJ [KJF] Indo-European, Indo-Iranian, Iranian, Western, Northwestern. Related to Kurdish and Talysh. Pronounced with 2 short or front a's. Different from Turkic Khalaj in Iran. See main entry under Iran.

KHINALUGH ***(KHINALUG, XINALUG, KHINALUGI)*** [KJJ] 1,500. Quba. North Caucasian, Northeast, Lezgian. The most divergent Lezgian language. Azerbaijani is used as the literary language. Used in everyday family communication. Traditional territory and way of life. Not a written language. Muslim.

KRYTS ***(KRYZ, KRYC, KRYZY, KATSY, DZEK, DZHEK, DZHEKI)*** [KRY] 6,000 (1975 SIL). Quba. North Caucasian, Northeast, Lezgian. Dialects: KRYTS, DZHEK, XAPUT (KHAPUT), YERGYUDZH, ALYK. Dialects are quite distinct; perhaps separate languages. Azerbaijani is used as the literary language. Used in daily family communication. Traditional territory and way of life. Not a written language. Sunni Muslim.

KURMANJI ***(NORTHERN KURDISH, KERMANJI, KIRMANJI, KIRDASI, KIRMÂNCHA)*** [KUR] 20,000 in Azerbaijan (1989 census). Southwest. Indo-European, Indo-Iranian, Iranian, Western, Northwestern, Kurdish. Muslim. NT 1872. See main entry under Turkey.

LEZGI ***(LEZGIAN, LEZGHI, LEZGIN, KIURINTY)*** [LEZ] 171,400 in Azerbaijan (1996). Near the northeastern border with Russia and on the southern slopes of the main Caucasus chain. North Caucasian, Northeast, Lezgian. Dialect: QUBA. Quba is considerably different from the standard dialect. Bilingualism in Azerbaijani. Muslim. Bible portions 1990-1996. See main entry under Russia.

TALYSH ***(TALISH, TALESH, TALYSHI)*** [TLY] 800,000 to 1,000,000 in Azerbaijan (1996). Population total both countries 800,000 to 2,000,000. Along the Caspian coast south of the Viliazh-Chai River. There may be speakers in Central Asia and Siberia. Also spoken in Iran. Indo-European, Indo-Iranian, Iranian, Western, Northwestern, Talysh. Dialects: ASTARA, LENKORAN, LERIK, MASSALI. Northern Talyshi is in Azerbaijan and Iran. Dialects in Azerbaijan are close. Close to Harzani. Azerbaijani is used as literary language. Speakers are bilingual in Azerbaijani. Now taught in schools up to grade 4. Dictionary. Grammar. Arabic script was used. Newspapers. Shi'a Muslim and Sunni Muslim.

TAT, MUSLIM ***(MUSSULMAN TATI, MUSLIM TAT, TATI)*** [TTT] 22,000 in Azerbaijan (1979 census). Population total both countries 30,000 (1994 UBS). It may be declining around Baku, but still widely used in the mountainous area around Qonaqkend. Also spoken in Iran. Indo-European, Indo-Iranian, Iranian, Western, Southwestern, Tat. Dialects: QUBA, DEVECHI, QONAQKEND, QYZYL QAZMA, ARUSKUSH-DAQQUSHCHU (KHYZY), ABSHERON, BALAKHANI, SURAKHANI, LAHYJ, MALHAM. Difficult intelligibility with Judeo-Tat. Close to Farsi. It has vowel harmony like Azerbaijani. The first 4 dialects listed are northern, the next is central, the last 5 are southern. It is not clear if this distinction is linguistic or geographic. Balakhani are recent exiles from Iran, and their language is very close to Farsi. Lahyj may be a separate language. Lahyi use Azerbaijani as a literary language. Different from Takestani of Iran. Taught up to grade 3 in schools. Shi'a Muslim.

TSAKHUR ***(SAKHUR, TSAXUR, TSAKHURY, CAXUR)*** [TKR] 13,000 in Azerbaijan (1989 census). Population total all countries 20,000 (1994 UBS). Northwest. Also spoken in Russia (Europe), Uzbekistan. North Caucasian, Northeast, Lezgian. Muslim.

UDI ***(UDIN, UTI)*** [UDI] 4,200 in Azerbaijan (Nic) (1995). Population total all countries 8,800. Qabala, Nic and Mirzabeyli villages, and Oghuz, Oghuz town. Most Udi are reported to have left Oghuz. Also spoken in Georgia, Russia (Asia), Turkmenistan. North Caucasian, Northeast, Lezgian. Dialects: OGHUZ (VARTASHEN), NIDZH (NIJ, NIC, NIZH), OKTOMBERI. Dialects are inherently intelligible, but to what degree is not known. Oktomberi is reported to be more different from Nic Udi than Oghuz Udi is. One of the most divergent of the Lesgian languages. Russian and sometimes Azerbaijani used as literary languages; in some areas they use Armenian or Georgian. In Nic the children attend Russian language schools. Udi is used for intragroup communication. Up to 1954 schooling was in Azerbaijani. New primers and folk tales have been prepared for publication. Dictionary. Grammar. Not officially a written language. New cyrillic orthography. Deciduous forest. Plains. Peasant agriculturalists: horticulture; animal husbandry: hogs, cattle. Christian. Bible portions 1902.

BAHRAIN

State of Bahrain. Dawlat al-Bahrayn. National or official language: Standard Arabic. 595,000 (1998 UN). Literacy rate 49% to 75%. Also includes Western Farsi 48,000, Korean, Kurmanji, Malayalam, Tamil, Telugu, Urdu 18,500, people from the Philippines 22,000 (1995). Information mainly from T. M. Johnstone 1967; J. A. Fischer and O. Jastrow 1980; M. Al-Tajir 1982; C. Holes 1990. Shi'a Muslim, Sunni Muslim, Christian, Hindu. Blind population 62. Deaf population 35,529. Data accuracy estimate: B. The number of languages listed for Bahrain is 3. Of those, all are living languages. Diversity index 0.53.

ARABIC, BAHARNA SPOKEN ***(BAHRAINI SHI'ITE ARABIC, BAHARNAH, BAHARNA)*** [AFH] 300,000 (1995). Population total both countries 310,000. Also spoken in Oman. Afro-Asiatic, Semitic, Central, South, Arabic. Bilingualism in Gulf Spoken Arabic. Their dialect is stigmatized. Shi'a Muslim.

ARABIC, GULF SPOKEN ***(KHALIJI, GULF ARABIC)*** [AFB] 100,000 in Bahrain (1995). Afro-Asiatic, Semitic, Central, South, Arabic. Dialect: BAHRAINI GULF ARABIC. Sunni Muslim. See main entry under Iraq.

ARABIC, STANDARD ***(MODERN LITERARY ARABIC, FASIH, HIGH ARABIC)*** [ABV] Middle East, North Africa. Afro-Asiatic, Semitic, Central, South, Arabic. Used for education, official purposes. National language. Newspapers. Bible 1984-1991. See main entry under Saudi Arabia.

BANGLADESH

People's Republic of Bangladesh. GaNa Prajãtantrï Bangladesh. Formerly East Pakistan. National or official language: Bengali. 124,774,000 (1998 UN). Population density 2,026 per square mile. 531,000 speakers of Tibeto-Burman languages, 125,000 speakers of Austro-Asiatic languages (1991 J. Matisoff). Literacy rate 24% to 25%. Also includes Gujarati, Hindi 346,000, Oriya 13,299, Eastern Panjabi 9,677, Sadri 200,000, Urdu 600,000. Information mainly from B. Comrie 1987; J. Matisoff et al. 1996. Muslim, Hindu, Buddhist. Blind population 1,085. Deaf population 7,596,511. Deaf institutions: 14. Data accuracy estimate: B. The number of languages listed for Bangladesh is 38. Of those, all are living languages. Diversity index 0.31.

ARAKANESE ***("MAGHI", "MOGH", "MAGH", MASH)*** [MHV] 185,000 in Bangladesh (1993 Johnstone), .1% of the population. Southeast, Chittagong Hills area. Marma is in the hills and Rakhine along the coast. Some possibly in China. Sino-Tibetan, Tibeto-Burman, Lolo-Burmese, Burmish, Southern. Dialects: MARMA (MORMA), RAKHINE (RAKHAIN, YAKHAIN). Related to Burmese. Educated speakers know and read standard Burmese. Many men can speak Bengali. People came to Bangladesh over a period of time. The Marma and Rakhine are ethnic Arakanese Buddhists who speak a dialect of Arakanese Burmese, but were born in southeastern Bangladesh. SOV. Tropical forest. Agriculturalists. Buddhist, Muslim, Christian. Bible portions 1914. See main entry under Myanmar.

ASSAMESE ***(ASAMBE, ASAMI)*** [ASM] Indo-European, Indo-Iranian, Indo-Aryan, Eastern zone, Bengali-Assamese. Bible 1833, in press (1999). See main entry under India.

BENGALI ***(BANGA-BHASA, BANGALA, BANGLA)*** [BNG] 100,000,000 in Bangladesh (1994 UBS), 98% of the population (1990 WA). Population total all countries 207,000,000 first language speakers (1999 WA), 211,000,000 including second language speakers (1999 WA). Western. Also spoken in India, Malawi, Nepal, Saudi Arabia, Singapore, UAE, United Kingdom, USA. Indo-European, Indo-Iranian, Indo-Aryan, Eastern zone, Bengali-Assamese. Languages or dialects in the Bengali group according to Grierson: Central (Standard) Bengali, Western Bengali (Kharia Thar, Mal Paharia, Saraki), Southwestern Bengali, Northern Bengali (Koch, Siripuria), Rajbangsi, Bahe, Eastern Bengali (East Central, including Sylhetti), Haijong, Southeastern Bengali (Chakma), Ganda, Vanga,

Chittagonian (possible dialect of Southeastern Bengali). National language. Bengali script used. Muslim. Bible 1809-1998.

BISHNUPRIYA ***(BISHNUPURIYA, BISNA PURIYA, BISHNUPRIA MANIPURI)*** [BPY] Indo-European, Indo-Iranian, Indo-Aryan, Eastern zone, Bengali-Assamese. See main entry under India.

BURMESE ***(BAMA, BAMACHAKA, MYEN)*** [BMS] 231,000 in Bangladesh (1993 Johnstone). Area bordering Myanmar. Sino-Tibetan, Tibeto-Burman, Lolo-Burmese, Burmish, Southern. Dialect: BOMANG. People in Bangladesh speak Bomang, not Standard Burmese. Buddhist. Bible 1835, in press (1995). See main entry under Myanmar.

CHAK [CKH] 909 in Bangladesh (1981 census). Chittagong Hills. Most in Arakan Blue Mts., Myanmar. Unclassified. Distinct from Chakma. Tropical forest. Agriculturalists. Traditional religion. See main entry under Myanmar.

CHAKMA ***(TAKAM)*** [CCP] 260,577 in Bangladesh (1991 UBS). Southeast, Chittagong Hills area, and Chittagong City. Indo-European, Indo-Iranian, Indo-Aryan, Eastern zone, Bengali-Assamese. 6 dialects. Educated speakers know Bengali. Many men can speak Bengali. A more assimilated hill people. Tropical forest. Hills. Agriculturalists: paddy rice; fishermen. Buddhist, Christian. NT 1926-1991. See main entry under India.

CHIN, ASHO ***(SHO, SHOA, KHYANG, KHYENG, QIN)*** [CSH] 1,422 in Bangladesh (1981 census). Arakan Hills, Myanmar. Not in China. Sino-Tibetan, Tibeto-Burman, Kuki-Chin-Naga, Kuki-Chin, Southern, Sho. Dialects: CHITTAGONG, LEMYO, MINBU, SANDOWAY, THAYETMYO. Tropical forest. Agriculturalists. NT 1954. See main entry under Myanmar.

CHIN, BAWM ***(BAWN, BAWNG, BOM, BAWM)*** [BGR] 5,773 in Bangladesh (1981 census). Chittagong Hills. Sino-Tibetan, Tibeto-Burman, Kuki-Chin-Naga, Kuki-Chin, Central. Tropical forest. Agriculturalists. Bible 1989. See main entry under India.

CHIN, FALAM ***(HALLAM CHIN, HALAM, FALLAM, FALAM)*** [HBH] Sino-Tibetan, Tibeto-Burman, Kuki-Chin-Naga, Kuki-Chin, Northern. Dialects: CHOREI, ZANNIAT. SOV. Bible 1991. See main entry under Myanmar.

CHIN, HAKA ***(HAKA, BAUNGSHE)*** [CNH] Sino-Tibetan, Tibeto-Burman, Kuki-Chin-Naga, Kuki-Chin, Central. Dialects: LAI, KLANGKLANG (THLANTLANG), ZOKHUA, SHONSHE. Shonshe may be a separate language. Bible 1978. See main entry under Myanmar.

CHIN, KHUMI ***(KHUMI, KHAMI, KHIMI, KHWEYMI, KHUNI)*** [CKM] 1,188 in Bangladesh (1981 census). Sino-Tibetan, Tibeto-Burman, Kuki-Chin-Naga, Kuki-Chin, Southern, Khumi. Dialects: KHIMI, KHAMI, YINDU (YINDI), MATU, NGALA. Khami and Ngala may be separate languages. Tropical forest. Agriculturalists. NT 1959. See main entry under Myanmar.

CHIN, MRO [CMR] A few villages across from Rakhine State, Myanmar. Sino-Tibetan, Tibeto-Burman, Kuki-Chin-Naga, Kuki-Chin. About 13% lexical similarity with Mru [MRO] of Bangladesh and Myanmar. See main entry under Myanmar.

CHITTAGONIAN ***(CHITTAGONIAN BENGALI)*** [CIT] 14,000,000 (1998 H. Ebersole). Population total both countries 14,000,000 or more. Chittagong region. Also spoken in Myanmar. Indo-European, Indo-Iranian, Indo-Aryan, Eastern zone, Bengali-Assamese. Dialect: ROHINGA (AKYAB). Not inherently intelligible with Bengali, although considered to be a nonstandard Bengali dialect. A continuum of dialects from north to south, with a larger religious distinction between Muslim and others. An ethnic Bengali Muslim who speaks the Muslim variety of Chittagonian Bengali and was born in Arakan state, Myanmar is called a 'Rohinga'. The dialect is intelligible to those born in southeastern Bangladesh. Village women without access to TV do not understand Bengali. Many educated people understand some Bengali, but are not comfortable using it. All education is in Standard Bengali. Used for religious instruction in village mosques. Lower literacy rate than most of the country. TV. Muslim, Hindu, Christian.

DARLONG ***(DALONG)*** [DLN] 9,000 in Bangladesh. Population total both countries 15,000. Also spoken in India. Sino-Tibetan, Tibeto-Burman, Kuki-Chin-Naga, Kuki-Chin, Central. Also reported to be related to Tipura. NT 1995.

GARO ***(GARROW, MANDE)*** [GRT] 102,000 in Bangladesh (1993). Northeastern, Mymensingh plains. Sino-Tibetan, Tibeto-Burman, Jingpho-Konyak-Bodo, Konyak-Bodo-Garo, Bodo-Garo, Garo. Dialects: ABENG, ACHIK. The Achik dialect predominates among several inherently intelligible dialects. The Abeng dialect is in Bangladesh. Closest to Koch. Bible 1924-1994. See main entry under India.

HAJONG ***(HAIJONG)*** [HAJ] Indo-European, Indo-Iranian, Indo-Aryan, Eastern zone, Bengali-Assamese. See main entry under India.

HO ***(LANKA KOL)*** [HOC] Austro-Asiatic, Munda, North Munda, Kherwari, Mundari. Distinct from Ho (Hani) of Myanmar, China, Viet Nam, Laos. NT 1997. See main entry under India.

INDIAN SIGN LANGUAGE [INS] Deaf sign language. Not related to French, Spanish, American sign languages, or their group. Some influence from British Sign Language in the fingerspelling system and a few other signs, but most signs are unrelated to European sign systems. It developed indigenously in India. The Indian manual English system is hardly understandable to American Signed English. See main entry under India.

KHASI ***(KAHASI, KHASIYAS, KHUCHIA, KYI, COSSYAH, KHASSEE, KHASIE)*** [KHI] 85,088 in Bangladesh (1961 census). Northern. Austro-Asiatic, Mon-Khmer, Northern Mon-Khmer, Khasian. Dialects: KHASI (CHERRAPUNJI), LYNGNGAM (LNGNGAM), WAR. Bible 1891. See main entry under India.

KOCH ***(KOC, KOCCH, KOCE, KOCHBOLI, KONCH)*** [KDQ] Sino-Tibetan, Tibeto-Burman, Jingpho-Konyak-Bodo, Konyak-Bodo-Garo, Bodo-Garo, Koch. Dialects: BANAI, HARIGAYA, SATPARIYA, TINTEKIYA, WANANG. Dialect or separate language: A'tong. See main entry under India.

KOK BOROK ***(TRIPURI, TRIPURA, TIPURA, MRUNG, USIPI)*** [TRP] 78,000 in Bangladesh (1993 Johnstone). Sino-Tibetan, Tibeto-Burman, Jingpho-Konyak-Bodo, Konyak-Bodo-Garo, Bodo-Garo, Bodo. Dialects: JAMATIA, NOATIA, RIANG (TIPRA), HALAM, DEBBARMA. Bible, in press (1998). See main entry under India.

KURUX ***(KURUKH, URAON, ORAOAN)*** [KVN] Dravidian, Northern. Distinct from Nepali Kurux. NT 1950-1997. See main entry under India.

LUSHAI ***(LUSHEI, LUSAI, SAILAU, HUALNGO, WHELNGO, LEI)*** [LSH] 1,041 in Bangladesh (1981 census). Mizo Hills. Sino-Tibetan, Tibeto-Burman, Kuki-Chin-Naga, Kuki-Chin, Central. Dialects: RALTE, DULIEN, NGENTE, MIZO. Related to Zahao, Hmar, Pankhu, Paang. Tropical forest. Agriculturalists. Bible 1959-1995. See main entry under India.

MEGAM ***(MIGAM)*** [MEF] Northeastern. Sino-Tibetan, Tibeto-Burman, Jingpho-Konyak-Bodo, Konyak-Bodo-Garo, Bodo-Garo, Garo. Called a dialect of Garo, but may be a separate language.

MEITEI ***(MEITHEI, MEITHE, MITEI, MITHE, MEITEIRON, MANIPURI, KATHE, KATHI, PONNA)*** [MNR] 92,800 in Bangladesh (1982). Sino-Tibetan, Tibeto-Burman, Meithei. Hindu, traditional religion, Muslim, Christian. Bible 1984. See main entry under India.

MRU ***(MRO, MURUNG, MRUNG, MARU, NIOPRENG)*** [MRO] 20,000 in Bangladesh (1999 ABWE). Population total all countries 41,200. Southeastern, Chittagong Hills; 200 villages. Also spoken in India, Myanmar. Sino-Tibetan, Tibeto-Burman, Mru. SOV. Tropical forest. Agriculturalists. Traditional religion with some Buddhist elements. NT 1994.

MUNDARI ***(MUNDA, MANDARI, MUNARI, HORO, MONDARI, COLH)*** [MUW] Austro-Asiatic, Munda, North Munda, Kherwari, Mundari. Dialects: HASADA', LATAR, NAGURI, KERA'. Bible 1910-1932. See main entry under India.

PANKHU ***(PANKHO, PANKO, PANGKHU)*** [PKH] 2,278 in Bangladesh (1981 census). Bandarban, Rangamati, Kagrachori, and some in Malumghat and Chittagong. Sino-Tibetan, Tibeto-Burman, Kuki-Chin-Naga, Kuki-Chin, Central. Education for the few in school is in Bengali and English. Tropical forest. Agriculturalists. See main entry under India.

RAJBANGSI ***(RAJBANSI, TAJPURI)*** [RJB] Districts of Jalpaiguri, Cooch Behar. Indo-European, Indo-Iranian, Indo-Aryan, Eastern zone, Bengali-Assamese. Dialect: BAHE. See main entry under India.

RIANG ***(REANG, KAU BRU)*** [RIA] 1,011 in Bangladesh. Sino-Tibetan, Tibeto-Burman, Jingpho-Konyak-Bodo, Konyak-Bodo-Garo, Bodo-Garo, Bodo. Not the same as Riang of Myanmar, a Mon Khmer language. NT 1990. See main entry under India.

SADRI, ORAON [SDR] 84,000 to 200,000 in Bangladesh(1994). Throughout Rajshahi Division; in Chittagong Division, Moulvibazar and Hobigani districts; and Khulna Division, Jhenaidah District (Jhenaidah Thana, Moheshpur Thana), Kushtia District (Mirpur Thana), Magura District (Magura Thana). Indo-European, Indo-Iranian, Indo-Aryan, Eastern zone, Bihari. Dialects: BORAIL SADRI, NURPUR SADRI, UCHAI SADRI, MOKKAN TILA SADRI. The dialects listed may need separate literature. Inherent intelligibility of 7 Sadri varieties on Borail ranges from 70% to 93%; of 8 varieties on Nurpur from 78% to 94%. Lexical similarity of 14 Sadri varieties with Borail Sadri ranges from 88% to 97%. Speakers' bilingual proficiency in Bengali is limited. Vigorous. The Oraon people came from India over 100 years ago. Sometime in the past some Oraon shifted from Kurukh, a Dravidian language, to Sadri, which is Indo-Aryan. Some Oraon people still speak Kurukh. Literacy rate in second language: Much lower than 25%. Agriculturalists. Traditional religion, Hindu.

SANTALI ***(HOR, SATAR, SANTHALI, SANDAL, SANGTAL, SANTAL, HAR, SONTHAL)*** [SNT] 157,000 in Bangladesh (1993 Johnstone). Austro-Asiatic, Munda, North Munda, Kherwari, Santali. Dialects: KARMALI (KHOLE), KAMARI-SANTALI, LOHARI-SANTALI, MAHALI (MAHLE), MANJHI, PAHARIA. Bible 1914-1992. See main entry under India.

SHENDU ***(KHYEN, KHYENG, KHIENG, SHANDU, SANDU)*** [SHL] 1,000 in Bangladesh (1980 UBS). Population total both countries 1,000 or more. Also spoken in India. Sino-Tibetan, Tibeto-Burman, Kuki-Chin-Naga, Kuki-Chin, Southern, Sho. Close to Mara Shin (Lakher). Also related to Sho, Khyang, Thayetmo, Minbu, Chinbon, Lemyo.

SYLHETTI ***(SYLHETI, SYLHETTI BANGLA)*** [SYL] 5,000,000 in Bangladesh. Population total both countries 5,100,000. District of Sylhet, about 100 miles north of Dacca. Also possibly in India. Also spoken in United Kingdom. Indo-European, Indo-Iranian, Indo-Aryan, Eastern zone, Bengali-Assamese. Approximately 70% lexical similarity with Bengali. Bilingualism in Bengali. Educated speakers can read Bengali. Few women are educated. Muslim. Bible portions 1993.

TANGCHANGYA ***(TANCHANGYA)*** [TNV] 17,695 (1981 census). Indo-European, Indo-Iranian, Indo-Aryan, Eastern zone, Bengali-Assamese. Closely related to Chakma. Tropical forest. Agriculturalists.

TIPPERA ***(TIPPERA-BENGALI, TIPPERAH, TIPRA, TIPURA, TRIPERAH, TIPPURAH, TRIPURA)*** [TPE] 105,000 (1993 Johnstone). Chittagong Hills. Indo-European, Indo-Iranian, Indo-Aryan, Unclassified. 36 dialects. Many men can speak Bengali. Tropical forest. Agriculturalists. Traditional religion with Hindu elements. NT 1995.

USUI ***(UNSHOI, UNSUIY, USHOI)*** [USI] 4,010 (1981 census). Chittagong Hills. Indo-European, Indo-Iranian, Indo-Aryan, Unclassified. Closely related to Tippera. Investigation needed: intelligibility with Tippera. Tropical forest. Agriculturalists. Hindu, traditional religion.

BHUTAN

Kingdom of Bhutan, Druk-Yul. National or official language: Dzongkha. 2,004,000 (1998 UN). Literacy rate 15% to 18%. Also includes Assamese 30,000, Western Gurung, Limbu, Eastern Magar, Santali, Sherpa, Eastern Tamang. Information mainly from V. H. Coelho 1967; J. C. White 1971; N. Singh 1972; J. Matisoff 1991; J. Matisoff et al. 1996; G. Van Driem 1993; E. Andvic 1993. Lamaistic Buddhist, Hindu. Deaf population 105,435. Data accuracy estimate: C. The number of languages listed for Bhutan is 24. Of those, all are living languages. Diversity index 0.82.

ADAP [ADP] South central, between Damphu and Shemgang, Ada village, Wangdue Phodrang District. Sino-Tibetan, Tibeto-Burman, Himalayish, Tibeto-Kanauri, Tibetic, Tibetan, Southern. 77% lexical similarity with Dzongkha, 62% to 65% with Bumthangkha, 41% with Tshangla. May be the same as Tapadamteng (see Dzongkha).

BROKKAT ***(BROKSKAD)*** [BRO] 300 (1993 Van Driem). Dur in central Bumthang District. Sino-Tibetan, Tibeto-Burman, Himalayish, Tibeto-Kanauri, Tibetic, Tibetan, Southern. A different language from Brokpake (1993 Van Driem).

BROKPAKE ***(MIRA SAGTENGPA, DAKPA, BROKPA, DAP, MERA SAGTENGPA, SAGTENGPA, MERAGSAGSTENGKHA)*** [SGT] 5,000 including 2,000 in and around Mera, 3,000 in and around Sagteng (1993 Van Driem). Sakteng Valley east of Trashigang District. Sino-Tibetan, Tibeto-Burman, Himalayish, Tibeto-Kanauri, Tibetic, Tibetan, Southern. Related to Monpa of Tawang in Arunachal Pradesh, India. Speakers are called 'Dakpa'. Agriculturalists: corn, barley, beets; butter producers. 3,000 meters.

BUMTHANGKHA ***(BUMTANP, BUMTHAPKHA, BUMTANG, KEBUMTAMP, BHUMTAM, BUMTHANG, BUMTANGKHA)*** [KJZ] 30,000 (1993 Van Driem). Central. Bumthang and in the whole of central Bhutan. Mangdikha is in Mangdi District around Tongsa. Tsamangkha is on the east northeast border of Kurto. Salabekha is in the Yangtse District and Tawang and southeast Tibet. Sino-Tibetan, Tibeto-Burman, Himalayish, Tibeto-Kanauri, Tibetic, Tibetan, Eastern. Dialects: URA, TANG, CHOGOR, CHUNMAT. Khengkha and Bumtangkha are reported by one source to be intelligible with each other. Cuona Monpa is the same as, or closely related to, Bumthangkha (see Moinba in India and China). 92% lexical similarity with Khengkha. 47% to 52% with Dzongkha, 62% to 65% with Adap, 40% to 50% with Sharchagpakha. Gungdekha is an archaic language today reluctantly joined politically to the Khen or Bhumtam group. Ucan script.

CHALIKHA ***(CHALI, TSHALI, CHALIPKHA, TSHALINGPA)*** [TGF] 1,000 (1993 Van Driem). In and around Chali area, Shongar District, east Bhutan, north of Monggar. Sino-Tibetan, Tibeto-Burman, Himalayish, Tibeto-Kanauri, Tibetic, Tibetan, Eastern. Related to Bumthangkha and Kurtopakha. Investigation needed: intelligibility with Kurteopkha.

CHOCANGACAKHA ***(MAPHEKHA, RTSAMANGPA'IKHA, TSAGKAGLINGPA'IKHA, KURSMADKHA)*** [CHK] 20,000 (1993 Van Driem). East of Dzongkha, in lower areas of Monggar District, Tsamang and Tsakaling villages, and Lhuntsi District, Kurmet village. Sino-Tibetan, Tibeto-Burman, Himalayish, Tibeto-Kanauri, Tibetic, Tibetan, Southern. Related to Dzongkha.

DAKPAKHA [DKA] 1,000 (1993 Van Driem). Near Brokpake. Sino-Tibetan, Tibeto-Burman, Himalayish, Tibeto-Kanauri, Tibetic, Tibetan, Eastern. May be a dialect of Brokpake. Has been influenced by Dzalakha, and Brokpake.

DZALAKHA ***(DZALAMAT, YANGTSEBIKHA)*** [DZL] 15,000 (1993 Van Driem). Northeastern in Lhüntsi, Kurto District. Sino-Tibetan, Tibeto-Burman, Himalayish, Tibeto-Kanauri, Unclassified. Dialect: KHOMAKHA.

DZONGKHA ***(DRUKKE, DRUKHA, DUKPA, BHUTANESE, JONKHA, BHOTIA OF BHUTAN, BHOTIA OF DUKPA, ZONGKHAR, RDZONGKHA)*** [DZO] 160,000 (1993 Van Driem). Population total both countries 160,000 or more. Ha, Paru, Punakha districts. Also spoken in Nepal. Sino-Tibetan, Tibeto-Burman, Himalayish, Tibeto-Kanauri, Tibetic, Tibetan, Southern. Dialects: WANG-THE (THIMPHU-PUNAKHA), HA, NORTHERN THIMPHU. As different from Lhasa Tibetan as Nepali is from Hindi. Partially intelligible with Sikkimese (Drenjoke). Names listed as dialects may be separate languages. 48% lexical similarity with Sharchagpakha, 47% to 52% with Kebumtamp, 77% with Adap. 'Lhoke' means 'southern language'. National language. Grammar. Literacy rate in first language: Below 1%. Literacy rate in second language: Below 5%. Ucan script. Common school language. Bible portions 1970.

GONGDUK ***(GONGDUBIKHA)*** [GOE] 2,000 (1993 Van Driem). Sino-Tibetan, Tibeto-Burman, Himalayish, Tibeto-Kanauri, Tibetic, Tibetan. Retain the complex verbal agreement system of Proto Tibeto- Burman. Said to belong to one of the ancient populations of Bhutan.

KHENGKHA ***(KHENKHA, KHEN, KENG, KEN)*** [XKF] 40,000 (1993 Van Driem). Central, Kheng, near Bumthangkha. Sino-Tibetan, Tibeto-Burman, Himalayish, Tibeto-Kanauri, Tibetic, Tibetan, Eastern. Much dialect diversity. Khengkha, Kurtokha, and Bumthangkha are partly intelligible with each other. 92% lexical similarity with Bumthangkha; 65% with Adap, 47% with Dzongkha, 40% with Sharchagpakha. Investigation needed: intelligibility with Bumthang.

KURTOKHA ***(GURTÜ, KURTOPAKHA, KÜRTHÖPKA, KURTEOPKHA, KURTHOPKHA, KURTOBIKHA)*** [XKZ] 10,000 (1993 Van Driem). Northeastern, especially in Kurto. The dialect around Tangmachu is more divergent. Sino-Tibetan, Tibeto-Burman, Himalayish, Tibeto-Kanauri, Tibetic, Tibetan, Eastern. Related to Bumthangkha and Khengkha. Investigation needed: intelligibility with Bumthangkha, Khengkha, Tshalingpakha.

LAKHA ***(TSHANGKHA)*** [LKH] 8,000 (1993 Van Driem). Sino-Tibetan, Tibeto-Burman, Himalayish, Tibeto-Kanauri, Tibetic, Tibetan, Southern. Mountain slope.

LAYAKHA [LYA] Northern Punakha District, around Laya. Sino-Tibetan, Tibeto-Burman, Himalayish, Tibeto-Kanauri, Tibetic, Tibetan, Southern. Closely related to Dzongkha, but many divergent grammatical features significantly limit intelligibility between them.

LEPCHA ***(LAPCHE, RONG, RONGKE, RONGPA, NÜNPA)*** [LEP] 2,000 in Bhutan (1993 Van Driem). Lower valleys in the west and south. Sino-Tibetan, Tibeto-Burman, Himalayish, Tibeto-Kanauri, Lepcha. Dialects: ILAMMU, TAMSANGMU, RENGJONGMU. Agriculturalists, pastoralists. Buddhist. NT 1989. See main entry under India.

LHOKPU ***(LHOBIKHA)*** [LHP] 2,500 (1993 Van Driem). Between Samtsi and Phuntsoling. Sino-Tibetan, Tibeto-Burman, Himalayish, Tibeto-Kanauri, Tibetic, Tibetan. Said to be one of the ancient populations of Bhutan.

LUNANAKHA [LUK] 700 (1998). North, northeastern quadrant of Punakha Dzongkhak District, community of Lunana, on the Pho Chhu River north from Punakha, on the right fork about half way up the valley. Sino-Tibetan, Tibeto-Burman, Himalayish, Tibeto-Kanauri, Tibetic, Tibetan, Southern. Closely related to Dzongkha, but many divergent grammatical features limit intelligibility between them. Speakers are called 'Lunape'. They often take their herds over to Gasa District, north from Punakha up the Mo Chhu River. Alpine yak herdsmen.

NEPALI ***(NEPALESE, GORKHALI, GURKHALI, KHASKURA, PARBATIYA, EASTERN PAHARI)*** [NEP] 156,000 in Bhutan (1993 Van Driem). In the foothills the entire length of Bhutan, especially south central. Indo-European, Indo-Iranian, Indo-Aryan, Northern zone, Eastern Pahari. People are called 'Paharia'. May be the majority language of the south. Many are Bhutanese citizens. Hindu. Bible 1914-1978. See main entry under Nepal.

NUPBIKHA [NUB] Around Trongsa town. Sino-Tibetan, Tibeto-Burman, Himalayish, Tibeto-Kanauri, Tibetic, Tibetan, Eastern. Related to Bumthangkha. Has phonoloogical similarities to Khengkha. Speakers view their language as different from Bumthangkha.

NYENKHA ***(HENKHA, LAP, MANGSDEKHA)*** [NEH] 10,000 (1993 Van Driem). Sephu Geo. The Black River passes below their villages. Sino-Tibetan, Tibeto-Burman, Himalayish, Tibeto-Kanauri, Tibetic, Tibetan, Eastern. Dialects: PHOBJIKHA, CHUTOBIKHA. Related to Bumthangkha. Mountain slope.

OLEKHA ***(MONPA, OLE MÖNPA)*** [OLE] 1,000 (1993 Van Driem). The 2 dialects have the Black Mountains between them, central Bhutan. Sino-Tibetan, Tibeto-Burman, Himalayish, Tibeto-Kanauri, Tibetic, Tibetan, Eastern. Retained complex verbal system of Proto Tibeto-Burman. 2 main dialects. Said to be one of the ancient populations of Bhutan. Grammar.

TIBETAN ***(BHOKHA)*** [TIC] 4,000 in Bhutan (1996). Sino-Tibetan, Tibeto-Burman, Himalayish, Tibeto-Kanauri, Tibetic, Tibetan, Central. Refugees from Tibet since 1959. People of Tibetan origin are referred to as 'Bhotia'. Lamaist. Bible 1948. See main entry under China.

TSEKU ***(TSUKU, TZUKU)*** [TSK] Sino-Tibetan, Tibeto-Burman, Himalayish, Tibeto-Kanauri, Tibetic, Tibetan, Central. This may be an alternate name for a language variety listed under another name, or it may only be in Tibet. See main entry under China.

TSHANGLA ***(SANGLA, SHARCHAGPAKHA, SARCHAPKKHA, SHACHOPKHA, SHACHOBIIKHA, TSANGLA, MENBA, MONPA)*** [TSJ] 138,000 in Bhutan (1993 Van Driem). Population total all countries 145,000. Eastern and southeastern Bhutan, especially in Tashigang and Dungsam. Also spoken in China, India. Sino-Tibetan, Tibeto-Burman, Himalayish, Tibeto-Kanauri, Tibetic, Bodish, Tshangla. 40% to 50% lexical similarity with Bumthangkha, 48% with Dzongkha, 41% with Adap. A speaker is called 'Schachop' in Dzongkha, 'Sharchhokpa' (pl.). Not the same as Tsanglo (Angami Naga) of Assam, India. It may also be classified as North Assam, Monpa. Literacy rate in first language: Below 1%. Literacy rate in second language: Below 5%. Ucan script. Bible portions.

BRUNEI

State of Brunei Darussalam. Negara Brunei Darussalam. National or official languages: English, Malay. 315,000 (1998 UN). Literacy rate 85% to 95%. Also includes Korean, Nepali, people from South Asia 4,200, others from the Philippines. Information mainly from R. Needham 1954; S. Wurm and S. Hattori 1981; K. Purnama 1991; P. Martin 1991; P. Martin, C. Oxog, and G. Poedjosoedarmo 1996. Muslim, Chinese traditional religion, Christian, traditional religion, Hindu. Data accuracy estimate: B. The number of languages listed for Brunei is 17. Of those, all are living languages. Diversity index 0.45.

BELAIT ***(BALAIT JATI, LEMETING, METING)*** [BEG] 700 (1995 P. Martin). Scattered areas in Belait District, Kampung Kiudang, in Tutong District. Austronesian, Malayo-Polynesian, Western Malayo-Polynesian, Borneo, Northwest, North Sarawakan, Berawan-Lower Baram, Lower Baram, Central, A. Related to Kiput, Baram and Tinjar. 54% lexical similarity with Tutong 2. Used more among those above 19 years old. Shift toward Brunei in progress. Recognized by the government as an indigenous group. The Muslim Belait are Malay in orientation. The non-Muslims retain their Belait identity more. Heavy intermarriage with Tutong 1, Bisaya, and Chinese. Muslim.

BISAYA, BRUNEI ***(BISAYAH, BISAYA BUKIT, VISAYAK, BEKIAU, LORANG BUKIT, BASAYA, BESAYA, BISAIA, JILAMA BAWANG, JILAMA SUNGAI, SOUTHERN BISAYA)*** [BSB] 600 (1984 Dunn). East of Tutong 1 and east to the coast, west of Seria, a few villages near the Sarawak border. Austronesian, Malayo-Polynesian, Western Malayo-Polynesian, Borneo, Northwest, Sabahan, Dusunic, Bisaya, Southern. 78% to 79% lexical similarity with Sarawak Bisaya, 57% to 59% with Sabah Bisaya, and about 50% with other Dusunic languages. Recognized by the government as an indigenous group.

BRUNEI ***(BRUNEI-KADAIAN, ORANG BUKIT)*** [KXD] 250,000 in Brunei (1984 SIL). Population total both countries 304,000 (1984 SIL). Brunei is in the capital, Brunei-Muara District, and the coastal strip. Kedayan is in West Brunei-Muara District and Tutong District. Also spoken in Malaysia (Sabah). Austronesian, Malayo-Polynesian, Western Malayo-Polynesian, Sundic, Malayic, Malayan, Local Malay. Dialects: BRUNEI MALAY, KEDAYAN (KADAIAN, KADAYAN, KADIAN, KADIEN, KADYAN, KARAYAN, KEDYAN, KEDIEN. KERAYAN), KAMPONG AYER. Brunei, Kadayan, and Kampong Ayer have 94% to 95% lexical similarity with each other, 80% to 82% lexical similarity with Standard Malay. Bilingualism in Malay. All ages. The de facto national dialect. Very vigorous use. Brunei is used by those in Bandar Seri Begawan and surroundings, and by young people, and educated older people from different language or dialect backgrounds. Brunei and Kadayan are both recognized by the government as indigenous groups. 'Orang Bukit' is the name of the people. Investigation needed: bilingual proficiency, attitudes toward Malay. Kadayan: agriculturalists, Kampong Ayer: fishermen and craftsmen in Water Village. Muslim.

CHINESE, HAKKA ***(HAKKA)*** [HAK] 3,000 in Brunei, 5.94% of ethnic Chinese (1979). 44,400 speakers of all Chinese languages (1989). Sino-Tibetan, Chinese. Bible 1916. See main entry under China.

CHINESE, MANDARIN [CHN] 15,000 in Brunei, 29.7% of ethnic Chinese (1979). Sino-Tibetan, Chinese. Bible 1874-1983. See main entry under China.

CHINESE, MIN DONG [CDO] 6,000 in Brunei, 11.88% of ethnic Chinese (1979). Sino-Tibetan, Chinese. Dialect: FOOCHOW. Bible 1884-1905. See main entry under China.

CHINESE, MIN NAN ***(MIN NAN, MINNAN)*** [CFR] 10,000 in Brunei (1979). Sino-Tibetan, Chinese. Dialects: CHAOCHOW (TIUCHIU, TEOCHOW), HAINAN, FUJIAN (HOKKIEN). Bible 1933. See main entry under China.

CHINESE, YUE ***(YUE, YUEH, CANTONESE)*** [YUH] 3,500 in Brunei, 6.93% of ethnic Chinese (1979). Sino-Tibetan, Chinese. Bible 1894-1981. See main entry under China.

ENGLISH [ENG] 8,000 in Brunei. 16% of ethnic Chinese speak English as first language. Probably other first language speakers. Indo-European, Germanic, West, English. Government, education. Used increasingly by educated speakers as first or second language. National language. Newspapers, TV. Bible 1535-1989. See main entry under United Kingdom.

IBAN ***(SEA DAYAK)*** [IBA] 15,000 in Brunei (1995 P. Martin). Rural areas of Belait and Tutong districts, and Temburong District. Austronesian, Malayo-Polynesian, Western Malayo-Polynesian, Sundic, Malayic, Malayic-Dayak, Ibanic. Dialects: BATANG LUPAR, BUGAU. Dictionary. SVO. Bible 1988. See main entry under Malaysia, Sarawak.

LUNDAYEH ***(LUN BAWANG, LUN DAYE, BRUNEI MURUT, SOUTHERN MURUT, MURUT)*** [LND] 300 in Brunei (1987 Langub). 7 villages in Temburong District. Austronesian, Malayo-Polynesian, Western Malayo-Polynesian, Borneo, Northwest, North Sarawakan, Dayic, Kelabitic. Dialect: TRUSAN. Not Murutic, although sometimes called Southern Murut. 'Murut' is recognized by the government as an indigenous group. Christian (Lunbawang, some Lundayeh), traditional religion (others). Bible 1982. See main entry under Indonesia, Kalimantan.

MALAY ***(STANDARD MALAY)*** [MLI] Austronesian, Malayo-Polynesian, Western Malayo-Polynesian, Sundic, Malayic, Malayan, Local Malay. Used only in formal domains, like religion, government. Official language. Taught in school through third grade. Used in the classroom through the final year. Newspapers, radio programs, TV. Sunni Muslim. Bible 1733-1993. See main entry under Malaysia, Peninsular.

MELANAU ***(MILANAU, MILANO, BELANA'U)*** [MEL] 200 Mukah in Brunei (1995 P. Martin). Around Kuala Belait town. Austronesian, Malayo-Polynesian, Western Malayo-Polynesian, Borneo, Northwest, Melanau-Kajang, Melanau. Dialect: MUKAH-OYA (MUKAH, MUKA, OYA, OYA', OGA). Bilingualism in Malay. Mukah is spoken in Brunei. Tropical forest. Agriculturalists: sago, rice, coconut, rubber; fishermen; loggers; animal husbandry: chickens, goats, water buffalos; traders with Iban. Muslim. See main entry under Malaysia, Sarawak.

PENAN, EASTERN ***("PUNAN")*** [PEZ] East of the Baram River, Apoh River district. Austronesian, Malayo-Polynesian, Western Malayo-Polynesian, Borneo, Punan-Nibong. Dialect: PENAN APOH. A distinct but closely related language to Western Penan and Kenyah, but not inherently intelligible to each others' speakers. See main entry under Malaysia, Sarawak.

PENAN, WESTERN [PNE] 50 in Brunei (1988 Lian). West of the Baram River. Austronesian, Malayo-Polynesian, Western Malayo-Polynesian, Borneo, Punan-Nibong. Dialects: NIBONG (NIBON, PENAN NIBONG), BOK PENAN (BOK), PENAN SILAT, PENAN GANG (GANG), PENAN LUSONG (LUSONG), SIPENG (SPENG), PENAN LANYING, JELALONG PENAN. Not closely related to other languages. Bilingualism in Iban. They consider "Punan", meaning 'to quarrel' to be derogatory. Traditionalists are nomadic and semi-nomadic; Muslims are settled. Schools. Tropical forest. Subsistence agriculturalists, hunter-gatherers. Muslim, traditional religion. NT 1974, out of print. See main entry under Malaysia, Sarawak.

TUTONG 1 ***(DUSUN)*** [TTX] 15,000 in Brunei (1995 P. Martin). Population total both countries 25,000 (1981 Wurm and Hattori). Central and interior Belait and Tutong districts, east of Bisaya, south of Tutong 2. May not be in Sarawak. Also spoken in Malaysia (Sarawak). Austronesian, Malayo-Polynesian, Western Malayo-Polynesian, Borneo, Northwest, Sabahan, Dusunic, Bisaya, Southern. Bilingualism in Brunei Malay. 72% of parents below 40 years old use Tutong with their children. In mixed marriages, 57% of parents use Brunei Malay with children. Distinct from Tutong 2 in Baram-Tinjar Subgroup. 'Dusun' is recognized by the government as an indigenous group. Muslim.

TUTONG 2 ***(TUTUNG)*** [TTG] 12,000 (1996 Martin, Ozog, and Poedjosoedarmo). Around Tutong town on the coast and central Tutong District. Austronesian, Malayo-Polynesian, Western Malayo-Polynesian, Borneo, Northwest, North Sarawakan, Berawan-Lower Baram, Lower Baram, Central, B. 54% lexical similarity with Belait. Bilingualism in Brunei Malay. 63% of parents below 40 years old use Tutong 2 with their children. In mixed marriages, 48% use Brunei Malay with their children. They have pride in their language, and use it for interethnic communication. Different from Tutong 1 in Dusunic, Bisaya Group. Tutong 2 is recognized by the government as an indigenous group. Dictionary. Muslim.

CAMBODIA

State of Cambodia. Formerly Kampuchea, Khmer Republic. National or official language: Central Khmer. 10,716,000 (1998 UN). 6,467,000 or 94.3% speakers of Austro-Asiatic languages, 125,000 or 1.9% speakers of Austronesian languages (1990). Literacy rate 48% to 50%. Also includes Mandarin Chinese 340,000, Lao 17,000, Vietnamese 600,000. Information mainly from F. Lebar, G. Hickey, J. Musgrave 1964; D. Thomas and R. Headley 1970; S. Wurm and S. Hattori 1981. Theravada Buddhist, secular, traditional religion, Muslim. Blind population 40,000 (1982 WCE). Deaf population 622,366.

Data accuracy estimate: B,C. The number of languages listed for Cambodia is 19. Of those, all are living languages. Diversity index 0.31.

BRAO ***(BRAOU, PROUE, BROU, LOVE, LAVE, LAVEH)*** [BRB] 5,286 in Cambodia (1980 Diffloth). Northeastern Cambodia on the Laos border, Rattanakiri Province. Austro-Asiatic, Mon-Khmer, Eastern Mon-Khmer, Bahnaric, West Bahnaric, Brao-Kravet. Closely related to Krung 2, Kravet, and Sou. See main entry under Laos.

CHAM, WESTERN ***(CAMBODIAN CHAM, TJAM, CHAM, NEW CHAM)*** [CJA] 220,000 in Cambodia (1992 govt. figure). Population total all countries 253,100 or more. Near the major cities and along the Mekong. Also spoken in Australia, France, Indonesia, Libya, Malaysia, Saudi Arabia, Thailand, USA, Viet Nam, Yemen. Austronesian, Malayo-Polynesian, Western Malayo-Polynesian, Sundic, Malayic, Achinese-Chamic, Chamic, South, Coastal, Cham-Chru. The language differs somewhat from Eastern Cham of central Viet Nam. Devanagari-based script. Roman script under discussion in USA and elsewhere. Muslim.

CHONG ***(CHAWNG, SHONG, XONG)*** [COG] 5,000 possibly in Cambodia. Population total both countries 8,000 (1981 Wurm and Hattori). Thai-Cambodia border southeast of Chantaburi, Pursat Province. Also spoken in Thailand. Austro-Asiatic, Mon-Khmer, Eastern Mon-Khmer, Pearic, Western, Chong. Somray in Cambodia is a separate but related language.

JARAI ***(DJARAI, GIA-RAI, JORAI, CHO-RAI, CHOR, MTHUR, CHRAI, GIO-RAI)*** [JRA] 15,000 or more (1998). Ratankiri Province, principally the districts of Bokeo, Andons, Meas, O Yadou, along northeast border near Viet Nam. Austronesian, Malayo-Polynesian, Western Malayo-Polynesian, Sundic, Malayic, Achinese-Chamic, Chamic, South, Plateau. Dialects: PUAN, HODRUNG (HDRUNG), JHUE, ARÁP, HABAU (HO-BAU), TO-BUAN, SESAN, CHUTY, PLEIKLY, GOLAR. Possibly largely Puan (To-Buan) dialect. A different script is used in Cambodia and Viet Nam. NT 1974, out of print. See main entry under Viet Nam.

KACO' ***(KACHAH')*** [XKK] 2,000 (1992 G. Diffloth). Rattanakiri Province. Austro-Asiatic, Mon-Khmer, Eastern Mon-Khmer, Bahnaric, Central Bahnaric. A distinct language, not intelligible to Tampuan speakers. Speakers are not bilingual.

KHMER, CENTRAL ***(KHMER, CAMBODIAN)*** [KMR] 5,932,800 in Cambodia, about 90% of the population (1990). Population total all countries 7,039,200. Including second language speakers: 8,000,000 (1999 WA). Throughout the country. Also spoken in China, France, Laos, USA, Viet Nam. Austro-Asiatic, Mon-Khmer, Eastern Mon-Khmer, Khmer. Distinct from Northern Khmer of Thailand. National language. Grammar. SVO. Bible 1954-1998.

KRAOL [RKA] 2,600 (1992 G. Diffloth). Kratie Province. Austro-Asiatic, Mon-Khmer, Eastern Mon-Khmer, Bahnaric, South Bahnaric, Sre-Mnong, Mnong, Southern-Central Mnong. A distinct language, not intelligible to Mnong speakers. Not bilingual. Different from the Kraol dialect of Kuy.

KRAVET ***(KOWET, KHVEK, KAVET)*** [KRV] 3,012 (1988 govt. figure). Northeastern. Austro-Asiatic, Mon-Khmer, Eastern Mon-Khmer, Bahnaric, West Bahnaric, Brao-Kravet. Investigation needed: intelligibility with Brao, Kru'ng.

KRU'NG 2 ***(KRUENG)*** [KRR] 9,368 (1982 G. Diffloth). Northeastern, Rattanakiri Province and eastern Stung Treng. Austro-Asiatic, Mon-Khmer, Eastern Mon-Khmer, Bahnaric, West Bahnaric, Brao-Kravet. Brao, Kravet, Krung 2 in Cambodia are inherently intelligible with each other. Central Khmer is known to a lesser extent than Lao for second language use. Different from Krung 1 dialect of Rade in Viet Nam.

KUY ***(KUAY)*** [KDT] 15,495 or more in Cambodia (1989). Northeastern Cambodia, all districts of Preah Vihear, eastern Siem Reap, northern Kampong Thom, western Stung Traeng, and several areas of Kratie Province. Austro-Asiatic, Mon-Khmer, Eastern Mon-Khmer, Katuic, West Katuic, Kuay-Yoe. Dialects: DAMREY, ANLOUR, O, KRAOL, ANTRA, NA NHYANG. Bilingualism in Central Khmer. A different script is used in Cambodia and Thailand. Literacy rate in first language: 1% to 5%. Literacy rate in second language: 50%. NT 1978. See main entry under Thailand.

LAMAM ***(LMAM)*** [LMM] 1,000 (1981 Wurm and Hattori). Near northeast corner on the Viet Nam border. Austro-Asiatic, Mon-Khmer, Eastern Mon-Khmer, Bahnaric, Central Bahnaric. Related to Bahnar, Tampuan, Alak 1.

MNONG, CENTRAL ***(PHONG, PHNONG, BUDONG, PHANONG)*** [MNC] 19,000 in Cambodia (1988 govt. figure). Northeastern, 80% of Mondolkiri Province, all districts. Austro-Asiatic, Mon-Khmer, Eastern Mon-Khmer, Bahnaric, South Bahnaric, Sre-Mnong, Mnong, Southern-Central Mnong. Dialects: BIAT, PREH, BU NAR, BU RUNG, DIH BRI, BU DANG. Biat is the main dialect of Cambodian Mnong. It may be a separate language from Central Mnong. Other dialect variation is slight. Central Khmer only spoken well by a few individuals. Others have limited ability. Investigation needed: intelligibility with Biat. Literacy rate in second language: Low. See main entry under Viet Nam.

PEAR ***(POR, KOMPONG THOM)*** [PCB] 1,300 (1988 govt. figure). Southwestern, Kompong Thom. Austro-Asiatic, Mon-Khmer, Eastern Mon-Khmer, Pearic, Eastern.

SAMRE [SCC] 200 (1981 Wurm and Hattori). Just north of Siemreap. Austro-Asiatic, Mon-Khmer, Eastern Mon-Khmer, Pearic, Western, Samre. Related to Sa'och, Suoy, Pear. Investigation needed: intelligibility with Suoy, Pear, Sa'och.

SA'OCH ***(SAUCH, SAOTCH)*** [SCQ] 500 (1981 Wurm and Hattori). Southwest near Kompong Som on the coast. Austro-Asiatic, Mon-Khmer, Eastern Mon-Khmer, Pearic, Western, Chong. Related to Samre, Suoy, Pear. Investigation needed: intelligibility with Suoy, Pear, Samre.

SOMRAY [SMU] 2,000 (1981 Wurm and Hattori). West; north, east, and west of Phum Tasanh, and Tanyong River around Phum Pra Moi; 2 areas. Austro-Asiatic, Mon-Khmer, Eastern Mon-Khmer, Pearic, Western, Samre. Related to Chong. Investigation needed: intelligibility with Chong.

STIENG, BULO ***(KAJIANG)*** [STI] 3,571 to 5,000 in Cambodia (1992 G. Diffloth). Eastern, Kratie Province, Snuol District, and southern Mondolkiri. Austro-Asiatic, Mon-Khmer, Eastern Mon-Khmer, Bahnaric, South Bahnaric, Stieng-Chrau. Dialects: BUDIP, BULACH, BULO. Bilingualism in Mnong, Khmer. Literacy rate in second language: Low. Bible portions 1971. See main entry under Viet Nam.

SUOY [SYO] 200 (1981 Wurm and Hattori). Central, northwest of Phnom Penh. Austro-Asiatic, Mon-Khmer, Eastern Mon-Khmer, Pearic, Western, Suoy. Related to Sa'och, Samre, Pear. Investigation needed: intelligibility with Samre, Pear, Sa'och.

TAMPUAN ***(TAMPHUAN, TAMPUEN, TAMPUON, KHA TAMPUON, CAMPUON, PROON, PROONS)*** [TPU] 25,000 (1998). Northeast border area, south of Brao, west of Jarai, Central Rattanakiri Province. Austro-Asiatic, Mon-Khmer, Eastern Mon-Khmer, Bahnaric, Central Bahnaric. Related to Bahnar, Lamam, Alak 1, but geographically separated. Closest to Kaco', a related but separate language. Central Khmer is known by some individuals, Lao by all or most. Exogamous clans, together with Kaco' and Jarai, that override ethnic and linguistic boundaries.

CHINA

People's Republic of China. Zhonghua Renmin Gongheguo. National or official language: Mandarin Chinese. 1,262,358,000 (1998 UN). 55 official minority nationalities total 91,200,314 or 6.5% of the population (1990). Han Chinese 1,033,057,000 or 93.5% (J. Matisoff). Also includes Central Khmer 1,000, Portuguese 2,000, Shan, Tai Dam 10,000, Tai Don 10,000. Information mainly from J. Dreyer 1976; S. Wurm et al. 1987; J-O Svantesson 1989, 1995; J. Janhumen 1989; J. Matisoff et al. 1996; J. Evans 1999. Secular, Chinese traditional religion, Buddhism, Taoism, Christian, Muslim, traditional religion. Blind population 2,000,000. Deaf population 3,000,000 (1986 Gallaudet University). Deaf institutions: 7. Data accuracy estimate: B. The number of languages listed for China is 202. Of those, 201 are living languages and 1 is extinct. Diversity index 0.48.

ACHANG ***(ACHUNG, ATSANG, ACH'ANG, ACANG, AHCHAN, NGACANG, NGATSANG, NGACHANG, NGAC'ANG, NGO CHANG, MÖNGHSA)*** [ACN] 27,708 in China (1990 census). Population total both countries 29,400 or more. Dehong Dai-Jingpo Autonomous Prefecture and Baoshan District, western Yunnan Province, along the Myanmar border. Also spoken in Myanmar. Sino-Tibetan, Tibeto-Burman, Lolo-Burmese, Burmish, Northern. Dialects: LONGCHUAN, LIANGHE, LUXI. Longchuan is more distinct from the other dialects, and has more Dai loan words. Lianghe and Luxi use many Chinese loan words. There are also Burmese loan words. Spoken Chinese and Dai are in common use as second languages. Written Chinese is also in use. An official nationality in China. Unidentified ethnic groups in the area: Ben Ren, Hknong. SOV, four tones. Literacy rate in second language: 39%. Not a written language. Agriculturalists: rice, craftsmen. Polytheist, Hinayana Buddhist. NT 1992.

AI-CHAM ***(JIAMUHUA, JINHUA, ATSAM)*** [AIH] 2,300 speakers (1986). 13 villages in Di'e and Boyao townships in Libo County of the Qiannan Buyi-Miao Autonomous Prefecture in southern Guizhou Province. Tai-Kadai, Kam-Tai, Kam-Sui. Dialects: DI'E, BOYAO. A separate language officially included under the Bouyei nationality. The two dialects listed have phonological differences, but are largely intelligible to each other's speakers. Similar to Mak. SVO, 6 tones.

AINU ***(AYNU, AINI, ABDAL)*** [AIB] 5,000 (1988). Yengixar (Shule) town, Hanalik and Paynap villages in the Kashgar area, and Gewoz village near Hoban; Hetian, Luopu, Moyu, Shache, Yingjisha and Shulekuche counties of southwestern Xinjiang Autonomous Region. Altaic, Turkic, Eastern. The language has the same grammar as Uyghur but much Persian vocabulary. Some consider it to be a dialect of Uyghur, others to be an Iranian language heavily influenced by Uyghur. The government counts them as Uyghur. They speak Aynu in the family, but Uyghur to outsiders. The Uyghur despise them and call them 'Abdal' or 'beggar'. They do not intermarry with the Uyghur. Different from the Ainu spoken in Russia and Japan. Caste of circumcisers.

AKHA ***(KAW, EKAW, KO, AKA, IKAW, AK'A, AHKA, KHAKO, KHA KO, KHAO KHA KO, IKOR, AINI, YANI)*** [AKA] 103,000 in China (1990). Southwest Yunnan. Sino-Tibetan, Tibeto-Burman, Lolo-Burmese, Loloish, Southern, Akha, Hani, Ha-Ya. 'Aini' may be the same as the Yani dialect of Hani. It is reported that, aside from loan word differences, the Akha of Thailand and Myanmar is virtually identical to the Yani dialect of Hani spoken in Xishuangbanna (Yunnan). Dictionary. SOV, 3 tones. Traditional religion, Christian. NT 1968-1987. See main entry under Myanmar.

AMDO ***(ANDUO, NGAMBO)*** [ADX] 809,500 including 538,500 Hbrogpa, 97,600 Rongba, 112,800 Rongmahbrogpa, 60,600 Rtahu (1987 Wurm et al.). Huangnan, Hainan, Haibei, and Guoluo (Golog) Tibetan Autonomous prefectures and the Haixi Mongolian-Tibetan-Kazakh Autonomous Prefecture of Qinghai Province; in the Gannan Tibetan Autonomous Prefecture and Tianzhu Autonomous County of southwestern Gansu Province, and in parts of the Ganzi and Aba (Ngawa) Tibetan Autonomous prefectures of western and northern Sichuan Province. Sino-Tibetan, Tibeto-Burman, Himalayish, Tibeto-Kanauri, Tibetic, Tibetan, Northern. Dialects: HBROGPA, RONGBA, RONGMAHBROGPA, RTAHU. Not intelligible with Central Tibetan or Kham varieties. Those listed as dialects may not be intelligible with each other. About 70% lexical similarity with Central Tibetan and Kham. All ages. Speakers in 'Golog' are called 'Golog', 'Ngolok', 'Mgolog', 'Ggolo'. SOV, many onset clusters, not tonal. Pastoral: yak, sheep; wool. Lamaist Buddhist.

ATUENCE ***(ATUENTSE, ANSHUENKUAN NYARONG, NYARONG, NGANSHUENKUAN)*** [ATF] 520,000. Yunnan-Tibet border. Sino-Tibetan, Tibeto-Burman, Himalayish, Tibeto-Kanauri, Tibetic, Tibetan, Central. Probably included officially under the Tibetan nationality. It may not be a separate language. It has been identified as Central Bodish (Shafer 1955, 1966), Archaic Nomad Dialect of Tibetan (Roerich 1931), or Central Tibetan (Voegelin and Voegelin 1977). This may be the same as the Rgalthangwas language in Yunnan on the Tibet Autonomous Region border. There is a town named 'Atuentze' in Dechen Tibetan Autonomous Prefecture, Yunnan, on the border of the Tibet Autonomous Region. Lamaist Buddhist, Christian.

AYI [AYX] Fugong and Gongshan counties, Nujiang Nu-Lisu Autonomous Prefecture of northwestern Yunnan. Sino-Tibetan, Tibeto-Burman, Unclassified. Subclassification unknown, perhaps Lolo. Spoken by members of the Nu nationality. SOV, 4 tones, 3-way obstruent distinction (voiced-voiceless-aspirated), voiced and voiceless nasals and liquids, inflecting. Loan words from Chinese, Lisu, Bai, Burmese, and Tibetan.

BA PAI ***(YAO MIN, ZAOMIN, DZAO MIN, YAU MIN)*** [BPN] 62,000 (1995 McConnell). Liannan and Yangshan counties of northern Guangdong Province, and Yizhang County of southern Hunan Province. Hmong-Mien, Mienic, Zaomin. Phonological and lexical differences from Mien of Thailand and Laos make communication difficult. Also different from Mian Jin and Biao Jiao. 61% lexical similarity with Iu Mien, 59% with Kim Mun, 58% with Biao-Jiao Mien. Officially in the Yao nationality. Mountain slope. Swidden agriculturalists: paddy rice. Daoist.

BAI ***(PAI, MINJIA, MINCHIA, MINKIA, LABBU, NAMA, LEME)*** [PIQ] 900,000 speakers (1990 J-O Svantesson), out of ethnic group of 1,594,827 (1990 census). Northwest Yunnan, between the Lancang (Mekong) and Jinsha rivers, on the Dali Plain. 85% of Bai are in Dali Bai Autonomous Prefecture, others elsewhere in Yunnan Province, some in Hunan, Sichuan, and Guizhou provinces. Sino-Tibetan, Tibeto-Burman, Bai. Dialects: DALI (TALI-XIANGYUN, XIANGYUN-DALI, SOUTHERN BAI), JIANCHUAN (CENTRAL BAI, HEQING-JIANCHUAN, HOKING-JIANCHUAN), BIIJIANG (LANBI, BIJIANG-LANPING, LANPING-BIJIANG, NORTHERN BAI). Classification difficult because of heavy borrowing (60% to 70%) from Chinese. The 3 dialects may be separate languages. An official nationality. Dictionary. Grammar. SVO, attributives precede heads, number classifier constructions follow heads, no consonant clusters, no checked syllables, has tense-lax vowel distinction, 5-8 tones. Literacy rate in second language: 70% Chinese, Jianchuan County, 1985. Roman orthography based on the Jianchuan dialect as spoken in Jinhuatownship in Jianchuan County, taking two other dialects into consideration. An old script dates from the 8th century, called 'Bowen' or 'Lao Baiwen', based on Chinese characters, but this was never standardized. Poetry, radio programs. Agriculturalists. 2,000 meters and higher. Polytheist, Buddhist, Daoist.

BAIMA ***(BAI MA, PE)*** [BQH] 110,000 (1995 EDCL). Pingwu County in north central Sichuan. Sino-Tibetan, Tibeto-Burman, Himalayish, Unclassified. Spoken by members of the Tibetan nationality. SOV; 4 tones; initial consonant clusters; no consonantal codas; mostly monosyllabic morphemes; loans from Chinese and Tibetan. Traditional religion.

BELA ***(PELA, PALA, BOLA, POLO)*** [BEQ] 2,000 to 3,000 in Luxi (1992 Edmondson). Yunnan Province, Dehong Prefecture, Luxi County, Santaishan Township, and Yingjang and Lianghe counties. May also be in Myanmar. Sino-Tibetan, Tibeto-Burman, Lolo-Burmese, Loloish, Unclassified. Live among the Jingpo majority and wear Jingpo clothing. Officially included in the Jingpo nationality. They regard themselves as different from Zaiwa and Jingpo and have different traditions. SOV; 4 tones; only voiceless affricates and stops; no consonant clusters; palatalized and nonpalatalized series of labials and velars; nasal and stop codas; tense-lax and nasal-unnasalized vowels; tone sandhi; Chinese, Jingpo, Dai, and Burmese loans. Agriculturalists: long grain rice.

BIAO MIEN *(BIAO MON, BIAOMAN)* [BMT] 21,500 (1993). Ruyuan County, Guangdong Province. Hmong-Mien, Mienic, Mian-Jin. Phonological and lexical differences from Mien of Thailand and Laos make communication difficult. Different from Biao Jiao or its dialect Biaomin, also called 'Biao Mien'. Officially in the Yao nationality. Mountain slope. Swidden agriculturalists: paddy rice. Daoist.

BIAO-JIAO MIEN *(BIAO CHAO, BYAU MIN)* [BJE] 40,000 (Pan Chengqian 1991:48). Northeastern Guangxi Zhuang Autonomous Region (Quanzhou, Gongcheng, and Guanyang counties, and southern Hunan Province, Lingling and Daoxian counties. Hmong-Mien, Mienic, Biao-Jiao. Dialects: BIAO MIN (BIAOMIN, BIAO MIEN, AO YAO), JIAOGONG MIAN (CHAO KONG MENG, JIAOGONG). Different from Biao Mien (Biaoman). 70% lexical similarity with Iu Mien, 67% with Kim Mun, 58% with Ba Pai. Officially included under the Yao (Mien) nationality in China. Grammar. Daoist.

BISU *(MBISU, MISU, MIBISU, MBI)* [BII] 6,000 in China (1991 Li Yongsui). Population total both countries 7,000 or more. Xishuangbanna area of southwestern Yunnan Province: in Mengzhe village of Menghai County, in the villages of Zhutang, Laba, Donglang, and Fubang in Lancang Couunty, in the villages of Jingxin, Fuyan, and Nanya in Menglian County, and in parts of Ximeng County. Also spoken in Thailand. Sino-Tibetan, Tibeto-Burman, Lolo-Burmese, Loloish, Southern, Phunoi. Closely related to Mpi, Pyen, and Phunoi. There are some dialect differences based on Dai versus Lahu loanwords. 36% lexical similarity with Hani, 32% with Lahu, 31% with Lisu. Most in China can also speak Dai, Lahu, or Chinese. Bisu in Menghai County are called 'Laopin' or 'Pin'; they call themselves 'Mbisu'; those in Lancang and Menglian are called 'Laomian'; those in Thailand call themselves 'Bisu', 'Misu', or 'Mbi'. Investigation needed: intelligibility with Mpi, Pyen, Phunoi. SVO; simple syllable structure; certain obstruent onsets may be prenasalized, aspirated, or palatalized, but otherwise no consonant clusters; syllables may be closed by stop or nasal; 3 tones, tone sandhi; words have 1 or 2 syllables; modifiers follow heads; loan words from Dai and Chinese. Traditional religion.

BIT *(KHABIT, PHSING, PHSIN)* [BGK] 500 in China (1990 J-O Svantesson). Southern Yunnan Province. Austro-Asiatic, Mon-Khmer, Northern Mon-Khmer, Khmuic, Khao. Not Khmuic but Palaungic (J-O Svantesson 1990). Related to Khao in Viet Nam. Investigation needed: intelligibility with Khao. See main entry under Laos.

BIYO *(BIO, BIYUE)* [BYO] 100,000 (J-O Svantesson). Yunnan, near the Hani. Sino-Tibetan, Tibeto-Burman, Lolo-Burmese, Loloish, Southern, Akha, Hani, Bi-Ka. A distinct language from Akha and Kado (Kaduo?). Emu may be a separate language. Officially included under the Hani nationality.

BLANG *(BULANG, PULANG, PULA, PLANG, KAWA, K'ALA, KONTOI)* [BLR] 24,000 in China (1990 J-O Svantesson), out of an official nationality of 82,280 (1990 census). Population total all countries 37,200. Southwestern Yunnan Province, Xishuangbanna Dai Autonomous Prefecture, and the Simao and Lincang regions. Most live in Menghai and Shuangjiang counties. Some are scattered, living among Va (Wa). Also spoken in Myanmar, Thailand. Austro-Asiatic, Mon-Khmer, Northern Mon-Khmer, Palaungic, Western Palaungic, Waic, Bulang. Dialects: PHANG, KEM DEGNE. Dialects listed may be separate languages. K'ala may be a separate language. Chinese sources list two dialects: Bulang (Blang Proper) and Awa (A'erwa). It is not known how these relate to the dialects listed above. Dai, Wa, and Chinese are in common use. An official nationality in China; it officially includes Blang, Lawa, and Angkuic languages, Puman, U, and 3 to 7 others. SVO; modifiers follow heads; voiceless nasal initials; 4 tones; singular-dual-plural pronoun distinction; rich in morphophonemic processes. 2 alphabetic scripts used: 'Totham' in the Xishuangbanna area, 'Tolek' from Dehong to Lincang. Agriculturalists. 1,500 meters and over. Hinayana Buddhist, some Christian.

BONAN *(BAO'AN, BOAN, PAOAN, PAONGAN, BAONAN)* [PEH] 12,212 (1990 census), including 6,000 Jishishan, 4,000 Tongren. East Qinghai Province and southwestern Gansu Province in the Jishishan Bao'an-Dongxiang-Sala Autonomous County of the Linxia Hui Autonomous Prefecture. Bonan-speaking Tu live in Tongren, eastern Qinghai Province. Altaic, Mongolian, Eastern, Mongour. Dialects: JISHISHAN (DAHEJIA, DAKHECZJHA), TONGREN (TUNGYEN). Jishishan subdialects are Ganhetan and Dadun; Tongren subdialects are Nianduhu, Guomari, Gajiuri, and Lower Bao'an village. Jishishan has been influenced by Chinese, Tongren by Tibetan. There are phonological and grammatical differences between the two, and inherent intelligibility may be low. Written Chinese is in common use. An official nationality. Investigation needed: intelligibility with dialects. SOV, no vowel harmony; vowel devoicing and nasalization processes; modifiers precede heads. Literacy rate in second language: 24%. Agriculturalists, forestry, crafts. Sunni Muslim, Lamaist Buddhist.

BOUYEI *(BUYI, BUI, BO-I, BUYEI, BUYUI, PUYI, PUI, PU-I, PU-JUI, PUJAI, PUYOI, DIOI, TUJIA, SHUIHU, ZHONGJIA, CHUNG-CHIA)* [PCC] 2,000,000 speakers or more out of a nationality of 2,545,059 in China (1990 census). Population total both countries 2,001,500. Guizhou-Yunnan plateau, mainly Buyi-Miao and Miao-Dong autonomous prefectures, Zhenning and Guanling counties, south and southwest Guizhou, and some in Yunnan Province, Luoping County, and Sichuan Province, Ningnan and Huidong counties. Also spoken in Viet Nam. Tai-Kadai, Kam-Tai, Be-Tai, Tai-Sek, Tai, Northern. Dialects: QIANNAN (SOUTHERN GUIZHOU, BOUYEI 1), QIANZHONG (CENTRAL GUIZHOU, BOUYEI 2), QIANXI (WESTERN GUIZHOU, BOUYEI 3). Dialect chain to Northern Zhuang. At times the name 'Buyi' is applied to all, or nearly all Northern Tai groups, including Northern Zhuang in Guangxi; the official division between the Zhuang and Buyi is determined by provincial borders. Those in Guizhou are the Buyi official nationality in China; officially includes the T'en, Ching, and Ai-cham languages. All Bouyei seem to understand the Buzmaadt dialect. Written Chinese is in common use. The name 'Quinnan hua' (Quinnan speech) also refers to a dialect of southwestern Mandarin spoken in Guizhou, and should not be confused with Qiannan Bouyei. An official nationality in Viet Nam. Dictionary. SVO; modifiers follow heads; highly monosyllabic in native vocabulary; 6 tone categories in open syllables and 4 (split of 2 categories according to vowel length) in closed syllables; loans from local Mandarin. Literacy rate in second language: 46%. Official Roman pan-dialectal orthography, based on Qiannan Bouyei spoken in Wangmo County. Mountain slope. Agriculturalists: oranges; batik dyers, textiles, tung oil, kapok. Polytheist, some Daoist.

BUGAN *(PUKAN, HUALO, HUAZU)* [BBH] 3,000 (1996 J. Edmondson). Southern Guangnan and northern Xichou counties in southeastern Yunnan Province, Laowalong, Xinwalong, Jiuping, Shibeipo, Xinzhai, Manlong, and Nala villages. Austro-Asiatic, Mon-Khmer, Unclassified. All in 1 dialect. Newly discovered. They live with Han Chinese in 3 villages, by themselves in 4. Traditionally enoganous. Colorful printed dresses. Prenasalized and plain stop and affricate initials; tense and lax vowel contrast; nasal and stop variation word final; tone sandhi; 6 tones. Mountain slope.

BUNU, BAHENG *(PA HNG, PA-HNG, PA NGNG, PAHENG, BAHENG, BAHENGMAI, PA THEN, TONG, MEO LAI, MAN PA SENG)* [PHA] 26,815 speakers in China (1995 McConnell). Population total both countries 33,700. Guizhou Province (Liping and Congjiang counties), northeastern Guangxi Zhuang Autonomous Region (Rongshui, Sanjiang, Longsheng, Rong'an and Lingui counties). Also spoken in Viet Nam. Hmong-Mien, Hmongic, Bunu. A separate language officially included under the Yao nationality. An official ethnic community in Viet Nam, although the variety spoken there may be a separate language. SVO; uvular onsets; no nasal-final syllables but has nasalized vowels. Mountain slope. Daoist.

BUNU, BU-NAO *(PUNU, BUNAO, PO-NAU)* [BWX] 258,000 speakers (1995 McConnell) out of an ethnic group of 439,000 (1982 census). 100,000 ethnic Bunu speak Zhuang as mother tongue. Western Guangxi Zhuang Autonomous Region (Du'an, Bama, Dahua, Lingyun, Nandan, Tiandong, Tianyang, Pingguo, Fengshan, Donglan, Hechi, Mashan, Bose, Tianlin, Leye, Tiandeng, Xincheng, Shanglin, Long'an, Debao, Laibin, Luocheng counties), Guizhou Province (Libo County), and Yunnan Province (Funing County). Hmong-Mien, Hmongic, Bunu. Dialects: DONGNU (TUNG NU), NUNU, BUNUO (PU NO), NAOGELAO (NAO KLAO), NUMAO (NU MHOU, HONG YAO). The dialects listed may be 5 languages (D. Strecker 1987), communication is difficult (McConnell 1995). Bilingualism in Zhuang, Chinese. Officially included under Yao (Mien) nationality in China. Dictionary. Grammar. SVO; modifiers follow heads; most dialects have 8 tones, the greatest number is 11; complex set of initials including pre-nasalized stops; relatively simple rhymes. Mountain slope. Daoist.

BUNU, JIONGNAI *(PUNU, QIUNGNAI, KIONG NAI, JIONGNAI, JIONGNAIHUA, HUALAN YAO)* [PNU] 1,116 (1995 McConnell). Longhua, Nanzhou, Dajin, Liuxiang, Mentou, Gubu, Ludan, Liutuan, and Chang'e in the Jinxiu Yao Autonomous County, southeast of Liuzhou City in eastern Guangxi Zhuang Autonomous Region. Hmong-Mien, Hmongic, Bunu. Thought to be linguistically in the middle between the Mien, Hmong, Bunu, and She languages. Very different from and unintelligible to speakers of surrounding Yao and other Bunu languages. 52% lexical similarity with Bu-Nao Bunu. Bilingualism in Zhuang, Chinese. Their own name is 'Kiang Nai'. The Han call them 'Hualan Yao' which means 'Flowery Blue Yao'. Ethnically Yao. Officially included under the Yao (Mien) nationality in China. 'Bunu' is a cover term for separate languages. Mountain slope. Daoist.

BUNU, WUNAI *(PUNU, WUNAI, NGNAI, HM NAI)* [BWN] 18,442 (1995 McConnell). Western Hunan Province, Longhui, Xupu, Tongdao, Chenxi, Dongkou, Cengbu, and Xinning counties. Hmong-Mien, Hmongic, Bunu. Bilingualism in Zhuang, Chinese. Officially included under Yao (Mien) nationality in China. 'Bunu' is a cover term for separate languages. SVO; has uvular onsets; only final nasal is velar. Daoist.

BUNU, YOUNUO *(PUNU, PU NO, YOUNUO, YUNUO, YUNO)* [BUH] 9,716 (1995 McConnell). Northeastern Guangxi Zhuang Autonomous Region, Xing'an and Longsheng counties. Hmong-Mien, Hmongic, Bunu. Bilingualism in Zhuang, Chinese. Officially included under Yao (Mien) nationality in China. 'Bunu' is a cover term for separate languages (D. Strecker 1989). SVO; relatively simple set of initials; 6 tones; many Chinese loans. Daoist.

BURIAT, CHINA *(BURYAT, BURIAT-MONGOLIAN, NORTHERN MONGOLIAN, NORTHEASTERN MONGOLIAN, BARGU BURIAT)* [BXU] 65,000 (1982 census), including 47,000 New Bargu, 14,000

Old Bargu, 4,500 Buriat. Hulun-Buyr District of Inner Mongolia, near Russian (Siberian) and Mongolian borders. Altaic, Mongolian, Eastern, Oirat-Khalkha, Khalkha-Buriat, Buriat. Dialects: BARGU (OLD BARGU, NEW BARGU), KHORI, AGA. Officially included under Mongolian in China. Differs from Buriat of Mongolia and Russia because of influences from different languages. Lamaist Buddhist.

BUXINHUA [BXT] 200 (1994). Mengla County, Xishuangbanna Dai Autonomous Prefecture, southwestern Yunnan Province. Austro-Asiatic, Mon-Khmer, Unclassified. SVO, no tones, simple syllable structure, complex morphology (prefixing), attributives follow heads, adverbials precede heads.

BUYANG [BYU] 2,000 to 3,000 (1990 Liang Min), including 200 at Ecun, 180 at Lagan, 200 at Maguan, 300 at Langjia, 50 at Nongna, 20 at Damen, 30 to 40 at Jinglong Township, and at a settlement in Guangnan County Diyu, and a village near Yiliang. Yunnan Province, Wenshan Zhuang-Miao Autonomous District, Guangnan County, one location, and Funing County, Gula Township. Yunnan Province, Wenshan Zhuang-Miao Autonomous District, Guangnan County, one location, and Funing County, Gula Township. Tai-Kadai, Kadai, Yang-Biao. A number of dialects. Some similarities grammatically with Kam-Sui. 38% lexical similarity with Pubiao, 34% with Lati, 32% with Northern Zhuang, 31% with Gelo, 28% with Dong, 24% with Laka, 23% with Hlai, 10% with Hmong, 6% with Mien. Most speakers can use Southwest Mandarin, except for children and the elderly. Those from 15 to 50 can speak the local kind of Zhuang. About half can speak Yerong. Buyang is used among themselves. Officially part of the Zhuang nationality. SVO; adjectives follow nouns; 6 tones (combining categories in checked and unchecked syllables).

CAO MIAO ***(MJIUNIANG, GRASS MIAO)*** [COV] 60,000 speakers (1994). Liping county of southeastern Guizhou Province, Tongdao Dong Autonomous County of southwestern Hunan Province, and Sanjiang Dong Autonomous County of northeastern Guangxi, near Southern Dong. Tai-Kadai, Kam-Tai, Kam-Sui. Closely related to Northern Dong and sometimes referred to as a special dialect of Dong. Bilingualism in Chinese. Used in daily communication. Chinese used in singing. Members of the Miao nationality. 6 tones.

CHINESE SIGN LANGUAGE [CSL] (3,000,000 deaf persons in China; 1986 Gallaudet Univ.). Also spoken in Malaysia, Taiwan. Deaf sign language. Dialect: SHANGHAI SIGN LANGUAGE. There are several dialects, of which Shanghai is the most influential. Few signs of foreign origin. Schools and workshops or farms for the deaf are channels of dissemination. Developed since the late 1950s. There are also Chinese character signs. Others use home sign languages. The first deaf school was begun by missionary C. R. Mills and wife in 1887, but American Sign Language did not influence Chinese Sign Language. Dictionary. Grammar. TV.

CHINESE, GAN ***(GAN, KAN)*** [KNN] 20,580,000 2% of the population (1984). Jiangxi and southeastern corner of Hubei including Dachi, Xianning, Jiayu, Chongyang, and parts of Anhui, Hunan, and Fujian provinces. Chang-Jing dialect includes the speech of Nanchang City, Xiuhui, and Jing'an; Yi-Liu includes Yichun (Ichun) in Jiangxi to Liuyang in Hunan. Sino-Tibetan, Chinese. Dialects: CHANG-JING, YI-LIU, JI-CHA, FU-GUANG, YING-YI. Marginally intelligible with Mandarin and Wu Chinese. Speakers are reported to be sufficiently bilingual in Standard Chinese (Mandarin) to use that literature. No written form apart from Standard Chinese.

CHINESE, HAKKA ***(HAKKA, HOKKA, KEJIA, KECHIA, KE, XINMINHUA, MAJIAHUA, TU GUANGDONGHUA)*** [HAK] 25,725,000 in mainland China, 2.5% of the population (1984). Population total all countries 33,000,000 (1999 WA). Spoken in many parts of mainland China side by side with other dialects. Greatest concentration of speakers in eastern and northeastern Guangdong, otherwise especially in Fujian, Jiangxi, Guangxi, Hunan, and Sichuan. Also spoken in Brunei, French Guiana, French Polynesia, Indonesia (Java and Bali), Malaysia (Peninsular), Mauritius, New Zealand, Panama, Singapore, South Africa, Suriname, Taiwan, Thailand, United Kingdom, USA. Sino-Tibetan, Chinese. Dialects: YUE-TAI (MEIXIAN, RAOPING, TAIWAN KEJIA), YUEZHONG (CENTRAL GUANGDONG), HUIZHOU, YUEBEI (NORTHERN GUANGDONG), TINGZHOU (MIN-KE), NING-LONG (LONGNAN), YUGUI, TONGGU. Meixian is now the standard dialect. Bible 1916.

CHINESE, HUIZHOU ***(HUIZHOU)*** [CZH] South Anhui Province and north Zhejiang Province. Sino-Tibetan, Chinese. Dialects: JIXI, XIUYI, QIDE, YANZHOU, JINGZHAN. Formerly considered to be part of the Jianghuai dialect of Mandarin, but now considered by many to be a separate major variety of Chinese. Dialects are reported to differ greatly from each other. Different from the Huizhou dialect of Hakka. Speakers are reported to be sufficiently bilingual in Standard Chinese to use that literature. No written form apart from Standard Chinese.

CHINESE, JINYU ***(JINYU)*** [CJY] 45,000,000 (1995 Milliken). Mainly in Shanxi Province, with some in Shaanxi and Henan provinces. Sino-Tibetan, Chinese. Formerly considered to be part of the Xibei Guanhua dialect of Mandarin, but now considered by many to be a separate major variety of Chinese. Unlike Mandarin in having contrastive glottal checked syllables and other distinctive features. Speakers are reported to be sufficiently bilingual in Standard Chinese to use that literature. No written form apart from Standard Chinese.

CHINESE, MANDARIN ***(MANDARIN, GUANHUA, BEIFANG FANGYAN, NORTHERN CHINESE, GUOYU, STANDARD CHINESE, PUTONGHUA)*** [CHN] 867,200,000 in mainland China (1999), 70% of the population, including 8,602,978 Hui (1990 census). Other estimates for Hui are 20,000,000 or more. 1,042,482,187 all Han in China (1990 census). Population total all countries 874,000,000 first language speakers, 1,052,000,000 including second language speakers (1999 WA). Covers all of mainland China north of the Changjiang River, a belt south of the Changjiang from Qiujiang (Jiangxi) to Zhenjiang (Jiangsu), Hubei except the southeastern corner, Sichuan, Yunnan, Guizhou, the northwestern part of Guangxi, and the northwestern corner of Hunan. Also spoken in Brunei, Cambodia, Indonesia (Java and Bali), Laos, Malaysia (Peninsular), Mauritius, Mongolia, Philippines, Russia (Asia), Singapore, Taiwan, Thailand, United Kingdom, USA, Viet Nam. Sino-Tibetan, Chinese. Dialects: HUABEI GUANHUA (NORTHERN MANDARIN), XIBEI GUANHUA (NORTHWESTERN MANDARIN), XINAN GUANHUA (SOUTHWESTERN MANDARIN), JINGHUAI GUANHUA (JIANGXIA GUANHUA, LOWER YANGZE MANDARIN). Wenli is a literary form. Written Chinese is based on the Beijing dialect, but has been heavily influenced by other varieties of Northern Mandarin. Putonghua is the official form taught in schools. Hezhouhoua is spoken in the Linxia Hui Autonomous Prefecture and Gannan Tibetan Autonomous Prefecture of southern Gansu Province, and in neighboring areas in Qinghai Province. The grammar is basically Altaic or Tibetan, while the vocabulary and phonology is basically Northwestern Mandarin, or a relexified variety of Tibetan. More investigation is needed. Putonghua is inherently intelligible with the Beijing dialect, and other Mandarin varieties in the northeast. Mandarin varieties in the Lower Plateau in Shaanxi are not readily intelligible with Putonghua. Mandarin varieties of Guilin and Kunming are inherently unintelligible to speakers of Putonghua. Taibei Mandarin and Beijing Mandarin are fully inherently intelligible to each other's speakers. The Hui are non-Turkic, non-Mongolian, Muslims who speak Mandarin as first language. Hui is a separate official nationality. The Hui correspond ethnically to 'Khoton', 'Hoton', or 'Qotong' in Mongolia, 20,000 Muslim Chinese in Taiwan, and the Hui in Thailand. Several hundred Chinese Jews in Kaifeng city, Henan Province are largely assimilated to the Han or Hui Chinese, and speak Mandarin. They are officially recognized. Investigation needed: intelligibility with varieties in Loess Plateau in Shaanxi, varieties in Guillin and Kunming. Official language. Dictionary. Grammar. SVO, SOV. If literate, they read Chinese. A few read Arabic. Chinese characters. Official language taught in all schools in Han China and Taiwan. Hui: agriculturalists (rural), traders (urban). Traditional Chinese religion, Buddhist, Muslim (Hui), Jewish, Christian, secular. Bible 1874-1983.

CHINESE, MIN BEI ***(NORTHERN MIN, MIN PEI)*** [MNP] 10,290,000 1.2% of the population (1984). Population total both countries 10,537,000. Northern Fujian Province in 7 counties around Jian'ou. Also spoken in Singapore. Sino-Tibetan, Chinese. The Chinese now divide Chinese Min into 5 major varieties: Min Nan, Min Bei, Min Dong, Min Zhong, and Pu-Xian. Others say there are at least 9 varieties which are inherently unintelligible to each others' speakers. NT 1934.

CHINESE, MIN DONG ***(EASTERN MIN)*** [CDO] Population total all countries 247,000 or more. Area from Fu'an in northeastern Fujian to Fuzhou in east central Fujian. Also spoken in Brunei, Indonesia (Java and Bali), Malaysia (Peninsular), Singapore, Thailand. Sino-Tibetan, Chinese. Dialect: FUZHOU (FUCHOW, FOOCHOW, GUXHOU). The prestige variety is that spoken in Fujian. Speakers are reported to be adequately bilingual in Standard Chinese. Highly literate in Chinese, and they use that literature. Bible 1884-1905.

CHINESE, MIN NAN ***(SOUTHERN MIN, MINNAN)*** [CFR] 25,725,000 in mainland China (1984), 2.5% of the population, including 1,000,000 Xiamen dialect (1988 census), 6,000,000 Quanzhou dialect (Quanzhoushi Fangyan Zhi). Population total all countries 45,000,000. Southern Fujian, Guangdong, south Hainan Island, southern Zhejiang, southern Jiangxi provinces. Xiamen is spoken in southern Fujian, Jiangxi, and Taiwan; Hainan dialect in Hainan; Leizhou on the Leizhou peninsula of southwestern Guangdong; Chao-Shan in the far eastern corner of Guangdong in the Chaozhou-Shantou area; Longdu is a dialect island in the area around Zhongshan City and Shaxi in Guangdong south of Guangzhou; Zhenan Min in southeastern Zhejiang Province around Pingyang and Cangnan and on the Zhoushan archipelago of northeastern Zhejiang. Also spoken in Brunei, Indonesia (Java and Bali), Malaysia (Peninsular), Philippines, Singapore, Taiwan, Thailand, USA. Sino-Tibetan, Chinese. Dialects: XIAMEN (AMOY), LEIZHOU (LEI HUA, LI HUA), CHAO-SHAN (CHOUSHAN), HAINAN (HAINANESE, QIONGWEN HUA, WENCHANG), LONGDU, ZHENAN MIN. Xiamen has subdialects Amoy, Fujian (Fukien, Hokkian, Taiwanese). Amoy is the prestige dialect. Amoy and Taiwanese are easily intelligible to each other. Chao-Shan has subdialects Chaoshou (Chaochow, Chaochow, Teochow, Teochew) and Shantou (Swatow). Chao-Shan, including Swatow, has very difficult intelligibility with Amoy. Sanjiang is somewhat difficult for other dialect speakers. Hainan is quite different from other dialects. Min Nan is the most widely distributed and influential Min variety. Bible 1933.

CHINESE, MIN ZHONG *(CENTRAL MIN)* [CZO] Area around Yong'an, Sanming, and Shaxian in central Fujian Province. Sino-Tibetan, Chinese. Speakers are reported to be adequately bilingual in Standard Chinese to use that literature. Highly literate in Chinese and they use that literature.

CHINESE, PU-XIAN [CPX] Population total all countries 6,000 or more. Putian and Xianyou counties of east central Fujian Province. Also spoken in Malaysia (Peninsular), Singapore. Sino-Tibetan, Chinese. Dialects: PUTIAN (PUTTEN, XINGHUA, HINGHUA, HENGHUA, HSINGHUA), XIANYOU (HSIENYU). Speakers are reported to be adequately bilingual in Standard Chinese. Highly literate in Chinese, and they use that literature. Bible 1912.

CHINESE, WU *(WU)* [WUU] 77,175,000 7.5% of the population (1984). Jiangsu south of the Changjiang River, east of Zhenjiang, on Chongming Island in the mouth of the Changjiang, and north of the Changjiang in the area around Nantong, Haimen, Qidong, and Qingjiang, and in Zhejiang Province as far south as Quzhou, Jinhua, and Wenzhou. Sino-Tibetan, Chinese. Dialects: TAIHU, JINHUA (KINHWA), TAIZHOU, OUJIANG, WUZHOU, CHUQU, XUANZHOU. Subdialects of the Taihu dialect are Piling, Su-Hu-Jia, Tiaoxi, Hangzhou, Lin-Shao, Yongjiang. Chuqu subdialects are Chuzhou, Longqu. Xuanzhou subdialects are Tongjing, Taigao, Shiling. Mandarin is used for news and official broadcasts. Radio programs, TV. Bible 1908-1914.

CHINESE, XIANG *(HUNAN, HUNANESE, XIANG, HSIANG)* [HSN] 36,015,000 3.5% of the population (1984). Hunan Province, over 20 counties in Sichuan, and parts of Guangxi and Guangdong provinces. Sino-Tibetan, Chinese. Dialects: CHANGYI, LUOSHAO, JISHU. Linguistically between Mandarin and Wu Chinese and marginally intelligible with them. Sufficiently bilingual in Standard Chinese to use that literature. Xiang has no written form apart from Standard Chinese.

CHINESE, YUE *(YUET YUE, GWONG DUNG WAA, CANTONESE, YUE, YUEH, YUEYU, BAIHUA)* [YUH] 52,000,000 in mainland China, 4.5% of the population (1984). Includes 498,000 in Macau. Population total all countries 71,000,000 (1999 WA). Spoken in Guangdong (except for the Hakka speaking areas especially in the northeast, the Min Nan speaking areas of the east, at points along the coast as well as Hainan Island), Macau, and in the southern part of Guangxi. Also possibly in Laos. Also spoken in Australia, Brunei, Canada, Costa Rica, Honduras, Indonesia (Java and Bali), Malaysia (Peninsular), Mauritius, Nauru, Netherlands, New Zealand, Panama, Philippines, Singapore, South Africa, Thailand, United Kingdom, USA, Viet Nam. Sino-Tibetan, Chinese. Dialects: YUEHAI (GUANGFU, HONG KONG CANTONESE, MACAU CANTONESE, SHATOU, SHIQI, WANCHENG), SIYI (SEIYAP, TAISHAN, TOISAN, HOISAN, SCHLEIYIP), GAOLEI (GAOYANG), QINLIAN, GUINAN. The Guangzhou variety is considered the standard. Subdialects of Yuehai are Xiangshan, spoken around Zhongshan and Shuhai, and Wanbao around Dongwan City and Bao'an County. Official language. Grammar. SVO; prepositions; genitives, relatives after noun heads; articles, adjectives, numerals before noun heads; word order mainly distinguishes subjects, objectives, indirect objects; passives usually indicated by adding a word in front of the verb; tonal. Outside of mainland China, many Cantonese-specific characters are used in the writing system. TV. Bible 1894-1981.

CHONI *(CHONA, CHONE, CONE, JONE)* [CDA] 22,710 (1993). Yunnan-Tibet border. Sino-Tibetan, Tibeto-Burman, Himalayish, Tibeto-Kanauri, Tibetic, Tibetan, Northern. Dialect: HBRUGCHU. Related to Amdo, Golog, and Kham. Possible dialects or related languages: Dpari (Dpalri, Dparus), Rebkong, Wayen, Horke.

CUN *(NGAO FON, CUNHUA, CUN-HUA)* [CUQ] 70,000 (1990 Jan-Olof Svantesson). South bank of Changhua River in north Dongfang county and north bank in Changjiang county, Hainan Island. Tai-Kadai, Kadai, Yang-Biao. 40% lexical similarity with Hlai. Many loan words from Chinese. A separate language officially under the Han (Chinese) nationality. The people are considered to be Han. Investigation needed: bilingual proficiency in Chinese. SVO, 10 tones (5 in checked syllables and 5 in unchecked syllables).

DARANG DENG *(DARANG)* [DAT] Chayu (Zayü) County along the Dulai River valley in southeastern Tibet. Sino-Tibetan, Tibeto-Burman, North Assam, Deng. Some believe them to be in the Jingpo branch. May be in the Tibetan nationality in China. SOV; 4 tones which are reported to vary considerably among speakers.

DAUR *(DAGUR, DAGUOR, DAWAR, DAWO'ER, TAHUR, TAHUERH)* [DTA] 84,950 speakers or 70% of the ethnic group of 121,357 (1990 census). Inner Mongolia and border of Heilongjiang Province, and northwest Xinjiang. Altaic, Mongolian, Eastern, Dagur. Dialects: BUTEHA (BATAXAN), HAILA'ER (HAILAR), QIQIHA'ER (QIQIHAR, TSITSIKHAR). Definitely distinct from other Mongolian languages (Voegelin and Voegelin). Some sources list Tacheng (spoken in Xinjiang) as a dialect. Some list Haila'er as a dialect of Evenki. Speakers are reported to have high and widespread levels of bilingualism in Chinese. An official nationality. Dictionary. Grammar. SOV; grammatical function marked mainly by suffixes; vowel harmony but not very strict; many consonant clusters, palatalized and labialized consonants; rich vocabulary related to hunting, fishing, animal husbandry; loans from Chinese, Manchu, Evenki. Literacy rate in second language: 81%. Some literacy in Mongolian among those 30 to 50 years old in Hala'er. A Daur script was used during the Qing dynasty, then experimental

Cyrillic script in 1957, then Latin based on Chinese orthography, but scholars are experimenting with a Latin orthography based on Pinyin. Written Manchu once used, now written Chinese used. Agriculturalists, pastoralists, hunters. Shamanism, Lamaist, Christian.

DONG, NORTHERN ***(KAM, GAM, TONG, TUNG, TUNG-CHIA)*** [DOC] 907,560 speakers out of 2,514,014 in the official nationality (1990 census). Population total both countries 907,560 or more. Area where southeastern Guizhou (Yuping Autonomous County), western Hunan, and northern Guangxi provinces meet, and Guangxi Zhuang Autonomous Region, 20 contiguous counties. Also spoken in Viet Nam. Tai-Kadai, Kam-Tai, Kam-Sui. Reported to be close to Mulam. 80% lexical similarity within Northern Dong, 71% between Northern Dong and Southern Dong. 49% lexical similarity with Northern Zhuang, 46% with Laka, 29% with Laqua, 28% with Buyang, 26% with Hlai, 24% with Gelo, 22% with Lati, 6% with Hmong, 4% with Mien. Speakers of Northern Dong are more bilingual than are those in Southern Dong. Speakers use Mandarin for literature. Dong is an official nationality in China. 'Kam' is their own name, 'Dong' is the Chinese name. Traditional way of life is relatively undisturbed. Investigation needed: intelligibility with S. Dong. 9 tones. Literacy rate in second language: 55%. Has an official orthography. Agriculturalists: rice, tung oil, tea oil; forestry. Polytheist.

DONG, SOUTHERN ***(KAM, GAM, TONG, TUNG, TUNG-CHIA)*** [KMC] 1,480,750 speakers out of 2,514,014 in the official nationality (1990 census). 62% of the 2,388,310 Dong speakers speak Southern Dong. Area where southeastern Guizhou (Yuping Autonomous County), western Hunan, and northern Guangxi provinces meet, and Guangxi Zhuang Autonomous Region, 20 contiguous counties. Tai-Kadai, Kam-Tai, Kam-Sui. Reported to be close to Mulam. 93% lexical similarity within Southern Dong, 71% between Northern Dong and Southern Dong. 49% lexical similarity with Northern Zhuang, 46% with Laka, 29% with Laqua, 28% with Buyang, 26% with Hlai, 24% with Gelo, 22% with Lati, 6% with Hmong, 4% with Mien. Speakers of Northern Dong are more bilingual than those of Southern Dong. Speakers use Mandarin for literature. An official nationality in China. 'Kam' is their own name, 'Dong' is the Chinese name. Traditional way of life is relatively undisturbed. Investigation needed: intelligibility with dialects, N. Dong. Dictionary. 9 tones. Has an official orthography. Magazines. Agriculturalists: rice, tung oil, tea oil; forestry. Polytheist.

DONGXIANG ***(TUNGHSIANG, SANTA, TUNG)*** [SCE] 373,872 (1990 census), about half in the Suonanba dialect. Southwest Gansu Province, mainly in Linxia Hui Autonomous Prefecture. Altaic, Mongolian, Eastern, Mongour. Dialects: SUONANBA, WANGJIAJI, SIJIAJI. Some intelligibility with Bonan. Minor dialect differences in pronunciation and borrowed words. Suonanba is considered to be the standard. Written Chinese is in common use. 30% of vocabulary borrowed from Chinese. The people call themselves 'Santa'. An official nationality. Dictionary. SOV; no vowel harmony or vowel length distinction; rich in consonants including uvulars; case marking. Literacy rate in second language: 12%. No official Dongxiang orthography. Agriculturalists, pastoralists. Sunni Muslim.

DRUNG ***(TRUNG, TULUNG, DULONG, QIU)*** [DUU] 11,300 speakers including 5,816 Drung (1990 census) and 5,500 ethnic Nung in the Nu nationality (1990 J-O Svantesson). About 6,000 in Nu River dialect, about 4,000 in Dulong River dialect. Dulong River dialect is spoken along both sides of the Dulong River in Gongshan Dulong-Nu Autonomous County in far northwestern Yunnan. Nu River dialect is spoken from Gongshan Dulong-Nu Autonomous County west to Chayu (Zayü) County in Tibet. Sino-Tibetan, Tibeto-Burman, Nungish. Dialects: DULONG RIVER, NU RIVER. The dialects are reported to be inherently intelligible. The Nu River Drung may be the same as the Tibeto-Burman 'Nung', which are also in Myanmar. Not the same as Rawang in Myanmar. Other possible dialect names are Melam, Metu, Tamalu, Tukiumu. An official nationality, called 'Dulong'. 'Qiuzu' is an old term for the people. Not a written language. SOV; 3 tones. Agriculturalists. Polytheist, Christian.

E ***(KJANG E, "WUSE HUA", "WUSEHUA")*** [EEE] 30,000 (1992 J. A. Edmondson). Northern Guangxi-Zhuang Autonomous Region, Rongshui Hmong Autonomous County, Yongle Township, and neighboring border areas of Luocheng Mulam Autonomous County. Yongle and nineteen surrounding villages. Tai-Kadai, Kam-Tai, Be-Tai, Tai-Sek, Tai, Central. Chinese is the second language (especially the Tuguai Hua variety of Cantonese, or Yue). A mixed language, with large amounts of Tuguai Hua (Chinese) vocabulary, tone category, voice quality, and some word structure. The grammar has been more resistant to Chinese influence. Officially under the Zhuang nationality in China, but the speakers do not speak Zhuang. "Wuse" is the Chinese name, with derogatory connotations. 'E' is their name for themselves. Tonal. Plains. Agriculturalists: paddy rice; skilled labor.

ERSU ***(DUOXU, ERHSU)*** [ERS] 13,000 (1995). South central Sichuan in the lower reaches of the Dadu River, Ya'an District. Sino-Tibetan, Tibeto-Burman, Tangut-Qiang, Qiangic. Dialects: ERSU (EASTERN ERSU), DUOXU (CENTRAL ERSU), LISU (WESTERN ERSU, LÜZÜ). Menia (Menya) is reported to be a dialect, but it is unclear how it relates to the other dialects. Dialect differences are reported to be great. Speakers belong to the Tibetan nationality. SOV; adjectives and number-classifier constructions follow noun heads; consonant cluster onsets; most morphemes monosyllabic; 3 tones. Has a pictographic script in which the color used is reported to play a role in expressing meaning.

EVENKI ***(EWENKE, EWENKI, OWENKE, SOLON, SUOLUN, KHAMNIGAN)*** [EVN] 20,000 speakers out of 34,000 in the ethnic population in China (1995 M. Krauss). Population total all countries 30,000. Hulunbuir Banners Ewenki, Moriadawa, Oronchon, Chen Bargu, Arong, Ergune East, and Huisuomu in Inner Mongolia; Nale Prefecture in Heilongjiang Province; and a few in Xinjiang. Also spoken in Mongolia, Russia (Asia). Altaic, Tungus, Northern, Evenki. Dialects: HAILA'ER, AOLUGUYA, CHENBA'ERHU. Significant dialect differences from Russia. It is not clear how dialect names Solon, Kakut, and Tungus relate to names listed above. Written Mongolian and Chinese used as literary languages. Herdsmen use Mongolian as second language, farmers use Chinese. They maintain native language and customs. It has official regional recognition in China. 'Solon' is their name for themselves in China, but they also now use the official name 'Ewenke'. 'Sulong' may be an alternate spelling. Investigation needed: intelligibility with Evenki of Russia. Literacy rate in second language: 81%. Mountain forests, marshlands. Nomadic pastoralists: reindeer; hunters, agriculturalists. Shamanism, Lamaist, Christian.

GAHRI ***(BUNAN, LAHULI OF BUNAN)*** [BFU] Sino-Tibetan, Tibeto-Burman, Himalayish, Tibeto-Kanauri, Western Himalayish, Kanauri. Related languages or dialects: Thebor, Kanam, Lippa, Sumtsu (Sumchu), Sungnam (Sungam), Zangram. Bible portions 1911-1923. See main entry under India.

GELAO ***(GELO, KELAO, KELEO, KEHLAO, KLAU, KLO, ILAO, KHI, CHILAO, LAO)*** [KKF] 6,400 speakers out of an ethnic group of 437,997 in China (1990 census), including 3,000 Qau, 1,500 A'ou, 1,700 Hagei, 1,200 Duoluo. Daozhen and Wuchuan counties, Anshun and Bijie prefectures of southwest Guizhou province, southern Yunnan (Zhuang-Miao Autonomous District at Maguan, Malipo, and nearby counties), Guangxi (Longlin Pan-Nationalities Autonomous County), and Hunan. The White Gelo are on the China-Viet Nam border at Tiechang and Yangwan townships, Wenshan Zhuang-Miao Autonomous District, Malipo County, Yunnan Province. They live dispersed among the Han, Miao, Bouyei, Zhuang, and Yi nationalities. Tai-Kadai, Kadai, Ge-Chi. Dialects: QAU (GAO), A'OU, HAGEI (HAKEI), DUOLUO. Phonologically close to Hmong, grammatically to Northern Zhuang and Bouyei. Anshun Gelo (Guizhou Anshun) and Sanchong Gelo (Guangxi Longlin) have 54% lexical similarity, and should be considered separate languages. 45% lexical similarity with Southern Zhuang and Dai, 40% with Dong, 36% with Lati, 32% with Laqua, 29% with Buyang, 24% with Northern Zhuang, 24% with Dong, 22% with Laka, 27% to 40% with Hlai, 10% to 15% with Hmong, 5% to 15% with Mien. The White Gelo retain their language. The Flowery Gelo have shifted to Chinese. An official nationality in China and Viet Nam. Called 'Gelo' in China. SVO; adjectives follow noun head; negative follows predicate but other adverbials precede predicate; 6 tones; only final consonants are alveolar and velar nasals; nasal-stop and some obstruent-lateral onset clusters. Agriculturalists. Polytheistic. See main entry under Viet Nam.

GEMAN DENG [GEN] Chayu (Zayü) County on the tablelands on either side of the lower reaches of the Chayu (Zayü) River in the southeastern corner of Tibet. Also spoken in India, Myanmar. Sino-Tibetan, Tibeto-Burman, North Assam, Deng. 'Kuman' may be an alternate name. EDCL calls it a separate language from Darang Deng. Some believe them to be in the Jingpo branch. May be in the Tibetan official nationality in China. SOV; 4 tones which are reported to have a low functional load.

GROMA ***(TROMOWA)*** [GRO] 12,840 in China (1993). Population total both countries 12,840 or more. Chambi Valley, between Sikkim and Bhutan, Tibet. Also spoken in India. Sino-Tibetan, Tibeto-Burman, Himalayish, Tibeto-Kanauri, Tibetic, Tibetan, Southern. Dialects: UPPER GROMA, LOWER GROMA. Possible dialects or related languages: Spiti, Tomo (Chumbi).

GUANYINQIAO ***(ZHONGZHAI, WESTERN JIARONG)*** [JIQ] 50,000 (1993 Lin). North central Sichuan, along the tributaries of the Jinchuan River in the southwestern tip of Maerkang County, northwestern Jinchuan County, and southeastern Rangtang County. Sino-Tibetan, Tibeto-Burman, Tangut-Qiang, rGyarong. Phonologically Western and Northern are fairly similar and differ greatly from Eastern. Western and Northern Jiarong have 60% lexical similarity. Under the Tibetan nationality. SOV, phonologically and lexically similar to Tibetan, grammatically more similar to Pumi and Qiang; complex consonant clusters; limited pitch contrast.

GUIQIONG [GQI] 7,000 (1995). Plateaus on both sides of the Dadu River north from Luding County in the Ganzi (Garzê) Tibetan Autonomous Prefecure in west central Sichuan, and nearby in northwest Tianquan County. One town is Wasigou. Sino-Tibetan, Tibeto-Burman, Tangut-Qiang, Qiangic. Phonological dialect differences, but communication is possible. Speakers belong to the Tibetan nationality. SOV; adjectives and number-classifier constructions follow noun heads; 4 tones.

HANI ***(HANHI, HAW, HANI PROPER)*** [HNI] 500,000 Hani speakers in China (1990 J-O Svantesson). The official nationality of 1,253,952 (1990 census) probably includes Kado, Mahei, Sansu, Akha, Biyo (Bio, Biyue), Honi, possibly Menghua and others. Population total all countries 722,500. Yuanjiang and Lancang (Mekong) River basins, Ailao Mountains, south Yunnan. None in Thailand. Also spoken in Laos, Myanmar, Viet Nam. Sino-Tibetan, Tibeto-Burman, Lolo-Burmese, Loloish, Southern, Akha,

Hani, Ha-Ya. Divided into three dialect groups depending on whether and to what degree they have vowels with 'clear-muddy' vowel contrasts (P. B. Denlinger 1974). Sang Kong (Sangkong; 2,000) in Jing Hong Xishuangbanna Dai Autonomous State, Yunnan, is officially under Hani, and may be a separate language. Kaduo is reported to be a separate language. Written Chinese is in common use. Taught at Kunming Institute. Hani ethnic groups include Pudu (Putu). An official nationality in China. The term 'Hani' has been applied to South, Central, and North Lolo languages. Investigation needed: intelligibility with Sang Kong, Kaduo. Dictionary. SOV, 3 tones. Roman script. Newspapers. Swidden agriculturalists: rice, millet, maize. 800 to 2,600 meters. Polytheist, ancestor worship.

HLAI ***(LI, DAI, DAY, LAI, LA, LOI, LE, DLI, BLI, KLAI, SLAI)*** [LIC] 747,000 speakers, including 432,000 Ha, 178,000 Qi, 52,000 Jiamao, 44,000 Bendi, 30,000 Meifu, out of an official nationality of 1,100,900 (1990 census). Mountains in central and south central Hainan Province, southern China. Tai-Kadai, Hlai. Dialects: HA (LUOHUA-HAYAN-BAOXIAN), QI (GEI, TONGSHI-QIANDUI-BAOCHENG), MEIFU (MOIFAU), BENDI (ZWN, BAISHA-YUANMEN). Divided into 5 groups: Ha Li, Meifu Li, Qi Li, Local Li, Detou Li. Some varieties listed as dialects may be separate languages. 30% lexical similarity with Northern Zhuang, 27% with Gelo, 26% with Dong and Laqua, 25% with Lati, 23% with Buyang. Spoken and written Chinese in common use. An official nationality, called 'Li'. Traditional culture. Literacy rate in second language: 54%. Official Roman orthography. Tropical forest. Agriculturalists: rice, coconut, betel nut, sisal, hemp, lemon grass, cocoa, coffee, rubber, palm oil, textiles; traditionally hunters. Polytheist.

HMONG DAW ***(WHITE MEO, WHITE MIAO, MEO KAO, WHITE LUM, PEH MIAO, PE MIAO, CHUAN MIAO, BAI MIAO)*** [MWW] 60,000 in China (1987). Population total all countries 165,000 or more. All Hmong in all countries: 6,000,000 (1999 WA). Central and western Guizhou, southern Sichuan, and Yunnan. Also spoken in France, Laos, Thailand, USA, Viet Nam. Hmong-Mien, Hmongic, Chuanqiandian. Dialects: HMONG GU MBA (HMONG QUA MBA, STRIPED HMONG), MONG LENG, PETCHABUN MIAO. Also spoken by the Hmong Qua Mba people; no significant dialect difference. Largely intelligible with Hmong Njua. Mong Leng is intelligible with Hmong Daw. Sociolinguistic factors require separate literature for Mong Leng. Dictionary. Literacy rate in second language: 42%. NT 1975-1984.

HMONG NJUA ***(CHUANQIANDIAN MIAO, CHUANCHIENTIEN MIAO, SICHUAN-GUIZHOU-YUNNAN HMONG, TAK MIAO, MEO, MIAO, WESTERN MIAO, WESTERN HMONG)*** [BLU] 1,000,000 in China (1982), including about 29,000 Bunu of the Yao nationality who speak it as mother tongue (1990 J-O Svantesson). Population total all countries 1,245,000 or more. The area where Guizhou, Sichuan, and Yunnan provinces meet. Also spoken in French Guiana, Laos, Myanmar, Thailand, USA, Viet Nam. Hmong-Mien, Hmongic, Chuanqiandian. Dialects: XIAO HUA MIAO (ATSE, SMALL FLOWERY MIAO), TAK MIAO (CHING MIAO, GREEN MIAO, BLUE MIAO). Corresponds more or less to Ma's Western and Northern groups, and Purnell's Central and Western groups. Hua, the Miao (Hmongic) group, consists of 30 to 40 varieties which are inherently unintelligible to each others' speakers (Joakim Enwall 1993:12). A distinct variety called 'Gejiahua' with 50,000 speakers in Huangping County and Kaili City is believed to belong to Hmong Njua. It has 6 tones. Another distinct variety called 'Xijiahua' or 'Haiba Miano' with 50,000 speakers in Huangping, Fuquan, Weng'an, Longli, and Guiding counties and Kaili City, is believed to belong to Hmong Njua. It has 3 tones. Another distinct variety called 'Dongjiahua' in Majiang, Longli, and Xiuwen counties and Kaili City is believed to belong to Hmong Njua. Speakers are called 'Dongjian', 'Duck-Raising Miano', or 'Duck-Raising Gedou'. It shares many characteristics with Gejiahua. Hmong is an official nationality in China. Village centered. Dictionary. SOV. Has an official orthography. Agriculturalists. Traditional religion, Christian. NT 1975-1983.

HMONG, CENTRAL HUISHUI ***(CENTRAL HUISHUI MIAO, MIAO)*** [HMC] 30,000 (1987 Wurm et al.). Gaopa, Huishui, Guiding, Changshun, Ziyun, and Pingba counties, Guiyang City region, central portion. Hmong-Mien, Hmongic, Chuanqiandian. Inherently unintelligible to speakers of other Hmong varieties. 30 to 40 different Hmong (Miao) languages in China. Linguistic differences are great (Joakim Enwall 1993). Village centered. Agriculturalists. Polytheist, Christian.

HMONG, CENTRAL MASHAN ***(CENTRAL MASHAN MIAO, MIAO)*** [HMM] 50,000 (1987 Wurm et al.). Southwestern Guizhou, Ziyun, Changshun, Luodian, Huishui, and Wangmo counties, central portion. Hmong-Mien, Hmongic, Chuanqiandian. Not inherently intelligible with other varieties of Hmong. Village centered. Reported to have 13 tones.

HMONG, CHONGANJIANG ***(CHONG'ANJIANG MIAO)*** [HMJ] 70,000 (1982), half in Chong'anjiang District. Kaili City, Chong'an township, Huangping county, east central Guizhou. Hmong-Mien, Hmongic, Chuanqiandian. Dialect: GEJIAHUA (GE, GEDOU MIAO, KEH-DEO, GETOU, GEDANG, HUADOU MIAO). Not inherently intelligible with other varieties of Hmong. Gedou may be separate from Chong'anjiang. Village centered. Traditional religion. Bible portions 1937.

HMONG, EASTERN HUISHUI ***(EASTERN HUISHUI MIAO, MIAO)*** [HME] 20,000 (1987 Wurm et al.). Gaopa, Huishui, Guiding, Changshun, Ziyun, and Pingba counties, Guiyang City region, eastern portion. Hmong-Mien, Hmongic, Chuanqiandian. Inherently unintelligible to speakers of other Hmong varieties. Village centered. Agriculturalists. Polytheist, Christian.

HMONG, EASTERN QIANDONG ***(EASTERN QIANDONG MIAO, HMU, MIAO, BLACK MIAO, CENTRAL MIAO, EASTERN EAST-GUIZHOU MIAO)*** [HMQ] 200,000 (1987 Zhang and Cao). Qiandongnan Miao Dong Autonomous Prefecture, Guizhou, and eastward into Hunan Province. Hmong-Mien, Hmongic, Qiandong. Not intelligible with other varieties of Hmong. Corresponds more or less to Ma's Central Miao and Purnell's Eastern Miao. Miao is an official nationality in China. Dictionary. Has an official orthography. Agriculturalists. Polytheist, Christian. Bible portions 1928.

HMONG, EASTERN XIANGXI ***(EASTERN XIANGXI MIAO, HSIANGHSI MIAO, RED MIAO, MEO DO, RED MEO, GHAO-XONG, EASTERN WEST-HUNAN MIAO)*** [MUQ] 70,000 (1987 Zhang and Cao). Western Hunan, Xiangxi Tujia Miao Autonomous Prefecture, and some places in Hubei. Hmong-Mien, Hmongic, Xiangxi. Not inherently intelligible with other varieties of Hmong (Miao). 'Maojiahua' is a variety of Chinese spoken by about 20,000 members of the Miao nationality in southwestern Hunan, Chengbu Miao Autonomous County, Xining and Suining, and in northeastern Guangxi, Longshen Pan-nationalities Autonomous County and the area around Ziyuan, with 7 tones. Polytheist, Christian.

HMONG, LUOPOHE ***(LUOBOHE MIAO, XIMAHE MIAO, XIJIA MIAO)*** [HML] 40,000 (1987 Wurm et al.). Fuquan, Guiding, Longli, Kaiyang, and Kaili counties east of Guiyang, central Guizhou. Hmong-Mien, Hmongic, Chuanqiandian. Not inherently intelligible with other varieties of Hmong. Village centered.

HMONG, NORTHEASTERN DIAN ***(A-HMAO, DIANDONGBEI, VARIEGATED MIAO, TA HUA MIAO, TA HWA MIAO, BIG FLOWERY MIAO, HUA MIAO, HWA MIAO, FLOWERY MIAO, NORTH-EASTERN YUNNAN MIAO)*** [HMD] 200,000 (1987 Wurm et al.). Northwestern Guizhou, northeast and central Yunnan provinces. Hmong-Mien, Hmongic, Chuanqiandian. Inherently unintelligible to speakers of other Hmong varieties. Village centered. Dictionary. Agriculturalists. Polytheist, Christian. NT 1917-1936.

HMONG, NORTHERN GUIYANG ***(NORTHERN GUIYANG MIAO, MIAO)*** [HUJ] 60,000 (1987 Wurm et al.). Suburbs of Guiyang City, Pingba, Zhenning, Kaiyang, Guiding, Qingzhen, and Anshun counties or towns, northern portion. Hmong-Mien, Hmongic, Chuanqiandian. Inherently unintelligible to speakers of other Hmong varieties. Village centered. Agriculturalists. Polytheist, Christian.

HMONG, NORTHERN HUISHUI ***(NORTHERN HUISHUI MIAO, MIAO)*** [HMN] 50,000 (1987 Wurm et al.). Gaopa, Huishui, Guiding, Changshun, Ziyun, and Pingba counties, Guiyang City region, northern portion. Hmong-Mien, Hmongic, Chuanqiandian. Inherently unintelligible to speakers of other Hmong varieties. Village centered. Agriculturalists. Polytheist, Christian.

HMONG, NORTHERN MASHAN ***(NORTHERN MASHAN MIAO)*** [HMO] 25,000 (1987 Wurm et al.). Southwestern Guizhou, Ziyun, northern portions of Changshun, Luodian, Huishui, and Wangmo counties. Hmong-Mien, Hmongic, Chuanqiandian. Not inherently intelligible with other varieties of Hmong. Reported to have 13 tones.

HMONG, NORTHERN QIANDONG ***(NORTHERN QIANDONG MIAO, CHIENTUNG MIAO, EAST GUIZHOU MIAO, HMU, MIAO, BLACK MIAO, HEH MIAO, HEI MIAO, CENTRAL MIAO, NORTHERN EAST-GUIZHOU MIAO)*** [HEA] 900,000 (1987 Zhang and Cao). Northeast Yunnan and upper Cingshuiho River area of southeast Guizhou (southeast, south, and southwest Guizhou Autonomous areas, Songtao County, Guanling County, Ziyun County). Hmong-Mien, Hmongic, Qiandong. Not intelligible with other varieties of Hmong. Corresponds more or less to Ma's Central Miao and Purnell's Eastern Miao. Hmu was chosen by the government as the standard variety. It is based on Yanghao, but with some similarities to other varieties. Miao is an official nationality in China. Dictionary. Has an official orthography. Agriculturalists. Polytheist, Christian. NT 1934.

HMONG, SOUTHERN GUIYANG ***(SOUTHERN GUIYANG MIAO, MIAO)*** [HMY] 20,000 (1987 Wurm et al.). Suburbs of Guiyang City, Pingba, Zhenning, Kaiyang, Guiding, Qingzhen, and Anshun counties or towns, southern portion. Hmong-Mien, Hmongic, Chuanqiandian. Inherently unintelligible to speakers of other Hmong varieties. Village centered. Agriculturalists. Polytheist, Christian.

HMONG, SOUTHERN MASHAN ***(SOUTHERN MASHAN MIAO, MIAO)*** [HMA] 7,000 (1987 Wurm et al.). Southwestern Guizhou, southern portions of Ziyun, Changshun, Luodian, Huishui, and Wangmo counties. Hmong-Mien, Hmongic, Chuanqiandian. Not inherently intelligible with other varieties of Hmong. Village centered. Reported to have 13 tones.

HMONG, SOUTHERN QIANDONG ***(SOUTHERN QIANDONG MIAO, HMU, MIAO, BLACK MIAO, CENTRAL MIAO, SOUTHERN EAST-GUIZHOU MIAO)*** [HMS] 300,000 (1987 Zhang and Cao). Qiandongnan Miao Dong Autonomous Prefecture, Guizhou Province, and southward into Guangxi Province. Hmong-Mien, Hmongic, Qiandong. Not intelligible with other varieties of Hmong. Corresponds more or less to Ma's Central Miao and Purnell's Eastern Miao. Miao is an official nationality in China. Dictionary. Has an official orthography. Agriculturalists. Polytheist, Christian.

HMONG, SOUTHWESTERN GUIYANG ***(SOUTHWESTERN GUIYANG MIAO, MIAO)*** [HMG] 50,000 (1987 Wurm et al.). Suburbs of Guiyang City, Pingba, Zhenning, Kaiyang, Guiding, Qingzhen, and Anshun counties or towns, southwestern portion. Hmong-Mien, Hmongic, Chuanqiandian. Inherently unintelligible to speakers of other Hmong varieties. Village centered. Agriculturalists. Polytheist, Christian.

HMONG, SOUTHWESTERN HUISHUI ***(SOUTHWESTERN HUISHUI MIAO, MIAO)*** [HMH] 40,000 (1987 Wurm et al.). Gaopa, Huishui, Guiding, Changshun, Ziyun, and Pingba counties, Guiyang City region, southwestern portion. Hmong-Mien, Hmongic, Chuanqiandian. Inherently unintelligible to speakers of other Hmong varieties. Village centered. Agriculturalists. Polytheist, Christian.

HMONG, WESTERN MASHAN ***(WESTERN MASHAN MIAO, MIAO)*** [HMW] 10,000 (1987 Wurm et al.). Southwestern Guizhou, Ziyun, Changshun, Luodian, Huishui, and Wangmo counties, western portion. Hmong-Mien, Hmongic, Chuanqiandian. Not inherently intelligible with other varieties of Hmong. Village centered. Reported to have 13 tones.

HMONG, WESTERN XIANGXI ***(RED MIAO, MEO DO, RED MEO, WESTERN XIANGSI MIAO, GHAO-XONG, HUAYUAN MIAO, HSIANGHSI MIAO, WEST HUNAN MIAO, WESTERN WEST-HUNAN MIAO)*** [MMR] 700,000 (1987 Zhang and Cao). Western Hunan, Xiangxi Tujia Miao Autonomous Prefecture, Songtao County in Guizhou, Xiushan County in Sichuan, and some places in Guangxi. Possibly also in Ha Tuyen Province, northern Viet Nam and in Thailand. Hmong-Mien, Hmongic, Xiangxi. Not inherently intelligible with other varieties of Hmong (Miao). Polytheist, Christian.

HONI ***(WONI, OUNI, UNI, HO, HAONI)*** [HOW] 100,000 (1990 J-O Svantesson). Yunnan, near the Hani. May also be in Viet Nam. Sino-Tibetan, Tibeto-Burman, Lolo-Burmese, Loloish, Southern, Akha, Hani, Hao-Bai. Dialect: BAIHONG. Officially included under the Hani nationality, but it is a distinct language. Baihong may be a separate language.

HORPA ***(HOR, HÓRSÓK, ERGONG, DANBA, WESTERN JIARONG, PAWANG, BAWANG)*** [ERO] 35,000 (1995). Danba (=Rongzhag), Daofu (Dawu), Luhuo, Xinlong (Nyagrong) counties of the Ganzi (Garzê) Tibetan Autonomous Prefecture of western Sichuan, and Jinchua (Quqên) County of the Aba (Ngawa) Tibetan-Qiang Autonomous Prefecture of northwestern Sichuan. Central and eastern Daofu County, Chengguan District, Wari, Xiajia, and Muru townships of Wari District, and Shazhong township of Bamei District; and central and northwestern Danba County, in Geshiza, Bianer, and Dandong townships of Dasang District, Donggu township in Chuangu District, Bawang and Jinchuan townships of Jinchuan District; of Ganzi Prefecture, an area traditionally known as the five parts of Horpa territory. Scattered communities are also in adjacent Luhuo (in Renda township of Xialatuo District, and Xinlong in Manqing, Zhuwo, and Duoshan townships of Hexi District. Sino-Tibetan, Tibeto-Burman, Tangut-Qiang, rGyarong. Dialects: DAOFU (DAOFUHUA, TAOFU), GESHIZA (GESHITSA). Speakers belong to the Tibetan nationality. SOV; adjectives and number-classifier constructions follow noun heads; affixation; compounding; reduplication; complex consonant cluster onsets; not tonal.

HU [HUO] 1,000 (1984 J. Svantesson). Southwestern Yunnan Province, Mengla, Jinghong, 5 villages. Austro-Asiatic, Mon-Khmer, Northern Mon-Khmer, Palaungic, Western Palaungic, Angkuic. Counted separately in 1982 census and combined into a group of 'Undetermined Minorities'. Investigation needed: intelligibility with Angkuic languages. Tonal, affixes.

ILI TURKI ***(T'URK, TUERKE)*** [ILI] 120 approximately, or at least 30 households in China (1980 R. F. Hahn). Population total both countries 120 or more. Ili Valley near Kuldja, Xinjiang. Probably some in Kazakhstan. Also spoken in Kazakhstan. Altaic, Turkic, Eastern. Reported to be a link between Chagatai and Kypchak (Uzbek dialect). Bilingualism in Kazakh, Uyghur. Spoken by older people. Younger people are intermarrying with neighboring groups. Ethnically and linguistically distinct, discovered in 1956. Their oral history says they came from the Ferghana Valley (Uzbekistan/ Kyrgyzstan) about 200 years ago. SOV; vowel harmony; influenced greatly by Kazakh and Uyghur; has Arabic, Persian, Chinese, and Russian loans.

IU MIEN ***(YOUMIAN, YIU MIEN, YAO, MIEN, MIAN, MYEN, HIGHLAND YAO, PAN YAO, BAN YAO)*** [IUM] 884,000 speakers in China (1999), out of 2,134,013 in the official nationality (1990 census). Population total all countries 1,329,000. Dayao Mountains, Guangxi Zhuang Autonomous Region, Guangdong, Yunnan, Hunan, and Guizhou provinces. In Guizhou Province Mien are in Rongjiang, Congjiang, and Libo counties; in Guangdong Province, in Ruyuan County. Also spoken in Belgium, Canada, Denmark, France, Laos, Myanmar, New Zealand, Switzerland, Taiwan, Thailand, USA, Viet Nam. Hmong-Mien, Mienic, Mian-Jin. Differences from other Mienic languages are in the tone system, consonants, vowel quality, vowel length. Chinese linguists consider the Iu Mien spoken in Changdong, Jinxiu Yao Autonomous County, Guangxi to be the standard. 78% lexical similarity with Kim Mun, 70% with Biao-Jiao Mien, 61% with Ba Pai. Spoken and written Chinese are also in use. The largest language in the Yao nationality. Ethnic groups: Hua Lan, Hua, Hung, Cao Long, Coc,

Khoc, Quan Coc, Quan Trang, Son Trang, Sung, Tien (Tiao Tchaine), Yaya. The Laka, Mun, Bunu languages, plus speakers of other Mienic and Hmongic languages, and ethnic Yao who speak Chinese, are officially included under the Yao nationality in China. 'Pingdi Yao' (Piongtuojo, Piongtoajeu) is a variety of Chinese with 1,000,000 speakers, half of whom are members of the Yao nationality, in Hunan-Guangxi border and Guangdong Province. It has 7 tones, and may be closest to Mandarin. Dictionary. Grammar. Roman orthography agreed on in 1984. Minor differences with orthography used in China and western countries. Trial use limited and possibly discontinued. Mountain slope and plains. Peasant agriculturalists: paddy rice; hunters, lumbermen, weavers, embroiderers. Daoist, ancestor veneration, traditional religion. NT 1975-1991.

JIAMAO ***(KAMAU, TAI)*** [JIO] 52,300 (1987 Wurm et al.). Near Wuzhi Mountain in southern Hainan Province, Baoting, Lingshui, and Qiongzhong counties. Tai-Kadai, Hlai. Very different from Hlai dialects in phonology, grammar, and vocabulary. Officially under the Li (Hlai) nationality.

JIARONG ***(JYARUNG, GYARONG, GYARUNG, RGYARONG, CHIARONG, JARONG)*** [JYA] 151,200 including 139,000 in Situ Jiarong, 12,197 in Chabao and Sidaba (1993 Lin). North central Sichuan. Situ is in the traditional territory of four chieftaincies: Zhuokeji, Suomo, Songgang, Dangba. Chabao is in the northeastern corner of Maerkang county, at Longerjia, Dazang, and Shaerzong townships in Chabao District. Sidaba is in Caodeng, Kangshan, and Ribu townships in Sidaba District of Maerkang County. Some outlier Sidaba communities are to the north in certain villages of Kehe and Rongan townships, at the southwesten corner of the Aba County, and to the west along the middle Duke River between Wuyi and Shili townships in Rangtang County, spilling over to a small area near the confluence of the Seda and Duke rivers in Seda County. Sino-Tibetan, Tibeto-Burman, Tangut-Qiang, rGyarong. Dialects: CHABAO (DAZANG, NORTHEASTERN JIARONG), SIDABA (CAODENG, NORTHWESTERN JIARONG), SITU (EASTERN JIARONG). Subdialects of Situ are: Maerkang, Lixian, Jinchuan, Xiaojin; of Sidaba Caodeng and Ribu. Phonologically Western and Northern are fairly similar and differ greatly from Eastern. Eastern and Northern Jiarong have 75% lexical similarity, Western and Northern 60%. Situ has 13% with Horpa. Under the Tibetan nationality. SOV, phonologically and lexically similar to Tibetan, grammatically more similar to Pumi and Qiang; complex consonant clusters; limited pitch contrast.

JINGPHO ***(JINGPO, JINGHPAW, CHINGPAW, CHINGP'O, KACHIN, MARIP, DASHANHUA)*** [CGP] 20,000 speakers (1990 J-O Svantesson) out of an ethnic group of 119,209 in China (1990 census). Western Yunnan, Dehong Dai-Jingpo Autonomous Prefecture, Yingjiang County (Shidan dialect; Enkun dialect elsewhere in Dehong Dai-Jingpo Autonomous Prefecture). Sino-Tibetan, Tibeto-Burman, Jingpho-Konyak-Bodo, Jingpho-Luish, Jingpho. Dialects: ENKUN, SHIDAN, HKAKU (HKA-HKU), KAURI (HKAURI, GAURI), DZILI (JILI), DULONG. Dialects in China are Enkun and Shidan. Dzili may be a separate language. Hkaku and Kauri are only slightly different from Jinghpo. Taught at Kunming Institute. 'Kachin' refers to the cultural rather than the linguistic group. An official nationality in China; includes 70,000 Atsi, and Maru and Lashi officially. Dictionary. SOV; 4 tones; adjectives and numbers follow nouns; singular, dual, and plural pronouns; tense-lax vowel distinction; 4 tones with relatively complex sandhi phenomena. Has a Pinyin alphabet in China. Orthography at Kunming Institute is based on Enkun dialect. Pastoralists, agriculturalists. Polytheist, some Buddhist, Christian. Bible 1927. See main entry under Myanmar.

JINUO, BUYUAN ***(JINO, BUYUAN)*** [JIY] 1,000 speakers (1994) out of an ethnic group of 18,021 (1990 census). South Yunnan, Xishuanbanna Dai Autonomous Prefecture, near Laos and Myanmar borders, 53 kms. east of Jinghong. Youle Mountains. 40 villages. Over 3,000 square kms. Sino-Tibetan, Tibeto-Burman, Lolo-Burmese, Loloish, Southern. The two 'dialects' (Buyuan and Youle) are not inherently intelligible with each other. Some bilingualism in Dai. Jinuo is an official nationality. SOV; 6 tones; initial consonant clusters (stop or nasal plus /r/; no syllable-final consonants; mostly monosyllabic words. Literacy rate in second language: 49%. The government sponsored the development and promotion of a Roman-script orthography in 1983. Forests. Agriculturalists: rice; hunter-gatherers traditionally. Worship of Kong Ming (a Chinese hero).

JINUO, YOULE ***(JINO, YOULE)*** [JIU] 10,000 speakers (1994) out of an ethnic group of 18,021 (1990 census). South Yunnan, Xishuanbanna Dai Autonomous Prefecture, near Laos and Myanmar borders, 53 kms. east of Jinghong. Youle Mountains. 40 villages. Over 3,000 square kms. Sino-Tibetan, Tibeto-Burman, Lolo-Burmese, Loloish, Southern. The two 'dialects' (Youle and Buyuan) are not inherently intelligible with each other. Some bilingualism in Dai. An official nationality. Investigation needed: intelligibility with dialects. SOV; 6 tones; initial consonant clusters (stop or nasal plus /r/; no syllable-final consonants; mostly monosyllabic words. Literacy rate in second language: 49%. The government sponsored the development and promotion of a Roman-script orthography in 1983. Forests. Agriculturalists: rice; hunter-gatherers traditionally. Worship of Kong Ming (a Chinese hero).

JURCHEN ***(NUZHEN, NUCHEN)*** [JUC] Altaic, Tungus, Southern, Southwest. Related to Manchu. It was spoken by the Nuzhen people. Extinct.

KADO ***(KADU, KATU, KATO, KUDO, GADO, ASAK, SAK, THET, THAT, MAWTEIK, PUTEIK)*** [KDV] 100,000 in China (1990 J-O Svantesson). South Yunnan. Sino-Tibetan, Tibeto-Burman, Jingpho-Konyak-Bodo, Jingpho-Luish, Luish. Dialects: KADU, GANAAN (GANAN), ANDRO, SENGMAI, CHAKPA, PHAYENG. Ganaan may be a separate language. Different from Katu, a Mon-Khmer language of Viet Nam and Laos. Bible portions 1939. See main entry under Myanmar.

KADUO ***(GAZHUO, KADO, KADU)*** [KTP] 4,000 to 6,200 in China (1994). South central Yunnan Province, Hexi District of Tonghai County. Sino-Tibetan, Tibeto-Burman, Burmese-Lolo, Lolo, Southern, Akha, Hani, Bi-Ka. No information on intelligibility with other Lolo languages. No significant dialect differences. Members of the Mongolian nationality. Remnants of an outpost dating back to the Yuan Dynasty. SOV; 8 tones; CV(V); a voiced-voiceless distinction only for fricatives; no tense or nasalized vowels; nouns mostly polysyllabic, other words mostly monosyllabic; many loan words from Chinese. See main entry under Laos.

KALMYK-OIRAT ***(OIRAT, WEILATE, XINJIANG MONGOLIAN, WESTERN MONGOL)*** [KGZ] 139,000 Oirat in China (1989 Wurm et al.), including 106,000 Torgut, 33,000 Kok Nur. Bayan Gool Autonomous Prefecture and Bortala Autonomous Prefecture. Altaic, Mongolian, Eastern, Oirat-Khalkha, Oirat-Kalmyk-Darkhat. Dialects: JAKHACHIN, BAYIT, MINGAT, OLOT (ÖÖLD, ELYUT, ELEUTH), KHOSHUT (KHOSHUUD). Dorbot dialect also reported to be in China. Other dialects are different from varieties of China Mongolian spoken by other Oirat peoples. Since 1982 schooling has been in Chahar Mongolian. People have high bilingualism in Chahar Mongolian in China. Officially under the Mongolian nationality in China. Official language. NT 1827-1894, out of print. See main entry under Russia.

KANG [KYP] 34,065 in China (1993). Southwest Yunnan. Tai-Kadai, Kam-Tai, Be-Tai, Tai-Sek, Tai, Unclassified. Related ethnic groups, dialects, or languages in the area: Chang Teo Fah, Kentse, Mengka (Mengkah). Officially under the Dai nationality. See main entry under Laos.

KAZAKH ***(KAZAK, KAZAX, HAZAKE)*** [KAZ] 1,111,718 in China (1990 census), including 830,000 Northeastern Kazakh, 70,000 Southwestern Kazakh (1982). North Xinjiang (Yili Kazakh Autonomous Prefecture), east Xinjiang (Mulei Kazakh Autonomous County and Balikun Kazakh Autonomous County), northwest Gansu (Akesai Kazakh Autonomous County), and northwest Qinghai provinces. Altaic, Turkic, Western, Aralo-Caspian. Dialects: NORTHEASTERN KAZAKH, SOUTHWESTERN KAZAKH. An official nationality in China. SOV. Literacy rate in second language: 72%. Had an official Roman alphabet; since 1980 uses a modified Arabic script. Radio programs. Pastoralists, some agriculture. Sunni Muslim, some shamanism. NT 1820-1910, out of print. See main entry under Kazakhstan.

KEMIEHUA [KFJ] 1,000 (1991). Jinghong County, Xishuangbanna Dai Autonomous Prefecture, southwestern Yunnan Province. Austro-Asiatic, Mon-Khmer, Unclassified. SVO; most modifiers follow heads, although adverbial phrases precede heads; simple syllable structure; tonal.

KHAKAS ***(KHAKHAS, KHAKHASS, ABAKAN TATAR, YENISEI TATAR)*** [KJH] 10 fluent speakers out of 875 in ethnic group in China (1982 census). Fuyu County, north of Qiqihar, in Heilongjiang Province. Altaic, Turkic, Northern. Dialects: SAGAI, BELTIR, KACHA, KYZYL, SHOR, KAMASSIAN. Bilingualism in Mongolian, Chinese. Only about 10 very old people speak fluently, others use some words, but mainly Mongolian. The young people are monolingual in Chinese. It was counted as Kirghiz in the 1982 Chinese census. People came from the Altay Mts. in Russia in 1761. See main entry under Russia.

KHAMS ***(KHAMS-YAL, KHAMS BHOTIA, KAM, KHAMBA, KHAMPA, KANG)*** [KHG] 1,487,000 (1994), including 996,000 Eastern, 135,000 Southern, 158,000 Western, 91,000 Northern, 77,000 Jone, 30,000 Hbrugchu. Northeastern Tibet, Changdu (Qamdo) and Naqu (Nagqu) districts; Ganzi (Garzê) Tibetan Autonomous Prefecture in western Sichuan; Diqing (Dêqên) Tibetan Autonomous Prefecture in northwestern Yunnan Province; and Yushu Tibetan Autonmous Prefecture in southwestern Qinghai Province. Sino-Tibetan, Tibeto-Burman, Himalayish, Tibeto-Kanauri, Tibetic, Tibetan, Northern. Dialects: EASTERN KHAMS, SOUTHERN KHAMS, WESTERN KHAMS, NORTHERN KHAMS, HBRUGCHU, JONE. Dialects listed may be separate languages; differences are reported to be large. 80% lexical similarity with Dbusgtsang (Central Tibetan). Different from Takale, Nisi, Sheshi, Maikoti, and Gamale Kham of Nepal. Included officially under the Tibetan nationality. Investigation needed: intelligibility with dialects. SOV; 4 tones. Traditional religion.

KHMU ***(KAMMU, KHAMU, KHMU', KHAMUK, KAMHMU, KAMU, KEMU, KHOMU, MOU, LAO TERNG, POUTENG, THENG)*** [KJG] 1,600 in China (1990). Mengla and Jinghong counties of Xishuangbanna Prefecture, southwestern Yunnan. Austro-Asiatic, Mon-Khmer, Northern Mon-Khmer, Khmuic, Mal-Khmu', Khmu'. Khmu was counted separately in the 1982 census and combined into a group of 'Undetermined Minorities'. It may soon be recognized as an official nationality. Phsing (Bit) is regarded as Khmu in China, but is in the Palaungic branch (J-O Svantesson 1990). Those in Mengla have no script, but those in Jinghong use a classical script called 'Duota'. Bible portions 1918. See main entry under Laos.

KHUEN ***(KWEEN, KHWEEN, KHOUEN)*** [KHF] 1,000 in China (1993). Austro-Asiatic, Mon-Khmer, Northern Mon-Khmer, Khmuic, Mal-Khmu', Khmu'. See main entry under Laos.

KIM MUN ***(MUN, KEM MUN, GEM MUN, JIM MUN, JINMEN, KIMMUN, MEN, MAN LANTIEN, LANTEN, LAN TIN, LOWLAND YAO, CHASAN YAO, SHANZI YAO, HAINAN MIAO)*** [MJI] 107,000 in China (1982), including 41,000 in Hainan Province (1982). Population total all countries 280,000. Qiongzhong, Qionghai, and Baoting counties of Hainan Province, and neighboring areas of surrounding counties (Jinmen); Guangxi Zhuang Autonomous Region (Xilin, Baise, Napo, Bama counties), Guizhou Province, and Yunnan Province (Malipo, Maguan, Guangnan counties). They may also be in Thailand and Myanmar. Also spoken in Laos, Viet Nam. Hmong-Mien, Mienic, Mian-Jin. 78% lexical similarity with Iu Mien, 67% with Biao-Jiao Mien, 59% with Ba Pai. Officially included under Yao (Mien) nationality in China, except for those on Hainan Island, who are under the Miao nationality. The largest Yao group after Iu Mien. Dictionary. Daoist.

KIRGHIZ ***(KIRGIZ, KARA, KE'ERKEZ)*** [KDO] 141,549 in China (1990 census), including 50,000 in North Kirghiz, 50,000 in South Kirghiz. West and southwest Xinjiang. Altaic, Turkic, Western, Aralo-Caspian. Two dialects, divided by Kyzyl Su River. An official nationality in China. SOV. Literacy rate in second language: 59%. Uses a modified Arabic script in China. Agriculturalists. Sunni Muslim, some shamanist traditions. NT 1991. See main entry under Kyrgyzstan.

KON KEU [ANG] Austro-Asiatic, Mon-Khmer, Northern Mon-Khmer, Palaungic, Western Palaungic, Angkuic. May be in Myanmar or Laos. Under Blang minority in China.

KOREAN [KKN] 1,920,597 in China (1990 census). Inner Mongolia. 46% of Koreans in China live in Hyanbian Korean Autonomous District along Tumen River, Jilin (Kirin). Language Isolate. Considered one of the main official nationalities. 'Chaoxian' is the name used in China. High level of education. Radio programs. Agriculturalists. Buddhist, Christian. Bible 1911-1993. See main entry under Korea, South.

KUANHUA [QAK] 1,000 (1991). Jinghong County, Xishuangbanna Dai Autonomous Prefecture, southwestern Yunnan Province. Austro-Asiatic, Mon-Khmer, Unclassified. SVO.

KYERUNG [KGY] Tibet. Sino-Tibetan, Tibeto-Burman, Bodic, Bodish, Tibetan, Unclassified. Close to Tibetan (Lhasa). Apparently distinct from Jiarong (Gyarung). See main entry under Nepal.

LACHI ***(LA CHI, LATI, TAI LATI, LAJI, LIPULIO, I TO, Y TO, Y POONG, Y MIA, KU TE)*** [LBT] 1,153 speakers out of 1,634 in China in 306 households (1990 Liang Min), including 193 Bag Lachi in 37 households, 852 Han Lachi in 179 households, 157 Red Lachi in 27 households, 432 Flowery Lachi in 72 households. Yunnan Province, Wenshan Zhuang-Miao Autonomous Prefecture, southern Maguan County, several villages: Bag Lachi in Nanlao Township, Han Lachi in Renhe and Jiahanqing townships, Red Lachi in Xiaobazi Township, and Flowery Lachi in Jinchang. Tai-Kadai, Kadai, Ge-Chi. Dialects: LIPUTE (BAG LACHI), LIPUTCIO (HAN LACHI), LIPUKE (RED LACHI), LIPULIONGTCO (FLOWERY LACHI), LIPUTIÕ (BLACK LACHI), LIPUPI (LONG-HAIRED LACHI). Related to Gelo. The first five dialects listed are in China, the others in Viet Nam. Long-Haired Lachi of Viet Nam (4,806 speakers) has 80% lexical similarity with Flowery Lachi of China; White Lachi of Viet Nam (1,602) has 30% to 40% similarity with the others, and should be considered a separate language. 36% lexical similarity with Gelo, 33% with Laqua, 34% with Buyang, 28% with Northern Zhuang, 22% with Dong, 23% with Laka, 25% with Hlai. Those who do not speak Lachi speak Chinese. The Flowery Lachi also speak Chinese, most can speak Southern Zhuang, and some can speak Miao and Dai. Mixed families speak Chinese. They speak Lachi at home. Many younger than 20 cannot speak Lachi. Officially in the Yi nationality. See main entry under Viet Nam.

LADAKHI ***(LADAPHI, LADHAKHI, LADAK, LADWAGS)*** [LBJ] 12,000 in China (1995). Western Tibet. Sino-Tibetan, Tibeto-Burman, Himalayish, Tibeto-Kanauri, Tibetic, Tibetan, Western, Ladakhi. Dialects: LEH (CENTRAL LADAKHI), SHAMMA (SHAM, SHAMSKAT, LOWER LADAKHI), NUBRA LADAKHI. Perhaps 30% to 40% intelligibility with Tibetan. Lexical similarity among 5 main dialects: 84% to 94%; 71% to 83% with Purik, 53% to 60% with Tibetan. Officially included under the Tibetan nationality. Grammar. SOV; postpositions; genitives, relatives before noun heads; articles, adjectives numerals after noun heads; suffixes indicate case of noun phrase; ergative; causatives; comparative; CCVCC or CCCVV maximum; nontonal. Mountain valleys. Agriculturalists: wheat, barley; pastoralists: yaks, goats, sheep (cashmere wool). 8,250 to 16,500 feet. Lamaist Buddhist. Bible portions 1904-1919. See main entry under India.

LAHU ***(LOHEI, LAHUNA, LAKU, KAIXIEN, NAMEN, MUSSUH, MUHSO, MUSSO, MUSSAR, MOSO)*** [LAH] 411,476 in China (1990 census), including 240,000 Na, probably including Kutsung and Laopang. Population total all countries 580,000 (1981 Wurm and Hattori). Lancang Lahu Autonomous County, Gengma, and Menglian counties, southwestern Yunnan. Also spoken in Laos,

Myanmar, Thailand, Viet Nam. Sino-Tibetan, Tibeto-Burman, Lolo-Burmese, Loloish, Southern, Akha, Lahu. Dialects: NA (BLACK LAHU, MUSSER DAM, NORTHERN LAHU, LOHEIRN), NYI (RED LAHU, SOUTHERN LAHU, MUSSEH DAENG, LUHISHI, LUHUSHI), SHEHLEH. Black Lahu and Lahu Shi (Yellow Lahu, Kutsung) have difficult intelligibility. (See separate entry for Lahu Shi.) Mossu is in Laos. Taught at Kunming Institute. An official nationality in China. Dictionary. SOV. Pinyin (Roman) alphabet used in China. Subtropical forest. Mountain slope. Agriculturalists: rice, maize; some hunters. Some Christian. Bible 1989.

LAHU SHI ***(LAHU XI, KUTSUNG, KUCONG, KUR, SHI, YELLOW LAHU, KWI)*** [KDS] 5,000 in China (1984). Southern Yunnan. Sino-Tibetan, Tibeto-Burman, Lolo-Burmese, Loloish, Southern, Akha, Lahu. Difficult intelligibility with Black Lahu. A distinct language from Nyi (Red Lahu). SOV. See main entry under Laos.

LAKKIA ***(LAKKJA, LAKJA, LAKIA, LAJIA, TAI LAKA, LAKA, CHASHAN YAO, TEA MOUNTAIN YAO)*** [LBC] 8,703 speakers (1995 McConnell) out of 11,503 ethnic Lakkia. Jinxiu Yao Autonomous County of eastern Guangxi Zhuang Autonomous Region. Tai-Kadai, Kam-Tai, Lakkja. Officially under the Yao (Mien) nationality, but the language is Tai-Kadai (J-O Svantesson). Phonetically similar to Mien, word order to Bunu. Not intelligible with Hmong or Bunu. Minimal variation within Lakkia. All varieties are inherently intelligible to each other's speakers. 45% lexical similarity with Dong, 44% with Northern Zhuang, 24% with Buyang, 23% with Lati and Laqua, 22% with Gelo. Different from Lashi, which is also called Chashan(hua). 'Lajia' is the same name used for the Yayao variety of the Siyi dialect of Cantonese spoken in Heshan County, Guangdong. Grammar. SVO; modifiers follow heads; consonant clusters and palatalized and labialized onsets; voiced and voiceless nasal onsets; long-short vowel distinction; 6 basic tone categories in unchecked syllables and 2 in checked with further split in checked syllables according to vowel length. Mountain slope. Daoist.

LAQUA ***(PUBIAO, PUPEO, PU PÉO, KA BIAO, KA BAO, KA BEO, KABEO, QABIAO)*** [LAQ] 307 in China, or 58 households (1990 Zhang Junru). Yunnan Province, Wenshan Zhuang-Miao Autonomous Prefecture, Malipo County, Tiechang, Matong, Punong, Pucha, and Pufeng towns. Tai-Kadai, Kadai, Yang-Biao. At all locations they can communicate with each other without difficulty. 38% lexical similarity with Gelo, 33% with Lati, 38% with Buyang, 30% with Northern Zhuang, 29% with Dong, 23% with Laka, 26% with Hlai, 10% with Hmong, 7% with Mien. Generally everyone can also speak Southwestern Mandarin. Those at Pialong can speak Southern Zhuang. Those near Matong can speak Hmong. Nearly 30% of the younger generation speak Laqua. Ka Biao is their name for themselves. Classified officially under the Yi nationality. See main entry under Viet Nam.

LASHI ***(LASI, LEQI, LETSI, LACHIKWAW, CHASHANHUA, ACYE)*** [LSI] Luxi, Longchuan, Yingjiang, and Ruili counties, Dehong Dai-Jingpo Autonomous Prefecture, western Yunnan. Sino-Tibetan, Tibeto-Burman, Lolo-Burmese, Burmish, Northern. Officially included under Jingpo in China. SOV; 4 tones; final nasals and stops; vowel length and tense-lax distinction. See main entry under Myanmar.

LAWA, WESTERN ***(WA, WA PROPER, LAVA, LUWA, LUA, L'WA, LAVUA, LAVÜA, MOUNTAIN LAWA)*** [LCP] 75,000 in China, including 30,000 in the Blang nationality, 45,000 in the Va nationality (1990 J-O Svantesson). Population total both countries 82,000. Southwest Yunnan Province. Also spoken in Thailand. Austro-Asiatic, Mon-Khmer, Northern Mon-Khmer, Palaungic, Western Palaungic, Waic, Lawa. Unintelligible to speakers of Eastern Lawa in Thailand. Some dialects are unintelligible to each other's speakers. Related to Wa and Parauk in Myanmar and China. Traditional religion, Buddhist. NT 1972.

LHOMI ***(LHOKET, SHING SAAPA)*** [LHM] 1,000 in Tibet. Tibet. Sino-Tibetan, Tibeto-Burman, Himalayish, Tibeto-Kanauri, Tibetic, Tibetan, Central. Dialect may be different from Nepal. Probably officially included under Tibetan in China. Agriculturalists, pastoralists. Traditional religion, Lamaist. NT 1995. See main entry under Nepal.

LINGAO ***(VO LIMKOU, LIMKOW, LINKOW, ONGBE, ONG-BE, BÊ)*** [ONB] 520,000 (1982 census) in the ethnic group, including 350,000 Lincheng, 170,000 Qiongshan. The number of speakers is unclear (A. Diller). North central coast of Hainan, entire Lingao county, parts of Danxian, Chengmai, and Qiongshan counties, and suburbs of Haikou city. Tai-Kadai, Kam-Tai, Be-Tai, Be. Dialects: LINCHENG (LINGAO PROPER-DENGMAI), QIONGSHAN. Classified as in Tai or Kadai family. Urban members are bilingual in Hainan dialect of Min Nan Chinese. Most think of themselves as Han (Chinese) nationality. Investigation needed: bilingual proficiency in Hainan Chinese, Zhuang. Dictionary. Grammar. SVO; linguistically similar to Zhuang and Dai. Lincheng reported to have 7 tone categories, Qiongshan 13. Loans from Cantonese and Hainan variety of Min Nan Chinese.

LIPO ***(EASTERN LISU, TAKU LISU, HE LISU, BLACK LISU, TAKU)*** [TKL] 60,068 (1993). Around Taku, east Yunnan, highland areas. Sino-Tibetan, Tibeto-Burman, Lolo-Burmese, Loloish, Northern, Lisu. Not intelligible with Lisu. Use a different script from Lisu. NT 1951.

LISU ***(LISSU, LISAW, LI-SHAW, LI-HSAW, LU-TZU, LESUO, LI, LISHU, LISO, LEISU, LESHUOOPA, LOISU, SOUTHERN LISU, YAO YEN, YAW-YEN, YAW YIN, YEH-JEN, CHUNG, CHELI, CHEDI,***

LIP'A, LUSU, KHAE) [LIS] 515,000 in China (1990). Population total all countries 657,000. West Yunnan, upper reaches of the Salween and Mekong rivers, and Sichuan. Also spoken in India, Myanmar, Thailand. Sino-Tibetan, Tibeto-Burman, Lolo-Burmese, Loloish, Northern, Lisu. Dialects: HUA LISU (FLOWERY LISU), PAI LISU (WHITE LISU), LU SHI LISU. Dialect differences are not great. Taught at Kumning Institute. An official nationality in China. The official orthography is with Roman script. There are 2 older alphabetic orthographies and 1 indigenous script. Agriculturalists, animal husbandry. Polytheist, Christian. Bible 1968-1986.

LÜ ***(TAI LU, LUE, LY, LU, DAI LE, XISHUANGBANNA DAI, SIPSONGPANNA DAI, PAI-I, PAI'I', SHUI-PAI-I)*** [KHB] 250,000 in China (1990 J-O Svantesson) to possibly 770,000 or 75% of the Dai (1990 A. Diller). Population total all countries 551,700. South Yunnan, Jinghong (Chiang Hung, Chien Rung), Xishuangbanna Dai Autonomous Prefecture, west of the Lixianjiang (Black) River. Also spoken in Laos, Myanmar, Thailand, Viet Nam. Tai-Kadai, Kam-Tai, Be-Tai, Tai-Sek, Tai, Southwestern, East Central, Northwest. Mu'ang Yong and dialects in the Lanna area may converge phonologically with Lanna (Diller 1990). Different from Tai Nüa, each having their own traditions. Officially included under Dai nationality in China. An official nationality in Viet Nam. Dictionary. SVO; modifiers follow heads. Old Lü script is used. Has a different script than Tai Nüa. Traditional religion, Buddhist. NT 1933.

LUOBA, BOGA'ER ***(LHOBA, LHO-PA, BOGA'ER, BENGNI-BOGA'ER, BOKAR, ADI-BOKAR, ADI, ABOR)*** [ADI] 3,000 in China (1994). Lhunze and Mainling counties in southeast Tibet, south of the Yaluzangjiang River in the Luoyu area. Sino-Tibetan, Tibeto-Burman, North Assam, Tani. The same as Adi in India. A different language from Yidu Lhoba. Barely intelligible with Yidu Lhoba. Luoba is an official nationality. Different from Lopa (Loba) in Nepal. Not a written language. SOV; particles indicate grammatical relations; long-short vowel distinction; no contrastive tone; most words polysyllabic; loans mainly from Tibetan. 27% attended school, 31% have some degree of literacy, .8% have a university degree. Tibetan. Evergreen and bamboo forest. Mountain slope. Swidden agriculturalists: rice, maize, barley, cotton; hunters, forestry, animal husbandry, fishermen. Traditional religion, Lamaist Buddhist. NT 1988. See main entry under India.

LUOBA, YIDU ***(LHOBA, LHO-PA, YIDU, IDU MISHMI, CHULIKATA)*** [CLK] 7,000 in China (1994). Lhunze and Mainling counties in southeast Tibet, in the Danba River valley and adjoining mountain slopes, near the Bhutan border. Sino-Tibetan, Tibeto-Burman, North Assam, Tani. A different language from Boga'er Lhoba. Same as Idu in India. May be a dialect of Miri in India. Luoba is an official nationality. Different from Lopa (Loba) in Nepal. Not a written language. 27% attended primary school, 31% have some degree of literacy, .8% have a university degree. Tibetan. Evergreen and bamboo forest. Mountain valley, mountain slope. Swidden agriculturalists: rice, maize, barley, cotton; forestry, animal husbandry, hunters, fishermen. Traditional religion, Lamaist Buddhist. See main entry under India.

MACANESE ***(MACAO CREOLE PORTUGUESE, MACAENSE)*** [MZS] 4,000 in Hong Kong (1977 Voegelin and Voegelin) and a few in Macau (1996 Ian Watts), out of 8,500 in the ethnic group (1985). Hong Kong and Macau. Possibly in USA. Creole, Portuguese based.

MAK ***(MO, MOHUA, MO-HUA, CHING, MOJIAHUA, MOCHIAHUA)*** [MKG] 10,000 or more (1982 census). Yangfeng, Fangcun, Jialiang, and Di'e villages in northwestern Libo County in Guizhou Province, and some in neighboring Dushan County, Guizhou. Tai-Kadai, Kam-Tai, Kam-Sui. Dialects: MAK, CHI, CHING (CHAM), HWA, LYO. Dialect differences are minor. Similar to Ai-Cham. Local Chinese and Bouyei are used as second languages. Officially included under the Bouyei nationality. Traditional religion.

MAN MET ***(MANMIT, MANMI)*** [MML] 900 (1984 J. Svantesson). Southwestern Yunnan Province, 5 communities in Xishuangbanna near the Hu. Austro-Asiatic, Mon-Khmer, Northern Mon-Khmer, Palaungic, Western Palaungic, Angkuic. Counted separately in 1982 census and combined into a group of 'Undetermined Minorities'. Reported to be similar to Hu. Investigation needed: intelligibility with Angkuic languages. Tonal; affixes. Mountain slope.

MANCHU ***(MAN)*** [MJF] 20 to 70 speakers (1995 M. Krauss) out of 1,821,180 in the ethnic group (1990 census). Heilongjiang, a few Manchu-speaking villages in Aihui and Fuyu counties. The ethnic group is in Heilongjiang, Jilin, and Liaoning provinces. There may also be members of the ethnic group in North Korea and Siberia. Altaic, Tungus, Southern, Southwest. The nonspeakers of Manchu in the ethnic group speak Mandarin. Now written Chinese in common use. All speakers over 70 years old (1986). An official nationality. Dictionary. Literacy rate in second language: 82%. Written Manchu was once in use with old Manchu script. Agriculturalists. Chinese traditional religion, shamanism, Buddhist. NT 1835.

MANG ***(MANG U, XAMANG, CHAMAN, MANBU, BA'E)*** [MGA] 500 in China. Yunnan, Jinping County, Hani-Yi Autonomous Prefecture. Austro-Asiatic, Mon-Khmer, Northern Mon-Khmer, Mang. Counted separately in 1982 census and combined into a group of 'Undetermined Minorities'. Dai, Hani, and

Kutsung call them 'Chaman', 'Manbu', 'Ba'e'. An official ethnic community in Viet Nam. Thick forests. Mountain slope. Agriculturalists: maize, rice; hunters. See main entry under Viet Nam.

MAONAN ***(AI NAN)*** [MMD] 37,000 speakers out of an ethnic group of 71,968 (1990 census). Xianan area of Huanjiang Maonan Autonomous County in north central Guangxi Zhuang Autonomous Region. A few in nearby Hechi, Yishan, Nandan, and Du'an counties. Tai-Kadai, Kam-Tai, Kam-Sui. Spoken Chinese and Zhuang and written Chinese in use. An official nationality. SVO; numbers and adjectives follow nouns; reduplication; glottalized, pre-nasalized, palatalized, and labialized onsets; nasal and stop finals; 6 tone categories in unchecked syllables, 2 in checked (split into 4 according to vowel length); many Chinese loans. Chinese script. Agriculturalists. Daoist, Christian.

MARU ***(MATU, MALU, LAWNG, LAUNGWAW, LAUNGAW, LANGSU, LANG'E, NYKY, DISO, ZI, LHAO VO)*** [MHX] (Over 10,000 households in China; 1999). Western Yunnan, Luxi, Longchuan, Yingjiang, Ruili, and Lianghe counties of the Dehong Dai-Jingpo Autonomous Prefecture. Sino-Tibetan, Tibeto-Burman, Lolo-Burmese, Burmish, Northern. Officially included under Jingpo in China. Different from the Matu variety of Khumi Chin. SOV; 3 tones; tense-lax vowel distinction; loans from Jingpo, Dai Burmese, and Chinese. NT 1985. See main entry under Myanmar.

MOINBA ***(MENBA, CUONA MENBA, CUONA MONPA, MENPA, MONPA, MONBA, MOMPA, MOMBA)*** [MOB] 30,000 speakers in China (1990 J-O Svantesson), although the 1990 census gives only 7,475 in the official nationality. To the east of Bhutan, partly in southeastern Tibet, mainly on the Yarlung-Zanbo River, Medog, Nyinchi, Cuona counties. There may be speakers in Bhutan. Sino-Tibetan, Tibeto-Burman, Himalayish, Mahakiranti, Kiranti, Eastern. Dialects: NORTHERN CUONA, SOUTHERN CUONA. There are more speakers of Southern Cuona. More Chinese loans in Southern Cuona, and a different number of tones from Northern Cuona. Cuona differs from Tshangla in phonology, vocabulary, and grammar. Cuona is the same as, or closely related to, Bumthangkha of Bhutan. May also be classified as North Assam, Monpa. Written Tibetan is used. An official nationality. Tshangla (7,000) is also officially included in the Moinba nationality. Investigation needed: intelligibility with 2 dialects. 2 tones (Northern), 4 tones (Southern). Agriculturalists: rice, maize, bananas, peppers, leeks, ginger, millet; cattle. 6,500 meters. Lamaist Buddhism. See main entry under India.

MONGOLIAN, PERIPHERAL ***(MONGOL, MONGGOL, MENGGU, SOUTHERN-EASTERN MONGOLIAN, INNER MONGOLIAN)*** [MVF] 3,381,000 (1982 estimate), 4,806,849 including Buriat and Tuvin (1990 census). 299,000 Chakhar, 317,000 Bairin, 1,347,000 Khorain, 593,00 Karachin, 123,000 Ordos, 34,000 Ejine (1982 census). Population total both countries 3,381,000 or more. Inner Mongolia, Liaoning, Jilin, and Heilongjiang provinces, Urumchi to Hailar. Also spoken in Mongolia. Altaic, Mongolian, Eastern, Oirat-Khalkha, Khalkha-Buriat, Mongolian Proper. Dialects: CHAHAR (CHAHA'ER, CHAKHAR, QAHAR), ORDOS (E'ERDUOSITE), TUMUT (TUMET), SHILINGOL (UJUMCHIN), ULANCHAB (URAT, MINGAN), JO-UDA (BAIRIN, BALIN, NAIMAN, KESHIKTEN), JOSTU (KE'ERQIN, KHARCHIN, KHARACHIN, KHARCHIN-TUMUT, EASTERN TUMUT), JIRIM (KALAQIN, KHORCHIN, JALAIT, GORLOS), EJINE. Largely intelligible with Halh standard dialect of Mongolia, but there are phonological and important loan differences. Written Chinese is in use. One of the five main official nationalities. The government includes Buriat, Tuvin, Oirat, and other varieties under the Mongolian official nationality. In Xinjiang, the Torgut, Oold, Korbet, and Hoshut peoples are known as the 'Four tribes of Oirat'. Language of wider communication. SOV. Literacy rate in second language: 71%. Standard Inner Mongolian script. Radio programs. Agriculturalists, pastoralists. Buddhist, Lamaist, shamanism. NT 1952.

MULAM ***(MULAO, MOLAO, MULOU, MULIAO, MULAO MIAO, ABO, AYO)*** [MLM] 159,328 (1990 census). Luocheng Mulam Autonomous County (90% in Dongmen and Siba communes), and adjacent counties in north central Guizhou Province; and in Majiang and Kaili City in Guizhou Province. Tai-Kadai, Kam-Tai, Kam-Sui. Close to Kam. 65% lexical similarity with Dong (probably Southern Dong); 53% with Zhuang (probably Northern Zhuang). Chinese is used as second language. Written Chinese in common use. Many use Northern Zhuang. Most Mulam people use Mulam extensively. Many Han Chinese and Zhuang are bilingual in Mulam. An official nationality. They live close to the Han, Zhuang, Dong, Hmong, and Mien. They call themselves 'Mulam'. Some around Luocheng call themselves 'Kyam'. SVO; reduplication; aspirated, palatalized, labialized, voiceless nasal, lateral onsets; nasal and stop finals; 6 tone categories in unchecked syllables, 2 in checked (split into 4 according to vowel length); many Chinese loans. Literacy rate in second language: 65%. Agriculturalists. Buddhist.

MUYA ***(MIYAO, MINYAK, MANYAK)*** [MVM] 15,000 (1995). West central Sichuan (Kangbo and Juilong (Gyaisi) in the Ganzi (Garzê) Tibetan Autonomous Prefecture and Simian County in the Ya'an District. Sino-Tibetan, Tibeto-Burman, Tangut-Qiang, Qiangic. 'Muyak' may be an alternate name. Speakers belong to the Tibetan nationality. SOV; adjectives and number-classifier constructions follow noun heads; compounding; affixation; reduplication; consonant cluster onsets; tense-lax vowel distinction; nasalized vowels; 4 tones.

NAMUYI ***(NAMUZI)*** [NMY] 5,000 (1982). Mianning, Muli, Xichang, and Yanyuan counties of the Liangshan Yi Autonomous Prefecture, and Jiulong (Gyaisi) County in the Ganzi (Garzê) Tibetan Autonomous

Prefecture of southwestern Sichuan. Sino-Tibetan, Tibeto-Burman, Tangut-Qiang, Qiangic. Speakers belong to the Tibetan nationality. They call themselves 'Namuzi'. SOV; adjectives and number-classifier constructions follow noun heads; compounding; affixation; consonant cluster onsets but no consonantal codas; tense-lax vowel distinction; nasalized and retroflexed vowels; 4 tones.

NANAI ***(GOLDI, GOLD, SUSHEN, JUCHEN)*** [GLD] 40 speakers out of 4,245 in the ethnic group in China (1990 census). Sanjiang plain in the northeastern corner of Heilongjiang Province, near where the Heilong, Songhua, and Wusuli rivers merge, with most in Tongjiang county, Bacha and Jiejinkou villages and in Sipai village in Raohe County. Altaic, Tungus, Southern, Southeast, Nanaj. Dialects: HEZHEN (HEZHE, HECHE), QILENG (KILI, KILEN). Written Chinese in common use. All speakers are elderly. Younger generation in China speaks Chinese. An official nationality in China. Formerly called 'Sushen'. Literacy rate in second language: 84%. Agriculturalists, fishermen, hunters. Shamanism. Bible portions 1884. See main entry under Russia.

NAXI ***(NAHSI, NASI, NAKHI, LOMI, MU, "MOSO", "MOSSO", "MO-SU")*** [NBF] 278,009 (1990 census) including 225,000 in Yunnan, 20,000 in Sichuan. Most (200,000) in Lijiang Naxi Autonomous County, northwestern Yunnan. Some scattered through Weixi, Zhongdian, Ninglang, Deqing, Yongsheng, Heqing, Jianchuan, and Lanping counties. Some in Yanyuan, Yanbian, and Muli counties of Sichuan Province. A few in Mangkang county, southeastern Tibet. Possibly also in Myanmar. Sino-Tibetan, Tibeto-Burman, Lolo-Burmese, Naxi. Dialects: LICHIANG (LIJIANG), LAPAO, LUTIEN. The western dialect is reported to be fairly uniform, and is considered to be the standard (from Dayan in Lijiang County). Eastern has some internal differences, and intelligibility may be low within it. Written Chinese in common use. People resent the older term "Moso". One of the official nationalities in China. The 8,000 or so 'Eastern' Naxi in the Lugu Lake area are matriarchal. Most Naxi are patriarchal. Dictionary. SOV; no checked syllables; 4 tones. Literacy rate in second language: 62%. Roman alphabet developed in the 1950s and revised in 1984. An ideographic writing system called 'Dongba' is not practical for everyday use, but is a system of prompt-illustrations for reciting classic texts. 2 syllabary scripts called 'Geba' and 'Malimasa' are also used in Weixi County. Agriculturalists, animal husbandry. Lamaist Buddhist, Daoist, Christian. Bible portions 1932.

NUSU [NUF] 9,000 speakers (1994), including 2,000 in Northern Nusu, 3,000 in Southern Nusu, and 4,000 in Central Nusu. Bijiang County in Nujiang Prefecture of northwestern Yunnan. Sino-Tibetan, Tibeto-Burman, Lolo-Burmese, Loloish, Unclassified. Dialects: NORTHERN NUSU, SOUTHERN NUSU, CENTRAL NUSU. May be Nungish or a variety of Yi (Matisoff et al. 1996:74). Some bilingualism with Lisu. A separate language officially under the Nu nationality with Ayi, Zauzou (1,500), and 5,500 speakers of Drung. SOV; grammatical relations indicated mainly by word order and particles; 4 tones with relatively complex sandhi; loans from Lisu, Chinese, and a few from Burmese.

OROQEN ***(OROCHON, ORONCHON, OLUNCHUN, ELUNCHUN, ULUNCHUN)*** [ORH] 2,240 speakers (1982) out of 6,965 in official nationality (1990 census). Huma, Aihui, Sunko districts, Great Xingan Ridge, Heilongjiang Province. Possibly eastern Siberia. Altaic, Tungus, Northern, Evenki. Maintain native language and customs. An official nationality. Not a written language. Literacy rate in second language: 84%. Dense mountain forests. Hunters, lumbermen, agriculturalists. Shamanism, ancestor worship.

PALAUNG, PALE ***(DLANG, NGWE PALAUNG, SILVER PALAUNG, PALE, PALAY, BULAI, PULEI, SOUTHERN TA'ANG)*** [PCE] 5,000 in China (1995). Western Yunnan, Luxi County, just east of Rumai. Austro-Asiatic, Mon-Khmer, Northern Mon-Khmer, Palaungic, Eastern Palaungic, Palaung. Dialects: BULEI, RAOJIN. Some intelligibility with Riang, and close to Shwe. Not intelligible with Rumai. 50% of the De'ang speak Pale. Officially under De'ang in China. See main entry under Myanmar.

PALAUNG, RUMAI ***(RUMAI, RUOMAI, HUMAI)*** [RBB] 2,000 in China (1995). Far western Yunnan, Longchuan and Ruili counties. Austro-Asiatic, Mon-Khmer, Northern Mon-Khmer, Palaungic, Eastern Palaungic, Palaung. Not intelligible with Pale. 20% of the De'ang speak Rumai. Officially under De'ang in China. See main entry under Myanmar.

PALAUNG, SHWE ***(TA-ANG PALAUNG, GOLDEN PALAUNG, SHWE)*** [SWE] 2,000 in China (1995 SIL). Yunnan. Austro-Asiatic, Mon-Khmer, Northern Mon-Khmer, Palaungic, Eastern Palaungic, Palaung. Officially included under De'ang in China. Hinayana Buddhist. See main entry under Myanmar.

PALYU ***(PALJU, BOLYU, LAI)*** [PLY] 10,000 (1993). Other reports say 150 (1995), and 800 (1996). Far western Guangxi on the Guizhou border, Xilin and Longlin counties, in 2 groups. There may be some in Yunnan. Austro-Asiatic, Mon-Khmer, Palyu. Recently discovered. Called 'Lai' in Chinese. SVO; modifiers follow heads; grammatical relations marked mainly by word order and particles; reported to have long and half long versus short vowel distinction; uvular stops; 6 tone categories in unchecked syllables plus 5 in checked syllables. Shows similarities to Kadai languages.

PANANG ***(PANAGS, PANAKHA, PANANAG, BANAG, BANANG, SBANAG, SBRANAG)*** [PCR] Tibet. Sino-Tibetan, Tibeto-Burman, Himalayish, Tibeto-Kanauri, Tibetic, Tibetan, Central. Probably included officially under Tibetan. May not be a separate language.

PARAUK ***(WA, PRAOK, BARAOG, BAROKE)*** [PRK] 180,000 speakers (1990) out of 351,974 in the official Wa nationality in China (1990 census). Awa Mountains, southwest Yunnan as far east as the Lancang (Mekong) River. Austro-Asiatic, Mon-Khmer, Northern Mon-Khmer, Palaungic, Western Palaungic, Waic, Wa. A large and powerful group. Traditional culture. Taught at Kunming Institute. Part of the Wa official nationality, which includes 3 languages: Parauk, Vo, and Western Lawa. Parauk is the largest and the standard. Parauk has an orthography. Mountain slope. Agriculturalists: potatoes, cotton, hemp, tobacco, sugarcane, tea, rice, beans, buckwheat, maize; some hunters. Hinayana Buddhist, some Christian. NT 1938. See main entry under Myanmar.

PUMI, NORTHERN ***(P'UMI, PIMI, PRIMMI, PRUUMI, P'ÖMI, P'ROME, CH'RAME)*** [PMI] 35,000 speakers (1999): 24,000 in the Pumi nationality, 30,000 in the Tibetan nationality (1994). Southwestern Sichuan, Muli, Yanyuan, and Kiulong counties; and northwestern Yunnan, Yongning District of Ninglang County. Sino-Tibetan, Tibeto-Burman, Tangut-Qiang, Qiangic. Dialect: TAOBA. Northern Pumi has 5 subdialects. Intelligibility with Southern Pumi is difficult. Lexical similarity between Northern and Southern is 60%, grammatical differences minor. Pumi is an official nationality. No written form. SOV; adjectives and numbers follow noun heads; 3 tones; no uvular obstruents; no initial /s/ or consonant clusters; different vowels from S. Pumi; loans mainly from Tibetan (10% of the vocabulary). Literacy rate in second language: 39%. Agriculturalists. Lamaist.

PUMI, SOUTHERN ***(P'UMI, PIMI, PRIMMI, PRUUMI, P'ÖMI, P'ROME)*** [PUS] 19,000 speakers (1999): 24,000 in the Pumi nationality, 30,000 in the Tibetan nationality (1994). Northwestern Yunnan Province, Lanping, Weixi, Yongsheng and Lijiang counties, and Xinyingpan District of Ninglang County. Sino-Tibetan, Tibeto-Burman, Tangut-Qiang, Qiangic. Dialect: QINGHUA. Southern Pumi has 5 subdialects. Intelligibility with Northern Pumi is difficult. Lexical similarity between Northern and Southern is 60%, grammatical differences minor. Pumi is an official nationality. No written form. SOV; adjectives and numbers follow noun heads; 2 tones; uvular obstruents; initial /s/ + consonant clusters; different vowels from N. Pumi; loans mainly from Chinese (making up 15% of the vocabulary). Literacy rate in second language: 39%. Agriculturalists. Lamaist.

QIANG, NORTHERN ***(CH'IANG)*** [CNG] 57,800 (1999). 130,000 speakers in all Qiang languages, including 80,000 in the Qiang nationality and 50,000 in the Tibetan nationality (1990 J-O Svantesson). 198,252 ethnic population in the Qiang nationality (1990 census). North central Sichuan Province, Heishuihe River basin northward through most of Heishui County. Sino-Tibetan, Tibeto-Burman, Tangut-Qiang, Qiangic. Dialects: YADU, WEIGU, CIMULIN, LUHUA. Written Chinese is in use. Qiang is an official nationality. No tones; more consonants than Southern Qiang. Agriculturalists, some animal husbandry. Lamaist, polytheist.

QIANG, SOUTHERN ***(CH'IANG)*** [QMR] 81,300 (1999 Jonathan Evans). Speakers in all Qiang languages, including 80,000 in the Qiang nationality and 50,000 in the Tibetan nationality; 1990 J-O Svantesson.) 198,252 people in the Qiang nationality (1990 census). North central Sichuan Province, along the Minjiang River basin between Zhenjiangguan in Songpan County to the north and Wenchuan and Li counties to the south, as far east as Beichuan County. Sino-Tibetan, Tibeto-Burman, Tangut-Qiang, Qiangic. Dialects: DAJISHAN, TAOPING, LONGXI, MIANCHI, HEIHU, SANLONG, JIAOCHANG. Related to Manyak, Menia, Muli. Written Chinese is in use. Qiang is an official nationality. 2 to 6 tones, depending on location. Agriculturalists, some animal husbandry. Lamaist, polytheist.

QUEYU ***(ZHABA)*** [QEY] 7,000 (1995). Xinlong (Nyagrong), Yajiang (Nyagquka) and Litang counties in the Ganzi (Garzê) Tibetan Autonomous Prefecture of western Sichuan. Sino-Tibetan, Tibeto-Burman, Tangut-Qiang, Qiangic. Closely related to Zhaba. Speakers belong to the Tibetan nationality. The term 'Zhaba' is used in Tuanjie township of Yajiang county. Different from the Zhaba language in Zhamai District. SOV; adjectives and number-classifier constructions follow noun heads; consonant cluster initials; 4 tones.

RIANG ***(RIANG-LANG, LIANG, YANG SEK, YANG WAN KUN, YIN, YANGLAM)*** [RIL] 3,000 in China (1995). Western Yunnan, vicinities of Zhenkang and Baoshan. Austro-Asiatic, Mon-Khmer, Northern Mon-Khmer, Palaungic, Eastern Palaungic, Riang. Close to Pale Palaung. May be the same as Shwe Palaung. Officially under De'ang in China. SVO. Bible portions 1950. See main entry under Myanmar.

RUSSIAN ***(OLOSSU, ELUOSI, RUSS, RUSSKI)*** [RUS] 13,504 in China (1990 census). North Xinjiang, including Urumqi, and Heilongjiang. Indo-European, Slavic, East. An official nationality in China. Agriculturalists, animal husbandry. Christian. Bible 1680-1993. See main entry under Russia.

SALAR ***(SALA)*** [SLR] 55,000 speakers (1982) out of 87,697 in the official nationality (1990 census). Xunhua Salar Autonomous County and Hualong Hui Autonomous County in Qinghai Province, Jishishan Autonomous County in Gansu Province, and Yining in Xinjiang. Altaic, Turkic, Southern.

Dialects: JIEZI, MENGDA. Reinhard F. Hahn says Salar is spoken by descendants of an Oghuz-Turkic-speaking sub-tribe that, in the 15th century area of Samarkand, split off a main tribe and 'returned eastward', eventually settling in Western China. Their language has an Oghuz Turkic base, has taken on a medieval Chaghatay Turkic stratum through Central Asian contacts and finally acquired a stratum of features from local languages. The people use Chinese as literary language. Bilingualism is reported high in Chinese, Uyghur, and Tibetan. An official nationality. SOV. Literacy rate in second language: 27%. Agriculturalists, animal husbandry, commerce. Sunni Muslim.

SAMEI [SMH] Small. Yunnan. Sino-Tibetan, Tibeto-Burman, Lolo-Burmese, Loloish, Northern. Children do not speak Mandarin. May be officially under Yi.

SAMTAO *(SAMTAU, SAMTUAN)* [STU] 100 in China (1993). Austro-Asiatic, Mon-Khmer, Northern Mon-Khmer, Palaungic, Western Palaungic, Angkuic. Different from Blang. See main entry under Myanmar.

SARIKOLI *(SARYKOLY, TAJIK, TADZIK, TAJIKI)* [SRH] 20,500 (1982 estimate), out of 33,538 'Tajik' (1990 census). Southwest Xinjiang, in and around Taxkorgan (Tashkurghan), Sarikol Valley. Indo-European, Indo-Iranian, Iranian, Eastern, Southeastern, Pamir, Shugni-Yazgulami. Not intelligible with Shughni of Russia and Afghanistan. Written Uyghur is used. Chinese is also used. The majority of Tajiks in China speak Sarikoli, the remainder speak Wakhi. An official nationality, called 'Tajik' in China. Different from Tajiki of Tajikistan, Afghanistan, and Iran. The label 'Tajik' is used in different ways in different countries. SOV. Literacy rate in second language: 15% to 52%. Mountain slope, plateau. Pastoralists; agriculturalists: wheat, barley, peas. Ismaili Muslim.

SHANGZHAI *(WESTERN JIARONG)* [JIH] North central Sichuan, near the confluence of the Duke River and its tributary Zhongke River in Shili, Zongke, and Puxi townships, Shangzhai District, southern Rangthang County. Sino-Tibetan, Tibeto-Burman, Tangut-Qiang, rGyarong. Dialects: DAYILI, ZONGKE, PUXI. Phonologically Western and Northern are fairly similar and differ greatly from Eastern. Eastern and Northern Jiarong have 75% lexical similarity, Western and Northern 60%. Under the Tibetan nationality. SOV, phonologically and lexically similar to Tibetan, grammatically more similar to Pumi and Qiang; complex consonant clusters; limited pitch contrast.

SHE *(HUO NTE, HO NTE)* [SHX] 965 speakers including 579 Luofu, 386 Lianhua (1995 McConnell) out of ethnic group of 630,378 (1990 census), including 270,000 in Fujian and a smaller group in Guangdong. Southeastern Guangdong Province, (Lianhua dialect in Haifeng and Huidong counties; Luofu dialect in Boluo and Zengcheng counties). Hmong-Mien, Ho Nte. Dialects: LUOFU (EASTERN SHE), LIANHUA (WESTERN SHE). Major linguistic differences with Mien. Closest to Jiongnai Bunu. Dialects are inherently intelligible. Classification within Hmong-Mien is in dispute (McConnell 1995:1320). People use Hakka or Min Chinese as second language. Written Chinese is in common use. 'Shehua' refers to the variety of Hakka spoken by the She. Children are predominantly monolingual in She, adults predominantly bilingual. An official nationality. Grammar. SVO; 8 tones; modifiers precede heads; mainly monosyllabic roots, but mainly compound words; loans from Hakka and Cantonese Chinese. Mountain slope. Agriculturalists. Daoist.

SHERPA *(SHARPA, SHARPA BHOTIA, XIAERBA, SERWA)* [SCR] 800 speakers in China (1994). Tibet. Sino-Tibetan, Tibeto-Burman, Himalayish, Tibeto-Kanauri, Tibetic, Tibetan, Southern. Officially under the Tibetan nationality in China. Lamaist. Bible portions 1977. See main entry under Nepal.

SHIXING [SXG] Muli Tibetan Autonomous County in the Liangshan Yi Autonomous Prefecture of southwestern Sichuan. Sino-Tibetan, Tibeto-Burman, Tangut-Qiang, Qiangic. Speakers belong to the Tibetan nationality. SOV; adjectives and number-classifier constructions follow noun heads; consonant cluster initials; 4 tones.

SUI *(SHUI, AI SUI, SUI LI, SUIPO)* [SWI] 345,993 in China (1990 census). Population total both countries 346,000. Districts of Sandu and Libo in Guizhou and District of Nandan in Guangxi, dispersed in Guangxi and northeastern Yunnan. Also spoken in Viet Nam. Tai-Kadai, Kam-Tai, Kam-Sui. Dialects: SANDONG (SAN TUNG), YANG'AN, PANDONG. Dialect differences are minor. That spoken in Yunnan is reported to be more different. Bilingualism is low in the main areas. Written Chinese is in use. An official nationality. Literacy rate in second language: 37%. Agriculturalists. Polytheist.

TAI HONGJIN [TIZ] 150,000 (1995 Luo Meizhen). Scattered communities in Honghe, Jinshajiang, Yuanyang, Yuanjiang, Xinping, Maguan, Wuting, and Sichuan north of the Yangtze at Huili and Takou. Tai-Kadai, Kam-Tai, Be-Tai, Tai-Sek, Tai, Southwestern, Unclassified. Only recently known and described. Traditional religion.

TAI NÜA *(DAI NUEA, TAI NEUA, TAI NUE, TAI NÜ, DAI NA, DEHONG DAI, DEHONG, TAI DEHONG, TAI LE, TAI-LE, DAI KONG, TAI-KONG, TAI MAO, CHINESE SHAN, CHINESE TAI, YUNANNESE SHAN, YUNNAN SHANT'OU)* [TDD] 250,000 in China (1990 J-O Svantesson) out of 1,025,128 in the official nationality (1990 census). Population total all countries 442,400. Dehong Prefecture, southwest of Dali near the Lancang (Mekong) River in south central Yunnan. Also possibly in northern Viet Nam. Also spoken in France, Laos, Myanmar, Switzerland, Thailand. Tai-Kadai, Kam-Tai, Be-Tai, Tai-Sek, Tai, Southwestern, East Central, Northwest. Dialects: DEHONG,

TAI PONG (LA, YOU, YA, KA, TAI KA, SAI), YONGREN. The Laos dialect is different. 65% lexical similarity with Northern Zhuang, 29% with Laqua, 27% with Buyang and Lati, 22% with Gelo. Northern Shan-like varieties referred to collectively as 'Tai Nüa'. Officially included under Dai in China; called 'Dehong Dai'. Language taught at Kunming Institute. They have their own traditions. Investigation needed: intelligibility with dialects. Dictionary. SVO; modifiers follow heads. Own script called 'Liek'. Agriculturalists: paddy rice, sugar, Pu'er tea, bananas, coconuts, papayas, rubber. Hinayana Buddhist, polytheist. Bible portions 1931-1948.

TAI YA ***(TAI-CUNG, TAI-CHUNG, TAI CUNG, CUNG, DAIYA, YA)*** [CUU] 34,000 or more (1982). Central Yunnan Province, Xinping Yi-Dai Autonomous County, Mosha District. Tai-Kadai, Kam-Tai, Be-Tai, Tai-Sek, Tai, Southwestern, Unclassified. Probably not intelligible with other varieties of Dai. Closely related to Tai Nüa. Called 'Daiya' in China. Dictionary. Grammar. SVO; 6 tone categories in unchecked syllables, 2 (split into 4 according to vowel length) in checked syllables; nasal and stop finals. Bible portions 1922.

TAKPA ***(DWAGS)*** [TKK] Sino-Tibetan, Tibeto-Burman, Himalayish, Tibeto-Kanauri, Tibetic, Tibetan, Western, Ladakhi.

TATAR ***(TARTAR, TATA'ER)*** [TTR] 1,000 speakers out of 4,873 in the official nationality in China (1990 census). North Xinjiang, mainly in Yining (Ghulja, Kulja), Qvqek, and Ür|üqi. Altaic, Turkic, Western, Uralian. Speech in different areas is influenced by Uyghur and Kazakh. Written Uyghur and Kazakh are used as literary languages; nearly all use them. An official nationality in China. SOV. Traders, craftsmen, agriculturalists. Sunni Muslim. Bible portions 1864-1995. See main entry under Russia.

T'EN ***(THEN, YANGHUANG)*** [TCT] 20,000 (1982 census). A few villages in Huishui, just south of Guiyang, and Pingtang and Dushan counties, Guizhou. Tai-Kadai, Kam-Tai, Kam-Sui. Close to Sui. Local Chinese and Bouyei are used as second languages. Officially under the Buyi nationality.

TIBETAN ***(WEI, WEIZANG, CENTRAL TIBETAN, BHOTIA, ZANG, PHOKE, DBUS, DBUSGTSANG, U)*** [TIC] 1,066,200 in China (1990 census), including 570,000 Dbus, 460,000 Gtsang, 40,000 Mngahris out of 4,593,000 in the official nationality. Population total all countries 1,254,000. Tibet, Sichuan, Qinghai. Also spoken in Bhutan, India, Nepal, Norway, Switzerland, Taiwan, USA. Sino-Tibetan, Tibeto-Burman, Himalayish, Tibeto-Kanauri, Tibetic, Tibetan, Central. Dialects: GTSANG (TSANG), DBUS, MNGAHRIS (NGARI). Drokba: do not know Chinese. Xifan (Hsifan) and Bhotia are general terms for Tibetan. One of the main official nationalities, called 'Zang' in China. Probably officially includes many separate languages: Atuence, Choni, Groma, Niarong, Lhomi, Panang, Sherpa, Tseku, Tinan Lahul, Khams. Nomads in central and northern Tibet in Phala on the 15,000 foot Chang Tang plateau are known as 'Drokba'. They number around 500,000 (National Geographic June 1989:752-781). Dictionary. SOV; 4 tones. Literacy rate in second language: 30%. Motivation is high. Written Tibetan is reported to be based on a southern dialect. 2 scripts are known: U-chan is a common script used by all, the other is a less-widely known and more priestly script. Agriculturalists, pastoralists: yak, sheep, goats; weavers, salt traders (Drokba). Lamaist Buddhism, some Muslim. Bible 1948.

TINANI ***(LAHULI TINAN, BHOTIA OF LAHUL, LAHAULI, LAHOULI, RANGLOI, GONDLA)*** [LBF] 450 to 1,600 in China (1977 Voegelin and Voegelin). Western Tibet border. Sino-Tibetan, Tibeto-Burman, Himalayish, Tibeto-Kanauri, Western Himalayish, Kanauri. Different from Bunan and Pattani in India. It is probably officially included under Tibetan in China. Bible portions 1908-1915. See main entry under India.

TSAT ***(UTSAT, UTSET, HUIHUI, HUI, HAINAN CHAM)*** [HUQ] 4,500 (1991 I. Maddieson). Southern Hainan, villages of Huixin and Huihui in the Yanglan suburban district of Sanya City. Austronesian, Malayo-Polynesian, Western Malayo-Polynesian, Sundic, Malayic, Achinese-Chamic, Chamic, North. The phonology suggests a history of some independence from other Chamic languages (Maddieson). Their name for themselves is 'Utsat', for their language 'Tsat'. 'Huihui' or 'Hui' is the Chinese name. Tonal. Fishermen. Muslim.

TSEKU ***(TSUKU, TZUKU)*** [TSK] Tibet. Possibly only in Tibet. Also spoken in Bhutan, Nepal. Sino-Tibetan, Tibeto-Burman, Himalayish, Tibeto-Kanauri, Tibetic, Tibetan, Central. Probably officially under Tibetan in China.

TSHANGLA ***(SANGLA, TSANGLA, CANGLUO MENBA, MOTUO MENBA, MENBA, MONBA, MONPA, CENTRAL MONPA)*** [TSJ] 7,000 in China (1967). Southeastern Tibet, Motuo (Medoz) and Linzhi (Ngingchi) counties, including Padma-bkot (Pemak), just north of (and possibly on both sides of) the McMahon line, and clustered near the Tshangpo (Siang) River. Sino-Tibetan, Tibeto-Burman, Himalayish, Tibeto-Kanauri, Tibetic, Bodish, Tshangla. Their speech is nearly identical to that of eastern Bhutan, except for the loss of initial voicing and tonogenesis in Tibet. Differs from Cuona Menba in phonology, vocabulary, and grammar. Not the same as Tsanglo (Angami Naga) of India. Officially in the Moinba nationality in China. SOV; numbers and adjectives follow their noun; not tonal; singular-dual-plural personal pronouns. Agriculturalists: rice. Buddhist. Bible portions. See main entry under Bhutan.

TU ***(MONGOUR, MONGOR)*** [MJG] 90,000 speakers (1982) out of 191,624 in the official nationality (1990 census). East Qinghai Province. Altaic, Mongolian, Eastern, Mongour. Dialects: HUZHU, MINHE. Said to be the most divergent of all the Mongolian languages. Intelligibility is reported to be low between dialects. written Chinese or Tibetan is used. An official nationality. An unwritten language. Investigation needed: intelligibility with dialects. Dictionary. Literacy rate in second language: 42%. Agriculturalists. Lamaist Buddhism.

TUJIA, NORTHERN ***(TUCHIA, TUDJA)*** [TJI] 170,000 to 200,000 speakers (1982) out of 5,704,223 in the official nationality (1990 census). Northwest Hunan, Hubei, Guizhou in Yingjiang and Yanhe counties. Sino-Tibetan, Tibeto-Burman, Tujia. Dialects: LONGSHAN, BAOJING. There are also phonological and grammatical differences with Southern Tujia. 40% lexical similarity with Southern Tujia. Spoken and written Chinese are in use. An official nationality. SOV; 4 tones; no voiced stops or affricates. Agriculturalists.

TUJIA, SOUTHERN ***(TUCHIA)*** [TJS] 4,000 speakers (1994) out of 5,704,223 in the official nationality (1990 census). Northwest Hunan, Hubei, Guizhou in Yingjiang and Yanhe counties. Sino-Tibetan, Tibeto-Burman, Tujia. There are phonological and grammatical differences with Northern Tujia. 40% lexical similarity with Northern Tujia. Spoken and written Chinese are in use. Tujia is an official nationality. SOV; 4 tones; voiced stops and affricates. Agriculturalists.

TUVIN ***(DIBA, KÖK, MUNGAK, TUWA)*** [TUN] 400 in China (1990). Burjin, Habahe, Fuyun, and Altay counties of Altay Prefecture, Yinjiang Autonomous Region. Altaic, Turkic, Northern. Chahar Mongolian used in education. More than 90% are bilingual in Kazakh, 30% also know Kalmyk-Oirat. Included under the Mongolian official nationality in China. Lamaist Buddhist mixed with shamanism. Bible portions 1996. See main entry under Russia.

U ***(PUMAN, P'UMAN)*** [UUU] 3,000 (1990 J-O Svantesson). Southwestern Yunnan Province. Austro-Asiatic, Mon-Khmer, Northern Mon-Khmer, Palaungic, Western Palaungic, Angkuic. Not very closely related to Blang (Svantesson). Officially included under the Blang nationality. Investigation needed: intelligibility with Angkuic languages.

UYGHUR ***(UIGHUR, UYGUR, UIGUR, UIGHUIR, UIGUIR, WEIWUER, WIGA)*** [UIG] 7,214,431 in China (1990 census), including 4,700,000 Central Uyghur, 1,150,000 Hotan, 25,000 Lop. Population total all countries 7,595,512 or more. Throughout the Xinjiang Autonomous Region. Also spoken in Afghanistan, Australia, Germany, India, Indonesia, Kazakhstan, Kyrgyzstan, Mongolia, Pakistan, Saudi Arabia, Taiwan, Tajikistan, Turkey (Asia), USA, Uzbekistan. Altaic, Turkic, Eastern. Dialects: CENTRAL UYGHUR, HOTAN (HETIAN), LOP (LUOBU). The Akto Türkmen speak a dialect of Uyghur with 500 different seldom-used words. They have different appearance and customs. They say they originated in Samarkand, and are listed as Kirghiz by the government. There are 2,000 in two villages, Kösarap and Oytak in Akto County, south of Kashgar, Xinjiang. Dolan is a dialect spoken around the fringes of the Taklimakan desert in Xinjiang. Chinese linguists recognize 3 dialects. Others have used the following dialect names: Kashgar-Yarkand (Kashi-Shache), Yengi Hissar (Yengisar), Khotan-Kerya (Hotan-Yutian), Charchan (Qarqan, Qiemo), Aksu (Aqsu), Qarashahr (Karaxahar), Kucha (Kuqa), Turfan (Turpan), Kumul (Hami), Ili (Kulja, Yining, Taranchi), Urumqi (Urumchi), Lopnor (Lopnur), Dolan, Akto Türkmen. One of the five main official nationalities in China. Those in the north are more influenced by modern Chinese culture. SOV; postpositions; genitives, adjectives, numerals, relatives before noun heads; question words initial; a few prefixes; 3 suffixes on nouns; 6 suffixes on verbs; word order distinguishes subjects and indirect objects, topic and comment; 8 noun cases shown by suffixes; verb suffixes mark subject person, number, 2nd person marks plural and 3 levels of respect; passive, reflexive, reciprocal and causative; comparatives; CV, CVC, CVCC; nontonal. Literacy rate in second language: 56%. Based on Central Uyghur as spoken in the area between Yili (Ili) and Urumqi. It had a Roman script in China. A new Arabic script was introduced in 1987. Cyrillic script has been used. Radio programs. Desert, oases. Valleys. Agriculturalists: grain, fruit, grapes, vegetables, cotton; traders; craftsmen. Sunni Muslim. Bible 1950.

UZBEK, NORTHERN ***(OZBEK, OUZBEK, USBEKI, USBAKI)*** [UZB] 3,000 speakers out of 14,502 in the official nationality in China (1990 census). North and west Xinjiang; Urumqi, Kashgar, and Yining (Ghulja) cities, especially Ili. Altaic, Turkic, Eastern. Different from Southern Uzbek of Afghanistan, Pakistan, and Turkey. They use Uyghur and Kazakh as literary languages. All are bilingual in Uyghur and can write Uyghur. An official nationality in China. SOV; has lost its historical vowel harmony and its vowel system now resembles that of Tajiki. Literacy rate in second language: 79%. It has an alphabetic script based on Arabic. Agriculturalists, some traders. Sunni Muslim. NT 1992-1995. See main entry under Uzbekistan.

VIETNAMESE ***(JING, GIN, KINH, CHING, ANNAMESE)*** [VIE] 6,000 speakers out of 18,915 in the official nationality in China (1990 census). On the Shanxin, Wanwei, and Wutou peninsulas in the Jiangping region of the Fangcheng Pan-Nationality Autonomous County on the south coast of

Guangxi Province. Austro-Asiatic, Mon-Khmer, Viet-Muong, Vietnamese. Intelligibility with Viet Nam Vietnamese is high. Use Chinese as a written language. Bilingualism in Yue Chinese of Guanxi is reported to be high. An official nationality in China, called 'Jing'. Do not use Vietnamese alphabet in China. Not written in China. Fishermen, agriculturalists. Christian, Daoist. Bible 1916-1994. See main entry under Viet Nam.

VO ***(AWA, WA, K'AWA, KAWA, WA PWI, WAKUT)*** [WBM] 60,000 in China (1990 J-O Svantesson). Awa Mountains, southwest Yunnan as far east as the Lancang (Mekong) River. Austro-Asiatic, Mon-Khmer, Northern Mon-Khmer, Palaungic, Western Palaungic, Waic, Wa. The Wa language is related to the Lawa and Parauk languages, also under the Wa nationality in China. Traditional culture. Officially under Wa nationality in China. Dictionary. Mountain slope. Agriculturalists: potatoes, cotton, hemp, tobacco, sugarcane, tea, rice, beans, buckwheat, maize. Traditional religion. See main entry under Myanmar.

WAKHI ***(VAKHAN, WAKHANI, WAKHIGI, KHIK)*** [WBL] 6,000 in China. Taxkorgan Tajik Autonomous County (especially Daftar), and in the mountains south of Pishan, Xinjiang. Indo-European, Indo-Iranian, Iranian, Eastern, Southeastern, Pamir. Dialect: EASTERN WAKHI. Dialect intelligibility is reported to not be a problem, even with those in other countries. Bilingualism in Chinese. Included under the Tajik nationality (mainly Sarikoli) in China. SOV. Pastoralists: sheep, cattle; agriculturalists: barley, wheat, peas. Ismaili Muslim. See main entry under Pakistan.

WAXIANGHUA ***(XIANGHUA, WOGANG)*** [WXA] 300,000 (1995 Milliken). A 6,000 square km. area in western Hunan Province, Wuling Mts., including Yuanling, Chunxi, Jishou, Guzhang, and Dayong. Unclassified. It differs greatly from both Southwestern Mandarin (Xinan Guanhua) and Xiang Chinese (Hunanese), but is relatively uniform within itself. Neighboring Han Chinese, Miao and Tujia people do not understand it. Some view it as a special variety of Chinese, others as a minority language, perhaps related to Miao. Mountain slope.

WUTUNHUA ***(WUTUN)*** [WUH] 2,000 (1995). Eastern Qinghai Province, Huangnan Tibetan Autonomous Prefecture, Tongren County, Longwu township, Upper and Lower Wutun villages and Jiangchama village. Mixed Language, Chinese-Tibetan-Mongolian. Reported to be a variety of Chinese heavily influenced by Tibetan or perhaps a Tibetan language undergoing relexification with Chinese forms. Also described as Chinese which converged to an agglutinative language, using only Chinese material, towards Tibetan-Mongolian. Neighboring Tibetans refer to the Wutun people as 'Sanggaixiong', meaning 'center of the lion'. Known for their paintings of Buddha. Some consider themselves members of the Tu nationality, others Han Chinese. SOV; adjectives follow nouns; adverbials precede predicate; case and number marked on nouns; prenasalized consonants; 11 different syllable-final consonants; tone and stress have low functional load; most words polysyllabic; 60% Chinese, 20% Tibetan vocabulary with the rest having mixed Chinese and Tibetan elements. Agriculturalists.

XIANDAOHUA [XIA] 100 (1994). Xiandao and Meng'e villages, Manmian Township, Jiemao District, Yingjiang County in the Dehong Dai-Jingpo Autonomous Prefecture in extreme western Yunnan. Sino-Tibetan, Tibeto-Burman, Lolo-Burmese, Burmish, Unclassified. Subclassification unknown. Spoken by members of the Achang nationality, and some consider it to be a dialect of Achang. SOV, 4 tones, voiced and voiceless nasals and laterals. Loan words from Chinese, Jingpo, Dai, and Burmese.

XIBE ***(SIBO, XIBO, SIBE)*** [SJO] 27,364 speakers (1995 McConnel) out of 33,082 in ethnic Xibe in Xinjiang Province, 172,847 in the nationality (1990 census). 50,000 ethnic Xibe in northeast China speak Chinese as mother tongue. Mainly in Ili region of Xinjiang Province, and some in Ürümqi City and Tacheng region of Xinjiang Province. Altaic, Tungus, Southern, Southwest. Colloquial Manchu. Reported to be inherently intelligible with Manchu. Many prefer Chinese as a literary language. Some can speak or write Uyghur Kazakh, English, or Russian. All ages in rural areas. Descendants of an 18th century Qing dynasty military garrison. An official nationality. Loans from Uyghur, Kazakh, and Chinese. Dictionary. Grammar. SOV; genitives, articles, adjectives, numerals precede noun heads; question word initial; complex vowel harmony. Literacy rate in first language: 30%. Literacy rate in second language: 52%. Uses a modified Manchu script. Desert, savannah. Plains. Peasant agriculturalists, stock farming. 1,000 to 3,000 meters. Traditionally shamanistic, today largely atheistic.

YERONG ***(DABAN YAO)*** [YRN] 300 to 400 (1990 Liang Min). Western Guangxi Zhuang Autonomous Region, Napo County, Longhe Township and Pohe Township, just northeast of where Yunnan, Guangxi, and Viet Nam meet. Tai-Kadai, Kadai, Bu-Rong. Officially under the Yao nationality. 'Yeyong' may refer to this.

YI, CENTRAL [YIC] 460,000 (1991 EDCL). 6,572,173 in the official Yi nationality (1990 census). Covering much of central Yunnan, including Chuxiong Yi Autonomous Prefecture, Dali Bai Autonomous Prefecture, and Simao District. Sino-Tibetan, Tibeto-Burman, Lolo-Burmese, Loloish, Northern, Yi. Dialects: DAYAO (NORTH CENTRAL YI), NANHUA (SOUTH CENTRAL YI). A separate language in the Yi official nationality. The 2 dialects are reported to be 80% similar. SOV; 4 tones. Yi syllabary script is not used. Mountain slopes.

YI, GUIZHOU ***(EASTERN YI, SOUTHEASTERN YI)*** [YIG] 800,000 (1991 EDCL). 6,572,173 in official Yi nationality (1990 census). Guizhou Province, Weining Yi-Hui-Miao Autonomous County, Dafang Autonomous County, Hezhang County, Pan County; some in the Baise District of western Guangxi. Sino-Tibetan, Tibeto-Burman, Lolo-Burmese, Loloish, Northern, Yi. Dialects: DIAN-QIAN (YUNNAN-GUIZHOU, PAN COUNTY), DIAN DONGBEI (NORTHEASTERN YUNNAN). Distinct from other Yi. Intelligibility between dialects is reported to be low. 50% lexical similarity between Yi varieties. Fairly large differences within the varieties also. Dictionary. SOV.

YI, SICHUAN ***(NORTHERN YI, I, "LOLO", "NORTHERN LOLO", SEN NOSU, GNI, NYI)*** [III] 1,600,000 speakers (1991 EDCL), out of 6,572,173 in official nationality (1990 census). Mainly in Greater and Lesser Liangshan Mountains, southern Sichuan, southeast Xizang (Xichang). Yangshan is a cultural center. Yi in Gulin County are reported to no longer speak Yi. In northwestern Yunnan. Spoken in over 40 counties. Sino-Tibetan, Tibeto-Burman, Lolo-Burmese, Loloish, Northern, Yi. Dialects: NORTHERN SICHUAN YI, SOUTHERN SICHUAN YI. Yi is an official nationality, including at least 6, and possibly 20, languages. The Northern dialect of Sichuan Yi has subdialects Yinuohua, Shengzhahua and Tianbahua. Shengzhahua is said to be understood by 85% of speakers. Differences in phonology, vocabulary, and grammar among the Yi languages. Written Chinese is also used. Yi is the official term for what was formerly called Lolo and other names, all derogatory. 'Yi' is used in a broad sense, even at times including languages like the Lisu. At other times it is used in a more narrow sense for only those north of Kunming, Yunnan, and in the Great Cool and Small Cool Mountains of Sichuan. Black Lolo (Hei-I, Hei Kutou) and White Lolo (Pei-I) are caste names and do not refer to linguistic distinctions. Dictionary. Has an official script, the Yi syllabary based on Shenzhahua area, used in the Liangshan area. Plains. Swidden agriculturalists, some animal husbandry. Polytheist, some Christian.

YI, SOUTHEASTERN [YIE] 240,000 (1991 EDCL) including 90,000 Sani, 60,000 to 70,000 Axi, 30,000 to 40,000 Axhebo, 20,000 or more Awu (1999). Eastern and southeastern Yunnan in the Qujing District and in Honghe Hani-Yi Autonomous Prefecture and Wenshan Zhuang-Miao Autonomous Prefecture. The Sani dialect is in Shilin County just east of Kunming and surrounding counties; the Axi dialect is mainly in Mile County southeast of Kunming. Sino-Tibetan, Tibeto-Burman, Lolo-Burmese, Loloish, Northern, Yi. Dialects: SANI, AXI (MILE, AHI), AWU, AXHEBO. Intelligibility between dialects is reported to be low. 2 dialects are also called Huami and Wenxi, but it is not known how they correspond to Awu and Axhebo. A major variety of Yi, one of 6 to 20 separate Yi languages. The Samei, an Eastern Yi group east of Kunming in the Guandu region call themselves Sani, but are not part of the Sani in Shilin. Tones differ on the two names, [sa^{21} ni^{53}] versus [sa^{21} ni^{21}]. An Eastern Yi group with a similar name call themselves Sanyie, immediately to the west of Kunming in the Xishan region and in Anning County. Plains. Animal husbandry: goats, cattle. Polytheist.

YI, WESTERN [YIW] 300,000 (1991 EDCL). 6,572,173 in official Yi nationality (1990 census). West central Yunnan, over 20 counties. Sino-Tibetan, Tibeto-Burman, Lolo-Burmese, Loloish, Northern, Yi. Dialects: DONGSHAN, XISHAN. A separate language in the Yi official nationality. Vocabulary is reported to be relatively uniform between dialects. Bilingualism in Chinese is reported to be high, especially among young people. Yi syllabary not used.

YI, YUNNAN ***(SOUTHERN YI, SOUTHERN NOSU, SHUI NOSU, NOSU, NASU, NASÖ, NYI, GNI, I)*** [NOS] 800,000 or slightly fewer (1991 EDCL). Central Yunnan, in Yuxi and Simao districts and Honghe Hani-Yi Autonomous Prefecture. Sino-Tibetan, Tibeto-Burman, Lolo-Burmese, Loloish, Northern, Yi. Dialects: SHIJIAN, YUANJIN, EXIN. One of 6 to 20 separate languages in the Yi nationality. There is some dialect variation in Yunnan Yi, but communication is claimed to be possible with all locations. Lexical similarity within Yunnan Yi at least 85%. High bilingualism in Chinese is reported among young people. Derogatory names are "Lolo", "Minchia", "Ichia", "Keikutou", "Peikutou". 'Nosu' originally referred to eastern Yi, an elite caste, endogamous, who raised horses; slaves and serfs in a separate caste. Plains. Swidden agriculturalists, some animal husbandry. Polytheist, some Christian. NT 1948.

YUGUR, EAST ***(SHIRA YUGUR, SHERA YOGUR, EASTERN YOGOR, YOGOR, YÖGUR, YUGU, YUGAR)*** [YUY] 3,000 (1991 EDCL). Northwest Gansu Province. Altaic, Mongolian, Eastern, Mongour. Written Chinese is in use. Chinese is used as a lingua franca with West Yugur. An official nationality together with West Yugur, a Turkic language. Literacy rate in second language: 59%. Pastoralists. Shamanism, Lamaist Buddhist.

YUGUR, WEST ***(SARYGH UYGUR, SARIG, YA LU, YELLOW UIGHUR, SARI YOGUR, YUKU, YUGU, SARY-UIGHUR)*** [YBE] 4,600 speakers out of ethnic group of 12,297 (1990 census). Sunan Yugur Autonomous County near Zhangye (Kanchow) in northwest Gansu Province. Altaic, Turkic, Eastern. About one-third of the ethnic group speaks Chinese as first language. Written Chinese is in use. Chinese is used as a lingua franca with East Yugur. An official nationality together with East Yugur, which is a Mongolian language. SOV. Literacy rate in second language: 59%. Animal husbandry. Lamaist Buddhist, shamanism.

ZAIWA ***(TSAIWA, ATSI, ATZI, AJI, ATSHI, ACI, AZI, ATSI-MARU, SZI, XIAOSHANHUA)*** [ATB] 70,000 in China (1990 J-O Svantesson). Population total both countries 100,000. Yunnan Province, Luxi, Ruili, Longchuan, Yingjiang, Bangwa Districts in Dehong Dai-Jingpo Autonomous Prefecture. Also spoken in Myanmar. Sino-Tibetan, Tibeto-Burman, Lolo-Burmese, Burmish, Northern. Dialects: ZAIWA, LANGWA, POLO. Closely related to Maru, Lashi, and Bela. Dialects have only minor phonological differences. They call themselves 'Tsaiva'. Officially under the Jingpo nationality in China. Distinct from the Ahi group under Yi. SOV; 3 tone categories in unchecked syllables and 2 in checked. A Roman script orthography was developed in 1957, based on the speech of Longzhun in the Xishan District of Luxi County. Polytheist. Bible portions 1939-1951.

ZAUZOU ***(ROUROU, RAOROU, JAOJO)*** [ZAL] 1,500 (1990 J-O Svantesson). Northwestern Yunnan Province, Lanping and Lushui counties. Sino-Tibetan, Tibeto-Burman, Lolo-Burmese, Loloish, Unclassified. A separate language officially under the Nu nationality with Ayi, Nusu, and 5,500 ethnic Nung who are Drung speakers. SOV; no consonant clusters; no checked syllables; tense-lax and nasalized-unnasalized vowel distinctions; 6 tones.

ZHABA [ZHA] 7,700 (1995). Zhamai District of Yajiang (Nyagquka) County and Zhaba District of Daofu (Dawu) County, which are in the Ganzi (Garzê) Tibetan Autonomous Prefecture of western Sichuan. Sino-Tibetan, Tibeto-Burman, Tangut-Qiang, Qiangic. Closely related to Queyu. 'Zaba' may be an alternate spelling. Different from Queyu, also called 'Zhaba'. Speakers belong to the Tibetan nationality.

ZHUANG, NORTHERN ***(CHUANG, TAI CHUANG, VAH CUENGH, CANGVA)*** [CCX] 10,000,000 speakers (1992 J. A. Edmondson) out of 15,489,630 in the Zhuang nationality (1990 census), including Yongbei 1,600,000, Youjiang 732,000, Guibian 522,000, Liujiang 1,300,000, Guibei 1,300,000, Hongshuihe 2,700,000, Qiubei (not available). Northern Guangxi Zhuang Autonomous Region, Wenshan Zhuang-Miao Autonomous Prefecture. Guizhou Province, Congjiang County, southwestern Hunan and northeastern Guangdong in Lianshan Zhuang-Yao Autonomous County. Yongbei is north of the Yongjiang and Youjiang rivers in the area from Hengxian to Pingguo; Hongshuihe is along the Red Water River; Liujiang around the town of Liujiang west of Liuzhou city; Youjiang straddles the Youjiang River in the area from Tiandong to Baise; Guibian in the northwesternmost region of Guangxi (Guibian lies across north central Guangxi); and Quibei around the town of Qiubei in Yunnan. Tai-Kadai, Kam-Tai, Be-Tai, Tai-Sek, Tai, Northern. Dialects: YONGBEI (YUNGPEI), LIUJIANG (LIUCHIANG), YOUJIANG (YUCHIANG), GUIBIAN (KUEIPIEN), QIUBEI (CHIUPEI), HONGSHUIHE, GUIBEI. Dialect chain to Bouyei. 'Biao' (Pumen) is a special variety spoken in Lianshan area of northwestern Guangdong and in eastern Guangxi around He Xian. 75% to 86% lexical similarity between the dialects; average 65% between Northern and Southern Zhuang; Northern Zhuang has 49% with Dong, 44% with Laka, 32% with Buyang, 30% with Laqua and Hlai, 28% with Lati, 25% with Gelo. In a Mandarin-speaking area, but some also speak Cantonese. Many in more developed locations control a variety of Chinese to some useful degree, but the majority in the countryside do not. Everywhere except in major cities the clear preference is to speak Zhuang, even in sizable towns. One of the five main official nationalities. Dictionary. SVO; modifiers follow heads; Wuming dialect has 6 tone categories in unchecked syllables and 2 (split into 4 according to vowel length) in checked syllables; most dialects lack aspirated stop series; rich in reduplicating modifiers and sound symbolism employing vowel gradation; several historical layers of borrowing from Chinese. Literacy rate in second language: 67%. Literacy generally low except in major towns and cities. Roman script based on the pronunciation of the Yongbei dialect spoken in Wuming County. May be difficult for some dialect speakers to use. Traditional ideographic script based on Chinese characters. Not standardized or widely used for general purposes. Mountain slope. Agriculturalists: paddy rice. Polytheist. Bible portions 1904.

ZHUANG, SOUTHERN [CCY] 4,000,000 speakers (1990 J-O Svantesson) out of 15,489,630 in the Zhuang nationality (1990 census), including Yongnan 1,400,000, Zuojiang 1,400,000, De-Jing 980,000, Yan-Guang (not available), Wen-Ma 100,000. Southwest Guangxi and southern Wenshan Zhuang-Miao Autonomous Prefecture of southeastern Yunnan Province. Yongnan is south of the Yongjiang River from Yongning in the east to Long'an in the west; Zuojiang is in southwestern Guangxi around Tiandeng, Daxin, Chongzuo, Longzhou, Pingxiang, and Ningming, down to the Viet Nam border; De-Jing is in southwestern Guangxi around Debao, Jingxi, and Napo, down to the Yunnan and Viet Nam borders; Wen-Ma is in southeastern Yunnan Province south of Wenshan and Malipo, but excluding an area west of Maguan; Yan-Guang is in southeastern Yunnan Province north of Wenshan and Malipo, including Yanshan and north to Guangnan, and west of Maguan along the Viet Nam border. Tai-Kadai, Kam-Tai, Be-Tai, Tai-Sek, Tai, Central. Dialects: YONGNAN (YUNGNAN), ZUOJIANG (TSOCHIANG), DE-JING (TECHING), YAN-GUANG (YENKUANG), WEN-MA. Dialect chain into Vietnam. Speakers of the varieties between the Youjiang River and the Vietnam border (particularly Zuojiang and De-Jing) refer to their language as 'Tho', share many regional characteristics, and are intelligible with the Tay ("Tho") of Vietnam. The Yan-Guang and De-Jing varieties are intelligible with Nung (and Tay) of Vietnam, and refer to their language as 'Nong'. Man Cao Lan may be close to the Yan-Guang dialect (if found in China, that name is not used) of Viet Nam. Dialects share about 70% lexical similarity, about 65% with Northern Zhuang. Similar to Northern Zhuang, but has aspirated stop series.

CYPRUS

National or official languages: Greek, Turkish. 7710200 (1998 UN). Republic of Cyprus, Kypriaki Dimokratia, Kibris Cumhuriyeti. Literacy rate 95% to 99%. Also includes North Levantine Spoken Arabic, Assyrian Neo-Aramaic. Information mainly from A. Borg 1985. Christian, Muslim, secular. Deaf population 49,259. Deaf institutions: 2. Data accuracy estimate: B. The number of languages listed for Cyprus is 4. Of those, all are living languages. Diversity index 0.37.

ARABIC, CYPRIOT SPOKEN ***(CYPRIOT MARONITE ARABIC, MARONITE, SANNA)*** [ACY] 1,300 speakers out of 6,000 in the Cypriot Maronite ethnic group, 140 Maronites in Kormatiki, 80 to 100 in Limassol, the rest in the Maronite community in Nicosia. Kormakiti, one of 4 Maronite villages in the mountains of northern Cyprus, and in refugee communities in Nicosia and Limassol. Afro-Asiatic, Semitic, Central, South, Arabic. No diglossia with Standard Arabic. Those in Kormatiki are bilingual in Greek or possibly Turkish. Those in southern Cyprus are bilingual in Greek. All speakers over 30. 140 mainly elderly in Kormatiki. A hybrid language with roots in the Arabic of both the Anatolia and the Levant. Many borrowings from Syriac and Greek. People are called 'Maronites'. Christian: Maronite Catholic.

ARMENIAN ***(HAIEREN, SOMKHURI, ERMENICE, ARMJANSKI)*** [ARM] 2,740 in Cyprus (1987). Indo-European, Armenian. Dialect: WESTERN ARMENIAN. Most speak Greek. The older ones speak Turkish. Urban population. Christian. Bible 1853-1978. See main entry under Armenia.

GREEK [GRK] 578,000 in Cyprus (1995), 75% of the population. Nearly all in southern Cyprus. Indo-European, Greek, Attic. Dialect: CYPRIOT GREEK. The dialect is reported to be closer to Classical Greek than that spoken in Greece in some vocabulary and grammar, and to have many Arabic and Turkish loan words. National language. Christian. Bible 1840-1994. See main entry under Greece.

TURKISH ***(OSMANLI)*** [TRK] 177,000 in Cyprus (1995), 20% of the population. Nearly all in northern Cyprus. Altaic, Turkic, Southern, Turkish. National language. Muslim. Bible 1827-1941. See main entry under Turkey.

GEORGIA

National or official language: Georgian. 5,059,000 (1998 UN). Formerly part of USSR. Capital: Tbilisi. 26,911 square miles. Literacy rate 99%. Also includes Armenian 448,000, North Azerbaijani 308,000, Chechen, Greek 38,000, Judeo-Crimean Tatar, Kurmanji 33,000, Lak 246, Lezgi 3,650, Lishan Didan 50, Pontic 120,000, Russian 372,000, Tatar 3,102, Turkish 3,102, Udi, Ukrainian 52,000. Information mainly from T. Sebeok 1963; E. Haby 1975, A. Kibrik 1991. Data accuracy estimate: B. The number of languages listed for Georgia is 11. Of those, all are living languages. Diversity index 0.57.

ABKHAZ ***(ABXAZO)*** [ABK] 101,000 in Georgia (1993), 94% speak it as mother tongue. Population total all countries 105,000 (1993 UBS). Abkhaz ASSR within Georgia, Black Sea coast. Also spoken in Turkey (Asia), Ukraine. North Caucasian, Northwest, Abkhaz-Abazin. Dialects: BZYB, ABZHUI, SAMURZAKAN. Christian. Bible portions 1912-1981.

ASSYRIAN NEO-ARAMAIC ***(AISORSKI)*** [AII] 3,000 in Georgia (1999) out of an ethnic population of 14,000. Erevan and scattered throughout Transcaucasia. Afro-Asiatic, Semitic, Central, Aramaic, Eastern, Central, Northeastern. The Assyrian and Chaldean separated denominationally during the 16th century. Close linguistically to other Northeastern Aramaic varieties. Most speakers are elderly now. Many use Russian as primary language. 'Aisor' is the Russian name for the people. Syriac script is used. Christian (Nestorian). Bible 1852-1911. See main entry under Iraq.

BATS ***(BATSI, BATSAW, TSOVA-TUSH, TUSH, BATSBI, BAC, BATSBIITSY)*** [BBL] 2,500 to 3,000 (1975 SIL). Georgia, spoken by about half the inhabitants of Zemo-Alvani. North Caucasian, North Central, Batsi. Not intelligible with other related languages. Georgian is used as the literary language. Used in daily family communication. Traditional territory and way of life. Grammar. Sunni Muslim.

BOHTAN NEO-ARAMAIC [BHN] 1,000 in Georgia (1999 Samuel Ethan Fox). Population total both countries 1,000 or more. Mainly in Garbadani village, Georgia. Also spoken in Russia (Asia). Afro-Asiatic, Semitic, Central, Aramaic, Eastern, Central, Northeastern. Most over 60. Younger generations tend to shift to Georgian or Russian. Originally spoken by villagers in Anatolia, Ottoman Empire, east of the Tigris River (present-day southeastern Turkey). They fled to Russia during World War I. Christian.

GEORGIAN ***(KARTULI, GRUZINSKI)*** [GEO] 3,901,380 speakers (98%), out of 3,981,000 in the ethnic group in Georgia (1993 UBS). Population total all countries 4,103,000. 69,700 square miles. Also spoken in Armenia, Azerbaijan, Iran, Kazakhstan, Kyrgyzstan, Russia (Asia), Tajikistan, Turkey (Asia), Turkmenistan, Ukraine, USA, Uzbekistan. South Caucasian, Georgian. Dialects: IMERETIAN, RACHA-LEXCHXUM (LECHKHUM), GURIAN, ADZHAR (ACHARIAN), IMERXEV KARTLIAN, KAXETIAN (KAKHETIAN), INGILO, TUSH, XEVSUR (KHEYSUR), MOXEV (MOKHEV), PSHAV, MTIUL, FEREJDAN, MESKHUR-JAVAKHURI. Imerxev is in Turkey, Ferejdan in Iran. The Meskhi are ethnically Georgian, speak Georgian, are Eastern Orthodox, and live in southwestern Georgia. Adzhai Muslims are in Armenia. South Caucasian is also called 'Kartvelian'. National language. Grammar. SVO. Its own script is called Mkhedruli. Georgian Orthodox Church, some Sunni and Shi'a Muslim (Acharian dialect). Bible 1743-1989.

JUDEO-GEORGIAN [JGE] 20,000 in Georgia (1995). Some have gone elsewhere in the former USSR and to other countries. South Caucasian, Georgian. May not be a separate language from Georgian, but a dialect using various Hebrew loan words. Oriental and Ashkenazic Jews in Georgia live separately. Judeo-Georgian speakers live separately from non-Jewish Georgian speakers. Jewish. See main entry under Israel.

LAZ ***(LAZE, CHAN, CHANZAN, ZAN, CHANURI)*** [LZZ] 2,000 in Georgia (1982 estimate). Adjar, Georgia, a couple of villages. South Caucasian, Zan. Dialects: XOPA (HOPA), CHXALA (CKHALA), VICE-ARXAVA (VITAL-ARKHAVA), ATINA, SAMURZAKAN-ZUGDIDI, SENAKI. Officially considered to be a single language with Mingrelian, called 'Zan', although linguists recognize that they are not inherently intelligible with each other. Georgian used as literary language. Their name for their language is 'Lazuri'. Not a written language in Georgia or Turkey. Muslim. See main entry under Turkey.

MINGRELIAN ***(MARGALURI, MEGREL, MEGRULI)*** [XMF] 500,000 (1989 B. G. Hewitt). Lowland west Georgia. South Caucasian, Zan. Officially considered to be a single language with Laz, called Zan, but linguists recognize that they are not inherently intelligible with each other. Georgian used as a literary language. Their name for themselves is 'Margaluri'. Not a written language. Christian.

OSETIN ***(OSSETE)*** [OSE] 164,000 in Georgia (1993 Johnstone). Population total all countries 593,000. Also spoken in Azerbaijan, Germany, Hungary, Kazakhstan, Russia (Asia), Tajikistan, Turkey (Asia), Turkmenistan, Ukraine, Uzbekistan. Indo-European, Indo-Iranian, Iranian, Eastern, Northeastern. Dialects: DIGOR, TAGAUR, KURTAT, ALLAGIR, TUAL, IRON. Cyrillic script. Sunni Muslim (Digor), Christian (Iron). NT 1993.

SVAN ***(LUSHNU, SVANURI)*** [SVA] 35,000 (1975). South Caucasian, Svan. Dialects: UPPER BAL, LOWER BAL, LASHX, LENTEX. Georgian and Russian are used as literary languages. Svan is used in daily family communication. Proficiency limited among young people. Reports indicate that speakers want to remain separate from Georgian. Their name for their language is 'Lushnu'. Not a written language. Traditional territory and way of life. Christian, Jewish (Lakhamul).

URUM [UUM] Most in Georgia (1985 B. Podolsky). Caucasus. In recent years there has been emigration of Urum speakers from Georgia to Greece. Also spoken in Greece, Ukraine. Altaic, Turkic. Related to Crimean Tatar. A number of inherently intelligible dialects. Spoken by ethnic 'Greeks'. Investigation needed: intelligibility with Crimean Tatar.

INDIA

Republic of India, Bharat. National or official languages: Assamese, Bengali, Gujarati, Hindi, Kannada, Kashmiri, Malayalam, Marathi, Oriya, Panjabi, Sanskrit, Sindhi, Tamil, Telugu, Urdu, English (Associate Official). 1,000,000,000 (1999 IMA). 7% classified as tribals. Indo-Aryan languages: 491,087,116, 74.24%, Dravidian languages: 157,836,723, 23.86%, Austro-Asiatic languages 7,705,011, 1.16%, Tibeto-Burman languages 4,071,701, .62% (1987 Mahapatra). 15 national languages. 1,683 'mother tongues' (official figure). An estimated 850 languages in daily use (Todd and Hancock 1986). Literacy rate 36% to 52%. Also includes Judeo-Iraqi Arabic, Armenian 560, Burushaski, Western Farsi 18,000, Geman Deng, Lisu 1,000, Northern Pashto 15,000, Portuguese 250,000, Russian 1,036, Thami, Chitwania Tharu, Kathoriya Tharu, Uyghur, Walungge, Arabic, Chinese. Information mainly from G. Marrison 1967; R. Hugoniot 1970; C. Masica 1991; K. S. Singh 1994, 1995; J. Matisoff et al. 1996; R. Breton 1997; R. Burling ms. (1999). Hindu, Muslim, Christian, Sikh, traditional religion, Buddhist. Blind population 9,000,000. Deaf population 1,500,000 to 55,773,718 (1998). Deaf institutions: 149. Data accuracy estimate: B, C. The number of languages listed for India is 398. Of those, 387 are living languages and 11 are extinct. Diversity index 0.93.

A-PUCIKWAR ***(PUCIKWAR, PUCHIKWAR)*** [APQ] 36 (1997 CIIL). Andaman Islands, Boratang Island, south coast of Middle Andaman Island, northeast coast of South Andaman Island. Andamanese, Great Andamanese, Central. Bilingualism in Hindi. Language shift to Hindi taking place. CIIL working to revive A-Pucikwar. Other languages in the Central Andamanese group are extinct. Great Andamanese is classified as a Scheduled Tribe in India, and Puchikwar is a subtribe. Dictionary. Grammar. Literacy rate in first language: Below 1%. Nearly extinct.

AARIYA [AAR] Madhya Pradesh. Unclassified.

ABUJMARIA ***(ABUJHMADIA, ABUJMARIYA, ABUJHMARIA, ABUJMAR MARIA, HILL MARIA)*** [ABJ] 47,000 including 16,000 in Narayanpur District (1981 GR), 31,000 in Gadchiroli District (1961 census). Some officials estimate up to 100,000 Hill Maria (1998). Maharashtra, Gadchiroli District; Madhya Pradesh, Bastar District, Narayanpur and Bijapur tahsils. In Narayanpur, an administrative block of 200 villages is known as 'Abujhmar block'. Dravidian, South-Central, Gondi-Kui, Gondi. May be intelligible with Maria of Bhamragarh. A Scheduled Tribe. Gatte Maria is an ethnic group that seems to not be distinctive linguistically from Abujmaria. A separate language from Muria, Dandami Maria, Gondi of Adilabad, and Koya. Investigation needed: intelligibility with Maria (Bhamragarh). Dictionary. Literacy rate in first language: 5% men, 0% women. Literacy help urgently requested. High interest in literacy. Hills. Shifting cultivation.

ADI ***(ABOR, ARBOR, LHOBA, LUOBA, BOGA'ER LUOBA)*** [ADI] 110,000 in India (1997 BSI). Population total both countries 113,000. Assam, north hills of Assam Valley, between Bhutan and the Buruli River; Arunachal Pradesh, East and West Siang districts. Also spoken in China. Sino-Tibetan, Tibeto-Burman, North Assam, Tani. Dialects: PADAM (STANDARD ADI), MINYONG, GALONG (GALLONG, GALO, GALLO), BOKAR (BOGA'ER LUOBA), MILANG. Sun (1993) lists Tani languages and dialects as Apatani, Milang, Bokar, Damu, Mising, Padam, Bangni, Tagin, Sagli, south Aya, Leli, and perhaps Pailibo, Ramo, Asing, Bori, Pasi, Panggi, Simong, Minyong, Karok, Hill Miri, and some northern and western dialects of Nisi. Bilingualism in Assamese, Hindi, Nepali. Adi is a Scheduled Tribe in India with several subgroups: Ashing, Bokar, Bori, Galong, Karko, Komkar, Milang, Minyong, Padam, Pailibo, Pangi, Pasi, Ramo, Shimong, Tangam. These are different speech varieties. 'Adi' has been used as a cover term for the eastern Tani group of languages. Agriculturalists: rice, grain, beans, fruit, eggs; hunters. Traditional religion, Christian. NT 1988.

AGARIYA ***(AGHARIA, AGORIA)*** [AGI] 55,757 (1981 census). Madhya Pradesh, Mandla, Bilaspur, Rewa districts, Maikal hills; Bihar; Maharashtra; Orissa. Austro-Asiatic, Munda, North Munda, Kherwari. A Scheduled Tribe in India. Literacy rate in second language: 5% (1981 census). Traditional religion, Hindu.

AHIRANI ***(AHIRI)*** [AHR] 779,000 (1997 IMA). Maharashtra; Gujarat. Indo-European, Indo-Iranian, Indo-Aryan, Central zone, Khandesi. Preliminary findings are that it is distinct from Khandesi. Investigation needed: intelligibility with Khandesi.

AHOM ***(TAI AHOM)*** [AHO] Assam. Tai-Kadai, Kam-Tai, Be-Tai, Tai-Sek, Tai, Southwestern, East Central, Northwest. No longer spoken in daily life, but used in religious chants and literary materials. Former language of the Tai-Ahom King. Possibly 8,000,000 Assamese speakers claim to be of Ahom descent (A. Diller 1990). Extinct.

AIMOL [AIM] 1,862 (1981 census). Assam; Manipur, Chandel, Senapati districts. Sino-Tibetan, Tibeto-Burman, Kuki-Chin-Naga, Kuki-Chin, Northern. Dialect: LANGRONG. Langrong may be a separate language. Related to Chiru, Purum. A Scheduled Tribe in India. Literacy rate in second language: 35% (1981 census). Roman. Plains, foothills. Shifting cultivation. Christian.

AITON ***(AITONIA)*** [AIO] Several thousand speakers and semi-speakers (1990 A. Diller). Assam. Tai-Kadai, Kam-Tai, Be-Tai, Tai-Sek, Tai, Southwestern, East Central, Northwest. Related to Shan of Myanmar. Literacy rate in first language: Below 1%.

AKA-BEA ***(BEA, BEADA, BIADA, AKA-BEADA, BOJIGNIJI, BOGIJIAB, BOJIGYAB)*** [ACE] Andaman Islands, coasts of South Andaman Island except northeast coast, and north and east interiors; coastal Rutland Island except south coast; small islands southeast of Rutland; and Labyrinth Islands. Andamanese, Great Andamanese, Central. Extinct.

AKA-BO ***(BO, BA)*** [AKM] Andaman Islands, east central coast of North Andaman Island, and North Reef Island. Andamanese, Great Andamanese, Northern. Extinct.

AKA-CARI ***(CARI, CHARIAR)*** [ACI] Andaman Islands, north coast of North Andaman Island, Landfall Island, and other nearby small islands. Andamanese, Great Andamanese, Northern. Extinct.

AKA-JERU ***(JERU, YERAWA)*** [AKJ] Andaman Islands, interior and south North Andaman Island, and Sound Island. Andamanese, Great Andamanese, Northern. Extinct.

AKA-KEDE ***(KEDE)*** [AKX] Andaman Islands, central and north central Middle Andaman Island. Andamanese, Great Andamanese, Central. Extinct.

AKA-KOL ***(KOL)*** [AKY] Andaman Islands, southeast Middle Andaman Island. Andamanese, Great Andamanese, Central. Extinct.

AKA-KORA ***(KORA)*** [ACK] Andaman Islands, northeast and north central coasts of North Andaman Island, and Smith Island. Andamanese, Great Andamanese, Northern. Extinct.

AKAR-BALE ***(BALE, BALWA)*** [ACL] Andaman Islands, Ritchie's Archipelago, Havelock Island, Neill Island. Andamanese, Great Andamanese, Central. Extinct.

ALLAR ***(CHATANS)*** [ALL] 350. Kerala, Palghat District. Dravidian, Unclassified. Literacy rate in first language: Below 1%.

AMWI [AML] Austro-Asiatic, Mon-Khmer, Northern Mon-Khmer, Khasian. A distinct language from Khasi. Jirang is similar, and may be a dialect. Investigation needed: bilingual proficiency in Khasi. Literacy rate in first language: Below 1%.

ANAL ***(NAMFAU)*** [ANM] 15,000 in India (1997 IMA). Population total both countries 15,000 or more. Southeast Manipur. Also possibly Bangladesh. Also spoken in Myanmar. Sino-Tibetan, Tibeto-Burman, Kuki-Chin-Naga, Kuki-Chin, Northern. Dialects: LAIZO, MULSOM, MOYON-MONSHANG. A Scheduled Tribe in India. Declared themselves Nagas (ethnically) 1963. SOV. Literacy rate in first language: Below 1%. Forest. Christian (1981 census). NT 1983.

ANDH ***(ANDHA, ANDHI)*** [ANR] 80,000 (1991 IMA). Maharashtra, Nanded, Parbhani, Yeotmal districts; Andhra Pradesh; Madhya Pradesh. Unclassified. A Scheduled Tribe in India. People speak Marathi as mother tongue. Investigation needed: bilingual proficiency in Marathi. Literacy rate in first language: Below 1%. Cultivation. Hindu (1981 census).

ANGIKA ***(ANGA, ANGIKAR, CHHIKA-CHHIKI)*** [ANP] 725,000 (1997 IMA). Northern Bihar. Indo-European, Indo-Iranian, Indo-Aryan, Eastern zone, Bihari. 79% inherent intelligibility with Brahmin Maithili. Angika has 81% (Brahmin) to 87% (non-Brahmin) lexical similarity with Darbhanga Maithili. Hindi is used for trading, government, praying. Angika is used in most traditional domains (home, community, children playing, young people talking together). All ages. Angika is looked at as inferior to Maithili. Investigation needed: bilingual proficiency in Hindi. Radio programs.

APATANI ***(APA)*** [APT] 23,000 (1997 IMA). Assam; Arunachal Pradesh, Subansiri District, 7 villages in and around Hapoli and Zirol; Nagaland. Sino-Tibetan, Tibeto-Burman, North Assam, Tani. It may be intelligible with Nisi. A Scheduled Tribe in India. Literacy rate in first language: Below 1%. Agriculturalists: wet rice. Traditional religion.

ARAKANESE ***(MOGH, MOG, MAGH, MAGHI, MORMA, YAKAN, YAKHAING, RAKHAIN, MARMA)*** [MHV] 24,000 in India (1997 IMA). Assam; Tripura; Mizoram; West Bengal. Sino-Tibetan, Tibeto-Burman, Lolo-Burmese, Burmish, Southern. Bilingualism in Bengali. Mag is a Scheduled Tribe in India. Literacy rate in first language: 10% to 30%. Bible portions 1914. See main entry under Myanmar.

ARANADAN ***(ERANADANS)*** [AAF] 236 (1981 census). Tamil Nadu; Karnataka; Kerala, Calicut and Palghat Districts. Dravidian, Southern, Tamil-Kannada, Tamil-Kodagu, Tamil-Malayalam, Malayalam. Bilingualism in Malayalam. A Scheduled Tribe in India. Literacy rate in first language: Below 1%. Literacy rate in second language: 20% in Kerala (1981 census). Wage laborer, animal husbandry. Hindu.

ARE ***(ADE BHASHA, ARAY, ARREY, ARYA, KALIKA ARYA BHASHA)*** [AAG] 2,591 (1961 census). Andhra Pradesh; Maharashtra; Karnataka. Indo-European, Indo-Iranian, Indo-Aryan, Southern zone, Unclassified. Literacy rate in first language: Below 1%.

ASSAMESE ***(ASAMBE, ASAMI, ASAMIYA)*** [ASM] 15,334,000 in India (1997 IMA). Population total all countries 15,334,000 or more. Assam; Meghalaya; Arunachal Pradesh. Also spoken in Bangladesh, Bhutan. Indo-European, Indo-Iranian, Indo-Aryan, Eastern zone, Bengali-Assamese. Dialects: JHARWA (PIDGIN), MAYANG, STANDARD ASSAMESE, WESTERN ASSAMESE. National language. Bengali script. Bible 1833, in press (1999).

ASURI ***(ASHREE, ASURA, ASSUR)*** [ASR] 5,819. Bihar, Gumla and Lohardaga districts of Chotanagpur Plateau; east Madhya Pradesh, Raigarh District, Jashpur area; Maharashtra; Orissa, Sambalpur District; West Bengal. Austro-Asiatic, Munda, North Munda, Kherwari, Mundari. Dialects: BRIJIA (BIRJIA, KORANTI), MANJHI. Asur and Birjia are both Scheduled Tribes in India. Investigation needed: intelligibility with Mundari. Literacy rate in first language: Below 1%. Hindu, traditional religion, Christian (1981 census).

A'TONG [AOT] Assam. Sino-Tibetan, Tibeto-Burman, Jingpho-Konyak-Bodo, Konyak-Bodo-Garo, Bodo-Garo, Koch. Most closely related to Koch and Rabha. Not inherently intelligible with Garo, but many A'tong speak Garo as second language.

AWADHI ***(ABADI, ABOHI, AMBODHI, AVADHI, BAISWARI, KOJALI, KOSALI)*** [AWD] 20,000,000 in India (1999 IBS). Population total both countries 20,540,000. Bihar; Madhya Pradesh; Uttar Pradesh, Kanpur District; Delhi. Also spoken in Nepal. Indo-European, Indo-Iranian, Indo-Aryan, East Central zone. Dialects: GANGAPARI, MIRZAPURI, PARDESI, UTTARI. Awadhi is the standard for literature.

There is considerable epic literature. 'Kosali' is a name used for the Eastern Hindi group. Literacy rate in first language: 50% to 75%. Hindu, Muslim, Christian. NT 1996.

BADAGA ***(BADAG, BADAGU, BADUGU, BADUGA, VADAGU)*** [BFQ] 171,000 to 300,000 (1997). Tamil Nadu, Madras-Nilgiri, Kunda hills. 200 villages. Dravidian, Southern, Tamil-Kannada, Kannada. NT 1999.

BAGHELI ***(BAGELKHANDI, BHUGELKHUD, MANNADI, RIWAI, GANGGAI, MANDAL, KEWOT, KEWAT, KAWATHI, KENAT, KEVAT BOLI, KEVATI, KEWANI, KEWATI, NAGPURI MARATHI)*** [BFY] 396,000 in India (1997 IMA). Population total both countries 396,000 or more. Northeast Madhya Pradesh; Maharashtra; Uttar Pradesh. Also spoken in Nepal. Indo-European, Indo-Iranian, Indo-Aryan, East Central zone. Dialects: MARARI, OJHI (OJABOLI, OJHA, OJHE, OZA, OZHA), POWARI, BANAPARI, GAHORE, TIRHARI, GODWANI (MANDLAHA), SONPARI. The Ojhi are semi-nomadic. Investigation needed: intelligibility with dialects. Hindu, traditional religion (Ojhi). NT 1821, out of print.

BAGRI ***(BAGARI, BAGRIA, BAGRIS, BAORIAS, BAHGRI)*** [BGQ] 1,807,000 in India (1997 IMA). Population total both countries 2,007,000. Punjab; Rajasthan; Haryana; Madhya Pradesh. Also spoken in Pakistan. Indo-European, Indo-Iranian, Indo-Aryan, Central zone, Rajasthani, Unclassified. A Scheduled Caste in India. Singh 1993 reports they speak Malvi in Madhya Pradesh, Bagri in Rajasthan. Hindu.

BALOCHI, EASTERN ***(BALOCHI, BALUCI, BALOCI)*** [BGP] 5,000 in India (1977 Voegelin and Voegelin). Indo-European, Indo-Iranian, Iranian, Western, Northwestern, Balochi. Distinct from Western Balochi of Pakistan, Afghanistan, Iran, Turkmenistan; and Southern Balochi of Pakistan, Iran, Oman, United Arab Emirates. Sunni Muslim. Bible portions 1815-1906. See main entry under Pakistan.

BALTI ***(SBALT, BALTISTANI, BHOTI OF BALTISTAN)*** [BFT] 67,000 in India (1997 IMA). Jammu and Kashmir. Sino-Tibetan, Tibeto-Burman, Himalayish, Tibeto-Kanauri, Tibetic, Tibetan, Western. Chorbat is the most divergent dialect. 87% to 100% lexical similarity among dialects, 78% to 85% with Purik. Some Shina is used as second language. Urdu proficiency is reported to be high in some places. Women and uneducated people have little knowledge of Urdu. Many Purik have shifted to Balti. Speakers call themselves and their language 'Balti'. A Scheduled Tribe in India. Perso-Arabic script is the accepted one. Shi'ah Muslim. Bible portions 1903-1940. See main entry under Pakistan.

BARELI ***(BAREL, PAURI, PAWRI, PAWARI)*** [BGD] 695,000 including 394,000 Barela and 301,000 Paura (1997 IMA). Madhya Pradesh, Khargone, Dewas, Khandwa districts; Maharashtra, northern Dhule and Jalgaon districts. Indo-European, Indo-Iranian, Indo-Aryan, Central zone, Bhil. Dialects: RATHWI BARELI, BARLI (BARELI), PALYA BARELI (PALI), RATHWI PAURI, BARELI PAURI, NOIRI PAURI. Bareli Pauri and Rathwi Pauri not intelligible with Vasavi or Bhilori. 87% to 93% lexical similarity among Bareli dialects; 73% to 79% between Bareli Pauri and Rathwi Pauri dialects (closest). Bilingualism in Hindi (for the Barela) and Marathi (for the Paura) is limited. A Scheduled Tribe in India. Speakers are called 'Barela' and 'Paura'. Investigation needed: intelligibility with Bareli dialects, Bhilali. Literacy rate in second language: Low. Literacy effort in Bareli is needed. Traditional religion, Hindu, Christian. Bible portions 1986.

BATERI [BTV] 800 or about 200 families in India. Jammu and Kashmir, near Srinagar. Indo-European, Indo-Iranian, Indo-Aryan, Northwestern zone, Dardic, Kohistani. Closer to Indus Kohistani than to Shina, but distinct from both. See main entry under Pakistan.

BAURIA ***(BADAK, BABRI, BASRIA, BAWARI, BAWARIA, BHORIA, VAGHRI, BAORI)*** [BGE] 247,872 (1999 IMA). Punjab; Himachal Pradesh; Delhi; Haryana; Chandigarh; Rajasthan; Uttar Pradesh. Indo-European, Indo-Iranian, Indo-Aryan, Central zone, Bhil. A Scheduled Caste in India. In Punjab (only) they speak "a particular dialect named after the community" with population 62,624 (Singh 1993). Literacy rate in first language: Below 1%. Traditional religion, Sikh.

BAZIGAR [BFR] 100 (1951). Gujarat; Himachal Pradesh; Jammu and Kashmir; Madhya Pradesh; Karnataka. Dravidian, Unclassified. Literacy rate in first language: Below 1%.

BELLARI [BRW] Dravidian, Southern, Tulu. Related to Tulu and Koraga. Literacy rate in first language: Below 1%.

BENGALI ***(BANGALA, BANGLA, BANGLA-BHASA)*** [BNG] 70,561,000 in India (1997 IMA). West Bengal and neighboring states. Indo-European, Indo-Iranian, Indo-Aryan, Eastern zone, Bengali-Assamese. Dialects: BARIK, BHATIARI, CHIRMAR, KACHARI-BENGALI, LOHARI-MALPAHARIA, MUSSELMANI, RAJSHAHI, SAMARIA, SARAKI, SIRIPURIA (KISHANGANJIA). Spoken by some Koda as mother tongue. Investigation needed: intelligibility with dialects. National language, official language. Literacy rate in first language: 85%. Bengali script. Muslim, Hindu, Christian. Bible 1809-1998. See main entry under Bangladesh.

BHADRAWAHI ***(BADERWALI, BADROHI, BHADERBHAI JAMU, BHADERWALI PAHARI, BHADRAVA, BHADRI, BAHI)*** [BHD] 69,000 (1997 IMA). Jammu and Kashmir. Indo-European, Indo-Iranian,

Indo-Aryan, Northern zone, Western Pahari. Dialects: BHALESI, PADARI. Pangi is reported to be nearly the same as Bhadrawahi. Hindu, Muslim.

BHALAY [BHX] Maharashtra, Amravati District. Indo-European, Indo-Iranian, Indo-Aryan, Southern zone, Unclassified. Bilingualism in Hindi. Investigation needed: intelligibility with dialects, bilingual proficiency in Hindi.

BHARIA ***(BHAR, BHARAT, BHUMIA, BHUMIYA, PALIHA)*** [BHA] 196,512 (1981 census). Madhya Pradesh, Bilaspur, Chhatarpur, Chhindwara, Datia, Durg, Jabalpur, Mandla, Panna, Rewa, Sidhi, Surguja, Tikamgarh districts; Uttar Pradesh; West Bengal. Dravidian, Unclassified. Singh 1993 reports they speak a variety of Hindi. A Scheduled Tribe in India. Devanagari. Forest. Hindu.

BHATOLA [BTL] Madhya Pradesh. Unclassified.

BHATRI ***(BHATTRI, BHATTRA, BHATRA, BASTURIA, BHOTTADA, BHOTTARA)*** [BGW] 178,000 (1997 IMA). Andhra Pradesh; Madhya Pradesh, Bastar District, Jagdalpur tahsil; Maharashtra; Orissa, Koraput District, Kotpad tahsil. Indo-European, Indo-Iranian, Indo-Aryan, Eastern zone, Oriya. All dialects understand each other at 88%. Closely related to Halbi. 70% to 90% lexical similarity between dialects, 58% with Adwasi Oriya. Communities in Madhya Pradesh have limited bilingual proficiency in Hindi. Those in Orissa have limited proficiency in Oriya. 1/3 of the speakers have enhanced understanding of Halbi because of closeness to the Halbi-speaking area. Bhatri is preferred in home and religious domains. Vigorous. Positive attitude toward Bhatri. A Scheduled Tribe in India. Investigation needed: intelligibility with Adivasi Oriya. Literacy rate in second language: 7.5% (1981 census). Oriya script. Plains. Agriculturalists. Hindu (1981 census).

BHATTIYALI ***(BHATEALI, BHATIALI PAHARI, BHATIYALI)*** [BHT] 102,252 (1991 census). Himachal Pradesh, Chamba District, Bhattiyat Tahsil, Sihunta Sub-Tahsil. Indo-European, Indo-Iranian, Indo-Aryan, Northern zone, Western Pahari. 86% lexical similarity with Chambeali, 83% with Palampur Kangri, 76% with Bilaspuri. Bilingualism in Hindi, Panjabi, Urdu. All ages. SOV. Literacy rate in first language: Below 1%. Mountain slope, valley. Agriculturalists: rice, maize, millet. 300 to 1,350 meters. Hindu, Muslim, Sikh, Buddhist, Christian.

BHILALI ***(BHILALA)*** [BHI] 500,000 (1998). Madhya Pradesh, Khargone, southern Jhabua and southern Dhar districts; Maharashtra, Chule District: some in Gujarat; Karnataka; Rajasthan. Indo-European, Indo-Iranian, Indo-Aryan, Central zone, Bhil. A Scheduled Tribe in India. They call their language 'Bhili' in some areas, but it is a different language from Bhili. Investigation needed: intelligibility with subgroups, Bareli, bilingual proficiency in Hindi, Nimadi, attitudes. Agriculturalists, wage laborers. Hindu.

BHILI ***(BHILBARI, BHILBOLI, BHILLA, BHIL, VIL, BHAGORIA, LENGOTIA)*** [BHB] 1,300,000 including 1,000,000 Bhil plus 300,000 Patelia in Madhya Pradesh. 12,688 Kotvali (1994 IMA), 5,624,000 in languages in the Bhil family (1994 IMA). Madhya Pradesh, Jhabua, Char, Ratlam districts; Gujarat, Panchmahals and Dahod districts; Rajasthan; Maharashtra; some in Jammu and Kashmir; Andhra Pradesh; Karnataka; Punhab; Bihar; Tripura; mountainous areas. Indo-European, Indo-Iranian, Indo-Aryan, Central zone, Bhil. Dialects: AHIRI, ANARYA (PAHADI), BAORI, BAREL, BHIM, CHARANI, CHODHRI, DEHAWALI, CHODIA, DUBLI, GAMTI, GIRASIA, HABURA, KONKANI, KOTALI, KOTVALI (KOTWALIA), MAGRA KI BOLI, MAWCHI, NAHARI (BAGLANI) NAIKDI, PANCHALI, PARDHI, PAWRI, RANAWAT, RANI BHIL, RATHVI, SIYALGIR, WAGDI. Patelia in Gujarat is inherently intelligible with Bhili. Bhili of Ratlam District in Madhya Pradesh is inherently intelligible with Wagdi. Connecting link between Gujarati and Rajasthani (Marwari). Bhili is a Scheduled Tribe in Rajasthan, Gujarat, Maharashtra, Madhya Pradesh, Tripura; Kotwalia a Scheduled Tribe in Gujarat and Maharashtra. Limited proficiency in Hindi. Spoken as mother tongue by the Patelia in Madhya Pradesh. Connecting link between Gujarati and Rajasthani. 'Bhil' is an ethnic designation (caste or tribe). Dewali (Dehawali) is a cover term for Vasavi and Kotali, among others. Investigation needed: intelligibility with, bilingual proficiency, attitudes toward Kotwalia, Tadvi, Valvi, Naikda, Dhodia, Dubla, Charan, Rani with Bhili, Gujarati. Grammar. Literacy rate in first language: 1% to 5%. Literacy rate in second language: 10%. There are efforts being made in literature development. TV, videos. Traditional religion. Tadavi Bhil are Muslim. NT 1930, out of print.

BHILORI ***(BHILODI, PATELIA)*** [BQI] 100,000 (1998). Maharashtra, northern Dhule District, around Dhadgaon; Gujarat. Indo-European, Indo-Iranian, Indo-Aryan, Central zone, Bhil. Dialects: BHILODI, NOIRI (SATPUDA NOIRI). Noiri may be the same as Nora. 60% intelligibility with Marathi, 50% with Vasavi. Might be intelligible with Dungra Bhil. Bhilori has 95% lexical similarity with the Noiri dialect of the Satpuda, 70% to 64% with Bareli Pauri, 50% to 53% with Rathwi Pauri, 66% to 70% with Vasavi. Limited bilingual proficiency in Marathi. Spoken as mother tongue by the Patelia in Gujarat. Literacy rate in second language: Low. Agriculturalists, coolies. Hindu, traditional religion.

BHOJPURI ***(BHOJAPURI, BHOZPURI, BAJPURI, BIHARI)*** [BHJ] 24,544,000 in India (1997 IMA). Population total all countries 26,254,000. Bihar, Purnea area; Uttar Pradesh; Assam; Delhi; Madhya Pradesh; West Bengal. Also spoken in Mauritius, Nepal. Indo-European, Indo-Iranian, Indo-Aryan, Eastern zone, Bihari. Dialects: NORTHERN STANDARD BHOJPURI (GORAKHPURI, SARAWARIA, BASTI),

WESTERN STANDARD BHOJPURI (PURBI, BENARSI), SOUTHERN STANDARD BHOJPURI (KHARWARI), THARU, MADHESI, DOMRA, MUSAHARI. May be more than one language. Extent of dialect variation in India and Nepal not yet determined. The cover term 'Bihari' (Behari) is used for Bhojpuri, Maithili, and Magahi. Investigation needed: intelligibility with dialects. Literacy rate in first language: 5% to 30%. Literacy rate in second language: 50% to 75%. Kaithi script. Agriculturalists. Hindu, Muslim, Christian. Bible portions 1911-1982.

BHUNJIA ***(BUNJIA, BHUMJIYA, BHUNJIYA)*** [BHU] 18,601 (1981 census). Madhya Pradesh, Raipur, Hoshangabad districts; Orissa, Sambalpur, Kalshandi districts, Sunabera Plateau area; Maharashtra. Indo-European, Indo-Iranian, Indo-Aryan, Eastern zone, Oriya. Called a more divergent dialect of Halbi. A Scheduled Tribe in India. Agriculturalists. Hindu (1981 census).

BIETE ***(BETE, BIATE)*** [BIU] 19,000 (1997 IMA). Meghalaya, Jaintia Hills District; Mizoram northeast; Assam, Cachar Hills. Sino-Tibetan, Tibeto-Burman, Kuki-Chin-Naga, Kuki-Chin, Northern. Closest to Hrangkhol. A Scheduled Tribe in India. An ethnic subgroup of the Mizo (see Lushai). Literacy rate in first language: 56%. Christian. NT 1985-1991.

BIJORI ***(BINJHIA, BIRIJIA, BRIJIA, BURJA, BIRJIA)*** [BIX] 2,391 (1961 census). Bihar, Cowerdaga and Ranchi districts; West Bengal, Darjeeling and Jalpaiguri districts; Madhya Pradesh; Orissa. Austro-Asiatic, Munda, North Munda, Kherwari. A Scheduled Tribe in India. The ethnic group is called 'Birjia'. Literacy rate in second language: 10% Hindi. Agriculturalists: shifting cultivation. Hindu, Christian (1981 census).

BILASPURI ***(BILASPURI PAHARI, PACCHMI, KAHLURI, KEHLURI, KEHLOORI PAHARI)*** [KFS] 295,387 (1991 census). Himachal Pradesh, Bilaspur District. Indo-European, Indo-Iranian, Indo-Aryan, Northern zone, Western Pahari. 95% intelligibility of Mandeali, 94% of Kangri. 90% lexical similarity with Kangri of Palampur, 86% with Mandeali, 84% with Chambeali. Hindi is used for instruction in school and politics. Middle-aged and older women have limited understanding of Hindi. Some speak Panjabi as second language. Urdu is spoken by middle-aged and older educated people as second language. Spoken for home, community, agricultural and religious topics. Hindi is used for instruction in school and politics. All ages. 'Kahluri' is based on the old name for the princely state. SOV. Radio programs. Mountain slope, valley. Agriculturalists: rice, maize, millet. 300 to 1,350.

BIRHOR ***(BIHOR, BIRHAR, BIRHORE, MANKIDI, MANKIDIA)*** [BIY] 10,000 (1998 GR). Bihar, Hazaribagh, Singbhum, and Ranchi districts; Madhya Pradesh, Raigarh District; Orissa, Sundgarh, Kalahandi, Keonijhar, Mayurbhanj, Sambalpur districts; West Bengal; Maharashtra. Austro-Asiatic, Munda, North Munda, Kherwari, Mundari. 55% to 72% lexical similarity with Santhali, Ho, Mundari. Second languages Sadri, Santhali, Ho, Mundari, Hindi, Oriya used in market. Birhor used in most domains. Vigorous. No indication of language shift. Positive attitude toward Birhor. A Scheduled Tribe in India. Traditionally nomadic. Investigation needed: intelligibility with central, southern Bihar varieties, Bagdamal Birhor. Literacy rate in first language: 0.02% (1971 census). Literacy rate in second language: 10% Hindi. Rope makers, hunter-gathers, fishermen, agriculturalists. Hindu, traditional religion.

BISHNUPRIYA ***(BISHNUPURIYA, BISNA PURIYA, BISHNUPRIA MANIPURI)*** [BPY] 75,000 (1997 IMA). Population total both countries 75,000 or more. Manipur; Assam, Cachar District; Tripura. Also spoken in Bangladesh. Indo-European, Indo-Iranian, Indo-Aryan, Eastern zone, Bengali-Assamese. Related to Bengali and Assamese. Though once regarded as a Bengali-Meithei creole, it retains pre-Bengali features (Masica 1991). Bilingualism in Hindi. Valley.

BODO ***(BORO, BODI, BARA, BORONI, MECHI, MECHE, MECH, MECI, KACHARI)*** [BRX] 600,000 in India (1997 IMA). Population total both countries 601,000. Assam, South Bank; West Bengal; Manipur, Tengnoupal District. Also spoken in Nepal. Sino-Tibetan, Tibeto-Burman, Jingpho-Konyak-Bodo, Konyak-Bodo-Garo, Bodo-Garo, Bodo. Dialects: CHOTE, MECH. Related to Dimasa, Tripuri, Lalunga. Vigorous Bodo language and culture. Most Mech in Assam speak Assamese as mother tongue (R. Breton 1997:24). 3 Scheduled Tribes: Mech, Boro-Kachari, Plains Kachari. Literacy rate in second language: 40% Assamese. Agriculturalists. Spiritist, traditional religion, Hindu, Christian. Bible 1981.

BODO PARJA ***(BODO PARAJA, PARJI, PARJA, PAROJA, POROJA, JHODIA PARJA, SODIA PARJA, PARJHI, PARAJHI, HARJA, JHARIA, JHALIYA)*** [BDV] 50,000 (1995). Orissa, Koraput District. Indo-European, Indo-Iranian, Indo-Aryan, Eastern zone, Oriya. Phonology and grammar show Indo-European relationship, not related to Dravidian Duruwa Parji. 76% to 86% lexical similarity between Bodo Parja and Jhodia Parja, 70% to 89% between Bodo Parja, Jhodia Parja, and Desia. Adivasi Oriya mainly used in the market, but proficiency is limited. Bodo is higher caste than Jhodia, showing some signs of negative attitudes, despite high intelligibility. Paroja is a Scheduled Tribe in India. Investigation needed: intelligibility with 609,646 Bodo Parja in Mayughanj District, NE Orissa. Literacy program needed. Oriya script. Scrub forest. Mountain valley. Peasant agriculturalists, laborers. 200 to 1,000 meters. Hindu, traditional religion, Christian.

BONDO ***(PORAJA KATHA, BHONDA BHASHA, BONDO-PORAJA, REMO, REMOSUM, BONDA, NANQA POROJA)*** [BFW] 8,000, including 4,500 Upper Bondo and 3,500 Lower Bondo (1991 census). Orissa, Koroput District, Malkangiri subdivision, Khairput block, Bondo Hills. Austro-Asiatic, Munda, South Munda, Koraput Munda, Gutob-Remo-Geta', Gutob-Remo. Dialects: UPPER BONDO, LOWER BONDO. Closest to Didayi, Gutob Gadaba, Parenga. 70% to 94% lexical similarity with other Bondo varieties, 45% to 51% with Gadaba Gutob, 22% to 32% with Upper Gata' (Didayi). Few Lower Bondo are monolingual. Many speak Adivasi Oriya for trade and interactions with surrounding communities. Few Upper Bondo are bilingual. A Scheduled Tribe in India. Non-vegetarians who occasionally eat meat. Investigation needed: intelligibility with dialects. Literacy rate in second language: 0.76% female, 6.81% male, 3.61% total (1981 census). Hills. Shifting agriculturalists, hunter-gatherers. 3,000 feet. Traditional religion, Hindu (1981 census).

BRAJ BHASHA ***(BRAJ, BRAJ BHAKHA, BRIJ BHASHA, ANTARBEDI, ANTARVEDI, BIJBHASHA, BRI, BRIJU, BRUJ)*** [BFS] 44,000 (1997 IMA). Uttar Pradesh, Agra region; Rajasthan, Bharatpur, Sawai Madhopur districts; Haryana, Gurgaon District; Bihar; Madhya Pradesh; Delhi. Indo-European, Indo-Iranian, Indo-Aryan, Central zone, Western Hindi, Unclassified. Dialects: BRAJ BHASHA, ANTARBEDI, BHUKSA, SIKARWARI, JADOBAFI, DANGI. Bhuksa is sometimes mentioned as a dialect of Kanauji. NT 1824-1999.

BROKSKAT ***(BROKPA, BROKPA OF DAH-HANU, DOKSKAT, KYANGO)*** [BKK] 3,000 (1981 census). Jammu and Kashmir, along the Indus River in Ladakh and Kargil districts, northern Kashmir, villages around Garkhon, including Darchiks, Chulichan, Gurgurdo, Batalik, and Dah, and formerly in Hanu. Indo-European, Indo-Iranian, Indo-Aryan, Northwestern zone, Dardic, Shina. Broq-pa is a Scheduled Tribe in India. A very divergent variety of Shina. Minaro is an alternate ethnic name. 'Brokpa' is the name given by the Ladakhi for the people. 'Brokskat' is the language. Literacy rate in first language: Below 1%. Balti script. Buddhism, traditional religion, some Muslim.

BUKSA [TKB] 43,000 (1999 IMA). Uttar Pradesh, southwestern Nainital District, along a diagonal from Ramnagar to Keneshpur. 130 villages in Kichha and Kashipur tahsils, and small numbers in Bijnor and Garhwal districts. Indo-European, Indo-Iranian, Indo-Aryan, Eastern zone, Unclassified. Speakers tested at 95% intelligibility of Rana Tharu. 58% to 79% lexical similarity with western Tharu varieties, 58% with Chitwania Tharu, 83% with Hindi. Investigation needed: intelligibility, bilingual proficiency in Kathoriya. Agriculturalists, pastoralists. Traditional religion.

BUNDELI ***(BUNDEL KHANDI)*** [BNS] 644,000 (1997 IMA) to 8,000,000 or more (1997). Uttar Pradesh, Jalaun, Jhansi, Hamirpur, Banda districts; Madhya Pradesh, Balaghat, Chhindwara, Hoshangabad, Sagar, Sehore, Panna, Satna, Chhatarpur, Tikamgarh, Shivpuri, Guna, Bhind, Morena, Gwalior, Lalitpur, Narsinghpur, Seoni, Datia districts; Maharashtra, Bhandara, Nagpur districts; Rajasthan; Gujarat; Andhra Pradesh. Indo-European, Indo-Iranian, Indo-Aryan, Central zone, Western Hindi, Bundeli. Dialects: STANDARD BUNDELI, PAWARI (POWARI), LODHANTI (RATHORA), KHATOLA, BANAPHARI, KUNDRI, NIBHATTA, TIRHARI, BHADAURI (TOWARGARHI), LODHI, KOSTI, KUMBHARI, GAOLI, KIRARI, RAGHOBANSI, NAGPURI HINDI, CHHINDWARA BUNDELI. Intelligibility testing of Standard varieties gave 83%, 92%, and 98%. Chhatapur dialect is widely understood. Other dialects listed by Grierson are Standard Braj of Mathura, Aligarh, western Agra; Standard Braj of Bulandshahr; Standard Braj of eastern Agra, southern Morena, southern Bharatpur; Braj merging into Kanauji in Etah, Mainpuri, Budaun, and Bareilly; Braj merging into the Bhadauri subdialect in northern Morena; Braj merging into Jaipuri (Rajasthani) in northern Bharatpur and Sawai Uradhopur; Bhuksa in southern Nainital. Chhindwara has 65% to 85% lexical similarity with Standard Bundeli, and 41% with Nagpuri Hindi. The uneducated have limited ability in Hindi. Bundeli is used in the home. There is ethnic pride in the language and culture. Favorable attitudes toward Chhatapur dialect. Investigation needed: intelligibility, attitudes. Radio programs. Plains. Agriculturalists. Hindu, Buddhist.

BYANGSI ***(BYANSHI, BYANSI, BYANGKHO LWO)*** [BEE] Population total both countries 1,314 and more. Uttar Pradesh, in the Kuthi Yangti River valley high in the Himalayas on the border with Tibet and Nepal. Also spoken in Nepal. Sino-Tibetan, Tibeto-Burman, Himalayish, Tibeto-Kanauri, Western Himalayish, Almora. Related to Rangkas, Darmiya, Chaudangsi. Devidatta Sharma 1989 suggests that Chaudangsi and Byangsi are varieties of one language. Considered to be dialects of one language with Chaudangsi and dialects in Chhanguru and Tinker districts of Nepal. Cultural center seems to be India. Investigation needed: intelligibility with Chaudangsi, dialects. Grammar.

CHAKMA ***(TAKAM, CHAKAMA)*** [CCP] 300,000 in India (1987 ABWE). Population total both countries 560,000. Mizoram, southwestern part along Karnafuli River; Tripura, northern; Assam, Karbi, Anglong, North Cachar, Cachar districts; West Bengal; Manipur. Also spoken in Bangladesh. Indo-European, Indo-Iranian, Indo-Aryan, Eastern zone, Bengali-Assamese. A Scheduled Tribe in India. Forest. Agriculturalists: shifting cultivation. Buddhist. NT 1926-1991.

CHAMARI ***(CHAMAR, CHAMBHAR BOLI, CHAMBHARI)*** [CDG] 5,324 (1971 census). Madhya Pradesh; Uttar Pradesh; Maharashtra. Indo-European, Indo-Iranian, Indo-Aryan, Central zone, Western Hindi, Unclassified. Literacy rate in first language: Below 1%.

CHAMBEALI ***(CHAMAYA, CHAMBIALI, CHAMBIYALI, CHAMIYALI PAHARI, CHAMYA, CAMEALI)*** [CDH] 129,654 (1991 census). Himachal Pradesh, Chamba District, Chamba Tahsil; Jammu and Kashmir. Indo-European, Indo-Iranian, Indo-Aryan, Northern zone, Western Pahari. Dialects: BANSBALI, BANSYARI, GADI CHAMEALI. 91% intelligibility of Mandeali, 87% by Kangri. 90% lexical similarity with Palumpur Kangri, 86% with Bhattiyali, 84% with Bilaspuri, 83% with Mandeali, 79% with Gaddi, 78% with Churahi. Bilingualism in Hindi, Panjabi, Urdu. All ages. SOV. Radio programs. Mountain slope, valley. Agriculturalists: rice, maize millet, fruit. 900 to 3,000 meters. Bible portions 1883-1979.

CHANGTHANG ***(CHANGTANG, CHANGTANG LADAKHI, CHANGS-SKAT, BYANGSKAT, BYANSKAT, RONG, RUPSHU, STOTPA, UPPER LADAKHI)*** [CNA] Jammu and Kashmir, Tibetan border area, ChangThang region east and southeast of Leh. Sino-Tibetan, Tibeto-Burman, Himalayish, Tibeto-Kanauri, Tibetic, Tibetan, Western, Ladakhi. May be intelligible with Ladakhi. Some multilingualism in Ladakhi, Urdu, Kashmiri, Hindi, or English. Champa is a Scheduled Tribe. People are called 'Champas'. Nomadic. They barter for grain from the Zangskari. Noted for music and dance. Investigation needed: intelligibility with Ladakhi. Bodhi script. Plateau. Pastoralists: sheep (cashmere wool), goats; traders: wool, salt. 4,000 to 5,000 meters. Buddhist.

CHAUDANGSI ***(TSAUDANGSI)*** [CDN] Population total both countries 1,500 (1977 Voegelin and Voegelin). Uttar Pradesh, facing the Nepal border along the Mahakali Valley. May only be in India. Also spoken in Nepal. Sino-Tibetan, Tibeto-Burman, Himalayish, Tibeto-Kanauri, Western Himalayish, Almora. Related to Rangkas, Darmiya, Byangsi. Literacy rate in first language: Below 1%.

CHAURA ***(CHOWRA, TUTET)*** [CHO] Nicobar Islands, Chaura Island. Austro-Asiatic, Mon-Khmer, Nicobar, Chowra-Teressa. Investigation needed: intelligibility.

CHENCHU ***(CHENCHUCOOLAM, CHENCHWAR, CHENSWAR, CHONCHARU)*** [CDE] 28,754 (1981 census). Andhra Pradesh, highest concentration in Kurnool District, Nallamalla Hills; Karnataka; Orissa. Dravidian, South-Central, Telugu. Entirely monolingual. A Scheduled Tribe in India. Literacy rate in second language: 9.7% (1981 census). Telugu. Tropical forest. Agriculturalists. Hindu (1981 census).

CHHATTISGARHI ***(LARIA, KHALTAHI)*** [HNE] 11,535,000 including 11,456,000 Chhattisgarhi (1997 IMA), 79,000 Laria (1997 IMA). Madhya Pradesh; Bihar; Orissa; and possibly in Maharashtra, Uttar Pradesh, and Tripura. Surgujia is in the Surguja and Raigarh districts of Madhya Pradesh; Sadri Korwa spoken by Korwa people of Jashpur district; Baigani in Balaghat, Raipur, and Bilaspur districts of Madhya Pradesh, and Sambalpur District of Orissa; Binjhwari in Raipur and Raigarh districts of Madhya Pradesh; Kalanga and Bhulia in Patna District of Bihar; Chhattisgarhi Proper in Raipur, Durg, Bilaspur and other districts of Madhya Pradesh. Indo-European, Indo-Iranian, Indo-Aryan, East Central zone. Dialects: SURGUJIA, SADRI KORWA, BAIGANI (BAIGA, BEGA, BHUMIA, GOWRO), BINJHWARI, KALANGA, BHULIA, CHHATTISGARHI PROPER, KAVARDI, KHAIRAGARHI. Most closely related to Awadhi and Bagheli. Limited proficiency in Hindi. Oriya also used. Used in nearly all domains. Spoken as mother tongue by the Kawari. Positive attitude toward Chhattisgarhi. Investigation needed: intelligibility with dialects. Devanagari script. Poetry, newspapers, radio programs, TV. Arid plains. Traditional religion, Hindu, Muslim. Bible portions 1904-1952.

CHIN, BAWM ***(BAWM, BAWNG, BAWN, BOM)*** [BGR] Population total all countries 9,000 (1990 UBS). Mizoram, Chhimtuipui, Lunglei, and Aizawl districts; Assam. Also spoken in Bangladesh, Myanmar. Sino-Tibetan, Tibeto-Burman, Kuki-Chin-Naga, Kuki-Chin, Central. Regard themselves correctly as a subgroup of the Laizou (Anal) (Matisoff et al. 1996:8). Bilingualism in Lushai. A Scheduled Tribe in India. Bible 1989.

CHIN, FALAM ***(HALAM CHIN, HALLAM, FALLAM, TIPURA)*** [HBH] 25,367 in India (1994 IMA), including 7,000 Ranglong. Assam; Tripura; Mizoram; West Bengal. Sino-Tibetan, Tibeto-Burman, Kuki-Chin-Naga, Kuki-Chin, Northern. Dialects: CHOREI, CHARI CHONG, HALAM, KAIPANG, KALAI (KOLOI), KHELMA, MURSUM (MOLSOM), RUPINI, SHEKASIP, RANGLONG. Other dialect or clan names are: Ranglong, Choral, Ranjkho, Molsom, Kaipeng, Sankachep, Bong, Bongcher, Langkai, Moosephang. They are collectively called 'Baro Halam'. Rupini and Koloi are said to be quite different from the others. Halam is a Scheduled Tribe in India. Many ethnic Halam speak Kokborok as mother tongue. SOV. Bible 1991. See main entry under Myanmar.

CHIN, HAKA ***(HAKA, BAUNGSHE)*** [CNH] 345,000 Lai speakers in India (1996 UBS). Mizoram, Chhimtuipui and Aizawi District, southernmost tip; Assam; Meghalaya. Sino-Tibetan, Tibeto-Burman, Kuki-Chin-Naga, Kuki-Chin, Central. Dialects: LAI (LAI PAWI, LAI HAWLH), KLANGKLANG (THLANTLANG), ZOKHUA, SHONSHE. Shonshe may be a separate language. Lai Pawi is a Scheduled Tribe in India. Forest. Hills. Agriculturalists: shifting cultivation. Christian. Bible 1978. See main entry under Myanmar.

CHIN, KHUMI ***(KHUMI, KHAMI, KAMI, KUMI, KHWEYMI, KHUNI, ARENG, AWA)*** [CKM] Assam. Sino-Tibetan, Tibeto-Burman, Kuki-Chin-Naga, Kuki-Chin, Southern, Khumi. Dialects: KHIMI, MATU (MATUPI), YINDI (YINDU), KHAMI. Called Khami Chin in India. Tropical forest. Traditional religion, Christian. NT 1959-1991. See main entry under Myanmar.

CHIN, MARA ***(LAKHER, ZAO, MARAM, MIRA, MARA)*** [MRH] 22,000 in India (1997 IMA). Population total both countries 42,000. Assam, Lushai hills; Mizoram, southern. Also spoken in Myanmar. Sino-Tibetan, Tibeto-Burman, Kuki-Chin-Naga, Kuki-Chin, Southern. Dialects: TLONGSAI (TLOSAI-SIAHA), HLAWTHAI. Close to Shendu. Reported to be affiliated with Lai (Haka Chin). A Scheduled Tribe in India. A subgroup of Mizo (Lushai). SOV. Roman script. Christian nearly. Bible 1956.

CHIN, PAITE ***(PAITE, PAITHE, PARTE, HAITHE)*** [PCK] 45,000 in India (1997 IMA). Population total both countries 53,900. Assam; Manipur, southern; Mizoram, Aizaw District, Champhai subdivision; Tripura. Also spoken in Myanmar. Sino-Tibetan, Tibeto-Burman, Kuki-Chin-Naga, Kuki-Chin, Northern. Related to Tedim Chin, Zomi. A Scheduled Tribe in India. Dictionary. Grammar. Roman script. Christian. Bible 1971.

CHIN, TEDIM ***(TEDIM, TIDDIM)*** [CTD] 155,000 in India (1990 BAP). Mizoram, Chin Hills, Upper Chindwin, Chin State, Tiddim area. Sino-Tibetan, Tibeto-Burman, Kuki-Chin-Naga, Kuki-Chin, Northern. Dialects: SOKTE, KAMHAU (KAMHOW, KAMHAO). Other Chin languages or dialects of this area are Saizang, Teizang, Zo. Trade language. SOV. Bible 1983, in press (1996). See main entry under Myanmar.

CHIN, THADO ***(THADOU, THADO-UBIPHEI, THADO-PAO, KUKI, KUKI-THADO, THAADOU KUKI)*** [TCZ] 125,100 in India. Population total both countries 200,000 (1993 UBS). Assam; Manipur, Tengnoupal District; Nagaland; Mizoram; Tripura. Also spoken in Myanmar. Sino-Tibetan, Tibeto-Burman, Kuki-Chin-Naga, Kuki-Chin, Northern. Dialects: BAITE, CHANGSEN, JANGSHEN, KAOKEEP, KHONGZAI, KIPGEN, LANGIUNG, SAIRANG, THANGNGEN, HAWKIP, SHITHLOU, SINGSON (SHINGSOL). Some of those listed as dialects are separate languages. A Scheduled Tribe in India. SOV. Christian mainly. Bible 1971-1994.

CHINALI ***(CHINAL, CHANA, DAGI, SHIPI, HARIJAN, CHANNALI)*** [CIH] 500 to 1,000 speakers (1996). Himachal Pradesh, throughout Lahul Valley, especially in Pattan Valley, Gushal village. Indo-European, Indo-Iranian, Indo-Aryan, Unclassified. Speakers say their language is closely related to Sanskrit. Spoken by the Chinal caste. Many are well educated. Investigation needed: intelligibility with dialects in Chamba and Kinnaur by Sippi, Dagi, Hali castes, bilingual proficiency in Hindi. Literacy program needed. Devanagari.

CHIRU ***(CHHORI)*** [CDF] 3,774 (1981 census). Assam; Manipur; Nagaland. Scattered. Sino-Tibetan, Tibeto-Burman, Kuki-Chin-Naga, Kuki-Chin, Northern. Related to Aimol, Purum, Langrong, Koireng. A Scheduled Tribe in India. Literacy rate in second language: 40% (1981 census). Roman and Bengali scripts. Agriculturalists: shifting and wet cultivation. Christian.

CHODRI ***(CHAUDRI, CHODHARI, CHAUDHARI, CHOUDHARY, CHOUDHARA)*** [CDI] 226,534 (1994 IMA). Mainly in Gujarat, Broach and Dangs districts. Some in Maharashtra, Karnataka, Rajasthan. Indo-European, Indo-Iranian, Indo-Aryan, Central zone, Bhil. A Scheduled Tribe in India. Ethnically Bhil. Literacy rate in second language: 20% Gujarati, Hindi (1977). Traditional religion, Hindu. Bible portions 1991.

CHURAHI ***(CHURAHI PAHARI, CHAURAHI, CHURAI PAHARI)*** [CDJ] 110,552 (1991 census). Himachal Pradesh, Chamba district, Chaurah and Saluni tahsils, Bhalai Sub-tahsil. Indo-European, Indo-Iranian, Indo-Aryan, Northern zone, Western Pahari. 90% intelligibility of Mandeali, 83% of Kangri, 85% of Chambeali. 78% lexical similarity with Chambeali (closest), 70% with Palampur Kangri and Bhattiyali, 67% to 69% with Gaddi, 65% with Mandeali and Bilaspuri, 64% with Pangi. Bilingualism in Hindi, Panjabi, Urdu. All ages. SOV; postpositions; genitives after noun heads; adjectives, numerals before noun heads; question word initial; verb suffixes mark person, number, gender of subject. Mountain slope, valley. Agriculturalists: rice, maize millet, wheat, barley. 1,500 to 3,000 meters.

DARLONG ***(DALONG)*** [DLN] 6,000 in India (1998 Thanglura Darlong). Tripura. Sino-Tibetan, Tibeto-Burman, Kuki-Chin-Naga, Kuki-Chin, Central. Literacy rate in first language: Below 1%. Literacy rate in second language: 45%. NT 1995. See main entry under Bangladesh.

DARMIYA ***(DARIMIYA)*** [DRD] 1,750 (1977 Voegelin and Voegelin). Uttar Pradesh, facing the Nepal border along the Mahakali Valley. Not in Nepal (Bradley 1997). Sino-Tibetan, Tibeto-Burman, Himalayish, Tibeto-Kanauri, Western Himalayish, Almora. Related to Rangkas, Chaudangsi, Byangsi. Literacy rate in first language: Below 1%.

DECCAN ***(DESI, DEKINI, DECCANI)*** [DCC] 10,709,800 (1990). Central Maharashtra, Deccan Plateau. Indo-European, Indo-Iranian, Indo-Aryan, Southern zone, Unclassified. Dialects: KALVADI (DHARWAR), BIJAPURI. Distinct from Deccan (Dakhini, Mirgan) dialect of Urdu. Arid. Plateau. Muslim.

DEGARU ***(DHEKARU)*** [DGR] Bihar; West Bengal. Indo-European, Indo-Iranian, Indo-Aryan, Eastern zone, Unclassified.

DEORI ***(CHUTIYA, DEURI, DEWRI, DRORI, DARI)*** [DER] 19,000 (1997 IMA). Assam, North Lakhimpur, Dibrugarh, Sibsagar, Jorhat, Sonitpur districts; Arunachal Pradesh, Lohit District; Nagaland. Sino-Tibetan, Tibeto-Burman, Jingpho-Konyak-Bodo, Konyak-Bodo-Garo, Bodo-Garo, Bodo. Deori may constitute its own subgroup under Bodo-Garo. Not close to other languages. Some Deori speak Assamese as mother tongue. A Scheduled Tribe in India. Agriculturalists. Hindu, traditional religion.

DHANKI ***(DHANKA, DANGI, DANGRI, DANGS BHIL, TADAVI, TADVI BHIL, KAKACHHU-KI BOLI)*** [DHN] 138,000 (1997 IMA). Gujarat, Dangs District; Maharashtra, Jalgaon District; Karnataka; Rajasthan. Indo-European, Indo-Iranian, Indo-Aryan, Central zone, Khandesi. Bilingualism in Gujarati. Dhankia and Tadvi Bhil are both Scheduled Tribes. Chanka of Rajasthan reportedly speak Hindi as mother tongue. Dhanka of Maharashtra reportedly speak Gujarati as mother tongue. The Tadvi Bhil reportedly speak Bhil as mother tongue. The people are called 'Dhanka'. Trade language. Agriculturalists. Hindu mainly.

DHANWAR ***(DHANVAR, DANUWAR)*** [DHA] 104,195 (1981 census). Madhya Pradesh, Bilaspur, Raigarh, Sarguja districts; Maharashtra, Akola, Amraoti, Yavatmal, Nagpur, Wardha, Chandrapur districts. Indo-European, Indo-Iranian, Indo-Aryan, East Central zone. A Scheduled Tribe in India. In Madhya Pradesh they are reported to speak Chhattisfarhi as mother tongue, and in Maharashtra Marathi. A distinct language from Danuwar Rai in Nepal. Shepherds; cattle breeders and sellers; blanket weavers. Hindu, traditional religion.

DHODIA ***(DHORI, DHORE, DHOWARI, DORIA)*** [DHO] 139,000 (1997 IMA). Gujarat, Surat and Valsad districts, Daman and Diu, Dadra and Nagar Haveli; Madhya Pradesh; Maharashtra; Karnataka; Rajasthan. Indo-European, Indo-Iranian, Indo-Aryan, Central zone, Bhil. Bilingualism in Gujarati. A Scheduled Tribe in India. Not the same as Dori in Pakistan. Agriculturalists; fishermen. Hindu.

DIGARO ***(DIGARU, TAAON, TARAON, TAYING, MISHMI)*** [MHU] 33,000 (1997 IMA). Arunachal Pradesh, Lohit District, Hayuliang, Changlagam, Goiliang circles; Assam. Sino-Tibetan, Tibeto-Burman, North Assam, Tani. Closely related language: Idu. They may not be in the Tani group, but are related to the Tani group. Bilingualism in Assamese. A Scheduled Tribe in India. Traditional religion.

DIMASA ***(DIMASA KACHARI)*** [DIS] 106,000 (1997 IMA). Assam, North Cachar district and Cachar Hills, Karbi Anglong, Nowgong districts; Nagaland, Haflong District. Sino-Tibetan, Tibeto-Burman, Jingpho-Konyak-Bodo, Konyak-Bodo-Garo, Bodo-Garo, Bodo. Dialects: DIMASA, HARIAMBA. Related to Kachari, but separate. Kachar Barman and Kachar Hoja speak Dimasa as mother tongue. Some Dimasa speak other languages as mother tongue: Mikir, Bengali, Assamese. Dictionary. Grammar. Literacy rate in second language: Low. 3 scripts. Bible portions 1905-1908.

DOGRI-KANGRI ***(DOGRI, DHOGARYALI, DOGARI, DOGRI JAMMU, DOGRI PAHARI, DONGARI, HINDI DOGRI, TOKKARU, DOGRI-KANGRA)*** [DOJ] 2,200,000 including 2,105,000 Dogri (1997 IMA), 95,000 Kangri (1997 IMA). The home area is in the outer hills and strip of plain at their feet in Jammu and Kashmir between the Ravi and Chenab Rivers. Central states from north to south; Chandigarh; Himachal Pradesh, Kangra and Hamirpur districts; West Bengal. Indo-European, Indo-Iranian, Indo-Aryan, Northern zone, Western Pahari. Dialects: BHATBALI, EAST DOGRI, KANDIALI, KANGRI (KANGRA), NORTH DOGRI, DOGRI. Palampur Kangri has 90% lexical similarity with Bilaspuri and Chambeali, 89% with Mandeali, 83% with Bhattiyali, 80% with MacLeod Ganj Gaddi. Urdu (middle-aged and older), Hindi (school, shops. cities), and Panjabi (shops) are spoken as second languages for certain purposes. All ages. Dogri formerly considered a Panjabi dialect, but now promoted as a written language in India. Dhogri is a Scheduled Caste in Himachal Pradesh and Punjab. They reportedly speak Chambeali in Himachal Pradesh. Investigation needed: intelligibility with Kangri dialects, Chotti Bangal, Bara Kangal, Kullui Kangri, Mandeali, Bhattiyali, Chambeali, Churahi, Gaddi. SOV. Literacy rate in second language: 18% to 19%. Nastaliq script used for Dogri in Jammu, Devanagari used for Kangri in Himachal Pradesh. Radio programs. Mountain slope, valley. Agriculturalists: rice, maize, millet, fruit. 300 to 1,350 meters. Hindu, Muslim, Sikh, Buddhist, Christian. NT 1826, out of print.

DOMARI [RMT] Bihar, Saran and Champaran districts. Indo-European, Indo-Iranian, Indo-Aryan, Central zone, Dom. Dialects: DOMAKI, WOGRI-BOLI. A Gypsy language partly used for in-group identification. Muslim. See main entry under Iran.

DUBLI ***(DUBALA, DUBLA, RATHOD, TALAVIA)*** [DUB] 202,000 (1991 IMA). Gujarat, Surat, Valsad, Bharuch, Vadodara districts; Maharashtra, Thana District, Talasari and Dahanu areas; Dadra and Nagar Haveli; Daman and Diu; Karnataka: Rajasthan. Indo-European, Indo-Iranian, Indo-Aryan, Central zone, Bhil. A Scheduled Tribe in India. Language name is 'Dubli', people's name 'Dubla'. Reports they speak Gujarati have not been confirmed. Literacy rate in second language: 10%. Hindu, Christian, Muslim.

DUNGRA BHIL [DUH] 200,000 (1998). Gujarat, Baroda District; Madhya Pradesh; Maharashtra. Indo-European, Indo-Iranian, Indo-Aryan, Central zone, Bhil. 84% to 89% intelligibility with Bhilori of

Maharashtra. 86% lexical similarity between subgroups, 71% to 87% with Bhilori and Noiri Bhili, below 53% with Girasia. A Scheduled Tribe in Gujarat. A Bhil subgroup. 'Dungra Bhil' is sometimes used as an alternate name for Adivasi Girasia and Rajput Girasia but probably refers to more than one group living in the hills ('Dungra' means 'hill'). Settled agriculturalists.

DURUWA ***(DHURWA, DHRUVA, DURVA, PARJI, PARJHI, PARAJA, PARAJHI, THAKARA, TAGARA, TUGARA)*** [PCI] 90,000 speakers out of 100,000 in the ethnic group (1986), 2/3 in Bastar, 1/3 in Koraput. Madhya Pradesh, Bastar Disctrict, southeast Jagdalpur Tahsil; Orissa, Koraput District. Dravidian, Central, Parji-Gadaba. Dialects: TIRIYA, NETHANAR, DHARBA, KUKANAR. All dialects are inherently intelligible. Nethanar dialect is central. Dialects have 90% to 96% lexical similarity. Dialects have 70% to 82% lexical similarity with Halbi. Monolinguals include children. Halbi is the second language. Part of the ethnic group speaks Halbi as first language (around Jagdalpur, Bastar district); 1% speak Oriya; less than 2% use Bhatri (northern Bastar District). Hindi is the state language, but it is not well known except by the educated. 90% of the ethnic group speaks Parji as mother tongue. Parji is spoken by the Madiya for communicating with the Dhurwa people. A Scheduled Tribe in India. Name of the people is 'Dhurwa', the language 'Parji'. Literacy rate in first language: Below 1%. Literacy rate in second language: 15% to 25%. Devanagari and Oriya scripts. Forest. Plains. Lumbermen, hunter-gatherers, agriculturalists.

ENGLISH [ENG] Second language speakers: 11,021,610 (1961 census). Indo-European, Germanic, West, English. Official language. Bible 1535-1989. See main entry under United Kingdom.

GADABA, BODO ***(GADBA, GUTOB, GUTOP, GUDWA, GODWA, GADWA, BOI GADABA)*** [GBJ] 32,500 (1977 Voegelin and Voegelin). At least 7,460 mother tongue speakers in Lamtaput Block, Koraput, and 1,080 in Khairaput Block, Koraput (1995). Andhra Pradesh, Visakhapatnam District; Orissa, Koraput District. Lamtaput block in Koraput is the largest concentration. Austro-Asiatic, Munda, South Munda, Koraput Munda, Gutob-Remo-Geta', Gutob-Remo. Dialects: MUNDA ORISSA GADABA, MUNDA ANDHRA PRADESH GADABA. Some intelligibility testing showed inadequate comprehension. Lexical similarity among 7 varieties of Orissa was 69% to 89%; between 2 in Andhra Pradesh 73%, others 30% to 37%. Adivasi Oriya is used as second language. Low bilingualism in Oriya in Orissa. Speakers use Telugu in Andhra Pradesh as second language. Some migrant communities may be shifting to Adivasi Oriya. Positive attitudes toward Gadaba and language maintenance. A Scheduled Tribe in India. Some ethnic Gadaba in Madhya Pradesh speak Bhatri as mother tongue. Different from Dravidian Gadaba. Nonvegetarian. Investigation needed: intelligibility, bilingual proficiency, attitudes. Literacy rate in second language: 6.53%. Literacy program needed. Oriya script. Rolling hills. Agriculturalists: shifting cultivation; gathering forest produce. Hindu, traditional religion.

GADABA, OLLAR, POTTANGI ***(OLLAR GADABA, OLLARI, OLLARO, HALLARI, ALLAR, HOLLAR GADBAS, SAN GADABA, GADBA, SANO, KONDEKAR, KONDKOR)*** [GDB] 15,000 (1997), 4,000 to 7,000 in Pottangi Block, Koraput District (1995). Orissa, Koraput District, Pottangi and Nandapur blocks. Dravidian, Central, Parji-Gadaba. 4 varieties investigated in Orissa had 69% to 80% lexical similarity, and with one in Andhra Pradesh 42% to 47%; 52% to 62% with Gadaba Salur in Andhra Pradesh. Adivasi Oriya is the main second language. Bilingual proficiency in Oriya is limited. Telugu is also used. Positive attitude toward Gadaba. Gabada is a Scheduled Tribe. Different from Gadaba in Munda family, also spoken in Koraput. Investigation needed: intelligibility, bilingual proficiency, attitudes. Literacy rate in second language: 6.53%. Oriya script in Orissa, Telugu script in Andhra Pradesh. Rolling hills. Hindu, traditional religion.

GADABA, OLLAR, SALUR [GAU] 10,000 (1996). Andhra Pradesh, Vizianagaram, Vishakapatnam, and Srikakulam districts. Dravidian, Central, Parji-Gadaba. 93% to 98% intelligibility among dialects. 84% to 94% lexical similarity between dialects, 42% to 47% with Dravidian Gadaba in Pottangi, Orissa. Bilingual proficiency in Telugu is limited. Used at home, in the village, for religion. Positive attitudes toward Gabada. A Scheduled Tribe in India. Nonvegetarian. Investigation needed: bilingual proficiency in Telugu, attitudes toward Telugu. Literacy rate in second language: 6.53%. Literacy program needed and wanted. Telugu script. Plains. Agriculturalists: shifting cultivation.

GADDI ***(BHARMAURI BHADI, PAHARI BHARMAURI, PANCHI BRAHMAURI RAJPUT, GADDYALI, GADIALI, GADI)*** [GBK] 120,000 (1997 IMA). Himachal Pradesh, Chamba District, Brahmaur Tahsil and Holi Sub-Tahsils; Uttar Pradesh; Jammu and Kashmir. Higher elevations in summer, lower in winter. Indo-European, Indo-Iranian, Indo-Aryan, Northern zone, Western Pahari. Dialect: BHARMAURI. 93% intelligibility of Mandeali, 97% of Kangri, 83% of Chambeali. 74% to 80% lexical similarity with Palamur Kangri, 79% with Chambeali, 67% to 73% with Mandeali. Hindi is used for instruction in school, in shops, and cities. A Scheduled Tribe in India. SOV. Radio programs. Mountain slope. Nomadic shepherds. 1,340 to 5,882 meters. Hindu.

GAHRI ***(GHARA, LAHULI OF BUNAN, BOONAN, PUNAN, POONAN, ERANKAD, KEYLONG BOLI, BUNAN)*** [BFU] 4,000 (1997). Population total both countries 4,000 or more. Himachal Pradesh,

Gahr Valley. Also spoken in China. Sino-Tibetan, Tibeto-Burman, Himalayish, Tibeto-Kanauri, Western Himalayish, Kanauri. Also related to Tukpa and Kanashi. 39% lexical similarity with Sunam, 26% to 39% with varieties of Chamba Lahuli, 37% with Tinan Lahuli, 26% to 34% with varieties of central Tibetan, 34% with Jangshung and Shumcho, 31% with Puh, 30% with Chitkuli and Nesang, 24% with Lhasa Tibetan, 23% with Kanauri. Gahri used in all domains, including the home. Speakers are called 'Gahri', and call themselves 'Lahuli'. Bodh caste, but they speak a different language from the Bodhs of Mayar, Khoksar, and Stod valleys. They consider themselves to be different from Bodhs of the north, whom they call Tibetans. Literacy rate in first language: Below 1%. Agriculturalists: cultivators. Buddhist. Bible portions 1911-1923.

GAMIT ***(GAMATI, GAMTI, GAMTA, GAVIT, GAMITH, GAMETI)*** [GBL] 233,000 (1997 IMA). Gujarat, mainly Surat District, some in Bharuch, Dangs, and Valsad districts. Indo-European, Indo-Iranian, Indo-Aryan, Central zone, Bhil. Similar to Mawchi. A Scheduled Tribe in India. Most speakers have high school or college education. Barati script. Traditional religion, Hindu, Christian. NT 1982.

GANGTE ***(GANTE)*** [GNB] 11,000 or more (1997 IMA). Population total both countries 11,000 or more. Manipur, southern districts; Megalaya; Assam. Also spoken in Myanmar. Sino-Tibetan, Tibeto-Burman, Kuki-Chin-Naga, Kuki-Chin, Northern. Related to Thado Chin. A Scheduled Tribe in India. Agriculturalists. Christian (1981 census). Bible 1991.

GARASIA, ADIWASI ***(ADIWASI GIRASIA, GIRASIA, ADIWASI GUJARATI)*** [GAS] 100,000 (1988 Williams). Northern Gujarat, Banaskantha and Sabarkantha districts. Indo-European, Indo-Iranian, Indo-Aryan, Central zone, Bhil. Not intelligible with Rajput Girasia or Dungari Garasia. Dialects have 89% to 96% lexical similarity with each other; 75% to 93% with dialects of Rajput Girasia; 79% to 92% with dialects of Patelia; 79% to 93% with Wagdi; 76% to 87% with Marwari dialects. Gujarati proficiency is limited. Speakers are Bhils. Literacy rate in second language: 15% to 25%. Hindu, traditional religion. Bible portions.

GARASIA, RAJPUT ***(RAJPUT GARASIA, GIRASIA, GRASIA, DUNGRI GRASIA, DHUNGRI GARASIA, DUNGARI GARASIA)*** [GRA] 62,000 (1997 IMA). Rajasthan, Sirchi, Pali, and Udaipur districts; Gujarat. Indo-European, Indo-Iranian, Indo-Aryan, Central zone, Bhil. Not intelligible with Adiwasi Garasia. Dialects in Gujarat and Rajasthan have 94% to 99% lexical similarity; 75% to 93% with Adiwasi Girasia dialects; 76% to 84% with Pateliya dialects; 79% to 86% with Wagdi; 67% to 84% with Marwari dialects. Proficiency in Hindi and Gujarati is limited. Positive attitude toward Garasia. Some negative attitudes toward Adiwasi Garasia and Bhil. A Scheduled Tribe in Rajasthan. Speakers are of the warrior caste. Literacy rate in second language: 15% to 25%. Primers in 2 scripts. Gujarati and Devanagari scripts. Hindu, traditional religion. Bible portions 1998.

GARHWALI ***(GADHAVALI, GADHAWALA, GADWAHI, GASHWALI, GODAULI, GORWALI, GURVALI, PAHARI GARHWALI, GIRWALI)*** [GBM] 2,186,000 (1997 IMA). Kashmir; Uttar Pradesh. Indo-European, Indo-Iranian, Indo-Aryan, Northern zone, Garhwali. Dialects: SRINAGARIA, TEHRI, BADHANI, DESSAULYA, LOHBYA, MAJH-KUMAIYA, BHATTIANI, NAGPURIYA, RATHI, SALANI. Literacy rate in first language: 30% to 60%. Literacy rate in second language: 50% to 75%. Mountain slope. NT 1827-1994.

GARO ***(GARROW, MANDE)*** [GRT] 575,000 in India (1997 IMA). Population total both countries 650,000. Meghalaya, Garo Hills District; West Assam, Goalpara, Kamrup, Karbi Anglong districts; Nagaland, Kohima District; Tripura, South Tripura District; West Bengal, Jalpaiguri and Cooch Behar districts. Also spoken in Bangladesh. Sino-Tibetan, Tibeto-Burman, Jingpho-Konyak-Bodo, Konyak-Bodo-Garo, Bodo-Garo, Garo. Dialects: A'BENG (A'BENGYA, AM'BENG), A'CHICK (A'CHIK), A'WE, CHISAK, DACCA, GANCHING, KAMRUP, MATCHI. A Scheduled Tribe in India. Dictionary. Grammar. Roman script. Christian mainly. Bible 1924-1994.

GATA' ***(GATAQ, GETAQ, GETA', GTA', GTA ASA, DIDEI, DIDAYI, DIRE)*** [GAQ] 3,055 (1991 census). Orissa, Koraput and Malkangiri districts, Kudumulgumma and Chitrakonda blocks, south of the Bondo Hills. Some communities in the Khairput block. 47 villages. Austro-Asiatic, Munda, South Munda, Koraput Munda, Gutob-Remo-Geta', Geta'. Dialects: PLAINS GETA', HILL GETA'. Ruhlen treats Plains Geta' and Hill Geta' as separate languages. 68% to 93% lexical similarity with other Gata' varieties, 27% to 37% with Bondo varieties, 22% to 28% with Gadaba Gutob. Many speak Desiya for market. A Scheduled Tribe in India. They call themselves 'Gntre'. They are occasional nonvegetarians. Investigation needed: intelligibility with dialects. Literacy rate in second language: 0.5% female, 5.99% male, 3.19% total. Shifting cultivation, hunter-gatherers. Traditional religion, Hindu.

GONDI, NORTHERN ***(GONDI, GAUDI, GONDIVA, GONDWADI, GOONDILE, GOUDWAL, GHOND, GODI, GONDU, GOUDI)*** [GON] 1,954,000 Betul (1997 BSI). 2,632,000 all Gondi (1997 IMA). Madhya Pradesh, Betul, Chindwara, Seoni, Mandla, Balaghat districts; Maharashtra State, Amravati, Wardha, Nagpur, Bhandara, Yavatmal districts. Dravidian, South-Central, Gondi-Kui, Gondi. Dialects: BETUL, CHINDWARA, MANDLA, SEONI, AMRAVATI, BHANDARA, NAGPUR, YAVATMAL. Inherent intelligibility between dialects 94% to 97%. Speakers tested in some other dialects understood Amravati 94% to 97%; Betul 83% to 96%, and Seoni 82% to 97%. 58% to 78% intelligibility of Southern Gondi. A separate language from Muria, Maria of Garhichiroli, Abujmaria, Dandami Maria, and Koya. Lexical similarity among 'dialects' 58% to 90%. Some bilingualism in Hindi in Madhya Pradesh, and Marathi in Maharashtra, but proficiency is not very high. All ages. Positive attitude toward Gondi. The people are called 'Gond'. Investigation needed: intelligibility, bilingual proficiency in Hindi, Marathi. Literacy rate in first language: 1% to 5%. Literacy rate in second language: 25% to 50%. Forest. Agriculturalists, city dwellers. Traditional religion, Hindu. NT 1996.

GONDI, SOUTHERN *(TELUGU GONDI)* [GGO] 600,000 to 700,000 (1993). Andhra Pradesh, Adilabad District; Maharashtra, southern Yavatmal, southern Chandrapur and southeastern Garhichiroli districts. Dravidian, South-Central, Gondi-Kui, Gondi. Dialects: SIRONCHA, NIRMAL (ADILABAD), BHAMRAGARH, UTNOOR, AHERI, RAJURA, ETAPALLY GONDI. Sironcha is the dialect understood best by the others, with 90% to 98% intelligibility. 49% to 58% intelligibility of Northern Gondi. 64% to 90% lexical similarity among dialects. Speakers are called 'Gond'. Literacy rate in second language: 25% to 50%. Telugu script. Tropical forests, deforested agricultural lands. Plains, hills. Swidden agriculturalists, hunters, fishermen. Traditional religion, Hindu. Bible portions 1962.

GOWLAN [GOJ] Maharashtra, Amravati District, and in some cases in the same communities as Korku tribal people. Also in Hoshangabad District. Some reported in northern Karnataka. Indo-European, Indo-Iranian, Indo-Aryan, Southern zone, Unclassified. Dialects in Maharashtra and Karnataka reported to be different. May be closer to Hindi (Central zone) than to Marathi (Southern zone). Bilingualism in Hindi is low in at least the Chikli area. Positive language attitudes toward Gowlan and Hindi. Only some want their children to learn Marathi. Surrounded by Korku. Belong to Gowli caste. Investigation needed: bilingual proficiency in Hindi. Pastoralists: cattle.

GOWLI *(NAND)* [GOK] 35,000 (1997 IMA). Madhya Pradesh; Maharashtra, Amravati District. Indo-European, Indo-Iranian, Indo-Aryan, Central zone, Western Hindi, Unclassified. Dialects: NAND, RANYA, LINGAAYAT, KHAMLA. Nand subdialects have 93% or higher intelligibility of the Khamla dialect. Dialect used in Madhya Pradesh appears closer to Marathi (Southern zone) than to Hindi (Central zone). Ranya has 84% to 92% lexical similarity with Nand. Many have some understanding of Marathi and Hindi. Nand Gowli is the primary language used in the home. Surrounded by Korku. Speakers belong to Gowli caste. There are 12 and a half subgroups; Nand Gowli the highest, Musalman (the 'half tribe') the lowest. Investigation needed: intelligibility with Ranya. Literacy rate in first language: Below 1%. Literacy rate in second language: 5% to 15%. Tropical forest. Mountain slope. Agriculturalists, laborers. Hindu, traditional religion.

GROMA *(TROMOWA)* [GRO] Sikkim. Sino-Tibetan, Tibeto-Burman, Himalayish, Tibeto-Kanauri, Tibetic, Tibetan, Southern. Dialects: UPPER GROMA, LOWER GROMA. See main entry under China.

GUJARATI *(GUJRATHI, GUJERATI, GUJERATHI)* [GJR] 45,479,000 in India (1997 IMA). Population total all countries 46,100,000 or more. Gujarat; Maharashtra; Rajasthan; Karnataka; Madhya Pradesh. Also spoken in Bangladesh, Fiji, Kenya, Malawi, Mauritius, Oman, Pakistan, Réunion, Singapore, South Africa, Tanzania, Uganda, United Kingdom, USA, Zambia, Zimbabwe. Indo-European, Indo-Iranian, Indo-Aryan, Central zone, Gujarati. Dialects: STANDARD GUJARATI (SAURASHTRA STANDARD, NAGARI, BOMBAY GUJARATI, PATNULI), GAMADIA (GRAMYA, SURATI, ANAWLA, BRATHELA, EASTERN BROACH GUJARATI, CHAROTARI, PATIDARI, VADODARI, AHMEDABAD GAMADIA, PATANI), PARSI, KATHIYAWADI (JHALAWADI, SORATHI, HOLADI, GOHILWADI, BHAWNAGARI), KHARWA, KAKARI, TARIMUKI (GHISADI). Spoken as mother tongue by the Keer. National language. Grammar. Literacy rate in second language: 30% (1974). Gujarati script. Hindu. Bible 1823-1998.

GUJARI *(GUJURI, GUJER, GUJAR, GUJJARI, GURJAR, GOJRI, GOGRI, KASHMIR GUJURI, RAJASTHANI GUJURI, GOJARI)* [GJU] 600,000 to 700,000 in India (1996). Population total all countries 1,400,000. Himachal Pradesh; Madhya Pradesh; Uttar Pradesh; Jammu and Kashmir; Haryana. Northwestern India, and into Pakistan and northeastern Afghanistan. Also spoken in Afghanistan, Pakistan. Indo-European, Indo-Iranian, Indo-Aryan, Central zone, Rajasthani, Unclassified. Dialect: AJIRI OF HAZARA. Poonch may be understood by others and form the basis for a standard dialect. Lexical similarity between Uttar Pradesh and Pakistan average about 60%, with Poonch 76%. Bilingualism in Hindi. Urdu, Kumauni, Garwhali, Kullu, Jaunsari, Kashmiri, Dogri also used. At home, with other Gujars, about 50% for religion. In general, the Hindu agriculturalists have not retained the Gujari language and culture, whereas the Muslim Gujari have. They perceive Gujari as one people and one language. Positive attitude toward Gujari, and toward second languages if it is advantageous to use them. A Scheduled Tribe in India. Literacy rate in second language: 5% to 15%. Nastaliq and Devanagari. Poetry, magazines, radio programs, TV. Mountain slope, hills. Muslim Gujari are transhument pastoralists: Bakarwal goats and sheep, Dodhi buffalo. Hindu Gujari are agriculturalists. Hindu, Muslim.

GURUNG, WESTERN ***(GURUNG KURA)*** [GVR] 82 in India (1961 census). West Bengal, Darjeeling. Also possibly in Myanmar. Sino-Tibetan, Tibeto-Burman, Himalayish, Tibeto-Kanauri, Tibetic, Tamangic. Related to Thakali. NT 1982. See main entry under Nepal.

HAJONG ***(HAIJONG, HAZONG)*** [HAJ] 19,000 in India (1997 IMA) to 60,000 (1998 Karotemprel). Population total both countries 19,000 or more. Meghalaya, West Garo Hills District, western side, West Khasi Hills; Assam, Goalpara and Nowgong districts; West Bengal. Also spoken in Bangladesh. Indo-European, Indo-Iranian, Indo-Aryan, Eastern zone, Bengali-Assamese. Formerly a Tibeto-Burman language, but culturally and linguistically Hinduized and Bengalized (Breton 1997). A Scheduled Tribe in India. Agriculturalists. Traditional religion, Hindu.

HALBI ***(BASTARI, HALBA, HALVAS, HALABI, HALVI, MAHARI, MEHARI)*** [HLB] 736,000 (1994 IMA). Madhya Pradesh, open plains in Bastar District; Maharashtra; Orissa; Andhra Pradesh. Indo-European, Indo-Iranian, Indo-Aryan, Eastern zone, Bengali-Assamese. Dialects: ADKURI, BASTARI, CHANDARI, GACHIKOLO, MEHARI, MURI (MURIA), SUNDI. Bhunjia, Nahari, Kawari are considered to be more divergent dialects. Reported to be a creole language. Grierson called it a dialect of Marathi for convenience, but noted similarities to Bhatri, a dialect of Oriya. Men who have been to school use Hindi as second language for trading and common topics. Some use Bhatri as second language. A Scheduled Tribe in India. Trade language. SOV, postpositions; genitives, articles, adjectives, numerals before noun heads; 2 or 3 affixes per word; word order distinguishes given and new information; noun affixes indicate case; verb affixes mark person, number, gender of subject; passives; causatives; comparatives; CV, CVC, CVV; nontonal. Literacy rate in second language: Very low. Government literacy program. Scrub forest, semi-tropical. Plains. Pastoralists (sedentary), peasant agriculturalists. 600 meters. Hindu. Bible portions 1989.

HARAUTI ***(HADAUTI, HADOTI, HADOTHI, PIPLODA)*** [HOJ] 572,000 (1997 IMA). Rajasthan, Kota District; Madhya Pradesh. Indo-European, Indo-Iranian, Indo-Aryan, Central zone, Rajasthani, Unclassified. Dialects: SIPARI, HARAUTI. Mother tongue of the ethnic Saharia of Rajasthan. Saharia is a Scheduled Tribe in India. NT 1822, out of print.

HARYANVI ***(BANGARU, BANGER, BANGRI, BANGRU, HARYANI, HARIYANI, HARIANI, DESARI, CHAMARWA)*** [BGC] 13,000,000 or 85% of Haryan population of 16,000,000 (1992 SIL), including 107,000 Haryanvi proper (1997 IMA). Haryana; Punjab; Karnataka; Delhi; Himachal Pradesh; Uttar Pradesh. Indo-European, Indo-Iranian, Indo-Aryan, Central zone, Western Hindi, Unclassified. Dialects: BANGARU PROPER, DESWALI, BAGDI, MEWATI. 'Bagdi' is the variety used around Fatehabad and Sirsa, and south of Bhiwani (distinct from the Wagdi language in southern Rajasthan). Needs comparison with Bagri. Intelligibility among dialects is good, but Haryanvi is not intelligible with Hindi, the closest language. Closest to Braj Bhasha. 92% lexical similarity between dialects. Hindi is used as second language; proficiency higher among educated speakers than uneducated ones. Some bilingual ability in all social groups for education and contact with non-Haryanvi speakers. At home and for religion. All ages. Positive attitudes toward Haryanvi. 'Bangru' now used for speakers in Jind area. 'Khadar' is used by speakers in Jind to refer to the speech of Rohtak and Sonipat. Investigation needed: intelligibility, attitudes toward north Rajasthan. Dictionary. Literacy rate in second language: 55% Hindi. Plains. Hindu, Muslim.

HINDI ***(KHARI BOLI, KHADI BOLI)*** [HND] 180,000,000 in India (1991 UBS), 363,839,000 or nearly 50% of the population including second language users in India (1997 IMA). Population total all countries 366,000,000 first language speakers (1999 WA), 487,000,000 including second language users (1999 WA). Throughout northern India: Delhi; Uttar Pradesh; Rajasthan; Punjab; Madhya Pradesh; northern Bihar; Himachal Pradesh. Also spoken in Bangladesh, Belize, Botswana, Germany, Kenya, Nepal, New Zealand, Philippines, Singapore, South Africa, Uganda, UAE, United Kingdom, USA, Yemen, Zambia. Indo-European, Indo-Iranian, Indo-Aryan, Central zone, Western Hindi, Hindustani. Formal vocabulary is borrowed from Sanskrit, de-Persianized, de-Arabicized. Literary Hindi, or Hindi-Urdu, has four varieties: Hindi (High Hindi, Nagari Hindi, Literary Hindi, Standard Hindi); Urdu; Dakhini; Rekhta. State language of Delhi, Uttar Pradesh, Rajasthan, Madhya Pradesh, Bihar, Himachal Pradesh. Languages and dialects in the Western Hindi group are Hindustani, Haryanvi, Braj Bhasha, Kanauji, Bundeli; see separate entries. Spoken as mother tongue by the Saharia in Madhya Pradesh. Hindi, Hindustani, Urdu could be considered co-dialects, but have important sociolinguistic differences. National language. Grammar. SOV. Devanagari script. Hindu. Bible 1818-1987.

HINDURI ***(HANDURI)*** [HII] 138 (1961 census). Himachal Pradesh, Shimla and Solan districts. Indo-European, Indo-Iranian, Indo-Aryan, Northern zone, Western Pahari. May be a dialect of Mahasu Pahari. Masica (1991) says it is "transitional between Panjabi and West Pahari of Mahasui type" (p. 429). Investigation needed: intelligibility with Mahasu Pahari, bilingual proficiency in Hindi.

HMAR ***(HAMAR, MHAR, HMARI)*** [HMR] 50,000 (1997 IMA). Assam, North Cachar and Cachar districts; Manipur; Mizoram. Sino-Tibetan, Tibeto-Burman, Kuki-Chin-Naga, Kuki-Chin, Central. Close to Zomi.

Bilingualism in Assamese. A Scheduled Tribe in India. Ethnic Hmar living in Mozoram speak Mizo (Lushai) as mother tongue. Literacy rate in second language: 90%. Christian mainly. Bible 1968-1987.

HO ***(LANKA KOL, BIHAR HO)*** [HOC] 1,077,000 in India (1997 IMA), including 444,000 in Singhbhum, 200,000 in Oriya (1990 UBS). Population total both countries 1,077,000 or more. Bihar, mainly in Singhbhum District; Orissa, Mayurbhanj and Koenjhar districts; West Bengal. Also spoken in Bangladesh. Austro-Asiatic, Munda, North Munda, Kherwari, Mundari. Dialects: LOHARA, CHAIBASA-THAKURMUNDA. Most speakers understand the Chaibasa and Thakurmunda dialects well, at 90% to 92% on narrative discourse. 'Kherwari' (Khanwar, Kharar, Kharoali, Kharwari) is a group name for Ho, Mundari, and Santali, which are closely related languages, and some other smaller languages or dialects. Most dialects have 85% lexical similarity with each other, except for three on the southern and eastern edges of the Ho area. Oriya, Santali, and Hindi are used in limited domains. Vigorous in home and community in most areas. Positive attitudes toward Ho. A Scheduled Tribe in India. Different from Ho (Hani) of Myanmar, China, Viet Nam, Laos. Investigation needed: intelligibility with Mundari, Bhumij. Dictionary. Grammar. Literacy rate in first language: 1% to 5%. Literacy rate in second language: 25% to 50%. Literacy program in progress. Devanagari script used in Bihar, Oriya script in Orissa. Forest. Agriculturalists, hunters. Traditional religion. NT 1997.

HOLIYA ***(HOLAR, HOLARI, HOLE, HOLIAN, HOLU, GOLARI-KANNADA, GOHLLARU)*** [HOY] 8,000 (1984 GR). Madhya Pradesh; Maharashtra; Karnataka. Dravidian, Southern, Tamil-Kannada, Kannada. It is reported that 50% of Holiya speakers speak some Telugu as second language: 60% adults, 30% children. A Scheduled Caste in Madhya Pradesh. Literacy rate in first language: Below 1%. Literacy rate in second language: 5% Kannada. Hunter-gatherers, mixed commerce. Hindu, traditional religion.

HRANGKHOL ***(RANGKHOL)*** [HRA] 18,000 in India (1997 IMA). Manipur; Assam; Tripura. Sino-Tibetan, Tibeto-Burman, Kuki-Chin-Naga, Kuki-Chin, Northern. Dialect: HADEM. SOV. Literacy rate in first language: Below 1%. NT, in press (1997). See main entry under Myanmar.

HRUSO ***(AKA, HRUSSO, ANGKA, ANGKAE, TENAE)*** [HRU] Arunachal Pradesh, between Monpa on the west and the Tani languages on the east. Sino-Tibetan, Tibeto-Burman, Unclassified. Dialects: HRUSO, DHAMMAI (MIJI), LEVAI (BANGRU). No wider affiliation within Tibeto-Burman is apparent. These varieties are sometimes grouped under Tibeto-Burman as 'Hruish'. The names listed as dialects may be separate languages.

IDU ***(CHULIKATA, CHULIKOTTA, MIDHI, MIDU, IDA, YIDU LUOBA)*** [CLK] 8,569 (1981 census). Population total both countries 15,569. Assam; Arunachal Pradesh, Dibang Valley District; West Bengal. Also spoken in China. Sino-Tibetan, Tibeto-Burman, North Assam, Tani. Closest to Digaro. May not be in the Tani group, but is related to the Tani group. Bilingualism in Assamese. Mishmi Idu is a Scheduled Tribe in India. Exogamous clans: Mega, Pulu, Mendo, Lingi, Michichi. Investigation needed: intelligibility with Digaro. Literacy rate in first language: Below 1%. Hills. Hunter-gatherers; swidden agriculturalists: millet, maize, rice, wheat, sweet potatoes; fishermen; animal husbandry: pigs, chicken, goats, mithun (high altitude cattle); weavers. 5,000 feet. Traditional religion.

INDIAN SIGN LANGUAGE [INS] 1,500,000 or more users (1986 Gallaudet Univ.) Population total all countries 1,500,000 or more. All over the country. Also spoken in Bangladesh, Pakistan. Deaf sign language. Dialects: DELHI SIGN LANGUAGE, CALCUTTA SIGN LANGUAGE, BANGALORE-MADRAS SIGN LANGUAGE, BOMBAY SIGN LANGUAGE. Over 75% of signs from all regions are related. Dialects are not related to deaf school usage. Delhi dialect is the most influential. Not related to French, Spanish, or American sign languages, or their group. Some influence from British Sign Language in the fingerspelling system and a few other signs, but most are unrelated to European sign systems. Developed indigenously in India. The Indian manual English system is hardly intelligible to American Signed English. Related to Nepalese Sign Language. Over 1,000,000 deaf adults, and about 500,000 deaf children (1986). Deaf schools mainly do not use ISL, but vocational programs often do. Less than 5% of deaf people attend deaf schools. Investigation needed: intelligibility with Pakistan Sign Language.

INDO-PORTUGUESE [IDB] 700 monolingual speakers in Korlai (1977 Theban). Maharashtra, Korlai near Bombay, Daman and Diu; Vypeen Island, and Cochin area. Creole, Portuguese based. Active use among Catholic citizens in Daman (1982 Jackson). Some communities in India have become extinct. SOV. NT 1826-1852. See main entry under Sri Lanka.

IRULA ***(ERAVALLAN, ERUKALA, IRAVA, IRULAR, IRULAR MOZHI, IRULIGA, IRULIGAR, KORAVA, KAD CHENSU)*** [IRU] 75,000. Tamil Nadu, Nilgiri, Coimbatore, Periyar, Salem, Chengai Anna districts; Karnataka; Kerala, Palghat District; Andhra Pradesh. Dravidian, Southern, Tamil-Kannada, Tamil-Kodagu, Tamil-Malayalam, Tamil. Dialects: MELE NADU IRULA, VETTE KADA IRULA, IRULA PALLAR, NORTHERN IRULA, URALI. Vette Kada had 73% intelligibility with Mele Nadu, Northern Irula had 83% intelligibility with Mele Nadu. Irula is not inherently intelligible with Tamil. Mele Nadu varieties have 78% to 86% lexical similarity with each other, 67% to 70% with Northern Irula, 64% to

66% with Vette Kada, 47% to 50% with Tamil. Nearly all speak some Tamil, 44% Kannada, 32% Badaga. Tamil proficiency limited. Irula is used in the home, village, in market and politics with other Irula people, and for praying. Positive attitude toward Irula, and literature development. A Scheduled Tribe in India. Called 'Kad Chensu' in Andhra Pradesh. Some people called 'Irula' speak Tamil as mother tongue. Investigation needed: intelligibility with Irula outside of Nilgiri. SOV, postpositions, nontonal. Literacy rate in first language: Below 1%. Literacy rate in second language: 5% to 15%. Subtropical forest. Mountain slope, plains. Peasant agriculturalists, coffee and tea laborers. 1,000 to 6,500 feet. Hindu, traditional religion.

JANGSHUNG ***(JANGRAMI, ZANGRAM, ZHANG-ZHUNG, JANGIAM, THEBOR, THEBÖR SKADD, THEBARSKAD, CENTRAL KINNAURI)*** [JNA] 1,990 or 4% of the population of Kinnaur District (1998). Himachal Pradesh, Kinnaur District, Jangi, Lippa, and Asrang villages in Morang Tahsil. Sino-Tibetan, Tibeto-Burman, Himalayish, Tibeto-Kanauri, Western Himalayish, Kanauri. Closest to Shumcho and Sunam. 70% lexical similarity with Shumcho, 65% with Sunam, 51% with Chitkuli, 49% with Lower Kinnauri. Investigation needed: intelligibility with Shumcho, Sunam, bilingual proficiency, attitudes toward Kinnauri. Mountain slope, valleys. Pastoralists (sedentary), peasant agriculturalists. 5,000 to 6,770 meters. Traditional religion, Hindu, Lamaistic Buddhist.

JARAWA [ANQ] 200 (1997 CIIL). Andaman Islands, interior and south central Rutland Island, central interior and south interior South Andaman Island. Andamanese, South Andamanese. Different from Önge and Sentinel. Completely monolingual. They are semi-nomadic. Dictionary. Grammar. Literacy rate in first language: Below 1%. Hunter-gatherers. Traditional religion.

JAUNSARI ***(JAUNSAURI, JANSAURI, PAHARI)*** [JNS] 97,000 (1997 IMA). Uttar Pradesh, Jaunsar, Dehra Dun District, Chakrata tahsil; Himachal Pradesh, Jansar-Bawar Division. Indo-European, Indo-Iranian, Indo-Aryan, Northern zone, Western Pahari. May be intelligible with Mahasui Pahari. Grierson said it was also close to western Hindi, and had some similarity to Garhwali to the east. A Scheduled Tribe in India. Investigation needed: intelligibility with Mahasui. Literacy rate in first language: Below 1%. Literacy rate in second language: 15% to 25%. Hindu. Bible portions 1895-1904.

JUANG ***(PUTTOOAS, PATUA, PATRA-SAARA, JUANGO)*** [JUN] 40,000 (1996 A. Matthew). Orissa, southern Keonjhar, northern Angul, and eastern Dhenkanal districts. Austro-Asiatic, Munda, South Munda, Kharia-Juang. Not closely related to other languages. 20% to 22% lexical similarity with Kharia. Understanding and use of Oriya is limited. Proficiency is higher among men and the educated. Juang used in home, family, community. Positive attitude toward Juang. A Scheduled Tribe in India. Grammar. Literacy rate in second language: 7.99% (14.48% males, 1.71% females). Forest. Hill slope, plateau, plain. Agricultural laborers, basket makers, firewood traders. Traditional religion.

JURAY [JUY] Orissa. Austro-Asiatic, Munda, South Munda, Koraput Munda, Sora-Juray-Gorum, Sora-Juray. Closest to Sora. Investigation needed: intelligibility with Sora.

KACHARI ***(CACHARI)*** [QKC] 56,413 (1994 IMA). Assam, North Cachar District and the Cachar Hills; Nagaland. Sino-Tibetan, Tibeto-Burman, Jingpho-Konyak-Bodo, Konyak-Bodo-Garo, Bodo-Garo, Bodo. Fewer than 1/3 of ethnic Kachari speak it as mother tongue. Most Kachari speak Assamese as mother tongue. A Scheduled Tribe in India. Mountain slope.

KACHCHI ***(KACHCHHI, KUTCHCHI, CUCHI, CUTCH, KUTCHIE, KACHI, KATCH, KAUTCHY, KATCHI)*** [KFR] 806,000 in India (1997 IMA). Population total all countries 866,000 or more. Gujarat, Kutch area; Andhra Pradesh; Madhya Pradesh; Uttar Pradesh; Assam; Kerala; Tamil Nadu; Maharashtra; Karnataka; Orissa. Also spoken in Kenya, Malawi, Pakistan, Tanzania. Indo-European, Indo-Iranian, Indo-Aryan, Northwestern zone, Sindhi. Dialect: JADEJI. Closely related to Sindhi. Most Kachchi do not understand Gujarati. Agriculturalists; mixed commerce. Hindu, Muslim. Bible portions 1834.

KADAR ***(KADA, KADIR)*** [KEJ] 2,265 (1981 census). Kerala, Ernakulam, Palghat, and Trichur districts; Andhra Pradesh; Tamil Nadu, Coimbatore District. Dravidian, Southern, Tamil-Kannada, Tamil-Kodagu, Tamil-Malayalam, Malayalam. Close to Malayalam, but a separate language (Thundyil 1975.246). Close to Tamil (Singh 1994). They speak Malayalam or Tamil with outsiders. A Scheduled Tribe in India. Literacy rate in first language: Below 1%. Forest. Hills. Hunter-gatherers traditionally, now some settled cultivators, agricultural laborers. Hindu (1981 census).

KAIKADI ***(KOKADI, KAIKAI, KAIKADIA)*** [KEP] 11,846 (1971 census). Maharashtra, Jalgaon District; Karnataka. Dravidian, Southern, Tamil-Kannada, Tamil-Kodagu, Tamil-Malayalam, Tamil. Nomadic. Mountain slope. Hunter-gatherers, mixed commerce. Traditional religion, Hindu.

KAMAR [KEQ] 23,456 (1981 census). Madhya Pradesh, Raipur and Rewa districts; Maharashtra. Dravidian, Unclassified. Singh 1994 reports they speak Chhatisgarhi among themselves and Hindi with others. A Scheduled Tribe in India. Shifting cultivation. Hindu (1981 census).

KANASHI ***(KANASI)*** [QAS] 1,000 (1977 Voegelin and Voegelin). Himachal Pradesh, Kullu District, Kullu Tahsil, glen of the Bios Valley, around the village of Malana (Malani). Sino-Tibetan, Tibeto-Burman, Himalayish, Tibeto-Kanauri, Western Himalayish, Kanauri. Not known how different it is from dialects spoken in Lahul and Spiti to the north and east. Surrounded by speakers of Indo-Aryan languages. Investigation needed: intelligibility, bilingual proficiency in neighboring languages.

KANAUJI ***(BHAKHA, BRAJ KANAUJI, BRAJ)*** [BJJ] 6,000,000 (1977 Voegelin and Voegelin). Uttar Pradesh. Indo-European, Indo-Iranian, Indo-Aryan, Central zone, Western Hindi, Unclassified. Dialects: KANAUJI PROPER, TIRHARI, TRANSITIONAL KANAUJI. Transitional Kanauji dialect is between Kanauji and Awadhi. Literacy rate in first language: Below 1%. NT 1821.

KANIKKARAN ***(KANIKKAR, KANNIKAN, KANNIKARAN, KANNIKHARAN, MALAMPASHI)*** [KEV] 25,000 (1982 GR). Kerala, Calicut, Ernakulam, Quilon, Trivandrum districts, Neyyattinkara and Nedumangadu taluks; Tamil Nadu, Tirunelveli District. Dravidian, Unclassified. 90% of the people use Malayalam as second language, 10% use Tamil. A Scheduled Tribe in India. Malaryan may be the same. Literacy rate in second language: 20% Malayalam. Hills. Hunter-gatherers, Agriculturalists. Hindu, traditional religion.

KANJARI ***(KAGARI, KANGAR BHAT, KANGRI, KANJRI)*** [KFT] 55,386 (1971 census). Andhra Pradesh; Madhya Pradesh; Uttar Pradesh, Aligarh, Farrukhabad, Etawah, Sitapur, Kheri districts; Rajasthan. Indo-European, Indo-Iranian, Indo-Aryan, Unclassified. Dialect: KUCHBANDHI. It may be in the Panjabi group. Sometimes called a 'Gypsy' language. They are reported to use certain linguistic means of disguising their language to make it unintelligible to outsiders. Hunters, mat making of Sirki reed, ropes, brushes.

KANNADA ***(KANARESE, CANARESE, BANGLORI, MADRASSI)*** [KJV] 35,346,000 (1997 IMA). 44,000,000 including second language users (1999 WA). Karnataka; Andhra Pradesh; Tamil Nadu; Maharashtra. Dravidian, Southern, Tamil-Kannada, Kannada. Dialects: BIJAPUR, JEINU KURUBA, AINE KURUBA. About 20 dialects; Badaga may be one. National language. SOV. Literacy rate in first language: 60%. Literacy rate in second language: 60%. Kannada script is similar to Telugu script. Hindu, Muslim, Christian. Bible 1831-1998.

KASHMIRI ***(KESHUR, KASCHEMIRI, CASHMIRI, CASHMEEREE, KACMIRI)*** [KSH] 4,391,000 in India including 4,370,000 Kashmiri, 21,000 Kishtwari (1997 IMA). 52.29% of the population of Jammu and Kashmir. Population total all countries 4,511,000. Jammu and Kashmir; Punjab; Uttar Pradesh; Delhi; Kashmir Valley. Also spoken in Pakistan, United Kingdom. Indo-European, Indo-Iranian, Indo-Aryan, Northwestern zone, Dardic, Kashmiri. Dialects: BAKAWALI, BUNJWALI, STANDARD KASHMIRI, KISHTWARI (KASHTAWARI, KISTWALI, KASHTWARI, KATHIAWARI), MIRASKI, POGULI, RAMBANI, RIASI, SHAH-MANSURI, SIRAJI OF DODA, SIRAJI-KASHMIRI, ZAYOLI, ZIRAK-BOLI. Bilingualism in Urdu, English. Literature can be traced to the 1400s, and poetry is important. Not used in primary education. National language. Grammar. SVO. Literacy rate in second language: Men 36.29%, women 15.88%; rural 21.63%, urban 45.56% (1981 census). Another source: Kashmiri 5%, Urdu 5%. Persian-based script. Mountain slope, valleys. Agriculturalists: rice, wheat, maize; craftsmen (weaving, carpets, carving, furniture, papier mache). 6,000 feet. Muslim, Christian. Bible 1899, out of print.

KATKARI ***(KATARI, KATAKARI, KATHODI, KATVADI)*** [KFU] 4,951 (1961 census). Maharashtra, Raigad and Thane districts, along the foothills of the Sahayadri Range; Rajasthan, northwest, Onga, Samicha Parebati, Mubusha, Jhadol police station areas; Gujarat, Surat, Bharuch, Sabarkantha, Dang districts; Dadra and Nagar Haveli, Amboli and Dapada Panchayat areas. Indo-European, Indo-Iranian, Indo-Aryan, Southern zone, Konkani. A Scheduled Tribe. Singh (1994: 475-9) reports their mother tongue in Maharashtra is Marathi, in Dadra and Nagar Haveli is Kokni, in Gujarat is a variety of Marathi, in Rajasthan is Kathodi, a variety of Marathi. Agriculturalists. Traditional religion, Hindu.

KHALING ***(KHALINGE RAI, KHAEL BRA, KHAEL BAAT)*** [KLR] Darjeeling and Sikkim, scattered. Sino-Tibetan, Tibeto-Burman, Himalayish, Mahakiranti, Kiranti, Western. NT 1994. See main entry under Nepal.

KHAMTI ***(KHAM-TAI, HKAMTI, KHAMPTI, KHAMTI SHAN, KHANTIS, TAI KHAM TI)*** [KHT] 6,181 in India (1981 census). Assam, Lakimpur District; Arunachal Pradesh, Siang and Lohit districts. Also possibly in China. Tai-Kadai, Kam-Tai, Be-Tai, Tai-Sek, Tai, Southwestern, East Central, Northwest. Dialects: ASSAM KHAMTI, NORTH BURMA KHAMTI, SINKALING HKAMTI. Related languages in Assam: Phakaes, Aiton, Khamjang, Turung. A Scheduled Tribe in India. Resembles Mon script. Buddhist, Hinayana sect. See main entry under Myanmar.

KHAMYANG ***(KHAMJANG)*** [KSU] 812 (1981 census). Assam, Rowai Mukh village; Arunachal Pradesh, Lohit and Tirap districts. Tai-Kadai, Kam-Tai, Be-Tai, Tai-Sek, Tai, Southwestern, East Central, Northwest. Similar to Phake of Assam and Shan of Myanmar. Being replaced by the Assamese language and script. A Scheduled Tribe in India. Close affinity to the Khampti of Arunachal. Several thousand Assamese speakers may still use the name for their ethnic group. Literacy rate in second language: 58% Assamese (1981 census). Buddhist. Nearly extinct.

KHANDESI ***(KHANDESHI, KHANDISH, DHED GUJARI)*** [KHN] 1,579,000 (1997 IMA). Maharashtra; Gujarat. Indo-European, Indo-Iranian, Indo-Aryan, Central zone, Khandesi. Dialects: KUNBI (KUNBAU), RANGARI, KHANDESI, KOTALI BHIL. See also Dhanki. Investigation needed: intelligibility with Ahirani.

KHARIA ***(HARIA, KHARVI, KHATRIA, KHERIA, KHADIA, KHARIYA)*** [KHR] 278,500 (1994 IMA). Population total both countries 278,500 or more. Primarily Bihar, Ranchi District; also Madhya Pradesh, Raigarh District, Jashpur tahsil; Orissa, Sundargarh District; Assam; Tripura; West Bengal; Andaman and Nicobar Islands. Also spoken in Nepal. Austro-Asiatic, Munda, South Munda, Kharia-Juang. Dialects: DHELKI KHARIA, DUDH KHARIA, MIRDHA-KHARIA. A Scheduled Tribe in India. Literacy rate in second language: 15% Hindi. Christian, Hindu (1981 census). NT Y.

KHARIA THAR [KSY] Bihar, Manbhum. Indo-European, Indo-Iranian, Indo-Aryan, Eastern zone, Bengali-Assamese.

KHASI ***(KAHASI, KHASIYAS, KHUCHIA, KASSI, KHASA, KHASHI)*** [KHI] 865,000 in India (1997 IMA). Population total both countries 950,000. Assam; Meghalaya, Khasi-Jaintia hills; Manipur; West Bengal. Also spoken in Bangladesh. Austro-Asiatic, Mon-Khmer, Northern Mon-Khmer, Khasian. Dialects: BHOI-KHASI, LYNGNGAM (MEGAM), KHASI, WAR, CHERRAPUNJI (SOHRA). Bhoi in East Khasi Hills, Nongpoh block, and Nonglung in East Khasi Hills, Umksning block, are very different from standard Khasi, with different word order. Lyngngam dialect in West Khasi Hills, Mawshynrut block is divergent, and may not be a dialect (Abbi 1997). Many varieties called dialects have only partial inherent intelligibility with each other by their speakers. Amwi is a separate language (B. Comrie 1989). Used in government, courts, mass media in Meghalaya. A Scheduled Tribe in India. Lyngngam is a former Garo clan, but do not mix with the Garo, and consider themselves to be Khasi (R. Breton 1997). Investigation needed: intelligibility with dialects. Official language. Dictionary. SVO. Roman script. Radio programs, TV. Traditional religion, Christian. Bible 1891.

KHIRWAR ***(KHIRWARA, KHERWARI)*** [KWX] 34,251. Madhya Pradesh. Dravidian, South-Central, Gondi-Kui, Gondi.

KINNAURI ***(KINNAURA YANUSKAD, KANOREUNU SKAD, KANORUG SKADD, LOWER KINNAURI, KINORI, KINNER, KANAURI, KANAWARI, KANAWI, KUNAWARI, KUNAWUR, TIBAS SKAD, KANORIN SKAD, KANAURY ANUSKAD, KOONAWURE, MALHESTI, MILCHANANG, MILCHAN, MILCHANG))*** [KFK] 48,778 in Kinnaur District in India, 72% of the population of the District (1991 census). 15,000 to 20,000 second language speakers in Kinnaur District. Himachal Pradesh, Kinnaur and Lahul-Spiti districts, from Chauhra to Sangla and north along the Satluj River to Morang and several villages of the upper Ropa River Valley; Uttar Pradesh; Punjab; Kashmir. Sino-Tibetan, Tibeto-Burman, Himalayish, Tibeto-Kanauri, Western Himalayish, Kanauri. Nichar has 79% inherent intelligibility with Sangla. All other varieties have functional intelligibility with each other. Related languages: Kanashi, Chitkuli, Tukpa, Jangshung. 76% to 90% lexical similarity among varieties. Proficiency in Hindi is limited. In 1981 there were 14 high schools, 19 middle schools, 134 primary schools. A Scheduled Tribe in India. Trade language. Dictionary. Grammar. Literacy rate in second language: 37%: men 51.5%, women 21.8%. Mountain slope, valley. Peasant agriculturalists, pastoralists (sedentary). 5,000 to 6,770 meters. Hindu, Lamaist Buddhist, traditional religion. Bible portions 1909-1917.

KINNAURI, BHOTI ***(NYAMSKAD, MYAMSKAD, MYAMKAT, NYAMKAT, BUD-KAT, BOD-SKAD, SANGYAS, SANGS-RGYAS, BHOTEA OF UPPER KINNAURI)*** [NES] 6,000 (1998). Himachal Pradesh, Kinnaur District, Morang Tahsil, upper Kinnauri Sutlej River basin where it turns into the Spiti River, Nesang village in Morang Tahsil, Puh village in Puh Tahsil. It may also be spoken in Kuno and Charang villages. Sino-Tibetan, Tibeto-Burman, Himalayish, Tibeto-Kanauri, Western Himalayish, Kanauri. May constitute more than one language. 63% lexical similarity with Mane village, 59% with Darcha village, 54% with Lhasa Tibetan. Kinnaura is a Scheduled Tribe. Investigation needed: intelligibility with dialects Bhoti area, attitudes toward Tibetan. Grammar. Mountain slope, valleys. Pastoralists (sedentary), peasant agriculturalists. 5,000 to 6,770 meters. Traditional religion, Hindu, Lamaistic Buddhist.

KINNAURI, CHITKULI ***(CHITKULI, CHITKHULI, TSÍHULI, TSITKHULI, KINNAURI, KANAURI, THEBARSKAD)*** [CIK] 1,060 or 2% of the population of Kinnaur District (1998). Himachal Pradesh, Kinnaur District, Chitkul and Rakchham villages along the Baspa River in the Sangla Valley. Sino-Tibetan, Tibeto-Burman, Himalayish, Tibeto-Kanauri, Western Himalayish, Kanauri. 46% lexical similarity with Kinnauri, 51% with Jangshung, 43% with Shumcho, 38% with Sunam. Bilingualism in Kinnauri. Kinnaura is a Scheduled Tribe in India. Investigation needed: bilingual proficiency in Kinnauri, attitudes toward Kinnauri. Grammar. Literacy rate in first language: Below 1%. Mountain slope, valleys. Pastoralists (sedentary), peasant agriculturalists. 5,000 to 6,770 meters. Traditional religion, Hindu, Lamaistic Buddhist.

KINNAURI, HARIJAN ***(HARIJAN BOLI, ORES BOLI CHAMANG BOLI, SONAR BOLI)*** [KJO] 6,331 (1998). Himachal Pradesh, spoken by Scheduled Caste communities in villages throughout Kinnaur

District. Indo-European, Indo-Iranian, Indo-Aryan, Northern zone, Western Pahari. Spoken by different scheduled castes. Not spoken by all Harijans in India. Investigation needed: intelligibility with dialects, bilingual proficiency in Hindi, Pahari.

KOCH ***(KOC, KOCCH, KOCE, KOCHBOLI, KONCH)*** [KDQ] 23,000 in India (1997 IMA). Population total both countries 35,000 (1973 MARC). Meghalaya, West Garo Hills District; Assam; Tripura. Also spoken in Bangladesh. Sino-Tibetan, Tibeto-Burman, Jingpho-Konyak-Bodo, Konyak-Bodo-Garo, Bodo-Garo, Koch. Dialects: BANAI, HARIGAYA, SATPARIYA, TINTEKIYA, WANANG. A Scheduled Tribe in India. Assamese script. Agriculturalists. Hindu, traditional religion.

KODAGU ***(COORGE, KADAGI, KHURGI, KOTAGU, KURJA, KURUG, KODAVA THAK)*** [KFA] 122,000 (1997 IMA). Karnataka, Coorg (Kodagu) District, around Mercara, bordering on Malayalam to the south. Dravidian, Southern, Tamil-Kannada, Tamil-Kodagu, Kodagu. May be more than one language. 66% intelligibility of Malappuram Paniya. 72% lexical similarity with Malappuram Paniya. 80% of speakers use Kannada as second language. Investigation needed: intelligibility with dialects. Kannada script. Newspapers. Agriculturalists. Hindu. Bible portions.

KOIRENG ***(KWOIRENG, KOIRNG, QUOIRENG, LIYANG, LIYANGMAI, LIANGMAI, LIANGMEI, LYENGMAI)*** [NKD] 2,000 (1991). Manipur, Senapati District, Saikul and Kangpokpi subdivisions, Lamphal in the Imphal Valley; Nagaland. Sino-Tibetan, Tibeto-Burman, Kuki-Chin-Naga, Naga, Zeme. Bilingualism in Meithei. Different than Liangmai Naga. A Scheduled Tribe. Assigned to be under three different Naga groups politically. Literacy rate in first language: Below 1%. Christian (1981 census).

KOK BOROK ***(TRIPURI, TIPURA, USIPI MRUNG, TRIPURA, KAKBARAK, KOKBARAK)*** [TRP] 691,000 in India (1997 IMA). Population total both countries 769,000. Assam; eastern Tripura. Also spoken in Bangladesh. Sino-Tibetan, Tibeto-Burman, Jingpho-Konyak-Bodo, Konyak-Bodo-Garo, Bodo-Garo, Bodo. Dialects: JAMATIA, NOATIA, RIANG (TIPRA), HALAM, DEBBARMA. 13 dialects. Debbarma is spoken by the royal family, and is the medium of communication with the other dialects. It is understood by all, but not vice versa. Jamatia, Noatia, Riang, Halam, and Tripuri are Scheduled Tribes in India. Bengali and Roman scripts. Traditional religion, Hindu. Bible, in press (1998).

KOLAMI, NORTHWESTERN ***(KOLAMBOLI, KULME, KOLAM, KOLMI, KOLAMY)*** [KFB] 50,000 (1989 F. Blair). 115,000 all Kolami (1997 IMA). Maharashtra, Yavatmal, Wardha, and Nanded districts; Andhra Pradesh; Madhya Pradesh. Dravidian, Central, Kolami-Naiki. Dialects: MADKA-KINWAT, PULGAON, WANI, MAREGAON. Northwestern and Southeastern Kolami are not inherently intelligible. Kolami is probably not intelligible with Parji, Gadaba, or Ollar Pottangi. 61% to 68% lexical similarity with Southeastern Kolami. Nearly all adults are somewhat bilingual in Marathi, Telugu, or Gondi. Proficiency is very limited in Marathi; actually a nonstandard Marathi, also used by mother tongue Marathi speakers in the region. Kolami is used within the caste; the state language for outside communication. People are called 'Kolavar' or 'Kolam'. Kolam is a Scheduled Tribe in India. Investigation needed: attitudes toward Wani, Maregaon. Literacy rate in first language: 4.21%. Hills, plains. Agriculturalists, forest laborers. Traditional religion, Hindu.

KOLAMI, SOUTHEASTERN [NIT] 10,000 (1989 F. Blair). Andhra Pradesh, Adilabad District; Maharashtra, Chandrapur, and Nanded districts. Dravidian, Central, Kolami-Naiki. Dialects: METLA-KINWAT, UTNUR, ASIFABAD, NAIKI. Not intelligible with Northwestern Kolami. Rao (1950) reports another dialect in Chinnoor and Sirpur taluks of Adilabad District. Naiki is different from Naikri (Zvelebil 1970.13). 85% to 88% lexical similarity between Naiki and other Southeastern Kolami dialects; 83% between Metla-Kinwat and Utnur; 86% between Asifabad and Utnur; 60% to 74% with Northwestern Kolami. People in Maharashtra are not functionally bilingual in Telugu or Marathi. The Arakh speak the Naiki dialect as mother tongue. Literacy rate in second language: Low.

KOLI, KACHI ***(KUCHI, KACHI, KATCHI, KOLI, KOHLI, KOLHI, KORI, VAGARI, VAGARIA, KACHI GUJARATI)*** [GJK] 400,000 in India including 100,000 Kachi Koli, 250,000 Rabari, 50,000 or more Vagri Meghwar, Katai Meghwar, and Zalavaria Koli (1998). There may be a group in India, concentrated in their ancestral homeland centered around Bhuj, in the Rann of Kach, Gujarat. Indo-European, Indo-Iranian, Indo-Aryan, Central zone, Gujarati. Dialects: KACHI, RABARI (RAHABARI), KACHI BHIL, VAGRI (KACHI MEGHWAR), KATAI MEGHWAR, ZALAVARIA KOLI. Intermediate between Sindhi and Gujarati; it is becoming more like Sindhi. Kachi has 89% lexical similarity with Rabari, 96% with Kachi Bhil, 86% with Vagri, 92% with Katai Meghwar, 88% with Zalavaria Koli, 78% lexical similarity with Gujarati, 76% with Tharadari Koli. Hindu. Bible portions 1834-1995. See main entry under Pakistan.

KOLI, WADIYARA ***(WADARIA, WADHIARA)*** [KXP] 175,000 to 180,000 in India possibly (1998). Indo-European, Indo-Iranian, Indo-Aryan, Central zone, Gujarati. See main entry under Pakistan.

KOM ***(KOM REM)*** [KMM] 14,000 (1997 IMA). East and central Manipur, Churachandandpur, tamenglong, and Senapati districts. Sino-Tibetan, Tibeto-Burman, Kuki-Chin-Naga, Kuki-Chin, Northern. Dialect: KOLHRENG. Kolhreng may be a separate language. A Scheduled Tribe in India. Literacy rate in second language: 42% (1981 census). Roman script. Christian (1981 census). Bible 1996.

KONDA-DORA ***(PORJA)*** [KFC] 32,000 (1997 IMA). Konda-Dora in Andhra Pradesh, Visianagaram, Srikakulam, East Godavari districts; Kubi in Orissa, Koraput District; Assam. Dravidian, South-Central, Gondi-Kui, Konda-Kui, Konda. Dialects: KONDA-DORA (KONDA), KUBI. Konda and Kubi are inherently intelligible with each other. 83% lexical similarity between Konda and Kubi, 28% to 36% with Telugu. Bilingualism is very limited in Telugu. Many speakers along roads through Araku are competent in Adiwasi Oriya, others are more limited. A Scheduled Tribe in India. Language is called 'Konda-Dora', people are 'Porja'. Many ethnic Konda-Kora have adopted Telugu as mother tongue. Investigation needed: intelligibility with Konda in Aruku Valley with Paderu, Chintapali, farther north in Orissa. Literacy program needed. Agriculturalists: settled cultivation. 3,080 feet. Hindu mainly.

KONKANI ***(KONKAN STANDARD, BANKOTI, KUNABI, NORTH KONKAN, CENTRAL KONKAN, CONCORINUM, CUGANI, KONKANESE)*** [KNK] 4,000,000 (1999 WA), including 99,000 Thakuri (1991 IMA). North and central coastal strip of Maharashtra; Karnataka; Dadra and Nagar Haveli; Kerala. Indo-European, Indo-Iranian, Indo-Aryan, Southern zone, Konkani. Dialects: PARABHI (KAYASTHI, DAMANI), KOLI, KIRISTAV, DHANAGARI, BHANDARI, THAKURI (THAKARI, THAKRI, THAKUA, THAKURA), KARHADI, SANGAMESVARI (BAKOTI, BANKOTI), GHATI (MAOLI), MAHARI (DHED, HOLIA, PARVARI). The dialects listed are closely related. More distinct dialects or closely related languages: Katkari (Kathodi, Katvadi), Varli, Vadval, Phudagi, Samvedi, Mangelas. Others speak nonstandard Konkani. NT 1970, in press (1995).

KONKANI, GOANESE ***(GOMATAKI, GOAN)*** [GOM] Population total all countries 2,000,000 (1977 Voegelin and Voegelin). Southern coastal strip of Maharashtra, primarily in the districts of Ratnagari and Goa; Karnataka; Kerala. Also spoken in Kenya, UAE. Indo-European, Indo-Iranian, Indo-Aryan, Southern zone, Konkani. Dialects: STANDARD KONKANI (GOANESE), BARDESKARI (GOMANTAKI), SARASVAT BRAHMIN, KUDALI (MALVANI), DALDI (NAWAITS), CHITAPAVANI (KONKANASTHS), MANGALORE. Daldi and Chitapavani are transitional dialects between Goanese and Standard Konkani. Agriculturalists, mixed commerce. NT 1818-1976.

KORAGA, KORRA ***(KORAGAR, KORAGARA, KORANGI, KORRA)*** [KFD] Total ethnic Koraga: 16,665 (1981 census). Karnataka, Dakshin Kannad District; Kerala, Cannanore and Kasargod districts; Tamil Nadu. Dravidian, Southern, Tulu, Koraga. Related to Tulu and Bellari. Not intelligible with Mudu Koraga, Tulu, or Kannada. Structural differences in phonology with Mudu Koraga. Koraga is a Scheduled Tribe. Hindu.

KORAGA, MUDU ***(MU:DU)*** [VMD] Total ethnic Koraga: 16,665 (1981 census). Kerala. Dravidian, Southern, Tulu, Koraga. Not intelligible with Korra Koraga, Tulu, or Kannada. Structural differences in phonology with Korra Koraga. Koraga is a Scheduled Tribe. Hindu.

KORAKU [KSZ] Madhya Pradesh, Surguja district. Austro-Asiatic, Munda, North Munda, Kherwari. Possibly related to Korwa. Separate dialect or language from Korku.

KORKU ***(BONDEYA, BOPCHI, KORKI, KURKU, KURI, RAMEKHERA, KURKU-RUMA)*** [KFQ] 478,000 (1997 IMA). Southern Madhya Pradesh, southern Betul District, north of and around Betul city, Hoshangabad District, East Nimar (Khandwa) District; northern Maharashtra, Amravati, Buldana, Akola districts. Austro-Asiatic, Munda, North Munda, Korku. Dialects: BOURIYA, BONDOY, RUMA, MAWASI (MUWASI, MUASI). Dialects in northern Maharashtra and south central Madhya Pradesh constitute one language; 82% to 97% intelligibility among them. Bouriya is most widely understood. Lexical similarity of dialects with Laki Bouriya is 76% to 82%. Bilingualism in Hindi and Marathi is low. Different from Koraku. A Scheduled Tribe in India. Investigation needed: intelligibility with Mawasi, other dialects. Literacy rate in first language: 1% to 5%. Literacy program in some villages in Chikaldard field. Devanagari script. Hills, plains. Traditional religion, Hindu. Bible portions 1900-1981.

KORLAI CREOLE PORTUGUESE [VKP] 750 (1998 J. C. Clements). Maharashtra, Korlai, 200 km. south of Bombay, west coast. Creole, Portuguese based. Recently discovered. Originated around 1520. Originally cut off from Hindu and Muslim neighbors by social and religious barriers, lost virtually all Portugese contact as well after 1740. Situation now rapidly changing, with intense cultural pressure from the surrounding Marathi-speaking population.

KORWA ***(ERNGA, SINGLI)*** [KFP] 66,000 (1997 IMA). Bihar, Palamau and Gumla districts; Madhya Pradesh, Surguja, Raigarh, Bilaspur districts; Orissa, Mayurbhanj and Sundargarh districts; Uttar Pradesh, Mirazpur District; West Bengal; Andhra Pradesh; Maharashtra. Austro-Asiatic, Munda, North Munda, Kherwari, Mundari. Dialect: MAJHI-KORWA. Ethnic Kodaku speak Korwa as mother tongue. Some ethnic Korwa speak Sadri or Chhattisgarhi as mother tongue. Rapid assimilation to Sadri. A Scheduled Tribe in India. Literacy rate in first language: Below 1%. Hindu.

KOTA ***(KOTTA, KOWE-ADIWASI, KOTHER-TAMIL)*** [KFE] 2,000 (1992). Tamil Nadu, Madras; Nilgiri Hills, Trichikadi village and a few others around Kokkal Kotagiri. Dravidian, Southern, Tamil-Kannada, Tamil-Kodagu, Toda-Kota. Dialect: KO BASHAI. A Scheduled Tribe in India. Endogamous within the ethnic group. Literacy rate in first language: Below 1%. Tamil script. Mountains. Agriculturalists. Hindu.

KOYA ***(KOI, KOI GONDI, KAVOR, KOA, KOITAR, KOYATO, KAYA, KOYI, RAJ KOYA)*** [KFF] 330,000 (1997 IMA), including 24,320 Dorli (1972 census). Estimates up to 10,000,000 speakers. Andhra Pradesh, south of the Godavari River and in adjoining districts north of the river; Maharashtra; Madhya Pradesh, Bastar District; Orissa, Koraput District, Malkangiri subdivision; 300 km. east to west, 200 km. north to south. Dravidian, South-Central, Gondi-Kui, Konda-Kui, Manda-Kui, Kui-Kuvi. Dialects: MALAKANAGIRI KOYA, PODIA KOYA (GOTTE KOYA), CHINTOOR KOYA (DORLA KOITUR), JAGANATHAPURAM KOYA (GOMMU KOYA, GODAVARI KOYA), DORLI (KORLA, DORA, DOR KOI, DORA KOI, DORLA KOITUR, DORLA KOYA). Chintoor is the linguistic center. The Malakanagiri and Podia varieties are more divergent. A separate language from Gondi. Telugu is their second language but bilingual proficiency is low. Different from Kui and Kuvi. A Scheduled Tribe in India. Investigation needed: attitudes toward Podia. Literacy rate in second language: 7%. Literacy centers. Some Telugu materials available. Telugu, Oriya, and Devanagari scripts. Roman script reportedly preferred by Koya leaders. Swidden agriculturalists, peasant agriculturalists. Traditional religion, Hindu. NT 1997.

KUDIYA [KFG] 2,462 (1981 census). Kerala, Cannanore District; Karnataka, Coorg and South Kannara districts; Tamil Nadu. Dravidian, Southern, Tulu. Tulu, Kodagu, Kannada, Malayalam spoken with outsiders. A Scheduled Tribe in India. Literacy rate in second language: 30% (1981 census). Kannada and Malayalam scripts. Hindu.

KUDMALI ***(KURMALI, KURUMALI, KURMALI THAR, BEDIA, DHARUA)*** [KYW] 37,000 (1997 IMA). Bihar; West Bengal; Orissa; Assam. Indo-European, Indo-Iranian, Indo-Aryan, Eastern zone, Bihari. Related to Sadri. Possibly the same as Panchpargania. Spoken by some Scheduled Tribes and Castes, including Bedia of West Bengal and Dharua. 'Mahato' could be an alternate name.

KUI ***(KANDH, KHONDI, KHOND, KHONDO, KANDA, KODU, KODULU, KUINGA, KUY)*** [KXU] 717,000 (1997 IMA). Orissa, Phulbani, Koraput, Ganjam districts, Udayagiri area in Ganjam; Andhra Pradesh; Madhya Pradesh; Tamil Nadu. Dravidian, South-Central, Gondi-Kui, Konda-Kui, Manda-Kui, Kui-Kuvi. Dialects: KHONDI, GUMSAI. Spoken by the Dal and Sitha Kandha as mother tongue. Different from Kuvi and Koya (Koi). Kondh is a Scheduled Tribe. Christian, traditional religion. NT 1954-1975.

KUKNA ***(KANARA, KOKNA, KOKNI)*** [KEX] 570,419 (1981 census), plus 100,000 second language speakers (1998). Gujarat, Dangs and Valsad districts; Maharashtra, Dhule, Nasik, and Thane districts; Dadra and Nagar Haveli; Karnataka, Kanara; Rajasthan. Indo-European, Indo-Iranian, Indo-Aryan, Southern zone, Konkani. Trade language. Literacy rate in first language: 10% to 30%. Some literacy work being done. Gujarat and Devanagari scripts. Agriculturalists. Hindu (1981 census), Christian. NT 1977.

KULUNG ***(KHULUNGE RAI, KULU RING, KHULUNG, KHOLUNG)*** [KLE] Dehradun, Sikkim; Buthan, Dalpiguri, West Bengal. Sino-Tibetan, Tibeto-Burman, Himalayish, Mahakiranti, Kiranti, Eastern. See main entry under Nepal.

KUMARBHAG PAHARIA ***(MALTO, MALTI, MALTU, MALER, MAL, MAD, PAHARIA, PAHARIYA, KUMAR)*** [KMJ] 12,000 to 14,000 plus several thousand in West Bengal (1994). Central eastern Bihar, central part of former Santhal Pargana District, Sundar Pahari Block of Godda District, and all but southernmost block of Pakaur District. Reported in at least Bankura, Barddhaman, and Murshidabad districts of West Bengal; Orissa, Mayurbhanj. Dravidian, Northern. Inherent intelligibility with Mal Paharia is inadequate. Related to Kurux. 80% lexical similarity with Mal Paharia. Low bilingualism in Hindi and Bengali. Kumarbhag actively used in all domains. Positive attitude toward Kumarbhag. Part of the Malto ethnic group. Investigation needed: intelligibility with dialects in West Bengal, Bangladesh. They want literature in Kumarbhag. Forest. Hills, plains. Subsistence agriculturalists: rice, maize, wheat, sugarcane, lentils, vegetables; firewood gatherers; fishermen; hunters. 1,000 to 2,000 feet. Traditional religion.

KUMAUNI ***(KAMAONI, KUMAONI, KUMAU, KUMAWANI, KUMGONI, KUMMAN, KUNAYAONI)*** [KFY] 2,360,000 in India (1998). Population total both countries 2,360,000 or more. Uttar Pradesh, Almora, Nainital, Pithoragarh, Bageshwar, Udhamsingh Nagar districts; Assam; Bihar; Delhi; Madhya Pradesh; Maharashtra; Nagaland. Central Kumauni is in Almora and northern Nainital, Northeastern Kumauni is in Pithoragarh, Southeastern Kumauni is in Southeastern Nainital, Western Kumauni is west of Almora and Nainital. It may not be in Nepal. Also spoken in Nepal. Indo-European, Indo-Iranian, Indo-Aryan, Northern zone, Central Pahari. Dialects: CENTRAL KUMAUNI, NORTHEASTERN KUMAUNI, SOUTHEASTERN KUMAUNI, WESTERN KUMAUNI, ASKOTI, BHABARI OF RAMPUR, CHAUGARKHIYA, DANPURIYA, GANGOLA, JOHARI, KHASPARJIYA, KUMAIYA PACHHAI, PASHCHIMI, PHALDAKOTIYA, RAU-CHAUBHAISI, SIRALI, SORIYALI. All dialects listed are functionally intelligible to each other's speakers for all purposes. People report the eastern dialects to be different. Names sometimes listed for dialects or subgroups are: Askoti, Bhabari of Rampur, Chaugarkhiya, Danpuriya, Gangola, Johari, Khasparjiya, Kumaiya Pachhai,

Pashchimi, Phaldakotiya, Kumaoni, Rau-Chaubhaisi, Sirali, Soriyali. Most closely related to Garwhali and Nepali. Hindi used in towns and markets. Spoken by most men, the few women who have been to school, and school-aged children. Men can converse about common topics, some women only about trade. Used in homes and villages. All ages. The Southeast dialect is reported to be 'sweet'. The Central one is the most accepted. Hindi valued as the language of education and progress. English valued as the gateway to success. Dictionary. Grammar. Literacy rate in second language: 58%, 73% men, 41% women. Literacy effort needed. Motivation not high. Kumauni script slightly different from Devanagari in Hindi. Poetry, magazines, radio programs. Mountain slope. 1,500 to 2,500 meters. Hindu. Bible portions 1825-1876.

KUPIA ***(VALMIKI)*** [KEY] 4,000 (1983 SIL). Andhra Pradesh, Visakhapatnam and East Godavari districts. Indo-European, Indo-Iranian, Indo-Aryan, Eastern zone, Oriya. A Scheduled Tribe in India. People called 'Valmiki'. Ethnic Valmiki are not the same as mother tongue Kupia speakers. Agriculturalists. Traditional religion, Christian. NT 1983.

KURICHIYA ***(KURICHIA, KURICHCHIA)*** [KFH] 29,375 (1981 census). Kerala, Wynad, Cannanore districts; Tamil Nadu, Dharampuri District. Dravidian, Unclassified. Language shift taking place to Malayalam in Kerala and Kannada in Tamil Nadu. The CIIL lists this as an endangered language. Further study is being done at Annamalai University. A Scheduled Tribe in India. Consider themselves higher caste than Brahmin. Grammar. Forest. Settled agriculturalists. Hindu, Christian (1981 census).

KURUMBA ***(KORAMBAR, KURAMWARI, KURUMAR, KURUMBAR, KURUBA, KURUMVARI, KUREMBAN, KURUBAS KURUBAN, KURUBAR, KURUMA, KURUMAN, KURUMANS, KURUMBAS, KURUMBAN, PALU KURUMBA, NONSTANDARD KANNADA, SOUTHERN KANNADA, CANARESE)*** [KFI] 150,000 to 200,000 (1998). Tamil Nadu, Coimbatore District, Pollachi, Western Fields, Western Gate Hills; Dharmapuri, South Arcot and Chengalpet districts; in pockets in Salem and North Arcot districts; Theni District, Cumbari Valley; Dindukat District, Sirumalai, Senkuruchi Hillocks, Palani; Karnataka; Andhra Pradesh. Dravidian, Southern, Tamil-Kannada, Tamil-Kodagu, Kodagu. Dialects are inherently intelligible to each other's speakers. Limited bilingual proficiency in Tamil and Standard Kannada. There are reported to be 3 groups of Gowda, Okkili, Anuppa and Kurumba. These may be languages or dialects of one language. Sometimes referred to as Alu or Palu Kurumba, but it is a different language from Alu Kurumba in the hills. Kurumba and Kuruman are different Scheduled Tribes. Younger generation over 50% literate, older generation less. Plains. Agriculturalists, pastoralists, urban jobs. Traditional religion, Hindu.

KURUMBA, ALU ***(ALU KURUMBA NONSTANDARD KANNADA, PAL KURUMBA, HAL KURUMBA)*** [QKA] 2,500 (1997). Tamil Nadu, eastern side of Nilgiri Hills. Dravidian, Southern, Tamil-Kannada, Tamil-Kodagu, Kodagu. Alu and Pal have 80% lexical similarity. Limited bilingualism in Tamil, Standard Kannada, and Southern Nonstandard Kannada. A Scheduled Tribe in India. Literacy rate in first language: Below 1%. Literacy rate in second language: 15% to 25%. Hunter-gatherers, tea and coffee laborers, beekeepers, horticulturalists. Hindu, traditional religion.

KURUMBA, BETTA ***(BETTA KURUMBA NONSTANDARD TAMIL, KADU KURUMBA, URALI KURUMBA)*** [QKB] 10,000 (1994). Tamil Nadu, Nilgiri District; Karnataka, Mysore District, north side of Nilgiri Hills, just east of Kerala border; Kerala, Wynad District. Dravidian, Southern, Tamil-Kannada, Tamil-Kodagu, Tamil-Malayalam, Tamil. A nonstandard variety of Tamil or Kannada. May or may not be the same as Betta Kuruba in Coorg District. 59% to 77% lexical similarity among groups that are called 'Betta Kurumba'. The CIIL lists Urali Kurumba as endangered. It is being studied by Annamalai University. 'Kadu Kurumba' means 'Jungle Shepherds'. 'Betta Kurumba' means 'Hill Shepherds'. There are 3 subdivisions: Ane (Elephant) Kurumba, Bevina (neem tree) Kurumba, and Kolli (fire-brand) Kurumba. May or may not be the same as Betta Kuruba in Coorg District. A Scheduled Tribe in India. Investigation needed: intelligibility with dialects, Tamil, Kannada. Grammar. Literacy rate in second language: 15% to 25%. Favorable attitude toward literacy. Tropical forest. Swidden agriculturalists, basket makers, laborers. Hindu, traditional religion.

KURUMBA, JENNU ***(JENNU KURUMBA NONSTANDARD KANNADA, JEN KURUMBA, TEN KURUMBA, JENNU NUDI, NAIKAN, KATTU NAYAKA, NAIK KURUMBA)*** [QKJ] 35,000 (1997 IMA). North side of Nilgiri Hills on the border between Tamil Nadu and Karnataka, just east of the Kerala border, Mysore and Kodagu districts of Karnataka; Kerala, Wynad District. Dravidian, Southern, Tamil-Kannada, Tamil-Kodagu, Kodagu. May or may not be the same as Jeinu Kuruba, a variety of Kannada. 61% to 83% lexical similarity among varieties called 'Jennu Kurumba', less than 60% lexical similarity with Betta Kurumba dialects. Limited bilingual proficiency in Kannada, Malayalam and Tamil. Positive attitude toward Kurumba. Jennu Kurumba means 'Honey Shepherds'. A Scheduled Tribe in India. Investigation needed: intelligibility with nonstandard Kannada varieties. Literacy rate in second language: Low. Literacy effort needed. Attitudes favorable. Tropical forest. Hunter-gatherers, day laborers, agriculturalists. Hindu, traditional religion.

KURUMBA, MULLU [KPB] 6,000 (1994 Singh). Tamil Nadu, Nilgiri District; Kerala, Wynad District. Dravidian, Southern, Tamil-Kannada, Tamil-Kodagu, Kodagu. 34% to 41% lexical similarity with other Kurumba languages. A Scheduled Tribe in India. Investigation needed: intelligibility with dialects. Favorable motivation toward literacy. Hunters, agriculturalists, field laborers. Hindu, traditional religion.

KURUX *(URAON, KURUKH, KUNRUKH, KADUKALI, KURKA, ORAON, URANG, KISAN, KUNHA, KUNHAR, KUNUK, KUNNA, KUDA, KORA, KODA, KOLA, MORVA, BIRHOR)* [KVN] 2,053,000 in India, including 1,834,000 Oraon, 219,000 Kisan (1997 IMA). Population total both countries 2,053,000 or more. Bihar; Madhya Pradesh; West Bengal; Orissa; Assam; Tripura. Also spoken in Bangladesh. Dravidian, Northern. Dialects: ORAON, KISAN. Kisan and Oraon have 73% intelligibility. Oraon beoming standardized. Related to Malto. Kisan and Oraon are Scheduled Tribes in India. Different from Nepali Kurux. Investigation needed: intelligibility with Kisan in Bihar. Literacy rate in first language: 23% Oraon, 17% Kisan. NT 1950-1997.

KUVI *(KUWI, KUVINGA, KUVI KOND, KOND, KHONDI, KHONDH, JATAPU)* [KXV] 300,000 (1990 UBS). Orissa, mainly Koraput District, also Kalahandi, Ganjam, and Phulbani districts; Andhra Pradesh, Visakhapatnam, Vizianagaram, Srikakkulam districts. Dravidian, South-Central, Gondi-Kui, Konda-Kui, Manda-Kui, Kui-Kuvi. The Dongria and Kuvi subgroups speak Kuvi as mother tongue. Kondh is a Scheduled Tribe in India. Distinct from Kui and Koi (Koya). Hindu (1981 census). NT 1987.

LADAKHI *(LADAPHI, LADHAKHI, LADAK, LADWAGS)* [LBJ] 102,000 in India (1997 IMA) including 29,800 to 33,300 Shamma (Voegelin and Voegelin 1977.328). Population total both countries 114,000. Jammu and Kashmir, Ladakh District. Leh is in Leh and surrounding areas. Zanskari is in Zanskar Tahsil to the south of Leh in Ladakh District. Changtang is in the Changtang region east and southeast of Leh to the Tibetan border. Shamma is west of Leh along the Indus Valley and to the south of Khaltse. Nubra is in Nubra Tahsil north of Leh. 250 villages and hamlets. Also spoken in China. Sino-Tibetan, Tibeto-Burman, Himalayish, Tibeto-Kanauri, Tibetic, Tibetan, Western, Ladakhi. Dialects: LEH (CENTRAL LADAKHI), SHAMMA (SHAM, SHAMSKAT, LOWER LADAKHI), NUBRA LADAKHI. Perhaps 30% to 40% intelligibility with Tibetan. Leh is used as the medium of communication. Leh speakers understand Zanskar and Changtang at more than 90% on recorded text tests. Not known if speakers of all dialects understand Leh well. Lexical similarity among 5 main dialects: 84% to 94%; 71% to 83% with Purik, 53% to 60% with Tibetan. Many people in urban areas have some bilingualism in Urdu, Hindi, or English, but rural speakers are mainly monolingual in Ladakhi. All ages. Investigation needed: intelligibility with Leh with Zanskar and Changtang. Compare with Purik. Grammar. SOV; postpositions; genitives, relatives before noun heads; articles, adjectives numerals after noun heads; suffixes indicate case of noun phrase; ergative; causatives; comparative; CCVCC or CCCVV maximum; nontonal. Literacy rate in second language: Men: 36%, women: 12% in Hindi, Urdu, Tibetan, or English (1991). Tibetan script used. It is difficult to use, but desired by the people. Mountain valleys. Agriculturalists: wheat, barley; pastoralists: yaks, goats, sheep (cashmere wool); cottage industries: weaving, jewelry making, religious artifact production. 8,250 to 16,500 feet. Buddhist, Muslim, Christian. Bible portions 1904-1919.

LALUNG *(DOWYAN)* [LAX] 23,000 (1997 IMA). Assam, Nowgong, Karbi Anglong, Kamrup, Sibsagar, Lakhimpur districts; Meghalaya, Khasi Hills District. Sino-Tibetan, Tibeto-Burman, Jingpho-Konyak-Bodo, Konyak-Bodo-Garo, Bodo-Garo, Bodo. Most ethnic Lalung speak Lalung as mother tongue; in the plains they use Assamese primarily, in the hills Lalung. A Scheduled Tribe in India. Grammar. Literacy rate in second language: 21.5% (31.5% males, 11.2% females). Agriculturalists. Traditional religion.

LAMBADI *(LAMANI, LAMADI, LAMBANI, LABHANI, LAMBARA, LAVANI, LEMADI, LUMADALE, LABHANI MUKA, BANJARA, BANJARI, BANGALA, BANJORI, BANJURI, BRINJARI, GOHAR-HERKERI, GOOLA, GURMARTI, GORMATI, KORA, SINGALI, SUGALI, SUKALI, TANDA, VANJARI, WANJI)* [LMN] 2,867,000 including 1,961,000 Lambadi (1994 IMA), plus 769,120 Banjari. Andhra Pradesh; Madhra Pradesh; Himachal Pradesh; Gujarat; Tamil Nadu; Maharashtra; Karnataka; Orissa; West Bengal. Indo-European, Indo-Iranian, Indo-Aryan, Central zone, Rajasthani, Unclassified. Dialects: MAHARASHTRA LAMANI, KARNATAKA LAMANI (MYSORE LAMANI), ANDHRA PRADESH LAMANI (TELUGU LAMANI). Bilingualism in Telugu, Kannada, Marathi. A Scheduled Tribe in Orissa, a Scheduled Caste in Karnataka, Haryana, Punjab, Himachal Pradesh. 'Gormati' is self name. SOV. Literacy rate in second language: 18% Marathi. Each of the three dialects needs a different script: Maharashtra uses Devanagari script, Karnataka uses Kannada script, Andhra Pradesh uses Telugu script. Agriculturalists, laborers. Traditional religion, Hindu, Christian. NT 1999.

LAMKANG *("LAMGANG", "HIROI-LAMGANG", LAMKAANG)* [LMK] 10,000 (1996 UBS). Southeast Manipur, 26 villages in Chandel District; Nagaland, Thamlakhuren. Sino-Tibetan, Tibeto-Burman, Kuki-Chin-Naga, Kuki-Chin, Northern. Closest to Anal Naga. A Scheduled Tribe in India. "Lamgang" and "Hiroi-Lamgang" are not correct names. Literacy rate in second language: 15% Manipuri. Literacy help requested. Agriculturalists. Christian (1981 census). NT, in press (1997).

LEPCHA ***(LAPCHE, RONG, RONGKE, RONGPA, NÜNPA)*** [LEP] 38,000 in India (1997 IMA). Population total all countries 41,300. Sikkim, Dzongu District; West Bengal, Darjeeling District, Kalimpong. Also spoken in Bhutan, Nepal. Sino-Tibetan, Tibeto-Burman, Himalayish, Tibeto-Kanauri, Lepcha. Dialects: ILAMMU, TAMSANGMU, RENGJONGMU. Has been classified both in Himalayan and Naga groups. Classification still uncertain. Sikkim, all ages. Some younger generation speak Nepali as mother tongue. Vigorous in Sikkim. A Scheduled Tribe in India. 'Lepcha' is the name of both people and language. Has own script. Language of instruction in some schools in Sikkim. Agriculturalists, pastoralists. Up to 4,000 feet. Buddhist. NT 1989.

LHOMI ***(LHOKET, SHING SAAPA)*** [LHM] 1,000 in India. West Bengal, Darjeeling. Sino-Tibetan, Tibeto-Burman, Himalayish, Tibeto-Kanauri, Tibetic, Tibetan, Central. Literacy rate in first language: Below 1%. Literacy rate in second language: 5% to 25% (men). Traditional religion, Lamaist. NT 1995. See main entry under Nepal.

LIMBU ***(LIMBO, LUMBU)*** [LIF] 28,000 in India (1997 IMA). Sikkim, West Bengal, Darjeeling district. Sino-Tibetan, Tibeto-Burman, Himalayish, Mahakiranti, Kiranti, Eastern. Related to Lohorong, Yakha. There may be 5 or 6 dialects; 1 or 2 of which may not be inherently intelligible to each other's speakers. Roman, Devanagari, Limbu scripts. See main entry under Nepal.

LODHI ***(LODHA, LODI, LOHI, LOZI)*** [LBM] 75,000 (1997 IMA). Orissa, Mayurghanj and Baleswar districts; West Bengal, Midnapore District. Austro-Asiatic, Munda, South Munda, Koraput Munda, Sora-Juray-Gorum, Sora-Juray. Related to Sora. They are reported to be fluent in Bengali. Lodha is a Scheduled Tribe in India. Literacy rate in second language: 9% (1981 census). Hindu, Christian (1981 census).

LOHAR, GADE ***(GADULIYA LOHAR, LOHPITTA RAJPUT LOHAR, BAGRI LOHAR, BHUBALIYA LOHAR, LOHARI, GARA, DOMBA, DOMBIALI, CHITODI LOHAR, PANCHAL LOHAR, BELANI, DHUNKURIA KANWAR KHATI)*** [GDA] 500 to 750 (1997). Rajasthan; Gujarat; Madhya Pradesh; Maharashtra; Uttar Pradesh; Delhi; Haryana; Punjab. Indo-European, Indo-Iranian, Indo-Aryan, Central zone, Rajasthani, Unclassified. No significant dialect differences. May be the same as Loarki [LRK] listed in Pakistan. Considered by others to be low caste. 'Gade Lohar' refers to people who travel in bullock carts and are blacksmiths. Literacy rate in second language: 39.97% (1981 census). Devanagari script. Nomadic blacksmiths, carpentry, construction, agriculturalists, animal husbandry. Hindu.

LOHAR, LAHUL ***(GARAS, LOHAR)*** [LHL] 750 (1996). Himachal Pradesh, Lahul Valley. Indo-European, Indo-Iranian, Indo-Aryan, Unclassified. A different language from Gade Lohar. Bilingualism in Hindi. Lohar is a Scheduled Caste in Himachal Pradesh, all of whom do not speak this language. Similar name, occupation to Gade Lohar. Investigation needed: intelligibility with Lohar of Kullu Valley, bilingual proficiency in Hindi. Literacy program needed. Devanagari script. Metalsmiths.

LUSHAI ***(DULIEN, DUHLIAN TWANG, LUSAI, LUSEI, LUSHEI, LUKHAI, LUSAGO, LE, SAILAU, HUALNGO, WHELNGO)*** [LSH] 529,000 in India (1997 IMA). Population total all countries 542,500. Mizoram; Assam; Manipur; Nagaland; Tripura, Jampui Hill range. Also spoken in Bangladesh, Myanmar. Sino-Tibetan, Tibeto-Burman, Kuki-Chin-Naga, Kuki-Chin, Central. Dialects: FANNAI, MIZO, NGENTE, PANG (PAANG), TLAU. Related to Hmar, Pankhu, Zahao (Falam Chin). Mizo is a Scheduled Tribe in India with subgroups listed as dialects. Christian (1981 census). Bible 1959-1995.

MAGAHI ***(MAGADHI, MAGAYA, MAGHAYA, MAGHORI, MAGI, MAGODHI, BIHARI)*** [MQM] 11,362,000 (1997 IMA). Southern districts of Bihar, eastern Patna District, northern Chotanagpur Division; West Bengal, Malda District. Indo-European, Indo-Iranian, Indo-Aryan, Eastern zone, Bihari. Dialects: SOUTHERN MAGAHI, NORTHERN MAGAHI, CENTRAL MAGAHI. Also used as a religious language. Literacy rate in first language: 30%. Hindu, traditional religion, Jainism. NT 1826, out of print.

MAGAR, EASTERN ***(MAGARI, MANGGAR, MANGARI, MAGARKURA)*** [MGP] 1,136 in India (1961 census). Sikkim. Sino-Tibetan, Tibeto-Burman, Himalayish, Mahakiranti, Kham-Magar-Chepang-Sunwari, Magar. Mountain slope. Agriculturalists: rice, corn, wheat; hunters. NT 1991. See main entry under Nepal.

MAHALI ***(MAHILI, MAHLI, MAHLE)*** [MJX] 66,000 (1991 IMA). Bihar, Chotanagpur region; Orissa, Balasore, Mayurbhanj, Keonjhargarh districts; West Bengal; Assam. Austro-Asiatic, Munda, North Munda, Kherwari, Santali. Possible dialect of Santali. Mahli is a Scheduled Tribe, reported speaking Sadri as mother tongue in Bihar, Thar in Orissa, and Bengali in West Bengal.

MAITHILI ***(MAITLI, MAITILI, METHLI, TIRAHUTIA, BIHARI, TIRHUTI, TIRHUTIA, APABHRAMSA)*** [MKP] 22,000,000 in India (1981). Population total both countries 24,191,900. Northern Bihar, from Muzaffarpur on the west, past the Kosi on the east to western Purnia District, to the districts of Munger and Bhagalpur in the south, and the Himalayan foothills on the north. Cultural and linguistic center are the towns of

Madhubani and Darbhanga. Janakpur also important culturally and religiously. Delhi, Calcutta, Bombay have thousands. Many have settled abroad. Also spoken in Nepal. Indo-European, Indo-Iranian, Indo-Aryan, Eastern zone, Bihari. Dialects: STANDARD MAITHILI, SOUTHERN STANDARD MAITHILI, EASTERN MAITHILI (KHOTTA, KORTHA), WESTERN MAITHILI, JOLAHA, CENTRAL COLLOQUIAL MAITHILI (SOTIPURA), KISAN, DEHATI. Caste variation more than geographic variation in dialects. Functional intelligibility among all dialects, including those in Nepal. Closest to Magahi. Brahmin and non-Brahmin dialects average 91% lexical similarity. Hindi, Nepali, English, Bhojpuri, Bengali used mainly for business or social interaction outside the home by men or working women with various degrees of proficiency from marketing only to fluency. In cities some may use Hindi, Nepali, or English in the home. Used in home, village, town, or cities with other Maithili speakers. Spoken by Brahmin and other high caste or educated Hindus, who influence the culture and language, and other castes. There is a Maithili Academy. Linguistics and literature are taught at the L. N. Mithila University in Darbhanga and Patna University. Language attitudes are influenced by caste, ranging from superiority to resentment. Non-Brahmin speech viewed as inferior. Hindi considered superior, Nepali generally accepted. Dictionary. Grammar. SOV; postpositions; genitives, articles, numerals before noun heads, adjectives before and after noun heads; 1 prefix, 1 suffix; object marked by position; person, gender, animate distinguished, obligatory for subject; transitives; passives; causatives; comparatives; V, VC, VCC, CV, CVC, CVV, CCV, CVCC, CCVCC; nontonal. Literacy rate in first language: 25% to 50%. Literacy rate in second language: 25% to 50%. If they can read Nepali or Hindi, they can read Maithili. The educated read Hindi, Nepali, or English books with pleasure. Literacy effort needed. Devanagari. Poetry, magazines, radio programs, TV. Tropical forest, gallery forest. Plains. Peasant agriculturalists: rice. 80 meters. Hindu, Muslim.

MAJHI ***(MANJHI)*** [MJZ] 246 in Sikkim (1981 census). Bihar; Sikkim, South District, Majhigaon near Jorethang, East District, Majhitar near Rangpol. Indo-European, Indo-Iranian, Indo-Aryan, Eastern zone, Bihari. Bilingualism in Nepali. Distinct from Majhi dialect of Panjabi or Bote-Majhi of Nepal. Devanagari. Business, contract work. See main entry under Nepal.

MAJHWAR ***(MAJHVAR, MANJHI, MANJHIA)*** [MMJ] 27,958. Madhya Pradesh, Bilaspur District, Katghora tahsil; Uttar Pradesh, Allahabad, Varanasi, Mirapur districts; Sikkim. Unclassified. Possibly a dialect of Asuri. A Scheduled Tribe in Madhya Pradesh, speaking Chhattisgarhi as mother tongue. A Scheduled Caste in Uttar Pradesh, speaking Hindi as mother tongue. Hindu.

MAL PAHARIA ***(MALTO, MALTI, MALTU, MALER, MALPAHARIA, MARPAHARIA, MAL PAHARIYA, MAL, MAR, MAW, MAWDO, MAWER, MAWER NONDI, MAD, MADER, DEHRI, PAHARIA, PARSI)*** [MKB] 51,000 to 71,000 plus possibly 40,000 in West Bengal (1994). Central eastern Bihar, southern part of former Santhal Pargana District, Ramgarh Hills. Mainly in Dumka District, but many villages are in Pakaur, southern Godda, and Deoghar districts, and a few as far north as Depart village north of Borio in Sahibganj District. Reported in at least Bankura, Barddhaman, and Murshidabad districts of West Bengal. Possibly in Bangladesh. Indo-European, Indo-Iranian, Indo-Aryan, Eastern zone, Bengali-Assamese. Not inherently intelligible with Kumarbhag Paharia, Sauria Paharia, Bengali, or Hindi. Part of the Malto ethnic group. Speak a variety similar to Kharia Thar of Manbhum (Bihar). Dialects have 85% or higher lexical similarity with each other, but 59% with Mal Paharia Barmasiya and 55% with Khorta Babudoha. Some have shifted to Bengali or Khorta. All domains. Vigorous. A Scheduled Tribe in India. Investigation needed: intelligibility with West Bengal. Literacy rate in second language: 12.8% male, 2.3% female, average 7.6% (1981). Forest. Hills, plains. Firewood gatherers; subsistence agriculturalists. 1,000 to 2,000 feet. Traditional religion, Christian. NT, in press (1997).

MALANKURAVAN ***(MALAIKURAVAN, MALE KURAVAN, MALANKUDI)*** [MJO] 7,339 (1981 census). Tamil Nadu, Kanyakumari District; Kerala. Dravidian, Unclassified. Dialect: MALAYADIARS. Bilingualism in Tamil. A Scheduled Tribe in India. Reported to speak Malayalam as mother tongue. Traditional religion, Hindu.

MALAPANDARAM ***(MALAPANTARAM, MALEPANTARAM, HILL PANTARAM, PANDARAM BASHA)*** [MJP] 3,147 (1981 census). Kerala, Kottayam, Ernakulam, and Quilon districts; Tamil Nadu. Dravidian, Southern, Tamil-Kannada, Tamil-Kodagu, Tamil-Malayalam, Malayalam. A Scheduled Tribe in India. Investigation needed: intelligibility with Malayalam. Hindu, traditional religion.

MALARYAN ***(MALAI ARAYAN, MALEY ARAYAN, MALE ARAYANS, MALAYARAYAN, ARAYANS, KARINGAL, VAZHIYAMMAR)*** [MJQ] 27,716 (1981 census). Kerala, Ernakulam, Kottayam, and Trichur districts; Tamil Nadu. Dravidian, Southern, Tamil-Kannada, Tamil-Kodagu, Tamil-Malayalam, Malayalam. Bilingualism in Malayalam. A Scheduled Tribe in India. They are reported to speak a variety of Malayalam as mother tongue. Possibly the same as Kanikkaran. Literacy rate in second language: 76% Malayalam. Agriculturalists: settled. Hindu, Christian (1981 census).

MALAVEDAN ***(MALAVETAN, TOWETAN, VEDANS)*** [MJR] 9,533 (1981 census). Kerala, Ernakulam, Kottayam, Quilon, Trivandrum districts; Tamil Nadu, Kanyakumari and Tirunelveli districts. Dravidian, Southern, Tamil-Kannada, Tamil-Kodagu, Tamil-Malayalam, Malayalam. Dialects: VETAN, VETTUVAN. Bilingualism in Tamil. A Scheduled Tribe in India. They are reported to speak Malayalam as mother tongue.

Nomadic. Literacy rate in second language: 32% (1981 census). Hunter-gatherers. Hindu, Christian (1981 census).

MALAYALAM ***(ALEALUM, MALAYALANI, MALAYALI, MALEAN, MALIYAD, MALLEALLE, MOPLA)*** [MJS] 35,351,000 in India (1997 IMA). Population total all countries 35,706,000 or more. Kerala, Laccadive Islands, and neighboring states. Also spoken in Bahrain, Fiji, Israel, Malaysia, Qatar, Singapore, UAE, United Kingdom. Dravidian, Southern, Tamil-Kannada, Tamil-Kodagu, Tamil-Malayalam, Malayalam. Dialects: MALABAR, NAGARI-MALAYALAM, MALAYALAM, SOUTH KERALA, CENTRAL KERALA, NORTH KERALA, KAYAVAR, NAMBOODIRI, MOPLAH, PULAYA, NASRANI, NAYAR. Caste and communal dialects: Namboodiri, Nayar, Moplah, Pulaya, Nasrani. State language of Kerala. The Cochin Jews in Kerala speak Malayalam. National language. Malayalam script. Saivite Hindu, Muslim, Christian, Jewish. Bible 1841-1998.

MALDIVIAN ***(MALIKH, MAHL, MALKI, DEVEHI, DIVEHLI, DIVEHI BAS)*** [SNM] 4,500 in India (1997 CIIL). Minicoy Island in the Laccadive Islands in India. Indo-European, Indo-Iranian, Indo-Aryan, Sinhalese-Maldivian. No transitional dialects to Sinhalese, which is a separate language. Bilingualism in Arabic. Literacy rate in first language: 60% to 100%. Literacy rate in second language: 75% to 100%. Tana. Fishermen. Sunni Muslim, traditional religion. See main entry under Maldives.

MALVI ***(MALWADA, MALLOW, UJJAINI, MALWI, MALAVI)*** [MUP] 1,102,000 (1997 IMA). Northwest Madhya Pradesh; Maharashtra; Rajasthan; Gujarat. Indo-European, Indo-Iranian, Indo-Aryan, Central zone, Rajasthani, Unclassified. Dialects: BACHADI, BHOYARI, DHOLEWARI, HOSHANGABAD, JAMRAL, KATIYAI, MALVI PROPER, PATVI, RANGARI, RANGRI, SONDWARI (SOUDHWARI). Considered the standard dialect of Southeastern Rajasthani. Investigation needed: intelligibility with dialects, Nimade, Bhil of Maheshwar. NT 1826.

MANDA [MHA] Orissa, Kalahandi District. Dravidian, South-Central, Gondi-Kui, Konda-Kui, Manda-Kui, Manda-Pengo. Discovered in 1964. Investigation needed: intelligibility with Pengo.

MANDEALI ***(MANDI, PAHARI MANDIYALI, MANDIALI)*** [MJL] 776,372 (1991 census). Himachal Pradesh, Mandi District. Indo-European, Indo-Iranian, Indo-Aryan, Northern zone, Western Pahari. Preliminary survey suggests Mandeali speakers have functional intelligibility with Dogri-Kangri. 89% lexical similarity with Palampur Kangri, 83% with Chambeali. Speakers use Hindi for instruction in school, shops, in cities; Panjabi, shops; or Urdu, middle-aged or older. All ages. Grammar. SOV. Radio programs. Mountain slope, valley. Agriculturalists: rice, maize, millet, fruit. 300 to 3,000 meters. Hindu. Bible portions 1970.

MANNA-DORA [MJU] 18,964 (1981 census). Andhra Pradesh, East Godavari, Srikakulam, Visakhapatnam districts; Tamil Nadu. Dravidian, South Central, Telugu. A Scheduled Tribe in India. Reported to speak Telugu as mother tongue. Literacy rate in second language: 6.8% Telugu (1981 census). Telugu script. Agriculturalists: cultivation. Hindu.

MANNAN ***(MANNE, MANNYOD)*** [MJV] 58,028 including 5,852 in the Scheduled Tribe, 52,176 in the Scheduled Caste (1981 census). Kerala, Idukki District, Devikulam taluk; Tamil Nadu, Kanyakumari and Tirunelvgeli districts. Dravidian, Southern, Tamil-Kannada, Tamil-Kodagu, Tamil-Malayalam. 70% intelligibility with Malayalam. A Scheduled Tribe in India, A Scheduled Caste in Kerala and Tamil Nadu. Conflicting reports that they speak a dialect of Tamil or Malayalam as mother tongue. Literacy rate in second language: 30% Malayalam. Tropical forest. Mountain slope. Hunter-gatherers, agriculturalists. Hindu.

MARATHI ***(MAHARASHTRA, MAHARATHI, MALHATEE, MARTHI, MURUTHU)*** [MRT] 68,022,000 (1997 IMA). Population total all countries 68,022,000 or more. Including second language speakers: 71,000,000 (1999 WA). Maharashtra and adjacent states. Also spoken in Israel, Mauritius. Indo-European, Indo-Iranian, Indo-Aryan, Southern zone. 42 dialects. The dialect situation throughout the greater Marathi speaking area is complex. Dialects bordering other major language areas share many features with those languages. See separate entries for dialects or closely related languages: Konkani, Goanese, Deccan, Varhadi-Nagpuri, Ikrani, Gowlan. There is a dialect in Thanjavur District and elsewhere in Tamil Nadu, which has been influenced by Tamil and Kannada words, with at least 100,000 speakers. State language of Maharashtra. Spoken by the Mangelas as mother tongue. The Bene Israel are a Marathi-speaking Jewish group of Bombay. The Habshi are descended from East African slaves brought to western India, and are Muslim. Investigation needed: intelligibility with dialects. National language. SOV. Literacy rate in first language: 34%. Literacy rate in second language: 34%. Devanagari script. Hindu, Muslim, Sikh, Christian, Jain, Jewish (Bene Israel). Bible 1821-1998.

MARIA ***(MADI, MADIYA, MADIA, MODH, MODI)*** [MRR] 134,000 (1997 IMA). Maharashtra, Garhichiroli (Chanda) District; Madhya Pradesh. Dravidian, South-Central, Gondi-Kui, Gondi. Dialects: BHAMANI MARIA (BHAMANI), ADEWADA, ETAPALLY MARIA. Etapally Maria is apparently understood by all. A separate language from Muria, Dandami Maria, Northern Gondi, Southern Gondi, and Koya. 76% to 77% intelligibility of other Gondi varieties. May be intelligible with Abujmaria. 53% to 83% lexical similarity among dialects. Use in all domains nearly always. Speakers have negative attitudes toward the varieties mentioned above. A Scheduled Tribe in India. Investigation needed: intelligibility with Abujmaria. Literacy rate in first language: Below 1%. Literacy rate in second language: 25% to 50%. Hindu, traditional religion.

MARIA, DANDAMI ***(BISON HORN MARIA, MARIA GOND, MADIYA, DHURU, DANDAMI MADIYA)*** [DAQ] 150,000 (1992 UBS). Madhya Pradesh, central and southern Bastar District, Dantewara tahsil. Dravidian, South-Central, Gondi-Kui, Gondi. Dialects: GEEDAM, SUKMA (SUKA). Geedam and Bailadila have 95% to 98% intelligibility with each other, 81% of Sukma, but 18% to 21% of Maria, 18% to 45% of Muria. Speakers in Sukma understood Geedam at 81% or lower; those in Bailadila understood Sukma at 92%. May be more than one language. A separate language from Northern Gondi, Southern Gondi, Abujmaria, and Koya. All ages. A Scheduled Tribe in India. Speakers are called 'Maria'. Investigation needed: intelligibility with Sukma, other dialects. Grammar. Primers with literacy program in progress. Degraded forests, tropical forest. Plains, hills. Swidden agriculturalists, peasant agriculturalists, hunter-gatherers. Traditional religion.

MARWARI ***(RAJASTHANI, MERWARI, MARVARI)*** [MKD] 12,963,000 including 8,068,000 Marwari, 3,583,000 Rajasthani, 265,000 Dhundhari, 47,000 Shekawati (1997 IMA). Population total both countries 12,963,000 or more. Gujarat; Rajasthan; Madhya Pradesh; Punjab; Delhi; Haryana; Uttar Pradesh; thoughout India. Also spoken in Nepal. Indo-European, Indo-Iranian, Indo-Aryan, Central zone, Rajasthani, Marwari. Dialects: STANDARD MARWARI, JAIPURI, SHEKAWATI, DHUNDHARI, BIKANERI. The standard form of Rajasthani. 23 dialects. It is not clear if Mewari is a dialect of Marwari or separate language—see Mewari language entry. Different from Mewati, dialect of Haryanvi. May or may not be different from Marwari of Pakistan. 80% to 85% lexical similarity among some Gujarat and Rajasthan Marwari Bhil dialects; 75% to 80% with Wagdi; 75% to 83% with some Patelia dialects; 67% to 87% with Adiwasi Girasia dialects; 67% to 84% with Rajput Girasia dialects. Literacy rate in first language: 5% to 10%. Literacy rate in second language: 50% to 75%. Devanagari script. Hindu, traditional religion. NT 1820-1821, out of print.

MAWCHI ***(MAUCHI, MAVCHI, MAWACHI, MOWCHI, MAWCHI BHIL)*** [MKE] 76,000 (1997 IMA). Southwest Gujarat; Maharashtra, Dhule District. Indo-European, Indo-Iranian, Indo-Aryan, Central zone, Bhil. Dialects: GAMTI, MAWCHI, PADVI. A Scheduled Tribe in Maharashtra. Literacy rate in first language: 5% to 10%. Literacy rate in second language: 25% to 50%. Agriculturalists. Traditional religion. NT 1989.

MEITEI ***(MEITHEI, MEITHE, MITHE, MITEI, MEITEIRON, MANIPURI, MENIPURI, KATHE, KATHI, PONNA)*** [MNR] 1,240,000 in India (1997 IMA). Population total all countries 1,648,000 (1996 UBS). Manipur (most); Assam, Kankan; Nagaland; Tripura; Uttar Pradesh; West Bengal. Also spoken in Bangladesh, Myanmar. Sino-Tibetan, Tibeto-Burman, Meithei. Dialects: MEITEI, LOI, PANGAL. Bilingualism in Hindi. Mainly rural. 7 clans (Ningthonia, Luwang, Angom, Moirang, Khabanaganba, Chonglei). Trade language. Literacy rate in second language: 24%. They had an earlier script called 'Meitei Mayek'. Valley. Agriculturalists (rice and vegetables) and fishermen 60%, government 20%, technical 10%, business 10%, weaving, wood products. Hindu, traditional religion (Sana Mahi), Muslim, Christian. Bible 1984.

MEMBA [MMC] 2,000 (2000 Roland Breton). Northern Arunachal Pradesh, West Siang District, up near Pemak in China. Sino-Tibetan, Tibeto-Burman, Himalayish, Tibeto-Kanauri, Tibetic, Unclassified. May or may not be the same as Moinba (Menba, Monba, Monpa), Tshangla, or other varieties referred to as 'Monpa'. A Scheduled Tribe in India. Sparce forest. Agriculturalists: shifting and wet cultivation. Lamaistic Buddhist (1981 census).

MEWARI ***(MEWATI, MEWADI)*** [MTR] 1,220,000 including 1,058,000 Mewari and 162,000 Mewati (1997 IMA). Rajasthan, Udaipur, Bhilwara, Chitorgarh districts. Indo-European, Indo-Iranian, Indo-Aryan, Central zone, Rajasthani, Marwari. It is not clear if Mewari is a dialect of Marwari or separate language—see Marwari language entry. A Scheduled Tribe in India, Bhil Gametia and 7 Scheduled Castes. Different from Mewati, dialect of Haryanvi. Devanagari script. Hindu, traditional religion. Bible portions 1815.

MIJU ***(KAMAN, MISHMI, MIJI)*** [MXJ] 3,662 (1981 census). Assam; Arunachal Pradesh, Lohit District. Sino-Tibetan, Tibeto-Burman, North Assam, Tani. Conflicting reports about Miju closeness to Idu and Digaro. They are ethnically related, but may not be linguistically close. A Scheduled Tribe in India, subgroup of Mishmi. Different from the Miji who speak Sajalong. Investigation needed: intelligibility with Idu, Digaro. Roman script. Forest. Hills. Agriculturalists: shifting cultivation. Traditional religion, Hindu.

MIKIR ***(MANCHATI, MIKIRI, KARBI, KARBI KARBAK, ARLENG ALAM)*** [MJW] 478,000 including 341,000 Mikir (1997 IMA), 137,000 Amri (1997 IMA). Assam, Karbi Anglong District, Mikir and Rengma hills; Arunachal Pradesh, Lower Subansiri District, Balijan circle; Meghalaya, Jaintia and East Khasi Hills districts; Nagaland, foothills around Dimapur. Sino-Tibetan, Tibeto-Burman, Mikir. Dialects: AMRI (AMRI KARBI), BHOI MYNRI. Bhoi Mynri is intelligible only with difficulty. Speakers of all ages use Assamese as second language. Some other groups speak Mikir as mother tongue, including some Dimasa. A Scheduled Tribe in India. Their name for themselves is 'Karbi', outsiders' name is 'Mikir'. Investigation needed: intelligibility with Bhoi Mynri. Grammar. Literacy rate in second language: 17% (1971). Roman script. Agriculturalists: wet rice. Hindu (mainly), Christian. Bible 1952.

MINA [MYI] 900,000 (1991 IMA), or 2,087,075 (1981 census). Madhya Pradesh, Gwalior, Shiypuri, Guna, Rajgarh districts, Vidisha District, Sironj subdivision; Rajasthan, Jaipur, Alwar, Bharatpur, Sawai Madhopur, Tonk, Bundi districts. Indo-European, Indo-Iranian, Indo-Aryan, Unclassified. A Scheduled Tribe in India. It is reported that their mother tongue is Dhundhari in Rajasthjan and Braj Bhasha in Madhya Pradesh. Agriculturalists, animal husbandry. Hindu.

MIRGAN ***(PANIKA, PANKA, MIRKAN, MIRGAMI)*** [QMK] 12,000 including 10,000 in Orissa, 2,000 in Madhya Pradesh (1992). Madhya Pradesh, Bastar District; Orissa, Koraput District. Indo-European, Indo-Iranian, Indo-Aryan, Eastern zone, Bengali-Assamese. Dialects have good intelligibility. Not functionally intelligible with Halbi. Dialects have 83% to 95% lexical similarity. Limited proficiency in Oriya. Oriya and Adivasi Oriya are used in Orissa, Hindi and Halbi in Madhya Pradesh. Home, religion. Vigorous. Positive attitudes toward speaking Mirgan. Declared a General Caste by the government. Literacy rate in second language: 10% Oriya. Literacy program needed in Oriya script. Oriya, Telugu. Scrub forest, semi-tropical. Rolling hills, plains. Traditionally weavers, peasant agriculturalists, sedentary pastoralists, city workers. 200 to 1,000 meters. Hindu, Kabirpanthi.

MIRI ***(MISHING, MISING)*** [MRG] 400,000 (1998 BSI). Assam, North Lakhimpur, Dibrugarh, Sibsagar, Darrang districts; Arunachal Pradesh, a few villages near Pasighat. The Hill Miri are in Arunachal Pradesh, the Plain Miri are in Assam. Sino-Tibetan, Tibeto-Burman, North Assam, Tani. Idu may be a dialect. Bilingualism in Assamese. A Scheduled Tribe in India. Assamese and Devanagari scripts. Mountain slope, plains. Agriculturalists: shifting cultivation. Hindu, traditional religion.

MOINBA ***(MONBA, MOMPA, MONPA, MOMBA, MENBA, KHAMBA)*** [MOB] 46,000 in India (1997 IMA). Population total both countries 76,000. Arunachal Pradesh, Tawang and Kameng districts. Also spoken in China. Sino-Tibetan, Tibeto-Burman, Himalayish, Mahakiranti, Kiranti, Eastern. Dialects: MATCHOPA NAGNOO (BUT), CHUG, SANGLA (DIRANG), KALAKTANG, KISHPIGNAG (LISH), MONKIT (TAWANG). The Lish, But, and Chug dialects differ from the others, resembling Aka, Miji, and Sherdukpen languages. Officially recognized nationality in China. A Scheduled Tribe in India. 'Monpa' is used for Tshangla ('Central Monpa'), and other languages. May be the same as 'Memba'. Dictionary. Mountain slope. Agriculturalists. Lamaist Buddhist.

MRU ***(MRO, MURUNG, NIOPHENG, MRUNG)*** [MRO] 1,231 in India (1981 census). West Bengal, Nadia and Hoogly districts. Sino-Tibetan, Tibeto-Burman, Mru. SOV. Traditional religion with some Buddhist elements. NT 1994. See main entry under Bangladesh.

MUKHA-DORA ***(REDDI-DORA, CONTA-REDDI, REDDI, RIDDI, NOOKA DORA, MUKHA DHORA)*** [MMK] 17,456 (1981 census). Andhra Pradesh, Visakhapatnam, Srikakulam, Vizianagaram districts. Unclassified. Possibly Dravidian. May be a dialect of Telugu. A Scheduled Tribe in India. Reported that they speak Telugu as mother tongue. Agriculturalists: shifting cultivation. Hindu.

MUNDARI ***(MANDARI, MUNARI, MUNDA, MONDARI, HORO, COLH)*** [MUW] 2,069,000 in India (1997 IMA), including 1,022,000 Mundari, 519,000 Munda, 528,000 Bhumij. Population total all countries 2,075,000 or more. Assam; Bihar, mainly in southern and western parts of Ranchi District; Himachal Pradesh; Madhya Pradesh; Orissa; Tripura; West Bengal; Andaman and Nicobar Islands. Also spoken in Bangladesh, Nepal. Austro-Asiatic, Munda, North Munda, Kherwari, Mundari. Dialects: HASADA', LATAR, NAGURI, KERA', BHUMIJ (SADAR BHUMIJ, BHUMIJ MUNDA, BHUMIJ THAR). Related to Ho and Santali, but a separate language. 75% intelligibility with Ho. 70% to 84% lexical similarity with Bhumij. There is Bhumij literature and a Bhumij Society. A Scheduled Tribe in India. Investigation needed: intelligibility with Ho, Mundari of Ranchi, Mundari of Mayurbhanj, Bhumij. Literacy rate in first language: 10% to 30%. Literacy rate in second language: 50% to 75%. Plateau. Agriculturalists. 2,000 feet. Traditional religion, Hindu. Bible 1910-1932.

MURIA, EASTERN [EMU] Madhya Pradesh, Northeastern Bastar District, northwestern Koraput District. Dravidian, South-Central, Gondi-Kui, Gondi. Dialects: RAIGARH, LANJODA. 95% intelligibility between dialects; 73% to 83% of Western Muria; 19% to 34% of Northern Gondi; 35% of Dandami Maria. All domains. All ages. Speakers are called 'Muria'. A Scheduled Tribe in India. Degraded forest, tropical forest. Plains, hills. Swidden agriculturalists, peasant agriculturalists, hunter-gatherers. Traditional religion, Hindu.

MURIA, FAR WESTERN [FMU] Maharashtra, northern Garhichiroli District, Kurkhed Taluk. Dravidian, South-Central, Gondi-Kui, Gondi. 79% to 88% intelligibility of other Muria languages; 74% of Dandami Maria, 0% to 34% of Northern Gondi, 6% to 50% of Southern Gondi, 2% to 70% of Maria. All domains. All ages. Speakers are called 'Muria' or 'Gond'. A Scheduled Tribe in India. Degraded forest, tropical forest. Plains, hills. Swidden agriculturalists, peasant agriculturalists, hunter-gatherers. Traditional religion, Hindu.

MURIA, WESTERN ***(JHORIA, MUDIA, MURIA GONDI)*** [MUT] 12,898 (1971 census). Madhya Pradesh, northern and western Bastar District. Dravidian, South-Central, Gondi-Kui, Gondi. Dialects: SONAPAL, BANCHAPAI, DHANORA. 80% to 96% intelligibility among dialects, 69% to 73% with Eastern Muria; 51% to 78% with Far Western Muria. Not inherently intelligible with Dandami Maria, Northern Gondi, Southern Gondi, or Maria. All domains. All ages. Speakers are called 'Muria'. A Scheduled Tribe in India. Degraded forest, tropical forest. Plains, hills. Swidden agriculturalists, peasant agriculturalists, hunter-gatherers. Traditional religion, Hindu.

MUTHUVAN ***(MUDAVAN, MUDUVAR, MUDUGAR, MUTUVAR, MUDUVAN, MUDUVA)*** [MUV] 12,219 (1981 census). Andhra Pradesh; Kerala, Calicut, Cannanore, Ernakulam, Kottayam, and Trichur districts; Tamil Nadu, Coimbatore District, Anaimalai Hills. One source says the Mudugar live in Kerala, Palghat District, Pudar and Agali panchayats. Dravidian, Unclassified. 80% intelligibility with Malayalam. A Scheduled Tribe in India. Tropical forest. Mountain slope. Hunter-gatherers, agriculturalists. Hindu.

NAGA PIDGIN ***(NAGAMESE, NAGA-ASSAMESE, NAGA CREOLE ASSAMESE, KACHARI BENGALI, BODO)*** [NAG] Used by most of the 500,000 speakers of 29 Naga languages as second language (1989 J. Holm). Nagaland, especially Kohima District, Dimapur Subdivision; bordering areas of Arunachal Pradesh. Creole, Assamese based. A variety farthest from Assamese is spoken by the Yimchenger Naga, and varieties closest to Assamese by the Angami Naga, and around Dimapur and Kohima. Mother tongue for the Kachari in and around Dimapur, a small community, and among children of interethnic marriages. Classroom textbooks (1992). Trade language. Grammar. An official medium of instruction in schools. Mountains.

NAGA, ANGAMI ***(GNAMEI, NGAMI, ANGAMIS, TSOGHAMI, TSUGUMI, MONR, TSANGLO, TENDYDIE)*** [NJM] 109,000 (1997 IMA). Western Nagaland, Kohima District; Manipur; Maharashtra. Sino-Tibetan, Tibeto-Burman, Kuki-Chin-Naga, Naga, Angami-Pochuri. Dialects: KOHIMA, DZUNA, KEHENA, KHONOMA, CHAKROMA (WESTERN ANGAMI), MIMA, NALI, MOZOME, TENGIMA, TENYIDIE (TENYIDYE). Kohima dialect is now standard Angami. Naga Chokri and Naga Kezhama are eastern Angami groups with their own dialects. A Scheduled Tribe in India. Trade language. Roman script. Christian (1981 census). Bible 1970.

NAGA, AO ***(AORR, PAIMI, CHOLIMI, NOWGONG, HATIGORIA, URI, AO)*** [NJO] 141,000 (1997 IMA). Northeastern Nagaland, central Mokokchung District, Assam. Sino-Tibetan, Tibeto-Burman, Kuki-Chin-Naga, Naga, Ao. Dialects: MONGSEN KHARI, CHANGKI, CHONGLI (CHUNGLI), DORDAR (YACHAM), LONGLA. A Scheduled Tribe in India. Christian (1981 census). Bible 1964.

NAGA, CHANG ***(CHANG, MOJUNG, MACHONGRR, MOCHUMI, MOCHUNGRR, CHANGYANGUH)*** [NBC] 31,000 (1997 IMA). Assam; east central Nagaland, Tunsang District. Sino-Tibetan, Tibeto-Burman, Jingpho-Konyak-Bodo, Konyak-Bodo-Garo, Konyak. Close to Wancho Naga. Christian (1981 census), traditional religion. NT 1982.

NAGA, CHOKRI ***(EASTERN ANGAMI, CHAKRIMA NAGA, CHAKRU, CHOKRI, CHAKHESANG)*** [NRI] 20,000 (1991). Nagaland, Cheswezumi is the main village. Sino-Tibetan, Tibeto-Burman, Kuki-Chin-Naga, Naga, Angami-Pochuri. Some bilingual ability in Angami Naga and English. An eastern Angami tribe with its own language. Chokri, Khezha, and Sangtam-Pochuri make up the Chakhesang Naga community (see separate entries). Chakhesang Naga is a Scheduled Tribe in India. Literacy rate in second language: 27% English or Angami Naga. Tropical forest. Mountain slope. Agricultural, mixed commerce. Christian, traditional religion.

NAGA, CHOTHE ***(CHOTHE, CHOWTE, CHAWTE)*** [NCT] 2,852 (1988 Y. Hunem CNBA). Southeast Manipur, Chandel District; Nagaland, near Myanmar border. Sino-Tibetan, Tibeto-Burman, Kuki-Chin-Naga, Kuki-Chin, Northern. Closest to Tarao Naga. Bilingualism in Meitei. A Scheduled Tribe in India. Roman and Bengali scripts. Agriculturalists. Christian (1981 census).

NAGA, KABUI ***(KABUI, KAPWI, KOBOI, KUBAI)*** [NKF] 48,268 (1994). Manipur, Imphal city, Satar Hills, Nagaland; Assam. Sino-Tibetan, Tibeto-Burman, Kuki-Chin-Naga, Naga, Zeme. Close to Rongmei Naga, but not inherently intelligible to speakers. Manipuri and English are languages of instruction at school. Manipuri Bible is difficult for Kabui speakers to understand well. Spoken at home. Children learn it first. Speakers want Kabui to be written. Speakers are known as 'Inbui'. Winemakers. Christian.

NAGA, KHEZHA ***(KEZAMI, KHEZHAMA, KHEZHA)*** [NKH] 23,000 (1997 IMA). Eastern Nagaland, Kohima District, Khezhakhonoma. Sino-Tibetan, Tibeto-Burman, Kuki-Chin-Naga, Naga, Angami-Pochuri. An eastern Angami group with its own language. Bilingualism in Angami Naga. The speakers of Khezha belong to the Chakhesang Naga community. Investigation needed: bilingual proficiency in Angami Naga. Grammar.

NAGA, KHIAMNIUNGAN ***(KHIAMNGAN, KHIAMNIUNGAN, KHIENMUNGAN, KHEMUNGAN, KEMMUNGAM, KALYOKENGNYU, MAKWARE, NOKAW, PARA, PONYO, AOSHEDD, WELAM)*** [NKY] 25,000 in India (1997 IMA). Population total both countries 25,000 or more. Nagaland, east central part of Tuensang District. Also spoken in Myanmar. Sino-Tibetan, Tibeto-Burman,

Jingpho-Konyak-Bodo, Konyak-Bodo-Garo, Konyak. A divergent member of the Konyak subgroup. In Myanmar the alternate names are Makware, Nokaw, Para, Ponyo, and Welam. A Scheduled Tribe in India. SOV. Christian (mainly). NT 1981.

NAGA, KHOIBU MARING ***(KHOIBU, KHOIBU MARING)*** [NKB] 20,000 (1987 A. Hongsha). Manipur, southeast, Laiching. Sino-Tibetan, Tibeto-Burman, Kuki-Chin-Naga, Naga, Tangkhul. NT 1988.

NAGA, KHOIRAO ***(KHOIRAO, KOIRAO, KOLYA, MAYANGKHANG, MIYANG-KHANG, NGARI, THANGGAL, THANGAL, TUKAIMI)*** [NKI] 20,000 (1992 K. Tombing). North Manipur, Senapati District, hill ranges of East and West Sadar Hills subdivisions. Most are east of Barak Valley groups. 250 square miles. Sino-Tibetan, Tibeto-Burman, Kuki-Chin-Naga, Naga, Zeme. A Scheduled Tribe in India. Literacy rate in second language: 90% Meitei, English. Roman and Bengali scripts. Mountain slope. Agriculturalists. Christian (1981 census). NT, in press (1998).

NAGA, KONYAK ***(KANYAK, KONYAK)*** [NBE] 105,000 (1997 IMA). Assam, Sibsagar District; northeast Nagaland, Mon District. Sino-Tibetan, Tibeto-Burman, Jingpho-Konyak-Bodo, Konyak-Bodo-Garo, Konyak. Dialects: ANGPHANG, HOPAO, CHANGNYU, CHEN, CHINGKAO, CHINGLANG, CHOHA, GELEKIDORIA, JAKPHANG, KONGON, LONGCHING, LONGKHAI, LONGMEIN, LONGWA, MOHUNG, TABLENG, MON, MULUNG, NGANGCHING, SANG, SHANLANG, SHUNYUO, SHENGHA, SIMA, SOWA, SHAMNYUYANGA, TABU, TAMKHUNGNYUO, TANG, TOBUNYUO, TOLAMLEINYUA, TOTOK. Tableng is standard dialect spoken in Wanching and Wakching. Close to Phom Naga. A Scheduled Tribe in India. Literacy rate in first language: 13% (1994 Singh). Roman script. Hunter-gatherers, agriculturalists. Christian (1981 census). Bible 1992.

NAGA, LIANGMAI ***(LIYANG, LIANGMAI, LYENGMAI, LIANGMEI, LYANGMAY)*** [NJN] 20,000 (1997 BSI). Nagaland, upper Barak Valley. Sino-Tibetan, Tibeto-Burman, Kuki-Chin-Naga, Naga, Zeme. Now merged ethnically with the Zeme and Rongmei Naga to form the Zeliang community. Bible, in press (1995).

NAGA, LOTHA ***(CHIZIMA, CHOIMI, HLOTA, LHOTA, MIKLAI, TSINDIR, LUTHA, LOTHA, TSONTSII)*** [NJH] 80,000 (1997 IMA). Nagaland, west central, Workha District. Sino-Tibetan, Tibeto-Burman, Kuki-Chin-Naga, Naga, Ao. Dialects: LIVE, TSONTSU, NDRENG, KYONG, KYO, KYON, KYOU. A Scheduled Tribe in India. Grammar. Christian (1981 census). Bible 1967.

NAGA, MAO ***(MAO, SPOWAMA, SOPVOMA, MAIKEL, MEMI, SOPFOMO, EMELA)*** [NBI] 81,000 (1997 IMA). Northwest Manipur; Nagaland. Sino-Tibetan, Tibeto-Burman, Kuki-Chin-Naga, Naga, Angami-Pochuri. Dialect: PAOMATA. Related to Angami. Mao is a Scheduled Tribe in India. Dictionary. Literacy rate in second language: 25% Meitei, English. Mountain slope. Hunter-gatherers, agriculturalists. Bible 1995.

NAGA, MARAM ***(MARAM)*** [NMA] 15,000 (1993 UBS). Assam; north Manipur, Barak Valley, 5 locations. Sino-Tibetan, Tibeto-Burman, Kuki-Chin-Naga, Naga, Zeme. A Scheduled Tribe in India. Christian (1981 census), traditional religion. NT, in press (1998).

NAGA, MARING ***(MARING)*** [NNG] 16,000 (1997 IMA). Manipur, southeast, Laiching. Sino-Tibetan, Tibeto-Burman, Kuki-Chin-Naga. Naga, Tangkhul. A Scheduled Tribe in India. Tropical forest. Mountain slope. Christian (mainly), traditional religion. NT, in press (1997).

NAGA, MELURI ***(MELURI, MELUORY, ANYO)*** [NLM] 4 (1961 census). Nagaland. Sino-Tibetan, Tibeto-Burman, Kuki-Chin-Naga, Naga, Angami-Pochuri. Called 'Eastern Rengma', but the Rengma speak a different language.

NAGA, MONSANG ***(MOSHANG, MONSHANG, MUSHANG, MAWSHANG)*** [NMH] 2,550 (1988 Th. Kotha MNBCA). Manipur, Chandel District; Northern Nagaland, near Myanmar border. Sino-Tibetan, Tibeto-Burman, Kuki-Chin-Naga, Kuki-Chin, Northern. Closest to Moyon Naga and Anal. Bilingualism in Meitei. A Scheduled Tribe in India. Roman script. Christian (1981 census).

NAGA, MOYON ***(MOYON, MAYON NAGA, MAYOL)*** [NMO] 2,970 (1988 W. Roel MYNBA). Nagaland, near Myanmar border; Manipur State, Chandel District. Sino-Tibetan, Tibeto-Burman, Kuki-Chin-Naga, Kuki-Chin, Northern. Related to Monsang Naga and Anal. A Scheduled Tribe in India. Bengali and Roman scripts. Agriculturalists: shifting cultivation. Christian (1981 census).

NAGA, MZIEME ***(MZIEME)*** [NME] 29,000 (1997 IMA). Southwestern Nagaland, northeast of Zeme. Sino-Tibetan, Tibeto-Burman, Kuki-Chin-Naga, Naga, Zeme. Different from Zeme Naga. Bible 1992.

NAGA, NOCTE ***(NOCTE, BORDURIA, JAIPURIA, PANIDURIA, MOHONGIA, NAMSANGIA)*** [NJB] 33,000 (1997 IMA). Northern Nagaland, Namsang, Jaipur in Lakhimpur district and neighboring parts of Tirap Division; southeastern Arunachal Pradesh, Tirap District; Assam. Sino-Tibetan, Tibeto-Burman, Jingpho-Konyak-Bodo, Konyak-Bodo-Garo, Konyak. Dialects: LAJU, PONTHAI, TOTCHA. Closely related to Tase Naga. A Scheduled Tribe in India. Literacy rate in second language: 11.7% (1971).

NAGA, NTENYI ***(NTENYI, NTHENYI)*** [NNL] 6,600 (1980 UBS). West central Nagaland, northern section of Rengma. Kotsenyu is chief village of Ntenyi. Sino-Tibetan, Tibeto-Burman, Kuki-Chin-Naga, Naga, Angami-Pochuri. A distinct language from Rengma. NT 1979.

NAGA, PHOM ***(PHOM, PHON, TAMLU NAGA, CHINGMENGU, TAMLU)*** [NPH] 34,000 (1997 IMA). Northeastern Nagaland, Tuensang District, Longleng subdivision, and Assiringia village. Sino-Tibetan, Tibeto-Burman, Jingpho-Konyak-Bodo, Konyak-Bodo-Garo, Konyak. Dialect: YONGYASHA. Closely related to Konyak. A Scheduled Tribe in India. Literacy rate in second language: 35% adults. Mountain slope. Hunter-gatherer. Christian (1981 census). NT 1978, in press (1997).

NAGA, POCHURI ***(POCHURI, POCHURY)*** [NPO] 13,000 (1997 IMA). Southeast Nagaland. All villages are in the Meluri subdivision of Phek District. Sino-Tibetan, Tibeto-Burman, Kuki-Chin-Naga, Naga, Angami-Pochuri. Close to Meluri. A Scheduled Tribe in India. Mountain slope. Hunter-gatherers. Christian, traditional religion. NT 1994.

NAGA, POUMEI ***(POUMEI, PAUMEI)*** [PMX] 51,000 (1997 IMA). Manipur. Sino-Tibetan, Tibeto-Burman, Kuki-Chin-Naga, Naga, Angami-Pochuri. Close to Mao. NT 1992.

NAGA, PUIMEI ***(PUIMEI)*** [NPU] 2,500 in Manipur (1991). Manipur; Assam. Sino-Tibetan, Tibeto-Burman, Kuki-Chin-Naga, Naga, Unclassified. Were assigned to be under the Rongmei. Christian, traditional religion.

NAGA, RENGMA ***(RENGMA, MOZHUMI, MOIYUI, MON, UNZA, NZONG, NZONYU, INJANG)*** [NRE] 34,000 including 21,000 in Southern Rengma (1997 IMA), 13,000 in Northen Rengma (1997 IMA). West central Nagaland; Assam; Manipur. Tseminyu is the main center for the principal dialect. Sino-Tibetan, Tibeto-Burman, Kuki-Chin-Naga, Naga, Angami-Pochuri. Dialects: KETENENEYU, AZONYU (NZONYU, SOUTHERN RENGMA). Southern Rengma and Northern Rengma are reported to be inherently unintelligible to each other's speakers. A Scheduled Tribe in India. Christian (1981 census). Bible, in press (1996).

NAGA, RONGMEI ***(MARUONGMAI, NRUANGHMEI, RONGMEI, RONGMAI)*** [NBU] 59,000 (1997 IMA). Northwest Manipur; Nagaland; Assam, Cachar District. Sino-Tibetan, Tibeto-Burman, Kuki-Chin-Naga, Naga, Zeme. Dialect: SONGBU. Songbu is the principal division of Rongmei. Merged with Zeme and Liangmei Naga to form the Zeliang community. Bible 1989.

NAGA, SANGTAM ***(SANGTAM, ISACHANURE, LOPHOMI)*** [NSA] 39,000 (1997 IMA). Southeast Nagaland. Sino-Tibetan, Tibeto-Burman, Kuki-Chin-Naga, Naga, Ao. Dialects: KIZARE, PIRR (NORTHERN SANGTAM), PHELONGRE, THUKUMI (CENTRAL SANGTAM), PHOTSIMI, PURR (SOUTHERN SANGTAM). Kizare spoken north of Meluri. It is not known how much it differs from other Sangtam. Chokri, Khezha, and Sangtam-Pochuri make up the Chakhsang Naga community. A Scheduled Tribe in India. Literacy rate in second language: 20% Assamese, English. Kizare: woodwork. Christian (mainly), traditional religion. Bible 1995.

NAGA, SUMI ***(SEMA, SIMI, SUMI)*** [NSM] 132,000 (1997 IMA). Central and southern Nagaland; Assam. Dayang is by the Dayang River. Sino-Tibetan, Tibeto-Burman, Kuki-Chin-Naga, Naga, Angami-Pochuri. Dialects: DAYANG (WESTERN SUMI), LAZEMI, ZHIMOMI, ZUMOMI. A Scheduled Tribe in India. Literacy rate in second language: 50% Assamese, English. Agriculturalists. Christian (mainly), traditional religion. Bible 1985.

NAGA, TANGKHUL ***(TANGKHUL, TAGKHUL, THANGKHULM, CHAMPHUNG, LUHUPPA, LUPPA, SOMRA)*** [NMF] 110,000 (1997 IMA). Manipur, Ukhrul District; Nagaland; Tripura. Sino-Tibetan, Tibeto-Burman, Kuki-Chin-Naga, Naga, Tangkhul. Dialects: UKHRUL, KHUNGGOI, KHANGOI, KUPOME, PHADANG. Ukhrul is principal dialect. A Scheduled Tribe in India. Literacy rate in second language: 70% Meitei, English. Mountain slope, plains. Agriculturalists. Christian (1981 census). Bible 1976, in press (1998).

NAGA, TARAO ***(TARAO, TARAU, TARAOTRONG)*** [TRO] 570 (1988 K. Mohon TRNBA). Southeast Manipur. Sino-Tibetan, Tibeto-Burman, Kuki-Chin-Naga, Kuki-Chin, Northern. Closest to Chothe Naga, 70% intelligibility. Literacy rate in second language: 30% Meitei, English. Agriculturalists. Christian.

NAGA, TASE ***(TASEY, TANGSA, RANGPAN, CHAM CHANG)*** [NST] 17,000 in India (1997 IMA). Population total both countries 17,000 or more. Southeastern Arunachal Pradesh, Changlang District. Also spoken in Myanmar. Sino-Tibetan, Tibeto-Burman, Jingpho-Konyak-Bodo, Konyak-Bodo-Garo, Konyak. Dialects: LONGPHI, YOGLI, HAVE, KHEMSING, LUNGCHANG, LUNGRI, MOKLUM, PONTHAI, RONGRANG, RONRANG, TAIPI, TIKHAK, SANKE (SHANGGE), SANGCHE. Some dialects are widely divergent. Close to Nocte Naga. 'Tase' is the name of the language; 'Tangsa' of the people. 'Tangsa' means 'hill people'. A Scheduled Tribe in India. SOV. Literacy rate in second language: 20%. Traditional religion, Christian (some). NT 1992.

NAGA, WANCHO ***(WANCHO, BANPARA NAGA, JOBOKA)*** [NNP] 45,000 (1997 IMA). Assam; Nagaland; southeastern Arunachal Pradesh, Tirap District. Sino-Tibetan, Tibeto-Burman, Jingpho-Konyak-Bodo, Konyak-Bodo-Garo, Konyak. Dialects: CHANGNOI, BOR MUTHUN (BOR MUTONIA), HORU MUTHUN, KULUNG MUTHUN (MITHAN). Close to Chang Naga. The younger generation speaks Hindi or Assamese as second language. A Scheduled Tribe in India. Literacy rate in second language: Low. Roman and Devanagari scripts. Swidden agriculturalists. Traditional religion. Bible portions.

NAGA, YIMCHUNGRU ***(YIMCHUNGRU, YIMCHUNGER, YIMCHUNGRE, TOZHUMA, YACHUMI)*** [YIM] 37,000 (1997 IMA). Nagaland, northern between Namchik and Patkoi, Tuensang District. Sino-Tibetan, Tibeto-Burman, Kuki-Chin-Naga, Naga, Ao. Dialects: TIKHIR, WAI, CHIRR, MINIR, PHERRONGRE, YIMCHUNGRU. The last three dialects listed are southern. A Scheduled Tribe in India. Christian (1981 census). NT 1981-1989.

NAGA, ZEME ***(KACHCHA, KACHA, KUTCHA, MEZAMA, SANGRIMA, SENGIMA, ARUNG, EMPUI, JEME, ZEMI)*** [NZM] 27,000 (1994 IMA). Manipur; Nagaland; Assam, large upper Barak Valley. Sino-Tibetan, Tibeto-Burman, Kuki-Chin-Naga, Naga, Zeme. Dialects: PAREN, NJAUNA. Called 'Zeliang' together with Liangmei and Rongmei. A Scheduled Tribe in India. NT 1978-1992.

NAGARCHAL ***(NAGAR, NAGARCHI)*** [NBG] 7,090 (1971 census). Madhya Pradesh; Maharashtra; Rajasthan. Dravidian, South-Central, Gondi-Kui, Gondi.

NAHARI ***(NAHALI)*** [NHH] 108 (1961 census). Madhya Pradesh, Raipur, Bilaspur districts; Orissa, Sambalpur District. Indo-European, Indo-Iranian, Indo-Aryan, Eastern zone, Bengali-Assamese. A more divergent variety, related to Halbi. A Scheduled Tribe in India. Singh 1994 reports they speak Nimadi as mother tongue.

NEPALI ***(NEPALESE, GORKHALI, GURKHALI, KHASKURA, PARBATIYA, EASTERN PAHARI)*** [NEP] 6,000,000 in India (1984 Far Eastern Economic Review). West Bengal, Darjeeling area; Assam; Arunachal Pradesh; Bihar; Haryana; Himachal Pradesh; Uttar Pradesh. Indo-European, Indo-Iranian, Indo-Aryan, Northern zone, Eastern Pahari. Dialects: GORKHALI, PALPA, NEPALI. People are called 'Paharia'. Literacy rate in first language: 30% to 100%. Literacy rate in second language: 25% to 75%. Hindu. Bible 1914-1978. See main entry under Nepal.

NEWARI [NEW] Some in Bettiah, Bihar. Sino-Tibetan, Tibeto-Burman, Himalayish, Mahakiranti, Newari. NT 1986. See main entry under Nepal.

NICOBARESE, CAR ***(PU, CAR)*** [CAQ] 30,000 (1997 IMA). North Nicobar Islands, Car Island. Austro-Asiatic, Mon-Khmer, Nicobar, Car. A Scheduled Tribe in India. Bible 1969.

NICOBARESE, CENTRAL ***(NICOBAR)*** [NCB] 2,200 (1981), 800 Nancowry, 1,400 closely related dialects (1981 Radhakrishnan). 22,100 in all six Nicobarese languages (1981 Wurm and Hattori). Nicobar Islands, Katchal, Camorta, Nancowry, and Trinket islands. Austro-Asiatic, Mon-Khmer, Nicobar, Nancowry. Dialects: CAMORTA (KAMORTA), KATCHAL (KACHEL, TEHNU), NANCOWRY (NANCOURY), TRINKUT (TRINKAT). Car, Chaura, Shom Peng, Southern Nicobarese, and Teressa are separate but closely related languages. Bible portions 1884-1890.

NICOBARESE, SOUTHERN ***(NICOBARA)*** [NIK] Nicobar Islands, Little Nicobar and outer Great Nicobar islands. Austro-Asiatic, Mon-Khmer, Nicobar, Great Nicobar. Dialects: CONDUL, GREAT NICOBAR, LITTLE NICOBAR, MILO.

NIHALI ***(NIHAL, NAHALI, NAHAL, KALTO, NAHALE)*** [NHL] 5,000 (1987). Madhya Pradesh, Khandwa District, mainly around Temi (Tembi) village in Nimar District; Maharashtra, Buldana, Akola, Amravati, Jalgaon districts; 12 hamlets around Toranmal. Language Isolate. Nahale north of Amalwadi in Jalgaon District speak a language similar to Ahirani (Indo-European). Nihali and Nahali may be different languages. Nihal in Chikaldara taluk and Akola District have 25% lexical similarity with Korku (Munda). Nahal near Toranmal have 51% to 73% lexical similarity with several Bhil languages (Indo-European). They live in or near Korku villages, and identify closely with the Korku. Investigation needed: intelligibility with nearby Bhili languages, bilingual proficiency in Korku (Munda), Hindi, Marathi. Tropical forest. Mountain slope.

NIMADI ***(NEMADI, NIMARI, NIMIADI)*** [NOE] 1,359,000 (1997 IMA). Madhya Pradesh; Uttar Pradesh; Maharashtra. Indo-European, Indo-Iranian, Indo-Aryan, Central zone, Rajasthani, Unclassified. Dialect: BHUANI. Investigation needed: intelligibility with Malvi, Bhil of Maheshwar Tahsil Khargone District, Mhow Tahsil Indore District, east Dhar District, Madhya Pradesh.

NISI ***(DAFLA, DAPHLA, NISSI, NISHI, NYISING, NYISHI, BANGNI, LEL)*** [DAP] 261,000 (1997 IMA). Assam, Darrang District; Arunachal Pradesh, Subansiri District. Sino-Tibetan, Tibeto-Burman, North Assam, Tani. Dialects: AKA LEL, TAGIN, NISHANG. Related to Apatani, Adi, Yano, possibly Lepcha. Tagin may be a separate language. Apatani may be a dialect of Nisi. Nishi and Tagin are both Scheduled Tribes in India. 'Nishi' has been used as a cover term for the western Tani languages. Investigation needed: intelligibility with Tagin, Apatani. Literacy rate in second language: 10% Assamese. Agriculturalists: shifting cultivation. Traditional religion. NT, in press (1998).

NUKA-DORA [NUK] Andhra Pradesh, near Adiwasi Oriya. Dravidian, South-Central, Gondi-Kui, Konda-Kui, Konda. Bilingualism in Adiwasi Oriya. Speakers live scattered throughout the Adiwasi Oriya area. Speakers and language are called Nuka-Dora. Distinct from Mukha-Dora.

OKO-JUWOI ***(OKU-JUWOI, JUWOI, JUNOI)*** [OKJ] Andaman Islands, west central and southwest interior Middle Andaman Island. Andamanese, Great Andamanese, Central. Extinct.

ÖNGE ***(ONG)*** [OON] 96 (1997 CIIL). Southern Andaman Islands, Dugong Creek and South Bay islands. Andamanese, South Andamanese. A distinct language from Sentinelese. Speakers are mainly monolingual. Reserved toward outsiders. A Scheduled Tribe in India. Dictionary. Hunter-gatherers, fishermen. Traditional religion.

ORIYA ***(URIYA, UTKALI, ODRI, ODRUM, OLIYA, ORISSA, VADIYA, YUDHIA)*** [ORY] 31,666,000 in India (1997 IMA). Population total both countries 32,000,000. Orissa; Bihar; West Bengal; Assam; Andhra Pradesh. Also spoken in Bangladesh. Indo-European, Indo-Iranian, Indo-Aryan, Eastern zone, Oriya. Dialects: MUGHALBANDI (ORIYA PROPER, STANDARD ORIYA), SOUTHERN ORIYA, BHATRI, NORTHWESTERN ORIYA, WESTERN ORIYA (SAMBALPURI), NORTH BALASORE ORIYA, MIDNAPORE ORIYA, HALBI, KORAPUT ORIYA (DESIA ORIYA). Some of the larger dialects have many subdialects. Sambalpuri around Sambalpur and Sundargh needs intelligibility testing with Standard Oriya. Spoken as mother tongue by the Bathudi, Bhuiya, some Koda, and the Mali. Investigation needed: intelligibility with Sambalpuri, other dialects. National language. Literacy rate in first language: 30% to 60%. Literacy rate in second language: 25% to 50%. Oriya script. Hindu. Bible 1815-1998.

ORIYA, ADIVASI ***(TRIBAL ORIYA, DESIYA, DESIA, DESHIA, KOTIYA, KOTIA ORIYA, ADIWASI ORIYA)*** [ORT] 300,000 mother tongue speakers, 150,000 in Andhra Pradesh, 150,000 in Orissa (1991 U. Gustafsson), 200,000 second language users (1998 U. Gustafsson). Andhra Pradesh, Visakhapatnam District, Araku Valley; Orissa, Koraput District. Indo-European, Indo-Iranian, Indo- Aryan, Eastern zone, Oriya. Dialects: ADIVASI ORIYA, VALMIKI ADIVASI ORIYA. Andhra Pradesh varieties 38% to 42% lexical similarity with Standard Oriya; 80% to 85% with Desiya dialects in Orissa. Kotia is a Scheduled Tribe in India. The language is called 'Adivasi Oriya' (Tribal Oriya); the people are called 'Kotia'. The name 'Adivasi Oriya' is used in Andhra Pradesh; 'Desiya' in Koraput District. Trade language. Dictionary. Literacy rate in first language: 7.3%. Literacy materials for Orissa in Oriya script needed. Current materials in Telugu script. Telugu script used in Andhra Pradesh; 100,000 Tribal Oriya speakers in Orissa use Oriya script. Agriculturalists, mixed commerce. Traditional religion, Hindu, Christian. Bible portions 1977-1982.

PAHARI, KULLU ***(KULUI, KULLUI, KAULI, KULU BOLI, KULU PAHARI, PAHARI, PAHARI KULLU, PHARI KULU, KULVI, KULWALI)*** [KFX] 109,000 in Kullu (1997 IMA). 2,173,000 all Pahari (1997 IMA). Himachal Pradesh, Kullu District. Indo-European, Indo-Iranian, Indo-Aryan, Northern zone, Western Pahari. Dialects: INNER SIRAGI (INNER SERAJI, SIRAGI, SIRAJI, SARAJI), KLLUI, OUTER SERAJI. Dialects are inherently intelligible. Inner Siraji is apparently different from Siraji-Kashmiri. 85% lexical similarity or higher among dialects. Limited bilingualism in Hindi. Panjabi, Urdu, Lahuli, and Nepali are also used. Dictionary. Literacy program needed. Devanagari script. Radio programs. Mountain slope. Bible portions 1932-1980.

PAHARI, MAHASU ***(MAHASUI)*** [BFZ] 500,000 (1992 estimate), including 3,976 Baghati (1961 census). Himachal Pradesh, Shimla (Simla) and Solan districts. Indo-European, Indo-Iranian, Indo- Aryan, Northern zone, Western Pahari. Dialects: LOWER MAHASU PAHARI (KIUNTHALI, SIRMAURI, BAGHATI, BAGHLIANI), UPPER MAHASU PAHARI (SHIMLA SIRAJI, SODOCHI, RAMPURI, ROHRURI). The Kiunthali subdialect appears to be understood by speakers of the other varieties, and their attitude toward it is favorable. The Rampuri subdialect is also called 'Kochi'; the Rohrui subdialect also called 'Soracholi'. Intelligibility among dialects is above 85%. 74% to 82% lexical similarity among upper dialects, 74% to 95% among lower dialects. Bilingual level estimates for Hindi are 0 0%, 1 40%, 2 30%, 3 15%, 4 10%, 5 5%. Hindi is used as second language with non-Pahari speakers. Those with more than 5 years of schooling are more proficient. Used at home and in religion. All ages. Speakers are called 'Pahari'. Investigation needed: intelligibility with dialects. Dictionary. SOV, postpositions, genitives after noun heads, nontonal. Literacy rate in second language: Less than 40% in Hindi. Radio programs. Mountain slope, valleys. Peasant agriculturalists. Hindu (majority), Muslim (small), Christian (small).

PALI [PLL] Also spoken in Myanmar, Sri Lanka. Indo-European, Indo-Iranian, Indo-Aryan, Unclassified. Used as the literary language of the Buddhist scriptures. Buddhist. Extinct. NT 1835.

PALIYAN ***(PALAYA, PALAYAN, PALIYAR, PALLIYAR, POLIYAR, PALLEYAN, PALANI, MAKKAL, MALAI, SERAMAR)*** [PCF] 5,438 (1981 census). Kerala, Idukki District; Tamil Nadu, Nadyraum Tahavur, Pudukkotai, Tiruneveli, Coimbatore districts. Dravidian, Southern, Tamil-Kannada, Tamil-Kodagu, Tamil-Malayalam, Malayalam. A Scheduled Tribe in India. It is reported that they speak Tamil as mother tongue (Singh 1994). Agriculturalists, plantation laborers. Traditional religion, Hindu.

PANCHPARGANIA ***(TAMARIA, TAIR, TAMARA, TEMORAL, TUMARIYA, TANTI, CHIK BARIK, BEDIA, PAN, PAN SAWASI)*** [TDB] 274,000 (1997 IMA). Bihar, Ranchi, Singhbhum districts; West Bengal. Indo-European, Indo-Iranian, Indo-Aryan, Eastern zone, Bihari. Related to Sadri. Possibly the same as Kudmali. Spoken by the Bedia of Bihar and Chik Barik of West Bengal. Traditional religion.

PANGWALI ***(PAHARI, PANGI, PANGWALI PAHARI)*** [PGG] 17,000 (1997 IMA). Himachal Pradesh, Lahul-Spiti District, Udaipur down the Chenab (Chandra-Bhaga) River to the Chamba border at Purthi, and possibly from Tandi to the Sanch Pass. Another dialect over the pass; Chamba District, Pangi Tahsil. Indo-European, Indo-Iranian, Indo-Aryan, Northern zone, Western Pahari. Reported to be nearly the same as Bhadrawahi. 64% inherent intelligibility of Mandeali, 52% of Kangri, 44% of

Chambeali. 55% lexical similarity with Hindi, 77% with Kullui Pahari. Hindi is the language of education and government; it is used as second language by men who have travelled, anyone with 5th grade education or higher, some women who have an educated person in the home. Second language Hindi speakers can handle marketing in Hindi, and some men can discuss common topics. Those with a college education have learned English, and speak it outside Pangi and in educated circles. Speakers are called 'Pangwala' or 'Pangi'. A Scheduled Tribe in India. Investigation needed: intelligibility with Bhadrawah. Literacy rate in second language: 9% men, 1% women. In 1981 9% of the men had a 5th grade education, 1% of the women; 3% of the men had an 8th grade education, .3% of the women. In 1987 Pangi had 40 primary schools, 4 middle schools, 4 high schools. Alpine forest. Mountain slope. Agriculturalists: wheat, barley, maize, ragi, millet, potatoes, pulses; animal husbandry: cattle, yaks, sheep, goats. 5,000 to 12,000 feet. Hindu.

PANIYA ***(PANIA, PANIYAN, PANYAH, NIL)*** [PCG] 63,827 (1981 census) including 56,952 in Kerala, 6,393 in Tamil Nadu, 482 in Karnataka. Kerala, Wynad, Kozhikode, Cannanore, Malapuram districts; Tamil Nadu, west of Nilgiris Hillls; Karnataka. Dravidian, Southern, Tamil-Kannada, Tamil-Kodagu, Tamil-Malayalam, Malayalam. Intelligibility of Malappura Paniya by Kodagu is 66%. Dialects have 79% to 88% lexical similarity with Malappura Paniya, Kodagu has 71%. State languages: Malayalam, Tamil, or Kannada used with non-Paniya speakers. Paniya used with Paniya speakers at home and for religion. Christians pray in Malayalam. A Scheduled Tribe in India. Investigation needed: intelligibility with Kodagu. Literacy rate in second language: 11% (1981 census). Malayalam in Kerala, Tamil in Tamil Nadu, Kannada in Karnataka. Forest. Mountain slope, hills, coast. Agricultural workers, woodcutters, fishermen. Hindu, traditional religion, Christian.

PANJABI, EASTERN ***(PUNJABI, GURMUKHI, GURUMUKHI)*** [PNJ] 27,125,000 in India, including 26,975,000 Panjabi, 16,000 Majhi (1997 IMA), 134,000 Bhatneri (1991 IMA). Population total all countries 27,125,000 or more. Punjab, Majhi in Gurdaspur and Amritsar districts, Bhatyiana in South Ferozepore District; Rajasthan, Bhatyiana in north Ganganagar District; Haryana; Delhi; Jammu and Kashmir. Also spoken in Bangladesh, Canada, Fiji, Kenya, Malaysia, Mauritius, Singapore, UAE, United Kingdom, USA. Indo-European, Indo-Iranian, Indo-Aryan, Central zone, Panjabi. Dialects: PANJABI PROPER, MAJHI, DOAB, BHATYIANA (BHATNERI, BHATTI), POWADHI, MALWA, BATHI. Western Panjabi is distinct from Eastern Panjabi, although there is a chain of dialects to Western Hindi (Urdu). Bhatyiana considered to be a mixture of Panjabi and Rajasthani. See separate entry for Dogri-Kangri. Gurumukhi is associated with Sikhs. Different from Majhi in India and Nepal. Investigation needed: intelligibility with dialects. National language. Grammar. Gurmukhi script, a variant of Devanagari; Bhatyiana uses Devanagari script. Sikh, Muslim (Bhatneri). Bible 1959-1984.

PANJABI, MIRPUR ***(MIRPURI)*** [PMU] 98 in Jammu and Kashmir (1961 census). Population total both countries 20,000 to 30,000 or more. Kashmir, Mirpur area, near Pakistan border. Also possibly in Pakistan. Also spoken in United Kingdom. Indo-European, Indo-Iranian, Indo-Aryan, Northwestern zone, Lahnda. Distinct from Western Panjabi, although closely related.

PANJABI, WESTERN ***(WESTERN PUNJABI, LAHNDA, LAHANDA, LAHNDI)*** [PNB] 52,000 in India (1991 IMA). Jammu and Kashmir; Delhi; Haryana. Indo-European, Indo-Iranian, Indo-Aryan, Northwestern zone, Lahnda. Dialect: MAJHI. There is a continuum of varieties between Eastern and Western Panjabi, and with Western Hindi and Urdu. 'Lahnda' is a name given earlier for Western Panjabi; an attempt to cover the dialect continuum between Hindko, Pahari-Potwari, and Western Panjabi in the north and Sindhi in the south. Several dozen dialects. Perso-Arabic script is used, but not often written in Pakistan. Films. Muslim; Christian. NT 1819-1952. See main entry under Pakistan.

PANKHU ***(PANKHO, PANKO, PANGKHU)*** [PKH] Population total all countries 2,278 or more. Mizoram. Also spoken in Bangladesh, Myanmar. Sino-Tibetan, Tibeto-Burman, Kuki-Chin-Naga, Kuki-Chin, Central. Tropical forest. Agriculturalists.

PAO ***(PABRA)*** [PPA] 7,223 (1981 census). Madhya Pradesh, Satna district. Sino-Tibetan, Tibeto-Burman, Unclassified. May not be Tibeto-Burman. Bilingualism in Hindi. A Scheduled Tribe in India. Singh 1994 reports they speak Bagheli as mother tongue. Agriculturalists. Hindu.

PARDHAN ***(PRADHAN, PRADHANI)*** [PCH] 116,919 (1981 census). Andhra Pradesh, Adilbad District; Madhya Pradesh, Seoni, Mandla, Chhindawara, Hoshangabad, Betual, Balaghat, Raipur, Bislapur districts; Maharashtra, Vidarbha region. Dravidian, South-Central, Gondi-Kui, Gondi. Probably more than 1 language. Most speak Hindi in Madhya Pradesh, Marathi in Maharashtra. Singh 1994 says Gondi is their mother tongue. Investigation needed: intelligibility with dialects. Agriculturalists. Hindu.

PARDHI ***(BAHELIA, CHITA PARDHI, LANGO PARDHI, PAIDIA, PARADI, PARIA, PHANS PARDHI, TAKANKAR, TAKIA)*** [PCL] 18,000 (1997 IMA). Andhra Pradesh; Madhya Pradesh; Gujarat; Maharashtra; scattered over wide area. Indo-European, Indo-Iranian, Indo-Aryan, Central zone, Bhil. Dialects: NEELISHIKARI, PITTALA BHASHA, TAKARI. Probably more than 1 language (Lango). Reported they speak Gujarati and Hindi as mother tongue in Madhya Pradesh. A Scheduled Tribe in

India, Scheduled Caste in Madhya Pradesh. Different from Paradhi, who speak Kachchi. Investigation needed: intelligibility with Lango, dialects. Plains. Hunter-gatherers, mixed commerce, agriculturalists.

PARENGA ***(PARENGI, PARENG, PARENGA PARJA, PARENJI, POROJA, GORUM, GORUM SAMA)*** [PCJ] 4,281 (1992 Albert). Orissa, Koraput District; Andhra Pradesh. Austro-Asiatic, Munda, South Munda, Koraput Munda, Sora-Juray-Gorum, Gorum. People are rapidly shifting to Adivasi Oriya. Reported as endangered by CIIL. Study being done at Telugu University. A Scheduled Tribe in India. Erroneously called Gadaba. Grammar.

PARSI ***(PARSEE)*** [PRP] 60,000 to 150,000 in India (1999). Population total all countries 230,000 or more. Gujarat; Maharashtra. Also reported to be in Australia, Bangladesh, Canada, Germany, Hong Kong, Kazakhstan, Kyrgyzstan, Malaysia, New Zealand, Singapore, Switzerland, Tajikistan, Uzbekistan, southern and western Africa, elsewhere in Europe. Also spoken in Pakistan, United Kingdom, USA. Indo-European, Indo-Iranian, Iranian, Western, Northwestern, Central Iran. Parsi is reported to not be inherently intelligible with Parsi-Dari, from whom they separated 600 to 700 years ago or more. Other reports say they came to India 1300 years ago. Related to Dari [GBZ] in Iran. Many are reported to not speak other languages well. 'Parsee' is the name of the ethnic group. Literacy rate in second language: 90% in English. Well educated. Zoroastrian.

PATTANI ***(MANCHATI, MANCHAD, PATNI, CHAMBA, CHAMBA LAHULI, LAHULI, SWANGLA, CHANGSAPA BOLI)*** [LAE] 11,000 mother tongue speakers, 5,000 second language speakers (1997). Himachal Pradesh, Lahul Valley, Pattan, Chamba-Lahul, and lower Mayar valleys. Sino-Tibetan, Tibeto-Burman, Himalayish, Tibeto-Kanauri, Western Himalayish, Kanauri. Dialects: CHAMBA-LAJULI (WESTERN PATTANI), EASTERN PATTANI, CENTRAL PATTANI. Western Pattani has 63% to 55% lexical similarity with Tinan Lahuli, 39% to 26% with Bunan, 37% with Shumcho, 35% with Jangshung, 33% with Sunam, 31% with Chitkuli and Kanauri, 25% with Puh and Kinnaur District varieties of Tibetan, 22% with Nesang, 18% with Lhasa Tibetan, 14% to 15% with the Spiti and Stod varieties of Tibetan. Hindi is the state language. Used in home, village, religion. Hindi is used in education and trade. Positive attitude toward Pattani. Lahaula and Swangla are both Scheduled Tribes in India. Language of wider communication. Literacy rate in second language: High. Poetry. Hindu. Bible portions 1907-1914.

PENGO ***(PENGU, HENGO)*** [PEG] 1,254 (1961 census). Orissa, Koraput District, Kashipur, Pappadahandi, Nowrangapur, and Nandapur tahsils, Kalahandi District. Dravidian, South-Central, Gondi-Kui, Konda-Kui, Manda-Kui, Manda-Pengo. Dialects: INDI, AWE, MANDA. They consider themselves to be separate from Jhodia Poraja. Agriculturalists: shifting cultivation. Traditional religion, Hindu.

PHAKE ***(PHAKIAL, PHAKEY, FAAKE)*** [PHK] Several thousand (A. Diller ANU 1990). Assam, villages along the Dihing River. Tai-Kadai, Kam-Tai, Be-Tai, Tai-Sek, Tai, Southwestern, East Central, Northwest. Similar to Shan of Myanmar.

PHUDAGI ***(VADVAL)*** [PHD] Maharashtra. Indo-European, Indo-Iranian, Indo-Aryan, Southern zone, Konkani. A more divergent dialect of, or closely related language to, Konkani.

PNAR [PBV] 84,000 (1991 IMA). Assam, Khasi and Jaintia Hills; Maehalaya; Mizoram, northern Aizawi District. Austro-Asiatic, Mon-Khmer, Northern Mon-Khmer, Khasian. Dialects: JAINTIA (SYNTENG), NONGTUNG. Formerly considered to be a dialect of Khasi, but it is separate. A Scheduled Tribe in India. Roman script. Radio programs. Hunter-gatherers. Christian.

PURIK ***(PURIGSKAD, BURIG, PURIG, PURKI, PURIK BHOTIA, BURIGSKAT)*** [BXR] 132,000 (1991 IMA). North Kashmir, Kargil District. Suru Valley is the main population center. It is the dominant group in Suru, a sizeable minority is in Dras Valley, and a minority is in the western Himalayas. Sino-Tibetan, Tibeto-Burman, Himalayish, Tibeto-Kanauri, Tibetic, Tibetan, Western. Closely related to Balti. Level of education and bilingual proficiency in Urdu is low. Uneducated men speak little Urdu. Dominant language in Kargil District. Women tend to speak only Purik. People are called 'Purig-pa'. 'Purig' means 'of Tibetan origin'. People prefer to be culturally and linguistically identified with Tibet, although religiously with Islam. A Scheduled Tribe in India. Persian-Arabic script of Urdu used unless they have been to the university. Almost totally Shi'a Muslim. NT 1950.

RABHA ***(RAVA)*** [RAH] 31,000 (1997 IMA). West Assam, Darrang, Goalpara, Kamrup districts; Nagaland; West Bengal, Jalpaiguri and Koch Bihar districts; Meghalaya, East Garo Hills District. Sino-Tibetan, Tibeto-Burman, Jingpho-Konyak-Bodo, Konyak-Bodo-Garo, Bodo-Garo, Koch. Dialects: MAITARIA, RANGDANIA. The majority of the ethnic group speak Assamese as mother tongue; the rest speak Rabha as mother tongue. A Scheduled Tribe in India. Dictionary. Assamese script. Agriculturalists: settled agriculturalists. NT, in press (1997).

RAJBANGSI ***(RAJBANSI, RAJBANSHI, TAJPURI)*** [RJB] 2,258,760 in India (1981 census). Population total all countries 2,350,000. West Bengal, Jalpaiguri, Cooch Behar, Darjeeling districts. Also spoken in Bangladesh, Nepal. Indo-European, Indo-Iranian, Indo-Aryan, Eastern zone, Bengali-Assamese. Dialect: BAHE. A Scheduled Caste in India. Singh 1994 says they speak Bengali as mother tongue. Agriculturalists. Hindu.

RALTE [RAL] 170 in India (1971 census). Assam; Mizoram, mainly Aizawi District, scattered in Lunglei and Chhimtuipui districts. Sino-Tibetan, Tibeto-Burman, Kuki-Chin-Naga, Kuki-Chin, Northern. Related to Tiddim, Paite, Thado, Zo. Bilingualism in Lushai. A Scheduled Tribe in India. A subgroup of the Mizo. SOV. Agriculturalists. Christian. See main entry under Myanmar.

RANGKAS [RGK] Uttar Pradesh, facing the Nepal border along the Mahakali Valley. Sino-Tibetan, Tibeto-Burman, Himalayish, Tibeto-Kanauri, Western Himalayish, Almora. Related to Darmiya, Chaudangsi, Byangsi. May only be in India. See main entry under Nepal.

RATHAWI ***(KOHELIA, BAL-LA)*** [RTW] 308,640 (1981 census). Gujarat, Baroda and Panchmahals districts. Indo-European, Indo-Iranian, Indo-Aryan, Central zone, Bhil. 76% intelligibility with Bhilali. There is a dialect continuum from Bhilali to Rathawa, but the extremes have limited intelligibility with each other. 83% lexical similarity with Bhilali. Bilingualism in Gujarati. A Scheduled Tribe in India. Investigation needed: intelligibility with dialects, Bareli, bilingual proficiency in Gujarati, attitudes. Literacy rate in second language: 12%, 21% males, 3% females. Agriculturalists. Hindu.

RAVULA ***(ADIYA, ADIYAN, YORUBA, YERAVA, PANJIRI YERAVA)*** [YEA] 27,413 (1981) including 19,261 Yerava in Karnataka (1981 census), and 8,152 Adiya in Kerala (1981 census). Karnataka, Coorg (Kodagu) District; Kerala, Wayanad and Cannanore districts. Dravidian, Southern, Tamil-Kannada, Tamil-Kodagu, Tamil-Malayalam, Malayalam. 93% to 94% dialect intelligibility between Yerava and Adiya. 83% to 98% lexical similarity among Yerava and Adiya varieties, 5% to 61% with Standard Malayalam, 35% to 40% with Badaga, 32% to 42% with Colloquial Kannada. Bilingual proficiency in Kannada (in Karnataka) and Malayalam (in Kerala) is limited. Vigorous. Language attitudes positive toward Ravula. Speakers are called 'Ravula' or 'Panjiri Yerava' in Karnataka, and 'Ravula' or 'Adiya' in Kerala. They prefer 'Ravula' in both places. Adiyan are a Scheduled Tribe in Karnataka and Tamil Nadu. Yerava is a Scheduled Tribe in Karnataka. Investigation needed: attitudes toward Kerala on Panjiri Yerava, scripts. Literacy rate in second language: 6.35%, male 8.62%, female 4% (Karnataka); 15%, Male 21%, female 9.3% (Kerala). Literacy program needed in 2 scripts. Good motivation for literature, literacy. Kannada script, Karnataka; Malayalam script, Kerala. Tropical forest. Hills. Agricultural workers. 700 to 2,100 meters. Hindu (mainly), Muslim, Buddhist, Christian.

RAWANG ***(NUNG RAWANG, GANUNG-RAWANG, HKANUNG, NUMG, KRANGKU, TARON, KIUTZE, CH'OPA, CHIUTSE)*** [RAW] The Kunlang dialect is in India. Sino-Tibetan, Tibeto-Burman, Nungish. Dialect: KUNLANG. 75 to 100 'dialects', some of which are inherently unintelligible to each other's speakers. Five major divisions: Longmi, Mutwang, Serwang, Tangsarr, Kwinpang (Nung); each has 20 to 30 subdialects. Kunglang is in India; communication with Myanmar dialects was cut off in the 1950s. Dialects near the Tibet border are more difficult to understand. Speakers of most dialects understand Mutwang, the central, written dialect. The Chinese name is 'Kiutze' or 'Qiuze'. The Lisu name is 'Ch'opa'. SOV. Bible 1986. See main entry under Myanmar.

RAWAT ***(JANGGALI, JANGALI, JHANGAR, DZANGGALI, RAUT)*** [JNL] 2,000 to 3,000 in India (1991). Uttar Pradesh, Pithorgarh District, north of Askot Maila. Sino-Tibetan, Tibeto-Burman, Himalayish, Tibeto-Kanauri, Western Himalayish, Janggali. Bilingualism in Kumauni. Raji is a Scheduled Tribe in India. Literacy rate in first language: Below 1%. Hindu (1981 census), traditional religion. See main entry under Nepal.

RELI ***(RELLI)*** [REI] 19,000 (1997 IMA). Andhra Pradesh, near Adiwasi Oriya; Orissa, Koraput District. Indo-European, Indo-Iranian, Indo-Aryan, Eastern zone, Oriya. Speakers known by Adiwasi Oriya people. A Scheduled Caste in India. Hindu.

RIANG ***(REANG, KAU BRU)*** [RIA] 139,000 in India (1997 IMA). Population total both countries 139,000 or more. Assam, Karimgani District; central Tripura; Mizoram, Aizawi, Lunglei, Chhimtuipui districts. Also spoken in Bangladesh. Sino-Tibetan, Tibeto-Burman, Jingpho-Konyak-Bodo, Konyak-Bodo-Garo, Bodo-Garo, Bodo. Considered to be a dialect of Kok Borok. A Scheduled Tribe in India. Different from Riang of Myanmar, a Mon-Khmer language. Roman script. Traditional religion, Hindu, Christianity. NT 1990.

RUGA [RUH] Meghalaya, near the Garo. Sino-Tibetan, Tibeto-Burman, Jingpho-Konyak-Bodo, Konyak-Bodo-Garo, Bodo-Garo, Koch. Most closely related to A'tong, Koch, and Rabha. Not inherently intelligible with Garo. Most Ruga are more fluent in Garo than Ruga. Over 50 years old. Children are not learning Ruga. Nearly extinct.

SADRI ***(SADANI, SADANA, SADATI, SADARI, SADHAN, SADNA, SADRIK, SANTRI, SIDDRI, SRADRI, SADHARI, SADAN, NAGPURIA, NAGPURI, CHOTA NAGPURI, DIKKU KAJI, GAWARI, GANWARI, GOARI, GAUUARI)*** [SCK] 1,965,000 including 1,381,000 Sadani (1997 IMA), 574,000 Nagpuria (1997 IMA). Population total both countries 1,965,000 or more. Assam; Bihar; Madhya Pradesh; West Bengal; Orissa; Andaman Islands; Nagaland. Also spoken in Bangladesh. Indo-European, Indo-Iranian, Indo-Aryan, Eastern zone, Bihari. Intelligibility of all dialects with each other is high, except for Sadri of Bangladesh, where it is 77%. Speakers name 3 kinds of Sadri: Sadani (finer, respectful, formal), Common

Sadri (Nagpuri), and Lower Sadri (rough). Dialects have 77% to 96% lexical similarity, 58% to 71% with Hindi, 47% to 54% with Oriya, 45% to 61% with Bengali. Hindi, Oriya, and Bengali used as official languages. Hindi used in market, with leaders, for prayer and worship, but proficiency limited. Spoken by Scheduled Tribes, Scheduled Castes, and other communities. Spoken by the Chero as mother tongue. Positive attitude toward Sadri, including for religious literature. Investigation needed: intelligibility with Assam, Andaman Islands, Nagaland. Language of wider communication. Dictionary. Literacy rate in second language: 15% to 25%. Devanagari script. Magazines, radio programs. Agriculturalists, laborors: tea estates, rice. Hindu, traditional religion, Christian, Muslim. NT 1931-1986.

SAJALONG ***(MIJI)*** [SJL] 4,000 (1999 Breton). Arunachal Pradesh, West Kemang District, Bichom and Pakesa River valley. Sino-Tibetan, Tibeto-Burman, Unclassified. Generally considered to be in the Mirish subgroup. Bilingualism in Aka, Moinba, Assamese, Hindi. A Scheduled Tribe in India. Roman script. Forest. Hills, mountain slope. Agriculturalists: shifting cultivation. Traditional religion.

SAMVEDI [SMV] Maharashtra. Indo-European, Indo-Iranian, Indo-Aryan, Southern zone, Konkani. A more divergent dialect of, or closely related language to Konkani. Shares many features with Gujarati.

SANSKRIT [SKT] 6,106 (1981 census). 194,433 second language users (1961 census). Indo-European, Indo-Iranian, Indo-Aryan. Literary and liturgical language. National language. Literacy rate in first language: 60% to 100%. Literacy rate in second language: 15% to 25% literate. Bible 1822.

SANTALI ***(HOR, HAR, SATAR, SANTHALI, SANDAL, SANGTAL, SANTAL, SENTALI, SAMTALI, SANTHIALI, SONTHAL)*** [SNT] 5,959,000 in India (1997 IMA). Population total all countries 6,050,000. Assam; Bihar; Orissa; Tripura; West Bengal. Also spoken in Bangladesh, Bhutan, Nepal. Austro-Asiatic, Munda, North Munda, Kherwari, Santali. Dialects: KARMALI (KHOLE), KAMARI-SANTALI, LOHARI-SANTALI, MAHALI (MAHLE), MANJHI, PAHARIA. Closely related to Ho and Mundari, but a separate language. Santali is a Scheduled Tribe in India. Investigation needed: intelligibility with dialects. Literacy rate in first language: 10% to 30%. Literacy rate in second language: 25% to 50%. Agriculturalists, laborers. Hindu, traditional religion, Christian (some). Bible 1914, in press (1994).

SARAIKI ***(MULTANI, MUTANI, SIRAIKI, SOUTHERN PANJABI, REASATI, RIASATI, BAHAWALPURI)*** [SKR] 59,640 including 59,000 Multani (1997 IMA), 640 Bahawalpuri in India (1961 census). Punjab; Maharashtra; Andhra Pradesh; Madhya Pradesh; Uttar Pradesh; Rajasthan; Delhi; Gujarat. Indo-European, Indo-Iranian, Indo-Aryan, Northwestern zone, Lahnda. Dialects: JAFRI, SIRAIKI HINDKI, THALI, JATKI, BAHAWALPURI (BHAWALPURI, RIASATI, REASATI). 80% intelligibility of Dogri. May be intelligible with Bahawalpuri. A new literary language based on south Lahnda dialects, especially Multani and Bahawalpuri. Investigation needed: intelligibility with dialects. Literacy rate in first language: Below 1%. Literacy rate in second language: 15% Urdu, Marathi. Tropical forest. Mountain slope. Muslim. NT 1819, out of print. See main entry under Pakistan.

SAURASHTRA ***(SAURASHTRI, SOURASHTRA, SOWRASHTRA, PATNULI)*** [SAZ] 310,000 (1997 IMA). The districts mentioned each have communities of at least 5,000 speakers. Tamil Nadu, Madurai, Thanjavur, Dindugul Quaid-E. Milleth, Ramanathapuram, Chengai-Annai, Salem, Tiruchchirappalli, Tirunelveli, North Arcot districts, Madras, Deccan, Madurai, Thanjavur, Salem cities; Karnataka; Andhra Pradesh. Indo-European, Indo-Iranian, Indo-Aryan, Central zone, Gujarati. Dialects: SOUTHERN SAURASHTRA, NORTHERN SAURASHTRA. Indo-Aryan elements in its deep structure reveal Gujarati relationship. Has borrowed some structure from Dravidian, lexicon from Telugu and Tamil. An Indo-European island surrounded by Dravidian languages. The 3 main populations in Salem, Thanjavur, and Madurai cities had between 67% and 97% inherent intelligibility. All varieties sampled had 77% to 96% lexical similarity. The 3 main populations in Salem, Thanjavur, and Madurai cities had 84% to 96%. Southern dialects have 83% or higher lexical similarity with Thanjavur dialect. Most adults speak Tamil in public. Used at home and in prayer. Most adults speak Saurashtra in private. Vigorous. The nonweavers are generally better educated. System of exogamous clans. Investigation needed: intelligibility with dialects. Dictionary. Literacy program needed. Has had its own script for centuries. A modern version developed in the late 1800s. Since the end of the 19th century, books have been printed using Telugu, Tamil, Devanagari, and Saurashtra scripts. Currently an adapted Tamil script is most commonly employed, using superscript numbers and a colon to show sounds not used in Tamil. Traditionally silk weavers 40% to 70%, business, professions. Hindu (Brahmin). NT, in press (1999).

SAURIA PAHARIA ***(MALTO, MALTI, MALTU, MALER, SAWRIYA MALTO)*** [MJT] 74,000 to 86,000 (1994). Central eastern Bihar, northern part of former Santhal Pargana District, Rajmahal hills proper, mainly in Sahibganj and Godda districts, Litipara Block of Pakaur District; West Bengal, Bankura, Barddhaman, and Murshidabad districts. Dravidian, Northern. Dialects: SAHIBGANJ, GODDA, HIRANPUR, LITIPARA (CHATGAM). Inherent intelligibility with Kumarbhag Paharis is inadequate. Related to Kurux. 80% lexical similarity with Kumarbhag Paharia. Part of the Malto ethnic group. A Scheduled Tribe in India. Literacy rate in second language: 6.9%. Forest. Hills, plains. Swidden agriculturalists: rice, maize, wheat, sugarcane, lentils, vegetables; animal husbandry: dairy cattle, goats, pigs, chickens; fishermen; hunters; firewood gatherers. 1,000 to 2,000 feet. Traditional religion, Christian. NT 1998.

SAVARA [SVR] Andhra Pradesh; Orissa. Dravidian, South-Central, Telugu. Distinct from Sora (Savara). Savara indigenous, Oriya, Telugu scripts.

SENTINEL ***(SENTINELESE)*** [STD] 50(?) (1981 Wurm and Hattori). Southeastern Andaman Islands, Sentinel Island. Andamanese, South Andamanese. Similar to Önge, but a distinct language. A Scheduled Tribe in India. Reserved toward outsiders. Hunter-gatherers, fishermen. Traditional religion.

SHENDU ***(KHYEN, KHIENG, SHANDU, SANDU)*** [SHL] Assam, Lushai Hills. Sino-Tibetan, Tibeto-Burman, Kuki-Chin-Naga, Kuki-Chin, Southern, Sho. Close to Asho, Khyang, Thayetmo, Minbu, Chinbon, Lemyo. See main entry under Bangladesh.

SHERDUKPEN ***(NGNOK)*** [SDP] 1,144 (1982 Hale) to 4,000 (1999 Breton). Assam; Arunachal Pradesh, Kameng District, mainly Rupa, Shargang, Jigang villages. Sino-Tibetan, Tibeto-Burman, Himalayish, Tibeto-Kanauri, Tibetic, Tibetan, Unclassified. Bugun (Khoa), Lishpa, and Butpa might be related, but are little-known languages (Sun Tianshin Jackson 1993). Sulung may also be related. A Scheduled Tribe in India. Agriculturalists: shifting cultivation. Lamaistic Buddhist.

SHERPA ***(SHARPA, SHARPA BHOTIA, XIAERBA, SERWA)*** [SCR] 20,000 in India (1997 IMA). West Bengal, Darjeeling District; Sikkim; Arunachal Pradesh. Sino-Tibetan, Tibeto-Burman, Himalayish, Tibeto-Kanuari, Tibetic, Tibetan, Southern. A Scheduled Tribe in India. 'Sharpa' means 'easterner', so the term used in different countries may not always refer to this language. Tibetan script. Lamaist. See main entry under Nepal.

SHINA ***(SHINAKI, SINA)*** [SCL] 21,000 in India (1997 IMA). Northern Kashmir, Dras Valley and Gurais area in Kishenganga Valley near the cease fire line. Indo-European, Indo-Iranian, Indo-Aryan, Northwestern zone, Dardic, Shina. Dialects: DRASI, GUREZI. Brokskat is very different. Many in Dras Valley also speak Purik, but there are villages in Dras Valley that are pure Shina-speaking. Speakers are called 'Shin'. People are open to education and jobs outside the area. Gurezi and Dras are Sunni and Shi'a Muslim. Bible portions 1929. See main entry under Pakistan.

SHOBANG [SSB] Andaman and Nicobar Islands; West Bengal, Calcutta. Unclassified. Probably a variant spelling of Shom Peng.

SHOLAGA ***(SHOLIGA, SHOLIGAR, KADU SHOLIGAR, SOLIGA, SOLAGA, SOLIGAR)*** [SLE] 24,000 (1984 GR). Karnataka, Mysore District, Biligiri Rangana Hills; Tamil Nadu. Dravidian, Southern, Tamil-Kannada, Tamil-Kodagu, Tamil-Malayalam, Tamil. 65% lexical similarity with Kannada. A Scheduled Tribe in India. May be in the Kannada group. Tropical forest. Hunter-gatherers, agriculturalists: cultivators. Hindu, traditional religion.

SHOM PENG ***(SHOM PEN, SHOMPENG)*** [SII] 214 (1982 census). Nicobar Islands, interior Great Nicobar Island. Austro-Asiatic, Mon-Khmer, Nicobar, Shom Peng. A distinct language from other Nicobarese languages. Speakers are mainly monolingual. A Scheduled Tribe in India. Shobang may be a variant spelling of Shom Peng. Dictionary. Hunter-gatherers, fishermen. Traditional religion.

SHUMCHO ***(SUMCHU, SUMTSU, SHUMCU, THEBOR, THEBÖR SKADD, THEBARSKAD, CENTRAL KINNAURI, SUMCHO)*** [SCU] 2,174 5% of the population of Kinnaur District (1998). Himachal Pradesh, Kinnaur District, Kanam, Labrang, Spilo, Shyaso, Taling, and Rushkaling villages of Puh Tahsil. Sino-Tibetan, Tibeto-Burman, Himalayish, Tibeto-Kanauri, Western Himalayish, Kanauri. 70% lexical similarity with Jangshung, 67% with Sunam, 45% with Lower Kinnauri, 43% with Chitkuli. Investigation needed: intelligibility with Sunam, Jangshung, bilingual proficiency, attitudes toward Kinnauri. Mountain slope, valleys. Pastoralists (sedentary), peasant agriculturalists. 5,000 to 6,770 meters. Traditional religion, Hindu, Lamaistic Buddhist.

SIKKIMESE ***(SIKKIM BHOTIA, SIKKIM BHUTIA, DANDZONGKA, DANJONGKA, DANYOUKA, DENJONG, DENJONGKHA, DENJONGPA, DENJONKE, DENJONKA, LACHENGPA, LACHUNGPA, SIKAMI)*** [SIP] 28,600 (1996). Sikkim, all districts; West Bengal, Darjeeling. Possibly also in Tibet. Sino-Tibetan, Tibeto-Burman, Himalayish, Tibeto-Kanauri, Tibetic, Tibetan, Southern. Partially intelligible with Dzongkha of Bhutan. 65% with Dzongkha of Bhutan, 42% with Tebetan. Nepali used for education and trade. A few can speak Tibetan, which is viewed as appropriate for religion. Strong. Positive attitude toward Sikkimese, which they also think is appropriate for religion. Investigation needed: bilingual proficiency in Nepali. Agriculturalists, pastoralists. Buddhist.

SIMTE [SMT] 20,000 (1993 UBS). Southwest Manipur. Sino-Tibetan, Tibeto-Burman, Kuki-Chin-Naga, Kuki-Chin, Northern. Related to Thado and Zome. Singh 1994 says this is an alternate name for Paite. A Scheduled Tribe in India. Bible 1992.

SINDHI [SND] 2,812,000 in India (1997 IMA). Gujarat; Maharashtra; Rajasthan; Andhra Pradesh; Bihar; Delhi; Madhya Pradesh; Orissa; Tamil Nadu; Uttar Pradesh. Indo-European, Indo-Iranian, Indo-Aryan, Northwestern zone, Sindhi. Dialects: BHATIA, JADEJI, KAYASTHI, LARI, LASI, THARELI,

THARI, VICCHOLI, VISHOLI. Kachchi may be a dialect. National language. Dictionary. Arabic and Gurumukhi scripts. Hindu, Sikh, Muslim. Bible 1954. See main entry under Pakistan.

SINGPHO ***(SING-FO, KACHIN)*** [SGP] 3,000 (1997 R. Breton). Assam, Tinsukia District, Margherita Subdivision; Arunachal Pradesh, Lohit and Tirap districts. Sino-Tibetan, Tibeto-Burman, Jingpho-Konyak-Bodo, Jingpho-Luish, Jingpho. 50% lexical similarity with Jinghpo of Myanmar. Many loans from Khamti. 'Kachin' refers to a cultural rather than a linguistic group. A Scheduled Tribe in India. Agriculturalists. Polytheist, some Buddhist, Christian. Bible portions 1907.

SIRMAURI ***(SIRMOURI, SIRMURI)*** [SRX] 14,542 (1971 census). Himachal Pradesh, Shimla (Simla) and Solan districts. Indo-European, Indo-Iranian, Indo-Aryan, Northern zone, Western Pahari. Dialects: GIRIPARI, DHARTHI. May be a dialect of Mahasu Pahari. Investigation needed: intelligibility with Mahasu Pahari, bilingual proficiency in Hindi. Grammar. Takri script, special variety used informally.

SORA ***(SAORA, SAONRAS, SHABARI, SABAR, SAURA, SAVARA, SAWARIA, SWARA, SABARA)*** [SRB] 288,000 (1997 IMA). South Orissa, mainly in the Ganjam District, also in the Koraput and Phulbani districts; Andhra Pradesh, Srikakulam District; Madhya Pradesh; Bihar; Tamil Nadu; West Bengal; the Plains Division of Assam. Austro-Asiatic, Munda, South Munda, Koraput Munda, Sora-Juray-Gorum, Sora-Juray. A Scheduled Tribe in India. Investigation needed: intelligibility with dialects. Hindu (mainly), Christian. Bible 1992.

STOD BHOTI ***(STOD, TOD, TOD-KAD, STOD-KAD, LAHUL BHOTI)*** [SBU] 2,500 (1996). Himachal Pradesh, Lahul region, Stod, Khoksar, and upper Mayar valleys. Sino-Tibetan, Tibeto-Burman, Himalayish, Tibeto-Kanauri, Tibetic, Tibetan, Central. Dialects: STOD (KOLONG), KHOKSAR (KHOKSAR BHOTI), MAYAR (MAYAR BHOTI, MAYARI). 85% intelligibility of Stod Bhoti by Khoksar, 75% by Mayar, 62% of Khoksar by Mayar, 95% of Khoksar by Stod Bhoti. Many speak Hindi, but their understanding is lower than that of other Lahul communities. Used for home, community, and religion, Hindi for trade and education. Attitudes good among speakers toward dialects and with Ladakhi. Investigation needed: intelligibility with Lahuli, Spiti Tibetan. Desire for literacy in Stod Bhoti. Devanagari, Tibetan scripts. Buddhist.

SULUNG [SUV] 4,227 (1981 census). Arunachal Pradesh, east Kameng and lower Subansire districts, a remote corner of the eastern Himalayas. Sino-Tibetan, Tibeto-Burman, North Assam, Tani. A divergent language which some suggest is not Sino-Tibetan but possibly Austro-Asiatic. A "satellite relationship" to the Nisi and Bangni, "bonded economically". A Scheduled Tribe in India. Dictionary. Literacy rate in second language: 2%. Hills. High. Traditional religion.

SUNAM ***(SUNGAM, SUNGNAM, THEBOR, THEBÖR SKADD, THEBARSHAD, CENTRAL KINNAURI, SANGNAUR)*** [SSK] 558 or less than 2% of the population of Kinnaur District (1998). Himachal pradesh, Kinnaur District, Sunam village in Puh Tahsil. Sino-Tibetan, Tibeto-Burman, Himalayish, Tibeto-Kanauri, Western Himalayish, Kanauri. 67% lexical similarity with Shumcho, 65% with Jangshung, 38% with Lower Kinnauri and Chitkuli Kinnauri. Investigation needed: intelligibility with Shumcho, Jangshung, bilingual proficiency, attitudes toward Kinnauri. Mountain slope, valleys. Pastoralists (sedentary), peasant agriculturalists. 5,000 to 6,770 meters. Traditional religion, Hindu, Lamaistic Buddhist.

SURAJPURI ***(SURAIJI, CHOUPAL, CHAUPAL)*** [SJP] 273,000 (1997 IMA). Bihar. Indo-European, Indo-Iranian, Indo-Aryan, Eastern zone, Bihari. May be a dialect of Maithili.

TAMANG, EASTERN [TAJ] 14,000 (1997 IMA). Darjeeling, Sikkim; Arunachal Pradesh. Sino-Tibetan, Tibeto-Burman, Himalayish, Tibeto-Kanauri, Tibetic, Tamangic. Distinct from Western Tamang. They migrate from Nepal. See main entry under Nepal.

TAMIL ***(TAMALSAN, TAMBUL, TAMILI, TAMAL, DAMULIAN)*** [TCV] 61,527,000 in India (1997 IMA). Population total all countries 66,000,000 first language speakers; 74,000,000 including second language users (1999 WA). Tamil Nadu and neighboring states. Also spoken in Bahrain, Fiji, Germany, Malaysia (Peninsular), Mauritius, Netherlands, Qatar, Réunion, Singapore, South Africa, Sri Lanka, Thailand, UAE, United Kingdom. Dravidian, Southern, Tamil-Kannada, Tamil-Kodagu, Tamil-Malayalam, Tamil. Dialects: ADI DRAVIDA, AIYAR, AIYANGAR, ARAVA, BURGANDI, KASUVA, KONGAR, KORAVA, KORCHI, MADRASI, PARIKALA, PATTAPU BHASHA, TAMIL, SRI LANKA TAMIL, MALAYA TAMIL, BURMA TAMIL, SOUTH AFRICA TAMIL, TIGALU, HARIJAN, SANKETI, HEBBAR, MANDYAM BRAHMIN, SECUNDERABAD BRAHMIN. Kasuva is a jungle tribe dialect. Burgandi speakers are nomadic. Aiyar and Aiyangar are Brahmin dialects. CIIL has prepared syllabus for hearing-impaired children. National language. SOV. Tamil script. Hindu, Muslim. Bible 1727-1995.

TEHRI ***(GANGAPARIYA)*** [THB] Uttar Pradesh, Garhwal District. Indo-European, Indo-Iranian, Indo-Aryan, Northern zone, Garhwali. Close to Garhwali. Investigation needed: intelligibility with Garhwali. Bible portions 1914.

TELUGU ***(TELEGU, ANDHRA, GENTOO, TAILANGI, TELANGIRE, TELGI, TENGU, TERANGI, TOLANGAN)*** [TCW] 69,634,000 in India (1997 IMA). Population total all countries 69,666,000 or more. Including second language speakers: 75,000,000 (1999 WA). Andhra Pradesh and neighboring states. Also spoken in Bahrain, Fiji, Malaysia, Mauritius, Singapore, UAE. Dravidian, South-Central, Telugu. Dialects: BERAD, DASARI, DOMMARA, GOLARI, KAMATHI, KOMTAO, KONDA-REDDI, SALEWARI, TELANGANA, TELUGU, VADAGA, VADARI, SRIKAKULA, VISHAKAPATNAM, EAST GODAVERI, RAYALSEEMA, NELLORE, GUNTUR. Yanadi and Bagata are ethnic groups speaking Telugu as mother tongue. National language. SOV. Telugu script. Bible 1854-1998.

TERESSA ***(TAIH-LONG)*** [TEF] Nicobar Islands, Teressa and Bompoka islands. Austro-Asiatic, Mon-Khmer, Nicobar, Chowra-Teressa. Dialect: BOMPOKA (BOMPAKA, PAUHUT).

THARU, DANGAURA ***(DANG, DANGORA, DANGURA, DANGALI, DANGHA)*** [THL] 31,000 in India (1981 census). Uttar Pradesh, along the border in Nighasan Tahsil of Kheri District and Tulsipur Tahsil of Gonda District. Indo-European, Indo-Iranian, Indo-Aryan, Central zone, Unclassified. 63% to 72% lexical similarity with Rana Tharu, 74% to 79% with Kathoriya Tharu, 58% to 65% with Hindi. Hindi bilingual proficiency is limited among the 70% to 90% who are uneducated. Tharu is a Scheduled Tribe in India. Investigation needed: intelligibility with dialects. Literacy rate in second language: 20% to 25% (census). Hindu, traditional religion. See main entry under Nepal.

THARU, KOCHILA ***(SAPTARI)*** [THQ] Indo-European, Indo-Iranian, Indo-Aryan, Eastern zone, Unclassified. Dialect: MORANGIA. Traditional religion with Hindu overlay. See main entry under Nepal.

THARU, RANA ***(RANA THAKUR)*** [THR] 64,000 in India (1981 census). Border with Nepal, Uttar Pradesh, near Nighasan Tahsil of Kheri District, Khatima, Sitargani, Kiccha, and Haldwani tahsils of Nainital District, and Pilibhit districts, Uttar Pradesh. Indo-European, Indo-Iranian, Indo-Aryan, Eastern zone, Unclassified. 73% to 79% lexical similarity with Buksa, 66% to 79% with Kathoriya Thatu, 63% to 72% with Dangaura Tharu, 68% to 71% with Hindi. Hindi bilingual proficiency is limited among the 70% to 90% who are uneducated. Tharu is a Scheduled Tribe in India. Investigation needed: intelligibility with dialects. Literacy rate in second language: 20% to 25% (census). Hindu, traditional religion. See main entry under Nepal.

THULUNG ***(THULUNGE RAI)*** [TDH] 3,313 in India (1961 census). Sikkim; Uttar Pradesh. Sino-Tibetan, Tibeto-Burman, Himalayish, Mahakiranti, Kiranti, Western. Agriculturalists, pastoralists. Hindu. See main entry under Nepal.

TIBETAN ***(CENTRAL TIBETAN, BHOTIA, POHBETIAN, TEBILIAN, TIBATE)*** [TIC] 124,280 in India (1994 IMA). Tibet border, Himachal Pradesh; Arunachal Pradesh; Assam; Delhi; Sikkim. The Darjeeling-Kalimpong area of West Bengal has been heavily settled by Tibetans since at least 1900. Sino-Tibetan, Tibeto-Burman, Himalayish, Tibeto-Kanauri, Tibetic, Tibetan, Central. Dialects: KONGBO, SPITI. In Himalayan countries 'Bhotiya' means 'people of Tibetan origin' and is applied to those speaking various languages. Dialects or closely related languages: Aba (Batang), Dartsemdo (Tatsienlu), Dru, Garhwal, Gtsang, Hanniu, Jad (Dzad), Lhoskad (Hloka), Ngambo (Amdo), Nganshuenkuan (Anshuenkuan Nyarong), Panakha-Panags, Paurong, Kumaun, Spiti, Takpa (Dwags). Spiti and Stod have 74% lexical similarity. Tibetan is a Scheduled Tribe in India. Lamaist. Bible 1948. See main entry under China.

TINANI ***(LAHAULI, LAHOULI, RANGLOI, TINAN LAHULI, LAHULI, TEENAN, GONDLA, GONDHLA)*** [LBF] 2,000 in India (1996). Population total both countries 2,400 to 3,600. Himachal Pradesh, Lahul and Spiti Subdivision, lower Chandra Valley (Tinan or Rangloi Valley). Gondhla is the main village. Also spoken in China. Sino-Tibetan, Tibeto-Burman, Himalayish, Tibeto-Kanauri, Western Himalayish, Kanauri. Closely related to Pattani. 63% to 56% lexical similarity with Chamba Lahuli, 32% to 37% with Bunan, 21% with the Spiti and Stod varieties of central Tibetan, 62% with Tandi village, 34% with Shumcho, 32% with Jangshung, 31% with Kanauri and Sunam, 13% with Lhasa Tibetan. Bilingualism in Hindi. Used in home and village, infrequently in religion. 'Lahuli' as applied to the inhabitants of Lahul and Spiti refers primarily to the language of a place. It is not a tight linguistic designation. Speakers are well educated. Literacy rate in second language: High. Mountain slope, valleys. 3,700 to 7,000 meters. Buddhism, some Hindu. Bible portions 1908-1915.

TODA ***(TODI, TUDA)*** [TCX] 1,006 (1981 census). Orissa; Tamil Nadu, Nilgiri Hills, Kunda hills. Dravidian, Southern, Tamil-Kannada, Tamil-Kodagu, Toda-Kota. Toda is a Scheduled Tribe in India. Traditional religion, Christian. Bible portions 1897-1910.

TOTO [TXO] 20,000 (1994 King). West Bengal, Subhapara, Dhunchipara, Panchayatpara hillocks on the Indo-Bhutan border. Sino-Tibetan, Tibeto-Burman, Himalayish, Tibeto-Kanauri, Tibetic, Dhimal. Not inherently intelligible with Dhimal of Nepal. Low lexical similarity with Dhimal. Hindi is also used. The Toto can converse in Bengali and Nepali. Toto is a Scheduled Tribe in India. SOV; postpositions; genitives, demonstratives, relatives before noun heads; nontonal. Devanagari, Bengali. Agriculturalists; animal husbandry: poultry, pigs. Traditional religion, Hindu.

TSHANGLA ***(TSANGLA, SANGLA, CANGLOU MENBA, MENBA, MONBA, MONPA, MOTUO, CENTRAL MONPA)*** [TSJ] Western Arunachal Pradesh, Bishing and several other villages. Sino-Tibetan, Tibeto-Burman, Himalayish, Tibeto-Kanauri, Tibetic, Bodish, Tshangla. They claim to have come from Bhutan. Many young people attend school. Agriculturalists: rice. Buddhist. See main entry under Bhutan.

TUKPA ***(NESANG)*** [TPQ] 723 (1998). Himachal Pradesh, Kinnaur District, Nesang, Charang, and Kunnu villages. Sino-Tibetan, Tibeto-Burman, Himalayish, Tibeto-Kanauri, Western Himalayish, Kanauri. Related to Bhoti Kinnauri, Chitkuli Kinnauri, and Kanashi. Investigation needed: intelligibility with dialects.

TULU ***(TAL, THALU, TILU, TULUVA BHASA, TULLU, THULU)*** [TCY] 1,949,000 (1997 IMA). Andhra Pradesh; Kerala; Tamil Nadu; Maharashtra; Karnataka; Meghalaya. Dravidian, Southern, Tulu. Dialects: TULU, BELLARI. Bellari may be a separate language. Literacy rate in second language: 20% Kannada, Malayalam. Mixed commerce, fishermen. Hindu, Christians. NT 1847-1892.

TURI [TRD] 2,000 to 4,000 (1977 Voegelin and Voegelin) out of an ethnic population of 150,000 (1981 census). Bihar, Ranchi, Gumla, Lohardaga districts, Chotanagpur area; Madhya Pradesh, Raigarh District; Orissa, Sambalpur and Sundargarb districts; West Bengal, Birbhum, Nadia, Murshidabad, Bankura districts. Austro-Asiatic, Munda, North Munda, Kherwari, Santali. A Scheduled Caste in India. Singh 1993 reports they speak Sadri as mother tongue in Bihar, Mundari in West Bengal, Oriya in Orissa.

TURUNG [TRY] Assam. Tai-Kadai, Kam-Tai, Be-Tai, Tai-Sek, Tai, East Central, Northwest. May be extinct. Nearly extinct.

ULLATAN ***(KATAN, KATTALAN, KOCHUVELAN, ULLADAN)*** [ULL] 12,687 (1981 census). Kerala, palghat, Trichur, Ernakulam, Kottayam, Quilon, Alleppey, Trivandrum districts. Dravidian, Southern, Unclassified. Ulladan and Kochu Velan are both Scheduled Tribes in India. Singh reports their mother tongue is Malayalam. Animal husbandry, salaried jobs, wage labor. Hindu.

URALI ***(OORAZHI, URALY, URLI)*** [URL] 18,257 (1981 census). Tamil Nadu, Periyar District, Sathayamangalam area, east of Nilgiri District; Kerala, Idukki, Wynad districts. Dravidian, Southern, Tamil-Kannada, Kannada. Reported to be a distinct speech variety, sharing features with Tamil, Irula, and Kannada (Mohan Lal 1991). A Scheduled Tribe in India. Singh 1994 reports they speak Malayalam as mother tongue. Investigation needed: intelligibility with Mele Nadu Irula, bilingual proficiency. Literacy rate in second language: Low. Hunter-gatherers, agriculturalists. Hindu, Christian (1981 census).

URDU ***(ISLAMI, UNDRI, URUDU)*** [URD] 48,062,000 in India (1997 IMA). Jammu and Kashmir and by Muslims in many parts of India. Indo-European, Indo-Iranian, Indo-Aryan, Central zone, Western Hindi, Hindustani. Dialects: DAKHINI (DAKANI, DECCAN, DESIA, MIRGAN), PINJARI, REKHTA (REKHTI). Dakhini is freer of Persian and Arabic loans than Urdu. Rekhta is a form of Urdu used in poetry. National language. Arabic script for both Urdu and Dakhini. Muslim. Bible 1843-1998. See main entry under Pakistan.

VAAGRI BOOLI ***(NARAKUREAVAR, NARIKKORAVA, KURUVIKKARAN, KARIKKORAVA, HAKKIPIKKARU, HAKI PIKI, GUVVALOLLU, SHIKARUANAM, RATTIYAN, MARATTIYAN)*** [VAA] 10,000 or more (1970 Varma. Tamil Nadu, Arcot District. Indo-European, Indo-Iranian, Indo-Aryan, Unclassified. Hakkipikki is a Scheduled Tribe in India. The name of the language means 'bird catchers'. Hindu. Bible portions 1975.

VAIPHEI ***(BHAIPEI, VAIPEI, VEIPHEI)*** [VAP] 21,000 (1997 IMA). Assam; south Manipur; Meghalaya; Tripura. Sino-Tibetan, Tibeto-Burman, Kuki-Chin-Naga, Kuki-Chin, Northern. A Scheduled Tribe in India. Reported to be a subgroup of Zomi. Mountain slope. Agriculturalists, mixed commerce. Christian. NT 1957-1989.

VARHADI-NAGPURI ***(MADHYA PRADESH MARATHI, BERARI, BERAR MARATHI, DHANAGARI, KUMBHARI)*** [VAH] 463 including 186 Dahngari, 271 Kumbhari, 6 Warhadi (1961 census). Maharashtra. Indo-European, Indo-Iranian, Indo-Aryan, Southern zone, Unclassified. Dialects: BRAHMANI, KUNBI, RAIPUR, JHADPI, GOVARI, KOSTI (RANGARI), KUNBAN (KOHLI), MAHARI (DHEDI). More distinct dialects or languages are Marheti, Natakani, Katia (Katiyai). Bible portions 1834.

VARLI ***(WARLI)*** [VAV] 470,000 including 33,971 in Maharashtra (1981 census) and 126,108 in Gujarat (1971 census). Maharashtra, northern Thane District, especially Dahanu and Talasari taluks, and some in Nasik and Dhule districts; Gujarat, Valsad District, especially Dharampur taluk; Dadra and Nagar Haveli. Davari dialect in far north Thane District and southern Gujarat; Nihiri elsewhere. Indo-European, Indo-Iranian, Indo-Aryan, Southern zone, Konkani. Dialects: DAVARI, WESTERN NIHIRI, EASTERN NIHIRI. Some classify this as a dialect of Gujarati or Bhili. 61% to 93% lexical similarity among dialects. Bilingualism in Marathi and Gujarati is limited. Each dialect group is endogamous. Patrilocal. A Scheduled Tribe in India. Investigation needed: intelligibility with dialects, bilingual proficiency in Marathi. Forest. Hills. Agriculturalists: rice; cattle raising; fishermen. 1,604 meters. Traditional religion, Hindu influences.

VASAVI ***(VASAVE, VASAVA, VASAVA BHIL)*** [VAS] 900,000 or more (1997 BSI). Maharashtra, small villages and hamlets around the Tapti River; Gujarat, Surat and Bharuch districts, north of the Tapti River in the southern areas of Akkalkuwa and Akrani tahsils on a narrow belt of land between the Satpudas the the Tapti banks; some in the Satpudas; south of the Tapti in the central and northern Nandurbar and Nawapur tahsils. Indo-European, Indo-Iranian, Indo-Aryan, Central zone, Gujarati.

Dialects: DEHVALI (AMBODI), DUNGRI (DOGRI). Not intelligible with Pauri or Bhilori. 77% to 93% intelligibility between Dogri, Khatali, Dehwali, Dubli, and Kotni varieties. Bilingual proficiency in Marathi is limited. Subgroup of Bhil ethnic group. 'Vasavi' is the name of the language; 'Vasava' the people. Speakers in different locations are known as Adiwasi Bhil, Dhogri Bhil, Keski Bhil, Bhilori, Padwi Bhilori, Ambodia Bhil, Vasave Bhil. A Scheduled Tribe in India. Investigation needed: intelligibility with dialects. Literacy rate in second language: Low. Literacy program needed in Vasavi. Gujarati and Marathi scripts. Agriculturalists. Bible portions 1998.

VISHAVAN ***(MALARKUTI)*** [VIS] 150. Kerala, Ernakulam, Kottayam, Trichur districts. Dravidian, Unclassified.

WADDAR ***(VADARI, WERDERS)*** [WBQ] 61,000 (1997 IMA). Andhra Pradesh; Karnataka; Maharashtra, Jalgaon District. Dravidian, South-Central, Telugu. Some are literate in Telugu or Marathi. Traditional religion, Hindu.

WAGDI ***(WAGADI, VAGDI, VAGADI, VAGARI, VAGERI, VAGED, VAGI, WAGARI, WAGHARI, WAGRI, WAGHOLI, MINA BHIL, BHILI)*** [WBR] 1,621,000 (1997 IMA). Rajasthan, southern Udaipur District, Dungarpur and Banswara; Gujarat, Sabarkantha and Panch Mahals; Andhra Pradesh, Hyderabad. Indo-European, Indo-Iranian, Indo-Aryan, Central zone, Bhil. Dialects: KHERWARA, SAGWARA, ADIVASI WAGDI. Intelligibility among dialects is above 95%. 84% lexical similarity with Patelia dialects; 75% to 80% with Marwari dialects; 79% to 93% with Adiwasi Girasia dialects; 79% to 87% with Rajput Girasia dialects. Second language is Hindi; proficiency is adequate for market and other common topics; used with people not speakers of Wagdi. A regional language in Vagad Desh. Merchants and government workers use it as second language. No feeling of inferiority attached to Wagdi. Speakers are called 'Bhil'. Vagri is a Scheduled Tribe in India. Investigation needed: intelligibility with Bhil, bilingual proficiency in Hindi. Language of wider communication. SOV, postpositions, genitivies after noun heads, nontonal. Literacy rate in first language: Below 1%. Literacy rate in second language: 25% to 50%. Devanagari script. Radio programs. Desert. Plains, hills. Peasant agriculturalists. Hindu, traditional religion.

YAKHA ***(YAKKHA, YAKKHABA)*** [YBH] Among British Gurkhas in Sikkim. Sino-Tibetan, Tibeto-Burman, Himalayish, Mahakiranti, Kiranti, Eastern. Related to Lohorong, Limbu. Buddhist, Hindu. See main entry under Nepal.

YERUKULA ***(YERUKALA, YARUKULA, YERKULA, YERUKLA, ERUKALA, KORAVA, YERUKALA-KORAVA, YERUKULA-BHASHA, ERUKU BHASHA, KORCHI, KURUTHA, KURRU BHASHA)*** [YEU] 300,000 (1997). Andhra Pradesh, Rayalseema, Telengana and Andhra regions; Tamil Nadu, Nilgiri, Coimbatore, Periyar, Salem, Chengai Anna; Karnataka; Kerala; Maharashtra. Dravidian, Southern, Tamil-Kannada, Tamil-Kodagu, Tamil-Malayalam, Tamil. Dialects: PARIKALA, SANKARA-YERUKALA. Closely related to Ravula and Irula. Lexical similarity among varieties ranges from 53% to 81%, with Irula from 33% to 38%, with Ravula from 28% to 45%, with Tamil from 27% to 45%. Some regions have low bilingual proficiency in Telugu-higher in Andhra Pradesh and among educated adults. In Andhra Pradesh, increasing use in home, friends, religion. In Rayalseema and Telengana regions it is even greater. Fairly vigorous language use. Strong positive attitude toward Yerukula. Some people called 'Yerukula' speak Telugu as mother tongue. Traditionally nomadic. A Scheduled Tribe in India. Investigation needed: intelligibility with dialects. Literacy rate in second language: 14.55%. Most want Yerukula books, but script decision is sensitive. Telugu. Subtropical forest. Mountain slope, plains. Basketmakers; animal husbandry: pigs. 1,000 to 6,500 feet. Hindu.

ZAKHRING [ZKR] Arunachal Pradesh, Lohit District, hilly terrain and banks of the Lohit River in the Walong and Kibithoo area. Sino-Tibetan, Tibeto-Burman, Unclassified. Dialects: LOWER ZYPHE, UPPER ZYPHE. Bilingualism in Hindi. A Scheduled Tribe in India. Buddhist.

ZANGSKARI ***(ZANSKARI, ZASKARI)*** [ZAU] 8,000 to 10,000 (1984 Dayton and Wilson). Kashmir, Zaskar Mts.; southernmost end of Kargil District. Between Himalayas and Indus River Valley. Next to Leh-Ladakhi area and Kargil-Purik area. Possibly Tibet. Sino-Tibetan, Tibeto-Burman, Himalayish, Tibeto-Kanauri, Tibetic, Tibetan, Western. Closer linguistically to ChangThang than to Ladakhi. People are somewhat bilingual in Leh dialect of Ladakhi; inherent and learned comprehension needs investigation. Small primary schools throughout Zanskar, lower high schools in Karsha and Zangla, high school in Padum. 90% of students are male. Nearly all teachers are from outside the area. People trade grain with ChangThang to acquire wool and salt. Investigation needed: intelligibility with Ladakhi, ChangThang. Literacy rate in second language: Highest rate in Tibetan script in Ladakh. Tibetan script. Buddhist. Bible portions 1945-1951.

ZOME ***(ZORNI, ZOMI, ZOLI, ZO, ZOU)*** [ZOM] 17,000 in India (1997 IMA). Manipur, Chandel and southern districts; Assam. Sino-Tibetan, Tibeto-Burman, Kuki-Chin-Naga, Kuki-Chin, Northern. 'Zome' is the general name for all Chin, but also refers to this specific group. Zou is a Scheduled Tribe in India. Literacy rate in second language: 33%: males 42%, females 24% (1981 census). Roman script. Agriculturalists: shifting cultivation. Christian (1981 census). Bible 1992. See main entry under Myanmar.

ZYPHE *(ZOPHEI)* [ZYP] Mizoram, Lakher District. Sino-Tibetan, Tibeto-Burman, Kuki-Chin-Naga, Kuki-Chin, Southern. Dialects: LOWER ZYPHE, UPPER ZYPHE. Close to Mara Chin. Many are bilingual in Haka Chin, Lakher, or Mara, depending on location. See main entry under Myanmar.

INDONESIA

Republic of Indonesia, Republik Indonesia. National or official language: Indonesian. 206,338,000 (1998 UN). Literacy rate 78% to 85%. Also includes Western Cham, Dutch, Portuguese, Uyghur, Arabic, people from India, Europe. Information mainly from R. Blust 1983-1984; S. Wurm and S. Hattori 1981; D. T. Tryon 1995. Muslim, Christian, traditional religion, Hindu, Buddhist, secular. Blind population 1,000,000. Deaf population 2,000,000 or more (1993). Deaf institutions: 94. The number of languages listed for Indonesia is 731. Of those, 726 are living languages, 2 are second languages without mother tongue speakers, and 3 are extinct. Diversity index 0.83.

INDONESIA (IRIAN JAYA)

1,641,000 (1995). Information mainly from C. Roesler 1972; C. L. Voorhoeve 1975; M. Donohue 1998-1999; SIL 1975-1999. Data accuracy estimate: A2, B. The number of languages listed for Indonesia (Irian Jaya) is 265. Of those, 263 are living languages and 2 are second languages without mother tongue speakers. Diversity index 0.94.

ABINOMN *(AVINOMEN, "BASO", FOYA, FOJA)* [BSA] 300 (1999 Clouse and Donohue). Lakes Plain area, from the mouth of the Baso River just east of Dabra at the Idenburg River to its headwaters in the Foya Mts., Jayapura Kabupaten, Mamberamo Hulu Kecamatan. Language Isolate. Completely unrelated to any language in the area. Very eager for literacy. Want to make their own dictionary and write their traditional stories. They strongly dislike the name "Baso". SOV. Schooling is very low.

ABUN *(YIMBUN, A NDEN)* [KGR] 3,000 (1995 SIL). North coast and interior of central Bird's Head, north and south of Tamberau ranges. Sorong Kabupaten, Ayamaru, Sausapor, and Moraid kecamatans. About 20 villages. West Papuan, Bird's Head, North-Central Bird's Head, North Bird's Head. Dialects: ABUN TAT (KARON PANTAI), ABUN JI (MADIK), ABUN JE. Literacy rate in first language: 5% to 15%. Bible portions 1991-1995.

AGHU [AHH] 3,000 (1987 SIL). South coast area along the Digul River west of the Mandobo language, Merauke Kabupaten, Jair Kecamatan. Trans-New Guinea, Main Section, Central and Western, Central and South New Guinea-Kutubuan, Central and South New Guinea, Awyu-Dumut, Awyu, Aghu. Different from Aghu of Australia. Grammar.

AIRORAN *(AERORAN, ADORA, IRIEMKENA)* [AIR] 400 (1991 SIL). North coast area on the lower Apauwer River. Subu, Motobiak, Isirania and other villages, Jayapura Kabupaten, Mamberamo Hilir and Pantai Barat kecamatans. Trans-New Guinea, Main Section, Central and Western, Dani-Kwerba, Northern, Kwerba. Coastal, river.

AMBAI *(AMBAI-MENAWI)* [AMK] 9,000 to 10,000 (1991 SIL). On Ambai Island in Cenderawasih Bay, south of Serui Island, along the south coast of Serui Island from 136.20' to 136.45', Yapen Waropen Kabupaten, Yapen Selatan and Yapen Timur kecamatans. 10 villages. Austronesian, Malayo-Polynesian, Central-Eastern, Eastern Malayo-Polynesian, South Halmahera-West New Guinea, West New Guinea, Cenderawasih Bay, Yapen, Central-Western. Dialects: RANDAWAYA, AMBAI (WADAPI-LAUT), MANAWI. Closely related to Serui-Laut (77% lexical similarity), Ansus, Woi, Pom, Wabo, Wandamen (71%), Marau, Papuma, Munggui, Kurudu. Children are bilingual in Indonesian. Serial verbs, complex directional demonstrative system. Literacy rate in first language: 25% to 50%. Literacy rate in second language: 50% to 75%. Bible portions 1994.

ANASI *(BAPU)* [BPO] 2,000 (1993 R. Doriot UFM). North coast area along the west bank of the lower Mamberamo River. Jayapura Kabupaten, Mamberamo Hilir Kecamatan. Geelvink Bay, East Geelvink Bay.

ANSUS [AND] 4,600 (1987 SIL). Miosnum Island and the south coast of Serui Island, from 135.35' to 135.50', Yapen Waropen Kabupaten, Yapen Barat Kecamatan, Ansus, Kairawi, Aibondeni, and Yenusi villages. Austronesian, Malayo-Polynesian, Central-Eastern, Eastern Malayo-Polynesian, South Halmahera-West New Guinea, West New Guinea, Cenderawasih Bay, Yapen, Central-Western. 82% lexical similarity with Marau Papuma, 77% with Wandamen.

ANUS [AUQ] 100 (1975 SIL). Island off north coast east of the Tor River, Jayapura Kabupaten, Bonggo Kecamatan. Austronesian, Malayo-Polynesian, Central-Eastern, Eastern Malayo-Polynesian, Oceanic, Western Oceanic, North New Guinea, Sarmi-Jayapura Bay, Sarmi.

ARANDAI ***(YABAN, JABAN, DOMBANO, SEBYAR)*** [JBJ] 1,000 (1987 SIL). Southern Bird's Head, east and west of the Wariaga River and around the Sebyar (Timoforo) River, Manokwari Kabupaten, Bintuni Kecamatan. Trans-New Guinea, South Bird's Head-Timor-Alor-Pantar, South Bird's Head, South Bird's Head Proper, Eastern. Dialects: KEMBERANO (TOMU), DOMBANO (ARANDAI). Related to Kampong Baru. Kemberano and Dombano appear to have 71% lexical similarity with each other in preliminary word lists; probably 2 separate languages.

ARGUNI ***(ARGOENI)*** [AGF] 200 (1977 Voegelin and Voegelin). Northwest coast of Bomberai Peninsula on an island in the Maccluer Gulf. Austronesian, Malayo-Polynesian, Central-Eastern, Central Malayo-Polynesian, North Bomberai.

AS [ASZ] 250 (1988 SIL). West Bird's Head, north coast, villages of Asbakin (main center), Maklaumkarta, and Mega. Austronesian, Malayo-Polynesian, Central-Eastern, Eastern Malayo-Polynesian, South Halmahera-West New Guinea, West New Guinea, Cenderawasih Bay, Raja Ampat. 60% lexical similarity with some dialects on Misool Island. Bilingualism in Moi, Indonesian. Reported to originate from Gag Island, west of Waigeo Island.

ASMAT, CASUARINA COAST ***(KAWEINAG)*** [ASC] 9,000 (1991 SIL), including 5,200 in Matia and 3,400 in Sapan. Casuarina coast from the Ewta River in the north to the Kuti River in the south, inland as far as 25 km. from the coast in some places. Merauke Kabupaten, Pantai Kasuari Kecamatan. Trans-New Guinea, Main Section, Central and Western, Central and South New Guinea-Kutubuan, Central and South New Guinea, Asmat-Kamoro. Dialects: MATIA, SAPAN (SAFAN).

ASMAT, CENTRAL ***(MANOWEE, JAS, YAS)*** [AST] 7,000 in Central Asmat (1972 Roesler TEAM). 50,000 all Asmat (1987 Roesler). On the south coast from the Owap River in the northwest to the Farec River in the southwest, inland toward the foothills to 210 kms. from the coast in some areas. Merauke Kabupaten, Sawa-Erma, Agats, Atsy, and Pantai Kasuari kecamatans. Between the Kamoro and Sawi languages. Trans-New Guinea, Main Section, Central and Western, Central and South New Guinea-Kutubuan, Central and South New Guinea, Asmat-Kamoro. Dialects: SIMAI (SIMAY), MISMAN, AJAM (AYAM). North Asmat is the most distinct dialect. Related to the Sempan language north of the rivers. Close to Kamoro and Citak. Many are becoming bilingual in Indonesian; some in neighboring languages. Traditional religion. NT 1985.

ASMAT, NORTH ***(KEENOK)*** [NKS] 1,000 (1991 SIL). Near the headwaters of the Paterle Cocq River to the west, to the Unir River to the east, to the foothills in some places, Merauke Kabupaten, Sawa-Erma Kecamatan. Trans-New Guinea, Main Section, Central and Western, Central and South New Guinea-Kutubuan, Central and South New Guinea, Asmat-Kamoro.

ASMAT, YAOSAKOR ***(YAOSAKOR)*** [ASY] 2,000 (1991 SIL). South coast along the Sirac River, Merauke Kabupaten, Agats and Atsy kecamatans. Trans-New Guinea, Main Section, Central and Western, Central and South New Guinea-Kutubuan, Central and South New Guinea, Asmat-Kamoro. NT 1995.

ATOHWAIM ***(KAUGAT)*** [AQM] 1,000 (1987 SIL). South coast on the Cook and Kronkel rivers, between the Sawi and Kaygir languages. Merauke Kabupaten, Pantai Kasuari Kecamatan. Trans-New Guinea, Main Section, Central and Western, Kayagar. About 50% bilingual in Indonesian, Sawi, or Kaygir.

AUYE ***(AUWJE)*** [AUU] 350 (1995 SIL). Central Highlands, Siriwo River, mountains southeast of Cenderawasih Bay. Paniai Kabupaten, Napan Kecamatan. Trans-New Guinea, Main Section, Central and Western, Wissel Lakes-Kemandoga, Ekari-Wolani-Moni. Related to Ekari, but a distinct language. Distinct from Awyi (Awye) in Taikat group. Literacy rate in first language: 5% to 15%. Mountain slope.

AWBONO [AWH] 100 or fewer (1999 D. Clouse SIL). South of Tokuni on the Modera River. Kvolyab is on the south coast, northwest of Korowai. Bayono-Awbono. Dialect: KVOLYAB. Not related to Ok, Asmat, Awyu-Dumut, Momuna, or highland languages like Dani or Mek. 55% lexical similarity with Bayono. No bilinguals among the Kvolyab. The Kvolyab are frequently at war with the Tokuni, Kopkaka, and Korowai. SOV.

AWERA [AWR] 100 approximately (1987 SIL). Village at the mouth of the Wapoga River, east side of Cenderawasih Bay, Yapen Waropen Kabupaten, Waropen Bawah Kecamatan. Same community with 100 Ansus-speaking people. Geelvink Bay, Lakes Plain, Awera. Ansus and Indonesian are used widely in the community. Awera is used in home and interaction with other Awera.

AWYI ***(AWYE, AWJE, AWJI, NYAO, NJAO)*** [AUW] 400 (1978 SIL). Northeast near Papua New Guinea border, just south of Jayapura, Jayapura Kabupaten, Arso Kecamatan. Trans-New Guinea, Northern, Border, Taikat. Distinct from Auye in Ekari-Wolani-Moni group.

AWYU, MIARO ***(MIARO, PISA)*** [PSA] 3,500 (1987 SIL). South coast area, southwest of Wildeman River and east of Kampong River, inland from Pirimapun. Trans-New Guinea, Main Section, Central and Western, Central and South New Guinea-Kutubuan, Central and South New Guinea, Awyu-Dumut, Awyu. Closely related to Siagha-Yenimu. A separate language from Nohon Awyu.

AWYU, NOHON ***(AUYU, AWYA, AWJU, AJAU, AVIO, NOHON)*** [AWJ] 18,000 (1987 SIL). South coast east of Bipim, northwest of Yaqay, west of Tanamerah, southwest of Boma. Merauke Kabupaten; Edera, Pantai Kasuari, Kouh, Mandobo, Asgon, and Kepi kecamatans. Trans-New Guinea, Main Section, Central and Western, Central and South New Guinea-Kutubuan, Central and South New Guinea, Awyu-Dumut, Awyu. A separate language from Miaro Awyu. About 9 dialects. Many becoming bilingual in Indonesian. Traditional religion.

BAGUSA ***(KAPESO, SUASESO)*** [BQB] 300 (1987 SIL). East of Mamberamo, Lake Rombebai, north of Kauwera language. Jayapura Kabupaten, Mamberamo Tengah Kecamatan. Trans-New Guinea, Main Section, Central and Western, Dani-Kwerba, Northern, Kwerba. All ages. Vigorous. Tropical forest, swamp. Hunter-gatherers. Traditional religion, Christian.

BAHAM ***(PATIMUNI)*** [BDW] 1,100 (1987 SIL). West Bomberai Peninsula east of the Iha language. Fakfak Kabupaten, Kaimana, Fakfak, and Kokas kecamatans. Trans-New Guinea, Main Section, Central and Western, West Bomberai, West Bomberai Proper. Close to Iha.

BARAPASI ***(BAROPASI)*** [BRP] 2,500 (1995 SIL). East side of Cenderawasih Bay just east of the Waropen language, along the Barapasi River and its tributaries. Yapen Waropen Kabupaten, Waropen Atas Kecamatan. Geelvink Bay, East Geelvink Bay. Dialects: SIPISI, MARIKAI. Literacy rate in second language: 15% to 25%.

BAUZI ***(BAUDI, BAURI, BAUDJI, BAUDZI)*** [PAU] 1,500 (1991 SIL). Around Lake Holmes near the mid Mamberamo River, Danau Bira area, northeast, Kasonoweja north of Kustera. Jayapura and Yapen Waropen kabupatens, Mamberamo Tengah and Waropen Atas kecamatans; Vakiadi, Noiadi, Danau Bira, Solom, Kustera, Neao, Itaba villages. Geelvink Bay, East Geelvink Bay. Dialects: GESDA DAE, NEAO, AUMENEFA. Bilingual level estimates for Eritai are 0 90%, 1 5%, 2 5%, 3 0%, 4 0%, 5 0%. Vigorous. Investigation needed: intelligibility with Gesda Doe. Literacy rate in first language: 10% to 25%. Bible portions 1983-1994.

BAYONO [BYL] 100 or fewer (1999 D. Clouse SIL). South of Tokuni on the Steenboom River. Bayono-Awbono. Not related to Ok, Asmat, Awyu-Dumut, Momuna, or highlands languages like Dani or Mek. 55% lexical similarity with Awbono. SOV.

BEDOANAS [BED] 250 (1977 Voegelin and Voegelin). Northwest coast, Bomberai Peninsula, Fakfak Kabupaten, Kokas Kecamatan. Austronesian, Malayo-Polynesian, Central-Eastern, Eastern Malayo-Polynesian, South Halmahera-West New Guinea, West New Guinea, Bomberai.

BERIK ***(BERRIK, BERICK, UPPER TOR)*** [BER] 1,200 (1994 SIL). North coast area along the mid and upper Tor River, inland from Sarmi. Jayapura Kabupaten, Tor Atas Kecamatan; Bora Bora, Waf, Doronta, Beu, Togonfo, Dangken, Kondirjan, Somanente, Tenwer, Sewan, Safrontani, and Taminambor villages. Trans-New Guinea, Northern, Tor, Tor. 45% lexical similarity with Keder. Bilingual level estimates for Irianese Malay are 0 10%, 1 30%, 2 25%, 3 20%, 4 10%, 5 5%. Formerly the trade language of the Tor area. Traditional religion, Christian. NT 1993.

BETAF [BFE] 400 (1973 R. Sterner SIL). North coast area east of Sarmi, Jayapura Kabupaten, Pantai Timur Kecamatan. Unclassified.

BIAK ***(BIAK-NUMFOR, NOEFOOR, MAFOOR, MEFOOR, NUFOOR, MAFOORSCH, MYFOORSCH)*** [BHW] 40,000 native speakers, quite a few thousand second language users (1981 Wurm and Hattori). Islands of Biak and Numfor to the north and on numerous small islands east and west of the Bird's Head, including Mapia Island. Biak Numfor Kabupaten. Austronesian, Malayo-Polynesian, Central-Eastern, Eastern Malayo-Polynesian, South Halmahera-West New Guinea, West New Guinea, Cenderawasih Bay, Biakic. Dialects: ARIOM, BO'O, DWAR, FAIRI, JENURES, KORIM, MANDUSIR, MOFU, OPIF, PADOA, PENASIFU, SAMBERI, SAMPORI (MOKMER), SOR, SORENDIDORI, SUNDEI, WARI, WADIBU, SORIDO, BOSNIK, KORIDO, WARSA, WARDO, KAMER, MAPIA, MIOS NUM, RUMBERPON, MONOARFU, VOGELKOP. Some consider Biak and Numfor to be two languages. Vigorous. Investigation needed: intelligibility with Biak, Numfor. Christian. NT 1990.

BIKSI ***(INISINE, BIAKSI)*** [BDX] 200 in Irian Jaya (1978 SIL). Population total both countries 400. Headwaters of Upper Sepik, Jayawijaya Kabupaten, Kiwirok Kecamatan. Many villages south of Gunung. Also spoken in Papua New Guinea. Sepik-Ramu, Sepik, Biksi. Very close to Yetfa, if not the same language.

BIRITAI ***(ATI, ALIKI)*** [BQQ] 250 (1988 SIL). Lakes Plain just north of mid Rouffaer River, village of Biri. Geelvink Bay, Lakes Plain, Tariku, East. SOV, tonal.

BONERIF ***(BENERAF)*** [BNV] 4 (1994 Westrum SIL). North coast area on east side of the upper Tor River, north of Mander and south of Berik and Kwesten languages, village of Beneraf. Jayapura Kabupaten, Pantai Timur Kecamatan. Trans-New Guinea, Northern, Tor, Tor. Speakers intermarry with the Berik and use Berik as second language. Nearly extinct.

BONGGO ***(ARMOPA, BGU, BOGU, BONGO)*** [BPG] 432 (1975 SIL). Northeast coast east of Sarmi and west of Demta near Betaf; villages of Taronta, Tarawasi, Armopa. Jayapura Kabupaten, Bonggo

Kecamatan. Austronesian, Malayo-Polynesian, Central-Eastern, Eastern Malayo-Polynesian, Oceanic, Western Oceanic, North New Guinea, Sarmi-Jayapura Bay, Sarmi.

BURATE [BTI] 100 approximately (1987 SIL). Near mouth of the Wapoga River, Yapen Waropen Kabupaten, Waropen Bawah Kecamatan. Geelvink Bay, East Geelvink Bay. Semi-nomadic.

BURMESO ***(TAURAP, BOROMESO, BORUMESSO, BURUMESO, MONAU, MONAO, MANAU)*** [BZU] 250 (1998 Donohue). Burmeso village and isolated temporary houses along nearby rivers, mid Mamberamo River between Trimuris and Sikari northeast of Danau Bira (Lake Holmes). Jayapura Kabupaten, Mamberamo Tengah Kecamatan. Language Isolate. Less than 5% lexical similarity with any other languages. Many proficient in Indonesian, more than surrounding groups. Many understand nearby languages. All domains. All ages. Vigorous. Interest in language strong. Not spoken by outsiders. Pride in ethnic identity. Dictionary. Fishermen, hunters, sago horticulturalists, animal husbandry: chickens, ducks. 200 meters. Christian.

BURUMAKOK [AIP] 40 or more (1994 Kroneman). Lowlands area south of the main ranges, southeast of Sumo and Dekai, south of Langda and Bomela, Jayawijaya Kabupaten, Kurima Kecamatan, village of Burumakok, south of Sumtanon, east of Siradala. Trans-New Guinea, Main Section, Central and Western, Central and South New Guinea-Kutubuan, Central and South New Guinea, Ok, Western. Some bilingual ability. All ages.

BURUWAI ***(ASIENARA, ASIANARA, KARUFA, MADIDWANA, SABAKOR)*** [ASI] 700 (1978 SIL). South Bomberai Peninsula along the southwest part of Kamrau Bay, Fakfak Kabupaten, Kaimana Kecamatan; Yarona, Kuna, Esania, Marobia, Guriasa, Tairi, Hia, and Gaka villages. Trans-New Guinea, Main Section, Central and Western, Central and South New Guinea-Kutubuan, Central and South New Guinea, Asmat-Kamoro.

BUSAMI [BSM] 700 (1993 R. Doriot UFM). South and north coast, Serui Island near 136', villages of Kamanap, Masiaroti, Kaonda. Yapen Waropen Kabupaten, Yapen Barat and Yapen Selatan kecamatans. Austronesian, Malayo-Polynesian, Central-Eastern, Eastern Malayo-Polynesian, South Halmahera-West New Guinea, West New Guinea, Cenderawasih Bay, Yapen, Central-Western. Three dialects. 71% lexical similarity with Ansus, 63% with Serui-Laut.

CITAK ***(CICAK, TJITAK, TJITJAK, KAUNAK, AMAT DARAT)*** [TXT] 8,000 (1985 M. Stringer TEAM). South coast area, west of the upper Digul River, north of Awyu, east of Asmat, Senggo and north, 19 villages. Merauke Kabupaten, Citak-Mitak Kecamatan. Trans-New Guinea, Main Section, Central and Western, Central and South New Guinea-Kutubuan, Central and South New Guinea, Asmat-Kamoro. Dialects: SENGGO, KOMASMA, BUBIS, ESAUN, PIRABANAK, VAKAM, TIAU. A closely related language to Asmat. Bilingual level estimates for Indonesian are 0 90%, 1 10%, 2 0%, 3 0%, 4 0%, 5 0%. Vigorous. NT 1995.

CITAK, TAMNIM ***(TAMNIM, ASMAT DARAT)*** [TML] 290 (1993 R. Doriot UFM). Near Senggo, villages of Tamnim, Epem, Zinak, Wowi. Merauke Kabupaten, Citak-Mitak Kecamatan. Trans-New Guinea, Main Section, Central and Western, Central and South New Guinea-Kutubuan, Central and South New Guinea, Asmat-Kamoro. May be linguistically closer to Asmat, but the speakers want to be called Citak, not Asmat. Vigorous.

DABE ***(MANGAMBILIS)*** [DBE] 200(?) (1993 R. Doriot UFM). Upper Tor River area, north coast east of Sarmi, village of Dabe. Jayapura Kabupaten, Pantai Timur Kecamatan. Trans-New Guinea, Northern, Tor, Tor.

DAMAL ***(UHUNDUNI, AMUNG, AMUNG KAL, AMUNGME, AMUY, ENGGIPILOE, HAMUNG, OEHOENDOENI)*** [UHN] 14,000 (1991 UBS). Central highlands west of the Western Dani, east of Ekari, southeast of the source of the Kemandoga River, all around Puncak Jaya, northern and southern Carstens Mts. Paniai Kabupaten, Ilaga and Beoga kecamatans. Trans-New Guinea, Main Section, Central and Western, Wissel Lakes-Kemandoga, Uhunduni. Dialects: DAMAL, AMUNG, ENGGIPILU. Related to Ekari, Moni, Wolani. Tonal. NT 1988.

DANI, LOWER GRAND VALLEY [DNI] 20,000 (1996). Central highlands, Baliem Grand Valley and upper gorge. Trans-New Guinea, Main Section, Central and Western, Dani-Kwerba, Southern, Dani. Dialects: LOWER GRAND VALLEY HITIGIMA (DANI-KURIMA, KURIMA), UPPER BELE, LOWER BELE, LOWER KIMBIN (KIBIN), UPPER PYRAMID. Christian, traditional religion. NT 1989-1994.

DANI, MID GRAND VALLEY ***(TULEM, CENTRAL GRAND VALLEY DANI, BALIEM VALLEY DANI)*** [DNT] 50,000 (1990 UBS). Baliem Valley. Trans-New Guinea, Main Section, Central and Western, Dani-Kwerba, Southern, Dani. Agriculturalists: sweet potatoes; animal husbandry: pigs. NT 1990.

DANI, UPPER GRAND VALLEY [DNA] 20,000 (1996). Central highlands, Baliem Grand Valley and upper gorge. Trans-New Guinea, Main Section, Central and Western, Dani-Kwerba, Southern, Dani. Christian, traditional religion. NT 1992.

DANI, WESTERN ***(DANI BARAT, ILAGA WESTERN DANI, LANI, LAANY, OERINGOEP, TIMORINI)*** [DNW] 180,000 (1993 census). Central highlands, west of Baliem Grand Valley and east from upper Kemandoga Valley. Trans-New Guinea, Main Section, Central and Western, Dani-Kwerba, Southern,

Dani. Dialects: WESTERN DANI OF PYRAMID, WESTERN DANI OF BOKONDINI. Many other dialects are not as distinct as those listed. Literacy rate in second language: 10% semi-literate. NT 1981.

DAO [DAZ] 250 (1991 SIL). West central highlands, Paniai kabupaten, Napan Kecamatan, east of Cenderawasih Bay along the Dao River. Trans-New Guinea, Main Section, Central and Western, Wissel Lakes-Kemandoga, Ekari-Wolani-Moni.

DEM ***(LEM, NDEM)*** [DEM] 1,000 (1987 SIL). Western highlands along upper Rouffaer River north of Damal, northeast of Western Dani. Trans-New Guinea, Main Section, Central and Western, Dem.

DEMISA [DEI] 500 (1993 R. Doriot UFM). First language in Desawa and Muyere villages along the coast in Waropen Bawah District, and Botawa village in the interior along the Wonoi River. Reported to be the lingua franca of most of the eastern side of Cenderawasih Bay, and of semi-nomadic people in interior Waropen Bawah. Geelvink Bay, East Geelvink Bay. Trade language.

DEMTA ***(MURIS)*** [DMY] 836 (1975 SIL). North coast west of Tanamerah Bay, villages of Demta, Muris Besar, Muris Kecil, Ambora, Yougafsa. Trans-New Guinea, Main Section, Central and Western, Sentani.

DIUWE [DIY] 100 (1999 D. Clouse SIL). 12 miles southwest of Sumo, east of the Catalina River. Trans-New Guinea, Main Section, Central and Western, Central and South New Guinea-Kutubuan, Central and South New Guinea, Asmat-Kamoro.

DOUTAI ***(TAORI-SO, TAORI, TOLITAI)*** [TDS] 335 (1993 R. Doriot UFM). Lakes Plain area at Toli-Dou village, west and south of Taiyeve. Geelvink Bay, Lakes Plain, Tariku, East.

DUBU [DMU] 130 (1978 SIL). Border area south of Jayapura, south of Waris, east of Emumu, north of Towei languages, villages of Affi, Dobu, Yambe. Trans-New Guinea, Pauwasi, Western.

DURIANKERE ***(ESARO, SAILEN, DURIANKARI)*** [DBN] 100 (1988 SIL). On a small island in the Raja Ampat Islands in the strait between Salawati Island and the west end of Bird's Head. Trans-New Guinea, South Bird's Head-Timor-Alor-Pantar, South Bird's Head, Inanwatan. Reported that the only speakers are elderly.

DUSNER ***(DUSNIR)*** [DSN] 6 (1978 SIL). Around the town of Dusner, west coast of Cenderawasih Bay, Wandamen Bay area. Only one village. Austronesian, Malayo-Polynesian, Central-Eastern, Eastern Malayo-Polynesian, South Halmahera-West New Guinea, West New Guinea, Cenderawasih Bay, Biakic. Nearly extinct.

DUVLE ***(DUVELE, WIRI, DUVDE, DUVRE)*** [DUV] 800 to 1,000 (1996 UFM). Lakes Plain area south of Van Daalen River and north of Mulia, Paniai. Eastern dialect along Dagai River, western dialect along Fedide and Wedi rivers. Geelvink Bay, Lakes Plain, Tariku, Duvle. Dialects: EASTERN DUVLE, WESTERN DUVLE. Closest to Kaiy. Little difference between dialects. Wano is the trade language. Vigorous.

EDOPI ***(ELOPI, DOU, DOUFOU)*** [DBF] 1,000 (1995 SIL). Around the juncture of the Tariku (Rouffaer) and Kliki (Fou) rivers. Geelvink Bay, Lakes Plain, Tariku, Central. SOV, tonal. Literacy rate in first language: Below 5%. Literacy rate in second language: Below 5%.

EIPOMEK ***(EIPO, T-VALLEY)*** [EIP] 3,000 (1987 SIL). Eastern highlands area, Eipo River, east of Nalca. Trans-New Guinea, Mek, Eastern. 80% lexical similarity with Una.

EKARI ***(KAPAUKU, EKAGI, MEE MANA, TAPIRO)*** [EKG] 100,000 (1985 Marion Doble CMA). West central highlands, Paniai, 135.25-137 E, 3.25-4.10 S. Trans-New Guinea, Main Section, Central and Western, Wissel Lakes-Kemandoga, Ekari-Wolani-Moni. Dialects: SIMORI, YABI (JABI), MAPIYA-KEGATA. Closest to Wolani. Slight dialect difference with Mapiya-Kegata. Bilingual level estimates for Indonesian are 0 10%, 1 40%, 2 20%, 3 15%, 4 10%, 5 5%. They call themselves 'Me'. The Moni call them 'Ekari'. 'Kapauku' is used for them by their southern neighbors. Tropical forest, pine forest, savannah, swamps. Rugged mountain chains, deep valleys. 1,500 meters. NT 1963-1985.

ELSENG ***("MORWAP", JANGGU, DJANGGU, TABU, SAWA)*** [MRF] 300 (1991 SIL). Jayapura kabupaten, Arso, Abepura, Kemtuk Gresi, Senggi kecamatans, south of Jayapura, northeast of the Kaure. Trans-New Guinea, Morwap. Not closely related to any other language. Reported minimal ability in Indonesian. Vigorous. Almost no influence from outside. "Morwap" means 'what is that?' and is vigorously rejected by speakers and government officials. Lowland sago palm. Sago hunter-horticulturalists.

EMUMU ***(KIAMEROP)*** [ENR] 1,100 (1987 SIL). Border area south of Jayapura, 11 villages. Trans-New Guinea, Pauwasi, Eastern.

ERITAI ***(EDITODE EDAI, ERAI, ERI, BARUA, BABURIWA, BABIRUWA, BABRUWA, BABRUA, ALIKI, HAYA)*** [BAD] 400 to 450 (1987 D. L. Martin WT). West of the Mamberamo River, Lakes Plain area in low mountains just south of Danau Bira (Lake Holmes), around the Kustera airstrip, to the villages of Erai to the east, Kustera, and Haya to the south. Jayapura Kabupaten, Mamberamo Tengah and Mamberamo Hulu kecamatans. Geelvink Bay, Lakes Plain, Tariku, East. The dialect in Obogwi village is close but not the same. Also related to Kaiy, Doutai, Biritai. 76% lexical similarity with Obokuitai, 50% with Sikaritai. Some people at Kustera are bilingual in Bauzi, but not those in other villages. Vigorous. SOV, tonal.

EROKWANAS [ERW] 250 (1977 Voegelin and Voegelin). Northwest coast of Bomberai Peninsula, north of Baham language. Austronesian, Malayo-Polynesian, Central-Eastern, Eastern Malayo-Polynesian, South Halmahera-West New Guinea, West New Guinea, Bomberai.

FAYU *(SEHUDATE)* [FAU] 400 (1991 SIL). West of juncture of Tariku (Rouffaer) and Kliki (Fou) rivers, west of the Kirikiri language. Geelvink Bay, Lakes Plain, Tariku, West. 4 nomadic groups.

FOAU [FLH] 232 (1975 SIL). Foa and Mudiay village, east Lakes Plain area just north of lower Idenburg River. Geelvink Bay, Lakes Plain, East Lakes Plain. Closely related to Dabra and Taworta.

GRESI *(GRESIK, KLESI)* [GRS] 2,500 (1987 SIL). West of Lake Sentani, southeast of Genyem, in villages of Hawa, Bring, Tabangkwari, Yansu, Ibub, Sunna, Klaysu. Trans-New Guinea, Nimboran. 80% lexical similarity with Kemtuik. Bilingualism in Indonesian.

HATAM *(HATTAM, ATAM, TINAM, MIRIEI, MOI, ADIHUP, URAN, BORAI, MANSIM)* [HAD] 16,000 (1993 TEAM). Eastern Bird's Head, northeast of Manikion, south and southwest of Manokwari. Manokwari Kabupaten; Warmare, Ransiki, and Oransbari kecamatans. West Papuan, Hattam. Dialects: MOI (MOIRE), TINAM, MIRIEI, ADIHUP, URAN. Mountain slope. Traditional religion, Christian. NT 1993.

HUPLA *(SOBA)* [HAP] 3,000 or more (1982 WT). Central highlands area near east side of Baliem gorge. Trans-New Guinea, Main Section, Central and Western, Dani-Kwerba, Southern, Dani. Closely related to Lower Grand Valley Dani. NT 1994.

IAU *(FOI, URUNDI, URURI, YAU, TURU, IAW)* [TMU] 1,000 to 1,200 (1991 SIL). Waropen, Paniai, Mulia, Lakes Plain area between Rouffaer and upper Van Daalen rivers, villages of Barere, Fawi, and Taiyai. Poi dialect on Rouffaer River, Turu dialect on Van Daalen River. Geelvink Bay, Lakes Plain, Tariku, Central. Dialects: FOI, TURU, IAU. Closely related to Edopi. Distinct from Turu (Yawa). The varieties listed as dialects above may be separate languages. Bilingual level estimates for Indonesian are 0 98%, 1 2%, 2 0%, 3 0%, 4 0%, 5 0%. Investigation needed: intelligibility with dialects. Literacy rate in first language: 5% to 15%. Bible portions 1985-1993.

IHA *(KAPAUR)* [IHP] 5,500 (1987 SIL). Bomberai Peninsula, far west end around Fak Fak and north. Trans-New Guinea, Main Section, Central and Western, West Bomberai, West Bomberai Proper. Closely related to Baham.

IHA BASED PIDGIN [IHB] Bomberai Peninsula, far west end around Fak Fak and north. Pidgin, Iha based. Trade language. Second language only.

IRARUTU *(IRAHUTU, IRUTU, KASIRA, ARGUNI BAY, KAITERO)* [IRH] 4,000 (1987 SIL). East Bomberai Peninsula southwest from Arguni Bay north to Bintuni Bay, 44 villages. Austronesian, Malayo-Polynesian, Central-Eastern, Unclassified. 6 or 7 dialects. Literacy rate in second language: 15% to 25%. Tropical forest. Coastal swamp. Fishermen. Bible portions 1992.

IRESIM [IRE] 100 (1977 Lincoln). South Cenderawasih Bay, west of Nabire and around Yamur Lake. Austronesian, Malayo-Polynesian, Central-Eastern, Eastern Malayo-Polynesian, South Halmahera-West New Guinea, West New Guinea, Cenderawasih Bay, Iresim.

ISIRAWA *(SAWERI, SABERI, OKWASAR)* [SRL] 2,000 (1993 R. Doriot UFM). Jayapura, north coast, around Sarmi and to the west, the villages of Mararena, Kamenawari, Amsira, Siaratesa, Perkami, Martewar, Arsania, Nisero, Arabais, Webro, Wari, Nuerawar, and Waim. Trans-New Guinea, Main Section, Central and Western, Dani-Kwerba, Northern, Isirawa. Dialects: WESTERN ISIRAWA, EASTERN ISIRAWA. Close to Kwerba. The dialects are very close. Bilingual level estimates for Indonesian are 0 0%, 1 30%, 2 40%, 3 30%, 4 0%, 5 0%. Vigorous. Trade language. Literacy rate in first language: 5% to 15%. Bible portions 1977-1992.

ITIK *(ITTIK, BETEF, ITTIK-TOR)* [ITX] 100 (1978 SIL). North coast east of Tor River, along upper Biri River. Trans-New Guinea, Northern, Tor, Tor. Dialects: ITTIK, ITTIK-TOR. Ethnic group: Borto.

IWUR *(IWOER)* [IWO] 1,000 (1987 SIL). Border area in valley of Iwur River, Ok Iwur and east to Ok Denom. Trans-New Guinea, Main Section, Central and Western, Central and South New Guinea-Kutubuan, Central and South New Guinea, Ok, Lowland.

JAIR *(DYAIR, DJAIR, YAIR, AWYU)* [YIR] 1,500 (1987 SIL). South coast west side of Digul River, south of Kombai, east of Awyu. Trans-New Guinea, Main Section, Central and Western, Central and South New Guinea-Kutubuan, Central and South New Guinea, Awyu-Dumut, Awyu.

KABURI [UKA] 600 (1986 Gravelle SIL). Southern Bird's Head, east of Kemberano and Arandai languages, north of Kokoda and Fakfak, Manokwari Kabupaten, Merdei, Inanwatan Kecamatans. Trans-New Guinea, South Bird's Head-Timor-Alor-Pantar, South Bird's Head, South Bird's Head Proper, Western.

KAIS *(AISO, ATORI, MINTAMANI, KAMPUNG BARU)* [KZM] 700 (1993 R. Doriot UFM). South Bird's Head area inland along Kais River, 8 villages. Trans-New Guinea, South Bird's Head-Timor-Alor-Pantar, South Bird's Head, South Bird's Head Proper, Western.

KAIY *(TAORI-KAIY, TAORI-KEI, KAI, TODI)* [TCQ] 250 (1991). Lakes Plain area around airstrip of Kaiy on lower Rouffaer River, villages of Kaiy and Kokou. Geelvink Bay, Lakes Plain, Tariku, East.

KALABRA ***(BERAUR)*** [KZZ] 2,100 (1975). West Bird's Head, south of Madik language, east of Moi. West Papuan, Bird's Head, West Bird's Head. Closest to Tehit.

KAMBERATARO ***(DERA, MANGGUAR, DRA)*** [KBV] 1,000 in Irian Jaya (1987 SIL). Population total both countries 1,700. Northeast Irian Jaya, south of Jayapura, near Waris; 13 villages. Also spoken in Papua New Guinea. Trans-New Guinea, Senagi.

KAMBERAU ***(KAMRAU, IRIA)*** [IRX] 1,570 (1993 R. Doriot UFM). Southeast Bomberai Peninsula around Kamrau Bay, villages of Ubia-Seramuku, Bahomia, Waho, Wamoma, Inari, Tanggaromi, Koi, Wamesa, Coa. Trans-New Guinea, Main Section, Central and Western, Central and South New Guinea-Kutubuan, Central and South New Guinea, Asmat-Kamoro. Closely related to Buruwai.

KAMORO ***(KAMORA, MIMIKA, LAKAHIA, NAGRAMADU, UMARI, MUKAMUGA, NEFERIPI, NEFARPI, NAFARPI, KAOKONAU)*** [KGQ] 8,000 (1987 SIL). South coast from Etna Bay to Mukamuga River. Trans-New Guinea, Main Section, Central and Western, Central and South New Guinea-Kutubuan, Central and South New Guinea, Asmat-Kamoro. Dialects: TARYA, YAMUR. Four other dialects. Many becoming bilingual in Indonesian. Different from Yeretuar (Umari).

KANUM, BÄDI ***(ENKELEMBU, KNWNE, KENUME)*** [KHD] 10 (1996 Mark Donohue). South coast border area, east of Merauke, bordering Southeast Marind on the east: Yanggandur, Tomer, Tomerau, Sota, Kondo, Onggaya, north and west of Smärky language. Trans-New Guinea, Trans-Fly-Bulaka River, Trans-Fly, Morehead and Upper Maro Rivers, Tonda. Intelligible to other Kanum variety speakers only with difficulty. Closely related to Yei. It has also been classified as Australian, Pama-Nyungan. They use Moraori or Indonesian as trade languages, Indonesian for official purposes. They use Kanum at home and in hunting camps. All ages. One ethnic group with other Kanum varieties. Clan marriages common, and much ritual exchange. Literacy rate in second language: 5%. Christian. Nearly extinct.

KANUM, NGKÂLMPW ***(ENKELEMBU, KNWNE, KENUME)*** [KCD] 150 (1996 Mark Donohue). South coast border area, east of Merauke, bordering Southeast Marind on the east: Yanggandur, Tomer, Tomerau, Sota, Kondo, Onggaya. to the north and west of Smärky language. Trans-New Guinea, Trans-Fly-Bulaka River, Trans-Fly, Morehead and Upper Maro Rivers, Tonda. The Kanum varieties are separate languages, intelligible to each other's speakers only with difficulty. Closely related to Yei. It has also been classified as Australian, Pama-Nyungan. They use Moraori or Indonesian as trade languages, Indonesian for official purposes. They use Kanum at home and in hunting camps. All ages. One ethnic group with the other Kanum varieties. Clan marriages common, and much ritual exchange. Literacy rate in second language: 5%. Christian.

KANUM, SMÄRKY ***(ENKELEMBU, KNWNE, KENUME)*** [KXQ] 80 or more (1996 Mark Donohue). South coast border area, east of Merauke, bordering Southeast Marind on the east: Yanggandur, Tomer, Tomerau, Sota, Kondo, Onggaya, bordering PNG. Trans-New Guinea, Trans-Fly-Bulaka River, Trans-Fly, Morehead and Upper Maro Rivers, Tonda. Intelligible to other speakers Kanum varieties only with difficulty. Closely related to Yei. It has also been classified as Australian, Pama-Nyungan. They use Moraori or Indonesian as trade languages, Indonesian for official purposes. They use Kanum at home and in hunting camps. All ages. One ethnic group with other Kanum varieties. Clan marriages common, and much ritual exchange. Literacy rate in second language: 5%. Christian.

KANUM, SOTA ***(ENKELEMBU, KNWNE, KENUME)*** [KRZ] 100 or more (1996 Mark Donohue). Population total both countries 100 or more. South coast border area, east of Merauke, bordering Southeast Marind on the east: Yanggandur, Tomer, Tomerau, Sota, Kondo, Onggaya, north and west of Smärky language. Also spoken in Papua New Guinea. Trans-New Guinea, Trans-Fly-Bulaka River, Trans-Fly, Morehead and Upper Maro Rivers, Tonda. Intelligible to other Kanum variety speakers only with difficulty. Closely related to Yei. It has also been classified as Australian, Pama-Nyungan. They use Moraori or Indonesian as trade languages, Indonesian for official purposes. They use Kanum at home and in hunting camps. All ages. One ethnic group with other Kanum varieties. Clan marriages common, and much ritual exchange. Literacy rate in second language: 5%. Christian.

KAPORI ***(KAPAURI)*** [KHP] 60 (1978 SIL). Village of Pagai on north bank of upper Idenburg River. Trans-New Guinea, Kaure.

KARAS [KGV] 200 (1978 SIL). Karas Island, off southwest coast of Bomberai Peninsula, southeast from Fak Fak. Trans-New Guinea, Main Section, Central and Western, West Bomberai, Karas.

KARON DORI ***(MAIYACH, MEON)*** [KGW] 5,000 (1987 SIL). Central Bird's Head north of Brat, villages of Pef, Asses, Sunopi, Siakwa. West Papuan, Bird's Head, North-Central Bird's Head, Central Bird's Head. Closely related to Mai Brat.

KAURE ***(KAUREH)*** [BPP] 450 (1995 SIL). Southwest of Lake Sentani along Nawa River, in villages of Lereh, Harna, Wes, Masta, Aurina. Trans-New Guinea, Kaure, Kaure Proper. SOV. Bible portions 1990.

KAUWERA ***(KAUWERAWEC, KAUWERAWETJ, KAOWERAWEDJ)*** [QKX] 400 or more (1987 SIL). East of mid Mamberamo, north and south of Kasonaweja. Trans-New Guinea, Main Section, Central and Western, Dani-Kwerba, Northern, Kwerba. Vigorous. Tropical forest. Hunters, horticulturalists. Traditional religion, Christian.

KAWE [KGB] 300 (1978 SIL). West end of Waigeo Island off west coast of Bird's Head, Raja Ampat Islands, villages of Salio, Selepele, Bianci, Menyefun. Austronesian, Malayo-Polynesian, Central-Eastern, Eastern Malayo-Polynesian, South Halmahera-West New Guinea, West New Guinea, Cenderawasih Bay, Raja Ampat. Related dialects or languages: Maya, Maden, Palamul, Matbat.

KAYAGAR ***(KAYGIR, KAJAGAR)*** [KYT] 10,000 (1993 WT). South coast near Pirimapun and Sawi, Merauke area. Trans-New Guinea, Main Section, Central and Western, Kayagar. Literacy rate in second language: 10% semi-literate in Indonesian.

KAYUPULAU ***(KAJUPULAU)*** [KZU] 573 (1978 SIL). Villages of Kayubatu and Kayupulau in Jayapura harbor. Austronesian, Malayo-Polynesian, Central-Eastern, Eastern Malayo-Polynesian, Oceanic, Western Oceanic, North New Guinea, Sarmi-Jayapura Bay, Jayapura Bay. Not a dialect of Tobati (Yotafa). Only those 30 and older speak it. Declining in use.

KEDER [KDY] 200 to 600 (1973 SIL). North coast east of Tor River mouth. Trans-New Guinea, Northern, Tor, Tor. 45% lexical similarity with Berik.

KEHU [KHH] Area between Auye and Dao who live in the foothills, and the Wapoga River. Unclassified. Lowland swamps.

KEMBERANO ***(KALITAMI)*** [BZP] 1,500 (1987 SIL). Southern Bird's Head along the coast, east of Komundan River, south of Arandai language. Several villages also northwest Bomberai Peninsula, south from Kalitami across Bintuni Bay. Trans-New Guinea, South Bird's Head-Timor-Alor-Pantar, South Bird's Head, South Bird's Head Proper, Eastern. Dialects: BARAU, WERIAGAR.

KEMBRA [XKW] 30 (1991 SIL). Jayawijaya Kabupaten, Okbibab Kecamatan, east of the Sogber River. Unclassified. Nearly extinct.

KEMTUIK ***(KEMTUK, KAMTUK)*** [KMT] 2,500 (1987 SIL). West of Lake Sentani, villages of Mamdayawang, Meikari, Merem, Yanim, Braso, Aib, Sabransamon, Mamda, Sabeyap, Sabeyap Kecil, Sekorup, Aimbe, Sabron Yaru. East of Gresi language. Trans-New Guinea, Nimboran. Kemtuik and Gresi are 80% lexically similar. Bilingualism in Indonesian. All ages. Literacy rate in first language: 25% to 50%. Literacy rate in second language: 25% to 50%. Bible portions 1980-1993.

KETENGBAN ***(KUPEL, OKTENGBAN)*** [KIN] 12,000 to 14,000 (1998 Sims SIL). Scattered slopes in eastern highlands area east of Eipomek and west of Ngalum language near Papua New Guinea border. Trans-New Guinea, Mek, Eastern. Dialects: OKBAP, OMBAN, BIME, ONYA. Literacy rate in first language: 15% to 30%. Tropical forest. Hunter-gatherers; gardeners. NT 1997.

KIMAAMA ***(KIMAGHAMA, KALADDARSCH, TERI-KALWASCH)*** [KIG] 3,000 (1987 SIL). Kolopom (Frederik Hendrik) Island west of southeast Irian Jaya. Ngolar II, village 10 km. east of Marauke, is all Kimaama. Trans-New Guinea, Kolopom.

KIMKI ***(AIPKI, KIMGI, SUKUBATOM, SUKUBATONG)*** [SBT] 350 or fewer (1978 UFM). Border area where Sepik River enters Irian Jaya. Sepik-Ramu, Sepik, Biksi. Investigation needed: intelligibility with Biksi.

KIRIKIRI ***(KIRIRA)*** [KIY] 250 (1982 SIL). West of juncture of the Tariku (Rouffaer) and Kliki (Fou) rivers, villages at Dofu Wahuka, Paniai. Geelvink Bay, Lakes Plain, Tariku, West. Dialects: KIRIKIRI, FAIA. Most are functionally bilingual in Fayu or Edopi. No Indonesian spoken. All ages. Vigorous. SOV, tonal. Literacy rate in first language: Below 5%. Literacy rate in second language: Below 5%. Lowland swamps. Hunter-gatherers, sago.

KOFEI [KPI] 100 approximately (1987 SIL). East side of Geelvink Bay, recently moved to Sauri-Sirami village. There may be more living semi-nomadically in the interior. Geelvink Bay, East Geelvink Bay.

KOKODA ***(SAMALEK, ODERAGO, KOMUDAGO, NEBES, TAROF)*** [QKW] 3,700 (1991 SIL). Bird's Head, south coast on Maccluer Gulf, east of Inanwatan. Trans-New Guinea, South Bird's Head-Timor-Alor-Pantar, South Bird's Head, South Bird's Head Proper, Central. Dialects: KASUWERI (KOMUDAGO), NEGRI BESAR (NEGERI BESAR), TAROF. Wurm and Hattori 1981 list Kasuweri and Tarof as separate languages. Kasuweri 86% lexical similarity with Tarof, Negri Besar 82% with Tarof. Investigation needed: intelligibility with dialects.

KOMBAI ***(KOMBOY)*** [KGU] 5,000 including 4,000 Kombai (1991 SIL), 1,000 Wanggom (1978 SIL). South coast area east of Senggo around Boma. Trans-New Guinea, Main Section, Central and Western, Central and South New Guinea-Kutubuan, Central and South New Guinea, Awyu-Dumut, Dumut. Dialects: WANGGOM (WANGGO, WANGOM), CENTRAL KOMBAI, TAYAN. Closely related to Wambon, Mandobo.

KONDA ***(OGIT)*** [KND] 500 or more (1988 SIL). Southwest Bird's Head along lower Waromge River south of Teminabuan, villages of Konda and Teminabuan District. Trans-New Guinea, South Bird's Head-Timor-Alor-Pantar, South Bird's Head, Konda-Yahadian.

KONERAW [KDW] 300 (1978 SIL). South coast of Frederik Hendrik Island. Trans-New Guinea, Main Section, Central and Western, Central and South New Guinea-Kutubuan, Central and South New Guinea, Mombum.

KOPKAKA ***(KOPKA)*** [OPK] 250 (1988 Kroneman and Peckham SIL). Lowlands area south of the main ranges, southeast of Sumo and Dekai, south of Langda and Bomela, Jayawijaya Kabupaten, Kurima Kecamatan, villages of Siradala and Burungmakok. Trans-New Guinea, Main Section, Central and Western, Central and South New Guinea-Kutubuan, Central and South New Guinea, Ok, Western. Closely related to Kwer. No bilingual ability.

KOROWAI [KHE] 700 (1998 M. Donohue). South coast area, north of Boma, east of Senggo. Trans-New Guinea, Main Section, Central and Western, Central and South New Guinea-Kutubuan, Central and South New Guinea, Awyu-Dumut, Unclassified. Lowland swamp.

KOROWAI, NORTH [KRG] 100 (1998 M. Donohue). North of Korowai area, southeast of Siradala, west of Awimbon. Trans-New Guinea, Main Section, Central and Western, Central and South New Guinea-Kutubuan, Central and South New Guinea, Awyu-Dumut, Unclassified.

KORUPUN-SELA ***(KORAPUN, KIMYAL OF KORUPUN)*** [KPQ] 8,000 (1996 E. Young). Eastern highlands on upper reaches of Erok River, southwest of Nalca, east of Yali of Ninia, Jayawijaya District, Kurima region. Trans-New Guinea, Mek, Western. Dialects: KORUPUN (DURAM), DAGI, SISIBNA (GOBUGDUA), DEIBULA, SELA. Related to Nalca. Bilingual level estimates for Nipsan are 0 98%, 1 0%, 2 0%, 3 0%, 4 1.5%, 5 .5%. Bible portions 1980-1985.

KOSADLE ***(KOSARE)*** [KIQ] 250 (1993 R. Doriot UFM). Hulu Atas just west of juncture of Nawa and Idenburg rivers. Trans-New Guinea, Kaure, Kaure Proper.

KOWIAI ***(KOIWAI, KAIWAI, KUIWAI, AIDUMA, KAYUMERAH, KAJUMERAH)*** [KWH] 600 (1984 SIL). Bomberai Peninsula; southwest coast at Kaimana and in Kamrau Bay on several islands, villages of Keroi, Adijaya, Namatota, Waikala, Kayumerah. Austronesian, Malayo-Polynesian, Central-Eastern, Central Malayo-Polynesian, South Bomberai. Dialects: ADI, NAMATOTA (NAMATOTE). Blust says this appears to be Central Malayo-Polynesian. Bilingual level estimates are Indonesian: 0 0%, 1 0%, 2 60%, 3 34%, 4 5%, 5 1%; Irianese Malay: 0 0%, 1 0%, 2 1%, 3 99%, 4 0%, 5 0%. Tropical forest. Mountain slope, limestone karst, coral islands. Fishermen. 0 to 20 feet. Muslim.

KURI ***(MODAN, NABI)*** [NBN] 500 (1982 SIL). Southwest Bomberai Peninsula, along Nabi (Kuri) River west from Wandamen Bay, 16 villages. Austronesian, Malayo-Polynesian, Central-Eastern, Unclassified. Closely related to Irarutu. 'Nabi' is a name used by outsiders, 'Kuri' by insiders.

KURUDU [KJR] 2,180 (1993 R. Doriot UFM). Kurudu Island between eastern tip of Serui Island and mainland of Irian Jaya to east, villages of Kaipuri, Poiwai. Austronesian, Malayo-Polynesian, Central-Eastern, Eastern Malayo-Polynesian, South Halmahera-West New Guinea, West New Guinea, Cenderawasih Bay, Yapen, East. Kaipuri dialect has highest lexical similarity with Yapen group. 71% lexical similarity with Woriasi, 46% with Western Serui. Vigorous.

KWER [KWR] 100 (1998 M. Donohue). Lowlands area south of the main ranges, southeast of Sumo and Dekai, south of Langda and Bomela, Jayawijaya Kabupaten, Kurima Kecamatan, village of Kwer. Trans-New Guinea, Main Section, Central and Western, Central and South New Guinea-Kutubuan, Central and South New Guinea, Ok, Western. Closely related to Kopkaka. All ages.

KWERBA ***(AIRMATI, NAIBEDJ, TEKUTAMESO)*** [KWE] 2,500 (1996 SIL). Upper Tor River area, northeast, headwaters of Apauwer River inland from Sarmi east to Berik language, villages of Aurime, Munukania, Wamariri, Tatsewalem around Apiaweti. Trans-New Guinea, Main Section, Central and Western, Dani-Kwerba, Northern, Kwerba. Dialects: SERIKENAM, SASAWA, NOGUKWABAI. Literacy rate in first language: Below 5%. Tropical forest. Hunter-gatherers; some agriculturalists. Traditional religion, Christian. Bible portions 1986-1991.

KWERBA MAMBERAMO ***(NOPUKW, NOPUK, NOBUK)*** [NOB] 300(?) (1993 R. Doriot UFM). East of Mamberamo River, in the mountains between the villages of Kwerba, Edifalen, and Marinafalen, south of Kasonaweja. Trans-New Guinea, Main Section, Central and Western, Dani-Kwerba, Northern, Kwerba. All ages. Vigorous. 'Nopukw' means 'language' in the Kwerba family, and does not distinguish a particular variety. Tropical forest. Mountain slope. Hunter-gatherers. Traditional religion, Christian.

KWERISA [KKB] 55 (1993 R. Doriot UFM). At village of Kaiy on lower Rouffaer River. Geelvink Bay, Lakes Plain, Tariku, East. Bilingualism in Kaiy. There may be a few older speakers (1987). Most or all now speak Kaiy. Nearly extinct.

KWESTEN [KWT] 2,000 (1987 SIL). Lower Tor River, north coast area inland east of Sarmi, villages of Holmhaven, Mafenter, Arare, Omte. Trans-New Guinea, Northern, Tor, Tor. 40% lexical similarity with Berik.

LEGENYEM ***(LAGANYAN)*** [LCC] 300(?) (1993 R. Doriot UFM). Raja Ampat Islands, Waigeo Island in northwest end of main bay and on south coast, villages of Beo, Lempintol and Wawiai. Austronesian, Malayo-Polynesian, Central-Eastern, Eastern Malayo-Polynesian, South Halmahera-West New Guinea, West New Guinea, Cenderawasih Bay, Raja Ampat.

LEPKI [LPE] 530 (1991 SIL). Jayawijaya kabupaten, Okbibab kecamatan, on the Sogber River, east and north of the Ketengban. Unclassified. Some speakers at Luban have some ability in Ketengban. SOV, head and dependent marking, tonal.

LIKI ***(MOAR)*** [LIO] 100 (1998 M. Donohue). Islands off north coast of Sarmi, Jayapura Kabupaten, Sarmi Kecamatan. Austronesian, Malayo-Polynesian, Central-Eastern, Eastern Malayo-Polynesian, Oceanic, Western Oceanic, North New Guinea, Sarmi-Jayapura Bay, Sarmi. Used in church by local leaders. Reported to be the same as Sobei. Investigation needed: intelligibility with Sobei.

MADEN ***(SAPRAN)*** [XMX] 400(?) (1981 Wurm and Hattori). Raja Ampat Islands, northwestern Salawati Island. Austronesian, Malayo-Polynesian, Central-Eastern, Eastern Malayo-Polynesian, South Halmahera-West New Guinea, West New Guinea, Cenderawasih Bay, Raja Ampat. Possibly the same as Maya.

MAI BRAT ***(AYAMARU, AJAMARU, BRAT, MAIBRAT, MEY BRAT)*** [AYZ] 20,000 or more (1987 SIL). Central Bird's Head around Ayamaru Lakes, about 40 villages. West Papuan, Bird's Head, North-Central Bird's Head, Central Bird's Head. Dialects: MAISAWIET, MAIYAH, MAIMAKA, MAITE, MAISEFA. 10% lexical similarity with Tehit, Mpur, Abun, its closest neighbors. 5,000 to 7,000 are in cities and are very bilingual, some highly educated. Maibrat is used in church. All ages. 'Ayamaru' is name of the people, 'Mai Brat' of language. SVO, heavy verb serialization. Literacy rate in first language: 25% to 50%. Literacy rate in second language: 25% to 50%. Bible portions 1990-1994.

MAIRASI ***(FARANYAO, KANIRAN)*** [FRY] 3,300 (1996 L. Peckham). Bomberai Peninsula, southwest coast of neck, east and northeast from Kaimana, Wasior, Triton Bay. Trans-New Guinea, Main Section, Central and Western, Mairasi-Tanahmerah, Mairasi. Dialect: NORTHEASTERN MAIRASI. Close to Semimi. Northeastern Mairasi may be a separate language. Bilingual level estimates for Indonesian are 0 5%, 1 20%, 2 30%, 3 20%, 4 23%, 5 2%. Some speak some Kowiai and Indonesian. Literacy rate in second language: 15% to 25%. Bible portions 1986-1987.

MAKLEW ***(MAKLEU)*** [MGF] 120. South coast area, east side of Marianne strait, west of Marind and east of Yelmek languages. Trans-New Guinea, Trans-Fly-Bulaka River, Bulaka River.

MANDER [MQR] 20 (1991 SIL). North coast area on the upper Bu River, a tributary of the Upper Tor River. Trans-New Guinea, Northern, Tor, Tor. Speakers intermarry with the Berik, and speak Berik as second language. Nomadic. Nearly extinct.

MANDOBO ***(NUB, DUMUT, "KAETI", MANDOBBO)*** [KZH] Population total both countries 10,000 (1987 SIL). Border area near Fly River on east side of Digul River between Tanahmerah and Mindiptanah. Also spoken in Papua New Guinea. Trans-New Guinea, Main Section, Central and Western, Central and South New Guinea-Kutubuan, Central and South New Guinea, Awyu-Dumut, Dumut. "Kaeti" is an offensive name.

MANEM ***(YETI, JETI, WEMBI, SKOFRO)*** [JET] 400 in Irian Jaya (1978 SIL). Northeast border area south of Jayapura, villages of Wembi, Yeti, Kibai, Uskuar, Griku, Skotiaho, Skofro. Trans-New Guinea, Northern, Border, Waris. 50% lexical similarity with Waris. Bilingualism in Indonesian. Literacy rate in second language: Significant level. See main entry under Papua New Guinea.

MANIKION ***(MANTION, SOUGB, SOGH)*** [MNX] 12,000 (1987 SIL). East Bird's Head, east of Meyah, south of Manokwari, about 50 villages. East Bird's Head. Four dialects. NT 1996.

MAPIA ***(MAPIAN)*** [MPY] 1 speaker on Mapia Island. Mapia Islands, about 180 miles north of Manokwari. Austronesian, Malayo-Polynesian, Central-Eastern, Eastern Malayo-Polynesian, Oceanic, Central-Eastern Oceanic, Remote Oceanic, Micronesian, Micronesian Proper, Ponapeic-Trukic, Trukic. Speaker is elderly. Ethnic group went to Micronesia, and presumably speak a language from there, probably either Palauan, Sonsorol, or Tobian. Nearly extinct.

MARAU [MVR] 1,700 (1987 SIL). South coast of Serui Island, 5 villages. Austronesian, Malayo-Polynesian, Central-Eastern, Eastern Malayo-Polynesian, South Halmahera-West New Guinea, West New Guinea, Cenderawasih Bay, Yapen, Central-Western. Dialect: WARABORI (NATABUI, WAREMBORI). 82% lexical similarity with Pom, Munggui, Papuma, Ansus.

MAREMGI ***(MARENGGE)*** [MRX] 47 (1975 SIL). North coast inland from Bonggo language, village of Marengge. Trans-New Guinea, Northern, Tor, Tor. Unintelligible to speakers in neighboring settlements including Bonggo.

MARIND [MRZ] 7,000 (1987 SIL). South coast around Merauke, 2 villages. Trans-New Guinea, Main Section, Central and Western, Marind, Marind Proper. Dialects: GAWIR, SOUTHEAST MARIND, TUGERI, HALIFOERSCH. Four or more dialects. Significant differences between inland and coastal dialects, but speakers report intelligibility. Vigorous. Children in towns have passive ability. Positive language attitudes. Dictionary. Grammar. Seasonal savannah. Bible portions.

MARIND, BIAN ***(BOVEN-MBIAN, BIAN, NORTHWEST MARIND)*** [BPV] 900 (1977 Voegelin and Voegelin). Bian River area near Merauke, Merauke Kabupaten, Muting Kecamatan, and Sanayu village on Maro River. Trans-New Guinea, Main Section, Central and Western, Marind, Marind Proper. Not inherently intelligible with Marind.

MARUB [MJB] 100 or fewer (1999 D. Clouse SIL). Between Kwer and Tokuni on the west bank of the Sirec River. Trans-New Guinea, Main Section, Central and Western, Central and South New Guinea-Kutubuan, Central and South New Guinea, Ok, Western.

MASIMASI [ISM] 200 (1973 SIL). Island off north coast east of the Tor River mouth, Jayapura Kabupaten, Pantai Timur Kecamatan. Austronesian, Malayo-Polynesian, Central-Eastern, Eastern Malayo-Polynesian, Oceanic, Western Oceanic, North New Guinea, Sarmi-Jayapura Bay, Sarmi.

MASSEP ***(MASEP)*** [MVS] 40 (1978 SIL). North coast east of Mamberamo River mouth and west of Sarmi, near Apauwer River. Trans-New Guinea, Main Section, Central and Western, Dani-Kwerba, Northern, Massep.

MATBAT ***(ME, BIGA)*** [XMT] 550 (1991 SIL). Raja Ampat Islands, Misool Island, Segaf Islands. Austronesian, Malayo-Polynesian, Central-Eastern, Eastern Malayo-Polynesian, South Halmahera-West New Guinea, West New Guinea, Cenderawasih Bay, Raja Ampat.

MAWES [MGK] 693 (1975 SIL). Northeast coast east of Sarmi near mouth of Wirowai River, villages of Mawes, Mawesweres, Mawesdai. Trans-New Guinea, Northern, Tor, Mawes.

MA'YA ***(SALAWATI, SAMATE, SAILOLOF)*** [SLZ] 1,600 (1991 SIL). Raja Ampat Islands, central Waigeo Island and central Salawati Island. Austronesian, Malayo-Polynesian, Central-Eastern, Eastern Malayo-Polynesian, South Halmahera-West New Guinea, West New Guinea, Cenderawasih Bay, Raja Ampat. Dialects: MA'YA, KAWIT, BANLOL, BATANTA ISLAND.

MEKWEI ***(MENGGEI, MUNGGAI, MUNGGE, DEMENGGONG-WAIBRON-BANO, MENGGWEI, MUNKEI, MOOI, MOI, WAIPU)*** [MSF] 1,200 (1987 SIL). West of Lake Sentani, villages of Maribu, Waibrong, Kendate, Sabron Dosay. Trans-New Guinea, Nimboran. 60% lexical similarity with Kemtuik. Bilingualism in Indonesian. Different from Moi (Mosana).

MEOSWAR ***(WAR)*** [MVX] 250(?) (1993 R. Doriot UFM). Meoswar Island, west Cenderawasih Bay. Austronesian, Malayo-Polynesian, Central-Eastern, Eastern Malayo-Polynesian, South Halmahera-West New Guinea, West New Guinea, Cenderawasih Bay, Biakic.

MER ***(MURI, MIERE)*** [MNU] 100 to 300 (1988 L. Peckham SIL). Central Bird's Head, headwaters of Wosimi and Uremo River. Trans-New Guinea, Main Section, Central and Western, Mairasi-Tanahmerah, Mairasi.

MEYAH ***(MEAX, MEYACH, MEAH, MEJAH, MEJACH)*** [MEJ] 15,000 to 20,000 (1995 G. Gravelle SIL). East Bird's Head, north coast, west of Manokwari, north of Hattam language, and scattered locations. East Bird's Head, Meax. Closest to Sougb. Many are becoming bilingual in Indonesian. Literacy rate in first language: 25% to 50%. Literacy rate in second language: 25% to 50%. NT 1997.

MLAP ***(KWANSU, KWANSU-BONGGRANG, KUANGSU-BONGGRANG, KWANGSU-BONGGRANG)*** [KJA] 350 (1977 SIL). West of Lake Sentani, just north of Gresi language. Trans-New Guinea, Nimboran. 60% lexical similarity with Kemtuik. Most speakers use Indonesian as second language. Many or most speak or understand Kemtuik. There is a lot of intermarriage with Kemtuik speakers. 'Kwansu' is an obsolete village name.

MOI ***(MOSANA)*** [MXN] 4,600 (1993 R. Doriot UFM). Salawati Island, west Bird's Head around Sorong, 9 villages. West Papuan, Bird's Head, West Bird's Head. Different from Mekwei (Moi).

MOLOF ***(AMPAS)*** [MSL] 200 (1978 SIL). South of Jayapura, west of Waris. Trans-New Guinea, Molof. Not closely related to any other language.

MOMBUM ***(KEMELOM)*** [MSO] 250 (1993 R. Doriot UFM). Island next to southeast coast of Fredrik Hendrik Island. Trans-New Guinea, Main Section, Central and Western, Central and South New Guinea-Kutubuan, Central and South New Guinea, Mombum. Closest to Koneraw.

MOMINA [MMB] 200 (1998M. Donohue). Lowlands just south of main ranges extending from south of Silimo east to south of Una language, Samboka village. Trans-New Guinea, Main Section, Central and Western, Central and South New Guinea-Kutubuan, Central and South New Guinea, Momuna.

MOMUNA ***(SOMAHAI, SOMAGE, SUMOHAI)*** [MQF] 2,700 (1987 SIL). Lowlands just south of main ranges extending from south of Silimo east to south of Una language. Trans-New Guinea, Main Section, Central and Western, Central and South New Guinea-Kutubuan, Central and South New Guinea, Momuna. No bilinguals. They have contact with Dani who are learning Momuna. Literacy rate in first language: 5% to 15%. Bible portions 1985-1987.

MONI ***(MIGANI, DJONGGUNU, JONGGUNU)*** [MNZ] 20,000 (1991 SIL). Central highlands, 10 to 70 miles northeast of Lake Paniai. Trans-New Guinea, Main Section, Central and Western, Wissel Lakes-Kemandoga, Ekari-Wolani-Moni. Dialect: AWEMBAK (AWEMBIAK). NT 1990.

MOR [MHZ] 700 (1987 SIL). Mor Islands in east Cenderawasih Bay near Nabire. Austronesian, Malayo-Polynesian, Central-Eastern, Eastern Malayo-Polynesian, South Halmahera-West New Guinea, West New Guinea, Cenderawasih Bay, Mor. Different from Trans-New Guinea Mor. Tonal.

MOR [MOQ] 60 (1977 Voegelin and Voegelin). Northwest Bomberai Peninsula, coast of Bintuni Bay. Trans-New Guinea, Main Section, Central and Western, Mor. Distinct from Austronesian Mor.

MORAID [MSG] 1,000 or fewer (1988 SIL). West Bird's Head, east of Moi and south of Madik languages, villages of Sailala, Makbon, Luwelala, Seni. West Papuan, Bird's Head, West Bird's Head.

MORORI ***(MORAORI, MOARAERI, MORARI, MARORI)*** [MOK] 50 out of an ethnic population of 250 (1998 M. Donohue). South coast border area 20 km. east of Merauke, east of Marind, west of Kanum. Trans-New Guinea, Trans-Fly-Bulaka River, Trans-Fly, Moraori. Menge dialect remembered as the language of ceremony, though the last Menge speaker died in 1997. All use Irianese Malay or Indonesian as second language. Many proficient in Marind. Over 30. Rainforest. Coastal swamp.

MOSKONA ***(SABENA, MENINGGO, MENINGO)*** [MTJ] 8,000 (1996 G. Gravelle SIL). Southeast Bird's Head, south of Meyah and west of Manikion. East Bird's Head, Meax. 85% lexical similarity with Meyah. Also related to Manikion.

MPUR ***(KEBAR, AMBERBAKEN, EKWARE, DEKWAMBRE)*** [AKC] 7,000 (1993 R. Doriot UFM). North coast of Bird's Head, west of Manokwari, and Kebar Valley. West Papuan, Kebar. Dialects: SIRIR, AJIW. Literacy rate in second language: 15% to 25%.

MUNGGUI ***(NATABUI)*** [MTH] 800 (1982 SIL). North coast of Serui Island near 135.50', villages of Munggui, Windesi, Murui, Asei Puramati. Austronesian, Malayo-Polynesian, Central-Eastern, Eastern Malayo-Polynesian, South Halmahera-West New Guinea, West New Guinea, Cenderawasih Bay, Yapen, Central-Western. 82% lexical similarity with Marau, Papuma.

MURKIM [RMH] Jayawijaya kabupaten, Kiwirok kecamatan, border area around the Mot airstrip, near the headwaters of the Sepik River. Unclassified.

NAFRI [NXX] 1,630 (1975 SIL). Nafri village, southeast end of Yotafa Bay, Jayapura area. Trans-New Guinea, Main Section, Central and Western, Sentani, Sentani Proper.

NAKAI [NKJ] 700 (1999 Mark Donohue). East of the upper Digul River, Awimbom village in the center of 5 other villages extending toward Ok Sibil to the northeast, and a little way to the south-west toward Iwur. No settlement on the west side of the Digul River, with a large unpopulated area between Nakai and Burumakok. Trans-New Guinea, Main Section, Central and Western, Central and South New Guinea-Kutubuan, Central and South New Guinea, Ok, Mountain. They report difficulty in understanding Indonesian or Malay. Lowlands. Sago hunters.

NALCA ***(HMANGGONA, NALTJE, NALTYA, HMONONO, KIMYAL, KIMJAL)*** [TVL] 8,000 to 10,000 (1987 SIL). Eastern highlands area on north slopes of ranges northeast of Korupun and southeast of Nipsan. Trans-New Guinea, Mek, Western. Distinct from Korupun (Kimyal). Literacy rate in second language: Below 1% semi-literate. Bible portions.

NARAU [NXU] 100(?) (1993 R. Doriot UFM). Kecamatan Kaureh, Jayapura area. Trans-New Guinea, Kaure, Kaure Proper.

NDOM [NQM] 450 (1977 Voegelin and Voegelin). Kolopom (Frederik Hendrik) Island. Trans-New Guinea, Kolopom. Closest to Kimaama, Riantana.

NDUGA ***(NDUGWA, NDAUWA, DAUWA, DAWA, PESECHEM, PESECHAM, PESEGEM)*** [NDX] 10,000 (1985 Mary Owen CMA). Jayawijaya, Tiom, central highlands, south of high ranges, south of Western Dani, north of Asmat. Widely scattered. Trans-New Guinea, Main Section, Central and Western, Dani-Kwerba, Southern, Ngalik-Nduga. Dialects: SINAK NDUGA, HITADIPA NDUGA. Bilingual level estimates for Dani are 0 60%, 1 10%, 2 20%, 3 0%, 4 0%, 5 10%. Some speak Damal, Moni, Indonesian. NT 1984.

NGALUM [SZB] 10,000 in Indonesia (1987 SIL). Population total both countries 18,000 (1981 Wurm and Hattori). Valleys of Ok Sibil, Ok Tsop, and perhaps Ok Bon, border area in main range north of Muyu (Yongkom) and Iwur languages, northeast of Nakai. Also spoken in Papua New Guinea. Trans-New Guinea, Main Section, Central and Western, Central and South New Guinea-Kutubuan, Central and South New Guinea, Ok, Mountain. Dialects: NGALUM, APMISIBIL, SIBIL. NT 1992.

NGGEM [NBQ] 3,000 (1991 SIL). Along the middle Haflifoeri River, north of Wamena. Trans-New Guinea, Main Section, Central and Western, Dani-Kwerba, Southern, Dani. Closely related to Walak. 50% lexical similarity with Western Dani. SOV clause chaining. Bible portions 1982.

NIMBORAN ***(NAMBRONG)*** [NIR] Ethnic population: 3,500 (1987 SIL). North Irian Jaya, due west of Lake Sentani, about 26 villages. Trans-New Guinea, Nimboran. 40% lexical similarity with Kemtuik. Bilingualism in Irianese Malay. Restricted to older people. Children learn Irianese Malay exclusively. Bible portions 1982-1985.

NINGGERUM ***(NINGGRUM, NINGGIRUM, NINGGEROEM, KATIVA, KASIWA, ORGWO, MUYU)*** [NXR] 1,000 in Irian Jaya. Border area and in Papua New Guinea between the Ok Birim and Ok Tedi Rivers. Trans-New Guinea, Main Section, Central and Western, Central and South New Guinea-Kutubuan, Central and South New Guinea, Ok, Lowland. Speakers are called 'Muyu'. See main entry under Papua New Guinea.

NIPSAN ***(SOUTHERN JALE, YALE-NIPSAN)*** [NPS] 2,500 (1993 R. Doriot UFM). Jayawijaya, Kurima, just west of Hmanggona. Trans-New Guinea, Mek, Western. 78% lexical similarity with Yale-Kosarek. Distinct from Yali of Ninia, Yali of Angguruk, and Yali of Pass Valley.

NISA ***(BONEFA, KEREMA)*** [NIC] 500 (1987 SIL). Inland from east side of Geelvink Bay around Danau Nisa. Geelvink Bay, East Geelvink Bay. Vigorous.

OBOKUITAI ***(OBOGWITAI, ATI, ALIKI)*** [AFZ] 130 (1996 SIL). Lakes Plain just north of mid Rouffaer River, village of Obogwi. Geelvink Bay, Lakes Plain, Tariku, East. Different from Doutai, Biritai, Sikaritai, but related. 76% lexical similarity with Eritai. Ati means 'language'. SOV, tonal. Literacy rate in first language: 15%. Bible portions 1994.

ONIN [ONI] 600 (1978 SIL). North and northwest Bomberai Peninsula. Austronesian, Malayo-Polynesian, Central-Eastern, Central Malayo-Polynesian, North Bomberai. Dialects: NIKUDA, OGAR, PATIPI, SEPA. Muslim mainly.

ONIN BASED PIDGIN [ONX] Onin Peninsula. Pidgin, Onin based. Second language only.

ORMU [ORZ] 600 (1995 SIL). North coast area just west of Jayapura, villages of Ormu Besar and Ormu Kecil, north of the Cyclops Mountains. Austronesian, Malayo-Polynesian, Central-Eastern, Eastern Malayo-Polynesian, Oceanic, Western Oceanic, North New Guinea, Sarmi-Jayapura Bay, Jayapura Bay. May use Indonsian as second language.

ORYA ***(URIA, WARPOK)*** [URY] 1,600 (1985 Philip Fields SIL). Immediately southwest of Nimboran, north of Lereh, Jayapura district, Unurum-Guay, villages of Nembonton, Bwasom, Guay, Dore, Suma, Santosa, Taja, Witi, Orya. 140.83 E to 139.47 E, 02.40.66 S to 02.37 S. 44 nautical miles from Sentani, 22 from Genyem. Trans-New Guinea, Northern, Tor, Orya. Dialects: BARAT (WEST ORYA), TIMUR (EAST ORYA), YAPSI-TAJA. Slight dialect differences. Bilingual level estimates for Indonesian are 0 0%, 1 55%, 2 23%, 3 19%, 4 2%, 5 1%. 'Uria' is a misspelling used earlier. 'Warpok' is the Nimboran name. Literacy rate in first language: 15% to 25%. Tropical forest. Interfluvial. Swidden agriculturalists. 1,200 feet to about 300 feet. Bible portions 1987-1995.

PALAMUL [PLX] 200(?) (1981 Wurm and Hattori). Raja Ampat Islands, southwestern Salawati Island around Sailolof. Austronesian, Malayo-Polynesian, Central-Eastern, Eastern Malayo-Polynesian, South Halmahera-West New Guinea, West New Guinea, Cenderawasih Bay, Raja Ampat.

PAPASENA [PAS] 400 (1982 SIL). Lakes Plain area on lower Idenburg River just east of juncture with Rouffaer River. Geelvink Bay, Lakes Plain, Tariku, East. 23% lexical similarity with Sikaritai.

PAPUMA [PPM] 600 (1982 SIL). South coast of Serui Island near 135.50', village of Papuma. Austronesian, Malayo-Polynesian, Central-Eastern, Eastern Malayo-Polynesian, South Halmahera-West New Guinea, West New Guinea, Cenderawasih Bay, Yapen, Central-Western. 82% lexical similarity with Munggui, Marau, Ansus. Vigorous.

PODENA [PDN] 200 (1954 A. C. van der Leeden ms.). Island off north coast of Biri River, Jayapura Kabupaten, Bonggo Kecamatan. Austronesian, Malayo-Polynesian, Central-Eastern, Eastern Malayo-Polynesian, Oceanic, Western Oceanic, North New Guinea, Sarmi-Jayapura Bay, Sarmi.

POM [PMO] 2,000 (1987 SIL). Miosnum Island and west Serui Island, villages of Pom, Serewen, Mias Endi. Austronesian, Malayo-Polynesian, Central-Eastern, Eastern Malayo-Polynesian, South Halmahera-West New Guinea, West New Guinea, Cenderawasih Bay, Yapen, Central-Western. Dialect: JOBI.

PURAGI ***(MOGAO)*** [PRU] 700 (1991 SIL). Southwest Bird's Head along Maccluer Gulf, inland around Matamani River. Trans-New Guinea, South Bird's Head-Timor-Alor-Pantar, South Bird's Head, South Bird's Head Proper, Western.

RASAWA [RAC] 200 or more (1987 SIL). Two villages near the southern coast of Waropen Bawah District. Geelvink Bay, Lakes Plain, Rasawa-Saponi.

RIANTANA [RAN] 1,100 (1977 Voegelin and Voegelin). Frederik Hendrik Island. Trans-New Guinea, Kolopom.

ROON ***(RON)*** [RNN] 1,100 (1993 R. Doriot UFM). Roon Island west of Cenderawasih Bay, north of Wandamen Peninsula. Austronesian, Malayo-Polynesian, Central-Eastern, Eastern Malayo-Polynesian, South Halmahera-West New Guinea, West New Guinea, Cenderawasih Bay, Yapen, Central-Western.

SAMAROKENA ***(SAMARKENA, KARFASIA, TAMAYA, TAMAJA)*** [TMJ] 400 (1982 SIL). North coast inland just east of Apawar River, west of Sarmi, villages of Karfasia, Samarkena, Maseb, Tamaya. Trans-New Guinea, Main Section, Central and Western, Dani-Kwerba, Northern, Samarokena. Speakers bilingual in Airoran, Isirawa, and some in Kwerba. Coastal.

SAPONI [SPI] 10 or fewer (1987 SIL). Botawa village, interior Waropen Bawah District. Geelvink Bay, Lakes Plain, Rasawa-Saponi. Nearly extinct.

SAURI [SAH] 100 (1987 SIL). East side of Cenderawasih Bay near Waropen language, in Sauri-Sirami village, near Sirami River. Geelvink Bay, East Geelvink Bay.

SAUSE ***(SEUCE)*** [SAO] 300 (1993 SIL). Southwest of Sentani, northwest of Lereh, villages of Ures, Mubararon, Sause-Bokoko, Witti-Yadow, Lidya, Puaral. Trans-New Guinea, Northern, Tor, Unclassified.

SAWERU [SWR] 300 (1991 SIL). Central Serui Island, Serui Waropen kabupaten, Yapen Selatan kecamatan, on an island south of Yapen Island near Serui. Geelvink Bay, Yawa. Coastal.

SAWI ***(SAWUY, AEJAUROH)*** [SAW] 3,500 (1993 R. Doriot UFM). Merauke, Atsy, near south coastal lowland, between Kronkel and Ayip rivers and upper Fayit River area, villages of Kamur, Esebor, Wiagas, Minahai, Comoro. Trans-New Guinea, Main Section, Central and Western, Central and

South New Guinea-Kutubuan, Central and South New Guinea, Awyu-Dumut, Sawi. Closest to Awyu. Bilingual level estimates for Indonesian are 0 75%, 1 25%, 2 0%, 3 0%, 4 0%, 5 0%. Literacy rate in second language: 5% semi-literate. NT 1973-1994.

SEGET [SBG] 1,200 (1988 SIL). West Bird's Head southwest of Sorong, west and southwest of Moi language, villages of Walian, Sailolof, Segum, Seget. West Papuan, Bird's Head, West Bird's Head.

SEKAR *(SEKA)* [SKZ] 450 (1977 Voegelin and Voegelin). Northwest Bomberai Peninsula on coast and one small island. Austronesian, Malayo-Polynesian, Central-Eastern, Central Malayo-Polynesian, North Bomberai. Arguni has the highest percentage of lexical similarity with Sekar.

SEMIMI *(ETNA BAY)* [ETZ] 1,000 (1991 L. Peckham SIL). Bomberai Peninsula close to Kaniran, south part of neck extending west to Triton Bay. Trans-New Guinea, Main Section, Central and Western, Mairasi-Tanahmerah, Mairasi.

SEMPAN *(NARARAPI)* [SEM] 1,000 (1987 SIL). Middle south coast, between Kokonao and Agats, east of Kamoro and west of Asmat languages. Trans-New Guinea, Main Section, Central and Western, Central and South New Guinea-Kutubuan, Central and South New Guinea, Asmat-Kamoro. Close to Kamoro and Nefarpi.

SENGGI [SNU] 120 (1978 SIL). Border area south of Jayapura, villages of Senggi and Tomfor. Trans-New Guinea, Northern, Border, Waris.

SENTANI *(BUYAKA)* [SET] 30,000 (1996 SIL). Around Lake Sentani, about 30 villages. Trans-New Guinea, Main Section, Central and Western, Sentani, Sentani Proper. Dialects: EAST SENTANI, WEST SENTANI, CENTRAL SENTANI. 'Buyaka' is their name for themselves. Dictionary. Grammar. Literacy rate in first language: 50% to 75%. Literacy rate in second language: 50% to 75%. Fishermen, agriculturalists. Traditional religion, Christian. NT 1997.

SERUI-LAUT *(ARUI)* [SEU] 1,200 (1987 SIL). South central Serui Island and Nau Island south of Serui, 5 villages. Austronesian, Malayo-Polynesian, Central-Eastern, Eastern Malayo-Polynesian, South Halmahera-West New Guinea, West New Guinea, Cenderawasih Bay, Yapen, Central-Western. 82% lexical similarity with Ansus, 77% with Ambai. Vigorous.

SIAGHA-YENIMU *(SIAGHA, SYIAGHA, SJIAGHA, SIJAGHA, OSER, YENIMU, JENIMU)* [OSR] 3,000 (1987 SIL). Southeast near coast, north of lower Digul River. Trans-New Guinea, Main Section, Central and Western, Central and South New Guinea-Kutubuan, Central and South New Guinea, Awyu-Dumut, Awyu.

SIKARITAI *(AIKWAKAI, TORI AIKWAKAI, SIKARI)* [TTY] 800 (1993 R. Doriot UFM). Lakes Plain area just north of junction of Idenburg and Rouffaer rivers, along Mamberamo River, and west 15 miles, south 10 miles, villages of Sikari, Haya, Iri. Geelvink Bay, Lakes Plain, Tariku, East. Vigorous.

SILIMO *(SOUTH NGALIK, PAIYAGE)* [WUL] 5,000 (1987 SIL). Central highlands south of the range immediately west of the Baliem River, Amo, Kiniage valleys. Trans-New Guinea, Main Section, Central and Western, Dani-Kwerba, Southern, Ngalik-Nduga. Dialect: LOWER SAMENAGE. NT 1992.

SKOU *(SKO, SKOUW, SKOW, SEKOU, TUMAWO, TE MAWO)* [SKV] 700 (1999 M. Donohue). North coast border area east of Jayapura, at the mouth of the Tami River, villages of Sko-Yambe, Sko-Mabu, Sko-Sai. Sko, Vanimo. Related to Vanimo, Wutung, Yako. Most people use Irianese Malay or Indonesian, Wutung of Papua New Guinea or Vanimo to speakers of those languages. Comprehension is limited. All domains. All ages. Some older Wutung people use Sko as their second or third language. They have reservations about Indonesian. Dictionary. Literacy rate in first language: 10%. Literacy rate in second language: 10% Indonesian. Literacy motivation high, program in progress. Sago palms. Coastal, swamps. Christian.

SOBEI *(BIGA, IMASI)* [SOB] 1,850 (1987 SIL). North coast area east of Sarmi, Jayapura Kabupaten, Sarmi Kecamatan. Austronesian, Malayo-Polynesian, Central-Eastern, Eastern Malayo-Polynesian, Oceanic, Western Oceanic, North New Guinea, Sarmi-Jayapura Bay, Sarmi. Reported to be the same as, or intelligible with, Liki. Children bilingual in Indonesian. Irianese Malay is used with people from other language groups. Bilingual evaluation needed with adequate sampling of community and degrees of proficiency investigated. Government schools through entire area. Intermarriage with other language groups increasing. Investigation needed: bilingual proficiency in Indonesian, Irianese Malay.

SOWANDA *(WAINA, WINA, WANYA, WANJA)* [SOW] A few. Northeast border area south of Jayapura. Trans-New Guinea, Northern, Border, Waris. See main entry under Papua New Guinea.

SUABO *(SUABAU, INANWATAN)* [SZP] 1,100 (1987 SIL). South Bird's Head along Maccluer Gulf, 15 villages. Trans-New Guinea, South Bird's Head-Timor-Alor-Pantar, South Bird's Head, Inanwatan. Closest to Duriankere.

TABLA *(TEPERA, TANAH MERAH, TABI)* [TNM] 3,750 (1990 UBS). Jayapura, Demta, Depapre, 13 villages on north coast east and west of Tanahmerah Bay. Trans-New Guinea, Main Section, Central and Western, Sentani, Sentani Proper. Dialects: YOKARI, TEPERA, YEWENA-YONGSU. Yokari dialect understood by other dialects at 80% to 95%, others have 95% to 100% intelligibility with each other. Tabla has 30% lexical similarity with Sentani (closest). Bilingual level estimates for Indonesian are 0 1%, 1 1%, 2 8%, 3 85%, 4 5%, 5 0%. Distinct from Tanahmerah (Sumeri) of Bomberai Peninsula. 'Tepera' is their name for themselves. Bible portions 1986.

TAIKAT ***(TAJKAT, ARSO)*** [AOS] 600 (1978 SIL). Northeast border area, straight south of Jayapura. Trans-New Guinea, Northern, Border, Taikat. Closest to Awyi.

TAMAGARIO ***(BURU, TAMARAW, WAGOW)*** [TCG] 3,500 (1987 SIL). South coast area between Gondu and Bapai rivers. Trans-New Guinea, Main Section, Central and Western, Kayagar.

TANAHMERAH ***(SUMERI, SUMERINE)*** [TCM] 500 (1978 SIL). North Bomberai Peninsula along the Gondu and Bapai rivers. Trans-New Guinea, Main Section, Central and Western, Mairasi-Tanahmerah, Tanahmerah. Distinct from Tanahmerah (Tabla) of Sentani branch.

TANDIA [TNI] 2 (1991 SIL). Bird's Head neck area just south of Wandamen Peninsula along Wohsimi River. Austronesian, Malayo-Polynesian, Central-Eastern, Eastern Malayo-Polynesian, South Halmahera-West New Guinea, West New Guinea, Cenderawasih Bay, Tandia. Bilingualism in Wandamen. Most Tandia people speak Wandamen. Nearly extinct.

TARPIA ***(KAPTIAUW, KAPITIAUW)*** [SUF] 564 (1978 SIL). North coast area near Demta, villages of Tarfia and Kaptiau, Jayapura Kabupaten, Demta and Bonggo kecamatans. Austronesian, Malayo-Polynesian, Central-Eastern, Eastern Malayo-Polynesian, Oceanic, Western Oceanic, North New Guinea, Sarmi-Jayapura Bay, Sarmi. Dialects: SUFRAI, TARPIA (TARFIA). Closest to Bonggo.

TAUSE ***(DOA, DARHA)*** [TAD] 350 (1993 R. Doriot UFM). Around Deraposi, southwest of Danau Bira, northeast of Fayu language, northwest of Edopi language, western Lakes Plain (Paniai). Geelvink Bay, Lakes Plain, Tariku, West. Dialects: TAUSE, WEIRATE, DEIRATE. Related to Fayu and Kirikiri, but a separate language. Bilingual level estimates for Fayu are 0 75%, 1 15%, 2 7%, 3 2%, 4 0%, 5 1%. No Indonesian spoken. There is a trade language spoken with nearby language speakers. First contact with outside world in 1982.

TAWORTA ***(TAWORTA-AERO, TARIA, DABRA, BOK)*** [TBP] 150 (1993 R. Doriot UFM). Lakes Plain area on the south side of the Idenburg River east of Taiyeve, Jayapura Kabupaten, Mamberamo Hulu Kecamatan. Geelvink Bay, Lakes Plain, East Lakes Plain.

TEFARO ***(DEMBA)*** [TFO] 100 approximately (1987 SIL). East side of Cenderawasih Bay, in villages of Tefaro and Demba. Geelvink Bay, East Geelvink Bay.

TEHIT ***(TEHID, KAIBUS)*** [KPS] 8,800 (1993 R. Doriot). Southwest Bird's Head, kecamatan Teminabuan, about 35 villages. West Papuan, Bird's Head, West Bird's Head. Dialects: TEHIT JIT, MBOL FLE, SAIFI, IMYAN, SFA RIERE, FKAR, SAWIAT SALMEIT. Closest to Kalabra. Literacy rate in second language: 15% to 25%.

TOBATI ***(JOTAFA, YOTAFA, YAUTEFA, HUMBOLDT JOTAFA, JAYAPURA, ENGGROS, TOBWADIC)*** [TTI] 350 (1998 M. Donohue). Jayapura Bay, close to Jayapura, villages of Tobati, Enggros, Entrop, Kota Raja, Tanah Hitam. Austronesian, Malayo-Polynesian, Central-Eastern, Eastern Malayo-Polynesian, Oceanic, Western Oceanic, North New Guinea, Sarmi-Jayapura Bay, Jayapura Bay. Formerly classified as Papuan. Tobati villagers have mainly assimilated to Indonesian culture and language. Enggros maintains stronger language use, but is completely bilingual in Irianese Malay. Mud flats and pile houses in water.

TOFANMA ***(TOFAMNA)*** [TLG] 100(?) (1993 R. Doriot UFM). Tofanma village, south of Jayapura just east of Nawa River. Trans-New Guinea, Tofanma. Not closely related to any other language.

TOKUNI [TKO] 100 or fewer (1999 M. Donohue). Lowlands just south of main ranges, south of Momina and Kopkaka, Tokuni village. Trans-New Guinea, Main Section, Central and Western, Central and South New Guinea-Kutubuan, Central and South New Guinea, Ok, Western. Dialect chain running east and west. Closely related to Kopkaka. No bilingual speakers.

TOWEI ***(TOWE)*** [TTN] 115 (1975 SIL). Border area south of Jayapura, south of Dubu, west of Emumu languages, in and around Towe. Trans-New Guinea, Pauwasi, Western.

TRIMURIS [TIP] 300 (1999 SIL). East bank of the Mamberamo River between Kauwera and Bagusa languages, Jayapura Kabupaten, Mamberamo Tengah Kecamatan. Trans-New Guinea, Main Section, Central and Western, Dani-Kwerba, Northern, Kwerba. They do not understand Kwerba very well. About 70% lexical similarity with Kauwera and 60% with Kwerba. All ages. Vigorous. Tropical forest, swamp. Hunter-gatherers. Traditional religion, Christian.

TSAKWAMBO ***(KOTOGÜT, TSOKWAMBO)*** [KVZ] 500 (1991 SIL). South coast area on upper Digul River north of Mandobo language. Trans-New Guinea, Main Section, Central and Western, Central and South New Guinea-Kutubuan, Central and South New Guinea, Awyu-Dumut, Awyu, Aghu. Dialects or related languages: Ederah, Kia, Upper Digul, Upper Kaeme.

TUNGGARE ***(TARUNGGARE, TURUNGGARE)*** [TRT] 500 (1993 R. Doriot UFM). North central, inland from Waropen group, west of Mamberamo River, east Geelvink Bay near Nabire. Geelvink Bay, East Geelvink Bay. Most closely related to Bauzi. 70% lexical similarity with Bauzi.

UNA ***(GOLIATH, MT. GOLIATH, ORANJE-GEBERGTE, LANGDA)*** [MTG] 4,000 (1991 SIL). Eastern highlands on south slopes of main ranges east of Sela Valley, west of Ngalum, Bidabuh, east Weip Valley, Yay Valley, around Langda, Bomela, Sumtamon. Trans-New Guinea, Mek, Eastern. 80% lexical similarity with Eipomek. SOV, clause chaining, switch reference, split ergative. Literacy rate in first language: 5% to 15%.

URUANGNIRIN ***(FAUR, TUBIRUASA)*** [URN] 250 (1977 Voegelin and Voegelin). Two small islands between Karas Island and mainland of southwest Bomberai Peninsula. Austronesian, Malayo-Polynesian, Central-Eastern, Central Malayo-Polynesian, North Bomberai. Blust says this appears to be Central Malayo-Polynesian.

USKU [ULF] 150 (1991 SIL). Usku village, south of Jayapura, just south of Pauwasi. Trans-New Guinea, Usku. Not closely related to any other language.

WABO ***(WORIASI, NUSARI)*** [WBB] 1,500 (1987 SIL). North and south coast of east end of Serui Island, near 136.45' to 136.55', 6 villages. Austronesian, Malayo-Polynesian, Central-Eastern, Eastern Malayo-Polynesian, South Halmahera-West New Guinea, West New Guinea, Cenderawasih Bay, Yapen, East. 71% lexical similarity with Kurudu, 46% with Western Serui.

WAIGEO ***(AMBER, AMBERI, WAIGIU)*** [WGO] 300 (1978 SIL). North central Waigeo Island off western Bird's Head, Sorong Kabupaten, Waigeo Selatan Kecamatan, Warsanbin, Selegop, Waifoi, Go, Kabilol, Kabare, and Nyandesawai villages. Austronesian, Malayo-Polynesian, Central-Eastern, Eastern Malayo-Polynesian, South Halmahera-West New Guinea, West New Guinea, Cenderawasih Bay, Raja Ampat. Dialects: AMBER, SAONEK.

WAKDE [WKD] 400 (1980 SIL). Wakde Islands off the north coast just east of the Tor River, Jayapura Kabupaten, Pantai Timur Kecamatan. Austronesian, Malayo-Polynesian, Central-Eastern, Eastern Malayo-Polynesian, Oceanic, Western Oceanic, North New Guinea, Sarmi-Jayapura Bay, Sarmi.

WALAK ***(LOWER PYRAMID, WODO)*** [WLW] 1,500(?) (1993 R. Doriot UFM). Villages of Ilugwa, Wodo, Bugi, Mogonik, Wurigelebut. Trans-New Guinea, Main Section, Central and Western, Dani-Kwerba, Southern, Dani.

WAMBON [WMS] 3,000 (1987 SIL). South coast area northeast of Mandobo language. Trans-New Guinea, Main Section, Central and Western, Central and South New Guinea-Kutubuan, Central and South New Guinea, Awyu-Dumut, Dumut.

WANDAMEN ***(WANDAMEN-WINDESI, WINDESI, WINDESSI, BINTUNI, BENTUNI, BENTOENI, WAMESA)*** [WAD] 5,000 (1993 R. Doriot UFM). Wasior, Manokwari, west Cenderawasih Bay along Wandamen Bay extending west to east end of Bintuni Bay. Austronesian, Malayo-Polynesian, Central-Eastern, Eastern Malayo-Polynesian, South Halmahera-West New Guinea, West New Guinea, Cenderawasih Bay, Yapen, Central-Western. Dialects: WINDESI, BINTUNI, WAMESA, WASIOR, AMBUMI, DASENER, AIBONDENI. Bilingualism in Indonesian. Literacy rate in first language: 25%. Literacy rate in second language: 50%. Bible portions 1937-1994.

WANO [WNO] 3,500 (1993 R. Doriot UFM). Central highlands area on upper Rouffaer River basin north of Damal, northwest of Dem, south of Kirikiri. Trans-New Guinea, Main Section, Central and Western, Dani-Kwerba, Southern, Wano. Bible portions 1989.

WAREMBORI ***(WARENBORI, WAREMBOIVORO)*** [WSA] 600 (1998 SIL). North coast, mouth of Mamberamo River and west to Poiwai, villages of Warembori, Tamakuri, and Bonoi. Lower Mamberamo. Close to Yoke. About 33% lexical similarity with Yoke, and about 30% resembles Austronesian. Most are proficient in Irianese Malay. Indonesian and Yoke also spoken. Most are 20 and older, but there are speakers below 20. About 20 people use it as their second or third language. Much typology resembles Austronesian. Dictionary. SVO; prepositions; genitives before noun heads; articles, adjectives, numerals, relatives after noun heads; 1 prefix, 6 or more suffixes on a word; word order distinguishes subject, object, indirect object; topic (SVO) is for pragmatic salience; affixes do not indicate case of noun phrase; obligatory subject agreement, optional object agreement shown by verb affixes; the scope of a serialized quantifier shows a trace of ergativity; causative shown by verbs 'make' and 'give'; CV; nontonal. Literacy rate in second language: 30% in Indonesian. Swamp. Riverine. Swidden agriculturalists. Sea level. Christian.

WARES [WAI] 200(?) (1993 R. Doriot UFM). North coast area inland from Kwesten language on upper Biri River, south side, village of Mauswares. Trans-New Guinea, Northern, Tor, Tor. Distinct from Waris or Wari.

WARIS ***(WALSA)*** [WRS] 1,500 in Irian Jaya. Northeast Irian Jaya south of Jayapura. Trans-New Guinea, Northern, Border, Waris. NT, in press (1999). See main entry under Papua New Guinea.

WARITAI ***(WERETAI, WARI)*** [WBE] 300(?) (1993 R. Doriot UFM). Lakes Plain area around Taiyeve. Geelvink Bay, Lakes Plain, Tariku, East. Related language: Doutai. Different from Waris or Wares.

WARKAY-BIPIM ***(BIPIM AS-SO, BIPIM)*** [BGV] 300 (1993 R. Doriot UFM). South coast area bordering Asmat to east and Sawi to west, lower Eilanden River, 3 villages. Trans-New Guinea, Main Section, Central and Western, Marind, Yaqay. 50% of speakers somewhat bilingual in Indonesian or Asmat.

WAROPEN ***(WONTI, WORPEN)*** [WRP] 6,000 (1987 SIL). East Cenderawasih Bay, south coast of Serui Island. Austronesian, Malayo-Polynesian, Central-Eastern, Eastern Malayo-Polynesian, South Halmahera-West New Guinea, West New Guinea, Cenderawasih Bay, Waropen. Dialects: WAROPEN KAI, NAPAN, MO'OR. Literacy rate in second language: 25%.

WOI ***(WO'OI)*** [WBW] 1,300 (1987 SIL). Miosnum and west Serui Islands, villages of Wooi and Wainap. Austronesian, Malayo-Polynesian, Central-Eastern, Eastern Malayo-Polynesian, South Halmahera-West New Guinea, West New Guinea, Cenderawasih Bay, Yapen, Central-Western. 77% lexical similarity with Pom, Marau, Ansus.

WOLANI ***(WODANI, WODA, WODA-MO)*** [WOD] 5,000 (1992 UBS). Western central highlands along Kemandoga and Mbiyandogo rivers, north of Ekari language 75 miles northeast of Lake Paniai, north of Wissel Lakes and northwest of the Moni. Trans-New Guinea, Main Section, Central and Western, Wissel Lakes-Kemandoga, Ekari-Wolani-Moni. NT, in press (1995).

WORIA [WOR] 12 approximately (1987 SIL). Interior Waropen Bawah, Botawa village. Geelvink Bay, East Geelvink Bay. Botawa is a Demisa and Waropen speaking village. Nearly extinct.

YAFI ***(JAFI, YAFFI, WAGARINDEM, WARGARINDEM)*** [WFG] 175 (1975 SIL). Northeast Irian Jaya, border area south of Jayapura near Ampas, villages of Yaffri, Sungguar, Tainda, Abiu, Tokondo. Trans-New Guinea, Pauwasi, Eastern.

YAHADIAN ***(NERIGO, JAHADIAN)*** [NER] 500 (1991 SIL). South Bird's Head, between lower Mintamani River and Sekak River along Maccluer Gulf. Trans-New Guinea, South Bird's Head-Timor-Alor-Pantar, South Bird's Head, Konda-Yahadian.

YALE, KOSAREK ***(KOSAREK, YALE-KOSAREK, WANAM, INLOM)*** [KKL] 2,300 (1993 R. Doriot UFM). Eastern highlands, just east of Yali of Ninia, northwest of Nipsan, east of Dani, a little north of Yali of Angguruk. Trans-New Guinea, Mek, Western. Dialects: KOSAREK, GILIKA (KILIKA), TIPLE. Closely related to Nipsan, Nalca, and Gilika. The term 'In Lom' refers to only half the group. Bible portions 1992.

YALI, ANGGURUK ***(NORTHERN YALI, ANGGURUK, YALIMO)*** [YLI] 15,000 (1991 UBS). Central highlands area northwest of Nalca, east of Grand Valley Dani. Trans-New Guinea, Main Section, Central and Western, Dani-Kwerba, Southern, Ngalik-Nduga. Different from Yali of Ninia and Yali of Pass Valley, but related. NT 1988.

YALI, NINIA ***(NINIA, SOUTHERN YALI, JALY, JALÈ, NORTH NGALIK)*** [NLK] 10,000 to 12,000 (1999 J. D. Wilson WT). Central highlands area south of Angguruk, east of Soba, west of Korupun, including Ninia, Holuwon, and Lolat villages. Several hundred at Elelim, transmigrated by government in 1989 following earthquake. More than 50 villages. Trans-New Guinea, Main Section, Central and Western, Dani-Kwerba, Southern, Ngalik-Nduga. Different from Yali of Pass Valley, Yali of Angguruk, and Hupla, but closely related. Literacy rate in first language: 20%. Literacy program since 1990. Southern watershed of Jayawijaya Mts. Christian. Bible, in press (1999).

YALI, PASS VALLEY ***(WESTERN YALI, PASS VALLEY, ABENDAGO)*** [YAC] 5,000 or fewer (1988 SIL). Central highlands, east of Angguruk and northwest of Naltya, Jayawijaya, Kurulu, and Kurima. Trans-New Guinea, Main Section, Central and Western, Dani-Kwerba, Southern, Ngalik-Nduga. Dialects: PASS VALLEY, LANDIKMA, APAHAPSILI. Different from Yali of Ninia and Yali of Angguruk, but related. NT 1977.

YAMNA [YMN] 250 (1980 SIL). Island off the north coast east of the Tor River, Jayapura Kabupaten, Pantai Timur Kecamatan. Austronesian, Malayo-Polynesian, Central-Eastern, Eastern Malayo-Polynesian, Oceanic, Western Oceanic, North New Guinea, Sarmi-Jayapura Bay, Sarmi.

YAQAY ***(YAQAI, JAKAI, SOHUR, MAPI, JAQAI)*** [JAQ] 10,000 (1987 SIL). South coast area north of Odamun River and along Miwamon River southeast of Sawuy and Kaygir languages. Trans-New Guinea, Main Section, Central and Western, Marind, Yaqay. Dialects: OBA-MIWAMON, NAMBLOMON- MABUR, BAPAI. Many becoming bilingual in Indonesian.

YARSUN [YRS] 200 (1991 SIL). Island off the north coast east of the Biri River, Jayapura Kabupaten, Bonggo Kecamatan. Austronesian, Malayo-Polynesian, Central-Eastern, Eastern Malayo-Polynesian, Oceanic, Western Oceanic, North New Guinea, Sarmi-Jayapura Bay, Sarmi.

YAUR ***(JAUR)*** [JAU] 350 (1978 SIL). Lower end of Cenderawasih Bay, west of Iresim. Austronesian, Malayo-Polynesian, Central-Eastern, Eastern Malayo-Polynesian, South Halmahera-West New Guinea, West New Guinea, Cenderawasih Bay, Yaur.

YAWA ***(YAPANANI, MORA, TURU, MANTEMBU, YAVA, IAU)*** [YVA] 6,000 (1987 SIL). Central Serui Island, Serui Waropen, Serui Selatan, Timur Barat, 8 north coast villages, 2 interior villages, 18 south coast villages. Geelvink Bay, Yawa. Dialects: CENTRAL YAWA (MORA), WEST YAWA, SOUTH YAWA, NORTH YAWA, EAST YAWA. Distinct from Iau in Lakes Plain area. Literacy rate in first language: 15% to 25%. Bible portions 1989-1990.

YEI ***(YEY, JEI, JE, YEI-NAN)*** [JEI] Population total both countries 900 out of an ethnic population of 1,100 (1996 Donohue). Border area of south coast, east of Marind along Maro River, 6 villages. Also spoken in Papua New Guinea. Trans-New Guinea, Trans-Fly-Bulaka River, Trans-Fly, Morehead and Upper Maro Rivers, Yey. Dialects: UPPER YEI, LOWER YEI. The dialects are inherently intelligible with each other only with difficulty. Most are proficient in Irianese Malay or Marind. Different cultural group from Marind. Investigation needed: intelligibility with dialects.

YELMEK ***(JELMEK, JAB, JABSCH)*** [JEL] 400 (1978 SIL). South coast area on east side of Marianne Strait between Kolopom (Frederik Hendrik) Island and mainland. Trans-New Guinea, Trans-Fly-Bulaka River, Bulaka River. Closest to Maklew.

YERETUAR ***(GONI, UMAR, UMARI)*** [GOP] 250 (1978 SIL). Lower Cenderawasih Bay, south of Wandamen language. Austronesian, Malayo-Polynesian, Central-Eastern, Eastern Malayo-Polynesian, South Halmahera-West New Guinea, West New Guinea, Cenderawasih Bay, Yeretuar. Distinct from Kamoro.

YETFA [YET] 1,000 (1996 UFM). Jayawijaya kabupaten, Okbibab kecamatan, border area east and north of the Sogber River. Sepik-Ramu, Sepik, Biksi. Very closely related to, if not identical with, Biksi. Trade language in the area, extending to PNG border.

YOKE ***(YOKI, YAUKE, JAUKE, PAUWI)*** [YKI] 200 (1998 Donohue). East of Warembori east of the Mamberamo River, Jayapura Kabupaten, Mantarbori village. Recently moved to coastal location from the interior. Lower Mamberamo. About 33% lexical similarity with Warembori. Almost no ability in Indonesian. Some ability in Warembori, though more Warembori speak Yoke than vice versa. All ages. Vigorous.

YONGKOM ***(YONGOM, YONGGOM)*** [YON] 2,000 in Irian Jaya (1987 SIL). South coast border area just north of where Fly River forms border between Irian Jaya and Papua New Guinea. Trans-New Guinea, Main Section, Central and Western, Central and South New Guinea-Kutubuan, Central and South New Guinea, Ok, Lowland. Dialects: NORTHERN MUYU (NORTH KATI, NORTH MOEJOE, NIINATI, NINATIE, KATI-NINANTI, KATAUT), SOUTHERN MUYU (SOUTH KATI, SOUTH MOEJOE, DIGOEL, DIGUL, METOMKA, KATI METOMKA, OK BARI). 80% lexical similarity with Northern Muyu, 70% with Southern Muyu, 30% with Ninggerum. Bible portions 1965-1988. See main entry under Papua New Guinea.

INDONESIA (JAVA AND BALI)

107,600,000 in Java (1993), 2,778,000 in Bali (1993). Data accuracy estimate: B. The number of languages listed for Indonesia (Java and Bali) is 19. Of those, all are living languages. Diversity index 0.66.

BADUI [BAC] 5,000 (1989). West Java, Mount Kendeng, Kabupaten Rangkasbitung, Pandeglang, and Sukabumi. Austronesian, Malayo-Polynesian, Western Malayo-Polynesian, Sundic, Sundanese. Sometimes considered a dialect of Sunda. A separate socio-religious group. 'Inner' and 'outer' Badui refer to location and status within tribal religion. Traditional religion with Hindu or Buddhist influences.

BALI ***(BALINESE)*** [BZC] 3,800,000 (1993 Johnstone), 2.1% of the population (1987 UBS). Island of Bali, northern Nusapenida, western Lombok Islands, and east Java. 7,000 in south Sulawesi. Austronesian, Malayo-Polynesian, Western Malayo-Polynesian, Sundic, Bali-Sasak. Dialects: LOWLAND BALI (KLUNGKUNG, KARANGASEM, BULELENG, GIANYAR, TABANAN, JEMBRANA, BADUNG), HIGHLAND BALI ("BALI AGA"), NUSA PENIDA. Reported to be two distinct dialects: High Balinese is used in religion, but those who can handle it are diminishing. There are speech strata in several lowland varieties (Clynes 1989, personal communication). The term "Bali Aga" is considered derogatory by those who are called that. The variety spoken on Nusa Penida Island is associated with Bali Aga. It is a scattering of villages with minimal influence from the former Majapahit empire. Hindu. Bible 1990.

BALI SIGN LANGUAGE [BQY] 2,200 in the village, out of 50 deaf people and 2,150 hearing people (1995 T. Friedman). 1 village in Bali. Deaf sign language. The majority of the hearing people learn and use the sign language. This might not be the correct name.

BETAWI ***(JAKARTA MALAY, BETAWI MALAY, BATAVI, BATAWI, MELAYU JAKARTE)*** [BEW] 2,700,000 (1993 Johnstone). Jakarta, Java. Creole, Malay based. "A Malay based creole which is quite distinct from both standard Indonesian and from other Malay-based pidgins and creoles." It had evolved by the mid-19th century. Unique phonological, morphological, and lexical traits. There are also influences from Peranakan Chinese and Bali. Often not intelligible to Indonesian speakers not familiar with it (R. B. Allen, Jr. 1989). Functions as a 'low' variety in a diglossic situation, but is a prestige variety when used by the upper class. The people are called 'Betawi Asli' or 'Betawi'. Grammar.

CHINESE, HAKKA [HAK] 640,000 speakers (1982 CCCOWE). Sino-Tibetan, Chinese. Bible 1916. See main entry under China.

CHINESE, MANDARIN [CHN] 460,000 speakers (1982 CCCOWE). Scattered throughout Indonesia. Sino-Tibetan, Chinese. Of the five to six million ethnic Chinese in Indonesia (1979 CCCOWE; 5,500,000 in 1976 or 4% of total population according to United Nations), 65% (3,500,000 to 4,000,000) speak Indonesian in the home, 35% (2,000,000) speak 5 Chinese languages in the home. Bible 1874-1983. See main entry under China.

CHINESE, MIN DONG ***(MIN DONG)*** [CDO] 20,000 in Indonesia (1982 CCCOWE). Sino-Tibetan, Chinese. Dialect: XINGHUA (HSINGHUA). Bible 1884-1905. See main entry under China.

CHINESE, MIN NAN ***(MINNAN, MIN NAN)*** [CFR] 700,000 speakers in Indonesia (1982 CCCOWE). Pontianak (West Borneo) and elsewhere. Sino-Tibetan, Chinese. Dialects: FUJIAN (HOKKIEN), CHAOCHOW (TIU CHIU). Bible 1933. See main entry under China.

CHINESE, YUE ***(CANTONESE, YUE, YUEH)*** [YUH] 180,000 in Indonesia (1982 CCCOWE). Sino-Tibetan, Chinese. Bible 1894-1981. See main entry under China.

INDONESIAN ***(BAHASA INDONESIA)*** [INZ] 17,000,000 to 30,000,000 mother tongue speakers; over 140,000,000 second language users with varying levels of speaking and reading proficiency. Population total all countries 17,050,000 to 30,000,000. Used in all regions of Indonesia. Also spoken in Netherlands, Philippines, Saudi Arabia, Singapore, USA. Austronesian, Malayo-Polynesian, Western Malayo-Polynesian, Sundic, Malayic, Malayan, Local Malay. Reported to be modeled on Riau Malay of northeast Sumatra. Has regional variants. Over 80% cognate with Standard Malay. National language. Grammar. Roman and Arabic scripts. Muslim. Bible 1974-1985.

INDONESIAN SIGN LANGUAGE [INL] (At least 2,000,000 deaf people; 1993). Deaf sign language. 94 schools for the deaf use the oral method for instruction. A blend of Malaysian Sign Language and indigenous signs. ASL not used.

INDONESIAN, PERANAKAN ***(CHINESE INDONESIAN, BABA INDONESIAN, PERANAKAN)*** [PEA] Many thousands of speakers (1981 Wurm and Hattori). East and central Java. Creole, Indonesian based. It is based in Indonesian and Javanese. It has Mandarin elements, in contrast to Baba Malay, which has Hokkien elements. Monolinguals are over 70 years old. Developed at the beginning of the 17th century among Low Malay speaking Chinese traders from Fukien who married Javanese women. Investigation needed: intelligibility with Baba Malay, bilingual proficiency in Indonesian, Javanese.

JAVANESE ***(JAWA, DJAWA)*** [JAN] 75,200,000 in Indonesia, 42% of the population (1989), including 500,000 Banten, 2,500,000 Cirebon. About 25,000 in south Sulawesi. Population total all countries 75,500,800. Central Java, eastern third of west Java, southwestern half of east Java. Also resettlements in Irian Jaya, Sulawesi, Maluku, Kalimantan, and Sumatra. Also spoken in Malaysia (Sabah), Netherlands, Singapore. Austronesian, Malayo-Polynesian, Western Malayo-Polynesian, Sundic, Javanese. Dialects: JAWA HALUS, CIREBON (TJIREBON, CHERIBON), TEGAL, INDRAMAYU, SOLO, TEMBUNG, PASISIR, SURABAYA, MALANG-PASURUAN, BANTEN, MANUK. West Javanese dialects: Banten, Cirebon, Tegal; central Javanese dialect: Solo in Yogyakarta; East Javanese dialects: Surabaya, Malang-Pasuruan. High Javanese (Jawa Halus) is the language of religion, but the number of people that can control that form is diminishing. The Javanese in Suriname and that in New Caledonia have changed sufficiently to be only partially intelligible with difficulty. Javanese in New Caledonia are reported to not be able to use High Javanese (Koentjaraninggrat). Investigation needed: intelligibility with Cirebon. SVO. Traditional Javanese script. Muslim, Christian. Bible 1854-1994.

KANGEAN [KKV] Eastern Madura area. Austronesian, Malayo-Polynesian, Western Malayo-Polynesian, Sundic, Madurese. Barely intelligible with East Madura. A separate language (Stevens 1968). 75% lexical similarity with Madura. Investigation needed: bilingual proficiency.

MADURA ***(MADURESE, MADHURA, BASA MATHURA)*** [MHJ] 13,694,000 (1995), or 7% of the population (1987 UBS), including 70,000 Bawean. Population total both countries 13,694,000 or more. Island of Madura, Sapudi Islands, northern coastal area of eastern Java. Also spoken in Singapore. Austronesian, Malayo-Polynesian, Western Malayo-Polynesian, Sundic, Madurese. Dialects: BAWEAN (BOYANESE), BANGKALAN (BANGKALON), PAMEKESAN (PAMEKASAN), SAMPANG, SAPUDI, SUMENEP. There is a dialect continuum. Reports differ about inherent intelligibility among dialects, but some speakers of Sumenep and Sampang report that they cannot understand Pamekasan or Sumenep. Difficult intelligibility with Kangean. 75% lexical similarity with Kangean. About 60% of men and 40% of women speak 'passable' Indonesian to outsiders. All domains. East Madurese, especially Sumenep, is considered 'high' or 'standard Madurese'. Sumenep is isolated culturally and geographically. Bangkalon, spoken in Surabaya is important economically, because that is the city with the most outside and trade contact. It is the most urbanized and affected by Bahasa Indonesia. Mainly rural. Literacy rate in second language: 40%. Literacy higher among Bangkalon speakers. Muslim, Christian. Bible 1994.

OSING ***(BANYUWANGI)*** [OSI] 200,000 to 500,000 (1981 C. and B. Grimes SIL). East and northeast coast of east Java. Austronesian, Malayo-Polynesian, Western Malayo-Polynesian, Sundic, Javanese. Related to East Javanese. Have their own script, which is a modified Javanese script. Muslim.

PETJO ***(PETJOH, PECOK)*** [PEY] Djakarta (Batavia), Java. Creole, Dutch based. Influences from Dutch, Javanese, and Betawi. Little is known of this language. May be a pidgin or mixed language, rather than a creole.

SUNDA ***(SUNDANESE, PRIANGAN)*** [SUO] 27,000,000 or 13.6% of the population (1990 Clynes). Western third of Java Island. Austronesian, Malayo-Polynesian, Western Malayo-Polynesian, Sundic, Sundanese. Dialects: BANTEN, BOGOR (KRAWANG), PRINGAN, CIREBON. 60% use Indonesian and 5% use Dutch as second language. Muslim, Christian, traditional religion. Bible 1891-1991.

TENGGER ***(TENGGERESE)*** [TES] 500,000 (1989). East Java, on the slopes of Mt. Bromo up to the crater. Austronesian, Malayo-Polynesian, Western Malayo-Polynesian, Sundic, Javanese. May be marginally intelligible with Javanese. Javanese is used as second language. 20% use Indonesian. Ethnically distinct. Investigation needed: intelligibility with Javanese. Literacy rate in second language: 20%. Volcano slope. Vegetable growers. Hindu, Muslim, Christian.

INDONESIA (KALIMANTAN)

9,110,000 (1995). 4 provinces. Also includes Tringgus. Information mainly from A. A. Cense and E. M. Uhlenbeck 1958; R. Blust 1974. Data accuracy estimate: B. The number of languages listed for Indonesia (Kalimantan) is 82. Of those, all are living languages. Diversity index 0.78.

AHE ***(AHE DAYAK, DAYAK AHE)*** [AHE] 30,000 (1990 UBS). Austronesian, Malayo-Polynesian, Western Malayo-Polynesian, Borneo, Land Dayak.

AMPANANG [APG] 30,000(?) (1981 Wurm and Hattori). East central, southeast of Tunjung, around Jambu and Lamper. Austronesian, Malayo-Polynesian, Western Malayo-Polynesian, Borneo, Barito, Mahakam.

AOHENG ***(PENIHING)*** [PNI] 2,630 (1981 Wurm and Hattori). North central near Sarawak border. Austronesian, Malayo-Polynesian, Western Malayo-Polynesian, Borneo, Kayan-Murik, Muller-Schwaner 'Punan'.

BAHAU [BHV] 3,200 (1981 Wurm and Hattori). Northeast, north and southeast of Busang. Austronesian, Malayo-Polynesian, Western Malayo-Polynesian, Borneo, Kayan-Murik, Kayan.

BAKUMPAI ***(BARA-JIDA)*** [BKR] 40,000 or more (1981 Wurm and Hattori). Kapuas and Barito rivers, northeast of Kualakapuas. Austronesian, Malayo-Polynesian, Western Malayo-Polynesian, Borneo, Barito, West, South. Dialects: BAKUMPAI, MENGKATIP (MANGKATIP, OLOH MENGKATIP). Related to Ngaju, Kahayan, Katingan.

BANJAR ***(BANJARESE, BANDJARESE, BANJAR MALAY)*** [BJN] 2,100,000 in Indonesia (1993 Johnstone). Population total both countries 3,000,000 (1993 J. Collins). Around Banjarmasin in the south and east, and one pocket on east coast south of the Kelai River mouth. Also spoken in Malaysia (Sabah). Austronesian, Malayo-Polynesian, Western Malayo-Polynesian, Sundic, Malayic, Malayan, Local Malay. Dialects: KUALA, HULU. Strongly influenced by Javanese. Settled 800 to 1000 A. D. Investigation needed: intelligibility with Malay, Indonesian. Muslim.

BASAP [BDB] 17,000(?) (1981 Wurm and Hattori). Eastern Kalimantan, scattered throughout Bulungan, Sangkulirang, and Kutai. Austronesian, Malayo-Polynesian, Western Malayo-Polynesian, Borneo, Northwest, Rejang-Sajau. Dialects: JEMBAYAN, BULUNGAN, BERAU, DUMARING, BINATANG, KARANGAN. Cave-dwellers. Traditional religion, Christian.

BEKATI' ***(BAKATIQ)*** [BAT] 4,000 (1986 UBS). Northwestern near Sarawak border, around Sambas and Selvas. Austronesian, Malayo-Polynesian, Western Malayo-Polynesian, Borneo, Land Dayak. Bible portions 1986.

BENYADU' [BYD] 45,000 possibly (1981 Wurm and Hattori). Northwestern near Sarawak border, around Tan, Darit. Austronesian, Malayo-Polynesian, Western Malayo-Polynesian, Borneo, Land Dayak.

BIATAH ***(BIDEYU, SIBURAN, LUNDU, LANDU, PUEH)*** [BTH] Northwest Kalimantan, on Sarawak border. Mainly in Sarawak. Austronesian, Malayo-Polynesian, Western Malayo-Polynesian, Borneo, Land Dayak. May be distinct from Biatah of Sarawak. Christian, traditional religion. NT 1963. See main entry under Malaysia, Sarawak.

BOLONGAN ***(BULUNGAN)*** [BLJ] 15,000 (1989). Northeast, around Tanjungselor, lower Kayan River. Austronesian, Malayo-Polynesian, Western Malayo-Polynesian, Borneo, Northwest, North Sarawakan, Dayic, Murutic, Tidong. May be a dialect of Tidong or Segai. Classification uncertain. Traditional religion.

BUKAR SADONG ***(SADONG, TEBAKANG, BUKA, BUKAR, SERIAN, SABUTAN)*** [SDO] Austronesian, Malayo-Polynesian, Western Malayo-Polynesian, Borneo, Land Dayak. Dialects: BUKAR SADONG, BUKAR BIDAYUH (BIDAYUH, BIDAYAH). See main entry under Malaysia, Sarawak.

BUKAT [BVK] 400 (1981 Wurm and Hattori). North central near Sarawak border, Kapuas River, southeast of Mendalam, 3 areas. Austronesian, Malayo-Polynesian, Western Malayo-Polynesian, Borneo, Kayan-Murik, Muller-Schwaner 'Punan'.

BUKITAN ***(BAKITAN, BAKATAN, BEKETAN, MANGKETTAN, MANKETA, PAKATAN)*** [BKN] Iwan River, on the Sarawak border. Austronesian, Malayo-Polynesian, Western Malayo-Polynesian, Borneo, Northwest, Melanau-Kajang, Kajang. Dialects: PUNAN UKIT, PUNAN BUSANG. Christian. See main entry under Malaysia, Sarawak.

BURUSU [BQR] 6,000(?) (1981 Wurm and Hattori). Northeast, around Sekatakbunyi, north of Sajau Basap language. Austronesian, Malayo-Polynesian, Western Malayo-Polynesian, Borneo, Northwest, Rejang-Sajau.

DAYAK, LAND [DYK] 57,619 (1981). Western Kalimantan. Austronesian, Malayo-Polynesian, Western Malayo-Polynesian, Borneo, Land Dayak. Dialects: KARAGAN (KARANGAN), SIDIN (SIDING, SINDING), MERATEI (MERETEI), SAU (SAUH, BIRATAK), SERMAH (BIONAH), BERANG, SABUNGO, SANTAN, GURGO, SINAN, SUMPO, BUDANOH, SERING, GUGU, MATAN, TEMILA, BEHE, IPOH, MANYUKAI (MENJUKE, MENYUKAI, MANYUKE, MANUKAI), PUNAN (BUNAN, MURANG PUNAN, PENYABUNG PUNAN, BUSANG, DJULOI), KATI, BETA. There may be several languages represented among the dialects listed. All Land Dayak in Sarawak are covered by separate listings. Bible portions 1935.

DJONGKANG [DJO] 45,000 possibly (1981 Wurm and Hattori). Northwest, south of Balai Sebut. Austronesian, Malayo-Polynesian, Western Malayo-Polynesian, Borneo, Land Dayak.

DOHOI ***(OT DANUM, UUT DANUM, UUD DANUM)*** [OTD] 80,000(?) (1981 Wurm and Hattori) including 2,700 Ulu Ai'. Extensive area south of the Schwaner Range on the upper reaches of south Borneo rivers. The Ulu Ai' are on the Mandai River with 7 villages. Austronesian, Malayo-Polynesian, Western Malayo-Polynesian, Borneo, Barito, West, North. Dialects: OT BALAWAN, OT BANU'U, OT MURUNG 1 (MURUNG 1, PUNAN RATAH), OT OLANG, OT TUHUP, SARAWAI (MELAWI), DOHOI, ULU AI' (DA'AN). Dohoi and Murung 1 may be separate languages. Traditional religion, Christian.

DUSUN DEYAH ***(DEAH, DEJAH)*** [DUN] 20,000(?) (1981 Wurm and Hattori). Southeast, Tabalong River northeast of Bongkang. Austronesian, Malayo-Polynesian, Western Malayo-Polynesian, Borneo, Barito, East, Central-South, Central.

DUSUN MALANG [DUQ] 10,000(?) (1981 Wurm and Hattori). East central, west of Muarainu, northeast of Muarateweh. Austronesian, Malayo-Polynesian, Western Malayo-Polynesian, Borneo, Barito, East, Central-South, South. Closest to Ma'anyan, Paku, Dusun Witu, and Malagasy.

DUSUN WITU [DUW] 25,000(?) (1981 Wurm and Hattori). Southeast, regions of Pendang and Buntokecil; south of Muarateweh. Austronesian, Malayo-Polynesian, Western Malayo-Polynesian, Borneo, Barito, East, Central-South, South. Closest to Ma'anyan, Paku, Dusun Malang, Malagasy.

EMBALOH ***(MBALOH, MALOH, MALO, MEMALOH, MATOH, PARI, PALIN, SANGAU, SANGGAU)*** [EMB] 10,000 (1991 NTM). West central, Hulu Kapuas Regency, just south of the Sarawak border, upper Kapuas River: Embaloh, Leboyan, Lauh, Palin, Nyabau, Mandai, and Kalis tributaries. Austronesian, Malayo-Polynesian, Western Malayo-Polynesian, Sundic, Mbaloh. Dialect: KALIS (KALIS MALOH, KALIS DAYAK). Complex of ethnic groups: Taman of upper Kapuas Rer, Suai, Taman Mendalem, Taman Sibau, Palin, Lauk, Leboyan, Kalis Dayak. Traditional religion, Christian. NT 1998.

HOVONGAN ***(PUNAN BUNGAN)*** [HOV] 1,000 (1991 NTM). North central near Sarawak border, 2 areas. Austronesian, Malayo-Polynesian, Western Malayo-Polynesian, Borneo, Kayan-Murik, Muller- Schwaner 'Punan'. Dialects: HOVONGAN, SEMUKUNG UHENG. Traditional religion, Christian.

IBAN ***(SEA DAYAK)*** [IBA] Western and northern Kalimantan. Austronesian, Malayo-Polynesian, Western Malayo-Polynesian, Sundic, Malayic, Malayic-Dayak, Ibanic. Dialects: BATANG LUPAR, BUGAU, SEBERUANG, KANTU', DESA, KETUNGAU (AIR TABUN, SIGARAU, SEKALAU, SEKAPAT, BANJUR, SEBARU', DEMAM, MAUNG). Seberuang (20,000 speakers on the Kapuas River) may be a separate language. Investigation needed: intelligibility with Seberiamg. SVO. Traditional religion, Christian. Bible 1988. See main entry under Malaysia, Sarawak.

KAHAYAN ***(KAHAIAN, KAHAJAN)*** [XAH] 45,000 (1981 Wurm and Hattori). Kapuas and Kahayan rivers, south central, northeast of Ngaju. Austronesian, Malayo-Polynesian, Western Malayo-Polynesian, Borneo, Barito, West, South. Related to Ngaju, Katingan, and Bakumpai.

KATINGAN [KXG] 45,000(?) (1981 Wurm and Hattori). Katingan River, south central. Austronesian, Malayo-Polynesian, Western Malayo-Polynesian, Borneo, Barito, West, South. Related to Ngaju, Kahayan, and Bakumpai.

KAYAN MAHAKAM [XAY] 1,300 (1981 Wurm and Hattori). North central, Mahakam River, 2 areas. Austronesian, Malayo-Polynesian, Western Malayo-Polynesian, Borneo, Kayan-Murik, Kayan. A mixture of Kayan and Ot Danum (Dohoi).

KAYAN, BUSANG ***(KAJAN, KAJANG, BUSANG)*** [BFG] 3,000 (1981 Wurm and Hattori). On the upper Mahakam, Oga, and Belayan rivers. Austronesian, Malayo-Polynesian, Western Malayo-Polynesian, Borneo, Kayan-Murik, Kayan. Dialects: MAHAKAM BUSANG, BELAYAN, LONG BLEH. Christian, traditional religion.

KAYAN, KAYAN RIVER ***(KAYAN RIVER KAJAN, KAJANG)*** [XKN] 2,000(?) (1981 Wurm and Hattori). Northeast, Kayan River, 2 areas. Austronesian, Malayo-Polynesian, Western Malayo-Polynesian, Borneo, Kayan-Murik, Kayan. Dialects: UMA LAKAN, KAYANIYUT KAYAN.

KAYAN, MENDALAM ***(MENDALAM KAJAN)*** [XKD] 1,500 (1981 Wurm and Hattori). North central, northeast of Putus Sibau, Mendalam River. Austronesian, Malayo-Polynesian, Western Malayo-Polynesian, Borneo, Kayan-Murik, Kayan.

KAYAN, WAHAU ***(WAHAU KAJAN)*** [WHU] 500(?) (1981 Wurm and Hattori). Northeast, north of Muara Wahau. Austronesian, Malayo-Polynesian, Western Malayo-Polynesian, Borneo, Kayan-Murik, Kayan.

KELABIT ***(KALABIT, KERABIT)*** [KZI] Remote mountains, on Sarawak border, northwest of Longkemuat. Mainly in Sarawak. Austronesian, Malayo-Polynesian, Western Malayo-Polynesian, Borneo, Northwest, North Sarawakan, Dayic, Kelabitic. Dialect: LON BANGAG. Mountain slope. Agriculturalists: paddy and hill rice. Part Christian. Bible portions 1965. See main entry under Malaysia, Sarawak.

KEMBAYAN [XEM] 45,000 possibly (1981 Wurm and Hattori). Northwest, near Sarawak border, around Balaikarangan, Kembayan, Landak River. Austronesian, Malayo-Polynesian, Western Malayo-Polynesian, Borneo, Land Dayak.

KENDAYAN ***(BAICIT, KENDAYAN-AMBAWANG, KENDAYAN DAYAK)*** [KNX] 150,000(?) (1981 Wurm and Hattori). Kalimantan Barat, northeast of Bengkayang in the Ledo area, extending into the jungle area of Madi and Papan. Austronesian, Malayo-Polynesian, Western Malayo-Polynesian, Sundic, Malayic, Malayic-Dayak. Dialects: AMBAWANG, KENDAYAN. Indonesian is well understood only by the few who have had at least a 6th grade education.

KENINJAL ***(KANINJAL DAYAK, DAYAK KANINJAL, KANINJAL)*** [KNL] 35,000 (1990 UBS). West central, Sayan and Melawi rivers, around Nangapinoh, Nangaella, Nangasayan, Gelalak. Austronesian, Malayo-Polynesian, Western Malayo-Polynesian, Sundic, Malayic, Malayic-Dayak.

KENYAH, BAHAU RIVER ***(BAHAU RIVER KENYA)*** [BWV] 1,500(?) (1981 Wurm and Hattori). Northeast, on Sarawak border, around Longkemuat, Iwan River. Austronesian, Malayo-Polynesian, Western Malayo-Polynesian, Borneo, Northwest, North Sarawakan, Kenyah, Main Kenyah. Dialects: LONG ATAU, LONG BENA, LONG PUYUNGAN.

KENYAH, BAKUNG ***(BAKUNG, BAKUNG KENYA, BAKONG)*** [BOC] Population total both countries 2,000 (1981 Wurm and Hattori). Northeast, near the Sarawak border, Oga River and southeast of Datadian, and around Kubumesaai. Also spoken in Malaysia (Sarawak). Austronesian, Malayo-Polynesian, Western Malayo-Polynesian, Borneo, Northwest, North Sarawakan, Kenyah. Dialects: BOH BAKUNG, OGA BAKUNG, KAYAN RIVER BAKUNG. Muslim.

KENYAH, KAYAN RIVER ***(KAYAN RIVER KENYA, KENYA, KENJA, KENYAH, KINJIN, KINDJIN, KEHJA)*** [KNH] 6,000(?) (1981 Wurm and Hattori). Northeast, Apo Kayan highlands where Kayan River begins, Iwan River, and around Longbia. Austronesian, Malayo-Polynesian, Western Malayo-Polynesian, Borneo, Northwest, North Sarawakan, Kenyah, Main Kenyah. Dialects: LOWER KAYAN KENYAH, LONGBIA, KAYANIYUT KENYAH, LONG NAWAN, LONG KELAWIT. Christian. NT 1978.

KENYAH, KELINYAU ***(KELINYAU, KELINJAU, KENJA, KENYAH, KENYA, KINJIN, KINDJIN, KEHJA)*** [XKL] 1,200(?) (1981 Wurm and Hattori). Northeast, Kinjau River, around Long Laes, and Telen River. Austronesian, Malayo-Polynesian, Western Malayo-Polynesian, Borneo, Northwest, North Sarawakan, Kenyah, Main Kenyah. Dialects: UMA BEM, UMA TAU, LEPO' KULIT, UMA JALAM.

KENYAH, MAHAKAM ***(MAHAKAM KENYA, KENYA, KENJA, KENYAH, KINJIN, KINDJIN, KEHJA)*** [XKM] 7,000 (1981 Wurm and Hattori). Northeast, east of Bahau, and on Mahakam River, 5 areas. Austronesian, Malayo-Polynesian, Western Malayo-Polynesian, Borneo, Northwest, North Sarawakan, Kenyah, Main Kenyah. Dialects: MAHAKAM KENYAH, BOH.

KENYAH, UPPER BARAM ***(UPPER BARAM KENJA, KENJA, KENYAH, KINJIN, KANYAY, KINDJIN)*** [UBM] Border with Sarawak, northwest of Longkemuat. Austronesian, Malayo-Polynesian, Western Malayo-Polynesian, Borneo, Northwest, North Sarawakan, Kenyah, Main Kenyah. See main entry under Malaysia, Sarawak.

KENYAH, WAHAU ***(WAHAU KENYA)*** [WHK] 1,000(?) (1981 Wurm and Hattori). Northeast, north of Muara Wahau and Wahau Kayan. Austronesian, Malayo-Polynesian, Western Malayo-Polynesian, Borneo, Northwest, North Sarawakan, Kenyah. Dialect: UMA TIMAI.

KEREHO-UHENG ***(PUNAN KERIAU)*** [XKE] 200 (1981 Wurm and Hattori). North central near Sarawak border, south of Bukat and Hovongan. Austronesian, Malayo-Polynesian, Western Malayo-Polynesian, Borneo, Kayan-Murik, Muller-Schwaner 'Punan'.

LARA' ***(LURU)*** [LRA] Population total both countries 12,000 (1981 CBFMS). Upper Lundu and Sambas rivers, around Bengkayang east of Gunung Pendering, and farther north, Pejampi and two other villages. Also spoken in Malaysia (Sarawak). Austronesian, Malayo-Polynesian, Western Malayo-Polynesian, Borneo, Land Dayak. Traditional religion.

LAWANGAN ***(LUWANGAN, NORTHEAST BARITO)*** [LBX] 100,000 (1981 Wurm and Hattori). Around the Karau River in east central Kalimantan. Austronesian, Malayo-Polynesian, Western Malayo-Polynesian, Borneo, Barito, East, North. Dialects: TABUYAN (TABOYAN, TABOJAN, TABOJAN TONGKA), AJUH, BAKOI (LAMPUNG), BANTIAN (BENTIAN), BANUWANG, BAWU, KALI, KARAU (BELOH), LAWA, LOLANG, MANTARAREN, NJUMIT, PURAI, PURUNG, TUWANG, PASIR, BENUA. At least 17 dialects. Tawoyan may be inherently intelligible.

LENGILU [LGI] 10(?) (1981 Wurm and Hattori). Northeast, between Sa'ban and Lundayeh. Austronesian, Malayo-Polynesian, Western Malayo-Polynesian, Borneo, Northwest, North Sarawakan, Dayic, Kelabitic. Nearly extinct.

LUNDAYEH ***(SOUTHERN MURUT, LUN DAYE, LUN DAYAH, LUN DAYA, LUN DAYOH, LUNDAYA)*** [LND] 25,000 in Kalimantan (1987). Population total all countries 38,100. Interior about 4 degrees north from Brunei Bay to headwaters of Padas River, to headwaters of Baram and into Kalimantan, Indonesian mountains where tributaries of Sesayap River arise. Also spoken in Brunei, Malaysia (Sarawak). Austronesian, Malayo-Polynesian, Western Malayo-Polynesian, Borneo, Northwest, North Sarawakan, Dayic, Kelabitic. Dialects: LUN DAYE, PAPADI, LUN BAWANG (LONG BAWAN, SARAWAK MURUT). Not Murutic, although sometimes called Southern Murut. Christian (Lunbawang, some Lundayeh), traditional religion (others). Bible 1982.

MA'ANYAN ***(MAANYAK DAYAK, MA'ANJAN, SIANG)*** [MHY] 70,000 (1981 Wurm and Hattori). South around Tamianglayang, area of the drainage of Patai River. Austronesian, Malayo-Polynesian, Western Malayo-Polynesian, Borneo, Barito, East, Central-South, South. Dialects: SAMIHIM (BULUH KUNING), SIHONG (SIONG), DUSUN BALANGAN. Related to Malagasy in Madagascar, Africa. Traditional religion. NT, in press (1996).

MALAY, BERAU ***(BERAU, MERAU MALAY)*** [BVE] 20,000(?) (1981 Wurm and Hattori). East central coastal area, Tanjungreder and Muaramalinau in the north to Sepinang in the south. Austronesian, Malayo-Polynesian, Western Malayo-Polynesian, Sundic, Malayic, Malayan, Local Malay. Shares phonological innovations with Kutai Malay, Banjar, and Brunei.

MALAY, BUKIT ***(BUKIT, MERATUS)*** [BVU] 50,000 (1981 Wurm and Hattori). Southeastern, Sampanahan River, northwest of Limbungan. Austronesian, Malayo-Polynesian, Western Malayo-Polynesian, Sundic, Malayic, Malayan, Local Malay. Traditional religion.

MALAY, KOTA BANGUN KUTAI [MQG] 80,000 (1981 Wurm and Hattori). Central Mahakam River basin. Austronesian, Malayo-Polynesian, Western Malayo-Polynesian, Sundic, Malayic, Malayan, Local Malay. Not intelligible with Tenggarong Kutai Malay. May be intelligible with Northern Kutai. Investigation needed: intelligibility with dialects.

MALAY, TENGGARONG KUTAI ***(KUTAI, TENGGARONG)*** [VKT] 210,000 including 100,000 in Tenggarong, 60,000 in Ancalong, 50,000 in Northern Kutai (1981 Wurm and Hattori). Mahakam River basin, east central coastal area, from Sepinang and Tg. Mangkalihat in the north to Muarabadak and Samarinda in the south. Austronesian, Malayo-Polynesian, Western Malayo-Polynesian, Sundic, Malayic, Malayan, Local Malay. Dialects: TENGGARONG KUTAI, ANCALONG KUTAI, NORTHERN KUTAI. Many dialects. Tenggarong and Kota Bangun are not inherently intelligible. Shares phonological innovations with Berau Malay, Banjar, and Brunei. Investigation needed: intelligibility with dialects.

MALAYIC DAYAK [XDY] 520,000 including 300 Tapitn, 100,000(?) Banana', 100,000(?) Kayung, 200,000 Delang, 10,000 Semitau, 10,000 Suhaid, 20,000 Mentebah-Suruk (1981 Wurm and Hattori). Banana' and Tapitn are western, between Singakawang, Bengkayang, Darit, and Sungairaya; Kayung and Delang are southern, between Sandai, Muarakayang, Pembuanghulu, Sukamara, and Sukaraja; Semitau, Suhaid, and Mentebah-Suruk are eastern, southeast of Kapuas River from Sintang to Putus Sibau. Austronesian, Malayo-Polynesian, Western Malayo-Polynesian, Sundic, Malayic, Malayic-Dayak. Dialects: TAPITN, BANANA', KAYUNG (KAYONG), DELANG, SEMITAU, SUHAID, MENTEBAH-SURUK. May constitute 3 or more languages. Related to Selako, Kendaya, and Keninjal.

MODANG [MXD] 15,300 (1981 Wurm and Hattori). Around Segah, Kelinjau, and Belayan rivers in northeast Kalimantan, 5 areas. Austronesian, Malayo-Polynesian, Western Malayo-Polynesian, Borneo, Kayan-Murik, Modang. Dialects: KELINGAN (LONG WAI, LONG WE), LONG GLAT, LONG BENTO', BENEHES, NAHES, LIAH BING.

MUALANG [MTD] 10,000 (1981 Wurm and Hattori). Along the Ayak and Belitang Rivers, about 200 miles upstream from Pontianak. Austronesian, Malayo-Polynesian, Western Malayo-Polynesian, Sundic, Malayic, Malayic-Dayak, Ibanic. Closely related to Iban. Investigation needed: intelligibility with Iban.

NGAJU ***(NGADJU, NGAJU DAYAK, BIADJU, SOUTHWEST BARITO)*** [NIJ] 250,000 (1981 Wurm and Hattori). Kapuas, Kahayan, Katingan, and Mentaya rivers, south. Austronesian, Malayo-Polynesian, Western Malayo-Polynesian, Borneo, Barito, West, South. Dialects: PULOPETAK, KAPUAS (NGAJU, BARA-DIA), BA'AMANG (BARA-BARE, SAMPIT), MANTANGAI (OLOH MANGTANGAI). Related to Katingan, Kahayan, Bakumpai. Trade language for most of Kalimantan, from the Barito to the Sampit rivers, east of the Barito languages, and north in the Malawi River region. Trade language. Bible 1858-1955.

NYADU ***(NJADU, BALANTIANG, BALANTIAN)*** [NXJ] 9,000. West and north Kalimantan, Landak, tributary of Sambas River. Austronesian, Malayo-Polynesian, Western Malayo-Polynesian, Borneo, Land Dayak. Similar to Lara' spoken along upper Lundu and Sambas rivers. Bible portions 1952.

OKOLOD ***(KOLOD, KOLOUR, KOLUR, OKOLOD MURUT)*** [KQV] Northeast along Sabah border, east of Lumbis, north of Lundayeh. Primarily Kalimantan and Sarawak, some in Sabah. Austronesian, Malayo-Polynesian, Western Malayo-Polynesian, Borneo, Northwest, North Sarawakan, Dayic, Murutic, Murut. Traditional religion, Christian. See main entry under Malaysia, Sarawak.

PAKU [PKU] 20,000(?) (1981 Wurm and Hattori). Southeast, south of Ampah. Austronesian, Malayo-Polynesian, Western Malayo-Polynesian, Borneo, Barito, East, Central-South, South. Closest to Ma'anyan, Malagasy, Dusun Malang, Dusun Witu.

PUNAN APUT ***(APUT)*** [PUD] 370 (1981 Wurm and Hattori). Northeast, west and north of Mt. Menyapa. Austronesian, Malayo-Polynesian, Western Malayo-Polynesian, Borneo, Kayan-Murik, Muller-Schwaner 'Punan'.

PUNAN MERAH [PUF] 137 (1981 Wurm and Hattori). Northeast, Mahakam River, east of Ujohhilang. Austronesian, Malayo-Polynesian, Western Malayo-Polynesian, Borneo, Kayan-Murik, Muller-Schwaner 'Punan'. Distinct from Punan Merap.

PUNAN MERAP [PUC] 200(?) (1981 Wurm and Hattori). Northeast, east of Longkemuat. Austronesian, Malayo-Polynesian, Western Malayo-Polynesian, Borneo, Northwest, Rejang-Sajau. Distinct from Punan Merah.

PUNAN TUBU [PUJ] 2,000 (1981 Wurm and Hattori). Northeast, Malinau, Mentarang, and Sembakung rivers, 8 locations. Austronesian, Malayo-Polynesian, Western Malayo-Polynesian, Borneo, Northwest, North Sarawakan, Kenyah. May not be a Kenyah language. Blust 1974, 'penan' is a generic term for nonagricultural peoples. It does not reflect language differences; there are no "Penan" languages as a distinguishable subgrouping.

PUTOH [PUT] 6,000 (1981 Wurm and Hattori). Northeast, east of Lundayeh and Sa'ban, Mentarang River, around Longberang, Mensalong, and Bangalan. Austronesian, Malayo-Polynesian, Western Malayo-Polynesian, Borneo, Northwest, North Sarawakan, Dayic, Kelabitic. Dialects: PA KEMBALOH, ABAI.

RIBUN [RIR] 45,000 possibly (1981 Wurm and Hattori). Northwest, south of Kembayan. Austronesian, Malayo-Polynesian, Western Malayo-Polynesian, Borneo, Land Dayak.

SA'BAN [SNV] Population total both countries 1,000 (1981 Wurm and Hattori). Northeast on Sarawak border, south of Lundayeh. Also spoken in Malaysia (Sarawak). Austronesian, Malayo-Polynesian, Western Malayo-Polynesian, Borneo, Northwest, North Sarawakan, Dayic, Kelabitic. Bible portions 1969.

SAJAU BASAP ***(SAJAU, SUJAU)*** [SAD] 6,000(?) (1981 Wurm and Hattori). Northeast, northeast of Muaramalinau. Austronesian, Malayo-Polynesian, Western Malayo-Polynesian, Borneo, Northwest, Rejang-Sajau. Dialects: PUNAN SAJAU, PUNAN BASAP, PUNAN BATU 2. Distinct from Basap, but related.

SANGGAU [SCG] 45,000 possibly (1981 Wurm and Hattori). Northwestern, around Sanggau, Kapuas River. Austronesian, Malayo-Polynesian, Western Malayo-Polynesian, Borneo, Land Dayak.

SARA [SRE] Smaller than Lara. Near Sanggau-Ledo northeast of Ledò. Austronesian, Malayo-Polynesian, Western Malayo-Polynesian, Borneo, Land Dayak. Some dialect differences but one written form can serve.

SEBERUANG [SBX] 20,000 (1993 UBS). Kapuas River. Austronesian, Malayo-Polynesian, Western Malayo-Polynesian, Sundic, Malayic, Malayic-Dayak, Ibanic. SVO. Traditional religion, Christian.

SEGAI [SGE] 2,000 (1981 Wurm and Hattori). Northeast, Kelai River and around Longlaai. Austronesian, Malayo-Polynesian, Western Malayo-Polynesian, Borneo, Kayan-Murik, Modang. Dialects: KELAI, SEGAH. Bolongan may be a dialect.

SELAKO ***(SELAKO DAYAK, SALAKAU, SILAKAU)*** [SKL] 100,000 in Kalimantan(?) (1981 Wurm and Hattori). Population total both countries 103,800. Northwest, around Pemangkat. Also spoken in

Malaysia (Sarawak). Austronesian, Malayo-Polynesian, Western Malayo-Polynesian, Sundic, Malayic, Malayic-Dayak. Mainly traditional religion.

SELUNGAI MURUT [SLG] Along the upper reaches of the Sembakung River, east of Lumbis. Austronesian, Malayo-Polynesian, Western Malayo-Polynesian, Borneo, Northwest, North Sarawakan, Dayic, Murutic, Murut. See main entry under Malaysia, Sabah.

SEMANDANG [SDM] 30,000 (1981 Wurm and Hattori). West central, around Balaiberkuwak, north of Sandai. Austronesian, Malayo-Polynesian, Western Malayo-Polynesian, Borneo, Land Dayak. Dialects: SEMANDANG, GERAI, BEGINCI, BIHAK. Traditional religion, Christian. Bible portions 1982.

SEMBAKUNG MURUT ***(SIMBAKONG, SEMBAKOENG, SEMBAKONG, TINGGALAN, TINGGALUM, TINGALUN)*** [SMA] Population total both countries 5,000(?) (1981 Wurm and Hattori). Along the Sembakung River in northern Kalimantan, from the mouth, into Sabah. Also spoken in Malaysia (Sabah). Austronesian, Malayo-Polynesian, Western Malayo-Polynesian, Borneo, Northwest, North Sarawakan, Dayic, Murutic, Tidong.

SIANG ***(OT SIANG)*** [SYA] 60,000(?) (1981 Wurm and Hattori). Central, east of Dohoi. Austronesian, Malayo-Polynesian, Western Malayo-Polynesian, Borneo, Barito, West, North. Dialects: SIANG, MURUNG 2. Related to Dohoi.

TAGAL MURUT ***(SUMAMBU-TAGAL, SUMAMBU, SUMAMBUQ, SEMEMBU, SEMAMBU)*** [MVV] 2,000 Alumbis in Kalimantan. Along the Pegalan Valley, Alumbis River. Austronesian, Malayo-Polynesian, Western Malayo-Polynesian, Borneo, Northwest, North Sarawakan, Dayic, Murutic, Murut. Dialects: RUNDUM (ARUNDUM), TAGAL (TAGOL, NORTH BORNEO MURUT, SABAH MURUT), SUMAMBU (SEMEMBU, SUMAMBUQ), TOLOKOSON (TELEKOSON), SAPULOT MURUT (SAPULUT MURUT), PENSIANGAN MURUT (PENTJANGAN, TAGAL, TAGUL, TAGOL, TAGGAL, LAGUNAN MURUT), ALUMBIS (LUMBIS, LOEMBIS), TAWAN, TOMANI (TUMANIQ), MALIGAN (MAULIGAN, MELIGAN, BOL MURUT, BOLE MURUT). NT 1984-1991. See main entry under Malaysia, Sabah.

TAMAN ***(TAMAN DAYAK, DAYAK TAMAN)*** [TMN] 5,000 to 6,000 (1991 NTM). North central, Kapuas River in the area directly upriver from Putussibau, and the Mendalam and Sibau tributaries. Austronesian, Malayo-Polynesian, Western Malayo-Polynesian, Sundic, Mbaloh. Traditional religion, Christian.

TAUSUG ***(TAW SUG, SULU, SULUK, TAUSOG, MORO JOLOANO, SOOLOO, TAOSUG, JOLOANO SULU)*** [TSG] 12,000 in Kalimantan (1981 Wurm and Hattori). Settlements along the coast of northeastern Kalimantan, immigrants from the Sulu Archipelago in the Philippines. Austronesian, Malayo-Polynesian, Western Malayo-Polynesian, Meso Philippine, Central Philippine, Bisayan, South, Butuan-Tausug. Fishermen. Muslim. NT 1985. See main entry under Philippines.

TAWOYAN ***(TAWOYAN DAYAK, TABOYAN, TABUYAN, TABOJAN, TABOJAN TONGKA)*** [TWY] 20,000(?) (Wurm and Hattori 1981). East Central around Palori. Austronesian, Malayo-Polynesian, Western Malayo-Polynesian, Borneo, Barito, East, North. Investigation needed: intelligibility with Lawangan.

TIDONG ***(CAMUCONES, TIDUNG, TEDONG, TIDOENG, TIRAN, TIRONES, TIROON, ZEDONG)*** [TID] Population total both countries 25,000 (1981 Wurm and Hattori). Population center is along Sembakung and Sibuka Rivers of eastern Kalimantan, coast and islands around Tarakan and interior, Malinau River. Also spoken in Malaysia (Sabah). Austronesian, Malayo-Polynesian, Western Malayo-Polynesian, Borneo, Northwest, North Sarawakan, Dayic, Murutic, Tidong. Dialects: NONUKAN (NUNUKAN), PENCHANGAN, SEDALIR (SALALIR, SADALIR, SARALIR, SELALIR), TIDUNG, TARAKAN (TERAKAN), SESAYAP (SESAJAP), SIBUKU.

TUNJUNG ***(TUNJUNG DAYAK)*** [TJG] 50,000(?) (1981 Wurm and Hattori). East central, between Adas, Dempar, Melak, and east around the lake; south around Muntaiwan. Austronesian, Malayo-Polynesian, Western Malayo-Polynesian, Borneo, Barito, Mahakam. Dialects: TUNJUNG (TUNJUNG TENGAH), TUNJUNG LONDONG, TUNJUNG LINGGANG, PAHU.

INDONESIA (MALUKU)

1,500,000 to 1,700,000 (1987). Information mainly from K. Whinnom 1956; K. Polman 1981; J. Collins 1983; C. and B. D. Grimes 1983; E. Travis 1986; R. Bolton 1989, 1990; P. Taylor 1991; M. Taber 1993. Data accuracy estimate: A2, B. The number of languages listed for Indonesia (Maluku) is 131. Of those, 128 are living languages and 3 are extinct. Diversity index 0.94.

ALUNE ***(SAPALEWA, PATASIWA ALFOEREN)*** [ALP] 13,000 to 15,000 (1987 SIL). 5 villages in Seram Barat District, and 22 villages in Kairatu and Taniwel districts, west Seram, central Maluku. 27 villages total. Austronesian, Malayo-Polynesian, Central-Eastern, Central Malayo-Polynesian, Central Maluku, East, Seram, Nunusaku, Three Rivers, Amalumute, Northwest Seram, Ulat Inai.

Dialects: KAIRATU, CENTRAL WEST ALUNE (NINIARI-PIRU-RIRING-LUMOLI), SOUTH ALUNE (RAMBATU-MANUSSA-RUMBERU), NORTH COASTAL ALUNE (NIKULKAN-MURNATEN-WAKOLO), CENTRAL EAST ALUNE (BURIAH-WETH-LATURAKE). Rambatu dialect is reported to be prestigious. Kawe may be a dialect. Related to Nakaela and Lisabata-Nuniali. 77% to 91% lexical similarity among dialects, 64% with Lisabata-Nuniali, 63% with Hulung and Naka'ela. The largest language in west Seram. The people in the interior, who are the majority, use the language daily. Usage in the coastal villages is not as vigorous. The southern dialect in Kairatu village is nearly extinct. Literacy rate in first language: 50% to 65%. Literacy rate in second language: 40% to 55%. Christian. Bible portions 1991-1997.

AMAHAI ***(AMAHEI)*** [AMQ] 50 speakers (1987 SIL). 4 villages near Masohi, southwest Seram, central Maluku. Austronesian, Malayo-Polynesian, Central-Eastern, Central Malayo-Polynesian, Central Maluku, East, Seram, Nunusaku, Piru Bay, East, Seram Straits, Uliase, Hatuhaha, Elpaputi. Dialects: MAKARIKI, RUTAH, SOAHUKU. Language chain with Iha and Kaibobo. Also related to Elpaputih and Nusa Laut. 87% lexical similarity between the villages of Makariki and Rutah; probably two languages, 59% to 69% with Saparua, 59% with Kamarian, 58% with Kaibobo, 52% with Piru, Luhu, and Hulung, 50% with Alune, 49% with Naka'ela, 47% with Lisabata-Nunialiand South Wemale, 45% with North Wemale and Nuaulu, 44% with Buano and Saleman. Muslim, Christian. Nearly extinct.

AMBELAU ***(AMBLAU)*** [AMV] 5,700 (1989 C. Grimes SIL 1989). Ambelau Island off the southeastern coast of Buru Island. Wae Tawa village on the coast of Buru, opposite Ambelau. 8 villages. Central Maluku. Austronesian, Malayo-Polynesian, Central-Eastern, Central Malayo-Polynesian, Central Maluku, Ambelau. Schools through junior high on Island. Wild pigs and rocky terrain on Ambelau make cultivation impossible; that is done in Wae Tawa village on Buru Island. Literacy rate in first language: Below 1%. Island, rocky, flat. Clove cultivation; agriculturalists: vegetables, tubers; copra production. Muslim.

APUTAI ***(ILPUTIH, OPOTAI, TUTUNOHAN)*** [APX] 150 (1990 Hinton SIL). Wetar Island, Ilputih village, south central Wetar coast, and Lurang village, north central Wetar coast, south Maluku. Austronesian, Malayo-Polynesian, Central-Eastern, Central Malayo-Polynesian, Timor, Southwest Maluku, Wetar. Dialect: WELEMUR. 79% lexical similarity with Perai, 74% with Tugun, 69% with Iliun, 57% with Talur. Ilputih speakers use Talur as second language. Welemur dialect is extinct. Literacy rate in first language: Below 1%. Coastal.

ASILULU [ASL] 8,756 (1987 SIL). Asilulu, Ureng, Negeri Lima villages, northwest Ambon Island, and some families in villages on the south coast of the Hoamoal Peninsula in West Seram. Spoken as second language in northwest Ambon, north and west Seram, Manipa, Boano, Kelang islands. Austronesian, Malayo-Polynesian, Central-Eastern, Central Malayo-Polynesian, Central Maluku, East, Seram, Nunusaku, Piru Bay, West, Asilulu. Dialects: ASILULU, URENG, NEGERI LIMA (LIMA, HENALIMA). 88% lexical similarity between Asilulu and Negeri Lima, 78% to 82% with Hila-Kaitetu, 72% to 73% with the Wakal dialect of Hitu, 67% to 72% with Larike-Wakasihu, 71% to 73% with Luhu on Seram. Trade language. Literacy rate in first language: Below 1%. Literacy rate in second language: 15% to 25%. Coastal. Muslim.

BABAR, NORTH [BCD] 1,500 (1989 Taber SIL) in 6 villages. North Babar Islands, east of Timor, south Maluku. 6 villages. Austronesian, Malayo-Polynesian, Central-Eastern, Central Malayo-Polynesian, Babar, North. Reported dialect variation. Bilingualism in Malay. Vigorous. Literacy rate in first language: Below 1%. Coastal. Agriculturalists: maize, cosbi; fishermen. Christian.

BABAR, SOUTHEAST [VBB] 3,325 (1989 Taber SIL). Southeast Babar Island, south Maluku. Austronesian, Malayo-Polynesian, Central-Eastern, Central Malayo-Polynesian, Babar, South, Masela-South Babar. Literacy rate in first language: Below 1%.

BANDA [BND] 3,000 (1987 SIL). West and northeastern side of Kei Besar Island in Kei Islands, villages of Banda-Eli and Banda-Elat, south Maluku. There may be a third village. The people originally came from the Banda Islands, but the language is no longer spoken there. Austronesian, Malayo-Polynesian, Central-Eastern, Central Malayo-Polynesian, Central Maluku, East, Banda-Geser. Dialects: ELI, ELAT. Different from other languages of south Maluku. Bilingualism in Kei. Banda used for all purposes among themselves. Literacy rate in first language: Below 1%. Muslim.

BARAKAI ***(WORKAI)*** [BAJ] 4,300 (1995 J. Hughes). Barakai Island, southeast Aru Islands; 4 villages on Barakai Island (Longgar, Apara, Bemun, and Mesiang) and one on Gomo-Gomo Island northeast of Barakai, south Maluku. Austronesian, Malayo-Polynesian, Central-Eastern, Central Malayo-Polynesian, Aru. Dialects: BARAKAI, MESIANG. Closely related to Karey. 70% lexical similarity with Batuley. Vigorous. Investigation needed: intelligibility with Batuley, Karey. Literacy rate in first language: Below 1%. Christian, Muslim, traditional religion.

BATI ***(GAH)*** [BVT] 3,500 (1989 Loski). Eastern Seram Island along the coast between Kian Darat and Keleser, and in the interior. Austronesian, Malayo-Polynesian, Central-Eastern, Central Malayo-Polynesian, Central Maluku, East, Banda-Geser, Geser-Gorom. Related to Geser and Watubela.

Many claim to be bilingual in Geser. Strong separation of ethnolinguistic identity with Geser. Literacy rate in first language: Below 1%. Muslim.

BATULEY ***(WATULAI, GWATALEY)*** [BAY] 3,840 excluding Mariri (1995 J. Hughes). 7 villages in Aru on small islands off the east coast of Wokam Island, south Maluku. Austronesian, Malayo-Polynesian, Central-Eastern, Central Malayo-Polynesian, Aru. Fairly closely related to Kompane to the north and Lola to the south, slightly more distant from Dobel. 70% lexical similarity with Barakai and Karey, 81% with Mariri. Vigorous. Batuley speakers consider Mariri to be a separate language. Investigation needed: intelligibility with Barakai, Karey. Literacy rate in first language: Below 1%. Muslim (5 southern villages), Christian (3 northern villages).

BENGGOI ***(BENGOI, KOBI-BENGGOI, UHEI-KACLAKIN, UHEI KACHLAKAN, UHEI-KAHLAKIM, ISAL)*** [BGY] 350 (1989 Loski and Loski SIL). North coast, Werinama and Bula districts, east Seram, central Maluku, 3 villages (Benggoi, Balakeo, Lesa). Austronesian, Malayo-Polynesian, Central-Eastern, Central Malayo-Polynesian, Central Maluku, East, Seram, Manusela-Seti. Dialects: LESA, BENGGOI, BALAKEO. 70% lexical similarity among 'dialects'; 54% to 66% with Liana-Seti, 46% to 50% with Salas Gunung, 32% to 46% with Manusela. 'Isal' was given by Salzner in the area where Benggoi is located; the name is not used now. Investigation needed: intelligibility with dialects, bilingual proficiency. Literacy rate in first language: Below 1%. Christian, Muslim.

BOANO ***(BUANO)*** [BZN] 3,240 (1982). Boano Island west of Seram, mainly in North Buano village, central Maluku. Austronesian, Malayo-Polynesian, Central-Eastern, Central Malayo-Polynesian, Central Maluku, East, Seram, Nunusaku, Piru Bay, West, Hoamoal, East. Related to Larike-Wakasihu. 60% lexical similarity with Luhu, 61% with Lisabata-Nuniali (closest). Vigorous in north Boano. South Boano may be extinct. Muslim (northern Boano), Christian (southern Boano).

BOBOT ***(WERINAMA, HATUMETEN, ATIAHU, AHTIAGO, NTAU)*** [BTY] 4,500 (1989 Loski and Loski SIL). Southeast Seram, Werinama District, from the village of Atiahu to Kota Baru, and Tunsai village in the Liana area, central Maluku. Austronesian, Malayo-Polynesian, Central-Eastern, Central Malayo-Polynesian, Central Maluku, East, Seram, Bobot. 44% lexical similarity with Sepa and Teluti, 42% with Atamanu. Atiahu is a village name, not a dialect. Literacy rate in first language: Below 1%. Coastal. Muslim.

BULI [BZQ] 1,800 to 2,000 (1983 C. Grimes SIL). North Maluku, central Halmahera, east coast, three villages. Austronesian, Malayo-Polynesian, Central-Eastern, Eastern Malayo-Polynesian, South Halmahera-West New Guinea, South Halmahera, Southeast. Dialects: BULI, WAYAMLI (WAJAMLI, JAWANLI). Several communities of over 100 dwellings. Investigation needed: intelligibility with Maba, Sawai, Weda. Literacy rate in first language: Below 1%. Coconut plantations. Muslim, Christian.

BURU ***(BOEROE, BURUESE)*** [MHS] 32,980 including 6,622 Wae Sama, 9,600 Masarete, 14,258 Rana, 500 Fogi, and 2,000 in Ambon (1989 C. Grimes SIL). Population total both countries 33,000. South, southeast, and central Buru Island, central Maluku, Ambon, Jakarta. Also spoken in Netherlands. Austronesian, Malayo-Polynesian, Central-Eastern, Central Malayo-Polynesian, Central Maluku, Buru. Dialects: MASARETE (SOUTH BURU), WAE SAMA (WAESAMA), CENTRAL BURU (RANA, WAE GEREN, WAE KABO), FOGI (LI EMTEBAN, TOMAHU). Li Garan is a special taboo dialect spoken by the Rana people (3,000 to 5,000 users). 90% lexical similarity between Masarete and Wae Sama, 88% between Masarete and Rana, 80% between Wae Sama and Rana, 68% between Li Enyorot (Lisela) and Masarete, 48% between Liliali and Masarete, 45% between Kayeli and Masarete, 44% between Ambelau and Masarete, 27% to 33% between Buru and the languages of Sula. Bilingual level estimates are Ambonese Malay: 0 15%, 1 20%, 2 50%, 3 10%, 4 5%, 5 0%; Indonesian: 0 15%, 1 40%, 2 35%, 3 7%, 4 3%, 5 0%. All ages. Vigorous in most areas. Fogi has apparently undergone complete shift to Ambonese Malay. There are word taboos and complex intermarriage patterns on the island. Grammar. SVO; prepositions; genitives before nouns; predominantly head marking; CV, CVC, V, VC; nontonal. Roman. Tropical forest, savannah. Coastal, mountain slope. Swidden agriculturalists, cloves, copra. 0 to 5,000 feet. Traditional religion, Muslim, Christian. Bible portions 1904-1997.

DAI [DIJ] 808 (1981 Wurm and Hattori). South, Dai and Babar islands. Dai is 15 miles north of Babar. 3 villages. Austronesian, Malayo-Polynesian, Central-Eastern, Central Malayo-Polynesian, Babar, North. No dialect variation. 72% lexical similarity with Dawera-Daweloor (closest), 71% with Nakarahamto, 49% with Masela-South Babar, 48% with Tepa (Luang). Bilingualism in Malay. Vigorous. Literacy rate in first language: Below 1%. Mountain slope. Agriculturalists: maize, cassava; fishermen. Sea level. Christian.

DAMAR, EAST ***(SOUTH DAMAR)*** [DMR] 2,800 (1990 SIL). Six villages along the east side of Damar Island, north and east of Roma Island, north of the eastern tip of Timor Island, south Maluku. Austronesian, Malayo-Polynesian, Central-Eastern, Central Malayo-Polynesian, Timor, Southwest Maluku, East Damar. Not intelligible with West Damar. Literacy rate in first language: Below 1%.

DAMAR, WEST ***(NORTH DAMAR)*** [DRN] 800 (1987 SIL). Two villages on the north side of Damar Island, north of the eastern tip of Timor Island, south Maluku, Indonesia. Austronesian, Malayo-Polynesian,

Central-Eastern, Central Malayo-Polynesian, West Damar. Not intelligible with East Damar. Literacy rate in first language: Below 1%.

DAWERA-DAWELOOR ***(DAVELOR)*** [DDW] 1,500 or fewer (1989 Taber SIL). South Maluku, six villages on Dawera and Daweloor islands. The islands are 11 miles northeast of Babar Island. Austronesian, Malayo-Polynesian, Central-Eastern, Central Malayo-Polynesian, Babar, North. Minor dialect differences. Bilingualism in Malay. Vigorous. Literacy rate in first language: Below 1%. Coastal. Agriculturalists: maize, cosbi; fishermen. Sea level. Christian.

DOBEL ***(KOBRO'OR, KOBROOR, DOIBEL)*** [KVO] 7,000 (1995 J. Hughes). Aru Islands, along the whole east coast of Kobror Island, one village in southeast Wokam Island, 4 villages on both sides of the eastern half of Barakai Strait (on both Kobror Islands and Koba Island), and 2 villages in central Kobror Island. 18 villages. Southeast Maluku. Austronesian, Malayo-Polynesian, Central-Eastern, Central Malayo-Polynesian, Aru. Dialects: INLAND DOBEL, SOUTHEAST DOBEL, NORTHEAST DOBEL. At least three dialects. Related to Lola and Lorang. Koba has 78% to 86% lexical similarity with Dobel. Ambonese Malay is used with outsiders. Some pre-school children do not know Ambonese Malay. Vigorous. Investigation needed: intelligibility. Literacy rate in first language: Below 1%. Literacy rate in second language: 25% to 50%. Christian, Muslim. Bible portions 1991.

ELPAPUTIH ***(ELPAPUTI)*** [ELP] West Seram, central Maluku. Austronesian, Malayo-Polynesian, Central-Eastern, Central Malayo-Polynesian, Central Maluku, East, Seram, Nunusaku, Piru Bay, East, Seram Straits, Uliase, Hatuhaha, Elpaputi. Closest to Nusalaut, Amahai. Investigation needed: intelligibility with Nusalaut, Amahai.

EMPLAWAS [EMW] 250 (1989 Taber SIL). Emplawas village, southwest Babar Island, south Maluku. Austronesian, Malayo-Polynesian, Central-Eastern, Central Malayo-Polynesian, Babar, South, Southwest Babar. Literacy rate in first language: Below 1%.

FORDATA ***(LARAT, VAI TNEBAR)*** [FRD] 50,000 including 25,000 in the language area, 25,000 throughout Indonesia (1995 SIL). Southeast Maluku, northern Tanimbar Islands of the Fordata, Larat, the Molu-Maru group, a few villages on the northwest part of Yamdena, and on Seira off the west coast of Yamdena. 30 villages. Austronesian, Malayo-Polynesian, Central-Eastern, Central Malayo-Polynesian, Southeast Maluku, Kei-Tanimbar, Kei-Fordata. Dialects: FODATA-LARAT I, FORDATA-LARAT II, MOLO-MARU, SEIRA (SERA). Seira is the most divergent dialect. 68% lexical similarity with Kei. Nearly everyone is bilingual to some degree in Ambonese Malay, the trade language. They are less bilingual in Standard Indonesian, usually the third language learned. Less than 1% monolingual. Vigorous. Elementary schools in nearly every village, secondary schools for every 3 or 4 villages. Trade language. Literacy rate in first language: 1% to 5%. Literacy rate in second language: 50% to 75%. Coastal, many with reef ecosystems. Swidden agriculturalists: diversification of crops and planting cycles. Muslim, Christian. Bible portions 1996.

GALELA [GBI] 79,000 including 41,000 Kadai, 10,000 Kadina, 24,000 Morotai, and 4,000 Sopi (1990 SIL). North Maluku, Galela Bay and north of Tobelo to the northern tip of Halmahera, Morotai Island except southeast quadrant, islands of Gunage and Moari near Kayoa, Bacan, Obi, scattered along the southwest coast of Halmahera. West Papuan, North Halmahera, North, Galela-Loloda. Dialects: KADAI, KADINA, MOROTAI, SOPI. Laba may be a dialect. Speakers have 65% intelligibility of Loloda, Loloda 85% of Galela. Bilingualism in Indonesian. Vigorous use in daily communication. Investigation needed: intelligibility with Laba. Dictionary. Grammar. Literacy rate in first language: 5% to 10%. Literacy rate in second language: 50% to 75%. Agriculturalists, fishermen. Christian, Muslim. Bible portions 1990-1991.

GAMKONORA [GAK] 1,500 (1987 Voorhoeve and Visser). North Halmahera, a few villages along the coast to the south of the Ibu area, north Maluku. West Papuan, North Halmahera, North, Sahu. 81% lexical similarity with Waioli. Investigation needed: intelligibility with Sahu subgroup. Literacy rate in first language: Below 1%. Muslim, Christian.

GANE ***(GANI, GIMAN)*** [GZN] 2,900 (1982 Teljeur). North Maluku, Halmahera Island, south part of southern peninsula. Austronesian, Malayo-Polynesian, Central-Eastern, Eastern Malayo-Polynesian, South Halmahera-West New Guinea, South Halmahera, East Makian-Gane. Close to East Makian and Kayoa. Language attitudes are positive. Investigation needed: intelligibility with East Makian, Kayoa. Literacy rate in first language: Below 1%. Muslim.

GEBE ***(GEBI)*** [GEI] 1,000 to 3,000 in four villages (1983 C. and B. D. Grimes SIL). North Maluku, Gebe, Yoi'umiyal, and Gag islands between southern Halmahera and Waigeo Island (Irian Jaya). Austronesian, Malayo-Polynesian, Central-Eastern, Eastern Malayo-Polynesian, South Halmahera-West New Guinea, West New Guinea, Cenderawasih Bay, Raja Ampat. Dialect: UMERA. 44% lexical similarity with Patani. Bilingualism in Indonesian increasing because of mining operation and schools. Language used in daily communication. A school in each village. Investigation needed: intelligibility with Raja Ampat Islands, Irian Jaya. Literacy rate in first language: Below 1%. Muslim.

GESER-GOROM ***(GESER, GESA, GOROM, GORAM, GORAN, GORONG, SERAM, SERAN, SERAN LAUT)*** [GES] 36,500 (1989 Loski and Loski SIL). Eastern end of Seram, and the Gorom Islands. Austronesian, Malayo-Polynesian, Central-Eastern, Central Malayo-Polynesian, Central Maluku, East, Banda-Geser, Geser-Gorom. Dialects: GORAM LAUT, MINA MINA GORONG, KELIMURI. 73% to 93% lexical similarity among dialects, 51% to 61% with Watubela. Watubela speakers use this as second language. Literacy rate in first language: Below 1%. Literacy rate in second language: 50% to 75%. Muslim.

GORAP [GOQ] 1,000 (1992 SIL). North Maluku, Morotai Island, Pilowo and Waringin villages; Central Halmahera, Bobane and Igo villages. Austronesian, Malayo-Polynesian, Unclassified. Reported to be a mixed language, including Ternate and Malay words, with different word order from other languages of north Halmahera or the Austronesian languages. 85% lexical similarity with Indonesian, but understanding is limited. Reported to be in daily use. Speakers consider Sulawesi to be their ancestral homeland.

HARUKU [HRK] 18,219 (1989 SIL). Haruku Island, Lease Islands, central Maluku. Austronesian, Malayo-Polynesian, Central-Eastern, Central Malayo-Polynesian, Central Maluku, East, Seram, Nunusaku, Piru Bay. Dialects: HULALIU, PELAUW, KAILOLO, ROHOMONI. Each village is a separate dialect. 81% to 92% lexical similarity among dialects. 74% to 76% lexical similarity with Tulehu, 67% to 71% with Saparua. Bilingualism in Ambonese Malay. Literacy rate in first language: Below 1%. Muslim, Christian.

HITU [HIT] 15,965 (1987 SIL). 5 villages: Wakal, Hitu, Mamala, Morela, and Hila; Hitu Peninsula, Ambon Island. Austronesian, Malayo-Polynesian, Central-Eastern, Central Malayo-Polynesian, Central Maluku, East, Seram, Nunusaku, Piru Bay, East, Seram Straits, Ambon. Dialects: WAKAL, MORELA, MAMALA, HITU, HILA. 67% to 82% lexical similarity with Seit-Kaitetu, 74% to 82% with Tulehu. Moderate to vigorous. Literacy rate in first language: Below 1%. Muslim, Christian.

HORURU [HRR] Seram, central Maluku. Austronesian, Malayo-Polynesian, Central-Eastern, Central Malayo-Polynesian, Central Maluku, East, Seram, Nunusaku, Three Rivers, Amalumute, Northwest Seram. Hulung may be related. This may be an alternate name for another language.

HOTI [HTI] 10 speakers possibly (1987 SIL). East Seram, central Maluku. Austronesian, Malayo-Polynesian, Central-Eastern, Central Malayo-Polynesian, Central Maluku, East, Seram, East Seram. All are elderly (1987).

HUAULU ***(ALAKAMAT, BAHASA ASLI)*** [HUD] 300 (1987 SIL). East Seram, central Maluku, northwest of Manusela, 10 villages. Austronesian, Malayo-Polynesian, Central-Eastern, Central Malayo-Polynesian, Central Maluku, East, Seram, Manusela-Seti. 64% to 72% lexical similarity with Manusela dialects. Culturally distinct from Manusela. Traditional religion.

HUKUMINA ***(BAMBAA)*** [HUW] 1 (1989 C. Grimes SIL). Formerly spoken in Hukumina, Palumata, and Tomahu districts of northwest Buru Island. The present speaker is from the former village of Hukumina that used to be located behind the present village of Masarete, near the fort at Kayeli in northeast Buru. Austronesian, Malayo-Polynesian, Unclassified. The one speaker was 80 years old in 1989. 'Bambaa' in Hukumina means 'there isn't any'. Nearly extinct.

HULUNG [HUK] 10 or fewer (1991 Y. Taguchi SIL). Hulung village, and Sauweli hamlet, west Seram, central Maluku. Austronesian, Malayo-Polynesian, Central-Eastern, Central Malayo-Polynesian, Central Maluku, East, Seram, Nunusaku, Three Rivers, Amalumute, Northwest Seram, Hulung. 67% lexical similarity with Lisabata-Nuniali, 66% with Naka'ela and South Wemale, 63% with Alune, 59% with North Wemale. Christian. Nearly extinct.

IBU [IBU] A few speakers (1987 Voorhoeve and Visser). 50 to 200 in the ethnic group (1984). North Maluku, northern Halmahera Island, mouth of Ibu River, villages of Gamlamo and Gamici. West Papuan, North Halmahera, North, Sahu. May be inherently intelligible with Sahu. All are elderly (1987). Nearly extinct.

ILIUN ***(HAHUTAU, HAHUTAN, LIMERA, ILMAUMAU, ERAI)*** [ILU] 1,400 or more (1990 Hinton SIL). Wetar Island, villages of Telemar, Karbubu, Klishatu, Ilmaumau, Erai (Eray), Nabar, and Esulit on the west end of Wetar, and Istutun village on Lirang Island off the southwest tip of Wetar, south Maluku. Austronesian, Malayo-Polynesian, Central-Eastern, Central Malayo-Polynesian, Timor, Southwest Maluku, Wetar. All speakers now speak the Iliun dialect. 73% lexical similarity with Tugun, 69% with Aputai, 67% with Perai, 51% with Talur. Jeh and Juru are extinct. Literacy rate in first language: Below 1%.

IMROING ***(IMROIN)*** [IMR] 450 (1989 Taber SIL). Village of Imroing, southwest Babar Island, south Maluku. Austronesian, Malayo-Polynesian, Central-Eastern, Central Malayo-Polynesian, Babar, South, Southwest Babar. Literacy rate in first language: Below 1%.

KADAI [KZD] 300 to 500 (1982 SIL). North Maluku, Sula Islands, Taliabu Island, interior mountains. Possibly also in the mountains of Mangole Island. Austronesian, Malayo-Polynesian, Central-Eastern, Central

Malayo-Polynesian, Central Maluku, Sula, Taliabo. May be intelligible with Taliabu. The government wants to resettle them along the coast. Investigation needed: intelligibility with Taliabu dialects. Traditional religion.

KAIBOBO *(KAIBUBU)* [KZB] 500 (1983 Collins and Voorhoeve). Kaibobo, Hatusua, Waisamu, Kamarian, Seruawan, Tihulale, and Rumahkay villages in Kairatu District; 8 villages total, Piru Bay, west Seram, central Maluku. Austronesian, Malayo-Polynesian, Central-Eastern, Central Malayo-Polynesian, Central Maluku, East, Seram, Nunusaku, Piru Bay, East. Dialects: KAIBOBO, HATUSUA. Related to Lisabata-Nuniali. 82% to 88% lexical similarity between Kaibobo and Hatusua, 75% with Kamarian, 62% to 65% with Saparua, 62% with Piru, 58% to 62% with Luhu, 61% with Naka'ela. Bilingualism in Ambonese Malay. Language use may be shifting to Ambonese Malay in some villages. Investigation needed: bilingual proficiency in Ambonese Malay. Christian.

KAMARIAN *(KAMARIANG, SERUAWAN)* [KZX] 10 or fewer out of village population of 6,000 (1987 SIL). West Seram, central Maluku, Kamarian village on the south coast of Seram, at the eastern end of Piru Bay. Austronesian, Malayo-Polynesian, Central-Eastern, Central Malayo-Polynesian, Central Maluku, East, Seram, Nunusaku, Piru Bay, East, Seram Straits, Uliase, Kamarian. 75% lexical similarity with Kaibobo, 67% with Saparua, 60% with Lisabata-Nuniali, 59% with Amahai, Piru, Naka'ela, and Hulung. Nearly extinct.

KAO *(KAU, KA'U)* [KAX] 200 to 400 possibly (1983 C. Grimes SIL). North Maluku, interior North Halmahera, around the town of Kao, near the mouth of the Kao River. West Papuan, North Halmahera, North, Kao River. Could be a marginal dialect of Pagu, but relates uniquely to other languages in the Kao River subbranch. Investigation needed: intelligibility with Kao River subbranch, Pagu. Literacy rate in first language: Below 1%. Literacy rate in second language: 50% to 75%.

KAREY *(KEREI, KREI)* [KYD] 950 (1995 J. Hughes). Village of Karey, east coast of Tarangan Island, southern Aru Islands, south Maluku. Austronesian, Malayo-Polynesian, Central-Eastern, Central Malayo-Polynesian, Aru. 70% lexical similarity with East Tarangan and Batuley. Vigorous. Investigation needed: intelligibility with Barakai. Literacy rate in first language: Below 1%. Christian, Muslim.

KAYELI *(KAJELI, CAJELI, CAELI, GAELI)* [KZL] 3 speakers out of 800 in the ethnic group (1995). Not used for 3 decades by the speakers (1989 C. Grimes SIL). Southern Namlea Bay, north Buru Island, central Maluku. Austronesian, Malayo-Polynesian, Central-Eastern, Central Malayo-Polynesian, Central Maluku, East, Seram, Nunusaku, Kayeli. Dialects: KAYELI, LELIALI (LILIALI), LUMAETE (LUMAITI, MUMAITE, LUMARA). Bilingualism in Ambonese Malay. Speakers are over 60 years old. Others have completely shifted to Ambonese Malay as first language. Lumaete became extinct recently and Leliali became extinct in March, 1989. The ethnic group continues to function. Muslim. Nearly extinct.

KEI *(EVAV, KAI)* [KEI] 86,000 (1990 SIL). Kei Kecil, Kei Besar, and surrounding islands, except the villages of Banda Eli and Banda Elat on Kei Besar, and the Kur Islands, where Kei is used as a lingua franca. About 207 villages. Southeast Maluku. Austronesian, Malayo-Polynesian, Central-Eastern, Central Malayo-Polynesian, Southeast Maluku, Kei-Tanimbar, Kei-Fordata. Dialects: KEI KECIL, KEI BESAR, TAYANDO, TANIMBAR KEI (ATNEBAR), TA'AM. Tanimbar Kei is closer to Fordata than the other Kei dialects. 60% lexical similarity with Fordata. 5% monolingual. Used in everyday life. Trade language. Dictionary. Grammar. Literacy rate in first language: 1% to 5%. Literacy rate in second language: 50% to 75%. Morphophonemic orthography, approved by local Kei conference 1990. Agriculturalists: millet. Muslim, Christian, traditional religion.

KISAR *(MEHER, YOTOWAWA)* [KJE] 20,000 (1995 SIL). Kisar Island northeast of Timor Island, 19 villages, villages of Hila and Likagraha (Solath) on Roma Island, 3 villages on Wetar Island (Amau, Naumatan, Hi'ai), and several hundred in Ambon city, Dili and Kupang. Used as a second language by a handful of Oirata speakers on Kisar. South Maluku. Austronesian, Malayo-Polynesian, Central-Eastern, Central Malayo-Polynesian, Timor, Southwest Maluku, Kisar-Roma. Not related to Oirata, which has sometimes been called a dialect. Called Yotowawa or Meher locally. Trade language. Literacy rate in first language: Below 1%. Literacy rate in second language: 25% to 50%. Christian. Bible portions 1995.

KOBA [KPD] 520 (1995 SIL). Aru Islands, southeast Maluku. Austronesian, Malayo-Polynesian, Central-Eastern, Central Malayo-Polynesian, Aru. Intelligibility of Dobel is limited. 78% to 86% lexical similarity with Dobel.

KOLA *(WARILAU, KULAHA, MARLASI)* [KVV] 7,700 (1995 J. Hughes). North Aru Islands, all around the coast of Kola Island and adjacent islands, south Maluku. 22 villages. Austronesian, Malayo-Polynesian, Central-Eastern, Central Malayo-Polynesian, Aru. Intelligibility testing showed Marlasi is intelligible to Kompane speakers, but with some possible adaptation of literature needed. 77% lexical similarity with Kompane, 70% with Ujir. Vigorous. Outsiders want to learn it. Literacy rate in first language: Below 1%. Literacy rate in second language: 25% to 50%.

KOMPANE *(KOMFANA, KONGAMPANI)* [KVP] 330 (1995 J. Hughes). Northeast Aru in Kompane village on the east coast of Kongan Island, south of Kola and north of Wokam islands, south Maluku. Austronesian, Malayo-Polynesian, Central-Eastern, Central Malayo-Polynesian, Aru. Closely related to Kola, linguistically between Kola and Batuley. Intelligibility of Kola is good, but some adaptation of literature may be needed. Vigorous. Investigation needed: intelligibility with Kola. Muslim.

KUR [KUV] 2,000 to 3,000 possibly (1985 J. Hughes SIL). Kur Island and nearby islands, western Kei Kecil District, south Maluku. Austronesian, Malayo-Polynesian, Central-Eastern, Central Malayo-Polynesian, Teor-Kur. Separate language from Kei. Survey needed to determine boundaries of intelligibility with dialects to the north and the central dialect, and with Teor. 47% to 50% lexical similarity with Kei, 71% to 83% with Teor, 41% with Watubela, 38% with Geser. Vigorous. Muslim.

LABA *(SOUTH LOLODA, KEDI)* [LAU] 2,000 (1991 H. Shelden SIL). North Maluku, 4 villages to the interior of the south end of Loloda District. West Papuan, North Halmahera, North, Galela-Loloda. Phonology like Galela, 70% intelligibility, 75% with Loloda. 75% lexical similarity with Galela, 78% with Loloda. Christian.

LAHA *(CENTRAL AMBON)* [LAD] 3,894 (1987 SIL). Laha village, and several nearby smaller villages, south central coast of Ambon Island, central Maluku. Austronesian, Malayo-Polynesian, Central-Eastern, Central Malayo-Polynesian, Central Maluku, East, Seram, Nunusaku, Piru Bay, East, Seram Straits, Ambon. Related to Seram languages, but distinct from Manusela. 64% to 66% lexical similarity with Asilulu and Hila-Kaitetu (closest). Bilingualism in Ambonese Malay. All ages. Parents encourage children to speak Laha. Muslim, Christian.

LARIKE-WAKASIHU [ALO] 12,557 (1987 SIL). Larike, Wakasihu, Tapi, Allang, and Lai villages, southwest Hitu Peninsula, Ambon Island. Austronesian, Malayo-Polynesian, Central-Eastern, Central Malayo-Polynesian, Central Maluku, East, Seram, Nunusaku, Piru Bay, West, Hoamoal, East. Dialects: ALLANG, WAKASIHU, LARIKE. Wakasihu may need separate literature from Larike. The western end of the Ambon dialect chain. 81% lexical similarity between Allang and Larike and Wakasihu, 92% between Larike and Wakasihu. 68% to 71% with Asilulu, 67% to 72% with Negeri Lima. Vigorous use in Larike and Wakasihu, weak in Allang. Only older people in Allang, Allang Asaude, Uraur, and Urusana still speak Allang, but apparently do not use it. Investigation needed: intelligibility with Wakasihu. Literacy rate in first language: 1% to 5%. Literacy rate in second language: 50% to 75%. Muslim (Larike, Wakasihu), Christian (Allang).

LATU [LTU] 2,134 (1982 SIL). Latu village, Elpaputih Bay, southwest Seram Island, central Maluku. Austronesian, Malayo-Polynesian, Central-Eastern, Central Malayo-Polynesian, Central Maluku, East, Seram, Nunusaku, Piru Bay, East, Seram Straits, Uliase, Hatuhaha, Saparua. 82% to 84% lexical similarity with Saparua dialects. Investigation needed: intelligibility with Saparua.

LETI [LTI] 7,500 (1995 M. Taber). Leti Island. Austronesian, Malayo-Polynesian, Central-Eastern, Central Malayo-Polynesian, Timor, Southwest Maluku, Luang. Marginal intelligibility with Luang. They have difficulty with written Luang. 89% lexical similarity with Luang. They share a historical and cultural heritage with Luang, but maintain their own identity and local pride. Matrilineal. Literacy rate in first language: Below 1%. Literacy rate in second language: 25% to 50%. Christian.

LIANA-SETI *(LIANA, LIANAN, UHEI KACLAKIN, UHEI KACHLAKAN, UHEI KAHLAKIM, TEULA, LIAMBATA-KOBI)* [STE] 3,000 (1989 Loski and Loski SIL). Eastern Teluti Bay to the north coast, districts of Seram, Bula, Werinama, and Tehoru, central Maluku, 8 villages. Austronesian, Malayo-Polynesian, Central-Eastern, Central Malayo-Polynesian, Central Maluku, East, Seram, Manusela-Seti. Dialects: "SETI", WAHAKAIM, KOBI. Lexical similarity between Seti (westernmost and interior), and Wahakaim (near coast) is 66% to 74%, Kobi and Seti 69% to 78%, Kobi and Wahakaim 70%; 42% to 61% with Manusela; 54% to 66% with Benggoi; 48% to 58% with Salas Gunung. Seti use Teluti as second language. Vigorous. Speakers use the name 'Liana'; "Seti" is derogatory. Investigation needed: intelligibility with Seti, Wahakaim, Kobi. Literacy rate in first language: Below 1%. Literacy rate in second language: 25% to 50%. Christian.

LISABATA-NUNIALI *(LISABATA, NUNIALI, NONIALI)* [LCS] 1,830 or more (1982). Spread across the north coast of West and North Seram, 5 villages, central Maluku. Austronesian, Malayo-Polynesian, Central-Eastern, Central Malayo-Polynesian, Central Maluku, East, Seram, Nunusaku, Three Rivers, Amalumute, Northwest Seram. Dialects: LISABATA-TIMUR, NUNIALI, SUKARAJA, KAWA. Lexical similarity between Kawa (far western) and Lisabata Timur (far eastern) is 85%; 72% with Naka'ela, 67% with Hulung, 63% with Alune. Bilingualism in Ambonese Malay. Vigorous except in Kawa. Muslim, Christian (Nuniali).

LISELA *(BURU, NORTH BURU, LI ENYOROT, LIET ENJOROT, WAYAPO)* [LCL] 11,922 (1989 C. Grimes SIL). Northern, northeastern, north central coastal strips, and northwestern Buru Island, lower Wae Geren and Vae Apo valleys of Buru Island, central Maluku. Some in Ambon. Austronesian, Malayo-Polynesian, Central-Eastern, Central Malayo-Polynesian, Central Maluku, Buru. Dialects: LISELA (LICELA, LICELLA), TAGALISA. Bilingualism in Ambonese Malay. Not vigorous; a shift to Ambonese Malay is taking place. Tropical forest, savannah. Coastal, mountains. Swidden agriculturalists, eucalyptus oil. 0 to 1,500 feet. Muslim, traditional religion.

LOLA [LCD] 830 (1995 J. Hughes). 3 villages of Lola, Warabal, and Jambuair on 3 islands east of Kobroor and Baun Islands, Aru Islands, southeast Maluku. Austronesian, Malayo-Polynesian, Central-Eastern, Central Malayo-Polynesian, Aru. Dialects: LOLA, WARABAL. Linguistically between Batuley and Dobel; close to Koba. In Lola some young people use Ambonese Malay among themselves. In Jambuair there are many non-Aru people, so Ambonese Malay is in common use. Most vigorous in Warabal. Investigation needed: intelligibility with Koba. Muslim.

LOLODA ***(LODA, NORTH LOLODA)*** [LOL] 15,000 including 2,000 Bakun (1991 SIL). North Maluku, northwest coast of Halmahera. West Papuan, North Halmahera, North, Galela-Loloda. Dialect: BAKUN. Intelligibility with Laba is very limited. Speakers have 85% intelligibility of Galela, Galela has 65% of Loloda. Vigorous. Investigation needed: bilingual proficiency in Galela. Grammar. Literacy rate in first language: Below 1%. Literacy rate in second language: 50% to 75%. Christian, Muslim. Bible portions 1915.

LORANG [LRN] 325 (1995 J. Hughes). Village of Lorang, center of Aru, on Koba Island. Southeast Maluku. Austronesian, Malayo-Polynesian, Central-Eastern, Central Malayo-Polynesian, Aru. Closely related to Koba, and to a lesser extent to Dobel. Some similarities with Manombai, but intelligibility is lower than might be expected. Lorang people can speak several local languages to some degree, and speak Dobel from childhood. Vigorous. Investigation needed: intelligibility with Dobel. Christian.

LOUN [LOX] Few speakers. North central Seram, central Maluku. Austronesian, Malayo-Polynesian, Central-Eastern, Central Malayo-Polynesian, Central Maluku, East, Seram, Nunusaku, Three Rivers, Amalumute, Northwest Seram, Loun. Nearly extinct.

LUANG ***(LETRI LGONA, LITERI LAGONA, LGONA)*** [LEX] 20,000 (1995 Taber). Moa, Lakor, Luang, Sermata, Wetan, northwest Babar Islands east of Timor, south Maluku. Austronesian, Malayo-Polynesian, Central-Eastern, Central Malayo-Polynesian, Timor, Southwest Maluku, Luang. Dialects: LUANG, WETAN (WETANG), MOA, LAKOR. Intelligibility with Leti is marginal. 89% lexical similarity with Leti. Matrilineal. Investigation needed: intelligibility with Wetan. Literacy rate in first language: 15%. Literacy rate in second language: 15% to 25%. Christian. Bible portions 1995-1997.

LUHU [LCQ] 6,500 (1983 Collins and Voorhoeve). Luhu village on Hoamoal Peninsula, west Seram Island, and Boano and Kelang islands, off of west Seram. Austronesian, Malayo-Polynesian, Central-Eastern, Central Malayo-Polynesian, Central Maluku, East, Seram, Nunusaku, Piru Bay, West, Hoamoal, West. Dialects: LUHU, BATU MERAH, KELANG. Related to Manipa. 77% lexical similarity with Piru, 71% to 73% with Asilulu. Vigorous. Batu Merah dialect spoken on Ambon Island is nearly extinct. Historically one language with Piru. Investigation needed: intelligibility with Waesala, Kelang. Muslim.

MABA ***(BITJOLI, BICOLI, INGLI)*** [MQA] 3,000 to 7,000 (1983 C. and B. D. Grimes SIL). North Maluku, northern coast of southeastern peninsula of Halmahera, and in Wasilei area. Austronesian, Malayo-Polynesian, Central-Eastern, Eastern Malayo-Polynesian, South Halmahera-West New Guinea, South Halmahera, Southeast. Investigation needed: intelligibility with Patani, Buli. Literacy rate in first language: Below 1%. Literacy rate in second language: 25% to 50%. Muslim.

MAKIAN, EAST ***(MAKIAN TIMUR, MAKIAN DALAM)*** [MKY] 20,000 including 18,000 or more in East Makian, 2,000 or more in Kayoa (1983 C. and B. D. Grimes SIL). Eastern Makian Island, southern Mori Island, Kayoa Islands, west coast of south Halmahera, Bacan, and Obi islands, north Maluku. Transmigration project near Kao. Austronesian, Malayo-Polynesian, Central-Eastern, Eastern Malayo-Polynesian, South Halmahera-West New Guinea, South Halmahera, East Makian-Gane. Dialects: EAST MAKIAN, KAYOA (KAJOA). Close to Gane. Language attitudes are positive. Literacy rate in first language: Below 1%. Literacy rate in second language: 25% to 50%. Muslim.

MAKIAN, WEST ***(MAKIAN BARAT, MAKIAN LUAR)*** [MQS] 12,000 including 7,000 on Makian Island, 5,000 on Kayoa Islands (1977 Voegelin and Voegelin). Western Makian Island, some of the Kayoa Islands, areas along the west coast of southern Halmahera, north Maluku. West Papuan, North Halmahera, North, West Makian. Language isolate within north Halmahera. Formerly classified as Austronesian. Literacy rate in first language: Below 1%. Literacy rate in second language: 25% to 50%. Muslim.

MALAY, AMBONESE ***(MELAYU AMBON, AMBONESE)*** [ABS] 200,000 first language speakers, other second language speakers in Indonesia (1987 J. Collins). Population total all countries 245,000. Central Maluku, Ambon, Haruku, Nusa Laut, Saparua islands, along the coastal areas of Seram, and southern Maluku. Also spoken in Netherlands, USA. Creole, Malay based. Marginal intelligibility with Indonesian. Difficult intelligibility with Ternate Malay; speakers switch to Indonesian. 81% lexical similarity with Standard Malay. Bilingualism in Indonesian is high around Ambon city, Some Dutch is known. Developed from Bazaar Malay and still reflects some archaic forms. Further diverged by adapting to the vernaculars of central Maluku. Considered to be a Malay-based creole by B. D. Grimes (1988, 1991) and J. Holm (1989:581-3). Trade language. Grammar. Literacy rate in first language: 1% to 5%. Literacy rate in second language: 50% to 75%. Christian (since early 16th century), Muslim. NT 1877-1883.

MALAY, BACANESE ***(BACAN, BATJAN)*** [BTJ] 2,500 mother tongue speakers (1991 H. Shelden SIL). Over 1,000 in Labuha (1987 J. Collins). North Maluku, Bacan Island west of southern Halmahera. Centered around the site of the former palace in Labuha, 1 village within about 5 km. walking distance from Labuha, another 1 hour by dugout (Indomut), and half the population of Waya and Lele villages on Mandioli Island. Austronesian, Malayo-Polynesian, Western Malayo-Polynesian, Sundic, Malayic, Malayan, Local Malay. No second language speakers. No evidence of an earlier indigenous language (J. Collins). The Portuguese cut off Bacan from other Malay in 1515. No historic connection with Borneo since. Junior high school in Labuha. Literacy rate in first language: 1% to 5%. Literacy rate in second language: 50% to 75%. Agriculturalists (rural speakers). Muslim.

MALAY, NORTH MOLUCCAN ***(TERNATE MALAY)*** [MAX] A few hundred mother tongue speakers (1987 J. Collins). North Maluku, Halmahera, Sula, and Obi islands. Mother tongue speakers in one neighborhood of Labuha (Christian), and some other families with parents of different ethnic origins. Austronesian, Malayo-Polynesian, Western Malayo-Polynesian, Sundic, Malayic, Malayan, Local Malay. A few small communities speak it as mother tongue. Most speakers use it as a second language. Many bilinguals are competent in it at Foreign Service Institute levels 2 or 3. Used between speakers of different languages. Used orally, not written. Investigation needed: intelligibility with Indonesian, Menadonese Malay. Trade language. Literacy rate in first language: 1% to 5%. Literacy rate in second language: 50% to 75%. Muslim, Christian.

MANGOLE ***(MANGOLI, SULA MANGOLI)*** [MQC] 4,000 to 7,000 (1983 C. and B. D. Grimes SIL). North Maluku, southern coast of Mangole Island and northern tip of Sulabesi of the Sula Islands. Austronesian, Malayo-Polynesian, Central-Eastern, Central Malayo-Polynesian, Central Maluku, Sula. Investigation needed: intelligibility with Sula dialects. Muslim.

MANIPA ***(SOOW HUHELIA)*** [MQP] 1,500 (1983 Collins and Voorhoeve). Manipa Island west of Seram, central Maluku, 4 villages. Austronesian, Malayo-Polynesian, Central-Eastern, Central Malayo-Polynesian, Central Maluku, East. 72% lexical similarity with Luhu, 64% with Piru, 60% to 62% with Hitu, 60% to 61% with Tulehu and Asilulu, 58% to 61% with Hila-Kaitetu, 55% to 60% with Larike-Wakasihu, 56% with Boano and Kaibobo. Muslim.

MANOMBAI ***(MANOBAI, WOKAM, WAMAR)*** [WOO] 7,475 (1995 J. Hughes). West coast of Wokam Island, from Wokam village southwards, in 21 villages along both sides of Manombai Strait (Sungai) as far as Wakua, and in Benjina on Kobror Island, and Gardakau on Maikor Island at the western end of Barakai Strait, and small village of Kobamar on east coast of Wokam Island. It may be no longer spoken on Wamar Island. Aru Islands, Southeast Maluku. Austronesian, Malayo-Polynesian, Central-Eastern, Central Malayo-Polynesian, Aru. Not inherently intelligible with Dobel. 76% lexical similarity with Lorang. Vigorous. Investigation needed: intelligibility with West Tarangan, dialects. Christian, some Muslim.

MANUSELA ***(WAHAI, WAHINAMA)*** [WHA] 7,000 (1989 Loskii SIL). 30 villages, Manusela mountains of north Seram, and along Teluti Bay in south Seram, central Maluku. Austronesian, Malayo-Polynesian, Central-Eastern, Central Malayo-Polynesian, Central Maluku, East, Seram, Manusela-Seti. Dialects: KANIKEH, HATUOLU, MANEO, SOUTH MANUSELA. Kanikeh has 66% to 74% lexical similarity with other varieties, Hatuolo 67% to 75%, Maneo 64% to 86%, Maneoratu 66% to 86%, South Manusela 67% to 80%; dialects have 64% to 72% with Huaulu, 42% to 61% with Liana, 45% with Saleman. Bilingualism in Teluti. Vigorous. Investigation needed: intelligibility with dialects, Huaulu. Grammar. Mountain slope. Traditional religion, Christian, Hindu.

MARIRI ***(MAIRIRI)*** [MQI] 390 (1995 J. Hughes). Eastern Aru on Mariri Island east of Kobroor Island, 1 village, south Maluku. Austronesian, Malayo-Polynesian, Central-Eastern, Central Malayo-Polynesian, Aru. 81% lexical similarity with Batuley. Vigorous. Investigation needed: intelligibility with Batuley. Muslim.

MASELA, CENTRAL ***(CENTRAL MARSELA, MARSELA-SOUTH BABAR)*** [MKH] 511 (1980 de Jonge). 3 villages on Marsela Island, south Maluku. Austronesian, Malayo-Polynesian, Central-Eastern, Central Malayo-Polynesian, Babar, South, Masela-South Babar. Literacy rate in first language: Below 1%. Christian.

MASELA, EAST ***(EAST MARSELA)*** [VME] 519 (1980 de Jonge). 3 villages on Marsela Island, south Maluku. Austronesian, Malayo-Polynesian, Central-Eastern, Central Malayo-Polynesian, Babar, South, Masela-South Babar. Literacy rate in first language: Below 1%. Christian.

MASELA, WEST ***(WEST MARSELA)*** [MSS] 850 (1980 de Jonge). 5 villages on Marsela Island, south Maluku. Austronesian, Malayo-Polynesian, Central-Eastern, Central Malayo-Polynesian, Babar, South, Masela-South Babar. Literacy rate in first language: Below 1%. Christian.

MASIWANG ***(BONFIA)*** [BNF] 1,000 (1989 Loski and Loski SIL). Seram Island, Waru Bay area, Bula District, central Maluku. Austronesian, Malayo-Polynesian, Central-Eastern, Central Malayo-Polynesian,

Central Maluku, East, Seram, Masiwang. 44% lexical similarity with Bobot, 43% with Salas Gunung, 39% with Sepa and Teluti, 36% with Liana and Atamanu. Some use Geser as second language. Used by Salas as second languge. Investigation needed: bilingual proficiency in Geser. Grammar.

MODOLE ***(MADOLE)*** [MQO] 2,000 (1983 C. and B. D. Grimes SIL). North Maluku, interior north Halmahera Island, headwaters of Kao River. West Papuan, North Halmahera, North, Kao River. Dialects: NORTH MODOLE, SOUTH MODOLE. Minimal differences between north and south Modole. Language attitudes are positive. Some intermarriage with the Tobaru. Investigation needed: intelligibility with Pagu dialects. Christian.

MOKSELA ***(MAKSELA, OPSELAN)*** [VMS] Central Maluku, possibly east Buru Island, near Kayeli. Austronesian, Malayo-Polynesian, Central-Eastern, Central Malayo-Polynesian, Central Maluku, Buru. Last speaker died in 1974. Extinct.

NAKA'ELA [NAE] 5 (1985 Y. Taguchi SIL). Kairatu village, northwest Seram, central Maluku. Austronesian, Malayo-Polynesian, Central-Eastern, Central Malayo-Polynesian, Central Maluku, East, Seram, Nunusaku, Three Rivers, Amalumute, Northwest Seram, Ulat Inai. 71% lexical similarity with Lisabata- Nuniali, 66% with Hulung, 63% with Alune. Formerly lived in mountains. Reportedly decreased in number after moving down to Kairatu. Christian. Nearly extinct.

NILA [NIL] 1,800 (1989 Taber SIL). Transmigration area on south central Seram Island, central Maluku. 6 villages. (Originally Nila Island in south central Maluku). Austronesian, Malayo-Polynesian, Central-Eastern, Central Malayo-Polynesian, Timor, Southwest Maluku, Teun-Nila-Serua, Nila-Serua. Close to Serua. Not intelligible with Teun. They have been moved to Seram because of volcanic activity on their island. Literacy rate in first language: Below 1%.

NUAULU, NORTH ***(NUAULU, PATAKAI, FATAKAI)*** [NNI] 500 (1990 Bolton SIL). Two villages on the north coast of central Seram Island, central Maluku. Austronesian, Malayo-Polynesian, Central-Eastern, Central Malayo-Polynesian, Central Maluku, East, Seram, Sawai-Nuaulu. 67% lexical similarity with South Nuaulu, 64% with Saleman. A distinct language from Huaulu.

NUAULU, SOUTH ***(NUAULU, PATAKAI, FATAKAI)*** [NXL] 1,500 (1995 Taber). 6 villages on the south coast and interior of Amahai District, Seram Island, central Maluku. Austronesian, Malayo-Polynesian, Central-Eastern, Central Malayo-Polynesian, Central Maluku, East, Seram, Sawai-Nuaulu. 67% lexical similarity with North Nuaulu, 50% with South Wemale, Hulung, and Naka'ela, 48% with Saleman. Many use Sepa as second language. Some people do not speak Indonesian. Vigorous. Different from Huaulu. Literacy rate in first language: Below 1%. Literacy rate in second language: 5% to 15%. Christian, traditional religion. Bible portions 1991-1995.

NUSA LAUT ***(NUSALAUT)*** [NUL] 10 speakers possibly out of an ethnic group of 2,226 (1989 SIL). Titawai village, Nusa Laut Island, Lease Islands, central Maluku. Austronesian, Malayo-Polynesian, Central-Eastern, Central Malayo-Polynesian, Central Maluku, East, Seram, Nunusaku, Piru Bay, East, Seram Straits, Uliase, Hatuhaha, Elpaputi. 69% lexical similarity with Saparua, 65% with Amahai. Barely used, and only by a few older people. Christian. Nearly extinct.

OIRATA ***(MAARO)*** [OIA] 1,221 (1987 SIL). 2 villages in east and west Oirata in southeast Kisar Island, south Maluku, and in Ambon city (several hundred). Trans-New Guinea, South Bird's Head-Timor-Alor-Pantar, Timor-Alor-Pantar, Oirata. Not related to other languages on Oirata or central Maluku languages. Related to languages in Timor Lorosae, but not closely. SOV. Literacy rate in first language: Below 1%. Christian.

PAGU ***(PAGO, PAGOE)*** [PGU] 2,000 to 3,000 (1983 C. and B. D. Grimes SIL). North Maluku, interior North Halmahera south of the Modole language area out to the mouth of the Kao River. West Papuan, North Halmahera, North, Kao River. Dialects: ISAM, PAGU, TOLIWIKU (TOLILIKO). Investigation needed: intelligibility with Modole, Kao. Literacy rate in first language: Below 1%. Literacy rate in second language: 25% to 50%. Muslim, Christian.

PALUMATA ***(PALAMATA, BALAMATA)*** [PMC] Central Maluku, northwest Buru Island. Austronesian, Malayo-Polynesian, Central-Eastern, Central Malayo-Polynesian, Central Maluku, Buru. Extinct.

PATANI [PTN] 7,000 to 9,000 (1983 C. and B. D. Grimes SIL). North Maluku, the entire narrow tip of the southeastern peninsula of Halmahera, extending west along coast of peninsula. Nine villages: Patani, Peniti, Tepeleu, Gemya, Kipai, Wailegi, Yeisowo, Banemo, Moreala, Sibenpopu (with some Tobelo speakers). Austronesian, Malayo-Polynesian, Central-Eastern, Eastern Malayo-Polynesian, South Halmahera-West New Guinea, South Halmahera, Southeast. Vigorous use in daily communication. Schools. Investigation needed: intelligibility with Maba. Literacy rate in first language: Below 1%. Literacy rate in second language: 25% to 50%. Swidden agriculturalists, loggers. Muslim.

PAULOHI [PLH] 50 possible speakers (1982). Central Maluku, West Seram, western shore of Elpaputih Bay in south central Seram Island, 2 villages, Kecamatan Amahai. Austronesian, Malayo-Polynesian, Central-Eastern, Central Malayo-Polynesian, Central Maluku, East, Seram, Nunusaku, Piru Bay, East, Seram Straits, Solehua. Experienced a severe earthquake and tidal wave. Nearly extinct.

PERAI ***(TUTUNOHAN)*** [WET] 278 (1990 Hinton). Wetar Island, north of Timor, south Maluku, Uhak, and Moning villages on the northeast coast. Austronesian, Malayo-Polynesian, Central-Eastern, Central Malayo-Polynesian, Timor, Southwest Maluku, Wetar. 79% lexical similarity with Aputai, 76% with Tugun, 67% with Iliun, 51% with Talur. Literacy rate in first language: Below 1%.

PIRU [PPR] 10 or fewer (1985 Y. Taguchi SIL). 1 village, west Seram Island, central Maluku. Austronesian, Malayo-Polynesian, Central-Eastern, Central Malayo-Polynesian, Central Maluku, East, Seram, Nunusaku, Three Rivers, Amalumute, Northwest Seram. 72% lexical similarity with Luhu. People use Ambonese Malay as first or second language. Christian. Nearly extinct.

ROMA ***(ROMANG)*** [RMM] 1,700 (1991 SIL). Jerusu village, Roma Island, north of Timor Island, south Maluku. Austronesian, Malayo-Polynesian, Central-Eastern, Central Malayo-Polynesian, Timor, Southwest Maluku, Kisar-Roma. Literacy rate in first language: Below 1%. Literacy rate in second language: 25% to 50%. Christian.

SAHU ***(SA'U, SAU, SAHU'U)*** [SUX] 7,500 including 3,500 in Tala'i, 4,000 in Pa'disua (1987 Voorhoeve and Visser). North Maluku, southwestern north Halmahera Island. West Papuan, North Halmahera, North, Sahu. Dialects: PA'DISUA (PALISUA), TALA'I. Close to Waioli and Gamkonora. Vigorous use in daily communication. Investigation needed: intelligibility with Sahu group. Dictionary. Grammar. Literacy rate in first language: Below 1%. Literacy rate in second language: 25% to 50%. Christian, Muslim.

SALAS ***(LIAMBATA, LENKAITAHE, SALAS GUNUNG)*** [SGU] 50 (1989 Loski and Loski SIL). Salas Gunung village, Seram Island, Waru Bay, central Maluku. Austronesian, Malayo-Polynesian, Central-Eastern, Central Malayo-Polynesian, Central Maluku, East, Seram, Manusela-Seti. 48% to 58% lexical similarity with Liana, 46% to 50% with Benggoi, 35% to 46% with Manusela. Most use Masiwang as second language. Christian.

SALEMAN ***(SAWAI, SELEMAN, HATUE, WAHAI)*** [SAU] 4,800 (1989 Loski and Loski SIL). 5 villages (Saleman, Pasanea, Sawai, Besi, Wahai), north central Seram, central Maluku. Austronesian, Malayo-Polynesian, Central-Eastern, Central Malayo-Polynesian, Central Maluku, East, Seram, Sawai-Nuaulu. 64% lexical similarity with North Nuaulu, 48% with South Nuaulu. Vigorous except in Wahai. Investigation needed: intelligibility with dialects. Muslim.

SAPARUA [SPR] 10,216 (1989 SIL), including 4,519 or more in Iha. Kulur, Iha, and Siri-Sori villages on Saparua Island, and Iha, Kulur, Latu, Hualoy, and Tomalehu villages on Seram Island, Lease Islands, central Maluku. Also spoken by hundreds of Latu people in Kairatu village. Austronesian, Malayo-Polynesian, Central-Eastern, Central Malayo-Polynesian, Central Maluku, East, Seram, Nunusaku, Piru Bay, East, Seram Straits, Uliase, Hatuhaha, Saparua. Dialects: KULUR, IHA-SAPARUA, IHA-SERAM, SIRI-SORI. Each village is a dialect. 86% to 89% lexical similarity among dialects; 82% to 84% with Latu, 69% with Amahai, 67% with Kamarian, 68% to 71% with Haruku, 65% with Kaibobo, 62% to 66% with Tulehu, 54% to 62% with Luhu, 49% with Piru, 54% with Naka'ela. Investigation needed: intelligibility with dialects. Literacy rate in first language: Below 1%. Muslim, Christian.

SAWAI ***(WEDA, WERE, WEDA-SAWAI)*** [SZW] 12,000 (1989 SIL). North Maluku, coastal area between southern and southeastern peninsulas of Halmahera. Austronesian, Malayo-Polynesian, Central-Eastern, Eastern Malayo-Polynesian, South Halmahera-West New Guinea, South Halmahera, Southeast. Dialects: WEDA, SAWAI, KOBE. 64% lexical similarity with North Nuaulu. Different from Saleman (Sawai). Literacy rate in first language: 10%. Literacy rate in second language: 25% to 50%. Muslim, Christian. Bible portions 1994.

SEIT-KAITETU ***(HILA-KAITETU)*** [HIK] 10,171 (1987 SIL). Seit (Seith) and Kaitetu villages, north coast of Ambon Island, central Maluku. Austronesian, Malayo-Polynesian, Central-Eastern, Central Malayo-Polynesian, Central Maluku, East, Seram, Nunusaku, Piru Bay, West, Asilulu. Dialects: SEIT (SEITH), KAITETU. 85% lexical similarity between Kaitetu and Seit. 78% to 82% lexical similarity with Asilulu, 67% to 74% with Tulehu. Bilingualism in Ambonese Malay. Vigorous. Muslim, Christian.

SELARU ***(SALARU)*** [SLU] 7,000 to 9,000 (1989 Coward SIL). Tanimbar, six of seven villages on Selaru Island, half of the village of Latdalam on Yamdena Island, and Lingada village on Nus-Wotar Island off the west coast of Yamdena. 8 villages. South Maluku. Austronesian, Malayo-Polynesian, Central-Eastern, Central Malayo-Polynesian, Southeast Maluku, Southern. Dialect: KANDAR. Slight dialect differences. Not closely related to other nearby languages. Vigorous. Literacy rate in first language: Below 1%. Literacy rate in second language: 25% to 50%. Christian.

SELUWASAN ***(SELVASA, SELWASA)*** [SWH] 2,839 including 739 in Makatian, 2,100 in Seluwasan (1980 government report). Southwest coast of Yamdena Island, south Maluku. Three villages: Wermatang, Batu Putih, and Marantutul. Austronesian, Malayo-Polynesian, Central-Eastern, Central Malayo-Polynesian, Southeast Maluku, Southern. Dialects: SELUWASAN, MAKATIAN. Distinct language and culture. Makatian is quite different. Hunters. Christian.

SEPA ***(TAMILOUW)*** [SPB] 2,600 (1989 Loski and Loski SIL). Sepa village, Seram Island, central Maluku. Austronesian, Malayo-Polynesian, Central-Eastern, Central Malayo-Polynesian, Central Maluku, East, Seram, Nunusaku, Piru Bay, East. 79% lexical similarity between Sepa and Tamilouw, 69% to 78% with Teluti, 50% with Atamanu. Used as a second language by South Nuaulu speakers. Investigation needed: intelligibility with Tamilouw, Teluti. Trade language.

SERILI [SVE] 328 (1980 de Jonge). Northeast Marsela Island, south Maluku. Austronesian, Malayo-Polynesian, Central-Eastern, Central Malayo-Polynesian, Babar, South, Masela-South Babar. Literacy rate in first language: Below 1%. Christian.

SERUA [SRW] 2,000 (1990 SIL). Transmigration area in south central Seram Island, central Maluku. 4 villages. (Originally Serua Island in south central Maluku). Austronesian, Malayo-Polynesian, Central-Eastern, Central Malayo-Polynesian, Timor, Southwest Maluku, Teun-Nila-Serua, Nila-Serua. Close to Nila. Not intelligible with Teun. Moved by the government to Seram because of volcanic activity on their island. Investigation needed: intelligibility with Nila. Literacy rate in first language: Below 1%.

SULA ***(SANANA)*** [SZN] 20,000 (1983 C. and B. D. Grimes SIL). North Maluku, Sula Islands, Sulabesi Island and scattered communities on the eastern and western ends and north coast of Mangole Island, and northeast coast of Buru Island. Austronesian, Malayo-Polynesian, Central-Eastern, Central Malayo-Polynesian, Central Maluku, Sula. Dialects: FAGUDU, FALAHU, FACEI (FACÉ). Mangole is closely related. Vigorous in daily communication. Literacy rate in first language: Below 1%. Muslim.

TABARU ***(TOBARU)*** [TBY] 15,000 (1991 Kotynski SIL). North Maluku, Ibu, Jailolo, and Oba districts. West Papuan, North Halmahera, North, Tobaru. Dialects: ADU, NYEKU. The northern dialect is the main one. The two dialects are inherently intelligible with each other. Literacy rate in first language: Below 1%. Literacy rate in second language: 25% to 50%. Christian.

TALIABU ***(TALIABO)*** [TLV] 2,500 to 5,500, including 500 to 1,500 in Mangei (1991 C. Grimes SIL). North Maluku, Taliabu Island and northwestern Mangole, Sula Islands. Austronesian, Malayo-Polynesian, Central-Eastern, Central Malayo-Polynesian, Central Maluku, Sula, Taliabo. Dialects: PADANG (SAMADA), MANANGA, MANGEI (MANGE'E, MANGE, MANG, SOBOYO, SOBOJO). Dialects share lexical similarities in the upper 90% range. Language attitudes are positive. Talo, Seho, Biha, Bono (Mbono) are place names. Traditional religion, Christian.

TALUR ***(ILWAKI, ILIWAKI, GALOLENG, LIR TALO, ILMEDU)*** [ILW] 675 (1990 B. Hinton SIL). Hiay, Ilputih, and Ilwaki villages in south central Wetar Island, north of Timor Island, south Maluku. Austronesian, Malayo-Polynesian, Central-Eastern, Central Malayo-Polynesian, Timor, Southwest Maluku, Wetar. 86% lexical similarity with Galoli on east Timor, 57% with Aputai, 52% with Tugun, 51% with Perai and Iliun. Investigation needed: intelligibility with Galoli. Literacy rate in first language: Below 1%.

TARANGAN, EAST ***(EAST TRANGAN, TARANGAN TIMUR)*** [TRE] 3,784 (1987 Maluku Dalam Angka). East coast of Tarangan Island, south Aru Islands, and villages in Maikor Strait (Sungai Maikor), 13 villages. South Maluku. Austronesian, Malayo-Polynesian, Central-Eastern, Central Malayo-Polynesian, Aru. 71% lexical similarity with West Tarangan. Vigorous. Investigation needed: intelligibility with dialects. Literacy rate in first language: Below 1%. Christian, Muslim.

TARANGAN, WEST ***(WEST TRANGAN, TARANGAN BARAT)*** [TXN] 6,478 (Maluku Dalam Angka). West coast of Tarangan Island, southern Aru Islands, south Maluku. Largest language in the Aru Islands. Austronesian, Malayo-Polynesian, Central-Eastern, Central Malayo-Polynesian, Aru. Dialects: SOUTH-WESTERN TARANGAN, NORTH CENTRAL TARANGAN. 2 sharply distinct dialect groups, with minor variation within them. 70% lexical similarity with East Tarangan and Wokam. Vigorous. Trade language. Literacy rate in first language: 10% to 70%. Literacy rate in second language: 60% to 70%. Christian, Muslim.

TELA-MASBUAR ***(TELA'A, MASBUAR-TELA)*** [TVM] 1,050 (1990 SIL). Villages of Tela and Masbuar, southwest Babar Island, south Maluku. Austronesian, Malayo-Polynesian, Central-Eastern, Central Malayo-Polynesian, Babar, South, Southwest Babar. Literacy rate in first language: Below 1%.

TELUTI ***(TALUTI, TIHORU, TEHORU, SILEN, WOLU)*** [TLT] 17,000 (1989 Loski and Loski SIL). Central Maluku, south Seram Island, Teluti Bay. Austronesian, Malayo-Polynesian, Central-Eastern, Central Malayo-Polynesian, Central Maluku, East, Seram, Nunusaku, Piru Bay, East. Dialects: WEST TELUTI (HAYA, WOLU, TEHORU, TEHUA), LAHA SERANI. 74% to 89% lexical similarity among dialects, 69% to 78% with Sepa, 50% with Atamanu. Used as second language by many Manusela and Seti speakers in the area. Investigation needed: intelligibility with dialects. Trade language. Mostly Muslim, some Christian.

TEOR ***(TIO'OR)*** [TEV] 1,100 (1986 SIL). Teor and Ut islands, South Maluku. Austronesian, Malayo-Polynesian, Central-Eastern, Central Malayo-Polynesian, Teor-Kur. Dialects: GAUR KRISTEN, UT. Speakers say they understand Kur. 79% lexical similarity between Gaur Kristen and Ut, 71% to 83%

with Kur, 41% with Watubela, 38% with Geser. Investigation needed: intelligibility with Kur. Muslim, some Christian.

TERNATE [TFT] 42,000 native speakers and 20,000 or more second language users (1981 Wurm and Hattori). North Maluku, islands of Ternate, Kayoa, Bacan, Obi, and coastal communities on western north Halmahera. Lingua franca in northern and northeastern Halmahera. West Papuan, North Halmahera, South. Close to Tidore. Vigorous use in daily communication. Investigation needed: intelligibility with Tidore. Trade language. Literacy rate in first language: 1% to 5%. Literacy rate in second language: 25% to 50%. Muslim.

TERNATEÑO *(TERNATENYO)* [TMG] North Maluku, Ternate Island, west of Halmahera Island. Creole, Portuguese based. Spanish relexification. Historical relationship with Chavacano and dialects, which are still spoken in the Philippines. Varieties of creole Portuguese were also spoken in Banda and Ambon. The Jakarta variety of creole Portuguese survived in Tugu until recent times (Wurm and Hattori 1981). Other varieties were also spoken in Larantuka, Flores; Adonara (Vure), Solor; Sumatra, Kalimantan, and Sulawesi. See also Timor Pidgin in Timor Lorosae, Indo-Portuguese in Sri Lanka, and Malaccan Creole Portuguese in Peninsular Malaysia. Extinct.

TE'UN [TVE] 1,200 (1990 SIL). Transmigration area in south central Seram Island, central Maluku. 4 villages. (Originally Teun Island in south central Maluku). Austronesian, Malayo-Polynesian, Central-Eastern, Central Malayo-Polynesian, Timor, Southwest Maluku, Teun-Nila-Serua, Teun. Moved by the government because of volcanic activity on their island. Investigation needed: intelligibility. Literacy rate in first language: Below 1%.

TIDORE [TVO] 26,000 native speakers, 20,000 or more second language users (1981 Wurm and Hattori). North Maluku, islands of Tidore, Maitara, Mare, northern half of Moti, and some areas of west coast of Halmahera. West Papuan, North Halmahera, South. Close to Ternate. Language attitudes are positive. Investigation needed: intelligibility with Ternate. Literacy rate in first language: 1% to 5%. Literacy rate in second language: 25% to 50%. Muslim.

TOBELO [TLB] 20,000 to 25,000 (1987 SIL). North Maluku, north Halmahera Island, Tobelo, Kao, and Jailolo districts, and Maba and Wasile districts, Harmahera Tengah; northern half of Morotai, all coastal areas of Kao Bay and inland, Patani, Weda, Gane, Bacan, Obi, Ambon, Raja Ampat islands of Irian Jaya, Sorong, Irian Jaya. West Papuan, North Halmahera, North, Tobelo. Dialects: DODINGA, BOËNG, TOBELO (HELEWORURU). Bilingualism in Indonesian. Language attitudes are positive. Tobelo taught in middle school in Tobelo town. Investigation needed: intelligibility with dialects, Tugutil. Dictionary. Literacy rate in first language: 1% to 5%. Literacy rate in second language: 25% to 50%. Traditional religion, Christian. NT 1993.

TUGUN *(TUTUNOHAN, MAHUAN)* [TZN] 1,200 or more (1990 Hinton SIL). Wetar Island, north of Timor, south Maluku; Mahuan, Masapun, Tomliapat, Ilpokil, Kahailin, Ilway, Arwala villages, on the southeast end of Wetar. Austronesian, Malayo-Polynesian, Central-Eastern, Central Malayo-Polynesian, Timor, Southwest Maluku, Wetar. Dialect: ARWALA. 76% lexical similarity with Perai, 74% with Aputai, 73% with Iliun, 52% with Talur. There are word taboos. Literacy rate in first language: Below 1%. Literacy rate in second language: 15% to 25%.

TUGUTIL [TUJ] 1,000 to 3,000 (1984 C. and B. D. Grimes SIL). North Maluku, north Halmahera Island, inland around Kusuri, inland in Kecamatan Tobelo, around Taboulamo in Kecamatan Kao, in the pass between Lolobata and Buli in Kecamatan Wasilei, along the Dodaga and Tutuling rivers, and along the Akelamo and Mabulan rivers in Kecamatan Maba, Tanjung Lili, villages of Miaf, Bebseli, and Marasibno. A few along the Lili, Waisango, and Afu rivers, and reports of other places. West Papuan, North Halmahera, North, Tobelo. Dialects: TELUK LILI, KUSURI. Possibly several dialects separated by large distances. Intelligibility with Tobelo dialects is inadequate. Bilingualism in Indonesian. Language attitudes are positive. Ethnically distinct from Tobelo. A group of forest peoples who have contact with village people for selling copra and purchasing supplies. Literacy rate in first language: Below 1%. Literacy rate in second language: 5% to 15%. Traditional religion, Christian.

TULEHU *(NORTHEAST AMBON)* [TLU] 18,843 (1987 SIL). 4 villages on the coast of northeast Ambon Island, central Maluku. Austronesian, Malayo-Polynesian, Central-Eastern, Central Malayo-Polynesian, Central Maluku, East, Seram, Nunusaku, Piru Bay, East, Seram Straits, Ambon. Dialects: TULEHU, LIANG, TENGAH-TENGAH, TIAL. Each dialect is in a separate village. Eastern end of Ambon dialect chain. 84% to 90% lexical similarity among dialects, 74% to 82% lexical similarity with Hitu, 72% to 76% with Haruku. Vigorous. Muslim, Christian.

UJIR *(UDJIR)* [UDJ] 975 (1995 J. Hughes). 2 villages, Ujir on Ujir Island and Samang on the end of western peninsula on Wokam Island, in northwest Aru Islands, south Maluku. Austronesian, Malayo-Polynesian, Central-Eastern, Central Malayo-Polynesian, Aru. 75% lexical similarity with Kola in north Aru, and slightly less with Kulaha on the west coast of Kola Island. Bilingualism in Malay.

Language use is declining in Ujir because of the influence of Malay used by an increasing number of outsiders. Use is reported to be less in Samang than in Ujir. Muslim.

WAIOLI ***(WAJOLI, WAYOLI)*** [WLI] 3,000 (1987 Voorhoeve and Visser). North Halmahera, between Sahu and Ibu languages, north Maluku. West Papuan, North Halmahera, North, Sahu. Intelligibility testing needed with all languages in Sahu subgroup. 81% lexical similarity with Gamkonora. Investigation needed: intelligibility with Sahu group. Christian, Muslim.

WATUBELA ***(SNABI WATUBELA, KASIUI, KESUI, KASUI, WESI, ESIRIUN, MATABELLO)*** [WAH] 4,000 (1990 R. Loski SIL). Watubela Islands, east central Maluku, north of Kur Island. Austronesian, Malayo-Polynesian, Central-Eastern, Central Malayo-Polynesian, Central Maluku, East, Banda-Geser, Geser-Gorom. Dialects: TAMHER TIMUR, SULMELANG. 77% lexical similarity between dialects, 51% to 61% with Geser-Gorom, 41% with Teor and Kur, 37% with Bobot, 34% with Masiwang. Many claim to use Geser-Gorom as second language. Investigation needed: bilingual proficiency in Geser-Gorom. Muslim, some Christian.

WEMALE, NORTH [WEO] 4,929 (1982). Spread along the north coast of Taniwel District, east of Taniwel, and in the westernmost part of East Seram District, 24 villages. Austronesian, Malayo-Polynesian, Central-Eastern, Central Malayo-Polynesian, Central Maluku, East, Seram, Nunusaku, Three Rivers, Wemale. Dialects: HORALE, KASIEH, UWENPANTAI. Kawe may be a dialect. Lexical similarity between east and central dialects is 80%, 72% with South Wemale, 59% with Hulung. Language used in church. Vigorous. Literacy rate in first language: Below 1%. Christian, Muslim (Kanikeh village).

WEMALE, SOUTH ***(TALA, HONITETU)*** [TLW] 3,726 (1987 SIL). Central Maluku, west Seram, 15 villages; 13 in Kairatu, mainly in the interior, and two westernmost coastal villages of Amahai District. Austronesian, Malayo-Polynesian, Central-Eastern, Central Malayo-Polynesian, Central Maluku, East, Seram, Nunusaku, Three Rivers, Wemale. Dialect chain between Horale, Kasieh, Uwenpantai, and Honitetu. Kawe may be a dialect. Lexical similarity between Horale and Kasieh, and between Uwenpantai and Honitetu is 80%, 72% with North Wemale, 66% with Hulung, 47% with Atamanu. Vigorous. Investigation needed: intelligibility with dialects. Literacy rate in first language: Below 1%. Christian.

YALAHATAN ***(ATAMANU, JAHALATAN, JAHALATANE, AWAIYA)*** [JAL] 800 including 400 in each village (1991 SIL). West Seram, villages of Yalahatan and Haruru, central Maluku. Austronesian, Malayo-Polynesian, Central-Eastern, Central Malayo-Polynesian, Central Maluku, East, Seram, Nunusaku, Three Rivers. Slight dialect differences reported between the two villages. 50% to 52% lexical similarity with Sepa, 49% to 50% with Teluti. Speakers are not familiar with the name 'Atamanu'. Literacy rate in first language: Below 1%. Literacy rate in second language: 15% to 25%.

YAMDENA ***(JAMDENA, JAMDEN)*** [JMD] 25,000 active speakers out of an ethnic group of 35,000 to 40,000 (1991 T. Mettler SIL). Southeast Maluku, eastern coast of Yamdena, Adaut village on northern tip of Selaru, and one of the two languages spoken in Latdalam village, southwest Yamdena. 35 villages. Austronesian, Malayo-Polynesian, Central-Eastern, Central Malayo-Polynesian, Southeast Maluku, Kei-Tanimbar, Yamdena. Dialects: NORTH YAMDENA, SOUTH YAMDENA. Dialect chaining from north to south with 90% lexical similarity between the extremes, but with considerable morphological and phonological differences. The southern dialect is more prestigious. 90% lexical similarity between the north and south dialects, 47% lexical similarity with Fordata. Bilingualism in Ambonese Malay, Indonesian. Vigorous except for some villages, especially in the north. Investigation needed: intelligibility with dialects. Dictionary. Grammar. Literacy rate in first language: 2% to 5%. Literacy rate in second language: 80%. Morhophonemic orthography. Christian.

INDONESIA (NUSA TENGGARA)

7,387,000 including 3,370,000 in West Nusa Tenggara (1993), 3,269,000 in East Nusa Tenggara (1993). Information mainly from C. Grimes, T. Therik, B. D. Grimes, and M. Jacob 1997. Data accuracy estimate: A2, B, C. The number of languages listed for Indonesia (Nusa Tenggara) is 68. Of those, all are living languages. Diversity index 0.85.

ABUI ***(BARUE, "BARAWAHING", NAMATALAKI)*** [ABZ] 16,000(?) in the ethnic group (1981 Wurm and Hattori). Central and western Alor in the Lesser Sundas. Trans-New Guinea, South Bird's Head-Timor-Alor-Pantar, Timor-Alor-Pantar, Makasai-Alor-Pantar, Alor. Dialects: ATIMELANG, KOBOLA, ALAKAMAN. Much dialect diversity. The Alakaman dialect may be a dialect of Kamang (Woisika). May be more than one language. "Barawahing" is a derogatory name.

ADANG ***(ALOR)*** [ADN] Northwestern (Bird's Head) Alor Island in the Lesser Sundas. Trans-New Guinea, South Bird's Head-Timor-Alor-Pantar, Timor-Alor-Pantar, Makasai-Alor-Pantar, Alor. Dialect: AIMOLI.

On the basis of linguistic differences and social identity, it is best considered a separate language from Kabola. Christian.

ADONARA ***(NUSA TADON, WAIWERANG, VAIVERANG, SAGU)*** [ADA] Adonara Island, and eastern Solor Island, between Flores and Lembata. Austronesian, Malayo-Polynesian, Central-Eastern, Central Malayo-Polynesian, Timor, Flores-Lembata. Dialects: WEST ADONARA, EAST ADONARA, EAST SOLOR. Lamaholot is used as a language of wider communication. Muslim, Christian.

ALOR ***(ALORESE)*** [AOL] 25,000 (1997 Grimes, Therik, Grimes, Jacob). West and south of Bird's Head of Alor, north Ternate Island, pockets along northern Pantar and adjacent islands. Austronesian, Malayo-Polynesian, Central-Eastern, Central Malayo-Polynesian, Timor, Flores-Lembata. Speakers oriented toward Lembata and Adonara, but Alor is not inherently intelligible with those languages. Speakers use Lamaholot as language of wider communication, so it was formerly thought to be a dialect of Lamaholot. Muslim, Christian.

AMARASI ***(TIMOR AMARASI)*** [AAZ] 50,000 (1997 C. Grimes, Therik, B. D. Grimes, Jacob). Southwestern tip, Timor Island. Austronesian, Malayo-Polynesian, Central-Eastern, Central Malayo-Polynesian, Timor, Nuclear Timor, West. Dialects: AMARASI BARAT (WEST AMARASI), AMARASI TIMUR (EAST AMARASI). Closest to Atoni, but a separate language with differences in phonology, vocabulary, and discourse, with semantic shifts. Limited bilingualism in Indonesian. They live interspersed with Helong speakers. Christian.

ANAKALANGU ***(ANAKALANG)*** [AKG] 14,000 in the ethnic group (1981 Wurm and Hattori). Sumba Island, southwest coast, east of Wanukaka. Austronesian, Malayo-Polynesian, Central-Eastern, Central Malayo-Polynesian, Bima-Sumba. Closely related to, but unintelligible to speakers of Wejewa, Mamboru, Wanukaka, and Lamboya.

ATONI ***(UAB METO, METO, UAB ATONI PAH METO, UAB PAH METO, TIMOR, TIMORESE, TIMOL, TIMOREESCH, TIMOREEZEN, DAWAN, TIMOR DAWAN, RAWAN, ORANG GUNUNG)*** [TMR] 586,000 in West Timor (1997 Grimes, Therik, Grimes, Jacob). Population total both countries 600,000. Western Timor Island. Also spoken in Timor Lorosae. Austronesian, Malayo-Polynesian, Central-Eastern, Central Malayo-Polynesian, Timor, Nuclear Timor, West. Dialects: AMFOAN-FATULE'U-AMABI (AMFOAN, AMFUANG, FATULE'U, AMABI), AMANUBAN-AMANATUN (AMANUBAN, AMANUBANG, AMANATUN), MOLLO-MIOMAFO (MOLLO, MIOMAFO), BIBOKI-INSANA (BIBOKI, INSANAO), AMBENU (AMBENO, VAIKENU, VAIKINO, BAIKENU, BIKENU, BIQUENO), KUSA-MANLEA (KUSA, MANLEA). Much dialect variation, requiring speakers several weeks to adjust, for effective communication to take place. Ethnological and linguistic differences in nearly every valley. Close to Amarasi. 'Uab Meto' is speakers' name for their own language. Investigation needed: intelligibility with dialects. Christian (Atoni). NT 1948-1984.

BIMA ***(BIMANESE)*** [BHP] 500,000 (1989). Sunda Islands, eastern Sumbawa Island, east of the isthmus. Austronesian, Malayo-Polynesian, Central-Eastern, Central Malayo-Polynesian, Bima-Sumba. Dialects: KOLO, SANGAR (SANGGAR), TOLOWERI, BIMA, MBOJO. Muslim, Christian.

BLAGAR ***(BELAGAR, TARANG)*** [BEU] 11,000(?) in ethnic group (1981 Wurm and Hattori). Eastern Pantar, northern Pura, southern Ternate islands, Lesser Sundas. Trans-New Guinea, South Bird's Head-Timor-Alor-Pantar, Timor-Alor-Pantar, Makasai-Alor-Pantar, Pantar. Dialects: APURI, LIMARAHING, BAKALANG, PURA. The Retta variety on south Pura is thought to be a separate language by 2 Alorese. Investigation needed: intelligibility with Tereweng.

BUNAK ***(BUNA', BUNAKE, BUNAQ)*** [BUA] Central interior Timor Island, south coast. Trans-New Guinea, South Bird's Head-Timor-Alor-Pantar, Timor-Alor-Pantar, Bunak. Not closely related to other languages. Some small groups are scattered among other languages. Grammar. Traditional religion. See main entry under Timor Lorosae.

ENDE ***(ENDEH)*** [END] 87,000 including 78,000 Ende, 9,000 Nga'o (1981 Wurm and Hattori). South central Flores, west of Sikka, Lesser Sundas. Austronesian, Malayo-Polynesian, Central-Eastern, Central Malayo-Polynesian, Bima-Sumba, Ende-Lio. Dialects: ENDE (ENDEH, JA'O, DJAU), NGA'O (NGAO, WEST ENDE). Dialect chain. Li'o is on the border between a separate language or dialect of Ende. Investigation needed: intelligibility with dialects, Li'o. Christian.

HAMAP [HMU] 1,000 to 1,500 in ethnic group (1997 Grimes, Therik, Grimes, Jacob). Kalabahi Bay, across from Kalabahi city, around Moru town. 2 villages. Migration in 1947 from Mo'eng, a few kms. to the south. Still on their traditional land, but now in an interethnic community with Kui speakers. 18 km. by road from Kalabahi. Trans-New Guinea, South Bird's Head-Timor-Alor-Pantar, Timor-Alor-Pantar, Makasai-Alor-Pantar, Alor. Said to be intelligible with the Adang-Aimoli dialect of Kabola, but 'Kabola' is associated with the Bird's Head area of Alor. Structural and lexical differences with Kabola. Separate socio-political history from Kabola. Some intermarriage. Investigation needed: intelligibility with Kabola. Verb final, contrast between close and open [e], vowel-initial and glottal-initial words. Christian.

HELONG ***(HELON, SEMAU, KUPANG)*** [HEG] 14,000 (1997 Grimes, Therik, Grimes, Jacob). Western tip of Timor Island near the port of Tenau (4 villages), in and around Kupang, extending across the island to the Amarasi region, and several villages on Semau Island. Austronesian, Malayo-Polynesian, Central-Eastern, Central Malayo-Polynesian, Timor, Helong. Dialects: HELONG PULAU (ISLAND HELONG), HELONG DARAT (LAND HELONG). 2 groups which have minor dialect differences: Helong Darat on the Timor mainland, and Helong Pulau on Semau Island. Speakers are in contact with Rote, Sabu, Ndao, Atoni, Kupang Malay, and Standard Indonesian. Helong is used for daily domestic and rural routine and traditional ceremonies. Helong Darat speakers are reported to be beginning to shift to Kupang Malay under the influence of people from Rote and Savu. Unlike many surrounding languages, does not inflect V-initial verb roots for person or number; has long and short vowels; glottal stop, metathesis. Christian, traditional religion.

ILE APE ***(NUSA TADON)*** [ILA] North Lembata (Lomblen Island), including Ile Ape volcanic peninsula and nearby mainland Lembata. North Ile Ape is on the peninsula, South Ile Ape is on the mainland. Austronesian, Malayo-Polynesian, Central-Eastern, Central Malayo-Polynesian, Timor, Flores-Lembata. Dialects: NORTH ILE APE, SOUTH ILE APE. Bilingualism in Lamaholot.

KABOLA [KLZ] 3,900 (1995 N. Johnston). Northwestern (Bird's Head) Alor Island in the Lesser Sundas. Trans-New Guinea, South Bird's Head-Timor-Alor-Pantar, Timor-Alor-Pantar, Makasai-Alor-Pantar, Alor. Dialects: PINTUMBANG, TANG'ALA, MEIBUIL, OTVAI, KEBUN KOPI. The names and locations of the dialect in Wurm and Hattori (1981) are disputed by native speakers. May be more than one language. On the basis of linguistic differences and social identity, is best considered a separate language from Adang. Investigation needed: intelligibility with Hamap. Christian, Muslim.

KAFOA ***(JAFOO, RUILAK, AIKOLI, FANATING, PAILELANG)*** [KPU] 1,000(?) in ethnic group (1981 Wurm and Hattori). Southwest Alor Island, north of Aluben, between Abui and Kelong languages. Trans-New Guinea, South Bird's Head-Timor-Alor-Pantar, Timor-Alor-Pantar, Makasai-Alor-Pantar, Alor. The name 'Jafoo' is suggested by some Alorese. The name 'Kafoa' is not known locally.

KAMANG ***(WOISIKA, WAISIKA)*** [WOI] 12,000 in the ethnic group (1981 Wurm and Hattori). Alor Island, east central, between Abui and Tanglapui. 'Woisika' is the name of 1 village. The Kamang dialect is spoken there and in 2 other villages. Apui is reported as a place name, not a dialect. Trans-New Guinea, South Bird's Head-Timor-Alor-Pantar, Timor-Alor-Pantar, Makasai-Alor-Pantar, Alor. Dialects: LEMBUR (LIMBUR, KAWEL), SIBO, KAMANG, TIAYAI, WATANG, KAMANA-KAMANG. Probably more than one language. It is reported that 'Kamang' is preferred by speakers as the language name.

KAMBERA ***(SUMBANESE, EAST SUMBANESE, OOST-SUMBAAS, HUMBA, HILU HUMBA, EAST SUMBA, SUMBA)*** [SMI] 200,000 in the ethnic group (1989). Eastern half of Sumba Island, south of Flores, Lesser Sundas. Austronesian, Malayo-Polynesian, Central-Eastern, Central Malayo-Polynesian, Bima-Sumba. Dialects: KAMBERA, MELOLO, UMA RATU NGGAI (UMBU RATU NGGAI), LEWA, KANATANG, MANGILI-WAIJELO (WAI JILU, WAIDJELU, RINDI, WAIJELO), SOUTHERN SUMBA. Dialect network. Kambera dialect is widely understood. Speakers of Lewa and Uma Taru Nggai have difficulty understanding those from Mangili in many speech domains. Distinct from Sumbawa in the Bali-Sasak group. Dictionary. Grammar. Christian, traditional religion. Bible 1995.

KEDANG ***(DANG, KDANG, KÉDANG, KEDANGESE)*** [KSX] 30,000 (1997 N. Johnston). Northeast Lembata (Lomblen) Island, Lesser Sundas. All modern villages located on a ring road around the base of a volcano. Austronesian, Malayo-Polynesian, Central-Eastern, Central Malayo-Polynesian, Timor, Flores-Lembata. Christian, Muslim.

KELON ***(KELONG, KALONG)*** [KYO] 6,000 (1997 Grimes, Therik, Grimes, Jacob). Southwestern Alor Island, Lesser Sundas. Trans-New Guinea, South Bird's Head-Timor-Alor-Pantar, Timor-Alor-Pantar, Makasai-Alor-Pantar, Alor. Dialects: PROBUR, HALERMAN, GENDOK, PANGGAR.

KEMAK ***(EMA)*** [KEM] North central Timor Island, border area between West Timor and Timor Lorosae, mostly on eastern side. Austronesian, Malayo-Polynesian, Central-Eastern, Central Malayo-Polynesian, Timor, Nuclear Timor, East. Dialects: NOGO (NOGO-NOGO), KEMAK. Closely related to Tetun. Most closely related to Mambae and Tukudede. Also related to Atoni. Morris 1992 counts Nogo as a separate language from Kemak. Investigation needed: intelligibility with dialects. OSV. Traditional religion, Christian. See main entry under Timor Lorosae.

KE'O ***(NAGE-KEO)*** [XXK] 50,000 (1993 Forth). South central Flores, east of Ngad'a, south of Nage, south and southeast of the volcano Ebu Lobo. Austronesian, Malayo-Polynesian, Central-Eastern, Central Malayo-Polynesian, Bima-Sumba, Ende-Lio. Investigation needed: intelligibility.

KEPO' ***(KEPOQ)*** [KUK] Central Flores, between Manggarai and Rembong, with a separate enclave between Manggarai and Wae Rana. Austronesian, Malayo-Polynesian, Central-Eastern, Central Malayo-Polynesian, Bima-Sumba. May be intelligible with one of the surrounding languages. Investigation needed: intelligibility with surrounding languages.

KODI ***(KUDI)*** [KOD] 40,000 (1987 UBS). West Sumba, Lesser Sundas. Austronesian, Malayo-Polynesian, Central-Eastern, Central Malayo-Polynesian, Bima-Sumba. Dialects: KODI BOKOL, KODI BANGEDO, NGGARO (NGGAURA). May be closest to Wejewa. Traditional religion, Christian.

KOMODO [KVH] Komodo Island and west coast of Flores. Not on Timor. Austronesian, Malayo-Polynesian, Central-Eastern, Central Malayo-Polynesian, Bima-Sumba. Considered a separate language from Manggarai by Verheijen.

KUI ***(LERABAIN, MASIN-LAK)*** [KVD] 5,000(?) in the ethnic group (1981 Wurm and Hattori). Alor Island in scattered enclaves. Kui dialect is on the south coast in Lerabaing and Buraga; Batulolong dialect is in Sibera and Kapebang. Kui is also in Moru in Kalabahi Bay, interspersed with Hamap speakers. Trans-New Guinea, South Bird's Head-Timor-Alor-Pantar, Timor-Alor-Pantar, Makasai-Alor-Pantar, Alor. Dialects: KUI (LERABAING, BURAGA), KIRAMANG (KRAMANG), BATULOLONG. 'Masin-Lak' is speakers' own name for their language. Muslim, Christian.

KULA ***(LANTOKA, TANGLAPUI, LAMTOKA, KOLA)*** [TPG] 5,000 (1997 Grimes, Therik, Grimes, Jacob). Eastern quarter of Alor Island, between Kamang and Sawila. Naumang is an old village. Other villages are the result of recent migrations from older locations. Most are in higher elevations, but the villagers of Maukuru, Takala, Koilela, Peisaka, and Kiralela on the north coast also speak Kula. Trans-New Guinea, South Bird's Head-Timor-Alor-Pantar, Timor-Alor-Pantar, Tanglapui. Dialects: IRAMANG, KULA, KULATELA, WATENA, LARENA, KULA WATENA, SUMANG, ARUMAKA. Not closely related to other languages. Intelligibility with Sawila is marginal. Investigation needed: intelligibility with dialects. Mountain slope, coastal. Christian, traditional religion.

LAMAHOLOT ***(SOLOR, SOLORESE)*** [SLP] 150,000(?) (1997 Grimes, Therik, Grimes, Jacob). Lesser Sundas. Used as mother tongue on the eastern tip of Flores, east of the Sika language, and on western Solor. Used as language of wider communication on all of Solor. Adonara Lembata (except the Kedang area) and in enclaves on the northern coast of Pantar, northwest Alor, and surrounding islands. Austronesian, Malayo-Polynesian, Central-Eastern, Central Malayo-Polynesian, Timor, Flores-Lembata. Dialects: WEST LAMAHOLOT (MUHANG, PUKAUNU), LAMAHOLOT (TAKA, LEWOLAGA, ILE MANDIRI, TANJUNG BUNDA, LARANTUKA, RITAEBANG), WEST SOLOR. Wide variation among dialects. Possibly up to 10 languages. Keraf (1978) reports 18 distinct languages. The area around Larantuka is multi-ethnic and some people have shifted to Malay. 'Lamaholot-Alor' is used to refer to (1) a lingua franca, (2) any of several Austronesian varieties spoken from eastern Flores to Alor. Language of wider communication. Grammar. Traditional religion, Muslim, Christian.

LAMALERA ***(MULAN, KAWELA, LEBATUKAN)*** [LMR] South coastal Lembata (Lomblen) Island, about 4 villages. Austronesian, Malayo-Polynesian, Central-Eastern, Central Malayo-Polynesian, Timor, Flores-Lembata. Bilingualism in Lamaholot. Grammar. Traditionally whale hunters.

LAMATUKA ***(LAMATOKA)*** [LMQ] Central Lembata (Lomblen) Island, between Ile Ape and Lewo Eleng. Several villages. Villages near the north coast are the result of recent government-induced migrations. Austronesian, Malayo-Polynesian, Central-Eastern, Central Malayo-Polynesian, Timor, Flores-Lembata. Lewo Eleng is probably the most closely related language. Bilingualism in Lamaholot. Mountain slope. Harvesting candlenut. Christian, traditional religion.

LAMBOYA [LMY] 25,000 (1997 Grimes, Therik, Grimes, Jacob). Sumba Island, southwest coast, southwest of Waikabubak. Austronesian, Malayo-Polynesian, Central-Eastern, Central Malayo-Polynesian, Bima-Sumba. Dialects: LAMBOYA, NGGAURA. Closely related to, but unintelligible to speakers of Wejewa, Mamboru, Wanukaka, and Anakalangu. Investigation needed: bilingual proficiency.

LAMMA ***(LEMMA, LAMMA', MAUTA)*** [LEV] 10,000(?) in ethnic group. Southwestern and western Pantar, Lesser Sundas. Trans-New Guinea, South Bird's Head-Timor-Alor-Pantar, Timor-Alor-Pantar, Makasai-Alor-Pantar, Pantar. Dialects: KALONDAMA, TUBAL (TUBE, MAUTA), BIANGWALA.

LAURA ***(LAORA)*** [LUR] 10,000 (1997 Grimes, Therik, Grimes, Jacob). Northwest Sumba between Kodi and Mamboru. Austronesian, Malayo-Polynesian, Central-Eastern, Central Malayo-Polynesian, Bima-Sumba. Dialects: LAURA, MBUKAMBERO (BUKAMBERO). Not intelligible with Kodi.

LEMBATA, SOUTH [LMF] South Lembata (Lomblen) Island, between Lamalera and Lamatuka. Austronesian, Malayo-Polynesian, Central-Eastern, Central Malayo-Polynesian, Timor, Flores-Lembata. Bilingualism in Lamaholot.

LEMBATA, WEST ***(MINGAR, LABALEKAN)*** [LMJ] Western end of Lembata (Lomblen) Island, west of Levuka. Both mountain and coastal villages around the base of a volcano. Austronesian, Malayo-Polynesian, Central-Eastern, Central Malayo-Polynesian, Timor, Flores-Lembata. Bilingualism in Lamaholot.

LEVUKA ***(LEWUKA, LEMBATA, PAINARA, LEWOKUKUN)*** [LVU] West central Lembata (Lomblen) Island, between Ile Ape and Lamalera. Austronesian, Malayo-Polynesian, Central-Eastern, Central Malayo-Polynesian, Timor, Flores-Lembata. Dialects: LEVUKA, KALIKASA. Different from other

Lembata languages. Bilingualism in Lamaholot. Recent road to Lamalera. Mountain slope. Christian, traditional religion.

LEWO ELENG [LWE] East central Lembata (Lomblen) Island, between Lamatuka and Kedang. Several villages. Villages near the north coast are the result of recent government-induced migrations. Austronesian, Malayo-Polynesian, Central-Eastern, Central Malayo-Polynesian, Timor, Flores-Lembata. Lamatuka is probably the most closely related language. Bilingualism in Lamaholot. Investigation needed: intelligibility with Lamatuka. Mountain slope. Harvesting candlenut. Christian, traditional religion.

LEWOTOBI *(SOUTHWEST LAMAHOLOT)* [LWT] Eastern Flores, south of Lamaholot and east of Sika. Austronesian, Malayo-Polynesian, Central-Eastern, Central Malayo-Polynesian, Timor, Flores-Lembata. Bilingualism in Lamaholot.

LI'O *(LIO, AKU, TANAH KUNU, LIONESE)* [LJL] 130,000 (1981 Wurm and Hattori). Central Flores, west of Sikka around Paga and Dondo, Lesser Sundas. Austronesian, Malayo-Polynesian, Central-Eastern, Central Malayo-Polynesian, Bima-Sumba, Ende-Lio. Dialect chain with Ende, difficult intelligibility at ends. Palu'e is borderline between language and dialect with Li'o. Investigation needed: intelligibility with Ende. Christian.

MALAY, KUPANG *(KUPANG)* [MKN] 200,000 mother tongue speakers (1997 Max Jacob). Others use it as a second language. Kupang and surrounding towns, West Timor. Creole, Malay based. Dialect: AIR MATA. 2 dialects. Some preachers preach in it. Loan words from Rote, Portuguese, Chinese, Uab Meto (Atoni), Sabu, Spanish, Dutch, English. Newspapers, radio programs. Christian. Bible portions 1999.

MAMBORU *(MEMBORO)* [MVD] 16,000 (1981 Wurm and Hattori). Northwest Sumba Island, coast around Memboro. Austronesian, Malayo-Polynesian, Central-Eastern, Central Malayo-Polynesian, Bima-Sumba. Closely related to, but unintelligible to speakers of Wejewa, Wanukaka, Lamboya, and Anakalangu.

MANGGARAI [MQY] 500,000 (1989). Western third of Flores Island, Lesser Sundas. Austronesian, Malayo-Polynesian, Central-Eastern, Central Malayo-Polynesian, Bima-Sumba. Dialects: WESTERN MANGGARAI, CENTRAL MANGGARAI (RUTENG), WEST-CENTRAL MANGGARAI, EASTERN MANGGARAI. Around 43 subdialects. Closely related to Riung. Dictionary. Christian, Muslim.

NAGE *(NAGÉ, NAGE-KEO)* [NXE] 50,000 (1993 Forth). Central Flores, northeast of Ngad'a, on the northern and western slopes of Ebu Lobo volcano. Austronesian, Malayo-Polynesian, Central-Eastern, Central Malayo-Polynesian, Bima-Sumba, Ende-Lio.

NDAO *(NDAONESE, NDAUNDAU, DAO)* [NFA] 5,000 (1997 Dr. Ayub Ranoh). Island of Ndao, scattered on Rote, and Timor. Austronesian, Malayo-Polynesian, Central-Eastern, Central Malayo-Polynesian, Bima-Sumba. Related to Sabu, but a distinct language. Difficult phonology. Silversmiths. Men leave the island for long periods of seasonal work. Women are well known as weavers of traditional cloth. Christian.

NEDEBANG *(BALUNGADA, NÉDEBANG)* [NEC] 1,000(?) in the ethnic group (1981 Wurm and Hattori). North central Pantar, south and southwest of Kabir. Trans-New Guinea, South Bird's Head-Timor-Alor-Pantar, Timor-Alor-Pantar, Makasai-Alor-Pantar, Pantar.

NGAD'A *(NGADHA, NGADA, NAD'A, NGA'DA, BAJAVA, BADJAVA, BAJAWA, ROKKA)* [NXG] 60,000 (1995). South central Flores, between Manggarai and Ende and Li'o. Austronesian, Malayo-Polynesian, Central-Eastern, Central Malayo-Polynesian, Bima-Sumba. Dialects: CENTRAL NGADA, BAJAWA, SOUTH NGADA. Dialect diversity. Investigation needed: intelligibility with Soa. Grammar. Christian.

NGAD'A, EASTERN *(SOUTHEAST NGADA)* [NEA] 5,000 (1994). South central Flores, between Ngad'a and Nage in Kecamatan Golewa in the administrative villages of Sara Sedu, Taka Tunga, Sanga Deto, and in Kecamatan Boawae in desa Rowa, all in Kabupaten Ngada. Austronesian, Malayo-Polynesian, Central-Eastern, Central Malayo-Polynesian, Bima-Sumba. Minor dialect variation. Christian.

PALU'E *(PALUE, LU'A, PALUQE)* [PLE] 10,000 (1997 Grimes, Therik, Grimes, Jacob). Palu Island, north of central Flores. Also the village of Nangahure on the north coast of the Flores mainland northwest of Maumere. Austronesian, Malayo-Polynesian, Central-Eastern, Central Malayo-Polynesian, Bima-Sumba. Dialect chain with Ende-Lio; marginal intelligibility with Li'o. Christian, traditional religion.

RAJONG *(RAZONG)* [RJG] Central Flores, 2 enclaves between Manggarai, Wae Rana, Ngad'a, and Rembong. Austronesian, Malayo-Polynesian, Central-Eastern, Central Malayo-Polynesian, Bima-Sumba.

REMBONG [REB] North central Flores, between Eastern Manggarai and Riung. Austronesian, Malayo-Polynesian, Central-Eastern, Central Malayo-Polynesian, Bima-Sumba. Dialects: REMBONG, WANGKA, NAMU.

RETTA [RET] Southern Pura Island at mouth of Kalabahi Bay, and southern part of Ternate Island. Trans-New Guinea, South Bird's Head-Timor-Alor-Pantar, Timor-Alor-Pantar, Makasai-Alor-Pantar, Pantar. Not intelligible with languages on north Pura.

RIUNG ***(FAR EASTERN MANGGARAI)*** [RIU] 14,000 (1981 Wurm and Hattori). North central Flores Island, Kecamatan Riung in Kaupaten Ngada, Lesser Sundas. Austronesian, Malayo-Polynesian, Central-Eastern, Central Malayo-Polynesian, Bima-Sumba. Closely related to Manggarai; but marginal intelligibility. Investigation needed: bilingual proficiency.

RONGGA [ROR] South central Flores, between Manggarai and Ngad'a, and south of Wae Rana. Austronesian, Malayo-Polynesian, Central-Eastern, Central Malayo-Polynesian, Bima-Sumba.

ROTE ***(ROTI, ROTTI, ROTINESE)*** [ROT] 123,000 to 133,000 in ethnic group (1981 Wurm and Hattori). Rote Island southwest of Timor and on adjacent Timor Island around Kupang and Semau Island. Austronesian, Malayo-Polynesian, Central-Eastern, Central Malayo-Polynesian, Timor, Nuclear Timor, West. Dialects: ROTE-TIMUR (LANDU, ROTE-RINGGOU, RINGGOU, RENGGOU, OEPAO, LANDU-RINGGOU-OEPAO, RIKOU), BILBA-DIU-LELENUK (BILBA, DIU, LELENUK, BELUBAA), ROTE-TENGAH (TERMANU, PADA, TALAE, KEKA, TERMANU-TALAE-KEKA, BOKAI, KORBAFO, KORBAFFO, KOLBAFFO, LELAIN), BA'Ä-LOLEH (BADÄ BA'A, LOLEH, LOLE), TII (TI, THIE). Significant linguistic blockages to intelligibility among Rote varieties, and attitudes which hinder acceptance of each other's varieties, but social factors favor considering them one. Speakers from different Rote varieties often communicate by using Malay. Christian. Bible portions 1895.

ROTE, WESTERN ***(ROTE BARAT, WEST ROTE)*** [ROW] Western Rote Island. Austronesian, Malayo-Polynesian, Central-Eastern, Central Malayo-Polynesian, Timor, Nuclear Timor, West. Dialects: OENALE-DELHA (OENALE, UNALE, DELHA), DENGKA. Christian, traditional religion.

SABU ***(HAWU, HAVUNESE, SAVU, SAWU, SAWUNESE, SAVUNESE)*** [HVN] 110,000 (1997), including 15,000 to 25,000 outside of Sawu (1981 Wurm and Hattori). Islands of Sawu and Raijua south of Flores and west of Timor, and in Sumba (especially in Waingapo and Melolo), in Ende on Flores, and the Kupang area of Timor. Administratively in Kabupaten Kupang. Airstrip is served irregularly. Austronesian, Malayo-Polynesian, Central-Eastern, Central Malayo-Polynesian, Bima-Sumba. Dialects: SEBA (HEBA), TIMU (DIMU), LIAE, MESARA (MEHARA), RAIJUA (RAIDJUA). Related to Ndao. Grammar. Complex phonetics with implosives, glottal, long and short vowels, diphthongs, long and short consonants. Christian, traditional religion (Jengetiu). Bible portions 1976-1997.

SASAK ***(LOMBOK)*** [SAS] 2,100,000 1.2% of the population (1989). Lombok Island. Austronesian, Malayo-Polynesian, Western Malayo-Polynesian, Sundic, Bali-Sasak. Dialects: KUTO-KUTE (NORTH SASAK), NGETO-NGETE (NORTHEAST SASAK), MENO-MENE (CENTRAL SASAK), NGENO-NGENE (CENTRAL EAST SASAK, CENTRAL WEST SASAK), MRIAK-MRIKU (CENTRAL SOUTH SASAK). Complex dialect network. Some 'dialects' have difficult intelligibility with each other. Related to Sumbawa and Balinese. Subgroups: Waktu Lima, Waktu Telu. Most Waktu Telu own farms, most Waktu Lima are landless, travel more, and have diverse occupations. Many Balinese also on Lombok Island, especially in the west. Waktu Telu: agriculturalists. Muslim, Christian, traditional religion (Waktu Telu). NT, in press (1996).

SAWILA ***(TANGLAPUI)*** [SWT] 3,000 (1997 Grimes, Therik, Grimes, Jacob). Eastern Alor Island between Kula and Wersing. Many current village locations are the result of recent migrations from older locations. Trans-New Guinea, South Bird's Head-Timor-Alor-Pantar, Timor-Alor-Pantar, Tanglapui. Dialects: SAWILA, LONA, SALIMANA, LALAMANA, SILEBA. Intelligibility with Kula is marginal, and the historical ethnic identities are distinct. Mountain slope, coastal. Christian, traditional religion.

SIKA ***(SARA SIKKA, SIKKANESE, SIKKA, KROWE, MAUMERE)*** [SKI] 175,000 (1990 E. D. Lewis). Eastern Flores Island, between Li'o and Lamaholot, Lesser Sundas. Austronesian, Malayo-Polynesian, Central-Eastern, Central Malayo-Polynesian, Timor, Flores-Lembata. Dialects: SARA KROWE (CENTRAL SIKKA), SIKKA NATAR (SOUTH COAST SIKKA, KANGAÉ), TANA AI. Wide variation within language and culture. Investigation needed: intelligibility with dialects. Grammar. Christian.

SO'A ***(SOA)*** [SSQ] 10,000(?) (1994). Central Flores, central Kabupaten Ngada, between Ngad'a and Riung. Austronesian, Malayo-Polynesian, Central-Eastern, Central Malayo-Polynesian, Bima-Sumba. Closely related to Ngad'a. Christian.

SUMBAWA ***(SEMAWA, SUMBAWARESE)*** [SMW] 300,000 (1989). Western end of Sumbawa Island, west of the isthmus. Austronesian, Malayo-Polynesian, Western Malayo-Polynesian, Sundic, Bali-Sasak. Different from Sumba (Kambera).

TEREWENG [TWG] 800 in the ethnic group(?) (1997 Grimes, Therik, Grimes, Jacob). Tereweng Island off southeast Pantar. 2 villages on the northern side of the island and one on Pantar mainland. Water and gardens on Pantar. Trans-New Guinea, South Bird's Head-Timor-Alor-Pantar, Timor-Alor-Pantar, Makasai-Alor-Pantar, Pantar. There is disagreement over whether this is a dialect of Blagar or a separate language. Grouped by Stokhof (1975) with Blagar, by Vatter (1932) with Kelong, and by van Gaalen (1945) as distinct. Distinct ethnic identity from Blagar. Investigation needed: intelligibility with Blagar, Kelong.

TETUN ***(TETUM, TETTUM, TETO, TETU, TETUNG, BELU, BELO, FEHAN, TETUN BELU)*** [TTM] 450,000 (1997). Population total both countries 450,000 or more. Central Timor corridor from the north to the south coasts, east of Atoni, west of Bunak (in Batagude) around Batibo and in from the south coast around Viqueque and Soibada. Also spoken in Timor Lorosae. Austronesian, Malayo-Polynesian, Central-Eastern, Central Malayo-Polynesian, Timor, Nuclear Timor, East. Dialects: EASTERN TETUN (SOIBADA, NATARBORA, LAKLUTA, TETUN LOOS, TETUN LOS), SOUTHERN TETUN (LIA FEHAN, PLAIN TETUN, TASI MANE, BELU SELATAN, SOUTH BELU, SOUTH TETUN), NORTHERN TETUN (LIA FOHO, HILL TETUN, TASI FETO, BELU UTARA, NORTH BELU, TETUN TERIK, TETUN THERIK). Wide variation in morphology and syntax among major dialects, and variation in social structure. Investigation needed: intelligibility with dialects. Grammar. Christian, traditional religion. Bible portions 1997.

TEWA [TWE] 5,000(?) in the ethnic group (1981 Wurm and Hattori). Central Pantar. Trans-New Guinea, South Bird's Head-Timor-Alor-Pantar, Timor-Alor-Pantar, Makasai-Alor-Pantar, Pantar. Dialects: DEING, MADAR, LEBANG.

WAE RANA ***(WAERANA)*** [WRX] South central Flores, between Manggarai and Ngad'a. Austronesian, Malayo-Polynesian, Central-Eastern, Central Malayo-Polynesian, Bima-Sumba.

WANUKAKA ***(WANOKAKA)*** [WNK] 10,000 (1981 Wurm and Hattori). Sumba Island, southwest coast, east of Lamboya. Austronesian, Malayo-Polynesian, Central-Eastern, Central Malayo-Polynesian, Bima-Sumba. Dialects: WANUKAKA, RUA. Closely related to, but unintelligible to speakers of, Wejewa, Mamboru, Lamboya, and Anakalangu. Intelligibility with varieties in east Sumba and Kambera uncertain. Investigation needed: intelligibility with Kambera, east Sumba.

WEJEWA ***(WEWEWA, WAJEWA, WEWJEWA, WAIDJEWA, WEST SUMBANESE, WEYEWA, VEVEVA)*** [WEW] 65,000 (1997 Grimes, Therik, Grimes, Jacob). Interior of western Sumba Island, Lesser Sundas. Austronesian, Malayo-Polynesian, Central-Eastern, Central Malayo-Polynesian, Bima-Sumba. Dialects: WEYEWA, LAULI (LOLI), TANA RIGHU. Traditional religion. NT 1970.

WERSING ***(KOLANA-WERSIN, KOLANA, WERSIN, WARSINA)*** [KVW] 3,700 in ethnic group (1997 Grimes, Therik, Grimes, Jacob). Alor Island, east coast around Kolana, southeast coast at Pietoko and Pureman, 2 enclaves on north central north coast. Trans-New Guinea, South Bird's Head-Timor-Alor-Pantar, Timor-Alor-Pantar, Kolana. Dialects: KOLANA, MANETA, LANGKURU (PUREMAN, MADEMANG). Closely related to Kamang. Cultural and historical relationship with Liquisa area in Timor Lorosae. Said to have migrated from Timor mainland prior to 1500, first to Pureman on the south coast, then Kolana on the east coast, then on the north coast near Taramana. The former king was at Kolana. Coastal. Christian, traditional religion.

INDONESIA (SULAWESI)

12,000,000 (1989). 4 provinces. Information mainly from T. Sebeok 1971; J. C. Anceaux 1978; S. Kaseng 1978, ms. (1983); C. Salombe, D. Barr, and S. Barr 1979; B. H. Bhurhanuddin ms. (1979); J. N. Sneddon 1981, 1988; C. E. and B. D. Grimes 1987; T. Friberg 1987; T. Friberg and T. Laskowske 1988; R. Van den Berg 1988; M. Martens 1989; N. P. Himmelmann 1990. Data accuracy estimate: A2. B. The number of languages listed for Indonesia (Sulawesi) is 114. Of those, all are living languages. Diversity index 0.87.

ANDIO ***(MASAMA, ANDIO'O, IMBAO'O, "BOBONGKO")*** [BZB] 1,700 (1991 R. Busenitz SIL). Central Sulawesi, Banggi District, Lamala Subdistrict, eastern peninsula, Taugi and Tangeban villages. Austronesian, Malayo-Polynesian, Western Malayo-Polynesian, Sulawesi, Central Sulawesi, Eastern. Related to Balantak, Saluan. The name "Bobongko" is derogatory. 'Masama' is the preferred local name. Muslim.

ARALLE-TABULAHAN [ATQ] 12,000 (1984 SIL). South Sulawesi, Mambi Subdistrict, between Mandar and Kalumpang. Austronesian, Malayo-Polynesian, Western Malayo-Polynesian, Sulawesi, South Sulawesi, Northern, Pitu Ulunna Salu. Dialects: ARALLE, TABULAHAN, MAMBI. Aralle has 84% to 89% lexical similarity with other dialects listed, 75% to 80% with dialects of Pitu Ulunna Salu, Pannei, Ulumandak. Investigation needed: intelligibility with dialects. Christian, Muslim.

BADA ***(BADA', TOBADA')*** [BHZ] 10,000 (1991 R. Hanna SIL). South central portion of central Sulawesi, in 14 villages of Lore Selatan Subdistrict, two mixed villages of Pamona Selatan Subdistrict, four mixed villages of Poso Pesisir Subdistrict, part of Lemusa village in Parigi Subdistrict, and Ampibabo Subdistrict. Ako village is in northern Mamuju District, Pasangkayu Subdistrict. 23 villages or parts of villages. Members of the ethnic group in south Sulawesi, headwaters of the Budong-Budong River in Budong-Budong Subdistrict, Mamuju District no longer speak the language. One speaker spoke some, with influences from other languages. Austronesian, Malayo-Polynesian, Western Malayo-Polynesian, Sulawesi, Central Sulawesi, West Central, Kaili-Pamona,

Pamona. Dialects: BADA, AKO. The Hanggira dialect is no longer distinguished from Bada. Bada and Besoa have 85% lexical similarity; Besoa and Napu 91%; Bada and Napu 80%. The three are geographically, politically, culturally, and lexically distinct. Speakers use Indonesian as second language with varying proficiency. They speak Bada in the home and at work. 'Tobada' means 'Bada person'. Agriculturalists: rice. 2,500 feet. Christian, Muslim.

BAHONSUAI [BSU] 200 (1991 D. Mead SIL). Central Sulawesi, Bungku Tengah Subdistrict, Bahonsuai village on the east coast. Austronesian, Malayo-Polynesian, Western Malayo-Polynesian, Sulawesi, Central Sulawesi, West Central, Bungku-Mori-Tolaki, Mori. 71% lexical similarity with Tomadino, 68% with Mori Atas, Mori Bawah, and Padoe. Investigation needed: intelligibility with Tomadino. Coastal. Muslim.

BAJAU, INDONESIAN ***(BADJAW, BADJO, BAJO, BAJAO, BAYO, GAJ, LUAAN, LUTAOS, LUTAYAOS, SAMA, ORANG LAUT, TURIJE'NE')*** [BDL] 50,000 (1977 Pallesen SIL) including 25,000 in central Sulawesi (1979 D. Barr), 8,000 to 10,000 in south Sulawesi (1983 C. Grimes), 5,000 or more in north Maluku (1982 C. Grimes), several thousand in Nusa Tenggara (1981 Wurm and Hattori). In south Sulawesi in Selayar, Bone, and Pangkep districts. On the east coast of southeast Sulawesi on Wowonii, Muna, northern Buton, Kabaena, and northern Tukangbesi islands. Widely distributed throughout Sulawesi, north Maluku (Bacan, Obi, Kayoa, and Sula islands), Kalimantan, and the islands of the East Sunda Sea. Other Bajau languages are in Sabah, Malaysia, and the southern Philippines. Austronesian, Malayo-Polynesian, Western Malayo-Polynesian, Sama-Bajaw, Sulu-Borneo, Borneo Coast Bajaw. Dialects: JAMPEA, SAME', MATALAANG, SULAMU, KAJOA, ROTI, JAYA BAKTI, POSO, TONGIAN 1, TONGIAN 2, WALLACE. Vigorous in north Maluku. Known as Bayo and Turijene in the language of Macassar. Known as Bajo in Buginese. It may include several languages. There are schools in some villages. They live in houses on stilts over water. Investigation needed: intelligibility with dialects. Coastal inlets, islands, reefs, sand bars. Seamen. Muslim, traditional religion.

BALAESAN ***(BALAESANG, BALAISANG, PAJO)*** [BLS] 4,000 (1979 Barr). Central Sulawesi, Balaesang Subdistrict, 5 villages on the Manimbayu Peninsula. Austronesian, Malayo-Polynesian, Western Malayo-Polynesian, Sulawesi, Central Sulawesi, West Central, Balaesan. Not closely related to other languages. Investigation needed: bilingual proficiency. Muslim.

BALANTAK ***(KOSIAN)*** [BLZ] 25,000 (1991 Busenitz SIL). East central Sulawesi; Banggai District, Luwuk, Balantak, Tinangkung, and Lamala subdistricts, eastern peninsula; 49 villages or parts of villages. Austronesian, Malayo-Polynesian, Western Malayo-Polynesian, Sulawesi, Central Sulawesi, Eastern. Related to Andio, Saluan. Muslim, Christian, traditional religion. Bible portions 1991.

BAMBAM ***(PITU-ULUNNA-SALU)*** [PTU] 22,000 (1988 SIL). South Sulawesi, watershed of the Maloso and Mapilli rivers in Mambi Subdistrict of western Polmas District, overlapping into Majene and Mamuju districts. Austronesian, Malayo-Polynesian, Western Malayo-Polynesian, Sulawesi, South Sulawesi, Northern, Pitu Ulunna Salu. Dialects: BUMAL, BAMBANG (HULU), MEHALA'AN-EASTERN RANTEBULAHAN, WEST RANTEBULAHAN (RANTEBULAWAN), PATTAE (GALUNG), MATANGNGA, ISSILITA', SALU MUKANAM, PAKKAU. Complex dialect chain. Bumal has 83% to 94% lexical similarity with all dialects listed, 85% to 80% lexical similarity with dialects of Aralle-Tabulahan, Pannei, and Ulumandak. All ages. Vigorous. Grammar. Mountains, river valleys. Agriculturalists: wet rice, coffee, cacao. Christian (north), Muslim (south), traditional religion. Bible portions 1994-1998.

BANGGAI ***(AKI)*** [BGZ] 100,000 (1995 SIL). Central Sulawesi; Banggai, Liang, Bulagi, Buko, Totikum, Tinangkum, Labobo Bangkurung subdistricts; Banggai Islands off the eastern peninsula; 157 villages or parts of villages. Austronesian, Malayo-Polynesian, Western Malayo-Polynesian, Sulawesi, Central Sulawesi, Banggai. Dialects: EAST BANGGAI, WEST BANGGAI. Dictionary. Grammar. Muslim, Christian. NT 1993.

BANTIK [BNQ] 11,000 (1981 Wurm and Hattori). Northeast section of the northern peninsula of Sulawesi; three villages, within Manado city limits. Austronesian, Malayo-Polynesian, Western Malayo-Polynesian, Sulawesi, Sangir-Minahasan, Sangiric. Christian.

BARAS ***(ENDE)*** [BRS] 250 or 50 households (1987 SIL). South Sulawesi, Mamuju District, south Pasangkayu and north Budong-Budong subdistricts, a few villages, mainly in Desa Baras, between the Lariang and Budong-Budong rivers. Austronesian, Malayo-Polynesian, Western Malayo-Polynesian, Sulawesi, Central Sulawesi, West Central, Kaili-Pamona, Kaili. 84% lexical similarity with Da'a, 85% with Inde, 80% or more with other Kaili varieties, 64% with Uma. Some think the language will die out. Investigation needed: intelligibility with Da'a, attitudes. Muslim.

BENTONG ***(DENTONG)*** [BNU] 25,000 (1987 SIL). South Sulawesi, northwest corner of the southern tip of the peninsula; inland parts of Maros, Bone, Pangkep, and Barru districts. Austronesian, Malayo-Polynesian, Western Malayo-Polynesian, Sulawesi, South Sulawesi, Makassar. Closest to Konjo. Investigation needed: intelligibility with Konjo. Muslim over, Christian.

BESOA ***(BEHOA)*** [BEP] 3,000 (1991 R. Hanna SIL). Central Sulawesi, Lore Utara Subdistrict, Napu Valley, 8 villages. Austronesian, Malayo-Polynesian, Western Malayo-Polynesian, Sulawesi, Central Sulawesi, West Central, Kaili-Pamona, Pamona. Geographically, politically, culturally, and lexically distinct from Bada and Napu. Nearly everyone can speak Indonesian at some level. Agriculturalists: rice. 3,700 feet. Christian over, Muslim.

BINTAUNA [BNE] 6,000 (1981 Wurm and Hattori). Northeast Sulawesi, around Bintauna. Austronesian, Malayo-Polynesian, Western Malayo-Polynesian, Sulawesi, Mongondow-Gorontalo, Gorontalic. Muslim.

BOLANGO ***(BULANGA, BULANGA-UKI, DIU)*** [BLD] 20,000 including 5,000 in Bolango, 15,000 in Atinggola (1981 Wurm and Hattori). Northeastern Sulawesi. Bolango is on the south coast of the peninsula around Molibagu, and Atinggola on the north central coast around Atinggola, between Kaidipang and Gorontalo. Austronesian, Malayo-Polynesian, Western Malayo-Polynesian, Sulawesi, Mongondow-Gorontalo, Gorontalic. Dialects: BOLANGO, ATINGGOLA. Separate language from Gorontalo (J. Little). Muslim.

BOLANO ***(BOANO, DJIDJA)*** [BZL] 2,350 (1990 N. P. Himmelmann). Central Sulawesi, Montong Subdistrict, Bolano village, on the south coast. Austronesian, Malayo-Polynesian, Western Malayo-Polynesian, Sulawesi, Central Sulawesi, West Central, Tomini. 83% lexical similarity with Tolitoli. Muslim.

BONERATE [BNA] 9,500 (1987 T. Friberg SIL). South Sulawesi, Bonerate, Madu, Kalaotoa, and Karompa islands. Austronesian, Malayo-Polynesian, Western Malayo-Polynesian, Sulawesi, Muna-Buton, Tukangbesi-Bonerate. Dialects: BONERATE, KAROMPA. 79% to 81% lexical similarity with Tukangbesi South, 31% with Kalao, 25% with Laiyolo. Muslim.

BUDONG-BUDONG ***(TANGKOU, TONGKOU)*** [TGK] 70 speakers or fewer, 5 households, plus a few individuals (1988). Tongkou village, Mamuju District, Budong-Budong Subdistrict, on the Budong-Budong River. Austronesian, Malayo-Polynesian, Western Malayo-Polynesian, Sulawesi, South Sulawesi, Seko. Closer to Aralle-Tabulahan and Ulumandak. 56% lexical similarity with Mamuju and Seko Padang, 61% with Seko Tengah, 72% with Panasuan. Some speakers are becoming bilingual in Topoiyo through intermarriage and geographical proximity. Muslim.

BUGIS ***(BUGINESE, BUGI, BOEGINEESCHE, BOEGINEZEN, UGI, DE', RAPPANG BUGINESE)*** [BPR] 3,500,000 (1991 SIL). Population total both countries 3,500,000 or more. Including second language users: 4,000,000 (1999 WA). South Sulawesi, 3.5' to 5' South, other areas of the coastal swamp such as Bulukumba, Luwu, Polewali in Polmas, Pasangkayu in Mamuju districts. On the western coast of southeast Sulawesi in Kolaka, Wundulako, Rumbia, and Poleang districts. Also in major towns of Sulawesi. Large enclaves also in other provinces of Sulawesi, Kalimantan, Maluku, Irian Jaya, and Sumatra. Also spoken in Malaysia (Sabah). Austronesian, Malayo-Polynesian, Western Malayo-Polynesian, Sulawesi, South Sulawesi, Bugis. Dialects: BONE (PALAKKA, DUA BOCCOE, MARE), PANGKEP (PANGKAJENE), CAMBA, SIDRAP (SIDENRANG, PINRANG UTARA, ALITTA), PASANGKAYU (UGI RIAWA), SINJAI (ENNA, PALATTAE, BULUKUMBA), SOPPENG (KESSI), WAJO, BARRU (PARE-PARE, NEPO, SOPPENG RIAJA, TOMPO, TANETE), SAWITTO (PINRANG), LUWU (LUWU', BUA PONRANG, WARA, MALANGKE-USSU). The Bone or Soppeng dialects are central. Vigorous. Investigation needed: intelligibility with Sawitto, Luwu, Sinjai, Barru dialects with Soppeng central dialect. Bugis Lontara syllabary is still in use. Coastal swamp, rolling hills. Agriculturalists: wet rice; famous as seafarers, merchants. Muslim, Christian. Bible 1900-1996.

BUNGKU ***(NAHINE)*** [BKZ] 21,500 (1995 SIL), including 100 Routa, 16,400 Bungku, 2,500 Torete, 1,000 Tulambatu, 800 Landawe, 650 Waia (1991 D. Mead SIL). Central Sulawesi, Bungku Utara, Bungku Tengah, and Bungku Selatan subdistricts, along east coast; 45 villages or parts of villages. Also Tulambatu dialect in northern Southeast Sulawesi, Kendari District, Asera, Soropia, and Lasolo subdistricts, where there is difficult access. Austronesian, Malayo-Polynesian, Western Malayo-Polynesian, Sulawesi, Central Sulawesi, West Central, Bungku-Mori-Tolaki, Bungku. Dialects: BUNGKU, ROUTA, TULAMBATU, TORETE (TO RETE), LANDAWE, WAIA. Bungku and Routa have 82% lexical similarity; 81% with Torete, Waia, Tulambatu, and Landawe, 38% with Pamona dialects. Tulambatu has 88% with Landawe, 84% with Waia, 82% wih Torete, 74% wih Wawonii, 66% with Taloki, Kulisusu, and Koroni, 65% with Moronene, 54% with the Mori and Tolaki groups. Bungku was a language of wider communication before independence. Torete is not becoming extinct as reported earlier. Muslim.

BUOL ***(BUAL, BWO'OL, DIA)*** [BLF] 75,000 (1989). Central Sulawesi; Paleleh, Bunobogu, Bokat, Momunu, Biau, Baolan subdistricts; north coast near the border with north Sulawesi, 68 villages. Austronesian, Malayo-Polynesian, Western Malayo-Polynesian, Sulawesi, Mongondow-Gorontalo, Gorontalic. 61% lexical similarity with Tolitoli. Muslim.

BUSOA [BUP] 500 (1991 René van den Berg SIL). Southeast Sulawesi, Batauga Subdistrict, southwest coast of Buton Island, south of the Katobengke-Topa-Sulaa-Lawela area. Austronesian, Malayo-Polynesian, Western Malayo-Polynesian, Sulawesi, Muna-Buton, Muna. Kambe-Kambero shares some innovations with Kaimbulawa, and may not be a Busoa dialect. 84% lexical similarity with Kambe-Kambero, 70% to 79% with Muna dialects, 71% with Muna, 76% with Lantoi. Muslim.

CAMPALAGIAN ***(TALLUMPANUAE, TJAMPALAGIAN, TASING)*** [CML] 30,000 (1986 K. Stromme SIL). South Sulawesi, Majene Kabupaten, Polmas, south coast. Austronesian, Malayo-Polynesian, Western Malayo-Polynesian, Sulawesi, South Sulawesi, Bugis. Dialects: CAMPALAGIAN, BUKU. 50% to 58% lexical similarity with Mandar, 50% to 62% with Bugis, 55% with Bugis Bone, 62% with Bugis Pangkajene, Bugis Sidrap. Vigorous. Coastal plain. Merchants, fishermen, agriculturalists. Muslim.

CIA-CIA ***(SOUTH BUTON, SOUTHERN BUTUNG, BUTON, BUTUNG, BUTONESE, BOETONEEZEN)*** [CIA] 15,000 (1986 SIL). Southeast Sulawesi, south Buton Island. Austronesian, Malayo-Polynesian, Western Malayo-Polynesian, Sulawesi, Muna-Buton, Buton. Dialects: KAESABU, SAMPOLAWA (MAMBULU-LAPORO), WABULA, MASIRI. Wabula dialect has subdialects Wabula, Burangasi, Wali, Takimpo, Kondowa, Holimombo. 93% lexical similarity with Masiri, 74% with Kambe-Kambero, 69% with Busoa, 67% with Lantoi, 66% with Liabuku, 61% with Wolio, 60% with Muna. Bilingualism in Wolio. "Cia-Cia" is the generally used name, although it is a negative term. Muslim.

DAKKA [DKK] 1,500 (1986 SIL). South Sulawesi, Polewali-Mamasa District, Wonomulyo Subdistrict. Austronesian, Malayo-Polynesian, Western Malayo-Polynesian, Sulawesi, South Sulawesi, Northern, Pitu Ulunna Salu. 72% to 77% lexical similarity with Pannei and Pitu Ulunna Salu. Investigation needed: bilingual proficiency. Muslim.

DAMPAL [DMP] Fewer than 100 in the ethnic group (1990 N. P. Himmelmann). Central Sulawesi, Dampelas Sojol and Dampal Selatan subdistricts. Austronesian, Malayo-Polynesian, Western Malayo-Polynesian, Sulawesi, Central Sulawesi, West Central, Tomini. The older generation is hardly able to give basic lexical information. Most Dampal have intermarried with speakers of other languages and do not use their language at home. Nearly extinct.

DAMPELASA ***(DIAN, DAMPELAS)*** [DMS] 13,000 (1991 D. Andersen SIL). Central Sulawesi; Dampelas Sojol and Balaesang subdistricts, 8 villages. Austronesian, Malayo-Polynesian, Western Malayo-Polynesian, Sulawesi, Central Sulawesi, West Central, Tomini. Muslim.

DONDO [DOK] 15,000 or fewer (1991 D. Andersen SIL). Central Sulawesi; Tolitoli Buol District, Tolitoli Utara, Baolan, Dondo, Galang, and Dampal Utara subdistricts on the north coast; 25 villages or parts of villages. Austronesian, Malayo-Polynesian, Western Malayo-Polynesian, Sulawesi, Central Sulawesi, West Central, Tomini. Speakers consider Dondo a separate language from Tolitoli. It is probably separate from Tomini. Investigation needed: intelligibility with Tolitoli, Tomini. Muslim, Christian.

DURI ***(MASENREMPULU, MASSENREMPULU)*** [MVP] 95,000 including 90,000 in Enrekang District (1991 SIL). South Sulawesi, northern Enrekang District, and in Ujung Pandang and elsewhere in South Sulawesi. Austronesian, Malayo-Polynesian, Western Malayo-Polynesian, Sulawesi, South Sulawesi, Northern, Masenrempulu. Dialects: CAKKE, KALOSI. Vigorous. Duri is the prestige language of the Masenrempulu group. VSO, split ergative. Mountains. Agriculturalists: vegetables, coffee, wet rice. Muslim, Christian.

ENREKANG ***(ENDEKAN, ENDEKAN TIMUR)*** [PTT] 50,000 (1991 SIL). South Sulawesi, Enrekang and Pinrang districts. Austronesian, Malayo-Polynesian, Western Malayo-Polynesian, Sulawesi, South Sulawesi, Northern, Masenrempulu. Dialects: ENREKANG, RANGA, PATTINJO (LETTA-BATULAPPA-KASSA). Foothills, plains. Agriculturalists: maize, wet rice, cassava, vegetables. Muslim.

GORONTALO ***(HULONTALO)*** [GRL] 900,000 .5% of the population (1989). Northwestern Sulawesi, southern coast of northern peninsula. Austronesian, Malayo-Polynesian, Western Malayo-Polynesian, Sulawesi, Mongondow-Gorontalo, Gorontalic. Dialects: EAST GORONTALO, GORONTALO, WEST GORONTALO, TILAMUTA. Muslim, Christian. NT, in press (1996).

KAIDIPANG ***(KAIDIPAN, DIO)*** [KZP] 22,000 (1981 Wurm and Hattori). Northern Sulawesi, northern coast on both sides of Bolang Itang. Austronesian, Malayo-Polynesian, Western Malayo-Polynesian, Sulawesi, Mongondow-Gorontalo, Gorontalic. Dialects: KAIDIPAN, BOLAANG ITANG (BOLANG ITANG). Muslim.

KAILI, DA'A ***(DA'A, BUNGGU)*** [KZF] 55,000 including 35,000 Da'a and Inde together, 20,000 Unde (1979 Barr, Barr, and Salombe). 3,000 to 5,000 Da'a and Inde are in south Sulawesi. Central Sulawesi. 'Bunggu' is the name used for Da'a and Inde in south Sulawesi, Mamuju District, Pasangkayu Subdistrict, near Palu. Austronesian, Malayo-Polynesian, Western Malayo-Polynesian, Sulawesi, Central Sulawesi, West Central, Kaili-Pamona, Kaili. Dialects: DA'A (PEKAWA, PEKAVA, PAKAWA), INDE, UNDE (BANAWA, BANAVA). There is some intelligibility with Ledo and other Kaili varieties, but with major sociolinguistic differences. Da'a and Inde have 98% lexical similarity. Investigation needed: intelligibility with Unde, Baras. Christian (Da'a, Inde), Muslim (Unde). NT 1998.

KAILI, LEDO ***(LEDO, PALU, PALOESCH)*** [LEW] 233,500 including 128,000 Ledo, Doi, Ado, and Edo together, 7,500 Ija and Taa together, 55,000 Rai and Raio together, 43,000 Tara (1979 Barr, Barr, and Salombe). 8,000 to 10,000 are in south Sulawesi. Central and south Sulawesi. Austronesian, Malayo-Polynesian, Western Malayo-Polynesian, Sulawesi, Central Sulawesi, West Central, Kaili-Pamona, Kaili. Dialects: LEDO (PALU), DOI, ADO, EDO, TADO, TARA (PARIGI), RAI (SINDUE-TAWAILI, TAWAILI-SINDUE), RAIO (KORI), IJA (SIGI), TAA. Doi is intelligible with Ledo, Edo and Ado the next most intelligible, Tado a little less. Some intelligibility with Da'a, but there are major sociolinguistic differences. Ledo has 80% to 88% lexical similarity with Ado, Edo, Doi, and Lindu. Ledo is the lingua franca throughout the West Toraja area; the largest and most prestigious of the Kaili varieties. The Tado dialect is different from 'Tado', used as an alternate name for Lindu. Investigation needed: intelligibility with dialects: Tado, Ija, Taa, Tara, Rai, Raio. Trade language. Coastal plain, mountain slope. Copra, swidden and peasant agriculturalists: wet rice. Muslim, Christian. NT 1999.

KAIMBULAWA [ZKA] 1,500 (1991 René van den Berg SIL). Southeast Sulawesi, part of Siompu Island. Austronesian, Malayo-Polynesian, Western Malayo-Polynesian, Sulawesi, Muna-Buton, Muna. Dialects: LANTOI, KAMBE-KAMBERO. A separate language; not a dialect of Muna or Cia-Cia. 96% lexical similarity with Lantoi, 75% with Busoa, 64% to 74% with Muna dialects, 64% with Muna, 70% with Liabuku, 66% with Cia-Cia, 58% with Wolio, 45% with Kaledupa. Muslim.

KALAO ***(KALAOTOA)*** [KLY] 500 (1988 T. Friberg SIL). South Sulawesi, eastern Kalao Island south of Selayar Island. Austronesian, Malayo-Polynesian, Western Malayo-Polynesian, Sulawesi, Muna-Buton, Kalao. Related to Laiyolo (76% lexical similarity) and Wotu. Muslim.

KALUMPANG ***(MAKKI, MANGKI, MAKI, MA'KI, MANGKIR, GALUMPANG)*** [KLI] 12,000 (1991 SIL). South Sulawesi, southeast Mamuju District, Kalumpang Subdistrict. Austronesian, Malayo-Polynesian, Western Malayo-Polynesian, Sulawesi, South Sulawesi, Northern, Toraja-Sa'dan. Dialects: KARATAUN, MABLEI, MANGKI (E'DA), BONE HAU (TA'DA). There are other small dialects not listed. 78% lexical similarity with Mamasa, 78% with Rongkong, 74% with Toraja-Sa'dan. Between Karataun and Bone Hau dialects: average 82%. Vigorous. Mountain slope, river valleys. Agriculturalists: rice; coffee. Christian, Muslim.

KAMARU [KGX] 2,000 (1979 Bhurhanuddin). Southeastern Buton Island, southeast Sulawesi. Austronesian, Malayo-Polynesian, Western Malayo-Polynesian, Sulawesi, Muna-Buton, Buton. 68% lexical similarity with Lasalimu, 67% with Wolio, 54% with Cia-Cia, 51% with Pancana, 49% with Tukangbesi, 45% with Muna. Muslim.

KIOKO [UES] 1,000 (1991 René van den Berg SIL). Southeast Sulawesi, Kulisusu Subdistrict on Buton Island. Austronesian, Malayo-Polynesian, Western Malayo-Polynesian, Sulawesi, Muna-Buton, Muna. Dialects: KIOKO, KAMBOWA. Reported to be a separate language. It might be part of the Pancana language. 82% lexical similarity with Kambowa, 81% with Laompo dialect of Muna, 74% with Muna, 75% with Liabuku and Busoa. Muslim.

KODEOHA ***(KONDEHA)*** [VKO] 1,500 (1991 D. Mead SIL). Southeast Sulawesi, Kolaka District, Lasusua Subdistrict, west coast of Kolaka. 4 villages. Austronesian, Malayo-Polynesian, Western Malayo-Polynesian, Sulawesi, Central Sulawesi, West Central, Bungku-Mori-Tolaki, Tolaki. 75% lexical similarity with Rahambuu; 70% with Tolaki, Mekongga, and Waru; 54% with the Mori and Bungku groups. Bilingualism in Bugis. Investigation needed: bilingual proficiency in Bugis. Muslim.

KONJO, COASTAL ***(KONDJO, TIRO)*** [KJC] 125,000 including 50,000 Kajang, 10,000 Tiro (1991 SIL). South Sulawesi, southeast corner of the southern tip of the peninsula; parts of Sinjai, Bulukumba, and Bantaeng districts. Austronesian, Malayo-Polynesian, Western Malayo-Polynesian, Sulawesi, South Sulawesi, Makassar. Dialects: KONJO PESISIR (ARA, BIRA), TANA TOA (TANA TOWA, BLACK KONJO, KAJANG, KADJANG), BANTAENG (BONTHAIN). Tana Toa is at the northern end of the dialect chain. 76% lexical similarity with Makassar. Tana Toa is within 10% lexical similarity of the other coastal dialects. Vigorous by all Konjo. Tana Towa resist modern ways, contact with outsiders. Coastal. Agriculturalists, fishermen, boat builders. Muslim, traditional religion (Tana Towa).

KONJO, HIGHLAND ***(KONJO PEGUNUNGAN, KONYO)*** [KJK] 150,000 (1991 SIL). South Sulawesi, central mountain area, Sinjai, Bone, Gowa, Bulukumba districts. Austronesian, Malayo-Polynesian, Western Malayo-Polynesian, Sulawesi, South Sulawesi, Makassar. 75% lexical similarity with Coastal Konjo. Mountain slope. Agriculturalists: wet rice, fruit, vegetables, coffee. Muslim, Christian.

KORONI [XKQ] 500 (1991 D. Mead SIL). Central Sulawesi, Bungku Tengah Subdistrict, Unsongi village on the east coast 12 km. south of Bungku town. Austronesian, Malayo-Polynesian, Western Malayo-Polynesian, Sulawesi, Central Sulawesi, West Central, Bungku-Mori-Tolaki, Bungku. 75% lexical similarity with Taloki and Kulisusu, 66% with Wawonii, Bungku, Tulambatu; 65% with Moronene. Investigation needed: intelligibility with Taloki, Kulisusu. Coastal. Muslim.

KULISUSU ***(KALISUSU, KOLINSUSU, KOLENSUSU)*** [VKL] 22,000 (1995 SIL). Southeast Sulawesi, Kulisusu and Bonegunu subdistricts on the northeast corner of Buton Island. Austronesian, Malayo-Polynesian, Western Malayo-Polynesian, Sulawesi, Central Sulawesi, West Central, Bungku-Mori-Tolaki, Bungku. 81% lexical similarity between dialects, 77% with Taloki, 75% with Koroni, 66% with Wawonii and the Bungku group, 65% with Moronene, 54% with the Mori and Tolaki groups. Investigation needed: intelligibility with dialects, Taloki, Koroni. Muslim.

KUMBEWAHA ***('UMBEWAHA)*** [XKS] 250 (1993 Mark Donohue). Sulawesi Tenggara Province, Buton District, Lasalimu Subdistrict in southeast Buton Island, Kumbewaha village. Austronesian, Malayo-Polynesian, Western Malayo-Polynesian, Sulawesi, Muna-Buton, Buton, Lasilimu-Kumbewaha. Not close enough to other languages to have inherent intelligibility with their speakers. They use Indonesian for school, official purposes, Lasilimu if they have family ties, Tukang Basi for trade or family. They use Kumbewaha for all domains. All ages. Literacy rate in second language: 20%. Muslim.

KWANDANG [KJW] Northern peninsula of Sulawesi between the Bolaang Mongondow and Toli-Toli, mostly on the Gorontalo Plain. Austronesian, Malayo-Polynesian, Western Malayo-Polynesian, Sulawesi, Mongondow-Gorontalo, Gorontalic. Investigation needed: intelligibility with Gorontalo.

LAIYOLO ***(DA'ANG, BARANG-BARANG)*** [LJI] 800 including 250 Laiyolo, 550 Barang-Barang (1997 SIL). South Sulawesi, Laiyolo in villages of Lembang Mate'ne in Desa Laiyolo, and a few in Kilotepo' and Sangkeha'. Barang-Barang in Barang-barang village in Desa Lowa, southern tip of Selayar Island. Austronesian, Malayo-Polynesian, Western Malayo-Polynesian, Sulawesi, Muna-Buton, Kalao. Dialects: BARANG-BARANG (LOA, LOA', LOWA), LAIYOLO (LAJOLO, LAYOLO). Barang-Barang may need separate literature. 86% lexical similarity between Laiyolo and Barang-Barang, 76% with Kalao, 65% with Buton, 53% with Wotu, 39% with Muna. Selayar is second language used. Indonesian used little. Children in Laiyolo villages are reported to not be using Laiyolo. Vigorous in Barang-Barang dialect. Dry coastal hills. Agriculturalists: maize, cassava cultivation, copra. Muslim, some Christian.

LASALIMU [LLM] 2,000 (1979 Bhurhanuddin). Southeastern part of Buton Island, Lasalimu Subdistrict, southeast Sulawesi. Austronesian, Malayo-Polynesian, Western Malayo-Polynesian, Sulawesi, Muna-Buton, Buton, Lasilimu-Kumbewaha. 68% lexical similarity with Kamaru, 64% with Cia-Cia, 57% with Tukangbesi, 51% with Pancana, 50% with Wolio and Muna. Muslim.

LAUJE ***(LAUDJE, TINOMBO, AMPIBABO)*** [LAW] 45,000 (1991 D. Andersen SIL). Central Sulawesi, Dampelas Sojol, Dondo, Tinombo, Tomini, and Ampibabo subdistricts, along Tomini Bay, Sidoan River area. Austronesian, Malayo-Polynesian, Western Malayo-Polynesian, Sulawesi, Central Sulawesi, West Central, Tomini. Investigation needed: intelligibility with Tomini dialects. Muslim, Christian, traditional religion. Bible portions.

LEMOLANG ***(BAEBUNTA)*** [LEY] 2,000 (1995 SIL). South Sulawesi, Luwu District, inland from the northeast coast, centered in the villages of Sassa and Salassa, with other scattered speakers in Sabbang Subdistrict, and possibly Baebunta. Austronesian, Malayo-Polynesian, Western Malayo-Polynesian, Sulawesi, South Sulawesi, Lemolang. 41% lexical similarity with Mori Bawah, 39% with Mori Atas, 38% with Bungku, 39% with Buton, 31% with Seko Padang, 30% with Rampi, 29% with Toraja-Sa'dan, 26% with Muna, 25% with Wotu, 24% with Bugis. Bilingual level estimates for Indonesian are 0 0%, 1 3%, 2 75%, 3 22%, 4 0%, 5 0%. Tae' Luwu is the dominant language of the area. There are reports that some children do not speak Lemolang, however, of 25 children questioned in 1990, 76% said they spoke it well. Base of foothills. Muslim.

LIABUKU [LIX] 500 to 1,500 possibly (1991 R. van den Berg SIL). Southeast Sulawesi, one village north of Bau-Bau in Bungi and Kapontori districts, south Buton Island. Austronesian, Malayo-Polynesian, Western Malayo-Polynesian, Sulawesi, Muna-Buton, Muna. Quite divergent from other Muna varieties. 82% lexical similarity with the Burukene dialect of Muna, 72% to 76% with other Muna dialects, 72% with Muna, 75% with Kioko. Investigation needed: intelligibility with Pancana. Muslim.

LIMBOTO ***(LIMBOTTO)*** [LJO] Northern peninsula. Austronesian, Malayo-Polynesian, Western Malayo-Polynesian, Sulawesi, Mongondow-Gorontalo, Gorontalic. Investigation needed: intelligibility with Gorontalo.

LINDU ***(LINDUAN, TADO)*** [KLW] 2,000 (1990 SIL). Central Sulawesi, Kulawi Subdistrict; villages of Anca, Tomado, Langko, near Lake Lindu. Austronesian, Malayo-Polynesian, Western Malayo-Polynesian, Sulawesi, Central Sulawesi, West Central, Kaili-Pamona, Kaili. 'Tado' as an alternate name for Lindu is different from the Tado dialect of Ledo Kaili. Christian.

LOLAK [LLQ] Northeastern Sulawesi, villages of Lolak, Mongkoinit, and Motabang. Austronesian, Malayo-Polynesian, Western Malayo-Polynesian, Sulawesi, Mongondow-Gorontalo, Gorontalic. Structurally related to Gorontalo, but with heavy lexical borrowing from Mongondow. 79% lexical similarity with Mongondow, 66% with Ponosakan, 63% with Kaidipang. Surrounded by Mongondow, which is the second language of speakers. Muslim.

MAIWA ***(MASENREMPULU)*** [WMM] 50,000 (1990 SIL). South Sulawesi, Enrekang and Sidenrang districts. Austronesian, Malayo-Polynesian, Western Malayo-Polynesian, Sulawesi, South Sulawesi, Northern, Masenrempulu. Lowlands. Pastoralists, fruit, palm sugar. Muslim.

MAKASAR ***(MAKASSAR, MACASSARESE, MACASSAR, MAKASSA, MAKASSARESE, TAENA, TENA, GOA, MENGKASARA, MANGASARA, MAKASSAARSCHE)*** [MSR] 1,600,000 .9% of the population (1989). South Sulawesi, southwest corner of the peninsula, most of Pangkep, Maros, Gowa, Bantaeng, Jeneponto, and Takalar districts. Austronesian, Malayo-Polynesian, Western Malayo-Polynesian, Sulawesi, South Sulawesi, Makassar. Dialects: GOWA (GOA, LAKIUNG), TURATEA (JENEPONTO), MAROS-PANGKEP. The Gowa dialect is prestigious. Dialects form a chain. Vigorous. Many ethnic Chinese speak Makassar as first language. Trade language. Lontara script is a Bugis-Makasar syllabary still in use. Coastal plain, foothills. Fishermen; agriculturalists: wet rice, corn, cassava, vegetables; salt harvest. Muslim, Christian. Bible 1900, in press (1996).

MALAY, MENADONESE ***(MANADO MALAY, MANADONESE MALAY, MENADO MALAY, MINAHASAN MALAY)*** [XMM] Many mother tongue speakers, and millions of second language speakers (1994:411 Prentice). North Sulawesi, Minahasa District, west coast around the Port of Manado. Used as second language in many in North Sulawesi. Austronesian, Malayo-Polynesian, Western Malayo-Polynesian, Sundic, Malayic, Malayan, Local Malay. Its closest relative is North Moluccan Malay. Also close to Sri Lankan Malay. Bilingualism in Indonesian. An important, growing lingua franca in many parts of Sulawesi. Influences from Portuguese and Ternate. Investigation needed: intelligibility with Indonesian, other Malay varieties. Trade language. Dictionary. Christian, some Muslim.

MALIMPUNG [MLT] 5,000 (1995 SIL). South Sulawesi, Pinrang District, Patampanua Subdistrict, Malimpung area. Austronesian, Malayo-Polynesian, Western Malayo-Polynesian, Sulawesi, South Sulawesi, Northern, Masenrempulu. 80% lexical similarity with Maiwa, 70% with Enrekang. They view themselves as distinct from Bugis and Enrekang. Muslim.

MAMASA [MQJ] 100,000 (1991 SIL). South Sulawesi, Polmas District, Polewali Subdistrict, along the Mamasa River. Austronesian, Malayo-Polynesian, Western Malayo-Polynesian, Sulawesi, South Sulawesi, Northern, Toraja-Sa'dan. Dialects: NORTHERN MAMASA, CENTRAL MAMASA, PATTAE' (SOUTHERN MAMASA, PATTA' BINUANG, BINUANG, TAE', BINUANG-PAKI-BATETANGA-ANTEAPI). 78% lexical similarity with Toraja-Sa'dan. Vigorous. River valleys. Wet rice cultivation, coffee. Christian, Muslim (Pattae'), traditional religion. Bible portions 1995.

MAMUJU ***(MAMUDJU, UDAI, MAMOEDJOE, MAMOEDJOESCH)*** [MQX] 60,000 (1991 SIL) including 50,000 in Mamuju dialect. South Sulawesi, Mamuju District, on the coast of Mamuju, Kalukku, and Budong-Budong subdistricts. Austronesian, Malayo-Polynesian, Western Malayo-Polynesian, Sulawesi, South Sulawesi, Northern, Mamuju. Dialects: MAMUJU, SUMARE-RANGAS, PADANG, SINYONYOI. The Mamuju dialect is prestigious. Language attitudes are positive. Trade language. Coastal plain, foothills. Copra, cocoa, cloves, maize, cassava, rattan; fishermen. Muslim.

MANDAR ***(ANDIAN, MANJAR, MANDHARSCHE)*** [MHN] 200,000 (1985). South Sulawesi, Majene and Polewali-Mamasa districts, a few settlements in Mamuju District, on the islands of Pangkep District, and at Ujung Lero near Pare-Pare. Austronesian, Malayo-Polynesian, Western Malayo-Polynesian, Sulawesi, South Sulawesi, Northern, Mandar. Dialects: MAJENE, BALANIPA (NAPO-TINAMBUNG), MALUNDA, PAMBOANG, SENDANA (CENRANA, TJENDANA). Mandar is a complex dialect grouping; there may be more dialects than those listed. Balanipa and Sendana may each be more than one dialect. Balanipa is the prestige dialect. Mandar, Mamuju, and Pitu Ulunna Salu are separate languages in a language chain. Dictionary. Textbooks in primary schools use the Lontara syllabary script. Coastal lowlands, hills. Fishermen, agriculturalists: cacao, copra, maize, cassava. Muslim.

MOMA ***(KULAWI)*** [MYL] 5,500 (1985 D. Barr SIL). Central Sulawesi, northern Kulawi Subdistrict, primarily around Kulawi and Toro towns. Austronesian, Malayo-Polynesian, Western Malayo-Polynesian, Sulawesi, Central Sulawesi, West Central, Kaili-Pamona, Kaili. Historically a 'dialect' of Kaili, but strong influences from Uma. Lexically similar to Uma, but grammatically similar to Lindu. Christian over, Muslim. Bible portions 1939.

MONGONDOW ***(BOLAANG MONGONDOW, MONGONDOU, MINAHASSA)*** [MOG] 900,000 .5% of the population (1989). Northeast Sulawesi, between Tontemboan and Gorontalo. Austronesian, Malayo-Polynesian, Western Malayo-Polynesian, Sulawesi, Mongondow-Gorontalo, Mongondowic. Dialects: LOLAYAN, DUMOGA, PASI. Traditional religion, Muslim, Christian. Bible portions 1932-1939.

MORI ATAS ***(WEST MORI, UPPER MORI)*** [MZQ] 12,000 to 18,000 (1995 SIL). Central Sulawesi at the neck of the southeastern peninsula, Mori Atas, Lembo, and Petasia subdistricts. Also in south Sulawesi. 25 villages or parts of villages. Austronesian, Malayo-Polynesian, Western Malayo-Polynesian, Sulawesi, Central Sulawesi, West Central, Bungku-Mori-Tolaki, Mori. Dialect: AIKOA. 73% to 86% lexical similarity with Mori Bawah and Padoe. Christian, Muslim. NT 1948, out of print.

MORI BAWAH ***(EAST MORI, LOWER MORI, NAHINA)*** [XMZ] 12,000 to 18,000 (1995 SIL). Central Sulawesi at the neck of the southeastern peninsula; Petasia and Lembo subdistricts; 24 villages or parts of villages. Also in south Sulawesi. Austronesian, Malayo-Polynesian, Western Malayo-Polynesian, Sulawesi, Central Sulawesi, West Central, Bungku-Mori-Tolaki, Mori. Dialects: TAMBE'E, NAHINA, PETASIA, SOROAKO, KARONSIE. 73% to 86% lexical similarity with Mori Atas, 75% with Padoe. Christian, Muslim.

MORONENE ***(MARONENE)*** [MQN] 31,000 including 20,000 in Moronene, 11,000 in Tokotu'a (1991 D. Mead SIL). Southeast Sulawesi, Buton District. Tokotu'a dialect is on Kabaena Island, Wita Ea is on the mainland portion of Buton District opposite Kabaena, with Rumbia subdialect in Rubia Subdistrict, and Poleang subdialect in Poleang, Poleang Timur, and Watubangga Subdistrict of Kolaka District. Austronesian, Malayo-Polynesian, Western Malayo-Polynesian, Sulawesi, Central Sulawesi, West Central, Bungku-Mori-Tolaki, Bungku. Dialects: WITA EA (RUMBIA, POLEANG, MORONENE), TOKOTU'A (KABAENA). Moronene dialect has 80% lexical similarity with Tokotu'a; 68% with Wawonii-Menui, 66% with Kulisusu, 65% with Taloki, Koroni, Tulambatu, 64% with Bungku, and 57% with Tolaki. Bilingual level estimates for Indonesian are 0 5%, 1 15%, 2 67%, 3 12.5%, 4 .5%, 5 0%. Formerly a kingdom. Muslim, Christian.

MUNA ***(WUNA, MOUNAN)*** [MYN] 227,000 (1989 van den Berg), including 600 in Ambon (1985 SIL). 150,000 Standard Muna, 10,000 Tiworo, 7,000 Siompu, 60,000 Gumas (1989 van den Berg). Muna Island off southeast Sulawesi, northwest coast of Buton Island, and Ambon, central Maluku. Austronesian, Malayo-Polynesian, Western Malayo-Polynesian, Sulawesi, Muna-Buton, Muna. Dialects: STANDARD MUNA (NORTHERN MUNA), GUMAS (SOUTHERN MUNA), SIOMPU, TIWORO (EASTERN MUNA). Subdialects of Standard Muna are: Tungkuno, Kabawo, Lawa, Katobu, Tobea Besar; of Gumas are: Gu, Mawasangka, Lakudo, Wale-Ale, Lawama, Kadatua, Lowu-Lowu, Kalia-Lia, Katobengke, Topa, Salaa, Lawela, Laompo, Burukene. 71% lexical similarity with Pancana, 62% with Cia-Cia, 52% with Wolio, 50% with Lasalimu, 47% with Tukangbesi, 45% with Kamaru. 'Wuna' is their self-name. Muslim, Christian. Bible portions 1993.

NAPU ***(PEKUREHUA)*** [NAP] 6,000 (1995). Central Sulawesi, Lore Utara Subdistrict, Napu Valley, 10 villages. Austronesian, Malayo-Polynesian, Western Malayo-Polynesian, Sulawesi, Central Sulawesi, West Central, Kaili-Pamona, Pamona. Closest linguistically to Besoa. Nearly all speakers use Indonesian as second language with varying proficiency. Agriculturalists: rice. 3,300 feet. Christian over, Muslim. Bible portions 1995.

PADOE ***(SOUTH MORI, PADOÉ, ALALAO)*** [PDO] 6,000 (1991 D. Andersen). South Sulawesi, eastern Luwu District in Nuha, Malili, and Mangkutana subdistricts; Central Sulawesi, Banggai District, 2 villages in Mori Atas Subdistrict and 1 village in Pamona Utara Subdistrict. Austronesian, Malayo-Polynesian, Western Malayo-Polynesian, Sulawesi, Central Sulawesi, West Central, Bungku-Mori-Tolaki, Mori. Two dialects. 73% to 86% lexical similarity with Mori Atas, 75% with Mori Bawah. Bilingual level estimates for Indonesian are 0 0%, 1-2 82%, 2+ 33%, 3 17%, 4 1%, 5 0%. Vigorous. Investigation needed: intelligibility with Mori. Christian, Muslim.

PAMONA ***(BARE'E, BAREE, POSO, TAA, WANA)*** [BCX] 106,000 (1979 Barr), including 100,000 in central Sulawesi, 6,000 to 10,000 in south Sulawesi. Central Sulawesi; Poso District, Poso Kota, Poso Pesisir, Parigi, Lage, Pamona Utara, Pamona Selatan, Tojo, Ulubongko, Ampana Kota, Ampanatete, Una-Una, Mori Atas, Petasia, Bungku Utara, Bungku Tengah subdistricts; 193 villages. South Sulawesi in Mangkutana Subdistrict and north Wotu and Bone-Bone subdistricts in Luwu District. Austronesian, Malayo-Polynesian, Western Malayo-Polynesian, Sulawesi, Central Sulawesi, West Central, Kaili-Pamona, Pamona. Dialects: PAMONA (BARE'E), LAIWONU (IBA), BATUI, SINOHOAN (DAIDO, IDO, IDORE'E), MBELALA (BARIA, BELA, BELALA), RAPANGKAKA (ARIA), TOMONI, TOBAU (TOBAO, TOBALO, BARE'E), TOKONDINDI, TOPADA, TAA (WANA, TOPOTAA). Laiwonu, Batui, Sinohoan, Mbelala, and Rapangkaka may be separate languages. Pamona speakers in Bungku Utara recognize five ethnic groups with minor dialect differences: Pusangke, Kajumorangka, Tokasiala, Burangas, Topotaa. The first four are mountain dwellers in the interior; the Topotaa live along the coast. Speakers in Bungku Tengah recognize five varieties: Topotaa (the same as Taa), Tobau, Tokondindi, Topada, and Tombelala. Dialects have 76% (Taa) to 90% lexical similarity with each other, except for Tombelala, which has 66% to 76% lexical similarity with other Bungku Tengah dialects, and is considered to be a separate language. Bilingualism in Indonesian. They call themselves Taa or Wana. Mountain slope, foothills, coast. Swidden agriculturalists, copra. Christian. NT 1933-1992.

PANASUAN ***(TO PANASEAN, TO PAMOSEAN)*** [PSN] 900 or more (1988 T. Laskowske). South Sulawesi, northeast of Kalumpang-speaking area and west of Seko area merging into Kalumpang area in Mamuju District. 2 villages. Austronesian, Malayo-Polynesian, Western Malayo-Polynesian, Sulawesi, South Sulawesi, Seko. 67% lexical similarity with Seko Tengah, 63% with Seko Padang, 72% with Tangkou. Christian.

PANCANA ***(PANTJANA)*** [PNP] 15,000 (1979 Bhurhanuddin). Southeast Sulawesi, near Muna, central Buton Island. Austronesian, Malayo-Polynesian, Western Malayo-Polynesian, Sulawesi, Muna-Buton, Muna. Dialects: KAPONTORI, KALENDE (LAWELE), LABUANDIRI. Dialect names are also place names. May be more than one language. 71% lexical similarity with Muna, 57% with Cia-Cia. Bilingualism in Wolio. Investigation needed: intelligibility with dialects. Muslim.

PANNEI ***(TAPANGO)*** [PNC] 9,000 (1986 SIL). South Sulawesi, Polewali-Mamasa District, Wonomulyo Subdistrict. Austronesian, Malayo-Polynesian, Western Malayo-Polynesian, Sulawesi, South Sulawesi, Northern, Pitu Ulunna Salu. Dialects: TAPANGO, BULO. Bulo has 87% to 93% lexical similarity with all dialects. Lexical similarity 75% to 80% with dialects of Ulumandak, Pitu Ulunna Salu, Aralle-Tabulahan. Investigation needed: intelligibility with Ulumandak, Pitu Ulunna Salu, dialects. Muslim.

PENDAU ***(NDAU, NDAOE, UMALASA)*** [UMS] 2,000 to 5,000 (1991 P. Quick SIL). Central Sulawesi, Balaesang Subdistrict, villages of Walandano and part of Sibayu, and Simatang Island; and Dampelas Sojol, Ampibabo, Sirenja, Tinombo subdistricts, close to and north of Tajio. Austronesian, Malayo-Polynesian, Western Malayo-Polynesian, Sulawesi, Central Sulawesi, West Central, Tomini. Muslim, Christian.

PONOSAKAN ***(PONASAKAN)*** [PNS] 3,000 (1981 Wurm and Hattori). Northeast Sulawesi around Belang. Austronesian, Malayo-Polynesian, Western Malayo-Polynesian, Sulawesi, Mongondow-Gorontalo, Mongondowic. 75% lexical similarity with Mongondow, 66% with Lolak. Muslim.

RAHAMBUU ***(WIAU, WIAOE)*** [RAZ] 5,000 (1991 SIL). Southeast Sulawesi, Kolaka District, Pakue Subdistrict, west coast north of the Kodeoha. Austronesian, Malayo-Polynesian, Western Malayo-Polynesian, Sulawesi, Central Sulawesi, West Central, Bungku-Mori-Tolaki, Tolaki. 87% lexical similarity between dialects, 75% with Kodeoha, 70% with Tolaki, Mekongga, and Waru; 54% with the Mori and Bungku groups. Investigation needed: intelligibility with dialects, Kodeoha. Muslim.

RAMPI ***(LEBONI, RAMPI-LEBONI, HA'UWA)*** [LJE] 8,000 2,300 in South Sulawesi, 5,700 in Central Sulawesi (1991 SIL). South Sulawesi, 6 villages in an isolated mountain area of Masamba Subdistrict in Luwu District; also in Sabbang Limbong, Wotu, and Mangkutana subdistricts; and about 15 villages in Poso and Donggala districts of Central Sulawesi. Rato speakers have moved elsewhere. Austronesian, Malayo-Polynesian, Western Malayo-Polynesian, Sulawesi, Central Sulawesi, West Central, Kaili-Pamona, Pamona. Dialects: RAMPI (LAMBU), RATO. Leboni is the prestige dialect. Vigorous. Mountain slope. Swidden agriculturalists. Christian, some Muslim.

RATAHAN ***(BENTENAN, PASAN)*** [RTH] 30,000 (1989). Northeastern section of the northern peninsula of Sulawesi, around Ratahan and to the southeast coast of the northern peninsula. Austronesian, Malayo-Polynesian, Western Malayo-Polynesian, Sulawesi, Sangir-Minahasan, Sangiric. Traditional religion, Christian.

SALUAN, COASTAL ***(LOINANG, LOINDANG, MADI)*** [LOE] 74,000 (1979 Barr). East central Sulawesi; Luwuk, Balantak, Lamala, Buko, Totikum, Kintom, Batui, Pagimana, Bunta subdistricts; 136 villages. Loinang dialect is in the mountains. Austronesian, Malayo-Polynesian, Western Malayo-Polynesian, Sulawesi, Central Sulawesi, Eastern. Related to Kahumamahon Saluan, Balantak, Andio. The name 'Saluan' is preferred over 'Loinang' by the speakers. Muslim, traditional religion, Christian. NT, in press (1996).

SALUAN, KAHUMAMAHON ***(INTERIOR SALUAN, KAHUMAMAHON)*** [SLB] 1,500 to 2,000 (1995 SIL). East central Sulawesi. Austronesian, Malayo-Polynesian, Western Malayo-Polynesian, Sulawesi, Central Sulawesi, Eastern. Related to Coastal Saluan, Balantak, Andio. Traditional religion, Christian. Bible portions.

SANGIR ***(SANGIHÉ, SANGIRESE, SANGI, SANGIH)*** [SAN] 200,000 in Indonesia (1995 Indonesian Consul, Davao, Philippines), including 50,000 Siau. Population total both countries 255,000. North Sulawesi, Great Sangir Island, and north Maluku. Also spoken in Philippines. Austronesian, Malayo-Polynesian, Western Malayo-Polynesian, Sulawesi, Sangir-Minahasan, Sangiric. Dialects: SIAU, MANGANITU, TAMAKO, NORTH TABUKANG (TABUKANG, TABUKAN), SOUTH TABUKANG, CENTRAL TABUKANG, KANDAR, TARUNA, TAGULANDANG (TAHULANDANG). Christian, Muslim. NT 1883-1993.

SARUDU ***(DODA')*** [SDU] 4,000 (1990 SIL). South Sulawesi, south Pasangkayu District, Mamuju Subdistrict. Austronesian, Malayo-Polynesian, Western Malayo-Polynesian, Sulawesi, Central Sulawesi, West Central, Kaili-Pamona, Kaili. Dialects: NUNU', KULU (LARIANG). 75% lexical similarity with Uma, 80% with Benggaulu. They have contact with Bugis and Kaili speakers. Investigation needed: intelligibility with Uma. Lowland coastal swamp. Sago palm, fishermen. Muslim.

SEDOA ***(TAWAELIA)*** [TVW] 600 (1979 Barr). East central Sulawesi, Lore Utara and Poso Pesisir subdistricts; villages of Sedoa, and parts of Tambarona and Pinedapa. Austronesian, Malayo-Polynesian, Western Malayo-Polynesian, Sulawesi, Central Sulawesi, West Central, Kaili-Pamona, Kaili. A distinct language; not a dialect of nearby Napu or Kaili. Vigorous. Christian.

SEKO PADANG ***(SEKO, WONO, SUA TU PADANG)*** [SKX] 5,000 of whom 2,300 are in the Seko area (1991 T. Laskowske SIL). South Sulawesi, northeast section of Limbong Subdistrict in Luwu District. About half the speakers have resettled in Palolo Valley of central Sulawesi. Austronesian, Malayo-Polynesian, Western Malayo-Polynesian, Sulawesi, South Sulawesi, Seko. Dialects: LODANG, HONO' (WONO). Bilingualism in Indonesian. Vigorous. Many primary schools. Sua Tu Padang is self name. Plains. Subsistence agriculturalists: coffee, wet rice, corn, cassava. They provide their own meat and fish. 1,150 meters. Christian, Muslim.

SEKO TENGAH ***(SEKO, POHONEANG, PEWANEAN, PEWANEANG)*** [SKO] 2,500 (1995 SIL). Northern south Sulawesi, western part of Limbong Subdistrict along the Betue River. Austronesian, Malayo-Polynesian, Western Malayo-Polynesian, Sulawesi, South Sulawesi, Seko. 71% lexical similarity with Seko Padang, 67% with Panasuan. Bilingualism in Indonesian. Mountain slope, high plateau. Agriculturalists: dry rice, coffee, corn, cassava. Christian, Muslim.

SELAYAR ***(SALAYAR, SALAJAR, SALAYER, SILAJARA, SILADJA, SALEIER)*** [SLY] 90,000 (1983 SIL). South Sulawesi, Selayar Island. Austronesian, Malayo-Polynesian, Western Malayo-Polynesian, Sulawesi, South Sulawesi, Makassar. 69% lexical similarity with Makassar. Bilingual level estimates for Bugis are 0 28%, 1-2 51%, 3 17%, 4 4%, 5 0%. Indonesian also used. Vigorous. Mountain slope, coastal strip. Copra plantations, maize, cassava. Muslim, Christian.

SUWAWA ***(BUNDA, SUWAWA-BUNDA)*** [SWU] 10,000 (1981 Wurm and Hattori). Northeastern Sulawesi, around Suwawa and Pinogu, east of Gorontalo town and Lake Limboto. Austronesian, Malayo-Polynesian, Western Malayo-Polynesian, Sulawesi, Mongondow-Gorontalo, Gorontalic. Dialect: BUNDA. Separate language from Gorontalo. Muslim.

TAE' ***(RONGKONG, RONGKONG KANANDEDE, TO RONGKONG, LUWU, TORAJA TIMUR, EAST TORAJA, SADA, TOWARE, SANGANGALLA', TAEQ, TAE' TAE')*** [ROB] 250,000 (1992 SIL). South Sulawesi, southeast Limbong and Sabbang subdistricts of Luwu District. Also an enclave in Wasuponda, Nuha Subdistrict near the town of Soroako. Rongkong Atas is the upper river system in Limbong and in Seko Lemo. Rongkong Bawah is the lower river system in Sabbang. Austronesian, Malayo-Polynesian, Western Malayo-Polynesian, Sulawesi, South Sulawesi, Northern, Toraja-Sa'dan. Dialects: RONGKONG, NORTHEAST LUWU, SOUTH LUWU, BUA. 92% lexical similarity among dialects, over 86% with the northern dialects, 80% with Toraja-Sa'dan. Vigorous. Coastal plain, upland valleys. Agriculturalists: wet rice, coffee, vegetables. Rongkong Bawah is predominantly Muslim, Rongkong Atas has a Christian minority. Muslim over, Christian.

TAJE ***(PETAPA)*** [PEE] 400 (1981 R. McKenzie). Central Sulawesi, village of Tanampedagi in Ampibabo Subdistrict; also near Sipeso in Sindue Subdistrict. Austronesian, Malayo-Polynesian, Western Malayo-Polynesian, Sulawesi, Central Sulawesi, West Central, Tomini. Muslim.

TAJIO ***(KASIMBAR, TADJIO, TA'ADJIO, ADJIO)*** [TDJ] 18,000 (1991 R. McKenzie). Central Sulawesi; Ampibabo, Tinombo, and Sindue subdistricts; 21 villages or parts of villages. Austronesian, Malayo-Polynesian, Western Malayo-Polynesian, Sulawesi, Central Sulawesi, West Central, Tomini. Self name is Tajio. Kasimbar is the name of the main town. Muslim, Christian.

TALAUD ***(TALAUT, TALODDA)*** [TLD] 60,000 (1981 UBS). North Sulawesi, Talaud Islands northeast of the Sangihe Islands. Austronesian, Malayo-Polynesian, Western Malayo-Polynesian, Sulawesi, Sangir-Minahasan, Sangiric. Dialects: KABURUANG, SOUTH KARAKELONG (KARAKELONG, KARAKELANG), NENUSA-MAINGAS, ESSANG, ARANGKA'A, DAPALAN (RIUNG), AWIT, BEO, LIRANG (SALIBABU, SALEBABU). Christian. NT 1993.

TALOKI ***(TALUKI)*** [TLK] 500 (1995 SIL). Southeast Sulawesi, northwest coast Buton Island, Wakorumba Subdistrict, Maligano village, and possibly some on south Buton Island, Kapontori Subdistrict, Wakalambe village. Austronesian, Malayo-Polynesian, Western Malayo-Polynesian, Sulawesi, Central Sulawesi, West Central, Bungku-Mori-Tolaki. 77% lexical similarity with Kulisusu; 75% with Koroni; 66% with Wawonii, Bungku, Tulambatu; 65% with Moronene. Speakers are reported to have a high bilingualism in Muna. Investigation needed: intelligibility with Kulisusu, Koroni, bilingual proficiency in Muna. Muslim.

TALONDO' [TLN] 500 speakers, 1 village (1986 SIL). Talondo and Pedasi villages, Mamuju District, Kalumpang Subdistrict. Austronesian, Malayo-Polynesian, Western Malayo-Polynesian, Sulawesi, South Sulawesi, Northern, Toraja-Sa'dan. They claim to understand the Bone Hau dialect of Kalumpang, but Kalumpang speakers cannot understand Talondo'. May be in the Seko subgroup. 80% lexical similarity with Kalumpang. Investigation needed: bilingual proficiency in Bone Hau (Kalumpang). Christian, Muslim.

TOALA' ***(TOALA, TOALA-PALILI, LUWU', TORAJA TIMUR, EAST TORAJA, SADA, TOWARE, SANGANGALLA')*** [TLZ] 30,000 (1983 SIL). South Sulawesi, Luwu District from Masamba to the southern tip of the district. Toala' dialect is from the foothills up to the divide. Palili' dialect is on a narrow coastal strip overlapping with Bugis Luwu. Austronesian, Malayo-Polynesian, Western Malayo-Polynesian, Sulawesi, South Sulawesi, Northern, Toraja-Sa'dan. Dialects: TOALA', PALILI'. Probably at least 4 dialects. 74% lexical similarity with Toraja-Sa'dan. Vigorous. Coastal plain, mountain slope. Copra plantations, swidden agriculturalists. Muslim.

TOLAKI ***(TO'OLAKI, LOLAKI, LALAKI, LAKI, KOLAKA, "NOIE", "NOIHE", "NEHINA", "NOHINA", "NAHINA", "AKIDO")*** [LBW] 281,000 including 230,000 Konawe, 50,000 Mekongga, 650 Asera, fewer than 100 Wiwirano, 200 Laiwui (1991 D. Mead SIL). Southeast Sulawesi, Kendari and Kolaka districts. Mekongga are in the Mekongga Mts. on the western edge of the group near Soroako. Austronesian, Malayo-Polynesian, Western Malayo-Polynesian, Sulawesi, Central Sulawesi, West Central, Bungku-Mori-Tolaki, Tolaki. Dialects: WIWIRANO, ASERA, KONAWE (KENDARI), MEKONGGA (BINGKOKAK), NORIO, KONIO, TAMBOKI (TAMBBUOKI), LAIWUI (KIOKI). Wiwirano has 88% lexical similarity with Asera, 84% with Konawe, 85% with Mekongga, 81% with Laiwui, 78% with Waru, 70% with Rahambuu and Kodeoha, 54% with the Mori and Bungku groups. Mekongga has 86% with Konawe, 80% with Laiwui. Wiwirano dialect is spoken only by older people. Negative names are no longer in use. Investigation needed: intelligibility with dialects, Mekongga, Laiwui, Waru;, attitudes toward dialects. Dictionary. Grammar. Muslim, Christian.

TOLITOLI ***(TONTOLI, TOTOLI, GAGE)*** [TXE] 28,000 (1991 D. Andersen SIL). Central Sulawesi, Tolitoli Utara, Galang, Baolan, Dondo, subdistricts on the north coast; 29 villages or parts of villages. Austronesian, Malayo-Polynesian, Western Malayo-Polynesian, Sulawesi, Central Sulawesi, West Central, Tomini. Muslim.

TOMADINO [TDI] 600 (1991 D. Mead SIL). Central Sulawesi, Bungku Tengah Subdistrict, Sakita village on the east coast, outskirts of Bungku town. Austronesian, Malayo-Polynesian, Western Malayo-Polynesian, Sulawesi, Central Sulawesi, West Central, Bungku-Mori-Tolaki, Mori. 71% lexical similarity with Bahonsuai, 68% with Mori Atas, Mori Bawah, and Padoe. Bilingualism in Bungku. Investigation needed: intelligibility with Bahonsuai. Coastal. Muslim.

TOMBELALA [TTP] 1,100 (1995 SIL). Central Sulawesi, Bungku Tengah Subdistrict, 4 villages. Austronesian, Malayo-Polynesian, Western Malayo-Polynesian, Sulawesi, Central Sulawesi, West Central, Kaili-Pamona, Pamona. They have 66% to 76% lexical similarity with Pamona varieties, and 38% with Bungku. Bilingualism in Indonesian. Speakers consider themselves part of Pamona. Muslim.

TOMBULU ***(TOMBULU', TOMBULA, TOUMBULU, TOMBALU, MINAHASA, MINHASA)*** [TOM] 60,000 (1981 Wurm and Hattori). Northeastern Sulawesi, around Tanawangko and Tomohon. Austronesian, Malayo-Polynesian, Western Malayo-Polynesian, Sulawesi, Sangir-Minahasan, Minahasan. Dialects: TARATARA, TOMOHON. Closest to Tondano and Tonsea. Traditional religion, Christian. Bible portions 1933.

TOMINI ***(TIADJE, TIALO)*** [TXM] 42,000 (1992 D. Andersen). Central Sulawesi; Moutong, Tomini, Tinombo subdistricts along Tomini Bay; 42 villages. Austronesian, Malayo-Polynesian, Western Malayo-Polynesian, Sulawesi, Central Sulawesi, West Central, Tomini. Muslim.

TONDANO ***(TONDANOU, TOLOU, TOLOUR, TOULOUR)*** [TDN] 92,000 in Indonesia (1981 Wurm and Hattori). Population total both countries 92,000 or more. Northeastern Sulawesi around Tondano and to the southeast coast of the northern peninsula. Also spoken in USA. Austronesian, Malayo-Polynesian, Western Malayo-Polynesian, Sulawesi, Sangir-Minahasan, Sangiric. Dialects: TONDANO, KAKAS (KA'KAS), REMBOKEN. Closest to Tombulu and Tonsea. Christian.

TONSAWANG ***(TOMBATU)*** [TNW] 20,000 (1981 Wurm and Hattori). Northeastern Sulawesi around Tombatu. Austronesian, Malayo-Polynesian, Western Malayo-Polynesian, Sulawesi, Sangir-Minahasan, Minahasan. Christian.

TONSEA ***(TONSEA')*** [TXS] 90,000 (1989). Northeastern tip of Sulawesi. Austronesian, Malayo-Polynesian, Western Malayo-Polynesian, Sulawesi, Sangir-Minahasan, Sangiric. Dialects: MAUMBI, AIRMADIDI, LIKUPANG, KAUDITAN, KALABAT ATAS. Traditional religion, Christian.

TONTEMBOAN ***(TOMPAKEWA, TOUNTEMBOAN, PAKEWA)*** [TNT] 150,000 (1990). Northeastern coast of Minahasa Peninsula from Sonder to around Motoling and Tompasobaru. Austronesian, Malayo-Polynesian, Western Malayo-Polynesian, Sulawesi, Sangir-Minahasan, Minahasan. Dialects: LANGOAN, TOMPASO (MAKELAI, MAKELA'I-MAOTOW), SONDER (MATANAI, MATANA'I-MAORE'). Christian. Bible portions 1852.

TOPOIYO [TOY] 2,000 (1988 T. Laskowske). South Sulawesi, Budong-Budong Subdistrict in Mamuju District, inland along Budong-Budong River. Austronesian, Malayo-Polynesian, Western Malayo-Polynesian, Sulawesi, Central Sulawesi, West Central, Kaili-Pamona, Kaili. 66% lexical similarity with Sarudu and Da'a, 56% with Ledo, 54% with the Parigi dialect of Kaili. Vigorous. Recent settlers from elsewhere and rubber plantation development have brought new language contacts. Riverine. Swidden agriculturalists, rubber plantation workers. Muslim.

TORAJA-SA'DAN ***(SA'DAN, SADAN, SADANG, TORAJA, TORADJA, TAE', TA'E, SOUTH TORAJA, SA'DANSCHE)*** [SDA] 500,000 (1990 UBS). South Sulawesi, Tana Toraja District with large enclaves in Luwu District. Several thousand also in Ujung Pandang city. Also on west coast of southeast Sulawesi in

Kolaka and Wundulako districts. Austronesian, Malayo-Polynesian, Western Malayo-Polynesian, Sulawesi, South Sulawesi, Northern, Toraja-Sa'dan. Dialects: MAKALE (TALLULEMBANGNA), RANTEPAO (KESU'), TORAJA BARAT (WEST TORAJA, MAPPA-PANA). Rantepao is prestige dialect. River valleys. Agriculturalists: wet rice, coffee. Christian over, some traditional religion, Muslim. Bible 1960-1995.

TUKANGBESI NORTH ***(WAKATOBI, BUTON)*** [KHC] 120,000 including 60,000 in Maluku (1995 SIL). Population total both countries 120,000 or more. Northern islands of Tukangbesi Archipelago, Kaledupa and Wanci, off Southeast Sulawesi; several hundreds in Singapore and Baubau city; on Bacan, Taliabu, Mongole, Buru, Sulabesi, Seram, and Ambon islands in Maluku; Irian Jaya; and Sumbawa. Most speakers in Nusa Tenggara and Maluku have a lot of movement and are mixed with Tukangbesi South. Also spoken in Singapore. Austronesian, Malayo-Polynesian, Western Malayo-Polynesian, Sulawesi, Muna-Buton, Tukangbesi-Bonerate. Dialects: KALEDUPA (KAHEDUPA), WANCI (WANJI, WANTJI, WANJE, WANGI-WANGI). 80% lexical similarity between Kaledupa and Wanci; they may be separate languages. 70% to 75% with Tukangbesi South, 48% with Lasalimu, 47% with Cia-Cia, 40% with Kamaru, an average of 35% with other nearby languages. Investigation needed: intelligibility with dialects. Grammar. Muslim.

TUKANGBESI SOUTH ***(TUKANG-BESI, WAKATOBI, BUTON)*** [BHQ] 130,000 including 100,000 in Maluku (1995 SIL). Southern islands of Tukangbesi archipelago, (Binongko and Tomea islands) off the southeast Sulawesi; Taliabu, Mongole, Sulabesi, Buru, Seram, Ambon, and Alor islands in Maluku; Bonerate dialect in Bonerate, Madu, Kalaotoa, and Karompa islands in Selayar District, South Sulawesi; numerous settlements throughout western Irian Jaya. Austronesian, Malayo-Polynesian, Western Malayo-Polynesian, Sulawesi, Muna-Buton, Tukangbesi-Bonerate. Dialects: BINONGKO, TOMEA (TOMIA). Binongko has 85% lexical similarity, with Tomea 81% with Bonerate, Tomea 79% with Bonerate. 70% to 75% with Tukangbesi North, 48% with Cia-Cia, 49% with Lasalimu, average of 35% with other nearby languages. Bilingualism in Wolio. Grammar. Pronominal indexing, grammatical status of subject, morphological case, causative, Philippine and Oceanic type language features. Muslim.

ULUMANDA' ***(ULUMANDAK, OELOEMANDA, ULUNDA, TUBBI, BOTTENG-TAPPALANG, AWO-SUMAKUYU, KADO)*** [ULM] 30,000 including 18,000 in Polmas and Majene (1986 SIL). South Sulawesi, Majene, Mamuju, and Polewali-Mamasa districts. Austronesian, Malayo-Polynesian, Western Malayo-Polynesian, Sulawesi, South Sulawesi, Northern, Pitu Ulunna Salu. Dialects: SONDOANG, TAPPALANG, BOTTENG. About 6 dialects. Lexical similarity 75% to 80% with dialects of Pitu Ulunna Salu, Aralle-Tabulahan, Pannei. Investigation needed: intelligibility with dialects, related varieties. Muslim.

UMA ***(PIPIKORO, OEMA)*** [PPK] 20,000 including 15,000 in the region, 5,000 outside (1990 M. Martens SIL), 500 in Benggaulu (1990 SIL). The Uma homeland is Pipikoro, 'banks of the Koro', along the Lariang, 'Koro', River in central Sulawesi, Donggala District, southern half of Kulawi Subdistrict. 32 villages. Bana dialect is in south Sulawesi, enclave within the Seko Padang dialect area, Kabupaten Luwu. Benggaulu is in south Sulawesi, south Pasangkayu District, Mamuju Subdistrict. Other Uma have migrated to Gimpu and Palolo valleys, Palu and Pani'i, about 120 km. north of Palu. Austronesian, Malayo-Polynesian, Western Malayo-Polynesian, Sulawesi, Central Sulawesi, West Central, Kaili-Pamona, Kaili. Dialects: WINATU (NORTHERN UMA), TOBAKU (WESTERN UMA, DOMPA, OMPA), TOLEE' (EASTERN UMA), KANTEWU (CENTRAL UMA), SOUTHERN UMA (ARIA), BENGGAULU (BINGKOLU), BANA. Most Uma speak Indonesian fluently. Most children living outside the homeland learn Indonesian as first language. Kantewu is the prestige dialect. Use of Uma is vigorous in the Uma homeland. Among those living outside (e.g., in Palu, Palolo, Gimpu), use of Uma is vigorous among adults. Investigation needed: intelligibility with Sarudu. Grammar. Swidden agriculturalists. 600 to 1,000 meters. Christian, Muslim (Benggaulu). NT 1996.

WARU ***(MOPUTE, MAPUTE)*** [WRU] 350 (1991 SIL). Southeast Sulawesi, Kendari District, Asera Subdistrict, Mopute village by the Lindu River. Austronesian, Malayo-Polynesian, Western Malayo-Polynesian, Sulawesi, Central Sulawesi, West Central, Bungku-Mori-Tolaki, Tolaki. Dialects: WARU, LALOMERUI. Waru dialect has 86% lexical similarity with Lalomerui, 79% with Tolaki dialects and Mekongga, 70% with Rahambuu and Kodeoha, 54% with the Mori and Bungku groups. Investigation needed: intelligibility with Tolaki. Muslim.

WAWONII ***(WOWONII)*** [WOW] 22,000 including 14,000 Wawonii, 7,500 Menui (1991 D. Mead SIL). Southeast Sulawesi, Wawonii and Menui islands near Kendari. Austronesian, Malayo-Polynesian, Western Malayo-Polynesian, Sulawesi, Central Sulawesi, West Central, Bungku-Mori-Tolaki, Bungku. Dialects: WAWONII, MENUI. 75% lexical similarity with Bungku and Tulambatu; 66% with Taloki, Kulisusu, and Koroni; 65% with Moronene. Investigation needed: intelligibility with Bungku, Tulambatu. Muslim.

WOLIO ***(BAUBAU)*** [WLO] 25,000 to 35,000 (1990). Population total both countries 25,000 to 35,000. Southwestern Buton Island in Bau-Bau, southeast Sulawesi. Also spoken in Malaysia (Sabah). Austronesian, Malayo-Polynesian, Western Malayo-Polynesian, Sulawesi, Muna-Buton, Buton. Dialect survey is needed in south and central Buton, Bungi, Sorawolio, Kapontori, Pasar Wajo, Sampolawa, Betoambari, and Batauga districts. 61% lexical similarity with Cia-Cia, 60% with Masiri and Lantoi. Wolio is the former court language of the Sultan at Baubau and a few surrounding communities, and formerly used by the nobility in the region. Official regional language. The name 'Buton' is usually used generically inside southeast Sulawesi to refer to Wolio; outside southeast Sulawesi it refers to people from southeast Sulawesi, or is sometimes confused with Bajau people as sailors. Trade language. Had an Arabic based script. Muslim.

WOTU [WTW] 5,000 (1987 C. and B. D. Grimes SIL). South Sulawesi, town of Wotu, Wotu Subdistrict, Luwu District. Austronesian, Malayo-Polynesian, Western Malayo-Polynesian, Sulawesi, Muna-Buton, Buton. 58% lexical similarity with Wolio, 53% with Barang-Barang (Laiyolo), average 43% with South Sulawesi Group, 43% with Kaili-Pamona Subgroup, 41% with Seko Padang, 39% with Tae' Luwu, 36% to 43% with Bungku-Mori-Tolaki Subgroup, 37% with Toraja-Sa'dan, 33% with Bugis, 31% with Rampi, 25% with Lemolang. Bilingual level estimates for Indonesian are 0 0%, 1 8%, 2 83%, 3 9%, 4 0%, 5 0%. Bugis-Luwu is the dominant second language. Muslim.

INDONESIA (SUMATRA)

36,455,000 (1995). 7 provinces. Information mainly from P. Voerhoeve 1955; D. Walker 1976. Data accuracy estimate: B, C. The number of languages listed for Indonesia (Sumatra) is 52. Of those, all are living languages. Diversity index 0.86.

ABUNG [ABL] 500,000 (1976 D. Walker). South. Austronesian, Malayo-Polynesian, Western Malayo-Polynesian, Sundic, Lampungic, Abung. Dialects: JABUNG, MENGGALA (NORTHEAST LAMPUNG), KOTA BUMI (NORTHWEST LAMPUNG). Many differences in vocabulary and phonology with Pesisir. Dialects have 77% lexical similarity, some phonological differences. Menggala has 72% lexical similarity with Kalianda, a dialect of Southern Pesisir. Investigation needed: intelligibility with dialects. Muslim.

ACEH ***(ATJEH, ATJEHNESE, ACHINESE, ACHEHNESE)*** [ATJ] 3,000,000, 1.6% of the population (1999 WA). Northern, Aceh Province, northern and southern coasts around the tip of Sumatra. Austronesian, Malayo-Polynesian, Western Malayo-Polynesian, Sundic, Malayic, Achinese-Chamic, Achinese. Dialects: BANDA ACEH, BARUH, BUENG, DAJA, PASE, PIDIE (PEDIR, TIMU), TUNONG. Bilingualism in Indonesian. Dictionary. Grammar. SVO. Coastal. Muslim, Christian. NT 1996.

BATAK ALAS-KLUET ***(ALAS-KLUET BATAK)*** [BTZ] 80,000 (1989). Northern, northeast of Tapaktuan and around Kutacane. Austronesian, Malayo-Polynesian, Western Malayo-Polynesian, Sundic, Sumatra, Batak, Northern. Dialect: ALAS. Reported to not be Batak. Investigation needed: intelligibility with Dairi, Karo. Muslim.

BATAK ANGKOLA ***(ANAKOLA, ANGKOLA)*** [AKB] 750,000 (1991 UBS). North central, Sipirok area. Austronesian, Malayo-Polynesian, Western Malayo-Polynesian, Sundic, Sumatra, Batak, Southern. Closely related to Mandailing Batak, but distinct sociolinguistically. Christian, Muslim. Bible 1991.

BATAK DAIRI ***(DAIRI, PAKPAK, PAKPAK DAIRI)*** [BTD] 1,200,000 (1991 UBS). Northern, southwest of Lake Toba around Sidikalang. Austronesian, Malayo-Polynesian, Western Malayo-Polynesian, Sundic, Sumatra, Batak, Northern. Diari and Pakpak are sociolinguistically distinct. Christian. Bible, in press (1995).

BATAK KARO ***(KARO BATAK)*** [BTX] 600,000 (1991 UBS). Central and northern, west and northwest of Lake Toba. Austronesian, Malayo-Polynesian, Western Malayo-Polynesian, Sundic, Sumatra, Batak, Northern. Dialect: SINGKIL. Grammar. Christian, traditional religion. Bible 1987-1995.

BATAK MANDAILING ***(MANDAILING BATAK, BATTA)*** [BTM] 400,000 (1989). Northern. Austronesian, Malayo-Polynesian, Western Malayo-Polynesian, Sundic, Sumatra, Batak, Southern. Sociolinguistically different from Angkola. A general form of Batak common to a wider area than Angkola. Muslim.

BATAK SIMALUNGUN ***(TIMUR, SIMELUNGAN)*** [BTS] 800,000 (1977 Hayes). Northern, northeast of Lake Toba. Austronesian, Malayo-Polynesian, Western Malayo-Polynesian, Sundic, Sumatra, Batak, Simalungan. Bible 1976.

BATAK TOBA ***(TOBA BATAK, BATTA)*** [BBC] 2,000,000 (1991 UBS). Samosir Island and east, south, and west of Toba Lake in north Sumatra. Austronesian, Malayo-Polynesian, Western Malayo-Polynesian, Sundic, Sumatra, Batak, Southern. Closely related to Angkola Batak. Traditional Batak script. Christian. Bible 1894-1989.

BENGKULU ***(BENKULAN, BENCOOLEN)*** [BKE] 55,000 (1989). Small area around Benkulu city, western end of southern Sumatra. Austronesian, Malayo-Polynesian, Western Malayo-Polynesian, Sundic, Malayic, Malayan, Local Malay. Muslim.

ENGGANO ***(ENGGANESE)*** [ENO] 1,000 (1981 Wurm and Hattori). Enganno Island, southwest of Sumatra and on four smaller nearby islands. Austronesian, Malayo-Polynesian, Western Malayo-Polynesian, Sundic, Sumatra, Enggano. Not closely related to other languages.

ENIM [ENI] 70,000 (1989). Southern Sumatra, south of Muaraenim, east and southeast of Lahat. Austronesian, Malayo-Polynesian, Western Malayo-Polynesian, Sundic, Malayic, Malayan, Local Malay. Investigation needed: intelligibility with Malay varieties. Muslim.

GAYO ***(GAJO)*** [GYO] 180,000 (1989). Mountain region of north Sumatra around Takengon, Genteng, and Lokon. Austronesian, Malayo-Polynesian, Western Malayo-Polynesian, Sundic, Gayo. Dialects: DOROT, BOBASAN, SERBODJADI, TAMPUR. Not closely related to other languages. Muslim, traditional religion.

KAUR ***(KA'UR, BINTUHAN)*** [VKK] 20,000 (1989). Southwestern Sumatra, South Bengkulu, Southern Kaur area, and Northern Kaur area. Austronesian, Malayo-Polynesian, Western Malayo-Polynesian, Sundic, Malayic, Malayan, Local Malay. Related to Serawai. Investigation needed: intelligibility with Malay varieties. Muslim, traditional religion.

KAYU AGUNG [VKY] 45,000 (1989). Southern Sumatra, around Kayuagung. Austronesian, Malayo-Polynesian, Western Malayo-Polynesian, Sundic, Malayic, Malayan, Local Malay. Investigation needed: intelligibility with Malay varieties. Muslim.

KERINCI ***(KERINCHI, KERINTJI, KINCHAI)*** [KVR] 300,000 (1989). Western mountains around Sungaipenuh and north and west. Austronesian, Malayo-Polynesian, Western Malayo-Polynesian, Sundic, Malayic, Malayan, Local Malay. Dialects: ULU, MAMAQ, AKIT, TALANG, SAKEI. Distinct from Kerinci-Minangkabau dialect of Minangkabau. Investigation needed: intelligibility with Malay dialects, bilingual proficiency in Minangkabau. Traditional script. Muslim.

KOMERING ***(KOMERIN, NJO)*** [KGE] 700,000 (1989) including 20,000 in Jakarta (1992). Southeastern Sumatra, Martapura, Kangkung, nearly to Kayuagung, and east to the coast. Austronesian, Malayo-Polynesian, Western Malayo-Polynesian, Sundic, Lampungic, Pesisir. 70% lexical similarity with Kalianda, 74% with Sungkai (closest). Bilingualism in Indonesian. Called Njo together with Krui. Lowland swamps. Agriculturalists: wet rice. Shafi Sunni Muslim.

KRUI ***(KROE, KRU'I, WESTERN LAMPUNG, NJO)*** [KRQ] 20,000 to 30,000 (GEKISUS 1985). Southern, south Benkulu Province around Krui, Sanggi, Kotajawa, and possibly into Lampung Province. Austronesian, Malayo-Polynesian, Western Malayo-Polynesian, Sundic, Lampungic, Pesisir. Related to Komering. Vocabulary differences with other Pesisir languages. 84% lexical similarity between Krui and Ranau. Called Njo together with Komering. Investigation needed: intelligibility with Ranau, Komering. Muslim.

KUBU [KVB] 10,000 (1989). Spread across Jambi, Riau in south Sumatra, eastern swamp region. Austronesian, Malayo-Polynesian, Western Malayo-Polynesian, Sundic, Malayic, Malayan, Local Malay. Dialects: LALANG, BAJAT, ULU LAKO, TUNGKAL, TUNGKAL ILIR, DAWAS, SUPAT, DJAMBI, RIDAN, NOMADIC KUBU. Related to Lubu. Forest dwellers. Swamp forest. Traditional religion, Muslim, Christian.

LAMPUNG ***(API, LAMPONG)*** [LJP] 1,500,000 (1981 Wurm and Hattori). Southern Sumatra, entire province of Lampung. Austronesian, Malayo-Polynesian, Western Malayo-Polynesian, Sundic, Lampungic, Pesisir. The majority can speak some Indonesian, which is used in schools, and increasingly in the city as first language by Lampung people. Outside of the city Lampung is used daily in home and village. Teachers must use Lampung to communicate with children, especially in lower grades. Grammar. Roman script for modern use, Lampung script, developed from Devanagari, is used traditionally. Muslim.

LEMATANG ***(LEMANTANG)*** [LMT] 150,000 (1989). Southern Sumatra, around Muaraenim and another pocket southeast of Sarolangun. Austronesian, Malayo-Polynesian, Western Malayo-Polynesian, Sundic, Malayic, Malayan, Local Malay. Investigation needed: intelligibility with Malay varieties. Muslim.

LEMBAK ***(LINGGAU)*** [LIW] 50,000 (1989). Interior south Sumatra around Lubuklinggau and east of Bengkulu; 2 areas. Austronesian, Malayo-Polynesian, Western Malayo-Polynesian, Sundic, Malayic, Malayan, Local Malay. Dialects: LEMBAK BLITI (BLITI), LEMBAK SINDANG. Investigation needed: intelligibility with Malay varieties. Muslim.

LINTANG [LNT] 70,000 (1989). Southern Sumatra, between Lahat and Kapahiang. Austronesian, Malayo-Polynesian, Western Malayo-Polynesian, Sundic, Malayic, Malayan, Local Malay. Investigation needed: intelligibility with Malay varieties. Muslim.

LOM ***(BELOM, MAPOR, MAPORESE)*** [MFB] 50 (1981 Wurm and Hattori), or 850 including Bangka Malay (1989 Olaf H. Smedal). Sumatra, northeast Bangka Island, Belinyu District. Austronesian, Malayo-Polynesian, Western Malayo-Polynesian, Sundic, Sumatra, Lom. Not closely related to other languages. The people are called 'Lom' or 'Mapur'.

LONCONG ***(LONTJONG, LONCHONG, ORANG LAUT)*** [LCE] East coast on both sides of the mouths of the Kampat and Inderagiri rivers, nearby islands, and coasts of Bangka and Belitung islands.

Austronesian, Malayo-Polynesian, Western Malayo-Polynesian, Sundic, Malayic, Malayan, Local Malay. It may be two languages. Other languages have been called Orang Laut: Lawta of Myanmar and Indonesian Bajau (see Sulawesi).

LUBU [LCF] 30,000 (1981 Wurm and Hattori). Central region of east Sumatra. Austronesian, Malayo-Polynesian, Western Malayo-Polynesian, Sundic, Malayic, Malayan, Local Malay. Related to Kubu. Lubu people consider the name 'Kerinci' an insult. Muslim.

MALAY ***(MELAYU, MALAYU, MELAJU, BAHASA MELAYU, BAHASA MALAYU, STANDARD MALAY)*** [MLI] 10,000,000 in Indonesia (1981 Wurm and Hattori) including 2,000,000 in Riau, 40,000 in Bangka, 170,000 in Belitung. Also in Kalimantan, Java, Maluku, Sulawesi, Irian Jaya. Austronesian, Malayo-Polynesian, Western Malayo-Polynesian, Sundic, Malayic, Malayan, Local Malay. Dialects: RIAU (RIOUW-LINGGA, JOHOR), JAKARTA, SAMBAS, DELI, MELAYU PASAR (BAZAAR MALAY, PASIR), BORNEO (SINTANG), KOTA-WARINGIN, SUKADANA, MAKAKAU, IRIANESE, MAKASSARESE, MANADONESE (MENADONESE), LABU (LEBU, LABU BASAP), RITOK (SIANTAN, PONTIANAK), BALIKPAPAN, SAMPIT, BAKUMPAI, WEST BORNEO COAST MALAY, BELIDE, LENGKAYAP, AJI, DAYA, MULAK, BANGKA, BELITUNG, LARANTUKA (ENDE MALAY), BASA KUPANG (KUPANG), PERANAKAN. See separate entries for Kalimantan: Kutai Malay, Berau Malay, Bukit; Maluku: Ambonese Malay, Bacan Malay, North Moluccan Malay; Nusa Tenggara: Kupang Malay; Sumatra: Enim, Kaur, Kayu Agung, Lematang, Lembak, Jambi Malay, Lintang, Penesak, Rawas, Sindang Kelingi. Some listed as dialects are probably not inherently intelligible with Standard Malay or Indonesian. Kupang Malay and Larantuka Malay in Nusa Tenggara are very similar to each other. Over 80% cognate with Indonesian (J. Echols). Investigation needed: intelligibility with dialects. Sunni Muslim. Bible 1733-1993. See main entry under Malaysia, Peninsular.

MALAY, JAMBI [JAX] 800,000 (1989). Southern Sumatra. Austronesian, Malayo-Polynesian, Western Malayo-Polynesian, Sundic, Malayic, Malayan, Local Malay. Investigation needed: intelligibility with Malay varieties. Muslim.

MENTAWAI ***(MENTAWEI, MENTAWI)*** [MWV] 50,000 (1992 UBS). Mentawai Islands off the west coast of Sumatra. Austronesian, Malayo-Polynesian, Western Malayo-Polynesian, Sundic, Sumatra, Mentawai. Dialects: SIMALEGI, SAKALAGAN, SILABU, TAIKAKU, SAUMANGANJA, NORTH SIBERUT, SOUTH SIBERUT, SIPURA, PAGAI. Christian, traditional religion. NT 1987-1996.

MINANGKABAU ***(MINANG, PADANG)*** [MPU] 6,500,000 including 500,000 in Jakarta. 3.3% of the population (1981 Moussay). West central Sumatra around Padang, and throughout the Indonesian archipelago. Nearly half live outside of central Sumatra. Austronesian, Malayo-Polynesian, Western Malayo-Polynesian, Sundic, Malayic, Malayan, Para-Malay. Dialects: AGAM, PAJOKUMBUH, TANAH, SI JUNJUNG, BATU SANGKAR-PARIANGAN, SINGKARAK, ORANG MAMAK, ULU, KERINCI-MINANGKABAU. Not intelligible with Indonesian. Muko-Muko and Pekal may be intelligible with Minang. There is literature. Investigation needed: intelligibility with Muko-Muko, Pekal. SVO. There is instruction in Minang in 1st and 2nd grade, although texts are in Indonesian. Newspapers, radio programs. Sunni Muslim. NT 1996.

MUKO-MUKO ***(MOKOMOKO)*** [VMO] 30,000 (1989). Southern Sumatra, west coast around Mukomuko. Austronesian, Malayo-Polynesian, Western Malayo-Polynesian, Sundic, Malayic, Malayan, Para-Malay. Related to Minangkabau with strong influences from Rejang. Investigation needed: intelligibility with Minangkabau, Pekal, Rejang. Muslim.

MUSI [MUI] 150,000 (1989). Interior south Sumatra, both sides of the Musi River northwest of Sekayu and to the Palembang language. Austronesian, Malayo-Polynesian, Western Malayo-Polynesian, Sundic, Malayic, Malayan, Local Malay. Investigation needed: intelligibility with Malay varieties. Muslim.

NIAS ***(BATU)*** [NIP] 480,000 (1989). Nias and Batu Islands off the west coast of Sumatra. Austronesian, Malayo-Polynesian, Western Malayo-Polynesian, Sundic, Sumatra, Northern. Dialects: NIAS, BATU. Investigation needed: intelligibility with Sikule. Christian. Bible 1911, in press (1996).

OGAN [OGN] 300,000 (1989). South Sumatra around Baturaja, Pagerdewa, and north and west of Kayuagung. Austronesian, Malayo-Polynesian, Western Malayo-Polynesian, Sundic, Malayic, Malayan, Local Malay. Investigation needed: intelligibility with Pasemah, Serawai, Palembang, Malay varieties. Muslim.

PALEMBANG [PLM] 500,000 (1989). Southeast Sumatra, Palembang area. Austronesian, Malayo-Polynesian, Western Malayo-Polynesian, Sundic, Malayic, Malayan, Local Malay. Investigation needed: intelligibility with Malay varieties. Swamp. Coast. Muslim.

PASEMAH ***(BESEMAH)*** [PSE] 400,000 (1989). Central Bukit Barisan highlands. Austronesian, Malayo-Polynesian, Western Malayo-Polynesian, Sundic, Malayic, Malayan, Local Malay. Investigation needed: intelligibility with Serawai, Malay varieties. Mountain slope. Muslim.

PEKAL [PEL] 30,000 (1989). Southern Sumatra, west coast from north of Ipuh to Tembesi River, to near Argamakmur in the south. Austronesian, Malayo-Polynesian, Western Malayo-Polynesian, Sundic, Malayic, Malayan, Para-Malay. Related to Minangkabau with strong Rejang influences. Investigation needed: intelligibility with Minangkabau, Muko-Muko, Rejang. Muslim.

PENESAK ***(PENASAK)*** [PEN] 20,000 (1989). Southern Sumatra, around Prabumulih. Austronesian, Malayo-Polynesian, Western Malayo-Polynesian, Sundic, Malayic, Malayan, Local Malay. Investigation needed: intelligibility with Malay varieties. Muslim.

PESISIR, SOUTHERN [PEC] 400,000 (1976 D. Walker). South Sumatra. Austronesian, Malayo-Polynesian, Western Malayo-Polynesian, Sundic, Lampungic, Pesisir. Dialects: KOTA AGUNG (SOUTHWEST LAMPUNG), WAY LIMA, KALIANDA (SOUTHEAST LAMPUNG), TELUKBETUNG, TALANG PADANG. 79% lexical similarity between Kota Agung and Kalianda, 70% between Kalianda and Komering, 78% between Kota Agung and Pubian, 78% between Kota Agung and Krui, 78% between Way Lima and Kalianda, 72% between Kalianda and Menggala (Abung). Investigation needed: intelligibility with dialects. Muslim.

PUBIAN [PUN] 400,000 (1976 D. Walker). South Sumatra. Austronesian, Malayo-Polynesian, Western Malayo-Polynesian, Sundic, Lampungic, Pesisir. 76% to 81% lexical similarity with other Pesisir languages.

RANAU [RAE] 60,000 (1989). Southern Sumatra, south of Muaradua, near headwaters of Kanan River. Austronesian, Malayo-Polynesian, Western Malayo-Polynesian, Sundic, Malayic, Malayan, Local Malay. 84% lexical similarity with Krui. Distinct from Ranau dialect of Central Dusun in Sabah, Malaysia. Investigation needed: intelligibility with Malay varieties, Krui. Muslim.

RAWAS [RAJ] 150,000 (1989). Southern Sumatra, around Ambacang and along Musi River. Austronesian, Malayo-Polynesian, Western Malayo-Polynesian, Sundic, Malayic, Malayan, Local Malay. Investigation needed: intelligibility with Malay varieties. Muslim.

REJANG ***(REDJANG, REJANG-LEBONG, JANG, DJANG, DJANG BELE TEBO)*** [REJ] 1,000,000 (1981 Wurm and Hattori). Southwest highlands, north Bengkulu Province, around Argamakmur, Muaraaman, Curuo, and Kapahiang. Austronesian, Malayo-Polynesian, Western Malayo-Polynesian, Sundic, Malayic, Malayan, Para-Malay. Dialect: LEBONG (DJANG LEBONG). Subgroups: Jang Lebong, Jang Musai, Jang Lai, Jang Bekulau, Abeus. 85% live in remote rural areas. Very different from Serawai. Different from Rejang-Baram group of languages on Borneo. Grammar. Literacy rate in second language: 45%. Traditional script. Muslim.

SEKAYU [SYU] 400,000 (1989). Southern Sumatra. Austronesian, Malayo-Polynesian, Western Malayo-Polynesian, Sundic, Unclassified. Muslim.

SEMANG, LOWLAND ***(ORANG BENUA, SAKAI)*** [ORB] 10,000 (1989). Bintan Island, in the Riau Islands southeast of Singapore. Austro-Asiatic, Mon-Khmer, Aslian, North Aslian, Western. Dialect: ORANG BENUA (NEWBOLD'S SEMANG). There seem to be 2 or 3 groups in different locations which share this name, and one is Malayic. Muslim.

SEMENDO [SMN] 105,000 (1989). Interior south Sumatra; two areas: west of Baturaja and south of Pajarbulan. Austronesian, Malayo-Polynesian, Western Malayo-Polynesian, Sundic, Malayic, Malayan, Local Malay. Investigation needed: intelligibility with Malay varieties. Muslim.

SERAWAI ***(SERAWAJ, SERAWI)*** [SRJ] 225,000 (1989). South Bengkulu coast. Austronesian, Malayo-Polynesian, Western Malayo-Polynesian, Sundic, Malayic, Malayan, Local Malay. The two dialects may not be very different. Related to Pasemah. Muslim, traditional religion, Christian. NT 1995.

SIKULE ***(SICHULE, WALI BANUAH, SIKHULE)*** [SKH] 20,000. Central Simeulue Island. Austronesian, Malayo-Polynesian, Western Malayo-Polynesian, Sundic, Sumatra, Northern. Dialects: LEKON, TAPAH. Closely related to Nias. Investigation needed: intelligibility with Nias.

SIMEULUE ***(SIMALUR, SIMULUL, SIMEULOË, LONG BANO)*** [SMR] 100,000 (1981 Wurm and Hattori). West and east ends of Simeulue Island, Babi and Banjak islands. Austronesian, Malayo-Polynesian, Western Malayo-Polynesian, Sundic, Sumatra, Northern. Related to Sikule and Nias. Muslim.

SINDANG KELINGI ***(KELINGI)*** [SDI] 50,000 (1989). Southern Sumatra, around Muaraklingi, south, east, and north. Austronesian, Malayo-Polynesian, Western Malayo-Polynesian, Sundic, Malayic, Malayan, Local Malay. Investigation needed: intelligibility with Malay varieties, bilingual proficiency in Indonesian. Muslim.

SUKU BATIN ***(BATIN)*** [SBV] 90,000 (1989). Southeastern Sumatra, Jambi Province, along the Tembesi, Batan Merangin, Batang Bungo, and Batang Masumai rivers. Austronesian, Malayo-Polynesian, Western Malayo-Polynesian, Sundic, Malayic, Malayan, Local Malay. Reported to have come from the Kerinci. Muslim, traditional religion.

SUNGKAI [SUU] South Sumatra, northeast of Krui, west of Abung. Austronesian, Malayo-Polynesian, Western Malayo-Polynesian, Sundic, Lampungic, Pesisir. 76% lexical similarity with Pubian (closest), 74% with Komering.

IRAN

Islamic Republic of Iran, Jomhouri-e-Eslami-e-Irân. National or official language: Western Farsi. 65,758,000 (1998 UN). Literacy rate 70% to 75% among those 6 years old and over (1995-996 Iran Statistical Center). Also includes Hulaula 300, Turkish 2,570, people from Afghanistan 1,500,000, Kurds from Iraq 120,000, Shi'a Arabs from Iraq. Information mainly from E. Drowser 1939; R. Macuch 1965; I. Garbell 1965; T. Sebeok 1969, 1970; G. Doerfer et al. 1971; R. Oberling 1974; D. L. Stilo 1981; R. D. Hoberman 1988a, b. Shi'a Muslim (official), Sunni Muslim, Baha'i, Christian. Blind population 200,000 (1982 WCE). Deaf population 3,978,055. Deaf institutions: 50. Data accuracy estimate: B, C. The number of languages listed for Iran is 71. Of those, 69 are living languages and 2 are extinct. Diversity index 0.76.

AIMAQ [AIQ] 170,000 (1993 Johnstone). Mazanderan Province. Indo-European, Indo-Iranian, Iranian, Western, Southwestern, Persian. Dialect: TEIMURI (TEIMURTASH). See main entry under Afghanistan.

ALVIRI-VIDARI [AVD] Near Saveh. Indo-European, Indo-Iranian, Iranian, Western, Northwestern, Talysh. Dialects: ALVIR (ALVIRI), VIDAR (VIDARI). Related to Gozarkhani and Vafsi. Muslim.

ARABIC, GULF SPOKEN *(KHALIJI, GULF ARABIC)* [AFB] 200,000 in Iran (1993). Southern coast. Afro-Asiatic, Semitic, Central, South, Arabic. Dialect: AL-HASAA. See main entry under Iraq.

ARABIC, MESOPOTAMIAN SPOKEN *(MESOPOTAMIAN GELET ARABIC)* [ACM] 1,200,000 in Iran. Khuzestan Province, southwest side of Zagros Mts., along the bank of the Shatt al Arab and the Tigris. Afro-Asiatic, Semitic, Central, South, Arabic. SVO. Shi'a Muslim. See main entry under Iraq.

ARMENIAN *(HAIEREN, SOMEKHURI, ERMENICE, ARMJANSKJ)* [ARM] 170,800 in Iran (1993). Northern Iran, Azerbaijan around Khoi, Shahpur, Ahar, Tabriz, Tehran, Esfahan, Shiraz. Indo-European, Armenian. Dialects: EASTERN ARMENIAN, AGULIS, ASTRAKHAN, EREVAN, JOLFA (DZHULFA), KARABAGH SHAMAKHI, TBILISI (TIFLIS), ARTVIN, KHOI-SALMST (KHVOY), URMIA-MARAGHEH. Dialects listed are Eastern. Eastern Armenian is spoken in Armenia and its Turkish and Iranian borderlands; Western Armenian is spoken elsewhere. Western Armenian is understood only by some in Iran. Christian. Bible 1883-1994. See main entry under Armenia.

ASHTIANI *(ASTIANI)* [ATN] Tafres area. Indo-European, Indo-Iranian, Iranian, Western, Northwestern, Central Iran. Transitional between central Iranian dialects and Talysh. Very close to Vafsi. Speakers are bilingual in Farsi. Muslim.

ASSYRIAN NEO-ARAMAIC [AII] 10,000 to 20,000 in Iran (1994) out of a reported population of 80,000. Reza'iyeh (Rizaiye, Urmia, Urmi). Most in Tehran. Afro-Asiatic, Semitic, Central, Aramaic, Eastern, Central, Northeastern. Dialect: IRANIAN KOINE (GENERAL URMI). The Assyrian separated denominationally from the Chaldean in the 16th century. Syriac script used. Christian (Nestorian) mainly. Bible 1852-1911. See main entry under Iraq.

AVESTAN *(PAZEND, AVESTA)* [AVS] Indo-European, Indo-Iranian, Iranian, Eastern, Northeastern. The language of the Zoroastrian scriptures, from 600 B.C. Zoroastrian. Extinct.

AZERBAIJANI, SOUTH *(AZERI)* [AZB] 23,500,000 in Iran (1997), or 37.3% of the population (1997), including 290,000 Afshar, 5,000 Aynallu, 7,500 Baharlu, 1,000 Moqaddam, 3,500 Nafar 1,000 Pishagchi, 3,000 Qajar, 2,000 Qaragozlu, 130,000 Shahsavani (1993). Population total all countries 24,364,000. East and west Azerbaijan, Zanjan, and part of central provinces. Many in a few districts of Tehran. Some Azerbaijani-speaking groups are in Fars Province and other parts of Iran. Also spoken in Afghanistan, Azerbaijan, Iraq, Jordan, Syria, Turkey (Asia), USA. Altaic, Turkic, Southern, Azerbaijani. Dialects: AYNALLU (INALLU, INANLU), KARAPAPAKH, TABRIZ, AFSHARI (AFSHAR, AFSAR), SHAHSAVANI (SHAHSEVEN), MOQADDAM, BAHARLU (KAMESH), NAFAR, QARAGOZLU, PISHAGCHI, BAYAT, QAJAR. Distinctive dialect differences between the Azerbaijani of the former USSR (North) and Iranian Azerbaijani (South) in phonology, lexicon, morphology, syntax, and loan words. Teimurtash (7,000 in Mazandaran; possibly the same as Teimuri, Timuri, Taimouri) and Salchug (in Kerman Province) may be dialects. Qashqai is probably a dialect. They feel that North and South Azerbaijani are spoken by one people, one ethnic group, but recognize that there are differences in both the spoken and written language. Each has problems accepting the written form of the other. People called 'Turki' (Turks). Language of wider communication. Arabo-Persian script. Poetry, newspapers. Agriculturalists, pastoralists. Shi'a Muslim.

BALOCHI, SOUTHERN *(BALUCHI, BALUCI, BALOCI)* [BCC] 405,000 in Iran. Southern Baluchistan Province. Indo-European, Indo-Iranian, Iranian, Western, Northwestern, Balochi. Dialect: MAKRANI (LOTUNI). Sunni Muslim. Bible portions 1992-1994. See main entry under Pakistan.

BALOCHI, WESTERN *(BALUCHI, BALUCI, BALOCI)* [BGN] 451,000 in Iran, 1% of the population (1986). Northern Baluchistan Province. Half are settled in cities and villages, half are nomadic. Indo-European, Indo-Iranian, Iranian, Western, Northwestern, Balochi. Dialects: RAKHSHANI (RAXSHANI), SARAWANI. Strongly influenced by Fars, but not intelligible with Farsi. Few speak Farsi. Distinct from Eastern and

Southern Balochi. Ethnic group: Yarahmadza. Sunni Muslim. Bible portions 1984. See main entry under Pakistan.

BASHKARDI [BSG] Indo-European, Indo-Iranian, Iranian, Western, Northwestern, Balochi. Muslim.

BRAHUI ***(BRAHUDI, BIRAHUI, KUR GALLI)*** [BRH] 10,000 in Iran (1983). Eastern. Dravidian, Northern. Dialects: JHARAWAN, KALAT, SARAWAN. Kalat is standard dialect, Jharawan is lowland. Brahui in Iran are reported to speak Western Baluchi now. Pastoralists. Muslim. Bible portions 1905-1978. See main entry under Pakistan.

DARI ***("GABRI", "GABAR")*** [GBZ] 8,000 to 15,000 (1999). Yezd and Kerman areas. Indo-European, Indo-Iranian, Iranian, Western, Northwestern, Central Iran. Related to Parsi-Dari. All use Western Farsi as second language. Spoken by Persian Zoroastrians in their personal communications as a private language. A different language from Dari (Eastern Farsi [PRS]) of Afghanistan, although both names come from Darius, the ancient Emperor, whom they both relate to. Many Zoroastrians speak Parsi-Dari, and do not know this language. "Gabri" and "Gabar" are derogatory names. Zoroastrian.

DOMARI ***(MIDDLE EASTERN ROMANI, TSIGENE, GYPSY)*** [RMT] 80,000 in Iran (1929). Population total all countries 500,000 (1980 Kenrick). Kurbati dialect is in western Iran, Karachi in northern Iran. Also spoken in Afghanistan, Egypt, India, Iraq, Israel, Jordan, Libya, Palestinian West Bank and Gaza, Russia (Europe), Syria, Turkey (Europe), Uzbekistan. Indo-European, Indo-Iranian, Indo-Aryan, Central zone, Dom. Dialects: KURBATI (GHORBATI), QINATI, YÜRÜK, KOLI, KARACHI, LULI, MAZNOUG, NAWAR. Arabic influenced. Muslim.

DZHIDI ***(JUDEO-PERSIAN, DJUDI, JUDI)*** [DZH] (60,000 in Israel; 1995). Indo-European, Indo-Iranian, Iranian, Western, Southwestern, Persian. Close to Bukharic, Western Farsi. Jewish. See main entry under Israel.

ESHTEHARDI [ESH] Eshtehard and environs, Karaj District, Central Province. Indo-European, Indo-Iranian, Iranian, Western, Northwestern, Talysh. Close to Takestani. Muslim.

FARS [FAC] Indo-European, Indo-Iranian, Iranian, Western, Southwestern, Fars. Related to Lari. Distinct from Farsi. Muslim.

FARSI, WESTERN ***(PERSIAN, PARSI)*** [PES] 22,000,000 in Iran, or 35.92% of the population (1997), including 800,000 Dari in Khorasan, Gilan, Tat, Bakhtiyari, Lor. Population total all countries 24,280,000. Central and south central Iran. Also spoken in 26 other countries including Australia, Austria, Azerbaijan, Bahrain, Canada, Denmark, France, Germany, Greece, India, Iraq, Israel, Netherlands, Oman, Qatar, Saudi Arabia, Spain, Sweden, Tajikistan. Indo-European, Indo-Iranian, Iranian, Western, Southwestern, Persian. Dialects: QAZVINI, MAHALLATI, HAMADANI, KASHANI, ISFAHANI, SEDEHI, KERMANI, ARAKI, SHIRAZI, JAHROMI, SHAHRUDI, KAZERUNI, MASHADI (MESHED), BASSERI. The literary language is virtually identical in Iran and Afghanistan, with very minor lexical differences. Zargari may be a dialect used by goldsmiths (also see Balkan Romani in Iran). Dialect shading into Dari in Afghanistan and Tajiki in Tajikistan. National language. Grammar. SOV. All schools use Farsi. Radio programs. Mainly Shi'a Muslim. Bible 1838-1995.

GAZI [GZI] Indo-European, Indo-Iranian, Iranian, Western, Northwestern, Central Iran. Muslim.

GEORGIAN ***(KARTULI, GRUZIN)*** [GEO] 1,000 to 10,000 in Iran. South Caucasian, Georgian. Dialect: FEREYDAN (FEREJDAN). Ferejdan dialect is or was in Iran; there may not be any now. In Iran they may not be able to read Mkhedruli script, which they use in Georgia. Muslim. Bible 1743-1989. See main entry under Georgia.

GILAKI ***(GELAKI, GILANI, GUILAKI, GUILANI)*** [GLK] 3,265,000 (1993), including 2,000 Galeshi (1991 WA). Gilan region, coastal plain, south of Talish. Galeshi is a mountain dialect. Indo-European, Indo-Iranian, Iranian, Western, Northwestern, Caspian. Dialect: GALESHI. Close to Mazanderani. Speakers use Western Farsi as second language. The educated can read Farsi well. Not in written form. Agriculturalists, fishermen. Shi'a Muslim, Christian.

GOZARKHANI [GOZ] Alamut area. Indo-European, Indo-Iranian, Iranian, Western, Northwestern, Talysh. Close to Maraghei. Muslim.

HARZANI [HRZ] West Azerbaijan Province, Qalingie, betweenf Marand and Jolfa, northwest of Tabriz. Indo-European, Indo-Iranian, Iranian, Western, Northwestern, Talysh. Very close to Karingani. Muslim.

HAWRAMI ***(HAWRAMANI, GURANI, GORANI, MÂCHO MÂCHO)*** [HAC] West part of Kordestan Province, near Iraq border. Indo-European, Indo-Iranian, Iranian, Western, Northwestern, Zaza-Gorani. Closest to Dimli of Turkey. Both are different from Kurdish. Yazdani. See main entry under Iraq.

HAZARAGI ***(HAZARA, HEZAREH, HEZARE'I)*** [HAZ] 283,000 in Iran (1993). Indo-European, Indo-Iranian, Iranian, Western, Southwestern, Persian. They speak a dialect related to Dari; possibly distinct from Dari. Ethnic group names are (Central) Dai Kundi, Dai Zangi, Behsud, Yekaulang, (Southern) Polada, Urusgani, Jaguri, Ghazni Hazaras, Dai Miradad. Agriculturalists, semi-sedentary pastoralists. Muslim: Imami Shi'a, Ismaili, some Sunni. See main entry under Afghanistan.

HERKI [HEK] Indo-European, Indo-Iranian, Iranian, Western, Northwestern, Kurdish. Possibly a dialect of Kurmanji. Muslim. See main entry under Iraq.

JADGALI ***(JATGALI, JATKI, JAT)*** [JAV] Indo-European, Indo-Iranian, Indo-Aryan, Northwestern zone, Sindhi. People called Jats. Different from Jakati of Afghanistan, Moldova, Ukraine, and Russian Central Asia. Muslim. See main entry under Pakistan.

KABATEI [XKP] Rudbar District, Gilan Province. Indo-European, Indo-Iranian, Iranian, Western, Northwestern, Talysh. Dialects: KALAS, KABATE. Close to Upper Taromi. Muslim.

KAJALI [XKJ] Khalkhal District in Eastern Azerbaijan Province, Kaqazkonan District, Kajal. Indo-European, Indo-Iranian, Iranian, Western, Northwestern, Talysh. Close to Shahrudi and Koresh-e Rostam. Muslim.

KARINGANI [KGN] East Azerbaijan Province, Dizmar District, Keringan village, and Hasanu District, northeast of Tabriz. Indo-European, Indo-Iranian, Iranian, Western, Northwestern, Talysh. Various dialects. Very close to Harzani. Muslim.

KAZAKH ***(KAZAK, KAZAKHI, GAZAQI)*** [KAZ] 3,000 in Iran (1982 estimate). Gorgan City, Mazandaran Province. Altaic, Turkic, Western, Aralo-Caspian. Any who are literate would use Arabic script. Muslim. NT 1820-1910, out of print. See main entry under Kazakhstan.

KHALAJ [KJF] Also spoken in Azerbaijan. Indo-European, Indo-Iranian, Iranian, Western, Northwestern. Related to Kurdish and Talysh. Pronounced with 2 short or front a's. Different from Turkic Khalaj in Iran.

KHALAJ [KLJ] 17,000 and decreasing (1968). Northeast of Arak in Central Province. Altaic, Turkic, Southern, Azerbaijani. Not a dialect of Azerbaijani, as previously supposed. An independent language distinct from other extant Turkish languages (Doerfer 1971). Most are bilingual in Farsi. Some children know only Farsi. Pronounced with two long or back a's. Different from Indo-Iranian Khalaj. Muslim.

KHOINI [XKC] Khoin District, Zanjan Province. Indo-European, Indo-Iranian, Iranian, Western, Northwestern, Talysh. Various dialects. Related to Kabatei and Takestani. Muslim.

KHORASANI TURKISH ***(QUCHANI)*** [KMZ] 400,000 possibly (1977 Doerfer). Northeast Iran, in the northern part of Khorasan Province, especially northwest of Mashhad. West dialect in Bojnurd region; north dialect in Quchan region (probably the largest), south dialect around Soltanabad near Sabzevar. Altaic, Turkic, Southern, Turkish. Dialects: WEST QUCHANI (NORTHWEST QUCHANI), NORTH QUCHANI (NORTHEAST QUCHANI), SOUTH QUCHANI. Midway linguistically between Azerbaijani and Turkmen, but not a dialect of either. Oghuz-Uzbek in Uzbekistan is reported to be a dialect of this. Bilingualism in Farsi. Not a literary language, but the government broadcasts in Quchani. Different from Khorasani, a local Persian dialect in Khorasan. Muslim.

KHUNSARI [KFM] Indo-European, Indo-Iranian, Iranian, Western, Northwestern, Central Iran. Distinct from Kumzari of Oman. Muslim.

KORESH-E ROSTAM [OKH] Eastern Azerbaijan Province, Koresh-e Rostam District. Indo-European, Indo-Iranian, Iranian, Western, Northwestern, Talysh. Related to Shahrudi and Kajali. Muslim.

KOROSHI [KTL] 160 to 200, or 40 to 50 families (Mohamedi). Indo-European, Indo-Iranian, Iranian, Western, Northwestern, Balochi. Appears to be Baluchi with some features of Farsi. They work for the Qashqai people. Camel keepers.

KURDI ***(KURDY, SOUTHERN KURDISH, SORANI, KORKORA, WÂWÂ)*** [KDB] 3,250,000 in Iran. Northwest Iran, primarily Kordestan, Kermanshahan, West Azerbaijan provinces; also a large number in northeast Iran, in the very north of Khorasan Province. Indo-European, Indo-Iranian, Iranian, Western, Northwestern, Kurdish. Dialects: KERMANSHAHI, MUKRI, JAFI. 90% are settled in cities or villages, 10% are nomadic. Jafi may be a separate language. Taught at 2 universities. Language of wider communication. Literacy rate in second language: All people: 1%, boys: 15%. Arabic script used in Iran and Iraq. Muslim (mainly Sunni, some Shi'a), Christian. NT 1994. See main entry under Iraq.

KURMANJI ***(NORTHERN KURDISH, KERMANJI, KIRMANJI)*** [KUR] 200,000 in Iran (1983 estimate). Mountain villages along the Turkey border region in the west of West Azerbaijan Province. Indo-European, Indo-Iranian, Iranian, Western, Northwestern, Kurdish. Teaching Kurmanji is prohibited in Iranian schools (Time 4/1/91). Roman script used in Turkey; Arabic in Syria, Iran, Iraq; Cyrillic in Russia. Armenian script not used now. Muslim. NT 1872. See main entry under Turkey.

LARI ***(LARESTANI)*** [LRL] Indo-European, Indo-Iranian, Iranian, Western, Southwestern, Fars. Muslim.

LASGERDI [LSA] In Lasgerd. Indo-European, Indo-Iranian, Iranian, Western, Northwestern, Semnani. Related to Sorkhei. Dictionary. Muslim.

LURI ***(LUR, LOR, LORI)*** [LRI] 4,280,000 in Iran (1993) including 680,000 Bakhtiari (1989). Population total all countries 4,280,000 or more. Southwestern Iran, Lorestan and Ilam. Khorramabad is an important political and economic center. Borujerd is also a center. The Bakhtiari migrate mainly from Bakhtiari and Esfahan provinces (summer) to Khuzestan (winter). Mamasani and Kurdshuli in Fars Province; Bovir-Ahmadi in Boyer-Ahmadi Kohgiluyeh Province. Also spoken in Iraq, USA. Indo-European, Indo-Iranian, Iranian, Western, Southwestern, Luri. Dialects: LURI, FEYLI, LEKI (LAKI,

ALAKI), BAKHTIARI, KELHURI. Closely related to Kumzari. Bilingualism in Farsi. Ethnic groups: Lor, Bakhtiari (Haftlang, Chaharlang), Mamasani (perhaps 75,000 in 1982), Bovir-Ahmadi and Kuhgiluyeh (200,000 in 1982). Posht-Kuh: nomadic, Pish-Kuh: agriculturalists, Bakhtiari Haft-Lang: nomadic pastoralists: sheep, Bakhtiari Cahr-Lang: settled. Shi'a Muslim.

MANDAIC ***(MANDAEAN, NEO-MANDAIC, MODERN MANDAIC, MANDA:YI, MANDI, SUBBI, SA'IBA)*** [MID] 800 to 1,000 speakers in Iran, out of an ethnic group of 5,000 in Khuzistan, Iran who speak Western Farsi. 23,000 ethnic Mandaeans in Iraq all speak Arabic (1994 H. Mutzafi), but some people are reported to be bilingual in Mandaic. Population total both countries 800 to 1,000. Khuzistan. Speakers reported in Khuzistan in the 1960s. Ethnic Mandaeans in Iraq now do not speak Mandaic. Assyrians in the USA report Mandaic speakers there, whom they call 'Yokhananaye'. Also spoken in Iraq. Afro-Asiatic, Semitic, Central, Aramaic, Eastern, Mandaic. Dialects: AHWAZ (AHVAZ), SHUSHTAR, IRAQI NEO-MANDAIC. Little dialect variation. Bilingualism in Western Farsi. Speakers are older bilingual people. Iraqi Neo-Mandaic is extinct. Shustar may be extinct. Mandaic script used. Mandaism (Gnostic).

MANDAIC, CLASSICAL ***(CLASSICAL MANDAEAN)*** [MYZ] Also used in Iraq and small communities in the USA and Australia (300 Mandaeans in Sydney in 1995). Afro-Asiatic, Semitic, Central, Aramaic, Eastern, Mandaic. Appears to be the direct ancestor of Modern Mandaic. The liturgical language used by followers of the Mandaean religion. Mandaic script used. Mandaism. Extinct.

MARAGHEI [VMH] Upper Rudbar area (Rudbare Alamut). Indo-European, Indo-Iranian, Iranian, Western, Northwestern, Talysh. Dialect: DIKINI. Various dialects. Close to Gozarkhani. Muslim.

MAZANDERANI ***(TABRI)*** [MZN] 3,265,000, or 4.7% of the population (1993). Northern Iran near Caspian Sea, southern half of Mazandaran Province. Indo-European, Indo-Iranian, Iranian, Western, Northwestern, Caspian. Related to Gilaki. Qadikolahi (Ghadikolahi) and Palani may be dialects. Bilingualism in Farsi. The educated can read Farsi well. Agriculturalists, fishermen. Shi'a Muslim.

NATANZI [NTZ] Indo-European, Indo-Iranian, Iranian, Western, Northwestern, Central Iran. Muslim.

NAYINI [NYQ] Indo-European, Indo-Iranian, Iranian, Western, Northwestern, Central Iran. Muslim.

PARSI-DARI ***(PARSEE-DARI)*** [PRD] Population total both countries 350,000 or more. Also spoken in Afghanistan. Indo-European, Indo-Iranian, Iranian, Western, Northwestern, Central Iran. Parsi-Dari is reported to not be inherently intelligible with Parsi of India, Pakistan, and other countries, but linguistically and ethnically related. Separated 600 to 700 years ago or more from that. It is related to Dari [GBZ]. Many are reported to not speak other languages well. 'Parsee' is the name of the ethnic group. Zoroastrian.

PASHTO, SOUTHERN ***(PASHTU, PAKTU)*** [PBT] 113,000 in Iran (1993). Khorasan on Afghanistan border east of Qa'en. Indo-European, Indo-Iranian, Iranian, Eastern, Southeastern, Pashto. Different from Northern Pashto of Pakistan and India. Sunni Muslim. See main entry under Afghanistan.

PERSIAN SIGN LANGUAGE [PSC] Deaf sign language. Dictionary.

QASHQA'I ***(QASHQAY, QASHQAI, KASHKAI)*** [QSQ] 1,500,000 (1997), or 2.38% of the population (1997). Southwestern Iran, Fars Province; southern pasture in winter, northern in summer. Shiraz is a center. Altaic, Turkic, Southern, Azerbaijani. Very close to Azerbaijani. Many are bilingual in Farsi. Nomadic. Many can read Farsi well. Desert. Rug weavers, pastoralists: sheep, donkeys, camels. Shi'a Muslim.

RASHTI [RSH] Rasht city, the provincial capital of Gilan. Indo-European, Indo-Iranian, Iranian, Western, Northwestern, Caspian. Closely related to Gilaki, but significantly different enough to need separate literature. 'Real' Gilaki of the countryside is not intelligible to speakers of Rashti. Speakers are fairly bilingual in Farsi. Heavy influence from Farsi.

RAZAJERDI [RAT] Qazvin Kuhpaye area, Razajerd. Indo-European, Indo-Iranian, Iranian, Western, Northwestern, Talysh. Various dialects. Related to Takestani. Muslim.

ROMANI, BALKAN [RMN] Indo-European, Indo-Iranian, Indo-Aryan, Central zone, Romani, Balkan. Dialect: ZARGARI. Also see Western Farsi in Iran concerning a Zargari. Muslim. Bible portions 1912-1937. See main entry under Yugoslavia.

RUDBARI [RDB] Sefid Rud Valley. Indo-European, Indo-Iranian, Iranian, Western, Northwestern, Talysh. Various dialects. Transitional to Caspian languages and related to Vafsi. Muslim.

SALCHUQ [SLQ] Altaic, Turkic, Southern, Azerbaijani. Probably a dialect of Azerbaijani. Investigation needed: intelligibility with Azerbaijani. Muslim.

SANGISARI ***(SANGESARI)*** [SGR] Indo-European, Indo-Iranian, Iranian, Western, Northwestern, Semnani. Dictionary. Muslim.

SEMNANI [SMJ] Indo-European, Indo-Iranian, Iranian, Western, Northwestern, Semnani. Dictionary. Muslim.

SENAYA ***(SENA:YA, CHRISTIAN NEO-ARAMAIC, SHAN SRAY, LSHAN SRAY, SORAY, SRAY, SHAN GYANAN)*** [SYN] 60 in Iran (1997 H. Mutzafi). Population total all countries 500. Teheran and Qazwin. Originally in Sanandaj, Iranian Kurdistan. Some in western Europe. Also spoken in Australia, USA. Afro-Asiatic, Semitic, Central, Aramaic, Eastern, Central, Northeastern. The variety in Qazwin is slightly different from that spoken by Sanandaj-born people. Bilingualism in Assyrian Neo-Aramaic. Gradually becoming extinct. Syriac script used. Christian (Chaldean).

SHAHMIRZADI [SRZ] Shahmirzad. Indo-European, Indo-Iranian, Iranian, Western, Northwestern, Caspian. Close to Mazanderani and Gilaki. Dictionary.

SHAHRUDI [SHM] Khalkhal District in Eastern Azerbaijan Province, Shahrud District, Shal, Kolur, Lerd. Indo-European, Indo-Iranian, Iranian, Western, Northwestern, Talysh. Close to Kajali and Koresh-e Rostam. Not a Western Farsi dialect. Muslim.

SHIKAKI [SHF] Indo-European, Indo-Iranian, Iranian, Western, Northwestern, Kurdish. Possibly a dialect of Kurmanji. Muslim. See main entry under Iraq.

SIVANDI [SIY] Indo-European, Indo-Iranian, Iranian, Western, Northwestern, Central Iran. Muslim.

SOI [SOJ] Indo-European, Indo-Iranian, Iranian, Western, Northwestern, Central Iran. Muslim.

SORKHEI [SQO] In Sorkhe. Indo-European, Indo-Iranian, Iranian, Western, Northwestern, Semnani. Related to Lasgerdi. Dictionary. Muslim.

TAKESTANI *(TAKISTANI)* [TKS] 220,000. Various towns and villages in the mainly Azerbaijani- speaking region from Khalkhal to Saveh, especially in Takestan and villages to the south and southeast. Indo-European, Indo-Iranian, Iranian, Western, Northwestern, Talysh. Dialects: KHALKHAL, TAROM, ZANJAN, KHARAQAN, RAMAND (TAKESTAN). Close to Talysh, especially Khalkhal dialect. Bilingualism in Farsi. Different from Tat of Russia, Azerbaijan, and Iran. Muslim.

TALYSH *(TALISH, TALESH, TALISHI)* [TLY] 112,000 in Iran (1993). Along the Caspian Sea up to Kepri-chal, northwest Gilan Province along coastal plain. Northern Talyshi is centered around Astara and the Caspian littoral in Azerbaijan; Central Talyshi is centered around the Asalem-Hashtpar area along the Caspian littoral in northwestern Iran; Southern Talyshi is centered around Shandermen, Masal, Masule, and surrounding mountainous areas in Gilan Province. Indo-European, Indo-Iranian, Iranian, Western, Northwestern, Talysh. Dialects: NORTHERN TALYSHI, CENTRAL TALYSHI, SOUTHERN TALYSHI. The dialects listed may be separate languages. Close to Harzani. Agajani and Sasani may be dialects. Bilingualism in Farsi. Muslim. See main entry under Azerbaijan.

TAROMI, UPPER [TIB] Upper Tarom of Zanjan Province, Hazarrud, Siavarud. Indo-European, Indo-Iranian, Iranian, Western, Northwestern, Talysh. Various dialects. Close to Kabatei. Muslim.

TAT, MUSLIM *(MUSSULMAN TATI)* [TTT] 8,000 in Iran. Indo-European, Indo-Iranian, Iranian, Western, Southwestern, Tat. Difficult intelligibility with Judeo-Tat. There may be a Christian dialect. They use Azerbaijani as a literary language in Azerbaijan. Not written. Different from Takestani of Iran. Shi'a Muslim. See main entry under Azerbaijan.

TURKMEN *(TORKOMANI)* [TCK] 2,000,000 in Iran (1997), or 3.17% of the population (1997). Northeast, mainly in Mazandaran Province, along the Turkmenistan border; important centers are Gonbad-e Kavus and Pahlavi Dezh. Altaic, Turkic, Southern, Turkmenian. Dialects: ANAULI, KHASARLI, NEREZIM, NOKHURLI (NOHUR), CHAVDUR, ESARI (ESARY), GOKLEN (GOKLAN), SALYR, SARYQ, TEKE (TEKKE), YOMUD (YOMUT), TRUKMEN. Bilingualism in Farsi. Not a literary language in Iran. Many are semi-nomadic. Ethnic groups: Yomut, Goklan. They could read Arabic script. Radio programs. Agriculturalists: cotton, wheat, barley; cattle. Hanafi Sunni and Shi'a Muslim; Goklan and Yomut: Shi'a Muslim. Bible portions 1880-1982. See main entry under Turkmenistan.

VAFSI [VAF] Central Province, Arak District, Vafs, Tafres area. Indo-European, Indo-Iranian, Iranian, Western, Northwestern, Central Iran. Various dialects. Transitional between central Iranian dialects and Talysh; very close to Ashtiani. Bilingualism in Western Farsi. Muslim.

IRAQ

Republic of Iraq, al Jumhouriya al'Iraqia. National or official languages: Standard Arabic, Kurdi. 21,800,000 (1998 UN). Literacy rate 60% to 70%. Also includes Egyptian Spoken Arabic 450,000, Mandaic, Syriac, Turkish 3,000, Turkmen 227,000, Turoyo 3,000. Information mainly from A. M. Maclean 1893; T. Sebeok 1963; T. M. Johnstone 1967; H. Kloss and G. McConnell 1974; O. Jastrow 1978; W. Fischer and O. Jastrow 1980; B. Ingham 1982; R. D. Hobermann 1988a, b; M. Izadi 1993. Shi'a Muslim, Sunni Muslim, Yezidi, Christian. Blind population 75,000 (1982 WCE). Deaf population 1,205,930. Deaf institutions: 5. Data accuracy estimate: C. The number of languages listed for Iraq is 23. Of those, all are living languages. Diversity index 0.65.

ADYGHE *(WEST CIRCASSIAN, ADYGEY)* [ADY] 19,000 in Iraq (1993). North Caucasian, Northwest, Circassian. Sunni Muslim. NT 1992. See main entry under Russia.

ARABIC, GULF SPOKEN *(KHALIJI, GULF ARABIC)* [AFB] 40,000 in Iraq. Population total all countries 2,440,000 (1995). In and around Zubair and on the Fau Peninsula. Also spoken in Bahrain, Iran, Kuwait, Oman, Qatar, Saudi Arabia, UAE, Yemen. Afro-Asiatic, Semitic, Central, South, Arabic. Dialect: ZUBAIR-FAAU ARABIC.

ARABIC, JUDEO-IRAQI ***(IRAQI JUDEO-ARABIC, JEWISH IRAQI-BAGHDADI ARABIC, ARABI, YAHUDIC)*** [YHD] 100 to 150 in Iraq (1992 H. Mutzafi). Most in Israel. Afro-Asiatic, Semitic, Central, South, Arabic. Not intelligible with Judeo-Arabic of Libya, Judeo-Arabic of Tunisia, or Morocco. Close to North Mesopotamian Arabic. All are elderly (1992). Jewish. See main entry under Israel.

ARABIC, MESOPOTAMIAN SPOKEN ***(MESOPOTAMIAN QELTU ARABIC, MESOPOTAMIAN GELET ARABIC, BAGHDADI ARABIC, IRAQI ARABIC, FURATI)*** [ACM] 11,500,000 in Iraq. Population total all countries 13,900,000. Tigris and Euphrates clusters are in Iraq. Also spoken in Iran, Jordan, Syria, Turkey (Asia). Afro-Asiatic, Semitic, Central, South, Arabic. Dialects: ANATOLIAN CLUSTER, TIGRIS CLUSTER, EUPHRATES CLUSTER. Geographical and sectarian divisions correlate with Iraqi dialects. The vernacular standard is forming based on Baghdad speech. There are also Bedouin dialects. Nearly unintelligible to speakers of certain other vernacular Arabic varieties. National language. SVO. Radio programs, TV. Shi'a Muslim, Sunni Muslim, Christian, Jewish, Yazidi.

ARABIC, NAJDI SPOKEN [ARS] 900,000 in Iraq. Central Najdi is spoken by bedouin in the western desert, North Najdi by bedouin in the south between the rivers up to the Syrian border. Afro-Asiatic, Semitic, Central, South, Arabic. Dialects: NORTH NAJDI (SHAMMAR), CENTRAL NAJDI. See main entry under Saudi Arabia.

ARABIC, NORTH MESOPOTAMIAN SPOKEN ***(SYRO-MESOPOTAMIAN VERNACULAR ARABIC, MOSLAWI, MESOPOTAMIAN QELTU ARABIC)*** [AYP] 5,400,000 in Iraq. Population total all countries 6,300,000 (1992). Along most of the Tigris and part of the Euphrates valleys north of Baghdad. Also spoken in Jordan, Syria, Turkey (Asia). Afro-Asiatic, Semitic, Central, South, Arabic. Very close to Judeo-Iraqi Arabic, but there are important sociolinguistic differences. Muslim, Christian.

ARABIC, STANDARD [ABV] Middle East, North Africa. Afro-Asiatic, Semitic, Central, South, Arabic. Used for education, official purposes. National language. Newspapers. Bible 1984-1991. See main entry under Saudi Arabia.

ARMENIAN [ARM] 60,000 in Iraq. Indo-European, Armenian. Dialect: WESTERN ARMENIAN. Christian. Bible 1853-1978. See main entry under Armenia.

ASSYRIAN NEO-ARAMAIC ***(LISHANA ATURAYA, SURET, SURETH, SURYAYA SWADAYA, ASSYRIAN, NEO-SYRIAC, ASSYRISKI, AISORSKI, ASSYRIANCI)*** [AII] 30,000 in Iraq (1994) out of up to a reported 2,000,000 ethnic population. Population total all countries 210,000 or more speakers. 4,250,000 reported ethnic population. Northern Iraq, Baghdad, Basrah, Karkuk, Arbil. Also spoken in 25 other countries including Armenia, Australia, Austria, Azerbaijan, Belgium, Brazil, Canada, Cyprus, France, Georgia, Germany, Greece, Iran, Italy, Lebanon, Netherlands, New Zealand, Russia (Europe), Sweden. Afro-Asiatic, Semitic, Central, Aramaic, Eastern, Central, Northeastern. Inherent intelligibility is hard to estimate due to intense exposure of most speakers throughout the Assyrian diaspora to many dialects, especially to Urmi and Iraqi Koine. Only because of this exposure is actual intelligibility between different dialects as high as 80% to 90%. Subdialects of the Urmian group: Urmi, Sipurghan, Solduz; of the Northern Group: Salamas, Van, Jilu, Gavar, Qudshanis, Upper Barwari, Dez, Baz; of the Central Group: Mar Bishu, Nochiya (Shamezdin), Tergawar, Anhar; of the Western Group: Upper Tiari, Lower Tiari, Tkhuma, Lower Barwari, Tal, Lewin. Standard literary Assyrian is based on Urmi. Many speakers have left the original areas and have developed a common spoken and written form based on the prestigious Urmi dialect as spoken by those from Iraq living in Baghdad, Chicago, and elsewhere (Iraqi Koine). Most Christians understand it. The Urmi subdialect of this language is different from the Urmi subdialect of Lishán Didán. In some countries young people speak the language of that country, not Assyrian Neo-Aramaic. The Assyrian and Chaldean separated denominationally in the 16th century. Radio programs. Christian: Nestorian (vast majority), also other sects or denominations. Bible 1852-1919.

AZERBAIJANI, SOUTH [AZB] 300,000 to 900,000 or more in Iraq (1982 estimate). Kirkuk city, Arbil, Rowanduz, towns and villages southeast from Kirkuk as far as Al Miqdadiyah, Khanaqin, and Mandali; also several places in the Mosul region. Altaic, Turkic, Southern, Azerbaijani. Dialect: KIRKUK. Significant differences from North Azerbaijani in Azerbaijan. They speak South Azerbaijani at home and within their own group. There is little literature. They are called 'Turkmen' or 'Turks' in Iraq and Syria. Many read Arabic or Kurdish. Most are illiterate in South Azerbaijani. Written in Arabic script. Muslim. See main entry under Iran.

BAJELAN ***(BAJALANI, GURANI, SHABAK, CHICHAMACHU)*** [BJM] 20,000 (1976 Sara). Indo-European, Indo-Iranian, Iranian, Western, Northwestern, Zaza-Gorani. Closer to Dimli than to Kurdish. Muslim.

BEHDINI ***(BAHDINI, BANDINANI, KURDISH BANDINANI)*** [BDF] Also spoken in Germany. Indo-European, Indo-Iranian, Iranian, Western, Northwestern, Kurdish. Muslim.

CHALDEAN NEO-ARAMAIC ***(CHALDEAN, KILDANI, KALDAYA, NEO-CHALDEAN, MODERN CHALDEAN, SURETH, LISHANA KALDAYA, FELLIHI, FALLANI)*** [CLD] 100,000 to 120,000 in Iraq (1994). Population total all countries 200,000 (1994 H. Mutzafi). Originally in central western and northern Iraqi Kurdistan and some in bordering Turkey. Now in Mosul, Baghdad, Basrah, southeastern Iraqi Kurdistan. Also spoken in Australia, Belgium, Canada, Germany, Lebanon, Netherlands, Sweden, Syria, Turkey (Asia), USA. Afro-Asiatic, Semitic, Central, Aramaic, Eastern, Central, Northeastern. Dialects: MANGESH, ALQOSH, TEL KEPE, TISQOPA, BARTILLE, SHIRNAK-CHIZRE (BOHTAN), ARADHIN, DIHOK. High intelligibility with Lishana Deni and Ashirat (western dialect group of Assyrian Neo-Aramaic); low to none with other Northeastern Aramaic varieties. Comprehension among all of these improves with contact. The ethnic group is distinct denominationally from speakers of other Northeastern Aramaic varieties; separated from the Assyrian during the 16th century. The names 'Chaldean' and 'Assyrian' are sometimes each used in a popular sense to include both groups. Syriac script used. Christian (Chaldean, Uniate Catholic, Syrian Orthodox). Bible portions 1992.

DOMARI ***(MIDDLE EASTERN ROMANI)*** [RMT] 50,000 in Iraq (1970). Indo-European, Indo-Iranian, Indo-Aryan, Central zone, Dom. People called 'Zott'. Muslim. See main entry under Iran.

FARSI, WESTERN ***(PERSIAN)*** [PES] 227,000 in Iraq (1993), 1.2% of the population (1989). Indo-European, Indo-Iranian, Iranian, Western, Southwestern, Persian. Muslim. Bible 1838-1995. See main entry under Iran.

HAWRAMI ***(HAWRAMANI, GURANI, GORANI)*** [HAC] Also spoken in Iran. Indo-European, Indo-Iranian, Iranian, Western, Northwestern, Zaza-Gorani. Closest to Dimli of Turkey. Both are different from Kurdish languages. Yazdani.

HERKI [HEK] Also spoken in Iran, Turkey (Asia). Indo-European, Indo-Iranian, Iranian, Western, Northwestern, Kurdish. Considered a dialect of Kurmanji. Muslim.

KOY SANJAQ SURAT ***(KOI SANJAQ SOORIT, KOY SANJAQ SOORET)*** [KQD] 800 to 1,000 (1995 H. Mutzafi). Northern Iraq, town of Koi-Sanjaq and nearby village of Armota. Afro-Asiatic, Semitic, Central, Aramaic, Eastern, Central, Northeastern. Related in certain morphological and lexical respects to Senaya. Speakers call their language 'Surat'. Investigation needed: intelligibility. Syriac script. Christian (Chaldean, Uniate Catholic).

KURDI ***(KURDY, SOUTHERN KURDISH, SORANI, SURANI)*** [KDB] 2,785,500 in Iraq, 18% of population including all Kurdish in Iraq, most of whom speak Kurdi (1986). Population total all countries 6,036,000. All Kurd speakers in all countries: 11,000,000 (1999 WA). In and around Sulamanya. Also spoken in Iran, USA. Indo-European, Indo-Iranian, Iranian, Western, Northwestern, Kurdish. Dialects: ARBILI, KHUSHNAW, PIZHDAR, MUKRI, GARRUSI (BIJBRI), ARDAIÂNI (SANANDAJI), SULAYMÂNI (SULEIMANIYE), WARMÂWA, GARMIYÂNI, KOLYÂ'I, ZANGANA, KIRMÂNSHÂHI. Sorani is mainly in Iraq. Official language. Literacy rate in second language: 27%. Other reports are that many are well educated. Sunni and Shi'a Muslim; Ahl-e-haqq groups in 3 districts in south and southeast Kurdistan, mainly around Kermanshah and Kerkuk; 50,000 Yezidis in northern Iraq near Mosul and in the Sinjar Hills. NT 1994.

KURMANJI ***(NORTHERN KURDISH, KERMANJI, KIRMANJI)*** [KUR] Indo-European, Indo-Iranian, Iranian, Western, Northwestern, Kurdish. Dialects: HAKARI, JEZIRE (BOTAN). A distinct language from Kurdi (Southern Kurdish). Language of wider communication. Roman script used in Turkey; Arabic script in Syria, Iran, and Iraq; Cyrillic script in former USSR. Armenian script is not used now. Muslim. NT 1872. See main entry under Turkey.

LURI ***(LUR, LORI)*** [LRI] Indo-European, Indo-Iranian, Iranian, Western, Southwestern, Luri. Dialects: LURI, FEYLI, LEKI, BAKHTIARI. Closely related to Kumzari of Oman. Muslim. See main entry under Iran.

SHIKAKI [SHF] Also spoken in Iran, Turkey (Asia). Indo-European, Indo-Iranian, Iranian, Western, Northwestern, Kurdish. Considered a dialect of Kurmanji. Muslim.

SURCHI [SUP] Indo-European, Indo-Iranian, Iranian, Western, Northwestern, Kurdish. Possibly a dialect of Kurmanji. Also shares features with Kurdi.

ISRAEL

State of Israel, Medinat Israel. National or official languages: Hebrew, Standard Arabic, English. 5,984,000 (1998 UN), including 4,700,000 Jewish (1997), 805,000 Muslim, 160,000 Christian, 95,000 Druze, 300 Samaritan (1995 Central Statistics Dept., Israel). About half the Jewish people are Sephardi and half Ashkenazi. Literacy rate 88% to 92% (Jewish), 70% (Arab). Also includes Egyptian Spoken Arabic 25,000, Levantine Bedawi Spoken Arabic 50,000, North Levantine Spoken Arabic 100,000, Bulgarian, Czech, Dutch 1,680, Western Farsi, French 40,000, Italian 5,435, Malayalam 8,000, Marathi 8,000, Samaritan, Samaritan Aramaic, Spanish 60,000, Turkish 30,000, Northern Uzbek, Many other languages. Information mainly from D. Gold 1974; H. Kloss and G. McConnell 1974; H. Paper 1978; W. Fischer and O. Jastrow 1980; T. K. Harris 1994; J. Fishman 1985, 1991; J. Chetrit 1985; D. Cohen 1985; B. Comrie 1987; A. Saenz-Badillos 1993; P. E. Miller 1993; Y. Mutzafi 1992-1999. Jewish, Muslim,

Christian, Druze. Blind population 5,285. Deaf population 4,500 to 306,242 (1998). Deaf institutions: 31. The number of languages listed for Israel is 36. Of those, 33 are living languages and 3 are extinct. Diversity index 0.65.

ADYGHE ***(WEST CIRCASSIAN, ADYGEY)*** [ADY] 3,000 in Israel (1987). Kafr Kama and Rehaniya, small border villages. North Caucasian, Northwest, Circassian. Very slight dialect differences between the two villages. They understand radio programs in Adyghe from Jordan. Closest to Kabardian. Bilingualism in South Levantine Arabic. They came about 100 years ago from the Caucasus (now Russia). They call themselves 'Circassian'. SOV. Sunni Muslim. NT 1992. See main entry under Russia.

AMHARIC [AMH] 40,000 in Israel (1994 H. Mutzafi). Afro-Asiatic, Semitic, South, Ethiopian, South, Transversal. Bilingualism in Hebrew. Spoken by Jews of Ethiopian origin. They call themselves 'Beta Israel', and consider "Falasha" pejorative. Radio programs. Jewish. Bible 1840-1988. See main entry under Ethiopia.

ARABIC, JUDEO-IRAQI ***(IRAQI JUDEO-ARABIC, JEWISH IRAQI-BAGHDADI ARABIC, ARABI, YAHUDIC)*** [YHD] 100,000 to 120,000 in Israel (1994 H. Mutzafi). Population total all countries 105,000 to 125,000. Originally from Iraq. Also spoken in India, Iraq, United Kingdom. Afro-Asiatic, Semitic, Central, South, Arabic. Not intelligible with Judeo-Tripolitanian Arabic, Judeo-Tunisian Arabic, or Judeo-Moroccan Arabic. Close to Baghdadi Arabic. Speakers in Israel are reported to be bilingual in Hebrew. Over 40 years old (1994 H. Mutzafi). The term 'Yahudic' is used by a few scholars to denote all Judeo-Arabic languages. Investigation needed: intelligibility with North Mesopotamian Arabic. Hebrew script used. Jewish.

ARABIC, JUDEO-MOROCCAN [AJU] 250,000 in Israel (1992 H. Mutzafi). Population total all countries 254,000. Also spoken in Canada, France, Morocco. Afro-Asiatic, Semitic, Central, South, Arabic. Many dialects. Much intelligibility with Tunisian Judeo-Arabic, some with Judeo-Tripolitanian Arabic, but none with Judeo-Iraqi Arabic. Speakers in Israel are reported to be bilingual in Hebrew. Large number of borrowings from Spanish, Ladino, French. Investigation needed: intelligibility with Tunisian Judeo-Arabic, Moroccan Spoken Arabic, bilingual proficiency in Hebrew. Hebrew script used. Radio programs. Jewish.

ARABIC, JUDEO-TRIPOLITANIAN ***(TRIPOLITANIAN JUDEO-ARABIC, JEWISH TRIPOLITANIAN-LIBYAN ARABIC, TRIPOLITA'IT, YUDI)*** [YUD] 30,000 in Israel, most over 40 (1994 H. Mutzafi). Population total both countries 35,000. Originally from Tripolitania, Libya. None left in Libya. Also spoken in Italy. Afro-Asiatic, Semitic, Central, South, Arabic. Not intelligible with Judeo-Iraqi Arabic. Medium intelligibility with Judeo-Tunisian Arabic and Judeo-Morocco Arabic. Speakers in Israel are reported to be bilingual in Hebrew. Hebrew script used. Jewish.

ARABIC, JUDEO-TUNISIAN [AJT] 45,000 in Israel (1995 H. Mutzafi). Population total all countries 45,500. Also spoken in France, Italy, Spain, Tunisia, USA. Afro-Asiatic, Semitic, Central, South, Arabic. A lexicon of 5,000 words in 1950 had 79% words of Arabic origin, 15% Romance loan words, 4.4% Hebrew loan words, 1.6% others (D. Cohen 1985.254). In Israel the generation of immigrants is reported to be bilingual in Hebrew. Older speakers. Younger generation has only passive knowledge of Judeo-Tunisian Arabic. Investigation needed: intelligibility with Judeo-Moroccan Arabic, Tunisian Spoken Arabic. Hebrew script used. Jewish. Bible portions 1897-1937.

ARABIC, JUDEO-YEMENI ***(JUDEO-YEMENI, YEMENITE JUDEO-ARABIC)*** [JYE] 50,000 in Israel (1995 Y. Kara). Population total both countries 51,000. Also spoken in Yemen. Afro-Asiatic, Semitic, Central, South, Arabic. Dialects: SAN<A, <ADEN, BE:DA, HABBAN. Language varieties are all markedly different from their coterritorial Muslim ones. Hebrew script used. Jewish.

ARABIC, SOUTH LEVANTINE SPOKEN ***(LEVANTINE, PALESTANIAN-JORDANIAN ARABIC)*** [AJP] 910,000 in Israel. Afro-Asiatic, Semitic, Central, South, Arabic. Dialects: MADANI, FELLAHI. Distinct from North Levantine Arabic. Bilingualism in Hebrew. A few hundred speakers are of Gypsy origin. Literacy rate in second language: 90% in Arabic, 60% in Hebrew. Muslim, Christian, Jews, Druze. Bible portions 1940-1973. See main entry under Jordan.

ARABIC, STANDARD [ABV] Middle East, North Africa. Afro-Asiatic, Semitic, Central, South, Arabic. Used for education and communication among Arabic speaking countries. National language. Bible 1984-1991. See main entry under Saudi Arabia.

ARMENIAN ***(HAIEREN, SOMKHURI, ERMENICE, ARMJANSKI)*** [ARM] 3,000 in Israel (1971 The Armenian Review). Jerusalem. Indo-European, Armenian. Dialect: WESTERN ARMENIAN. Bilingualism in South Levantine Arabic. Eastern Armenian is spoken in Armenia, Turkey, and Iran; Western in other countries, including Israel. SVO. Christian. Bible 1853-1978. See main entry under Armenia.

BABYLONIAN TALMUDIC ARAMAIC [BYA] Afro-Asiatic, Semitic, Central, Aramaic, Eastern, Central, Northeastern. The language of the Babylonian Talmud and other sacred Jewish works. Familiar among students of Judaism in both religious and scholarly realms, and studied diligently by most Orthodox Jewish young men. Used widely in Jewish culture and life. Extinct.

BIJIL NEO-ARAMAIC ***(LISHANID JANAN)*** [BJF] About 10 semi-speakers (1998 Hezy Mutzafi). Afro-Asiatic, Semitic, Central, Aramaic, Eastern, Central, Northeastern. The last vigorous speaker died in 1998, age over 80. All the other speakers are over 60, her relatives, and still have varying competence in this language. They heard it from one parent, while the other parent was a Kurdish or Arabic native speaker. In 1951 it was spoken among the 8 Jewish families of Bijil, a village in Iraqi Kurdistan. All imigrated to Israel in 1951. They are all competent in Hebrew and Kurdish, which they speak as their primary languages, and some speak other Neo-Aramaic languages. Extinct.

BUKHARIC ***(BOKHARIC, BUKHARIAN, BOKHARAN, BUKHARAN, JUDEO-TAJIK)*** [BHH] 50,000 in Israel (1995 H. Mutzafi). Population total all countries 60,000. Also spoken in USA, Uzbekistan. Indo-European, Indo-Iranian, Iranian, Western, Southwestern, Persian. Related to Tajiki Persian. May be easily intelligible with Tajiki or Farsi. Also close to Judeo-Persian. Many are recent immigrants (1995). Investigation needed: intelligibility, bilingual proficiency. Hebrew script used. Radio programs. Jewish.

DOMARI ***(DOM, NEAR-EASTERN GYPSY)*** [RMT] 2,000 including Palestinian West Bank and Gaza (1997 Yaron Matras). Mainly Jerusalem (Old City), Bir Zeit near Ramallah, and Gaza. Indo-European, Indo-Iranian, Indo-Aryan, Central zone, Dom. Dialect: NAWARI. Not intelligible to Romani speakers. Bilingualism in South Levantine Spoken Arabic. The first language of children in some places. They call themselves 'Dom'. A large number of loan words from Arabic, Kurdish, and some other Iranian languages. Grammar. Muslim. See main entry under Iran.

DZHIDI ***(JUDEO-PERSIAN)*** [DZH] 60,000 in Israel (1995). Population total both countries 60,000 or more. Also spoken in Iran. Indo-European, Indo-Iranian, Iranian, Western, Southwestern, Persian. Close to Bukharic, Western Farsi. Many are speakers of Western Farsi. Jewish.

ENGLISH ***(ANGLIT)*** [ENG] 100,000 in Israel (1993). Indo-European, Germanic, West, English. Official language. Bible 1535-1989. See main entry under United Kingdom.

HEBREW ***(IVRIT)*** [HBR] 4,847,000 in Israel (1998), or 81% of the population (1995). Population total all countries 5,150,000. Also spoken in Australia, Canada, Germany, Palestinian West Bank and Gaza, Panama, United Kingdom, USA. Afro-Asiatic, Semitic, Central, South, Canaanite. Dialects: STANDARD HEBREW (GENERAL ISRAELI, EUROPEANIZED HEBREW), ORIENTAL HEBREW (ARABIZED HEBREW, YEMENITE HEBREW). Not a direct offspring from Biblical or other varieties of Ancient Hebrew, but an amalgamation of different Hebrew strata plus intrinsic evolution within the living speech. Some who use it as primary language now in Israel, learned it as their second language originally. Spoken by all Israelis as first or second language. There is a Hebrew Language Academy. National language. Dictionary. Grammar. SVO. Jewish. Bible 1599-1877.

HEBREW, ANCIENT ***(OLD HEBREW)*** [HBO] Afro-Asiatic, Semitic, Central, South, Canaanite. Used as a liturgical language, and for the text of the Jewish Bible. Jewish. Extinct. Bible portions c. 2000-400 B.C.

HULAULÁ ***(JUDEO-ARAMAIC, LISHANA NOSHAN, LISHANA AXNI, JABALI, KURDIT, GALIGLU, 'ARAMIT, <ARAMIT, HULA HULA)*** [HUY]10,000 in Israel (1999 H. Mutzafi). Population total all countries 10,000 or more. Also spoken in Iran, USA. Afro-Asiatic, Semitic, Central, Aramaic, Eastern, Central, Northeastern. Dialects: SAQIZ, KEREND, SANANDAJ, SULEIMANIYA. Very different and not intelligible with the Christian Aramaic languages or Lishana Deni. 60% to 70% intelligibility with Lishanan and Lishanid Noshan. Many speakers use Hebrew as second language. The older speakers use Kurdish as second language. Originally from Iranian Kurdistan and adjoining areas of Iraq. Investigation needed: intelligibility with Arbil. Hebrew script used. Jewish.

HUNGARIAN [HNG] 70,000 in Israel (1998 H. Mutzafi). Uralic, Finno-Ugric, Ugric, Hungarian. Bilingualism in Hebrew. Elderly speakers use Hebrew as second language but prefer Hungarian. Jewish. Bible 1590-1991. See main entry under Hungary.

ISRAELI SIGN LANGUAGE [ISL] 5,000 users including some hearing persons (1986 Gallaudet Univ.) Deaf sign language. Not derived from and relatively little influence from other sign languages. No special signs have been introduced from outside by educators. Minor dialect variation. Not all deaf use ISL. Interpreters are provided in courts. Some interpretation for college students. Sign language instruction for parents of deaf children. Many sign language classes for hearing people. There is a committee on national sign language, and an organization for sign language teachers. The sign language used in classrooms and that by deaf adults outside is different. The first deaf school was established in Jerusalem in 1934. A fingerspelling system was developed in 1976. Dictionary. Grammar. Employs the Eshkol-Wachmann movement notation system. Films, TV, videos. Jewish.

JUDEO-BERBER [JBE] 2,000 speakers (1992 Podolsky). Formerly High Atlas range, Tifnut and other communities. Speakers went to Israel from 1950 to 1960. Afro-Asiatic, Berber, Northern, Atlas. Monolingual communities may have disappeared before 1930 in Morocco. Speakers also used Judeo-Arabic (J. Chetrit 1985). All are elderly (1992). Hebrew script used. Jewish.

JUDEO-GEORGIAN [JGE] 40,000 to 50,000 in Israel (1995 H. Mutzafi). Population total both countries 60,000 to 70,000. Some have gone elsewhere in the former USSR and to other countries. Also spoken in Georgia. South Caucasian, Georgian. Oriental and Ashkenazic Jews in Georgia live separately. Judeo-Georgian speakers live separately from non-Jewish Georgian speakers. May not be a separate language from Georgian, but a dialect using various Hebrew loan words. Jewish.

JUDEO-TAT ***(JUDEO-TATIC, JEWISH TAT, BIK, DZHUHURIC, JUWRI, JUHURI)*** [TAT] 70,000 in Israel (1998). Population total all countries 101,000. Sderot, Haderah, and Or Akiva, Israel. None in Iran. They are emigrating from the Caucasus Mts. to Israel at the rate of 2,000 a year. Also spoken in Azerbaijan, Russia (Europe). Indo-European, Indo-Iranian, Iranian, Western, Southwestern, Tat. Dialect: DERBEND. Several dialects. Difficult intelligibility with Mussulman Tat. There may also be a Christian dialect. Speakers of Judeo-Tat are called 'Bik'. They call their language 'Juwri' or 'Juhuri'. They are called 'Gorskiye Yevreyi', or 'Mountain Jews' in the Caucasus. Speakers consider the label "Tati" to be pejorative. Tradition says that they have lived in the Caucasus since 722 B.C. Different from Takestani of Iran. Recently private literature uses Hebrew script. Cyrillic script used in Russia. Roman alphabet was used there officially from 1920 to 1940. Agriculturalists: marena grass for dying (traditionally), merchants. Jewish. Bible portions 1980.

KARAIM [KDR] Ethnic group has 20,000 in Israel (1996 Philip E. Miller). Altaic, Turkic, Western, Ponto-Caspian. Close to Karachay and Kumyk. National language of the Karaim. They are descended from a medieval sect of Judaism which rejected the authority of the Talmud and the rabbinic tradition. Cyrillic and Hebrew scripts. Karaim Jewish. Bible portions 1842. See main entry under Lithuania.

LADINO ***(JUDEO SPANISH, SEFARDI, DZHUDEZMO, JUDEZMO, SPANYOL, HAQUETIYA)*** [SPJ] 100,000 or more in Israel (1985). Population total all countries 160,000 or fewer (1992). Ethnic group members also in Salonica, Greece; Sofia, Bulgaria; Yugoslavia. Formerly also in Morocco. Also spoken in Puerto Rico, Turkey (Europe), USA. Indo-European, Italic, Romance, Italo-Western, Western, Gallo-Iberian, Ibero-Romance, West Iberian, Castilian. Dialects: JUDEZMO (JUDYO, JIDYO), LADINO, HAQUETIYA (HAKETIA, HAKETIYA, HAKITIA). The Balkan dialect is more influenced by Turkish and Greek. The North African dialect is more influenced by Arabic and French. There are no monolinguals. It is not the dominant language for most speakers. Formerly the main language of Sefardic Jewry. The name 'Dzhudezmo' is used by Jewish linguists and Turkish Jews; 'Judeo-Spanish' by Romance philologists; 'Ladino' by laymen, especially in Israel; 'Hakitia' by Moroccan Jews; 'Spanyol' by some others. Different from Ladin in the Rhaeto-Romansch group. The Hebrew (Rashi) alphabet does not work well because of the need to differentiate vowels. Yet there are texts in Hebrew script. Newspapers, radio programs. Jewish. Bible 1829, in progress (1999).

LISHÁN DIDÁN ***(LISHANÁN, LISHANID NASH DIDÁN, PERSIAN AZERBAIJAN JEWISH ARAMAIC, LAKHLOKHI, GALIHALU)*** [TRG] 3,000 to 4,000 in Israel (1999 H. Mutzafi). Population total all countries 3,050 to 4,300. Jerusalem and Tel-Aviv area mainly. Originally Iranian Azerbaijan and southeast Turkey. Also spoken in Azerbaijan, Georgia. Afro-Asiatic, Semitic, Central, Aramaic, Eastern, Central, Northeastern. Dialects: NORTHERN CLUSTER LISHÁN DIDÁN, SOUTHERN CLUSTER LISHÁN DIDÁN. 60% to 70% intelligibility with Hulaulá and Lishanid Noshan, but not with other Aramaic languages. Northern cluster subdialects are Urmi, Salmas, Anatolia; southern cluster dialects are Naghada, Ushno, Mahabad. The Urmi subdialect of Lishán Didán is different than the Urmi subdialect of Assyrian Neo-Aramaic. Hebrew is the second language. Some are multilingual. Many are married to nonspeakers. Most speakers older than 50, few below 40. Many loan words from Kurdish, Turkish, Arabic, Persian, Hebrew, and several European languages. Sometimes erroneously called 'Judeo-Kurdish' or 'Azerbaijani Kurdish'. Hebrew script used. Jewish. Bible portions 1950s.

LISHANA DENI ***(JUDEO-ARAMAIC, LISHAN HUDAYE, LISHAN HOZAYE, KURDIT)*** [LSD] 7,000 to 8,000 (1999 H. Mutzafi). Jerusalem and vicinity, including Maoz Tsiyon. Originally from northwest Iraqi Kurdistan. Afro-Asiatic, Semitic, Central, Aramaic, Eastern, Central, Northeastern. Dialects: ZAKHO, AMADIYA, NERWA, DOHUK, ATRUSH, BÉTANURE, SANDU. Resembles Chaldean Neo-Aramaic, but there are differences in morphology and other features. Inherent intelligibility is high between them. Low intelligibility with Ashirat dialects of Assyrian New-Aramaic; not intelligible with other Neo-Aramaic varieties. All over 50 years old (1998). Investigation needed: intelligibility with Chaldean Neo-Aramaic. Hebrew script is used. Jewish. Bible portions.

LISHANID NOSHAN ***(ARBILI NEO-ARAMAIC, LISHANA DIDÁN, HULANI, KURDIT, GALIGALU, JBELI, HULA'ULA)*** [AIJ] 2,000 to 2,500 (1994 H. Mutzafi). Originally eastern and southern Iraqi Kurdistan. Afro-Asiatic, Semitic, Central, Aramaic, Eastern, Central, Northeastern. Dialects: WESTERN CLUSTER LISHANID NOSHAN, EASTERN CLUSTER LISHANID NOSHANARBIL, DOBE, KOY SANJAQ, QALADZE, RWANDUZ, RUSTAQA. 60% to 70% inherent intelligibility with Lishanan and Hulaulá. Very different and not inherently intelligible with the Christian Aramaic languages and Lishana Deni. Western cluster subdialects are Arbil, Dobe, Eastern cluster subdialects are Southeastern varieties: Koy Sanjaq, Qaladze; Northeastern varieties: Rwanduz, Rustaqa. All over 40. Investigation needed: intelligibility with Hulaula, Assyrian, Chaldean, Salamas. Hebrew script used. Jewish.

POLISH ***(POLSKI)*** [PQL] 100,000 speakers out of 272,000 people of Polish origin (1992 H. Mutzafi). Indo-European, Slavic, West, Lechtic. All speakers use Hebrew as second language but prefer Polish. Many other people of Polish origin speak Yiddish or Hebrew as first or second language. Jewish. Bible 1561-1965. See main entry under Poland.

ROMANIAN [RUM] 250,000 in Israel (1993 Statistical Abstract of Israel). Indo-European, Italic, Romance, Eastern. Bilingualism in Hebrew. Elderly speakers use Hebrew as second language but prefer Romanian. Radio programs. Jewish. Bible 1688-1989. See main entry under Romania.

RUSSIAN ***(RUSSIT, RUSSKI)*** [RUS] 750,000 in Israel (1999 H. Mutzafi). Indo-European, Slavic, East. Most speakers use Hebrew as second language but prefer Russian. Radio programs. Jewish. Bible 1860-1993. See main entry under Russia.

TIGRIGNA ***(TIGRINYA)*** [TGN] 10,000 in Israel (1994 H. Mutzafi). Afro-Asiatic, Semitic, South, Ethiopian, North. Bilingualism in Amharic, Hebrew. Called "Falashas", which they consider to be pejorative. They call themselves 'Beta Israel'. Their liturgy is written in Geez. Ethiopic script. Radio programs. Jewish. Bible 1956. See main entry under Ethiopia.

YEVANIC ***(JUDEO-GREEK, YEVANITIKA)*** [YEJ] 35 possibly in Israel. There were a few semi-speakers left in 1987, and may be none now. Population total both countries 50 or fewer. There may be a handful of elderly speakers still in Turkey. Also spoken in USA. Indo-European, Greek, Attic. Jews gave it up in Rome by 4th century, Spain by 6-7th centuries, Crimea by 8th century. After 1000 A.D. almost entirely in Greece, some in the Balkans (Wexler 1985). Jewish. Nearly extinct.

YIDDISH SIGN LANGUAGE [YDS] Deaf sign language. Apparently distinct from Israeli Sign Language. Jewish.

YIDDISH, EASTERN ***(JUDEO-GERMAN, YIDDISH)*** [YDD] 215,000 in Israel, 5% of the population (1986). Population total all countries 3,000,000 (J. A. Fishman 1991:194). Southeastern dialect in Ukraine and Romania, Mideastern in Poland and Hungary, Northeastern dialect in Lithuania and Belarus. Also spoken in Argentina, Australia, Belarus, Belgium, Canada, Estonia, Hungary, Latvia, Lithuania, Moldova, Panama, Poland, Puerto Rico, Romania, Russia (Europe), South Africa, Ukraine, Uruguay, USA. Indo-European, Germanic, West, High German, Yiddish. Dialects: SOUTHEASTERN YIDDISH, MIDEASTERN YIDDISH, NORTHEASTERN YIDDISH. Has many loans from Hebrew and local languages where spoken. Eastern Yiddish originated east of the Oder River through Poland, extending into Belarus, Russia (to Smolensk), Lithuania, Latvia, Hungary, Rumania, Ukraine, and pre-state British-Mandate Palestine (Jerusalem and Safed). Western Yiddish originated in Germany, Holland, Switzerland, Alsace (France), Czecholovakia, western Hungary, and is nearing extinction. It branched off medieval High German (mainly Rhenish dialects) and received Modern German influences during the 19th and early 20th centuries. Eastern and Western Yiddish have difficult inherent intelligibility, because of differing histories and influences from other languages. There are some Western Yiddish speakers in Israel too (M. Herzog 1977). The vast majority speak Eastern Yiddish. SVO. Usually written in Hebrew character. Radio programs. Jewish. Bible 1821-1936.

JAPAN

Nippon. National or official language: Japanese. 126,281,000 (1998 UN). Also includes English 70,000, Orok 3, Chinese 150,000, from the Philippines 36,000, from Pakistan, Iran, Bangladesh, Thailand, Malaysia over 300,000. Information mainly from S. Wurm and S. Hattori 1981; M. Shibatani 1990. Shinto-Buddhist, secular, Christian. Blind population 256,700. Deaf population 317,000 to 7,585,237 (1998). Deaf institutions: 131. Data accuracy estimate: A2. The number of languages listed for Japan is 15. Of those, all are living languages. Diversity index 0.03.

AINU ***(AINU ITAK)*** [AIN] 15 active speakers (1996 Alexander Vovin). In the ethnic group: 15,000 in Japan. Population total both countries 15 or more. Kuril Islands (Tsishima), Hokkaido. Formerly also on south Sakhalin Island, Russia. Also spoken in Russia (Asia). Language Isolate. Dialects: TSISHIMA, SAKHALIN. The last speaker of Sakhalin dialect died in 1994. There were at least 19 dialects. Bilingualism in Japanese. Most of the people speak only Japanese and are integrated into Japanese culture. The Ainu in China is a different, unrelated language. SOV. Nearly extinct. NT 1897.

AMAMI-OSHIMA, NORTHERN ***(NORTHERN AMAMI-OSIMA, OSHIMA, OSIMA, OOSIMA)*** [RYN] Northwestern Okinawa; northern Amami-oshima Island. Japanese, Ryukyuan, Amami-Okinawan, Northern Amami-Okinawan. Dialects: NAZE, SANI. Inherent intelligibility is generally impossible or very difficult with other Ryukyuan languages and Japanese. The younger the generation, the more fluently they speak Japanese (Hattori in Wurm and Hattori 1981). Those under 20 are mainly monolingual in Japanese (T. Fukuda SIL 1989). Those over 50 use the vernacular among themselves, but understand and use Standard Japanese. Those 20 to 50 understand the vernacular, but mainly use Japanese.

AMAMI-OSHIMA, SOUTHERN ***(SOUTHERN AMAMI-OSIMA)*** [AMS] Northern Okinawa; southern Amami-oshima, Kakeroma, Yoro, and Uke islands. Japanese, Ryukyuan, Amami-Okinawan, Northern Amami-Okinawan. Inherent intelligibility is generally impossible or very difficult with other Ryukyuan languages and Japanese. The younger the generation, the more fluently they speak Japanese (Hattori in Wurm and Hattori 1981). Those under 20 are monolingual in Japanese. Those over 50 use the vernacular at home among themselves but understand and use Standard Japanese. Those 20 to 50 understand the vernacular, but mainly speak Japanese.

JAPANESE [JPN] 121,050,000 in Japan (1985). Population total all countries 125,000,000 first language speakers (1999 WA); 126,000,000 including second language speakers (1999 WA). Throughout the country. Also spoken in 26 other countries including American Samoa, Argentina, Australia, Belize, Brazil, Canada, Dominican Republic, Germany, Guam, Mexico, Micronesia, Mongolia, New Zealand, Northern Mariana Islands, Palau, Panama, Paraguay, Peru, Philippines. Japanese, Japanese. Dialects: WESTERN JAPANESE, EASTERN JAPANESE. Possibly related to Korean. The Kagoshima dialect is 84% cognate with Tokyo dialect. National language. Grammar. SOV; postpositions; demonstrative, numeral, adjective, possessive, relative clause, proper noun precede noun head; adverb precedes verb; sentence final question particle; CV. Hiragana, Katakana, and Kanji (Chinese character) writing systems. Buddhist, Shintoist. Bible 1883-1987.

JAPANESE SIGN LANGUAGE ***(SHUWA, TEMANE)*** [JSL] Hearing impaired: 317,000 (1986 Gallaudet Univ.). Deaf sign language. Related to Taiwanese and Korean sign languages. Over 95% of the deaf understand Japanese Sign Language. 107 deaf schools. The first school was in Kyoto in 1878. 'Temane' is the former name. Pidgin Signed Japanese is different. Pidgin Signed Japanese is used often in formal situations, lectures, speeches. 80% of the deaf understand finger spelling. TV.

KIKAI [KZG] Northeastern Okinawa; Kikai Island. Japanese, Ryukyuan, Amami-Okinawan, Northern Amami-Okinawan. Dialect: ONOTSU. Inherent intelligibility is generally impossible or very difficult with other Ryukyuan languages and Japanese. The younger the generation, the more fluently they speak Japanese (Hattori in Wurm and Hattori 1981). Those under 20 are mainly monolingual in Japanese (T. Fukuda SIL 1989). Those over 50 use Kikai at home among themselves but can understand and use Japanese. Those 20 to 50 can understand Kikai, but mainly speak Japanese.

KOREAN [KKN] 670,000 in Japan, .5% of the population (1988). Language Isolate. Bilingualism in Japanese. Buddhist, Christian. Bible 1911-1993. See main entry under Korea, South.

KUNIGAMI [XUG] Central Okinawa; central and northern Okinawa Island, Iheya, Izena, Ie-jima, Sesoko islands. Japanese, Ryukyuan, Amami-Okinawan, Southern Amami-Okinawan. Dialect: NAGO. Inherent intelligibility is generally impossible or very difficult with other Ryukyuan languages and Japanese. Ryukyu languages are 62% to 70% cognate with Tokyo dialect of Japanese. The younger the generation, the more fluently they speak Japanese (1981 Hattori in Wurm and Hattori). Those under 20 are mainly monolingual in Japanese (T. Fukuda SIL 1989). Those over 50 use Kunigami at home among themselves but can understand and use Japanese. Those 20 to 50 can understand Kunigami, but mainly use Japanese at home and work.

MIYAKO [MVI] Southern Okinawa; Miyako, Ogami, Ikema, Kurima, Irabu, Tarama, Minna islands. Japanese, Ryukyuan, Sakishima. Dialects: MIYAKO-JIMA (HIRARA, OGAMI), IRABU-JIMA, TARAMA-MINNA. Inherent intelligibility is generally impossible or very difficult with other Ryukyuan languages and Japanese. The dialects listed have noticeable differences, but not impossible communication. The younger the generation, the more fluently they speak Japanese (Hattori in Wurm and Hattori 1981). Those under 20 are mainly monolingual in Japanese (T. Fukuda SIL 1989). Those over 50 use Miyako at home but can understand and speak Japanese. Those 20 to 50 can understand Miyako, but mainly use Japanese at home and work. Dictionary. Grammar.

OKI-NO-ERABU [OKN] North central Okinawa; Oki-no-erabu Island. Japanese, Ryukyuan, Amami-Okinawan, Southern Amami-Okinawan. Dialects: EAST OKI-NO-ERABU, WEST OKI-NO-ERABU. Inherent intelligibility is generally impossible or very difficult with other Ryukyuan languages and Japanese. Dialect differences are noticeable, but communication is not impossible. Ryukyu languages are 62% to 70% cognate with Tokyo dialect of Japanese. The younger the generation, the more fluently they speak Japanese (1981 Hattori in Wurm and Hattori). Those under 20 are monolingual in Japanese (T. Fukuda SIL 1989). Those over 50 use the vernacular at home among themselves but can understand and use Standard Japanese. Those 20-50 can understand the vernacular, but use Japanese at home and work.

OKINAWAN, CENTRAL ***(OKINAWAN, LUCHU)*** [RYU] 900,000 all Ryukyuan languages. Central Okinawa; southern Okinawa Island, Kerama Islands, Kume-jima, Tonaki, Aguna islands, and islands east of Okinawa Island. Japanese, Ryukyuan, Amami-Okinawan, Southern Amami-Okinawan. Dialects: SHURI,

NAHA, TORISHIMA, KUDAKA. Inherent intelligibility is generally impossible or very difficult with other Ryukyuan languages and Japanese. Ryukyu languages are 62% to 70% cognate with Tokyo dialect of Japanese. The younger the generation, the more fluently they speak Japanese (1981 Hattori in Wurm and Hattori). Those under 20 are mainly monolingual in Japanese (T. Fukuda SIL 1989). Those over 50 use Okinawan at home among themselves, but can understand and use Standard Japanese. Those 20 to 50 can understand Okinawan, but use Japanese at home and work. Bible portions 1855-1858.

TOKU-NO-SHIMA [TKN] Northern Okinawa; Toku-no-shima Island. Japanese, Ryukyuan, Amami-Okinawan, Northern Amami-Okinawan. Dialect: KAMETSU. Inherent intelligibility is generally impossible or very difficult with other Ryukyuan languages and Japanese. The younger the generation, the more fluently they speak Japanese (Hattori in Wurm and Hattori 1981). Those under 20 are monolingual in Japanese (T. Fukuda SIL 1989). Those over 50 use the vernacular at home among themselves but understand and use Standard Japanese. Those 20-50 understand the vernacular but use Japanese at home and work.

YAEYAMA *(YAYEYAMA)* [RYS] Southern Okinawa; Ishigaki, Iriomote, Hatoma, Kohama, Taketomi, Kuroshima, Hateruma, Aregusuku islands. Japanese, Ryukyuan, Sakishima. Dialects: ISHIGAKI, KABIRA, SHIRAHO, TAKETOMI, KOHAMA, HATOMA, SONAI, KUROSHIMA, HATERUMA. Inherent intelligibility is generally impossible or very difficult with other Ryukyuan languages and Japanese. The younger the generation, the more fluently they speak Japanese (Hattori in Wurm and Hattori 1981). Those under 20 are monolingual in Japanese (T. Fukuda SIL 1989). Those over 50 use Yaeyama at home among themselves but can understand and use Standard Japanese. Those 20-50 can understand Yaeyama but mainly use Japanese at home and work.

YONAGUNI [YOI] Southern Okinawa; Yonaguni Island. Japanese, Ryukyuan, Sakishima. Inherent intelligibility is generally impossible or very difficult with other Ryukyuan languages and Japanese. The younger the generation, the more fluently they speak Japanese (Hattori in Wurm and Hattori 1981). Those under 20 are monolingual in Japanese (T. Fukuda SIL 1989). Those over 50 speak Yonaguni at home among themselves but can understand Japanese. Those 20-50 can understand Yonaguni, but mainly use Japanese at home and work (T. Fukuda SIL 1989).

YORON [YOX] North central Okinawa; Yoron Island. Japanese, Ryukyuan, Amami-Okinawan, Southern Amami-Okinawan. Inherent intelligibility is generally impossible or very difficult with other Ryukyuan languages and Japanese. Ryukyu languages are 62% to 70% cognate with Tokyo dialect of Japanese. The younger the generation, the more fluently they speak Japanese (1981 Hattori in Wurm and Hattori). Those under 20 are monolingual in Japanese (T. Fukuda SIL 1989). Those over 50 use Yoron at home among themselves, but also understand and use Standard Japanese. Those from 20 to 50 understand Yoron but mainly speak Standard Japanese at home and work.

JORDAN

Hashemite Kingdom of Jordan, al Mamlaka al Urduniya al Hashemiyah. National or official language: Standard Arabic. 6,304,000 (1998 UN). Literacy rate 71% to 80%. Also includes Egyptian Spoken Arabic 10,000, Mesopotamian Spoken Arabic 500,000, North Mesopotamian Spoken Arabic 200,000, South Azerbaijani 4,000, Greek, Kurmanji 4,000, people from Pakistan, Philippines 5,000 (1995). Information mainly from T. Sebeok 1963; T. M. Johnstone 1967; W. Fischer and O. Jastrow 1980; B. Ingham 1982. Sunni Muslim, Christian, secular. Blind population 9,000 (1982 WCE). Deaf population 240,155. Deaf institutions: 2. Data accuracy estimate: B. The number of languages listed for Jordan is 9. Of those, all are living languages. Diversity index 0.48.

ADYGHE *(WEST CIRCASSIAN, ADYGEY)* [ADY] 44,280 in Jordan, 1.2% of the population (1986). North Caucasian, Northwest, Circassian. City dwellers. Radio programs. Sunni Muslim. NT 1992. See main entry under Russia.

ARABIC, LEVANTINE BEDAWI SPOKEN *(BEDAWI)* [AVL] 700,000 in Jordan. Throughout Jordan, but especially in the east. Afro-Asiatic, Semitic, Central, South, Arabic. Dialects: SOUTH LEVANTINE BEDAWI ARABIC, NORTH LEVANTINE BEDAWI ARABIC, EASTERN EGYPTIAN BEDAWI ARABIC. The language of Jordan before Palestinian refugees arrived. It remains the language of the army. TV. Sunni Muslim, Christian. See main entry under Egypt.

ARABIC, NAJDI SPOKEN [ARS] 50,000 in Jordan. Far eastern Jordan. Afro-Asiatic, Semitic, Central, South, Arabic. See main entry under Saudi Arabia.

ARABIC, SOUTH LEVANTINE SPOKEN *(LEVANTINE ARABIC, SOUTH LEVANTINE ARABIC, PALESTINIAN-JORDANIAN ARABIC)* [AJP] 3,500,000 in Jordan (1996). Population total all countries 6,155,000. Also spoken in Argentina, Egypt, Israel, Kuwait, Palestinian West Bank and Gaza, Puerto Rico, Syria. Afro-Asiatic, Semitic, Central, South, Arabic. Dialects: MADANI, FELLAHI. There are differences from village to village of which speakers are aware. There is a newly emerging urban standard dialect based on Amman. Used in drama. Radio programs, TV. Muslim, Christian. Bible portions 1940-1973.

ARABIC, STANDARD [ABV] Middle East, North Africa. Afro-Asiatic, Semitic, Central, South, Arabic. Used for education, official purposes, communication among Arabic speaking countries. Education officials promoting this variety among students. Regional varieties have been used in classrooms, but this is changing. National language. Newspapers, TV. Bible 1984-1991. See main entry under Saudi Arabia.

ARMENIAN [ARM] 8,000 in Jordan (1971 The Armenian Review). Indo-European, Armenian. Dialect: WESTERN ARMENIAN. Christian. Bible 1853-1978. See main entry under Armenia.

CHECHEN [CJC] 3,000 in Jordan (1993 Johnstone). In 2 or 3 villages mixed among Adygey and Arabic speakers. North Caucasian, North Central, Chechen-Ingush. Sunni Muslim: Sufi. Bible portions 1986-1995. See main entry under Russia.

DOMARI *(MIDDLE EASTERN ROMANI, TSIGENE, GYPSY)* [RMT] Indo-European, Indo-Iranian, Indo-Aryan, Northwestern zone, Dom. Dialects: NAWAR, KURBAT, BARAKE. Arabic influence. Muslim. See main entry under Iran.

JORDANIAN SIGN LANGUAGE [JOS] Deaf sign language.

KAZAKHSTAN

National or official language: Kazakh. 16,319,000 (1998 UN). Formerly part of USSR. Capital Akmola (Agmola). 1,000,000 square miles. Also includes Armenian 19,000, Avar 959, North Azerbaijani 90,000, Bashkir 21,442, Belarusan 183,000, Chechen, Chuvash 22,871, Dargwa 636, Dungan, Erzya 34,371, Gagauz, Georgian 7,700, Greek 47,000, Judeo-Crimean Tatar, Karachay-Balkar 2,714, Karakalpak, Kirghiz 9,612, Korean 103,000, Kumyk 554, Kurmanji 25,000, Lak 617, Lezgi 2,570, Lithuanian 10,964, Low Mari 9,089, Nogai 155, Osetin 3,491, Polish 61,445, Pontic, Romanian 33,000, Russian 6,227,000, Tabassaran 225, Tajiki 26,000, Tatar 328,000, Turkish, Turkmen 3,265, Udmurt 15,786, Ukrainian 898,000, Northern Uzbek 332,000. Information mainly from T. Sebeok 1963; Z. Xiangru and R. F. Hahn 1989. Muslim, Jewish (27,689). The number of languages listed for Kazakhstan is 6. Of those, all are living languages. Diversity index 0.70.

GERMAN, STANDARD [GER] 958,000 in Kazakhstan excluding Plautdietsch. 57% of ethnic Germans speak it as mother tongue. Indo-European, Germanic, West, High German, German, Middle German, East Middle German. Bible 1466-1982. See main entry under Germany.

ILI TURKI *(T'URK, TUERKE)* [ILI] Ili Valley near Kuldja, Xinjiang, China. There may be none in Kazakhstan. Altaic, Turkic, Eastern. The language is linguistically distinct, a link between Chagatai and Kypchak (Uzbek dialect). Their oral history says their ancestors came from the Ferghana Valley (Uzbekistan and Kyrgyzstan) about 200 years ago. Speakers are older. Younger people understand Ili Turki, but are adopting Kazakh or Uyghur, and intermarrying with neighboring groups. See main entry under China.

KAZAKH *(KAZAK, KAISAK, KOSACH, QAZAQ)* [KAZ] 5,293,400 in Kazakhstan (1979 census), 40% of the population, 98% speak Kazakh as mother tongue. Population total all countries 8,000,000 (1999 WA). Kazakhstan, northern Soviet Middle Asia and into western Siberia. Also spoken in Afghanistan, China, Germany, Iran, Kyrgyzstan, Mongolia, Russia (Asia), Tajikistan, Turkey (Asia), Turkmenistan, Ukraine, Uzbekistan. Altaic, Turkic, Western, Aralo-Caspian. Dialects: NORTHEASTERN KAZAKH, SOUTHERN KAZAKH, WESTERN KAZAKH. Minor dialect differences. Many speak Russian or Uzbek as second language. Increasing ethnic pride and feelings of Islamic brotherhood. Semi-nomadic. The names 'Eastern Kirghiz' and 'Western Kirghiz' have been erroneously applied to Kazakh. Official language. SOV. Cyrillic script. Increasing education in Kazakh. Radio programs. Traditionally pastoralists, now agriculturalists, industrialists. Sunni Muslim. NT 1820-1910, out of print.

PLAUTDIETSCH *(LOW GERMAN)* [GRN] 100,000 in Russia and Kazakhstan (1986). Various locations including Alma Ata near the China border, beyond Tashkent, and Kazakhstan. Indo-European, Germanic, West, Low Saxon-Low Franconian, Low Saxon. 50% speak Russian as second language. Christian. NT 1987. See main entry under Canada.

ROMANI, SINTE *(SINTI, TSIGANE, MANUCHE, MANOUCHE)* [RMO] Kazakhstan (formerly Volga area until 1941). Indo-European, Indo-Iranian, Indo-Aryan, Central zone, Romani, Northern. Not intelligible with Vlax Romani. Ethnic group: Sasítka Romá. Christian. Bible portions 1875-1995. See main entry under Yugoslavia.

UYGHUR *(UIGHUR, UIGUIR, UYGUR, NOVOUYGUR)* [UIG] 300,000 in Kazakhstan (1993), 86% speak it as mother tongue. Taranchi dialect in Kazakhstan, Kashgar-Yarkand dialect in Uzbekistan. Altaic, Turkic, Eastern. Dialects: TARANCHI (KULJA), KASHGAR-YARKAND. There are significant dialect differences between China, Kazakhstan, Kyrgyzstan, and Uzbekistan. Cyrillic script. Agriculturalists. Sunni Muslim. Bible 1950. See main entry under China.

KOREA, NORTH

Democratic People's Republic of Korea, Chosun Minchu-chui Inmin Konghwa-guk. National or official language: Korean. 23,348,000 (1998 UN). Literacy rate 91% to 99%. Also includes Chinese 51,000. Information mainly from B. Comrie 1987. Secular, Buddhist-Confucianist, Christian. Blind population 110,000 (1982 WCE). Data accuracy estimate: A2. The number of languages listed for North Korea is 1. Diversity index 0.00.

KOREAN [KKN] 20,000,000 in North Korea (1986). Language Isolate. Dialects: HAMGYONGDO (NORTH HAMGYONGDO, SOUTH HAMGYONGDO), P'YONG'ANDO (NORTH P'YONG'ANDO, SOUTH P'YONG'ANDO), HWANGHAEDO. Dialect boundaries generally correspond to provincial boundaries. Some dialects are not easily intelligible with others (Voegelin and Voegelin 1977). National language. SOV. Korean script (Hangul). Buddhist-Confucianist, Christian. Bible 1911-1993. See main entry under Korea, South.

KOREA, SOUTH

Republic of Korea, Taehan Min'guk. National or official language: Korean. 46,109,000 (1998 UN). Literacy rate 92%. Also includes English, Sherpa, Chinese 24,000. Information mainly from B. Comrie 1987. Buddhist, Christian, secular, Confucianist, synchretism. Blind population 48,000 (1982 WCE). Deaf institutions: 28. Data accuracy estimate: A2. The number of languages listed for South Korea is 2. Of those, both are living languages. Diversity index 0.00.

KOREAN ***(HANGUOHUA, HANGUK MAL)*** [KKN] 42,000,000 in South Korea (1986). Population total all countries 78,000,000 (1999 WA). Also spoken in 31 other countries including American Samoa, Australia, Bahrain, Belize, Brazil, Brunei, Canada, China, Germany, Guam, Japan, Kazakhstan, Korea, North, Kyrgyzstan, Mauritania, Mongolia, New Zealand, Northern Mariana Islands. Language Isolate. Dialects: SEOUL (KANGWONDO, KYONGGIDO), CH'UNGCH'ONGDO (NORTH CH'UNGCH'ONG, SOUTH CH'UNGCH'ONG), KYONGSANGDO (NORTH KYONGSANGDO, SOUTH KYONGSANGDO), CHOLLADO (NORTH CHOLLADO, SOUTH CHOLLADO), CHEJU ISLAND. There is a difference of opinion among scholars as to whether or not Korean is related to Japanese. Some scholars suggest that both languages are possibly distantly related to Altaic. Dialect boundaries generally correspond to provincial boundaries. Some dialects are not easily intelligible with others (Voegelin and Voegelin 1977). The suffix -do on dialect names means 'province'. Comprehension of Standard Korean may be lower on Cheju Island. National language. Grammar. SOV. Higher adult illiteracy is reported on Cheju Island. Korean script (Hangul) used. The McCune-Reischauer system is the official Roman orthography in South Korea used for maps and signs. Buddhist, Christian. Bible 1911-1993.

KOREAN SIGN LANGUAGE [KVK] Deaf sign language. Related to Japanese and Taiwanese sign languages, but distinct. Used since 1889. Signed interpretation required in court, used at important public events, in social services programs. There is sign language instruction for parents of deaf children. Many sign language classes for hearing people. There is a manual system for spelling. Dictionary. Elementary schools for deaf children using sign language since 1908. TV.

KUWAIT

State of Kuwait, Dowlat al-Kuwait. National or official language: Standard Arabic. 1,811,000 (1998 UN). Literacy rate 71% to 79%. Also includes Egyptian Spoken Arabic 20,000, Najdi Spoken Arabic 200,000, South Levantine Spoken Arabic 85,000, Kurmanji, Balochi, people from India, Pakistan, the Philippines 50,000 (1995), the West. Information mainly from T. M. Johnstone 1967; B. Ingham 1982; C. Holes 1990. Sunni Muslim, Shi'a Muslim, Christian, Hindu. Deaf population 110,285. Deaf institutions: 1. Data accuracy estimate: B. The number of languages listed for Kuwait is 3. Of those, all are living languages. Diversity index 0.54.

ARABIC, GULF SPOKEN ***(KHALIJI)*** [AFB] 500,000 in Kuwait, 85% of the population (1986). Afro-Asiatic, Semitic, Central, South, Arabic. Dialect: KUWAITI HADARI ARABIC. Muslim. See main entry under Iraq.

ARABIC, STANDARD [ABV] Middle East, North Africa. Afro-Asiatic, Semitic, Central, South, Arabic. Used for education, official purposes. National language. Newspapers. Bible 1984-1991. See main entry under Saudi Arabia.

MEHRI ***(MAHRI)*** [MHR] 3,537 in Kuwait (1965 government report). Scattered individuals in Kuwait. Afro-Asiatic, Semitic, South, South Arabian. Bathari and Hobyot may be Mehri dialects. Muslim. Bible portions 1902. See main entry under Yemen.

KYRGYZSTAN

Kyrgyz Republic. National or official language: Kirghiz. 4,643,000 (1998 UN). Formerly part of USSR. Capital: Bishkek (Biskeck). 76,642 square miles. Literacy rate 99%. Also includes Armenian 3,285, North Azerbaijani 17,207, Bashkir 3,250, Belarusan 7,676, Chechen, Chuvash 2,092, Crimean Turkish 38,000, Dargwa 1,419, Erzya 5,390, Georgian 1,002, Standard German 101,057, Kalmyk-Oirat, Karachay-Balkar 1,973, Karakalpak, Kazakh 37,000, Korean 18,000, Kurmanji 14,000, Lak 257, Lezgi 1,599, Lithuanian 430, Halh Mongolian, Romanian 1,375, Russian 1,408,800, Tajiki 34,000, Tatar 70,000, Turkish, Turkmen 352, Ukrainian 109,000, Uyghur 37,000, Northern Uzbek 657,440. Information mainly from T. Sebeok 1963. Muslim, Jewish (7,680), Christian. Data accuracy estimate: B. The number of languages listed for Kyrgyzstan is 2. Of those, both are living languages. Diversity index 0.67.

DUNGAN ***(DZHUNYAN, TUNGAN, HUIZU, ZWN'JAN, KWUIZWU)*** [DNG] 38,000 in Kyrgyzstan (1993 Johnstone). Mother tongue speakers were 95% out of an ethnic population of 52,000 in the former USSR (1979 census). Population total all countries 49,400 out of an ethnic population of 100,000. The Gansu dialect is mainly in Prschewalsk and Osh, Kyrgyzstan, the Shaanxi dialect in Kazakhstan, and in Fergana, Uzbekistan. Also spoken in Kazakhstan, Tajikistan, Turkmenistan, Uzbekistan. Sino-Tibetan, Chinese. Dialects: GANSU, SHAANXI (SHENSI), YAGE. Dungan has three tones (Standard Mandarin tones 1 and 2 are merged), but they are not indicated in writing. Also different from Mandarin in phonology and lexicon. Bilingualism in Russian. Those under 50 to 55 are reported to speak Russian as mother tongue. The people call themselves 'Huizu'. Cyrillic script. Sunni Muslim.

KIRGHIZ ***(KARA-KIRGIZ, KIRGIZ)*** [KDO] 2,448,220 in the former USSR (1993 UBS), 98% of the 2,539,000 Kirghiz speak it as mother tongue. Population total all countries 2,631,420. Throughout the country. Also spoken in Afghanistan, China, Kazakhstan, Tajikistan, Turkey (Asia), Uzbekistan. Altaic, Turkic, Western, Aralo-Caspian. Dialects: NORTHERN KIRGIZ, SOUTHERN KIRGIZ. 29% speak Russian as second language. The Ichkilik are a Kirghiz-speaking people of non-Kirghiz origin. Books, theater. The names 'Eastern Kirghiz' and 'Western Kirghiz' have been erroneously applied to Kazakh. Increasing education. Increasing feelings of Islamic brotherhood. Cyrillic script. Schools in Kirghiz. Newspapers, radio programs, films, TV. Mountain slope. Sunni Muslim, some Lamaism. NT 1991.

LAOS

Lao People's Democratic Republic, Sathanalat Paxathipatai Paxaxon Lao. National or official language: Lao. 5,163,000 (1998 UN) including 2,769,000 or 71% speakers of Daic languages, 1,100,000 or 24.1% Austro-Asiatic languages, 175,000 or 4% Miao-Yao languages, 42,500 or 1% Tibeto-Burman languages (1991 J. Matisoff). Literacy rate 43% to 45%. Also includes Mandarin Chinese, Central Khmer 10,400, Sedang, Vietnamese 76,000, Chinese 25,000 (1984 MARC). Information mainly from F. Lebar, G. Hickey, J. Musgrave 1967; D. Thomas and R. Headley 1970; S. Wurm and S. Hattori 1981; J. Matisoff et al. 1996; J. Edmondson and D. Solnit 1997; R. Burling ms. (1998). Buddhist, traditional religion, secular, Christian, Muslim. Blind population 10,000 (1982 WCE). Data accuracy estimate: B, C. The number of languages listed for Laos is 82. Of those, all are living languages. Diversity index 0.56.

AHEU ***(KHA TONG LUANG, THAVUNG, PHON SOUNG, SO)*** [THM] 200 to 300 in Laos (1996 Ferlus). The Thavung live near Lak Sao, Khamkeut District in Pak Sane Province. Austro-Asiatic, Mon-Khmer, Viet-Muong. See main entry under Thailand.

AKHA ***(KAW, EKAW, KO, AKA, IKAW, AK'A, AHKA, KHAKO, HKA KO, KHAO KHA KO, IKOR, AINI, YANI)*** [AKA] 58,000 in Laos (1995 Nguyen Duy Thieu). Extreme northern and northwest Laos. Sino-Tibetan, Tibeto-Burman, Lolo-Burmese, Loloish, Southern, Akha, Hani, Ha-Ya. SOV. Traditional religion, Christian. NT 1968-1987. See main entry under Myanmar.

ALAK ***(HRLAK)*** [ALK] 4,000 (Bradley). Southern Laos, mainly in Saravan Province. Austro-Asiatic, Mon-Khmer, Eastern Mon-Khmer, Bahnaric, Central Bahnaric. Included under Bahnaric as closest to Bahnar, Tampuan, Lamam. Also included under Katuic.

AREM ***(CHOMRAU, CHOMBRAU, UMO)*** [AEM] West central, both sides of the Viet Nam-Laos border, west of Phuc Trach. Austro-Asiatic, Mon-Khmer, Viet-Muong, Chut. May and Ruc are closely related. Investigation needed: intelligibility with May, Ruc. Nearly extinct. See main entry under Viet Nam.

BIT ***(KHABIT, KHBIT, PHSING, PHSIN)*** [BGK] 1,530 in Laos (1985 F. Proschan). Population total both countries 2,000. Near the northern border with China, southeast of Nam Tha and south of Boun Neua; 2 areas. Also spoken in China. Austro-Asiatic, Mon-Khmer, Northern Mon-Khmer, Khmuic, Khao. Not Khmuic but Palaungic (J-O Svantesson 1990). Related to Khao in Viet Nam. Investigation needed: intelligibility with Khao.

BO [BGL] 2,000 (1981 Wurm and Hattori). Central Laos inland from the bend of the Mekong, Nhang River, around Nape and Lak Sao. Austro-Asiatic, Mon-Khmer, Viet-Muong, Muong.

BRU, EASTERN ***(BROU, VANKIEU)*** [BRU] 69,000 in Laos (1999). Population total all countries 114,000. Eastern Savannehkhet Province: Tchepone area east of Vietnamese border, and Saravan Province, on the Viet Nam border. Also spoken in Thailand, Viet Nam. Austro-Asiatic, Mon-Khmer, Eastern Mon-Khmer, Katuic, West Katuic, Brou-So. Dialect: TRI (SO TRI, SO TRII, CHALI). It is partially intelligible with Western Bru of Thailand. Literacy rate in first language: 1% to 5%. Literacy rate in second language: 15% to 25%. NT 1981.

CHUT ***(MAY, RUC, SACH, SALANG)*** [SCB] Khammouan Province, near the Viet Nam border at about the latitude of the Mu Gia Pass. Austro-Asiatic, Mon-Khmer, Viet-Muong, Chut. Dialects: MAY, RUC. Semi-nomadic. See main entry under Viet Nam.

CON [CNO] 1,000 (1981 Wurm and Hattori). Northwestern corner, southwest of Vieng Pou Kha. Austro-Asiatic, Mon-Khmer, Northern Mon-Khmer, Palaungic, Western Palaungic, Lametic. Investigation needed: intelligibility with Lamet.

HALANG DOAN ***(HALANG DUAN, DUAN, DOAN)*** [HLD] 1,000 in Laos (1962 Lafont). Austro-Asiatic, Mon-Khmer, Eastern Mon-Khmer, Bahnaric, North Bahnaric, West, Duan. Investigation needed: intelligibility with Takua, Kayong, Halang Daksut, Rengao. See main entry under Viet Nam.

HANI ***(HANHI, HAW)*** [HNI] 30,000 in Laos (1994). Scattered along the Yunnan border. None in Thailand. Sino-Tibetan, Tibeto-Burman, Lolo-Burmese, Loloish, Southern, Akha, Hani, Ha-Ya. An official nationality in China. Polytheist, ancestor worship. See main entry under China.

HMONG DAW ***(WHITE MEO, WHITE MIAO, MEO KAO, WHITE LUM, BAI MIAO)*** [MWW] Hmong-Mien, Hmongic, Chuanqiandian. Dialects: HMONG GU MBA (HMONG QUA MBA, STRIPED HMONG), MONG LENG. Also spoken by the Hmong Qua Mba people, no significant dialect difference. Largely intelligible with Hmong Njua. Mong Leng is intelligible with Hmong Daw, but sociolinguistic factors require separate literature. NT 1975-1984. See main entry under China.

HMONG NJUA ***(BLUE MEO, BLUE MIAO, TAK MEO, HMONG NJWA, HMONG LENG, MIAO, MEO)*** [BLU] 100,000 in Laos (1975 Katzner). Hmong-Mien, Hmongic, Chuanqiandian. Closer to Hmong Daw in Laos than the two are to varieties in Thailand. Dictionary. NT 1975-1983. See main entry under China.

HUNG [HNU] 2,000 to 3,000 in Laos (1996 Ferlus). Population total both countries 2,700 to 3,700. Borikhamsay Province. The Toum live northeast of Nape and south of the Phong. Also spoken in Viet Nam. Austro-Asiatic, Mon-Khmer, Viet-Muong, Cuoi. Dialects: TOUM (TUM), PHONG (PONG, POONG, PONG 1, PONG 2).

IR ***(IN, YIR)*** [IRR] 10,000 together with Ong (1981 Wurm and Hattori). Saravane Province, east of Saravane. Austro-Asiatic, Mon-Khmer, Eastern Mon-Khmer, Katuic, Central Katuic, Ta'oih. Closest to Ong. Investigation needed: intelligibility with Ong.

IU MIEN ***(MIEN, MAN, YAO, MYEN, HIGHLAND YAO)*** [IUM] 30,000 in Laos (1999 H. Purnell). Hmong-Mien, Mienic, Mian-Jin. The language is the same as Thailand and Viet Nam Mien. Not all ethnic Yao speak the language. Almost all refugees in the West have come from Laos. Daoist, ancestor veneration, traditional religion. NT 1975-1991. See main entry under China.

JEH ***(DIE, YEH, GIE)*** [JEH] Basin of Poko, Se Kamane, and Dak Main rivers in southern Laos. Austro-Asiatic, Mon-Khmer, Eastern Mon-Khmer, Bahnaric, North Bahnaric, West, Jeh-Halang. Dialects: JEH BRI LA, JEH MANG RAM. The language is closely related to Halang. Literacy rate in first language: 1% to 5%. Literacy rate in second language: 15% to 25%. Bible portions 1967-1978. See main entry under Viet Nam.

JENG ***(CHENG, CENG)*** [JEG] 5,400 (1981). North of Attopeu. Austro-Asiatic, Mon-Khmer, Eastern Mon-Khmer, Bahnaric, West Bahnaric, Oi-The. Related to Oy, Sapuan, Sok. Investigation needed: intelligibility.

KADO ***(KADU, KATU, ASAK, SAK, GADU, THET)*** [KDV] Sino-Tibetan, Tibeto-Burman, Jingpho-Konyak-Bodo, Jingpho-Luish, Luish. Dialects: KADU, GANAAN (GANAN), ANDRO, SENGMAI, CHAKPA, PHAYENG. Kado and Ganaan may be separate languages. Different from Katu, a Mon-Khmer language of Viet Nam and Laos. See main entry under Myanmar.

KADUO ***(GAZHUO)*** [KTP] 5,000 in Laos (1981 Wurm and Hattori). Population total both countries 9,000 to 11,200. North central on the China border, north of Mong Ou Tay. Also spoken in China. Sino-Tibetan, Tibeto-Burman, Lolo-Burmese, Loloish, Southern, Akha, Hani, Bi-Ka. Different from Kado and Katu. Investigation needed: intelligibility.

KANG [KYP] Population total both countries 34,065 or more. Also spoken in China. Tai-Kadai, Kam-Tai, Be-Tai, Tai-Sek, Tai, Unclassified.

KASSENG ***(KOSENG, KASENG, KRASENG)*** [KGC] 7,000 (Bradley). Southern Laos near Viet Nam border, Boloven Plateau area north of Attopeu, and between the Jeh, Alak, Laven, and Tareng peoples. Austro-Asiatic, Mon-Khmer, Eastern Mon-Khmer, Katuic, East Katuic, Kaseng. Also classified as West Bahnaric. Investigation needed: intelligibility.

KATAANG ***(KATANG)*** [KGD] 10,000 (1981 Wurm and Hattori). Southern Laos near the Ta'oih and Bru peoples, around Muong Nong, in Saravan, Savannakhet, Sekong, and Champassak. Austro-Asiatic, Mon-Khmer, Eastern Mon-Khmer, Katuic, Central Katuic, Ta'oih. Not intelligible with Ta'oih. Investigation needed: intelligibility. Literacy rate in first language: Below 1%. Literacy rate in second language: 25% to 50%.

KATU, WESTERN [KUF] 14,700 (1998). Upper Xe Kong River, high basin of Song Boung River along watershed along the border, Xe Kong, Saravan, and Champasak provinces. Austro-Asiatic, Mon-Khmer, Eastern Mon-Khmer, Katuic, East Katuic, Katu-Pacoh. A different language variety and orthography from Viet Nam. Has its own script, called 'Liek'.

KHLOR ***(KLOR, LOR)*** [LLO] 6,000 (1981 Wurm and Hattori). Saravan Province, south of Ir and Ong. Austro-Asiatic, Mon-Khmer, Eastern Mon-Khmer, Katuic, East Katuic, Ngeq-Nkriang. Closest to Ngeq. Investigation needed: intelligibility with Ngeq.

KHMU ***(KMHMU, KHMU', KHAMU, KAMU, KAMMU, KHAMUK, KAMHMU, KHOMU, MOU, POUTENG, PU THENH, TENH, THENG, LAO TERNG)*** [KJG] 389,694 in Laos (1985 F. Proschan). Population total all countries 500,000 (1996 F. Proschan). Scattered through northern Laos. Also spoken in China, France, Myanmar, Thailand, USA, Viet Nam. Austro-Asiatic, Mon-Khmer, Northern Mon-Khmer, Khmuic, Mal-Khmu', Khmu'. Dialects: YUAN, KHROONG (KRONG), LUANG PRABANG, SAYABURY, LYY, ROK, U, HAT. SVO. Traditional religion. Bible portions 1918.

KHUA [XHU] East central; northwest of Boualapha. Austro-Asiatic, Mon-Khmer, Eastern Mon-Khmer, Katuic, West Katuic, Brou-So. Related to Bru, Mangkong, Leun. Different from Cua. Investigation needed: intelligibility with Eastern Bru, Mangkong, Leun. See main entry under Viet Nam.

KHUEN ***(KWEEN, KHWEEN, KHOUEN)*** [KHF] 8,000 in Laos (Chazee). Population total all countries 9,000. Near the Lamet people. Also spoken in China, USA. Austro-Asiatic, Mon-Khmer, Northern Mon-Khmer, Khmuic, Mal-Khmu', Khmu'.

KIM MUN ***(MUN, LAN TIN, LANTEN, MAN LAN-TIEN, LOWLAND YAO, JIM MUN)*** [MJI] 3,600 in Laos, 770 families (1995). Northwestern Laos, Nam Tha District and Province; Huay Sai Province; Nam Moh District, Udom Sai Province; Long District, Luang Nam Tha Province. Hmong-Mien, Mienic, Mian-Jin. A few know Lahu, Mien, Lao. See main entry under China.

KIORR ***(SAAMTAAV, SAMTAO, SAMTAO 2, CON, COL)*** [XKO] 2,359 in Laos (1985 F. Proschan). Population total both countries 2,359 or more. Louang Nam Tha and Bokeo provinces, 6 villages. Also spoken in Myanmar. Austro-Asiatic, Mon-Khmer, Northern Mon-Khmer, Palaungic, Western Palaungic, Angkuic. Investigation needed: intelligibility with Angkuic languages.

KUAN [UAN] Khammouan Province. Tai-Kadai, Kam-Tai, Be-Tai, Tai-Sek, Tai, Unclassified. Some classification problems, possibly because of migration.

KUY ***(SUI, SUAI, SUAY, SUOI, SOAI, SUEI, AOUEI, KUOY, KUI, DUI, KHAMEN-BORAN, CUOI)*** [KDT] 64,000 in Laos (1993 Johnstone). Saravan, Sedone provinces. A large group on both sides of the Mekong in southern Laos, Cambodia. Austro-Asiatic, Mon-Khmer, Eastern Mon-Khmer, Katuic, West Katuic, Kuay-Yoe. Dialects: ANTRA, NA NHYANG. 80% monolingual. A different script is used in Cambodia. Literacy rate in first language: 1% to 5%. NT 1978. See main entry under Thailand.

LAHU ***(MUSEU, MUSSUH, MUHSO, MUSSO)*** [LAH] 2,000 to 2,500 in Laos (1973 Matisoff). Nam Tha. Sino-Tibetan, Tibeto-Burman, Lolo-Burmese, Loloish, Southern, Akha, Lahu. Dialects: NA (BLACK LAHU, MUSSER DAM, NORTHERN LAHU, LOHEIRN), NYI (RED LAHU, SOUTHERN LAHU, MUSSEH DAENG, LUHISHI, LUHUSHI), SHEHLEH. Black Lahu, Red Lahu, and Shehleh dialects are close. Lahu Shi (Yellow Lahu, Kutsung) is distinct. Bible 1989. See main entry under China.

LAHU SHI ***(KUTSUNG, KUCONG, YELLOW LAHU, SHI, KUI, KWI)*** [KDS] 20,000 in Laos (1998). Population total all countries 62,000. Kentung District. Also spoken in China, Myanmar, Thailand, USA, Viet Nam. Sino-Tibetan, Tibeto-Burman, Lolo-Burmese, Loloish, Southern, Akha, Lahu. Difficult intelligibility with Black Lahu. A distinct language from Nyi (Red Lahu). SOV.

LAMET ***(LEMET, KHA LAMET, KHAMET, KHAMED, RMEET)*** [LBN] 14,355 in Laos (1985 F. Proschan). Population total all countries 14,480. Northwestern Laos, in the midst of the Khmu, Namthat area. Also spoken in Thailand, USA. Austro-Asiatic, Mon-Khmer, Northern Mon-Khmer, Palaungic, Western Palaungic, Lametic. Dialects: UPPER LAMET, LOWER LAMET. Called 'Lamet' in Laos and 'Khamet' in Thailand. Literacy rate in first language: Below 1%. Literacy rate in second language: 25% to 50%.

LAO ***(LAOTIAN TAI, LAOTIAN, PHOU LAO, EASTERN THAI, LUM LAO, LAO WIANG, LAO KAO, RONG KONG, TAI LAO, LAO-TAI, LÀO, LAO-LUM, LAO-NOI)*** [NOL] 3,000,000 in Laos (1991 UBS). Population total all countries 3,188,000 or more. Including second language speakers: 4,000,000 (1999 WA). Mekong River Valley from Luang Prabang south to the Cambodian border. The Lao Kao went to Thailand and are in Nan, Loei, Saraburi, and elsewhere; the Lao-Khrang are in the Nakhonsawan and Nakhon Pathom area. May also be in Viet Nam. Also spoken in Cambodia, Canada, Thailand, USA. Tai-Kadai, Kam-Tai, Be-Tai, Tai-Sek, Tai, Southwestern, East Central, Lao-Phutai. Dialects: LUANG PRABANG, VIENTIANE (WIANG JAN), SAVANNAKHET (SUWANNAKHET), PAKSE, LAO-KAO, LAO-KHRANG. Dialect continuum with Northeastern Tai of Thailand. 100% monolingual. National language. SOV. Literacy rate in first language: 30% to 60%. Literacy rate in second language: 50% to 75%. Buddhist, traditional religion. Bible 1932, in press (1997).

LAOS SIGN LANGUAGE [LSO] Deaf sign language. Related to sign languages in Viet Nam and earlier ones in Thailand. May be more than one sign language.

LAVE ***(BRAO, BRAOU, BRAU, PROUE, BROU, LOVE, LAVEH, RAWE)*** [BRB] 12,750 in Laos (1984). Population total all countries 18,381. Stung Treng and Ratanakiri provinces, Laos-Cambodian border. Also spoken in Cambodia, France, USA, Viet Nam. Austro-Asiatic, Mon-Khmer, Eastern Mon-Khmer, Bahnaric, West Bahnaric, Brao-Kravet. Dialect: PALAU. Closely related to Krung 2 and Kravet in Cambodia. Called 'Lave' in Laos.

LAVEN ***(LOVEN, BOLOVEN, BORIWEN, LAWEENJRU, JARU)*** [LBO] 32,000 (1993 Johnstone). Population total both countries 32,000 or more. Southwestern Laos, Boloven Plateau, near the Alak. Also spoken in USA. Austro-Asiatic, Mon-Khmer, Eastern Mon-Khmer, Bahnaric, West Bahnaric, Laven. Different from Brao.

LÜ ***(LUE, LU, PAI-I, SHUI-PAI-I)*** [KHB] 20,000 in Laos (1993 Johnstone). Western Phong Saly, north and west Haut Mekong, Luang Prabang, and along Nam Tha and Nam Beng. Tai-Kadai, Kam-Tai, Be-Tai, Tai-Sek, Tai, Southwestern, East Central, Northwest. Traditional religion, Buddhist. NT 1933. See main entry under China.

MAL ***(KHATIN, T'IN, HTIN, THIN, TIN)*** [MLF] 13,977 in Laos (1985 F. Proschan). Population total all countries 17,000 to 18,000. Oudomsay Province. Also spoken in Thailand, USA. Austro-Asiatic, Mon-Khmer, Northern Mon-Khmer, Khmuic, Mal-Khmu', Mal-Phrai. Not intelligible with Lua, Phai, or Pray 3. 'Mal' and 'Madl' are self names. 'T'in' is an ethnic name used in Thailand. NT 1994.

MALENG ***(MALIENG, MALANG)*** [PKT] 800 in Laos (1996 Ferlus). Population total both countries 1,000. Khammouan Province, Nam Theun Valley. Also spoken in Viet Nam. Austro-Asiatic, Mon-Khmer, Viet-Muong, Chut. Dialects: MALENG, PAKATAN (KHA PAKATAN), MALANG, HAREME.

MLABRI ***(MLA, MLA-BRI, MABRI, MRABRI, YUMBRI, MA KU, YELLOW LEAF)*** [MRA] 24 in Laos (1985 F. Proschan). Laos border area. Austro-Asiatic, Mon-Khmer, Northern Mon-Khmer, Khmuic, Mlabri. Nomadic. Mlabri are different from Kha Tong Luang (Phi Tong Luang, Yellow Leaf), which are Western Viet-Muong (Wurm and Hattori 1981). Forest. See main entry under Thailand.

NGEQ ***(NGEH, NGE', KRIANG, NKRIANG)*** [NGT] 4,000 (1981 Wurm and Hattori). Southern Laos, in the Muong Phine-Bung Sai area. Austro-Asiatic, Mon-Khmer, Eastern Mon-Khmer, Katuic, East Katuic, Ngeq-Nkriang. Closest to Khlor. Related to Alak 2. 70% monolingual. "Kha Koh" means '(derogatory) mountain people'. 'Nkriang' is their name for themselves. Literacy rate in first language: Below 1%. Literacy rate in second language: 15% to 25%.

NUNG ***(NONG)*** [NUT] A few in Laos. Tai-Kadai, Kam-Tai, Be-Tai, Tai-Sek, Tai, Central. Different from Chinese Nung (Cantonese in Viet Nam) and Tibeto-Burman Nung. An official ethnic community in Viet Nam. Bible portions 1971-1975. See main entry under Viet Nam.

NYAHEUN ***(NHA HEUN, NYAH HEUNY, HOEN, NIA HOEN, HUN, HIN, NIAHON, NYAHÖN, YAHEUN)*** [NEV] 4,000 (1981 Wurm and Hattori). Eastern part of Boloven Plateau near Saravan and Paksong. Austro-Asiatic, Mon-Khmer, Eastern Mon-Khmer, Bahnaric, West Bahnaric, Nyaheun. Literacy rate in first language: Below 1%. Literacy rate in second language: 15% to 25%.

O'DU ***(O DU, IDUH, 'IDUH, "TAY HAT", HAT, HAAT)*** [TYH] 194 in Laos (1989 F. Proschan 1996). Northern. Austro-Asiatic, Mon-Khmer, Northern Mon-Khmer, Khmuic, Mal-Khmu', Khmu'. An official ethnic community in Viet Nam. Speakers call themselves 'O Du'. See main entry under Viet Nam.

ONG [OOG] (10,000 together with Ir; 1981 Wurm and Hattori). Saravan Province, north of Saravan. Austro-Asiatic, Mon-Khmer, Eastern Mon-Khmer, Katuic, Central Katuic, Ta'oih. Closest to Ir. Investigation needed: intelligibility with Ir.

OY ***(HUEI, OI)*** [OYB] 10,600 (1981). South, foot of Boloven Plateau and Pakse. Austro-Asiatic, Mon-Khmer, Eastern Mon-Khmer, Bahnaric, West Bahnaric, Oi-The. Dialects: RIYAO, TAMAL EUY, INN TEA, KRANYEU. Related to Jeng, Sapuan, Sok, The. 80% monolingual. Investigation needed: intelligibility with Jeng, Sapuan, Sok, The. Traditional religion.

PACOH ***(BO RIVER VAN KIEU, POKOH)*** [PAC] Austro-Asiatic, Mon-Khmer, Eastern Mon-Khmer, Katuic, East Katuic, Katu-Pacoh. Dialect: PAHI. Related to Phuong. 'Koh' in 'Pacoh' means 'mountain'.

Literacy rate in first language: Below 1%. Literacy rate in second language: 15% to 25%. Bible portions 1965-1969. See main entry under Viet Nam.

PHAI ***(THUNG CHAN PRAY, PHAY, KHA PRAY, PRAY 1, PRAI)*** [PRT] West of B. Na Sing. Austro-Asiatic, Mon-Khmer, Northern Mon-Khmer, Khmuic, Mal-Khmu', Mal-Phrai. Distinct from Lua, Mal, and Pray 3. See main entry under Thailand.

PHANA' ***(PANA', BANA')*** [PHN] 5,000 (1981 Wurm and Hattori). One village in north Laos. Larger number near Yunnan border. Sino-Tibetan, Tibeto-Burman, Lolo-Burmese, Loloish, Southern, Akha. Adults speak some Lahu.

PHONG-KNIANG ***(PONG 3, KHANIANG, KENIENG, KENENG, LAO PHONG)*** [PNX] 1,000 (1981 Wurm and Hattori). Southern Hua Phan and northern Xieng Khwang provinces. Austro-Asiatic, Mon-Khmer, Northern Mon-Khmer, Khmuic, Xinh Mul. Related to Puoc and Khang. Phong is the exonymn of the Kenieng and is not to be confused with Kha Phong, a dialect of Maleng, nor with the autonym Pong as applied to one of the dialects of Hung (Ferlus 1996:16, 19). Investigation needed: intelligibility with Puoc, Khang. Many are educated.

PHU THAI ***(PUTAI, PHUTAI, PUTHAY)*** [PHT] 128,000 in Laos (1993 Johnstone). Also possibly in China. Tai-Kadai, Kam-Tai, Be-Tai, Tai-Sek, Tai, Southwestern, East Central, Lao-Phutai. Various dialects. Close to Lao. Bilingualism in Laotian. Agriculturalists. See main entry under Thailand.

PHUAN ***(LAO PHUAN, PHU UN)*** [PHU] 96,000 in Laos (1993 Johnstone). Bolikhamxai, Vientiane, Xieng Khoang, and Houaphan. Tai-Kadai, Kam-Tai, Be-Tai, Tai-Sek, Tai, Southwestern, East Central, Chiang Saeng. Closest to Northern Tai, Song, Tai Dam; close to Lao. The name is also used for Lao speakers in Thailand. Investigation needed: intelligibility. See main entry under Thailand.

PHUNOI ***(PHOUNOY, PHU NOI, PUNOI, CÔÔNG)*** [PHO] 20,000 in Laos (1993 Johnstone). Population total all countries 32,000 (1981 Wurm and Hattori). North central, around Phony Saly. Also spoken in Thailand, Viet Nam. Sino-Tibetan, Tibeto-Burman, Lolo-Burmese, Loloish, Southern, Phunoi. Dialects: BLACK KHOANY, WHITE KHOANY, MUNG, HWETHOM, KHASKHONG. Bisu, Pyen, and Mpi are closely related. Those listed as dialects may be separate languages. Called 'Phunoi' or 'Phounoy' in Laos, 'Côông' in Viet Nam. "Kha Punoi" is derogatory.

PU KO ***(POKO)*** [PUK] 2 villages. Tai-Kadai, Kam-Tai, Be-Tai, Tai-Sek, Tai, Southwestern. Two villages.

PUOC ***(KHA PUHOC, PUHOC, PUOK, POU HOK, XINH MUL, XIN MUL, XING MUN, KSING MUL, LAO MUH, KHA NIANG)*** [PUO] 2,164 in Laos (1985 F. Proschan). Northeast, Hua Phan and Xieng Khouang, Het River, along the Viet Nam border. Austro-Asiatic, Mon-Khmer, Northern Mon-Khmer, Khmuic, Xinh Mul. Related to Khang and Pong 3. Investigation needed: intelligibility with Khang, Pong 3. Buddhist. See main entry under Viet Nam.

RIEN [RIE] Tai-Kadai, Kam-Tai, Be-Tai, Tai-Sek, Tai, Unclassified.

SAEK ***(SEK, TAI SEK, SET)*** [SKB] More than half in Laos (1990 A. Diller ANU). Population total both countries 25,000. Central Laos near the Viet Nam border. Upper Nam Noy and Nam Pheo areas in Khammouan Province and the village of Na Kadok in Khamkeut District, Borikhamxay Province. Also spoken in Thailand. Tai-Kadai, Kam-Tai, Be-Tai, Tai-Sek, Sek. Dialects: NA KADOK, KHAMMOUAN. Closely related to Tai Mène. Bilingualism in Lao. The Saek of Na Kadok claim to have come originally from Phu Quan, Ban Pho Quang, Duc Tho District, in what is now Ha Tinh Province, Viet Nam. The Khammouan dialect speakers are originally from Nakai District, and is still spoken in Toeng, Nam Meo, Na Moey, and Beuk.

SALANG ***(HALANG)*** [HAL] 2,000 to 4,000 in Laos. Attopeu Province, southern Laos. Austro-Asiatic, Mon-Khmer, Eastern Mon-Khmer, Bahnaric, North Bahnaric, West, Jeh-Halang. Closely related to Jeh. Halang in Viet Nam may be a separate language. Literacy rate in first language: 5% to 10%. Literacy rate in second language: 25% to 50%. Traditional religion. Bible portions 1970-1972. See main entry under Viet Nam.

SAPUAN ***(SAPOUAN)*** [SPU] 2,400 (1981). Banks of the Se Kong and Se Kamane, Attopeu Province, southern Laos. Austro-Asiatic, Mon-Khmer, Eastern Mon-Khmer, Bahnaric, West Bahnaric, Oi-The. Related to Oy, Sok, Jeng. Investigation needed: intelligibility. Traditional religion.

SILA [SLT] 19,000 in Laos (1993 Johnstone). Population total both countries 19,600. North central, north of Muong Hai. Also spoken in Viet Nam. Sino-Tibetan, Tibeto-Burman, Lolo-Burmese, Loloish, Southern, Akha, Hani. An official ethnic community in Viet Nam.

SÔ ***(MANGKONG, MANG-KOONG, MAKONG, SO MAKON, MANKOONG, MANG CONG, BRU, KAH SO, THRO)*** [SSS] 102,000 in Laos. Population total both countries 157,000. Both sides of the Mekong River in Thakhek and Savannakhet Provinces in Laos and Thailand. Also spoken in Thailand. Austro-Asiatic, Mon-Khmer, Eastern Mon-Khmer, Katuic, West Katuic, Brou-So. Dialects: SO TRONG, SO SLOUY, SO PHONG, CHALI (CHARI, SHARI), KALEU. Because of contact with the Laotian Tai, they speak Tai dialects. Called 'Mangkong' and 'Bru' in Laos. The name 'So' is not used in Laos. Mangkong is a separate ethnic group. Literacy rate in first language: Below 1%. Literacy rate in second language: 15% to 25%. Bible portions 1980.

SOK ***(SORK, SAWK)*** [SKK] 1,600 (1981). Attopeu Province, southern Laos. Austro-Asiatic, Mon-Khmer, Eastern Mon-Khmer, Bahnaric, West Bahnaric, Oi-The. Related to Oy, Sapuan, Jeng. Investigation needed: intelligibility.

SOU ***(SUQ, SOUK, SU, SU')*** [SQQ] 1,000 (1962 Lafont). Attopeu Province, southern Laos. Austro-Asiatic, Mon-Khmer, Eastern Mon-Khmer, Bahnaric, West Bahnaric, Brao-Kravet. Investigation needed: intelligibility with Brao, Kravet, Krung 2.

TAI DAENG ***(RED THAI, THAI DO, THAI DANG, TAI DENG, DAENG)*** [TYR] 25,000 in Laos (CMA 1991). Northeastern Laos, near the Viet Nam border. Tai-Kadai, Kam-Tai, Be-Tai, Tai-Sek, Tai, Southwestern, East Central, Chiang Saeng. Part of the official Thai ethnic community in Viet Nam. See main entry under Viet Nam.

TAI DAM ***(BLACK TAI, TAI NOIR, THAI DEN)*** [BLT] Khammouan Province. Tai-Kadai, Kam-Tai, Be-Tai, Tai-Sek, Tai, Southwestern, East Central, Chiang Saeng. Dialect: TAI MUOI (TAI MUEI, TAY MUEAI, MEUAY). They live mixed with Tai Don. The two are not inherently intelligible, but are very closely related. Part of the Dai official nationality in China and the Thai official nationality in Viet Nam. Bible portions 1982-1993. See main entry under Viet Nam.

TAI DÓN ***(TAI BLANC, THÁI TRẮNG, TAI LAI, TAI KAO, WHITE TAI)*** [TWH] Northeastern Laos. Tai-Kadai, Kam-Tai, Be-Tai, Tai-Sek, Tai, Southwestern, East Central, Chiang Saeng. Not intelligible with Tai Dam. Those who have had prolonged contact with Tai Dam have become bilingual in it. Many have not had that contact. A large influential group. Part of the Thai official ethnic community in Viet Nam. Bible portions 1969. See main entry under Viet Nam.

TAI LOI ***(LOI, TAILOI, WAKUT, MONGLWE)*** [TLQ] Doi is in the northwest corner near the Myanmar and Chinese borders. Tai Loi is across the border in Myanmar. Tai Loi may also be in China. Austro-Asiatic, Mon-Khmer, Northern Mon-Khmer, Palaungic, Western Palaungic, Angkuic. Dialects: TAI LOI, DOI. Investigation needed: intelligibility with Doi. See main entry under Myanmar.

TAI LONG [THI] Tai-Kadai, Kam-Tai, Be-Tai, Tai-Sek, Tai, Southwestern. May be the same as Mao (Tai-Long, Tai-Mao, Maw, Mau) on the Burma-Yunnan border, a variety of Dai in China.

TAI MÈNE ***(TAI MAEN, TAI-MAEN, TAY MÈNÈ, TAI MENE, TAI MAN)*** [TMP] Borikhamxay Province, Vieng Thong District, several villages; Khamkeut District, many villages: Lak Xao, Khamkeut, Na Heuang, Nam Sak, Sop Chat, Ka'ane, Phon Thoen, Sop Pone, and Tha Veng. Tai-Kadai, Kam-Tai, Be-Tai, Tai-Sek, Tai, Northern. Closely related to Saek. They claim to have come from Xieng Lip and Ban Pot in Nghe An, Viet Nam.

TAI NÜA ***(CHINESE SHAN, TAI NEUA, TAI NUEA)*** [TDD] 120,000 in Laos (1990 A. Diller). Northwestern Laos. Also possibly in north Viet Nam. Tai-Kadai, Kam-Tai, Be-Tai, Tai-Sek, Tai, Southwestern, East Central, Northwest. A different dialect than in China. Called 'Dehong Dai' or 'Shan' in China. Investigation needed: intelligibility with dialects. Bible portions 1931-1948. See main entry under China.

TAI PAO [TPO] Khammouan Province. Tai-Kadai, Kam-Tai, Be-Tai, Tai-Sek, Tai, Unclassified. Classification problems, possibly due to migration.

TALIENG ***(TALIANG, TARIANG)*** [TDF] Muong Phine-Bung Sai area, Savannakhet Province. Austro-Asiatic, Mon-Khmer, Eastern Mon-Khmer, Bahnaric, North Bahnaric, West. Related to Trieng or Hre in Viet Nam; may be the same as Trieng. Apparently different from Tareng, which is East Katuic. 'Tariang' means 'headhunters'. Investigation needed: intelligibility with Trieng, Hre.

TA'OIH, LOWER ***(TONG)*** [TTO] Saravan. Austro-Asiatic, Mon-Khmer, Eastern Mon-Khmer, Katuic, Central Katuic, Ta'oih. Dialects: TONG, HANTONG'. Not intelligible with Upper Ta'oih. Some are bilingual in Upper Ta'oih.

TA'OIH, UPPER ***(TA-OY, TA-OI, TAU OI, TA HOI, KANTUA)*** [TTH] Population total all countries 30,000 (1981 Wurm and Hattori). Saravan Province, Laos. Also spoken in USA, Viet Nam. Austro-Asiatic, Mon-Khmer, Eastern Mon-Khmer, Katuic, Central Katuic, Ta'oih. Dialects: PASOOM, KAMUAN', PALEE'N, LEEM, HA'AANG (SA'ANG). Not intelligible with Lower Ta'oih until speakers have had at least 2 weeks' contact. 70% monolingual.

TARENG ***(TARIANG)*** [TGR] 5,000 (1981 Wurm and Hattori). Just west of Viet Nam border, east of Kayong, north of Chavane and Thia. Austro-Asiatic, Mon-Khmer, Eastern Mon-Khmer, Katuic, East Katuic, Katu-Pacoh. Distinct from Talieng, which is North Bahnaric.

TAY KHANG [TNU] Small. Khammouan Province. Possibly also in Viet Nam. Tai-Kadai, Kam-Tai, Be-Tai, Tai-Sek, Tai, Unclassified. Some problem in classification and confusion with Khang of Viet Nam.

THAI, NORTHERN ***(LANNA, LAN NA, LANATAI, LANNATAI, "YUAN", "YOUON", "YOUANNE", MYANG, MUANG)*** [NOD] 3,000 to 5,000 in Laos (1962 Lafont). Haut Mekong and Sayaboury provinces, Laos. Daic, Tai, Southwestern, East Central, Chiang Saeng. Dialect: NAN. Bible 1927, out of print. See main entry under Thailand.

THE ***(THAE)*** [THX] 1,500 (1962 Lafont). Attopeu Province, southern Laos. Austro-Asiatic, Mon-Khmer, Eastern Mon-Khmer, Bahnaric, West Bahnaric, Oi-The. Investigation needed: intelligibility with Oy.

YOY ***(YOI, YOOI, YOOY)*** [YOY] Daic, Tai, Unclassified. Bilingualism in Lao. May be the same as Tai Yo of Khamouan Province, a Northern Tai language. See main entry under Thailand.

LEBANON

Republic of Lebanon, al-Jumhouriya al-Lubnaniya. National or official languages: Standard Arabic, French. 3,191,000 (1998 UN). Literacy rate 70% to 75%. Also includes Assyrian Neo-Aramaic 1,000, Chaldean Neo-Aramaic, Kurmanji 70,000, Turoyo. Information mainly from T. Sebeok 1963; H. Fleisch 1974; W. Fischer and O. Jastrow 1980. Shi'a Muslim, Sunni Muslim, Christian, Druze, secular. Blind population 5,000. Deaf population 219,480. Deaf institutions: 13. Data accuracy estimate: B. The number of languages listed for Lebanon is 5. Of those, all are living languages. Diversity index 0.14.

ARABIC, NORTH LEVANTINE SPOKEN ***(LEVANTINE ARABIC, LEBANESE-SYRIAN ARABIC, SYRO-LEBANESE ARABIC)*** [APC] 3,900,000 in Lebanon, 93% of the population (1991). Throughout Lebanon. Afro-Asiatic, Semitic, Central, South, Arabic. Dialects: NORTH LEBANESE ARABIC, NORTH-CENTRAL LEBANEE ARABIC, SOUTH-CENTRAL LEBANESE ARABIC, SOUTH LEBANESE ARABIC, CENTRAL SYRIAN ARABIC (SHAMI). National language. Muslim, Christian, Druze. Bible portions 1973. See main entry under Syria.

ARABIC, STANDARD [ABV] Middle East, North Africa. Afro-Asiatic, Semitic, Central, South, Arabic. Used for education, official purposes, communication among Arabic speaking countries. National language. Dictionary. Bible 1984-1991. See main entry under Saudi Arabia.

ARMENIAN ***(ERMENICE, ARMANSKI, HAIEREN, SOMKHURI)*** [ARM] 234,600 in Lebanon, 6% of the population (1986). Indo-European, Armenian. Dialect: WESTERN ARMENIAN. Eastern dialect (4,341,000) spoken in Armenia and in its Turkish and Iranian borderlands. Western dialect (879,612) spoken elsewhere. Language of wider communication. Christian. Bible 1853-1978. See main entry under Armenia.

ENGLISH [ENG] Indo-European, Germanic, West, English. Has been used to some extent since the founding of the American University of Beirut in 1866. Many English language publications. Not spoken on the street or in Lebanese homes. Bible 1535-1989. See main entry under United Kingdom.

FRENCH [FRN] Indo-European, Italic, Romance, Italo-Western, Western, Gallo-Iberian, Gallo-Romance, Gallo-Rhaetian, Oïl, French. An estimated 20% of the population speak French in their daily lives, and up to 65% of the population can read and converse in French. A number of government and private universities teach in French. Official language. The language of instruction in most schools. Newspapers, magazines. Bible 1530-1986. See main entry under France.

MALAYSIA

National or official language: Malay. 21,410,000 (1998 UN). Also includes Burmese, Western Cham, Chinese Sign Language, Malayalam 37,000, Eastern Panjabi 43,000, Telugu 30,000, people from Indonesia, Pakistan, the Philippines, Sri Lanka, Thailand, United Kingdom. Information mainly from S. Wurm and S. Hattori 1981. Deaf population 31,000 (1980). Deaf institutions: 5. Data accuracy estimate: B, C. The number of languages listed for Malaysia is 140. Of those, 139 are living languages and 1 is extinct. Diversity index 0.75.

MALAYSIA (PENINSULAR)

10,115,000 (1979). 6,396,790 speakers of Austronesian languages, 3,399,000 speakers of Chinese languages, 44,610 speakers of Austro-Asiatic languages (1991 J. Matisoff), 1,090,000 speakers of Dravidian languages. Information mainly from W. G. Shellabear 1913; F. Lebar, G. Hickey, J. Musgrave 1967; R. K. Dentan 1968; I. Hancock 1969; S. Lim 1981; B. Comrie 1987; A. Baxter 1988; J. Holm 1989. Blind population 22,300. Data accuracy estimate: B, C. The number of languages listed for Malaysia (Peninsular) is 39. Of those, all are living languages. Diversity index 0.65.

BATEK ***(BATEQ, BATEG, BATOK, KLEB, TOMO, NONG)*** [BTQ] 700 (1981 Wurm and Hattori). Northern Pahang, Kelantan, Trengganu. Austro-Asiatic, Mon-Khmer, Aslian, North Aslian, Eastern. Dialects: BATEK TEQ (TEQ), BATEK DE' (DEQ), BATEK IGA, BATEK NONG (NONG). Deq and Nong may be separate languages. Investigation needed: intelligibility with Mintil.

BESISI ***(MAH MERI, CELLATE)*** [MHE] 1,356 (1981 Wurm and Hattori). Selangor coast, Malacca. Austro-Asiatic, Mon-Khmer, Aslian, South Aslian. Dialects: KUALA LANGOT BESISI, MALAKKA BESISI, ULU LANGAT ORANG BUKIT, SELANGOR SAKAI, BETISE' (BETISEK), SISI. One other dialect became extinct in late 19th century. NT 1933.

CHEWONG ***(CHEQ WONG, CHE'WONG, SIWANG, BERI, CHUBA)*** [CWG] 270 (1975 SIL). Just south of Semai, Pahang. Austro-Asiatic, Mon-Khmer, Aslian, North Aslian, Chewong.

CHINESE, HAKKA [HAK] 985,635 in Malaysia, including 786,097 in Peninsular Malaysia, 109,060 in Sarawak, 90,478 in Sabah (1980 census). Sino-Tibetan, Chinese. Bible 1916. See main entry under China.

CHINESE, MANDARIN [CHN] 417,070 in Malaysia (1970 census). Peninsular Malaysia, Sabah, and Sarawak. Sino-Tibetan, Chinese. Speakers are primarily urban, in business. Bible 1874-1983. See main entry under China.

CHINESE, MIN DONG [CDO] 206,013 in Malaysia, including 85,368 in Peninsular Malaysia, 120,645 in Sarawak (1979, including Pu-Xian Chinese. Sino-Tibetan, Chinese. Dialect: FOOCHOW (FUZHOU). Bible 1884-1905. See main entry under China.

CHINESE, MIN NAN ***(MIN NAN, MINNAN)*** [CFR] 1,946,698 in Malaysia, including 1,824,741 in Peninsular Malaysia, 7,990 Teochew, 5,083 Hainanese, 24,604 Hokkien in Sabah (1980 census) 84,280 in Sarawak (1979). Sino-Tibetan, Chinese. Dialects: FUKIENESE (AMOY, FUJIANESE, HOKKIEN), HAINANESE, CHAOCHOW (TEOCHOW, TEOCHEW). Bible 1933. See main entry under China.

CHINESE, PU-XIAN [CPX] Peninsular Malaysia and Sarawak. Sino-Tibetan, Chinese. Dialect: XINGHUA (HSINGHUA, HINGHUA). Bible 1912. See main entry under China.

CHINESE, YUE ***(CANTONESE, YUE, YUEH)*** [YUH] 748,010 in Malaysia, including 704,286 in Peninsular Malaysia, 24,640 in Sarawak, 19,184 in Sabah (1980 census). Sino-Tibetan, Chinese. Dialects: CANTONESE, TOISHANESE. Bible 1894-1981. See main entry under China.

DUANO' ***(ORANG KUALA, DESIN DOLA')*** [DUP] 1,922 (1981 Wurm and Hattori). South coast around Pontian Kecil and northwest. Austronesian, Malayo-Polynesian, Western Malayo-Polynesian, Sundic, Malayic, Malayan, Para-Malay.

ENGLISH [ENG] Indo-European, Germanic, West, English. Bible 1535-1989. See main entry under United Kingdom.

JAH HUT ***(JAH HET)*** [JAH] 2,442 (1981 Wurm and Hattori). Just south of main body of Semai, Kuala Krau, Pahang. Austro-Asiatic, Mon-Khmer, Aslian, Jah Hut. Dialects: KERDAU, KRAU, KETIAR KRAU (TENGGANU), KUALA TEMBELING, PULAU GUAI, ULU CERES (CHERES), ULU TEMBELING.

JAKUN ***(JAKU'D, JAKUD'N, JAKOON, DJAKUN, ORANG HULU)*** [JAK] 9,799 (1981 Wurm and Hattori). East coast and inland, Pairang River, Pekan to Sri Gading, east to Benut, northwest to around middle Muat River. Austronesian, Malayo-Polynesian, Western Malayo-Polynesian, Sundic, Malayic, Malayan, Aboriginal Malay.

JEHAI ***(JAHAI, PANGAN)*** [JHI] 1,250 (1981 Wurm and Hattori). Northeastern Perak and western Kelantan. Austro-Asiatic, Mon-Khmer, Aslian, North Aslian, Eastern. Dialects: JEHAI, BATEK TEH. Investigation needed: intelligibility with Menriq.

KENSIU ***(KENSEU, KENSIEU, KENSIW, SEMANG, MONIQ, MONIK, MENDI, NEGRITO, NGOK PA, ORANG BUKIT, ORANG LIAR)*** [KNS] 3,000 in Malaysia. Population total both countries 3,300 (1984 D. Hogan). Northeast Kedah, near Thai border. Overlaps slightly into southern Yala Province of Thailand. Also spoken in Thailand. Austro-Asiatic, Mon-Khmer, Aslian, North Aslian, Western. Dialects: IJOH (IJOK), JARUM, JEHER (SAKAI TANJONG OF TEMONGOH), KEDAH (QUEDAH), PLUS, ULU SELAMA, KENSIU BATU, KENSIU SIONG, KENTAQ NAKIL. 'Semang' means 'debt slave' in Khmer, used more for primitive Negritos. 'Semang' is used to differentiate western groups from eastern ones, called Pangan. Orang Asli means 'aborigine' in Malay. Tropical forest. Nomadic.

KINTAQ ***(KENTA, KINTAK, KINTAQ BONG, BONG)*** [KNQ] Population total both countries 100 (1975 SIL). Kedah-Perak border area, Thai border. Overlaps slightly into Southern Yala Province of Thailand. Also spoken in Thailand. Austro-Asiatic, Mon-Khmer, Aslian, North Aslian, Western.

KUALA LUMPUR SIGN LANGUAGE ***(KLSL)*** [KGI] Kuala Lumpur and elsewhere in Peninsular Malaysia. Deaf sign language. American signs were introduced in the late 1960s to a class for deaf children. They were promoted by the club for deaf adults which was started at the YMCA in 1973. Many former users of Penang Sign Language now use KLSL. Uses predominantly American signs in a mixture of English and Malay word order. Investigation needed: bilingual proficiency in Malaysian Sign Language.

LANOH ***(JENGJENG)*** [LNH] 260 (1975 SIL). North central Perak. Austro-Asiatic, Mon-Khmer, Aslian, Senoic.

MALACCAN CREOLE MALAY ***(CHITTIES CREOLE MALAY)*** [CCM] Malacca Straits. Creole, Malay based. May be historically related to Sri Lankan Creole Malay. Spoken since the 16th century by descendants of Tamil merchants who intermarried with other groups. The speakers are called 'Chitties' (Lim 1981:126-8; Holm 1989:580). Has not been studied in detail. Investigation needed: intelligibility with Sri Lankan Creole Malay.

MALACCAN CREOLE PORTUGUESE ***(MALAYSIAN CREOLE PORTUGUESE, MALACCAN, PAPIA KRISTANG, KRISTANG, PORTUGUESE PATOIS, SERANI, BAHASA SERANI, BAHASA***

GERAGAU, MALAQUEIRO, MALAQUENSE, MALAQUÊS, MALAQUENHO, PORTUGUÊS DE MALACA, MALAYO-PORTUGUESE) [MCM] 5,000 (1997 Col. Timothy D'Souza, Eurasian Association). Population total both countries 5,000 or more (1997). Trankera and Hilir, Melaka, Straits of Malacca, Malacca city and the southwest coast of the Malaysian Peninsula. Related varieties in parts of Kuala Lumpur and Singapore. Variety in Pulau Tikus, Penang is now virtually extinct. Also spoken in Singapore. Creole, Portuguese based. Most speakers also know local varieties of Bazaar Malay and Malaysian English. Some Creole people speak only English. Some older female speakers have limited English. Most people over 20 speak Kristang, and 1/3 of those under 20. Also spoken as second language by some Chinese shopkeepers in Hilir. Used by Creole people more in 1997 than in 1987. 'Kristang' is their name for the language, people, and religion. Trade language. Dictionary. Grammar. Fishermen. Bible portions 1884.

MALAY *(BAHASA MALAYSIA, BAHASA MALAYU, MALAYU, MELAJU, MELAYU, STANDARD MALAY)* [MLI] 7,181,000 or 47% of the population (1986), including 248,757 in Sarawak (1980 census), 2,000,000 in Kelantan and Trengganu, and 1,000,000 in other parts of Malaysia; 10,000,000 in Malaysia including second language speakers (1977 SIL). Population total all countries 18,000,000 or more. All districts of Peninsular Malaysia, Sabah, and Sarawak. Also spoken in Brunei, Indonesia (Sumatra), Myanmar, Singapore, Thailand, UAE, USA. Austronesian, Malayo-Polynesian, Western Malayo-Polynesian, Sundic, Malayic, Malayan, Local Malay. Dialects: TRENGGANU, KELANTAN, KEDAH, PERAK (SOUTHERN MALAY), SARAWAK MALAY, BAZAAR MALAY (LOW MALAY, PASAR MALAY, PASIR MALAY, TRADE MALAY). 'Bazaar Malay' is used to refer to many regional nonstandard dialects. Over 80% cognate with Indonesian. Bilingualism in English, Chinese, Tamil. National language. Grammar. SVO. Roman and Arabic (Jawi) scripts. Agriculturalists: wet and dry rice, rubber, fruits, vegetables; fishermen. Bible 1733-1993.

MALAY, BABA *(STRAITS MALAY, CHINESE MALAY)* [BAL] 5,000 in Malacca or 3% of the Chinese population (1979 Tan Chee Beng). Melaka Tengah, Malacca Straits, Peninsular Malaysia. Creole, Malay based. Regional variants between Malacca and Singapore. Partially intelligible with Standard Malay. It is different from Peranakan Indonesian. Much bilingualism in Standard Malay. The only monolinguals are over 70 years old. It developed since the 15th century from Low Malay with many Hokkien Chinese borrowings. Lim (1981) and Holm (1989) treat it as a Malay-based creole. NT 1913, out of print. See main entry under Singapore.

MALAYSIAN SIGN LANGUAGE *(BAHASA MALAYSIA KOD TANGAN)* [XML] Deaf sign language. It is manually coded Bahasa Malaysia; it is easier than manual codes for other languages because Bahasa Malaysia is comparatively noninflected. It has input from local and American signs and structure. Under development by the Ministry of Education since 1978, and used in government programs. Words without signs are fingerspelled using the international version of the American manual alphabet.

MINRIQ *(MENRIQ, MENRIK, MENDRIQ, MENRAQ)* [MNQ] 125 (1981 Wurm and Hattori). Southeast Kelantan. Austro-Asiatic, Mon-Khmer, Aslian, North Aslian, Eastern. Investigation needed: intelligibility with Jehai.

MINTIL *(MITIL)* [MZT] 40 (1975 SIL). Tamun River, Pahang. Austro-Asiatic, Mon-Khmer, Aslian, North Aslian, Eastern. Investigation needed: intelligibility with Batek.

NEGERI SEMBILAN MALAY *(MALAYSIAN MINANGKABAU, ULU MUAR MALAY, ORANG NEGERI)* [ZMI] 300,000 (1981 Wurm and Hattori). Southeast of Kuala Lumpur, Ulu Muar District. Austronesian, Malayo-Polynesian, Western Malayo-Polynesian, Sundic, Malayic, Malayan, Para-Malay. Related to Minangkabau in Sumatra, Indonesia. People call themselves 'Orang Negeri' or use their district name, and call Minangkabau immigrants, who have come during the last 60 to 80 years, 'Minang'. Sunni Muslim.

ORANG KANAQ [ORN] 34 (1981 Wurm and Hattori). Southeast and northeast of Mawai. Austronesian, Malayo-Polynesian, Western Malayo-Polynesian, Sundic, Malayic, Malayan, Aboriginal Malay.

ORANG SELETAR [ORS] Population total both countries 541 (1981 Wurm and Hattori). Southeast coast around Kukuo, Jahore Bahru, east and north, and the north coast of Singapore. Also spoken in Singapore. Austronesian, Malayo-Polynesian, Western Malayo-Polynesian, Sundic, Malayic, Malayan, Aboriginal Malay. Coastal.

PENANG SIGN LANGUAGE [PSG] Penang. Deaf sign language. Deaf school established in 1954, where only oral method was used. Sign language evolved outside the classroom. Use declined in the late 1970s due to spread of other sign languages, but there are still users.

SABÜM [SBO] North central Perak. Austro-Asiatic, Mon-Khmer, Aslian, Senoic. Closest to Lanoh and Semnam; but not the same as Lanoh.

SEMAI *(CENTRAL "SAKAI", SENOI, SENGOI)* [SEA] 18,327 (1981 Wurm and Hattori). Northwest Pahang and southern Perak, Selangor, Negri Sembilan, central mountain area. Austro-Asiatic, Mon-Khmer, Aslian, Senoic. Dialects: JELAI, ORANG TANJONG OF ULU LANGAT, SUNGKAI, PERAK I, PERAK II,

CAMERON, TELOM, BIDOR, BETAU, LIPIS, BIL, ULU KAMPAR (KAMPAR). Bilingualism in Malay. Sakai means 'slave'. The west Semai are more acculturated to Malay society than the east Semai. Tropical forest. Mountain slope. Agriculturalists: rice, sweet potatoes, bananas, fruit, rubber. 2,500 to 3,000 feet. Bible portions 1951-1962.

SEMAQ BERI ***(SEMAQ BRI, SEMOQ BERI)*** [SZC] 2,080 (1981 Wurm and Hattori). Pahang, Trengganu, Kelantan. Austro-Asiatic, Mon-Khmer, Aslian, South Aslian. Two dialects.

SEMELAI [SZA] 2,682 (1981 Wurm and Hattori). Between Segamat (Johore) and the Pahang River. Austro-Asiatic, Mon-Khmer, Aslian, South Aslian. Two dialects became extinct in the early 20th century. Investigation needed: intelligibility with Temoq.

SEMNAM [SSM] North central Perak. Austro-Asiatic, Mon-Khmer, Aslian, Senoic. Close to Lanoh and Sabüm.

TAMIL [TCV] 1,060,000 in Malaysia (1993). Dravidian, Southern, Tamil-Kannada, Tamil-Kodagu, Tamil-Malayalam, Tamil. Bilingualism in Malay, English. Together with speakers of Hindi, Telugu, Malayalam, Urdu, Gujarati, Sindhi, Panjabi they total 10% of the population or 1,528,000. Some are plantation workers. Bible 1727-1995. See main entry under India.

TEMIAR ***(TEMER, NORTHERN SAKAI, SEROQ, PIE)*** [TMH] 11,593 (1981 Wurm and Hattori). Mostly in Perak and Kelantan; also Pahang. Austro-Asiatic, Mon-Khmer, Aslian, Senoic. Dialects: GRIK, KENDERONG, KENERING, PO-KLO (SAKAI BUKIT OF TEMONGOH), SAKAI OF PLUS KORBU, SUNGAI PIAH, TANJONG RAMBUTAN, TEMBE' (TEMBI), ULU KINTA (KINTA SAKAI), LANOH KOBAK. Semi-nomadic. Grammar.

TEMOQ [TMO] 350 (1981 Wurm and Hattori). Jeram River, southeast Pahang. Austro-Asiatic, Mon-Khmer, Aslian, South Aslian. Investigation needed: intelligibility with Semelai.

TEMUAN ***(BENUA, NIAP)*** [TMW] 9,312 (1981 Wurm and Hattori). Southern extension of the main range in the southern half of the peninsula, Selangor, Pahang, Jahore, Negri Sembilan, Kuala Langat, scattered settlements. Austronesian, Malayo-Polynesian, Western Malayo-Polynesian, Sundic, Malayic, Malayan, Aboriginal Malay. Dialects: BEDUANDA (BIDUANDA), BELANDA (BELANA, BLANDA, LANDA, BELANAS, BELANDAS), BEREMBUN (BIRMUN), MANTRA (MENTERA, MINTRA), TEMUAN, UDAI. Also classified as Malacca group of Austro-Asiatic phylum. Beduanda is sometimes considered to be a separate language. Traditional religion.

TONGA ***(MOS)*** [TNZ] Northwest tip north of Kaki. Austro-Asiatic, Mon-Khmer, Aslian, North Aslian, Tonga. Dialect: SATUN. Probably close to Kensiu. See main entry under Thailand.

MALAYSIA (SABAH)

1,002,608 (1980). Literacy rate 58%. Information mainly from C. P. Miller 1981-1982, 1987; J. K. King and J. W. King 1984; A. K. Pallesen 1984; J. Walton and D. Moody 1984; P. R. Kroeger 1985, 1986; M. and A. Boutin 1985; M. Boutin 1986; C. Sather 1997. Data accuracy estimate: A1, A2. The number of languages listed for Malaysia (Sabah) is 54. Of those, all are living languages. Diversity index 0.73.

ABAI SUNGAI [ABF] 500 (1982 SIL). Lower reaches of the Kinabatangan River. Austronesian, Malayo-Polynesian, Western Malayo-Polynesian, Borneo, Northwest, Sabahan, Paitanic. Distinct from other Paitanic languages (Upper Kinabatangan, Tombonuwo). 1 school. Investigation needed: bilingual proficiency, attitudes. Fishermen.

BAJAU, WEST COAST ***(LAND BAJAW, WEST COAST BAJAO)*** [BDR] 40,000 (1982), 97,124 Bajau and Sama in Sabah (1980 census). Kuala Penyu to Kudat, northern and some eastern areas, west coast of Sabah. Austronesian, Malayo-Polynesian, Western Malayo-Polynesian, Sama-Bajaw, Sulu-Borneo, Borneo Coast Bajaw. Dialects: KOTA BELUD, KAWANG, PUTATAN, PAPAR, BANGGI, SANDAKAN BAJAU, PITAS BAJAU. Diversified in structure more than other Borneo languages. Related to, but a distinct language from, Sama (East Coast Bajau) groups of Malaysia and Philippines, and Indonesian Bajau (K. Pallesen 1977). 60% intelligibility of Sama. Papar dialect used in national broadcasting. May be more than one language. Radio programs. Fishermen, agriculturalists: rice, fruit, vegetables; animal husbandry: chickens, goats, water buffaloes, ponies.

BANJAR ***(BANJARESE, BANDJARESE, BANJAR MALAY)*** [BJN] 900,000 in Sabah (1993). Tawau. Austronesian, Malayo-Polynesian, Western Malayo-Polynesian, Sundic, Malayic, Malayan, Local Malay. Separated from Brunei-Kedayan for at least 400 years. Investigation needed: intelligibility with Malay, Indonesian. See main entry under Indonesia, Kalimantan.

BAUKAN ***(BAUKAN MURUT)*** [BNB] 1,800 to 2,100 or more (1985 SIL), including 300 or more Tengara. Keningau and Kinabatangan districts around the headwaters of the Sook and Kinabatangan rivers. Austronesian, Malayo-Polynesian, Western Malayo-Polynesian, Borneo, Northwest, North Sarawakan, Dayic, Murutic, Northern. Dialects: BAUKAN (BAOKAN, BOKAN, BOOKAN, BOKEN, BOKUN, BUKUN, BOKON, ULUN-NO-BOKON, ULUN-NO-BOKAN, PINGAS), KOKOROTON MURUT, TENGARA

(TUNGARA, TINGARA, TENGGARAQ, TANGARA', TANGGARAQ, KINABATANGAN MURUT). Closely related to Keningau Murut, Timugon, and Tagal.

BISAYA, SABAH ***(BASAYA, BESAYA, BISAIA, BISAYAH, JILAMA BAWANG, JILAMA SUNGAI)*** [BSY] 10,000 to 12,000 (1985 SIL). On the coast north of and around Brunei Bay, mainly in west Beaufort along Padas River, south of Weston, and south Kuala Penyu districts to coast. Austronesian, Malayo-Polynesian, Western Malayo-Polynesian, Borneo, Northwest, Sabahan, Dusunic, Bisaya. 90% intelligibility with Tatana. 58% lexical similarity with Sarawak Bisaya, 57% to 59% with Brunei Bisaya ('Dusun'). Negative attitudes toward Tatana and Coastal Kadazan. Both North and South Bisaya are in Sabah (Wurm and Hattori 1981). Most people are educated to primary level, not many to secondary.

BONGGI ***(BANGGI, BANGAY, BANGGI DUSUN)*** [BDG] 1,400 (1990 UBS). Banggi Island in Kudat District, 15 villages. Austronesian, Malayo-Polynesian, Western Malayo-Polynesian, Meso Philippine, Palawano. Closest to Molbog of the Philippines, although not very close. Bilingualism in Sabah Malay. Bible portions 1992.

BRUNEI ***(BRUNEI-KADAIAN, ORANG BUKIT)*** [KXD] 54,000 in Malaysia (46,500 in Sabah, 7,500 in Sarawak). Upper Balait and Tutau rivers, northern coast, 4th and 5th Divisions, Sarawak; Sabah in Beaufort, Kuala Penyu, Labuan, Labuk-Sugut, Papar, Sipitang, Sandakan, and Tenom Districts. Austronesian, Malayo-Polynesian, Western Malayo-Polynesian, Sundic, Malayic, Malayan, Local Malay. Dialects: BRUNEI, KADAIAN (KADAYAN, KADIAN, KADIEN, KADYAN, KARAYAN, KEDYAN, KEDAYAN, KEDIEN, KERAYAN). Dialect variations are regional, not ethnic. 73% to 80% lexical similarity with Standard Malay. Bilingualism in Malay. Investigation needed: bilingual proficiency, attitudes toward Malay. Agriculturalists (Kedayan), fishermen (Brunei). See main entry under Brunei.

BUGIS ***(BUGINESE)*** [BPR] Austronesian, Malayo-Polynesian, Western Malayo-Polynesian, Sulawesi, South Sulawesi, Bugis. Bible 1900, in press (1995). See main entry under Indonesia, Sulawesi.

CHAVACANO [CBK] One village in Semporna. Creole, Spanish based. NT 1981. See main entry under Philippines.

DUMPAS ***(DOOMPAS)*** [DMV] 500 to 1,000 (1985 SIL). Perancangan village in Labuk-Sugut District. Austronesian, Malayo-Polynesian, Western Malayo-Polynesian, Borneo, Northwest, Sabahan, Dusunic, Unclassified. May be Paitanic. Comprehension of Tombonuo 87%, Eastern Kadazan 57%, Coastal Kadazan 44%. Bilingualism in Tambanua. Language dying out because of intermarriage with other groups. Investigation needed: bilingual proficiency, attitudes.

DUSUN, CENTRAL ***(DUSUN, DUSAN, DUSUM, DUSUR, KADAYAN, KEDAYAN, KADASAN, CENTRAL KADAZAN)*** [DTP] 140,500 (1991 SIL), including 50,000 Ranau (1989 UBS), 70,000 Bundu (1990 UBS), 500(?) Kuala Monsok Dusun (1981 Wurm and Hattori). Beaufort, Kota Belud, Kota Kinabalu, Kota Marudu, Kinabatangan, Keningau, Labuk-Sugut, Penampang, Papar, Ranau, Tambunan, Tenom, Tuaran, and Tawau districts. Austronesian, Malayo-Polynesian, Western Malayo-Polynesian, Borneo, Northwest, Sabahan, Dusunic, Dusun, Central. Dialects: DUSUN SINULIHAN (SINULIHAN), KADAZAN-TAGARO (TAGARO), KIUNDU, PAHU', SOKID, TINDAL, MENGGATAL (KIULU, TELIPOK), RANAU, BUNDU (TAGINAMBUR), BEAUFORT, LUBA, KUALA MONSOK DUSUN. Ranau dialect is different from Ranau in Sumatra, Indonesia. Dictionary. Bible 1990.

DUSUN, SUGUT ***(DUSUN, SUGUT, SUGUT KADAZAN, KADAYAN, TANGGAL, TILAU-ILAU)*** [KZS] 8,000 to 9,000 (1985 SIL). Headwaters of the Sugut River, Labuk-Sugut District. Austronesian, Malayo-Polynesian, Western Malayo-Polynesian, Borneo, Northwest, Sabahan, Dusunic, Dusun, Central. Dialects: TINAGAS, TALANTANG. Bilingualism in Central Dusun. Comprehension testing needed with Central Dusun, Minokok, and Kimaragang. Investigation needed: intelligibility.

DUSUN, TAMBUNAN ***(TAMBUNAN)*** [KZT] Throughout Tambunan District and parts of Keningau. Austronesian, Malayo-Polynesian, Western Malayo-Polynesian, Borneo, Northwest, Sabahan, Dusunic, Dusun, Central. Agriculturalists: rice.

DUSUN, TEMPASUK ***(TINDAL, KEDAMAIAN DUSUN, TAMPASUK, TAMPASSUK, TAMPASOK, TEMPASOK)*** [TDU] 6,000(?) (1981 Wurm and Hattori). Area around Tempasuk village, Kota Belud. Austronesian, Malayo-Polynesian, Western Malayo-Polynesian, Borneo, Northwest, Sabahan, Dusunic, Dusun, Central. Investigation needed: intelligibility with Central Dusun.

GANA ***(GANAQ, GANA', MINANSUT, KENINGAU DUSUN)*** [GNQ] 2,000 (1985 SIL). Minusut and Kuangoh, Keningau District along the Baiaya River, a tributary of the Pegalan River, north of Keningau town. Austronesian, Malayo-Polynesian, Western Malayo-Polynesian, Borneo, Northwest, Sabahan, Dusunic, Dusun. Bilingualism in Sabah Malay, Central Dusun, Bahasa Malaysia. People seldom use Gana.

IDA'AN ***(ERAANS, BULUD UPI, IDAAN, IDAHAN, IDAN, IDAYAN)*** [DBJ] 6,000 (1987 SIL), including 1,500 Begahak. East coast of Sabah, Lahad Datu, Kinabatangan, and Sandakan districts. Austronesian, Malayo-Polynesian, Western Malayo-Polynesian, Borneo, Northwest, Sabahan, Ida'an. Dialects: BEGAK

(BEGAHAK, BAGAHAK), SUBPAN (SUPAN, SUNGAI), IDA'AN. Not closely related to other languages. Bible portions 1987-1997.

ILANUN ***(ILLANUN, ILLANOAN, ILLANOON, IRANON MARANAO, IRANUM, IRANUN, LANOON, YLANOS, LANUN, ILLANOS)*** [ILL] 6,000 (1981 Wurm and Hattori). 17 villages around Lahad Datu and Kota Belud districts; also reported to be in Kudat and Marudu. Austronesian, Malayo-Polynesian, Western Malayo-Polynesian, Southern Philippine, Danao, Maranao-Iranon. Most closely related to Maranao of the Philippines (85% intelligibility). Related to, but distinct from, Iranun and Magindanao of the Philippines. They claim to have come from Mindanao, Philippines in 1850. Different from Lahanan (Lanun) of Sarawak. Investigation needed: intelligibility. Fishermen; agriculturalists: rice, fruit trees.

JAVANESE ***(JAWA)*** [JAN] 300,000 in Sabah (1981 Wurm and Hattori). Austronesian, Malayo-Polynesian, Western Malayo-Polynesian, Sundic, Javanese. Several dialects in Sabah. SVO. Bible 1854-1994. See main entry under Indonesia, Java and Bali.

KADAZAN, COASTAL ***(PENAMPANG KADAZAN, PAPAR KADAZAN, MEMBAKUT KADAZAN)*** [KZJ] 60,000 (1986 SIL). West coast of Sabah, Penampang and Papar districts. Austronesian, Malayo-Polynesian, Western Malayo-Polynesian, Borneo, Northwest, Sabahan, Dusunic, Dusun. Dictionary. VSO. Bible portions 1986.

KADAZAN, KLIAS RIVER [KQT] 1,000 (1984 SIL). Klias River area, Beaufort District. Austronesian, Malayo-Polynesian, Western Malayo-Polynesian, Borneo, Northwest, Sabahan, Dusunic, Dusun. Low intelligibility with Coastal Kadazan. 77% lexical similarity with Tatana. Investigation needed: bilingual proficiency in Tatana. Agriculturalists.

KADAZAN, LABUK-KINABATANGAN ***(EASTERN KADAZAN, LABUK KADAZAN, SOGILITAN, TINDAKON, TOMPULUNG)*** [DTB] 21,000 to 24,000 including 14,000 to 16,000 Labuk (1987 SIL), 7,000 to 8,000 Sungai (1982 SIL). Northeast Sabah, Sandakan, Labuk-Sugut, and Kinabatangan districts. Austronesian, Malayo-Polynesian, Western Malayo-Polynesian, Borneo, Northwest, Sabahan, Dusunic, Dusun, Eastern. Dialects: MANGKAAK (MANGKAHAK, MANGKOK, MANGKAK), SUKANG, LABUK, LAMAG SUNGAI (SUNGEI). Bilingualism in Sabah Malay. Investigation needed: intelligibility with Kinabatangan Sungai. VSO, prepositions, genitives after nouns, question word initial, nontonal. NT 1996.

KALABAKAN ***(KALABAKAN MURUT, TAWAU MURUT, TIDUNG)*** [KVE] 1,500 to 2,000 (1989 SIL). Tawau District along the Kalabakan River. Austronesian, Malayo-Polynesian, Western Malayo-Polynesian, Borneo, Northwest, North Sarawakan, Dayic, Murutic, Tidong.

KENINGAU MURUT ***(CENTRAL MURUT)*** [KXI] 4,000 to 5,200 (1982 SIL), including 1,000 to 1,200 Dusun Murut (1985 SIL). 34,282 all Murut in Sabah (1980 census). Keningau District within a 10-mile radius to the north of Keningau town along the Pegalan River. Austronesian, Malayo-Polynesian, Western Malayo-Polynesian, Borneo, Northwest, North Sarawakan, Dayic, Murutic, Murut. Dialects: NABAY (NABAI, NEBEE, DABAY, DABAI, RABAY, RABAI), AMBUAL, DUSUN MURUT. Closely related to Baukan and Timugon. No one under 20 uses Nabay as first language. Investigation needed: intelligibility, bilingual proficiency in Baukan.

KIMARAGANG ***(KIMARAGAN, KIMARAGANGAN, MARAGANG, MARIGANG)*** [KQR] 10,000 (1987 SIL), including 6,000 Tandek, 2,000 Sonsogon. Kota Marudu and Pitas districts. Austronesian, Malayo-Polynesian, Western Malayo-Polynesian, Borneo, Northwest, Sabahan, Dusunic, Dusun. Dialects: TANDEK (GARO), PITAS KIMARAGANG, SANDAYO, SONSOGON. Dandun is somewhat different. Intelligibility of Sandayo with other dialects needs testing. Agriculturalists: paddy rice, cocoa, cash crops. Bible portions 1996.

KINABATANGAN, UPPER [DMG] 5,300 to 6,400 (1987 SIL), including 500 Dusun Segama and 800 to 900 Sinabu' (1985 SIL). Primarily the upper reaches of the Kinabatangan River, also Lahad Datu and Sandakan districts, Maligatan, Minusu, and Tongud. Austronesian, Malayo-Polynesian, Western Malayo-Polynesian, Borneo, Northwest, Sabahan, Paitanic, Upper Kinabatangan. Dialects: KALABUAN (KOLOBUAN), MAKIANG, DUSUN SEGAMA (SAGA-I, SOGHAI, SEGAI), SINABU' (SINABU). Dialects have 87% intelligibility. All dialects have over 90% lexical similarity, except Makiang and Sinabu' with 80%. Agriculturalists, rattan gatherers, lumbermen. Bible portions 1984-1995.

KOTA MARUDU TALANTANG [GRM] 800 to 1,000 (1985 SIL). Kota Marudu District, in Talantang 1 and Talantang 2. Austronesian, Malayo-Polynesian, Western Malayo-Polynesian, Borneo, Northwest, Sabahan, Dusunic, Dusun. Bilingualism in Kimaragang. Agriculturalists: wet rice.

KOTA MARUDU TINAGAS [KTR] 1,250 (1985 SIL). Southern Kota Marudu and Parong, a migrant village in northern Kota Marudu. Austronesian, Malayo-Polynesian, Western Malayo-Polynesian, Borneo, Northwest, Sabahan, Dusunic, Dusun, Central. Investigation needed: intelligibility with Central Kadazan (Ranau), Kimaragang, Sugut, Talantang.

KUIJAU ***(KIJAU, KUJAU, KWIJAU, MINANSUT, KULIOW, KUIYOW, KURIYO, KOIJOE, MENINDAL, TINDAL, MENINDAQ, TIDUNG, HILL DUSUN)*** [DKR] 5,000 to 6,000 (1985 SIL). Keningau District to the west and north of Keningau town within a 12-mile radius. Austronesian, Malayo-Polynesian,

Western Malayo-Polynesian, Borneo, Northwest, Sabahan, Dusunic, Dusun. They also use Central Dusun.

LOBU, LANAS [RUU] 2,800 including 2,000 in Lobu, 800 in Rumanau (1986 SIL). Lobu in Keningau District near Lanas, Rumanau in Masaum, Mangkawagu, Minusu, Kinabatangan District. Austronesian, Malayo-Polynesian, Western Malayo-Polynesian, Borneo, Northwest, Sabahan, Paitanic, Upper Kinabatangan. Dialects: LOBU, RUMANAU (RUMANAU ALAB, ROMANAU, ROOMARROWS). Investigation needed: intelligibility with Upper Kinabatangan. Agriculturalists.

LOBU, TAMPIAS [LOW] 1,800 (1985 SIL). 3 villages in Ranau around Tampias. Austronesian, Malayo-Polynesian, Western Malayo-Polynesian, Borneo, Northwest, Sabahan, Paitanic, Upper Kinabatangan. High intelligibility with Upper Kinabatangan. 73% lexical similarity with Lanas Lobu. High bilingualism in Central Dusun. Plantation agriculturalists.

LOTUD *(LATOD, LATUD, SUANG LOTUD, TUARAN DUSUN)* [DTR] 5,000 (1985 SIL). Tuaran District, just north of Kota Kinabalu, a 10-mile radius around Tuaran town. Austronesian, Malayo-Polynesian, Western Malayo-Polynesian, Borneo, Northwest, Sabahan, Dusunic, Dusun. Agriculturalists: rice. Bible portions 1992.

MALAY, COCOS ISLANDS *(COCOS, KOKOS, KUKUS)* [COA] 3,000 in Sabah (1975 SIL). Population total both countries 4,000. Tawau and Lahad Datu. From the Cocos Islands (Keeling Islands), an Australian territory. Also spoken in Australia. Austronesian, Malayo-Polynesian, Western Malayo-Polynesian, Sundic, Malayic, Malayan, Local Malay. Investigation needed: intelligibility with Standard Malay, Indonesian.

MALAY, SABAH *(BAZAAR MALAY, PASAR MALAY)* [MSI] Austronesian, Malayo-Polynesian, Western Malayo-Polynesian, Sundic, Malayic, Malayan, Local Malay. A few mother tongue speakers in urban areas, especially children of parents who have different mother tongues. Used mainly as a contact language, so it is not yet fully developed. Speakers shift to various other languages they know to fill in expressions in domains where Sabah Malay is lacking. For at least this reason, if the only form of Malay a person knows is Sabah Malay, he will have difficulty understanding Standard Malay in other domains. 'Bazaar Malay' is used to refer to many regional nonstandard varieties of Malay. Trade language. Dictionary. SVO. Agriculturalists: wet and dry rice, rubber, fruits, vegetables; fishermen; shopkeepers; small traders.

MAPUN *(SAMA MAPUN, JAMA MAPUN, CAGAYAN DE SULU, CAGAYANON, BAJAU KAGAYAN, ORANG CAGAYAN, KAGAYAN)* [SJM] East coast of Sabah, concentrated in Sandakan, west coast of Sabah: Banggi, Marudu, Kudat, Kota Kinabalu. Austronesian, Malayo-Polynesian, Western Malayo-Polynesian, Sama-Bajaw, Sulu-Borneo, Borneo Coast Bajaw. Bible portions 1979-1985. See main entry under Philippines.

MINOKOK [MQQ] 2,000(?) (1981 Wurm and Hattori). Headwaters of Kinabatangan River. Austronesian, Malayo-Polynesian, Western Malayo-Polynesian, Borneo, Northwest, Sabahan, Dusunic, Dusun, Central. Closest to Labuk-Kinabatangan Kadazan and Kimaragang.

MOLBOG [PWM] Banggi Island. Austronesian, Malayo-Polynesian, Western Malayo-Polynesian, Meso Philippine, Palawano. Brooke's Point Palawano 27% intelligibility; South Palawano 55% intelligibility. Quezon Palawano (Central) 69% lexical similarity. Bible portions 1977. See main entry under Philippines.

PALUAN [PLZ] 4,000 to 5,000 (1990 SIL), including 3,000 Paluan, 1,000 to 2,000 Pandewan. Sabah, Tenom, Keningau, and Pensiangan districts along some tributaries of the Padas River, and along the Dalit, Keramatoi, Nabawan, Pamentarian, and Mesopo rivers, and the lower Sook River valley, and the headwaters of the Talankai and Sapulut rivers. Austronesian, Malayo-Polynesian, Western Malayo-Polynesian, Borneo, Northwest, North Sarawakan, Dayic, Murutic, Murut. Dialects: PALUAN (PELUAN), DALIT MURUT, SOOK MURUT, TAKAPAN, MAKAHEELIGA (MAKIALIGA), PANDEWAN (PANDEWAN MURUT). Closest to Tagal Murut. Speakers are also fluent in Tagal.

PAPAR *(BAJAU BUKIT)* [DPP] 600 to 800 (1985 SIL). Kuala Penyu District. Austronesian, Malayo-Polynesian, Western Malayo-Polynesian, Borneo, Northwest, Sabahan, Dusunic, Dusun. High comprehension of Tatana. Much intermarriage with Tatana, Bisaya, Bajau, Brunei Kedayan speakers.

RUNGUS *(DUSUN DAYAK, MELOBONG RUNGUS, MEMAGUN, MEMOGUN, MOMOGUN, ROONGAS, RUNGUS DUSUN)* [DRG] 15,000 (1991 UBS). Kudat, Pitas, and Labuk-Sugut districts. Austronesian, Malayo-Polynesian, Western Malayo-Polynesian, Borneo, Northwest, Sabahan, Dusunic, Dusun. Dialects: NULU, GONSOMON, RUNGUS. Dictionary. NT 1981.

SAMA, BALANGINGI *(BALANGINGI BAJAU, BAANGINGI', NORTHERN SINAMA, BALANIAN, BALAGNINI, BALANINI, BALIGNINI, BINADAN, BANADAN)* [SSE] 30,000 in all East Coast Bajau (Sama), including Kagayan (Sama Mapun) and Southern Sama (1977 K. Pallesen SIL). East coast of Sabah. Austronesian, Malayo-Polynesian, Western Malayo-Polynesian, Sama-Bajaw, Sulu-Borneo, Inner Sulu Sama. Bible portions 1981-1982. See main entry under Philippines.

SAMA, CENTRAL ***(SIASI SAMA, CENTRAL SINAMA, SAMAL, SINAMA)*** [SML] Southeastern Sabah, especially Semporna District. Austronesian, Malayo-Polynesian, Western Malayo-Polynesian, Sama-Bajaw, Sulu-Borneo, Inner Sulu Sama. NT 1987. See main entry under Philippines.

SAMA, SOUTHERN ***(SAMA SIBUTU', SOUTHERN BAJAU)*** [SIT] 20,000 or more in Sabah. East, north, and west coasts: Banggi, Kota Belud, Gaya Island, Kuala Penyu. Austronesian, Malayo-Polynesian, Western Malayo-Polynesian, Sama-Bajaw, Sulu-Borneo, Inner Sulu Sama. Dialects: BAJAU BANARAN, BAJAU DARAT, BAJAU LAUT (MANDELAUT, PALA'AU, SAMA LAUT, SAMA MANDELAUT, SAMA PALA'AU, SEA BAJAU, SEA GYPSIES), BAJAU SEMPORNA (BAJAU ASLI, KUBANG, SAMA KUBANG), LAMINUSA (LAMINUSA SINAMA), SIBUTU (SIBUTUQ, SAMA SIBUTU, SAMAH-SAMAH, SAMAH LUMBUH), SIMUNUL (SAMA SIMUNUL), SIKUBUNG (KUBUNG, SAMA KUBUNG), SAMA (A'A SAMA, SAMA', SAMAH, SAMAL, SAMAR), UBIAN (OBIAN, SAMA UBIAN, TAU UBIAN). Bible portions 1979-1981. See main entry under Philippines.

SELUNGAI MURUT [SLG] 300 in Sabah (1990 SIL). Population total both countries 800 (1981 Wurm and Hattori). Pensiangan District, 1 village, along the Sapulut River from the confluence with the Pensiangan River south to the Indonesian border. Also spoken in Indonesia (Kalimantan). Austronesian, Malayo-Polynesian, Western Malayo-Polynesian, Borneo, Northwest, North Sarawakan, Dayic, Murutic, Murut.

SEMBAKUNG MURUT ***(TINGGALAN, TINGGALUM, TINGALUN, SIMBAKONG, SEMBAKOENG, SEMBAKONG, TIDONG, TIDOENG, TIDUNG)*** [SMA] Along the Sembakung River in northern Kalimantan, Indonesia, from the mouth upstream possibly as far as Sabah. Austronesian, Malayo-Polynesian, Western Malayo-Polynesian, Borneo, Northwest, North Sarawakan, Dayic, Murutic, Tidong. See main entry under Indonesia, Kalimantan.

SERUDUNG MURUT ***(SERUDONG, TAWAU MURUT, TIDUNG)*** [SRK] 1,000 (1989 SIL). Tawau District along the Serudung River and one village 12 miles from Tawau town. Austronesian, Malayo-Polynesian, Western Malayo-Polynesian, Borneo, Northwest, North Sarawakan, Dayic, Murutic, Tidong.

TAGAL MURUT [MVV] 28,000 to 48,000 in Sabah, Malaysia (1987 SIL). Population total both countries 30,000 to 50,000. Pensiangan, Keningau, Tenom, Sipitang districts over the whole southwestern portion of Sabah, south into Kalimantan, Indonesia. Also spoken in Indonesia (Kalimantan). Austronesian, Malayo-Polynesian, Western Malayo-Polynesian, Borneo, Northwest, North Sarawakan, Dayic, Murutic, Murut. Dialects: RUNDUM (ARUNDUM), TAGAL (TAGGAL, TAGUL, TAGOL, NORTH BORNEO MURUT, SABAH MURUT), SUMAMBU (SEMEMBU, SEMAMBU, SUMAMBUQ), TOLOKOSON (TELEKOSON), SAPULOT MURUT (SAPULUT MURUT), PENSIANGAN MURUT (PENTJANGAN, LAGUNAN MURUT), SALALIR (SADALIR, SEDÁLIR, SARALIR), ALUMBIS (LUMBIS, LOEMBIS), TAWAN, TOMANI (TUMANIQ), MALIGAN (MAULIGAN, MELIGAN, BOL MURUT, BOLE MURUT). Closest to Paluan. Literacy rate in second language: 20%. NT 1984-1991.

TATANA ***(TATANA', TATANAQ)*** [TXX] 5,500 (1982 SIL). Kuala Penyu District. Austronesian, Malayo-Polynesian, Western Malayo-Polynesian, Borneo, Northwest, Sabahan, Dusunic, Bisaya.

TAUSUG ***(TAW SUG, SULU, SULUK, SOOLOO, TAUSOG, TAOSUG, MORO, JOLOANO, JOLOANO SULU)*** [TSG] 110,000 in Sabah, Malaysia (1982 SIL). Sempurna, Sandakan, Tawau, Lahad Datu, Labuk-Sugut, Kudat districts. Austronesian, Malayo-Polynesian, Western Malayo-Polynesian, Meso Philippine, Central Philippine, Bisayan, South, Butuan-Tausug. Immigrants from the Sulu Archipelago in the Philippines. Known as 'Suluk' in Sabah. Malay-Arabic script used. Agriculturalists: dry and wet rice, maize, millet, cassava, yam, bananas, fruit, coconuts; fishermen; animal husbandry: goats, cattle, water buffaloes, chickens, geese, ducks. NT 1985. See main entry under Philippines.

TEBILUNG ***(TABILONG, TOBILANG, TOBILUNG)*** [TGB] 2,000 or more (1984 SIL). Kota Marudu District, on the road from Kota Belud to Kudat, and in Kota Belud. Austronesian, Malayo-Polynesian, Western Malayo-Polynesian, Borneo, Northwest, Sabahan, Dusunic, Dusun. Low intelligibility with Central Kadazan, Kimaragang.

TIDONG ***(CAMUCONES, NONUKAN, TEDONG, TIDOENG, TIRAN, TIRONES, TIROON, ZEDONG)*** [TID] 9,800 in Sabah (1982 SIL). Sabah, Labuk-Sugut, Sandakan, and Tawau Districts. Population center is along northeast coast of Kalimantan, Indonesia. Austronesian, Malayo-Polynesian, Western Malayo-Polynesian, Borneo, Northwest, North Sarawakan, Dayic, Murutic, Tidong. Dialects: TARAKAN (TERAKAN), SESAYAP (SESAJAP). Investigation needed: intelligibility with Tarakan in Kalimantan. See main entry under Indonesia, Kalimantan.

TIMUGON MURUT ***(TIMUGON, TIMOGUN, TIMIGAN, TIMIGUN, TIMOGON, TUMUGUN, TEMOGUN, TENOM MURUT)*** [TIH] 7,200 to 8,700 (1982 SIL), including 1,200 to 1,700 in Beaufort Murut (1982 SIL). Tenom District along the Padas River from Melalap to Batu, and Beaufort District along the Bukau and lower Padas rivers. Austronesian, Malayo-Polynesian, Western Malayo-Polynesian, Borneo, Northwest, North Sarawakan, Dayic, Murutic, Murut. Dialects: KAPAGALAN, POROS, BEAUFORT MURUT (BINTA'), TIMUGON, SANDIWAR (SANDEWAR), DABUGUS, LOWER MURUT, MURUT PADAASS, BUKAU (BUKOW). NT 1998.

TOMBONUWO ***(TOMBONUO, TOMBONUVA, TAMBANUO, TAMBANUA, TAMBANUVA, TAMBANWAS, TAMBENUA, TAMBUNWAS, TEMBENUA, TUNBUMOHAS, TUMBUNWHA, PAITAN, SUNGAI, SUNGEI, LOBU)*** [TXA] 20,000 (1991 UBS), including 3,000 Lingkabau. Labuk-Sugut, Kota Marudu, and Pitas districts. Austronesian, Malayo-Polynesian, Western Malayo-Polynesian, Borneo, Northwest, Sabahan, Paitanic. Dialect: LINGKABAU SUGUT (LINKABAU). Bible portions 1987-1998.

WOLIO ***(BUTON, BUTUNG, BUTONESE)*** [WLO] Austronesian, Malayo-Polynesian, Western Malayo-Polynesian, Sulawesi, Muna-Buton, Buton. The name 'Buton' is often used generically outside southeast Sulawesi for people from southeast Sulawesi, or is confused with Bajau people as sailors. The varieties spoken in Sabah may be Cia-Cia, Tukangbesi, Indonesian Bajau, or some other. See main entry under Indonesia, Sulawesi.

YAKAN ***(YACAN)*** [YKA] 5,000 to 10,000 in Sabah (1985). Austronesian, Malayo-Polynesian, Western Malayo-Polynesian, Sama-Bajaw, Yakan. Mainly temporary workers. NT 1984. See main entry under Philippines.

MALAYSIA (SARAWAK)

1,294,000 (1979). Information mainly from A. A. Cense and E. M. Uhlenbeck 1958; R. Blust 1974; P. Sercombe 1997. Data accuracy estimate: B. The number of languages listed for Malaysia (Sarawak) is 47. Of those, 46 are living languages and 1 is extinct. Diversity index 0.44.

BALAU ***(BALA'U)*** [BUG] 5,000 (1981 Wurm and Hattori). Southwest Sarawak, southeast of Simunjan. Austronesian, Malayo-Polynesian, Western Malayo-Polynesian, Sundic, Malayic, Malayic-Dayak, Ibanic. Investigation needed: intelligibility with Iban.

BERAWAN [LOD] 870 (1981 Wurm and Hattori). Tutoh and Baram rivers in the north. Austronesian, Malayo-Polynesian, Western Malayo-Polynesian, Borneo, Northwest, North Sarawakan, Berawan-Lower Baram, Berawan. Dialects: BATU BLA (BATU BELAH), LONG PATA, LONG JEGAN, WEST BERAWAN, LONG TERAWAN. It may be two languages: West Berawan and Long Terawan, versus East-Central Berawang: Batu Belah, Long Teru, and Long Jegan (Blust 1974).

BIATAH ***(KUAP, QUOP, BIKUAB, SENTAH)*** [BTH] Population total both countries 20,100 (1981 Wurm and Hattori). Sarawak, 1st Division, Kuching District, 10 villages. Also spoken in Indonesia (Kalimantan). Austronesian, Malayo-Polynesian, Western Malayo-Polynesian, Borneo, Land Dayak. Dialects: SIBURAN, STANG (SITAANG, BISITAANG), TIBIA. Speakers cannot understand Bukar Sadong, Silakau, or Bidayuh from Indonesia. 71% lexical similarity with Singgi. Siburan is the prestige dialect. 'Bidayuh' is a cover term for all Sarawak Land Dayak groups plus Selako. 'Siburan' is the speakers' name for themselves. Literacy rate in second language: 45%. Radio programs. Agriculturalists: sago, wet rice, vegetables, fruit, rubber, pepper; animal husbandry: pigs, poultry; government employees. NT 1963.

BINTULU [BNY] 4,200 (1981 Wurm and Hattori). Northeast coast around Sibuti, west of Niah, around Bintulu, and two enclaves west. Austronesian, Malayo-Polynesian, Western Malayo-Polynesian, Borneo, Northwest, North Sarawakan, Bintulu. Could also be classified as in Baram-Tinjar Subgroup or as an isolate within the Rejang-Baram Group. Blust classifies as an Isolate with North Sarawakan. Not close to other languages. Investigation needed: bilingual proficiency. Coastal.

BISAYA, SARAWAK ***(BISAYAH, BISAYA BUKIT, VISAYAK, BEKIAU, LORANG BUKIT)*** [BSD] 7,000 (1984 SIL). Southeast of Marudi, 5th Division. Austronesian, Malayo-Polynesian, Western Malayo-Polynesian, Borneo, Northwest, Sabahan, Dusunic, Bisaya, Southern. Dialects: LOWER BISAYA, MID BISAYA, UPPER BISAYA. 58% lexical similarity with Sabah Bisaya, 78% to 79% with Brunei Bisaya, and lower with other Dusunic languages or any other language in Sabah. Radio programs. Agriculturalists: hill and wet rice, fruit, vegetables, rubber; sago palm; animal husbandry: water buffalo; fishermen. Bible portions 1938.

BUKAR SADONG ***(SADONG, BUKA, BUKAR, TEBAKANG, SERIAN, SABUTAN, SEPUTAN, SAPUTAN)*** [SDO] Population total both countries 34,600 (1981 Wurm and Hattori). Serian 1st Division, Sarawak, 30 or more villages. Also spoken in Indonesia (Kalimantan). Austronesian, Malayo-Polynesian, Western Malayo-Polynesian, Borneo, Land Dayak. Dialects: BUKAR BIDAYUH (BIDAYUH, BIDAYAH), BUKAR SADONG, MENTUH TAPUH. 57% lexical similarity with Bahasa Malaysia. Radio programs.

BUKITAN ***(BAKITAN, BAKATAN, BEKETAN, MANGKETTAN, MANKETA, PAKATAN)*** [BKN] Population total both countries 410 (1981 Wurm and Hattori). Kapit, 7th Division. Also spoken in Indonesia (Kalimantan). Austronesian, Malayo-Polynesian, Western Malayo-Polynesian, Borneo, Northwest, Melanau-Kajang, Kajang. Investigation needed: intelligibility with Ukit, Sian, Puna Batu 1.

DARO-MATU [DRO] 7,600 including 4,800 Matu, 2,800 Daro (1981 Wurm and Hattori). Matu River from north channel of Rejang River to the sea, around Daro and Matu. Austronesian, Malayo-Polynesian,

Western Malayo-Polynesian, Borneo, Northwest, Melanau-Kajang, Melanau. Dialects: DARO, MATU. Investigation needed: intelligibility with Melanau.

IBAN *(SEA DAYAK)* [IBA] 400,000 in Sarawak (1995 P. Martin). Population total all countries 415,000 (1995 P. Martin), 1,000,000 including second language users (1999 WA). From Sadong River north to Bintulu, Sibu, one village in Tawau District of Sabah. Also spoken in Brunei, Indonesia (Kalimantan). Austronesian, Malayo-Polynesian, Western Malayo-Polynesian, Sundic, Malayic, Malayic-Dayak, Ibanic. Dialects: BATANG LUPAR, BUGAU, SKRANG, DAU, LEMANAK, ULU AI, UNDUP. Dialect of Second Division is the norm for literature. Largest language group in Sarawak. Grammar. SVO. Iban taught in some primary schools. Radio programs. Agriculturalists: dry and wet rice, fruit, rubber; fishermen. Bible 1988.

JAGOI *(SARAWAK DAYAK, JAGGOI, BAU-JAGOI)* [SNE] 19,000 (1981 Wurm and Hattori). Bau, 1st Division, Sadong, Samarahan and Lundu rivers, about 50 villages. Austronesian, Malayo-Polynesian, Western Malayo-Polynesian, Borneo, Land Dayak. Dialects: GROGO (GROGOH), STENGGANG JAGOI, KROKONG, GUMBANG, SERAMBAU (SERAMBU, SERAMBO), EMPAWA, ASSEM, SINGGE (SINGGAI, SINGGI, SINGGIE, SINGHI, BISINGAI), SUTI, TENGOH, DONGAY, TAUP (TAHUP). Gumbang may not be a Jagoi dialect, but closer to Tringus. Related to Tringus. 69% lexical similarity with Bukar Sadong, 53% between Bukar Sadong and Singgai. Radio programs.

KAJAMAN *(KAYAMAN, KEJAMAN)* [KAG] 500 (1981 Wurm and Hattori). Near Belaga on the Baloi River in central Sarawak, 7th Division. Austronesian, Malayo-Polynesian, Western Malayo-Polynesian, Borneo, Northwest, Melanau-Kajang, Kajang. Limited comprehension of Iban. Investigation needed: intelligibility with Sekapan.

KANOWIT [KXN] 170 (1981 Wurm and Hattori). Middle Rejang River, below Tanjong language, 3rd Division. Austronesian, Malayo-Polynesian, Western Malayo-Polynesian, Borneo, Northwest, Melanau-Kajang, Melanau. Bilingualism in Iban. Being absorbed by Iban. Investigation needed: bilingual proficiency in Iban.

KAYAN, BARAM *(BARAM KAJAN)* [KYS] 4,150 (1981 Wurm and Hattori). Baram River area, Upper Sarawak. Not in Brunei. Austronesian, Malayo-Polynesian, Western Malayo-Polynesian, Borneo, Kayan-Murik, Kayan. Dialects: LONG ATIP, LONG AKAHSEMUKA. Trade language. Agriculturalists: wet and dry rice, sweet potatoes, bananas, tobacco, sugarcane, maize, rubber; hunters; fishermen; rattan sellers, beeswax, camphor. Bible 1990.

KAYAN, MURIK [MXR] 1,120 (1981 Wurm and Hattori). Below Long Miri (Banyuq) and below Lio Mato (Semiang) on the Baram River. Austronesian, Malayo-Polynesian, Western Malayo-Polynesian, Borneo, Kayan-Murik, Murik. Dialects: LONG BANYUQ (BANYUQ), LONG SEMIANG (SEMIANG). Not closely related to other languages.

KAYAN, REJANG *(REJANG KAJAN)* [REE] 3,030 (1981 Wurm and Hattori). Rejang, Balui river areas. Austronesian, Malayo-Polynesian, Western Malayo-Polynesian, Borneo, Kayan-Murik, Kayan. Dialects: MA'AGING, LONG BADAN, UMA DARO, LONG KEHOBO (UMA POH), UMA JUMAN, LONG MURUN, LONG GENG, LEMENA, LISUM. Limited comprehension of Baram Kayan. Different from Rejang in Sumatra.

KELABIT *(KALABIT, KERABIT)* [KZI] Population total both countries 1,650 (1981 Wurm and Hattori). Northern Sarawak, in the remotest and highest of Borneo mountains. Also spoken in Indonesia (Kalimantan). Austronesian, Malayo-Polynesian, Western Malayo-Polynesian, Borneo, Northwest, North Sarawakan, Dayic, Kelabitic. Dialects: BRUNG, LIBBUNG, LEPU POTONG, BARIO, LON BANGAG. Long Napir, Long Seridan, Pa'Dalih, Long Leilang, Bruang may also be dialects (Blust 1974). Speakers strongly independent. Agriculturalists: paddy and hill rice, maize, tapioca, pineapple, pumpkin, cucumber, beans, fruits; hunters; fishermen. Bible portions 1965.

KENYAH, BAKUNG *(BAKUNG, BAKONG, BAKUNG KENYA)* [BOC] South central, near Kalimantan border. Austronesian, Malayo-Polynesian, Western Malayo-Polynesian, Borneo, Northwest, North Sarawakan, Kenyah. Dialect: OGA BAKUNG. See main entry under Indonesia, Kalimantan.

KENYAH, SEBOB *(SIBOP, SEBOP, SEBOB, SABUP, SAMBUP)* [SIB] 1,730 (1981 Wurm and Hattori). On the upper Tinjar River in northern Sarawak, 4th Division, between the Rejang and Baram rivers, several large villages. Austronesian, Malayo-Polynesian, Western Malayo-Polynesian, Borneo, Northwest, North Sarawakan, Kenyah, Sebob. Dialects: TINJAR SIBOP, LIRONG, LONG POKUN, BAH MALEI (BA MALI), LONG ATUN, LONG EKANG (LONG IKANG), LONG LUYANG. Not closely related to other languages.

KENYAH, TUTOH *(TUTOH KENYA)* [TTW] 600 (1981 Wurm and Hattori). Northeast, Tutoh River. Austronesian, Malayo-Polynesian, Western Malayo-Polynesian, Borneo, Northwest, North Sarawakan, Kenyah. Dialects: LONG WAT, LONG LABID, LUGAT. Not closely related to other languages.

KENYAH, UPPER BARAM *(UPPER BARAM KENJA, KENJA, KENYAH, KINJIN, KINDJIN, KANYAY)* [UBM] Population total both countries 2,660 (1981 Wurm and Hattori). Upper Baram River near the Kalimantan border. Not in Brunei. Also spoken in Indonesia (Kalimantan). Austronesian,

Malayo-Polynesian, Western Malayo-Polynesian, Borneo, Northwest, North Sarawakan, Kenyah, Main Kenyah. Long Anap may be a dialect (Blust 1974).

KENYAH, WESTERN ***(WESTERN KENYA, KENJA, KINJIN, KINDJIN, KANYAY)*** [XKY] 1,250 (1981 Wurm and Hattori). Balui, Belaga, Kalua, and Kemena rivers. Austronesian, Malayo-Polynesian, Western Malayo-Polynesian, Borneo, Northwest, North Sarawakan, Kenyah, Main Kenyah. Dialects: LONG BANGAN, KEMENA PENAN, KAKUS PENAN, UMA BAKAH (LONG BULAN), LUNAN. Madang may be a dialect. 80% lexical similarity between Madang and Lepu Kulit. Agriculturalists: wet and dry rice, sweet potatoes, bananas, tobacco, sugar cane, maize, rubber; hunters; fishermen.

KIPUT [KYI] 2,460 (1981 Wurm and Hattori). Northeast around Marudi. Not in Brunei. Austronesian, Malayo-Polynesian, Western Malayo-Polynesian, Borneo, Northwest, North Sarawakan, Berawan-Lower Baram, Lower Baram, Central, A. Dialects: LONG KIPUT, LONG TUTOH (KUALA TUTOH), LEMITING. Related to Narom, Lelak, Tutong 2, Belait, and Berawan.

LAHANAN ***(LANUN, LANAN)*** [LHN] 350 (1981 Wurm and Hattori). Central, east of Belaga, southwest of Long Murum. Austronesian, Malayo-Polynesian, Western Malayo-Polynesian, Borneo, Northwest, Melanau-Kajang, Kajang. Closest to Kayaman. Not the same as Illanun of Sabah or Iranun of the Philippines.

LARA' ***(LURU)*** [LRA] Two small villages on Pasir River, Lundu, 1st Division. Austronesian, Malayo-Polynesian, Western Malayo-Polynesian, Borneo, Land Dayak. Related to Bukar-Sadong. See main entry under Indonesia, Kalimantan.

LELAK [LLK] 220 (1981 Wurm and Hattori). Northeast, east of Sibuti (Dali) and the Tinjar River (Lelak). Austronesian, Malayo-Polynesian, Western Malayo-Polynesian, Borneo, Northwest, North Sarawakan, Berawan-Lower Baram, Lower Baram, Central, B. Dialects: LELAK, DALI. Related to Narom, Kiput, Tutong 2, Berawan. They may now speak only Belait.

LUNDAYEH ***(LUN DAYAH, LUN DAYE, LUN DAYEH, LUN DAYA, LUN DAYOH, LUNDAYA, LUN LOD, SOUTHERN MURUT)*** [LND] 12,800 including 10,000 in Lun Bawang dialect in Sarawak (1987), 2,800 in Lun Daye in Sabah (1982 SIL). Southwestern border of Sabah and Sarawak. Austronesian, Malayo-Polynesian, Western Malayo-Polynesian, Borneo, Northwest, North Sarawakan, Dayic, Kelabitic. Dialects: LUN BAWANG (SARAWAK MURUT), LUN DAYAH, ADANG, BALAIT (TABUN, TRENG), KOLUR, PADAS, TRUSAN (LAWAS, LIMBANG), LEPU POTONG. Not Murutic, although sometimes called Southern Murut. Radio programs. Agriculturalists: wet and dry rice, coffee, sugar cane, maize, cucumber, pumpkin, tapioca, coconut, banana, pomelo, papaya, durian, mango; animal husbandry: chicken, pigs, buffaloes; hunters, fishermen. Bible 1982. See main entry under Indonesia, Kalimantan.

MADANG ***(BADANG, MEDANG, MALANG, LEPO TAU KENYAH, LEPO TAU KENYA, LEPU TAU)*** [MQD] Tinjar River, 4th Division. Austronesian, Malayo-Polynesian, Western Malayo-Polynesian, Borneo, Northwest, North Sarawakan, Kenyah, Sebob. Investigation needed: intelligibility with Sebob Kenyah, Lepu Tau, Lepu Anan, Long Aki. Literacy rate in second language: 25%. NT 1978.

MELANAU ***(MILANAU, MILANO, BELANA'U)*** [MEL] 25,120. Population total both countries 25,320 (1981 Wurm and Hattori). Coastal area of the Rejang delta up to the Balingian River, 3rd Division. Also spoken in Brunei. Austronesian, Malayo-Polynesian, Western Malayo-Polynesian, Borneo, Northwest, Melanau-Kajang, Melanau. Dialects: MUKAH-OYA (MUKAH, MUKA, OYA, OYA', OGA), BALINGIAN, BRUIT, DALAT (DALAD), IGAN, SARIKEI, SEGAHAN, PREHAN, SEGALANG, SITENG. Bilingualism in Malay. Literacy rate in second language: 52%. Tropical forest. Agriculturalists: sago, rice, coconut, rubber; fishermen; loggers; animal husbandry: chickens, goats, water buffalos; traders with Iban.

MILIKIN ***(MILLIKIN, REMUN)*** [MIN] 3,500 (1999 Peter Cullip). Serian District, Kuching Division, and dialects in 13 villages southeast of Serian to Balai Ringin. Austronesian, Malayo-Polynesian, Western Malayo-Polynesian, Sundic, Malayic, Malayic-Dayak, Ibanic. Iban reported to be intelligible only with difficulty. Some bilingualism in Iban, Bahasa Malaysia, Sarawak Malay, English, Bidayuh. All ages. Attitudes toward Iban and Malay go from indifferent to unfriendly. The people's name for their language is 'Remun', and for themselves is 'Remun Iban'. Christian, traditional religion, Baha'i.

NAROM ***(NARUM)*** [NRM] 2,420 (1981 Wurm and Hattori). South of the mouth of the Baram River around Miri and to the south. Austronesian, Malayo-Polynesian, Western Malayo-Polynesian, Borneo, Northwest, North Sarawakan, Berawan-Lower Baram, Lower Baram, Central, B. Dialects: NAROM, MIRI.

OKOLOD ***(KOLOUR, KOLUR, KOLOD, OKOLOD MURUT)*** [KQV] 1,100 to 1,200, including 1,000 in Sarawak, 100 to 200 in Sabah (1987 SIL). Population total both countries 2,000 to 3,500 (1985 SIL). Sabah southwest of Tenom and Sipitang districts on some of the plantation estates and some along the headwaters of the Padas River. Primarily in Sarawak and Kalimantan, Indonesia. Also spoken in Indonesia (Kalimantan). Austronesian, Malayo-Polynesian, Western Malayo-Polynesian, Borneo, Northwest, North Sarawakan, Dayic, Murutic, Murut. 82% lexical similarity with Okolod of Sabah; 70% with Pensiangan Murut (Tagal), 34% with Lundayeh. 1 school in Sarawak.

PENAN, EASTERN ***("PUNAN")*** [PEZ] East of the Baram River, Apoh River district. Also spoken in Brunei. Austronesian, Malayo-Polynesian, Western Malayo-Polynesian, Borneo, Punan-Nibong. Dialect: PENAN APOH. A distinct but closely related language to Western Penan and Kenyah, but not inherently intelligible to each others' speakers.

PENAN, WESTERN ***(NIBONG, NIBON, "PUNAN")*** [PNE] 9,000 in Sarawak (1988 Lian). Population total both countries 9,050. Upper Baram and Balui rivers around Mt. Dulit, 3 villages, 4th to 7th divisions, and Nibong branch of the Lobong River, a tributary of the Tinjar River. Also spoken in Brunei. Austronesian, Malayo-Polynesian, Western Malayo-Polynesian, Borneo, Punan-Nibong. Dialects: NIBONG, BOK PENAN (BOK), PENAN SILAT, PENAN GANG (GANG), PENAN LUSONG (LUSONG), PENAN APO, SIPENG (SPENG), PENAN LANYING, JELALONG PENAN. Not closely related to other languages. Traditionalists are nomadic and semi-nomadic. Tropical forest. Subsistence agriculturalists, hunter-gatherers. NT 1974, out of print.

PUNAN BAH-BIAU [PNA] 450 (1981 Wurm and Hattori). Central, around Merit, Rejang River, 7th Division. Austronesian, Malayo-Polynesian, Western Malayo-Polynesian, Borneo, Northwest, Rejang-Sajau. Dialects: PUNAN BAH (PUNAN BA), PUNAN BIAU. Nomadic. They get salt from the Kayan. Hunter-gatherers.

PUNAN BATU 1 [PNM] 50 (1981 Wurm and Hattori). Central, west of Long Geng, southeast of Belaga. Austronesian, Malayo-Polynesian, Western Malayo-Polynesian, Borneo, Northwest, Melanau-Kajang, Kajang. Different from Punan Batu 2, a dialect of Sajau Basap in Kalimantan. Nomadic. They get salt from the Kayan. Investigation needed: intelligibility with Bukitan. Hunter-gatherers.

SA'BAN [SNV] Northeast on the Kalimantan border, northeast of Ramudu, Upper Baram, 4th Division, including Long Banga'. Austronesian, Malayo-Polynesian, Western Malayo-Polynesian, Borneo, North-west, North Sarawakan, Dayic, Kelabitic. Bible portions 1969. See main entry under Indonesia, Kalimantan.

SEBUYAU ***(SIBUYAU, SABUYAU, SIBUIAN, SIBUYAN, SABUYAN)*** [SNB] 9,000 (1981 Wurm and Hattori). Lundu, 1st Division, mouth of the Lupa River, west bank around Sebuyau. Austronesian, Malayo-Polynesian, Western Malayo-Polynesian, Sundic, Malayic, Malayic-Dayak, Ibanic. Investigation needed: intelligibility with Iban.

SEKAPAN ***(SEKEPAN)*** [SKP] 750 (1981 Wurm and Hattori). Belaga, 7th Division. Austronesian, Malayo-Polynesian, Western Malayo-Polynesian, Borneo, Northwest, Melanau-Kajang, Kajang. Investigation needed: intelligibility with Kajaman.

SELAKO ***(SELAKAU, SALAKAU, SILAKAU)*** [SKL] 3,800 in Sarawak (1981 Wurm and Hattori). Saak, Lundu, 1st Division, 22 villages. Austronesian, Malayo-Polynesian, Western Malayo-Polynesian, Sundic, Malayic, Malayic-Dayak. Gradually being adopted by the younger speakers of Lara'. See main entry under Indonesia, Kalimantan.

SERU [SZD] Kabong, 2nd Division. Austronesian, Malayo-Polynesian, Western Malayo-Polynesian, Borneo, Northwest, Melanau-Kajang, Melanau. Extinct.

SIAN ***(SIHAN)*** [SPG] 70 (1981 Wurm and Hattori). Belaga, 7th Division. Austronesian, Malayo-Polynesian, Western Malayo-Polynesian, Borneo, Northwest, Melanau-Kajang, Kajang. May be intelligible with Bukitan, Ukit, Punan Batu 1. Investigation needed: intelligibility with Bukitan, Ukit, Punan Batu 1.

SIBU ***(SIDUAN, SIDUANI, SEDUAN-BANYOK)*** [SDX] 420 (1981 Wurm and Hattori). Sibu, 3rd Division, Rejang River. Austronesian, Malayo-Polynesian, Western Malayo-Polynesian, Borneo, Northwest, Melanau-Kajang, Melanau. Dialects: SEDUAN, BANYOK. May be intelligible with Melanau. Investigation needed: intelligibility with Melanau.

TANJONG [TNJ] 100 (1981 Wurm and Hattori). Rejang River above the Kanowit language area, below Song village, Kapit, 7th Division. Austronesian, Malayo-Polynesian, Western Malayo-Polynesian, Borneo, Northwest, Melanau-Kajang, Melanau.

TRING [TGQ] Long Terawan village, lower Tutoh River. Austronesian, Malayo-Polynesian, Western Malayo- Polynesian, Borneo, Northwest, North Sarawakan, Dayic, Kelabitic. Not the same as Tringgus.

TRINGGUS ***(TRINGUS)*** [TRX] 350 (1981 Wurm and Hattori). Population total both countries 350 or more. Southwest of Kuching, south of the Jagoi, on the Kalimantan border. Also spoken in Indonesia (Kalimantan). Austronesian, Malayo-Polynesian, Western Malayo-Polynesian, Borneo, Land Dayak. Dialects: TRINGGUS, MBAAN (SEMBAAN, BIMBAAN). Each dialect has a few villages. Closer to Biatah than to Jagoi. Gumbang may be a Tringgus dialect rather than a Jagoi dialect. A different language from Tring. Investigation needed: intelligibility with Jagoi.

TUTONG 1 [TTX] 10,000. Along the lower Limbang River. Austronesian, Malayo-Polynesian, Western Malayo-Polynesian, Borneo, Northwest, Sabahan, Dusunic, Bisaya, Southern. Distinct from Tutong 2 in Baram-Tinjar Subgroup. May not be in Sarawak. See main entry under Brunei.

UKIT [UMI] 120 (1981 Wurm and Hattori). Upper Rajom and Tatau rivers, Baleh, 7th Division. Austronesian, Malayo-Polynesian, Western Malayo-Polynesian, Borneo, Northwest, Melanau-Kajang, Kajang. Different from the Punan Ukit dialect of Bukitan. Investigation needed: intelligibility with Bukitan, Punan Batu 1, Sian.

MALDIVES

Republic of Maldives. National or official language: Maldivian. 271,000 (1998 UN). 1,200 islands; 203 inhabited. Literacy rate 93% to 95.4%. Also includes Sinhala 1,400, Arabic 300, people from India 1,000. Information mainly from J. Gair 1980. Muslim, mainly Sunni. Deaf population 15,278. Data accuracy estimate: B. The number of languages listed for Maldives is 1. Diversity index 0.01.

MALDIVIAN ***(MALIKH, MAHL, MALKI, DIVEHI, DIVEHLI, DIVEHI BAS)*** [SNM] 213,215 in Maldives (1991 Statistical Yearbook of Maldives). Population total both countries 220,000. Throughout the country. Also spoken in India. Indo-European, Indo-Iranian, Indo-Aryan, Sinhalese-Maldivian. No transitional dialects to Sinhalese, which is a separate language. Bilingualism in Arabic. National language. Tana, based on Arabic script. Tropical forest. Coral island. Fishermen, tourist industry. Sea level. Sunni Muslim, traditional religion.

MONGOLIA

Mongolian People's Republic, Bügd Nayramdakh Mongol Ard Uls. National or official language: Halh Mongolian. 2,579,000 (1998 UN). Literacy rate 89% to 90%. Also includes Japanese, Korean, people from the West. Information mainly from T. Sebeok 1967; N. Poppe 1970. Secular, Lamaist Buddhist, Muslim. Blind population 10,000 to 40,000 visually handicapped (1997). Deaf population 10,000 to 147,330. Data accuracy estimate: A2. The number of languages listed for Mongolia is 12. Of those, all are living languages. Diversity index 0.30.

BURIAT, MONGOLIA ***(BURYAT, BURIAT-MONGOLIAN, NORTHERN MONGOLIAN, MONGOLIAN BURIAT, BUR:AAD)*** [BXM] 64,900 (1995), 2.5% of the population (1985 estimate). Northeast, especially bordering Buryat ASSR. Altaic, Mongolian, Eastern, Oirat-Khalkha, Khalkha-Buriat, Buriat. Dialects: KHORI, AGA. Buriat in Mongolia is a variety of Khori, and differs considerably from Buriat of China and Russia. The language has been influenced by Standard (Halh) Mongolian. Halh Mongolian is used as a literary language. There are some books in Buriat. Not a literary language in Mongolia. Literacy rate in second language: High in Halh. Traditionally shamanist and Buddhist Lamaist; now largely atheist.

CHINESE, MANDARIN ***(HOTON, QOTONG, HUI-ZU, HUI, XUI, NORTHERN CHINESE, MANDARIN, HYTAD)*** [CHN] 35,000 in Mongolia (1993 Johnstone), including 2,000 Qotong (1982 estimate). Northwestern Mongolia, Uvs Aimag. Sino-Tibetan, Chinese. Bilingualism in Halh Mongolian. Literacy rate in second language: High in Halh or Mandarin. Those who are traditionally Sunni Muslim in China (Hui) are known as 'Qotong' (Hoton) in Mongolia, 'Dungan' in Kyrgyzstan, 'Hui' in Thailand. The majority of Chinese in Mongolia are not Muslim. Distinct from Khoton (Hoton) of Mongolia. Secular, Maoism, Confucian, Muslim. Bible 1874-1983. See main entry under China.

DARKHAT [DAY] 4,500 (1956 census). Hövsgöl Aimag, north Mongolia, around Lake Khubsugul. Altaic, Mongolian, Eastern, Oirat-Khalkha, Oirat-Kalmyk-Darkhat. Speakers are fully bilingual in Halh Mongolian. One of the Oirat peoples. Influences from Oirat and possibly the Buriat languages. Distinct from Darkhan, which refers to southern Khalkha people in Ulanchab league, Inner Mongolia, China, and to Khorchin people in eastern Inner Mongolia. Literacy rate in second language: High in Halh. Originally shamanist, then Lamaist Buddhist, now largely atheist.

EVENKI ***(KHAMNIGAN, TUNGUS, SOLON)*** [EVN] 1,000 in Mongolia (1995 M. Krauss). Selenge Aimag, north Mongolia. Altaic, Tungus, Northern, Evenki. Bilingualism in Halh Mongolian. Literacy rate in second language: In Halh Mongolian. Shamanist, Lamaist Buddhist. See main entry under China.

KALMYK-OIRAT ***(OIRAT, WESTERN MONGOL)*** [KGZ] 205,500 in Mongolia, including 139,000 Oirat, 55,100 Dorbot, 11,400 Torgut. Altaic, Mongolian, Eastern, Oirat-Khalkha, Oirat-Kalmyk-Darkhat. Dialects: JAKHACHIN, BAYIT, MINGAT, OLOT (ÖÖLD, ELYUT, ELEUTH), KHOSHUT (KHOSHUUD), URIANKHAI, KHOTON (HOTON). Khoton (Hoton) were originally of Turkic origin (G. Kara). They were once Muslim. Different from the Chinese-speaking Qotong (Hoton). NT 1827-1894, out of print. See main entry under Russia.

KAZAKH ***(KAZAKHI, QAZAQ, QAZAQI, KAZAX, KAISAK, KOSACH)*** [KAZ] 120,000 (1993 Johnstone), 4% of population in Mongolia (1991). Bayan-Olgiy Aimag, northwest Mongolia, mining communities east of the capital, and in far east around Choibalsan. Altaic, Turkic, Western, Aralo-Caspian. Cyrillic script used. Traditionally Muslim, but now largely atheist with Muslim traditions and occultism. NT 1820-1910, out of print. See main entry under Kazakhstan.

MONGOLIAN SIGN LANGUAGE [QMM] Unknown number of users out of 10,000 to 147,330 deaf (1998). Deaf sign language. Different from Russian Sign Language and other sign languages.

MONGOLIAN, HALH ***(HALH, KHALKHA MONGOLIAN, MONGOL, CENTRAL MONGOLIAN)*** [KHK] 2,329,000 in Mongolia (1995), 89.7% of the population, including 32,300 Dariganga. Population total all countries 2,330,000. Buryat ASSR of Russia and Issyk-Kul Oblast of Kyrgyzstan. Also spoken in Kyrgyzstan, Russia (Asia), Taiwan. Altaic, Mongolian, Eastern, Oirat-Khalkha, Khalkha-Buriat, Mongolian Proper. Dialects: HALH (KHALKHA), DARIGANGA, KHOTOGOIT, SARTUL, TSONGOL. Ethnic Zahchin (Dzakhachin, Jakhachin 24,700 or 1.3%), Mingat (possibly 4,000; 1984), Bayad (Bayit, Bait, 39,900 or 2.1%), Oold (Oolet, Olot, 11,400 or .6%), are bilingual and literate in Halh Mongolian. National language. Cyrillic script. Traditionally pastoralists, now many industrialists. Originally shamanist, then Lamaist Buddhist, now largely atheist. NT 1990.

MONGOLIAN, PERIPHERAL ***(SOUTHERN-EASTERN MONGOLIAN)*** [MVF] Altaic, Mongolian, Eastern, Oirat-Khalkha, Khalkha-Buriat, Mongolian Proper. Dialects: UJUMCHIN (UZEMCHIN, UJUMUCHIN), JOSTU (KHARCHIN, KHARACHIN), TUMUT (TUMET), JIRIM (KHORCHIN), URAT, ORDOS. Bilingualism in Halh Mongolian. Literacy rate in second language: In Halh Mongolian. NT 1952. See main entry under China.

RUSSIAN ***(RUSSKI)*** [RUS] 4,000 in Mongolia (1993 Johnstone). Indo-European, Slavic, East. Russians who are permanent residents are called 'Mectny Oros'. Widely taught in schools and for higher education. Mainly atheist, many occultist. Bible 1680-1993. See main entry under Russia.

TUVIN ***(URIANKHAI, URYANKHAI-MONCHAK, TUVINIAN, TUVA, TUBA, TANNU-TUVA, SOYON, SOYOD, SOYOT, TUVAN, TUVIA, DIBA, KÖK, MUNGAK, TUVA-URIANKHAI, TUWA-URIANKHAI)*** [TUN] 27,000 (1993 Johnstone), 1.3% of the population in Mongolia (1985 estimate). Hövsgöl and Hovd Aimags, north and west Mongolia. Altaic, Turkic, Northern. Dialects: KOKCHULUTAN, KHÖWSÖGÖL UIGUR. Sharp dialect differences. Bilingualism in Halh Mongolian. Literacy rate in second language: In Halh Mongolian. Buddhist. Bible portions 1996. See main entry under Russia.

UYGHUR ***(UYGUR, UIGHUR, UIGUR, UIGHUIR, UIGUIR)*** [UIG] 1,000 in Mongolia (1982 estimate). Hövsgöl Aimag, north Mongolia. Altaic, Turkic, Eastern. Literacy is in Halh in Mongolia and the Uyghur are generally assimilated to Halh culture. Sunni Muslim. Bible 1950. See main entry under China.

MYANMAR

Union of Myanmar, Pyeidaungzu Myanma Naingngandaw. Formerly Burma. National or official language: Burmese. 44,497,000 (1998 UN). Speakers of Tibeto-Burman languages: 28,877,000 or 78% of the population, Daic languages 2,778,900 or 9.6%, Austro-Asiatic languages 1,934,900 or 6.7%, Hmong-Mien languages 6,000 (1991 J. Matisoff). Literacy rate 66% to 78%; 78.5% over 15 years old (1991). Also includes Geman Deng, Iu Mien, Malay 21,000, Eastern Tamang, Chinese 1,015,000, people from Bangladesh and India 500,000. Information mainly from F. Lebar, G. Hickey, J. Musgrave 1967; A. Hale 1982; B. Comrie 1987; R. B. Jones 1988; J. Matisoff et al. 1996; R. Burling ms. (1998). Buddhist, Christian, Muslim, traditional religion, Hindu. Blind population 214,440. Deaf population 2,684,514. Deaf institutions: 1. Data accuracy estimate: C. The number of languages listed for Myanmar is 108. Of those, 107 are living languages and 1 is extinct. Diversity index 0.64.

ACHANG ***(ANCHAN, CHUNG, ATSANG, ACANG, NGAC'ANG, NGACHANG, NGO CHANG, MÖNGHSA, TAI SA')*** [ACN] 1,700 Maingtha in Myanmar (1983 estimate), and many others. West of the Irrawaddy River in Katha District, near Banmauk. Along the China border. Sino-Tibetan, Tibeto-Burman, Lolo-Burmese, Burmish, Northern. Dialect: MAINGTHA. Related to Phun, Maru, Lashi, Tsaiwa. Not a literary language. Literacy rate in first language: Below 1%. Literacy rate in second language: 5% to 15%. Polytheist, Hinayana Buddhist. NT 1992. See main entry under China.

AKHA ***(KAW, EKAW, KO, AKA, IKAW, AK'A, AHKA, KHAKO, KHA KO, KHAO KHA KO, IKOR, AINI, YANI)*** [AKA] 103,600 in Myanmar (1991 UBS). Population total all countries 450,000. Eastern part of Kengtung Shan State. Also spoken in China, Laos, Thailand, Viet Nam. Sino-Tibetan, Tibeto-Burman, Lolo-Burmese, Loloish, Southern, Akha, Hani, Ha-Ya. Dialects: AKO, ASONG. SOV. Traditional religion, some Christian, Buddhist. NT 1968-1987.

ANAL ***(NAMFAU)*** [ANM] Also possibly in Bangladesh. Sino-Tibetan, Tibeto-Burman, Kuki-Chin-Naga, Kuki-Chin, Northern. Closest to Lamgang (Kuki Naga). SOV. NT 1983. See main entry under India.

ANU [ANL] 700. Sino-Tibetan, Tibeto-Burman, Unclassified. May be the same as Anal, Nung of Rawang, or some other language. SOV.

ARAKANESE ***(MAGHI, MORMA, YAKAN, YAKHAING, RAKHAIN, MOGH, MAGH, MARMA, MASH, RAKHINE)*** [MHV] 1,875,000 in Myanmar (1993 Johnstone). Population total all countries 2,083,000. Southwest, Arakan Province. Also possibly in China. Also spoken in Bangladesh, India. Sino-Tibetan, Tibeto-Burman, Lolo-Burmese, Burmish, Southern. One of the better known varieties of nonstandard

Burmese with profound pronunciation and vocabulary differences from Burmese. The people wear Burmese dress. SOV. Buddhist, Muslim, Hindu. Bible portions 1914.

BLANG ***(BULANG, PULANG, PULA, KAWA, K'ALA, PLANG, KONTOI)*** [BLR] 12,000 in Myanmar (1994). Eastern Shan State, Mong Yang area, and Kengtung. Austro-Asiatic, Mon-Khmer, Northern Mon-Khmer, Palaungic, Western Palaungic, Waic, Bulang. Some are becoming urbanized in Myanmar, Thailand, and China. An official nationality in China. Agriculturalists. Hinayana Buddhist, some Christian. See main entry under China.

BURMESE ***(BAMA, BAMACHAKA, MYEN)*** [BMS] 21,553,000 first language speakers (1986), 58.41% of the population. 3,000,000 second language speakers (1977 Voegelin and Voegelin). Population total all countries 32,000,000 (1999 WA). South, central, and adjacent areas. Also spoken in Bangladesh, Malaysia, Thailand, USA. Sino-Tibetan, Tibeto-Burman, Lolo-Burmese, Burmish, Southern. Dialects: MERGUESE (MERGUI, BEIK), YAW, DANU (TARUW), BURMESE, PALAW. Native speakers of Burmese seldom speak a second indigenous language. If they have one, it is usually English. Burmese is the second language of many educated speakers of other languages. Burmese dominates the nation's publishing production. Myanma is the largest ethnic group; another is Baramagyi (Barua). Educated speech has many Pali borrowings. The Rawang people call them 'Myen'. National language. SOV. Burmese script. Scrub forest. Alluvial plains. Peasant agriculturalists, fishermen, craftsmen, industrialists. Sea level and higher. Buddhist. Bible 1835, in press (1995).

CHAK [CKH] Population total both countries 910 or more. Most in Arakan Blue Mts., Myanmar. Also spoken in Bangladesh. Unclassified. Distinct from Chakma. Tropical forest. Agriculturalists. Traditional religion.

CHAUNGTHA [CCQ] 121,700 (1983 estimate). Sino-Tibetan, Tibeto-Burman, Lolo-Burmese, Burmish, Southern. Related to Burmese. Their name means 'People of the valley' or 'People of the stream'. Investigation needed: intelligibility with Burmese. SOV.

CHIN, ASHO ***(QIN, ASHO, ASHU, SHOA, SHO, KHYANG, KYANG)*** [CSH] 10,000 in Myanmar (1991 UBS). Population total both countries 11,500 or more. Irrawaddy River, lowlands. Not in China. Also spoken in Bangladesh. Sino-Tibetan, Tibeto-Burman, Kuki-Chin-Naga, Kuki-Chin, Southern, Sho. Dialects: THAYETMYO (THAYETMO), MINBU, LEMYO, KHYANG. Closely related to Saingbaung Chin. Also related to Shendu and Chinbon. Lemyo, Thayetmo, Minbu, and Khyang may be separate languages. Speakers are quite bilingual in Burmese. SOV. NT 1954.

CHIN, BAWM ***(BAWM, BAWN, BAWNG, BOM)*** [BGR] Falam area, Chin Hills. Sino-Tibetan, Tibeto-Burman, Kuki-Chin-Naga, Kuki-Chin, Central. SOV. Bible 1989. See main entry under India.

CHIN, CHINBON ***(ÜTBÜ, CHINDWIN CHIN, SHO, CHINBON)*** [CNB] 19,600 (1983 estimate). Kanpetlet, Yaw, Seidoutia, and Paletwa townships. Sino-Tibetan, Tibeto-Burman, Kuki-Chin-Naga, Kuki-Chin, Southern, Sho. About 50% lexical similarity with Asho Chin. Buddhist.

CHIN, DAAI ***(DAAI, DAI, M'KAANG)*** [DAO] 30,000 (1994 UBS). Matupi, Paletwa, Kanpetiet townships. Sino-Tibetan, Tibeto-Burman, Kuki-Chin-Naga, Kuki-Chin, Southern. Sometimes called 'Mün' or 'Ütbü' ethnically, but those groups are linguistically distinct. They have in the past called themselves 'Mün', 'Ütbü', and 'Khyo' (Hyo, Sho, Zo) for higher status. SOV. Tropical forest. Mountain slope. Swidden agriculturalists. 2,700 to 5,700 feet. NT 1996.

CHIN, FALAM ***(HALLAM CHIN, HALAM, FALLAM, FALAM)*** [HBH] 100,000 in Myanmar (1991 UBS), including 9,000 Tashon, 16,000 Zanniat, 7,000 Khualshim, 4,000 Lente, 14,400 Zahao 18,600 in Laizao (1983 estimate). Population total all countries 125,370 or more. Falam District, Chin Hills. Also spoken in Bangladesh, India. Sino-Tibetan, Tibeto-Burman, Kuki-Chin-Naga, Kuki-Chin, Northern. Dialects: ZANNIAT, TASHON (TASHOM, SHUNKLA, SUNKHLA), LAIZO (LAISO, LAIZAO, LAIZO-SHIMHRIN), ZAHAO (ZAHAU, YAHOW, ZAHAU-SHIMHRIN, LYEN-LYEM), KHUALSHIM (KWELSHIN), LENTE (LYENTE), CHOREI. Chorei may be a separate language. An important language. SOV. Christian. Bible 1991.

CHIN, HAKA ***(HAKA, HAKHA, BAUNGSHE)*** [CNH] 100,000 in Myanmar (1991 UBS), including 2,000 Zokhua, 60,100 Lai (1983 estimate). Population total all countries 445,000. Chin Hills, Haka area. Also spoken in Bangladesh, India. Sino-Tibetan, Tibeto-Burman, Kuki-Chin-Naga, Kuki-Chin, Central. Dialects: LAI, KLANGKLANG (THLANTLANG), ZOKHUA, SHONSHE. Shonshe may be a separate language. Bible 1978.

CHIN, KHUMI ***(KHUMI, KHAMI, KHWEYMI, KHIMI, KHUNI)*** [CKM] 76,700 in Myanmar (1983 estimate) including 40,000 Matu Chin (1990 UBS). Population total all countries 78,000 or more. Arakan Hills, Akyab area. Matu are in Southern Chin State, Matupi, Mindat, and Paletwa townships, western Myanmar. A few in India. Also spoken in Bangladesh, India. Sino-Tibetan, Tibeto-Burman, Kuki-Chin-Naga, Kuki-Chin, Southern, Khumi. Dialects: KHIMI, MATU (MARU, DAI-PATU), YINDI (YINDU), KHAMI, NGALA. Bilingualism in Burmese. Khami and Ngala may be separate languages. SOV, genitives, articles, adjectives, numerals after noun heads. Literacy rate in second language: 60%.

Tropical forest. Mountain slope. Peasant agriculturalists. 4,000 feet. Christian, traditional religion, Buddhist. NT 1959-1991.

CHIN, KHUMI AWA [CKA] Arakan Hills, coast areas. Sino-Tibetan, Tibeto-Burman, Kuki-Chin-Naga, Kuki-Chin, Southern, Khumi. The coastal dialect differs from the inland Khumi. SOV. Bible portions 1939.

CHIN, MARA ***(MARA, LAKHER, ZAO, MARAM, MIRA)*** [MRH] 20,000 in Myanmar (1994 IMA). Lushai Hills. Sino-Tibetan, Tibeto-Burman, Kuki-Chin-Naga, Kuki-Chin, Southern. Dialects: TLONGSAI, HLAWTHAI, SABEU. Close to Shendu. SOV. Bible 1956. See main entry under India.

CHIN, MRO [CMR] 100,000 to 200,000 in Myanmar (1999). Population total both countries 100,000 to 200,000. Rakhine State. Also spoken in Bangladesh. Sino-Tibetan, Tibeto-Burman, Kuki-Chin-Naga, Kuki-Chin. About 13% lexical similarity with Mru [MRO] of Bangladesh and Myanmar.

CHIN, MÜN ***(MÜN, NG'MEN, CHO, YAWDWIN, MINDAT, "CHINBOK")*** [MWQ] 30,000 (1991 UBS, 1990 E. Hang). Chin Hills, western. Sino-Tibetan, Tibeto-Burman, Kuki-Chin-Naga, Kuki-Chin, Southern. Dialect: NITU. Related to Daai Chin. "Chinbok", "Tsinbok", "Chinme", "Chinbe" are derogatory names for this group, and not separate languages. SOV. NT, in press (1995).

CHIN, NGAWN ***(NGAWN, NGORN, NGON)*** [CNW] 15,000 (1984). Chin Hills, Falam area. Sino-Tibetan, Tibeto-Burman, Kuki-Chin-Naga, Kuki-Chin, Central. SOV. Bible portions 1951.

CHIN, PAITE ***(PAITE, PAITHE, OARTE, HAINTE, VUITE)*** [PCK] 8,900 in Myanmar (1983 estimate). Tiddim District, Chin Hills. Sino-Tibetan, Tibeto-Burman, Kuki-Chin-Naga, Kuki-Chin, Northern. Related to Thado Chin, Tedim Chin, Ralte, Zomi. SOV. Bible 1971. See main entry under India.

CHIN, SENTHANG ***(SENTHANG, HSEMTANG)*** [SEZ] 18,200 (1983 estimate). Haka, Chin Hills. Sino-Tibetan, Tibeto-Burman, Kuki-Chin-Naga, Kuki-Chin, Central. A very different Chin language. SOV.

CHIN, SIYIN ***(SIYIN, SIYANG, SIZANG)*** [CSY] 10,000 (1991 UBS). Chin Hills. Sino-Tibetan, Tibeto-Burman, Kuki-Chin-Naga, Kuki-Chin, Northern. Close to Paite Chin. SOV. NT 1995.

CHIN, TAWR ***(TAWR, TORR)*** [TCP] 700 (D. Van Bik). Falam, Haka, Chin Hills. Sino-Tibetan, Tibeto-Burman, Kuki-Chin-Naga, Kuki-Chin, Central. A completely distinct language. SOV.

CHIN, TEDIM ***(TEDIM, TIDDIM)*** [CTD] 189,100 in Myanmar (1990 BAP). Population total both countries 344,100. Chin Hills, Upper Chindwin, Chin State, Tiddim area. Also spoken in India. Sino-Tibetan, Tibeto-Burman, Kuki-Chin-Naga, Kuki-Chin, Northern. Dialects: SOKTE, KAMHAU (KAMHOW, KAMHAO). Other Chin languages or dialects of this area are Saizang, Teizang, Zo (Zome). Trade language of the Tiddim political subdivision. SOV. Bible 1983, in press (1996).

CHIN, THADO ***(THADOU, THADO-UBIPHEI, THADO-PAO, KUKI, KUKI-THADO)*** [TCZ] 26,200 in Myanmar (1983 estimate). Sino-Tibetan, Tibeto-Burman, Kuki-Chin-Naga, Kuki-Chin, Northern. Dialects: BAITE, CHANGSEN, JANGSHEN, KAOKEEP, KHONGZAI, KIPGEN, LANGIUNG, SAIRANG, THANGNGEN, HAWKIP. Related to Kamhau, Ralte, Paite, Zo. SOV. Bible 1971-1994. See main entry under India.

CHIN, ZOTUNG ***(ZOTUNG, BANJOGI, BANDZHOGI)*** [CZT] 40,000 (1990 UBS). Chin Hills, Haka area. Sino-Tibetan, Tibeto-Burman, Kuki-Chin-Naga, Kuki-Chin, Central. Zotung is reported to be intelligible with Haka. Bible portions 1951.

CHITTAGONIAN [CIT] Arakan state. Indo-European, Indo-Iranian, Indo-Aryan, Eastern zone, Bengali-Assamese. Dialect: ROHINGA (AKYAB). Not inherently intelligible with Bengali, although considered to be a nonstandard Bengali dialect. An ethnic Bengali Muslim who speaks the Muslim dialect of Chittagonian Bengali and was born in Arakan state, Myanmar is called a 'Rohinga'. The dialect is intelligible to those born in southeastern Bangladesh. Not intelligible with Bengali. They migrated from Bangladesh several generations ago. 250,000 refugees went back to Bangladesh recently, but most have been repatriated back to Myanmar by the United Nations Commission on Repatriation. Muslim. See main entry under Bangladesh.

DANAU ***(DANAW)*** [DNU] 10,000 (1984). Austro-Asiatic, Mon-Khmer, Northern Mon-Khmer, Palaungic, Eastern Palaungic, Danau. Closest to Riang-Lang and Pale Palaung. It may be in Thailand or China rather than, or in addition to, Myanmar. Investigation needed: intelligibility with Riang-Lang, Pale Palaung.

GANGTE ***(GANTE)*** [GNB] Sino-Tibetan, Tibeto-Burman, Kuki-Chin-Naga, Kuki-Chin, Northern. Related to Thado Chin. Bible 1991. See main entry under India.

HANI ***(HANHI, HAW)*** [HNI] 180,000 in Myanmar (1994). North Shan State. None in Thailand. Sino-Tibetan, Tibeto-Burman, Lolo-Burmese, Loloish, Southern, Akha, Hani, Ha-Ya. Distinct from the Ho of India, which is Munda. Hani ethnic group: Pudu (Putu). An official nationality in China. SOV. Muslim. See main entry under China.

HMONG NJUA ***(BLUE MEO, GREEN MIAO, TAK MEO, HMONG NJWA, HMONG LENG)*** [BLU] 10,000 in Myanmar (1987 Haiv Hmoob). Hmong-Mien, Hmongic, Chuanqiandian. Largely intelligible with Hmong Daw. Dictionary. SOV. NT 1975-1983. See main entry under China.

HPON *(HPÖN, PHUN, PHÖN, PHON, MEGYAW, SAMONG)* [HPO] 1,700 (1983 estimate). Sino-Tibetan, Tibeto-Burman, Lolo-Burmese, Burmish, Northern.

HRANGKHOL *(RANGKHOL)* [HRA] Population total both countries 18,000 or more (1997). Also spoken in India. Sino-Tibetan, Tibeto-Burman, Kuki-Chin-Naga, Kuki-Chin, Northern. Closest to Biete. SOV. NT, in press (1997).

INTHA *(INNTHA)* [INT] 141,100 (1983 estimate). Near Inle Lake in the southern Shan State. Sino-Tibetan, Tibeto-Burman, Lolo-Burmese, Burmish, Southern. One of the better known varieties of nonstandard Burmese with profound pronunciation and vocabulary differences from Burmese. Investigation needed: bilingual proficiency. SOV. Fishermen, agriculturalists. Buddhist, traditional religion.

JINGPHO *(KACHIN, JINGHPAW, CHINGPAW, CHINGP'O, MARIP)* [CGP] 625,000 in Myanmar (1993 Johnstone). Population total both countries 645,000. Kachin State. Also spoken in China. Sino-Tibetan, Tibeto-Burman, Jingpho-Konyak-Bodo, Jingpho-Luish, Jingpho. Dialects: HKAKU HKA-HKU, KAURI (HKAURI, GAURI), DZILI (JILI), DULONG. Dzili may be a separate language. Hkaku and Kauri are only slightly different from Jinghpo. 50% lexical similarity with Singhpo of India. Serves as lingua franca for Zaiwa, Lashi, and Maru. 'Kachin' refers to the cultural rather than the linguistic group. Called 'Aphu' or 'Phu' by the Rawang people. SOV, 4 tones. Literacy rate in first language: 60% to 100%. Literacy rate in second language: 50% to 75%. Pastoralists, agriculturalists. Polytheist, some Buddhist, Christian. Bible 1927.

KADO *(KADU, KATU, KATO, KUDO, ASAK, SAK, GADU, THET, THAT, MAWTEIK, PUTEIK, WONI)* [KDV] 128,500 in Myanmar including 90,300 Kado, 38,200 Ganaan (1983 estimate). Population total all countries 228,500 or more. Also spoken in China, Laos. Sino-Tibetan, Tibeto-Burman, Jingpho-Konyak-Bodo, Jingpho-Luish, Luish. Dialects: KADU, GANAAN (GANAN), ANDRO, SENGMAI, CHAKPA, PHAYENG. Kadu, Ganaan, Andro, Sengmai, Chakpa, and Phayeng may be separate languages. Different from Katu, a Mon-Khmer language of Viet Nam, China, and Laos. Bible portions 1939.

KAREN, BREK *(BREK, BREC, BRE, PRAMANO, PRE, LAKU)* [KVL] 16,600 (1983 estimate). 2,600,000 in all Karen languages in Myanmar. Southwestern Kayah State. Sino-Tibetan, Tibeto-Burman, Karen, Sgaw-Bghai, Brek. Reported to be a separate language. 'Brek' and 'Bwe' are variant names of a dialect cluster that extends from southwest Kayah State to northeast Karen State. 'Brek' or 'Bre' usually refers to varieties in Kayah State. Mostly Christian.

KAREN, BWE *(BGHAI KAREN, BAGHI, BWE)* [BWE] 15,700 (1983 estimate). Kyèbogyi area of Kayah State. A few in Thailand. Sino-Tibetan, Tibeto-Burman, Karen, Sgaw-Bghai, Bghai, Unclassified. 'Kayin' is Burmese for all Karen, 'Yang' is Thai for all Karen. SVO. Literacy rate in first language: Below 1%. Bible portions 1857-1862.

KAREN, GEBA *(GEBA, KABA, KARENBYU, KAYINBYU, WHITE KAREN, EASTERN BWE)* [KVQ] 40,100 (1983 estimate). Northern Kayah State and southern Shan State. Sino-Tibetan, Tibeto-Burman, Karen, Sgaw-Bghai, Bghai, Western. Reported to be a separate language, but probably is part of the same dialect continuum with Bwe and Brek. There is some literature in Geba. Mostly Christian.

KAREN, GEKO *(GEK'O, GHEKO, GEKHO, GHEKHOL, GHEKHU, KEKU, KEKHONG, KEKAUNGDU, GAIKHO, PADAUNG)* [GHK] 9,500 (1983 estimate). Yamethin, Toungoo Districts, Mobyè State of the southern Shan States. Sino-Tibetan, Tibeto-Burman, Karen, Sgaw-Bghai, Bghai, Unclassified. SVO. Mostly Christian.

KAREN, LAHTA *(LAHTA, TARU, TARULAKHI, KHAHTA, PEU)* [KVT] Southern Shan State. Sino-Tibetan, Tibeto-Burman, Karen, Sgaw-Bghai, Bghai, Eastern. Reported to be a separate language.

KAREN, MANUMANAW *(MANUMANAW, MONU, MANÖ)* [KXF] 3,000 or more (1965). Western Kyèbogyi part of Kayah State. Sino-Tibetan, Tibeto-Burman, Karen, Sgaw-Bghai, Kayah. Reported to be a separate language. Mostly Christian.

KAREN, PADAUNG *(PADAUNG, KAYANG)* [PDU] 40,900 in Myanmar (1983 estimate). Population total both countries 41,000. Kayah State, Mobyè State, town of Phekon in the southern Shan States, and hills east of Toungoo. A few villages in Thailand. Also spoken in Thailand. Sino-Tibetan, Tibeto-Burman, Karen, Sgaw-Bghai, Bghai, Eastern. A separate language. Literacy rate in first language: Below 1%. Literacy rate in second language: Below 5%. Traditional religion, Buddhist, Christian.

KAREN, PAKU *(PAKU, PAGU, MONNEPWA, MONEBWA, MOPWA, MOPHA, MOPAGA, MOGPHA, MOGWA, THALWEPWE)* [KPP] 5,300 (1983 estimate). Southern hills east of Taungoo in Kayah State. Sino-Tibetan, Tibeto-Burman, Karen, Sgaw-Bghai, Sgaw. Dialects: BILICHI, DERMUHA. Closely related to S'gaw. Some reports indicate Paku and Mopwa are separate languages. SVO.

KAREN, PA'O *(NORTHERN TAUNGTHU, BLACK KAREN, PA-U, PA'O, PA OH, PA-O)* [BLK] 560,000 in Myanmar (1983). Population total both countries 560,600. Southwestern Shan State and east of the Gulf of Martaban in Tenasserim. Also spoken in Thailand. Sino-Tibetan, Tibeto-Burman, Karen, Pa'o.

Dialects: SOUTHERN PA'O, NORTHERN PA'O. Southern Pa'o is in Myanmar, Northern Pa'o in Thailand. SVO. Buddhist, traditional religion. Bible portions 1912-1964.

KAREN, PWO EASTERN ***(PHLOU, MOULMEIN PWO KAREN)*** [KJP] 1,000,000 in Myanmar (1998). Population total both countries 1,050,000. Karen State, Mon State, Tensserim Division. Also spoken in Thailand. Sino-Tibetan, Tibeto-Burman, Karen, Pwo. Dialects: PA'AN (MOULMEIN, INLAND PWO EASTERN KAREN), KAWKAREIK (EASTERN BORDER PWO KAREN), TAVOY (SOUTHERN PWO KAREN). Not intelligible with other Pwo Karen varieties. 91% to 97% lexical similarity among dialects, 63% to 65% with other Pwo Karen varieties. SVO. Monastic Burmese, Mon-based script being developed for Myanmar and Thailand; Christian script Burmese based; Leke script.

KAREN, PWO WESTERN ***(MUTHEIT, DELTA PWO KAREN, BASSEIN PWO KAREN, PHLONG SHO)*** [PWO] 210,000. Irrawaddy Delta. Sino-Tibetan, Tibeto-Burman, Karen, Pwo. Dialects: BASSEIN, TUAN TET, MAUBIN. SVO. Burmese-based script. Traditional religion, Christian, Buddhist. Bible 1883-1885.

KAREN, S'GAW ***(S'GAW, S'GAU, S'GAW KAYIN, KANYAW, PAGANYAW, PWAKANYAW, WHITE KAREN, BURMESE KAREN, YANG KHAO, PCHCKNYA, KYETHO)*** [KSW] 1,284,700 in Myanmar (1983 estimate). Population total both countries 2,000,000 (1990 UBS). Irrawaddy delta area, Tenasserim, the Pegu range between the Irrawaddy and Sittang, the eastern hills. Also spoken in Thailand. Sino-Tibetan, Tibeto-Burman, Karen, Sgaw-Bghai, Sgaw. Dialects: PANAPU, PALAKHI (PALACHI). Closely related to Paku. SVO. Bible 1853-1995.

KAREN, YINBAW ***(YINBAW, YEINBAW)*** [KVU] 7,300 (1983 estimate). Shan Plateau of eastern Shan State. Sino-Tibetan, Tibeto-Burman, Karen, Sgaw-Bghai, Kayah. Reported to be a variety of Padaung. Buddhist, Christian, traditional religion.

KAREN, YINTALE ***(YINTALE, YINTALET, YANGATALET, YANGTADAI, TALIAK)*** [KVY] Bawlakhè part of Kayah State. Sino-Tibetan, Tibeto-Burman, Karen, Sgaw-Bghai, Kayah. Reported to be a variety of Kayah. Buddhist, traditional religion.

KAREN, ZAYEIN ***(ZAYEIN, KHAUNGTOU, GAUNGTOU)*** [KXK] 9,300 (1983 estimate). Between the towns of Mobyè and Phekon in the southern Shan State. Sino-Tibetan, Tibeto-Burman, Karen, Unclassified. Reported to be a separate language, similar to Sawntung, Padang, Banyang.

KAYAH, EASTERN ***(RED KAREN, KARENNI, KAYAY, KAYAH)*** [EKY] Population total both countries 77,900. Maehongson, east of the Salween River. Also spoken in Thailand. Sino-Tibetan, Tibeto-Burman, Karen, Sgaw-Bghai, Kayah. Distinct from but related to Bwe Karen (Bghai), forming a continuous chain of dialects. Speakers have difficulty understanding Western Kayah of Myanmar. Literacy rate in first language: 1% to 5%. Literacy rate in second language: 50% to 75%.

KAYAH, WESTERN ***(KAYAH LI, KARENNI, KARENNYI, RED KAREN, YANG DAENG, KARIENG DAENG)*** [KYU] 210,000 (1987). Kayah and Karen states, west of the Pong River. Sino-Tibetan, Tibeto-Burman, Karen, Sgaw-Bghai, Kayah. Different from but related to Bwe Karen, forming a continuous chain of dialects from Thailand (Eastern Kayah) to western Kayah State. Dictionary. Literacy rate in first language: 1% to 5%. Christian, traditional religion.

KHAMTI ***(HKAMTI, KHAMPTI, KHAMTI SHAN, KHAMPTI SHAN, KHANDI SHAN, KAM TI, TAI KAM TI, TAI-KHAMTI)*** [KHT] Population total both countries 70,000 (1990 A. Diller ANU). Northwestern Myanmar. Also possibly in China. Also spoken in India. Tai-Kadai, Kam-Tai, Be-Tai, Tai-Sek, Tai, Southwestern, East Central, Northwest. Dialects: ASSAM KHAMTI, NORTH BURMA KHAMTI, SINKALING HKAMTI. Related to Shan but distinct. Some similarities to northern Shan. Bilingualism in Burmese, Jingpo. SOV, postpositional case-marking particle. Distinctive script called Lik-Tai. Buddhist.

KHMU ***(KMHMU, KHMU', KAMU, KAMMU, KHAMUK, KAMHMU, KHOMU, MOU, POUTENG, PU THENH, TENH, THENG, LAO TERNG)*** [KJG] Austro-Asiatic, Mon-Khmer, Northern Mon-Khmer, Khmuic, Mal-Khmu', Khmu'. Bible portions 1918. See main entry under Laos.

KHÜN ***(HKUN, KHUN SHAN, KHYN, GON SHAN, TAI KHUN, KHUEN, TAI-KHUEN)*** [KKH] Population total both countries 100,000 (1990 A. Diller ANU). Main Kentung Valley in the center of Shan State. Possibly not in Thailand. Also spoken in Thailand. Tai-Kadai, Kam-Tai, Be-Tai, Tai-Sek, Tai, Southwestern, East Central, Northwest. Closely related to Lü and Northern Tai or southern Shan. Lanna and Khun spoken dialects are considered close by their speakers. Different from Khouen (Khuen), a Mon-Khmer language of Laos. Script close to that of the Lanna. Buddhist. Bible portions 1938.

KIORR ***(SAAMTAAV, CON, COL)*** [XKO] Austro-Asiatic, Mon-Khmer, Northern Mon-Khmer, Palaungic, Western Palaungic, Angkuic. Investigation needed: intelligibility with Angkuic varieties. See main entry under Laos.

LAHU ***(LOHEI, LAHUNA, LAUNA, MUSEU, MUSSUH, MUHSO, MUSSO)*** [LAH] 125,000 in Myanmar (1993 Johnstone). Shan State, Kentung area. Sino-Tibetan, Tibeto-Burman, Lolo-Burmese, Loloish, Southern, Akha, Lahu. Dialects: NA (BLACK LAHU, MUSSER DAM, NORTHERN LAHU, LOHEIRN),

NYI (RED LAHU, SOUTHERN LAHU, MUSSEH DAENG, LUHISHI, LUHUSHI), SHEHLEH. Black Lahu and Lahu Shi (Yellow Lahu, Kutsung) have difficult intelligibility. Red Lahu (Nyi) and Yellow Lahu are distinct. See separate entry for Lahu Shi. SOV. Tropical forest, scrub forest. Mountain slope. Swidden agriculturalists. Some Christian. Bible 1989. See main entry under China.

LAHU SHI ***(KUTSUNG, KUCONG, YELLOW LAHU, SHI, KUI, KWI)*** [KDS] 10,000 in Myanmar (1998). Kentung District. Sino-Tibetan, Tibeto-Burman, Lolo-Burmese, Loloish, Southern, Akha, Lahu. Difficult intelligibility with Black Lahu. A distinct language from Nyi (Red Lahu). SOV. See main entry under Laos.

LAMA [LAY] 3,000 (1977 Voegelin and Voegelin). Sino-Tibetan, Tibeto-Burman, Nungish. Dialect or closely related language to Norra. SOV.

LAOPANG ***(LAOPA)*** [LBG] Sino-Tibetan, Tibeto-Burman, Lolo-Burmese, Loloish, Unclassified. Possibly same as Laba, a group of Lahu near Lao-Thai border (Mundhenk 1973). SOV.

LASHI ***(LASI, LETSI, LECHI, LEQI, LASHI-MARU, CHASHAN, LACHIKWAW, AC'YE, LACID)*** [LSI] 55,500 in Myanmar (1983 estimate). Population total both countries 55,500 or more. Htawgaw Subdivision, Kachin State. Also spoken in China. Sino-Tibetan, Tibeto-Burman, Lolo-Burmese, Burmish, Northern. SOV. Literacy rate in first language: Below 1%. Literacy rate in second language: 5% to 15%.

LISU ***(LISAW, LI-SHAW, LI-HSAW, LU-TZU, SOUTHERN LISU, YAO YEN, YAW-YEN, YAW YIN, YEH-JEH, CENTRAL LISU)*** [LIS] 126,000 in Myanmar (1987 estimate). Around Lashio, in Wa State, around Myitkyina and Bhamo, around Putar towards Assam border, around Loilem area in Shan States. Sino-Tibetan, Tibeto-Burman, Burmese-Lolo, Lolo, Northern, Lisu. Dialects: HWA LISU (FLOWERY LISU), WHITE LISU, LU SHI LISU. All four dialects are in Myanmar. Black Lisu is the most different. Burmese and Thai Lisu have difficulties in communicating because of dialect differences. Yawgin, Tangsir, Hkwinhpang are dialects or ethnic groups. SOV. Literacy rate in first language: 30% to 60%. Literacy rate in second language: 50% to 75%. Polytheist, Christian. Bible 1968-1986. See main entry under China.

LOPI [LOV] Possibly also in China. Sino-Tibetan, Tibeto-Burman, Lolo-Burmese, Loloish, Unclassified. SOV.

LÜ ***(PAI-I, SHU-AI-I, LUE, TAI LU)*** [KHB] 200,000 in Myanmar (1981). Kengtung District. Tai-Kadai, Kam-Tai, Be-Tai, Tai-Sek, Tai, Southwestern, East Central, Northwest. Traditional religion, Buddhist. NT 1933. See main entry under China.

LUI ***(LOI)*** [LBA] Small. Sino-Tibetan, Tibeto-Burman, Unclassified. 'Loi' means 'mountain' in Shan, and many groups are called that.

LUSHAI ***(HUALNGO, WHELNGO, LE, LUSHEI, LUSAI)*** [LSH] 12,500 in Myanmar (1983 estimate). Western Myanmar. Sino-Tibetan, Tibeto-Burman, Kuki-Chin-Naga, Kuki-Chin, Central. Dialects: DULIEN, NGENTE, MIZO. SOV. Bible 1959-1995. See main entry under India.

MAHEI ***(MAHE, MABE)*** [MJA] 12,000. Sino-Tibetan, Tibeto-Burman, Lolo-Burmese, Loloish, Southern, Akha. Ethnic group or dialect of Hani or Akha. SOV.

MARU ***(MATU, MALU, LAWNG, LAUNGWAW, LAUNGAW, LANSU, LANG, MULU, DISO, ZI, LHAO VO)*** [MHX] 103,600 in Myanmar (1983 census). Over 10,000 households in China (1999). Population total both countries 103,600 or more. Kachin State, eastern border area, north Myanmar. Also spoken in China. Sino-Tibetan, Tibeto- Burman, Lolo-Burmese, Burmish, Northern. Dialects: DAGO' LAWNG BIT, ZAGARAN MRAN, GAWAN NAW', HLO'LAN, LAKING, WA KHAWK, LAWNG HSU. Lawng Hsu may have difficult intelligibility with the other dialects. Different from the Matu variety of Khumi Chin. Culture similar to Kachin. SOV. Literacy rate in first language: Below 1%. Literacy rate in second language: 25% to 50%. Bible portions 1940-1985, NT 1994.

MEITEI ***(MEITHEI, MEITHE, MITHE, MITEI, MEITEIRON, MANIPURI, MENIPURI, KATHE, KATHI, PONNA)*** [MNR] 6,000 in Myanmar (1931). Sino-Tibetan, Tibeto-Burman, Meithei. Hindu, traditional religion, Muslim, Christian. Bible 1984. See main entry under India.

MOKEN ***(MAWKEN, BASING, SELUNG, SELONG, SALONG, SALON, CHAU KO')*** [MWT] 7,000 in Myanmar (1993 Johnstone). Population total both countries 7,000 or more. Mergui Archipelago, Dung and other islands in south Myanmar. Also spoken in Thailand. Austronesian, Malayo-Polynesian, Western Malayo-Polynesian, Sundic, Malayic, Moklen. Dialects: DUNG, JA-IT, L'BE. Closest to Moklen. Related to Urak Lawoi. They live primarily on boats, but occasionally settle on islands in the area. SVO. Tropical forest. Islands. Marine products. Sea level. Traditional religion, Muslim. Bible portions 1913.

MON ***(TALAING, MUN, PEGUAN)*** [MNW] 835,100 in Myanmar (1983 estimate). Population total both countries 900,000 to 935,000. Eastern delta region from east of Rangoon as far as Ye and Thailand; south Martaban, adjacent area. Also spoken in Thailand. Austro-Asiatic, Mon-Khmer, Monic. Dialects: MATABAN-MOULMEIN (CENTRAL MON, MON TE), PEGU (NORTHERN MON, MON TANG), YE (SOUTHERN MON, MON NYA). The Mon can read Burmese and are generally bilingual in Burmese.

Many young people use only Burmese. Remnants of a nation that once spread over southern Myanmar and western Thailand. SVO. Ancient script, Indic-based derived from Pali. Bible 1928.

MRU ***(MRO, MURUNG, NIOPRENG, MRUNG)*** [MRO] 20,000 in Myanmar (1999 ABWE). Arakan Hills and adjacent area. Sino-Tibetan, Tibeto-Burman, Mru. SOV. Traditional religion with some Buddhist elements. NT 1994. See main entry under Bangladesh.

NAGA, KHIAMNIUNGAN ***(KHIAMNGAN, KHIAMNIUNGAN, KALYOKENGNYU, MAKWARE, NOKAW, PARA, PONYO, WELAM)*** [NKY] Northwestern. Sino-Tibetan, Tibeto-Burman, Jingpho-Konyak-Bodo, Konyak-Bodo-Garo, Konyak. SOV. NT 1981. See main entry under India.

NAGA, TASE ***(TASE, TASEY, CHAM CHANG, TANGSA, RANGPAN)*** [NST] Northwestern Myanmar. Sino-Tibetan, Tibeto-Burman, Jingpho-Konyak-Bodo, Konyak-Bodo-Garo, Konyak. Dialects: GASHAN, HKALUK, SANGCHE, SAUKRANG, LANGSHIN, MAWRANG, MYIMU, SANGTAI, TULIM, LONGRI. Some dialects are widely divergent. SOV. NT 1992. See main entry under India.

NORRA ***(NORA, NOZA, NURRA)*** [NOR] 10,000 (1951). Myanmar-Tibet border. Sino-Tibetan, Tibeto-Burman, Nungish. Dialects: NORA, BYABE, KIZOLO. Lama (3,000) may be a dialect. SOV.

NUNG ***(ANUNG, ANOONG, ANU, NU, LU, LUTZU, LUTZE, KIUTZE, KHANUNG, KWINP'ANG, KHUPANG, KWINGSANG, FUCH'YE)*** [NUN] North Myanmar. Salween (Nu) River. Sino-Tibetan, Tibeto-Burman, Nungish. Dialects: CHOLO, GWAZA, MIKO. 15 or 16 dialects, mostly inherently intelligible with each other. They understand the Mutwang dialect of Rawang. They may be the same as the Nu River Drung in China. 70% lexical similarity with Rawa. Different from Nung (Tai family) of Viet Nam, Laos, and China, and from Chinese Nung (Cantonese) of Viet Nam. SOV. Agriculturalists. Polytheist, Christian, Lamaist.

PALAUNG, PALE ***(DI-ANG, NGWE PALAUNG, SILVER PALAUNG, PALE, PALAY)*** [PCE] 190,000 to 290,000 in Myanmar. Population total all countries 200,000 to 300,000. Southern Shan State area near Kalaw. 10,000 square mile area. Also spoken in China, Thailand. Austro-Asiatic, Mon-Khmer, Northern Mon-Khmer, Palaungic, Eastern Palaungic, Palaung. Closely related to Shwe Palaung and Rumai Palaung, but a distinct language. SVO. Literacy rate in first language: Below 1%. Literacy rate in second language: Below 5%. Evergreen forest. Rocky, steep mountain slope. Peasant agriculturalists. 4,000 feet. Buddhist.

PALAUNG, RUMAI ***(RUMAI)*** [RBB] 137,000 in Myanmar. Population total both countries 139,000 (1977 Voegelin and Voegelin). Northern Shan State. Also spoken in China. Austro-Asiatic, Mon-Khmer, Northern Mon-Khmer, Palaungic, Eastern Palaungic, Palaung. Closely related to Shwe Palaung and Pale Palaung, but a distinct language. Officially included De'ang nationality in China. SVO.

PALAUNG, SHWE ***(TA-ANG PALAUNG, GOLDEN PALAUNG, SHWE)*** [SWE] 148,000 in Myanmar (1982). Population total both countries 150,000 (1982). Northern Shan State, centered in Nam Hsan. Also spoken in China. Austro-Asiatic, Mon-Khmer, Northern Mon-Khmer, Palaungic, Eastern Palaungic, Palaung. 15 Palaung dialects in Myanmar. Pale Palaung and Rumai are closely related but distinct languages. Shan is the lingua franca for intercommunication among Palaung groups with marked dialect differences and between Palaung and Shan, Kachin, and smaller groups such as Lisu. Included under De'ang official nationality in China. SVO. Mainly Buddhist.

PALI [PLL] Indo-European, Indo-Iranian, Indo-Aryan, Unclassified. Used as the literary language of the Buddhist Scriptures. Buddhist. Extinct. NT 1835. See main entry under India.

PALU [PBZ] Sino-Tibetan, Tibeto-Burman, Unclassified. May be the same as a language listed under another name. SOV.

PANKHU ***(PANKHO, PANKO, PANGKHU)*** [PKH] Falam area, Chin Hills. Sino-Tibetan, Tibeto-Burman, Kuki-Chin-Naga, Kuki-Chin, Central. Tropical forest. Agriculturalists. See main entry under India.

PARAUK ***(WA, PRAOK, PHALOK, BARAOG)*** [PRK] 348,400 in Myanmar (1983 estimate). Population total both countries 528,400. Shan State, upper Salween River area. Also spoken in China. Austro-Asiatic, Mon-Khmer, Northern Mon-Khmer, Palaungic, Western Palaungic, Waic, Wa. Related to Lawa and Vo in Thailand and China. A large and powerful group. The standard form for the Wa official nationality in China. Traditional culture. Mountain slope. Hinayana Buddhist, some Christian. NT 1938.

PURUM ***(PURAM)*** [PUB] 300 (1977 Voegelin and Voegelin). Sino-Tibetan, Tibeto-Burman, Kuki-Chin-Naga, Kuki-Chin, Northern. Related to Chiru, Aimol, Langrong. SOV.

PYEN [PYY] 800 (1981 Wurm and Hattori). East central, 2 enclaves very near the Laos border, near the Kha River. Sino-Tibetan, Tibeto-Burman, Lolo-Burmese, Loloish, Southern, Phunoi. Closely related to Phunoi, Bisu, and Mpi.

RALTE [RAL] 16,830 in Myanmar. Population total both countries 17,000 (1977 Voegelin and Voegelin). Also spoken in India. Sino-Tibetan, Tibeto-Burman, Kuki-Chin-Naga, Kuki-Chin, Northern. SOV.

RAWANG ***(NUNG RAWANG, GANUNG-RAWANG, HKANUNG, NUNG, KRANGKU, TARON, KIUTZE, CH'OPA, CHIUTSE)*** [RAW] Population total both countries 100,000 or more (1980 Seindang Sakram). Kachin State, highlands. Serwang is close to the Tibet border. Wadamkong is in Myanmar. Also spoken in

India. Sino-Tibetan, Tibeto-Burman, Nungish. Dialects: RAWANG, AGU, HPUNGSI, HTISELWANG, MATWANLY, MUTWANG, SERHTA, SERWANG, WADAMKONG, WAHKE, TARON, TANGSARR, LONGMI (LUNGMI), ZITHUNG, KUNLANG. 75 to 100 dialects, some of which are inherently unintelligible to each others' speakers. Five major divisions: Longmi, Mutwang, Serwang, Tangsarr, Kwinpang (Nung); each has 20 to 30 subdialects. Dialect continuum with Nu nationality in China. Dialects near the Tibet border are harder to understand. Kunglang in India; communication cut off in 1950s. Most dialects understand Mutwang, the central, written dialect. Related, but not the same as Drung in China. Their second language is Burmese, third is English. Some speak Lisu and Kachin. The Chinese name is 'Kiutze' or 'Qiuze'. The Lisu name is 'Ch'opa'. 'Krangku' is a regional name of Rawang. SOV. Literacy rate in first language: 30% to 60%. Literacy rate in second language: 75% to 100%. Bible 1986.

RIANG ***(BLACK KAREN, YANGLAM, BLACK YANG, RIANG-LANG, YIN, YANG, LIANG SEK, YANG WAN KUN)*** [RIL] 20,000 in Myanmar (1955). Population total both countries 23,000 or more. Shan State, southeastern Myanmar. Also spoken in China. Austro-Asiatic, Mon-Khmer, Northern Mon-Khmer, Palaungic, Eastern Palaungic, Riang. Bilingualism in Shan. Not related to the Tripuri speaking Riang of India and Bangladesh. Not related to Black (Pa'o) Karen which is Sino-Tibetan. Officially included under De'ang nationality in China. SVO. Bible portions 1950.

SAMTAO ***(SAMTAU, SAMTUAN)*** [STU] Population total both countries 100 or more. Eastern Shan State. Also spoken in China. Austro-Asiatic, Mon-Khmer, Northern Mon-Khmer, Palaungic, Western Palaungic, Angkuic. Different from Blang.

SANSU [SCA] Sino-Tibetan, Tibeto-Burman, Lolo-Burmese, Loloish, Southern, Akha, Hani. May not be a distinct language. Investigation needed: intelligibility with Hani dialects. SOV.

SHAN ***(SHA, TAI SHAN, SAM, THAI YAI, TAI YAI, GREAT THAI, TAI LUANG, "NGIO", "NGIOW", "NGIAW", "NGIAO", "NGEO")*** [SJN] 2,920,000 in Myanmar (1993 Johnstone), 6% of the population (1986). Population total all countries 3,000,000 (1999 WA). 350,000 Tai Mao (1990 A. Diller ANU). Shan States, southeast Myanmar. Kokant Shan is in the Kokant area in northern Wa State in the Shan States. Tai Mao is on the Burma-Yunnan border, centered at Mu'ang Mao Long or Namkham, Myanmar. Also spoken in China, Thailand. Tai-Kadai, Kam-Tai, Be-Tai, Tai-Sek, Tai, Southwestern, East Central, Northwest. Dialects: KOKANT SHAN, TAI MAO (MAO, MAW, MAU, TAI LONG, NORTHERN SHAN). Burmese Shan is spoken with regional dialect differences, but dialects are close linguistically. Tai-Khae (Khe) may be a dialect. A large, civilized group. Tai Mao have own script. Southern Shan traditionally written with a Burmese-like script which does not distinguish tone or some vowels. Plains. Paddy rice, artisans (gold, silver, blacksmiths), shopkeepers. Buddhist. Bible 1892.

TAI LOI ***(LOI, TAILOI, WAKUT, MONGLWE)*** [TLQ] Population total both countries 1,500 (1981 Wurm and Hattori). Namkham, in the northeast corner near the Laos and Chinese borders. Doi is across the border in Laos. Also spoken in Laos. Austro-Asiatic, Mon-Khmer, Northern Mon-Khmer, Palaungic, Western Palaungic, Angkuic. Dialects: TAI LOI, DOI. Closest to Pale Palaung, but with a lot of sound changes, separating it from Palaung in China also. Investigation needed: intelligibility with Doi. Nontonal. Mountain slope.

TAI NÜA ***(TAI NEUA, CHINESE SHAN, TAI KONG)*** [TDD] 72,400 in Myanmar (1983 estimate). Also possibly in northern Viet Nam. Tai-Kadai, Kam-Tai, Be-Tai, Tai-Sek, Tai, Southwestern, East Central, Northwest. The Laos dialect is different. Called 'Dehong Dai' in China. Bible portions 1931-1948. See main entry under China.

TAMAN [TCL] 10,000. Sino-Tibetan, Tibeto-Burman, Jingpho-Konyak-Bodo, Jingpho-Luish, Jingpho. SOV.

TAUNGYO ***(TARU, TAVOYA, TAVOYAN, DAWE, DAWAI, TAWE-TAVOY, TORU)*** [TCO] 443,400 (1983 estimate). Vicinity of Taunggyi, Shan State southward to Tavoy, Tenasserim State. Sino-Tibetan, Tibeto-Burman, Lolo-Burmese, Burmish, Southern. Related to Burmese. SOV.

TAVOYAN [TVN] Southeast. Sino-Tibetan, Tibeto-Burman, Lolo-Burmese, Burmish, Southern. One of the better known varieties of nonstandard Burmese with profound pronunciation and vocabulary differences from Burmese. SOV. Buddhist.

VO ***(WA, K'AWA, KAWA, VA, WA PWI, WAKUT)*** [WBM] 558,000 in Myanmar (1993 Johnstone). Population total both countries 618,000. Shan State, upper Salween River area. Kentung Wa are in or around Kentung City in southern Wa area. Also spoken in China. Austro-Asiatic, Mon-Khmer, Northern Mon-Khmer, Palaungic, Western Palaungic, Waic, Wa. Dialects: WA LON, WU, KENTUNG WA, SON, EN, LA. Related to Lawa and Parauk in Thailand and China. Kentung Wa is more closely related to Lawa than are the northern dialects. En and Son are very different from each other. Son, En, and La may be separate languages. 'Kawa' may refer to Blang. An official nationality in China. 'Wa pwi' means 'Wa people'. Investigation needed: intelligibility with Lawa, Parauk, Son, En, La. SVO. Defoliated into scrub forest. Mountain slope, plateau. Swidden agriculturalists. 3,000 to 6,000 feet. Traditional religion, Christian, Buddhist.

WELAUNG [WEL] Sino-Tibetan, Tibeto-Burman, Kuki-Chin-Naga, Kuki-Chin, Southern. SOV.

WEWAW ***(WEWAU)*** [WEA] Toungoo District. Sino-Tibetan, Tibeto-Burman, Karen, Sgaw-Bghai, Sgaw. SOV.

YANGBYE ***(YANBE, YANGYE, YANBYE)*** [YBD] 810,300 (1983 estimate). Sino-Tibetan, Tibeto-Burman, Lolo-Burmese, Burmish, Southern. SOV.

YINCHIA ***(STRIPED KAREN, YINNET, BLACK RIANG, RANEI)*** [YIN] 4,000 (1974 Hackett). Shan State south. Austro-Asiatic, Mon-Khmer, Northern Mon-Khmer, Palaungic, Eastern Palaungic, Riang. Related to Riang Lang and Wa. Not Karen linguistically. SVO.

YOS ***(YO, YOTE)*** [YOS] 3,400 (1983 estimate). Sino-Tibetan, Tibeto-Burman, Kuki-Chin-Naga, Kuki-Chin, Northern. Different from Mizo Chin. SOV.

ZAIWA ***(TSAIWA, ATSI, ATSHI, ATZI, AZI, ACI)*** [ATB] 30,000 in Myanmar (1997). Kachin State, Sedan, Kentung. Sino-Tibetan, Tibeto-Burman, Lolo-Burmese, Burmish, Northern. Closely related to Lashi and Maru. Also related to Phun, Achang. Dialects have only minor phonological differences. They use Jingpo as lingua franca. SOV. Literacy rate in first language: Below 1%. Literacy rate in second language: 50% to 75%. Tropical forest. Mountain slope, interfluvial. Peasant agriculturalists. Bible portions 1939-1951. See main entry under China.

ZOME ***(ZORNI, ZOMI, ZOU, ZO, KUKI CHIN)*** [ZOM] 30,000 in Myanmar. Population total both countries 46,400. Chin State, Tiddim, Chin Hills. Also spoken in India. Sino-Tibetan, Tibeto-Burman, Kuki-Chin-Naga, Kuki-Chin, Northern. 'Zomi' is a general name for all Chin, but is also used for this specific group. SOV. Bible 1992.

ZYPHE ***(ZOPHEI)*** [ZYP] Population total both countries 20,000 (1994 IMA). Chin State, Thantlang Township. Also spoken in India. Sino-Tibetan, Tibeto-Burman, Kuki-Chin-Naga, Kuki-Chin, Southern. Dialects: LOWER ZYPHE, UPPER ZYPHE. Close to Mara Chin. Many are bilingual in Haka Chin, Lakher, or Mara, depending on location.

NEPAL

Kingdom of Nepal, Sri Nepala Sarkar. National or official languages: Nepali, Gurung. 22,847,000 (1998 UN). 2,423,840 speakers of Tibeto-Burman languages (1991 J. Matisoff). Literacy rate 20% to 29%. Also includes Kharia, Urdu 202,208. Information mainly from R. Hugoniot 1970; D. B. Bista 1972; S. Toba 1976, 1983, 1991; A. Hale 1982; W. Winter 1991; K. Ebert 1994; J. Matisoff et al. 1996; R. Burling ms. (1998). Hindu, Buddhist, Muslim, Christian. Blind population 100,000. Deaf population 1,275,776. Deaf institutions: 3. Data accuracy estimate: A2, B. The number of languages listed for Nepal is 121. Of those, 120 are living languages and 1 is extinct. Diversity index 0.69.

ATHPARIYA ***(ATHAPRE, ATHPARE, ARTHARE, ARTHARE-KHESANG)*** [APH] 2,000 (1995 Karen Ebert), 439,312 all Rai languages (1991 census). Kosi Zone, Dhankuta District, north of the Tamur, between the Dhankutakhola in the west and the Tangkhuwa in the east; Dhankuta and Bhirgaon panchayats. Sino-Tibetan, Tibeto-Burman, Himalayish, Mahakiranti, Kiranti, Eastern. Athpare from Dhankuta and from Belhara are very similar, but not inherently intelligible to each other's speakers (Bickel 1996:21). Reported to be close to Limbu, but not inherently intelligible with it. The term 'Kiranti' covers about 21 dialects, of which fewer than half are even partially intelligible to each other. Low bilingualism in Nepali. All ages. Used by all, including educated speakers. 'Athpare' refers to the ethnic unit formed by close cultural ties between the Belhare and the autochthonous inhabitants of neighboring Dhankuta bazaar. People from each recognize the linguistic difference, and distinguish them by calling the Dhankuta people 'Noupagari' and the Belhare people 'Athpagari' (Bickel 1996:21). 'Rai' and 'Kiranti' are partially overlapping terms and subject to many interpretations (Austin Hale SIL 1977, personal communication). Grammar. SOV; postpositions; genitives, adjectives, numerals before noun heads; polar questions marked with a suffix attached to the verb sentence final; content questions can have the same word order as assertive sentences, or the question word occurs directly before the verb; maximum number of suffixes 9; affixes indicate case of noun phrase; verb affixes mark person, number, object-obligatory; split ergative; comparatives with Nepali 'Bhanda'; CV, CVC, CVCC; nontonal.

AWADHI ***(ABADI, ABADHI, ABOHI, AMBODHI, AVADHI, BAISWARI, KOJALI, KOSALI)*** [AWD] 374,638 in Nepal, 2.03% of the population (1991 census). Lumbini Zone, Kapilbastu District; Bheri Zone, Banke and Bardiya districts. Indo-European, Indo-Iranian, Indo-Aryan, East Central zone. Dialects: BAGHELI, GANGAPARI, MIRZAPURI, PARDESI, THARU, UTTARI. Literacy rate in second language: 50% to 75%. NT 1996. See main entry under India.

BAGHELI ***(BAGELKHANDI, BHUGELKHUD, MANNADI, RIWAI, GANGGAI, MANDAL, KEWOT, KEWAT, KAWATHI, KENAT, KEVAT BOLI, KEVATI, KEWANI, KEWATI, NAGPURI MARATHI)*** [BFY] Morang District, Koshi Zone. Indo-European, Indo-Iranian, Indo-Aryan, East Central zone. Dialects: MARARI, OJHI, POWARI, BANAPARI, GAHORE, TIRHARI, GODWANI (MANDLAHA), SONPARI. Trade language. NT 1821, out of print. See main entry under India.

BAHING ***(RUMDALI, BAINGE RAI, BAING, BAYING, BAYUNG, BAHING LO, BAYUNG LO)*** [RAR] 7,000 to 10,000 (1991 W. Winter). Sagarmatha Zone, Okhaldunga District, south of the Solu River in the Nachedanda ranges, east of the Melung River to the Thatan River and its tributaries in the west. Sino-Tibetan, Tibeto-Burman, Himalayish, Mahakiranti, Kham-Magar-Chepang-Sunwari, Sunwari. Dialects: NAMBER SACHA, ROKHUNG, KHALING, BANENGE, DOBO LO, PROCA LO. The Khaling dialect of Bahing is distinct from the Khaling language. More homogenous than most Kiranti languages. Related to Sunwar. Agriculturalists, pastoralists.

BANTAWA ***(BANTAWA RAI, BANTABA, BONTAWA, BANTAWA YÜNG, BANTAWA YONG, BANTAWA DUM)*** [BAP] 35,000 or more (1985 N. K. Rai), 50,700 to 70,000 including second language users (1991 W. Winter). 'Intermediate Bantawa' represents most groups (Hansson in Winter 1991:7). Morang, Dhankuta, Bhojpur districts, Koshi Zone, and western Dhankuta District, Khotang District. Amchoke is in Limbuwan, especially in Ilam District; Udaipur District, Sagarmatha Zone; Japa District, Mechi Zone. Many villages. Sino-Tibetan, Tibeto-Burman, Himalayish, Mahakiranti, Kiranti, Eastern. Dialects: NORTHERN BANTAWA (DILPALI), SOUTHERN BANTAWA (HANGKHIM), EASTERN BANTAWA (DHANKUTA), WESTERN BANTAWA, CHHINTANG, DUNGMALI (DUNMALI), WALING (WALUNG, WALÜNG), RUNGCHENBUNG, AMCHOKE (AMCHAUKE), YANGMA. Southern and Northern Banatawa are the most similar, and could be united as 'Intermediate Bantawa'. Dozens of dialects reported to be inherently intelligible with each other. Sorung and Saharaja are Amchoke subdialects. In some regions young people prefer Nepali. Some varieties are used as the traditional lingua franca among Rai minorities in Limbuwan, Sikkim India, and Bhutan, and as first language among Rai of other origin. This seems to have been happening for some time, and is reflected by dialect diversity. It is currently happening among the Lambichong, Mugu, and Chhintang (Bradley 1996). Dictionary. Grammar. SOV; postpositions; genitives, adjectives, numerals before noun heads; polar questions marked only with rising intonation; content questions same word order as assertive sentences or question word directly before the verb; affixes indicate case of noun phrases; verb affixes mark person, number, object-obligatory; split ergative; comparatives use Nepali word bhanda; CV, CVC, CVCC; nontonal. Mountain slope, plains. Agriculturalists, pastoralists. Traditional religion.

BARAAMU ***(BARHAMU, BRAHMU, BHRAMU, BRAMU, BARAM)*** [BRD] 2,000 (1998) out of 6,580 in the ethnic group (1996 Thapa). Gandaki Zone, North Gorkha District, Takhu village up the Doraundi Khola on the east side above Chorgate, near Kumhali, about 7 villages. They may be in Dhading District. Sino-Tibetan, Tibeto-Burman, Himalayish, Tibeto-Kanauri, Western Himalayish, Eastern. Related to Thami (Grierson-Konow). Most people know some Nepali. Spoken mainly by older people, perhaps those over 40 years. Baraamu may be going out of use. OV (Subject position varies); postpositions; genitives, articles, adjectives, numerals before noun heads; Maximum number of suffixes 3; word order does not distinguish subjects, objects, or indirect objects; affixes indicate case of noun phrase; verb affixes mark person, number-obligatory; ergative; passives, causatives, comparatives; simple syllable patterns; nontonal. Mountain slope. Peasant agriculturalists. 500 to 1,500 meters. Traditional religion, Hindu.

BARAGAUNLE ***(BARAGAUN, BARAGAON, BHOTI GURUNG)*** [BON] 1,600 to 2,200 or more, including 650 in Kagbeni, 530 to 1,140 in Jharkot, 400 in Purang (1990). Dhaulagiri Zone, Mustang District, 18 villages in the Kali Gandaki Valley and on the hillsides north of Jomosom up to Kagbeni, and east to Muktinath; on the plains and along the river. Sino-Tibetan, Tibeto-Burman, Himalayish, Tibeto-Kanauri, Tibetic, Tibetan, Central. Dialects: JHARKOT, KAGBENI. Apparently in the Tibetan rather than the Gurung subgroup. Some intelligibility with Lopa, but virtually none with Thakali. 78% lexical similarity with Lopa; 70% with Dolpo; 69% with Lhomi; 66% with Olangchung Gola; 65% with Kyerung; 64% with Helambu Sherpa; 63% with Kutang Bhotia; 60% with Lhasa Tibetan; 59% with Jirel; 58% with Sherpa. Less than 20% lexical similarity with Thakali, the closest Gurung language. The two dialects have 85% lexical similarity, 95% with Mustang, 80% with Kham. 80% understand Nepali, 90% Kham Tibetan, 80% Mustang. There are schools in Kagbeni and Purang. Investigation needed: intelligibility with Lopa. Literacy rate in second language: 50% Nepali. Buddhist, Bon-po.

BELHARIYA ***(BELHARE, ATHPARIYA, ATHPAHARIYA, ATHPARE, ATHPAGARI)*** [BYW] 500 (1995 Karen Ebert) to 2,000 (1996 Bickel). Kosi Zone, Dhankuta District, Belhara village and hill west of Dhankuta Bajar. Sino-Tibetan, Tibeto-Burman, Himalayish, Mahakiranti, Kiranti, Eastern. Different from Athpariya, although also called that, and closely related to it (W. Winter 1991). Not intelligible with Athpariya (Bickel 1996:21). Appears to be between Athpariya, Yakkha, and Chhilling linguistically. All speakers are bilingual in Nepali (Bickell 1996). Belhare is preferred and the standard means of communication in most households. At least part of the younger generation, as well as the older generation. 'Athpare' refers to the ethnic group made up of Belhare and Athpariya. They have close cultural ties, but recognize their linguistic differences. They can clarify by calling the Dhankuta people 'Noupagari' and the Belhare people 'Athpagari' (Bickel 1996:21). 1,150 meters.

BENGALI ***(BANGALA, BANGLA, BANGLA-BHASA)*** [BNG] 27,712 in Nepal, 0.15% of the population (1991 census). Mechi Zone, Jhapa District; Koshi Zone, Morang and Sunsari districts; Sagarmatha Zone, Saptari District. Indo-European, Indo-Iranian, Indo-Aryan, Eastern zone, Bengali-Assamese. Dialects: BARIK, BHATIARI, CHIRMAR, KACHARI-BENGALI, LOHARI-MALPAHARIA, MUSSELMANI, RAJSHAHI, SAMARIA, SARAKI, SIRIPURIA. Literacy rate in second language: 51.2%. Hindu. Bible 1809-1998. See main entry under Bangladesh.

BHOJPURI ***(BHOJAPURI, BHOZPURI, BAJPURI)*** [BHJ] 1,379,717 in Nepal, 7.46% of population (1991 census). Main concentration in Narayani Zone, Rautahat, Para, and Parsa districts. And near the India border in Lumbini Zone, Nawalparasi District; Janakpur Zone, Sarlahi District; Koshi Zone, Morang District; Mechi Zone, Jhapa District. Indo-European, Indo-Iranian, Indo-Aryan, Eastern zone, Bihari. Dialects: BHOJPURI THARU, TELI. The extent of dialect variation among speakers in India and Nepal has not been determined. Bhojpuri Tharu is a dialect of Bhojpuri spoken by the Tharu caste in Nepal. It is distinct from Chitwan and other Tharu. Bilingualism in Hindi, Maithili, Nepali, Awadhi. Literacy rate in first language: 5% to 30%. Literacy rate in second language: 50% to 75%. 40% literate in Nepali, Hindi. Hindu, Muslim, Christian. Bible portions 1911-1982. See main entry under India.

BODO ***(BORO, BODI, BARA, BORONI, MECHE, MECHI, MECI, MECH, MACHE)*** [BRX] 938 in Nepal (1961 census). Mechi Zone, Jhapa District. Sino-Tibetan, Tibeto-Burman, Jingpho-Konyak-Bodo, Konyak-Bodo-Garo, Bodo-Garo, Bodo. Bible 1981. See main entry under India.

BOTE-MAJHI ***(KUSHAR)*** [BMJ] 11,000 (1991 census). Mainly Chitawan District, Narayani Zone, near Kumhali. Indo-European, Indo-Iranian, Indo-Aryan, Eastern zone, Unclassified. Boatmen along various rivers, fishermen.

BUJHYAL ***(GHARTI, BUJHEL, BUJAL, WESTERN CHEPANG)*** [GOR] 5,000 (1998). Gandaki Zone, East Tanahun, south side of Chimkesori Peak, behind Yangchok, near the Magar. Separated from the Chepang by the Trisuli (Narayani) River. Sino-Tibetan, Tibeto-Burman, Himalayish, Mahakiranti, Kham-Magar-Chepang-Sunwari, Chepang. Pronominal affix differences hinder intelligibility. More like the East Himalayish languages. 98% lexical similarity with Chepang. Bilingual level estimates for Nepali are 0 5%, 1 30%, 2 40%, 3 15%, 4 10%, 5 0%. Young people sometimes speak Nepali to each other. People over 5 know some Nepali, which is learned in school. Men can talk about most common and political topics. Women know greetings and how to trade in Nepali. Buhhyal used at home and with other Gharti people. All ages. Not a high view of Bujhyal. Chepang viewed as superior. Nepali viewed for education. Distinct from slave Gharti. Similar culturally to Chepang. OV (S varies); postpositions; genitives, articles, adjectives, numerals, before noun heads; relatives before or without noun heads; question word final; maximum number of suffixes 8; word order does not distinguish subjects, objects, indirect objects; affixes indicate case of noun phrase; verb affixes mark person, number, subject, object-obligatory; passives, causatives, comparatives, CV to CCCVCCC with certain restrictions, semitonal. Literacy rate in second language: 15% in Nepal. Tropical to subtropical. Mountain slope. Swidden agriculturalists. 450 to 1,500 meters. Traditional religion, Hindu.

BYANGSI ***(BYANSHI, BYANSI, BYANGKHO LWO)*** [BEE] 1,314 in Nepal or 0.01% of the population (1991 census). Mahakali Zone, Darchula District. Sino-Tibetan, Tibeto-Burman, Himalayish, Tibeto-Kanauri, Western Himalayish, Almora. Related to Rangkas, Darmiya, Chaudangsi. Devidatta Sharma 1989 suggests that Chaudangsi and Byangsi are varieties of one language. Cultural center seems to be India. Grammar. See main entry under India.

CAMLING ***(CHAMLING, CHAMLINGE RAI)*** [RAB] 10,000 or fewer (1995 Karen Ebert). Rawa Valley, Khotang District, Sagarmatha Zone. Sino-Tibetan, Tibeto-Burman, Himalayish, Mahakiranti, Kiranti, Eastern. Closest to Bantawa and Puma linguistically. Many people speak a variety mixed with Nepali. Many ethnic Camling are not fluent in Camling. Learned by children only in a remote area of Udaypur. Many ethnic subgroups, but linguistically homogeneous. 'Rodong' means 'Kiranti', not 'Camling'. Some Bantawa call their language 'Camling'.

CHANTYAL ***(CHENTEL, CHANTEL)*** [CHX] 2,000 speakers out of 10,000 in the ethnic group (1997 Michael Noonan). Dhaulagiri Zone, Myagdi District, Kali Gandaki River valley. Ethnic Chantel also in Baglung District. Sino-Tibetan, Tibeto-Burman, Himalayish, Tibeto-Kanauri, Tibetic, Tamangic. Related to Gurung, Manang, Tamang, and Thakali (Noonan). Everyone speaks Nepali as second language. Nepali always used to non-Chantel people. Chantel always used to Chantel people. The majority speak Chantel in their home villages (Noonan 1997). Chantel not used for singing. Chantel appears to be decreasing in use and Nepali increasing. In Baglung, Chantel ceased to be spoken in the 19th century, and only Nepali is used (Noonan 1997). Some speakers believe Chantel will be replaced soon (Noonan 1995:257, 260). Outsiders often regard it as Magar, but they claim a Thakuri origin, (Anne de Sales in G. L. Toffin 1993). A lot of lexical borrowing from Nepali. Dictionary.

CHAUDANGSI ***(TSAUDANGSI, BANGBA LWO)*** [CDN] Mahakali Zone, far western. Sino-Tibetan, Tibeto-Burman, Himalayish, Tibeto-Kanauri, Western Himalayish, Almora. Related to Rangkas,

Darmiya, Byangsi. Devidatta Sharma 1989 suggests that Chaudangsi and Byansi are varieties of one language. May only be in India (Bradley 1997:14). Investigation needed: intelligibility with Byangsi. Grammar. See main entry under India.

CHEPANG ***(TSEPANG)*** [CDM] 34,000 or 0.14% of the population (1997). Inner Terai; Narayani Zone, Makwanpur, Chitwan, and South Dhading districts; Gandaki Zone, South Gorkha District. Sino-Tibetan, Tibeto-Burman, Himalayish, Mahakiranti, Kham-Magar-Chepang-Sunwari, Chepang. Dialects: EASTERN CHEPANG, WESTERN CHEPANG. Bujhel can be considered a dialect close to Western Chepang, but has difficult intelligibility with Chepang, different morphology. Dialects differ in verb forms. Similar in morphology to Kiranti languages. 98% lexical similarity with Bujhel. Bilingual level estimates for Nepali are 0 5%, 1 30%, 2 40%, 3 15%, 4 10%, 5 0%. People over 5 know some Nepali. It is often learned in school. Men can talk about most common topics and political affairs. Women know greetings and vocabulary for trade. Young people may sometimes speak Nepali to each other. Chepang used at home and to other Chepang. All ages. Bujhel have more contacts with outsiders, think of themselves as superior to eastern varieties, do not mix with them, and may not accept their written materials. They see Nepali as the language of education and written materials. Do not have a high view of Chepang. Investigation needed: intelligibility with Bujhel. Dictionary. Grammar. OV (Subject position varies); postpositions; genitives, articles, adjectives, numerals before noun heads; relatives before or without noun heads; question word final; maximum number of suffixes 8; word order does not distinguish subjects, objects, or indirect objects; affixes indicate case of noun phrase; verb affixes mark person, number, subject, and object-obligatory; ergative; passives, causatives, comparatives; CV to CCCVCCC with certain restrictions; semitonal. Literacy rate in first language: 1% to 5%. Literacy rate in second language: 40% men, 15% women in Nepali; 13.9% ethnic group (1991 census). Difficulties in reading Chepang: long words, consonant clusters. They do not know how to write it. Written Chepang has lower prestige than Nepali. Motivation high for Nepali. Devanagari. Newspapers, radio programs. Tropical to subtropical. Mountain slope. Swidden agriculturalists. 450 to 1,500 meters, especially 450 to 1,500. Traditional religion, Hindu overlay.

CHHINTANG ***(CHHINTANGE, TELI, CHINTANG RÛNG, CHINTANG)*** [CTN] 100 or fewer (1991 W. Winter). Lower Arun region, Dhankuta District, Chhintang panchayat, Sambhung and Pokhare, and Ankhisalla panchayat, Dandagaon. Sino-Tibetan, Tibeto-Burman, Himalayish, Mahakiranti, Kiranti, Eastern. Bilingualism in Bantawa, Nepali. Speakers are mainly older. The ethnic group has largely shifted to Bantawa or Nepali (Bradley 1996). Nearly extinct.

CHHULUNG ***(CHULUNG, CHÜLÜNG, CHHÛLÛNG RÛNG, CHHOLUNG, CHHILLING)*** [CUR] 1,000 or fewer (1991 W. Winter). Ankhisalla Panchayat, Dhankuta District, end of Chhintang Panchayat. Sino-Tibetan, Tibeto-Burman, Himalayish, Mahakiranti, Kiranti, Eastern. Speakers know a moderate amount of Nepali.

CHOURASE ***(TSAURASYA, CHAURASIA, CHAURASYA, CHOURASIA, UMBULE, AMBULE, OMBULE)*** [TSU] 5,000 or more (1991 W. Winter). Sagarmatha Zone, Udayapur and Okhaldhunga districts. Sino-Tibetan, Tibeto-Burman, Himalayish, Mahakiranti, Kiranti, Western. Dialects: BONU, UBU. All dialects appear to have adequate inherent intelligiblity with each other. Closest to Jerung. Nepali is used. Some bilingualism in Bahing resulting from intermarriage. All ages. Strong language retention. Literacy rate in second language: 10%. Mountain slope. Agriculturalists.

CHUKWA ***(CUKWA RING, POHING, POHING KHA)*** [CUW] 100 or fewer (1991 W. Winter). Kulung Panchayat, Bhojpur District. Sino-Tibetan, Tibeto-Burman, Himalayish, Mahakiranti, Kiranti, Eastern. Bilingualism in Nepali. Linguistically between Kulung-Nachering-Sangpang and Meohang-Saam. Nearly extinct.

DARAI [DRY] 7,000 (1991 census). Inner Terai, Narayani Zone, Chitawan District. Indo-European, Indo-Iranian, Indo-Aryan, Unclassified. Bilingualism in Nepali. Typological affinities with Northwestern zone, Dardic group.

DHANWAR ***(DHANVAR, DANUWAR RAI, DANUWAR, DENWAR)*** [DHW] 16,000 (1993 Johnstone). Eastern hills and plain, inner Terai and Terai south of Kathmandu, Sindhuli Garhi, Makwanpur District, Narayani Zone. Indo-European, Indo-Iranian, Indo-Aryan, Unclassified. Danuwar Done in Makwanpur and India and Danuwar Kachariya in Rautahat and elsewhere are probably distinct languages from Danuwar Rai. Typological affinities with Northwestern zone, Dardic group. 70% to 75% monolingual. Others use Nepali as second language.

DHIMAL [DHI] 15,014 or 0.08% of the population (1991 census). Mechi Zone, Jhapa District; Koshi Zone, Morang District. Sino-Tibetan, Tibeto-Burman, Himalayish, Tibeto-Kanauri, Tibetic, Dhimal. Dialects: EASTERN DHIMAL, WESTERN DHIMAL. Toto in India is a separate language with no inherent intelligibility between them. Low lexical similarity with Toto. Most are partially bilingual in Nepali, men more than women. Hindi is also used. Dictionary. SOV; postpositions; genitives, demonstratives, relatives before noun heads; nontonal. Literacy rate in second language: 39.2% (1991 census). Devanagari. Plains.

DOLPO ***(PHOKE DOLPA, DOLPA TIBETAN)*** [DRE] 5,000 to 10,000 (1998). Dolpa, northern, Karnali Zone, villages of Goomatara, Kola, Tachel, Kani, Bajebara, Laun, Chilpara, Bantari, Byas, above Dolpa up to Tibet. It is beyond the mountains west of the upper Kali Gandaki River valley. Confined by the Dhaulagire Himal on the south and Tibet on the north. Includes the headwaters of the Karnali River. About 24 small villages scattered over 500 square miles in Namgang, Panzgang, Tarap, and Chharbung subdistricts. Sino-Tibetan, Tibeto-Burman, Himalayish, Tibeto-Kanauri, Tibetic, Tibetan, Central. Dho Tarap, Phoksumdo Lake, Barbung River, and Charka-Dolpo Chu River areas are slightly different, but inherent intelligibility is very good. Closest language is Lopa. Reported to be close to Tichurong. 78% lexical similarity with Lopa; 70% with Baragaunle; 69% with Lhomi; 68% with Lhasa Tibetan, Olungchung Gola, and Kyerung; 67% with Kutang Bhotia; 66% with Helambu Sherpa; 62% with Jirel and Sherpa. Dolpo used in home and with other Dolpo. Dho Tarap speech may have highest prestige. Speakers call themselves and their language 'Dolpo'. SOV. Mountain valley. Agriculturalists: local consumption only; pastoralists: local homes but some members may be away tending herds 10 months every year. 2,500 to 4,500 meters. Buddhist, Bon.

DUMI ***(DUMI BO'O, DUMI BRO, RO'DO BO', LSI RAI, SOTMALI)*** [DUS] 1,000 to 2,000 (1991 W. Winter). Northern Khotang District, hills near the middle of the Rawakhola Valley. Sino-Tibetan, Tibeto- Burman, Himalayish, Mahakiranti, Kiranti, Western. Dialects: BRASMI, KHARBARI, LAMDIJA, MAKPA. Closest to Khaling and Koi. Bilingualism in Nepali. Spoken mainly by older people.

DUNGMALI ***(DUNGMALI PÛK, DUNGMALI-BANTAWA, ARTHARE, ARTHARE-KHESANG)*** [RAA] 3,000 to 5,000 (1991 W. Winter). East of central Bhojpur District, northeast of the Singtang lekh, bend of the Arun River between its confluence with the Piukhuwa and the first confluence with the Piluwa River. Sino-Tibetan, Tibeto-Burman, Himalayish, Mahakiranti, Kiranti, Eastern. Dialect: KHESANG (KHESANGE). The term 'Kiranti' covers about 21 dialects, of which fewer than half are even partially intelligible. Local names which may not be dialects: Chhinamkhang, Hangbang, Khandung, Pungwai, Roktulung, Tuncha, Waitpang.

DZONGKHA ***(JONKHA, BHOTIA OF BHUTAN, ZONGKHAR, DRUKKE, DRUKHA, BHUTANESE)*** [DZO] Some in Kathmandu. Sino-Tibetan, Tibeto-Burman, Himalayish, Tibeto-Kanauri, Tibetic, Tibetan, Southern. 'Lhoke' means 'southern language'. Traders, shopkeepers. Bible portions 1970. See main entry under Bhutan.

GHALE, KUTANG ***(BHOTTE)*** [GHT] 1,300 (1992). Gandaki Zone, Northern Gorkha District, Buri Gandaki Valley from Nyak, up to and including Prok. Sino-Tibetan, Tibeto-Burman, Himalayish, Tibeto-Kanauri, Tibetic, Tamangic. Dialects: BIHI, CHAK, RANA. Barpak Ghale is understood fairly well farther north. There is a smaller difference between Uiya and Philim than between Barpak and either Uiya or Philim. Dialects have 62% to 76% lexical similarity with each other. Rana is the most diverse. 39% to 49% lexical similarity with Southern Ghale, 45% to 61% with Northern Ghale, 18% with Banspur Gurung, 16% to 23% with Tamang varieties, 13% to 31% with Nubri, 23% to 27% with Tsum, 22% to 27% with Kyerung, 19% to 24% with Tibetan. Speakers in Bihi village have minimal bilingual proficiency in Tibetan and Nepali. Nepali used for communicating with Northern and Southern Ghale speakers. Kutang Ghale used exclusively in nearly every domain. Vigorous. Some Tibetan religious books have been translated into Kutang Ghale by priests who speak the language. Attitude toward their language is positive and strong. Tibetan viewed favorably for religious use, Nepali for education and advancement. They call their language 'thieves language' because they think of it as a mixture of nearby languages. Investigation needed: intelligibility with dialects. Literacy rate in first language: Some can read Kutang Ghale in Tibetan script. Literacy rate in second language: 5%. Tibetan script is preferred and used for Tibetan religious book translations. Gallery forest. Mountain slope. Swidden and peasant agriculturalists. 2,000 to 4,100 meters. Lamaist Buddhist.

GHALE, NORTHERN [GHH] 2,500 (1991 Smith). Gandaki Zone, Gorkha District, Buri Gandaki Valley. Sino-Tibetan, Tibeto-Burman, Himalayish, Tibeto-Kanauri, Tibetic, Tamangic. Dialects: KHORLA, UIYA, JAGAT, PHILIM, NYAK. Nyak is the most diverse dialect. Philim people have 94% intelligibility of Uiya. Speakers have 75% to 79% intelligibility of Barpak in Southern Ghale. Dialect chain runs north and south. Dialects have 73% to 89% lexical similarity with each other. 65% to 81% lexical similarity with Southern Ghale, 45% to 61% with Kutang Ghale, 29% to 37% with Western Tamang, 21% to 27% with Nubri, 22% to 25% with Tsum, 19% to 23% with Kyerung, 19% to 21% with Tibetan. Speakers in Philim, Lho, and Bihi have no more than basic bilingual proficiency in Nepali. Ghale used nearly exclusively in every domain. N. and S. Ghale use mother tongue for communicating with each other, but Nepali for talking to Kutang Ghale and others. Vigorous. Positive attitudes toward N. Ghale. Nepali seen as good for use with government and other groups. Uiya and Barpak are the centers, Barpak has the most prestige. Gallery forest. Mountain slope, valley. Swidden and peasant agriculturalists. 2,000 to 4,100 meters.

GHALE, SOUTHERN ***(GALLE GURUNG)*** [GHE] 12,000 (1975 Nishi). Gandaki Zone, Gorkha District, hills south of Macha Khola. Sino-Tibetan, Tibeto-Burman, Himalayish, Tibeto-Kanauri, Tibetic, Tamangic. Dialects: BARPAK, KYAURA, LAPRAK. Some intelligibility between N. and S. Ghale. Dialect chain. Glover (1974:8-12) has a Ghale branch under Bodish intermediate between the Tibetan and Gurung branches. 75% to 78% lexical similarity among dialects. 65% to 81% lexical similarity with Northern Ghale, 39% to 49% with Kutang Ghale, 27% to 30% with Banspur Gurung, 31% with Western Tamang, 20% with Nubri and Tsum, 18% with Tibetan. 30% to 40% monolingual. Others use Nepali, Hindi, or English as second languages. Nepali used with Kutang Ghale and other groups. Ghale used in every domain, and between N. and S. Ghale. Vigorous. Positive attitudes toward Southern Ghale. Barpak is the most prestigious center. Nepali is viewed as useful for intergroup commerce and government. Investigation needed: intelligibility with dialects. Dictionary. Literacy rate in second language: 5% to 15%. Gallery forest. Mountain slope, valley. Swidden and peasant agriculturalists. 600 to 1,800 meters. Hindu, Buddhist. NT 1992.

GURUNG, EASTERN [GGN] 105,000 or more, 1.23% of the population (1991 census). 227,918 all Gurung languages in Nepal (1991 census). Western Dev. Region, Gandaki Zone, mainly Lamjung, Tanahu, and western Gorkha districts. Possibly some in Manang District. Sino-Tibetan, Tibeto-Burman, Himalayish, Tibeto-Kanauri, Tibetic, Tamangic. Dialects: LAMJUNG GURUNG, GORKHA GURUNG, TAMU KYI. Eastern and Western Gurung do not have adequate intelligibility to handle complex and abstract discourse. Daduwa town seems central linguistically. All sexes and ages use Nepali. Most people can talk about common topics. Some English is known by graduates from school. Gurung used at home and to other Gurung. All ages. Language reinforces ethnic membership. Nepali viewed as essential, English as economically advantageous. SOV; postpositions; genitives, adjectives, relatives before noun heads; numerals after noun heads; rising intonation in bipolar questions; 1 prefix on negative verbs; maximum number of suffixes 3; case of noun phrase shown by preposition; no subject or object referencing in verbs; split ergative system according to tense; causatives; benefactives; CV, CCV, CCCV; tonal. Literacy rate in first language: 30%. Literacy rate in second language: 30%. Devanagari. Radio programs. Mountain slope, foothills. Peasant agriculturalists, pastoralists. 1,500 to 3,000 meters. Buddhist, Hindu.

GURUNG, WESTERN ***(GURUNG, TAMU KYI)*** [GVR] 72,000 in Nepal (1991 census). Northwestern dialect is the largest. 227,918 all Gurung languages in Nepal, 1.23% of the population (1991 census). Population total all countries 72,000 or more. Gandaki Zone, Kaski, Syangia, and Parbat districts, Dhaulagiri. Also possibly in Myanmar. Also spoken in Bhutan, India. Sino-Tibetan, Tibeto-Burman, Himalayish, Tibeto-Kanauri, Tibetic, Tamangic. Dialects: SOUTHERN GURUNG (SYANGJA GURUNG), NORTHWESTERN GURUNG (KASKI GURUNG). Dialect speakers may have enough inherent intelligibility of each other to understand complex and abstract discourse. Not enough with Eastern Gurung. All ages and sexes use Nepali. Most people can talk about common topics in Nepali. Nepali is viewed as necessary. School graduates speak some English, which is viewed as economically advantageous. Gurung used at home and to other Gurung. All ages. Language reinforces ethnic membership. Investigation needed: intelligibility with Southern Gurung. Official language. Dictionary. Grammar. SOV; postpositions; genitives, adjectives, relatives before noun heads; numerals after noun heads; rising intonation marks bipolar questions; one negative prefix on verbs; maximum number of suffixes is 3; case of noun phrases is indicated by postpositions; no subject or object referencing in verbs; split ergative system according to tense; causatives; benefactives; CV, CCV, CCCV; tonal. Literacy rate in first language: 30%. Literacy rate in second language: 30%. Devanagari. Radio programs. Mountain slope, foothills. Peasant agriculturalists, pastoralists. 1,500 to 3,000 meters. Buddhist, Hindu. NT 1982, out of print.

HELAMBU SHERPA ***(YOHLMU TAM)*** [SCP] 5,000 to 10,000 (1998). Nuwakot and Sindhupalchok districts, Bagmati Zone, Helambu area. Sino-Tibetan, Tibeto-Burman, Himalayish, Tibeto-Kanauri, Tibetic, Tibetan, Central. Dialects: EASTERN HELAMBU SHERPA, WESTERN HELAMBU SHERPA. Melamchi River divides the dialects. Speakers understand other dialect even for abstract and complex subjects, including possibly Tarke Ghyang, Khang-Kharka, Pahndang, but not Kagate. 66% lexical similarity with Dolpo and Olangchung Gola; 65% with Lhasa Tibetan, Baragaunle, Jirel, and Kyerung; 63% with Lopa and Sherpa; 61% with Kutang Bhotia; 60% with Lhomi. Most people can talk about common topics in Nepali. Men know more than women. In Kathmandu Nepali is used in more domains. Helambu Sherpa used at home and in-group. All ages in homeland. In Kathmandu parents tend to speak Nepali to children. Helambu Sherpa is more prestigious than Kagate, has more of the original culture preserved. Shermathang-Chhimi area in the east is prestigious. Many lamas live there. Not much contact with Kagate, attitudes indifferent toward it. Nepali is viewed as useful. They go to India as laborers. Dictionary. SOV; postpositions; genitives, relatives before noun heads; articles, adjectives, numerals mostly after noun heads; maximum number of prefixes 1; maximum number of suffixes 2-3; word order distinguishes subject, object, indirect object some, but normally marked by postpositions; case of noun phrase indicated by postposition; split ergativity; impersonal voice; causatives; comparatives; CV, CVC, CVV, CCV, CCVV, CVVC; tonal. Literacy rate in first language: Below 1%.

Literacy rate in second language: 15% to 25%. Literacy motivation not high, except in English. Devanagari script. A few lamas know the Tibetan script. Radio programs. Mountain slope. Peasant agriculturalists. 2,000 to 3,000 meters. Buddhist, Lamaist.

HINDI [HND] 170,997 in Nepal, or 0.92% of the population (1991 census). Southern strip of low country. Indo-European, Indo-Iranian, Indo-Aryan, Central zone, Western Hindi, Hindustani. Language of wider communication. Hindu. Bible 1818-1987. See main entry under India.

HUMLA BHOTIA *(DANGALI, PHOKE)* [HUT] Bajura District, Seti Zone; Humla District, Karnali Zone. Sino-Tibetan, Tibeto-Burman, Himalayish, Tibeto-Kanauri, Tibetic, Tibetan, Central. Probably a separate language from Tibetan. Literacy rate in second language: Low in Tibetan. Buddhist.

JERUNG *(JERO, JERUM, JERUNGE, JHERUNG, JERO MALA, ZERO, ZERUM, ZERO MALA)* [JEE] 1,000 to 2,000 (1991 W. Winter). Around and above the mouth of the Melungkhola River. Sino-Tibetan, Tibeto-Burman, Himalayish, Mahakiranti, Kiranti, Western. Dialects: MADHAVPUR, BALKHU-SISNERI, RATNAWATI (SINDHULI). Linguistically closest to Chourase. Bilingualism in Nepali. Older people. Young people appear to not speak Jerung.

JIREL *(ZIRAL, JIRI, JIRIAL)* [JUL] 8,000 to 10,000 (1998). Janakpur Zone, Dolakha District, Jiri and Sikri valleys, eastern hills. Jiri is the main area. Others include Chhyatrapa; Lumbini and Nawalparasi districts. Sino-Tibetan, Tibeto-Burman, Himalayish, Tibeto-Kanauri, Tibetic, Tibetan, Southern. Accent differences, but not real dialects. Some comprehension of Lhasa Tibetan and some Tibetan dialects. 67% lexical similarity with Sherpa; 65% with Helambu Sherpa; 62% with Dolpo and Lopa; 60% with Baragaunle and Kyerung; 57% with Kutang Bhotia, Lhomi, and Olangchung Gola; 54% with Lhasa Tibetan. Bilingual level estimates for Nepali are 0 few, 1 5%, 2 40%, 3 <50%, 4 <10%, 5 0%. A few know some Sherpa, very few some Tamang and Sunwar. Some know enough Nepali only for trade (mainly women). Jirel used with Jirel speakers, Nepali to others. All ages. Karsa and Kharok accents are more prestigious, more educated. Nepali viewed as prestigious, needed for education, work, talking to non-Jirel people. SOV; postpositions; genitives, demonstratives, adjectives before noun heads; numerals after noun heads; relatives before and without noun heads; content question word initial or medial; polar question word final; maximum number of prefixes 1, maximum number of suffixes 4; subjects, objects, indirect objects distinguished by case marker; affixes indicate case of noun phrases; verb affixes mark person; ergative; causatives; CV, CVC, V, VC; tonal. Literacy rate in first language: 25% to 30% adults, 60% younger people. Literacy rate in second language: 25% to 30% adults, 60% younger people (1991 census). People literate in Nepali can read Jirel. Devanagari. Mountain slope. Peasant agriculturalists. 1,700 to 2,000 meters. Hindu, Buddhist. NT 1992.

KAGATE *(SHUBA, SHYUBA, SYUBA, KAGATE BHOTE)* [SYW] 800 to 1,000 (1998). Janakpur Zone, Ramechhap District, on one of the ridges of Likhu Khola. Sino-Tibetan, Tibeto-Burman, Himalayish, Tibeto-Kanauri, Tibetic, Tibetan, Central. Differs from Helambu Sherpa by using less the honorific system in verbs. People can talk about most common topics in Nepali. More Nepali used in Kathmandu. Kagate normally used at home and to other Kagate. All ages. Attitude toward Helambu Sherpa is indifferent—not much contact because of distance. Reserved attitude toward Nepali people and language. SOV; postpositions; genitives, adjectives, relatives before noun heads; numerals after noun heads; maximum number of prefixes 1; maximum number of suffixes 3; subject, object, indirect object, case of noun phrase indicated by postpositions; split ergativity; impersonal voice; causatives; comparatives; CV, CVC, CVV, CCV, CCVV, CVVC; tonal. Literacy rate in second language: Few. Devanagari. Mountain slope. Peasant agriculturalists. 2,000 meters. Buddhist, Lamaist. Bible portions 1977.

KAIKE *(TARALI KHAM)* [KZQ] 2,000 (1997 Bradley). Karnali Zone, Dolpa District; Daulagiri Zone. Sino-Tibetan, Tibeto-Burman, Himalayish, Tibeto-Kanauri, Kanauri. They view Kaike in low regard because it is felt to be unsophisticated and unexpressive, very low cultural self-esteem (Fisher 1987:130). Hunter-gatherers.

KAYORT [KYV] Koshi Zone, Morang District, Dakuwa Danga, near Rajbangsi language. Indo-European, Indo-Iranian, Indo-Aryan, Eastern zone, Bengali-Assamese. Separate language, related to Bengali.

KHALING *(KHALINGE RAI, KHAEL BRA, KHAEL BAAT)* [KLR] 15,000 to 20,000 (1975). Population total both countries 15,000 to 20,000. SoluKhumbu, Khotang, Bhujpur, Sankhuwasabha, Terathum, Pachtar, and Ilam districts. Also spoken in India. Sino-Tibetan, Tibeto-Burman, Himalayish, Mahakiranti, Kiranti, Western. Closest to Dumi and Koi. Bilingual level estimates for Nepali are 0 0%, 1 1%, 2 5%, 3 50%, 4 30%, 5 14%. All ages. Dictionary. SOV; postpositions; articles, adjectives, numerals, relatives before noun heads; question word initial; maximum number of prefixes 1; word order distinguishes subject, object, indirect object; affixes indicate case of noun phrase; verb affixes mark person and number of subject-obligatory; ergative; causatives; comparatives; C, V, CCV, tonal. Literacy rate in first language: Below 1%. Literacy rate in second language: 5% to 15%. Scrub forest: dwarf or stunted trees and shrubs. Mountain valley: long depression between mountains, usually with an outlet. Peasant agriculturalists: adapted marginally to market system. 1,300 to 2,300 meters. Traditional religion.

KHAM, GAMALE ***(GAMALE)*** [KGJ] 10,000 (1988). Gam Khola, western hills, Rukum and Rolpa districts, Rapti Zone. Sino-Tibetan, Tibeto-Burman, Himalayish, Mahakiranti, Kham-Magar-Chepang-Sunwari, Kham. Dialects: TAMALI, GHUSBANGGI. 71% lexical similarity with Takale Kham (closest), 55% with Nisi and Sheshi, 54% with Maikoti-Hukam, 45% with Bhujel. People have limited bilingualism in Nepali. Vigorous. Literacy rate in first language: 1% to 5%. Literacy rate in second language: 5% to 15%.

KHAM, MAIKOTI ***(MAIKOTI)*** [ZKM] 2,500 (1993). Western hills, Rukum and Rolpa districts, Rapti Zone. Sino-Tibetan, Tibeto-Burman, Himalayish, Mahakiranti, Kham-Magar-Chepang-Sunwari, Kham. Different from Takale and other Kham. Literacy rate in first language: Below 1%. Literacy rate in second language: Below 5%.

KHAM, NISI ***(NISI, NISEL, NISHEL KHAM, EASTERN PARBATE)*** [KIF] 3,000 (1988). Western hills, Rukum and Rolpa districts, Rapti Zone. Sino-Tibetan, Tibeto-Burman, Himalayish, Mahakiranti, Kham-Magar-Chepang-Sunwari, Kham. Dialect: BHUJEL KHAM. Partially intelligible with Western Parbate dialects. 79% lexical similarity with Bhujel Kham (closest), 71% with Takale, 69% with Maikoti-Hukam, 55% with Gamale, 44% with Sheshi. Limited Nepali is used as second language. Vigorous. Investigation needed: intelligibility with Bhujel Kham. Literacy rate in first language: Below 1%. Literacy rate in second language: Below 5%.

KHAM, SHESHI ***(SHESHI)*** [KIP] 7,500 (1988). Western hills, Rukum and Rolpa districts, Rapti Zone. Sino-Tibetan, Tibeto-Burman, Himalayish, Mahakiranti, Kham-Magar-Chepang-Sunwari, Kham. Dialects: TAPNANGGI, JANGKOTI. 55% lexical similarity with Gamale Kham (closest), 51% with Takale, 46% with Bhujel, 45% with Maikoti-Hukam, 44% with Nisi. Limited Nepali is used as second language. Vigorous. Literacy rate in first language: Below 1%. Literacy rate in second language: Below 5%.

KHAM, TAKALE ***(KHAM-MAGAR, TAKALE, WESTERN PARBATE)*** [KJL] 40,000 to 50,000 (1998). Rapti Zone, Rukum, Rolpa districts, west central Nepal. Taka-Shera is the center. Some in Dhaulagiri Zone, Baglung District. Sino-Tibetan, Tibeto-Burman, Himalayish, Mahakiranti, Kham-Magar-Chepang-Sunwari, Kham. Dialects: TAKALE, LUKUMEL, WALE, THABANGGI. Greatest similarities between Eastern and Western Parbate. The Parbate, Sheshi, and Gamale groups are all inherently unintelligible. Mahatale and Miruli are 2 dialects whose position within the Kham linguistic group has not been decided. 71% lexical similarity with Gamale Kham, Maikoti-Hukam, Nisi; 58% with Bhujel Kham, 51% with Sheshi. About 25% lexical similarity with Magar and Gurung, slightly below 25% with the Tibetan group, 15% with the Rai and Limbu groups. People use Nepali only when outside their homeland. Young males are most proficient, elderly women the least. People can discuss most common topics in Nepali. Kham used in all domains. All ages. Different from the Khams of eastern Tibet as spoken by the Khampa. People migrate in summer to the foot of glaciers on the western end of the Dhaulagiri massif, and in winter to the southern hills of Rolpa District. Trade language. SOV; postposition; genitives, adjectives, numerals, relatives before noun heads; maximum number for nouns: 1 prefix, 8 suffixes; for verbs: 5 prefixes, 7 suffixes; objects and indirect objects partially marked by word order; case marked on NPs by affixes; verb affixes mark person and number of subject and object-obligatory; split ergative; detransitivization common, some of which is passive-like; a kind of semantic inverse marked in verb morphology; causatives; applicatives; (C)V(V)(C) where the second V is a dipthong or long vowel; tonal. Literacy rate in first language: Some. Literacy rate in second language: Some. Extensive literacy effort needed. Devanagari. Northern type forests on north facing slopes, grassland on south facing slopes. Mountain slope in village areas, alpine in grazing areas. Semi-nomadic pastoralists: sheep, goats; subsistence agriculturalists, peasants. 1,800 to 2,500 meters. Traditional religion.

KOI ***(KOYU, KOHI, KOYI, KOI BO'O, KOYU BO')*** [KKT] 200 to 300 (1991 W. Winter). Sagarmatha Zone, south Khotang District, Sungdel Panchayat near the headwaters of the Rawakhola. Sino-Tibetan, Tibeto-Burman, Himalayish, Mahakiranti, Kiranti, Western. Dialects: SUNGDEL, BEHERE. Closest to Dumi and Khaling. Bilingualism in Nepali. Some people called 'Koi' who live scattered in other language areas speak only Nepali.

KULUNG ***(KHULUNGE RAI, KULU RING, KHULUNG, KHOLUNG)*** [KLE] 15,000 (1991 W. Winter) to 70,000. Population total both countries 15,000 to 70,000. Solu Khumbu District, Sagarmatha Zone, eastern hills, Hongu Valley, Mahakulung region, Sankhuwa Sabha, Terathum, Pachthar, Ilam. In Solu Khumbu they live primarily along the Hongu Khola in villages of Bumng (Bung), Pilmu, Cheskam Sadhi, Gudel, and Namlu. In Sankhuwa Sabha District in villages of Baliyamnang, Phedi Khola, Wasepla, Mangtewa, Yaphu, Chayeng, Walung, and Sheduwa. These areas are mainly in the drainages of the Sangkhuwa and Siswa rivers which flow into the Arun River. Also in some Terai areas. Also spoken in India. Sino-Tibetan, Tibeto-Burman, Himalayish, Mahakiranti, Kiranti, Eastern. Dialects: SOTANG (SOTARING, SOTTARING), MAHAKULUNG, TAMACHHANG, PIDISOI, CHHAPKOA, PELMUNG, NAMLUNG, KHAMBU. Intelligibility between Kulung and Sota Ring is 100% because only some words are pronounced differently. Related to Sangpang and Nachereng. Up to 50% of the population can understand some Nepali at a basic level. Only Kulung who live on the border with other language groups speak the other language. Attitudes among dialects from positive to hostile. Exogamous clan marriage. The high number of Kulung reflect the tendency of smaller groups to consider themselves Kulung, but they are by origin not Kulung. The Kulung possibly absorb smaller groups. Dictionary. Grammar. Case, ergative. Literacy rate in second language: 10% to 50% adults, 10% women. Extensive literacy effort needed. Motivation reported to be high. Devanagari. Scrub forest: dwarf or stunted trees and shrubs. Mountain valley. Agriculturalists: millet, maize; hunters; fishermen. 1,400 to 3,300 meters. Traditional religion, Hindu and Buddhist influences.

KUMAUNI ***(KUMAON)*** [KFY] Mahakali zone. Indo-European, Indo-Iranian, Indo-Aryan, Northern zone, Central Pahari. Bible portions 1825-1876. See main entry under India.

KUMHALI ***(KUMHALE, KUMBALE, KUMKALE)*** [KRA] 1,413 (1991 census). Nawalpur, Gorkha District, Gandaki Zone. Indo-European, Indo-Iranian, Indo-Aryan, Unclassified. Some are partially bilingual in Nepali. Lowlands, along rivers. Agriculturalists, pastoralists, fishermen. Hindu, traditional religion.

KURUX, NEPALI ***(DHANGAR, JHANGER, JANGHARD, JANGAD, URAON, ORAU, ORAON)*** [KXL] Eastern Terai, Janakpur Zone, Dhanusa District. Dravidian, Northern. Different from Kurux of India and Bangladesh. Bilingualism in whatever Indo-Aryan language is spoken in area, as Maithili, Nagpuri, Bhojpuri, Assamese, etc. The alternate names are used for the people. Bible portions 1977.

KUSUNDA ***(KUSANDA)*** [KGG] Tanahun District, Gandaki Zone, western hills, Satto Bhatti west of Chepetar and possibly jungle south of Ambhu. Kireni, near Kumhali. Sino-Tibetan, Tibeto-Burman, Himalayish, Mahakiranti, Kham-Magar-Chepang-Sunwari, Chepang. 3 speakers reported in 1970. Last speaker reported to have died in 1985. Their descendants do not speak the language. Verb pronominalization with subject agreement. Hunters. Extinct.

KYERUNG ***(KYIRONG, GYIRONG)*** [KGY] Rasuwa District, Bagmati Zone, Langtang region, Rasua Garbi, Birdim, Thangjet, Syabru, and Syabrubensi villages; and large concentrations in Kathmandu. Also spoken in China. Sino-Tibetan, Tibeto-Burman, Himalayish, Tibeto-Kanauri, Tibetic, Tibetan, Central. 68% lexical similarity with Dolpo, Olungchung Gola, Lhomi, and Lopa; 66% with Baragaunle; 65% with Kutang Bhotia and Tibetan (Lhasa); 63% with Helambu Sherpa; 60% with Jirel; 57% with Sherpa. Investigation needed: intelligibility with Tibetan.

LAMBICHHONG ***(LAMBICHONG, LAMBICCHONG, LAMBITSHONG)*** [LMH] 500 (1991 W. Winter). Eastern bank of the Arun River, in a strip between Mugakhola and Sinuwakhola; Muga and Pakhribas panchayats, Dhankuta District. Sino-Tibetan, Tibeto-Burman, Himalayish, Mahakiranti, Kiranti, Eastern. Ethnically related to the Bantawa. Bilingualism in Bantawa. Mainly older generation. Being replaced by Bantawa (D. Bradley 1996). Sometimes incorrectly called 'Mugali' or 'Yakkha'.

LEPCHA ***(RONG, RONGKE, LAPCHE, RONGPA, NÜNPA)*** [LEP] 1,272 in Nepal (1961 census). Ilam District, Mechi Zone. Sino-Tibetan, Tibeto-Burman, Himalayish, Tibeto-Kanauri, Lepcha. Dialects: ILAMMU, TAMSANGMU, RENGJONGMU. Many of the younger generation in Nepal speak Nepali as mother tongue, and do not speak Lepcha. Linguistic position within Tibeto-Burman still under discussion. Agriculturalists, pastoralists. Buddhist. NT 1989. See main entry under India.

LHOMI ***(LHOKET, SHING SAAPA, KATH BHOTE, KAR BHOTE)*** [LHM] 4,000 in Nepal. Population total all countries 6,000. Eastern hills, Sankhuwasawa District, Koshi Zone, near the Arun River, about 6 villages, and a few in Kathmandu. Also spoken in China, India. Sino-Tibetan, Tibeto-Burman, Himalayish, Tibeto-Kanauri, Tibetic, Tibetan, Central. The dialect may be different across the Tibet border. 69% lexical similarity with Baragaunle and Dolpo; 68% with Lopa; 66% with Olangchung Gola; 65% with Lhasa Tibetan and Kyerung; 64% with Kutang Bhotia; 60% with Helambu Sherpa; 58% with Sherpa; 57% with Jirel. Bilingualism in Nepali. SOV. Literacy rate in first language: Below 1%. Literacy rate in second language: 5% to 25% (men). Agriculturalists, pastoralists. Traditional religion, Lamaist. NT 1995.

LIMBU ***(YAKTHUNG PAN)*** [LIF] 238,088 in Nepal, 1.37% of the population (1991 census). There are 16,000 Chattare (1998). Population total all countries 266,000 or more. Limbuwan (preferred term for the Limbu area), Eastern hills, east of the Arun River; Koshi Zone, Dhankuta, Sankhuwasabha, Tehrathum, Dhankuta, and Morang districts; Mechi Zone, Taplejung, Panchthar, Ilam, and Jhapa districts. There may be migrant workers in Myanmar. Also spoken in Bhutan, India. Sino-Tibetan, Tibeto-Burman, Himalayish, Mahakiranti, Kiranti, Eastern. Dialects: TAPLEJUNGE (TAMORKHOLE, TAPLEJUNG), PANTHARE (PANTHAREY, PANCHTHARE, PANCHTHAR, PANTHARE-YANGGROKKE-CHAUBISE-CHARKHOLE), PHEDAPPE, CHATTARE (CHHATTARE, CHHATHAR, CHATTHARE, CHATTHARE YAKTHUNGBA PAN, YAKTHUNG PAN). Related to Lohorong and Yakha. Chaubise dialect is similar to Panthare, and Phedappe to Taplejunge. Chattare is poorly understood by speakers of the other dialects. Inherent intelligibility among the dialect speakers is 80% to 90%. Lexical similarity among the dialects is above 80%. 28% of adult speakers (24% of men and 3% of women) have completed 5 years of school, and have good general proficiency in Nepali. 62% of the Limbu have no more than basic proficiency.

There is a trend toward more use of Nepali, especially among young people, but it is not replacing Limbu in any domain. Limbu used in home, with other Limbu of all ages, in worship. All Ages. Vigorous. One of the main groups in eastern Nepal. Attitudes toward Limbu are positive. Panthare dialect is dominant in size, prestige, and language development. People prefer their own dialect, but are not negative toward others. Common Limbu is called 'Tajengpan'. The priestly high language, also known by some older people, is called 'Mundumban'. Dictionary. Grammar. SOV; postpositions; genitives, articles, adjectives, numerals before noun heads; content question word initial; bipolar question word final; maximum of 3 prefixes, 6 suffixes; affixes indicate case of noun phrases; verb affixes mark subjects, objects, indirect objects-obligatory; split ergativity; reflexes conjugated intrasitively can be used as a kind of passive; antipassives; causatives; comparatives; V, CV, CVC, CCV, CCVC; nontonal. Literacy rate in first language: 1% in Sirijangga script, 40% in Devanagari. Literacy rate in second language: 46.8% among the Limbu ethnic group (1991 census). Extensive literacy effort needed. Motivation high among all. It would be easier to read Limbu in Devanagari, but attitudes strongly positive toward Sirijannga script being taught. Have own script, 'Sirijangga' or 'Kirati', dating to early 18th century. Not fully standardized. Poetry, newspapers, magazines, radio programs, TV. Gallery forest. Mountain slope. Peasant agriculturalists. 2,500 to 5,000 feet. Kiranti traditional religion.

LINGKHIM ***(LIMKHIM, LINKHIM, LINGKHIM RAI)*** [LII] 1 (1991 W. Winter). Ilam District, Sumbek Panchayat Yokpi. Original homeland was apparently near the lower Dudhkosi River. Sino-Tibetan, Tibeto-Burman, Himalayish, Mahakiranti, Kiranti, Western. Bilingualism in Bantawa. Little information available. Nearly extinct.

LOPA ***(LOYU, LOBA, MUSTANG, LO MONTANG)*** [LOY] 26,000 (1998). Dhawalagiri Zone, Dolpa, Mustang districts, north central. Sino-Tibetan, Tibeto-Burman, Himalayish, Tibeto-Kanauri, Tibetic, Tibetan, Central. Dialects: LO, SEKE. Lo dialect has 78% lexical similarity with Baragaunle and Dolpo; 68% with Olungchung Gola, Kyerung, and Lhomi; 65% with Lhasa Tibetan and Kutang Bhotia; 63% with Helambu Sherpa; 62% with Jirel and Sherpa. The inhabitants of Lo are called 'Lopa'. Their capital is Manthang, called Mustang by outsiders. Manthang has 200 houses, many gombas, and a Nepali medium school up to grade ten. Distinct from Lhoba in China and India, a Mirish language. Investigation needed: intelligibility with Baragaunle. Salt traders, agriculturalists, pastoralists. Buddhist.

LORUNG, NORTHERN ***(LOHORONG, LOHRUNG, LOHRUNG KHANAWA)*** [LBR] 7,000 to 10,000 (1991 W. Winter). Between the middle Arun Valley and the Sabhakhola, middle Sankhuwasawa District, Koshi Zone. Sino-Tibetan, Tibeto-Burman, Himalayish, Mahakiranti, Kiranti, Eastern. Dialect: BIKSIT (BIKSHI). A Rai group. Related to Yamphu, Yamphe, Southern Lorung, and Yakkha, but a separate language. Ethnic subgroups are Kipa and Loke Lorung, but they do not appear to speak different dialects. Agriculturalists, pastoralists. Hindu, traditional religion.

LORUNG, SOUTHERN ***(LOHORONG, LOHRUNG, LOHRUNG KHAP, LOHRUNG KHATE, YAKKHABA LORUNG)*** [LRR] 3,000 to 5,000 (1991 W. Winter). Dhankuta District, in a small strip south of the Tamorkhola, between the Jaruwakhola in the east and the Raghuwkhola in the west, Bodhe, Maunabuduke, and Rajarani panchayats. Sino-Tibetan, Tibeto-Burman, Himalayish, Mahakiranti, Kiranti, Eastern. Dialect: GESS. A Rai group. Related to Yamphu, Yamphe, Northern Lorung, and Yakkha, but a separate language. Sometimes incorrectly called 'Yakkha'. Agriculturalists, pastoralists. Hindu, traditional religion.

LUMBA-YAKKHA ***(YAKKHABA CEA)*** [LUU] 1,000 (1991 W. Winter). North Dhankuta District, Arkhaule Jitpur and Marek Katahare panchayats, around Lakhshmikhola. Sino-Tibetan, Tibeto-Burman, Himalayish, Mahakiranti, Kiranti, Eastern. Related to Yakkha, Chhulung, Chhintang, and Lambichhong, but a separate language.

MAGAR, EASTERN ***(MAGARI, MANGGAR)*** [MGP] 288,383 in Nepal (1994). Population total all countries 290,000. Central mountains, east of Bagmati River, Tanahu District, Gandaki Zone. A few main centers are Okhaldhunga, Taplejung, Bhojpur, Dhankuta, Chainpur, Terhathum, Ollam, and Letang. Also spoken in Bhutan, India. Sino-Tibetan, Tibeto-Burman, Himalayish, Mahakiranti, Kham-Magar-Chepang-Sunwari, Magar. Bilingual level estimates for Nepali are 0-2 >70%, 2+-5 <30%. Nepali bilingualism in the Nawalparasi Hills is quite low; among the 70% to 80% who are uneducated, there is only a basic proficiency. Magar is the language of daily life. One of the main groups in the central mountains. Literacy rate in first language: 1% to 5%. Literacy rate in second language: 25% to 50%. Mountain slope. Agriculturalists: rice, corn, wheat; hunters; pastoralists; army. Hindu, traditional religion. NT 1991.

MAGAR, WESTERN ***(MAGAR, MAGARI, MANGGAR, MAGAR NUWAKOT)*** [MRD] 210,000 (1994). West of Pokhara, Tansen highway, Surkhet, Banke, and Dialekh districts, Bheri Zone; Pokhara and Syangja districts, Morang and Dhankuta districts, Koshi Zone, Nawalparasi District, Lumbini Zone. The center is Surkhet District. Sino-Tibetan, Tibeto-Burman, Himalayish, Mahakiranti,

Kham-Magar-Chepang-Sunwari, Magar. Partially bilingual in Nepali. Literacy rate in first language: Below 1%. Literacy rate in second language: 5% to 15%. Agriculturalists, pastoralists. Hindu.

MAITHILI *(APBHRAMSA, BIHARI, MAITLI, MAITILI, METHLI, TIRAHUTIA, TIRHUTI, TIRHUTIA)* [MKP] 2,191,900 (1998 census), 11.85% of the population (1998). Rautahat District, Narayani Zone; Sarlahi, Mahottari, Dhanusa districts, Janakpur Zone; Sirha , Saptari districts, Sagarmatha Zone; Sunsari District, Koshi Zone. Indo-European, Indo-Iranian, Indo-Aryan, Eastern zone, Bihari. Dialects: BANTAR, BAREI, BARMELI, KAWAR, KISAN, KYABRAT, MAKRANA, MUSAR, SADRI, TATI, DEHATI. More caste variation than geographical. Intelligibility good among all, including in India. Second languages used by men or working women mostly only for business, social interaction outside the home. In cities some may use Hindi, Nepali, or English even at home and with other Maithili. Bhojpuri or Bengali are used with friends from those groups. Bilingual ability varies greatly, from being limited to using them for trade, to being highly fluent. Maithili used in home, village, towns, cities with other Maithili. All ages. Spoken by a wide variety of castes, both 'high' and 'low'. There is a Maithili Academy in Patna. Bihar Maithili is taught at several universities including L. N. Mithila University in Karbhanga, Patna University and Janakpur Campus of Tribhuvan University. Brahmin speech considered to be standard. Brahmins consider themselves superior, varying from friendly to domineering. Others vary toward Brahmins from friendly to resentment. Hindi and its speakers considered close, culturally similar; Nepali accepted. Dictionary. Grammar. SOV; postpositions; genitives, articles, numerals before noun heads; adjectives before and after noun heads; maximum number of prefixes or suffixes 1; animate objects marked by postposition; person, gender distinguished in subject-obligatory; causatives; comparatives; V, VC, VCC, CV, CVC, CVV, CCV, CVCC, CCVCC; nontonal. Literacy rate in first language: 20%. Literacy rate in second language: 25% to 50%. The educated read a lot of Hindi, Nepali, or English. If they can read Hindi or Nepali, they can read Maithili. Several high schools. Poetry, newspapers, radio programs, films, TV. Tropical forest, gallery forest. Plains. Peasant agriculturalists. Hindu, Muslim. See main entry under India.

MAJHI *(MANJHI)* [MJZ] 11,322 in Nepal, 0.06% of the population (1991 census). Population total both countries 11,322 or more. Janakpur Zone, Sindhuli and Ramechhap districts; Narayani Zone; Lumbini Zone. Also spoken in India. Indo-European, Indo-Iranian, Indo-Aryan, Eastern zone, Bihari. Distinct from Majhi in Panjabi group or Bote-Majhi. 'Majhi', 'Bote', and 'Kushar' all are used by hill peoples.

MANANGBA *(MANANG, MANANGI, NYESHANG, NYISHANG, NORTHERN GURUNG, MANANGBOLT, MANANGBHOT)* [NMM] 3,736 (1988 Pohle). Gandaki Zone, Manang District, Nyeshang area, 7 villages, Marsyangdi River. Sino-Tibetan, Tibeto-Burman, Himalayish, Tibeto-Kanauri, Tibetic, Tamangic. Dialect: PRAKAA. Manangba may be distinct from Northern Gurung, which is spoken in Manang District. Very different from Eastern Gurung. Language has Tibetan influence. Mountain slope. Traders. 3,200 to 3,700 meters. Buddhist.

MARWARI *(MARWADI)* [MKD] 16,514 in Nepal, 0.09% of the population (1991 census). Mechi Zone, Jhapa District; Koshi Zone, Morang and Sunsari districts; Narayani Zone, Parsa District, some in Kathmandu. Indo-European, Indo-Iranian, Indo-Aryan, Central zone, Rajasthani, Marwari. The standard form of Rajasthani. Literacy rate in second language: 88%. Devanagari script. Hindu. NT 1820-1821, out of print. See main entry under India.

MEOHANG, EASTERN *(NEWANG, NEWAHANG, NEWANGE RAI, NEWAHANG JIMI, MEWAHANG)* [EMG] Sankhuwasawa District, Koshi Zone, upper Arun Valley east of the river, eastern Nepal. One dialect is in Sunsari District, Bhaludhunga, Bishnupaduka Panchayat; Dibum (Dibung) in Mangtewa Panchayat, Mulgaon-Wangtang in Yaphu Panchayat. Sino-Tibetan, Tibeto-Burman, Himalayish, Mahakiranti, Kiranti, Eastern. Dialects: SUNSARI, DIBUM, MULGAON-WANGTANG. Bilingualism in Nepali. Structurally different from Western Meohang. May be extinct or nearly extinct linguistically, being replaced by Nepali. Agriculturalists, pastoralists.

MEOHANG, WESTERN *(NEWANG, NEWAHANG, NEWANGE RAI, NEWAHANG JIMI, MEWAHANG)* [RAF] 2,000 to 5,000 (1991 W. Winter). Sankhuwasawa District, Koshi Zone, upper Arun Valley west of the river, eastern Nepal. Bala is in Bala village, Sankhuwasawa Panchayat; Bumdemba in Sishuwakhola Panchayat. 2 villages. Sino-Tibetan, Tibeto-Burman, Himalayish, Mahakiranti, Kiranti, Eastern. Dialects: BALA (BALALI), BUMDEMBA. Structurally different from Eastern Meohang. Many speakers use Kulung as a second language. Agriculturalists, pastoralists.

MUGU *(MUGALI)* [MUK] 3,557 (1998). Karnali Zone, Mugu, Humla, Jumla, Dolpa, Surket, Baihang, Bajura districts. Sino-Tibetan, Tibeto-Burman, Himalayish, Tibeto-Kanauri, Tibetic, Tibetan, Central. Dialect: MUGALI KHAM. 90% intelligibility with Mugali Kham. Close to Humla Bhotia. Not closely related to Takale, Nisi, Maikoti, Sheshi, or Gamale Kham. Nepali used for outside contacts such as trading, communicating with officials, and in school. Basic or limited Nepali ability for uneducated people, routine or good ability for the educated. Tibetan rarely used, though sometimes by Lamas in religious ceremonies. Mugu at home and with other Mugu. Literacy rate in second language: Up to

21.65% Nepali. Men have higher literacy than women and children. Devanagari. Mountain slope. Agriculturalists, pastoralists, traders. 1,500 to 3,000 meters. Buddhist.

MUNDARI ***(MUNDA, MANDARI, MONDARI, MUNARI, HORO)*** [MUW] 5,700 in Nepal (1993 Johnstone). Austro-Asiatic, Munda, North Munda, Kherwari, Mundari. Dialects: HASADA, LATAR, NAGURI, KERA. Bible 1910-1932. See main entry under India.

MUSASA ***(MUSAHAR)*** [SMM] Sindhuli Garhi District, Morang District, Koshi Zone, Dolakha District, Janakpur Zone. Indo-European, Indo-Iranian, Indo-Aryan, Eastern zone, Bihari.

NAAPA ***(NAWA SHERPA, NABA, NAAPAA)*** [NAO] 500 (1985). Sankhuwasawa District, Koshi Zone. Their own villages are interspersed among the Lhomi. Sino-Tibetan, Tibeto-Burman, Himalayish, Tibeto-Kanauri, Tibetic, Tibetan, Unclassified. Some bilingualism between Naapa and Lhomi; little intermarriage. The Lhomi consider the Naaket people a distinct group.

NACHERING ***(NACERING RA, NACHEṚING TÛM, MATHSERENG, NACCHHERING, NASRING, BANGDALE, BANGDEL TÛM, BANGDILE)*** [NCD] 2,000 (1991 W. Winter). Upper northeastern Khotang District near the Rawakhola Valley, on the slopes around the Lidim Khola River from the headwaters and its tributaries down to Aiselukharke to the south. Sino-Tibetan, Tibeto-Burman, Himalayish, Mahakiranti, Kiranti, Eastern. Dialects: DIMALI, PARALI, HEDANGPA (SANGPANG), BANGDALE (HACHERO, ACHERO, HANGKULA), KHARLALI, RAKHELI. Related to Kulung and Sangpang. The Hedangpa dialect is nearly extinct. It is not the same as the Sangpang language, although it is sometimes called 'Sangpang'.

NAR PHU ***(NAR-PHU)*** [NPA] 533 (1988 Pohle). Gandaki Zone, Manang District, Nar Valley north of Manang Valley, Nar (Nargaon) and Phu (Phugaon) villages. Sino-Tibetan, Tibeto-Burman, Himalayish, Tibeto-Kanauri, Tibetic, Tamangic. Dialects: NAR (NAR-MÄ, LOWER NAR), PHU (NAR-TÖ, UPPER NAR). Many men are fluent in Tibetan. Many men are literate in Classical Tibetan. 4,000 to 4,200 meters.

NEPALESE SIGN LANGUAGE [NSP] Deaf sign language. Developed from local signs and introduced signs. Related to Indian and Pakistan Sign Languages. Used by USA Peace Corps.

NEPALI ***(NEPALESE, GORKHALI, GURKHALI, KHASKURA, PARBATIYA, EASTERN PAHARI)*** [NEP] 9,900,000 in Nepal (1993 Johnstone), 58.3% of the population (1985). Population total all countries 16,056,000. Eastern region and adjacent south central region. Also spoken in Bhutan, Brunei, India. Indo-European, Indo-Iranian, Indo-Aryan, Northern zone, Eastern Pahari. Dialects: BAITADI, BAJHANGI, BAJURALI (BAJURA), DOTELI, SORADI, ACCHAMI, JUMLELI (JUMLA, SINGJA, SIJALI), DARJULA. Dialects listed may be quite distinct from Standard Nepali. 4 castes: Brahmin (highest or priestly), Chetri (warrior), Vaishya (trader and farmer), Shudra (untouchable or lowest). People are called 'Paharia'. National language. Hindu, Buddhist, Muslim. Bible 1914-1978.

NEWARI ***(NEPAL BHASA, NEWAR)*** [NEW] 690,000 in Nepal, 3.73% of the population (1991 census). Population total both countries 690,000 or more. Kathmandu Valley and in all towns and bigger villages thoughout Nepal. Fewer in the far west. Also spoken in India. Sino-Tibetan, Tibeto-Burman, Himalayish, Mahakiranti, Newari. Dialects: DOLKHALI (DOLAKHA), SINDHUPALCHOK PAHRI (PAHRI, PAHARI), TOTALI, CITLANG, KATHMANDU-PATHAN-KIRTIPUR, BAKTAPUR, BAGLUNG. Dolkhali of Dolakha and Pahri of Sindhupalchok may be separate languages (Genetti 1994:2-3). Dolakha, Totali, and Pahari are conservative linguistically. Kirtipur is close to Kathmandu. Baktapur people can mostly understand Kathmandu. There are some vocabulary differences between Hindus and Buddhists. Many women are monolingual. All ages. Language loss is greater among Hindus than among Buddhists. Dolakha and Totali people are reserved toward outsiders. Kathmandu is the prestige dialect; most published materials are in this dialect. Many attitudes are linked with political groupings. English is highly valued; there are mixed feelings about Hindi; Tibetan doesn't have high prestige. People learn whichever language will help them economically: Nepali, English, Hindi, and others. Dictionary. Grammar. SOV; postpositions; genitives, adjectives, demonstratives before noun heads; relatives before and without noun heads; in polar questions there is a particle sentence finally; maximum number of prefixes 2; maximum number of suffixes 4; affixes or clitics indicate case of noun phrases; ergative; causatives; comparatives; CVC; nontonal. Literacy rate in first language: 60.4% (1991 census). Literacy rate in second language: 60.4% (1991 census). There are enough Newari teachers. Devanagari script. Newari has a complex history of scripts. Newspapers, magazines, radio programs, films. Urban. Mountain valley. Jyapu intensive agriculturalists (farming caste); full range of occupations. 300 to 2,000 meters. Buddhist (Patan mainly), Hindu (Bhaktapur mainly). NT 1986.

NUBRI ***(KUTANG BHOTIA, LARKYE)*** [KTE] 3,200 (1992). Gandaki Zone, North Gorkha District, along the upper reaches of the Buri Gandaki River, west of and including Prok village, between Himal Chuli and Manaslu Himal on the west and Ganesh Himal on the east. The local people view Sama as regional center. Sino-Tibetan, Tibeto-Burman, Himalayish, Tibeto-Kanauri, Tibetic, Tibetan, Central. Dialects: SAMA, LHO, NAMRUNG, PROK. Only moderately intelligible with Kyirong Tibetan (74%) and Tsum (32%). 78% to 93% lexical similarity among dialects. Prok is more distinct. 71% to 78% with Tsum, 66% to 74% with Kyirong Tibetan; 67% with Dolpo; 65% with Lopa, 59% to 64% with

Lhasa Tibetan; 64% with Olangchung Gola and Lhomi; 63% with Baragaunle; 61% with Helambu Sherpa; 57% with Jirel; 55% with Sherpa, 21% to 27% with Northern Ghale, 20% to 23% with Southern Ghale, 14% to 31% with Kutang Ghale, 14% with Eastern Gorkha Tamang, Western Gurung, and Banspur Tamang. Speakers have minimal bilingual proficiency in Nepali and Tibetan. Nubri is used in nearly every domain, even to Tsum speakers, but otherwise Nepali is used to outsiders. Vigorous. Positive attitudes toward Nubri. Tibetan viewed favorably in the religious domain, Nepali for education and potential advancement. Women from Prok marry men from Nubri area primarily and some from Kutang area. People trade with Gorkha District and Tibet. Most villages have primary schools. "Bhotia" or "Bhote" refers to people of Tibetan origin; in at least some contexts it is derogatory. Investigation needed: intelligibility with dialects, Tsum. Literacy rate in second language: Below 10%. Gallery forest. Mountain slope, valley. Swidden and peasant agriculturalists. 2,000 to 4,000 meters. Lamaist Buddhist.

PALPA ***(PAHARI-PALPA)*** [PLP] 3,002 (1961 census). Western, town of Palpa. Indo-European, Indo-Iranian, Indo-Aryan, Northern zone, Eastern Pahari. This language stands midway between Nepali (Eastern Pahari) and Kumauni (Central Pahari). Sometimes considered a Kumauni or Nepali dialect. There is also a dialect of Newari called Pahari. The term literally means 'of the hills'. NT 1827, out of print.

PANCHGAUNLE [PNL] Mustang District, Dhawalagiri Zone. Sino-Tibetan, Tibeto-Burman, Himalayish, Tibeto-Kanauri, Tibetic, Tamangic. May be a dialect of Thakali.

PHANGDUWALI ***(PHANGDUWALI POTI, PHANGDUVALI)*** [PHW] Phangduwa village, Pakhribas Panchayat, Chankuta District, directly above the headwaters of the Mugakhola (W. Winter 1991:79). Sino-Tibetan, Tibeto-Burman, Himalayish, Mahakiranti, Kiranti, Eastern. Linguistically between Yakkha and Belhariya. It may be nearly extinct.

PONGYONG ***(PONYON KULUNG, SAMAKULUNG, KULUNG PUN)*** [PGY] Ilam District, Kannyam Panchayat, Ambikau. Sino-Tibetan, Tibeto-Burman, Himalayish, Mahakiranti, Kiranti, Eastern. Closest to Kulung and Sangpang. Nearly extinct.

PUMA ***(PUMA PIMA, PUMA LA, PUMA KALA)*** [PUM] 3,000 (1991 W. Winter). Northwestern slopes of the Rapcha Range from the highest peaks to the Shwahkola Valley, directly south of the Khotang Bajar. Sino-Tibetan, Tibeto-Burman, Himalayish, Mahakiranti, Kiranti, Eastern. Still spoken by most young people.

RAJBANGSI ***(RAJBANSI, TAJPURI, KOCH, KOCHE)*** [RJB] 85,558 in Nepal, 0.46% of the population (1991 census. Mechi Zone, Jhapa District; Koshi Zone, Morang District. Indo-European, Indo-Iranian, Indo-Aryan, Eastern zone, Bengali-Assamese. Dialect: KURTHA. 30% of the population use Nepali as second language, 30% Hindi, 60% Khavas Tharu. Literacy rate in second language: 37.7% (1991 census). Agriculturalists, pastoralists. Hindu, Muslim. See main entry under India.

RAJI ***(RAJIBAR)*** [RJI] 3,000 or more (1998). Bheri Zone, Surkhet and Bardia districts, Seti Zone, Kailaki District. Sino-Tibetan, Tibeto-Burman, Himalayish, Mahakiranti, Kham-Magar-Chepang-Sunwari, Magar. Closely related to Rawat and Raute. Devidatta Sharma (1990) concludes that Raji in India is a Munda language with borrowing from Tibeto-Burman and Indo-Aryan. Bilingualism in Nepali. Raji used at home, with Raji speakers, Nepali with outsiders. Moderately vigorous. Has been a nomadic group, but has now settled. Grammar. Literacy rate in second language: 21.5% (1991 census). Riverine. Swidden agriculturalists. Traditional religion, Hindu.

RANGKAS ***(RANGKHAS)*** [RGK] Population total both countries 600 (1977 Voegelin and Voegelin). Mahakali Zone, far western. Also spoken in India. Sino-Tibetan, Tibeto-Burman, Himalayish, Tibeto-Kanauri, Western Himalayish, Almora. Related to Darmiya, Chaudangsi, Byangsi. It may only be in India. Not the same as the Johar (Rangkhas) who live west of the Darmiya, but their Tibeto-Burman language has recently been completely replaced by the local Indic language.

RAUTE ***(RAUTYE, HARKA GURUNG, KHAMCHI)*** [RAU] 475, including 130 nomadic Raute (1997 Singh). Mainly in western Nepal, Seti, Rapti, Bheri, Karnali, and Dhaulagiri zones; Surkhet, Pyuthan, Jajakot, Achham, Doti, Jumla, Dolpa, Banke districts. Sino-Tibetan, Tibeto-Burman, Himalayish, Mahakiranti, Kiranti, Western. A separate language. More people use Nepali as second language among the settled Raute. Among the nomadic Raute, only the leaders have contact with outsiders. All ages. The nomadic Raute are secretive about their language; the settled Raute are not. Some youth in Nepal speak Nepali or Hindi among themselves in front of outsiders. The Raute are viewed as low caste by others. Migratory cycle is reported to be about 2 years. They may have been joined to the Rawat and Raji, but those groups are now settled. Singh 1997 reports they communicate with the Rawat in the 'Khamchi' language. Literacy rate in second language: 25.5% (1991 census). Hunter-gatherers. 125 to 3,000 meters. Traditional religion.

RAWAT ***(JANGGALI, JANGALI, JHANGAR, DZANGGALI)*** [JNL] 15,175 in Nepal, 0.98% of the population (1991 census). Population total both countries 17,175 to 18,175 or more. Mainly in 2 or 3 resettlement villages in the Nepal lowlands, and some in Mahakali Zone, Darchula, Baitadi, and

Dandeldhura districts. Also spoken in India. Sino-Tibetan, Tibeto-Burman, Himalayish, Tibeto-Kanauri, Western Himalayish, Janggali. Very close to Raute and Raji. Bilingualism in Nepali. Called 'Rawat' in India. OV (S varies); postpositions; genitives, articles, adjectives, numerals before noun heads; maximum number of suffixes 3; affixes indicate case of noun phrases; verb affixes mark person, number-obligatory; passives; causatives; comparatives; CV, CVC; nontonal. Mountain slope. Swidden agriculturalists. 300 to 1,500 meters. Traditional religion, Hindu.

SAAM ***(SAAM RAI, SAMAKHA, SAAMA KHA)*** [RAQ] Southern Ilam District. Sino-Tibetan, Tibeto-Burman, Himalayish, Mahakiranti, Kiranti, Eastern. Dialects: BUNGLA, SAMBYA. Bilingualism in Nepali, Bantawa. A few elderly speakers. Appears to be in process of replacement by Nepali or Bantawa. Other groups called 'Saam' may be Kulung, Limkhim, or Pongyong speakers. Nearly extinct.

SANGPANG ***(SAMPANG, SAMPANGE RAI, SANGPANG KHA, SANGPANG GUN, SANGPANG GÎN)*** [RAV] 5,000 to 7,000 (1991 W. Winter). From Dingla, Bhojpur District in the northeast to Kharpa in the southwest. The upper ridges south and east of the Rawakhola Valley and adjoining ridges in the northeast where the headwaters of the main tributaries of the lower and middle Arun River. Sino-Tibetan, Tibeto-Burman, Himalayish, Mahakiranti, Kiranti, Eastern. Dialects: TANA, HALUMBUNG (WAKCHALI), SAMARUNG, BHALU, TONGECCHA, PHALI, KHARTAMCHE, KHOTANG.

SANTALI ***(SATAR, SANTHALI, SONTHAL, SANDAL, SANGTAL, SANTAL, SENTALI, SAINTI, HOR, HAR)*** [SNT] 33,332 in Nepal (1991 census). Koshi Zone, Morang District; Mechi Zone, Jhapa District. Austro-Asiatic, Munda, North Munda, Kherwari, Santali. Some bilingualism in Maithili and Nepali. Dictionary. Grammar. Literacy rate in first language: Few. Literacy rate in second language: Few. Hunter-gatherers, agriculturalists. Hindu. Bible 1914-1992. See main entry under India.

SHERPA ***(SHARPA, SHARPA BHOTIA, XIAERBA, SERWA)*** [SCR] 30,000 in Nepal (1998). Population total all countries 49,895. Solu Khumbu District, northern mountains. Khumbu extends north from Namche Bazaar. Solu is the southern region including the villages of Gumdi, Sete, Junbesi, Phaplu, and Sallery. Around Rolwaling, northern border of Janakpur District, and Taplejung, Mechi District. There may be some around Lukla. Also spoken in Bhutan, China, India, Korea, South, USA. Sino-Tibetan, Tibeto-Burman, Himalayish, Tibeto-Kanauri, Tibetic, Tibetan, Southern. Dialects: SOLU, KHUMBU, RAMECHAAP. Solu and Khumbu dialects have 90% lexical similarity. 67% lexical similarity with Jirel; 63% with Helambu Sherpa; 62% with Lopa and Dolpo; 58% with Lhomi, Baragaunle, and Lhasa Tibetan; 57% with Kyerung; 55% with Kutang Bhotia and Walungge. Preschool age and over 40 years most are monolingual. Some use Nepali, Tibetan, English, as second language. Lamas are fluent in Tibetan. Guides learn trekkers languages: German, Korean, French, etc. All ages. They are proud of their language, but ashamed that it isn't developed more. In schools children are teased if they use Sherpa. In Kathmandu parents use Nepali with school age children. Grammar. SOV. Literacy rate in first language: Below 1%. Literacy rate in second language: 5% to 15%. In Kathmandu people are about 20% more literate than in Sherpa country. Devanagari, Tibetan. Radio programs. Lamaist, Tibetan Buddhist.

SONHA ***(SONAHAA)*** [SOI] 10,000 (1985). Along Karnali River in western Nepal, Kailali District, Seti Zone; Bheri River, Bheri Zone, Mahakali River, Mahakali Zone. Indo-European, Indo-Iranian, Indo-Aryan, Central zone, Unclassified. Close to Dangura Tharu; 80% intelligibility. Gold panners, agriculturalists.

SUNWAR ***(SUNUWAR, SUNBAR, SUNWARI, MUKHIYA, KWOICO LO)*** [SUZ] 30,000 to 40,000 (1998). Eastern hills, Ramechhap District, Janakpur Zone, and northwestern Okhaldhunga District. Sino-Tibetan, Tibeto-Burman, Himalayish, Mahakiranti, Kham-Magar-Chepang-Sunwari, Sunwari. Dialect: SUREL. Related to Bahing, and more distantly to Thulung, Chourase, and Jerung. Hayu is closest to Sunwar. Younger people speak more Nepali for trade. If people are addressed in Nepali they answer in Nepali, and use it for official purposes and with speakers from other languages. Proficiency not good enough to discuss abstract and complex concepts. Dictionary. SOV; portpositions; genitives after noun heads; relatives before noun heads; question word initial; maximum number of prefixes 1; suffixes 3; verb affixes mark person, number; causatives; comparatives; CV, CVC CVV, CCV, CCVC, V, VC; tonal. Literacy rate in first language: Young people 90%. Literacy rate in second language: Males 15% in villages, 20% in Kathmandu. Literacy effort needed for women. Poetry. Subtropical grassland, valley. Rocky hills with steep sloping sides, mountain slopes. Sedentary pastoralists, sedentary hunter-gatherers, peasant agriculturalists. 1,500 meters. Traditional religion, Hindu.

TAMANG, EASTERN [TAJ] 584,097 to 718,048 in Nepal, 3.26% of the population (1991 census). 904,456 all Tamang languages (1991 census). Another estimate is 2,500,000 to 3,000,000 all Tamang speakers (1994 Tamang Society representative). 23,645 second language speakers of all Tamang (1991 census). Tamang is the largest Tibeto-Burman language in Nepal. Population total all countries 584,097 to 718,048 or more. Kathmandu and to the northeast, east, and south. Outer-Eastern Tamang is in eastern Sindhu Palchowk, Ramechhap, Dolakha districts, and in most districts in eastern Nepal and parts of northeastern India. Central-Eastern Tamang is in most of Kabhre District, western Sindhu Palchowk,

Lalitput, Bhaktapur, Kathmandu, eastern Nuwakot districts, and districts south of those. Southwestern Tamang is in western Makwanpur and Chitwan districts, and districts south and southwest of those. Also spoken in Bhutan, India, Myanmar. Sino-Tibetan, Tibeto-Burman, Himalayish, Tibeto-Kanauri, Tibetic, Tamangic. Dialects: OUTER\EASTERN TAMANG, CENTRAL-EASTERN TAMANG, SOUTHWESTERN TAMANG. Central-Eastern Tamang is the most widely understood variety among all those tested to date: 85% by both Trisuli and Rasuwa Western Tamang, 93% to 98% by Outer-Eastern, 87% by Southwestern Tamang. Understanding of Outer-Eastern Tamang was 58% by Western Rasuwa Tamang, 64% to 75% by Western Trisuli Tamang, 67% to 54% by Southwestern Tamang, 88% to 93% by Central-Eastern Tamang, and 90% to 98% among its own varieties. Southwestern Tamang may be a bridge between Eastern and Western Tamang. Outer-Eastern Tamang varieties have 88% to 99% lexical similarity with each other; Central-Eastern varieties have 89% to 100% with each other. Outer-Eastern varieties have 79% to 93% with Central-Eastern varieties, and 77% to 82% with Southwestern Tamang. Southwestern has 86% to 93% with Central-Eastern. All Eastern varieties have 74% to 80% with Western Trisuli Tamang, 69% to 82% with Western Rasuwa Tamang, 72% to 80% with Northwestern Dhading Tamang, 63% to 77% with Eastern Gorkha Tamang. Those who have been to school or travelled often speak routine to good Nepali, others have limited proficiency, especially women, elderly, children. Home, indigenous religious use, social gatherings, market with other speakers, officials who understand, literature. All ages. Vigorous. There is a Tamang Language and Literature Council, and a Nepal Tamang Student Group. Attitudes correlate with understanding, but none are negative toward other Tamang varieties. Investigation needed: intelligibility with Southwestern Tamang. Dictionary. Grammar. SOV; postpositions, genitives after nouns; question word medial; ergative; CV, CVC, CCV, V, CCVC; tonal. Literacy rate in first language: 1% to 5%. Literacy rate in second language: 25% to 50%. Some literacy materials and classes conducted. Devanagari, Tibetan, some presently developing unique script. Poetry, magazines, radio programs, films, videos. Gallery forest. Mountain slope, valley. Swidden and peasant agriculturalists. Traditional religion, Buddhist, Hindu.

TAMANG, EASTERN GORKHA [TGE] 3,000 to 4,000 (1992). North Gorkha District, Gandaki Zone, south and east of Jagat. Sino-Tibetan, Tibeto-Burman, Himalayish, Tibeto-Kanauri, Tibetic, Tamangic. Dialects: KASIGAON, KEROUNJA. Dialects have 89% lexical similarity with each other, 76% to 77% with Northwestern (Dhading) Tamang, 77% to 79% with Western (Trisuli) Tamang, 72% to 73% with Western (Rasuwa) Tamang, 70% to 73% with Southwestern Tamang, 63% to 73% with Eastern Tamang dialects, 50% with Banspur Gurung, 31% to 37% with Northern and Southern Ghale, 18% to 23% with Kutang Ghale, 14% to 16% with Nubri, Tsum, and Kyerung, 12% to 14% with Tibetan. Speakers refer to themselves as 'Gurung', but recognize that their language is different. A few primary schools. The nearest middle and secondary schools are in Arughat. Investigation needed: intelligibility, attitudes. Literacy rate in second language: Below 10%. Gallery forest. Mountain slope, valley. Swidden and peasant agriculturalists. 600 to 1,800 meters. Traditional religion, Buddhist, Hindu.

TAMANG, NORTHWESTERN [TMK] 55,000 or more, 0.30% of population (based on 1991 census). Bagmati Zone, Nuwakot District, central mountainous strip. Migrations to the Terai. Sino-Tibetan, Tibeto-Burman, Himalayish, Tibeto-Kanauri, Tibetic, Tamangic. Dialect: DHADING. 94% lexical similarity with Western Trisuli Tamang, 82% to 83% with Western Rasuwa Tamang, 76% to 78% with Southwestern Tamang, 76% to 77% with Eastern Gorkha Tamang, 72% to 80% with Eastern Tamang. Investigation needed: intelligibility, attitudes. SOV, postpositions, genitives after nouns, relatives before nouns, question word medial, CV, CVC, CCV, V, CCVC, CVCCC, tonal. Literacy rate in first language: 1% to 10%. Literacy rate in second language: 25% to 75%. Gallery forest. Mountain slope, valley. Swidden and peasant agriculturalists. Traditional religion, Buddhist, Hindu.

TAMANG, SOUTHWESTERN [TSF] 109,051 or 0.59% of the population (1991 census). Western Makwanpur and Chitwan districts, and south and southwest of those districts. It may extend to the western and northwestern parts of Kathmandu District. Migrations to Terai. Sino-Tibetan, Tibeto-Burman, Himalayish, Tibeto-Kanauri, Tibetic, Tamangic. Preliminary results: 86% intelligibility by Western Trisuli Tamang, 87% by Central-Eastern Tamang, 54% to 67% by Outer-Eastern Tamang. Relationship within Tamang still needs evaluation. Southwestern Tamang has 80% lexical similarity with Western Trisuli Tamang, 76% to 78% with Western Rasuwa dialect, 78% with Northwestern Tamang, 70% to 73% with Eastern Gorkha Tamang, 77% to 93% with Eastern Tamang. Investigation needed: intelligibility, attitudes. SOV; postpositions; genitives after nouns; relatives before nouns; question word medial; CV, CVC, CCV, V, CCVC, CVCCC; tonal. Literacy rate in first language: 1% to 10%. Literacy rate in second language: 25% to 75%. Gallery forest. Mountain slope, valley. Swidden and peasant agriculturalists.

TAMANG, WESTERN ***(MURMI)*** [TDG] 186,408 to 320,350, 1% to 1.73% of population (based on 1991 census). Bagmati Zone, western Nuwakot, Rasuwa, Dhading, and parts of Gorkha districts, and other districts to the west and possibly southwest, central mountainous strip. Migrations to the Terai. Sino-Tibetan, Tibeto-Burman, Himalayish, Tibeto-Kanauri, Tibetic, Tamangic. Dialects: TRISULI

(NUWAKOT), RASUWA. Preliminary results showed 86% intelligibility of Western by Rasuwa, 81% to 88% by Central-Eastern, 78% to 88% by Outer-Eastern, 86% by Southwestern; 80% of Rasuwa by Trisuli, 13% by Outer-Eastern. Trisuli has 94% lexical similarity with Northwestern Tamang, 82% to 83% with Rasuwa Tamang, 80% with Southwestern Tamang, 77% to 79% with Eastern Gorkha Tamang. Rasuwa has 82% to 83% with Northwestern, 78% with Southwestern, 72% with Eastern Gorkha Tamang. All Western varieties have 69% to 81% with Eastern Tamang varieties. 'Murmi' is an archaic term used only in old British writings. No one uses it now. Investigation needed: intelligibility, attitudes. SOV, postpositions, genitives after nouns, relatives before nouns, question word medial, CV, CVC, CCV, V, CCVC, CVCCC, tonal. Literacy rate in first language: 1% to 10%. Literacy rate in second language: 25% to 75%. Some literacy materials and classes have been conducted. Devanagari, Tibetan. Gallery forest. Mountain slope, valley. Swidden and peasant agriculturalists. Traditional religion, Buddhist, Hindu. NT 1990.

THAKALI ***(TAPAANG, THAKSYA)*** [THS] 7,113 or 0.04% of the population (1991 census). Dhaulagiri Zone, Mustang District, Thak Khola, the mid Kali Gandaki Valley, with Annapurna Himal on one side and Dhaulagiri Himal on the other, from Tatopani village in the south to Jomosom in the north. Many live outside the area. Tukche is the cultural center. Tukche dialect is in all Southern Thak Khola and Jomosom, Syang in Syang, Thini, and Chimang. Sino-Tibetan, Tibeto-Burman, Himalayish, Tibeto-Kanauri, Tibetic, Tamangic. Dialects: TUKCHE (THAKALI), MARPHA, SYANG. Thakali dialects have 91% to 97% inherent intelligibility. Tukche is most easily understood by others. 41% to 46% lexical similarity with Gurung, 46% to 51% with Tamang. Thakali dialects in 4 villages have 75% to 86% lexical similarity with each other. 39% of the adult population (45% of men and 33% of women) have good, general proficiency in Nepali; others are less proficient. All ages except some educated ones under 30 who will probably speak it fluently later. The younger generation in Tukche is maintaining Thakali strongly. Elsewhere the younger generation uses less Thakali, but will develop it more fully as they grow older. Tukche is the prestige dialect. Marpha dialect is in an endogamous village. Literacy rate in second language: 62.2% (1991 census). Traders. Buddhist, Jhankrism, Bonpo, Hindu.

THAMI ***(THANGMI)*** [THF] 14,400 (1991 census). Population total both countries 14,400 or more. Most in Janakpur Zone, Dolakha District; villages in Sindhupalchok west of the Sun Kosi; a few villages in Ramechaap along the Sailung Khola. Also spoken in India. Sino-Tibetan, Tibeto-Burman, Himalayish, Tibeto-Kanauri, Western Himalayish, Eastern. Dialects: EASTERN THAMI, WESTERN THAMI. Related to Baraamu (Grierson-Konow). Bilingualism in Nepali. Dr. N. K. Rai says ethnic Thami outside Dolakha no longer speak Thami. Dictionary. Literacy rate in second language: 10%. Poetry, TV. Stone cutters and transporters, hunters, agriculturalists, pastoralists. Traditional religion, Buddhist, Hindu.

THARU, CHITWANIA ***(CHITUAN THARU, CHITAWAN THARU)*** [THE] 80,000 or more (based on 1991 census). 993,388 all Tharu, 5.32% of the population (1991 census). Population total both countries 80,000 or more. Narayani Zone, Chiatwan District, Lumbini Zone, Nawalparasi District. Also spoken in India. Indo-European, Indo-Iranian, Indo-Aryan, Eastern zone, Unclassified. Bilingualism in Nepali, Hindi, Bhojpuri Tharu. Literacy rate in first language: Below 1%. Literacy rate in second language: 27.7% (1991 census). Plains. Traditional religion, Hindu overlay. Bible portions 1977.

THARU, DANGAURA ***(DANG THARU)*** [THL] 300,000 or more in Nepal (1991 census). 993,388 all Tharu, 5.37% of the population (1991 census). Population total both countries 343,000. Rapti Zone, Dang District. Also in other areas of the Tarai, like Bardiya, Banke, Kailali, and Kanchanpur districts. Also spoken in India. Indo-European, Indo-Iranian, Indo-Aryan, Central zone, Unclassified. 68% to 91% intelligibility of Rana, 95% to 97% of Kathoriya. Some varieties listed as dialects have only 71% to 79% intelligibility of others. Some intelligibility difficulty with speakers from India. Closest to Mari Tharu. Possibly Eastern Hindi Group. 74% to 79% lexical similarity with Kathoriya, 72% to 74% with Sunha, 63% to 72% with Rana Thakur, 61% to 67% with Chitwan, 58% to 65% with Hindi. Educated people tend to be more bilingual in Nepali, men more than women, young people more than older people. Hindi and Maithili are also used. Dangaura is used almost exclusively in the family, with older people, children, and mainly with village leaders. They usually use Tharu with other Tharu, but sometimes Nepali. All ages. Vigorous. The Rana Tharu and Dangaura Tharu are well known, but the Kathoriya Tharu and other smaller groups are often unknown. Dang and Dangora are separate clans. Investigation needed: intelligibility with Deokuri, Kathoriya. Dictionary. SOV; postpositions; genitives after noun heads; adjectives, numerals before noun heads; CV, CVC, CCV; nontonal. Literacy rate in first language: Below 1%. Literacy rate in second language: 27.7% all Tharu (1991 census). Devanagari. Radio programs. Subtropical. Hill, valley. Agriculturalists. 600 to 900 meters. Traditional religion, Hindu overly.

THARU, DEOKHURI ***(DEOKHAR, DEOKRI)*** [THG] 80,000 (1981 census). Rapti Zone, Dang District. Indo-European, Indo-Iranian, Indo-Aryan, Eastern zone, Unclassified. May be a dialect of Dangauru Tharu.

Bilingualism in Nepali. Literacy rate in first language: Below 1%. Literacy rate in second language: 27.7% (1991 census). Agriculturalists, pastoralists. Traditional religion, Hindu overlay.

THARU, KATHORIYA ***(KATHARIYA)*** [TKT] 60,000 (1981). Population total both countries 60,000 or more. Seti Zone, Kailali District. Also spoken in India. Indo-European, Indo-Iranian, Indo-Aryan, Central zone, Unclassified. There appear to be differences in speech between Nepal and India dialects. Possibly Eastern Hindi Group. 79% lexical similarity with Dangaura and Rana, 66% with Hindi, 66% to 69% with Buksa, 63% with Chitwania. Bilingualism in Nepali. Hindi also used. Literacy rate in second language: 27.7% (1991 census). Traditional religion, Hindu overlay.

THARU, KOCHILA ***(SAPTARI)*** [THQ] 250,000 or more (1991 census). Population total both countries 250,000 or more. Koshi Zone, Morang and Sunsari districts; Sagarmatha Zone, Saptari, Udayapur, and Siraha districts; Janakpur Zone, Mahottari District. Also spoken in India. Indo-European, Indo-Iranian, Indo-Aryan, Eastern zone, Unclassified. Dialect: MORANGIA. Other Tharu in Siraha, Udayapur, and Saparti districts who call themselves 'Kochila' but do not speak Kochila can be distinguished by dress, customs, and language. They have adopted Maithili culture. Bilingualism in Nepali. Maithili also used. Family, older people, children, village leaders (mainly), sometimes Nepali with non-Tharu. Vigorous. Investigation needed: intelligibility with Morangia. Literacy rate in first language: Below 1%. Literacy rate in second language: 27.7% (1991 census). Traditional religion with Hindu overlay.

THARU, MAHOTARI ***(MAHOTTARI)*** [THN] 32,000 (1981 census). Janakpur Zone, Mahottari District. Indo-European, Indo-Iranian, Indo-Aryan, Eastern zone, Unclassified. May be part of Kochila Tharu. Bilingualism in Nepali. Literacy rate in first language: Below 1%. Literacy rate in second language: 27.7% (1991 census). Traditional religion, Hindu overlay.

THARU, RANA ***(RANA THAKUR)*** [THR] 200,000 in Nepal (1991 census). Population total both countries 264,000. Mahakali Zone, Kanchanpur District; Seti Zone, Kailali District. Also spoken in India. Indo-European, Indo-Iranian, Indo-Aryan, Eastern zone, Unclassified. Speakers appear to have 96% to 99% intelligibility among dialects, 90% with Kathoriya, 51% to 88% reported of Dangaura. Differences with India dialects. 83% to 97% lexical similarity among dialects, 73% to 79% with Buksa, 74% to 79% with Kathoriya, 70% to 73% with Sunha, 63% to 71% with Dangaura, 56% to 60% with Chitwania, 68% to 72% with Hindi. Bilingualism in Nepali. Hindi also used. Family, older people, children, mainly in village, Nepali with non-Tharu people. Vigorous. Some possible negative attitudes toward Dangaura Tharu. Investigation needed: intelligibility with dialects, bilingual proficiency in Kathoriya. Literacy rate in first language: Below 1%. Literacy rate in second language: 27.7% (1991 census). Agriculturalists, pastoralists. Traditional religion with Hindu overlay.

THUDAM BHOTE [THW] Mechi Zone, Taplejung District, northern. Sino-Tibetan, Tibeto-Burman, Himalayish, Tibeto-Kanauri, Tibetic, Tibetan, Unclassified.

THULUNG ***(THULUNGE RAI, DEUSALI, DEOSALI, THULU LUWA, THULULOA, THULUNG LA, THOLONG LO, THULUNG JEMU, TOAKU LWA)*** [TDH] 25,000 in Nepal (1991 W. Winter). Population total both countries 28,300. Eastern hills, southeast Solukumbu District. 6 to 7 villages in Okhaldhunga District and 1 in Bhojpur District. West of the highest ridges of the slopes to Dudhkosi, north of the Nechedanda and Halesidanda ranges, east of the upper Solu River, and south of the Kakukhola and the confluence of Ingkhukhola and Dudhkosi. Also spoken in India. Sino-Tibetan, Tibeto-Burman, Himalayish, Mahakiranti, Kiranti, Western. Dialect: LANNACHYO. Related to Lingkhim. 'Lancho' may be an alternate name for Lannachyo. Agriculturalists, pastoralists. Hindu.

TIBETAN ***(BHOTIA, ZANG)*** [TIC] 60,000 in Nepal (1973 SIL). Kathmandu. Sino-Tibetan, Tibeto-Burman, Himalayish, Tibeto-Kanauri, Tibetic, Tibetan, Central. Three dialects in Nepal. Agriculturalists, pastoralists, weavers. Lamaist. Bible 1948. See main entry under China.

TICHURONG ***(TICHERONG)*** [TCN] 1,500 (1980). Dolpa District, Karnali Zone, in the basin of the Bheri River. Sino-Tibetan, Tibeto-Burman, Himalayish, Tibeto-Kanauri, Tibetic, Tibetan, Central. Close to Dolpa Tibetan, but a separate language.

TILUNG ***(TILING, TILLING, TILUNG BLAMA)*** [TIJ] 1,000 or fewer (1991 W. Winter). Halesidanda Range in the outer west of Khotang District, between Dudhkosi and Sunkosi. Sino-Tibetan, Tibeto-Burman, Himalayish, Mahakiranti, Kiranti, Western. Dialects: CHOSKULE, DORUNKECHA. Choskule and Dorungkecha may be dialects or related languages; no linguistic data available. Little information available. Mountain slope.

TSEKU ***(TSUKU, TZUKU)*** [TSK] Mechi zone far east. Sino-Tibetan, Tibeto-Burman, Himalayish, Tibeto-Kanauri, Tibetic, Tibetan, Central. May not be in Nepal. See main entry under China.

TSUM ***(TSUMGE)*** [TTZ] 2,200 to 3,500 (1980). Gandaki Zone, northern Gorkha District, Tsum area, the region drained by the Shiar Khola north of Ganesh Himal. Chekampar (Chokong) is the prestige village. Sino-Tibetan, Tibeto-Burman, Himalayish, Tibeto-Kanauri, Tibetic, Tibetan, Central. 71% to 78% intelligibility with Nubri, 66% with Kyerung; 60% to 66% with Lhasa Tibetan; 22% to 25% with Northern Ghale, 22% with Southern Ghale, 23% to 27% with Kutang Ghale, 14% to 16% with

Eastern Gorkha Tamang, 14% with Western Gurung, 15% with Banspur Tamang. Divided into upper region, 'Yarba', and lower region, 'Ushug'. Speakers have minimal bilingualism in Nepali. Nepali used only to those who do not understand Tsum. Tsum used in nearly every domain. Vigorous. A few primary schools. Tibetans in Kathmandu call the people 'Tsumba' and the language 'Tsumge'. Investigation needed: intelligibility with Nubri. Literacy rate in second language: 10% or less. Gallery forest. Mountain slope, valley. Agriculturalists, traders. Lamaist Buddhist.

WALING *(WALUNG, WALÜNG)* [WLY] Khairang Panchayat, Bhojpur District. Sino-Tibetan, Tibeto-Burman, Himalayish, Mahakiranti, Kiranti, Eastern. Related to Dungmali. Probably extinct linguistically.

WALUNGGE *(OLANGCHUNG GOLA, WALUNGCHUNG GOLA, WALUNG, WALUNGGI KECCYA)* [OLA] 10,000 to 15,000, including 3,500 in the original area. Population total both countries 10,000 to 15,000. Taplejung District, 5 main villages: Walungchung, Yangma, Gunsa, Lilip, and Lungtung, and 6 or 7 smaller villages. Speakers also in Lungthung, Amjilesa, and Kambachen. Also spoken in India. Sino-Tibetan, Tibeto-Burman, Himalayish, Tibeto-Kanauri, Tibetic, Tibetan, Central. 71% lexical similarity with Lhasa Tibetan; 68% with Dolpo, Lopa, and Kyerung; 66% with Lhomi, Helambu Sherpa, and Baragaunle; 64% with Kutang Bhotia; 57% with Jirel; 55% with Sherpa. Young people in Kathmandu losing the language. In all areas except Kathmandu there is a strong sense of cultural identity revolving around their religion and language. The people are called 'Walungba'. Each of the main villages has a school. Cut off from the Lhomi, more links to Tibet. Some intermarriage with Lhomi and Tibetan speakers. Animal husbandry, traders.

WAYU *(HAYU, VAYU, WAYO)* [VAY] 1,500 (1974). Janakpur Zone, Ramechhap and Sindhuli districts, on the hills on both sides of the Sun Kosi River. Sino-Tibetan, Tibeto-Burman, Himalayish, Mahakiranti, Kham-Magar-Chepang-Sunwari, Chepang. Different from Chepang. Now no monolingual children (Matisoff 1991). Hodgson said it was becoming extinct in the mid-19th century, but it has survived until the end of the 20th century (Michailovsky 1988). Now strong Nepali influences in phonology, lexicon, and grammar (J. Matisoff 1991). 1,000 to 1,500 meters.

YAKHA *(YAKKHA, YAKKHABA, YAKKHABA CEA, YAKKHABA SALA, DEWANSALA)* [YBH] 8,000 to 10,000 in Nepal (1991 W. Winter). Population total both countries 8,000 to 10,000 or more. Tehrathum District, Sankhuwasawa District, Koshi Zone, Dhankuta District. East of the middle Arun River between the Hinuwankhola in the north and the Leguwakhola in the south. Northern Yakha is in the south of Sankhuwasabha District, and the adjoining strip of language in extreme northern Dhankuta District. Southern Yakha is in Dhankuta District. Eastern Yakha is in Ilam and Panchthar districts. Also spoken in India. Sino-Tibetan, Tibeto-Burman, Himalayish, Mahakiranti, Kiranti, Eastern. Dialects: NORTHERN YAKHA, SOUTHERN YAKHA, EASTERN YAKHA. Dialects have minimum diversity. Related to Lumba-Yakkha, Phangduwali, Mugali, Chhintang, Chhulung, Belhariya, and Athpahariya. Agriculturalists, pastoralists. Buddhist, Hindu.

YAMPHE *(YAMPHU, NEWAHANG YAMPHE, YAMPHE KHA)* [YMA] 3,000 to 5,000 (1991 W. Winter). Makalu Panchayat, both sides of the upper Arun River, northern Sankhuwasawa. To the south, the Jaljale Himal east of the Arun and the Apsuwakhola west of the Arun; to the north as far as the Leksuwakhola and Barun rivers. Sino-Tibetan, Tibeto-Burman, Himalayish, Mahakiranti, Kiranti, Eastern. Dialects: SIBAO-YAMPHE, PA-O. Related to Yamphu, but distinct in grammar and phonology. Still spoken by many young people. Sometimes called 'Yakkha' or 'Yamphu', but it is a distinct language. High mountain slopes.

YAMPHU *(YAMPHU RAI, YAMPHU KHA, YANPHU, YAMPHE)* [YBI] 5,000 (1997 Bradley, ed.). Eastern hills, upper Arun Valley, Matsayapokhari Panchayat, Sankhuwasawa District, extreme north of the Northern Lorung area, directly southwest of the Jaljale Mountains, Koshi, Mechi zones. Sino-Tibetan, Tibeto-Burman, Himalayish, Mahakiranti, Kiranti, Eastern. Related to Yamphe but different gramatically and phonologically. Dialects of Southern Lorung and the Yamphe language are also called 'Yamphu'. High mountain slope. Hindu.

OMAN

Sultanate of Oman, Saltanat <Uman. National or official language: Standard Arabic. 2,382,000 (1998 UN), of which 535,000 are expatriates (1993 census). Literacy rate 59.75% (1993 census). Also includes Baharna Spoken Arabic 10,000, Shihhi Spoken Arabic 10,000, Gujarati, Portuguese, Sindhi, Somali, Swahili 22,000, Urdu 30,000, people from Bangladesh 88,000, Egypt 33,000, India 268,000, Jordan 8,000, Pakistan 63,000, Philippines 10,000, Sri Lanka 25,000, Sudan 9,000, other Gulf States 6,000, other Arab 10,000, United Kingdom 7,000. Information mainly from T. M. Johnstone 1967; C. Holes 1988, 1990. Ibadi Muslim, Shi'a Muslim, Sunni Muslim, Hindu, secular, Christian. Deaf population 103,131. Data accuracy estimate: B. The number of languages listed for Oman is 11. Of those, all are living languages. Diversity index 0.68.

ARABIC, DHOFARI SPOKEN ***(DHOFARI, ZOFARI)*** [ADF] 70,000 (1996). In Salala and its nearby coastal regions. Afro-Asiatic, Semitic, Central, South, Arabic. Related to Hadromi Spoken Arabic and Gulf Spoken Arabic. Different from Omani Spoken Arabic.

ARABIC, GULF SPOKEN ***(OMANI BEDAWI ARABIC, BEDAWI, GULF ARABIC, KHALIJI)*** [AFB] 441,000 in Oman (1995). Most coastal regions and most border regions with the UAE. Afro-Asiatic, Semitic, Central, South, Arabic. Muslim. See main entry under Iraq.

ARABIC, OMANI SPOKEN ***(OMANI HADARI ARABIC)*** [ACX] 720,000 in Oman (1996). Population total all countries 1,010,000. Mainly in the Hajar Mts. highlands and a few coastal regions. Also spoken in Kenya, Tanzania, UAE. Afro-Asiatic, Semitic, Central, South, Arabic.

ARABIC, STANDARD [ABV] Middle East, North Africa. Afro-Asiatic, Semitic, Central, South, Arabic. Used for education, official purposes, formal speeches. National language. Newspapers. Bible 1984-1991. See main entry under Saudi Arabia.

BALOCHI, SOUTHERN ***(BALUCHI, BALUCI, BALOCI)*** [BCC] 130,300 out of 312,000 ethnic population in Oman (1993). Most were in Mutrah, but have dispersed a bit up the coast. Indo-European, Indo-Iranian, Iranian, Western, Northwestern, Balochi. Dialects: MAKRANI (LOTUNI, ZADGAALI), BARAHUWI, BASHGAADI, HUUTI. Ethnic Baloch who immigrated long ago are Omani citizens, but no longer speak Balochi. Speakers come from Pakistan. The majority are not Omani citizens. Sunni Muslim. Bible portions 1992-1994. See main entry under Pakistan.

FARSI, WESTERN ***(PERSIAN)*** [PES] 25,000 in Oman (1993). Scattered in cities along the coast. Many in a community in Jabroo, on the way out of Mutrah, going toward Ruwi. Indo-European, Indo-Iranian, Iranian, Western, Southwestern, Persian. Many women speak only Farsi. Men who go outside the community speak Arabic as second language, and many know 2 or 3 other languages. Shi'a Muslim. Bible 1838-1995. See main entry under Iran.

HARSUSI ***(HERSYET, HARSI <AFORIT)*** [HSS] 1,000 to 2,000 (1998 H. Mutzafi). Jiddat al-Harasis, Dhofar Province. Afro-Asiatic, Semitic, South, South Arabian. Close to Mehri, but usually considered to be a separate language. It is reported that they are increasing in use of Mehri and proficiency in it, and also bilingual in Arabic. Spoken by the Harasis and <Ifar (<Afar).

HOBYÓT ***(HEWBYÓT, HOBI, KALAM RIFI)*** [HOH] 100 or fewer (1998 Hezy Mutsafi). Population total both countries 100 or fewer. Near the Yemen border. Also spoken in Yemen. Afro-Asiatic, Semitic, South, South Arabian. A separate language from Jibbali. Related to Mehri-may be inherently intelligible with Mehri. They define themselves as belonging to the Mahra tribe. Investigation needed: intelligibility with Mehri. Muslim.

JIBBALI ***(GEBLET, SHERET, SHEHRI, SHAHARI, JIBALI, EHKILI, QARAWI)*** [SHV] 25,000 based on 1993 census. Another estimate gives 34,800 rural and 31,000 to 70,000 urban speakers, including bilinguals, largely in Dhofari Arabic. Dofar, in the mountains north of Al-Salala. Afro-Asiatic, Semitic, South, South Arabian. Dialects: CENTRAL JIBBALI, EASTERN JIBBALI, WESTERN JIBBALI. Eastern Jibbali includes Kuria Muria ('Baby' Jibbali). Speakers are reported to be increasingly bilingual in Dhofari Arabic. Spoken by the Qara (Ehkeló, Ahkló), Shahra (Sheró, Shahara), Barahama, Bait Ash-Shaik, and some Batahira. Muslim.

KUMZARI ***(KUMZAI)*** [ZUM] 3,000. Spoken only on the Musandam Peninsula of northern Oman. Indo-European, Indo-Iranian, Iranian, Western, Southwestern, Luri. Distinct from Khunsari of Iran. Investigation needed: intelligibility with Luri. Fishermen. Muslim.

LUWATI [LUV] 5,000 (1996). In a walled quarter of Mutrah, facing the old harbor, and in Muscat and other cities. Indo-European, Indo-Iranian, Unclassified. The people are called 'Luwathiya'. Their ancestors are reported to have migrated from Iran to Hyderabad, then to Mutrah. Sometimes called 'Persians'. Businessmen. Shi'a Muslim.

MEHRI ***(MAHRI)*** [MHR] 15,000 in Oman including 1,000 Bathari (1993). Dhofar Province. Nagdi is in Oman, Bathari in Dhofar Province of Oman, coast north from Salala. Afro-Asiatic, Semitic, South, South Arabian. Dialects: NAGDI, BATHARI (BAUTAHARI, BAT-HARI, BOTHARI). Hobyót may be a Mehri dialect. Bathari may be a separate language. Spoken by the Mahra and Bil Haf. Bathari is spoken by the Batahira (Botahara). The Bait Kathir speak Arabic. Investigation needed: intelligibility with Bathari, Hobyot. Muslim. Bible portions 1902. See main entry under Yemen.

PAKISTAN

Islamic Republic of Pakistan, Islam-i Jamhuriya-e Pakistan. National or official languages: Urdu, Sindhi, English. 148,166,000 (1998 UN). Literacy rate 26%. Also includes Indian Sign Language, Parsi 20,000, Turkmen, Uyghur, Southern Uzbek 50,000, Arabic 122,000, Chinese 6,000. Information mainly from R. F. Strand 1973; G. Morgenstierne 1974; C. Shackle 1979, 1980; J. C. Sharma 1982; J. S. Addleton 1986; J. R. Payne 1987; C. P. Masica 1991; C. O'Leary 1992. Muslim, Hindu, Christian (1981 census).

Blind population 1,500,000. Deaf population 7,398,329. Deaf institutions: 31. Data accuracy estimate: B. The number of languages listed for Pakistan is 69. Of those, all are living languages. Diversity index 0.83.

AER [AEQ] 100 to 200 (1998). Lower Sindh, Jikrio Goth near Kunri around Deh 333, Hyderabad, and at Jamesabad. Others are reported to have migrated to India at Partition in 1947, living in the Kach Bhuj area in Gujarat. Indo-European, Indo-Iranian, Indo-Aryan, Central zone, Gujarati. Dialects: JIKRIO GOTH AER, JAMESABAD AER. 78% lexical similarity with Katai Meghwar and Kachi Bhil, 75% to 77% with Rabari, 76% with Kachi Koli. They also speak Sindhi (adult men only for common topics), Panjabi (adult men of Jikrio Goth only for common topics), and have worship songs in Gujarati. Women are monolingual. 100% of boys and 25% of girls attend Sindhi medium schools. All ages. Aer is used within the group. Unusual interrogative word suggests possible historical connection with Western Rajasthani group. Speakers in Pakistan are running out of marriage possibilities and may have to move to India. The group in India is the most influential. Other Aer people in Nawabshah, Sindh are reported to speak a different language, dress differently, and do not intermarry with this group. Investigation needed: intelligibility with Aer in India, Aer speaking a different language in Pakistan. Literacy rate in second language: 15% in Sindhi. Sindhi-based script. Hindu.

BADESHI [BDZ] Upper reaches of Bishigram (Chail) Valley, east of Madyan, Swat Kohistan. One village. Indo-European, Indo-Iranian, Unclassified. Bilingualism in Pashto. Existence unconfirmed. The Torwali say they speak Ushojo, and the Ushojo say they speak Torwali. May be a family name of people who came from Badakhshan. Sunni Muslim.

BAGRI ***(BAGARI, BAGRIA, BAGRIS, BAORIAS, BAHGRI, BAWRI)*** [BGQ] 200,000 in Pakistan, including 100,000 in Sind Province (1998). In the Sindh and Punjab. Indo-European, Indo-Iranian, Indo-Aryan, Central zone, Rajasthani, Unclassified. Related to Bhil groups and Marwari. Does not seem close to any other language. 76% lexical similarity with Marwari Bhil of Jodhpur, 74% with Jandavra. They speak some Sindhi and understand some Urdu. Different from Vaghri. Nomadic. They practice begging. Literacy rate in first language: Below 1%. Literacy rate in second language: Below 5%. Begging. See main entry under India.

BALOCHI, EASTERN ***(BALUCHI, BALUCI, BALOCI)*** [BGP] 1,800,000 in Pakistan (1998). Population total both countries 1,805,000. Including second language users of all Balochi languages: 5,000,000 (1999 WA). Northeastern Balochistan Province, northwestern Sind, southwestern Punjab. Also spoken in India. Indo-European, Indo-Iranian, Iranian, Western, Northwestern, Balochi. One of the major languages in Pakistan. Distinct from Western Balochi and Southern Balochi. Balochi has a small body of literature. Literacy rate in first language: Below 1%. Literacy rate in second language: 5% to 15%. Urdu script used. Radio programs. Sunni Muslim. Bible portions 1815-1906.

BALOCHI, SOUTHERN ***(BALUCHI, BALUCI, BALOCI, MAKRANI)*** [BCC] 2,765,000 in Pakistan (1998). Population total all countries 3,400,000. Southern Balochistan, southern Sind, Karachi. Also spoken in Iran, Oman, UAE. Indo-European, Indo-Iranian, Iranian, Western, Northwestern, Balochi. Dialects: COASTAL BALOCHI, KECHI, MAKRANI (LOTUNI). Distinct from Eastern Balochi and fairly distinct from Western Balochi. Literacy rate in first language: Below 1%. Literacy rate in second language: 5% to 15%. Urdu script used. Sunni Muslim, and about 700,000 Zigri (Zikri) sect (semi-Muslim). Bible portions 1992-1994.

BALOCHI, WESTERN ***(BALUCHI, BALOCI, BALUCI)*** [BGN] 1,116,000 in Pakistan (1998). Population total all countries 1,800,000. Northwestern Balochistan Province. Also spoken in Afghanistan, Iran, Tajikistan, Turkmenistan. Indo-European, Indo-Iranian, Iranian, Western, Northwestern, Balochi. Dialects: RAKHSHANI (RAXSHANI), SARAWANI. Balochi is the official spelling in Pakistan. It has a small body of literature. Literacy rate in first language: 1% to 5%. Literacy rate in second language: 5% to 15%. Urdu script used. Radio programs. Sunni Muslim. Bible portions 1984.

BALTI ***(SBALTI, BALTISTANI, BHOTIA OF BALTISTAN)*** [BFT] 270,000 in Pakistan or 90% of the Baltistan population (1992). Population total both countries 333,640. Primarily northeastern Pakistan: Baltistan District, Skardu, Rondu, Shigar, Khapalu, Kharmang, and Gultari valleys. Also spoken in India. Sino-Tibetan, Tibeto-Burman, Himalayish, Tibeto-Kanauri, Tibetic, Tibetan, Western. Chorbat is the most divergent dialect. 87% to 100% lexical similarity among dialects, 78% to 85% with Purik. Some Shina is used as second language. Urdu proficiency is reported to be high in some places. Women and uneducated people have little knowledge of Urdu. Many Purik have shifted to Balti. Speakers call themselves and their language 'Balti'. Literacy rate in second language: 3% to 5% in Urdu. Perso-Arabic script is the accepted one. Shi'ah Muslim. Bible portions 1903-1940.

BATERI ***(BATERI KOHISTANI, BATERA KOHISTANI, BATERAWAL, BATERAWAL KOHISTANI)*** [BTV] 20,000 to 30,000 in Pakistan (1992). Population total both countries 22,000 to 45,000 or more. Extreme southern corner, Kohistan District, small pocket on the east bank of the Indus River, north of Besham; Batera area. Also spoken in India. Indo-European, Indo-Iranian, Indo-Aryan, Northwestern zone, Dardic, Kohistani. 58% to 61% lexical similarity with Indus Kohistani, 60% with Gowro, 54%

with Chilisso, 29% with Shina and Torwali, 27% with Kalami. Bilingualism in Some: Pashto, Shina. Vigorous.

BHAYA [BHE] 70 to 700 (1998). Lower Sindh: Kapri Goth near Samaro, near Khipro, Jamesabad, Mir ke goth, Mirpurkhas, Phuladia, a few families in Hyderabad. There may be more in India. Indo-European, Indo-Iranian, Indo-Aryan, Central zone, Western Hindi, Unclassified. Similarity of key morphemes: The possessive postposition with g- contrasts with all other languages in the area. Gender endings match Rajasthani. This might be the same as Bhoyari [BHY] in India. It may be in the Western Hindi group. Lexical similarity: Marwari sweeper 84%, Malhi 75%, Bhat 73%, Goaria 72% to 73%, Sindhi Meghwar 70% to 73%, Mogi 63% to 72%, Sindhi Bhil 63% to 71%, Urdu 70%.

BRAHUI ***(BRAHUIDI, BIRAHUI, BRAHUIGI, KUR GALLI)*** [BRH] 2,000,000 in Pakistan (1998), 1.2% of the population. Population total all countries 2,210,000. South central, Quetta and Kalat region, east Baluchistan and Sind provinces. Also spoken in Afghanistan, Iran, Turkmenistan. Dravidian, Northern. Dialects: JHARAWAN, KALAT, SARAWAN. Kalat is the standard dialect, Jharawan is lowland. Some bilingualism in Western Balochi. Literacy rate in first language: Below 1%. Literacy rate in second language: Below 5%. Nastaliq script used. Pastoralists. Muslim. Bible portions 1905-1978.

BURUSHASKI ***(BRUSHASKI, BURUSHAKI, BURUCAKI, BURUSHKI, BURUCASKI, BILTUM, KHAJUNA, KUNJUT)*** [BSK] 55,000 to 60,000 (1981). Population total both countries 55,000 to 60,000. Hunza-Nagar area and Yasin area in Gilgit District, Northern Areas. Scattered speakers also in Gilgit, Kashmir, and various cities. Also spoken in India. Language Isolate. Dialects: NAGAR (NAGIR), HUNZA, YASIN (WERCHIKWAR). Werchikwar is geographically separated from other dialects. Nagar and Hunza dialects have 91% to 94% lexical similarity. Werchikwar has 67% to 72% lexical similarity with Hunza, 66% to 71% with Nagar, and may be a separate language. Werchikwar speakers are somewhat bilingual in Khowar. Knowledge of Urdu is limited among women and some others. People are called Burusho. SOV. Literacy rate in second language: 20%. Ismaili Muslim, Shi'a Muslim (Nagar).

CHILISSO ***(CHILISS, GALOS)*** [CLH] 1,600 to 3,000 (1992 SIL). All may not be speakers. Scattered families in the Koli, Palas, Jalkot area of the Indus Kohistan, east bank of the Indus River. Indo-European, Indo-Iranian, Indo-Aryan, Northwestern zone, Dardic, Kohistani. 70% lexical similarity with Indus Kohistani, 65% to 68% with Gowro, 54% with Bateri, 48% to 56% with Shina. 26% with Torwali, 25% with Kalami. Socially integrated with the Kohistani Shina, and most or all speak that as first or second language.

DAMELI ***(DAMEL, DAMEDI, DAMIA, GUDOJI)*** [DML] 5,000 (1992 SIL). In the Damel Valley, about 32 miles south of Drosh in southern Chitral District, on the east side of the Kunar River. 11 villages. Indo-European, Indo-Iranian, Indo-Aryan, Northwestern zone, Dardic, Kunar. Two groups: Shintari and Swati, but no significant dialect variation. 44% lexical similarity with Gawar-Bati, Savi, and Phalura, 33% with Kamviiri, 29% with Kati. A few men use Urdu as second language. Few women know Pashto. Dameli is used in the home and for in-group communication. Vigorous. They are reported to have come from Afghanistan several hundred years ago. The language has been influenced by Nuristani languages. Mountain valleys. Pastoralists. Sunni Muslim.

DEHWARI ***(DEGHWARI)*** [DEH] 13,000 possibly (1998). Central Balochistan, in Kalat and Mastung. Indo-European, Indo-Iranian, Iranian, Western, Southwestern, Persian. Influenced by Brahui. Literacy rate in first language: Below 1%. Literacy rate in second language: Below 5%.

DHATKI ***(DHATI)*** [MKI] 200,000 (1919 Grierson), 100,000 in Sind (1987), probably many more. Lower Sind in Tharparkar and Sanghar districts. Indo-European, Indo-Iranian, Indo-Aryan, Central zone, Rajasthani, Marwari. Dialects: EASTERN DHATKI, SOUTHERN DHATKI, CENTRAL DHATKI, BARAGE, MALHI. Varies considerably from northern Marwari, although they claim to understand one another. The Malhi are an ethnic group living in 3 main areas. Those in the Kunri-Pithoro-Noakot-Mithi area speak a dialect with 80% lexical similarity to Dhatki, 74% to Sindhi, and work as water-drawers. 80% to 83% lexical similarity with Marwari dialects. Dhatki of Rajasthan and Dhatki of Thar are 88% lexically similar. People also speak some Sindhi and Urdu. Dhatki of Rajasthan and Dhatki of Thar are 88% lexically similar. Literacy rate in first language: Below 5%. Literacy rate in second language: Below 5%. Sindhi-based script. Hindu, Muslim, Christian.

DOMAAKI ***(DUMAKI, DOMA)*** [DMK] 500 (1989). Gilgit District, Northern Areas, mainly in Hunza Valley, Mominabad village, a few households in Big Nagar, Shishkat (Gojal), Dumial in Gilgit, Oshkandas (east of Gilgit), and Bakor village in Punyal. Indo-European, Indo-Iranian, Indo-Aryan, Northwestern zone, Dardic, Shina. It has loan words from Shina and Burushaski, but is not intelligible to speakers of those languages. 40% lexical similarity with Gilgit Shina. Bilingualism in Burushaski is fairly high, especially among young people. Shina and Urdu also used as second languages. Domaaki is used in the home. The people are called 'Bericho', 'Dom', or 'Doma'. Musicians and blacksmiths. Muslim.

ENGLISH [ENG] Indo-European, Germanic, West, English. Mainly second language speakers in Pakistan. Official language. Bible 1535-1989. See main entry under United Kingdom.

FARSI, EASTERN ***(DARI, TAJIK, MADAGLASHTI, BADAKHSHI)*** [PRS] 1,000,000 in Pakistan, plus 1,400 in Madaglasht, and many refugees (1992 SIL). Southeast Chitral, Madaglasht village of Shishi Koh Valley, Peshawar, Rawalpindi, Lahore, Karachi, other large cities. Indo-European, Indo-Iranian, Iranian, Western, Southwestern, Persian. Madaglasht community came from Badakhshan, Afghanistan 200 years ago. Other communities have been in Pakistan for many generations. Muslim. NT 1982-1985. See main entry under Afghanistan.

GAWAR-BATI ***(GOWAR-BATI, GOWARI, ARANDUI, SATRE, NARSATI, NARISATI)*** [GWT] 1,500 in Pakistan plus refugees (1992). Southern Chitral, Arandu, and several villages along the Kunar River south of Arandu. Indo-European, Indo-Iranian, Indo-Aryan, Northwestern zone, Dardic, Kunar. A distinct language from its neighbors. 47% lexical similarity with Shumashti, 44% with Dameli, 42% with Savi and Grangali. Some use Pashto as second language. Used in the home and for in-group communication. Vigorous. Mountain valleys. Sunni Muslim. See main entry under Afghanistan.

GHERA ***(SINDHI GHERA, BARA)*** [GHR] 10,000 or fewer (1998). A single colony in Hyderabad, between the main bus stop and the railway station. Speakers say more than 90% of the people remained in Surat and Ahmedabad, India. Indo-European, Indo-Iranian, Indo-Aryan, Central zone, Western Hindi, Unclassified. Quite different grammatically from Gurgula and similar to Urdu. 87% lexical similarity with Gurgula, 70% with Urdu. Widespread multilingualism among both sexes with both Sindhi and Urdu. 25% of boys and some girls attend Sindhi medium schools. Almost totally urbanized. Investigation needed: intelligibility, bilingual proficiency in India group. Literacy rate in second language: 20% Sindhi. Sellers of ceramic dishes and used clothing. Hindu.

GOARIA [GIG] 20,000 to 25,000 (1998). All towns in Sindh Province except Karachi: including Larkana, Sukkur, Moro, Badin, Umerkot. They claim to have come from Jodhpur Rajasthan, India, where there may be more. Indo-European, Indo-Iranian, Indo-Aryan, Central zone, Rajasthani, Marwari. This might be the same as Gawari [GBO] in India. 75% to 83% lexical similarity with Jogi, 76% to 80% with Marwari sweeper, 72% to 78% with Marwari Meghwar, 70% to 78% with Loarki. Adults speak Sindhi and other local languages for trade, Hindi for worship. All ages. Goaria used in all domains except religion. Literacy rate in second language: Below 1% in Sindhi. Sindhi-based script. Dessert. Plains. Women sell trinkets, men transport people by horse cart and goods by donkey or donkey cart. 0 to 100 meters. Hindu.

GOWRO ***(GABARO, GABAR KHEL)*** [GWF] 200 or fewer (1990). Indus Kohistan on the eastern bank, Kolai area, Mahrin village. Indo-European, Indo-Iranian, Indo-Aryan, Northwestern zone, Dardic, Kohistani. 65% to 68% lexical similarity with Chilisso, 62% with Indus Kohistani, 60% with Bateri, 40% to 43% with Shina, 25% with Torwali, 24% with Kalami. Bilingualism in Shina. Different from Gawri, an alternate name for Kalami.

GUJARATI [GJR] Lower Punjab, Sindh. Indo-European, Indo-Iranian, Indo-Aryan, Central zone, Gujarati. Some Pakistani dialects are closer to standard Gujarati than others. Pakistani Gujarati is probably a subdialect of Patani (Voegelin and Voegelin 1977). The Memoni ethnic group in Karachi, Hyderabad, Sukkur, and other parts of Pakistan are reported to speak a variety closer to Gujarati, while those in India are reported to speak a variety of Kachchi. All Parsi (5,000), many Ismaili Muslims, and many Hindu sweepers (10,000 to 100,000) speak Gujarati. Many Parsi and Ismaili Muslims are literate in Gujarati. There seems to be a shift to Urdu among many Gujarati-speaking sweepers. Newspapers, radio programs. Bible 1823-1998. See main entry under India.

GUJARI ***(GUJURI, GUJURI RAJASTHANI, GUJER, GOJRI, GOGRI, GOJARI, GUJJARI, KASHMIR GUJURI)*** [GJU] 300,000 or more in Pakistan (1992) including 2,910 in Chitral (1969), 20,000 in Swat Kohistan (1987), 200,000 to 700,000 in Azad Jammu and Kashmir (1989). Throughout northern Pakistan, mainly in the east in Hazara District, NWFP, in Kaghan Valley, Azad Jammu, and Kashmir. Scattered communities in southern Chitral, Swat Kohistan, and Dir Kohistan, NWFP, and Gilgit Agency, Northern Areas. Indo-European, Indo-Iranian, Indo-Aryan, Central zone, Rajasthani, Unclassified. Dialects: WESTERN GUJARI, EASTERN GUJARI. Eastern Gujari appears closer to Northern Hindko or Pahari-Potwari. Western Gujari speakers appear to understand the Eastern dialect better than vice versa. Comparison with India varieties is needed. 64% to 94% lexical similarity among dialects. It is reported that most Gujars in Pakistani Punjab have shifted to Panjabi. Spoken in some pockets of Punjab by immigrants from elsewhere. Some unpublished literature. Some speakers move with herds up in summer, down in winter. Radio programs. Pastoralists, dairy, nomadic, some settled agriculturalists. Muslim. See main entry under India.

GURGULA ***(MARWARI GHERA)*** [GGG] 30,000 to 35,000 (1998). Sindh Province, largest concentration in Bhens Colony, Karachi, others in smaller urban centers through Sindh, including Mirpur Khas, Shahdadpur, Panj, Moro, Sabura and Tando Allahyar. Indo-European, Indo-Iranian, Indo-Aryan, Central zone, Rajasthani, Unclassified. Ghera is quite different gramatically. 87% lexical similarity with Ghera. Widespread multilingualism in Sindhi, Urdu, some Gujarati among all ages and sexes as needed, with men being the most proficient. They speak Gurgula among themselves. They are proud of Gurgula. Literacy rate in second language: 5% in Urdu. Sindhi-based script. Dessert with irrigation. Plains. Itinerant sellers. Below 100 meters. Hindu.

HAZARAGI ***(AZARGI, HAZARA, HEZAREH)*** [HAZ] 110,000 to 220,000 in Pakistan, including many recent refugees from Afghanistan (1998). Quetta (100,000 to 200,000, Karachi and Islamabad (10,000), some villages in rural Sindh. Indo-European, Indo-Iranian, Iranian, Western, Southwestern, Persian. They speak a language related to Eastern Farsi (Dari). The alternate names listed refer to the people. Tribal or regional names are (Central) Dai Kundi, Dai Zangi, Behsud, Yekaulang, (Southern) Polada, Urusgani, Jaguri, Ghazni Hazaras, Dai Miradad, Kabul. Literacy rate in first language: Below 10%. Literacy rate in second language: 10% to 30% Urdu, Dari or Farsi. Radio programs. Laborers, civil servants, tradesmen, shop keepers, traders. Imami Shi'a Muslim. See main entry under Afghanistan.

HINDKO, NORTHERN ***(HAZARA HINDKO, HINDKI, KAGHANI, KAGANI)*** [HNO] 1,875,000 (1981 census). Both Hindko languages had 305,505 households, 2.4% of the population (1981 census). Total Hindko in Pakistan 3,000,000 (1993). Hazara Division, Mansehra and Abbotabad districts, Indus and Kaghan valleys and valleys of Indus tributaries, NWFP. Rural and urban. Indo-European, Indo-Iranian, Indo-Aryan, Northwestern zone, Lahnda. Also related to Panjabi, Siraiki, and Pahari-Potwari; which have all been called 'Greater Panjabi', forming part of 'Lahnda'. Lexical similarities within Northern Hindko dialects are 82% to 92%; between Northern and Southern Hindko varieties 67% to 82%. Second languages are Urdu for the educated, with varied proficiency, and Pashto or Panjabi. Bilingual proficiency is generally limited. Literacy rate in second language: Below 20%. Perso-Arabic script used. Poetry, radio programs, TV. Plains, low hills. Sunni Muslim. NT 1991.

HINDKO, SOUTHERN [HIN] 625,000 (1981 census). Attock District, Punjab Province, and into the southernmost portion of Hazara Division, NWFP; Kohat and Peshawar districts, NWFP. Rural and urban. Indo-European, Indo-Iranian, Indo-Aryan, Northwestern zone, Lahnda. Dialects: PESHAWAR HINDKO (PESHAWARI), ATTOCK HINDKO (ATTOCK-HARIPUR HINDKO), KOHAT HINDKO (KOHATI), RURAL PESHAWAR HINDKO. The dialect in Dera Ismail Khan, sometimes called 'Hindko', is apparently closer to Siraiki. Most people have limited bilingual proficiency in Urdu, Pashto, Panjabi, or other languages. Urdu is known by educated speakers. Perso-Arabic script used. Radio programs, TV. Plains, low hills. Sunni Muslim.

JADGALI ***(JATGALI, JATKI, JAT)*** [JAV] 100,000 (1998). Population total both countries 100,000 or more. Southeast Balochistan Province, southwest Sind. Also spoken in Iran. Indo-European, Indo-Iranian, Indo-Aryan, Northwestern zone, Sindhi. People called Jats. Different from Jakati of Afghanistan, Moldova and Ukraine. Literacy rate in first language: Below 1%. Literacy rate in second language: Below 5%. Muslim.

JANDAVRA ***(JHANDORIA)*** [JND] 5,000 (1998). Southern Sindh Province from Hyderabad to east of Mirpur Khas. Reported to be many more in Jodhpur, Rajasthan, India. Indo-European, Indo-Iranian, Indo-Aryan, Central zone, Gujarati. 74% lexical similarity with Bagri and Katai Meghwar, 68% with Kachi Koli. Men tend to be conversant in Sindhi and Urdu, at least on a basic level, but women are not. All ages. Literacy rate in second language: No literates. Desert. Plains. Beggars, scavengers. 0 to 100 meters. Hindu.

KABUTRA ***(NAT, NATRA)*** [KBU] 1,000 (1998). Sindh, some concentrations around Umerkot, Kunri, and Nara Dhoro. Speakers say that 90% of the people remain in the Zal area of Marwar, India. Indo-European, Indo-Iranian, Indo-Aryan, Central zone, Western Hindi, Hindustani, Sansi. Speakers report they have inherent intelligibility of Sansi and Sochi, and use Kabutra when speaking to them. 74% lexical similarity with the Sochi language variety. All ages and sexes speak Urdu for most common topics, some Sindhi. Women speak Urdu better than in most Hindu groups. They speak Kabutra among themselves. Investigation needed: intelligibility with Sansi, Sochi. Literacy rate in second language: 5% in Urdu. Entertainers, dancers. Hindu.

KACHCHI ***(KACHCHHI, KUTCHCHI, CUCHI, CUTCH, KUTCHIE, KACHI, KATCH, KAUTCHY, KATCHI)*** [KFR] 50,000 or more in Pakistan (1998). Karachi. Indo-European, Indo-Iranian, Indo-Aryan, Northwestern zone, Sindhi. Dialect: JADEJI. Most Kachchi do not understand Gujarati. Bible portions 1834. See main entry under India.

KALAMI ***(GARWI, GAWRI, GOWRI, GARWA, GAAWRO, KALAMI KOHISTANI, KOHISTANI, KOHISTANA, BASHKARIK, BASHGHARIK, DIR KOHISTANI, DIRI, DIRWALI)*** [GWC] 40,000 (1987). Upper Swat Kohistan from between Peshmal and Kalam north to upper valleys above Kalam, also in Dir Kohistan, in Thal, Lamuti (Kinolam), Biar (Jiar), and Rajkot (Patrak) villages. People at Khata Khotan, China, are reported to be related, recognized by their clothing and language. Indo-European, Indo-Iranian, Indo-Aryan, Northwestern zone, Dardic, Kohistani. Dialects: KALAM, USHU, THAL, LAMUTI (LAMTI), RAJKOTI (PATRAK), DASHWA. Dialect differences do not hinder communication, except that speakers of other dialects have difficulty with Rajkot. 90% to 93% lexical similarity among the main dialects; Rajkoti has 75% with Kalami; Dashwa has 77% with Kalami, and 74% with Rajkoti. The most widely understood indigenous language in northern Swat and Dir

Kohistan. Men are fairly bilingual in Pashto; women are more limited. Rajkoti men have high bilingualism in Pashto. Uneducated men and women are limited in Urdu. There appear to be few active speakers of Dashwa. Kalami and Ushu speakers indicate some negative attitudes toward each other's speech. Dashwa is a clan name of people originally from around Rajkot; little information available. About one-third migrate in winter to Mingora, Mardan, Peshawar, or the Punjab in search of work. Speakers of Pashto, Gujari, Khowar, and other Kohistani languages live among them, but they are generally in the majority. Patrilineal descent groups are: Drekhel, Nilor (Niliyor), Jaflor (Jafalor). The Drekhel are divided into the Kalamkhel, Akarkhel, and Chinorkhel. The Mullakhel are Pashtoons from Lower Swat who now speak Pashto as first language, but speak, understand, and identify with Kalami. Muslim.

KALASHA ***(KALASHAMON, KALASH)*** [KLS] 2,900 to 5,700 (1992). Southern Chitral District. The largest village is Balanguru in Rumbur Valley. Southern Kalasha is in Urtsun Valley; Northern Kalasha in Rumbur, Bumboret, and Birir valleys. Indo-European, Indo-Iranian, Indo-Aryan, North-western zone, Dardic, Chitral. Dialects: SOUTHERN KALASHA (URTSUN), NORTHERN KALASHA (RUMBUR, BUMBORET, BIRIR). There may be an eastern dialect on the east side of the Chitral River south of Drosh. Related to Khowar. The southern dialect has 75% lexical similarity with the northern dialects, and there seems to be little contact between them. Proficiency in Khowar is limited; in Birir some men do not speak Khowar. Women are learning Khowar, and some learning Urdu. Kalasha is used in the home and for in-group communication in the north. In the south Khowar or Kati are sometimes used in the home and within the group. SOV. Pastoralists: goats, sheep, cattle; agriculturalists: wheat, barley, corn, apples, mulberries, walnuts, grapes. Traditional religion (north), Muslim (south).

KALKOTI [XKA] 4,000 or more (1990). Dir Kohistan, NWFP, in Kalkot village. A little more than half the people in the village are speakers. Indo-European, Indo-Iranian, Indo-Aryan, Northwestern zone, Dardic, Kohistani. 69% lexical similarity with Kalami. Kalami is used as second language. Kalami do not understand Kalkoti. All men and most women are reported to speak Pashto as second language. Muslim.

KAMVIRI ***(KAMDESHI, KAMIK, LAMERTIVIRI, SHEKHANI)*** [QMV] 1,500 to 2,000 in Pakistan plus refugees (1992). Southern Chitral District, Langorbat or Lamerot, Badrugal, and the Urtsun Valley. Indo-European, Indo-Iranian, Indo-Aryan, Nuristani. Dialects: KAMVIRI, SHEKHANI. Some bilingualism in Pashto. This Shekhani is different from the Kati dialect also called 'Shekhani'. Mountain valley. See main entry under Afghanistan.

KASHMIRI ***(KASCHEMIRI, KACMIRI, KESHURI, CASHMIRI, CASHMEEREE)*** [KSH] 105,000 in Pakistan (1993). Jammu and Kashmir, south of Shina. Indo-European, Indo-Iranian, Indo-Aryan, North-western zone, Dardic, Kashmiri. Transitional dialects to Panjabi. Kashtawari dialect is standard, other dialects are influenced by Dogri. Attitude of people toward own language is poor. Institute of Kashmir Studies in Muzaffarabad does some language promotion. May need different script for Pakistan. Radio programs. Bible 1899, out of print. See main entry under India.

KATI ***(KATIVIRI, BASHGALI, NURISTANI)*** [BSH] 3,700 to 5,100 Eastern Kativiri in Pakistan, plus refugees (1992). Eastern Kativiri is in the Chitral District; in Gobar in the Lutkuh Valley, Kunisht in the Rumbur Valley, Shekhanan Deh in the Bumboret Valley, and in the Urtsun Valley. Indo-European, Indo-Iranian, Indo-Aryan, Nuristani. Dialects: EASTERN KATIVIRI (SHEKHANI), WESTERN KATIVIRI, MUMVIRI. Mumviri may be a separate language. Eastern Kativiri is often called 'Shekhani' in Pakistan, but is different from the Kamviri which is also called 'Shekhani' in Southern Chitral. Mountain valleys. See main entry under Afghanistan.

KHETRANI [QKT] A few thousand (1987). Northeast Balochistan Province. Indo-European, Indo-Iranian, Indo-Aryan, Northwestern zone, Lahnda. Related to Siraiki. Influenced by Balochi. Literacy rate in first language: Below 1%. Literacy rate in second language: Below 5%. Muslim.

KHOWAR ***(KHAWAR, CHITRALI, CITRALI, CHITRARI, ARNIYA, PATU, QASHQARI, KASHKARI)*** [KHW] 222,800 (1992). Chitral; Shandur Pass to Fupis in Ghizr Valley, Yasin and Ishkhoman valleys in Gilgit Agency, Ushu in northern Swat Valley, and large communities in Peshawar and Rawalpindi. Indo-European, Indo-Iranian, Indo-Aryan, Northwestern zone, Dardic, Chitral. Dialects: NORTH KHOWAR, SOUTH KHOWAR, EAST KHOWAR, SWAT KHOWAR. The northern dialect is considered to be more 'pure'. Related to Kalasha, but different. 86% to 98% lexical similarity among dialects. Urdu schools; some girls go through fifth grade or higher. Different second languages used in different areas: Pashto in the south, Shina and Burushaski in the Gilgit Agency, Kalami and some Pashto in Swat, Urdu and English among the educated. The most important language of Chitral. Monthly journal in Khowar. 'Kho' means 'people', 'war' means 'language'. Trade language. SOV. Literacy rate in second language: 15% to 20% men, 1% women. Radio programs. Mountain valleys. Sunni and Ismaili Muslim.

KOHISTANI, INDUS ***(KOHISTANI, KOHISTE, KHILI, MAIYON, MAIR, MAIYÃ, SHUTHUN)*** [MVY] 220,000 (1993). Indus Kohistan District on the western bank of the Indus River. Indo-European, Indo-Iranian, Indo-Aryan, Northwestern zone, Dardic, Kohistani. Dialects: INDUS (MANI, SEO, PATTAN, JIJAL), DUBER-KANDIA (MANZARI, KHILI). A separate language from nearby varieties (Bateri, Chilisso, Gowro, Shina, Torwali, Kalami). The names 'Mani' and 'Manzari' are not used by speakers for the dialects, but refer to legendary brothers whose descendants settled in the two dialect areas. Lexical similarity among dialects is 90%. 70% lexical similarity with Chilisso, 61% with Gowro, 58% with Bateri, 49% with Shina, 28% with Kalami and Torwali.

KOLI, KACHI ***(KUCHI, KACHI, KATCHI, KOLI, KOHLI, KOLHI, KORI, VAGARI, VAGARIA, KACHI GUJARATI)*** [GJK] 170,000 or more in Pakistan including 80,000 to 100,000 Kachi Koli, 5,000 to 6,000 Rabari, 10,000 Kachi Bhil, 50,000 Vagri, 10,000 Katai Meghwar, 1,000 Zalavaria Koli (1998). Population total both countries 570,000 or more. Lower Sindh in an area bordered by Sakrand and Nawabshah in the north, Matli in the south, and east beyond Mirpur Khas and Jamesabad. Concentrated in an area around the towns of Tando Allahyar and Tando Adam. There may be an equal number in India, concentrated in their ancestral homeland centered around Bhuj, in the Rann of Kach, Gujarat. Also spoken in India. Indo-European, Indo-Iranian, Indo-Aryan, Central zone, Gujarati. Dialects: KACHI, RABARI (RAHABARI), KACHI BHIL, VAGRI (KACHI MEGHWAR), KATAI MEGHWAR, ZALAVARIA KOLI. Intermediate between Sindhi and Gujarati; it is becoming more like Sindhi. Kachi has 89% lexical similarity with Rabari, 96% with Kachi Bhil, 86% with Vagri, 92% with Katai Meghwar, 88% with Zalavaria Koli, 78% lexical similarity with Gujarati, 76% with Tharadari Koli. Complex situation: people with basically the same language are socially quite distinct. Literacy rate in first language: Below 1%. Literacy rate in second language: Below 5%. Based on Sindhi, based in turn on Arabic. Some older people use Gujarati script, related to Devanagri. Sharecropper agriculturalists. Hindu, Christian. Bible portions 1834-1995.

KOLI, PARKARI ***(PARKARI)*** [KVX] 250,000 (1995). Centered in Tharparkar District, especially the town of Nagar Parkar in the southeastern tip of Sindh bordering India. It covers most of the lower Thar desert and west as far as the Indus River, bordered in the north and west by Hyderabad, and down to the south and west of Badin. An unknown (probably small) population in India. Indo-European, Indo-Iranian, Indo-Aryan, Central zone, Gujarati. 77% to 83% lexical similarity with Marwari Bhil; 83% with Tharadari Koli. Literacy rate in first language: Below 1%. Literacy rate in second language: Below 5%, mostly in Sindhi, a few in Urdu, very few in Gujarati. Based on Sindhi, based in turn on Arabic. Agriculturalists: sharecroppers in irrigated area, subsistence and stockbreeders in desert (east). Hindu, Christian. NT 1996.

KOLI, WADIYARA ***(WADARIA, WADHIARA)*** [KXP] 175,000 to 180,000 in Pakistan, including 75,000 Wadiyara, 5,000 to 10,000 Mewasi and Nairya, 30,000 Tharadari, 45,000 Hasoria, 20,000 Rardro (1998). Population total both countries 350,000 to 360,000. Sind in an area bounded by Hyderabad, Tando Allahyar and Mirpur Khas in the north, and Matli and Jamesabad in the south. Also spoken in India. Indo-European, Indo-Iranian, Indo-Aryan, Central zone, Gujarati. Dialects: MEWASI (MAYVASI KOLI), WADIYARA KOLI, NAIRYA KOLI, THARADARI KOLI, THARADARI BHIL, HASORIA KOLI, HASORIA BHIL, RARDRO BHIL. Mewasi and Wadiyara are almost the same linguistically, and are coming together as a caste. Dialects listed are distinct sociolinguistic endogamous ethnic groups. 78% lexical similarity with Kachi Koli. There is gradual beginning of breakdown of some strict caste rules concerning intermarriage and interdining: possibly 'lower' groups wishing to move 'up', and barriers in 'close' castes breaking down. Investigation needed: intelligibility with Kachi Koli, Wadiyara dialects. Literacy rate in first language: Below 1%. Literacy rate in second language: Below 5%.

LASI ***(LASSI)*** [LSS] 15,000 (1998). Southeast Balochistan Province, Las Bela District, about 80 miles north northwest of Karachi. Indo-European, Indo-Iranian, Indo-Aryan, Northwestern zone, Sindhi. Influenced by Balochi. Literacy rate in first language: Below 1%. Literacy rate in second language: Below 5%. Muslim.

LOARKI [LRK] 20,000 to 25,000 in Pakistan (1998). Sindh Province, rural. 500 to 750 in India. Indo-European, Indo-Iranian, Indo-Aryan, Central zone, Rajasthani, Marwari. Probably the same as Gade Lohar [GDA] in Rajasthan, India, a Rajasthani language. 82% lexical similarity with Jogi, 80% with Marwari. All ages and sexes speak Sindhi, the educated or those working outside the community speak Urdu for most common topics. Loarki is used for all in-group functions. All ages. Alternate names for the people are: Loar, Lohar, Gadlia, Gadolia Rajput, Gadolia Rajput Loar, Karia, Sisudia Rajput, Sisudia Loar. Literacy rate in second language: 25% boys, some older men, no girls or women in Sindhi, some Urdu. Desert. Plains. Craftsmen. 0 to 100 meters. Hindu.

MARWARI ***(MERWARI, RAJASTHANI, MARWARI MEGHWAR, JAISELMER, MARAWAR, MARWARI BHIL)*** [MRI] 220,000 including 100,000 Northern Marwari, 120,000 or more Southern Marwari (1998). The latter includes 100,000 Marwari Bhil, 10,000 Marwari Meghwar, 12,000 to 13,000 Marwari Bhat. Northern Marwari: South Punjab and northern Sindh, north of Dadu and Nawabshah; Southern Marwari:

Sindh and southern Punjab provinces, between Tando Mohammed Khan and Tando Ghulam Ali to the south, Dadu and Nawabshab to the north. Indo-European, Indo-Iranian, Indo-Aryan, Central zone, Rajasthani, Marwari. Dialects: NORTHERN MARWARI, SOUTHERN MARWARI, MARWARI BHIL, MARWARI MEGHWAR, MARWARI BHAT. Northern and Southern Marwari are inherently intelligible to speakers. May or may not be the same as Marwari in Rajasthan, India. 79% to 83% lexical similarity with Dhatki, 87% between Southern and Northern Marwari, 78% with Marwari Meghwar and Marwari Bhat. Speakers are moderately bilingual in Sindhi. Educated speakers are trilingual in Urdu. The literary language of Rajasthan is Hindi. One sweeper community of 10,000 to 100,000 identifies itself as Marwari, but is undergoing rapid shift to Urdu. Marwari is not usually written. The name 'Rajasthani' is a linguistic cover term for a group of languages. Speakers tend to be urban and educated. Northern Bhil tribes: Marwari-Thori, Gulguli, Shikari, Jogi, Sochi. Literacy rate in first language: Below 1%. Literacy rate in second language: Below 5% in Sindhi or Urdu. Sindhi and Urdu scripts. Newspapers. Hindu, Muslim, Christian. Bible portions 1969-1991.

MEMONI [MBY] Karachi. Indo-European, Indo-Iranian, Indo-Aryan, Unclassified. Memoni language appears to have similarities to Sindhi and Gujarati. They learn Urdu, Sindhi, or Gujarati as second language. The younger generation might not learn it as mother tongue. All speakers in Pakistan came from India at the time of the partition. It is reported that 500 to 600 years ago they moved from a Sindhi-speaking area to a Gujarati-speaking area. They tend to be highly educated. It is unwritten, but could be written in Gujarati script. Muslim.

OD ***(OAD, ODKI)*** [ODK] 50,000 (1998). Widely scattered in the Sindh and a few in southern Punjab. May also be in Rajasthan, India. Indo-European, Indo-Iranian, Indo-Aryan, Unclassified. Resembles Marathi with Gujarati features and borrowings from Marwari and Panjabi. 86% to 88% lexical similarity among dialects in Dadu, Shikarpur, and Pithoro. 70% to 78% lexical similarity with Marwari, Dhatki, and Bagri. 80% are bilingual in Sindhi; 10% are trilingual in Urdu, Sindhi, and Odki. Sindhi. Brickmakers, builders.

ORMURI ***(URMURI, ORMUR, ORMUI, BARGISTA, BARAKS, BARAKI)*** [ORU] 3,000 or more in Pakistan (1992). Population total both countries 3,050 or more. Kaniguram, a pocket in Mahsud Pashto area northwest of Dera Ismail Khan, Wazirstan. Also spoken in Afghanistan. Indo-European, Indo-Iranian, Iranian, Western, Northwestern, Ormuri-Parachi. Dialects: KANIGURAMI, LOGAR. 27% lexical similarity with Waneci, 25% to 33% with Pashto dialects. The Kanigurami retain the language.

PAHARI-POTWARI ***(POTWARI, POTHOHARI, POTOHARI, CHIBHALI, DHUNDI-KAIRALI)*** [PHR] Murree Hills north of Rawalpindi, and east to Azad Kashmir. To the north in the lower half of the Neelum Valley. Poonchi is east of Rawalakot. Potwari is in the plains around Rawalpindi. Punchhi and Chibhali are reported to be in Jammu and Kashmir. Indo-European, Indo-Iranian, Indo-Aryan, Northern zone, Western Pahari. Dialects: PAHARI (DHUNDI-KAIRALI), POTHWARI (POTWARI), CHIBHALI, PUNCHHI (POONCHI), MIRPURI. Pahari means 'hill language' referring to a string of divergent dialects, some of which may be separate languages. A dialect chain with Panjabi and Hindko. Closeness to western Pahari is unknown. 76% to 83% lexical similarity among varieties called 'Pahari', 'Potwari', and some called 'Hindko' in Mansehra, Muzzaffarabad, and Jammun. Investigation needed: intelligibility with Pahadi, Panjabi. Muslim.

PAKISTAN SIGN LANGUAGE ***(ISHARON KI ZUBANN)*** [PKS] Deaf sign language. Related to Nepalese Sign Language; may be the same language as Indian Sign Language. Used in urban centers with some regional variation in vocabulary. The National Institute of Special Education encourages a total communication approach, including the teaching of PSL. Dictionary. Grammar.

PANJABI, WESTERN ***(WESTERN PUNJABI, LAHNDA, LAHANDA, LAHNDI)*** [PNB] 30,000,000 to 45,000,000 in Pakistan (1981 census). Population total all countries 30,000,000 to 45,000,000. Mainly in the Punjab area of Pakistan. Also spoken in Afghanistan, Canada, India, UAE, United Kingdom, USA. Indo-European, Indo-Iranian, Indo-Aryan, Northwestern zone, Lahnda. Dialect: MAJHI. There is a continuum of varieties between Eastern and Western Panjabi, and with Western Hindi and Urdu. 'Lahnda' is a name given earlier for Western Panjabi; an attempt to cover the dialect continuum between Hindko, Pahari-Potwari, and Western Panjabi in the north and Sindhi in the south. Grierson said Majhi is the purest form of Panjabi. Several dozen dialects. The Balmiki (Valmiki) sweeper caste in Attock District speak a dialect of Panjabi. Perso-Arabic script used, but not often written in Pakistan. Radio programs, films, TV. Mainly Muslim; Christian. NT 1819-1952.

PASHTO, CENTRAL ***(MAHSUDI)*** [PST] Wazirstan, Bannu, Karak, southern tribal territories and adjacent areas. Indo-European, Indo-Iranian, Iranian, Eastern, Southeastern, Pashto. Dialects: WACIRI (WAZIRI), BANNUCHI (BANNOCHI, BANNU). Lexical comparison and interviews indicate this is distinct from Northern and Southern Pashto. Dictionary. Grammar. Sunni Muslim.

PASHTO, NORTHERN ***(PAKHTO, PUSHTO)*** [PBU] 9,585,000 in Pakistan or 8.47% of population, including Southern Pashto (1993 estimate). Population total all countries 9,685,000. Along Afghanistan border, most of NWFP, Yusufzai and Peshawar. Also spoken in Afghanistan, India, UAE, United Kingdom. Indo-European,

Indo-Iranian, Iranian, Eastern, Southeastern, Pashto. Dialects: NINGRAHARIAN PASHTO, NORTHEASTERN PASHTO. A good deal of similarity with Northwestern Pashto in Afghanistan. Subdialects of Northeastern Pashto are Kohat (Khatak), Yusufzai (Peshawar), Afridi, Shinwari, Mohmand, Shilmani. There is generally an 80% lexical similarity between Northeastern and Southwestern Pashto. Rich literary tradition. The Powinda are a nomadic Pashto-speaking group. Dictionary. Literacy rate in second language: Low. Modified Perso-Arabic script used. Used in schools and media in NWFP and adjacent tribal territories. Newspapers, radio programs, films, TV. Sunni Muslim, some Shi'a. Bible 1895.

PASHTO, SOUTHERN ***(PUSHTO, PUSHTU)*** [PBT] 1,000,000 to 1,500,000 in Pakistan (1992). Baluchistan, Quetta area. Indo-European, Indo-Iranian, Iranian, Eastern, Southeastern, Pashto. Dialects: SOUTHEASTERN PASHTO, QUETTA PASHTO. 80% lexical similarity with Northern Pashto, 76% with Central Pashto. Some Pashto speakers educated in Urdu medium schools mix Urdu into their Pashto speech. Perso-Arabic script used. Muslim. See main entry under Afghanistan.

PHALURA ***(PALULA, PALOLA, PHALULO, DANGARIK, BIYORI)*** [PHL] 8,600 (1990). 7 villages on the east side of the lower Chitral Valley, possibly 1 village in Dir Kohistan; Purigal, Ghos, the Biori Valley, Kalkatak, and Ashret. Indo-European, Indo-Iranian, Indo-Aryan, Northwestern zone, Dardic, Shina. Dialects: ASHRETI, NORTHERN PHALURA. Ashreti has 92% lexical similarity with Northern Phalura. 56% to 58% lexical similarity with Savi in Afghanistan, 38% to 42% with Shina. Bilingualism in Khowar. Speakers are called 'Phalulo'. Sunni Muslim.

SANSI ***(BHILKI)*** [SSI] 10,000 (1998). Northern Sindh Province, main town, and some in Karachi. The Sochi live throughout Sindh. Indo-European, Indo-Iranian, Indo-Aryan, Central zone, Western Hindi, Hindustani, Sansi. Dialect: SOCHI. The Sochi (100,000) speak a related variety. They sometimes identify themselves as Sansi or Marwari. 71% lexical similarity with Urdu, 83% with the Sochi language variety. Second language is Sindhi, followed by Urdu, Panjabi, and Saraiki. Bhils by caste. Investigation needed: bilingual proficiency in Sindhi, Urdu, Panjabi, Saraiki. Literacy rate in first language: Below 1%. Literacy rate in second language: Below 5%. Begging, sharecroppers, cobblers (Sochi). Hindu.

SARAIKI ***(RIASITI, BAHAWALPURI, MULTANI, SOUTHERN PANJABI, SIRAIKI)*** [SKR] 15,000,000 to 30,000,000 in Pakistan (1998), 9.8% of the population. Population total all countries 15,059,000 to 30,000,000. Southern Punjab and northern Sind, Indus River Valley, Jampur area. Derawali is in Dera Ismail Khan, Tank, Bannu, and Dera Ghazi Khan. Jangli is in Sahiwal area. Also spoken in India, United Kingdom. Indo-European, Indo-Iranian, Indo-Aryan, Northwestern zone, Lahnda. Dialects: DERAWALI, MULTANI (KHATKI), BAHAWALPURI (RIASATI, REASATI), JANGLI, JATKI. Dialects blend into each other, into Panjabi to the east, and Sindhi to the south. Until recently it was considered to be a dialect of Panjabi. 85% lexical similarity with Sindhi; 68% with Dhatki, Odki, and Sansi. Dictionary. Grammar. Literacy rate in first language: Below 1%. Literacy rate in second language: 5% to 15%. Radio programs, TV. Muslim, Hindu. NT 1819, out of print.

SAVI ***(SAWI, SAUJI, SAU)*** [SDG] Some might still live in refugee camps near Timargarha in Dir, Pakistan and near Drosh in Chitral, Pakistan. Probably most have returned to Afghanistan. Indo-European, Indo-Iranian, Indo-Aryan, Northwestern zone, Dardic, Shina. Bilingualism in Pashto. Investigation needed: bilingual proficiency in Pashto. Literacy rate in first language: Below 1%. Literacy rate in second language: 5% to 15%. Muslim. See main entry under Afghanistan.

SHINA ***(SINA, SHINAKI, BROKPA)*** [SCL] 300,000 in Pakistan (1981 census). Population total both countries 320,000. Northern Areas including Gilgit District, scattered villages in Yasin and Ishkoman valleys, Punial, Gilgit, Haramosh, lower Hunza Valley; Diamer District, Chilas area, Darel and Tangir valleys, Astor Valley; scattered areas of Baltistan District, Satpara, Kharmang, Kachura, and other small valleys; NWFP, east part of Kohistan District, Sazin, Harban. Also spoken in India. Indo-European, Indo-Iranian, Indo-Aryan, Northwestern zone, Dardic, Shina. Dialects: GILGITI (GILGIT, PUNIAL, HUNZA-NAGAR, BAGROTE, HARAMOSH, RONDU, BUNJI), ASTORI (ASTOR, GUREZI, DRAS, SATPARA, KHARMANGI), CHILASI KOHISTANI (CHILAS, DAREL, TANGIR, SAZIN, HARBAN). Gilgit functions as the language standard. Shina is the primary language in Gilgit and Diamer districts. 79% to 99% lexical similarity within the Gilgiti (Northern) dialect cluster, 81% to 96% among the Astori (Eastern) cluster, 84% to 98% among the Chilas (Diamer) cluster. 'Brokpa' is the name used for Shina speakers in Baltistan and Ladakh. 'Brokskat' refers to their language. 'Brokskat' is used semi-officially in India to refer to a highly divergent variety of Shina spoken by Buddhists. Muslim, some Shi'a, some Sunni. Bible portions 1929.

SHINA, KOHISTANI ***(PALASI-KOHISTANI, KOHISTANI, KOHISTYO)*** [PLK] 200,000 (1981 census). East bank of the Indus in Kohistan District, NWFP, in the Jalkot, Palas, and Kolai valleys and surrounding areas. Indo-European, Indo-Iranian, Indo-Aryan, Northwestern zone, Dardic, Shina. Dialects: PALASI, JALKOTI, KOLAI. A somewhat divergent variety of Shina linguistically and socially. Closer to Shina of Chilas, but more different from that of Gilgit. Mainly Sunni Muslim.

SINDHI [SND] 16,992,000 in Pakistan (1993 Johnstone), including 1,200,000 Hindu Sindhi (1986). Population total all countries 19,720,000 or more. Sindh. Also possibly United Arab Emirates. Also spoken in India, Oman, Philippines, Singapore, United Kingdom, USA. Indo-European, Indo-Iranian, Indo-Aryan, Northwestern zone, Sindhi. Dialects: KACHCHI, LARI, LASI, THARELI, VICHOLO (VICHOLI, VICCHOLI, CENTRAL SINDHI), MACHARIA, DUKSLINU (HINDU SINDHI), SINDHI MUSALMANI (MUSLIM SINDHI). Some southern Bhil groups speak dialects of Sindhi. Katiavari Kachi has 77% lexical similarity with Sindhi. 100,000 speakers in rural Sindh came originally from the Kathiawar Peninsula in India. They are solidly Muslim, have widespread bilingualism in Sindh, and are almost completely assimilated with the Sindhi people. Some Hindu speakers are first language speakers, most are second language speakers. Shikari (hunter) Bhils are a nomadic group of 2,000 to 3,000 who live in southern Sindh Province, centered around Badin, and have adopted the Sindhi language. Some are Hindu, others are Muslim. They are not literate. Official language. Dictionary. Arabic script used in Pakistan. Muslim, Hindu, Christian (a few). Bible 1954.

SINDHI BHIL [SBN] 10,000 to 50,000 (1998). Sindh Province, Mohrano, Badin-Matli-Thatta, Ghorabari (on west). Sindhi Meghwar are scattered in an area from Badin-Matli to Tando Allahyar. Indo-European, Indo-Iranian, Indo-Aryan, Northwestern zone, Sindhi. Dialects: SINDHI BHIL, MOHRANO, BADIN, SINDHI MEGHWAR. Badin is close to Sindhi. Mohrani has 82% lexical similarity with Sindhi; Sindhi Bhil has 89% with Sindhi Meghwar. They can converse in Sindhi, those in Mohrano area also in Dhatki. Women use Sindhi Bhil when talking to Sindhi and Dhatki speakers. Speakers consider the Mohrano dialect to be different from Sindhi and Dhatki. There is a positive attitude toward its use in traditional ceremonies. They have positive attitudes toward the Dhatki Bhil and Marwari Bhil, and there is intermarriage with them. The Dhatki Bhil tend to look down on the Sindhi Bhil. The Sindhi Bhil look with favor on the idea of literature in their language. Investigation needed: intelligibility with Sindhi, Dhatki. Sindhi or Dhatki orthographies acceptable. Hindu (mainly, Mohrano area), Muslim (more in Badin area).

TORWALI ***(TURVALI)*** [TRW] 60,000 (1987). Swat Kohistan, on both sides of Swat River from just beyond Madyan north to Asrit (between Mankjal and Peshmal), and in Chail Valley east of Madyan, Bahrain and Chail are centers. Indo-European, Indo-Iranian, Indo-Aryan, Northwestern zone, Dardic, Kohistani. Dialects: BAHRAIN, CHAIL. 44% lexical similarity with Kalkoti and Kalami, 89% between Behrain and Chail. Men are fairly bilingual in Pashto, more limited in Urdu. Women are limited in use of Pashto, and know almost no Urdu. Sunni Muslim.

URDU [URD] 10,719,000 mother tongue speakers in Pakistan (1993), 7.57% of the population. Population total all countries 60,290,000 or more. Including second language speakers: 104,000,000 (1999 WA). Also spoken in Afghanistan, Bahrain, Bangladesh, Botswana, Fiji, Germany, Guyana, India, Malawi, Mauritius, Nepal, Norway, Oman, Qatar, Saudi Arabia, South Africa, Thailand, UAE, United Kingdom, Zambia. Indo-European, Indo-Iranian, Indo-Aryan, Central zone, Western Hindi, Hindustani. Intelligible with Hindi, but has formal vocabulary borrowed from Arabic and Persian. The second or third language of most Pakistanis for whom it is not the mother tongue. National language. Grammar. Arabic script in Nastaliq style with several extra characters used. Muslim. Bible 1843-1998.

USHOJO ***(USHUJI)*** [USH] 2,000 (1992). Upper reaches of Bishigram (Chail) Valley, east of Madyan, Swat Kohistan. 12 villages. Indo-European, Indo-Iranian, Indo-Aryan, Northwestern zone, Dardic, Shina. 50% lexical similarity with Kolai Shina, 48% with Palas Shina, 42% with Gilgiti Shina, 35% with Chail Torwali, 31% with Biori Phalura, 27% with Bateri, 23% with Kalami, 22% with Kalkoti. Pashto seems to be influencing some adult speech. Pashto appears to be the main second language used. Education in Urdu is limited. Torwali is also used. Children are learning Ushojo in the home. Not known by linguists until 1989. Reportedly came from Kolai, Indus Kohistan several hundred years ago. SOV. Mountain valleys. Sunni Muslim.

VAGHRI ***(VAGHRI KOLI, SALAVTA, BAVRI)*** [VGR] 10,000 in Pakistan (1998). Sindh, in Sukkur, Karachi (Bhes Colony), Nawabshah, Sakrand, Hala, Sanghar, Tando Adam, Tando Mohammed Khan, Badin, Matli, Tando Ghulam Ali, Digri, Noakot, Jang Sai, Mirpur Khas, and Tando Allahyar. Possibly 90,000 in India. Indo-European, Indo-Iranian, Indo-Aryan, Central zone, Gujarati. Reported to be related to the language spoken by the Kukar people living near Chanesar Halt, Mehmoodabad in Karachi. 78% lexical similarity with Wadiyari Koli. They speak some Sindhi, Urdu, and Gujarati. People are urbanized. Literacy rate in first language: Below 1%. Literacy rate in second language: Below 5%. Masons, fruit vendors. Hindu.

WAKHI ***(WAKHANI, WAKHIGI, VAKHAN, KHIK)*** [WBL] 9,100 in Pakistan including 4,500 to 6,000 Gojal, 2,000 Ishkoman, 200 Yasin, 900 Yarkhun (1992), plus refugees. Population total all countries 29,000. Northeasternmost part of Chitral, called Baroghil area; in glacier neighborhood. Gojal is in the upper Hunza valley from Gulmit to the Chinese and Afghanistan borders, and the Shimshal and Chupursan valleys; also in upper Yarkhun valley of Chitral, and upper Ishkoman valley. Also spoken in Afghanistan, China, Tajikistan. Indo-European, Indo-Iranian, Iranian, Eastern, Southeastern, Pamir. Dialects: GOJAL, ISHKOMAN, YASIN, YARKHUN. Dialect intelligibility is reported to not be a problem even with those in other countries. Ishkoman and Gojal have 84% lexical similarity, Yasin and Gojal 89%, Ishkoman and Yasin 91%. Men and young people are fairly bilingual in Urdu. Fewer than half the women, and few older people in remote areas speak Urdu. Older people and those who live in mixed villages in Gojal can use Burushaski. Speakers have a positive language attitude toward Wakhi and Urdu. The people are called 'Guhjali' in upper Hunza, but call themselves 'Khik'. Valleys. Pastoralists: sheep, goats, cattle, yak, camels; agriculturalists: barley. Ismaili Muslim.

WANECI ***(WANECHI, WANETSI, VANECHI, TARINO, CHALGARI)*** [WNE] 95,000 (1998). Northeastern Balochistan Province, Harnai area. Indo-European, Indo-Iranian, Iranian, Eastern, Southeastern, Pashto. 71% to 75% lexical similarity with Southern Pashto, 63% to 72% with other Pashto varieties, 27% with Ormuri. Literacy rate in first language: Below 1%. Literacy rate in second language: Below 5%. Muslim.

YIDGHA ***(YUDGHA, YUDGA, YIDGA, LUTKUHWAR)*** [YDG] 5,000 to 6,000 (1991). Upper Lutkuh Valley of Chitral, west of Garam Chishma. Indo-European, Indo-Iranian, Iranian, Eastern, Southeastern, Pamir. No significant dialect variation within Yidgha. Lexical similarity with Munji in Afghanistan is estimated at 56% to 80%. Yidgha is used in many homes and for much in-group communication, and speakers have positive attitudes toward it. Khowar is the main second language used, although with much Yidgha language influence, and proficiency among women is limited. Mountain valleys. 7,600 to 7,900 feet. Ismaili Muslim.

PALESTINIAN WEST BANK AND GAZA

National or official language: Standard Arabic. 1,036,000 (1998 UN). Recognized by the United Nations during the interim period, based on the Israeli-Palestinian Declaration of Principles of 1993. Also includes Armenian, Hebrew 200,000. Information mainly from W. Fischer and O. Jastrow 1980. Muslim, Christian, Samaritan. Data accuracy estimate: B. The number of languages listed for Palestinian West Bank and Gaza is 6. Of those, 4 are living languages and 2 are extinct. Diversity index 0.21.

ARABIC, LEVANTINE BEDAWI SPOKEN ***(BEDAWI)*** [AVL] 10,000 in Palestinian West Bank and Gaza (1996). Judean desert and along the Jordan River. Afro-Asiatic, Semitic, Central, South, Arabic. Dialects: SOUTH LEVANTINE BEDAWI ARABIC, NORTH LEVANTINE BEDAWI ARABIC, EASTERN EGYPTIAN BEDAWI ARABIC. Sunni Muslim. See main entry under Egypt.

ARABIC, SOUTH LEVANTINE SPOKEN ***(BEDAWI)*** [AJP] 1,600,000 in Palestinian West Bank and Gaza (1996). Afro-Asiatic, Semitic, Central, South, Arabic. Dialects: MADANI, FELLAHI. Bilingualism in Hebrew. Distinct from North Levantine (Lebanese-Syrian) Arabic. Muslim, Christian. Bible portions 1940-1973. See main entry under Jordan.

ARABIC, STANDARD [ABV] Middle East, North Africa. Afro-Asiatic, Semitic, Central, South, Arabic. Used for education, official purpose, formal speeches. Newspapers. Bible 1984-1991. See main entry under Saudi Arabia.

DOMARI ***(DOM, NEAR-EASTERN GYPSY)*** [RMT] (2,000 including Israel; 1997). Gaza and Bir Zeit near Ramallah. Indo-European, Indo-Iranian, Indo-Aryan, Central zone, Dom. Dialect: NAWARI. Not intelligible to Romani speakers. Bilingualism in South Levantine Spoken Arabic. The first language of children in some places. They call themselves 'Dom'. A large number of loan words from Arabic, Kurdish, and some other Iranian languages. Grammar. Muslim. See main entry under Iran.

SAMARITAN ***(SAMARITAN HEBREW)*** [SMP] (620 ethnic Samaritans; 1999 H. Mutzafi). West bank near Nablus and in Tel Aviv, Israel. Also spoken in Israel. Afro-Asiatic, Semitic, Central, South, Canaanite. They use Samaritan Hebrew mainly and Samaritan Aramaic secondarily as liturgical languages. About one-third live near Nablus and speak Palestinian Arabic as mother tongue. Others live near Tel Aviv and speak Hebrew as mother tongue. They call themselves 'Shamerim'. Samaritan-Hebrew script used. Samaritan religion, related to Judaism. Extinct. Bible 1853.

SAMARITAN ARAMAIC [SRA] (620 ethnic Samaritans; 1999 H. Mutzafi). West bank near Nablus and in Tel Aviv, Israel. Also spoken in Israel. Afro-Asiatic, Semitic, Central, Aramaic, Western. The language ceased to be spoken as mother tongue in the 10th to 12th centuries A.D. They use Samaritan Hebrew mainly and Samaritan Aramaic secondarily as liturgical languages. About one-third live near Nablus and speak Palestinian Arabic as mother tongue. Others live near Tel Aviv and speak Hebrew as mother tongue. They call themselves 'Shamerim'. Samaritan religion, related to Judaism. Extinct.

PHILIPPINES

Republic of the Philippines. National or official languages: Tagalog (Pilipino, Filipino), English. 72,944,000 (1998 UN). Literacy rate 88% to 89%. Also includes Basque, Dutch 506, French 698, Standard German 961, Hindi 2,415, Indonesian 2,580, Italian 97, Japanese 2,899, Korean, Sindhi

20,000, Vietnamese, Arabic. Information mainly from L. A. Reid 1971; SIL 1954-1999. Christian, Muslim, secular, traditional religion. Blind population 1,144,500. Deaf population 100,000 to 4,232,519 (1998). Deaf institutions: 17. Data accuracy estimate: A1, A2. The number of languages listed for Philippines is 172. Of those, 169 are living languages and 3 are extinct. Diversity index 0.85.

ADASEN ***(ADDASEN TINGUIAN, ADDASEN, ADASEN ITNEG)*** [TIU] 4,000 (NTM). Luzon, northeastern Abra Province. Austronesian, Malayo-Polynesian, Western Malayo-Polynesian, Northern Philippine, Northern Luzon, Northern Cordilleran, Ibanagic, Isnag. Dialects: EASTERN ADDASEN, WESTERN ADDASEN. Comprehension of Isnag 74%. Very bilingual in Ilocano. NT 1990.

AGTA, ALABAT ISLAND ***(ALABAT ISLAND DUMAGAT)*** [DUL] 50 (1979 SIL). East of Quezon Province, Luzon. Austronesian, Malayo-Polynesian, Western Malayo-Polynesian, Northern Philippine, Northern Luzon, Northern Cordilleran, Dumagat, Southern. Bilingualism in Tagalog.

AGTA, CAMARINES NORTE ***(MANIDE, AGIYAN)*** [ABD] 200 (1979 SIL). Luzon, Santa Elena and Labo, Camarines Norte. Austronesian, Malayo-Polynesian, Western Malayo-Polynesian, Northern Philippine, Northern Luzon, Northern Cordilleran, Dumagat, Southern. 67% lexical similarity with Alabat Agta, 35% with Mt. Iriga Agta. Investigation needed: bilingual proficiency in Tagalog.

AGTA, CASIGURAN DUMAGAT ***(CASIGURAN DUMAGAT)*** [DGC] 580 (1998 T. Headland). East coast of Luzon, Aurora Province. Austronesian, Malayo-Polynesian, Western Malayo-Polynesian, Northern Philippine, Northern Luzon, Northern Cordilleran, Dumagat, Northern. Intelligibility of Paranan 83%. Bilingualism in Tagalog. Negrito. Literacy rate in first language: 2.4%. Literacy rate in second language: 2.4%. Hunter-gatherers. NT 1979.

AGTA, CENTRAL CAGAYAN [AGT] 700 to 800 (1998 SIL). Northeast Luzon. Austronesian, Malayo-Polynesian, Western Malayo-Polynesian, Northern Philippine, Northern Luzon, Northern Cordilleran, Dumagat, Northern. Negrito. Literacy rate in first language: 6%. Literacy rate in second language: 6%. Christian. NT 1992.

AGTA, DICAMAY ***(DICAMAY DUMAGAT)*** [DUY] Luzon, Isabela Province, near Jones. Austronesian, Malayo-Polynesian, Western Malayo-Polynesian, Northern Philippine, Northern Luzon, Northern Cordilleran, Dumagat, Northern. Extinct.

AGTA, DUPANINAN ***(EASTERN CAGAYAN AGTA)*** [DUO] 1,200 (1986 SIL). Northeast Luzon, from below Divilacan Bay in the south to Palaui Island in the north. Austronesian, Malayo-Polynesian, Western Malayo-Polynesian, Northern Philippine, Northern Luzon, Northern Cordilleran, Dumagat, Northern. Dialects: YAGA, TANGLAGAN, SANTA ANA-GONZAGA, BARONGAGUNAY, PALAUI ISLAND, CAMONAYAN, VALLEY COVE, BOLOS POINT, PEÑABLANCA, ROSO (SOUTHEAST CAGAYAN), SANTA MARGARITA. Yaga and Central Cagayan Agta are 63% intelligible. Central Cagayan Agta and Tanglagan have 51% lexical similarity; Yaga and Central Cagayan Agta have 66%. A small sample of speakers of Yaga had 70% comprehension of Ilocano. Literacy rate in first language: Below 1%. Literacy rate in second language: Below 1%. Hunter-gatherers. Bible portions 1986.

AGTA, ISAROG [AGK] (1,000 in ethnic group; 1984 SIL). Mt. Isarog east of Naga City, Bicol Province, Luzon. Austronesian, Malayo-Polynesian, Western Malayo-Polynesian, Meso Philippine, Central Philippine, Bikol, Coastal, Naga. Bilingualism in Central Bicolano. Nearly extinct.

AGTA, MT. IRAYA ***(INAGTA OF MT. IRAYA, RUGNOT OF LAKE BUHI EAST, LAKE BUHI EAST, ITBEG RUGNOT)*** [ATL] 200 (1979 SIL). East of Lake Buhi, Bicol Province, Luzon. Austronesian, Malayo-Polynesian, Western Malayo-Polynesian, Meso Philippine, Central Philippine, Bikol, Coastal, Naga. 54% to 86% comprehension of Naga (Central) Bicolano, 94% comprehension of Mt. Iriga Agta, Iriga City dialect. Four dialects 93% lexically similar with each other. 85% to 90% lexical similarity with Bicolano, 70% with Mt. Iriga Agta, Iriga City dialect. A population sample had 45% comprehension of Tagalog narrative. Heavy borrowing from Legaspi (Central) Bicolano.

AGTA, MT. IRIGA ***(SAN RAMON INAGTA, LAKE BUHI WEST, MT. IRIGA NEGRITO)*** [AGZ] 1,500 (1979 SIL). East of Iriga City, west of Lake Buhi, Bicol Province, Luzon. Austronesian, Malayo-Polynesian, Western Malayo-Polynesian, Meso Philippine, Central Philippine, Bikol, Inland. 86% intelligibility of Iriga City Bicolano, 82% of Mt. Iraya, 72% of Central Bicolano (Naga). It is doubtful whether Naga Bicolano is adequately understandable to Mt. Iriga Agta speakers. 76% lexical similarity of Iriga City Bicolano, 66% of Mt. Iraya, 66% lexical similarity of Central Bicolano (Naga). Moderate comprehension of Tagalog. Iriga City Bicolano has higher prestige. Iriga City inhabitants regard Naga as true Bicolano.

AGTA, REMONTADO ***(HATANG-KAYEY, SINAUNA)*** [AGV] 1,000 to 2,000 (1977 SIL). Luzon; Santa Inez, Rizal Province; Paimohuan, General Nakar, Quezon Province. Austronesian, Malayo-Polynesian, Western Malayo-Polynesian, Northern Philippine, Bashiic-Central Luzon-Northern Mindoro, Central Luzon, Sinauna. 73% lexical similarity with Tagalog, 37% with Umiray Dumaget. Fairly bilingual in Tagalog. No schools.

AGTA, UMIRAY DUMAGET ***(UMIREY DUMAGAT, UMIRAY AGTA)*** [DUE] 3,000 (1994 SIL). Quezon Province, Luzon. Austronesian, Malayo-Polynesian, Western Malayo-Polynesian, Northern Philippine, Northern Luzon, Northern Cordilleran, Dumagat, Southern. Dialects: PALAUI ISLAND AGTA, ANGLAT AGTA. Fairly fluent in Tagalog. Literacy rate in first language: 5% to 10%. Literacy rate in second language: 5% to 10%. Hunter-gatherers. NT 1977.

AGTA, VILLA VICIOSA [DYG] Luzon, Abra Province. Austronesian, Malayo-Polynesian, Western Malayo-Polynesian, Northern Philippine, Northern Luzon, Northern Cordilleran, Ibanagic, Ibanag. Bilingualism in Ilocano. Investigation needed: intelligibility with Adasen Itneg, Isnag, bilingual proficiency in Ilocano.

AGUTAYNEN ***(AGUTAYNON, AGUTAYNO)*** [AGN] 10,384 (1990 census). Agutaya Island, five smaller surrounding islands, and the municipalities of Roxas, San Vicente, and Brooke's Point, Palawan. A few also in Taytay, Linapacan, on Mindoro, and in Manila. Austronesian, Malayo-Polynesian, Western Malayo-Polynesian, Meso Philippine, Kalamian. 52% lexical similarity with Cuyonon; 71% with Calamian Tagbanwa. Limited bilingual proficiency by most speakers in Cuyonon, Tagalog, or English. Culturally lowland. Literacy rate in first language: 90%. Literacy rate in second language: 90%. Videos. Subsistence agriculturalists: rice; fishermen. Bible portions 1989-1993.

AKLANON ***(AKLAN, AKLANO, PANAY, AKLANON-BISAYAN)*** [AKL] 394,545 (1990 census). Aklan Province, northern Panay. Austronesian, Malayo-Polynesian, Western Malayo-Polynesian, Meso Philippine, Central Philippine, Bisayan, West, Aklan. 66% intelligibility of Hiligaynon. 68% lexical similarity with Hiligaynon. Bilingualism in Hiligaynon. Literacy rate in first language: 69.7%. Literacy rate in second language: 69.7%. Bible portions 1990-1993.

ALANGAN [ALJ] 6,000 to 7,000 (1991 SIL). North central Mindoro. Austronesian, Malayo-Polynesian, Western Malayo-Polynesian, Northern Philippine, Bashiic-Central Luzon-Northern Mindoro, Northern Mindoro. NT 1989.

ALTA, NORTHERN ***(EDIMALA, BALER NEGRITO, DITAYLIN ALTA, DITAYLIN DUMAGAT)*** [AQN] 240 speakers, 60 families (1992 L. Reid). Eastern Luzon, Aurora Province, Bayanihan, San Luis; Diteki, the first settlement along the road after coming through the mountains from Cabanatuan. Austronesian, Malayo-Polynesian, Western Malayo-Polynesian, Northern Philippine, Northern Luzon, Alta. Not close to other languages (Laurence Reid). 34% lexical similarity with Southern Alta. Investigation needed: bilingual proficiency.

ALTA, SOUTHERN ***(KABULUEN, KABULUWEN, KABULUWAN, KABULOWAN, KABOLOAN, BALUGA, PUGOT, ITA)*** [AGY] 1,000 (1982 SIL). Eastern Nueva Ecija, Sierra Madre and coast areas of Quezon Province, town of San Miguel, and a large community in a remote part of San Miguel, Bulacan Province. North of the Umiray Dumaget. Austronesian, Malayo-Polynesian, Western Malayo-Polynesian, Northern Philippine, Northern Luzon, Alta. Not close to other languages. A distinct language from Northern Alta (34% lexical similarity). Bilingualism in Tagalog. Speakers at Angat Dam in Bulacan are mixed with Umiray Dumaget Agta and call themselves 'Kaboloan'. Investigation needed: bilingual proficiency in Tagalog. Agriculturalists: maize. Bible portions 1970.

ARTA [ATZ] 16 or 17 speakers, including 12 in Villa Santiago, 1 in Villa Gracia, 3 or 4 in Nagtipunan (1992 L. Reid). Quirino Province, town of Aglipay, Villa Santiago and Villa Gracia, and town of Nagtipunan. Austronesian, Malayo-Polynesian, Western Malayo-Polynesian, Northern Philippine, Northern Luzon, Arta. Not linguistically close to any other language (Lawrence Reid). Other families are intermarried with Ilocano speakers or are bilingual in Casiguran Dumagat Agta. Negrito. Three families speak Arta in the home.

ATA [ATM] Nine or more families (1973 SIL). Mabinay, Negros Oriental. Austronesian, Malayo-Polynesian, Western Malayo-Polynesian, Meso Philippine, Central Philippine. Probably very bilingual in Cebuano. Different from Ata Manobo or the Atta languages. May be extinct. Nearly extinct.

ATI ***(INATI)*** [ATK] 1,500 (1980 SIL). Panay Island, small groups in all provinces. Austronesian, Malayo-Polynesian, Western Malayo-Polynesian, Meso Philippine, Central Philippine, Bisayan, Central, Peripheral. Dialects: MALAY, BAROTAC VIEJO NAGPANA. Bilingual level estimates are Hiligaynon: 1-3 5%, 3+ 11%, 4 50%, 4+ 32%, 5 2%; Kinaray-a: 1-3 9%, 3+ 30%, 4 61%. Hiligaynon is used for school, contact with outsiders, outside culture topics, jobs, religion. Ati is used in the home and with close friends. The Malay people mainly speak Malaynon. Malay Ati dialect is nearly extinct. Barotac Viejo Nagpana is the prestige dialect. Negrito.

ATTA, FAIRE ***(SOUTHERN ATTA)*** [ATH] 400 to 550 or 136 families (1981 SIL). Near Faire-Rizal, Cagayan Province, Luzon. Austronesian, Malayo-Polynesian, Western Malayo-Polynesian, Northern Philippine, Northern Luzon, Northern Cordilleran, Ibanagic, Ibanag. Lexical similarity relationships: Pudtol Atta 81%; Isnag 60%; Central Cagayan Agta 66%; Pamplona Atta 82%; Rizal Atta 90%; Ibanag 72%. Fairly bilingual in Ibanag and Pamplona Atta. Negrito. Literacy work needed for Sinundungan Valley: 100 families.

ATTA, PAMPLONA ***(NORTHERN CAGAYAN NEGRITO)*** [ATT] 1,000 (1998 SIL). Northwestern Cagayan Province, Luzon. Austronesian, Malayo-Polynesian, Western Malayo-Polynesian, Northern

Philippine, Northern Luzon, Northern Cordilleran, Ibanagic, Ibanag. Intelligibility of Ibanag North 97%, 52% of Itawit. 91% lexical similarity of Ibanag North; 63% with Ilocano; 69% lexical similarity with Itawit. Bilingualism in Ilocano. Literacy rate in first language: 20% to 25%. Literacy rate in second language: 20% to 25%. NT 1996.

ATTA, PUDTOL [ATP] 500 to 700, or 171 families (1991 SIL). Luzon, Kalinga-Apayao Province, Pudtol, on the Abulog River south of Pamplona. Austronesian, Malayo-Polynesian, Western Malayo-Polynesian, Northern Philippine, Northern Luzon, Northern Cordilleran, Ibanagic, Ibanag. Lexical similarity relationships: Pamplona Atta 86%; Ibanag 75%; Isnag 63%; Faire Atta 81%; Ilocano 42%. Fairly bilingual in Ibanag and Pamplona Atta. Negrito.

AYTA, ABENLEN ***(ABENLEN, AYTA ABENLEN SAMBAL, ABURLIN NEGRITO)*** [ABP] 6,850 (1985 SIL). Luzon, Tarlac Province, Maontoc, Labnay, Maamot, San Pedro, Dalayap, Pilyen, Tangan-Tangan. Austronesian, Malayo-Polynesian, Western Malayo-Polynesian, Northern Philippine, Bashiic-Central Luzon-Northern Mindoro, Central Luzon, Sambalic. 28% intelligibility with Botolan Sambal, 48% with Tina Sambal. 66% lexical similarity with Botolan Sambal, 49% with Tina Sambal, 38% to 44% with Ilocano, Pangasinan, Tagalog, Pampanga. Some in remote areas are nearly monolingual. Literacy rate in first language: 3%. Literacy rate in second language: 3%. Mountain slope.

AYTA, AMBALA ***(AMBALA AGTA, AMBALA SAMBAL)*** [ABC] 1,657 (1986 SIL). A few barrios of San Marcelino, Zambales, several of Subic City, Zambales, a few of Olongapa, Zambales, a few of Castillejos, Zambales, a few of Dinalupinan, Bataan Province, Luzon. Affected by Mt. Pinatubo eruption. Austronesian, Malayo-Polynesian, Western Malayo-Polynesian, Northern Philippine, Bashiic-Central Luzon-Northern Mindoro, Central Luzon, Sambalic. Intelligibility of Botolan Sambal 60%, 54% with Ayta Indi Sambal, 60% with Ayta Anchi Sambal, 70% with Bataan Sambal. 70% lexical similarity with Botolan Sambal, 55% with Tagalog. Bilingualism in Tagalog. They do not mix with other Ayta groups. Literacy rate in first language: 25%. Literacy rate in second language: 25%.

AYTA, BATAAN ***(MARIVELES AYTA, BATAAN SAMBAL, BATAAN AYTA)*** [AYT] 572 (1986 SIL). Mariveles, Bataan Province, Luzon. Austronesian, Malayo-Polynesian, Western Malayo-Polynesian, Northern Philippine, Bashiic-Central Luzon-Northern Mindoro, Central Luzon, Sambalic. 63% lexical similarity with Botolan Sambal and Tagalog. Fairly bilingual in Tagalog. Negrito. Investigation needed: bilingual proficiency in Tagalog.

AYTA, MAG-ANCHI ***(MAG-ANCHI SAMBAL)*** [SGB] 8,200 (1992 SIL). East side of mountain, Botolan Sambal area, close to Tarlac-Pampanga border, several barrios of Capas, Tarlac, several of Bamban, Tarlac, several of San Marcelino, Zambales, 2 of Castillejos, Zambales, 2 of Mabalacat, Pampanga, several of Sapang Bato, Angeles City, central Luzon. People affected by Mt. Pinatubo eruption. Austronesian, Malayo-Polynesian, Western Malayo-Polynesian, Northern Philippine, Bashiic-Central Luzon-Northern Mindoro, Central Luzon, Sambalic. 77% intelligibility with Ayta Indi Sambal, 65% with Ayta Ambala Sambal, 46% with Pampangan. 76% lexical similarity with Botolan Sambal, 50% with Tagalog, 46% with Pampangan. People scattered because of Mt. Pinatubo eruption. Literacy rate in first language: 10%. Literacy rate in second language: 10%. Bible portions 1995.

AYTA, MAG-INDI ***(BALOGA, MAG-INDI SAMBAL, INDI AYTA)*** [BLX] 5,000 (1998 SIL). A few barrios of Florida Blanca, several of Porac, Pampanga Province, several of San Marcelino, Zambales, Luzon. People affected by Mt. Pinatubo eruption. Austronesian, Malayo-Polynesian, Western Malayo-Polynesian, Northern Philippine, Bashiic-Central Luzon-Northern Mindoro, Central Luzon, Sambalic. 46% intelligibility with Botolan Sambal, 50% with Ayta Ambala Sambal, 59% with Pampangan, 32% with Ayta Anchi Sambal. 66% to 73% lexical similarity with Botolan Sambal, 44% with Tagalog, 73% to 81% with Ayta Anchi Sambal. Literacy rate in first language: Below 10%. Literacy rate in second language: Below 10%. Mountain slope.

AYTA, SORSOGON [AYS] 40 (1984 SIL). Prieto Diaz, Sorsogon Province. Austronesian, Malayo-Polynesian, Western Malayo-Polynesian, Meso Philippine, Central Philippine. Frequent intermarriage with other groups. Nearly extinct.

AYTA, TAYABAS [AYY] Tayabas, Quezon Province, Luzon. Austronesian, Malayo-Polynesian, Western Malayo-Polynesian, Meso Philippine, Central Philippine. No longer spoken; completely assimilated to Tagalog. Negrito. Extinct.

BALANGAO ***(BALANGAO BONTOC, BALANGAW, FARANGAO)*** [BLW] 6,560 (1975 census). Eastern Bontoc Province, Luzon. Austronesian, Malayo-Polynesian, Western Malayo-Polynesian, Northern Philippine, Northern Luzon, South-Central Cordilleran, Central Cordilleran, Nuclear Cordilleran, Balangao. Literacy rate in first language: 42.2%. Literacy rate in second language: 42.2%. Agriculturalists: rice. Traditional religion, Christian. NT 1982.

BANTOANON ***(BANTON, BANTUANON, ASIQ, SIMARANHON, CALATRAVANHON)*** [BNO] 70,000 to 100,000 (1998 SIL). Banton, Simara, Maestro de Campo, and Tablas Islands, Romblon Province, between Masbate and Mindoro. Austronesian, Malayo-Polynesian, Western Malayo-Polynesian, Meso Philippine, Central Philippine, Bisayan, Banton. Dialects: SIBALENHON (SIBALE), ODIONGANON.

63% intelligibility of Hiligaynon; 92% of Loocnon. Odionganon dialect is preferred for literature. 83% lexical similarity with Romblomanon (Zorc 1977). Tagalog is used for some politics, education, and with non-Bantuanon speakers. Over 95% of Bantuanon people use the vernacular in the majority of social situations; with family, friends, at work, and with Bantuanon officials and school teachers. Literacy rate in first language: 80% to 90%. Literacy rate in second language: 80% to 90%. Agriculturalists, forestry, fishermen. Bible portions 1992.

BATAK ***(BABUYAN, TINITIANES, PALAWAN BATAK)*** [BTK] 2,041 (1990 census). North central Palawan. Austronesian, Malayo-Polynesian, Western Malayo-Polynesian, Meso Philippine, Palawano. Bilingualism in Tagalog. Negrito. VOS. Bible portions 1972.

BICOLANO, ALBAY [BHK] 480,000 (1975 census). Western Albay Province and Buhi, Camarines Sur, Luzon. Austronesian, Malayo-Polynesian, Western Malayo-Polynesian, Meso Philippine, Central Philippine, Bikol, Inland, Buhi-Daraga. Dialects: BUHI (BUHI'NON), DARAGA, LIBON, OAS, LIGAO. Somewhat bilingual in Central Bicolano.

BICOLANO, CENTRAL ***(BIKOL)*** [BKL] 2,500,000 about 7% of the population speak Bikol languages; 3,519,236 all Bikol languages (1990 census). Southern Catanduanes, Northern Sorsogon, Albay, Camarines Norte and Sur, Luzon. Naga City and Legaspi City are centers. Austronesian, Malayo-Polynesian, Western Malayo-Polynesian, Meso Philippine, Central Philippine, Bikol, Coastal, Naga. Dialects: NAGA, LEGASPI. Trade language. Bible 1915, in press (1992).

BICOLANO, IRIGA ***(RINCONADA BICOLANO)*** [BTO] 180,000 (1975 census). Iriga City, Baao, Nabua, Bato, Camarines Sur, Luzon. Austronesian, Malayo-Polynesian, Western Malayo-Polynesian, Meso Philippine, Central Philippine, Bikol, Inland, Iriga. Investigation needed: bilingual proficiency in Central Bicolano, Tagalog.

BICOLANO, NORTHERN CATANDUANES ***(PANDAN)*** [CTS] 65,000 (1975 census). Luzon, Northern Catanduanes, east of Bicol. Austronesian, Malayo-Polynesian, Western Malayo-Polynesian, Meso Philippine, Central Philippine, Bikol, Pandan. Comprehension of Central Bicolano of Naga 68%. A population sample had 66% comprehension of Tagalog narrative. Investigation needed: intelligibility with Southern Catanduanes, bilingual proficiency in Central Bicolano.

BICOLANO, SOUTHERN CATANDUANES ***(VIRAC)*** [BLN] 85,000 (1981 Newell SIL). Luzon, Southern Catanduanes, east of Bicol. Austronesian, Malayo-Polynesian, Western Malayo-Polynesian, Meso Philippine, Central Philippine, Bikol, Coastal, Virac. Northern Catanduanes intelligibility 91%. Virac dialect is preferable for literature. Population samples had 85% comprehension of Central Bicolano and Tagalog narrative. Investigation needed: bilingual proficiency.

BINUKID ***(BINUKID MANOBO, BINOKID, BUKIDNON)*** [BKD] 100,000 (1987 SIL). North central Mindanao, southern Bukidnon, northeastern Cotabato, Agusan del Sur. Austronesian, Malayo-Polynesian, Western Malayo-Polynesian, Southern Philippine, Manobo, North. Literature should serve Kalabugao, Bukidnon, Minalowang, Esperanza, and Agusan del Sur. Closely related to Higaonon. Literacy rate in first language: 63%. Literacy rate in second language: 63%. Lowland, mountain slope. NT 1986.

BLAAN, KORONADAL ***(KORONADAL BILAAN, BILANES, BIRAAN, BARAAN, TAGALAGAD)*** [BIK] 100,000 (1981 SIL). South Cotabato Province, Mindanao. Austronesian, Malayo-Polynesian, Western Malayo-Polynesian, South Mindanao, Bilic, Blaan. The people have limited bilingualism in Cebuano. Literacy rate in first language: 20%. Literacy rate in second language: 20%. Traditional religion, Christian. NT 1995.

BLAAN, SARANGANI ***(BILAAN, BALUD, TUMANAO)*** [BIS] 75,000 to 100,000 (1998 SIL). South Cotabato Province, Sarangani, Davao Del Sur Province, Mindanao. Austronesian, Malayo-Polynesian, Western Malayo-Polynesian, South Mindanao, Bilic, Blaan. Literacy rate in first language: 28%. Literacy rate in second language: 28%. Videos. Traditional religion, Christian. NT 1981, in press (1999).

BOLINAO ***(BOLINAO SAMBAL, BOLINAO ZAMBAL)*** [SMK] 50,000 (1990). West Pangasinan Province, Luzon. Austronesian, Malayo-Polynesian, Western Malayo-Polynesian, Northern Philippine, Bashiic-Central Luzon-Northern Mindoro, Central Luzon, Sambalic. Half the people have some bilingual proficiency in Tagalog, Ilocano, and Pangasinan. Literacy rate in first language: 86.8%. Literacy rate in second language: 86.8%. High literacy rate in Ilocano and Tagalog. Bible portions 1963-1984.

BONTOC, CENTRAL ***(BONTOK, IGOROT)*** [BNC] 40,000 (1994 SIL). Central Mountain Province, Luzon. Austronesian, Malayo-Polynesian, Western Malayo-Polynesian, Northern Philippine, Northern Luzon, South-Central Cordilleran, Central Cordilleran, Nuclear Cordilleran, Bontok-Kankanay, Bontok. Dialects: SADANGA, GUINAANG BONTOC, BAYYU. Intelligibility of Ilocano 58%, Eastern Bontoc 56%. Bilingualism in Ilocano. Literacy rate in first language: 35%. Literacy rate in second language: 35%. NT 1992.

BONTOC, EASTERN ***(SOUTHERN BONTOC, KADAKLAN-BARLIG BONTOC)*** [BKB] 5,000 (1998 SIL). Central Mountain Province, Luzon. Austronesian, Malayo-Polynesian, Western Malayo-Polynesian, Northern Philippine, Northern Luzon, South-Central Cordilleran, Central Cordilleran, Nuclear Cordilleran, Bontok-Kankanay, Bontok. Dialects: LIAS, BARLIG, KADAKLAN. Intelligibility of Ilocano 53%; Balangao

49%. Bilingualism in Ilocano. Literacy rate in first language: 67%. Literacy rate in second language: 67%. Traditional religion. Bible portions 1977-1986.

BUHID ***(BUKIL, BANGON, BATANGAN)*** [BKU] 8,000 (1991 OMF). Southern Mindoro. Austronesian, Malayo-Polynesian, Western Malayo-Polynesian, Meso Philippine, South Mangyan, Buhid-Taubuid. NT 1988.

BUTUANON [BTW] 34,547 (1990 census). Butuan City, Mindanao. Austronesian, Malayo-Polynesian, Western Malayo-Polynesian, Meso Philippine, Central Philippine, Bisayan, South, Butuan-Tausug. 70% lexical similarity with Kamayo; 69% with Surigaonon. Fairly bilingual in Cebuano.

CALUYANUN ***(CALUYANEN, CALUYANHON)*** [CAU] 30,000 (1994 SIL). Caluya Islands, Antique. Austronesian, Malayo-Polynesian, Western Malayo-Polynesian, Meso Philippine, Central Philippine, Bisayan, West. Dialect: SEMIRARA. A sample of speakers scored 69% on Hiligaynon narrative comprehension; 62% on Cuyonon. Bilingualism in Hiligaynon. Literacy rate in first language: 67%. Literacy rate in second language: 67%. NT 1990.

CAPIZNON ***(CAPISANO, CAPISEÑO)*** [CPS] 445,716 (1975 census). Northeast Panay. Austronesian, Malayo-Polynesian, Western Malayo-Polynesian, Meso Philippine, Central Philippine, Bisayan, Central, Peripheral. A population sample had 91% comprehension of Hiligaynon narrative. Tagalog is also used.

CEBUANO ***(SUGBUHANON, SUGBUANON, VISAYAN, BISAYAN, BINISAYA, SEBUANO)*** [CEB] 14,713,220 in the Philippines (1990 census), about 24.4% of the population. Population total both countries 15,000,000. Negros, Cebu, Bohol, Visayas and parts of Mindanao. Also spoken in USA. Austronesian, Malayo-Polynesian, Western Malayo-Polynesian, Meso Philippine, Central Philippine, Bisayan, Cebuan. Dialects: CEBU, BOHOLANO, LEYTE, MINDANAO VISAYAN. Boholano is sometimes considered a separate language. Bilingualism in Tagalog. Language of wider communication. Dictionary. Grammar. Christian. Bible 1917-1981.

CHAVACANO ***(ZAMBOANGUEÑO, CHABAKANO)*** [CBK] 292,630 (1990 census), including 155,000 Zamboangueño (1989 J. Holm), 27,841 Caviten, 3,750 Ternateño (1975 census), 5,473 Cotabato Chavacano (1981 Wurm and Hattori). Population total both countries 292,630 or more. Zamboanga, Basilan, Kabasalan, Siay, Margosatubig, Ipil, Malangas, Lapuyan, Buug, Tungawa, Alicia, Isabela, Lamitan, Maluso, Malamawi, Cotabato city, Mindanao; Cavite, Ternate, and Ermita near Manila. The 1970 census listed speakers in 60 of the 66 provinces. Also spoken in Malaysia (Sabah). Creole, Spanish based. Dialects: CAVITEQO, TERNATEÑO (TERNATEÑO CHAVACANO), ERMITAÑO (ERMITEÑO), DAVAWENYO ZAMBOANGUENYO (ABAKAY SPANISH, DAVAO CHAVACANO, DAVAOEÑO, DAVAWEÑO), COTOBATO CHAVACANO, ZAMBOANGUEÑO (CHAVACANO). A creole with predominantly Spanish vocabulary and Philippine-type grammatical structure. Davawen Zamboangueño may be extinct. Nearly all Caviten speak Tagalog, but many still speak Caviteño. The major language of Zamboanga city. Ermiteño is extinct. Literacy rate in first language: 80%. Literacy rate in second language: 80%. Used in primary education. Newspapers, radio programs. NT 1981.

CHINESE, MANDARIN [CHN] 500 to 600 or 0.1% of Chinese population, including Chaochow dialect of Min Nam (1982 CCCOWE). All ethnic Chinese are 53,273 (1990 censu), or 1.3% of the population (1993 Johnstone). Sino-Tibetan, Chinese. Bible 1874-1983. See main entry under China.

CHINESE, MIN NAN ***(MIN NAN)*** [CFR] 493,500 to 592,200 or 98.7% of Chinese population in Philippines (1982 CCCOWE). Sino-Tibetan, Chinese. Dialect: CHAOCHOW. Bible 1933. See main entry under China.

CHINESE, YUE [YUH] 6,000 to 7,200 or 1.2% of Chinese population (1982 CCCOWE). Sino-Tibetan, Chinese. Bible 1894-1981. See main entry under China.

CUYONON ***(CUYONO, CUYUNON, CUYO, KUYUNON, KUYONON)*** [CYO] 123,384 (1990 census). Palawan coast, Cuyo Islands between Palawan and Panay. Austronesian, Malayo-Polynesian, Western Malayo-Polynesian, Meso Philippine, Central Philippine, Bisayan, West, Kuyan. Close to Ratagnon. Trade language. NT 1982.

DAVAWENYO ***(MATINO, DAVAOEÑO, DAVAWEÑO)*** [DAW] 147,279 (1990 census). Davao Oriental, Davao del Sur, Mindanao. Austronesian, Malayo-Polynesian, Western Malayo-Polynesian, Meso Philippine, Central Philippine, Mansakan, Davawenyo. Synthesis of Tagalog, Cebuano, other Visayan dialects. Some Spanish words. Not a Spanish Creole. Different from Davaweño which is dialect of Chavacano. Two dialects: East Coast with 90% of speakers, and Davao City and environs (Whinnom 1956). Speakers of Lowland Davaweño have 89% intelligibility of Kamayo. Speakers of Lowland Davawen are bilingual in Cebuano 91% to 97%. Of highland Davawenyo, they have much lower comprehension of Cebuano.

ENGLISH [ENG] 32,802 in Philippines (1990 census). 52% of the population said they could speak it as a second language (1980 census). Indo-European, Germanic, West, English. National language. Bible 1535-1989. See main entry under United Kingdom.

GA'DANG ***(BALIWON, GINABWAL, KALINGA)*** [GDG] 17,500 (1993 SIL). Paracelis, foothills, Mt. Province, Luzon. Austronesian, Malayo-Polynesian, Western Malayo-Polynesian, Northern Philippine, Northern Luzon, Northern Cordilleran, Ibanagic, Gaddang. Different from Gaddang. Related to Itawit, Yogad, Gaddang, Ibanag. Not very bilingual. An upland group. Literacy rate in first language: 40%. Literacy rate in second language: 40%. Traditional religion. Bible portions 1976-1981.

GADDANG ***(CAGAYAN)*** [GAD] 30,000 (1984 M. Walrod SIL). Central Isabela, and Bagabag, Solano, and Bayombong in Nueva Vizcaya, Luzon. Austronesian, Malayo-Polynesian, Western Malayo-Polynesian, Northern Philippine, Northern Luzon, Northern Cordilleran, Ibanagic, Gaddang. Less than 80% intelligibility with Ga'dang. 80% lexical similarity with Ga'dang. Bilingualism in Ilocano. A lowland group. 'Gaddang' refers to those in Nueva Vizcaya, 'Cagayan' to those in central Isabela. Dictionary. Grammar. Christian.

GIANGAN ***(BAGOBO, JANGAN, GUANGA, GULANGA, CLATA, ETO, ATTO)*** [BGI] 55,040 (1990 census). Davao City, Mindanao; eastern slopes of Mt. Apo, Davao del Sur. Austronesian, Malayo-Polynesian, Western Malayo-Polynesian, South Mindanao, Bagobo. 69% intelligibility with Tagabawa Manobo; 79% with Obo Manobo. 34% lexical similarity with Tagabawa Manobo, 35% with Obo Manobo; 43% with Blaan. Marginally bilingual in Cebuano. Different from Manobo.

HANUNOO ***(HANONOO)*** [HNN] 10,000 to 12,000 (1991 OMF). Southern Oriental Mindoro. Austronesian, Malayo-Polynesian, Western Malayo-Polynesian, Meso Philippine, South Mangyan, Hanunoo. Dialects: GUBATNON (GUBAT, SORSOGONON), BINLI, KAGANKAN, WAIGAN, WAWAN, BULALAKAWNON. NT 1985.

HIGAONON ***(MISAMIS HIGAONON MANOBO)*** [MBA] 30,000 (1996 NTM). Misamis Oriental, south of Ginoog City, north central Mindanao. Austronesian, Malayo-Polynesian, Western Malayo-Polynesian, Southern Philippine, Manobo, North. Related to Binukid; 77% to 81% intelligibility. Comprehension of Cebuano is limited. Bible portions 1987.

HILIGAYNON ***(ILONGGO, HILIGAINON)*** [HIL] 7,000,000 in the Philippines, about 10% of the population (1995). Population total both countries 7,000,000 or more (1995 WA). Iloilo and Capiz provinces, Panay, Negros Occidental, Visayas. Also spoken in USA. Austronesian, Malayo-Polynesian, Western Malayo-Polynesian, Meso Philippine, Central Philippine, Bisayan, Central, Peripheral. Dialects: HILIGAYNON, KAWAYAN, BANTAYAN. Bilingualism in Tagalog. Language of wider communication. Christian. Bible 1912-1982.

I-WAK ***(IWAAK)*** [IWK] 2,000 to 3,000 (1987 SIL). Reported to live in the following villages: Tojongan, Bakes, Lebeng, Domolpos, Bujasjas, Kayo-ko, Salaksak (in Kayapa), extreme eastern Itogon, Benguet Province, Luzon. I-wak people also live in Capintalan in Nueva Ecija, but speak only Kallahan. Austronesian, Malayo-Polynesian, Western Malayo-Polynesian, Northern Philippine, Northern Luzon, South-Central Cordilleran, Southern Cordilleran, Pangasinic, Benguet, Iwaak. Related to Karao, Ibaloi, and Kallahan. Less acculturated to outside culture than other mountain groups. Mountain slope.

IBALOI ***(IBALOY, IBADOY, INIBALOI, NABALOI, BENGUET-IGOROT, IGODOR)*** [IBL] 111,449 (1990 census). Central and southern Benguet Province, western Nueva Vizcaya Province, Luzon. Austronesian, Malayo-Polynesian, Western Malayo-Polynesian, Northern Philippine, Northern Luzon, South-Central Cordilleran, Southern Cordilleran, Pangasinic, Benguet, Ibaloi-Karao. Dialects: DAKLAN, KABAYAN, BOKOD. Literacy rate in first language: 75% to 100%. Literacy rate in second language: 75% to 100%. NT 1978.

IBANAG ***(YBANAG)*** [IBG] 500,000 (1990 SIL). Isabela and Cagayan provinces, Luzon. Austronesian, Malayo-Polynesian, Western Malayo-Polynesian, Northern Philippine, Northern Luzon, Northern Cordilleran, Ibanagic, Ibanag. Dialects: NORTH IBANAG, SOUTH IBANAG. 69% intelligibility of Itawit. Bilingual level estimates for Ilocano are 0 5%, 1 25%, 2 30%, 3 25%, 4 10%, 5 5%. Speakers also use Tagalog as second language. Speakers have pride in their language. VSO, genitives after nouns, adjectives and numerals before nouns, CV, CVC, nontonal. Literacy rate in first language: 75% to 100%. Literacy rate in second language: 75% to 100%. NT 1911-1989.

IBATAN ***(BABUYAN, IBATAAN, IVATAN)*** [IVB] 1,000 (1996 SIL). Babuyan Island, north of Luzon. Austronesian, Malayo-Polynesian, Western Malayo-Polynesian, Northern Philippine, Bashiic-Central Luzon-Northern Mindoro, Bashiic, Ivatan. Intelligibility of Itbayaten Ivatan 64%; Basco Ivatan 31%. 72% lexical similarity of Itbayaten Ivatan; Basco Ivatan 74% lexical similarity. Literacy rate in first language: 60%. Literacy rate in second language: 60%. NT 1996.

IFUGAO, AMGANAD ***(AMGANAD)*** [IFA] 27,000 (1981 SIL). 167,503 all Ifugao (1990 census). Ifugao Province, Luzon. Austronesian, Malayo-Polynesian, Western Malayo-Polynesian, Northern Philippine, Northern Luzon, South-Central Cordilleran, Central Cordilleran, Nuclear Cordilleran, Ifugao. Dialects: BURNAY IFUGAO, BANAUE IFUGAO. Burnay has 81% intelligibility of Amganad. Burnay has 83% lexical similarity of Amganad. Literacy rate in first language: 65%. Literacy rate in second language: 65%. Traditional religion, Christian. NT 1980-1987.

IFUGAO, BATAD ***(BATAD)*** [IFB] 43,000 (1987 SIL). Ifugao Province, Luzon. Austronesian, Malayo-Polynesian, Western Malayo-Polynesian, Northern Philippine, Northern Luzon, South-Central Cordilleran, Central Cordilleran, Nuclear Cordilleran, Ifugao. Dialects: AYANGAN IFUGAO, BATAD IFUGAO, DUCLIGAN IFUGAO. Intelligibility of Batad: Ayangan 87%; Mayoyao 86% to 94%. Lexical similarity with Batad: Ayangan 81%; Ducligan 89%; Mayoyao 79%. Dictionary. Literacy rate in first language: 55% to 60%. Literacy rate in second language: 55% to 60%. Traditional religion, Christian. NT 1977.

IFUGAO, MAYOYAO ***(MAYOYAO, MAYAOYAW)*** [IFU] 40,000 (1998 SIL). Ifugao Province, Luzon. Austronesian, Malayo-Polynesian, Western Malayo-Polynesian, Northern Philippine, Northern Luzon, South-Central Cordilleran, Central Cordilleran, Nuclear Cordilleran, Ifugao. 86% to 94% intelligibility of Batad. Grammatical markers are different. 79% lexical similarity with Batad Ifugao, 85% with Ayangan. Secondary schools. Literacy rate in first language: 50% to 60%. Literacy rate in second language: 50% to 60%. Mountain slope. Agriculturalists: wet rice. Traditional religion, Christian. Bible portions 1994.

IFUGAO, TUWALI ***(KIANGAN IFUGAO, QUIANGAN, GILIPANES, TUWALI)*** [IFK] 25,000 (1981 SIL). Ifugao Province, Luzon. Austronesian, Malayo-Polynesian, Western Malayo-Polynesian, Northern Philippine, Northern Luzon, South-Central Cordilleran, Central Cordilleran, Nuclear Cordilleran, Ifugao. Dialects: HAPAO IFUGAO, HUNGDUAN IFUGAO, LAGAWE IFUGAO. 77% intelligibility of Amganad Ifugao, 78% of Batad. Hapao has 88% intelligibility of Kiangan, Hungduan has 85% of Kiangan. 80% lexical similarity with Amganad Ifugao, 72% with Batad Ifugao, 78% with Hapao, 86% with Hungduan. Some speakers are bilingual in English, Ilocano, Tagalog, or Amganad Ifugao. Those over 35 are more bilingual in English than others. Kiangan is the place, Tuwali is the language. VSO, prepositions; genitives, relatives after noun heads; articles, adjectives, numerals before noun heads; question word initial; one suffix, two infixes; passives, causatives, comparatives; V, CV, CVC. Literacy rate in first language: 60%. Literacy rate in second language: 60%. Tropical forest. Mountain slope. Peasant agriculturalists, intensive agriculturalists. 500 to 900 meters. Traditional religion, Christian. NT 1991.

ILOCANO ***(ILOKO, ILOKANO)*** [ILO] 8,000,000 (1991 UBS). About 11.1% of the population. Population total both countries 8,000,000 or more. Northwestern Luzon, La Union and Ilocos provinces, Cagayan Valley, Babuyan, Mindoro, Mindanao. Also spoken in USA. Austronesian, Malayo-Polynesian, Western Malayo-Polynesian, Northern Philippine, Northern Luzon, Ilocano. There is a Pidgin Ilocano used in northern Luzon highlands. Language of wider communication. Roman script. Christian. Bible 1909-1996.

ILONGOT ***(BUGKALUT, BUKALOT, LINGOTES)*** [ILK] 50,786 (1990 census). Eastern Nueva Vizcaya, Western Quirino, Luzon. Austronesian, Malayo-Polynesian, Western Malayo-Polynesian, Northern Philippine, Northern Luzon, South-Central Cordilleran, Southern Cordilleran, Ilongot. Dialects: ABAKA (ABACA), EGONGOT, IBALAO (IBILAO), ITALON, IYONGUT. NT 1982.

INONHAN ***(LOOCNON, LOOKNON, "UNHAN")*** [LOC] 65,000 to 80,000 (1991 E. Talamisan TAP). Southern Tablas Island, Romblon Province, Mindoro Oriental and Mindoro Occidental. Austronesian, Malayo-Polynesian, Western Malayo-Polynesian, Meso Philippine, Central Philippine, Bisayan, West, North Central. Dialects: BULALAKAW, DISPOHOLNON, LOOKNON, ALCANTARANON. 70% lexical similarity with Odionganon (Bantuanon), 93% with Aklanon, 86% with Caluyanun. Speakers are fairly bilingual in Hiligaynon. Loocnon is the name of a town. "Unhan" is derogatory.

IRAYA [IRY] 10,000 (1991 OMF). Northern Mindoro. Austronesian, Malayo-Polynesian, Western Malayo-Polynesian, Northern Philippine, Bashiic-Central Luzon-Northern Mindoro, Northern Mindoro. Dialects: ABRA-DE-ILOG, ALAG-BAKO, PAGBAHAN, PALAUAN-CALAVITE, PAMBUHAN, SANTA CRUZ. Many speak Tagalog in the home. NT 1991.

ISINAI ***(INSINAI, ISINAY, ISNAY, INMEAS)*** [INN] 5,524 (1990 census). Luzon: Bambang, Dupax, and Aritao, Nueva Vizcaya. Austronesian, Malayo-Polynesian, Western Malayo-Polynesian, Northern Philippine, Northern Luzon, South-Central Cordilleran, Central Cordilleran, Isinai. Not close to other languages. 47% lexical similarity with Ilocano. Speakers appear to have general bilingual proficiency in Ilocano. People prefer Isinai for all purposes except speaking to outsiders.

ISNAG ***(DIBAGAT-KABUGAO-ISNEG, ISNEG, MARAGAT)*** [ISD] 30,000 (1994 SIL). Northern Apayao, Luzon. Austronesian, Malayo-Polynesian, Western Malayo-Polynesian, Northern Philippine, Northern Luzon, Northern Cordilleran, Ibanagic, Isnag. Dialects: BAYAG, DIBAGAT-KABUGAO, CALANASAN, KARAGAWAN (DARAGAWAN), TALIFUGU-RIPANG (TAWINI). Intelligibility testing: Calanasan: 94% of Dibagat, 88% of Ilocano; Talifugu-Ripang: 89% of Dibagat, 71% of Ilocano. Bilingualism in Ilocano. Literacy rate in first language: 50%. Literacy rate in second language: 50%. NT 1980.

ITAWIT ***(ITAWIS, TAWIT, ITAWES)*** [ITV] 134,126 including 119,584 Itawit, 14,542 Malaweg (1990 census). Luzon, southern Cagayan. Austronesian, Malayo-Polynesian, Western Malayo-Polynesian, Northern Philippine, Northern Luzon, Northern Cordilleran, Ibanagic, Ibanag. Dialects: MALAWEG (MALAUEG), ITAWIS. Related to Ibanag. 72% intelligibility of South Ibanag; 68% of Ilocano. 53% lexical similarity with Ilocano. Bilingualism in Ilocano. NT 1992.

ITNEG, BINONGAN ***(TINGUIAN, TINGGUIAN)*** [ITB] 7,000 (1982 SIL). 46,405 in all Itneg varieties (1990 census). Ba-ay Valley and Licuan Abra Province, Luzon. Austronesian, Malayo-Polynesian, Western Malayo-Polynesian, Northern Philippine, Northern Luzon, South-Central Cordilleran, Central Cordilleran, Kalinga-Itneg, Itneg. 69% lexical similarity with Ilocano, 86% with Masadiit Itneg. Bilingualism in Ilocano. Bible portions 1967.

ITNEG, INLAOD [ITI] Northern Luzon, southwest of Binongan Itneg, northwest of Masadiit Itneg. Austronesian, Malayo-Polynesian, Western Malayo-Polynesian, Northern Philippine, Northern Luzon, South-Central Cordilleran, Central Cordilleran, Kalinga-Itneg, Itneg. Reported to be bilingual in Ilocano. Investigation needed: bilingual proficiency, attitudes.

ITNEG, MASADIIT [TIS] 7,500. Sallapadan and Bucloc, Abra Province, Luzon. Austronesian, Malayo-Polynesian, Western Malayo-Polynesian, Northern Philippine, Northern Luzon, South-Central Cordilleran, Central Cordilleran, Kalinga-Itneg, Itneg. 62% lexical similarity with Ilocano, 70% with Guinaang Kalinga, 86% with Binongan Itneg. Reported to be bilingual in Ilocano. Investigation needed: bilingual proficiency in Ilocano.

ITNEG, SOUTHERN ***(LUBA-TIEMPO ITNEG)*** [ITT] Luzon, southern Abra Province. Austronesian, Malayo-Polynesian, Western Malayo-Polynesian, Northern Philippine, Northern Luzon, South-Central Cordilleran, Central Cordilleran, Kalinga-Itneg, Itneg. Investigation needed: bilingual proficiency in Ilocano, Northern Kankanay.

IVATAN [IVV] 35,000 (1998 SIL), including 554 Itbayatan (1990 census). Batanes Islands. Manu relocated on Mindanao near boundary of Bukidnon, Lanao del Sur, and Cotabato; some in Manila, Luzon, Palawan, other countries. Austronesian, Malayo-Polynesian, Western Malayo-Polynesian, Northern Philippine, Bashiic-Central Luzon-Northern Mindoro, Bashiic, Ivatan. Dialects: ITBAYATEN, BASCO IVATAN, SOUTHERN IVATAN. Literacy rate in first language: 91.8%. Literacy rate in second language: 91.8%. Christian. NT 1984.

KAGAYANEN ***(CAGAYANO CILLO, CAGAYANCILLO)*** [CGC] 23,000 (1992 SIL). Cagayan Island, between Negros and Palawan, and communities on the coast of Palawan. Austronesian, Malayo-Polynesian, Western Malayo-Polynesian, Southern Philippine, Manobo, North. Lowland. Literacy rate in first language: 75%. Literacy rate in second language: 75%. Bible portions 1983-1994.

KALAGAN [KQE] 21,402 (1990 census). Along east and west shores of Davao Gulf in Davao del Sur and Davao Oriental. Austronesian, Malayo-Polynesian, Western Malayo-Polynesian, Meso Philippine, Central Philippine, Mansakan, Western. Dialects: ISAMAL, PISO, TUMUAONG, LACTAN. Piso dialect may be the prestige dialect. Piso has 91% intelligibility of Kagan; 65% intelligibility of Tagakaulu, 92% intelligibility of Mansaka. Piso has 72% lexical similarity with Kagan, 74% lexical similarity with Mansaka; 83% lexical similarity with Sangab Mandaya. A population sample scored 87% on Cebuano narrative text. VSO. Literacy rate in first language: 80%. Literacy rate in second language: 80%. Muslim.

KALAGAN, KAGAN ***(KAAGAN, KAGAN KALAGAN)*** [KLL] 6,000 (1981 SIL). Davao City, Mindanao. Austronesian, Malayo-Polynesian, Western Malayo-Polynesian, Meso Philippine, Central Philippine, Mansakan, Western. Related to Kalagan; 82% intelligibility of Piso dialect. Bilingualism in Cebuano. Strong ethnic identity. Preference is for Kalagan language over Cebuano. Literacy rate in second language: Perhaps 60%. Bible portions 1980.

KALAGAN, TAGAKAULU ***(TAGAKAOLO)*** [KLG] 50,000 to 70,000 (1992 SIL). Southern Mindanao, South Cotabato, south of Kalagan. Austronesian, Malayo-Polynesian, Western Malayo-Polynesian, Meso Philippine, Central Philippine, Mansakan, Western. Related to Mandaya. 84% intelligibility of Piso dialect (Kalagan); 78% of Cebuano; 54% of Kagan Kalagan. Bilingualism in Cebuano. Literacy rate in first language: 20% to 30%. Literacy rate in second language: 20% to 30%. Bible portions 1964-1981.

KALANGUYA, KELEY-I ***(ANTIPOLO IFUGAO, KELEYQIQ IFUGAO, KELEY-I)*** [IFY] 5,000 (1980 SIL). Napayo, Kiangan Ifugao Province, northwest of Aritao, Nueva Vizcaya, Luzon. Austronesian, Malayo-Polynesian, Western Malayo-Polynesian,Northern Philippine, Northern Luzon, South-Central Cordilleran, Southern Cordilleran, Pangasinic, Benguet, Kallahan. Dialect: BAYNINAN. Literacy rate in second language: 70% to 75%. NT 1980.

KALINGA, BUTBUT ***(BUTBUT)*** [KYB] 4,000 (1981 PBS). 91,208 all Kalinga (1990 census). Luzon, Butbut, Tinglayan, Kalinga-Apayao Province. Austronesian, Malayo-Polynesian, Western Malayo-Polynesian, Northern Philippine, Northern Luzon, South-Central Cordilleran, Central Cordilleran, Kalinga-Itneg, Kalinga. 72% intelligibility of Limos Kalinga; 44% of Ilocano; 70% of Guinaang, 47% of Tanudan, 74% of Bangad (Southern) Kalinga. 82% lexical similarity with Bangan Kalinga, 78% of Guinaang and Tanudan,.

KALINGA, LIMOS ***(LIMOS-LIWAN KALINGA, NORTHERN KALINGA)*** [KMK] 20,000 (1977 SIL). Luzon, Kalinga-Apayao Province. Austronesian, Malayo-Polynesian, Western Malayo-Polynesian, Northern Philippine, Northern Luzon, South-Central Cordilleran, Central Cordilleran, Kalinga-Itneg, Kalinga. Literacy rate in first language: 55%. Literacy rate in second language: 80%. Bible portions 1977-1985.

KALINGA, LOWER TANUDAN ***(LOWER TANUDAN)*** [KML] 11,243 (1998 SIL). Luzon, southern Kalinga-Apayao Province. Austronesian, Malayo-Polynesian, Western Malayo-Polynesian, Northern Philippine, Northern Luzon, South-Central Cordilleran, Central Cordilleran, Kalinga-Itneg, Kalinga. Intelligibility of Limos Kalinga 79%, Guinaang 66%. Literature may serve Pangul. 87% lexical similarity with Pangul, 80% with Madukayang. Literacy rate in first language: 50%. Literacy rate in second language: 50%. Bible portions 1980.

KALINGA, LUBUAGAN [KNB] 12,000 to 15,000 (1998 SIL). Eastern Abra and Kalinga-Apayao provinces, Luzon. Austronesian, Malayo-Polynesian, Western Malayo-Polynesian, Northern Philippine, Northern Luzon, South-Central Cordilleran, Central Cordilleran, Kalinga-Itneg, Kalinga. Dialects: GUINAANG, BALBALASANG, BANAO ITNEG, LUBUAGAN, ABLEG-SALEGSEG. Intelligibility of Balbalasang 81%, Sumadel 82%, Limos 70%. 81% lexical similarity with Balbalasang and Limos. A population sample averaged 48% comprehension on Ilocano narrative. Literacy rate in first language: 70%. Literacy rate in second language: 70%. Bible portions 1970-1984.

KALINGA, MABAKA VALLEY ***(MABAKA ITNEG, KAL-UWAN)*** [KKG] Luzon, southeastern Kalinga-Apayao Province. Austronesian, Malayo-Polynesian, Western Malayo-Polynesian, Northern Philippine, Northern Luzon, South-Central Cordilleran, Central Cordilleran, Kalinga-Itneg, Kalinga. Bilingual in Limos Kalinga—79% average comprehension among the speakers tested.

KALINGA, MADUKAYANG ***(MADUKAYANG)*** [KMD] 1,500 (1990 SIL). Southern Mountain Province, Luzon. Austronesian, Malayo-Polynesian, Western Malayo-Polynesian, Northern Philippine, Northern Luzon, South-Central Cordilleran, Central Cordilleran, Kalinga-Itneg, Kalinga. 83% intelligibility of Limos and Balangao, 86% of Mangali. 80% lexical similarity with Tanudan Kalinga, 68% of Limos, 65% of Balangao, 80% of Mangali. A population sample averaged 68% comprehension on an Ilocano narrative test.

KALINGA, SOUTHERN ***(SUMADEL-TINGLAYAN KALINGA)*** [KSC] 12,000 (1981 SIL). Southern Kalinga-Apayao Province, Luzon. About 12 villages. Austronesian, Malayo-Polynesian, Western Malayo-Polynesian, Northern Philippine, Northern Luzon, South-Central Cordilleran, Central Cordilleran, Kalinga-Itneg, Kalinga. Dialects: MALLANGO, SUMADEL, BANGAD. Intelligibility of Guinaang Kalinga 63%, Mangali 51%. A population sample averaged 42% on an Ilocano narrative text. Literacy rate in first language: 65%. Literacy rate in second language: 65%. Mountain slope. NT 1986.

KALINGA, UPPER TANUDAN ***(UPPER TANUDAN)*** [KGH] 3,000 (1991 S. Brainard SIL). Luzon, Kalinga-Apayao Province, southern end of the Tanudan Valley. Austronesian, Malayo-Polynesian, Western Malayo-Polynesian, Northern Philippine, Northern Luzon, South-Central Cordilleran, Central Cordilleran, Kalinga-Itneg, Kalinga. Language attitudes require separate literature from Lower Tanudan Kalinga. Literacy rate in first language: 52%. Literacy rate in second language: 70% to 75%.

KALLAHAN, KAYAPA ***(KAYAPA, KALANGOYA, KALANGUYA, KALKALI, IKALAHAN, KALANGOYA-IKALAHAN, AKAB)*** [KAK] 15,000 (1991 UBS). Western Nueva Vizcaya, northeastern Pangasinan, western Ifugao, Luzon. Austronesian, Malayo-Polynesian, Western Malayo-Polynesian, Northern Philippine, Northern Luzon, South-Central Cordilleran, Southern Cordilleran, Pangasinic, Benguet, Kallahan. NT 1983.

KALLAHAN, TINOC ***(TINOC KALANGOYA)*** [TNE] Tinoc, a barrio of Hungduan in Luzon. Austronesian, Malayo-Polynesian, Western Malayo-Polynesian, Northern Philippine, Northern Luzon, South-Central Cordilleran, Southern Cordilleran, Pangasinic, Benguet, Kallahan. Intelligibility of Akab 95%, Tinoc 89%. Literature from other areas is probably not acceptable to the people. Investigation needed: bilingual proficiency, attitudes.

KAMAYO [KYK] Surigao del Sur between Marihatag and Lingig, Mindanao. Austronesian, Malayo-Polynesian, Western Malayo-Polynesian, Meso Philippine, Central Philippine, Mansakan, Northern. Dialects: NORTH KAMAYO, SOUTH KAMAYO. Intelligibility of Surigaonon 92%, of Butuanon 87%, of Mansaka 82%. 66% lexical similarity with Surigaonon, 70% with Butuanon. Fairly bilingual in Cebuano. Investigation needed: bilingual proficiency in Cebuano.

KANKANAEY ***(CENTRAL KANKANAEY, KANKANAI, KANKANAY)*** [KNE] 150,000 (1991 SIL). 218,279 all Kankanai (1990 census). Northern Benguet Province, southwestern Mountain Province, southeastern Ilocos Sur, northeastern La Union, Luzon. Austronesian, Malayo-Polynesian, Western Malayo-Polynesian, Northern Philippine, Northern Luzon, South-Central Cordilleran, Central Cordilleran, Nuclear Cordilleran, Bontok-Kankanay, Kankanay. Dialects: MANKAYAN-BUGUIAS, KAPANGAN, BAKUN-KIBUNGAN, GUINZADAN. Literacy rate in first language: 75%. Literacy rate in second language: 78%. Mountain slope. Agriculturalists: rice, vegetables. Traditional religion, Christian. NT 1990.

KANKANAY, NORTHERN ***(SAGADA IGOROT, WESTERN BONTOC)*** [KAN] 70,000 (1987 SIL). Western Mountain Province, southeastern Ilocos Sur, Luzon. Austronesian, Malayo-Polynesian, Western Malayo-Polynesian, Northern Philippine, Northern Luzon, South-Central Cordilleran, Central Cordilleran, Nuclear Cordilleran, Bontok-Kankanay, Kankanay. Grammar. Literacy rate in first language: 65% to 70%. Literacy rate in second language: 65% to 70%. NT 1984.

KARAO *(KARAW)* [KYJ] 1,400 (1998 SIL). Karao and Ekip, Bokod, eastern Benguet Province, Luzon. Austronesian, Malayo-Polynesian, Western Malayo-Polynesian, Northern Philippine, Northern Luzon, South-Central Cordilleran, Southern Cordilleran, Pangasinic, Benguet, Ibaloi-Karao. Limited comprehension testing showed Kayapa Kallahan 85%; Ilocano 78%. 90% lexical similarity with Ibaloi. Bilingual level estimates for Ibalo are 1-2 47%, 3 18%, 3+ 22%, 4 13%, 5 0%. Literacy rate in first language: 80% to 90%. Literacy rate in second language: 80% to 90%.

KAROLANOS [KYN] Mid-central Negros. Austronesian, Malayo-Polynesian, Western Malayo-Polynesian, Meso Philippine, Central Philippine. Present size, location need investigation. Investigation needed: bilingual proficiency in Cebuano, Hiligaynon.

KASIGURANIN *(CASIGURANIN)* [KSN] 10,000 (1975 SIL). Casiguran, Aurora Province, Luzon. Austronesian, Malayo-Polynesian, Western Malayo-Polynesian, Northern Philippine, Northern Luzon, Northern Cordilleran, Dumagat, Northern. 82% intelligibility of Paranan. 52% lexical similarity with Tagalog, 75% with Paranan. Fairly bilingual in Tagalog.

KATABAGA [KTQ] Bondoc Peninsula, Luzon. Austronesian, Malayo-Polynesian, Western Malayo-Polynesian, Unclassified. An assimilated group. Speak Tagalog. Negrito. Extinct.

KINARAY-A *(HINARAY-A, KINIRAY-A, KARAY-A, ANTIQUEÑO, HAMTIKNON, SULUD, ATI, PANAYANO)* [KRJ] 377,529 (1994 SIL). Iloilo and Antique provinces, western Panay. Austronesian, Malayo-Polynesian, Western Malayo-Polynesian, Meso Philippine, Central Philippine, Bisayan, West, Kinarayan. Dialects: PANDAN, HAMTIK, ANINI-Y, POTOTAN, LAMBUNAO, MIAG-AO, GUIMARAS ISLAND (GIMARAS). Antique has 67% comprehension of Tagalog; 61% of Hiligaynon; Iloilo has 78% of Hiligaynon; 85% of Antique. Bilingualism in Hiligaynon. Bible portions 1982-1985.

MAGAHAT *(BUKIDNON, ATA-MAN)* [MTW] Southwestern Negros, Mt. Amiyo near Bayawan. Austronesian, Malayo-Polynesian, Western Malayo-Polynesian, Meso Philippine, Central Philippine. Investigation needed: bilingual proficiency in Cebuano, Hiligaynon.

MAGINDANAON *(MAGUINDANAO, MAGINDANAW)* [MDH] 1,000,000 (1999 WA) including 766,565 Magindanaon (1990 census), 241,000 Iranun (1981 SIL), 1.7% of the population. Maguindanao, North Cotabato, South Cotabato, Sultan Kuderat, and Zamboanga del Sur provinces; Iranun also in Bukidnon, Mindanao. Austronesian, Malayo-Polynesian, Western Malayo-Polynesian, Southern Philippine, Danao, Magindanao. Dialects: LAYA, ILUD, BIWANGAN, SIBUGAY, IRANUN (ILANON, ILLANON, ILANUM, IRANON), TAGAKAWANAN. 84% intelligibility of Iranun, 60% of Maranao. Iranun has 98% intelligibility of Maguindanaon; 96% of Illanun of Sabah, Malaysia and 95% of Maranao. Subdialects of Iranun: Iranun and Isebanganen. Comprehension of Tagalog is low. Trade language. Dictionary. Literacy rate in first language: 60%. Literacy rate in second language: 60%. Muslim, Christian. Bible portions 1946-1995.

MALAYNON [MLZ] 8,500 (1973 SIL). Malay, northwest Aklan Province, lowland, Panay. Austronesian, Malayo-Polynesian, Western Malayo-Polynesian, Meso Philippine, Central Philippine, Bisayan, West, Aklan. 93% lexical similarity with Aklanon. Vigorous.

MAMANWA *(MAMANWA NEGRITO, MINAMANWA)* [MMN] 5,152 (1990 census). Agusan del Norte and Surigao provinces, Mindanao. Austronesian, Malayo-Polynesian, Western Malayo-Polynesian, Meso Philippine, Central Philippine, Mamanwa. Literacy rate in first language: 7%. Literacy rate in second language: 7%. NT 1982.

MANDAYA, CATAELANO *(CATEELENYO)* [MST] 19,000 (1980 census). 34,317 all Mandaya (1990 census). Town of Cateel, Davao Oriental, Mindanao. Austronesian, Malayo-Polynesian, Western Malayo-Polynesian, Meso Philippine, Central Philippine, Mansakan, Eastern, Mandayan. Fairly bilingual in Mansaka.

MANDAYA, KARAGA *(CARRAGA MANDAYA, MANAY MANDAYAN, MANGARAGAN MANDAYA)* [MRY] 3,000 (1982 SIL). Lamiyawan area, Davao Oriental, Mindanao. Austronesian, Malayo-Polynesian, Western Malayo-Polynesian, Meso Philippine, Central Philippine, Mansakan, Eastern, Caraga. 89% lexical similarity with Mansaka. Fairly bilingual in Mansaka.

MANDAYA, SANGAB *(SANGAB)* [MYT] Head of Carraga River, Banlalaysan area, highland, Davao del Norte, Mindanao. Austronesian, Malayo-Polynesian, Western Malayo-Polynesian, Meso Philippine, Central Philippine, Mansakan, Eastern, Mandayan. 77% intelligibility of Mansaka. 83% lexical similarity with Tumuwaong (Kalagan), 79% with Boston, 72% with Boso. Limited bilingualism in Cebuano.

MANOBO, AGUSAN *(AGUSAN)* [MSM] 40,000 (1981 SIL). 157,408 all Manobo (1990 census). Agusan del Norte, Agusan del Sur, Surigao del Sur, Mindanao. Austronesian, Malayo-Polynesian, Western Malayo-Polynesian, Southern Philippine, Manobo, Central, East. Dialects: UMAYAM, ADGAWAN, SURIGAO. 83% intelligibility of Dibabawon. Omayamnon has 80% lexical similarity with the other dialects, 85% with Dibabawon, 80% with Cebuano. Literacy rate in first language: 54.3%. Literacy rate in second language: 55% to 60%. Bible portions 1962-1992.

MANOBO, ATA *(ATAO MANOBO, ATA OF DAVAO, LANGILAN)* [ATD] 15,000 to 20,000 (1981 SIL). Mindanao, northwestern Davao. Austronesian, Malayo-Polynesian, Western Malayo-Polynesian,

Southern Philippine, Manobo, Central, South, Ata-Tigwa. Different from Ata of Mabinay, Negros Oriental, and Atta languages. A Negrito people. Literacy rate in first language: 25%. Literacy rate in second language: 25% to 30%. Bible portions 1974-1981.

MANOBO, CINAMIGUIN ***(CINAMIGUIN, KINAMIGIN, KAMIGIN)*** [MKX] 60,000 (1973 SIL). Camiguin Island, north of Mindanao. Austronesian, Malayo-Polynesian, Western Malayo-Polynesian, Southern Philippine, Manobo, North. Bilingualism in Cebuano.

MANOBO, COTABATO [MTA] 15,000 (1991 SIL). South Cotabato, Limulan Valley, Mindanao. Austronesian, Malayo-Polynesian, Western Malayo-Polynesian, Southern Philippine, Manobo, South. Dialects: TASADAY, BLIT. Dictionary. Literacy rate in first language: 15% to 20%. Literacy rate in second language: 15% to 20%. NT 1988.

MANOBO, DIBABAWON ***(MANDAYA, DIBABAON, DEBABAON)*** [MBD] 10,000 (1978 SIL). Manguagan, Davao del Norte, Mindanao. Austronesian, Malayo-Polynesian, Western Malayo-Polynesian, Southern Philippine, Manobo, Central, East. Dialect: MANGUAGAN MANOBO. Literacy rate in first language: 23%. Literacy rate in second language: 23%. NT 1978.

MANOBO, ILIANEN ***(ILIANEN)*** [MBI] 12,000 to 15,000 (1996 SIL). Northern Cotabato, Mindanao. Austronesian, Malayo-Polynesian, Western Malayo-Polynesian, Southern Philippine, Manobo, Central, West. Dialects: LIVUNGANEN, PULENIYAN. Literacy rate in first language: 15% to 20%. Literacy rate in second language: 15% to 20%. NT 1989.

MANOBO, MATIGSALUG ***(MATIG-SALUG MANOBO)*** [MBT] 15,000 (1998 SIL). Davao del Norte, southeast Bukidnon, Mindanao. Austronesian, Malayo-Polynesian, Western Malayo-Polynesian, Southern Philippine, Manobo, Central, South, Ata-Tigwa. Dialects: KULAMANEN, TIGWA, TALA INGOD, MATIG-SALUD. Tigwa has marginal intelligibility with Matigsalug. Tala Ingod may have adequate intelligibility with Matigsalug. People are becoming more bilingual in Cebuano. Investigation needed: intelligibility with Tigwa, Tala Ingod. Literacy rate in first language: 10%. Literacy rate in second language: 25%. Mountain slope. Bible portions 1972-1984.

MANOBO, OBO ***(OBO BAGOBO, BAGOBO, KIDAPAWAN MANOBO)*** [OBO] 80,000 to 100,000 (1998 SIL). Northeastern slope of Mt. Apo, between Davao del Sur and North Cotabato, Mindanao. Austronesian, Malayo-Polynesian, Western Malayo-Polynesian, Southern Philippine, Manobo, Central, South, Obo. 69% intelligibility of Tigwa (Matig-Salug Manobo; closest), 60% of Tagabawa Manobo, 13% of Ilianen Manobo. 63% lexical similarity with Tagabawa Manobo and Ilianen Manobo; 35% lexical similarity with Cebuano. Limited bilingualism in Cebuano. Literacy rate in second language: 40% (1994). Bible portions 1941-1993.

MANOBO, RAJAH KABUNSUWAN ***(RAJAH KABUNGSUAN MANOBO)*** [MQK] Southern Surigao del Sur. Austronesian, Malayo-Polynesian, Western Malayo-Polynesian, Southern Philippine, Manobo, Central, East. Intelligibility of Dibabawon Manobo 80%, San Miguel Calatugan Agusan 81% intelligibility. 82% lexical similarity with Dibabawon Manobo, 76% with Sagunto Agusan Manobo and San Miguel Calatugan Agusan Manobo. Low bilingualism in Cebuano, some in Dibabawon and Agusan Manobo. Investigation needed: bilingual proficiency in Dibabawon Manobo, Agusan Manobo.

MANOBO, SARANGANI [MBS] 35,000 (1987 SIL). Southern and eastern Davao, Mindanao. Austronesian, Malayo-Polynesian, Western Malayo-Polynesian, Southern Philippine, Manobo, South. Dialect: GOVERNOR GENEROSO MANOBO. Literacy rate in first language: 44%. Literacy rate in second language: 44%. NT 1982.

MANOBO, TAGABAWA ***(TAGABAWA, TAGABAWA BAGOBO)*** [BGS] 43,000 (1998 SIL). Mindanao, Davao City, slopes of Mt. Apo. Austronesian, Malayo-Polynesian, Western Malayo-Polynesian, Southern Philippine, Manobo, South. 45% intelligibility of Tigwa Manobo; low comprehension of Cebuano. 62% lexical similarity with Sarangani Manobo; 34% with Bagobo (Giangan). The official name is Tagabawa. Literacy rate in second language: 90%. Bible portions 1952-1992.

MANOBO, WESTERN BUKIDNON [MBB] 10,000 to 15,000 (1981 SIL). Mindanao, southern Bukidnon Province. Austronesian, Malayo-Polynesian, Western Malayo-Polynesian, Southern Philippine, Manobo, Central, West. Dialects: ILENTUNGEN, KIRIYENTEKEN, PULANGIYEN. Literacy rate in first language: 45%. Literacy rate in second language: 45%. Tropical forest. Mountain slope. Formerly swidden agriculturalists: upland rice; hunter-gatherers. Presently peasant agriculturalists: maize. NT 1978.

MANSAKA ***(MANDAYA MANSAKA)*** [MSK] 30,000 to 35,000 (1975 SIL). Eastern Davao and Davao Oriental Provinces, Mindanao. Austronesian, Malayo-Polynesian, Western Malayo-Polynesian, Meso Philippine, Central Philippine, Mansakan, Eastern, Mandayan. 80% lexical similarity with Bislig-Mati, 89% with Karaga Mandaya, 84% with Mati, 74% with Piso (Kalagan). NT 1975.

MAPUN ***(SAMA MAPUN, JAMA MAPUN, CAGAYAN DE SULU, CAGAYANON, KAGAYAN, BAJAU KAGAYAN, ORANG CAGAYAN, CAGAYANO)*** [SJM] 35,000 to 40,000 in the Philippines (1996 SIL). Population total both countries 35,000 to 40,000. Cagayan de Sulu and Palawan islands. Also spoken in Malaysia (Sabah). Austronesian, Malayo-Polynesian, Western Malayo-Polynesian, Sama-Bajaw, Sulu-Borneo, Borneo Coast Bajaw. 59% intelligibility of Central Sama. Somewhat bilingual in Tausug. Literacy rate in first language: 65% to 70%. Literacy rate in second language: 65% to 70%. Muslim. Bible portions 1979-1985.

MARANAO ***(RANAO, MARANAW)*** [MRW] 776,169 (1990 census), 1.4% of the population. Mindanao, Lanao del Norte and Lanao del Sur provinces. Austronesian, Malayo-Polynesian, Western Malayo-Polynesian, Southern Philippine, Danao, Maranao-Iranon. 87% intelligibility of Iranun (see Magindanaon); 52% of Magindanaon. Dictionary. Literacy rate in second language: 20%. Muslim, Christian. NT 1981.

MASBATENYO ***(MINASBATE, MASBATEÑO)*** [MSB] 600,000 first language speakers (1996 SIL), 150,000 to 200,000 second language speakers (1986 E. Wolfenden SIL). Masbate Province, three islands. Austronesian, Malayo-Polynesian, Western Malayo-Polynesian, Meso Philippine, Central Philippine, Bisayan, Central, Peripheral. Related to Hiligaynon and Capiznon. 79% lexical similarity with Capiznon, 76% with Hiligaynon. Masbatenyo used in the home, market, at work, on the street. Language of wider communication. Literacy rate in first language: 86.8%. Literacy rate in second language: 86.8%. NT 1993.

MOLBOG ***(MOLBOG PALAWAN)*** [PWM] 6,680 (1990 census). Population total both countries 6,680 or more. Balabac Island, southern Palawan, and Banggi Island, Sabah, Malaysia. Also spoken in Malaysia (Sabah). Austronesian, Malayo-Polynesian, Western Malayo-Polynesian, Meso Philippine, Palawano. Brooke's Point Palawano has 27% intelligibility; South Palawano 55% intelligibility. Quezon Palawano (Central) has 69% lexical similarity. Sama Mapun is used as second language, and 20% use Tagalog. Literacy rate in first language: 5%. Literacy rate in second language: 7%. Bible portions 1977.

PALAWANO, BROOKE'S POINT ***(PALAWAN, BROOKE'S POINT PALAWAN, PALAWEÑO, PALAWANUN)*** [PLW] 15,000 to 20,000 (1998 SIL). Southeastern Palawan. Austronesian, Malayo-Polynesian, Western Malayo-Polynesian, Meso Philippine, Palawano. Dialect: SOUTH PALAWANO (BUGSUK PALAWANO). Of Quezon Palawano (Central) 76% intelligibility, of Southwest Palawano 68%, of South Palawano 87% intelligibility. 82% lexical similarity with Quezon Palawano (Central), 85% with Southwest Palawano, 83% with South Palawano. Comprehension of Tagalog is low. Literacy rate in first language: 10%. Literacy rate in second language: 10%. Bible portions 1992.

PALAWANO, CENTRAL ***(QUEZON PALAWANO, PALAWANEN, PALAWEÑO)*** [PLC] 12,000 (1981 UBS). 40,549 all Palawano (1990 census). Central Palawan. Austronesian, Malayo-Polynesian, Western Malayo-Polynesian, Meso Philippine, Palawano. Of Brooke's Point Palawano 95% intelligibility, of Southwest Palawano 46% intelligibility. 82% lexical similarity with Brooke's Point Palawano, 78% of Southwest Palawano. Comprehension of Tagalog low. NT 1964.

PALAWANO, SOUTHWEST [PLV] 3,000 (1985 UBS). Southwest Palawan from Canipaan to Canduaga. Austronesian, Malayo-Polynesian, Western Malayo-Polynesian, Meso Philippine, Palawano. Intelligibility of Quezon Palawano (Central) 75%, Brooke's Point 76% intelligibility. 85% lexical similarity of Brooke's Point Palawano, 78% with Quezon Palawano (Central). Low comprehension of Tagalog.

PAMPANGAN ***(PAMPANGO, PAMPANGUEÑO, KAPAMPANGAN)*** [PMP] 1,897,378 (1990 census), about 3.4% of the population. Pampanga, Tarlac, and Bataan provinces, Luzon. Austronesian, Malayo-Polynesian, Western Malayo-Polynesian, Northern Philippine, Bashiic-Central Luzon-Northern Mindoro, Central Luzon, Pampangan. Dominant language in Pampanga Province. Language of wider communication. Bible 1917-1994.

PANGASINAN [PNG] 1,164,586 (1990 census), about 2.3% of the population. Pangasinan Province, Luzon. Austronesian, Malayo-Polynesian, Western Malayo-Polynesian, Northern Philippine, Northern Luzon, South-Central Cordilleran, Southern Cordilleran, Pangasinic. Grammar. Bible 1915-1983.

PARANAN ***(PALANENYO, PLANAN)*** [AGP] 14,220 to 15,220 including 13,220 Lowland Paranan, 1,000 to 2,000 Palanan Agta (1998 TAP). East coast, Isabela Province, Luzon; surrounded by hills. Isolated. Austronesian, Malayo-Polynesian, Western Malayo-Polynesian, Northern Philippine, Northern Luzon, Northern Cordilleran, Dumagat, Northern. Dialect: PALANAN DUMAGAT (PALANAN VALLEY AGTA, PALANAN VALLEY DUMAGAT). Paranan intelligibility of Casiguran Dumagat 76%. Palanan Dumagat intelligibility of Paranan 98%, of Casiguran Dumagat 94%. 85% lexical similarity with Palanan Dumagat. 87% lexical similarity with Casiguran Dumagat. Paranan speakers have moderate comprehension of Tagalog, low of Ilocano. Palanan Dumagat speakers have low comprehension of Tagalog and Ilocano. Lowland. Negrito. Literacy rate in first language: 75% (lowlanders), 1% to 3% (Negritos). Literacy rate in second language: 75% (lowlanders), 1% to 3% (Negritos). Accredited public school promised (1995). Tropical forest. Coastal. Bible portions 1988.

PHILIPPINE SIGN LANGUAGE ***(LOCAL SIGN LANGUAGE, FILIPINO SIGN LANGUAGE, FSL)*** [PSP] (100,000 deaf persons; 1986 Gallaudet Univ.). Deaf sign language. Reported to be very similar to ASL. American Sign Language is well-known as a second language. Total communication is used in deaf schools, with teachers both speaking and signing. Used by USA Peace Corps.

POROHANON ***(CAMOTES)*** [PRH] 23,000. Camotes Islands. Austronesian, Malayo-Polynesian, Western Malayo-Polynesian, Meso Philippine, Central Philippine, Bisayan, Central, Peripheral. Barely intelligible with Cebuano (J. Wolff 1967). Closer to Masbatenyo and Hiligaynon. 87% lexical similarity with Cebuano (J. Wolff 1967). Bilingual level estimates for Cebuano are 1-3 25%, 3+ 29%, 4 46%, 5 0%. Investigation needed: bilingual proficiency.

RATAGNON ***(DATAGNON, LATAGNUN, LATAN, LACTAN, ARADIGI)*** [BTN] 2,000 speakers (1997 SIL). Southern tip of western Mindoro. Austronesian, Malayo-Polynesian, Western Malayo-Polynesian, Meso Philippine, Central Philippine, Bisayan, West, Kuyan. Dialects: RATAGNON, SANTA TERESA. Close to Cuyonon. Rapidly assimilating to Tagalog.

ROMBLOMANON ***(ROMBLON)*** [ROL] 200,000 (1987 SIL). Romblon and Sibuyan Islands, parts of eastern Tablas Island, north of Panay. Austronesian, Malayo-Polynesian, Western Malayo-Polynesian, Meso Philippine, Central Philippine, Bisayan, Central, Romblon. Dialects: SIBUYAN, ROMBLON, BASIQ. Sibuyan Island has 70% intelligibility of Aklanon, 73% of Hiligaynon, 94% of Romblon. A sample population had 70% comprehension on Tagalog narrative.

SAMA, ABAKNON ***(ABAKNON, INBAKNON, INABAKNON, CAPUL, CAPULEÑO, KAPUL)*** [ABX] 20,000 to 30,000 (1997 SIL), including 11,000 on Capul, 5,000 elsewhere in the Philippines. Capul Island near San Bernardino Strait, Northwest Samar. Austronesian, Malayo-Polynesian, Western Malayo-Polynesian, Sama-Bajaw, Abaknon. Literacy rate in first language: 75% to 80%. Literacy rate in second language: 75% to 80%. Christian. NT 1996.

SAMA, BALANGINGI ***(BAANGINGI', BANGINGI SAMA, NORTHERN SAMA, NORTHERN SINAMA)*** [SSE] 60,000 in Philippines (1981 SIL), including 11,000 Sibuco-Vitali, 500 Sibuguey, 10,000 to 20,000 Balangingi. Population total both countries 90,000. Sulu Archipelago northeast of Jolo, Zamboanga coast, Basilan Island, western Mindanao. Some Balangingi may be on Luzon. Northern Sama speakers are at White Beach on Luzon near Subic Bay. Also spoken in Malaysia (Sabah). Austronesian, Malayo-Polynesian, Western Malayo-Polynesian, Sama-Bajaw, Sulu-Borneo, Inner Sulu Sama. Dialects: LUTANGAN (LUTANGO), SIBUCO-VITALI (SIBUKU), SIBUGUEY (BATUAN), BALANGINGI, DAONGDUNG, KABINGA'AN. Most Lutangan speakers (2,000 to 3,000, Olutangga Island, western Mindanao) understand Balangingi, the prestige dialect. Intelligibility of Central Sama is 71%, of Lutangan is 83%, of Sibuco-Vitali is 85%. 77% lexical similarity of Lutangan, 75% of Sibuco-Vitali. People have good bilingual comprehension of Tausug. Literacy rate in first language: 40% to 45%. Literacy rate in second language: 40% to 45%. Most urban men are literate. Coastal. Fishermen, traders, agriculturalists, professional. Muslim. Bible portions 1979-1988.

SAMA, CENTRAL ***(SIASI SAMA, CENTRAL SINAMA, SAMAL, SINAMA)*** [SML] 120,000 to 150,000 (1997 SIL). Population total both countries 120,000 to 150,000. Sulu Province. Also spoken in Malaysia (Sabah). Austronesian, Malayo-Polynesian, Western Malayo-Polynesian, Sama-Bajaw, Sulu-Borneo, Inner Sulu Sama. Dialect: DILAUT-BADJAO. 59% intelligibility of Tausug; 79% of Balangingi. Literacy rate in first language: 15%. Literacy rate in second language: 15%. Muslim, Christian. NT 1987.

SAMA, PANGUTARAN [SLM] 25,000 to 40,000 (1996 SIL). West central Sulu, west of Jolo, Mindanao. Also southern Palawan, Cagayan de Tawi-Tawi. Reported that there are also 145 in Sabah, Malaysia, Look Banga village of 620, Lahad Datu. Austronesian, Malayo-Polynesian, Western Malayo-Polynesian, Sama-Bajaw, Sulu-Borneo, Western Sulu Sama. 65% intelligibility of Central Sama. Moderate bilingualism in Tausug by 80% of speakers, and 20% use Tagalog. Literacy rate in first language: 25% to 30%. Literacy rate in second language: 25% to 30%. Agriculturalists. Muslim. NT 1994.

SAMA, SOUTHERN ***(SAMA SIBUTU', SOUTHERN BAJAU)*** [SIT] 30,000 or more in Philippines, including 6,652 Obian (1990 census). Population total both countries 50,000 to 100,000. Archipelago next to Borneo, southern Sulu. Tawi-Tawi Island group includes Tawi-Tawi, Simunul, Sibutu, and other major islands. Also spoken in Malaysia (Sabah). Austronesian, Malayo-Polynesian, Western Malayo-Polynesian, Sama-Bajaw, Sulu-Borneo, Inner Sulu Sama. Dialects: SIBUTU' (SIBUTU), SIMUNUL, TANDUBAS, OBIAN. Sibutu intelligibility: 77% of Sama Central; 89% of Simunul. Simunul intelligibility: 77% of Sama Central; 80% of Sibutu. Moderate bilingualism in Tausug by Sibutu and Simunul speakers. Literature may not be acceptable to other dialect speakers because of marginal intelligibility. Literacy rate in first language: 65% to 70%. Literacy rate in second language: 65% to 70%. Muslim. Bible portions 1979-1996.

SAMBAL, BOTOLAN ***(AETA NEGRITO, BOTOLAN ZAMBAL)*** [SBL] 31,500 (1975 census). Central Luzon, Zambales Province. People were affected by Mt. Pinatubo eruption. Austronesian, Malayo-Polynesian, Western Malayo-Polynesian, Northern Philippine, Bashiic-Central Luzon-Northern Mindoro, Central Luzon, Sambalic. Limited bilingualism in Tagalog. Literacy rate in first language: 90% lowlanders, 30% Negritos. Literacy rate in second language: 90% lowlanders, 30% Negritos. NT 1982.

SAMBAL, TINA ***(TINA, SAMBALI)*** [SNA] 70,000 (1998 SIL). Luzon, northern Zambales Province. Austronesian, Malayo-Polynesian, Western Malayo-Polynesian, Northern Philippine, Bashiic-Central Luzon-Northern Mindoro, Central Luzon, Sambalic. Tina has 70% intelligibility of Botolan. Moderate comprehension of Tagalog. Dictionary. Literacy rate in first language: 98%. Literacy rate in second language: 98%. Bible portions 1938-1979.

SANGIL ***(SANGIRI, SANGGIL)*** [SNL] 15,000 (1996 SIL). Balut Island, off Mindanao. Austronesian, Malayo-Polynesian, Western Malayo-Polynesian, Sulawesi, Sangir-Minahasan, Sangiric. Dialects: SARANGANI, MINDANAO. Speakers have limited bilingualism in Cebuano. Literacy rate in first language: 50%. Literacy rate in second language: 50%. Muslim, Christian. Bible portions 1979.

SANGIR ***(SANGIHÉ, SANGIRESE)*** [SAN] 55,000 in Philippines (1981 SIL). Balut and Sarangani islands off of Mindanao. Austronesian, Malayo-Polynesian, Western Malayo-Polynesian, Sulawesi, Sangir-Minahasan, Sangiric. NT 1883-1994. See main entry under Indonesia, Sulawesi.

SORSOGON, MASBATE ***(NORTHERN SORSOGON, SORSOGON BICOLANO)*** [BKS] 85,000 (1975 census). Luzon, Sorsogon, Casiguran and Juban, Sorsogon Province. Austronesian, Malayo-Polynesian, Western Malayo-Polynesian, Meso Philippine, Central Philippine, Bisayan, Central, Warayan. People with less than high school education are highly bilingual in Tagalog and Naga Bicolano.

SORSOGON, WARAY ***(SOUTHERN SORSOGON, BIKOL SORSOGON, GUBAT)*** [SRV] 185,000 (1975 census). Southern Sorsogon Province. Austronesian, Malayo-Polynesian, Western Malayo-Polynesian, Meso Philippine, Central Philippine, Bisayan, Central, Warayan, Gubat. Closely related to Waray-Waray. Bilingual in Tagalog, Central Bicolano, Masbatnyo. Comprehension of Masbaten: 63% to 91%; Central Bicolano (Naga): 71% to 82%; Tagalog 85% to 91%.

SPANISH [SPN] 2,658 (1990 census). Mainly in Manila. Indo-European, Italic, Romance, Italo-Western, Western, Gallo-Iberian, Ibero-Romance, West Iberian, Castilian. Formerly the official language. Used by a few families as mother tongue. Christian. Bible 1553-1979. See main entry under Spain.

SUBANEN, CENTRAL ***(SINDANGAN SUBANUN)*** [SUS] 120,000 to 150,000 (1998 SIL). Eastern Zamboanga Peninsula, Mindanao, Sulu Archipelago. Austronesian, Malayo-Polynesian, Western Malayo-Polynesian, Southern Philippine, Subanun, Eastern. Dialect: EASTERN KOLIBUGAN (EASTERN KALIBUGAN). 71% intelligibility of Lapuyan. 79% lexical similarity with Siocon. High comprehension of Cebuano. Literacy rate in first language: 50%. Literacy rate in second language: 50%. Traditional religion, Christian, Muslim. NT 1992.

SUBANEN, NORTHERN ***(TUBOY SUBANON)*** [STB] 10,000 (1985 SIL). Tuboy: Sergio Osmeña, Mutia; Zamboanga del Norte; Salog: Misamis Occidental, Mindanao. Austronesian, Malayo-Polynesian, Western Malayo-Polynesian, Southern Philippine, Subanun, Eastern. Dialects: DAPITAN, SALOG (SALUG), DIKAYU. 63% intelligibility of Sindanga, 40% of Lapuyan. 87% lexical similarity of Sindanga. Limited comprehension of Cebuano.

SUBANON, KOLIBUGAN ***(KOLIBUGAN, CALIBUGAN, KALIBUGAN)*** [SKN] 20,000 (1998 Bill Hall SIL). Mindanao, Zamboanga Peninsula, southern Zamboanga del Norte and Zamboanga del Sur provinces. Austronesian, Malayo-Polynesian, Western Malayo-Polynesian, Southern Philippine, Subanun, Kalibugan. Close to Western Subanon, but there are limitations on inherent intelligibility between the two. Lexical and grammatical differences. Culture and attitudes require Kolibugan to be viewed as separate from Western Subanon. Literacy rate in first language: 39%. Literacy rate in second language: 39%. Muslim, traditional religion.

SUBANON, WESTERN ***(SIOCON)*** [SUC] 75,000 (1997 SIL). Mindanao, Zamboanga Peninsula. Austronesian, Malayo-Polynesian, Western Malayo-Polynesian, Southern Philippine, Subanun, Kalibugan. Dialect: WESTERN KOLIBUGAN (WESTERN KALIBUGAN). Siocon and Western Kolibugan have 89% lexical similarity. Literacy rate in first language: 39%. Literacy rate in second language: 39%. Christian. NT 1996.

SUBANUN, LAPUYAN ***(LAPUYEN, MARGOSATUBIG, SUBANEN)*** [LAA] 25,000 (1978 Brichoux SIL). Sub-peninsulas of eastern Zamboanga del Sur, Mindanao. Austronesian, Malayo-Polynesian, Western Malayo-Polynesian, Southern Philippine, Subanun, Eastern. Lapuyan Subanun speakers understand Sindangan (85%), but not vice versa. Low comprehension of Cebuano. NT 1982.

SULOD ***(BUKIDNON, MONDO)*** [SRG] 14,000 (1980 SIL). Tapaz, Capiz Province; Lambunao, Iloilo Province; Valderrama, Antique Province, Panay. Austronesian, Malayo-Polynesian, Western Malayo-Polynesian, Meso Philippine, Central Philippine. Investigation needed: bilingual proficiency in Higaynon, Kinaray-a.

SURIGAONON [SUL] 344,974 (1990 census). Surigao, Carrascal, Cantilan, Madrid, Lanusa. Austronesian, Malayo-Polynesian, Western Malayo-Polynesian, Meso Philippine, Central Philippine, Bisayan, South, Surigao. Dialects: JAUN-JAUN, CANTILAN (KANTILAN), NATURALIS, SURIGAONON. 82% lexical similarity with Dibabawon Manobo, 81% with Agusan Manobo, 69% with Butuanon. Speakers are reported to have a high rate of bilingualism in Cebuano. Investigation needed: bilingual proficiency in Cebuano.

TADYAWAN ***(PULA, TADIANAN, BALABAN)*** [TDY] 3,000 to 5,000 (1998 OMF). East central Mindoro. Austronesian, Malayo-Polynesian, Western Malayo-Polynesian, Northern Philippine, Bashiic-Central Luzon-Northern Mindoro, Northern Mindoro. Most Tadyawan understand Tawbuid. A lot of intermarriage with the Tawbuid.

TAGALOG ***(FILIPINO, PILIPINO)*** [TGL] 16,911,871 first language speakers (1990 census), about 23.8% of the population. Used to some degree by 39,000,000 (1991 WA). Population total all countries 17,000,000. Including second language speakers: 57,000,000 (1999 WA). Manila, most of Luzon, and Mindoro. Also spoken in Canada, Guam, Midway Islands, Saudi Arabia, UAE, United Kingdom, USA. Austronesian, Malayo-Polynesian, Western Malayo-Polynesian, Meso Philippine, Central Philippine, Tagalog. Dialects: LUBANG, MANILA, MARINDUQUE, BATAAN, BATANGAS, BULACAN, TANAY-PAETE, TAYABAS. Pilipino is presently the national language. Filipino is to be developed from it to replace it. National language. Grammar. Roman script. Used in the schools. Christian. Bible 1905, in press (1998).

TAGBANWA ***(APURAHUANO, ABORLAN TAGBANWA)*** [TBW] 8,000 (1981 SIL). 13,386 probably including Central Taganwa (1990 census). Central and northern Palawan, around Lamane. Austronesian, Malayo-Polynesian, Western Malayo-Polynesian, Meso Philippine, Palawano. Intelligibility of Quezon Palawano (Central) 66%, of Cuyonon 77%. 65% lexical similarity with Quezon Palawano, 71% with Batak, 54% with Cuyonon. Speakers have low comprehension of Tagalog. Dictionary. Literacy rate in first language: 36%. Literacy rate in second language: 36%. Fishermen, agriculturalists. NT 1992.

TAGBANWA, CALAMIAN ***(KALAMIAN, CALAMIANO, KALAMIANON, KARAMIANANEN)*** [TBK] 8,472 (1990 census). Coron Island, north of Palawan, northern Palawan and Busuanga. Baras is on eastern coast of Palawan opposite Dumaran Island. Austronesian, Malayo-Polynesian, Western Malayo-Polynesian, Meso Philippine, Kalamian. Dialect: BARAS. Baras has 94% intelligibility of Calamian. Baras has 80% lexical similarity of Calamian. Literacy rate in first language: 40% to 50%. Literacy rate in second language: 40% to 50%. Bible portions 1968-1994.

TAGBANWA, CENTRAL [TGT] 2,000 (1985 SIL), about 235 families. Northern Palawan. Austronesian, Malayo-Polynesian, Western Malayo-Polynesian, Meso Philippine, Kalamian. Intelligibility of Tagbanwa (Lamane) 29%, 56% of Calamian Tagbanwa, 61% of Cuyonon. 56% lexical similarity with Tagbanwa (Lamane), 57% with Calamian Tagbanwa, 48% with Cuyonon, 40% with Tagalog. Low comprehension of Tagalog.

TAUSUG ***(TAW SUG, SULU, SULUK, TAUSOG, MORO JOLOANO)*** [TSG] 651,808 in the Philippines (1990 census). Population total all countries 764,000. Jolo, Sulu Archipelago. Also spoken in Indonesia (Kalimantan), Malaysia (Sabah). Austronesian, Malayo-Polynesian, Western Malayo-Polynesian, Meso Philippine, Central Philippine, Bisayan, South, Butuan-Tausug. Language of wider communication. Dictionary. Literacy rate in first language: 50%. Literacy rate in second language: 50%. Fishermen. Muslim, Christian. NT 1985-1998.

TAWBUID, EASTERN ***(BANGON, BATANGAN, TABUID, TAUBUID, TIRON, SURI, BARANGAN, BINATANGAN)*** [BNJ] 10,000 to 12,000 including Eastern and Western Tawbuid (1991 OMF). Central Mindoro. Austronesian, Malayo-Polynesian, Western Malayo-Polynesian, Meso Philippine, South Mangyan, Buhid-Taubuid. Western Tawbuid is different enough to need separate literature. NT, in press (1995).

TAWBUID, WESTERN ***(WESTERN TAUBUID)*** [TWB] (10,000 to 12,000 including Eastern Tawbuid; 1991 OMF). Central Mindoro. Austronesian, Malayo-Polynesian, Western Malayo-Polynesian, Meso Philippine, South Mangyan, Buhid-Taubuid. Different enough from Eastern Tawbuid to need separate literature.

TBOLI ***(TIBOLI, T'BOLI, "TAGABILI")*** [TBL] 80,000 to 100,000 (1997 SIL). South Cotabato, Mindanao. Austronesian, Malayo-Polynesian, Western Malayo-Polynesian, South Mindanao, Bilic, Tboli. Dialects: SINALON, KIAMBA, UBU. The Tboli dislike the name "Tagabili" formerly used for them. Literacy rate in first language: 15% to 20%. Literacy rate in second language: 15% to 20%. They operate their own government school. NT 1979-1992.

TIRURAY ***(TIRURAI, TEDURAY)*** [TIY] 34,340 (1975 census). Upi, Cotabato, Mindanao. Austronesian, Malayo-Polynesian, Western Malayo-Polynesian, South Mindanao, Tiruray. Literacy rate in first language: 49%. Literacy rate in second language: 49%. NT 1983, out of print.

WARAY-WARAY ***(SAMAREÑO, SAMARAN, SAMAR-LEYTE, WARAY, BINISAYA)*** [WRY] 2,437,688 (1990 census), about 4.6% of the population. Northern and eastern Samar-Leyte. Austronesian, Malayo-Polynesian, Western Malayo-Polynesian, Meso Philippine, Central Philippine, Bisayan, Central, Warayan, Samar-Waray. Dialects: WARAY, SAMAR-LEYTE, NORTHERN SAMAR. Several dialects. Investigation needed: intelligibility with dialects. Language of wider communication. Bible 1937-1984.

YAKAN ***(YACAN)*** [YKA] 105,545 (1990 census). Population total both countries 105,545 or more. Sulu Archipelago, Basilan Island, western Mindanao. Also spoken in Malaysia (Sabah). Austronesian, Malayo-Polynesian, Western Malayo-Polynesian, Sama-Bajaw, Yakan. 95% use Tausug, 10% use Chavacano as second language. Literacy rate in first language: 25%. Literacy rate in second language: 25%. Agriculturalists. Muslim. NT 1984.

YOGAD [YOG] 16,043 (1990 census). Echague, Isabela Province, Luzon. Austronesian, Malayo-Polynesian, Western Malayo-Polynesian, Northern Philippine, Northern Luzon, Northern Cordilleran, Ibanagic, Ibanag. Related to Ibanag and Gaddang. 52% lexical similarity with Ilocano, 66% with Itawis, 63% with Ibanag. Highly bilingual in Ilocano. Investigation needed: bilingual proficiency in Ilocano. 77% literacy in Isabela in 1955.

QATAR

State of Qatar, Dawlet al-Qatar. National or official language: Standard Arabic. 579,000 (1998 UN). Literacy rate 60% to 76%. Also includes Malayalam, Tamil, Urdu 19,950, Balochi, people from the Philippines 25,000 (1995), Sri Lanka. Sunni Muslim, Shi'a Muslim, Christian, Hindu. Deaf population 31,103. Data accuracy estimate: B. The number of languages listed for Qatar is 3. Of those, all are living languages. Diversity index 0.57.

ARABIC, GULF SPOKEN ***(KHALIJI, QATARI, GULF ARABIC)*** [AFB] 103,600 in Qatar, 56% of the population (1986). Afro-Asiatic, Semitic, Central, South, Arabic. Dialects: NORTH QATARI ARABIC, SOUTH QATARI ARABIC. Muslim. See main entry under Iraq.

ARABIC, STANDARD [ABV] Middle East, North Africa. Afro-Asiatic, Semitic, Central, South, Arabic. Used for education, official purposes, formal speeches. National language. Newspapers. Bible 1984-1991. See main entry under Saudi Arabia.

FARSI, WESTERN ***(PERSIAN)*** [PES] 73,000 in Qatar (1993), 23% of the population (1986). Indo-European, Indo-Iranian, Iranian, Western, Southwestern, Persian. Muslim. Bible 1838-1995. See main entry under Iran.

RUSSIA (ASIA)

See Russia in Europe for the list of languages in Europe. Also includes North Azerbaijani 336,000, Mandarin Chinese, Georgian 130,000, Kazakh 636,000, Korean, Lomavren, Osetin 402,000, Plautdietsch, Baltic Romani 20,000, Tajiki 38,000, Turkish, Turkmen, Udi 4,000, Ukrainian 4,363,000, Northern Uzbek 61,588. Data accuracy estimate: B. The number of languages listed for Russia (Asia) is 44. Of those, 42 are living languages and 2 are extinct. Diversity index 0.60.

AINU [AIN] South Sakhalin Island and southern Kuril Islands. Language Isolate. Dialects: SAKHALIN (SAGHILIN), TARAIKA, HOKKAIDO (EZO, YEZO), KURIL (SHIKOTAN). Ainu has not been determined to be related linguistically to any other language. Sources list up to 19 dialects. The last speaker of Sakhalin dialect died in 1994. Except for 15 speakers (1996), the Ainu in Japan speak Japanese. The Ainu spoken in China is a different, unrelated language. Nearly extinct. NT 1897. See main entry under Japan.

ALEUT ***(UNANGANY, UNANGAN, UNANGHAN)*** [ALW] 5 speakers of Bering Island Atkan (1995 M. Krauss). Nikolskoye settlement, Bering Island, Commander (Komandor) Islands. Eskimo-Aleut, Aleut. Dialect: BERINGOV (BERING, ATKAN). Bilingualism in Russian. All speakers of Bering Island Atkan are 60 years old and older (1995 M. Krauss). Aleut is taught in school until the fourth grade. Most ethnic group members in Russia speak Russian as mother tongue. From 1820 to 1840 dozens of Aleut families were brought from various islands to the Komandor Islands. Until the 1960s there were two villages on Bering and Medny islands. From the 1950s to the 1980s children were sent by the state to boarding schools. Dictionary. Grammar. Christian. Bible portions 1840-1903. See main entry under USA.

ALTAI, NORTHERN ***(TELEUT, TELENGUT)*** [ATV] (71,600 including Southern Altai; 1993 UBS). Gorno-Altai AO mountains, bordering on Mongolia and China. Altaic, Turkic, Northern. Not intelligible with Southern Altai. Considered a separate language outside the region. Bilingualism in Russian. Southern Altai is rejected by children. Traditional religion, secularist.

ALTAI, SOUTHERN ***(OIROT, OYROT, ALTAI)*** [ALT] 71,600 mother tongue speakers (86%) out of the ethnic population, including Northern Altai (1993 UBS). Gorno-Altai AO mountains, bordering on Mongolia and China. Altaic, Turkic, Northern. Dialects: ALTAI PROPER (ALTAI-KIZHI, ALTAJ KIZI, MAINA-KIZHI, SOUTHERN ALTAI), TALANGIT (TALANGIT-TOLOS, CHUY). Northern Altai and Southern Altai are not inherently intelligible, although there is a dialect continuum between them. Russian is used as the second language by all except older people as a contact language, for literature, and urban professional and cultural life. Altai is used in the familiar sphere and with speakers of other Turkic varieties. Written Altai is based on Southern Altai, but is rejected by Northern Altai children. Teleut is considered a separate language outside the AO. Different from Oirat (Kalmyk-Oirat), a Mongolian language. Cyrillic script.

Mountain slope. Cattle raisers, agriculturalists, hunters. Traditional religion, secularist. Bible portions 1910-1996.

ALUTOR ***(ALYUTOR, ALIUTOR, OLYUTOR)*** [ALR] 200 speakers out of 2,000 in the ethnic group (1997 M. Krauss). Koryak National District, northeast Kamchatka Peninsula, many in Vyvenka and Rekinniki villages, and individual families in Tilichiki, Ossora, and Palana. Some speakers are separated at considerable distances and without regular contact. Chukotko-Kamchatkan, Northern, Koryak-Alyutor. Dialects: ALUTORSKIJ, KARAGINSKIJ, PALANSKIJ. Considered a dialect of Koryak until recently. Bilingualism in Russian. The elderly speak Alutor actively and some are monolinguals; the middle-aged know it passively; those younger than 35 know only Russian (1997). Endangered. Children were sent to boarding schools during the 1950s to the 1970s.

BOHTAN NEO-ARAMAIC [BHN] Afro-Asiatic, Semitic, Central, Aramaic, Eastern, Central, Northeastern. Most over 60. Younger generations tend to shift to Georgian or Russian. Originally spoken by villagers in Anatolia, Ottoman Empire, east of the Tigris River (present-day southeastern Turkey). They fled to Russia during World War I. Christian. See main entry under Georgia.

BURIAT, RUSSIA ***(BURYAT, BURIAT-MONGOLIAN, NORTHERN MONGOLIAN)*** [MNB] 318,000 mother tongue speakers (90%) out of an ethnic population of 422,000 (1990 National Geographic). Buryat-Mongol ASSR, east of Lake Baikal, Siberia, bordering on Mongolia. Ulan Ude is the capital. Altaic, Mongolian, Eastern, Oirat-Khalkha, Khalkha-Buriat, Buriat. Dialects: EKHIRIT, UNGA, NINZNE-UDINSK, BARGUZIN, TUNKA, OKA, ALAR, BOHAAN (BOKHAN), BULAGAT. The Buriat in newspapers is that of the area around Irkutsk, west of Lake Baikal. The Buriat east of the lake is less influenced by Russian and is more like that in Mongolia. The literary dialect differs considerably from those spoken in Mongolia and China, which are influenced by other languages. Khori is the main dialect in Russia. Speakers in Russia apparently understand each other well. The younger generation in cities are fluent in Russian, which is the contact language with the outside world. Buriat is used with Buriat people. Heavily influenced by Russian. Literacy rate in second language: Those on both sides of the lake are fully literate in the literary style. Cyrillic. Newspapers. East: cattle, horse raisers; west: agriculturalists. Buddhist Lamaist (east), traditional religion (west). Bible 1846.

CHUKOT ***(CHUKCHA, CHUCHEE, CHUKCHEE, LUORAVETLAN, CHUKCHI)*** [CKT] 10,000 mother tongue speakers out of an ethnic population of 15,000 (1997 M. Krauss), Maritime Chukchi 25% of population, Raindeer Chukchi 75%. Chukchi Peninsula, Chukot and Koryak National Okrug, northern Yakut ASSR, northeastern Siberia. Chukotko-Kamchatkan, Northern, Chukot. Dialects: UELLANSKIJ, PEVEKSKIJ, ENMYLINSKIJ, NUNLIGRANSKIJ, XATYRSKIJ, CHAUN, ENURMIN, YANRAKINOT. Bilingualism in Russian, Yakut, Lamut, Yukagir. Nomadic groups have adult and some children speakers. Settled groups have few or no children speakers. Although those under 50 speak Russian with varying proficiency, nomadic groups resist Russian language and culture. School at Anadyr. Chukchi in Magadan area are nomadic. Reindeer herdsmen. Shamanism.

CHULYM ***(CHULYM-TURKISH, CHULIM, MELETS TATAR, CHULYM TATAR)*** [CHU] Basin of the Chulym River north of the Altay Mts., a tributary of the Ob River. Altaic, Turkic, Western, Uralian. Dialects: LOWER CHULYM, MIDDLE CHULYM. Closely related to Shor; some consider them one language. The government considers them separate. Bilingualism in Russian. Spoken in villages. Also spoken by the Kacik (Kazik, Kuarik).

DOLGAN [DLG] 5,000 (1994 UBS). Yakut ASSR. Altaic, Turkic, Northern. Bilingualism in Russian. A separate language from Yakut. Dolgan is the contact language on the Tajmyr Peninsula, and is spoken also by Evenki, Nganasan, and long-term Russian residents. Several publications in Dolgan. 2 Cyrillic orthographies: one based on Yakut and one on Russian. Traditional religion, shamanism.

ENETS ***(YENISEI SAMOYEDIC)*** [ENE] 90 speakers (1989 Juha Janhunen) out of an ethnic group of 200 (1990 census). 40 speakers in Forest Enets, 30 or fewer in Tundra Enets (1995 M. Krauss). Taimyr National Okrug. Along the Yenisei River's lower course, upstream from Dudinka. The 'Forest' dialect is in the Potapovo settlement of the Dudinka region, 'Tundra' in the Vorontzovo settlement of the Ust-Yenisei region. Uralic, Samoyedic, Northern Samoyedic. Dialects: BAY (PE-BAE, FOREST ENETS), MADU (SOMATU, TUNDRA ENETS). Two 'dialects' barely intelligible to each other's speakers. It is transitional between Yura and Nganasan. For a time it was officially considered part of Nenets. All speakers are bilingual or trilingual. Youngest speakers are in their 30s or 40s. About half of the ethnic middle-aged speak Enets, but no children or adolescents. In summer they wander between the left bank of the Yenisei River and the Yenisei Gulf; in winter in the grove tundras between the left tributaries of the Yenisei and Pyasino Lake on the Kheta River on the Taimyr Peninsula. Russian and Nenets people also live in some settlements. Those who assimilate with the Nenets keep the traditional way of life, those with the Russians are acculturating to modern ways. Intermarriage with other ethnic groups is uncommon. Grammar. Taught in school.

EVEN ***(LAMUT, EWEN, EBEN, ORICH, ILQAN)*** [EVE] 7,170 mother tongue speakers (56%) out of an ethnic population of 12,800 (1979 census). Yakutia and the Kamchatka Peninsula, widely scattered over the entire Okhotsk Arctic coast. Altaic, Tungus, Northern, Even. Dialects: ARMAN, INDIGIRKA, KAMCHATKA, KOLYMA-OMOLON, OKHOTSK, OLA, TOMPON, UPPER KOLYMA, SAKKYRYR, LAMUNKHIN. Ola dialect is not accepted by speakers of other dialects. A dialect continuum. It was incorrectly reported to be a Yukagir dialect. Bilingualism in Russian, Yakut. Youngest speakers may be in their 30s. Use of Even indicates solidarity. Some literature available. Reindeer herdsmen, hunters. Christian: Russian Orthodox. Bible portions 1880.

EVENKI ***(EWENKI, TUNGUS, CHAPOGIR, AVANKI, AVANKIL, SOLON, KHAMNIGAN)*** [EVN] 9,000 mother tongue speakers out of an ethnic population of 30,000 in Russia (1997 M. Krauss). Evenki National Okrug, Sakhalin Island. Capital is Ture. Altaic, Tungus, Northern, Evenki. Dialects: YERBOGOCEN, NAKANNA, ILIMPEYA, TUTONCANA, PODKAMENNAYA TUNGUSKA, CEMDALSK, VANAVARA, EAYKIT, POLIGUS, UCHAMA, CIS-BAIKALIA, SYM, TOKMO-UPPER LENA, NEPA, LOWER NEPA TUNGIR, KALAR, TOKKO, ALDAN TIMPTON, TOMMOT, JELTULAK, UCHUR, AYAN-MAYA, KUR-URMI, TUGURO-CHUMIKAN, SAKHALIN, ZEYA-BUREYA. Manegir may be a dialect or related language. Significant dialect differences from China. Bilingualism in Russian, Yakut, Buriat. Grammar. Literacy rate in second language: Nearly all. Shamanist, Lamaist, Christian. See main entry under China.

GILYAK ***(NIVKH, NIVKHI)*** [NIV] 400 or slightly more mother tongue speakers (1991) out of an ethnic population of 4,400 (1996 G. A. Otaina). 100 Amur speakers out of 2,000 population; 300 Sakhalin speakers out of 2,700 population (1995 M. Krauss). Sakhalin Island, many in Nekrasovka and Nogliki villages, small numbers in Rybnoe, Moskalvo, Chir-Unvd, Viakhtu, and other villages, and along the Amur River in Aleevka village. Language Isolate. Dialects: AMUR, EAST SAKHALIN GILYAK, NORTH SAKHALIN GILYAK. The Amur and East Sakhalin dialects have difficult inherent intelligibility with each other. North Sakhalin is between them linguistically. All members of the ethnic group are reported to be bilingual or monolingual in Russian. Most speakers are older than 50 years. The language has been written. Forced resettlement has weakened language use. Some are scattered and without regular contact with other speakers. Endangered. Taught through second grade in settlements at Nogliki and Nekrasovka. Not taught at Amur. Fishermen, agriculturalists (recently).

ITELMEN ***(ITELYMEM, WESTERN ITELMEN, KAMCHADAL, KAMCHATKA)*** [ITL] 100 or fewer speakers out of an ethnic population of 1,500 (1991 A. E. Kibrik). Southern Kamchatka Peninsula, Koryak Autonomous District, Tigil region, primarily in Kovran and Upper Khairiuzovo villages, west coast of the Kamchatka River. Chukotko-Kamchatkan, Southern. Dialects: SEDANKA, KHARYUZ, ITELMEN, XAJRJUZOVSKIJ, NAPANSKIJ, SOPOCNOVSKIJ. Bilingualism in Russian. Speakers are primarily the older generation. From the 1950s to the 1980s the state sent all children to boarding schools. All are reported to be acculturated. Taught in school through fourth grade. Shamanism. Bible portions 1996.

KAMAS ***(KAMASSIAN)*** [XAS] Sayan Mts., Abalakovo village. Uralic, Samoyedic, Southern Samoyedic. Dialects: KAMASSIAN, KOIBAL. Originally spoken in Siberia. Different from the Kamassian dialect of Khakas. Extinct.

KARAGAS ***(TOFA, TOFALAR, SAYAN SAMOYED, KAMAS, KARAGASS)*** [KIM] 600 (1959 census). Siberia. Altaic, Turkic, Northern. Bilingualism in Russian. The official name is Tofa or Tofalar. Grammar. Christian: Russian Orthodox.

KEREK [KRK] 2 speakers out of an ethnic population of 400 (1997 M. Krauss). There were 200 to 400 speakers in 1900. Cape Navarin, in Chukot villages. Chukotko-Kamchatkan, Northern, Koryak-Alyutor. Dialects: MAINYPILGINO (MAJNA-PIL'GINSKIJ), KHATYRKA (XATYRSKIJ). Kerek is now classified as a separate language. Previously it had been considered a dialect of Chukot. Speakers are now assimilated into Chukot. All are elderly. Nearly extinct.

KET ***(YENISEI OSTYAK, YENISEY OSTIAK, IMBATSKI-KET)*** [KET] 550 to 990 mother tongue speakers (80% to 85%) out of an ethnic population of 1,100 to 1,200 (1995, M. Krauss, 1991 A. E. Kibrik). Upper Yenisei Valley, Krasnoyarski drai, Turukhansk and Baikitsk regions, Sulomai, Bakhta, Verkhneimbatsk, Kellog, Kangatovo, Surgutikha, Vereshchagino, Baklanikha, Farkovo, Goroshikha, and Maiduka villages. East of the Khanti and Mansi, eastern Siberia. Yenisei Ostyak. Bilingualism in Russian. Youngest speakers are children or people 25 to 35 years old. No other extant related languages: the Arin, Assan, and Kott peoples became extinct in the 19th century. Traditional way of life has changed. Taught in 5 schools. Traditional religion.

KHAKAS ***(KHAKHAS, KHAKHASS, ABAKAN TATAR, YENISEI TATAR)*** [KJH] 64,800 mother tongue speakers (81%) out of an ethnic population of 80,000 in Russia (1993 UBS). Population total both countries 64,800 or more. Khakassia, north of the Altai Mts., and a few north of the Oblast. Ababan is the capital. Also spoken in China. Altaic, Turkic, Northern. Dialects: SAGAI (SAGAJ), BELTIR, KACHA (KACA), KYZYL, SHOR, KAMASSIAN. Bilingualism in Russian. Cyrillic script. Animal husbandry: sheep, goats, cattle, horses; industrialists. Traditional religion, Russian Orthodox. Bible portions 1995.

KHANTY ***(KHANTI, HANTY, XANTY, OSTYAK)*** [KCA] 12,000 mother tongue speakers out of an ethnic population of 21,000 (1994 Salminen, 1994 Janhunen). Northern Khanty has 9,000 speakers out of

15,000, Eastern Khanty has 3,000 speakers out of 5,000, Southern Khanty has few or no speakers out of 1,000. Khanty-Mansi National Okrug. Farther east than the Mansi, along the Ob River. Uralic, Finno-Ugric, Ugric, Ob Ugric. Dialects: NORTHERN KHANTI, EASTERN KHANTI, SOUTHERN KHANTI, VACH (VASYUGAN). Intelligibility is difficult between geographically distant dialects. Three dialect groups. Vach is an 'archaic' dialect. The dialect used in writing is rejected by many speakers. Russian is used in school. Hunters, fishermen, cattle raisers. Traditional religion. Bible portions 1868.

KORYAK ***(NYMYLAN)*** [KPY] 3,500 speakers out of an ethnic population of 7,000 (1997 M. Krauss). Koryak National Okrug, south of the Chukot; northern half of Kamchatka Peninsula and adjacent continent. Chukotko-Kamchatkan, Northern, Koryak-Alyutor. Dialects: CAVCUVENSKIJ (CHAVCHUVEN), APOKINSKIJ (APUKIN), KAMENSKIJ (KAMEN), XATYRSKIJ, PAREN, ITKAN, PALAN, GIN. Chavchuven, Palan, and Kamen are apparently not inherently intelligible. Bilingualism in Russian. A few children speak Koryak. Taught in school. Coast: fishermen, hunters; inland: cattle raisers. Traditional religion, Christian.

MANSI ***(VOGUL, GOGULICH, MANSIY, VOGULY)*** [MNS] 3,184 mother tongue speakers out of an ethnic population of 8,500 (1990 census). Northern Mansi has 3,000 speakers out of 7,000, Eastern Mansi has 100 speakers out of 1,000 population. Western Siberia between Komi-Zyrian and west of the Urals, between Urals and Ob River. Uralic, Finno-Ugric, Ugric, Ob Ugric. Dialects: NORTHERN VOGUL (SOS'VA, SOSYVIN, UPPER LOZYVIN), SOUTHERN VOGUL (TAVDIN), WESTERN VOGUL (PELYM, VAGILY, MIDDLE LOZYVIN, LOWER LOZYVIN), EASTERN VOGUL (KONDIN). Intelligibility between geographically distant dialects is difficult. May be 4 languages. Closest to Hungarian. Russian is used in education. Eastern Mansi is used only by the older generation. Southern Mansi has been extinct since about 1950. Western Mansi is nearly extinct or extinct. Hunters, fishermen, cattle raisers. Traditional religion. Bible portions 1868-1882.

MATOR [MTM] Sayan Mountains region. Uralic, Samoyedic, Southern Samoyedic. Dialects: MATOR, TAIGI, KARAGAS. Became extinct at the beginning of the 19th century. Extinct.

MEDNYJ ALEUT ***(MEDNY, COPPER, COPPER ISLAND ALEUT, ATTUAN, COPPER ISLAND ATTUAN, CREOLIZED ATTUAN)*** [MUD] 10 (1995 M. Krauss). Copper Island, Komandor Islands. Mixed Language, Russian-Aleut. Bilingualism in Russian. Aleut is taught in school until the fourth grade. Most ethnic group members in Russia speak Russian as mother tongue. From 1820 to 1840 dozens of Aleut families were brought from various islands to the Komandor Islands. Until the 1960s there were two villages on Bering and Medny islands. From the 1950s to the 1980s children were sent by the state to boarding schools. Christian. Nearly extinct.

MONGOLIAN, HALH ***(HALH, KHALKHA MONGOLIAN, MONGOL, CENTRAL MONGOLIAN)*** [KHK] 1,774 in Russia (1959). Buryat ASSR. Altaic, Mongolian, Eastern, Oirat-Khalkha, Khalkha-Buriat, Mongolian Proper. Dialects: KHALKHA (HALH), DARIGANGA, URAT, UJUMUCHIN. Halh serves as the basis for modern literary Mongolian. Buddhist. NT 1990. See main entry under Mongolia.

NANAI ***(NANAJ, GOLD, GOLDI, HEZHEN, HEZHE, HECHE)*** [GLD] 5,760 or fewer mother tongue speakers (48.5%) out of an ethnic population of 11,877 in Russia (1990 census). Population total both countries 5,760 or fewer. In the extreme Soviet far east, confluence of the Amur and Ussuri rivers, scattered in Ussuri Valley and Sikhote-Alin, settled more densely in the Amur Valley below Khabarovsk. Also spoken in China. Altaic, Tungus, Southern, Southeast, Nanaj. Dialects: SUNGGARI, TORGON, KURO-URMI, USSURI, AKANI, BIRAR, KILA, SAMAGIR. The dialects are quite distinct. Bilingualism in Russian, Chinese. Youngest speakers are over 30, with most over 50. Older people use Chinese. Shamanism. Bible portions 1884.

NEGIDAL ***(NEGIDALY, NEGHIDAL)*** [NEG] 100 to 170 or fewer speakers out of 500 in the ethnic group (1995 M. Krauss). Lower reaches of the Amur River, in two regions of the Khabarovsk krai (Ulch (Kamenka settlement and Im), and in the Paulina Osipenko region. Altaic, Tungus, Northern, Negidal. Dialects: NIZOVSK, VERKHOVSK. Elderly adults have a good command of the language, younger adults can understand it, children speak and understand only Russian. Endangered. From the 1950s to the 1980s the state sent all children to boarding schools. Traditional way of life. Contacts and inter-marriage with the Ulch, Nanai, and Nivkh in the Amur area. Dictionary. Grammar. Traditional religion.

NENETS ***(NENEC, NENTSE, NENETSY, YURAK, YURAK SAMOYED)*** [YRK] 26,300 mother tongue speakers out of an ethnic population of 27,000 (1994 Salminen). 1,300 Forest Nenets speakers out of 2,000; 25,000 Tundra Nenets. Northwest Siberia, tundra area from the mouth of the northern Dvina River in northeastern Europe to the delta of the Yenisei in Asia, and a scattering on the Kola Peninsula; Nenets, Yamalo-Nenets, and Taimyr national okrugs. Uralic, Samoyedic, Northern Samoyedic. Dialects: FOREST YURAK, TUNDRA YURAK. Bilingualism in Russian. 80% use Nenets in daily life. Speakers are mainly nomadic. Reindeer herdsmen. Christian, traditional religion.

NGANASAN ***(TAVGI SAMOYED)*** [NIO] 500 to 1,000 mother tongue speakers out of an ethnic population of 1,300 (1995 M. Krauss, 1989 census). Taimyr National Okrug, Taimyr Peninsula,

Siberia, Ust-Avam village in the Dudinka region; Volochanka and Novaya villages in the Khatang region. They are the northernmost people in Russia, near the Yakut, Dolgan, and Evenki peoples. Uralic, Samoyedic, Northern Samoyedic. Dialects: AVAM, KHATANG. Russian is used as second language. Dolgan is a separate language, but is also used by Nganasan speakers. They formerly had passive bilingualism or trilingualism with Tundra Enets and Nenets. The older and middle and a third of the younger generations have full command of the language. It is even more so in Volochanka. Few children are speakers. Ethnic pride is expressed. Status is enhanced by knowledge of the Nganasan language. Two ethnic groups: Avam and Vadeyev. They were resettled in several villages they had formerly used as winter quarters or trading posts along their migratory routes in the 1940's. Before that they had intermittent contact with the Tundra Enets and the Nenets. They were formerly officially considered to be part of Nenets. Resettlement has brought close contact with Russian, Ukrainian, Belorussian, and Tatar peoples. Nganasan is taught in school to ethnic Nganasan who do not use it as mother tongue. Traditional religion, shamanism.

OROCH *(OROCHI)* [OAC] 100 to 150 or fewer mother tongue speakers (1995 M. Krauss) out of an ethnic population of 900 (1990 census). Eastern Siberia in the Khabarovski krai along the rivers that empty into the Tatar Channel, on Amur River not far from the city of Komsomolsk-na-Amure. Many live in the Vanino region in Datta and Uska-Orochskaya settlements. Some live among the Nanai. Altaic, Tungus, Southern, Southeast, Udihe. Dialects: KJAKELA (KJAKAR, KEKAR), NAMUNKA, ORICHEN, TEZ. Bilingualism in Russian. The older and middle-aged speak Oroch, but not those up to 20 years old, who speak Russian. The larger of the two groups lives in the region of Sovetskaja Gavan' on the rivers flowing into the Tatar Strait separating Sakhalin Island from the mainland. Not taught in school. Russians, Ukrainians, and Evenki live among them. For a time it was officially considered part of Udihe. Different from Orok. The same writing system as the Udihe. Traditional religion, Buddhism, Christian.

OROK *(OROC, ULTA, UJLTA)* [OAA] 30 to 82 speakers out of 250 to 300 in the ethnic group (1995 M. Krauss). Population total both countries 33 to 85. Sakhalin Island, Poronajsk District, Poronajsk town, Gastello and Vakhrushev settlements; Nogliki District, Val village, Nogliki settlement. Also spoken in Japan. Altaic, Tungus, Southern, Southeast, Nanaj. Dialects: PORONAISK (SOUTHERN OROK), VAL-NOGLIKI (NOGLIKI-VAL, NORTHERN OROK). Significant differences between dialects. For a while Orok was officially considered part of Nanai. Prevalent intermarriage with Russians, Nivkh, Nanai, Evenksi, Negidal, and Korean people. The older generation has high proficiency in Orok, the middle generation partial proficiency, children and adolescents no ability in Orok. Youngest fluent speakers are over 50. Endangered. Speakers have been scattered and have relinquished their traditional way of life. Different from Oroch.

SELKUP *(OSTYAK SAMOYED)* [SAK] 1,570 mother tongue speakers out of an ethnic population of 3,600 (1994 Salminen, 1994 Janhunen). Northern Sel'kup has 1,400 speakers out of 1,700, Central Sel'kup has 150 speakers out of 1,700, Southern Sel'kup has 20 speakers out of 200. Tom Oblast, Yamalo-Nenets Autonomous District, Krasnoyarski krai and Tomskaya oblast. The northern dialect is spoken in Krasnoselkup region, Krasnoselkup, Sidorovsk, Tolka, Ratta, and Kikiyakki villages; part of the Purovsk region, Tolka Purovskaya village; adjacent regions of the Krasnoyarski krai; Kureika village, Kellog, and Turukhan River basin and Baikha. The southern dialect (Tym) is spoken in a range of villages in the northern part of the Tomskaya oblast. Uralic, Samoyedic, Southern Samoyedic. Dialects: TAZ (NORTHERN SEL'KUP, TAZOV-BAISHYAN), TYM (CENTRAL SELK'UP, KETY), NARYM (CENTRAL SEL'KUP), SREDNYAYA OB-KET (SOUTHERN SEL'KUP). A dialect continuum with difficult or impossible intelligibility between the extremes. Speakers in the south are separated from others. Bilingualism in Russian. Northern dialect: spoken by 90% of the Selkup, with young adults and younger not having mastered it. Southern dialect: spoken by 30% of the Selkup, with 10% speaking it fluently. Selkup was formerly used as lingua franca by the Ket, Evenki, Nenets, and Khanty. The writing system has been updated. The northern dialect is taught in the schools through fourth grade. Christian, shamanism.

SHOR *(SHORTSY, ABA, KONDOMA TATAR, MRAS TATAR, KUZNETS TATAR, TOM-KUZNETS TATAR)* [CJS] 9,760 mother tongue speakers (61%) out of an ethnic population of 16,000 (1979 census). Altai Krai, Khakass AO and Gorno-Altai AO, on the River Tomy. Altaic, Turkic, Northern. Dialects: MRASSA, KONDOMA. Some sources combine Shor and Chulym. Before 1927 literary norms were developing, it was taught in school, literature was published, and the language and culture were studied. After 1937 it was no longer written or taught in school for 50 years, and the culture was damaged. There is now a revival of study (I. A. Nevskaya 1996). A language association has been formed, and a chair of Shor was formed at the Pedagogical Institute in Novokuzneck. Shor is different from the Shor dialect of Khakas. Grammar. Altai missionaries worked out the first alphabet in the middle of the 19th century. Mountain slope. Christian: Russian Orthodox.

TUVIN ***(TUVA, TUVAN, TUVIA, TYVA, TOFA, TOKHA, SOYOT, SOYON, SOYOD, TANNU-TUVA, TUBA, TUVINIAN, URIANKHAI, URIANKHAI-MONCHAK, URYANKHAI, DIBA, KÖK MUNGAK)*** [TUN] 206,000 in Russia (1993 Johnstone), 99% speak it as mother tongue. Population total all countries 233,400. Tuvin AO. Capital is Kyzl. Also spoken in China, Mongolia. Altaic, Turkic, Northern. Dialects: CENTRAL TUVIN, WESTERN TUVIN, NORTHEASTERN TUVIN (TODZHIN), SOUTHEASTERN TUVIN, TUBA-KIZHI. Sharp dialect differences. Speakers use Russian as second language, and Mongolian near the border. Until 1944 Tuva was a formally independent state. Literacy rate in second language:. Cyrillic script. Hunters; pastoralists: cattle, horses, sheep, goats, camels, reindeer. Lamaist Buddhist. Bible portions 1996.

UDIHE ***(UDEKHE, UDEGEIS)*** [UDE] 100 speakers out of 1,600 in the ethnic group (1991 A. E. Kibrik). Siberian far east; Khabarovski krai, Gvasiugi settlement, Lazo region; Arsenievo settlement, Nanai region; Primorski krai, Krasny Yar settlement in the Pozharsk region, Agzu settlement in the Terneisk region. Altaic, Tungus, Southern, Southeast, Udihe. Dialects: KHUNGARI, KHOR, ANJUSKI, SAMARGIN, BIKIN, IMAN, SIKHOTA ALIN. Dialect differences are not great. All are 50 years old and older (1991). They were resettled into artificial villages, in a Russian-speaking region, with some Ukrainian and Nanai people. Children were sent to boarding schools. 'Hezhe' in China may refer to this. Same as Orok. Shamanism. Nearly extinct.

ULCH ***(ULCHI, ULCHA, ULYCH, OLCH, OLCHA, OLCHIS, HOCHE, HOL-CHIH)*** [ULC] 500 to 1,000 (1995 M. Krauss) out of 3,200 in the ethnic group (1990 census). Ulch region of the Khabarosvki krai along the Amur River and its tributaries, along the coast of the Tatar Channel. Bogorodskove is the capital. Also at Bulava, Dudi, Kalinovka, Mariinskoe, Nizhnaya Gavan, Savinskoe, Mongol, Solontsy, Kolchom, Sofiyskoe, Tur, and Ukhta. Altaic, Tungus, Southern, Southeast, Nanaj. Bilingualism in Russian. The older generation knows the language, middle-aged less well, adolescents and young adults passively, children under 20 do not speak it. Close contact with Russian, Ukrainian, Nanai, Nivkh (Gilyak), Negidal, and others. Taught in first grade.

YAKUT ***(SAKHA, YAKUT-SAKHA)*** [UKT] 363,000 mother tongue speakers (95%) out of an ethnic population of 382,000 (1993 UBS)). Yakutia, near the Arctic Ocean, nearly the entire length of the basin of the middle Lena River and the Aldan and Kolyma rivers; 2,000 miles long. Jakutsk (Yakutsk) is the capital. Altaic, Turkic, Northern. Russian is used in higher education. It is used as second language by some Evenki, Even, and Yukaghir people. A town koine has developed in Jakutsk, which older speakers rejected. A higher percentage of teachers and officials come from this group than from nearby languages. Yakut is preferred by most speakers for most purposes. Grammar. Cyrillic script. Nomadic, fishermen, hunters, agriculturalists. Traditional religion, secular, Christian: Russian Orthodox. Bible portions 1858-1995.

YUGH ***(YUG)*** [YUU] 2 or 3 semi-speakers out of an ethnic group of 10 to 15 (1991 G. K. Verner in Kibrik). Turukhan region of the Krasnoyarsk krai at the Vorogovo settlement. Previously they lived along the Yenisei River from Yeniseisk to the mouth of the Dupches. Yenisei Ostyak. No published descriptions of the language (1991). Nearly extinct.

YUKAGHIR, NORTHERN ***(YUKAGIR, JUKAGIR, ODUL, TUNDRA, TUNDRE, NORTHERN YUKAGIR)*** [YKG] 30 to 150 Tundra out of 230 to 1,100 in the ethnic group (1995 M. Krauss, 1989 census). Yakutia and the Kamchatka Peninsula. Yukaghir. Not inherently intelligible with Southern Yukaghir (Kolyma). It may be distantly related to Altaic or Uralic. Even is the literary language used. Speakers below 50 years use Russian as second language. All can speak Yakut. Reindeer herdsmen and some other families can speak Even. Chukot is also used. Most speakers over 50 years old. Endangered. No sense of ethnic identity between speakers of the two Yukaghir varieties. In the 19th century their territory shrank because of merging clans, military clashes, assimilation with the Even, and later, collectivization. From the 1950s to the 1980s the state sent all children to boarding school. 'Odul' is their name for themselves. SOV; postpositions; genitives, articles, adjectives, numerals, relatives before noun heads; question word not initial or final; 2 prefixes, 6 suffixes; word order focus preverbal, subjects and topics tend to be initial; affixes indicate case of noun phrases; person and number of subject indicated by obligatory verb phrases; split intransitivity: intransitive subjects encoded as transitive when nonfocus; focus marked the same way for intransitive subjects and direct objects, and only those, otherwise rather accusative; resultative; reflexive; reciprocal; causative; comparative; CV, CVCCVV; nontonal. Taught through fourth grade in the Adnriushkino settlement, and as an elective through eighth grade in Nelemnoye. Pine and deciduous forest. Riverine. Swidden agriculturalists; heavy dependence on the support of the government. Christian, traditional religion.

YUKAGHIR, SOUTHERN ***(YUKAGIR, JUKAGIR, ODUL, KOLYMA, KOLYM, SOUTHERN YUKAGIR)*** [YUX] 10 to 50 speakers out of 130 in the ethnic group (1995 M. Krauss, 1989 census). Yakutia and the Kamchatka Peninsula. Yukaghir. Not inherently intelligible with Northern Yukaghir. All can speak Russian as second language, especially those below 40. Those above 35 can speak Yakut, and those over 60 can speak Even. Russian is used as a literary language. All over 35 to 40 years old

(1989). SOV; postpositions, genitives, articles, adjectives, numerals, relatives before noun heads; question word not initial or final; 2 prefixes, 6 suffixes; focus is preverbal, subjects and topics tend to be initial; affixes indicate case of noun phrases; person and number of subject is obligatory; split intransitivity: intransitive subjects encode as transitive when nonfocus, focus marked the same for intransitive subjects and direct objects, and only for those; otherwise rather accusative; resultative; reflexive; reciprocal; causative; comparative; CV, CVCCVV; nontonal. Pine and deciduous forest. Riverine. Swidden agriculturalists; heavy dependence on the support of the government. Christian, traditional religion.

YUPIK, CENTRAL SIBERIAN *(YOIT, YUK, YUIT, ASIATIC ESKIMO, SIBERIAN YUPIK)* [ESS] 300 speakers out of 1,200 to 1,500 population in Russia (1991 A. E. Kibrik). Chukchi National Okrug, coast of the Bering Sea, Wrangel Island. The Chaplino live in Providenie region in Novo-Chaplino and Providenie villages. Eskimo-Aleut, Eskimo, Yupik, Siberian. Dialects: AIWANAT, NOOHALIT (PEEKIT), WOOTEELIT, CHAPLINO. Chaplino and Naukan speakers have 60% to 70% inherent intelligibility with each other. Sirenik is a separate language. Older people have active command of the language, those 35 to 50 have passive knowledge, children know what they have learned in school. Resettlement has weakened language use, but recent contacts with Alaska have increased prestige. School at Anadyr. Chaplino is taught in schools through fourth grade. Shamanism. Bible portions 1974-1998. See main entry under USA.

YUPIK, NAUKAN *(NAUKAN, NAUKANSKI)* [YNK] 75 (1990 L. D. Kaplan) to 100 speakers (1991 A. E. Kibrik) out of an ethnic population of 350. Chukota region, Laurence, Lorino, and Whalen villages, scattered. Formerly spoken in Naukan village and the region surrounding East Cape, Chukot Peninsula, but they have been relocated. Eskimo-Aleut, Eskimo, Yupik, Siberian. 60% to 70% intelligibility with Chaplino.

YUPIK, SIRENIK *(SIRENIK, SIRENIKSKI, OLD SIRENIK, VUTEEN)* [YSR] 1 fluent speaker (1995 M. Krauss). Chukot Peninsula, Sireniki village. Eskimo-Aleut, Eskimo, Yupik, Siberian. The speaker is elderly (1996). Other Eskimo residents of Sirenik village now speak Central Siberian Yupik. Nearly extinct.

SAUDI ARABIA

Kingdom of Saudi Arabia, al-Mamlaka al-<Arabiya as-Sa<udiya. National or official language: Standard Arabic. 17,181,000 (1998 UN). Literacy rate 38%, 50% men. Also includes Egyptian Spoken Arabic 300,000, Sudanese Spoken Arabic, Bengali 15,000, Western Cham 100, English, Western Farsi 102,000, French, Indonesian 37,000, Italian, Kabardian, Korean 66,000, Somali, Tagalog, Urdu 382,000, Uyghur, Chinese 58,000, from India 120,000, from the Philippines 700,000 (1995), others from Nigeria. Information mainly from M. Bateson 1967; T. M. Johnstone 1987; B. Comrie 1987; A. S. Kaye 1988; C. Holes 1990; B. Ingham 1994. Sunni Muslim, Shi'a Muslim, Ismaili. Blind population 140,000. Deaf population 1,103,284. Data accuracy estimate: B. The number of languages listed for Saudi Arabia is 5. Of those, all are living languages. Diversity index 0.56.

ARABIC, GULF SPOKEN *(GULF SPOKEN)* [AFB] 200,000 in Saudi Arabia. Northern and southern Eastern Province. Afro-Asiatic, Semitic, Central, South, Arabic. Dialect: AL-HASAA. See main entry under Iraq.

ARABIC, HIJAZI SPOKEN *(HIJAZI, WEST ARABIAN COLLOQUIAL ARABIC)* [ACW] 6,000,000 (1996). Population total both countries 6,000,000 or more. Red Sea coast and adjacent highlands. Also spoken in Eritrea. Afro-Asiatic, Semitic, Central, South, Arabic. Dialects: NORTH HIJAZI, SOUTH HIJAZI, VALLEY TIHAAMAH, COASTAL TIHAAMAH. North Hijazi has 4 subdialects, South Hijazi 16.

ARABIC, NAJDI SPOKEN [ARS] 8,000,000 in Saudi Arabia. Population total all countries 9,800,000. Also spoken in Canada, Iraq, Jordan, Kuwait, Syria, USA. Afro-Asiatic, Semitic, Central, South, Arabic. Dialects: NORTH NAJDI (SHAMMARI, BANI KHAALID, DAFIIR), CENTRAL NAJDI (RWALA, HAAYIL, AL-QASIIM, SUDAIR, RIYADH, HOFUF, BIISHAH, NAJRAAN, WILD <ALI, <AWAAZIM, RASHAAYDA, MUTAIR, <UTAIBA, <AJ MAAN), SOUTH ANJDI (AAL MURRAH, NAJRAN). Some dialects are spoken by Bedouins. SVO. Muslim.

ARABIC, STANDARD *(HIGH ARABIC, AL FUS-HA, AL ARABIYA)* [ABV] Middle east, north Africa, other Muslim countries. Also spoken in 24 other countries including Algeria, Bahrain, Chad, Comoros Islands, Egypt, Eritrea, Iraq, Israel, Jordan, Kuwait, Lebanon, Libya, Morocco, Oman, Palestinian West Bank and Gaza, Qatar, Somalia, Sudan, Syria. Afro-Asiatic, Semitic, Central, South, Arabic. Dialects: MODERN STANDARD ARABIC (MODERN LITERARY ARABIC), CLASSICAL ARABIC (KORANIC ARABIC, QURANIC ARABIC). Used for education, official purposes, written materials, and formal speeches. Classical Arabic is used for religion and ceremonial purposes, having archaic vocabulary. Modern Standard Arabic is a modernized variety of Classical Arabic. In most Arab countries only the well educated have adequate proficiency in Standard Arabic, while over 100,500,000 do not. National language. VSO. Not a mother tongue, but taught in schools. Bible 1984-1991.

SAUDI ARABIAN SIGN LANGUAGE [SDL] Deaf sign language.

SINGAPORE

Republic of Singapore. National or official languages: Bengali, Mandarin Chinese, Malay, Tamil, English. 3,476,000 (1998 UN). Total ethnic Chinese are 2,227,000 or 76.4% of the population. Literacy rate 87% to 90%. Also includes Hindi 5,000, Indonesian, Japanese 20,000, Korean 5,200, Sindhi 5,000, Telugu 300, Thai 30,000, Tukangbesi North, people from the Philippines 50,000. Chinese traditional religion, Muslim, secular, Christian, Hindu. Blind population 1,442. Deaf institutions: 3. Data accuracy estimate: B. The number of languages listed for Singapore is 21. Of those, all are living languages. Diversity index 0.74.

BENGALI [BNG] 600 speakers in Singapore (1985), out of 12,000 in the ethnic group in Singapore (1993 Johnstone). Indo-European, Indo-Iranian, Indo-Aryan, Eastern zone, Bengali-Assamese. National language. Bengali script. Hindu, Muslim. Bible 1809-1998. See main entry under Bangladesh.

CHINESE, HAKKA ***(KHEK, KEK, KEHIA, KECHIA, KE, HOKKA)*** [HAK] 69,000 speakers in Singapore (1980), or 2.9% of the population, out of 151,000 in the ethnic group (1993). Sino-Tibetan, Chinese. Bible 1916. See main entry under China.

CHINESE, MANDARIN ***(HUAYU, GUOYU)*** [CHN] 201,000 speakers, 7.9% of population, and 880,000 second language users (literate in Mandarin) in Singapore (1985 estimate). Sino-Tibetan, Chinese. Increasing use. 44% also use other Chinese varieties at home; 12% use English at home. National language. Taught in schools. Bible 1874-1983. See main entry under China.

CHINESE, MIN BEI ***(MIN PEI)*** [MNP] 4,000 speakers of Hokchia out of 11,000 in ethnic group in Singapore (1985). Sino-Tibetan, Chinese. Dialect: HOKCHIA (HOCKCHEW). NT 1934. See main entry under China.

CHINESE, MIN DONG [CDO] 15,000 speakers of Foochow out of 31,391 in ethnic group in Singapore (1985). Mainly in China. Sino-Tibetan, Chinese. Dialect: FUZHOU (FUCHOW, FOOCHOW, GUXHOU). Bible 1884-1905. See main entry under China.

CHINESE, MIN NAN ***(MIN NAM, SOUTHERN MIN)*** [CFR] 1,170,000 speakers in Singapore (1985), out of 1,482,000 in the ethnic group (1993), including 736,000 speakers of Hokkien, 28.8% of the population, out of 884,000 in the ethnic group (1993), 360,000 speakers of Teochew (1985), 14.2% of the population out of 452,000 in the ethnic group (1993); 74,000 speakers of Hainanese (1985), 2.9% of the population out of 146,000 in the ethnic group (1993). Sino-Tibetan, Chinese. Dialects: HOKKIEN (FUKIENESE, FUJIAN, AMOY, XIAMEN), TEOCHEW (CHAOCHOW, CHAOZHOU, TAECHEW), HAINANESE. Speakers report Hokkien and Teochew to be intelligible with each other, but not Hainanese. Mandarin, English, and other Chinese varieties are also used at home. Hokkien is the most widely understood language in Singapore (Kuo 1979). Trade language. Bible 1933. See main entry under China.

CHINESE, PU-XIAN [CPX] 6,000 speakers of Henghua in Singapore, out of 12,902 in ethnic group (1985). Sino-Tibetan, Chinese. Dialect: HENGHUA (HINGHUA, XINGHUA). Bible 1912. See main entry under China.

CHINESE, YUE ***(CANTONESE, YUE, YUEH, GUANGFU)*** [YUH] 314,000 speakers in Singapore (1985), 12.3% of the population, out of 338,000 in the ethnic group (1993). Sino-Tibetan, Chinese. Bible 1894-1981. See main entry under China.

ENGLISH [ENG] 227,000 speakers, 8.9% of population, 729,000 second language users (literate in English) in Singapore, 28.5% of population (1985 estimate). Indo-European, Germanic, West, English. Ethnic groups which use English: Chinese 154,000, 68%; European and Eurasian 34,000, 15%; Indian 32,000, 14%; Malay 6,000, 3%. Chinese varieties and Tamil also used at home. National language. Bible 1382-1989. See main entry under United Kingdom.

GUJARATI ***(GUJERATHI, GUJERATI)*** [GJR] 800 speakers out of 1,619 ethnic group (1985 estimate). Indo-European, Indo-Iranian, Indo-Aryan, Central zone, Gujarati. Hindu. Bible 1823-1998. See main entry under India.

JAVANESE ***(JAWA, DJAWA)*** [JAN] 800 in Singapore out of 21,230 in ethnic group (1985 estimate). Austronesian, Malayo-Polynesian, Western Malayo-Polynesian, Sundic, Javanese. SVO. Traditional Javanese script. Muslim. Bible 1854-1994. See main entry under Indonesia, Java and Bali.

MADURA ***(MADURESE, MADHURA)*** [MHJ] 900 speakers in Singapore out of 14,292 in the ethnic group (1985 estimate). Austronesian, Malayo-Polynesian, Western Malayo-Polynesian, Sundic, Madurese. Dialect: BAWEAN (BOYANESE). Muslim. Bible 1994. See main entry under Indonesia, Java and Bali.

MALACCAN CREOLE PORTUGUESE ***(MALAYSIAN CREOLE PORTUGUESE, MALACCAN, PAPIA KRISTANG)*** [MCM] Trankera and Hilir, Melaka, Straits of Malacca. Related varieties in parts of Kuala Lumpur and Singapore. Variety in Pulau Tikus, Spoken more in 1997 than in 1987. Penang is now virtually extinct. Creole, Portuguese based. Also spoken as second language by some Chinese shopkeepers in Hilir. Used in RC church services until World War II. Trade language. Fishermen. Christian. See main entry under Malaysia, Peninsular.

MALAY ***(BAHASA MALAY, MELAYU)*** [MLI] 396,000 in Singapore (1985 estimate), 15.5% of the population. Austronesian, Malayo-Polynesian, Western Malayo-Polynesian, Sundic, Malayic, Malayan, Local Malay. Mandarin and Hokien are used as second languages by some, and 70% use English. Ethnic groups who speak Malay: Malay 339,000, 85%; Javanese 21,000, 5%; Indians 14,000, 3.5%; Bawean Madurese 14,000, 3.5%; Arabs 2,500, .6%; Bugis 500, .1%. English used at home by 7%. National language. Literacy rate in second language: 85%. Sunni Muslim, Christian. Bible 1733-1993. See main entry under Malaysia, Peninsular.

MALAY, BABA ***(CHINESE MALAY, BABA, STRAITS MALAY)*** [BAL] 10,000 or more in Singapore (1986 A. Pakir). Estimates of ethnic Baba are from 250,000 to 400,000. Population total both countries 15,000. Mainly in the Katong District on the east coast and the surrounding districts of Geylang and Jao Chiat. Also spoken in Malaysia (Peninsular). Creole, Malay based. It developed since the 15th century from Low Malay with many Hokkien Chinese borrowings. Regional variants between Malacca and Singapore. Partially intelligible with Standard Malay. It is generally believed that the Baba of Malaysia is more 'refined', and that of Singapore more 'rough'. Most have learned Standard Malay and English in school. Lim (1981) and Holm (1989) treat it as a Malay-based creole. It is different from Peranakan Indonesian. Some who grew up with Chinese neighbors know Hokkien, Teochew, and Cantonese. Children now learn Mandarin in school rather than Standard Malay. Baba is mainly used in the home and with other Babas. The only monolinguals are over 70 years old. NT 1913, out of print.

MALAYALAM ***(ALEALUM, MALAYALANI, MALAYAL, MALEAN, MALIYAD, MALLEALLE, MOPLA)*** [MJS] 10,000 speakers in Singapore, .4% of the population, out of 14,000 in the ethnic group (1993). Dravidian, Southern, Tamil-Kannada, Tamil-Kodagu, Tamil-Malayalam, Malayalam. Malayalam script. Christian. Bible 1841-1998. See main entry under India.

ORANG SELETAR [ORS] North coast of Singapore, and opposite coast of Malaysia. Austronesian, Malayo-Polynesian, Western Malayo-Polynesian, Sundic, Malayic, Malayan, Aboriginal Malay. Coastal. See main entry under Malaysia, Peninsular.

PANJABI, EASTERN [PNJ] 9,500 speakers in Singapore (1987), .4% of the population, out of 14,000 in the ethnic group (1993). Indo-European, Indo-Iranian, Indo-Aryan, Central zone, Panjabi. Sikh. Bible 1959-1984. See main entry under India.

SINGAPORE SIGN LANGUAGE [SLS] Deaf sign language. Dictionary.

SINHALA ***(SINHALESE, SINGHALESE, CHINGALESE)*** [SNH] 852 speakers in Singapore (1987), out of 12,000 in the ethnic group (1993). Indo-European, Indo-Iranian, Indo-Aryan, Sinhalese-Maldivian. A great difference between the literary and colloquial language. SOV. Sinhalese script. Buddhist. Bible 1823-1982. See main entry under Sri Lanka.

TAMIL [TCV] 90,000 speakers in Singapore (1985), 3.5% of the population, out of 111,000 in the ethnic group (1993). Dravidian, Southern, Tamil-Kannada, Tamil-Kodagu, Tamil-Malayalam, Tamil. 19% speak English at home. National language. Hindu. Bible 1727-1995. See main entry under India.

SRI LANKA

Democratic Socialist Republic of Sri Lanka. Sri Lanka Prajathanthrika Samajavadi Janarajaya. Formerly Ceylon. National or official language: Sinhala. 18,455,000 (1998 UN). Literacy rate 86% to 87%. Information mainly from J. Gair 1990; J. Holm 1989. Buddhist, Hindu, Muslim, Christian. Blind population 13,800. Deaf population 3,459 to 1,093,340 (1998). Deaf institutions: 14. Data accuracy estimate: B. The number of languages listed for Sri Lanka is 8. Of those, 7 are living languages and 1 is extinct. Diversity index 0.31.

ENGLISH [ENG] 97,000 first language speakers in Sri Lanka (1962). Indo-European, Germanic, West, English. Bible 1535-1989. See main entry under United Kingdom.

INDO-PORTUGUESE [IDB] 30 to 2,250 in Sri Lanka (1971 Ian Smith), including 250 families in Batticaloa (1984 Ian Smith), but possibly only about 30 speakers left (1992 P. Baker). Population total all countries 730 to 3,000. Colombo, Kandy, Trincomalee, Galle, Batticaloa. Also spoken in

Australia, India. Creole, Portuguese based. Similar to Tamil in phonology and syntax. Varieties of creole Portuguese were also spoken in Myanmar, Bangladesh, Thailand, Indonesia, Malaysia, China. See also Malaccan Creole Portuguese (Peninsular Malaysia), Macao Creole Portuguese (Macau, Hongkong), Ternateño (Maluku, Indonesia), Timor Pidgin (Nusa Tenggara, Indonesia). Everyone is fluent in Tamil. Older speakers are also bilingual in English; some younger ones in Sinhalese. The creole is used at home only. Most of the Burgher caste speak it at home. Many in the ethnic group may not know the creole well. Virtually no contact with Goa or Portugal since 1656. NT 1826-1852.

PALI [PLL] Indo-European, Indo-Iranian, Indo-Aryan, Unclassified. The literary language of the Buddhist scriptures. Monks from different countries may speak Pali to each other. Sri Lankan history has been recorded in Pali. Buddhist. Extinct. NT 1835. See main entry under India.

SINHALA *(SINHALESE, SINGHALESE, SINGHALA, CINGALESE)* [SNH] 13,190,000 in Sri Lanka, 72% of the population (1993) to 15,000,000 possibly including second language users (1997). Population total all countries 13,220,000. All parts of Sri Lanka except some districts in the north, east, and center. Also spoken in Canada, Maldives, Midway Islands, Singapore, Thailand, UAE. Indo-European, Indo-Iranian, Indo-Aryan, Sinhalese-Maldivian. Dialect: RODIYA. There is a great difference between the literary and the colloquial language. The Rodiya dialect is spoken by low caste Rodiya people. National language. Dictionary. Grammar. SOV; 7 long vowels, 7 short vowels, 24 consonants, including 4 which are prenasalized; gender, number, and case agreement between subject and verb in literary Sinhala. Sinhalese script, which is syllabic. Earliest writing dates to 3rd century B.C. Buddhist. Bible 1823-1982.

SRI LANKAN CREOLE MALAY *(SRI LANKAN MALAY, MELAYU BAHASA)* [SCI] 50,000 speakers, .29% of the population (1986 Hussainmiya, Prentice 1994:411). Especially the cities of Colombo, Kandy, Badulla, Hambantota. Creole, Malay based. Not intelligible with standard Malay because of phonological and syntactic differences, and strong influence from Tamil. May be close to Malaccan Creole Malay (S. Lim 1981). Most or all may speak Tamil, but second language proficiency needs investigation. The creole is used at home and among friends. All ages. There are current efforts to revive the older literature. Widely used. Malay vocabulary with grammatical structure based on Sri Lankan Moor Tamil. Investigation needed: intelligibility with Malaccan Creole Malay, bilingual proficiency in Tamil. SOV, postpositions, case, adjectives and genitives precede noun heads. Roman script used. Jawi (Arabic) script used earlier. Newspapers, radio programs.

SRI LANKAN SIGN LANGUAGE [SQS] (12,800 deaf persons; 1986 Gallaudet Univ.). Deaf sign language. 14 deaf schools. Several sign languages used by different schools. British English fingerspelling also used. Investigation needed: intelligibility.

TAMIL [TCV] 3,000,000 in Sri Lanka (1993). North and northeast coasts, a few pockets in the south. Dravidian, Southern, Tamil-Kannada, Tamil-Kodagu, Tamil-Malayalam, Tamil. Tamil script. Hindu, Muslim. Bible 1727-1995. See main entry under India.

VEDDAH *(VEDDHA, VEDA, WEDA, WEDDO, BEDA, BEDDA, VAEDDA)* [VED] 300 (1993 Johnstone). All may not be speakers. Eastern mountains, Badulla and Polonnaruwa districts. Indo-European, Indo-Iranian, Indo-Aryan, Sinhalese-Maldivian. Bilingualism in Sinhalese. The language is being replaced by Sinhalese.

SYRIA

Syrian Arab Republic, al-jamhouriya al Arabia as-Souriya. National or official language: Standard Arabic. 15,333,000 (1998 UN). Literacy rate 65%, 78% males. Also includes South Levantine Spoken Arabic, Chaldean Neo-Aramaic 5,000, Chechen. Information mainly from T. Sebeok 1963; W. Fischer and O. Jastrow 1980; B. Ingham 1982. Sunni Muslim, Alawi Muslim, Ismaili Muslim, Christian, Druze, secular. Blind population 152. Deaf population 902,598. Deaf institutions: 1. Data accuracy estimate: C. The number of languages listed for Syria is 17. Of those, 15 are living languages and 2 are extinct. Diversity index 0.50.

ADYGHE *(WEST CIRCASSIAN, ADYGEY)* [ADY] 25,000 in Syria. North Caucasian, Northwest, Circassian. Sunni Muslim. NT 1992. See main entry under Russia.

ARABIC, LEVANTINE BEDAWI SPOKEN *(BEDAWI)* [AVL] 70,000 in Syria. Southwest corner, Hawran region, from the border to within 20 miles of Damascus. Afro-Asiatic, Semitic, Central, South, Arabic. Sunni Muslim, Christian. See main entry under Egypt.

ARABIC, MESOPOTAMIAN SPOKEN *(NORTH SYRIAN ARABIC, FURATI, MESOPOTAMIAN GELET ARABIC)* [ACM] 1,800,000 in Syria. Eastern Syria. Afro-Asiatic, Semitic, Central, South, Arabic. Dialect: EUPHRATES CLUSTER. SVO. Muslim, Christian, Jewish. See main entry under Iraq.

ARABIC, NAJDI SPOKEN *(BEDAWI)* [ARS] 500,000 in Syria, including 100,000 North Najdi, 100,000 Central Najdi (1995). Syrian desert. Afro-Asiatic, Semitic, Central, South, Arabic. Spoken by bedouins. Investigation needed: intelligibility with Gulf Arabic, Mesopotamian Arabic. See main entry under Saudi Arabia.

ARABIC, NORTH LEVANTINE SPOKEN *(LEVANTINE ARABIC, NORTH LEVANTINE ARABIC, LEBANESE-SYRIAN ARABIC, SYRO-LEBANESE ARABIC)* [APC] 8,800,000 in Syria, including 6,000,000 in Lebanese-Central Syrian, 1,000,000 in North Syrian (1991). Population total all countries 15,000,000. Also spoken in Antigua and Barbuda, Argentina, Belize, Cyprus, Dominican Republic, French Guiana, Israel, Jamaica, Lebanon, Mali, Puerto Rico, Suriname, Trinidad and Tobago, Turkey (Asia). Afro-Asiatic, Semitic, Central, South, Arabic. There is an urban standard dialect based on Damascus speech. Beiruti dialect is well accepted here. Aleppo dialect shows Mesopotamian (North Syrian) influence. Used in drama. Radio programs, TV. Muslim, Christian, Druze, Jewish.

ARABIC, NORTH MESOPOTAMIAN SPOKEN *(MOSLAWI, SYRO-MESOPOTAMIAN ARABIC, MESOPOTAMIAN QELTU ARABIC)* [AYP] 300,000 in Syria. Far eastern Syria. Afro-Asiatic, Semitic, Central, South, Arabic. Muslim, Christian. See main entry under Iraq.

ARABIC, STANDARD [ABV] Middle East, North Africa. Afro-Asiatic, Semitic, Central, South, Arabic. Used for education, official purposes, formal speeches. National language. Newspapers. Bible 1984-1991. See main entry under Saudi Arabia.

ARMENIAN *(HAIEREN, SOMKHURI, ERMENICE, ARMJANSKI)* [ARM] 320,000 in Syria (1993), 2.8% of the population (1986). Indo-European, Armenian. Dialect: WESTERN ARMENIAN. Eastern dialect spoken in Armenia and its Turkish and Iranian borderlands. Western dialect spoken elsewhere. In Syria, people in Kessaberen (northeastern mountain village of Kessab) and the village of Musa Dagh (now relocated to Lebanon) speak related varieties which other Western Armenian speakers do not understand. Most speakers of Kessaberen have now learned Western Armenian. Language of wider communication. Christian. Bible 1853-1978. See main entry under Armenia.

ASSYRIAN NEO-ARAMAIC *(LISHANA ATURAYA, SURET, SURETH, SURYAYA SWADAYA, ASSYRIAN, NEO-SYRIAC, ASSYRISKI, AISORSKI)* [AII] 30,000 in Syria (1995) out of a reported 700,000 population. Over 30 villages on the banks of the Khabur River, northern Syria. Afro-Asiatic, Semitic, Central, Aramaic, Eastern, Central, Northeastern. All dialects of Western, Northern, and Central Assyrian are spoken in Syria. Christian: Nestorian, a few Chaldeans (Uniate Catholic). Bible 1852-1911. See main entry under Iraq.

AZERBAIJANI, SOUTH [AZB] 30,000 in Syria (1961 census). Homs and Hama. Altaic, Turkic, Southern, Azerbaijani. The dialect spoken in Syria is different from Kirkuk of Iraq, and may be closer to Turkish (Osmanli) than to Azerbaijani. Bilingualism in Arabic. They are called 'Turkmen' or 'Turkomen' in Syria and Iraq. Not a written language in Syria. Muslim. See main entry under Iran.

DOMARI *(MIDDLE EASTERN ROMANI, TSIGENE, GYPSY)* [RMT] 10,000 in Syria (1961). Turkey to India; Nawar is in Palestine, Syria, and Egypt; Kurbat in Syria and western Iran; Helebi in Egypt and Libya; Karachi in north Turkey, the Caucasus of Russia; and north Iran; Domaki and Wogri-Boli in India; Barake in Syria; Luli and Maznoug in Uzbekistan; other groups in Iran; Churi-Wali in Afghanistan. Indo-European, Indo-Iranian, Indo-Aryan, Northwestern zone, Dom. Dialects: NAWAR, KURBATI, BEIRUT, NABLOS, BARAKE. Arabic influence. Muslim. See main entry under Iran.

KURMANJI *(NORTHERN KURDISH, KERMANJI, KIRMANJI)* [KUR] 938,000 in Syria (1993), 6.3% of the population. Northern Syria. Indo-European, Indo-Iranian, Iranian, Western, Northwestern, Kurdish. Differen from Kurdi (Southern Kurdish). Bilingualism in Arabic. A few urbanites and nomads. Kurmanji is prohibited in Syrian schools (Time 4/1/91). Language of wider communication. Arabic script used in Syria, Iran, and Iraq. Roman or Cyrillic used elsewhere. Mainly agriculturalists. Muslim. NT 1872. See main entry under Turkey.

LOMAVREN *(ARMENIAN BOSHA, ARNEBUAB BISA, BOSHA, BOSA)* [RMI] Indo-European, Armenian. Restructured Armenian. See main entry under Armenia.

MLAHSÖ *(SURYOYO)* [QMQ] Qamishli town. Originally in Mlahsó and <Ansha villages, Diyarbakir Province, Turkey. Afro-Asiatic, Semitic, Central, Aramaic, Eastern, Central, Northwestern.Close to Turoyo. The last speaker died in 1998. His daughter knows Mlahso well, but is nearly deaf and has no one to speak it to (1999). Mlahso was still spoken by a handful of people during the 1970s. 'Suryoyo' is their own name. A different language from Turoyo, also called 'Suryoyo'. Christian (Jacobite). Extinct.

SYRIAC *(CLASSICAL SYRIAC, ANCIENT SYRIAC, SURYAYA, SURYOYO)* [SYC] Turkey, Iraq, and Syria. Afro-Asiatic, Semitic, Central, Aramaic, Eastern. Dialects: WESTERN SYRIAC, EASTERN SYRIAC. The Syrian churches (Eastern (Nestorian), Syrian Orthodox (Jacobite), Syrian Catholic (Melkite, Maronite) developed a vast literature based on the Edessa (currently Sanliurfa, southeastern Turkey) variety of the Syrian dialect. The Assyrian group (see Assyrian Neo-Aramaic in Iraq and elsewhere) separated denominationally from the Chaldean (see Chaldean Neo-Aramaic in Iraq) and

Suryoyo (see Turkey and Syria) in the Middle Ages. Became extinct in the 10th to 12th centuries. Still used as a literary secular language among followers of the churches listed, although rarely. Neo-Eastern Aramaic languages spoken by Christians are often dubbed 'Neo-Syriac', although not directly descended from Syriac. Christian: Nestorian, Jacobite, Melkite, Maronite, Syrian Orthodox. Extinct. Bible 1645-1891. See main entry under Turkey.

TUROYO *(SURYOYO, SYRYOYO, TURANI)* [SYR] 7,000 speakers in Syria (1994), of 20,000 in the ethnic group. Afro-Asiatic, Semitic, Central, Aramaic, Eastern, Central, Northwestern. Related to, but different from Northeastern Aramaic. Western Syriac used in church, Arabic in schools and trade. Turoyo used at home. Religious capital is in Damascus; formerly at Tur <Abdin, Turkey. Christian (Jacobite). Bible portions 1983. See main entry under Turkey.

WESTERN NEO-ARAMAIC *(MAALULA, SIRYON, LOGHTHA SIRYANOYTHA, NEO-WESTERN ARAMAIC)* [AMW] 15,000 speakers including 8,000 in Maaloula (1996 Maalula Home Page, Internet). Qalamoun mts., 30 miles north of Damascus. Villages of Ma<lula, Bakh<a, and Jubb <Adin. Only in Syria. Afro-Asiatic, Semitic, Central, Aramaic, Western. Dialects: MA<LULA (MAALULA, MAALOULA, MA<LU:LA), BAKH<A (BAX<A), JUB-<ADIN (JUBB <ADI:N). Little dialect variation. Bilingualism in Syrian Arabic. They use Aramaic in homes and as a literary and religious language. There are members of the ethnic group in the USA who now speak Arabic. Mountain slope. Peasant agriculturalists, vineyards, orchards. 1,500 meters. Christian (Melchite, 1 village), Sunni Muslim (2 villages).

TAIWAN

Republic of China, Chung-hua Min-kuo. Formerly Formosa. National or official language: Mandarin Chinese. 21,507,000 (1995). 349120 tribal people, or 2% of the population, Han Chinese 97.8%. Literacy rate 90% to 92%. Also includes Chinese Sign Language, Iu Mien, Kalmyk-Oirat, Halh Mongolian 6,000, Tibetan 2,000, Uyghur, people from the Philippines 50,000. Information mainly from T. Sebeok 1971; S. Tsuchida 1976; S. Wurm and S. Hattori 1981; P. Li 1987; D. T. Tryon 1995. Chinese traditional religion, secular, Christian, tribal traditional religion, Muslim. Deaf population 30,000 to 1,302,969 (1998). Deaf institutions: 8. Data accuracy estimate: A2. The number of languages listed for Taiwan is 29. Of those, 22 are living languages and 7 are extinct. Diversity index 0.49.

AMIS *(AMI, AMIA, PAGCAH, PANGTSAH, BAKURUT, LAM-SI-HOAN, MARAN, SABARI, TANAH)* [ALV] 130,000 (1986 Virginia Fey TEAM). Plains in the valley along the railroad between Hualien and Taitung, and on the east coast near the sea between Hualien and Taitung. Austronesian, Formosan, Paiwanic. Dialects: CENTRAL AMIS (HAIAN AMI, HSIUKULAN AMI), TAVALONG-VATAAN (KWANGFU, KUANGFU), SOUTHERN AMIS (PEINAN, HENGCH'UN AMIS, TAITUNG), CHENGKUNG-KWANGSHAN, NORTHERN AMIS (NANSHI AMIS). The Chengkung-Kwangshan dialect is closest to Central Amis. Bilingualism in Japanese, Mandarin. 'Amis' is their name for themselves; 'Ami' is the Chinese name. Traditionally matrilineal. Many are migrating to cities and industrial areas. Dictionary. Roman script used. Plains. Agriculturalists: rice. NT 1972-1981.

AMIS, NATAORAN [AIS] Villages in the Hualien area and north of Fenglin. Austronesian, Formosan, Paiwanic. Dialect: SAKIZAYA (SAKIRAY). Not generally understood by other Amis. Sakizaya is even more divergent from Central Amis. About 50% lexical similarity with Central Amis. It is on the verge of extinction. Investigation needed: bilingual proficiency.

ATAYAL *(TAYAL, TYAL, TAIYAL, ATAIYAL, ATTAYAL, TAIJYAL, BONOTSEK, SHABOGALA, TAKONAN, TANGAO, YUKAN)* [TAY] 63,000 speakers (1993 Johnstone), 78,957 in ethnic group (1989 govt. figure). Mountains in the northeast, south of the Ketagalan area. Austronesian, Formosan, Atayalic. Dialects: SQOLEQ (SQULIQ), TS'OLE' (CI'ULI). People in some areas are quite bilingual. In some areas Atayal is in active use. NT 1974.

BABUZA *(BABUSA, FAVORLANG, FAVORLANGSCH, JABORLANG, POAVOSA)* [BZG] A few speakers (1987 I. Dyen). West central coast and inland, Tatu and Choshui rivers and beyond, around 24'N. Austronesian, Formosan, Paiwanic. Dialect: POAVOSA. Sinicized. Nearly extinct. Bible portions.

BASAY *(KAWANUWAN, BASAI)* [BYQ] North around Tam Shui to near Kungliao, Fengtzulin, Taipei, Sangchung, and northeast around Suao and east of Ilan. Austronesian, Formosan, Paiwanic. Dialects: TROBIAWAN, LINAW-QAUQAUL. Sinicized. Older people can remember a few words. Extinct.

BUNUN *(BUNTI, VONUN, BUNAN, BUBUKUN, VUNUM, VUNUN, VUNUNG, BUNUM)* [BNN] 34,000 speakers (1993 Johnstone), 38,267 in ethnic group (1989 govt. figure). East central plain, south of the Sediq (Taroko). Austronesian, Formosan, Paiwanic. Dialects: RANDAI, TONDAI, SHIBUKUN (SIBUKUN, SIBUKAUN, SIBUCOON, SIVUKUN), NORTH BUNUN (TAKITUDU, TAKETODO, TAKEBAKHA, TAKIBAKHA), CENTRAL BUNUN (TAKBANUAO, TAKIVATAN, TAKEVATAN),

SOUTH BUNUN (ISHBUKUN), TAKOPULAN. Also spoken by the Kanakanabu and the Saaroa in everyday life. NT 1973.

CHINESE, HAKKA [HAK] 2,366,000 in Taiwan (1993), 11% of the population. Taoyuan, Hsinchu, Miaoli, Pingtung counties. Shi Xien is in northern and southern Taiwan, Hi-Lu is central and north central. Sino-Tibetan, Chinese. Dialects: HAILU (HOILUK, HOILLUK, HI-LU), SANHSIEN (SHIGEN, SHIXIEN, SHI XIEN). Sanhsien closely resembles Yuetai of Mainland China. Hailu closely resembles Yong-Ting or Yuqui of Mainland China. Settled in Taiwan for 200 years. Bible 1916. See main entry under China.

CHINESE, MANDARIN ***(KUOYU, MANDARIN, PUTONGHUA, GUOYU)*** [CHN] 4,323,000 in Taiwan (1993), 20.1% of the population. Spoken as a second language by over 15,000,000. Mainly in Taipei and 5 provincial cities. Sino-Tibetan, Chinese. Dialect: TAIBEI MANDARIN. Fully inherently intelligible with Putonghua in China, but intelligible with Benjing dialect with some difficulty. Nearly all mother tongue speakers in Taiwan speak with Min-influenced grammar and various degrees of Min-influenced pronunciation. Many of the educated strive to cultivate standard pronunciation. Grammatical differences of the Taiwan variety often appear in writing. Many of the 30 to 50 year-old generation in Taiwan are also fluent in Taiwan Min. National language. Putonghua taught in all schools. Traditional Chinese, Buddhist, Christian, Secular. Bible 1874-1983. See main entry under China.

CHINESE, MIN NAN ***(MIN NAN, MINNAN)*** [CFR] 15,000,000 in Taiwan (1997 A. Chang), 66.7% of the population (1993). Tainan, Penghu Archipelago, cities on the east coast, western plain except for a few Hakka pockets. Sino-Tibetan, Chinese. Dialect: AMOY (TAIWANESE, FORMOSAN). Taiwanese is close to Amoy dialect; intelligibility is not very difficult. There are two subdialects in Taiwan: Sanso and Chaenzo, with some difficulty in intelligibility. Mandarin is used as second language. Those over 60 also speak Japanese. The Taiwanese people are called Hoklo or Holo. Chinese traditional religion, Buddhist Christian, secular. Bible 1884-1933. See main entry under China.

HOANYA ***(HOANNYA, KALI)*** [HON] West central, from Taihsi to Peimen to Tsou language area, south of 24'N. Austronesian, Formosan, Paiwanic. Dialects: LLOA (LOA), ARIKUN, HOANYA. Sinicized. Extinct.

JAPANESE [JPN] 10,000 in Taiwan (1993). Japanese, Japanese. Used among a few elderly aboriginal speakers and some Chinese as second language. Trade language. Bible 1883-1987. See main entry under Japan.

KANAKANABU ***(KANABU, KANAKANAVU)*** [QNB] (160 in 1977; Lincoln). Central Taiwan around Minchuan. Austronesian, Formosan, Tsouic, Southern. Bilingualism in Bunun, Taiwanese. A few older people know Kanakanabu. On the verge of extinction in 1990. The people speak Bunun in daily life. Older people speak Taiwanese mainly. Nearly extinct.

KAVALAN ***(KUWARAWAN, KIWARAWA, KUVARAWAN, KIBALAN, KIWARAW, KUVALAN, KAVARAUAN, KVALAN, SHEKWAN, CABARAN, KABALAN, KABARAN, KAMALAN, KAVANAN, KBALAN)*** [CKV] 100 or fewer (1987). Northeast coast, above Toucheng to Ilan, nearly to Suao, and inland to Tayal language area. No longer spoken in the original area; a few migrants to the east coast, Hualien, one small village (1990). Austronesian, Formosan, Paiwanic. Dialect: KAREOVAN (KAREOWAN). Used only as a home language in 1930. Still spoken in Atayal territory (1987). Sinicized. Dictionary. Nearly extinct.

KETANGALAN ***(KETAGALAN, TANGALAN)*** [KAE] North central, around Panchiao and to the northwest, west, and southeast. Austronesian, Formosan, Paiwanic. Sinicized. Extinct.

KULUN ***(KULON)*** [KNG] North central, between Taoyuan and Panchiao. Austronesian, Formosan, Paiwanic. Sinicized. Extinct.

PAIWAN ***(PAIUAN, PAYOWAN, LI-LI-SHA, SAMOBI, SAMOHAI, SAPREK, TAMARI, KADAS, KALE-WHAN, KAPIANGAN, KATAUSAN, BUTANGLU, STIMUL)*** [PWN] 53,000 speakers (1981 Wurm and Hattori), 60,434 in ethnic group (1989 govt. figure). Southern, southeastern mountains. Austronesian, Formosan, Paiwanic. NT 1973-1993.

PAPORA ***(BUPURAN, HINAPAVOSA, VUPURAN, PAPOLA)*** [PPU] North central coast around Lishui, Chingshui, Shalu, and inland to Taichung. Austronesian, Formosan, Paiwanic. Sinicized. Extinct.

PAZEH ***(PAZZEHE, PAZEHE, PAZEX, PAZEH-KAHABU, SHEKHOAN, SEK-HWAN, LEKWHAN)*** [PZH] Near the west coast just north of 24'N, east of Tayal, around Cholan, Houli, Fengyuan, Tantzu, Taichung, Tungshih. Austronesian, Formosan, Paiwanic. Dialects: KAHABU, PAZEH. Known only by a couple of old people in 1990 (P. Li). Used only as a home language in 1930. Sinicized. Nearly extinct.

PYUMA ***(PUYUMA, PILAM, PELAM, PIYUMA, PANAPANAYAN, KADAS, TIPUN)*** [PYU] 7,225 speakers (1973 census), 8,132 in ethnic group (1989 govt. figure). Along the east coast south of Taitung and inland. Austronesian, Formosan, Paiwanic. Dialects: NANWANG, PINAN. The people speak Pyuma in daily life.

RUKAI ***(DRUKAY, DRUKAI, DYOKAY, DUKAI, RUTKAI, TSARISEN, TSALISEN, SARISEN, BANGA, BANTALANG, BANTAURANG, TALOMA, KADAS)*** [DRU] 8,000 (1994 UBS), 8,007 in ethnic group

(1989 govt. figure). South central mountains, west of the Pyuma, 11 villages around Ping Tung, and 2 or 3 villages near Taitung. Austronesian, Formosan, Tsouic. Dialects: BUDAI, LABUAN, TANAN, MAGA, TONA, MANTAURAN. 3 dialects are reported to be divergent. Some speak Pyuma. Some older people speak Japanese. Some older people are monolingual in Rukai. Speakers of most dialects speak Rukai in daily life. Budai people speak Taiwanese in every day life. Some linguists classify it as Paiwanic. There is Paiwanic influence. Grammar. VSO.

SAAROA ***(SAROA, SAARUA, RARUA, LA'ALUA, PACHIEN, PAICHIEN, SISYABAN)*** [SXR] 370 (1977 Lincoln). West central mountains, south and southeast of Minchuan, along the Laonung River. Austronesian, Formosan, Tsouic, Southern. Bilingualism in Bunun. Some older people know Saaroa. On the verge of extinction in 1990. The people speak Bunun in everyday life. Older people speak Taiwanese. Nearly extinct.

SAISIYAT ***(SAISET, SEISIRAT, SAISETT, SAISIAT, SAISIETT, SAISIRAT, SAISYET, SAISYETT, AMUTOURA, BOUIOK)*** [SAI] 3,200 (1978), 4,194 in ethnic group (1989 govt. figure). Western mountains, west of the Atayal. Austronesian, Formosan, Paiwanic. Dialects: TAAI (NORTH SAISET), TUNGHO (SOUTH SAISET). Many young people speak Hakka Chinese. Atayal is also used. Tungho: more active use, Taai: a few speakers, but nearly assimilated to Atayal.

SIRAIYA ***(FORMOSAN, SIRAIA, SIRAYA, SIDEIA, SIDEIS, SIDEISCH, BAKSA, PEPOHOAN, PEPOHWAN)*** [FOS] Southwestern, around present-day Tainan, from Peimen to Hengchun to Tapu. Austronesian, Formosan, Paiwanic. Dialects: SIRAYA, MAKATAO (MAKATTAO, TAKARAYA, TTA'O), PANGSOIA-DOLATOK, TAIVOAN (TEVORANG), LAMAI. It was still spoken in 1908. Sinicized. Dictionary. Extinct. Bible portions 1661.

TAIWANESE SIGN LANGUAGE ***(ZIRAN SHOUYU)*** [TSS] 30,000 users (1986 Gallaudet Univ.). Deaf sign language. Dialects: TAIPEI, TAINAN. 2 major dialects. The sources from which the sign language developed were indigenous sign systems before 1895, Japanese occupation and education 1895-1946, Mainland Chinese Sign Language brought by refugees in 1949 and some from Hong Kong since. 50% lexical similarity with Japanese Sign Language. Quite different from (Mainland) Chinese Sign Language; only a few signs are the same or similar. Not related to Taiwanese languages. Some signs are borrowed from Mandarin through palmwriting. There is also a Signed Mandarin (Wenfa Shouyu).

TAOKAS ***(TAOKA, TAOKAT)*** [TOA] Northwest coast and inland, Touchien River to Taan River and beyond. Austronesian, Formosan, Paiwanic. Sinicized. Extinct.

TAROKO ***(TARUKU, TOROKO, TRUKU, TODA, SEDIQ, SAEDIQ, SEEDIK, SEJIQ, SEDEQ, SEEDEK, SEEDEQ, SHEDEKKA, SEDEK, SEDIAKK, SEDIK, SAZEK, BU-HWAN, CHE-HWAN, DAIYA-ATAIYAL, HOGO, IBOHO, PARAN)*** [TRV] 28,000 (1993 Johnstone). Central, eastern and coastal; northern mountains in the Puli area and along the coast south of Hualien, south of the Atayal. Austronesian, Formosan, Atayalic. The people are called 'Sediq', the language 'Taroko'. NT 1963-1981. Bible nearing completion (1999).

THAO ***(SAU, SAO, SHAO, CHUIHWAN, CHUI-HUAN, VULUNG)*** [SSF] A few speakers out of 248 in the ethnic group (1989). Central, around Sun Moon Lake, 1 village. Austronesian, Formosan, Paiwanic. Dialects: BRAWBAW, SHTAFARI. Bilingualism in Taiwanese Chinese. Speakers are older (1989). Sinicized. The people speak Taiwanese in daily life. There is cooperation with the Bunun, and intermarriage with Bunun women, loan words from Bunun. Nearly extinct.

TSOU ***(TSU-U, TSOO, TSUOU, TSU-WO, TZO, TSO, NAMAKABAN, NIITAKA, TIBOLA, TIBOLAH, TIBOLAK, TIBOLAL)*** [TSY] 5,000 speakers (1982 McGill), 5,797 in ethnic group (1989 govt. figure). West central mountains southeast of Kagi around Mt. Ali. Austronesian, Formosan, Tsouic, Northern. Dialects: DUHTU, LUHTU, TAPANGU, TFUEA, IIMUTSU. Bilingualism in Mandarin. Iimutsu is extinct (1981 Wurm and Hattori). The people speak Tsou in daily life. Young people speak Mandarin. Some linguistic work has been done.

YAMI ***(BOTEL TABAGO, BOTEL TOBAGO, LANYU)*** [YMI] 3,000 speakers (1994 UBS), 4,335 in ethnic group (1989 govt. figure). Orchid Island, Botel Tobago (Lanyu) Island, southeast coast. Austronesian, Malayo-Polynesian, Western Malayo-Polynesian, Northern Philippine, Bashiic-Central Luzon-Northern Mindoro, Bashiic, Yami. Closely related to Ivatan of northern Philippines. Bilingualism in Mandarin. People prefer to be called 'Lanyu'. Traditional religion, Christian. NT 1994.

TAJIKISTAN

National or official language: Tajiki. 6,015,000 (1998 UN). Formerly part of USSR. Capital: Dushanbe. 54,019 square miles. Literacy rate 99%. Also includes Aimaq, Armenian 6,000, Western Balochi 4,842, Bashkir 5,412, Belarusan, Dungan, Georgian 808, Standard German, Hazaragi, Kazakh 9,606, Kirghiz 64,000, Korean 13,000, Lak 861, Lithuanian 472, Osetin 8,000, Southern Pashto 4,000, Romanian 580,

Russian 237,000, Tatar 80,000, Turkish, Turkmen 13,991, Ukrainian 41,000, Uyghur 3,581, Northern Uzbek 873,000. Information mainly from T. Sebeok 1963; S. Akiner 1983; B. Comrie 1987; A. Kibrik 1991. Muslim, Jewish (14,667). Data accuracy estimate: B. The number of languages listed for Tajikistan is 9. Of those, all are living languages. Diversity index 0.48.

ARABIC, TAJIKI SPOKEN ***(JUGARI, BUKHARA ARABIC, BUXARA ARABIC, TAJIJI ARABIC, CENTRAL ASIAN ARABIC)*** [ABH] 1,000 in Tajikistan. Population total all countries 6,000. Villages in Vakhsh Valley of Khatlon Province, and communities in Kuliab and Leninabad cities. They mainly live in small villages. Some in Uzbekistan. Also spoken in Afghanistan, Uzbekistan. Afro-Asiatic, Semitic, Central, South, Arabic. The language is close to Mesopotamian Spoken Arabic. Sharp dialect differences between Bukhara and Kashkadarya regions. Bukhara is strongly influenced by Tajiki; Kashkadarya by Uzbek and other Turkic languages. Speakers use Tajiki to communicate with each other, and as literary language. Few members of the ethnic group now speak Arabic. Others speak Tajiki as mother tongue. No diglossia with Modern Standard Arabic. They are endogamous and do not mix with speakers of other languages. Agriculturalists; cattle raisers. Hanafi Sunni Muslim.

FARSI, WESTERN ***(PERSIAN)*** [PES] 31,000 in Tajikistan (1993 Johnstone), 31% speak it as mother tongue. Indo-European, Indo-Iranian, Iranian, Western, Southwestern, Persian. Dialect blending into Tajiki. Not a literary language in Tajikistan. Shi'a Muslim. Bible 1838-1995. See main entry under Iran.

PARYA ***(AFGHANA-YI NASFURUSH, AFGHANA-YI SIYARUI, LAGHMANI, PBHARYA)*** [PAQ] 1,000 in Tajikistan and Uzbekistan (1960). Population total all countries 1,000 or more. Hissar Valley in Tajikistan and some in the upper part of the Surkhandarya Valley in Uzbekistan. Also spoken in Afghanistan, Uzbekistan. Indo-European, Indo-Iranian, Indo-Aryan, Central zone, Unclassified. It may be a dialect of Marwari, related to Panjabi, or the Laghman dialect of Southeast Pashayi of Afghanistan. Subgroups: Kalu, Jitain, Juni, Maggar, Bisiyan, Mussali, Shuiya. Bilingualism in Tajiki. Parya remains the exclusive language within the home. Uzbek and Tajiki men who marry Parya women learn Parya and become assimilated into the community. They came to Tajikistan from Laghman, Afghanistan in 1880. They refer to themselves as 'Changgars'. Subgroup names are similar to those of the Changgars of Lahore, and to names used for groups mistakenly called 'Gypsies'. Collective farm workers. Sunni Muslim.

SANGLECHI-ISHKASHIMI [SGL] 500 in Tajikistan. Population total both countries 2,500. Tajikistan. Also spoken in Afghanistan. Indo-European, Indo-Iranian, Iranian, Eastern, Southeastern, Pamir. Dialects: ISHKASHIMI (ISHKASHIM, ESHKASHMI), ZEBAK (ZEBAKI), SANGLICH. Dialects listed may be separate languages. Speakers are bilingual in Tajiki, which is used as literary language. Used in daily family communication. Traditional territory and way of life. Not a written language. Ismaili Muslim.

SHUGHNI ***(SHUGNAN-RUSHAN)*** [SGH] 35,000 to 40,000 in Tajikistan including 20,000 Shugan, 1,500 to 2,000 Oroshor, 15,000 Rushan (1975 SIL). Population total both countries 55,000 to 60,000. Tajikistan, Gorno-Bagakhshan, Pamir Mts. Also spoken in Afghanistan. Indo-European, Indo-Iranian, Iranian, Eastern, Southeastern, Pamir, Shugni-Yazgulami. Dialects: RUSHANI (RUSHAN, ROSHANI, OROSHANI), BARTANGI (BARTANG), OROSHOR, KHUFI (KHUF, CHUF), SHUGHNI (SHUGAN, SHUGNAN, SHIGHNI, KHUGNI). Khufi and Bartangi may be separate languages. Oroshani may be separate from Rushani. Not intelligible with Sarikoli (called 'Tajiki' in China). Tajiki is used as a literary language. Used in daily family communication. Traditional territory and way of life. Mountain slope. Pastoralists. Ismaili Muslim.

TAJIKI ***(TADZHIK, TAJIKI PERSIAN, GALCHA)*** [PET] 3,344,720 in Tajikistan (1991), 98% speak it as mother tongue. Population total all countries 4,380,000. Also spoken in Kazakhstan, Kyrgyzstan, Russia (Asia), Turkmenistan, Ukraine, Uzbekistan. Indo-European, Indo-Iranian, Iranian, Western, Southwestern, Persian. Four groups of small dialects; no distinct boundaries. Dialect blending into Dari Persian in Afghanistan. Most Tajiki are trilingual in Northern Uzbek, Russian, and Tajiki. There is some literature. Russian sources refer to all Persian dialects in Afghanistan as 'Tajiki'. So-called 'Tajiki' in China is actually Shugni or Wakhi. There are Tajiki-speaking Gypsy communities in Soviet central Asia. National language. Cyrillic script used. Agriculturalists. Sunni Muslim. Bible 1992.

WAKHI ***(VAKHAN, WAKHANI, WAKHIGI, GUHJALI, KHIK)*** [WBL] 7,000 in Tajikistan (1993 UBS). Gorno-Badakhshan, Pamir Mts. Indo-European, Indo-Iranian, Iranian, Eastern, Southeastern, Pamir. Dialects: WESTERN WAKHI, CENTRAL WAKHI, EASTERN WAKHI. Dialects are inherently intelligible. Tajiki is used as a literary language. Not a written language. Speakers are called 'Guhjali'. Ismaili Muslim. See main entry under Pakistan.

YAGNOBI ***(YAGNOB)*** [YAI] 2,000 (1975 SIL). A high mountain valley of the Yagnob River. Indo-European, Indo-Iranian, Iranian, Eastern, Northeastern. Dialects: WESTERN YAGNOBI, EASTERN YAGNOBI. Tajiki is used as literary language. Russian also used. Used in daily family communication. Not a written language. People were resettled in the 1960s to southern Tajikistan; a change from cool mountain valleys with water to irrigated desert plains. Sunni Muslim.

YAZGULYAM *(IAZGULEM, YAZGULAM, YAZGULYAMI)* [YAH] 4,000 (1994 UBS). Along the Yazgulyam River, Gorno-Badakhshan AO. Indo-European, Indo-Iranian, Iranian, Eastern, Southeastern, Pamir, Shugni-Yazgulami. Dialects: UPPER YAZGULYAM, LOWER YAZGULYAM. Little dialect difference. Speakers are bilingual in Tajiki, which is used as literary language. Used in daily family communication. Traditional territory and way of life. Not a written language. Ismaili Muslim.

THAILAND

Kingdom of Thailand, Muang Thai or Prathet Thai. National or official language: Thai. 60,300,000 (1998 UN). 45,815,000 or 93.5% Daic languages, 1,037,650 or 2% Austro-Asiatic languages, 1,009,500 or 2% Austronesian languages, 533,500 or 1% Tibeto-Burman languages, 100,000 or .2% Hmong-Mien languages (1991 J. Matisoff). Literacy rate 89%. Also includes Burmese, Japanese, Padaung Karen 150, Lao, Sinhala, Tai Daeng, Tamil, Urdu, Vietnamese. Information mainly from F. Lebar, G. Hickey, J. Musgrave 1967; H. C. Purnell 1970; W. Smalley 1976; S. Wurm and S. Hattori 1981; J. Matisoff 1991, J. Matisoff et al. 1996; P. Prachakij-karacak 1995. Buddhist, Muslim, Chinese traditional religion, Christian, tribal traditional religion. Blind population 210,000 (1982 WCE). Deaf institutions: 22. Data accuracy estimate: A2, B. The number of languages listed for Thailand is 75. Of those, all are living languages. Diversity index 0.75.

AHEU *(PHON SOUNG, SO)* [THM] 750 in Thailand (1996 Ferlus). Population total both countries 1,000. The Thavung live in Sakon Nakhon Province, Song Daw District, 3 villages. The Phon Soung live about 100 km. south of the Thavung. Also spoken in Laos. Austro-Asiatic, Mon-Khmer, Viet-Muong, Thavung. Called 'So' in Thailand.

AKHA *(KAW, EKAW, KO, AKA, IKAW, AK'A, AHKA, KHAKO, KHA KO, KHAO KHA KO, IKOR, AINI, YANI)* [AKA] 60,000 in Thailand (1998). Chiangmai, Chiangrai, Maehongson provinces. 250 villages. Sino-Tibetan, Tibeto-Burman, Lolo-Burmese, Loloish, Southern, Hani, Ha-Ya. SOV. Literacy rate in first language: 1% to 5%. Literacy rate in second language: 1% to 50%. Traditional religion, Christian. NT 1968-1987. See main entry under Myanmar.

BAN KHOR SIGN LANGUAGE [BLA] Northeastern Thailand, a few villages. Deaf sign language. Not related to the original sign languages of Thailand, but there is some similarity.

BISU *(MBISU, MIBISU)* [BII] 1,000 or fewer in Thailand (1987 E. Purnell). Southwest Chiangrai, North Lampang. Two main villages, the largest with 100 houses. Sino-Tibetan, Tibeto-Burman, Lolo-Burmese, Loloish, Southern, Phunoi. Closely related to Mpi, Pyen, and Phunoi. All ages. Vigorous. Investigation needed: intelligibility with Mpi, Pyen, Phunoi. Literacy rate in first language: Below 1%. Literacy rate in second language: Below 5%. Traditional religion. See main entry under China.

BLANG *(SEN CHUN, HKAWA, KAWA, K'WA, K'ALA, BULANG, PULANG, PULA, PLANG, WA, KHON DOI, KONTOI)* [BLR] 1,200 in Thailand (1998 SIL). Chiangrai; 1,000 live outside Mae Sai near the northern border, a village of 200 to 300 is near Mae Chan. About 200 live west of Bangkok and work in gardens. Austro-Asiatic, Mon-Khmer, Northern Mon-Khmer, Palaungic, Western Palaungic, Waic, Bulang. Close to Wa. The group from Mae Sai came from Sipsongpanna, Yunnan, China, stayed in Myanmar for a while, and have been in Thailand since 1974. There are 6 to 10 dialects represented in one refugee village in Thailand. Samtao of Myanmar and China is not intelligible with Blang, but is closely related to Blang and Wa. Literacy rate in first language: Below 1%. Literacy rate in second language: Below 10%. Horticulturalists. Hinayana Buddhist, some Christian. See main entry under China.

BRU, EASTERN *(BROU, VANKIEU)* [BRU] 5,000 in Thailand (1983 SIL). Sakon Nakhon Province, about 12 villages. Austro-Asiatic, Mon-Khmer, Eastern Mon-Khmer, Katuic, West Katuic, Brou-So. Dialects: TRI (SO TRI, SO TRII), BRU KOK SA-AT. It is partially intelligible with Western Bru. Tri young people in Thailand do not speak the language. NT 1981. See main entry under Laos.

BRU, WESTERN *(BRUU, B'RU, BARU)* [BRV] 20,000 or more (1991). Population total both countries 20,000 or more. Dong Luang District of Mukdahand Province, one village in Amnat Charoen Province, 2 villages in Khong Chiam District, Ubon Province. Also spoken in USA. Austro-Asiatic, Mon-Khmer, Eastern Mon-Khmer, Katuic, West Katuic, Brou-So. It is partially intelligible with Eastern Bru. Literacy rate in first language: 1% to 5%. Literacy rate in second language: 80%.

CHAM, WESTERN *(CAMBODIAN CHAM, TJAM, CHAM, NEW CHAM)* [CJA] 4,000 in Thailand. Ban Khrue, Bangkok, and possibly in refugee camps. Austronesian, Malayo-Polynesian, Western Malayo-Polynesian, Sundic, Malayic, Achinese-Chamic, Chamic, South, Coastal, Cham-Chru. The language differs somewhat from Eastern Cham of central Viet Nam. Recognized fairly recently as Cham. They are thought to be remnants of Cham who fought in the Thai army about 200 years ago. There are conflicting reports about whether the people in Thailand still speak Cham or have shifted to Central Thai. Austro-Asiatic influences. Old Devanagari-based script used. Roman script being discussed in USA and elsewhere. Muslim. See main entry under Cambodia.

CHIANGMAI SIGN LANGUAGE ***(CHIENGMAI SIGN LANGUAGE)*** [CSD] Chiangmai. Deaf sign language. Related to present sign languages in Laos and Viet Nam (Haiphong, Hanoi, Ho Chi Minh City). A distinct language from Thai Sign Language. Still remembered by signers over 45 years old in Chiangmai. Younger signers use Modern Thai Sign Language. Investigation needed: bilingual proficiency in Thai Sign Language, attitudes.

CHINESE, HAKKA ***(HAKKA)*** [HAK] 58,800 in Thailand, 1% of Chinese-speaking Chinese in Thailand (1984 estimate). Cities. Sino-Tibetan, Chinese. Business class. Bible 1916. See main entry under China.

CHINESE, MANDARIN [CHN] 5,880 in Thailand, .1% of the Chinese population in Thailand (1984 estimate). Bangkok, provincial towns, and Kra Peninsula in the south. Sino-Tibetan, Chinese. Dialect: HO (HAW, CIN HAW, YUNNANESE, WESTERN MANDARIN, HUI, HUI-TZE, HWEI, PANGHSE, PANTHA, PANTHE, PATHEE). Chinese folk religion; Hui: Muslim. Bible 1874-1983. See main entry under China.

CHINESE, MIN DONG ***(EASTERN MIN)*** [CDO] Sino-Tibetan, Chinese. Dialect: FUZHOU (FUCHOW, FOOCHOW). Bible 1884-1905. See main entry under China.

CHINESE, MIN NAN ***(MIN NAN, MINNAN)*** [CFR] 1,081,920 in Thailand or 18.4% of Chinese-speaking population in Thailand, including 1,058,400 Chaochow (18%), 17,640 Fujian (.3%), 5,880 Hainanese (.1%) (1984 estimate). Cities. Sino-Tibetan, Chinese. Dialects: CHAOZHOU (CHAOCHOW, TIUCHIU, TEOCHOW, TECHU), SHANTOU (SWATOW), HAINAN, FUJIAN (FUKIEN, HOKKIEN). Most Min Nan speakers in Thailand speak Chaochow. Business, industrialists, clerks, sales, service, agriculturalists, professionals. Buddhist, Chinese folk religion, secular, Christian. Bible 1933. See main entry under China.

CHINESE, YUE ***(CANTONESE, YUE, YUEH)*** [YUH] 29,400 in Thailand, .5% of Chinese-speaking Chinese in Thailand (1984 estimate). Sino-Tibetan, Chinese. Bible 1894-1981. See main entry under China.

CHONG ***(SHONG, XONG, CHAWNG)*** [COG] 500 possibly in Thailand. Chantaburi, four villages, Trat Province, northwest of Par. Austro-Asiatic, Mon-Khmer, Eastern Mon-Khmer, Pearic, Western, Chong. Closely related to Somray of Cambodia. See main entry under Cambodia.

HMONG DAW ***(WHITE MEO, WHITE MIAO, MEO KAO, WHITE LUM, PEH MIAO, PE MIAO, CHUAN MIAO, BAI MIAO)*** [MWW] 25,000 to 30,000 in Thailand (1984 OMF). Petchabun, Tak, Maehongson, Chiangmai, Nan, Chiangrai, Pitsanalok, Loei, Sukhothai, Kamphaengphet, Prae, Phayao, Uttaradit, Lampang. Hmong-Mien, Hmongic, Chuanqiandian. Dialects: HMONG GU MBA (HMONG QUA MBA, STRIPED HMONG, MIAO LAI), MONG LENG, PETCHABUN MIAO. Also spoken by the Hmong Qua Mba people, an ethnic subgroup who live in Hmong Daw or Hmong Njua villages, except possibly in Nan Province, with no significant dialect differences. Largely intelligible with Hmong Njua. Mong Leng is intelligible with Hmong Daw, but sociolinguistic factors require separate literature. Probably the same as Peh Miao (White Miao) of China. Traditional religion, Christian. NT 1975-1984. See main entry under China.

HMONG NJUA ***(CHUANQIANDIAN MIAO, CHUANCHIENTIEN MIAO, SICHUAN-GUIZHOU-YUNNAN HMONG, TAK MIAO, MEO, MIAO, WESTERN MIAO)*** [BLU] 33,000 in Thailand (1987). Tak, Nan, Chiangmai, Maehongson, Petchabun, Chiangrai, Phayao, Phrae, Loei, Sukhothai, Kamphaengphet, Uthai provinces. Hmong-Mien, Hmongic, Chuanqiandian. Largely intelligible with Hmong Daw. Dictionary. SOV. Agriculturalists. Traditional religion, Christian. NT 1975-1983. See main entry under China.

IU MIEN ***(MIEN, YAO, MIAN, MYEN, YIU MIEN, YOUMIAN, HIGHLAND YAO, PAN YAO)*** [IUM] 40,000 in Thailand (1999). Chiangmai, Chiangrai, Phayao, Lampang, Kampaengphet, Nan, and Sukhothai provinces, 159 villages. Hmong-Mien, Mienic, Mian-Jin. Dialect: CHIANGRAI. Relatively little dialect variation. All 'Yao' and 'Mien' in Thailand are Iu Mien. Bilingualism in Northern Tai. Swidden agriculturalists: rice; hunters, weavers, embroiderers. Daoist, ancestor veneration, traditional religion. NT 1975-1991. See main entry under China.

KAREN, PA'O ***(TAUNGTU, BLACK KAREN, PA-U, PA'0, PA OH)*** [BLK] 600 in Thailand (1975 SIL). Maehongson. Sino-Tibetan, Tibeto-Burman, Karen, Pa'o. Bible portions 1912-1964. See main entry under Myanmar.

KAREN, PWO NORTHERN ***(PHLONG)*** [PWW] 60,000 (1983 SIL). Mae Sarieng town in northwest Thailand, Mae Ngaw along the Salween River, 15 to 25 villages, Hot to Mae Sarieng (Highway 1099 which runs south to Omkoi). Sino-Tibetan, Tibeto-Burman, Karen, Pwo. Dialects: MAE PING, OMKOI (HOD), MAE SARIENG. Three dialects are intelligible with each other. The Pwo Karen of Phrae, Kanchanaburi, and Hua Hin are not intelligible with these. 87% lexical similarity with Phrae Province Pwo Karen of Thailand, 68% to 73% with other Pwo Karen. Little knowledge of Thai in Hot to Mae Sarieng area. SVO. Literacy rate in first language: Below 1%. Literacy rate in second language: 25% to 50%. Thai-based script. Traditional religion, Christian. Bible portions 1995.

KAREN, PWO WESTERN THAILAND *(PHLOU, SOUTHERN PWO KAREN)* [KJP] 50,000 in Thailand (1998). Tak (Mae Sot south), Ulthaithani, Suphanburi, Kanchanaburi, Ratchaburi, Phetchaburi, and Prachuapkhirikhan (Hushin District) provinces. Kanchanaburi dialect is northern, Ratchaburi-Phetchaburi dialect is southern. Sino-Tibetan, Tibeto-Burman, Karen, Pwo. Dialects: KANCHANABURI PWO KAREN, RATCHABURI PWO KAREN (PHETCHABURI PWO KAREN). Not intelligible with other Pwo Karen varieties. 91% to 97% lexical similarity among dialects, 63% to 65% with other Pwo Karen varieties. SVO. Literacy rate in first language: Below 1%. Literacy rate in second language: 15% to 50%. Thai-based script. See main entry under Myanmar.

KAREN, PWO, PHRAE *(PWO PHRAE, PHRAE, PRAE, NORTHEASTERN PWO KAREN)* [KJT] Northern Thailand, eastern provinces including Phrae Province. Sino-Tibetan, Tibeto-Burman, Karen, Pwo. Not intelligible with other Pwo Karen languages. 87% lexical similarity with Northern Pwo Karen of Thailand, 67% to 71% with other Pwo Karen varieties. Most use Northern Thai and S'gaw Karen as second languages. Literacy rate in first language: Below 1%. Literacy rate in second language: 50% to 75%.

KAREN, S'GAW *(S'GAW, S'GAU, S'GAW KAYIN, KANYAW, PAGANYAW, PWAKANYAW, WHITE KAREN, BURMESE KAREN, YANG KHAO)* [KSW] 300,000 in Thailand (1987 E. Hudspith). Tak, Maehongsong, Chiangmai, and Chiangrai provinces, near the Myanmar border. Sino-Tibetan, Tibeto-Burman, Karen, Sgaw-Bghai, Sgaw. Dialects: PANAPU, PALAKHI (PALACHI). Closely related to Paku. SVO. Literacy rate in first language: 10% to 30%. Literacy rate in second language: 25% to 50%. Traditional religion, Christian. Bible 1853-1995. See main entry under Myanmar.

KAYAH, EASTERN *(RED KAREN, KARENNYI, KAYAY, KAYAH)* [EKY] 77,900 (1983). Maehongson Province, east of the Salween River. Sino-Tibetan, Tibeto-Burman, Karen, Sgaw-Bghai, Kayah. Distinct from but related to Bwe Karen (Bghai), forming a continuous chain of dialects. Speakers have difficulty understanding Western Kayah of Myanmar. They have a strong ethnic feeling that all Kayah are the same ethnic group. Literacy rate in first language: 1% to 5%. Literacy rate in second language: 60% in Thai. See main entry under Myanmar.

KENSIU *(KENSE, KENSIEU, KENSEU, KENSIW, SAKAI, MONIQ, MONIK, MANIQ, MONI, MENIK, MENI, NEGRITO, NGOK PA, ORANG BUKIT, ORANG LIAR, MOS, MENGO, TIONG, MAWAS, BELUBN)* [KNS] 300 in Thailand. Southern Yala Province, Phattaloong, Satun, Narathiwat provinces, Thai-Malay border. Some in a resettlement camp in Yala. Austro-Asiatic, Mon-Khmer, Aslian, North Aslian, Western. Negrito pygmies, nomads, small bands. Literacy rate in first language: Below 1%. Literacy rate in second language: 5% to 15%. Tropical forest. Traditional religion. See main entry under Malaysia, Peninsular.

KHMER, NORTHERN [KXM] 1,000,000 (1991 SIL). Northeastern Thailand, mainly Surin, Sisaket, Buriram, Korat Provinces. Austro-Asiatic, Mon-Khmer, Eastern Mon-Khmer, Khmer. Dialects: BURIRAM, SURIN, SISAKET. Different from Central Khmer. Dialects are intelligible with each other. Bilingualism in Thai. SVO; prepositions; genitives, modifiers, relatives after noun heads; 1 prefix; CV, CVC, CCV; nontonal. Literacy rate in first language: Below 1%. Literacy rate in second language: 50% to 75%. Scrub forest. Plains. Peasant and intensive agriculturalists, craftsmen, educators, officials. 500 meters. Buddhist, Christian. NT 1996.

KHMU *(KMHMU, KHAMU, KHMU', KHAMUK, KAMHMU, KAMU, KHA KHMU, KAMMU, TMOOY, MOU, LUU, POUTENG)* [KJG] 15,000 to 40,000 in Thailand (1984). Scattered through Thailand, Chiangrai, Nan, Phayao. Austro-Asiatic, Mon-Khmer, Northern Mon-Khmer, Khmuic, Mal-Khmu', Khmu'. Traditional religion, Christian. Bible portions 1918. See main entry under Laos.

KHUN *(HKUN, KHUN SHAN, GON SHAN, TAI KHUN, KHUEN)* [KKH] Chiangrai, Chiangmai. May not be in Thailand. Tai-Kadai, Kam-Tai, Be-Tai, Tai-Sek, Tai, Southwestern, East Central, Northwest. Closely related to Lü. Different from Khouen (Khuen), a Mon-Khmer language of Laos. Buddhist. Bible portions 1938. See main entry under Myanmar.

KINTAQ *(KENTA, KINTK, KINTAQ BONG)* [KNQ] Kedah-Perak border area, Thai border. Overlaps slightly into Southern Yala Province of Thailand. Austro-Asiatic, Mon-Khmer, Aslian, North Aslian, Western. Negrito pygmies, nomadic. Hunter-gatherers. Traditional religion. See main entry under Malaysia, Peninsular.

KOREAN [KKN] Bangkok. Language Isolate. Buddhist, Christian. Bible 1911-1993. See main entry under Korea, South.

KUY *(SUI, SUAI, SUAY, SUOI, SOAI, SUEI, CUOI, KUI SOUEI, KUI, KUOY, KHAMEN-BORAN)* [KDT] 300,000 in Thailand (1992 Diffloth). Population total all countries 380,000. East central Thailand; Buriram, Surin, Sisaket, Ubon, Roi Et. Also spoken in Cambodia, Laos. Austro-Asiatic, Mon-Khmer, Eastern Mon-Khmer, Katuic, West Katuic, Kuay-Yoe. Dialects: DAMREY, ANLOUR, O, KRAOL, ANTRA, CHANG (SUAI CHANG). The first 5 dialects listed are in Cambodia. A different script is used in Cambodia. Literacy rate in first language: Below 1%. Literacy rate in second language: 25% to 50%. Traditional religion, Buddhist. NT 1978.

LAHU ***(LOHEI, MUHSUR, MUSSUH, MUHSO, MUSSO, MUSSER)*** [LAH] 28,000 in Thailand (1993 Johnstone). Chiangmai, Chiangrai, Maehongson, Lampang, Tak provinces, 119 known villages. There has been some migration from Myanmar and Laos. Sino-Tibetan, Tibeto-Burman, Lolo-Burmese, Loloish, Southern, Akha, Lahu. Dialects: NA (BLACK LAHU, MUSSER DAM, NORTHERN LAHU, LOHEIRN), NYI (RED LAHU, SOUTHERN LAHU, MUSSEH DAENG, LUHISHI, LUHUSHI), SHEHLEH. Black Lahu, Red Lahu, and Shehleh dialects are close. Lahu Shi (Yellow Lahu, Kutsung) is distinct. Dictionary. Grammar. Literacy rate in first language: 30% to 60%. Literacy rate in second language: 5% to 15%. Traditional religion, Christian. Bible 1989. See main entry under China.

LAHU SHI ***(KUTSUNG, KUCONG, KUI, KWI, SHI, YELLOW LAHU, MUSSEH KWI, MUSSEH LYANG)*** [KDS] 20,000 in Thailand (1998). In refugee camps near Laos border; formerly in Chiang Kham camp, but now in camps near Pua, Nan, or elsewhere. Sino-Tibetan, Tibeto-Burman, Lolo-Burmese, Loloish, Southern, Akha, Lahu. Difficult intelligibility with Black and Red Lahu. Distinct from Kui (Kuy, Suoi), which is Mon-Khmer. Literacy rate in first language: Below 1%. Literacy rate in second language: 5% to 15%. See main entry under Laos.

LAMET ***(KHA LAMET, KHAMET, KAMET, LEMET)*** [LBN] 100 in Thailand. Lampang, Chiangrai. Austro-Asiatic, Mon-Khmer, Northern Mon-Khmer, Palaungic, Western Palaungic, Lametic. Dialects: UPPER LAMET, LOWER LAMET. Called 'Khamet' in Thailand and 'Lamet' in Laos. Traditional religion. See main entry under Laos.

LAWA, EASTERN ***(WIANG PAPAO LUA, NORTHERN LAWA)*** [LWL] 7,000 (1987 D. Schlatter). Northern; Chiangmai, Chiangrai, one village: Wiang Papao. Austro-Asiatic, Mon-Khmer, Northern Mon-Khmer, Palaungic, Western Palaungic, Waic, Lawa. Dialects: PHALO, PHANG. Not intelligible with Western Lawa. Phalo (100) and Phang (100) are treated as distinct languages in Wurm and Hattori 1981. Bilingualism in Northern Tai. Literacy rate in first language: Below 1%. Literacy rate in second language: 25% to 50%. Traditional religion, Buddhist.

LAWA, WESTERN ***(LAVA, LUWA, LUA, L'WA, LAVUA, LAVÜA, MOUNTAIN LAWA)*** [LCP] 7,000 in Thailand (1987 D. Schlatter). Numerous villages in Chiangmai and Maehongson provinces of northern Thailand. Austro-Asiatic, Mon-Khmer, Northern Mon-Khmer, Palaungic, Western Palaungic, Waic, Lawa. Dialect: LA-OOR. Unintelligible to speakers of Eastern Lawa. Some dialects are unintelligible to each others' speakers. La-oor is becoming the standard for literature. Bilingualism in Northern Tai. Literacy rate in first language: 1% to 5%. Literacy rate in second language: 25% to 50%. Traditional religion, Buddhist. NT 1972. See main entry under China.

LISU ***(LISAW, LI-SHAW, LI-HSAW, LU-TZU, SOUTHERN LISU, YAO YEN, YAW-YEN, YAW YIN, YEH-JEN, LISO)*** [LIS] 16,000 in Thailand (1993 Johnstone). Chiangmai, Chiangrai, Maehongson, Tak, Sukhothai, Kamphaeng Phet provinces. Some have migrated to northwest Thailand from Myanmar. Sino-Tibetan, Tibeto-Burman, Burmese-Lolo, Lolo, Northern, Lisu. Dialect: LU SHI LISU. Literacy rate in first language: 5% to 10%. Literacy rate in second language: 50% to 75%. Traditional religion, Christian. Bible 1968-1986. See main entry under China.

LÜ ***(LUE, TAI LUE, THAI LU, TAI LU, LU, PAI-I, PAI-YI, SHUI-PAI-I)*** [KHB] 78,000 in Thailand (1993 Johnstone). Chiangrai, Payao, Lamphun, Nan, Chiang Kham, and throughout northern Thailand. Tai-Kadai, Kam-Tai, Be-Tai, Tai-Sek, Tai, Southwestern, East Central, Northwest. Most closely related to Khun. 88% lexical similarity with Northern Thai; 74% with Central Thai. Central Thai is used in schools and on the radio. Northern Thai is the language used in town for trade, employment, and with Northern Thai speakers. Many thousands of Lü people including men and women, younger and older people understand very little Central Thai. Lü is used exclusively in talking to other Lü people; in the home, with friends, children, in the market, fields, in arguments, for telling stories, for counting. All ages. The Lü are proud of their language and eager to be identified as Lü. Literacy rate in first language: 1% to 5%. Literacy rate in second language: 50% to 75%. High in Central Thai in Thai script. Extensive literature in old Lü script, which no one reads now. Tropical forest. Valleys. Agriculturalists: wet rice; fishermen. Traditional religion, Buddhist. NT 1933. See main entry under China.

LUA' ***(EAST PUA PRAY, PRAY 2)*** [PRB] East of Pua District in Nan Province. Also on Laos-Thailand border. Austro-Asiatic, Mon-Khmer, Northern Mon-Khmer, Khmuic, Mal-Khmu', Mal-Phrai. Distinct from Mal, Phai, and Pray 3. Some Christian. Bible portions 1984.

MAL ***(T'IN, HT'IN, THIN, TIN, KHATIN)*** [MLF] 3,000 to 4,000 in Thailand (1982 SIL). East of Pua District and Chiang Kam, valley near northern Laos border, Nan Province. Austro-Asiatic, Mon-Khmer, Northern Mon-Khmer, Khmuic, Mal-Khmu', Mal-Phrai. Not intelligible with Lua, Phai, or Pray 3. 'Mal' and 'Madl' are self names. 'T'in' is an ethnic name used in Thailand. Literacy rate in first language: Below 1% literate. Literacy rate in second language: 1% to 15%. NT 1994. See main entry under Laos.

MALAY ***(BAHASA MALAY, MELAYU)*** [MLI] Some villages in Ranong, south Thailand. Austronesian, Malayo-Polynesian, Western Malayo-Polynesian, Sundic, Malayic, Malayan, Local Malay. Shafi Muslim. Bible 1733-1993. See main entry under Malaysia, Peninsular.

MALAY, KEDAH [MEO] A few villages near Satun. Isolated. Austronesian, Malayo-Polynesian, Western Malayo-Polynesian, Sundic, Malayic, Malayan, Local Malay. Apparently distinct from Pattani Malay or Standard Malay. Bilingualism in Central Thai. More people in the area speak Thai than Pattani. Most outside contacts are with centers of Thai population in Songkhla, Phattalung, and Haad Yai; with west coast Malay states of Perlis and Kedah. Culturally Malay. Tropical forest. Muslim.

MALAY, PATTANI ***(THAI ISLAM)*** [MFA] 3,100,000 including 2,600,000 in southern Thailand, 500,000 in Bangkok and elsewhere (1998). Chana (Chenok) region of Songkhla (Singgora) Province in the north, traversing southward through Pattani, Narathiwat, Yala, Saiburi, Tak Bai. Austronesian, Malayo-Polynesian, Western Malayo-Polynesian, Sundic, Malayic, Malayan, Local Malay. Different from Kedah Malay and Standard Malay. Bilingualism in Central Thai. Investigation needed: intelligibility with Trengganu, Kelantan. Muslim, Christian. NT 1981.

MANG ***(MANG U, XAMANG, CHAMAN, MANBU, BA'E)*** [MGA] 5 in Thailand. 1 village in the north. Austro-Asiatic, Mon-Khmer, Northern Mon-Khmer, Mang. See main entry under Viet Nam.

MLABRI ***(MLA, MLA BRI, MABRI, MRABRI, YUMBRI, MA KU, YELLOW LEAF, PHI THONG LUANG)*** [MRA] 300 (1982 E. R. Long). Population total both countries 324. Laos border area. Phayao, Nan, Phrae, Utaradit, Phitsanuloke, Loey, and perhaps other provinces. Also spoken in Laos. Austro-Asiatic, Mon-Khmer, Northern Mon-Khmer, Khmuic, Mlabri. They speak or understand some Hmong and Northern Thai. Mlabri are different from the Kha Tong Luang (Phi Tong Luang, Yellow Leaf) in Laos, which are Western Viet-Muong (Wurm and Hattori 1981). Speakers are sometimes employed by the Hmong. Some are nomadic. Literacy rate in first language: Below 1%. Literacy rate in second language: 0 to 1%. Tropical forest. Agriculturalists: rice, maize; hunter-gatherers. Traditional religion.

MOK ***(AMOK, HSEN-HSUM)*** [MQT] 7 (1981 Wurm and Hattori). Northwest; east northeast of Chiang Mai, on Wang River. Austro-Asiatic, Mon-Khmer, Northern Mon-Khmer, Palaungic, Western Palaungic, Angkuic. Nearly extinct.

MOKEN ***(MAWKEN, BASING, SELUNG, SELONG, SALONG, SALON, CHAU KO')*** [MWT] West coast of south Thailand, Phuket, Phangnga, Krabi, Ranong. Austronesian, Malayo-Polynesian, Western Malayo-Polynesian, Sundic, Malayic, Moklen. Dialects: DUNG, JA-IT, L'BE. Closest to Moklen. Related to Urak Lawoi. They live primarily on boats, but occasionally settle on islands in the area. Traditional religion, Muslim. Bible portions 1913. See main entry under Myanmar.

MOKLEN ***(CHAU POK)*** [MKM] 1,500 or fewer (1984 D. Hogan). West coast of south Thailand, Phuket, Phangnga. Austronesian, Malayo-Polynesian, Western Malayo-Polynesian, Sundic, Malayic, Moklen. Heavy Thai and Mon-Khmer influence. Traditional religion, Muslim.

MON ***(TALAING, TALENG, ALENG, MUN, PEGUAN, TAKANOON)*** [MNW] 70,000 to 100,000 in Thailand (1983 SIL). On the Myanmar border, Kanchanaburi, Pathum Thani, Rat Buri, Surat Thani, Lopburi, Khorat; north and south of Bangkok. Austro-Asiatic, Mon-Khmer, Monic. In some areas they have apparently integrated with the Thai, in other areas they are separate. Traditional religion, Buddhist. Bible 1928. See main entry under Myanmar.

MPI ***(MPI-MI)*** [MPZ] 2,000 (1981 Wurm and Hattori). Phrae, Phayao, two villages. Sino-Tibetan, Tibeto-Burman, Lolo-Burmese, Loloish, Southern, Phunoi. Closely related to Bisu, Pyen, and Phunoi. Investigation needed: intelligibility with Bisu, Pyen, Phunoi. Traditional religion.

NYAHKUR ***(NYAH KUR, NYAKUR, NIAKUOL, NIAKUOLL, "CHAOBON", "CHAODON", LAWA)*** [CBN] 300 (1983 SIL) to 10,000 (1981 Wurm and Hattori). Central Thailand, Korat, Petchabun, Chayaphum, a few villages, from north of B. Khum Chieo to south of Ban Kao, Thakhong, and other rivers. Austro-Asiatic, Mon-Khmer, Monic. Their name for themselves is 'Nyahkur'. "Chaobon" is the Thai name and is derogatory. Literacy rate in first language: Below 1%. Literacy rate in second language: 75% to 100%. Buddhist.

NYAW ***(YO, NYO)*** [NYW] 50,000 (1990 A. Diller ANU). Sakorn Nakorn, Ta Bo', Nong Khai; Tha Uthen, Nakorn Panom. Tai-Kadai, Kam-Tai, Be-Tai, Tai-Sek, Tai, Southwestern, East Central, Lao-Phutai. Closely related to Isan (Northeastern Thai) and Luang Prabang Lao. Bilingualism in Isan. Maw may be an alternate name. Buddhist.

NYEU ***(YEU, YOE)*** [NYL] Small. Sisaket. Austro-Asiatic, Mon-Khmer, Eastern Mon-Khmer, Katuic, West Katuic, Kuay-Yoe. Literacy rate in first language: Below 1%. Literacy rate in second language: 25% to 50%.

PALAUNG, PALE ***(DI-ANG, NGWE PALAUNG, SILVER PALAUNG, PALE, PALAY, SOUTHERN TA-ANG)*** [PCE] 5,000 in Thailand (1989). Austro-Asiatic, Mon-Khmer, Northern Mon-Khmer, Palaungic, Eastern Palaungic, Palaung. A distinct language from Shwe Palaung and Rumai Palaung. Literacy rate in first language: Below 1%. Literacy rate in second language: Below 5%. See main entry under Myanmar.

PHAI ***(PHAY, THUNG CHAN PRAY, KHA PHAY, PRAY 1, PRAI)*** [PRT] 31,000 in Thailand (1993 Johnstone). Population total both countries 31,000 or more. Thung Chang District of Nan Province. Also spoken in Laos. Austro-Asiatic, Mon-Khmer, Northern Mon-Khmer, Khmuic, Mal-Khmu', Mal-Phrai. More Pray speakers have recently come from Laos to refugee camps, which could represent additional dialects. Different from Lua, Mal, and Pray 3.

PHU THAI ***(PUTHAI, PUTAI, PHUU THAI, PHUTAI)*** [PHT] 156,000 in Thailand (1993). Population total all countries 434,000. Kham Chai, Nakorn Panom, Ubon, Kalasin, Sakorn Nakorn. Also spoken in Laos, USA, Viet Nam. Tai-Kadai, Kam-Tai, Be-Tai, Tai-Sek, Tai, Southwestern, East Central, Lao-Phutai. Little dialect differentiation. Close to Tai Dam and Tai Don. Bilingualism in Isan. Literacy rate in first language: Below 1%. Literacy rate in second language: 75% to 100%. Buddhist.

PHUAN ***(LAO PHUAN, PHU UN)*** [PHU] Population total both countries 96,000 or more. Uthai Thani, Phichit, Petchabun, Lopburi, Singburi, Suphanburi, Saraburi, Nakorn Nayok, Phrachinburi, Udon, Loei, and one village south of Bangkok. Also spoken in Laos. Tai-Kadai, Kam-Tai, Be-Tai, Tai-Sek, Tai, Southwestern, East Central, Chiang Saeng. Closely related to Northern Tai, Tai Dam, Song, Lao. Vigorous. Strong sense of identity. A socially prominent group. They were relocated to Thailand from 1827 to 1890. The name is also used for Lao speakers in Thailand. There is an annual Phuan celebration in Bangkok. Investigation needed: intelligibility. Buddhist.

PHUNOI ***(PHU NOI, PUNOI, PHOUNOY, CÔÔNG)*** [PHO] Some in Chiangrai. Sino-Tibetan, Tibeto-Burman, Lolo-Burmese, Loloish, Southern, Phunoi. Dialects: BLACK KHOANY, WHITE KHOANY, MUNG, HWETHOM, KHASKHONG. Closely related to Bisu, Pyen, and Mpi. Those listed as dialects may be separate languages. Known as 'Côông' in Viet Nam. Literacy rate in second language: 50% to 75%. See main entry under Laos.

PRAY 3 [PRY] Interspersed in Thung Chang and Pua districts among the Mal. Austro-Asiatic, Mon-Khmer, Northern Mon-Khmer, Khmuic, Mal-Khmu', Mal-Phrai. One dialect is more distinct. Separate from Phai and Lua. People speak Mal fairly well. Investigation needed: intelligibility with dialects, Mal. Literacy rate in first language: Below 1%. Literacy rate in second language: 25% to 50%.

SAEK ***(SEK, TAI SEK)*** [SKB] 11,000 in Thailand (1993 Johnstone). Northeastern, Nakorn Panom. Tai-Kadai, Kam-Tai, Be-Tai, Tai-Sek, Sek. Bilingualism in Lao. Buddhist. See main entry under Laos.

SHAN ***(SHA, TAI SHAN, SAM, TAI YAY, THAI YAY, GREAT THAI, TAI LUANG, "NGIO", "NGIOW", "NGIAW", "NGIAO", "NGEO")*** [SJN] 56,000 in Thailand (1993 Johnstone). Maehongson, Myuang Haeng, Chiangrai, Chiangmai, Maesai, Tak, on northwestern border. Tai-Kadai, Kam-Tai, Be-Tai, Tai-Sek, Tai, Southwestern, East Central, Northwest. Plains. Paddy rice, artisans (gold, silver, blacksmiths), shopkeepers. Buddhist, traditional religion, Christian. Bible 1892. See main entry under Myanmar.

SÔ ***(KHA SO, THRO)*** [SSS] 55,000 in Thailand (1993 Johnstone). Nakorn Panom, Sakorn Nakorn, Nong Kai, Kalasin. Both sides of Mekong River in northeastern Thailand. 53 villages in Thailand. Austro-Asiatic, Mon-Khmer, Eastern Mon-Khmer, Katuic, West Katuic, Brou-So. Dialects: SO TRONG, SO SLOUY, SO PHONG, SO MAKON. They came from Laos, and the same dialect is spoken there. Closely related to Bru. They also speak Lao. They are adjusting to Thai culture and gradually becoming bilingual in Thai. People speak So in the home. All ages. Literacy rate in first language: Below 1%. Literacy rate in second language: 25% to 50%. Plains. Agriculturalists: wet rice. Buddhist, traditional religion, Christian. Bible portions 1980. See main entry under Laos.

SONG ***(THAI SONG, LAO SONG, LAO SONG DAM)*** [SOA] 20,000 to 30,000 (1982 SIL). Kanchanaburi, Phetburi, Pitsanulok, Nakorn Sawaan, Nakorn Pathom, Suphanaburi. Tai-Kadai, Kam-Tai, Be-Tai, Tai-Sek, Tai, Southwestern, East Central, Chiang Saeng. Only slight dialect differences. Closely related to Tai Dam. Traditional religion. Bible portions.

TAI DAM ***(JINPING DAI, TAI NOIR, THAI DEN, BLACK TAI)*** [BLT] 20,000 in Thailand (1991 J. Matisoff). Widely scattered in Nongkhai, Korat, Loei, and Saraburi. Tai-Kadai, Kam-Tai, Be-Tai, Tai-Sek, Tai, Southwestern, East Central, Chiang Saeng. Related to Tai Don. Bible portions 1982-1993. See main entry under Viet Nam.

TAI NÜA ***(CHINESE SHAN, TAI NEUA, TAI MAN, DEHONG DAI)*** [TDD] Also possibly in northern Viet Nam. Tai-Kadai, Kam-Tai, Be-Tai, Tai-Sek, Tai, Southwestern, East Central, Northwest. Bible portions 1931-1948. See main entry under China.

THAI ***(CENTRAL TAI, STANDARD THAI, THAIKLANG, SIAMESE)*** [THJ] 20,000,000 to 25,000,000 in Thailand (1990 A. Diller), including 400,000 Khorat (1984), 4,704,000 mother tongue Thai speakers who are ethnic Chinese, or 80% of the Chinese (1984). Population total all countries 20,047,000 to 25,000,000. Central Thailand, centered in Bangkok. Khorat dialect in Ratchasima. Also spoken in Midway Islands, Singapore, UAE, USA. Tai-Kadai, Kam-Tai, Be-Tai, Tai-Sek, Tai, Southwestern, East Central, Chiang Saeng. Dialect: KHORAT THAI (KORAT). People sometimes called 'Siamese'. Official language. Grammar. SVO. Thai script. Radio programs. Buddhist, Christian. Bible 1883-1990.

THAI SIGN LANGUAGE [TSQ] 51,000 profoundly, prelingually deaf people in Thailand (1997 Charles B. Reilly). 20% of deaf children go to school, where they get the opportunity to learn this language. Major regional centers and Bangkok. Deaf sign language. The first deaf school was established in 1951, with influence from Gallaudet University in the USA. It uses a combination of indigneous signs and ASL. Before 1950 Chiangmai and Bangkok had their own separate but related sign languages, and probably other 'urban' areas had their own sign languages, related to present sign languages in parts of Laos and Vietnam, including Haiphong. The signs used at the deaf school at Tak are reported to be very different. Bilingualism in Central Thai. All deaf born since 1951, and some older ones. Total communication used in school: speaking and signing. Reported to be high mobility among most deaf people today. The sign language used in the classroom and that by deaf adults outside is different. There is a manual system for spelling. Dictionary. Literacy rate in second language: Fewer than 10%. Educated deaf people have some Thai literacy skills, but limited. TV. Buddhist.

THAI, NORTHEASTERN ***(ISAN, ISAAN, ISSAN)*** [TTS] 15,000,000 (1983 SIL) to 23,000,000 including Lao, at least 1,000,000 in Bangkok. Kalerng has a few thousand speakers (1990 A. Diller ANU). Northeastern; 17 provinces. Kalerng is in Sakon Nakhon and Nakhon Phanom. Tai-Kadai, Kam-Tai, Be-Tai, Tai-Sek, Tai, Southwestern, East Central, Lao-Phutai. Dialects: NORTHERN ISAN, CENTRAL ISAN (KALERNG, KALEUNG), SOUTHERN ISAN, KORAT. The Korat dialect is quite different, and may be a separate language. 88% use Isan in the home, 1% use Central Thai, 11% use both. The people are called 'Isan'. Investigation needed: intelligibility with Korat. SVO. Thai script used. Buddhist.

THAI, NORTHERN ***(LANNA, LAN NA, LANATAI, "YUAN", PHYAP, PHAYAP, PAYAP, KAMMÜANG, KAMMYANG, MYANG, KAM MU'ANG, MU'ANG, KHON MUNG, KHON MYANG, TAI NYA, LA NYA, NORTHERN THAI, WESTERN LAOTIAN)*** [NOD] 6,000,000 in Thailand (1983 SIL). Population total both countries 6,003,000. Chiangmai, Chiangrai, Lamphun, Lampang, Maehongson, Hot, Nan, Phayao, Phrae, Uttaradit, Tak provinces. Also spoken in Laos. Tai-Kadai, Kam-Tai, Be-Tai, Tai-Sek, Tai, Southwestern, East Central, Chiang Saeng. Dialects: NAN, BANDU, TAI WANG. The Nan dialect is more distinct. Rural or uneducated speakers have limited bilingualism in Central Thai. 87.5% use Northern Tai in the home, 3% use Central Thai, 9.5% use both. People are called 'Khon Mung', but do not like the name "Yuan". Has had Yuan script for a long time, in which are written Buddhist sermons, inscriptions, the Bible. Not used much now. Few can read it. Thai script has been used for literature in Northern Thai also, although it lacks some necessary contrasts. Newspapers. Buddhist. Bible 1927, out of print.

THAI, SOUTHERN ***(PAK THAI, PAK TAI, PAKTAY, DAMBRO)*** [SOU] 5,000,000 (1990 A. Diller ANU), including 1,500,000 Muslim Tai (1981 Wurm and Hattori). Chumphon, Nakorn Srithammerat; 14 provinces total. Muslim Tai in provinces of Chumporn, Nakorn Srithammerat, Phattalung, Songkhla, Ranong, Phanga, Phuket, Krabi, Trang, Satun. Tai-Kadai, Kam-Tai, Be-Tai, Tai-Sek, Tai, Southwestern, Southern. Dialects: TAK BAI (TAI TAK BAI), THAI MALAY (TAI ISLAM). A group of dialects more distantly related to other Tai languages. The border dialects are quite distinct from others. 81% use Southern Tai in the home, 8.5% use Central Tai, 10.5% use both. Muslim Tai ('Thai Malay') speak only Southern Tai. Investigation needed: bilingual proficiency in Central Thai. Buddhist, Muslim, Christian.

TONGA ***(MOS)*** [TNZ] Population total both countries 300 (1981 Wurm and Hattori). Two areas in the south. Also spoken in Malaysia (Peninsular). Austro-Asiatic, Mon-Khmer, Aslian, North Aslian, Tonga. Dialect: SATUN. Probably close to Kensiu.

UGONG ***(LAWA, 'UGONG, GONG, UGAWNG)*** [UGO] 100 (1991 D. Bradley) to 1,000 (1993). Kanchanaburi, Uthai Thani, Suphanaburi. None in Myanmar. Sino-Tibetan, Tibeto-Burman, Lolo-Burmese, Loloish, Southern. Dialects: KOK CHIANG, SUPHANABURI. Not closely related to other languages. All speak some variety of Thai. Reported to be used by 100 adults as language of the home. Adult speakers. Children speak Thai as mother tongue. Distinct from Lawa in the Palaung-Wa branch of Mon-Khmer.

URAK LAWOI' ***(ORAK LAWOI', LAWTA, CHAW TALAY, CHAWNAM, LAWOI)*** [URK] 3,000 (1984 D. Hogan). Phuket and Langta islands, west coast of southern Thailand. Not in Malaysia. Austronesian, Malayo-Polynesian, Western Malayo-Polynesian, Sundic, Malayic, Malayan, Para-Malay. Aboriginal Malays who speak a unique Malay language. Strand dwellers. Traditional religion, Christian. NT 1998.

YONG ***(NYONG)*** [YNO] Chiangrai, Chiangmai, Lamphun. May also be in Muang Yong, northern Myanmar. Tai-Kadai, Kam-Tai, Be-Tai, Tai-Sek, Tai, Southwestern, Unclassified. Phonology similar to Lü. Bilingualism in Northern Tai. Buddhist.

YOY ***(YOI, YOOI, YOOY)*** [YOY] 5,000 in Thailand (1990 A. Diller ANU). Population total both countries 5,000 or more. Sakorn Nakorn. Also spoken in Laos. Tai-Kadai, Kam-Tai, Be-Tai, Tai-Sek, Tai, Unclassified. Bilingualism in Northeastern Tai.

TIMOR LOROSAE

East Timor, Timor Timur, Timor L'este. 857,000 (1998 UN). National language: Tetun. Official language: Portuguese. Information mainly from Grimes, Therik, Grimes, and Jacob 1997. Christian, traditional religion. The number of languages listed for Timor Lorosae is 20. Of those, 19 are living languages and 1 is extinct. Diversity index 0.88.

ADABE ***(ATAURA, ATAURU, ATAURO, RAKLU-UN, RAKLU UN)*** [ADB] 1,000(?) in ethnic group (1981 Wurm and Hattori). Atauro Island, north of Dili on Timor Island. Austronesian, Malayo-Polynesian, Central-Eastern, Unclassified. Dialect: MUNASELI PANDAI. Reported to be different from Galoli dialects on Atauro. Investigation needed: intelligibility with Timor mainland languages.

ATONI ***(UAB METO, METO, UAB ATONI PAH METO, UAB PAH METO, TIMOR, TIMORESE, TIMOL, TIMOREESCH, TIMOREEZEN, DAWAN, TIMOR DAWAN, RAWAN, ORANG GUNUNG)*** [TMR] 14,000 in Ambenu (1989). Ambenu, western Timor Island, but politically part of Timor Lorosae. Austronesian, Malayo-Polynesian, Central-Eastern, Central Malayo-Polynesian, Timor, Nuclear Timor, West. Dialect: AMBENU (AMBENO, VAIKENU, VAIKINO, BAIKENU, BIKENU, BIQUENO). Much dialect variation, requiring speakers several weeks to adjust, for effective communication to take place. Ethnological and linguistic differences in nearly every valley. Close to Amarasi. Tetum Prasa not widely known as second language. 'Uab Meto' is speakers' name for their own language. Investigation needed: intelligibility with dialects. Traditional religion (Ambenu). NT 1948-1984. See main entry under Indonesia, Nusa Tenggara.

BUNAK ***(BUNA', BUNAKE, BUNAQ)*** [BUA] 50,000 in the ethnic group (1977 Voegelin and Voegelin). Population total both countries 50,000 or more. Central interior Timor Island, south coast. Also spoken in Indonesia (Nusa Tenggara). Trans-New Guinea, South Bird's Head-Timor-Alor-Pantar, Timor-Alor-Pantar, Bunak. Not closely related to other languages. Some small groups are scattered among other languages. Grammar. Traditional religion.

FATALUKU ***(DAGAGA, DAGODA', DAGADA)*** [DDG] 30,000 in the ethnic group (1989). Eastern tip of Timor Island around Los Palos. Trans-New Guinea, South Bird's Head-Timor-Alor-Pantar, Timor-Alor-Pantar, Fataluku. May be related to Oirata on nearby Kisar Island. Some speakers cannot function at all in Indonesian, Portuguese, or Tetum Prasa. Verb final. Traditional religion, Christian.

GALOLI ***(GALOLE)*** [GAL] 50,000(?) in the ethnic group (1981 Wurm and Hattori). North coast between Mambae and Makasae, regions of Laklo, Manatutu, Laleia, and We-Masin, Wetar Island. Austronesian, Malayo-Polynesian, Central-Eastern, Central Malayo-Polynesian, Timor, Nuclear Timor, East. Dialects: NA NAHEK, EDI, DADUA, GALOLI, BABA, HAHAK. Talur on Wetar in Maluku may be inherently intelligible.

HABU [HBU] 1,000(?) in the ethnic group (1981 Wurm and Hattori). East Timor Island, northeast of Laclubar and the Idate language. Austronesian, Malayo-Polynesian, Central-Eastern, Central Malayo-Polynesian, Timor, Nuclear Timor, Waima'a. Many loan words from Trans-New Guinea languages similar to Makasae, but with Austronesian structure. Related to Waima'a and Kairui. Classification needs further investigation.

IDATÉ [IDT] 5,000(?) in ethnic group (1981 Wurm and Hattori). Central east Timor Island, mountains of part of the Laclubar area, surrounded by the Mambae, Galoli, Kairui, and Tetun. Austronesian, Malayo-Polynesian, Central-Eastern, Central Malayo-Polynesian, Timor, Nuclear Timor, East. Closest to Lakalei and Galoli. Mountain slope.

KAIRUI-MIDIKI ***(CAIRUI, MIDIKI)*** [KRD] 2,000(?) in the ethnic group (1981 Wurm and Hattori). Central East Timor Island, small mountainous area surrounded by Makasae, Waima'a, Tetun, Galoli. Austronesian, Malayo-Polynesian, Central-Eastern, Central Malayo-Polynesian, Timor, Nuclear Timor, Waima'a. Dialects: KAIRUI, MIDIKI (MIDIK). Vocabulary is predominantly Trans-New Guinea, structure is Austronesian. Related to Waima'a and Habu. Classification needs further investigation. Mountain slope.

KEMAK ***(EMA)*** [KEM] 50,000 or more in the ethnic group (1981 Wurm and Hattori). Population total both countries 50,000 or more. North central Timor Island, border area between east and west Timor, mostly on eastern side. Also spoken in Indonesia (Nusa Tenggara). Austronesian, Malayo-Polynesian, Central-Eastern, Central Malayo-Polynesian, Timor, Nuclear Timor, East. Dialects: NOGO (NOGO-NOGO), KEMAK. Closely related to Tetun. Most closely related to Mambae and Tukudede. Also related to Atoni. Morris 1992 counts Nogo as a separate language from Kemak. Investigation needed: intelligibility with dialects. OSV. Traditional religion, Christian.

LAKALEI [LKA] 5,000(?) in ethnic group (1981 Wurm and Hattori). Central Timor Island, north of Same, northeast of Ainaro. Austronesian, Malayo-Polynesian, Central-Eastern, Central Malayo-Polynesian, Timor, Nuclear Timor, East. Closely related to Idate, Tetun, and Galoli. Many loanwords from Tetun, Mambae, and Idate.

MAKASAE ***(MAKASSAI, MACASSAI, MA'ASAE, MAKASAI)*** [MKZ] 70,000 in the ethnic group (1989). Timor Island, eastern end around Baucau and inland, west of Fataluku, from northern to southern coast in a dialect chain. Trans-New Guinea, South Bird's Head-Timor-Alor-Pantar, Timor-Alor-Pantar, Makasai-Alor-Pantar, Makasai. Dialects: MAKLERE, MAKASAI. Not closely related to other languages. Some speakers cannot function at all in Indonesian, Portuguese, or Tetum Prasa. Traditional religion, Christian.

MAKU'A ***(LOVAEA, LOVAIA)*** [LVA] 50 in ethnic group (1981 Wurm and Hattori). Northeast tip of Timor Island, around Tutuala. Trans-New Guinea, South Bird's Head-Timor-Alor-Pantar, Timor-Alor-Pantar, Maku'a. Spoken only by some elderly people. Almost completely assimilated with Fataluku. Nearly extinct.

MAMBAE ***(MAMBAI, MANBAE)*** [MGM] 80,000 in the ethnic group (1981 Wurm and Hattori). Population total both countries 80,000 or more. Mountains of central Timor Island, around Ermera, Aileu, and Ainaro. One of the dominant groups among Timorese communities in Australia. Also spoken in Australia. Austronesian, Malayo-Polynesian, Central-Eastern, Central Malayo-Polynesian, Timor, Nuclear Timor, East. Dialects: DAMATA, LOLEI, MANUA, MAMBAI. Some speakers cannot function at all in Indonesian, Portuguese, or Tetum Prasa. Second most widely spoken language of Timor Lorosae. Mountain slope. Traditional religion, Christian.

NAUETE ***(NAUHETE, NAUETI, NAUOTE, NAUOTI)*** [NXA] 1,000(?) in ethnic group (1981 Wurm and Hattori). South coast, eastern tip of Timor Island, west of Tiomar. The main town is Uato Lari. Austronesian, Malayo-Polynesian, Central-Eastern, Central Malayo-Polynesian, Timor, Nuclear Timor. Dialects: NAUMIK, OSO MOKO. Not closely related to any other language. Many loan words from Trans-New Guinea languages like Makasae.

PIDGIN, TIMOR ***(TIMOR CREOLE PORTUGUESE)*** [TVY] Timor Island, around Bidau, Dili and Lifan. Creole, Portuguese based. Dialects: PORTUGUÊS DE BIDAU, MACAÍSTA. Extinct.

PORTUGUESE ***(PORTUGUÊS)*** [POR] Indo-European, Italic, Romance, Italo-Western, Western, Gallo-Iberian, Ibero-Romance, West Iberian, Portuguese-Galician. Probably 2% of the population from Timor Lorosae worldwide can function in it, including about 9,000 people living overseas. Dictionary. Grammar. Christian. Bible 1751, in press (1993). See main entry under Portugal.

TETUM PRASA ***(TETUM PRAÇA, DILI TETUM, TETUM DILI)*** [TDT] 50,000(?) (1995). First language speakers concentrated in and around Dili on the north coast of Timor Lorosae. Fluent second language speakers scattered widely throughout the western 2/3 of Timor Lorosae. Creole, Tetun based. Speakers of North and South Tetun [TTM] have significant difficulty understanding it in many speech domains, and vice versa. Some first language speakers of Tetum Prasa consider themselves to be bilingual in Tetun because of contact, but when pressed, admit there are domains in which communication is completely blocked. There are important differences with Tetun in parts of the grammar, morphology, functors, and much of the lexicon. There is heavy influence of Portuguese and some Indonesian or Malay loans in Tetum Prasa. Growing in its role as a language of wider communication, functioning as a symbol of inter-ethnic solidarity in the region, predominantly in urban areas. There are 3 second-language varieties spoken by different people: (1) fluent Tetum Prasa spoken throughout the western 2/3 of Timor Lorosae, primarily by those who have lived in Dili for one or more years, (2) occasional Dili residents with significant influence from their own local mother tongues, and (3) people originally from Timor Lorosae who are overseas residents in Portugal or Australia, with higher portion of inflected Portuguese vocabulary and almost complete lack of Indonesian or Malay loans. There is also 'Tetum Ibadat' or 'liturgical Tetum' which is not spoken by anyone for everyday communication, nor as mother tongue, with a lot of vocabulary and some grammar that is not understood widely. Cultural rituals and themes in Tetun are not as deeply rooted in Tetum Prasa. Heavy Portuguese and Mambae influence. Language of wider communication. Compared to Tetun: many more Portuguese loan words; does not inflect V-initial verb roots for person or number; uses more periphrastic constructions than morphological constructions (e.g., causatives); differences in possessive constructions and negatives. Christian. Bible portions 1996.

TETUN ***(TETUM, TETTUM, TETO, TETU, TETUNG)*** [TTM] Western Timor Lorosae on the south coast from Suai to Viqueque. East of Atoni, west of Bunak (in Batagude) around Batibo and in from the south coast around Viqueque and Soibada. Austronesian, Malayo-Polynesian, Central-Eastern, Central Malayo-Polynesian, Timor, Nuclear Timor, East. Dialect: TETUN TERIK (TETUN THERIK). One dialect in Timor Lorosae, and two in West Timor. Wide variation in morphology and syntax among major dialects, and variation in social structure. Spoken by some Bunak around Suai as second language. Investigation needed: intelligibility with dialects. Grammar. Christian, traditional religion. Bible portions 1997. See main entry under Indonesia, Nusa Tenggara.

TUKUDEDE ***(TUKUDE, TOKODEDE, TOKODÉ, TOCOD)*** [TKD] 50,000 in the ethnic group (1981 Wurm and Hattori). Timor Island, north coast, regions of Maubara and Liquisa from the banks of the Lois River to Dili. Austronesian, Malayo-Polynesian, Central-Eastern, Central Malayo-Polynesian, Timor, Nuclear Timor, East. Dialects: KEHA (KEIA), TUKUDEDE. Christian.

WAIMA'A ***(UAI MA'A, WAIMAHA, WAIMOA, UAIMO'A)*** [WMH] 3,000(?) in ethnic group (1981 Wurm and Hattori). Northeast coast Timor Island, enclave within Makasae-speaking area. Austronesian, Malayo-Polynesian, Central-Eastern, Central Malayo-Polynesian, Timor, Nuclear Timor, Waima'a. Many Trans-New Guinea loan words similar to Makasae. Related to Habu and Kairui. Classification needs further investigation.

TURKEY

Republic of Turkey, Turkiye Cumhuriyeti. National or official language: Turkish. 64,479,000 including both Europe and Asia sections (1998 UN). Literacy rate 76% to 90%. Also includes Refugees from Central Asia 50,000. Information mainly from T. Sebeok 1963, 1970; O. Jastrow 1971, 1988; A.. Nakano 1986; B. Comrie 1987; P. A. Andrews 1989; M. Izadi 1993. Muslim (Alevite Muslim 17,000,000 to 20,000,000), Christian, Jewish. Blind population 38,178. Deaf population 316,839. Deaf institutions: 12. Data accuracy estimate: C. The number of languages listed for Turkey is 36. Of those, 34 are living languages and 2 are extinct. Diversity index 0.25.

TURKEY (ASIA)

Also see Turkey in Europe for a listing of languages in Europe. Also includes Mesopotamian Spoken Arabic 100,000, North Levantine Spoken Arabic 500,000, Assyrian Neo-Aramaic, Avar, Chaldean Neo-Aramaic, Chechen 8,000, Dargwa, Western Farsi 500,000, Lak 300, Lezgi 1,200, Northern Uzbek. Data accuracy estimate: C. The number of languages listed for Turkey (Asia) is 25. Of those, 24 are living languages and 1 is extinct. Diversity index 0.23.

ABAZA ***(ABAZIN, TAPANTA, ABAZINTSY, AHUWA)*** [ABQ] 10,000 in Turkey (1995). North Caucasian, Northwest, Abkhaz-Abazin. Dialects: TAPANTA, ASHKARAUA, BEZSHAGH. Bilingualism in Turkish. Has literary status in Russia. Roman script used in Turkey. Muslim. See main entry under Russia.

ABKHAZ ***(ABXAZO)*** [ABK] 4,000 first language speakers (1980), out of 35,000 in Turkey (1993 Johnstone). Coruh in northeast Turkey, and some in northwest. Mainly villages in Bolu and Sakarya provinces. North Caucasian, Northwest, Abkhaz-Abazin. Dialects: BZYB, ABZHUI, SAMURZAKAN. 96% bilingual in Turkish. Agriculturalists. Sunni Muslim. Bible portions 1912-1981. See main entry under Georgia.

ADYGHE ***(ADYGEY, CIRCASSIAN, CHERKES)*** [ADY] 71,000 first language speakers out of 130,000 in ethnic group in Turkey, 6,409 monolinguals (1965 census). Villages in Kayseri, Tokat, Karaman Maras, and many other provinces in central and western Anatolia. North Caucasian, Northwest, Circassian. 94% bilingual in Turkish. Roman script. Agriculturalists. Sunni Muslim. NT 1992. See main entry under Russia.

ARABIC, NORTH MESOPOTAMIAN SPOKEN ***(SYRO-MESOPOTAMIAN VERNACULAR ARABIC)*** [AYP] 400,000 in Turkey. Mardin and Siirt provinces. Afro-Asiatic, Semitic, Central, South, Arabic. Men are quite bilingual in Turkish. They do not read Arabic. Agriculturalists, small shops and businesses. Muslim, Christian. See main entry under Iraq.

AZERBAIJANI, SOUTH ***(AZERI)*** [AZB] 530,000 or more in Turkey. Kars Province. Altaic, Turkic, Southern, Azerbaijani. Dialect: KARS. There is a gradual transition of dialects from Turkish to Azerbaijani from central to western Turkey. The people of Kars Province speak Azerbaijani but use Turkish as the literary language. Muslim. See main entry under Iran.

CRIMEAN TURKISH ***(CRIMEAN TATAR)*** [CRH] It is not known how many still speak it in Turkey, though there are definitely some Crimean Tatar villages, such as Karakuyu in Polatli District of Ankara Province. Altaic, Turkic, Southern. Dialects: NORTHERN CRIMEAN (CRIMEAN NOGAI, STEPPE CRIMEAN), CENTRAL CRIMEAN, SOUTHERN CRIMEAN. Muslim. NT 1666-1825. See main entry under Uzbekistan.

DIMLI ***(DIMILI, ZAZAKI, SOUTHERN ZAZA, ZÂÂ)*** [ZZZ] Population total both countries 1,000,000 (1999 WA). East central, mainly in Elazig, Bingol, and Diyarbakir provinces, upper courses of the Euphrates, Kizilirmaq, and Murat rivers. Also spoken in Germany. Indo-European, Indo-Iranian, Iranian, Western, Northwestern, Zaza-Gorani. Dialects: SIVEREKI, KORI, HAZZU (HAZO), MOTKI (MOTI), SHABAK, DUMBULI. Several dialects. Closest to Hawrami. Not a Kurdish language. Not intelligible with Kurmanji. Speakers from the southeast know some Kurmanji, but others do not. Some in Germany are publishing a magazine. The speakers are called 'Zaza', and the language 'Zazaki'. 'Dimli' is used for both speakers and language. Mountain slope, plains. Agriculturalists, pastoralists: sheep, goats, cattle. Sunni Muslim, Yazdani.

GEORGIAN ***(KARTULI, GRUZIN)*** [GEO] 40,000 first language speakers out of 91,000 in ethnic group of Imerxev in Turkey (1980 estimate), 4,042 monolinguals (1965 census). Villages in Artvin, Ordu, Sakarya, and other provinces of north and northwest Anatolia. South Caucasian, Georgian. Dialect: IMERXEV. Imerxev is the western dialect of Georgian. 95% are bilingual in Turkish. Sunni Muslim. Bible 1743-1989. See main entry under Georgia.

HERKI [HEK] Indo-European, Indo-Iranian, Indo-Aryan, Western, Northwestern, Kurdish. Considered a dialect of Kurmanji. Muslim. See main entry under Iraq.

HÉRTEVIN [HRT] Several hundreds, perhaps over 1,000 (1999 H. Mutzafi). Originally Siirt Province. They have left their villages, most emigrating to the West, but some may still be in Turkey. Afro-Asiatic, Semitic, Central, Aramaic, Eastern, Central, Northeastern. Dialects: HÉRTEVIN PROPER (ARTON), UMRAYA, JINET. Considerable differences from other Northeastern Aramaic varieties, and not intelligible with any or most of them. Speakers are bilingual in Kurdish, and some are multilingual. Syriac script used. Christian (Chaldean).

KABARDIAN [KAB] 202,000 in Turkey (1993 Johnstone). Most around Kayseri. 1,000 villages of Kabardian and Adyghe in Turkey. North Caucasian, Northwest, Circassian. Close to Adygey, but a separate language. Sunni Muslim. NT 1993. See main entry under Russia.

KAZAKH ***(KAZAKHI, QAZAQI, KAZAX, KOSACH, KAISAK)*** [KAZ] 600 or more in Turkey (1982). Salihli town in Manisa Province, and an unknown number in Istanbul city; 308 in Kayseri Province; refugees from Afghanistan, now Turkish citizens. Altaic, Turkic, Western, Aralo-Caspian. Roman script used in Turkey. Muslim. NT 1820-1910, out of print. See main entry under Kazakhstan.

KIRGHIZ [KDO] 1,137 in Turkey (1982). Van and Kars provinces. Altaic, Turkic, Western, Aralo-Caspian. Refugees from Afghanistan; now Turkish citizens. Speakers in Turkey read Roman, but not Cyrillic, script. Sunni Muslim. NT 1991. See main entry under Kyrgyzstan.

KIRMANJKI ***(ZAZA, NORTHERN ZAZA, ZAZAKI, ALEVICA, DIMILKI, DERSIMKI, SO-BÊ, ZONÊ MA)*** [QKV] 140,000 in Turkey including 100,000 in 182 villages in Tunceli Province, 40,000 in 13 or more villages in Erzincan Province (1972). Population total all countries 1,500,000 possibly or more (1992). Tunceli Province, Tunceli Merkez, Hozat, Nazmiye, Pülümür, and Ovacik subprovinces; Erzincan Province, Erzincan and Cayirli subprovinces; 8 or more villages in Elazig Province, Elazig Merkez and Karakoqan subprovinces; 3 villages in Bingöl Province, Kigi and Karkiova subprovinces; 46 villages in Mush Province, Varto Subprovince; 15 or more villages in Sivas Province, Zara, Imranli, Kangal, and Divrigi subprovinces; 11 or more villages in Erzerum Province, Hinis and Tekman subprovinces; and in many major cities of Turkey. Also spoken in Austria, Denmark, France, Germany, Netherlands, Sweden, Switzerland, United Kingdom. Indo-European, Indo-Iranian, Iranian, Western, Northwestern, Zaza-Gorani. Dialects: TUNCELI, VARTO. Closest to Dimli. 70% lexical similarity with Dimli. Turkish is used for religious ceremonies and for official purposes. Most men know some Turkish, and some know some Kurmanji. Abroad they use Turkish for religious ceremonies, wedding celebrations, and conversations with some people. All who live abroad learn the national languages to some degree and use them for communication with nationals. In Turkey Kirmanjki is used for conversations with family, friends, and neighbors. All ages, most between 20 and 50. Women over 50 in outlying villages in Tunceli Province and children under 7 are monolingual. Some Kurmanji know Kirmanjki as second language. Abroad they use Kirmanjki for close relationships. People from different ethnic groups or places call themselves 'Shar Ma', 'Sar Ma', 'Dimil' or 'Kirmandz'. SOV; pre- and postpositions; genitives, articles, adjectives' relatives after noun heads; numerals before noun heads; question word replaces content word in content questions; 2 prefixes, 2 suffixes, word order distinguishes subject, object, indirect object; noun affixes indicate case; verb affixes indicate person, number, gender; ergativity; passives; causatives; comparatives; V, VC, VCC, CV, CVC, CVCC; nontonal. Literacy rate in first language: 100 people. Literacy rate in second language: School-age children to 30 years old, Turkish. Deciduous forest. Mountain mesa, slope, valley. Pastoralists (transhumance), peasant agriculturalists. 1,000 to 3,000 meters. Alevi Muslim.

KUMYK ***(KUMUK, KUMUKLAR, KUMYKI)*** [KSK] A few villages. Altaic, Turkic, Western, Ponto-Caspian. Dialects: KHASAV-YURT, BUINAK, KHAIDAK. Dialects apparently quite diverse. Different from the Kumux dialect of Lak. Language of wider communication. Cyrillic script. Muslim. Bible portions 1888-1897. See main entry under Russia.

KURMANJI ***(NORTHERN KURDISH, KERMANJI, KIRMANJI, KIRDASI, KIRMÂNCHA, BÂHDINÂNI)*** [KUR] 3,950,000 first language speakers (1980), out of 6,500,000 in the ethnic group in Turkey (1993 Johnstone). Population total all countries 7,000,000 to 8,000,000. The majority are in the provinces of Hakkari, Siirt, Mardin, Agri, Diyarbakir, Bitlis, Bingol, Van, Adiyaman, and Mus. Also many in Urfa, Elazig, Kars, Tunceli, Malatya, Erzurum, Karaman Maras, Sivas, Ankara, and other provinces. Also spoken in 25 other countries including Armenia, Australia, Austria, Azerbaijan, Bahrain, Belgium, France, Georgia, Germany, Iran, Iraq, Jordan, Kazakhstan, Kuwait, Kyrgyzstan, Lebanon, Netherlands, Norway, Sweden. Indo-European, Indo-Iranian, Iranian, Western, Northwestern, Kurdish. Dialects: GUWII, HAKKÂRI, JEZIRE (BOTAN, BOHTÂNI, BUHTÂNI), URFI, BÂYAZIDI, SURCHI, QOCHÂNI, BIRJANDI, ALBURZ,

SANJÂRI, JUDIKÂNI. Differences in speaking among dialects, but all use the same written form. Distinct from Kurdi (Southern Kurdish). Not many are very bilingual in Turkish. Ethnic names also include Doudjik, Kizibakh. Language of wider communication. Grammar. Literacy rate in second language: 28%. Roman script used in Turkey; Arabic script in Syria, Iraq, and Iran; Cyrillic script in former USSR. Armenian script not used now. Mountain slope. Traditionally pastoralists, now agriculturalists. Muslim (Sunni and Alevi), some Yezidi, secular. NT 1872.

LAZ *(LAZURI, LAZE, CHAN, CHANZAN, ZAN, CHANURI)* [LZZ] 30,000 first language speakers out of 92,000 in the ethnic group in Turkey (1980 estimate). Population total all countries 33,000 or more. Rize in northeast, towns of Kemer, Atin, Artasen, Vitse, Arkab, Hopa, Sarp; and villages in Artvin, Sakarya, Kocaeli, and Bolu provinces. Also spoken in Belgium, France, Georgia, Germany, USA. South Caucasian, Zan. Linguists recognize that Laz and Mingrelian are inherently unintelligible with each other's speakers. Reported to be 95% bilingual in Turkish, with only the older people not being bilingual. Their name for their language is 'Lazuri'. Not a written language in Turkey. Fishermen. Muslim.

OSETIN *(OSSETE)* [OSE] The Digor dialect is reported to be in Bitlis and another small town in the west. Iron dialect in cities or towns of Sarikamis and Erzerum. Also in Mugla, Kars, Antalya. May also be in Syria. Indo-European, Indo-Iranian, Iranian, Eastern, Northeastern. Dialects: DIGOR, TAGAUR, KURTAT, ALLAGIR, TUAL, IRON. Russian Orthodox, Sunni Muslim. NT 1993. See main entry under Georgia.

SHIKAKI [SHF] Indo-European, Indo-Iranian, Iranian, Western, Northwestern, Kurdish. See main entry under Iraq.

SYRIAC *(CLASSICAL SYRIAC, ANCIENT SYRIAC, SURYAYA, SURYOYO, LISHANA ATIGA)* [SYC] Turkey, Iraq, and Syria. Also spoken in Iraq, Syria. Afro-Asiatic, Semitic, Central, Aramaic, Eastern. Dialects: WESTERN SYRIAC, EASTERN SYRIAC. The Syrian churches (Eastern (Nestorian), Syrian Orthodox (Jacobite), Syrian Catholic (Melkite, Maronite) developed a vast literature based on the Edessa (currently Sanliurfa, southeastern Turkey) variety of the Syrian dialect. The Assyrian group (see Assyrian Neo-Aramaic in Iraq and elsewhere) separated denominationally from the Chaldean (see Chaldean Neo-Aramaic in Iraq) and Jacobite (see Turoyo in Turkey and Syria) in the Middle Ages. Neo-Eastern Aramaic languages spoken by Christians are often dubbed 'Neo-Syriac', although not directly descended from Syriac. Became extinct in the 10th to 12th centuries. Still used as a literary secular language among followers of the churches listed, although rarely. Christian: Nestorian, Jacobite, Melkite, Maronite, Syrian Orthodox. Extinct. Bible 1645-1891.

TURKISH *(TÜRKÇE, TÜRKISCH, ANATOLIAN)* [TRK] 46,278,000 in Turkey, 90% of the population (1987). Population total all countries 61,000,000 (1999 WA). Spoken throughout Turkey as first or second language. Also spoken in 35 other countries including Australia, Austria, Azerbaijan, Belgium, Bosnia-Herzegovina, Bulgaria, Canada, Cyprus, Denmark, El Salvador, Finland, France, Georgia, Germany, Greece, Honduras, Iran, Iraq, Israel. Altaic, Turkic, Southern, Turkish. Dialects: DANUBIAN, ESKISEHIR, RAZGRAD, DINLER, RUMELIAN, KARAMANLI, EDIRNE, GAZIANTEP, URFA. Danubian is western; other dialects are eastern. The Karamanli are Turkish-speaking Greeks. National language. Dictionary. Grammar. SOV. Roman script now used. Muslim. Bible 1827-1941.

TURKISH SIGN LANGUAGE [TSM] Deaf sign language.

TURKMEN *(TRUKHMEN)* [TCK] 925 in Turkey (1982). Tokat Province. Altaic, Turkic, Southern, Turkmenian. Refugees from Afghanistan; now Turkish citizens. Sunni Muslim. Bible portions 1880-1982. See main entry under Turkmenistan.

TUROYO *(SURYOYO, SYRYOYO, TURANI, SÜRYANI)* [SYR] 3,000 in Turkey (1994) out of 50,000 to 70,000 population. Population total all countries 70,000 (1994 Hezy Mutzafi). Southeastern Turkey, Mardin Province (originally). Also spoken in Argentina, Australia, Belgium, Brazil, Canada, Germany, Iraq, Lebanon, Netherlands, Sweden, Syria, USA. Afro-Asiatic, Semitic, Central, Aramaic, Eastern, Central, Northwestern. Dialects: MIDYAT, MIDIN, KFARZE, <IWARDO, ANHIL, RAITE. Related to, but distinct from Northeastern Aramaic varieties. Turoyo subdialects exhibit a cleavage between Town Turoyo (Midyat Turoyo), Village Turoyo, and Mixed (Village-Town) Turoyo. The latter is spoken mainly by the younger generation outside Tur <Abdin, Turkey, the language's original location, and is gaining ground thoughout the Jacobite diaspora in other countries. All speakers are bilingual in their national languages or local lingua francas, and some are multilingual. Known among scholars almost exclusively as 'Tûrôyo'. 'Suryoyo' is a popular name. 'Western Syriac' refers to the Classical Western Syriac liturgy and orthography used by Turoyo speakers. Syriac script. Christian (Syrian Orthodox=Jacobite). Bible portions 1983.

UYGHUR *(UIGHUR, UYGUR, UIGUR)* [UIG] 500 or more first language speakers in Turkey (1981). Kayseri city, and an unknown number in Istanbul. Possibly in Iran. Altaic, Turkic, Eastern. Roman script used. Sunni Muslim. Bible 1950. See main entry under China.

UZBEK, SOUTHERN [UZS] 1,981 in Turkey (1982). Hatay, Gaziantep, and Urfa provinces. Also possibly in Germany. Altaic, Turkic, Eastern. Refugees from Afghanistan; now Turkish citizens.

Distinct from Northern Uzbek of Uzbekistan and China. Sunni Muslim. See main entry under Afghanistan.

TURKMENISTAN

National or official language: Turkmenistan. 4,309,000 (1998 UN). Formerly part of USSR. Capital: Ashgabat. 188,417 square miles. Literacy rate 98%. Also includes Armenian 32,000, North Azerbaijani 33,000, Bashkir 2,607, Belarusan 5,289, Brahui, Dargwa 1,599, Dungan, Erzya 3,488, Western Farsi 8,000, Georgian 1,047, Karakalpak 2,542, Kazakh 88,000, Korean 3,493, Kurmanji 2,933, Lak 1,590, Lezgi 10,400, Lithuanian 224, Osetin 1,887, Romanian 1,561, Russian 349,000, Tabassaran 177, Tajiki 1,277, Tatar 40,434, Udi 20, Ukrainian 37,118, Northern Uzbek 317,000. Information mainly from T. Sebeok 1963. Muslim, Jewish (3,494), Christian. Data accuracy estimate: B. The number of languages listed for Turkmenistan is 2. Of those, 1 is a living language and 1 is extinct. Diversity index 0.38.

BALOCHI, WESTERN ***(BALOCI, BALUCHI, BALUCI)*** [BGN] 28,000 in Turkmenistan (1993). Indo-European, Indo-Iranian, Iranian, Western, Northwestern, Balochi. Turkmen is used as the literary language in Turkmenistan. Distinct from Eastern and Southern Balochi. Muslim. Bible portions 1984. See main entry under Pakistan.

CHAGATAI ***(CHAGHATAY, JAGATAI)*** [CGT] Altaic, Turkic, Eastern. Extinct.

TURKMEN ***(TURKOMANS, TURKMENLER, TURKMANIAN, TRUKHMEN, TRUKHMENY, TURKMANI)*** [TCK] 3,430,000 in Turkmenistan (1995), 99% of the ethnic group of 3,465,000 (1995). Population total all countries 6,400,000. Also spoken in Afghanistan, Germany, Iran, Iraq, Kazakhstan, Kyrgyzstan, Pakistan, Russia (Asia), Tajikistan, Turkey (Asia), USA, Uzbekistan. Altaic, Turkic, Southern, Turkmenian. Dialects: NOKHURLI, ANAULI, KHASARLI, NEREZIM, YOMUD, TEKE (TEKKE), GOKLEN, SALYR, SARYQ, ESARI, CAWDUR. Some dialects differ from Teke. 50% claim a good knowledge of Russian. The so-called 'Turkmen' in Syria, and possibly Iraq and Jordan, actually speak an ancient form of Turkmen; so-called 'Turkmen' in Tibet may speak a different Turkic language. National language. Dictionary. Grammar. Cyrillic script. Radio programs. Sand desert, narrow oases. Agriculturalists: cotton; stock breeders: sheep; carpet weavers; traditionally pastoralists: sheep; gas, oil workers. Sunni Muslim. Bible portions 1880-1982.

UNITED ARAB EMIRATES

Ittihad al-Imarat al-Arabiyah, UAE. Formerly called Trucial States. National or official language: Standard Arabic. 2,353,000 (1998 UN). Literacy rate 68% to 78%. Also includes Egyptian Spoken Arabic 100,000, Omani Spoken Arabic 80,000, Bengali 70,000, Danish 156, Dutch 785, English 100, French 250, Standard German 1,300, Greek 100, Hindi, Italian 400, Japanese 1,300, Goanese Konkani, Malay, Malayalam 300,000, Bokmaal Norwegian 200, Eastern Panjabi, Western Panjabi, Polish 100, Serbo-Croatian 100, Sinhala 25,000, Somali 100,000, Swahili 2,500, Swedish 113, Tagalog 80,000, Tamil, Telugu, Thai 3,000, Turkish 750, Urdu, Chinese 100, from India including Telugu 120,000, and temporary residents from other countries. Information mainly from T. Sebeok 1970. Sunni Muslim, Shi'a Muslim, Christian, Hindu, Buddhist, secular. Deaf population 109,218. Data accuracy estimate: A2. The number of languages listed for United Arab Emirates is 6. Of those, all are living languages. Diversity index 0.78.

ARABIC, GULF SPOKEN ***(KHALIJI, GULF ARABIC)*** [AFB] 744,000 in UAE. Gulf Bedu or village peoples. Afro-Asiatic, Semitic, Central, South, Arabic. Government officials, oil administration, business leaders, military, police, university professors, sports coaches. Muslim. See main entry under Iraq.

ARABIC, SHIHHI SPOKEN ***(SHIHHI, SHIHU, SHIHUH, AL-SHIHUH)*** [SSH] 5,000 in UAE (1995). Population total both countries 15,000. In the Musandam Peninsula in UAE and Oman. Also spoken in Oman. Afro-Asiatic, Semitic, Central, South, Arabic. Not a written language. Most Shihuh speak Shihhi, but the Kumazirah subdivision of Shihuh, like the Dhahuriyin tribe, speak Kumzari. Influenced by Farsi. 'Shihuh' is the name of the people. Some may be literate in Arabic. Muslim.

ARABIC, STANDARD [ABV] Middle East, North Africa. Afro-Asiatic, Semitic, Central, South, Arabic. Used for education, official purposes, formal speeches. National language. Newspapers. Bible 1984-1991. See main entry under Saudi Arabia.

BALOCHI, SOUTHERN ***(BALUCHI, BALUCI, BALOCI)*** [BCC] 100,000 in UAE. Indo-European, Indo-Iranian, Iranian, Western, Northwestern, Balochi. Dialect: MAKRANI (LOTUNI). Speakers come from Oman, Iran, and Pakistan. Unskilled laborers, police, military. Sunni Muslim. Bible portions 1992-1994. See main entry under Pakistan.

FARSI, WESTERN ***(PERSIAN)*** [PES] 80,000, or 4.9% of population in UAE (1986). Indo-European, Indo-Iranian, Iranian, Western, Southwestern, Persian. Merchants, traders. Muslim. Bible 1838-1995. See main entry under Iran.

PASHTO, NORTHERN ***(PUSTO, PASHTU, PASSTOO, PAKHTOO, PUSHTO)*** [PBU] 100,000 in UAE (1986). Indo-European, Indo-Iranian, Iranian, Eastern, Southeastern, Pashto. People called Pathans. Speakers have come from Pakistan. Modified Urdu script used. Unskilled laborers, drivers. Muslim. Bible 1895. See main entry under Pakistan.

PASHTO, SOUTHERN ***(PAKTU, PAKHTU, PAKHTOO, AFGHAN)*** [PBT] Thousands in UAE. Indo-European, Indo-Iranian, Iranian, Eastern, Southeastern, Pashto. Speakers have come from Afghanistan. Unskilled laborers, drivers, shopkeepers. Mainly Sunni Muslim. See main entry under Afghanistan.

UZBEKISTAN

National or official language: Northern Uzbek. 23,574,000 (1998 UN). Formerly part of USSR. Capital: Tashkent. 172,700 square miles. Literacy rate 99%. Also includes Tajiki Spoken Arabic, Armenian 50,000, North Azerbaijani 44,000, Bashkir 35,000, Belarusan 29,000, Chechen, Chuvash 8,868, Dargwa 1,337, Domari, Dungan 1,400, Erzya 14,176, Western Farsi 31,300, Georgian 4,088, Standard German 40,000, Ingush, Karachay-Balkar 254, Kazakh 808,000, Kirghiz 175,776, Korean 183,000, Lak 1,762, Lezgi 1,585, Lithuanian 1,040, Nogai 151, Osetin 6,000, Parya, Romanian 3,152, Russian 1,661,000, Tabassaran 224, Tajiki 934,000, Tatar 468,000, Tsakhur 73, Turkmen 228,000, Ukrainian 153,000, Uyghur 36,000. Information mainly from T. Sebeok 1963; H. Paper 1978; S. Akiner 1983. Muslim, Jewish (102,855). Data accuracy estimate: B. The number of languages listed for Uzbekistan is 7. Of those, all are living languages. Diversity index 0.44.

ARABIC, UZBEKI SPOKEN ***(JUGARI, KASHKADARYA ARABIC, UZBEKI ARABIC, CENTRAL ASIAN ARABIC)*** [AUZ] 700 members of the ethnic group or speakers. Uzbekistan, Bukhara Province; middle and lower Zerafshan Valley in Samarkand Province, and a few in Katta-Kurgan town. They mainly live in small villages. Afro-Asiatic, Semitic, Central, South, Arabic. The language is close to North Mesopotamian Spoken Arabic. Sharp dialect differences between Bukhara and Kashkadarya regions. Bukhara is strongly influenced by Tajiki; Kashkadarya by Uzbek and other Turkic languages. Speakers use Northern Uzbek to communicate with each other, and as literary language. Few members of the ethnic group now speak Arabic. Others speak Uzbek as mother tongue. No diglossia with Modern Standard Arabic. They are endogamous and do not mix with speakers of other languages. Agriculturalists; cattle raisers. Hanafi Sunni Muslim.

BUKHARIC ***(BUKHARAN, JUDEO-TAJIK, BOKHARIC, BUKHARIN, BOKHARIAN)*** [BHH] 10,000 in Uzbekistan (1995). Various parts of Uzbekistan. The cultural center is Bokhara (Buchara). Indo-European, Indo-Iranian, Iranian, Western, Southwestern, Persian. Related to Tajiki Persian. It may be easily intelligible with Tajiki or Farsi. Also close to Judeo-Persian. Hebrew script used. Jewish. See main entry under Israel.

CRIMEAN TURKISH ***(CRIMEAN TATAR)*** [CRH] 189,000 in Uzbekistan (1993). Population total all countries 460,000 or more. Removed from southern shore of Crimean Peninsula to Uzbekistan in 1944. Also spoken in Bulgaria, Kyrgyzstan, Moldova, Romania, Turkey (Asia), Ukraine, USA. Altaic, Turkic, Southern. Dialects: NORTHERN CRIMEAN (CRIMEAN NOGAI, STEPPE CRIMEAN), CENTRAL CRIMEAN, SOUTHERN CRIMEAN. The census counted them with the Tatar, but the languages are distinct. Cyrillic script. Muslim. NT 1666-1825.

JUDEO-CRIMEAN TATAR ***(JUDEO-CRIMEAN TURKISH, KRIMCHAK)*** [JCT] Uzbekistan (most), Georgia, Kazakhstan. Also spoken in Georgia, Kazakhstan. Altaic, Turkic, Western, Ponto-Caspian. There are only individual speakers left (T. Salminen 1993). Jewish. Nearly extinct.

KARAKALPAK ***(KARAKLOBUK, TCHORNY, KLOBOUKI)*** [KAC] 407,000 mother tongue speakers (96%) out of an ethnic population of 424,000 in the former USSR (1993 UBS). Population total all countries 409,000. Karakalpak ASSR, Uzbekistan, along the lower Amu Darya and around the southern part of the Aral Sea. Also spoken in Afghanistan, Kazakhstan, Kyrgyzstan, Turkmenistan. Altaic, Turkic, Western, Aralo-Caspian. Dialects: NORTHEASTERN KARAKALPAK, SOUTH-EASTERN KARAKALPAK. Bilingualism in Uzbek, Russian. Some literature. Cyrillic script. Fishermen in Aral Sea, agriculturalists, craftsmen. Sunni Muslim. Bible portions 1996.

TURKISH ***(OSMANLI)*** [TRK] 197,000 estimate in Uzbekistan, Tajikistan, Kazakhstan, and Kyrghyzstan (based on 1979 census, not counting 56,000 'Turks of Fergana', who speak an Uzbek dialect). Altaic, Turkic, Southern, Turkish. Dialects: DANUBIAN, ESKISEHIR, RAZGRAD, DINLER, RUMELIAN, KARAMANLI, EDIRNE, GAZIANTEP, URFA. The Danubian dialect is western, other dialects are eastern. Bilingualism in Azerbaijani. Some speak Turkish; others Azerbaijani. Meskhetian Georgians,

Khemshel Armenians, and Kurds in Uzbekistan speak Turkish. Sunni Muslim. Bible 1827-1941. See main entry under Turkey.

UZBEK, NORTHERN *(ÖZBEK)* [UZB] 16,539,000 in Uzbekistan (1995 UN). Population total all countries 18,466,000. Uzbekistan and throughout Asian republics of the former USSR. East of the Amu Darya and around the southern Aral Sea. Possibly in Munich, Germany. Also spoken in Australia, China, Israel, Kazakhstan, Kyrgyzstan, Russia (Asia), Tajikistan, Turkey (Asia), Turkmenistan, Ukraine, USA. Altaic, Turkic, Eastern. Dialects: KARLUK (QARLUG), KIPCHAK (KYPCHAK), OGHUZ. Distinct from Southern Uzbek of Afghanistan and Turkey. Russian influences in grammar, use of loan words, script. Oghuz may be a dialect of Khorasani Turkish (see Turkey) rather than Uzbek. 49% of speakers are bilingual in Russian, but rural people have limited proficiency. All ages. Children speak Uzbek at home. Vigorous. Used in theater. Turks of Fergana and Samarkand speak Uzbek. There are Uzbek-speaking Gypsy communities in Soviet central Asia. Increasing ethnic pride. People are about one-third urbanized. Much Persian influence in language and culture. Patrilineal. 'Sart' is an obsolete name for sedentary Uzbek, possibly those who are ethnically Tajik. Official language. Dictionary. Grammar. Literacy rate in second language: High. Cyrillic script used. Arabic and Roman scripts used formerly. Used in school. Radio programs, TV. Desert, semi-arid; fertile valleys. Agriculturalists: cotton, fruit, vegetables, grain; pastoralists: sheep; silk production; technicians, professionals, industrialists, communications, medicine, educators, administrators. Hanafi Sunni Muslim. NT 1992-1995.

VIET NAM

Socialist Republic of Vietnam. Cong Hoa Xa Hoi Chu Nghia Viet Nam. National or official language: Vietnamese. 77,562,000 (1998 UN). 54 official ethnic communities. 56,849,370 or 94% speakers of Austro-Asiatic languages, 2,255,450 or 3.7% speakers of Daic languages, 679,000 or 1.1% speakers of Miao-Yao languages, 492,000 or 0.8% speakers of Austronesian languages, 40,000 speakers of Tibeto-Burman languages (1991 J. Matisoff). Literacy rate 78% to 88%. Also includes Mandarin Chinese, Northern Dong, Sui 55. Information mainly from C. P. Miller 1964, 1966; M. Barker 1966; D. Thomas 1966, 1969, 1976, 1980; D. Thomas and R. Headley, Jr. 1970; F. Lebar, G. Hickey, J. Musgrave 1967; K. Smith 1968; J. A. Edmondson and D. B. Solnit 1997. Buddhist, secular, Christian, traditional religion, Muslim. Blind population 200,000 (1982 WCE). Deaf institutions: 1. Data accuracy estimate: A2, B. The number of languages listed for Viet Nam is 94. Of those, 93 are living languages and 1 is extinct. Diversity index 0.20.

AKHA *(KAW, EKAW, IKAW, AKA, AK'A, AHKA, KO, KHAKO, KHA KO, KHAO IKOR, AINI, YANI)* [AKA] 1,261 in Viet Nam (1995 Institute for Southeast Asian Studies, Hanoi). Binh Tri Thien, east central, both sides of the Viet Nam-Laos border, northeast of Phuc Trach. Sino-Tibetan, Tibeto-Burman, Lolo-Burmese, Loloish, Southern, Akha, Hani, Ha-Ya. SOV. Traditional religion, Christian. NT 1968-1987. See main entry under Myanmar.

AREM *(A-REM, CHOMRAU, CHOMBRAU, UMO)* [AEM] 20 adult speakers out of 100 in the ethnic group in Viet Nam (1996 Ferlus). Population total both countries 20 or more. Tan Trach and one or two families of Thuong Trach in Bo Trach Distyrict, Quang Binh Province. Also spoken in Laos. Austro-Asiatic, Mon-Khmer, Viet-Muong, Chut. Other dialects or ethnic names: Tu-vang, Pa-leng, Xo-lang, To-hung, Chà-cu, Tac-cui, Nhà Chút. Bilingualism in Vietnamese. Chút is an official ethnic community in Viet Nam, including Sách, Mày, Ruc, and Arem. Nearly extinct.

BAHNAR *(BANA)* [BDQ] 137,000 (1993 Dang Nghiem Van). Population total both countries 137,000 or more. Southeastern Gia Lai-Cong Tum, Nghia Binh, Phu Khanh provinces, central highlands. Also spoken in USA. Austro-Asiatic, Mon-Khmer, Eastern Mon-Khmer, Bahnaric, Central Bahnaric. Dialects: TOLO, GOLAR, ALAKONG (A-LA CONG), JOLONG (GIO-LANG, Y-LANG), BAHNAR BONOM (BOMAM), KONTUM, KREM. Other dialects or ethnic names: Roh, Kpang Cong. Closest to Alak 1, Tampuan, and Lamam. An official ethnic community in Viet Nam. Literacy rate in first language: 10% to 30%. Literacy rate in second language: 50% to 75%. Mountain slope. Traditional religion, Christian. NT 1977.

BOUYEI *(BO-Y, BO-I, BUYI, PU-I, PUYI, PUI, CHANG CHÁ, TRONG GGIA, TU-DÍ, TU-DÌN)* [PCC] 1,450 in Viet Nam (1993 Dang Nghiem Van). Hoàng Lien Son and Hà Tuyen provinces. Tai-Kadai, Kam-Tai, Be-Tai, Tai-Sek, Tai, Northern. Close to Nhang. An official nationality in Viet Nam and China. Polytheist, some Daoist. See main entry under China.

BRAO *(BRAU, BRAOU, PROUE, BROU, LOVE, LAVE, LAVEH, RAWE)* [BRB] 250 in Viet Nam (1993 Dang Nghiem Van). Gia Lai-Cong Tum Province, Cambodia-Laos border area. Austro-Asiatic, Mon-Khmer, Eastern Mon-Khmer, Bahnaric, West Bahnaric, Brao-Kravet. Dialect: PALAU. Traditional religion, Christian. See main entry under Laos.

BRU, EASTERN ***(BRŨ, BROU, VAN KIEU, QUANG TRI BRU)*** [BRU] 40,000 in Viet Nam (1993 Dang Nghiem Van). Bl'nh Tri Thien Province. Austro-Asiatic, Mon-Khmer, Eastern Mon-Khmer, Katuic, West Katuic, Brou-So. Dialect: MANGKONG. Partially intelligible with Western Bru of Thailand. Related to Khua. Mangkong in Viet Nam and eastern Laos is a dialect of Eastern Bru, different linguistically from the Mangkong that are the same as So of Thailand. Mangkong is an ethnic group. The name 'Bru' means 'minority people'. So of Laos call themselves 'Bru'. Literacy rate in first language: 1% to 5%. Literacy rate in second language: 15% to 25%. Traditional religion, Christian. NT 1981. See main entry under Laos.

BUNU, BAHENG ***(PA HNG, PAHENG, BAHENG, BAHENGMAI, PÀ HUNG, PÀ THEN, TÓNG, MÈO LÀI, MÁN PA SENG, PATENG, NA-E, NA'E, IAO HOA, FLOWERY MIAO)*** [PHA] 3,700 in Viet Nam (1993 Dang Nghiem Van). Tuyên Quang and Hà Giang provinces. Hmong-Mien, Hmongic, Bunu. Na-e (Pateng) in Viet Nam may be a separate language from Pa Hng (Baheng), either Hmongic, related to Baheng, or a separate branch within Hmong-Mien. An official ethnic community in Viet Nam. Culturally Yao (Mien). Traditional religion. See main entry under China.

CHAM, EASTERN ***(TJAM, CHIEM, CHIEM THÀNH, BHAMAM)*** [CJM] 35,000 in Viet Nam (1990 govt. figure). 99,000 all Cham in Viet Nam (1993 Dang Nghiem Van). Population total both countries 35,000 or more. Thuan Hai, An Giang, Thành phó Hò Chi Minh, Nghia Bình, and Phú Khánh provinces. Also spoken in USA. Austronesian, Malayo-Polynesian, Western Malayo-Polynesian, Sundic, Malayic, Achinese-Chamic, Chamic, South, Coastal, Cham-Chru. An official ethnic community in Viet Nam. Remnants of a once powerful kingdom. Austro-Asiatic influences. Literacy rate in first language: 5% to 10%. Literacy rate in second language: 60%. Agriculturalists. Traditional religion, Christian. Bible portions 1973.

CHAM, WESTERN ***(CAMBODIAN CHAM, TJAM, CHAM, NEW CHAM, CHIEM)*** [CJA] 25,000 in Viet Nam including 4,000 in Saigon (1990 govt. figure). Near Chau Doc and Tay Ninh and 4,000 in Saigon Cholon. Austronesian, Malayo-Polynesian, Western Malayo-Polynesian, Sundic, Malayic, Achinese-Chamic, Chamic, South, Coastal, Cham-Chru. The language differs somewhat from Eastern Cham of central Viet Nam. Muslim. See main entry under Cambodia.

CHINESE, YUE ***(SUÒNG PHÓNG, QUANG DONG, HAI NAM, HA XA PHANG, MINH HUONG, CHINESE NUNG, NUNG, LOWLAND NUNG, HOA, HAN, TRIÈU CHAU, PHÚC KIÉN, LIEM CHAU, SAMG PHANG)*** [YUH] 900,000 in Viet Nam (1993 Dang Nghiem Van). Thành Phó Hò Chí Minh, Hà Noi, Hau Giang, Hai Phòng, Cuu Long provinces. Sino-Tibetan, Chinese. Renowned fighters. Came from Canton, China as railroad workers and soldiers several decades ago. They are not the same as the Nung in the Tai family or the Tibeto-Burman Nung (Nu) of China and Myanmar. Chinese calligraphy. Daoist, Christian. Bible 1894-1981. See main entry under China.

CHRAU ***(CHAURO, CHORO, RO, TAMUN)*** [CHR] 15,000 (1993 Dang Nghiem Van). Dòng Nai Province. The Tamun group live in Tayninh and Binhlong provinces. Austro-Asiatic, Mon-Khmer, Eastern Mon-Khmer, Bahnaric, South Bahnaric, Stieng-Chrau. Dialects: JRO, DOR (DORO), PRANG, MRO, VOQTWAQ, VAJIENG, CHALAH, CHALUN, TAMUN. The name Chrau means 'mountain dweller'. Literacy rate in first language: 5% to 10%. Literacy rate in second language: 50% to 75%. Traditional religion, Christian. NT 1982.

CHRU ***(CHURU, CHORU, CHU RU, CHU, CRU, KRU, CHRAU HMA, CADOE LOANG, SEYU)*** [CJE] 11,000 (1993 Dang Nghiem Van). Population total all countries 11,000 or more. Lam Dong and Thuan Hai provinces. Also spoken in France, USA. Austronesian, Malayo-Polynesian, Western Malayo-Polynesian, Sundic, Malayic, Achinese-Chamic, Chamic, South, Coastal, Cham-Chru. Dialects: RAI, NOANG (LA-DANG). Closely related to Cham. Bilingualism in Vietnamese. Literacy rate in first language: 5% to 10%. Literacy rate in second language: 25% to 50%. Bible portions 1955.

CHUT ***(SACH, SALANG, RUC, MAY)*** [SCB] 1,500 (1996 Ferlus). Population total both countries 1,500 or more. Quang Binh Province, Thuong Hoa, Hoa Son, Dan Hoa communes, near the Laos border at the same latitude as Mu Gia Pass. Also spoken in Laos. Austro-Asiatic, Mon-Khmer, Viet-Muong, Chut. Dialects: SACH, MAY, RUC (KHA MU GIA, TAC CUI). Tu-vang, Pa-leng, Xo-lang, To-hung, Chàcu, Tac-cui may be dialects or related names in Viet Nam. Part of the Chut official ethnic community, together with Arem, May, and Ruc. Upland rice cultivation (Sach, Salang), semi-nomads (Ruc, May). Traditional religion.

CUA ***(BONG MIEW, BÒNG MIEU)*** [CUA] 23,000 (1993 Dang Nghiem Van). Nghia Bình, Quang Nam-Da Nang provinces. Austro-Asiatic, Mon-Khmer, Eastern Mon-Khmer, Bahnaric, North Bahnaric, East, Cua-Kayong. Dialects: KOL (KOR, COR, CO, COL, DOT, YOT), TRAW (TRÀU, DONG). Traditional religion, Christian. Bible portions 1973.

EN ***(NUNG VEN)*** [ENC] 200 (1998 J. A. Edmondson). Cao Bang Province, Noi Thon village, about 20 km. directly east on foot from Ho Quang City, Ho Quang District. Tai-Kadai, Kadai, Yang-Biao. Related to Laha, Laqua, Lachi, Gelao, Buyang, and Hlai. Shares less than 50% common vocabulary with Laha, Laqua, Lachi, Gelao, Buyang, Hlai. No uvular consonants. Has its own number system.

GELAO ***(CO LAO, KELAO, KELEO, KEH-LAO, GELO, CHILAO, LAO, ILAO, QUÔC LAO, CÁC LAO, THU, THIL)*** [KKF] 1,500 in Viet Nam (1993 Dang Nghiem Van). Population total both countries 7,900. North, Hà Tuyen Province. Also spoken in China. Tai-Kadai, Kadai, Ge-Chi. Dialects: WHITE GELAO (TÚ DU, SOUTHWESTERN GELAO), RED GELAO (VOA DÊ), GREEN GELAO (HO KI, NORTH CENTRAL GELAO), CAPE DRAPING GELAO (KLAU, QAU, CENTRAL GELAO), MOUNTAIN GELAO (PUYUI, WESTERN GELAO). The three dialect groups of Viet Nam are distinguished by the color of their dress. An official nationality in Viet Nam and China. The Red Gelao are shifting to Mandarin. Sororate. Agriculturalists: rice. Polytheistic.

HAIPHONG SIGN LANGUAGE [HAF] Haiphong. Deaf sign language. Related to sign languages in Hanoi, Ho Chi Minh City, Laos, and earlier sign languages in Thailand.

HALANG ***(SALANG, KOYONG)*** [HAL] 10,000 in Viet Nam. Population total both countries 12,000 (1973 SIL). Gia Lai-Cong Tum Province. Also spoken in Laos. Austro-Asiatic, Mon-Khmer, Eastern Mon-Khmer, Bahnaric, North Bahnaric, West, Jeh-Halang. Close to Jeh. Salang in Laos may be a different but related language. Literacy rate in first language: 5% to 10%. Literacy rate in second language: 25% to 50%. Traditional religion. Bible portions 1970-1972.

HALANG DOAN ***(HALANG DUAN, DUAN, DOAN)*** [HLD] Population total both countries 2,000 (1981 Wurm and Hattori). Gia Lai-Cong Tum Province, between the Sedang and the Cua. Also spoken in Laos. Austro-Asiatic, Mon-Khmer, Eastern Mon-Khmer, Bahnaric, North Bahnaric, West, Duan. May be intelligible with Takua, Kayong, Halang Daksut, or Rengao. Investigation needed: intelligibility with Takua, Kayong, Halang Daksut, Rengao.

HANI ***(HÀNHÌ, HAW, UNI, U NÍ, XAUNI, XÁ U NÍ)*** [HNI] 12,489 in Viet Nam (1995 Nguyen Duy Thieu). Lai Châu, Hoàng Liên Son provinces in northern Viet Nam. One variety is east, one west of Muong Te City. Not in Thailand. Sino-Tibetan, Tibeto-Burman, Lolo-Burmese, Loloish, Southern, Akha, Hani, Ha-ya. Two close varieties in Viet Nam differ only in phonology and lexicon. An official nationality in Viet Nam and China. Speakers call themselves 'Hà Nhì'. Polytheist, ancestor worship. See main entry under China.

HANOI SIGN LANGUAGE [HAB] Hanoi. Deaf sign language. Related to sign languages in Haiphong, Ho Chi Minh City, Laos, and earlier sign languages in Thailand.

HAROI ***(HRWAY, HROI, HROY, HOI, AROI, BAHNAR CHAM)*** [HRO] 35,000 (1998). Binh Dinh and Phu Yen provinces. Austronesian, Malayo-Polynesian, Western Malayo-Polynesian, Sundic, Malayic, Achinese-Chamic, Chamic, South, Plateau.

HMONG DAW ***(WHITE MEO, MEO KAO, WHITE LUM, MÁN TRÁNG, BAI MIAO)*** [MWW] All Hmong in Viet Nam: 556,000 (1993 Dang Nghiem Van). Hà Tuyen Province, northern Viet Nam. Hmong-Mien, Hmongic, Chuanqiandian. Largely intelligible with Hmong Njua. No significant difference between White and Striped Hmong. Traditional religion, Christian. NT 1975-1984. See main entry under China.

HMONG NJUA ***(BLUE MEO, GREEN MIAO, TAK MEO, HMONG NJWA, HMONG LENG)*** [BLU] Hà Tuyen Province, northern Viet Nam. Hmong-Mien, Hmongic, Chuanqiandian. Largely intelligible with Hmong Daw. Dictionary. Traditional religion, Christian. NT 1975-1983. See main entry under China.

HO CHI MINH CITY SIGN LANGUAGE [HOS] Ho Chi Minh City. Deaf sign language. Related to sign languages in Hanoi, Haiphong, Laos, and earlier sign languages in Thailand.

HRE ***(DAVAK, DAVACH, MOI DA VACH, MOI, MOI LUY, CHAM-RE, CHOM, TACHOM)*** [HRE] 94,000 (1993 Dang Nghiem Van). Nghia Bình Province. Austro-Asiatic, Mon-Khmer, Eastern Mon-Khmer, Bahnaric, North Bahnaric, West, Sedang-Todrah, Sedang. Dialects: RABAH (TAVA), CREQ (KARE, KRE), HRE. Closest to Sedang. An official ethnic community in Viet Nam. Literacy rate in first language: 1% to 5%. Literacy rate in second language: 15% to 25%. Traditional religion, Christian. Bible portions 1967-1975.

HUNG ***(CUÓI, K'KATIAM-PONG-HOUK)*** [HNU] 700 in Viet Nam (1996 Ferlus). Pong dialect in Tam Thai commune, Tuong Duong District, Nghe An Province, and Dan Lai and Ly Ha dialects in Mon Son and Luc Da communes, Con Cuong District. Austro-Asiatic, Mon-Khmer, Viet-Muong, Cuoi. Dialects: PONG (POONG, PHONG, TAY PONG, TOUM PHONG, KHONG KHENG, XA LA VANG, PONG 1, PONG 2), DAN LAI, LY HA. See main entry under Laos.

IU MIEN ***(YU MIEN, MIEN, MÁN, YAO, MYEN, HIGHLAND YAO, DAO, DONG, TRAI, XÁ, DÌU)*** [IUM] 350,000 in Viet Nam (1999 H. Purnell). All Mien in Viet Nam: 474,000 (1993 Dang Nghiem Van). Hà Tuyen, Hoàng Lien Son, Cao Bang, Lang Son, Bac Thái, Lai Chau, Son La, Hà Son Binh, Vinh Phú, Hà Bac, Thanh Hóa, Quang Ninh provinces. Hmong-Mien, Mienic, Mian-Jin. Dialects: MAN DO, DEO TIEN, CHAM, QUAN CHET, QUAN TRANG. The language is the same as in Thailand and Laos. Not all ethnic Yao speak Mien; many speak Chinese. Part of the population figure given for Viet Nam may be for Kim Mun. An official ethnic community in Viet Nam. Daoist, ancestor veneration, traditional religion. NT 1975-1991. See main entry under China.

JARAI ***(DJARAI, GIA-RAI, JORAI, CHO-RAI, CHOR, MTHUR, CHRAI, GIO-RAI)*** [JRA] 242,000 (1989 census). Population total all countries 257,000 or more. Gia Lai-Cong Tum Province. Also spoken in Cambodia, USA. Austronesian, Malayo-Polynesian, Western Malayo-Polynesian, Sundic, Malayic, Achinese-Chamic, Chamic, South, Plateau. Dialects: PUAN, HODRUNG (HDRUNG), JHUE, ARÁP, HABAU (HO-BAU), TO-BUAN, SESAN, CHUTY, PLEIKLY, GOLAR. An official ethnic community in Viet Nam. A different script used in Viet Nam and Cambodia. Literacy rate in first language: 10% to 30%. Literacy rate in second language: 50% to 75%. Mountain slope. Traditional religion, Christian. NT 1974, out of print.

JEH ***(DIE, YEH, GIE)*** [JEH] 10,000 in Viet Nam (1973 SIL). Population total both countries 10,000 or more. Quang Nam-Da Nang and Gia Lai-Cong Tum provinces. Also spoken in Laos. Austro-Asiatic, Mon-Khmer, Eastern Mon-Khmer, Bahnaric, North Bahnaric, West, Jeh-Halang. Dialects: JEH BRI LA (BRI-LA), JEH MANG RAM. Literacy rate in first language: 1% to 5%. Literacy rate in second language: 15% to 25%. Bible portions 1967-1978.

KATU, EASTERN ***(HIGH KATU)*** [KTV] 37,300 (1998). Quang Nam and Thua Thien provinces. Austro-Asiatic, Mon-Khmer, Eastern Mon-Khmer, Katuic, East Katuic, Katu-Pacoh. A different language variety and orthography in Laos. Literacy rate in first language: Below 1%. Literacy rate in second language: 5% to 15%. Traditional religion, Christian. NT 1978.

KATUA ***(CA TUA)*** [KTA] 3,000 (1981 Wurm and Hattori). Gia Lai-Cong Tum Province, around Mang Buk, west of the Kayong language. Austro-Asiatic, Mon-Khmer, Eastern Mon-Khmer, Bahnaric, North Bahnaric.

KAYONG ***(KAGIUONG, CA GIONG, KATANG)*** [KXY] 2,000 (1981 Wurm and Hattori). Remote mountains of Cong Tum Province. Austro-Asiatic, Mon-Khmer, Eastern Mon-Khmer, Bahnaric, North Bahnaric, East, Cua-Kayong. Close to Takua and Cua. Mountain slope.

KHANG ***(KHAANG, TAYHAY, TAY HAY, XA, XÁ KHAO, XA XUA, XA DON, XA DANG, XA HOC, XA AI, XA BUNG, QUANG LAM, HANG, BREN, KSAKAUTENH, PUTENH, POUTENG, TENG, THENG)*** [KJM] 3,921 (1985 F. Proschan). Scattered through the northwest Tai provinces and in western Nghe Tinh Province of northern Viet Nam. Austro-Asiatic, Mon-Khmer, Northern Mon-Khmer, Khmuic, Xinh Mul. Dialects: KHANG CLAU, KHANG AI (XA KHAO, XA CAU, SAKAU). Related to Puoc and Phong-Kniang in Laos. An official ethnic community. Investigation needed: intelligibility with Puoc, Phong-Kniang. Traditional religion.

KHAO [XAO] 10,000 (1981 Wurm and Hattori). Northwest, near the Ma River, north of Pa Ma. Austro-Asiatic, Mon-Khmer, Northern Mon-Khmer, Khmuic, Khao. Related to Bit in Laos and China. May be the same as Xa Khao (Khla Phlao, Laha). Investigation needed: intelligibility with Bit.

KHMER, CENTRAL ***(CAMBODIAN, KHO ME, CUR CUL, CU THO, VIET GO MIEN, KHOME, KROM)*** [KMR] 895,000 in Viet Nam (1993 Dang Nghiem Van). Hau Giang, Cuu Long, Kien Giang, Minh Hai, Thành phó Hò Chí minh, Song Bé, Tay Ninh provinces, Mekong Delta of southwestern Viet Nam. Austro-Asiatic, Mon-Khmer, Eastern Mon-Khmer, Khmer. Dialects: CENTRAL KHMER, SOUTHERN KHMER. Buddhist, Christian. Bible 1954-1998. See main entry under Cambodia.

KHMU ***(KMHMU, KHOMU, KHAMU, MUN XEN, XA CAU, KHA CAU, CAM MU)*** [KJG] 42,853 in Viet Nam (1989 F. Proschan). Nghe Tinh, Son La, Lai Chau, Hoàng Lien Son provinces. Austro-Asiatic, Mon-Khmer, Northern Mon-Khmer, Khmuic, Mal-Khmu', Khmu'. Traditional religion, Christian. Bible portions 1918. See main entry under Laos.

KHUA [XHU] Population total both countries 5,000 (1981 Wurm and Hattori). West central; southeast of Giap Tam. Also spoken in Laos. Austro-Asiatic, Mon-Khmer, Eastern Mon-Khmer, Katuic, West Katuic, Brou-So. Related to Bru, Mangkong, Leun. Distinct from Cua. Investigation needed: intelligibility with Eastern Bru, Mangkong.

KIM MUN ***(MUN, LANTEN, LAN TEN, LANTIN, MAN LAN-TIEN, LOWLAND YAO, COC MUN, JINMEN)*** [MJI] 170,000 in Viet Nam (1999 J. Edmondson UTA). Hmong-Mien, Mienic, Mian-Jin. The variety at Lao Cai to the northwest of Lao City and Ha Giang at Na Khe village are very different phonetically. Part of the population figure given for Iu Mien in Viet Nam may be for Kim Mun. See main entry under China.

KOHO ***(COHO, KOHOR)*** [KPM] 92,000 (1993 Dang Nghiem Van). Population total both countries 92,000 or more. Lam Dòng and Thuan Hai provinces. Also spoken in USA. Austro-Asiatic, Mon-Khmer, Eastern Mon-Khmer, Bahnaric, South Bahnaric, Sre-Mnong, Sre. Dialects: CHIL (KIL), TRING (TRINH), SRE, KALOP, SOP, LAYA, RION, NOP (XRE NOP, TU-LOP), TALA (TO LA), KODU (CO-DON), PRU, LAC (LAT, LACH). An official ethnic community. Literacy rate in first language: 10% to 30%. Literacy rate in second language: 50% to 75%. Christian, traditional religion. NT 1967.

LACHI ***(LA CHI, LACHÍ, LAJI, LATI, TAI LATI, LIPULIO, Y TO, Y PÍ, Y PÓNG, Y MIA, CÙ TE, CU-TÊ)*** [LBT] 7,863 in Viet Nam (1990 census), including 3,990 women, in 1,450 households (1990 Liang Min), including Black Lachi 2,500 in 550 households, Long-Haired Lachi 4,500 in 900 households. Population total both countries 9,016. Hà Tuyen Province, mostly west of Há Giang in the upper

Clear River valley (Riviere Claire) on the China border: Black Lachi at Manyou, Long-Haired Lachi at Manpeng. Also spoken in China. Tai-Kadai, Kadai, Ge-Chi. Dialects: LIPUTIÕ (BLACK LACHI), LIPUPI (LONG-HAIRED LACHI), LIPUTE (BAG LACHI), LIPUTCIO (HAN LACHI), LIPUKE (RED LACHI), LIPULIONGTCO (FLOWERY LACHI). The first two dialects listed are in Viet Nam, the others in China. Related to Gelo. Long-Haired Lachi of Viet Nam have 80% lexical similarity with Flowery Lachi of China. White Lachi of Viet Nam has 30% to 40% lexical similarity with the others, and should be considered a separate language. Bilingualism in Zhuang, Miao, Chinese. Those in Viet Nam retain their language. 'Red', 'Flowery', etc., refer to clothing color or other features of physical appearance. Agriculturalists: wet rice; livestock. Traditional religion.

LACHI, WHITE ***(WHITE LACHI, LIPUPÕ)*** [LWH] 1,602 in 300 households (1990 Liang Min). Hà Tuyen Province, northern Viet Nam south of Maguan in China, Manbang and Manmei. Tai-Kadai, Kadai, Ge-Chi. 30% to 40% lexical similarity with other Lachi. They retain their language. Tonal.

LAGHUU ***(LAOPA)*** [LGH] 1,000 (1997 J. A. Edmondson and Lama Ziwo). Northwestern Viet Nam. Lao Cai Province, Sa Pa District, Nam Sa village. 15 km. south and east of Sa Pa City, in the valley below the highest mountain in Viet Nam, Phan Si Pan (3,198 meters). Sino-Tibetan, Tibeto-Burman, Lolo-Burmese, Loloish, Northern, Yi. It is not known how this relates to Laopang (Laopa) of Myanmar, also in the Lolo group.

LAHA ***(XÁ KHAO, KHLÁ PHLAO, KLÁ DONG, KHLÁ DON, KHLÁ DUNG, KHLÁ LIIK, LA HA UNG, LA HA, XÁ CHIEN, XÁ LAY)*** [LHA] 2,000 (1994 Hoàng Luong in Edmondson). Northwestern, Ha Tuyen, Son La, and Lao Cay provinces, along the Red and Black rivers. Tai-Kadai, Kadai, Yang-Biao. Closely related to Laqua. Those under 50 speak Thái and dress like the Tai Dam. Those under 50 seldom speak Laha. An official nationality. They live together with the Thai and Khang. Agriculturalists: wet and dry rice. Traditional religion.

LAHU ***(LOHEI, LAHUNA, LAUNA, LAKU, KAIXIEN, NAMEN, MUSSUH, MUHSO, MUSSO, MUSSAR, MOOSO)*** [LAH] 5,400 in Viet Nam (1993 Dang Nghiem Van). Northwestern border of Viet Nam with Laos. Black Lahu are north of Muong Te City near the China border, at Ban Kiem Tra, Phu Nam Ma, Phu Nam Cau, Phu Nam Ha. White Lahu are in one village just to the east of Nha Ca in Muong Te. Sino-Tibetan, Tibeto-Burman, Lolo-Burmese, Loloish, Southern, Akha, Lahu. Dialects: NA (BLACK LAHU, MUSSER DAM), NYI (RED LAHU, MUSSEH DAENG), SHEHLEH. One source called them White Lahu. It is not clear if these are the same as Red Lahu, Black Lahu, or different. An official ethnic community in Viet Nam. Distinct from Lahu Shi (Yellow Lahu). Traditional religion. Bible 1989. See main entry under China.

LAHU SHI ***(KUTSUNG, KUCONG, KHUTSHO, YELLOW LAHU, SHI, KUI, KWI, NE THU, LA HU SI)*** [KDS] 5,000 in Viet Nam (1998). Just to the west of Muong Te City on the Son Da (Black River). Sino-Tibetan, Tibeto-Burman, Lolo-Burmese, Loloish, Southern, Akha, Lahu. Difficult intelligibility with Black Lahu. A distinct language from Nyi (Red Lahu). SOV. See main entry under Laos.

LAQUA ***(KA BEO, KA BAO, KA BIAO, QABIAO, PUBIAO, PUPEO, PU PÉO, PEN TI LOLO, BENDI LOLO)*** [LAQ] 382 in Viet Nam (1994 Hoàng Luong in Edmondson). Population total both countries 689. Hà Tuyen Province, Viet Nam-Yunnan-Kwangsi border, upper Clear River valley, Dunshi, Pugao, Pula, Pubang, Manong; Phô Là and Sung Chang villages, Dông Van District, and Yên Minh and Mèo Vac districts, Hà Giang Province. Also spoken in China. Tai-Kadai, Kadai, Yang-Biao. They call themselves 'Ka Beo' or 'Qa Beo'. An official ethnic community in Viet Nam. Sororate. Traditional religion.

LÜ ***(PAI-I, SHUI-PAI-I, LUE, TAI LU, NHUON, DUON)*** [KHB] 3,700 in Viet Nam (1993 Dang Nghiem Van). Lai Chau Province, northern Viet Nam in the Binh Lu area. Tai-Kadai, Kam-Tai, Be-Tai, Tai-Sek, Tai, Southwestern, East Central, Northwest. An official nationality in Viet Nam. Traditional religion, Buddhist. NT 1933. See main entry under China.

MAA ***(MAAQ, MA, MAA', CHAUMA, MA NGAN, CHE MA, MA XOP, MA TO, MA KRUNG)*** [CMA] 25,000 (1993 Dang Nghiem Van). Lam Dong, Dong Nai, and Thuan Hai provinces, spread over a wide area. Austro-Asiatic, Mon-Khmer, Eastern Mon-Khmer, Bahnaric, South Bahnaric, Sre-Mnong, Sre. Sometimes considered a Koho dialect. An official ethnic community. Literacy rate in first language: 10% to 30%. Literacy rate in second language: 50% to 75%. Traditional religion, Christian.

MALENG ***(MALIENG, MALANG)*** [PKT] 200 in Viet Nam (1996 Ferlus). Malieng in Thanh Hoa and Lam Hoa communes,Tuyen Hoa District, Dan Hoa in Minh Hoa District, northern Quang Binh Province; Huong Lien commune in Huong Khe District, Ha Tinh Province, 2 or 3 villages bordering Laos, and another to the southeast. Austro-Asiatic, Mon-Khmer, Viet-Muong, Chut. Dialects: MALIENG (PA LENG), KHA PHONG (MALENG KARI, MALENG BRO, KHA NAM OM). See main entry under Laos.

MAN CAO LAN ***(CAO LAN, CAOLAN, SAN CHAY, SAN CHI, MAN CAO-LAN, SÁN-CHI, MÁN, CAO LAN-SÁN CHI)*** [MLC] 114,000 (1993 Dang Nghiem Van). Bac Thái, Quang Ninh, Hà Bac, Cao Bang, Lang Son, and Hà Tuyen provinces, northern Viet Nam-China border. Tai-Kadai, Kam-Tai, Be-Tai, Tai-Sek, Tai, Central. Related to Tu Dí. May be close to some varieties of Southern Zhuang in China. The official San Chay nationality in Viet Nam. Speakers are said to have come from China in the 19th century. Traditional religion.

MANG ***(MANG U, XÁ MANG, XÁ Ó, NIENG Ó, CHAMAN, MANBU, BA'E, XÁ LÁ VÀNG)*** [MGA] 2,300 in Viet Nam (1993 Dang Nghiem Van). Population total all countries 2,800. Lai Chau Province, in villages in a triangle-shaped area between the Song Da (Black River) and the Nam Na at places such as Nam Nghe, Nam Xung, Nam Ban, Ban Nam Voi. Also spoken in China, Thailand. Austro-Asiatic, Mon-Khmer, Northern Mon-Khmer, Mang. An official ethnic community in Viet Nam. The linguistic subclassification of Mang is uncertain. Traditional religion.

MANTSI ***(LOLO, FLOWERY LOLO)*** [MUS] Ha Giang Province at Meo Vac and Dong Van districts. Sino-Tibetan, Tibeto-Burman, Lolo-Burmese, Loloish, Northern, Yi. Called 'Southeast Vernacular' type of Yi. May be related to what is called Southeastern Yi or Guizhou Yi in China. Not intelligible with Sichuan Yi (Nosu). Many uvular consonants, tense-lax voice quality, 5 tones. Yi script.

MNONG, CENTRAL ***(PNONG, BUDONG, BUDANG, PHANONG)*** [MNC] 50,000 or more in Viet Nam (1992 Diffloth). Population total both countries 69,000. All Mnong 186,000 (1981 Wurm and Hattori). Southwest of the Rade, mainly in Song Bé and western Dac Lac provinces. Also spoken in Cambodia. Austro-Asiatic, Mon-Khmer, Eastern Mon-Khmer, Bahnaric, South Bahnaric, Sre-Mnong, Mnong, Southern-Central Mnong. Dialects: PRÉH (PRE), BIAT (BHIÉT), BU NAR, BU RUNG, DIH BRI (DI-PRI), BU DANG. Biat may be a separate language related to Eastern Mnong. Mnong is an official ethnic community in Viet Nam. Investigation needed: intelligibility with Biat. Mountain slope. Traditional religion, Christian.

MNONG, EASTERN [MNG] 48,000 (1981). Population total both countries 48,000 or more. Southeast of the Rade in Dac Lac and Lam Dòng provinces. Also spoken in USA. Austro-Asiatic, Mon-Khmer, Eastern Mon-Khmer, Bahnaric, South Bahnaric, Sre-Mnong, Mnong, Eastern Mnong. Dialects: MNONG ROLOM (ROLOM, ROLAM, RLAM, RALAM), MNONG GAR (GAR), MNONG KWANH, CHIL. Biat may be closer to Eastern Mnong than to Central Mnong. Investigation needed: intelligibility with Biat. Bible portions 1977.

MNONG, SOUTHERN [MNN] 48,000 (1981). Mostly in Song Bé Province south of the Central Mnong and north of the Stieng. Austro-Asiatic, Mon-Khmer, Eastern Mon-Khmer, Bahnaric, South Bahnaric, Sre-Mnong, Mnong, Southern-Central Mnong. Dialects: BUNONG (NONG, PNONG), PRANG (PO RANG). Ra-Ong, Bu Sre, Bu Dip, and Kuenh are possibly subgroups. Probably the same as Pnong (Phnong) in Cambodia. Investigation needed: intelligibility with Chrau, Central Mnong.

MONOM ***(BONOM, MENAM, MONAM)*** [MOO] 5,000 (1973 SIL). Eastern Gia Lai-Cong Tum Province. Austro-Asiatic, Mon-Khmer, Eastern Mon-Khmer, Bahnaric, North Bahnaric, West, Sedang-Todrah, Todrah-Monom.

MUONG [MTQ] 914,000 (1993 Dang Nghiem Van). Hoa Bình, Thanh Hóa, Vinh Phú, Yen Bai, Son La, and Ninh Binh provinces, mostly in the mountains of north central Viet Nam. Austro-Asiatic, Mon-Khmer, Viet-Muong, Muong. Dialects: THANG, WANG, MOL, MUAL, MOI 1, BOI BI (MOI BI), AO TÁ (AU TÁ). Sach, May, Ruc, Arem, Thavung, Pakatan are related. An official ethnic community. Investigation needed: intelligibility with Sach, May, Ruc, Arem, Thavung, Pakatan. Literacy rate in first language: 1% to 5%. Literacy rate in second language: 50% to 70%. Mountain slope. Traditional religion, Christian. Bible portions 1963.

NGUÔN ***(NGOUAN)*** [NUO] 2,000 (1981 Wurm and Hattori). Minh Hoa District, northeastern Quang Binh Province. Austro-Asiatic, Mon-Khmer, Viet-Muong, Muong. Diffloth (1992) groups Nguon as a separate language close to Vietnamese, but Doi (1996) and Ferlus (1996) group it with Muong.

NHANG ***(NHAANG, NYANG, NIANG, YAI, YAY, GIAI, GIANG, GIÁY, DANG, DIOI, PAU THIN, PÚ NÀ, PU-NAM, CÙI CHU, XA CHUNG CHÁ, CHUNG CHA, SA)*** [NHA] 38,000 in Viet Nam (1993 Dang Nghiem Van). Population total all countries 38,105 or more. Hoàng Lien Son, Hà Tuyen, Lai Chau provinces. Also probably in Laos. Also spoken in France, USA. Tai-Kadai, Kam-Tai, Be-Tai, Tai-Sek, Tai, Northern. Close to Bouyei. Included under the Zhuang nationality in China; possibly a dialect or alternate name for Southern Zhuang. An official nationality in Viet Nam. Traditional religion.

NUNG ***(NONG, BU-NONG, HIGHLAND NUNG, TAI NUNG, TAY, TÀY NÙNG)*** [NUT] 705,000 in Viet Nam (1993 Dang Nghiem Van). Population total all countries 705,000 or more. Cao Bang, Lang Son, Bac Thái, Hà Tuyen, Hà Bac, Hoàng Lien Son, Quang Ninh, Thành phó Hò Chí Minh, Lam Dòng provinces. They have mixed with Chinese Nung. Also spoken in Australia, Canada, Laos, USA. Tai-Kadai, Kam-Tai, Be-Tai, Tai-Sek, Tai, Central. Dialects: XUÒNG, GIANG, NÙNG AN, NÙNG PHAN SLÌNH (NÙNG FAN SLIHNG), NÙNG CHÁO, NÙNG LÒI, NÙNG QÚY RIN (GUIREN), KHEN LÀI, NÙNG INH. Closely related to Tày and Southern Zhuang (Ningming, Longzhou varieties). Dialect continuum with Southern Zhuang in China. They have preserved their language and culture more than the Tày. Different from Chinese Nung (Cantonese) and Tibeto-Burman Nung (Nu). An official nationality in Viet Nam. Dictionary. Literacy rate in first language: 1% to 5%. Literacy rate in second language: 50% to 75%. Bible portions 1971-1975.

O'DU ***(O DU, IDUH, 'IDUH, "TAY HAT", HAT, HAAT)*** [TYH] 100 in Viet Nam (1993 Dang Nghiem Van). Population total both countries 294. Nghe Tinh Province in northern Viet Nam. Also spoken in Laos. Austro-Asiatic, Mon-Khmer, Northern Mon-Khmer, Khmuic, Mal-Khmu', Khmu'. An official ethnic community in Viet Nam. Speakers call themselves 'O Du'. Traditional religion.

PACOH ***(PACO, POKOH, BO RIVER VAN KIEU)*** [PAC] 15,000 (1973 SIL). Population total both countries 15,000 or more. Bình Tri Thien Province. Also spoken in Laos. Austro-Asiatic, Mon-Khmer, Eastern Mon-Khmer, Katuic, East Katuic, Katu-Pacoh. Dialect: PAHI (BA-HI). Investigation needed: intelligibility with Phuong. Literacy rate in first language: Below 1%. Literacy rate in second language: 15% to 25%. Bible portions 1965-1969.

PHU THAI ***(PUTAI, PHUTAI, PUTHAY, PUTHAI)*** [PHT] 150,000 in Viet Nam (1993 Johnstone). Northern. Tai-Kadai, Kam-Tai, Be-Tai, Tai-Sek, Tai Southwestern, East Central, Lao-Phutai. Part of the Thai official ethnic community in Viet Nam. See main entry under Thailand.

PHULA ***(PHU LA, PHU KHLA, FU KHLA)*** [PHH] A few speakers out of an ethnic population of 5,000 (1999 J. Edmondson UTA). Lai Chau Province, near Lao Cai City and one village in Xin Mun District of Ha Giang Province. Sino-Tibetan, Tibeto-Burman, Lolo-Burmese, Unclassified. Related to Laghuu. An official minority nationality. Endangered. Most have shifted to Vietnamese.

PHUNOI ***(CÔÔNG, PHU NOI, PUNOI, PHOUNOY, CONG, XA COONG, XA XAM KHOONG, XA XENG)*** [PHO] 1,300 in Viet Nam (1989 census). Lai Chau Province, Muong Te District, east of Sila, south of Mang. 4 villages at Ban Nam Luong in Xa Can Ho, Bo Lech in Xa Can Ho, Nam Kha Co area at Ban Bo, Muong Tong at Nam Ke near the Lao border. Sino-Tibetan, Tibeto-Burman, Lolo-Burmese, Loloish, Southern, Phunoi. Dialects: BLACK KHOANY, WHITE KHOANY, MUNG, HWETHOM, KHASKHONG. The northern and southern varieties in Viet Nam are different, but inherently intelligible to speakers. Bisu, Pyen, and Mpi are closely related. Those listed as dialects may be separate languages. Speakers in the southern villages dress like the White Thai. Some visit relatives in Laos. One of the official ethnic groups in Viet Nam. Called 'Côông' in Viet Nam, 'Phunoi' or 'Phounoy' in Laos. "Kha Punoi" is derogatory. See main entry under Laos.

PHUONG ***(PHUANG, PHUONG CATANG)*** [PHG] 15,000. Quang Nam-Da Nang and Gia Lai-Cong Tum provinces, southeast of the Pacoh language. Austro-Asiatic, Mon-Khmer, Eastern Mon-Khmer, Katuic, East Katuic, Katu-Pacoh. Part of the Katu official ethnic community. Investigation needed: intelligibility with Pacoh.

PUOC ***(KHA PUHOC, PUHOC, PUOK, PUA, XINH MUL, XINH-MUN, XIN MUL, SING MUN, KSING MUL)*** [PUO] 11,000 in Viet Nam (1993 Dang Nghiem Van). Population total both countries 13,000. Lai Chau and Son La provinces in northern Viet Nam, along the Laos border. Also spoken in Laos. Austro-Asiatic, Mon-Khmer, Northern Mon-Khmer, Khmuic, Xinh Mul. Related to Khang and Pong 3. An official ethnic community in Viet Nam.

RADE ***(RHADE, RADAY, RDE, E-DE, EDEH, DE)*** [RAD] 195,000 (1993 Dang Nghiem Van). Population total both countries 195,000 or more. Dac Lac and part of Phú Khánh provinces, centered around Banmethuot. Possibly also Cambodia. Also spoken in USA. Austronesian, Malayo-Polynesian, Western Malayo-Polynesian, Sundic, Malayic, Achinese-Chamic, Chamic, South, Plateau. Dialects: BIH, NDHUR (MDHUR), ADHAM (A-DHAM), BLO, KODRAO (KDRAO), KRUNG 1, RDE KPA (KPA). Bih (1,000) may be a separate language. The Krung 1 dialect is different from the Bahnaric language Krung 2, in Cambodia. Other names of dialects or ethnic groups: Ktul, Dlie, Rue, E-pan, Dong Kay, Arul, Kah. An official ethnic community in Viet Nam. Investigation needed: intelligibility with Bih. Literacy rate in first language: 10% to 30%. Literacy rate in second language: 50% to 75%. Christian, traditional religion. NT 1964.

RENGAO ***(RO-NGAO)*** [REN] 15,000 (1973 SIL). Cong Tum Province, from northwest of Dak To to southeast of Kontum city between Sedang and Bahnar. Austro-Asiatic, Mon-Khmer, Eastern Mon-Khmer, Bahnaric, North Bahnaric, West, Rengao. Dialects: WESTERN RENGAO, SEDANG-RENGAO, BAHNAR-RENGAO. Investigation needed: intelligibility with Halang Doan. Grammar. Literacy rate in first language: 5% to 10%. Literacy rate in second language: 25% to 50%. Bible portions 1977.

ROGLAI, CACGIA ***(RA-GLAI)*** [ROC] 2,000 (1973 SIL). 72,000 all Roglai in Viet Nam (1993 Dang Nghiem Van). Thuan Hai Province, on the coast northeast of Phan Rang. Austronesian, Malayo-Polynesian, Western Malayo-Polynesian, Sundic, Malayic, Achinese-Chamic, Chamic, South, Coastal, Roglai. It is considerably different from other Roglai dialects.

ROGLAI, NORTHERN ***(RADLAI, ADLAI, RAYGLAY, RA-GLAI, RANG GLAI, NOANG, LA-OANG)*** [ROG] 25,000 (1981 Wurm and Hattori). Thuan Hai and Phú Khánh provinces, in the mountains west and south of Nhatrang, and some near Dalat. Austronesian, Malayo-Polynesian, Western Malayo-Polynesian, Sundic, Malayic, Achinese-Chamic, Chamic, South, Coastal, Roglai. Roglai is an official ethnic community. Literacy rate in first language: 5% to 10%. Literacy rate in second language: 25% to 50%. Traditional religion, Christian. Bible portions 1966-1973.

ROGLAI, SOUTHERN ***(RAI)*** [RGS] 20,000 (1981 Wurm and Hattori). Thuan Hai Province, southern Viet Nam. Austronesian, Malayo-Polynesian, Western Malayo-Polynesian, Sundic, Malayic, Achinese-Chamic, Chamic, South, Coastal, Roglai. Dialect: RAI. Closely related to Chru and Northern Roglai. Roglai is an official ethnic community. Investigation needed: intelligibility with Northern Roglai, Chru. Traditional religion.

ROMAM [ROH] 250 (1993 Dang Nghiem Van). On the Viet Nam-Cambodian border. Austro-Asiatic, Mon-Khmer, Eastern Mon-Khmer, Bahnaric, Central Bahnaric. An official ethnic community. Traditional religion.

SEDANG ***(HADANG, HDANG, HOTEANG, ROTEANG, ROTEA, HOTEA, XODANG, XA DANG, CADONG, TANG, KMRANG)*** [SED] 40,000 in Viet Nam (1973 SIL). Population total both countries 40,000 or more. Cong Tum Province. Also spoken in Laos. Austro-Asiatic, Mon-Khmer, Eastern Mon-Khmer, Bahnaric, North Bahnaric, West, Sedang-Todrah, Sedang. Dialects: CENTRAL SEDANG, GREATER SEDANG, DAK SUT SEDANG, KOTUA SEDANG, KON HRING SEDANG. Closest to Hre. SaKau or Xa Cau may be an alternate name. Literacy rate in first language: 5% to 10%. Literacy rate in second language: 25% to 50%. Traditional religion, Christian.

SILA [SLT] 600 in Viet Nam (1993 Dang Nghiem Van). Lai Chau Province, Cú Dè Xù, Khá Pé. 3 villages: Ban Xeo Hai in Xa Can Ho, Xi Thao Chai of Pa Ha, Nam Xin of Muong Nhe. Sino-Tibetan, Tibeto-Burman, Lolo-Burmese, Loloish, Southern, Akha, Hani. An official ethnic community in Viet Nam. They say they came from Laos. Traditional religion. See main entry under Laos.

STIENG, BUDEH ***(LOWER STIENG, SOUTHERN STIENG)*** [STT] Southern Stieng area. Austro-Asiatic, Mon-Khmer, Eastern Mon-Khmer, Bahnaric, South Bahnaric. Different enough from Bulo Stieng that intelligibility is not functional.

STIENG, BULO ***(XTIENG, XA-DIENG, BUDÍP, RANGAH, UPPER STIENG, NORTHERN STIENG)*** [STI] 50,000 in Viet Nam for all Stieng (1993 Dang Nghiem Van). Population total both countries 53,571 all Stieng. Song Bé an Tay Ninh provinces. Also spoken in Cambodia. Austro-Asiatic, Mon-Khmer, Eastern Mon-Khmer, Bahnaric, South Bahnaric, Stieng-Chrau. Stieng is an official ethnic community in Viet Nam. Literacy rate in first language: Below 1%. Literacy rate in second language: 15% to 25%. Christian, traditional religion. Bible portions 1971.

TAI DAENG ***(RED TAI, TAI ROUGE, THAI DO, THAI DANG, TAI DENG, DAENG, TÁY-MÔC-CHÂU, MÔC-CHÂU)*** [TYR] 100,000 in Viet Nam (1990 A. Diller). Population total all countries 125,000. North central Viet Nam in the area of Thanh Hoa Province, south of Sam Nuea. Also spoken in Laos, Thailand, USA. Tai-Kadai, Kam-Tai, Be-Tai, Tai-Sek, Tai, Southwestern, East Central, Chiang Saeng. Part of the Thai official nationality in Viet Nam. Speakers in Viet Nam tend to identify with Tai Dam, and deny they are 'Red Tai'.

TAI DAM ***(TAI NOIR, THÁI DEN, TÁY-DAM, BLACK TAI, TAI DO)*** [BLT] 500,000 or more in Viet Nam (1990 A. Diller). Population total all countries 534,000 or more. Northern Viet Nam along the Red and Black rivers. Some moved south and are settled in Tung Nghia (Tuyenduc), Tho Thanh (Darlac), Pleiku, and elsewhere. Also spoken in Australia, China, France, Laos, Thailand, USA. Tai-Kadai, Kam-Tai, Be-Tai, Tai-Sek, Tai, Southwestern, East Central, Chiang Saeng. Dialect: TÁY MU'Ò'I (TAI MUEAI, MEUAY). Close to Song. It is part of the Thai official nationality in Viet Nam (760,000 in 1984; official figure), which also includes Tai Kao and Tai Daeng. Officially included under Dai in China. Literacy rate in first language: 1% to 5%. Literacy rate in second language: 50% to 75%. Traditional religion. Bible portions 1982-1993.

TAI DÓN ***(TAI DÓN, TAI BLANC, THÁI TRÁNG, TAI LAI, TAI KAO, TÁY KHAO, WHITE TAI)*** [TWH] 190,000 in Viet Nam (1984 official figure). Population total all countries 400,000 (1990 A. Diller ANU). North Viet Nam along the Red and Black rivers. Some are settled in southern Viet Nam, mainly in Tung Nghia (Tuyen Duc). Also spoken in China, France, Laos. Tai-Kadai, Kam-Tai, Be-Tai, Tai-Sek, Tai, Southwestern, East Central, Chiang Saeng. Not intelligible with Tai Dam. Lao has influenced the speech of some Tai Dón speakers. Those who have had prolonged contact with Tai Dam have become bilingual in it. Many have not had that contact. They have different customs from the Tai Dam. Tai Dón have strong ethnic pride. Part of the Thai official nationality in Viet Nam. Distinctive writing system. Traditional religion, Buddhism. Bible portions 1969.

TAI HANG TONG ***(HÀNG TONG, TÀY MUÒNG)*** [THC] Small. Northern Viet Nam. Tai-Kadai, Kam-Tai, Be-Tai, Tai-Sek, Tai, Southwestern, Unclassified. Part of the Thái official ethnic community, related to White Thai, Tai Dam, Pu Thay, Tay Thanh, and Tho Da Bac.

TAI MAN THANH ***(TÁY THANH, MAN THANH)*** [TMM] Small. Northern Viet Nam. Tai-Kadai, Kam-Tai, Be-Tai, Tai-Sek, Tai, Southwestern, Unclassified. Part of the Thái official ethnic community, related to White Thai, Tai Dam, Tai Hang Tong, Pu Thay, and Tho Da Bac.

TAKUA ***(QUANG TIN KATU, LANGYA)*** [TKZ] 5,000 to 10,000 (1973 SIL). Quang Nam-Da Nang Province. Austro-Asiatic, Mon-Khmer, Eastern Mon-Khmer, Bahnaric, North Bahnaric, East, Takua. Closest to Cua and Kayong.

TA'OIH, UPPER ***(T-OY, TÀ-OI, TAU OI, TA HOI, TOI-OI, KANTUA)*** [TTH] 26,000 in Viet Nam (1993 Dang Nghiem Van). Dòng Nai Province, east of A Tuc. Austro-Asiatic, Mon-Khmer, Eastern Mon-Khmer, Katuic, Central Katuic, Ta'oih. Dialects: PASOOM, KAMUAN', PALEE'N, LEEM, HA'AANG (SA'ANG). Not intelligible with Lower Ta'oih until speakers have had at least 2 weeks' contact. 70% monolingual. An official ethnic community in Viet Nam. Investigation needed: intelligibility with dialects. Literacy rate in first language: Below 1%. Literacy rate in second language: 5% to 15%. Traditional religion, Christian. See main entry under Laos.

TÀY ***("THÔ", THU LAO, T'O, TAI THO, NGAN, PHEN, PA DI)*** [THO] 1,190,000 in Viet Nam (1993 Dang Nghiem Van). Population total all countries 1,190,000 or more. Cao Bàng, Lang Son, Hà Giang, Tuye Quang, Bác Thái, Hoàng Lien Son, Quang Ninh, Hà Bac, and Lam Dòng provinces, central and northeastern Viet Nam near the China border. Some moved south and settled in Tung Nghia and Song Mao. Also possibly in Laos. Also spoken in France, USA. Tai-Kadai, Kam-Tai, Be-Tai, Tai-Sek, Tai, Central. Dialects: CENTRAL TÀY, EASTERN TÀY, SOUTHERN TÀY, NORTHERN TÀY. Dialect continuum to Southern Zhuang in China. Closely related to Nung. High degree of bilingualism and acculturation in Vietnamese. "Tho" is a derogatory name. An official nationality in Viet Nam. Dictionary. Literacy rate in first language: 1% to 5%. Literacy rate in second language: 50% to 75%. Traditional religion, Christian. Bible portions 1938-1963.

TAY BOI ***(TAY BOY, ANNAMITE FRENCH, VIETNAMESE PIDGIN FRENCH)*** [TAS] Was used in the major ports of French Indo-China. Pidgin, French based. Developed beginning in 1862. Influences from Vietnamese, French, English, Javanese, and Portuguese. It was used between French and Vietnamese until 1954, and in lower levels of administration, in the military, and by police. No longer spoken (1981 Wurm and Hattori). Extinct.

TAY JO ***(TAY-JO)*** [TYJ] Small. Northern Viet Nam. Tai-Kadai, Kam-Tai, Be-Tai, Tai-Sek, Tai, Unclassified. It may be the same as Tay Yo of Khamouan Province, Laos.

TAY TAC [TYT] Northwestern Viet Nam, Muong Tâc District in eastern Son La Province. Tai-Kadai, Kam-Tai, Be-Tai, Tai-Sek, Tai, Southwestern, East Central, Chiang Saeng. Related to Tai Dam, Tai Dón, and Tai Daeng. Part of the Thai official nationality in Viet Nam. The women's blouse is similar to that worn by White Tai women of Lai Châu, without the silver buttons. CN(C) in which N=V + tone, 22 consonants, 13 vowels, 6 tones on open syllables and those ending with a continuant, 3 tones on syllables ending with a stop.

THO ***(CUOI, CUOI CHAM, KEO, HO MUONG MERIDIONAL)*** [TOU] 30,000 (1996 Ferlus). Northern Nghe An Province, highland areas. Cuoi Cham is in Tan Hop commune, Tan Ky District. Austro-Asiatic, Mon-Khmer, Viet-Muong, Cuoi. Dialects: CUOI CHAM (UY LO), MON. An official ethnic community. Associated culturally with other principal local ethnonyms Keo, Mon, Cuoi, Ho, Dan, Lai-Ly Ha, and Tay Poong.

TODRAH ***(TODRÁ, DIDRAH, DIDRA, PODRA, MODRA, KODRA)*** [TDR] 5,000 (1973 SIL). Gia Lai-Cong Tum Province, northeast of Kontum city from Kon Hring to Kon Braih. Austro-Asiatic, Mon-Khmer, Eastern Mon-Khmer, Bahnaric, North Bahnaric, West, Sedang-Todrah, Todrah-Monom. Didra may be a separate language. Investigation needed: intelligibility with Didra.

TRIENG ***(STRIENG, GIE-TRIENG, TAREH, TRENG, TA-RIENG, TALIENG, DGIÉH, GIANG RAY, PIN)*** [STG] 27,000 (1993 Dang Nghiem Van). Quang Nam-Da Nang and Gia Lai-Cong Tum provinces, northwest of Dak Rotah. Austro-Asiatic, Mon-Khmer, Eastern Mon-Khmer, Bahnaric, North Bahnaric, West. May be related to Jeh or Talieng in Laos. An official ethnic community in Viet Nam. Traditional religion, Christian.

TS'ÜN-LAO ***(LAO)*** [TSL] 10,000 (1993 Dang Nghiem Van). Lai Chau Province, northwestern Viet Nam. Tai-Kadai, Kam-Tai, Be-Tai, Tai-Sek, Tai, Central. Official ethnic community, with associated names Lào Bóc and Lào Noi. Traditional religion.

VIETNAMESE ***(KINH, GIN, JING, CHING, VIET, ANNAMESE)*** [VIE] 65,051,000 in Viet Nam, 86.7% of the population (1993). Population total all countries 68,000,000 (1999 WA). The entire country. Also spoken in Australia, Cambodia, Canada, China, Côte d'Ivoire, Finland, France, Germany, Laos, Martinique, Netherlands, New Caledonia, Norway, Philippines, Senegal, Thailand, United Kingdom, USA, Vanuatu. Austro-Asiatic, Mon-Khmer, Viet-Muong, Vietnamese. Dialects: NORTHERN VIETNAMESE (TONKINESE, HANOI), CENTRAL VIETNAMESE (HUE), SOUTHERN VIETNAMESE. Numerous dialects, including the principal ones listed above. People are called 'Kinh'. National language. Grammar. SVO; prepositions; genitives, articles, adjectives, numerals, relatives before noun heads; question word initial. Literacy rate in first language: 65%. Literacy rate in second language: 80%. Roman script used. Buddhist, Christian. Bible 1916-1994.

YEMEN

Republic of Yemen, al-Jumhurïyah al-Yamaniyah. National or official language: Standard Arabic. 16,887,000 (1998 UN). Literacy rate 25% to 39%. Also includes Egyptian Spoken Arabic 10,000, Gulf Spoken Arabic 10,000, Western Cham, Hindi 232,760, Hobyót, Somali 290,000, people from Africa 28,000, India and Pakistan 65,000. Information mainly from T. Sebeok 1970; R. F. Nyrop 1986; T. M. Johnstone 1987. Sunni Muslim, Zaydi Muslim, Ismaili Muslim, Christian, Hindu, secular, Jewish. Deaf population 1,052,571. Data accuracy estimate: B. The number of languages listed for Yemen is 7. Of those, all are living languages. Diversity index 0.56.

ARABIC, HADRAMI SPOKEN ***(HADROMI, HADRAMI)*** [AYH] 300,000 in Yemen (1995). Population total all countries 410,000. Hadramaut. Also spoken in Eritrea, Kenya. Afro-Asiatic, Semitic, Central, South, Arabic. Distinct from Ta'izzi-Adeni Spoken Arabic and Sanaani Spoken Arabic. Literacy rate in second language: 10%. Muslim.

ARABIC, JUDEO-YEMENI ***(JUDEO-YEMENI, YEMENITE JUDEO-ARABIC)*** [JYE] 1,000 in Yemen (1995 H. Mutzafi). Afro-Asiatic, Semitic, Central, South, Arabic. Dialects: SAN<A, <ADEN, BE:DA, HABBAN. All dialects are markedly different from their co-territorial non-Judeo-Yemeni dialects. Jewish. See main entry under Israel.

ARABIC, SANAANI SPOKEN ***(NORTHERN YEMENI ARABIC)*** [AYN] 7,600,000 (1996). Extends as far south as Dhamar, about 14.4 degrees north. Afro-Asiatic, Semitic, Central, South, Arabic. Distinct from Hadrami and Ta'izzi-Adeni Arabic. Literacy rate in second language: 10%. Zaydi Muslim.

ARABIC, STANDARD [ABV] Afro-Asiatic, Semitic, Central, South, Arabic. Used for education, official purposes, formal speeches. National language. Newspapers. Bible 1984-1991. See main entry under Saudi Arabia.

ARABIC, TA'IZZI-ADENI SPOKEN ***(SOUTHERN YEMENI SPOKEN ARABIC)*** [ACQ] 6,760,000 in Yemen (1996). Population total all countries 6,840,000. All provinces except 2 eastern and the northeastern ones. Probably a few in UAE, Somalia, Egypt, and Saudi Arabia. Also spoken in Djibouti, Eritrea, Kenya, United Kingdom. Afro-Asiatic, Semitic, Central, South, Arabic. Dialects: TA'IZZI, ADENI. Ta'izzi dialect is the one best-accepted throughout Yemen. Different from Hadromi and Sanaani Arabic Arabic. Literacy rate in second language: 10%. Zaydi Muslim.

MEHRI ***(MAHRI)*** [MHR] 58,000 in Yemen. Population total all countries 100,000 (1997 Hetzron). Mahrah State, scattered individuals. Both dialects are in Yemen. Also spoken in Kuwait, Oman. Afro-Asiatic, Semitic, South, South Arabian. Dialects: WESTERN MEHRI (MEHRIYET), EASTERN MEHRI (MEHRIYOT). The dialect of Qishn town is very prestigious. Within the main dialects there are also differences between bedouin and city or village varieties. Bathari and Hobyot may be Mehri dialects. Many ethnic Mehri in Yemen are Arabic mother tongue speakers. Spoken by the Mahra and Beyt Kathir (Bilhari?) Dictionary. Muslim. Bible portions 1902.

SOQOTRI ***(SAQATRI, SOKOTRI, SUQUTRI, SOCOTRI)*** [SQT] 70,000 (1990 census). Mainly in Soqotra Island, hundreds in <Abd al-Kuri island, and about a dozen in Samha Island in the Gulf of Aden. Afro-Asiatic, Semitic, South, South Arabian. Dialects: <ABD AL-KURI, SOUTHERN SOQOTRI, NORTHERN SOQOTRI, CENTRAL SOQOTRI, WESTERN SOQOTRI.North Soqotri includes North Central and Northwest Central (highland) Soqotri. Mostly monolingual in Soqotri. Women are forbidden to leave the islands, so there are no Soqotri communities on the mainland. Muslim. Bible portions 1902.

Europe

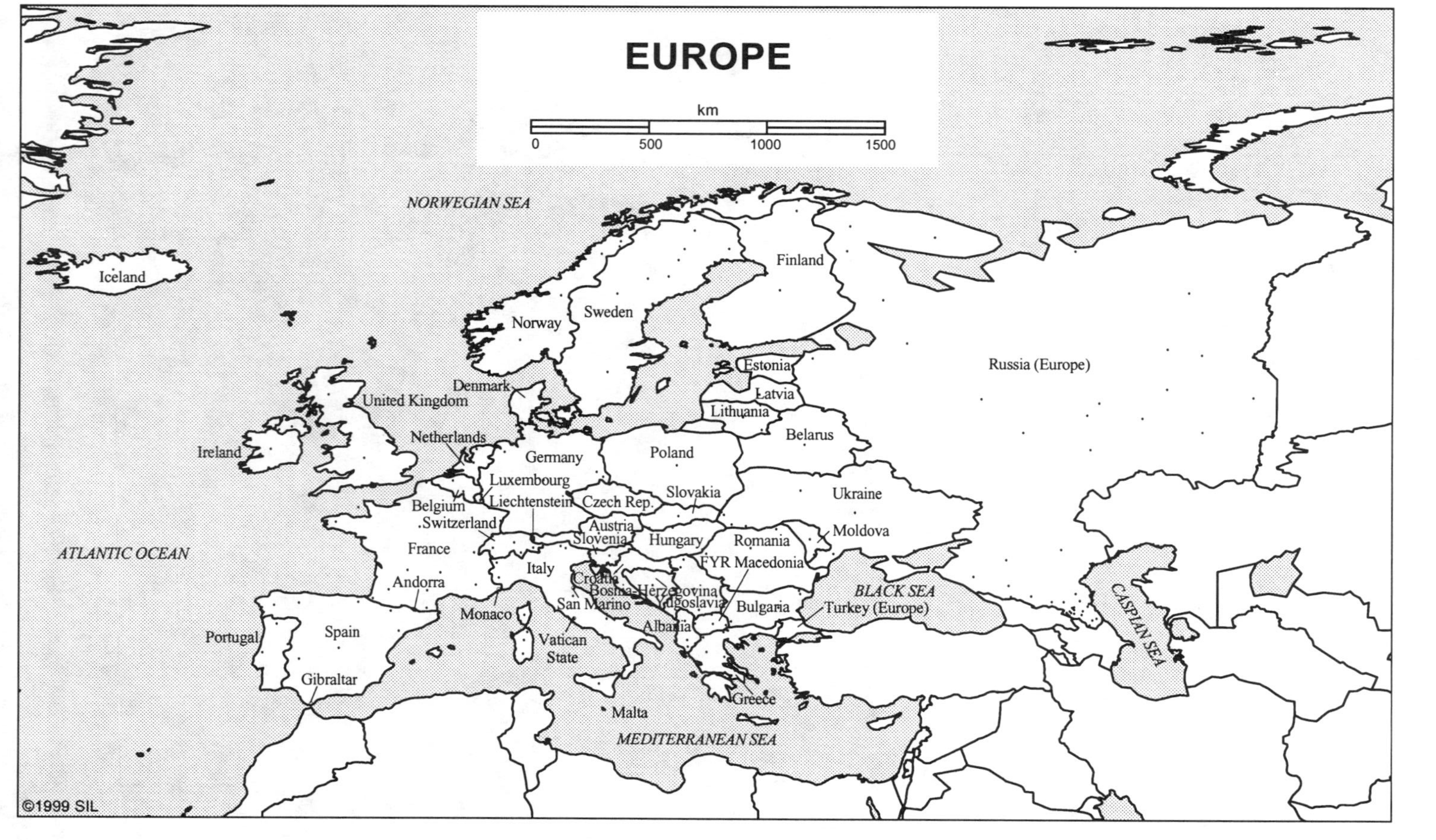
EUROPE
km
0
500
1000
1500
NORWEGIAN SEA
Iceland
Norway
Sweden
Finland
Russia (Europe)
Estonia
Latvia
Lithuania
Belarus
Denmark
United Kingdom
Ireland
Netherlands
Germany
Poland
Luxembourg
Belgium
Liechtenstein
Czech Rep.
Slovakia
Ukraine
Switzerland
Austria
Slovenia
Hungary
Romania
Moldova
ATLANTIC OCEAN
France
Italy
Croatia
FYR Macedonia
Andorra
Bosnia-Herzegovina
Yugoslavia
Bulgaria
BLACK SEA
Turkey (Europe)
San Marino
Monaco
Albania
Portugal
Spain
Vatican State
CASPIAN SEA
Gibraltar
Greece
Malta
MEDITERRANEAN SEA

ALBANIA

Republic of Albania. Republika e Shqipërisë. National or official language: Tosk Albanian. 3,119,000 (1998 UN). Literacy rate 85% (1991 National Geographic). Information mainly from G. Messing 1980; B. Comrie 1987; L. Newmark. Secular, Muslim, Christian. Blind population 2,000. Deaf population 204,565 (1998). Data accuracy estimate: B. The number of languages listed for Albania is 7. Of those, all are living languages. Diversity index 0.26.

ALBANIAN, GHEG ***(GEG, GHEG, SHOPNI, GUEGUE)*** [ALS] 300,000 in Albania. Northern Albania. Indo-European, Albanian, Gheg. Dialects: MANDRICA, SHIP (KOSOVE), SCUTARI, ELBASAN-TIRANA. Speakers may be bilingual in Standard Albanian. Predominantly Muslim except in the northwest around Scutari and the Mirdita, which are RC. NT 1869-1990. See main entry under Yugoslavia.

ALBANIAN, TOSK ***(TOSK, ARNAUT, SHKIP, SHQIP, SKCHIP, SHQIPERË, ZHGABE)*** [ALN] 2,900,000 in Albania (1989). 3,202,000 in Albania including Gheg (1989), 98% of the population (1989). Population total all countries 3,000,000 for Tosk, 5,000,000 for all Albanian (L. Newmark and WA 1999). Mainly south Albania to the Shkumbi River. Also spoken in Belgium, Canada, Egypt, Germany, Sweden, Turkey (Europe), Ukraine, USA. Indo-European, Albanian, Tosk. Dialects: ARBANASI (ZADAR), SREM (SYRMIA), CAMERIJA, KORCA. Reported to be inherently unintelligible with Gheg Albanian and partially intelligible with Arvanitika Albanian of Greece. Not intelligible with Arbëreshë of Italy. Tosk has been the basis of the official language for Standard Albanian since 1952. It is used in schools. The Jevgjit claim to be Egyptians, but may be assimilated Roma. National language. Grammar. SVO. Deciduous forest. Coastal, mountain slope. Peasant agriculturalists; animal husbandry: sheep, petroleum workers. Sea level to 800 meters. Muslim, Christian (Orthodox). Bible 1993.

GREEK [GRK] 60,000 in Albania, 1.8% of the population (1989). South. Indo-European, Greek, Attic. Bible 1840-1994. See main entry under Greece.

MACEDONIAN ***(SLAVIC, MACEDONIAN SLAVIC)*** [MKJ] 30,000 in Albania (1993 Johnstone). Indo-European, Slavic, South, Eastern. Called 'Slavic' in Greece. Bible 1990. See main entry under Macedonia.

ROMANI, VLAX [RMY] 60,000 in Albania (1991). Indo-European, Indo-Iranian, Indo-Aryan, Central zone, Romani, Vlax. Dialect: SOUTHERN VLAX ROMANI. Ethnic groups are Mechkaria, Kurtofia, Chergaria, and Kabuzia. Christian. NT 1984-1995. See main entry under Romania.

ROMANIAN, MACEDO ***(MACEDO-RUMANIAN, ARUMANIAN, ARUMUN, AROMUNIAN, ARMINA, VLACH)*** [RUP] 50,000 (1995 T. J. Winnifrith) or more out of up to 400,000 in the ethnic group in Albania. South Albania, especially in Korçë, Lushnjë, Pernët, Gjirokastër, Sarandë, Berat, Durrës, Kavajë, and Tiranë. Indo-European, Italic, Romance, Eastern. Structurally a distinct language from Romanian (F. Agard). Inherent intelligibility with Romanian is very low. It split from the other three Romanian languages between 500 and 1000 A.D. No Arumanian language teaching, press, or television. A church in Korçë holds services in Arumanian. 'Armini' refers to the people. Bible portions 1881-1889. See main entry under Greece.

SERBO-CROATIAN ***(MONTENEGRIN)*** [SRC] Southwest Albania, 2 or 3 villages, and some in the city. Indo-European, Slavic, South, Western. Montenegrins. Mainly Muslim. Bible 1804-1968. See main entry under Yugoslavia.

ANDORRA

Principality of Andorra. Principat d'Andorra. National or official languages: Catalan-Valencian-Balear, French. 72,000 (1998 UN). Literacy rate 92% to 99%. Also includes English 770, Portuguese 2,100. Christian. Deaf population 3,880. Data accuracy estimate: B. The number of languages listed for Andorra is 3. Of those, all are living languages. Diversity index 0.57.

CATALAN-VALENCIAN-BALEAR ***(CATALÀ, CATALÁN, BACAVÈS)*** [CLN] 31,000 in Andorra (1990), 61% of the population (1990). Indo-European, Italic, Romance, Italo-Western, Western, Gallo-Iberian, Ibero-Romance, East Iberian. National language. Literacy rate in first language: 75% to 100%. Literacy rate in second language: 75% to 100%. Christian. Bible 1478-1993. See main entry under Spain.

FRENCH [FRN] 2,400 in Andorra, 6% of the population (1986). Indo-European, Italic, Romance, Italo-Western, Western, Gallo-Iberian, Gallo-Romance, Gallo-Rhaetian, Oïl, French. National language. Bible 1530-1986. See main entry under France.

SPANISH *(CASTILIAN)* [SPN] 24,600 in Andorra, 60% of population (1986). Indo-European, Italic, Romance, Italo-Western, Western, Gallo-Iberian, Ibero-Romance, West Iberian, Castilian. Bible 1553-1979. See main entry under Spain.

AUSTRIA

Republic of Austria. Republik Österreich. National or official languages: Standard German, Slovenian (regional). 8,140,000 (1998 UN). Literacy rate 99% to 100%. Also includes Assyrian Neo-Aramaic, Czech 7,100, Western Farsi 2,000, French 15,000, Greek 12,000, Kirmanjki, Kurmanji 23,000, Polish 39,000, Turkish 68,000, Yeniche, Arabic 3,000, Chinese 1,200. Information mainly from M. Stephens 1976; B. Comrie 1987. Christian, secular, Muslim. Blind population 11,005. Deaf population 482,311. Deaf institutions: 17. Data accuracy estimate: A2, B. The number of languages listed for Austria is 9. Of those, all are living languages. Diversity index 0.14.

ALEMANNISCH *(ALEMANNIC)* [GSW] 300,000 in Austria (1991 Annemarie Schmidt). Western Austria, Vorarlberg. Indo-European, Germanic, West, High German, German, Upper German, Alemannic. Dialect: HIGH ALEMANNISCH (HOCHALEMANNISCH). Similar to Swabian. Called 'Schwyzerdütsch' in Switzerland and 'Alsatian' in southeastern France. NT 1984. See main entry under Switzerland.

AUSTRIAN SIGN LANGUAGE *(AUSTRO-HUNGARIAN SIGN LANGUAGE)* [ASQ] Deaf sign language. Partially intelligible with French Sign Language. Related to Russian Sign Language. The sign language used in class and that used by adults outside class are different. Deaf people go to different schools, each using a different sign language. Sign language interpreters are used some in court. Professionals are required to know sign language in job training and social services programs. There is little research. There are a few classes for hearing people. Originated 1870. There is a manual alphabet for spelling. Dictionary. Films, TV, videos.

BAVARIAN *(BAYERISCH, BAIRISCH, BAVARIAN AUSTRIAN, OST-OBERDEUTSCH)* [BAR] Central Bavarian is in the Alps and Lower Austria and Salzburg; North Bavarian in the north of Regensburg, to Nuremburg and Western Bohemia, Czech Republic; South Bavarian in the Bavarian Alps, Tyrol, Styria, including the Heanzian dialect of Burgenland, Carinthia, northern Italy, and part of Gottschee. Also spoken in Czech Republic, Germany, Hungary, Italy. Indo-European, Germanic, West, High German, German, Upper German, Bavarian-Austrian. Dialects: CENTRAL BAVARIAN, NORTH BAVARIAN, SOUTH BAVARIAN. School is compulsory for 9 years, and is taught in Standard German. However, one report indicated that active competence in Standard German is limited for some speakers. News broadcasts in German are understood poorly by some of the population. Not endangered. SVO; prepositions; genitives, articles, adjectives, numerals, relatives before noun heads; question word initial; 2 prefixes, 3 to 4 suffixes on a word; word order distinguishes subjects, objects, indirect objects; affixes indicate case of noun phrase; obligatory verb affixes mark person and number of subject, other suffixes can mark gender of subject and person, number, and gender of object; causatives; comparatives; CV, CVC, CVV, CCV. Bible 1998.

GERMAN, STANDARD [GER] 7,500,000 in Austria (J. A. Hawkins in B. Comrie 1987), 98% of the population (1990 WA). Indo-European, Germanic, West, High German, German, Middle German, East Middle German. National language. Bible 1466-1982. See main entry under Germany.

HUNGARIAN *(MAGYAR)* [HNG] 22,000 in Austria (1995). Vienna, Lower Austria, Styria, Burgenland. Uralic, Finno-Ugric, Ugric, Hungarian. Dialect: OBERWART. Speakers of Standard Hungarian have difficulty understanding Oberwart dialect. Taught at primary levels in schools where there are larger numbers of speakers in Burgenland. Used regularly by REF and RC churches. Bible 1590-1991. See main entry under Hungary.

ROMANI, SINTE *(ROMMANES, SINTE, SINTI)* [RMO] 500 in Austria (1990 D. Holzinger). Indo-European, Indo-Iranian, Indo-Aryan, Central zone, Romani, Northern. Christian. Bible portions 1875-1995. See main entry under Yugoslavia.

SERBO-CROATIAN [SRC] 103,000 or more in Austria (1991). Burgenland and Vienna. Indo-European, Slavic, South, Western. Dialect: BURGENLAND CROATIAN. The form of Croat spoken in Burgenland differs extensively from that spoken in the Republic of Croatia and intelligibility is difficult. Some dialects are heavily influenced by German. Bilingualism in Standard German. About 40 primary schools teach bilingually through Croat and German. Croat is used extensively by the RC church. Rapid assimilation with the German-speaking population. Investigation needed: bilingual proficiency in Standard German. Literacy rate in first language: Few. Christian. Bible 1804-1968. See main entry under Yugoslavia.

SLOVENIAN *(SLOVENE)* [SLV] 20,000 to 40,000 in Austria (1993 T. Priestly), including at least several thousand Windisch speakers (1995). Carinthia (Kärnten) and Steiermark (Styria), southwest Austria. Indo-European, Slavic, South, Western. Dialect: WINDISCH. Separated by the Karawanken Mts. from the larger group of Slovenes in Slovenia. They and their speech are called 'Windisch', an archaic form of Slovene, heavily influenced by German. The dialects of Slovene, generally, tend to differ from one another very much. No one has made any kind of a measured dialect analysis, so it is not possible at this time (1995) to say how different any of the dialects are from the standard (T. Priestly, U. of Alberta, personal communication 1995). Some speakers speak Standard Slovene well; some use it only in church. Some of the ethnic group are able to speak the dialects, some are losing their command of them. Many speakers go to church, where they hear Standard Slovene. Speakers are bilingual or trilingual in the Slovenian dialect (Windisch), a German regional variety (Kärntnerisch or Steierisch), or Standard German. Most speakers educated since 1945 speak Standard German reasonably well. Most do not consider themselves to be Slovenians, but Carinthians, belonging to the German culture. Investigation needed: intelligibility with Standard Slovenian. Official language. Bible 1584-1996. See main entry under Slovenia.

WALSER *(WALSCHER)* [WAE] 5,000 to 10,000 in Austria (1995 C. Buchli). Vorarlberg (Grosses Walsertal: Blons, Fontanella, Raggal, St. Gerold, Sonntag, Thnringerberg); Kleinwalsertal (Mittleberg); Brandnertal (Brand); Montafon (Silbertal); Reintal (Laterns); Tannberg (Schricken, Lech, Warth); Tirol: Paznauntal (Galtnr). 14 communities in Austria. Indo-European, Germanic, West, High German, German, Upper German, Alemannic. Ancestors came from the Wallis Canton between the 12th and 13th centuries. Close but different from Schwytzertusch. Different from Cimbrian, Mocheno, or Bavarian. See main entry under Switzerland.

BELARUS

National or official language: Belarusan. 10,315,000 (1998 UN). Formerly part of USSR. Capital: Minsk. 80,200 square miles. Literacy rate 99%. Also includes Latvian 1,000, Lithuanian 10,031, Polish 403,000, Baltic Romani, Russian 1,134,000, Tatar 12,000, Ukrainian 291,000, Eastern Yiddish 231,000, Possibly Yiddish 112,000 to 231,000, Romani. Data accuracy estimate: B. The number of languages listed for Belarus is 1. Diversity index 0.36.

BELARUSAN *(BELARUSIAN, BELORUSSIAN, BIELORUSSIAN, WHITE RUSSIAN, WHITE RUTHENIAN, BYELORUSSIAN)* [RUW] 7,905,000 in Belarus, 98% of the population (1993 Johnstone). Population total all countries 10,200,000. 74% of the ethnic group from the former USSR speak it as mother tongue. Also spoken in Azerbaijan, Canada, Estonia, Kazakhstan, Kyrgyzstan, Latvia, Lithuania, Moldova, Poland, Russia (Europe), Tajikistan, Turkmenistan, Ukraine, USA, Uzbekistan. Indo-European, Slavic, East. Dialects: NORTHEAST BELARUSAN (POLOTS, VITEB-MOGILEV), SOUTHWEST BELARUSAN (GRODNEN-BARANOVICH, SLUTSKO-MOZYR, SLUTSKA-MAZYRSKI), CENTRAL BELARUSAN. Linguistically between Russian and Ukrainian, with transitional dialects to both. National language. Cyrillic script used. Christian, Muslim (Tatar). Bible 1973.

BELGIUM

Kingdom of Belgium. Koninkrijk België. Royaume de Belgique. National or official languages: Dutch, French, Standard German. 10,141,000 (1998 UN). Literacy rate 98%. Also includes Tosk Albanian 3,000, Algerian Spoken Arabic 10,800, Moroccan Spoken Arabic 105,000, Tunisian Spoken Arabic 8,900, Assyrian Neo-Aramaic, Catalan-Valencian-Balear, Chaldean Neo-Aramaic, Italian 280,000, Iu Mien 200, Kabyle, Kurmanji 22,000, Laz, Portuguese 80,000, Spanish 70,000, Turkish 63,600, Turoyo 2,000, Eastern Yiddish, Chinese 14,000; people from DRC 10,000. Information mainly from M. Stephens 1976; B. Comrie 1976. Christian, secular, Muslim. Blind population 4,779. Deaf population 610,119. Deaf institutions: 26. Data accuracy estimate: A2, B. The number of languages listed for Belgium is 8. Of those, 7 are living languages and 1 is a second language without mother tongue speakers. Diversity index 0.65.

BELGIAN SIGN LANGUAGE [BVS] Deaf sign language. Dialects: NORTH BELGIUM SIGN LANGUAGE, SOUTH BELGIUM SIGN LANGUAGE. A variety of regional dialects which have their roots in different deaf schools. The dialect in the Flemish region is closer to that in the Walloon region than it is to Dutch Sign Language. Adopted signs from the old French sign language directly and indirectly. It began in 1825. Different sign languages are used in the classroom and by adults outside the classroom. Limited influence from Signed Dutch. Signed French and Signed Dutch are used some for intercommunication with hearing people. 3 deaf schools in Brussels have trained about one-third of the deaf in Belgium. There are 26 deaf institutions. Sign language interpreters are required in court. Some interpreters are available for college students. Some interpreters are provided for job training and mental health programs. There is sign language instruction for parents of deaf children. There is a committee on national sign language. Little research on the language.

There are sign language classes for hearing people. There have been schools for deaf people since 1825. Dictionary. Films, TV, videos.

DUTCH *(NEDERLANDS)* [DUT] 4,620,150 in Belgium (1990 WA). The language of provinces of West Vlaanderen, Oost Vlaanderen, Antwerpen, Limburg, Vlaams-Brabant, and the bilingual part (10% to 20%) of Brussels. Indo-European, Germanic, West, Low Saxon-Low Franconian, Low Franconian. Dialects: BRABANTS, OOST-VLAAMS. The variety of Dutch (not Vlaams) spoken in Belgium is only slightly different from the variety spoken in the Netherlands. Called 'Vlaams' in Belgium, even though it is different from the (West) Vlaams spoken there. In the Dutch linguistic area there are minority rights for French-speaking persons in Drogenbos, Kraainem, Linkebeek, Sint-Genesius-Rode, Wemmel, Wezembeek-Oppem, Mesen, Spiere-Helkijn, Ronse, Bever, Herstappe, Voeren. Official language. Radio programs, TV. Bible 1522-1988. See main entry under Netherlands.

EUROPANTO [EUR] Brussels, European Union buildings. Artificial language. A mixture of elements from some of the main European languages, for use among members of the European Union. Second language only.

FRENCH *(FRANÇAIS)* [FRN] 4,000,000 in Belgium (M. Harris in B. Comrie 1988), 33% of the population (1990 WA). Official language in provinces of Hainaut, Namur, Liège, Luxembourg, Brabant-Walloon, southern hills, and the bilingual part of Brussels. Indo-European, Italic, Romance, Italo-Western, Western, Gallo-Iberian, Gallo-Romance, Gallo-Rhaetian, Oïl, French. Dialects: WALLOON (WALLON), PICARD. The eastern subdialect of Walloon is considered to be more difficult to understand within Belgium. The following municipalities have minority rights for Dutch-speaking persons: Comines-Warneton, Mouscron, Enghien, Floubecques; and for German-speaking persons: Malmèdy, Weismes, Welkenraedt. Official language. Bible 1530-1986. See main entry under France.

GERMAN, STANDARD [GER] 150,000 in Belgium (J. A. Hawkins in B. Comrie 1988), 1.5% of the population. Official language in Liège Province, cantons of Eupen and Sankt-Vith, municipalities: Eupen, Kelmis, Lontzen, Raeren, Amel, Bnlingen, Bntchenbach, Sankt-Vith, and Burg-Reuland. Indo-European, Germanic, West, High German, German, Middle German, East Middle German. Official language. Bible 1466-1982. See main entry under Germany.

LUXEMBOURGEOIS *(LETZBURGISCH)* [LUX] 30,000 in Belgium (1998). Area of Arlon and Bastogne, Luxembourg Province. Indo-European, Germanic, West, High German, German, Middle German, Moselle Franconian. See main entry under Luxembourg.

PICARD *(ROUCHI, CHTIMI)* [PCD] Most of Hainaut Province (Tournai, Mons, Ath). Indo-European, Italic, Romance, Italo-Western, Western, Gallo-Iberian, Gallo-Romance, Gallo-Rhaetian, Oïl, French. Dialect: BELGIAN PICARD. All dialects, including those in France are inherently intelligible to speakers. French is spoken at school, in court, for administration, with outsiders. Home, family, friends, in local stores. The Belgian government recognizes Picard officially as an indigenous regional language. The European Bureau for Lesser Used Languages considers it as a language. Some reports used and edited by the French government consider it a separate language from French. No standardized writing system. Poetry. See main entry under France.

VLAAMS *(FLAMAND, VLAEMSCH)* [VLA] 1,070,000, over 89% of the inhabitants of West Flanders in Belgium (1998 U. of Ghent). Population total all countries 1,300,000 (1998 University of Ghent) including 220,000 in Zeeuws, 1,100,000 in West Vlaams and Frans Vlaams. Large parts of the Province of West Flanders. Also spoken in France, Netherlands. Indo-European, Germanic, West, Low Saxon-Low Franconian, Low Franconian. Dialect: WEST VLAAMS (VLAEMSCH). Bilingualism in French, some English. All ages. Speakers attitude toward French was hostile, but has normalized. Speakers are called 'Vlamingen', language 'Vlaemsch'. Dictionary. SOV. The spelling systems in the 3 countries differ so as to make acceptance of written materials difficult among them. Christian.

BOSNIA-HERZEGOVINA

National or official languages: Bosnian, Croatian, Serbian. 3,675,000 (1998 UN). Part of Yugoslavia until 1992. Literacy rate 92%. Also includes Standard German, Italian, Macedo Romanian, Turkish, Albanian. Muslim, Orthodox, Roman Catholic, other. Data accuracy estimate: B. The number of languages listed for Bosnia-Herzegovina is 2. Of those, both are living languages. Diversity index 0.00.

BOSNIAN [SRC] 4,000,000 in Bosnia-Herzegovina (1995). Indo-European, Slavic, South, Western. Dialects: BOSNIAN, CROATIAN, SERBIAN. There are influences from Turkish and Arabic. Macedonian and Montenegrin are ethnic minorities speaking varieties of this language. Official language. Dictionary. SVO. Literacy rate in second language: 97%. Roman script used. Muslim, Christian, Jewish. Bible 1804-1999. See main entry under Yugoslavia.

ROMANI, VLAX ***(TSIGENE, DANUBIAN, GYPSY, VLAX)*** [RMY] Indo-European, Indo-Iranian, Indo-Aryan, Central zone, Romani, Vlax. Dialects: SERBO-BOSNIAN (MACHWAYA, MACHVANO), KALDERASH, SOUTHERN VLAX. Vlax and Kalderash are understood by the Lovari. Ethnic group: Gurbéti. Christian. NT 1984-1995. See main entry under Romania.

BULGARIA

Republic of Bulgaria. Narodna Republika Bulgaria. National or official languages: Bulgarian, Turkish. 8,336,000 (1998 UN). Literacy rate 90% to 98%. Also includes Armenian 27,000, Czech 9,000, Greek 11,000, Russian 18,000, Serbo-Croatian 9,000. Information mainly from B. Comrie 1987. Christian, secular, Muslim. Blind population 3,312. Deaf population 533,544. Deaf institutions: 19. Data accuracy estimate: B. The number of languages listed for Bulgaria is 12. Of those, 11 are living languages and 1 is extinct. Diversity index 0.22.

ALBANIAN, GHEG [ALS] 1,000 in Bulgaria (Newmark). Indo-European, Albanian, Gheg. Not intelligible with Tosk Albanian. NT 1869-1990. See main entry under Yugoslavia.

BULGARIAN ***(BALGARSKI)*** [BLG] 7,986,000 in Bulgaria, 85% of the population (1986). Population total all countries 9,000,000 (1999 WA). Also spoken in Canada, Greece, Hungary, Israel, Moldova, Romania, Turkey (Europe), Ukraine, USA, Yugoslavia. Indo-European, Slavic, South, Eastern. Dialect: PALITYAN (PALITIANI, BOGOMIL). Palityan is functionally intelligible with Standard Bulgarian. The Sopa are of Petecheneg origin and speak Bulgarian. National language. Grammar. SVO. Christian. Bible 1864-1923.

BULGARIAN SIGN LANGUAGE [BQN] Deaf sign language. Different sign languages are used in the classroom and by adults outside. One sign language which has been used since 1920. There have been elementary schools for deaf people since 1898. Since 1945 sign language has been allowed in the classroom. Sign language interpreters are required in court. Some are available for college students. There is sign language instruction for parents of deaf children. There is a committee on national sign language. Little research on the sign language. There are few sign language classes for hearing people. There is a manual alphabet for spelling. Dictionary. Films, TV, videos.

CRIMEAN TURKISH ***(CRIMEAN TATAR)*** [CRH] 6,000 in Bulgaria (1990). Northeast Bulgaria. Altaic, Turkic, Southern. Dialects: NORTHERN CRIMEAN (CRIMEAN NOGAI, STEPPE CRIMEAN), CENTRAL CRIMEAN, SOUTHERN CRIMEAN. Muslim. NT 1666-1825. See main entry under Uzbekistan.

GAGAUZ ***(GAGAUZI)*** [GAG] 12,000 in Bulgaria (1982 estimate). Varna coastal region. Altaic, Turkic, Southern, Turkish. Dialects: BULGAR GAGAUZ, MARITIME GAGAUZ. Gagauz might be considered a dialect of Turkish, except for the use of Orthodox Christian religious vocabulary. Christian. Bible portions 1927-1996. See main entry under Moldova.

GOTHIC [GOF] Bulgaria and central Europe. Indo-European, Germanic, East. Dialects: CRIMEAN GOTHIC, OSTROGOTH, VISIGOTH. Some settlements survived in the Crimea until the 18th century (Bloomfield 1933). Extinct. Bible 520. See main entry under Ukraine.

MACEDONIAN [MKJ] An undetermined number of inhabitants of the Pirin region in Bulgaria claim Macedonian as mother tongue, bordering the former Yugoslav Republic of Macedonia (Prof. Wayles Brown, 1998, Cornell University). Indo-European, Slavic, South, Eastern. Bible 1990. See main entry under Macedonia.

ROMANI, BALKAN ***(GYPSY)*** [RMN] 187,900 in Bulgaria, 2% of the population (1986), including 100,000 Arlija, 20,000 Dzambazi, 10,000 Tinsmiths, 10,000 East Bulgarian, 200,000 including second language speakers (1985 Gunnemark and Kenrick). Between Sofia and the Black Sea (Central dialect). The Tinsmiths dialect is in central and northwest Bulgaria; Arlija is in the Sofia region. Indo-European, Indo-Iranian, Indo-Aryan, Central zone, Romani, Balkan. Dialects: ARLIJA, TINNERS ROMANI, GREEK ROMANI, DZAMBAZI, EAST BULGARIAN ROMANI, PASPATIAN, IRONWORKER ROMANI. Ethnic groups: Jerlídes (western Bulgaria), Drindári (central Bulgaria). Muslim. Bible portions 1912-1937. See main entry under Yugoslavia.

ROMANI, VLAX [RMY] 500 Kalderash in Bulgaria. Indo-European, Indo-Iranian, Indo-Aryan, Central zone, Romani, Vlax. Christian. NT 1984-1995. See main entry under Romania.

ROMANIAN, MACEDO ***(MACEDO-RUMANIAN, ARUMANIAN, AROMANIAN, ARMINA)*** [RUP] 2,000 to 3,000 (Sofia Aromanian Society). Communities have associations in Peshtera, Velingrad, Dupnitsa, Rakitovo, and Blagoevgrad. Indo-European, Italic, Romance, Eastern. Structurally a distinct language from Romanian (F. Agard). 'Armini' refers to the people. Their relatives emigrated from Macedonia and northern Greece between 1850 and 1914. The Romanian Cultural Institute has been closed since 1948. Bible portions 1881-1889. See main entry under Greece.

RUSSIAN SIGN LANGUAGE [RSL] Deaf sign language. Related to Austrian and French sign languages, but different. Originated 1806. See main entry under Russia.

TURKISH *(OSMANLI, TURKI)* [TRK] 845,550 in Bulgaria, 9% of the population (1986). Kurdzhali Province and neighboring areas of South Bulgaria, along the Danube, and various regions of East Bulgaria. Altaic, Turkic, Southern, Turkish. Dialects: DANUBIAN, RAZGRAD, DINLER, MACEDONIAN TURKISH. The Turkish language is gradually being replaced by Bulgarian, although Islam and ethnic identity remain strong. Natural growth has been balanced by emigration to Turkey. Official language. Muslim. Bible 1827-1941. See main entry under Turkey.

CROATIA

National or official languages: Croatian, Italian. 4,481,000 (1998 UN). Part of Yugoslavia until 1991. Literacy rate 97%. Also includes Sinte Romani, Slovenian. Information mainly from B. Comrie 1987. Data accuracy estimate: B. The number of languages listed for Croatia is 6. Of those, 5 are living languages and 1 is extinct. Diversity index 0.07.

CROATIAN *(HRVATSKI)* [SRC] 4,800,000 in Croatia (1995). Indo-European, Slavic, South, Western. Dialects: KAYKAVSKI, CHAKAVSKI, SHTOKAVSKI. Shtokavski is the official dialect, but the others are recognized as valid dialects, with a large body of literature. Other dialects in other countries, like Burgenland Croatian in Austria, are less intelligible. Bilingualism in English, German. Official language. SVO. Literacy rate in second language: 90%. Roman script. Christian, Muslim. Bible 1831-1968. See main entry under Yugoslavia.

DALMATIAN *(RAGUSAN, VEGLIOTE)* [DLM] Coast near Dubrovnik. Indo-European, Italic, Romance, Italo-Western, Italo-Dalmatian. Recently extinct, late nineteenth century. A dialect of Croatian is now spoken in the area. Extinct.

ISTRIOT [IST] 1,000 or fewer (1994 Tapani Salminen). Western coast of Istrian Peninsula, now only in the towns of Rovinj (Rovigno) and Vodnjan (Dignano). Indo-European, Italic, Romance, Italo-Western, Italo-Dalmatian. Reported to be an archaic Romance language, often confused with Istro-Rumanian. Perhaps closer to Friulian or Dalmatian than to Istro-Rumanian. Few children speakers.

ITALIAN [ITN] 70,000 in Croatia whose mother tongue is Italian or Venetian, including 30,000 ethnic Italian and 40,000 ethnic Croats and Istrian people (1998 Eugen Marinov). Istria. Indo-European, Italic, Romance, Italo-Western, Italo-Dalmatian. Official language. Bible 1471-1985. See main entry under Italy.

ROMANIAN, ISTRO *(ISTRO-ROMANIAN)* [RUO] 555 to 1,500 (1994). Northeast Istrian Peninsula, Zejane village and a few villages to the south. Indo-European, Italic, Romance, Eastern. Structurally a separate language from Romanian (F. B. Agard). Split from the other 3 Romanian languages between 500 and 1000 A.D. Not the same as the Istriot language. Few children speakers.

VENETIAN [VEC] 100,000 in Croatia and Slovenia (1994 Tapani Salminen). See also Italian in Croatia. Istrian Peninsula and Dalmatia. Indo-European, Italic, Romance, Italo-Western, Western, Gallo-Iberian, Gallo-Romance, Gallo-Italian. Dialects: ISTRIAN, TRETINE, VENETIAN PROPER. Very different from Standard Italian. Vigorous. Investigation needed: bilingual proficiency, attitudes. Bible portions 1859. See main entry under Italy.

CZECH REPUBLIC

National or official language: Czech. 10,282,000 (1998 UN). Officially separated from Slovakia January 1, 1993. Literacy rate 99%. Also includes Russian. Information mainly from B. Comrie 1987. Christian, secular. Blind population 10,000 in former Czechoslovakia. Deaf population 63,037. Deaf institutions: 51 in former Czechoslovakia. Data accuracy estimate: B. The number of languages listed for Czech Republic is 9. Of those, 8 are living languages and 1 is extinct. Diversity index 0.06.

BAVARIAN *(BAYERISCH, BAVARIAN AUSTRIAN)* [BAR] North Bavarian is in Western Bohemia and in the north of Regensburg to Nuremburg; Central Bavarian is in the Alps and Lower Austria and Salzburg; South Bavarian is in the Bavarian Alps, Tyrol, Styria, including the Heanzian dialect of Burgenland, Carinthia, northern Italy, and part of Gottschee. Indo-European, Germanic, West, High German, German, Upper German, Bavarian-Austrian. Dialects: CENTRAL BAVARIAN, NORTH BAVARIAN, SOUTH BAVARIAN. Investigation needed: intelligibility with dialects, bilingual proficiency, attitudes. Bible 1998. See main entry under Austria.

CZECH *(CESTINA, BOHEMIAN)* [CZC] 10,004,800 in Czech Republic (1990 WA). Population total all countries 12,000,000 (1999 WA). Western, Bohemia, Moravia, Silesia. Also spoken in Austria, Bulgaria, Canada, Israel, Poland, Slovakia, Ukraine, USA. Indo-European, Slavic, West, Czech-Slovak. Dialects: CENTRAL BOHEMIAN, CZECHO-MORAVIAN, HANAK, LACH (YALACH), NORTHEAST BOHEMIAN, SOUTHWEST BOHEMIAN. All Czech and Slovak dialects are inherently intelligible to each other's speakers. National language. Grammar. SVO. Christian. Bible 1380-1980.

CZECH SIGN LANGUAGE [CSE] Deaf sign language. Partially intelligible with French Sign Language. Used since 1786 when deaf schools began. Sign language used in school different from that used by adults outside. Signed interpretation required in court. Some provided for college students and at important public events. There is sign language instruction for parents of deaf children. Many sign language classes for hearing people. There is a committee on national sign language. More than one sign language used in the country. There is a manual alphabet for spelling. Dictionary. Films, TV, videos.

GERMAN, STANDARD [GER] 50,000 in Czech Republic (1998). In the Erzgebirge, a mountain range along the border of Czech Republic. Indo-European, Germanic, West, High German, German, Middle German, East Middle German. Dialect: ERZGEBIRGISCH. Bilingualism in Czech. Bible 1466-1982. See main entry under Germany.

KNAANIC *(CANAANIC, LESHON KNAAN, JUDEO-SLAVIC)* [CZK] Indo-European, Slavic, West, Czech-Slovak. Dialect: JUDEO-CZECH. Became extinct in late Middle Ages. The name 'Knaanic' applied mainly to Judeo Czech, but also to other Judeo-Slavic varieties. Jewish. Extinct.

POLISH *(POLSKI)* [PQL] 50,000 in Czech Republic. Indo-European, Slavic, West, Lechitic. Christian. Bible 1561-1965. See main entry under Poland.

ROMANI, CARPATHIAN *(BASHALDO, ROMUNGRO, HUNGARIAN-SLOVAK ROMANI)* [RMC] 220,000 in Czech Republic and Slovakia (1980 UBS). Population total all countries 241,000 or more. Central, Bohemia, and Moravia. Also spoken in Hungary, Poland, Romania, Slovakia, Ukraine, USA. Indo-European, Indo-Iranian, Indo-Aryan, Central zone, Romani, Northern. Dialects: MORAVIAN ROMANI, EAST SLOVAKIAN ROMANI, WEST SLOVAKIAN ROMANI. Not intelligible with Vlach Romani or Angloromani. Speakers do not interact socially with speakers of Vlach Romani or Angloromani. Ethnic groups: Sárvika Romá (northern and eastern Slovakia), Ungrike Romá (southern Slovakia). The people are called 'Karpacki Roma'. Dictionary. Grammar. Christian. Bible portions 1936-1996.

ROMANI, SINTE *(ROMMANES, SINTE, SINTI, TSIGANE)* [RMO] Indo-European, Indo-Iranian, Indo-Aryan, Central zone, Romani, Northern. Dialect: LALLERE. Not intelligible with Vlach Romani. The Lallere are those whose ancestors came from the Czech Republic. Ethnic group: Sasítka Romá. Christian. Bible portions 1875-1995. See main entry under Yugoslavia.

SILESIAN, LOWER *(LOWER SCHLESISCH)* [SLI] Indo-European, Germanic, West, High German, German, Middle German, East Middle German. Different than Upper Silesian, a dialect of Polish. See main entry under Poland.

DENMARK

Kingdom of Denmark, Kongeriget Danmark. National or official languages: Danish, Standard German. 5,313,000 (1998 UN), including 43,000 on Faroe Islands (1998 UN). Also see Greenland. Greenland and Faroe Islands both have home rule. Literacy rate 99%. Also includes English 10,000, Western Farsi 9,000, Western Frisian, Iu Mien, Kirmanjki, Turkish 30,000, Romani 3,000, from the former Yugoslavia 10,000, from India or Pakistan 4,000. Information mainly from M. Stephens 1976; B. Comrie 1987; I. Hancock 1991. Christian, secular, Muslim. Blind population 9,350. Deaf population 3,500 to 314,548 (1998). Deaf institutions: 20. Data accuracy estimate: A2, B. The number of languages listed for Denmark is 8. Of those, all are living languages. Diversity index 0.05.

DANISH *(DANSK, CENTRAL DANISH, SJAELLAND)* [DNS] 5,000,000 in Denmark (1980). Population total all countries 5,326,000. Also spoken in Canada, Germany, Greenland, Norway, Sweden, UAE, USA. Indo-European, Germanic, North, East Scandinavian, Danish-Swedish, Danish-Bokmal, Danish. See separate entries for Skåne, often called 'Eastern Danish' and Jutish, often called 'Western Danish'. Also see Norwegian, Riksmal. National language. Dictionary. Grammar. SVO. Christian. Bible 1550, in press (1993).

DANISH SIGN LANGUAGE [DSL] (3,500 deaf in Denmark; 1986 Gallaudet Univ.). Deaf sign language. Some signs are related to French Sign Language. Intelligible with Swedish and Norwegian sign languages with only moderate difficulty. Not intelligible with Finnish Sign Language. Used in all 5 state schools for the deaf. Signed interpretation required in court, college classes, at important public events, in job training, social services, and mental health programs. Instruction provided for parents of deaf children, for other hearing people. There is a committee on national sign language, an organization for sign language teachers. A lot of research. Signed Danish is distinct, but used in intercommunication with some hearing people. The first school was begun in 1807. Dictionary. Grammar. Films, TV, videos.

FAROESE ***(FØROYSKT)*** [FAE] 47,000 (1976 Stephens). Faroe Islands. Indo-European, Germanic, North, West Scandinavian. Not inherently intelligible with Icelandic. Not endangered. The Faroe Islands are self-governing in most matters. Bible 1948-1961.

GERMAN, STANDARD [GER] 23,000 first language speakers (1976 Stephens). North Slesvig (Sydjylland). Indo-European, Germanic, West, High German, German, Middle German, East Middle German. There are German schools. Official language. Bible 1466-1982. See main entry under Germany.

INUKTITUT, GREENLANDIC ***(GREENLANDIC ESKIMO, GREENLANDIC, KALAALLISUT)*** [ESG] 7,000 on Denmark mainland (1990 L. D. Kaplan). Eskimo-Aleut, Eskimo, Inuit. Radio programs. Bible 1900. See main entry under Greenland.

JUTISH ***(JUTLANDISH, JYSK, WESTERN DANISH)*** [JUT] German-Danish border area, Southern Jutland on the Danish side, and in northern Schleswig, Schleswig-Holstein, Germany. Also spoken in Germany. Indo-European, Germanic, North, East Scandinavian, Danish-Swedish, Danish-Bokmal, Danish. The westernmost and southernmost dialects differ so much from Standard Danish, that many people from the Eastern Islands have great difficulty understanding it. From the viewpoint of inherent intelligibility, it could be considered a separate language (Norbert Strade). All inhabitants in Rudbol village are reported to be able to speak 5 languages: Danish, Jutish, North Frisian, Low Saxon, and German.

SKÅNE ***(SKÅNSKA, SCANIAN, EASTERN DANISH)*** [SCY] Bornholm Island. Indo-European, Germanic, North, East Scandinavian, Danish-Swedish, Swedish. Dialects: HALLAENDSKA, SKÅNSKA, BLEKINGSKA, BORNHOLM. Speakers are highly bilingual in Swedish or Danish. The language has had no recognition since Sweden obtained Scania from Denmark in 1658. It is called 'Southern Swedish' in Sweden, and 'Eastern Danish' in Denmark. Bible 1523. See main entry under Sweden.

TRAVELLER DANISH ***(RODI, ROTWELSCH)*** [RMD] Indo-European, Germanic, North, East Scandinavian, Danish-Swedish, Danish-Bokmal, Danish. An independent language based on Danish with heavy lexical borrowing from Northern Romani. Not inherently intelligible with Angloromani. It may be intelligible with Traveller Norwegian and Traveller Swedish. There are reported to be few speakers. It may be linguistically extinct (D. Kenrick 1986). Romani people were transported to Denmark by James IV of Scotland in July 1505.

ESTONIA

Republic of Estonia, Eesti Vabariik. National or official language: Estonian. 1,476,301 (1996 Statistical Yearbook of Estonia). Independence from USSR in 1991. 17,413 square miles. Capital Tallinn. Literacy rate 99%. Also includes Armenian 837, North Azerbaijani 869, Belarusan 8,841, Chuvash 563, Finnish 5,155, Standard German 1,249, Latvian 1,794, Lithuanian 1,610, Polish 601, Baltic Romani 465, Russian 468,216, Swedish 29, Tatar 2,248, Ukrainian 21,320, Eastern Yiddish 570, Many with from 1 to 663 speakers each (1989 census). Information mainly from B. Comrie 1987. Deaf population 1,600 (1998). Data accuracy estimate: B. The number of languages listed for Estonia is 2. Of those, both are living languages. Diversity index 0.48.

ESTONIAN ***(EESTI)*** [EST] 953,032 in Estonia out of 963,281 (93%) ethnic group (1989 census). Population total all countries 1,100,000. Also spoken in Australia, Canada, Finland, Latvia, Russia (Europe), Sweden, United Kingdom, USA. Uralic, Finno-Ugric, Finno-Permic, Finno-Cheremisic, Finno-Mordvinic, Finno-Lappic, Baltic-Finnic. Dialects: TALLINN (REVAL), TARTU (DORPAT), MULGI, VÔRU (WERRO), SETO (SETU). Dialects are grouped into three: Northeastern Coastal Estonian (between Tallinn and Narva), North Estonian (island, western, central, and eastern dialects), and South Estonian (Mulgi, Tartu, Vôru). Vôru, Setu (a subdialect of Vôru), and island are clearly distinct from standard Estonian. All the other dialects are assimilated into standard Estonian. Those over 60 and under 20 speak little Russian. It is spoken less in rural areas and in southern areas. 75% to 80% of the population in the northeast are Russian speakers. Those over 60 know some German. Most in the north speak Finnish for common topics. Estonian has remained the language of education, including universities. Some linguistic influences from Russian, German, Swedish, Latvian, Lithuanian, and Finnish. National language. Dictionary. Grammar. SVO; 14 cases: affixes indicate case of noun phrases; verb affixes mark person and number of subject and agreement (obligatory); genitives, adjectives, numerals before noun heads; question word initial; 1 prefix maximum; 5-6 suffixes maximum; word order distinguishes given and new information; active and passive voice; 4 moods in both voices: indicative, imperative, conditional, oblique; 2 infinitives for all verbs; 4 tenses in both voices and all moods: present, past, perfect, pluperfect; 3 degrees of comparison: positive, comparative, superlative; V, CV, CVC, CVCCC, CVV, CVVC, VC, VCCC, VV,

VVC, CCV, CCVV, CCVC, CCVCC, CCVVCC, CCVCCC; nontonal; stress on first syllable; possible secondary stress on third syllable. Literacy rate in second language: North Estonian, central dialect. Roman script used. TV. Christian. Bible 1739-1995.

ESTONIAN SIGN LANGUAGE *(VIIPEKEEL)* [ESO] 4,500 users out of 1,600 deaf and 20,000 hearing impaired. 2,000 persons need regular help from interpreters (1998 Urmas Sutrop). Throughout Estonia, especially Tallinn and Pärnu. Deaf sign language. Some local dialects. The dialect in Pärnu is the most archaic. Apparent influences from Finnish and Russian Sign Languages. Some people can use both Estonian and Russian Sign Languages. Russian Sign Language is used in Tallinn by deaf Russians. In other regions Russians use some pidginized versions of Russian Sign Language mixed with Estonian Sign Language. Systematic teaching and research since 1990 at the Dept. of Special Education at Tartu University. Sign language instruction for parents of deaf children in Tallinn. Classes for hearing people in Tallinn and Pärnu. Classes for interpretars. Schools for children with hearing impairments. Many children with hearing impairments in ordinary schools. Oral and signed teaching. There is a Society of the Interpreters of Estonian Sign Language. Centers for interpreters in Tallinn, Tartu, Pärnu, at the Association of Deaf People. Local authorities pay for interpreters for 36 hours for each deaf person per year. Some grants for students who need interpreters. Courts accept signed interpretation and pay for interpreters. Dictionary. Grammar. TV, videos.

FINLAND

Republic of Finland, Suomen Tasavalta. National or official languages: Finnish, Swedish. 5,154,000 (1998 UN). Literacy rate 100%. Also includes English 4,500, Standard German, Polish, Romanian 1,000, Russian 10,000, Somali 1,300, Spanish, Tatar 1,000, Turkish 1,000, Vietnamese, Arabic, Chinese. Information mainly from M. Stephens 1976; B. Comrie 1987; T. Salminen 1987-1998. Christian, secular. Blind population 3,345. Deaf population 8,000 to 307,333 (1986 Gallaudet University). Deaf institutions: 44. Data accuracy estimate: A2, B. The number of languages listed for Finland is 12. Of those, 11 are living languages and 1 is extinct. Diversity index 0.14.

ESTONIAN [EST] 6,000 in Finland (1993). Traditionally on the southern coast. Uralic, Finno-Ugric, Finno-Permic, Finno-Cheremisic, Finno-Mordvinic, Finno-Lappic, Balto-Finnic. Dialects: TALLINN (REVAL, NORTHERN ESTONIAN), TARTU (DORPAT, TATU, SOUTHERN ESTONIAN), SETU, MULY (MULGI), VYRUS (VORU). North and South Estonian may be separate languages. The traditional community was assimilated to the Swedish-speaking community. Present speakers are refugees from World War II or recent immigrants. SVO. Roman script used. Christian. Bible 1739-1995. See main entry under Estonia.

FINNISH *(SUOMI, SUOMEA)* [FIN] 4,700,000 in Finland, 93.5% of population (1993), including 30,000 speakers of Tornedalen Finnish. Population total all countries 6,000,000 (1999 WA). Also spoken in Canada, Estonia, Norway, Russia (Europe), Sweden, USA. Uralic, Finno-Ugric, Finno-Permic, Finno-Cheremisic, Finno-Mordvinic, Finno-Lappic, Baltic-Finnic, Finnic. Dialects: SOUTHWESTERN FINNISH, HÄME (TAVAST), SOUTH POHJANMAA, CENTRAL AND NORTH POHJANMAA, PERÄPOHJA, SAVO (SAVOLAX), SOUTHEASTERN FINNISH (FINNISH KARJALA, FINNISH KARELIAN). Southeastern dialects called 'Karelian' in colloquial Finnish are distinct from true Karelian (T. Salminen). Finnish is closely related to Karelian and Olonetsian. About 300,000 are bilingual in Swedish. National language. Grammar. SVO. Christian. Bible 1642-1991.

FINNISH SIGN LANGUAGE *(VIITTOMAKIELI)* [FSE] 5,000 users out of 8,000 deaf persons (1986 Gallaudet Univ.). Deaf sign language. 2 major dialects from the Finnish (17 schools) and Swedish (1 school) communities. Apparent influence from Swedish Sign Language merged with local indigenous varieties. Not intelligible with Danish Sign Language. The government pays interpreters to accompany the deaf to hospitals, college, church, etc. Signed interpretation required in court. Sign language instruction for parents of deaf children. Many classes for hearing people. There is a committee on national sign language. The first deaf school was founded in the 1850s. Signed Finnish is distinct, but used by some teachers of the deaf. Dictionary. Grammar. Films, TV, videos. Bible portions 1989.

FINNISH, TORNEDALEN [FIT] 30,000 in Finland (1997 Birger Winsa). Uralic, Finno-Ugric, Finno-Permic, Finno-Cheremisic, Finno-Mordvinic, Finno-Lappic, Balto-Finnic, Finnic. Bible portions 1993-1995. See main entry under Sweden.

KARELIAN *(KARELY, KARELIAN PROPER)* [KRL] 10,000 in Finland (1994). There are two villages in Oulu Province, close to the Russian border (Northern Karelian), and others scattered around Finland (Southern Karelian). Uralic, Finno-Ugric, Finno-Permic, Finno-Cheremisic, Finno-Mordvinic, Finno-Lappic, Balto-Finnic. Dialects: NORTHERN KARELIAN, SOUTHERN KARELIAN, NORGOROD,

TVER (KALININ). Ludic is a separate language (Juha Janhunen 1990). All are now apparently completely competent in Finnish (T. Salminen). Northern Karelian is traditionally spoken in Oulu, though decreasingly. Southern Karelian speakers were resettled from areas ceded to the former USSR from 1940 to 1944. Literacy rate in first language: 75% to 100%. Literacy rate in second language: 75% to 100%. Bible portions 1820-1993. See main entry under Russia.

LIVVI ***(OLONETSIAN, OLONETS, LIVVIKOVIAN, LÍVÕNKÉL, AUNUS)*** [OLO] Scattered around Finland. Uralic, Finno-Ugric, Finno-Permic, Finno-Cheremisic, Finno-Mordvinic, Finno-Lappic, Balto-Finnic. Close to Karelian and Finnish. Ludic is transitional between Livvi and Veps. A distinct language from Karelian and Ludic. They now appear to be completely competent in Finnish (T. Salminen). Speakers were resettled from areas ceded to the former USSR from 1940 to 1944. Literacy rate in first language: 75% to 100%. Literacy rate in second language: 75% to 100%. See main entry under Russia.

ROMANI, KALO FINNISH ***(FÍNTIKA RÓMMA, GYPSY)*** [RMF] 4,000 to 6,000 speak the language out of 8,000 Gypsies in Finland (1980). Western and southern. Also spoken in Sweden. Indo-European, Indo-Iranian, Indo-Aryan, Central zone, Romani, Northern. Not inherently intelligible with Traveller Swedish, Traveller Norwegian, Traveller Danish, or Angloromani. Speakers originally came from Scotland. Literacy rate in first language: 10% to 30%. Literacy rate in second language: 50% to 100%. Christian. Bible portions 1971.

SAAMI, INARI ***(INARI "LAPPISH", ANAR, "FINNISH LAPP", "LAPP", SÁMI, SAMIC, SAAM, SAAME)*** [LPI] 250 speakers out of 700 population (1995 M. Krauss). 4,700 all Saami in Finland (1995). Lapland, above 68.00N Lat., in an area about 15,400 square miles between Lake Inari and the Norway border. They are in the majority around the border town of Utsjoki. Uralic, Finno-Ugric, Finno-Permic, Finno-Cheremisic, Finno-Mordvinic, Finno-Lappic, Lappic, Eastern. Finnish Saami all know Finnish and speak it for all purposes outside their work as reindeer herdsmen. Instruction in schools is in Finnish. Few children speakers. The name "Lapp" is derogatory. Some literature. Literacy rate in first language: 30% to 100%. Literacy rate in second language: 75% to 100%. Pastoralists: reindeer. Bible portions 1903-1980.

SAAMI, KEMI ***(SÁMI, SAMI, "LAPP")*** [LKS] Lapland Province, Sodankyla and Kuolajarvi (Salla) counties. Formerly south as far as Kuusamo County. Uralic, Finno-Ugric, Finno-Permic, Finno-Cheremisic, Finno-Mordvinic, Finno-Lappic, Lappic, Central. Extinct.

SAAMI, NORTHERN ***(NORTHERN LAPP, DAVVIN, "LAPP", SAAME, SAME)*** [LPR] 2,000 speakers out of 3,500 population (1995 M. Krauss). Utsjoki, Enontekio, and Sodankyla. Uralic, Finno-Ugric, Finno-Permic, Finno-Cheremisic, Finno-Mordvinic, Finno-Lappic, Lappic, Northern. Dialects: RUIJA, TORNE, SEA LAPPISH. The most widely spoken Saami language in Finland. Literacy rate in first language: 30% to 100%. Literacy rate in second language: 75% to 100%. Bible 1895. See main entry under Norway.

SAAMI, SKOLT ***(SKOLT LAPPISH, RUSSIAN LAPP, "LAPP", SAAME, SAME, LOPAR, KOLTA, KOLTTA)*** [LPK] 300 speakers out of 500 population in Finland (1995 M. Krauss). Population total both countries 320 to 330. Northwest of Inari Saami. Also spoken in Russia (Europe). Uralic, Finno-Ugric, Finno-Permic, Finno-Cheremisic, Finno-Mordvinic, Finno-Lappic, Lappic, Central. Many use Finnish as second language. Youngest in their 30s. They moved here from Russia during World War II. Literacy rate in first language: 10% to 60%. Literacy rate in second language: 75% to 100%. Roman script with diacritics used. Pastoralists: reindeer; fishermen, hunters. Christian. Bible portions 1878-1988.

SWEDISH [SWD] 296,000 in Finland, 5.7% of the population (1997). Coasts of the provinces of Central Ostrobothnia, Ostrobothnia (Vasa), Southwest Finland, Uusimaa (Helsinki), Aland Islands, Kymenlaakso. Indo-European, Germanic, North, East Scandinavian, Danish-Swedish, Swedish. Dialects: STANDARD SWEDISH, OSROBOTHNIAN, ALAND ISLANDS SWEDISH, SOUTHWEST FINLAND SWEDISH, UUSIMAA SWEDISH. Swedish Finns have a distinctive pronunciation compared to the dialect in Sweden, but no apparent difficulty in intelligibility. Some Ostrobothnian dialects are intelligible to others with difficulty. Perhaps 3/4 of speakers are fluent in Finnish, 1/4 are totally bilingual. National language. Bible 1541-1999. See main entry under Sweden.

FRANCE

French Republic, République Francaise. National or official language: French. 58,683,000 (1998 UN). Literacy rate 99% (1991 WA). Also includes Adyghe, Algerian Spoken Arabic 660,000, Judeo-Moroccan Arabic, Judeo-Tunisian Arabic, Moroccan Spoken Arabic 492,700, Tunisian Spoken Arabic 212,900, Armenian 70,000, Assyrian Neo-Aramaic, Brao 5, Western Cham 1,000, Chru 1, Western Farsi 40,000, Standard German, Hmong Daw 10,000, Iu Mien 700, Kabuverdianu 8,000, Kabyle 537,000, Central

Khmer 50,000, Khmu 500, Kirmanjki, Kurmanji, Laz, Lesser Antillean Creole French 150,000, Mandjak, Nhang 100, Tachelhit, Tai Dam 1,000, Tai Don, Tai Nüa, Central Atlas Tamazight 150,000, Tarifit, Tay, Turkish 135,000, Vietnamese 10,000, Wolof 34,500, Yeniche, Western Yiddish. Information mainly from M. Stephens 1976; P. Blanchet 1986; B. Comrie 1987. Christian, secular, Muslim, Jewish. Blind population 43,000 (1982 WCE). Deaf population 3,506,839. Deaf institutions: 99. Data accuracy estimate: A2, B. The number of languages listed for France is 32. Of those, 29 are living languages, 1 is a second language without mother tongue speakers, and 2 are extinct. Diversity index 0.24.

ALEMANNISCH ***(ALEMANNIC)*** [GSW] 1,500,000 in France (J. A. Hawkins in B. Comrie 1988). Northeastern France, Alsace-Lorraine. Indo-European, Germanic, West, High German, German, Upper German, Alemannic. Dialect: ALSATIAN (ALSACIEN, ELSAESSISCH). No standard form of Alsatian, but a variety of village dialects. All speakers do not necessarily understand or read Standard German, but most are bilingual in French. Bilingualism in Standard French varies from 79% to 90% of the population in the different regions. Standard German is taught in some primary schools, and used in local newspapers. Called 'Schwyzerdütsch' in Switzerland and 'Alemannisch' in Austria and parts of Germany. Christian. NT 1984. See main entry under Switzerland.

AUVERGNAT ***(AUVERNHAS, AUVERNE, OCCITAN)*** [AUV] Auvergne; Haut-Auvergnat in Cantal and south of Haute-Loire; Bas-Auvergnat in the north of Haute-Loire and in Puy-de-Dome. Indo-European, Italic, Romance, Italo-Western, Western, Gallo-Iberian, Ibero-Romance, Oc. Dialects: HAUT-AUVERGNAT, BAS-AUVERGNAT. Highly fragmented dialect situation, with limited intelligibility between northern and southern varieties. Bilingualism in French. More vigorous use in the south. Attitudes are strong and differ about how different the Oc varieties are from each other. Investigation needed: intelligibility with northern and southern varieties. Bible portions 1831.

BASQUE, NAVARRO-LABOURDIN ***(NAVARRO-LABOURDIN)*** [BQE] 67,500 speakers (1991), including 45,000 Labourdin, 22,500 Lower Navarro. Total Basque speakers in France estimated at 80,000 (1991 L. Trask, U. of Sussex). Reported to be 730,000 ethnic Basque in France (1993 Johnstone). French-Spanish border, 800 square miles surrounding Bayonne, Labourd (Lapurdi), and Basse-Navarre departments. Basque. Dialects: LABOURDIN (LAPURDIERA), EASTERN LOW NAVARRESE (BENAFFARERA, BAJO NAVARRO ORIENTAL), WESTERN LOW NAVARRESE (BAJO NAVARRO OCCIDENTAL). Navarro-Labourdin is diverse from other Basque dialects, and needs separate literature. Bilingualism in French. Dictionary. Grammar. Christian. Bible 1856.

BASQUE, SOULETIN ***(SOULETIN, SOULETINO, SULETINO, XIBEROERA, ZUBEROERA, SUBEROAN)*** [BSZ] 8,700 (1991). French-Spanish border, 800 square miles surrounding Bayonne, Soule, Pyrénées Atlantiques Province. Basque. Souletin is more diverse and speakers have difficulty understanding other varieties, especially for complex and abstract discourse. Separate literature desired and needed. Dictionary. Grammar. Christian. Bible portions 1856-1888.

BRETON ***(BREZHONEG)*** [BRT] 500,000 speakers for whom it is the daily language in France (1989 ICDBL). 1,200,000 know Breton who do not regularly use it. Population total both countries 500,000 or more. Western Brittany, and dispersed in Eastern Brittany and Breton emigrant communities throughout the world. Also spoken in USA. Indo-European, Celtic, Insular, Brythonic. Dialects: LEONAIS, TREGORROIS, VANNETAIS, CORNOUAILLAIS. Some claim to be monolingual in Breton. 18,000 speakers are children under 14 years; 56,250 between 15 and 24; 423,000 between 25 and 64; 168,000 over 65 (1974). No official status. Strong nationalistic movement demanding recognition, a place in the schools, media, and public life. VSO; prepositions; genitives, adjectives, relatives after noun heads; articles, numerals before noun heads; question word initial; probably 2 prefixes, 2 or 3 suffixes on a word; topic or focus first, verb second; verb affixes mark person, number of subject; passives; causatives and comparatives shown lexically; up to 3 consonants syllable initially, and 3 finally, one vowel; nontonal. Literacy rate in first language: 25% can read and write Breton. Radio programs, TV. Bible 1866-1985.

CALÓ ***(GITANO, IBERIAN ROMANI)*** [RMR] 10,000 to 20,000 in France. Southern France. Indo-European, Italic, Romance, Italo-Western, Western, Gallo-Iberian, Ibero-Romance, West Iberian, Castilian. Dialects: BASQUE CALO, CATALONIAN CALO, SPANISH CALO. Related to Spanish. Bilingualism in Spanish, Portuguese. Christian. Bible portions 1837-1872. See main entry under Spain.

CATALAN-VALENCIAN-BALEAR [CLN] 100,000 in France (1996). Catalonian France. Indo-European, Italic, Romance, Italo-Western, Western, Gallo-Iberian, Ibero-Romance, East Iberian. Population given above may be the ethnic group, not mother tongue speakers. Bible 1478-1993. See main entry under Spain.

CORSICAN ***(CORSU, CORSO, CORSE, CORSI)*** [COI] 281,000 in Corsica (1993 Johnstone). Population total all countries 341,000 or more (1976). Corsica, Paris, Marseilles. Also spoken in Bolivia, Canada, Cuba, Italy, Puerto Rico, Uruguay, USA, Venezuela. Indo-European, Italic, Romance, Southern, Corsican. Dialects: SARTENAIS, VICO-AJACCIO, NORTHERN CORSICAN (CAPE CORS, BASTIA),

VENACO. Corsican is in the Tuscan group of Italian varieties. Southern Corsican is closer to northern Sardinian or Gallurese than other Corsican dialects (R. A. Hall, Jr.). Dialects of Bastia, Venaco, Vico, and Sartene have 79% to 89% lexical similarity. Bonifacio on the southern tip of the island has 78% lexical similarity (highest) with Bastia at extreme north. Ajaccio dialect is central and prestigious. Speakers are bilingual in French but many are not fluent in it. There is a movement for bilingual education. Corsican has been recognized as a separate language by the French government. Not endangered. Bible portions 1861-1994.

DUTCH [DUT] 80,000 in Westhoek. Westhoek in the northeast corner of France between the Artois Hills and the Belgium border. Indo-European, Germanic, West, Low Saxon-Low Franconian, Low Franconian. Not used in schools. Usage is reported to be diminishing. Bible 1522-1988. See main entry under Netherlands.

ESPERANTO *(LA LINGVO INTERNACIA)* [ESP] 200 to 2,000 people who speak it as first language (1996); 2,000,000 users (1999 WA). Speakers in about 115 countries, used most widely in central and eastern Europe, China and other countries in eastern Asia, certain areas of South America and southwest Asia. Artificial language. All ages. Was developed from 1872 to 1885 by L. L. Zamenhof of Warsaw Poland for intercommunication by mother tongue speakers of other languages. SVO; prepositions; genitives, relatives after noun heads, articles, adjectives, numerals before noun heads; question word initial; accusative *-n*, dative *-al*; affixes mark tense; passive with *esti* = passive participle, causative *-ig*; comparative word, nontonal. Christian, Baha'i, Jewish, Muslim, Hindu, Sikh, Buddhist, Shinto, Taoist, tribal religions, none. Bible 1900-1910.

FRANCO-PROVENÇAL *(PATOIS)* [FRA] Population total all countries 77,000 or more. Savoie, southeastern France, near the Italian and Switzerland borders. Also spoken in Italy, Switzerland. Indo-European, Italic, Romance, Italo-Western, Western, Gallo-Iberian, Gallo-Romance, Gallo-Rhaetian, Oïl, Southeastern. Dialects: DAUPHINOIS, LYONNAIS, NEUCATELAIS, SAVOYARD. Structurally separate language from Provençal, French, Piemontese, and Lombard (F. B. Agard). Bilingualism in French. Bible portions 1830.

FRENCH *(FRANÇAIS)* [FRN] 51,000,000 first language speakers in France. Population total all countries 77,000,000 first language speakers (1999 WA), 128,000,000 including second language speakers (1999 WA). Also spoken in 53 other countries including Algeria, Andorra, Austria, Belgium, Benin, Burkina Faso, Burundi, Cameroon, Canada, CAR, Chad, Comoros Islands, Congo, Côte d'Ivoire, DRC, Djibouti, French Guiana, French Polynesia, Gabon. Indo-European, Italic, Romance, Italo-Western, Western, Gallo-Iberian, Gallo-Romance, Gallo-Rhaetian, Oïl, French. Dialects: STANDARD FRENCH, NORMAN (NORMAND), PICARD (ROUCHI, CHTIMI), WALLON (WALLOON), ANGEVIN, BERRICHON, BOURBONNAIS, BOURGUIGNON, FRANC-COMTOIS, GALLO, LORRAINE, POITEVIN, SANTONGEAIS. 89% lexical similarity with Italian, 80% with Sardinian, 78% with Rheto-Romance, 75% with Portuguese, Romanian, and Spanish, 29% with German, 27% with English. Investigation needed: intelligibility with Walloon, Picard Jèrrais. National language. Dictionary. Grammar. SVO. Deciduous forest. Intensive agriculturalists, industry, business. 80 meters. Christian. Bible 1530-1995.

FRENCH SIGN LANGUAGE *(LANGUE DES SIGNES FRANÇAISE, LSF, FSL)* [FSL] 50,000 to 100,000 primary users in France (1986 Gallaudet Univ.) 1,000 users of Marseille Sign Language (1975 Sallagooty). Population total both countries 50,000 to 100,000. Southern FSL is used in Marseille, Toulon, La Ciotat, and Salon de Provence. Also spoken in Togo. Deaf sign language. Dialect: MARSEILLE SIGN LANGUAGE (SOUTHERN FRENCH SIGN LANGUAGE). Many sign languages have been influenced by this, but are not necessarily intelligible with it. Reported to be partially intelligible with sign languages from Austria, Czech Republic, and Italy, at least. 43% lexical similarity with ASL in an 872-word list. First sign language in the western world to gain recognition as a language (1830). Originated in 1752. Sign languages were known in France in the 16th century, and probably earlier. Different from Signed French and Old French Sign Language.

GASCON *(OCCITAN)* [GSC] 250,000 speakers in France (1990 P. Blanchet), The population in the Béarn region of southern Gasconha, France is 400,000 (1982); 51% speak Gascon, 70% understand it, 85% are in favor of saving it. Population total both countries 254,800. Gascogne Province, from Médoc to the Pyrénées, from the Atlantic to the Catalan area. Béarnese is spoken by a strong majority in the Béarn. Also spoken in Spain. Indo-European, Italic, Romance, Italo-Western, Western, Gallo-Iberian, Ibero-Romance, Oc. Dialects: LANDAIS, BÉARNAIS (BIARNESE), ARIÉGEOIS, ARANESE. Gascon, Languedocien, and Limousin are structurally separate languages (F. B. Agard). Gascon speakers have some intelligibility of Provençal; some or limited intelligibility of Languedocien (reports differ). Inherently intelligible with Aranese Gascon in Spain, which is a dialect. Literacy rate in first language: Much lower than in Spain. Bible portions 1583-1983.

GREEK [GRK] Corsica. Indo-European, Greek, Attic. Dialect: CARGESE. The Greek of Italy and that of Corsica are probably separate languages (R. Zamponi 1992). The last native speaker died about 1982 (Nick Nicalas 1997). The ethnic group speaks French. Bible 1840-1994. See main entry under Greece.

INTERLINGUA ***(INTERLINGUA DE IALA)*** [INR] Artificial language. A latinate language devised by Alexander Gode around 1950, and published by the International Auxiliary Language Association (IALA). Second language only.

ITALIAN [ITN] 1,000,000 in France (1977 Voegelin and Voegelin). Indo-European, Italic, Romance, Italo-Western, Italo-Dalmatian. Few, if any, speakers of Italian dialects in France do not know French. Bible 1471-1985. See main entry under Italy.

LANGUEDOCIEN ***(LENGADOUCIAN, LANGUEDOC, LANGADOC, OCCITAN, OCCITANI)*** [LNC] Fluent speakers are 10% of the population in the region. About 20% more have some knowledge of it. Languedoc Province, from Montpellier to Toulouse, Bordeaux, Rodez, and Albi. Indo-European, Italic, Romance, Italo-Western, Western, Gallo-Iberian, Ibero-Romance, Oc. Dialects: BAS-LANGUEDOCIEN, LANGUEDOCIEN MOYEN, HAUT-LANGUEDOCIEN, GUYENNAIS. A separate language from Provençal (P. Blanchet 1990). Gascon speakers have limited intelligibility of Languedocien. Everyone speaks French as first or second language. To family and close friends. Mainly spoken in rural communities by people over 50. Attempts to standardize Languedocien for all languages of southern France have not been accepted by speakers of those languages. Attitudes are strong and differ about how different the Oc varieties are from each other. Languedocien resembles most the literary variety of Middle Occitan used in the Troubadours of the Middle Ages. Literacy rate in second language: 99%. Toulouse orthography is different from Ron. Poetry, newspapers. Bible portions 1888.

LIGURIAN ***(LIGURE)*** [LIJ] Bonifacio, Corsica, and between the Italian border and Monaco. Indo-European, Italic, Romance, Italo-Western, Western, Gallo-Iberian, Gallo-Romance, Gallo-Italian. Dialect: GENOESE (GENOAN, GENOVESE). Bible portions 1860. See main entry under Italy.

LIMOUSIN ***(LEMOSIN, OCCITAN)*** [LMS] Spoken by 10% to 20% of the population of the region. Limousin Province. Haut-Limousin around Limoges, Guéret, and Nontron in Charente; Bas-Limousin around Correze and Périgord. Indo-European, Italic, Romance, Italo-Western, Western, Gallo-Iberian, Ibero-Romance, Oc. Dialects: HAUT-LIMOUSIN, BAS-LIMOUSIN. Limousin, Languedocien, and Gascon are structurally separate languages (F. B. Agard). Partially intelligible to Provençal. In the north of the province people use a transition dialect with certain Oïl (north French) features. People speak French as first or second language. Few children speakers. Attitudes are strong and differ about how different the Oc varieties are from each other.

LUXEMBOURGEOIS ***(FRANKISH, PLATT)*** [LUX] Spoken along the border with Germany and Luxemburg in the Moselle Department, Thionville, France. Indo-European, Germanic, West, High German, German, Middle German, Moselle Franconian. As distinct from Standard German as is Dutch (Stephens 1976), and not inherently intelligible with it. The common language of French and German coal miners. See main entry under Luxembourg.

LYONS SIGN LANGUAGE [LSG] Deaf sign language. 250 miles from Paris, but difficult and little intelligibility with French Sign Language.

PICARD ***(ROUCHI, CHTIMI)*** [PCD] Most of the Region de Picardie (Amiens, Abbeville, Beauvais, St. Quentin), the Region Nord-Pas-de-Calais (Lille, Douai, Cambrai, Arras, Valenciennes, Boulogne sur Mer, Calais), except the Dunkerque District, and a little eastern zone (border with Picardie of the Region de Haute Normandie near Dieppe). Also spoken in Belgium. Indo-European, Italic, Romance, Italo-Western, Western, Gallo-Iberian, Gallo-Romance, Gallo-Rhaetian, Oïl, French. Dialects: PONTHIEU, VIMEU, HAINAUT, ARTOIS, LILLOIS, BOULONNAIS, SANTERRE, CALAISIS, CAMBRESIS, VERMANDOIS, AMIENOIS. All dialects, including those in Belgium are inherently intelligible to speakers. French is spoken at school, in court, for administration, with outsiders. Home, family, friends, in local stores. The Belgian government recognizes Picard officially as an indigenous regional language. The European Bureau for Lesser Used Languages considers it as a language. Some reports used and edited by the French government consider it a separate language from French. No standardized writing system. Poetry.

PORTUGUESE [POR] 750,000 in France (1989 National Geographic). Indo-European, Italic, Romance, Italo-Western, Western, Gallo-Iberian, Ibero-Romance, West Iberian, Portuguese-Galician. Literacy rate in second language: Relatively low. Bible 1751, in press (1993). See main entry under Portugal.

PROVENÇAL ***(PROUVENÇAU, MISTRALIEN)*** [PRV] 250,000 fluent speakers in France, 800,000 with some knowledge (1990 P. Blanchet). Population total all countries 354,500. Southeastern France, province of Provence, south of Dauphiné, region of Nimes in Languedoc. Also spoken in Italy, Monaco. Indo-European, Italic, Romance, Italo-Western, Western, Gallo-Iberian, Ibero-Romance, Oc. Dialects: TRANSALPIN, NIÇARD (NIÇOIS), MARITIME PROVENÇAL (MARSEILLAIS, TOULONNAIS, VAROIS), GAVOT (ALPIN, VALEIEN, GAPIAN, FORCALQUIEREN), RHODANIEN (NIMOIS), DAUPHINOIS (DROMOIS). Gascon, Languedocien, and Limousin are structurally separate languages (F. Agard). Provençal and Languedocien (Occitan) are separate languages (P. Blanchet 1990). No Provençal variety is universally accepted as the standard literary form. Niçard and Northern Gavot (Valeien and Gapian) are more difficult for other dialect speakers to understand. Through increased contact in army and school, most speakers are actively bilingual in French. Literary French is sometimes difficult for speakers with less school education. Regional French has a lot of Provençal influence. Most speakers are over 50 years old. There is regional pride and increasing status as a literary language. Strong demand for teaching in school and books in Provençal. Attitudes are strong and differ about how different the Oc varieties are from each other. The Nobel Prize laureate Frederic Mistal wrote in Provençal. Two orthographies in use: Ron and Toulousse. Bible portions 1824-1975.

ROMANI, BALKAN [RMN] 10,500 in France, including 10,000 Arlija, 500 Dzambazi. Indo-European, Indo-Iranian, Indo-Aryan, Central zone, Romani, Balkan. Dialects: ARLIJA, DZAMBAZI. Muslim. Bible portions 1912-1937. See main entry under Yugoslavia.

ROMANI, SINTE ***(SINTI, ROMMANES, TSIGANE)*** [RMO] 10,000 to 30,000 in France. Indo-European, Indo-Iranian, Indo-Aryan, Central zone, Romani, Northern. Dialect: MANOUCHE (MANUCHE, MANUSH). Not intelligible with Vlach Romani. Ethnic group: Sasítka Romá. Christian. Bible portions 1875-1995. See main entry under Yugoslavia.

ROMANI, VLAX ***(ROMENES, ROM, TSIGANE, VLAX)*** [RMY] 10,000 in France, including 8,000 Kalderash, 2,000 Lovari. Indo-European, Indo-Iranian, Indo-Aryan, Central zone, Romani, Vlax. Dialects: KALDERASH, LOVARI. Vlax and Kalderash are understood by the Lovari. Christian. NT 1984-1995. See main entry under Romania.

SHUADIT ***(SHUADI, JUDEO-PROVENÇAL, JUDEO-COMTADINE)*** [SDT] Department of Vaucluse in southern France, and city of Avignon. Indo-European, Italic, Romance, Italo-Western, Western, Gallo-Iberian, Ibero-Romance, Oc. It became extinct in 1977. May still be used in Passover song. Jewish. Extinct.

SPANISH ***(CASTILLIAN)*** [SPN] Indo-European, Italic, Romance, Italo-Western, Western, Gallo-Iberian, Ibero-Romance, West Iberian, Castilian. Bible 1553-1979. See main entry under Spain.

VLAAMS ***(FLAMAND, FLEMISH, VLAEMSCH)*** [VLA] 10,000 in France (1984 Menheere, 1993 Evenhuis). Westhoek (French Flanders). Indo-European, Germanic, West, Low Saxon-Low Franconian, Low Franconian. Dialect: FRANS VLAAMS (VLAEMSCH). Close to Dutch, English, Frisian. Dutch is not understood in France, but Vlaams dialects in Belgium and the Netherlands are understood. Bilingualism in French, some English. Used for informal situations. Speakers are over 50 years old. Speakers view Dutch as a completely different, friendly language. Speakers in France are called 'Vlamingen', the language called 'Vlaemsch'. Speakers sometimes refer to Dutch as 'Vlaams'. Dictionary. SOV. Different orthographies used in the 3 countries. Christian. See main entry under Belgium.

ZARPHATIC ***(JUDEO-FRENCH)*** [ZRP] Indo-European, Italic, Romance, Italo-Western, Western, Gallo-Iberian, Gallo-Romance, Gallo-Rhaetian, Oïl, French. Jewish. Extinct.

GERMANY

Federal Republic of Germany, Bundesrepublik Deutschland. National or official language: Standard German. 82,133,000 (1998 UN) including 5,241,801 without German citizenship (1990 official figures). Literacy rate 99%. Also includes Abaza 80, Adyghe 2,000, Tosk Albanian 25,000, Algerian Spoken Arabic 26,000, Moroccan Spoken Arabic 44,200, Tunisian Spoken Arabic 26,000, Assyrian Neo-Aramaic, Behdini, Catalan-Valencian-Balear, Chaldean Neo-Aramaic 3,000, Chechen, Dimli, Dutch 101,000, English 110,000, Western Farsi 90,000, Western Frisian, Greek 314,000, Hausa, Hebrew, Hindi 24,500, Italian 548,000, Japanese 20,000, Jutish, Kabuverdianu 3,000, Kalmyk-Oirat, Kazakh, Kirmanjki, Korean 14,000, Kurmanji 480,000, Latvian 8,000, Laz 1,000, Osetin, Portuguese 78,000, Russian 360,000, Serbo-Croatian 652,000, Spanish 134,000, Tamil 35,000, Turkish 2,107,426, Turkmen, Turoyo 20,000, Urdu 23,000, Uyghur, Vietnamese 60,000, Chinese 40,000, people from Afghanistan 29,000, possibly Northern Uzbek. Information mainly from M. Stephens 1976; B. Comrie 1987; S. Barbour and P. Stevenson 1990. Christian, secular, Muslim. Blind population 82,000 in western Germany, including 51,000 blind, 31,000 severely visually handicapped (1989 SB). Deaf population 50,000 to 8,000,000 (1986 Gallaudet University). Deaf institutions: 141. Data accuracy estimate: B. The number of languages listed for Germany is 27. Of those, 25 are living languages and 2 are extinct. Diversity index 0.18.

ALEMANNISCH ***(ALEMANNIC)*** [GSW] Southwestern, southern Baden-Wuerttemberg. Indo-European, Germanic, West, High German, German, Upper German, Allemanic. Dialects: LOW ALEMANNISCH, HIGH ALEMANNISCH. Varieties in Germany include Low and High Alemannisch. Approximately 40% inherent intelligibility with Standard German. Close to 'Schwyzerdütsch' in Switzerland. 'Alsatian' in northeastern France. Similar to Swabian. Speakers are bilingual in Standard German. NT 1984. See main entry under Switzerland.

BAVARIAN ***(BAIRISCH, BAYERISCH, BAVARIAN AUSTRIAN)*** [BAR] North Bavarian is north of Regensburg, to Nuremburg and Western Bohemia, Czech Republic; Central Bavarian is in the Alps and Lower Austria and Salzburg; South Bavarian is in the Bavarian Alps, Tyrol, Styria, including the Heanzian dialect of Burgenland, Carinthia, northern Italy, and part of Gottschee in Slovenia. Indo-European, Germanic, West, High German, German, Upper German, Bavarian-Austrian. Dialects: CENTRAL BAVARIAN, NORTH BAVARIAN, SOUTH BAVARIAN. Bilingualism in Standard German, Czech. School is taught in Standard German. Bible 1998. See main entry under Austria.

DANISH ***(DÄNISCH, DANSK)*** [DNS] 50,000 in Germany (1976 Stephens). South Schleswig. Indo-European, Germanic, North, East Scandinavian, Danish-Swedish, Danish-Bokmal, Danish. There are Danish schools. Bible 1550, in press (1993). See main entry under Denmark.

FRANKISH ***(FRÄNKISCH, OLD FRANKISH)*** [FRK] Indo-European, Germanic, West, High German, German. Different from present day German language varieties. Extinct. Bible portions 1758-1827.

FRISIAN, EASTERN ***(OSTFRIESISCH, SATERLANDIC FRISIAN, SEELTERSK FRISIAN)*** [FRS] 11,000 (1976 Stephens). Language of the home for 1,500 to 2,000 (1977 SIL). Population total both countries 11,000 or more. Schleswig-Holstein, Ostfriesland, the area around the towns of Emden and Oldenburg in Lower Saxony, and Saterland, Jeverland, and Butjadingen in 1976. Reported to be used only in Saterland, Eastern Frisia in 1998. Also spoken in USA. Indo-European, Germanic, West, Frisian. Not intelligible with Western Frisian of the Netherlands or Northern Frisian (E. Matteson SIL 1978). 77% lexical similarity with Standard German, 74% with Western Frisian. Speakers are mainly the older generation. Investigation needed: bilingual proficiency, attitudes.

FRISIAN, NORTHERN ***(NORDFRIESISCH)*** [FRR] 10,000 speakers out of 60,000 population (1976 Stephens). Language of the home for 10,000 (1977 SIL). Schleswig-Holstein, on the coastal strip between the rivers Eider in the south and Wiedau in the north, and adjacent islands of Föhr, Amrum, Sylt, Norstrand, Pellworm, the ten islands of the Halligen group, and Helgoland. Indo-European, Germanic, West, Frisian. Dialects: MOORINGER (MOORINGA, MAINLAND FRISIAN), FERRING (FOHR-AMRUM), SÖLRENG (SYLT), HELGOLAND. The first 3 dialects listed are different enough that more than one set of literature would be needed. Ferring dialect is actively used. Not intelligible to Eastern Frisian of Germany or Western Frisian of the Netherlands except to a few educated bilingual speakers of West Frisian. Mooringer has 70% lexical similarity with Standard German, 55% with English, 66% with Eastern Frisian; Föhr has 69% with Standard German, 62% with English, 68% with Western Frisian, 73% with Eastern Frisian, 86% with Mooringer, 91% with Amrum; Sylt has 64% with Standard German, 61% with English, 79% with Mooringer, 85% with Föhr. Standard German, Low Saxon, and some English are used as second languages, but fluency is limited. Few children speakers. The Sölreng dialect is nearly extinct. There is ethnic pride, efforts to revive Frisian literature and bilingual education. Education is in Standard German only. Business and church services in German. Investigation needed: intelligibility with 3 dialects, bilingual proficiency in German, Low Saxon. Grammar. Literacy rate in first language: Few read Frisian. Bible portions 1954.

GERMAN SIGN LANGUAGE ***(DEUTSCHE GEBÄRDENSPRACHE, DGS)*** [GSG] (50,000 deaf persons; 22,000 members of German Deaf Association; 1986 Gallaudet Univ.). Western Germany. Deaf sign language. Many regional lexical variations, but dialects are easily inherently intelligible. Some similarity to French and other European sign languages. Relation to sign languages of eastern Germany, Austria, and Switzerland is not known. More than one sign language used in eastern Germany. Bible portions 1998.

GERMAN, STANDARD ***(DEUTSCH, HOCHDEUTSCH, HIGH GERMAN)*** [GER] 75,300,000 in Germany (1990). Population total all countries 100,000,000 first language speakers (1999 WA); 128,000,000 including second language speakers (1999 WA). Also spoken in 40 other countries including Argentina, Australia, Austria, Belgium, Bolivia, Bosnia-Herzegovina, Brazil, Canada, Chile, Czech Republic, Denmark, Ecuador, Estonia, Finland, France, Hungary, Italy, Kazakhstan, Kyrgyzstan. Indo-European, Germanic, West, High German, German, Middle German, East Middle German. Dialect: ERZGEBIRGISCH. Major related language areas are Bavarian, Schwäbisch, Allemannisch, Mainfränkisch, Hessisch, Palatinian, Rheinfränkisch, Westfälisch, Saxonian, Thuringian, Brandenburgisch, and Low Saxon. Many varieties are not inherently intelligible with each other. Our present treatment in this edition is incomplete. Standard German is one High German variety, which developed from the chancery of Saxony, gaining acceptance as the written standard in the 16th and 17th centuries. High German refers to dialects and languages in the upper Rhine region. 60% lexical similarity with English, 29% with French. National language. Dictionary. Grammar. Poetry, newspapers, radio programs, films, TV, videos. Christian. Bible 1466-1982.

KÖLSCH [KOR] 250,000 (1997 Holger Jakobs). Cologne (Köln) and surrounding areas. Indo-European, Germanic, West, High German, German, Middle German, West Middle German, Ripuarian Franconian. Nearly all use Standard German as second language. Used in theaters, literature, and an academy for teaching it. All ages. Literacy rate in second language: 99%. Christian. Bible portions 1992.

LUXEMBOURGEOIS ***(LUXEMBURGIAN, LETZBURGISCH, LËTZEBUERGESCH, MOSELLE FRANCONIAN)*** [LUX] A few. Bitburg area in western Germany. Indo-European, Germanic, West, High German, German, Middle German, West Middle German, Moselle Franconian. See main entry under Luxembourg.

MAINFRÄNKISCH ***(FRANCONIAN)*** [VMF] Spoken mostly along the River Main, including the city of Mainz, thus not far west of Frankfurt. Indo-European, Germanic, West, High German, German, Middle German, West Middle German, Moselle Franconian. Approximately 40% inherently intelligible with Standard German. Bilingualism in Standard German.

PFAELZISCH ***(PFÄLZISCHE, PFÄLZISCH)*** [PFL] Southwest Palatinate, Rheinpfalz. Indo-European, Germanic, West, High German, German, Middle German, West Middle German, Rhenisch Fraconian. Various dialects. Bilingualism in Standard German. There is literature published in the language. Dictionary.

PLAUTDIETSCH [GRN] 90,000 possibly (1996 Reuben Epp). Indo-European, Germanic, West, Low Saxon-Low Franconian, Low Saxon. NT 1987. See main entry under Canada.

POLABIAN [POX] North of the Wend language area. Indo-European, Slavic, West, Lechitic. Extinct.

POLISH ***(POLSKI, POLNISCH)*** [PQL] 241,000 in Germany. Indo-European, Slavic, West, Lechitic. Christian. Bible 1561-1965. See main entry under Poland.

ROMANI, BALKAN [RMN] 3,500 in Germany including 2,000 Arlija and 1,500 Dzambazi. Indo-European, Indo-Iranian, Indo-Aryan, Central zone, Romani, Balkan. Dialects: ARLIJA (ERLI), DZAMBAZI. The Arlija dialect is understood by Dzambazi speakers. Muslim. Bible portions 1912-1937. See main entry under Yugoslavia.

ROMANI, SINTE ***(ROMMANES, ZIGUENER, SINTÍ, SINTE)*** [RMO] 30,500 in Germany (1990 D. Holzinger). Hamburg and colonies in the south. Indo-European, Indo-Iranian, Indo-Aryan, Central zone, Romani, Northern. Dialects: GADSCHKENE, ESTRACHARIA, KRANTIKI, KRANARIA, EFTAWAGARIA, PRAISTIKI. All dialects in Germany are inherently intelligible, but possibly not with Yugoslavian dialects. Not intelligible with Vlach Romani. Most use Sinte. The Gadschkene are those whose ancestors came from north Germany. Semi-nomadic. Christian. Bible portions 1875-1995. See main entry under Yugoslavia.

ROMANI, VLAX [RMY] 5,000 to 6,500 in Germany including 2,500 Lovari, 2,500 to 4,000 Kalderash. Indo-European, Indo-Iranian, Indo-Aryan, Central zone, Romani, Vlax. Dialects: LOVARI, KALDERASH. Christian. NT 1984-1995. See main entry under Romania.

SAXON, LOW ***(NEDDERSASSISCH, NIEDERSAECHSISCH, NEDERSAKSISCH, LOW GERMAN, PLATTDNNTSCH, NEDDERDNNTSCH)*** [SXN] An estimated 10,000,000 understand it in Germany, but much fewer are native speakers (1996 Reinhard F. Hahn). Northern Germany. The dialects listed are northwest, southwest, south central, northeast, and southeast, respectively. Lower Rhine region below a line from Aachen to Witenberg. Indo-European, Germanic, West, Low Saxon-Low Franconian, Low Saxon. Dialects: NORTHERN LOW SAXON, EASTPHALIAN (OSTFAELISCH, OSTFÄLISCH), MECKLENBURG-ANTERIOR POMERANIA (MECKLENBURGISCH-VORPOMMERSCH), MARK-BRANDENBURG (MAERKISCH-BRANDENBURGISCH, MÄRKISCH-BRANDENBURGISCH). The dialects listed are in Germany. The first three dialects listed are Western Low Saxon, the other two are Eastern Low Saxon. Not intelligible to speakers of Standard German. A direct descendant of Old Saxon, related to English. 20 to 30 dialects with differing inherent intelligibility, depending on geographic distance. They did not experience the second consonantal shift of the 8th and 9th centuries (J. Thiessen, U. of Winnipeg 1976). Its modern forms have been largely suppressed until recently, and have received much German, Dutch, or Frisian influence, depending on the area. Pomerano is used in Latin America. Westphaelian and Plautdietsch also have separate entries. Most speakers in Germany are bilingual in Standard German. Officially recognized as a regional (separate) language in 8 states of Germany and in the northeastern provinces of the Netherlands. Recognized as a regional (separate) language by the European Charta on Languages. Printed fairly widely outside Europe, particularly in North and Latin America, Australia, Southern Africa, Eastern Europe (Siberia, Kazakhstan). Dictionary. Bible 1478-1534.

SAXON, UPPER [SXU] 2,000,000 or more (1998 Andreas Thomsen). Eastern Germany, southeast, Sachsen with Dresden, Leipzig, Chemnitz, Halle in Sachsen-Anhalt. Indo-European, Germanic, West, High German, German, Middle German, East Middle German. Bilingualism in Standard German. Spoken by 'several millions'.

SILESIAN, LOWER ***(LOWER SCHLESISCH)*** [SLI] Gorlitz, eastern Germany. Indo-European, Germanic, West, High German, German, Middle German, East Middle German. Bilingualism in Standard German. Spoken by younger people. There is literature by Gerhard Hauptmann. Different from Upper Silesian, a dialect of Polish. See main entry under Poland.

SORBIAN, LOWER *(NIEDERSORBISCH, BAS SORABE, WENDISH, LUSATIAN, LOWER LUSATIAN, DOLNOSERBSKI, DELNOSERBSKI)* [WEE] 14,000 or fewer speakers (1991 Elle) out of a larger ethnic group. Niederlausitz (Dolna Luzica) in eastern Germany, Cottbus (Chosebuz) the main town. The ethnic group has over 60 towns and villages. Indo-European, Slavic, West, Sorbian. Almost exclusively older generation. Their own name for the language is 'Dolnoserbski'. High school, Sorbian language school. Newspapers. Bible 1796-1824.

SORBIAN, UPPER *(OBERSORBISCH, HAUT SORABE, UPPER LUSATIAN, WENDISH, HORNJOSERBSKI, HORNOSERBSKI)* [WEN] 55,000 (1991 Elle). 15,000 are reported to be primary users. 40,000 to 45,000 others have some knowledge of it (1996). Upper Saxony, eastern Germany, principal towns Bautzen (Budysin, Catholic) and Kamenz (Protestant). Perhaps a few in Texas, USA. Indo-European, Slavic, West, Sorbian. Dialects: BAUTZEN, KAMENZ. Nearly all are bilingual in German. Mainly older speakers. Most of the monolinguals are the very young (Stephens 1976). Zgusta (1974) says Upper Sorbian and Lower Sorbian are two standard languages. Use of Sorbian is authorized in local government and schools. Increasing literature production. Now accepted as a minority language. Newspapers, radio programs, TV. Bible 1728-1797.

SWABIAN *(SCHWÄBISCH, SUABIAN, SCHWAEBISCH)* [SWG] Southwest, Wuerttemberg, the eastern part of Baden-Wuerttemberg, Schwaben, western Bavaria. Indo-European, Germanic, West, High German, German, Upper German, Alemannic. A variety of Highest Alemannisch. More distinct than Bavarian from Standard German. 40% inherently intelligible with Standard German (estimate). Swabian of the Black Forest is different from Swabian in the Alb (H. Kloss 1978). Bilingualism in Standard German. Dictionary. Bible portions.

WESTPHALIEN *(WESTFAELISCH, WESTFÄLISCH)* [WEP] Northwestern, Westphalia. Indo-European, Germanic, West, Low Saxon-Low Franconian, Low Saxon. Bilingualism in Standard German. See also Low Saxon entry.

YENICHE *(JENISCH, YENISHE, GERMAN TRAVELLERS)* [YEC] Also spoken in Austria, France, Netherlands, Switzerland. Mixed Language, German-Yiddish-Romani-Rotwelsch. German with a heavy cryptolectal lexical influsion from Rotwelsch, Yiddish, Romani, and Hebrew. The first language of some (The Carrier Pidgin 1977). A blend language of certain urban nomadic groups. Not Gypsies. Possibly arose as a result of those who were dispossessed because of the Hanseatic laws (I. Hancock). They are a distinct ethnic group.

YIDDISH, WESTERN *(YIDDISH, YIDISH, JUDEO-GERMAN)* [YIH] Southwestern dialect in southern Germany, Switzerland, and Alsace France, Midwestern dialect in central Germany and parts of the former Czechoslovakia, Northwestern dialect is northern Germany and the Netherlands. Also spoken in France, Hungary, Netherlands, Switzerland. Indo-European, Germanic, West, High German, Yiddish. Dialects: SOUTHWESTERN YIDDISH, MIDWESTERN YIDDISH, NORTHWESTERN YIDDISH. Western Yiddish originated in Germany, Holland, Switzerland, Alsace (France), Czechoslovakia, western Hungary. "The variety of Western Yiddish in Hungary is probably the most readily intelligible to Yiddish speakers in Romania, the Baltic, and the Slavic countries in the East. The Western Yiddish variety in Holland less so; the Western Yiddish in Alsace [France] and Switzerland, least so" (M. Herzog 1997). On the eve of the Holocaust it was spoken by several tens of thousands. Hebrew characters. Nearly extinct.

GIBRALTAR

National or official language: English. 25,000 (1998 UN). A British dependency. Literacy rate 80%. Also includes Moroccan Spoken Arabic 2,900, From India or Pakistan 360. Christian, Muslim, Jewish, Hindu. The number of languages listed for Gibraltar is 2. Of those, both are living languages. Diversity index 0.50.

ENGLISH [ENG] 3,300 in Gibraltar (1993 Johnstone). Indo-European, Germanic, West, English. Dialect: YANITO. Yanito is spoken by most Gibraltarians among themselves. It is a dialect of English with a strong Spanish influence, with over 500 words coming from Genoese (Ligurian) and Hebrew. Official language. Bible 1535-1989. See main entry under United Kingdom.

SPANISH [SPN] Indo-European, Italic, Romance, Italo-Western, Western, Gallo-Romance, Ibero-Romance, West Iberian, Castilian. Bible 1553-1979. See main entry under Spain.

GREECE

Hellenic Republic, Elliniki Dimokratia. National or official language: Greek. 10,600,000 (1998 UN). Literacy rate 94% to 96%. Also includes Armenian 20,000, Assyrian Neo-Aramaic 2,000, Balkan Gagauz Turkish, English 8,000, Western Farsi 10,000, Russian, Serbo-Croatian, Urum, Arabic 28,000. Information mainly from R. Dawkins 1916; P. Trudgill and G. Tzavaras 1977; B. Comrie 1987; W. Browne 1989, 1998. Christian, Muslim. Blind population 13,000 (1982 WCE). Deaf population 42,600 to 634,565 (1986 Gallaudet University). Deaf institutions: 17. Data accuracy estimate: B. The number of languages listed for Greece is 15. Of those, 13 are living languages and 2 are extinct. Diversity index 0.14.

ALBANIAN, ARVANITIKA ***(ARVANITIKA, ARVANITIC, ARBERICHTE)*** [AAT] 50,000 (Newmark) to 140,000 possible speakers (1977 Trudgill and Tzavaras). Attica (Attiki), Bocotia (Viotia), southern Euboea (Evia), and the island of Salamis (Salamina); Epyrus region and Athens. Mainly rural. Indo-European, Albanian, Tosk. Dialects: THRACEAN ARVANITIKA, NORTHWESTERN ARVANITIKA, SOUTH CENTRAL ARVANITIKA. Arvanitika is partially intelligible to speakers of Tosk. Dialects are perceived as unintelligible to speakers of other dialects. Bilingualism in Greek. Speakers are older people. Young people are migrating to Athens and assimilating as Greeks. Some cultural revival since the 1980s. Speakers are called 'Arvanites'. The language is heavily influenced by Greek. Greek or Roman script. Christian. NT 1827.

BULGARIAN [BLG] 30,000 in Greece (1998 Greek Helsinki Monitor). Western Thrace, 3 departments, including Xanthi. Indo-European, Slavic, South, Eastern. Dialect: POMAK (POMAKCI, POMAKIKA). Pomak is close to Serbian and Bulgarian; geographical dialect shading toward each. Bilingualism in Turkish, Greek. They speak Pomak at home. Also referred to locally as 'Macedonian' and 'Vlach'. The term 'Vlach' is applied variously to varieties of Bulgarian, Romani, and Romanian in Romania, Greece, Albania, and Yugoslavia. Many Greek loan words and others from the dead language, Thraco-Illyrian. Viewed as Turks in Greece. Muslim. Bible 1864-1923. See main entry under Bulgaria.

CAPPADOCIAN GREEK [CPG] Resettled to various locations in Greece in 1922. Formerly in central Turkey (Cappadocia). Sille was in Sille town near Konya, Western Cappadocian was in villages south of Kayseri, Pharasa was in Pharasa (Faràs) and surrounding villages. Indo-European, Greek, Attic. Dialects: SILLE, WESTERN CAPPADOCIAN, PHARASA. Closest to Pontic. Even more distinct from Standard Greek than Pontic is. Language was under extensive attrition from Turkish at the time of the population exchanges in 1922, and has now died out since the 1960s under pressure from Standard Greek (N. Nicholas 1997, Costakis). Different from the ancient Anatolian language spoken in Cappadocia. Dictionary. Christian. Extinct.

GREEK ***(ELLINIKA, GREC, GRAECAE, ROMAIC, NEO-HELLENIC)*** [GRK] 9,859,850 in Greece, 98.5% of the population (1986). Population total all countries 12,000,000 (1999 WA). Thoughout the country. Also spoken in 35 other countries including Albania, Armenia, Australia, Austria, Bahamas, Bulgaria, Canada, Congo, Cyprus, DRC, Djibouti, Egypt, France, Georgia, Germany, Hungary, Italy, Jordan, Kazakhstan. Indo-European, Greek, Attic. Dialects: KATHAREVOUSA, DIMOTIKI, SARACATSAN. Katharevousa is an archaic literary dialect, Dimotiki is the spoken literary dialect and now the official dialect. The Saracatsan are nomadic shepherds of northern Greece. Greeks in Russia and Ukraine speak either Greek or Turkish and are called 'Urums'. The Karamanli were Orthodox Christian Turks who came from central Turkey. National language. Dictionary. Grammar. SVO. Bible 1840-1955.

GREEK SIGN LANGUAGE [GSS] 42,600 or more users (1986 Gallaudet Univ.). Deaf sign language. 12,000 children and 30,000 active adult users (1996). Roots in American and French sign languages and various indigenous sign languages, which came together in the 1950s.

GREEK, ANCIENT [GKO] Indo-European, Greek, Attic. Dialects: KOINE GREEK, CLASSICAL GREEK. Koine Greek is used as a religious language by the Greek Orthodox Church. The language of the text of the Christian New Testament. Extinct. Bible c. 42-98 A.D.

PONTIC ***(PONTIC GREEK)*** [PNT] 200,000 in Greece (1993 Johnstone). Population total all countries 320,000 or more. The majority of speakers live in Salonica, borough of Kalamaria, and the rest of Macedonia in Greece. There may still be speakers on the Black Sea coast of Turkey. Also spoken in Azerbaijan, Canada, Georgia, Kazakhstan, USA. Indo-European, Greek, Attic. Speakers of Standard Greek cannot understand Pontic, and Pontic speakers are reported to not understand or speak Standard Greek. Pontic clubs and centers exist in the Athens-Peiraeus suburbs. Young people may speak Standard Greek as their first language. Speakers in North America are reported to hold onto their language more zealously than those in Greece. Ethnic Greeks in Georgia called 'Rumka' speak Pontic Greek. Brought to Greece in the 1920s and 1930s by immigrants from the Black Sea coast, which had been inhabited by Greeks since antiquity.

ROMANI, BALKAN [RMN] 40,000 in Greece including 10,000 Arlija, 30,000 Greek Romani. About 500 families in Agia Varvara (1996 Birgit Igla). Agia Varvara, a suburb of Athens. Indo-European, Indo-Iranian, Indo-Aryan, Central zone, Romani, Balkan. Dialects: GREEK ROMANI, ARLIJA (ERLI). Bilingualism in Greek. Dictionary. Grammar. Christian, Muslim. Bible portions 1912-1937. See main entry under Yugoslavia.

ROMANI, VLAX ***(ROMANÉS, TSINGANI, ROM)*** [RMY] 1,000 Lovari in Greece. Indo-European, Indo-Iranian, Indo-Aryan, Central zone, Romani, Vlax. Dialect: LOVARI. They can understand Manus (Manuche) only with difficulty. Settled Gypsies are bilingual. Speakers call themselves 'Rom'. Settled

Gypsies accept being called 'Tsingani'. They call the nonsettled Gypsies 'Yifti'. Distinct from Rumanovlach, a variety of Rumanian. Christian. NT 1984-1995. See main entry under Romania.

ROMANIAN, MACEDO ***(MACEDO-RUMANIAN, ARUMANIAN, AROMANIAN, ARMINA, VLACH)*** [RUP] 200,000 in Greece (1995 Greek Monitor of Human and Minority Rights 1.3 Dec. 1995), out of possibly 700,000 in the ethnic group (Association of French Aromanians). Population total all countries 260,000 to 378,000. Northwest Salonika, and northern Greece, Pindus Mts., around Trikala. Also spoken in Albania, Bosnia-Herzegovina, Bulgaria, Macedonia, Romania, Yugoslavia. Indo-European, Italic, Romance, Eastern. Structurally a distinct language from Romanian (F. Agard). It split from the other 3 Rumanian languages between 500 and 1000 A.D. Many dialects. Bilingualism in Greek. People over 50 are fluent in Aromanian, many between 25 to 50 are passive speakers with limited knowledge of vocabulary and grammar. Some younger ones know the language. Rapid assimilation to Greek culture; children attend Greek schools. 20% live traditionally. No legal status in Greece. Not taught in school except for one course at the University of Salonica. Some revival of the culture in progress since the 1980s. 'Armini' refers to the people. Roman or Greek alphabet used. Traditionally shepherds and woodworkers. Christian. Bible portions 1881-1889.

ROMANIAN, MEGLENO ***(MEGLENITIC, MEGLENITE)*** [RUQ] 12,000 (1995). Meglen region, north of Salonika. Indo-European, Italic, Romance, Eastern. Structurally a distinct language from Romanian, Macedo Romanian, and Istro Romanian (F. Agard). The 4 Romanian languages split between 500 and 1000 A.D.

ROMANO-GREEK ***(HELLENOROMANI)*** [RGE] Indo-European, Greek, Attic. Structured on Greek with heavy Romani lexicon.

SLAVIC ***(MACEDONIAN SLAVIC, MACEDONIAN)*** [MKJ] 41,017 mother tongue speakers in Greece, 0.537% of the population (1951 census). Macedonia region in Greece. Indo-European, Slavic, South, Eastern. Speakers are bilingual in Greek, which is used for education and religion. Called 'Slavic' in Greece, where 'Macedonian' refers only to people living in Macedonia, a region in Greece. Bible 1990. See main entry under Macedonia.

TSAKONIAN ***(TSAKONIA)*** [TSD] (300 shepherds; 1981 J. Werner) Towns of Kastanitsa, Sitena, Prastos, Leonidi, Pramatefti, Sapounakeika, Tyros,Melana, possibly Korakovunio; eastern coast of Peloponnesos. Isolated in summer in the mountains west of Leonidi in the eastern Peloponnesus; in winter they descend to Leonidi and neighboring towns. Indo-European, Greek, Doric. Dialects: NORTHERN TSAKONIAN (KASTANISTA-SITENA), SOUTHERN TSAKONIAN (LEONIDIO-PRASTOS), PROPONTIS TSAKONIAN (VATKA-HAVOUTSI). Derived from the Doric dialect spoken in Lakonia by ancient Spartans. Northern and Southern are reported to be intelligible to each other's speakers, but Propontis was more distinct, and closer to Standard Greek. Not inherently intelligible with modern Greek (Voegelin and Voegelin). All use Greek as second language. There were monolingual speakers in 1927. Few speakers of Northern Tsakonian. Speakers use Southern Tsakonian. Propontis Tsakonian has become extinct since 1970. Children attend Greek schools in winter, including kindergarten. Dictionary. Grammar. Pastoralists. Christian.

TURKISH ***(OSMANLI)*** [TRK] 128,380 in Greece (1976 WA). Thrace and Aegean regions. Altaic, Turkic, Southern, Turkish. The number of Turks in Greece remains fairly constant, because growth is offset by a steady flow of emigration to Turkey. Muslim, Christian. Bible 1827-1941. See main entry under Turkey.

HUNGARY

Republic of Hungary. Magyar Köztársaság. National or official language: Hungarian. 10,116,000 (1998 UN). Literacy rate 98% to 99%. Also includes Armenian, Bulgarian, Greek, Macedonian, Polish 21,000, Ukrainian 300,000, Eastern Yiddish, Western Yiddish, Chinese 30. Information mainly from I. Hancock 1979, 1987, 1988; B. Comrie 1987. Christian, secular, Jewish. Blind population 25,000 (1973 estimate); 10,000 (1982 WCE). Deaf population 625,640. Deaf institutions: 17. Data accuracy estimate: B. The number of languages listed for Hungary is 12. Of those, all are living languages. Diversity index 0.14.

BAVARIAN ***(BAYERISCH, BAVARIAN-AUSTRIAN)*** [BAR] Indo-European, Germanic, West, High German, German, Upper German, Bavarian-Austrian. Standard German used by educated people. Hungarian, Standard German used in professions. Used at home. Investigation needed: intelligibility, bilingual proficiency, attitudes. Bible 1998. See main entry under Austria.

GERMAN, STANDARD [GER] 250,000 in Hungary (J. A. Hawkins in B. Comrie 1988) .5% of the population. Indo-European, Germanic, West, High German, German, Middle German, East Middle German. Germans in Hungary speak other Germanic varieties than Standard German at home. Bible 1466-1982. See main entry under Germany.

HUNGARIAN ***(MAGYAR)*** [HNG] 10,298,820 in Hungary (1995), 98% of the population (1986). Population total all countries 14,500,000. Also spoken in Australia, Austria, Canada, Israel, Romania, Slovakia, Slovenia, Ukraine, USA, Yugoslavia. Uralic, Finno-Ugric, Ugric, Hungarian. Dialects: ALFOLD, WEST DANUBE, DANUBE-TISZA, KING'S PASS HUNGARIAN, NORTHEAST HUNGARIAN, NORTHWEST HUNGARIAN, SZEKELY, WEST HUNGARIAN. Closest to Vogul (Mansi) of Russia. 'Magyar' is the Hungarian name. National language. Grammar. SVO. Bible 1590-1991.

HUNGARIAN SIGN LANGUAGE ***(MAGYAR JELVNYELV)*** [HSH] 60,000 deaf (1999 National Association for Deaf and Hard-of-Hearing). 300,000 hard-of-hearing people use it as second language. Used throughout Hungary. May also be used in western Romania. Deaf sign language. Dialects: BUDAPEST, SOPRON, MISKOLC, DEBRECEN, SZEGED, EGER. Related to Austrian Sign Language and German Sign Language. May be related to Yugoslavian Sign Language. Dialects have some different signs for lexical items, similar or same grammar. All ages. Budapest dialect is viewed as the standard. Dictionary. Extensive literacy effort needed.

ROMANI, BALKAN ***(CIGÁNY)*** [RMN] In Hungary, 150,000 Gypsies speak a variety of Romani as first language (1995 Z. Réger). 450,000 to 800,000 all Gypsies in Hungary. Indo-European, Indo-Iranian, Indo-Aryan, Central zone, Romani, Balkan. This variety may not be in Hungary. Bible portions 1912-1937. See main entry under Yugoslavia.

ROMANI, CARPATHIAN ***(CIGÁNY)*** [RMC] 3,000 in Hungary (1980 UBS). Three divisions are recognized: Nograd County north of Budapest, overlapping into Slovakia; in Budapest and towns along the Danube such as Baja, Dunaszekcso, Kalocsa, Mohacs, Pecs, and Versend as far south as the Yugoslav border; and travelers with carnivals. One dialect is in east Hungary, south Poland, and Galicia; another in Transylvania, Romania; others in Czech Republic and Slovakia; Ukraine, USA. Indo-European, Indo-Iranian, Indo-Aryan, Central zone, Romani, Northern. Dialects: GALICIAN, TRANSYLVANIAN. Ethnic group: Ungrike Romá (northern). Medicinal herb collectors and sellers, factory workers, basketmakers, wood merchants, horse dealers, rag-and-bone merchants, carnival workers, knife grinders, brick makers, professionals. Christian. Bible portions 1936-1996. See main entry under Czech Republic.

ROMANI, SINTE [RMO] Eastern Hungary. Indo-European, Indo-Iranian, Indo-Aryan, Central zone, Romani, Northern. Not intelligible with Vlach Romani. A Gypsy language. Christian. Bible portions 1875-1995. See main entry under Yugoslavia.

ROMANI, VLAX ***(GYPSY, TSIGENE, CIGÁNY, ROMUNGRE)*** [RMY] 5,000 to 20,000 Lovari in Hungary. Indo-European, Indo-Iranian, Indo-Aryan, Central zone, Romani, Vlax. Dialects: LOVARI, CHURARI. Vlax in Hungary and Slovakia are called 'Romungre'. Christian. NT 1984-1995. See main entry under Romania.

ROMANIAN ***(RUMANIAN, DACO-ROMANIAN, MOLDAVIAN)*** [RUM] 100,000 in Hungary (1995 Iosif Bena). Indo-European, Italic, Romance, Eastern. Dialect: BAYASH ROMANIAN. The Bayash are ex-slave Roma who worked in houses, and were forbidden to speak Romani. The Bayash speak a very distinctive kind of Romanian. Substantial literature in Bayash. Radio programs. Bible 1688-1989. See main entry under Romania.

SERBO-CROATIAN [SRC] 32,130 in Hungary, .3% of the population (1986). Southern border area. Indo-European, Slavic, South, Western. Dialects: CROATIAN, SERBIAN. Roman script used by Croats. Croats tend to be RC Christian. Bible 1804-1968. See main entry under Yugoslavia.

SLOVAK [SLO] 10,000 to 12,000 in Hungary (1990 Slovak Information Agency). Indo-European, Slavic, West, Czech-Slovak. Western and central dialects of Slovak are inherently intelligible to Czech speakers. Bible 1832-1926. See main entry under Slovakia.

SLOVENIAN ***(SLOVENE)*** [SLV] 4,205 in Hungary (1970). Near Slovenian border. Indo-European, Slavic, South, Western. Dialect: PREKMURSKI. Bible 1584-1996. See main entry under Slovenia.

ICELAND

Republic of Iceland, Lýdveldio Island. National or official language: Icelandic. 276,000 (1998 UN). Literacy rate 100%. Christian, secular. Blind population 43. Deaf population 16,006. Deaf institutions: 2. Data accuracy estimate: B. The number of languages listed for Iceland is 2. Of those, both are living languages. Diversity index 0.00.

ICELANDIC ***(ÍSLENSKA)*** [ICE] 230,000 in Iceland (1980 WA). Population total all countries 250,000. Also spoken in Canada, USA. Indo-European, Germanic, North, West Scandinavian. No appreciable dialect differences (Nida 1972). Not inherently intelligible with Faroese. National language. SVO. Bible 1584-1981.

ICELANDIC SIGN LANGUAGE [ICL] Deaf sign language. Until 1910 Icelandic deaf people were sent to school in Denmark. The sign language is based on Danish Sign Language, but has changed and developed since then, so it is not the same today. Signed interpretation provided for college students. Instruction for parents of deaf children. There is a committee on national sign language. There is a manual spelling system. Dictionary. TV.

IRELAND

Éire. National or official languages: Irish Gaelic, English. 3,681,000 (1998 UN). Literacy rate 99%. Information mainly from M. Stephens 1976; R. McCrum, W. Cran, R. MacNeil 1986; J. Fishman 1991. Christian. Deaf population 214,569. Deaf institutions: 36. Data accuracy estimate: B. The number of languages listed for Ireland is 5. Of those, all are living languages. Diversity index 0.17.

ENGLISH [ENG] 2,600,000 in Ireland (1983 estimate). Indo-European, Germanic, West, English. Dialects: SOUTH HIBERNO ENGLISH, NORTH HIBERNO ENGLISH. National language. Bible 1535-1989. See main entry under United Kingdom.

GAELIC, IRISH *(IRISH, ERSE, GAEILGE)* [GLI] 260,000 fluent or native speakers (1983 census), 13% of the population (1983 census). 13% of the population over 3 claim to be Irish speakers (1981 census). Population total all countries 260,000 or more. Western isles northwest and southwest coasts; Galway, part of Mayo, Kerry, Donegal, Meath, Cork, Waterford, Scotland (Albain), Isle of Mann. Also spoken in Brazil, Canada, United Kingdom, USA. Indo-European, Celtic, Insular, Goidelic. Dialects: MUNSTER, CONNACHT, DONEGAL, LEINSTER, ULSTER. Bilingualism in English. It is taught as an official language in schools and encouraged by the government. National language. VSO. Bible 1685-1989.

IRISH SIGN LANGUAGE [ISG] Dublin and elsewhere. Deaf sign language. In 1816 British signs were brought in. In 1846 Irish signs developed in the girls' school, in 1857 Irish signs brought into the boys' school. Related to French Sign Language. There are informal male and female sign systems. Females learn the male system during dating and marriage. The informal system is referred to as 'Deaf Sign Language'. Irish Sign Language is a new unified system, a manual code for English. It has structural features such as directional verbs. It has influenced sign languages in South Africa and Australia. It originated between 1846-1849. Several deaf schools with 750 to 800 students in each. There is a committee on national sign language, and an organization for sign language teachers. TV.

SCOTS [SCO] Donegal County. Indo-European, Germanic, West, English. English is considered to be the language of education and religion. Used with family and friends. All ages. Christian. NT 1901-1984. See main entry under United Kingdom.

SHELTA *(THE CANT, CANT, IRISH TRAVELER CANT, SHELDRU, GAMMON)* [STH] 6,000 in Ireland. Population total all countries 86,000. Also spoken in United Kingdom, USA. Indo-European, Celtic, Insular, Goidelic. The secret language, or cryptolect, of Travellers in the British Isles. Based largely on Irish. Not Gypsies.

ITALY

Italian Republic, Repubblica Italiana. National or official languages: Italian, French (regional), Standard German (regional), Serbo-Croatian. 57,369,000 (1998 UN). Literacy rate 97% to 98%. Also includes Judeo-Tripolitanian Arabic 5,000, Judeo-Tunisian Arabic, Assyrian Neo-Aramaic, English 29,000, Kabuverdianu 10,000, Maltese 28,000, Somali, Chinese 40,000, people from Eritrea, the Philippines. Information mainly from R. A. Hall 1974; M. Stephens 1976; F. B. Agard 1984; B. Comrie 1987. Christian, secular. Blind population 100,000. Deaf population 3,524,906. Deaf institutions: 80. Data accuracy estimate: B. The number of languages listed for Italy is 33. Of those, all are living languages. Diversity index 0.59.

ALBANIAN, ARBËRESHË *(ARBËRESHË)* [AAE] 80,000 (L. Newmark) to 100,000 speakers (N. Vincent in B. Comrie 1987), out of a population of 260,000 (1976 M. Stephens). Southern; Calabria, Apulia, Basilicata, Molise, Sicily. Indo-European, Albanian, Tosk. Dialects: SICILIAN ALBANIAN, CALABRIAN ALBANIAN, CENTRAL MOUNTAIN ALBANIAN, CAMPO MARINO ALBANIAN. Speakers say the four Italian dialects are not inherently intelligible with each other. 45% lexical similarity with Tosk Albanian. Speakers are bilingual in Italian and regional Italian varieties in varying degrees; one report says they are highly bilingual. Albanian is the language of the home. Strong position in some districts. Not used in schools. No official status. Descendents of 15th century mercenaries. Some literature. Investigation needed: bilingual proficiency in Italian, attitudes toward Italian. Farmers, shepherds. Christian. Bible portions 1868-1869.

BAVARIAN ***(BAYERISCH, BAVARIAN AUSTRIAN)*** [BAR] South Bavarian is in the Bavarian Alps, Tyrol, Styria, including Heanzian dialect of Burgenland, Carinthia, northern Italy, and part of Gottschee; Central Bavarian is in the Alps and Lower Austria and Salzburg; North Bavarian in the north of Regensburg, to Nuremburg and Western Bohemia, Czech Republic. Indo-European, Germanic, West, High German, German, Upper German, Bavarian-Austrian. Dialects: CENTRAL BAVARIAN, NORTH BAVARIAN, SOUTH BAVARIAN. School in South Tyrol is taught in Standard German. Investigation needed: intelligibility with Standard German, bilingual proficiency in Italian, attitudes toward German, Italian. Bible 1998. See main entry under Austria.

CATALAN-VALENCIAN-BALEAR [CLN] 20,000 in Alghero (1996). Alghero, northwest coast on Sardinia. Indo-European, Italic, Romance, Italo-Western, Western, Gallo-Iberian, Ibero-Romance, East Iberian. Dialect: ALGHERESE. Italian or Logudorese Sardinian are used as second language by many. Bible 1478-1993. See main entry under Spain.

CIMBRIAN ***(TZIMBRO, ZIMBRISCH)*** [CIM] 2,230 including 500 in Lusernese Cimbrian in Trentino Alto Oolige 40 km. southeast from Trento, plus 1,500 Sette Comuni Cimbrian (40% of Roana (Rowan), 70% of Messaselva di Roana Rotzo) in Veneto around 60 km. north of Vicenza (1978 H. Kloss), and 230 or 65% of Giazza (Ijetzan) Veneto, 43 km. northeast of Verona (1992 R. Zamponi). There were 22,700 speakers in Sieben Gemainde and 12,400 in Dreizehn Gemeinde in 1854. Northeast Italy, Sette and Tredici Comuni (Sieben and Dreizehn Gemainde) south of Trent, towns of Giazza (Glietzen, Ljetzen), Roana (Rabam), Lusern, some in Venetia Province. Indo-European, Germanic, West, High German, German, Upper German, Bavarian-Austrian. Dialects: LUSERNESE CIMBRIAN, TREDICI COMMUNI CIMBRIAN (TAUCH), SETTE COMUNI CIMBRIAN. Structural and intelligibility differences indicate that the 3 dialects listed could be considered separate languages. Lusernese Cimbrian is heavily influenced by Italian. Heavily influenced by Bajuwarisch dialects. It is sometimes considered to be a dialect of south Bavarian. Different from Bavarian, Walser, and Mocheno. No written influence from Standard German. Speakers are all bilingual in Standard Italian and Venetian (Trentine), and many know Standard German. Pastors preached in Cimbrian until the late 19th century. Attempts to promote it have been increasing in recent decades. It is taught in some classes and is scheduled to become required. Newspapers.

CORSICAN ***(CORSO, CORSU, CORSE, CORSI)*** [COI] Maddalena Island, northeast coast of Sardinia. Indo-European, Italic, Romance, Southern, Corsican. Southern Corsican is closer to Gallurese Sardinian than to other Corsican dialects (R. A. Hall, Jr.). Bible portions 1861. See main entry under France.

EMILIANO-ROMAGNOLO ***(EMILIANO, EMILIAN, SAMMARINESE)*** [EML] 3,531,780 speakers in Emilia-Romagna (1987) Maurizio Masetti). About 10% of the people in the province come from elsewhere, and do not speak the language. Population total both countries 3,551,892. Northwest Italy, region of Piacenza to that of Ravenna, and between the Po and the Adriatic and the Apennines, in the territories of Emilia and Romagna, southern Pianura Padana (all provinces), southern Lombardia (Provinces Mantova and Pavia), northern Toscana (Lunigiana), northern Marche (Province Pesaro). Also spoken in San Marino. Indo-European, Italic, Romance, Italo-Western, Western, Gallo-Iberian, Gallo-Romance, Gallo-Italian. Dialects: WESTERN EMILIANO, CENTRAL EMILIANO, EASTERN EMILIANO, NORTHERN ROMAGNOLO, SOUTHERN ROMAGNOLO, MANTOVANO, VOGHERESE-PAVESE, LUNIGIANO. A structurally separate language from Italian (F. B. Agard). Related to Lombard (R. A. Hall 1974:29, S. Fleischman in OIEL 3.339:1992). Adults use Italian as second language. Not endangered. SVO. Literacy rate in second language: 100%. Christian. Bible portions 1862-1995.

FRANCO-PROVENÇAL [FRA] 70,000 in Italy (1971 census), including 700 Faetar speakers (1995 Naomi Nagy). Northwest Italy, Aosta Valley. A small speech community also in Faeto and Celle S. Vito in the Province of Foggia in Apulia, and Guardia Piemontese in Calabria, Cosenza. Covers a huge area. Indo-European, Italic, Romance, Italo-Western, Western, Gallo-Iberian, Gallo-Romance, Gallo- Rhaetian, Oïl, Southeastern. Dialects: VALLE D'AOSTA (PATOÉ VALDOTEN, VALDOTAIN, VALDOSTANO), FAETO (FAETAR), CELLE SAN VITO. A structurally separate language from Provençal, French, Piemontese, and Lombard (F. B. Agard). Bilingualism in Italian, Piemontese. Most occasions. Bible portions 1830. See main entry under France.

FRENCH ***(FRANÇAIS)*** [FRN] 100,000 in Italy (M. Harris in B. Comrie 1987). Aosta Valley. Indo-European, Italic, Romance, Italo-Western, Western, Gallo-Iberian, Gallo-Romance, Gallo-Rhaetian, Oïl, French. Official language. Bible 1530-1986. See main entry under France.

FRIULIAN ***(FURLAN, FRIOULAN, FRIOULIAN, PRIULIAN, FRIULANO)*** [FRL] 600,000 (1976 Stephens). Northeast and adjacent areas, northern Friuli-Venezia-Giulia on the borders of the Austrian province of Corinthia and the Republic of Slovenia. Indo-European, Italic, Romance, Italo-Western, Western, Gallo-Iberian, Gallo-Romance, Gallo-Rhaetian, Rhaetian. Dialects: EAST CENTRAL FRIULIAN, WESTERN FRIULIAN, CARNICO. Friulian, Ladin, and Romansch are separate languages (R. A. Hall, Jr. 1978, personal communication). F. B. Agard considers it to be structurally closer to Italian than to Romansch (personal communication 1981). Most speakers know Standard Italian. Some are cultivating Friulian as a literary language. In the area of Gorizia all the Slovenes speak it as a second or third language. Germans in the area also speak it. Regional pride. NT 1972.

GERMAN, STANDARD [GER] 225,000 in Italy (N. Vincent in B. Comrie 1987). Northern, Trentino-Alto Adige, South Tyrol, Province of Bolzano. Indo-European, Germanic, West, High German, German, Middle German, East Middle German. German used in schools. Official language. Bible 1466-1982. See main entry under Germany.

GREEK [GRK] 20,000 in Italy (N. Vincent in B. Comrie 1987). Southern, east of Reggio; Salento (Colimera, Sternatía, Zollino) and Aspromonte (Bova, Condofuri, Palizzi, Roccoforte, Roghudi). Indo-European, Greek, Attic. Dialects: SALENTO, ASPROMONTE. The Greek spoken in Italy and that of Corsica are probably two separate languages (R. Zamponi 1992). Mainly older speakers. Not used in schools. Investigation needed: intelligibility with Greek of Greece, Corsica. Bible 1840-1994. See main entry under Greece.

ITALIAN *(ITALIANO)* [ITN] 55,000,000 mother tongue speakers, some of whom are native bilinguals of Italian and regional varieties, and some of whom may use Italian as second language. Population total all countries 62,000,000. Also spoken in 29 other countries including Argentina, Australia, Belgium, Bosnia-Herzegovina, Brazil, Canada, Croatia, Egypt, Eritrea, France, Germany, Israel, Libya, Liechtenstein, Luxembourg, Paraguay, Philippines, Puerto Rico, San Marino. Indo-European, Italic, Romance, Italo-Western, Italo-Dalmatian. Dialects: TUSCAN, ABRUZZESE, PUGLIESE, UMBRIAN, LAZIALE, CENTRAL MARCHIGIANO, CICOLANO-REATINO-AQUILANO, MOLISANO. Regional varieties coexist with the standard language; some are inherently unintelligible (Nida) to speakers of other varieties unless they have learned them. Aquilano, Molisano, and Pugliese are very different from the other Italian 'dialects'. Piemontese and Sicilian are distinct enough to be separate languages (F. B. Agard 1981, personal communication). Venetian and Lombard are also very different (Philippe Cousson 1981, personal communication). Neapolitan is reported to be unintelligible to speakers of Standard Italian. Northern varieties are closer to French and Occitan than to standard or southern varieties (Agard, N. Vincent). 89% lexical similarity with French, 87% with Catalan, 85% with Sardinian, 82% with Spanish, 78% with Rheto-Romance, 77% with Rumanian. Most Italians use varieties along a continuum from standard to regional to local according to what is appropriate. Possibly nearly half the population do not use Standard Italian as mother tongue. Only 2.5% of Italy's population could speak standard Italian when it became a unified nation in 1861. Investigation needed: intelligibility with Pugliese with Standard Italian. National language. Grammar. SVO. Bible 1471-1985.

ITALIAN SIGN LANGUAGE *(LINGUA ITALIANA DEI SEGNI, LIS)* [ISE] Deaf sign language. Partially intelligible with French Sign Language. Not intelligible with ASL. Regional differences, but signers from different regions seem to communicate fluently. Used in families, clubs, and schools outside the classroom, but not in the classroom.

JUDEO-ITALIAN *(ITALKIAN)* [ITK] A tiny number who speak it fluently. Perhaps 4,000 occasionally use elements of it in their speech (1/10th of Italy's 40,000 Jews). Indo-European, Italic, Romance, Italo-Western, Italo-Dalmatian. More commonly spoken two generations ago. Used in Passover song. Hebrew script. Jewish. Nearly extinct. Bible portions.

LADIN *(DOLOMITE)* [LLD] 30,000 to 35,000 in Italy (1976 Stephens). Population total both countries 30,000 to 35,000. Southern Tyrol in the Alto Adige and the Dolomites, principally in Badia Valley in the autonomous province of Bolzano, also in the provinces of Trento and Belluno, in the parishes of Valle Moena, Cortina d'Ampezzo, Pieve-di-Livinallongo and Colle-Santa-Lucia, Cles, Val di Non. Also spoken in USA. Indo-European, Italic, Romance, Italo-Western, Western, Gallo-Iberian, Gallo-Romance, Gallo-Rhaetian, Rhaetian. Dialects: ATESINO, CADORINO, NONES (NONES BLOT, NONESH, PARLATA TRENTINA, NONESE), GARDENA (GARDENESE, GRÜDNO), FASSANO, BADIOTTO, MAREBBANO, LIVINALLESE, AMPEZZANO. Friulian, Ladin, and Romansch are separate languages (R. A. Hall, Jr. 1978, personal communication). Seven dialects. The dialect of Val di Fassa is taught in schools. Distinct from Ladino (Dzhudezmo, Judeo-Spanish). Most people know Standard Italian, but have pride in their language. Written since 1700. Investigation needed: attitudes toward Italian.

LIGURIAN *(LÍGURU, LIGURE)* [LIJ] 1,853,578 (1976). Population total all countries 1,856,680 or more. Liguria, northern Italy; east and west of Genoa long the Riviera and mountain hinterland, St. Pietro and St. Antioch, islands off southwest coast of Sardinia, cities of Carloforte and Calasetta in Sardinia. Also spoken in France, Monaco. Indo-European, Italic, Romance, Italo-Western, Western, Gallo-Iberian, Gallo-Romance, Gallo-Italian. Dialect: GENOESE (GENOAN, GENOVESE). Very different from Standard Italian. Speakers may all be adequately bilingual in Standard Italian. Not endangered. Bible portions 1860.

LOMBARD *(LOMBARDO)* [LMO] 8,671,210 in Italy (1976). Population total all countries 8,974,000. Milan, Lombardy, 3 valleys of Graubnnden (Val Mesolcina, Val Bregaglia, Val Poschiavo), northern

Italy. Western Lombard varieties also in Sicily. Ticino is in Switzerland. Also spoken in Switzerland, USA. Indo-European, Italic, Romance, Italo-Western, Western, Gallo-Iberian, Gallo-Romance, Gallo-Italian. Dialects: MILANESE, EASTERN LOMBARD, WESTERN LOMBARD (PIAZZA ARMERINA, NOVARA, NICOSIA, SAN FRATELLO), ALPINE LOMBARD, NOVARESE LOMBARD, TRENTINO WESTERN, LATIN FIAMAZZO, LATIN ANAUNICO, BERGAMASCO, TICINESE (TICINO). A group of dialects, some of which may be separate languages. Western Lombard dialects (of Ticino and Graubnnden) are inherently intelligible to each other's speakers. Speakers in more conservative valleys may have to use some kind of 'standard' dialect to communicate with speakers of other dialects of Lombard. Very different from Standard Italian. Speakers may all be adequately bilingual in Standard Italian. Not endangered. Investigation needed: intelligibility with dialects, bilingual proficiency in Italian. Bible portions 1859-1860.

MÓCHENO [QMO] 1,900 including 400 Fierozzo, 1,000 Palú, 460 Gereut (1992 Raoul Zamponi). Valle del Fersina (Trentino). Indo-European, Germanic, West, High German, German, Upper German, Bavarian-Austrian. Dialects: FIEROZZO (FLORUTZ), PALÚ (PALAI), FRASSILONGO (GEREUT). Speakers can partially understand Bavarian, Cimbrian, or Standard German. Investigation needed: bilingual proficiency in Italian.

NAPOLETANO-CALABRESE *(NEAPOLITAN-CALABRESE)* [NPL] 7,047,399 (1976). Campania and Calabria provinces, southern Italy. Indo-European, Italic, Romance, Italo-Western, Italo-Dalmatian. Dialects: NAPOLETANO (NEAPOLITAN, TIRRENIC), NORTHERN CALABRESE-LUCANO (LUCANIAN, BASILICATAN). Limited inherent intelligibility with Standard Italian. Neapolitan and Calabrese are reported to be very different from each other. Southern Calabrian is reported to be a dialect of Sicilian. Bilingualism in Italian. Vigorous. Not endangered. A large literature. It might be in Southern Romance instead of Italo-Western. Investigation needed: intelligibility with Neapolitan, Southern Calabrian with Sicilian. Bible portions 1861-1862.

PIEMONTESE *(PIEMONTÈIS, PIEDMONTESE)* [PMS] 3,000,000 (1976). Population total all countries 3,000,000 or more. Northwest Italy, Piedmont, except for the Provençal- and Franco-Provençal-speaking Alpine valleys. Also spoken in Australia, USA. Indo-European, Italic, Romance, Italo-Western, Western, Gallo-Iberian, Gallo-Romance, Gallo-Italian. Dialects: HIGH PIEMONTESE, LOW PIEMONTESE. Distinct enough from Standard Italian to be considered a separate language. Considerable French influence. Speakers may all be highly bilingual in Standard Italian. NT 1835.

PROVENÇAL *(PROVENZALE)* [PRV] 100,000 in Italy (1990 P. Blanchet). Upper valleys of the Italian Piedmont (Val Mairo, Val Varacho, Val d'Esturo, Entraigas, Limoun, Vinai, Pignerol, Sestriero), Guardia Piemonese in Calabria. Indo-European, Italic, Romance, Italo-Western, Western, Gallo-Iberian, Ibero-Romance, Oc. Dialect: TRANSALPIN. Bilingualism in Piemontese, Italian. All ages. It is widely spoken. Bible portions 1824-1975. See main entry under France.

ROMANI, BALKAN [RMN] 5,000 Arlija in Italy. Indo-European, Indo-Iranian, Indo-Aryan, Central zone, Romani, Balkan. Dialect: ARLIJA (ERLI). Muslim. Bible portions 1912-1937. See main entry under Yugoslavia.

ROMANI, SINTE [RMO] 14,000 in Italy including 10,000 Manouche, 4,000 Slovenian-Croatian. North Italy. Indo-European, Indo-Iranian, Indo-Aryan, Central zone, Romani, Northern. Dialects: PIEDMONT SINTÍ, SLOVENIAN-CROATIAN, MANOUCHE. Not intelligible with Vlach Romani. Christian. Bible portions 1875-1995. See main entry under Yugoslavia.

ROMANI, VLAX [RMY] 2,000 to 4,000 in Italy including 1,000 to 3,000 Kalderash, 1,000 Lovari. Indo-European, Indo-Iranian, Indo-Aryan, Central zone, Romani, Vlax. Dialects: KALDERASH, LOVARI. Christian. NT 1984-1995. See main entry under Romania.

SARDINIAN, CAMPIDANESE *(SARDU, CAMPIDANESE, CAMPIDESE, SOUTH SARDINIAN)* [SRO] Southern Sardinia. Indo-European, Italic, Romance, Southern, Sardinian. Dialects: CAGLIARE (CAGLIARI, CAGLIARITAN), ARBORENSE, SUB-BARBARICINO, WESTERN CAMPIDENESE, CENTRAL CAMPIDANESE, OGLIASTRINO, SULCITANO, MERIDIONALE, SARRABENSE. Cagliaritan is the dialect of Cagliari, the capital of Sardinia. Campidanese is quite distinct from the other Sardinian languages. Cagliare has 62% lexical similarity with Standard Italian, 73% with Logudorese, 66% with Gallurese. It is in general use in the south. A movement is growing to recognize Sard as an important part of their linguistic and cultural heritage. Bible portions 1860-1900.

SARDINIAN, GALLURESE *(NORTHEASTERN SARDINIAN, GALLURESE)* [SDN] Gallurese is in northeastern Sardinia. Indo-European, Italic, Romance, Southern, Sardinian. 83% lexical similarity with Standard Italian; 81% with Sassarese; 70% with Logudorese, 66% with Cagliare. A growing movement to recognize Sard as an important part of their cultural and linguistic heritage. Influenced by Corsican and Tuscan (Standard Italian). They call Campidanese and Logudorese 'Sard', and the people 'Sards', but do not include themselves or their language in those terms. Bible portions 1861-1862.

SARDINIAN, LOGUDORESE ***(SARD, SARDARESE, LOGUDORESE, CENTRAL SARDINIAN)*** [SRD] 1,500,000 including all Sardinian languages (1977 M. Ibba, Rutgers University). Central Sardinia. Indo-European, Italic, Romance, Southern, Sardinian. Dialects: NUORESE, NORTHERN LOGUDORESE, BARBARICINO, SOUTHWESTERN LOGUDORESE. No one form of Sardinian is selected as standard for literary purposes. Logudorese is quite different from other Sardinian varieties. 68% lexical similarity with Standard Italian, 73% with Sassarese and Cagliarese, 70% with Gallurese. 'Sardinian' has 85% lexical similarity with Italian, 80% with French, 78% with Portuguese, 76% with Spanish, 74% with Rumanian and Rheto-Romance. Italian is used for literary and teaching purposes. Farmers and housewives over 35 use almost no Italian. Sardinian is in general use in central and southern areas. It has prestige equal to Italian in some contexts including writing. There is a growing movement to recognize Sard as an important part of their linguistic and cultural heritage. Christian. Bible portions 1858-1861.

SARDINIAN, SASSARESE ***(NORTHWESTERN SARDINIAN, SASSARESE)*** [SDC] Northwestern Sardinia. Indo-European, Italic, Romance, Southern, Sardinian. 81% lexical similarity with Gallurese, 76% with Standard Italian. There is a growing movement to recognize Sard as an important part of their cultural and linguistic heritage. Influenced by Ligurian and Pisan (Pisa, northwest coast of Italy). They call Campidanese and Logudorese 'Sard', and the people 'Sards', but do not include themselves or their language in those terms. Bible portions 1863-1866.

SERBO-CROATIAN [SRC] 3,500 in Italy (N. Vincent in B. Comrie 1987). Molise, southern, villages of Montemitro, San Felice del Molise, Acquaviva-Collecroce. Indo-European, Slavic, South, Western. Dialect: CROATIAN. They are reviving the use of Serbo-Croatian literature. Descendents of 15th and 16th century refugees. Official language. Christian, Muslim. Bible 1804-1968. See main entry under Yugoslavia.

SICILIAN ***(CALABRO-SICILIAN)*** [SCN] 4,680,715 (1976). Sicily, an island off the southern mainland. Indo-European, Italic, Romance, Italo-Western, Italo-Dalmatian. Dialects: WESTERN SICILIAN (PALERMO, TRAPANI, CENTRAL-WESTERN AGRIGENTINO), CENTRAL METAFONETICA, SOUTHEAST METAFONETICA, EASTERN NONMETAFONETICA, MESSINESE, ISOLE EOLIE, PANTESCO, SOUTHERN CALABRO. Distinct enough from Standard Italian to be considered a separate language. Pugliese (see Italian) and Southern Calabrese are reported to be dialects of Sicilian. Bilingualism in Italian. Vigorous. Not endangered. French influence. It may be Southern Romance instead of Italo-Western. Investigation needed: intelligibility with Pugliese, Southern Calabrian, bilingual proficiency in Italian. Bible portions 1860.

SLOVENIAN ***(SLOVENE)*** [SLV] 100,000 in Italy (N. Vincent in B. Comrie 1987). The provinces of Trieste and Gorizia in northeast near Slovenia border. Indo-European, Slavic, South, Western. Dialects: PRIMORSKI, CIVIDALE, RESIA. Some dialects are very diverse. The Slovene have their own schools. Bible 1584-1996. See main entry under Slovenia.

VENETIAN ***(VENETO)*** [VEC] 2,109,502 in Italy (1976). Population total all countries 2,210,000. Northern Italy, city of Venice, area of the Tre Venezie; Venezia Eugànea westward to Verona, southward to the Po, and eastward to the border of the Fruili; Venezia Tridentina, in the Adige valley and neighboring mountain regions to the north of Trent; and Venezia Giulia, east of the Friuli, and including Trieste. Bisiacco is spoken in Gorizia Province. Also spoken in Croatia, Slovenia. Indo-European, Italic, Romance, Italo-Western, Western, Gallo-Iberian, Gallo-Romance, Gallo-Italian. Dialects: ISTRIAN, TRIESTINO, VENETIAN PROPER, BISIACCO. Very different from Standard Italian. Bilingualism in Italian. Vigorous. Not endangered. Investigation needed: bilingual proficiency in Italian, attitudes. Bible portions 1859.

WALSER ***(WALSCHER)*** [WAE] 3,400 in Italy (1978 Fazzini). Valle d'Aosta: Val Lesa (Gressoney, Issime, Gaby); Piemonte: Valsesie (Alagna, Rima S. Siuseppe, Rimelle), Novara: Valle Anzacxa (Macugnage); Val Formazza (Formazza, Pomatt). 9 communities in Italy, and 4 former ones. Indo-European, Germanic, West, High German, German, Upper German, Alemannic. Ancestors came from the Wallis Canton between the 12th and 13th centuries. Close but different from Schwytzertusch. Different from Cimbrian, Mocheno, or Bavarian. All ages. Used for children's services in church. In Valle d'Aosta it has been influenced by Franco-Provençal and Piemontese; elsewhere in Italy by Italian. Investigation needed: bilingual proficiency in Italian. See main entry under Switzerland.

LATVIA

Republic of Latvia, Latvijas Republika. National or official language: Latvian. 2,424,000 (1998 UN). 1,394,000 or 54.5% are Latvians (1994 V. Zeps). Independence from USSR 1991. 24,695 square miles. Capital: Riga. Literacy rate 99%. Also includes Belarusan 105,000, Estonian 3,000, Lithuanian 35,000,

Polish 57,000, Russian 861,600, Tatar 5,000, Ukrainian 78,000. Information mainly from V. Zeps 1986-1995; A. E. Kibrik 1991; T. Salminen 1998. Christian, Jewish (40,000). Data accuracy estimate: B. The number of languages listed for Latvia is 5. Of those, all are living languages. Diversity index 0.60.

LATVIAN ***(LATVISKA, "LETTISH", "LETTISCH")*** [LAT] 1,394,000 in Latvia including over 500,000 Latgalians. Population total all countries 1,500,000 (1995 V. Zeps). Also spoken in Australia, Belarus, Brazil, Canada, Estonia, Germany, Lithuania, New Zealand, Russia (Europe), Sweden, Ukraine, United Kingdom, USA, Venezuela. Indo-European, Baltic, Eastern. Dialects: WEST LATVIAN (CENTRAL LATVIAN), EAST LATVIAN (HIGH LATVIAN, LATGALIAN). Tamian is a subdialect of Central Latvian. Latvians do not like the term "Lettish." National language. Grammar. Roman script. Christian. Bible 1689-1995.

LATVIAN SIGN LANGUAGE [LSL] Deaf sign language.

LIV ***(LIVONIAN)*** [LIV] 15 to 20 active speakers (1995 V. Zeps), 150 to 400 speakers (1986 V. Zeps), 1,500 who have some knowledge of it (1979 Valt). 8 coastal villages west of Kolkasrags in Kurzeme and a dispersed population elsewhere, mostly in Riga. Uralic, Finno-Ugric, Finno-Permic, Finno-Cheremisic, Finno-Mordvinic, Finno-Lappic, Baltic-Finnic. Dialects: WESTERN LIVONIAN (KURZEME, RAANDALIST), EASTERN LIVONIAN (VIDZEME). Bilingualism in Latvian, Russian. Endangered. Eastern Livonian is now extinct. Christian. NT 1942.

ROMANI, BALTIC [ROM] 8,000 in Latvia (1995 V. Zeps). Indo-European, Indo-Iranian, Indo-Aryan, Central zone, Romani, Northern. Dialects: LATVIAN ROMANI (LETTISH ROMANI), NORTH RUSSIAN ROMANI, WHITE RUSSIA ROMANI, ESTONIAN ROMANI, POLISH ROMANI. Ethnic groups: Rúska Romá (northern Russian SFSR), Lotfítka Romá (western Latvia, Estonia), Lajenge Romá (eastern Estonia). Christian. Bible portions 1933-1996. See main entry under Poland.

YIDDISH, EASTERN ***(JUDEO-GERMAN)*** [YDD] 40,000 (1991). Indo-European, Germanic, West, High German, Yiddish. Of the 1,811,000 Jewish people listed in the 1979 USSR census, the majority spoke Russian as their first language and virtually all others spoke Russian as their second language. About 50,000 Jews spoke Georgian, Tat, or Tajiki as their first language. There may be no Yiddish speakers in Latvia now (1995). Had literary status, but very little literature. Jewish. Bible 1821-1936. See main entry under Israel.

LIECHTENSTEIN

Principality of Liechtenstein, Fürstentum Liechtenstein. National or official language: Standard German. 32,000 (1998 UN). Literacy rate 100% (1989 WA). Also includes Italian 800. Christian, secular. Deaf population 1,818. The number of languages listed for Liechtenstein is 3. Of those, all are living languages. Diversity index 0.13.

ALEMANNISCH ***(ALEMANNIC, SCHWYZERDÜTSCH, SCHWYTZERTUETSCH)*** [GSW] 29,000. Indo-European, Germanic, West, High German, German, Upper German, Alemannic. Dialect: HIGH ALEMANNISCH. Bilingualism in Standard German. Spoken by the majority of the people in the country. NT 1984. See main entry under Switzerland.

GERMAN, STANDARD [GER] Indo-European, Germanic, West, High German, German, Middle German, East Middle German. German dialects vary. National language. Bible 1466-1982. See main entry under Germany.

WALSER ***(WALSCHER)*** [WAE] 1,300 in Liechtenstein (1995 C. Buchli). Triesenberg, including Saminatal and Malbun. 1 community in Liechtenstein. Indo-European, Germanic, West, High German, German, Upper German, Allemannic. Ancestors came from the Wallis Canton in Switzerland. Close but different from Schwytzertusch. Different from Cimbrian, Mocheno, or Bavarian. See main entry under Switzerland.

LITHUANIA

Republic of Lithuania, Lietuvos Respublika. National or official language: Lithuanian. 3,694,000 (1998 UN). Independence from USSR 1991. 26,173 square miles. Capital Vilnius. Literacy rate 99%. Also includes Belarusan 63,000, Latvian 5,000, Polish 258,000, Russian 344,000, Tatar 5,100, Ukrainian 45,000, Eastern Yiddish, Also possibly Yiddish. Christian, Jewish. Data accuracy estimate: B. The number of languages listed for Lithuania is 4. Of those, all are living languages. Diversity index 0.34.

KARAIM ***(KARAITE)*** [KDR] 535 mother tongue speakers (16%) out of an ethnic population of 3,340 (1979 census). Population total all countries 535 or more. Also spoken in Israel, Ukraine. Altaic, Turkic, Western, Ponto-Caspian. Dialects: EASTERN KARAIM, NORTHWESTERN KARAIM, TRAKAY, GALITS. Close to Karachay and Kumyk. One report says few children speakers. National language of the Karaim. Cyrillic and Hebrew scripts. Karaim Jewish: they say their religion is 'Karaim', not Judaism, celebrate the same religious holidays as the Jews, but their prayer services, held in Turkic, bear little resemblance to Jewish services (Philip E. Miller). Bible portions 1842.

LITHUANIAN ***(LIUTUVISKAI, LIETUVI, LITOVSKIY, LITEWSKI, LITAUISCHE)*** [LIT] 2,955,200 in Lithuania (including 3,460 Tatar) or about 80% of the population (1998). Population total all countries 4,000,000 (1993 UBS). Lithuania. Capital is Vilnius. Also spoken in Argentina, Australia, Belarus, Brazil, Canada, Estonia, Kazakhstan, Kyrgyzstan, Latvia, Poland, Russia (Europe), Sweden, Tajikistan, Turkmenistan, United Kingdom, Uruguay, USA, Uzbekistan. Indo-European, Baltic, Eastern. Dialects: AUKSHTAITISH (AUKSHTAICHIAI, AUKSTAITISKAI, HIGHLAND LITHUANIAN), DZUKISH (DZUKISKAI), SHAMAITISH (SAMOGITIAN, ZHEMAITISH, ZEMAITIS, ZEMAITISKAI, ZEMACHIAI, LOWLAND LITHUANIAN), SUVALKIETISKAI. Aukstaitiskai speakers can understand Suvalkai easily, Dzukai with a little difficulty, and vice versa. Zemaitiskai is difficult for all others to understand. Second languages Russian or English used with foreigners. All domains. All ages. Highlanders look down on lowlanders. Some speakers have reserved attitudes toward Russian and Polish. National language. Dictionary. Grammar. Postpositions; genitives, relatives after noun heads. Literacy rate in first language: 99%. Roman script. Christian, Muslim (Tatar). Bible 1735-1998.

LITHUANIAN SIGN LANGUAGE [LLS] Deaf sign language. Dictionary.

ROMANI, BALTIC [ROM] Indo-European, Indo-Iranian, Indo-Aryan, Central zone, Romani, Northern. Dialect: LITHUANIAN ROMANI. Bible portions 1933-1996. See main entry under Poland.

LUXEMBOURG

Grand Duchy of Luxembourg, Grand-Duché de Luxembourg. National or official languages: French, Standard German, Luxembourgeois. 422,000 (1998 UN). Literacy rate 100%. Also includes Italian 20,800, Kabuverdianu 3,000, Portuguese 100,000. Information mainly from M. Stephens 1976. Christian. Blind population 204. Deaf population 24,373. Deaf institutions: 1. The number of languages listed for Luxembourg is 3. Of those, all are living languages. Diversity index 0.53.

FRENCH [FRN] 13,100 or more (1993 Johnstone). Indo-European, Italic, Romance, Italo-Western, Western, Gallo-Iberian, Gallo-Romance, Gallo-Rhaetian, Oïl, French. Used mainly by intellectuals, professionals, authorities. Taught in school as a third language. Used for streets, shops, travel tickets, hotel registries, menus. National language. Bible 1530-1986. See main entry under France.

GERMAN, STANDARD [GER] 9,200 or more (1993 Johnstone). Indo-European, Germanic, West, High German, German, Middle German, East Middle German. Used as a second language by industrial workers and rural people. Taught in school as a second language. National language. Bible 1466-1982. See main entry under Germany.

LUXEMBOURGEOIS ***(LUXEMBURGISH, LUXEMBURGIAN, LUXEMBOURGISH, LETZBURGISCH, LËTZEBUERGESCH, MOSELLE FRANCONIAN, FRANKISH)*** [LUX] 250,000 first language speakers in Luxembourg, perhaps 50,000 as second language (1998). Population total all countries 300,000. Also spoken in Belgium, France, Germany, USA. Indo-European, Germanic, West, High German, German, Middle German, Moselle Franconian. As distinct from Standard German as is Dutch (Stephens 1976), and not inherently intelligible with it. A Moselle variety of Frankish-German origin, related to varieties of Mitteldeutsch of Belgium. Bilingual level estimates for French are 0 0%, 1 10%, 2 25%, 3 40%, 4 15%, 5 10%. Speakers learn French and German mainly in school. Younger well-educated people speak English. Most written statements are in French (official) or German (less official, TV, newspaper). French used in high school, for speaking to foreigners at work. German used in school for technical terms, speaking to tourists, commuters from Germany. Everyday life, home, school for explanations, court, parliament. All ages. Vigorous use. The mother tongue of most of the population. Taught in school. For most people it is the language of creativity. Literature flourishes at a modest level. Pride in ethnic identity and language. West and Central varieties considered to be more sophisticated, North considered more rural, peasant-like. The variety used by older Belgian-border inhabitants is considered old-fashioned and riddled with French words, but perfectly intelligible. German is considered to be a foreign language, not to be used with others who speak Luxembourgeois. National language. Dictionary. Grammar. SVO; prepositions; genitives, articles, adjectives, numerals, relatives before noun heads; question word initial; 3 prefixes, 2 suffixes on a word; rigid word order; passives; nontonal. Literacy rate in second language: 99% German, French. Written Luxembourgeois not taught in school, so use depends on individual. Letters often written in it. Newspapers, radio programs, TV. Christian.

MACEDONIA

The former Yugoslav Republic of Macedonia (FYROM). National or official language: Macedonian. 1,999,000 (1998 UN). Capital: Skopje. Part of Yugoslavia until 1992. Different from the region of Greece with the name Macedonia. Also includes Greek. Information mainly from B. Comrie 1987; W. Browne 1989, 1996. Data accuracy estimate: B. The number of languages listed for Macedonia is 8. Of those, all are living languages. Diversity index 0.49.

ADYGHE ***(WEST CIRCASSIAN, ADYGEY)*** [ADY] A few villages in Macedonia. North Caucasian, Northwest, Circassian. Sunni Muslim. NT 1992. See main entry under Russia.

ALBANIAN, GHEG ***(GEG)*** [ALS] 242,250 in Macedonia (1992). Indo-European, Albanian, Gheg. Shiptars: Sunni and Bektashi Muslim. NT 1869-1990. See main entry under Yugoslavia.

BALKAN GAGAUZ TURKISH ***(BALKAN TURKIC)*** [BGX] 4,000 in Macedonia and Greece. Macedonian Gagauz dialect in the Kumanovo area, Yuruk dialect in the Bitola area. Altaic, Turkic, Southern, Turkish. Dialects: MACEDONIAN GAGAUZ, YURUK (YORUK, KONYAR). A different language from Gagauz of Moldova, Bulgaria, and Romania. Nomadic shepherds (Yuruk). Christian (Macedonian Gagauz, Yuruk), Muslim (Yuruk). See main entry under Turkey.

MACEDONIAN ***(MAKEDONSKI, SLAVIC, MACEDONIAN SLAVIC)*** [MKJ] 1,386,000 in Macedonia (1986). Population total all countries 2,000,000 (1999 WA). The northern dialect is in Kumanovo-Kratovo region; the southeastern dialect around Gevgelija, Strumica, and Lake Dojran; the western dialect has one subdialect in the Veles, Prilep, Kichevo, and Bitola region, and another in the Debar-Galchnik region. Also spoken in Albania, Bulgaria, Canada, Greece, Hungary, Slovenia. Indo-European, Slavic, South, Eastern. Dialects: NORTHERN MACEDONIAN, SOUTHEASTERN MACEDONIAN, WESTERN MACEDONIAN. The standard dialect was recognized in 1944. Sociopolitical attitudes are strong: called 'Slavic' in Greece, considered to be a dialect of Bulgarian by some in Bulgaria. National language. Grammar. Newspapers, radio programs. Bible 1990.

ROMANI, BALKAN [RMN] 120,000 in Macedonia and Yugoslavia, including 100,000 Arlija, 20,000 Dzambazi. Balkans. Indo-European, Indo-Iranian, Indo-Aryan, Central zone, Romani, Balkan. Dialects: ARLIJA, DZAMBAZI, TINNERS ROMANI. The Arlija dialect (252,000 to 367,000 total) is understood by Greek Romani and Dzambazi speakers. Ethnic group: Jerlídes (Macedonia, southern Serbia). Muslim. Bible portions 1912-1937. See main entry under Yugoslavia.

ROMANIAN, MACEDO ***(ARUMANIAN, AROMUNIAN, ARMINA, MACEDO-RUMANIAN)*** [RUP] 8,467 (1994 official figures) to 100,000 (1994 British Helsinki Human Rights Group). Concentrated in the regions of Skopje, Stip, Bitola, Krusevo, and Struga, and in Ohrid, Kocani-Vinica, Sveti Nikole, Kumanovo, and Gevgelija. Indo-European, Italic, Romance, Eastern. Structurally a distinct language from Romanian (F. Agard). Split from the other 3 Romanian languages between 500 and 1000 A.D. 'Armini' refers to the people. Bible portions 1881-1889. See main entry under Greece.

SERBO-CROATIAN [SRC] Indo-European, Slavic, South, Western. Dialect: SERBIAN. SVO. Roman script used. Christian. Bible 1831-1968. See main entry under Yugoslavia.

TURKISH ***(OSMANLI)*** [TRK] 250,000 in Macedonia and Yugoslavia (1982 estimate). Altaic, Turkic, Southern, Turkish. Dialects: MACEDONIAN, DINLER. Sunni and Bektashi Muslim. Bible 1827-1941. See main entry under Turkey.

MALTA

Repubblika Ta'Malta. National or official languages: Maltese, English. 384,000 (1998 UN). Literacy rate 90% to 96%. Also includes Arabic 250. Information mainly from M. Bateson 1967. Christian, secular. Blind population 565. Deaf population 20,799. Deaf institutions: 3. Data accuracy estimate: B. The number of languages listed for Malta is 3. Of those, all are living languages. Diversity index 0.02.

ENGLISH [ENG] 2,400 speakers in Malta (1993 Johnstone). Indo-European, Germanic, West, English. National language. Bible 1535-1989. See main entry under United Kingdom.

MALTESE ***(MALTI)*** [MLS] 300,000 in Malta (1975 Katzner). Population total all countries 330,000 or more. Also spoken in Australia, Canada, Italy, Tunisia, United Kingdom, USA. Afro-Asiatic, Semitic, Central, South, Arabic. Dialects: STANDARD MALTESE, PORT MALTESE, RURAL WEST MALTESE, RURAL EAST MALTESE, RURAL CENTRAL MALTESE, ZURRIEQ, GOZO. It is descended from Maghrebi Arabic but has borrowed heavily from Italian; it is a separately developed form with different syntax and phonology. No diglossia with Standard Arabic. Not endangered. National language. Grammar. Roman script. Bible 1932-1984.

MALTESE SIGN LANGUAGE [MDL] Deaf sign language.

MOLDOVA

National or official language: Romanian (Moldovan). 4,378,000 (1998 UN). Formerly part of USSR. Capital: Chisincu. 13,012 square miles. Literacy rate 99%. Also includes Belarusan 20,000, Crimean Turkish 1,859, Standard German 7,000, Vlax Romani, Russian 562,000, Tatar, Ukrainian 600,000, Eastern Yiddish. Information mainly from T. Sebeok 1963. Christian. Data accuracy estimate: B. The number of languages listed for Moldova is 4. Of those, all are living languages. Diversity index 0.59.

BULGARIAN [BLG] 361,000 in Moldova (1979 census), 68% speak it as mother tongue. Indo-European, Slavic, South, Eastern. Christian. Bible 1864-1923. See main entry under Bulgaria.

GAGAUZ ***(GAGAUZI)*** [GAG] 173,000 in Moldova (1979 census), 89% speak it as mother tongue. Population total all countries 198,000 (1993 UBS). Cultural center is Kishinev. Also spoken in Bulgaria, Kazakhstan, Romania, Ukraine. Altaic, Turkic, Southern, Turkish. Dialects: BULGAR GAGAUZI, MARITIME GAGAUZI. Close to Turkish, but uses Russian Orthodox Christian religious vocabulary in contrast to the Islamic vocabulary of Turkish. Speakers have proclaimed autonomy from Moldova and appealed to Turkey for protection (1992 Time). Cyrillic script introduced in 1957. Christian. Bible portions 1927-1996.

ROMANI, BALKAN ***(GYPSY)*** [RMN] 12,000 in Moldova (1993 Johnstone). Moldova; Crimean Peninsula, Ukraine. Indo-European, Indo-Iranian, Indo-Aryan, Central zone, Romani, Balkan. Ethnic groups: Ursári (Moldova), Karamítika (Ukraine), Romá (Crimean Peninsula). Muslim. Bible portions 1912-1937. See main entry under Yugoslavia.

ROMANIAN ***(MOLDAVAN, ROUMANIAN, RUMANIAN)*** [RUM] 2,664,000 in Moldova (1979 census). Moldova, and throughout the country. Indo-European, Italic, Romance, Eastern. Dialects: MOLDAVAN (MOLDOVIAN, MOLDOVEAN), MUNTENIAN (WALACHIAN, MUNTEAN), BANAT, BAYASH, CHRISHANA, MARAMURESH, OLTENIA-LESSER WALLACHIA (OLTEAN). Little dialect variation. The Bayash are Gypsies who speak a dialect based on Banat, but influenced by Romani and Hungarian. Many Gypsies in Moldova and southern Ukraine speak Moldavan as mother tongue. Called 'Moldavan' in Moldova. National language. Cyrillic script was replaced by Roman script in 1989. Christian. Bible 1688-1984. See main entry under Romania.

MONACO

Principality of Monaco. National or official language: French. 33,000 (1998 UN). Literacy rate 99%. Information mainly from R. Arveiller 1967. Christian, Jewish. Deaf population 1,879. Data accuracy estimate: B. The number of languages listed for Monaco is 3. Of those, all are living languages. Diversity index 0.52.

FRENCH ***(FRANÇAIS)*** [FRN] 17,400 in Monaco, 58% of the population (1988). Indo-European, Italic, Romance, Italo-Western, Western, Gallo-Iberian, Gallo-Romance, Gallo-Rhaetian, Oïl, French. National language. Bible 1530-1986. See main entry under France.

LIGURIAN ***(LIGURE)*** [LIJ] 5,100 in Monaco, 17% of the population (1988). Indo-European, Italic, Romance, Italo-Western, Western, Gallo-Iberian, Gallo-Romance, Gallo-Italian. Dialects: GENOESE (GENOAN, GENOVESE), MONÉGASQUE (MUNEGASC, VENTIMIGLIESE). Ligurian is closer to Piemontese, Lombard, and French than to Standard Italian. Monégasque was nearly extinct in the 1970s. Compulsory learning in schools has revived it. Bible portions 1860. See main entry under Italy.

PROVENÇAL [PRV] 4,500 in Monaco, 15% of the population (1988). Indo-European, Italic, Romance, Italo-Western, Western, Gallo-Iberian, Ibero-Romance, Oc. Dialect: NIÇARD (NIÇOIS). Speakers come from Nice and Cannes. Bible portions 1824-1975. See main entry under France.

NETHERLANDS

Kingdom of the Netherlands, Koninkrijk der Nederlanden. National or official languages: Dutch, West Frisian, Drents, Gronings, Westerwolds. 15,678,000 (1998 UN). Literacy rate 95% to 99%. Also includes Adyghe, Algerian Spoken Arabic 60,000, Moroccan Spoken Arabic 100,000, Tunisian Spoken Arabic 60,000, Assyrian Neo-Aramaic, Buru, Chaldean Neo-Aramaic, Yue Chinese 70,000, Western Farsi 5,000, Caribbean Hindustani, Indonesian 10,000, Javanese 7,500, Kabuverdianu 8,000, Kirmanjki, Kurmanji 40,000, Ambonese Malay 45,000, Papiamentu 80,000, Sranan, Tamil 7,000, Tarifit, Turkish 192,000, Turoyo 4,000, Vietnamese 8,000, Yeniche, Western Yiddish, from the former Yugoslavia 16,000. Information mainly from M. Stephens 1976; B. Comrie 1987; R. Hahn 1996-1998; D. Meijer 1996-1998; M. Evenhuis 1998. Christian, secular, Muslim, Hindu. Blind population 8,000 (1982 WCE).

Deaf population 28,000 to 931,761 (1998). Deaf institutions: 44. Data accuracy estimate: B. The number of languages listed for Netherlands is 16. Of those, all are living languages. Diversity index 0.20.

ACHTERHOEKS ***(ACHTERHOEK, AACHTERHOEKS)*** [ACT] Northeastern, Gelderland Province. Indo-European, Germanic, West, Low Saxon-Low Franconian, Low Saxon. Bilingualism in Dutch. Official language.

DRENTS ***(DRENTE)*** [DRT] Drenthe Province, northeastern Netherlands near German border. Indo-European, Germanic, West, Low Saxon-Low Franconian, Low Saxon. Dialects: NORTH DRENTE (NOORD-DRENTS), SOUTH DRENTE (ZUID-DRENTS). Bilingualism in Dutch. Official language. Dictionary.

DUTCH ***(NEDERLANDS, HOLLANDS)*** [DUT] 13,400,000 in the Netherlands (1976 WA). Population total all countries 20,000,000 or more (1988 J. G. Kooij in B. Comrie). Also spoken in Aruba, Australia, Belgium, Canada, France, Germany, Indonesia, Israel, Netherlands Antilles, Philippines, Suriname, UAE, USA. Indo-European, Germanic, West, Low Saxon-Low Franconian, Low Franconian. Dialects: BREDAS, VENLOS. The name 'Dutch' is resented by some speakers. National language. Dictionary. Grammar. SOV. Bible 1522-1988.

DUTCH SIGN LANGUAGE ***(SIGN LANGUAGE OF THE NETHERLANDS, SLN)*** [DSE] 20,000 deaf use Dutch Sign Language. There are 400,000 hearing impaired, 28,000 deaf (1986 Gallaudet Univ.). Deaf sign language. All users listed are adults (1986). There are 5 varieties associated with 5 schools for the deaf, each with about 1,500 students. There have been elementary schools for the deaf since 1790. Developed from French Sign Language, some features similar to American and British sign languages. Currently in transition. Distinct from Signed Dutch. There is a manual system for spelling. Dictionary. TV.

FRISIAN, WESTERN ***(FRYSK, FRIES)*** [FRI] 700,000 in the Netherlands, including 400,000 in Friesland, 300,000 elsewhere (1976 Stephens). Population total all countries 730,000 or more. Friesland, northern Netherlands. Also spoken in Canada, Denmark, Germany, USA. Indo-European, Germanic, West, Frisian. Dialect: TOWN FRISIAN. Linguistically between Dutch and English. Not intelligible with Eastern and Northern Frisian of Germany (E. Matteson SIL 1978). 71% lexical similarity with Standard German, 61% with English, 74% with Eastern Frisian. Most speakers are bilingual in Dutch. Over 70% of those in Friesland still speak Western Frisian. Town Frisian is a mixed language. National language. Literacy rate in first language: Speakers not generally literate in Frisian. Bilingual education is compulsory in Friesland but speakers are not generally literate in Frisian. Has an official orthography in the Netherlands. Bible 1943-1978.

GRONINGS ***(GRONINGEN, GRUNNINGS)*** [GOS] Groningen Province. Indo-European, Germanic, West, Low Saxon-Low Franconian, Low Saxon. Dialects: WEST GRONINGEN (WEST GRONINGS), GRONINGEN-EAST FRISIAN (GRONINGS-OOSTFRIES). Most use Dutch as second language. The primary language of many rural people. Official language. Dictionary. Bible portions 1955-1956.

ROMANI, SINTE [RMO] 500 to 1,000 Manouche in the Netherlands. Indo-European, Indo-Iranian, Indo-Aryan, Central zone, Romani, Northern. Dialect: MANOUCHE. Christian. Bible portions 1875-1995. See main entry under Yugoslavia.

ROMANI, VLAX [RMY] 1,000 in the Netherlands including 500 Kalderash, 500 Lovari. Indo-European, Indo-Iranian, Indo-Aryan, Central zone, Romani, Vlax. Dialects: KALDERASH, LOVARI. Christian. NT 1984-1986. See main entry under Romania.

SALLANDS ***(SALLAND, SALLAN)*** [SNK] Northeastern, Overijssels Province. Sallands in the Center. Indo-European, Germanic, West, Low Saxon-Low Franconian, Low Saxon. Bilingualism in Dutch. Official language.

STELLINGWERFS ***(STELLINGWERFSTELLINGWARFS)*** [STL] Northeastern, Stellingwerven region, Friesland Province. Centers are Oosterwoolde and Wolvege. Indo-European, Germanic, West, Low Saxon-Low Franconian, Low Saxon. Bilingualism in Dutch. Official language.

TWENTS ***(TWENTE)*** [TWD] Northeastern, Overijssels Province. Twents is in the east. Indo-European, Germanic, West, Low Saxon-Low Franconian, Low Saxon. Bilingualism in Dutch. Official language.

VEENKOLONIAALS ***(VEEN COLONY)*** [VEK] Northeastern. Indo-European, Germanic, West, Low Saxon-Low Franconian, Low Saxon. Bilingualism in Dutch. Official language.

VELUWS, EAST ***(EAST VELUWE)*** [VEE] Northeastern, Gelderlaand Province. Indo-European, Germanic, West, Low Saxon-Low Franconian, Low Saxon. Bilingualism in Dutch. Official language.

VELUWS, NORTH ***(NOTH VELUWE)*** [VEL] Northeastern. Indo-European, Germanic, West, Low Saxon-Low Franconian, Low Saxon. Bilingualism in Dutch. Official language.

VLAAMS ***(FLAMAND, FLEMISH)*** [VLA] 222,000, or 60% of the 370,000 inhabitants of Zeeland in the Netherlands (1998 U. of Ghent). Holland: Province of Zeeland, and southernmost island of the Province of South Holland: Goeree-Overflakkee. Every island in the Rhine-Scheldt delta has its own dialect. Indo-European, Germanic, West, Low Saxon-Low Franconian, Low Franconian. Dialects: ZEEUWS (ZEAWS), WEST VLAAMS, FRANS VLAAMS (VLAEMSCH). Close to Dutch, English,

Frisian. Subdialects of Zeeuws include: Goerees, Flakkees, Schouws, Duvelands, Fluplands, Bevelands, Walchers, Axels, Kezands. Speakers have difficulty understanding nearby Brabant dialect of Dutch. Bilingualism in Dutch, English, German. Used for informal situations. Varies locally from all ages to over 40. Speakers have Vlaams as first and sometimes only language. 50,000 speak it as second language. Speakers sometimes refer to Dutch as 'Vlaams'. They view Dutch as the language of trade, tourism, school. Dictionary. SOV. Literacy rate in second language: 99% Dutch. There is a magazine, drama, folk music. Christian. See main entry under Belgium.

WESTERWOLDS *(WESTERWOLD)* [WEV] Northeastern. Indo-European, Germanic, West, Low Saxon-Low Franconian, Low Saxon. Bilingualism in Dutch. Official language.

NORWAY

Kingdom of Norway, Kongeriket Norge. National or official languages: Bokmal Norwegian, Nynorsk Norwegian. 4,419,000 (1998 UN). Literacy rate 96% to 100%. Also includes Danish 12,000, English, Finnish 4,000, Kurmanji 3,000, Russian 3,000, Spanish 6,500, Swedish 21,000, Tibetan, Urdu, Vietnamese 99,000, Chinese 3,000, from Africa 7,000, from Pakistan 17,000. Information mainly from M. Stephens 1976; B. Comrie 1987; I. Hancock 1991; J. Hupli 1998; B. Winsa 1998. Christian, secular. Blind population 4,000 (1982 WCE). Deaf population 4,000 to 261,618 (1998). Deaf institutions: 12. Data accuracy estimate: B. The number of languages listed for Norway is 11. Of those, all are living languages. Diversity index 0.08.

FINNISH, KVEN *(KVEN, NORTH FINNISH)* [FKV] 5,000 to 8,000 (1998 The Federation of Norwegian Kven People). Northern Norway, Tromso and Finnmark counties, Ruija, Kveeniland; city of Tromso, and in Oteren, Skibotn, Storslett, Kvaenangsbotn, Nordreisa, Alta, Borselv, Neiden, Bygoynes, Vadso. Uralic, Finno-Ugric, Finno-Permic, Finno-Cheremisic, Finno-Mordvinic, Finno-Lappic, Balto-Finnic, Finnic. Standard Finnish speakers generally understand most of it, except for some vocabulary. Closer to Tornedalen Finnish (see Sweden) than to Standard Finnish. Various dialects: northern west coast varieties differ from eastern ones. Kven has integrated Norwegian loans, whereas Tornedalen has integrated Swedish loans. Bilingualism in Norwegian, Finnish. Only older people, most in their 70s, speak Kven. There are a few books about Kven culture. Study at the University of Tromso, Institute of Finnish. Accepted from 1997 as a second language in Norway. It is now taught in schools 3 hours a week. The language and culture have been suppressed until the recent past, and are endangered. Considered to be 'Old Finnish'. Speakers of Tornedalen and Kven recognize the differences between the two. Literacy rate in second language: Over 90% in Finnish. Newspapers. Christian: Laestadian.

NORWEGIAN SIGN LANGUAGE [NSL] 4,000 deaf users out of about 4,000 deaf (1986 Gallaudet Univ.). Deaf sign language. Dialects: HOLMESTRAND, OSLO, TRONDHEIM. Intelligible with Danish and Swedish sign languages with only moderate difficulty. Not intelligible with Finnish Sign Language. Used since 1815. The first deaf school was begun in 1825, first club in 1878. It is passed to the next generation mainly through the schools. 3 dialects are associated with 3 schools. Signed Norwegian is used by teachers; pupils use Norwegian Sign Language among themselves. Signed interpretation required in court, provided some for college students, in mental health programs. Sign language instruction provided for parents of deaf children. Many classes for hearing people. There is a committee on national sign language. There is a manual system for spelling. Films, TV, videos.

NORWEGIAN, BOKMAAL *(BOKMAAL, RIKSMAAL, DANO-NORWEGIAN, NORWEGIAN)* [NRR] 4,250,000 including Nynorsk, 99.5% of population (1991 WA). Population total all countries 5,000,000 (1999 WA). Also spoken in Canada, Ecuador, Sweden, UAE, USA. Indo-European, Germanic, North, East Scandinavian, Danish-Swedish, Danish-Bokmal, Bokmal. Dialects: WESTERN NORWEGIAN (COASTAL NORWEGIAN), CENTRAL NORWEGIAN (MIDLAND NORWEGIAN), EASTERN NORWEGIAN (OSTLANDET), NORTHERN NORWEGIAN (TRONDELAAG, NORDLAND). Norwegian form of Danish and based on urban dialects. One of the two norms for written Norwegian. Spoken Norwegian has many dialects, grouped as shown under the dialect list. It was reported in 1971 that 82.5% of the pupils used Riksmaal as their main written language. Primarily urban. National language. Dictionary. Grammar. SVO. Bible 1834-1978.

NORWEGIAN, NYNORSK *(LANDSMAAL, NEW NORSE, NYNORSK, NORWEGIAN)* [NRN] Indo-European, Germanic, North, West Scandinavian. The linguist Ivar Aasen founded this written variety in the 1850s from spoken Norwegian and Old Norse. Primarily rural and based on rural dialects. One of the two norms for written Norwegian. In 1971 30% of the people used Nynorsk as their main written language. National language. SVO. Bible 1921-1938.

ROMANI, VLAX [RMY] 500 Lovari in Norway. Reported to be 3,500 Gypsies in Norway (1993 Johnstone). Indo-European, Indo-Iranian, Indo-Aryan, Central zone, Romani, Vlax. Dialect: LOVARI. Literacy rate in first language: 30% to 60%. Literacy rate in second language: 75% to 100%. Christian. NT 1984-1986. See main entry under Romania.

SAAMI, LULE ***(LULE, SAAME)*** [LPL] 500 speakers out of 1,000 to 2,000 population in Norway (1995 M. Krauss). 31,600 to 42,600 ethnic Saami in Norway (1995). Tysfjord, Hamaroy, and Folden, Norway. Uralic, Finno-Ugric, Finno-Cheremisic, Finno-Mordvinic, Finno-Lappic, Lappic, Southern. Few children speakers. Literacy rate in first language: 30% to 60%. Literacy rate in second language: 75% to 100%. Traditionally hunters, fishermen, reindeer herders. NT 1903. See main entry under Sweden.

SAAMI, NORTHERN ***("NORTHERN LAPPISH", "NORWEGIAN LAPP", SAAMI, SAME, SAMIC, "LAPP")*** [LPR] 15,000 speakers out of 30,000 to 40,000 population in Norway (1995 M. Krauss). Population total all countries 21,000 to 25,000. Finnmark, Troms, Nordland, Ofoten. Also spoken in Finland, Sweden. Uralic, Finno-Ugric, Finno-Permic, Finno-Cheremisic, Finno-Mordvinic, Finno-Lappic, Lappic, Northern. Dialects: RUIJA, TORNE, SEA LAPPISH. Two-thirds of all Saami speak Ruija. The people were formerly called "Finns", which they consider to be derogatory. The name "Lapp" is derogatory. Literacy rate in first language: 30% to 60%. Literacy rate in second language: 75% to 100%. Use in schools is now encouraged. Bible 1895.

SAAMI, PITE ***("LAPP", PITE)*** [LPB] Between Saltenfjord and Ranenfjord in Norway. Uralic, Finno-Ugric, Finno-Permic, Finno-Cheremisic, Finno-Mordvinic, Finno-Lappic, Lappic, Southern. Nearly extinct. See main entry under Sweden.

SAAMI, SOUTHERN ***("NORTHERN LAPPISH", "NORWEGIAN LAPP", SAAMI, SAME, SAMIC)*** [LPC] 300 speakers out of 600 population in Norway (1995 M. Krauss). Hatfjelldal and Wefsen, south to Elga. Uralic, Finno-Ugric, Finno-Permic, Finno-Cheremisic, Finno-Mordvinic, Finno-Lappic, Lappic, Southern. Few children speakers. Literacy rate in first language: 30% to 60%. Literacy rate in second language: 75% to 100%. See main entry under Sweden.

TAVRINGER ROMANI ***(ROMMANI, SVENSK ROMMANI, TRAVELLER SWEDISH, "TATTARE")*** [RMU] 6,000 in Norway (1998 Hallman). In eastern and northern Norway. Indo-European, Germanic, North, East Scandinavian, Danish-Swedish, Swedish. Not intelligible with Angloromani. Speakers are fluent in Swedish or Norwegian. Used mainly as a secret language by the speakers (D. Kenrick 1985). An independent language based on Swedish with heavy lexical borrowing from Northern Romani. Romani people arrived in Sweden via Denmark in 1512. A Gypsy group. See main entry under Sweden.

TRAVELLER NORWEGIAN ***(RODI, NORWEGIAN TRAVELLER)*** [RMG] Indo-European, Germanic, North, West Scandinavian. An independent language based on Norwegian with heavy lexical borrowing from Northern Romani and German Rotwelsch. Not intelligible with Angloromani. Still very much alive (1997). Spoken by the Fanter, who are not Gypsies, but have intermarried with Gypsies and Yeniche (German Travellers). The Romani influence comes from speakers who are descended from the first diaspora from India. Romani people were abandoned on the coast of Norway from British ships from 1544 onwards.

POLAND

Republic of Poland. National or official language: Polish. 38,718,000 (1998 UN). Literacy rate 98% to 99%. Also includes Czech, Greek 114,000, Lithuanian 30,000, Russian 60,000, Slovak 38,000, Eastern Yiddish. Information mainly from A. Schenker and E. Stankiewicz 1980; B. Comrie 1987. Christian, secular. Blind population 21,523. Deaf population 50,000 to 2,342,493 (1998). Deaf institutions: 11. Data accuracy estimate: B. The number of languages listed for Poland is 12. Of those, 11 are living languages and 1 is extinct. Diversity index 0.12.

BELARUSAN ***(BYELORUSSIAN, WHITE RUSSIAN)*** [RUW] 230,000 in Poland (1993 Johnstone). Indo-European, Slavic, East. Cyrillic alphabet. Bible 1973. See main entry under Belarus.

GERMAN, STANDARD [GER] 500,000 in Poland (1998). Silesia and elsewhere. Indo-European, Germanic, West, High German, German, Middle German, East Middle German. Bible 1466-1982. See main entry under Germany.

KASHUBIAN ***(KASZUBSKI, CASHUBIAN, CASSUBIAN)*** [CSB] A few thousand speakers. Most of the ethnic group of over 100,000 speak a regional variety of Polish (1993 Tapani Salminen). Population total both countries 3,000 or more. The left bank of the Lower Vistula in north central Poland, near the Baltic coast, west of the Bay of Gdansk, and a narrow strip inland, southwest from Gdynia. Also spoken in Canada. Indo-European, Slavic, West, Lechitic. Dialects: KASHUBIAN PROPER, SLOVINCIAN. German influences in the language. There are transitional dialects between Kashubian Proper, Slovenian, and Polish. Few children speakers of Kashubian Proper. The Slovincian dialect is extinct. NT 1995.

POLISH ***(POLSKI, POLNISCH)*** [PQL] 36,554,000 in Poland, 98% of the population (1986). Population total all countries 44,000,000 (1999 WA). Also spoken in Australia, Austria, Azerbaijan, Belarus, Canada, Czech Republic, Estonia, Finland, Germany, Hungary, Israel, Kazakhstan, Latvia, Lithuania, Romania, Russia (Europe), Slovakia, Ukraine, UAE, USA. Indo-European, Slavic, West, Lechitic. Dialect: UPPER SILESIAN. National language. SVO. Roman script. Christian, Muslim. Bible 1561-1965.

POLISH SIGN LANGUAGE [PSO] (50,000 deaf, 25,000 members of Polish Association of the Deaf; 1986 Gallaudet Univ.). Deaf sign language. Various regional dialects. Not intelligible with ASL. 5,000 deaf children in deaf schools, plus 1,000 who attend school with hearing children. There is a committee for the unification of Polish Sign Language. Used since 1889. Elementary schools for deaf children since 1817. Signed interpretation required in court, provided for some college students and in important public events. Sign language instruction for parents of deaf children. Many sign language classes for hearing people. There is a committee on national sign language. There is a manual system for spelling. Dictionary. Grammar. Films, TV, videos.

PRUSSIAN ***(OLD PRUSSIAN)*** [PRG] East Prussia, formerly in Germany, now in Poland and Russia. Indo-European, Baltic, Western. Among other extinct Baltic languages are: Selonian, Yotvingian, Semigallian, Curonian. Became extinct the end of the 17th or beginning of the 18th century. Extinct.

ROMANI, BALTIC [ROM] 30,000 in Poland. Reported to be 81,000 Rom in Poland (1993 Johnstone). Population total all countries 100,000. Baltic region, central and southern parts. Also spoken in Belarus, Estonia, Latvia, Lithuania, Russia (Asia), Ukraine. Indo-European, Indo-Iranian, Indo-Aryan, Central zone, Romani, Northern. Dialects: LATVIAN ROMANI (LETTISH ROMANI), NORTH RUSSIAN ROMANI, WHITE RUSSIAN ROMANI, ESTONIAN ROMANI, POLISH ROMANI. Ethnic groups: Pólska Foldítka, Romá. Christian. Bible portions 1933-1996.

ROMANI, CARPATHIAN [RMC] One dialect is in south Poland, east Hungary, and Galicia; another in Transylvania, Romania; others in Czech Republic and Slovakia; Ukraine, USA. Indo-European, Indo-Iranian, Indo-Aryan, Central zone, Romani, Northern. Dialects: GALICIAN, TRANSYLVANIAN. Christian. Bible portions 1936-1996. See main entry under Czech Republic.

ROMANI, SINTE ***(SINTI, TSIGANE)*** [RMO] Indo-European, Indo-Iranian, Indo-Aryan, Central zone, Romani, Northern. Dialect: MANUCHE (MANOUCHE). Not intelligible with Vlach Romani. Ethnic group: Sasítka Romá. Christian. Bible portions 1875-1995. See main entry under Yugoslavia.

ROMANI, VLAX [RMY] 5,000 Lovari in Poland. Indo-European, Indo-Iranian, Indo-Aryan, Central zone, Romani, Vlax. Dialect: LOVARI. Christian. NT 1984-1995. See main entry under Romania.

SILESIAN, LOWER ***(LOWER SCHLESISCH)*** [SLI] Dolny Slask (Lower Silesia). Also spoken in Czech Republic, Germany. Indo-European, Germanic, West, High German, German, Middle German, East Middle German. Bilingualism in Polish. Even spoken by younger people. There is literature by Gerhard Hauptmann. Different than Upper Silesian, a dialect of Polish.

UKRAINIAN [UKR] 1,500,000 in Poland. Indo-European, Slavic, East. The largest minority language group in Poland. Christian. Bible 1903-1962. See main entry under Ukraine.

PORTUGAL

Republic of Portugal, República Portuguesa. National or official language: Portuguese. 9,869,000 (1998 UN). Literacy rate 83% to 84%. Also includes Kabuverdianu 50,000, Arabic 27,000, from Goa India 20,000, Timor Indonesia 3,000, Brazil 103,000, Angola or Mozambique 100,000, Cape Verde 3,000, elsewhere in Africa 800,000. Information mainly from R. A. Hall 1977; F. B. Agard 1984; B. Comrie 1987. Christian, secular. Blind population 8,225. Deaf population 8,000 to 638,070 (1998). Deaf institutions: 16. Data accuracy estimate: B. The number of languages listed for Portugal is 7. Of those, all are living languages. Diversity index 0.02.

ASTURIAN ***(ASTURIAN-LEONESE)*** [AUB] Miranda do Douro. Indo-European, Italic, Romance, Italo-Western, Western, Ibero-Romance, North, Central. Dialects: WEST ASTURIAN, CENTRAL ASTURIAN (BABLE). As different from Spanish as Galician or Catalan; more different than Murcian and Andalusian. Close to Leonese. About 80% intelligibility with Spanish (R. A. Hall, Jr. 1989); enough to cause disruption of communicative ability (T. Erickson SIL 1992). Intelligibility among the dialects is adequate. Central Asturian is considered the model, and has the most speakers. Children 6 to 16 are required to study it in school. It is voluntary for those 16-19. They use Spanish in formal situations and with outsiders. There is literature, both popular and literary, since the 17th century; poetry, and traditional ballads and chivalric novels of oral tradition. The Academy of the Asturian Language was formed in 1981, to revive the academy of the 18th century. The Vaqueros ethnic group speaks Western Asturian. Dictionary. Western Asturian may need orthography adaptation. NT 1997. See main entry under Spain.

CALÓ ***(CALÃO, GITANO, IBERIAN ROMANI)*** [RMR] 5,000 in Portugal. Indo-European, Italic, Romance, Italo-Western, Western, Gallo-Iberian, Ibero-Romance, West Iberian, Castilian. Dialects: SPANISH CALO, PORTUGUESE CALÃO (CALÃO, LUSITANO-ROMANI), CATALONIAN CALO, BASQUE CALO, BRAZILIAN CALÃO. A Gypsy language very different from other Romani. Calão of Portugal is structured on Portuguese regional dialects where the overlap is not distinct between Spanish and Portuguese. Bilingualism in Portuguese. Christian. Bible portions 1837-1872. See main entry under Spain.

GALICIAN ***(GALEGO, GALLEGO)*** [GLN] 15,000 in Tras Os Montes (1994 D. and N. Burns). Northern provinces of Entre-Minho-e-Douro and Trazoz-Montes (Tras Os Montes). Indo-European, Italic, Romance, Italo-Western, Western, Gallo-Iberian, Ibero-Romance, West Iberian, Portuguese-Galician. Galician is between Portuguese and Spanish, but closer to Portuguese. There is an Academy of the Galician Language. There is tension between those in Tras Os Montes Portugal and Spain over dialect differences and identity. There is tension between those in Tras Os Montes Portugal and Spain over orthography. Bible 1989-1992. See main entry under Spain.

MIRANDA DO DOURO ***(MIRANDESA, MIRANDES)*** [MWL] 10,000 (1995 SIL). Northeast Portugal, southeastern tip of Tras Os Montes area, on the Spain border, at the latitude of Zamora, city of Miranda. Indo-European, Italic, Romance, Italo-Western, Western, Gallo-Iberian, Ibero-Romance, West Iberian, Asturo-Leonese. Related to Asturian and Leonés. Probably separated from them at the time of the invasion of the Moors. A folklore group is promoting the language and culture. The language has been introduced into the schools. The people have a different style of dress from their neighbors (black, handwoven cloth). Official language. Agriculturalists.

PORTUGUESE ***(PORTUGUÊS)*** [POR] 10,000,000 in Portugal. Population total all countries 176,000,000 first language speakers (1999 WA), 191,000,000 including second language speakers (1999 WA). Iberia, Azores, Madeira. Also spoken in 33 other countries including Andorra, Angola, Antigua and Barbuda, Belgium, Brazil, Canada, Cape Verde Islands, China, Congo, France, Germany, Guinea-Bissau, Guyana, India, Indonesia, Jamaica, Luxembourg, Malawi, Mozambique. Indo-European, Italic, Romance, Italo-Western, Western, Gallo-Iberian, Ibero-Romance, West Iberian, Portuguese-Galician. Dialects: BEIRA, GALICIAN, MADEIRA-AZORES, ESTREMENHO, BRAZILIAN PORTUGUESE. Standard Portuguese of Portugal is based on Southern or Estremenho dialect (Lisbon and Coimbra). Official language. Dictionary. Grammar. SVO. Literacy rate in second language: 83% to 84%. Christian. Bible 1751, in press (1993).

PORTUGUESE SIGN LANGUAGE ***(LINGUA GESTUAL PORTUGUESA)*** [PSR] (Used by a considerable portion of the 8,000 deaf persons; 1986 Gallaudet Univ.). Deaf sign language. Dialects: LISBON, OPORTO. Not derived from Portuguese. Different dialects in 2 different deaf schools in Lisbon and Oporto. Related to Swedish Sign Language. Signed Portuguese has similar signs to Signed Swedish. It began in 1823.

ROMANI, VLAX [RMY] 500 Kalderash in Portugal. Indo-European, Indo-Iranian, Indo-Aryan, Central zone, Romani, Vlax. Dialect: KALDERASH. Christian. NT 1984-1986. See main entry under Romania.

ROMANIA

National or official language: Romanian. 22,474,000 (1998 UN). Literacy rate 96% to 98%. Also includes Gheg Albanian, Slovak 34,000, Ukrainian 67,000, Eastern Yiddish, Possibly Rusyn. Information mainly from R. A. Hall 1977; I. Hancock 1979, 1987, 1988; F. B. Agard 1984; B. Comrie 1987. Christian, secular, Muslim. Blind population 15,918. Deaf population 1,405,464. Deaf institutions: 20. Data accuracy estimate: B. The number of languages listed for Romania is 15. Of those, all are living languages. Diversity index 0.20.

BULGARIAN [BLG] 10,439 (1966 census). Romanian Banat. The Palityan dialect is also in Bulgaria and Hungary. Indo-European, Slavic, South, Eastern. Dialect: PALITYAN (PALITIANI, BOGOMIL). The Palityan dialect is apparently intelligible with other Bulgarian dialects. In Romania it is a recognized minority language. Christian. Bible 1864-1923. See main entry under Bulgaria.

CRIMEAN TURKISH ***(CRIMEAN TATAR)*** [CRH] 25,000 in Romania (1982 estimate). Eastern Romania. Altaic, Turkic, Southern. Dialects: NORTHERN CRIMEAN (CRIMEAN NOGAI, STEPPE CRIMEAN), CENTRAL CRIMEAN, SOUTHERN CRIMEAN. Muslim. NT 1666-1825. See main entry under Uzbekistan.

GAGAUZ ***(GAGAUZI)*** [GAG] Altaic, Turkic, Southern, Turkish. Dialects: BULGAR GAGAUZ, MARITIME GAGAUZ. Christian. Bible portions 1927-1996. See main entry under Moldova.

GERMAN, STANDARD [GER] 150,000 in Romania (1993). Transylvania. Indo-European, Germanic, West, High German, German, Middle German, East Middle German. Dialect: TRANSYLVANIA.

Over 70% of the 500,000 1988 population has emigrated to Germany since 1988 (1993 Johnstone). The people are known as 'Saxons'. Bible 1466-1982. See main entry under Germany.

GREEK [GRK] Indo-European, Greek, Attic. The Karakatchan are Romanian nomadic shepherds who speak Greek. Bible 1840-1955. See main entry under Greece.

HUNGARIAN ***(MAGYAR)*** [HNG] 1,700,000 to 3,000,000 in Romania (1998). Trans-Carpathian provinces. Uralic, Finno-Ugric, Ugric, Hungarian. Bilingualism in Romanian. Newspapers. Bible 1590-1991. See main entry under Hungary.

POLISH ***(POLSKI)*** [PQL] 10,000 in Romania. Indo-European, Slavic, West, Lechitic. Christian. Bible 1561-1965. See main entry under Poland.

ROMANI, BALKAN [RMN] Black sea region. Indo-European, Indo-Iranian, Indo-Aryan, Central zone, Romani, Balkan. Dialect: URSÁRI (USARI). Many have gone to Germany since 1989. Muslim. Bible portions 1912-1937. See main entry under Yugoslavia.

ROMANI, CARPATHIAN [RMC] One dialect is in Transylvania. Indo-European, Indo-Iranian, Indo-Aryan, Central zone, Romani, Northern. Dialects: GALICIAN, TRANSYLVANIAN. Christian. Bible portions 1936-1996. See main entry under Czech Republic.

ROMANI, VLAX ***(GYPSY, TSIGENE, ROMANESE, VLAX ROMANY, DANUBIAN)*** [RMY] 200,000 to 250,000 in Romania. Population total all countries 1,500,000 (1986). 6,000,000 to 11,000,000 all Gypsies in the world (1987 Ian Hancock). Also spoken in 27 other countries including Albania, Argentina, Bosnia-Herzegovina, Brazil, Bulgaria, Canada, Chile, Colombia, France, Germany, Greece, Hungary, Italy, Mexico, Moldova, Netherlands, Norway, Poland, Portugal. Indo-European, Indo-Iranian, Indo-Aryan, Central zone, Romani, Vlax. Dialects: SEDENTARY ROMANIA, KALDERASH (KELDERASHÍCKO, COPPERSMITH), UKRAINE-MOLDAVIA, EASTERN, CHURARI (CHURARÍCKO, SIEVEMAKERS), LOVARI (LOVARÍCKO), MACHVANO (MACHVANMCKO), NORTH ALBANIAN, SOUTH ALBANIAN, SERBO-BOSNIAN, ZAGUNDZI, SEDENTARY BULGARIA, GHAGAR, GREKURJA (GRECO). Vlax developed from the Romani spoken when they were slaves in Romania for 500 years. There were migrations out of Romania from the mid-14th to mid-19th centuries. Those who left earlier have less Romanian influence in their dialects. Kalderash, Ursari, Churari are occupational ethnonyms; Machvano is a geographical one. Other names are Argintari 'silversmith', and Lingurari 'spoonmakers'. Machvano and Serbian Kalderash have a south Slavic superstratum; Russian Kalderash is influenced by east Slavic, mainly Russian; Lovari is influenced by Hungarian; Grekurja is probably Turkish influenced and is distinct from the Greek Romani dialect of Balkan Romani. All 20 or more Vlax dialects are inherently intelligible; the differences are mainly lexical and sociolinguistic (I. Hancock). Ethnic groups: Chache, Kaldarari, Lovári. The people are called Rroma. Grammar. Christian. NT 1984-1995.

ROMANIAN ***(RUMANIAN, MOLDAVIAN, DACO-RUMANIAN)*** [RUM] 20,520,000 in Romania, 90% of the population (1986). Population total all countries 26,000,000 (1999 WA). Moldavian is in Moldova to the northeast, and Muntenian in Muntenia, or Wallachia in the southeast, other dialects in the north and west, including much of Transylvania. Also spoken in Australia, Azerbaijan, Canada, Finland, Hungary, Israel, Kazakhstan, Kyrgyzstan, Moldova, Russia (Europe), Tajikistan, Turkmenistan, Ukraine, USA, Uzbekistan, Yugoslavia. Indo-European, Italic, Romance, Eastern. Dialects: MOLDAVIAN, MUNTENIAN (WALACHIAN), TRANSYLVANIAN, BANAT, BAYASH. Romanian has 77% lexical similarity with Italian, 75% with French, 74% with Sardinian, 73% with Catalan, 72% with Portuguese and Rheto-Romance, 71% with Spanish. The Bayash are Gypsies who have lost their language and now speak Romanian based on the Banat dialect with Romani and Hungarian influences. National language. Grammar. SVO. Deciduous forest. Mountain slope. Peasant agriculturalists, other. Christian. Bible 1688-1989.

ROMANIAN SIGN LANGUAGE [RMS] Deaf sign language.

ROMANIAN, MACEDO ***(AROMANIAN)*** [RUP] 28,000 (official Romanian figure) to 150,000 (World Union of Aromanian Women), or 200,000 (President of the Aromanian Youth Foundation). Southeastern Romania, especially Dobrudja (75%), but also in major cities such as Bucharest and Constanta, and other places. Indo-European, Italic, Romance, Eastern. The educational structure is being set up to teach in Aromanian. Speakers are officially related to the Romanians rather than classified as a minority. Newspapers, radio programs, TV. See main entry under Greece.

SERBO-CROATIAN ***(SERBIAN)*** [SRC] 80,000 in Romania (1993 Johnstone). Indo-European, Slavic, South, Western. Several dialects. Christian, Muslim. Bible 1804-1968. See main entry under Yugoslavia.

TURKISH ***(OSMANLI)*** [TRK] 150,000 in Romania (1993 Johnstone). Along the Danube in southeast Romania. Altaic, Turkic, Southern, Turkish. Dialect: DANUBIAN. Muslim. Bible 1827-1941. See main entry under Turkey.

RUSSIA

National or official language: Russian. 147,434,000 including Europe and Asia regions (1998 UN). Formerly part of the Union of Soviet Socialist Republics. See Russia, Europe and Russia, Asia for languages in the European and Asian regions, respectively. Literacy rate 98% to 99%. Information mainly from T. Sebeok 1963; B. Comrie 1987; A. E. Kibrik 1991. Secular, Christian, Muslim, Jewish. Blind population 350,000 in the former USSR (1982 WCE). Deaf institutions: 22. Data accuracy estimate: A2, B. The number of languages listed for Russia is 103. Of those, 100 are living languages and 3 are extinct. Diversity index 0.27.

RUSSIA (EUROPE)

See Russia in Asia for information about languages in Asia. Also includes Armenian 532,000, Assyrian Neo-Aramaic 10,000, Belarusan 1,206,000, Estonian 56,000, Standard German 896,000, Greek 105,000, Latvian 29,000, Lithuanian 70,000, Polish 94,000, Romanian 178,000, Eastern Yiddish 701,000. Data accuracy estimate: B. The number of languages listed for Russia (Europe) is 59. Of those, 58 are living languages and 1 is extinct. Diversity index 0.21.

ABAZA ***(ABAZIN, ABAZINTSY, ASHUWA)*** [ABQ] 34,800 in Russia (1989 census), about 95% speak it as mother tongue. Population total all countries 44,900. Karachay-Cherkess Republic. Also spoken in Germany, Turkey (Asia), USA. North Caucasian, Northwest, Abkhaz-Abazin. Dialects: TAPANTA, ASHKARAUA, BEZSHAGH. Some dialects are partially intelligible with Abkhaz. 69.5% are fluent in Russian. More vigorous in Russia than Turkey. 'Abaza' is their name for themselves. 'Abazin, Abazintsy, Abazinskiy' are Russian names for them. Dictionary. Grammar. SOV; ergative-absolutive agreement on the verb. Modified Cyrillic script. Newspapers, radio programs, TV. Muslim.

ADYGHE ***(CIRCASSIAN, LOWER CIRCASSIAN, KIAKH, KJAX, WEST CIRCASSIAN, ADYGEI, ADYGEY)*** [ADY] 125,000 in Russia (1993 UBS), 96% speak it as mother tongue. Population total all countries 300,000. Adygea Republic. Maikop is the capital. Also spoken in Australia, Egypt, France, Germany, Iraq, Israel, Jordan, Macedonia, Netherlands, Syria, Turkey (Asia), USA. North Caucasian, Northwest, Circassian. Dialects: SHAPSUG (SAPSUG), XAKUCHI, BEZHEDUKH (BZEDUX, BZHEDUG, BEZHEHUX-TEMIRGOI, TEMIRGOJ, CHEMGUI), ABADZEX (ABADEKH, ABADZEG), NATUZAJ (NATUKHAI). Some literature. Dictionary. Grammar. SOV. Cyrillic script used. Used for instruction in schools. Sunni Muslim. NT 1992.

AGHUL ***(AGUL, AGHULSHUY, AGULY)*** [AGX] 19,000 in Russia, 98% speak it as mother tongue (1979 census). Population total both countries 19,000 or more. Southern Dagestan ASSR. Also spoken in Azerbaijan. North Caucasian, Northeast, Lezgian. Dialects: KOSHAN, KEREN, GEKXUN, AGUL. Lezgi is used as the literary language. Not a literary language. Sunni Muslim.

AKHVAKH ***(AXVAX)*** [AKV] 5,000 (1975 Ruhlen). Southern Dagestan ASSR. North Caucasian, Northeast, Avaro-Andi-Dido, Andi. Dialects: KAXIB, NORTHERN AKHVAKH, SOUTHERN AKHVAKH (TLYANUB, TSEGOB). 'Dialects' are diverse; speakers communicate in Avar. Avar is used as the literary language. Not a written language. Muslim.

ANDI ***(ANDII, QWANNAB, ANDIY)*** [ANI] 10,000 (1993 UBS). Southern Dagestan ASSR. North Caucasian, Northeast, Avaro-Andi-Dido, Andi. Dialects: MUNIN, RIKVANI, KVANXIDATL, GAGATL, ZILO. Dialects appear to be quite divergent. Avar is used as the literary language. Not a written language. Muslim.

ARCHI ***(ARCHIN, ARCHINTSY)*** [ARC] 859 (1975 Ruhlen). Southern Dagestan ASSR. North Caucasian, Northeast, Lezgian. One of the most divergent of the Lezgian languages. Avar is used as the literary language. Used in everyday family communication. Live in native territory. Traditional way of life. Not a written language. Muslim.

AVAR ***(AVARO, DAGESTANI)*** [AVR] 556,000 in Russia (1989 census). Population total all countries 601,000. Southern Dagestan ASSR and Terek and Sulak river areas. Also spoken in Azerbaijan, Kazakhstan, Turkey (Asia). North Caucasian, Northeast, Avaro-Andi-Dido, Avar. Dialects: SALATAV, KUNZAKH (XUNZAX, NORTHERN AVAR), KELEB, BACADIN, UNTIB, SHULANIN, KAXIB, HID, ANDALAL-GXDATL, KARAX (KARAKH), BATLUX, ANCUX (ANTSUKH), ZAKATALY (CHAR). Bilingualism in Russian. North Caucasian is also called 'Caucasian'. Trade language. Cyrillic script used. Education in it for the first two years, except in cities. Newspapers. Sunni Muslim. Bible portions 1979-1996.

BAGVALAL ***(KVANADIN, KVANADA, BAGULAL, BAGVALIN, BARBALIN)*** [KVA] 5,500 (1962 Maxwell). Southern Dagestan ASSR. North Caucasian, Northeast, Avaro-Andi-Dido, Andi. Dialect:

TLISI. Close to Tindin but probably not inherently intelligible. Avar is used as a literary language. Not a written language. Muslim.

BASHKIR ***(BASQUORT)*** [BXK] 901,150 or 67% of the ethnic group in Russia (1993 Johnstone). Population total all countries 1,000,000 (1999 WA). Baskir ASSR, between the Volga River and Ural Mountains, and beyond the Urals. Ufa is the capital. Over 61% of the people live in cities. Also spoken in Kazakhstan, Kyrgyzstan, Tajikistan, Turkmenistan, Ukraine, Uzbekistan. Altaic, Turkic, Western, Uralian. Dialects: KUVAKAN (MOUNTAIN BASHKIR), YURMATY (STEPPE BASHKIR), BURZHAN (WESTERN BASHKIR). Close to Tatar. Bilingualism in Tatar. The people call themselves 'Bashkort'. Cyrillic script. Oil workers, agriculturalists; traditionally cattle raisers. Sunni Muslim. Bible portions 1899-1995.

BEZHTA ***(BEZHITA, BEZHETA, BEZHTI, BEXITA, BECHITIN, KAPUCHA, KUPUCA, KAPUCHIN)*** [KAP] 3,000 (1993 UBS). Southern Dagestan ASSR. North Caucasian, Northeast, Avaro-Andi-Dido, Dido. Dialects: BEZHTA, TLYADALY, KHOCHARKHOTIN. A separate language from Hunzib (B. Comrie 1989). Avar is used as the literary language; bilingual proficiency undetermined. Not a written language. Muslim.

BOTLIKH ***(BOTLIX)*** [BPH] 3,500 including Godoberi (1962 Maxwell). Southern Dagestan ASSR. North Caucasian, Northeast, Avaro-Andi-Dido, Andi. Dialects: BOTLIKH, ZIBIRKHALIN. Close to Andi. Godoberi is a separate language (B. Comrie 1989). Avar is used as literary language; bilingual proficiency undetermined. Not a written language. Muslim.

CHAMALAL ***(CAMALAL, CHAMALIN)*** [CJI] 5,500 (1962 Maxwell). Southern Dagestan ASSR. North Caucasian, Northeast, Avaro-Andi-Dido, Andi. Dialects: GADYRI (GACHITL-KVANKHI), GAKVARI (AGVALI-RICHAGANIK-TSUMADA-URUKH), GIGATL. Dialects are quite distinct. Avar is used as literary language. Not a written language. Muslim.

CHECHEN ***(NOKHCHIIN, NOKCHIIN MUOTT, GALANCHO)*** [CJC] 944,600 speakers out of an ethnic population of 956,879 (1989 census). The population of Chechnya is 1,200,000 (1994). Population total all countries 1,000,000. Chechnya, north Caucasus. The capital is Syelzha Ghaala (Chechen name) or Grozny (Groznii; Russian name). 80% live in rural areas. Also spoken in Georgia, Germany, Jordan, Kazakhstan, Kyrgyzstan, Syria, Turkey (Asia), Uzbekistan. North Caucasian, North Central, Chechen-Ingush. Dialects: PLOSKOST, ITUMKALA (SHATOI), MELKHIN, KISTIN, CHEBERLOI, AKKIN (AUX). Melkhi is the transitional dialect to Ingush. Chechen is at least partially intelligible with Ingush-more so with contact. Most speakers are quite fluent in Russian. The largest North Caucasian language. Used in publishing. They call themselves 'Nakhchuo' (sg.) or 'Nokhchi' (pl.). There are many Russians, Ingush, Ossetins, and other peoples living among them. From 1944 to 1957 they were deported to Kazakhstan and Siberia, losing 1/4 to 1/2 of their population, and have lost much land, economic resources, and civil rights. They have been largely removed from the productive lowlands. Dictionary. Grammar. Ergative case system; many consonants and vowels; extensive inflectional morphology, many nominal cases, several gender classes; complex sentences by chaining participial clauses; verbs have gender agreement with the direct object or intransitive subject, but no person agreement (Johanna Nichols). Cyrillic script used. Used in schools. Newspapers, radio programs. Alpine forest (highlands). Mountain slope, foothills, plains. Shepherds, agriculturalists: grain. Sunni Muslim: Sufi. Bible portions 1986-1995.

CHUVASH ***(BULGAR)*** [CJU] 1,774,000 in Russia (1993 Johnstone). Population total all countries 1,809,000. Possibly including second language users: 2,000,000 (1999 WA). Chuvashia, east of Moscow, near the Volga River. Cheboksary is their capital. About half live in towns (1995). Also spoken in Estonia, Kazakhstan, Kyrgyzstan, Uzbekistan. Altaic, Turkic, Bolgar. Dialects: ANATRI, VIRYAL. The only extant language in the Bolgar branch of Turkic. About 80% can use Russian as second language. Chuvash magazines. Cyrillic script. Newspapers, radio programs, TV. Agriculturalists. Christian: Russian Orthodox; traditional religion. NT 1904-1911.

DARGWA ***(DARGIN, DARGINTSY, KHIURKILINSKII)*** [DAR] 365,000 in the former USSR (1993 UBS), 98% speak it as mother tongue. Population total all countries 371,000. Southern Dagestan ASSR. Also spoken in Azerbaijan, Kazakhstan, Kyrgyzstan, Turkey (Asia), Turkmenistan, Ukraine, Uzbekistan. North Caucasian, Northeast, Lak-Dargwa. Dialects: CUDAXAR (TSUDAKHAR), AKUSHA (URKARAX, URAKHA-AKHUSH, AKKHUSHA), URAXA-AXUSHA, KAJTAK (XAJDAK, KAITAK, KAYTAK), KUBACHI (KUBACHIN, KUBACHINTSY, UGHBUG), DEJBUK, XARBUK, MUIRIN, SIRXIN. Kaytag and Kubachin were previously considered separate languages from Dargwa. Cyrillic script used. Newspapers. Mountain slope. Agriculturalists. Sunni and some Shi'a Muslim. Bible portions 1996.

DIDO ***(DIDOI, TSEZ, CEZ, TSEZY, TSUNTIN)*** [DDO] 7,000 (1994 UBS). Southern Dagestan ASSR. North Caucasian, Northeast, Avaro-Andi-Dido, Dido. Dialect: SAGADIN. Sagadin dialect is most distinct. Slight dialect differences from village to village. Avar is used as the literary language. Not a written language. Muslim.

DOMARI [RMT] Karachi dialect is in the Caucasus, Luli and Maznoug in Uzbekistan. Indo-European, Indo-Iranian, Indo-Aryan, Central zone, Dom. Dialects: KARACHI, LULI, MAZNOUG. Muslim. See main entry under Iran.

ERZYA *(MORDVIN-ERZYA, MORDVIN, ERZIA)* [MYV] 440,000 in Russia. Population total all countries 500,000 (1994 Tapani Salminen). Northern Mordvin ASSR. They are spread out, but there are compact groups of speakers. Also spoken in Azerbaijan, Kazakhstan, Kyrgyzstan, Turkmenistan, Ukraine, Uzbekistan. Uralic, Finno-Ugric, Finno-Permic, Finno-Cheremisic, Finno-Mordvinic, Mordvinic. Quite different from Moksha. Speakers are quite acculturated to national culture and the Russian language. Christian: Russian Orthodox, traditional religion. NT 1824.

FINNISH [FIN] 31,570 speakers out of 77,000 in the ethnic group in Russia (1979 census). 41% speak it as mother tongue. St. Petersburg area, Ingria region. Uralic, Finno-Ugric, Finno-Permic, Finno-Cheremisic, Finno-Mordvinic, Finno-Lappic, Balto-Finnic, Finnic. Eastern dialects merge gradually into Karelian. Bilingualism in Russian. Christian. Bible 1642-1991. See main entry under Finland.

GHODOBERI *(GODOBERI, GODOBERIN)* [GDO] 3,000 (1996). Southern Dagestan ASSR. North Caucasian, Northeast, Avaro-Andi-Dido, Andi. Close to Andi. A separate language from Botlikh (B. Comrie 1989). Avar is used as literary language. Used in daily family communication. Not a written language. Traditional territory and way of life. Muslim.

HINUKH *(GINUKH, GINUX, GINUKHTSY, HINUX)* [GIN] 200 (A. E. Kibrik 1991). Southern Dagestan ASSR. North Caucasian, Northeast, Avaro-Andi-Dido, Dido. Close to Tsez (Dido) but probably not inherently intelligible. Avar is used as the literary language. Hinukh remains the language of the family. Vigorous. Hinukh has high prestige. Not a written language. Hinukh men marry Dido women. Hinukh women marry men from other ethnic groups. Muslim.

HUNZIB *(GUNZIB, XUNZAL, KHUNZALY, KHUNZAL, ENZEB)* [HUZ] 2,000 (1995 H. Ven den Berg). Southern Dagestan ASSR. North Caucasian, Northeast, Avaro-Andi-Dido, Dido. A separate language from Bezhta (B. Comrie 1989). Avar is used as the literary language; bilingual proficiency undetermined. Not a written language. Grammar. 27 consonants, 16 vowels, word stress generally linked to prefinal vowel, 5 noun classes, agreement between nouns and coreferent adjectives, pronouns, verbs, and adverbs marked by prefixes, nominative-ergative system, demonstratives. Muslim.

INGRIAN *(IZHOR)* [IZH] 302 speakers (1989 census) out of 10,000 to 15,000 in the ethnic group. Baltic area, Kingisepp and Lomonosov areas of St. Petersburg Oblast. Uralic, Finno-Ugric, Finno-Permic, Finno-Cheremisic, Finno-Mordvinic, Finno-Lappic, Baltic-Finnic. Dialects: SOYKIN, KHAVA, LOWER LUZH, OREDEZH (UPPER LUZH). Close to Karelian but the government considers them separate languages. Bilingualism in Russian. Few children speakers. Endangered. Christian.

INGUSH *(GHALGHAY, INGUS)* [INH] 230,315 mother tongue speakers (97%) out of an ethnic population of 237,438 (1989 census). Population total both countries 230,315 or more. Chechen Ingushetia, northern Caucasus, west of the Chechen. Vladikavkaz (Ordzhhonikidze) is the main city. Nazran in the lowlands is an important market town. 64.6% live in rural areas. Since 1992 up to 60,000 Ingush refugees are reported to be in Ingushetia. Also spoken in Uzbekistan. North Caucasian, North Central, Chechen-Ingush. Somewhat intelligible with Chechen—more so with contact. Many speak Russian as second language. 'Ghalghay' is their name for themselves. From 1944 to 1957 they were deported to Kazakhstan and Siberia, losing 1/4 to 1/2 of their population, and have lost much land, economic resources, and civil rights. Many Russians, Ossetins, and Georgians live in Vladikavkaz—the Ingush were removed from there in late 1992. Grammar. Cyrillic script. Alpine highlands, plains. Mountain slope, foothills, lowlands. Hanafi Sunni Muslim.

JUDEO-TAT *(JUDEO-TATIC, HEBREW TAT, JEWISH TAT, BIK, DZHUHURIC, JUWRI, JUHURI)* [TAT] 7,000 in Russia (1989 census). Dagestan ASSR, Nalchik in Kabardino-Balkar ASSR, in villages and ancient cities of the Caucasus mountains (Derbent, Makhachkale, Nalchik, Majalis, Pyatigorsk). Until recently they were in Grozny in Checheno-Ingush. None in Iran. Indo-European, Indo-Iranian, Iranian, Western, Southwestern, Tat. Dialect: DERBEND. Difficult intelligibility with Mussulman Tat. There may also be a Christian dialect. Speakers of Judeo-Tat are called 'Bik'. They are known as 'Mountain Jews'. They call their language 'Juwri' or 'Juhuri'. Tradition says that they have lived in the Caucasus since 722 B.C. Different from Takestani of Iran. Cyrillic script. Literature produced officially from 1920 to 1940 in Roman script. Recent private literature uses Hebrew script. Radio programs. Mountain slope. Agriculturalists: marena grass for dying (traditionally), fruit, cattle; hides; merchants. Jewish. Bible portions 1980. See main entry under Israel.

KABARDIAN *(BESLENEI, UPPER CIRCASSIAN, EAST CIRCASSIAN, KABARDINO-CHERKES, KABARDO-CHERKES)* [KAB] 443,000 including 46,000 Cherkes in Russia (1993 UBS), 97% speak it as mother tongue. Population total all countries 647,000. Kabardino-Balkaria and Karachai-Cherkessia. Naltshik is the capital. Also spoken in Saudi Arabia, Turkey (Asia), USA. North Caucasian,

Northwest, Circassian. Dialects: GREATER KABARDIAN, BAKSAN, LESSER KABARDIAN, MALKA, MOZDOK, KUBAN, CHERKES, BESLENEI (BESLENEJ). Cyrillic alphabet. Sunni Muslim. NT 1993.

KALMYK-OIRAT ***(KALMUK, KALMUCK, KALMACK, QALMAQ, KALMYTSKII JAZYK, KHAL:MAG, OIRAT, VOLGA OIRAT, EUROPEAN OIRAT, WESTERN MONGOLIAN)*** [KGZ] 174,000 Kalmyk in Russia (1993 UBS), 91% speak it as mother tongue. Population total all countries 518,000. The Kalmyk are in Kalmykia, the steppes between the Don and Volga rivers, lower Volga region, now the Astrakhan Province. The capital is Elista. The Dorbot and Torgut live between the Volga and the Don, east of the Caspian and north of the Caucasus, in Kalmyk ASSR. Also spoken in China, Germany, Kyrgyzstan, Mongolia, Taiwan, USA. Altaic, Mongolian, Eastern, Oirat-Khalkha, Oirat-Kalmyk-Darkhat. Dialects: BUZAWA, OIRAT, TORGUT (TORGUUD, TORGHUD, TORGHOUD), DÖRBÖT (DÖRBÖD, DERBET), SART QALMAQ. Their language has diverged from other Mongolian languages and they are called 'Kalmyk' in Russia; 'Oirat' in China and Mongolia. In USA Kalmyk has not been heavily influenced by Russian as it has been in Russia. Different from other varieties in China called Oirat, which are sometimes called 'Asiatic Oirat'. Tibetan is used as religious language. Russian is used as second language for other purposes. In 1628 the Oirat moved from Dzungaria, Eastern Turkistan (Xinjiang, China) to the Volga, north and west of the Caspian Sea. Cyrillic script used by the Dorbot and Torgut. Lamaist Buddhist. NT 1827-1894, out of print.

KARACHAY-BALKAR ***(KARACHAY, KARACHAI, KARACHAYLA, KARACHAITSY, KARACAYLAR)*** [KRC] 236,000 mother tongue speakers in Russia, 97% of the ethnic population, including 156,000 Karachay, 85,000 Balkar (1993 UBS). Population total all countries 241,000. Karachi-Cherkessia and Kabardino-Balkaria. Karachaevsk-Cherkessk is the capital. The Balkar are isolated. Also spoken in Armenia, Azerbaijan, Kazakhstan, Kyrgyzstan, USA, Uzbekistan. Altaic, Turkic, Western, Ponto-Caspian. Dialects: BALKAR, KARACHAY. Balkar and Karachay are almost identical. From 1944 to 1957 they were deported to Kazakhstan and Siberia, losing 1/4 to 1/2 of their population, and have lost much land, economic resources, and civil rights. Cyrillic script. Sunni Muslim. NT 1994.

KARATA ***(KARATIN, KIRDI, KARATAI)*** [KPT] 6,000 (1962 Maxwell). Southern Dagestan ASSR. North Caucasian, Northeast, Avaro-Andi-Dido, Andi. Dialects: TOKITA (TOKITIN), ANCHIX. Karatin and Tokitin are quite different. Avar is used as the literary language. Not a written language. Muslim.

KARELIAN ***(KARELY, KARELIAN PROPER, SOBSTVENNO-KAREL'SKIJ-JAZYK, SEVERNO-KAREL'SKIJ, KAREL'SKOGO JAZYKA)*** [KRL] 118,000 mother tongue speakers out of an ethnic population of 172,000 in Russia (1993 Johnstone). Population total both countries 128,000. Karelia, Tver (Kalinin), St. Petersburg, and Murmansk oblasts. Petrozavodsk is the capital. Also spoken in Finland. Uralic, Finno-Ugric, Finno-Permic, Finno-Cheremisic, Finno-Mordvinic, Finno-Lappic, Baltic-Finnic. Dialects: NORTHERN KARELIAN, SOUTHERN KARELIAN, NOVGOROD, TVER (KALININ). Ludic and Livvi are separate languages. Many are bilingual in Russian, but those over 50 have difficulty understanding Russian. Some use Finnish as second language. A primer was recently produced in Tver Karelian. Dictionary. Agriculturalists, animal husbandry, wood industry. Bible portions 1820-1996.

KHVARSHI ***(XVARSHI, KHVARSHIN)*** [KHV] 1,800 (Maxwell 1962). Southern Dagestan ASSR. North Caucasian, Northeast, Avaro-Andi-Dido, Dido. Dialects: XVARSHI, INXOKVARI. Dialects are quite distinct. Avar is used as the literary language. Used in daily family communication. Traditional territory and way of life. Not a written language. Muslim.

KOMI-PERMYAK ***(PERMYAK, KOMI-PERMYAT, KAMA PERMYAK, KOMI-PERM)*** [KOI] 116,000 mother tongue speakers (77%) out of an ethnic population of 151,000 (1979 census). Komi-Permyak National Okrug, west of the central Ural Mountains, south of Komi-Zyrian. Uralic, Finno-Ugric, Finno-Permic, Permic. Dialects: ZYUDIN, NORTH PERMYAK (KOCHIN-KAM), SOUTH PERMYAK (INYVEN). Possible difficulty in understanding among dialects. 80% cognate with Komi-Zyrian and Udmurt. Bilingualism in Russian. Some literature available. Ancient literary and cultural traditions. More densely populated and mixed, higher education, and more assimilated to national culture than Komi-Zyrian. Agriculturalists, some industrialists. Christian: Russian Orthodox, traditional religion. Bible portions 1866-1882.

KOMI-ZYRIAN ***(KOMI)*** [KPV] 262,200 mother tongue speakers (76%) out of an ethnic population of 345,000 (1993 UBS). Komi ASSR, 60' N. Lat., nearly to the Arctic Ocean. South of Yurak, west of the Vogul (Mansi) peoples. Capital is Syktywkar. Uralic, Finno-Ugric, Finno-Permic, Permic. Dialect: YAZVA. 80% lexical similarity with Komi-Permyat and Udmurt. Some use Nenets in the north. Russian is also used. Komi is used in the Institute for Language and Literature of the Komi branch of the Academy of Science. Pastoralists: reindeer; hunters, fishermen, lumbermen, traders. Christian: Russian Orthodox, traditional religion. NT 1979.

KUMYK ***(KUMUK, KUMUKLAR, KUMYKI)*** [KSK] 282,000 in Russia (1993 UBS). Population total all countries 282,500. Southern Dagestan ASSR, northern and eastern Caucasian plain. Also spoken in Kazakhstan, Turkey (Asia). Altaic, Turkic, Western, Ponto-Caspian. Dialects: KHASAVYURT,

BUINAKSK, KHAIKENT. Dialects are apparently quite divergent. Most speakers use Russian as second language. Education is in Russian, with some in Kumyk in heavily populated Kumyk areas. Different from the Kumux dialect of Lak. Dictionary. Grammar. Literacy rate in first language: Higher in Kumyk where the majority speak Kumyk. Literacy rate in second language: High in Russian. Cyrillic script. Newspapers, radio programs. Plains. Sunni Muslim. Bible portions 1888-1996.

LAK ***(LAKI, KAZIKUMUKHTSY)*** [LBE] 112,100 mother tongue speakers (95%) out of an ethnic population of 118,000 in Russia. Population total all countries 130,000. Southern Dagestan ASSR. Also spoken in Azerbaijan, Georgia, Kazakhstan, Kyrgyzstan, Tajikistan, Turkey (Asia), Turkmenistan, Ukraine, Uzbekistan. North Caucasian, Northeast, Lak-Dargwa. Dialects: KUMUX (KUMKH), VICXIN (VITSKHIN), VIXLIN (VIKHLIN), ASHTIKULIN, BALXAR-CALAKAN (BALKAR-TSALAKAN). Dialects are close. Cyrillic script. Sunni Muslim. Bible portions 1996.

LEZGI ***(LEZGIAN, LEZGHI, LEZGIN, KIURINSTY)*** [LEZ] 257,000 in Russia (1996). Population total all countries 451,000. Southern Dagestan ASSR, the western Caspian Sea coast, central Caucasus. Also spoken in Azerbaijan, Georgia, Kazakhstan, Kyrgyzstan, Turkey (Asia), Turkmenistan, Ukraine, Uzbekistan. North Caucasian, Northeast, Lezgian. Dialects: KIURI, AKHTY, KUBA, GJUNEJ, GARKIN, ANYX, STAL. Some dialects are reported to not be inherently intelligible with others. Cyrillic script. Mountain slope. Agriculturalists. Sunni and some Shi'a Muslim. Bible portions 1990-1996.

LIVVI ***(OLONETSIAN, OLONETS, LIVVIKOVIAN, LIVVIKOVSKIJ JAZYK, SOUTHERN KARELIAN)*** [OLO] 80,000 out of an ethnic population of 140,000 (1992). Population total both countries 80,000 or more. Karelian Republic. 'Olonets' is the Russian name of their capital, which they call 'Anus', or 'Aunus' in Finnish. Also spoken in Finland. Uralic, Finno-Ugric, Finno-Permic, Finno-Cheremisic, Finno- Mordvinic, Finno-Lappic, Baltic-Finnic. Bilingualism in Russian. Ludic is transitional between Livvi and Veps. A distinct language from Karelian Proper and Ludic. Primers, textbooks, poetry. Dictionary. Poetry, newspapers, radio programs, TV. Bible portions 1992-1995.

LUDIAN ***(LYUDIKOVIAN, LYUDIC, LUDIC)*** [LUD] Karelian ASSR. Uralic, Finno-Ugric, Finno-Permic, Finno-Cheremisic, Finno-Mordvinic, Finno-Lappic, Baltic-Finnic. Ludian is transitional between Livvi and Veps. A separate language from Karelian (Juha Janhunen 1990). May be separate from Livvi. Bilingualism in Russian. Few children speakers.

MARI, HIGH ***(CHEREMISS, MARI-HILLS, GORNO-MARIY)*** [MRJ] 66,000 (1993 UBS). Mari ASSR, Gorno-Mariy, and some in Bashkortostan. Capital is Joschkar-Ola. Uralic, Finno-Ugric, Finno-Permic, Finno-Cheremisic, Cheremisic. Dialects: KOZYMODEMYAN, YARAN. Speakers have difficulty reading Low Mari because of lexical differences. There are also phonological and morphological differences. Bilingualism in Russian, Low Mari. Agriculturalists, lumbermen. Christian, traditional religion. NT 1824.

MARI, LOW ***(CHEREMIS, MARI, MARI-WOODS, EASTERN MARI, LUGOVO MARI)*** [MAL] 525,480 mother tongue speakers (87%) out of an ethnic population of 604,000 (1993 UBS). Population total both countries 534,000. Mari ASSR, left bank of Volga, Bashkir, Tatar, Udmurt ASSR, Perm, Sverov, Kirov Oblasts. Capital is Yoshkar-Ola, 500 km. east of Moscow. Also spoken in Kazakhstan. Uralic, Finno-Ugric, Finno-Permic, Finno-Cheremisic, Cheremisic. Dialect: GRASSLAND MARI (SERNUR-MORKIN, YOSHKAR-OLIN, VOLGA). Bilingualism in Russian. Books. Used in schools. Newspapers, radio programs. Christian: Russian Orthodox, traditional religion. NT 1986.

MOKSHA ***(MORDVIN-MOKSHA, MORDOV, MORDOFF, MOKSHAN)*** [MDF] 428,333 (1970). Mordovia, southern. Saramsk is the capital. Uralic, Finno-Ugric, Finno-Permic, Finno-Cheremisic, Finno-Mordvinic, Mordvinic. Considerable difference with Erzya. Bilingualism in Russian. The Tengushen are Erzya ethnically, but speak Moksha. Christian. Bible portions 1879-1996.

NOGAI ***(NOGAY, NOGHAY, NOGHAI, NOGHAYLAR, NOGAITSY, NOGALAR)*** [NOG] 67,500 mother tongue speakers (90%) out of an ethnic population of 75,000 (1993 UBS). Population total all countries 68,000. Northern Caucasus, Cherkes AO. Also spoken in Kazakhstan, Uzbekistan. Altaic, Turkic, Western, Aralo-Caspian. Dialects: WHITE NOGAI (AK), BLACK NOGAI (KARA), CENTRAL NOGAI. Dialect differences are slight. Bilingualism in Russian. Cyrillic script. Sunni Muslim. Bible portions 1996.

ROMANI, VLAX [RMY] 10,000 Kalderash in Russia, Ukraine, and Moldova. Russian SFSR, Odessa, Transcarpathia. Indo-European, Indo-Iranian, Indo-Aryan, Central zone, Romani, Vlax. Dialects: CENTRAL VLAX ROMANI, KALDERASH. Vlax from the former USSR are called 'Rusurja'. Ethnic groups: Sárvi (left-bank Ukraine), Volóxuja (right-bank Ukraine), Chache (Moldavia), Kalderari (Moldavia, Ukraine, Odessa, Transcarpathia), Lovári (Ukraine). About 300,000 Gypsies from the former USSR speak a variety of Romani, Lomavren, or Domari as first or second language (Gunnemarck and Kenrick). Christian. NT 1984-1986. See main entry under Romania.

RUSSIAN ***(RUSSKI)*** [RUS] 153,655,000 in the republics of the former USSR. Population total all countries 167,000,000 first language speakers (1999 WA); 277,000,000 including second language users (1999 WA). Also spoken in 30 other countries including Armenia, Azerbaijan, Belarus, Bulgaria, Canada, China, Czech Republic, Estonia, Finland, Georgia, Germany, Greece, India, Israel, Kazakhstan, Kyrgyzstan, Latvia, Lithuania, Moldova. Indo-European, Slavic, East. Dialects: NORTH RUSSIAN, SOUTH RUSSIAN. The Chuvan are a Yukagiric people now speaking Russian. The Meshcheryak are ethnically Erzya, but speak Russian. The Teryukhan are ethnically Erzya in Gorkiy, but speak Russian. National language. Dictionary. Grammar. SVO; prepositions; genitives after noun heads; articles, adjectives, numerals before noun heads; question word initial; 1 prefix on a word; recursive addition of suffixes allowed; nontonal. Christian. Bible 1680-1993.

RUSSIAN SIGN LANGUAGE [RSL] Moscow, Armavir, Gorky, Kazan, Kirov, Kolomna, Kujbyshev, St. Petersburg, Novosibirsk, Rostov on Don, Sverdlovsk have schools for the deaf. Also spoken in Bulgaria. Deaf sign language. Related to Austrian and French sign languages, but different. There are deaf associations and athletic clubs. Signed interpretation required in court, and used at important public events. Many sign language classes for hearing people. There is an organization for sign language teachers. Originated in 1806. There is a manual system for spelling. Dictionary. Elementary schools for deaf children since 1878. Films, TV, videos.

RUTUL ***(RUTAL, RUTULY, RUTULTSY, MYKHANIDY, CHAL, MUKHAD)*** [RUT] 20,000 in Russia (1993 UBS), 99% speak it as mother tongue. Population total both countries 20,000 or more. Southern Dagestan ASSR. Also spoken in Azerbaijan. North Caucasian, Northeast, Lezgian. Dialects: SHINA, BORCH, IXREKO-MUXREK. Dialects are not sharply defined. Lezgin is used as the literary language. Not a literary language. Sunni Muslim.

SAAMI, AKKALA ***(AHKKIL, BABINSK)*** [SIA] 7 speakers out of 100 population (1995 M. Krauss). Southwest Kola Peninsula. Uralic, Finno-Ugric, Finno-Permic, Finno-Cheremisic, Finno-Mordvinic, Finno-Lappic, Lappic, Central. Recently recognized as a separate language. Closest to Skolt. Nearly extinct.

SAAMI, KILDIN ***("KILDIN LAPPISH", "LAPP", SAAM)*** [LPD] 650 speakers out of 1,000 population (1995 M. Krauss). 1,900 Saami in Russia (1995 M. Krauss). Uralic, Finno-Ugric, Finno-Permic, Finno-Cheremisic, Finno-Mordvinic, Finno-Lappic, Lappic, Central. Many are bilingual in Russian. Few children speakers. The name "Lapp" is derogatory; 'Saami' is preferred. Have own literacy. Have their own writing system.

SAAMI, SKOLT ***("SKOLT LAPPISH", "RUSSIAN LAPP", "LAPP", SAAM, LOPAR, KOLTA, SKOLT)*** [LPK] 20 to 30 speakers out of 400 population in Russia (1995 M. Krauss). Northern and western Kola Peninsula around Petsamo. Uralic, Finno-Ugric, Finno-Permic, Finno-Cheremisic, Finno-Mordvinic, Finno-Lappic, Lappic, Central. Dialects: NOTOZER, YOKAN. Many in Russia are bilingual in Russian. Few children speakers. The name "Lapp" is derogatory; 'Saami' is preferred. Christian. Bible portions 1878-1988. See main entry under Finland.

SAAMI, TER ***("TER LAPPISH", "LAPP", SAAM)*** [LPT] 6 speakers out of 400 population (1995 M. Krsuss). Uralic, Finno-Ugric, Finno-Permic, Finno-Cheremisic, Finno-Mordvinic, Finno-Lappic, Lappic, Central. Many are bilingual in Russian. The name "Lapp" is derogatory; 'Saami' is preferred. Nearly extinct.

SERBO-CROATIAN ***(SERBIAN)*** [SRC] 5,000 in Russia (1959 census). Indo-European, Slavic, South, Western. Cyrillic script. Christian, Muslim. Bible 1804-1968. See main entry under Yugoslavia.

SLAVONIC, OLD CHURCH [SLN] Indo-European, Slavic, South, Eastern. Used as liturgical language of various Orthodox and Byzantine Catholic churches. Christian. Extinct. Bible 1581-1751.

TABASSARAN ***(TABASARAN, TABASARANTSY, GHUMGHUM)*** [TAB] 95,000 mother tongue speakers (97%) out of an ethnic population of 98,000 in Russia (1993 UBS). Population total all countries 96,000. Southern Dagestan ASSR. Also spoken in Azerbaijan, Kazakhstan, Turkmenistan, Uzbekistan. North Caucasian, Northeast, Lezgian. Dialects: SOUTH TABASARAN, NORTH TABASARAN (KHANAG). Cyrillic alphabet. Sunni Muslim. Bible portions 1996.

TATAR ***(TARTAR)*** [TTR] 5,715,000 speakers (86%) out of an ethnic group of 6,645,588 in the former USSR (1989 census), including 6,017,000 ethnic Tatar, of whom 86% speak Tatar as mother tongue, and an additional 370,000 Bashkir speak it as mother tongue. Population total all countries 7,000,000. Tatarstan, from Moscow to eastern Siberia. Capital is Kazan (Kasan), on the Volga River. Also spoken in Afghanistan, Azerbaijan, Belarus, China, Estonia, Finland, Georgia, Kazakhstan, Kyrgyzstan, Latvia, Lithuania, Moldova, Tajikistan, Turkey (Europe), Turkmenistan, Ukraine, USA, Uzbekistan. Altaic, Turkic, Western, Uralian. Dialects: MIDDLE TATAR (KAZAN), WESTERN TATAR (MISHER), EASTERN TATAR (SIBERIAN TATAR). Eastern Tatar is divided into 3: Tobol-Irtysh, Baraba, and Tom. Tobol-Irtysh is divided into 5: Tyumen, Tobol, Zabolotny, Tevriz, and Tara (Tumasheva). Mixed dialects are: Astrakhan, Kasimov, Tepter, and Ural (Poppe). 43,000 Astrakhan have assimilated to the Middle dialect. Kasim (5,000) is between Middle and Western Tatar. Tepter (300,000) is reported to be between the Tatar and Bashkir languages. Uralic Tatar (110,000) is spoken by the Kerashen Tatar. The Karatai are ethnically Erzya, who speak Tatar. Not endangered. Different from Crimean Tatar (Crimean Turkish). Literacy rate in second language: High. Cyrillic script. Agriculturalists, oil workers, coal miners. Sunni Muslim, some Christian. Bible portions 1864-1995.

TINDI ***(TINDAL, TINDIN)*** [TIN] 5,000 (1962 Maxwell). Southern Dagestan ASSR. North Caucasian, Northeast, Avaro-Andi-Dido, Andi. Bagvalal is closely related, but probably not inherently intelligible. Avar is used as the literary language. Used in daily family communication. Traditional territory and way of life. Not a written language. Muslim.

TSAKHUR ***(TSAXUR, CAXUR, TSAKHURY)*** [TKR] 7,000 in Russia. Southern Dagestan ASSR and Azerbaijan. North Caucasian, Northeast, Lezgian. Dialects: KIRMICO-LEK, MIKIK, MISLES. Bilingualism in Avar. A written language. The most widely scattered of the smaller ethnic groups. Muslim. See main entry under Azerbaijan.

UDMURT ***(VOTIAK, VOTYAK)*** [UDM] 550,000 mother tongue speakers (77%) out of an ethnic population of 750,000 in the former USSR (1989 census). Population total both countries 566,000. Udmurtia, 1,000 km. northeast of Moscow, bounded by the Kama and Cheptsa rivers, near the Ural Mts. Izhyevsk (Ischewsk) is the capital. Also spoken in Kazakhstan. Uralic, Finno-Ugric, Finno-Permic, Permic. Dialects: NORTH UDMURT (VESERMYAN, UDMURT), SOUTH UDMURT (SOUTHWESTERN UDMURT). Bilingualism in Russian. The Besermyan are Udmurt-speaking Tatar. Agriculturalists. Christian, traditional religion, secular. Bible portions 1847-1995.

VEPS ***(VEPSIAN, "CHUDY", "CHUHARI", "CHUKHARI")*** [VEP] 2,320 speakers (1979 census) out of 13,500 in the ethnic group (1989 census). The remaining persons speak Russian as first language. Other reports indicate the number of speakers is higher. Among Russian speakers, on the boundary between St. Petersburg and Vologda oblasts and in Karelian Republic. Half reportedly went to Finland during World War II. Uralic, Finno-Ugric, Finno-Permic, Finno-Cheremisic, Finno-Mordvinic, Finno-Lappic, Baltic-Finnic. Dialects: SOUTHERN VEPS, CENTRAL VEPS, PRIONEZH (NORTH VEPS). Bilingualism in Russian. Few children speakers. A growing sense of ethnic identity and desire to revive Veps. Dictionary. Grammar. Taught in some primary schools, but not compulsory. Book of poems, school primers for grades 1-3. Poetry, newspapers, radio programs, TV. Christian. Bible portions 1992-1996.

VOD ***(VOTIAN, VOTE, VODIAN, VOTISH, VOTIC)*** [VOD] 25 (1979 Valt). Kingisepp area of St. Petersburg. Uralic, Finno-Ugric, Finno-Permic, Finno-Cheremisic, Finno-Mordvinic, Finno-Lappic, Baltic-Finnic. Dialects: EAST VOD, WEST VOD. Intelligible with Estonian of the northeast coast. Nearly extinct.

SAN MARINO

Most Serene Republic of San Marino, Serenissima Repubblica di San Marino. National or official language: Italian. 26,000 (1998 UN). Literacy rate 97% to 98%. Christian, secular. Deaf population 1,455. The number of languages listed for San Marino is 2. Of those, both are living languages. Diversity index 0.00.

EMILIANO-ROMAGNOLO [EML] 20,112 in San Marino (1993), 83% of the population (1993 Johnstone). Indo-European, Italic, Romance, Italo-Western, Western, Gallo-Iberian, Gallo-Romance, Gallo- Italian. Dialect: SAMMARINESE. See main entry under Italy.

ITALIAN [ITN] Indo-European, Italic, Romance, Italo-Western, Italo-Dalmatian. National language. Bible 1471-1985. See main entry under Italy.

SLOVAKIA

National or official language: Slovak. 5,377,000 (1998 UN). Officially separated from Czech Republic January 1, 1993. Literacy rate 99%. Also includes Czech, Russian. Information mainly from B. Comrie 1987; I. Hancock 1990. Christian, secular, other, (Jewish 3,500 or more). Blind population 10,000 in former Czechoslovakia. Deaf institutions: 51 in former Czechoslovakia. Data accuracy estimate: B. The number of languages listed for Slovakia is 10. Of those, all are living languages. Diversity index 0.25.

GERMAN, STANDARD [GER] 5,900 in Czech Republic (1991 census) to 15,000 (1999). Indo-European, Germanic, West, High German, German, Middle German, East Middle German. Bilingualism in Slovakian, Hungarian. Christian. Bible 1466-1982. See main entry under Germany.

HUNGARIAN ***(MAGYAR)*** [HNG] 597,400 in Slovakia (1993), 11.2% of the population. In the south. Uralic, Finno-Ugric, Ugric, Hungarian. Bible 1590-1991. See main entry under Hungary.

POLISH ***(POLSKI)*** [PQL] 50,000 in Slovakia. Indo-European, Slavic, West, Lechitic. Christian. Bible 1561-1965. See main entry under Poland.

ROMANI, CARPATHIAN *(BASHALDO, ROMUNGRO, HUNGARIAN-SLOVAK ROMANI)* [RMC] (220,000 in Slovakia and Czech Republic; 1980 UBS). Northern, eastern, and southern Slovakia. Indo-European, Indo-Iranian, Indo-Aryan, Central zone, Romani, Northern. Dialects: MORAVIAN ROMANI, EAST SLOVAKIAN ROMANI, WEST SLOVAKIAN ROMANI. Not intelligible with Vlach Romani or Angloromani, and speakers do not interact socially with speakers of those languages. Ethnic groups: Sárvika Romá (northern and eastern Slovakia), Ungrike Romá (southern Slovakia). The people are called Karpacki Rom. Dictionary. Grammar. Christian. Bible portions 1936-1996. See main entry under Czech Republic.

ROMANI, VLAX [RMY] 500 Lovari in Slovakia. Indo-European, Indo-Iranian, Indo-Aryan, Central zone, Romani, Vlax. Dialects: LOVARI, KALDERASH (KALDARÁRI). Kalderash is reported to be understood by the Lovari. Vlax from Hungary and Slovakia are called 'Romungre'. Christian. NT 1984-1995. See main entry under Romania.

RUSYN *(RUTHENIAN, CARPATHIAN, CARPATHO-RUSYN)* [RUE] 50,000 in Slovakia (1991 census). Northeast Slovakia, Preshov region. Indo-European, Slavic, East. Dialect: LEMKO. Rusyn is sometimes called a dialect of Ukrainian, but speakers are reported to consider themselves distinct from Ukrainians. Nearly two-thirds have assimilated culturally and linguistically with the Slovaks. Some ethnic Rusyns in Yugoslavia are reported to speak Eastern Slovak, Sarish dialect, not Rusyn. In 1995 it was declared a normative, codified language in Slovakia, can formally be taught in schools, used for publications, school textbooks. Investigation needed: intelligibility with Ukrainian, bilingual proficiency in Slovak. Dictionary. Radio programs, TV. Christian. See main entry under Ukraine.

SERBO-CROATIAN [SRC] Indo-European, Slavic, South, Western. Dialect: CROATIAN. Latin script used by Croats, Cyrillic by Serbs and Montenegrins. Christian, Muslim. Bible 1804-1968. See main entry under Yugoslavia.

SLOVAK *(SLOVAKIAN)* [SLO] 4,865,450 in Slovakia (1990 WA). Population total all countries 5,606,000. Western upland country around Bratislava. Also spoken in Canada, Hungary, Poland, Romania, Ukraine, USA, Yugoslavia. Indo-European, Slavic, West, Czech-Slovak. Western and central dialects of Slovak are inherently intelligible with Czech. National language. Grammar. Christian. Bible 1832-1926.

SLOVAKIAN SIGN LANGUAGE [SVK] Deaf sign language. Dictionary.

UKRAINIAN [UKR] 100,000 in Slovakia. Indo-European, Slavic, East. Christian. Bible 1903-1962. See main entry under Ukraine.

SLOVENIA

National or official languages: Slovenian, Hungarian, Italian. 1,993,000 (1998 UN). Part of Yugoslavia until 1991. Literacy rate 98%. Also includes Gheg Albanian 4,022, Standard German 1,543, Macedonian 4,603, Sinte Romani 2,847, Serbo-Croatian 155,013, Venetian. Information mainly from M. Stephens 1976: B. Comrie 1987; T. Priestley 1995; W. Browne 1996. Christian, Muslim, Jewish, atheist. Data accuracy estimate: B. The number of languages listed for Slovenia is 4. Of those, all are living languages. Diversity index 0.17.

HUNGARIAN *(MAGYAR)* [HNG] 9,240 (1991 census). Eastern Slovenia. Uralic, Finno-Ugric, Ugric, Hungarian. Acknowledged as autochtonous communities and protected by the constitution. Official language. SVO. Bible 1590-1991. See main entry under Hungary.

ITALIAN [ITN] 4,009 in Slovenia (1991 census). Indo-European, Italic, Romance, Italo-Western, Italo-Dalmatian. Acknowledged as autochtonous communities and protected by the constitution. Official language. Bible 1471-1985. See main entry under Italy.

SLOVENIAN *(SLOVENSCINA, SLOVENE)* [SLV] 1,727,360 in Slovenia (1991 census). Population total all countries 2,000,000 (1999 WA). Carniola and southern parts of Styria and Carinthia; Lower Carniola in Dolenjsko, Upper Carniola in Gorenjska, Primorski in West Slovenia, Stajerski in Styria. Also spoken in Argentina, Australia, Austria, Canada, Croatia, Hungary, Italy, USA, Yugoslavia. Indo-European, Slavic, South, Western. Dialects: LOWER CARNIOLA, UPPER CARNIOLA, STAJERSKI, PRIMORSKI. The literary dialect is between the two main dialects, based on Dolenjsko. Dialects are diverse. National language. Grammar. SVO. Radio programs. Bible 1584-1996.

YUGOSLAVIAN SIGN LANGUAGE [YSL] Deaf sign language. Dialect: SLOVENIAN SIGN LANGUAGE. Related to Austrian and Hungarian sign languages. See main entry under Yugoslavia.

SPAIN

España. National or official languages: Spanish, Basque, Galician, Gascon (Aranese), Catalan (regional). 39,652,742 (1996 census). Literacy rate 93% to 97%. Also includes Judeo-Tunisian Arabic, Fa D'ambu, Western Farsi 25,000, Kabuverdianu 10,000, Portuguese, Vlax Romani 500, Arabic 200,000, Chinese 20,000, from Latin America 150,000. Information mainly from M. Stephens 1976; P. Blanchet 1986; B. Comrie 1987; J. Fishman 1991. Christian, Jewish, Muslim, secular. Blind population 30,000 (1982 WCE). Deaf population 120,000 to 2,383,940. Deaf institutions: 129. Data accuracy estimate: B. The number of languages listed for Spain is 15. Of those, 13 are living languages and 2 are extinct. Diversity index 0.44.

ARAGONESE *(ARAGOIERAZ, ALTOARAGONÉS, ARAGONÉS, FABLA ARAGONESA, PATUÉS, HIGH ARAGONESE)* [AXX] 11,000 or more active speakers. An additional 20,000 people use it as second language (1993 Counsel of the Aragonese Language). The majority speak Eastern Aragonese. 2,000,000 in the ethnic group. Zaragoza, Uesca Province. The northern limit is the Pyrenean border, separating Aragon from Occitania; the western limit is the border of Navarra; the eastern limit is north of Montsó. Western Aragonese includes the towns of Ansó, Echo, Chasa, Berdún, and Chaca; Central Aragonese the towns of Panticosa, Biescas, Torla, Broto, Bielsa, Yebra, and L'Ainsa; Eastern Aragonese the towns of Benás (Benasque, Benasc, Patués), Plan, Bisagorri, Campo, Perarruga, Graus, Estadilla; Southern Aragonese the towns of Agüero, Ayerbe, Rasal, Bolea, Lierta, Uesca, Almudébar, Nozito, Labata, Alguezra, Angüés, Pertusa, Balbastro, Nabal. Indo-European, Italic, Romance, Italo-Western, Western, Pyrenean-Mozarabic, Pyrenean. Dialects: WESTERN ARAGONESE (ANSOTANO, CHESO), CENTRAL ARAGONESE (BELSETÁN, CHISTABINO, TENSINO, PANDICUTO, BERGOTÉS), EASTERN ARAGONESE (BENASQUÉS, GRAUSINO, RIBAGORZANO, FOBANO, CHISTABINO), SOUTHERN ARAGONESE (AYERBENSE, SEMONTANÉS). There are local varieties. Different from the local variety of Spanish (also called 'Aragonese', which is influenced by High Aragonese). Eastern Aragonese is transitional to Catalan. Similarities to Catalan, Occitan, and Gascón. Speakers use Spanish (Castilian) in varying degrees, depending on their education; generally they use it well. Used with outsiders. Speakers include 500 elderly monolinguals (1993). There is an Aragonese Speakers' League (Ligallo de Fablans de l'Aragonés) in Zaragoza, and a Council of the Aragonese Language (Consello d'a Fabla Aragonesa) in Uesca. There are 5 magazines in Aragonese, and at least 6 organizations of mother tongue speakers working in the language. The written language is based on Central and Eastern Aragonese. Official language. Grammar. Literacy rate in second language: Nearly 100%. Christian.

ASTURIAN *(ASTUR-LEONESE, ASTURIAN-LEONESE, ASTURIANU)* [AUB] 100,000 first language speakers, plus 450,000 second language speakers able to speak or understand it (1994 F. F. Botas). 50,000 in Central Asturian, 30,000 in Western Asturian, 20,000 in Eastern Asturian. 550,000 in the ethnic group. Population total both countries 100,000 or more. Princedom of Asturias except for the most western section where Galician is spoken, the western part of Cantabria and Leon, and northern Castilla-Leon. In Cantabria and Las Peñamelleras (Asturies) people speak Montañes, a Spanish dialect with Asturian influence. Leonese associations promote their language variety. There are Leonese minorities in Portugal. Also spoken in Portugal. Indo-European, Italic, Romance, Italo-Western, Western, Gallo-Iberian, Ibero-Romance, West Iberian, Asturo-Leonese. Dialects: LEONESE (LLEONES), WESTERN ASTURIAN, CENTRAL ASTURIAN (BABLE), EASTERN ASTURIAN. As different from Spanish as Galician or Catalan; more different than Murcian and Andalusian. Close to Leonese. About 80% intelligibility with Spanish (R. A. Hall, Jr. 1989); enough to cause disruption of communicative ability (T. Erickson SIL 1992). The Vaqueiros ethnic group speaks Western Asturian. Intelligibility among the three dialects is functional. Central Asturian is considered the model, and has the most speakers. Closely related to Mirandés in Portugal. Leonese may be a separate language. Bilingualism in Spanish. May be studied in school by ages 6 to 19 if teachers and books are available. They use Spanish in formal situations and with outsiders. There is literature, both popular and literary, since the 17th century; poetry, and traditional ballads and chivalric novels of oral tradition. The Academy of the Asturian Language was formed in 1981, to revive the academy of the 18th century. About 43% of the population in the region have immigrated into the region from the south since the 1950s, and they have not absorbed the Asturian culture or language. Official language. Dictionary. Western Asturian may need orthography adaptation. NT 1997.

BASQUE *(VASCUENSE, EUSKERA)* [BSQ] 580,000 in Spain (1991 L. Trask U. of Sussex). There are 2,000,000 residents of the 3 provinces of Basque territory; 25% were born outside the territory, 40% in the territory were born to Basque parents. 4,400,000 in Spain have a Basque surname; 19% live in Basque country. Population total all countries 580,000 or more. French-Spanish border, 3 Basque provinces: Alava (Araba), Biskaia (Biskay), and Gipuzkoa of the Autonomous Basque Community (CAV); in the northern area of the Autonomous Region of Navarra (Nafarroa) of north central Spain.

Also spoken in Australia, Costa Rica, Mexico, Philippines, USA. Basque. Dialects: GUIPUZCOAN (GUIPUZCOANO, GIPUZKOAN), ALTO NAVARRO SEPTENTRIONAL (HIGH NAVARRESE, UPPER NAVARRAN), ALTO NAVARRO MERIDIONAL, BISCAYAN (VIZCAINO), AVALAN. Batua is based on Guipuzcoan, the central and most widely known dialect. A fair amount of inherent intelligibility among all regional varieties except Souletin. Regional varieties are sometimes preferred for oral use, but in Spain there is also a fairly strong desire for the Batua unified standard. Bilingualism in Castillian, Catalan sometimes. Ages 2 to 20 and over 50 as first language, all ages as first or second language in mainly Basque-speaking areas. 'Euzkadi' is the name of the Basque region, not for the language. Official language. Dictionary. Grammar. SOV; prepositions; genitives, articles, adjectives, numerals, relatives after noun heads; question word initial; verb affix gender agreement obligatory; prefix marks causative; comparative shown lexically. Batua uses a unified orthography. Deciduous forest. Mountain slope, coastal, riverine. Sea level to 1,000 meters. Christian. Bible 1855-1994.

CALÓ ***(GITANO, IBERIAN ROMANI, HISPANOROMANI)*** [RMR] 40,000 to 140,000 in Spain. Population total all countries 65,000 to 170,000. Also spoken in Brazil, France, Portugal. Indo-European, Italic, Romance, Italo-Western, Western, Gallo-Iberian, Ibero-Romance, West Iberian, Castilian. Dialects: SPANISH CALÓ, PORTUGUESE CALÃO (CALÃO, LUSITANO-ROMANI), CATALONIAN CALO, BASQUE CALO, BRAZILIAN CALÃO. A cryptological variety of Spanish (I. Hancock 1995). McLane found 300 to 400 words based on Romani, but no individual was acquainted with more than 100. The Iberian base for Calo is regional dialects, where the overlap is not distinct between Spanish and Portuguese. Bilingualism in Spanish. There is a movement to revive the defunct inflected Spanish Romani, and a book has been printed in it (I. Hancock 1990). Grammar. Christian. Bible portions 1837-1872.

CATALAN-VALENCIAN-BALEAR ***(CATALÀ, CATALÁN, BACAVÈS, CATALONIAN)*** [CLN] 6,472,828 mother tongue speakers (1996), plus 5,000,000 second or third language speakers in Spain (1994 La Generalitat de Catalunya). Population total all countries 6,565,000 or more. Including second language users: 10,000,000 (1999 WA). Northeastern Spain, around Barcelona; Catalonia, Valencia Provinces, Balearic Islands, region of Carche, Murcia Province. Menorquin is on Menorca. Pallarese, a subdialect of Northwestern Catalan, is in Pallars. Ribagorçan, another subdialect extends from the Valley of Aran to the south of Tamarit, and from the Noguera Ribagorçana to the border with Aragonese. Also spoken in Algeria, Andorra, Argentina, Belgium, Brazil, Chile, Colombia, Cuba, Dominican Republic, France, Germany, Italy, Mexico, Switzerland, Uruguay, USA, Venezuela. Indo-European, Italic, Romance, Italo-Western, Western, Gallo-Iberian, Ibero-Romance, East Iberian. Dialects: CATALAN-ROUSILLONESE (NORTHERN CATALÁN), VALENCIAN (VALENCIANO, VALENCIÀ), BALEARIC (BALEAR, INSULAR CATALAN, MALLORQUI, MENORQUI, EIVISSENC), CENTRAL CATALAN, ALGHERESE, NORTH-WESTERN CATALAN (PALLARESE, RIBAGORÇAN, LLEIDATÀ, AIGUAVIVAN). The standard variety is a literary composite which no one speaks, based on several dialects. Pallarese and Ribogorçan dialects are less similar to standard Catalan. Benasquese and Aiguavivan people live in isolated valleys and have a distinct phonology from their neighbors. Tortosin may be closer to Valencian. Central Catalan has about 90% to 95% inherent intelligibility to speakers of Valencian (R. A. Hall, Jr., 1989). Written Catalan is closest to Barcelona speech. Central Catalan has 87% lexical similarity with Italian, 85% with Portuguese and Spanish, 76% with Rheto-Romance, 75% with Sardinian, 73% with Rumanian. Bilingualism in Spanish, French, Italian, Sard, Occitan. All domains. All ages. Official language. Dictionary. Grammar. Literacy rate in first language: 60%. Literacy rate in second language: 96%. The high literacy in Catalan (60%) is recent. Pallarese and Ribogorçan speakers have less education, less contact with the standard, and live in high valleys of the Pyrenees. Some Valencian speakers desire separate literature. Radio programs, TV. Christian, secular. Bible 1478-1993.

CATALONIAN SIGN LANGUAGE [CSC] 18,000 (1994 estimate). Catalonia. Deaf sign language. An indigenous sign language, quite distinct from Spanish Sign Language. About 50% intelligibility by users of Spanish Sign Language.

EXTREMADURAN ***(EXTREMEÑO, EHTREMEÑU, CAHTÚO, CAHTÚÖ)*** [EXT] 200,000 active speakers, plus 500,000 able to use it, including some monolinguals (1994 T. Erickson). Most speakers are in the northern dialect. 1,100,000 in the ethnic group. Autonomous region of Extremadura (except the Fala-speaking valley in the northwest, Portuguese dialect-speaking strips in the west, and Spanish-speaking strip in the east), and a few neighboring areas. Indo-European, Italic, Romance, Italo-Western, Western, Gallo-Iberian, Ibero-Romance, West Iberian, Castilian. Dialects: NORTHERN EXTREMADURAN (ARTU EHTREMEÑU), CENTRAL EXTREMADURAN (MEYU EHTREMEÑU), SOUTHERN EXTREMADURAN (BAHU EHTREMEÑU). Related to the eastern dialect of Tur-Leonese. Dialects are inherently intelligible to each others' speakers. Those who have gone to school speak Spanish in formal situations and to outsiders. Most speakers are over 30 years old (1994). They use Extremaduran in all contexts. SVO. Literacy rate in second language: 90%. 2 orthographies, one

Castilian-like, developed around the turn of the century by the famous poet José María Gabriel y Galán, the other more recent and more phonetic.

FALA ***(A FALA DE XÁLIMA, A FALA DO XÃLIMA, GALAICO-EXTREMADURAN, "CHAPURREÁU")*** [FAX] 10,500 including 5,500 active speakers in the language area; 5,000 outside, many of whom return each summer (1994 T. Erickson). Northwest corner of the autonomous region of Extremadura, an isolated valley on the Portuguese border called Val de Xalima or Val du riu Ellas, towns of Valverdi du Fresnu, As Ellas and Sa Martín de Trebellu. Indo-European, Italic, Romance, Italo-Western, Western, Gallo-Iberian, Ibero-Romance, West Iberian, Portuguese-Galician. Dialects: VALVIDEIRU, MAÑEGU, LAGARTEIRU. Dialects are inherently intelligible to each others' speakers. Not easily intelligible with the surrounding language varieties. Intelligible to speakers of Galician. They speak Spanish in school, church, and with outsiders. Spoken in all contexts except school, church, and contacts with outsiders. All ages. Vitality is high. The speakers do not identify with the Galicians. Literacy rate in second language: Nearly 100%. Speakers do not want orthography to be like Galician.

GALICIAN ***(GALEGO, GALLEGO)*** [GLN] 3,173,400 in Spain, 8.2% of the population (1986). Population total both countries 4,000,000 (1999 WA). Northwest Spain, Autonomous Region of Galicia. Also spoken in Portugal. Indo-European, Italic, Romance, Italo-Western, Western, Gallo-Iberian, Ibero-Romance, West Iberian, Portuguese-Galician. Galician is between Portuguese and Spanish, but closer to Portuguese. Portuguese has about 85% intelligibility to speakers of Galician (R. A. Hall, Jr., 1989). Many dialects. Bilingualism in Spanish. There is an Academy of the Galician Language. It has had many decades of development as a language of serious literature, including poetry, essays on novel, ideological, philosophical, and sociological topics, and for all levels of education, including higher education. A growing sense of ethnic identity and of the Galician language. Investigation needed: intelligibility with dialects on the border with Asturian. Official language. Bible 1989-1992.

GASCON, ARANESE ***(ARANÉS, ARANESE, ARNAIS, GASCON, ARANESE OCCITAN)*** [GSC] 3,814 speakers, plus 1,283 who understand it in Spain (1991 linguistic census) out of 5,922 in the valley (1991 census). Aran Valley, headwaters of the Garona River in the northwest corner of the autonomous region of Catalonia, Pyrenees Mts. Indo-European, Italic, Romance, Italo-Western, Western, Gallo-Iberian, Ibero-Romance, Oc. Dialects: BAISH ARANÉS, MIJARANÉS ARANÉS, NAUT ARANÉS. Some regional variation. Inherently intelligible with Commingese Gascon of France. Not as close to Limousin, Auvergnat, Languedocien, or Provençal, related languages of France. Over half the speakers are fluent in French, Spanish, Catalan, or Occitan. Catalan and Spanish are taught in school. About half of those in Spain also speak French because of commercial traffic both ways across the border. Most occasions. Speakers in Spain: 532 ages 2-14, 775 15-29, 733 30-44, 750 45-64, 609 over 65, 9 without age indicated. The Aranese magazine 'Toti' is published monthly. The Center of Linguistic Normalization is dedicated to the promotion of its use. Called 'Aranese' in France. Aranese is influenced by Catalan and Spanish more than French. Official language. Literacy rate in first language: 32% Aranese. Literacy rate in second language: Nearly 100% in Spanish, 50% in Catalan. Own orthography in Spain. Taught regularly in school since 1984. Newspapers. Bible portions 1583-1983. See main entry under France.

GUANCHE [GNC] Canary Islands. Afro-Asiatic, Berber, Guanche. Extinct in the 16th century. Its relation to Berber has been questioned. Extinct.

MOZARABIC [MXI] Indo-European, Italic, Romance, Italo-Western, Western, Pyrenean-Mozarabic, Mozarabic. A Romance language with Arabic influences. It is still used liturgically by 2 churches in Toledo. Used by Christians during the Moorish occupation of Spain in the Middle Ages. Christian. Extinct.

QUINQUI [QUQ] Many live on the edge of towns. Unclassified. A blend language of certain urban ex-nomadic groups. It contains elements of Calo and Germania argot. They used to be tinsmiths—their name comes from 'quincalleria' meaning ironmongery. It is thought they came originally from Germany. They are blond. They prefer to be called 'mercheros'. Not Rom or Gypsies.

SPANISH ***(ESPAÑOL, CASTELLANO, CASTILIAN)*** [SPN] 28,173,600 in Spain, 72.8% of the population (1986). Population total all countries 322,200,000 to 358,000,000 first language users (1999 WA-source for the second figure), 417,000,000 including second language users (1999 WA). Central and southern Spain and the Canary Islands. Also spoken in 43 other countries including Andorra, Argentina, Aruba, Australia, Belgium, Belize, Bolivia, Canada, Cayman Islands, Chile, Colombia, Costa Rica, Cuba, Dominican Republic, Ecuador, El Salvador, Equatorial Guinea, Finland, France. Indo-European, Italic, Romance, Italo-Western, Western, Gallo-Iberian, Ibero-Romance, West Iberian, Castilian. Dialects: ANDALUSIAN, MURCIAN, ARAGONESE, NAVARRESE, CASTILIAN, CANARY ISLANDS SPANISH, AMERICAN SPANISH. Leonese has similarities to Asturian, and may be extinct. 89% lexical similarity with Portuguese, 85% with Catalan, 82% with Italian, 76% with Sardinian, 75% with French, 74% with Rheto-Romance, 71% with Rumanian. Most mother tongue speakers of other languages in Spain use Spanish as second language. The Aragonese dialect of Spanish is different from the Aragonese language. Official language. Dictionary. Grammar. SVO; prepositions; genitives, relatives after noun heads; articles, numerals before noun heads; adjectives before or after noun heads depending on whether it is evaluative or descriptive; question word initial; (C(C))V(C); nontonal. Christian. Bible 1553-1979.

SPANISH SIGN LANGUAGE *(MÍMICA)* [SSP] 102,000 (1994). 20,000 members of deaf associations (1986 Gallaudet University). Deaf sign language. Small differences throughout Spain with no difficulties in intercommunication, except in Catalonia. Origin unknown, but it is reported that there are influences from American, French, and Mexican sign languages. Some signed interpretation used in court, at important public events. There is sign language instruction for parents of deaf children. Many sign language classes for hearing people. There is a committee on national sign language. There is a manual system for spelling. Dictionary. Literacy rate in second language: 20% to 30%. Films, TV, videos.

SWEDEN

Kingdom of Sweden, Konungariket Sverige. National or official language: Swedish. 8,875,000 (1998 UN). Literacy rate 99%. Also includes Tosk Albanian 4,000, Amharic, Assyrian Neo-Aramaic, Chaldean Neo-Aramaic, Danish 35,000, Estonian 1,560, Western Farsi 35,000, Greek 50,000, Kirmanjki, Kurmanji 10,000, Latvian 450, Lithuanian 310, Bokmaal Norwegian 28,000, Serbo-Croatian 120,000, Somali, Spanish 35,000, Turkish 20,000, Turoyo 20,000, Chinese, people from Iraq 6,000, Eritrea, North Africa. Information mainly from B. Comrie 1987; I. Hancock 1991; E. Haugen 1992; O. Dahl 1996; B. Winsa 1998. Christian, secular. Blind population 15,716. Deaf population 8,000 to 532,210 (1998). Deaf institutions: 72. The number of languages listed for Sweden is 15. Of those, all are living languages. Diversity index 0.37.

DALECARLIAN *(DALSKA, DALMAAL)* [DLC] 1,500 (1996 Oesten Dahl). Upper Dalecarlia (Oevre Dalarna), especially Aelvdalen (Elfdal). Indo-European, Germanic, North, East Scandinavian, Danish-Swedish, Swedish. Quite deviant from other varieties. Various dialects, some of which are reported to be unintelligible to each others' speakers. Bilingualism in Swedish.

FINNISH *(SUOMI, SUOMEA)* [FIN] 200,000 in Sweden (1997 Birger Winsa). 'Swedish-Finns' were 446,134 in 1999, which counts those born in Finland and first generation born in Sweden, but not others, even if the mother tongue is Finnish. Uralic, Finno-Ugric, Finno-Permic, Finno-Cheremisic, Finno-Mordvinic, Finno-Lappic, Balto-Finnic, Finnic. 1st to 3rd generation immigrants, apart from speakers of Tornedalen Finnish. Christian. Bible 1642-1991. See main entry under Finland.

FINNISH, TORNEDALEN *(TORNEDALEN (MEÄNKIELI, TORNE VALLEY FINNISH, TORNEDALS-FINSKA, NORTH FINNISH))* [FIT] 60,000 to 80,000 in Sweden, including 40,000 to 70,000 in the main region (1997), and including 20,000 who speak it in the home (1996). Population total both countries 90,000 to 110,000. Northeast Sweden, County of Norrbotten, municipalities of Gellivare, Kiruna, Pajala, Övertorneä, and Haparanda. Also spoken in Finland. Uralic, Finno-Ugric, Finno-Permic, Finno-Cheremisic, Finno-Mordvinic, Finno-Lappic, Balto-Finnic, Finnic. Dialects: TORNE VALLEY FINNISH, VITTANGI FINNISH, GELLIVARE FINNISH. Standard Finnish is not entirely intelligible to speakers of Tornedalen, especially abstract and complex discourse. Swedish is used as second language, and some speak Standard Finnish. The dominant mother tongue speakers are 30 years and older. Quarterly magazine in Finnish, Tornedalen Finnish, and Swedish. 30 children's books. There is a Swedish Tornedalian Association with 5,000 members. Many Saami speak it as second language. Torne Valley dialect has the highest prestige because of its size and closeness to Finland. Gellivare dialect has the lowest prestige because of its high percentage of Swedish and Saami loan words and deviant morphophonology. Somewhat negative attitudes toward Standard Finnish, and weak motivation to learn it, although it is partially intelligible to Tornedalen speakers. Some speakers refer to it as 'Finnish'. It has influences from Swedish. Finnish speakers settled here in the 12th century. Dictionary. Grammar. SVO, postpositions, genitives after noun heads, articles, adjectives, numerals before noun heads, question word initial. Literacy rate in first language: 20% to 30%. Christian: Lutheran, Laestadian. Bible portions 1993-1995.

JAMSKA *(JAMTSKA)* [JMK] 30,000 or more who speak it fluently, plus 60,000 or more second language speakers (2000 J. Persson). Jämtland and scattered elsewhere in Sweden. Indo-European, Germanic, North, West Scandinavian. Perhaps 95% lexical similarity to other Norwegian or Swedish dialects, other loans from German, Danish, French. Many parents do not teach it to their children.

ROMANI, KALO FINNISH *(FÍNTIKA RÓMMA)* [RMF] 1,000 to 2,000 in Sweden. Indo-European, Indo-Iranian, Indo-Aryan, Central zone, Romani, Northern. Christian. Bible portions 1971. See main entry under Finland.

ROMANI, VLAX *(ZIGENARE)* [RMY] 500 Kalderash, 1,000 Lovari in Sweden. Indo-European, Indo-Iranian, Indo-Aryan, Central zone, Romani, Vlax. Dialects: KALDERASH, LOVARI. Christian. NT 1984-1986. See main entry under Romania.

SAAMI, LULE *(LULE, "LAPP")* [LPL] 1,500 speakers out of 6,000 population in Sweden (1995 M. Krauss). 14,600 ethnic Saami in Sweden (1995). Population total both countries 2,000 or more Lule. 52,800 to 63,800 all ethnic Saami. Lapland along the Lule River in Gällivare and Jokkmokk. Also spoken in Norway. Uralic, Finno-Ugric, Finno-Permic, Finno-Cheremisic, Finno-Mordvinic, Finno-Lappic, Lappic, Southern. Lule Saami is quite distinct from other Saami. Few children speakers. The name "Lapp" is derogatory. Literacy rate in first language: 1% to 5%. Literacy rate in second language: 75% to 100%. NT 1903.

SAAMI, NORTHERN *(NORWEGIAN SAAMI, "LAPP", SAAME, SAME, SAMIC, NORTHERN LAPPISH)* [LPR] 4,000 speakers (1995 M. Krauss) out of 5,000 population in Sweden (1994 SIL). Karesuando and Jukkasjärvi. Uralic, Finno-Ugric, Finno-Permic, Finno-Cheremisic, Finno- Mordvinic, Finno-Lappic, Lappic, Northern. Dialects: RUIJA, TORNE, SEA LAPPISH. Literacy rate in first language: 10% to 30%. Literacy rate in second language: 75% to 100%. Bible 1895. See main entry under Norway.

SAAMI, PITE *("LAPP", PITE)* [LPB] 50 or fewer speakers out of 2,000 population in Sweden (1995 M. Krauss). Population total both countries 50 or fewer. Lapland along Pite River in Arjeplog and Arvidsjaur. Also spoken in Norway. Uralic, Finno-Ugric, Finno-Permic, Finno-Cheremisic, Finno-Mordvinic, Finno-Lappic, Lappic, Southern. Pite Saami is very distinct. Literacy rate in first language: Below 1%. Literacy rate in second language: 75% to 100%. Nearly extinct.

SAAMI, SOUTHERN *("LAPP", SOUTHERN LAPP)* [LPC] 300 speakers out of 600 population in Sweden (1995 M. Krauss). Population total both countries 600. Vilhelmina in Lapland, in Jämtland, Härjedalen, and Idre in Dalarna. Also spoken in Norway. Uralic, Finno-Ugric, Finno-Permic, Finno-Cheremisic, Finno-Mordvinic, Finno-Lappic, Lappic, Southern. Few children speakers. Literacy rate in first language: 1% to 5%. Literacy rate in second language: 75% to 100%. Bible portions.

SAAMI, UME *("LAPP", UME)* [LPU] 50 speakers out of 1,000 population (1995 M. Krauss). Lycksele, Mala, Tärna, and Sorsele, along the Ume River. Probably no speakers in Norway. Uralic, Finno-Ugric, Finno-Permic, Finno-Cheremisic, Finno-Mordvinic, Finno-Lappic, Lappic, Southern. Literacy rate in first language: Below 1%. Literacy rate in second language: 75% to 100%. Bible 1811.

SKÅNE *(SKÅNSKA, SCANIAN, SKÅNSK)* [SCY] 1,500,000 (1998 Scanian Regional Institute). Population total both countries 1,500,000 or more. Blekinge, Halland, Skåne in Sweden. The main regional city is Malmö. Also spoken in Denmark. Indo-European, Germanic, North, East Scandinavian, Danish-Swedish, Swedish. Dialects: HALLAENDSKA, SKÅNSKA, BLEKINGSKA, BORNHOLM. Speakers are highly bilingual in Swedish. The language has had no recognition since Sweden obtained Scania from Denmark in 1658. It is called 'Southern Swedish' in Sweden, and 'Eastern Danish' in Denmark. Today it is heavily influenced by Swedish in Sweden. Dictionary. Literacy rate in second language: 100% Swedish. Bible 1523.

SWEDISH *(SVENSKA, RUOTSI)* [SWD] 7,825,000 in Sweden, 93% of the population (1986), including 5,000 speakers of Gutniska (1998 Sven Hakansson). Gutniska has 10,000 second language speakers. Population total all countries 9,000,000 (1999 WA). The Göta dialect group is southern, including parts of Småland, south Swedish provinces, Värmland, Västergvtland; the Svea dialect group is northern, including Hälsingland, parts of Östergotland and Uppland, and the Swedish-speaking parts of Finland. Southern Swedish is in Skaåne, Blekinge, southern Småland, southern Halland. Northern Swedish is from northern Hälsingland and Jämtland and northwards. Eastern Swedish is in Finland, Estonia, and Gammalsvenskby, Ukraine. Gutnic is in southeastern Isle of Gotland and Faaroe. Nearly extinct in Estonia. Also spoken in Canada, Estonia, Finland, Norway, UAE, USA. Indo-European, Germanic, North, East Scandinavian, Danish-Swedish, Swedish. Dialects: NORTHERN SWEDISH (NORRLAND), EASTERN SWEDISH (FINLAND SWEDISH, ESTONIAN SWEDISH), SVEA, GUTNISKA (GUTAMAL, GOTLANDIC, GUTNIC). 'Proper' Swedish is considered to be spoken in Svealand. Dialect investigation is needed of diverse varieties Gutniska, Överkalixmål, Nörpes, Pitemål, provinces around the Bothnic Sea (Västerbotten and Norbotten in Sweden, and Oesterbotten in Finland), and the island of Gotland. Gutniska is descended from Forngutniska (Old Gotlandic), which is ranked as a separate language. A mixed variety, with Turkish influence, Rinkebysvenska, is used among immigrants. There are, or were, Swedish varieties spoken in Estonia and Ukraine which are now more or less extinct. See separate listing for Skåne, often called Southern Swedish. Investigation needed: intelligibility with Gutniska, Överkalixmål, Pitemål, Nörpes, Skåne. National language. Bible 1541-1999, NT 1526-1996.

SWEDISH SIGN LANGUAGE [SWL] 8,000 deaf primary users, and the first language of many hearing children of deaf parents (1986 Gallaudet Univ.). Deaf sign language. No origins from other sign languages, but it has influenced Portuguese and Finnish sign languages. Intelligible with Norwegian and Danish sign languages with only moderate difficulty. Not intelligible with Finnish Sign Language.

Today the deaf are regarded as a bilingual minority. Sign language used since 1800. The first deaf school was established in 1809. There are 5 deaf schools, and they use Swedish Sign Language for instruction in all subjects. Also taught at the University of Stockholm. Many sign language classes for hearing people. Government interpreters assist the deaf in contacts with official and private institutions. There is an organization for sign language teachers. Signed Swedish is distinct. Much research. Dictionary. Grammar. TV, videos.

TAVRINGER ROMANI ***(ROMMANI, SVENSK ROMMANI, TRAVELLER SWEDISH, "TATTARE")*** [RMU] 25,000 in Sweden (1998 Hallman). Population total both countries 31,000. Scattered all over Sweden. Also spoken in Norway. Indo-European, Germanic, North, East Scandinavian, Danish-Swedish, Swedish. Not intelligible with Angloromani. Speakers are fluent in Swedish or Norwegian. Used mainly as a secret language by the speakers (D. Kenrick 1985), a Gypsy group in Sweden. An independent language based on Swedish with heavy lexical borrowing from Northern Romani. Romani people arrived in Sweden via Denmark in 1512. Investigation needed: intelligibility with Traveller Norwegian, Traveller Danish, bilingual proficiency in Swedish.

SWITZERLAND

Swiss Confederation. National or official languages: French, Standard German, Italian, Rheto-Romance. 7,299,000 (1998 UN). Literacy rate 99%. Also includes Assyrian Neo-Aramaic, Catalan-Valencian-Balear, English, Iu Mien, Kirmanjki, Kurmanji 13,000, Portuguese 86,000, Serbo-Croatian 142,000, Spanish 117,000, Tai Nüa, Tibetan 200, Turkish 53,000, Yeniche, Western Yiddish. Information mainly from M. Stephens 1976; W. Moulton 1985; B. Comrie 1987; C. Buchli 1999. Christian, secular, Muslim. Blind population 9,000. Deaf population 7,200 to 426,835 (1998). Deaf institutions: 45. Data accuracy estimate: B. The number of languages listed for Switzerland is 12. Of those, all are living languages. Diversity index 0.53.

ALEMANNISCH ***(ALEMANNIC, SCHWYZERDÜTSCH)*** [GSW] 4,215,000 in Switzerland, 63.6% of the population (1990 census). Population total all countries 6,044,000 or more. Central, south central, north central, northeast, and eastern cantons. Also spoken in Austria, France, Germany, Liechtenstein. Indo-European, Germanic, West, High German, German, Upper German, Alemannic. Dialects: BERN (BÄRNDÜTSCH), ZURICH, LUCERNE, BASEL, OBWALD, APPENZEL, ST. GALLEN, GRAUBENDEN-GRISONS (VALSERISCH), WALLIS. Swiss varieties are High Alemannisch (most) and Highest Alemannisch (several in central Switzerland). Not functionally intelligible to speakers of Standard German. Each canton has a separate variety, many of which are unintelligible to each others' speakers. Only a few of the 20 to 70 varieties are listed as dialects (subdialects). Close to Schwäbish in south central Germany. All speakers are actively or passively bilingual in Standard German. Standard German is the language of instruction in school. There is an important literature. Used in some schools and churches. 93.3% of German speakers in Switzerland speak a Swiss German dialect, and 66.4% speak dialect only, and no High German (1990 census). 72% of the entire population of Switzerland speak Schwyzerdütsch every day (1990 census). They have a strong social function, being used to maintain the borders of regions or cantons, or even to keep one village different from another. They also draw the line between Germans, Swiss, and Austrians. Called 'Schwytzertütsch' in Switzerland, and 'Alsatian' in France. Grammar. NT 1984.

FRANCO-PROVENÇAL ***(PATOIS)*** [FRA] 7,000 in Valais Canton, Switzerland (1998). French cantons of Valais, Fribourg, and Vaud. Indo-European, Italic, Romance, Italo-Western, Western, Gallo-Iberian, Gallo-Romance, Gallo-Rhaetian, Oïl, Southeastern. Dialects: SAVOYARD, NEUCH-TELOIS, VALAISAN, VAUDOIS. A structurally separate language from Provençal, French, Piemontese, and Lombard (F. B. Agard). Every canton in Switzerland has its own dialect, with no standardization. Difficult intelligibility among the dialects, and especially with Fribourg. Bilingualism in French. Valais Canton: young and old in Evolène commune; communes of Hérémence, Vex, Saint-Martin, Savièse, Nendaz, Cermignon, Fully, Arbaz, Ayent, Vissole, and other smaller villages in the central Valais, and persons in towns like Sion and Sierre, spoken by persons 50 and older, understood by persons 35-40. Fribourg Canton: rural areas as Gruyère. Dictionary. Bible portions 1830. See main entry under France.

FRENCH ***(FRANÇAIS)*** [FRN] 1,272,000 in Switzerland, 19.2% of the population (1990 census). Western Switzerland. Indo-European, Italic, Romance, Italo-Western, Western, Gallo-Iberian, Gallo- Romance, Gallo-Rhaetian, Oïl, French. Dialect: FRANCHE-COMTOIS (JURASSIEN, FRIBOURGOIS). 33% of the population of Switzerland speak French every day (1990 census). Official language. Used for education in French-speaking areas. Bible 1530-1986. See main entry under France.

GERMAN, STANDARD [GER] Indo-European, Germanic, West, High German, German, Middle German, East Middle German. Not used as mother tongue by many. Official language. Main language used in education in Schwyzerdütsch- (German) and Rheto-Romansch-speaking areas. Bible 1466-1982. See main entry under Germany.

ITALIAN [ITN] 195,000 in Switzerland (1990). Indo-European, Italic, Romance, Italo-Western, Italo-Dalmatian. People in all of the Italian cantons speak Italian as first or second language. Used for education in Italian- and Ticino- (Lombard) speaking areas. Official language. Bible 1471-1985. See main entry under Italy.

LOMBARD [LMO] 303,000 or fewer (1995). Ticino Canton and Graubunden in the Mesolcina District and two districts south of St. Moritz, central southeast Switzerland. Indo-European, Italic, Romance, Italo-Western, Western, Gallo-Iberian, Gallo-Romance, Gallo-Italian. Dialect: TICINESE (TICINO, TESSINIAN, TICINES, TICINEES). No intelligibility with Standard Italian. Speakers are adequately bilingual in Standard Italian. Ticinese is the form of Lombard used in the home in Italy. Used more extensively in Switzerland than in Italy. 14.5% of the population of Switzerland speak 'Italian' every day (1990 census). Dictionary. Radio programs, TV. Bible portions 1859-1860. See main entry under Italy.

ROMANI, SINTE [RMO] 21,000 in Switzerland (1993 Johnstone). Indo-European, Indo-Iranian, Indo-Aryan, Central zone, Romani, Northern. Christian. Bible portions 1875-1995. See main entry under Yugoslavia.

ROMANSCH ***(RHETO-ROMANCE, RHAETO-ROMANCE, ROMANSH, ROMANCHE)*** [RHE] 40,000 or 0.6% of the population (1990 census). Borders of Switzerland, Austria, Italy; Graubünden Canton, Grisons valley of Surselva, valley of Voderrhein; Engadin and Val Mustair, southeast Switzerland. Indo-European, Italic, Romance, Italo-Western, Western, Gallo-Iberian, Gallo-Romance, Gallo-Rhaetian, Rhaetian. Dialects: LOWER ENGADINE (PUTER-LOWER ENGADINE, GRISONS), UPPER ENGADINE (VALLADER-UPPER ENGADINE), SURSILVAN (SURSELVA, SUTSILVAN-HINTERRHEIN), SURSILVAN-OBERLAND, SURMIRAN-ALBULA. Friulian, Ladin, and Romansch are separate languages (R. A. Hall, Jr., personal communication 1978). 78% lexical similarity with Italian and French, 76% with Catalan, 74% with Spanish, Sardinian, and Portuguese, 72% with Romanian. Speakers are bilingual. Standard German is the language of instruction in school. An official written language is in common use now, called Grischuna. Official language. All dialects taught in school. Newspapers. Bible 1679-1953.

SWISS-FRENCH SIGN LANGUAGE ***(LANGAGE GESTUELLE)*** [SSR] 1,000 (1986 Gallaudet Univ.). Deaf sign language. Some regional lexical variations in the French area are tied to specific schools. There are local Swiss signs and imported French signs. Sign language is now taught in a bilingual program in Geneva. The status of signing has been low, but is now improving. French Sign Language is used some in the French area. TV.

SWISS-GERMAN SIGN LANGUAGE ***(NATÜRLICHE GEBÄRDE)*** [SGG] 6,000 (1986 Gallaudet Univ.). Deaf sign language. Some regional lexical variations in German areas are tied to specific schools. The status of signing has been low, but is now improving. In schools in the German area there is a strong oralist tradition.

SWISS-ITALIAN SIGN LANGUAGE [SLF] 200 (1986 Gallaudet Univ.). Deaf sign language. The status of signing has been low, but is now improving.

WALSER ***(WALSCHER)*** [WAE] 10,000 to 20,000 speakers in Switzerland out of 21,900 population (1980 C. Buchli). Population total all countries 20,000 to 40,000. Bosco-Gurin, Canton Ticino; Wallis, Simplon; Graubunden, Obersaxen; Valsertal (Vals, St. Martin); Safiental (Valendas, Versam, Tenna, Safien); Rheinwald (Medels, Nufenen, Splngen, Sufers, Hinterrhein, Avers); Schanfigg (Arosa, Langwiesn); Albula (Mutten, Schmitte Wiesen); Landquart (Davos, Klosters, Furna, Says, St. Antonien, Valzeina). 26 communities in Switzerland, and 7 former ones. Also spoken in Austria, Italy, Liechtenstein. Indo-European, Germanic, West, High German, German, Upper German, Alemannic. Ancestors came from the Wallis Canton between the 12th and 13th centuries. Close but different from Schwytzertusch spoken in Wallis Canton in Switzerland. Different from Cimbrian, Mocheno, or Bavarian.

TURKEY (EUROPE)

Also see Turkey in Asia for a listing of languages in Asia. Data accuracy estimate: C. The number of languages listed for Turkey (Europe) is 11. Of those, 10 are living languages and 1 is extinct. Diversity index 0.66.

ALBANIAN, TOSK [ALN] 15,000 first language speakers (1980), out of 65,000 in Turkey (1993 Johnstone), 1,075 monolinguals (1965 census). Scattered in western Turkey. Indo-European, Albanian, Tosk. 96% of speakers can use Turkish as second language. Sunni Muslim. Bible 1993. See main entry under Albania.

ARMENIAN *(HAIEREN, SOMKHURI, ERMENICE, ARMJANSKI)* [ARM] 40,000 first language speakers out of 70,000 ethnic group in Turkey (1980 estimate), 1,022 monolingual speakers (1965 census). Many in Istanbul, and a few scattered across eastern Turkey. The Hemshin (Hamshen) are Armenian Muslims, living near the Laz. Indo-European, Armenian. Dialect: EASTERN ARMENIAN. Eastern dialect spoken in Armenia and its Iranian and Turkish borderlands. Western dialect spoken elsewhere. Western (Turkish) Armenian and Ararat (Russian) are easily intelligible. 96% bilingual in Turkish. Christian. Bible 1883-1994. See main entry under Armenia.

BALKAN GAGAUZ TURKISH *(BALKAN TURKIC)* [BGX] 327,000 in Turkey, including 7,000 Surguch (1965) and 320,000 Yuruk (1993 Johnstone). Population total all countries 331,000. Yuruk dialect on the west coast in Macedonia. Also spoken in Greece, Macedonia. Altaic, Turkic, Southern, Turkish. Dialects: GAJOL, GERLOVO TURKS, KARAMANLI, KYZYLBASH, SURGUCH, TOZLUK TURKS, YURUK (YORUK, KONYAR). Distinct from Gagauz of Moldova, Bulgaria, and Romania. Muslim.

BULGARIAN *(POMAK)* [BLG] 270,000 in Turkey, including refugees from Bulgaria (1993 Johnstone). Scattered in Edirne and other western provinces. Indo-European, Slavic, South, Eastern. Dialect: POMAK. 93% bilingual in Turkish. Spoken by Muslim Pomaks in Turkey and Greece. Sunni Muslim. Bible 1864-1923. See main entry under Bulgaria.

DOMARI *(MIDDLE EASTERN ROMANI, TSIGENE, GYPSY)* [RMT] 20,000 perhaps in Turkey (1982 estimate). Mainly in western Turkey, some in eastern Turkey. Indo-European, Indo-Iranian, Indo-Aryan, Northwestern zone, Dom. Dialects: KARACHI, BELUDJI, MARASHI. 500,000 Gypsies in Turkey speak Domari or varieties of Romani (Gunnemark and Kenrick 1985). Muslim. See main entry under Iran.

GREEK [GRK] 4,000 in Turkey (1993). Istanbul city. Indo-European, Greek, Attic. Nearly all Greeks have now emigrated from Turkey. There were 1,500,000 in Turkey in 1900. Bible 1840-1994. See main entry under Greece.

LADINO *(DZHUDEZMO, JUDEO SPANISH, SEFARDI, JUDEZMO, HAKITIA, HAKETIA, SPANYOL)* [SPJ] 8,000 or fewer first language speakers out of 15,000 people in Turkey (1976). Mainly in Istanbul; some in Izmirin. Indo-European, Italic, Romance, Italo-Western, Western, Gallo-Iberian, Ibero-Romance, West Iberian, Castilian. Nearly all are bilingual in Turkish. Chief language of Sefardic Jews. The Donme are a Ladino-speaking group in Turkey, adherents of Shabbetai Zevi (Zvi). Roman. Newspapers. Jewish. Bible 1829. See main entry under Israel.

ROMANI, BALKAN [RMN] 25,000 to 40,000 Arlija in Turkey. Indo-European, Indo-Iranian, Indo-Aryan, Central zone, Romani, Balkan. Dialect: ARLIJA (ERLI). Muslim. Bible portions 1912-1937. See main entry under Yugoslavia.

SERBO-CROATIAN *(BOSNIAN)* [SRC] 20,000 first language speakers (1980), out of 61,000 in Turkey (1980 estimate), 2,345 monolinguals (1965 census). Scattered in western Turkey. Indo-European, Slavic, South, Western. 95% bilingual in Turkish. Muslim. Bible 1804-1968. See main entry under Yugoslavia.

TATAR [TTR] Istanbul and perhaps other places. Altaic, Turkic, Western, Uralian. Muslim. Bible portions 1864-1995. See main entry under Russia.

UBYKH *(UBYX, PEKHI, OUBYKH)* [UBY] Haci Osman village, near the Sea of Marmara, near Istanbul. North Caucasian, Northwest, Ubyx. The last fully competent speaker, Tevfik Esen, of Haci Osman, died in Istanbul 10/92. A century ago there were 50,000 speakers in the Caucasus valleys east of the Black Sea. Most migrated to Turkey in 1894. The ethnic group now speaks a distinct dialect of Adyghe. Extinct.

UKRAINE

National or official language: Ukrainian. 50,861,000 (1998 UN). Formerly part of USSR. Capital: Kiev. 233,100 square miles. Literacy rate 99%. Also includes Abkhaz 476, Tosk Albanian 5,000, Armenian 54,000, Bashkir 3,672, Belarusan 440,000, Bulgarian 234,000, Crimean Turkish 200,000, Czech 21,000, Dargwa 634, Erzya 19,000, Gagauz, Georgian 24,000, Standard German 38,000, Greek 104,000, Kazakh 7,555, Lak 574, Latvian 2,600, Lezgi 1,708, Osetin 4,554, Polish 1,151,000, Balkan Romani, Baltic Romani, Russian 11,335,000, Serbo-Croatian 5,000, Slovak 12,000, Tajiki 2,215, Tatar 90,542, Turkish, Northern Uzbek 10,563, Eastern Yiddish 634,000. Information mainly from B. Podolsky 1985; B. Comrie 1987. Christian, Muslim, Jewish (634,000). Data accuracy estimate: B. The number of languages listed for Ukraine is 11. Of those, 10 are living languages and 1 is extinct. Diversity index 0.48.

GOTHIC [GOF] Bulgaria and central Europe. Also spoken in Bulgaria. Indo-European, Germanic, East. Dialects: CRIMEAN GOTHIC, OSTROGOTH, VISIGOTH. Some settlements survived in Crimea until the 18th century (Bloomfield 1933). Extinct. Bible 520.

HUNGARIAN *(MAGYAR)* [HNG] 187,000 in Ukraine (1993 Johnstone), 95% speak it as mother tongue. Transcarpathian Ukraine. Uralic, Finno-Ugric, Ugric, Hungarian. Closest to Vogul (Mansi) of Russia. Christian. Bible 1590-1991. See main entry under Hungary.

JAKATI *(JATI, JATU, JAT, JATAKI, KAYANI, MUSALI)* [JAT] 156,000 in former USSR (1979). Population total both countries 157,000. Kabul (25 families); Jalalabad (50 families); Charikar (15 families). Also spoken in Afghanistan. Indo-European, Indo-Iranian, Indo-Aryan, Northwestern zone, Lahnda. Related to Western Panjabi. Spoken by the Jats ('Gypsies' of Afghanistan). Different from Jadgali of Pakistan. Nomadic. Ironsmiths, fortune tellers. Muslim.

KARAIM [KDR] Southwest, small communities in the Crimean Peninsula, city of Galiche. Altaic, Turkic, Western, Ponto-Caspian. Karaim Jewish. Bible portions 1842. See main entry under Lithuania.

ROMANI, CARPATHIAN [RMC] Ukraine, Transcarpathia. One dialect is in east Hungary, south Poland, and Galicia; another in Transylvania, Romania; others in Czech Republic and Slovakia, USA. Indo-European, Indo-Iranian, Indo-Aryan, Central zone, Romani, Northern, Vlax. Ethnic group: Ungrike Romá (Ukraine). Christian. Bible portions 1936-1996. See main entry under Czech Republic.

ROMANI, VLAX [RMY] Eastern and western Ukraine, Odessa, Transcarpathia. Indo-European, Indo-Iranian, Indo-Aryan, Central zone, Romani, Vlax. Dialects: UKRAINIAN VLAX ROMANI, CENTRAL VLAX ROMANI, KALDERASH. Vlax from the former USSR are called 'Rusurja'. Ethnic groups: Sárvi (left-bank Ukraine), Volóxuja (right-bank Ukraine), Chache (Moldavia), Kalderari (Moldavia, Ukraine, Odessa, Transcarpathia), Lovári (Ukraine). Christian. NT 1984-1995. See main entry under Romania.

ROMANIAN *(RUMANIAN, MOLDAVIAN, DACO-ROMANIAN)* [RUM] 250,000 or fewer in Ukraine (1999). Historically the regions of Bucovina and southern Basarabia (Chernowitz or Cernauti regions) were incorporated into the USSR from Romania by the Ribentrop-Molotov treaty in 1939. Indo-European, Italic, Romance, Eastern. Mountain slope. Bible 1688-1989. See main entry under Romania.

RUSYN *(RUTHENIAN, CARPATHIAN, CARPATHO-RUSYN)* [RUE] Population total both countries 50,000 or more. Transcarpathian Oblast of Ukraine. Also possibly in Romania. Also spoken in Slovakia. Indo-European, Slavic, East. Rusyn is called a dialect of Ukrainian, but speakers are reported to consider themselves distinct from Ukrainians. Standard Ukrainian used for literature, signs. Investigation needed: bilingual proficiency in Ukrainian. Radio programs, TV. Christian.

UKRAINIAN [UKR] 31,058,000 in Ukraine (1993), 83% of 37,419,000 in the ethnic group (1993 Johnstone). 75% of the population is ethnic Ukrainian. Population total all countries 47,000,000 (1999 WA). Western Ukraine, adjacent republics. Also spoken in 25 other countries including Argentina, Armenia, Azerbaijan, Belarus, Brazil, Canada, Estonia, Georgia, Hungary, Kazakhstan, Kyrgyzstan, Latvia, Lithuania, Moldova, Paraguay, Poland, Romania, Russia (Asia), Slovakia. Indo-European, Slavic, East. Dialects: NORTHWEST UKRAINIAN, SOUTHWEST UKRAINIAN, EAST UKRAINIAN. Dialect differences are slight. Official language. Grammar. Cyrillic script. Christian. Bible 1903-1962.

UKRAINIAN SIGN LANGUAGE [UKL] Deaf sign language.

URUM [UUM] A few villages in the Donetsk Oblast of southeastern Ukraine. 10 villages total. Altaic, Turkic. Related to Crimean Tatar. A number of inherently intelligible dialects. Spoken by ethnic 'Greeks'. Investigation needed: intelligibility with Crimean Tatar. See main entry under Georgia.

UNITED KINGDOM

United Kingdom of Great Britain and Northern Ireland. National or official languages: English, Welsh, French (regional). 58,649,000 (1998 UN). Literacy rate 97% to 99%. Also includes Judeo-Iraqi Arabic, Moroccan Spoken Arabic, Taizzi-Adeni Spoken Arabic, Assyrian Neo-Aramaic 5,000, Bengali, Hakka Chinese, Mandarin Chinese, Yue Chinese, Estonian, Western Farsi 12,000, Greek 200,000, Gujarati 140,000, Hebrew, Hindi, Italian 200,000, Japanese 12,000, Kashmiri 115,000, Kirmanjki, Kurmanji 6,000, Latvian, Leeward Caribbean Creole English, Lithuanian, Malayalam, Maltese, Eastern Panjabi, Mirpur Panjabi 20,000, Western Panjabi, Parsi 75,000, Northern Pashto, Southern Pashto 87,000, Portuguese, Saraiki, Shelta 30,000, Sindhi 25,000, Somali, Southwestern Caribbean Creole English, Sylhetti 100,000, Tagalog 74,000, Tamil, Turkish 60,000, Urdu, Vietnamese 22,000, Yoruba, people from Ghana, Nigeria, Guyana, West Indies. Information mainly from I. Hancock 1974, 1984, 1986; M. Stephens 1976; R. McCrum, W. Cran, R. MacNeil 1986; B. Comrie 1987. Christian, secular, Muslim, Jewish, Hindu. Blind population 116,414. Deaf population 909,000 to 3,524,725 (1998). Deaf institutions: 468 in England, 2 in Northern Ireland, 14 in Scotland, 34 in Wales. Data accuracy estimate: B. The number of languages listed for United Kingdom is 17. Of those, 12 are living languages, 2 are second languages without mother tongue speakers, and 3 are extinct. Diversity index 0.07.

ANGLOROMANI ***(ENGLISH ROMANI, ROMANI ENGLISH, ROMANICHAL, POGADI CHIB, POSH 'N' POSH)*** [RME] 90,000 in Britain (1990 I. Hancock). Population total all countries 170,000 to 270,000. England, Wales, Scotland. Also spoken in Australia, South Africa, USA. Indo-European, Germanic, West, English. Angloromani not inherently intelligible with Welsh Romani, Traveller Swedish, Traveller Norwegian, or Traveller Danish. The grammar is basically English with heavy Romani lexical borrowing. Many dialects. It has been spoken in the United Kingdom for 500 years. "The Romanichal population must be considered as being more actively determined to retain the ethnic language than some other British minorities" (I. Hancock).

BRITISH SIGN LANGUAGE ***(BSL)*** [BHO] 40,000 mother tongue users (1984 Deuchar), out of 909,000 deaf, of which the majority probably have some degree of sign language competence (1977 Deuchar). United Kingdom including Northern Ireland, Scotland. Deaf sign language. Not inherently intelligible to users of ASL. The deaf community is cohesive, so communication is good despite regional differences. However, there are many reports of different sign languages which are inherently unintelligible to users as close as approximately every 50 miles. Good regional and national organizations for the deaf. Signed interpretation is required in court, and provided in some other situations. Sign language instruction for parents of deaf children. Many sign language classes for hearing people. There is an organization for sign language teachers. There is a committee on national sign language. Sign language was used before 1644. Deaf schools were established in the late 18th century. There is increasing desire to train deaf children in BSL. British Signed English is different from American Signed English. Dictionary. Grammar. Films, TV, videos.

CORNISH ***(KERNOWEK, KERNEWEK, CURNOACK)*** [CRN] A number of people under 20 years of age are first language speakers. There are 1,000 speakers who use Cornish as their everyday language, and about 2,000 others who speak it fluently (1999). Duchy of Cornwall, southwest of England. Indo-European, Celtic, Insular, Brythonic. Bilingualism in English. Some children grow up bilingual. Church services are held in Cornish. There are evening classes, correspondence courses, summer camps, children's play groups. There is a Cornish Language Board. It became extinct as a first language in 1777, but is being revived. Two spelling systems are in use. Taught in some schools. Bible portions 1936.

ENGLISH [ENG] 55,000,000 first language speakers in United Kingdom (1984 estimate). Population total all countries 341,000,000 first language speakers (1999 WA), 508,000,000 including second language speakers (1999 WA). Also spoken in 104 other countries including American Samoa, Andorra, Anguilla, Antigua and Barbuda, Aruba, Australia, Bahamas, Barbados, Belize, Bermuda, Botswana, British Indian Ocean Territory, British Virgin Islands, Brunei, Cameroon, Canada, Cayman Islands, Cook Islands, Denmark. Indo-European, Germanic, West, English. Dialects: COCKNEY, SCOUSE, GEORDIE, WEST COUNTRY, EAST ANGLIA, BIRMINGHAM (BRUMMY, BRUMMIE), SOUTH WALES, EDINBURGH, BELFAST, CORNWALL, CUMBERLAND, CENTRAL CUMBERLAND, DEVONSHIRE, EAST DEVONSHIRE, DORSET, DURHAM, BOLTON LANCASHIRE, NORTH LANCASHIRE, RADCLIFFE LANCASHIRE, NORTHUMBERLAND, NORFOLK, NEWCASTLE NORTHUMBERLAND, TYNESIDE NORTHUMBERLAND, LOWLAND SCOTTISH, SOMERSET, SUSSEX, WESTMORLAND, NORTH WILTSHIRE, CRAVEN YORKSHIRE, NORTH YORKSHIRE, SHEFFIELD YORKSHIRE, WEST YORKSHIRE. 60% lexical similarity with German, 27% with French, 24% with Russian. National language. Dictionary. Grammar. SVO; prepositions; genitives after noun heads; articles, adjectives, numerals before noun heads; question word initial; word order distinguishes subject, object, indirect objects, given and new information, topic and comment; active and passive; causative; comparative; consonant and vowel clusters; nontonal. Deciduous forest. Island, plains, hills. Industrial, fishermen, craftsman. Christian. Bible 1382-1989.

FRENCH [FRN] 14,000 in England (1976 Stephens). Channel Islands. Indo-European, Italic, Romance, Italo-Western, Western, Gallo-Iberian, Gallo-Romance, Gallo-Rhaetian, Oïl, French. Dialects: JERRIAIS, DGERNESIAIS. French is only spoken by about 11% of the population of Channel Islands, mainly older people. Official language. Bible 1530-1986. See main entry under France.

GAELIC, IRISH ***(IRISH, ERSE)*** [GLI] Belfast and counties of Fermanagh and Armagh, Northern Ireland. Indo-European, Celtic, Insular, Goidelic. Grammar. Bible 1685-1989. See main entry under Ireland.

GAELIC, SCOTS ***(GÀIDHLIG, GAELIC)*** [GLS] 88,892 including 477 monolinguals, 88,415 bilinguals in Scotland (1971 census). Population total all countries 94,000. North and central counties of Ross, Islands of Hebrides and Skye. Also spoken in Australia, Canada, USA. Indo-European, Celtic, Insular, Goidelic. Dialect: EAST SUTHERLANDSHIRE. Church Gaelic is based on the Perthshire dialect of 200 years ago, and is at a distance from spoken dialects. East Sutherlandshire dialect is so different from other spoken dialects as to be a barrier to communication. In some communities it is primarily used in the home, in church, and for social purposes. Books and journals are produced on various topics. Resurgence of interest in Scots Gaelic in the 1990s has been given a boost by the establishing of Scotland's own Parliament, for the first time in 300 years. Investigation needed:

intelligibility with East Sutherlandshire. VSO. Literacy rate in first language: 50% (1971 census). In bilingual areas Gaelic is usually the first language of instruction for most primary subjects. Gaelic Medium Education schools have been set up. Newspapers, radio programs. Bible 1801-1991.

MANX ***(GAELG, GAILCK, MANX GAELIC)*** [MJD] On the Isle of Man: 77,000 residents (1998 UN). Isle of Man, part of the British Isles, a Crown Dependency, with its own Parliament, laws, currency, and taxation. The United Kingdom represents the Isle of Man at the United Nations. Indo-European, Celtic, Insular, Goidelic. It became extinct during this century as a first language. There are efforts to revive it. Second language for 200 to 300 who have mainly learned it as adults. Used for some public functions. It was supplanted by Manx Vernacular English, which in turn is now being supplanted by other varieties of English. Grammar. Extinct. Bible 1773.

NORN [NON] Shetland and Orkney Islands. Indo-European, Germanic, North, West Scandinavian. Became extinct after the islands were ceded to Scotland in the 15th century. Extinct.

OLD KENTISH SIGN LANGUAGE [OKL] Kent. Deaf sign language. The apparent ancestor of Martha's Vineyard Sign Language. Extinct.

POLARI ***(PARLARE)*** [PLD] Unclassified. An in-group language among theatrical and circus people. Second language only.

ROMANI, VLAX ***(ROMENES, ROM, TSIGANE)*** [RMY] Indo-European, Indo-Iranian, Indo-Aryan, Central zone, Romani, Vlax. Dialects: KALDERASH, LOVARI. Vlax and Kalderash are understood by the Lovari. Christian. NT 1984-1995. See main entry under Romania.

ROMANI, WELSH [RMW] England and Wales. Indo-European, Indo-Iranian, Indo-Aryan, Central zone, Romani, Northern. Not inherently intelligible with Angloromani. Ethnic groups: Volshanange, Kalá. Christian.

SCOTS [SCO] 100,000 (1999 Billy Kay) including 60,000 in Lallans, 30,000 in Doric, 10,000 in Ulster. Population total both countries 100,000 or more. All of Scotland except highlands: lowlands: Aberdeen to Ayrshire. Northern Ireland. Doric dialect in northeastern Scotland, Lallans in South Scotland lowlands, Ulster in Northern Ireland. Also spoken in Ireland. Indo-European, Germanic, West, English. Dialects: DORIC, LALLANS, ULSTER. Difficult intelligibility among dialects. Northern Scots on the Scottish Islands is considered by some to be a different language (Shetlandic or Orcadian). Doric and Ulster are inherently intelligible to speakers, but difficulties are common in speech and writing. Lallans is the main literary dialect. Ulster Scots has its own development group. Scots is closest to English and Frisian. English is considered to be the language of education and religion. Used with family and friends. All ages. 1,500,000 speak it as second language. Dictionary. SVO; prepositions; gentivies, articles, adjectives, numerals before noun heads; relatives without noun heads; question word initial; 2 prefixes, 1 suffix; word order distinguishes subjects, objects, indirect objects, given and new information, topic and comment; affixes indicate genitive case of noun phrase; passives; comparatives; CVC; nontonal. Literacy rate in second language: 97% English. Poetry, magazines. Christian. NT 1901-1984.

TRAVELLER SCOTTISH ***(SCOTTISH CANT, SCOTTISH TRAVELLER CANT)*** [TRL] 4,000 in Scotland. Population total all countries 4,000 or more. Also spoken in Australia, USA. Unclassified. A blend language of High Romani and Elizabethan Cant. The earliest texts go back to the sixteenth century. Not Gypsies. Nomadic in Scotland. In USA they travel but have a fixed base.

WELSH ***(CYMRAEG)*** [WLS] 508,098 speakers (1991 census). Out of 575,102 speakers in 1971, it included 32,700 monolinguals, 542,402 bilinguals (1971 census). Population total all countries 580,000. Northern, western, and southern Wales. Also spoken in Argentina, Canada. Indo- European, Celtic, Insular, Brythonic. Dialects: NORTHERN WELSH, SOUTHERN WELSH, PATAGONIAN WELSH. 44,600 between 5 and 9 years old and speak Welsh, 47,100 between 10 and 14 years old (1991). 19% of the Welsh population speak the language, and 33% able to understand it (1998). Literature being produced. The Royal National Eisteddfod meets annually. 88% of those questioned believe they should be proud of Welsh, and that it should be treated equally with English. There is an increase in the number of parents choosing a Welsh-medium education for their children. Official language. Dictionary. Grammar. VSO. 525 Welsh primary and secondary schools provide Welsh-medium education to over 82,000 children (1999). Compulsory in most Welsh schools. Magazines, radio programs, TV. Bible 1588-1988.

YINGLISH [YIB] Indo-European, Germanic, West, English. Bilingualism in English. Professor Joshua A. Fishman says, "'Yinglish' is a variety of English influenced by Yiddish (lexically, particularly, but also grammatically and phonetically). Any good English dictionary will now include 50-100 (or more) 'borrowings from Yiddish' (=Yinglish)....Since the variety is only used...(by speakers who can always speak 'proper English') Yinglish is never a mother tongue acquired by the usual process of intergenerational transmission. French, Spanish, and Russian counterparts (also a Hebrew counterpart) also exist(s), but are more restricted in nature, both in size as well as in availability to non-Jews." Jewish. Second language only. See main entry under USA.

VATICAN STATE

The Holy See. National or official language: Latin. 480 (1998 UN). Information mainly from B. Comrie 1987. The number of languages listed for Vatican State is 3. Of those, 1 is a living language, 1 is a second language without mother tongue speakers, and 1 is extinct. Diversity index 0.00.

ITALIAN [ITN] Indo-European, Italic, Romance, Italo-Western, Italo-Dalmatian. Bible 1471-1985. See main entry under Italy.

LATIN *(LATINA)* [LTN] Indo-European, Italic, Latino-Faliscan. Used in Roman Catholic liturgy. There is an effort to revive it. The Vatican Latin Foundation was established in 1976. National language. Dictionary. Radio programs. Extinct. Bible 1385-1906.

MONASTIC SIGN LANGUAGE [MZG] Monastic communities, especially in Europe. Sign language. A second language means of communicating while maintaining vows of silence. Not a deaf sign language. Second language only.

YUGOSLAVIA

Federal Republic of Yugoslavia, Federativna Republika Jugoslavija. National or official languages: Serbian, Hungarian (regional). 10,635,000 (1998 UN). Now includes Serbia and Montenegro republics. Literacy rate 90% to 93%. Also includes Slovenian, Turkish, Ukrainian 22,896. Information mainly from M. Stephens 1976; B. Comrie 1987. Christian, secular, Muslim. Blind population 23,000 in the former larger Yugoslavia (1982 WCE). Deaf population 60,000 (1986 Gallaudet University). Deaf institutions: 56. Data accuracy estimate: B. The number of languages listed for Yugoslavia is 11. Of those, all are living languages. Diversity index 0.32.

ALBANIAN, GHEG *(GEG)* [ALS] 1,372,750 to 1,800,000 in Yugoslavia (1992). Ethnic Albanians are 90% of Kosovo's 2,000,000 people (1998 Los Angeles Times). Population total all countries 2,000,000 (1980 UBS). Kossovo-Metohija (Kosmet). Also spoken in Albania, Bulgaria, Macedonia, Romania, Slovenia, USA. Indo-European, Albanian, Gheg. Books are published in Gheg in Yugoslavia. Restrictions on Albanian at Kossovo's university since 1990. Not endangered. Speakers are called 'Kossovar' in Yugoslavia. Official language. Newspapers. Shiptars: Muslim. NT 1869-1990.

BULGARIAN [BLG] Dmitrovgrad and Bosiljgrad districts. Indo-European, Slavic, South, Eastern. Catholic Bulgarians are in Yugoslav and Romanian Banat. Bible 1864-1923. See main entry under Bulgaria.

HUNGARIAN *(MAGYAR)* [HNG] 450,500 in Yugoslavia (1986). Vojvodine. Uralic, Finno-Ugric, Ugric, Hungarian. Closest to Vogul (Mansi) of Russia. Official language. Bible 1590-1991. See main entry under Hungary.

ROMANI, BALKAN [RMN] 120,000 in Yugoslavia and Macedonia including 100,000 Arlija, 20,000 Dzambazi. Population total all countries 1,000,000 (1980 UBS). Balkans, Kossovo. Also spoken in Bulgaria, France, Germany, Greece, Hungary, Iran, Italy, Macedonia, Moldova, Romania, Turkey (Europe), Ukraine, USA. Indo-European, Indo-Iranian, Indo-Aryan, Central zone, Romani, Balkan. Dialects: ARLIJA, DZAMBAZI, TINNERS ROMANI. The Arlija dialect (252,000 to 367,000 total) is understood by Greek Romani and Dzambazi speakers. Ethnic group: Jerlídes (Macedonia, southern Serbia). Muslim. Bible portions 1912-1937.

ROMANI, SINTE *(ROMMANES, SINTE, SINTI)* [RMO] 31,000 in Yugoslavia including 30,000 Serbian, 1,000 Manouche. Population total all countries 200,000 (1980 UBS). Kossovo. Also spoken in Austria, Croatia, Czech Republic, France, Germany, Hungary, Italy, Kazakhstan, Netherlands, Poland, Slovenia, Switzerland. Indo-European, Indo-Iranian, Indo-Aryan, Central zone, Romani, Northern. Dialects: ABBRUZZESI, SLOVENIAN-CROATIAN ROMANI, SERBIAN ROMANI. Croatian, Slovenian, and Serbian Romani speakers understand each other. Those varieties may be quite distinct from the German varieties. Sinte is characterized by German influence. 'Rommanes' is the self-name. Ethnic group: Sasítka Romá. Investigation needed: intelligibility with German Sinte varieties. Christian. Bible portions 1875-1995.

ROMANIAN *(RUMANIAN, MOLDAVIAN, DACO-RUMANIAN)* [RUM] 200,000 to 300,000 in Yugoslavia (1995 Iosif Bena). Vojvodina and the Timoc Valley. Indo-European, Italic, Romance, Eastern. Radio programs, TV. Bible 1688-1989. See main entry under Romania.

ROMANIAN, MACEDO [RUP] Up to 15,000 (Society of Aromanians). Belgrade, Vojvodina and Kosovo. Indo-European, Italic, Romance, Eastern. See main entry under Greece.

ROMANO-SERBIAN ***(TENT GYPSY)*** [RSB] Serbia. Indo-European, Slavic, South, Western. Related linguistically to Serbian with influences from Romani.

SERBO-CROATIAN ***(SERBIAN, MONTENEGRIN)*** [SRC] 10,200,000 in Yugoslavia and Macedonia (1981 WA). Population total all countries 21,000,000 (1999 WA). Serbia, Kossovo, and Montenegro. Also spoken in 23 other countries including Albania, Australia, Austria, Bosnia-Herzegovina, Bulgaria, Canada, Croatia, Germany, Greece, Hungary, Italy, Macedonia, Romania, Russia (Europe), Slovakia, Slovenia, Sweden, Switzerland, Turkey (Europe). Indo-European, Slavic, South, Western. Dialects: CHAKAVIAN, KAJKAVIAN, STOKAVIAN, TORLAKIAN. Speakers are Serbs, Croatians, Bosnians, Montenegrins. National language. Grammar. SVO; postpositions; genitives, articles, adjectives, numerals, relatives after noun heads; question word initial; 1 suffix; case determines subject, object; obligatory verb affixes mark person, number, gender of subject, object, other noun phrase; passive for each tense, today not commonly used; causatives marked by separate words; comparatives marked by prefix; CCVCVC, nontonal. Roman script used by Croats, both Cyrillic and Roman by Serbs and Montenegrins. Orthodox (most Serbs). Bible 1804-1968.

SLOVAK [SLO] 80,000 in Yugoslavia (1996 W. Brown). Vojvodine. Indo-European, Slavic, West, Czech-Slovak. Western and central dialects of Slovak are inherently intelligible to Czech speakers. Official language. Bible 1832-1926. See main entry under Slovakia.

YUGOSLAVIAN SIGN LANGUAGE [YSL] 30,000 users out of 60,000 deaf persons in the former larger Yugoslavia (1986 Gallaudet Univ.). Population total both countries 30,000 or more (1986 Gallaudet University). Also spoken in Slovenia. Deaf sign language. Dialect: SERBIAN SIGN LANGUAGE. Origin from deaf schools in Austria and Hungary. There are regional variants, but no problem in comprehension. Since 1979 there have been efforts to standardize. Slovenian Sign Language used in Slovenia is a dialect. First deaf school in 1840, but sign language is not used in schools. Interpreters are furnished in court. TV.

The Pacific

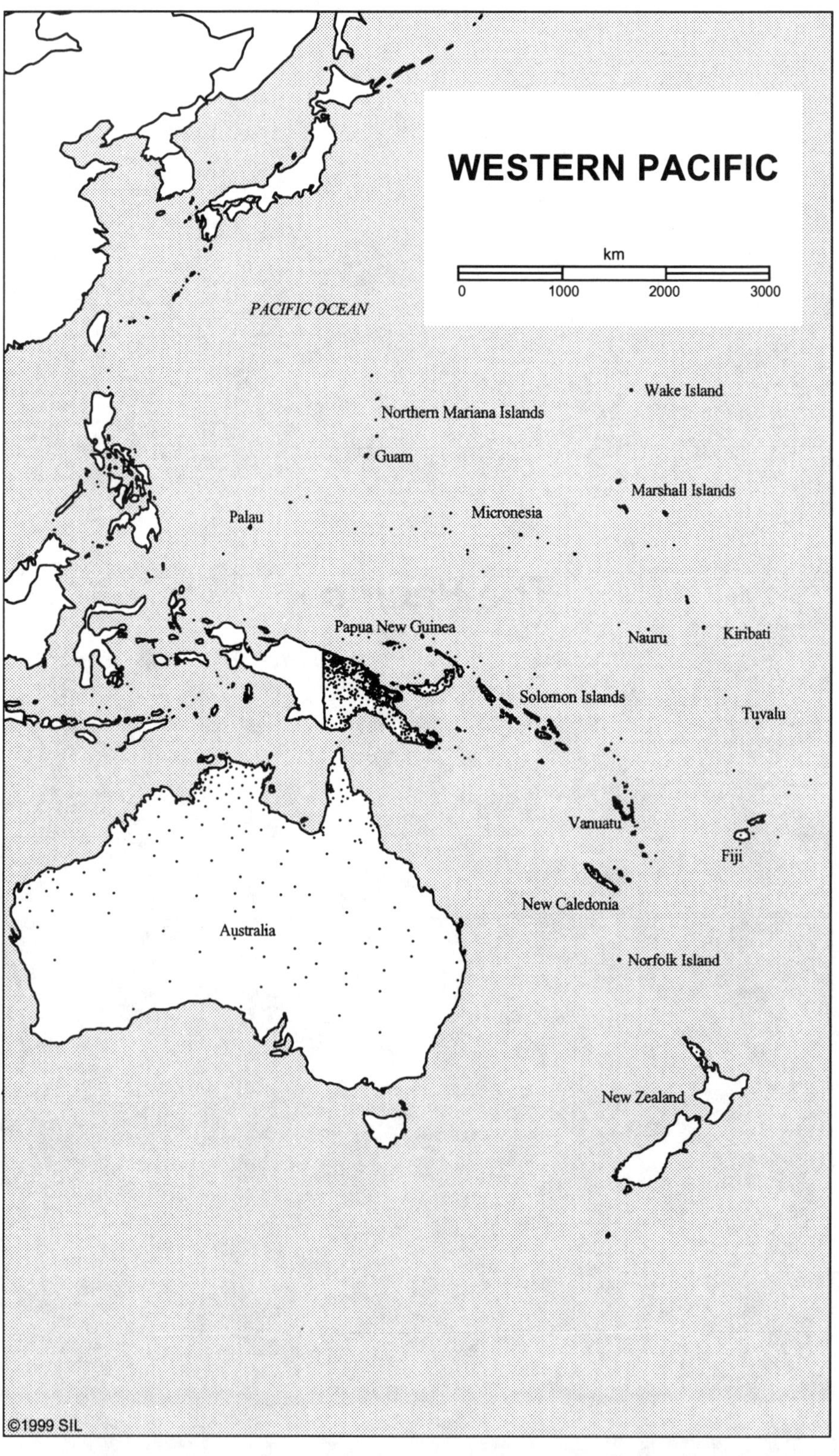
WESTERN PACIFIC
km
0
1000
2000
3000
PACIFIC OCEAN
Wake Island
Northern Mariana Islands
Guam
Marshall Islands
Palau
Micronesia
Papua New Guinea
Nauru
Kiribati
Solomon Islands
Tuvalu
Vanuatu
Fiji
New Caledonia
Australia
Norfolk Island
New Zealand
©1999 SIL

EASTERN PACIFIC

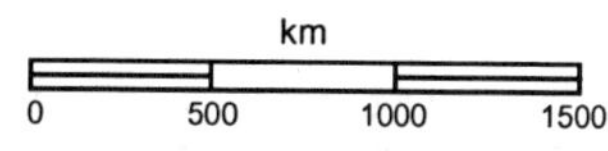

Midway Islands

Hawaiian Islands (USA)

PACIFIC OCEAN

Kiribati

Tokelau

Western Samoa

American Samoa

Wallis and Futuna

Cook Islands

French Polynesia

Niue

Tonga

Pitcairn

Easter Island (Chile)

AMERICAN SAMOA

National or official language: English. 63,000 (1998 UN). A USA territory. 6 islands: Tutuila, Aunuu, Manua Islands (Tau, Iosega, Ofu), Rose, Swain's. Also includes Tokelau 100 (1970), Tongan 800, Korean and Japanese 1,500. Literacy rate 98%. Also includes Japanese 1,500, Korean, Tokelauan 100, Tongan 800. Information mainly from S. Wurm and S. Hattori 1981; N. Besnier OIEL 1992. Christian. The number of languages listed for American Samoa is 2. Of those, both are living languages. Diversity index 0.12.

ENGLISH [ENG] 1,248 first language speakers in American Samoa, foreign born (1970 census), 15,050 mainly second language speakers, representing 75% of the native born population. Indo-European, Germanic, West, English. Official language. Bible 1535-1989. See main entry under United Kingdom.

SAMOAN [SMY] 56,700 in American Samoa (1999), 90% of the population. Austronesian, Malayo-Polynesian, Central-Eastern, Eastern Malayo-Polynesian, Oceanic, Central-Eastern Oceanic, Remote Oceanic, Central Pacific, East Fijian-Polynesian, Polynesian, Nuclear, Samoic-Outlier, Samoan. There are only minor regional dialect differences, but great phonological and lexical differences between formal and colloquial speech. Speakers in American Samoa are highly bilingual in English. Fishermen, canning. Christian. Bible 1855-1970. See main entry under Western Samoa.

AUSTRALIA

Commonwealth of Australia. National or official language: English. 18,520,000 (1998 UN). 170,000 or about 1% of the population is of Aboriginal descent, of whom 47,000 have some knowledge of an Aboriginal language. Includes Cocos Islands (569 in 1981), Christmas Island (3,000 in 1983), and Norfolk Island (1,800 in 1985). Literacy rate 99%. Also includes Adyghe, Afrikaans 12,655, Assyrian Neo-Aramaic 30,000, Basque, Chaldean Neo-Aramaic, Western Cham, Yue Chinese, Dutch 47,955, Estonian, Western Farsi 11,000, Scots Gaelic, Standard German 135,000, Greek 106,677, Hebrew, Fijian Hindustani, Hungarian 5,764, Indo-Portuguese, Italian 500,000, Japanese 12,000, Korean 37,000, Kurmanji 11,000, Latvian 25,000, Lithuanian 10,000, Maltese, Mambae, Nung, Piemontese, Polish 13,782, Pukapuka 140, Romanian, Senaya, Serbo-Croatian 38,753, Slovenian, Spanish, Tai Dam, Traveller Scottish, Turkish 40,000, Turoyo 2,000, Unserdeutsch, Uyghur, Northern Uzbek, Vietnamese 35,000, Eastern Yiddish, Malay and Indonesian 35,000, Arabic 250,000, Chinese 190,000, many other languages of Europe. Information mainly from W. J. and L. F. Oates 1970; S. Wurm and S. Hattori 1981; P. Black 1983; J. Hudson 1987; B. Waters 1989; A. Schmidt 1990. Christian, secular, Muslim. Blind population 28,000. Deaf population 9,000 to 1,096,008 (1998). Deaf institutions: 116. Data accuracy estimate: A2, B. The number of languages listed for Australia is 268. Of those, 235 are living languages, 2 are second languages without mother tongue speakers, and 31 are extinct. Diversity index 0.13.

ADYNYAMATHANHA ***(WAILPI, WAILBI, WALJBI, WIPIE, AD'N'AMADANA, ANJIMATANA, ANJIWATANA, ARCHUALDA, BENBAKANJAMATA, BINBARNJA, GADJNJAMADA, JANDALI, KANJIMATA, KEYDNJMARDA, MARDALA, NIMALDA, NURALDA, UNYAMOOTHA, UMBERTANA)*** [ADT] 20 or more (1990 Schmidt). Flinders Ranges area, South Australia. Australian, Pama-Nyungan, South-West, Yura. Related to Guyani, Banggarla, Nugunu, and Narungga, which may be extinct. Bilingualism in English.

AGHU THARNGGALU [GGR] Queensland, Cape York Peninsula, Laura. Australian, Pama-Nyungan, Paman, Rarmul Pama. Recently extinct. Extinct.

AGWAMIN [AWG] Queensland, south central Cape York Peninsula, Einasleigh River. Australian, Pama-Nyungan, Paman, Southern Pama. Ruhlen (1987) says this is extinct. Extinct.

ALAWA ***(KALLANA, LEEALOWA)*** [ALH] 17 to 20 fluent and 4 partial first language speakers (1991 M. Sharpe). Roper River, Arnhem Land, Northern Territory. Australian, Maran, Alawic. All speakers are bilingual in Kriol. Young people speak Kriol and understand only a little Alawa. Nearly extinct.

ALNGITH [AID] 3(?) (1981 Wurm and Hattori). Queensland, northeast Cape York Peninsula just north of Weipa. Australian, Pama-Nyungan, Paman, Northern Pama. Nearly extinct.

ALYAWARR ***(ALYAWARRA, ALYAWARRE, ALJAWARA, ILIAURA, YOWERA)*** [ALY] 1,500 or more (1991 Hoogenrad). Sandover and Tennant Creek areas, Northern Territory and Queensland. Australian, Pama-Nyungan, Arandic, Urtwa. Related to Arrernte, Arrernte Akerre, Anmatyerre, and Kaytetye. Speakers are somewhat bilingual in English. Dictionary. Grammar. Literacy rate in second language: 40%. Roman. Bible portions 1996.

AMARAG ***(WUREIDBUG, AMURAG)*** [AMG] A few speakers. Goulburn Island, Oenpelli, Northern Territory. Australian, Yiwaidjan, Amaragic. A few elderly people use it as second language. May be extinct (Black 1983). Nearly extinct.

AMI ***(AME, AMIJANGAL)*** [AMY] 30 to 35 fluent speakers (1983 Black). Northern Territory, Coast along Anson Bay, southwest of Darwin. Australian, Daly, Bringen-Wagaydy, Wagaydy. May be intelligible with Wadjiginy. Bilingualism in Kriol. Investigation needed: intelligibility with Wadjiginy.

ANDEGEREBINHA [ADG] 10(?) (1981 Wurm and Hattori). Northern Territory, Hay River, Pituri Creek area, east of Alyawarra. Australian, Pama-Nyungan, Arandic, Urtwa. Nearly extinct.

ANGLOROMANI ***(ROMANICHAL, ENGLISH ROMANI, POGADI CHIB)*** [RME] 5,000 in Australia. Indo-European, Germanic, West, English. A variety of English with heavy Romani lexical borrowing. See main entry under United Kingdom.

ANINDILYAKWA ***(ANDILJANGWA, ANDILYAUGWA, ENINDILJAUGWA, INGURA, WAN-INDILYAUGWA, GROOTE EYLANDT, ENINDHILYAGWA)*** [AOI] 1,000 or more (1983 Black). Groote Eylandt, Northern Territory, Gulf of Carpenteria. Australian, Enindhilyagwa. Most young people are bilingual in English. SOV. Scrub forest. Coastal, island. Hunter-gatherers traditionally. 0 to 200 meters. Bible portions 1976-1993.

ANMATYERRE ***(ANMATJIRRA)*** [AMX] 800 (1983 Black). Northern Territory, Mt. Allen, Northwest Alice Springs Region. Australian, Pama-Nyungan, Arandic, Urtwa. Dialects: EASTERN ANMATYERRE, WESTERN ANMATYERRE (KALENTHELKWE, KELENTHWELKERE, KELENTHEYEWELRERE). Investigation needed: intelligibility, bilingual proficiency. Dictionary.

ANTAKARINYA ***(ANDAGARINYA)*** [ANT] 50 possibly (1981 Wurm and Hattori), or few (1983 Black). Northeast area of South Australia. Australian, Pama-Nyungan, South-West, Wati. Closest to Warnman and Western Desert Language. People generally speak Kriol.

ARABANA [ARD] 8 possibly (1981 Wurm and Hattori). Birdsville, west side of Lake Eyre to Stuart Range, South Australia. Australian, Pama-Nyungan, Karnic, Arabana-Wangganguru. Nearly extinct.

AREBA [AEA] 2(?) (1981 Wurm and Hattori). Queensland, southwestern Cape York Peninsula, Bilbert River, northeast of Normanton. Australian, Pama-Nyungan, Paman, Norman Pama. Nearly extinct.

ARRARNTA, WESTERN ***(ARANDA, ARUNTA)*** [ARE] 1,000 (1981 Wurm and Hattori). Northern Territory, Alice Springs area, Hermannsburg. Australian, Pama-Nyungan, Arandic, Urtwa. Dialects: WESTERN ARANDA, AKERRE (AKARA), SOUTHERN ARANDA. Closely related to Alyawarra and Gaididj. Wurm and Hattori (1981) and Ruhlen (1987) treat Western Arrartna and Eastern Arrernte as separate languages. Southern Aranda is nearly extinct. Investigation needed: intelligibility with Andegerebinha, Anmatjirra. SOV. Savannah. Plains. Hunter-gatherers. NT 1956.

ARRERNTE, EASTERN ***(EASTERN ARANDA, ARUNTA)*** [AER] 1,500 to 2,000 (1995 Neil Broad). Northern Territory, Alice Springs area, Santa Teresa, Hats Range. Australian, Pama-Nyungan, Arandic, Urtwa. Related to Mparntwe Arrernte, Alyawarr, Arrernte Akarre, Anmatyerre, Kaytetye, Western Arrarnta. English bilingual program in operation at a school at Santa Teresa. Dictionary. Grammar. SOV. Literacy rate in first language: 10%. Literacy rate in second language: 50%. Savannah. Plains. Hunter-gatherers.

ATAMPAYA [AMZ] 4(?) (1981 Wurm and Hattori). Queensland, extreme northern Cape York Peninsula, Eliot Creek. Australian, Pama-Nyungan, Paman, Northern Pama. Nearly extinct.

AUSTRALIAN ABORIGINES SIGN LANGUAGE [ASW] Southern, central, and western desert regions, coastal Arnhem Land, some islands of north coast, western side of Cape York Peninsula, islands of Torres Strait. Deaf sign language. Not related to Australian Sign Language. Several different sign languages are also used by deaf persons. Also used by hearing Aborigines as an alternate form of communication with speakers of other languages. Other non-deaf sign languages are used by some groups, such as Aranda, Warlpiri, Warumungu, during periods of mourning or hunting.

AUSTRALIAN SIGN LANGUAGE ***(AUSLAN)*** [ASF] 14,000 users possibly (1991 Hyde and Power). Deaf sign language. Related to British Sign Language, with influences also from Irish and American sign languages. Australian Signed English is different. It is a manual system for English spelling, used by hearing people for communication with the deaf. It is used in teaching the deaf, and officially so in New South Wales. The earliest schools for the deaf were established by British deaf immigrants in 1860. Many agencies for the deaf. Some signed interpretation in court, for college students, at important public events. There is sign language instruction for parents of deaf children. There is a committee on national sign language. Dictionary. Grammar. Films, TV, videos.

AWABAKAL ***(AWABAGAL)*** [AWK] Lake Macquarie, south from Newcastle, New South Wales. Australian, Pama-Nyungan, Yuin-Kuric, Kuri. Recently extinct. Extinct. Bible portions 1891.

AYABADHU [AYD] 6(?) (1981 Wurm and Hattori). Queensland, Cape York Peninsula, north of the Coleman River, south of Coen. Australian, Pama-Nyungan, Paman, Middle Pama. Nearly extinct.

BAADI ***(BARD, BARDI, BADI)*** [BCJ] 20 (1999 Claire Bowern) including 16 Bardi, 3 Jawi. One Arm Point Aboriginal Community, Lombadina Aboriginal Community, Broome, Derby, Western Kimberley Region,

Western Australia. Australian, Nyulnyulan. Dialects: BARDI, JAWI. Intelligibility is adequate between Bardi and Jawi dialects. Related to Nyigina, Warwa, Djawi, Nimanbur, Nyulnyul, Dyaberdyaber, Dyugun, Yawuru, which may be extinct. No monolinguals. English and Kriol are the second languages. English is generally spoken in the community, Kriol with Aboriginals from farther east. Children and adolescents can understand Bardi, but never seem to speak it. They appear to use English as their language. Speakers are over 40 years old. Dictionary. Literacy rate in second language: 60% in English. There is a feeling that English or Bardi are the languages that should be written, not Kriol. Christian. Nearly extinct.

BADIMAYA ***(WIDIMAYA)*** [BIA] Western Australia. Australian, Pama-Nyungan, South-West, Wadjari. Related to Wajarri. Not extinct, but endangered. Linguists at Yamaji Language Centre working on a draft dictionary and wordlist. Nearly extinct.

BANDJALANG ***(BANDJELANG, BOGGANGER, BUNDALA, GIDABAL, YUGUMBE)*** [BDY] 10 speakers (1983 R. M. W. Dixon). New South Wales, northeastern, Woodenbong. Australian, Pama-Nyungan, Bandjalangic. Dialects: GIDABAL (GIDHABAL), YUGUMBIR. All speakers are bilingual in English. Dictionary. Bible portions.

BANDJIGALI [BJD] 1(?) (1981 Wurm and Hattori). New South Wales, northwest, north and west of White Cliffs. Australian, Pama-Nyungan, Baagandji. Nearly extinct.

BANGGARLA ***(BANGALA, BANGGALA, BAHANGA-LA, BUNGEHA, BUNGELA, PANGKALA, PAKARLA, PANKALLA, PARNKALA, PARNKALLA, PUNKALLA, KORTABINA)*** [BJB] South Australia, Port Lincoln to the head of Spencer Gulf. Australian, Pama-Nyungan, South-West, Yura. Ruhlen (1987) says it is extinct. Extinct.

BARROW POINT [BPT] 1(?) (1981 Wurm and Hattori). Queensland, Cape York Peninsula, Barrow Point on Princess Charlotte Bay and inland. Australian, Pama-Nyungan, Barrow Point. Nearly extinct.

BAYALI ***(BIYALI, DARAMBAL, ORAMBUL, CHARUMBUL, DARAWAL, DARUMBAL, KOOIN-MARBURRA, KUINMURBARA, NINGEBAL, TARUMBAL, THARUMBAL, URAMBAL, WARABAL, YETIMARALA)*** [BJY] Queensland, from the mouth of the Fitzroy River inland to Boomer Range at Marlborough, Yeppon, Yamba, and Rockhampton. Australian, Pama-Nyungan, Waka-Kabic, Kingkel. Extinct.

BAYUNGU ***(BAIONG, BAIUNG, BIONG, BAJUNGU, PAJUNGU, PAYUNGU, GIONG, MULGARNOO)*** [BXJ] 6 (1981 Wurm and Hattori). Western Australia, lower Lyndon and Minilya rivers, West Pilbara. Australian, Pama-Nyungan, South-West, Kanyara. Dictionary. Nearly extinct.

BIDYARA ***(BITJARA, BITHARA)*** [BYM] 20(?) (1981 Wurm and Hattori). Queensland, between Tambo and Augathella, Warrego River and Langlo River. Australian, Pama-Nyungan, Maric, Mari. Bilingualism in English. Ruhlen (1987) says it is extinct. Nearly extinct.

BIRI [BZR] 5(?) (1981 Wurm and Hattori). Queensland southeast of Charters Towers. Australian, Pama-Nyungan, Maric, Mari. Ruhlen (1987) says it is extinct. Nearly extinct.

BROOME PEARLING LUGGER PIDGIN ***(BROOM CREOLE, KOEPANG TALK, MALAY TALK, JAPANESE PIDGIN ENGLISH)*** [BPL] (40 to 50 speakers, mainly Aborigines). Broome, Lombardinie, Beagle Bay, La Grange, One Arm Point, Derby. Pidgin, Malay based. Used as a lingua franca on pearling boats to communicate between Malays, Japanese, Chinese, and Aborigines. Some Japanese and Aboriginal creole or pidgin English words. Second language only.

BUNABA ***(PUNAPA, BUNUBA)*** [BCK] 50 to 100 (1990 Schmidt). Fitzroy Crossing area, Western Australia. Australian, Bunaban. Bilingualism in Kriol. Only old people speak Bunaba. Children only know a few words; their first language is Kriol (Hudson 1987:16).

BURARRA ***(BURADA, BUREDA, BURERA, GUJINGALIA, GUJALABIYA, GUN-GURAGONE, BARERA, BAWERA, JIKAI, TCHIKAI)*** [BVR] 400 to 600 (1990 Schmidt). Maningrida, Arnhem Land, Northern Territory. Australian, Burarran. Gunardba is a related language which may be extinct. SOV. Scrub forest. Coastal. Hunter-gatherers. NT 1991.

BURDUNA ***(BUDUNA, BOORDOONA, BUDINA, BUDOONA, PURDUNA, PINNEEGOOROO, POODENA, POORDOONA, PURDUMA)*** [BXN] 3 (1981 Wurm and Hattori). Henry and upper Lyndon rivers. Australian, Pama-Nyungan, South-West, Kanyara. Nearly extinct.

DARLING ***(KULA, BAAGANDJI, SOUTHERN BAAGANDJI)*** [DRL] 5 or more fluent speakers, but Bagundji dialect is widely understood by others (1970 Oates). Darling River Basin, New South Wales. Australian, Pama-Nyungan, Baagandji. Dialects: KULA, WILJAKALI (WILYAGALI), BAGUNDJI (BAAGANDJI, BAGANDJI). Nearly extinct.

DAYI ***(DHAY'YI, DHA'I)*** [DAX] 200 (1983 Black). Arnhem Land, Roper River, Yirrkala, Lake Evella, Galiwinku, Numbulwam, Northern Territory. Australian, Pama-Nyungan, Yuulngu. Dialects: DHALWANGU, DJARRWARK. Bilingualism in Djambarrpuyngu, Gumatj, All or nearly all: Dhuwal, English. The clans are active, but the position of the language is weak because of scattering and children speaking other languages, such as Djambarrpuyngu. Nearly extinct.

DHALANDJI ***(TALANDJI, DALANDJI, DALENDI, DJALENDI, TALLAINGA, TALANDI, TALAINDJI, TALANGEE, TALOINGA, THALANYJI)*** [DHL] 20 (1981 Wurm and Hattori). Western Australia, head of Exmouth Gulf, inland to Ashburton River, West Pilbara. Australian, Pama-Nyungan, South-West, Kanyara. Speakers are reported to be highly bilingual in English. Dictionary.

DHANGU ***(DANGU, DHANGU'MI, DJANGU)*** [GLA] 350 including 200 in Gaalpu, 150 in Wangurri (1983 Black). Elcho Island, Arnhem Land, Northern Territory. Australian, Pama-Nyungan, Yuulngu. Dialects: DHANGU-DJANGU, GAALPU (KALBU), WANGURRI, NGAYMIL, RIRRATJINGU, GOLUMALA. Speakers are bilingual in Djambarrpuyngu. Yolngu-Matha means 'people language'. SVO, SOV if O is a pronoun or deictic. Scrub forest. Coastal, insular. Hunter-gatherers, fishermen. Bible portions 1977.

DHARGARI ***(TARGARI, DAL'GARI, TARKARRI, THARGARI, THARRGARI)*** [DHR] 6 (1981 Wurm and Hattori). Western Australia, Kennedy Range, upper Minilya and lower Lyons rivers, West Pilbara. Australian, Pama-Nyungan, South-West, Kanyara. Ruhlen classifies it in a separate Mantharda group. Dictionary. Nearly extinct.

DHURGA ***(DHU'RGA, DURGA, THOORGA)*** [DHU] New South Wales, Bermagui to Jervis Bay. Australian, Pama-Nyungan, Yuin-Kuric, Yuin. Ruhlen (1987) says it is extinct. Extinct.

DHUWAL ***(DUALA, DUAL, WULAMBA)*** [DUJ] 500 fluent first language speakers (1983 Black), including 200 Djapu, 160 Liyagalawumirr (clan names). Roper River, Arnhem Land, Northern Territory. Australian, Pama-Nyungan, Yuulngu, Dhuwal. Dialects: DHUWAYA, DHUWAL, LIYAGAWUMIRR, MARRANGU, MARRAKULU, DJAPU, LIYAGALAWUMIRR, DATIWUY. Bilingualism in Djambarrpuyngu.

DIERI ***(DIYARI)*** [DIF] South Australia, Leigh Creek. Australian, Pama-Nyungan, Karnic, Karna. Related to Garuwali, Marrula, Midhaga, Yarluyandi, all of which may be extinct. Extinct. NT 1897.

DIRARI [DIT] 1 (1981 Wurm and Hattori). South Australia, east of Lake Eyre North. Australian, Pama-Nyungan, Karnic, Karna. Nearly extinct.

DJAMBARRPUYNGU ***(DJAMBARBWINGU, JAMBAPUING, JAMBAPUINGO)*** [DJR] 450 fully fluent first language speakers (1983 Black). Lingua franca for 2,000 (1990 UBS). Elcho Island, Northern Territory. Australian, Pama-Nyungan, Yuulngu, Dhuwal. Bible portions 1977-1993.

DJAMINDJUNG ***(JAMINJUNG)*** [DJD] 30 (1990 Schmidt). Victoria River, Northern Territory. Australian, Djamindjungan. Dialect: NGALIWURU (NGALIWERRA). Reports indicate that Djamindjung and Ngaliwuru are so close as to be one language; only some elderly people can distinguish the difference. No monolinguals. Ngarinman or Kriol are the second languages.

DJANGUN ***(DJANGGUN, ADHO-ADHOM, BUTJU, CHUNGKI, CHUNKUMBERRIES, CHUNKUNBURRA, KOKO-MUDJU, MUTYU, NGAIGUNGO, KOKO-TYANKUN)*** [DJF] 1(?) (1981 Wurm and Hattori). Queensland, from Mt. Mulligan south to Alma-den, east to Dimbula, west to Mungana. Australian, Pama-Nyungan, Yalandyic. Nearly extinct.

DJAUAN ***(JAWAN, ADOWEN, KUMERTUO, JAWONY)*** [DJN] 100 possibly (1983 Black). Bamyili settlement, Northern Territory, and Katherine. Australian, Gunwingguan, Djauanic. Speakers are bilingual in limited English, some in Ngalkbon, probably all in Kriol. They live in the center of the Kriol speaking area. All education is in Kriol and English. Djauan is used only rarely by people over 50.

DJAWI [DJW] 1(?) (1981 Wurm and Hattori). Western Australia, islands from King Sound to Brunswick Bay. Australian, Nyulnyulan. Nearly extinct.

DJEEBBANA ***(NDJÉBBANA, GUNAVIDJI)*** [DJJ] 100 fluent speakers and 100 partial second language speakers (1991). West Arnhem Land, north coast around Maningrida. Australian, Burarran. Not closely related to other languages. Most speakers also speak Gunwinjku and another Burarran language. Gunavidji is the name of the people, Ndjéebana of the language. Different from Gunawitji, an alternate name for Gunwinggu. Investigation needed: attitudes.

DJINANG ***(JANDIJINUNG)*** [DJI] 250 or more (1982 B. Waters SIL). Ramingining, Goyder, and Blyth rivers, Arnhem Land, Northern Territory. Australian, Pama-Nyungan, Yuulngu. Dialects: DJADIWITJIBI, MILDJINGI, WULAKI, BALURBI, MURRUNGUN, MANYARRING. There are varying degrees of bilingualism in Ganalbingu (Djinba dialect), Gupapuyngu, Djambarrpuyngu, Chuwal, or Dhuwala. There is limited use of English. Wulaki people are bilingual in Burarra. Speakers intermarry with the Djinba. Scrub forest. Coastal, river plains. Hunter-gatherers (formerly). Bible portions 1985-1987.

DJINBA [DJB] 60 to 90 speakers (1989 Waters), including 70 Ganalbingu (1983 Black). Dabi is nearly extinct (1991 SIL). Ngangalala, Arnhem Land, Northern Territory, southeast adjoining Djinang area. Australian, Pama-Nyungan, Yuulngu. Dialects: GANALBINGU, DABI, MANDJALPINGU. Not intelligible with Djinang. 60% lexical similarity with Djinang. Some use Djinang as second language, some Djambarrpuyngu. Some Ritarungo use this as second language. Speakers intermarry with the Djinang. Scrub forest. River plains.

DJINGILI ***(JINGALI, TJINGILU, CHINGALEE, DJINGILA, LEE, CHUNGULOO, TCHINGALEE, JINGULU)*** [JIG] 10 fluent first language speakers (1997). Newcastle Waters, Ash Burton Range area, Elliott, Northern Territory, Elsey Station. Australian, West Barkly, Jingalic. Bilingualism in Kriol. Nearly extinct.

DJIWARLI ***(DJWARLI)*** [DJL] 1 (1981 Wurm and Hattori). Western Australia, northwest, north of Mount Augustus. Australian, Pama-Nyungan, South-West, Coastal Ngayarda. Ruhlen (1987) classifies it in a separate Mantharda group. Nearly extinct.

DYAABUGAY ***(DYABUGAY, TJAPUKAI, BULUM-BULUM, CHECK-CULL, CHEWLIE, DJABUGAI, HILEMAN, KODGOTTO, KIKONJUNKULU, KOKONYUNGALO, KOKO-TJUMBUNDJI, NGARLKAJIE, ORLOW, TJABAKAI-THANDJI, TJABOGAIJANJI, TJANKIR, TJANKUN, TJAPUNKANDJI, TJUNBUNDJI)*** [DYY] 3(?) (1981 Wurm and Hattori). Queensland, Barron River from south of Mareeba to Kuranda, north to Port Douglas on a plateau. Australian, Pama-Nyungan, Yidinic. Dialects: NJAKALI (NYAKALI, NYAGALI), DYAABUGAY, GULAY. Dictionary. Nearly extinct.

DYABERDYABER ***(NYULNYUL)*** [DYB] 3(?) (1981 Wurm and Hattori). Western Australia, coast south of Beagle Bay and inland. Australian, Nyulnyulan. Nearly extinct.

DYANGADI ***(DAINGGATI, BOORKUTTI, BURGADI, DANGADI, DANGATI, DANGGADI, DANGGETTI, GHANGATTY, TANGETTI, THANGATTI, THANGATTY)*** [DYN] 5(?) (1981 Wurm and Hattori). New South Wales, Kempsey area, Armidale, Macleay River. Australian, Pama-Nyungan, Yuin-Kuric, Kuri. Ruhlen (1987) says it is extinct. Nearly extinct.

DYIRBAL ***(DJIRUBAL)*** [DBL] 40 to 50 (1983 R. M. W. Dixon). Northeast Queensland, Herberton south to headwaters of Herbert River, to Cashmere, at Ravenshoe, Millaa Millaa and Woodleigh, east to Tully Falls. Australian, Pama-Nyungan, Dyirbalic. There are about 30 speakers of related Yara languages: 3 Nawagi, 12 Keramai, 3 Gulngui, 1 Djiru, 6 Mamu, 5 Ngatjan. Nearly extinct.

DYUGUN ***(JUKUN)*** [DYD] 2(?) (1981 Wurm and Hattori). Western Australia, coast around Broome and inland. Australian, Nyulnyulan. Nearly extinct.

ENGLISH [ENG] 15,682,000 in Australia (1987), 95% of population (1980 WA). Indo-European, Germanic, West, English. Dialects: AUSTRALIAN STANDARD ENGLISH, ABORIGINAL ENGLISH, NEO-NYUNGAR (NOONGA, NOONGAR, NOOGAR). Minor regional dialect differences. Neo-Nyungar is the community dialect of the Nyungar people. National language. Dictionary. Bible 1382-1989. See main entry under United Kingdom.

ERRE ***(ERE, ARI)*** [ERR] 1(?) (1981 Wurm and Hattori). Northern Territory, Red Lily area west of Oenpelli; around East Alligator River, Mt. Howship. Australian, Mangerrian, Urninganggic. Nearly extinct.

FLINDERS ISLAND [FLN] 3(?) (1981 Wurm and Hattori). Queensland, Cape York Peninsula, Flinders Island, Princess Charlotte Bay. Australian, Pama-Nyungan, Flinders Island. Nearly extinct.

GADJERAWANG ***(GADJERONG, KAJIRRAWUNG)*** [GDH] 3(?) (1981 Wurm and Hattori). Western Australia and Northern Territory, north coast from Wyndham to mouth of Victoria River and inland. Australian, Djeragan, Miriwungic. Nearly extinct.

GAGADU ***(GAGUDJU, KAKDJUAN, KAKDJU, KAKADU, ABDEDAL, ABIDDUL, KAKAKTA)*** [GBU] 6 (1981 Wurm and Hattori). Northern Territory, Oenpelli. Australian, Gagudjuan. All are bilingual in another Aboriginal language. Nearly extinct.

GAMBERA ***(GAMBRE, GAMGRE, GUWAN, KAMBERA)*** [GMA] 6(?) (1981 Wurm and Hattori). Western Australia, Admiralty Gulf, far northern Kimberleys area. Australian, Wororan, Wunambalic. Nearly extinct.

GANGGALIDA ***(GANGGALITA, JUGULA, JAKULA, YUKALA, YUKULTA, YUGULDA, YOKULA)*** [GCD] 5 possibly (1981 Wurm and Hattori). Near Bourketown, Queensland. Australian, Pama-Nyungan, Tangic. Only elderly speakers. Nearly extinct.

GANGULU [GNL] Queensland around Isaac River, west of Marlborough. Australian, Pama-Nyungan, Maric, Mari. Ruhlen (1987) says it is extinct. Extinct.

GARAWA ***(KARAWA, LEEARRAWA)*** [GBC] 200 or more (1990 Schmidt). Borroloola, Northern Territory and Doomadgee, Queensland. Australian, Garawan. Dialect: WANJI (WAINYI, WAANYI). Bilingualism in Kriol. Speakers intermarry with the Yanyuwa. Bible portions 1983.

GAYARDILT ***(GAJADILT, GAJARDILD, GAYADILT, KAIADILT, KAYARDILD, MALUNUNDA)*** [GYD] 50(?) (1981 Wurm and Hattori). Queensland, Bentinck Island, Gulf of Carpentaria. Australian, Pama-Nyungan, Tangic. Bilingualism in English. Dictionary.

GIYUG [GIY] 2(?) (1981 Wurm and Hattori). Peron Islands in Anson Bay, southwest of Darwin. Australian, Daly, Bringen-Wagaydy, Wagaydy. Nearly extinct.

GOONIYANDI ***(GUNIAN, KUNIAN, KUNIYAN, GUNIYAN, GUNIYN, KUNAN, GUNIANDI, KONEYANDI, KONEJANDI)*** [GNI] 100 (1990 Schmidt). Gogo, Fossil Downs, Louisa, and Margaret River stations, Western Australia. Australian, Bunaban. Bilingualism in Kriol. Peile says it is nearly extinct. People generally speak Kriol. Investigation needed: intelligibility with Bunaba.

GUGADJ [GGD] 1(?) (1981 Wurm and Hattori). Queensland, north coast from west of Karumba inland on Norman River. Australian, Pama-Nyungan, Paman, Flinders Pama. Nearly extinct.

GUGU BADHUN [GDC] 2(?) (1981 Wurm and Hattori). Queensland, west of Ingham and Abergowrie almost to Einasleigh. Australian, Pama-Nyungan, Maric, Mari. Nearly extinct.

GUGU WARRA ***(GUGUWARRA)*** [WRW] Queensland, Cape York Peninsula, west bank of Normanby River. Australian, Pama-Nyungan, Paman, Lamalamic. Ruhlen (1987) says it is extinct. Extinct.

GUGUBERA ***(KUKUBERA, KOKO BERA, KOKO PERA, BERANG, PAPERYN)*** [KKP] 15 fluent speakers (1991 SIL), out of an ethnic group of 50 (1990 Schmidt). Around the mouth of Mission River,

Mitchell River, Queensland. Australian, Pama-Nyungan, Paman, Coastal Pama. Most use Kunjen as second language, some use Torres Strait Creole. The ethnic group has poor understanding of English.

GUGUYIMIDJIR ***(KUKUYIMIDIR, KOKO IMUDJI, GUGU YIMIJIR, GUUGU YIMITHIRR)*** [KKY] 20 to 30 fluent speakers, 200 to 300 know and understand the language but prefer English (1991 Wayne Rosendale), 400 in the ethnic group (1990 Schmidt). Hopevale, Queensland. Australian, Pama-Nyungan, Yalandyic. Bilingualism in English. Children understand Guguyimidjir, but only speak a little, and mainly speak Aboriginal English. Bible portions 1940.

GUMATJ ***(GOMADJ, GUMAIT, GUMAJ)*** [GNN] 300 or more fully fluent first language speakers (1983 Black). Yirrkala, Northern Territory. Australian, Pama-Nyungan, Yuulngu, Dhuwala. Dialect: MANGALILI. Many are bilingual in Gupapuyngu, some in English. SOV. Scrub forest. Coastal. Hunter-gatherers. NT 1985.

GUNGABULA [GYF] 2(?) (1981 Wurm and Hattori). Queensland, around Injune. Australian, Pama-Nyungan, Maric, Mari. Nearly extinct.

GUNWINGGU ***(GUNAWITJI, MAYALI, KUNWINJKU)*** [GUP] 400 first language speakers (1983 Black), 900 including second language speakers (1983 Black; 1990 Schmidt). Oenpelli, Arnhem Land, Northern Territory, Maningrida, Croker Island. Australian, Gunwingguan, Gunwinggic. Dialects: GUMADIR, MURALIDBAN, GUNEI, GUNDJEIPME, NAIALI. Some Ngalkbun use this as a second language. Bible portions 1942-1993.

GUNYA [GYY] 3(?) (1981 Wurm and Hattori). Queensland, around Wyandra. Australian, Pama-Nyungan, Maric, Mari. Nearly extinct.

GUPAPUYNGU ***(GOBABINGO, GUBABWINGU)*** [GUF] 450 fully fluent first language speakers, 950 including second language users (1983 Black), plus 500 in other Dhuwal varieties besides those listed. Milingimbi, Arnhem Land, Northern Territory, and Elcho Islands. Australian, Pama-Nyungan, Yuulngu, Dhuwala. Dialects: GUPAPUYNGU, MADARRPA, MANGGALILI, MUNYUKU, WUBULKARRA, WALANGU. About 45 related dialects. Close to Gumatj. Children are learning Djambarrpuyngu. Others use that, Gumaj or other Aboriginal languages as second language. SOV, OVS. Scrub forest. Coastal. Hunter-gatherers. 0 to 50 meters. Bible portions 1967.

GURAGONE ***(GURROGONE, GOROGONE, GUN-GURAGONE, GUNGOROGONE, GUNAGORAGONE, GUTJERTABIA)*** [GGE] 20 (1990 Schmidt). Arnhem Land, south of Maningrida, along the Mann River, northwest of the Rembarrnga language, east of the Gunwinygu language. Australian, Burarran. All speakers are bilingual in Burarra or Gunwingku.

GURDJAR ***(KURTJJAR)*** [GDJ] 30 possibly (1981 Wurm and Hattori). Northeastern side of Norman River, Normanton, western Queensland. Australian, Pama-Nyungan, Paman, Norman Pama. Speakers say it is similar to Kunggar. Bilingualism in English. Gurdjar is in daily use by older people, but children prefer English. Nearly extinct.

GURENG GURENG [GNR] Queensland, southeast, around Abercorn. Australian, Pama-Nyungan, Waka-Kabic, Than. Ruhlen (1987) says it is extinct. Guweng may be a dialect. Related to Daribalang and Gabi, which may be extinct. Extinct.

GURINJI ***(GURINDJI)*** [GUE] 250 fully fluent first language speakers, 400 including partial speakers (1983 Black). Victoria River and Wave Hill, Kalkaringi, Northern Territory. Australian, Pama-Nyungan, South-West, Ngumbin. Dialects: MALNGIN, WANYJIRRA (WANDJIRA). All are bilingual in Kriol. There is a mixed 'Gurinji children's language' formed from Gurinji and Kriol. Bible portions 1981-1986.

GUWAMU [GWU] 1(?) (1981 Wurm and Hattori). Queensland, between St. George, Moonie River, Surat, Maranoa River. Australian, Pama-Nyungan, Maric, Mari. Nearly extinct.

IWAIDJA ***(IWAIDJI, IBADJO, EIWAJA, JIWADJA, LIMBA, KARADJEE)*** [IBD] 180 (1983 SIL). Croker Island, Northern Territory. Australian, Yiwaidjan, Yiwaidjic. Bilingualism in English.

JARNANGO ***(YAN-NHANGU, NANGU, YANANGU)*** [JAY] 40 possibly (1983 Black). Two of the most western Crocodile Islands, adjacent to Cape Stewart, Maningrida and Milingimbi, Northern Territory. Australian, Pama-Nyungan, Yuulngu. Dialects: GARMALANGGA, GURJINDI. Bilingualism in Djambarrpuyngu, Gupapuyngu, Burarra. People generally speak Djambarrpuyngu, Gupapuyngu, or Burarra. Nearly extinct.

JARU ***(DJARU, JAROO, TJARU)*** [DDJ] 250 (1981 Wurm and Hattori). Halls Creek, Ringers Soak, south-eastern Kimberley region, Western Australia. Australian, Pama-Nyungan, South-West, Ngumbin. Dialects: NYININY, DJARU. Nyininy is inherently intelligible with Jaru (Black 1983). Bilingualism in Kriol, Aboriginal English. Children speak Kriol or Aboriginal English. Dictionary.

KALA LAGAW YA ***(KALA YAGAW YA, YAGAR YAGAR, MABUIAG, KALA LAGAU LANGGUS, LANGUS, KALA LAGAW)*** [MWP] 3,000 to 4,000 fluent speakers (1990 Schmidt). Western Torres Strait Islands, Queensland; including Mabuiag, Badu, Moa, Kubin, Saibai, Boigu, Dauan, Yam, Sue, Yorke, Coconut, Thursday, Bamaga Islands; Townsville. Australian, Pama-Nyungan, Kala Lagaw Ya. Dialect: KALAW KAWAW. Outside the language area those younger than 30 are likely to speak Torres Strait Creole. SOV. Tropical island; trade wind dry season, monsoon wet; moderate rainfall.

Islands: volcanic, coral, river deposits. Hunters, fishermen, agriculturalists. 0 to 400 meters. NT 1994.

KALARKO ***(MALPA, MALBA, GALAAGU, KALAKO, KALAKUL, KALAKU)*** [KBA] Fraser and Bremer ranges area, Western Australia. Australian, Pama-Nyungan, South-West, Mirning. Recently extinct. Extinct.

KALKUTUNG ***(GALGADUUN, GALGADUNGU, KALKATUNGU, KALKADOON)*** [KTG] Mt. Isa area, Queensland. Australian, Pama-Nyungan, Galgadungic. All speak English. Recently extinct. Extinct.

KAMILAROI ***(CAMILEROI, GAMILARAAY, GAMILAROI)*** [KLD] 3 or more (1997 Coonabarabran Public School). Barwon, Bundarra, Balonne Rivers, Liverpool Plains and upper Hunter River, central northern New South Wales. Australian, Pama-Nyungan, Wiradhuric. At least one family still speak the language and teach in schools as community visitors. Dictionary. Nearly extinct.

KAMU ***(GAMOR)*** [QKY] 2 (1967). Northern Territory, south of Darwin, east of Daly River. Australian, Daly, Malagmalag, Daly Proper. Possibly extinct. Nearly extinct.

KANJU ***(KANDJU, KAANTYU, GANDJU, GANDANJU, KAMDHUE, KANDYU, KANYU, KARNU, JABUDA, NEOGULADA, YALDIYE-HO)*** [KBE] 50 possibly (1981 Wurm and Hattori). Central Cape York, Queensland. Australian, Pama-Nyungan, Paman, Northeastern Pama. Nearly extinct.

KARADJERI ***(KARAJARRI, KARRAJARRA, GARADJIRI, GARADYARI, GURADJARA, GARD'ARE)*** [GBD] 12 speakers (1991 Geytenbeek SIL). Roebuck Bay to seventy miles inland, Broome, Western Australia, La Grange mission. Australian, Pama-Nyungan, South-West, Marngu. Bilingualism in Aboriginal English. The children speak Aboriginal English. Nearly extinct.

KARIYARRA ***(KARIERA, KARRIARA, GARIERA)*** [VKA] Western Australia, south of Port Hedland. Australian, Pama-Nyungan, South-West, Coastal Ngayarda. No speakers left (1991). Some people know some vocabulary. Extinct.

KAYTETYE ***(KAIDITJ, KAITITJ, GAIDIDJ)*** [GBB] 200 (1983 Black). North of Alice Springs, Northern Territory. Australian, Pama-Nyungan, Arandic, Artuya. Related to Alyawarra. People generally speak Kriol.

KITJA ***(KIJA, GIDJA, KIDJA)*** [GIA] 100 or more (1983 Black). Near Hall's Creek and Turkey Creek, Western Australia. Australian, Djeragan, Kitjic. Closest to Miriwung. Related to Kuluwarrang (Guluwarin, Guluwarung). Bilingualism in Kriol. Kriol is Kitja children's mother tongue, and adults are bilingual in Kriol. Nomadic. SOV. Savannah. Hills. Hunter-gatherers. 100 to 400 meters. Bible portions 1978.

KOKATA ***(GUGADA, KOKITTA, KOOCATHO, KOOGURDA, KOKATHA, KUGURDA, KUKATA, MADUTARA, MADUWONGA, WANGGAMADU, WONGAMARDU)*** [KTD] 3 possibly (1981 Wurm and Hattori). South Australia, Pimba, Mt. Eba, Coober Peby. Australian, Pama-Nyungan, South-West, Wati. People may adequately understand Pintupi or Pitjantjatjara. Nearly extinct.

KRIOL ***(ROPER-BAMYILI CREOLE)*** [ROP] 10,000 or more fluent first language speakers (1991 B. Borneman SIL), 20,000 or more including second language users (1991 SIL). Roper River, Katherine areas, Ngukurr, Northern Territory; Kimberley Region, Western Australia; Gulf Country, Lower Cape York Peninsula, Queensland. Creole, English based, Pacific. Dialects: ROPER RIVER KRIOL (ROPER RIVER PIDGIN), BAMYILI CREOLE, BARKLY KRIOL, FITZROY VALLEY KRIOL, DALY RIVER KRIOL. Kimberley Kriol has many differences with Ngukkur Kriol. Both Kriol and Torres Strait Creole are spreading, and are nearly overlapping in Queensland. There are many first language Kriol speakers who are not fully bilingual in English or in Aboriginal languages. Preschool children may not be bilingual in another language. SVO. Savannah, scrub forest. Coastal, plains. Pastoralists, hunter-gatherers. 0 to 1,000 meters. NT 1991.

KUKATJA ***(KUKAJA, GUGADJA)*** [KUX] 300 (1983 Black). Balgo, Lake Gregory and area to the east, south of Halls Creek, Western Australia. Australian, Pama-Nyungan, South-West, Wati. Bilingual in Pintupi-Luritja, Ngaanyatjarra, Martu Wangka, or Walmajarri. Different from Kokata.

KUKU-MANGK ***(KUGU-MANGK)*** [XMQ] 1 (1981 Wurm and Hattori). Queensland, Cape York Peninsula, east coast south of Aurukun. Australian, Pama-Nyungan, Paman, Middle Pama. Nearly extinct.

KUKU-MU'INH ***(KUGU-MU'INH)*** [XMP] 7 (1981 Wurm and Hattori). Queensland, Cape York Peninsula, east coast south of Aurukun. Australian, Pama-Nyungan, Paman, Middle Pama. Nearly extinct.

KUKU-MUMINH ***(KUGU-MUMINH, WIK MUMINH, WIK-MUMIN)*** [XMH] 31 (1981 Wurm and Hattori). Queensland, Cape York Peninsula, east coast south of Aurukun. Australian, Pama-Nyungan, Paman, Middle Pama.

KUKU-UGBANH ***(KUGU-UGBANH)*** [UGB] 6 (1981 Wurm and Hattori). Queensland, west coast Cape York Peninsula below Aurukun. Australian, Pama-Nyungan, Paman, Middle Pama. Nearly extinct.

KUKU-UWANH ***(KUGU-UWANH)*** [UWA] 40 (1981 Wurm and Hattori). Queensland, Cape York Peninsula, east coast south of Aurukun. Australian, Pama-Nyungan, Paman, Middle Pama.

KUKU-YALANJI ***(GUGUYALANJI, KOKO-YALANJI, KUKU-YALANGI)*** [GVN] 300 or more (1981 Wurm and Hattori). Wujal-Wujal, Bloomfield River, Queensland, between Cooktown and Mossman. Australian, Pama-Nyungan, Yalandyic. Some are bilingual in English. Dictionary. SOV. Scrub forest. Coastal, mountain slope. Hunter-gatherers formerly, now laborers. NT 1985.

KUMBAINGGAR ***(GUMBAINGARI, GUMBAYNGGIR, KUMBAINGERI)*** [KGS] 1 possibly (1981 Wurm and Hattori). New South Wales, Grafton and north coast. Australian, Pama-Nyungan, Gumbaynggiric. Nearly extinct.

KUNBARLANG ***(GUNBALANG, WALANG, WARLANG, GUNGALANG)*** [WLG] 50 to 100 (1983 Black). Oenpelli, Maningrida, and Goulburn Island, Northern Territory. Australian, Gunwingguan, Gunwinggic. People generally speak Gunwinggu.

KUNGARAKANY ***(GUNGARAGAN, GUNERAKAN, KANGARRAGA, KUNGARAKAN)*** [GGK] Northern Territory, Finniss River. South of Darwin around Darwin River and Rum Jungle. Australian, Gungaraganyan. The last speaker died in 1989. Extinct.

KUNGGARA ***(GUNGGARA, KUNGGERA, GOOM-GHARRA)*** [KVS] Few speakers (SIL). Normanton, Delta, Queensland. Australian, Pama-Nyungan, Paman, Norman Pama. Possibly extinct. Nearly extinct.

KUNGGARI ***(COONGURRI, UNGORRI, GUNGARI, GUNGGARI)*** [KGL] Very few. Upper Nebine and Mungallala creeks, Queensland. Australian, Pama-Nyungan, Maric, Kapu. Related to Birria, which may be extinct. Possibly extinct. Nearly extinct.

KUNJEN ***(GUGUMINJEN, KUKUMINDJEN)*** [KJN] 20 to 25 fluent speakers, 40 with some knowledge, about 300 in the ethnic group (1991 Bruce Sommer). Wrotham Park, Kowanyama, Edward River, Queensland. Australian, Pama-Nyungan, Paman, Central Pama. Dialects: ULKULU, OYKANGAND (OLGOL, OLGEL, OGONDYAN). Most are bilingual in other Aboriginal languages, English, or Kriol. Ethnic group members mainly speak Torres Strait Creole. Bible portions 1967.

KURRAMA ***(KURAMA, GURAMA, KARAMA, KORAMA)*** [VKU] 50(?) (1981 Wurm and Hattori). Western Australia, northwest, southeast of Pannawonica. Australian, Pama-Nyungan, South-West, Coastal Ngayarda. Bilingualism in English.

KUTHANT [QKD] 3(?) (1981 Wurm and Hattori). Queensland, southwest Cape York Peninsula, north of Karumba and Normanton. Australian, Pama-Nyungan, Paman, Norman Pama. Ruhlen (1987) says it is extinct. Nearly extinct.

KUUKU-YA'U ***(YA'O, KOKO-JA'O, KOKOYAO, BAGADJI, PAKADJI)*** [QKL] 100(?) (1981 Wurm and Hattori). Queensland, northeastern Cape York Peninsula south of Temple Bay. Australian, Pama-Nyungan, Paman, Northeastern Pama. Bilingualism in Torres Strait Creole.

KUWAMA ***(PUNGUPUNGU)*** [QKU] 2(?) (1981 Wurm and Hattori). Near mouth of Muldiva River, southwest of Darwin. Australian, Daly, Bringen-Wagaydy, Wagaydy. Nearly extinct.

KWINI ***(GWINI, GWIINI, CUINI, GUNIN, WUNAMBAL, GOONAN, KUNAN)*** [GWW] 50 or more (1979 Black). Kalumburu, Western Australia. Australian, Wororan, Wunambalic. Bilingualism in Aboriginal English. Children may know some of the language, but most speak Aboriginal English as first language. Known in the area as 'Kwini', the name of the people. 'Goonan' (Kunan) is the name of the language. 'Gwini' is the Wunambal word for 'east' and was used by some people to refer to the Gunin and Yeidji.

LAMU-LAMU ***(LAMULAMUL, LAMALAMA)*** [LBY] 1 possibly (1981 Wurm and Hattori). Bamiga, Queensland, and Coen. Australian, Pama-Nyungan, Paman, Lamalamic. Ethnic groups include Baganambia, Gan-Ganda, Wurangung. Nearly extinct.

LARAGIA ***(LARAKIA, LARAKIYA, LARAGIYA)*** [LRG] Few (1983 Black). Darwin area, Northern Territory. Australian, Laragiyan. All speak English. Nearly extinct.

LARDIL ***(LADIL, LARDILL, LAIERDILA, KUNANA)*** [LBZ] 50 possibly (1981 Wurm and Hattori). Mornington Island, Queensland. Australian, Pama-Nyungan, Tangic. Related to Gayardilt, Nyangga, Yugulda. All apparently use English more than Lardil. Nearly extinct.

LENINGITIJ ***(LINNGITHIG, LINNGITHIGH)*** [LNJ] Winduwinda area, Queensland. Australian, Pama-Nyungan, Paman, Northern Pama. Recently extinct. Extinct.

LIMILNGAN ***(MANADJA, MINITJI)*** [LMC] 3(?) (1981 Wurm and Hattori). Northern Territory, Arnhem Land, between Mary River and W. Alligator River, from coast and inland. Australian, Unclassified. It may be the same as Lemil (Norweilimil; Oates 1970:29) or Manaidja (Manatja, Mandatja; Oates 1970:220). Nearly extinct.

MADNGELE ***(MATNGALA, WARAT, MADNGELA, MAANGELLA, MANDELLA, MUTTANGULLA)*** [ZML] 15 to 20 (1983 Black). Northern Territory, south of Darwin and Daly River, west bank of Muldiva River. Australian, Daly, Malagmalag, Daly Proper. Related to Kamu and Yunggor, which may be extinct. Nearly extinct.

MAGADIGE [ZMG] 30(?) (1983 Black). Inland from Anson Bay, south of Maridjabin, southwest of Darwin. Australian, Daly, Bringen-Wagaydy, Bringen. Nearly extinct.

MALAY, COCOS ISLANDS ***(COCOS, KOKOS, KUKUS)*** [COA] 1,000 including 495 in Cocos Islands (1987), 558 on Christmas Island (1987). Cocos (Keeling) Islands, and Christmas Island. Austronesian, Malayo-Polynesian, Western Malayo-Polynesian, Sundic, Malayic, Malayan, Local Malay. Young people are bilingual in English, but as the age increases the knowledge of English decreases. Vigorous. Grammar study requested. Investigation needed: intelligibility with Standard Malay, Indonesian. Orthography study requested. Muslim. See main entry under Malaysia, Sabah.

MALGANA ***(MALJANNA, MALDJANA, MALKANA)*** [VML] Western Australia, Shark Bay, south of Wooramel River to near Hamelin Pool. Australian, Pama-Nyungan, South-West, Kardu. Extinct.

MANDA [ZMA] 25(?) (1983 Black). Northern Territory, coast southwest of Anson Bay, southwest of Darwin. Australian, Daly, Bringen-Wagaydy, Wagaydy. Bilingualism in Kriol, English. Nearly extinct.

MANDANDANYI [ZMK] 1(?) (1981 Wurm and Hattori). Queensland, around Roma from Maranoa River to near Miles and Wandoan. Australian, Pama-Nyungan, Maric, Mari. Nearly extinct.

MANGALA ***(MANGALAA, MANGARLA, MANALA, MINALA, DJAWALI, DJUWALI, JIWALI, JIWARLI, KOALGURDI, YALMBAU)*** [MEM] 20 possibly (1981 Wurm and Hattori). Broome, Jurgurra Creek, Edgar Range, southwest Fitzroy, West Pilbara, Western Australia. Australian, Pama-Nyungan, South-West, Marngu. Bilingualism in Kriol. Only elderly speakers. Children know a few words, but speak Kriol or Aboriginal English. Dictionary. Nearly extinct.

MANGARAYI ***(MUNGERRY, MANGARAI, MANGGARAI, MUNGARAI)*** [MPC] 50 or fewer (1983 Black). Mataranka and Elsey stations, Northern Territory. Australian, Gunwingguan, Mangarayic. People generally speak Kriol. Different from Mangerr (Mangerei).

MANGERR ***(MENGERRDJI, MANGEREI, MENNAGI, MANGERI)*** [ZME] 1(?) (1981 Wurm and Hattori). Arnhem Land around Oenpelli. Australian, Mangerrian, Mangerric. Intelligible with Urningangg (Black). Nearly extinct.

MARA ***(LEELALWARRA, LEELAWARRA, MALA, MARRA)*** [MEC] 15 or fewer (1991 M. Sharpe). Roper River area, Arnhem Land, Northern Territory. Australian, Maran, Mara. Related to Yugul, which may be extinct. Most speak Kriol or English as second language. Speakers intermarry with the Yanyuwa. Nearly extinct.

MARANUNGGU [ZMR] 15 to 20 (1983 Black). Southwest of Darwin, inland from Anson Bay, east of Manda. Australian, Daly, Bringen-Wagaydy, Wagaydy. Young people speak Kriol. Nearly extinct.

MARGANY [ZMC] 1(?) (1981 Wurm and Hattori). Queensland, between Quilpie and Wyandra, Bulloo River and Paroo River. Australian, Pama-Nyungan, Maric, Mari. Nearly extinct.

MARGU ***(AJOKOOT, JAAKO, TERUTONG, YAAKO, YAKO)*** [MHG] 4 possibly (1981 Wurm and Hattori). Croker Island, Northern Territory. Australian, Yiwaidjan, Margic. Nearly extinct.

MARIDAN ***(MERADAN)*** [ZMD] 20(?) (1981 Wurm and Hattori). Southwest of Darwin, north of Moyle River, east of Magadige. Australian, Daly, Bringen-Wagaydy, Bringen. Nearly extinct.

MARIDJABIN ***(MARETYABIN, MARIDYERBIN, MAREDYERBIN)*** [ZMJ] 20 (1970 Oates). Northern Territory, inland from Anson Bay, south of Mariyedi and Manda, southwest of Darwin. Australian, Daly, Bringen-Wagaydy, Bringen. May be intelligible with Marithiel or Maringarr. Bilingualism in Kriol. Investigation needed: intelligibility with Marithiel, Maringarr.

MARIMANINDJI ***(MARAMARANDJI, MARAMANANDJI, MARIMANINDU, MURINMANINDJI, MARRAMANINJSJI)*** [ZMM] 15(?) (1983 Black). Northern Territory, south of Darwin and Daly River, west of Muldiva River, near headwaters. Australian, Daly, Bringen-Wagaydy, Bringen. Nearly extinct.

MARINGARR ***(MARENGGAR, MARINGA)*** [ZMT] 30 to 40 (1983 Black). Northern Territory south of Moyle River, southwest of Darwin. Australian, Daly, Bringen-Wagaydy, Bringen. Dialect: MARANUNGGU (MARRANUNGA, MARAMANUNGGU, MERRANUNGGU, WARRGAT). May be intelligible with other Bringen languages. 40% lexical similarity with MullukMulluk and Murrinh-Patha. Bilingualism in Kriol. Investigation needed: intelligibility with Maridjabin, Marithiel.

MARITHIEL ***(MARIDHIYEL, MARITHIYEL, MARRITHIYEL, MARIDHIEL, "BRINKEN", "BRINGEN", BERRINGEN)*** [MFR] 25 fluent speakers, 50 second language users (1983 Black). 30 to 50 miles south of Daly River and central Daly River; Daly River Mission, Bagot, Delissaville, Roper River Mission, Northern Territory. Australian, Daly, Bringen-Wagaydy, Bringen. Dialects: MARITHIEL, NGANYGIT, MARE-AMMU. People generally speak Kriol. The people dislike the name "Brinken". Nearly extinct.

MARIYEDI [ZMY] 20(?) (1981 Wurm and Hattori). Inland from Anson Bay, south of Manda, southwest of Darwin. Australian, Daly, Bringen-Wagaydy, Bringen. Nearly extinct.

MARTU WANGKA [MPJ] 720 (1991 J. Marsh SIL), 100 In Wankajunga (1991). Western Australia, Jigalong area, western side of Lake Disappointment, Great Sandy Desert. Australian, Pama-Nyungan, South-West, Wati. Dialects: MANYJILYJARA (MANTJILTJARA), KARTUJARRA (KARTUTJARA, KARDUTJARA, KADADDJARA, KARDUTJARRA, KIADJARA, GARDUDJARA, GAGUDJARA), PUDITARA (BUDIDJARA, PUTUJARA), YULPARITJA (YILPARITJA, YULBARIDJA), WANGKAJUNGA (WANGKAJUNGKA). Mantjiltjara and Kartutjara are two tribal groups speaking almost identical dialects. High inherent intelligibility between Yulparitja and Wangkajunga. Speakers of the 4 dialects can use the same written language with possible minor adjustments, including vocabulary change, partly needed because of cultural identity factors. Bilingualism in Walmajarri, Kukatja, Kriol. Puditara dialect is extinct. Dictionary. Bible portions 1981-1994.

MARTUYHUNIRA [VMA] 5(?) (1981 Wurm and Hattori). Western Australia, northwest coast southwest of Dampier and inland. Australian, Pama-Nyungan, South-West, Coastal Ngayarda. Nearly extinct.

MAUNG ***(GUNMARUNG, MANAGARI)*** [MPH] 200 (1983 Black). Goulburn Island, Arnhem Land, Northern Territory. Australian, Yiwaidjan, Yiwaidjic. Speakers are bilingual in English or Gunwinggu with some limitations. Bible portions 1960.

MAYAGUDUNA ***(MAYI-KUTUNA)*** [XMY] 2(?) Queensland, near north coast, inland between Leichhardt River and Flinders River. Australian, Pama-Nyungan, Paman, Mayabic. Ruhlen (1987) says it is extinct. Nearly extinct.

MAYKULAN ***(MAYI-KULAN)*** [MNT] Canobie, Queensland. Australian, Pama-Nyungan, Paman, Mayabic. Extinct.

MBARA [VMB] 2(?) (1981 Wurm and Hattori). Queensland, north of Stawell River. Australian, Pama-Nyungan, Paman, Southern Pama. Ruhlen (1987) says it is extinct. Nearly extinct.

MBARIMAN-GUDHINMA [ZMV] 3(?) (1981 Wurm and Hattori). Queensland, Cape York Peninsula, southwest coast of Princess Charlotte Bay. Australian, Pama-Nyungan, Paman, Lamalamic. Nearly extinct.

MERIAM ***(MIRIAM-MIR, MIRIAM, MER, MIR)*** [ULK] 300 to 400 active speakers (1991 Rod Kennedy). Murray Island, Eastern Torres Strait Islands, Queensland. Not in Papua New Guinea. Trans-New Guinea, Trans-Fly-Bulaka River, Trans-Fly, Eastern Trans-Fly. Dialects: BOIGU, BULGAI, BUGLIAL, TAGOTA. Most people are bilingual in Torres Strait Creole. No literacy programs have been run for more than a generation. Bible portions 1879-1902.

MIRIWUNG ***(MIRUNG, MERONG, MIRIWUN, MIRIWOONG)*** [MEP] 10 to 20 fluent first language speakers (1990 Schmidt), possibly 350 partial speakers (1983:20 Black). Kununurra, Western Australia, and Turkey Creek. Australian, Djeragan, Miriwungic. Some older people speak Miriwung. The young people use only Kriol. Most older people speak Kriol. Nearly extinct.

MIWA ***(BAGU)*** [VMI] 4(?) (1981 Wurm and Hattori). Western Australia, Drysdale River, far northern Kimberleys area. Australian, Wororan, Wunambalic. Nearly extinct.

MUDBURA ***(MUDBURRA)*** [MWD] 50 possibly (1983 Black). Victoria River to Barkly Tablelands, Northern Territory. Australian, Pama-Nyungan, South-West, Ngumbin. Most speakers are bilingual in English and other Aboriginal languages. Very few monolinguals.

MULLUKMULLUK ***(MALAK-MALAK, MALAGMALAG, NGOLAK-WONGA, NGULUWONGGA)*** [MPB] 9 to 11 fully fluent speakers (1988 Ellis SIL). Northern bank of Daly River, Northern Territory. Australian, Daly, Malagmalag, Malagmalag Proper. Tryon says it is a dying language. People generally speak Kriol. Nearly extinct.

MULURIDYI ***(BINJARA, KOKOMOLOROIJ, KOKOMOLOROITJI, KOOKANOONA, MOLLOROIDYI, MOOLOROIJI, MULARITCHEE, MULLRIDGEY, MULURUTJI, WALURIDJI)*** [VMU] 1(?) (1981 Wurm and Hattori). Queensland, headwaters of Mitchell River, to Mt. Carbine, Rumula, Mareeba, Woodville. Australian, Pama-Nyungan, Yalandyic. Nearly extinct.

MURRINH-PATHA ***(MURINBADA, MURINBATA, GARAMA)*** [MWF] 900 or more (1990 Schmidt). Port Keats area, Wadeye, Northern Territory. Australian, Daly, Murrinh-Patha. Dialects: MURRINHPATHA, MURRINHKURA, MURRINHDIMININ. Related to Ngan'gitjemerri, which may be extinct. Bilingualism in Port Keats about 90% of speakers: English, other Aboriginal languages. SOV. Tropical savannah. Coastal. Hunter-gatherers, fishermen (traditionally). 50 to 100 meters. Bible portions 1982.

MURUWARI ***(MURAWARI)*** [ZMU] 1(?) (1981 Wurm and Hattori). Queensland and New South Wales from Bollon, Dirranbandi, Weilmoringle, Bourke, almost to Cunnamulla. Australian, Pama-Nyungan, Muruwaric. Dictionary. Nearly extinct.

NAKARA ***(KOKORI, NAGARA, NAKKARA)*** [NCK] 75 to 100 (1983 Black). Maningrida, Arnhem Land, Northern Territory, Goulburn Island. Australian, Burarran. People generally speak Burarra or Djeebbana.

NANGIKURRUNGGURR ***(NGENKIKURRUNGGUR, NGANGIKARANGURR, NGANKIKURRUNKURR, NANGIKURUNGGURR)*** [NAM] 275 (1988 J. Ellis SIL), including 40 Ngenkiwumerri (1983 Black). Junction of Flora and Daly rivers, Daly River Mission, Tipperary Station, Northern Territory. Australian, Daly, Moil. Dialects: TYEMERI (MOIL, NGANKIKURRUNKURR), NGENKIWUMERRI (NANGUMIRI, NANGIOMERI, ANGOMERRY, MAREWUMIRI, NANGIMERA, NGANGOMORI). 84% lexical similarity with Ngenkiwumerri dialect. Bilingualism in Kriol, English. Main language in Daly River group.

NARRINYERI ***(NGARINYERI)*** [NAY] South Australia. Australian, Pama-Nyungan, Ngarinyeric-Yithayithic. Recently extinct. Extinct. Bible portions 1864.

NARUNGGA ***(NARANGGA, NANUNGA, NARANGA, NARRANGA, NARRANGGU, NARRANGU)*** [NNR] 1(?) (1981 Wurm and Hattori). South Australia, south Yorke Peninsula. Australian, Pama-Nyungan, South-West, Yura. Dialects: ADJABDURAH (ADJAHDURAH), TURRA. May have become extinct in 1936. Nearly extinct.

NGAANYATJARRA ***(NYANGANYATJARA, NGAANYATJARA)*** [NTJ] 1,200 (1995 D. Hackett). Warburton Ranges, Western Australia. Australian, Pama-Nyungan, South-West, Wati. Bilingualism in English. Grammar. Literacy rate in first language: 11%. NT 1991.

NGADJUNMAYA ***(BADONJUNGA, BARDOJUNGA, NGADJU, NGADJUNMAIA, NGADJUMAJA, NGATJUMAY, TCHAAKALAAGA)*** [NJU] 10(?) (1981 Wurm and Hattori). Western Australia, Eyre's Sand Patch, Goddard Creek to Port Malcolm, to Fraser Range, to Naretha and Point Culver, at Mount Andres, Russell Range, and Balladonia. Australian, Pama-Nyungan, South-West, Mirning. Related to Kalarko and Mirning. Nearly extinct.

NGALAKAN ***(HONGALLA, NGALANGAN)*** [NIG] 10 possibly (1981 Wurm and Hattori). Roper River area, Northern Territory. Australian, Gunwingguan, Ngalakanic. Related to Ngalkbun and Rembarranga. Nearly extinct.

NGALKBUN ***(NGALKBON, DALABON, BUIN, BOUN, BUAN, BOUIN, BUWAN, GUNDANGBON, NALABON, DANGBON)*** [NGK] 100 to 200 (1983 Black). Oenpelli, Arnhem Land, Northern Territory, Katherine area. Australian, Gunwingguan, Gunwinggic. Most speak Kriol, and some speak Rembarrnga or Gunwinggu as second language. Some Rembarunga use this as a second language.

NGAMINI [NMV] 2(?) (1981 Wurm and Hattori). South Australia around Narburton Creek. Australian, Pama-Nyungan, Karnic, Karna. Nearly extinct.

NGANDI [NID] Upper Wilton River, Northern Territory. Australian, Gunwingguan, Ngandic. Extinct.

NGANYAYWANA [NYX] New South Wales, northeastern, between Inverell, Ashford, and Glen Innes. Australian, Pama-Nyungan, Yuin-Kuric, Kuri. Ruhlen (1987) says it is extinct. Extinct.

NGARINMAN ***(AIRIMAN, HAINMAN, NGAIMAN, NGRARMUN)*** [NBJ] 170 possibly (1983 Black). Victoria River around Jasper Creek, Northern Territory. Australian, Pama-Nyungan, South-West, Ngumbin. Dialect: BILINARA. People generally speak Kriol.

NGARINYIN ***(UNGARINYIN, UNGARINJIN)*** [UNG] 82 possibly (1981 Wurm and Hattori). Derby to King River, Kimberley, Western Australia. Australian, Wororan, Ungarinjinic. Dialects: WILAWILA, WOLYAMIDI, GUWIDJ, WURLA (WORLA, WORLAJA, WULA, OLA, WALAR, WULADJA, WULA-DJANGARI). Bilingualism in Kriol. Children may know some of the language. Most children speak Kriol as first language. A different Wurla is described by Alan Rumsey 1990, reported to still be spoken. Semi-nomadic. OSV, VOS. Savannah. Interfluvial, coastal. Hunter-gatherers. Now station hands and country town workers.

NGARLA [NLR] 8 fluent speakers, 10 partial speakers (1991 B. Geytenbeek SIL). Western Australia, Port Hedland area. Australian, Pama-Nyungan, South-West, Inland Ngayarda. Nearly extinct.

NGARLUMA ***(NGALUMA, GNALOUMA, GNALLUMA, NGALLOOMA)*** [NRL] 70 (1970 C. G. von Brandenstein). Western Australia, northwest coast around Roebourne and inland. Australian, Pama-Nyungan, South-West, Coastal Ngayarda. Bilingualism in English.

NGARNDJI [NJI] 3(?) (1981 Wurm and Hattori). Northern Territory, Barkly Tableland, northeast of Lake Woods. Australian, West Barkly, Wambayan. Nearly extinct.

NGAWUN [NXN] 1(?) (1981 Wurm and Hattori). Queensland, southwest of Croydon, between Flinders River and Norman River. Australian, Pama-Nyungan, Paman, Mayabic. Nearly extinct.

NGURA [NBX] 6 possibly, including 1 Punthamara, 4 Wongkumara, 2 Badjiri, and 1 Kalali (1981 Wurm and Hattori). Northwestern New South Wales and southwestern Queensland. Australian, Pama-Nyungan, Karnic, Ngura. Dialects: PUNTHAMARA (BUNDHAMARA), KALALI (GARLALI), WONGKUMARA (WANGKUMARA, WANGUMARRA), BADJIRI, BIDJARA, DHIRAILA, GARANDALA, MAMBANGURA, MINGBARI, NGURAWARLA, YARUMARRA. Wurm and Hattori list the dialects as separate languages. Nearly extinct.

NGURMBUR ***(NGORMBUR, GNORMBUR, GNUMBU, KOARNBUT, NGUMBUR, OORMBUR)*** [NRX] 1(?) (1981 Wurm and Hattori). Northern Territory, Arnhem Land, between West and South Alligator Rivers, northeast of Umbugarla. Australian, Unclassified. Nearly extinct.

NHUWALA [NHF] 10(?) (1981 Wurm and Hattori). Western Australia, northwest, Barrow and Monte Bello Islands and nearby coast. Australian, Pama-Nyungan, South-West, Coastal Ngayarda. Wordick says it may be extinct. Nearly extinct.

NIJADALI ***(NJIJAPALI, NYIYABALI, BAILKO, BALYGU, PALJGU, BALGU, JAUNA)*** [NAD] 6 (1990 B. Geytenbeek SIL). Western Australia, Marblebar, and possibly some at Nulagine. Australian, Pama-Nyungan, South-West, Wati. People generally speak Aboriginal English or Nyangumarta. Two groups: Bailko and Jauna. Nearly extinct.

NIMANBUR [NMP] 2(?) (1981 Wurm and Hattori). Western Australia, southwest of King Sound and inland. Australian, Nyulnyulan. Nearly extinct.

NUGUNU ***(NUKUNA, DOORA, NJUGUNA, NOKUNNA, NOOCOONA, NOOKOONA, NUGUNA, NUKANA, NUKUNNU, NUKUNU, PUKUNNA, TJURA, TYURA, WALLAROO, WARRA, WONGAIDYA)*** [NNV] 1(?) (1981 Wurm and Hattori). South Australia, south of Gugada people to coast west to Fowler's Bay and east to Streaky Bay, eastern Spencer Gulf. Australian, Pama-Nyungan, South-West, Yura. Dictionary. Nearly extinct.

NUNGALI [NUG] 2 possibly (1981 Wurm and Hattori). Upper Daly River area, Northern Territory. Australian, Djamindjungan. Nearly extinct.

NUNGGUBUYU *(NUNGGUBUJU)* [NUY] 300 fluent speakers, 400 partial or second language speakers (1991 M. Hore ANG). Numbulwar, east Arnhem Land, Northern Territory. Australian, Gunwingguan, Nunggubuan. Not intelligible with other languages. Bilingualism in Kriol. Children understand Nunggubuyu, but speak Kriol. Most Ritharrngu speakers around Numbulwar understand it fairly well. Hunter-gatherers. Coastal. 0 to 30 meters. Bible portions 1946-1993.

NYAMAL *(GNAMO, NAMEL, NJAMAL, NJAMARL, NYAMEL)* [NLY] 20 to 30 (1991 B. Geytenbeek SIL). Western Australia, northwest, around Bamboo Creek, Marble Bar, Nullagine, to coast just east of Port Hedland. Australian, Pama-Nyungan, South-West, Inland Ngayarda. Bilingualism in Nyangumarta, English. Children speak Nyangumarta or English.

NYANGGA *(JANGA, JANGAA, JANGGA, NJANGGA, YANGGAL, JANG-KALA, NJANGGALA, YANGARELLA, YUCKAMURRI)* [NNY] 1(?) (1981 Wurm and Hattori). Queensland, head of Gilbert River, south of Forsayth to Gledswood and Gregory Range to Oak Park and Glenora; Northern Territory, coast east of Robinson River. Australian, Pama-Nyungan, Tangic. Reported to be the same as Ganggalida (Yugulda, Jakula). Nearly extinct.

NYANGUMARTA *(NYANGUMARDA, NYANGUMATA)* [NNA] 520 (1991 B. Geytenbeek SIL). Marble Bar, Port Hedlund, Tjalku Wara, Western Australia. Australian, Pama-Nyungan, South-West, Marngu.

NYAWAYGI [NYT] 1(?) (1981 Wurm and Hattori). Queensland coast between Ingham and Townsville. Australian, Pama-Nyungan, Nyawaygic. Related to Wulguru, Bindal, and Yuru, which may be extinct. Nearly extinct.

NYIGINA *(NYIKINA)* [NYH] 50 possibly (1981 Wurm and Hattori). Lower Fitzroy River, Western Australia. Australian, Nyulnyulan. Most speak Walmatjari, Kriol, or English as second language. Children speak Kriol or Aboriginal English as first language.

NYULNYUL [NYV] 3(?) (1981 Wurm and Hattori). Western Australia, coast around Beagle Bay. Australian, Nyulnyulan. Nearly extinct.

NYUNGA *(NYUNGAR)* [NYS] Southwest Australia. Australian, Pama-Nyungan, South-West, Nyungar. Recently extinct. Former Nyungar languages: Tjapanmay, Karlamay, Pipelman, Ngatjumay, Kwetjman, Mirnong, Kaniyang. There are about 8,000 people who are descended from the Nyunga and speak a mixture of English and Nyunga. They are sometimes called 'Noonga', 'Noongar', or 'Noogar', and their speech 'Neo-Nyunga'. Extinct.

PAKANHA [PKN] 10(?) (1981 Wurm and Hattori). Queensland, central Cape York Peninsula, south of Coleman River. Australian, Pama-Nyungan, Paman, Middle Pama. Nearly extinct.

PANYTYIMA *(PANDJIMA, BANDJIMA, PANJIMA, PANYJIMA, BANJIMA)* [PNW] 50 (1972 B. Geytenbeek). Western Australia, northwest, east southeast of Tom Price. Australian, Pama-Nyungan, South-West, Inland Ngayarda. Related to Yinawongga, Ngarlawangga, Ngarla, Tjurruru, which may be extinct, and Nyamal. Bilingualism in Yindjibarndi, English.

PINI *(PINIRITJARA, PIRNIRITJARA, BINI, BIRNI)* [PII] Few speakers. Three Rivers, Western Australia. Australian, Pama-Nyungan, South-West, Wati. Possibly extinct. Nearly extinct.

PINIGURA *(BINIGURA)* [PNV] 5(?) (1981 Wurm and Hattori). Western Australia, northwest, inland on Duck Creek. Australian, Pama-Nyungan, South-West, Coastal Ngayarda. Nearly extinct.

PINTIINI *(PINDIINI, WANGADA, WANGGAJI, WANGKATJA, WONGA, WONGAI-I, WONGGAII)* [PTI] 200 to 300 (1983 Black). Western Australia, northern margin of Nullabor Plain from north of Hughes. Australian, Pama-Nyungan, South-West, Wati. Bilingualism in Pitjantjatjara, Ngaanyatjarra.

PINTUPI-LURITJA *(PINTUBI, BINDDIBU, LORIDJA)* [PIU] 800 or more (1983 Black). Papunya settlement, Yuendumu and Kintore, Northern Territory, and Balgo Hills, Western Australia. Australian, Pama-Nyungan, South-West, Wati. About 10% are bilingual in English, 90% monolingual. NT 1981.

PIRLATAPA *(BILADABA)* [BXI] South Australia, around Lake Blanche and Lake Callabonn. Australian, Pama-Nyungan, Karnic, Karna. It was close to Diyari. The language became extinct in the 1960s. Extinct.

PITCAIRN-NORFOLK *(PITCAIRN ENGLISH)* [PIH] Some second language users. Cant, English-Tahitian. An in-group language used to assist in the preservation of identity. The people speak Standard English as mother tongue. There may be no speakers on the Australian mainland. Christian. Second language only. See main entry under Norfolk Island.

PITJANTJATJARA *(PITJANTJARA)* [PJT] 2,500 speakers, including dialects (1995 Paul Eckert), 3,000 including second language speakers (1995 Paul Eckert). Pitjantjatjara Freehold lands, northwest South Australia, surrounding areas, and Yalata. Australian, Pama-Nyungan, South-West, Wati. Dialects: YANKUNYTJATJARA, PITJANTJATJARA. Pitjantjatjara is one of the many varieties of the 'Western Desert language'. About 20% are bilingual in English, 80% monolingual. Dictionary.

Grammar. Literacy rate in first language: 50% to 70%. Literacy rate in second language: 10% to 15%. Roman. Bible portions 1949-1995.

PITTA PITTA ***(PITA PITA, BIDHABIDHA, BIDA-BIDA)*** [PIT] 2 possibly (1981 Wurm and Hattori). Boulia, Queensland. Australian, Pama-Nyungan, Karnic, Palku. Related to Gangalanya, Garanya, Lhanima, Ngurlubulu, Ragaya, Rangwa, Yurlayurlanya, which may be extinct, and Wanggamala. Distinct from Pita Pita. Nearly extinct.

REMBARUNGA ***(REMBARRANGA, REMBARRNGA, RAINBARGO)*** [RMB] 150 (1983 Black). Roper River area, Maningrida and outstations, Katherine area, Northern Territory. Australian, Gunwingguan, Rembargic. Bilingualism in Many: Kriol, Ngalkbun, Gunwinggu. Few children seem to be learning the language.

RITARUNGO ***(RITARNUGU, RITHARNGU, RIDHARRNGU, RIDARNGO, WAGELAK, WAWILAG)*** [RIT] 300 or more (1983 Black). Eastern Arnhem Land (Rose River, Roper River), Northern Territory. Australian, Pama-Nyungan, Yuulngu. Some are bilingual in Kriol, some in Djinba.

THAYORE ***(KUUK THAAYOORE, KUUK THAAYORRE, THAAYORE, THAYORRE, TAIOR, GUGUDAYOR, KUKTAYOR, KUKUDAYORE, BEHRAN)*** [THD] 150 speakers (1991 SIL) out of 350 in the ethnic group (1982 A. Hall). Between Edward and Coleman rivers, Western Cape York, Queensland. Australian, Pama-Nyungan, Paman, Western Pama. Related to Kuuk-Yak and Yir Thangedl, which may be extinct. Dictionary. SVO. Desert, savannah, scrub forest. Coastal plains. Hunter-gatherers, fishermen. Sea level. Bible portions 1981.

THAYPAN [TYP] 2(?) (1981 Wurm and Hattori). Queensland, central Cape York Peninsula, Coleman River. Australian, Pama-Nyungan, Paman, Rarmul Pama. Nearly extinct.

THURAWAL ***(DHARAWAL, DHARAWAAL, TURRUBUL)*** [TBH] Port Hacking to Shoalhaven River, New South Wales. Australian, Pama-Nyungan, Yuin-Kuric, Yuin. Dialect: WADIWADI (WODIWODI). Recently extinct. People now speak English or Aboriginal English. Extinct.

TIWI [TIW] 1,500 including nonfluent speakers (1983 Black). Bathurst and Melville Islands, Nguiu, Northern Territory. Australian, Tiwian. Bilingualism in English. SVO. Scrub forest. Coastal, islands. Hunter-gatherers formerly; now laborers, craftsmen. Sea level. Bible portions 1979-1985.

TJURRURU [TJU] Western Australia, northwest, Hardey River, southwest of Tom Price. Australian, Pama-Nyungan, South-West, Inland Ngayarda. Ruhlen (1987) says it is extinct. Extinct.

TORRES STRAIT CREOLE ***(TORRES STRAIT PIDGIN, TORRES STRAIT BROKEN, CAPE YORK CREOLE, LOCKHART CREOLE)*** [TCS] 23,400 or fewer (1989 J. Holm). Others are second language users. Torres Strait Islands, towns on upper Cape York and some towns on the east coast of north Queensland. Creole, English based, Pacific. Dialects: AP-NE-AP, MODERN LANGUS. 80% lexical similarity with English. A creolization of Tok Pisin or Bislama and Kala Lagau Langgus. Trade language.

TYARAITY ***(DYERAIDY, DAKTJERAT, TJERAIT, DJERADJ, DJERAG, KUWEMA)*** [WOA] Few (1983 Black). Delissaville, Northern Territory. They were originally near the mouth of the Reynold River. Australian, Daly, Malagmalag, Malagmalag Proper. All or most are bilingual in English. Nearly extinct.

UMBINDHAMU [UMD] 6(?) (1981 Wurm and Hattori). Queensland, Cape York Peninsula, north of Coen. Australian, Pama-Nyungan, Paman, Lamalamic. Nearly extinct.

UMBUGARLA ***(MBAKARLA)*** [UMR] 3(?) (1981 Wurm and Hattori). Northern Territory, Arnhem Land, southeast of Limilngan, between Mary River and South Alligator River. Australian, Unclassified. Nearly extinct.

UMBUYGAMU [UMG] 7(?) (1981 Wurm and Hattori). Queensland, Cape York Peninsula, east coast of Princess Charlotte Bay. Australian, Pama-Nyungan, Paman, Lamalamic. Nearly extinct.

UMPILA [UMP] 100 possibly (1981 Wurm and Hattori). Cape Sidmouth and north nearly to Night Island, Queensland. Australian, Pama-Nyungan, Paman, Northeastern Pama. Only a few older people know Umpila. The middle generation has varying proficiency. The younger generation speak Torres Strait Creole.

URADHI [URF] 2(?) (1981 Wurm and Hattori). Queensland, northeast Cape York Peninsula, North Alice Creek. Australian, Pama-Nyungan, Paman, Northern Pama. Nearly extinct.

URNINGANGG ***(UNINGANGK, WUNINGAK)*** [URC] Few (1983 Black). Arnhem Land, northwest; upper reaches of Alligator River. Australian, Mangerrian, Urninganggic. Intelligible with Mangerr. Nearly extinct.

WADJIGINY ***(WOGAITY, WAGAYDY)*** [WDJ] 12 fluent speakers (1988 J. Ellis SIL). Southwest of Darwin along coast and inland along Finniss River. Australian, Daly, Bringen-Wagaydy, Wagaydy. Dialect: PUNGUPUNGU (KUWAMA). The people speak Kriol, but understand Wadjiginy when the older people speak it. Nearly extinct.

WADJIGU [WDU] 1(?) (1981 Wurm and Hattori). Queensland, southwest of Fairbairn Reservoir. Australian, Pama-Nyungan, Maric, Mari. Nearly extinct.

WAGAYA ***(WAKAYA, WAAGAI, WAAGI, WAGAI, WAGAJA, WAGGAIA, WAKAJA, WAKKAJA, WARKYA, WORGAI, WORGAIA, WORKIA, LEEWAKYA, UKKIA)*** [WGA] Few (1983 Black). Northern

Territory, Avon Downs, Camooweal, Austral Downs, area north of Lake Nash. Australian, Pama-Nyungan, Wagaya-Warluwaric, Wagaya. Nearly extinct.

WAGEMAN ***(WOGEMAN, WAGIMAN)*** [WAQ] 50(?) (1983 Black). South of Pine Creek, Tipperary Station, and Bagot, Northern Territory. Australian, Gunwingguan, Yangmanic, Wagiman. People generally speak Kriol.

WAJARRI ***(WATJARI, WATJARRI, WADJARI, WADJERI)*** [WBV] 50 or fewer fluent speakers out of an ethnic group of fewer than 200 (1981 W. Douglas). Mt. Magnet to Geraldton, Western Australia. Australian, Pama-Nyungan, South-West, Wadjari. Related to Badimay. People generally speak English.

WAKAWAKA ***(WAKKA, WAGA, WAGAWAGA, ENIBURA, NUKUNUKUBARA)*** [WKW] 3 possibly (1981 Wurm and Hattori). Nanango north to Mt. Perry, west to Boyne River, at Kingaroy, Murgon, and Gayndah, Queensland. Australian, Pama-Nyungan, Waka-Kabic, Miyan. Dialects: DUUNGIDJAWU, WAGAWAGA. Related to Wuliwuli, Barunggam, Gayabara, Muringam, which may be extinct. Most speak English as second language. Nearly extinct.

WALMAJARRI ***(WALMATJARI, WALMATJIRI, WALMAJIRI, WOLMERI)*** [WMT] 1,000 (1990 Schmidt). Area along the Fitzroy River valley, Lake Gregory and La Grange, Western Australia. Australian, Pama-Nyungan, South-West, Ngumbin. Dialect: DJUWARLINY (JUWALINY). The western group speaks Juwaliny. Bilingualism in Kriol. Some children understand and respond to Walmajarri, but their first language is Kriol. Dictionary. SOV. Semi-desert. Plains. Hunter-gatherers. Bible portions 1978-1985.

WAMBAYA ***(WAMBAIA, WAMBAJA, WOMBYA, WOM-BY-A, UMBAIA, YUMPIA)*** [WMB] 12(?) including dialects (1981 Wurm and Hattori). Up to 80 (1983 Black). Northern Territory, Barkly Tableland, headwaters of Limmen Bight and McArthur rivers, and east of Lake Woods. Australian, West Barkly, Wambayan. Dialects: WAMBAYA, BINBINGA, GUDANDJI. Black (1983) says the dialects are inherently intelligible. Bilingualism in Kriol. Nearly extinct.

WAMIN [WMI] 1(?) (1981 Wurm and Hattori). Queensland, northwest of Einasleigh. Australian, Pama-Nyungan, Paman, Southern Pama. Nearly extinct.

WANDARANG ***(WANDARAN, WARNDARANG)*** [WND] Arnhem Land, Roper River area, Northern Territory. Australian, Maran, Mara. People now speak Kriol. Extinct.

WANGAAYBUWAN-NGIYAMBAA [WYB] 12(?) (1981 Wurm and Hattori). New South Wales, Darling River, Barwon River River, Yanda Creek, Bogan River. Australian, Pama-Nyungan, Wiradhuric. Dialects: WANGAAYBUWAN (WONGAIBON, WOMBUNGEE, WONGAGIBUN, WONGHIBON, WONGHI, WONJHIBON), NGIYAMBAA (GIAMBA, NARRAN, NOONGABURRAH, NGEUMBA, NGIAMBA, NGIUMBA, NGJAMBA, NGUMBARR), WAYILWAN (WALJWAN). Nearly extinct.

WANGGAMALA [WNM] 1(?) (1981 Wurm and Hattori). Northern Territory, Hay River, south of Andegerebinha. Australian, Pama-Nyungan, Karnic, Palku. Nearly extinct.

WANGGANGURU [WGG] 8 (1981 Wurm and Hattori). Northern Territory, southeast corner. Australian, Pama-Nyungan, Karnic, Arabana-Wangganguru. Nearly extinct.

WANMAN ***(WARNMAN)*** [WBT] 20 (1973 B. Geytenbeck SIL). Marble Bar area, Western Australia. Australian, Pama-Nyungan, South-West, Wati. Bilingualism in Kriol. People generally speak English, Martu Wangka, or Nyangumarta.

WARAY ***(WARRAI, ARWUR, AWARAI, AWARRA)*** [WRZ] 4(?) (1981 Wurm and Hattori). Adelaide River area, Northern Territory. Australian, Gunwingguan, Warayan. Nearly extinct.

WARDAMAN ***(WADAMAN, WADERMAN, WADUMAN, WARDA'MAN, WARDUMAN, WARTAMAN, WARDMAN, WORDAMAN)*** [WRR] 50(?) (1983 Black). Northern Territory, upper Daly River. Australian, Gunwingguan, Yangmanic, Yibwan. Bilingualism in Kriol. People generally speak Kriol. Investigation needed: bilingual proficiency in Kriol.

WARIYANGGA ***(WARRIYANGKA)*** [WRI] Western Australia, southeast of Mount Augustus, West Pilbara. Australian, Pama-Nyungan, South-West, Inland Ngayarda. Ruhlen (1987) classifies it in a separate Mantharda group. Dictionary. Extinct.

WARLMANPA ***(WALMALA)*** [WRL] 50(?) (1981 Wurm and Hattori). Northern Territory, Mount Leichhardt area. Australian, Pama-Nyungan, South-West, Ngarga. People generally speak Kriol.

WARLPIRI ***(WALBIRI, ELPIRA, ILPARA, WAILBRI, WALPIRI)*** [WBP] 3,000 (1990 Schmidt). Northern Territory, Yuendumu, Ali Curung Willowra, Alice Springs, Katherine, Darwin, and Lajamanu. Australian, Pama-Nyungan, South-West, Ngarga. Related to Warlmanpa, Ngardi (Ngarti, Ngari, Ngati, Ngadi), and Kartangaruru. SOV. Desert. Plains. Hunter-gatherers, nomadic. NT, in press (1999).

WARLUWARA ***(MAULA, MAUULA, MAWULA, WALOOKERA, WALUGERA, WALUWARA, WOLLEGARA, YUNNALINKA)*** [WRB] 3(?) (1981 Wurm and Hattori). Queensland, Roxborough Downs. Australian, Pama-Nyungan, Wagaya-Warluwaric, Warluwara-Thawa. Nearly extinct.

WARRGAMAY [WGY] 3(?) (1981 Wurm and Hattori). Queensland, coast south of Hinchinbrook Island, and inland along Herbert River. Australian, Pama-Nyungan, Dyirbalic. Nearly extinct.

WARUMUNGU ***(WARRAMUNGA)*** [WRM] 200 (1983 Black). Tennant Creek area, Northern Territory. Australian, Pama-Nyungan, Warumungic. Bilingualism in Kriol. People generally speak Kriol.

WARUNGU [WRG] 2(?) (1981 Wurm and Hattori). Queensland, northeast of Einasleigh. Australian, Pama-Nyungan, Maric, Mari. Nearly extinct.

WIK-EPA [WIE] 3(?) (1981 Wurm and Hattori). Queensland, Cape York Peninsula, southeast of Aurukun. Australian, Pama-Nyungan, Paman, Middle Pama. Nearly extinct.

WIK-IIYANH [WIJ] 40 (1981 Wurm and Hattori). Queensland, central Cape York Peninsula, southwest of Coen. Australian, Pama-Nyungan, Paman, Middle Pama.

WIK-KEYANGAN [WIF] 3 (1981 Wurm and Hattori). Queensland, Cape York Peninsula, southeast of Aurukun. Australian, Pama-Nyungan, Paman, Middle Pama. Nearly extinct.

WIK-ME'ANHA [WIH] 12 (1981 Wurm and Hattori). Queensland, Cape York Peninsula, southeast of Aurukun. Australian, Pama-Nyungan, Paman, Middle Pama. Nearly extinct.

WIK-MUNGKAN ***(WIK-MUNKAN, MUNKAN)*** [WIM] 400 to 1,000 including second language speakers (1990 Schmidt). Edward River to Aurukun, Queensland. Australian, Pama-Nyungan, Paman, Middle Pama. Some are bilingual in English. NT 1985.

WIK-NGATHANA [WIG] 126 (1981 Wurm and Hattori). Queensland, Cape York Peninsula, west coast below Aurukun. Australian, Pama-Nyungan, Paman, Middle Pama.

WIKALKAN ***(WIKNGATARA, WIK-NGATHARA, WIK-NGATHARRA)*** [WIK] 86 (1981 Wurm and Hattori). Aurukun, Queensland. Australian, Pama-Nyungan, Paman, Middle Pama. Dialects: WIK-NGANDJARA (NGANDJARA), NGADANJA. Bilingualism in Wik-Mungkan. Young people speak Wik-Mungkan.

WIKNGENCHERA ***(NGANDJARA, NANTJARA, NGANTJERI, WIK-NANTJARA, WIK NJINTURA)*** [WUA] 50 (1970 Oates). Aurukun, Queensland. Australian, Pama-Nyungan, Paman, Middle Pama. Related to Wikngathara (Wikalkan). Bilingualism in Wik-Mungkan. All young people speak Wik-Mungkan. Nearly extinct.

WILAWILA ***(WILA-WILA)*** [WIL] 2(?) (1981 Wurm and Hattori). Western Australia, central Kimberleys. Australian, Wororan, Ungarinjinic. Nearly extinct.

WIRADHURI ***(WIRADJURI, BERREMBEEL, WARANDGERI, WEROGERY, WIIRATHERI, WIRA-ATHOREE, WIRADURI, WIRAJEREE, WIRASHURI, WIRATHERI, WIRRACHAREE, WIRAIDYURI, WIRRAI'YARRAI, WOORAGURIE, WORDJERG)*** [WRH] 3(?) (1981 Wurm and Hattori). New South Wales, from Murray River to Macquarie River, along Lachlan River from junction with Murrumbidgee River to Parkes. Australian, Pama-Nyungan, Wiradhuric. Nearly extinct.

WIRANGU ***(NJANGGA, NYANGGA, WARRANGOO, WIRONGU, WIRONGUWONGGA, WIRRUNG, WIRRUNGA)*** [WIW] 2(?) (1981 Wurm and Hattori). South Australia, coast between head of Bight and Streaky Bay and inland to Ooldea region. Australian, Pama-Nyungan, South-West, Wati. Nearly extinct.

WORIMI ***(KATTANG, GADHANG, GADANG)*** [KDA] Between Hunter and Hastings rivers, from Port Macquarie to Hawkesbury River, New South Wales. Australian, Pama-Nyungan, Yuin-Kuric, Kuri. All speak English. Recently extinct. Extinct.

WORORA ***(WORRORRA)*** [UNP] 20 fluent speakers (1990 Schmidt), 150 second language speakers (1983 R. M. W. Dixon). Derby area, Collier Bay, Western Australia. Australian, Wororan, Wororic. Dialects: WORORA, UNGGUMI. Many are bilingual in English, Aboriginal English, or Kriol. Children may know some of the language. Bible portions 1930-1943.

WULIWULI [WLU] Queensland, southwestern, Dawson River, Baralaba, Banana, Theodore. Australian, Pama-Nyungan, Waka-Kabic, Miyan. Ruhlen says it is extinct. Extinct.

WULNA [WUX] 1 (1981 Wurm and Hattori). Arnhem Land around Darwin, mouth of Adelaide River and inland. Australian, Laragiyan. Nearly extinct.

WUNAMBAL ***(UNAMBAL, WUMNABAL, WUNAMBULLU, YEIDJI, YEITHI, JEIDJI, JEITHI)*** [WUB] 20 (1990 A. Schmidt). Kalumburu, Wyndham and Mowanjum, Western Australia. Australian, Wororan, Wunambalic. Dialects: WUNAMBAL, GAMBERA, MIWA. Bilingualism in Kriol, Aboriginal English, Standard Australian English. People generally speak Kriol. Children may know some of the language, but most speak Kriol, Aboriginal English or Standard Australian English as mother tongue. Different from Kwini. 'Yeidji' means 'talk, speech'. Nearly extinct.

YALARNNGA [YLR] Queensland around Burke River and Dajarra. Australian, Pama-Nyungan, Galgadungic. Ruhlen (1987) says it is extinct. Extinct.

YANDRUWANDHA [YND] 2(?) (1981 Wurm and Hattori). South Australia around Moomba, and east into Queensland. Australian, Pama-Nyungan, Karnic, Karna. Nearly extinct.

YANGMAN ***(JUNGMAN)*** [JNG] 10 fluent speakers, 50 in the ethnic group (1983 Black). Elsey Creek, Northern Territory, and Katherine. Australian, Gunwingguan, Yangmanic, Nolgin. Related to Dagoman, which may be extinct. People now speak English or Kriol. Nearly extinct.

YANKUNYTJATJARA ***(YANKUNTATJARA, JANGKUNDJARA, KULPANTJA)*** [KDD] 200 to 300 (1985 Cliff Goddard). Yalata, Musgrave, and Everard Ranges, and the eastern part of Pitjantjatjara freehold lands and surrounding areas, South Australia. Australian, Pama-Nyungan, South-West, Wati. Bilingualism in Pitjantjatjara. Dictionary. Grammar.

YANYUWA ***(YANYULA, JANJULA, ANYULA, WADIRI, YANULA, ANIULA, ANULA, LEEANUWA)*** [JAO] 70 to 100 (1990 Schmidt). Borroloola, Northern Territory and Doomadgee, Queensland. Australian, Pama-Nyungan, Yanyuwan. All speak Kriol or English, and some speak Garawa as second language. Speakers intermarry with the Garawa or Mara. Wives learn the husband's language, but use their own with members of their own group. Children usually speak the mother's language, but boys at puberty learn and then speak the father's language. SVO. Savannah, scrub forest. Coastal, plains. Hunter-gatherers traditionally. Bible portions 1980.

YAWARAWARGA [YWW] 1(?) (1981 Wurm and Hattori). South Australia and Queensland, north of Cooper Creek, southeast of Lake Yamma Yamma. Australian, Pama-Nyungan, Karnic, Karna. Nearly extinct.

YAWURU [YWR] Western Australia, coast south of Broome and inland. Australian, Nyulnyulan. Ruhlen (1987) says it is extinct. Extinct.

YIDINY ***(IDINJI, BOOLBOORA, DEBA, ENEBY, GERRAH, GIJOW, GILLAH, GUWAMAL, IDIN IDINDJI, IDIN-WUDJAR, INDINDJI, JIDINDJI, KITBA, MAIMBIE, MUNGERA OHALO, PEGULLO- BURA, WARRA-WARRA, WARRYBOORA, WOGGIL, YETINJI, YIDDINJI, YIDIN, YIDINDJI, YITINTYI, YUKKABURRA)*** [YII] 12(?) (1981 Wurm and Hattori). Queensland, formerly Atherton region. A few now at Palm Island Babinda, north to Gordonvale. Australian, Pama-Nyungan, Yidinic. Dialects: GUNGGAY, YIDINY, MADYAY. Nearly extinct.

YINDJIBARNDI ***(JINDJIBANDI)*** [YIJ] 500 to 600 (1990 Schmidt). Roebourne, Western Australia, surrounding towns and stations. Australian, Pama-Nyungan, South-West, Coastal Ngayarda. Bilingualism in English, Aboriginal English. SVO. Desert. Coastal, riverine. Hunter-gatherers, fishermen. 0 to 200 meters.

YINDJILANDJI [YIL] 1(?) (1981 Wurm and Hattori). Northern Territory, northeast of Wonarah. Australian, Pama-Nyungan, Wagaya-Warluwaric, Warluwara-Thawa. Nearly extinct.

YINGGARDA ***(INGGARDA, INGARA, INGARDA, INGARRA, INGARRAH, INPARRA, JINGGARDA, YINGKARTA, KAKARAKALA)*** [YIA] 5 (1981 Wurm and Hattori). Western Australia, coast at Shark Bay between Gascoyne and Wooramel rivers, inland to Red Hill, West Pilbara. Australian, Pama-Nyungan, South-West, Kardu. Related to Malgana which is extinct, Nhanda which is nearly extinct (handful of speakers, Blevins 1995), and Bulinya which may be extinct. Ruhlen (1987) says it is extinct. Dictionary. Nearly extinct.

YIR YORONT ***(YIR YIRONT, JIR JORONT, GWANDERA, KOKOMINDJEN, MANDJOEN, MILLERA, MIND'JANA, MUNDJUN, MYUNDUNO)*** [YIY] 15 fluent speakers, some second language speakers (1991 Bruce Sommer). Queensland, west central Cape York Peninsula, just southeast of Edward River. Australian, Pama-Nyungan, Paman, Western Pama. Dialects: DANGEDL (DHANU'UN, DJUDJAN, DUDJYM), GORMINANG, JIR'JOROND (JIRMEL MEL-JIR, NGAMBA'WANDH, YIRMEL, YIRTANGETTLE, YIRTUTIYM). Understanding of English is poor. Most members of the ethnic group speak Torres Strait Creole. Nearly extinct.

YUGAMBAL ***(YUGUMBAL, JUGUMBIR, JUKAMBA, MANALDJALI, MINJANBAL)*** [YUB] Queensland, Logan and Albert river basins from Jimboomba to MacPherson Range. Australian, Pama-Nyungan, Yuin-Kuric, Kuri. Ruhlen (1987) says it is extinct. Extinct.

COOK ISLANDS

National or official language: English. 19,000 (1998 UN). A New Zealand self-governing territory. 15 islands including Danger, Manahiki, Rakahanga, Penrhyn (Tongareva), Pukapuka islands. Literacy rate 92% to 94%. Also includes Niue 23. Information mainly from S. Wurm and S. Hattori 1981; N. Besnier OIEL 1992. Christian, Baha'i. Data accuracy estimate: B. The number of languages listed for Cook Islands is 5. Of those, all are living languages. Diversity index 0.37.

ENGLISH [ENG] 683 in Cook Islands (1966 UN report). Indo-European, Germanic, West, English. National language. Bible 1535-1989. See main entry under United Kingdom.

PENRHYN ***(TONGAREVA, MANGARONGARO, PENRHYNESE)*** [PNH] 600 on Penrhyn Island (1981 Wurm and Hattori). Northern Cook Islands, Penrhyn Island. Austronesian, Malayo-Polynesian, Central-Eastern, Eastern Malayo-Polynesian, Oceanic, Central-Eastern Oceanic, Remote Oceanic, Central Pacific, East Fijian-Polynesian, Polynesian, Nuclear, East, Central, Tahitic. Almost intelligible with Rarotongan. Bilingualism in Rarotongan. Disappearing rapidly. The language spoken on Palmerstone Island is reported to be a mixture of Penrhynese and Yorkshire English. Unwritten.

PUKAPUKA ***(BUKABUKAN, PUKAPUKAN)*** [PKP] 840 speakers out of 1,200 in the ethnic group (1997). Population total all countries 2,030. Pukapuka and Nasau islands, northern Cook Islands; some in Rarotonga. Also spoken in Australia, New Zealand. Austronesian, Malayo-Polynesian, Central-Eastern, Eastern Malayo-Polynesian, Oceanic, Central-Eastern Oceanic, Remote Oceanic, Central Pacific, East Fijian-Polynesian, Polynesian, Nuclear, Samoic-Outlier, Pukapuka. Not intelligible with Rarotongan or other Cook Islands languages. Related to Samoan. Unwritten. VSO, VOS. Fishermen, agriculturalists, copra.

RAKAHANGA-MANIHIKI ***(MANIHIKI-RAKAHANGA)*** [RKH] 2,500 in Cook Islands (1981 Wurm and Hattori). Population total both countries 5,000. Northern Cook Islands, Rakahanga an Manihiki islands. Also spoken in New Zealand. Austronesian, Malayo-Polynesian, Central-Eastern, Eastern Malayo-Polynesian, Oceanic, Central-Eastern Oceanic, Remote Oceanic, Central Pacific, East Fijian-Polynesian, Polynesian, Nuclear, East, Central, Tahitic. Limited intelligibility with Rarotongan. Unwritten. Fishermen; agriculturalists: taro, coconuts.

RAROTONGAN ***(COOK ISLAND, COOK ISLANDS MAORI, MAORI, KUKI AIRANI, RAROTONGAN-MANGAIAN)*** [RRT] 16,800 in Cook Islands, possibly including second language speakers (1979 Government report). Population total all countries 43,000. 13 inhabited Cook Islands. Also spoken in French Polynesia, New Zealand. Austronesian, Malayo-Polynesian, Central-Eastern, Eastern Malayo-Polynesian, Oceanic, Central-Eastern Oceanic, Remote Oceanic, Central Pacific, East Fijian-Polynesian, Polynesian, Nuclear, East, Central, Tahitic. Dialects: MITIARO, MAUKE, ATIU, MANGAIA, RAROTONGA, AITUTAKI. 83% lexical similarity with Paumotu, 79% with Hawaiian, 75% with Mangarevan, 73% with Marquesas. Trade language. Prepositions. The government is deciding on the orthography (1987). Fishermen, agriculturalists: arrowroot, coconut, sweet potato, yam, taro, banana, citrus fruit, pineapple, papaya, mango, chestnut. Christian. Bible 1851-1888.

EASTER ISLAND

A dependency of Chile. See Chile.

FIJI

Republic of Fiji. National or official languages: Fijian, Fijian Hindustani, English. 796,000 (1998 UN), including 46.2% ethnic Fijian, 48.6% Indian, 5.2% Chinese and European. 325 islands, 100 inhabited. Land area 7,000 square miles. Literacy rate 80% to 90%. Also includes Gujarati, Malayalam, Eastern Panjabi, Pitcairn-Norfolk, Samoan 300, Tamil, Telugu, Tongan 300, Tuvaluan 357, Urdu, Wallisian, Chinese 5,500. Information mainly from A. J. Schütz 1972; S. Wurm and S. Hattori 1981; P. Geraghty 1983. Christian, Hindu, Muslim, Sikh. Blind population 392. Deaf population 46,321. Data accuracy estimate: B. The number of languages listed for Fiji is 10. Of those, all are living languages. Diversity index 0.60.

ENGLISH [ENG] 4,929 Europeans in Fiji (1976 census). An additional 10,276 or 1.8% of population (1976 census) are part-European, and speak English and Fijian. Indo-European, Germanic, West, English. Also used by many urban Chinese (4,652 in 1976), Rotuman, occasionally by Indians, rarely by Fijians (P. Geraghty 1981). Main language of commerce, education, government. There are also reports of a Fijian Pidgin English. National language. Newspapers, radio programs. Bible 1535-1989. See main entry under United Kingdom.

FIJIAN ***(FIJI, STANDARD FIJIAN, EASTERN FIJIAN, NADROGA, NADRONGA)*** [FJI] 330,441 in Fiji or 46.2% of the population (1996 census) including 10,000 in Kadavu (1,500 Nabukelevu), 20,000 in Northeast Viti Levu. 650,000 including second language users (1991 UBS). Population total all countries 350,000 or more. Eastern half of Viti Levu and its eastern offshore islands, Kadavu Island, Vanua Levu and its offshore islands, Nayau, Lakeba, Oneata, Moce, Komo, Namuka, Kabara, Vulaga, Ogea, Vatoa islands as mother tongue; other areas of Fiji as second language. Also spoken in Nauru, New Zealand, Vanuatu. Austronesian, Malayo-Polynesian, Central-Eastern, Eastern Malayo-Polynesian, Oceanic, Central-Eastern Oceanic, Remote Oceanic, Central Pacific, East Fijian-Polynesian, East Fijian. Dialects: KADAVU (ONO, TAVUKI, NABUKELEVU), SOUTHEAST VITI LEVU (WAIDINA, LUTU, NANDRAU, NAIMASIMASI), BAU (BAUAN, MBAU), NORTHEAST VITI LEVU (TOKAIMALO, NAMENA, LOVONI), CENTRAL VANUA LEVU (BAARAVI, SEAQAAQAA, NABALEBALE, SAVUSAVU), NORTHEAST VANUA LEVU (LABASA, DOGOTUKI SAQANI, KOROLAU), SOUTHEAST VANUA LEVU (NAVATU-C, TUNULOA, NAWENI, BAUMAA), WEST VANUA LEVU (NAVATU-B, SOOLEVU, BUA, NAVAKASIGA). The southern part of Vanua Levu has several dialects similar to Bau. On the northern part of Vanua Levu and adjacent islands people speak a variety somewhat related to Bau. Bau is very similar to Standard Fijian, used as traditional lingua franca among Fijians. National language. Dictionary. Grammar. VOS. Newspapers, radio programs. Lumbermen; agriculturalists: taro, yams, breadfruit, bananas; sugar cane, molasses, copra, coconut oil; miners: gold, copper; fishermen. Christian, traditional religion. Bible 1864, in press (1997).

FIJIAN, WESTERN ***(FIJI, NADROGA, NADRONGA)*** [WYY] 57,000 including 38,500 in Waya (Waya and Ba-Navosa), 18,500 in Nadroga (1977 Lincoln). Fiji Islands, western half of Viti Levu, Waya Islands.

Austronesian, Malayo-Polynesian, Central-Eastern, Eastern Malayo-Polynesian, Oceanic, Central-Eastern Oceanic, Remote Oceanic, Central Pacific, West Fijian-Rotuman, West Fijian. Dialects: NUCLEAR WESTERN FIJIAN (NADROGAA, TUBANIWAI, BAARAVI), WAYA (NAKOROBOYA, NOIKORO, MAGODRO).

GONE DAU ***(GONEDAU)*** [GOO] 500 (1977 Lincoln). Eastern Fiji, Gone and Dau islands off western Vanua Levu. Austronesian, Malayo-Polynesian, Central-Eastern, Eastern Malayo-Polynesian, Oceanic, Central-Eastern Oceanic, Remote Oceanic, Central Pacific, East Fijian-Polynesian, East Fijian. Dialect chain to Bau (Standard) Fijian at the opposite end. Speakers learn Standard Fijian; it is not functionally intelligible to them. Investigation needed: bilingual proficiency in Fiji.

HINDUSTANI, FIJIAN ***(FIJIAN HINDI)*** [HIF] 380,000 (1991 UBS) or 48.6% of the population (1987 Honolulu Star-Bulletin). Population total all countries 380,000 or more. Also spoken in Australia, USA. Indo-European, Indo-Iranian, Indo-Aryan, East Central zone. No significant regional variation. A type of Awadhi, also Influenced by Bhojpurl. Spoken by all of Indian ancestry in Fiji, including ethnic Tamil (6,663), Gujarati (6,203), Urdu, Telugu (2,008), Gurmukhi (Panjabi, 1,167), Bengali (17,875), Malayalam. A small Gujarati community speak Gujarati at home, and a few others, mainly older people, speak their traditional languages. Speakers were brought by the British to work as indentured laborers from 1879 until the 1920s. Official language. SOV; verb conjugations have been simplified from Standard Hindi. Literacy rate in second language: 85%. Newspapers, radio programs. Agriculturalists: sugar cane, rice, vegetables; shopkeepers, small businessmen, professional people. Hindu, Muslim, Christian, Sikh. Bible portions.

KIRIBATI ***(GILBERTESE, IKIRIBATI)*** [GLB] 5,300 in Fiji, including 3,000 or more Banaban (1988). Austronesian, Malayo-Polynesian, Central-Eastern, Eastern Malayo-Polynesian, Oceanic, Central-Eastern Oceanic, Remote Oceanic, Micronesian, Micronesian Proper, Ikiribati. Dialect: BANABAN. Christian. Bible 1893-1954. See main entry under Kiribati.

LAUAN ***(LAU)*** [LLX] 16,000 (1981 P. Geraghty). Eastern Fiji Islands, Lau, Nayau, Lakeba, Oneata, Moce, Komo, Namuka, Kabara, Vulaga, Ogea, Vatoa islands. Austronesian, Malayo-Polynesian, Central-Eastern, Eastern Malayo-Polynesian, Oceanic, Central-Eastern Oceanic, Remote Oceanic, Central Pacific, East Fijian-Polynesian, East Fijian. Dialects: LAU, VANUA BALAVU. In the middle of the East Fijian dialect chain; a cluster of dialects. Has some similarities to Bau Fijian; may be inherently intelligible with it. Agriculturalists: yams, taro, breadfruit, sugar cane, coconut; fishermen. Traditional religion.

LOMAIVITI [LMV] Islands east of Viti Levu: Koro, Makogai, Levuka, Ovalau, Batiki, Nairai, Gau. Austronesian, Malayo-Polynesian, Central-Eastern, Eastern Malayo-Polynesian, Oceanic, Central-Eastern Oceanic, Remote Oceanic, Central Pacific, East Fijian-Polynesian, East Fijian.

NAMOSI-NAITASIRI-SERUA ***(NAMOSI-NAITAASIRI-SEERUA)*** [BWB] Namosi, Serua, Naitasiri provinces. Austronesian, Malayo-Polynesian, Central-Eastern, Eastern Malayo-Polynesian, Oceanic, Central-Eastern Oceanic, Remote Oceanic, Central Pacific, West Fijian-Rotuman, West Fijian. Dialects: BATIWAI, TUBAI, NALEA. Namosi is a divergent variety of West Fijian. The dialects listed may be separate languages. Investigation needed: intelligibility, bilingual proficiency.

ROTUMAN ***(ROTUNA, RUTUMAN)*** [RTM] 9,000 (1991 UBS) or 1.2% of the population (1981 Wurm and Hattori). 2,500 on Rotuma, 300 overseas (1990 J. Vamarasi). Rotuma Island. Austronesian, Malayo-Polynesian, Central-Eastern, Eastern Malayo-Polynesian, Oceanic, Central-Eastern Oceanic, Remote Oceanic, Central Pacific, West Fijian-Rotuman, Rotuman. Dictionary. Grammar. Agriculturalists, fishermen, copra. Bible 1999.

FRENCH POLYNESIA

French Overseas Territory of French Polynesia. National or official languages: French, Tahitian. 227,000 (1998 UN). Includes Marquesas Islands, Gambier Islands, Austral Islands, Tuamotu Archipelago, Tahiti and the Society Islands. Literacy rate 82% to 95%. Also includes Rapa Nui, Rarotongan 869. Information mainly from S. Wurm and S. Hattori 1981; N. Besnier 1992. Christian, secular. Data accuracy estimate: B. The number of languages listed for French Polynesia is 9. Of those, all are living languages. Diversity index 0.56.

AUSTRAL ***(TUBUAI-RURUTU)*** [AUT] 8,000 (1987), 5% of the population. Austral (Tubuai) Islands. Austronesian, Malayo-Polynesian, Central-Eastern, Eastern Malayo-Polynesian, Oceanic, Central-Eastern Oceanic, Remote Oceanic, Central Pacific, East Fijian-Polynesian, Polynesian, Nuclear, East, Central, Tahitic. Dialects: RAIVAVAE, RIMATARA, RURUTU, TUBUAI. The dialects are all inherently intelligible. Speakers seem to be shifting to Tahitian. Speakers on Raivavae may be less bilingual. Investigation needed: bilingual proficiency in Raivavae in Tahitian.

CHINESE, HAKKA *(HAKKA)* [HAK] 19,200 in French Polynesia (1987), 2% of the population. Sino-Tibetan, Chinese. Many are shifting to Tahitian. Buddhist, Christian, Chinese traditional religion. Bible 1916. See main entry under China.

FRENCH [FRN] 15,338 first language speakers in French Polynesia, foreign born (1977). 50,215 attending French schools, second language users (1978). Indo-European, Italic, Romance, Italo-Western, Western, Gallo-Iberian, Gallo-Romance, Gallo-Rhaetian, Oïl, French. National language. Bible 1530-1986. See main entry under France.

MANGAREVA *(MANGAREVAN)* [MRV] 1,600 (1987), 1% of the population. Gambier Islands, Mangareva Island, Rikitea settlement. Austronesian, Malayo-Polynesian, Central-Eastern, Eastern Malayo-Polynesian, Oceanic, Central-Eastern Oceanic, Remote Oceanic, Central Pacific, East Fijian-Polynesian, Polynesian, Nuclear, East, Central, Marquesic. 75% lexical similarity with Rarotongan, 73% with Marquesan, 72% with Paumotu, 50% to 68% with Tahitian. Some bilingualism in Tahitian; 65% average comprehension of those tested. Agriculturalists: breadfruit, coconut, banana, plantain, sugar cane, taro, sweet potato, yam, arrowroot, turmeric, pandanus; fishermen. 441 meters. Traditional religion. Bible portions 1908.

MARQUESAN, NORTH [MRQ] 3,400 (1981 Wurm and Hattori). Marquesas Islands: Hatutu, Nuku Hiva, Ua Huka, Ua Pou islands. Austronesian, Malayo-Polynesian, Central-Eastern, Eastern Malayo-Polynesian, Oceanic, Central-Eastern Oceanic, Remote Oceanic, Central Pacific, East Fijian-Polynesian, Polynesian, Nuclear, East, Central, Marquesic. Dialects: HATUTU, NUKU HIVA, UA HUKA, UA POU. Wurm and Hattori (1981) list North Marquesas and South Marquesas as two languages. The dialects of North Marquesas are all inherently intelligible. 50% intelligibility of Tahitian. 45% to 67% lexical similarity with Tahitian, 73% with Mangareva and Rarotonga, 70% with Hawaiian, 29% with Paumotu. Fishermen, agriculturalists: breadfruit, coconut, banana, manioc, taro, melon, sweet potato, lettuce, tomato, orange, grapefruit, coffee; copra production. NT 1995.

MARQUESAN, SOUTH [QMS] 2,100 (1981 Wurm and Hattori). Marquesas Islands: Hiva Oa, Tahuta, Fatu Hiva islands. Austronesian, Malayo-Polynesian, Central-Eastern, Eastern Malayo-Polynesian, Oceanic, Central-Eastern Oceanic, Remote Oceanic, Central Pacific, East Fijian-Polynesian, Polynesian, Nuclear, East, Central, Marquesic. Dialects: HIVA OA, TAHUTA, FATU HIVA. The dialects listed are inherently intelligible. Wurm and Hattori (1981) list North Marquesan as a separate language. Fishermen, agriculturalists. Bible portions 1858-1905.

RAPA *(RAPAN)* [RAY] 521 (1998 Kenji Rutter, U. of Hawaii). Austral Islands, Rapa (Rapa Iti) Island, 2 villages, Ha'urei and 'Area. Austronesian, Malayo-Polynesian, Central-Eastern, Eastern Malayo-Polynesian, Oceanic, Central-Eastern Oceanic, Remote Oceanic, Central Pacific, East Fijian-Polynesian, Polynesian, Nuclear, East, Central. May be a dialect of Tubuai-Rurutu (Austral). Tahitian is used in church. School attendance is required to age 14; instruction is in French. French proficiency is limited. Children seem more comfortable speaking French. Speak French among themselves. Some children are monolingual in French. School teachers desire to preserve Rapa. Investigation needed: intelligibility with Austral, bilingual proficiency in Tahitian. Agriculturalists: taro, coconut, orange, banana, coffee; fishermen; livestock: goats, cattle. Up to 2,000 feet. Christian.

TAHITIAN [THT] 117,000 in French Polynesia (1977 census) including several thousand non-Tahitians. Population total all countries 125,000. Society Islands and some islands in the Tuamotus including the Mihiroa group. Also spoken in New Caledonia, New Zealand, Vanuatu. Austronesian, Malayo-Polynesian, Central-Eastern, Eastern Malayo-Polynesian, Oceanic, Central-Eastern Oceanic, Remote Oceanic, Central Pacific, East Fijian-Polynesian, Polynesian, Nuclear, East, Central, Tahitic. 85% lexical similarity with Rarotongan, 76% with Hawaiian. National language. Dictionary. Agriculturalists: taro, yam, sweet potato, corn, eggplant, tomato, melon, lettuce, coconut, breadfruit, Tahitian chestnut, mango, banana, coffee; fishermen; livestock: pigs, cattle. Bible 1838-1913.

TUAMOTUAN *(PA'UMOTU)* [PMT] 14,400 (1987), 9% of the population, including 6,700 on Tuamotu (1977 census), 2,000 in Tahiti (1977 Voegelin and Voegelin). Tuamotu, Tahiti. Austronesian, Malayo-Polynesian, Central-Eastern, Eastern Malayo-Polynesian, Oceanic, Central-Eastern Oceanic, Remote Oceanic, Central Pacific, East Fijian-Polynesian, Polynesian, Nuclear, East, Central, Tahitic. Dialects: VAHITU, TAPUHOE, NAPUKA, REAO, FANGATAU (TUPITIMOAKE), PARATA (PUTAHI), MARANGAI. 83% lexical similarity with Rarotongan, 77% with Hawaiian. Dialect variations are being leveled out as people become more bilingual in Tahitian. Speakers on Napuka and Reao may be less bilingual. Investigation needed: bilingual proficiency in Napuka, Reao with Tahitian.

GUAM

National or official languages: Chamorro, English. 161,000 (1998 UN). USA territory. Geographically southernmost of the Mariana Islands. Literacy rate 96%. Also includes Chuukese, Japanese 2,500,

Korean 4,000, Palauan, Pingelapese, Tagalog 24,000, Chinese 2,000, people from the Philippines 30,000. Information mainly from Byron Bender 1971, 1996; K. Rehg 1991, 1996; J. Ellis 1996. Christian, secular, Baha'i. Data accuracy estimate: A2. The number of languages listed for Guam is 2. Of those, both are living languages. Diversity index 0.64.

CHAMORRO ***(TJAMORO)*** [CJD] 62,500 in Guam (1991 Bender and Rehg), about 50% of the population. About 80% of ethnic Chamorros have some command of the language (1997 Honolulu Advertiser). Population total both countries 78,000. Also spoken in Northern Mariana Islands. Austronesian, Malayo-Polynesian, Western Malayo-Polynesian, Chamorro. Dialects: CHAMORRO, ROTANESE CHAMORRO. Active language use. Language gaining in importance. Taught at the University of Guam. Influence from Spanish. National language. Grammar. SVO, VSO. Tropical. Coral plateau in north, volcanic in south. 500 to 1,334 feet. Christian. Bible portions 1908-1992.

ENGLISH [ENG] 28,800 in Guam (1987). Indo-European, Germanic, West, English. USA military and dependents. National language. Bible 1535-1989. See main entry under United Kingdom.

HAWAIIAN ISLANDS

See USA.

KIRIBATI

Repubic of Kiribati. Formerly Gilbert Islands, part of the British Gilbert and Ellice Islands Colony. National or official languages: Kiribati, English. 81,000 (1998 UN). 38 islands and atolls; land area is 32.5 square miles, spread over nearly 2 million square miles of ocean at the equator. Literacy rate 90%. Also includes Tuvaluan 500. Information mainly from B. Bender 1996; K. Rehg 1996. Christian, Baha'i. Data accuracy estimate: B. The number of languages listed for Kiribati is 2. Of those, both are living languages. Diversity index 0.03.

ENGLISH [ENG] 338 in Kiribati (1978 census). Indo-European, Germanic, West, English. National language. Bible 1535-1989. See main entry under United Kingdom.

KIRIBATI ***(GILBERTESE, IKIRIBATI)*** [GLB] 58,320 in Kiribati (1987), 97.2% of the population. Population total all countries 67,200. Also spoken in Fiji, Nauru, Solomon Islands, Tuvalu, Vanuatu. Austronesian, Malayo-Polynesian, Central-Eastern, Eastern Malayo-Polynesian, Oceanic, Central-Eastern Oceanic, Remote Oceanic, Micronesian, Micronesian Proper, Ikiribati. Dialect: BANABAN. North-south dialect division. 26% lexical similarity with Ponapean. Only 30% of the speakers are effectively bilingual in Kiribati and English. Active language use. National language. Dictionary. VOS. Most are literate in Kiribati, but little material is available. Fishermen, sailors, agriculturalists, copra production. Christian. Bible 1893-1954.

MARSHALL ISLANDS

Formerly part of U.S. Trust Territory of the Pacific Islands. National or official language: Marshallese. 60,000 (1998 UN). Capital: Majuro. Double chain of 1,225 islands and reefs, 68 square miles of land. Literacy rate 85%. Information mainly from B. W. Bender 1996; K. L. Rehg 1996; J. Ellis 1996. Data accuracy estimate: A. The number of languages listed for Marshall Islands is 2. Of those, both are living languages. Diversity index 0.00.

ENGLISH [ENG] Indo-European, Germanic, West, English. Bible 1535-1989. See main entry under United Kingdom.

MARSHALLESE ***(EBON)*** [MZM] 43,900 in Marshall Islands (1979 Bender). Population total both countries 43,900 or more. Also spoken in Nauru. Austronesian, Malayo-Polynesian, Central-Eastern, Eastern Malayo-Polynesian, Oceanic, Central-Eastern Oceanic, Remote Oceanic, Micronesian, Micronesian Proper, Marshallese. Dialects: RÄLIK, RATAK. Two inherently intelligible dialects. Speech on Ujelang, the westernmost island, is slightly less homogeneous. 33% lexical similarity with Ponapean. Active language use. National language. Dictionary. Grammar. Copra production, coconut oil. Bible 1982.

MICRONESIA

Federated States of Micronesia. Formerly part of the U.S. Trust Territory of the Pacific Islands. National or official languages: Chuuk, Kosraean, Ponapean, Yapese, English. 114,000 (1998 UN). It includes the states of Yap, Chuuk (Truk), Pohnpei (Ponape), and Kosrae (Kusaie). 607 islands, 270.8 square miles of land, spread over more than 1 million square miles of ocean. Capital: Palikir. Literacy rate 85%. Also includes Japanese, Chinese. Information mainly from B. W. Bender 1996; K. L. Rehg 1996; J. Ellis 1996. Christian. Data accuracy estimate: A2. The number of languages listed for Micronesia is 17. Of those, all are living languages. Diversity index 0.78.

CHUUKESE ***(CHUUK, TRUK, TRUKESE, RUK, LAGOON CHUUKESE)*** [TRU] 38,341 (1989 census). 45,000 including second language users (1991 UBS). Population total both countries 38,341 or more. Chuuk Lagoon, Caroline Islands, some on Ponape. Also spoken in Guam. Austronesian, Malayo-Polynesian, Central-Eastern, Eastern Malayo-Polynesian, Oceanic, Central-Eastern Oceanic, Remote Oceanic, Micronesian, Micronesian Proper, Ponapeic-Trukic, Trukic. Dialects: EAST LAGOON, FAYICHUCK. Mortlockese has 80% to 85% lexical similarity with Chuuk, 81% with Puluwat, 79% with Satawal, 78% with Carolinian, 75% with Woleaian, 67% with Ulithi. Active language use. National language. Dictionary. Grammar. Island. Agriculturalists, copra production. Bible 1989, in press (1998).

ENGLISH [ENG] 3,540 first language speakers in Micronesia, foreign born (1970 census). Indo-European, Germanic, West, English. National language. Bible 1535-1989. See main entry under United Kingdom.

KAPINGAMARANGI ***(KIRINIT)*** [KPG] 3,000 (1995 SIL), including 1,500 on Kapingamarangi and 1,500 in Porakiet village on Ponape. Kapingamarangi and Ponape islands, Caroline Islands. Austronesian, Malayo-Polynesian, Central-Eastern, Eastern Malayo-Polynesian, Oceanic, Central-Eastern Oceanic, Remote Oceanic, Central Pacific, East Fijian-Polynesian, Polynesian, Nuclear, Samoic-Outlier, Ellicean. 55% lexical similarity with Nukuoro, 54% with Rarotongan, 53% with Samoan, 51% with Paumotu, 50% with Tahitian. Active language use. There is intermarriage with Nukuoro people. Dictionary. SVO, VSO. Agriculturalists: taro, breadfruit, banana, coconut, pandanus; fishermen; livestock: pigs, poultry; woodcarvers.

KOSRAEAN ***(KUSAIE, KOSRAE)*** [KSI] 6,900 in Micronesia (1993 Johnstone). Population total both countries 6,900 or more. Kusaie Island, Caroline Islands. Also spoken in Nauru. Austronesian, Malayo-Polynesian, Central-Eastern, Eastern Malayo-Polynesian, Oceanic, Central-Eastern Oceanic, Remote Oceanic, Micronesian, Micronesian Proper, Kusaiean. Dialects: LELU-TAFUNSAK, MALEN-UTWE. Dialects are inherently intelligible to each other's speakers. 26% lexical similarity with Ponapean. Active language use. National language. Dictionary. Grammar. Bible 1928.

MOKILESE ***(MOKIL, MWOAKILESE, MWOAKILOA)*** [MNO] 1,050 (1979 Bender). Fewer than 500 on Mokil Atoll. Mokil (Mwoakiloa) Atoll, east of Carolines, and on Pohnpei Island. Austronesian, Malayo-Polynesian, Central-Eastern, Eastern Malayo-Polynesian, Oceanic, Central-Eastern Oceanic, Remote Oceanic, Micronesian, Micronesian Proper, Ponapeic-Trukic, Ponapeic. 79% lexical similarity with Pingelapese, 75% with Ponapean. Bilingualism in Ponapean. Active language use. Investigation needed: intelligibility with Pingelapese, bilingual proficiency in Ponapean, attitudes. Dictionary. Grammar.

MORTLOCKESE ***(MORTLOCK, NOMOI)*** [MRL] 5,904 (1989 census), including 1,692 in Upper Mortlock, 1,757 in Mid Mortlock, 2,455 in Lower Mortlock, about 1,000 elsewhere. Mortlock Islands, 70 miles southeast of Truk, Caroline Islands. A large group of Lower Mortlock speakers are on Ponape Island. Austronesian, Malayo-Polynesian, Central-Eastern, Eastern Malayo-Polynesian, Oceanic, Central-Eastern Oceanic, Remote Oceanic, Micronesian, Micronesian Proper, Ponapeic-Trukic, Trukic. Dialects: UPPER MORTLOCK, MID MORTLOCK, LOWER MORTLOCK. 75% intelligibility of Pulapese, 18% of Satawal, 8% of Woleaian. 80% to 85% lexical similarity with Chuuk, 83% with Puluwat, 82% with Satawal, 81% with Carolinian, 78% with Woleaian, 72% with Ulithi. Active language use. NT 1883.

NAMONUITO ***(NAMON WEITE)*** [NMT] 944 (1989 census). Magur, Ono, Onari, Piserarh, Ulul islands, Carolines. Austronesian, Malayo-Polynesian, Central-Eastern, Eastern Malayo-Polynesian, Oceanic, Central-Eastern Oceanic, Remote Oceanic, Micronesian, Micronesian Proper, Ponapeic-Trukic, Trukic. Very active language use.

NGATIK MEN'S CREOLE ***(NGATIKESE MEN'S LANGUAGE, NGATIKESE)*** [NGM] 700 including 500 on atoll (1983 Poyer), 200 on Ponape. Ngatik (Sapuahfik) Atoll, east of the Caroline Islands. Creole, English based, Pacific. A creolized language from the Sapuahfik dialect of Ponapean and English whose genesis is the direct result of a massacre in 1837 of adult males on Ngatik by British traders. Spoken by adult males who are also native bilinguals of the Sapuahfik dialect of Ponapean. Adult male speakers. Women and children understand it. Agriculturalists: coconut; fishermen; pig raisers.

NUKUORO ***(NUKORO, NUGUOR)*** [NKR] 860 (1993 Johnstone) including 125 on Ponape. Nukuoro Island, Caroline Islands. Austronesian, Malayo-Polynesian, Central-Eastern, Eastern Malayo-Polynesian, Oceanic, Central-Eastern Oceanic, Remote Oceanic, Central Pacific, East Fijian-Polynesian, Polynesian, Nuclear, Samoic-Outlier, Ellicean. 55% lexical similarity with Kapingamarangi. Many older speakers are bilingual in Ponapean. Active language use. SVO, VSO. Fishermen (net, spear, rod); agriculturalists: taro; copra production; animal husbandry. NT 1986.

PÁÁFANG [PFA] 1,318 (1989 census). Hall Islands (Nomwin, Fananu, Marilo, Ruo), Carolines. Austronesian, Malayo-Polynesian, Central-Eastern, Eastern Malayo-Polynesian, Oceanic, Central-Eastern Oceanic, Remote Oceanic, Micronesian, Micronesian Proper, Ponapeic-Trukic, Trukic. Indications of convergence with Chuukese. Highly bilingual in Chuukese. Active language use. No published dictionary or grammar.

PINGELAPESE ***(PINGELAP, PINGILAPESE)*** [PIF] 2,500 including 500 on Pingelap, about 2,000 on Ponape. Population total all countries 3,000. Pingelap and Ponape. Also spoken in Guam, USA. Austronesian, Malayo-Polynesian, Central-Eastern, Eastern Malayo-Polynesian, Oceanic, Central-Eastern Oceanic, Remote Oceanic, Micronesian, Micronesian Proper, Ponapeic-Trukic, Ponapeic. 81% lexical similarity with Ponapean, 79% with Mokilese. Bilingualism in Ponapean. Active language use. Investigation needed: bilingual proficiency in Ponapean, Mokilese, attitudes.

POHNPEIAN ***(PONAPEAN)*** [PNF] 27,700 (1993 Johnstone) including 24,000 on Pohnpei, 3,425 on outer islands, 275 elsewhere. Pohnpei Island, Caroline Islands. Austronesian, Malayo-Polynesian, Central-Eastern, Eastern Malayo-Polynesian, Oceanic, Central-Eastern Oceanic, Remote Oceanic, Micronesian, Micronesian Proper, Ponapeic-Trukic, Ponapeic. Dialects: KITI, PONAPEAN, SAPWUAHFIK. 81% lexical similarity with Pingalap, 75% with Mokilese, 36% with Chuuk. Active language use. National language. Dictionary. Grammar. Bible 1994.

PULUWATESE ***(PULUWAT)*** [PUW] 1,364 (1989 census). Polowat, Pollap, Houk (Pulusuk), and Tamtam islands, Carolines. Austronesian, Malayo-Polynesian, Central-Eastern, Eastern Malayo-Polynesian, Oceanic, Central-Eastern Oceanic, Remote Oceanic, Micronesian, Micronesian Proper, Ponapeic-Trukic, Trukic. Dialects: PULUWATESE, PULAPESE, PULUSUKESE. 64% intelligibility of Satawalese, 40% of Woleaian, 21% of Ulithian. Pulap speakers may need separate literature. 88% lexical similarity with Satawalese and Carolinian, 83% with Mortlock, 82% with Woleaian, 81% with Chuukese, 72% with Ulithian. Speakers have limited bilingualism in English. Active language use. Dictionary.

SATAWALESE [STW] 458 (1987 Yap census). Satawal Island, Carolines. Austronesian, Malayo-Polynesian, Central-Eastern, Eastern Malayo-Polynesian, Oceanic, Central-Eastern Oceanic, Remote Oceanic, Micronesian, Micronesian Proper, Ponapeic-Trukic, Trukic. 60% intelligibility of Ulithian and Woleaian. 95% lexical similarity with Carolinian, 88% with Woleaian and Puluwat, 82% with Mortlockese, 79% with Chuukese, 77% with Ulithian. Active language use. No published dictionary or grammar.

ULITHIAN [ULI] 3,000 (1987 UBS). Ulithi, Ngulu, Sorol, Fais islands, eastern Caroline Islands. Austronesian, Malayo-Polynesian, Central-Eastern, Eastern Malayo-Polynesian, Oceanic, Central-Eastern Oceanic, Remote Oceanic, Micronesian, Micronesian Proper, Ponapeic-Trukic, Trukic. 85% intelligibility with Woleaian, 57% with Satawalese, very low intelligibility of Pulapese and Chuuk. 74% to 80% lexical similarity with Woleaian, 77% with Satawalese, 74% with Carolinian, 72% with Puluwatese and Mortlockese, 68% with Chuuk. Semi-official status. Active language use. Grammar. Christian, traditional religion. NT 1995.

WOLEAIAN [WOE] 1,631 (1987 Yap census). Woleai (Wottegai), Falalus, Seliap (Sulywap), Falalop (Falalap), Tegailap (Tagalap), Paliau, Mariang, Eauripik, Faraulep, Elato, Lamotrek, Ifaluk islands, eastern Caroline Islands. The first 5 listed are inhabited. 22 islands total, Yap State. Austronesian, Malayo-Polynesian, Central-Eastern, Eastern Malayo-Polynesian, Oceanic, Central-Eastern Oceanic, Remote Oceanic, Micronesian, Micronesian Proper, Ponapeic-Trukic, Trukic. Dialects: WOLEAIAN, LAMOTREK. 84% intelligibility of Satawalese, 81% of Ulithian, 50% of Sonsorol, very low of Pulapese and Chuukese. 88% lexical similarity with Satawalese and Carolinian, 82% with Puluwatese, 80% with Ulithian, 78% with Mortlockese, 75% with Chuukese. Speakers have limited bilingualism in English. Active language use. Lamotrek speakers desire their own literature. Dictionary. Grammar.

YAPESE [YPS] 6,592 (1987 Yap census). Yap Island, 10 islands, Caroline Islands. Austronesian, Malayo-Polynesian, Western Malayo-Polynesian, Yapese. Active language use. National language. Dictionary. Grammar. VSO. Mangrove swamps, coconut groves. Mountain, plateau, coral reef, volcanic. Agriculturalists: yam, banana, betel nut, breadfruit, Tahitian chestnut, mango, papaya, cassava, sweet potato, sugar cane, turmeric, pigs, chicken; fishermen. 15 to 590 feet. Traditional religion, Christian. NT 1973.

MIDWAY ISLANDS

National or official language: English. 180 to 200 (1996). USA possession. Two islands: Sand and Eastern. Also includes Sinhala, Tagalog, Thai. The number of languages listed for Midway Islands is 1. Diversity index 0.00.

ENGLISH [ENG] 2,256 in Midway (1975 WA). Indo-European, Germanic, West, English. National language. 99% USA military. Bible 1535-1989. See main entry under United Kingdom.

NAURU

Republic of Nauru. Naoero. National or official languages: Nauruan, English. 11,000 (1998 UN). One coral island, 9 square miles. Literacy rate 99%. Also includes Yue Chinese 626, Fijian 180, Kiribati 1,700, Kosraean, Marshallese, Tuvaluan 607. Information mainly from B. Bender and K. Rehg 1991. Christian, Chinese traditional religion, secular, Baha'i. Data accuracy estimate: B. The number of languages listed for Nauru is 3. Of those, all are living languages. Diversity index 0.57.

CHINESE PIDGIN ENGLISH [CPE] Pidgin, English based, Pacific. Currently spoken.

ENGLISH [ENG] 564 first language speakers, 7,254 including second language users (1979 Government figures). Indo-European, Germanic, West, English. National language. Bible 1535-1989. See main entry under United Kingdom.

NAURUAN [NRU] 6,000 (1991 Bender and Rehg), 50% of the population, 7,000 including second language users (1991 UBS). Nauru Island, Pleasant Island, isolated atoll west of Kiribati. Austronesian, Malayo-Polynesian, Central-Eastern, Eastern Malayo-Polynesian, Oceanic, Central-Eastern Oceanic, Remote Oceanic, Micronesian, Nauruan. Almost all people are bilingual in English. Children apparently not learning Nauru. Active use. Used as a second language by the Kiribati, Tuvalu, Kosraean, Marshallese. School attendance is required from age 6 to 17. National language. Fishermen, phosphate mining. Christian. Bible 1918.

NEW CALEDONIA

National or official language: French. 206,000 (1998 UN). 45% Melanesian. A French territory. Literacy rate 85% among Melanesians. Also includes Tahitian 7,000, Vietnamese 5,000, Chinese 500. Information mainly from S. Wurm and S. Hattori 1981; S. Schooling 1990; P. A. Geraghty 1988; D. T. Tryon 1995. Christian, secular, Muslim. Blind population 30. Data accuracy estimate: B. The number of languages listed for New Caledonia is 40. Of those, 38 are living languages and 2 are extinct. Diversity index 0.84.

AJIË *(HOUAILOU, WAILU, WAI, ANJIE)* [AJI] 5,000 (1982 SIL). Houailou: east coast Monéo to Kouaoua and inland valleys. Austronesian, Malayo-Polynesian, Central-Eastern, Eastern Malayo- Polynesian, Oceanic, Central-Eastern Oceanic, Remote Oceanic, New Caledonian, Southern, South, Wailic. Regional language and 'church language'. Language of wider communication. Grammar. NT 1922.

ARHÂ *(ARA)* [ARN] 250 (1974 census). Poya, upper valleys. Austronesian, Malayo-Polynesian, Central-Eastern, Eastern Malayo-Polynesian, Oceanic, Central-Eastern Oceanic, Remote Oceanic, New Caledonian, Southern, South, Wailic. Different from Arho. Reported to be bilingual in Ajië. Investigation needed: bilingual proficiency in Ajië.

ARHÖ *(ARO)* [AOK] 10 to 100 (1982 SIL). Poya, Cradji and Nékliai villages. Austronesian, Malayo-Polynesian, Central-Eastern, Eastern Malayo-Polynesian, Oceanic, Central-Eastern Oceanic, Remote Oceanic, New Caledonian, Southern, South, Wailic. Bilingualism in Ajië. Reported to be nearing extinction. Different from Arhâ. Investigation needed: bilingual proficiency in Ajië.

BISLAMA *(BICHELAMAR)* [BCY] 1,200 in New Caledonia (1982 SIL). Mainly in Noumea. All from Vanuatu. Creole, English based, Pacific. Bible, in press (1996). See main entry under Vanuatu.

BWATOO [BWA] 300 (1982 SIL). Voh-Kone: Baco, Gatope, Oundjo; Poya: Népou. Austronesian, Malayo-Polynesian, Central-Eastern, Eastern Malayo-Polynesian, Oceanic, Central-Eastern Oceanic, Remote Oceanic, New Caledonian, Northern, North, Hmwaveke. May be a dialect of Haveke. Wurm and Hattori treat it as a dialect of Voh-Kone. Investigation needed: intelligibility with Haveke.

CAAC *(MOENEBENG)* [MSQ] 750 (1982 SIL). Pouébo, northeast coast. Austronesian, Malayo-Polynesian, Central-Eastern, Eastern Malayo-Polynesian, Oceanic, Central-Eastern Oceanic, Remote Oceanic, New Caledonian, Northern, Extreme Northern. Dialects: POUÉBO (PWEBO), LA CONCEPTION (ST. LOUIS).

CEMUHÎ *(CAMUHI, CAMUKI, TYAMUHI, WAGAP)* [CAM] 2,500 (1982 SIL). Touho: east coast from Congouma to Wagap and inland valleys. Austronesian, Malayo-Polynesian, Central-Eastern, Eastern Malayo-Polynesian, Oceanic, Central-Eastern Oceanic, Remote Oceanic, New Caledonian, Northern, Central. Dictionary. Grammar. Tonal.

DEHU *(DE'U, DREHU, LIFOU, LIFU)* [DEU] 15,000 (1991 UBS). Lifou, Loyalty Islands. Austronesian, Malayo-Polynesian, Central-Eastern, Eastern Malayo-Polynesian, Oceanic, Central-Eastern Oceanic, Remote Oceanic, Loyalty Islands. Dialects: LOSI, WETE. Min is an old language of respect. Dictionary. Grammar. Word order depends on tense. Bible 1890.

DUMBEA ***(NDUMBEA, NAA DUBEA, DUBEA, DRUBEA)*** [DUF] 1,400 (1982 SIL). Paita on the west coast, Ounia on the east coast. Austronesian, Malayo-Polynesian, Central-Eastern, Eastern Malayo-Polynesian, Oceanic, Central-Eastern Oceanic, Remote Oceanic, New Caledonian, Southern, Extreme Southern. Dictionary. Grammar. Tonal.

FRENCH [FRN] 53,400 first language speakers in New Caledonia (1987), 35.6% of the population. Mainly Noumea. Indo-European, Italic, Romance, Italo-Western, Western, Gallo-Iberian, Gallo-Romance, Gallo-Rhaetian, Oïl, French. National language. Bible 1530-1986. See main entry under France.

FUTUNA, EAST ***(FUTUNIAN)*** [FUD] 3,000 in New Caledonia (1986). Austronesian, Malayo-Polynesian, Central-Eastern, Eastern Malayo-Polynesian, Oceanic, Remote Oceanic, Central Pacific, East Fijian-Polynesian, Polynesian, Nuclear, Samoic-Outlier, Futunic. Not intelligible with Wallisian. Bilingualism in French. Different from Futuna-Aniwa (West Futuna) in Vanuatu. Dictionary. Migrant workers. See main entry under Wallis and Futuna.

FWÂI ***(POAI, YENGEN, YEHEN)*** [FWA] 1,000 (1982 SIL). Hiènghène on the east coast; Ouenguip to Pindache and lower valleys. Austronesian, Malayo-Polynesian, Central-Eastern, Eastern Malayo-Polynesian, Oceanic, Central-Eastern Oceanic, Remote Oceanic, New Caledonian, Northern, North, Nemi. Dictionary.

HAEKE ***(AEKE, 'AEKE)*** [AEK] 100 or fewer (1982 SIL). Voh-Kone: Baco. Austronesian, Malayo-Polynesian, Central-Eastern, Eastern Malayo-Polynesian, Oceanic, Central-Eastern Oceanic, Remote Oceanic, New Caledonian, Haekic. Wurm and Hattori treat it as a dialect of Voh-Kone. Speakers are reported to be bilingual in a neighboring dialect. Nearly extinct.

HAVEKE ***(AVEKE, 'AVEKE)*** [AVE] 300 (1982 SIL). Voh-Kone: Gatope, Oundjo, Tiéta. Austronesian, Malayo-Polynesian, Central-Eastern, Eastern Malayo-Polynesian, Oceanic, Central-Eastern Oceanic, Remote Oceanic, New Caledonian, Northern. Bwatoo may be a dialect. Wurm and Hattori treat it as a dialect of Voh-Kone. Investigation needed: intelligibility with Bwatoo.

HMWAVEKE ***('MOAVEKE, CETA, FAA CETA)*** [MRK] 300 (1982 SIL). Voh: Tiéta. Austronesian, Malayo-Polynesian, Central-Eastern, Eastern Malayo-Polynesian, Oceanic, Central-Eastern Oceanic, Remote Oceanic, New Caledonian, Northern, North, Hmwaveke. Wurm and Hattori treat it as a dialect of Voh-Kone.

IAAI ***(IAI, YAI)*** [IAI] 2,200 (SIL 1982). Ouvéa Island, Loyalty Islands. Austronesian, Malayo-Polynesian, Central-Eastern, Eastern Malayo-Polynesian, Oceanic, Central-Eastern Oceanic, Remote Oceanic, Loyalty Islands. Grammar. VOS. Bible 1901.

JAVANESE, NEW CALEDONIAN [JAS] 6,750 (1987), 4.5% of the population. Noumea. Austronesian, Malayo-Polynesian, Western Malayo-Polynesian, Sundic, Javanese. Bilingualism in French. Young people understand Javanese, but speak French. Migrant workers who came primarily between 1900 and 1938. Since World War II there has been continuing migration in both directions by individuals and families. The language is influenced by French, in contrast to the Javanese of Indonesia, which is influenced by Indonesian. Sunni Muslim.

JAWE ***(NJAWE, DIAHOUE, OUBATCH, UBACH)*** [JAZ] 900 (1982 SIL). Northeast coast from Tchamboenne to Tao and upper valleys. Austronesian, Malayo-Polynesian, Central-Eastern, Eastern Malayo-Polynesian, Oceanic, Central-Eastern Oceanic, Remote Oceanic, New Caledonian, Northern, North, Nemi. Dictionary.

KUMAK ***(KOUMAC, FWA-GOUMAK)*** [NEE] 900 (1982 SIL). Northwest coast of Koumac (Kumak dialect) and Poum (Nenema dialect). Austronesian, Malayo-Polynesian, Central-Eastern, Eastern Malayo-Polynesian, Oceanic, Central-Eastern Oceanic, Remote Oceanic, New Caledonian, Northern, Extreme Northern. Dialects: KUMAK, NENEMA (NELEMA). Grammar.

MEA ***(HA MEA, HAMEHA)*** [MEG] 300 (1982 SIL). La Foa: upper valleys. Austronesian, Malayo-Polynesian, Central-Eastern, Eastern Malayo-Polynesian, Oceanic, Central-Eastern Oceanic, Remote Oceanic, New Caledonian, Southern. Some influences from Tiri. Wurm and Hattori treat it as a dialect of Tiri. Investigation needed: intelligibility with Tiri. Dictionary.

NEKU [NEK] 200 (1982 SIL). Bourail, lower valley. Austronesian, Malayo-Polynesian, Central-Eastern, Eastern Malayo-Polynesian, Oceanic, Central-Eastern Oceanic, Remote Oceanic, New Caledonian, Southern, South, Wailic.

NEMI [NEM] 600 (1982 SIL). East coast: upper valleys north of Hiènghène, and west coast at Voh: Ouélis and upper valley. Austronesian, Malayo-Polynesian, Central-Eastern, Eastern Malayo-Polynesian, Oceanic, Central-Eastern Oceanic, Remote Oceanic, New Caledonian, Northern, North, Nemi. Dictionary.

NENGONE ***(MARÉ, IWATENU)*** [NEN] 6,050 (1982 SIL). Mare, Loyalty Islands. Austronesian, Malayo-Polynesian, Central-Eastern, Eastern Malayo-Polynesian, Oceanic, Central-Eastern Oceanic, Remote Oceanic, Loyalty Islands. Iwatenu is a dialect of respect. Dictionary. Grammar. Word order depends on tense. Bible 1903.

NUMEE ***(NAA NUMEE, KAPONE, TOUAOURU, OUEN, KWENYII, KUNIE, TUAURU, DUAURU, UEN, WEN, NAA-WEE)*** [KDK] 1,800 (1982 SIL). Yate, Touaouru and Goro on main island south coast (Numee dialect), Isle Ouen (Ouen dialect), and Isle of Pines (Kwenyii). Austronesian, Malayo-Polynesian, Central-Eastern, Eastern Malayo-Polynesian, Oceanic, Central-Eastern Oceanic, Remote Oceanic, New Caledonian, Southern, Extreme Southern. Dialects: NUMEE (TOUAOURU), OUEN, KWENYII (KUNIE). Distinct from Nume of Vanuatu. Grammar. Tonal.

NYÂLAYU [YLY] 1,400 (1988). North coast, Belep Island, Arama and Balade. Austronesian, Malayo-Polynesian, Central-Eastern, Eastern Malayo-Polynesian, Oceanic, Central-Eastern Oceanic, Remote Oceanic, New Caledonian, Northern, Extreme Northern. Dialects: YALAYU, BELEP.

OROWE ***(BOEWE)*** [BPK] 750 (1982 SIL). Bourail upper valleys: Ni, Pothé, Bouirou, Azareu. Austronesian, Malayo-Polynesian, Central-Eastern, Eastern Malayo-Polynesian, Oceanic, Central-Eastern Oceanic, Remote Oceanic, New Caledonian, Southern, South, Wailic.

PAICÎ ***(PATI, PAACI, CI, PONERIHOUEN)*** [PRI] 5,500 (1982 SIL). East coast between Poindimié and Ponérihouen and inland valleys. Austronesian, Malayo-Polynesian, Central-Eastern, Eastern Malayo-Polynesian, Oceanic, Central-Eastern Oceanic, Remote Oceanic, New Caledonian, Northern, Central. Dictionary. Tonal. Bible portions 1998.

PIJE ***(PINJE, PINDJE)*** [PIZ] 100 (1982 SIL). Hiènghène: Tipindjé, Tiendanite, and Pouépaï. Austronesian, Malayo-Polynesian, Central-Eastern, Eastern Malayo-Polynesian, Oceanic, Central-Eastern Oceanic, Remote Oceanic, New Caledonian, Northern, North, Nemi. Dictionary.

PWAAMEI ***(POAMEI)*** [PME] 325 (1974 census). Voh: Ouélis, Témala, Tiéta. Austronesian, Malayo-Polynesian, Central-Eastern, Eastern Malayo-Polynesian, Oceanic, Central-Eastern Oceanic, Remote Oceanic, New Caledonian, Northern, North.

PWAPWA ***(POAPOA)*** [POP] 130 (1982 SIL). Voh: Boyen. Austronesian, Malayo-Polynesian, Central-Eastern, Eastern Malayo-Polynesian, Oceanic, Central-Eastern Oceanic, Remote Oceanic, New Caledonian, Northern, North.

TAYO ***("KALDOSH", "CALDOCHE", PATOIS, PATOIS DE ST-LOUIS)*** [CKS] 2,000 (1996 C. Corne). Southern, Ploum, Mont-Dore, and especially Saint Louis, near Noumea, and Paita. Creole, French based. Not intelligible with French. Used as first language by some who are also bilingual in French, and as second language by others, mainly Wallis Islanders. Investigation needed: bilingual proficiency, attitudes. Grammar. The only known writing is personal letters using French orthography.

TIRI ***(CIRI, HA-TIRI, TINRIN)*** [CIR] 600 (1982 SIL). La Foa: lower valleys. Austronesian, Malayo-Polynesian, Central-Eastern, Eastern Malayo-Polynesian, Oceanic, Central-Eastern Oceanic, Remote Oceanic, New Caledonian, Southern, South, Zire-Tiri. Speakers have some understanding of Mea. Investigation needed: intelligibility with Mea. Dictionary. Grammar. SVO, VOS.

UVEAN, WEST ***(FAGA-UVEA)*** [UVE] 1,870 (1982 SIL). Northern and southern parts of Ouvea Atoll, Loyalty Islands. Austronesian, Malayo-Polynesian, Central-Eastern, Eastern Malayo-Polynesian, Oceanic, Central-Eastern Oceanic, Remote Oceanic, Central Pacific, East Fijian-Polynesian, Polynesian, Nuclear, Samoic-Outlier, Futunic. Different from East Uvean on Uvea Island in the Wallis Islands. Dictionary. may be VSO. Atoll. Fishermen; agriculturalists: taro, sweet potato; hunters.

VAMALE ***('MOAEKE, HMWAEKE, PAMALE)*** [MKT] 150 (1982 SIL). East coast: (Vamale dialect) Téganpaïk, Tiouandé; west coast: (Hmwaeke dialect) Voh, Tiéta. Austronesian, Malayo-Polynesian, Central-Eastern, Eastern Malayo-Polynesian, Oceanic, Central-Eastern Oceanic, Remote Oceanic, New Caledonian, Northern. Dialects: VAMALE, HMWAEKE. Wurm and Hattori treat it as a dialect of Voh-Kone. Hmwaeke dialect nearly extinct.

WAAMWANG ***(WAMOANG)*** [WMN] Voh, north. Austronesian, Malayo-Polynesian, Central-Eastern, Eastern Malayo-Polynesian, Oceanic, Central-Eastern Oceanic, Remote Oceanic, New Caledonian, Northern, North, Hmwaveke. Extinct.

WALLISIAN ***(UVEAN, EAST UVEAN, WALLISIEN)*** [WAL] 9,000 in New Caledonia (1982). Noumea. Austronesian, Malayo-Polynesian, Central-Eastern, Eastern Malayo-Polynesian, Oceanic, Remote Oceanic, Central Pacific, East Fijian-Polynesian, Polynesian, Nuclear, Samoic-Outlier, East Uvean-Niuafo'ou. Dialect divergence from Wallis Islands Wallisian is becoming apparent. Limited intelligibility with Tongan. Speakers are originally from Uvea Island in Wallis and Futuna. It has borrowed heavily from Tongan. Tongan is increasingly influenced by English and Wallisian by French. Bible portions 1971. See main entry under Wallis and Futuna.

XÂRÂCÙÙ ***(XARACII, ANESU, HARANEU, KANALA, CANALA)*** [ANE] 3,500 (1982 SIL). Canala, east coast and inland valleys. Austronesian, Malayo-Polynesian, Central-Eastern, Eastern Malayo-Polynesian, Oceanic, Central-Eastern Oceanic, Remote Oceanic, New Caledonian, Southern, South, Xaracuu-Xaragure. Dictionary. SVO, VOS.

XARAGURE ***(ARAGURE, 'ARAGURE, HARAGURE, THIO)*** [ARG] 950 (1982 SIL). Thio, east coast, and Ouinane on west coast. Austronesian, Malayo-Polynesian, Central-Eastern, Eastern Malayo-Polynesian,

Oceanic, Central-Eastern Oceanic, Remote Oceanic, New Caledonian, Southern, South, Xaracuu-Xaragure. SVO, VOS.

YUAGA ***(YUANGA, THUANGA, JUANGA, NUA, NYUA)*** [NUA] 2,000 (1991 UBS). Inland valleys between Gomen (Thuanga dialect) and Bondé (Juanga dialect). Austronesian, Malayo-Polynesian, Central-Eastern, Eastern Malayo-Polynesian, Oceanic, Central-Eastern Oceanic, Remote Oceanic, New Caledonian, Northern, Extreme Northern. Dialects: THUANGA, JUANGA. Grammar.

ZIRE ***(ZIRA, SIRHE, SICHE, SÎSHËË, NERË)*** [SIH] Bourail, coastal plain. Austronesian, Malayo-Polynesian, Central-Eastern, Eastern Malayo-Polynesian, Oceanic, Central-Eastern Oceanic, Remote Oceanic, New Caledonian, Southern, South, Zire-Tiri. Zire is reported to be extinct. No mother tongue speakers. There are apparently a few who learned it as second language. Grammar. Extinct.

NEW ZEALAND

National or official languages: English, Maori. 3,796,000 (1998 UN). Two main islands, several smaller ones. Literacy rate 99%. Also includes Afrikaans, Assyrian Neo-Aramaic, Hakka Chinese, Yue Chinese 20,000, Fijian 6,671, Hindi 11,200, Iu Mien 35, Japanese 3,000, Korean, Latvian, Niue 5,688, Pukapuka 1,050, Rakahanga-Manihiki 2,500, Rarotongan 25,000, Samoan 50,000, Tahitian 262, Tokelauan 1,737, Tongan 3,965, Tuvaluan 500, Arabic 4,000, other Chinese 600, 15,000 others from India. Information mainly from S. Wurm and S. Hattori 1981; N. Besnier 1992; D. T. Tryon 1995. Christian, secular. Blind population 3,687. Deaf institutions: 29. Data accuracy estimate: A2. The number of languages listed for New Zealand is 4. Of those, 3 are living languages and 1 is a second language without mother tongue speakers. Diversity index 0.10.

ENGLISH [ENG] 3,213,000 in New Zealand (1987), 90% of the population. Indo-European, Germanic, West, English. National language. Bible 1382-1989. See main entry under United Kingdom.

MAORI ***(NEW ZEALAND MAORI)*** [MBF] 50,000 to 70,000 speakers (1991 Fishman, p. 231), 100,000 who understand it, but do not speak it, out of 310,000 or more Maori people (1995 Maori Language Commission). Far north, east coast, North Island. Austronesian, Malayo-Polynesian, Central- Eastern, Eastern Malayo-Polynesian, Oceanic, Central-Eastern Oceanic, Remote Oceanic, Central Pacific, East Fijian-Polynesian, Polynesian, Nuclear, East, Central, Tahitic. Dialects: NORTH AUCKLAND, SOUTH ISLAND, TARANAKI, WANGANUI, BAY OF PLENTY, ROTORUA-TAUPO, MORIORI. Formerly fragmented into a number of regional dialects, some of which diverged quite radically from what has become the standard dialect. 71% lexical similarity with Hawaiian, 57% with Samoan. All or most use English as second language. 30,000 to 50,000 adult speakers over 15 years old (1995 Maori Language Commission). 33% of fluent speakers are over 60 years old, 38% are between 45 and 59. Until the 20th century spoken throughout New Zealand. The Moriori dialect in the Chatham Islands is extinct. Official language. VSO. 322 government-funded Maori language schools, including for pre-schoolers. Volcanic plateau. Christian. Bible 1858-1952.

NEW ZEALAND SIGN LANGUAGE [NZS] Deaf sign language. The first school for the deaf was established in 1878. Sign language used since the 1800s. It developed informally among deaf people because the oralist method only was used in schools. It has some features in common with British sign languages and some from other countries. Some signed interpretation used in court and at important public events. There is a committee on national sign language. There is a manual system for spelling. Investigation needed: intelligibility with British Sign Language, Australian Sign Languages. Dictionary. Grammar. TV.

PITCAIRN-NORFOLK ***(PITCAIRN ENGLISH)*** [PIH] Cant, English-Tahitian. Developed from mutineers settling on Pitcairn in 1790. Some people were removed to Norfolk in 1859. An in-group language used to assist in the preservation of identity. People speak standard English as mother tongue. Christian. Second language only. See main entry under Norfolk Island.

NIUE

National or official language: English. 2,082 (1997 Honolulu Advertiser). One coral island, 100 square miles. A New Zealand self-governing territory. Literacy rate 99% to 100%. Information mainly from N. Besnier 1992. Christian, Baha'i. Data accuracy estimate: B. The number of languages listed for Niue is 2. Of those, both are living languages. Diversity index 0.00.

ENGLISH [ENG] Second language speakers in Niue: 2,082. Indo-European, Germanic, West, English. National language. Bible 1535-1989. See main entry under United Kingdom.

NIUE ***(NIUEAN, "NIUEFEKAI")*** [NIQ] 2,240 in Niue (1991), 97.4% of the population. Population total all countries 8,000. Also spoken in Cook Islands, New Zealand, Tonga. Austronesian, Malayo-Polynesian, Central-Eastern, Eastern Malayo-Polynesian, Oceanic, Central-Eastern Oceanic, Remote Oceanic,

Central Pacific, East Fijian-Polynesian, Polynesian, Tongic. Linguistically close to Tongan. Christian. Bible 1904.

NORFOLK ISLAND

National or official language: English. 1,700 (1994 Honolulu Advertiser). An External Territory of Australian. Information mainly from M. Adler 1977. The number of languages listed for Norfolk Island is 2. Of those, 1 is a living language and 1 is a second language without mother tongue speakers. Diversity index 0.00.

ENGLISH [ENG] 1,678 in Norfolk Island (1980 Government report). Indo-European, Germanic, West, English. National language. Bible 1535-1989. See main entry under United Kingdom.

PITCAIRN-NORFOLK ***(PITCAIRN ENGLISH)*** [PIH] (580 on Norfolk Island; 1989 Holm). Norfolk Island, Pitcairn Island. There are some second generation Pitcairn Islanders in Australia and New Zealand. Also spoken in Australia, Fiji, New Zealand, Pitcairn. Cant, English-Tahitian. Dialect: NORFOLK ENGLISH. Slightly different variety than in Pitcairn. An in-group language used to assist in the preservation of identity. People speak Standard British English as mother tongue. Developed from mutineers settling on Pitcairn in 1790. Some were removed to Norfolk in 1859. Agriculturalists: breadfruit, banana, pineapple, passion fruit, watermelon, mango, custard apple, orange, lime, lemon, grapefruit. Second language only.

NORTHERN MARIANA ISLANDS

Commonwealth of the Northern Mariana Islands (USA). National or official languages: Carolinian, Chamorro, English. 70,000 (1998 UN). Capital: Saipan. Includes Rota, Aguiguan, Tinian, Saipan, Farallon de Medinilla, Anatahan, Sariguan, Guguan, Alamagan, Pagan, Agrihan, Asuncion, Maug Islands, Farallon de Pajaros. Also includes Japanese 1,600, Korean 5,200, Sonsorol, Chinese 5,800, people from the Philippines 28,000. Information mainly from F. Jackson 1983; B. Bendor 1971, 1996; K. Rehg 1991, 1996; J. Ellis 1996-1999. Data accuracy estimate: B. The number of languages listed for Northern Mariana Islands is 4. Of those, all are living languages. Diversity index 0.58.

CAROLINIAN ***(SAIPAN CAROLINIAN, SOUTHERN CAROLINIAN)*** [CAL] 3,000 (1990 census). Saipan, Anatahan, and Agrihan islands, Carolines. Austronesian, Malayo-Polynesian, Central-Eastern, Eastern Malayo-Polynesian, Oceanic, Central-Eastern Oceanic, Remote Oceanic, Micronesian, Micronesian Proper, Ponapeic-Trukic, Trukic. Southern Carolinian has 95% lexical similarity with Satawalese, 88% with Woleaian and Puluwatese; 81% with Mortlockese; 78% with Chuukese, 74% with Ulithian. All speakers on Saipan are bilingual in Chamorro. Most also speak English. Semi-official status. Active language use. No published grammar. National language. Dictionary. Fishermen mainly; agriculturalists: vegetables; livestock: cattle, pigs, goats.

CHAMORRO ***(TJAMORO)*** [CJD] 14,205 in Northern Mariana Islands (1990), including 11,466 on on Saipan (1990), 1,502 on Rota (1990), 1,231 on Tinian (1990); 62,500 on Guam (1991 Bender and Rehg); 90,000 including second language users (1987 UBS). Alamagan Island. Austronesian, Malayo-Polynesian, Western Malayo-Polynesian, Chamorro. Slight dialect differences. Some bilingualism in English. It is a trade language on Saipan. National language. Dictionary. Grammar. Christian. Bible portions 1908-1992. See main entry under Guam.

ENGLISH [ENG] Indo-European, Germanic, West, English. National language. Bible 1535-1989. See main entry under United Kingdom.

TANAPAG ***(NORTHERN CAROLINIAN, TALLABWOG)*** [TPV] West central coast of Saipan, Tanapag community. Austronesian, Malayo-Polynesian, Central-Eastern, Eastern Malayo-Polynesian, Oceanic, Central-Eastern Oceanic, Remote Oceanic, Micronesian, Micronesian Proper, Ponapeic-Trukic, Trukic. Close to Namonuito of Micronesia. Speakers have limited bilingual proficiency in English or Chamorro. Members of the ethnic group under 30 do not speak Tanapag, but Chamorro. They are working to promote Tanapag.

PALAU

Republic of Palau. Republic of Belaw. Formerly part of U.S. Trust Territory of the Pacific Islands. National or official languages: Palauan, English. 19,000 (1998 UN). Capital: Koror. 200 islands. Literacy rate 85%. Also includes Japanese, Chinese, other people from Asia and the Pacific. Information mainly from B. W. Bender 1996; K. L. Rehg 1996; J. Ellis 1996. Data accuracy estimate: A2. The number of languages listed for Palau is 4. Of those, all are living languages. Diversity index 0.07.

ENGLISH [ENG] Indo-European, Germanic, West, English. National language. Bible 1535-1989. See main entry under United Kingdom.

PALAUAN ***(BELAUAN, PALAU)*** [PLU] Population total both countries 15,000 (1991 UBS). Palau Islands and Guam, west Carolines. Also spoken in Guam. Austronesian, Malayo-Polynesian, Western Malayo-Polynesian, Palauan. Little dialect variation. Active language use. National language. Dictionary. Grammar. SVO. Agriculturalists: taro, cassava; fishermen; government employees; merchants. NT 1964, in press (1996).

SONSOROL ***(SONSOROLESE)*** [SOV] 600 (1981 Wurm and Hattori). Approximately 60 on the outer islands: Sonsoral 29, Pulo Anna 25, Merir 5. The number of outer islanders resident on the main island of Palau is unclear from the 1990 census. Population total both countries 600 or more. Pulo Anna, Merir, Helen, and Sonsorol islands. Also spoken in Northern Mariana Islands. Austronesian, Malayo-Polynesian, Central-Eastern, Eastern Malayo-Polynesian, Oceanic, Central-Eastern Oceanic, Remote Oceanic, Micronesian, Micronesian Proper, Ponapeic-Trukic, Trukic. Dialects: SONSOROLESE, PULO ANNA. There are significant linguistic differences between the Tobian variety and Sonsorolese; similar to or greater than differences between, e.g., Puluwat and Namonuito. 50% intelligibility with Woleaian, less with the remainder of the Trukic continuum. 69% lexical similarity with Ulithi. Reported to be completely bilingual in Palauan. Investigation needed: intelligibility with Tobian, bilingual proficiency in Palauan, attitudes. Grammar.

TOBIAN ***(TOBI, HATOBOHEI)*** [TOX] 22 or more (1995 J. Ellis SIL). Tobi (Hatobohei) Island and near the capitol. Austronesian, Malayo-Polynesian, Central-Eastern, Eastern Malayo-Polynesian, Oceanic, Central-Eastern Oceanic, Remote Oceanic, Micronesian, Micronesian Proper, Ponapeic-Trukic, Trukic. There are significant linguistic differences between Tobian and Sonsorolese, although they are often treated as one language. Reported to be highly bilingual in Palauan and bicultural. Investigation needed: bilingual proficiency in Palauan.

PAPUA NEW GUINEA

National or official languages: Hiri Motu, Tok Pisin, English. 4,600,000 (1998 UN), 78% Papuan, 20% Melanesian. 600 islands. Literacy rate 32% to 43%. Also includes Chinese, people from the Philippines, India. Information mainly from J. C. Anceaux 1961; A. Healey 1964; K. Franklin 1968; G. Sankoff 1968; J. A. Z'Graggen 1969, 1971, 1975; K. McElhanon 1970, 1978; B. Hooley 1971; B. Hooley and K. McElhanon 1970; R. D. Shaw 1973, 1981; S. Wurm and S. Hattori 1981; M. Ross 1988; L. Carrington 1996; SIL 1971-1999. Christian, traditional religion, cargo cult, Baha'i. Blind population 12,500. Data accuracy estimate: A2. The number of languages listed for Papua New Guinea is 832. Of those, 823 are living languages and 9 are extinct. Diversity index 0.99.

ABAGA [ABG] 5 (1994 SIL). Ethnic group: 1,200 (1975 SIL). Eastern Highlands Province, Goroka District. Trans-New Guinea, Main Section, Central and Western, Huon-Finisterre, Finisterre, Abaga. Bilingualism in Kamano, Benabena. Nearly extinct.

ABASAKUR [ABW] 761 (1981 Wurm and Hattori). Madang Province. Trans-New Guinea, Madang-Adelbert Range, Adelbert Range, Pihom-Isumrud-Mugil, Pihom, Omosan. Related language: Koguman.

ABAU ***(GREEN RIVER)*** [AAU] 4,545 (1981 Wurm and Hattori) in 28 villages. Sandaun Province, Green River District, Sepik and Green rivers. Not in Irian Jaya, Indonesia. Sepik-Ramu, Sepik, Upper Sepik, Abau. Grammar. Bible portions 1990.

ABU ***(ADJORA, ADJORIA, AZAO)*** [ADO] 2,400 (1986 PBT). Madang Province, East Sepik Province, Ramu River. Sepik-Ramu, Ramu, Ramu Proper, Grass, Grass Proper. Bible portions 1969.

ADZERA ***(AZERA, ATZERA, ACIRA)*** [AZR] 20,675 (1988 Holzknecht), including 367 Ngariawan (1978 McElhanon), 497 Sarasira (1988 Holzknecht), 990 Sukurum (1990). Morobe Province, Markham Valley, Kaiapit District, Leron River. Austronesian, Malayo-Polynesian, Central-Eastern, Eastern Malayo-Polynesian, Oceanic, Western Oceanic, North New Guinea, Huon Gulf, Markham, Upper, Adzera. Dialects: YARUS, AMARI, AZERA, NGAROWAPUM, TSUMANGGORUN, GURUF-NGARIAWANG (NGARIAWAN), SARASIRA (SIRASIRA), SUKURUM. The dialects form a chain. Bilingualism in Tok Pisin. Grammar. NT 1976.

AEKYOM ***(AWIN, AIWIN, AKIUM, WEST AWIN)*** [AWI] 8,000 (1987 UBS). Western Province, Kiunga area. Trans-New Guinea, Main Section, Central and Western, Central and South New Guinea-Kutubuan, Central and South New Guinea, Awin-Pare. Dialects: NORTH AWIN, SOUTH AWIN, EAST AWIN. Literacy rate in first language: Less than 5%. Literacy rate in second language: 5% to 15%. NT 1987.

AGARABI ***(AGARABE, BARE)*** [AGD] 20,000 (1998 SIL). Eastern Highlands Province, Kainantu District. Trans-New Guinea, Main Section, Central and Western, East New Guinea Highlands, Eastern, Gadsup-Auyana-Awa. Close to Gadsup. Grammar. SOV. Literacy rate in first language:

Less than 5%. Literacy rate in second language: 15% to 25%. Savannah. Mountain slope. Swidden agriculturalists. 1,640 meters. Bible portions 1970.

AGI [AIF] 700 (1993 SIL). Sandaun Province. Torricelli, Wapei-Palei, Palei.

AGOB *(DABU)* [KIT] 3,500 (1990 SIL). Western Province, along the Pahoturi River and southern coast. Trans-New Guinea, Trans-Fly-Bulaka River, Trans-Fly, Pahoturi. Dialects: AGOB, ENDE, KAWAM. One end of a dialect chain stretching to Idi. Ende and Kawam are closest to Agob. Distinct from, but related to Idi (Tame) and Waia. 3 government schools. SOV. Literacy rate in first language: Less than 5%. Literacy rate in second language: 5% to 15%. Savannah, lowland forest, palm swamp. Riverine, Coastal. Swidden agriculturalists, hunters. 0 to 5 meters.

AIKLEP *(MOEWEHAFEN, EKLEP, AGERLEP, LOKO)* [MWG] 3,697 (1991 SIL). West New Britain Province, southwest coast and inland, A Viklo Island near Kandrian. Austronesian, Malayo-Polynesian, Central-Eastern, Eastern Malayo-Polynesian, Oceanic, Western Oceanic, North New Guinea, Ngero-Vitiaz, Vitiaz, Southwest New Britain, Arawe-Pasismanua, Arawe, West Arawe. Dialect chain with Gimi and Apalik. Investigation needed: intelligibility with Gimi, Apalik.

AIKU *(MINENDON, MENANDON, MALEK)* [MZF] 750 to 900 (1990 SIL). Sandaun Province, Maimai Namblo Division, Wemil village, and more in West Palei Division. Torricelli, Wapei-Palei, Palei.

AIMELE *(KWARE)* [AIL] 500 (1981 Shaw). Southwest corner of Southern Highlands Province around Mt. Bosavi; Western Province around Lake Campbell. Most have moved to Wawoi Falls area of Western Province. Trans-New Guinea, Main Section, Central and Western, Central and South New Guinea-Kutubuan, Central and South New Guinea, Bosavi.

AINBAI [AIC] 110 to 250 (1993 SIL). Sandaun Province, Vanimo District, south of Bewani station. 2 villages. Trans-New Guinea, Northern, Border, Bewani. 30% lexical similarity with Manem, 25% with Pagi.

AIOME *(AYOM)* [AKI] 751 (1981 Wurm and Hattori). Madang Province, 70 miles west of Madang city, scattered houses. Sepik-Ramu, Ramu, Ramu Proper, Annaberg, Aian. Mountain slope, valleys. Agriculturalists: sweet potato, pigs, sugar cane, bananas. 50 to 100 meters. Traditional religion.

AION [AEW] 857 (1981 Wurm and Hattori). East Sepik Province. Sepik-Ramu, Ramu, Ramu Proper, Grass, Grass Proper.

AK [AKQ] 83 (1981 Wurm and Hattori). Sandaun Province. Sepik-Ramu, Sepik, Yellow River. Closest to Namia and Awun.

AKOLET [AKT] 954 (1982 SIL). West New Britain Province, southwest coast, including Pililo, Kambun, and Sauren. Austronesian, Malayo-Polynesian, Central-Eastern, Eastern Malayo-Polynesian, Oceanic, Western Oceanic, North New Guinea, Ngero-Vitiaz, Vitiaz, Southwest New Britain, Arawe-Pasismanua, Arawe, East Arawe. Dialect chain. Bilingualism in Pidgin, English. 3 primary schools, provincial high school, vocational school. Investigation needed: bilingual proficiency in Arove, intelligibility with Arove. Tropical forest. Raised coral coast.

AKOYE *(AKOINKAKE, LOHIKI, OBI, MAI-HEA-RI, MAIHIRI, ANGOYA, AKOYI)* [MIW] 800 (1998 SIL). Gulf Province, Kaberofe District, valleys between the Nabo Range and the Albert Mountains, Lohiki River. The largest group is living in a settlement in Kerema. Trans-New Guinea, Main Section, Central and Western, Angan, Angan Proper. Similar to Tainae. SOV; postpositions. Literacy rate in first language: Less then 5%. Literacy rate in second language: Less than 5%. Tropical forest. Mountain slope, coastal plain. Agriculturalists. 0 to 3,000 feet. Traditional religion.

AKRUKAY [AFI] 191 (1981 Wurm and Hattori). Madang Province. Sepik-Ramu, Ramu, Ramu Proper, Goam, Tamolan.

ALAMBLAK [AMP] 1,500 (1987 SIL). 9 villages (900 speakers) on Middle Karawari and Wagupmeri rivers. Another dialect has 4 villages (400 speakers) near Kuvanmas Lake. East Sepik Province, Angoram District. Sepik-Ramu, Sepik, Sepik Hill, Alamblak. Dialects: KUVENMAS, KARAWARI. Karawari is distinct from Karawari in the Pondo branch. Grammar. Literacy rate in first language: 15% to 25%. Literacy rate in second language: 15% to 25%. Traditional religion, Christian. Bible portions 1974-1998.

ALATIL *(ARU, ERU)* [ALX] 125 (1981 Wurm and Hattori). Sandaun Province. Torricelli, Wapei-Palei, Palei.

ALEKANO *(GAHUKU, GAFUKU, GAHUKU-GAMA)* [GAH] 25,000 (1999 E. Deibler SIL). Eastern Highlands Province, Goroka District, centered around the town of Goroka. Trans-New Guinea, Main Section, Central and Western, East New Guinea Highlands, East-Central, Gahuku-Benabena. Close to Tokano, Dano, Yaweyuha, Siane, Benabena. All speakers are probably fluent in Tok Pisin. They use it in the market or streets along with Alekano. Those under 35 who have had extensive schooling may know English, but do not use it on the streets. About 1/3 of speakers do not teach the language to their children. Grammar. Literacy rate in first language: 25% to 50%. Literacy rate in second language: 50% to 75%. Christian. NT 1973-1986.

AMA *(SAWIYANU)* [AMM] 475 (1990 census). East Sepik Province, Ambunti District, Waniap Creek, south of the Sepik River, south of Namia. Villages: Ama (Wopolu I, Wopolu II (Nokonufa), Kauvia (Kawiya), Yonuwai; all on hills rising from the swamp. Left May. Dialects have converged into one. Semi-nomadic. SOV. Literacy rate in first language: 25% to 50%. Literacy rate in second language: 15% to 25%. Hunter-gatherers; sago. 100 to 200 meters. Christian, traditional religion. NT 1990.

AMAIMON [ALI] 366 (1981 Wurm and Hattori). Madang Province. Trans-New Guinea, Madang-Adelbert Range, Adelbert Range, Pihom-Isumrud-Mugil, Pihom, Amaimon.

AMAL *(ALAI)* [AAD] 388 (1981 Wurm and Hattori). Sandaun Province, on Wagana River, near the confluence with Wanibe Creek. Sepik-Ramu, Sepik, Upper Sepik, Iwam.

AMANAB [AMN] 4,000 (1982 SIL). Sandaun Province, Amanab District. Not in Irian Jaya. Trans-New Guinea, Northern, Border, Waris. Grammar. SOV. Literacy rate in first language: 25% to 50%. Literacy rate in second language: 25% to 50%. Tropical forest. Mountain slope. Swidden agriculturalists. 300 to 600 meters. Traditional religion, Christian. Bible portions 1996-1997.

AMARA *(LONGA, BIBLING)* [AIE] 200 (1998 SIL). West New Britain Province, northwest coast. Austronesian, Malayo-Polynesian, Central-Eastern, Eastern Malayo-Polynesian, Oceanic, Western Oceanic, North New Guinea, Ngero-Vitiaz, Vitiaz, Southwest New Britain, Amara. Related to Mouk-Aria and Lamogai. Close to 100% bilingualism with Bariai. Because of intermarriage, most children learn Bariai first, and many never become proficient in Amara. Also high bilingualism in Tok Pisin. Investigation needed: bilingual proficiency in Bariai. Dictionary.

AMBULAS *(ABULAS, ABELAM)* [ABT] 44,000 (1991 SIL), including 27,000 in Wosera (1991 SIL), 9,000 in Maprik (1991 SIL), 8,000 in Wingei (1991 SIL). East Sepik Province, Maprik District. Sepik-Ramu, Sepik, Middle Sepik, Ndu. Dialects: MAPRIK, WINGEI, WOSERA-KAMU, WOSERA-MAMU. OSV. Literacy rate in first language: 25% to 50%. Literacy rate in second language: 50% to 75%. Tropical forest. Riverine, narrow valleys. Swidden agriculturalists. 250 to 500 meters. Traditional religion, Christian. NT 1983-1996.

AMELE *(AMALE)* [AMI] 5,300 (1987 SIL). Madang Province, Madang District, in the hills up from Astrolabe Bay, between the Gum and Gogol rivers. 40 hamlets. Trans-New Guinea, Madang-Adelbert Range, Madang, Mabuso, Gum. Dialects: HUAR, JAGAHALA, HAIJA. Related languages: Gumalu, Sihan, Isebe, Bau, Panim. Grammar. SOV. Literacy rate in first language: 75% to 100%. Literacy rate in second language: 75% to 100%. NT 1997.

AMPEELI-WOJOKESO *(AMPALE, AMPELE, AMBARI, SAFEYOKA)* [APZ] 2,388 (1980 census). Morobe Province, Kaiapit, Lae-Wamba, and Menyamya districts. Trans-New Guinea, Main Section, Central and Western, Angan, Angan Proper. Dialects: AIEWOMBA, WAJAKES (WOJOKESO). Bilingualism in Tok Pisin, Yabem. Grammar. SOV. Literacy rate in first language: 5% to 15%. Literacy rate in second language: 25% to 50%. Tropical forest. Mountain slope. Swidden agriculturalists. 1,000 to 1,500 meters. Traditional religion, Christian. NT 1989.

AMTO *(KI, SIWAI, SIAWI, SIAFLI)* [AMT] 230 (1981 Wurm and Hattori). Sandaun Province, Amanab District and Rocky Peak District, south of the Upper Sepik River, toward the headwaters of the Left May River on the Samaia River. Villages: Amto, Habiyon (Sernion). Amto-Musan. Dialects: AMTO, SIAWI. Acculturating rapidly. SOV. Literacy rate in first language: 30% to 35%. Literacy rate in second language: 50% to 60%. Tropical forest. Mountain slope, foothills. Hunter-gatherers. 230 to 500 feet. Traditional religion, Christian. Bible portions 1992-1998.

ANAM *(PONDOMA)* [PDA] 684 (1990 census). Madang Province, villages around Josephstaal. Trans-New Guinea, Madang-Adelbert Range, Adelbert Range, Josephstaal-Wanang, Josephstaal, Pomoikan. Bilingualism in Anamgura, Mum, Tok Pisin. Different villages are shifting to Anamgura, Mum, or Tok Pisin. Investigation needed: bilingual proficiency in Anamgura, Mum, Tok Pisin. Mountain slope, riverine. Swidden agriculturalists, sago.

ANAMGURA *(IKUNDUN, MINDIVI)* [IMI] 1,253 (1990 census). Madang Province, northwest of Josephstaal. Trans-New Guinea, Madang-Adelbert Range, Adelbert Range, Josephstaal-Wanang, Josephstaal, Pomoikan.

ANDARUM [AOD] 1,084 (1981 Wurm and Hattori). Madang Province. Sepik-Ramu, Ramu, Ramu Proper, Goam, Ataitan. Related to Igom.

ANDRA-HUS *(AHUS, HA'US)* [ANX] 810 (1977 Lincoln). Manus Province, Andra and Hus islands. Austronesian, Malayo-Polynesian, Central-Eastern, Eastern Malayo-Polynesian, Oceanic, Admiralty Islands, Eastern, Manus, East. Investigation needed: bilingual proficiency in Kurti, intelligibility with Ponam.

ANEM *(KARAIAI)* [ANZ] 500 to 600 (1991 SIL). West New Britain Province, northwest coast and inland. East Papuan, Yele-Solomons-New Britain, New Britain, Anem. Speakers in one village among the Bariai use Bariai as second language. Investigation needed: bilingual proficiency in Bariai.

ANEME WAKE *(ABIE, ABIA)* [ABY] 650 (1990 SIL). Oro Province, Afore District, both sides of Owen Stanley Range, Central Province; north from Ianu along Foasi and Domara creeks. Trans-New

Guinea, Main Section, Eastern, Central and Southeastern, Yareban. Dialects: MORI, BUNIABURA, AUWAKA, JARI, DOMA. 65% to 73% lexical similarity with Moikodi (closest). Bilingualism in Motu, Yareba. Foothills. NT 1988.

ANGAATIHA ***(LANGIMAR, ANGATAHA, ANGAATIYA, ANGAATAHA)*** [AGM] 1,200 (1991 SIL). Morobe Province, Menyamya District. Trans-New Guinea, Main Section, Central and Western, Angan. Grammar. SOV. Tropical forest. Mountain slope. Swidden agriculturalists. 1,400 to 1,600 meters. Bible portions 1976-1980.

ANGAL ***(EAST ANGAL, MENDI)*** [AGE] 10,000 (1971 ACTNM). Southern Highlands Province, Mendi area, north into Mendi Valley, west into Lai Valley, east bank, west of Mt. Glouwe. Trans-New Guinea, Main Section, Central and Western, East New Guinea Highlands, West-Central, Angal-Kewa. SOV, Time-Subject-Object-Location-Verb. Highland forest. Mountain slope. Swidden agriculturalists. 4,500 to 8,500 feet. Bible portions 1990.

ANGAL ENEN ***(SOUTH ANGAL HENENG, SOUTH MENDI, NEMBI)*** [AOE] 22,000 (1995 UBS). Southern Highlands Province, 10 to 12 km. south of Nipa, north of the Erave River, east of Lake Kutubu, west of Lai Valley. Trans-New Guinea, Main Section, Central and Western, East New Guinea Highlands, West-Central, Angal-Kewa. Dialect: MEGI. Grammar. SOV, Time-Subject-Object-Location-Verb. Highland forest. Mountain slope. Swidden agriculturalists. 4,500 to 8,500 feet. Bible portions 1968-1996.

ANGAL HENENG ***(AUGU, WEST MENDI, WEST ANGAL HENENG, AGARAR, WAGE, KATINJA)*** [AKH] 40,000 (1994 V. Schlatter SPIM). Southern Highlands Province, south of Margarima and Kandep, north of Lake Butubu, west of the Lai Valley. Trans-New Guinea, Main Section, Central and Western, East New Guinea Highlands, West-Central, Angal-Kewa. Dialects: WAOLA (WALA), AUGU, NIPA. SOV, Time-Subject-Object-Location-Verb. Highland forest. Mountain slope. Swidden agriculturalists. 4,500 to 8,500. NT 1978.

ANGOR ***(WATAPOR, SENAGI, ANGGOR)*** [AGG] 1,266 including 836 in Nai, 430 in Samanai(1990 census). Sandaun Province, Amanab District. 11 villages. Trans-New Guinea, Senagi. Dialects: NAI (CENTRAL ANGOR), SAMANAI (SOUTHERN ANGOR). Grammar. SOV. Literacy rate in second language: 15% to 25%. Tropical forest. Lowland foothills. Swidden agriculturalists. 150 to 500 meters. NT, in press (1999).

ANGORAM ***(PONDO, TJIMUNDO, OLEM)*** [AOG] 6,200 (1981 Wurm and Hattori). East Sepik Province, along lower Sepik River, Angoram District. Sepik-Ramu, Nor-Pondo, Pondo. Bilingualism in Tok Pisin.

ANJAM ***(BOGATI, BOM, BOGAJIM, BOGADJIM, LALOK)*** [BOJ] 1,300 (1986 SIL). Madang Province, Astrolabe Bay District. Trans-New Guinea, Madang-Adelbert Range, Madang, Rai Coast, Mindjim. SOV. Tropical forest. Coastal. Swidden agriculturalists. Sea level. Christian, traditional religion, cargo cult. Bible portions 1987-1989.

ANKAVE ***(ANGAVE)*** [AAK] 1,600 (1987 SIL). Gulf Province, Kerema District, in the valleys of the Mbwei and Swanson rivers. Trans-New Guinea, Main Section, Central and Western, Angan, Angan Proper. Dialects: SAWUVE, WIYAGWA, WUNAVAI, MIYATNU, ANKAI, BU'U. Literacy rate in first language: Less than 5%. Literacy rate in second language: Less than 5%. Traditional religion. NT 1991.

ANOR [ANJ] 574 (1975 Z'Graggen). Madang Province. Sepik-Ramu, Ramu, Ramu Proper, Annaberg, Aian.

ANUKI ***(GABOBORA)*** [AUI] 542 (census). North coast, Cape Vogel, Milne Bay Province. Austronesian, Malayo-Polynesian, Central-Eastern, Eastern Malayo-Polynesian, Oceanic, Western Oceanic, Papuan Tip, Nuclear, North Papuan Mainland-D'Entrecasteaux, Anuki. 49% to 57% lexical similarity with Gapapaiwa (closest).

AP MA ***(KAMBOT, AP MA BOTIN, BOTIN)*** [KBX] 7,000 (1990 UBS). Angoram District, East Sepik Province. Sepik-Ramu, Ramu, Ramu Proper, Grass, Grass Proper. Dialect: KAMBARAMBA. Bible portions 1994.

APALI ***(EMERUM, APAL)*** [ENA] 600 (1992 M. Wade PBT). Madang Province, upper Ramu River area, Aiome District. Trans-New Guinea, Madang-Adelbert Range, Adelbert Range, Josephstaal-Wanang, Wanang, Emuan. Dialects: AKI, ACI. Literacy rate in first language: 5% to 25%. Literacy rate in second language: 25% to 50%. Bible portions 1993.

APALIK ***(PALIK, AMBUL)*** [PLI] 374 (1979 census). West New Britain Province, southwest coast and inland. Austronesian, Malayo-Polynesian, Central-Eastern, Eastern Malayo-Polynesian, Oceanic, Western Oceanic, North New Guinea, Ngero-Vitiaz, Vitiaz, Southwest New Britain, Arawe-Pasismanua, Arawe, West Arawe. In a dialect chain with Gimi and Aiklep. Investigation needed: intelligibility with Gimi, Aiklep.

APOS ***(KWANGA, GAWANGA, WOMSAK)*** [APO] 500 (1996 SIL). East Sepik Province, extending beyond the western boundary of Maprik District; Makru-Klaplei Division, Nuku District. Sepik-Ramu, Sepik, Middle Sepik, Nukuma. Dialects: TAU, BONGOMAISI (BONGAMAISE). OSV. Literacy rate in first language: 5% to 15%. Literacy rate in second language: 15% to 25%. Tropical forest. Plains. Swidden agriculturalists. 50 to 60 meters.

ARAFUNDI ***(ALFENDIO)*** [ARF] 733 (1981 Wurm and Hattori). East Sepik Province, on the Arafundi River. Sepik-Ramu, Ramu, Ramu Proper, Arafundi. Dialect: MEAKAMBUT. Meakambut may be a separate language.

ARAMMBA ***(ARAMBA, SERKISETAVI, UPPER MOREHEAD, SERKI)*** [STK] 900 (1998 SIL). Western Province, Morehead Subprovince, southwest of Suki. Trans-New Guinea, Trans-Fly-Bulaka River, Trans-Fly, Morehead and Upper Maro Rivers, Tonda. 2 community schools. Literacy rate in first language: Less than 5%. Literacy rate in second language: Less than 5%. Swamp, savannah. Below 300 meters.

ARAPESH, BUMBITA ***(WERI)*** [AON] 4,000 (1994 R. Conrad SIL) in 13 villages (1986 PBT). East Sepik Province, Maprik District, Torricelli Mountains, south of Wom. Torricelli, Kombio-Arapesh, Arapesh. Dialects: BONAHOI, URITA, TIMINGIR, WERIL, WERIR. Weril and Werir are inherently intelligible to each other's speakers. 21% lexical similarity with Southern Arapesh, 30% with Bukiyip. Bilingualism in Tok Pisin. Middle-aged and older speakers use Bumbita, and in 2 villages younger members use it. Elsewhere younger members mainly use Tok Pisin. Literacy rate in first language: 15% to 25%. Literacy rate in second language: 25% to 50%. For beginning literacy Weril and Werir use different materials. Mountain slope. Agriculturalists: taro, tobacco; animal husbandry: pigs.

ARAWUM [AWM] 75 (1981 Wurm and Hattori). Madang Province. Trans-New Guinea, Madang-Adelbert Range, Madang, Rai Coast, Kabenau. Related languages: Siroi, Pulabu, Kolom, Lemio. Investigation needed: intelligibility.

ARE ***(MUKAWA)*** [MWC] 1,231 (1973 SIL). Milne Bay Province, tip of Cape Vogel. Austronesian, Malayo-Polynesian, Central-Eastern, Eastern Malayo-Polynesian, Oceanic, Western Oceanic, Papuan Tip, Nuclear, North Papuan Mainland-D'Entrecasteaux, Are-Taupota, Are. Close to Gapapaiwa. 47% to 55% lexical similarity with Doga (closest). Grammar. Bible 1925.

ARI [AAC] 80 to 100 (1976 G. Reesink SIL). Ari and Serea villages, Aramia River area, Western Province. Trans-New Guinea, Main Section, Central and Western, Gogodala-Suki, Gogodala. Bilingualism in Gogodala. Investigation needed: bilingual proficiency in Gogodala.

ARIBWATSA ***(LAE, LAHE)*** [LAZ] Morobe Province, lower Wamped River, living in Bukawa villages of Butibum and Kamkumun at Lae. Austronesian, Malayo-Polynesian, Central-Eastern, Eastern Malayo-Polynesian, Oceanic, Western Oceanic, North New Guinea, Huon Gulf, Markham, Lower, Busu. No speakers left (1995). The ethnic group now speaks Bukawa. Extinct.

ARIBWAUNG ***(ARIBWAUNGG, YALU, JALOC)*** [YLU] 1,000 (1994 Eckerman LBT). Morobe Province, lower Markham Valley, Yalu village. Austronesian, Malayo-Polynesian, Central-Eastern, Eastern Malayo-Polynesian, Oceanic, Western Oceanic, North New Guinea, Huon Gulf, Markham, Lower, Busu. Closely related to Musom, Guwot, Sirak, Wampar. Jaloc is the Yabem spelling of the village name. Investigation needed: intelligibility with Musom, Guwot, Sirak.

ARIFAMA-MINIAFIA ***(MINIAFIA-ARIFAMA)*** [AAI] 2,147 (1977 Wurm). Four locations along the coast of Cape Nelson and Collingwood Bay, Oro Province, Tufi District. 20 to 25 villages. Austronesian, Malayo-Polynesian, Central-Eastern, Eastern Malayo-Polynesian, Oceanic, Western Oceanic, Papuan Tip, Nuclear, North Papuan Mainland-D'Entrecasteaux, Are-Taupota, Are. Dialects: ARIFAMA, MINIAFIA. 39% lexical similarity with Ubir. Bilingualism in English, Motu. Arifama speakers are shifting to nearby languages. SOV. Literacy rate in second language: 10%. Tropical forest, mangrove swamp. Coastal. Fishermen, swidden agriculturalists. 0 to 200 meters. Bible portions 1990.

AROP-LOKEP ***(SIASI, SIASSI, TOLOKIWA, MOROMIRANGA, LUKEP)*** [APR] 2,200 (1991 SIL). 3 islands in the Siassi chain in the Vitiaz Strait. Arop dialect on Long Island, Madang Province, Saidor District. Lokep dialect on Tolokiwa Island and the north tip of Umboi Island, Morobe Province, Siassi District. Austronesian, Malayo-Polynesian, Central-Eastern, Eastern Malayo-Polynesian, Oceanic, Western Oceanic, North New Guinea, Ngero-Vitiaz, Vitiaz, Korap. Dialects: AROP (POONO), LOKEP (LUKEP, LOKEWE). Different from Arop-Sissano in Sandaun Province. SVO. Literacy rate in first language: 75% to 100%. Literacy rate in second language: 50% to 75%. Bible portions 1990-1993.

AROP-SISSANO ***(AROP)*** [APS] 1,150 (1998). Sandaun Province, Aitape District, Arop village. Austronesian, Malayo-Polynesian, Central-Eastern, Eastern Malayo-Polynesian, Oceanic, Western Oceanic, North New Guinea, Schouten, Siau. Related to Sissano, Malol, and Sera, but different enough to be a separate language. 863 people killed in July 1998 tsunami. Literacy rate in first language: 15% to 25%. Literacy rate in second language: 25% to 50%. Bible portions 1988-1994.

ARUAMU ***(MIKAREW, ARIAWIAI, MAKARUP, MAKARUB, MIKARUP, MIKAREW-ARIAW)*** [MSY] 8,000 (1990 UBS). Madang Province, west of Bogia. Sepik-Ramu, Ramu, Ramu Proper, Ruboni, Misegian. Literacy rate in first language: 5% to 25%. Literacy rate in second language: 50% to 75%. Bible portions 1996.

ARUEK ***(DJANG)*** [AUR] 614 (1981 Wurm and Hattori). Sandaun Province, north of Kombio. Torricelli, Kombio-Arapesh, Kombio.

ARUOP ***(LAUISARANGA, LAU'U)*** [LSR] 700 (1991 SIL). Sandaun Province, 6 villages. Torricelli, Wapei-Palei, Palei. 1 community school. Mountain ridge. 2,500 feet.

ASARO'O ***(MORAFA)*** [MTV] 672 (1981 Wurm and Hattori). Madang Province, southeast of Saidor. At least 4 villages. Trans-New Guinea, Main Section, Central and Western, Huon-Finisterre, Finisterre, Warup. Related languages: Asat, Bulgebi, Degenan, Forak, Guiarak, Gwahatike, Yagomi. Morafa is a clan name. Coastal, mountain slope. Sea level to 400 meters.

ASAS ***(KOW)*** [ASD] 333 (1981 Wurm and Hattori). Madang Province. Trans-New Guinea, Madang-Adelbert Range, Madang, Rai Coast, Evapia. Related languages: Sinsauru, Sausi, Kesawai, Dumpu.

ASAT ***(MURATAIK)*** [ASX] 1,047 (1980 census). Madang Province, Rai Coast District, east of Saidor. Trans-New Guinea, Main Section, Central and Western, Huon-Finisterre, Finisterre, Warup. Related languages: Asaro'o, Bulgebi, Degenan, Forak, Guiarak, Gwahatike, Yagomi. People in Yagomi villages are said to speak Asat. Coastal, mountain slope. Sea level to 1,200 meters.

ATEMBLE ***(ATEMPLE-APRIS, ATEMPLE)*** [ATE] 65 (1981 Wurm and Hattori). Madang Province. Trans-New Guinea, Madang-Adelbert Range, Adelbert Range, Josephstaal-Wanang, Wanang, Atan.

ATURU ***(ATURA, ADULU, MAKAEYAM)*** [AUP] 220 (1981 Wurm and Hattori). Western Province, Sumogi Island in Fly Estuary, Adulu, Lewada, and Suame villages. Trans-New Guinea, Trans-Fly-Bulaka River, Trans-Fly, Tirio. 78% lexical similarity with Lewada-Dewara.

AU [AVT] 5,000 (1991 SIL). Sandaun Province, Lumi District, 19 villages in the foothills of the Torricelli Mountains. Torricelli, Wapei-Palei, Wapei. 20% monolingual. Others use Tok Pisin as second language. Grammar. SVO, extensive agreement system. Literacy rate in second language: 25% to 50%. Tropical forest. Mountain slope. Hunter-gatherers. 200 to 600 meters. NT 1982.

'AUHELAWA ***(NUAKATA, KURADA, 'URADA)*** [KUD] 1,200(1998 SIL). Milne Bay Province, Normanby Island, Sehuleya District. Austronesian, Malayo-Polynesian, Central-Eastern, Eastern Malayo-Polynesian, Oceanic, Western Oceanic, Papuan Tip, Nuclear, Suauic. 52% lexical similarity with Duau (closest). 30% monolingual. Others use Dobu as second language. Literacy rate in first language: 85%. Literacy rate in second language: 85%. Tropical forest. Large volcanic islands. Agriculturalists: yam; fishermen. 0-1,000 feet. Christian, traditional religion. Bible portions 1986-1993.

AUNALEI ***(ONELE, ONE, ONI)*** [AUN] 2,206 (1981 Wurm and Hattori). 40% live north of the mountains, 60% south. Sandaun Province. Lumi and Aitape districts, Toricelli Mts. 11 villages. Torricelli, West Wapei. Dialects: NORTH AUNALEI, CENTRAL AUNALEI, SOUTH AUNALEI. Speakers have routine bilingual proficiency in Tok Pisin. Literacy rate in second language: 25% to 50%. Mountain slope.

AUWE ***(SIMOG)*** [SMF] 400 (1993 SIL). Sandaun Province, Amanab District, Simog and Watape villages. Trans-New Guinea, Northern, Border, Waris. Literacy rate in second language: 50% to 75%.

AVAU ***(AWAU)*** [AVB] 6,000 (1982 SIL). West New Britain Province, southwest, inland from Gasmata. Austronesian, Malayo-Polynesian, Central-Eastern, Eastern Malayo-Polynesian, Oceanic, Western Oceanic, North New Guinea, Ngero-Vitiaz, Vitiaz, Southwest New Britain, Arawe-Pasismanua, Arawe, East Arawe. Bilingualism in Tok Pisin, English. Tropical forest.

AWA ***(MOBUTA)*** [AWB] 1,789 (1981 Wurm and Hattori). Okapa and Kainantu districts, Eastern Highlands Province. Trans-New Guinea, Main Section, Central and Western, East New Guinea Highlands, Eastern, Gadsup-Auyana-Awa. Dialects: TAUNA, ILAKIA, NORTHEAST AWA, SOUTH AWA. Dictionary. Grammar. SOV. Literacy rate in first language: 25% to 50%. Literacy rate in second language: 25% to 50%. Tropical forest. Mountain slope. Swidden, peasant agriculturalists. 1,700 to 1,800 meters. NT 1974-1997.

AWAD BING ***(BILIAU, SENGAM, BING)*** [BCU] 700 (1991 SIL). Madang Province, 7 villages west of Saidor, Astrolabe Bay area. Austronesian, Malayo-Polynesian, Central-Eastern, Eastern Malayo-Polynesian, Oceanic, Western Oceanic, North New Guinea, Ngero-Vitiaz, Vitiaz, Bel, Astrolabe. Dialects: BILIAU, YAMAI, SUIT, GALEG. Distinct from, but closely related to, Mindiri and Wab. Four dialects. Bible portions 1992.

AWAR [AYA] 572 (1975 Z'Graggen). Madang Province. Sepik-Ramu, Ramu, Ramu Proper, Ruboni, Ottilien. Dialects: AWAR, NUBIA.

AWARA [AWX] 1,627 (1994 govt. figure). Morobe Province, Lae District, near the Wantoat. Trans-New Guinea, Main Section, Central and Western, Huon-Finisterre, Finisterre, Wantoat. There is some dialect variation within Awara. Wantoat, Wapu, and Awara are part of a language chain, with Awara being the western end. 60% to 70% lexical similarity with Wantoat and Wapu. Tok Pisin is used as second language. Use of Wantoat is passive. 35% monolingual. SOV. Literacy rate in first language: Less than 1%. Literacy rate in second language: 3%. Tropical forest, savannah. Mountain ridge, plateau. Swidden agriculturalists: coffee. 3,500 to 6,000 feet.

AWIYAANA ***(AUYANA)*** [AUY] 6,500 (1975 SIL). Kainantu, Okapa districts, Eastern Highlands Province. 15 villages. Trans-New Guinea, Main Section, Central and Western, East New Guinea Highlands, Eastern, Gadsup-Auyana-Awa. SOV. Tropical forest. Mountain ridge. Agriculturalists. 1,208 to 1,988 meters. NT 1984.

AWTUW ***(KAMNUM, AUTU)*** [KMN] 394 (1979 census). Sandaun Province. Sepik-Ramu, Sepik, Ram. Related languages: Karawa, Pouye. Investigation needed: intelligibility with Karawa, Pouye. Grammar. Tropical forest. Sago gatherers. 300 to 400 meters.

AWUN ***(AWON)*** [AWW] 384 (1981 Wurm and Hattori). Sandaun Province, east of Namia. Sepik-Ramu, Sepik, Yellow River. Related to Namia and Ak.

BAGUPI [BPI] 58 (1981 Wurm and Hattori). Madang Province. Trans-New Guinea, Madang-Adelbert Range, Madang, Mabuso, Hanseman. Related languages: Rapting, Wamas, Samosa, Murupi, Saruga, Nake, Mosimo, Garus, Yoidik, Rempi, Silopi, Utu, Mawan, Baimak, Matepi, Gal, Garuh, Kamba.

BAHINEMO ***(BAHENEMO, GAHOM, WOGU, YIGAI, INARU)*** [BJH] 550 (1998 NTM). East Sepik Province, Ambunti District, Hunstein Range, south of the Sepik River. 4 villages. Sepik-Ramu, Sepik, Sepik Hill, Bahinemo. Bilingualism in Tok Pisin. Literacy rate in first language: 5% to 15%. Literacy rate in second language: 15% to 25%. Tropical forest. Low mountains. Hunter-gatherers, sago palm. 60 to 1,000 meters. Christian, traditional religion. Bible portions 1973-1983.

BAIBAI [BBF] 271 (1981 Wurm and Hattori). Sandaun Province, Amanab District. Kwomtari-Baibai, Baibai.

BAIMAK [BMX] 441 (1981 Wurm and Hattori). Madang Province, 20 miles west of Madang city. Trans-New Guinea, Madang-Adelbert Range, Madang, Mabuso, Hanseman. Related to Gal.

BAINAPI ***(PIKIWA, DIBIASU, TURUMASA)*** [PIK] 400 (1981 Wurm and Hattori). Western Province, villages of Makapa, Pikiwa, and Bamustu, via Balimo. Trans-New Guinea, Main Section, Central and Western, Central and South New Guinea-Kutubuan, Central and South New Guinea, Bosavi. Literacy rate in first language: Less than 5%. Literacy rate in second language: Less than 5%.

BALUAN-PAM [BLQ] 1,000 (1982 SIL). Manus Province, Baluan and Pam islands. Austronesian, Malayo-Polynesian, Central-Eastern, Eastern Malayo-Polynesian, Oceanic, Admiralty Islands, Eastern, Southeast Islands. Dialects: BALUAN, PAM. Two close dialects; Baluan is the larger one. Speakers are moderately bilingual in Lou or Titan. SVO. Win Nesien cult.

BAMU ***(BAMU KIWAI)*** [BCF] 5,000 (1998 SIL). Western Province from the mouth of the Bamu River to 50 miles upriver. Trans-New Guinea, Trans-Fly-Bulaka River, Trans-Fly, Kiwaian. Dialects: GAMA, LOWER BAMU, SISIAME, UPPER BAMU (MIDDLE BAMU), NUHIRO. Gama dialect may be a separate language. Closely related to Wabuda Kiwai. Gama dialect is below 80% lexically similar to Lower Bamu, the closest other Bamu dialect. Literacy rate in first language: 5% to 10%. Literacy rate in second language: 5% to 15%. Swamp on tidal river. Hunter-gatherers. 0-2 meters. Bible portions 1952.

BANARO ***(BANAR, BANARA)*** [BYZ] 2,484 (1991 SIL). Madang and East Sepik provinces. 2 villages. Sepik-Ramu, Ramu, Ramu Proper, Grass, Banaro. Literacy rate in first language: 5% to 25%. Literacy rate in second language: 50% to 75%. Traditional religion, Christian.

BANONI ***(TSUNARI)*** [BCM] 1,000 (1977 Lincoln). North Solomons Province, southwestern Bougainville. Austronesian, Malayo-Polynesian, Central-Eastern, Eastern Malayo-Polynesian, Oceanic, Western Oceanic, Meso Melanesian, New Ireland, South New Ireland-Northwest Solomonic, Piva-Banoni. Grammar.

BARAI [BCA] 2,000 (1998 SIL). Inland Oro Province, Afore District, on the Managalas Plateau. Birarie dialect is in Umuate, Naokanane, Itokama, Madokoro villages. Namiae dialect is in Kuae, Kokoro, Tahama, Sorefuna, Ubuvara villages. Trans-New Guinea, Main Section, Eastern, Central and South-eastern, Koiarian, Baraic. Dialects: BIRARIE, NAMIAE. Birarie and Namiae are major dialects, Muguani is minor. 50% lexical similarity with Managalsi. Barai on the southern slopes of the Owen Stanley Mountains in the Central Province is a separate language. SOV. Literacy rate in first language: 50%. Literacy rate in second language: 50% to 60%. Tropical forest. Interfluvial. Swidden agriculturalists. 700 to 900 meters. Christian, traditional religion. NT 1994.

BARAMU [BMZ] 478 (1979 census). Western Province, Baramula and Tirio villages. Trans-New Guinea, Trans-Fly-Bulaka River, Trans-Fly, Tirio. Different from Aturu, Tirio, or Were.

BARGAM ***(MUGIL, BUNU, SAKER)*** [MLP] 3,500 to 4,000 (1987 M. Hepner). Madang Province, Madang District, north coast just opposite Karkar Island. Trans-New Guinea, Madang-Adelbert Range, Adelbert Range, Pihom-Isumrud-Mugil, Mugil. The name 'Mugil' refers to an RC station. 'Bunu' is a village name. Bible portions 1989-1991.

BARIAI ***(KABANA)*** [BCH] 1,380 (1998 SIL). West New Britain Province, east of Cape Gloucester, northwest coast. Austronesian, Malayo-Polynesian, Central-Eastern, Eastern Malayo-Polynesian, Oceanic, Western Oceanic, North New Guinea, Ngero-Vitiaz, Ngero, Bariai. 72% lexical similarity with Kove, 76% with Lusi. Bilingualism in Tok Pisin. 'Kabana' is a name acceptable to the three eastern villages, but offensive to the majority of the population. 'Bariai' is more commonly accepted as the language name. SVO, prepositions, 14% of syllables are closed, morphologically less complex than most Austronesian languages. Literacy rate in first language: 40.5% (adults). Literacy rate in second language: 82.5% (adults). Tropical forest. Coastal. Swidden agriculturalists, fishermen. Bible portions 1998.

BARIJI ***(AGA BEREHO)*** [BJC] 256 (1973 SIL). Oro Province, on the south bank of the Bariji River. Trans-New Guinea, Main Section, Eastern, Central and Southeastern, Yareban. 49% lexical similarity with Moikodi. Speakers are bilingual in Hiri Motu and reported to know Moikodi or Yareba.

BARIM [BBV] 450 (1991 SIL). Morobe Province, 4 villages on mainland near Wasu and 3 on southwestern Umboi Island. Austronesian, Malayo-Polynesian, Central-Eastern, Eastern Malayo-Polynesian, Oceanic, Western Oceanic, North New Guinea, Ngero-Vitiaz, Vitiaz, Korap. Malasanga is a separate language. Coastal.

BAROK ***(KOMALU, KANAPIT, KULUBI, KOLUBE, KANALU)*** [BJK] 2,116 (1985 AIL). New Ireland, south central, east and west coasts. 15 villages. Austronesian, Malayo-Polynesian, Central-Eastern, Eastern Malayo-Polynesian, Oceanic, Western Oceanic, Meso Melanesian, New Ireland, Madak. Dialects: USEN, BAROK. Bible portions 1929.

BARUGA [BBB] 1,500 (1998 SIL) including about 600 Tapota Baruga, 400 to 500 Mado, 400 Bareji Baruga (1998 SIL), and 119 Doghoro (1981 Wurm and Hattori). Oro Province, Tufi District, in the Musa and Bariji (Bareji) River flood plains. The Gaina, Bariji and Yareba border them to the south. The Okeina dialect of Ewage-Notu, Ambe Tofo, Korafe-Mokorua, Miniafia-Arifama, Ubir, and Maisin border them to the east. Dyke Ackland Bay is to the north. Trans-New Guinea, Main Section, Eastern, Binanderean, Binanderean Proper. Dialects: BAREJI, BARUGA, MADO, TAPOTA BARUGA, DOGHORO. 56% to 61% with Korafe and Gaina (Dutton 1971), 43% with Ewage dialect of Ewage-Notu. Some speakers are bilingual in Hiri Motu, Tok Pisin, and English. SOV. Literacy rate in first language: about 60%. Literacy rate in second language: about 60%. Tropical forest. Riverine, coastal. Swidden agriculturalists; fishermen; hunters. 0 to 60 meters. Bible portions 1995.

BARUYA ***(BARUA, YIPMA)*** [BYR] 6,600 (1990 census). Eastern Highlands Province, Marawaka District. Trans-New Guinea, Main Section, Central and Western, Angan, Angan Proper. Dialects: WANTAKIA, BARUYA, GULICHA, USIRAMPIA (DOGORO). 'Yipma' is the name most acceptable to speakers of most dialects. Dictionary. SOV. Literacy rate in first language: 10% to 20%. Literacy rate in second language: 15% to 25%. Tropical forest, savannah. Mountain slope. Swidden agriculturalists. 1,040 to 3,459 meters. NT 1992.

BAU [BBD] 1,789 (1975 Z'Graggen). Madang Province. Trans-New Guinea, Madang-Adelbert Range, Madang, Mabuso, Gum. Related languages: Sihan, Gumalu, Isebe, Amele, Panim. Different from Bao in New Britain, an Oceanic language.

BAUWAKI ***(BAWAKI)*** [BWK] 398 (1980 census). Most are at Amau (Mori River), Central Province, extending into Oro Province. Trans-New Guinea, Main Section, Eastern, Central and Southeastern, Mailuan. Dutton says this is a bridge language between the Mailuan and Yareban families. 66% lexical similarity with Abia (closest), 39% with Domu. 85% to 100% of speakers are bilingual in Magi, Suau, Motu, or English.

BEAMI ***(BEDAMINI, BEDAMUNI, MOUGULU)*** [BEO] 4,200 (1981 Wurm and Hattori). Western Province, east of Nomad, extending into Southern Highlands Province. Trans-New Guinea, Main Section, Central and Western, Central and South New Guinea-Kutubuan, Central and South New Guinea, Bosavi. Dialects: KOMOFIO, NORTH BEAMI. Literacy rate in first language: 5% to 15%. Literacy rate in second language: 15% to 25%. NT 1991.

BEBELI ***(BENAULE, BANAULE, KAPORE, BELI)*** [BEK] 1,050 (1982 SIL). West New Britain Province, Stettin Bay, Cape Hoskins area. Austronesian, Malayo-Polynesian, Central-Eastern, Eastern Malayo-Polynesian, Oceanic, Western Oceanic, North New Guinea, Ngero-Vitiaz, Vitiaz, Southwest New Britain, Arawe-Pasismanua, Arawe, East Arawe. Different from Beli in Sandaun Province.

BELI ***(MUKILI, AKUWAGEL, MAKARIM)*** [BEY] 1,453 including 1,400 in area and 53 outside (1978 census). Sandaun Province, west of Mehek. Torricelli, Maimai, Beli. Different from Bebeli (Beli) in West New Britain.

BEMAL ***(KEIN)*** [BMH] 700 (1987 SIL). Madang Province, Trans-Gogol District. Trans-New Guinea, Madang-Adelbert Range, Madang, Mabuso, Kokon. Related languages: Girawa, Munit. SOV. Tropical forest. Interfluvial. Agriculturalists. above 40 meters.

BENABENA ***(BENA)*** [BEF] 45,000 (1998 NTM). Eastern Highlands Province, Goroka District. Trans-New Guinea, Main Section, Central and Western, East New Guinea Highlands, East-Central, Gahuku-Benabena. Grammar. Literacy rate in first language: 25% to 50%. Literacy rate in second language: 50% to 75%. Savannah, tropical forest. Mountain valley. Swidden agriculturalists. 1,500 to 2,000 meters. Traditional religion, Christian. NT 1983.

BEPOUR [BIE] 57 (1981 Wurm and Hattori). Madang Province. Trans-New Guinea, Madang-Adelbert Range, Adelbert Range, Pihom-Isumrud-Mugil, Pihom, Kumilan. Related languages: Mauwake, Moere.

BIANGAI [BIG] 1,400 (1991 SIL). Morobe Province, Wau District, headwaters of the Bulolo River. 7 villages. Trans-New Guinea, Main Section, Eastern, Central and Southeastern, Goilalan, Kunimaipa. Dialects: NGOWIYE, YONGOLEI. 50% monolingual. Others use Tok Pisin as second language. SOV. Literacy rate in first language: 50%. Literacy rate in second language: 75% to 100%. The literacy rate remains high because of the number of children attending school. The vernacular literacy rate has dropped because of the deaths of adult readers and the shift of children to Tok Pisin. Mixed forests. Interfluvial below mountain slopes. Swidden agriculturalists. 950 to 1,100 meters. NT 1985.

BIEM *(BAM)* [BMC] 1,455 (1981 Wurm and Hattori). East Sepik Province, Viai, Blupblup, Kadovar, and Bam islands east of Wewak. Austronesian, Malayo-Polynesian, Central-Eastern, Eastern Malayo-Polynesian, Oceanic, Western Oceanic, North New Guinea, Schouten, Kairiru-Manam, Manam. Investigation needed: intelligibility with Manam.

BIKARU *(PIKARU, BUGALU)* [BIC] 100 (1981 Wurm and Hattori). East Sepik Province, headwaters of April River. Sepik-Ramu, Sepik, Sepik Hill, Sanio. Nomadic. Literacy rate in first language: Less than 5%. Literacy rate in second language: 5% to 15%. Traditional religion.

BIKSI *(INISINE, BIAKSI)* [BDX] 200 in Papua New Guinea (1992 SIL). South of the Green River, and into Irian Jaya. Sepik-Ramu, Sepik, Biksi. See main entry under Indonesia, Irian Jaya.

BILAKURA [BQL] 34 (1981 Wurm and Hattori). Madang Province. Trans-New Guinea, Madang-Adelbert Range, Adelbert Range, Pihom-Isumrud-Mugil, Pihom, Numugenan. Related languages: Usan, Yaben, Yarawata, Parawen, Ukuriguma. Nearly extinct.

BILBIL *(BILIBIL)* [BRZ] 700 (1981 Wurm and Hattori). Madang Province, coast just south of Madang town. Austronesian, Malayo-Polynesian, Central-Eastern, Eastern Malayo-Polynesian, Oceanic, Western Oceanic, North New Guinea, Ngero-Vitiaz, Vitiaz, Bel, Nuclear Bel, Northern.

BILUR *(BIRAR)* [BXF] 1,447 (1979 census). East New Britain Province, Gazelle Peninsula, 9 villages southeast of Cape Gazelle. Austronesian, Malayo-Polynesian, Central-Eastern, Eastern Malayo-Polynesian, Oceanic, Western Oceanic, Meso Melanesian, New Ireland, South New Ireland-Northwest Solomonic.

BIMIN [BHL] 2,000 (1991 SIL). Sandaun Province, Bak-Bimin District, and Western Province. Trans-New Guinea, Main Section, Central and Western, Central and South New Guinea-Kutubuan, Central and South New Guinea, Ok, Mountain. Closely related to Faiwol. Much intermarriage and cultural exchange with Oksapmin. Literacy rate in first language: Less than 5%. Literacy rate in second language: 5% to 15%.

BINA [BMN] (2 nonprimary speakers left; 1981 Wurm and Hattori). Central Province, north of Baibara. Austronesian, Malayo-Polynesian, Central-Eastern, Eastern Malayo-Polynesian, Oceanic, Western Oceanic, Papuan Tip, Peripheral, Central Papuan, Oumic, Magoric. Extinct.

BINAHARI [BXZ] 764 (1980 census). Central Province, both sides of a range of hills inland from Cloudy Bay. Trans-New Guinea, Main Section, Eastern, Central and Southeastern, Mailuan. Dialects: NEME (NEMEA), MA. 70% lexical similarity with Morawa (closest). 80% to 100% bilingual in Magi, Suau, Hiri Motu, or English.

BINANDERE *(IOMA BINANDERE)* [BHG] 6,700 (1991 SIL), including 1,200 in Ambasi (1981 Wurm and Hattori). Oro Province, along the Eia, Gira, Ope, Mambere, and Kumusi rivers, between Zia and Ambasi; a few in Morobe Province. Trans-New Guinea, Main Section, Eastern, Binanderean, Binanderean Proper. Dialects: AEKA (AIGA), AMBASI (TAIN-DAWARE, DAVARI, DAWARI), BINANDERE. 50% to 54% lexical similarity with Suena and Zia, 67% with Ambasi. Speakers who live near the coast are more bilingual. Grammar. SOV. Literacy rate in first language: 25% to 50%. Literacy rate in second language: 25% to 50%. Sago swamp, plains. Fishermen; hunters; swidden agriculturalists: tobacco; wood carvers; potters. Sea level to 300 feet. Christian, traditional religion. Bible portions 1912-1949.

BINE *(ORIOMO, PINE)* [ORM] 2,000 (1987 SIL). Western Province, Daru District, south of Fly River. Trans-New Guinea, Trans-Fly-Bulaka River, Trans-Fly, Eastern Trans-Fly. Dialects: KUNINI, BOZE-GIRINGAREDE, SOGAL, MASINGLE, TÄTE, IRUPI-DRAGELI, SEBE. SOV. Literacy rate in first language: 50% to 75%. Literacy rate in second language: 25% to 50%. Tropical forest, mangrove swamp, savannah. Coastal, riverine. Fishermen, swidden agriculturalists. Sea level. NT 1993.

BINUMARIEN *(BINUMARIA, BINAMARIR)* [BJR] 360 (1990 census). Eastern Highlands Province, Kainantu District. Trans-New Guinea, Main Section, Central and Western, East New Guinea Highlands, Eastern, Tairora. SOV. Literacy rate in first language: 75% to 100%. Literacy rate in second language: 75% to 100%. Tropical forest. Mountain slope. Swidden agriculturalists. 1,350 meters. NT 1983.

BIPI *(SISI-BIPI)* [BIQ] 1,200 (1990 SIL). Manus Province, west coast, Maso, Matahei, and Salapai villages, Bipi and Sisi islands. Austronesian, Malayo-Polynesian, Central-Eastern, Eastern Malayo-Polynesian, Oceanic, Admiralty Islands, Eastern, Manus, West. Close to Loniu. Investigation needed: intelligibility with Loniu. SVO.

BISIS ***(YAMBIYAMBI)*** [BNW] 500 (1986 W. Dye SIL). East Sepik Province, Hunstein Range, Ambunti District, next to the Bahinemo, between the Lower Salumei River and Chambri Lake. 3 villages. Sepik-Ramu, Sepik, Sepik Hill, Bahinemo. Highly bilingual in Tok Pisin. Investigation needed: bilingual proficiency in Tok Pisin. Tropical forest. Low mountains. Hunter-gatherers, sago palm. Traditional religion, Christian.

BISORIO ***(INYAI-GADIO-BISORIO, INIAI)*** [BIR] 230 to 280 (1983 SIL), including 50 to 100 Pikaru. East Sepik Province, headwaters of the Karawari, Wagupmeri, and Korosameri rivers; villages of Bisorio, Iniai, Gadio. Trans-New Guinea, Main Section, Central and Western, East New Guinea Highlands, West-Central, Enga. Dialect: PIKARU (BIKARU). 70% lexical similarity with Nete. NT 1993.

BITARA [BIT] 256 (1983 SIL). East Sepik Province, April River. Several villages. Sepik-Ramu, Sepik, Sepik Hill, Bahinemo. Dialect: APOWASI (KAKIRU). Speakers are moderately bilingual in Tok Pisin.

BIWAT ***(MUNDUGUMOR, MUNDUGUMA)*** [BWM] 1,642 (1975 SIL). East Sepik Province, lower and middle Yuat River. Sepik-Ramu, Ramu, Yuat-Waibuk, Yuat-Maramba, Yuat. Related to Kyenele, Changriwa, Mekmek, Miyak, Bun.

BIYOM ***(SASIME)*** [BPM] 379 (1981 Wurm and Hattori). Madang Province, southeast of Gende. Trans-New Guinea, Madang-Adelbert Range, Adelbert Range, Brahman. Related languages: Isabi, Tauya, Faita. Investigation needed: intelligibility.

BLAFE ***(TONDA, INDORODORO)*** [IND] 600 (Wurm and Hattori 1981). Western Province, west of Nambu language. Indorodoro town is center. Trans-New Guinea, Trans-Fly-Bulaka River, Trans-Fly, Morehead and Upper Maro Rivers, Tonda. Different from Ara (Rouku), although related. Literacy rate in first language: 5% to 5%. Literacy rate in second language: 5% to 15%.

BO ***(PO, SORIMI)*** [BPW] 85 (1998 NTM). Sandaun Province, the heart of the western range; Bo, Kobaru, Kaumifi, Nigyama Umarita villages. Western range, close to the border of West Sepik Province, near Right May River, East Sepik Province. Left May. Dialects: KABORU, NIKIYAMA, UMURUTA. The area is seldom entered by outsiders. Unconfirmed as a separate language. Literacy rate in second language: 50% Tok Pisin. Tropical forest. Mountain slope, valley. Hunters-gatherers. 475 feet. Traditional religion.

BOAZI ***(BOADJI, BWADJI)*** [KVG] 2,000 (1990 SIL). Western Province, Lake Murray District. None now in Irian Jaya (1978 SIL). Trans-New Guinea, Main Section, Central and Western, Marind, Boazi. Dialects: KUNI, NORTH BOAZI, SOUTH BOAZI. Related to Zimakani. Some are educated. Literacy rate in second language: 30% to 40%. Low sand ridges between swamps and lagoons.

BOGAYA ***(POGAYA, BOGAIA)*** [BOQ] 300 (1981 Wurm and Hattori). Western Province, some also in base of northern neck of Southern Highlands Province. Trans-New Guinea, Main Section, Central and Western, Central and South New Guinea-Kutubuan, Central and South New Guinea, Duna-Bogaya. Literacy rate in first language: Less than 5%. Literacy rate in second language: Less than 5%.

BOHUAI ***(PAHAVAI, PELIPOWAI, BOWAI, POHUAI, BOHUAI-TULU, TULU-BOHUAI)*** [RAK] 1,400 (1982 SIL). Manus Province, Bohuai, Peli Island, Pelipowai. Austronesian, Malayo-Polynesian, Central-Eastern, Eastern Malayo-Polynesian, Oceanic, Admiralty Islands, Eastern, Manus, West. Dialects: KELI, BOHUAI, TULU (TULUN, TJUDUN). Close to Levei-Ndrehet. Bilingualism in Kurti, Titan, Ere. Investigation needed: bilingual proficiency in Kurti, Titan, Ere.

BOIKIN ***(BOIKEN, NUCUM, YANGORU, YENGORU)*** [BZF] 35,204 (1981 Wurm and Hattori). East Sepik Province, Yangoru District. Sepik-Ramu, Sepik, Middle Sepik, Ndu. Dialects: WEST BOIKIN, CENTRAL BOIKIN, EAST BOIKIN, MUNJI, HARIPMOR, KWUSAUN, KUNAI, ISLAND BOIKIN. 30% monolingual. Others use Tok Pisin as second language. Literacy rate in first language: 5% to 15%. Literacy rate in second language: 50% to 75%. Bible portions 1971-1979.

BOLA ***(BAKOVI, BOLA-BAKOVI)*** [BNP] 7,533 including 6,194 in Bola, 1,339 in Harua (1982 SIL). West New Britain Province, northeast coast, most of Willaumez Peninsula. Harua is on the east side of Kimbe. Austronesian, Malayo-Polynesian, Central-Eastern, Eastern Malayo-Polynesian, Oceanic, Western Oceanic, Meso Melanesian, Willaumez. Dialects: HARUA (KARUA, XARUA, GARUA, MAI), BOLA. Harua is a dialect that has developed as a result of a group of people being resettled on an oil palm plantation. 11 vernacular preparatory schools. NT 1934, out of print.

BONGOS ***(BONGOMASI, W'HAUKIA, APEKU, MASALAGA)*** [BXY] 3,000 (1994 SIL). East Sepik Province, extending beyond the western boundary of Maprik District; Makru-Klaplei Division, Nuku District; Sandaun Province, east of Mehek. 40 villages. Sepik-Ramu, Sepik, Middle Sepik, Nukuma. Dialects: BONGOS, APEKU. A dialect chain of 5 sub-dialects, 2 main dialects. OSV. Literacy rate in first language: 5% to 15%. Literacy rate in second language: 15% to 25%. Tropical forest. Plains. Swidden agriculturalists. 50 to 60 meters.

BONGU [BPU] 415 (1975 Z'Graggen). Madang Province, Astrolabe Bay, Rai Coast. Trans-New Guinea, Madang-Adelbert Range, Madang, Rai Coast, Mindjim.

BONKIMAN [BOP] 175 (1991 SIL). Madang and Morobe provinces. Trans-New Guinea, Main Section, Central and Western, Huon-Finisterre, Finisterre, Yupna. People's second language is Tok Pisin. Passive bilingualism with neighboring languages. 40% monolingual.

BOREI ***(GAMEI, GAMAI, MBOREI, MBORE)*** [GAI] 2,000 (1990 UBS). Madang Province, Bogia District. Sepik-Ramu, Ramu, Ramu Proper, Ruboni, Ottilien. Dialects: BOROI, BOREWAR, BOTBOT. Literacy rate in first language: 5% to 25%. Literacy rate in second language: 50% to 75%.

BOSILEWA [BOS] 350 (1972 census). Milne Bay Province, north shore of Fergusson Island. Austronesian, Malayo-Polynesian, Central-Eastern, Eastern Malayo-Polynesian, Oceanic, Western Oceanic, Papuan Tip, Nuclear, North Papuan Mainland-D'Entrecasteaux, Dobu-Duau. 61% lexical similarity with Galeya (closest). 30% monolingual. Others use Dobu as second language.

BOSNGUN ***(BOSMAN)*** [BQS] 717 (1975 Z'Graggen). Madang Province. Sepik-Ramu, Ramu, Ramu Proper, Ruboni, Ottilien. 20% monolingual. Others use Tok Pisin as second language.

BRAGAT ***(ALAUAGAT, YAUAN)*** [AOF] 400 (1991 SIL). Sandaun Province, 4 villages. Torricelli, Wapei-Palei, Palei. Most closely related to Aru. 1 community school. Investigation needed: intelligibility with Aru. Mountain ridge. 1,500 to 1,800 feet.

BREM ***(BAREM, BUNABUN, BUNUBUN, BUBUBUN)*** [BUQ] 498 (1975 Z'Graggen). Madang Province, including Bunabun village. Trans-New Guinea, Madang-Adelbert Range, Adelbert Range, Pihom-Isumrud-Mugil, Isumrud, Mabuan. Speakers refer to themselves as Brem or Barem.

BRERI ***(KUANGA)*** [BRQ] 1,100 (1986 PBT). Madang Province, lower Ramu Valley, 80 miles west of Madang City. Sepik-Ramu, Ramu, Ramu Proper, Goam, Tamolan. Related dialects or languages: Kominimung, Igana, Itutang. Swampy plain.

BUANG, MANGGA ***(MANGA BUANG, KAIDEMUI)*** [MMO] 3,000 (1986 SIL). Morobe Province, mid-upper Snake River area, Mumeng District. Austronesian, Malayo-Polynesian, Central-Eastern, Eastern Malayo-Polynesian, Oceanic, Western Oceanic, North New Guinea, Huon Gulf, South, Hote-Buang, Buang. Dialects: LAGIS, KWASANG. Bilingualism in Tok Pisin. SVO. Literacy rate in first language: 50% to 75%. Literacy rate in second language: 50% to 75%. Savannah. Mountain slope. Swidden agriculturalists. 670 to 1,830 meters. Christian, traditional religion. NT 1981.

BUANG, MAPOS ***(MAPOS, CENTRAL BUANG)*** [BZH] 6,666 (1978 McElhanon). Morobe Province, upper Snake River area, Mumeng District. 10 villages. Austronesian, Malayo-Polynesian, Central-Eastern, Eastern Malayo-Polynesian, Oceanic, Western Oceanic, North New Guinea, Huon Gulf, South, Hote-Buang, Buang. Dialects: WAGAU, MAMBUMP, BUWEYEU, WINS, CHIMBULUK, PAPAKENE, MAPOS. 61% lexical similarity between Mambump and Mangga. 30% monolingual. Others use Tok Pisin as second language. Grammar. SVO. Literacy rate in first language: 50% to 75%. Literacy rate in second language: 50% to 75%. Scrub forest, tropical forest. Mountain slope. Swidden agriculturalists. 1,500 to 2,000 meters. Christian, traditional religion. NT 1978.

BUDIBUD ***(NADA)*** [BTP] 170 (1972 census). Milne Bay Province, Lachlan Islands, 50 miles east of Woodlark Island. Austronesian, Malayo-Polynesian, Central-Eastern, Eastern Malayo-Polynesian, Oceanic, Western Oceanic, Papuan Tip, Peripheral, Kilivila-Louisiades, Kilivila. 65% lexical similarity with Muyuw. 15% monolingual. Speakers use Muyuw as second language but they prefer Budibud. The name 'Nada' is no longer used. Investigation needed: bilingual proficiency, attitudes toward Muyuw. Christian, traditional religion.

BUGAWAC ***(BUKAWA, BUKAUA, BUKAWAC, KAWA, KAWAC, YOM GAWAC)*** [BUK] 9,694 (1978 McElhanon). Morobe Province, coast of Huon Gulf. Austronesian, Malayo-Polynesian, Central-Eastern, Eastern Malayo-Polynesian, Oceanic, Western Oceanic, North New Guinea, Huon Gulf, North. Closely related to Yabem. 40% monolingual. Yabem bilingual proficiency is decreasing with those educated in Yabem up to the 1960s. Tok Pisin is the second language. Yabem is decreasingly used as church language. Literacy rate in first language: 15% to 25%. Literacy rate in second language: 15% to 25%.

BUHUTU ***(BOHUTU, BUHULU, YALEBA, SIASIADA)*** [BXH] 1,065 (1972 census). Eastern tip of Papua, Sagarai Valley, Milne Bay Province, Alotau District. Austronesian, Malayo-Polynesian, Central-Eastern, Eastern Malayo-Polynesian, Oceanic, Western Oceanic, Papuan Tip, Nuclear, Suauic. 68% lexical similarity with Suau. Many old people are bilinjgual in Suau or Tawala, but this has declined since the mission schools were replaced by an English medium government school.

BUIN ***(TELEI, TEREI, RUGARA)*** [BUO] 25,000 to 28,000 (1996 SIL). Southern North Solomons Province, Buin District. East Papuan, Bougainville, East, Buin. Closest to Uisai. Literacy rate in first language: 50% to 75%. Literacy rate in second language: 75% to 100%. Bible portions 1973-1978.

BUKIYIP ***(BUKIYÚP, MOUNTAIN ARAPESH)*** [APE] 14,000 (1998 SIL) including 8,000 Coastal Arapesh (1998 R. Conrad SIL). East Sepik Province, west Yangoru District, Torricelli Mountains. Torricelli, Kombio-Arapesh, Arapesh. Dialects: COASTAL ARAPESH, BUKIYIP (MOUNTAIN ARAPESH). 60% lexical similarity with Mufian. Grammar. SVO; 14 noun classes; noun phrase concordance. Literacy rate in first language: 15% to 25%. Literacy rate in second language: 25% to 50%. Scrub forest, tropical forest. Mountain slope. Swidden agriculturalists. 300 to 500 meters. NT 1994.

BULGEBI [BMP] 52 (1981 Wurm and Hattori). Madang Province, 10 miles southeast of Saidor. Trans-New Guinea, Main Section, Central and Western, Huon-Finisterre, Finisterre, Warup. Related to Asaro'o, Asat, Degenan, Forak, Guiarak, Gwahatike, Yagomi.

BULU [BJL] 566 (1982 SIL). West New Britain Province, Willaumez Peninsula. Austronesian, Malayo-Polynesian, Central-Eastern, Eastern Malayo-Polynesian, Oceanic, Western Oceanic, Meso Melanesian, Willaumez. Bilingualism in Bola.

BUN [BUV] 194 (1981 Wurm and Hattori). East Sepik Province. Sepik-Ramu, Ramu, Yuat-Waibuk, Yuat-Maramba, Yuat. Related languages: Changriwa, Mekmek, Biwat, Miyak. Investigation needed: intelligibility with Biwat. Literacy rate in second language: 25% to 50%.

BUNA [BVN] 500 to 1,000 (1994 SIL). East Sepik Province, Angoram District. Torricelli, Marienberg. Dialects: KASMIN, MASAN. Apparently 2 dialects: 1 in Kasmin, Boig, Waskurin, and Arapang villages, and 1 in Masan, Mangan, and Garien villages. Literacy rate in first language: Less than 5%. Literacy rate in second language: 15% to 25%.

BUNAMA [BDD] 4,000 (1993 SIL). Milne Bay Province, southern Normanby Island, Esa'ala District. Austronesian, Malayo-Polynesian, Central-Eastern, Eastern Malayo-Polynesian, Oceanic, Western Oceanic, Papuan Tip, Nuclear, North Papuan Mainland-D'Entrecasteaux, Dobu-Duau. Dialects: BUNAMA, BARABARA, SAWATUPWA, LOMITAWA, SIPUPU, WEYOKO, MEUDANA, KEROROGEA, KUMALAHU, KASIKASI, SAWABWALA. 66% lexical similarity with Mwateba, 75% with most Dobu dialects. Speakers use Dobu as second language, although proficiency is limited. Literacy rate in first language: 85%. Literacy rate in second language: 85%. Tropical forest. Volcanic islands. Agriculturalists: yams. 0 to 1,000 feet. Traditional religion, Christian. NT 1991.

BUNGAIN [BUT] 2,451 (1975 SIL). East Sepik Province. Yaugiba is one village. Torricelli, Marienberg. Literacy rate in second language: 50% to 75%.

BURUI [BRY] 150 (1975 SIL). East Sepik Province, Ambunti District. Sepik-Ramu, Sepik, Middle Sepik, Ndu. Bilingualism in Gaikundi. Most adults are fluent in Gaikundi. Literacy rate in first language: Less than 5%. Literacy rate in second language: 25% to 50%.

BURUM-MINDIK ***(BULUM, BURUM, MINDIK, SOMBA-SIAWARI)*** [BMU] 7,000 including 4,500 in Somba, 2,500 in Siawari (1989 SIL). Morobe Province, Finschhafen District, 30 villages in Central Huon Peninsula, south of Cromwell Range, Burum River valley and some western slopes of Kuat River. (Burum and Kuat are tributaries of the main Mongi River.) Many live in towns, 1,000 in Lae. 3 airstrips: Ogeramnang, Mindik, Nomanene. Trans-New Guinea, Main Section, Central and Western, Huon-Finisterre, Huon, Western. Dialects: SOMBA, SIAWARI. 92% lexical similarity between the dialects. Vigorous use of Burum-Mindik. 'Bulum' is the Kâte name for them. Kâte is the church language. Place of origin of cargo cults in Morobe Province. 7 community schools. There has been a self-help movement since 1975. SOV; postpositions. Literacy rate in first language: 75% to 100%. Literacy rate in second language: 75% to 100%. Tropical forest. Mountain slope. Swidden agriculturalists. 500 to 1,700 meters. NT 1996.

BUSA [BHF] 307 (1994 SIL). Sandaun Province, Amanab District, north of Upper Sepik River, west of Namia. 3 villages. Yare is north and east, Abau is south and west, Biaka is northwest. Language Isolate. No schools. Some intermarriage with the Yale. Lowland swamps. Hunter-gatherers. 300 feet.

BWAIDOKA ***(BWAIDOGA)*** [BWD] 6,000 (1994 SIL). Milne Bay Province, southeast tip of Goodenough Island and west Fergusson Island, Bolubolu District. Austronesian, Malayo-Polynesian, Central-Eastern, Eastern Malayo-Polynesian, Oceanic, Western Oceanic, Papuan Tip, Nuclear, North Papuan Mainland-D'Entrecasteaux, Bwaidoga. Dialects: MATAITAI, WAGIFA, KILIA, LAUWELA, BWAIDOGA. 72% lexical similarity with Iduna (closest). 50% monolingual. Others use Dobu as second language. Bwaidoka speakers consider Iduna to be a less important language. Half of the children are in school. Trade language. Literacy rate in first language: 75% to 100%. Literacy rate in second language: 50% to 75%. Bible portions 1934-1994.

BWANABWANA ***(TUBETUBE)*** [TTE] 2,015 (1994 SIL). Milne Bay Province, Bwanabwana District, Engineer Islands, Laseinie Islands, Ware Island, Kitai Island and southeast peninsula of Basilaki Island. Austronesian, Malayo-Polynesian, Central-Eastern, Eastern Malayo-Polynesian, Oceanic, Western Oceanic, Papuan Tip, Nuclear, Suauic. Dialects: WALE (WARI, WARE), KWALAIWA. 52% lexical similarity with Duau (closest). 30% monolingual. Older people know Dobu, the traditional church language, and language of kula trade. Some people are bilingual in Dobu, Suau, Tawala, Duau, or Misima. Important language at the center of the trade route. Literacy rate in first language: 25% to 50%. Literacy rate in second language: 25% to 50%. Bible portions 1928-1994.

CHAMBRI ***(TSHAMBERI, TCHAMBULI)*** [CAN] 1,700 (1991). East Sepik Province, marsh dwellers east and north of Sepik Hill area, southeastern shore and island in Chambri Lake. 3 villages. Sepik-Ramu, Nor-Pondo, Pondo. Speakers are highly bilingual in Tok Pisin. Wealth comes from fishing. Investigation needed: bilingual proficiency in Tok Pisin. Literacy rate in first language: Less than 5%. Literacy rate in second language: 15% to 25%. Fishermen, poultry husbandry, turtle catching. Traditional religion.

CHANGRIWA [CGA] 498 (1981 Wurm and Hattori). East Sepik Province. Sepik-Ramu, Ramu, Yuat-Waibuk, Yuat-Maramba, Yuat. Related languages: Mekmek, Miyak, Biwat, Bun. Investigation needed: intelligibility.

CHENAPIAN ***(TSENAP, ZENAP, CHENAP)*** [CJN] 187 (1981 Wurm and Hattori). East Sepik Province, on the Sepik River west of Wogamusin. 1 village. Sepik-Ramu, Sepik, Upper Sepik, Wogamusin. Many Tok Pisin speakers. Some young people are learning English. Literacy rate in first language: Less than 5%. Literacy rate in second language: Less than 5%.

CHUAVE ***(TJUAVE)*** [CJV] 23,107 (1981 Wurm and Hattori), including 4,290 Sua (1962 Wurm). Simbu Province, Chuave District. Trans-New Guinea, Main Section, Central and Western, East New Guinea Highlands, Central, Chimbu. Dialects: ELIMBARI, KEBAI, GOMIA, CHUAVE, SUA. Kebai is more distinct, but intelligible. SOV. Literacy rate in first language: 50% to 75%. Literacy rate in second language: 25% to 50%. Savannah. Mountain mesa. Swidden agriculturalists. 1,500 to 2,200 meters. NT 1992-1994.

DADIBI ***(DARIBI, KARIMUI)*** [MPS] 10,000 (1988 SIL). Southern Simbu Province, Karimui District, eastern corner of Southern Highlands Province. 28 villages. Trans-New Guinea, Teberan-Pawaian, Teberan. Dialect: ERAVE. Those villages have minor dialect differences from standard Dadibi in the Karimui and Negabo areas. 10% or more monolingual. Speakers in 2 or 3 villages on the Erave River are heavily bilingual in Folopa. They also use Tok Pisin. Grammar. SOV. Literacy rate in first language: 50% to 75%. Literacy rate in second language: 50% to 75%. Tropical forest. Plateau. Swidden agriculturalists. 1,000 to 1,150 meters. Christian, traditional religion. NT 1987.

DAGA ***(DIMUGA, NAWP)*** [DGZ] 6,000 (1991 SIL). Milne Bay Province, Rabaraba District, and Central Province, Abau District. Trans-New Guinea, Main Section, Eastern, Central and Southeastern, Dagan. Related languages: Bagoi, Galeva, Swoiden, Kanamara, Makiara, Maneao, Moibiri, Pue, Tevi, Turaka. Grammar. Literacy rate in first language: 25% to 50%. Literacy rate in second language: 25% to 50%. NT 1974.

DAMBI [DAC] 445 (1979 census). Morobe Province, Mumeng District. Austronesian, Malayo-Polynesian, Central-Eastern, Eastern Malayo-Polynesian, Oceanic, Western Oceanic, North New Guinea, Huon Gulf, South, Hote-Buang, Buang, Mumeng. In the Mumeng language chain. Some intelligibility with Kumalu. Investigation needed: attitudes toward Kumalu. SVO. Literacy rate in first language: 15% to 25%. Literacy rate in second language: 25% to 50%. Tropical forest. Mountain slope. Swidden agriculturalists. 300 to 900 meters.

DANARU [DNR] 115 (1981 Wurm and Hattori). Madang Province. Trans-New Guinea, Madang-Adelbert Range, Madang, Rai Coast, Peka. Related languages: Usino, Urigina, Sumau. Investigation needed: intelligibility.

DANO ***(UPPER ASARO, ASARO)*** [ASO] 30,000 (1987 SIL). Eastern Highlands Province, Goroka District. Trans-New Guinea, Main Section, Central and Western, East New Guinea Highlands, East-Central, Gahuku-Benabena. Dialects: UPPER ASARO, LUNUBE MADO, BOHENA, AMAIZUHO, KONGI. SOV. Literacy rate in first language: 15% to 25%. Literacy rate in second language: 25% to 50%. Savannah. Mountain slope. Peasant agriculturalists. 1,500 to 2,300 meters. NT 1989.

DAONDA [DND] 200 (1993 SIL). Sandaun Province, Amanab District near Imonda. Trans-New Guinea, Northern, Border, Waris. Bilingualism in Waris. Adults can understand Waris.

DAWAWA ***(DAWANA)*** [DWW] 2,500 (1994 SIL). West and inland from Wedau in Milne Bay Province, Rabaraba District. Austronesian, Malayo-Polynesian, Central-Eastern, Eastern Malayo-Polynesian, Oceanic, Western Oceanic, Papuan Tip, Nuclear, North Papuan Mainland-D'Entrecasteaux, Kakabai. 58% lexical similarity with Kakabai. 20% monolingual. Older speakers know Wedau, and some English. Wedau is used primarily in church. Some Motu is known. Dawawa is used in home and village life. Mountain slope. Bible portions 1991-1992.

DEDUA [DED] 5,000 (1991 SIL). Morobe Province, Sialum District, headwaters of the Masaweng and Tewae rivers, south of Mt. Besenona. Trans-New Guinea, Main Section, Central and Western, Huon-Finisterre, Huon, Eastern. Dialects: DZEIGOC, FANIC. Literacy rate in first language: 80%. Literacy rate in second language: 80%. Mountain slope. Swidden agriculturalists. NT, in press (1999).

DEGENAN [DGE] 358 (1975 Z'Graggen). Madang Province. Trans-New Guinea, Main Section, Central and Western, Huon-Finisterre, Finisterre, Warup. Related languages: Asaro'o, Asat, Bulgebi, Forak, Guiarak, Gwahatike, Yagomi.

DENGALU [DEA] 140 (1978 McElhanon). Morobe Province. Austronesian, Malayo-Polynesian, Central-Eastern, Eastern Malayo-Polynesian, Oceanic, Western Oceanic, North New Guinea, Huon Gulf, South, Hote-Buang, Buang, Mumeng. In Mumeng dialect chain. Investigation needed: intelligibility with Mumeng.

DIA ***(ALU, METRU, GALU)*** [DIA] 1,880 (1973 Laycock). Sandaun Province. Torricelli, Wapei-Palei, Wapei.

DIMIR ***(BOSKIEN, BOSIKEN)*** [DMC] 1,700 (1986 PBT). Madang Province. Trans-New Guinea, Madang-Adelbert Range, Adelbert Range, Pihom-Isumrud-Mugil, Isumrud, Dimir.

DIODIO [DDI] 1,200 (1972 census). Milne Bay Province, west coast of Goodenough Island. Austronesian, Malayo-Polynesian, Central-Eastern, Eastern Malayo-Polynesian, Oceanic, Western Oceanic, Papuan Tip, Nuclear, North Papuan Mainland-D'Entrecasteaux, Bwaidoga. Dialects: IAUIAULA, UTALO, AWALE, CENTRAL DIODIO. 66% lexical similarity with Bwaidoka (closest). 20% monolingual. Speakers are bilingual in Bwaidoka. Bwaidoka is the church language. Literacy rate in second language: Many speakers.

DOBU [DOB] 10,000 (1998 SIL). Lingua franca for 100,000 (1987 SIL). Milne Bay Province, Esa'ala District, Sanaroa, Dobu, and parts of Fergusson and Normanby islands. 500 villages. Austronesian, Malayo-Polynesian, Central-Eastern, Eastern Malayo-Polynesian, Oceanic, Western Oceanic, Papuan Tip, Nuclear, North Papuan Mainland-D'Entrecasteaux, Dobu-Duau. Dialects: GALUBWA, SANAROA, UBUIA, CENTRAL DOBU, LOBODA (ROBODA, DAWADA-SIAUSI). 56% lexical similarity with Morima (closest). 60% monolingual. Speakers are somewhat bilingual in Motu, English, adjacent languages. Many schools. Trade language. Dictionary. SOV. Literacy rate in first language: 90%. Literacy rate in second language: 90%. Tropical forest. Large volcanic islands. Agriculturalists: yams. 0 to 1,000 feet. Bible 1928.

DOGA *(MAGABARA)* [DGG] 200 (1975 SIL). Milne Bay Province, north coast of Cape Vogel. Austronesian, Malayo-Polynesian, Central-Eastern, Eastern Malayo-Polynesian, Oceanic, Western Oceanic, Papuan Tip, Nuclear, North Papuan Mainland-D'Entrecasteaux, Are-Taupota, Are. 47% to 55% lexical similarity with Are (closest). 60% of young people know English, others Anuki and Dima. Literacy rate in second language: Most young people.

DOM [DOA] 12,000 (1994 NTM). Simbu Province, mainly south of the Wahgi River from Kundiawa west of the Sinasina area. Trans-New Guinea, Main Section, Central and Western, East New Guinea Highlands, Central, Chimbu. Dialect: ERA. Bible portions.

DOMU *(DOM)* [DOF] 593 (1979 census). Central Province, coast east of Cape Rodney and inland. Trans-New Guinea, Main Section, Eastern, Central and Southeastern, Mailuan. 66% lexical similarity with Bauwaki (closest). 85% to 100% of the speakers are bilingual in Mailu, Suau, Hiri Motu, English.

DOMUNG [DEV] 2,000 (1991 SIL). Tapen, Madang Province. Trans-New Guinea, Main Section, Central and Western, Huon-Finisterre, Finisterre, Yupna.

DOROMU *(DORAM)* [KQC] 1,200 (1993 SIL). Central Province, south of Mt. Obree, west of Mt. Brown. Trans-New Guinea, Main Section, Eastern, Central and Southeastern, Manubaran. Dialects: KOKILA, KORIKO, KOKI (DOROMU). 63% lexical similarity with Maria (closest).

DOSO [DOL] 700 (1973 D. Shaw). Western Province, Aramia River and Wawoi Falls areas, near the Kamula. Unclassified. A separate language from Kamula.

DOURA [DON] 800 (1981 Wurm and Hattori). Central Province, around Galley Reach. Austronesian, Malayo-Polynesian, Central-Eastern, Eastern Malayo-Polynesian, Oceanic, Western Oceanic, Papuan Tip, Peripheral, Central Papuan, West Central Papuan, Nuclear. 54% lexical similarity with Motu (closest). Many know Motu and Hiri Motu. Investigation needed: bilingual proficiency in Motu, Hiri Motu.

DUAU [DUA] 3,550 (1991 SIL). Milne Bay Province, Sawabwala, Normanby islands. Austronesian, Malayo-Polynesian, Central-Eastern, Eastern Malayo-Polynesian, Oceanic, Western Oceanic, Papuan Tip, Nuclear, North Papuan Mainland-D'Entrecasteaux, Dobu-Duau. Dialects: MWALUKWASIA, SOMWADINA, GULEGULEU (GURAGUREU), DAWADA, SIAUSI. Dialects are diverse. No central or dominant dialect. 75% lexical similarity with Bunama, 52% with Mwatebu, Auhelawa, and Tubetube. 20% monolingual. Others use Dobu as second language. Trade language. There are many schools, but many speakers are illiterate. Christian, traditional religion.

DUDUELA [DUK] 469 (1981 Wurm and Hattori). Madang Province. Trans-New Guinea, Madang-Adelbert Range, Madang, Rai Coast, Nuru. Related languages: Kwato, Ogea, Uya, Rerau, Jilim, Yangulam. Investigation needed: intelligibility.

DUMPU *(WATIFA, WATIWA)* [WTF] 261 (1981 Wurm and Hattori). Madang Province, two villages: Bebei and Dumpu. Trans-New Guinea, Madang-Adelbert Range, Madang, Rai Coast, Evapia. Related languages: Sinsauru, Asas, Sausi, Kesawai. All men use Tok Pisin as second language. Investigation needed: intelligibility.

DUMUN *(BAI)* [DUI] 42 (1981 Wurm and Hattori). Madang Province. Trans-New Guinea, Madang- Adelbert Range, Madang, Rai Coast, Yaganon. Related languages: Yabong, Ganglau, Saep. Investigation needed: intelligibility.

DUNA *(YUNA)* [DUC] 11,000 (1991 SIL). Southern Highlands Province, Lake Kopiago and Koroba districts, some in Western Highlands Province. Trans-New Guinea, Main Section, Central and Western, Central and South New Guinea-Kutubuan, Central and South New Guinea, Duna-Bogaya. NT 1976.

DUWET *(GUWET, GUWOT, WAING)* [GVE] 398 (1988 Holzknecht). Morobe Province, Busu River area. Austronesian, Malayo-Polynesian, Central-Eastern, Eastern Malayo-Polynesian, Oceanic, Western Oceanic, North New Guinea, Huon Gulf, Markham, Lower, Busu.

EDOLO ***(ETORO, EDOLO ADO, ETOLO)*** [ETR] 1,300 (1995 Deiyo Bamo). Southern Highlands Province, Tari District, and Western Province, Nomad District; southwest of Mt. Sisa. Trans-New Guinea, Main Section, Central and Western, Central and South New Guinea-Kutubuan, Central and South New Guinea, Bosavi. Dialects: EASTERN EDOLO, WESTERN EDOLO. 38% lexical similarity with Beami. SOV; (C)V(V). Literacy rate in first language: 25% to 50%. Literacy rate in second language: 25% to 50%. Tropical forest. Mountain slope. Swidden agriculturalists. 365 to 1,000 meters. Bible portions 1997.

EITIEP [EIT] 394 (1981 Wurm and Hattori). East Sepik Province, southwest of Kombio, and partially in Sandaun Province, across Bongos River. Torricelli, Kombio-Arapesh, Kombio. Close to Kombio. Investigation needed: intelligibility with Kombio.

EIVO [EIV] 1,200 (1981 Wurm and Hattori). Mountains of south central North Solomons Province. East Papuan, Bougainville, West, Rotokas. Close to Kunua. Investigation needed: intelligibility with Kunua.

ELEPI ***(SAMAP)*** [ELE] 149 (1981 Wurm and Hattori). East Sepik Province, coast around Samap. Torricelli, Marienberg. Literacy rate in first language: Less than 5%. Literacy rate in second language: 25% to 50%.

ELKEI ***(OLKOI)*** [ELK] 1,590 (1988 SIL). Sandaun Province. Torricelli, Wapei-Palei, Wapei. At least 3 dialects.

ELU [ELU] 216 (1983 SIL). Manus Province, north coast of Manus Island. Austronesian, Malayo-Polynesian, Central-Eastern, Eastern Malayo-Polynesian, Oceanic, Admiralty Islands, Eastern, Manus, East. Most speakers are bilingual in Kurti. Investigation needed: bilingual proficiency in Kurti. SVO.

ENGA ***(CAGA, TSAGA, TCHAGA)*** [ENQ] 164,750 (1981 Wurm and Hattori), including 12,000 in Sau (1990 UBS). Enga Province. The Maramuni are nomadic, and are in the lower reaches of the central range. Trans-New Guinea, Main Section, Central and Western, East New Guinea Highlands, West-Central, Enga. Dialects: KANDEPE, LAYAPO, TAYATO, MAE (MAI, WABAG), MARAMUNI (MALAMUNI), KAINA, KAPONA, SAU (SAU ENGA, WAPI), YANDAPO, LAPALAMA 1, LAPALAMA 2, LAIAGAM, SARI. Mae is the standard dialect; all understand it. Layapo is between Mae and Kyaka. Trade language. Dictionary. SOV. Scrub forest. Mountain slope. Swidden agriculturalists. 1,200 to 2,700 meters. NT 1979-1988.

ENGLISH [ENG] 50,000 in Papua New Guinea (1987), 1.5% of the population. Indo-European, Germanic, West, English. Official language. Used in schools. Bible 1535-1989. See main entry under United Kingdom.

ERAVE ***(POLE, SOUTH KEWA, KEWA SOUTH)*** [KJY] 7,000 (1997 K. Franklin). Southern Highlands Province. Trans-New Guinea, Main Section, Central and Western, East New Guinea Highlands, West-Central, Angal-Kewa. NT 1993.

ERE ***(NANE, E)*** [TWP] 1,030 (1980 census). Manus Province, south coast, Drabitou, Lohe, Londru, Metawari, Pau, Piterait, Taui-Undrau, Hatwara, and Loi villages. Austronesian, Malayo-Polynesian, Central-Eastern, Eastern Malayo-Polynesian, Oceanic, Admiralty Islands, Eastern, Manus, East. Speakers are highly bilingual in Kele. SVO.

EWAGE-NOTU ***(NOTU, EWAGE)*** [NOU] 12,900 (1988 SIL). Oro Province, Popondetta District, on the coast between Bakumbari and Pongani. Trans-New Guinea, Main Section, Eastern, Binanderean, Binanderean Proper. Dialects: EWAGE-NOTU, YEGA (GONA, OKEINA, OKENA). Also spoken by the Soverapa people. People do not like the name 'Ewage' in the Ovo Bay, Dongani, and Ako areas. The name 'Ewage' is preferred in the Buna and Gona areas where the name 'Notu' is not liked. SOV. Literacy rate in first language: 75% to 100%. Literacy rate in second language: 75% to 100%. Tropical forest. Coastal. Fishermen, swidden agriculturalists. 0 to 60 meters. NT 1987.

FAITA [FAT] 57 (1981 Wurm and Hattori). Madang Province. Trans-New Guinea, Madang-Adelbert Range, Adelbert Range, Brahman. Related languages: Biyom, Isabi, Tauya. Investigation needed: intelligibility.

FAIWOL ***(FAIWOLMIN, FEGOLMIN, UNKIA, KAUWOL, KAWOL, KAVWOL)*** [FAI] 4,500 (1987 SIL). Western Province, Tabubil District, at the headwaters of the Fly and Palmer rivers. Not in Irian Jaya. Trans-New Guinea, Main Section, Central and Western, Central and South New Guinea-Kutubuan, Central and South New Guinea, Ok, Mountain. Dialects: WOPKEIMIN, ANKIYAKMIN. Many dialects. SOV. Literacy rate in first language: 25% to 50%. Literacy rate in second language: 50% to 75%. Gallery forest. Mountain slope. Swidden agriculturalists. 300 to 900 meters. NT 1995.

FAS ***(BEMBI)*** [FAS] 1,600 or more (1988 W. Baron SIL). Sandaun Province, Amanab and Aitape districts. Kwomtari-Baibai, Kwomtari. Dialects: EASTERN FAS, WESTERN FAS. Dialect differences are small. SOV. Tropical forest. Mountain slope, riverine. Hunter-gatherers, agriculturalists. 200 to 600 meters.

FASU ***(NAMOME)*** [FAA] 1,200 including 750 Fasu, 300 Namuni, 150 Some (1981 Wurm and Hattori). Southern Highlands Province, Nipa District. Trans-New Guinea, Main Section, Central and Western, Central and South New Guinea-Kutubuan, Kutubuan, West. Dialects: SOME, KAIBU (KAIPU), NAMOME (NAMUMI, NAMUNI). Wurm and Hattori treat Some and Namuni as separate languages.

Dictionary. Grammar. Literacy rate in first language: 75% to 100%. Literacy rate in second language: 75% to 100%. NT 1976-1995.

FEMBE ***(SINALE, AGALA)*** [AGL] 350 (1986 SIL). Western Province, Upper Strickland River. Trans-New Guinea, Main Section, Central and Western, Central and South New Guinea-Kutubuan, Central and South New Guinea, East Strickland. Closest to Kalamo and Konai. 'Fembe' is their own name. Bogala language speakers have moved into Fembe territory, dividing the Fembe into 2 geographical areas. Literacy rate in first language: Less than 5%. Literacy rate in second language: Less than 5%.

FINUNGWA ***(FINUNGWAN)*** [FAG] 469 (1978 McElhanon). Morobe Province. Trans-New Guinea, Main Section, Central and Western, Huon-Finisterre, Finisterre, Erap. Traditional religion.

FIWAGA ***(FIMAGA, FIWAGE)*** [FIW] 300 (1981 Wurm and Hattori). Southern Highlands Province, northeast of Tama. Trans-New Guinea, Main Section, Central and Western, Central and South New Guinea-Kutubuan, Kutubuan, East. Wurm and Hattori treat Fiwage and Foi as separate languages.

FOI ***(FOE, MUBI RIVER)*** [FOI] 2,800 (1980 UBS). Southern Highlands Province, east and south of Lake Kutubu and Mubi River. Trans-New Guinea, Main Section, Central and Western, Central and South New Guinea-Kutubuan, Kutubuan, East. Dialects: IFIGI, KAFA, KUTUBU, MUBI. NT 1978.

FOLOPA ***(PODOPA, POLOPA, PODOBA, FORABA)*** [PPO] 3,000 (1985 SIL). Gulf Province, Baimuru District, Kerabi Valley; also in Southern Highlands Province. 20 villages. Trans-New Guinea, Teberan-Pawaian, Teberan. Dialects: RO (KEAI, WORUGL), BARA (HARAHUI, HARAHU), SESA (MAMISA, SONGU, IBUKAIRU), KEWAH, TEBERA, AUREI, WARAGA, PUPITAU, BORO, SURI, SILIGI, SOPESE, KEBA-WOPASALI. Closest to Dadibi. SOV. Tropical forest. Mountain slope. Hunter-gatherers, agriculturalists. 600 to 1,000 meters. Bible portions 1978-1989.

FORAK [FRO] 163 (1981 Wurm and Hattori). Madang Province, Saidor District, Mamgak village, 5 miles west and inland from Seure on the coast. Trans-New Guinea, Main Section, Central and Western, Huon-Finisterre, Finisterre, Warup. Bilingualism in Asat, Asaro'o. Asaro'o, Asat, Bulgebi, Degenan, Guiarak, Gwahatike, Yagomi. Mountain slope.

FORE [FOR] 17,000 (1991 SIL). Eastern Highlands Province, Okapa District. Trans-New Guinea, Main Section, Central and Western, East New Guinea Highlands, East-Central, Fore. Dialects: PAMUSA (SOUTH FORE), NORTH CENTRAL FORE. Dictionary. Grammar. SOV. Literacy rate in first language: 25% to 50%. Literacy rate in second language: 25% to 50%. NT 1970-1974.

FUYUG ***(FUYUGE, FUYUGHE, MAFUFU)*** [FUY] 18,000 (1994 SIL). Central Province, Goilala District, Owen Stanley Range. Trans-New Guinea, Main Section, Eastern, Central and Southeastern, Goilalan. Dialects: CENTRAL UDAB, NORTHEAST FUYUG, NORTH-SOUTH UDAB, WEST FUYUG. 35% lexical similarity with Biangai, 33% with Kunimaipa, 29% with Weri, 27% with Tauade. Grammar. SOV, (C)V(C)(C); postpositions. Literacy rate in first language: 5%. Literacy rate in second language: 10%. Pandanus forest. Mountain valleys. 335 to 2,600 meters. Bible portions 1973-1994.

GABUTAMON [GAV] 302 (1981 Wurm and Hattori). Madang Province, 10 miles west southwest of Gali. Trans-New Guinea, Main Section, Central and Western, Huon-Finisterre, Finisterre, Yupna. Related to Yupna, Mebu.

GADSUP [GAJ] 10,000 (1996 SIL). Eastern Highlands Province, Kainantu District. Trans-New Guinea, Main Section, Central and Western, East New Guinea Highlands, Eastern, Gadsup-Auyana-Awa. Dialects: OYANA (OIYANA), GADSUP. Ontenu is a related but separate language. SOV. Literacy rate in first language: 25% to 50%. Literacy rate in second language: 50% to 75%. Tropical forest. Mountain slope. Swidden agriculturalists. 1,538 meters. NT 1981.

GAIKUNDI ***(GAIKUNTI)*** [GBF] 700 (1975 SIL). East Sepik Province, Ambunti District, Sepik Plains south of Maprik. Sepik-Ramu, Sepik, Middle Sepik, Ndu. Close to Sawos. Literacy rate in first language: Less than 5%. Literacy rate in second language: 25% to 50%. Bible portions 1978.

GAINA [GCN] 1,130 including 1,000 in Bareji, 130 in Gaina (1971 Dutton). Oro Province, next to the Baruga, the villages around Iwuji. Trans-New Guinea, Main Section, Eastern, Binanderean, Binanderean Proper. Dialects: BAREJI (BAREDJI), GAINA. 61% lexical similarity with Dogoro (closest). Sago swamp.

GAL ***(BAIMAK, WEIM)*** [GAP] 224 (1981 Wurm and Hattori). Madang Province, on the Gogol River. Trans-New Guinea, Madang-Adelbert Range, Madang, Mabuso, Hanseman.

GALEYA ***(GAREA)*** [GAR] 1,876 (1972 Govt. survey). Milne Bay Province, northeast coast, Fergusson Island. Austronesian, Malayo-Polynesian, Central-Eastern, Eastern Malayo-Polynesian, Oceanic, Western Oceanic, Papuan Tip, Nuclear, North Papuan Mainland-D'Entrecasteaux, Dobu-Duau. Dialects: WADALEI, GAMETA, URUA, BASIMA, SEBUTUIA, GAREA (GALEYA). 61% lexical similarity with Bosilewa (closest). Galeya and Basima dialects have 80% lexical similarity. 30% monolingual. Dobu is well known by others. Less than half of children are in school. Coastal. Christian, traditional religion.

GANGLAU [GGL] 154 (1981 Wurm and Hattori). Madang Province. Trans-New Guinea, Madang-Adelbert Range, Madang, Rai Coast, Yaganon. Related languages: Yabong, Dumun, Saep.

GANTS ***(GAJ)*** [GAO] 1,884 (1981 Wurm and Hattori). Madang Province. Trans-New Guinea, Main Section, Central and Western, East New Guinea Highlands, Kalam, Gants.

GAPAPAIWA ***(MANAPE, GAPA, PAIWA)*** [PWG] 3,000 including about 1,300 in western dialect, 1,700 in eastern (1998 SIL). Milne Bay Province, Makamaka District, south coast of Cape Vogel and inland along the Ruaba River. Austronesian, Malayo-Polynesian, Central-Eastern, Eastern Malayo-Polynesian, Oceanic, Western Oceanic, Papuan Tip, Nuclear, North Papuan Mainland-D'Entrecasteaux, Are-Taupota, Are. 73% lexical similarity with Ghaiyavi (Boanaki, closest). English is the church language. Only older people can speak Wedau. Tok Pisin is seldom heard, and men are more fluent than women. A number of well educated people. Dictionary. Grammar. SOV, CV, nontonal. Literacy rate in first language: 80%. Literacy rate in second language: 80%. Tropical and gallery forest. Coastal. Swidden agriculturalists: coconut palm; fishermen. 0 to 50 meters. Bible portions 1997.

GARUS ***(ATE, EM, KURUPI)*** [GYB] 1,394 (1980 census). Madang Province, Astrolabe Bay. Trans-New Guinea, Madang-Adelbert Range, Madang, Mabuso, Hanseman. Related languages: Bagupi, Matepi, Mosimo, Murupi, Rapting, Samosa, Silopi. Speakers are becoming more bilingual. Literacy rate in first language: less than 5%. Literacy rate in second language: 25% to 50%.

GASMATA [GSA] 200 (1981 Wurm and Hattori). West New Britain Province, southwest coast. Austronesian, Malayo-Polynesian, Central-Eastern, Eastern Malayo-Polynesian, Oceanic, Western Oceanic, North New Guinea, Ngero-Vitiaz, Vitiaz, Southwest New Britain, Arawe-Pasismanua, Arawe, East Arawe. Older speakers understand Avau, but it is not understood by others. Tropical forest. Raised coral coast.

GEDAGED ***(BEL, GRAGED, STAR, STAR-RAGETTA, TIARA, MITEBOG, RAGETTA, RIO, SEK, SZEAK-BAGILI)*** [GDD] 2,764 (1975 Z'Graggen). Madang Province; Sek, Yabob, Karkar, and Bagabag islands, Astrolabe Bay, and coastal villages around Madang. Austronesian, Malayo-Polynesian, Central-Eastern, Eastern Malayo-Polynesian, Oceanic, Western Oceanic, North New Guinea, Ngero-Vitiaz, Vitiaz, Bel, Nuclear Bel, Northern. Literacy rate in first language: 25% to 50%. Literacy rate in second language: 50% to 100%. NT 1960.

GENDE ***(BUNDI, GENE, GENDEKA)*** [GAF] 8,000 (1987 SIL). Madang Province, Bundi District near Bundi. Trans-New Guinea, Main Section, Central and Western, East New Guinea Highlands, East-Central, Gende. Bilingualism in Tok Pisin. Vigorous. Mountain slope. 4,000 to 6,500 feet. Traditional religion.

GETMATA [GET] West New Britain Province, Kandrian District. Austronesian, Malayo-Polynesian, Central-Eastern, Eastern Malayo-Polynesian, Oceanic, Western Oceanic, North New Guinea, Ngero-Vitiaz, Vitiaz, Southwest New Britain, Arawe-Pasismanua, Pasismanua. Dialect chain with Kaulong and Karore. May be extinct.

GHAYAVI ***(GALAVI, BOIANAKI, BOANAKI, BOINAKI, BOANAI)*** [BMK] 1,757 (1979 census). Milne Bay Province, Alotau District, Weraura Local Government Area, north coast along Goodenough Bay from Uga in the west to Wadobuna in the east, including Rabaraba. Austronesian, Malayo-Polynesian, Central-Eastern, Eastern Malayo-Polynesian, Oceanic, Western Oceanic, Papuan Tip, Nuclear, North Papuan Mainland-D'Entrecasteaux, Are-Taupota, Are. 76% lexical similarity with Gapapaiwa (closest), 46% with Wedau. Wedau, Gapapaiwa, and English are the second languages. Wedau people were traditional rivals, and there are reservations toward the use of Wedau. The alternate names given are all mistakes in reports written by outsiders. Investigation needed: intelligibility, attitudes toward Gapapaiwa. Most speakers are literate. There are adequate schools in the area, but Ghayavi does not seem to be used for instruction.

GIDRA ***(ORIOMO, JIBU, WIPI)*** [GDR] 1,800 (1976 SIL). Western Province, eastern third of area between Fly Delta, estuary, and south coast. Trans-New Guinea, Trans-Fly-Bulaka River, Trans-Fly, Eastern Trans-Fly. Dialects: DOROGORI, ABAM, PEAWA, UME, KURU, ZIM, WONIE, IAMEGA, GAMAEWE, PODARI, WIPIM, KAPAL, RUAL, GUIAM, YUTA. Literacy rate in first language: 25% to 50%. Literacy rate in second language: 25% to 50%.

GIMI [GIM] 22,463 (1981 Wurm and Hattori). Eastern Highlands Province, Okapa District. Trans-New Guinea, Main Section, Central and Western, East New Guinea Highlands, East-Central, Fore. Dialects: EAST GIMI, WEST GIMI (GOUNO). Literacy rate in first language: 5% to 15%. Literacy rate in second language: 5% to 15%. Traditional religion, Christian. NT 1994.

GIMI ***(LOKO)*** [GIP] 3,697 (1982 SIL). West New Britain Province, southwest coast and inland, Johanna River to Anu River. Austronesian, Malayo-Polynesian, Central-Eastern, Eastern Malayo-Polynesian, Oceanic, Western Oceanic, North New Guinea, Ngero-Vitiaz, Vitiaz, Southwest New Britain, Arawe-Pasismanua, Arawe, West Arawe. Dialect chain with Aiklep and Apalik. Different from Gimi in Eastern Highlands Province. Literacy rate in first language: 25% to 50%. Literacy rate in second language: 25% to 50%. Bible portions 1992.

GINUMAN ***(DIME)*** [GNM] 775 (1971 Dutton). Milne Bay Province, Mt. Simpson to coast at Naraka. Trans-New Guinea, Main Section, Eastern, Central and Southeastern, Dagan. 42% lexical similarity with Kanasi (Dombosaina village).

GIRA [GRG] 500 (1987 census). Madang Province. Trans-New Guinea, Main Section, Central and Western, Huon-Finisterre, Finisterre, Gusap-Mot.

GIRAWA ***(BEGASIN, BEGESIN, BAGASIN)*** [BBR] 4,003 (1981 Wurm and Hattori). Madang Province, Ramu District. Trans-New Guinea, Madang-Adelbert Range, Madang, Mabuso, Kokon. Related languages: Munit, Bemal. SOV. Literacy rate in first language: 25% to 50%. Literacy rate in second language: 25% to 50%. Tropical forest. Mountain slope. Swidden agriculturalists. 300 to 1,000 meters. NT 1994.

GITUA ***(GITOA, KELANA)*** [GIL] 483 (1978 McElhanon). Morobe Province, north coast of Huon Peninsula. Austronesian, Malayo-Polynesian, Central-Eastern, Eastern Malayo-Polynesian, Oceanic, Western Oceanic, North New Guinea, Ngero-Vitiaz, Ngero, Tuam.

GIZRA [TOF] 1,100 (1998 SIL). Western Province, South Fly Area, north-northeast of the Torres Strait island of Saibai, villages of Kulalae, Ngomtono, Barnap, Kupere, and Waidoro. Trans-New Guinea, Trans-Fly-Bulaka River, Trans-Fly, Eastern Trans-Fly. Dialects: WESTERN GIZRA, WAIDORO. SOV. Literacy rate in first language: 15% (including semiliterates). Literacy rate in second language: 80% (including semiliterates). Savannah, wooded freshwater swamp, mangroves. Coastal plains, interfluvial. Swidden agriculturalists. 3 to 12 meters. Christian, traditional religion.

GNAU [GNU] 980 (1981 Wurm and Hattori). Sandaun Province, Namblo Census Division, northwest of Maimai. Torricelli, Wapei-Palei, Wapei.

GOBASI [GOI] 1,100 (1993 ECP). Western Province. Trans-New Guinea, Main Section, Central and Western, Central and South New Guinea-Kutubuan, Central and South New Guinea, East Strickland. Dialects: GOBASI (BIBO), HONIBO, OIBAE (OIBA). Related to Samo and Kubo. Literacy rate in first language: Less than 5%. Literacy rate in second language: Less than 5%.

GOGODALA ***(GOGODARA)*** [GOH] 10,000 (1991 UBS). Western Province, north bank of Fly River, Aramia River. 301 villages. Trans-New Guinea, Main Section, Central and Western, Gogodala-Suki, Gogodala. Closest to Ari. Literacy rate in first language: 15% to 25%. Literacy rate in second language: 25% to 50%. NT 1981.

GOLIN ***(GOLLUM, GUMINE)*** [GVF] 51,105 (1981 Wurm and Hattori). Simbu Province, Gumine District. Trans-New Guinea, Main Section, Central and Western, East New Guinea Highlands, Central, Chimbu. Dialects: YURI, KIA (KIARI), GOLIN, KERI, MARIGL. Close to Dom. Nondiri is not a language, but a village where the Mian bush people live. They speak Golin. Grammar. Literacy rate in first language: 25% to 50%. Literacy rate in second language: 25% to 50%. NT 1980.

GORAKOR [GOC] 2,741 (1979 census). Morobe Province, Mumeng District, including Yanta. Austronesian, Malayo-Polynesian, Central-Eastern, Eastern Malayo-Polynesian, Oceanic, Western Oceanic, North New Guinea, Huon Gulf, South, Hote-Buang, Buang, Mumeng. In the Mumeng language chain. Some intelligibility with Patep. Investigation needed: intelligibility, attitudes toward Patep. SVO. Literacy rate in first language: 15% to 25%. Literacy rate in second language: 25% to 50%. Tropical forest. Mountain slope. Swidden agriculturalists. 300 to 900 meters.

GOROVU ***(GOROVA, YERANI)*** [GRQ] 50 (1981 Wurm and Hattori). East Sepik Province, Bangapela village, Ramu River. Sepik-Ramu, Ramu, Ramu Proper, Grass, Grass Proper. Bilingualism in Banaro. Banaro is replacing the language. Nearly extinct.

GUHU-SAMANE ***(PAIAWA, TAHARI, MURI, BIA, MID-WARIA)*** [GHS] 6,289 (1978 McElhanon). Morobe Province, Lae District, and a few in Oro Province, from Kanoma and Sidema villages northward. Trans-New Guinea, Main Section, Eastern, Binanderean, Guhu-Samane. Dialect: SEKARE. 18% lexical similarity with Suena and Zia (closest). Literacy rate in first language: 50% to 75%. Literacy rate in second language: 50% to 75%. NT 1975-1983.

GUIARAK [GKA] 131 (1981 Wurm and Hattori). Madang Province, 10 to 15 miles west of Seure. Trans-New Guinea, Main Section, Central and Western, Huon-Finisterre, Finisterre, Warup. Related to Asaro'o, Asat, Bulgebi, Degenan, Forak, Gwahatike, Yagomi.

GUMALU [GMU] 271 (1981 Wurm and Hattori). Madang Province. Trans-New Guinea, Madang-Adelbert Range, Madang, Mabuso, Gum. Related languages: Sihan, Amele, Isebe, Bau, Panim. Investigation needed: intelligibility.

GUMAWANA ***(GUMASI, DOMDOM)*** [GVS] 367 (1996 census). Milne Bay Province, Esa'ala District, Amphlett Islands; a group of about 25 islands north of Fergusson. 7 villages. Austronesian, Malayo-Polynesian, Central-Eastern, Eastern Malayo-Polynesian, Oceanic, Western Oceanic, Papuan Tip, Nuclear, North Papuan Mainland-D'Entrecasteaux, Gumawana. 48% lexical similarity with Galeya, 47% with Dobu (closest). 50% monolingual. Others use Dobu or Kilivila as second language. People do not mix with others. Grammar. Literacy rate in first language: 75% to 100%. Literacy rate in second language: 75% to 100%. Christian. Bible portions 1992.

GUNTAI [GNT] 168 (1980 census). Western Province, Morehead District. Trans-New Guinea, Trans-Fly-Bulaka River, Trans-Fly, Morehead and Upper Maro Rivers, Tonda.

GURAMALUM [GRZ] 3 or 4 speakers (1987 SIL). New Ireland Province. Austronesian, Malayo-Polynesian, Central-Eastern, Eastern Malayo-Polynesian, Oceanic, Western Oceanic, Meso Melanesian, New Ireland, South New Ireland-Northwest Solomonic, Patpatar-Tolai. Nearly extinct.

GURIASO [GRX] 350 (1993 SIL). Sandaun Province, Amanab District. Kwomtari-Baibai, Kwomtari. Distinct language from Kwomtari.

GUSAN [GSN] 794 (1980 census). Morobe Province. Trans-New Guinea, Main Section, Central and Western, Huon-Finisterre, Finisterre, Erap.

GWAHATIKE ***(GWATIKE, DAHATING)*** [DAH] 1,200 (1995 SIL). Madang Province, Saidor District, several villages south of Saidor. Trans-New Guinea, Main Section, Central and Western, Huon-Finisterre, Finisterre, Warup. Dialects: GWAHATIKE, GWAHAMERE, GORA, GWAPTI. Related languages: Asaro'o, Asat, Bulgebi, Degenan, Forak, Guiarak, Yagomi. No monolinguals. Tok Pisin is the second language. SOV. Literacy rate in first language: 0% to 5%. Literacy rate in second language: 70%. Foothills. Swidden agriculturalists. 1,800 feet. Christian, traditional religion, cargo cult. Bible portions 1992.

GWEDA ***(GARUWAHI)*** [GRW] 10 to 20 (1998 SIL). Milne Bay Province, Alotau District, Maramatana Local Council Area, Garuwahi village. Austronesian, Malayo-Polynesian, Central-Eastern, Eastern Malayo-Polynesian, Oceanic, Western Oceanic, Papuan Tip, Nuclear, North Papuan Mainland-D'Entrecasteaux, Are-Taupota, Taupota. 71% lexical similarity with Wa'ema, 69% with Taupota, 68% with Naura, 67% with Kapulika, 64% with Topura, 63% with Tawala, 53% with Wedau. Except for 1 or 2 elderly people, all use Wedau, Taupota, Motu, or English as second language. Nearly extinct.

HAHON ***(HANON)*** [HAH] 1,300 (1977 Lincoln). Northwest North Solomons Province. Austronesian, Malayo-Polynesian, Central-Eastern, Eastern Malayo-Polynesian, Oceanic, Western Oceanic, Meso Melanesian, New Ireland, South New Ireland-Northwest Solomonic, Nehan-North Bougainville, Saposa-Tinputz. Dialects: KURUR, RATSUA, ARAVIA. Moderate acculturation.

HAIGWAI ***(NAURA, KAPULIKA)*** [HGW] 942 (1990 census). Milne Bay Province, Alotau District, Huhu Local Government Area, inland from the head of Milne Bay between Hagita and Waigani estates and the mountains to the west. Austronesian, Malayo-Polynesian, Central-Eastern, Eastern Malayo-Polynesian, Oceanic, Western Oceanic, Papuan Tip, Nuclear, North Papuan Mainland-D'Entrecasteaux, Are-Taupota, Taupota. Dialects: NAURA, KAPULIKA. Naura and Gweda agree that Gweda is the closest to Haigwai. Naura has 68% lexical similarity with Gweda, Kapulika has 65% with Taupota, both dialects have 52% with Wedau, 48% with Maiwala. Fewer than 20% are monolingual. Some speakers know some Suau, Tawala, Wedau, English, or Motu. Strong support for Haigwai language. One vernacular elementary school, and one primary school.

HAKÖ ***(HAKU)*** [HAO] 5,000 (1982 SIL). North Solomons Province, North Bougainville District, northeastern Buka Island. Austronesian, Malayo-Polynesian, Central-Eastern, Eastern Malayo-Polynesian, Oceanic, Western Oceanic, Meso Melanesian, New Ireland, South New Ireland-Northwest Solomonic, Nehan-North Bougainville, Buka, Halia. Dialect: LONTES. SVO. Literacy rate in first language: 75% to 100%. Literacy rate in second language: 75% to 100%. Tropical forest, deciduous forest. Coastal, coral escarpment. Fishermen; intensive agriculturalists: cocoa, copra. 0 to 70 meters.

HALIA ***(TASI)*** [HLA] 20,000 or more (1994 J. Allen SIL). North Solomons Province, North Bougainville District, northeastern Buka Island. Austronesian, Malayo-Polynesian, Central-Eastern, Eastern Malayo-Polynesian, Oceanic, Western Oceanic, Meso Melanesian, New Ireland, South New Ireland-Northwest Solomonic, Nehan-North Bougainville, Buka, Halia. Dialects: HANAHAN, HANGAN, TOULOUN (TULON, TULUN), SELAU. Distinct from Tulun in Manus Province (see Bohuai). Dictionary. Grammar. SVO. Literacy rate in first language: 75% to 100%. Literacy rate in second language: 75% to 100%. Tropical forest, deciduous forest. Coastal, coral escarpment. Fishermen; intensive agriculturalists: cocoa, copra. 0 to 70 meters. NT 1978.

HAMTAI ***(HAMDAY, KAPAU, KAMEA, WATUT, "KUKUKUKU")*** [HMT] 45,000 (1998 Tom Palmer). Gulf Province, Kukipi District, along the Tauri River inland east to the Ladedamu River; Morobe Province, Lae District, Kodama Range into Bulolo-Watut divide, across to Mt. Grosse and north to Mt. Taylor. Trans-New Guinea, Main Section, Central and Western, Angan, Angan Proper. Dialects: WENTA, HOWI, PMASA'A, HAMTAI, KAINTIBA. The people dislike the name "Kukukuku". The name 'Kamea' is used in Gulf Province. 'Hamtai' is preferred elsewhere. Grammar. 1,500 to 6,000 feet. NT 1974, out of print.

HANGA HUNDI ***(KWASENGEN, WEST WOSERA)*** [WOS] 6,008 (1983 SIL). East Sepik Province, Pagwi District. 16 villages. Sepik-Ramu, Sepik, Middle Sepik, Ndu. Closely related to Ambulas. 3 community schools. Literacy rate in first language: 5% to 15%. Literacy rate in second language: 5% to 15%. Savannah, hills, swamp. 150 to 300 feet.

HARUAI ***(HARWAY, WAIBUK, WIYAW, WIYAU, WOVAN, TAMAN)*** [TMD] 1,000 speakers (1988 B. Comrie). Madang Province, southwest corner, southwest Mid-Ramu (Simbai) District, western Schrader Range, west of the Kobon. Trans-New Guinea, Main Section, East New Guinea Highlands, Piawi. Dialects: NORTH WAIBUK (HAMIL), CENTRAL WAIBUK (MAMBAR), SOUTH WAIBUK

(ARAMA). Related language: Pinai-Hagahai, though not inherently intelligible with Haruai. Word taboo is practiced, but does not seem to impede intelligibility among related language varieties. 37% lexical similarity with Aramo, 35% with Kobon. Young men are likely to know Tok Pisin or Kobon, many children speak good Tok Pisin, and many women are at least communicatively competent in Tok Pisin (Comrie). Many are monolingual. Speeches and sermons by outsiders are always translated into Haruai. All ages (1988). 'Haruai' is self name. Some similarities to Kalam languages due to borrowing (Comrie). More loan words from Kobon are used in the northern area. SOV; postpositions (few); genitives precede noun heads; possessives, adjectives, numerals, relative clauses follow noun heads; postclitic demonstratives; suffixes; V, CV, VC, CVC. Tropical forest. Mountain slope. Swidden agriculturalists. 2,000 to 6,000 feet.

HERMIT ***(AGOMES, LUF, MARON)*** [LLF] Western Manus Province, Luf and Maron islands in Hermit Islands. Austronesian, Malayo-Polynesian, Central-Eastern, Eastern Malayo-Polynesian, Oceanic, Admiralty Islands, Eastern, Manus, West. Extinct.

HEWA ***(SISIMIN)*** [HAM] 2,147 (1986 P. Vollrath SIL), including 290 in Yoliapi (1982 SIL). Southern Highlands Province, Koroba District; Enga Province, Lagaip District; Sandaun Province, Telefomin District. Lagaip River area, in the mountains north of Duna and Ipili. Sepik-Ramu, Sepik, Sepik Hill, Sanio. Dialects: UPPER LAGAIP, CENTRAL LAGAIP, LOWER LAGAIP, NORTH HEWA. Bilingual level estimates for Tok Pisin, English, Ipili, Duna, Oksapmin are Tok Pisin: 0 85%, 1 8%, 2 5%, 3 2%, 4 0%, 5 0%; English: 0 99%, 1 1%, 2-5 0%; Ipili: 0 98%, 1-5 2%; Duna: 0 96%, 1 2%, 2 1%, 3 1%, 4 0%, 5 0%; Oksapmin: 0 99%, 1-5 1%. Semi-nomadic. SOV. Literacy rate in first language: 5% to 15%. Literacy rate in second language: 5% to 15%. Tropical forest. Mountain slope. Swidden agriculturalists, hunter-gatherers traditionally. 480 to 1,700 meters. Traditional religion, Christian. Bible portions 1985.

HINIHON [HIH] 1,100 (1981 Wurm and Hattori). Madang Province, north central. Trans-New Guinea, Madang-Adelbert Range, Adelbert Range, Pihom-Isumrud-Mugil, Pihom, Tiboran. Related dialect or language: Kowaki.

HOTE ***(HO'TEI, HOTEC, MALEI)*** [HOT] 2,106 including 1,805 Hote and 301 Misim (1983 census). Morobe Province, Lae District, Francisco River area. Austronesian, Malayo-Polynesian, Central-Eastern, Eastern Malayo-Polynesian, Oceanic, Western Oceanic, North New Guinea, Huon Gulf, South, Hote-Buang, Hote. Dialects: HOTE, MISIM (MUSIM, OMBALEI). 90% lexical similarity between Hote and Misim, 70% with Yamap. Speakers consider them all to be one language. Investigation needed: intelligibility with Yamap. Literacy rate in first language: 30% to 50%. Literacy rate in second language: 40% to 65%. Bible portions 1988.

HULA ***(VULAA)*** [HUL] 3,000 (1987 SIL). Central Province, Hood Peninsula. Austronesian, Malayo-Polynesian, Central-Eastern, Eastern Malayo-Polynesian, Oceanic, Western Oceanic, Papuan Tip, Peripheral, Central Papuan, Sinagoro-Keapara. NT 1954.

HULI ***(HULI-HULIDANA, HURI)*** [HUI] 70,000 (1991 UBS). Southern Highlands Province around Tari, and southern fringe of Enga Province. Trans-New Guinea, Main Section, Central and Western, East New Guinea Highlands, West-Central, Huli. Grammar. Literacy rate in first language: 50% to 75%. Literacy rate in second language: 50% to 75%. NT 1983.

HUMENE [HUF] 438 (1966 census). Central Province, lower edge of Sogeri Plateau and adjacent plain between Gaire and Kapakapa villages. Manugoro is principal village. Trans-New Guinea, Main Section, Eastern, Central and Southeastern, Kwalean. Dialects: LAGUME (LAKUME, MANUKOLU), HUMENE. 65% to 74% lexical similarity with Kwale (closest). Some speakers know Hiri Motu and Motu, some English.

IAMALELE ***(YAMALELE)*** [YML] 2,800 (1987 SIL). Milne Bay Province, Bwaidoka District, west Fergusson Island. Austronesian, Malayo-Polynesian, Central-Eastern, Eastern Malayo-Polynesian, Oceanic, Western Oceanic, Papuan Tip, Nuclear, North Papuan Mainland-D'Entrecasteaux, Bwaidoga. Dialects: DIDIGAVU, GWABEGWABE, MASIMASI, CENTRAL YAMALELE, SOUTHERN YAMALELE. 64% lexical similarity with Kalokalo (closest). 40% monolingual. Some bilingualism in Bwaidoka and Dobu. Dictionary. SOV. Literacy rate in first language: 50% to 75%. Literacy rate in second language: 50% to 75%. Tropical forest. Coastal plains, mountain slopes. Swidden agriculturalists. 0 to 1,500 meters. NT 1984.

IATMUL ***(BIG SEPIK, NGEPMA KWUNDI, GEPMA KWUDI, GEPMA KWUNDI)*** [IAN] 12,000 (1986 SIL). East Sepik Province, Ambunti and Angoram districts, Sepik River villages from Tambunum to Japandai, Kundungay area. Sepik-Ramu, Sepik, Middle Sepik, Ndu. Dialects: NYAURA, PALIMBEI. Literacy rate in first language: 5% to 15%. Literacy rate in second language: 25% to 50%. Riverine. Fishermen, sago gatherers. NT 1975.

IDI ***(TA:ME, DIMSISI, DIMISI, DIBLAEG)*** [IDI] 2,000 (1990 census). Western Province, northwest of Agöb, east of Nambu language. Trans-New Guinea, Trans-Fly-Bulaka River, Trans-Fly, Pahoturi. Dialects: TAME, IDI. One end of a dialect chain stretching to Agöb. Distinct from but close to Agöb. Primary schools. Investigation needed: intelligibility with Tame. Literacy rate in first language: Less than 5%. Literacy rate in second language: 50%. Savannah, tropical forest, palm swamp. Lowland swamp. Hunters, swidden agriculturalists. 0 to 5 meters.

IDUNA ***(VIVIGANA, VIVIGANI)*** [VIV] 6,000 (1984 SIL). Milne Bay Province, north coast, Goodenough Island, Esa'ala District. Austronesian, Malayo-Polynesian, Central-Eastern, Eastern Malayo-Polynesian, Oceanic, Western Oceanic, Papuan Tip, Nuclear, North Papuan Mainland-D'Entrecasteaux, Bwaidoga. Dialects: WAIBULA, UFAUFA, IDAKAMENAI, BELEBELE, KALAUNA, GOIALA, UFUFU, CENTRAL VIVIGANI. 72% lexical similarity with Bwaidoka (closest). Three-quarters of the children are in school. Grammar. Literacy rate in first language: 75% to 100%. Literacy rate in second language: 75% to 100%. NT 1983.

IGANA [IGG] 114 (1981 Wurm and Hattori). Madang Province, west of Josephstaal. Sepik-Ramu, Ramu, Ramu Proper, Goam, Tamolan. Related languages: Romkun, Breri, Kominimung, Akrukay, Itutang, Inapang. Investigation needed: intelligibility.

IGOM [IGM] 1,082 (1981 Wurm and Hattori). Madang Province, west of Tanggu. Sepik-Ramu, Ramu, Ramu Proper, Goam, Ataitan. Related languages: Andarum, Tangu, Tanguat. Investigation needed: intelligibility.

IKOBI-MENA ***(KOPO-MONIA, KASERE, WAILEMI, MENI, IKOBI KAIRI)*** [MEB] 650 (1977 R. Lloyd SIL), including 350 Ikobi, 300 Mena (1981 Wurm and Hattori). Gulf Province, south of Kibirowi Island, around upper Omati River and around Middle Turama River. Trans-New Guinea, Turama-Kikorian, Turama-Omatian. Dialects: MENI, MENA, PIMURU, GORAU, UTABI. Closest language is Omati (Mini). Wurm and Hattori treat Ikobi and Mena as separate languages. Literacy rate in first language: Less than 5%. Literacy rate in second language: Less than 5%.

IMBONGU ***(IMBO UNGU, IBO UGU, IMBONGGO, AWA, AUA, AU, IMBO UNGO)*** [IMO] 16,000 (1985 SIL). Southern Highlands Province, Ialibu District. Trans-New Guinea, Main Section, Central and Western, East New Guinea Highlands, Central, Hagen, Kaugel. Literacy rate in first language: 25% to 50%. Literacy rate in second language: 15% to 25%. 5,500 to 7,000 feet. NT 1997.

IMONDA [IMN] 250 (1994 SIL). Sandaun Province, Amanab District, near Imonda airstrip. Trans-New Guinea, Northern, Border, Waris. A separate language from Waris. Grammar.

INAPANG ***(MIDSIVINDI)*** [MZU] 1,611 (1990 census). Madang Province, Josephstaal Subdistrict. Sepik-Ramu, Ramu, Ramu Proper, Goam, Tamolan.

INOKE-YATE ***(INOKE, YATE)*** [INO] 10,000 (1993 SIL). Eastern Highlands Province, Okapa District. Trans-New Guinea, Main Section, Central and Western, East New Guinea Highlands, East-Central, Kamano-Yagaria. Literacy rate in first language: 50% to 75%. Literacy rate in second language: 50% to 75%. NT 1992.

IPIKO ***(IPIKOI, HIGA, EPAI)*** [IPK] 200 (1977 SIL). Gulf Province, 5 miles up Pie River beyond Baimuri, villages of Ipiko and Pahemuba. Trans-New Guinea, Inland Gulf, Ipiko. Slightly related to Minanibai and Tao-Suamato. Vigorous. Semi-nomadic. Literacy rate in first language: Less than 5%. Literacy rate in second language: Less than 5%. Tropical forest. Lowland swamp. Below 300 meters.

IPILI ***(IPILI-PAIELA, IPILI-PAYALA)*** [IPI] 7,764 (1981 Wurm and Hattori). Enga Province around Porgera patrol post. Trans-New Guinea, Main Section, Central and Western, East New Guinea Highlands, West-Central, Enga. Dialect: TIPININI. Tipinini dialect is more like Enga. SOV. Tropical forest. Mountain slope. Swidden agriculturalists. 1,500 to 2,200 meters. Bible portions 1978.

ISABI ***(MARUHIA)*** [ISA] 280 (1981 Wurm and Hattori). Madang Province. Trans-New Guinea, Madang-Adelbert Range, Adelbert Range, Brahman. Related languages: Biyom, Tauya, Faita. Investigation needed: intelligibility.

ISEBE ***(BALAHAIM)*** [IGO] 913 (1981 Wurm and Hattori). Madang Province, northern bank of Gum River, west of Madang Town. Trans-New Guinea, Madang-Adelbert Range, Madang, Mabuso, Gum. Dialects: ISEBE, URUKUN, MIRKUK. Related languages: Sihan, Gumalu, Amele, Bau, Panim. Investigation needed: intelligibility. Mountain slope. Swidden agriculturalists. 60 to 250 meters. Christian, traditional religion, cargo cult.

ITERI ***(ALOWIEMINO)*** [ITR] 450 to 500 (1998 NTM). East Sepik Province. Left May. Area seldom entered by outsiders. The Iteri are called the 'Rocky Peak' people. Bible portions 1988-1998.

ITUTANG [ITU] 220 (1981 Wurm and Hattori). East Sepik Province. Sepik-Ramu, Ramu, Ramu Proper, Goam, Tamolan. Related languages: Romkun, Breri, Kominimung, Akrukay, Igana, Inapang. Investigation needed: intelligibility.

IWAL ***(KAIWA)*** [KBM] 1,500 (1987 SIL). Morobe Province, Lae District, between Wau and Salamaua. Austronesian, Malayo-Polynesian, Central-Eastern, Eastern Malayo-Polynesian, Oceanic, Western Oceanic, North New Guinea, Huon Gulf, South, Kaiwa. Close to Yabem. Literacy rate in first language: 15% to 25%. Literacy rate in second language: 25% to 50%. NT 1984.

IWAM ***(MAY RIVER)*** [IWM] 3,000 (1998 NTM). East Sepik Province, Ambunti District. Sepik-Ramu, Sepik, Upper Sepik, Iwam. Close to Amal and Sepik Iwam. Literacy rate in first language: 5% to 15%. Literacy rate in second language: 5% to 15%. Traditional religion. Bible portions 1990-1998.

IWAM, SEPIK ***(YAWENIAN)*** [IWS] 2,500 (1987 SIL). East Sepik Province, Ambunti District. Villages along the Sepik River, and on lagoons north and south of the River. Sepik-Ramu, Sepik, Upper Sepik, Iwam. Literacy rate in first language: 25% to 50%. Literacy rate in second language: 25% to 50%. Riverine. Sago gatherers, fishermen. NT 1989.

JILIM [JIL] 409 (1981 Wurm and Hattori). Madang Province. Trans-New Guinea, Madang-Adelbert Range, Madang, Rai Coast, Nuru. Related languages: Kwato, Ogea, Usu, Duduela, Rerau, Yangulam. Investigation needed: intelligibility.

JIMAJIMA ***(DIMA)*** [JMA] 542 (1971 Dutton). Milne Bay Province, along the coast east of Moi Bay almost to Midino, and along the Ruaba River. Trans-New Guinea, Main Section, Eastern, Central and Southeastern, Dagan. Dialects: WEST COASTAL JIMAJIMA, EAST INLAND JIMAJIMA. 41% lexical similarity with Daga (closest). Jimajima and Paiwa are spoken in villages in the same area.

KABADI ***(GABADI)*** [KBT] 1,500 (1975 SIL). Central Province, north of Galley Reach. Austronesian, Malayo-Polynesian, Central-Eastern, Eastern Malayo-Polynesian, Oceanic, Western Oceanic, Papuan Tip, Peripheral, Central Papuan, West Central Papuan, Gabadi. 49% lexical similarity with Doura (closest).

KAIAN ***(KAYAN)*** [KCT] 322 (1981 Wurm and Hattori). Madang Province. Sepik-Ramu, Ramu, Ramu Proper, Ruboni, Ottilien.

KAIEP ***(SAMAP)*** [KBW] 300 (1993 SIL). East Sepik Province, coast around Taul at Kaiep. Austronesian, Malayo-Polynesian, Central-Eastern, Eastern Malayo-Polynesian, Oceanic, Western Oceanic, North New Guinea, Schouten, Kairiru-Manam, Kairiru. Bilingualism in Manam. Investigation needed: intelligibility with Manam, Terebu. Literacy rate in second language: 50% to 75%.

KAIRAK [CKR] 750 (1988 SIL). East New Britain Province, Gazelle Peninsula. East Papuan, Yele-Solomons-New Britain, New Britain, Baining-Taulil. Many people are passively bilingual in Uramat. There is a primary school. Mountains and foothills.

KAIRIRU [KXA] 3,507 (1981 R. Wivell). East Sepik Province, Wewak District, Kairiru, Yuo, Karesau Islands, several coastal villages on the mainland between Cape Karawop and Cape Samein, and northern and western Mushu Island. Austronesian, Malayo-Polynesian, Central-Eastern, Eastern Malayo-Polynesian, Oceanic, Western Oceanic, North New Guinea, Schouten, Kairiru-Manam, Kairiru. Close to Kaiep. Speakers are highly bilingual in Tok Pisin. Investigation needed: bilingual proficiency in Tok Pisin. Dictionary. Grammar. Literacy rate in first language: Less than 5%. Literacy rate in second language: 25% to 50%.

KAKABAI ***(IGORA)*** [KQF] 816 (1990 census). Milne Bay Province, Alotau District, Weraura and Suau Local Government Areas, inland villages, eastern tip of Papua. Austronesian, Malayo-Polynesian, Central-Eastern, Eastern Malayo-Polynesian, Oceanic, Western Oceanic, Papuan Tip, Nuclear, North Papuan Mainland-D'Entrecasteaux, Kakabai. Dialects: NORTH KAKABAI, SOUTH KAKABAI. Less than 20% monolingual. Speakers have some degree of bilingualism in Wedau, Dawawa, English, or Motu.

KAKI AE ***(TATE, RAEPA TATI, TATI, LORABADA, LOU)*** [TBD] 310 (1993 SIL). Gulf Province, southeast of Kerema. Trans-New Guinea, Eleman, Tate. Different from Torricelli (Lou) in East Sepik Province or Lou in Manus Province. Bilingualism in Toaripi. Sea level to 15 meters.

KALAM ***(AFORO, KARAM)*** [KMH] 15,000 (1991 SIL). Madang Province, Ramu District, and in Western Highlands Province, Hagen District, along the north side of the Jimi River into the Kaironk Valley. Trans-New Guinea, Main Section, Central and Western, East New Guinea Highlands, Kalam, Kalam-Kobon. Related languages: Gants, Kobon. Grammar. SOV. Literacy rate in first language: Less than 5%. Literacy rate in second language: 15% to 25%. Savannah. Mountain slope. Swidden agriculturalists. 1,500 to 2,000 meters. NT 1992.

KALOU ***(YAWA)*** [YWA] 820 (1981 Wurm and Hattori). Sandaun Province, northwest of Hauna in the Sepik Iwam area. Sepik-Ramu, Sepik, Tama. Tropical forest. Lowland swamp.

KALULI ***(BOSAVI)*** [BCO] 2,500 (1994 Grosh SIL). Southern Highlands Province, extending into Western Province, on the northern and western slopes of Mt. Bosavi. Trans-New Guinea, Main Section, Central and Western, Central and South New Guinea-Kutubuan, Central and South New Guinea, Bosavi. Dialects: OLOGO, KALULI, WALULU, KUGENESI. No significant dialect differences. Closely related to but different from Kasua. Bilingual level estimates are Tok Pisin: 0 60%, 1 20%, 2 15%, 3 5%, 4 0%, 5 0%; English: 0 89%, 1 8%, 2-5 3%. Some speakers between 15 and 25 years old speak a little Tok Pisin for common topics. 'Bosavi' is a geographic name. SOV; prepositions; articles, adjectives, numerals after noun heads; question word initial; 1-4 prefixes; word order important; affixes indicate case; verb affixes mark person; ergativity; CV, CVC, CVV; tonal. Literacy rate in first language: 5%. Literacy rate in second language: 10%. Tropical forest. Mountain slope. Swidden agriculturalists. 800 meters. Traditional religion, Christian. Bible portions 1997-1998.

KAMANO ***(KAMANO-KAFE)*** [KBQ] 70,000 (1994 SIL). Eastern Highlands Province, Kainantu and Henganofi districts. Trans-New Guinea, Main Section, Central and Western, East New Guinea

Highlands, East-Central, Kamano-Yagaria. No major dialect differences. Dictionary. SOV. Literacy rate in first language: 25% to 50%. Literacy rate in second language: 25% to 50%. Savannah, scrub forest. Mountain slope. Swidden agriculturalists: coffee cash crop. 1,800 meters. NT 1977-1982.

KAMASA [KLP] 20 (1978 McElhanon). Morobe Province, in part of the Katsiong census unit. Trans-New Guinea, Main Section, Central and Western, Angan, Angan Proper. Nearly extinct.

KAMASAU *(WAND TUAN)* [KMS] 790 (1990 census). East Sepik Province, Wewak District. Segi is in Kamasau, Tring, and Wau villages, Hagi in Kenyari, Ghini in Yibab, Wandomi, and Wobu. Torricelli, Marienberg. Dialects: HAGI, SEGI, GHINI. Dictionary. Literacy rate in first language: 15% to 25%. Literacy rate in second language: 50% to 75%. NT 1998.

KAMBAIRA [KYY] 135 (1971 Wurm). Eastern Highlands Province, Kainantu District. Trans-New Guinea, Main Section, Central and Western, East New Guinea Highlands, Eastern, Kambaira. Bilingualism in Binumarien, Gadsup. Trilingual in Binumarien, Gadsup. Investigation needed: bilingual proficiency in Binumarien, Gadsup.

KAMBERATARO *(DERA, DRA, MANGGUAR, KOMBERATORO, KAMBERATORO)* [KBV] 687 in Papua New Guinea. Sandaun Province, Amanab District, both sides of the Faringi River. Trans-New Guinea, Senagi. Dialects: NORTH KAMBERATARO, SOUTH KAMBERATARO, MENGAU, LIHEN, DUKA-EKOR. See main entry under Indonesia, Irian Jaya.

KAMULA *(KAMURA, WAWOI)* [KHM] 800 (1998 SIL). Villages of Wasapea, Aramia River area, and villages of Keseki and Somokopa, Wawoi Falls area, Western Province. Trans-New Guinea, Main Section, Central and Western, Central and South New Guinea-Kutubuan, Central and South New Guinea, Awin-Pare. The closest language is Pare (G. Reesink SIL 1976). Speakers are basically monolingual. Literacy rate in first language: 25% to 50%. Literacy rate in second language: 15% to 25%. Bible portions 1996-1999.

KANASI *(SONA)* [SOQ] 2,200 (1998 SIL). Milne Bay Province, Rabaraba District, on both sides of the main range river valleys from Mt. Thomson. Trans-New Guinea, Main Section, Eastern, Central and South-eastern, Dagan. 51% lexical similarity with Ginuman (closest). Grammar. Literacy rate in first language: 15% to 25%. Literacy rate in second language: 15% to 25%. NT 1997.

KANDAS *(KING)* [KQW] 480 (1972 Beaumont). New Ireland Province, southwest coast, Watpi, King, and Kait villages. Austronesian, Malayo-Polynesian, Central-Eastern, Eastern Malayo-Polynesian, Oceanic, Western Oceanic, Meso Melanesian, New Ireland, South New Ireland-Northwest Solomonic, Patpatar-Tolai.

KANDAWO *(NARAKE)* [GAM] 5,000 (1994 SIL). Western Highlands Province, Hagen District in the upper Jimi headwaters, on the slopes of Mt. Wilhelm. Trans-New Guinea, Main Section, Central and Western, East New Guinea Highlands, Central, Jimi. Literacy rate in first language: Less than 5%. Literacy rate in second language: 5% to 15%. Mountain slope. Bible portions 1989.

KANIET [KTK] Manus Province, Anchorite and Kaniet Islands, western. Austronesian, Malayo-Polynesian, Central-Eastern, Eastern Malayo-Polynesian, Oceanic, Admiralty Islands, Western. Extinct since 1950. Extinct.

KANINGRA *(KANINGARA)* [KNR] 327 (2 villages). East Sepik Province, Blackwater River just south of Kuvanmas Lake. Sepik-Ramu, Sepik, Sepik Hill, Alamblak. Highly bilingual in Tok Pisin. Investigation needed: bilingual proficiency in Tok Pisin. Literacy rate in first language: Less than 5%. Literacy rate in second language: Less than 5%.

KANITE [KMU] 8,000 (1991 SIL). Eastern Highlands Province, Okapa District. Trans-New Guinea, Main Section, Central and Western, East New Guinea Highlands, East-Central, Kamano-Yagaria. Closely related to Keyagana, Inoke-Yate. Literacy rate in first language: 25% to 50%. Literacy rate in second language: 25% to 50%. NT 1980.

KANUM, SOTA *(ENKELEMBU)* [KRZ] Western Province, southwestern half of area between Fly River and coast. Trans-New Guinea, Trans-Fly-Bulaka River, Trans-Fly, Morehead and Upper Maro Rivers, Tonda. Dialects: NORTH KANUM (SOTA), SOUTH KANUM, CENTRAL KANUM (BRONGA, BERONK). 4 different languages. The variety in PNG may be different from Irian Jaya. Related to Ara, Aramba, Blafe, Bothar, Peremka. 4 primary schools. Savannah, tropical forest. Lowland swamp. Below 300 meters. See main entry under Indonesia, Irian Jaya.

KAPIN *(SAMBIO, TAIAK, TAYEK, KATUMENE)* [TBX] 2,351 (1979 census). Morobe Province, Mumeng District, Bulolo District, 5 villages in the hills southwest of Mumeng, and settlements in Wau and Lae. Austronesian, Malayo-Polynesian, Central-Eastern, Eastern Malayo-Polynesian, Oceanic, Western Oceanic, North New Guinea, Huon Gulf, South, Hote-Buang, Buang. Dialects: KAPIN, GARAWA (GAWAWA). May be part of the Mumeng language chain. Tok Pisin is used with others by all under the age of 40, and by men and half the women over 40. Tok Pisin is used in church; Yabem was the former church language. Kumalu and English are used some. Kapin is used with other Kapin speakers. All ages. SVO, prepositions, genitives before nouns, adjectives, numerals, relatives after noun heads, V, CV, CVC, CVV, CVVC, CVCC, VC, nontonal. Literacy rate in second language: Tok Pisin; possibly

10% are fluent readers, 25% halting. Tropical forest, gallery forest. Mountain valley. Swidden agriculturalists, coffee producers, gold traders. 1,600 to 3,500 feet. Traditional religion.

KAPRIMAN ***(WASARE, MUGUMUTE)*** [DJU] 1,450 in 6 villages (1986 PBT). East Sepik Province, Blackwater River and Korosameri River. Sepik-Ramu, Sepik, Sepik Hill, Bahinemo. Dialects: KAPRIMAN, KARAMBIT. Literacy rate in first language: Less than 5%. Literacy rate in second language: 5% to 15%.

KARA ***(LEMUSMUS, LEMAKOT)*** [LEU] 5,000 (1998 SIL). New Ireland Province, northern New Ireland District. Austronesian, Malayo-Polynesian, Central-Eastern, Eastern Malayo-Polynesian, Oceanic, Western Oceanic, Meso Melanesian, New Ireland, Lavongai-Nalik. Dialects: EAST KARA, WEST KARA. SVO. Tropical forest. Coastal. Swidden agriculturalists. 0 to 300 meters. NT 1997.

KARAMI [XAR] Gulf Province, on Western Province border, northeast of Tao-Suamoto. Trans-New Guinea, Inland Gulf, Minanibai. Extinct.

KARAWA ***(BULAWA)*** [QKR] 463 (1991 SIL). Sandaun Province. Sepik-Ramu, Sepik, Ram. Related languages: Awtuw, Pouye. 67% lexical similarity with Karawa. Pouye speakers consider Karawa to be part of their language. Investigation needed: intelligibility with Awtuw, Pouye.

KARE [KMF] 384 (1981 Wurm and Hattori). Madang Province. Trans-New Guinea, Madang-Adelbert Range, Madang, Mabuso, Kare. Literacy rate in first language: 25% to 50%. Literacy rate in second language: 50% to 75%.

KARKAR-YURI ***(YURI, KARKAR)*** [YUJ] 1,142 (1994 SIL). Sandaun Province, Amanab District, along the Irian Jaya border. Language Isolate. Dialects: NORTH CENTRAL YURI, AUIA-TARAUWI, USARI. No known relationships. SOV. Literacy rate in first language: 25% to 50%. Literacy rate in second language: 25% to 50%. Tropical forest. Mountain slope. Swidden agriculturalists. 100 to 700 meters. NT 1994.

KARORE [XKX] 500 to 600 (1995 SIL). West New Britain Province, Kandrian District. Austronesian, Malayo-Polynesian, Central-Eastern, Eastern Malayo-Polynesian, Oceanic, Western Oceanic, North New Guinea, Ngero-Vitiaz, Vitiaz, Southwest New Britain, Arawe-Pasismanua, Pasismanua. Dialect chain with Kaulong and Getmata.

KASUA [KHS] 600 in 6 villages (1990 SIL). Southern Highlands Province, east and south of Mt. Bosavi, and Western Province. Trans-New Guinea, Main Section, Central and Western, Central and South New Guinea-Kutubuan, Central and South New Guinea, Bosavi.

KÂTE ***(KAI, KÂTE DONG)*** [KMG] 6,125 (1978 McElhanon). Morobe Province, Finschhafen District. Trans-New Guinea, Main Section, Central and Western, Huon-Finisterre, Huon, Eastern. Dialects: MAGOBINENG (BAMOTA), WAMORA (WAMOLA), WEMO, PAREC, WANA. Those listed as dialects may be separate languages. Used by Lutherans as a religious language in the area for 80,000 (1980 UBS). Dictionary. Literacy rate in first language: 25% to 50%. Literacy rate in second language: 50% to 75%. Christian. Bible 1978.

KAULONG ***(PASISMANUA, KOWLONG)*** [PSS] 3,000 (1991 SIL). West New Britain Province, Kandrian District, southwest hinterland. Austronesian, Malayo-Polynesian, Central-Eastern, Eastern Malayo-Polynesian, Oceanic, Western Oceanic, North New Guinea, Ngero-Vitiaz, Vitiaz, Southwest New Britain, Arawe-Pasismanua, Pasismanua. Dialects: KAULONG, EAST INLAND KAULONG. Dialect chain. Miu, Bao, and Senseng are treated as dialects by Wurm and Hattori. SVO. Tropical forest. Mountain slope. Swidden agriculturalists. 25 to 500 meters. Bible portions 1992.

KAWACHA ***(KAWATSA)*** [KCB] 30 (1978 McElhanon). Morobe Province, east of Ampale, in part of the Katsiong census unit. Trans-New Guinea, Main Section, Central and Western, Angan, Angan Proper. Bilingualism in Yagwoia. Nearly extinct.

KELA ***(GELA, KELANA, LAUKANU)*** [KCL] 2,145 (1980 census). Morobe Province, southern coast of Huon Gulf, between Salamaua and Kui, Paiawa River. 10 villages. Austronesian, Malayo-Polynesian, Central-Eastern, Eastern Malayo-Polynesian, Oceanic, Western Oceanic, North New Guinea, Huon Gulf, North. Literacy rate in first language: 15% to 25%. Literacy rate in second language: 15% to 25%. Coastal.

KELE ***(GELE')*** [SBC] 600 (1982 SIL). Manus Province, south coast inland, Buyang, Droia, Kawaliap, Koruniat, Tingau. Austronesian, Malayo-Polynesian, Central-Eastern, Eastern Malayo-Polynesian, Oceanic, Admiralty Islands, Eastern, Manus, East. Bilingualism in Kurti, Ere. Investigation needed: bilingual proficiency in Kurti, Ere. SVO. Win Nesien cult.

KENATI ***(KENATHI, GANATI, AZIANA)*** [GAT] 950 (1990 census). Eastern Highlands Province, Wonenara District. All 3 villages are within ten miles of Wonenara. Trans-New Guinea, Main Section, Central and Western, East New Guinea Highlands, Kenati. Mountain slope. Agriculturalists: sweet potatoes, yams, bananas, coffee. Traditional religion, Christian. Bible portions 1989.

KEOPARA ***(KEAPARA, KEREPUNU)*** [KHZ] 16,423 (1975 SIL). Central Province, coast from east of Hood Peninsula to Lalaura west of Cape Rodney. 3 villages. Austronesian, Malayo-Polynesian, Central-Eastern, Eastern Malayo-Polynesian, Oceanic, Western Oceanic, Papuan Tip, Peripheral, Central Papuan, Sinagoro-Keapara. Dialects: BABAGA, KALO, KEOPARA, AROMA (ARONA, ALOMA,

GALOMA), MAOPA, WANIGELA, KAPARI, LALAURA. Dialect chain to Hula. High educational standard and income level. Coastal. Bible portions 1892-1905.

KEREAKA ***(KERIAKA)*** [KJX] 1,000 (1981 Wurm and Hattori). North Solomons Province, northwest Bougainville Island, south of Rapoisi. East Papuan, Bougainville, West, Keriaka. About 19% lexical similarity with Rapoisi. Few are bilingual in Tok Pisin. Traditional religion, Christian.

KEREWO ***(KEREWA, KEREWA-GOARI)*** [KXZ] 2,200 (1975 Wurm). Gulf Province, west bank of Omati River, east and inland to Samoa village. Trans-New Guinea, Trans-Fly-Bulaka River, Trans-Fly, Kiwaian. Dialect: GIBARIO (GOARIBARI). Literacy rate in first language: 15% to 25%. Literacy rate in second language: 5% to 15%. Bible portions 1926-1941.

KESAWAI ***(NAMUYA)*** [QKE] 538 (1981 Wurm and Hattori). Madang Province. Trans-New Guinea, Madang-Adelbert Range, Madang, Rai Coast, Evapia. Related languages: Sinsauru, Asas, Sausi, Dumpu. Investigation needed: intelligibility.

KEURU ***(KEURO, BELEPA, HAURA, HAURA HAELA)*** [QQK] 4,523 (1981 Wurm and Hattori). Gulf Province, from the mouth of the Purari River east to the Bairu River. Trans-New Guinea, Eleman, Eleman Proper, Western. Dialect: AHEAVE.

KEWA, EAST [KJS] 35,000 (1997 K. Franklin SIL). Southern Highlands Province, Ialibu and Kagua districts. Trans-New Guinea, Main Section, Central and Western, East New Guinea Highlands, West-Central, Angal-Kewa. Literacy rate in first language: 15% to 25%. Literacy rate in second language: 25% to 50%. Bible portions 1967-1988.

KEWA, WEST ***(PASUMA)*** [KEW] 35,000 (1997 K. Franklin SIL). Southern Highlands Province, Kagua and Mendi districts. Trans-New Guinea, Main Section, Central and Western, East New Guinea Highlands, West-Central, Angal-Kewa. Dictionary. Grammar. SOV. Tropical forest, some savannah, scrub forest. Mountain mesa. Swidden agriculturalists, some cash crops. Below 2,000 meters. NT 1973.

KEYAGANA ***(KEIGANA, KEIAGANA, KE'YAGANA)*** [KYG] 12,284 (1981 Wurm and Hattori). Okapa and Henganofi districts, Eastern Highlands Province. Trans-New Guinea, Main Section, Central and Western, East New Guinea Highlands, East-Central, Kamano-Yagaria. Literacy rate in first language: 15% to 25%. Literacy rate in second language: 25% to 50%. NT, in press (1996).

KHEHEK ***(LEVEI-DREHET, LEVEI-NDREHET)*** [TLX] 1,600 (1991 SIL). Manus Province, Soparibeu District. Ndrehet, Levei, and Bucho villages; Ndrehet is the center. Austronesian, Malayo-Polynesian, Central-Eastern, Eastern Malayo-Polynesian, Oceanic, Admiralty Islands, Eastern, Manus, West. Dialects: LEVEI (LEBEI, LEBEJ), DREHET (KHEHEK, CHEHEK, CHECHEK), BUCHO. Those in the Levei area speak a dialect closely related to that of Bucho in the south. A distinct language from Tulu and Bohuai.

KIBIRI ***(POROME, POLOME)*** [PRM] 1,100 (1977 SIL). Gulf Province, Kikori District, near Aird Hills, on several tributaries of Kikori River, villages of Tipeowo, Doibo, Paile, Babaguina, Ero, and Wowa. Language Isolate. Dialects: AIRD HILLS (KIBIRI), POROME. Unrelated to other languages in Gulf Province. Different from Kairi, which is also called Kibiri. Literacy rate in first language: 15% to 25%. Literacy rate in second language: 5% to 15%.

KILIVILA ***(KIRIWINA)*** [KIJ] 22,000 (1991 UBS). Milne Bay Province, Trobriand Islands. Austronesian, Malayo-Polynesian, Central-Eastern, Eastern Malayo-Polynesian, Oceanic, Western Oceanic, Papuan Tip, Peripheral, Kilivila-Louisiades, Kilivila. Dialects: KITAVA, VAKUTA, SINAKETA. Various dialects. 68% lexical similarity with Muyuw (closest). Kitava Island has 80% lexical similarity. 60% monolingual. Others use Dobu as second language. Many schools. Investigation needed: intelligibility with Kitava dialect. Dictionary. Grammar. Agriculturalists: yams, sweet potato, taro, cassava, greens, coconuts. Christian, traditional religion. NT 1985.

KILMERI ***(KILMERA)*** [KIH] 2,231 (1991 SIL). Sandaun Province, Vanimo District near Ossima. 15 villages. Trans-New Guinea, Northern, Border, Bewani. Dialects: WESTERN KILMERI (ISI), EASTERN KILMERI (OSSIMA). Bible portions 1880.

KINALAKNA [KCO] 219 (1978 McElhanon). Morobe Province. Trans-New Guinea, Main Section, Central and Western, Huon-Finisterre, Huon, Western.

KIRE ***(GIRE, GIRI, KIRE-PUIRE)*** [GEB] 2,000 (1986 PBT). Madang Province, lower Ramu, around Garati village. Sepik-Ramu, Ramu, Ramu Proper, Ruboni, Misegian. Literacy rate in first language: 5% to 25%. Literacy rate in second language: 50% to 75%. Bible portions 1992.

KIS [KIS] 216 (1977 Lincoln). East Sepik Province, 10 to 20 miles south southeast of Samap, inland from the coast. Austronesian, Malayo-Polynesian, Central-Eastern, Eastern Malayo-Polynesian, Oceanic, Western Oceanic, North New Guinea, Schouten, Kairiru-Manam, Manam.

KIWAI, NORTHEAST ***(GIBAIO)*** [KIW] 4,400 including 1,300 in Kope, 700 in Gibaio, 1,700 in Urama, 700 in Arigibi (1986 Foley). Gulf Province. Trans-New Guinea, Trans-Fly-Bulaka River, Trans-Fly, Kiwaian. Dialects: GIBAIO, KOPE (GOPE, ERA RIVER), URAMA, ARIGIBI (ANIGIBI). Wurm and

Hattori (1981) treat Arigibi as a separate language. Literacy rate in first language: 15% to 25%. Literacy rate in second language: 25% to 50%.

KIWAI, SOUTHERN [KJD] 9,700 (1975 Wurm), including 3,800 in Coast, 1,000 in Daru, 4,500 in Island Kiwai, 400 in Doumori. Western Province, Fly River Delta. Trans-New Guinea, Trans-Fly-Bulaka River, Trans-Fly, Kiwaian. Dialects: DOUMORI, COAST KIWAI, SOUTHERN COAST KIWAI, DARU KIWAI, EASTERN KIWAI, ISLAND KIWAI. Literacy rate in first language: 15% to 25%. Literacy rate in second language: 15% to 25%. NT 1960.

KOBON [KPW] 6,000 (1991 SIL). Madang Province, Middle Ramu District, and Western Highlands Province on Kaironk River in lower Jimi River area north of Mt. Hagen. Trans-New Guinea, Main Section, Central and Western, East New Guinea Highlands, Kalam, Kalam-Kobon. Grammar. SOV. Literacy rate in first language: 5% to 15%. Literacy rate in second language: 5% to 15%. Tropical forest. Mountain slope. Swidden agriculturalists. 1,000 to 2,000 meters. Bible portions 1988.

KOGUMAN [QKG] 943 (1981 Wurm and Hattori). Madang Province. Trans-New Guinea, Madang-Adelbert Range, Adelbert Range, Pihom-Isumrud-Mugil, Pihom, Omosan. Related language: Abasakur. Investigation needed: intelligibility with Abasakur.

KOIALI, MOUNTAIN ***(MOUNTAIN KOIARI)*** [KPX] 1,700 (1975 SIL). Central Province, Port Moresby District, north of Koita, Koiari, and Barai. One village is Efogi. Trans-New Guinea, Main Section, Eastern, Central and Southeastern, Koiarian, Koiaric. 50% to 57% lexical similarity with Grass Koiari (closest). 50% monolingual. Others use Motu as second language. Grammar. SOV. Literacy rate in second language: 25% to 50%. Tropical forest. Mountain slope. Swidden agriculturalists. 800 to 1,400 meters. NT 1981.

KOIARI, GRASS ***(KOIARI)*** [KBK] 1,800 (1973 SIL). Central Province, east of Port Moresby and to coast. Trans-New Guinea, Main Section, Eastern, Central and Southeastern, Koiarian, Koiaric. 60% to 65% lexical similarity with Koitabu (closest). 10% monolingual. Others use Hiri Motu or English as second language. Dictionary.

KOITABU ***(KOITA)*** [KQI] 3,000 (1989 SIL). Central Province, around Port Moresby. Trans-New Guinea, Main Section, Eastern, Central and Southeastern, Koiarian, Koiaric. Dialects: WEST KOITA, EAST KOITA. 60% to 65% lexical similarity with Grass Koiari (closest). Bilingual level estimates are Hiri Motu: 0 33%, 1 10%, 2 20%, 3 20%, 4 13%, 5 4%; Motu: 0 80%, 1 5%, 2 5%, 3 5%, 4 5%, 5 0%. Some speakers are bilingual in Hiri Motu, Motu, Tok Pisin, or English. Traditionally hunters, agriculturalists.

KOIWAT [KXT] 450 (1975 SIL). East Sepik Province, Ambunti District. Sepik-Ramu, Sepik, Middle Sepik, Ndu.

KOL ***(KOLE, KOLA)*** [KOL] 4,000 (1991 SIL), including 1,300 Sui, Kol (1987). East New Britain Province, Pomio District, Open Bay to the waterfall. Most are on the south side of the Island. East Papuan, Yele-Solomons-New Britain, New Britain. Dialects: SUI, KOL (NAKGAKTAI). SVO. Tropical forest. Mountain mesa. Swidden agriculturalists. 0 to 800 meters.

KOLOM [KLM] 209 (1981 Wurm and Hattori). Madang Province. Trans-New Guinea, Madang-Adelbert Range, Madang, Rai Coast, Kabenau.

KOLUAWAWA ***(KALOKALO, KOLUWA)*** [KLX] 900 (1998 SIL). Milne Bay Province, northwest tip of Fergusson Island. Austronesian, Malayo-Polynesian, Central-Eastern, Eastern Malayo-Polynesian, Oceanic, Western Oceanic, Papuan Tip, Nuclear, North Papuan Mainland-D'Entrecasteaux, Bwaidoga. 64% lexical similarity with Iamalele (closest), and then Bwaidoka. Bilingualism in Minaveha. Literacy rate in first language: 15% to 25%. Literacy rate in second language: 35% to 60%. 0 to 100 feet. Christian.

KOMBA [KPF] 12,235 (1978 McElhanon). Morobe Province, Kabwum District. Trans-New Guinea, Main Section, Central and Western, Huon-Finisterre, Huon, Western. Dialects: EAST KOMBA, CENTRAL KOMBA, WEST CENTRAL KOMBA, BORDER KOMBA, WEST KOMBA. SOV. Literacy rate in first language: 75% to 100%. Literacy rate in second language: 50% to 75%. Savannah. Mountain slope. Swidden agriculturalists. 1,330 to 2,000 meters. NT 1980.

KOMBIO ***(ENDANGEN)*** [KOK] 2,545 (1980 census). East Sepik Province, Dreikikir District, Torricelli Mts. 31 villages. Torricelli, Kombio-Arapesh, Kombio. Dialects: NORTH KOMBIO (AKWUN), WEST-CENTRAL KOMBIO (WAPUKUAMP), SOUTH KOMBIO (YANIMOI). SVO. Literacy rate in second language: 25% to 35%. Tropical rainforest. No significant natural water source but high water table. Foothills, mountain ridges. Agriculturalists: yams, sweet potato, coffee, cocoa; coconuts, sago. 900 to 3,000 feet.

KOMINIMUNG [QKM] 328 (1981 Wurm and Hattori). Madang Province. Sepik-Ramu, Ramu, Ramu Proper, Goam, Tamolan. Related languages: Romkun, Breri, Igana, Akrukay, Itutang, Inapang. Investigation needed: intelligibility.

KOMUTU [KLT] 510 (1978 McElhanon). Morobe Province, lower Timbe River valley. Trans-New Guinea, Main Section, Central and Western, Huon-Finisterre, Finisterre, Uruwa.

KONAI ***(MIRAPMIN)*** [KXW] 600 (1991 SIL). Western Province, west side of Upper Strickland River. Trans-New Guinea, Main Section, Central and Western, Central and South New Guinea-Kutubuan, Central and South New Guinea, East Strickland. Closest to Kalamo and Agala. Investigation needed:

intelligibility with Kalamo, Agala. Literacy rate in first language: Less than 5%. Literacy rate in second language: Less than 5%.

KONOMALA [KOA] 800 (1985 SIL). New Ireland Province, southeastern coast. 8 villages. Austronesian, Malayo-Polynesian, Central-Eastern, Eastern Malayo-Polynesian, Oceanic, Western Oceanic, Meso Melanesian, New Ireland, South New Ireland-Northwest Solomonic, Patpatar-Tolai. Dialects: LAKET, KONOMALA. People now apparently speak Siar. Investigation needed: bilingual proficiency in Siar.

KOPAR [QKO] 229 (1981 Wurm and Hattori). East Sepik Province. Sepik-Ramu, Nor-Pondo, Nor. Related language: Murik. Investigation needed: intelligibility with Murik.

KORAFE ***(KORAPE, KORAFI, KWARAFE, KAILIKAILI)*** [KPR] 2,800 to 3,000 (1997 J. Farr SIL). Oro Province, Tufi District, on the headlands (fiord system) of Cape Nelson. Trans-New Guinea, Main Section, Eastern, Binanderean, Binanderean Proper. Dialects: KORAFE, MOKORUA (YEGA, YEGHA). Yega dialect is distinct from Gona, also called 'Yega'. Gaina may also be a dialect. 56% to 61% lexical similarity with Baruga (closest), 50% with Ewage dialect of Ewage Notu (Dutton 1971). Some speakers are bilingual in English, Tok Pisin, or Hiri Motu. Investigation needed: intelligibility with Gaina. Dictionary. SOV. Literacy rate in first language: 75% to 100%. Literacy rate in second language: 75% to 100%. Tropical forest. Coastal. Fishermen, swidden agriculturalists. 0 to 300 meters. NT 1984.

KORAK [KOZ] 205 (1981 Wurm and Hattori). Madang Province. Trans-New Guinea, Madang-Adelbert Range, Adelbert Range, Pihom-Isumrud-Mugil, Isumrud, Kowan.

KORO [KXR] 400 (1983 SIL). Manus Province. Austronesian, Malayo-Polynesian, Central-Eastern, Eastern Malayo-Polynesian, Oceanic, Admiralty Islands, Eastern, Manus, East. Close to, and possibly intelligible with, Papitalai. Investigation needed: intelligibility with Papitalai. SVO.

KOROMIRA [KQJ] 1,562 including 1,448 Koromira and 114 Koianu (1990 C. Hurd SIL). North Solomons Province, Kieta District, central mountains and southeast coast. East Papuan, Bougainville, East, Nasioi. Dialects: KOROMIRA, KOIANU. Koianu may need separate literature. SOV. Tropical forest. Mountain slope, coastal. Swidden agriculturalists: cash crops.

KOSENA [KZE] 2,000 (1987 SIL). Eastern Highlands Province, Kainantu and Okapa districts. Trans-New Guinea, Main Section, Central and Western, East New Guinea Highlands, Eastern, Gadsup-Auyana-Awa. SOV. Literacy rate in first language: 5% to 15%. Literacy rate in second language: 5% to 15%. Tropical forest. Mountain ridges. Agriculturalists. 1,200 to 2,000 meters. NT 1980.

KOSORONG ***(NAAMA)*** [KSR] 2,000 (1998 SIL). Morobe Province, Finschhafen District, 5 villages and 5 hamlets in the central Huon Peninsula between the Kuat and Burum rivers, south of Mindik airstrip. Burum and Kuat are tributaries of the Mongi River. Many live in Lae and other towns. Trans-New Guinea, Main Section, Central and Western, Huon-Finisterre, Huon, Eastern. Dialects: KOSORONG, YANGEBORONG. Use of Tok Pisin is increasing and Kâte decreasing as second language. Vigorous. Kâte is the church language. SOV; postpositions; long and short vowels. Tropical forest. Mountain slope. Swidden agriculturalists. 500 to 1,500 to meters.

KOVAI ***(UMBOI, KOBAI, KOWAI)*** [KQB] 4,500 (1991 SIL). Morobe Province, Siassi District, Umboi or Rooke Island, 12 villages. Trans-New Guinea, Main Section, Central and Western, Huon-Finisterre, Huon, Kovai. Literacy rate in first language: 15% to 25%. Literacy rate in second language: 15% to 25%. Plateau. Traditional religion. Bible portions 1993.

KOVE [KVC] 6,750 (1994 SIL). West New Britain Province, northwest coast. 24 villages, most on small islands off the coast. Austronesian, Malayo-Polynesian, Central-Eastern, Eastern Malayo-Polynesian, Oceanic, Western Oceanic, North New Guinea, Ngero-Vitiaz, Ngero, Bariai. A separate language from Kaliai. Many highly educated people. Grammar. Coastal, coral islands. Swidden agricultualists; fishermen. Sea level.

KOWAKI [QKK] 31 (1981 Wurm and Hattori). Madang Province. Trans-New Guinea, Madang-Adelbert Range, Adelbert Range, Pihom-Isumrud-Mugil, Pihom, Tiboran. Related languages: Mawak, Hinihon, Musar, Wanambre. Investigation needed: intelligibility.

KRISA [KRO] 400 (1993 SIL). Sandaun Province near coast. Sko, Krisa. Related languages: Rawo, Puari, Warapu.

KUANUA ***(TOLAI, GUNANTUNA, TINATA TUNA, TUNA, BLANCHE BAY, NEW BRITAIN LANGUAGE)*** [KSD] 61,000 (1991 SIL), 80,000 including second language speakers (1985 UBS). East New Britain Province, Rabaul District, Gazelle Peninsula. Austronesian, Malayo-Polynesian, Central-Eastern, Eastern Malayo-Polynesian, Oceanic, Western Oceanic, Meso Melanesian, New Ireland, South New Ireland-Northwest Solomonic, Patpatar-Tolai. Dialects: VUNADIDIR, RAPITOK, RALUANA, VANUMAMI, LIVUAN, MATUPIT, KOKOPO, KABAKADA, NODUP, KININANGGUNAN, RAKUNEI, REBAR, WATOM, MASAWA. 'Tolai' is the name of the people; 'Kuanua' of the language. Trade language. Bible 1983.

KUBE ***(MONGI, HUBE)*** [KGF] 6,000 (1987 SIL). Morobe Province, Dindiu District, at the eastern headwaters of the Mongi River, on the eastern slopes of the lower Kua River valley and Foris River Valley.

Trans-New Guinea, Main Section, Central and Western, Huon-Finisterre, Huon, Eastern. Dialects: KURUNGTUFU, YOANGEN (YOANGGENG). Mountain slope. Swidden agriculturalists.

KUBO [JKO] 1,000. Western Province, Lake Murray District, northern half of Upper Strickland Census District, east of Strickland River, north of the Samo. Trans-New Guinea, Main Section, Central and Western, Central and South New Guinea-Kutubuan, Central and South New Guinea, East Strickland. A separate language from Samo and Gobasi, but related.

KUMALU ***(KUMARA)*** [KSL] 2,583 (1979 census). Morobe Province, Mumeng District. Austronesian, Malayo-Polynesian, Central-Eastern, Eastern Malayo-Polynesian, Oceanic, Western Oceanic, North New Guinea, Huon Gulf, South, Hote-Buang, Buang, Mumeng. In the Mumeng language chain. Some intelligibility with Dambi. SVO. Literacy rate in first language: 15% to 25%. Literacy rate in second language: 25% to 50%. Tropical forest. Mountain slope. Swidden agriculturalists. 300 to 900 meters.

KUMAN ***(CHIMBU, SIMBU)*** [KUE] 80,000 (1994 SIL). Simbu Province, northern third, overlapping into Minj Subprovince of Western Highlands Province. Trans-New Guinea, Main Section, Central and Western, East New Guinea Highlands, Central, Chimbu. Dialects: KUMAN, NAGANE (GENAGANE, GENOGANE). Major language of area. Trade language. Dictionary. SOV, clause chaining, auxiliary verbs with adjuncts. Literacy rate in first language: 10% to 15%. Literacy rate in second language: 25% to 40%. Tropical forest, savannah. Mountain valley. Swidden agriculturalists: coffee. 5,000 to 9,000 feet. Christian. Bible portions 1968-1995.

KUMUKIO ***(KUMOKIO)*** [KUO] 552 (1978 McElhanon). Morobe Province. Trans-New Guinea, Main Section, Central and Western, Huon-Finisterre, Huon, Western.

KUNI [KSE] 4,500 (1993 SIL). Central Province, Kairuku and southwest Goilala districts, towards Port Moresby, south of Mekeo. Austronesian, Malayo-Polynesian, Central-Eastern, Eastern Malayo-Polynesian, Oceanic, Western Oceanic, Papuan Tip, Peripheral, Central Papuan, West Central Papuan, Nuclear. 52% lexical similarity with Nara, 47% with Mekeo, 40% with Roro, the closest varieties. Literacy rate in first language: 25% to 50%. Literacy rate in second language: 25% to 50%.

KUNIMAIPA [KUP] 11,000 (1991 SIL), including 1,429 in Morobe Province (1978 McElhanon). Central Province, northern Goilala District; Morobe Province, Wau District. Trans-New Guinea, Main Section, Eastern, Central and Southeastern, Goilalan, Kunimaipa. Dialects: KARUAMA, KATE (HATE), GAJILI (GAJILA, GAZILI, HAZILI). Bilingualism in Tok Pisin. Grammar. SOV. Literacy rate in first language: 15% to 25%. Literacy rate in second language: 25% to 50%. Tropical forest. Mountain slope. Swidden agriculturalists. 1,500 to 2,000 meters. Traditional religion, Christian. NT 1990.

KUNJA ***(LOWER MOREHEAD, THUNDAI-KANZA, PEREMKA)*** [PEP] 223 (1980 census). Western Province, extreme southwest. Trans-New Guinea, Trans-Fly-Bulaka River, Trans-Fly, Morehead and Upper Maro Rivers, Tonda. Dialects: GAMBADI, SEMARIJI. Related to Kanum, Aramba, Bothar, Rouku. Swamp, savannah. Below 300 meters.

KUOT ***(KUAT, PANARAS)*** [KTO] 2,300 (1996 census). New Ireland Province, northwest coast. 9 villages. East Papuan, Yele-Solomons-New Britain, New Britain, Kuot. Bilingualism in Tok Pisin. Vigorous on the west coast. Literacy rate in first language: 75% to 85%. Literacy rate in second language: 75% to 95%. Coastal. Bible portions 1994.

KURTI ***(KURUTI, KURUTI-PARE, NDRUGUL)*** [KTM] 2,600 (1990 census). Manus Province, north central coast. Austronesian, Malayo-Polynesian, Central-Eastern, Eastern Malayo-Polynesian, Oceanic, Admiralty Islands, Eastern, Manus, East. SVO. Literacy rate in first language: 25%. Literacy rate in second language: 50% to 75%.

KWATO ***(WAUPE)*** [KOP] 778 (1981 Wurm and Hattori). Madang Province. Trans-New Guinea, Madang-Adelbert Range, Madang, Rai Coast, Nuru. Related languages: Uya, Ogea, Duduela, Rerau, Jilim, Yangulam.

KWOMA ***(WASHKUK)*** [KMO] 2,865 in about 12 villages (1981 Wurm and Hattori). East Sepik Province, Ambunti District, along the Sepik River, along the Sanchi River. Sepik-Ramu, Sepik, Middle Sepik, Nukuma. Dialects: KWOMA (WASHKUK), NUKUMA. Dictionary. Grammar. Literacy rate in first language: 5% to 15%. Literacy rate in second language: 15% to 25%. Low mountains, riverine. Swidden agriculturalists; sago; fishermen. 50 meters. NT 1975.

KWOMTARI [KWO] 600 (1998 SIL). Sandaun Province, Amanab District, north of Namia. 6 villages. Kwomtari-Baibai, Kwomtari. Dialects: WEST CENTRAL KWOMTARI, EKOS-YENABI-MARAGIN. Some men and boys and a few women can communicate in Tok Pisin. Kwomtari is used for home and village life. One school. Tropical forest. Swamp. Hunter-gatherers. 100 to 300 meters. Traditional religion, Christian.

KYAKA ***(BAIYER, ENGA-KYAKA)*** [KYC] 15,368 (1981 Wurm and Hattori). Enga Province. Trans-New Guinea, Main Section, Central and Western, East New Guinea Highlands, West-Central, Enga. NT 1973.

KYENELE ***(KEÑELE, KEYELE, KENEN BIRANG, KYENYING-BARANG, KENYING BULANG, MIYAK)*** [KQL] 1,000 (1986 UBS). East Sepik Province, Giling village, Yuat River. Sepik-Ramu, Ramu, Yuat-Waibuk, Yuat-Maramba, Yuat. Bible portions 1994.

LABEL [LBB] 144 (1979 census). New Ireland Province, southwest coast, Nasko and Tampakar villages. Austronesian, Malayo-Polynesian, Central-Eastern, Eastern Malayo-Polynesian, Oceanic, Western Oceanic, Meso Melanesian, New Ireland, South New Ireland-Northwest Solomonic, Patpatar-Tolai.

LABU ***(LABU', LABO, HAPA)*** [LBU] 1,600 including 800 in Labu-Butu (1989 SIL). Morobe Province, coast near the mouth of the Markham River. 3 communities: Labu-Butu, Labu-Miti, and Labu-Tali. Austronesian, Malayo-Polynesian, Central-Eastern, Eastern Malayo-Polynesian, Oceanic, Western Oceanic, North New Guinea, Huon Gulf, Markham, Lower, Labu. Bilingualism in Tok Pisin. Labu only used in the home, especially when older people are present. Children are taught Tok Pisin first; use of Tok Pisin is active. The culture seems in decline. Those who attend school learn English. Yabem was the church language, and there were schools in Yabem. The economy is strong. Grammar.

LAEKO-LIBUAT ***(LAEKO, LAEKO-LIMBUAT)*** [LKL] 538 including 518 in area and 20 outside (1978 census). Sandaun Province, Torricelli Mts., west of Mehek. Torricelli, Maimai, Laeko-Libuat.

LAK ***(SIAR, LAMBOM, LAMASSA)*** [SJR] 1,800 (1991 SIL). Southern New Ireland Province, Namatanai District. Austronesian, Malayo-Polynesian, Central-Eastern, Eastern Malayo-Polynesian, Oceanic, Western Oceanic, Meso Melanesian, New Ireland, South New Ireland-Northwest Solomonic, Patpatar-Tolai. Tok Pisin is second language. English used in schools. SVO. Coastal.

LAMOGAI ***(MULAKAINO, AKIURU)*** [LMG] 3,653 (1980 Johnston). West New Britain Province, northwest interior, and 2 regions on the south coast. Austronesian, Malayo-Polynesian, Central-Eastern, Eastern Malayo-Polynesian, Oceanic, Western Oceanic, North New Guinea, Ngero-Vitiaz, Vitiaz, Southwest New Britain, Bibling. Dialects: IBANGA (IVANGA), PULIE-RAUTO (RAUTO, ROTO), LOMOGAI, MUSEN, PARET. Tropical forest. Low mountain, valley, coastal plain. Agriculturalists, fishermen, hunter-gatherers. Christian, traditional religion. NT 1996.

LANGAM [LNM] 254 (1981 Wurm and Hattori). East Sepik Province. Sepik-Ramu, Ramu, Yuat-Waibuk, Mongol-Langam. Related languages: Mongol, Yaul. Investigation needed: intelligibility with Mongol, Yaul.

LANTANAI [LNI] 300 (1990 C. Hurd SIL). North Solomons Province, Kieta District, Piruneu' village. East Papuan, Bougainville, East, Nasioi. The language was quite different from others in the Nasioi group, but it may have converged to be more like Koromira or Nasioi.

LAUA ***(LABU)*** [LUF] 1 speaker (1987 SIL). Central Province, north and west of Laua. Trans-New Guinea, Main Section, Eastern, Central and Southeastern, Mailuan. Different from Austronesian Labu in Morobe Province. Nearly extinct.

LAVATBURA-LAMUSONG ***(LAMASONG)*** [LBV] 1,308 (1972 Beaumont). New Ireland Province, central. Austronesian, Malayo-Polynesian, Central-Eastern, Eastern Malayo-Polynesian, Oceanic, Western Oceanic, Meso Melanesian, New Ireland, Madak. Dialects: UGANA, KONTU, LAVATBURA, LAMUSONG (LAMASONG).

LEIPON ***(PITILU, PITYILU)*** [LEK] 650 (1977 Lincoln). Manus Province, Lolo village, Hauwai, Ndrilo, and Pityilu islands. Austronesian, Malayo-Polynesian, Central-Eastern, Eastern Malayo-Polynesian, Oceanic, Admiralty Islands, Eastern, Manus, East. Speakers are very bilingual in Lele. Investigation needed: bilingual proficiency in Lele. SVO.

LELE ***(LELE HAI, HAI, USIAI, MOANUS, MANUS, ELU-KARA)*** [UGA] 1,300 (1982 SIL). Manus Province, Manus Island. Austronesian, Malayo-Polynesian, Central-Eastern, Eastern Malayo-Polynesian, Oceanic, Admiralty Islands, Eastern, Manus, East. Dialect: SABON. SVO. Tropical forest. Coastal, island. Swidden agriculturalists: copra, rubber, cocoa; fishermen. Sea level. NT 1956.

LEMBENA [LEQ] 1,500 (1994 SIL). Enga Province, northeast corner, and into East Sepik Province. 10 villages. Trans-New Guinea, Main Section, Central and Western, East New Guinea Highlands, West-Central, Enga. Some bilingualism in Enga. SOV. Literacy rate in first language: Less than 5%. Literacy rate in second language: Less than 5%. Tropical forest. Rugged mountain slope. Swidden agriculturalists. 80 to 1,520 meters.

LEMIO [LEI] 175 (1981 Wurm and Hattori). Madang Province, several villages on coast near Saidor. Trans-New Guinea, Madang-Adelbert Range, Madang, Rai Coast, Kabenau.

LENKAU [LER] 250 (1982 SIL). Manus Province, southwest Rambutyo Island. 1 village only. Austronesian, Malayo-Polynesian, Central-Eastern, Eastern Malayo-Polynesian, Oceanic, Admiralty Islands, Eastern, Southeast Islands. Bilingualism in Titan, Penchal. SVO.

LESING-GELIMI ***(LESING-ATUI, ATUI)*** [LET] 929 (1982 SIL). Eastern end of West New Britain Province, south coast, Kaskas Island and Amio village (Lesing dialect), Atui Island and Paronga village (Gelimi dialect). Austronesian, Malayo-Polynesian, Central-Eastern, Eastern Malayo-Polynesian, Oceanic, Western Oceanic, North New Guinea, Ngero-Vitiaz, Vitiaz, Southwest New Britain, Arawe-Pasismanua, Arawe, East Arawe. Dialects: LESING, GELIMI. Speakers have receptive bilingualism in Mangseng. Tok Pisin is also used. 3 primary schools. Tropical forest. Raised coral coast.

LEWADA-DEWARA ***(LEWADA, DEWALA-LEWADA)*** [LWD] 450 (1981 Wurm and Hattori). Western Province, southern bank and hinterland of Fly Estuary, east of Tirio, and on Sumogi

Island around Dewala. Trans-New Guinea, Trans-Fly-Bulaka River, Trans-Fly, Tirio. Dialects: BALAMULA (MATARU), DEWALA, LEWADA. 78% lexical similarity with Aturu. Investigation needed: intelligibility with Aturu.

LIHIR ***(LIR)*** [LIH] 6,000 (1985 SIL). New Ireland Province, Lihir Island and 3 smaller islands. Austronesian, Malayo-Polynesian, Central-Eastern, Eastern Malayo-Polynesian, Oceanic, Western Oceanic, Meso Melanesian, New Ireland, Tabar. Traditional religion.

LIKUM [LIB] 100 (1977 Lincoln). Manus Province. Austronesian, Malayo-Polynesian, Central-Eastern, Eastern Malayo-Polynesian, Oceanic, Admiralty Islands, Eastern, Manus, West. Bilingualism in Lindrou. Investigation needed: bilingual proficiency in Lindrou. SVO.

LILAU ***(NGAIMBOM)*** [LLL] 449 (1981 Wurm and Hattori). Madang Province, Bogia District. Torricelli, Monumbo.

LONIU ***(LONIO, NDROKU)*** [LOS] 460 (1977 Lincoln). Manus Province, Lolak and Loniu villages, south coast of Los Negros Island. Austronesian, Malayo-Polynesian, Central-Eastern, Eastern Malayo-Polynesian, Oceanic, Admiralty Islands, Eastern, Manus, Mokoreng-Loniu. Close to Bipi. Moderate bilingualism in Lele and Papitalai. Dictionary. Grammar. SVO.

LOTE ***(UVOL)*** [UVL] 4,200 (1982 SIL). East New Britain Province, Pomio District, southeast coast and inland near Cape Dampier. Austronesian, Malayo-Polynesian, Central-Eastern, Eastern Malayo-Polynesian, Oceanic, Western Oceanic, North New Guinea, Ngero-Vitiaz, Vitiaz, Mengen. Literacy rate in second language: 50% to 75%. Bible portions 1993.

LOU [LOJ] 1,000 (1994 SIL). Manus Province, Lou Island. Austronesian, Malayo-Polynesian, Central-Eastern, Eastern Malayo-Polynesian, Oceanic, Admiralty Islands, Eastern, Southeast Islands. Dialect: REI. Three very similar dialects. Rei is dominant. Bilingualism in Baluan-Pam, Titan. Different from Torricelli (Lou) in East Sepik Province or Tate (Lou) in Gulf Province. SVO.

LUKEP ***(SIASI, SIASSI, TOLOKIWA, LOKEP)*** [LOA] 591 (1980 census). Morobe Province, Tolokiwa and north tip of Umboi Island. Austronesian, Malayo-Polynesian, Central-Eastern, Eastern Malayo-Polynesian, Oceanic, Western Oceanic, North New Guinea, Ngero-Vitiaz, Vitiaz, Korap. Close to Arop. Investigation needed: intelligibility with Arop. Bible portions 1993.

LUSI ***(KALIAI)*** [KHL] 2,000 (1994 SIL). West New Britain Province, northwest coast. Austronesian, Malayo-Polynesian, Central-Eastern, Eastern Malayo-Polynesian, Oceanic, Western Oceanic, North New Guinea, Ngero-Vitiaz, Ngero, Bariai. Dialect: KALIAI. A distinct language from Kove. Grammar.

MADAK ***(MANDAK, LELET)*** [MMX] 3,000 (1985 UBS). New Ireland Province, Central New Ireland District. Austronesian, Malayo-Polynesian, Central-Eastern, Eastern Malayo-Polynesian, Oceanic, Western Oceanic, Meso Melanesian, New Ireland, Madak. Dialects: DANU, KATINGAN, LELET, MESI, MALOM. NT 1995.

MAGORI [MDR] 200 (1971 Dutton). Central Province, eastern end of Table Bay, lower reaches of Bailebo-Tavenei River. Austronesian, Malayo-Polynesian, Central-Eastern, Eastern Malayo-Polynesian, Oceanic, Western Oceanic, Papuan Tip, Peripheral, Central Papuan, Oumic, Magoric. Vocabulary is heavily influenced by Mailu. Ouma, Yoba, and Bina are separate languages. 85% to 100% of speakers are bilingual or trilingual in Suau, the Gadaisu dialect of Suau, Mailu, or Hiri Motu. Probably extinct.

MAIA ***(SAKI, PILA, SUARO, TURUTAP, YAKIBA, MAYA, BANAR)*** [SKS] 2,500 (1987 SIL). Madang Province, Bogia District, on the mainland south of Manam Island. Trans-New Guinea, Madang-Adelbert Range, Adelbert Range, Pihom-Isumrud-Mugil, Pihom, Kaukombaran. Literacy rate in first language: 25% to 50%. Literacy rate in second language: 50% to 75%. Bible portions 1988.

MAIADOM [MZZ] 716 (1998 census). Milne Bay Province, Bwaidoka District, East Fergusson Island. Austronesian, Malayo-Polynesian, Central-Eastern, Eastern Malayo-Polynesian, Oceanic, Western Oceanic, Papuan Tip, Nuclear, North Papuan Mainland-D'Entrecasteaux, Bwaidoga. 62% lexical similarity with Iamelele, 35% with Bosilewa, 32% with Gameta, 20% with Dobu. Coastal, mountain slope. Agriculturalists, fishermen. Sea level to 600 meters.

MAIANI ***(TANI, BANARA, WAGIMUDA, MIANI SOUTH)*** [TNH] 2,496 (1981 Wurm and Hattori). Madang Province, Bogia District. Trans-New Guinea, Madang-Adelbert Range, Adelbert Range, Pihom-Isumrud-Mugil, Pihom, Kaukombaran. Different from Mala (Banara). Literacy rate in first language: 25% to 50%. Literacy rate in second language: 50% to 75%. Bible portions 1982-1988.

MAILU ***(MAGI)*** [MGU] 6,000 (1980 UBS). Central Province, south coast, Gadaisu to Baramata, Table Bay and Toulon Island. Trans-New Guinea, Main Section, Eastern, Central and Southeastern, Mailuan. Dialects: DOMARA, DARAVA, ASIAORO, DEREBAI, ISLAND, GEAGEA, BOREBO, ILAI, BAIBARA. Related language: Laua. Education standard above average. NT 1936-1979.

MAISIN ***(MAISAN)*** [MBQ] 3,000 (1996 John Barker). Oro Province, villages along coast of Collingwood Bay and Kosirava swamp. Austronesian, Malayo-Polynesian, Central-Eastern, Eastern Malayo-Polynesian, Oceanic, Western Oceanic, Papuan Tip, Nuclear, Maisin. Dialects: KOSIRAVA, MAISIN. No closely related languages. Dialects have 73% lexical similarity, but there is little interaction between the speakers. Many Maisin are fluent in Korafe, as well as Ubir and English. Grammar. SOV. Literacy varies from 20% to 80% in different areas. Coastal, swamps.

MAIWA [MTI] 1,400 (1998 SIL). Milne Bay Province, Rabaraba District, on the northern slopes and foothills of the Meneao Range eastward from the Mt. Tantam Valley of the Ruaba River; it reaches the coast of Moi Bin Bay, extending into Oro Province. Trans-New Guinea, Main Section, Eastern, Central and Southeastern, Dagan. Dialects: MAIWA, OREN, MANIGARA, GAIREN, GWARETA. Closest lexical similarity is with Mapena at 41%. Wedau is used as church language. Swamp and lowlands.

MAIWALA [MUM] 1,294 (1990 census). Milne Bay Province, Alotau District, Huhu Local Government Area, at the head of Milne Bay. Austronesian, Malayo-Polynesian, Central-Eastern, Eastern Malayo-Polynesian, Oceanic, Western Oceanic, Papuan Tip, Nuclear, North Papuan Mainland-D'Entrecasteaux, Are-Taupota, Taupota. Maiwala is the major dialect. 67% lexical similarity with Tawala at Diwala village (closest). Speakers know English, Suau, Tawala, some Motu. Two schools. They have a good Maiwala elementary school.

MAKOLKOL [ZMH] 7 (1988 SIL). East New Britain Province, Gazelle Peninsula. East Papuan, Yele-Solomons-New Britain, New Britain, Baining-Taulil. Nearly extinct.

MALA ***(MALALA, PAY, PAI, ALAM, BANARA, DAGOI, HATZFELDHAFEN, DAGUI)*** [PED] 769 (1981 Wurm and Hattori). Madang Province, Bogia District. Trans-New Guinea, Madang-Adelbert Range, Adelbert Range, Pihom-Isumrud-Mugil, Pihom, Kaukombaran. Increasing use of Tok Pisin. Distinct from Maiani (Banara), and from Pei (Pai) in Walio group. SOV. Literacy rate in first language: 25% to 50%. Literacy rate in second language: 50% to 75%. Savannah, scrub, tropical forest. Coastal. Swidden agriculturalists, fishermen. Sea level. Bible portions 1982-1988.

MALALAMAI ***(BONGA)*** [MMT] 341 (1977 Lincoln). Madang Province, Rai coast east and west of Saidor; Malalamai and Bonga villages. Austronesian, Malayo-Polynesian, Central-Eastern, Eastern Malayo-Polynesian, Oceanic, Western Oceanic, North New Guinea, Ngero-Vitiaz, Ngero, Bariai.

MALAS [MKR] 220 (1981 Wurm and Hattori). Madang Province near Tokain. Trans-New Guinea, Madang-Adelbert Range, Adelbert Range, Pihom-Isumrud-Mugil, Isumrud, Mabuan.

MALASANGA [MQZ] 435 (1991 SIL). Morobe Province, north coast, two villages: Malasanga and Singorakai. Austronesian, Malayo-Polynesian, Central-Eastern, Eastern Malayo-Polynesian, Oceanic, Western Oceanic, North New Guinea, Ngero-Vitiaz, Vitiaz, Korap. Dialects: MALASANGA, SINGORAKAI. Separate from Barim.

MALE ***(KOLIKU)*** [MDC] 393 (1981 Wurm and Hattori). Madang Province, coast south of Bom. Trans-New Guinea, Madang-Adelbert Range, Madang, Rai Coast, Mindjim. Related to Bongu and Anjam.

MALEU-KILENGE ***(IDNE)*** [MGL] 5,000 (1991 SIL), including 440 Kilenge (M. Ross 1988). West New Britain Province, Talasea District, western tip. Austronesian, Malayo-Polynesian, Central-Eastern, Eastern Malayo-Polynesian, Oceanic, Western Oceanic, North New Guinea, Ngero-Vitiaz, Vitiaz, Kilenge-Maleu. Dialects: MALEU, KILENGE (KAITAROLEA). Wurm and Hattori (1981) and M. Ross (1988) treat Maleu and Kilenge as separate languages. SVO. Literacy rate in first language: 25% to 50%. Literacy rate in second language: 50% to 75%. Savannah, tropical forest. Coastal, mountain slope, volcanic. Swidden agriculturalists. Bible portions 1990.

MALI ***(GAKTAI)*** [GCC] 2,200 (1988 SIL). East New Britain Province, eastern Gazelle Peninsula. East Papuan, Yele-Solomons-New Britain, New Britain, Baining-Taulil. A distinct language within the Baining ethnic group. Two dialects. Several primary schools. Mountains sloping to coastline.

MALINGUAT ***(TSHWOSH, TSHUOSH, KWARUWIKWUNDI, SEPIK PLAINS)*** [SIC] 9,000 (1986 PBT). East Sepik Province, Maprik District, Sepik Plains south of Maprik. Sepik-Ramu, Sepik, Middle Sepik, Ndu. Dialects: KOIWAT, BURUI, CHIMBIAN, CENTRAL SAWOS, EASTERN SAWOS. Close to Gaikundi.

MALOL ***(MALON, MALOLO)*** [MBK] 3,330. Sandaun Province, around Malol village. Austronesian, Malayo-Polynesian, Central-Eastern, Eastern Malayo-Polynesian, Oceanic, Western Oceanic, North New Guinea, Schouten, Siau. Distinct enough from Sissano, Arop-Sissano, and Sera that it will probably need separate literature.

MAMAA ***(MAMA)*** [MHF] 198 in one village (1978 McElhanon). Morobe Province. Trans-New Guinea, Main Section, Central and Western, Huon-Finisterre, Finisterre, Erap.

MAMUSI ***(KAKUNA)*** [KDF] 6,000 (1985 SIL). East New Britain Province, southeast coast, inland on the Melkoi and Torlu rivers. Inland villages are up to 40 km. from the coast. Austronesian, Malayo-Polynesian, Central-Eastern, Eastern Malayo-Polynesian, Oceanic, Western Oceanic, North New Guinea, Ngero-Vitiaz, Vitiaz, Mengen. Dialects: MAMUSI, MELKOI (KAKUNA). Bilingualism in Tok Pisin. Mamusi is used for home and village life. Scattered village schools. Literacy rate in second language: Only young people. Bushy area. 3,000 feet.

MANAGALASI ***(MANAGULASI)*** [MCQ] 5,000 (1982 SIL). Oro Province, Popondetta District, southeast of the Omie. Trans-New Guinea, Main Section, Eastern, Central and Southeastern, Koiarian, Baraic.

Dialects: MUATURAINA, CHIMONA, DEA, AKABAFA, NAMI, MESARI, AVERI, AFORE, MINJORI, OKO, WAKUE, NUMBA, JIMUNI, KARIRA. 50% monolingual. Others use Hiri Motu as second language. Dictionary. Mountains. Agriculturalists: taro, bananas, pineapple. Traditional religion. NT 1975-1999.

MANAM ***(MANUM)*** [MVA] 7,000 (1998 SIL). Manam and Boesa islands, Madang Province, Bogia District, and in Sepa and Wanami on the adjacent mainland. Austronesian, Malayo-Polynesian, Central-Eastern, Eastern Malayo-Polynesian, Oceanic, Western Oceanic, North New Guinea, Schouten, Kairiru-Manam, Manam. Dialect: WANAMI. Related to Wogeo, Biem, Sepa, Medebur. Different from Manem. Grammar. SOV. Tropical forest. Coastal. Swidden agriculturalists. 0 to 300 meters. NT 1996.

MANAMBU [MLE] 2,058 in 3 villages (1981 Wurm and Hattori). East Sepik Province, Ambunti Subprovince, villages along the Sepik River. Sepik-Ramu, Sepik, Middle Sepik, Ndu. Different from Manumbo in Madang Province. Literacy rate in first language: 5% to 15%. Literacy rate in second language: 15% to 25%. Riverine. Fishermen; sago. 50 meters. Traditional religion, Christian. NT 1979.

MANDARA ***(MADARA, TABAR)*** [TBF] 2,500 (1985 SIL). New Ireland Province, Simberi, Tatau, Tabar and one other island. Austronesian, Malayo-Polynesian, Central-Eastern, Eastern Malayo-Polynesian, Oceanic, Western Oceanic, Meso Melanesian, New Ireland, Lavongai-Nalik. Dialects: SIMBERI, TATAU, TABAR.

MANDI ***(IMANDI)*** [TUA] 162 (1981 Wurm and Hattori). East Sepik Province, coast about 15 miles south-east of Wewak. Torricelli, Marienberg.

MANDOBO ***("KAETI", KWEM)*** [KZH] Western Province, east of Fly River around Maporoan and Kwem. Trans-New Guinea, Main Section, Central and Western, Central and South New Guinea-Kutubuan, Central and South New Guinea, Awyu-Dumut, Dumut. Literacy rate in first language: Less than 5%. Literacy rate in second language: Less than 5%. See main entry under Indonesia, Irian Jaya.

MANEM ***(YETI, JETI, WEMBI, SKOFRO)*** [JET] 500 in Papua New Guinea (1993 SIL). Population total both countries 900. Sandaun Province, 1 village; Skotiau. Also spoken in Indonesia (Irian Jaya). Trans-New Guinea, Northern, Border, Waris. 50% lexical similarity with Waris (closest). Different from Manam. Significant literacy in Tok Pisin and Bahasa Indonesian.

MANGSENG ***(MANGSING, MASEGI, MASEKI)*** [MBH] 2,500 (1998 L. Milligan SIL). West New Britain and East New Britain provinces, area south of Commodore Bay (north coast, West New Britain), through to Montagu Harbor (south coast of East New Britain) on the east and through to Fulleborn Harbor (south coast of West New Britain) on the west. Austronesian, Malayo-Polynesian, Central-Eastern, Eastern Malayo-Polynesian, Oceanic, Western Oceanic, North New Guinea, Ngero-Vitiaz, Vitiaz, Southwest New Britain, Arawe-Pasismanua, Arawe. Dialects: UMUA, MARAPU. Arawe chain isolate, most closely related to West Arawe. Literacy rate in first language: 25% to 50%. Literacy rate in second language: 25% to 50%. NT, in press (1999).

MAPE [MLH] 5,117 (1978 McElhanon). Morobe Province along the Mape River. Trans-New Guinea, Main Section, Central and Western, Huon-Finisterre, Huon, Eastern. Dialects: NAGA, MAPE, NIGAC, FUKAC. Close to Kâte, which is the lingua franca. Bilingualism in Kâte. Naga and Nigac dialects may be extinct. Investigation needed: bilingual proficiency in Kâte.

MAPENA [MNM] 274 (1973 SIL). Milne Bay Province, around Mt. Gwoira. Trans-New Guinea, Main Section, Eastern, Central and Southeastern, Dagan. 51% lexical similarity with Daga (closest).

MARAMBA [MYD] 300 (1981 Wurm and Hattori). East Sepik Province. Sepik-Ramu, Ramu, Yuat-Waibuk, Yuat-Maramba, Maramba.

MARI ***(HOP)*** [HOB] 806 (1988 Holzknecht). Madang Province, upper Ramu River. 4 villages. Austronesian, Malayo-Polynesian, Central-Eastern, Eastern Malayo-Polynesian, Oceanic, Western Oceanic, North New Guinea, Huon Gulf, Markham, Upper, Mountain. Different from Mari of East Sepik Province and Mari of Western Province.

MARI [MBX] 120 (1981 Wurm and Hattori). East Sepik Province, near Mari Lake and on Salumei River. Sepik-Ramu, Sepik, Sepik Hill, Bahinemo. Speakers are highly bilingual in Tok Pisin. Different from Mari of Madang Province and Mari of Western Province. Investigation needed: bilingual proficiency in Tok Pisin.

MARI ***(DORRO)*** [MXW] 84 (1980 census). Western Province, south coast near Tais, and inland about 10 miles. 1 village. Trans-New Guinea, Trans-Fly-Bulaka River, Trans-Fly, Morehead and Upper Maro Rivers, Nambu. Closely related to Tais. Related to Kanum, Aramba, Bothar, Nambu, Peremka, Rouku. Different from Mari of East Sepik Province, and Mari of Madang Province. Literacy rate in first language: Less than 5%. Literacy rate in second language: Less than 5%.

MARIA ***(MANUBARA)*** [MDS] 870 (1980 census). Central Province, Marshall Lagoon to Mt. Brown; a remote area. Trans-New Guinea, Main Section, Eastern, Central and Southeastern, Manubaran. Dialects: DIDIGARU, MARIA, GEBI, OIBU, AMOTA, IMILA, UDERI. 63% lexical similarity with Doromu (closest).

MARIK ***(DAMI, HAM)*** [DAD] 3,500 (1998 SIL). Madang Province, Madang District, inland around Gogol River. 10 villages. Austronesian, Malayo-Polynesian, Central-Eastern, Eastern Malayo-Polynesian,

Oceanic, Western Oceanic, North New Guinea, Ngero-Vitiaz, Vitiaz, Bel, Nuclear Bel, Southern. Dialects: NORTHERN MARIK, WESTERN MARIK, SOUTHERN MARIK. The people have chosen 'Marik' as the name for their language. SOV. Tropical forest. Interfluvial. Agriculturalists. Above 40 meters. Bible portions 1989.

MARING ***(MARENG, YOADABE-WATOARE)*** [MBW] 11,000 (1998 SIL). Western Highlands Province, Hagen District. A small number are over the Bismarck Range in Madang Province. 18 villages. Trans-New Guinea, Main Section, Central and Western, East New Guinea Highlands, Central, Jimi. Dialects: CENTRAL MARING, EASTERN MARING, TIMBUNKI, TSUWENKI, KARAMBA, KAMBEGL. Speakers of all dialects understand the central one. Grammar. SOV. Literacy rate in first language: Less than 5%. Literacy rate in second language: Less than 5%. Tropical forest. Mountain slope. Swidden agriculturalists. 400 to 2,734 meters. Bible portions 1974-1979.

MATEPI [MQE] 238 (1981 Wurm and Hattori). Madang Province. Trans-New Guinea, Madang-Adelbert Range, Madang, Mabuso, Hanseman. Related languages: Rapting, Wamas, Samosa, Murupi, Saruga, Nake, Mosimo, Garus, Yoidik, Rempi, Silopi, Utu, Mawan, Baimak, Bagupi, Gal, Garuh, Kamba. Investigation needed: intelligibility.

MATO ***(NENAYA, NENGAYA, NINEIA)*** [NIU] 575 (1998 SIL). Morobe Province, north coast of Huon Peninsula, near Morobe-Madang provincial border, Uruwa River plain 38 km. west of Wasu, 20 km. north of Sapmanga, approximately 55 km. southeast of Saidor. Austronesian, Malayo-Polynesian, Central-Eastern, Eastern Malayo-Polynesian, Oceanic, Western Oceanic, North New Guinea, Ngero-Vitiaz, Vitiaz, Roinji-Nenaya. Dialects: BONEA, NANAYA. 67% lexical similarity with Ronji, 39% with Barim and Arop-Lokep, 38% with Malasanga, 29% with Sio, 23% with Tuam-Mutu. Speakers want 'Mato' for the language name. SVO. Literacy rate in first language: 4%. Literacy rate in second language: 41%. Savannah, tropical forest. Mountain slope, coastal plain. Swidden agruculturalists. 0 to 1,700 feet. Christian, traditional religion.

MATUKAR [MJK] 219 (1981 Wurm and Hattori). Madang Province, 40 miles north of Madang town around Matukar. Austronesian, Malayo-Polynesian, Central-Eastern, Eastern Malayo-Polynesian, Oceanic, Western Oceanic, North New Guinea, Ngero-Vitiaz, Vitiaz, Bel, Nuclear Bel, Northern. Related to Gedaged. Coastal.

MAUWAKE ***(ULINGAN, MAWAKE)*** [MHL] 2,000 (1987 SIL). Madang Province, Bogia District, east of Malala High School. Trans-New Guinea, Madang-Adelbert Range, Adelbert Range, Pihom-Isumrud-Mugil, Pihom, Kumilan. Related to Moere. Literacy rate in first language: 25% to 50%. Literacy rate in second language: 50% to 75%. Christian, traditional religion. NT 1998.

MAWAK [MJJ] 31 (1981 Wurm and Hattori). Madang Province, southwest of Mauwake. Trans-New Guinea, Madang-Adelbert Range, Adelbert Range, Pihom-Isumrud-Mugil, Pihom, Tiboran. Related to Hinahon.

MAWAN [MCZ] 269 (1981 Wurm and Hattori). Madang Province, Gogol River area. Trans-New Guinea, Madang-Adelbert Range, Madang, Mabuso, Hanseman.

MBO-UNG ***(TEMBALO, BO-UNG, MBOUNG)*** [MUX] 23,000 (1985 SIL), including 5,000 Miyemu (1990 UBS). Western Highlands Province, Hagen District. Some also in Tambul and Lower Kaugel districts. Trans-New Guinea, Main Section, Central and Western, East New Guinea Highlands, Central, Hagen, Kaugel. Dialects: MIYEMU (MIYEM), MARA-GOMU, TEMBALO (TEMBAGLO). Some people are bilingual in Medlpa. SOV. Mountain slope and valley. 3,500 to 8,000 feet. Bible portions 1989-1990.

MBULA ***(MANGAP-MBULA, MANGAABA, MANGAAWA, MANGAAVA, MANGAP, KAIMANGA)*** [MNA] 2,500 (1991 Bugenhagen SIL). Morobe Province, Siassi District, 6 villages on eastern Umboi Island, 1 village on Sakar Island. Austronesian, Malayo-Polynesian, Central-Eastern, Eastern Malayo-Polynesian, Oceanic, Western Oceanic, North New Guinea, Ngero-Vitiaz, Vitiaz, Mangap-Mbula. Dialects: MBULA (CENTRAL MBULA), NORTHERN MBULA, GAURU, SAKAR. Grammar. SVOX; prepositions, NP: (Inalienable Genitive) Nn (Quant) (Det) (Alienable Genitive) (RC) (DEM). Literacy rate in first language: 15% to 25%. Literacy rate in second language: 25% to 50%. Tropical forest. Coastal. Swidden agriculturalists. Sea level. Christian, traditional religion. NT 1997.

MEBU [MJN] 319 (1981 Wurm and Hattori). Madang Province, 10 to 20 miles southwest of Saidor. Trans-New Guinea, Main Section, Central and Western, Huon-Finisterre, Finisterre, Yupna. Related to Yupna, Gabutamon.

MEDEBUR [MJM] 429 (1981 Wurm and Hattori). Madang Province, coast just north of Sikor at Medebur. Austronesian, Malayo-Polynesian, Central-Eastern, Eastern Malayo-Polynesian, Oceanic, Western Oceanic, North New Guinea, Schouten, Kairiru-Manam, Manam. Related to Wogeo, Biem, Sepa, and Manam.

MEHEK ***(NUKU, ME'EK, DRIAFLEISUMA, INDINOGOSIMA)*** [NUX] 6,300 or more (1994 SIL). Sandaun Province, Nuku District, Makru-Klaplei area, lower foothills of Torricelli Mts., southeast of Siliput. 9 large villages. Sepik-Ramu, Sepik, Tama. 51% lexical similarity with Pahi (closest). Bilingualism in Tok Pisin.

Mehek is used in home and village life. Vigorous. Positive language attitude. 50% or more of the children are in primary school. Literacy rate in second language: 50% to 75%. Mountain slope.

MEKEO ***(MEKEO-KOVIO)*** [MEK] 18,000 to 20,000 (1998 SIL). Central Province, Kaiyuku District, inland, bounded on the west by the Waima, on the east by the Kuni and Kunimaipa. Extends into Gulf Province. Austronesian, Malayo-Polynesian, Central-Eastern, Eastern Malayo-Polynesian, Oceanic, Western Oceanic, Papuan Tip, Peripheral, Central Papuan, West Central Papuan, Nuclear. Dialects: EAST MEKEO, WEST MEKEO, NORTH MEKEO, NORTHWEST MEKEO (KOVIO). Kovio is a peripheral or aberrant 'dialect'. The four 'dialects' are mutually unintelligible to each others' speakers, except for North and West Mekeo, but most Mekeo are reported to have familiarity with neighboring 'dialects'. Kovio, however, is not contiguous to the other 'dialects'. Kovio has 81% lexical similarity with West Mekeo and North Mekeo, and 79% with East Mekeo. West and East Mekeo have 87% lexical similarity. North Mekeo has 99% lexical similarity with West Mekeo and 87% with East Mekeo. Mekeo has 41% with Waima. Prestigious language. Patrilineal descent groups. "Kovio" is perjorative in some contexts. The educational standard is above average. Investigation needed: intelligibility with dialects. Grammar. NT 1998.

MEKMEK [MVK] 1,036 (1981 Wurm and Hattori). East Sepik Province. Sepik-Ramu, Ramu, Yuat-Waibuk, Yuat-Maramba, Yuat. Related languages: Changriwa, Miyak, Biwat, Bun. Investigation needed: intelligibility.

MELPA ***(MEDLPA, HAGEN)*** [MED] 130,000 (1991 SIL). Western Highlands Province, Hagen District. Trans-New Guinea, Main Section, Central and Western, East New Guinea Highlands, Central, Hagen. Dialect: TEMBAGLA. Only slight dialect differences. Literacy rate in first language: 5% to 15%. Literacy rate in second language: 25% to 50%. Swidden agriculturalists: sweet potatoes, yams, taro, maize, coffee. Traditional religion, some Christian. NT 1965-1995.

MENDE ***(SEIM, TAU, KUBIWAT)*** [SIM] 7,600 (1996 SIL). Sandaun Province, Nuku District, east of Mehek. Sepik-Ramu, Sepik, Middle Sepik, Nukuma. Related to Yubanakor. 49% lexical similarity to nearest Kwanga village.

MENGEN ***(POENG)*** [MEE] 8,400 (1982 SIL). East New Britain Province, Pomio District, Jacquinot Bay and inland. 20 villages. Austronesian, Malayo-Polynesian, Central-Eastern, Eastern Malayo-Polynesian, Oceanic, Western Oceanic, North New Guinea, Ngero-Vitiaz, Vitiaz, Mengen. Dialects: NORTH COAST MENGEN (MAENG), SOUTH COAST MENGEN (POENG). Some linguists separate Poeng (Mengen 1, Bush Mengen) and Maeng (Mengen 2, Orford, Maenge) into two languages. SVO. Literacy rate in first language: 5% to 15%. Literacy rate in second language: 25% to 50%. Tropical forest. Coastal. Fishermen, swidden agriculturalists. 0 to 70 meters.

MENYA ***(MENYE, MENYAMA)*** [MCR] 20,000 (1998 SIL). Morobe Province, Menyamya District, from the Papua border north along the Tauri River and its tributaries. Trans-New Guinea, Main Section, Central and Western, Angan, Angan Proper. SOV. Literacy rate in first language: 5% to 15%. Literacy rate in second language: 15% to 25%. Tropical forest, savannah. Mountain slope. Swidden agriculturalists. 1,100 to 2,300 meters. Bible portions 1995.

MERAMERA ***(UBILI, MELAMELA)*** [MXM] 2,000 (1995 SIL). West New Britain Province, Bialla District, northwest coast. Austronesian, Malayo-Polynesian, Central-Eastern, Eastern Malayo-Polynesian, Oceanic, Western Oceanic, Meso Melanesian, Willaumez. Dialect: LOLOBAO. 5% monolingual. SVO. Literacy rate in first language: 0% to 5%. Literacy rate in second language: 50% to 75%. Coastal. Swidden agriculturalists: cocoa; fishermen; copra; oil palm. Sea level.

MESẼ ***(MESEM, MOMOLILI, MOMALILI)*** [MCI] 4,000 (1997 census). Morobe Province, Lae District, Boana Subdistrict, interior north of Lae. 14 villages: Samanzing, Biliman, Tusulu, Hobu, Zezegi, Momolili, Zitare, Malapipi, Kwamu, Busu, Nomenga, Zitale-Ogaw, Tuzing, Kaisia. Sambuen is a border community with both Nabak and Mesẽ speakers. Trans-New Guinea, Main Section, Central and Western, Huon-Finisterre, Huon, Western. Dialects: WEST-CENTRAL MESẼ, EAST MESẼ, MOMOLILI, ZEZAGI. Men 50 years old and older can speak either Yabem or Kâte. Most adults under 30 are bilingual in Tok Pisin. Community schools at Hobu and Samanzing. SOV, adjectives, numerals after noun heads, verb affixes mark number, CV, CVC, CVV, CCV, VC, V, nontonal. Literacy rate in first language: Less than 5%. Literacy rate in second language: 5% to 15%. Tropical forest. Mountain slope. Swidden agriculturalists: coffee. 2,000 to 5,600 feet. Christian, traditional religion. Bible portions 1996-1997.

MIAN ***(MIANMIN)*** [MPT] 2,200 (1981 Wurm and Hattori). Sandaun Province, Telefomin District, north part of the Fạk (Hak) and Aki River valleys, headwaters of the August River and upper May River. Villages: Nenebil, Suganga, Blimo, and Wagarabai. Trans-New Guinea, Main Section, Central and Western, Central and South New Guinea-Kutubuan, Central and South New Guinea, Ok, Mountain. Dialects: UPPER AUGUST RIVER, USAGE, MIANMIN. Dialects have 75% to 83% lexical similarity. 'Mian' is the language, 'Mianmin' the people. Literacy rate in first language: 25% to 50%. Literacy rate in second language: 25% to 50%. NT 1986.

MIANI ***(BONAPUTA-MOPU, TANI, MIANI NORTH)*** [PLA] 1,500 (1987 SIL). Madang Province, Bogia District, inland. Trans-New Guinea, Madang-Adelbert Range, Adelbert Range, Pihom-Isumrud-Mugil, Pihom, Kaukombaran. Literacy rate in first language: 25% to 50%. Literacy rate in second language: 50% to 75%. Bible portions 1982.

MIGABAC ***(MIGABA')*** [MPP] 1,300 (1990 SIL). Morobe Province, Masaweng River area. 5 villages divided among 3 dialects: Hudewa and Waringai; Ago; Butengka and Kapawa. Trans-New Guinea, Main Section, Central and Western, Huon-Finisterre, Huon, Eastern. Dialects: NORTH MIGABAC, SOUTH MIGABAC, CENTRAL MIGABAC. Bilingualism in Kâte. Kâte is the lingua franca.

MINANIBAI ***(PEPEHA, EME-EME, HEI)*** [MCV] 300 (1981 Wurm and Hattori). Ikobi Kairi and Goaribari Census Districts, near the mouth of the Omati River, Gulf Province. Trans-New Guinea, Inland Gulf, Minanibai. Related to Tao-Suamato. Might be extinct.

MINAVEHA ***(MINAVEGA, KUKUYA)*** [MVN] 1,600 (1994 SIL). Milne Bay Province, Bolubolu District, southwest tip of Fergusson Island near Mapamoiwa station. Austronesian, Malayo-Polynesian, Central-Eastern, Eastern Malayo-Polynesian, Oceanic, Western Oceanic, Papuan Tip, Nuclear, North Papuan Mainland-D'Entrecasteaux, Are-Taupota, Taupota. 60% lexical similarity with Iamelele (closest), Koluawa, and Bwaidoka. Some bilingualism in Dobu, which is the lingua franca. Dictionary. SOV. Literacy rate in first language: 15% to 25%. Literacy rate in second language: 15% to 25%. Coastal. Bible portions 1993-1995.

MINDIRI [MPN] 93 in one village (1981 Wurm and Hattori). Madang Province, along the Rai Coast west of Saidor. Austronesian, Malayo-Polynesian, Central-Eastern, Eastern Malayo-Polynesian, Oceanic, Western Oceanic, North New Guinea, Ngero-Vitiaz, Vitiaz, Bel, Astrolabe. Close to Biliau and Wab, but a distinct language.

MINIGIR ***(LUNGALUNGA)*** [VMG] 373 (1979 census). East New Britain Province, Gazelle Peninsula, Lungalunga village on Ataliklikun Bay. Austronesian, Malayo-Polynesian, Central-Eastern, Eastern Malayo-Polynesian, Oceanic, Western Oceanic, Meso Melanesian, New Ireland, South New Ireland-Northwest Solomonic, Mono-Uruava.

MISIMA-PANEATI ***(PANAIETI, PANAEATI, PANEYATE, PANEATE, PANAYETI)*** [MPX] 14,000 (1994 SIL). Milne Bay Province, Misima District, Misima Island, Panaieti and all the islands of the Calvados Chain to (not including) Panawina, Alcester, Ole, and Tewatewan islands, and Bowagis on Woodlark Island. 22 villages. Austronesian, Malayo-Polynesian, Central-Eastern, Eastern Malayo-Polynesian, Oceanic, Western Oceanic, Papuan Tip, Peripheral, Kilivila-Louisiades, Misima. Dialects: NASIKWABW (TOKUNU), TEWATEWA. 33% lexical similarity with Nimowa and Dobu (closest). 4,000 or 28.5% are monolingual. Others use English as second language. Trade language. SOV. Literacy rate in first language: 75% to 80%. Literacy rate in second language: 75% to 80%. Many schools. Many go to high school. Tropical forest. Coastal. Swidden agriculturalists. 0 to 1,000 meters. NT 1947-1998.

MIU ***(MYU)*** [MPO] 500 (1998 NTM). West New Britain Province, Gimi Rauto District, southwest interior. Austronesian, Malayo-Polynesian, Central-Eastern, Eastern Malayo-Polynesian, Oceanic, Western Oceanic, North New Guinea, Ngero-Vitiaz, Vitiaz, Southwest New Britain, Arawe-Pasismanua, Pasismanua. A separate language from Kaulong. The people live in hamlets of 1 or 2 families. SVO, some minor affixation. Literacy rate in first language: 20%. Literacy rate in second language: 20%. Tropical forest. Mountain slope, foothills. Agriculturalists: taro, sweet potato, cassava, cucumber, papaya, banana, pineapple, coconut, maize; animal husbandry: pigs. 300 to 1,500 feet. Traditional religion, Christian. Bible portions 1992-1998.

MOERE [MVQ] 56 (1981 Wurm and Hattori). Madang Province. Trans-New Guinea, Madang-Adelbert Range, Adelbert Range, Pihom-Isumrud-Mugil, Pihom, Kumilan. Related languages: Mauwake, Bepour. Investigation needed: intelligibility with Mauwake, Bepour.

MOIKODI ***(DORIRI)*** [DOI] 571 (1981 Wurm and Hattori). Oro Province, north slopes of Owen Stanley Range around Mt. Brown down to Komi west of Foasi Creek. Trans-New Guinea, Main Section, Eastern, Central and Southeastern, Yareban. Several dialects. 65% to 73% lexical similarity with Aneme Wake (closest). 50% are monolingual. Others use Hiri Motu as second language. Literacy rate in second language: Partially.

MOKERANG ***(MOKARENG, MOKORENG)*** [MFT] 200(?) (1981 Wurm and Hattori). Manus Province, north Los Negros Island and Ndrilo Island. Austronesian, Malayo-Polynesian, Central-Eastern, Eastern Malayo-Polynesian, Oceanic, Admiralty Islands, Eastern, Manus, Mokoreng-Loniu. SVO.

MOLIMA ***(EBADIDI, SALAKAHADI, MORIMA)*** [MOX] 3,186 (1972 census) including 416 in Fagululu, 600 in Salakahadi. Milne Bay Province, 'Esa'ala District, West Fergusson Island, inland villages of the Salakahadi and Ebadidi areas, central west coast (Fagululu) and central south coast (Molima). Austronesian, Malayo-Polynesian, Central-Eastern, Eastern Malayo-Polynesian, Oceanic, Western Oceanic, Papuan Tip, Nuclear, North Papuan Mainland-D'Entrecasteaux, Bwaidoga. Dialects: TALA'AI, AI'ALU, TOSILA'AI. One dialect is on the coast, two dialects are remote in the mountains.

56% lexical similarity with Dobu. Church leaders, community leaders, traders, and travellers are bilingual in Dobu. 'Molima' refers to the whole area, as well as the south coast only, 'Ebadidi', 'Salakahadi', and 'Fagululu' to parts of it. One dialect is mainly on the west coast, two on the south coast and remote in the mountains. Literacy rate in first language: 15% to 30%. Literacy rate in second language: 15% to 30%. Tropical forest. Mountain slope, coastal plain. Swidden agriculturalists, hunter-gatherers, fishermen. Sea level to 1,500 feet. Traditional religion, Christian. Bible portions 1996-1997.

MOMARE ***(MOMALE, MOMOLE)*** [MSZ] 500 to 800 (1990 SIL). Morobe Province, north of Masaweng River. Trans-New Guinea, Main Section, Central and Western, Huon-Finisterre, Huon, Eastern. People below middle-aged use Kâte. Elderly and middle-aged speakers only.

MONDROPOLON [MLY] 300 (1981 Wurm and Hattori). Manus Province, north central coast, Manus Island. Austronesian, Malayo-Polynesian, Central-Eastern, Eastern Malayo-Polynesian, Oceanic, Admiralty Islands, Eastern, Manus, West. Most speakers are bilingual in Kurti. Investigation needed: bilingual proficiency in Kurti. SVO.

MONGOL [MGT] 338 (1981 Wurm and Hattori). East Sepik Province. Sepik-Ramu, Ramu, Yuat-Waibuk, Mongol-Langam. Related languages: Langam, Yaul. Investigation needed: intelligibility with Langam, Yaul.

MONUMBO [MXK] 459 (1981 Wurm and Hattori). Madang Province, Bogia District. Torricelli, Monumbo.

MORAWA [MZE] 755 (1973 SIL). Central Province, south coast around Cloudy Bay. Trans-New Guinea, Main Section, Eastern, Central and Southeastern, Mailuan. 70% lexical similarity with Binahari (closest). 85% to 100% of the people are bilingual in Magi, Suau, Hiri Motu, or English.

MORESADA ***(MURISAPA, MURUSAPA-SAREWA)*** [MSX] 197 (1981 Wurm and Hattori). Madang Province. Trans-New Guinea, Madang-Adelbert Range, Adelbert Range, Josephstaal-Wanang, Josephstaal, Pomoikan.

MORIGI ***(MORIGI ISLAND, WARIADAI, TURAMA RIVER KIWAI, DABURA)*** [MDB] 700 (1975 Wurm). Gulf Province, Lower Turama Census Division. Trans-New Guinea, Trans-Fly-Bulaka River, Trans-Fly, Kiwaian. Literacy rate in first language: Less than 5%. Literacy rate in second language: Less than 5%.

MOSIMO [MQV] 58 (1981 Wurm and Hattori). Madang Province. Trans-New Guinea, Madang-Adelbert Range, Madang, Mabuso, Hanseman. Related languages: Rapting, Wamas, Samosa, Murupi, Saruga, Nake, Matepi, Garus, Yoidik, Rempi, Silopi, Utu, Mawan, Baimak, Bagupi, Gal, Garuh, Kamba. Investigation needed: intelligibility.

MOTU ***(TRUE MOTU, PURE MOTU)*** [MEU] 14,000 (1981 Wurm and Hattori). Central Province, in and around Port Moresby, villages along the coast from Manumanu, Galley Reach, to GabaGaba (Kapakapa). Austronesian, Malayo-Polynesian, Central-Eastern, Eastern Malayo-Polynesian, Oceanic, Western Oceanic, Papuan Tip, Peripheral, Central Papuan, Sinagoro-Keapara. Dialects: WESTERN MOTU, EASTERN MOTU. Government schools in all villages. Dictionary. Bible 1973.

MOTU, HIRI ***(POLICE MOTU, PIDGIN MOTU, HIRI)*** [POM] Interethnic second language speakers: 120,000 (1989 J. Holm). Very few mother tongue speakers (T. Dutton 1992). Central Province, in and around Port Moresby area, also throughout Oro, Central, Gulf, and part of Milne Bay provinces, some in Western Province. Pidgin, Motu based. Dialects: AUSTRONESIAN HIRI MOTU, PAPUAN HIRI MOTU. Linguistically a pidginization of True Motu. Also influenced by English, Tok Pisin, and Polynesian languages. Speakers of Hiri Motu cannot understand Motu. There are phonological and grammatical differences. 90% lexical similarity with Motu. Papuan Hiri Motu is more widespread and considered as the standard. Official language. Dictionary. Literacy rate in first language: Less than 5%. Bible 1994.

MOUK-ARIA ***(ARIA-MOUK)*** [MWH] 626 (1982 SIL). West New Britain Province, southeast coast to northwest coast, Kandrian District. Austronesian, Malayo-Polynesian, Central-Eastern, Eastern Malayo-Polynesian, Oceanic, Western Oceanic, North New Guinea, Ngero-Vitiaz, Vitiaz, Southwest New Britain, Bibling. Dialects: MOUK (MOK), TOURAI.

MUDUAPA ***(VITU, WITU)*** [WIV] 8,800 (1991 SIL). West New Britain Province, Talasea District, Vitu and Mudua islands off the northwest coast. Austronesian, Malayo-Polynesian, Central-Eastern, Eastern Malayo-Polynesian, Oceanic, Western Oceanic, Meso Melanesian, Bali-Vitu. 2 or 3 dialects. The variety spoken on Mudua Island may be a separate language. A separate language from Bali, but related. 'Vitu' is the name of the island, 'Muduapa' the language. Literacy rate in first language: 15% to 25%. Literacy rate in second language: 75% to 100%.

MUFIAN ***(SOUTHERN ARAPESH, MUHIANG, MUHIAN)*** [AOJ] 11,000 (1998 SIL), including 6,000 Filifita (1999 SIL). East Sepik Province, Maprik District, Torricelli Mountains, west of Maprik. 36 villages. Torricelli, Kombio-Arapesh, Arapesh. Dialects: SUPARI, BALIF, FILIFITA (ILAHITA), IWAM-NAGALEMB. SVO; 14 noun classes, noun phrase concordance. Literacy rate in first language: Filifita 15% to 25%; Mufian: 15% to 25%. Literacy rate in second language: Filifita 50% to 75%; Mufian 50% to 75%. Tropical forest. Plains. Swidden agriculturalists. 200 to 300 meters. NT 1988-1998.

MULAHA [MFW] Central Province, just southeast of Gaile on the coast. Trans-New Guinea, Main Section, Eastern, Central and Southeastern, Kwalean. Dialects: MULAHA, IAIBU. Coastal. Extinct.

MUM ***(KATIATI)*** [KQA] 3,286 (1981 Wurm and Hattori). Madang Province. Trans-New Guinea, Madang-Adelbert Range, Adelbert Range, Josephstaal-Wanang, Josephstaal, Sikan. Related language: Sileibi. Literacy rate in first language: 5% to 25%. Literacy rate in second language: 25% to 50%.

MUMENG [MZI] 4,584 including 2,210 Mumeng, 2,154 Yanta (1980 census), 220 Latep (1978 McElhanon). 9,186 in entire dialect chain (1995 SIL). Morobe Province, Mumeng District. Austronesian, Malayo-Polynesian, Central-Eastern, Eastern Malayo-Polynesian, Oceanic, Western Oceanic, North New Guinea, Huon Gulf, South, Hote-Buang, Buang, Mumeng. Dialects: MUMENG, YANTA, LATEP. The language chain includes Mumeng, Gorakor, Patep, Zenag, Kumalu, and Dambi. SVO. Literacy rate in first language: 15% to 25%. Literacy rate in second language: 25% to 50%. Tropical forest. Mountain slope. Swidden agriculturalists. 300 to 900 meters.

MUNIT [MTC] 345 (1981 Wurm and Hattori). Madang Province, Trans-Gogol District. Trans-New Guinea, Madang-Adelbert Range, Madang, Mabuso, Kokon. Related languages: Girawa, Bemal. Investigation needed: intelligibility with Girawa, Bemal.

MUNIWARA ***(MAMBE, TUMARA, TUMARU)*** [MWB] 826 (1975). East Sepik Province, about 20 miles south southeast of Wewak. Torricelli, Marienberg.

MUNKIP [MPV] 137 (1978 McElhanon). Morobe Province. Trans-New Guinea, Main Section, Central and Western, Huon-Finisterre, Finisterre, Erap.

MURIK ***(NOR, NOR-MURIK LAKES)*** [MTF] 1,476 (1977 SIL). East Sepik Province, Angoram District, on the coast west of the mouth of the Sepik River. Sepik-Ramu, Nor-Pondo, Nor. Related language: Kopar. Investigation needed: intelligibility with Kopar. Literacy rate in first language: Less than 5%. Literacy rate in second language: 25% to 50%.

MURUPI [MQW] 301 (1981 Wurm and Hattori). Madang Province. Trans-New Guinea, Madang-Adelbert Range, Madang, Mabuso, Hanseman. Related languages: Rapting, Wamas, Samosa, Mosimo, Saruga, Nake, Matepi, Garus, Yoidik, Rempi, Silopi, Utu, Mawan, Baimak, Bagupi, Gal, Garuh, Kamba. Investigation needed: intelligibility.

MUSAK [MMQ] 355 (1981 Wurm and Hattori). Madang Province, west of Astrolabe Bay on the Ramu River. Trans-New Guinea, Madang-Adelbert Range, Adelbert Range, Josephstaal-Wanang, Wanang, Emuan.

MUSAN ***(MUSIAN, MUSA)*** [MMP] 75 (1981 Wurm and Hattori). Sandaun Province, village east of Amto. Amto-Musan. 29% lexical similarity with Amto. Amto and Musan 3% lexical similarity with Busa, 18 miles north. Both average 7% lexical similarity with Left May languages. Frequent interaction with Amto. Investigation needed: bilingual proficiency in Amto.

MUSAR ***(AREGEREK)*** [MMI] 684 (1981 Wurm and Hattori). Madang Province, inland, west of Tokain. Trans-New Guinea, Madang-Adelbert Range, Adelbert Range, Pihom-Isumrud-Mugil, Pihom, Tiboran. Related languages: Kowaki, Mawak, Hinihon, Wanambre.

MUSOM ***(MISATIK)*** [MSU] 264 (1989 Holzknecht). Morobe Province, tributary of the Busu River. Austronesian, Malayo-Polynesian, Central-Eastern, Eastern Malayo-Polynesian, Oceanic, Western Oceanic, North New Guinea, Huon Gulf, Markham, Lower, Busu. In the Azera dialect chain. Investigation needed: intelligibility with Yalu, Suwot, Sirak.

MUSSAU-EMIRA ***(EMIRA-MUSSAU, MUSAU-EMIRA)*** [EMI] 4,200 to 5,000 (1992 SIL). New Ireland Province, St. Matthias Islands (Mussau and Emira), 150 km. northwest of Kavieng. About 1/3 of the people live outside the language area, the majority in Kavieng. Austronesian, Malayo-Polynesian, Central-Eastern, Eastern Malayo-Polynesian, Oceanic, Western Oceanic, St. Matthias. Dialects: EMIRA, WESTERN MUSSAU, SOUTHERN MUSSAU, EASTERN MUSSAU. Bilingualism in Tok Pisin, English. Dictionary. SVO. Literacy rate in first language: 90% to 100%. Literacy rate in second language: 90% to 100%. Tropical forest. Island. Swidden agriculturalists, fishermen. 0 to 200 meters. Christian.

MUTU ***(TUAM-MUTU, TUAM, TUOM)*** [TUC] 3,000 (1998 Bugenhagen SIL). Morobe Province, 6 villages on the 6 Siassi Islands south of Umboi Island: Mandok, Malai, Aronai, Tuam, Mutu Malau, and Aramot, and Yam village on Umboi Island. Austronesian, Malayo-Polynesian, Central-Eastern, Eastern Malayo-Polynesian, Oceanic, Western Oceanic, North New Guinea, Ngero-Vitiaz, Ngero, Tuam. Dialects: MUTU, TUAM, MALAI. SVOX; prepositions. Literacy rate in second language: 25%. Island, coastal. Fishermen, traders. Christian, traditional religion.

MUTUM ***(PASWAM, DUDI)*** [MCC] 400 (1975 Wurm). Western Province, southern bank and hinterland of Fly River. Trans-New Guinea, Trans-Fly-Bulaka River, Trans-Fly, Tirio. Distinct from Tirio (Dudi).

MUYUW ***(MUYU, MUYUA, MURUA, MURUWA, MUYUWA)*** [MYW] 6,000 including 1,000 to 1,200 Iwa (1998 church figures). Milne Bay Province, Losuia District, Woodlark Island. Austronesian, Malayo-Polynesian, Central-Eastern, Eastern Malayo-Polynesian, Oceanic, Western Oceanic, Papuan Tip, Peripheral, Kilivila-Louisiades, Kilivila. Dialects: YANABA, LOUGAW (GAWA), WAMWAN, NAWYEM,

IWA. The Iwa dialect is half way between Muyuw and Kilivila. 68% lexical similarity with Kilivila. 50% monolingual. Bilingualism is in Dobu, Kilivila, or Misima. Dictionary. SVO. Literacy rate in first language: 75%. Literacy rate in second language: 75%. 30% of the children are in government schools. Tropical forest. Islands, coral, volcanic. Swidden agriculturalists. 0 to 100 meters. NT 1976-1996.

MWATEBU [MWA] 166 (1972 census). Milne Bay Province, Normanby Island, north central coast, one village. Austronesian, Malayo-Polynesian, Central-Eastern, Eastern Malayo-Polynesian, Oceanic, Western Oceanic, Papuan Tip, Nuclear, North Papuan Mainland-D'Entrecasteaux, Dobu-Duau. 49% lexical similarity with Dobu (closest). 10% monolingual. Others use Duau or Dobu as second language. Literacy rate in second language: Low.

NAASIOI ***(NASIOI, KIETA, KIETA TALK, AUNGE)*** [NAS] 10,000 (1990 SIL). North Solomons Province, Kieta District, central mountains and southeast coast. East Papuan, Bougainville, East, Nasioi. Dialects: NAASIOI, KONGARA, ORAMI (GUAVA), PAKIA-SIDERONSI. SOV. Literacy rate in first language: 50% to 75%. Literacy rate in second language: 50% to 75%. Tropical forest. Mountain slope, coastal. Swidden agriculturalists: cash crops. 0 to 1,000 meters. Christian, traditional religion. NT 1994.

NABAK ***(NABA, WAIN)*** [NAF] 16,000 (1994 SIL). Morobe Province, Lae District, eastern headwaters of the Busu River. 52 villages and 30 settlements. Trans-New Guinea, Main Section, Central and Western, Huon-Finisterre, Huon, Western. SOV. Literacy rate in first language: 50% to 75%. Literacy rate in second language: 50% to 75%. Tropical forest. Mountain slope, coastal, interfluvial. Swidden agriculturalists. Christian, traditional religion. NT 1998.

NABI ***(MITANG, METAN, NAMBIEB W&H 1981)*** [MTY] 564 (1994 SIL). Sandaun Province. 3 villages. Torricelli, Wapei-Palei, Palei. Speakers in 2 villages prefer 'Nabi', in 1 they prefer 'Metan'.

NAFI ***(SIRAK)*** [SRF] 157 (1988 Holzknecht). Morobe Province, Busu River. Austronesian, Malayo-Polynesian, Central-Eastern, Eastern Malayo-Polynesian, Oceanic, Western Oceanic, North New Guinea, Huon Gulf, Markham, Lower, Busu.

NAGOVISI ***(SIBBE, NAGOVIS)*** [NCO] 5,000 (1975 SIL). North Solomons Province, Buin District. East Papuan, Bougainville, East, Nasioi. Moderate acculturation. Literacy rate in second language: 75% to 100%. Bible portions 1984.

NAHU ***(NAHO, NABU)*** [NCA] 6,000 (1991 SIL). Madang Province, Nahu and Rawa districts, bordering the east of the Rawa area. Trans-New Guinea, Main Section, Central and Western, Huon-Finisterre, Finisterre, Gusap-Mot. 54% lexical similarity with Rawa. Literacy rate in first language: Less than 5%. Literacy rate in second language: 25% to 50%.

NAI ***(BIAKA, AMINI)*** [BIO] 600 (1991 SIL). Sandaun Province, Amanab District, adjacent to and southeast of the Angor language. 3 large villages. Kwomtari-Baibai, Baibai. No schools, but speakers desire education. Literacy rate in first language: 5% to 15%. Literacy rate in second language: 5% to 15%. Hills, plain.

NAKAMA [NIB] 983 (1980 census). Morobe Province, 6 villages in rugged terrain west and northwest of Boana of the south side of Saruwaged Range. Trans-New Guinea, Main Section, Central and Western, Huon-Finisterre, Finisterre, Erap. Dialects: NORTH NAKAMA, SOUTH NAKAMA. Mountain slope. Swidden agriculturalists. 1,000 to 1,300 meters.

NAKANAI ***(NAKONAI)*** [NAK] 13,000 (1981 Wurm and Hattori). West New Britain Province, Hoskins District, northwest coast. 42 villages. Austronesian, Malayo-Polynesian, Central-Eastern, Eastern Malayo-Polynesian, Oceanic, Western Oceanic, Meso Melanesian, Willaumez. Dialects: LOSA (LOSO, AUKA), BILEKI (LAKALAI, MUKU, MAMUGA), VERE (VELE, TAROBI), UBAE (BABATA), MAUTUTU. Major language of the Nakanai family. Grammar. Agriculturalists: cocoa, bananas, sweet potatoes, copra, palm oil; pigs. Christian, traditional religion. NT 1983.

NAKE ***(ALE)*** [NBK] 173 (1981 Wurm and Hattori). Madang Province, northwest of Madang. Trans-New Guinea, Madang-Adelbert Range, Madang, Mabuso, Hanseman.

NAKWI [NAX] 250 to 300 (1998 NTM). East Sepik Province, south of Ama language. Villages; Nakwi-Amasu, Augot (Mumupra, Sari), Tiki, Uwau. Left May. 71% lexical similarity between Nakwi and Nimo. Village locations change frequently. Acculturation is slight. Literacy rate in second language: 1%. Tropical forest, swamp. Foothills. Hunter-gatherers, some gardens. 80 to 120 feet. Traditional religion.

NALI ***(YIRU)*** [NSS] 1,800 (1982 SIL). Manus Province, southeast Manus Island, and southwest coast, northwest of Titan. Austronesian, Malayo-Polynesian, Central-Eastern, Eastern Malayo-Polynesian, Oceanic, Admiralty Islands, Eastern, Manus, East. Dialect: OKRO. Speakers are moderately bilingual in Lele. SVO. Literacy rate in first language: 75% to 100%. Literacy rate in second language: 50% to 75%. Tropical forest. Coastal and inland hills. Subsistence agriculturalists; hunters; fishermen. 0 to 200 meters. Bible portions 1991.

NALIK ***(LUGAGON, FESOA, FESSOA)*** [NAL] 5,138 (1990 census). New Ireland Province, north central, 14 villages from 70 to 115 km. from Kavieng on the east coast, and 3 villages on the west coast. Some in urban areas. Austronesian, Malayo-Polynesian, Central-Eastern, Eastern

Malayo-Polynesian, Oceanic, Western Oceanic, Meso Melanesian, New Ireland, Lavongai-Nalik. SVO. Tropical forest. Coastal. Swidden agriculturalists, cocoa plantations; fishermen; oil palm. 0 to 300 meters.

NAMBU ***(NAMBO, ARUFE)*** [NCM] 2,000 (1987 UBS), including 25 in Iauga. Western Province, Morehead River. Trans-New Guinea, Trans-Fly-Bulaka River, Trans-Fly, Morehead and Upper Maro Rivers, Nambu. Dialects: IAUGA (PARB), TAIS. Bible portions 1974.

NAMIA ***(NAMIE, YELLOW RIVER, NEMIA, EDAWAPI)*** [NNM] 3,500 (1990 census). Sandaun Province (19 villages), Yellow River District, Panewai village, East Sepik Province (1 village). Areas are called Edwaki, Ameni, Wiyari, Lawo, Pabei, Iwane. Sepik-Ramu, Sepik, Yellow River. Closest to Ak and Awun. 13% lexical similarity with Abau, 12% with May River Iwam. Grammar. SOV; postpositions; consonant clusters; vowel glides; 6 phonemic vowels. Literacy rate in first language: 5% to 15%. Literacy rate in second language: 50% to 75%. Swamp, savannah. Hunter-gatherers: sago (primarily); subsistence agriculturalists (some). 0 to 50 meters. Bible portions 1996.

NANKINA [NNK] 2,500 (1991 SIL). Madang Province, Saidor District, in the upper Nankina River valley. Trans-New Guinea, Main Section, Central and Western, Huon-Finisterre, Finisterre, Yupna. SOV. Literacy rate in first language: 5% to 15%. Literacy rate in second language: 25% to 50%. Tropical forest. Mountain slope. Swidden agriculturalists. 1,000 to 2,000 meters. Traditional religion, Christian. Bible portions 1990.

NARA ***(LALA, NALA, 'ALA'ALA, POKAU)*** [NRZ] 7,627 (1981 Wurm and Hattori). Central Province, between Kuni and Roro, just inland from the coast and south of Yule Island. Austronesian, Malayo-Polynesian, Central-Eastern, Eastern Malayo-Polynesian, Oceanic, Western Oceanic, Papuan Tip, Peripheral, Central Papuan, West Central Papuan, Nuclear. 61% lexical similarity with Doura (closest). Many know Motu and Hiri Motu. Grammar.

NARAK [NAC] 5,000 (1990 UBS). Western Highlands Province, Hagen District, middle Jimi near Tabibuga. Trans-New Guinea, Main Section, Central and Western, East New Guinea Highlands, Central, Jimi. Close to Maring, North Wahgi, and Kandawo. No significant dialect differences. SOV. Literacy rate in first language: 15% to 25%. Literacy rate in second language: 5% to 15%. Tropical forest. Mountain slope. Swidden agriculturalists. 550 to 2,750 meters. NT 1981.

NAUNA ***(NAUNE)*** [NCN] 130 (1977 Lincoln). Manus Province, Nauna Island. 1 village. Austronesian, Malayo-Polynesian, Central-Eastern, Eastern Malayo-Polynesian, Oceanic, Admiralty Islands, Eastern, Southeast Islands. Bilingualism in Titan. SVO.

NAWARU ***(SIRIO)*** [NWR] 190 (1990 SIL). Oro Province, around upper Musa River valley. Trans-New Guinea, Main Section, Eastern, Central and Southeastern, Yareban. Very close to Yareba. Bilingualism in Hiri Motu, Yareba.

NEHAN ***(NISSAN, NIHAN)*** [NSN] 7,000 (1995 SIL). North Solomons Province, Nissan Island. Austronesian, Malayo-Polynesian, Central-Eastern, Eastern Malayo-Polynesian, Oceanic, Western Oceanic, Meso Melanesian, New Ireland, South New Ireland-Northwest Solomonic, Nehan-North Bougainville, Nehan. Dialects: NEHAN, PINIPEL (PINIPIN). Not closely related to other languages. Little acculturation. Grammar. Literacy rate in first language: 25% to 50%. Literacy rate in second language: 50% to 75%.

NEK [NIF] 1,500 (1991 SIL). Morobe Province, Nawaeb District, 5 villages in rugged terrain north of Boana on the south side of the Saruwaged Range. Trans-New Guinea, Main Section, Central and Western, Huon-Finisterre, Finisterre, Erap. Dialects: EAST NEK, WEST NEK. About 65% lexical similarity with Nuk, less than 60% with Nakama. Literacy rate in first language: 5% to 15%. Literacy rate in second language: 50% to 75%. Tropical forest. Mountain slope. Swidden agriculturalists. 1,000 to 1,300 meters. Christian.

NEKGINI [NKG] 430 (1981 Wurm and Hattori). Madang Province, west of Mot River. Trans-New Guinea, Main Section, Central and Western, Huon-Finisterre, Finisterre, Gusap-Mot. Bilingualism in Tok Pisin. Nekgini used in home and village life. One community school. Coastal and foothills.

NEKO [NEJ] 315 (1981 Wurm and Hattori). Madang Province, coast near Biliau. Trans-New Guinea, Main Section, Central and Western, Huon-Finisterre, Finisterre, Gusap-Mot. Bilingualism in Tok Pisin. Neko used in home and village life. One community school. Coastal and foothills.

NEND ***(NENT, ANGAUA)*** [ANH] 2,000 (1991 UBS). Madang Province, between the Ramu and Sogeram rivers, around Pasinkap village. Trans-New Guinea, Madang-Adelbert Range, Adelbert Range, Josephstaal-Wanang, Wanang, Atan. 'Nend' is the language name, 'Angaua' the people's name. Grammar. Literacy rate in first language: 5% to 25%. Literacy rate in second language: 25% to 50%. Mountain ridge, swamp. Swidden agriculturalists, sago, hunters. 50 to 300 meters. Traditional religion, Christian.

NETE ***(INIAI, MALAMAUDA)*** [NET] 1,000 possibly (1982 SIL). East Sepik Province, adjoining the Hewa area. 3 villages. Trans-New Guinea, Main Section, Central and Western, East New Guinea Highlands,

West-Central, Enga. 70% lexical similarity with Bisorio of East Sepik. Literacy rate in first language: 0%. Literacy rate in second language: Below 1%. 2,300 to 3,000 feet.

NGAING ***(SOR, MAILANG)*** [NNF] 3,000 (1994 SIL). Madang Province, 15 villages, foothills from coast to Finisterre Range, southwest of Saidor. Trans-New Guinea, Main Section, Central and Western, Huon-Finisterre, Finisterre, Gusap-Mot. Vigorous. 3 community schools. Tropical forest. Low foothills. Swidden agriculturalists. 0 to 1,000 meters. Christian, traditional religion, cargo cult.

NGALA ***(KARA, SOGAP, SWAGUP)*** [NUD] 136 (1981 Wurm and Hattori). East Sepik Province, one village in Ambunti District. Sepik-Ramu, Sepik, Middle Sepik, Ndu. Literacy rate in first language: Less than 5%. Literacy rate in second language: 15% to 25%.

NGALUM [SZB] 8,000 in Papua New Guinea (1981). Sandaun Province. Trans-New Guinea, Main Section, Central and Western, Central and South New Guinea-Kutubuan, Central and South New Guinea, Ok, Mountain. Dialects: NGALUM, APMISIBIL, SIBIL. NT 1992. See main entry under Indonesia, Irian Jaya.

NII ***(EK NII)*** [NII] 12,000 (1991 SIL). Western Highlands Province, Hagen District. Trans-New Guinea, Main Section, Central and Western, East New Guinea Highlands, Central, Wahgi. SOV. Pine forest, bamboo. Mountain slope, valley. Intensive agriculturalists. 1,500 meters. NT 1980.

NIKSEK ***(MEIYARI, SUMWARI)*** [GBE] 300 (1988 Conrad and Dye). East Sepik Province, at the headwaters of the eastern branch of the Leonhard Schultze and upper Niksek (April) rivers. 200 are at a new settlement at Niksek airport. Also at Sumwari, and a few in 2 other villages. Sepik-Ramu, Sepik, Sepik Hill, Sanio. Dialects: GABIANO (KABIANO), MEIYARI ("PAKA"), SETIALI. Patrolled from Oksapmin. The people have limited comprehension of oral or written Tok Pisin. SOV. Literacy rate in first language: Less than 5%. Literacy rate in second language: 5% to 15%. Tropical forest. Mountain slope. Swidden agriculturalists. 900 to 1,500 meters.

NIMI [NIS] 1,381 (1980 census). Morobe Province, upper Erap River, south of the Saruwaged Range. Trans-New Guinea, Main Section, Central and Western, Huon-Finisterre, Finisterre, Erap. Mountain slope. Swidden agriculturalists. 1,330 to 1,830 meters.

NIMO ***(NIMO-WASAWAI)*** [NIW] 350 (1998 NTM). East Sepik Province, southeast of Ama language. Villages; Nimo (Boyemo), Wasuai, Didipas (including Uburu site), Yuwaitri (moved from Aimi site to Wanawo site), Fowiom, Uwawi, Wamwiu, Binuto, Arakau. Left May. 71% lexical similarity between Nakwi and Nimo. Village locations change frequently. Acculturation is slight. Bible portions.

NIMOA ***(NIMOWA)*** [NMW] 1,100 (census). Milne Bay Province, Misima District, group of islands just west of Sud-Est. Austronesian, Malayo-Polynesian, Central-Eastern, Eastern Malayo-Polynesian, Oceanic, Western Oceanic, Papuan Tip, Peripheral, Kilivila-Louisiades, Nimoa-Sudest. Dialects: PANAWINA, SABARI, PANATINANI, WESTERN POINT. 44% lexical similarity with Tagula (closest). 40% monolingual. Others have good knowledge of Misima. Half of the children are in school. Bible portions 1979-1984.

NINGERA ***(NAGIRA, NEGIRA, NINGGERA)*** [NBY] 400 (1993 SIL). Sandaun Province, Vanimo District, east of Vanimo, north of Bewani and Ossima. Trans-New Guinea, Northern, Border, Bewani. Literacy rate in second language: 50% to 75%.

NINGGERUM ***(NINGGRUM, NINGGIRUM, NINGERUM, KATIVA, KASIWA, OBGWO, TEDI, TIDI)*** [NXR] 3,000 in Papua New Guinea. Population total both countries 4,000. Western Province between the Ok Birim and Ok Tedi rivers. Also spoken in Indonesia (Irian Jaya). Trans-New Guinea, Main Section, Central and Western, Central and South New Guinea-Kutubuan, Central and South New Guinea, Ok, Lowland. Dialects: KASUWA, DAUPKA. Bilingualism in Hiri Motu. Literacy rate in first language: Less than 5%. Literacy rate in second language: 5% to 15%. Tropical forest. Interfluvial. Swidden agriculturalists. below 300 to 1500 feet. Traditional religion, Christian.

NINGIL [NIZ] 523 (1981 Wurm and Hattori). Sandaun Province. Torricelli, Wapei-Palei, Wapei. Related languages: Olo, Yau, Yis, Valman. Investigation needed: intelligibility. Literacy rate in second language: 25% to 50%. 2000 feet.

NOBANOB ***(BUTELKUD-GUNTABAK, GARUH, NOBONOB, NOBNOB)*** [GAW] 2,400 (1991 SIL). Madang Province, Madang District. Trans-New Guinea, Madang-Adelbert Range, Madang, Mabuso, Hanseman. SOV. Literacy rate in first language: 25% to 50%. Literacy rate in second language: 25% to 75%. Tropical forest. Mountain slope. Swidden agriculturalists. 0 to 300 meters. NT 1992.

NOMANE [NOF] 4,645 (1981 Wurm and Hattori). Simbu Province. Trans-New Guinea, Main Section, Central and Western, East New Guinea Highlands, Central, Chimbu. Dialects: NOMANE, KIARI. Mountain slope. Swidden agriculturalists.

NOMU [NOH] 807 (1978 McElhanon). Morobe Province, northern coast, Huon Peninsula. Trans-New Guinea, Main Section, Central and Western, Huon-Finisterre, Huon, Western. Bilingualism in Ono. Investigation needed: bilingual proficiency in Ono.

NOTSI ***(NOCHI)*** [NCF] 1,600 (1991 SIL). New Ireland Province, Central New Ireland District, east coast. Austronesian, Malayo-Polynesian, Central-Eastern, Eastern Malayo-Polynesian, Oceanic, Western Oceanic, Meso Melanesian, New Ireland, Tabar. Bible portions 1995.

NUGURIA ***(NUKURIA, NAHOA, FEAD)*** [NUR] 200 (1981 Wurm and Hattori). North Solomons Province, Atolls District, northeast of Bougainville Island, Nukuria Atoll. Austronesian, Malayo-Polynesian, Central-Eastern, Eastern Malayo-Polynesian, Oceanic, Central-Eastern Oceanic, Remote Oceanic, Central Pacific, East Fijian-Polynesian, Polynesian, Nuclear, Samoic-Outlier, Ellicean. Distinct from Takuu and Nukumanu in PNG and Sikiana and Luanguia (Ontong Java) in Solomon Islands.

NUK [NOC] 1,009 (1980 census). Morobe Province, 8 villages in rugged terrain northeast of Boana on the south side of Saruwaged Range. Trans-New Guinea, Main Section, Central and Western, Huon-Finisterre, Finisterre, Erap. Dialects: NORTH NUK, SOUTH NUK. Mountain slope. Swidden agriculturalists. 1,000 to 1,500 meters.

NUKUMANU ***(TASMAN)*** [NUQ] 200 (1981 D. Tryon). North Solomons Province, Atolls District, Nukumanu Atoll. Austronesian, Malayo-Polynesian, Central-Eastern, Eastern Malayo-Polynesian, Oceanic, Central-Eastern Oceanic, Remote Oceanic, Central Pacific, East Fijian-Polynesian, Polynesian, Nuclear, Samoic-Outlier, Ellicean. Tryon says it is distinct from Takuu (Nuguria) in PNG and Luanguia (Ontong Java) in Solomon Islands. Speakers have contact with Luanguia.

NUMANGGANG ***(MANGGANG, NUMANGANG, NUMANGAN, BOANA, KAI, NGAIN, SUGU)*** [NOP] 2,274 (1978 McElhanon). Morobe Province, Lae District. 10 villages. Trans-New Guinea, Main Section, Central and Western, Huon-Finisterre, Finisterre, Erap. Dialects: EAST NUMANGGANG, WEST NUMANGGANG. SOV. Literacy rate in first language: 15% to 25%. Literacy rate in second language: 15% to 25%. Tropical forest. Mountain slope. Swidden agriculturalists. Bible portions 1984-1994.

NUMBAMI ***(SIBOMA, SIPOMA)*** [SIJ] 270 (1978 McElhanon). Morobe Province, Lae District, one village on the coast. Austronesian, Malayo-Polynesian, Central-Eastern, Eastern Malayo-Polynesian, Oceanic, Western Oceanic, North New Guinea, Huon Gulf, Numbami. The use of Yabem as church language is declining.

NYINDROU ***(LINDROU, LINDAU, SALIEN, NYADA)*** [LID] 4,200 (1998 SIL). Manus Province, Manus Island. 10 villages. Austronesian, Malayo-Polynesian, Central-Eastern, Eastern Malayo-Polynesian, Oceanic, Admiralty Islands, Eastern, Manus, West. Dialect: BABON. The Babon dialect is in 3 southern villages. Bilingual level estimates are Bipi: 0 73%, 1 8%, 2 19%, 3-5 0%; Harengam: 1 84%, 1 9%, 2 7%, 3-5 0%; Sori: 1 89%, 1 6%, 2 5%, 3-5 0%; Levei: 0 94%, 1 2%, 2 4%, 3-5 0%. SVO. Literacy rate in first language: 25% to 50%. Literacy rate in second language: 50% to 75%. Tropical forest. Coastal. Fishermen, hunters, agriculturalists. 0 to 30 meters. Bible portions 1984-1998.

ODOODEE ***(KALAMO, NOMAD, TOMU, TOMU RIVER, ODODEI)*** [KKC] 410 (1998 SIL). Western Province from south bank of middle Rentoul River past the middle Tomu River to Wawoi Falls. Villages of Tulusi (Hesif), Hasalibi, Wawoi Falls. Trans-New Guinea, Main Section, Central and Western, Central and South New Guinea-Kutubuan, Central and South New Guinea, East Strickland. Closest to Agala and Konai. 'Kalamo' is the name of one of the clans living at Wawoi Falls. The speakers call themselves 'Odoodee'. Literacy rate in first language: 15%. Literacy rate in second language: 15%.

OGEA ***(ERIMA, NURU)*** [ERI] 700 (1995 SIL). Madang Province, Astrolabe Bay. Trans-New Guinea, Madang-Adelbert Range, Madang, Rai Coast, Nuru. Related languages: Uya, Duduela, Kwato, Rerau, Jilim, Yangulam. SOV. Literacy rate in second language: 65%. Tropical forest. Coastal. Swidden agriculturalists. Sea level. Bible portions 1981.

OKSAPMIN [OPM] 8,000 (1991 SIL). Sandaun Province, Telefomin District, bordering on the southwest of the Sepik Hill languages. Trans-New Guinea, Oksapmin. Not closely related to any other language. Several dialects. Dictionary. SOV. Literacy rate in first language: 25% to 50%. Literacy rate in second language: 25% to 50%. Tropical forest. Mountain slope. Swidden agriculturalists. 1,300 to 2,300 meters. NT 1992.

OLO ***(ORLEI)*** [ONG] 12,000 (1987 SIL). Sandaun Province, Lumi District. 55 villages. Torricelli, Wapei-Palei, Wapei. Dialects: PAYI (PAY, NORTH OLO), WAPI (WAPE, SOUTH OLO). Related languages: Yis, Yau, Ningil, Valman. Different from Wapi in Enga Province. SVO. Tropical forest. Mountain slope, coastal. Swidden agriculturalists. 20 to 1,600 meters. NT 1997.

OMATI ***(MINI)*** [MGX] 800 or more (1977 SIL). Gulf Province, villages on Omati River: Gihiteri, Iba, Gibidai, Kiberi, Kamairo. Trans-New Guinea, Turama-Kikorian, Turama-Omatian. 53% lexical similarity with Ikobi-Mena. Each village also has Joso and Juko language speakers. One school. Lowland limestone pinnacle region.

ÖMIE ***(AOMIE, UPPER MANAGALASI)*** [AOM] 800 (1993 SIL). Oro Province, Kokoda, Upper Kumusi, and Afore districts, northwest of Managalasi, Mamama River and Upper Kumusi Valley. Trans-New Guinea, Main Section, Eastern, Central and Southeastern, Koiarian, Baraic. Dialects: ASAPA, ZUWADZA, GORA-BOMAHOUJI. 50% monolingual. Others use Hiri Motu or English as second language. Grammar. SOV. Literacy rate in first language: 25% to 50%. Literacy rate in second language: 25% to 50%. Tropical forest. Mountain slope, riverine, interfluvial. Swidden agriculturalists, pigs. 545 to 1,500 meters. NT 1991.

OMWUNRA-TOQURA [OMW] 2,000 in Omwunra-Toqura (1990 UBS). Eastern Highlands Province, Kainantu and Obura districts, south of Kainantu. Trans-New Guinea, Main Section, Central and Western, East New Guinea Highlands, Eastern, Tairora. About 5 dialects. Tairora, Binumarien, Kambaira, and Waffa are closely related. SOV. Savannah, forest. Hills, mountains. Hunters, agriculturalists. 4,000 to 5,200 feet. NT 1994.

ONJAB ***(ONJOB)*** [ONJ] 160 (1981 Wurm and Hattori). Oro Province, Koreat and Naukwate villages. Trans-New Guinea, Main Section, Eastern, Central and Southeastern, Dagan. 30% lexical similarity with Maiwa (closest). Bilingualism in English, Ubir. Literacy rate in second language: English, Ubir.

ONO [ONS] 5,500 (1993 SIL). Morobe Province, Finschhafen District. Trans-New Guinea, Main Section, Central and Western, Huon-Finisterre, Huon, Western. Dialects: ZIWE, AMUGEN. Spoken as a second language by 1,000 Nomu and Sialum (Voegelin and Voegelin 1977). SOV. Literacy rate in first language: 25% to 50%. Literacy rate in second language: 50% to 75%. Savannah, tropical forest, gallery forest. Coral steps to the foot of limestone mountains. Swidden agriculturalists. 0 to 2,000 meters. NT 1991.

ONOBASULU ***(ONABASULU)*** [ONN] 800 (1998 SIL). Southern Highlands Province midway between Mt. Sisa and Mt. Bosavi. Trans-New Guinea, Main Section, Central and Western, Central and South New Guinea-Kutubuan, Central and South New Guinea, Bosavi. SOV. Literacy rate in first language: 5% to 15%. Literacy rate in second language: 15% to 25%. Mountain slope. Swidden agriculturalists. 700 to 1,000 meters. Bible portions 1996.

ONTENU ***(ONTENA)*** [ONT] 3,000 (1996 SIL). Eastern Highlands Province, Kainantu District. Trans-New Guinea, Main Section, Central and Western, East New Guinea Highlands, Eastern, Gadsup-Auyana-Awa. Related to Gadsup, but a separate language. SOV. Tropical forest. Mountain slope. Swidden agriculturalists. 1,538 meters.

OPAO [OPO] 1,116 (1973 H. A. Brown). Gulf Province, near Orokolo and Keuru. Trans-New Guinea, Eleman, Eleman Proper, Western. Investigation needed: intelligibility.

OROKAIVA ***(ORAKAIVA)*** [ORK] 33,300 (1989 SIL) including 4,300 Hunjara (1973 SIL), 2,000 Aeka (1981 Wurm and Hattori). Oro Province, Popondetta District between the Hunjara, Notu, Binandere and Managalasi. 200 villages. Trans-New Guinea, Main Section, Eastern, Binanderean, Binanderean Proper. Dialects: KOKODA, HUNJARA, AJEKA, ETIJA (SOSE, SOHE), EHIJA (IHANE, IFANE), HARAVA, AEKA. Bilingualism in Motu. Grammar. SOV. Literacy rate in second language: 15% to 25%. Tropical forest. Interfluvial. Swidden agriculturalists. 200 to 800 meters. Christian, traditional religion. NT 1988.

OROKOLO ***(WEST ELEMA, KAIRU-KAURA, HAIRA, KAIPI, VAILALA, BAILALA, MURU, MURO)*** [ORO] 13,000 (1977 SIL). Gulf Province, from mouth of Purari River east to Bairu River. Kerema is a main town. Trans-New Guinea, Eleman, Eleman Proper, Western. Dictionary. Literacy rate in first language: 25% to 50%. Literacy rate in second language: 25% to 50%. NT 1963.

OUMA [OUM] Central Province, south coast around Labu. Austronesian, Malayo-Polynesian, Central-Eastern, Eastern Malayo-Polynesian, Oceanic, Western Oceanic, Papuan Tip, Peripheral, Central Papuan, Oumic. M. Ross says it is extinct. Extinct.

OUNE ***(OUNGE, DAPERA)*** [OUE] 1,900 (1990 C. Hurd SIL). North Solomons Province, Kieta District, central mountains and southeast coast. East Papuan, Bougainville, East, Nasioi. Most dialects are not functionally intelligible with Nasioi.

OWENIA ***(OWENA, OWENDA, WAIJARA, WAISARA)*** [WSR] 349 (1981 Wurm and Hattori). Eastern Highlands Province, Obura District. Trans-New Guinea, Main Section, Central and Western, East New Guinea Highlands, Eastern, Owenia.

OWINIGA ***(SAMO, BERO, TAINA)*** [OWI] 330 (1998 NTM). East Sepik Province, southeast of Nimo language. Villages: Yei, Amu, Inagri, Samo. Left May. Traditional culture. Traditional religion, Christian. Bible portions 1991.

OYA'OYA ***(KUIARO, SIMAGAHI, DAIOMUNI, LOANI)*** [OYY] 367 (1990 census). Milne Bay Province, Samarai-Murua District, Bwanabwana Local Government Area, southeast tip of the Papuan mainland facing China Strait. Austronesian, Malayo-Polynesian, Central-Eastern, Eastern Malayo-Polynesian, Oceanic, Western Oceanic, Papuan Tip, Nuclear, Suauic. Dialect chain. 61% lexical similarity with Wagawaga, 46% with Saliba, 31% with Tawala, 48% with Buhutu. No schools. Children travel by boat to various offshore islands for school. Investigation needed: intelligibility, attitudes toward Wagawaga.

PAGI ***(PAGEI, BEMBI)*** [PGI] 2,000 (1993 SIL). Sandaun Province, Vanimo District, Bewani Subdistrict, 5 villages, east and southeast of the Kilmeri. Trans-New Guinea, Northern, Border, Bewani. Dialects: WESTERN PAGI (BEWANI), EASTERN PAGI (IMBINIS). Related to Kilmeri and Ningera.

PAHI ***(LUGITAMA, WANSUM, RIAHOMA)*** [LGT] 578 including 566 in area and 12 elsewhere (1978 census). Sandaun Province, extending north in Maimai Namblo Division. Sepik-Ramu, Sepik, Tama. Related to Pasi, Kalou, Mehek, Yessan-Mayo.

PAK-TONG ***(TONG-PAK)*** [PKG] 970 (1977 Lincoln). Manus Province, Pak and Tong Islands. Austronesian, Malayo-Polynesian, Central-Eastern, Eastern Malayo-Polynesian, Oceanic, Admiralty Islands, Eastern, Pak-Tong. Dialects: PAK, TONG. Two nearly identical dialects; Pak is larger. SVO.

PANIM [PNR] 152 (1981 Wurm and Hattori). Madang Province just west of Madang city. Trans-New Guinea, Madang-Adelbert Range, Madang, Mabuso, Gum. Related languages: Gumalu, Sihan, Isebe, Bau, Amele.

PAPAPANA [PAA] 150 (1977 Lincoln). North Solomons Province. Austronesian, Malayo-Polynesian, Central-Eastern, Eastern Malayo-Polynesian, Oceanic, Western Oceanic, Meso Melanesian, New Ireland, South New Ireland-Northwest Solomonic, Nehan-North Bougainville, Papapana.

PAPI ***(PAUPE)*** [PPE] 75 (1981 Wurm and Hattori). Sandaun Province, middle Sepik region, one village on the Frieda River. Sepik-Ramu, Leonhard Schultze, Papi. 29% lexical similarity with Suarmin, closest. Nearly all speakers have some knowledge of Tok Pisin. Literacy rate in second language: 2% to 3%.

PAPITALAI [PAT] 520 (1977 Lincoln). Manus Province, Naringel and Papitalai, Los Negros Island. Austronesian, Malayo-Polynesian, Central-Eastern, Eastern Malayo-Polynesian, Oceanic, Admiralty Islands, Eastern, Manus, East. Three dialects. Close to Koro. Speakers are moderately bilingual in Loniu. Investigation needed: intelligibility with Koro. SVO. Shore dwellers. Fishermen, hunters, pig raisers.

PARAWEN ***(PARA)*** [PRW] 429 (1981 Wurm and Hattori). Madang Province. Trans-New Guinea, Madang-Adelbert Range, Adelbert Range, Pihom-Isumrud-Mugil, Pihom, Numugenan.

PARE ***(PA, AKIUM-PARE)*** [PPT] 2,000 (1990 UBS). Western Province. Trans-New Guinea, Main Section, Central and Western, Central and South New Guinea-Kutubuan, Central and South New Guinea, Awin-Pare. Literacy rate in first language: Less than 5%. Literacy rate in second language: 5% to 15%. Bible portions 1978-1980.

PASI ***(BESI)*** [PSI] 600 (1994 SIL). Sandaun Province, Wan Wan Division, 6 villages. Sepik-Ramu, Sepik, Tama. Close to Yessan-Mayo. Investigation needed: intelligibility with Yessan-Mayo.

PATEP ***(PTEP)*** [PTP] 1,700 (1987 SIL). 9,186 in Mumeng dialect chain. Morobe Province, Mumeng District. Austronesian, Malayo-Polynesian, Central-Eastern, Eastern Malayo-Polynesian, Oceanic, Western Oceanic, North New Guinea, Huon Gulf, South, Hote-Buang, Buang, Mumeng. In the Mumeng dialect chain. Some intelligibility with Gorakor and Zenag. Grammar. SVO. Tropical forest. Mountain slope. Swidden agriculturalists. 300 to 900 meters. NT 1986.

PATPATAR ***(GELIK, PATPARI)*** [GFK] 7,000 (1998 SIL). New Ireland Province, Namatanai District, south central. Austronesian, Malayo-Polynesian, Central-Eastern, Eastern Malayo-Polynesian, Oceanic, Western Oceanic, Meso Melanesian, New Ireland, South New Ireland-Northwest Solomonic, Patpatar-Tolai. Dialects: PALA, SOKIRIK, PATPATAR. Literacy rate in first language: 75% to 100%. Literacy rate in second language: 75% to 100%. NT 1997.

PAWAIA ***(PAVAIA, SIRA, AURAMA, TUDAHWE, YASA)*** [PWA] 4,000 (1991 SIL). Simbu Province, Karimui District, and Gulf Province, Purari River near Oroi. Some also in Eastern Highlands Province. Trans-New Guinea, Teberan-Pawaian, Pawaian. Dialects: AURAMA (TUROHA, URI), HAURUHA. Literacy rate in first language: Less than 5%. Literacy rate in second language: Less than 5%. Traditional religion, Christian. NT, in press (1998).

PAYNAMAR [PMR] 150 (1975 Z'Graggen). Madang Province. Trans-New Guinea, Madang-Adelbert Range, Adelbert Range, Josephstaal-Wanang, Wanang, Paynamar.

PEI ***(PAI)*** [PPQ] 208 (1981 Wurm and Hattori). Sandaun Province, middle Sepik region, Hauna and Walio (Leonhard Schultze) River. Sepik-Ramu, Leonhard Schultze, Walio. Closely related to Walio. Speakers are learning Walio. Very limited comprehension of Tok Pisin. Different from Mala (Pai) in Madang Province. Nearly all Christian.

PELE-ATA ***(WASI, UASE, UASI, UASILAU, PELEATA)*** [ATA] 1,900 (1991 SIL). West New Britain Province, Nakanai District, inland from Bongula Bay. East Papuan, Yele-Solomons-New Britain, New Britain, Wasi. Dialects: PELE, ATA. Bible portions 1992.

PENCHAL [PEK] 550 (1982 SIL). Manus Province, Rambutyo Island. Austronesian, Malayo-Polynesian, Central-Eastern, Eastern Malayo-Polynesian, Oceanic, Admiralty Islands, Eastern, Southeast Islands. 3 nearly identical dialects. Speakers are moderately bilingual in Titan languages. Investigation needed: bilingual proficiency in Titan. SVO.

PETATS [PEX] 2,000 (1975 SIL). 10,000 including second language users (1977 Voegelin and Voegelin). North Solomons Province, Buka Passage District, Petats, Pororan, and Hitau islands off the west coast of Buka Island. Austronesian, Malayo-Polynesian, Central-Eastern, Eastern Malayo-Polynesian, Oceanic, Western Oceanic, Meso Melanesian, New Ireland, South New Ireland-Northwest Solomonic, Nehan-North Bougainville, Buka. Dialects: HITAU-PORORAN, MATSUNGAN, SUMOUN. Sumoun may be a dialect. Trade language. Literacy rate in first language: 75% to 100%. Literacy rate in second language: 75% to 100%. Bible portions 1934-1978.

PIAME ***(BIAMI)*** [PIN] 100 (1981 Wurm and Hattori). Sandaun Province, middle Sepik region, headwaters of the Niksek (April) and Walio (Leonhard Schultz) rivers. Sepik-Ramu, Sepik, Sepik Hill, Sanio. About 3 speakers of Tok Pisin. First contact with outsiders in 1982. Literacy rate in first language: Less than 5%. Literacy rate in second language: Less than 5%.

PINAI-HAGAHAI ***(PINAYE, PINAI, HAGAHAI, WAPI, ARAMO, MIAMIA)*** [PNN] 600 (1997 M. Melliger SIL). Border area of Enga, Madang, Western Highlands, and East Sepik provinces. Trans-New Guinea, Main Section, East New Guinea Highlands, Piawi. Dialects: LUYA-GINAM-MAMUSI, PINAI. The dialects have 78% lexical similarity with each other. They have about 33% with Haruai, 19% with Kobon, 8% with Enga. Some speakers are partially bilingual in Enga, Tok Pisin, or Haruai. Speakers in Enga Province use 'Pinai' to refer to the entire language group. Those in Madang Province use 'Hagahai' to refer to themselves, suggested to them by a medical anthropologist. 'Wapi' or 'Miamia' are sometimes used by the Enga, 'Aramo' by Haruai speakers. Medical workers report widespread health problems. Mountain slope. Hunter-gatherers, swidden agriculturalists. 100 to 1300 meters.

PIU ***(SANBIAU, LANZOG, KURUKO)*** [PIX] 130 (1970 SIL). Morobe Province, upper Watut River, one village. Austronesian, Malayo-Polynesian, Central-Eastern, Eastern Malayo-Polynesian, Oceanic, Western Oceanic, North New Guinea, Huon Gulf, South, Hote-Buang, Buang. Distinct from Pyu in Sandaun Province.

PIVA ***(NAGARIGE)*** [TGI] 550 (1977 Lincoln). North Solomons Province, Piva River. Austronesian, Malayo-Polynesian, Central-Eastern, Eastern Malayo-Polynesian, Oceanic, Western Oceanic, Meso Melanesian, New Ireland, South New Ireland-Northwest Solomonic, Piva-Banoni. Dialect: AMUN.

PONAM [NCC] 420 (1977 Lincoln). Manus Province, Ponam Island. Austronesian, Malayo-Polynesian, Central-Eastern, Eastern Malayo-Polynesian, Oceanic, Admiralty Islands, Eastern, Manus, East. Close to Andra-Hus. Moderately bilingual in Kurti. Investigation needed: bilingual proficiency in Kurti. SVO.

POUYE ***(BOUYE)*** [BYE] 800 (1991 SIL). Sandaun Province. Sepik-Ramu, Sepik, Ram. Related to Awtuw and Karawa. 67% lexical similarity to Karawa.

PSOHOH [BCL] 1,105 (1982 SIL). West New Britain Province, southwest coast to northwest. Austronesian, Malayo-Polynesian, Central-Eastern, Eastern Malayo-Polynesian, Oceanic, Western Oceanic, North New Guinea, Ngero-Vitiaz, Vitiaz, Southwest New Britain, Arawe-Pasismanua, Pasismanua. Dialects: BAO, AIGON, SOKHOK (PSOKHOK, PSOKOK, PSOHOH). In the Kaulong dialect chain. Different from Bau in Madang Province.

PUARI [PUX] 371 (1981 Wurm and Hattori). Sandaun Province, coast around Puari. Sko, Krisa. Related languages: Rawo, Krisa, Warapu. Literacy rate in second language: 50% to 75%.

PULABU [PUP] 116 (1981 Wurm and Hattori). Madang Province. Trans-New Guinea, Madang-Adelbert Range, Madang, Rai Coast, Kabenau. Related languages: Siroi, Arawum, Kolom, Lemio.

PURARI ***(KORIKI, EVORRA, NAMAU, IAI, MAIPUA)*** [IAR] 7,000 (1991 UBS). Gulf Province, between Kapaina Inlet and Orokolo language, Purari River. Trans-New Guinea, Eleman, Purari. Dialect: IAI (NAMAU). Apparently unrelated to other languages of Gulf Province. Literacy rate in first language: Less than 5%. Literacy rate in second language: 5% to 15%. NT 1920.

PYU [PBY] 100 (1978 SIL). Village of Biake No. 2 on the October River just east of Irian Jaya border. Not in Irian Jaya. Kwomtari-Baibai, Pyu. Different from Austronesian Piu in Morobe Province.

QAQET ***(MAQAQET, KAKAT, MAKAKAT, BAINING)*** [BYX] 6,350 (1988 SIL). East New Britain Province, Rabaul District, Gazelle Peninsula. East Papuan, Yele-Solomons-New Britain, New Britain, Baining-Taulil. 2 dialects. Several primary schools. Mountains sloping to coastline. NT 1996.

RAMOAAINA ***(DUKE OF YORK, MALU, RAMUAINA)*** [RAI] 10,000 (1997 local govt. estimate). East New Britain Province, Kokopo District, Duke of York Islands. Austronesian, Malayo-Polynesian, Central-Eastern, Eastern Malayo-Polynesian, Oceanic, Western Oceanic, Meso Melanesian, New Ireland, South New Ireland-Northwest Solomonic, Patpatar-Tolai. Dialects: MAKADA, MOLOT (MAIN ISLAND), AALAWA (AALAWAA, ALAWA, MIOKO, ULU, SOUTH ISLANDS). SVO. Literacy rate in first language: 50% to 75%. Literacy rate in second language: 75% to 100%. Tropical forest. Coastal, coral islands. Fishermen, swidden agriculturalists. 0 to 40 meters. Bible portions 1882-1992.

RAO ***(ANNABERG, RAO BRERI)*** [RAO] 6,000 (1992 UBS). Madang Province, Keram River area, lower Ramu Valley, 80 miles west of Madang city. Sepik-Ramu, Ramu, Ramu Proper, Annaberg, Rao. Dialects: LI'O, NDRAMINI'O. Swampy plain. Traditional religion. Bible portions 1991-1995.

RAPOISI ***(KUNUA, KONUA)*** [KYX] 3,500 (1998 SIL). North Solomons Province, northwest Bougainville Island, Kunua District. Most villages are inland. East Papuan, Bougainville, West. Related to Eivo, Kereaka, and Rotokas. Tok Pisin used in schools. Vigorous. Christian, traditional religion. Bible portions 1994.

RAPTING [RAP] 332 (1981 Wurm and Hattori). Madang Province. Trans-New Guinea, Madang-Adelbert Range, Madang, Mabuso, Hanseman. Related languages: Murupi, Wamas, Samosa, Mosimo, Saruga, Nake, Matepi, Garus, Yoidik, Rempi, Silopi, Utu, Mawan, Baimak, Bagupi, Gal, Garuh, Kamba.

RAWA ***(RAUA, ERAWA, EREWA)*** [RWO] 11,500 including 7,000 Rawa and 4,500 Karo (1998 SIL). Madang Province, Upper Ramu District (Rawa dialect), Rai Coast District (Karo dialect). The two dialects are on opposite sides of the Finisterre Range. Trans-New Guinea, Main Section, Central and Western, Huon-Finisterre, Finisterre, Gusap-Mot. Dialects: RAWA, KARO. Rawa speakers migrated over the mountains looking for better land. Their dialect is considered to be inferior by Karo speakers. Grammar. SOV. Literacy rate in first language: 20% Rawa, below 1% Karo. Literacy rate in second language: 25% Rawa, 50% Karo. Tropical forest. Mountain slope. Swidden agriculturalists: sweet potatoes, cash crops (coffee and vegetables). Sea level to 7,000 feet. NT 1992.

RAWO [RWA] 506 (1981 Wurm and Hattori). Sandaun Province coast around Rawo and Leitre. Sko, Krisa. Related languages: Krisa, Puari, Warapu. Literacy rate in second language: 50% to 75%.

REMA ***(BOTHAR)*** [BOW] 68 (1980 census). Western Province, Morehead District. Not in Irian Jaya. Trans-New Guinea, Trans-Fly-Bulaka River, Trans-Fly, Morehead and Upper Maro Rivers, Tonda. Related to Aramba, Kanum. 4 primary schools. Investigation needed: intelligibility with Aramba, Kanum. Swamp, savannah. Below 300 meters.

REMPI ***(REMPIN, A'E, EREMPI)*** [RMP] 592 (1981 Wurm and Hattori). Madang Province. Trans-New Guinea, Madang-Adelbert Range, Madang, Mabuso, Hanseman.

RERAU [REA] 235 (1981 Wurm and Hattori). Madang Province. Trans-New Guinea, Madang-Adelbert Range, Madang, Rai Coast, Nuru. Related languages: Kwato, Ogea, Uya, Duduela, Jilim, Yangulam.

ROCKY PEAK ***(LARO, IYO, YINIBU)*** [ROK] 275 or more (1975 Conrad and Dye). Estimate may be too high (1995). Sandaun Province, Rocky Peak Mountains, Iwau, Agrame, Uwau, and at least two other villages (possibly Benato). Left May. 80% to 90% lexical similarity with Iteri. Speakers in Iwau and Agrame vilages are partly bilingual in Ama. Traditional culture.

ROMKUN ***(ROMKUIN)*** [RMK] 389 (1981 Wurm and Hattori). Madang Province. Sepik-Ramu, Ramu, Ramu Proper, Goam, Tamolan.

RONJI ***(ROINJI, GALI)*** [ROE] 227 (1981 Wurm and Hattori). 2 villages, one each in Madang and Morobe provinces, north coast of Huon Peninsula, 50 km. northwest of Wasu, 30 km. north-northwest of Sapmanga, about 45 km. southeast of Saidor. Austronesian, Malayo-Polynesian, Central-Eastern, Eastern Malayo-Polynesian, Oceanic, Western Oceanic, North New Guinea, Ngero-Vitiaz, Vitiaz, Roinji-Nenaya. 67% lexical similarity with Mato, 46% with Barim, 45% with Malasanga, 44% with Arop-Lokep, 33% with Sio, 28% with Tuam-Mutu. Mato language schools are operating in both villages. SVO. Savannah. Coastal. Swidden agriculturalists. Sea level. Christian, traditional religion.

RORO ***(WAIMA)*** [RRO] 8,000 (1991 SIL). Central Province, Bereina District, near Kairuku, shores of Hall Sound, between Yule Island and mainland, 65 miles northwest of Port Moresby. Austronesian, Malayo-Polynesian, Central-Eastern, Eastern Malayo-Polynesian, Oceanic, Western Oceanic, Papuan Tip, Peripheral, Central Papuan, West Central Papuan, Nuclear. Dialects: WAIMA (WEST RORO), BEREINA, RORO (EAST RORO), YULE-DELENA. Two main dialects. Waima is a lesser dialect. 45% lexical similarity with Kuni (closest). Many schools. Bible portions 1947-1995.

ROTOKAS [ROO] 4,320 (1981 Wurm and Hattori). North Solomons Province, Central Bougainville District, central mountains. 28 villages. East Papuan, Bougainville, West, Rotokas. Dialects: PIPIPAIA, AITA, ATSILIMA. Dictionary. SOV. Literacy rate in first language: 50% to 75%. Literacy rate in second language: 50% to 75%. Tropical forest. Mountain slope, coastal. Swidden agriculturalists, intensive agriculturalists: cocoa, cash crops. 0 to 700 meters. NT 1982.

RUMU ***(KAIRI, RUMUWA, DUMU, TUMU, KIBIRI, KAI-IRI)*** [KLQ] 1,000 (1985 UBS). Gulf Province, Kikori District, north of Kikori on the Kikori, Sirebi, and Tiviri rivers. Trans-New Guinea, Turama-Kikorian, Kairi. A distinct language from Kibiri (Porome). Literacy rate in first language: Less than 5%. Literacy rate in second language: 5% to 15%. Bible portions 1965-93.

SAEP [SPD] 584 (1981 Wurm and Hattori). Madang Province, Gowar River area, Rai coast, 75 miles east of Madang. Trans-New Guinea, Madang-Adelbert Range, Madang, Rai Coast, Yaganon. Related language: Dumun. Literacy rate in first language: Less than 5%. Coconuts.

SAKAM [SKM] 510 (1978 McElhanon). Morobe Province. Trans-New Guinea, Main Section, Central and Western, Huon-Finisterre, Finisterre, Uruwa. The most divergent Uruwa language.

SALIBA [SBE] 2,300 to 2,500 (1998 SIL). Sariba and Rogeia islands, China Strait, Milne Bay Province. Austronesian, Malayo-Polynesian, Central-Eastern, Eastern Malayo-Polynesian, Oceanic, Western Oceanic, Papuan Tip, Nuclear, Suauic. Dialects: SALIBA, LOGEYA. A separate language from Suau.

SALT-YUI ***(SALT, SALT-IUI, YUI, IUI)*** [SLL] 6,500 (1981 Wurm and Hattori). Simbu Province, Gumine District. 10 villages. Trans-New Guinea, Main Section, Central and Western, East New Guinea Highlands, Central, Chimbu. Close to Nondiri. NT 1978.

SAMBERIGI ***(SAU, SANABERIGI)*** [SSX] 3,125 (1981 Wurm and Hattori). Southern Highlands Province, Lake Kutubu District, east of Erave. Trans-New Guinea, Main Section, Central and Western, East New Guinea Highlands, West-Central, Angal-Kewa. NT 1993.

SAMO ***(DABA, NOMAD)*** [SMQ] 700 (1973 Shaw). Western Province, Lake Murray District, southern Upper Strickland Census District, east of the Strickland River, north of Nomad. Trans-New Guinea, Main Section, Central and Western, Central and South New Guinea-Kutubuan, Central and South New Guinea, East Strickland. Bilingualism in Hiri Motu. Literacy rate in first language: 5% to 15%. Literacy rate in second language: 5% to 15%. Traditional religion, Christian. Bible portions 1980.

SAMOSA [SMO] 94 (1981 Wurm and Hattori). Madang Province. Trans-New Guinea, Madang-Adelbert Range, Madang, Mabuso, Hanseman. Related languages: Murupi, Wamas, Rapting, Mosimo, Saruga, Nake, Matepi, Garus, Yoidik, Rempi, Silopi, Utu, Mawan, Baimak, Bagupi, Gal, Garuh, Kamba.

SANIYO-HIYEWE ***(SANIO-HIOWE, SANIO, SANIYO, HIOWE, HIYOWE)*** [SNY] 644 (1981 Wurm and Hattori). East Sepik Province, Ambunti District, foothills of the Wogamus River basin. Sepik-Ramu, Sepik, Sepik Hill, Sanio. Dialects: MAKABUKY, NAKIAI. Related to Niksek ("Paka"). Semi-nomadic. SOV. Literacy rate in first language: 5% to 15%. Literacy rate in second language: 15% to 25%. Tropical forest. Interfluvial. Hunter-gatherers, agriculturalists. 100 meters. Bible portions 1983-1984.

SAPOSA [SPS] 1,400 (1998 SIL). North Solomons Province, Buka District, chain of islands south of Buka Island off northwest coast of Bougainville. Austronesian, Malayo-Polynesian, Central-Eastern, Eastern Malayo-Polynesian, Oceanic, Western Oceanic, Meso Melanesian, New Ireland, South New Ireland-Northwest Solomonic, Nehan-North Bougainville, Saposa-Tinputz. Dialects: TAIOF, SAPOSA (FA SAPOSA). Literacy rate in first language: 75% to 100%. Literacy rate in second language: 75% to 100%. Bible portions 1985-1987.

SARUGA [SRP] 129 (1981 Wurm and Hattori). Madang Province. Trans-New Guinea, Madang-Adelbert Range, Madang, Mabuso, Hanseman.

SAUK [SKC] 605 (1978 McElhanon). Morobe Province. Trans-New Guinea, Main Section, Central and Western, Huon-Finisterre, Finisterre, Erap.

SAUSI ***(UYA)*** [SSJ] 495 (1981 Wurm and Hattori). Madang Province. Trans-New Guinea, Madang-Adelbert Range, Madang, Rai Coast, Evapia. Related languages: Sinsauru, Asas, Kesawai, Dumpu.

SEIMAT ***(NINIGO)*** [SSG] 1,000 (1992 SIL). Western Manus Province, on the Ninigo Islands and Anchorite Islands. Austronesian, Malayo-Polynesian, Central-Eastern, Eastern Malayo-Polynesian, Oceanic, Admiralty Islands, Western. SVO.

SELEPET ***(SELEPE)*** [SEL] 7,000 (1988 SIL). Morobe Province, Kabwum District, valleys of the Pumune and Kiari rivers. Trans-New Guinea, Main Section, Central and Western, Huon-Finisterre, Huon, Western. Dialects: NORTH SELEPET, SOUTH SELEPET. Dictionary. Grammar. Literacy rate in first language: 25% to 50%. Literacy rate in second language: 25% to 50%. Christian, traditional religion. NT 1986.

SENE [SEJ] 10 or fewer (1978 McElhanon). Morobe Province. Trans-New Guinea, Main Section, Central and Western, Huon-Finisterre, Huon, Eastern. Nearly extinct.

SENGO [SPK] 300 (1975 SIL). East Sepik Province. Sepik-Ramu, Sepik, Middle Sepik, Ndu. Bilingualism in Iatmul. Most adults are fluent in Iatmul. Investigation needed: bilingual proficiency in Iatmul.

SENGSENG ***(ASENGSENG)*** [SSZ] 1,500 to 2,000 (1998 NTM). West New Britain Province, southwest interior. Austronesian, Malayo-Polynesian, Central-Eastern, Eastern Malayo-Polynesian, Oceanic, Western Oceanic, North New Guinea, Ngero-Vitiaz, Vitiaz, Southwest New Britain, Arawe-Pasismanua, Pasismanua. Wurm and Hattori treat it as a dialect of Kaulong. Literacy rate in second language: 30%. 1,000 to 1,500 feet. Bible portions 1992.

SEPA [SPE] 268 (1981 Wurm and Hattori). Madang Province, coast south of Manam Island around Bogia. Austronesian, Malayo-Polynesian, Central-Eastern, Eastern Malayo-Polynesian, Oceanic, Western Oceanic, North New Guinea, Schouten, Kairiru-Manam, Manam. Related to Wogeo, Biem, Manam, and Medebur.

SEPEN [SPM] 428 (1981 Wurm and Hattori). Madang Province. Sepik-Ramu, Ramu, Ramu Proper, Ruboni, Misegian.

SERA ***(SSIA, SERRA)*** [SRY] 432 (1981 Wurm and Hattori). Sandaun Province, around Serai, one village. Austronesian, Malayo-Polynesian, Central-Eastern, Eastern Malayo-Polynesian, Oceanic, Western Oceanic, North New Guinea, Schouten, Siau. Literacy rate in second language: 50% to 75%. Coastal.

SETA [STF] 155 (1981 Wurm and Hattori). Sandaun Province. Torricelli, West Wapei. Literacy rate in second language: 50% to 75%.

SETAMAN [STM] 200 (1981 Wurm and Hattori). Sandaun Province. Trans-New Guinea, Main Section, Central and Western, Central and South New Guinea-Kutubuan, Central and South New Guinea, Ok, Mountain.

SETI [SBI] 113 (1981 Wurm and Hattori). Sandaun Province. Torricelli, West Wapei. Literacy rate in second language: 50% to 75%.

SEWA BAY ***(DUAU PWATA)*** [SEW] 1,516 (1972 census). Milne Bay Province, center of Normanby Island around Sewa Bay. Austronesian, Malayo-Polynesian, Central-Eastern, Eastern Malayo-Polynesian,

Oceanic, Western Oceanic, Papuan Tip, Nuclear, North Papuan Mainland-D'Entrecasteaux, Dobu-Duau. Dialects: MIADEBA, BWAKERA, MAIABARE, DARUBIA, SEWATAITAI, SIBONAI, CENTRAL SEWA BAY. The dialects are very diverse. 45% lexical similarity with Dobu (closest). 20% monolingual. Others use Dobu as second language. Christian, traditional religion.

SIALUM [SLW] 642 (1978 McElhanon). Morobe Province. Trans-New Guinea, Main Section, Central and Western, Huon-Finisterre, Huon, Western. Bilingualism in Ono. Investigation needed: bilingual proficiency in Ono.

SIANE ***(SIANI)*** [SNP] 27,000 (1994 SIL). Eastern Highlands Province, Watabung and Unggai census divisions (16,000), Goroka District. Simbu Province, Nambaiyufa Census Division (11,000). Trans-New Guinea, Main Section, Central and Western, East New Guinea Highlands, East-Central, Siane. Dialects: KOLEPA, YAMOFOWE, KOMONGU, KOMOIGALEKA, KEMANIMOWE, ONA, KETO, LAIYA, FOWE, OLUMBA, LAMBAU, ALANGO, YANDIME, WANDO. Separate literature in Komongu and Lambau dialects. SOV. Literacy rate in first language: 25% to 50%. Literacy rate in second language: 25% to 50%. Forest. Mountain slope. Agriculturalists, some cash crops: coffee, vegetables. 1,700 to 2,500 meters. NT 1991-1996.

SIHAN [SNR] 314 (1981 Wurm and Hattori). Madang Province. Trans-New Guinea, Madang-Adelbert Range, Madang, Mabuso, Gum. Related languages: Gumalu, Amele, Isebe, Bau, Panim.

SILEIBI [SBQ] 259 (1981 Wurm and Hattori). Madang Province. Trans-New Guinea, Madang-Adelbert Range, Adelbert Range, Josephstaal-Wanang, Josephstaal, Sikan. Related language: Katiati. Investigation needed: intelligibility with Katiati.

SILIPUT ***(MAI, MAIMAI, SOKOROK)*** [MKC] 263 including 242 in Makru-Klaplei plus 21 elsewhere (1978 census). Sandaun Province, Seleput village, Makru-Klaplei Division, Nuku District, north of Mehek. Torricelli, Maimai, Maimai Proper. 30% lexical similarity with Yahang. Different from Selepet. Literacy rate in second language: 25% to 50%.

SILOPI [SOT] 140 (1981 Wurm and Hattori). Madang Province. Trans-New Guinea, Madang-Adelbert Range, Madang, Mabuso, Hanseman. Related languages: Murupi, Wamas, Rapting, Mosimo, Saruga, Nake, Matepi, Garus, Yoidik, Rempi, Samosa, Utu, Mawan, Baimak, Bagupi, Gal, Garuh, Kamba.

SIMBALI [SMG] 350 (1988 SIL). East New Britain Province, Gazelle Peninsula. East Papuan, Yele-Solomons-New Britain, New Britain, Baining-Taulil. Many people are passively bilingual in Mali. Mountains and foothills.

SIMBARI ***(CHIMBARI)*** [SMB] 3,036 (1990 census). Eastern Highlands Province, Marawaka District. Trans-New Guinea, Main Section, Central and Western, Angan, Angan Proper. A government school teaches children in English and Tok Pisin. Swidden agriculturalists: sweet potatoes, cassava, coffee; hunter-gatherers; animal husbandry: pigs, chickens. Traditional religion, Christian.

SIMEKU [SMZ] 1,898 including 1,183 Koopei and 715 Mainoki (1980 SIL). North Solomons Province, Kieta District, central mountains. Mainoki is on the west slope and Koopei on the east slope. East Papuan, Bougainville, East, Nasioi. Dialects: MAINOKI (MAINOKE), KOOPEI (KOPEI). Not functionally intelligible with Nasioi. The people are culturally conservative.

SINAGEN ***(GALU, METRU)*** [SIU] 208 (1981 Wurm and Hattori). Sandaun Province. Torricelli, Wapei-Palei, Wapei.

SINASINA [SST] 50,079 (1981 Wurm and Hattori). Simbu Province. Trans-New Guinea, Main Section, Central and Western, East New Guinea Highlands, Central, Chimbu. Dialects: TABARE, GUNA. Close to Dom and Golin. NT 1975.

SINAUGORO ***(SINAGORO)*** [SNC] 15,000 (1991 SIL). Central Province, Rigo District, south of Kwikila. Austronesian, Malayo-Polynesian, Central-Eastern, Eastern Malayo-Polynesian, Oceanic, Western Oceanic, Papuan Tip, Peripheral, Central Papuan, Sinagoro-Keapara. Dialects: IKOLU, BALAWAIA, SAROA, BABAGARUPU, KWAIBIDA, TABORO, KWAIBO, ALEPA, OMENE, TUBULAMO, IKEGA, BOKU, BUAGA, WIGA, VORA, KUBULI, ORUONE. Many dialects; Boku may be most central. 70% to 75% lexical similarity with Kalo (closest), 65% to 70% with Hula. Motu and Hiri Motu fairly well known. Dictionary. Grammar. Literacy rate in second language: 50% to 75%. NT 1995.

SINSAURU ***(KOW)*** [SNZ] 476 (1981 Wurm and Hattori). Madang Province, near Dumpu. Trans-New Guinea, Madang-Adelbert Range, Madang, Rai Coast, Evapia. Dialect: SAIPA. Related languages: Asas, Sausi, Kesawai, Dumpu.

SIO ***(SIGAWA)*** [SIO] 3,500 (1987 SIL). Morobe Province, Wasu District, mainland near Sio Island. Austronesian, Malayo-Polynesian, Central-Eastern, Eastern Malayo-Polynesian, Oceanic, Western Oceanic, North New Guinea, Ngero-Vitiaz, Vitiaz, Sio. Literacy rate in first language: 50% to 75%. Literacy rate in second language: 50% to 75%. Swidden agriculturalists. NT 1995.

SIROI ***(SUROI)*** [SSD] 1,200 (1998 SIL). Madang Province, Saidor District. Kumisanger is one village; not a separate language. Trans-New Guinea, Madang-Adelbert Range, Madang, Rai Coast, Kabenau. Related languages: Arawum, Pulabu, Kolom, Lemio. Grammar. NT 1975.

SISSANO ***(SISANO, SINANO, SINAMA)*** [SSW] 4,776 (1990 census). Sandaun Province, Aitape District, around Sissano. Austronesian, Malayo-Polynesian, Central-Eastern, Eastern Malayo-Polynesian, Oceanic, Western Oceanic, North New Guinea, Schouten, Siau. Related languages: Arop-Sissano, Malol, Sera, Tumleo, Yakamul, Suain. SVO. Literacy rate in first language: 15% to 25%. Literacy rate in second language: 50% to 75%. Tropical forest. Coastal. Fishermen. Sea level.

SIWAI ***(MOTUNA)*** [SIW] 6,600 including 600 in Baitsi. North Solomons Province, southeastern. East Papuan, Bougainville, East, Buin. Dialect: BAITSI (SIGISIGERO). NT 1977.

SOLONG ***(AROVE, ARAWE, PILILO)*** [AAW] 2,200 (1981 Wurm and Hattori). West New Britain Province, southwestern coast. Austronesian, Malayo-Polynesian, Central-Eastern, Eastern Malayo-Polynesian, Oceanic, Western Oceanic, North New Guinea, Ngero-Vitiaz, Vitiaz, Southwest New Britain, Arawe-Pasismanua, Arawe, West Arawe. Dialect chain. Understood by all along the coast. Bilingualism in Tok Pisin, English. The language is called 'Solong', the people 'Arove'. 3 primary schools. Tropical forest. Raised coral coast.

SOLOS [SOL] 3,200 (1977 Lincoln). North Solomons Province, central and southwest Buka Island. Austronesian, Malayo-Polynesian, Central-Eastern, Eastern Malayo-Polynesian, Oceanic, Western Oceanic, Meso Melanesian, New Ireland, South New Ireland-Northwest Solomonic, Nehan-North Bougainville, Solos. Dialect: SOLOS. Literacy rate in first language: 50% to 75%. Literacy rate in second language: 50% to 75%.

SOM [SMC] 88 (1978 McElhanon). Morobe Province. Trans-New Guinea, Main Section, Central and Western, Huon-Finisterre, Finisterre, Uruwa.

SONGUM [SNX] 326 (1981 Wurm and Hattori). Madang Province, just inland and south of Bongu. Trans-New Guinea, Madang-Adelbert Range, Madang, Rai Coast, Mindjim.

SONIA [SIQ] 300 (1988 Shaw). Western Province and Southern Highlands Province, 10 to 20 miles west and southwest of Bosavi. Trans-New Guinea, Main Section, Central and Western, Central and South New Guinea-Kutubuan, Central and South New Guinea, Bosavi. Literacy rate in first language: Less than 5%. Literacy rate in second language: Less than 5%.

SORI-HARENGAN [SBH] 570 (1977 Lincoln). Manus Province, Sori is on the northwest coast of Manus Island and on the Sori and Harengan islands off the coast. Austronesian, Malayo-Polynesian, Central-Eastern, Eastern Malayo-Polynesian, Oceanic, Admiralty Islands, Eastern, Manus, West. Dialects: SORI, HARENGAN. Two nearly identical dialects. Speakers are moderately bilingual in Nyindrou. Investigation needed: bilingual proficiency in Nyindrou. SVO.

SOWANDA ***(WAINA, WINA, WANYA, WANJA)*** [SOW] 1,000 in Papua New Guinea (1982 SIL). Population total both countries 1,100 (1978 SIL). Sandaun Province, Amanab District. Also spoken in Indonesia (Irian Jaya). Trans-New Guinea, Northern, Border, Waris. Dialects: PUNDA-UMEDA (UMADA), WAINA. May be 2 languages. Little use of Tok Pisin.

SUARMIN ***(DURANMIN, AKIAPMIN)*** [SEO] 188 (1979 census). Sandaun Province, Telefomin District, a few hamlets on the Kenu River, a tributary of the Om River. Near Duranmin airstrip. Sepik- Ramu, Leonhard Schultze, Papi. 29% lexical similarity with Papi. Young people are quite bilingual in Telefol. Speakers middle-aged and older are not bilingual.

SUAU [SWP] 6,795 (1981 Wurm and Hattori). Lingua franca of 14,000 along part of the south coast. Milne Bay Province, southeastern extremity of the Papua mainland. Austronesian, Malayo-Polynesian, Central-Eastern, Eastern Malayo-Polynesian, Oceanic, Western Oceanic, Papuan Tip, Nuclear, Suauic. Dialects: DAUI (FIFE BAY), SINAKI (GAIDASU, GADAISU), LEILEIAFA, BONA BONA, DAHUNI, SUAU, BONARUA. 10% monolingual. Literacy rate in second language: Many. NT 1956-1962.

SUDEST ***(TAGULA, SUD-EST, VANGA, VANATINA)*** [TGO] 2,000 (1987 SIL). Milne Bay Province, Yama-Yele District, Tagula Island, west of Rossel Island, at the end of the Calvados chain. Austronesian, Malayo-Polynesian, Central-Eastern, Eastern Malayo-Polynesian, Oceanic, Western Oceanic, Papuan Tip, Peripheral, Kilivila-Louisiades, Nimoa-Sudest. Dialects: RAMBUSO (REWA), EASTERN POINT, PAMELA, GRIFFIN POINT (NINE HILLS, NANHIL), JELEWAGA. 44% lexical similarity with Nimowa (closest). 40% monolingual. Others use Misima or Nimowa as second language. Half of the children are in school. Dictionary. Literacy rate in first language: 50% to 70%. Literacy rate in second language: 75% to 90%. Island. Swidden agriculturalists; fishermen; some hunting. 0 to 800 feet.

SUENA ***(YEMA, YARAWE, YARAWI)*** [SUE] 2,272 (1978 McElhanon). Morobe Province, Lae District, north of Yekora. Trans-New Guinea, Main Section, Eastern, Binanderean, Binanderean Proper. Bilingualism in Tok Pisin, English. Grammar. Literacy rate in first language: 75% to 100%. Literacy rate in second language: 75% to 100%. Christian, traditional religion. NT 1978.

SUGANGA ***(WAGARABAI, NORTH MIANMIN)*** [SUG] 700 (1981 Wurm and Hattori). Sandaun Province, Amanab District. Trans-New Guinea, Main Section, Central and Western, Central and South New Guinea-Kutubuan, Central and South New Guinea, Ok, Mountain. Closely related to Mianmin. Investigation needed: intelligibility with Mianmim.

SUKI ***(WIRAM)*** [SUI] 2,000 (1990 UBS). Western Province, Lake Suki. Trans-New Guinea, Main Section, Central and Western, Gogodala-Suki, Suki. English used in schools, which go through 6th grade. Hiri Motu also used. Literacy rate in first language: 5% to 15%. Literacy rate in second language: 15% to 25%. NT 1982.

SULKA [SLK] 2,500 (1991 SIL). East New Britain Province, East Pomio District, Wide Bay coast. East Papuan, Yele-Solomons-New Britain, New Britain, Sulka. A dialect chain. Several primary schools. Literacy rate in first language: 25% to 50%. Literacy rate in second language: 75% to 100%. Swamps, flood plain. NT 1997.

SUMARIUP ***(SOGOBA, LATOMA)*** [SIV] 80 (1993 SIL). East Sepik Province, Upper Wagupmeri River. 1 village. Sepik-Ramu, Sepik, Sepik Hill, Bahinemo. Bilingualism in Alamblak, Tok Pisin. Literacy rate in second language: 5% to 15%.

SUMAU ***(KARI, GARIA, SUMAU-GARIA)*** [SIX] 2,509 (1981 Wurm and Hattori). Madang Province, low mountain ranges between the Ramu and Naru rivers. Trans-New Guinea, Madang-Adelbert Range, Madang, Rai Coast, Peka. Possibly 2 dialects. Related languages: Usino, Urigina, Danaru. SOV. Lowlands forest. Mountain ridge, river valley. Agriculturalists: taro. 500 to 3,000 feet.

SURSURUNGA [SGZ] 3,000 (1991 SIL). South central New Ireland Province, Namatanai District. Austronesian, Malayo-Polynesian, Central-Eastern, Eastern Malayo-Polynesian, Oceanic, Western Oceanic, Meso Melanesian, New Ireland, South New Ireland-Northwest Solomonic, Patpatar-Tolai. Literacy rate in first language: 75% to 100%. Literacy rate in second language: 50% to 75%. Bible portions 1979-1987.

SUSUAMI [SSU] 15 (1990 Geoff Smith). Morobe Province, Upper Watut Valley outside Bulolo. Trans-New Guinea, Main Section, Central and Western, Angan. Most closely related to Kamasa. Bilingualism in Angaatiha. Nearly extinct.

TABO ***(WAIA, KENEDIBI, KAWAKARUBI, TAKALUBI, TAKARUBI, HIWI, HIBARADAI)*** [KNV] 2,000 (1994 T. Schlatter ECP). Western Province, lower Aramia River villages of Waia, Saiwase, Gau, Alagi, Alikinapi; and Fly River villages of Kenedibi, Ulio, and Waguni-Salau. Trans-New Guinea, Trans-Fly-Bulaka River, Trans-Fly, Waia. Dialects: ARAMIA RIVER, FLY RIVER. The dialects have about 60% lexical similarity, but nearly identical syntax and grammar. Investigation needed: intelligibility with dialects. Literacy rate in first language: 12%. Literacy rate in second language: 15%. Bible portions 1992-1996.

TABRIAK ***(KARAWARI)*** [TZX] 1,500 (1991 SIL). East Sepik Province, near Chambri, lower Karawari River. 9 villages. Sepik-Ramu, Nor-Pondo, Pondo. Closest to Kopar (Watam). Distinct from the Karawari dialect of Alamblak. Speakers are highly bilingual in Tok Pisin.

TAI ***(TAY)*** [TAW] Fewer than 1,000 (1990 UBS). Madang Province, southwest, Dundrom village. Trans-New Guinea, Main Section, Central and Western, East New Guinea Highlands, Kalam, Unclassified. 4,000 feet. Bible portions 1995.

TAIAP ***(GAPUN)*** [GPN] 89 (1987 Kulick). East Sepik Province, Gapun village. Sepik-Ramu, Gapun. Not closely related to any other language. No speakers younger than 10 years old. 'Taiap' is the language, 'Gapun' the village. Investigation needed: bilingual proficiency. Literacy rate in first language: Less than 5%. Literacy rate in second language: 15% to 25%.

TAINAE ***(IVORI)*** [AGO] 1,000 (1991 SIL). Gulf Province, Ivori-Swanson District. The main villages are Pio, Famba, and Paiguna. Trans-New Guinea, Main Section, Central and Western, Angan, Angan Proper. Close to Angoya. Literacy rate in first language: Less than 5%. Literacy rate in second language: Less than 5%.

TAIRORA [TBG] 11,500 (1996 SIL) including 4,000 in Northern Tairora (1990 UBS). Eastern Highlands Province, Kainantu and Obura districts, south of Kainantu. Trans-New Guinea, Main Section, Central and Western, East New Guinea Highlands, Eastern, Tairora. Dialects: NORTHERN TAIRORA (NANTA, UKAU), VAIRA, VINAATA, VEQAURAA, HAAVIQINRA. Binumarien and Kambaira are closely related. Waffa is related to Haaviqinra. SOV. Literacy rate in first language: 15% to 25%. Literacy rate in second language: 15% to 25%. Savannah, forest. Hills, mountains. Hunters, agriculturalists. 4,000 to 5,200 feet. NT 1979.

TAIRUMA ***(UARIPI)*** [UAR] 4,000 (1993 SIL). Gulf Province, Uaripi and several other villages near Toaripi. Trans-New Guinea, Eleman, Eleman Proper, Eastern. Investigation needed: intelligibility with Toaripi. Literacy rate in first language: Less than 5%. Literacy rate in second language: 5% to 15%.

TAIS ***(DORRO)*** [TST] 66 (1980 census). Western Province, south coast near Mari. 1 village. Trans-New Guinea, Trans-Fly-Bulaka River, Trans-Fly, Morehead and Upper Maro Rivers, Nambu. Closely related to Mari. Related to Kanum, Aramba, Bothar, Nambu, Peremka, Ara. Literacy rate in first language: Less than 5%. Literacy rate in second language: Less than 5%.

TAKIA [TBC] 20,000 (1998 SIL). Southern half of Karkar Island, Bagabag Island, and coastal villages Megiar and Serang, Madang Province, Madang District. Austronesian, Malayo-Polynesian, Central-Eastern, Eastern Malayo-Polynesian, Oceanic, Western Oceanic, North New Guinea, Ngero-Vitiaz,

Vitiaz, Bel, Nuclear Bel, Northern. Dialects: MEGIAR, SERANG. Literacy rate in first language: 50% to 75%. Literacy rate in second language: 50% to 75%. NT 1999.

TAKUU *(TAUU, TAKU, TAU, MORTLOCK)* [NHO] 250 (1981 D. Tryon). North Solomons Province, Atolls District, northeast of Bougainville, Takuu Atoll, Mortlock village. Austronesian, Malayo-Polynesian, Central-Eastern, Eastern Malayo-Polynesian, Oceanic, Central-Eastern Oceanic, Remote Oceanic, Central Pacific, East Fijian-Polynesian, Polynesian, Nuclear, Samoic-Outlier, Ellicean. Distinct from Nukumanu and Nuguria in Papua New Guinea and Ontong Java and Sikaiana in Solomon Islands, although very closely related.

TAMI [TMY] 1,800 (1995 SIL). Morobe Province, Tami Islands and mainland villages south of Finschhafen. Austronesian, Malayo-Polynesian, Central-Eastern, Eastern Malayo-Polynesian, Oceanic, Western Oceanic, North New Guinea, Ngero-Vitiaz, Vitiaz, Tami. Dialects: WANAM, TAEMI. Older speakers are bilingual in Yabem, the church language. SVO. Literacy rate in first language: Less than 5%. Literacy rate in second language: 25% to 50%. Tropical forest. Coastal, island. Swidden agriculturalists; fishermen; wood carving. Sea level.

TANGGA *(TANGA)* [TGG] 5,800 (1990 SIL). New Ireland Province, Tanga Islands, Anir (Feni) Island, three villages on New Ireland. Austronesian, Malayo-Polynesian, Central-Eastern, Eastern Malayo-Polynesian, Oceanic, Western Oceanic, Meso Melanesian, New Ireland, South New Ireland-Northwest Solomonic, Patpatar-Tolai. Dialects: TANGA, ANIR (FENI), MAKET. Dictionary.

TANGGU *(TANGGUM, TANGU)* [TGU] 3,000 (1991 SIL). Madang Province, Bogia District. Sepik-Ramu, Ramu, Ramu Proper, Goam, Ataitan. Forests. Agriculturalists, hunter-gatherers. Bible portions 1993.

TANGUAT [TBS] 506 (1981 Wurm and Hattori). Madang Province. Sepik-Ramu, Ramu, Ramu Proper, Goam, Ataitan.

TAO-SUAMATO *(TAO-SUAME, DAUSAME, TA)* [TSX] 500 (1981 Wurm and Hattori). Western Province, northeastern corner, middle and lower Wawoi Rivers and Guavi River, villages of Parieme, Sipsi, Diwami, Kubeai, Warehou, Paueme, Ugu on Aramia River. Trans-New Guinea, Inland Gulf, Minanibai. 42% lexical similarity with Minanibai (closest). Literacy rate in first language: Less than 5%. Literacy rate in second language: Less than 5%. Forests. Lowland swamp.

TAUADE *(TAUATA)* [TTD] 11,000 (1991 SIL). Central Province, Goilala District toward the northeast. Trans-New Guinea, Main Section, Eastern, Central and Southeastern, Goilalan. 44% lexical similarity with Kunimaipa (closest). Literacy rate in first language: 15% to 25%. Literacy rate in second language: 5% to 15%. RC schools teach in Tauade. 3,000 feet or higher.

TAULIL-BUTAM [TUH] 826 (1982 SIL). East New Britain Province, Gazelle Peninsula. East Papuan, Yele-Solomons-New Britain, New Britain, Baining-Taulil. Dialects: TAULIL, BUTAM. Bilingualism in Kuanua. Butam is extinct (1981). Investigation needed: bilingual proficiency in Kuanua.

TAUPOTA [TPA] Milne Bay Province, Alotau District, Maramatana Local Government Area, on East Cape facing Goodenough Bay from Wamawamana to Garuwahi including Taupota village. Austronesian, Malayo-Polynesian, Central-Eastern, Eastern Malayo-Polynesian, Oceanic, Western Oceanic, Papuan Tip, Nuclear, North Papuan Mainland-D'Entrecasteaux, Are-Taupota, Taupota. Probably a dialect chain with Wa'ema to the south and Wedau to the west. 81% lexical similarity with Topura village of Wedau, 69% with central Wedau, 76% with Wa'ema, 56% with Tawala, 53% with Maiwala. Limited bilingual proficiency in Tawala and Wedau. Two schools.

TAUYA *(INAFOSA)* [TYA] 347 (1981 Wurm and Hattori). Madang Province. Trans-New Guinea, Madang-Adelbert Range, Adelbert Range, Brahman. Related languages: Biyom, Isabi, Faita. Grammar.

TAWALA *(TAWARA, TAVARA, TAVORA, TAVALA)* [TBO] 10,000 (1988 B. Ezard SIL). Milne Bay Province, Alotau District, from Awaiama to East Cape, north and south shores of Milne Bay, Sideia and Basilaki islands. Austronesian, Malayo-Polynesian, Central-Eastern, Eastern Malayo-Polynesian, Oceanic, Western Oceanic, Papuan Tip, Nuclear, North Papuan Mainland-D'Entrecasteaux, Are-Taupota, Taupota. Dialects: AWAYAMA (AWAIAMA, AWALAMA), HUHUNA, KEHELALA (KEHERARA, EAST CAPE), LELEHUDI, TAWALA (TAVARA, DIWINAI, DIVINAI), LABE (RABE), YALEBA (WAGAWAGA, GWAWILI, GWAVILI, EALEBA), BOHILAI (BOHIRA'I, BASILAKI), SIDEYA (SIDEIA). 40% monolingual. Others are somewhat bilingual in Dobu, Suau, Motu, Wedau. Many speakers know a little English. Trade language. Grammar. SVO. Literacy rate in first language: 50% to 75%. Literacy rate in second language: 50% to 75%. Tropical forest. Mountain slope, coastal. Fishermen, peasant agriculturalists. Sea level. NT 1985.

TELEFOL *(TELEFOMIN, TELEFOLMIN, TELEEFOOL)* [TLF] 5,400 (1994 SIL). Sandaun Province, Telefomin District. Trans-New Guinea, Main Section, Central and Western, Central and South New Guinea-Kutubuan, Central and South New Guinea, Ok, Mountain. Dialects: TELEFOL, FERAMIN. Dictionary. Grammar. SOV. Literacy rate in first language: 5% to 15%. Literacy rate in second language: 25% tto 50%. Tropical forest. Mountain slope. Swidden agriculturalists. 800 to 2,600 meters. NT 1988.

TENIS ***(TENCH)*** [TNS] 49 (1972 Beaumont). New Ireland Province, Tench Island. Austronesian, Malayo-Polynesian, Central-Eastern, Eastern Malayo-Polynesian, Oceanic, Western Oceanic, St. Matthias. Speakers are highly bilingual in Emira-Mussau. Investigation needed: bilingual proficiency in Emira-Mussau.

TEOP [TIO] 5,000 (1991 SIL). North Solomons Province, Tinputz District, northeastern. Austronesian, Malayo-Polynesian, Central-Eastern, Eastern Malayo-Polynesian, Oceanic, Western Oceanic, Meso Melanesian, New Ireland, South New Ireland-Northwest Solomonic, Nehan-North Bougainville, Saposa-Tinputz. Dialects: WAINANANA, LOSIARA (RAOSIARA), TAUNITA, MELILUP, PETSPETS. Raosiara may be a dialect. Literacy rate in first language: 75% to 100%. Literacy rate in second language: 75% to 100%. Bible portions 1958-1966.

TEREBU ***(TEREPU, TURUPU, TURUBU)*** [TRB] 150(?) (1981 Wurm and Hattori). East Sepik Province, coast southeast of Taul. Austronesian, Malayo-Polynesian, Central-Eastern, Eastern Malayo-Polynesian, Oceanic, Western Oceanic, North New Guinea, Schouten, Kairiru-Manam, Kairiru. Investigation needed: intelligibility with Kaiep. Coastal.

TIANG ***(DJAUL)*** [TBJ] 791 (1972 Beaumont). New Ireland Province, northern; also eastern Djaul Island. Austronesian, Malayo-Polynesian, Central-Eastern, Eastern Malayo-Polynesian, Oceanic, Western Oceanic, Meso Melanesian, New Ireland, Lavongai-Nalik. SVO. Tropical forest. Coastal. Swidden agriculturalists. 0 to 300 meters.

TIFAL ***(TIFALMIN)*** [TIF] 3,200 (1991 SIL). Sandaun Province, Telefomin District. Trans-New Guinea, Main Section, Central and Western, Central and South New Guinea-Kutubuan, Central and South New Guinea, Ok, Mountain. Dialects: TIFAL, ASBALMIN. SOV. Scrub forest, tropical forest. Mountain slope. Swidden agriculturalists. 1,600 to 2,300 meters. NT 1998.

TIGAK ***(OMO)*** [TGC] 6,000 (1991 SIL). Northern New Ireland Province, Kavieng District, and western Djaul Island. Austronesian, Malayo-Polynesian, Central-Eastern, Eastern Malayo-Polynesian, Oceanic, Western Oceanic, Meso Melanesian, New Ireland, Lavongai-Nalik. Dialects: ISLAND TIGAK, WEST TIGAK, CENTRAL TIGAK, SOUTH TIGAK. Grammar. SVO. Tropical forest. Coastal. Swidden agriculturalists. 0 to 300 meters. Bible portions 1912-1972.

TIMBE [TIM] 11,000 (1991 SIL). Morobe Province, Kabwum District, Timbe River valley and tributaries. Trans-New Guinea, Main Section, Central and Western, Huon-Finisterre, Huon, Western. Dialects: CENTRAL TIMBE, NORTH TIMBE, SOUTH TIMBE. SOV. Literacy rate in first language: 50% to 75%. Literacy rate in second language: 50% to 75%. Tropical forest. Mountain slope. Swidden agriculturalists. 1,000 meters. NT 1987.

TINPUTZ ***(VASUII, WASOI, TIMPUTS, VASUI)*** [TPZ] 3,900 (1991 SIL). North Solomons Province, Teop-Tinputz District. Austronesian, Malayo-Polynesian, Central-Eastern, Eastern Malayo-Polynesian, Oceanic, Western Oceanic, Meso Melanesian, New Ireland, South New Ireland-Northwest Solomonic, Nehan-North Bougainville, Saposa-Tinputz. Dialects: VASUI, VAVOEHPOA', VAENE', VADO-VAENE', VAPOPEO', VAPOPEO'-RAUSAURA, VADO. Moderate acculturation. Their name for themselves is 'Vasuii'. SVO. Literacy rate in first language: 50% to 75%. Literacy rate in second language: 50% to 75%. Tropical forest. Mountain slope. Swidden agriculturalists. 0 to 1,000 meters. Bible portions 1975-1983.

TIRIO ***(DUDI)*** [TCR] 950 (1981 Wurm and Hattori). Western Province, southern bank and hinterland of Fly Estuary. Trans-New Guinea, Trans-Fly-Bulaka River, Trans-Fly, Tirio. Closest to, but distinct from, Mutum (Dudi). Bible portions 1975.

TITAN ***(MANUS, MOANUS, TITO, M'BUNAI)*** [TTV] 3,850 (1992 SIL), 2,674 in the area. Manus Province, M'buke, Mouk, and Rambutyo islands. Austronesian, Malayo-Polynesian, Central-Eastern, Eastern Malayo-Polynesian, Oceanic, Admiralty Islands, Eastern, Manus, East. 2 dialects. The trading ring was described by Margaret Mead. SVO. Literacy rate in first language: 75% to 100%. Literacy rate in second language: 50% to 75%. Coconut trees. Coastal. Copra. Sea level.

TOARIPI ***(MOTUMOTU, EAST ELEMA)*** [TPI] 23,000 (1977 SIL). Gulf Province, Cape Possession to Cape Cupola. Kerema is a main town. Trans-New Guinea, Eleman, Eleman Proper, Eastern. Dialects: KAIPI (MELARIPI), TOARIPI (MORIPI-IOKEA, MOVEAVE), SEPOE. Literacy rate in first language: 15% to 25%. Literacy rate in second language: 15% to 25%. Bible 1983.

TOBO [TBV] 2,230 (1980 census). Morobe Province, upper Kuat River valley, south of Cromwell Range. Trans-New Guinea, Main Section, Central and Western, Huon-Finisterre, Huon, Western. Two community schools. Mountain slope. Swidden agriculturalists. 1,665 to 1,900 meters.

TOK PISIN ***(PISIN, PIDGIN, NEOMELANESIAN, NEW GUINEA PIDGIN ENGLISH, MELANESIAN ENGLISH)*** [PDG] 50,000 first language, 2,000,000 second language speakers (1982 SIL). Mainly in the northern half of the country. Creole, English based, Pacific. There are dialect differences between lowlands, highlands, and the islands. The highlands lexicon has more English influence (J. Holm). The native language of some people in mixed urban areas. The main means of communication between speakers of different languages. The most frequently used language in Parliament and commerce. Some second language users speak a 'broken' Pidgin. Official language. Dictionary. Grammar. Christian, traditional religion. Bible 1989.

TOKANO ***(TOKAMA, GAMUSO, ZUHUZUHO, ZUHOZUHO, YUFIYUFA, ZAKA)*** [ZUH] 6,000 (1982 SIL). Eastern Highlands Province, Goroka District. Trans-New Guinea, Main Section, Central and Western, East New Guinea Highlands, East-Central, Gahuku-Benabena. Dialects: LOWER ASARO, ZUHUZUHO. Bilingualism in Dano, Alekano, Tok Pisi. Bible portions 1979.

TOMOIP ***(TUMUIP, TUMIE, TOMOYP, TOMOIVE)*** [TUM] 700 (1982 SIL). East New Britain Province, Wide Bay to Waterfall Bay and interior. Austronesian, Malayo-Polynesian, Central-Eastern, Eastern Malayo-Polynesian, Oceanic, Western Oceanic, Meso Melanesian, New Ireland, Tomoip.

TORAU ***(ROROVANA)*** [TTU] 605 (1963 SIL). North Solomons Province, southeast coast, north of Kieta. Austronesian, Malayo-Polynesian, Central-Eastern, Eastern Malayo-Polynesian, Oceanic, Western Oceanic, Meso Melanesian, New Ireland, South New Ireland-Northwest Solomonic, Mono-Uruava. Speakers have declined in number during the last 150 years. Fairly acculturated. Literacy rate in first language: 75% to 100%. Literacy rate in second language: 75% to 100%. Swampy coast. Agriculturalists: sweet potatoes.

TORRICELLI ***(LOU, ANAMAGI)*** [TEI] 953 in 5 villages (1981 Wurm and Hattori). East Sepik Province, Maprik District and partially in Sandaun Province, west of Kombio. Torricelli, Kombio-Arapesh, Kombio. Dialects: WEST TORRICELLI, EAST TORRICELLI. Two dialects. Different from Lou in Manus Province or Tate (Lou) in Gulf Province. Investigation needed: intelligibility. Literacy rate in first language: Less than 5%. Literacy rate in second language: 15% to 25%.

TUMA-IRUMU ***(GUMIA, UPPER IRUMU, TUMA, IRUMU)*** [IOU] 1,500 (1998 SIL). Morobe Province, Kaiapot District, Wantoat Sub-district. Trans-New Guinea, Main Section, Central and Western, Huon-Finisterre, Finisterre, Wantoat. Literacy rate in first language: 75%. Literacy rate in second language: 75%. Mountain slope. Swidden agriculturalists. 1,000 to 1,350 meters. NT 1997.

TUMLEO [TMQ] 675 (1981 Wurm and Hattori). Sandaun Province, Tumleo Island, and coast around Aitape. Austronesian, Malayo-Polynesian, Central-Eastern, Eastern Malayo-Polynesian, Oceanic, Western Oceanic, North New Guinea, Schouten, Siau. Literacy rate in second language: 50% to 75%.

TUNGAG ***(TUNGAK, LAVONGAI, LAVANGAI, DANG)*** [LCM] 12,000 (1990 SIL). New Ireland Province, Lamet District, New Hanover Island, Tingwon and Umbukul Islands. Austronesian, Malayo-Polynesian, Central-Eastern, Eastern Malayo-Polynesian, Oceanic, Western Oceanic, Meso Melanesian, New Ireland, Lavongai-Nalik. Primary education in English. Tok Pisin and some Tungag used in church. Center of Johnson cargo cult. Grammar. SVO. Tropical forest. Coastal. Swidden agriculturalists. 0 to 300 meters. Christian, cargo cult. NT 1999.

TURAKA [TRH] 35 (1981 Wurm and Hattori). Milne Bay Province, 5 miles southwest of Radarada and Ruaba. Trans-New Guinea, Main Section, Eastern, Central and Southeastern, Dagan. Related languages: Daga, Bagoi, Galeva, Gwoiden, Kanamara, Makiara, Maneao, Moibiri, Pue, Tevi.

TUWARI [TWW] 122 (1981 Wurm and Hattori). Sandaun Province, middle Sepik region, upper Walio (Leonhard Schultze) River. A few also near Akiapmin south of the Central Range. Sepik-Ramu, Leonhard Schultze, Walio. Literacy rate in second language: 0%.

UARE ***(KWALE, KWARE)*** [KSJ] 1,300 (1996 SIL). Central Province, Rigo Inland District, on the coast south of Port Moresby, Kemp Welsh and Hunter rivers. Trans-New Guinea, Main Section, Eastern, Central and Southeastern, Kwalean. Dialects: GARIHE (GARIA), UARE (KWALE). 65% to 74% lexical similarity with Humeme (closest). Different from Kware in the Bosavi family, Western Province. Bible portions 1994.

UBIR ***(UBIRI, KUBIRI)*** [UBR] 2,000 (1993 UBS). Oro Province, Tufi District, coast of Collingwood Bay on the Kwagila River. Austronesian, Malayo-Polynesian, Central-Eastern, Eastern Malayo-Polynesian, Oceanic, Western Oceanic, Papuan Tip, Nuclear, North Papuan Mainland-D'Entrecasteaux, Are-Taupota, Are. 27% lexical similarity with Miniafia (closest). Also spoken by the Maisin and Miniafia speakers. NT 1997.

UFIM [UFI] 550 (1978 McElhanon). Morobe Province. Trans-New Guinea, Main Section, Central and Western, Huon-Finisterre, Finisterre, Gusap-Mot.

UISAI [UIS] 2,500 (1991 SIL). North Solomons Province, southern, Buin District. East Papuan, Bougainville, East, Buin. Literacy rate in first language: 50% to 75%. Literacy rate in second language: 50% to 75%. Bible portions 1986.

UKURIGUMA [UKG] 134 (1981 Wurm and Hattori). Madang Province. Trans-New Guinea, Madang-Adelbert Range, Adelbert Range, Pihom-Isumrud-Mugil, Pihom, Numugenan. Related languages: Wanuma, Yaben, Yarawata, Parawen, Bilakura.

ULAU-SUAIN ***(SUAIN)*** [SVB] 1,369 (1981 Wurm and Hattori). Sandaun Province, coast around Ulau 1, Ulau 2, and Suain. Austronesian, Malayo-Polynesian, Central-Eastern, Eastern Malayo-Polynesian, Oceanic, Western Oceanic, North New Guinea, Schouten, Siau. Literacy rate in second language: 25% to 50%.

UMANAKAINA ***(GWEDENA, GWEDA, GWEDE, GVEDE, UMANIKAINA)*** [GDN] 2,400 (1987 SIL). Milne Bay Province, Rabaraba District, on the coast of Goodenough Bay, inland between Mt. Gwoira and Mt. Simpson. Trans-New Guinea, Main Section, Eastern, Central and Southeastern, Dagan. Dialects: UPPER UGU RIVER, EAST UMANAKAINA. At least two dialects. 23% lexical similarity with Ginuman (closest). Some speak some English. 'Umanakaina' is the name used by the people. SOV. Literacy rate in first language: 25% to 50%. Literacy rate in second language: 15% to 25%. Tropical forest. Mountain slope. Swidden agriculturalists. 500 to 1,200 meters. NT, in press (1999).

UMBU-UNGU ***(UBU UGU, KAUGEL, KAUIL, GAWIGL, GAWIL, KAKOLI)*** [UMB] 31,000 (1998 SIL), including 9,000 Andelale (1998 SIL), 12,000 Kala (1998 SIL), 10,000 No-Penge (1998 SIL). Western Highlands Province, Tambul (No-Penge dialect) and Lower Kaugel (Kala dialect) districts, extending into Southern Highlands Province (Andelale dialect). Trans-New Guinea, Main Section, Central and Western, East New Guinea Highlands, Central, Hagen, Kaugel. Dialects: KALA (MENDO-KALA), NO-PENGE, ANDELALE. Some speakers understand Medlpa. SOV. Scrub forest. Mountain slope and valley. Swidden agriculturalists. 6,500 to 9,000 feet. NT 1995-1998.

UMEDA [UPI] 300 (1993 SIL). Sandaun Province, Amanda District, south of Imonda. Trans-New Guinea, Northern, Border, Bewani.

UNEAPA ***(BALI)*** [BBN] 10,000 (1998 SIL). West New Britain Province, Talasea District, Unea (Bali) Island off the northwest coast. Austronesian, Malayo-Polynesian, Central-Eastern, Eastern Malayo-Polynesian, Oceanic, Western Oceanic, Meso Melanesian, Bali-Vitu. Separate from Muduapa. 'Bali' is the outsiders' name for the island, which the people call 'Unea'. 'Uneapa' is their language name.

UNSERDEUTSCH ***(RABAUL CREOLE GERMAN)*** [ULN] 100 or fewer fluent speakers including 15 in New Britain, a few in other parts of PNG and the rest in southeastern Queensland, Australia (1981 C. Volker). Population total both countries 100 or fewer. West New Britain. Also spoken in Australia. Creole, German based. All speakers are fluent in at least two of the following: Standard German, English, or Tok Pisin. Some can also speak Kuanua. Most speakers are middle-aged or older, although many younger members of the community can understand it. The descendent of a pidginized form of Standard German which originated in the Gazelle Peninsula of New Britain during German colonial times among the Catholic mixed-race ('Vunapope') community. With increased mobility and intermarriage, it has been disappearing in the last few decades. Grammar. Nearly extinct.

URA ***(URAMÄT, URAMIT, URAMET, URAMOT, AURAMOT)*** [URO] 1,900 (1991 SIL). East New Britain Province, Rabaul District, Gazelle Peninsula. East Papuan, Yele-Solomons-New Britain, New Britain, Baining-Taulil. 'Ura' is the language name, 'Uramät' refers to the people. There are several primary schools. Literacy rate in first language: 15% to 25%. Literacy rate in second language: 15% to 25%. Mountains, foothills.

URAPMIN [URM] 394 (1979 census). Sandaun Province, Telefomin District. Trans-New Guinea, Main Section, Central and Western, Central and South New Guinea-Kutubuan, Central and South New Guinea, Ok, Mountain. Geographically and linguistically between Tifal and Telefol.

URAT [URT] 6,500 or more (1996 Barnes SIL). East Sepik Province, Dreikikir District, southwest of Wom, south of Kombio. 20 major villages and several hamlets. Torricelli, Wapei-Palei, Urat. Dialects: WASEP NAU (NORTH URAT), WUSYEP YEHRE (CENTRAL URAT), WASEP YAM (SOUTH URAT), WUSYEP TEP (EAST URAT). Literacy rate in first language: 50% to 75%. Literacy rate in second language: 25% to 50%. Bible portions 1993.

URI ***(URII, URI VEHEES, ERAP)*** [UVH] 2,500 (1991 SIL). Morobe Province, Boana District. Trans-New Guinea, Main Section, Central and Western, Huon-Finisterre, Finisterre, Erap. Dialects: EAST URII, WEST URII. SOV. Literacy rate in first language: 25% to 50%. Literacy rate in second language: 25% to 50%. Savannah, tropical forest. Mountain slope. Swidden agriculturalists. 200 to 1,000 meters. NT 1984.

URIGINA ***(URIGINAU, ORIGANAU)*** [URG] 1,404 (1981 Wurm and Hattori). Madang Province, 30 miles downstream. Trans-New Guinea, Madang-Adelbert Range, Madang, Rai Coast, Peka. Related languages: Usino, Danaru, Sumau. Cargo cult.

URIM ***(KALP)*** [URI] 3,200 (1991 SIL) in 13 villages (1971 Wurm). East Sepik Province, Maprik Subdistrict, extending into Sandaun Province, Nuku Subdistrict, southwest of Kombio. 16 villages. Torricelli, Urim. Dialects: KUKWO, YANGKOLEN. SVO. Literacy rate in first language: 25% to 50%. Literacy rate in second language: 50% to 75%. Tropical forest. Foothills of Torricelli Mts. Swidden agriculturalists. 450 to 500 meters. Christian, traditional religion. Bible portions 1981-1992.

URIMO ***(YAUGIBA)*** [URX] 835 (1981 Wurm and Hattori). East Sepik Province. Torricelli, Marienberg. Related language: Elepi. Literacy rate in first language: Less than 5%. Literacy rate in second language: 25% to 50%.

URUAVA [URV] North Solomons Province, southeastern coast. Austronesian, Malayo-Polynesian, Central-Eastern, Eastern Malayo-Polynesian, Oceanic, Western Oceanic, Meso Melanesian, New Ireland, South New Ireland-Northwest Solomonic, Mono-Uruava. Extinct.

USAN *(WANUMA)* [WNU] 1,400 (1991 SIL). Madang Province, Madang District. Trans-New Guinea, Madang-Adelbert Range, Adelbert Range, Pihom-Isumrud-Mugil, Pihom, Numugenan. Related languages: Yarawata, Bilakura, Ukuriguma. Grammar. SOV. Literacy rate in second language: 50% to 755. Tropical forest. Mountain slope. Swidden agriculturalists. 600 to 1,200 meters.

USARUFA *(USURUFA, UTURUPA)* [USA] 1,300 (1996 SIL). Eastern Highlands Province, Okapa District. Trans-New Guinea, Main Section, Central and Western, East New Guinea Highlands, Eastern, Gadsup-Auyana-Awa. Grammar. Literacy rate in first language: 25% to 50%. Literacy rate in second language: 15% to 25%. NT 1980.

USINO *(KARI, SOP)* [URW] 1,630 (1981 Wurm and Hattori). Madang Province. Trans-New Guinea, Madang-Adelbert Range, Madang, Rai Coast, Peka. Related languages: Sumau, Urigina, Danaru.

UTARMBUNG *(OSUM)* [OMO] 480 (1990 census). Madang Province. Trans-New Guinea, Madang-Adelbert Range, Adelbert Range, Josephstaal-Wanang, Josephstaal, Osum.

UTU [UTU] 583 (1981 Wurm and Hattori). Madang Province. Trans-New Guinea, Madang-Adelbert Range, Madang, Mabuso, Hanseman.

UYA *(USU)* [USU] 93 (1987 SIL). Madang Province, Trans-Gogol District. Trans-New Guinea, Madang-Adelbert Range, Madang, Rai Coast, Nuru. Related languages: Kwato, Ogea, Duduela, Rerau, Jilim, Yangulam.

VALMAN *(KOROKO)* [VAN] 800 (1993 SIL). Sandaun Province. Torricelli, Wapei-Palei, Wapei. Related languages: Olo, Yau, Ningil, Yis. Investigation needed: intelligibility.

VANIMO *(MANIMO, WANIMO, DUSO)* [VAM] 2,200 (1990 SIL). Sandaun Province, Vanimo District. 3 villages. Not in Irian Jaya. Sko, Vanimo. 2 dialects. Related language: Wutung. Many highly educated speakers. Coastal. 0 to 150 meters.

VEHES *(BUASI, VEHEES)* [VAL] 100 (1978 McElhanon). Morobe Province, one village near the coast between Salamaua and Lae. Austronesian, Malayo-Polynesian, Central-Eastern, Eastern Malayo-Polynesian, Oceanic, Western Oceanic, North New Guinea, Huon Gulf, South, Hote-Buang, Buang. 60% lexical similarity with Buang (closest).

WAB *(SOM)* [WAB] 142 (1977 Lincoln). Madang Province, north coast of Huon Peninsula. 2 villages next to Saidor: Wab and Saui. Austronesian, Malayo-Polynesian, Central-Eastern, Eastern Malayo-Polynesian, Oceanic, Western Oceanic, North New Guinea, Ngero-Vitiaz, Vitiaz, Bel, Astrolabe. Related to Mindiri and Biliau. Investigation needed: intelligibility.

WABUDA *(WABUDA KIWAI, WABODA)* [KMX] 2,000 (1993 SIL). Western Province, Wabuda Island, and the north bank of the Fly River mouth. Maipani, Tirere, Maduduo, Sagero, Wapi, Gesoa, Dameratamu, and Kabaturi villages. Trans-New Guinea, Trans-Fly-Bulaka River, Trans-Fly, Kiwaian. Literacy rate in first language: 5% to 15%. Literacy rate in second language: 15% to 25%.

WADAGINAM *(WADAGINAMB)* [WDG] 546 (1981 Wurm and Hattori). Madang Province. Trans-New Guinea, Madang-Adelbert Range, Adelbert Range, Josephstaal-Wanang, Josephstaal, Wadaginam.

WA'EMA *(WAIEMA)* [WAG] Milne Bay Province, Alotau District, Huhu Local Government Area, the area from Giligili Estates to Turnbull War Memorial, near the head of Milne Bay north to, but not crossing, the East Cape coastal range. Austronesian, Malayo-Polynesian, Central-Eastern, Eastern Malayo-Polynesian, Oceanic, Western Oceanic, Papuan Tip, Nuclear, North Papuan Mainland-D'Entrecasteaux, Are-Taupota, Taupota. Wa'ema seems to be in a dialect chain with Taupota. Tawala is not intelligible to Wa'ema speakers. 76% lexical similarity with Taupota, 69% with Maiwala, 54% with Tawala. Speakers know some Wedau, Tawala, English, and Motu. Investigation needed: intelligibility, attitudes toward Taupota. One Wa'ema elementary school.

WAFFA [WAJ] 1,000 (1978 McElhanon). Morobe Province, Kaiapit District, headwaters of Waffa River. Trans-New Guinea, Main Section, Central and Western, East New Guinea Highlands, Eastern, Tairora. Dictionary. Literacy rate in first language: 50% to 75%. Literacy rate in second language: 50% to 75%. NT 1975-1988.

WAGAWAGA *(BAEAULA, GAMADOUDOU, GIBARA, KILAKILANA)* [WGW] 1,294 (1990 census). Milne Bay Province, Alotau District, Huhu Local Government Area, south shore of Milne Bay. Austronesian, Malayo-Polynesian, Central-Eastern, Eastern Malayo-Polynesian, Oceanic, Western Oceanic, Papuan Tip, Nuclear, Suauic. Dialects: WAGAWAGA (BAEAULA), GAMADOUDOU. 61% lexical similarity with Oya'oya, 31% with Tawala, 55% with Buhutu. 10% monolingual. Others are fairly bilingual in Suau, Hiri Motu, and Tawala. Two schools. Investigation needed: intelligibility, attitudes toward Oya'oya.

WAGI *(FORAN, FURAN, KAMBA, MIS-KEMBA)* [FAD] 1,500 (1986 M. Leaders SIL). Madang Province, 7 miles northwest of Madang. 5 villages: Mis, Kamba, Foran, Kauris, and Silibob. Trans-New Guinea, Madang-Adelbert Range, Madang, Mabuso, Hanseman. May be closest to Nobanob. 30% lexical similarity with Ari. Bilingualism in Ari, Nobanob, Tok Pisin. Speakers call their language 'Wagi'. SOV, adjectives, numerals follow noun head, verb affixes mark person, number, CV, CVC, VC, V, nontonal. Literacy rate in first language: 5% to 25%. Literacy rate in second language: 50% to 75%. Tropical forest. Mountain slope, coastal. Swidden agriculturalists, marginally peasant: cacao, coconuts, coffee. 0 to 1,000 feet.

WAHGI ***(MID WAHGI)*** [WAK] 39,000 (1999 SIL). Western Highlands Province, Minj District, overlapping into Simbu Province, South of the Wahgi River. Trans-New Guinea, Main Section, Central and Western, East New Guinea Highlands, Central, Wahgi. Dialects: KUP-MINJ (KUMAI), PUKAMIGL-ANDEGABU, KUNJIP, KAMBIA, MID-WAHGI. Dictionary. Grammar. NT 1989.

WAHGI, NORTH [WHG] 47,000 (1999 SIL). Western Highlands Province, Minj District, overlapping into Simbu Province. North Wahgi is on the north side of the Wahgi River, and on both sides of the Sepik-Wahgi Divide. Trans-New Guinea, Main Section, Central and Western, East New Guinea Highlands, Central, Wahgi. Dialect: BANZ-NONDUGL. Between 2 to 5 dialects of North Wahgi.

WALIO [WLA] 142 (1981 Wurm and Hattori). East Sepik Province. Sepik-Ramu, Leonhard Schultze, Walio. 12% lexical similarity with Yabio.

WAMAS [WMC] 135 in ten villages (1977). Madang Province. Trans-New Guinea, Madang-Adelbert Range, Madang, Mabuso, Hanseman.

WAMPAR ***(LAEWOMBA, LAEWAMBA, LAIWOMBA)*** [LBQ] 5,150 (1990). Morobe Province, lower Markham and Wamped rivers. Austronesian, Malayo-Polynesian, Central-Eastern, Eastern Malayo-Polynesian, Oceanic, Western Oceanic, North New Guinea, Huon Gulf, Markham, Lower, Wampar. 50% lexical similarity with Adzera. NT 1984.

WAMPUR [WAZ] 360 (1990). Morobe Province, Wanton River. Austronesian, Malayo-Polynesian, Central-Eastern, Eastern Malayo-Polynesian, Oceanic, Western Oceanic, North New Guinea, Huon Gulf, Markham, Upper, Mountain. Closest to Mari. 50% lexical similarity with Adzera. Investigation needed: intelligibility with Mari.

WAMSAK ***(WOMSAK, SEIM, NIHAMBER, MENDE, SAMBU)*** [WBD] 5,000 to 7,000 (1993 SIL). Sandaun Province, north of Middle Sepik River. Sepik-Ramu, Sepik, Middle Sepik, Nukuma. Literacy rate in second language: 15% to 25%.

WANAMBRE ***(VANAMBERE)*** [WLN] 489 (1981 Wurm and Hattori). Madang Province. Trans-New Guinea, Madang-Adelbert Range, Adelbert Range, Pihom-Isumrud-Mugil, Pihom, Tiboran.

WANAP ***(KAYIK)*** [WNP] 1,000 (1994 SIL). Sandaun Province, north of Mehek, northeast of Siliput. Torricelli, Wapei-Palei, Palei. Related languages: Agi, Aru, Aruop, Bragat, Nabi.

WANIB ***(ARINUA, ARINWA, ARIMA, HEYO, LOLOPANI, WAN WAN, RURUHIP)*** [AUK] 1,711 (1987 SIL). Sandaun Province, Wan Wan Division. Torricelli, Maimai, Maimai Proper. 60% lexical similarity with Yahang. Older men use Tok Pisin with difficulty; older women are monolingual. One primary school where English is used. 'Wanib' is the name preferred by speakers. Yahang is also called 'Ruruhip'. Hills, plains, sago swamp.

WANTOAT [WNC] 8,201 (1978 McElhanon) including 393 Bam (1978 McElhanon) and 492 Yagawak (1981 Wurm and Hattori). Morobe Province, Kaiapit District, Wantoat, Leron, and Bam rivers. Trans-New Guinea, Main Section, Central and Western, Huon-Finisterre, Finisterre, Wantoat. Dialects: WAPU (LERON), CENTRAL WANTOAT, BAM, YAGAWAK (KANDOMIN). Saseng is a village; not a separate language. Investigation needed: intelligibility with dialects. Literacy rate in second language: 25% to 50%. NT 1975.

WÁRA ***(ROUKU, WÄRÄ, YUMBAR, UPPER MOREHEAD, KAMINDJO, TJOKWAI, TOKWASA, VARA, ARA)*** [TCI] 350 (1981 Wurm and Hattori). Western Province, near Morehead. Trans-New Guinea, Trans-Fly-Bulaka River, Trans-Fly, Morehead and Upper Maro Rivers, Tonda. 4 primary schools. Literacy rate in first language: 5% to 15%. Literacy rate in second language: 5% to 15%. Swamp, savannah. Below 300 meters. Traditional religion.

WARAPU [WRA] 1,602 including 442 nonresidents (1983 census). Sandaun Province, coast near Sera and Sissano, northwest peninsula of the Sissano lagoon, around Sumo and Ramu towns. Sko, Krisa. Related languages: Krisa, Rawo, Puari. Literacy rate in second language: 50% to 75%.

WARIS ***(WALSA)*** [WRS] 2,500 in Papua New Guinea. Population total both countries 4,000. Sandaun Province, Amanab District, around Wasengla. Also spoken in Indonesia (Irian Jaya). Trans-New Guinea, Northern, Border, Waris. Different from Wari or Wares. Dictionary. Literacy rate in first language: 5% to 15%. Literacy rate in second language: 5% to 15%. NT, in press (1999).

WARUNA [WRV] 600 or more (1991 SIL). Western Province, Aramia River area, Waruna village. Trans-New Guinea, Main Section, Central and Western, Gogodala-Suki, Gogodala. 50% lexical similarity with Ari. Bilingualism in Gogodala. Investigation needed: bilingual proficiency in Gogodala.

WASAMBU ***(KWANGA, GAWANGA, WOMSAK)*** [WSM] 450 (1996 SIL). East Sepik Province, extending beyond the western boundary of Maprik District; Makru-Klaplei Division, Nuku District; Sandaun Province, east of Mehek. 40 villages. Sepik-Ramu, Sepik, Middle Sepik, Nukuma. OSV.

Literacy rate in first language: 5% to 15%. Literacy rate in second language: 15% to 25%. Tropical forest. Plains. Swidden agriculturalists. 50 to 60 meters.

WASEMBO ***(GUSAP, YANKOWAN, BIAPIM)*** [GSP] 586 (1980 census). Morobe Province, west of Ufim. Trans-New Guinea, Madang-Adelbert Range, Adelbert Range, Pihom-Isumrud-Mugil, Pihom, Wasembo.

WASKIA ***(WOSKIA, VASKIA)*** [WSK] 12,000 (1987 SIL). Madang Province, Madang District, Karkar Island. Trans-New Guinea, Madang-Adelbert Range, Adelbert Range, Pihom-Isumrud-Mugil, Isumrud, Kowan. Closest to Korak. Dictionary. Grammar. Volcanic island, mountain slope. NT 1985.

WATAKATAUI ***(WAXE)*** [WTK] 350 (1998 NTM). East Sepik Province, on a branch of the middle Korosameri River. 2 villages. Sepik-Ramu, Sepik, Sepik Hill, Bahinemo. The people are highly bilingual in Tok Pisin. Literacy rate in first language: Less than 25%. Literacy rate in second language: 25% to 50%. Bible portions 1991.

WATALUMA [WAT] 190 (1972 census). Milne Bay Province, two hamlets north of Goodenough Island. Austronesian, Malayo-Polynesian, Central-Eastern, Eastern Malayo-Polynesian, Oceanic, Western Oceanic, Papuan Tip, Nuclear, North Papuan Mainland-D'Entrecasteaux, Are-Taupota, Are. 51% lexical similarity with Iduna (closest). 10% monolingual. Others use Bwaidoka or Iduna as second language.

WATAM ***(MARANGIS)*** [WAX] 376 (1981 Wurm and Hattori). Madang and East Sepik provinces, near the mouth of the Ramu River. Sepik-Ramu, Ramu, Ramu Proper, Ruboni, Ottilien.

WATUT, MIDDLE ***(SILISILI, MARALIINAN, MARALINAN, WATUT)*** [MPL] 1,350 (1990 SIL). Morobe Province, Mumeng District, lower Watut Valley, 7 villages. Austronesian, Malayo-Polynesian, Central-Eastern, Eastern Malayo-Polynesian, Oceanic, Western Oceanic, North New Guinea, Huon Gulf, Markham, Watut. Yabem is the church language. Middle Watut is used for home and village life. Swidden agriculturalists: cash crop betelnut; gold. Lowlands to 330 meters.

WATUT, NORTH ***(UNANK, ONANK, UNANGG, WATUT)*** [UNA] 465 (1988 Holzknecht). Morobe Province, Mumeng District, Kaiapit area, Waffa Valley. Austronesian, Malayo-Polynesian, Central-Eastern, Eastern Malayo-Polynesian, Oceanic, Western Oceanic, North New Guinea, Huon Gulf, Markham, Watut.

WATUT, SOUTH [MCY] 889 (1988 Holzknecht). Morobe Province, southern or lower Watut River. 5 villages. Austronesian, Malayo-Polynesian, Central-Eastern, Eastern Malayo-Polynesian, Oceanic, Western Oceanic, North New Guinea, Huon Gulf, Markham, Watut. Dialects: MARALANGO (MARALANGKO), DANGAL (DANGGAL). Holzknecht says Maralango and Dangal are one language.

WEDAU ***(WEDAUN, WEDAWAN)*** [WED] 1,942 (1990 census). Lingua franca for another 5,000 (1985 UBS). Milne Bay Province, Rabaraba District, Weraura Local Government Area, on the mainland from Kuvira Bay to Dogura along the north coast. Austronesian, Malayo-Polynesian, Central-Eastern, Eastern Malayo-Polynesian, Oceanic, Western Oceanic, Papuan Tip, Nuclear, North Papuan Mainland-D'Entrecasteaux, Are-Taupota, Taupota. Dialects: TOPURA, YAPOA, LAVORA, KWAMANA. 40% monolingual. Trade language. NT 1927-1980.

WELIKI ***(WELEKI, KARANGI)*** [KLH] 200 (1990 SIL). Morobe Province, lower Timbe River valley. 2 villages. Trans-New Guinea, Main Section, Central and Western, Huon-Finisterre, Finisterre, Uruwa. People in one village are completely bilingual in Timbe.

WERE [WEI] 291 (1979 census). Western Province, Dewara (Weredai) village. Trans-New Guinea, Trans-Fly-Bulaka River, Trans-Fly, Tirio. Different from Dewara-Lewada, Aturu, Tirio, or Baramu.

WERI ***(WELI, WELE)*** [WER] 4,163 (1978 McElhanon). Morobe Province, Wau District, headwaters of Biaru, Waria, and Ono rivers. Trans-New Guinea, Main Section, Eastern, Central and Southeastern, Goilalan, Kunimaipa. Dialects: SIM, BIARU-WARIA, ONO. Literacy rate in first language: 50% to 75%. Literacy rate in second language: 50% to 75%. NT 1984.

WIAKI ***(WIAKEI)*** [WII] 561 (1981 Wurm and Hattori). Sandaun Province, north of Beli, Laeko-Libuat. Torricelli, Maimai, Wiaki.

WIRU ***(WITU)*** [WIU] 15,292 (1981 Wurm and Hattori). Southern Highlands Province, Ialibu District. Trans-New Guinea, Main Section, Central and Western, East New Guinea Highlands, Wiru. Grammar. Literacy rate in first language: 50% to 75%. Literacy rate in second language: 25% to 50%. NT 1990.

WOGAMUSIN ***(WONGAMUSIN)*** [WOG] 700 (1998 SIL). East Sepik Province, Ambunti District. 4 villages. Sepik-Ramu, Sepik, Upper Sepik, Wogamusin. Many Tok Pisin speakers. Some young people learning English. Literacy rate in first language: Less than 5%. Literacy rate in second language: 15% to 25%.

WOGEO ***(UAGEO)*** [WOC] 1,237 (1981 Wurm and Hattori). Vokeo and Koil islands, East Sepik Province. Austronesian, Malayo-Polynesian, Central-Eastern, Eastern Malayo-Polynesian, Oceanic, Western Oceanic, North New Guinea, Schouten, Kairiru-Manam, Manam. Related to Manam, Biem, Sepa, and Medebur. Bilingualism in Tok Pisin. SOV. Literacy rate in first language: Less than 5%. Literacy rate in second language: 5% to 15%. Tropical forest. Coastal. Swidden agriculturalists.

WOM ***(WAM)*** [WMO] 1,885 in 5 areas (1981 Wurm and Hattori). East Sepik Province, east of Wara Sikau, Maprik District. 12 villages, foothills of Torricelli Mts., 22 km. west northwest of Maprik in Dreikikir District, Maprik Province. Torricelli, Kombio-Arapesh, Kombio. 2 slightly different dialects. Bilingualism in Tok Pisin. Vigorous. One school. Literacy rate in first language: Less than 5%. Literacy rate in second language: 50% to 75%. Cargo cult.

WUTUNG ***(UDUNG)*** [WUT] 410 (1981 Wurm and Hattori). Sandaun Province, Vanimo District, coast bordering Irian Jaya, including Sangke village. Sko, Vanimo. Literacy rate in second language: 50% to 75%. Coastal.

WUVULU-AUA ***(AUA-VIWULU, VIWULU-AUA)*** [WUV] 1,000 (1982 SIL). Western Manus Province, Aua, Durour, Maty, and Wuvulu islands. Austronesian, Malayo-Polynesian, Central-Eastern, Eastern Malayo-Polynesian, Oceanic, Admiralty Islands, Western. Dialects: AUA, WUVULU (WUU). Two nearly identical dialects. SVO. Low atolls. Subsistence agriculturalists; fishermen. 0 to 10 meters.

YABEM ***(LAULABU, JABEM, JABIM, YABIM)*** [JAE] 2,084 (1978 McElhanon). Morobe Province, Huon Peninsula, coast near Finschhafen. Austronesian, Malayo-Polynesian, Central-Eastern, Eastern Malayo-Polynesian, Oceanic, Western Oceanic, North New Guinea, Huon Gulf, North. Used by Lutherans as a religious language throughout the area for 60,000 (1981 UBS). Christian. NT 1924-1974.

YABEN [YBM] 702 (1981 Wurm and Hattori). Madang Province. Trans-New Guinea, Madang-Adelbert Range, Adelbert Range, Pihom-Isumrud-Mugil, Pihom, Numugenan. Related languages: Usan, Yarawata, Bilakura, Parawen, Ukuriguma.

YABONG [YBO] 370 (1970 SIL). Madang Province. Trans-New Guinea, Madang-Adelbert Range, Madang, Rai Coast, Yaganon.

YAGARIA [YGR] 21,116 (1982 SIL). Eastern Highlands Province, Goroka District. Trans-New Guinea, Main Section, Central and Western, East New Guinea Highlands, East-Central, Kamano-Yagaria. Dialects: KAMI-KULAKA, MOVE, OLOGUTI, DAGENAVA, KAMATE, HIRA, HUA (HUVA), KOTOM. Dictionary. Grammar. NT 1977.

YAGOMI [YGM] 137 (1981 Wurm and Hattori). Madang Province, Saidor District, Yagomi village, on the coast southeast of Seure. Trans-New Guinea, Main Section, Central and Western, Huon-Finisterre, Finisterre, Warup. May be the same as Asat. Investigation needed: intelligibility with Asat. Coastal.

YAGWOIA ***(KOKWAIYAKWA, YEGHUYE)*** [YGW] 9,000 (1987 SIL). Morobe Province, Menyamya District, extending into Gulf Province; Eastern Highlands Province, one section west of the Tauri River, the other north of Menye. Trans-New Guinea, Main Section, Central and Western, Angan, Angan Proper. SOV. Literacy rate in first language: 5% to 15%. Literacy rate in second language: 5% to 15%. Pine forest, deciduous forest. Mountain slope. Swidden agriculturalists. 1,200 to 2,000 meters.

YAHANG ***(YA'UNK, RURUHIP, RURUHI'IP)*** [RHP] 1,182 including 1,116 in area and 66 outside (1978 census). Sandaun Province, west of Mehek. Torricelli, Maimai, Maimai Proper. 60% lexical similarity with Heyo (Arinua). Arinua also called 'Ruruhip'.

YAKAIKEKE [YKK] 100 (1998 SIL). Milne Bay Province, Alotau District, Weraura Local Government Area, on Goodenough Bay between Wedau and Radava, Near Manubada at Diruna only. Austronesian, Malayo-Polynesian, Central-Eastern, Eastern Malayo-Polynesian, Oceanic, Western Oceanic, Papuan Tip, Nuclear, North Papuan Mainland-D'Entrecasteaux, Are-Taupota, Taupota. 65% lexical similarity with Wedau (closest), 58% with Kwamana, 48% with Ghayavi (at Radava). Investigation needed: bilingual proficiency in Wedau, Dawawa, Ghayavi.

YAKAMUL ***(ALI)*** [YKM] 2,118 (1981 Wurm and Hattori). Sandaun Province, coast between Paup and Yakamul, and Ali, Seleo, and Angel islands. Austronesian, Malayo-Polynesian, Central-Eastern, Eastern Malayo-Polynesian, Oceanic, Western Oceanic, North New Guinea, Schouten, Siau. Dialects: ALI, YAKAMUL. Literacy rate in second language: 50% to 75%. Coastal, islands.

YALE ***(NAGATMAN, NAGATIMAN, YARË, YADE)*** [NCE] 600 (1991 SIL). Sandaun Province, Amanab District, west of Namia. Kwomtari is north, Abau is south, Busa is southwest, Biaka is west, Anggor and Amanab are northwest. 6 villages. Language Isolate. 2 very similar dialects. Most men up to 35 years old have routine proficiency in Tok Pisin. There is some intermarriage with the Busa. 'Nagatman' is a corrupted name of 1 village, not a language name. SOV. Literacy rate in first language: 5% to 15%. Literacy rate in second language: 15% to 25%. Tropical forest. Sago swamps. Hunter-gatherers, some cultivation: sugar cane, tobacco, sweet potatoes, taro. 300 feet.

YAMAP [YMP] 670 (1980 census). Morobe Province, Francisco River area. Austronesian, Malayo-Polynesian, Central-Eastern, Eastern Malayo-Polynesian, Oceanic, Western Oceanic, North New Guinea, Huon Gulf, South, Hote-Buang, Hote. Close to Hote and Misim. Investigation needed: intelligibility with Hote, Misim.

YAMBES [YMB] 860 in 4 villages (1981 Wurm and Hattori). East Sepik Province, Maprik District, northwest of Wom, east and southeast of Kombio. Torricelli, Kombio-Arapesh, Kombio. Dialects: WEST

YAMBES, EAST YAMBES. Investigation needed: intelligibility. Literacy rate in first language: Less than 5%. Literacy rate in second language: 15% to 25%.

YANGULAM [YNL] 180 (1981 Wurm and Hattori). Madang Province. Trans-New Guinea, Madang-Adelbert Range, Madang, Rai Coast, Nuru. Related languages: Kwato, Ogea, Uya, Duduela, Rerau, Jilim.

YAPUNDA *(REIWO)* [YEV] 69 (1981 Wurm and Hattori). Sandaun Province. Torricelli, Wapei-Palei, Wapei.

YARAWATA [YRW] 98 (1981 Wurm and Hattori). Madang Province. Trans-New Guinea, Madang-Adelbert Range, Adelbert Range, Pihom-Isumrud-Mugil, Pihom, Numugenan. Related languages: Usan, Yaben, Bilakura, Parawen, Ukuriguma. Investigation needed: intelligibility.

YAREBA *(MIDDLE MUSA)* [YRB] 750 (1981 Wurm and Hattori). Oro Province, Popondetta District. Trans-New Guinea, Main Section, Eastern, Central and Southeastern, Yareban. Speakers are highly bilingual in Hiri Motu. Dictionary. Grammar. Literacy rate in first language: 75% to 100%. Literacy rate in second language: 50% to 75%. NT 1973.

YAU *(URUWA)* [YUW] 1,700 (1991 SIL). Morobe Province, Kabwum District. Villages include Worin, Yawan, Kotet, Mitmit, Mup, Sindamon. Trans-New Guinea, Main Section, Central and Western, Huon-Finisterre, Finisterre, Uruwa. Dialects: NORTHERN YAU, HEADWATERS YAU. The dialects listed are inherently intelligible, and are also names of villages. It is different from Yau which is Torricelli. Literacy rate in first language: 50% to 75%. Literacy rate in second language: 50% to 75%. Mountain slope. Swidden agriculturalists. 930 to 1,500 meters. NT 1997.

YAU [YYU] 165 (1983 census). Sandaun Province. 1 village. Torricelli, Wapei-Palei, Wapei. Related languages: Olo, Yis, Ningil, Valman. 63% lexical similarity with Olo and Yis. Different from Yau in Uruwa group and the Yau dialect of Yessan-Mayo. Literacy rate in second language: 50% to 75%. 4,000 to 5,000 feet.

YAUL [YLA] 814 (1981 Wurm and Hattori). East Sepik Province. Sepik-Ramu, Ramu, Yuat-Waibuk, Mongol-Langam. Related languages: Langam, Mongol. Investigation needed: intelligibility with Langam, Mongol.

YAWEYUHA *(YABIYUFA, YAWIYUHA)* [YBY] 2,000 (1991 SIL). Eastern Highlands Province, Goroka District. Trans-New Guinea, Main Section, Central and Western, East New Guinea Highlands, East-Central, Siane. NT 1982.

YAWIYO *(YABIO)* [YBX] 100 (1977 Voegelin and Voegelin). Sandaun Province, 10 miles east of Duranmin. 3 villages. Sepik-Ramu, Leonhard Schultze, Walio. 7% lexical similarity with Papi. Most use Saniyo-Hiyowe as second language.

YEI *(YEY, JEI, JE)* [JEI] Western Province, south between Fly River and coast, Sirisa village. Trans-New Guinea, Trans-Fly-Bulaka River, Trans-Fly, Morehead and Upper Maro Rivers, Yey. Dialects: NORTH YEI (BUPUL), SOUTH YEI. See main entry under Indonesia, Irian Jaya.

YEKORA [YKR] 1,000 (1995 SIL). Morobe Province, 2 villages near Morobe government station. Trans-New Guinea, Main Section, Eastern, Binanderean, Binanderean Proper. Close to Mawae. Bilingualism in Suena, Zia.

YELE *(YELEJONG, ROSSEL, YELA, YELETNYE)* [YLE] 3,750 (1998 Rossel Health Centres estimate). Milne Bay Province, Misima District, Rossel Island at eastern end of Calvados chain. East Papuan, Yele-Solomons-New Britain, Yele-Solomons, Yele. Dialects: DAMINYU, BOU, WULANGA, JINJO, ABALETTI, JARU. 8% lexical similarity with Daga (closest). Half the children have primary education in English. Dictionary. Grammar. SOV, postpositions. Literacy rate in first language: 50% to 75%. Literacy rate in second language: 75% to 100%. Tropical forest. Coastal, island. Swidden agriculturalists. 0 to 830 meters. NT 1987.

YELOGU *(KAUNGA, BUIAMANAMBU)* [YLG] 230 (1981 Wurm and Hattori). East Sepik Province, one village in Ambunti District. Sepik-Ramu, Sepik, Middle Sepik, Ndu.

YERAKAI *(YEREKAI)* [YRA] 390 in 2 villages (1981 Wurm and Hattori). East Sepik Province, Ambunti District, southeast near government station. Sepik-Ramu, Sepik, Middle Sepik, Yerakai. 6% lexical similarity with Middle Sepik languages. Literacy rate in second language: 25% to 50%. Hills. Traditional religion, Christian.

YESSAN-MAYO *(MAYO-YESAN, MAIO-YESAN, YASYIN, YESAN)* [YSS] 1,500 (1998 SIL). East Sepik Province, Ambunti District, Sandaun Province, Wan Wan Division, south of Mehek. 10 villages. Sepik-Ramu, Sepik, Tama. Dialects: YAWU (YAU, YAW, WARASAI), MAYO-YESSAN. Yawu is distinct from Yau which is Torricelli or Yau which is Trans-New Guinea. Grammar. Literacy rate in first language: 15% to 25%. Literacy rate in second language: 50% to 75%. Tropical forest. Riverine. Fishermen, swidden agriculturalists, hunter-gatherers. 50 meters. Christian, traditional religion. NT 1980-1996.

YIL [YLL] 2,476 (1983 census). Sandaun Province, northwest of Au. 16 villages. Torricelli, Wapei-Palei, Wapei. 23% lexical similarity with Au. Literacy rate in second language: 15% to 25%. Tropical forest. Mountain slope. 4,000 to 6,000 feet.

YIMAS [YEE] 350 (1981 Wurm and Hattori). East Sepik Province, near Chambri, Arafundi River, middle Karawari River. Sepik-Ramu, Nor-Pondo, Pondo. Related language: Karawari. Investigation needed:

intelligibility with Karawari. Literacy rate in first language: Less than 5%. Literacy rate in second language: 15% to 25%.

YIS [YIS] 492 (1983 census). Sandaun Province. 5 villages. Torricelli, Wapei-Palei, Wapei. Different dialects in each village. Related languages: Olo, Yau, Ningil, Valman. Investigation needed: intelligibility. Mountain slope.

YOBA [YOB] Central Province, north of Magori. Austronesian, Malayo-Polynesian, Central-Eastern, Eastern Malayo-Polynesian, Oceanic, Western Oceanic, Papuan Tip, Peripheral, Central Papuan, Oumic, Magoric. Related to Magori. 2 nonprimary speakers left (1981 Wurm and Hattori). Extinct.

YOIDIK [YDK] 266 (1981 Wurm and Hattori). Madang Province. Trans-New Guinea, Madang-Adelbert Range, Madang, Mabuso, Hanseman.

YONGKOM ***(YONGOM, YONGGOM)*** [YON] 4,000 in Papua New Guinea (1997 SIL). Population total both countries 6,000. Western Province along the Fly and Tedi (Alice) rivers and towards Lake Murray, across the border into Irian Jaya, on both sides of the Muyu River up to the Kawo (Kao) River. Also spoken in Indonesia (Irian Jaya). Trans-New Guinea, Main Section, Central and Western, Central and South New Guinea-Kutubuan, Central and South New Guinea, Ok, Lowland. Literacy rate in first language: 50% to 75%. Literacy rate in second language: 50% to 75%. Bible portions 1965-1988.

YOPNO ***(YUPNA)*** [YUT] 10,000 including 7,000 Yupna (1987 SIL), 820 Kewieng (1981), 1,669 Nokopo (1981), 517 Wandabong (1981). Madang Province and Morobe Province. Trans-New Guinea, Main Section, Central and Western, Huon-Finisterre, Finisterre, Yupna. Dialects: KEWIENG, NOKOPO, WANDABONG, ISAN. Related to Mebu, Gabutamon. SOV. Literacy rate in first language: 15% to 25%. Literacy rate in second language: 50% to 75%. Mountain slope. Swidden agriculturalists. Christian, traditional religion. Bible portions 1979-1993.

YUBANAKOR ***(DAINA, KWANGA)*** [YUO] 4,800 (1996 SIL). East Sepik Province, extending beyond the western boundary of Maprik District; Makru-Klaplei Division, Nuku District. Sepik-Ramu, Sepik, Middle Sepik, Nukuma. Literacy rate in first language: 5% to 15%. Literacy rate in second language: 15% to 25%. Tropical forest. Plains. Swidden agriculturalists. 50 to 60 meters. NT 1991.

ZENAG ***(ZENANG)*** [ZEG] 1,818 (1979 census). Morobe Province, Mumeng District. Austronesian, Malayo-Polynesian, Central-Eastern, Eastern Malayo-Polynesian, Oceanic, Western Oceanic, North New Guinea, Huon Gulf, South, Hote-Buang, Buang, Mumeng. In Mumeng dialect chain. Some intelligibility with Patep. Investigation needed: intelligibility, attitudes toward Patep. SVO. Tropical forest. Mountain slope. Swidden agriculturalists. 300 to 900 meters.

ZIA ***(TSIA, LOWER WARIA, ZIYA)*** [ZIA] 3,943 including 3,000 Zia (1991 SIL), 943 Mawae (1978 McElhanon). Morobe Province, Lae District near the mouth of the Waria River. Trans-New Guinea, Main Section, Eastern, Binanderean, Binanderean Proper. Dialects: ZIA, MAWAE. 68% lexical similarity with Yekora (closest). Literacy rate in first language: 75% to 100%. Literacy rate in second language: 75% to 100%. NT 1982.

ZIMAKANI ***(BAEGWA, DEA, BAGWA ZIMAKANI)*** [ZIK] 1,500 (1990 UBS). Western Province, south end of Lake Murray. Trans-New Guinea, Main Section, Central and Western, Marind, Boazi. Dialects: ZIMAKANI, BAGWA (BEGUA, MBEGU), DEA. Related to Kuni (Boazi). Literacy rate in first language: 5% to 15%. Literacy rate in second language: 15% to 25%. NT 1989.

PITCAIRN

National or official language: English. 46 (1998 UN). A British colony. Information mainly from M. Adler 1977. The number of languages listed for Pitcairn is 2. Of those, 1 is a living language and 1 is a second language without mother tongue speakers. Diversity index 0.00.

ENGLISH [ENG] Indo-European, Germanic, West, English. National language. Bible 1535-1989. See main entry under United Kingdom.

PITCAIRN-NORFOLK [PIH] (Fewer than 50 on Pitcairn; 1989 J. Holm). Pitcairn Island, Norfolk Island, Fiji, and some second generation Pitcairn Islanders in Australia and New Zealand. Cant, English-Tahitian. Dialect: PITCAIRN ENGLISH. Developed from mutineers settling on Pitcairn in 1790. Some were removed to Norfolk in 1859. Slightly different variety than in Norfolk. An in-group language to assist in the preservation of identity. People speak Standard British English as mother tongue. Christian. Second language only. See main entry under Norfolk Island.

SOLOMON ISLANDS

National or official language: English. 417,000 (1998 UN). 94% Melanesian, 4% Polynesian, 1.5% Micronesian. Double chain of 6 large islands and many smaller ones. Literacy rate 5% to 60%; average years of schooling 4.4. Also includes Chinese 1,000. Information mainly from E. M. Todd 1975; S. Wurm and S. Hattori 1981; D. T. Tryon and B. D. Hackman 1983; M. Ross 1988; D. T. Tryon 1995; SIL 1977-1999. Christian, traditional religion, cargo cult. Data accuracy estimate: A1, A2. The number of languages listed for Solomon Islands is 74. Of those, 69 are living languages and 5 are extinct. Diversity index 0.97.

AMBA ***(ABA, NEMBAO, UTUPUA)*** [UTP] 485 (1998 SIL). Aveta, Matembo, and Nembao villages, Utupua Island, Temotu Province. Austronesian, Malayo-Polynesian, Central-Eastern, Eastern Malayo-Polynesian, Oceanic, Central-Eastern Oceanic, Remote Oceanic, Eastern Outer Islands, Utupua. Bilingualism in Pijin. SVO. Literacy rate in first language: 10% to 30%. Literacy rate in second language: 25% to 50%. Tropical forest. Mountain slope, coast. Agriculturalists, fishermen. 0 to 350 meters.

ANUTA [AUD] 360 (1998 SIL). Anuta Island. Austronesian, Malayo-Polynesian, Central-Eastern, Eastern Malayo-Polynesian, Oceanic, Central-Eastern Oceanic, Remote Oceanic, Central Pacific, East Fijian-Polynesian, Polynesian, Nuclear, Samoic-Outlier, Futunic. Investigation needed: intelligibility with Tikopia. Literacy rate in first language: 10% to 30%. Literacy rate in second language: 25% to 50%.

'ARE'ARE ***(AREARE)*** [ALU] 17,300 (1998 SIL). South Malaita Island. Austronesian, Malayo-Polynesian, Central-Eastern, Eastern Malayo-Polynesian, Oceanic, Central-Eastern Oceanic, Southeast Solomonic, Malaita-San Cristobal, Malaita, Southern. Dialects: 'ARE'ARE, MARAU (MARAU SOUND). Marau is reported to be completely intelligible with 'Are'are. Investigation needed: intelligibility with Marau. SVO. Literacy rate in first language: 30% to 60%. Literacy rate in second language: 25% to 50%. Tropical forest. Mountain slope, coast. Hunters, agriculturalists. 100 to 1,000 meters. Bible portions 1957.

AROSI [AIA] 4,600 (1998 SIL). Northwest Makira (San Cristobal) Island. Austronesian, Malayo-Polynesian, Central-Eastern, Eastern Malayo-Polynesian, Oceanic, Central-Eastern Oceanic, Southeast Solomonic, Malaita-San Cristobal, San Cristobal. Dialects: WANGO, AROSI. Many dialects. Dictionary. Grammar. Literacy rate in first language: 30% to 60%. Literacy rate in second language: 25% to 50%. Active literacy program. Bible portions 1905-1921.

ASUMBOA ***(ASUMBUA, ASUMUO)*** [AUA] 75 (1998 SIL). Asumbuo village, Utupua Island, Temotu Province. Austronesian, Malayo-Polynesian, Central-Eastern, Eastern Malayo-Polynesian, Oceanic, Central-Eastern Oceanic, Remote Oceanic, Eastern Outer Islands, Utupua. Bilingual level estimates for Amba, Pijin, Nyisunggu are 1 0%, 2 0%, 3+ 33%, 4 67%, 5 0%. SVO. Literacy rate in first language: 10% to 30%. Literacy rate in second language: 25% to 50%. Tropical forest. Mountain slope, coast. Agriculturalists, fishermen. 0 to 350 meters.

AYIWO ***(AÏWO, GNIVO, NIVO, NIFILOLE, LOMLOM, REEF ISLANDS, REEFS)*** [NFL] 7,100 (1998 SIL). Santa Cruz Islands, eastern Solomons. East Papuan, Reef Islands-Santa Cruz. Literacy rate in first language: 30%. Literacy rate in second language: 25% to 50%.

BABATANA ***(MBAMBATANA, EAST CHOISEUL)*** [BAQ] 6,150 (1998 SIL). East Choiseul Island. Austronesian, Malayo-Polynesian, Central-Eastern, Eastern Malayo-Polynesian, Oceanic, Western Oceanic, Meso Melanesian, New Ireland, South New Ireland-Northwest Solomonic, Choiseul. Dialects: BABATANA, SENGAN (SENGGA, SISINGGA, SENGA), KUBORO (KUMBORO), KATAZI, LÖMAUMBI, AVASÖ. Kirunggela (2,626 speakers) may be a dialect. Related to Ririo. There are second language speakers. Trade language. NT 1960-1998.

BAEGGU ***(BAEGU, MBAENGGU)*** [BVD] 5,700 (1998 SIL). North Malaita Island. Austronesian, Malayo-Polynesian, Central-Eastern, Eastern Malayo-Polynesian, Oceanic, Central-Eastern Oceanic, Southeast Solomonic, Malaita-San Cristobal, Malaita, Northern. Baelelea and Baegu are about equally intelligible with To'abaita and Lau. SVO. Literacy rate in first language: 30% to 60%. Literacy rate in second language: 25% to 50%. Tropical forest. Mountain slope, coast. Hunters, agriculturalists. 100 to 1,000 meters.

BAELELEA ***(MBAELELEA)*** [BVC] 10,700 (1998 SIL). North Malaita Island. Austronesian, Malayo-Polynesian, Central-Eastern, Eastern Malayo-Polynesian, Oceanic, Central-Eastern Oceanic, Southeast Solomonic, Malaita-San Cristobal, Malaita, Northern. Baelelea and Baegu are about equally intelligible with To'abaita and Lau. SVO. Literacy rate in first language: 30% to 60%. Literacy rate in second language: 25% to 50%. Tropical forest. Mountain slope, coast. Hunters, agriculturalists. 100 to 1,000 meters.

BANIATA ***(MBANIATA, LOKURU)*** [BNT] 1,480 (1998 SIL). South Rendova Island, Western Province. East Papuan, Yele-Solomons-New Britain, Yele-Solomons, Central Solomons. Bilingualism of speakers in Roviana is decreasing.

BAURO ***(MARMAREGHO)*** [BXA] 4,620 including 2,475 in Bauro, 1,320 in Haununu, 825 in Rawo (1998 SIL). Central Makira (San Cristobal) Island. Austronesian, Malayo-Polynesian, Central-Eastern, Eastern Malayo-Polynesian, Oceanic, Central-Eastern Oceanic, Southeast Solomonic, Malaita-San Cristobal, San Cristobal. Dialects: HAUNUNU (HAUHUNU), BAURO, RAWO (RAVO). There is a deep linguistic division between Bauro and Arosi. The purported Mamaregho language has not been found (1986 G. Simons SIL). Investigation needed: intelligibility with Kahua. Literacy rate in first language: 10% to 30%. Literacy rate in second language: 25% to 50%. Bible portions 1922.

BILUA ***(MBILUA, VELLA LAVELLA)*** [BLB] 8,540 (1998 SIL). Vella Lavella Island, Western Province. East Papuan, Yele-Solomons-New Britain, Yele-Solomons, Central Solomons. There are second language users. 'Vella Lavella' is a geographical name used in some lists as a language name. Dictionary. Literacy rate in first language: 30% to 60%. Literacy rate in second language: 25% to 50%. NT 1995.

BIRAO ***(MBIRAO)*** [BRR] 6,650 (1998 SIL). Eastern Guadalcanal Island. Austronesian, Malayo-Polynesian, Central-Eastern, Eastern Malayo-Polynesian, Oceanic, Central-Eastern Oceanic, Southeast Solomonic, Gela-Guadalcanal, Guadalcanal.

BLABLANGA ***(GEMA, GOI)*** [BLP] 760 (1998 SIL). Santa Isabel Island, villages of Popoheo and Hovukoilo in Maringe District and from Ghove to Biluro on Hograno coast. Austronesian, Malayo-Polynesian, Central-Eastern, Eastern Malayo-Polynesian, Oceanic, Western Oceanic, Meso Melanesian, New Ireland, South New Ireland-Northwest Solomonic, Santa Isabel, Central. Slight dialect differences. Speakers are reported to converse in Cheke Holo (Maringe).

BUGHOTU ***(BUGOTO, BUGOTA, BUGOTU, MBUGHOTU, MAHAGA)*** [BGT] 3,100 (1998 SIL). Santa Isabel Island, southeast end from Suma to Horara, and on Furona Island off the northwest coast of Kia District. Austronesian, Malayo-Polynesian, Central-Eastern, Eastern Malayo-Polynesian, Oceanic, Central-Eastern Oceanic, Southeast Solomonic, Gela-Guadalcanal, Bughotu. Dialects: HAGEULU, VULAVA. Related to vernaculars on Guadalcanal. Close affinity to Gela. Literature in Bughotu will also reach Gao-a total of 2,191 speakers, or 2% of the Island. Different from other languages of Santa Isabel. Except for Gao, speakers of other Santa Isabel languages cannot communicate with Bughotu speakers except through Pijin. The church language used by COM on the island. Trade language. Dictionary. Grammar. Literacy rate in first language: 30% to 60%. Literacy rate in second language: 50% to 75%. NT 1914-1934.

CHEKE HOLO ***(A'ARA, KUBONITU, HOLO)*** [MRN] 9,860 (1998 SIL). 57% of the population of Santa Isabel Island. Central Santa Isabel Island, on Maringe side from village of Gnulahaghe southeast to Kuma'ihaui; on Hograno coast in several villages in Kia district; and scattered villages in Gao-Bughotu region. Austronesian, Malayo-Polynesian, Central-Eastern, Eastern Malayo-Polynesian, Oceanic, Western Oceanic, Meso Melanesian, New Ireland, South New Ireland-Northwest Solomonic, Santa Isabel, East. Dialects: MARINGE (MARINGHE), HOGRANO (HOGIRANO). Most important language of Santa Isabel apart from Bughotu. Second language of many speakers of other languages. Literature in this language could be used by the Blablanga and Gao; a total of 6,344 people, or 70% of the island. Trade language. Dictionary. Grammar. Literacy rate in first language: 30% to 35%. Literacy rate in second language: 30% to 35%. NT 1993.

DORI'O ***(KWAREKWAREO)*** [DOR] 1,485 (1998 SIL). West central Malaita Island. Austronesian, Malayo-Polynesian, Central-Eastern, Eastern Malayo-Polynesian, Oceanic, Central-Eastern Oceanic, Southeast Solomonic, Malaita-San Cristobal, Malaita, Southern. 71% lexical similarity with 'Are'are. Investigation needed: intelligibility with 'Are'are. SVO. Tropical forest. Mountain slope, coast. Hunters, agriculturalists. 100 to 1,000 meters.

DORORO ***(DORIRI)*** [DRR] New Georgia. East Papuan, Yele-Solomons-New Britain, Yele-Solomons, Kazukuru. May have been a Kazukuru dialect. Extinct.

DUKE ***(NDUKE, NDUGHORE, KOLOMBANGARA)*** [NKE] 2,500 (1998 SIL). Kolombangara Island, Western Province. Austronesian, Malayo-Polynesian, Central-Eastern, Eastern Malayo-Polynesian, Oceanic, Western Oceanic, Meso Melanesian, New Ireland, South New Ireland-Northwest Solomonic, New Georgia, West. Close to Lungga and Roviana. Bilingual level estimates for Roviana are 0 7%, 1 11%, 2 24%, 3 58%, 4 0%, 5 0%. They speak Pijin or Roviana, Marovo, or English for some purposes. For historical reasons they use Marovo for Scripture. Marovo is the SDA lingua franca-Roviana used by Methodists. Most are SDA. SDA schools teach English. They use Roviana to the Roviana, Marovo to the Marovo, English to tourists, Pijin domestically and to all others. Nduke used for all domestic purposes. All ages. They prefer to read English over Pijin. Dictionary and grammar in progress by Ian Scales of ANU. Literacy rate in second language: 40% fluently, 90% haltingly. Motivation for literacy high. Christian, Baha'i.

ENGLISH [ENG] Indo-European, Germanic, West, English. National language. Bible 1382-1989. See main entry under United Kingdom.

FAGANI ***(FAGHANI)*** [FAF] 500 including 166 in each dialect (1998 SIL). Northwest Makira Island. Austronesian, Malayo-Polynesian, Central-Eastern, Eastern Malayo-Polynesian, Oceanic, Central-Eastern Oceanic, Southeast Solomonic, Malaita-San Cristobal, San Cristobal. Dialects: FAGANI, RIHU'A, AGUFI. Tryon says this is separate from Arosi. Literacy rate in second language: 25% to 50%.

FATALEKA [FAR] 5,700 (1998 SIL). Malaita Island. Austronesian, Malayo-Polynesian, Central-Eastern, Eastern Malayo-Polynesian, Oceanic, Central-Eastern Oceanic, Southeast Solomonic, Malaita-San Cristobal, Malaita, Northern. Wurm and Hattori treat it as a dialect of To'abaita. Intelligibility of the Baegu variety of To'abaita is reported to be high, but of To'abaita is much less. 82% lexical similarity with Kwara'ae, 76% with Lau. Bilingual level estimates for Pijin, Kwara'ae, Lau are Pijin: 0 0%, 1 0%, 2 20%, 3 60%, 4 20%; Kwara'ae: 0 0%, 1 0%, 2 50%, 3 30%, 4 20%; Lau: 0 0%, 1 0%, 2 60%, 3 20%, 4 20%. Fataleka is used in the home. All ages. SVO. Literacy rate in first language: 30% to 60%. Literacy rate in second language: 25% to 50%. Tropical forest. Mountain slope, coast. Hunters, agriculturalists. 100 to 1,000 meters.

GAO ***(NGGAO)*** [GGA] 700 (1998 SIL). Central Isabel Island, from Tausese southeast to Floakora Point. The principal village is Poro. Austronesian, Malayo-Polynesian, Central-Eastern, Eastern Malayo-Polynesian, Oceanic, Western Oceanic, Meso Melanesian, New Ireland, South New Ireland-Northwest Solomonic, Santa Isabel, East. The Cheke Holo prayer book is used in church. Cheke Holo and Bughotu are used when communicating with people from those areas. All ages. Some speakers, including children, use Gao and some use Cheke Holo in the home. There are a number of mixed marriages.

GELA ***(NGGELA, FLORIDA ISLANDS)*** [NLG] 10,000 (1998 SIL). Gela, Florida Islands, Guadalcanal (immigrants), and Savo Islands, central Solomons. Austronesian, Malayo-Polynesian, Central-Eastern, Eastern Malayo-Polynesian, Oceanic, Central-Eastern Oceanic, Southeast Solomonic, Gela-Guadalcanal, Gela. Similar to Lengo in north Guadalcanal. Literacy rate in first language: 30% to 60%. Literacy rate in second language: 25% to 50%. Subsistence agriculturalists: root vegetables, coconut; fishermen; copra production. Christian. NT 1923.

GHANONGGA ***(GANONGGA, KUBOKOTA, KUMBOKOTA)*** [GHN] 3,600 (1998 SIL). North Ranonga Island, Western Province. Austronesian, Malayo-Polynesian, Central-Eastern, Eastern Malayo-Polynesian, Oceanic, Western Oceanic, Meso Melanesian, New Ireland, South New Ireland-Northwest Solomonic, New Georgia, West. A related but separate language to Lungga and Simbo.

GHARI ***(GARI, TANGARARE, SUGHU, WEST GUADALCANAL)*** [GRI] 10,045 including 5,180 Ghari, 800 Gae, 1,240 Geri, 1,740 Ndi, 400 Nginia, 685 Tandai-Nggaria (1998 SIL). Guadalcanal Island, west, northwest and north central coast. Austronesian, Malayo-Polynesian, Central-Eastern, Eastern Malayo-Polynesian, Oceanic, Central-Eastern Oceanic, Southeast Solomonic, Gela-Guadalcanal, Guadalcanal. Dialects: GAE (NGGAE), GERI (NGGERI), NDI (VATURANGA), NGINIA, TANDAI-NGGARIA (TANAGHAI), GHARI. Trade language. Literacy rate in first language: 30% to 60%. Literacy rate in second language: 25% to 50%. Bible 1998.

GULA'ALAA ***(KWAI, NGONGOSILA)*** [GMB] 1,600 (1998 SIL). Kwai and Ngongosila islands on the east side of Kwara'ae, Malaita. Austronesian, Malayo-Polynesian, Central-Eastern, Eastern Malayo-Polynesian, Oceanic, Central-Eastern Oceanic, Southeast Solomonic, Malaita-San Cristobal, Malaita, Northern. Might be intelligible with Lau or Kwara'ae. About 85% lexical similarity with Lau and Kwara'ae. The people call their language 'Gula'alaa'. Investigation needed: intelligibility with Lau, Kwara'ae. SVO. Salt water. Coral reef. Fishermen, craftsmen. 0 to 1 meter.

GULIGULI ***(GULILI)*** [GLG] New Georgia. East Papuan, Yele-Solomons-New Britain, Yele-Solomons, Kazukuru. Possibly was a Kazukuru dialect. Extinct.

HOAVA [HOA] 1,000 (1998 SIL). North Marovo Lagoon, New Georgia Island, Western Province. Austronesian, Malayo-Polynesian, Central-Eastern, Eastern Malayo-Polynesian, Oceanic, Western Oceanic, Meso Melanesian, New Ireland, South New Ireland-Northwest Solomonic, New Georgia, West. Close to Kusaghe. Bilingualism in Roviana.

KAHUA ***(ANGANIWAI, ANGANIWEI, WANONI, NARIHUA)*** [AGW] 7,700 including 3,000 Kahua, 4,700 Tawarafa (1998 SIL). South Makira (San Cristobal) Island. Austronesian, Malayo-Polynesian, Central-Eastern, Eastern Malayo-Polynesian, Oceanic, Central-Eastern Oceanic, Southeast Solomonic, Malaita-San Cristobal, San Cristobal. Dialects: TAWARAFA (STAR HARBOUR), SANTA ANA (OWA RAHA), SANTA CATALINA (OWA RIKI), KAHUA. There are second language users. Trade language. Literacy rate in first language: 30% to 60%. Literacy rate in second language: 25% to 50%. NT 1986.

KAZUKURU [KZK] New Georgia. East Papuan, Yele-Solomons-New Britain, Yele-Solomons, Kazukuru. Extinct.

KIRIBATI ***(GILBERTESE, IKIRIBATI)*** [GLB] 1,230 (1998 SIL). One area on Gizo Island, and one area on Choiseul Island. Austronesian, Malayo-Polynesian, Central-Eastern, Eastern Malayo-Polynesian, Oceanic, Central-Eastern Oceanic, Remote Oceanic, Micronesian, Micronesian Proper, Ikiribati. The

British relocated them here in the 1950s. Dictionary. Christian. Bible 1893-1954. See main entry under Kiribati.

KOKOTA [KKK] 1,020 (1998 SIL). Santa Isabel, villages of Sisiga and Ghoveo on the northeast coast and Hurepelo on southwest coast. Austronesian, Malayo-Polynesian, Central-Eastern, Eastern Malayo-Polynesian, Oceanic, Western Oceanic, Meso Melanesian, New Ireland, South New Ireland-Northwest Solomonic, Santa Isabel, Central. Speakers can converse in Cheke Holo and Zabana.

KUSAGHE ***(KUSAGE)*** [KSG] 2,020 (1998 SIL). North New Georgia Island, Western Province. Austronesian, Malayo-Polynesian, Central-Eastern, Eastern Malayo-Polynesian, Oceanic, Western Oceanic, Meso Melanesian, New Ireland, South New Ireland-Northwest Solomonic, New Georgia, West. Close to Roviana. Bilingual level estimates for Roviana are 0 0%, 1 14%, 2 38%, 3-5 0%. Roviana and Kusaghe used in church.

KWAIO ***(KOIO)*** [KWD] 16,700 (1998 SIL). Central Malaita Island. Austronesian, Malayo-Polynesian, Central-Eastern, Eastern Malayo-Polynesian, Oceanic, Central-Eastern Oceanic, Southeast Solomonic, Malaita-San Cristobal, Malaita, Northern. Closer to Kwara'ae than to 'Are'are. Dictionary. Grammar. SVO. Tropical forest. Mountain slope, coast. Hunters, agriculturalists: sweet potato. 100 to 1,000 meters. Traditional religion.

KWARA'AE ***(FIU)*** [KWF] 33,600 (1998 SIL). Central Malaita Island. Austronesian, Malayo-Polynesian, Central-Eastern, Eastern Malayo-Polynesian, Oceanic, Central-Eastern Oceanic, Southeast Solomonic, Malaita-San Cristobal, Malaita, Northern. Largest indigenous vernacular in the Solomons. Many second language users. SVO. Literacy rate in first language: 30% to 60%. Literacy rate in second language: 25% to 50%. Tropical forest. Mountain slope, coast. Hunters, agriculturalists. 100 to 1,000 meters. NT 1961.

LAGHU ***(LAGU, KATOVA)*** [LGB] 5 (1981 D. Tryon). Santa Isabel, villages of Baolo and Samasodu in the Kia District. Austronesian, Malayo-Polynesian, Central-Eastern, Eastern Malayo-Polynesian, Oceanic, Western Oceanic, Meso Melanesian, New Ireland, South New Ireland-Northwest Solomonic, Santa Isabel, West. Nearly extinct.

LANGALANGA [LGL] 7,850 (1998 SIL). West central Malaita Island. Austronesian, Malayo-Polynesian, Central-Eastern, Eastern Malayo-Polynesian, Oceanic, Central-Eastern Oceanic, Southeast Solomonic, Malaita-San Cristobal, Malaita, Northern. 56% lexical similarity with Kwaio; 66% with Kwara'ae. SVO. Coral reef. Fishermen, craftsmen. 0 to 1 meter.

LAU [LLU] 16,500 (1998 SIL). Northeast Malaita Island. Austronesian, Malayo-Polynesian, Central-Eastern, Eastern Malayo-Polynesian, Oceanic, Central-Eastern Oceanic, Southeast Solomonic, Malaita-San Cristobal, Malaita, Northern. Dialects: SUAFA, LAU, DAI (NDAI). Dictionary. SVO. Literacy rate in first language: 30% to 60%. Literacy rate in second language: 25% to 50%. Coral reef. Fishermen, craftsmen. 0 to 1 meter. NT 1929-1992.

LAVUKALEVE ***(LAUBE, LAUMBE, RUSSELL ISLAND)*** [LVK] 1,150 (1998 SIL Joel and Virginia Lee). Russell Islands, northwest of Guadalcanal, central Solomons. East Papuan, Yele-Solomons-New Britain, Yele-Solomons, Central Solomons.

LENGO ***(RUAVATU, TASEMBOKO)*** [LGR] 10,000 including 8,300 Lengo,1,100 Paripao, 600 Ghaimuta (1998 SIL). North and east central Guadalcanal Island. Austronesian, Malayo-Polynesian, Central-Eastern, Eastern Malayo-Polynesian, Oceanic, Central-Eastern Oceanic, Southeast Solomonic, Gela-Guadalcanal, Gela. Dialects: AOLA, PARIPAO, GHAIMUTA (GHUA), LENGO. Literacy rate in first language: 30% to 60%. Literacy rate in second language: 25% to 50%.

LONGGU ***(LOGU)*** [LGU] 1,240 (1998 SIL). East coast of Guadalcanal Island. Austronesian, Malayo-Polynesian, Central-Eastern, Eastern Malayo-Polynesian, Oceanic, Central-Eastern Oceanic, Southeast Solomonic, Malaita-San Cristobal, Malaita, Longgu. Brought over long ago by settlers from Malaita; probably not intelligible with Malaitan languages. Investigation needed: intelligibility with Malaita languages. Dictionary.

LUNGGA ***(LUGA, KUMBOKOLA)*** [LGA] 1,350 to 2,000 (1997 A. Zobule). South Ranonga Island, Western Province. Austronesian, Malayo-Polynesian, Central-Eastern, Eastern Malayo-Polynesian, Oceanic, Western Oceanic, Meso Melanesian, New Ireland, South New Ireland-Northwest Solomonic, New Georgia, West. Close to Duke (Nduke). Ghanongga, and Simbo are related but separate languages. Literacy rate in first language: 30% to 60%. Literacy rate in second language: 25% to 50%.

MALANGO [MLN] 3,400 (1998 SIL). Central Guadalcanal Island. Austronesian, Malayo-Polynesian, Central-Eastern, Eastern Malayo-Polynesian, Oceanic, Central-Eastern Oceanic, Southeast Solomonic, Gela-Guadalcanal, Guadalcanal. Investigation needed: intelligibility with Ghari, Lengo.

MAROVO [MVO] 8,740 (1998 SIL). South New Georgia Island, Marovo Lagoon, Vangunu Island, and Nggatokae Island; Western Province. Austronesian, Malayo-Polynesian, Central-Eastern, Eastern Malayo-Polynesian, Oceanic, Western Oceanic, Meso Melanesian, New Ireland, South New Ireland-Northwest Solomonic, New Georgia, East. Second most important language of the New Georgia group. Trade language. Literacy rate in first language: 30% to 60%. Literacy rate in second language: 25% to 50%. Bible 1956, out of print.

MONO *(ALU, MONO-ALU)* [MTE] 9,500 (1998 SIL). Treasury Island (Mono), Shortland Island (Alu, Alo), Fauro Island (Fauro). Austronesian, Malayo-Polynesian, Central-Eastern, Eastern Malayo-Polynesian, Oceanic, Western Oceanic, Meso Melanesian, New Ireland, South New Ireland-Northwest Solomonic, Mono-Uruava. Dialects: MONO, ALU (ALO), FAURO. Literacy rate in first language: 30% to 60%. Literacy rate in second language: 25% to 50%.

NANGGU [NAN] 450 (1998 SIL). Santa Cruz Island. East Papuan, Reef Islands-Santa Cruz. Most people are bilingual in Santa Cruz. Investigation needed: bilingual proficiency in Santa Cruz.

ONTONG JAVA *(LUANGIUA, LEUANGIUA, LORD HOWE)* [LUN] 1,800 (1998 SIL). Luangiua Atoll (Lord Howe Island), 130 miles from Santa Isabel Island. Austronesian, Malayo-Polynesian, Central-Eastern, Eastern Malayo-Polynesian, Oceanic, Central-Eastern Oceanic, Remote Oceanic, Central Pacific, East Fijian-Polynesian, Polynesian, Nuclear, Samoic-Outlier, Ellicean. Dialects: LUANGIUA, PELAU. Close to Sikaiana in the Solomon Islands, and to Takuu and Nukumanu in Papua New Guinea. Grammar. VSO, SVO. Literacy rate in first language: 30% to 60%. Literacy rate in second language: 25% to 50% literate. NT 1998.

OROHA *(MARA MA-SIKI, ORAHA)* [ORA] 160 (1998 SIL). South Malaita Island. Austronesian, Malayo-Polynesian, Central-Eastern, Eastern Malayo-Polynesian, Oceanic, Central-Eastern Oceanic, Southeast Solomonic, Malaita-San Cristobal, Malaita, Southern. Speakers appear to be bilingual in Sa'a. Investigation needed: bilingual proficiency in Sa'a. Dictionary.

PIJIN *(SOLOMONS PIDGIN, NEO-SOLOMONIC)* [PIS] 15,000 first language speakers, 300,000 second or third language speakers (1997 Beimers SIL). Creole, English based, Pacific. Basic vocabulary is closer to standard English than is Tok Pisin of Papua New Guinea. Grammar shows Melanesian features. Pronunciation varies according to local languages. Historically related to Tok Pisin of PNG and Bislama of Vanuatu. Intelligibility with Bislama is quite high. Creolization in progress. Language of wider communication. Dictionary. Literacy rate in first language: 60%. Literacy rate in second language: 50%. Recent efforts to standardize orthography. NT 1993.

PILENI *(PILHENI)* [PIV] 1,680 (1998 SIL). Matema, Taumako, Nupani, Nukapu, Pileni, Nifiloli in the Duff and Reef islands. Austronesian, Malayo-Polynesian, Central-Eastern, Eastern Malayo-Polynesian, Oceanic, Central-Eastern Oceanic, Remote Oceanic, Central Pacific, East Fijian-Polynesian, Polynesian, Nuclear, Samoic-Outlier, Futunic. Dialects: MATEMA, TAUMAKO (DUFF), NUPANI, NUKAPU, PILENI, AUA. The Pileni and Taumako dialects differ in significant ways. Investigation needed: intelligibility with Taumako. SVO. Literacy rate in first language: 30% to 60%. Literacy rate in second language: 25% to 50%.

RENNELL *(RENNELLESE-BELLONESE, RENNELLESE)* [MNV] 3,570 (1998 SIL). Rennell and Bellona Islands, Central Solomons. Austronesian, Malayo-Polynesian, Central-Eastern, Eastern Malayo-Polynesian, Oceanic, Central-Eastern Oceanic, Remote Oceanic, Central Pacific, East Fijian-Polynesian, Polynesian, Nuclear, Samoic-Outlier, Futunic. Dialects: MUNGGAVA (RENNELL, MUGABA), MUNGIKI (MUGIKI, BELLONESE, BELLONA). Dictionary. VSO. Literacy rate in first language: 30% to 60%. Literacy rate in second language: 25% to 50%. NT 1994.

RENNELLESE SIGN LANGUAGE [RSI] 1 (1986 Gallaudet University), other second language users. Rennell Island. Deaf sign language. Developed about 1915 by Kagobai, the first deaf person. Used by others. Nearly extinct.

RIRIO [RRI] 380 (1998 SIL). Choiseul Island. Austronesian, Malayo-Polynesian, Central-Eastern, Eastern Malayo-Polynesian, Oceanic, Western Oceanic, Meso Melanesian, New Ireland, South New Ireland-Northwest Solomonic, Choiseul. Close to Babatana. Investigation needed: intelligibility with Babatana.

ROVIANA *(ROBIANA, RUVIANA, RUBIANA)* [RUG] 10,250 (1998 SIL). 16,000 second language users (1987 UBS). North central New Georgia, Roviana Lagoon, Vonavona Lagoon; Western Province. Austronesian, Malayo-Polynesian, Central-Eastern, Eastern Malayo-Polynesian, Oceanic, Western Oceanic, Meso Melanesian, New Ireland, South New Ireland-Northwest Solomonic, New Georgia, West. Bilingualism in Pijin. Trade language previously in Western Province and as far north as Buka and Bougainville in Papua New Guinea. It is being replaced as a lingua franca by Pijin in Western Province, and is now used as a second language mainly by those over 30 years old. Trade language. Dictionary. VSO. Literacy rate in first language: 30% to 60%. Literacy rate in second language: 25% to 50%. NT 1953-1995.

SA'A *(SAA, SOUTH MALAITA, APAE'AA)* [APB] 10,700 (1998 SIL). South Malaita Island, Ulawa Island, Three Sisters Islands. Austronesian, Malayo-Polynesian, Central-Eastern, Eastern Malayo-Polynesian, Oceanic, Central-Eastern Oceanic, Southeast Solomonic, Malaita-San Cristobal, Malaita, Southern. Dialects: ULAWA, UKI NI MASI (UGI). Uki Ni Masi is nearly extinct. Dictionary. Grammar. SVO. Literacy rate in first language: 30% to 60%. Literacy rate in second language: 25% to 50%. Tropical forest. Mountain slope, coast. Hunters, agriculturalists: yam, taro, banana, coconut, breadfruit; fishermen; pig raisers. 100 to 1,000 meters. Traditional religion. NT 1911-1927.

SANTA ANA *(OWA RAHA, OWA)* [STN] 5,000 (1998 Greg Mellow SIL). Santa Ana and Santa Catalina islands. Austronesian, Malayo-Polynesian, Central-Eastern, Eastern Malayo-Polynesian, Oceanic,

Central-Eastern Oceanic, Southeast Solomonic, Malaita-San Cristobal, San Cristobal. Formerly thought to be a dialect of Kahua.

SANTA CRUZ ***(NATÖGU, NENDÖ, NAMBAKAENGÖ, MBANUA)*** [STC] 5,000 (1998 SIL). Santa Cruz Islands, Eastern Solomons. East Papuan, Reef Islands-Santa Cruz. Dialects: NDENI (DENI), TE MOTU, LONDAI, NEA, NOOLI, LVOVA (LWOWA), MBANUA. Speakers of most dialects understand Lwowa and Mbanua well. Nea and Nooli dialects may be sufficiently diverse to require adapted literature. Investigation needed: intelligibility with Nea, Nooli. Literacy rate in first language: 25% to 50%. Literacy rate in second language: 15% to 25%. Fishermen. Bible portions 1985-1991.

SAVOSAVO ***(SAVO ISLAND, SAVO)*** [SVS] 2,200 (1998 SIL). Savo Island, north of Guadalcanal, Central Solomons. East Papuan, Yele-Solomons-New Britain, Yele-Solomons, Central Solomons. Bilingualism in Pijin. Use of Savosavo may be declining among the younger generation.

SIKAIANA ***(SIKAYANA)*** [SKY] 920 (1998 SIL). Sikaiana Atoll, Central Solomons. Austronesian, Malayo-Polynesian, Central-Eastern, Eastern Malayo-Polynesian, Oceanic, Central-Eastern Oceanic, Remote Oceanic, Central Pacific, East Fijian-Polynesian, Polynesian, Nuclear, Samoic-Outlier, Ellicean. Close to Luangiua (Ontong Java), but a distinct language. Dictionary. SVO.

SIMBO ***(SIBO, MADEGGUSU, MANDEGHUGHUSU)*** [SBB] 3,200 (1998 SIL). Simbo (Eddystone) Island, Western Province. Austronesian, Malayo-Polynesian, Central-Eastern, Eastern Malayo-Polynesian, Oceanic, Western Oceanic, Meso Melanesian, New Ireland, South New Ireland-Northwest Solomonic, New Georgia, West. A separate language from Lungga and Ghanongga. Use of Roviana is decreasing.

TALISE ***(TALISI, TOLO)*** [TLR] 9,750 including 532 in Talise, 1,960 in Tolo, 1,533 in Moli, 2,025 in Poleo, 2,220 in Koo, 774 in Malagheti (1998 SIL). Guadalcanal Island, southeast to southwest coast. Austronesian, Malayo-Polynesian, Central-Eastern, Eastern Malayo-Polynesian, Oceanic, Central-Eastern Oceanic, Southeast Solomonic, Gela-Guadalcanal, Guadalcanal. Dialects: TALISE, TOLO, MOLI, POLEO, KOO (INAKONA), MALAGHETI. Investigation needed: intelligibility with Ghari, Birao. Dictionary. Grammar.

TANEMA ***(TANIMA)*** [TNX] Ethnic group has 190 (1998 SIL). Emua village, Vanikolo Island, Temotu Province. Austronesian, Malayo-Polynesian, Central-Eastern, Eastern Malayo-Polynesian, Oceanic, Central-Eastern Oceanic, Remote Oceanic, Eastern Outer Islands, Vanikoro. The people speak Pijin or Teanu. The language is no longer in use; old people remember a few words. SVO. Tropical forest. Mountain slope, coast. Agriculturalists, fishermen. 0 to 1,000 meters. Extinct.

TANIMBILI ***(NYISUNGGU)*** [TBE] 190 (1998 SIL). Tanimbili village, Utupua Island, Temotu Province. Austronesian, Malayo-Polynesian, Central-Eastern, Eastern Malayo-Polynesian, Oceanic, Central-Eastern Oceanic, Remote Oceanic, Eastern Outer Islands, Utupua. Bilingual level estimates for Pijin, Amba, Asumbuo are Amba: 0 27%, 1 0%, 2 0%, 3+ 40%, 4 33%; Pijin: 0 0%, 1 0%, 2 0%, 3 47%, 4 53%. Investigation needed: bilingual proficiency in Pijin. SVO. Tropical forest. Mountain slope, coast. Agriculturalists, fishermen. 0 to 350 meters.

TEANU ***(BUMA, PUMA)*** [TKW] 450 (1998 SIL). Puma, Lavaka, Emua, and Lale villages, Vanikolo Island, Temotu Province. Austronesian, Malayo-Polynesian, Central-Eastern, Eastern Malayo-Polynesian, Oceanic, Central-Eastern Oceanic, Remote Oceanic, Eastern Outer Islands, Vanikoro. Bilingualism in Pijin. Speakers include 170 adults (1989). Speakers prefer the name 'Teanu'. SVO. Literacy rate in first language: 30% to 60%. Literacy rate in second language: 25% to 50%. Tropical forest. Mountain slope, coast. Agriculturalists, fishermen. 0 to 1,000 meters.

TIKOPIA [TKP] 3,550 (1998 SIL). Tikopia Island. Austronesian, Malayo-Polynesian, Central-Eastern, Eastern Malayo-Polynesian, Oceanic, Central-Eastern Oceanic, Remote Oceanic, Central Pacific, East Fijian-Polynesian, Polynesian, Nuclear, Samoic-Outlier, Futunic. Related to Anuta. SVO, VSO. Literacy rate in first language: 30% to 60%. Literacy rate in second language: 25% to 50%. Agriculturalists: sago. Bible portions 1989.

TO'ABAITA ***(TO'AMBAITA, TO'ABAITA, MALU, MALU'U)*** [MLU] 13,100 (1998 SIL). North Malaita Island. Austronesian, Malayo-Polynesian, Central-Eastern, Eastern Malayo-Polynesian, Oceanic, Central-Eastern Oceanic, Southeast Solomonic, Malaita-San Cristobal, Malaita, Northern. Baelelea and Baegu are about equally intelligible with To'abaita and Lau. Dictionary. SVO. Literacy rate in first language: 30% to 60%. Literacy rate in second language: 25% to 50%. Tropical forest. Mountain slope, coast. Hunters, agriculturalists. 100 to 1,000 meters. NT 1923.

UGHELE ***(UGELE)*** [UGE] 1,070 (1998 SIL). North end of Rendova Island, Western Province. Austronesian, Malayo-Polynesian, Central-Eastern, Eastern Malayo-Polynesian, Oceanic, Western Oceanic, Meso Melanesian, New Ireland, South New Ireland-Northwest Solomonic, New Georgia, West. Bilingual level estimates for Roviana are 0 0%, 1 0%, 2 30%, 3-5 70%.

VAGHUA ***(TAVULA, TAVOLA, VAGUA)*** [TVA] 1,650 (1998 SIL). Tavula, Choiseul Island. Austronesian, Malayo-Polynesian, Central-Eastern, Eastern Malayo-Polynesian, Oceanic, Western Oceanic, Meso Melanesian, New Ireland, South New Ireland-Northwest Solomonic, Choiseul. Closely related to Varese. Investigation needed: intelligibility with Varese.

VANGUNU [MPR] 1,485 including 660 Bareke, 825 Vangunu (1998 SIL). North Vangunu Island (Bareke), southwest Vangunu Island (Vangunu), Western Province. Austronesian, Malayo-Polynesian, Central-Eastern, Eastern Malayo-Polynesian, Oceanic, Western Oceanic, Meso Melanesian, New Ireland, South New Ireland-Northwest Solomonic, New Georgia, East. Dialects: BAREKE (MBAREKE), VANGUNU. Bilingualism in Marovo. Investigation needed: intelligibility, attitudes toward Marovo.

VANO *(VANIKORO, VANIKOLO)* [VNK] Ethnic group has 140 (1998 SIL). Lale and Lavaka villages, Vanikolo Island, Temotu Province. Austronesian, Malayo-Polynesian, Central-Eastern, Eastern Malayo-Polynesian, Oceanic, Central-Eastern Oceanic, Remote Oceanic, Eastern Outer Islands, Vanikoro. The people speak Pijin or Teanu. The language is no longer in use; old people remember a few words. SVO. Tropical forest. Mountain slope, coast. Agriculturalists, fishermen. 0 to 1,000 meters. Extinct.

VARISI *(VARESE)* [VRS] 7,200 (1998 SIL). Northeast Choiseul Island. Austronesian, Malayo-Polynesian, Central-Eastern, Eastern Malayo-Polynesian, Oceanic, Western Oceanic, Meso Melanesian, New Ireland, South New Ireland-Northwest Solomonic, Choiseul. Dialects: GHONE, VARISI. Closely related to Vaghua. Bible portions 1995.

ZABANA *(JABANA, KIA)* [KJI] 1,650 (1998 SIL). Santa Isabel Island from Samasodu on the southwest side up to Kia village and down the northeast side to Baolo village. Austronesian, Malayo-Polynesian, Central-Eastern, Eastern Malayo-Polynesian, Oceanic, Western Oceanic, Meso Melanesian, New Ireland, South New Ireland-Northwest Solomonic, Santa Isabel, West. Links with New Georgia group (Roviana). Literature in this language would also reach Kokota and Zazao; a total of 1,240 speakers, or 14% of the island. 'Zabana' is the name usually preferred by speakers. Grammar. Literacy rate in first language: 30% to 60%. Literacy rate in second language: 25% to 50%.

ZAZAO *(JAJAO, KILOKAKA)* [JAJ] 210 (1998 SIL). Central Isabel Island, village of Kilokaka on Hograno coast. Austronesian, Malayo-Polynesian, Central-Eastern, Eastern Malayo-Polynesian, Oceanic, Western Oceanic, Meso Melanesian, New Ireland, South New Ireland-Northwest Solomonic, Santa Isabel, Central. Speakers can converse in Cheke Holo (Maringe) and Zabana.

TOKELAU

Formerly called Union Islands. National or official language: English. 1,000 (1998 UN). A New Zealand self-governing territory. Three atolls: Atafu, Nukunono, Fakaofo. Literacy rate 94%. Information mainly from N. Besnier 1992. Data accuracy estimate: B. The number of languages listed for Tokelau is 2. Of those, both are living languages. Diversity index 0.00.

ENGLISH [ENG] Indo-European, Germanic, West, English. Used in schools. National language. Bible 1535-1989. See main entry under United Kingdom.

TOKELAUAN *(TOKELAU)* [TOK] 1,680 in Tokelau (1987), 99% of the population. Population total all countries 4,500. 65% of all speakers are in New Zealand (1981 Wurm and Hattaro). Also spoken in American Samoa, New Zealand, USA. Austronesian, Malayo-Polynesian, Central-Eastern, Eastern Malayo-Polynesian, Oceanic, Central-Eastern Oceanic, Remote Oceanic, Central Pacific, East Fijian-Polynesian, Polynesian, Nuclear, Samoic-Outlier, Tokelauan. There are dialect differences among the three atolls. Intelligible with Tuvalu. Closely related to Samoan. Tokelauans read the Samoan Bible and some speak some Samoan. Most who live in Tokelau have very rudimentary knowledge of English as a second language. Tokelauan is used in the schools. Fishermen mainly; agriculturalists: coconut, taro, breadfruit, banana, arrowroot. Christian, traditional religion.

TONGA

Kingdom of Tonga. Pulèanga Tonga. National or official languages: Tongan, English. 98,000 (1998 UN). Constitutional monarchy. 169 islands, 36 inhabited. 270 square miles. Literacy rate 93% to 100%. Also includes Niue 27, Samoan 17, Chinese 200. Information mainly from S. Wurm and S. Hattori 1981; N. Besnier 1992. Christian, Mormon, Baha'i. The number of languages listed for Tonga is 4. Of those, 3 are living languages and 1 is extinct. Diversity index 0.01.

ENGLISH [ENG] Indo-European, Germanic, West, English. Official language. Bible 1535-1989. See main entry under United Kingdom.

NIUAFO'OU [NUM] 690 (1981 Schooling SIL) or more (1992 Besnier). Niuafo'ou and 'Eua islands. Austronesian, Malayo-Polynesian, Central-Eastern, Eastern Malayo-Polynesian, Oceanic, Central-Eastern Oceanic, Remote Oceanic, Central Pacific, East Fijian-Polynesian, Polynesian, Nuclear, Samoic-Outlier, East Uvean-Niuafo'ou. Probably a dialect of East Uvean (Wallisian). Investigation needed: intelligibility with Wallisian, bilingual proficiency in Tongan.

NIUATOPUTAPU [NKP] Ethnic group: 1,630 (1981). Niuatoputapu Island. Austronesian, Malayo-Polynesian, Central-Eastern, Eastern Malayo-Polynesian, Oceanic, Central-Eastern Oceanic, Remote Oceanic, Central Pacific, East Fijian-Polynesian, Polynesian, Nuclear, Samoic-Outlier. Known from a few words collected by Westerners in the 17th century. Became extinct before the 19th century. The ethnic group speaks Tongan. Extinct.

TONGAN ***(TONGA)*** [TOV] 103,200 in Tonga (1987), 98.3% of the population. Population total all countries 123,000 or more (1993). Also spoken in American Samoa, Fiji, New Zealand, USA, Vanuatu. Austronesian, Malayo-Polynesian, Central-Eastern, Eastern Malayo-Polynesian, Oceanic, Central-Eastern Oceanic, Remote Oceanic, Central Pacific, East Fijian-Polynesian, Polynesian, Tongic. Closely related to Niue. There are slight dialect differences from north to south. 86% lexical similarity with Wallisian, 66% with Samoan. The ethnic group is predominantly monolingual in Tongan (1997 J. Siegel). National language. Dictionary. VSO. Newspapers, radio programs. Agriculturalists. Bible 1862-1966.

TUVALU

Formerly Ellice Islands. National or official language: Tuvaluan. 11,000 (1998 UN). 9 islands. Literacy rate 96%. Information mainly from B. Bender and K. Rehg 1991. Christian, Baha'i. The number of languages listed for Tuvalu is 2. Of those, both are living languages. Diversity index 0.17.

KIRIBATI ***(GILBERTESE, IKIRIBATI)*** [GLB] 870 (1987). Nui, a northern island. Austronesian, Malayo-Polynesian, Central-Eastern, Eastern Malayo-Polynesian, Oceanic, Central-Eastern Oceanic, Remote Oceanic, Micronesian, Micronesian Proper, Ikiribati. Dialect: NUI (NUIAN). The Nui dialect is inherently intelligible with Kiribati, but has vocabulary and pronunciation differences. Active language use. A part of Tuvalu culture. VOS. Christian. Bible 1893-1954. See main entry under Kiribati.

TUVALUAN ***(ELLICE, ELLICEAN, TUVALU)*** [ELL] 8,440 in Tuvalu (1987), 97% of the population. Population total all countries 11,000 (1991 UBS). Tuvalu, 7 of the 9 inhabited islands. Also spoken in Fiji, Kiribati, Nauru, New Zealand. Austronesian, Malayo-Polynesian, Central-Eastern, Eastern Malayo-Polynesian, Oceanic, Central-Eastern Oceanic, Remote Oceanic, Central Pacific, East Fijian-Polynesian, Polynesian, Nuclear, Samoic-Outlier, Ellicean. Dialects: NORTH TUVALUAN (NANUMANGA, NANUMEA, NIUTAO), SOUTH TUVALUAN (NUKUFETAU, VAITUPU, FUNAFUTI, NUKULAELAE). Not intelligible with Samoan, which was formerly used as a mission language. Tuvalu is intelligible with Tokelau. The southern dialect is official. Vigorous language use. Official language. Literacy rate in first language: Most people. Little Tuvalu material is available. Christian. Bible 1987, in press (1997).

VANUATU

Republic of Vanuatu. Ripablik Blong Vanuatu. Formerly New Hebrides. National or official languages: Bislama, English, French. 182,000 (1998 UN) including 175,700 Melanesian (92%). Y-shaped chain of 80 islands. Land area 13,000 square kms. Literacy rate 61% to 90%. 85% to 90% of school age children attend school (1977 WA). Also includes Fijian 350, Kiribati 370, Tahitian, Tongan, Vietnamese 770, Wallisian 500, Chinese 300. Information mainly from D. T. Tryon 1971, 1976, 1978, 1995; S. Wurm and S. Hattori 1981. Christian, cargo cult, traditional religion. Data accuracy estimate: A2, B. The number of languages listed for Vanuatu is 110. Of those, 109 are living languages and 1 is extinct. Diversity index 0.97.

AKEI ***(TASIRIKI)*** [TSR] 650 (1981 Wurm and Hattori). Southwestern Santo. Austronesian, Malayo-Polynesian, Central-Eastern, Eastern Malayo-Polynesian, Oceanic, Central-Eastern Oceanic, Remote Oceanic, North and Central Vanuatu, Northeast Vanuatu-Banks Islands, West Santo. Closely related to Fortsenal. Complex dialect chaining. Bible portions 1909-1924.

AMBAE, EAST ***(OMBA, OBA, AOBA, WALURIGI, NORTHEAST AOBA, NORTHEAST AMBAE)*** [OMB] 5,000 (1991 UBS). Ambae (Leper's) Island. Austronesian, Malayo-Polynesian, Central-Eastern, Eastern Malayo-Polynesian, Oceanic, Central-Eastern Oceanic, Remote Oceanic, North and Central Vanuatu, Northeast Vanuatu-Banks Islands, East Vanuatu. Dialects: LOMBAHA (LOBAHA), LONGANA, LOLOKARO (LOLOKARA, LOLSIWOI). About 15 dialects. SVO. Christian. Bible portions 1971-1986.

AMBAE, WEST ***(OPA)*** [NND] 4,500 (1983 SIL). West Ambae (Aoba, Leper's) Island. Austronesian, Malayo-Polynesian, Central-Eastern, Eastern Malayo-Polynesian, Oceanic, Central-Eastern Oceanic, Remote Oceanic, North and Central Vanuatu, Northeast Vanuatu-Banks Islands, East Vanuatu. Dialects: WALAHA, NDUINDUI (DUINDUI). Many dialects. NT 1984.

AMBLONG [ALM] 150 (1983 SIL). South Santo. Austronesian, Malayo-Polynesian, Central-Eastern, Eastern Malayo-Polynesian, Oceanic, Central-Eastern Oceanic, Remote Oceanic, North and Central Vanuatu, Northeast Vanuatu-Banks Islands, West Santo. Closely related to Narango and Morouas.

AMBRYM, NORTH [MMG] 2,850 (1983 SIL). North Ambrym Island. Austronesian, Malayo-Polynesian, Central-Eastern, Eastern Malayo-Polynesian, Oceanic, Central-Eastern Oceanic, Remote Oceanic, North and Central Vanuatu, Northeast Vanuatu-Banks Islands, East Vanuatu. Dialects: MAGAM, OLAL. Volcanic island, rugged. Traditional religion.

AMBRYM, SOUTHEAST [TVK] 1,800 (1983 SIL). Southeast Ambrym Island. Austronesian, Malayo-Polynesian, Central-Eastern, Eastern Malayo-Polynesian, Oceanic, Central-Eastern Oceanic, Remote Oceanic, North and Central Vanuatu, Northeast Vanuatu-Banks Islands, East Vanuatu. Dialects: TAVEAK (TAVIAK), ENDU, TOAK, PENAPO. Links with Paama linguistically. Traditional religion. Bible portions 1949.

ANEITYUM ***(ANEITEUM, ANEITEUMESE, ANEJOM)*** [ATY] 600 (1983 SIL). Aneityum Island. Austronesian, Malayo-Polynesian, Central-Eastern, Eastern Malayo-Polynesian, Oceanic, Central-Eastern Oceanic, South Vanuatu, Aneityum. Some simplification of the subject marking system has occurred. Literacy rate in first language: 30% to 60%. Literacy rate in second language: 50% to 75%. Bible 1879.

AORE [AOR] 1 (1982 SIL). Mafea Island, East Santo. Austronesian, Malayo-Polynesian, Central-Eastern, Eastern Malayo-Polynesian, Oceanic, Central-Eastern Oceanic, Remote Oceanic, North and Central Vanuatu, Northeast Vanuatu-Banks Islands, West Santo. Closely related to Malo and Tutuba. Nearly extinct.

APMA ***(CENTRAL RAGA)*** [APP] 4,500 (1983 SIL). Central Pentecost (Raga). Austronesian, Malayo-Polynesian, Central-Eastern, Eastern Malayo-Polynesian, Oceanic, Central-Eastern Oceanic, Remote Oceanic, North and Central Vanuatu, Northeast Vanuatu-Banks Islands, East Vanuatu. Dialects: BWATNAPNI, LOLTONG, MELSISI, SURU-BO, SURU-MARANI. NT, in press (1996).

ARAKI [AKR] 105 (1983 SIL). Araki Island, south Santo. Austronesian, Malayo-Polynesian, Central-Eastern, Eastern Malayo-Polynesian, Oceanic, Central-Eastern Oceanic, Remote Oceanic, North and Central Vanuatu, Northeast Vanuatu-Banks Islands, West Santo.

AULUA ***(AULUA BAY)*** [AUL] 300 (1983 SIL). East Malekula. Austronesian, Malayo-Polynesian, Central-Eastern, Eastern Malayo-Polynesian, Oceanic, Central-Eastern Oceanic, Remote Oceanic, North and Central Vanuatu, Northeast Vanuatu-Banks Islands, Malekula Coastal. Dialects: ONESSO, BOINELANG. Bible portions 1894-1925.

AXAMB ***(AHAMB)*** [AHB] 525 (1983 SIL). South Malekula. Austronesian, Malayo-Polynesian, Central-Eastern, Eastern Malayo-Polynesian, Oceanic, Central-Eastern Oceanic, Remote Oceanic, North and Central Vanuatu, Northeast Vanuatu-Banks Islands, Malekula Coastal. Bible portions 1935.

BAETORA [BTR] 540 (1983 SIL). Maewo Island. Austronesian, Malayo-Polynesian, Central-Eastern, Eastern Malayo-Polynesian, Oceanic, Central-Eastern Oceanic, Remote Oceanic, North and Central Vanuatu, Northeast Vanuatu-Banks Islands, East Vanuatu. Dialects: NASAWA, TALISE, NAROVOROVO. Considerable dialect variation.

BAKI ***(BURUMBA, PAKI)*** [BKI] 200 (1981 Wurm and Hattori). West Epi. Austronesian, Malayo-Polynesian, Central-Eastern, Eastern Malayo-Polynesian, Oceanic, Central-Eastern Oceanic, Remote Oceanic, North and Central Vanuatu, Northeast Vanuatu-Banks Islands, Epi, Lamenu-Baki, Baki-Bierebo. Slight dialect variation. Many Bierebo use Baki as second language. Literacy rate in first language: Below 1%. Literacy rate in second language: 5% to 15%. Bible portions 1886-1987.

BIEREBO ***(BONKOVIA-YEVALI)*** [BNK] 450 (1983 SIL). West Epi, south of the Lamenu, north of the Baki. Austronesian, Malayo-Polynesian, Central-Eastern, Eastern Malayo-Polynesian, Oceanic, Central-Eastern Oceanic, Remote Oceanic, North and Central Vanuatu, Northeast Vanuatu-Banks Islands, Epi, Lamenu-Baki, Baki-Bierebo. Many speakers are bilingual in Baki. Investigation needed: intelligibility, bilingual proficiency in Baki.

BIERIA ***(BIERI, VOVO, WOWO)*** [BRJ] 170 including 100 in Vovo, 70 in Bieria (1981 Wurm and Hattori). South Epi, between the Maii and the Lewo. Austronesian, Malayo-Polynesian, Central-Eastern, Eastern Malayo-Polynesian, Oceanic, Central-Eastern Oceanic, Remote Oceanic, North and Central Vanuatu, Northeast Vanuatu-Banks Islands, Epi, Bieria-Maii. Dialects: BIERIA, VOVO (WOWO). Wurm and Hattori treat Bieria and Vovo as separate languages. Speakers may be bilingual in Baki. Investigation needed: bilingual proficiency in Baki. Literacy rate in first language: Below 1%. Literacy rate in second language: 5% to 15%. Bible portions 1898.

BISLAMA ***(BICHELAMAR)*** [BCY] The majority of the population of 128,000 understands and uses it as a lingua franca. There are some first language speakers. Population total both countries 1,200 or more. Also spoken in New Caledonia. Creole, English based, Pacific. Unlike Tok Pisin (Papua New Guinea) and Pijin (Solomon Islands) there are some French loan words. Partially intelligible with Pijin and Tok Pisin. Widely used in commerce, government, internal dealings. National language.

Dictionary. Grammar. Literacy rate in first language: 10% to 30%. Literacy rate in second language: 25% to 50%. Newspapers. Bible 1998.

BURMBAR ***(VARTAVO, BANAN BAY)*** [VRT] 525 (1983 SIL). Southeast Malekula. Austronesian, Malayo-Polynesian, Central-Eastern, Eastern Malayo-Polynesian, Oceanic, Central-Eastern Oceanic, Remote Oceanic, North and Central Vanuatu, Northeast Vanuatu-Banks Islands, Malekula Coastal. Some dialect differences.

BUTMAS-TUR ***(ATI)*** [BNR] 525 (1983 SIL). East central Santo. Austronesian, Malayo-Polynesian, Central-Eastern, Eastern Malayo-Polynesian, Oceanic, Central-Eastern Oceanic, Remote Oceanic, North and Central Vanuatu, East Santo, South.

DAKAKA ***(BAIAP, SOUTH AMBRYM)*** [BPA] 600 (1983 SIL). South Ambrym. Austronesian, Malayo-Polynesian, Central-Eastern, Eastern Malayo-Polynesian, Oceanic, Central-Eastern Oceanic, Remote Oceanic, North and Central Vanuatu, Northeast Vanuatu-Banks Islands, East Vanuatu. Dialect: SESIVI. Several dialects.

DIXON REEF [DIX] 50 (1982 SIL). Southwest Malekula. Austronesian, Malayo-Polynesian, Central-Eastern, Eastern Malayo-Polynesian, Oceanic, Central-Eastern Oceanic, Remote Oceanic, North and Central Vanuatu, Malekula Interior, Small Nambas.

EFATE, NORTH [LLP] 3,000 (1983 SIL). Northern Efate Island, Nguna, Tongoa, and several smaller islands, southeast Epi. Austronesian, Malayo-Polynesian, Central-Eastern, Eastern Malayo-Polynesian, Oceanic, Central-Eastern Oceanic, Remote Oceanic, North and Central Vanuatu, Northeast Vanuatu-Banks Islands, Central Vanuatu. Dialects: NGUNA (GUNA, TONGOA, NGUNESE), BUNINGA, SESAKE, EMAU, PAUNANGIS, LIVARA. SVO (for Nguna). Literacy rate in first language: 30% to 60%. Literacy rate in second language: 50% to 75%. Bible 1972.

EFATE, SOUTH ***(FATE, ERAKOR, SOUTHERN EFATE)*** [ERK] 3,750 (1983 SIL). Efate Island. Austronesian, Malayo-Polynesian, Central-Eastern, Eastern Malayo-Polynesian, Oceanic, Central-Eastern Oceanic, Remote Oceanic, North and Central Vanuatu, Northeast Vanuatu-Banks Islands, Central Vanuatu. Literacy rate in first language: 10% to 30%. Literacy rate in second language: 50% to 75%. NT 1889-1930.

EMAE ***(EMWAE, MAE, MWAE, EMAI, MAI)*** [MMW] 200 (1981 Wurm and Hattori). Emae; Three Hills Island, Sesake Island, two villages. Austronesian, Malayo-Polynesian, Central-Eastern, Eastern Malayo-Polynesian, Oceanic, Central-Eastern Oceanic, Remote Oceanic, Central Pacific, East Fijian-Polynesian, Polynesian, Nuclear, Samoic-Outlier, Futunic. No dialect variation. Speakers use North Efate (Tongoan) as second language. Investigation needed: bilingual proficiency in Tongoan. SVO. Literacy rate in first language: Below 1%. Literacy rate in second language: 50% to 75%.

ENGLISH [ENG] 1,900 in Vanuatu (1995), 1.1% of the population. Indo-European, Germanic, West, English. First language speakers are from the United Kingdom. National language. Bible 1535-1989. See main entry under United Kingdom.

ETON ***(EPWAU, EASTERN EFATE)*** [ETN] 500 (1989 census). Southeastern Efate Island at Eton, Pang Pang, and surrounding villages. Austronesian, Malayo-Polynesian, Central-Eastern, Eastern Malayo-Polynesian, Oceanic, Central-Eastern Oceanic, Remote Oceanic, North and Central Vanuatu, Northeast Vanuatu-Banks Islands, Central Vanuatu. Dialects: ETON, PANG PANG. Formerly thought to be a dialect of South Efate. 88% inherent intelligibility with Lelepa, 64% with South Efate. Bilingualism in Bislama, English, French, South Efate, Lelepa, North Efate. All ages. Pang Pang dialect is nearly extinct.

FORTSENAL [FRT] 150 (1983 SIL). Central Santo. Austronesian, Malayo-Polynesian, Central-Eastern, Eastern Malayo-Polynesian, Oceanic, Central-Eastern Oceanic, Remote Oceanic, North and Central Vanuatu, Northeast Vanuatu-Banks Islands, West Santo. Closely related to Akei.

FRENCH [FRN] 6,300 in Vanuatu (1995), 3.8% of the population. Indo-European, Italic, Romance, Italo-Western, Western, Gallo-Iberian, Gallo-Romance, Gallo-Rhaetian, Oïl, French. National language. Bible 1530-1986. See main entry under France.

FUTUNA-ANIWA ***(WEST FUTUNA-ANIWA, ERRONAN)*** [FUT] 600 (1981 Wurm and Hattori). (West) Futuna and Aniwa Islands, east of Tanna. Austronesian, Malayo-Polynesian, Central-Eastern, Eastern Malayo-Polynesian, Oceanic, Central-Eastern Oceanic, Remote Oceanic, Central Pacific, East Fijian-Polynesian, Polynesian, Nuclear, Samoic-Outlier, Futunic. Dialects: WEST FUTUNA (FOTUNA), ANIWA (ANEWA). There are significant differences between the West Futunan and Aniwan dialects. Distinct from (East) Futuna on Futuna Island in French Territory of Wallis and Futuna. SVO, VS. Literacy rate in first language: 30% to 60%. Literacy rate in second language: 50% to 75%. Fishermen; agriculturalists: taro, yam, sweet potato, coconut, fig, breadfruit, banana, native cabbage, sugar cane, chestnut, arrowroot; livestock: pigs, poultry. NT 1898.

HANO ***(RAGA, LAMALANGA, NORTH RAGA, VUNMARAMA, QATVENUA, BWATVENUA)*** [LML] 7,000 (1991 UBS). North Pentecost (Raga, Whitsuntide Island) and southern Maewo (Aurora) Island. Austronesian, Malayo-Polynesian, Central-Eastern, Eastern Malayo-Polynesian, Oceanic,

Central-Eastern Oceanic, Remote Oceanic, North and Central Vanuatu, Northeast Vanuatu-Banks Islands, East Vanuatu. Slight dialect differences. 'Hano' is the name preferred locally. Trade language. Bible portions 1908-1989.

HIW ***(TORRES, TORRES ISLAND)*** [HIW] 120 (1983 SIL). Torres Islands. Austronesian, Malayo-Polynesian, Central-Eastern, Eastern Malayo-Polynesian, Oceanic, Central-Eastern Oceanic, Remote Oceanic, North and Central Vanuatu, Northeast Vanuatu-Banks Islands, East Vanuatu. Bible portions 1894-1900.

IFO ***(UTAHA)*** [IFF] Erromanga Island, southern Vanuatu. Austronesian, Malayo-Polynesian, Central-Eastern, Eastern Malayo-Polynesian, Oceanic, Central-Eastern Oceanic, South Vanuatu, Erromanga. The last speaker died in 1954. Extinct.

KATBOL ***(TEMBIMBE-KATBOL, TAREMP, TISVEL)*** [TMB] 450 (1983 SIL). Central Malekula. Austronesian, Malayo-Polynesian, Central-Eastern, Eastern Malayo-Polynesian, Oceanic, Central-Eastern Oceanic, Remote Oceanic, North and Central Vanuatu, Malekula Interior, Malekula Central.

KORO [KRF] 105 (1983 SIL). Gaua Island of the Banks Islands, villages of Koro and Mekeon. Austronesian, Malayo-Polynesian, Central-Eastern, Eastern Malayo-Polynesian, Oceanic, Central-Eastern Oceanic, Remote Oceanic, North and Central Vanuatu, Northeast Vanuatu-Banks Islands, East Vanuatu.

KWAMERA [TNK] 2,500 (1989 SIL). Southeast Tanna. Austronesian, Malayo-Polynesian, Central-Eastern, Eastern Malayo-Polynesian, Oceanic, Central-Eastern Oceanic, South Vanuatu, Tanna. 2 main dialects. NT 1890.

LABO ***(MEWUN, MEAUN, NIDE)*** [MWI] 350 (1981 Wurm and Hattori). Southwest Bay, Malekula. Austronesian, Malayo-Polynesian, Central-Eastern, Eastern Malayo-Polynesian, Oceanic, Central-Eastern Oceanic, Remote Oceanic, North and Central Vanuatu, Malekula Interior, Labo. Hunters; fishermen; agriculturalists: yam. Traditional religion. Bible portions 1905.

LAKONA ***(LAKON, GAUA, GOG)*** [LKN] 300 (1983 SIL). Gaua Island, Banks Group. Austronesian, Malayo-Polynesian, Central-Eastern, Eastern Malayo-Polynesian, Oceanic, Central-Eastern Oceanic, Remote Oceanic, North and Central Vanuatu, Northeast Vanuatu-Banks Islands, East Vanuatu. English is used by the teachers and in classes only. Outside communications and business are in Bislama. Church services are in Lakona or Bislama, not English. Some monolinguals. Two primary schools.

LAMENU ***(LEWO, VARMALI)*** [LMU] 750 (1986 SIL). Lamenu Island and the northern tip of Epi Island, Varmali region. Austronesian, Malayo-Polynesian, Central-Eastern, Eastern Malayo-Polynesian, Oceanic, Central-Eastern Oceanic, Remote Oceanic, North and Central Vanuatu, Northeast Vanuatu-Banks Islands, Epi, Lamenu-Baki, Lamenu-Lewo. Literacy rate in first language: Below 1%. Literacy rate in second language: 15% to 25%. Bible portions 1987.

LAREVAT ***(LARAVAT)*** [LRV] 150 (1983 SIL). Central Malekula. Austronesian, Malayo-Polynesian, Central-Eastern, Eastern Malayo-Polynesian, Oceanic, Central-Eastern Oceanic, Remote Oceanic, North and Central Vanuatu, Malekula Interior, Malekula Central.

LEHALI ***(TEQEL, TEKEL)*** [TQL] 150 (1983 SIL). Ureparapara Island, Banks Group. Austronesian, Malayo-Polynesian, Central-Eastern, Eastern Malayo-Polynesian, Oceanic, Central-Eastern Oceanic, Remote Oceanic, North and Central Vanuatu, Northeast Vanuatu-Banks Islands, East Vanuatu. Close to Lehalurup.

LEHALURUP ***(UREPARAPARA, EAST UREPARAPARA)*** [URR] 90 (1983 SIL). Ureparapara Island, Banks Group. Austronesian, Malayo-Polynesian, Central-Eastern, Eastern Malayo-Polynesian, Oceanic, Central-Eastern Oceanic, Remote Oceanic, North and Central Vanuatu, Northeast Vanuatu- Banks Islands, East Vanuatu. Close to Lehali.

LELEPA ***(HAVANNAH HARBOUR)*** [LPA] 400 or more (1989 census). Lelepa Island, and Mangaliliu and Napkoa on western Efate Island. Austronesian, Malayo-Polynesian, Central-Eastern, Eastern Malayo-Polynesian, Oceanic, Central-Eastern Oceanic, Remote Oceanic, North and Central Vanuatu, Northeast Vanuatu-Banks Islands, Central Vanuatu. Formerly thought to be a dialect of North Efate. Also related to South Efate. 84% inherent intelligibility with Eton, 88% with South Efate. Bilingualism in Some in Bislama, South Efate, North Efate, English, French. All ages. SVO. Bible portions 1877-1883.

LENAKEL [TNL] 6,500 (1988 SIL). West central Tanna. Austronesian, Malayo-Polynesian, Central-Eastern, Eastern Malayo-Polynesian, Oceanic, Central-Eastern Oceanic, South Vanuatu, Tanna. Dialects: LOANATIT, NERAUYA, ITONGA, IKYOO. Complex dialect chain; up to 10 dialects (Wurm and Hattori). SVO. Bible portions 1900-1902.

LETEMBOI ***(SMALL NAMBAS)*** [NMS] 305 (1983 SIL). South Malekula. Austronesian, Malayo-Polynesian, Central-Eastern, Eastern Malayo-Polynesian, Oceanic, Central-Eastern Oceanic, Remote Oceanic, North and Central Vanuatu, Malekula Interior, Small Nambas.

LEWO ***(VARSU)*** [LWW] 750 (1986 SIL). East Epi Island, Varsu and Varmali regions. Austronesian, Malayo-Polynesian, Central-Eastern, Eastern Malayo-Polynesian, Oceanic, Central-Eastern Oceanic, Remote Oceanic, North and Central Vanuatu, Northeast Vanuatu-Banks Islands, Epi, Lamenu-Baki, Lamenu-Lewo. Dialects: TASIKO, MATE-NUL-FILAKARA. Literacy rate in first language: Below 1%. Literacy rate in second language: 5% to 15%. Bible portions 1892-1990.

LINGARAK ***(BUSHMAN'S BAY)*** [LGK] 210 (1983 SIL). Malekula. Austronesian, Malayo-Polynesian, Central-Eastern, Eastern Malayo-Polynesian, Oceanic, Central-Eastern Oceanic, Remote Oceanic, North and Central Vanuatu, Malekula Interior, Malekula Central.

LITZLITZ ***(LITZLITZ-VISELE)*** [LTZ] 330 (1983 SIL). Malekula. Austronesian, Malayo-Polynesian, Central-Eastern, Eastern Malayo-Polynesian, Oceanic, Central-Eastern Oceanic, Remote Oceanic, North and Central Vanuatu, Malekula Interior, Malekula Central.

LONWOLWOL ***(CRAIG COVE, FALI, FANTING)*** [CRC] 600 (1983 SIL). West Ambrym Island and several hundred in Maat village on Efate Island. Austronesian, Malayo-Polynesian, Central-Eastern, Eastern Malayo-Polynesian, Oceanic, Central-Eastern Oceanic, Remote Oceanic, North and Central Vanuatu, Northeast Vanuatu-Banks Islands, East Vanuatu. 2 main dialects. Bible portions 1899-1949.

LOREDIAKARKAR [LNN] 50 (1972). Central east coast, Santo Island. Austronesian, Malayo-Polynesian, Central-Eastern, Eastern Malayo-Polynesian, Oceanic, Central-Eastern Oceanic, Remote Oceanic, North and Central Vanuatu, East Santo, South. Closely related to the Shark Bay language.

MAE [MME] 750 including North Small Nambas (1983 SIL). Malekula. Austronesian, Malayo-Polynesian, Central-Eastern, Eastern Malayo-Polynesian, Oceanic, Central-Eastern Oceanic, Remote Oceanic, North and Central Vanuatu, Northeast Vanuatu-Banks Islands, Malekula Coastal. Dialect: NORTH SMALL NAMBAS.

MAEWO, CENTRAL ***(MAEVO, TANORIKI)*** [MWO] 350 (1981 Wurm and Hattori). Maewo (Aurora) Island. Austronesian, Malayo-Polynesian, Central-Eastern, Eastern Malayo-Polynesian, Oceanic, Central-Eastern Oceanic, Remote Oceanic, North and Central Vanuatu, Northeast Vanuatu-Banks Islands, East Vanuatu. Dialects: LOTORA, TANORIKI, PETERARA. Dialects or closely related dying languages: Arata, Bangoro. Bible portions 1906.

MAFEA ***(MAVEA)*** [MKV] 50 (1981 Wurm and Hattori). East Santo, Mafea Island. Austronesian, Malayo-Polynesian, Central-Eastern, Eastern Malayo-Polynesian, Oceanic, Central-Eastern Oceanic, Remote Oceanic, North and Central Vanuatu, Northeast Vanuatu-Banks Islands, West Santo.

MAII ***(MAE-MORAE, MAFILAU)*** [MMM] 100 (1981 Wurm and Hattori). Mafilau village, southwest Epi, north of the Bieria, south of the Baki. Austronesian, Malayo-Polynesian, Central-Eastern, Eastern Malayo-Polynesian, Oceanic, Central-Eastern Oceanic, Remote Oceanic, North and Central Vanuatu, Northeast Vanuatu-Banks Islands, Epi, Bieria-Maii. No dialect variation. Literacy rate in first language: Below 1%. Literacy rate in second language: 5% to 15%.

MALFAXAL ***(MALVAXAL-TOMAN ISLAND, TAMAN, TOMMAN)*** [MLX] 600 (1983 SIL). South Malekula. Austronesian, Malayo-Polynesian, Central-Eastern, Eastern Malayo-Polynesian, Oceanic, Central-Eastern Oceanic, Remote Oceanic, North and Central Vanuatu, Northeast Vanuatu-Banks Islands, Malekula Coastal. Dialect: ORIERH (NA'AHAI). Bible portions 1919.

MALO [MLA] 1,500 (1981 Wurm and Hattori). Malo Island, three adjacent small islands and south Tangoa. Austronesian, Malayo-Polynesian, Central-Eastern, Eastern Malayo-Polynesian, Oceanic, Central-Eastern Oceanic, Remote Oceanic, North and Central Vanuatu, Northeast Vanuatu-Banks Islands, West Santo. Dialects: AVUNATARI (NORTH MALO), ATARIPOE (SOUTH MALO). Closely related to Aore and Tutuba. Southern dialect reported to be extinct. Dictionary. NT 1954.

MALUA BAY ***(ESPIEGLE BAY, MIDDLE NAMBAS)*** [MLL] 300 (1983 SIL). Northwest coast of Malekula. Austronesian, Malayo-Polynesian, Central-Eastern, Eastern Malayo-Polynesian, Oceanic, Central-Eastern Oceanic, Remote Oceanic, North and Central Vanuatu, Northeast Vanuatu-Banks Islands, Malekula Coastal. Several dialects.

MARAGUS ***(MARAGAUS)*** [MRS] 10 (1971 Tryon). Central north Malekula. Austronesian, Malayo-Polynesian, Central-Eastern, Eastern Malayo-Polynesian, Oceanic, Central-Eastern Oceanic, Remote Oceanic, North and Central Vanuatu, Malekula Interior, Malekula Central. Nearly extinct.

MARINO ***(NAONE, NORTH MAEWO)*** [MRB] 180 (1983 SIL). North Maewo. Austronesian, Malayo-Polynesian, Central-Eastern, Eastern Malayo-Polynesian, Oceanic, Central-Eastern Oceanic, Remote Oceanic, North and Central Vanuatu, Northeast Vanuatu-Banks Islands, East Vanuatu.

MASKELYNES ***(KULIVIU, MASKELYNE ISLANDS)*** [KLV] 1,200 (1990 UBS). South Malekula, Maskelyne Islets. Austronesian, Malayo-Polynesian, Central-Eastern, Eastern Malayo-Polynesian, Oceanic, Central-Eastern Oceanic, Remote Oceanic, North and Central Vanuatu, Northeast Vanuatu-Banks Islands, Malekula Coastal. Some dialect differences. Bible portions 1906.

MELE-FILA ***(FILA-MELE)*** [MXE] 2,000 (1980 UBS). Over 1,000 in Mele village on Efate, 500 on Fila Island (1977 Voegelin and Voegelin). Fila Island in Vila Harbor, Mele village on South Efate. Austronesian, Malayo-Polynesian, Central-Eastern, Eastern Malayo-Polynesian, Oceanic, Central- Eastern Oceanic, Remote Oceanic, Central Pacific, East Fijian-Polynesian, Polynesian, Nuclear, Samoic-Outlier, Futunic. Dialects: FILA (EFIRA, FIRA, IFIRA), MELE. There are significant differences between the Mele and Fila dialects. Bilingualism in South Efate. Investigation needed: intelligibility with Fila. SVO. Literacy rate in first language: 5% to 10%. Literacy rate in second language: 75% to 100%. NT 1993.

MEREI ***(LAMETIN)*** [LMB] 400 (1997 J. Chung). Central Santo, north of Morouas, between the Lape and Ora rivers. Austronesian, Malayo-Polynesian, Central-Eastern, Eastern Malayo-Polynesian, Oceanic, Central-Eastern Oceanic, Remote Oceanic, North and Central Vanuatu, Northeast Vanuatu-Banks Islands, West Santo. Dialect: WINIV. Men and school children are able to speak Bislama. 'Merei' is the name used by speakers. Investigation needed: intelligibility with Tiale. Valley, highland. Christian.

MERLAV ***(MERELAVA, MERLAV-MERIG)*** [MRM] 1,350 including 1,200 Merlav, 150 Merig. Mere Lava Island and Merig Island, Banks Group. Austronesian, Malayo-Polynesian, Central-Eastern, Eastern Malayo-Polynesian, Oceanic, Central-Eastern Oceanic, Remote Oceanic, North and Central Vanuatu, Northeast Vanuatu-Banks Islands, East Vanuatu. Dialects: MWERIG (MERIG), WEST MWERELAWA, MATLIWAG.

MOROUAS ***(MORUAS)*** [MRP] 150 (1983 SIL). Central Santo. Austronesian, Malayo-Polynesian, Central-Eastern, Eastern Malayo-Polynesian, Oceanic, Central-Eastern Oceanic, Remote Oceanic, North and Central Vanuatu, Northeast Vanuatu-Banks Islands, West Santo. Several dialects. Possibly a dialect chain with Amblong and Narango. Investigation needed: intelligibility with Amblong, Narango.

MOSINA ***(MOSIN)*** [MSN] 400 (1981 Wurm and Hattori). Vanua Lava, Banks Group. Austronesian, Malayo-Polynesian, Central-Eastern, Eastern Malayo-Polynesian, Oceanic, Central-Eastern Oceanic, Remote Oceanic, North and Central Vanuatu, Northeast Vanuatu-Banks Islands, East Vanuatu. Dialects: VETUMBOSO, VURES (VURAS, VUREAS, AVREAS). Mosina and Vures have 88% lexical similarity. Vures dialect increasingly vigorous.

MOTA [MTT] 450 (1983 SIL). Mota (Sugarloaf) Island, Banks Group. Austronesian, Malayo-Polynesian, Central-Eastern, Eastern Malayo-Polynesian, Oceanic, Central-Eastern Oceanic, Remote Oceanic, North and Central Vanuatu, Northeast Vanuatu-Banks Islands, East Vanuatu. Formerly a lingua franca. Dictionary. Literacy rate in first language: 30% to 60%. Literacy rate in second language: 75% to 100%. Bible 1912.

MOTLAV ***(MOTALAVA)*** [MLV] 1,275 (1983 SIL). Mota Lava (Saddle) Island, Banks Group. Austronesian, Malayo-Polynesian, Central-Eastern, Eastern Malayo-Polynesian, Oceanic, Central-Eastern Oceanic, Remote Oceanic, North and Central Vanuatu, Northeast Vanuatu-Banks Islands, East Vanuatu. Dialect: VOLOW (VALUVA, VALUWA, VALUGA).

MPOTOVORO [MVT] 180 (1983 SIL). North tip of Malekula. Austronesian, Malayo-Polynesian, Central-Eastern, Eastern Malayo-Polynesian, Oceanic, Central-Eastern Oceanic, Remote Oceanic, North and Central Vanuatu, Northeast Vanuatu-Banks Islands, Malekula Coastal.

NAMAKURA ***(MAKURA)*** [NMK] 2,850 (1983 SIL). North Efate, Tongoa, Tongariki. Austronesian, Malayo-Polynesian, Central-Eastern, Eastern Malayo-Polynesian, Oceanic, Central-Eastern Oceanic, Remote Oceanic, North and Central Vanuatu, Northeast Vanuatu-Banks Islands, Central Vanuatu. Dialects: TONGOA ISLAND, TONGARIKI ISLAND, BUNINGA, MAKURA (EMWAE ISLAND), MATASO. Literacy rate in first language: Below 1%. Literacy rate in second language: 25% to 50%.

NAMBAS, BIG [NMB] 1,800 (1983 SIL). Northwest Malekula. Austronesian, Malayo-Polynesian, Central-Eastern, Eastern Malayo-Polynesian, Oceanic, Central-Eastern Oceanic, Remote Oceanic, North and Central Vanuatu, Malekula Interior, Malekula Central. Literacy rate in first language: Below 1%. Literacy rate in second language: 5% to 15%. NT 1986.

NARANGO [NRG] 160 (1981 Wurm and Hattori). South Santo Island. Austronesian, Malayo-Polynesian, Central-Eastern, Eastern Malayo-Polynesian, Oceanic, Central-Eastern Oceanic, Remote Oceanic, North and Central Vanuatu, Northeast Vanuatu-Banks Islands, West Santo. Several dialects. Closely related to Amblong and Morouas. Investigation needed: intelligibility with Amblong, Morouas.

NASARIAN [NVH] 20 (1983 SIL). Southwest coast of Malekula. Austronesian, Malayo-Polynesian, Central-Eastern, Eastern Malayo-Polynesian, Oceanic, Central-Eastern Oceanic, Remote Oceanic, North and Central Vanuatu, Malekula Interior, Malekula Central. Nearly extinct.

NAVUT [NSW] 525 (1983 SIL). West central Santo. Austronesian, Malayo-Polynesian, Central-Eastern, Eastern Malayo-Polynesian, Oceanic, Central-Eastern Oceanic, Remote Oceanic, North and Central Vanuatu, Northeast Vanuatu-Banks Islands, West Santo. Closely related to Malmariv. Investigation needed: intelligibility with Malmariv.

NOKUKU ***(NOGUGU)*** [NKK] 160 (1981 Wurm and Hattori). Northwest Santo. Austronesian, Malayo-Polynesian, Central-Eastern, Eastern Malayo-Polynesian, Oceanic, Central-Eastern Oceanic, Remote Oceanic, North and Central Vanuatu, Northeast Vanuatu-Banks Islands, West Santo. Bible portions 1901-1918.

NUME ***(TARASAG, GAUA)*** [TGS] 450 (1983 SIL). Gaua Island. Austronesian, Malayo-Polynesian, Central-Eastern, Eastern Malayo-Polynesian, Oceanic, Central-Eastern Oceanic, Remote Oceanic, North and Central Vanuatu, Northeast Vanuatu-Banks Islands, East Vanuatu. Distinct from Numee of New Caledonia. Literacy rate in first language: 1% to 5%. Literacy rate in second language: 50% to 75%.

PAAMA ***(PAAMA-LOPEVI, PAUMA, PAAMESE)*** [PMA] 6,000 (1996 SIL). Paama, one village on east Epi (Lopevi), a large group in Vila. Austronesian, Malayo-Polynesian, Central-Eastern, Eastern

Malayo-Polynesian, Oceanic, Central-Eastern Oceanic, Remote Oceanic, North and Central Vanuatu, Northeast Vanuatu-Banks Islands, East Vanuatu. Dialects: NORTH PAAMA, SOUTH PAAMA. Close to Southeast Ambrym linguistically. Dictionary. Grammar. Literacy rate in first language: 5% to 10%. Literacy rate in second language: 75% to 100%. NT 1944.

PIAMATSINA [PTR] 150 (1981 Wurm and Hattori). Northwest Santo Island. Austronesian, Malayo-Polynesian, Central-Eastern, Eastern Malayo-Polynesian, Oceanic, Central-Eastern Oceanic, Remote Oceanic, North and Central Vanuatu, Northeast Vanuatu-Banks Islands, West Santo. Close to Vunapu.

POLONOMBAUK [PLB] 225 (1983 SIL). Southeast Santo Island. Austronesian, Malayo-Polynesian, Central-Eastern, Eastern Malayo-Polynesian, Oceanic, Central-Eastern Oceanic, Remote Oceanic, North and Central Vanuatu, East Santo, South.

PORT SANDWICH [PSW] 750 (1983 SIL). Southeast Malekula Island. Austronesian, Malayo-Polynesian, Central-Eastern, Eastern Malayo-Polynesian, Oceanic, Central-Eastern Oceanic, Remote Oceanic, North and Central Vanuatu, Northeast Vanuatu-Banks Islands, Malekula Coastal. Several dialects.

PORT VATO [PTV] 750 (1983 SIL). Southwest Ambrym Island. Austronesian, Malayo-Polynesian, Central-Eastern, Eastern Malayo-Polynesian, Oceanic, Central-Eastern Oceanic, Remote Oceanic, North and Central Vanuatu, Northeast Vanuatu-Banks Islands, East Vanuatu. Bible portions 1899.

REPANBITIP [RPN] 90 (1983 SIL). East Malekula Island. Austronesian, Malayo-Polynesian, Central-Eastern, Eastern Malayo-Polynesian, Oceanic, Central-Eastern Oceanic, Remote Oceanic, North and Central Vanuatu, Malekula Interior, Small Nambas.

REREP ***(PANGKUMU, PANGKUMU BAY)*** [PGK] 375 (1983 SIL). East Malekula Island. Austronesian, Malayo-Polynesian, Central-Eastern, Eastern Malayo-Polynesian, Oceanic, Central-Eastern Oceanic, Remote Oceanic, North and Central Vanuatu, Northeast Vanuatu-Banks Islands, Malekula Coastal. Dialect: TISMAN. Bible portions 1892-1913.

RORIA [RGA] 150 (1983 SIL). Central Santo Island. Austronesian, Malayo-Polynesian, Central-Eastern, Eastern Malayo-Polynesian, Oceanic, Central-Eastern Oceanic, Remote Oceanic, North and Central Vanuatu, Northeast Vanuatu-Banks Islands, West Santo. Some dialect differences.

SA [SSA] 1,800 (1983 SIL). South Raga Island. Austronesian, Malayo-Polynesian, Central-Eastern, Eastern Malayo-Polynesian, Oceanic, Central-Eastern Oceanic, Remote Oceanic, North and Central Vanuatu, Northeast Vanuatu-Banks Islands, East Vanuatu. Dialects: PONORWAL (SOUTH RAGA), LOLATAVOLA, NINEBULO.

SAKAO ***(HOG HARBOUR, SANTO, SAKAU)*** [SKU] 1,500 (1983 SIL). Northeast Santo Island. Austronesian, Malayo-Polynesian, Central-Eastern, Eastern Malayo-Polynesian, Oceanic, Central-Eastern Oceanic, Remote Oceanic, North and Central Vanuatu, East Santo, North. Dialect: LIVARA (LIARA). Livara is extinct. More divergent linguistically with some Polynesian characteristics. Agriculturalists: yam, sweet potato, sugar cane, banana, coconut, breadfruit; fishermen; pig raisers. Bible portions 1905-1949.

SEKE [SKE] 300 (1983 SIL). Central Raga Island. Austronesian, Malayo-Polynesian, Central-Eastern, Eastern Malayo-Polynesian, Oceanic, Central-Eastern Oceanic, Remote Oceanic, North and Central Vanuatu, Northeast Vanuatu-Banks Islands, East Vanuatu.

SHARK BAY [SSV] 225 (1983 SIL). East Santo on Litaro (Pilot) Island and also on the coast at Shark Bay. Austronesian, Malayo-Polynesian, Central-Eastern, Eastern Malayo-Polynesian, Oceanic, Central-Eastern Oceanic, Remote Oceanic, North and Central Vanuatu, East Santo, South. Closely related to Lorediakarkar. Investigation needed: intelligibility with Lorediakarkar.

SIE ***(EROMANGA, ERROMANGA, ERRAMANGA)*** [ERG] 1,200 to 1,300 (1998 T. Crowley). Erromanga Island, southern Vanuatu. Austronesian, Malayo-Polynesian, Central-Eastern, Eastern Malayo-Polynesian, Oceanic, Central-Eastern Oceanic, South Vanuatu, Erromanga. Dialects: YOKU (ENYAU), POTNARIVEN, SIE (SORUNG). NT 1909.

SOUTH WEST BAY ***(SINESIP, SENIANG, NAAHAI)*** [SNS] 250 (1981 Wurm and Hattori). Southwest Malekula Island. Austronesian, Malayo-Polynesian, Central-Eastern, Eastern Malayo-Polynesian, Oceanic, Central-Eastern Oceanic, Remote Oceanic, North and Central Vanuatu, Northeast Vanuatu-Banks Islands, Malekula Coastal. Hunters; fishermen; agriculturalists: yam. Bible portions 1905.

SOWA [SWW] 20 (1971 Tryon). Central Raga Island. Austronesian, Malayo-Polynesian, Central-Eastern, Eastern Malayo-Polynesian, Oceanic, Central-Eastern Oceanic, Remote Oceanic, North and Central Vanuatu, Northeast Vanuatu-Banks Islands, East Vanuatu. Nearly extinct.

TAMBOTALO [TLS] 50 (1981 Wurm and Hattori). Southeast Santo, Tambotalo village. Austronesian, Malayo-Polynesian, Central-Eastern, Eastern Malayo-Polynesian, Oceanic, Central-Eastern Oceanic, Remote Oceanic, North and Central Vanuatu, Northeast Vanuatu-Banks Islands, West Santo.

TANGOA ***(SANTO)*** [TGP] 375 (1983 SIL). Tangoa Island, off south Santo. Austronesian, Malayo-Polynesian, Central-Eastern, Eastern Malayo-Polynesian, Oceanic, Central-Eastern Oceanic, Remote Oceanic, North and Central Vanuatu, Northeast Vanuatu-Banks Islands, West Santo. Distinct from Tongoa (Namakura and North Efate languages). Literacy rate in first language: 30% to 60%. Literacy rate in second language: 50% to 75%. Bible portions 1892-1923.

TANNA, NORTH [TNN] 2,000 (1988 SIL). North Tanna. Austronesian, Malayo-Polynesian, Central-Eastern, Eastern Malayo-Polynesian, Oceanic, Central-Eastern Oceanic, South Vanuatu, Tanna. Dialects: EAST TANNA, WEST TANNA, IMAFIN. Two major dialects. There is a dialect chain. Closely related to Whitesands. Bislama is used as second language, but many women and some men do not understand it. SVO. Literacy rate in first language: Below 1%. Literacy rate in second language: 5% to 15%. Agriculturalists: coconut; copra production. Bible portions 1990-1999.

TANNA, SOUTHWEST [NWI] 2,250 (1983 SIL). Southwest Tanna Island. Austronesian, Malayo-Polynesian, Central-Eastern, Eastern Malayo-Polynesian, Oceanic, Central-Eastern Oceanic, South Vanuatu, Tanna. Dialects: NOWAI, NVHAL. A complex dialect chain (Wurm and Hattori). Agriculturalists: coconut; copra production.

TASMATE [TMT] 150 (1983 SIL). West Santo Island. Austronesian, Malayo-Polynesian, Central- Eastern, Eastern Malayo-Polynesian, Oceanic, Central-Eastern Oceanic, Remote Oceanic, North and Central Vanuatu, Northeast Vanuatu-Banks Islands, West Santo. Some dialect differences.

TIALE ***(MALMARIV)*** [MNL] 150 (1983 SIL), or probably much bigger (1997 J. Stahl). North central Santo. Austronesian, Malayo-Polynesian, Central-Eastern, Eastern Malayo-Polynesian, Oceanic, Central-Eastern Oceanic, Remote Oceanic, North and Central Vanuatu, Northeast Vanuatu-Banks Islands, West Santo. Closely related to Navut. Does not appear to be endangered (J. Stahl 1997). Investigation needed: intelligibility with Navut, Merei.

TOGA ***(LO, LOH-TOGA, TORRES)*** [LHT] 315 (1983 SIL). Torres Islands. Austronesian, Malayo-Polynesian, Central-Eastern, Eastern Malayo-Polynesian, Oceanic, Central-Eastern Oceanic, Remote Oceanic, North and Central Vanuatu, Northeast Vanuatu-Banks Islands, East Vanuatu. Bible portions 1900.

TOLOMAKO ***(TOLOMAKO-JEREVIU, BIG BAY, MARINA)*** [TLM] 450 (1983 SIL). Big Bay, Santo Island. Austronesian, Malayo-Polynesian, Central-Eastern, Eastern Malayo-Polynesian, Oceanic, Central-Eastern Oceanic, Remote Oceanic, North and Central Vanuatu, Northeast Vanuatu-Banks Islands, West Santo. Slight dialect differences. Bible portions 1904-1909.

TUTUBA [TMI] 150 (1983 SIL). Tutuba Island, south Santo. Austronesian, Malayo-Polynesian, Central-Eastern, Eastern Malayo-Polynesian, Oceanic, Central-Eastern Oceanic, Remote Oceanic, North and Central Vanuatu, Northeast Vanuatu-Banks Islands, West Santo. Close to Aore and Malo. Investigation needed: intelligibility with Malo.

UNUA ***(ONUA)*** [ONU] 525 including 50 in Bush Unua. East Malekula Island. Austronesian, Malayo-Polynesian, Central-Eastern, Eastern Malayo-Polynesian, Oceanic, Central-Eastern Oceanic, Remote Oceanic, North and Central Vanuatu, Northeast Vanuatu-Banks Islands, Malekula Coastal. Dialect: BUSH UNUA. Several dialects. Bible portions 1892-1913.

URA [UUR] 6 (1998 T. Crowley). North Erromanga Island, southern Vanuatu. Austronesian, Malayo-Polynesian, Central-Eastern, Eastern Malayo-Polynesian, Oceanic, Central-Eastern Oceanic, South Vanuatu, Erromanga. All speakers are elderly. Dictionary. Grammar. Nearly extinct.

URIPIV-WALA-RANO-ATCHIN [UPV] 6,000 (1988 SIL). Northeast Malekula and nearby islands. Austronesian, Malayo-Polynesian, Central-Eastern, Eastern Malayo-Polynesian, Oceanic, Central-Eastern Oceanic, Remote Oceanic, North and Central Vanuatu, Northeast Vanuatu-Banks Islands, Malekula Coastal. Dialects: URIPIV, WALA-RANO, ATCHIN (NALE). Dialect chain from Uripiv in the south to Atchin in the north. 85% lexical similarity at the extremes of the dialect chain. Literacy rate in first language: 10% to 30%. Literacy rate in second language: 25% to 50%. Bible portions 1893-1989.

VALPEI ***(VALPEI-HUKUA, VALPAY)*** [VLP] 300 (1983 SIL). Northwest Santo Island. Austronesian, Malayo-Polynesian, Central-Eastern, Eastern Malayo-Polynesian, Oceanic, Central-Eastern Oceanic, Remote Oceanic, North and Central Vanuatu, Northeast Vanuatu-Banks Islands, West Santo.

VAO [VAO] 1,350 (1983 SIL). Vao Island, north Malekula. Austronesian, Malayo-Polynesian, Central-Eastern, Eastern Malayo-Polynesian, Oceanic, Central-Eastern Oceanic, Remote Oceanic, North and Central Vanuatu, Northeast Vanuatu-Banks Islands, Malekula Coastal. Agriculturalists: yam, banana, taro, pineapple, cabbage, coconut, breadfruit; fishermen; pig raisers.

VATRATA ***(VANUA LAVA)*** [VLR] 600 (1983 SIL). Vanua Lava Island. Austronesian, Malayo-Polynesian, Central-Eastern, Eastern Malayo-Polynesian, Oceanic, Central-Eastern Oceanic, Remote Oceanic, North and Central Vanuatu, Northeast Vanuatu-Banks Islands, East Vanuatu. Dialects: LEON, PAK (BEK), SASAR (LEM). Leon, Sasar, and Pak dialects are extinct.

VINMAVIS ***(LAMBUMBU)*** [VNM] 210 (1983 SIL). Central west Malekula Island. Austronesian, Malayo-Polynesian, Central-Eastern, Eastern Malayo-Polynesian, Oceanic, Central-Eastern Oceanic, Remote Oceanic, North and Central Vanuatu, Malekula Interior, Malekula Central. Dialect: WINIV.

VUNAPU [VNP] 375 (1983 SIL). Northwest Santo Island. Austronesian, Malayo-Polynesian, Central-Eastern, Eastern Malayo-Polynesian, Oceanic, Central-Eastern Oceanic, Remote Oceanic, North and Central Vanuatu, Northeast Vanuatu-Banks Islands, West Santo. Close to Piamatsina. Investigation needed: intelligibility with Piamatsina.

WAILAPA [WLR] 100 (1981 Wurm and Hattori). Southwest Santo Island. Austronesian, Malayo-Polynesian, Central-Eastern, Eastern Malayo-Polynesian, Oceanic, Central-Eastern Oceanic, Remote Oceanic, North and Central Vanuatu, Northeast Vanuatu-Banks Islands, West Santo. A dialect chain with Akei and Penantsiro at the extremes; they are not inherently intelligible.

WETAMUT [WWO] 70 (1972). Gaua Island of the Banks Group, villages of Dorig and Kweteon. Austronesian, Malayo-Polynesian, Central-Eastern, Eastern Malayo-Polynesian, Oceanic, Central-Eastern Oceanic, Remote Oceanic, North and Central Vanuatu, Northeast Vanuatu-Banks Islands, East Vanuatu. Slight dialect differences.

WHITESANDS ***(NAPUANMEN, WHITSANDS)*** [TNP] 3,500 (1988 SIL). Tanna Island, east coast. Austronesian, Malayo-Polynesian, Central-Eastern, Eastern Malayo-Polynesian, Oceanic, Central-Eastern Oceanic, South Vanuatu, Tanna. Dialects: WEASISI (WASSISI), LOMETIMETI. SVO. Literacy rate in first language: 1% to 5%. Literacy rate in second language: 5% to 15%. NT 1924.

WUSI ***(WUSI-KEREPUA)*** [WSI] 170 (1977 Lincoln). West Santo Island. Austronesian, Malayo-Polynesian, Central-Eastern, Eastern Malayo-Polynesian, Oceanic, Central-Eastern Oceanic, Remote Oceanic, North and Central Vanuatu, Northeast Vanuatu-Banks Islands, West Santo. Some dialect differences.

WAKE ISLAND

National or official language: English. 1,730 (1987). USA possession. The number of languages listed for Wake Island is 1. Diversity index 0.00.

ENGLISH [ENG] 1,730 on Wake Island (1987). Indo-European, Germanic, West, English. National language. 99% USA military. Bible 1535-1989. See main entry under United Kingdom.

WALLIS AND FUTUNA

French Overseas Territory of Wallis and Futuna. National or official language: French. 14,000 (1998 UN). Literacy rate 95%. Information mainly from B. Biggs 1980; S. Wurm and S. Hattori 1981; N. Besnier 1992. Christian. Data accuracy estimate: B. The number of languages listed for Wallis and Futuna is 3. Of those, all are living languages. Diversity index 0.45.

FRENCH [FRN] 120 in Wallis and Futuna (1993 Johnstone). Indo-European, Italic, Romance, Italo-Western, Western, Gallo-Iberian, Gallo-Romance, Gallo-Rhaetian, Oïl, French. National language. Bible 1530-1986. See main entry under France.

FUTUNA, EAST ***(FUTUNIAN)*** [FUD] 3,600 on Futuna (1987), 31.9% of the population. Population total both countries 8,000 (1991 UBS). Futuna Island. Different from Futuna Island (West Futuna) in Vanuatu. Also spoken in New Caledonia. Austronesian, Malayo-Polynesian, Central-Eastern, Eastern Malayo-Polynesian, Oceanic, Central-Eastern Oceanic, Remote Oceanic, Central Pacific, East Fijian-Polynesian, Polynesian, Nuclear, Samoic-Outlier, Futunic. Not intelligible with Wallisian (East Uvean). Bilingualism in French. Different from Futuna-Aniwa (West Futuna) in Vanuatu. Agriculturalists: coconut, taro, breadfruit, yam, sweet potato, sugar cane, banana, arrowroot; pig and chicken raisers; fishermen. Christian, traditional religion.

WALLISIAN ***(UVEAN, EAST UVEAN, WALLISIEN)*** [WAL] 7,500 in Wallis and Futuna (1987). Population total all countries 17,000. Uvea Island is their original home. Also spoken in Fiji, New Caledonia, Vanuatu. Austronesian, Malayo-Polynesian, Central-Eastern, Eastern Malayo-Polynesian, Oceanic, Central-Eastern Oceanic, Remote Oceanic, Central Pacific, East Fijian-Polynesian, Polynesian, Nuclear, Samoic-Outlier, East Uvean-Niuafo'ou. Some dialect divergence between Wallis Islands and New Caledonia. Not functionally intelligibile with Tongan. Bible portions 1971.

WESTERN SAMOA

Independent State of Samoa, Malotuto'atasi o Samoa i Sisifo. National or official languages: Samoan, English. 214,384 (1996 The World Factbook). 93% Samoan, 7% mixed. 2 large islands, several smaller ones. Literacy rate 97%. Information mainly from S. Wurm and S. Hattori 1981; N. Besnier OIEL 1992. Christian, Baha'i. Data accuracy estimate: B. The number of languages listed for Western Samoa is 2. Of those, both are living languages. Diversity index 0.00.

ENGLISH [ENG] Indo-European, Germanic, West, English. Official language. Bible 1535-1989. See main entry under United Kingdom.

SAMOAN [SMY] 199,377 in Samoa, 93% of population (1999). Population total all countries 426,394. Also spoken in American Samoa, Fiji, New Zealand, Tonga, USA. Austronesian, Malayo-Polynesian, Central-Eastern, Eastern Malayo-Polynesian, Oceanic, Central-Eastern Oceanic, Remote Oceanic,

Central Pacific, East Fijian-Polynesian, Polynesian, Nuclear, Samoic-Outlier, Samoan. No significant dialect variations, but important register-based distinctions in the phonology. The talking chiefs' dialect is very different; most Samoans have difficulty understanding it. 70% lexical similarity with Wallisian, 67% with Rarotongan, 66% with Tongan, 62% with Paumotu. Official language. Dictionary. VSO. Agriculturalists. Christian. Bible 1855-1970.

BIBLIOGRAPHY

Abas, Hussen, ed. 1985. Lontara: Majalah Universitas Hasanuddin No 28. Ujung Pandang: Percetakan Lembaga Penerbitan Universitas Hasanuddin.

Abrahams, R. G. 1967. The peoples of Greater Unyamwezi, Tanzania. London: International African Institute.

Acebes, Argentina. 1966. Indígenas en Argentina. XXXVI Congreso Internacional de Americanistas, España 1964: Actas y Memorias, Tomo 3, Sevilla, pp. 543-546.

Acton, Thomas and Donald Kenrick, eds. 1984. Romani Rokkeripen Todivvus. London: Romanestan Publications.

Addleton, Jonathan S. 1986. The importance of regional languages in Pakistan. Al-Mushir 28:2.55-80.

Adelaar, Karl Alexander. 1985. Proto-Malayic: The reconstruction of its phonology and part of its lexicon and morphology. Alblasserdam: Offsetdrukkerij Kanters B. V.

Adler, Max K. 1977. Pidgins, creoles, and lingua francas, a sociolinguistic study. Hamburg: Helmut Buske Verlag.

Adler, Max K. 1977. Welsh and the other dying languages in Europe. Hamburg: Helmut Buske Verlag.

Afido, Pedro, Gregório Firmino, John Heins, Samba Mbuub, and Manuel Trinta. 1989. Seminario sobre a padronização da ortografia de línguas Moçambícanas. Maputo: Faculdade de Letras, Universidade Eduardo Mondlane.

Agard, Frederick B. 1975. Toward a taxonomy of language split, Part One: Phonology. Leuvense Bijdragen 64.3-4:293-312.

Agard, Frederick B. 1984. A course in Romance linguistics, Vol. 2: A diachronic view. Washington, D.C.: Georgetown University Press.

Agesthialingom, S. and S. Sakthivel. 1973. A bibliography for the study of Nilgiri hill tribes. Annamalainagar: Annamalai University.

Akiner, Shirin. 1983. Islamic peoples of the Soviet Union. London: Kegan Paul International.

Ali, Salah Mohamed. 1986. The unity of the Somali language despite the barrier of regional language variants. In Annarita Puglielli, ed., Proceedings of the Third International Congress of Somali Studies, pp. 90-98.

Allen, Jerry and Conrad Hurd. 1963. Languages of the Bougainville District. Port Moresby: Summer Institute of Linguistics.

Allen, Jerry and Conrad Hurd. 1963. Languages of the Cape Hoskins Patrol Post Division of the Talasea Sub-district New Britain. Port Moresby: Summer Institute of Linguistics.

Alleyne, Mervyn C. 1980. Comparative Afro-American. Ann Arbor: Karoma.

Alleyne, Mervyn C. n.d. A linguistic perspective on the Caribbean. Washington, D.C.: The Woodrow Wilson International Center for Scholars.

Allin, Trevor. 1976. A grammar of Resígaro. Horsleys Green, United Kingdom: Summer Institute of Linguistics.

Al-Tajir, Mahdi Abdalla. 1982. Language and linguistic origins in Bahrain: The Baharnah dialect of Arabic. London: Kegan Paul International.

Anceaux, J. C. 1961. The linguistic situation in the Islands of Yapen, Kurudu, Nau, and Miosnum, New Guinea. The Hague: Martinus Nijhoff.

Anceaux, J. C. 1978. The linguistic position of Southeast Sulawesi: A preliminary outline. In S. A. Wurm and Lois Carrington, eds., Proceedings of the Second International Conference on Austronesian Linguistics, pp. 275-283.

Anderson, Franklin Scott. 1987. The lexicon of Fanagolo. Carbondale: Southern Illinois University.

Andersson, Lars-Gunnar and Tore Janson. 1997. Languages in Botswana: Language ecology in southern Africa. Gaborone: Longman Botswana.

Andrews, Peter Alford, ed. 1989. Ethnic groups in the Republic of Turkey. Wiesbaden, Germany: Dr. Ludwig Reichert Verlag.

Andrzejewski, B. W. 1975a. The role of indicator particles in Somali. Afroasiatic Linguistics 1.6:1-69.

Andrzejewski, B. W. 1975b. Verbs with vocalic mutation in Somali and their significance for Hamitico-Semitic comparative studies. In James and Theodora Bynon, eds., Hamitico-Semitica. The Hague: Mouton, pp. 361-367.

Andvik, Eric. 1993. Tshangla verb inflections. Linguistics of the Tibeto-Burman Area 16.1:75-136.

Antworth, Evan L. 1979. A grammatical sketch of Botolan Sambal. Philippine Journal of Linguistics, Special Publication No. 8.

Applegate, Joseph R. 1970. The Berber languages. In T. A. Sebeok. ed., 1970, pp. 586-661.

Arango Montoya, P. Francisco MXY. 1977. Colombia atlas indigenista. Bogotá: Ministerio de Educación Nacional.

Arbues, Lilia R. 1960. The Negritos as a minority group in the Philippines. Philippine Sociological Review 8.1/2.

Armstrong, Robert G. 1955. The Idoma. Peoples of the Niger-Benue Confluence. London: International African Institute, pp.77-155.

Armstrong, Robert G. 1955. The Igala. Peoples of the Niger-Benue Confluence. London: International African Institute, pp. 77-155.

Arnott, D. W. 1970. The nominal and verbal systems of Fula. Oxford: Clarendon Press.

Arveiller, R. 1967. Études sur le parler de Monaco. Thése de Paris, Monaco.

Aschmann, Richard P. 1993. Proto Witotoan. Summer Institute of Linguistics and the University of Texas at Arlington Publications in Linguistics 114. Dallas.

Atlas Linguistique de l'Afrique Central. 1984, 1988. Bangui: ACCT.

Atlas National du Senegal. 1977. Dakar.

Backstrom, Peter C. and Carla F. Radloff, eds. 1992. Languages of northern areas. Vol. 2 of Sociolinguistic survey of Northern Pakistan. Dallas: Summer Institute of Linguistics.

Bahuchet, Serge. 1985. Les Pygmées Aka et la Forêt Centrafricaine. Paris: SELAF.

Bailey, T. Grahame. 1915. Linguistic studies from the Himalayas. London: The Royal Asiatic Society.

Baker, Philip and R. Ramnak. 1985. Mauritian Bhojpuri: An Indo-Aryan language spoken in a predominantly creolphone society. In S. A. Wurm, ed., Papers in Pidgin and Creole Linguistics IV (Series A, no. 72).

Baker, Philip. 1972. Kreol: A description of Mauritian Creole. London: C. Hurst & Co.

Barbour, Stephen and Patrick Stevenson. 1990. Variation in German: A critical approach to German sociolinguistics. Cambridge: Cambridge University Press.

Barker, Milton E. 1966. Proto-Vietnamuong initial labial consonants. Van-hóa Nguyêt-san 12:491-500.

Barreteau, Daniel and Paul Newman. 1978. Les langues Tchadiques. In D. Barreteau, ed., pp. 291-330.

Barreteau, Daniel, ed. 1978 Inventaire des études linguistiques sur les pays d'Afrique Noire d'expression française. Paris: Conseil International de la Langue Française.

Barrett, David B., ed. 1982. World Christian encyclopedia: A comparative study of churches and religions in the modern world A.D. 1900-2000. Nairobi: Oxford University Press.

Barry, Abdoulaye. 1987. The Joola languages: Subgrouping and reconstruction. Ph. D. dissertation. University of London, School of African and Oriental Studies.

Bartholomew, Doris. 1965. The reconstruction of Otopamean (Mexico). Ph.D. dissertation, Chicago: University of Chicago.

Barz, R. and J. Siegel, eds., 1988. Language transplanted: the development of overseas Hindi. Wiesbaden: Otto Harrasowitz.

Barz, R. and Y. K. Yadav. 1993. An introduction to Hindi and Urdu, fifth edition. New Delhi: Munshiram Manoharlal.

Bastin, Yvonne. 1978. Les langues Bantoues. In D. Barreteau, ed.

Bateson, Mary Catherine. 1967. Arabic language handbook. Washington D.C.: Center for Applied Linguistics.

Baxter, Alan N. 1988. A grammar of Kristang (Malacca Creole Portuguese). Canberra: Australian National University, Pacific Linguistics, Series B-95.

Beaumont, C. L. 1972. History of research in Austronesian languages: New Ireland. Pacific Linguistics Series A, 35:1-41.

Behnstedt, Peter. 1985. Die nordjemenitischen Dialaekte. Teil 1: Atlas. Wiesbaden: Dr. Ludwig Reichert Verlag.

Behnstedt, Peter and Manfred Woidich. 1988. Die ägyptisch-arabischen Dialekte, 3 vols. Wiesbaden: Dr. Ludwig Reichert Verlag.

Beidelman, T. O. 1967. The matrilineal peoples of eastern Tanzania. London: International African Institute.

Beltran I Caballer, Joan S. 1986. L'estandard occidental: una proposta sobre l'estandard català a les terres del darrer tram de l'Ebre. Barcelona: Generalitat de Catalunya.

Bender, Byron and Kenneth L. Rehg. 1991. Micronesian languages in jeopardy? Presented at the Sixth International Conference of Austronesian Linguistics, May 1991, Honolulu, Hawaii.

Bender, Byron W. 1971. Micronesian languages. In T. A. Sebeok, ed.

Bender, M. Lionel. 1971. The languages of Ethiopia. Anthropological Linguistics 13.5:165-288.

Bender, M. Lionel. 1975. The Ethiopian Nilo-Saharans. Addis Ababa.

Bender, M. Lionel, ed. 1976. The non-Semitic languages of Ethiopia. Monograph No. 5, Occasional Papers Series, Committee on Ethiopian Studies. East Lansing: African Studies Center, Michigan State University.

Bender, M. Lionel. 1983a. Nilo-Saharan language studies. East Lansing: African Studies Center, Michigan State University.

Bender, M. Lionel. 1983b. Majang phonology and morphology. In M. L. Bender, ed., pp. 114-147.
Bender, M. Lionel. 1983c. Remnant languages. In M. L. Bender, ed., pp. 336-354.
Bender, M. Lionel. 1989. Eastern Jebel languages. In Topics in Nilo-Saharan Linguistics.
Bendor-Samuel, John. 1971. Niger-Congo, Gur. In T. A. Sebeok, ed., pp. 141-178.
Bendor-Samuel, John, ed. 1989. The Niger-Congo languages. Lanham, MD: University Press of America.
Benedict, Paul K. 1975. Austro-Thai: language and culture with a glossary of roots. New Haven: HRAF Press.
Besnier, Nico. 1992. Polynesian languages, in W. Bright, ed., vol. 3, pp. 245-251.
Bhurhanuddin, B. H. (1979 ms.) Bahasa-bahasa daerah di Sulawesi Tenggara. Kendari.
Biber, Douglas. 1984. Pragmatic roles in Central Somali narrative discourse. Studies in African Linguistics 15.1.
Bickerton, Derek and Aquilas Escalante. 1970. Palenquero: A Spanish-based creole of northern Colombia. Lingua 24:254-267.
Bickerton, Derek. 1974. Priorities in creole studies. In David De Camp and Ian F. Hancock, eds., pp. 85-87.
Biggs, Bruce. 1957. Testing intelligibility among Yuman languages. IJAL 23:57-62.
Biggs, Bruce. 1980. The position of East Uvean and Anutan in the Polynesian language family. Te Reo: Journal of the Linguistic Society of New Zealand 23:115-134.
Bimson, Kent D. 1978. Comparative reconstruction of Proto-Northern-Western Mande. Ph.D. dissertation. Los Angeles: University of California.
Bista, Dor Bahadur. 1972. The people of Nepal. Second edition. Kathmandu: Ratna Pustak Bhandar.
Black, Paul. 1983. Aboriginal languages of the Northern Territory. Darwin: School of Australian Linguistics, Darwin Community College.
Blair, Frank. 1990. Survey on a shoestring: A manual for small-scale language surveys. Summer Institute of Linguistics and the University of Texas at Arlington Publications in Linguistics 96. Dallas.
Blanchet, Phillippe. 1986. Idiome spécifique et culture populaire: Le Français régional de Provence. Doctoral dissertation, Paris: Sorbonne University.
Blust, Robert A. 1974. The Proto-North Sarawak vowel deletion hypothesis. Ph.D. thesis. Honolulu: University of Hawaii.
Blust, Robert A. 1977. The Proto-Austronesian pronouns and Austronesian subgrouping: A preliminary report. Working Papers in Linguistics 9.2:1-15. Honolulu: Department of Linguistics, University of Hawaii.
Blust, Robert A. 1981. The Soboyo reflexes of Proto-Austronesian *S. NUSA, Linguistic studies in Indonesian and languages in Indonesia 10:21-30.
Blust, Robert A. 1983-1984. More on the position of the languages of eastern Indonesia. Oceanic Linguistics 22/23:1-28.
Borg, Alexander. 1985. Cypriot Arabic. Stuttgart: Deutsch Morgenlaendische Gesellschaft.
Bourgue, François. 1976. Los caminos de los hijos del cielo. Estudio Socio-Territorial de los Kawillary del Cananarí y del Apaporis. Revista Colombiana de Antropología. Bogotá: Instituto Colombiano de Cultura, pp. 101-146.
Boutin, Michael E. 1986. Indigenous groups of Sabah: An annotated bibliography of linguistic and anthropological sources: Supplement I [Sabah Museum Monograph 1, part 2] Kota Kinabalu: Sabah Museum ix, 226 pp.
Boutin, Michael E. and Alanna Y. Boutin. 1985. Report on the languages of Banggi and Balambangan. Sabah Society Journal 8.1:89-92.
Boyeldieu, Pascal. 1977. Etudes phonologiques tchadiennes. Paris: SELAF.
Boyeldieu, Pascal. 1985. La Langue lua (niellim). Paris: SELAF.
Bradley, C. Henry. 1968. A method for determining dialectal boundaries and relationships. América Indígena 28:751-760.
Brenzinger, Matthias. 1997. Moving to survive: Kxoe communities in arid lands. Hunter-gatherers in transition: Language, identity, and conceptualization among the Khoisan.
Breton, Roland J. L. 1979. Ethnies et langues. In Georges Laclavère, ed., Atlas de la République Unie du Cameroun, pp. 31-35. Paris: Éditions Jeune Afrique
Breton, Roland J. L. 1981. Groupe A10: Lundu-Mbo, Oroko-Ngoe. Map of Oroko-Ngoe language group of SW Cameroon. Yaoundé: D.G.R.S.T., C.R.E.A.
Breton, Roland J. L. 1981. Les ethnies. Paris: Presses Universitaires de France.
Breton, Roland J. L. 1986. Cartes Linguistiques (Cameroun, Centrafrique, Congo, Gabon, Zaïre, Tchad) in Conference des Ministres de l'Education Nationale des Etats de'expression française.
Breton, Roland J. L. 1991 The handicaps of language planning in Africa. In Joshua A. Fishman Festschrift, No. 3: Language planning. Amsterdam: John Benjamins.

Breton, Roland J. L. 1991. Geolinguistics: Language dynamics and ethno-linguistic geography. Ottawa: University of Ottawa Press.

Breton, Roland J. L. 1993. Is there a Furu language group? An investigation on the Cameroon-Nigeria border. Journal of West African Languages, SLAO 23.2:97-118.

Breton, Roland J. L. 1996. The dynamics of ethno-linguistic communities as the central factor in language policy and planning. International Journal of the Sociology of Language. 118. New York: Walter de Gruyter.

Breton, Roland J. L. 1997. Atlas of the languages and ethnic communities of South Asia. New Delhi: Sage Publications India Pvt. Ltd.

Breton, Roland J. L. and D. Louder. 1993. The linguistic geography of Acadiana. In Dean Louder and Eric Waddell, eds., French America. Baton Rouge: Louisiana State University Press.

Bright, William, ed. 1992. International encyclopedia of linguistics. New York: Oxford University Press.

Bromley, Myron. 1967. The linguistic relationships of Grand Valley Dani: A lexico-statistical classification. Oceania 37.4:286-308.

Brown, J. M. 1965. From ancient Thai to modern dialects. Bangkok.

Bruhn, Thea C. 1989. Passages: Life, the universe, and language proficiency assessment. In Georgetown University Round Table on Languages and Linguistics, 1989. Washington, D. C.: Georgetown University Press, pp. 245-254.

Bryan, Margaret A. 1959. The Bantu languages of Africa. London: Oxford University Press.

Buddruss, Georg. 1960. Die Sprach von Wotapur und Katarqala. Bonn: Selbstverlag des Orientalischen Seminars der Universitat Bonn.

Bulakarima, Umara. 1986. Is Mobar a Kanuri dialect? Annals of Borno 3:81-90.

Bulletin of the Department of Anthropology. 1987. Calcutta: Anthropological Survey of India.

Bunn, Gordon and Graham Scott. 1963. Languages of the Mount Hagen Sub-district. Port Moresby: Summer Institute of Linguistics.

Burling, Robbins. ms. (1998). The Tibeto-Burman languages of Northeast India.

Burmeister, Jonathan L. 1976. A comparison of variable nouns in Anyi-Sanvi and Nzema. Annales 9:7-19.

Burnham, Eugene C. 1976. The place of Haroi in the Chamic languages. M.A. thesis, Arlington: University of Texas.

Busenitz, Robert L. 1991. Lexicostatistic and sociolinguistic survey of Balantak and Andio. In T. Friberg, ed., pp. 7-22.

Butt, Audrey J. 1966. The present state of ethnology in Latin America: the Guianas. XXXVI Congreso Internacional de Americanistas, España 1964: Actas y Memorias, Tomo 3. Sevilla, pp. 19-37.

Callaghan, Catherine A. 1998. More evidence for Yok-Utian: A re-analysis of the Dixon and Kroeber sets. Paper read at the SSILA at LSA meeting, 1/11/98, New York.

Campbell, Lyle and David Oltrogge. 1980. Proto-Tol (Jicaque). IJAL 46:205-223.

Campbell, Lyle and Marianne Mithun. 1979. The languages of native America: Historical and comparative assessment. Austin: University of Texas Press.

Capell, A. 1962. A linguistic survey of the southwestern Pacific. South Pacific Commission, Technical Paper No. 136. Noumea: South Pacific Commission.

Capell, A. 1962. Polynesian languages. Current Anthropology 3:4.

Capell, A. 1968. Lexicostatistical study of the languages of Choiseul Island, British Solomon Islands. Pacific Linguistics, Series A, Occasional Papers, No. 15.

Capo, Hounkpati B. C. 1986. Renaissance du Gbe, une language de l'Afrique Occidentale. Etude critique sur les langues ajatado: l'Ewe, le Fon, le Gen, l'Aja, le Gun, etc. Lomé: Institut National des Sciences de l'Education, Universite du Benin.

Caprile, Jean P., ed. 1977. Etudes phonologiques tchadiennes. Paris: SELAF.

Capron, Jean. 1973. Communautes villageoises Mali-Haute Volta Bwa, vol. 1. Paris: Institut d'Ethnologie.

Carr, Elizabeth Ball. 1972. Da Kine Talk: From Pidgin to Standard English in Hawaii. Honolulu: The University Press of Hawaii.

Carrington, Lawrence D. 1984. St. Lucian Creole: A descriptive analysis. Hanburg: Buske.

Carrington, Lois. 1996. A linguistic bibliography of the New Guinea area. Canberra: Australian National University.

Casad, Eugene H. 1974. Dialect intelligibility testing. Norman, Oklahoma: SIL Publications in Linguistics and Related Fields, No. 38.

Cassanelli, Lee V. 1982. The shaping of Somali society: Reconstructing the history of a pastoral people, 1600-1900. Philadelphia: University of Pennsylvania Press.

Cavalli-Sforza, Luigi Luca, ed. 1986. African Pygmies. Academic Press.

Cense, A. A. and E. M. Uhlenbeck. 1958. A critical survey of studies on the languages of Borneo, Bibliographical Series No. 2. The Hague: Martinus Nijhoff.

Central Institute of Indian Languages. 1973. Distribution of languages in India in states and union territories (inclusive of mother tongues). Mysore.

Cerron-Palomino, Rodolfo. 1976. Gramática quechua: Junín-Huanca. Lima, Perú: Ministerio de Educación.

Chafe, Wallace L. 1962. Estimates regarding the present speakers of North American Indian languages. IJAL 28:162-171.

Chafe, Wallace L. 1965. Corrected estimates regarding speakers of Indian languages. IJAL 31:345-346.

Chagnoux, H. and A. Haribou. 1980. Les Comores. Que sais-je? Paris: PUF.

Chamanga, M. A. and N. J. Gueunie. 1966-1967Recherches sur l'instrumentalisation du comorien. Cahiers d'Etudes Africaines, vol. 17. The Hague: Mouton.

Chamberlain, James R. 1984. The Tai dialects of Khammoun Province, Laos: Their diversity and origins. The Science of Language 4:62-95.

Chamberlain, James R. 1998. The origin of the Sek: Implications for Tai and Vietnamese history. Paper presented at the International Conference on Tai Studies, Institute of Language and Culture for Rural Development of Mahidol University, Bangkok, 7/29-31/1998.

Chamberlain, James R. Mene: A Tai dialect originally spoken in Nghe An (Nghe Tinh), Vietnam. Preliminary linguistic observations and historical implications. Journal of the Siam Society 79:103-123.

Chamberlain, James R., Charles Alton, Latsamay Silavong. 1996. Socio-economic and cultural survey: Nam Theun 2 Project Area. Part 2, Appendix 2, Be-Tai ethnolinguistic family. CARE International and Lao People's Democratic Republic.

Chase-Sardi, Miguel. 1987. Derecho consuetudinario Chamacoco. Asunción: Asociación Indigenista del Paraguay, RP Ediciones.

Chazee, Laurent. 1995. Atlas des ethnies et des sous-ethnies du Laos. Bangkok.

Chetric, Joseph. 1985. Judeo-Arabic and Judeo-Spanish in Morocco. In J. Fishman, ed., pp. 261-279.

Claassen, Oren and Kenneth McElhanon. 1970. Languages of the Finisterre Range-New Guinea. Pacific Linguistics, Series A, No. 23, pp. 45-78.

Clairis, Christos. 1982. Les Qawasqar. Thesis, Paris: Sorbonne.

Clammer, J. R. 1976. Literacy and social change: A case study of Fiji. Leiden: E. J. Brill.

Cloarec-Heiss, France. 1978. Étude preliminaire à une dialectologie banda. Études Comparatives. BSELAF 65. Paris: SELAF 65:11-42.

Clouse, Duane. A reconstruction and reclassification of the Lakes Plain languages of Irian Jaya. Submitted to Pacific Linguistics.

Coelho, V. H. 1967. Sikkim and Bhutan. New Delhi: Indraprastha Press.

Cohen, David. 1963. Le dialecte Arabe Hassaniya de Mauritanie. Paris: Librairie C. Klincksieck.

Cohen, David. 1985. Judeo-Arabic of North Africa. In J. Fishman, ed., pp. 246-260.

Cohen, Pedro I. and others. 1976. El inglés criollo de Panamá. Primeras Jornadas Lingüísticas. Panamá: Editorial Universitaria.

Collins, James. 1983. The historical relationships of the languages of central Maluku, Indonesia. Pacific Linguistics.

Comrie, Bernard, ed. 1987. The world's major languages. New York: Oxford University Press.

Connell, Bruce and K.B. Maison. 1994. A Cameroun homeland for the Lower Cross languages? Sprache und Geschichte in Afrika 15:47-90.

Connell, Bruce. 1994. The Lower Cross languages: A prolegomena to the classification of the Cross River languages. Journal of West African Languages 24.1:3-46.

Conrad, Robert and Wayne Dye. 1975. Some language relationships in the Upper Sepik Region of Papua New Guinea. Papers in New Guinea Linguistics No. 18. Pacific Linguistics, Series A, No. 40, pp.1-35.

Cook, Edwin A. 1966. Narak: Language or dialect? Journal of the Polynesian Society 75:437-444.

Coon, Carleton Stevens. 1931. Tribes of the Rif. Harvard African Studies, Vol. IX. Cambridge, Mass: Peabody Museum of Harvard University.

Cortina-Borja, Mario and Leopoldo Valiñas C. 1989. Some remarks on Uto-Aztecan classification. IJAL 55:2.214-239.

Creider, Chet A. 1981. The tonal system of proto-Kalenjin. In Schadeberg and Bender, eds., pp. 19-39.

Crozier, D. H. and R. M. Blench, eds. 1992. An index of Nigerian languages, Second Edition. Language Development Centre, Abuja; Department of Linguistics and Nigerian Languages, Ilorin; Summer Institute of Linguistics, Dallas.

Curnow, Timothy Jowan. 1998. Why Paez is not a Barbacoan language: The nonexistence of "Moguex" and the use of early sources. International Journal of American Linguistics.

Cusihuaman G., Antonio. 1976. Gramática quechua: Cuzco-Collao. Lima, Perú: Ministerio de Educación.

Dalby, T. D. P. 1962. Language distribution in Sierra Leone: 1961-1962. Sierra Leone Language Review 1:62-67.

Dan Nghiem Van, et al. 1993. Ethnic minorities of Vietnam. Hanoi: The Gioi Publishers.

Dawkins, R. M. 1916. Modern Greek in Asia Minor. Cambridge: Cambridge University Press.

Day, Richard R. 1974. Decreolization: Coexistent systems and the post-creole continuum. In David De Camp and Ian F. Hancock, eds., pp. 38-45.

De Camp, David and Ian F. Hancock, eds. 1974. Pidgins and creoles: Current trends and prospects. Washington, D.C.: Georgetown University Press.

De Camp, David. 1968. The field of creole language studies. Presented at the Conference on Pidginization and Creolization, April 9-12. Jamaica: University of the West Indies.

Decker, D. Kendall. 1992. Languages of Chitral. Vol. 5 of Sociolinguistic survey of Northern Pakistan. Dallas: Summer Institute of Linguistics.

Delafosse, Maurice. 1904. Vocabulaires comparatifs de plus de soixante langues ou dialectes parlés à la Côte d'Ivoire et dans les régions limitrophes. Paris: Laroux.

Demesse, L. 1978. Changements techno-économiques et sociaux chez les Pygmées Babinga (Nord-Congo et Sud-Centrafrique). Paris: SELAF.

Derbyshire, Desmond C. 1977. Word order universals and the existence of OVS languages. Linguistic Inquiry 8:590-599.

Derbyshire, Desmond C. 1979. Hixkaryana syntax. Ph.D. thesis. University of London.

Derbyshire, Desmond C. and Geoffrey K. Pullum, eds. 1986. Handbook of Amazonian Languages, Vol. 1, 1990 Vol. 2, 1991 Vol. 3. Berlin: Mouton de Gruyter.

Dieu, Michel and Patrick Renaud, eds. 1983. Atlas linguistique du Cameroun. Yaoundé: Délégation Générale à la Recherche Scientifique et Technique.

Dimmendaal, Gerrit J. 1983. Topics in a grammar of Turkana. In M. L. Bender, ed., pp. 239-271.

Dimmendaal, Gerrit J. 1989. On language death of Eastern Africa. In Nancy C. Dorian, ed.

Doerfer, Gerhard with Wolfram Hesche, Hartwig Scheinhardt, and Semih Tezcan. 1971. Khalaj materials. Uralic and Altaic series v.115, Indiana University Publications. Bloomington, Indiana.

Doornbos, Paul and M. Lionel Bender. 1983. Languages of Wadai-Darfur. In M. L. Bender, ed., pp. 42-79.

Dorian, Nancy C., ed. 1989. Investigating obsolescense: Studies in language contraction and death. Studies in the Social and Cultural Foundations of Language, 7. Cambridge: Cambridge University Press.

Douglas, Leonora Mosende, ed. 1986. World Christianity: Oceania. Monrovia: MARC.

Douglas, Wilfred. 1976. The Aboriginal languages of the South-West of Australia. Canberra: Australian Institute of Aboriginal Studies.

Dreyer, June Teufel. 1976. China's forty millions: Minority nationalities and national integration in the People's Republic of China. Harvard East Asia Series No. 87.

Drower, Ethel S. 1939. The Mandaeans of Iraq and Iran. Oxford University Press.

Duboc, Général. 1935. Mauritanie. Paris: L. Fournier.

Dupree, Louis. 1980. Afghanistan. Princeton: Princeton University Press.

Durbin, Marshall and Haydee Seijas. 1973. Proto Hianacoto: Guaque-Carijona-Hianacoto Umaua. IJAL 39:1.22-31.

Dutton, T. E. 1969. The peopling of Central Papua: Some preliminary observations. Pacific Linguistics, Series B, No. 9.

Dutton, T. E. 1970. Notes on the languages of the Rigo area of the Central District of Papua. Pacific Linguistics Series C, No. 13, pp. 879-983.

Dutton, T. E. 1971. Languages of southeast Papua; a preliminary report. Pacific Linguistics, Series A, No. 28, pp. 1-46.

Dwyer, David J. 1989. Mande. In J. Bendor-Samuel, ed.

Dye, W., P. Townsend, and W. Townsend. 1968. The Sepik Hill languages: A preliminary report. Oceania 39.2:146-156.

Dyen, Isidore. 1962. The lexicostatistical classification of the Malayopolynesian languages. Language 38:38-46.

Dyen, Isidore. 1963. The lexicostatistical classification of the Austronesian languages. New Haven: Yale University.

Dyen, Isidore. 1965. A lexicostatistical classification of the Austronesian languages. Indiana University publications in anthropology and linguistics, memoir 19; IJAL 31:1, supplement.

Ebert, Karen 1994. The structure of Kiranti languages, Comparative grammar and texts, Kiranti subordination in the South Asian areal context. Zurich: University of Zuerich.

Edmondson, Jerold A. and David Solnit, eds. 1988. Comparative Kadai: Linguistic studies beyond Tai. Summer Institute of Linguistics and the University of Texas at Arlington Publications in Linguistics 86. Dallas.

Edmondson, Jerold A. and David Solnit, eds. 1997. Comparative Kadai: The Tai branch. Summer Institute of Linguistics and the University of Texas at Arlington Publications in Linguistics 124. Dallas.

Edmondson, Jerold A., ed. 1990. Kadai: Discussions in Kadai and S.E. Asian Linguistics. Arlington: University of Texas.

Egerod, Søren C. 1974. Sino-Tibetan languages. In Encyclopaedia Britannica 16:796-806.

Egland, Steven, Doris Bartholomew, and Saul Cruz Ramos. 1983. La inteligibilidad interdialectal en México: Resultados de algunos sondeos. Mexico, D. F.: Instituto Lingüístico de Verano.

Elkins, Richard E. 1967. Major grammatical patterns of Western Bukidnon Manobo. Ph.D. thesis. Honolulu: University of Hawaii.

Ellis, Jim. 1991. Language intelligibility testing across Micronesia. Presented at the Sixth International Conference of Austronesian Linguistics.

Encyclopedic dictionary of Chinese Linguistics. 1991. Jiangxi Educational Publishing House.

Eriksen, Thomas H. 1990. Linguistic diversity and the quest for national identity: The case of Mauritius. Ethnic and Racial Studies 13.1:1-24.

Everett, Daniel L. 1983. Á língua pirahã e a teoria da sintaxe: descrição, perspectivas, e teoria. Ph.D. thesis. Universidade Estadual de Campinas.

Fagerberg, Sonja. ms. (1978-1979) A brief survey of Pulaar/Fulfulde dialects in West Africa. New York: United Bible Societies.

Farhadi, A. G. Raven. 1967. Languages. Kabul: Kabul Times Publishing Agency.

Fasold, Ralph. 1984. The sociolinguistics of society, Vol. I. Oxford: Basil Blackwell.

Ferlus, Michel. 1996. Langues et peuples viet-muong. Mon-Khmer Studies 16:7-28.Mahidol University, Salaya, Thailand and The Summer Institute of Linguistics, Dallas, TX, USA.

Fischer, Wolfdietrich and Otto Jastrow. 1980. Handbuch der arabischen Dialekte. Wiesbaden: Otto Harrassowitz.

Fishman, Joshua A., ed. 1985. Readings in the sociology of Jewish languages. Leiden: E. J. Brill.

Fishman, Joshua A. 1988. Language spread and language policy for endangered languages. In Peter H. Lowenberg, ed., Language spread and language policy: Issues, implications, and case studies. Washington, D.C.: Georgetown University Press, pp. 1-15.

Fishman, Joshua A. 1991. Reversing language shift. Clevedon: Multilingual Matters, Ltd.

Fishman, Joshua A., C. A. Ferguson, and J. Das Gupta, eds. 1968. Language problems of developing nations. New York: Wiley.

Fleisch, H. 1974. Études d'Arabe dialectal. Beyrouth.

Foley, William A. 1986. The Papuan languages of New Guinea. Cambridge: Cambridge University Press.

Forte, Janette. 1990. The populations of Guyanese Amerindian settlements. University of Guyana, Amerindian Research Unit.

Frank, David B. (to appear) Political, religious, and economic factors affecting language choice in St. Lucia. International Journal of the Sociology of Language.

Franklin, Karl. 1968. Languages of the Gulf District: A preview. Papers in New Guinea Linguistics 8. PL-A 16:19-44.

Friberg, Timothy and Thomas V. Laskowske. 1988. South Sulawesi languages, 1988. Presented at the Fifth International Conference on Austronesian Linguistics.

Friberg, Timothy, ed. 1987. South Sulawesi Sociolinguistic Surveys. Workpapers in Indonesian Languages and Cultures, Vol. 5. Ujung Pandang: Summer Institute of Linguistics.

Friberg, Timothy, ed. 1991. More Sulawesi sociolinguistic surveys, 1987-1991. Workpapers in Indonesian Linguistics (and Cultures) 11. Ujung Pandang: Summer Institute of Linguistics.

Frick, E. and M. Bolli. 1971. Inventaire préliminaire des langues et dialectes en Côte-d'Ivoire. Actes du Huitième Congrès International de Linguistique Africaine 1:395-416.

Fu Maoji, ed. 1991. Tibeto-Burman sounds and vocabulary. Beijing: Zhongguo Shihui Kexue Chubanshe.

Fussman, Gerard. 1972. Atlas linguistique des perlers dardes et kafirs. 2 vol. Paris: Ecole Française d'Extreme Orient.

Fussman, Gerard. 1989. Languages as a source for history. In A. H. Dani, ed., History of northern areas of Pakistan. Islamabad: National Institute of Historical and Cultural Research, pp. 43-58.

Gallman, Andrew F. 1983. Proto East Mindanao and its internal relationships. Ph.D. dissertation. Arlington: University of Texas.

Galtier, Gerard. 1980. Proble'mes dialectologiques et phonograhématiques del parlers mandingues. Thèse de 3ème Cycle. University of Paris.

Garbell, Irene. 1965. The Jewish Neo-Aramaic dialect of Persian Azerbaijan: Linguistic analysis and folkloristic texts. Janua Linguarum, series practica, III. The Hague: Mouton & Co. 342 pp. + map.

Geraghty, Paul A. 1983. The history of the Fijian languages. Oceanic Linguistics, Special Publication 19.

Geraghty, Paul A. 1988. Proto New Caledonian and its relationships. Presented at the Fifth International Conference on Austronesian Linguistics.

Gerteiny, Alfred G. 1967. Mauritania. New York: Frederick A. Praeger.

Gibson, Michael. 1988. The Munichi language: With particular reference to verb morphology. Thesis, Reading University.

Gloria, Heidi K. 1987. The Bagobos: Their ethnohistory and acculturation. Quezon City, Philippines: New Day Publishers.

Godfrey, Thomas James and Wesley M. Collins. 1987. Una encuesta dialectal en el area Mam de Guatemala. Guatemala: SIL, 416 pp.

Gohain, B. C., compiler. 1971. Annexure to the tribal map of India. Calcutta: Anthropological Survey of India.

Gold, David L. 1974. Jewish intralinguistics. Sociological Abstracts, Suppl. 47-1, p. 344.

Goldbert de Goodbar, Perla. 1975. Cuento tradicional araucano; transcripción fonológica, traducción, y análisis. Buenos Aires: Centro de Investigaciones en Ciencias de la Educación.

Goodman, Morris. 1964. A comparative study of creole French dialects. The Hague: Mouton.

Goyvaerts, D. L. 1983. Some aspects of Logo phonology and morphology. In M. L. Bender, ed., pp. 272-279.

Gran Enciclopèdia Catalana. 1978-1988. Barcelona: Enciclopèdia Catalana, S.A.

Greenberg, Joseph H. 1963. The languages of Africa. Indiana University Research Center in Anthropology, Folklore, and Linguistics, Publication 25. The Hague: Mouton.

Greenberg, Joseph H. 1987. Language in the Americas. Stanford: Stanford University Press.

Gregerson, Kenneth J. 1976. Tongue-root and register in Mon-Khmer. In Philip N. Jenner, Laurence C. Thompson, and Stanley Starosta, eds., Austroasiatic studies, part I. Oceanic Linguistics, special publication 13. pp. 323-369.

Grierson, G. A., ed. 1903-1928. Linguistic survey of India. 3 vols. Calcutta: Government of India, Central Publication Branch.

Grimes, Barbara D. 1988. Exploring the sociolinguistics of Ambonese Malay. Presented at the Fifth International Conference on Austronesian Languages.

Grimes, Barbara F. 1985. Comprehension and language attitudes in relation to language choice for literature and education in pre-literate societies. Journal of Multilingual and Multicultural Development 6.2:165-181.

Grimes, Barbara F. 1985. Language attitudes: Identity, distinctiveness, survival in the Vaupes. Journal of Multilingual and Multicultural Development 6.5:389-401.

Grimes, Barbara F. 1986. Regional and other nonstandard dialects of major languages. Notes on Linguistics 35:19-39.

Grimes, Barbara F. 1987. How bilingual is bilingual? Notes on Linguistics 40:3-23.

Grimes, Barbara F. 1988. Why test intelligibility? Notes on Linguistics 42:39-64.

Grimes, Barbara F. 1989. Special considerations for creole surveys. Notes on Linguistics 47:41-63.

Grimes, Barbara F. 1994. Evaluating the Hawaii Creole English situation. Notes on Literature in Use and Language Programs 39:39-60.

Grimes, Charles E. 1992. The Buru Language of eastern Indonesia. Ph.D. thesis. Canberra: Australian National University.

Grimes, Charles E. and Barbara D. Grimes. 1983. Languages of the North Moluccas: A preliminary lexicostatistic classification. Ambon: Pattimura University and the Summer Institute of Linguistics.

Grimes, Charles E. and Barbara D. Grimes. 1987. Languages of South Sulawesi. Pacific Linguistics, Series D-78.

Grimes, Charles E., Tom Therik, Barbara Dix Grimes, and Max Jacob. 1997. A guide to the people and languages of Nusa Tenggara. Center for Regional Studies, Paradigma, Series B, No. 1 Kupang: Artha Wacana Press.

Grimes, Joseph E. 1964. Measures of linguistic divergence. In H. G. Lunt, ed., Proceedings of the Ninth International Congress of Linguists. The Hague: Mouton, pp. 44-50.

Grimes, Joseph E. 1974. Dialects as optimal communication networks. Language 50:260-269.

Grimes, Joseph E. 1986. Area norms of language size. In B. F. Elson, ed., Language in global perspective. Papers in honor of the 50th anniversary of the Summer Institute of Linguistics. Dallas: Summer Institute of Linguistics, pp. 5-19.

Grimes, Joseph E. 1988. Correlations between vocabulary similarity and intelligibility. Notes on Linguistics 41:19-33.

Grimes, Joseph E. 1989. Interpreting sample variation in intelligibility tests. In Thomas J. Walsh, ed. 1989. Synchronic and diachronic approaches to linguistic variation and change (Georgetown University Round Table on Languages and Linguistics 1988). Washington D.C.: Georgetown University Press, pp. 138-146.
Grimes, Joseph E. 1995. Language endangerment in the Pacific. Oceanic Linguistics 34.1:-12.
Grimes, Joseph E. 1995. Language survey reference guide. Dallas: Summer Institute of Linguistics.
Grimes, Joseph E. and Frederick B. Agard. 1959. Measures of phonological divergence in Romance. Language 35:598-604.
Grjunberg, A. L. 1963. The language of the northern Azerbaijan Tats. Leningrad. [In Russian]
Grjunberg, A. L. 1968. Languages of the Eastern Hindu Kush. Moscow.
Grjunberg, A. L. 1971. A dialektologii Dardskix jazykov (Glangali i Zemiaki). Moscow.
Grünberg, Georg and Friedl. 1978. Los Guaraní occidentales. In Augusto Roa Bisto, ed., Las culturas condenadas. Siglo XXI Editorial in Mexico. pp. 178-193.
Güldemann, Tom. 1998. San languages for education: A linguistic short survey and proposal, on behalf of the Molteno Early Literacy and Language Development Project in Namibia. Okahandja: National Institute of Educational Development, Ministry of Basic Education and Culture.
Gudschinsky, Sarah C. 1953. Proto-Mazateco. [Ciencias sociales: MCCM 12] Mexico: Universidad Nacional Autónoma de México, pp. 171-174.
Gudschinsky, Sarah C. 1956. The ABC's of lexicostatistics (glottochronology). In Dell Hymes, ed., Language in culture and society. New York: Harper and Row.
Gudschinsky, Sarah C. 1959. Proto-Popotecan: A comparative study of Popolocan and Mixtecan. [IURC Memoir 15] Bloomington, IN: Indiana University, supplement to IJAL 25:2.
Gunn, H. D. 1953. Peoples of the Plateau region of northern Nigeria. London: International African Institute.
Gunn, H. D. 1956. Peoples of the central area of northern Nigeria. London: International African Institute.
Gunn, H. D. and F. P. Conant. 1960. Peoples of the middle Niger region of northern Nigeria. London: International African Institute.
Gunnemark, Erik and Donald Kenrick. 1985. A geolinguistic handbook. Sweden: Gunnemark.
Gurung, G. M. 1989. The Chepangs: A study in continuity and change. Kathmandu: Centre for Nepal and Asian Studies.
Guthrie, Malcolm. 1948. The classification of the Bantu languages. Oxford: Oxford University Press.
Guthrie, Malcolm. 1967-1971. Comparative Bantu. 4 vols. Farnborough: Gregg International Publishers.
Haacke, Wilfrid H.G. and Edward E. Elderkin, eds. 1997. Namibian Languages: Reports and papers. Namibian African Studies Vol. 4. Cologne: Rudiger Koppe Verlag
Haby, Eden. 1975. Les Assyriens d'Union Sovietique. Cahiers du Mohde Russe et Sovietique 176.
Hagège, C. 1973. Profil d'un parler arabe du Tchad. Paris.
Hahn, Reinhold F. 1990. An annotated sample of Ili Turki. Acta Orientalia Hungaricae 43.
Hale, Austin. 1982. Research on Tibeto-Burman Languages. In Werner Winter, ed., Trends in Linguistics: State-of-the-art report 14. Amsterdam: Mouton.
Hall, Edward. 1983. Ghanaian languages. Accra: Asempa.
Hall, Robert A., Jr. 1966. Pidgin and creole languages. Ithaca: Cornell University Press.
Hall, Robert A., Jr. 1974. External history of the Romance languages. New York: American Elsevier Publishing Co., Inc.
Hallberg, Daniel G. 1992. Pashto, Waneci, Ormuri. Vol. 4 of Sociolinguistic survey of Northern Pakistan. Dallas: Summer Institute of Linguistics.
Hancock, Ian F. 1969. The Malacca Creoles and their language. Afrasia 3:38-45.
Hancock, Ian F. 1974. Shelta: A problem of classification. In David De Camp and Ian F. Hancock, eds., pp. 130-137.
Hancock, Ian F. ed., 1979. Romani sociolinguistics. International Journal of the Sociology of Language 19. The Hague: Mouton.
Hancock, Ian F. 1984. Romani and Angloromani. In Trudgill, P., ed., Language in the British Isles. Cambridge: Cambridge University Press, pp. 367-383.
Hancock, Ian F. 1984. Shelta and Polari. In P. Trudgill, ed., Language in the British Isles. Cambridge: Cambridge University Press, pp. 384-403.
Hancock, Ian F. 1984. The social and linguistic development of Angloromani. In Acton and Kenrick, eds., pp. 89-122.
Hancock, Ian F. 1985. A preliminary classification of the Anglophone Atlantic creoles. In Glenn Gilbert, ed., Pidgin and creole languages: Essays in memory of John E. Reinecke. Honolulu: The University Press of Hawaii.
Hancock, Ian F. 1985. A preliminary structural sketch of Trinidad Creole French. Amsterdam Creole Studies 8:27-40.

Hancock, Ian F. 1986. On the classification of Afro-Seminole Creole. In Montgomery and Bailey, eds. pp. 85-101.

Hancock, Ian F. 1986. The cryptolectal speech of the American roads: Traveler Cant and American Angloromani. American Speech 61:206-220.

Hancock, Ian F. 1987. A preliminary classification of the Anglophone Atlantic creoles, with syntactic data from thirty-three representative dialects. In Gilbert, ed. pp. 264-334.

Hancock, Ian F. 1987. Componentiality and the origins of Gullah. In Mary W. Helms, ed., Sea and land. Proceedings of the Southern Anthropological Society, Vol. 21. Athens: University of Georgia Press.

Hancock, Ian F. 1987. Romani: The language of the Gypsies. Gamut 23.

Hancock, Ian F. 1987. The function of the Gypsy myth. Chandigarh, India: Roma 27:35-44.

Hancock, Ian F. 1988. The development of Romani linguistics. In A. Jazyery and W. Winter, eds., Languages and Cultures: Studies in honor of Edgar C. Polomé. The Hague: Mouton, pp. 183-223.

Hancock, Ian F. 1988. Creole language provenance and the African component. Presented at the International Round-Table on Africanisms in Afro-American Language Varieties. The University of Georgia, Athens, Georgia, February 25-27.

Hancock, Ian F. 1990. A grammar of the Hungarian-Slovak (Carpathian, Bashaldo, Romungro) Romani Language. Manchaca, Texas: International Romani Union.

Hancock, Ian F. 1991. The social and linguistic development of Scandoromani. In Ernst H. Jahr, ed., Language contact in Scandinavia. Proceedings of the Fifth International Tromso Symposium. Berlin: Mouton de Gruyter.

Hansford, Keir, John Bendor-Samuel, and Ron Stanford. 1976. An index of Nigerian languages. Studies in Nigerian Languages, No. 5. Accra, Ghana: Summer Institute of Linguistics.

Hanson, F. A. 1970. The society and history on a Polynesian island. Boston: Little, Brown and Co.

Harmon, David. 1995. Losing species, losing languages: Connections between biological and linguistic diversity. Presented at the Symposium on Language Loss and Public Policy, Albuquerque, New Mexico, June 30-July 2, 1995, submitted for publication to the Southwest Journal of Linguistics.

Harmon, David. 1995. The status of the world's languages as reported in Ethnologue. Presented at the Symposium on Language Loss and Public Policy, Albuquerque, New Mexico, June 30-July 2, 1995, submitted for publication to the Southwest Journal of Linguistics.

Harris, Tracy K. 1994. Death of a language. Newark: University of Delaware Press. 354 pp.

Haugen, Einar. 1992l. Scandinavian languages. In W. Bright, ed. Vol. 3, pp. 375-379.

Hayes, Curtis W., Jacob Ornstein, and William W. Gage 1977. ABC's of languages and linguistics. Appendix: Languages of the world. Silver Spring, Maryland: Institute of Modern Languages, Inc.

Headland, Thomas N. 1985. Imposed values and aid rejection among Casiguran Agta. In P. Bion Griffin and Agnes Estioko-Griffin, eds. The Agta of Northeastern Luzon: Recent Studies. Cebu City, Philippines: University of San Carlos, pp. 102-118.

Headland, Thomas N. 1987. Negrito religions: Negritos of the Philippine Islands. In Mircea Eliade, ed., The Encyclopedia of Religion, vol. 10, pp. 348-349. New York: Macmillan.

Healey, Alan. 1964. The Ok language family in New Guinea. Ph.D. dissertation. Australian National University.

Hedinger, Robert. 1984. A comparative-historical study of the Manenguba languages (Bantu A.15 MBO cluster) of Cameroon. Ph.D. dissertation. London: University of London.

Heijdra, Martin. 1998. Who were the Laka? A survey of Scriptures in the minority languages of southwest China. The East Asian Library Journal 8.1, Spring.

Heine, Bernd and Wilhelm J. G. Möhlig. 1980. Language and dialect atlas of Kenya, Vol. 1. Berlin: Deitrich Reimer Verlag.

Heine, Bernd. 1968. Die Verbreitung und Gliederung der Togorestsprachen. (Kölner Beiträge zur Afrikanistik, Band 1). Berlin: Dietrich Reimer.

Hetzron, Robert, ed., 1997. The Semitic languages. Routledge.

Hickerson, Harold, Glen D. Turner, and Nancy P. Hickerson. 1952. Testing procedures for estimating transfer of information among Iroquois dialects and languages. IJAL 18:1-8.

Himmelmann, Nikolaus P. 1990. Sourcebook on Tomini-Tolitoli languages. Köln: Department of Linguistics, Universität zu Köln.

Hoberman, Robert D. 1988. Emphasis harmony in a modern Aramaic dialect. Language 64.1:1-26.

Hobermann, Robert D. 1988. The syntax and semantics of verb morphology in modern Aramaic: A Jewish dialect of Iraqi Kurdistan. New Haven: American Oriental Society.

Hodgson, Brian Houghton. 1874. Sifán and Hórsók vocabularies. Journal of the Royal Asiatic Society of Bengal 22:117-151.

Holes, Clive. 1988. The typology of Omani Arabic dialects. In Proceedings of the BRIMES International Conference on Middle Eastern Studies. Leeds: University of Leeds.

Holes, Clive. 1990. Gulf Arabic. New York: Routledge.

Holm, John. 1989. Pidgins and Creoles, Vols. 1,2. Cambridge: Cambridge University Press.
Hombert, Jean-Marie. 1980. Le groupe noun. In Hyman and Voorhoeve, eds., Les classes nominales dans le bantou des Grassfields. L'expansion bantoue Vol. 1, pp. 143-163.
Hooley, Bruce A. 1971. Austronesian languages of the Morobe District, Papua New Guinea. Oceanic Linguistics 10:79-151.
Hooley, Bruce A. and Kenneth McElhanon. 1970. Languages of the Morobe District, New Guinea. In Stephen A. Wurm and D. C. Laycock, eds., Series C, No. 13, pp. 1065-1094.
Hopkins, Bradley Lynn. 1995. Contribution a une etude de la syntaxe Diola-Fogny. Ph.D. thesis. Dakar: Universite Cheikh Anta Diop de Dakar.
Hopper, Janice H., ed. 1967. Indians of Brazil in the Twentieth Century (ICR Studies 2). Washington D.C.: Institute for Cross-Cultural Research.
Hu, C. T. 1970. The education of national minorities in Communist China. Washington, D.C.: U. S. Government Printing Office, Catalog HE 5.214:141-146.
Hudson, Joyce. 1987. Languages of the Kimberley region. Broome, WA: Catholic Education Kimberly Regional Office.
Hugoniot, Richard D., ed. 1970. A bibliographical index of the lesser known languages and dialects of India and Nepal. Waxhaw: Summer Institute of Linguistics.
Hunter, Brian. 1995. The stateman's yearbook: Statistical and historical annual of the states of the world for the year 1995-1996. London: MacMillan.
Huntingford, G. W. B. 1953. The northern Nilo-Hamites. London: International African Institute.
Huntingford, G. W. B. 1953. The southern Nilo-Hamites. London: International African Institute.
Hussainmiya, B. A. 1986. Melayu Bahasa: Some preliminary observations on the Malay Creole of Sri Lanka. Sari 4. Kuala Lampur: Universiti Kebangsaan Malaysia.
Huttar, George L. 1981. Some Kwa-like features of Djuka syntax. Studies in African Linguistics 12:291-323.
Huttar, George L. 1983. On the study of Creole lexicons. In Lawrence D. Carrington, Dennis Craig, and Ramon T. Dandare, eds., Studies in Caribbean languages, pp. 82-89.
Hyman, Larry M. 1980. Babanki and the Ring Group. In Hyman and Voorhoeve, eds., Les classes nominales dans le bantou des Grassfields. L'expansion bantoue, Vol. 1, pp. 225-258. Paris: SELAF.
Hyman, Larry M. and Jan Voorhoeve. 1980. Les classes nominales dans le bantou des Grassfields. L'expansion bantoue, Vol. 1. Paris: SELAF.
Ingemann, Frances and John Duitsman. 1976. A survey of Grebo dialects in Liberia. Liberian Studies Journal VII.2:121-131.
Ingemann, Frances, John Duitsman, and William Doe. 1972. A survey of Krahn dialects in Liberia. University of Liberia Journal.
Ingham, Bruce. 1982. Northeast Arabian dialects. London: Kegan Paul International.
Ingham, Bruce. 1994. Najdi Arabic: Central Arabian. Amsterdam: John Benjamins.
Israr-ud-Din. ms. (1969) The people of Chitral: A survey of their ethnic diversity.
Iyanga Pendi, Agusto. 1991. Pristamo en la lengua Ndowe de Guinea Ecuatorial, NAU Libres, Periodista Badia 10.
Izadi, Mehrdad. 1993. The Kurds: A Concise Handbook. Cambridge: Harvard University Press.
Jackson, Frederick. 1983. The internal and external relationships of the Trukic languages of Micronesia. Ph.D. dissertation. Honolulu: University of Hawaii.
Jacquot, André. 1971. Les langues du Congo-Brazzaville: Inventaire et classification, in Cahiers ORSTROM, Série sciences humaines, Vol. VIII, No. 4.
Jacquot, André. 1978. Le Gabon. In D. Barreteau, ed., pp. 493-503.
Janhumen, Juha. 1989. A Sino-Finnish joint expedition to the minority nationalities of northern China. Suomalais-Ugrilaisen Seuran Aikakauskiria 82:277-279.
Jastrow, Otto. 1971. Ein neuaramaischen Dielekt aus dem Vilayet Siirt (Ustanatolien). ZDub 121:215-222.
Jastrow, Otto. 1978. Die Mesopotamisch-Arabishen qeltu-Dialekte. 2 vols. Wiesbaden: Kommissionsverlag Franz Steiner GMBH.
Jastrow, Otto. 1988. Der Neuaramaische dialect von Hertevin (Provinz Siirt). Wiesbaden: Karassowitz.
Jensen, Allen A. 1985. Sistemas indígenas de classificação de aves: aspectos comparativos, ecológicos e evolutivos. Ph.D. dissertation. Campinas: State University of Campinas.
Jernudd, Bjorn H. 1968. Linguistic integration and national development: A case study of the Jebel Mara area, Sudan. In Fishman, Ferguson, and Das Gupta, pp. 167-181.
Jernudd, Bjorn H. and Muhammad H. Ibrahim. 1986. International Journal of the Sociology of Language, 61. Berlin: Mouton de Gruyter, p.128.
Jha, Sudhakar. 1958. The formation of the Maithili language. London.
Johnstone, Patrick. 1993. Operation World. Grand Rapids: Zondervan Publishing House.

Johnstone, T. M. 1967. Eastern Arabian dialect studies. London: Oxford University Press.

Johnstone, T. M. 1987. Mehri lexicon and English-Mehri word-list. London: SOAS.

Jones, Robert B. 1988. Proto-Burmese as a test of reconstruction. In Caroline Duncan-Rose and Theo Vennemann, eds., On Language: Rhetorica, phonologica, syntactica. A festshrift for Robert P. Stockwell. London: Routledge, pp. 203-211.

Jones, Schuyler. 1974. Men of influence in Nuristan. London: Seminar Press.

Jungraithmayr, H. 1971. How many Mimi languages are there? Africana Marburgensia 4.2:62-69.

Jungraithmayr, H. 1978. A lexical comparison of Darfur and Wadai Daju. In Thelwall, ed., pp. 145-154.

Kakumasu, James Y. 1976. Urubú sign language. IJAL 34:275-281.

Kanyoro, Rachel Angogo. 1983. Unity in diversity: A linguistic survey of the Abaluhyia of western Kenya. Wien: Beitrage zur Afrikanistik.

Kaseng, Syahruddin, et al. ms. (1983) Pemetaan Bahasa di Sulawesi Tenggara. Ujung Pandang.

Kaseng, Syahruddin. 1978. Kedudukan dan fungsi bahasa Makassar di Sulawesi Selatan. Jakarta: Pusat Pembinaan dan Pengembangan Bahasa.

Kastenholtz, Raimund. 1996. Sprachgeschichte im West-Mande: Methoden und Rekonstruktionen, Vol. 2, Mande Languages and Linguistics, Wilhelm J.G. Mohlig, ed. Cologne: Rudiger, Koppe Verlag. P. 281.

Katzner, Kenneth. 1975. The languages of the world. New York: Funk and Wagnalls.

Kaye, Alan S. 1988. Review of Bjorn H. Jernudd and Muhammad H. Ibrahim, Aspects of Arabic sociolinguistics International Journal of the Sociolinguistics of Language 1986. Language 64.1:210.

Key, Mary Ritchie. 1979. The grouping of South American Indian languages. Tübingen: Gunter Narr Verlag.

Kibrik, Aleksandr E. 1991. The problem of endangered languages in the USSR. In Robins and Uhlenbeck, eds., pp. 257-273.

King, Julie K. and John Wayne King, eds. 1984. Languages of Sabah: A survey report. Pacific Linguistics C-78.

Kirk, Paul L. 1970. Dialect intelligibility testing: The Mazatec study. IJAL 36:205-211.

Klein, Harriet E. Manelis and Louisa R. Stark. 1977. Indian languages of the Paraguayan Chaco. Anthropological Linguistics 19:8.

Klein, Harriet E. Manelis and Louisa R. Stark. 1985. South American Indian languages. Austin: University of Texas Press.

Kloss, Heinz and Grant D. McConnell. 1974. Linguistic composition of the nations of the world, Vol. 1, Central and Western South Asia. Quebec: International Center for Research on Bilingualism.

Kloss, Heinz and Grant D. McConnell. 1978. Linguistic composition of the nations of the world, Vol. 2, North America. Quebec: International Center for Research on Bilingualsm.

Koentjaraningrat, ed. 1971. Manusia dan kebudayaan di Indonesia. Jakarta: Djambatan.

Krauss, Michael E. 1979. Na-Dene and Eskimo-Aleut. In Campbell and Mithun, eds., pp. 803-901.

Krauss, Michael E. 1995. The indigenous languages of the North: A report on their present state. Alaska Native Language Center: University of Alaska Fairbanks.

Kroeger, Paul R. 1985. Linguistic relations among the Dusunic groups in the Kota Marudu District. Borneo Research Bulletin 17.1:31-46.

Kroeger, Paul R. 1986. Intelligibility patterns in Sabah and the problem of prediction. In Papers from the Fourth International Congress on Austronesian Linguistics, 309-339 [PL-C-93]. Canberra: Australian National University.

Krupa, Viktor. 1973. Polynesian languages, a survey of research. The Hague: Mouton.

Kullavanajaya, Pranee and Theraphan L-Thongkum. 1998. Linguistic criteria for determining Tai ethnic groups: Case studies on Central and Southwestern Tais. Paper presented at The International Conference on Tai Studies , Institute of Language and Culture for Rural Development of Mahidol University, Bangkok 7/29-31/1998.

Kuter, Lois. 1989. Breton vs. French: Language and the opposition of political, economic, social, and cultural values. In Nancy C. Dorian, ed., Investigating obsolescence: Studies in language contraction and death. Cambridge: Cambridge University Press.

Ladefoged, Peter, Ruth Glick, and Clive Criper. 1972. Language in Uganda. London: Oxford University Press.

Lafarge, Francine. 1978. Etudes phonologiques des parlers kosop (Kim) et gerep (Djouman), groupe kim (Adamawa). Mayo Kebbi, Tchad (thèse 3e cycle, Université de Paris III).

Lamberti, Marcello. 1986. Map of Somali dialects in the Somali Democratic Republic. Hamburg: Helmut Buske Verlag.

Lamberti, Marcello. 1986. The origin of the Jiiddu of Somalia. In Annarita Puglielli, ed., Proceedings of the Third International Congress of Somali Studies. Il Pensiero Scientifico Editore, pp. 3-10.

Landaburu, John. El tratamiento gramatical de la verdad en la lengua andoque. Revista Colombiana de Antropología. Bogotá: Instituto Colombiano de Cultura, pp. 81-100.
Langdon, Margaret. 1968. The Proto-Yuman demonstrative system. Folia Linguistica 2.1:61-81.
Langdon, Margaret. 1974. Comparative Hokan-Coahuiltecan studies. The Hague: Mouton.
Larsen, Thomas W. 1984. Case markings and subjecthood in Kipeá Kirirí. Proceedings of the 10th Annual Meeting of the Berkeley Linguistic Society, pp. 189-205.
Law, Gail. 1982. Chinese Churches Handbook. Hong Kong: Chinese Coordination Centre of World Evangelism.
Laycock, D. C. 1965. The Ndu language family (Sepik District), New Guinea. Linguistic Circle of Canberra Publications, Series C, No.1.
Laycock, D. C. 1968. Languages of the Lumi Sub-district (West Sepik District), New Guinea. Oceanic Linguistics 7.1.
Laycock, D. C. 1973. Sepik languages checklist and preliminary classification. Pacific Linguistics Series B, No. 25.
Le Page, R. B. 1960. Jamaican creole: A historical introduction to Jamaican Creole, Creole Language Studies, No. 1. London: MacMillan.
Lebar, Frank M., ed. 1972. Ethnic groups of insular Southeast Asia, Vol. 1. New Haven: Human Relations Area Files Press.
Lebar, Frank M., Gerald C. Hickey, and John K. Musgrave. 1964. Ethnic groups of mainland Southeast Asia. New Haven: Human Relations Area Files Press.
Lehmann, Winfred P. 1975. Language and linguistics in the People's Republic of China. Austin: University of Texas Press.
Leroy, Jacqueline. 1980. The Ngemba group: Mankon, Bangangu, Mundum I, Bafut, Nkwen, Bambui, Pinyin, Awing. In Hyman and Voorhoeve, eds., Les classes nominales dans le bantou des Grassfields. L'expansion bantoue, Vol. 1, pp. 111-141. Paris: SELAF.
Li Fang-gui. 1973. Languages and dialects of China. Journal of Chinese Linguistics 1:1-13.
Li Fang-gui. 1977. A handbook of comparative Tai. Honolulu: University of Hawaii Press.
Li Rong, Xiong Zhenghui, Zhang Zehnxing, Fu Maoji, Wang Jun, Dob, S. A. Wurm, B. T'sou, and D. Bradley. 1988. The language atlas of China, Parts 1, 2.
Li, Paul. 1987. The preglottalised stops in Bunun. Pacific Linguistics, C.
Liang Min. 1987. The origins of the Kam-Sui peoples. Zhongguo Minzushi Yanjiu 1.2.
Liang Min. 1990. The Buyang language. In Jerold A. Edmondson, ed., pp. 13-21.
Lieberson, Stanley. 1981. Language diversity and language contact. Stanford: Stanford University Press.
Lim, S. 1977. Listing Austronesian languages, Parts 1,2.
Lim, S. 1981. Baba Malay, the language of the "Straits-born" Chinese. M.A. thesis, Monash University, Australia.
Liu Guangkun. 1998. Research on Mawo Qiang. Chengdu: Sichuan Minorities Press.
Loewen, Jacob A. 1963. Choco I: Introduction and bibliography. IJAL 29.3:239-263.
Loewen, Jacob A. 1963. Choco II: Phonological problems. IJAL 29.4:357-371.
Lokpari, Basa Vyalisha. 1981. Introduction aux langues de l'Ituri, Colloque sur l'Enseignement des langues caïroises, CANDIP et Institut Supérieure Pédagogique/Bunia.
Longacre, Robert. 1957. Proto-Mixtecan. IURC Publication 5. Bloomington, IN: Indiana University, supplement to IJAL 23.4.
Longacre, Robert. 1967. Systemic comparison and reconstruction. In Norman McQuown, ed., Handbook of Middle American Indians, Vol. 5. Austin: University of Texas Press, pp. 117-159.
Loos, Eugene E. 1973. Algunas implicaciones de la reconstrucción de un fragmento de la gramática del proto-pano. Estudios Peruanos 2, Serie Lingüística Peruana 11. Yarinacocha: Instituto Lingüístico de Verano, pp. 263-282.
Lopis, J. 1980. Phonologie et morphologie du noon, parler de Ngente. Thèse de 3e cycle, Paris III.
Lorenzino, Gerardo A. 1999. The Angolar Creole Portuguese of São Tomé: Its grammar and sociolinguistic history. Muenchen, Germany: Lincom.
Lorimer, D. L. R. 1922. The phonology of the Baktiari, Badakhshani, and Madaglashti dialects of Modern Persian. London: Royal Asiatic Society.
Loukotka, Çestmír. 1968. Classification of South American Indian Languages. Reference series Vol. 7. Johannes Wilbert, ed. Latin American Center, University of California, Los Angeles, California.
Lukas, Johannes. 1937. A study of the Kanuri language: Grammar and vocabulary. London: Oxford University Press.
Lyon, Patricia J. 1975. Dislocación tribal y clasificación lingüística en la zona del río Madre de Dios. XXXIX Congreso International de Americanistas: Actas y Memorias, Vol. 5:185-207.

Maclean, Arthur J. 1895. Grammar of the dialects of vernacular Syriac. Cambridge: Cambridge University Press, reprinted 1971 Amsterdam: Philo Press.
Macuch, Rudolf. 1965. Handbook of Classical and modern Mandaic. Berlin: DeGruyter.
Mahapatra, B. P. Malto. 1971. An ethnosemantic study. Mysore, India: Central Institute of Indian Languages.
Maho, J.F. 1998. Few people, many tongues: The languages of Namibia. Windhoek: Gamsberg Macmillan.
Manessy, Gabriel. 1961. Le Bwamu et ses dialectes. Publication de la Section de Langues et Litteraires, No. 9. Dakar: Universite de Dakar, Fac. des Lettres et Sciences Humaines.
Manessy, Gabriel. 1975. Les langues Oti-Volta. p. 4. Paris: SELAF.
Manessy, Gabriel. 1981. Langues voltaïques. In Jean Perrot, ed., Les langues dans le monde ancien et moderne (Vol.1, Les langues dans l'Afrique subsaharienne). Paris: CNRS.
Mansur, Abdalla Omar. 1986. A lexical aspect of Somali and East Cushitic languages. In Annarita Puglielli, ed., Proceedings of the Third International Congress of Somali Studies, pp. 11-18.
Mapes, Glynn. 1990. Linguistic Lazarus: Cornish language is back from the dead. The Wall Street Journal, May 16, 1990, p. A1.
Marcais, Ph. 1977. Esqisse grammaticale de L'Arabe Maghrebin. Paris: Librairie d'Amerique et d'Orient.
Marchese, Lynell. 1979. Atlas Linguistique des Langues Kru. Abidjan: Université d'Abidjan.
Marrison, Geoffrey Edward. 1967. The Classification of the Naga Languages of North East India. Vol. I, II. Ph.D. dissertation. London: University of London.
Martens, Michael. 1989. The Badaic languages of Central Sulawesi. Studies in Sulawesi Linguistics: Part I, NUSA 31.
Martin, Peter W. 1991. Whither the Indigenous languages of Brunei Darussalem?' Oceanic Linguistics 34.1:29,39.
Martin, Peter W., Conrad Oxog, and Gloria Poedjosoedarmo, eds. 1996. Language use and language change in Brunei Darussalam. Athens, Ohio: Ohio University Center for International Studies.
Marty, Paul. 1930. Les Nimadi, Maures sauvages et chasseurs. Herperis 11:119-124.
Masica, Colin P. 1991. The Indo-Aryan languages. Cambridge: Cambridge University Press.
Masyhuda, M. 1971. Bahasa Kaili Pamona. Palu: Yayasan Kebudayaan.
Mathis, Steve L., III, ed. 1980. International directory of services for the deaf. Washington, D.C.: Gallaudet University.
Matisoff, James A. 1991. Endangered languages of Mainland Southeast Asia. In Robins and Uhlenbeck, eds., pp. 189-228.
Matisoff, James A., Stephen P. Baron, and John B. Lowe. 1996. Languages and dialects of Tibeto-Burman. STEDT Monograph Series, No. 2, James A. Matisoff, General Editor, Center for Southeast Asia Studies. Berkeley: University of California Press.
Matteson, Esther, Alva Wheeler, Frances L. Jackson, Nathan E. Waltz, and Diana R. Christian. 1972. Comparative studies in Amerindian languages. The Hague: Mouton.
Maurer, Phillippe. 1995. L'Angolar. Un créole afro-portugais parlé à São Tomé; Notes de grammaire, textes, vocabulaires. Hamburg: Helmut Buske Verlag.
Maybury-Lewis, David and James Howe. 1979. The Indian peoples of Paraguay, problems and prospects. USAID Paraguay.
Mayers, Marvin K. 1960. The linguistic unity of Pocoman-Pocomchi. IJAL 26:290-300.
Mayers, Marvin K. 1965. Linguistic comparisons [between Mayan languages]. In M. K. Mayers, ed., pp. 272-305.
McAlpin, David W. 1981. Proto-Elamo-Dravidian: The evidence and its implications. Philadelphia: The American Philosophical Society.
McConnell, Grant D., ed., 1995. The written languages of the world: A survey of the degree and modes of use, Vol. 4: China. Quebec: Laval University Press.
McCrum, Robert, William Cran, and Robert MacNeil. 1986. The Story of English. New York: Elisabeth Sifton Books, Viking.
McElhanon, Kenneth A. 1967. Preliminary observations on Huon Peninsula languages. Oceanic Linguistics 6:1-45.
McElhanon, Kenneth A. 1971. Classifying New Guinea languages. Anthropos 66:120-144.
McElhanon, Kenneth A. 1978. A classification of the languages of the Morobe Province, Papua New Guinea with the linguistic situation of individual villages. Canberra: Department of Linguistics, Australian National University.
McFarland, Curtis D. 1980. A linguistic atlas of the Philippines. Tokyo: University of Foreign Studies, Institute for the Study of Languages and Cultures of Asia and Africa.
McGregor, William. 1988. Handbook of Kimberley Languages, Vol 1: General Information. Canberra: Pacific Linguistics, Series C-105.

McKaughan, Howard P. and Michael L. Forman. 1981. Pidgin in Hawaii: 'Da Kine' talk serves useful purposes. Ampersand 14:4.11-15.
McKinney, Carol V. 1985. The Bajju of central Nigeria: A case study of religious and social change. M.A. thesis. Ann Arbor: University of Michigan.
McQuown, Norman. 1955. The indigenous languages of Latin America. American Anthropologist 57:501-570.
McVey, Ruth T., ed. 1963. Indonesia. New Haven: Human Relations Area Files.
Meillet, Antoine and Marcel Cohen, eds. 1952. Les langues du monde. Paris: Campion.
Menges, K. H. 1968. The Turkic languages and peoples. Wiesbaden: Otto Harrassowitz.
Menkhaus, K. J. 1989. Rural transformation and the roots of underdevelopment in Somalia's lower Jubba valley. Ph.D. dissertation. Columbia: University of South Carolina.
Messing, Gordon M. 1980. Politics and national language in Albania. In Frans Van Coetsem and Linda R. Waugh, eds., Contributions to historical linguistics. Leiden: E. J. Brill, pp. 270-280.
Middleton, J. 1955. Notes on the political organization of the Madi of Uganda. African Studies 14.1.
Middleton, J. 1960. Lugbara religion: Ritual and authority among an East African people. London: Oxford University Press.
Middleton, John. 1965. The Lugbara of Uganda. NY: Holt, Rinehart and Winston.
Migliazza, Ernest C. ms. (1977) Languages of the Rio Branco-Rio Orinoco Region: Current status.
Miller, Philip E. 1993. Karaite separatism in nineteenth-century Russia. Cincinnati: Hebrew Union College Press.
Miller, Wick R. 1984. The classification of the Uto-Aztecan languages based on lexical evidence. IJAL 50.1:1-24.
Mills, R. F. 1975. Proto South Sulawesi and Proto Austronesian phonology. Ph.D. dissertation. Ann Arbor: University of Michigan.
Mills, R. F. 1981. Additional addenda. NUSA, Linguistic studies in Indonesian and languages in Indonesia 10:59-82.
Ministry of Development, Sultanate of Oman. 1996. General census of population, housing and establishments 1993-Detailed publication of the results of the census.
Minnich, R. Herbert. 1974. Mennonites in Latin America: Number and distribution. The Mennonite Quarterly Review, Vol. 48.
Mohan, Peggy and Paul Zador. 1986. Discontinuity in a Life Cycle: The death of Trinidad Bhojpuri. Language 62.2:291-319.
Monan, James and Daisy Y. Noval-Morales. 1979. A primer on the Negritos of the Philippines. Manila: Philippine Business for Social Progress.
Moñino, Yves, ed. 1988. Lexique comparatif des langues Oubanguiennes. Paris: Librairie Orientaliste Paul Geuthner S.A.
Morgenstierne, Georg. 1974. Languages of Nuristan and surrounding regions. In Karl Jettmas, ed., Cultures of the Hindu Kush: Selected papers from the Hindu-Kush cultural conference held in Moesgard 1970, pp. 1-10. Wiesbaden: Franz Steiner Verlag.
Moulton, William G. 1985. Mutual intelligibility among speakers of early German dialects. Presented at Germania Conference, Georgetown University.
Mühlhäusler, Peter. 1987. Identifying and mapping the pidgins and creoles of the Pacific. Duisburg: Linguistic Agency, University of Duisburg.
Muller, Siegfried H. 1964. The world's living languages. New York: Frederick Ungar.
Murane, Elizabeth, ed. 1975. Bibliography of the Summer Institute of Linguistics Papua New Guinea Branch 1956 to 1975. Ukarumpa: Summer Institute of Linguistics.
Murdock, George Peter. 1959. Africa: Its peoples and their culture history. New York: McGraw-Hill.
Naden, Tony. 1989. Gur. In J. Bendor-Samuel, ed., pp. 147-168.
Nagore, Francho. 1989. Grammática de la lengua Aragonesa, Fifth edition. Zaragoza: Mira Editores, S.A. 347 pp.
Nakano, A. 1986. The Turoyo language today. Chicago: Journal of Assyrian Academic Studies.
Needham, R. 1954. Penan and Punan. Journal of the Malayan Branch of the Royal Asiatic Society 27.I :73-83.
Newman, Paul. 1977. Chadic classification and reconstructions. Afroasiatic Linguistics 5:1-42. Malibu, California: Undena Publications.
Nicolai, Robert. 1979. Le Songhay Central. Niamey: Études Linguistiques 1:2.33-69.
Nicolai, Robert. 1981. Les dialectes du Songhay: contributions a l'etude des changements linguistiques. Ph.D. dissertation. Paris: SELAF.
Nicolai, Robert. 1983. Position, structure, and classification of Songay. In M. L. Bender, ed., pp. 11-41.
Nida, Eugene A. and Harold Fehderau. 1970. Indigenous pidgins and koines. IJAL 36:146-155.

Nida, Eugene A., ed. 1972. The book of a thousand tongues. Second edition. New York: United Bible Societies.

Nigam, R. C. 1972. Language handbook on mother tongue in census. Census of India 1971, Census centenary monograph no. 10. New Delhi: Office of the Registrar General, Government of India, Ministry of Home Affairs.

Noble, G. Kingsley. 1965. Proto-Arawakan and its descendants. Indiana University Publications in Anthropology and Linguistics No. 38.

Nurse, Derek. 1982. Segeju and Daisu: A case study of evidence from oral tradition and comparative linguistics. History in Africa, Vol. 9.

Nyrop, Richard F., et al. 1974. Area handbook for India. Washington, D.C.: American University.

Nyrop, Richard F. ed, 1986. The Yemens: country studies. Washington, D. C.: American University.

Oates, W. J. and Lynette F. Oates. 1970. A revised linguistic survey of Australia. Canberra: Australian Institute of Aboriginal Studies.

Oberling, Pierre. 1974. The Qashqa'i nomads of Fars. The Hague: Mouton.

Odden, David. Aspects of Didinga phonology and morphology. In M. L. Bender, ed., pp. 148-176.

Ohannessian, Sirarpi and Mubanga E. Kashoki, eds. 1978. Language in Zambia. London: International African Institute.

O'Leary, Clare F., ed. 1992. Sociolinguistic survey of Northern Pakistan. National Institute of Pakistan Studies Quaid-i-Azam University and Summer Institute of Linguistics. Dallas: Summer Institute of Linguistics.

O'Leary, Clare F., Calvin R. Rensch, Calinda E. Hallberg, and Clare F. O'Leary, eds. 1992. Vol. 3, Hindko and Gujari.

O'Leary, Clare F., Calvin R. Rensch, Sandra J. Decker, and Daniel G. Hallberg, eds. 1992. Vol. 1, Languages of Kohistan.

O'Leary, Clare F., Kendall D. Decker. 1992. Vol. 5, Languages of Chitral.

O'Leary, Clare F., Peter C. Backstrom and Carla F. Radloff, eds. 1992. Vol. 2, Languages of northern areas.

O'Leary, Clare F. and Daniel G. Hallberg 1992. Vol. 4, Pashto, Waneci, Ormuri.

Olson, Kenneth S. 1996. On the comparison and classification of Banda dialects. In Lisa M. Dobrin, Kora Singer, and Lisa McNair, eds., CLS 32, Papers from the Main Session. Chicago: Chicago Linguistic Society, pp. 267-283.

Oltrogge, David. 1977 Proto-Jicaque Subtiaba-Tequistlateco: A comparative reconstruction. M.A. thesis. Arlington: University of Texas.

Omar, Asmah Haji. 1983. The Malay peoples of Malaysia and their languages. Kuala Lumpur: Dewan Bahasa Dan Pustaka, Kementerian Pelajaran Malaysia.

Ottenheimer, H. J. and M. Ottenheimer. 1976. The classification of the languages of the Comoro Islands. Africana Linguistica 18.9:408-415.

Otterloo, Roger Van. 1979. A Kalenjin dialect study. Nairobi: Summer Institute of Linguistics.

Ouane, Adama. 1986. Aperçu sociolinguistique du Mali. In Promotion et Intégration des Langues Nationales dans les Systèmes Educatifs. CONFEMEN. Paris: Editions Champion.

Owens, Jonathan. 1985. Arabic dialects of Chad and Nigeria. Journal of Arabic Linguistics 14:45-61. Wiesbaden: Harrassowitz.

Painter, Colin. 1966. Linguistic field notes from Banda and language maps of the Guang speaking areas of Ghana, Togo, and Dahomey. Institute of African Studies No. 7.

Painter, Colin. 1967. The distribution of Guang in Ghana and a statistical pre-testing on twenty-five idiolects. Journal of West African Languages 4.1:25-78.

Pallesen, A. Kemp. 1984. Culture contact and language convergence. Ph.D. dissertation. Berkeley: University of California.

Paper, Herbert H., ed. 1978. Jewish languages: Theme and variation. Cambridge, Massachusetts: Association for Jewish Studies.

Parker, Gary J. 1976. Gramática quechua: Ancash-Huaylas. Lima, Perú: Ministerio de Educación.

Parker, Stephen. 1988. Some universal aspects of coalescence processes confirmed by Chamicuro phonology and morphology. M.A. thesis. Arlington: University of Texas.

Patai, Bridglal, ed., 1972. The early history of Malawi. London: Longman.

Pawley, Andrew and Lawrence A. Reid. 1980. The evolution of transitive constructions in Austronesian. In Paz Buenaventura Naylor, ed., Austronesian studies (Michigan papers on South and Southeast Asia, 15), pp. 103-130. Ann Arbor: University of Michigan.

Payne, David L. 1978. Phonology and morphology of Axininca (Apurucayali Campa). Ph.D. thesis. University of Texas at Arlington.

Payne, David L. 1985. The genetic classification of Resigaro. IJAL 51:222-231.

Payne, David L. 1988. On proposing deep genetic relationships in Amazonian languages: The case of Candoshi and Maipuran Arawakan languages. Presented at the Society for the Study of Indigenous Languages of the Americas.

Payne, David L. 1988. Una visión panorámica de la familia lingüística arawak. Actas del Tercer Seminario-Taller para el Estudio Preliminar del Atlas Etnolingüístico Colombiano.

Payne, David L. 1991. A classification of Maipuran (Arawakan) languages based on shared lexical retentions. Handbook of Amazonian Languages, vol. 3.

Payne, David L. Some morphological elements of Maipuran Arawakan: Agreement affixes and the genitive construction. Language Sciences 9:57-75.

Payne, Doris L. 1985. Aspects of the grammar of Yagua: A typological perspective. Ph.D. thesis. UCLA.

Payne, Doris L. 1985. -ta in Zaparoan and Peba-Yaguan. IJAL 51:529-531.

Payne, J. R. 1987. Iranian Languages. In Bernard Comrie, ed., pp. 514-522.

Payne, Ronald and Kalpana Vora. 1991. Radio brings Latin back from the dead. The European September 27, 1991.

Payne, Thomas E. 1985. Participant coding in Yagua discourse. Ph.D. thesis. UCLA.

Perrot, Jean, ed. 1981. Les langues dans le monde ancien et moderne. Paris: Centre National de la Recherche Scientifique.

Persson, Andrew. 1984. The relationships of the languages of the Sudan. Occasional Papers in the Study of Sudanese Languages 3. Juba: University of Juba, SIL, and IRL, pp. 1-5.

Phillips, Kathleen. 1979. The initial standardization of the Yambeta language. D.E.S. dissertation submitted at the University of Yaoundé, Cameroon.

Pinnow, Heinz-Jurgen. 1963. The position of the Munda languages within the Austroasiatic language family. In H. L. Shorto, ed., Linguistic comparison in South East Asia and the Pacific. London: School of Oriental and African Studies.

Platiel, S. 1978. Les langues Mandé. In D. Barreteau, ed., Inventaire des études linguistiques sur les pays d'Afrique noire d'expression française et sur Madagascar. Paris: Conseil International de la Langue Française.

Podolsky, Baruch. 1985. Notes on the Urum language. Rovanik Orientalistyczny, T 44, z.2, pp. 59-66.

Pollet, E. 1971. La société Soninké (Dyahunn, Mali). Brussels: Editions de l'Université de Bruxelles.

Polman, Katrien. 1981. The Central Moluccas: An annotated bibliography. KITLV Bibliographical Series 12. Dordrecht: Foris Publications.

Polomé, E. C. and C. P. Hill, eds. 1980. Language in Tanzania. London: Oxford University Press for the IAI.

Poppe, Nicholas. 1970. Mongolian language handbook. Washington: Center for Applied Linguistics.

Prachakij-karacak, Phraya. 1995. Some languages of Siam, translated and annotated by David Thomas and Sophana Srichampa. Institute of Language and Culture for Rural Development, Mahidol University.

Prochazka, Theodore, Jr. 1988. Saudi Arabian dialects. London: Kegan Paul International.

Purnama, Karyono. 1991. The sociolinguistic pattern of use of Standard Malay in Brunei Darussalam. Brunei Darussalam: Department of Malay Language and Linguistics, Universiti Brunei Darussalam (presented at 6ICAL, Honolulu).

Purnell, Herbert C. 1970. Toward a reconstruction of Proto-Miao-Yao. Ph.D. dissertation. Ithaca: Cornell University.

Quackenbush, Edward M. 1988. From Sonsoral to Truk: A dialect chain. Ph.D. dissertation. Ann Arbor: University of Michigan.

Quakenbush, John Stephen. 1989. Language use and proficiency in a multilingual setting: A sociolinguistic survey of Agutaynen speakers in Palawan, Philippines. Manila: Linguistic Society of the Philippines.

R. B. Boeder. Silent majority—A history of the Lomwe in Malawi. Pretoria: Africa Institute of South Africa.

Ramer, Alexis Manaster. 1995. On the subject of Malagasy imperatives. Oceanic Linguistics 34.1:203-210.

Ramponi, E. 1937. Religion and divination of the Logbara tribe of North-Uganda. Anthropos 32.

Ramsey, Robert. 1987. The languages of China. Princeton: Princeton University Press.

Ravines, Rogger y Rosalía Ávalos de Matos. 1988. Atlas etnolingüística del Perú. Lima: Instituto Andino de Artes Populares del Convenio Andrés Bello, Comisión Nacional del Perú.

Redinha, Jose. 1970. Distribuição étnica da Província de Angola. Sixth Edition. Centro de Informação e Turismo de Angola.

Reesink, G. 1976. Languages of the Aramia River Area. Pacific Linguistics Series A, 45:1-37.

Rehg, Kenneth L. and Byron W. Bender. 1988. Lexical transfer from Marshallese to Mokilese: A study in Intra-Micronesian Borrowing. Presented at the Fifth International Conference on Austronesian Linguistics.

Reid, Lawrence A. (ms.) The Alta languages of the Philippines. Honolulu: Social Science Research Institute, University of Hawaii.

Reid, Lawrence A. 1971. Philippine minor languages: Word lists and phonologies. Oceanic Linguistics, Special Publication 8.

Reid, Lawrence A. 1982. The demise of Proto-Philippines. In Amran Halim et al., eds., Papers from the Third International Conference on Austronesian Linguistics, Vol. 2, Tracking the travellers, pp. 201-216. Pacific Linguistics, C-75.

Rennie, John Keith. 1973. Christianity, colonialism and the origins of nationalism among the Ndau of Mozambique. Ph.D. dissertation. Chicago: Northwestern University.

Rensch, Calvin R. 1966. Comparative Otomanguean phonology. Ph.D. dissertation. Philadelphia: University of Pennsylvania.

Rensch, Calvin R. 1968. Proto Chinantec phonology. [Papeles de la Chinantla 6, Serie Científica 10] México: Museo Nacional de Antropología.

Rensch, Calvin R., Calinda E. Hallberg, and Clare F. O'Leary, eds. 1992. Hindko and Gujari. Vol. 3 of Sociolinguistic survey of Northern Pakistan. Dallas: Summer Institute of Linguistics.

Rensch, Calvin R., Sandra J. Decker, and Daniel G. Hallberg, eds. 1992. Languages of Kohistan. Vol. 1 or Sociolinguistic survey of Northern Pakistan. Dallas: Summer Institute of Linguistics.

Report of the Commission of Enquiry into South West African Affairs. 1962-1963. Pretoria.

Ribeiro, Darcy and Mary Ruth Wise. 1979. Grupos étnicos de la Amazonía Peruana. Comunidades y Culturas Peruanas No. 13. Lima, Perú: Instituto Lingüístico de Verano.

Ribeiro, Darcy. 1957. Culturas e linguas indígenas do Brasil. Educação e Ciencias Sociais 2.6.

Rickford, John R. 1974. The insights of the mesolect. In David De Camp and Ian F. Hancock, eds., pp. 92-117.

Riviere, Jean-Claude. 1982. Situation des langues d'Oc. L'information grammaticale, Paris 12:13.

Robins, R. H. and E. M. Uhlenbeck, eds. 1991. Endangered Languages. Oxford: Berg Publishers, Ltd.

Robles, Carlos. 1964. Investigaciones lingüísticas sobre los grupos indígenas del estado de Baja California. Anales del Instituto Nacional de Antropología e Historia. 17:275-301.

Rodrigues, Aryon D. 1958. Classification of Tupi-Guarani. IJAL 24:231-234.

Roesler, Calvin. 1972. The phonology of the Ajam dialect of Asmat. M.A. thesis. Hartford Seminary Foundation.

Romaine, Suzanne. 1988. Pidgin and creole languages. London: Longman.

Ross, Malcolm D. 1988. Proto Oceanic and the Austronesian languages of western Melanesia. Pacific Linguistics, C-98.

Rottland, Franz. 1981. The segmental morphology of proto-Southern Nilotic. In Schadeberg and Bender, eds., pp. 5-17.

Rottland, Franz. 1983. Southern Nilotic. In M. L. Bender, 1983a, pp. 208-238.

Ruhlen, Merritt. 1975. A guide to the languages of the world. Stanford University Language Universals Project.

Ruhlen, Merritt. 1987. A guide to the world's languages, Vol 1: Classification. Stanford: Stanford University Press.

Rutkis, J., ed. 1967. Latvia: Country and people. Stockholm: Latvian National Foundation.

Sacks, Oliver. 1989. Seeing voices. Berkeley: University of California Press.

Saeed, John I. 1982. Central Somali—A grammatical outline. Afroasiatic Linguistics 8.2:2-43.

Saenz-Badillos, Angel. 1993. A history of the Hebrew language. Cambridge: Cambridge University Press.

Salombe, C., Donald F. Barr, and Sharon G. Barr. 1979. Languages of Central Sulawesi. Ujung Pandang: Summer Institute of Linguistics and Hasanuddin University.

Salzner, Richard. 1960. Sprachenatlas des Indopazifischen Raumes. Wiesbaden: Otto Harrassowitz.

Samarin, William J. 1971. Adamawa-Eastern. In Thomas A. Sebeok, ed., vol. 7, pp. 213-244.

Sandager, Oliver K. 1986. Sign languages around the world. North Hollywood: Ok Publishing.

Sandefur, John R. 1984. A language coming of age: Kriol of North Australia. M.A. thesis. Perth: University of Western Australia.

Sandefur, John R. 1990. Kriol and Torres Strait Creole: Where do they meet? Darwin: Occasional Bulletin, Nungalinya College.

Sankoff, Gillian. 1968. Social aspects of multilingualism in New Guinea. Ph.D. dissertation. McGill University.

Sapir, J. David. 1971. West Atlantic: An inventory of the languages, their noun class systems and consonant alternation. In Sebeok, vol. 7, pp. 45-58.

Sara, Solomon I. 1974. A description of modern Chaldean. Moulton.
Sasse, Hans-Jürgen. 1987. Kuschitische Sprachen. Studium Linguistik 21:78-99.
Sather, Clifford. 1997. The Bajau Laut. Oxford: Oxford University Press.
Schadeberg, Thilo C. 1981. A survey of Kordofanian I: Heiban Group, (SUGIA Beiheft I). Hamburg: Buske Verlag.
Schadeberg, Thilo C. 1981. The classification of the Kadugli language group. In Schadeberg and Bender, eds., pp. 291-305.
Schadeberg, Thilo C. and M. Lionel Bender, eds. 1981. Nilo-Saharan. Dordrecht: Foris Publications.
Schenker, A. M. and E. Stankiewicz, eds. 1980. The Slavic Literary Languages: Formation and Development, Yale Concilium on International and Area Studies. New Haven, Conn.
Schmidt, Annette. 1990. The loss of Australia's Aboriginal language heritage. The Institute Report Series. Canberra: Aboriginal Studies Press.
Schooling, Stephen. 1990. Language maintenance in Melanesia: Sociolinguistics and social networks in New Caledonia. Summer Institute of Linguistics and the University of Texas at Arlington Publications in Linguistics 91. Dallas.
Schreck, Harley and David Barrett, eds. 1987. Unreached peoples: Clarifying the task. Monrovia: MARC.
Schütz, Albert J. 1972. The languages of Fiji. Oxford: Clarendon.
Scriptures of the world. 1996. New York: United Bible Societies.
Scruggs, Terri R. ms. (1982) Rapport linguistique de l'enquête menée à Bokito. Yaoundé: Société Internationale de Linguistique.
Sebeok, Thomas A., ed. 1963. Soviet and East European linguistics (Current Trends in Linguistics, Vol. 1). The Hague: Mouton.
Sebeok, Thomas A., ed. 1967. Linguistics in east Asia and Southeast Asia (Current Trends in Linguistics, Vol. 2). The Hague: Mouton.
Sebeok, Thomas A., ed. 1968. Ibero-American and Caribbean linguistics (Current Trends in Linguistics, Vol. 4). The Hague: Mouton.
Sebeok, Thomas A., ed. 1969. Linguistics in South Asia (Current Trends in Linguistics, Vol. 5). The Hague: Mouton.
Sebeok, Thomas A., ed. 1970. Southwest Asia and North Africa (Current Trends in Linguistics, Vol. 6). The Hague: Mouton.
Sebeok, Thomas A., ed. 1971. Linguistics in Oceania (Current Trends in Linguistics, Vol. 8). The Hague: Mouton.
Sebeok, Thomas A., ed. 1971. Linguistics in Sub-Saharan Africa (Current Trends in Linguistics, Vol. 7). The Hague: Mouton.
Sebeok, Thomas A., ed. 1977. Native languages of the Americas, Vols. 1, 2. New York: Plenum.
Seidensticker, Wilhelm and Gizachew Adamu. 1986. A bibliographical guide to Borno studies 1821-1983. Maiduguri: University of Maiduguri.
Shackle, C. 1979. Problems of classification in Pakistan Punjab. Transaction of the Philological Society, pp 191-210.
Shackle, C. 1980. Hindko in Kohat and Peshawar. Bulletin of the School of Oriental and African Studies 43.3:482-510.
Shafer, Robert. 1955. Classification of the Sino-Tibetan languages. Word 11:94-111.
Shapiro, Michael C. and Harold F. Schiffman. 1981. Language and Society in South Asia. Delhi: Motilal Banarsidass.
Sharma, Jagdish Chander. 1971. Pronouns in Gade Lohar dialect. In H. S. Biligiri, ed., Papers and Talks. Mysore, India: Central Institute of Indian Languages.
Sharma, Jagdish Chander. 1982. Gojri grammar. Mysore: Central Institute of Indian Linguistics.
Shaw, R. D. 1973. A tentative classification of the languages of the Mt. Bosavi Region. Pacific Linguistics Series C, 26:187-215.
Shaw, R. D. 1981. The Bosavi language family: An interim report. Presented at the 1981 Congress of the Linguistic Society of Papua New Guinea.
Shellabear, W. G. 1913. Baba Malay, an introduction to the language of the Straits-born Chinese. Journal of the Royal Asiatic Society (Straits Branch) 65:49-63.
Shnukal, Annette. 1982. Why Torres Strait "Broken English" is not English. In Jeanie Bell, ed., Aboriginal languages and the question of a national language policy. Alice Springs, NT: Aboriginal Language Association, pp. 25-35.
Showalter, Stuart D. 1991. Surveying sociolinguistic aspects of interethnic contact in rural Burkina Faso: An adaptive methodological approach. Ph.D. dissertation. Georgetown University.
Siegel, Jeff. 1991. Language maintenance of Overseas Hindi. Anuario del seminario de filologica vasca "Julio de Urquijo" 25.2:91-114.

Silzer, Peter J., Heljä Heikkinen, and Duane Clouse. 1986. Peta lokasi bahasa-bahasa daerah di propinsi Irian Jaya, Seri D, No. 1. Jayapura: Program Kerjasama Universitas Cenderawasih and Summer Institute of Linguistics.

Simmons-McDonald, Hazel. 1994. Comparative patterns in the acquisition of English negation by native speakers of (St. Lucian) French Creole and English, Language Learning 44.1:29-74.

Simons, Gary F. 1979. Language variation and limits to communication, Technical Report No. 3., NSF Grant No. BNS 76-06031. DMLL, Cornell University.

Simons, Gary F. 1982. Word taboo and comparative Austronesian linguistics. Pacific Linguistics C-76, pp. 157-226.

Simons, Linda. 1983. A comparison of the pidgins of Solomon Islands and Papua New Guinea. Pacific Linguistics A-65, pp. 121-137.

Singh, K. S. 1994. The scheduled tribes. Anthropological Survey of India. Calcutta: Oxford University Press.

Singh, K. S. 1995. The scheduled castes. Anthropological Survey of India. Calcutta: Oxford University Press.

Singh, Nagendra. 1972. Bhutan: A kingdom in the Himalayas. New Delhi: Thomson.

Sirk, Ü. 1981. The South Sulawesi group and neighbouring languages. Indonesia Circle 25:29-36.

Sirk, Ü. 1983. The Buginese language. Moscow: Nauka Publishing House.

Smalley, W. A. ed. 1976. Phonemes and orthography: Language planning in ten minority languages of Thailand. Canberra: Australian National University.

Smedal, Olaf H. 1987. Lom-Indonesia-English and English-Lom Wordlists, Accompanied by four Lom Texts, NUSA: Linguistic Studies of Indonesian and Other Languages in Indonesia, Vol. 28/29, Jakarta.

Smith, Kenneth D. 1968. Sedang dialects. M.A. thesis. Grand Forks: University of North Dakota.

Smith, Kenneth D. 1972. A phonological reconstruction of Proto-North-Bahnaric. [Language Data-Asia Pacific Studies 3] Santa Ana: Summer Institute of Linguistics.

Smith, Kenneth D. 1973. Eastern north Bahnaric: Cua and Kotua. Mon-Khmer Studies 4:113-118.

Sneddon, J. N. 1981. Sulawesi. In S. A. Wurm and Shirô Hattori, eds., No. 44.

Sneddon, J. N.. 1988. The position of Lolak. Presented at the Fifth International Congress of Austronesian Linguistics.

Sobelman, Harvey, ed. 1962. Arabic dialect studies: A selected bibliography. Washington, D.C.: Center for Applied Linguistics and Middle East Institute.

Soto Ruiz, Clodoaldo. 1976. Gramática quechua: Ayacucho-Chanca. Lima, Perú: Ministerio de Educación.

Southall, A. W. 1956. Alur society. Cambridge: W. Seffer & Sons, Ltd.

Sperl, Savitri Rambissoon.1980. From Indians to Trinidadians: A study of the relationship between language, behaviour, socio-economic and cultural factors in a Trinidad village. Ph. D. dissertation. University of York.

Sreedhar, M. V. 1974. Naga Pidgin: A sociolinguistic study of inter-lingual communication pattern in Nagaland. Mysore, India: Central Institute of Indian Languages.

Staalsen, P. 1975. The languages of the Sawos Region. Anthropos 70:6-16.

Stahl, Wilmar. 1982, 1986. Escenario Indígena Chaqueño pasado y presente. Filadelfia: Asociación de Servicios de Cooperación Indígena-Menonita.

Stallcup, Kenneth I. 1980a. La géographie linguistique des Grassfields. In Hyman and Voorhoeve, eds., Les classes nominales dans le bantou des Grassfields. L'expansion bantoue, Vol. 1, pp. 43-57. Paris: SELAF.

Stallcup, Kenneth I. 1980b. The Momo languages. In Hyman and Voorhoeve, eds., Les classes nominales dans le bantou des Grassfields. L'expansion bantoue, Vol. 1, pp. 194-223. Paris: SELAF.

Stallcup, Kenneth I. 1980c. Noun classes in Esimbi. In L. Hyman, ed., Noun classes in the Grassfields Bantu borderland. Southern California Occasional Papers in Linguistics No. 8. Los Angeles, California: University of Southern California.

Stampe, David L., ed. 1965-1966. Recent work in Munda linguistics. (parts I-IV in Abstracts and Translations section) IJAL 31.4, Part 1, pp. 332-341 (1965); 32.1, pp. 74-80 (1966); 32.2, pp. 164-168 (1966); 32.4, pp. 390-397 (1966).

Stanley, George Edward. 1968. The indigenous languages of South West Africa. Anthropological Linguistics 10:5-18.

Stephens, Meic. 1976. Linguistic minorities in western Europe. Llandysul, Wales: Gomer.

Stevenson, Roland C. 1956. A survey of the phonetics and grammatical structure of the Nuba Mountain languages, with particular reference to Otoro, Katcha and Nyimang. Afrika und Ubersee 40:110-112.

Stevenson, Roland C. 1981. Adjectives in Nyimang, with special reference to k- and t- prefixes. In Schadeberg and Bender, pp. 151-165.

Stevenson, Roland C. 1984. The Nuba people of Kordofan Province. Khartoum.

Steward, Julian Haynes, ed. 1946-1950. Handbook of South American Indians (seven volumes). Washington, D.C. : U. S. Government Printing Office.

Stewart, John Massie. 1971. Niger-Congo, Kwa. In Thomas A. Sebeok, ed., Vol.7.

Stewart, William A. 1962. Creole languages of the Caribbean. In Frank A. Rice, ed., Study of the role of second languages in Asia, Africa, and Latin America. Washington, D.C.

Stigand, C. H. 1925. Equatoria, the Lado Enclave. London: Constable and Co., Ltd., pp. 19, 89.

Stilo, D. L. 1981. The Tati languages group in the sociolinguistic context of Northwestern Iran and Transcaucasia. Iranian Studies 14.3-4:137-187.

Stokes, J. F. G. 1965. Language in Rapa. Journal of the Polynesian Society 64:315-340.

Stokoe, William and Rolf Kuschel. 1979. A field guide for sign language research. Silver Spring: Linstok Press, Inc.

Stoltzfus, Ronald Dean. 1974. Toward defining centers for indigenous literature programs: A problem of language communication. M.A. thesis. Cornell University.

Strand, Richard F. 1973. Notes on the Nuristani and Dardic languages. Journal of the American Oriental Society 93.3:297-305.

Strecker, David. 1987. The Hmong-Mien languages. Linguistics of the Tibeto-Burman Area 10.2:1-11.

Strecker, David. 1989. Hmongic noun prefixes. Presented at the Linguistic Society of America Annual Meeting, December 1989.

Summer Institute of Linguistics. 1987. Second language oral proficiency evaluation. Notes on Linguistics 40:24-54.

Sun Hongkai, Lu Shaozun, Zhang Jichuan, and Ouyang Jueya. 1980. The languages of the Menba, Luoba, and Deng peoples. Beijing: Chinese Social Science Publishing House.

Sun, Tianshin Jackson. 1993. A historical-comparative study of the Tan (Mirish) branch in Tibeto-Burman. Ph.D. dissertation. Berkeley: University of California.

Susnik, Branislava. 1986-1987. Los aborígenes del Paraguay, VII/1, Lenguas Chaquenas. Asuncion: Museo Etnográfico “Andres Barbero”.

Swift, Jeremy. 1975. The Sahara. Amsterdam: Time-Life International.

Taber, Mark. 1993. Towards a better understanding of the languages of Maluku. Oceanic Linguistics 32.2.

Tarpent, Marie-Lucie and Daythal Kendall. 1998. On the relationship between Takelma and Kalapuyan: Another look at ‘Takelman’. Paper presented at SSILA, LSA 1/10/98 New York.

Tax, Sol. 1960. Aboriginal languages of Latin America. Current Anthropology 1:430-436.

Taylor, Brian K. 1962. The Western Lacustrine Bantu. London: International African Institute.

Taylor, Carrie. ms. (1982) Les langues de l’arrondissement de Bokito: esquisse d’une enquête sociolinguistique. Yaoundé: Société Internationale de Linguistique.

Taylor, Douglas. 1977. Languages of the West Indies. Baltimore: Johns Hopkins University Press.

Taylor, Paul. 1991. The folk biology of the Tobelo people: A study in folk classification. Washington, D.C.: Smithsonian Institution Press.

Teeuw, A. 1961. A critical survey of studies on Malay and Bahasa Indonesia. (Bibliographical Series No. 5). The Hague: Martinus Nijhoff.

Thelwall, Robin, ed. 1978. Aspects of language in the Sudan. (Occasional Papers in Linguistics and Language Learning, No. 5) Coleraine: New University of Ulster.

Thelwall, Robin. 1981. Lexicostatistical subgrouping and lexical reconstruction of the Daju group. In Schadeberg and Bender, pp. 167-185.

Thelwall, Robin. 1983. Meidob Nubian: Phonology, grammatical notes and basic vocabulary. In M. L. Bender, ed., 1983a, pp. 97-113.

Thelwall, Robin. 1983. Twampa phonology. In M. L. Bender, ed., 1983a, pp. 323-335.

Thieberger, N. comp. 1990. Handbook of South Western Australian languages south of the Kimberley regions. Port Hedland, WA: Pilbara Aboriginal Language Centre.

Thiessen, Jack. 1963. Studien zum deutschsprachigen Wortschatz der kanadischen Mennoniten. Elwert Verlag, 3550 Marburg.

Thomas, Bertram. n.d. Four strange tongues from south Arabia: The Hadara group. Proceedings of the British Academy, Vol. XXIII. London: Humphrey Milford Amen House EC.

Thomas, David D. 1966. Mon-Khmer subgroupings in Vietnam. In N. Zide, ed., Studies in comparative Austroasiatic linguistics. The Hague: Mouton, pp. 194-202.

Thomas, David D. 1969. Mon-Khmer in North Vietnam. Mon-Khmer Studies 3:74-75.

Thomas, David D. 1976. South Bahnaric and other Mon-Khmer numeral systems. Linguistics 174:65-80.

Thomas, David D. 1980. The place of Alak, Tampuan, and West Bahnaric. Mon-Khmer Studies 8:171-186.

Thomas, David D. and Robert K. Headley, Jr. 1970. More on Mon-Khmer subgroupings. Lingua 25:398-418.

Thomas, Jacqueline M. C. and Serge Bahuchet, eds. 1983. Encyclopedia des Pygmées Aka. Paris: SELAF.

Thompson, E. David. 1983. Kunama: Phonology and noun phrase. In M. L. Bender, ed., pp. 281-322.

Tippett, A. R. 1970. Peoples of Southwest Ethiopia. Pasadena: William Carey Library.

Titiev, Mischa. 1951. Araucanian culture in transition. Occasional Contributions from the Museum of Anthropology of the University of Michigan, No. 15. Ann Arbor: University of Michigan Press.

Toba, Sueyoshi. 1976. National language and ethnic minority languages in Nepal. In Symposium Nepal, 1975, Vol. 4, pp. 30-36. Japan-Nepal Society [in Japanese].

Toba, Sueyoshi. 1983. A phonological reconstruction of Proto-Northern Rai. M.A. thesis. University of Texas at Arlington ix, 106 pp.

Toba, Sueyoshi. 1991. A bibliography of Nepalese languages and linguistics. Kathmandu: Linguistic Society of Nepal ix, 120 pp.

Todd, E. M. 1975. The Solomon language family. Pacific Linguistics, Series C, No. 38. Canberra: Australian National University.

Todd, Loreto and Ian Hancock. 1986. International English usage. London: Croom Helm.

Torero, Alfredo F. 1970. Lingüística e historia de la sociedad andina. Anales Científicos 8:3-4.231-264.

Tovar, Antonio. 1961. Catálogo de las lenguas de América del Sur. Buenos Aires: Editorial Sudamérica.

Tovar, Antonio. 1966. Notas de campo sobre el idioma Chorote. XXXVI Congreso Internacional de Americanistas, España 1964: Actas y Memorias, Tomo 2. Sevilla.

Tran Tri Doi. 1996. The languages that constitute the Viet-Muong group. Ngon-Ngu 3:28-34. Hanoi: Linguistics Institute of Vietnam.

Travis, Edgar W. 1986. A lexicostatistic survey of the languages indigenous to Ambon Island. Ambon: Pattimura University and the Summer Institute of Linguistics.

Troike, Rudolph C. 1969. The glottochronology of six Turkic languages. IJAL 35:183-191.

Troike, Rudolph C. 1970. The linguistic classification of Cochimí. Paper presented at the Hokan Conference, University of California, San Diego.

Trudgill, Peter and G. A. Tzavaras. 1977. Why Albanian-Greeks are not Albanians. In Howard Giles, ed. Language, ethnicity and intergroup relations. London: Academic Press, chapter 7.

Tryon, D. T. and B. D. Hackman. 1983. Solomon Islands Languages: An internal classification. Pacific Linguistics C72.

Tryon, Darrell T., ed. 1995. Comparative Austronesian Dictionary, Parts 1-4. Berlin: Mouton de Gruyter.

Tryon, Darrell T. 1971. The contemporary language situation in the New Hebrides. Presented at the 28th International Congress of Orientalists.

Tryon, Darrell T. 1976. New Hebrides languages: An internal classification. Pacific Linguistics C-50.

Tryon, Darrell T. 1978. The languages of the New Hebrides: Internal and external relationships. Pacific Linguistics C-61.

Tryon, Darrell T. 1981. Towards a classification of Solomon Islands languages. Presented at Third International Conference of Austronesian Linguistics.

Tsuchida, Shigeru. 1976. Reconstruction of Proto-Tsouic phonology. Tokyo: Institute of Asian and African Languages and Cultures, University of Foreign Language.

Tucker, Archibald N. 1967 (1940). The Eastern Sudanic languages. Vol. 1. London: Dawsons for IAI.

Tucker, Archibald N. and M. A. Bryan. 1957. Linguistic survey of the northern Bantu borderland. London: Oxford University Press.

Tucker, Archibald N. and M. A. Bryan. 1966. The non-Bantu languages of North-Eastern Africa. Handbook of African Languages, Part III. Oxford: Oxford University Press.

T'ung-ho, Tung et al. 1964. A descriptive study of the Tsou language, Formosa. Taipei: Institute of History and Philology, Academia Sinica.

Turnbull, Colin M. 1972. The mountain people. New York: Simon & Schuster, Inc.

Tuttle, Edward F. 1988. Review of Glauco Sanga, Dialettologia Lombarda, Lingue e culture popolari. Pavia: Universita di Pavia, Dipartimento di Scienza della Letterature (Aurora Edizione) 1984. Language 64:1.208-9.

Ubels, Edward H. 1975. An historical-comparative study of some West Bamileke dialects. M.A. thesis. University of Toronto.

Uhlenbeck, E. M. 1964. A critical survey of studies on the languages of Java and Madura (Bibliographical Series No. 7). The Hague: Martinus Nijhoff.

United Bible Societies. 1978-1997. World translations progress reports and supplements. London: United Bible Societies.

Unseth, Peter. 1988. The validity and unity of the 'Southeast Surma' language grouping. Northeast African Studies 10.2-3:151-163.

Unseth, Peter. 1990. Linguistic bibliography of the non-Semitic languages of Ethiopia. [Ethiopian Series Monograph 20] East Lansing and Addis Ababa: African Studies Center, Michigan State University and Institute of Ethiopian Studies, Addis Ababa University.

Urvoy, Y. 1942. Mémoire de L'IFAN No. 5: Petit Atlas Ethno-Demographique du Soudan entre Sénégal et Tchad. Paris V: Librairie Larose.

Valenzuela, Pilar. 1988. Clasificación de iñapari. Presented at the Symposium on Arawakan Linguistics, 46th International Congress of Americanists.

Van Cleve, John. 1986. Encyclopedia of deaf people and deafness. Washington, D.C.: Gallaudet University.

Van den Berg, René. 1988. Muna dialects and Munic languages: Towards a reconstruction. Presented at the Fifth International Conference on Austronesian Linguistics.

Van Driem, George. 1993. The grammar of Dzongkha. Dzongkha Development Commission, Royal Government of Bhutan.

VanBulck, Gaston and Peter Hackett. 1956. Report of the eastern team (Oubangui to Great Lakes). Linguistic Survey of the northern Bantu borderland, 1, pp. 63-122. London: Oxford University Press for International Africa Institute.

Vanderaa, Larry. 1991. A survey for Christian Reformed World Missions of missions and churches in West Africa. Grand Rapids: Christian Reformed World Missions.

Vansina, J. 1966. Regions culturelles du Congo. Introduction a l'Ethnolographic du Congo. Brussels: CRISP.

Verin, Pierre, Kottak, and Gorlin. 1969. The glottochronology of Malagasy speech communities. Oceanic Linguistics 8.1.

Vitale, A. J. 1980. Kisetla: Linguistic and sociolinguistic aspects of a Pidgin Swahili of Kenya. Anthropological Linguistics 22.2:47-65.

Voegelin, C. F. and F. M. Voegelin. 1965a. Languages of the World: Sino-Tibetan, Fascicles 4 and 5. Anthropological Linguistics 7.5 (May 1965), 7.6 (June 1965).

Voegelin, C. F. and F. M. Voegelin. 1965b. Languages of the World: Indo-European, Fascicle 1. Anthropological Linguistics 7.8 (November 1965).

Voegelin, C. F. and F. M. Voegelin. 1977. Classification and index of the world's languages. New York: Elsevier North Holland, Inc.

Voeltz, Erhardt. 1979. The languages and dialects of the Southwest Province of Cameroon. Presented at the Tenth Annual Conference on African Linguistics, University of Illinois, Urbana.

Von Fuerer-Haimendorf, Christoph. 1985. Tribes of India: The struggle for survival. Delhi: Oxford University Press.

Voorhoeve, C. L. 1968. The Central and South New Guinea Phylum. Pacific Linguistics, Series A, Occasional Papers, No. 16.

Voorhoeve, C. L. 1975. Languages of Irian Jaya: Checklist, preliminary classification, language maps, word lists. Pacific Linguistics, Series B, No. 31.

Voorhoeve, P. 1955. A critical survey of studies on the languages of Sumatra (Bibliographical Series No. 1). The Hague: Martinus Nijhoff.

Voroshil, Q. 1972. On the Trilingualism of the Udi, in problems of bilingualism and multilingualism. Moscow.

Vossen, Rainier. 1981. The Eastern Nilotes: Linguistic and historical reconstructions. Köln: University of Köln.

Vossen, Rainier. 1983. Comparative Eastern Nilotic. In M. L. Bender, ed., 1983a, pp. 177-207.

Vydrine, Valentin. To appear. Review of Kastenholz. Journal of African Languages and Linguistics.

Wagner, C. Peter and Edward R. Dayton, eds. 1979-1984. Unreached peoples. Elgin, Illinois: David C. Cook Publishing Co.

Walker, Dale F. 1976. A grammar of the Lampung language: the Pesisir dialect of Way Lima. Jakarta: Badan Penyelenggara Seri NUSA, Vol. II.

Walton, Janice R. and David C. Moody. 1984. The east coast Bajau languages. In J. K. King and J. W. King, pp. 113-123.

Wang Fushi. 1985. Sketch of the Miao language. Beijing: Nationalities Publishing House.

Ward, Jack. 1969. Working papers No. 4. Honolulu: Department of Linguistics, University of Hawaii.

Wares, Alan C. 1965. A comparative study of Yuman consonantism. Ph.D. dissertation. Austin: University of Texas; 1968 The Hague: Mouton.

Wares, Alan C. 1979, 1985, 1986. Bibliography of the Summer Institute of Linguistics 1935-1985, Vols. 1-3. Dallas: Summer Institute of Linguistics.

Waters, Bruce. 1989. Djinang and Djinba: A historical and grammatical perspective. Pacific Linguistics C-114. Xvi, 405 pp.

Watters, John R. 1981. A phonology and morphology of Ejagham-with notes on dialect variation. Ph.D. dissertation. Los Angeles: University of California.

Welmers, William E. 1971. Checklist of language and dialect names. In Thomas A. Sebeok, ed., Vol. 7, pp. 759-900.

Welmers, William E. 1971. Christian missions and language policies. In Sebeok, T. A. pp. 559-569.

Welmers, William E. 1971. Niger-Congo, Mande. In Sebeok, T. A., pp. 113-140.

Welmers, William E. 1973. African language structures. Berkley: University of California Press.

Westermann, Diedrich and M. A. Bryan. 1970. Handbook of African languages, Part II. Folkestone: Dawsons.

Whinnom, Keith. 1956. Spanish contact vernaculars in the Philippine Islands. Hong Kong: Hong Kong University Press.

White, John Claude. 1971. Sikhim and Bhutan: Twenty-one years on the North-East Frontier (1887-1908). Delhi: Vivek.

Whiteford, Scott. 1981. Workers from the north. Austin: University of Texas Press.

Whiteley, Wilfred H. 1969. Swahili: The rise of a national language. London: Methuen and Co. Ltd.

Whiteley, Wilfred H., ed. 1974. Language in Kenya. Nairobi: Oxford University Press, Dar es Salaam.

Widlok, Thomas. 1997. Akhoe pragmatics, Haiom identity and the Khoekhoe language. In Haacke and Elderkin, eds. pp., 117-153.

Williams, Gordon, ed. 1993. Enque^te sociolinguistique sur les langues Cangin de la région de Thiès au Sénégal. Dakar, Senegal: SIL, Cahiers de Recherche Linguistique No 3.

Williamson, Kay. 1971. The Benue-Congo languages and Ijo. In Thomas A. Sebeok, ed., Vol. 7, pp. 245-306.

Willis, Roy G. 1966. The Fipa and related peoples of south-west Tanzania and north-east Zambia. London: International African Institute.

Wilson, Darryl. 1969. The Binandere language family. Pacific Linguistics, Series A, Occasional Papers No. 18.

Wimbish, John. 1989. WORDSURV: A program for analyzing language survey word lists. Occasional Publications in Academic Computing 13. Dallas: Summer Institute of Linguistics.

Winer, Lise. 1993. Varieties of English around the world: Trinidad and Tobago. Amsterdam: John Benjamins.

Winsa, Birger. 1998. Language attitudes and social identity—Opression and revival of a minority language in Sweden. Canberra: Applied Linguistics Association of Australia.

Winter, Werner, ed. 1991. The Rai of eastern Nepal: Ethnic and linguistic grouping. Findings of the Linguistic Survey of Nepal. Kirtipur: Tribhuvan University.

Wise, Mary Ruth. 1976. Apuntes sobre la influencia Inca entre los amuesha: Factor que oscurece la clasificación de su idioma. Revista del Museo Nacional XLII:355-366.

Wise, Mary Ruth. 1983. Lenguas indígenas de la Amazonia Peruana, historia y estado presente. América Indígena 43:4.823-848.

Wise, Mary Ruth. 1988. Comparative morphosyntax and subgrouping of Maipuran Arawakan languages. Presented at the Symposium on Arawakan Linguistics, 46th International Congress of Americanists.

Wise, Mary Ruth. Valence-changing affixes in Maipuran Arawakan languages. Proceedings of the Working Conference on American Languages.

Wismann, Lynn and Margaret Walsh. 1987. Signs of Morocco. U.S. Peace Corps.

Wittmann, Henri, ed. 1991. Les langues Signées. Revue québécoise de linguistique théorique et appliquée 10.1.

Wonderly, William L. and Eugene A. Nida. 1963. Linguistics and Christian missions. Anthropological Linguistics 5:104-144.

World Almanac and Book of Facts. 1999. Mahwah, N.J.: World Almanac Books.

Wumbu, Indra, et al. 1973. Bahasa-bahasa di Sulawesi Tengah. Palu: Prasurvey Kebudayaan Propinsi Sulawesi Tengah.

Wurm, Stephen A. 1961. The linguistic situation in the Highlands Districts of Papua and New Guinea. Australian Territories 1.2:14-23.

Wurm, Stephen A. 1971. The Papuan linguistic situation. In Sebeok, T. A., ed., Vol. 8.

Wurm, Stepehn A. 1972. Languages of Australia and Tasmania. Janua Linguarum, Series Critica, 1. The Hague: Mouton.

Wurm, Stephen A. 1975. Papuan languages and the New Guinea linguistic scene. New Guinea area languages and language study, Vol. 2. Pacific Linguistics Series C, No. 38.

Wurm, Stephen A. and Shirô Hattori. 1981. Language atlas of the Pacific area. Canberra: The Australian Academy of the Humanities in collaboration with the Japan Academy.

Wurm, Stephen A., Liu Yongquan, Wang Gungwu, B. T'sou, D. Bradley, J. Hardy, Li Rong, Xiong Zhenghui, Zhang Zhenxing, Fu Maoji, Wang Jun, Dob, Junast, and Ma Xuelian. 1987. Language atlas of China. Hong Kong: Longman Group.

Young, Colville N. 1973. Belize Creole: A study of the creolized English spoken in the city of Belize, in its social and cultural setting. Ph.D. dissertation. University of York.

Young, Oliver Gordon. 1961. The hill tribes of northern Thailand, Second edition (Siam Society Monograph 1).

Zavadovskii, Yurii Nikolaevich. 1962. The Arabic dialects of the Maghrib. Moscow: The Publishing House of Eastern Literature. [in Russian]

Z'Graggen, J. A. 1969. Classificatory and typological studies in languages of the western Madang District New Guinea. Canberra: Australian National University.

Z'Graggen, J. A. 1971. Classificatory and typological studies in languages of the Madang District. Pacific Linguistics C-19.

Z'Graggen, J. A. 1975. The languages of the Madang District, Papua New Guinea. Pacific Linguistics B-41.

Zhao Xiangru and Reinhard F. Hahn, 1989. The Ili Turk people and their language. Central Asiatic Journal 33.3-4.

Zorc, R. David. 1986. The genetic relationships of Philippine languages. In Paul Geraghty, ed., FOCAL: Papers from the Fourth International Conference on Austronesian Linguistics, Vol. 2., pp. 147-173.

ABBREVIATIONS

Note: Some institutions may be listed under more than one name because of differences among our sources. Some names are incomplete, such as 'Episcopal' or 'Mennonite'.

ABWE	Association of Baptists for World Evangelism
ACTNM	Apostolic Christian Mission
AIM	African Inland Mission
ALCAM	Atlas Linguistique du Cameroun
AMC	Association of Malian Churches
ANG	Anglican
AO	Autonomous Okrug, Autonomous Oblast
AOG	Assemblies of God
AP	Associated Press
ASL	American Sign Language
ASSR	Autonomous Soviet Socialist Republic
BAP	Baptist
BIA	Bureau of Indian Affairs (USA)
BSROC	Bible Society in Republic of China
BTL	Bible Translation and Literacy
CAL	Center for Applied Linguistics, Washington, D.C.
CAM	CAM International
CAR	Central African Republic
CBFMS	Conservative Baptist Foreign Mission Society
CCCOWE	Chinese Coordination Centre of World Evangelism
CIIL	Central Institute of Indian Languages
CMA	Christian and Missionary Alliance
COM	Church of Melanesia (ANG)
CNL	Commission Nationale de Linguistique, Benin or Togo
DFM	Deaf Missions
DOM	Dorothea Mission
DRC	Democratic Republic of Congo
EDCL	Encyclopedic Dictionary of Chinese Linguistics
EELC	Église Évangélique Lutherienne du Cameroun
EFL	Église Fraternelle Lutherienne du Cameroun
EP	Episcopal
F	Society of Friends
FUNAI	National Indian Foundation, Brazil
GEKISUS	Christian Evangelical Church in South Sumatra
GILLBT	Ghana Institute of Linguistics, Literacy, and Bible Translation
GKI	Indonesian Christian Church
GMI	Global Mapping International
GR	Gospel Recordings
HRAF	Human Relations Area Files, Yale University
IBS	International Bible Society
ICDBL	International Committee for the Defense of the Breton Language
IEM	Indian Evangelical Mission
IJAL	International Journal of American Linguistics
IMA	India Missions Association
LBT	Lutheran Bible Translators
LGA	Local Government Area (Nigeria)
MARC	Missions Advanced Research and Communications Center
MCA	Missionary Church Association
MEN	Mennonite
MES	Misión Evangélica Suiza
MOR	Moravian
MPR	Mongolian People's Republic
N	Church of the Nazarene
NRC	Netherlands Reformed Congregations
NT	New Testament
NTM	New Tribes Mission
NWFP	Northwest Frontier Province, Pakistan
OIEL	Oxford International Encyclopedia of Linguistics
OMF	Overseas Missionary Fellowship
ORTH	Orthodox
OVS	Object-Verb-Subject
PBS	Philippine Bible Society
PBT	Pioneer Bible Translators
PC	Peace Corps (USA)
PDR	People's Democratic Republic of...
PNG	Papua New Guinea
PNGBTA	Papua New Guinea Bible Translation Association
PR	Presbyterian
RBMU	Regions Beyond Missionary Union
RC	Roman Catholic Church
REF	Reformed
SDA	Seventh Day Adventist
SFM	Swedish Free Mission
SFSR	Soviet Federal Socialist Republic
SIL	SIL International
SIM	SIM International
SOV	Subject-Object-Verb
SUM	Sudan United Mission
TEAM	The Evangelical Alliance Mission
TILL	The Institute for Liberian Languages
TISLL	The Institute for Sierra Leonean Languages
UAE	United Arab Emirates
UBS	United Bible Societies
UC	United Church
UFM	Unevangelized Fields Mission
UMN	United Mission to Nepal
UMS	United Missionary Society (see MCA)
UN	United Nations
UPUSA	United Presbyterian Church in the United States of America
USA	United States of America
USSR	Union of Soviet Socialist Republics
VOS	Verb-Object-Subject
WA	World Almanac
WC	The Wesleyan Church
WCE	World Christian Encyclopedia (Barrett 1982)
WT	World Team

LANGUAGES OF SPECIAL INTEREST

More information on each language is available under the country indicated.

CREOLE LANGUAGES (82):

AFRO-SEMINOLE CREOLE [AFS] USA
AMAPA CREOLE [AMD] Brazil
ANGOLAR [AOA] Sao Tome e Principe
ARABIC, BABALIA CREOLE [BBZ] Chad
ARABIC, SUDANESE CREOLE [PGA] Sudan
AUKAN [DJK] Suriname
BAHAMAS CREOLE ENGLISH [BAH] Bahamas
BAJAN [BJS] Barbados
BAY ISLANDS CREOLE ENGLISH [BYH] Honduras
BERBICE CREOLE DUTCH [BRC] Guyana
BETAWI [BEW] Indonesia
BISLAMA [BCY] Vanuatu
CAFUNDO CREOLE [CCD] Brazil
CHAVACANO [CBK] Philippines
CRIOULO, UPPER GUINEA [POV] Guinea-Bissau
CUTCHI-SWAHILI [CCL] Kenya
DUTCH CREOLE [DCR] U.S. Virgin Islands
FA D'AMBU [FAB] Equatorial Guinea
FERNANDO PO CREOLE ENGLISH [FPE] Equatorial Guinea
FRENCH GUIANESE CREOLE FRENCH [FRE] French Guiana
GUYANESE CREOLE ENGLISH [GYN] Guyana
HAITIAN CREOLE FRENCH [HAT] Haiti
HAWAII CREOLE ENGLISH [HAW] USA
INDO-PORTUGUESE [IDB] Sri Lanka
INDONESIAN, PERANAKAN [PEA] Indonesia
KABUVERDIANU [KEA] Cape Verde Islands
KARIPUNA CREOLE FRENCH [KMV] Brazil
KITUBA [KTU] Democratic Republic of Congo
KORLAI CREOLE PORTUGUESE [VKP] India
KRIO [KRI] Sierra Leone
KRIOL [ROP] Australia
KWINTI [KWW] Suriname
LEEWARD CARIBBEAN CREOLE ENGLISH [AIG] Antigua and Barbuda
LESSER ANTILLEAN CREOLE FRENCH [DOM] St. Lucia
LOUISIANA CREOLE FRENCH [LOU] USA
MACANESE [MZS] China
MALACCAN CREOLE MALAY [CCM] Malaysia
MALACCAN CREOLE PORTUGUESE [MCM] Malaysia
MALAY, AMBONESE [ABS] Indonesia
MALAY, BABA [BAL] Singapore
MALAY, KUPANG [MKN] Indonesia
MORISYEN [MFE] Mauritius
MUNUKUTUBA [MKW] Congo
NAGA PIDGIN [NAG] India
NGATIK MENS CREOLE [NGM] Micronesia
NORTHERN CENTRAL AMERICA CREOLE ENGLISH [BZI] Belize
NUBI [KCN] Uganda
OORLAMS [OOR] South Africa
PALENQUERO [PLN] Colombia
PAPIAMENTU [PAE] Netherlands Antilles
PETJO [PEY] Indonesia
PIDGIN, CAMEROON [WES] Cameroon
PIDGIN, NIGERIAN [PCM] Nigeria
PIDGIN, TIMOR [TVY] Indonesia
PIJIN [PIS] Solomon Islands
PRINCIPENSE [PRE] Sao Tome e Principe
REUNION CREOLE FRENCH [RCF] Reunion
SAMANA ENGLISH [SAX] Dominican Republic
SAN MIGUEL CREOLE FRENCH [SME] Panama
SANGO [SAJ] Central African Republic
SANGO, RIVERAIN [SNJ] Central African Republic
SAOTOMENSE [CRI] Sao Tome e Principe
SARAMACCAN [SRM] Suriname
SEA ISLAND CREOLE ENGLISH [GUL] USA
SESELWA CREOLE FRENCH [CRS] Seychelles
SKEPI CREOLE DUTCH [SKW] Guyana
SOUTHWESTERN CARIBBEAN CREOLE
SRANAN [SRN] Suriname
SRI LANKAN CREOLE MALAY [SCI] Sri Lanka
TAYO [CKS] New Caledonia
TERNATENO [TMG] Indonesia
TETUM PRASA [TDT] Indonesia
TOBAGONIAN CREOLE ENGLISH [TGH] Trinidad and Tobago
TOK PISIN [PDG] Papua New Guinea
TORRES STRAIT CREOLE [TCS] Australia
TRINIDADIAN CREOLE ENGLISH [TRF] Trinidad and Tobago
TSOTSITAAL [FLY] South Africa
TURKS AND CAICOS CREOLE ENGLISH [TCH] Turks and Caicos Islands
UNSERDEUTSCH [ULN] Papua New Guinea
VIRGIN ISLANDS CREOLE ENGLISH [VIB] U.S. Virgin Islands
WESTERN CARIBBEAN CREOLE ENGLISH [JAM] Jamaica
WINDWARD CARIBBEAN CREOLE ENGLISH [SVG] St. Vincent and the Grenadines

DEAF SIGN LANGUAGES (114):

ADAMOROBE SIGN LANGUAGE [ADS] Ghana
ALGERIAN SIGN LANGUAGE [ASP] Algeria
AMERICAN SIGN LANGUAGE [ASE] USA
ARGENTINE SIGN LANGUAGE [AED] Argentina
ARMENIAN SIGN LANGUAGE [AEN] Armenia

AUSTRALIAN ABORIGINES SIGN LANGUAGE [ASW] Australia
AUSTRALIAN SIGN LANGUAGE [ASF] Australia
AUSTRIAN SIGN LANGUAGE [ASQ] Austria
BALI SIGN LANGUAGE [BQY] Indonesia
BAMAKO SIGN LANGUAGE [BOG] Mali
BAN KHOR SIGN LANGUAGE [BLA] Thailand
BELGIAN SIGN LANGUAGE [BVS] Belgium
BOLIVIAN SIGN LANGUAGE [BVL] Bolivia
BRAZILIAN SIGN LANGUAGE [BZS] Brazil
BRITISH SIGN LANGUAGE [BHO] United Kingdom
BULGARIAN SIGN LANGUAGE [BQN] Bulgaria
CATALONIAN SIGN LANGUAGE [CSC] Spain
CHADIAN SIGN LANGUAGE [CDS] Chad
CHIANGMAI SIGN LANGUAGE [CSD] Thailand
CHILEAN SIGN LANGUAGE [CSG] Chile
CHINESE SIGN LANGUAGE [CSL] China
COLOMBIAN SIGN LANGUAGE [CSN] Colombia
COSTA RICAN SIGN LANGUAGE [CSR] Costa Rica
CZECH SIGN LANGUAGE [CSE] Czech Republic
DANISH SIGN LANGUAGE [DSL] Denmark
DOMINICAN SIGN LANGUAGE [DOQ] Dominican Republic
DUTCH SIGN LANGUAGE [DSE] Netherlands
ECUADORIAN SIGN LANGUAGE [ECS] Ecuador
ESTONIAN SIGN LANGUAGE [ESO] Estonia
ETHIOPIAN SIGN LANGUAGE [ETH] Ethiopia
FINNISH SIGN LANGUAGE [FSE] Finland
FRENCH SIGN LANGUAGE [FSL] France
GERMAN SIGN LANGUAGE [GSG] Germany
GHANAIAN SIGN LANGUAGE [GSE] Ghana
GREEK SIGN LANGUAGE [GSS] Greece
GUATEMALAN SIGN LANGUAGE [GSM] Guatemala
GUINEAN SIGN LANGUAGE [GUS] Guinea
HAIPHONG SIGN LANGUAGE [HAF] Viet Nam
HANOI SIGN LANGUAGE [HAB] Viet Nam
HAUSA SIGN LANGUAGE [HSL] Nigeria
HAWAII PIDGIN SIGN LANGUAGE [HPS] USA
HO CHI MINH CITY SIGN LANGUAGE [HOS] Viet Nam
HUNGARIAN SIGN LANGUAGE [HSH] Hungary
ICELANDIC SIGN LANGUAGE [ICL] Iceland
INDIAN SIGN LANGUAGE [INS] India
INDONESIAN SIGN LANGUAGE [INL] Indonesia
IRISH SIGN LANGUAGE [ISG] Ireland
ISRAELI SIGN LANGUAGE [ISL] Israel
ITALIAN SIGN LANGUAGE [ISE] Italy
JAMAICAN COUNTRY SIGN LANGUAGE [JCS] Jamaica
JAPANESE SIGN LANGUAGE [JSL] Japan
JORDANIAN SIGN LANGUAGE [JOS] Jordan
KENYAN SIGN LANGUAGE [XKI] Kenya
KOREAN SIGN LANGUAGE [KVK] Korea, South
KUALA LUMPUR SIGN LANGUAGE [KGI] Malaysia
LAOS SIGN LANGUAGE [LSO] Laos
LATVIAN SIGN LANGUAGE [LSL] Latvia
LIBYAN SIGN LANGUAGE [LBS] Libya
LITHUANIAN SIGN LANGUAGE [LLS] Lithuania
LYONS SIGN LANGUAGE [LSG] France
MALAYSIAN SIGN LANGUAGE [XML] Malaysia
MALTESE SIGN LANGUAGE [MDL] Malta
MARITIME SIGN LANGUAGE [NSR] Canada
MARTHAS VINEYARD SIGN LANGUAGE [MRE] USA
MEXICAN SIGN LANGUAGE [MFS] Mexico
MONGOLIAN SIGN LANGUAGE [QMM] Mongolia
MOROCCAN SIGN LANGUAGE [XMS] Morocco
MOZAMBICAN SIGN LANGUAGE [MZY] Mozambique
NAMIBIAN SIGN LANGUAGE [NBS] Namibia
NEPALESE SIGN LANGUAGE [NSP] Nepal
NEW ZEALAND SIGN LANGUAGE [NZS] New Zealand
NICARAGUAN SIGN LANGUAGE [NCS] Nicaragua
NIGERIAN SIGN LANGUAGE [NSI] Nigeria
NORWEGIAN SIGN LANGUAGE [NSL] Norway
OLD KENTISH SIGN LANGUAGE [OKL] United Kingdom
PAKISTAN SIGN LANGUAGE [PKS] Pakistan
PENANG SIGN LANGUAGE [PSG] Malaysia
PERSIAN SIGN LANGUAGE [PSC] Iran
PERUVIAN SIGN LANGUAGE [PRL] Peru
PHILIPPINE SIGN LANGUAGE [PSP] Philippines
POLISH SIGN LANGUAGE [PSO] Poland
PORTUGUESE SIGN LANGUAGE [PSR] Portugal
PROVIDENCIA SIGN LANGUAGE [PRO] Colombia
PUERTO RICAN SIGN LANGUAGE [PSL] Puerto Rico
QUEBEC SIGN LANGUAGE [FCS] Canada
RENNELLESE SIGN LANGUAGE [RSI] Solomon Islands
ROMANIAN SIGN LANGUAGE [RMS] Romania
RUSSIAN SIGN LANGUAGE [RSL] Russia
SALVADORAN SIGN LANGUAGE [ESN] El Salvador
SAUDI ARABIAN SIGN LANGUAGE [SDL] Saudi Arabia
SINGAPORE SIGN LANGUAGE [SLS] Singapore
SLOVAKIAN SIGN LANGUAGE [SVK] Slovakia
SOUTH AFRICAN SIGN LANGUAGE [SFS] South Africa
SPANISH SIGN LANGUAGE [SSP] Spain
SRI LANKAN SIGN LANGUAGE [SQS] Sri Lanka
SWEDISH SIGN LANGUAGE [SWL] Sweden
SWISS-FRENCH SIGN LANGUAGE [SSR] Switzerland

SWISS-GERMAN SIGN LANGUAGE [SGG] Switzerland
SWISS-ITALIAN SIGN LANGUAGE [SLF] Switzerland
TAIWANESE SIGN LANGUAGE [TSS] Taiwan
TANZANIAN SIGN LANGUAGE [TZA] Tanzania
THAI SIGN LANGUAGE [TSQ] Thailand
TUNISIAN SIGN LANGUAGE [TSE] Tunisia
TURKISH SIGN LANGUAGE [TSM] Turkey
UGANDAN SIGN LANGUAGE [UGN] Uganda
UKRAINIAN SIGN LANGUAGE [UKL] Ukraine
URUBU-KAAPOR SIGN LANGUAGE [UKS] Brazil
URUGUAYAN SIGN LANGUAGE [UGY] Uruguay
VENEZUELAN SIGN LANGUAGE [VSL] Venezuela
YIDDISH SIGN LANGUAGE [YDS] Israel
YUCATEC MAYA SIGN LANGUAGE [MSD] Mexico
YUGOSLAVIAN SIGN LANGUAGE [YSL] Yugoslavia
ZAMBIAN SIGN LANGUAGE [ZSL] Zambia
ZIMBABWE SIGN LANGUAGE [ZIB] Zimbabwe

GYPSY LANGUAGES (15):
ANGLOROMANI [RME] United Kingdom
CALO [RMR] Spain
DOMARI [RMT] Iran
LOMAVREN [RMI] Armenia
ROMANI, BALKAN [RMN] Yugoslavia
ROMANI, BALTIC [ROM] Poland
ROMANI, CARPATHIAN [RMC] Czech Republic
ROMANI, KALO FINNISH [RMF] Finland
ROMANI, SINTE [RMO] Yugoslavia
ROMANI, VLACH [RMY] Romania
ROMANI, WELSH [RMW] United Kingdom
ROMANO-GREEK [RGE] Greece
ROMANO-SERBIAN [RSB] Yugoslavia
TAVRINGER ROMANI [RMU] Sweden
TRAVELLER DANISH [RMD] Denmark

JEWISH LANGUAGES (27):
ARABIC, JUDEO-IRAQI [YHD] Israel
ARABIC, JUDEO-MOROCCAN [AJU] Israel
ARABIC, JUDEO-TRIPOLITANIAN [YUD] Israel
ARABIC, JUDEO-TUNISIAN [AJT] Israel
ARABIC, JUDEO-YEMENI [JYE] Israel
BUKHARIC [BHH] Israel
DZHIDI [DZH] Israel
HEBREW [HBR] Israel
HEBREW, ANCIENT [HBO] Israel
HULAULA [HUY] Israel
ISRAELI SIGN LANGUAGE [ISL] Israel
JUDEO-BERBER [JBE] Israel
JUDEO-CRIMEAN TATAR [JCT] Uzbekistan
JUDEO-GEORGIAN [JGE] Israel
JUDEO-ITALIAN [ITK] Italy
JUDEO-TAT [TAT] Israel
KARAIM [KDR] Lithuania
KNAANIC [CZK] Czech Republic
LADINO [SPJ] Israel
LISHAN DIDAN [TRG] Israel
LISHANA DENI [LSD] Israel
LISHANID NOSHAN [AIJ] Israel
SHUADIT [SDT] France
YEVANIC [YEJ] Israel
YIDDISH SIGN LANGUAGE [YDS] Israel
YIDDISH, EASTERN [YDD] Israel
ZARPHATIC [ZRP] France

MIXED LANGUAGES (8):
CAKCHIQUEL-QUICHE MIXED LANGUAGE [CKZ] Guatemala
CAMTHO [CMT] South Africa
MBUGU [MHD] Tanzania
MEDIA LENGUA [MUE] Ecuador
MEDNYJ ALEUT [MUD] Russia
MICHIF [CRG] USA
WUTUNHUA [WUH] China
YENICHE [YEC] Germany

PIDGIN LANGUAGES (17):
BARIKANCHI [BXO] Nigeria
BROOME PEARLING LUGGER PIDGIN [BPL] Australia
CHINESE PIDGIN ENGLISH [CPE] Nauru
CHINOOK WAWA [CRW] Canada
DELAWARE, PIDGIN [DEP] USA
FANAGOLO [FAO] South Africa
GIBANAWA [GIB] Nigeria
IHA BASED PIDGIN [IHB] Indonesia
LIBERIAN ENGLISH [LIR] Liberia
LINGUA FRANCA [PML] Tunisia
MASKOY PIDGIN [MHH] Paraguay
MOBILIAN [MOD] USA
MOTU, HIRI [POM] Papua New Guinea
NDYUKA-TRIO PIDGIN [NJT] Suriname
ONIN BASED PIDGIN [ONX] Indonesia
SETTLA [STA] Zambia
TAY BOI [TAS] Viet Nam

GEOGRAPHIC DISTRIBUTION OF LIVING LANGUAGES, 2000

	Total Living Languages	%
The Americas	1,013	15%
Africa	2,058	30%
Europe	230	3%
Asia	2,197	32%
The Pacific	1,311	19%
TOTALS	6,809	

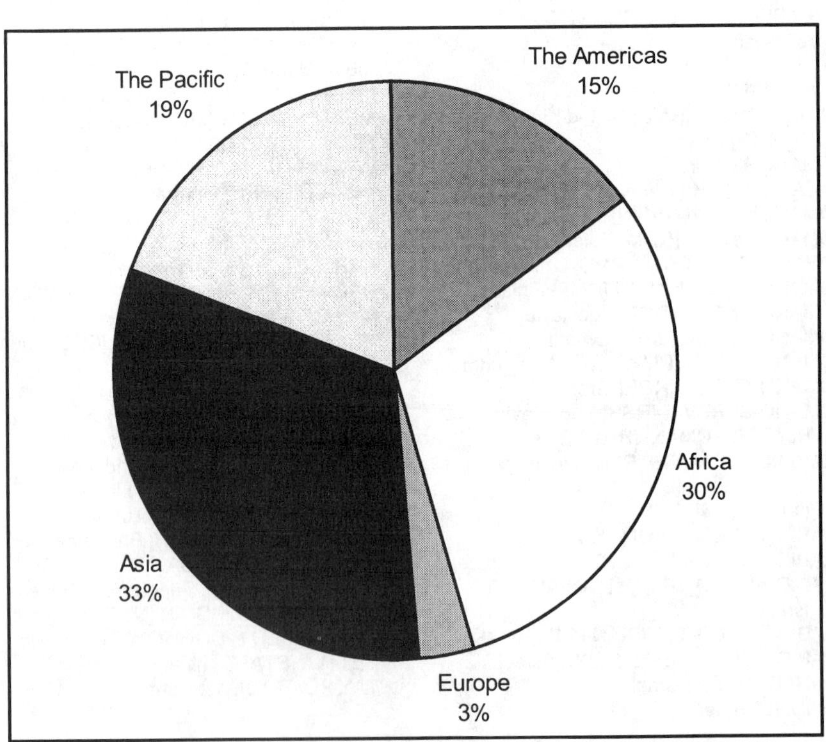

ETHNOLOGUE QUESTIONNAIRE

LANGUAGE UPDATE

If you are not able to answer all questions, please answer those you can. If the space given is not adequate, please answer in the space on the last page or on extra sheets, referring to the number of the question with your answer. Where there is multiple choice, please underline the ones that apply.

1. NAMES
(a) Name of language:
(b) If in 2000 Ethnologue, under what name?
(c) 3-letter identification code:
(d) Alternate names and spellings:
(e) Reason for preferred name:
(f) Name of people or ethnic group who speak it:

2. POPULATION
(a) Total number who speak it as first language (mother tongue), including all who speak dialects which are inherently intelligible (see No. 5):
(b) Source of the above number:
(c) Number in each dialect of (a):
(d) Age distribution of speakers:
(e) Number in each country where language is spoken (see 3a):
(f) Number who speak it as a second or third language:
(g) Number in ethnic group if different from first language speakers:

3. LOCATION
(a) Countries where spoken:
(b) Location in each country: towns, regions, states or provinces (draw a map if possible):
(c) Location of dialects:

4. LINGUISTIC AFFILIATION
(a) Family:
(b) Closely related languages:
(c) Closest language linguistically:

5. DIALECTS
(a) Names of dialects of the language:
(b) Names of ethnic subgroups if different from dialects:
(c) Comment on degree of intelligibility with specific dialects (give names of dialects): not intelligible, intelligible only with difficulty, not sufficient to understand complex and abstract discourse in the other dialect, possibly sufficient to understand complex and abstract discourse, definitely sufficient to understand complex and abstract discourse.
(d) Comment on the relative importance of each dialect in terms of size, prestige, economic, political, or religious factors.
(e) Attitudes between speakers of dialects: hostile, reserved, indifferent, friendly. Give reasons:
(f) If speakers could adequately understand complex discourse in another dialect (which?), is there any reason why they would not accept written materials in that dialect? Give reasons:
(g) If there are dialects in other countries, how intelligible are they to other dialects of the language?

6. MULTILINGUALISM
(a) What other languages do they speak?
(b) Who speaks them? (leaders only, men only, adults only, young people only, persons above age ______ only, persons below age ______ only, only those who have been to school, all ages and sexes)
(c) How well? (only greetings, weather, buying and selling, most common topics, sufficiently to discuss intimate personal problems, sufficiently to discuss abstract and complex concepts adequately)
(d) Attitudes toward other languages (which languages?): hostile, reserved, indifferent, friendly. Give reasons.

(e) If they can understand complex discourse adequately in another language (which?), is there any reason why they would not accept written materials in that language? Give reasons:
(f) Under what circumstances do they speak each language, including their first language?
(g) To whom do they speak each language?
(h) For what purposes do speakers of other languages use this language as their second or third language?

7. BIBLE TRANSLATION
(a) Bible published? Give dates: first ________, most recent ________:
(b) New Testament (NT) published? first ________, most recent ________:
(c) Scripture portions (whole books) published? Which? first ________, most recent ________:
(d) If the NT or Bible are in print, do they need revision or retranslation? Why?
(e) Is the Scripture out of print?
(f) Is Bible translation in progress? By whom (individual, organization, mother tongue speaker):
(g) If so, expected date of finished NT ________, Bible ________.
(h) If not, is the language sufficiently different from others that it would require its own translation of the Bible, if one were to be made? (definitely, probably, possibly, unlikely, no):
(i) If not, are most of the speakers fluent enough in another language to use Scriptures in that language? Which language?
(j) Are the Scriptures already in print in that language (i)?
(k) If not, are they now being translated?
(l) Is adaptation possible from a closely related language? Which?

8. LITERACY
(a) What percentage can read fluently? ______ haltingly? ______
(b) In what language?
(c) If in a second language, is the orthography or script different than for the first language?
(d) Is an extensive literacy effort needed?
(e) Motivation: high among all speakers, only among Christians, others, indifferent:
(f) Is a literacy program in progress? Government, church, private, other:
(g) Other literature available in the language:
(h) If the language is spoken in other countries, is a separate literacy effort needed? Different orthography or script? By whom? Problems:

9. RELIGION
(a) What religious affiliation(s) do the people claim?)
(b) What estimated percentages of the population are affiliated with each?

10. ORGANIZATIONS
(a) Work in the area, not among the people:
(b) Work among the people:
(c) Work in the vernacular language:
(d) Doing Bible translation:
(e) Work in national or trade language only (which language?)

11. OTHER COMMENTS, including corrections to 2000 Ethnologue:

12. SOURCE OF INFORMATION
(a) Person filling out update form:
(b) Address for further correspondence:
(c) Date:
(d) Type of contact with the language:
(1) Kind of work:
(2) Number of years:
(3) Most recent contact:
(4) Do you speak the language?
(5) Second hand from whom?
(6) What is his or her contact?
(7) From published source (give bibliographical reference):
(8) From correspondence with whom?
(9) What is his or her contact?

(e) Other published sources that should be checked:

Please return this update form to:

Editor, Ethnologue
c/o International Linguistics Center
7500 West Camp Wisdom Road
Dallas, Texas 75236 USA
or
ethnologue_editor@sil.org

SECOND LANGUAGE PROFICIENCY ESTIMATE OF VERNACULAR SPEAKERS

Name of language ______________________________ Country ______________________________

Number of speakers ____________________________ Date ________________________________

Second language ____________________ Other languages they speak____________________

Based on:
Person filling out form ____

second language oral proficiency testing [1] ________________

first hand familiarity ______________________________________

Please estimate the percentage of first language speakers between ages 10 and 70 years at each of the following levels. Remember that women probably constitute 50% of the speakers. Please do not include members of the ethnic group who are not mother tongue speakers of this language.

		PERCENTAGE
Level 0.	Unable to function in the spoken language. Oral production is limited to occasional isolated words. Has no communicative ability.	___________%
Level 1.	Able to satisfy minimum courtesy requirements and maintain very simple face-to-face conversations on familiar topics.	___________%
Level 2.	Able to satisfy routine social demands and limited requirements in other domains.	___________%
Level 3.	Able to speak the language with sufficient structural accuracy and vocabulary to participate effectively in most formal and informal conversations on practical, social, and occupational topics.	___________%
Level 4.	Able to use the language fluently and accurately on all levels normally pertinent to needs. The individual's language usage and ability to function are fully successful.	___________%
Level 5.	Speaking proficiency is functionally equivalent to that of a highly articulate well-educated native speaker and reflects the cultural standards of the country where the language is natively spoken.	___________%
	TOTAL	100%

[1] See SIL Second Language Oral Proficiency Evaluation 1987 for more detailed definitions of the levels and a description of oral proficiency testing.

LANGUAGE TYPOLOGY QUESTIONNAIRE

The following basic information about a language often points to a whole group of related features. Please underline the choices that apply or describe them briefly.

Name of language________________________Country_________________________

Date_________________Person filling out form________________________________

1. Basic constituent order; Subject (S), Object (O), Verb (V): SOV, SVO, VOS, VSO, OVS, or OSV.
2. Prepositions or postpositions.
3. Genitives before or after noun heads.
4. Articles, adjectives, numerals before or after noun heads.
5. Relatives before or after noun heads, or relatives without noun heads.
6. Question word position in sentence: initial, final, other.
7. Maximum number of prefixes that can occur together on a word. Maximum number of suffixes.
8. Does word order distinguish subjects, objects, and indirect objects? Given and new information? Topic and comment?
9. Do affixes indicate case of noun phrases?
10. Do verb affixes mark person, number, gender of subject, object, other noun phrase? Is this agreement obligatory?
11. Ergativity: Is the form of the object in a transitive clause the same as that of the subject of an intransitive clause? Does the subject of a transitive clause have a different form? In intransitive clauses are some subjects treated like transitive subjects, others like transitive objects?
12. Passives, other voice phenomena.
13. Causatives.
14. Comparatives.
15. Syllable patterns; Consonant (C), Vowel (V):CV, CVC, CVV, CCV,_______
16. Tonal, non-tonal.

ENVIRONMENTAL QUESTIONNAIRE

This is not intended to be a complete typology but a rough guide to the general physical setting and economic adaptation of the culture.

Name of language____________________Country______________________________

Date______________Person filling out form________________________________

1. Ecosystem type:____

Desert: arid region lacking moisture to support vegetation
Savannah: tropical or subtropical grassland, treeless or containing scattered trees and drought-resistant undergrowth
Scrub forest: dwarf or stunted trees and shrubs
Tropical forest: thick vegetation of tall trees with undergrowth of shorter trees, shrubs, and vines; in belts paralleling the equator to 23°27'
Tundra: level or rolling treeless plain in northern arctic regions
Deciduous forest: trees whose leaves fall off seasonally
Pine forest
Gallery forest: relatively narrow stretches of forest or jungle bordering rivers in predominantly savannah area. Peoples use them in conjunction with surrounding ecotypes
Semi-tropical: partially tropical vegetation

2. Geological type:____

Mountain mesa: flat-topped rocky hills with steep sloping sides
Mountain slope: cultivating or living on the sides of mountains
Mountain valley: long depression between mountains, usually with an outlet
Coastal: seashore or land nearby
Plains: broad stretches of land with few or no rises or depressions
Riverine: people live near major rivers, depend heavily on fishing (freshwater, not coastal), hunt the river environs, plant the floodplain, travel the waterways (usually by canoe); populations typically in large villages of more than 200
Interfluvial: zone away from major waterways, e.g. along small streams; usually small villages or family groups of 10 to 100, people rely on hunting, horticulture, travel by foot, frequently avoid major waterways
Islands: (volcanic, coral, other?)

3. Subsistence type:____

Pastoralists: (nomadic, sedentary?)
Hunter-gatherers: (nomadic, sedentary?)
Fishing culture, fishermen:
Swidden agriculturalists: people rely on a variety of resources: horticulture, collecting, hunting, fishing, slash and burn
Peasants: adapted marginally to market system, rely on balanced use of agriculture for subsistence and money for purchasing goods and some foodstuffs
Intensive agriculturalists: raise crops not for local consumption but almost exclusively for sale; cash used to buy most foodstuffs and goods
Coconut palm specialization
Craftsmen: only if major subsistence base (include cottage industry)
Industrial: only if large scale production

4. Altitude range (in meters) where people live:

____

5. Climate:____

INDEX OF COUNTRIES

SELECTED PUBLICATIONS FROM SIL INTERNATIONAL

Publications in Linguistics Series

Aspects of Western Subanon Formal Speech by William C. Hall, PL 81, 1988, 206 pp., ISBN 0-88312-093-3 $20.00

Aspects of Zaiwa Prosody: An Autosegmental Account by Mark W. Wannemaker, PL 129, 1999, 172 pp., ISBN 1-55671-054-2 $29.00

An Autosegmental Approach to Shilluk Phonology by Leoma G. Gilley, PL 103, 1992, 228 pp., ISBN 0-88312-106-9 $17.00

Babine and Carrier Phonology: A Historically Oriented Study by Gillian L. Story, PL 70, 1984, ISBN 0-88312-094-1 $7.81

Barasano Syntax: Studies in the Languages of Colombia 2 by Paula Jones; Wendell Jones, PL 101, 1991, 193 pp., ISBN 0-88312-807-1 $15.00

Beyond the Bilingual Classroom: Literacy Acquisition among Peruvian Amazon Communities by Barbara Trudell, PL 117, 1993, 176 pp., ISBN 0-88312-615-x $18.00

Case Grammar Applied by Walter A. Cook, PL 127, 1998, 290 pp., ISBN 1-55671-046-1 $29.00

Comparative Kadai: The Tai Branch edited by David B. Solnit; Jerold A. Edmondson, PL 124, 1997, 392 pp., ISBN 1-55671-005-4 $35.00

Comparative Kadai: Linguistic Studies beyond Tai edited by David B. Solnit; Jerold A. Edmondson, PL 86, 1989, 382 pp., ISBN 0-88312-066-6 $25.00

Cubeo Grammar: Studies in the Languages of Colombia 5 by Nancy Morse and Michael Maxwell, PL 130, 1999, 197 pp., ISBN 1-55671-044-5 $29.00

Current Trends and Issues in Hispanic Linguistics edited by Lenard Struderus, PL 80, 1987, 136 pp., ISBN 0-88312-012-7 $11.00

Desano Grammar: Studies in the Languages of Colombia 6 by Marion Miller, PL 132, 1999, 178 pp., ISBN 1-55671-076-3 $25.00

The Dinka Vowel System by Job Malou, PL 82, 1988, 104 pp., ISBN 0-88312-008-9 $20.00

A Discourse Analysis of First Corinthians by Ralph Bruce Terry, PL 120, 1995, 208 pp., ISBN 0-88312-707-5 $25.00

Discourse Features of Ten Languages of West-Central Africa edited by Steven H. Levinsohn, PL 119, 1995, 256 pp., ISBN 0-88312-619-2 $30.00

The Dong Language in Guizhow Province, China by Zheng Guoqiao; Long Yaohong; translated by D. Norman Geary, PL 126, 1998, 288 pp., ISBN 1-55671-051-8 $29.00

The Doyayo Language by Marinus Wiering; Elisabeth Wiering, PL 121, 1994, 320 pp., ISBN 0-88312-620-6 $28.00

The French Imparfait and Passé Simple in Discourse by Sharon R. Rand, PL 116, 1993, 152 pp., 0-88312-822-5 $15.00

The Function of Verb Prefixes in Southwestern Otomí by Henrietta Andrews, PL 115, 1993, 128 pp., ISBN 0-88312-605-2 $10.00

The Geometry and Features of Tone by Keith Snider, PL 133, 1999, 173 pp., ISBN 1-55671-077-1 $25.00

Grammatical Analysis by Evelyn G. Pike; Kenneth L. Pike, PL 53, 1982, 463 pp., ISBN 0-88312-085-2 $12.50

A Grammar of Sochiapan Chinantec by David P. Foris; 2000, PL 135, 412 pp., ISBN 1-55671-052-6 $29.00

Hixkaryana and Linguistic Typology by Desmond C. Derbyshire, PL 76, 1985, 284 pp., ISBN 0-88312-082-8 $24.00

Ika Syntax: Studies in the Languages of Colombia 1 by Paul Frank, PL 94, 1990, 160 pp., ISBN 0-88312-801-2 $11.00

Logical Relations in Discourse edited by Eugene Loos, 1999, 267 pp., ISBN 1-55671-040-2 $29.00

Mamaindé Stress: The Need for Strata by David Eberhard, PL 122, 1995, 176 pp., ISBN 1-55671-003-8 $25.00

Modes in Dényá Discourse by Samson N. Abangma, PL 79, 1987, 140 pp., ISBN 0-88312-007-0 $22.00

Phonological Studies in Four Languages of Maluku edited by Wyn D. Laidig; Donald A. Burquest, PL 108, 1992, 240 pp., ISBN 0-88312-803-9 $17.00

A Pragmatic Analysis of Norwegian Modal Particles by Erik E. Andvik, PL 113, 1992, 152 pp., ISBN 0-88312-188-3 $11.00

Proto Witotoan by Richard P. Aschmann, PL 114, 1993, 176 pp., ISBN 0-88312-189-1 $17.00

A Reference Grammar of the Northern Embera Languages by Charles A. Mortensen; 1999, PL134, 212 pp., ISBN 1-55671-081-X $29.00

A Reference Grammar of Southeastern Tepehuan by Thomas L. Willet, PL 100, 1991, 304 pp., ISBN 0-88312-802-0 $21.00

Retuara Syntax: Studies in the Languages of Colombia 3 by Clayton L. Strom, PL 112, 1992, 248 pp., 0-88312-181-6, $18.00

Senoufo Phonology, Discourse to Syllable: A Prosodic Approach by Elizabeth Mills, PL 72, 1984, ISBN 0-88312-102-6, $8.75

The Structure of Thai Narrative by Somsonge Burusphat, PL 98, 1991, 248 pp., ISBN 0-88312-805-5 $18.00

The Structure of Evidential Categories in Wanka Quechua by Rick Floyd, PL 131, 1999, 206 pp., ISBN 1-55671-066-6 $29.00

Switch Reference in Koasati Discourse by David P. Rising, PL 109, 1992, 104 pp., ISBN 0-88312-813-6 $8.00

Syntactic Change and Syntactic Reconstruction: A Tagmemic Approach by John R. Costello, PL 68, 1983, 79 pp., ISBN 0-88312-092-5 $9.00

Tense and Aspect of Obolo Grammar and Discourse by Uche Aaron, PL 128, 1999, 204 pp., ISBN 1-55671-063-1 $29.00

The Verbal Piece in Ebira by John R. Adive, PL 85, 1989, 180 pp., ISBN 0-88312-037-2 $13.00

Vietnamese Classifiers in Narrative Texts by Karen A. Daley, PL 125, 1998, 226 pp., ISBN 1-55671-021-6 $29.00

Why There Are No Clitics by Daniel L. Everett, PL 123, 1996, 200 pp., ISBN 1-55671-004-6 $25.00

Dictionaries and Language Data Series

Cheyenne Major Constituent Order by Elena Leman, 1999, 106 pp., ISBN 1-55671-015-1 $15.00

Chinantec Project CD ROM, Dictionary and Shoebox database by William R. Merrifield and Alfred E. Anderson, 2000, ISBN 1-55671-097-6 $29.00

Comanche Dictionary and Grammar by James Armagost; Lila W. Robinson, PL 92, 1994, 360 pp., ISBN 0-88312-715-6 $26.00

From Phonology to Discourse: Studies in Six Colombian Languages edited by Ruth M. Brend, LDAMI 9, 1985, 133 pp., ISBN 0-88312-091-7 $11.00

Index of Nigerian Languages edited by R. M. Blench; D. H. Crozier, 1992, 142 pp., ISBN 0-88312-611-7 $20.75

Libo Buyi Chinese-English Glossary $20.00

Mitla Zapotec Texts: Folklore Texts in Mexican Indian Languages 3 edited by Carol Stubblefield; Morris Stubblefield, LDAMI 12, 1995, 156 pp., ISBN 0-88312-700-8 $15.75

Modo-English Dictionary With Grammar $8.95

Mon-Khmer Studies 26: A Journal of Southeast Asian Languages edited by David Thomas, 1997, 448 pp., $38.00

Mon-Khmer Studies 27: A Journal of Southeast Asian Languages edited by David Thomas, 1997, 384 pp., $39.00

Mon-Khmer Studies 28: A Journal of Southeast Asian Languages edited by David Thomas, 1998, 238 pp. $29.00

Mon-Khmer Studies 29: A Journal of Southeast Asian Languages edited by David Thomas, 1999, 151 pp. $21.00

Naxi-Chinese-English Glossary (Naqxi-Habaq-Yiyu Geezheeq Ceeqhuil) Thomas Pinson, SIL, 1998 ISBN 1-55671-069-0 $25.00

The Niger-Congo Languages: A Classification and Description of Africa's Largest Language Family edited by Rhonda Hartell; John Bendor-Samuel, 1989, 518 pp., ISBN 0-81917-376-2 $38.00

Notes on Mada Phonology by Norman Price, LDAFS 23, 1989, 56 pp., ISBN 0-88312-600-1 $4.15

Occasional Papers / Sudanese #4 $9.40

Occasional Papers / Sudanese #5 $9.40

Occasional Papers / Sudanese #6 $9.40

Occasional Papers / Sudanese #7 $11.95

Ozumacín Chinantec Texts: Folklore Texts in Mexican Indian Languages 2 by Nadine Rupp; James E. Rupp, LDAMI 11, 1995, 86 pp., ISBN 0-88312-624-9 $12.50

Sounds & Tones Of Kalam Kohistani - Lang. Stud. N. Pakistan 1 $12.60

Languages Of Kohistan #1 (N. Pakistan Survey) $14.95

Languages Of Northern Areas #2 (N. Pakistan Survey) $17.95

Hindko & Gujari - #3 (N. Pakistan Survey) $16.95

Pashto, Waneci, Ormuri #4 (N. Pakistan Survey) $13.95

Languages Of Chitral #5 (N. Pakistan Survey) $14.95

A Phonological Study of the Gwari Lects by Heidi James Rosendall, LDAFS 24, 1992, 123 pp., ISBN 0-88312-186-7 $10.00

Sedang Dictionary with English, Vietnamese, and French Glossaries by Kenneth D. Smith; 2000, MKS Special Ed. #1, 616 pp. ISBN 1-55671-090-9 $29.00

Workpapers Concerning Waorani Discourse Features edited by Rachel Saint; Evelyn G. Pike, LDAMI 10, 1988, 170 pp., ISBN 0-88312-625-7 $15.50

Zapotec Oral Literature: El Folklore de San Lorenzo, Folklore Texts in Mexican Indian Lang.#4 by Chuck Speck, LDAMI 13, 1998, 254 pp., ISBN 1-55671-058-5 $29.00

Linguistic Computing Resources

AMPLE: A Tool for Exploring Morphology by Stephen R. McConnel; H. Andrew Black; David J. Weber, OPAC 12, 1988, 264 pp., ISBN 0-88312-635-4 $26.00

Conc Program (Concordance Generator), Disk, Mac, 1996, $5.00

Formatting Interlinear Text by Gary F. Simons; Stephen R. McConnel; Jonathan Kew, OPAC 17, 1990, 168 pp., ISBN 0-88312-743-1 $14.00

How To Use IT: A Guide to Interlinear Text Processing (version 1.2) by Larry Versaw; Gary F. Simons, 1992, 524 pp., ISBN 0-88312-735-0 $24.00

IT for Macintosh (Interlinear Text Ed.) V. 1.01R7 Disk, 1992, $10.00

HyperBIBTEX (HyperCard Bibliographic Database Man.), Disk, Mac, 1996, $5.00

Laptop Publishing for the Field Linguist: An Approach Based on Microsoft Word by Gary F. Simons; Priscilla M. Kew, OPAC 14, 1989, 160 pp., ISBN 0-88312-637-0 $13.00

PC-KIMMO: A Two-Level Processor for Morphological Analysis by Evan L. Antworth, OPAC 16, 1990, 331 pp., ISBN 0-88312-639-7 $24.00

Powerful Ideas for Text Processing by Gary F. Simons, 1984, 197 pp., ISBN 0-88312-930-2 $10.00

PRIMER: A Tool for Developing Early Reading Materials by B. Bryson; D. Weber; S. R. McConnel; D. Weber, OPAC 18, 1994, 288 pp., ISBN 0-88312-678-8 $26.00

The RAP Programming Language by Richard A. Strangfeld, OPAC 10, 1988, 250 pp., ISBN 0-88312-633-8 $22.75

STAMP: A Tool for Dialect Adaptation by Gary F. Simons; Alan Buseman; H. Andrew Black; Stephen R. McConnel; David J. Weber, OPAC 15, 1990, 232 pp., ISBN 0-88312-638-9 $20.00

Cultural Studies

Cashibo Folklore and Culture: Prose, Poetry, and Historical Background by Lila Wistrand-Robinson, PE 34, 1998, 195 pp., ISBN 1-55671-048-8 $29.00

The Cofan Art of Hammock Weaving by M. B. Borman, IMC 25, 1992, 36 pp., ISBN 0-88312-185-9 $5.00

Cognitive Studies of Southern Mesoamerica edited by Dean E. Arnold; Helen L. Neuenswander, IMC 3, 1977, 283 pp., ISBN 0-88312-152-2 $10.95

Current Concerns of Anthropologists and Missionaries by Karl Franklin, IMC 22, 1987, 164 pp., ISBN 0-88312-176-X $14.00

Five Amazonian Studies on Worldview and Cultural Change edited by William R. Merrifield, IMC 19, 1985, 96 pp., ISBN 0-88312-174-3 $11.00

Gods, Heroes, Kinsmen: Ethnographic Studies from Irian Jaya, Indonesia edited by Daniel C. Ajamiseba; Marilyn Gregerson; William R. Merrifield, IMC 17, 1983, ISBN 0-88312-112-3, $16.00

Grafting Old Rootstock: Studies in Culture and Religion of the Chamba, Duru, Fula, and Gbaya of Cameroun edited by Philip A. Noss, IMC 14, 1982, 264 pp., ISBN 0-88312-165-4 $12.00

Kinship and Social Organization in Irian Jaya edited by Joyce Sterner; Marilyn Gregerson, IMC 32, 1997, 254 pp., ISBN 1-55671-009-7 $28.00

Language Choice in Rural Development by Clinton D. Robinson, IMC 26, 1992, 64 pp., ISBN 0-88312-180-8 $5.00

A Look at Filipino Lifestyles by Marvin K. Mayers, IMC 8, 1980, 176 pp., ISBN 0-88312-158-1 $15.00

A Look at Latin American Lifestyles by Marvin K. Mayers, IMC 2, 1982, 130 pp., ISBN 0-88312-170-0 $12.50

Mice Are Men: Language and Society among the Murle of Sudan by Jonathan E. Arensen, IMC 27, 1992, 384 pp., ISBN 0-88312-606-0 $27.00

Nucleation in Papua New Guinea Cultures edited by Daniel D. Rath; Marvin K. Mayers, IMC 23, 1988, 120 pp., ISBN 0-88312-177-8 $22.00

Nuevo Destino: The Life Story of a Shipibo Bilingual Educator by Lucille Eakin, IMC 9, 1980, 56 pp., ISBN 0-88312-159-x $3.92

Peace Is Everything: World View of Muslims in the Senegambia by David E. Maranz, IMC 28, 1993, 320 pp., ISBN 0-88312-816-0 $32.00

People of the Drum of God—Come! by Paul L. Neeley, PE 35, 1999, 298 pp., ISBN 1-55671-013-5 $29.00

People of the Ucayali: The Shipibo and Conibo of Peru by Harry Boonstra; Erwin Lauriault; Lucille Eakin, IMC 12, 1986, 62 pp., ISBN 0-88312-163-8 $9.00

Proto Otomanguean Kinship by William R. Merrifield, IMC 11, 1981, 396 pp., ISBN 0-88312-161-1 $12.50

Ritual and Relationships in the Valley of the Sun: The Ketengban of Irian Jaya by Anne Sims; Andrew Sims, IMC 30, 1992, 176 pp., ISBN 0-88312-271-5 $12.00

Ritual, Belief, and Kinship in Sulawesi edited by Marilyn Gregerson, IMC 31, 1994, 206 pp., ISBN 0-88312-621-4 $25.00

South American Kinship: Eight Kinship Systems from Brazil and Colombia edited by William R. Merrifield, IMC 18, 1985, 122 pp., ISBN 0-88312-173-5 $12.00

Sticks and Straw: Comparative House Forms in Southern Sudan and Northern Kenya by Jonathan E. Arensen, IMC 13, 1983, 148 pp., ISBN 0-88312-164-6 $12.00

Symbolism and Ritual in Irian Jaya edited by Joyce Sterner; Marilyn Gregerson, IMC 33, 1998, 126 pp., ISBN 1-55671-025-9 $27.00

Tales from Indochina edited by Carol Zylstra; Doris Blood; Dorothy Thomas; Marilyn Gregerson, IMC 21, 1987, 115 pp., ISBN 0-88312-169-7 $11.00

The Value of the Person in the Guahibo Culture by Marcelino Sosa, IMC 36, 2000, 146 pp., ISBN 1-55671-085-2 $19.00

A View from the Islands: The Samal of Tawi-Tawi by Karen J. Allison, IMC 15, 1984, 50 pp., ISBN 0-88312-168-9 $6.90

Sociolinguistics

Assessing Ethnolinguistic Vitality: Theory and Practice, eds. Gloria Kindell & M. Paul Lewis, PS 3, 2000, 206 pp, ISBN 1-55671-087-9 $25.00

Bilingual Education: An Experience in Peruvian Amazonia edited by Patricia M. Davis; Mildred L. Larson, 1984, 417 pp., ISBN 0-88312-918-3 $12.00

Cognition and Learning: A Review of the Literature with Reference to Ethnolinguistic Minorities by Patricia M. Davis, 1996, 80 pp., ISBN 0-88312-100-x $6.00

The Early Days of Sociolinguistics: Memories and Reflections edited by G. Richard Tucker; Christina Bratt Paulston, PS 2, 1997, 374 pp., ISBN 1-55671-022-4 $37.00

English as a Second Language: Dimensions and Directions edited by Irwin Feigenbaum, 1984, 63 pp., ISBN 0-88312-929-9 $10.00

Proceedings of the International Language Assessment Conference ed. by Gloria Kindell, 1991, 215 pp., 0-88312-720-2 $15.00

Language Survey Reference Guide by Joseph E. Grimes, 1995, 88 pp., ISBN 0-88312-609-5 $9.50

Language Variation and Limits to Communication by Gary F. Simons, 1979, 228 pp., ISBN 0-88312-189-0 $10.00

Language Variation and Survey Techniques edited by Gary F. Simons; Richard Loving, 1986, 351 pp. $11.55

My Tongue is the Pen: How Audiocassettes Can Serve the Nonreading World by Marilyn Malmstrom, 1991, 224 pp., ISBN 0-88312-812-8 $17.00

North Sulawesi Language Survey by Scott Merrifield, PS 1, 1997, 336 pp., ISBN 1-55671-000-3 $28.00

Sentence Repetition Testing for Studies of Community Bilingualism by Carla F. Radloff, PL 104, 1992, 214 pp., ISBN 0-88312-667-2 $15.00

Survey on a Shoestring: A Manual for Small-Scale Language Survey by Frank Blair, PL 96, 1991, 152 pp., ISBN 0-88312-644-3 $11.00

Textbooks

Advanced Phonology with Workbook: A Hierarchical Approach by Eunice V. Pike, 1990 $5.60

Beginning Morphology and Syntax by Velma B. Pickett; Benjamin F. Elson, 1988, 248 pp., ISBN 0-88312-925-6 $21.00

Dictation Exercises in Phonetics by Eunice V. Pike, 1963, 194 pp., ISBN 0-88312-900-0, $9.00

English Phonetic Transcription by Charles-James N. Bailey, PL 74, 1985, 291 pp., ISBN 0-88312-000-3 $18.00

Globe Trotting in Sandals: A Field Guide to Cultural Research by Carol V. McKinney, 2000, 337 pp., ISBN 1-55671-086-0 $32.00

Introductory Grammar: A Stratificational Approach by Pamela Cope, 1994, 128 pp., ISBN 1-55671-001-1 $12.00

Introduction to Phonology: Course Syllabus , 1991, 186 pp. $13.00

Laboratory Manual for Morphology and Syntax edited by Gillian L. Story; Calvin R. Rensch; Constance M. Naish; William R. Merrifield, 1987, 292 pp., ISBN 0-88312-785-7 $18.75

Literacy Primers: The Gudschinsky Method by Ernest W. Lee, 1984, 448 pp., ISBN 0-88312-922-1 $24.00

Local Literacies: Theory and Practice by Glenys Waters, 1998, 437 pp., ISBN 1-55671-038-0 $39.00

Man and Message: A Guide to Meaning-Based Text Analysis, by Kathleen Callow, 1998, ISBN 0-7618-1128-1, 383 pp, $44.50

A Manual for Articulatory Phonetics by Norris McKinney; Anita C. Bickford, 1984, 124 pp. $12.00

Meaning-Based Translation, by Mildred L. Larson, 1998, 586 pp, ISBN 0-7618-0971-6, $40.50

Meaning-Based Translation Workbook-Biblical Exercises by Mildred L. Larson, 1998, 307 pp., ISBN 0-76180-948-1 $39.50

Phonological Analysis: A functional approach by Donald A. Burquest, 1998, 324 pp., ISBN 1-55671-067-4 $29.00

The Semantic Structure of Written Communication by John Beekman, John C. Callow, Michael F. Kopesec, 1981, 147 pp., $6.00

Sentence Initial Devices, ISBN 0-88312-096-8 $18.75

Studying and Describing Unwritten Languages by Jacqueline M. C. Thomas; Luc Bouquiaux; translated by James Roberts, 1992, 740 pp., ISBN 0-88312-814-4 $50.00

A Survey of Grammatical Structures: Second Edition by Charles W. Peck, 1981, 338 pp. $12.00

A Survey of Linguistic Theories: Third Edition by Donald A. Burquest; Jerold A. Edmondson, 1999, 254 pp., ISBN 1-55671-068-2 $29.00

Introduction to Semantics and Translation by Katharine Barnwell, 1984, 272 pp., ISBN 0-95036-515-9 $17.00

Tools for Analyzing the World's Languages: Morphology and Syntax by J. Albert Bickford, 1998, 410 pp., ISBN 1-55671-047-x $39.00

Workbook for Historical Linguistics by Winfred P. Lehmann, 1992, 167 pp., ISBN 0-88312-272-3, **$13.00**

A Workshop Guide for Primer Construction compiled by Katharine Barnwell, 1979, 189 pp. $15.00

Reference Books

Bibliography of the Summer Institute of Linguistics Hardcover by Alan C. Wares, 1993, 624 pp., ISBN 0-88312-824-1 $15.00

Bibliography of the Summer Institute of Linguistics Paperback by Alan C. Wares, 1993, 624 pp., ISBN 0-88312-821-7 $10.00

Living Languages of the Americas: Combined Volume by SIL, 1995, 456 pp. $30.00

Ethnologue: Volume 1 Languages of the World, 14th Edition, edited by Barbara F. Grimes, 2000, ISBN 1-55671-103-4 $44.00

Ethnologue: Volume 2 Maps and Indexes, 14th Edition, edited by Barbara F. Grimes, 2000, ISBN 1-55671-104-2 $36.00

Ethnologue: CD-ROM (containing Volumes 1 & 2), 14th Edition, edited by Barbara F. Grimes, 2000, ISBN 1-55671-105-0 $29.95

Ethnologue: Complete Set (including Volumes 1, 2 & CD-ROM), 14th Edition, edited by Barbara F. Grimes, 2000, ISBN 1-55671-106-9 $80.00

To inquire about these books, please contact:
International Academic Bookstore
7500 W. Camp Wisdom Road
Dallas, TX 75116 USA

Phone: 972-708-7404
FAX 972-708-7363
Email: academic_books@sil.org
Internet: www.sil.org (click on publications)

(Shipping and Handling is additional. Price and availability subject to change. Please check our website for current listings.)